Importers Manual USA

1995-96 Edition

Importers Manual USA

The Single Source Reference Encyclopedia for Importing to the United States

Edward G. Hinkelman

James L. Nolan, Ph.D. Karla C. Shippey, J.D.

Alexandra Woznick

United States Customs Service
Chansonette Buck Wedemeyer
George R. Tuttle, Sr., Esq.
Dale O. Torrence, Esq.
Dee Thompson
Swiss Bank Corporation
Hapag Lloyd Shipping Lines
Insurance Company of North America
International Chamber of Commerce
American Association of Exporters and Importers
United States Department of Agriculture, APHIS

Illustrations and graphics:
Rachel Zuniga, David Baker,
and Robert Wolchock
Cover Design: Brad Greene

IMPORTERS MANUAL USA
1995-96 Edition

World Trade Press
1505 Fifth Avenue
San Rafael, CA 94901, USA
Tel (415) 454-9934
Fax (415) 453-7980
Email WorldPress@aol.com
Order Line (800) 833-8586

Illustrations and maps: Rachel Zuniga, David Baker, and Robert Wolchock
Cover design: Brad Greene

Cataloging-in-Publication Data

Hinkelman, Edward G., 1947-

Importers Manual USA : the single source reference encyclopedia for importing to the United States / Edward G. Hinkelman. . . . [et al.] -- 1995-96 ed.

p. cm.

Includes bibliographical references and index.

ISSN 1065-5158

ISBN 1-885073-00-3

HF3035.H55 1995 658.8'48

QB192-2213

Printed in the United States of America

For Mela

my best friend, birthday mate, companion, supporter and wife.

ACKNOWLEDGEMENTS

Reference books are rarely the product of one individual. *Importers Manual USA* is the combined effort of literally hundreds of people in the United States and overseas. I owe a great debt of gratitude to those in the U.S. Customs Service, other U.S. governmental agencies, the U.S. foreign service, the foreign service of our trading partners, banks, law firms, shipping firms, and the insurance industry whose knowledge, expertise and support made this book possible.

First Incarnation

Special thanks to those who contributed to the first incarnation of this book: Mela Longo for her personalized, dedicated and faithful efforts, Carolyn McMahon, Bonnie Beijen, Hugh Grigsby, William Whittaker, and Bob Gandenberger for the germ of the idea for a reference book.

The 1993 Edition

Ed Zaccaro, Insurance Company of North America; C. von der Decken, Hapag Lloyd; Rachelle Bijou, ICC Publishing Corporation; Bonnie Sweeny, Swiss Bank Corporation; Dave Semling at Mill Valley Services; Carol at the Presentation Works; the folks at Desktop Publishing of Larkspur California; Jerry Fletcher for his understanding; Teddy Olwyler for her suggestions; Kelle Olwyler for her encouragement; David Garfinkel for his coaching; Lyn Lawton and Heidi Longo for their early work on the Country Index; Barry Schiller, California State Automobile Association, San Francisco; and Francis G. McFaul, U.S. Department of Commerce, International Trade Administration.

The 1995 Edition

U.S. Customs Service, San Francisco office; Annie Sutton, Public Affairs Specialist, and the veterinarian, agricultural, and legal consultants of U.S. Department of Agriculture's Animal and Plant Health Inspection Service(APHIS); Greg A. Pitkoff, Director of Communications, National Customs Brokers & Forwarders Association of America, Inc., New York, NY; Nick Orsini of the Foreign Trade Division, Bureau of the Census, at the U.S. Department of Commerce, Washington, DC.

Libraries

The San Francisco Public Library; the Marin County Civic Center Library; the Marin County Law Library; the San Rafael Public Library; the Sonoma Country Library, Main Branch; the U.S. Department of Commerce Library in San Francisco; and the Mill Valley Public Library.

Commodity Index

Seattle Customs Commodity Specialists: Steve Bailey, Helene Mikes, Roberta Choy, Don Schreiber, Bob Phillips, Connie Chancey, Georgann Falotico, Pat Hughes, Scott Johnson; San Francisco Customs Commodity Specialists: Dick Peltier, Jeff Nii, Carlton Roe, Doug Johnstone, Steve Goldberg, John Merillat; Don Kerlin, U.S. Coast Guard, Chief, Recreational Boating, Product Assurance Branch; Jim Summers, U.S. Food and Drug Administration, Center for Food Safety; Pete Pearson, American Presidents Line; Carmen L. Alston, Chief, U.S. Bureau of Alcohol, Tobacco and Firearms, Firearms and Explosives Imports Branch; Virginia Alford, U.S. Bureau of Alcohol, Tobacco and Firearms; William Marmura, U.S. Department of Energy, Office of Fossil Energy; Rick Foley, Federal Energy Regulatory Commission; Dr. Murphy, Animal and Plant Health Inspection Service; Dr. Garcia, Animal and Plant Health Inspection Service; Barbara Roth, Office of Solid Waste, U.S. Environmental Protection Agency; Henry P. Lau, Chief, Chemical Inventory Section, U.S. Environmental Protection Agency; Sheri Thomas, Federal Trade Commission; Nicole Collins, U.S. Department of Commerce Textile Unit; Naomi Goldberg, U.S. Department of Commerce Textile Unit; Michael Yanchulis, Office of Pesticide Programs, U.S. Environmental Protection Agency; Clive R. Van Orden, U.S. Department of Transportation, National Highway Traffic Safety Administration, Office of Vehicle Compliance; Bob Griffin, formerly of U.S. Department of Agriculture, Animal and Plant Health Inspection Service, Plant Protection and Quarantine (plants); Victor Harabin, U.S. Department of Agriculture, Animal and Plant Health Inspection Service, Plant Protection and Quarantine (plants); Deborah Knott, U.S. Department of Agriculture, Animal and Plant Health Inspection Service, Plant Protection and Quarantine (insects); James (Bud) Pedimarsh, U.S. Department of Agriculture, Animal and Plant Health Inspection Service, Plant Protection and Quarantine (plants); Polly Lehtonen, U.S. Department of Agriculture, Animal and Plant Health Inspection Service, Plant Protection and Quarantine (seed examination facility); Linda Wisniowski, U.S. Food and Drug Administration, Import Operations; Frank Krivda, U.S. Consumer Product Safety Commission, Compliance: bikes, toys; Patrician Fairall, U.S. Consumer Product Safety Commission, Compliance: FFA; Tims Jones, U.S. Consumer Product Safety Commission; John Lee, U.S. Department of Transportation, National Highway Traffic Safety Administration, Domestic Compliance; George Shifflett, U.S. Department of Transportation, National Highway Traffic Safety Administration, Import Compliance; Elizabeth Levy, U.S. Department of Commerce; Nancy Lee, Center for Disease Control; S. Marti-Volkoff, Federal Communications Commission; U.S. Customs; U.S. Department of Agriculture; U.S. Food and Drug Administration; U.S. Consumer Product Safety Commission; U.S. Department of Transportation, National Highway Traffic Safety Administration; U.S. Department of Commerce; Federal Trade Commission; U.S. Environmental Protection Agency; U.S. Fish and Wildlife Service; U.S. Bureau of Alcohol, Tobacco and Firearms; World Wildlife Fund: Allison Rogers and Ginette Hemley.

Edward G. Hinkelman
San Rafael, California
January 1995

DISCLAIMER

Material for this publication has been obtained from information supplied by U.S. government agencies, foreign government embassies, consulates and agencies, industry and trade organizations, from personal interview and by telephone and correspondence. We have diligently tried to ensure the accuracy of all of the information in this publication and to present as comprehensive a reference work as space would permit. The fluidity and fast pace of today's business world makes the task of keeping data current and accurate an extremely difficult one. Our purpose is to give you information so that you can become aware of importing issues and can discover resources most useful for your particular business. As you contact the resources within this book, you will no doubt learn of new and exciting business opportunities and of additional trading requirements that have arisen even within the short time since we published this edition. If we find errors, we will strive to correct them in preparing future editions. The publishers take no responsibility for inaccurate or incomplete information that may have been submitted to them in the course of research for this publication. The facts published indicate the result of those inquiries and no warranty as to their accuracy is given.

Table of Contents
Overview

InfoLists Contents

International Law

Contents

International Banking
Contents

U.S. Customs Entry and Clearance Contents

The following section is adapted from the U.S. Department of the Treasury, U.S. Customs Service publication *Importing to the United States* (March 1993 edition). We have updated for 1993-1994 laws— including revisions required by NAFTA, GSP, and the Customs Modernization Act, among others—and we have included the most current address and contact information available at publication.

Packing, Shipping, Insurance
Contents

Commodity Index Contents

Introduction

World Trade and The Global Economy

International trade is not new to the world, but the current scope of it is. International trade and commerce has historically led to great power and wealth for both the individuals and nations that see beyond their local shores to the opportunities that lie beyond the horizon.

Ancient Phoenicians, and later Venetian, traders boldly sailed small ships to ports of call throughout the Mediterranean, selling their products and buying what were to them exotic goods of foreign cultures. In the process, they established trade routes that are still in use today.

In the late 15th century and early 16th century, European demand for foreign products, especially spices, led to the great voyages of discovery of Christopher Columbus, Vasco da Gama, and Ferdinand Magellan.

Today, businessmen and women fly in jumbo jets to every corner of the world, selling their own products, buying raw materials to supply their factories, and buying finished goods for consumers who are as enamored of the exotic products of foreign cultures as were the Venetians of the 15th century.

In the last two decades, the world has truly become a global marketplace. Worldwide imports and exports have soared as most governments have come to realize that liberal trade policies are good for domestic consumers, workers, and businesses alike.

In those last two decades, combined U.S. imports and exports have risen from $84 billion in 1970 to $471 billion in 1980, to $889 billion in 1990, and to $1,046 billion in 1993! While imports have outpaced exports, U.S. exports have been surging in the past five years as world markets have opened, U.S. export restrictions have lessened, and U.S. exporters have become more aggressive.

Importing to the United States

Importing to the U.S. is the process of bringing goods from a foreign economy into the domestic U.S. economy. Rapid changes in the fast-paced global economy, as well as new rules—such as those found in the General Agreement on Tariffs and Trade (GATT), the North American Free Trade Agreement (NAFTA), and the 1993 Customs Modification Act (Mod Act), all of which are covered in the second edition of *Importers Manual USA*—can make this first step a daunting one for old hands and newcomers alike. Nevertheless, importing concerns are limited to the part of the operation aimed at clearing goods through U.S. Customs. Once goods are cleared, the importing process ends and the considerations of running a particular type of business begin.

Importing to the U.S. ranges from the small-time operator carrying a briefcase of costume jewelry or suitcase of leather jackets back from an overseas vacation trip to the large-scale corporate importers, with transactions measured in hundreds of millions of dollars.

Importing provides many benefits to the U.S. economy and U.S. consumers. Imported products offer the consumer a wider selection of products; competition between foreign producers and U.S. producers helps keep domestic prices more competitive; and, as we have seen in the automobile industry, competition has led to the design and production of better quality domestic products.

Furthermore, opening our domestic markets to friendly countries has generally led to the vitalization of their economies, resulting in greater demand for U.S. products. U.S. exports that have benefited significantly include pharmaceuticals; machine tools; aerospace, high-technology, and biotechnology products; entertainment items—films, video, and music; and a wide range of consumer products.

Why Import?

The first question an individual or business considering importing should ask is simply "Why import?" The process of importing is often complex and introduces a whole range of variables that do not exist when conducting business domestically.

When establishing your personal and corporate purposes, you will need to determine whether you are importing to satisfy a market demand for a product or, if you have a source for an item, to establish the market for the product in the U.S. On the other hand, you may want to travel the world specifically to find a product that inspires you to establish a new business in the U.S.

What are your strengths? Do you have experience as a buyer or purchasing agent? Do you have experience as a manufacturer of an item? Do you have experience in sales or marketing? Do you have general business expertise? The prospective importer needs to answer these questions to assess capabilities and establish his or her best position in the market chain running from the source to the ultimate consumer.

Before deciding to import, you should be able to identify distinct advantages to importing a foreign product over purchasing a domestic one. If you don't make this determination ahead of time, you could find yourself returning home from an expensive buying trip only to find that the goods you so laboriously sought out, purchased, and imported can be obtained in the U.S. from a wholesaler for less money than you paid for them overseas. In addition, not only must you, as an importer, handle the demands of your domestic business, you must also be able to do business in other countries. In effect, you will be dealing with the bureaucracies of two and possibly more countries. It is therefore of utmost importance to have good reasons to import a product.

For more information and ideas, refer to "18 Reasons to Go into Importing" and "18 Reasons Not to Go into Importing" on page 2.

Elements of the Import Process

While the level at which you import will determine the depth of understanding required for success in each of the subject areas, the general requirements for importing a product are the same whether you are a small- or large-scale importer. The following is an overview of the main steps involved in the import process.

Legal Considerations of International Trade

The greatest source of problems for U.S. businesspeople doing business internationally is the erroneous assumption that they can operate abroad according to the same rules that apply in the U.S. When you do business internationally, you are subject not only to U.S. law, but to the laws of any country involved in your business transaction. This may be the case even if you do not physically visit the other country.

The more complex your transactions, the more you travel abroad, the more you deal in product liability or in politically sensitive products, the more you obtain and extend credit, the more you trust others to follow through on their end of the bargain, the greater will be your chances of experiencing legal difficulties while conducting business internationally.

For a complete discussion of these issues refer to the "International Law" section, beginning on page 69.

Finding Suppliers

If you are planning to establish an ongoing importing business, it is advisable that you choose your foreign suppliers with even greater care than you would a domestic supplier. Your need to rely on individuals who are in a country 6,000 miles away, and who may be speaking another language, will be greater than when dealing with a domestic supplier who is only 500 miles away, who speaks your language, and who can easily be contacted by telephone.

There are numerous InfoLists beginning on page 1 that detail the process of securing suppliers. For example: "Finding Sources" on page 13, "26 Sources of Information" on page 14, "Buying from the Source" on page 13, "Letters of Request" on page 17, and "10 Tips About Suppliers" on page 18.

Also refer to the Commodity Index, beginning on page 325 for lists of the principal exporting countries for specific commodities.

Negotiating

Once you have secured an appropriate supplier, you will need to establish the terms and conditions of the sale. This is likely to involve communicating and negotiating with individuals of different nationalities, races, and cultural backgrounds. Be aware that you will be on their turf and that your established methods of communicating and dealing may not work at all. You may have to research and make special preparations to ensure successful negotiations.

Refer to the "10 Tips for Negotiating" on page 20 and "10 Tips for Negotiating in a Long-Term Relationship" on page 21.

Contracts for Purchase

You will need to know when a purchase contract is necessary and how it must be structured. When dealing with both U.S. and foreign laws, you will find it imperative to understand how they will affect you.

You and your supplier may agree to use the legal structure of either the U.S. or the supplier's country to govern your contract, or you may chose to settle conflicts through arbitration or mediation. In any case, all parties to the transaction should have well-defined responsibilities, and all terms of the purchase should be stated in the contract.

Refer to "Drafting the International Sales Contract" on page 88, and "Solving Contract Disputes" on page 95.

International Banking Letters of Credit

Your supplier will prefer that you prepay for your merchandise, while you will strive to establish 30-, 60-, 90-, or even 180-day, credit terms. The laws of some countries, however, require payment for goods before or as they are exported.

The political stability of the exporting country, the quality of its trade relationship with the U.S., and your relationship with your supplier will determine your ability to secure better payment terms for your purchases.

In most international transactions, the buyer and seller will agree to use a documentary letter of credit as the method of payment. You will need to know the different types of documentary credits and how they operate.

You will also need to understand at least a minimum about foreign exchange dealings. Otherwise you risk getting caught in currency fluctuations, which have the potential for destroying your profit margin.

Refer to "International Banking" on page 113, "Documentary Credits (Letters of Credit) on page 126, and "An Introduction to Foreign Exchange" on page 122.

Packing and Labeling

You should specify packing and labeling requirements for your goods in your purchase contract. First, specify how the merchandise is to be labeled to satisfy U.S. Customs and other government agency requirements. Second, specify how the merchandise is to be packed to withstand ocean or air shipment to the U.S. Third, consider specifying packaging in the country of origin, which will make the item ready for immediate retail stocking and sale in the U.S.

Refer to "Marking: Country of Origin" on page 215, "Packing of Goods—Commingling" on page 189, and the commodity specific "Marking and Labeling Requirements" subhead for your commodity in the Commodity Index section.

International Freight Transportation

The terms of your sale will determine whether you or your supplier is responsible for making shipping arrangements. Regardless of who is responsible, you will want to select an appropriate mode of transport as well as the best carrier, routing, container, and scheduling for your shipment. Consolidation, containerization, and intermodal transport may or may not save money. Cost-benefit analyses will help to establish the most desirable method.

Refer to Tab 5—"Packing, Shipping, Insurance" on page 257. Also, for explanation of terms of sale that include freight, insurance, etc., refer to "Drafting the International Sales Contract" on page 88.

Insurance

Your merchandise will have to be insured by you or the shipper. It is important to insure the full value of the shipment, which can include packing, shipping, cartage, storage, duties, and taxes. You can do this on an individual-policy basis through the freight forwarder or carrier, or on a term-policy basis with a broker or an insurance company, preferably in the U.S. Be certain that you are insured whenever you have an "insurable interest."

Refer to "Insurance" on page 81 and "Marine Insurance" on page 297.

Customs Entry and Clearance

Your first responsibility as an importer in dealing with U.S. Customs will be to know—*before* your purchase abroad—how your product is regulated by U.S. Customs and other U.S. government agencies. We cannot overestimate the advantages of understanding and knowing these requirements before negotiating contracts overseas.

Most importers employ the services of a customs broker to handle the Customs entry and clearance process. Customs brokers are licensed professionals who handle the clearance of goods through Customs on a day-to-day basis and are therefore experienced with documentation requirements.

Your knowledge, in concert with the efforts of a competent customs broker, will help to keep this very important part of your import operation running smoothly.

Your second responsibility will be to secure and present proper documentation, to your customs broker or to U.S. Customs. Each document required by U.S. Customs, except for those produced domestically in the U.S., should be specifically required of your foreign supplier in a contract. Your receipt of specified documentation should be established as a prerequisite for payment.

For information about entering goods through U.S. Customs, refer to Tab 4—U.S. Customs Entry and Clearance. For information about customs brokers, refer to "Selecting and Working with a Customs Broker" on page 50 and "Customs Brokers, Freight Forwarders, and Professional Associations" on page 51.

For specific regulatory information for your product, refer to Tab 6—Commodity Index.

Marketing

Once your goods have arrived in the U.S., it will be your job to get them to market. If you have an established wholesale or retail distribution system, this may be a predetermined matter. If you are seeking to establish a market, you will have many choices to make with regard to your merchandising. For most businesses, this step is where "the rubber meets the road" because no business becomes viable until it produces cash flow.

Basis of Success

Whether your import business is a success will depend on the range of your knowledge of each part of the process and your ability to absorb that knowledge and put it into practice.

The four major areas of knowledge and expertise that will be factors in your success are:

1. Knowledge of your product;
2. Knowledge of the import process itself;
3. Expertise in marketing your goods domestically; and
4. Expertise in the management of your business:

Importers Manual USA is primarily concerned with item #2, knowledge of the import process.

Importers Manual USA

Importers Manual USA is a desktop reference encyclopedia and source book for the process of importing into the United States. This reference is unique in that it addresses in one volume the specific how-to information you need to know:

- International legal issues
- International banking and letters of credit
- U.S. Customs entry and clearance
- Packing
- Shipping
- Insurance

In addition, the Commodity Index contains detailed articles on importing virtually all commodities, organized according to the Harmonized Tariff Schedule of the United States (HTSUS), which is the document Customs uses to classify and calculate duties on entries.

Importers Manual USA has been designed as an easy-to-use reference, the main purpose of which is to educate and, even more importantly, to save both the professional and small-time importer immense amounts of time, energy, money, and frustration.

Notes:

Notes:

THE DIRECTORY SOURCE 1994

InfoLists
Contents

InfoList #1

18 Reasons to Go into Importing

1. To obtain raw materials not available in the U.S.
2. To obtain products not manufactured in the U.S.
3. To obtain products and commodities directly from the source of supply, when that source is in a foreign country.
4. To obtain products and commodities at lower cost than in the U.S.
5. To add foreign products to your product line in an established retail, wholesale, mail-order, or other business in the U.S.
6. To take advantage of specific connections in a foreign country.
7. To exercise greater control over the supply of foreign-made products you have been purchasing in the U.S.
8. To arrange for contract manufacture of products overseas at a lower total cost.
9. To arrange for overseas contract manufacture of products requiring specialized labor not available in the U.S.
10. To take advantage of foreign government subsidies provided to those setting up manufacturing facilities designed to produce goods for export.
11. To take advantage of special financing deals provided by the exporting country or banks in the exporting country.
12. To earn a living while travelling and seeing the world.
13. You are an experienced designer of products you seek to have manufactured to your specifications at a specialized facility, or you simply wish to take advantage of lower materials or labor costs.
14. You are an experienced manufacturer who seeks to have products produced to your specifications at a specialized facility, or you simply wish to take advantage of lower materials or labor costs.
15. You have sales experience with imported products and seek to find your own overseas suppliers and start your own business.
16. You have a desire to operate internationally and are sophisticated enough to handle the complexities inherent in international trade and the import process.
17. You have knowledge of the price structure for the goods you seek to import and are confident that there is sufficient margin for the venture to be profitable.
18. You are an experienced businessperson who simply wants to expand your operations globally.

InfoList #2

18 Reasons Not to Go into Importing

1. You are not precise or detail-oriented enough to be able to handle the complexities of an import operation.
2. You lack business experience and/or have no business sense for buying and selling products.
3. You have no established or researched potential market for the goods you plan to import.
4. You have found no reliable source of supply even after conducting extensive research in all the likely countries of origin.
5. You are not emotionally prepared for the hassle of dealing overseas, with U.S. Customs, etc.
6. You are wildly undercapitalized for the venture you have in mind.
7. You are unfamiliar with the merchandise you are thinking of importing.
8. You are unfamiliar with the market for the goods you are interested in importing.
9. You are unfamiliar with the pricing structure for the goods you are interested in importing.
10. The margin differential between buying the goods in the U.S. versus the total landed cost of the goods from the country of origin does not justify establishing an import operation.
11. There may be better opportunities, with greater certainty, in the U.S.
12. Your views of the world and its people are narrow and you would find it difficult to by flexible and to operate outside your present frame of reference.
13. You are incapable of dealing with the differences of language and custom between yourself and foreign suppliers.
14. Your likely overseas source of supply is so undependable that you risk losing business to domestic competitors with more dependable domestic suppliers.
15. Shipping goods to the U.S. may take too long. You perhaps need a supplier closer to home.
16. You are unable to obtain the quality of product that your market or manufacturing process requires.
17. It may be impossible to personally manage production or to inspect the quality of products adequately from afar, or too expensive to hire someone else to do it for you.
18. Civil unrest and/or political instability in the exporting country make long-term business prospects uncertain.

InfoList #3

Key Elements of a Successful Import Operation

1. **General business knowledge and experience**
   The experience and/or ability to operate a business effectively.
2. **Knowledge of the import process**
   Experience with, or knowledge of the entire import process from finding suppliers to U.S. Customs entry and clearance.
3. **Knowledge of product**
   Thorough knowledge of the products you plan to import, based on experience or knowledge gained form being a broker, designer, manufacturer, retailer, wholesaler, or other experience related to the product.
4. **Knowledge of costs**
   Knowledge of all costs of obtaining and bringing the product to market.
5. **Access to low cost supply**
   Ability to obtain products or commodities at the source for the best (lowest) possible price.
6. **Relationship with supplier(s)**
   Ability to establish and maintain a good working relationship with your supplier.
7. **Ability to establish a market**
   Ability to successfully find or develop a market for the goods you import.
8. **Knowledge of price structure**
   Knowledge of the pricing structure for the imported goods which enables you to know how much to pay and how much to charge.
9. **Knowledge of market**
   Specialized knowledge of the wholesale, retail, mail-order, or other market for the product, based on actual experience or special knowledge.
10. **Ability to sell to a specific market efficiently**
    Past experience or special knowledge that enables you to sell your product or commodity for the best (highest) possible price once you have imported it.
11. **Working capital**
    An appropriate amount of working capital for the size and type of import operation you envision.
12. **Working relationship with "professional partners"**
    Your ability to establish and maintain good working relationships with your professional partners:
    - Customs broker
    - Freight forwarder
    - Banker
    - Attorney
    - Customs lawyer
    - Accountant

InfoList #4

13 Ways Import Businesses Fail

1. Individual does not have the required business knowledge or expertise to make a success of what is, first and foremost, a business.
2. Individual or company refuses to take the process of importing seriously. Thinks that importing from Africa or Asia is the same as ordering goods from the state next door. Never commits to acquiring the knowledge and expertise required to succeed in the new, specialized venture.
3. Importer is not familiar enough with the product to be able to discern differences in quality, specifications, or price that are meaningful to the intended market. Imports goods the domestic consumer market will simply not accept.
4. Failure to factor in all the costs of importing and bringing the product to market.
5. Inability to spot or guard against foreign exchange fluctuations which wipe out potential profit.
6. Inability to assess political changes occurring in the country of origin which might affect the relationship with a foreign supplier.
7. Inability to maintain a good working relationship with supplier.
8. Lack of understanding of the domestic market. Inability to sell goods cost-effectively in the U.S.
9. Inadequate working capital for the size and scope of the import operation.
10. Inability to establish and maintain good working relationships with the importer's "professional partners:"
    - Customs broker
    - Freight forwarder
    - Banker
    - Attorney
    - Customs lawyer
    - Accountant
11. Failure to meet strict U.S. Customs regulations for:
    - Marking and labeling
    - Quotas
    - Other requirements
12. Failure of goods to meet other U.S. governmental regulatory agency requirements for:
    - Product safety
    - Quality standards
    - Other standards
13. Goods arrive too late for seasonal sale.

InfoList #5

30 Easy-to-Import Products

The following products are relatively simple to import in that they are not subject to significant restrictions, prohibitions, permits, licenses, or documentation other than basic Customs requirements. Refer to the Commodity Index listing for each item for specific information.

1. **Appliances, Household.** Other than those producing radiation. Refer to Commodity Index Chapter 84: Large Mechanical Appliances and Machines, beginning on page 733; and Chapter 85: Electronics and Components, beginning on page 741.
2. **Art.** Specifically original works of art. Refer to Commodity Index Chapter 97: Works of Art, Collector's Pieces, and Antiques, beginning on page 799.
3. **Brushes.** Refer to Commodity Index Chapter 96: Miscellaneous Manufactured Articles, beginning on page 795.
4. **Cork.** Refer to Commodity Index Chapter 45: Cork and Articles of Cork, beginning on page 547.
5. **Cutlery.** Refer to Commodity Index Chapter 82: Metal Tools and Implements, beginning on page 727.
6. **Flowers, Artificial.** Refer to Commodity Index Chapter 67: Feathers, Down, Artificial Flowers, and Wigs, beginning on page 672.
7. **Fur, Artificial.** Refer to Commodity Index Chapter 43: Fur and Fur Products, beginning on page 536.
8. **Gems and Gemstones.** Refer to Commodity Index Chapter 71: Gems, Jewelry, and Related Products, beginning on page 692.
9. **Glass and Glass Products.** Refer to Commodity Index Chapter 70: Glass and Glassware, beginning on page 688.
10. **Jewelry.** Refer to Commodity Index Chapter 71: Gems, Jewelry, and Related Products, beginning on page 692.
11. **Leather Goods.** Other than those derived from endangered species. Refer to Commodity Index Chapter 42: Leather Articles, beginning on page 529.
12. **Leather Hides.** Other than those derived from endangered species. Refer to Commodity Index Chapter 41: Raw Hides, Skins, and Leather, beginning on page 524.
13. **Lighting Fixtures.** Refer to Commodity Index Chapter 94: Furnishings, beginning on page 782.
14. **Luggage.** Refer to Commodity Index Chapter 42: Leather Articles, beginning on page 529; and Chapter 46: Baskets and Wickerware, beginning on page 548.
15. **Machine Tools.** Refer to Commodity Index Chapter 84: Large Mechanical Appliances and Machines, beginning on page 733.
16. **Base Metals.** Refer to Commodity Index Chapters 72 through 81 on page 697 through page 727.
17. **Musical Instruments.** Refer to Commodity Index Chapter 92: Musical Instruments, beginning on page 775.
18. **Optics, Optical Goods.** Refer to Commodity Index Chapter 90: Optical, Medical, and Precision Instruments, beginning on page 764.
19. **Paper and Paper Products.** Refer to Commodity Index Chapter 47: Wood Pulp and Paper Waste, beginning on page 553; Chapter 48: Paper and Paperboard, beginning on page 554; and Chapter 49: Printed Materials, beginning on page 558.
20. **Pearls.** Refer to Commodity Index Chapter 71: Gems, Jewelry, and Related Products, beginning on page 692.
21. **Plastics and Plastic Products.** Refer to Commodity Index Chapter 39: Plastics and Articles Thereof, beginning on page 514.
22. **Rubber and Rubber Products.** Refer to Commodity Index Chapter 40: Rubber and Articles Thereof, beginning on page 519.
23. **Saddlery.** Refer to Commodity Index Chapter 42: Leather Articles, beginning on page 529.
24. **Sporting Goods.** Refer to Commodity Index Chapter 95: Toys, Games, and Sports Equipment, beginning on page 787.
25. **Stone and Stone Products.** Refer to Commodity Index Chapter 68: Articles of Stone and Related Products, beginning on page 681.
26. **Tile, Ceramic.** Refer to Commodity Index Chapter 69: Ceramic Products, beginning on page 684.
27. **Tools, Hand.** Refer to Commodity Index Chapter 82: Metal Tools and Implements, beginning on page 727 and Chapter 85: Electronics and Components, beginning on page 741.
28. **Umbrellas.** Refer to Commodity Index Chapter 66: Umbrellas and Related Items, beginning on page 670.
29. **Utensils.** Refer to Commodity Index Chapter 82: Metal Tools and Implements, beginning on page 727.
30. **Wallpaper.** Refer to Commodity Index Chapter 48: Paper and Paperboard, beginning on page 554.

InfoList #6

17 Difficult-to-Import Products

The following products are "difficult" to import because of stringent regulatory requirements by one or more U.S. governmental agency. With a very few exceptions, however, it is possible to import all the products listed below. Refer first to the Commodity Index listing for the product to get an overview of the regulations, then speak with a customs broker who has experience with the product. In some cases all that is required is an additional form which your broker presents with your Customs entry.

1. **Drugs**. Highly regulated by U.S. Food and Drug Administration (FDA); extensive requirements for drug quality and drug-producing establishments. FDA entry documentation required. Refer to Commodity Index Chapter 30: Pharmaceutical Products, beginning on page 467.
2. **Radioactive Materials**. Highly regulated by the Nuclear Regulatory Commission (NRC). NRC import authorization and licensing required. Refer to Commodity Index Chapter 84: Large Mechanical Appliances and Machines, beginning on page 733.
3. **Arms and Armaments**. Highly regulated by the Bureau of Alcohol, Tobacco, and Firearms (BATF). BATF import licensing and import permits required; stringent restrictions on the types of arms permissible. Refer to Commodity Index Chapter 93: Arms and Ammunition, beginning on page 778.
4. **Alcoholic Beverages**. Highly regulated by the Bureau of Alcohol, Tobacco, and Firearms (BATF). BATF import permit required; extensive labeling requirements, compliance with product standards of fill and identity, other federal, state, and municipal alcohol regulations, federal excise tax payable at entry. Refer to Commodity Index Chapter 22: Beverages, Spirits, and Vinegar, beginning on page 432.
5. **Dairy Products**. Highly regulated by the U.S. Food and Drug Administration (FDA) and the U.S. Department of Agriculture (USDA). Quotas, licensing, permits, quarantine restrictions, and entry and notification procedures apply depending upon the specific product and its point of origination. Refer to Commodity Index Chapter 4: Dairy Products, beginning on page 351.
6. **Poultry, Poultry Products, and Eggs**. Highly regulated by the U.S. Department of Agriculture (USDA). Import restrictions, port inspections, product certification, plant certification, and import permits apply. Refer to Commodity Index Chapter 2: Meat, beginning on page 339; and Chapter 4: Dairy Products, beginning on page 351.
7. **Meat and Meat Products**. Highly regulated by the U.S. Department of Agriculture (USDA). Import restrictions, port inspections, product certification, plant certification, and import permits apply. Refer to Commodity Index Chapter 2: Meat, beginning on page 339.
8. **Toys**. Highly regulated by the U.S. Consumer Product Safety Commission (CPSC): stringent safety standards apply, defect reporting requirements, recordkeeping for electrical toys or articles, extensive marking and labeling requirements. Refer to Commodity Index Chapter 95: Toys, Games, and Sports Equipment, beginning on page 787.
9. **Live Animals**. Highly regulated by the U.S. Fish and Wildlife Service (FWS), U.S. Public Health Service Centers for Disease Control (CDC), U.S. Department of Agriculture (USDA), and U.S. Food and Drug Administration (FDA), depending upon species. Restricted port of entry, quarantine, prior notification, license, import/export documentation, recordkeeping, etc. apply depending upon species. Refer to Commodity Index Chapter 1: Live Animals, beginning on page 331.
10. **Textiles and Textile Products**. Subject to complex quota restrictions, U.S. Customs country-of-origin declarations, labeling requirements, and flammability standards. Refer to Commodity Index Chapters 50 through 63 on page 562 through page 655.
11. **Motor Vehicles**. Stringent U.S. Department of Transportation (DOT) safety standards and U.S. Environmental Protection Agency (EPA) emission-control standards. Refer to Commodity Index Chapter 87: Vehicles, beginning on page 752.
12. **Aircraft and Aerospace Products**. Stringent Federal Aviation Administration (FAA) and National Aeronautics and Space Administration (NASA) standards. Refer to Commodity Index Chapter 88: Aircraft and Parts, beginning on page 758.
13. **Prepared Foods**. Subject to regulations of the U.S. Food and Drug Administration (FDA). Entry notification, certification, extensive labeling requirements, compliance with product standards, fill and identity standards, and entry notification. Refer to Commodity Index Chapters 16, 19, 20, and 21, beginning on pages 403, 420, 423, and 428, respectively.
14. **Radiation-Producing Goods and Radio Frequency Devices.** Subject to regulation and restrictions of the U.S Food and Drug Administration (FDA) and the U.S. Federal Communications Administration (FCC). Entries must comply with standards and entry notifications. Refer to Commodity Index Chapters 84, 85, 90, and 92 beginning on pages 733, 741, 764, and 775, respectively.
15. **Fertilizers.** Subject to compliance with U.S. Department of Agriculture (USDA) requirements for fertilizers of organic origin, U.S. Federal Trade Commission (FTC) and Consumer Products Safety Commission (CPSC) standards for products marketed to consumers, U.S. Environmental Protection Agency (EPA) regulation for products containing toxic or hazardous substances, and U.S. Department of Transportation (DOT) regulations on transport. Refer to Commodity Index Chapter 31: Fertilizers, beginning on page 478.
16. **Paints and Related Products.** Subject to U.S. Federal Trade Commission (FTC) and Consumer Product Safety Commission (CPSC) standards for consumer products, U.S. Environmental Protection Agency (EPA) requirements for toxic or hazardous substances, and compliance with U.S. Department of Transportation (DOT) regulations on transportation of hazardous and toxic substances. Refer to Commodity Index Chapter 32: Paints and Related Products, beginning on page 482.
17. **Explosives, Fireworks, and Other Combustibles.** Subject to compliance with U.S. Federal TRade Commission (FTC) and Consumer Product Safety Commission (CPSC) standards and U.S. Bureau of Alcohol, Tobacco, and Firearms (BATF) regulations and permit requirements, among others. Refer to Commodity Index Chapter 36: Explosives, Fireworks, and Other Combustibles, beginning on page 501.

InfoList #7

Top 50 Imports to the U.S.

Leading items in U.S. general imports (U.S. Customs value) worldwide in thousands of U.S. dollars

HTSUS commodity	1991	1992	1993	% change*
All commodities	483,778,301	525,091,414	574,862,928	18.83%
87—Automotive vehicles and parts	74,514,071	78,078,642	88,288,561	18.49%
84—Large mechanical appliances and machines	65,060,987	73,589,071	84,063,533	29.21%
85—Electric and electronic appliances and components	59,561,966	66,242,779	75,263,014	26.36%
27—Mineral fuels, oils, and waxes	54,177,820	54,014,357	54,852,568	1.25%
62—Apparel not knitted or crocheted	14,806,223	17,824,646	19,778,308	33.58%
90—Precision instruments	14,121,129	15,440,068	16,926,749	19.87%
71—Gems and jewelry	12,207,443	12,390,123	13,747,673	12.62%
64—Footwear	9,542,323	10,140,717	11,105,366	16.38%
95—Toys, games and sports equipment	8,177,147	10,101,730	10,939,890	33.79%
61—Knitted or crocheted articles	8,776,943	10,196,592	10,593,383	20.70%
29—Organic chemicals	8,721,644	9,773,624	9,556,446	9.57%
39—Plastics and articles thereof	7,006,711	7,981,492	8,921,823	27.33%
48—Paper and paperboard	8,069,919	8,051,189	8,700,174	7.81%
44—Wood and wood products	4,944,540	6,354,057	8,479,380	71.49%
72—Iron and steel	7,072,882	7,882,442	8,475,957	19.84%
94—Furniture	6,297,038	7,117,835	8,081,152	28.33%
73—Articles of iron or steel	6,487,111	6,057,146	6,842,910	5.48%
88—Aircraft and parts	7,522,984	7,294,653	6,346,846	-15.63%
40—Rubber and articles thereof	4,606,162	5,306,880	5,923,083	28.59%
03—Fish	4,699,568	4,796,593	5,004,273	6.48%
42—Leather articles	4,014,118	4,407,082	4,595,674	14.49%
76—Aluminum and articles thereof	3,199,724	3,417,124	4,178,343	30.58%
28—Inorganic chemicals	4,355,770	4,134,122	3,984,411	-8.53%
22—Beverages and spirits	3,381,436	3,883,147	3,797,610	12.31%
30—Pharmaceutical products	1,993,408	2,809,729	3,008,529	50.92%
97—Works of art, collectors' pieces, and antiques	1,969,793	2,067,655	2,661,412	35.11%
82—Metal tools	2,231,309	2,129,829	2,504,001	12.22%
91—Timepieces	2,172,070	2,219,505	2,447,389	12.68%
08—Fruit and nuts	2,340,909	2,443,141	2,427,366	3.69%
37— Photographic or cinematographic goods	1,943,219	2,197,837	2,375,825	22.26%
69—Ceramic products	1,949,418	2,212,147	2,348,435	20.47%
02—Meat	2,294,837	2,179,650	2,309,505	0.64%
74—Copper and articles thereof	1,978,281	2,071,322	2,228,727	12.66%
70—Glass and glassware	1,777,712	1,954,627	2,140,181	20.39%
83—Miscellaneous metal articles	1,596,465	1,854,582	2,013,708	26.14%
38—Miscellaneous chemical products	1,318,357	1,619,971	1,971,093	49.51%
49—Printed materials	1,649,099	1,813,154	1,961,647	18.95%
47—Wood pulp and paper waste	2,163,525	2,128,925	1,886,873	-12.79%
24—Tobacco products	935,336	1,759,928	1,837,281	96.43%
09—Coffee, tea, and spices	2,171,631	2,017,642	1,821,075	-16.14%
20—Vegetable, fruit, and nut preparations	1,839,729	1,960,289	1,759,957	-4.34%
96—Miscellaneous manufactured articles	1,467,891	1,593,303	1,721,555	17.28%
63—Other textile articles	1,393,222	1,552,638	1,712,329	22.90%
32—Paints and related products	1,431,754	1,621,937	1,697,592	18.57%
52—Cotton	1,407,851	1,626,827	1,674,816	18.96%
01—Live animals	1,174,050	1,434,447	1,538,747	31.06%
07—Vegetables and related products	1,217,106	1,145,113	1,435,428	17.94%
26—Ores, slag and ash	1,417,057	1,403,983	1,339,933	-5.44%
54—Man-made filaments	1,027,825	1,093,414	1,321,544	28.58%
33—Perfumes and cosmetics	999,154	1,227,361	1,296,853	29.80%

* % change from 1991 to 1993.
Compiled from official statistics of the U.S. Department of Commerce.
Top 40 commodities sorted by general imports, customs value in 1993.

InfoList #8

Top 50 Suppliers of U.S. Imports

General imports, U.S. Customs, millions of U.S. dollars

	1989	1990	1991	1992	1993	% change*
Canada	87,953	91,380	91,064	98,630	110,482	25.61%
Japan	93,553	89,684	91,511	97,414	106,162	13.48%
Mexico	27,162	30,157	31,130	35,211	38,667	42.36%
China	11,990	15,237	18,969	25,728	31,425	162.09%
Germany	24,971	28,162	26,137	28,820	28,103	12.54%
Taiwan	24,313	22,666	23,023	24,596	24,981	2.75%
United Kingdom	18,319	20,188	18,413	20,093	21,303	16.29%
South Korea	19,737	18,485	17,018	16,682	16,986	-13.94%
France	13,014	13,153	13,333	14,797	14,953	14.90%
Italy	11,933	12,751	11,764	12,314	13,056	9.41%
Singapore	9,003	9,800	9,957	11,313	12,744	41.55%
Malaysia	4,744	5,272	6,101	8,294	10,482	120.95%
Hong Kong	9,722	9,622	9,279	9,793	9,418	-3.13%
Thailand	4,379	5,289	6,122	7,529	8,539	95.00%
Saudi Arabia	7,157	10,021	10,900	10,371	7,815	9.19%
Venezuela	6,771	9,480	8,179	8,181	7,782	14.93%
Brazil	8,410	7,898	6,717	7,609	7,763	-7.69%
Switzerland	4,714	5,587	5,576	5,645	5,892	24.99%
Netherlands	4,810	4,952	4,811	5,300	5,406	12.39%
Indonesia	3,529	3,341	3,241	4,529	5,342	51.37%
Nigeria	5,284	5,982	5,168	5,103	5,306	0.42%
Belgium/Luxembourg	4,555	4,585	4,117	4,703	5,151	13.08%
Philippines	3,068	3,384	3,471	4,355	4,864	58.54%
India	3,314	3,197	3,192	3,780	4,536	36.87%
Sweden	4,892	4,937	4,524	4,716	4,447	-9.10%
Israel (incl. Gaza)	3,239	3,313	3,484	3,815	4,424	36.59%
Australia	3,873	4,447	3,988	3,688	3,268	-15.62%
Colombia	2,555	3,168	2,736	2,837	3,010	17.81%
Spain	3,317	3,311	2,848	3,002	2,964	-10.64%
Dominican Republic	1,646	1,752	2,008	2,373	2,667	62.03%
Ireland	1,566	1,755	1,948	2,262	2,480	58.37%
Angola	1,928	1,904	1,775	2,303	2,101	8.23%
Norway	1,991	1,830	1,624	1,969	1,959	-1.61%
South Africa	1,531	1,697	1,728	1,727	1,851	20.90%
Denmark	1,535	1,678	1,661	1,667	1,655	7.25%
Finland	1,370	1,262	1,085	1,185	1,604	17.08%
Algeria	1,829	2,626	2,103	1,586	1,590	-13.07%
Costa Rica	962	1,005	1,154	1,412	1,542	60.29%
Chile	1,292	1,313	1,302	1,388	1,449	12.15%
Austria	1,135	1,318	1,264	1,307	1,395	22.91%
Ecuador	1,474	1,376	1,327	1,344	1,389	-5.77%
Turkey	1,371	1,182	1,006	1,110	1,234	-9.99%
New Zealand	1,209	1,197	1,209	1,218	1,208	-0.08%
Argentina	1,391	1,511	1,287	1,256	1,189	-14.52%
Guatemala	609	794	899	1,081	1,178	93.43%
Sri Lanka	449	538	604	789	1,000	122.72%
Gabon	437	701	712	921	923	111.21%
Honduras	461	491	557	782	914	98.26%
Bangladesh	428	539	524	831	893	108.64%
Pakistan	523	610	662	866	887	69.60%

* % change from 1989 to 1993. Compiled from official statistics of the U.S. Department of Commerce. Sorted by general imports, customs value in 1993.

InfoList #9

Costs Associated with Importing a Product

The total costs of importing a product will generally be far greater than the selling price quoted by the foreign supplier at his or her place of business. When you think of cost you must think in terms of "total landed cost." Total landed cost is the total of *all* the costs of purchasing the product and getting it ready to sell at your place of business in the U.S.

The following list is intended to give you an idea of the types of costs associated with importing a product. Some items may not be relevant to your particular operation.

1. Product design costs
2. Model or sample costs
3. Dies, molds, patterns (note that in certain cases U.S. Customs duty must be paid on these items, even if these dies, etc. were produced and remain in the country of origin)
4. Manufacturing set-up costs (labor and materials)
5. Cost of goods manufactured (labor, materials, overhead, profit)
6. Buyer's agent fees
7. Facilitation payments
8. Export documentation fees
9. Export taxes or fees
10. Labeling of merchandise (for U.S. Customs)
11. Product packaging for retail or wholesale sale in the U.S.
12. Packing/crating for international shipment
13. Transportation to dock
14. Short-term warehousing at the dock
15. Ocean, rail, trucking, or air freight charges
16. Insurance
17. U.S. import duty
18. Customs broker fees
19. Import documentation fees
20. Costs associated with satisfying any additional U.S. regulatory agency requirements
21. International payment fees (letter of credit, etc.)
22. Foreign exchange fees
23. Transport to warehouse
24. Domestic short-term warehousing
25. Inspection fees
26. Transfer from port to your warehouse
27. Overseas travel and entertainment
28. Other overhead costs (attorney, interpreters, translators, international telephone, telex, fax, delivery services, etc.)

InfoList #10

Starting an Import Business with Little Capital

Almost any business can be started with a small amount of initial capitalization. However, importing presents problems for small-time operators because of the added costs of travel and transportation as well as the problems associated with governmental regulation of certain products. Nevertheless, many established importers started as small-time operators. Here are a number of tips for those who seek to start an import operation with restricted working capital:

1. **Start close to home**
   Start your business by importing goods from Mexico, Canada, Central America, or from anywhere you can get to inexpensively. In general, the closer the supplier, the more control you can exercise and the less expensive it will be to do business.
2. **Pre-sell merchandise**
   If you know what you're after, or know how to find what others want to buy, you might be able to pre-sell the merchandise. Consider whether it is more advantageous to quote a fixed price or a percentage commission on top of the total landed cost.
3. **Get prepayment for goods**
   If you are paid for the merchandise before you leave on your buying trip, you effectively increase your working capital. You may not even have to use your own money for anything beyond travel expenses.
4. **Import small amounts**
   You can gain valuable experience while limiting your risks by importing small amounts of easy-to-import products. Concentrate on those products which are least regulated by U.S. government agencies.
5. **Import products for an established market**
   It is best to start importing products for which you have an established market. For example, if you have a retail store, import goods which would sell there.
6. **Act as a buyer's agent**
   Many importers get their start by acting as an agent for a more established company. Many companies prefer to have someone act as their agent to avoid the costs of sending their own people overseas. You will be a good candidate for this if you have special qualifications, such as knowledge of the merchandise and/or knowledge of the country.
7. **Import as you travel on other business**
   Get your start by importing small quantities while overseas on vacation or on other business.
8. **Don't quit your "day job"**
   Start importing as a sideline while keeping your regular job to fund the import business.
9. **Use flight coupons to pay for travel**
   Many people who have jobs that require travel save their bonus flight coupons to pay for travel to the country of origin of the products they want to import.

InfoList #11

Product Requirements

The business of importing demands a stronger knowledge of the product than do most domestic merchandising businesses. The greater your overall knowledge of the product (and market), the greater will be your chances of success. Prior experience in the design, manufacturing, or marketing of the product is the ideal foundation for success in an import business. You need a high degree of knowledge at every stage of the process:

1. **Point of purchase**
   In order to get what you really want from your supplier, you must be clear about your product requirements and be able to communicate them. Otherwise you may find yourself getting what you ask for, which is not really what you want.
2. **Export requirements**
   You will need to know enough about your product to satisfy all applicable country-of-origin export requirements that may exist.
3. **Transport requirements**
   Many products need special handling in transport. You should know these requirements in order to effectively specify them to the shipper. In some cases, knowledge of the most cost-effective transport method for your merchandise makes the difference between profit and loss.
4. **U.S. Customs and other agency requirements**
   U.S. Customs and other agency requirements regarding entry, classification, valuation, marking and labeling, and requirements of other agencies can result in significant problems if you do not know exactly how they affect your product.
5. **Sales requirements**
   Reduced to its simplest terms, importing is basically the transfer of goods from one country's economy to that of another country. You will need to know the market for your product domestically. To successfully establish a marketing program, you will need to know your merchandise well.
6. **Seasonality of the product**
   Christmas products have to arrive in time for the complete holiday selling season. Some products sell in cold months, others only in warm months. You need to know both the seasonal aspect of your products and the lead time it takes to get them from the country of origin to your market on time.

InfoList #12

Know Your Product

The following list of questions is designed to get both prospective and established importers to think clearly about what they might need to learn about the products they seek to import. Some items on this list may not relate directly to your product. Often, the overall knowledge a person possesses about a product is what makes him or her successful.

General Information

1. What names does the product goes by, including its generic and trade names in the language of the exporting country?
2. What is the product's history of development?
3. What aspects of culture and/or folklore are associated with the product?
4. What nationalities and social/economic classes traditionally make, broker, or sell the product?

Specifications

5. What are the units of measure in which the product is bought and sold, including the foreign names of those units? Be aware that many products sold in the U.S. must adhere to specific standards of weight, fill, and size for that product.
6. What product models or variations are available? The product may have numerous models or variations for different markets. It may be that certain models of the product which are excellent sellers in the exporting country would be terrible sellers in the U.S. in general, or in specific regions of the U.S.
7. What design types are produced regionally?
8. What are the size variations? What are the sizes in which the product is normally available/manufactured? For example, an importer of garments or footwear must take into consideration that different nationalities have different body proportions. Be sure that you import your product in a size that is appropriate for the U.S. market. Garments and footwear are only obvious examples of size considerations. Other products may need to be specially sized for your market in the U.S.
9. What are the electrical or other technological requirements for U.S. usage? Certain products may be manufactured to operate only on 220v current in the country of origin and will need to be modified to operate on 110v in the United States.

Source

10. What is the product's traditional country of origin?
11. What are the emerging countries of origin for the product?
12. What are the product centers for the product or commodity within the country of origin?

Production

13. What are the product's component materials?
14. What countries export these component materials?
15. How are the component materials obtained by the local manufacturers?
16. What is the cost structure of the product's component materials?
17. What are the incremental mark-ups on the component materials from the original source to the manufacturer by percentage and actual cost?
18. What are the conditions of the manufacture of the product in the exporting country? Are they made in modern factories, small workshops, or by cottage or craft industry?
19. What types of individuals work in these factories and workshops? Are they unskilled, semi-skilled, or highly skilled workers, and how easily can the necessary skills be acquired?
20. What are workers' labor rates? Are they paid hourly, daily, monthly, or by the piece? What will these rates buy in essential commodities in the country of origin?
21. Does manufacture involve any unusual techniques?
22. How does workmanship vary from country to country, locale to locale, and factory to factory? "Quality" is a subjective valuation and varies from individual to individual and from culture to culture. The seller's idea of quality may not be yours. Be sure to buy the quality your market demands.
23. What is the capitalization required to establish a manufacturing facility for that product in the country of origin versus the United States?

Regulation of Product

24. What, if any, exporting country regulations and documentation affect the exportability of your product?
25. What transport regulations affect the product? Air or sea transport of certain hazardous products may be regulated or prohibited.
26. What special requirements of U.S. Customs and other U.S. governmental regulating agencies affect the importation, classification, valuation, or duty status of the product?
27. Are there any imminent export or import restrictions affecting the product?

Other

28. Are any pending technological changes expected to affect the product?

InfoList #13

Know Your Market

Knowledge of the merchandise is important, but by no means is it sufficient to establish a successful import operation. In order to succeed you must also know the buying and the selling market for your products.

1. Buying and Selling Experience

Nothing takes the place of active buying and selling experience. The most successful importers are constantly in touch with the market for their products and commodities. For example, department store buyers are required to spend a minimum amount of time working "the floor" as salespeople to get a feel for what people are buying and what they are asking for.

Learning the hard way. A small group of newly certified graduate gemologists from the Gemological Institute of America (GIA), one of the most prestigious gemological schools in the world, found out the hard way. Six months of intensive study had made these individuals quite knowledgeable about colored gem stones. They raised more than $30,000 (1975 dollars) from relatives and friends to finance a gem-purchasing trip to South America. After purchasing and importing high quality gemstones to the U.S. they discovered that they had paid altogether too much for gemstones for which they had no established market. Their error was not in knowledge of their product, but rather in knowledge of the price structure and market for that product. They were forced to liquidate their stock at a loss and start over.

2. Volatility of the Market

Changes in the market for goods can easily spell disaster to established ventures as well as to new ones. Many variables impact the market for merchandise and even experts can be caught off guard. Your job as an importer and a business person is to know as much about your market as possible. Be in tune with its variations: know when, how and why it changes.

In a fast-paced world, if you are only aware of the fluctuations in your regional market, you may be caught off guard by events, competition, or changes in foreign markets. For example, in an international situation where the price of a commodity is going up, the importer who buys last is at a disadvantage; whereas when the price is decreasing, the importer who buys last gains an edge.

3. Your Market's Quality Requirements

The buyer defines quality. Most markets for merchandise have exceedingly narrow ranges of acceptable quality.

Each market has its own minimum standards of acceptability and maximum price, no matter what the quality.

Before purchasing an item, you should know the tolerance for quality in your own market. Incremental quality increases of 10% can end up costing your customers 50% or more. Many consumers may not be able to discern the higher quality for which they are asked to pay substantially more. Your job is to know and assess the quality range your customers can discern, can afford, and will want.

Once you have established the quality and price range your market requires, make sure your suppliers understand that they have to come through with what you need. It is not enough to indicate that you want "quality." You must define quality, which is a very subjective matter. In actuality, you do not require an item of quality, you require an item that is produced according to your set of specifications. To get this you need to define and communicate your standards of quality in a technical way that does not leave room for interpretation.

4. Seasonality of Merchandise

Did you hear the one about the importer of Christmas ornaments whose merchandise arrived on December 26th? It isn't funny. As importer you must get your merchandise to market at the appropriate time to sell.

A great deal of merchandise such as wearing apparel, Christmas goods, and certain sporting goods are sold seasonally. Since orders of imported goods often require substantially more lead time than domestic orders, you need to know the seasonality of your merchandise. This becomes even more important if you supply component products to manufacturers of seasonal merchandise.

If you know when your clients need an item, you should schedule backwards from that date. For example, if you have an item to sell retail at Christmas, the retailer should have it in stock by the mid-November, Thanksgiving at the very latest.

The following movements of merchandise may each take from several days to several weeks to accomplish. You will have to allow for each in your planning.

- Retailer's warehouse to retail store shelves
- Importer's warehouse to retailer's warehouse
- Clearance through U.S. Customs
- Transport from overseas port to U.S. port of entry
- Transport from point of manufacture in exporting country to port of export
- Manufacturing time
- Preliminary research, planning, and design

The total process could take from several weeks to more than a year!

5. Conducting Market Research

You must constantly conduct some form of market research. It can range from highly structured research conducted by an outside consulting firm to a "seat-of-the-pants" approach, with you asking the right people the right questions.

Market research, whether called that, market assessment on a seasonal- or new-product basis, or something else is an integral part of good business planning. It should be conducted by every company on an ongoing basis. It is your means of setting goals for your business.

The importance of research cannot be overemphasized for any business, but it is especially crucial for importers. The greater the distance between product source and market, the greater the time and costs of getting it to the ultimate consumer. Domestic suppliers may be in a better position than importers to serve their customers on a timely basis. Therefore, importers need to be in tune with market trends, and stay ahead of the market.

Market research is a huge subject and beyond the scope of this publication. A number of excellent books on the subject are available in business libraries and bookstores. However, the best way to start a market research program is to establish a format for your research which takes into account the variables affecting your product, market and business.

6. Who is Your Market?

What type of individual and what type of business constitutes the natural target audience for the product you seek to import and sell?

1. Is the individual of a particular age, social, or economic group?
2. Is the individual more interested in fashion or more interested in quality and durability?
3. Is the individual interested in the snob appeal of your item?
4. Is the person interested in a bargain?
5. Is the person interested in the "story" that goes along with the item?
6. Is the person already buying the product or do you have to educate them to buy either a new product or your product specifically?
7. What needs are you filling with the product?

7. Where is Your Market?

Define the geographic location of your potential market. This can mean a neighborhood, a city, a metropolitan area, a country, a state, a region, or an entire country. A clear definition of your market area will keep your marketing efforts focused.

1. Who needs your product and why?
2. What makes your product different and desirable?
3. Where do you find the people who need your product?
4. What other criteria product lead to acceptance or rejection?
5. List prospective market areas which could support a sales program for your product.
6. Test the various prospective markets to determine where your marketing efforts will be most productive.

You may find it prohibitively expensive to reach a large market area in the beginning. The cost of making each sale often increases dramatically in proportion to the distance of the sale from your base of operation. You may find it more appropriate to deal in a small, local geographic area and achieve greater coverage. Alternatively, you may benefit from wider distribution and the economics of scale that result. Be aware of the point of diminishing return when expanding.

Also remember that certain parts of the country are more advanced stylistically than others.

8. Contact Potential Buyers/Customers

If you are established in a business, the best place to start your research is with your clients. You should be enough in tune with them to know their current product requirements as well as their future needs, and have enough rapport to be able to find out what you don't already know. If you know your market and your clients or customers well enough, you will always be in a position to offer them what they need rather than what you've got. It is always easier to supply demand than to create it.

If you are not yet in business, or want to change the scope of an established business, your question should be, "How do I know which import items will sell?" To find out, you need to know how to ask questions and listen to the responses.

You need to believe in your product. Nevertheless it is easier to import, or to bring to market, goods that the customers want to buy. If the goods you like are not what other people want, keep looking until you find a large enough market for the merchandise you prefer to deal in. Ultimately, however, you should be in business to serve your clients.

Seek out likely customers, develop good rapport, and ask them:

1. What do you need?
2. What are your customers asking for?
3. What is selling well?
4. What is hard or difficult to find?
5. What is costing you more than it really should?
6. What would you place an order for right now?
7. How much would you pay?
8. Would you pay C.O.D.?
9. What terms would you require?
10. Would you prepay for those goods?
11. I'm going to XYZ countries. What goods from those countries are in demand?
12. What stores and businesses are interested in goods from those countries?

Note: Don't be fooled by what is on display in either wholesale or retail businesses. Sometimes, what is on display is what's left because it didn't sell!

InfoList #14

Know Your Competition

Here are a number of questions you or your company might ask concerning your competition.

1. What products are competitive with ours?
2. Who and where are our competitors?
3. How are their products marketed?
4. How and why does their marketing work or fail to work?
5. What are the weak points in their marketing organization?
6. What are their short- and long-range plans?
7. What business problems are they facing?
8. Do they have any unusual advantages?
9. Are they efficient?
10. What is the extent and quality of their research and development effort?
11. What new products are they developing?
12. Who and where are their suppliers?
13. What are they paying for merchandise?
14. What supply problems do they have?
15. If they have labor problems, why?
16. What is the manufacturing cost of their goods?
17. How do our products compare with theirs?
18. How many middlemen handle their product before it reaches the consumer?
19. What are their sales terms, credit requirements, and commissions? What compensation terms are extended to distributors, to sales people, and to retailers of their goods?
20. How are their goods advertised?
    a. Promotion techniques?
    b. Media?
    c. Ad expenditures?

21\. How does the marketplace view our products compared to theirs?

21\. How good is their after-sales service?

23\. How does their pricing compare to ours?

24\. How are the above factors likely to change?

25\. How much does the competition know about you?

InfoList #15

Buying from the Source

As an importer you need to purchase as close to the product source as possible. You also need to bring the goods as close to the ultimate consumer as is economically feasible. The more you know about the market and price structure for your product, the better able you will be to insert yourself into the most profitable position in the market chain.

1. Middlemen

All economies worldwide rely on a series of middlemen to bring goods to market. Each middleman moves the merchandise one step further toward the ultimate consumer, adding both value and cost.

2. Flow Chart from Source to Ultimate Consumer

As an exercise, create a flow chart of the movement of your product from the source of the raw materials and component parts, through its processing and/or manufacture as a the final product, to its sale to the ultimate consumer.

In your analysis, describe the service or function each middleman provides, what makes this stop a necessary part of the structure, location where it occurs, how much the service costs, the provider's margin of profit, and your assessment of the strengths and weaknesses at every stage within the market.

Be aware that the price for which an item is on display in either a wholesale or retail situation may be either an inflated or deflated price. An item offered for sale at retail for $45 may have cost as little as $5 or as much as $40. Be careful when making assumptions about costs.

3. Where Are You Located in the Flow?

- What is your current position in the flow?
- What place in the market chain has the greatest strategic advantage?
- What are the most profitable positions to be in?
- Where would you like to be?

You may be in a position to cut out one of the intermediate suppliers and get closer to the source, or to cut out one of the middlemen at the other end and get closer to the ultimate consumer. Be careful: if it is easy to bump someone else out of the market flow, it may be equally easy for someone to bump you out next time. In any case, it may be unwarranted, or unprofitable to attempt to get closer to the source or to do the retail or wholesale distribution yourself. It just may be more profitable to leave that job to others.

InfoList #16

Finding Sources

One of the most treasured and protected secrets of any import operation is its list of suppliers. Importers will go to almost any length to maintain the confidentiality of their sources of supply of vital materials or products. Many importers see that the greater the shroud of mystery surrounding the business, and the more difficult it appears to those on the outside, the better. It is in the interests of these importers to not to cooperate with you, their potential competitor. The higher the entry barriers, the more secure their position.

There are many ways to find sources of supply. These depend upon product, country of origin, and the ability of the importer to research, plan ahead, and be patient.

You can either find overseas sources of supply while at home, or while on an overseas trip. Research done in the United States is the most cost-effective. Although some suppliers will be difficult to locate from the U.S., there will always be some preliminary research that is better done at home. For example, if you seek items available only from nomadic merchants in India whose shops are tents, you will not be able to locate them from the U.S. But you can ascertain the probable locations in India where such items are traditionally found before leaving the U.S.

Pre-planning allows you to set up a series of appointments with prospective suppliers before leaving the U.S. If these sources of supply turn out to be unacceptable, you will have at least gained some experience and a basis for comparison.

In all but the most primitive countries, research time costs three to 10 times as much as time spent conducting research from the U.S. Do your homework and save time and money.

InfoList #17

26 Sources of Information

1. Foreign government consulates in the U.S.
2. Commercial attachés of foreign governments in the U.S.
3. Foreign government embassies in the U.S.
4. Foreign chambers of commerce in the U.S. and in the exporting country
5. Domestic U.S. banks with international operations
6. Branches of overseas banks in the U.S.
7. Banks in the exporting country
8. Foreign trade development organizations with offices in the U.S. and in the foreign country
9. United Nations agencies
10. U.S.-based and foreign-based offices of export trade ministries of the country of origin
11. U.S. Department of Commerce libraries in major U.S. cities
12. U.S. Department of Commerce country desks, Washington, DC.
13. Other importers
14. U.S. exporters with experience and connections in the exporting country
15. Domestic U.S.- and foreign-trade publications
16. National airlines of the country of origin
17. Shipping companies
18. Customs brokers
19. Freight forwarders
20. Export trade associations of the exporting country
21. Yellow Pages in the country-of-origin
22. Travel agents
23. Church groups and missions
24. Travel guides
25. Ads placed in overseas publications
26. Foreign students in the U.S.

InfoList #18

How to Use Sources

1. Consulates/Commercial Attachés/ Embassies

The most efficient way to start a search for suppliers is to write a letter of request to the nearest consulate, embassy, or commercial attaché of the exporting country of the products you seek. Check your local telephone directory or call directory assistance to find out if there is a listing for a consulate of the country in which you are interested in your area. If not, call the embassy of the country in Washington, DC for a referral to the consulate serving your area.

Unless you are proposing a large and significant transaction, we recommend that you write a letter to the local consulate requesting information before writing to the commercial attaché at the embassy in Washington. Such letters are usually forwarded to the local consulate anyway.

Consular offices are usually established to promote the commercial interests of and protect the rights of their citizens in the host country. They also issue travel and business visas to citizens of the host country.

Consular officers are generally eager to assist with requests for sources of supply in their country. It is their job to promote home-country exports. Consular offices often have export directories for the home country that can refer you to sources. Some have the information on computer. Note that developing nations will not have the information as readily accessible, and often respond to such requests only if they have time.

It is possible to call these consular offices directly, but we recommend that you first write a formal letter of request for information. The written request is a clear communication, and it creates a positive record of the request. Make an initial call to obtain the name of the commercial officer or attaché so that your letter is properly addressed.

Although most industrialized countries have consular and trade offices throughout the U.S., some foreign countries do not. In that case write directly to their embassy in Washington, DC, addressing the inquiry to the commercial attaché.

Make a call to the consulate after you think your letter has arrived, to verify its arrival and to indicate your sincere interest in doing business. Be sure to note the name of the individual you speak to.

In all likelihood the consulate will send you a response letter within several weeks, with a list of names and addresses of businesses who are suppliers of items similar to the ones you requested. You should send letters immediately to each lead, giving more detailed information concerning the products you seek. Always mention the U.S.-based consulate and individual who referred the supplier to you. And while it can be safely assumed that every businessperson wants to respond quickly to a request for information on their products, these suppliers will take such a request even more seriously when names with titles (commercial attaché, etc.) are mentioned.

2. Chambers of Commerce

The various foreign chambers of commerce in the United States are excellent sources of information on overseas suppliers. Names and addresses of U.S.-based country-of-origin chambers of commerce for countries that export to the U.S. can be found by calling directory assistance in Washington, DC, New York, San Francisco and other major U.S. cities.

Chambers of commerce are essentially special-interest associations established to further the interests of their members. They assist U.S. importers in finding suppliers that among the members of their chamber. Some have been known to forward requests to other chambers and associations. In rare instances, they may refer you to suppliers who are not members. However, remember that they were not established with that purpose in mind.

The general exception to this rule is the *national* chamber of commerce of a country. Most chambers of commerce are private organizations, but many countries have national chambers which are actually government or quasi-governmental agencies. In some countries, all businesses must register with their national chamber of commerce as a prerequisite for being in business. This is a form of government control on their licensing and activities.

Chambers of commerce can be categorized in three groups. The first is the national or government chamber of commerce, which is an agency of the government. For example, in Great Britain it is the British Overseas Trade Board. An example of the second type of chamber of commerce is the British American Chamber of Commerce. This association is designed to promote British companies, i.e. exports from Britain to the United States. The American British Chamber of Commerce is an example of the third type. It is designed to promote U.S. companies, i.e. exports from the U.S. to the U.K.

Although each of these groups was established with different and often contradictory purposes and goals, useful commercial information can be obtained from all three types. All chambers of commerce have membership directories. Usually they have international divisions with specialized listings of exporters and importers. Their primary purpose will be to refer you to companies that are members of their organization. If they have a newsletter, they may be willing to publish your request in an import/export opportunities section.

Members of chambers of commerce are generally more established businesses. For certain products the more established company may not be your best opportunity. Old and established may mean that their products and styles are more rigid and/or dated, and may indicate a larger internal bureaucracy with more paperwork and more overhead. Nevertheless, they can also represent stability, something the importer looks for in an overseas source of supply.

3. Governmental Export Trade Ministries

These are the official governmental trade promotion agencies of countries. They often work closely with consulates in the host country. Some are extremely well organized, helpful, and efficient, and others are hopelessly uncoordinated and unresponsive. The purpose of these organizations is to promote their country's mercantile trade. The U.S. equivalent is the U.S. Department of Commerce. These agencies have export trade directories and sometimes computer or other data banks of information on products and suppliers. They often have bilingual staff to assist overseas businesspeople with requests. English is the most common second language for business. These agencies often have trade publications on how to do business in their country. Many are available free, while others are sold at a nominal cost. The names and addresses of many of these agencies are available from the U.S.-based consulates.

4. Product-Specific Export Associations

An excellent source of names and addresses of potential suppliers is the product-specific export trade association for your desired product in the exporting country. You will find that virtually every product group has its own trade association ready to do what it can to assist those who wish to do business with their members.

Start your search for these associations by contacting the consulate or embassy of the exporting country for the name and address of the associations which relate to your products.

5. Banks

International bankers are perhaps the best internationally connected individuals in the commercial realm. Since the vast majority of international trade goes through banks, bankers are in a good position to know what is going on. Many banks have special economic information services which can potentially assist the importer in finding suppliers. If unable to help in finding suppliers, they may be able to help by running credit checks on potential suppliers whose names are obtained from other sources.

When dealing with a bank, be sure to speak with someone who has international experience. Your personal/corporate bankers can often give an introduction to someone in the international department. It is a wise person indeed who cultivates banking relationships.

One sure way to get assistance here in the United States is to deal directly with a U.S. branch of a major overseas bank headquartered in the country of origin of the products you seek to import. For instance, when doing business in Switzerland, deal with the Swiss Bank Corporation; when doing business in Japan, deal with the Sumitomo Bank. These banks have far greater expertise, knowledge, and sources for their home country than would a U.S. bank with a branch in that country.

6. National Airline Companies

Most national airline companies of potential source countries, such as Japan Air Lines, Air France, Varig (Brazil), or Aerolineas Argentinas, have promotional departments that produce brochures and books extolling the virtues of visiting and doing business in their country. Some of these publications are excellent resources on the cultural aspects of doing business in the country and often contain valuable addresses.

Most airlines also conduct economic research for purposes of determining their market for freight services and might be willing to make some of this information available. While they may not give be able to give you actual names of sources of supply, they may tell you where to find the information. Start with a telephone call to the customer service or public relations department of the airline's local business office.

Another source of information within a given airline is the cargo or freight services headquarters. Since the air cargo section of the airline has a vested interest in boosting import/export trade, they might be willing to assist you in finding sources of supply.

7. Export Trade Directories

Export trade directories for specific countries are excellent sources of supplier information. These reference books are often 800 to 1200 pages in length, often with small print and advertising. They are usually organized so that you can obtain supplier information by company name alphabetically, by product or commodity, and by geographic location within the country of origin.

Export directories are found in the reference sections of larger libraries, especially business libraries or business sections of larger public libraries. Other sources for these directories are embassies and consulates of the country, foreign chambers of commerce and trade missions in the U.S., and U.S. Department of Commerce libraries in major U.S. cities.

8. Yellow Pages in the Exporting Country

One of the most overlooked sources of product information is the yellow pages. Yes, they do have yellow pages in Hong Kong, Bangkok, Paris, Rome, and just about everywhere else. To obtain a copy of the yellow pages directory of a major foreign city, first try contacting the consulate, or chamber of commerce of that country. The next line of inquiry involves calling your local Bell Telephone system office here in the U.S. and asking where you might find the specific directory.

If you plan to do business over a period of time in a city overseas, obtain a directory during your visit there. Almost every hotel will have a copy, and most hotel managers will help you obtain one.

While a great majority of business introductions are prearranged, once you are in the exporting country, don't hesitate to call a potential supplier directly. Identify yourself, your company, and your purpose. Once you are there, many suppliers may even arrange your transportation to their production facilities and showrooms.

9. Trade Journals

Most countries have trade journals for specific commodity groups. These may be independently published or be ancillary to a trade association. If you intend to concentrate on a particular commodity group, you should identify the journals that pertain to those commodities and obtain copies. Many will contain supplier advertisements that may be of help to you. You may also wish to place an advertisement yourself. A number of these journals have special sections listing import/export trade opportunities, often as a free service. Some of these publications come in the form of a book of products and producers consisting of paid advertisements. Product specific trade journals are also an excellent source for entrepreneurial importers looking for new ideas.

Contact the commercial section of the country's consulate, chamber of commerce, or export trade associations for information on such resources.

10. Business Libraries

Most major cities in the United States have public, university business, and commercial libraries. A number of these purchase export directories and subscribe to various trade publications of other countries. Business libraries are a much underutilized source of information in the U.S. Access to university libraries may be restricted, so it is always best to call in advance.

11. International Trade Shows, Fairs, and Exhibitions

Every major country in the world has trade fairs and exhibitions of its products. One type is the "national exposition" of general merchandise produced in that country. Another is the commodity specific trade show exhibiting one type of merchandise, such as jewelry, computers, or footwear.

Consulates and commercial attachés will almost always have trade fair and exhibition dates and information for their country. These events are excellent opportunities to view competitive merchandise from a large number of suppliers.

12. Religious Organizations in Emerging Countries

In a number of developing countries, religious organizations play a key role in the development of local businesses, such as handicraft cooperatives. These groups provide assistance to local people by establishing the organizational structure for cottage industries. Although they may be difficult to contact, and may require sleuthing even in the country of origin, these cooperatives sometimes produce very marketable merchandise, especially for the gift trade. Try contacting consulates, international religious organizations, such as the World Council of Churches, relief organizations, and the Peace Corps for leads.

InfoList #19
Letters of Request

Businesspeople in the U.S. (receptive to informality and immediacy) are accustomed to conducting business by telephone. This is less the common or even acceptable in international trade for a number of reasons. These include the high cost of international calls, language difficulties, and a desire for more formality. The most accepted form of business contact in foreign countries is through a formal letter of request via the post, fax, telex, or cable.

You will need at least two types of letters of request in seeking suppliers (both on your company letterhead). To obtain leads about potential suppliers, write a general letter of request for suppliers' names, sending one to each relevant consulate, chamber of commerce, and other third-party group whose purpose is to assist U.S. importers. Responses to these letters should give you a good beginning list of leads. Once you have the leads, you should write a formal business letter of request, with more details, to each supplier.

Your general letter of request should contain the following elements:

1. The nature of your business.
2. A statement to the effect that you are seeking suppliers of a particular type of merchandise. Be sure to describe the product in enough detail so that they can steer you in the right direction. However, avoid being overly technical. If the product you seek is unusual, you might include a photo or a sketch.
3. An estimate of the number of units per month or per year you are interested in purchasing.
4. The date you hope to have shipments begin. Including a date can motivate your source to expedite a response to your request.
5. A request for the names, complete addresses, and, if possible, telephone numbers of potential suppliers of the product in that country.
6. A request for the names of regions and geographic areas which produce the products you desire. Because many industries are grouped geographically, knowing the region may be half the battle.
7. The names and addresses of relevant product-specific export trade associations.
8. A request for printed information, brochures, pamphlets, etc. concerning the products in question, or on doing business in their country.
9. Thanks in advance for all the help they are sure to give you.
10. A bank reference; for example: Banker: Bank of America, 315 Montgomery Street, San Francisco, CA.

Letters of request made directly to potential suppliers should contain more detailed information and specifications of the product(s) you seek. Your ability to describe your product in technical terms will determine the adequacy of the supplier's response. Companies unable to supply your product may refer you to other possible suppliers.

InfoList #20
Sample Letter of Request for Sources

AB Leather Goods Company
123 Grant Avenue
San Francisco, California 94XXX
USA

Consulate General, Republic of Colombia
870 Market Street
San Francisco, California 94102

Dear Sirs:

We are wholesalers of fine leather goods. We have been in business for eight years and are interested in expanding our product line of imported wallets for men and women.

Would you please help us by providing the names and addresses of any trade organizations in Colombia that represent producers of leather goods, and any printed materials you have about doing business in Colombia, and about the Colombian leather industry in particular? Also, are there any specific geographic areas where leather goods are manufactured in Colombia?

We expect to be purchasing 1,000 wallets per month within six months. If you know of any producers in Colombia who have an existing product line, or who would be able to manufacture to our specification, please include their names, full addresses, and phone and fax numbers.

We look forward to a mutually beneficial business relationship with producers in Colombia. Thank you in advance for your gracious help in assisting us to locate suppliers.

Sincerely yours,

Bank reference: Bank of America, 315 Montgomery Street, San Francisco, California

InfoList #21

Sample Letter of Request to Potential Suppliers

AB Leather Goods Company
123 Grant Avenue
San Francisco, California 94XXX
USA

Manufacturas en Cuero de Medellin
Calle XX, No. XX-XX
Medellin, Colombia

Dear Sirs:

Your company name has been given to us by the Consulate General of Colombia in San Francisco, California, USA.

We are wholesalers of fine leather goods. We have been in business for eight years and are interested in expanding our product line of imported wallets for men and women.

We are looking for a producer of leather goods in Colombia that can manufacture a product line of fine wallets in calf skin on a contract basis to our exacting specifications.

We expect to purchase 1,000 wallets per month within five months. If your company is interested in supplying us, please forward a letter in response including any brochures or photographs of your existing product line and perhaps a sample of a small leather accessory in calf skin.

Our president, Mr. Edward Baker, will be in Colombia the first two weeks of March to interview potential suppliers. It would be helpful for us to have a response by the third week of February.

We thank you in advance for your assistance.

Sincerely yours,

Banker reference: Bank of America, 315 Montgomery Street, San Francisco, California

InfoList #22

10 Tips About Suppliers

1. Go to the Ultimate Source

As a buyer, one of your major goals is to purchase goods for the least cost possible. Generally, this means that you will want to purchase from the original producer of the product. A company that wants to supply your needs may seek a secondary supplier and become a middleman in the transaction. There are advantages and disadvantages to this. The advantage is that you get your product, sometimes for less trouble than if you went to the original source. The disadvantages include increased cost, longer lead time, and lessened control.

2. Export Trading Companies

The import/export regulations of some countries are so stringent that only specialized import/export trading houses are knowledgeable and connected enough to handle such transactions. For example, in Japan large conglomerate trading houses have a virtual monopoly on trade. Centrally planned socialist/communist countries, such as the People's Republic of China (PRC), set up a limited number of specialized corporations to serve as the sole importers and exporters. (In the case of the PRC more autonomy has been given to smaller trading houses and some individual firms during recent years.)

These trading houses often provide a worthwhile service, especially in countries whose import/export documentation and licensing is difficult. Also, they act as a go-between for smaller producers who may have difficulty communicating in English, or who may not have fax or telex equipment for easy international communication. Some of these organizations go so far as to finance and guarantee the export transaction.

3. Developing a Supplier Relationship

Ongoing overseas business relationships require the same considerations that guide domestic relationships. Contrary to popular belief, all overseas suppliers are not ready to drop what they are doing just to get an importer's product ready by the next morning. The dollar is no longer that almighty.

If you seek product quality and supplier reliability, pay particular attention to the manner in which you cultivate your business relationships. Every country has its own standards of business communication. To be effective you will need to learn them and be willing to go the extra mile to do so.

4. Established versus New Businesses

Be aware that there may be trade-offs between doing business with established businesses and new businesses. Established businesses may offer the best service, but may cost more. The younger, smaller companies often have less overhead and are able to supply a product for very competitive prices. However, they may be less able to offer you the type of service you need. A small company may be adequate if you do not require a high degree of after-sale service, or if you are personally making the overseas buying trips and making all arrangements yourself.

5. Keep in Touch

Call, write, visit, and/or fax your suppliers on a regular basis. Out of sight should not translate to out of mind. Keeping your suppliers advised of your business requirements on a regular basis will help them to serve you better.

6. Make It Easy for Your Supplier to Succeed

Become an expert at developing product specifications that your supplier can understand, and cannot help but succeed in fulfilling. Don't use U.S. slang—it does not translate.

7. Create the Desired Impression

1. Dress according to the requirements of your business and purpose.
2. Always be punctual, even if others are not.
3. Learn at least 10 phrases in the local language, especially the customary greetings.
4. Communicate your knowledge and appreciation of their country and customs.
5. Accommodate the values of your suppliers without disregarding your own.
6. Always follow through on your agreements.

8. Useful Attitudes toward Negotiations

1. Don't approach a seller with overt suspicion.
2. The seller needs to make a profit to survive to serve you the next time.
3. Learn the local business customs beforehand. Example: In much of North Africa, it is expected that you shout during negotiations, whereas in Thailand shouting is seen as a sign of weakness. Also, raising your hands above your head is considered an act of aggression in Thailand. Buy a copies of Do's and Taboos Around the World and Gestures, both by Roger E. Axtell, John Wiley & Sons publisher.
4. Don't be in too much of a rush. Business is usually conducted at a slower pace overseas.
5. Remember that the best route to a given end result may not be the shortest or most direct.
6. Allow yourself the opportunity to work within the framework of another person's or country's business style.
7. Remember that you are on their turf now and have to play by their rules.

9. Understand the Seller's Attitudes and Position

1. How well established is the seller in the local marketplace?
2. Is the seller the new business with the right single product at the right time, or the established supplier with many products and services to offer?
3. What are the seller's attitudes toward foreigners (that means YOU!)?
4. Is the seller in need of cash?
5. Does the timing of the sale affect the seller? (Prices are often cheaper when buying from traditional Chinese as the Chinese New Year approaches. Reason? It is good luck to have all your bills paid going into the new year!)
6. Does the seller start with a high price or does he have a best-offer-take-it-or-leave-it attitude?
7. Is entertainment part of the negotiation package?

10. Questions to Ask Before Committing to a Supplier

1. Is this a one-shot deal?
2. Is this going to be part of an ongoing relationship?
3. Is this supplier concerned about my well being or just about getting the most out of this transaction?
4. Am I getting the best possible price?
5. What do I have to do to get better terms?
6. Is the supplier saying "Yes" to everything just to please me, or is he or she going to follow through?
7. Am I really getting the goods I require?
8. Am I getting the quality my customers require?
9. If this transaction were to go bad, how would it go bad?
10. Have I asked for an impossible delivery date which the supplier cannot possibly adhere to?
11. Is there any leeway I can give the supplier either now or later to make it easier for him or her to follow through?
12. Am I getting all the documentation I need for export formalities, and for U.S. import formalities?

InfoList #23

Supplier Checklist

Use this checklist to determine if you are working with the right supplier. If you answer "No" to very many of the questions below, it would be wise to continue your search for another supplier.

	Yes	No
1. Has this supplier been in business long enough to know the business and be stable?	❑	❑
2. Have I received references concerning reliability and ethics?	❑	❑
3. Have I checked the references and found them to be good?	❑	❑
4. Does this person/company understand what I need?	❑	❑
5. Does the supplier understand my concept of quality?	❑	❑
6. Has the supplier been accommodating to our needs, and realistic in his or her promises?	❑	❑
7. Do I trust this person to follow through on the transaction as we have discussed it, and as it is in the contract?	❑	❑
8. Will the supplier make enough of a profit to service the account properly and want to do business with us in the future?	❑	❑
9. Is the supplier's plant properly equipped for production of the merchandise we are ordering?	❑	❑
10. Will this supplier be able to handle increases in production if the demand for the product increases?	❑	❑
11. Will this supplier let me know if there is a problem, or will he or she try and gloss over it until it becomes a disaster for me?	❑	❑
12. Is there someone at this place of business who is capable of properly handling the export and U.S. import documentation required?	❑	❑
13. Will this supplier be willing to work toward a solution when difficulties arise?	❑	❑
14. Am I dealing with this supplier because he or she is the right one for me, or because I cannot find any other?	❑	❑
15. Do I have a gut feeling that this is the right supplier for me?	❑	❑

InfoList #24

10 Tips for Negotiating

1. Don't let yourself get tied to having to do business with one supplier. Your attachment to a single deal will drive the price up, or keep it from coming down. Create the option for alternative opportunities even if you don't plan to use them.
2. Be prepared by knowing about the country-of-origin price structure as well as the U.S. price structure. Know how much you can afford to pay and still make an adequate margin of profit.
3. Price sheets usually serve as guidelines only. The quantity of an order, terms of payment, as well as personalities, will ultimately determine price.
4. Learn what the product costs your supplier. Although this may be impossible to find out precisely, you should be able to estimate it by knowing something about the material or component costs.
5. Does the supplier need money? It's hard to think of asking "Are you short of cash? If so, I'd like to make a ridiculously low offer for these goods!" This is something that you'll just have to sense from the seller's body language, the tone of the negotiations, the state and condition of the business and by asking the right questions.
6. Don't rush to fill conversational voids. If you make an offer that is low, just sit there. Don't squirm—let the others squirm. Many people give themselves away by making an offer, experiencing some silence, and then filling it by saying, "Well perhaps we could do better."
7. Get the seller to invest so much time in you that he or she would prefer to sell to you at a small profit than lose the sale to you and make no profit at all.
8. What might be considered unethical in our culture may be established business practice in others. Learn as much as you can about how business is conducted in the country you do business in and establish how you are going to respond to local practice.
9. Find two suppliers of the same goods. Remember that pricing is a matter of supply and demand. Let the suppliers know that you have alternatives. However, if you play one against the other be prepared to find that they are bosom buddies or for one to say "Fine! Buy it from the other supplier! I own that shop as well!"
10. Be prepared to walk away from a transaction if you cannot get what you need. This is perhaps the most difficult thing for some people to do. It is helpful to realize that very few opportunities are really the opportunity of a lifetime.

InfoList #25

10 Tips for Negotiating in a Long-Term Relationship

1. Look at the long-term consequences of any action you take with your supplier. Correct any errors that go against you, but also correct errors you find that go against your supplier.
2. Consider that if you make a tough deal today, taking advantage of your supplier's temporary weakness, it may come back to haunt you in the future, when your supplier may have the chance to get even.
3. Ask your supplier what he or she needs from you—besides money—to make the relationship run smoothly. Listen carefully and take careful note of the issues that come up. Many a supplier increases prices in subtle ways to compensate for problematic clients.
4. Establish what it is that you need in order to be successful. Differentiate between the window-dressing and your real issues. Let your supplier know what is important to you.
5. Negotiate a contract that gives you what you need in product and service and gives your supplier a fair price for supplying it. Consider the savings of not having to make as many trips to resolve problems, fewer defects, fewer missed shipment dates, etc.
6. Become friendly with your supplier. Be considerate of his or her family as well. In some cultures small gifts are appropriate. Although some prefer to keep everything on a business-only basis, you may find that having a personal relationship with your supplier will serve to cement the business relationship as well.
7. Consider negotiating for an exclusive supplier relationship, or perhaps an exclusive distributorship in your geographic area.
8. Actively look for ways in which you can support each other. Are there business opportunities you can share? Is there information you have that will help your supplier? Are you familiar with new equipment or manufacturing processes that will help your supplier? Do you have information about competitors that you can share?
9. Is it feasible or worthwhile for you to have an ownership position in the supplier company? Can you help by becoming a partner? Will such a relationship work over a period of time?
10. Keep lines of communication open with your supplier. Don't just communicate when you have an order and when you have a problem. Nearly every business has a fax machine. Send letters or short notes keeping them advised of your plans and progress. Think of your suppliers as partners in your business, who need to be kept current on what is going on.

InfoList #26

Business Meeting Pointers

1. Create a vision of what you want to accomplish as a result of the meeting.
2. Identify all the key components of what has to happen for the vision to become a reality.
3. Identify ahead of time all the objections, barriers, and problems the other side might have to your proposal or ideas.
4. Create a response to each possible objection.
5. Create a solution to each problem the other side might have with your proposal.
6. Learn enough about your counterpart on the other side of the bargaining table to be confident that you know how to reach him or her.
7. Put yourself in a positive mental state appropriate for the session.
8. Determine early on who has ultimate authority to set terms.
9. Don't be intimidated or overwhelmed by the seller's opening bravado. He or she is probably just as concerned about the outcome as you are.
10. Expect negative responses. Work around them by finding alternative solutions.
11. Learn how to operate in a context of no agreement.
12. Try not to put yourself in a position in which you have greater need to buy the commodity than the seller to sell it. The price you pay, given that position, will be higher. Establish alternative suppliers/deals.
13. Know what concessions you can and cannot make before the session starts.
14. Notice the seller's body language. Remember that body language means different things in different cultures.
15. Understand the seller's problems without taking them on as your own.
16. Be wary when your counterpart plays dumb.
17. Don't back the seller into a corner unless you really know what you are doing.
18. Don't brag. In most cultures bragging is a sign of weakness.
19. Be careful of the seller's pride. In some cultures, losing face is worse than losing money. Find a way to get a better price and terms without causing the seller to lose face.
20. Don't criticize the seller's merchandise if it doesn't meet your approval. Instead, explain that it is not right for your clients, that your clients will not buy it, or that your clientele cannot afford to pay the price, etc.
21. Speak clearly and don't use slang to communicate.
22. Don't become overly involved emotionally or agitated, unless it works for you.
23. Be prepared to walk away from any session if you can't get what you need.

24. Be prepared to back up your bluffs! If you don't mean it, don't say it.
25. Don't drink excessively.
26. Don't make phony promises.
27. Don't be belligerent.
28. Don't oppose the seller's belligerence. Just get out of the way of it, let it go by you.
29. Learn the seller's complete position.
30. Isolate problems when appropriate, group problems when appropriate.
31. Don't be impulsive. Impulsive decisions usually mean losing money.
32. Look for a variety of ways to give the seller what he wants without giving up what you need.
33. Be sure your tough questions are being answered, not side-stepped.
34. Verify statements that involve concessions.
35. Clarify all points made during the meeting by repeating the statement back to the others.
36. You can't insist on a delivery schedule based on a rate of production your supplier can't meet and expect no problems.
37. "No" does not always mean no.
38. "Yes" does not always mean yes.
39. It is always easier to get someone to say "Yes" than it is to get them to do what they said "Yes" to!
40. A contract is only as good as those who sign it.

InfoList #27

Tips for Attending Trade Fairs

Overseas trade fairs can be extremely effective for making face-to-face contacts and purchases, identifying suppliers, checking out competitors, and finding out how business really works in the host country. However, the cost of attending such fairs can be high. To maximize the return on your investment of time, money, and energy, you should be very clear about your goals for the trip and give yourself plenty of time for advance research and preparation.

You should also be aware of the limitations of trade fairs. The products on display probably do not represent the full range of goods available on the market. And while trade fairs give you an opportunity to make face-to-face contacts with many people, both exhibitors and buyers are rushed, which may make meaningful discussions and negotiations difficult.

Do Your Homework

Allow several months for preparation—more if you first need to identify the fair that you will attend. Even under ideal circumstances, you should begin laying the groundwork a year in advance. Don't forget that exhibiting at or attending a fair in a foreign country means more complex logistics: numerous faxes and phone calls involving you, the show operator, and local support people, plus customs and transportation delays.

Participating in international trade fairs should be considered a long-term investment. At domestic fairs, you may exhibit on a regular basis with short-term sales and marketing goals. But at foreign fairs, it is often best to participate to establish your company, make contacts for the future, and learn more about a market, its consumers, and products. New exporters may not generate high sales, but they often come away with information that assists them with future marketing and product development.

Selecting an Appropriate Trade Fair

Once you have identified some fairs, contact the organizers for literature and a show prospectus, attendee list, and exhibitor list. Ask lots of questions! Be sure not to neglect trade organizations in the host country, independent show-auditing firms, and attendees. Find out whether there are "must attend" fairs for your product group. Fairs that concentrate on other related, commodities might also be worthwhile. Be aware that there may be preferred seasons for trade in some products.

Your research needs to cover a number of points:

1. **Audience**
   Who is the intended audience? Is the fair open to the public or to trade professionals only? Are the exhibitors primarily foreigners looking for local buyers or locals looking for foreign buyers? (Many trade fairs are heavily weighted to one or the other.) Decide whether you are looking for an exposition of general merchandise produced in one region, a commodity-specific trade show, or both.

2. **Statistics**
   How many people attended the fair the last time it was held? What were the demographics? What volume of business was done? How many exhibitors were there? How big is the exhibition space? What was the ratio of foreign to domestic attendees and exhibitors?

3. **Specifics**
   Who are the major exhibitors? Are any particular publications or organizations associated with the fair? On what types of products does the fair focus? Does the fair have a theme that changes each time? How long has the fair been in existence? How often is it held? Is it always in the same location, or does it move around? How much does it cost to attend? Are there any separate or special programs connected with the event, and do they require additional fees? What does it cost to rent space?

Before You Go

1. If you have not already spoken with someone who has attended the fair, be sure to find someone who will give you advice, tips, and general information.
2. Make your reservations and travel arrangements well in advance, and figure out how you are going to get around once you get there. Even if the fair takes place in a large city, do not assume that getting around will be easy during a major trade fair. If the site is in a small city or a less-developed area, the transportation and accommodation systems are likely to become overburdened sooner than in metropolitan areas.
3. Will you need an interpreter for face-to-face negotiations? A translator to handle documents? Try to line up providers well in advance of your need for their services.
4. For printed materials, pay attention to language barriers and make preparations that will help you overcome them. Assess any literature and decide what should be available in translation or in bilingual editions. Have all translation work done by a true professional, particularly if technical terms are used. Consider having a bilingual business card, and add the country and international dialing code information to the address and telephone number. Find out from the show organizers which countries will be represented, and prepare information in the languages of those countries as well, if necessary.
5. Do you need hospitality suites and/or conference rooms? Reserve them as soon as you can.
6. Contact people you would like to meet before you go. Organize your appointments around the fair.
7. Familiarize yourself with the show's hours, locations (if exhibits and events are staged at multiple venues), and the schedule of events. Then prioritize.

While You Are There

1. Wear businesslike clothes that are comfortable. Find out what the norm is for the area and the season.
2. Immediately after each contact, write down as much information as you can. Do not depend on remembering it. Several companies now make inexpensive portable business card scanners with optical character recognition (OCR) software to read the information into a contact management program.
3. Be sensitive to the selling styles of the country you are in. Are hard-sell approaches taboo? Are you dealing with the right person? Status within one's company is often very important; someone may want to be clear about your position, and you will want to be sure your aren't causing offense by going to the wrong level.
4. Consider arriving a day early to get fully oriented, confirm appointments, and rest up.
5. It's common sense: make sure you take breaks, even if you have to schedule them. You'll end up having far more energy and being more effective.

After the Fair

1. Within a week after the fair, write letters to new contacts and follow up on requests for literature. If you have press releases and questionnaires, send them out quickly.
2. Write a report evaluating your experiences while they are still fresh in your mind. Even if you don't have to prepare a formal report, spend some time organizing your thoughts on paper for future reference. Aim to quantify the results. Did you meet your goals? Why or why not? What would you do differently? What unforeseen costs or problems arose?
3. With your new contacts and your experiences in mind, start preparing for your next trade fair.

As a Buyer You Should . . .

1. Familiarize yourself with customs regulations on the products that you seek to purchase and import into your own country or elsewhere. Be sure to get such information on any and all products that you might be interested in.
2. Set specific goals for supplier leads and for gathering industry information. For example, target the numbers of contacts made, leads converted to purchases, seminars and presentations attended, and booths visited. Other goals might be cost-to-return benefit ratio, amount of competitor information gathered, and percentage of projected purchases actually made.
3. List all the products that you seek to purchase, their specifications, and the number of units you plan to purchase of each.
4. Know the retail and wholesale market prices for the goods in your home country and in the country where you will be buying. List the highest price you can afford to pay for each item and still get a worthwhile return.
5. List the established and probable suppliers for each of the products or product lines that you plan to import. Include addresses and telephone numbers and note your source for the information. Before you go, contact suppliers to confirm who will attend and to make appointments.

InfoList #28

Overseas Buying Trips

Why Go?

If you are an importer considering an overseas buying trip, the first question you should ask is "Why go at all?" Much overseas travel is unnecessary. It takes time away from business and personal pursuits at home, may be filled with uncertainty, and can cost thousands of dollars.

Consider doing international business by mail, by fax, or by telephone as an alternative to travel. Also, a number of countries have export promotion groups which are set up to help facilitate and even guarantee trade transactions.

Consider hiring an agent in the exporting country. You may be able to establish a relationship with a buyer's agent who will be able to find the products you need.

Tip: Be careful how you legally structure an agency relationship: you may be setting yourself up for liability you never expected. Refer to "Agency" on page 78.

Consider sending a subordinate who has manufacturing or marketing knowledge of the product. Such a person may be in a better position to know what to buy anyway.

The benefits of the trip should outweigh the costs by a substantial margin.

Establish Clear Objectives Before You Go

Establishing clear objectives for your trip abroad should be your top priority. Plan each trip so that a number of diverse purposes can be served at the same time. Establish primary and secondary goals before you go.

Some Objectives for Business Travel

1. To locate a source of supply impossible to find from the U.S.
2. To establish a personal rapport with suppliers and/or buying and shipping agents.
3. To solve problems with suppliers, agents, and/or foreign government officials in person.
4. To render technical expertise in person or on site.
5. To supervise or train overseas personnel in specialized manufacturing procedures or techniques.
6. To personally supervise the selection of merchandise.
7. To seek new suppliers of products.
8. To view new product lines first-hand.
9. To view competitive merchandise from a number of suppliers at trade fairs.
10. To obtain legal counsel in the country of origin, or to be present during a legal proceeding.
11. To negotiate contracts in person.
12. To research the folklore and culture surrounding imported products.
13. To research and become more familiar with the marketing system.
14. To mix business with personal travel or to mix personal travel with business.

InfoList #29

Passports

When Required

A U.S. citizen needs a passport to depart or enter the U.S. and to enter and depart most foreign countries. Exceptions include short-term travel between the U.S. and Mexico, Canada, and some countries in the Caribbean. Your travel agent, airline, or the nearest embassy or consulate of the country you are traveling to can tell you if you need a passport.

Warning! Even if you are not required to have a passport to visit a country, U.S. Immigration requires you to prove your U.S. citizenship and identity when you reenter the U.S. Make certain that you take with you adequate documentation to pass through U.S. Immigration upon your return.

Note: A U.S. passport is the best proof of U.S. citizenship. Other documents to prove U.S. citizenship include an expired U.S. passport, a certified copy of your birth certificate, a Certificate of Naturalization, a Certificate of Citizenship, or a Report of Birth Abroad of a Citizen of the United States. To prove your identity, either a valid driver's license or a government identification card that includes a photo or a physical description is adequate.

With the number of international child custody cases on the rise, several countries have instituted passport requirements to help prevent child abductions. For example, Mexico has a law that requires a child traveling alone or with only one parent to carry written, notarized consent from the absent parent or parents. No authorization is needed if the child travels alone and is in possession of a U.S. passport. A child traveling alone with a birth certificate requires written, notarized authorization from both parents.

Beware of a passport that is about to expire. Certain countries will not permit you to enter and will not place a visa in your passport if the remaining validity is less than 6 months. If you return to the U.S. with an expired passport, you are subject to a passport waiver fee of $100, payable to U.S. Immigration at the port of entry.

All persons must have their own passport. Since January 1981, family members are not permitted to be included in each other's passports.

The Secretary of State has the statutory authority to invalidate U.S. passports for travel to countries with which the United States is at war, where armed hostilities are in progress, or where there is imminent danger to the public health and physical safety of U.S. travelers. Currently, the U.S. passport is not valid for travel to Libya, Lebanon, and Iraq.

Requests for an exception to this passport restriction, including biographical information concerning the individual, the specific reason for traveling to Lebanon, and any supporting documentation, should be forwarded to the Department of State, Office of Citizenship Appeals and Legal Assistance, Room 300, 1425 K Street, N.W., Washington, DC 20522-1705. The telephone number is (202) 326-6178.

How to Apply

It takes anywhere from two to several weeks to obtain a passport. However, it is best to apply two months in advance. Applications are processed according to the departure date indicated on the application form. If you give no departure date, the passport agency will assume you are not planning any immediate travel. Your passport will be returned to you by mail at the address you provided on your application.

It is best to apply through one of the 3,500 Clerks of Court or Post Offices which accepts passport applications. Passport Agencies tend to have extremely long lines during the busiest months which results in longer waiting times for people applying in person at a passport agency.

For your first passport, you must appear in person with a completed form DSP-11, *Passport Application*, at one of the 13 U.S. passport agencies or at one of the several thousand federal or state courts or U.S. post offices authorized to accept passport applications. A list of the U.S. passport agencies is at the end of this article.

If you have had a previous passport and wish to obtain another, you may be eligible to apply by mail. See below for information on applying by mail.

What to Bring When You Apply

1. A properly completed, but unsigned, passport application (DSP-11). Do not sign it!

   This form is available from passport agencies by mail or may be picked up and completed in person at the agency as you apply.

   Note: Although a Social Security number is not required for issuance of a passport, Section 603E of the Internal Revenue Code of 1986 requires passport applicants to provide this information. Passport Services will provide this information to the Internal Revenue Service (IRS) routinely. Any applicant who fails to provide the information is subject to a $500 penalty enforced by the IRS. All questions on this matter should be referred to the nearest IRS office.

2. Proof of U.S. citizenship (a, b, or c):

   a. Use your previously issued passport. If you are applying for a first passport, or cannot submit a previous passport, you must submit other evidence of citizenship.

   b. If you were born in the U.S., you should produce a certified copy of your birth certificate (a certified copy will have a registrar's raised, embossed, impressed, or multicolored seal and the date the certificate was filed with the registrar's office). If you cannot obtain a birth certificate, submit a notice from a state registrar stating that no birth record exists, accompanied by the best secondary evidence possible. This may include a baptismal certificate, a hospital birth record, notarized affidavits of older relatives having personal knowledge of the facts of your birth, or other documentary evidence such as early census, school records, family Bible records, and newspaper files.

   c. If you were born abroad, you can use:
   - A Certificate of Naturalization
   - A Certificate of Citizenship
   - A Report of Birth Abroad of a Citizen of the United States of America (Form FS-240)
   - A Certification of Birth (Form FS-545 or DS-1350)

   If you do not have any of these documents and are a U.S. citizen, you should take all available proof of citizenship to the nearest U.S. passport agency and request assistance in proving your citizenship.

3. Proof of identity

   You must also establish your identity to the satisfaction of the person accepting your application. The following items are generally acceptable documents of identity if they contain your signature and if they readily identify you by physical description or photograph:
   - A previous U.S. passport
   - A certificate of naturalization or citizenship
   - A valid driver's license
   - A government or military identification card
   - A corporate identification card

   The following are not acceptable: social security card, learner's or temporary driver's license, credit card, temporary or expired identity card or document, any document that has been altered or changed in any manner

4. Photographs

   The photos must be recent (taken within the past six months), identical, 2x2 inches, and in either color or black and white. They must show a front view, full face, on a plain, light (white or off-white) background. (Vending machine photographs are not acceptable.)

5. The correct fee

   The fee for an adult's (18 years of age and older) first-time, 10 year passport is $65.00. This includes the $55.00 passport fee and the $10.00 execution fee. The fee for the application for Passport by Mail for a person 18 years of age and older is $55.00. There is no execution fee and the passport is valid for 10 years.

Applying for a Passport by Mail

You may apply for your passport by mail if you already have a passport and that passport is your most recent passport, and it was issued within the past 12 years, and if you were over 18 years old at the time it was issued. Note: If the passport has been mutilated, altered, or damaged in any manner, you cannot apply by mail. You must apply in person and use Form DSP-11, present evidence of U.S. citizenship, and acceptable identification.

Ask the court, post office, or your travel agent for a DSP-82 *Application For Passport By Mail*. Fill it out, sign it, and date it. Attach to it:

a) Your most recent passport;

b) Two identical passport photographs (see previous section on passport photographs); and

c) A $55 fee. Make your check or money order payable to Passport Services. (The $10 execution fee is waived for those eligible to apply by mail.)

If your name has been changed, enclose the Court Order, Adoption Decree, Marriage Certificate, or Divorce Decree specifying another name for you to use. (Photocopies will not be accepted.) If your name has changed by any other means, you must apply in person.

Mail the completed DSP-82 application and attachments to:

National Passport Center
P.O. Box 371971
Pittsburgh, PA 15250-7971

Your previous passport will be returned to you with your new passport.

If you need faster service, you can use an overnight delivery service. If the service of your choice will not deliver to a post office box, send it to:

Mellon Bank
Attn: Passport Supervisor 371971
3 Mellon Bank Center, Rm. 153-2723
Pittsburgh, PA 15259-0001

Include the appropriate fee for overnight return of your passport.

Obtaining a Passport Quickly

Passport agencies will expedite issuance of passports for an additional fee. Effective October 1, 1994, a surcharge of $30 per passport was assessed for expedited service. The fee applies to expedited processing for all passport services, including issuance, amendment, extension of validity, and adding visa pages. Expedited passports will be processed within three business days of receipt by a Passport Agency, except when a passport must be denied or delayed. If the three-day processing deadline cannot be met, the expedite fee will be refunded. If desired, payment for overnight return of the issued passport should also be sent with the application.

Expedited processing is available only for travelers who are leaving in less than 10 days and can document their departure with plane tickets or confirmed reservations. Travelers who need to obtain foreign visas to depart within two to three weeks may also request expedited service. Expedited service is not available to travelers who cannot document their travel.

Travelers with very short deadlines may wish to apply directly at a Passport Agency (located in Boston, Chicago, Honolulu, Houston, Los Angeles, Miami, New Orleans, New York, Philadelphia, San Francisco, Seattle, Stamford (CT), and Washington, DC). However, many requests for expedited service can be handled by the more than 4,000 clerks of court and post offices which accept passport applications and forward them to Passport Services for issuance. If this option is selected, prepaid overnight delivery for each application is recommended both to and from the Passport Agency.

Expedited passport renewals by mail must include applicable passport fees, proof of imminent departure and $30 per passport. Mail applications to Passport Lockbox, P.O. Box 371971, Pittsburgh, PA 15250-7971; clearly mark the envelope "EXPEDITE." Mailed applications will be processed within three days of receipt at the National Passport Center in Portsmouth, NH.

If you are leaving on an emergency trip within five working days, apply in person at the nearest passport agency and present your tickets or travel itinerary from an airline, as well as the other required items. Or, apply at a court or post office and have the application sent to the passport agency through an overnight delivery service of your choice (you should include a self-addressed, prepaid envelope for the return of the passport). Be sure to include your dates of departure and travel plans on your application.

Additional Visa Pages

If you require additional visa pages before your passport expires, submit your passport to one of the passport agencies listed at the end of this section. If you travel frequently to countries that require visas, you may request a 48-page passport at the time you apply.

Change of Name

If you have changed your name, you will need to have your passport amended. Fill out Form DSP-19, *Passport Amendment/Validation Application*, which is available from any office that is authorized to accept passport applications. Submit the DSP-19 along with proof of the name change (Court Order, Adoption Decree, Marriage Certificate, or Divorce Decree) to the nearest passport agency. There is no fee for this service. If your name has changed by any other means, you must apply in person.

Altered or Mutilated Passport

If you mutilate or alter your U.S. passport in any way (other than changing the personal notification data), you may render it invalid, cause yourself much inconvenience, and expose yourself to possible prosecution under the law (22 US C 1543).

A passport that has been mutilated, altered, or damaged in any manner cannot be used for renewal by mail. You must apply in person and use Form DSP-11, present evidence of U.S. citizenship, and acceptable identification.

Loss or Theft of a U.S. Passport

Passport Services regards the loss of a passport as a serious matter. Lost or stolen passports can be, and are, used for fraudulent purposes. If your passport is lost or stolen in the U.S., report the loss or theft in writing to Passport Services, 1425 K Street, N.W., Department of State, Washington, DC 20522-1705, or to the nearest passport agency. If you are abroad, report the loss immediately to local police authorities and contact the nearest U.S. embassy or consulate.

If you wish to obtain another passport, you must execute a Form DSP-11 and you must submit a detailed statement explaining the circumstances surrounding the loss or theft of the passport and stating what efforts have been made to recover it. Brief notations such as "lost," "stolen," or "burned" are not sufficient. You must fill out a Form DSP-64, *Statement Regarding Lost or Stolen Passport*, or a statement containing the information requested on the DSP-64. You will be required to complete a Form DSP-11 in the prescribed manner, present acceptable identification, and submit two new photographs and the required fees. You should submit other acceptable evidence of citizenship in order to avoid delay in issuance of the replacement passport.

Passports issued to replace lost or stolen valid passports are normally issued for the full period of validity. However, there may occasionally be circumstances in which the replacement passport is limited to a shorter period of time. Upon conclusion of the initial period of validity, the bearer may request that the passport be extended by presenting it to Passport Services, a Passport Agency, or a U.S. consular post abroad. There is no fee charged for this extension. The bearer should submit a statement advising whether the previous passport has been recovered. This is usually done with a Form DSP-19, "Passport Amendment/Validation Application." (Caution: Extension of a passport while abroad may take several weeks for completion.) If the lost passport is subsequently recovered, it should be submitted to the nearest passport issuing office along with the limited passport. The recovered passport will normally be cancelled and the limited passport validated for use and returned to the bearer, unless the bearer specifically requests that the recovered passport be validated for use and returned.

Passport Agencies

24-hour information lines (indicated by *) give general passport information, passport agency location, hours of operation, and information regarding emergency passport services during nonworking hours.

Boston Passport Agency
Thomas P. O'Neill Fed. Bldg., Rm. 247
10 Causeway Street
Boston, MA 02222-1094
Recording: (617) 565-6998*; Inquiries: (617) 565-6990

Chicago Passport Agency
Suite 380, Kluczynski Federal Office Bldg.
230 South Dearborn Street
Chicago, IL 60604-1564
Recording: (312) 353-7155*

Honolulu Passport Agency
First Hawaii Tower
1132 Bishop Street, Suite 500
Honolulu, HI 96813-2809
Inquires: (808) 522-8283, 522-8286

Houston Passport Agency
Suite 1100, Mickey Leland Fed. Bldg.
1919 Smith Street
Houston, TX 77002-8049
Recording: (713) 653-3153*

Los Angeles Passport Agency
Room 13100, 11000 Wilshire Blvd.
Los Angeles, CA 90024-3615
Recording: (213) 575-7070*

Miami Passport Agency
3rd Floor, Claude Pepper Federal Office Bldg.
51 Southwest First Avenue
Miami, FL 33130-1680
Recording: (305) 536-4681*

New Orleans Passport Agency
Postal Service Building
701 Loyola Ave., Rm. T-12005
New Orleans, LA 70113-1931
Recording: (504) 589-6728*; Inquiries: (504) 589-6161/2

New York Passport Agency
Room 270, Rockefeller Center
630 Fifth Avenue
New York, NY 10111-0031
Recording: (212) 399-5290*

Philadelphia Passport Agency
Room 4426, Federal Bldg.
600 Arch Street
Philadelphia, PA 19106-1684
Recording: (215) 597-7480*

San Francisco Passport Agency
Suite 200, Tishman Speyer Bldg.
525 Market Street
San Francisco, CA 94105-2773
Recording: (415) 744-4444*; Inquiries: (415) 744-4010

Seattle Passport Agency
Room 992, Federal Office Bldg.
915 Second Avenue
Seattle, WA 98174-1091
Recording: (206) 220-7777*; Inquiries: (206) 220-7788

Stamford Passport Agency
One Landmark Square
Broad and Atlantic Streets
Stamford, CT 06901-2767
Recording: (203) 325-3530*

Washington Passport Agency
1111 19th Street, N.W.
Washington, DC 20522-1705
Recording: (202) 647-0518*

InfoList #30

Visas

A visa is an endorsement or stamp placed in your passport by a foreign government that permits you to visit that country for a specified purpose and a limited time—for example, a three-month tourist visa. It is advisable to obtain visas before you leave the U.S. because you will not be able to obtain visas for some countries once you have departed. Apply directly to the embassy or nearest consulate of each country you plan to visit, or consult a travel agent. U.S. passport agencies cannot help you obtain visas. Refer to "Visas and Work Permits" on page 70 for more information.

Foreign Entry Requirements

The U.S. Department of State Bureau of Consular Affairs publishes *Foreign Entry Requirements* annually (Department of State Publication 10137). It is available for 50 cents from the Consumer Information Center, Pueblo, CO 81009. However, it is advisable to verify the latest visa requirements with the embassy or consulate of each country you plan to visit.

Because a visa is stamped directly onto a blank page in your passport, you will need to give your passport to an official of each foreign embassy or consulate. You will also need to fill out a form, and you may need one or more photographs. Many visas require a fee. The process may take several weeks for each visa, so apply well in advance of your trip, especially if you need to apply for visas to visit several different countries.

Tourist Card

If the country you plan to visit only requires a tourist card, you can obtain one from the country's embassy or consulate. In some cases you may be able to obtain one from the airline serving the country or from your travel agent. Be sure to confirm the procedure before you show up at the airport.

However, a tourist card or tourist visa will not give you the right to conduct business in the country. Consult with the embassy or consulate for requirements for conducting business.

Proof of Citizenship

Check with the embassy or consulate of each country you plan to visit to learn what proof of citizenship is required of visitors. Even if a country does not require a visitor to have a passport, it will require some proof of citizenship and identity. Also remember that no matter what proof of citizenship a foreign country requires, U.S. Immigration has strict requirements for your reentry to the U.S.

InfoList #31

U.S. State Department Consular Information Sheets and Travel Warnings

The U. S. Department of State issues consular information sheets and travel warnings to inform travelers of conditions abroad which may affect them adversely. Warnings are issued when the State Department decides, based on all relevant information, to recommend that citizens avoid travel to a certain country. Countries where avoidance of travel is recommended will have Travel Warnings as well as Consular Information Sheets.

Consular Information Sheets are available for every country of the world. They include such information as locations of the U.S. Embassy and any Consulates in the subject country, unusual immigration practices, health conditions, minor political disturbances, unusual currency or entry regulations, crime and security information, and drug penalties. If an unstable condition exists in a country that is not severe enough to warrant a Warning, a description of the condition(s) may be included under an optional section entitled "Areas of Instability." On limited occasions, the State Department also restates in this section any Embassy advice given to official employees. Consular Information Sheets generally do not include advice, but present information in a factual manner so the traveler can make his or her own decisions concerning travel to a particular country.

How to Access Consular Information Sheets and Travel Warnings

By Telephone

Consular Information Sheets and Travel Warnings may be heard anytime by dialing the Citizens Emergency Center at (202) 647-5225 from a touchtone phone. The recording is updated as new information becomes available.

From U.S. Government Offices

Consular Information Sheets and Travel Warnings are available at any of the 13 regional passport agencies, field offices of the U.S. Department of Commerce, and U.S. embassies and consulates abroad, or, by writing and sending a self-addressed, stamped envelope to the Citizens Emergency Center, Bureau of Consular Affairs, Room 4811, N.S., U.S. Department of State, Washington, DC, 20520. Consular Affairs Bulletin Board (CABB).

By Computer Network

If you have a personal computer, modem and communications software, you can access the Consular Affairs Bulletin Board(CABB). This service is free of charge.

Modem Number: (202) 647-9225
Modem Speed: Will accommodate 300, 1200, 2300, 9600, or 14400 bps
Terminal Communications Program: Set to N-8-1 (No parity, 8 bits, 1 stop bit)

You can also access Consular Information Sheets and Travel Warnings through the Official Airlines Guide

(OAG). The OAG provides the full text of Consular Information Sheets and Travel Warnings on many online computer services. It is available through the following services: CompuServe (CompuServe subscribers may type GO STATE at any "!" prompt), Dialcom, Dialog, Dow Jones News/Retrieval, General Videotex-Delphi, NewsNet, GEnie, IP Sharp, iNet-America, iNet-Bell of Canada, Telenet, Western Union-Easylink. To obtain information on accessing Consular Information Sheets and Travel Warnings through OAG on any of the following computer services, call the OAG Electronic Edition at (800) 323-4000.

Infosys America Inc. also provides the full text of Consular Information Sheets and Travel Warnings through Travel Online BBS on the SmartNet International Computer Network in the U.S., Canada, and overseas. The modem telephone number for Infosys America is (314) 625-4054.

Interactive Office Services, Inc. offers online travel information in Travel+Plus through the following networks: Delphi, MCI (RCA Hotline), Unison, Bell South TUG, FTCC Answer Bank. For information on access, call Travel+Plus at (617) 876-5551 or (800) 544-4005.

The Overseas Security Electronic Bulletin Board provides State Department Consular Information Sheets and Travel Warnings as a free service (purchase of necessary software required) for American firms doing business overseas. Apply to the Executive Director, Overseas Security Advisory Council (DS/OSAC), Department of State, Washington, DC 20522-1003.

InfoList #32

Health Regulations for International Travel

Immunization

Under international health regulations adopted by the World Health Organization, a country may require international certificates of vaccination against yellow fever and cholera as a condition of entry. Typhoid vaccinations are not required for international travel, but are recommended for areas where there is risk of exposure. Smallpox vaccinations are no longer given. Check your healthcare records to insure that your measles, mumps, rubella, polio, diphtheria, tetanus, and pertusis immunizations are up-to-date. Medication to deter malaria and other preventative measures are advisable for certain areas. No immunizations are needed to return to the United States.

Information on immunization requirements, U.S. Public Health Service recommendations, and other health hints are included in the publication *Health Information for International Travel* (stock #017-023-00192-2), available for $6.50 from the Superintendent of Documents, U.S. Government Printing Office, Washington, DC 20402-9325, order line (202) 783-3238. You may also obtain such information from local and state health departments or physicians. This information is also available on the 24-hour International Travelers Hotline at the Centers for Disease Control: (404) 332-4559.

It is not necessary to be vaccinated against a disease you will not be exposed to and few countries will refuse to admit you if you arrive without the necessary vaccinations. Officials will either vaccinate you, give you a medical follow-up card, or, in rare circumstances, put you in isolation for the incubation period of the disease you were not vaccinated against. Check requirements before you depart.

If vaccinations are required, they must be recorded on approved forms, such as those in the booklet PHS-731, *International Certificate of Vaccination*. If your doctor or public health office does not have this booklet, it can be obtained from the Superintendent of Documents, U.S. Government Printing Office, Washington, DC 20402-9325, order line (202) 783-3238 or from any Government Printing Office bookstore. It must be signed by a licensed physician or by a person designated to sign the certificate. Keep it with your passport.

HIV Testing Requirements

Some countries require visitors to produce certification that they are free of the human immunodeficiency virus (HIV). Most often these regulations apply to applicants for residence or work permits, but they may apply to any visitors, or for some categories of temporary visitors. U.S. tests may be accepted, but you may be required to be tested on arrival. Check with the embassy or consulate of the countries you will visit for the latest information.

InfoList #33

U.S. Currency Declaration Regulations

It is not illegal to transport monetary instruments across the U.S. border, and there is no limit to the amount you may bring into or take out of the country. However, if you transport, attempt to transport, or cause to be transported (including by mail or other means) more than $10,000 in monetary instruments on any occasion into or out of the United States, you must file a report (Customs Form 4790) with Customs.

Monetary instruments include U.S. or foreign coin, currency, travelers checks, money orders, and negotiable instruments, or investments securities in bearer form.

Reporting is required under the Currency and Foreign Transactions Reporting Act (Public Law 97-258, 31 USC 5311 et seq.), as amended. Failure to comply can result in civil and criminal penalties and may lead to forfeiture of the monetary instruments.

If you have questions, contact a U.S. Customs Service office near you, or U.S. Customs Service, Washington DC 20229, Tel (202) 964-5607.

InfoList #34

Pre-Trip Product Planning

Planning your overseas buying trip (especially the first time around) can be more difficult and time-consuming than the trip itself. In a sense, it should be. Thorough predeparture planning should make the trip itself a matter of simply following through on well-made plans.

The following lists and comments are designed to assist in the planning of an overseas venture. Remember that time spent here in the U.S. is cheaper than time spent overseas. Calculate overseas time as three to 10 times more expensive. Thorough pre-planning makes good sense.

Product and Market

1. List all the products you seek to purchase.
2. List your established and highly probable customers for each product or product line you plan to import.
3. Establish and list, in detail, the product specifications for each item you seek to purchase. If the specifications are more subjective than objective, create some method of conveying the subjective quality to your product sheet.
4. List the quantities of each item you plan to purchase, with the number presold in parentheses and the number prepaid in double brackets. Example: bamboo living room sets 150 (64) ((15)), i.e. you want to purchase 150 sets of furniture, 64 have been ordered or presold, of which 15 have been prepaid.
5. List the "no later than" delivery dates for presold or ordered merchandise. For example, 100 units, November 15th. If you have standing orders, note the quantity requirements over time. For example, 65 units per month for six months.
6. Know and list the seasonality of each product you seek to purchase. Research and list customer seasonality requirements for each product. Research shipping time from point of origin to your customer. List latest dates for shipment from the country of origin.
7. Calculate the approximate shipping weight and volume required per unit of merchandise. This will enable you to know your shipping requirements for the merchandise.
8. Calculate (through use of a shipping agent or overseas freight forwarder) the shipping charges for various quantities of your commodity.
9. Know about U.S. Customs Service prohibitions or restrictions on the commodities you seek to purchase and import, including quotas. (Refer to the U.S. Customs section, beginning on page 175, for general information and to the Commodity Index section, beginning on page 325, for specific information on the commodity you seek to import; also contact a customs broker.)
10. List U.S. Customs Service packing, shipping, and labeling requirements, if any, for your commodity. (Refer to "Marking: Country of Origin" on page 215, "Special Marking Requirements" on page 217, and "Packing of Goods—Commingling" on page 189 for more information.)

11. Know and list required U.S. Customs documentation for the importation of your product or commodities. (Refer to "Entry Process" on page 182 and the Commodity Index section of this manual relevant to your product for specific documents required. Also speak to a customs broker about required documentation.)
12. Know about the U.S. Customs classification procedure for your product or commodity. There may be several potential classifications for your commodity, each of which may be subject to substantially different rates of duty. There may also be classifications with lower duty rates which can be satisfied with only minor alterations of your imported product. (Refer to "Classification—Liquidation" on page 207.)
13. Know the duties and tariffs which apply to your commodities. (Refer to a customs broker, the U.S. Customs Service, the Commodity Index of this manual for "Sample Duty Rates," or the Harmonized Tariff Schedules of the United States (HTSUS), available at most major city libraries, or from the U.S. Government Printing Office in Washington, DC.)
14. Know the retail/wholesale market prices for the goods in the U.S.
15. Know and list the maximum prices you can afford to pay and still get a worthwhile rate of return on your time and investment.
16. Analyze as thoroughly as possible the likelihood of being able to successfully import the commodity.

Potential Suppliers

1. For each potential supplier list the name, address, telephone, fax, telex number, and products.
2. List the source of the recommendation for each potential supplier.
3. Write letters to suppliers telling them that you plan to be in their country on certain dates.

   Refer to "Letters of Request" on page 17 to learn how to structure a letter of request.
4. Follow up on any references that the potential supplier has provided.
5. Get financial statements and references if possible. (Your banker may be able to help.)
6. Obtain and take notes on samples/specifications/catalog photos.
7. Collect price sheets.
8. Outline the sales and delivery terms of each supplier.
9. Note any guarantees or warranties on the products.
10. Sketch out an itinerary of which potential suppliers you plan to visit and in what sequence.

InfoList #35

Conducting Country Research

The scope of your analysis of the country in which you plan to travel will be determined by:

- The type of products you seek to purchase;
- The length of time to be spent in the country;
- The purpose and importance of the visit;
- The services you are likely to require; and
- The degree of your involvement.

Use the following list as a guideline for your country research. Information can be obtained from your public library, travel books, travel agents, airlines, international banks, chambers of commerce, consulates, embassies, the export trade ministries of exporting countries, the U.S. Department of Commerce, and many sources.

1. General Information

a. Business holidays
b. Business hours
c. Local time zones
d. Weather conditions
e. Clothing required
f. Electrical requirements for travel appliances
g. Weights and measures
h. Credit cards honored
i. Postal system
   1) Services available
   2) Reliability
   3) Rates
   4) Special cautions
j. Telephone system
   1) Availability
   2) Quality of service/reliability
      - Domestic
      - International
   3) How to get the best rates
   4) Procedure of use
      - Signals
      - Coins required
   5) Availability of "White & Yellow" Pages
   6) Fax machines
      - Availability
      - Use protocols
k. Telex
   1) Availability
   2) Nature of service/reliability
      - Domestic
      - International
   3) Rates
   4) Procedure of use
   5) Cautions
   6) Credit facilities
l. Banking facilities
   1) Local banks
   2) Your U.S. bank correspondent branch

2. Demographic and Economic Factors

a. Population of country
b. Major cities
c. Population of major cities
d. Median age of population
e. Percentage of population in work force
f. Salary of different types of workers
g. Standard of living
h. Major commercial centers
i. Major banking/financial centers
j. Major manufacturing/product centers
k. Major agricultural regions
l. Major ports
m. Major airports
n. Natural resources
o. Imports
p. Exports
q. Balance of payments
r. Gross national product/gross domestic product
s. Per capita income

3. Monetary Issues

a. Name of currency
b. Units of currency
c. Present exchange rate
d. History of exchange rate
e. Expected fluctuations (see your banker)
f. Recent devaluations
g. Exchange rate government fixed versus free floating
h. Discrepancies between "official" and free market exchange rates
i. History of inflation

4. Travel Requirements

a. Visa requirements (ask consulate or travel agent)
b. Immunization requirements (ask travel agent)
c. Onward ticket requirements (ask travel agent)
d. Minimum financial requirements to enter country (ask consulate or travel agent)
e. Police report required (some countries require proof of your good character—ask at consulate)

5. Business Practices, Services, and Facilities

a. Local business attitudes, etiquette, and practices
b. Degree of business formality
c. Acceptable dress (for your type of business)
d. Attitudes towards U.S. citizens
e. Procedure for appointing an agent
f. Special buying/selling seasons
g. Methods of business communication
h. Usual firmness of price/delivery quotations
i. Usual method of payment
j. Usual credit terms
k. Methods of debt collection
l. Patent and trademark protection
m. Banking services available
n. Local negotiation practices
o. Use of contracts
p. Contract enforcement
q. Settling of contract disputes
r. Use of arbitration
s. Local business services available
  1) Secretarial services
  2) Copy services
  3) Translation services
  4) Interpreter services
t. Importance of appointments; required timing: weeks, days, or hours ahead
u. Importance of letters of introduction and from whom
v. Business cards in local language
w. Strength of local trade organizations
x. Political sensitivity of your commodities
y. Duty free ports
z. Free trade zones
aa. Packing facilities
bb. Warehouse facilities
cc. Processing facilities
dd. Port facilities

6. Country-of-Origin Export Controls for Your Commodity

a. Restrictions and prohibitions
b. Documentation
c. Inspection
d. Licensing
e. Export quotas/visas (especially textiles)

7. Language

a. Language of the people
b. Language of business
c. Learn at least 10 phrases in local language
d. Availability of interpreters
e. Availability of translators

InfoList #36

International Travel Telephone Numbers

International Airline Reservations

AerLingus (Ireland) .... (800) 223-6537
Aeroflot (Russia).. (800) 995-5555
Aerolineas Argentinas .... (800) 327-0276
Aeromexico .... (800) 237-6639
Aeronica Airlines (Nicaragua)................ (800) 323-6422
Aeroperu.. (800) 777-7717
Air Afrique .... (800) 456-9192
Air Canada .... (800) 776-3000
Air France .... (800) 237-2747
Air India.. (800) 223-2420
Air Jamaica .... (800) 523-5585
Air Malta... (415) 362-2929
Air New Zealand....................................... (800) 262-1234
Alaska Airlines.. (800) 426-0333
Alitalia (Italy).. (800) 223-5730
All Nippon Airways (Japan).................... (800) 235-9262
ALM Antillean Airlines........................... (800) 327-7230
American Airlines .... (800) 433-7300
Argentina Airlines.................................... (800) 333-0276
Asiana Airlines (South Korea)................ (800) 227-4262
Austrian Airlines .... (800) 843-0002
Avianca Airlines (Columbia) .... (800) 284-2622
Aviateca (Guatemala).............................. (800) 327-9832
Bahamasair .... (800) 222-4262
British Airways .... (800) 247-9297
BWIA International (Trinidad & Tobago)(800) 327-7401
Canadian Airlines International............. (800) 426-7000
Cathay Pacific Airways (Hong Kong) .... (800) 233-2742
China Airlines (Taiwan)...........................(800) 227-5118
Continental Airlines................................. (800) 525-0280
Czechoslovak Airline............................... (800) 223-2365
Delta Airlines .... (800) 221-1212
Dominica Airlines (Dominican Rep.) ..... (800) 327-7240
Egyptair .... (800) 334-6787
El Al Israel Airlines .... (800) 223-6700
Ethiopian Airlines .... (800) 433-9677
EVA Airways (Taiwan) ....(800) 695-1188
Finnair.. (800) 950-5000
Garuda Indonesia..................................... (800) 342-7832
Gulf Air (Bahrain)..................................... (800) 223-1740
Guyana Airways.. (800) 327-8680
Hawaiian Airlines .... (800) 367-5320
Iberia Airlines (Spain).............................. (800) 772-4642
Icelandair .... (800) 223-5550
Japan Airlines.. (800) 525-3663
KLM Royal Dutch Airlines .... (800) 777-5553
Korean Airlines.. (800) 438-5000
Kuwait Airlines.. (800) 282-2064
Ladeco Chilean .... (800) 825-2332
LAN Chile Airlines .... (800) 735-5526
Lloyd Aereo Boliviano (LAB) .... (800) 327-7407
LOT Polish Airlines.................................. (800) 223-0593
LTU International Airways (Germany).. (800) 888-0200
Lufthansa... (800) 645-3880
Malaysia Airlines...................................... (800) 421-8641
Mexicana Airlines..................................... (800) 531-7921
Middle East Airlines (Lebanon)................ (415) 397-1834
Northwest Airlines .... (800) 447-4747
Olympic Airways (Greece)........................ (800) 223-1226
Pakistan International Airlines................. (800) 221-2552
Phillppine Airlines..................................... (800) 435-9725
Qantas Airlines (Australia)........................ (800) 227-4500
Royal Air Maroc... (800) 292-0081
Sabena Belgian World Airlines .... (800) 955-2000
SAS Scandinavian Airline Systems .... (800) 221-2350
Saudi Arabian Airlines.............................. (800) 472-8342
Singapore Airlines .... (800) 742-3333
South African Airways.............................. (800) 722-9675
Suriname Airways .... (800) 327-6864
Swissair .... (800) 221-4750
Taca International Airlines (Mexico)......... (800) 535-8780
TAP Air Portugal .... (800) 221-7370
Thai Airways .... (800) 426-5204
TWA International .... (800) 892-4141
United Airlines... (800) 241-6522
US Air .... (800) 428-4322
VARIG Brazilian Airways.......................... (800) 468-2744
VASP Brazilian .... (800) 732-8277
Viasa Venezuelan Airways .... (800) 468-4272
Virgin Air .... (800) 877-2537

International Car Rental Reservations

Alamo .... (800) 327-9633
Avis .... (800) 331-1084
Budget .... (800) 527-0700
Dollar.. (800) 800-4000
EuroDollar .... (800) 800-6000
Hertz... (800) 654-3001
National.. (800) 227-3876
Payless.. (800) 237-2804

International Hotel Reservations

Choice...(800) 4-CHOICE
Forte.. (800) 225-5843
Four Seasons.. (800) 332-3442
Hilton International..................................(800) HILTONS
Holiday Inn .... (800)465-4329
Hyatt.. (800) 233-1234
Intercontinental... (800) 327-0200
Kempinski .... (800) 426-3135
Leading Hotels... (800) 223-6800
Marriott .... (800) 228-9290
Nikko... (800) 645-5687
Novotel... (800) 221-4542
Omni...(800) THE-OMNI
Preferred Hotels & Resorts........................ (800) 323-7500
Regent International.................................. (800) 545-4000
Renaissance... (800) 228-9898
Sheraton .... (800) 325-3535
Stouffer...(800) HOTELS 1
Westin Hotels .... (800) 228-3000

InfoList #37

What Time Is It in . . .?

Use the chart below to determine what time it is in any of the listed countries. Use Column 1 as your reference if you live in the Eastern Time Zone (such as New York or Miami), or Column 2 as your reference if you live in the Pacific Time Zone (such as San Francisco or Los Angeles). Add or subtract the number of hours shown from your own time to find the time elsewhere.

Example: If you live in New York and want to find the time in France, note that Column 1 for France says +6, which means it is 6 hours later. When it is noon in New York, it is 6:00 PM in Paris. If you live in Los Angeles and want to find the time in Hong Kong, note that Column 2 for Hong Kong says +16, which means it is 16 hours later. When it is noon in Los Angeles, it is 4:00 AM the next day in Hong Kong.

The time differences shown are based on Standard Time, and may require adjustment if either you or the country you are looking up are following Daylight Savings Time (DST). Most of the United States is in DST from the first Sunday in April until the last Sunday in October. Many, but not all, countries north of the Tropic of Cancer also use daylight time during a similar period. Daylight time is not used in most tropical areas. Countries in the southern hemisphere that follow a daylight savings time (for example, Australia and Paraguay) use it during their summertime, often from mid-October through mid-March. The dates vary considerably from country to country and even from year to year. If you are in daylight savings and the county you are calling is not, *subtract* one hour.

A double dagger (††) following the name of a country indicates that its territory falls into more than one time zone. If most the major cities fall into one zone, only that information is given. If major cities fall into more than one zone, several representative cities are given.

	Column 1 New York EST	**Column 2** Los Angeles PST
Albania	+6	+9
Algeria	+6	+9
American Samoa	-6	-3
Andorra	+6	+9
Angola	+6	+9
Anguilla	+1	+4
Antigua & Barbuda	+1	+4
Argentina††	+2	+5
Armenia	+9	+12
Aruba	+1	+4
Australia††		
Adelaide	+14-1/2	+18-1/2
Brisbane	+15	+18
Canberra	+15	+18
Melbourne	+15	+18
Perth	+13	+16
Sydney	+15	+18
Austria	+6	+9
Bahamas	0	+3
Bahrain	+8	+11
Bangladesh	+11	+14
Barbados	+1	+4
Belarus	+7	+10
Belgium	+6	+9
Belize	-1	+2
Benin	+6	+9
Bermuda	+1	+4
Bhutan	+10-1/2	+13-1/2
Bolivia	+1	+4
Bosnia & Herzegovina	+6	+9
Botswana	+7	+10
Brazil††	+2	+5
Brunei	+13	+16
Bulgaria	+7	+10
Burundi	+7	+10
Cameroon	+6	+9
Canada††		
Calgary	-2	+1
Montreal	0	+3
Ottawa	0	+3
Toronto	0	+3
Winnipeg	-1	+2
Vancouver	-3	0
Cape Verde Islands	+4	+7
Cayman Islands	0	+3
Central African Rep.	+6	+9
Chad	+6	+9
Chile	+1	+4
China	+13	+16
Colombia	0	+3
Comoros	+8	+11
Congo	+6	+9
Costa Rica	-1	+2
Croatia	+6	+9
Cyprus	+7	+10
Czech Republic	+6	+9
Denmark	+6	+9
Djibouti	+8	+11
Dominica	+1	+4
Dominican Republic	+1	+4
Ecuador	0	+3
Egypt	+7	+10
El Salvador	-1	+2
Equatorial Guinea	+6	+9
Estonia	+7	+10
Ethiopia	+8	+11
Fiji	+17	+20
Finland	+7	+10
France	+6	+9
French Polynesia††	-5	-2
Gabon	+6	+9
Gambia	+5	+8
Georgia	+8	+11
Germany	+6	+9
Ghana	+5	+8
Greece	+7	+10
Greenland††	+2	+5
Grenada	+1	+4
Guam	+15	+18

	Column 1 New York EST	Column 2 Los Angeles PST
Guatemala	-1	+2
Guinea	+5	+8
Guyana	+1	+4
Haiti	0	+3
Honduras	-1	+2
Hong Kong	+13	+16
Hungary	+6	+9
Iceland	+5	+8
India	+10-1/2	+13-1/2
Indonesia††	+12	+15
Iran	+8-1/2	+11-1/2
Iraq	+8	+11
Ireland	+5	+8
Israel	+7	+10
Italy	+6	+9
Ivory Coast	+5	+8
Jamaica	0	+3
Japan	+14	+17
Jordan	+7	+10
Kampuchea	+12	+15
Kazakhstan	+11	+14
Kenya	+8	+11
Korea, South	+14	+17
Kuwait	+8	+11
Kyrgyzstan	+10	+13
Laos	+12	+15
Latvia	+7	+10
Lebanon	+7	+10
Lesotho	+7	+10
Liberia	+5	+8
Libya	+7	+10
Liechtenstein	+6	+9
Lithuania	+7	+10
Luxembourg	+6	+9
Macau	+13	+16
Macedonia	+6	+9
Madagascar	+8	+11
Malawi	+7	+10
Malaysia	+13	+16
Maldives	+10	+13
Malta	+6	+9
Mauritania	+5	+8
Mauritius	+9	+12
Mexico††		
Guadalajara	-1	+2
Mexico City	-1	+2
Monterrey	-1	+2
Tijuana	-3	0
Moldova	+7	+10
Monaco	+6	+9
Mongolia	+13	+16
Montenegro & Serbia	+6	+9
Montserrat	+1	+4
Morocco	+5	+8
Mozambique	+7	+10
Namibia	+7	+10
Nepal	+10-3/4	+13-3/4
Netherlands	+6	+9
Netherlands Antilles	+1	+4

	Column 1 New York EST	Column 2 Los Angeles PST
Nevis	+1	+4
New Caledonia	+16	+19
New Zealand	+17	+20
Nicaragua	-1	+2
Niger Republic	+6	+9
Nigeria	+6	+9
Norway	+6	+9
Oman	+9	+12
Pakistan	+10	+13
Panama	0	+3
Papua New Guinea	+15	+18
Paraguay	+1	+4
Peru	0	+3
Philippines	+13	+16
Poland	+6	+9
Portugal	+5	+8
Puerto Rico	+1	+4
Qatar	+8	+11
Romania	+7	+10
Russia††		
Moscow	+8	+11
Novosibirsk	+12	+15
St. Petersburg	+8	+11
Rwanda	+7	+10
St. Kitts	+1	+4
St. Lucia	+1	+4
Saudi Arabia	+8	+11
Senegal	+5	+8
Sierra Leone	+5	+8
Singapore	+13	+16
Slovakia	+6	+9
Slovenia	+6	+9
South Africa	+7	+10
Spain	+6	+9
Sri Lanka	+10-1/2	+13-1/2
Suriname	+2	+5
Swaziland	+7	+10
Sweden	+6	+9
Switzerland	+6	+9
Syria	+8	+11
Taiwan	+13	+16
Tanzania	+8	+11
Thailand	+12	+15
Togo	+5	+8
Trinidad & Tobago	+1	+4
Tunisia	+6	+9
Turkey	+7	+10
Turks & Caicos Islands	0	+3
Uganda	+8	+11
Ukraine††	+7	+10
United Arab Emirates	+9	+12
United Kingdom	+5	+8
Virgin Islands	+1	+4
Uruguay	+2	+5
Venezuela	+1	+4
Vietnam	+12	+15
Western Samoa	-6	-3
Yemen	+8	+11
Zaire	+6	+9

InfoList #38

Personal Travel

Travel Agents

If you plan to do a lot of international travel, it is best to establish an ongoing relationship with a good travel agent. Avoid agents who specialize in pleasure travel because they will be less attuned to your needs than will an experienced business travel agent.

Travel agents receive a commission paid by airlines and hotels. Usually there will be no added cost to you for using their services. Agents can:

1. Research and book transportation and accommodations;
2. Advise on visas, immunizations, etc.;
3. Answer many varied questions related to overseas travel;
4. Assist in locating sources of information; and
5. Modify your itinerary as required.

Air Transport from the U.S.

Air transport is the fastest and usually the least expensive means of international travel. In one day or less you can travel to almost any major capital of the world.

For many years the U.S. and other governments regulated the airline industry to insure passenger safety and often the financial stability of airlines. The association which acts for the international airline industry is "IATA" (International Air Transport Association). In conjunction with various governments, the airline industry has fixed prices on most routes. Prices used to be the same, no matter what airline you used. The only option for a reduced price was with charter companies.

Since deregulation, a degree of chaos has reigned in the marketplace for air fares. At this time there are dozens of air fares for the same route. Since these fares and the restrictions which apply to them change so rapidly, it is difficult to give a complete report that would be valid for any length of time. However, the general rule is: the fewer the restrictions, the higher the air fare.

For the lowest airfares consult with your travel agent and read the small display ads in the travel section of port city Sunday newspapers.

Tip: A number of agencies have sprung up offering low-cost tickets which are actually transfer of "mileage coupons." This is illegal. Many travellers have found themselves stranded at airports with worthless tickets.

Charters

The best deals on airfares are with charters offering special fares without restrictions on a first-come basis. Travel agents often do not suggest charters because of their relative unreliability and lower commission structure.

Charter flights leave from major U.S. cities and go almost everywhere. Sometimes the best opportunity is a charter to a major regional city such as Frankfurt or Hong Kong where you can get connections to other cities.

Some airline companies sponsor their own package charters. Look carefully at the package offered. A low air fare may be a loss leader offset by high cost ground packages for hotel, etc.

Charters almost always have specific departure and return dates, so be sure you can conduct your business in the time allotted. Some include hotel accommodations and can offer very attractive deals. Others include stays in several foreign capitals, such as Hong Kong, Taipei, Seoul, and Manila. Be sure to research the options and choose what is most appropriate for you.

The best procedure for finding an inexpensive charter is to:

1. Ask your travel agent;
2. Research other agents by telephone;
3. Read the Sunday travel supplement of a major city paper (especially in a port city);
4. Find a travel agent in a neighborhood which has a large ethnic population of the country you plan to visit. There is a high likelihood that such agents will know of special charters to accommodate their local clientele;
5. Fly local "bush" airlines in foreign countries which have less expensive fares, but may require a more "adventuresome" individual who is willing to put up with some discomforts along the way. Be aware that some such operations have deplorable safety records.

The situation is changing all the time, but sometimes it is less expensive to buy onward tickets overseas. For example, a few years ago, the standard fare for San Francisco–Hong Kong and return was $1,310.00, while the fare for Hong Kong–San Francisco and return was only $720.00.

Inter-European airfares are universally more expensive per kilometer than those for the same distance in the U.S. They are sometimes cheaper to purchase in the U.S., especially as part of a package.

Warning

There have been occasions when airlines or companies that sell charter flights or tour packages have gone out of business with little warning, stranding passengers overseas. If you know from the media or from your travel agent that an airline is in financial difficulty, ask your travel agent or airline what recourse you would have if the airline ceased to operate. Some airlines may honor the tickets of a defunct airline, but they usually do so with restrictions.

Before you purchase a charter flight or tour package, read the contract carefully. Unless it guarantees they will deliver services promised or give a full refund, consider purchasing trip insurance. If you are unsure of the reputation of a charter company or tour operator, consult your local Better Business Bureau, or the American Society of Travel Agents at 1101 King Street, Alexandria, VA 22314, Tel (703) 739-2782, to learn if the company has a complaint record.

Ocean Transport

In the fast-paced world of international business, ocean transport as a means of getting to your destination has become less and less viable. It takes longer and costs more, unless you work your way across as a crewmember (which has also become more difficult in recent years).

The attractions of traveling by ocean liner are simple: time to plan strategy, recuperate, and rest. Ocean travel is also best for those who do not like to fly. Travel by ship may also be the most reasonable way to return to the U.S. with an automobile purchased overseas. Consider the extra time spent on the way over as buying-strategy planning time and the way back as selling-strategy planning time, away from intense pressures. You will also not be subject to the jet lag of air transport.

Travel by Train

Rail transport overseas (especially in Europe) is more highly developed and relied upon than it is in the U.S. Fewer people overseas have access to automobiles and gasoline prices are significantly higher so governments have made great efforts to develop this efficient form of public inter-city transportation.

For short distances, air travel is often more trouble than it is worth—a false economy in time and expenditure. If the distances are not great, it may even take more time to get to an airport, wait, fly, and get from the airport to the destination than it does to take the train the whole distance. Furthermore, taking the train from city to city will give you time to relax and absorb what you have learned from your trip. Travel by train gives you the opportunity to see the countryside and is an infinitely better environment for meeting people than is traveling by air.

Some rail networks have unlimited 15-30-60-180 day use passes (e.g. Eurail Pass) which can be helpful if you plan a heavy schedule of travel in a short period of time. While they were actually designed for the student and tourist, business people can make use of them as well.

Tip: Be sure to research local train travel rules for each country. In Spain, for example, you must present a boarding card to enter the train, even if you have a Eurail Pass. Consult your travel agent for information and advice.

Buses

Buses are rarely a pleasant means of transport while overseas. More often than not they are extremely crowded, dirty, run on erratic schedules, and are difficult for someone unfamiliar with language to get around on. Do not expect to find many local equivalents of Greyhound in foreign countries (Europe excepted).

Taxis

Taxi services are usually well developed in most countries and provide excellent door-to-door service within a city. Some tips:

1. Be sure the meter is on and working, or settle on a price before you start out.
2. Ask at your hotel about appropriate tips if any.
3. Ask your travel agent beforehand about distances between airport and city, and best means of transport. (Tokyo airport to downtown Tokyo can cost US$150.00).
4. Have someone at the hotel write the name and address of your destination in the local language for you to show the taxi driver.

Automobile Travel

Driving or renting an automobile can be an excellent alternative to public transportation in a number of instances.

Advantages of Renting an Automobile

1. Freedom to come and go as you wish.
2. You will always have a place to lock things up (get an auto with locking trunk).
3. Useful for getting to out-of-the way places.
4. Useful for transporting small amounts of goods.

Notes About Renting an Automobile

1. Rentals require valid international or state drivers license (consult with travel agent or AAA) and often a valid major credit card or substantial cash deposits.
2. Additional fees may be required for mandatory insurance.
3. In some countries the safe driving condition of the rental car is your responsibility.
4. Rental cars are available in most countries but for an enormously wide range of prices, usually all expensive.

Driver's License

If you intend to drive overseas, check with the embassy or consulate of the countries you will visit to learn their driver's license, road permit, and auto insurance requirements. If possible, obtain road maps before you go.

Many countries do not recognize a U.S. driver's license. Most, however, accept an international driver's permit. Before departure, obtain one at a local office of an automobile association. You must be at least age 18, and you will need two passport-size photographs and your valid U.S. license. Certain countries require road permits instead of tolls to use their divided highways and will fine drivers without a permit.

Auto Insurance

Car rental agencies overseas usually provide auto insurance, but in some countries, the required coverage is minimal. A good rule of thumb when renting a car overseas is to purchase insurance coverage that is at least equivalent to that which you carry at home.

In general, your U.S. auto insurance does not cover you abroad. However, your policy may apply when you drive to countries that border the United States. Check with your insurer to see if your policy covers you in Canada, Mexico, or countries south of Mexico. Even if your policy is valid in one of these countries, it may not meet its minimum requirements. For instance, in most of Canada, you must carry at least $200,000 in liability insurance, and Mexico requires that if vehicles do not carry theft, third party liability, and comprehensive insurance, the owner must post a bond that could be as high as $20,000 based on the value of the vehicle. If you are under-insured for a country, auto insurance can usually be purchased on either side of the border.

InfoList #39

Accommodations

1. Many travelers wait until they reach their destination before making hotel reservations. However, you may be tired and unfamiliar with your surroundings on arrival and could have difficulty locating a hotel to meet your needs. Therefore, no matter what type of hotel you stay in, try to make confirmed reservations beforehand.
2. Be sure to research and know the busy or peak seasons in the cities you will be visiting. You may find it impossible to find hotel space for those seasons unless you book accommodations far in advance.
3. Ask your travel agent or consult a travel guide about customary tipping for each country you visit.
4. Be sure to know when the latest check-in time is—don't lose your reservation because of a delay.
5. Confirm reservations for lodging as you progress along on your trip from city to city.
6. Some train stations and airports have travel desks to assist you in finding lodging.
7. It is always best to have a hotel reservation for at least the first night you arrive in a foreign city.
8. Stay in a hotel appropriate for your type of business or mission overseas.
9. Try to arrange for commercial rates (business discounts of 5-40%) before you leave the U.S. A simple letter of request to the hotel management, stating that your company plans to use their hotel over a period of time may be sufficient.
10. Ask for commercial rates at the registration desk. You will be surprised how many times they will give it to you.
11. Most hotels have safe deposit boxes you can use for your valuables. Be careful, though. There have been reports of abuses involving hotel staff with access to both keys to the safe deposit box.
12. In a high rise hotel, always check the fire escape route.
13. If you are concerned about the hazard of fire in a high rise hotel, ask for a room on the first five stories of the hotel.
14. Do not leave valuables in plain sight in your hotel room. If the hotel does not have a safe and if you cannot take things with you, lock them into your suitcase. This will not prevent theft of your entire suitcase, but will keep housekeepers from pilfering what is openly available.

InfoList #40

13 Ways to Cut Travel Costs

1. Fly charter planes in coach class.
2. Find a package tour that fits your needs, even if it was designed for tourists.
3. Travel off-season to save on transportation and lodging costs.
4. Stay at small hotels or pensions outside of the commercial districts of cities. Do not stay at the international hotels.
5. When registering at hotels show business card and request commercial rate (after asking what the regular rate is).
6. Eat where the locals eat. Don't eat American-style meals, especially breakfast. Eat only when hungry.
7. Pay for your travel using credit cards that give you bonus miles toward free flights.
8. Take public transportation whenever possible.
9. Eat and drink nonimported food and liquor.
10. Smoke local cigarettes. Better yet, don't smoke at all.
11. Don't over-tip or double-tip. Many restaurants include a service charge in the bill.
12. Seek out discounts and bonuses offered to tourists, especially package deals.
13. For an extended stay, rent a house or an apartment.

InfoList #41

Managing Your Absence

1. If appropriate, give power of attorney to your attorney, accountant, business associate, or family member before you leave. Refer to "Power of Attorney" on page 78.
2. Pay existing bills and prepay bills that will come due during your absence, especially telephone, utilities, and payable-upon-presentation bills such as American Express and Diners Club.
3. Notify police, post office, and newspaper delivery services of your absence. Have all deliveries stopped.
4. Leave your itinerary with several people in your organization and/or family.
5. Leave a list of credit cards, travelers checks, passport information, and suitcase combination lock numbers with someone accessible by telephone in the U.S.
6. Make sure employees have enough work to keep busy during your absence.
7. Notify all those individuals who rely upon you or who should know of your whereabouts at all times.
8. Put valuables in a safe deposit box.

InfoList #42

Packing for Personal Travel

1. Travel light.
2. Quality molded suitcases will last longer and are worth the money, especially if you plan to travel frequently.
3. Leave enough room for articles purchased overseas and brought back with you. Consider packing a foldable canvas bag in your other baggage to handle the overflow on the way home.
4. If your suitcases use keys, be sure to keep one set on your person and another in your briefcase.
5. Pack clothing that is appropriate for the climate and your business.
6. Pack leisure clothing appropriate for the trip.
7. Be sure your medical kit is appropriate for the destination:
   a. Prescriptions to be filled while travelling
   b. Vitamins
   c. Prescription drugs
   d. Anti-diarrhea pills
   e. Anti-malarial pills
   f. Extra eyeglasses
   g. Extra pair of contact lenses plus accessories
   h. Water purification tablets
   i. Medical bracelet if appropriate
8. Documents:
   a. Passport
   b. International health certificate
   c. Visas
   d. Driver's license/international driver's license
   e. Travelers checks and personal checks
   f. Credit cards
   g. Extra passport photos
   h. Refund locations for travelers checks
   i. Travelers check numbers
   j. Birth certificate (if necessary)
   k. Address book (leave photo copy at home!)
   l. Letters of introductions from bank, businesses, local police, government official, etc.
   m. Tickets and vouchers
   n. Business cards
   o. Business brochures (if applicable)

InfoList #43

Documentation for Medications

Carry Your Prescription With You

If you have any preexisting medical problems and travel abroad, be sure to carry a letter from your doctor describing your condition and information on any prescription medicines you must take. You should also have the generic names of the drugs. Leave medicines in their original, labeled containers which should make Customs processing easier. A doctor's certificate may not suffice as authorization to bring all prescription drugs into all foreign countries. Travelers have been arrested for drug violations when carrying items not considered to be narcotics in the United States. To ensure you do not violate the drug laws of the countries you visit, consult the embassy or consulate of those countries for precise information before leaving the United States if you have any doubts regarding the status of your medication.

Medical Alert Bracelets

If you have allergies, reactions to certain medicines, or other unique medical problems, consider wearing a medical alert bracelet or carrying a similar warning.

Several private organizations provide listings of physicians to international travelers. Membership in these organizations is generally free, although a donation may he requested. Membership entitles the traveler to a number of traveler's medical aids, including a directory of physicians with their overseas locations, telephone numbers and doctors' fee schedules. The physicians are generally English-speaking and provide medical assistance 24 hours a day. The addresses of these medical organizations are in travel magazines or may be available from your travel agent.

InfoList #44

U.S. Customs Pre-Registration

Foreign-made personal articles taken abroad are subject to duty and tax on your return unless you have proof of prior possession such as a receipt, bill of sale, an insurance policy, or a jeweler's appraisal. If you do not have proof of prior possession, items such as foreign-made watches, cameras, or tape recorders that can be identified by serial number or permanent markings may be taken to the Customs office nearest you or at the port of departure for registration before departing the United States. The certificate of registration provided can expedite free entry of these items when you return.

InfoList #45

Handling Money Overseas

1. Before you leave the U.S. purchase US $50 to $200 worth of the local currency from your bank or a local foreign exchange-service such as Thomas Cook.
2. Purchase internationally recognized traveler's checks in a number of different denominations before you leave. Many banks will waive the 1% service charge for established customers. AAA (auto club) also waives traveler's checks fees for its members.
3. Be sure to keep the traveler's check purchase receipt (with check serial numbers) separate from the checks. Leave a copy of the receipt at your office in the U.S. as well.
4. Purchase traveler's checks in foreign currency denominations if you think the dollar is about to go down — or if you don't want to be at the mercy of the money changers overseas.
5. Be sure your credit cards are valid. Keep a copy of all your credit card numbers in another part of your luggage and with an associate, relative, or friend in the U.S. in case you need to report lost or stolen cards. American Express, Visa, and MasterCard are accepted almost everywhere in the world.
6. Banks in many countries now have automated teller machines (ATMs). Be sure to bring a credit or bank card that has a wide range of use.
7. There is little reason to carry large amounts of cash anymore. Travelers checks, access to cash machines, payment by credit card, etc. have made it possible to travel with relatively small amounts of cash.
8. Bring U.S. cash in larger denominations if you know you can get a better exchange rate or a better purchase price for cash in the country of destination. However, this is not recommended for the faint of heart. The risks are great. Other than the obvious risk of theft, currency exchange controls of the country may prohibit such a transaction. Also note #10 below.
9. Be sure to comply with U.S. Currency Export reporting rules for amounts of U.S. $10,000 or more in any monetary instrument. Contact Customs for details.
10. Money belts are good, but thieves are so familiar with them that they may ask for your belt after asking for your wallet and watch! The new way to hide your money is in a money pouch that secures to your ankle or around your waist inside your clothes. Check out different models of both at a good luggage store.
11. Note that a great deal of counterfeit U.S. currency in $100s, $50s, and $20s is being passed overseas. The advent of the color copier and more sophisticated offset lithography techniques has made this possible. Look carefully at any stack of bills that you are given. It is very easy to miss seeing a counterfeit $100 in a stack of twenty bills.

InfoList #46

As You Travel

Leaving the U.S.

1. Register personal items of foreign origin, such as camera, watch, etc., with U.S. Customs to avoid paying duty upon your return. It is best to carry U.S. receipts for these items with you just in case you need to prove that you bought them in the U.S.
2. Forward currency declaration forms to U.S. Customs if required.
3. Know where you will be staying.
4. Confirm flight and accommodations.
5. Know your arrival time.
6. Pre-plan transfer from airport to hotel.
7. Notify your potential suppliers of your arrival ahead of time. They may arrange to pick you up at the airport.
8. Have appointments already set up for the first few days after your arrival.

Managing Your Arrival

1. Plan on delays for health control, passport control, and customs clearance.
2. Be sure you are not carrying amounts of cigarettes, liquor, currency, or other items in excess of the specified travel allowance for the country in question.
3. Remember that certain countries ban items they find objectionable, such as obscene or seditious literature, or, in Islamic countries, alcohol.
4. Call your hotel to confirm reservations immediately after clearing customs, especially if your flight is late.
5. Complete a police registration card in countries that require one.
6. Register with the U.S. Embassy or Consulate if you expect to be in the country for some time or in countries where there is civil unrest.
7. After notifying any important parties of your arrival, sleep—or at least rest—to overcome effects of jet lag.
8. Immediately obtain a local map.
9. Immediately obtain local guide books to the country.

Expense Accounting and Receipts

1. Keep receipts of purchases so you can document your Customs declaration when you return to the U.S.
2. Account for all monies spent in the course of your business activities to make the job of expense accounting easier once you get back home.
3. Make sure your receipts indicate the type of currency.

InfoList #47

22 Health Suggestions

1. Don't eat food from street vendors.
2. Don't eat any raw foods except for fruit and vegetables you peel yourself.
3. Don't eat seafood away from the ocean.
4. Don't eat shellfish.
5. Eat in international hotel restaurants.
6. Don't eat unwashed food.
7. Eat only freshly cooked food.
8. Inspect the kitchen first, if possible. Draw your own conclusions!
9. Yogurt, cheeses, and fully cooked eggs are usually OK.
10. Don't drink tap water.
11. Drink bottled waters, soft drinks, hot tea, coffee, boiled milk, or bottled beer or wine; avoid hard liquor.
12. If you need to drink tap water, first let visible junk settle, skim off the top, boil for 10 minutes. Or, use chlorine or tincture of iodine. Aerate for taste.
13. Be careful of ice cubes—they are rarely made from purified water.
14. Drinking out of the bottle with a straw is usually better than drinking out of a glass that may have been rinsed in bad water.
15. Wear medical alert bracelets or other identification if you have a medical condition.
16. Always carry a supply of any needed prescription drug to last longer than your expected stay overseas.
17. Do not try to save money by avoiding medical attention.
18. All but the worst hotels will be able to refer you to a doctor.
19. Most large hotels will have a nurse or nurse practitioner on staff.
20. Do not undergo surgery overseas unless it is absolutely necessary.
21. Carry basic nausea as well as "turista" (diarrhea) medicine.
22. To find a competent doctor, consult
    a. International hotel
    b. U.S. Embassy
    c. U.S. consulates
    d. U.S. military base
    e. Recommendations from resident U.S. expatriates.

InfoList #48

13 Tips for Travel Safety

1. Before leaving the U.S., obtain a U.S. Department of State Consular Information Sheet for each country you plan to visit, and any Travel Warnings which may have been issued. Consular Information Sheets and Travel Warnings may be heard anytime by dialing the Citizens Emergency Center at (202) 647-5225 from a touchtone phone. Refer to "U.S. State Department Consular Information Sheets and Travel Warnings" on page 28 for information on other means of accessing the information.
2. Call the U.S. embassy or consular office upon arrival in a foreign country and ask if there are any special public safety or health hazards in the country you are visiting. Are U.S. citizens disliked or resented locally?
3. Be conservative in your dress and manners. Consider that you may be wearing watches, jewelry, and clothing worth 10 years' earnings to a local laborer. Don't flaunt your wealth. You could lose it, along with your life.
4. Leave your expensive and flashy jewelry at home. If you must take it with you, cover it up in public and display it only at appropriate social events. Leave it in the hotel safe when it is not in use.
5. Ask at the hotel about safety issues. Is it safe to walk certain streets by day? Safe by night? What are the safe areas? What are the dangerous areas?
6. Don't carry large amounts of cash on your person. Modern banking, credit cards, travelers checks, and other payment mechanisms make carrying substantial amounts of cash obsolete and risky.
7. Remember that when you are in a foreign country you are subject to local laws, not U.S. laws. It may be illegal to do things which are not illegal at home. By world standards the U.S. is a permissive society. Foreign laws are much tougher in many areas.
8. Know where you are going. Those who appear confused and indecisive are prime targets for con artists and muggers. The best protection against getting mugged is often an upright and purposeful posture.
9. Don't let your possessions out of your sight.
10. Use a money belt or money pouch which attaches to your ankle.
11. Beware of pickpockets in crowd situations.
12. It you use a shoulder bag, keep it on the side away from the street and hold it with your hand. Robbers on motorbikes grab bags as they speed by.
13. Travel with a small combination padlock in underdeveloped countries. It will come in handy.

InfoList #49

What to Do in Case of . . .

Loss of Passport

Your passport is your most important travel document. Keep it with you, or better yet leave it in the hotel safe and carry a photocopy of the relevant pages. If it is lost or stolen, report the loss immediately to the nearest U.S. Embassy or Consulate. You will need to apply for a new passport or travel document in person. You will need evidence of U.S. citizenship, two passport-sized photos, the application fee, a police report of the theft (if available), and an explanation of how it was lost or stolen. If you have no evidence of U.S. citizenship, the application process will be more complicated, but personnel will still be able to help you. A photocopy of the stolen passport is extremely helpful in these circumstances.

Loss of Credit Cards

Immediately call each of the issuing card companies and report the loss. Keep a list of the credit cards you carry and the emergency telephone numbers for reporting losses, separate from your credit cards. Register all your credit cards with an agency that notifies all credit card issuers in the case of a loss. Contact your issuing credit card company for details.

Major credit card issuers, especially American Express and large U.S. banks such as Bank of America, Citibank, etc. will be able to issue you a new card and a cash advance within a day or two.

Loss of All Funds

If your loss of funds does not include loss of your credit cards, go to a bank and ask for a cash advance.

If you don't have credit cards, or have lost them as well, call a relative or friend in the U.S. and ask that they send a bank wire transfer to you at a local bank.

If you have no credit cards, no checks, and no friends in the U.S. who can send money, and if you can't work something out with one of your suppliers in the country, go to the U.S. embassy or consulate. They are not authorized to advance funds to you, but they will help you with options.

Loss of Tickets

Loss of airline tickets is very problematic. Depending upon the type of ticket you have (had) you may not be able to get a replacement ticket at all. Start by immediately contacting the airline or other carrier. Don't wait until departure time to report the loss. You may be given a replacement, but don't count on it. You will probably have to buy a replacement ticket and file a lost ticket claim upon your return to the U.S. If you have a good relationship with your travel agent in the U.S., try calling them for help in getting things sorted out.

If the airline cannot or will not help you and if you have lost everything else as well (money, credit cards, etc.), go to the U.S. embassy or consulate. They may be able to supply you with a ticket home. (You do have to reimburse them!)

Illness

Don't wait until you are really sick. Call the U.S. Embassy or Consulate, or go to the reception desk of a good hotel, even if you are not registered there. Ask for the name of a doctor that speaks English, or simply a doctor they recommend that can help with the particular problem you have.

Political Unrest

Do your best to stay out of civil unrest in the countries you visit. Participating in demonstrations is asking for trouble. Your participation is about as welcome as would be a third party intervention in a dispute you are having with your spouse back home!

In the case of serious political unrest, it is best to know how to get out quickly. Americans have been used as pawns in political disputes they have nothing to do with. What happened to U.S. citizens in Iraq just as the Gulf War was breaking out provides a case in point.

Getting Arrested

Through any means possible, get word to the U.S. Embassy or Consulate that you have been arrested. Don't sign anything. U.S. federal law forbids a consular officer from acting as your legal representative. However, such officials can help get word to friends or relatives in the U.S. who can help.

Beyond notifying U.S. authorities there are two mutually exclusive strategies you could employ: Remain calm. Do not get huffy, telling your captors that they can't do this to you because you are a U.S. citizen. (The fact is, they can, and they have!) On the other hand, it may be tactically advantageous to get extremely huffy, express your outrage, argue with the arresting authorities, tell them you are a U.S. citizen and they will be in big trouble for having arrested you (however, NEVER physically touch a captor). You will have to decide based on your situation.

Auto Accident

When renting an automobile, make sure that you have complete insurance coverage. It is possible that your U.S. policy will cover some part of the insurance on a rental car in a foreign country. It is unlikely that it will cover everything, and it may not be in force at all outside the U.S. (For example, you will need separate coverage to drive in Mexico.)

Be sure to keep a copy of your insurance documents with you. You may need to present them to authorities before they will release you from the scene of an accident.

1. Check for injuries and call for medical assistance.
2. Ask for proof of driver's name and owner's name of the other vehicle.
3. Note the driver's license number and registration number of the other vehicle.
4. Note the number of people in the other vehicle, their approximate ages and genders.
5. Sketch the accident scene, take photos if possible.
6. Get the names of witnesses if possible.
7. Call the insurance carrier to report the accident.
8. Don't sign any document that might admit fault.
9. If the accident is serious, it is best to call the closest U.S. consulate or embassy.

InfoList #50

Help from U.S. Consuls Abroad

The Citizens Emergency Center

The Citizens Emergency Center deals with emergencies involving U.S. citizens abroad—including those who die, become destitute, get sick, disappear, have accidents, or get arrested. In addition to individual emergencies, the Citizens Emergency Center is also the State Department's focal point for major disasters involving U.S. nationals abroad: plane crashes, hijackings, natural disasters, terrorist incidents, etc.

The Citizens Emergency Center's telephone number is (202) 647-5225. The Center is open 8:15 am to 10:00 pm Eastern Time Monday through Friday, and 9:00 am to 3:00 pm Saturday. At other times, including holidays, a duty officer can be reached through the State Department's main number: (202) 634-3600.

Emergency assistance generally pertains to four categories: deaths, arrests, financial-medical problems, and welfare-whereabouts queries. The Citizens Emergency Center, working through U.S. embassies and consulates abroad, is a link between the citizen in distress and his or her family in the U.S.

When to Register with the U.S. Embassy

When you are traveling abroad, register at the Consular Section of the nearest U.S. embassy or consulate if:

- You find yourself in a country or area that is experiencing civil unrest, has an unstable political climate, or is undergoing a natural disaster, such as an earthquake or hurricane.
- You plan to go to a country where there are no U.S. officials. In such cases, register in an adjacent country, leave an itinerary, and ask about conditions in the country you will visit and what third country may represent U.S. interests there.
- You plan to stay in a country for longer than one month.

Registration makes your presence and whereabouts known in case it is necessary for a consular employee to contact you in an emergency. During a disaster overseas, U.S. consular officers offer assistance to U.S. nationals and can even assist in evacuation should that becomes necessary. However, they cannot help you if they can't find you. Registration also makes it easier to apply for a replacement passport if yours is lost or stolen.

If you are traveling with an escorted tour to areas experiencing political uncertainty or other problems, find out if registration is being taken care of by your tour operator. If it is not, or if you are traveling on your own, leave a copy of your itinerary at the nearest U.S. embassy or consulate soon after arrival.

What U.S. Consuls Can Do

U.S. consular officers are located at U.S. embassies and consulates in most countries overseas. They are available to advise and help you if you are in any serious trouble.

Destitution

If you become destitute abroad, the U.S. consul can help you get in touch with your family, friends, bank, or employer and tell you how to arrange for them to send funds for you. The State Department cannot advance you funds, but can sometimes serve as the intermediary for funds wired to you from home.

If Ill or Injured

Should you become ill while abroad, contact the nearest U.S. embassy or consulate for a list of local doctors, dentists, medical specialists, clinics, and hospitals. If your illness or injury is serious, the consul can help you find medical assistance from that list and, at your request, will inform your family or friends of your condition. If necessary, a consul can assist in the transfer of funds from the United States. Payment of hospital and other expenses is your responsibility. Neither can consular officers supply you with medications.

In an emergency when you are unable to communicate, the consul will check your passport for the name and address of any relative, friend, or legal representative whom you wish to have notified. Because the U.S. Government cannot pay for medical evacuations, it is advisable to have private medical insurance to cover this.

Marriage Abroad

U.S. diplomatic and consular officials do not have authority to perform marriages overseas. Marriages must he performed in accordance with local law. There are always documentary requirements, and in some countries, there is a lengthy residence requirement before a marriage may take place.

Before traveling, ask the embassy or consulate of the country in which you plan to marry about their regulations and how to prepare to marry abroad. Once abroad, the Consular Section of the nearest U.S. embassy or consulate may be able to answer some of your questions, but it is your responsibility to deal with local civil authorities.

Birth Abroad

A child born abroad to a U.S. citizen parent or parents generally acquires U.S. citizenship at birth. The U.S. parent or parents should contact the nearest U.S. embassy or consulate to have a Report of Birth Abroad of a Citizen of the United States of America prepared. This document serves as proof of acquisition of U.S. citizenship and is acceptable evidence for obtaining a U.S. passport and for most other purposes where one must show a birth certificate or proof of citizenship.

Adoption Abroad

The State Department and its embassies and consulates abroad have become increasingly concerned about international adoptions because of an increase in illegal activities by some intermediaries and adoption agencies. Illegal adoption practices can cause great difficulty, financial strain, and emotional stress for adopting parents. If you are a prospective adopting parent, beware of any agency or attorney claiming to be able to streamline established procedures. Because of irregular activities, foreign governments sometimes determine that an adoption in process is illegal and refuse to finalize and document the adoption.

For more information, you may write for a free pamphlet, *International Adoptions*. Send a self-addressed, triple-stamped 9" x 12" envelope to: Citizens Consular Services (CA/OCS/CCS), Room 4817, Department of State, Washington, DC 20520-4818. If you are planning to adopt from a particular country, mention that in your request, because Citizens Consular Services has specific information on the adoption process in certain countries.

Death Abroad

When a U.S. citizen dies abroad, the consular officer reports the death to the next of kin or legal representative and arranges to obtain from them the necessary private funds for local burial or return of the body to the United States. Before you begin your trip, complete the address page in the front of your passport. Provide the name, address, and telephone number of someone to be contacted in an emergency. Do not give the names of your traveling companions in case the entire party is involved in the same accident.

Because the U.S. Government cannot pay for local burial or shipment of remains to the United States, it is worthwhile to have insurance to cover this. Following a death, a Report of the Death of an American Citizen (Optional Form 180) is prepared by the consular officer to provide the facts concerning the death and the custody of the personal estate of the deceased. Under certain circumstances, a consular officer becomes the provisional conservator of a deceased U.S. citizen's estate and arranges for the disposition of those effects.

A Variety of Nonemergency Services

Consular officers provide nonemergency services as well. These include information on Selective Service registration, travel advisories, absentee voting, and the acquisition or loss of U.S. citizenship. They arrange for the transfer of Social Security and other federal benefits to beneficiaries residing abroad, provide U.S. tax forms, and notarize documents. Consuls can also provide information on how to obtain foreign public documents.

What U.S. Consuls Cannot Do

Consular officers will do their best to assist U.S nationals abroad. However, they must devote priority time and energies to those who find themselves in the most serious legal, medical, or financial difficulties.

Because of limited resources, consuls cannot provide routine or commercial-type services. They cannot act as travel agents, information bureaus, banks, or law enforcement officers. U.S. federal law forbids a consular officer from acting as your legal representative. Consular officers cannot: find you employment; get you visas, residence permits or driving permits; act as interpreters; search for missing luggage; call your credit card company or bank; replace stolen travelers checks; or settle disputes with hotel managers. However, they can advise you on how to get assistance in these and other matters.

InfoList #51

Coming Home

1. Reconfirm your return reservation at least 72 hours before departure. Whenever possible, obtain a written confirmation. If you do it by phone, record the time, day, and the agent's name who took the call.
2. Take some time to put all the brochures and slips of paper you collected on your trip into some sort of order. Throw out what you don't need to lug home.
3. Arrange sales slips for all personal purchases in a file. This will make it easier to make personal declarations when you go through U.S. Customs.
4. Make sure you have all U.S. Customs-required documentation for your commercial purchases, especially for hand-carried items you will clear through Customs on your way home.
5. If necessary, buy another suitcase for miscellaneous personal purchases, brochures, samples, and commercial goods you have purchased.
6. Pack all the goods you will need to declare at U.S. Customs in one suitcase. This will make your passage through Customs easier.
7. Learn in advance how long it takes to get to the airport and how much it costs.
8. Arrange for transport to the airport one to two days in advance.
9. Before going to the airport, call your airline and ask about baggage weight restrictions.
10. If you have excess baggage, it may be less expensive to ship via air freight. Airline's excess baggage charges are often disproportionately high.
11. If you are visiting a country that is suffering a period of social or political unrest, find out how you would be able to leave the country in a hurry.
12. Leave plenty of time to arrive at the airport and deal with immigration and security formalities. In some countries, if you do not arrive a full hour before flight time, you will be denied entry and boarding.
13. Go to the front desk of your hotel and ask to see your bill well before departure time. If the bill is inaccurate, it is likely to be in the hotel's favor. You may overlook incorrect charges if you are in a rush to get to the airport.
14. Some countries levy an airport departure tax on travelers that can be as high as $50 per person. Ask the airline or a travel agent about such departure taxes.
15. Few "duty free" shops at airports have really good prices on merchandise. Also, all merchandise that you bring back to the U.S. is subject to Customs regulations. Refer to "U.S. Customs Hints" on page 45 for information about personal exemptions for returning U.S. residents.
16. Always make a full and complete declaration to Customs upon your return to the U.S. Nondeclaration and undervaluing of merchandise is unprofessional, unethical, and illegal. U.S. Customs has vast powers of search and seizure. The consequences of getting caught are not worth the possible savings.

InfoList #52

U.S. Customs Hints

Basic information for returning U.S. residents about their personal Customs exemptions.

Duty-Free Exemptions

Articles valued at $400 (fair retail value in the country of acquisition) may be entered duty free provided:

- Articles are for personal use or gifts.
- Articles accompany you.
- You have been out of the country at least 48 hours. (Mexico and the U.S. Virgin Islands are exempt from the 48-hour limitation).
- You have not claimed the exemption within the preceding 30 days.

You may include in this duty-free exemption:

- 100 cigars and 200 cigarettes. Products of Cuban tobacco may be brought in only if acquired in Cuba.
- 1 liter (33.8 fl. oz.) wine, beer, or liquor, if 21 years of age or over. (Most states have restrictions on the amount of liquor or tobacco you can bring in).

Your exemption is $1,200 if you are returning from American Samoa, Guam, or the U.S. Virgin Islands. You may bring in 1,000 cigarettes. Of your $1,200 exemption, at least $600 worth of articles must have been purchased in the islands. Articles acquired in these islands need not accompany you but may be sent to the U.S. and claimed under your duty-free personal exemption if properly declared. Remember that shipping alcoholic beverages by mail is prohibited by U.S. postal laws.

If you are returning from any of the following 24 beneficiary countries, your customs exemption is $600: Antigua and Barbuda, Aruba, Bahamas, Barbados, Belize, Costa Rica, Dominica, Dominican Republic, El Salvador, Grenada, Guatemala, Guyana, Haiti, Honduras, Jamaica, Montserrat, Netherlands Antilles, Nicaragua, Panama, Saint Christopher/Kitts and Nevis, Saint Lucia, Saint Vincent and the Grenadines, Trinidad and Tobago, British Virgin Islands.

Your exemption is $25 (retail value) if you cannot claim the $400 , $600, or $1,200 exemption because of the 30-day or 48-hour minimum limitations. You may include 50 cigarettes, 10 cigars, 150 milliliters (5.1 fl. oz.) of alcoholic beverages, or 150 ml. of perfume containing alcohol. If the total is more than $25 duty is payable on the entire amount.

Gift packages may be sent to friends and relatives and received free of duty if the value does not exceed $50 (retail) or $100 if sent from the U.S. Virgin Islands, American Samoa, or Guam.

Other articles purchased abroad and sent to the U.S. are dutiable when received in this country. Duty cannot be prepaid. Do not list these items on your declaration when you return, except as indicated for the U.S. insular possessions.

Articles imported in excess of your exemptions will be subject to duty as indicated below unless an item is entitled to free entry.

Example: You acquire goods valued at $3,000 from:

	U. S. insular possessions	Other countries or locations
Personal exemption (free of duty)	Up to $1,200	Up to $400
Flat duty rate	Next $1,000 at 5%	Next $1,000 at 10%
Various rates of duty	Remaining $800	Remaining $1,600

Certain items made in designated developing countries and territories are admitted duty free under the Generalized System of Preferences and the Caribbean Basin Recovery Act, but must nevertheless be declared to Customs.

You must declare, at the price paid, everything acquired abroad that you bring home, including gifts given to you and articles worn or used. If you fail to declare or understate the value, penalties can be substantial.

If you take out of or bring into the U.S. more than $10,000 in currency or negotiable instruments, you must file a report (Customs Form 4790) with U.S. Customs.

It is wise to register foreign-made, serially-numbered articles (e.g. cameras, watches) with Customs before you leave, or take with you proof of prior possession (e.g. sales slip). All firearms should be registered with Customs, whether made in the U.S. or abroad.

Articles purchased in "duty-free" shops in foreign countries are subject to U.S. Customs duty and restrictions but may be included in your personal exemption. Articles purchased in U.S. "duty-free" shops are subject to U.S. Customs duty and I.R.S. tax if reentered into the U.S.

Caution: A "good buy" overseas on a brand-name product may be due to its being counterfeit and thus subject to seizure.

Please Note

Goods from countries that are under economic sanctions by the United States (Angola, Cuba, Iran, Iraq, Libya, North Korea, and the Federal Republic of Yugoslavia—Serbia and Montenegro) are generally prohibited. There are severe restrictions on travel and transportation transactions with these countries and special licenses—hardly ever issued—are required to import commercial goods. Foreign visitors may be allowed to bring in some small articles for personal use on a temporary basis. For more information, contact the Office of Foreign Assets Control, Department of the Treasury, Washington, DC 20220, (202) 622-2520.

Restricted or Prohibited Articles

Some items must meet certain requirements, require a license or permit, or may be prohibited entry. Among these are:

Absinthe • Biological materials • Books, audio and video tapes, and other recorded or printed materials protected by U.S. copyright if unauthorized foreign reprints • Candy, liquor-filled, where prohibited by state law • Ceramic tableware containing dangerous levels of lead • Copies of gold coins if not properly marked • Drug paraphernalia • Electronic products subject to radiation emissions standards. • Firearms and ammunition • Food, drugs, and certain other items not approved by the FDA • Fruit, plants, vegetables, and their products • Hazardous articles (e.g., fireworks, dangerous toys, toxic or poisonous substances) • Lottery tickets • Meats, poultry, and their products (e.g., sausage, paté, canned items) • Medicines and medical devices not approved by the FDA • Motor vehicles not conforming to safety and emission standards • Narcotics and dangerous drugs, including medicine containing same • Objects of Central and South American Pre-Columbian Indian cultures • Obscene articles and publications • Pets (e.g., dogs, birds, turtles, monkeys) • Seditious or treasonable matter • Trademarked items (e.g., certain cameras, watches, perfumes) • Switchblade knives (a one-armed person may import one with a blade less than three inches long for personal use) • Wildlife (e.g., birds, fish, animals) and endangered and protected species (e.g., pheasants; pelts; feathers, eggs, or skins of wild birds; articles of reptile skin, ivory, and whalebone).

Your Customs Declaration

You will receive a Customs Declaration on board your plane or vessel as you return to the United States. Before you enter the U.S., you must fill out the identification portion. Families returning together may prepare a joint declaration, with children claiming the same exemption as adults (except for liquor). Children born abroad, who have never lived in the United States, are considered nonresidents for Customs purposes.

Tip: Keep your receipts, sales slips, invoices, or other record of your purchases should there be a question concerning valuations. If you do not have specific supporting data, Customs will use standard price listings of goods from the country of acquisition to value the items in question.

In conformance with the simplified Customs Declaration form:

- You must complete a written declaration and include item #11 the total value of all goods acquired that are accompanying you if you arrive in the United States by aircraft or ocean vessel.
- If you exceed $1,400 per person ($400 tax-free exemption plus $1,000 dutiable at a flat 10% duty rate), you must list in writing all the articles acquired outside the United States and the price paid for each in U.S. currency or its equivalent in the country of acquisition. Repairs or alterations to articles taken abroad and returned must be declared, whether paid for or provided free of charge. State the fair retail value of acquisitions not purchased, such as gifts to you.

You must also list in writing your acquisitions when:

- You have exceeded the personal liquor or tobacco exemptions explained under "Duty-Free Exemptions." (Note that excess amounts of alcoholic beverages are subject to federal excise taxes in addition to import duties.)
- You bring in items for business purposes or for someone else.
- You send home items acquired in the U.S. Virgin Island, American Samoa, or Guam.
- You are asked to do so by the Customs Inspector.

You may make an oral declaration if you arrive in the United States from Canada or Mexico—by car, bus, train, or on foot—and you have less than $400 worth of items to declare.

Play It Safe

Customs will be glad to furnish you with detailed pamphlets: Refer to "U.S. Customs Brochures and Publications" on page 47. Contact your local Customs Office, or send a postcard to U.S. Customs Service, P.O. Box 7407, Washington, DC 20044, or the U.S. Customs Service National Distribution Center, P.O. Box 68912, Indianapolis, IN 46268.

InfoList #53

U.S. Customs Brochures and Publications

The following publications are available from U.S. Customs free of charge (except #1). Publications may be requested directly from:

U.S. Customs Service
National Distribution Center
P.O. Box 68912
Indianapolis, IN 46268

1. Global Trade Talk. Official U.S. Customs Service journal for the international trade community. Published bimonthly by the U.S. Customs Service. $8.50 per year. Contact the Superintendent of Documents, U.S. Government Printing Office, Washington, DC 20402.
2. Customs Map/Directory. Publication No. 500.
3. Currency Reporting Flyer. Publication No. 503.
4. Importing to the United States. Publication No. 504.
5. Pocket Hints for U.S. Residents. Publication No. 506. Note: Customs has not updated this brochure since 1988 and it is not current on existing limits and requirements)
6. Pets/Wildlife and U.S. Customs. Publication No. 509.
7. Tips for Visitors. (available in Chinese, Dutch, English, German, Italian, Japanese, Korean, Polish, Portuguese, and Spanish) Publication No. 511.
8. Know Before You Go. Customs Hints for Returning Residents. Publication No. 512.
9. U.S. Customs Guide for Private Flyers (General Aviation Pilots). Publication No. 513.
10. U.S. Customs International Mail Imports. Publication No. 514.
11. GSP and the Traveler. Information on bringing articles from developing countries under the Generalized System of Preferences. Publication No. 515.
12. United States Import Requirements. Publication No. 517.
13. U.S. Customs Highlights for Government Personnel. Publication No. 518.
14. Import Quotas. Publication No. 519.
15. Importing a Car. Publication No. 520.
16. Tips for Visitors. Publication No. 521.
17. Drawback. A Duty Refund on Certain Imports. Publication No. 525.
18. T.I.B. Temporary Importation Under Bond. Publication No. 527.
19. Travel Industry Tips. Publication No. 529.
20. 807 Guide. Import requirements on articles assembled abroad from U.S. Components. Publication No. 536.
21. Customs Bonded Warehouse. Publication No. 537.
22. Foreign Trade Zones. Publication No. 538.
23. Markings of Country of Origin. Publication No. 539.
24. District Rulings Program. Publication No. 542.
25. Pleasure Boats. (How to import your boat). Publication No. 544.
26. This Is Customs. Publication No. 545.
27. Tariff Classification of Prospective Imports. Publication No. 550.
28. ATA Carnet. Publication No. 566.
29. Customs from A to Z. Publication No. 567.
30. Harmonized Tariff Schedule of the United States—Questions and Answers. Publication No. 576.
31. Questions and Answers on Customs Bonds. Publication No. 590.
32. U.S./Canada Free Trade Agreement. Publication No. 592.
33. Pre-Class. U.S. Customs Service Pre-Entry Classification Program. No Publication No.
34. Customs Declaration (for individuals and families; available in Chinese, Dutch, English, French, German, Italian, Japanese, Korean, Polish, Portuguese, and Spanish). Customs Form 6059B (102584).
35. Currency Reporting Form CF 4790. (available in Arabic, Chinese, English, French, German, Italian, Japanese, Korean, Spanish).
36. Currency Reporting Flyer. (available in English, German, Italian, Spanish).

InfoList #54

Suggestions for Working with U.S. Customs

1. Learn as much as you can about importing your product from this manual and other information sources before you call Customs with your questions. Use Customs for clarification of fine points, not for your complete education.
2. Don't call Customs with questions that can only be answered by other regulatory agencies of the U.S. government. Generally speaking, agency expertise does not overlap. For example, U.S. Customs will not be able to answer questions about Bureau of Alcohol, Tobacco and Firearms (BATF) requirements not enforced by Customs.
3. Find out about necessary import documentation and other agency requirements before you actually start importing.
4. Customs has enforcement responsibility for the regulations of a number of U.S. governmental agencies. Their responsibility to these agencies and to the U.S. public is significant and they take it seriously. Be prepared. Know what you're doing at all times. Don't expect Customs to overlook something "just this one time."
5. If you have a problem handling paperwork and other details, don't make your own Customs entries. Hire a customs broker who does this professionally and make life easier for yourself.
6. If you plan on importing a specific commodity over a period of time, establish a good relationship with the U.S. Customs commodity specialist for that commodity in your district. Help your commodity specialist help you: know everything about your commodity that you can. Respect his/her time pressures by keeping your questions limited to his/her area of expertise. Always be courteous—recognize that the Customs person has many other people clamoring for his/her attention, and is usually under a lot of pressure. Remember that this specialist probably knows more about Customs entry and clearance of that commodity than you will ever know.
7. Customs inspections of shipments is usual, so don't panic. Don't make life difficult for the inspector lest he/she return the favor.
8. You and Customs may disagree on the classification of an imported product. The disagreement will likely be that they see it in a higher duty-rate category, while you see it in a lower duty-rate category. "Presenting your case" for the lower rate category works better than "making an argument" for the lower rate category. Generally, your customs broker should be making your case for you. If you run up against a brick wall and are convinced that you have a good case, refer the matter to a customs lawyer who can work administratively for you with Customs.

InfoList #55

Update on the Mod Act

What is the Mod Act?

The Customs Modernization Act, passed in December 1993, amends the Tariff Act of 1930 (19 USC 1202 et seq.). This Mod Act, as it is known, is designed to streamline and automate the commercial operations of the U.S. Customs Service. Subsidiary goals include improving compliance and enforcement and providing standards to ensure uniformity and due process in Customs procedures. The Act (Title VI) contains four main subtitles which revise existing statutes to accommodate electronic processing; establish the National Customs Automation program (NCAP); amend administrative procedures; and enact various miscellaneous conforming amendments. Most of the provisions either codify existing practice or implement anticipated technological changes.

In general, importers will see little immediate effect from most of the specific changes in the Act, although it will radically change the way they conduct their business as its full effects are felt over time. Customs brokers, shippers, and Customs Service agents will be the first to feel the specific changes. The cumulative effect—which is designed to streamline and speed up customs procedures—will come primarily from the computerization as the Customs Service becomes wired and goes on-line. There will also be a reorganization of customs operations, with a substantial number of ports of entry offices being closed once automation allows expedited remote electronic filing of materials that currently require physical transmission of papers at the site of entry.

Key Provisions for Importers

Recordkeeping

In one of the areas that directly affects importers, Subtitle A specifically authorizes Customs to make reasonable audits of records required for the entry of goods and increases the recordkeeping responsibilities for those involved in importing. The procedures adopted are designed to reduce the paperwork required of importers at the time of entry by encouraging Customs to waive production of records at the time of entry while retaining the right to demand their production at a later date. Records may now be demanded from any owner, importer, consignee, importer of record, entry filer, or other interested party involved in importing goods into the U.S., or one who files a drawback claim, transports or stores merchandise carried or stored under bond, or knowingly causes importation or transportation or storage of merchandise under bond. Records may also be demanded from any agent of these parties or other person whose activities require filing a declaration, entry, or both.

If you are involved in any of these activities, the law requires you to maintain certain records for a specified period of time. The specific period varies according to the type of document and transaction, but in no case exceeds five years (drawback records must be retained for three years after the date of the payment of a drawback claim).

Records that must be kept include, but are not limited to, commercial invoices, packing lists, certificates of origin, declarations of foreign manufacturers, and any additional documents required for the particular entry, either in paper form or as electrically-generated or machine readable material. All such documents consist of those usually kept in the ordinary course of business: there is no requirement to prepare separate, additional documents to comply with the law.

A party who fails to produce documents demanded is subject to a monetary fine. Willful failure to maintain or produce documents can subject the party to a fine of the lesser of $100,000 or 75% of the value of the goods in the transaction in question, while negligence can result in a fine of the lesser of $10,000 or 40% of the value of the goods in question. Rates of duty on the goods may also be increased. Penalties are discretionary, not mandatory, and may be avoided in cases in which the party cannot produce the materials because of factors beyond its control or if Customs already has the materials. Affected parties may participate in a voluntary Customs Recordkeeping Compliance Program through which they can be given an advance written warning rather than immediately assessed with noncompliance. Penalties may also be assessed for submission of fraudulent information and for fraudulent drawback claims.

Detentions

Subtitle A also provides that Customs must make a decision on the admissibility of a shipment within five working days. Any goods not released within that period are considered to have been detained. After no more than five days, the authorities must issue a formal notice of detention to the importer or other interested party, complete with specifics as to what is required to rectify the situation. If Customs fails to make a determination within 30 days after presentation, the shipment is presumed to have been excluded. This 30 day period may be waived or extended based on specific administrative action or in compliance with the governing rules of other interested agencies.

Testing and Other Procedures

The Act provides for Customs to establish sampling and testing procedures and license accredited private testing laboratories. Customs must now publish any precedent-setting decisions within 90 days instead of in 120 days. Provisions also enumerate merchandise subject to seizure and under what conditions.

NCAP

Subtitle B establishes the National Customs Automation Program (NCAP) which will ultimately allow remote location electronic filing of customs documents to be phased in by 1999. The subtitle also extends definitions on drawback rules and periods of eligibility and recapture and sets new manifest and invoice requirements designed to facilitate electronic filing. This subtitle also provides for electronic batch filing and periodic reconciliation of accounts. The new system will eventually allow importers to electronically file documentation for numerous entries as a group, as well as pay duties and fees on a monthly account basis rather than filing and paying separately for each entry as it occurs.

Other Provisions

Subtitle C consists of various administrative amendments aimed primarily at internal Customs procedures, such as allowing the waiver of fees on nonmaterial amounts, and technicalities affecting shippers. However, Section C also changes the rules under which goods may be seized and sold by Customs. Under the Act, the time that unclaimed merchandise must be held before it can be auctioned off is reduced from 12 to six months. Customs also has the option of appropriating the merchandise for its own use after giving the importer 30 days notice. And Customs may also dispose of merchandise immediately if it is unclaimed and officials deem that the cost of storing it is "disproportionate" to its value.

These procedures—designed to speed up operations in a computerized environment—become more important given that revamped liquidation procedures mandated elsewhere in the Act allow Customs more leeway to classify merchandise as unclaimed. These rules include entries submitted with incomplete paperwork as unclaimed along with truly unclaimed shipments lacking any paperwork.

Subtitle D consists of miscellaneous technical corrections designed to update and upgrade Customs authorization.

InfoList #56

Selecting and Working with a Customs Broker

Customs brokers are licensed by the Department of Treasury, U.S. Customs Service to conduct business with U.S. Customs on behalf of individual and corporate importers. For a fee, the customs broker will expedite your Customs entries.

Note: Don't go into a relationship with a Customs broker thinking that his or her job is to handle everything without your input. The most effective combination is that of an informed importer working in harmony with a knowledgeable and competent Customs broker.

1. Find a customs broker who has a large enough business to adequately handle the types of services you require. If you have a small operation importing non-regulated items, with no cargo forwarding, a small outfit will probably be just fine. If you are a larger-scale importer with offices in a number of locations making many, frequent entries, and/or importing heavily-regulated products, a larger, more established firm with multiple offices may be indicated.
2. What is the reputation of the brokerage? How many years has it been in business? Don't be afraid to ask for references. Actually follow up on them.
3. How many licensed brokers on are staff? In multi-office customs brokerage firms Customs only requires one licensed broker per district. Therefore, it is possible to have a local office that works off the license of someone far away. For example, the licensed broker for the district of Dallas may work out of the Dallas office, but be the central licensee for offices in northern Texas, and areas of Oklahoma and Kansas.
4. What is the financial stability of the brokerage? Customs regulations state that "The liability for duties, both regular and additional, attaching on importation, constitutes a personal debt due from the importer to the U.S." and "Payment to a broker covering duties does not relieve the importer of liability if the duties are not paid by the broker."

   Ask for a financial statement, financial references and/or their bank and bank officer's name. Follow up with your research until you feel comfortable in your choice of broker.
5. Does the broker have the technical expertise and knowledge of your specific product(s)? Does the broker specialize in your product(s)? This becomes more of an issue with highly-regulated items such as textiles and other quota products.
6. Do you get along well with the broker? Do you feel that you have good enough communication with the broker that you can work together as "partners?"
7. What are the fees for handling your types of Customs entries? Be sure to ask up front how much it will cost to handle your business. Note that charges can add up for each additional form that your broker completes for you. Always ask for all fees, not simply the basic entry fee.
8. Be prepared to submit a financial statement if you plan to ask for credit terms. Note that brokers are just like any other business in handling their accounts. The problem with credit terms is that Customs duties may amount to $3,000 on an entry the broker charges $320 for processing. Brokers are not at all thrilled about extending soft credit terms to their clients. Net 10 days with immediate cut-off of credit terms if you are slow to pay is common.
9. Be prepared to provide your broker with a power of attorney. This is a legal document that empowers your broker to act as an agent on your behalf with Customs. It authorizes them to sign your name to documents. Refer to "Power of Attorney" on page 78.
10. You will be required to purchase either a surety bond for each importation or a continuous bond to cover a series of ongoing importations.
11. Note that you can make checks for Customs duties payable to your customs broker or to Customs. If you have any unresolved concerns about your broker, make the check payable directly to Customs, forwarding it to your broker along with a separate check to cover their fees.
12. Your customs broker should be a major player on your team of "professional partners." You can almost always get insights on such additional questions as how you can save on international transportation, Customs duties, warehousing, cartage, etc. Ask to be kept informed of any changes in Customs regulations which affect your products.
13. Your customs broker does much more than clear goods through Customs. These professionals can also provide door-to-door delivery of freight to one or to many locations across the U.S. They can help advise you on issues and opportunities such as Foreign Trade Zones, Temporary Importation under Bond, warehousing, cartage, pre-clearance of cargo, marking and labeling, other agency requirements, etc.
14. You can find a customs broker by referring to the "Yellow Pages" of a port city under the listing "Customs Brokers."

    To locate a customs broker who is a member of a trade association for brokers, Refer to "Customs Brokers, Freight Forwarders, and Professional Associations" on page 51, which provides the names, addresses, and telephone numbers of customs brokers associations throughout the U.S.

InfoList #57

Customs Brokers, Freight Forwarders, and Professional Associations

Customs brokers are licensed by the U.S. Department of the Treasury and must demonstrate their knowledge of Customs regulations, procedures, tariffs, laws, and administrative rulings. The broker's task includes responsibility for assessing tariff classification, quota compliance, and anticipation of difficulties in the entry of the client's products. Brokers also often provide advice regarding shipping, including carriers, routes, and modes of transportation. Besides dealing with U.S. Customs, the customs broker must also keep current on the regulations of as many as 40 U.S. government agencies in order to represent clients before them.

Ocean freight forwarders are licensed by the Federal Maritime Commission (FMC), and international air cargo agents are licensed by the International Air Transportation Association (IATA). These forwarders advise clients on rates, routings, and modes of transport, assembling a customized package to cover the needs of the particular client, schedule, and commodity. Forwarders not only juggle the movements of specific shipments, but also must keep current on regulations such as those governing documentation, shipping, packaging, labeling, handling, licensing, and restrictions for both the U.S. and numerous foreign countries. Forwarders arrange for storage, disbursement, consolidation, bulk transit, and inland as well as international transport for door to door service. Forwarders can also help in preparing quotes, pro forma invoices, and other documents required for international payments.

The National Customs Brokers & Forwarders Association of America, Inc. (NCBFAA) represents customs brokers, international freight forwarders, and international air cargo agents in the U.S. Membership in this professional trade association includes 33 affiliated local and regional associations nationwide. Founded in 1897, the NBFAA represents the industry before Congress and regulatory agencies, maintaining national committees on policy and areas of industry concern. The national association operates educational programs and communications services for its members and the public aimed at disseminating information regarding current issues, as well as updates on rulings, decisions, and new and pending legislation.

You can find a customs broker or freight forwarder by referring to the Yellow Pages of a port city under the listing "Customs Brokers," "Freight Consolidating" or "Freight Forwarding." All customs brokers must be licensed by the U.S. Customs Service. If you wish to work with a customs broker who is also a member of a professional association, you can get references through the following list. Affiliated associations of the NCBFAA are organized into eight regions: Area 1 (Northern Border Area), Area 2 (New York Region), Area 3 (Northwest Region), Area 4 (Southeast Region, Area 5 (North Central Region), Area 6 (Pacific Region), Area 7 (South Central/Southwest Region), and Area 8 (Mexico-U.S. Border Region).

The National Association

National Customs Brokers & Forwarders Association of America, Inc. (NCBFAA)
1 World Trade Center, Suite 1153
New York, NY 10048
Tel (212) 432-0050, FAX (212) 432-5709

Atlanta

Independent Freight Forwarders & Customs House Brokers Association of Atlanta
President: Gayla Knowles
Division M
5139 Southridge Pkwy, Ste. 124, Atlanta, GA 30349
Tel (404) 991-2224, FAX (404) 991-9391

NAC Member: Janet Jenkins
J.V. Carr & Son
400 Tradeport Blvd., Ste. 408, Atlanta, GA 30354
Tel (404) 363-4090, FAX (404) 363-0085

Baltimore

Baltimore Customs Brokers & Forwarders Association
President: H. Nicholas Patronik
Patron Services, Inc.
908 Light St., Baltimore, MD 21230-4016

NAC Member: Louis G. Connor, Jr.
John S. Connor, Inc.
33 S. Gay St., Baltimore, MD 21202-4006
Tel (410) 332-4800, FAX (410) 547-6865

Boston

Boston Customs Brokers & International Forwarders Association
President: James W. Lawless
C.H. Powell Co.
One Inter-Continental Way, Peabody, MA 01960
Tel (508) 535-7073, FAX (508) 535-7028

Brownsville

Brownsville Customs Brokers Association
President: Angel A. Oliva-Hardison
Brownsville Customs Broker Association
265 E 12th St., Brownsville, TX 78520
Tel (210) 544-6934, FAX (210) 544-6999

NAC Member: Frank Parker, Jr.
Parker & Company
4694 Coffee Port Rd., Brownsville, TX 78522-0484
Tel (210) 831-2000, FAX (210) 831-4140

Charleston

Customs Brokers and Freight Forwarders Association of Charleston, SC, Inc.
President: Rosemary R. Downs
Frederick Richards, Inc.
P.O. Box 1267, Charleston, SC 29402
Tel (803) 769-2000, FAX (803) 769-2009

NAC Member: Jacqueline H. Adamson
John S. James Co.
P.O. Box 1017, Charleston, SC 29402
Tel (803) 554-6400, FAX (803) 554-4270

Charlotte

Independent Freight Forwarders & Customhouse Brokers Association of Charlotte, NC, Inc.
President & NAC Member: Maxine G. Kohlbacher
Maxine G. Kohlbacher, CHB, Division of MGK, Inc.
P.O. Box 19572, Charlotte, NC 28219
Tel (704) 359-8157, FAX (704) 359-0649

Chicago

Customs Brokers & Freight Forwarders Association of Chicago, Inc.
President & NAC Member: Pam Hynes
J.D.C. International, Inc.
945 N. Edgewood, Ste. G., Wood Dale, IL 60191
Tel (708) 616-7770, FAX (708) 616-7774

Columbia River

Columbia River Customs Brokers & Forwarders Association
President & NAC Member: Bob Coleman
Total Logistics Resources, Inc. (TLR)
5362 NE 112th Ave., Portland, OR 97220-1008
Tel (503) 257-6090, FAX (503) 254-6021

Executive Secretary: Doris Allen
Columbia River Customs Brokers & Forwarders Assn.
200 SW Market St., Ste 190, Portland, OR 97201
Tel (503) 228-4361, FAX (503) 295-3660

Connecticut

Connecticut Customs Brokers Association
President: Michael Silva
A.N. Deringer Co., Inc.
Rte. 20 Hazelwood Industrial Park, East Granby, CT 06026
Tel (203) 653-3450, FAX (203) 653-3450

NAC Member: William Connolly
Connecticut Customs Broker Association
Bradley International Airport, Cargo Complex A
Windsor Locks, CT 06096
Tel (203) 653-9040, FAX (203) 653-9640

Detroit

Detroit Customhouse Brokers & Foreign Freight Forwarders Association, Inc.
President: Tony Troja
PBB USA, Inc.
11700 Metro Airport Center Dr., Romulus, MI 48174
Tel (313) 942-7000, FAX (313) 942-7985

NAC Member: Martin W. Bloch
Intertrans Corporation
9770 Harrison Road, Romulus, MI 48174
Tel (313) 946-5210, FAX (313) 946-4017

El Paso

El Paso Customs Brokers Association
President and NAC Member: Raul A. Gomez
Rudolph Miles & Sons, Inc.
P.O. Box 11057, El Paso, TX 79983-1057
Tel (915) 778-3636, FAX (915) 778-7401

Florida

Florida Customs Brokers & Forwarders Association., Inc.
President: Aleida Fontao
Aleida Customs Brokers
7938 NW 66th St., Miami, FL 33166
Tel (305) 477-2235, FAX (305) 477-2615

NAC Member: Jose Aguirre
Miami Int'l Forwarders
1801 NW 82nd Ave., Miami, FL 33126
Tel (305) 5934-0038, FAX (305) 593-0431

Executive Vice Present: Barbara Reilly-Lang
Florida Customs Brokers & Forwarders Association
Cargo Clearance Center, P.O. Box 52-2022, Miami, FL 33152
Tel (305) 871-7177, FAX (305) 871-2712

Hidalgo

Port of Hidalgo Customs Brokers Association
President: Sergio Alvarez
Port of Hidalgo Customs Brokers Association
P.O. Box 800, Hidalgo, TX 78557
Tel (210) 843-9722, FAX (210) 843-7480

NAC Member: Jimmy Santos
Jimmy Santos, Inc.
P.O. Box 800, Hidalgo, TX 78557
Tel (210) 843-2711, FAX (210) 843-8838

Executive Director: Diana Rodriguez
P.O. Box 800, Hidalgo, TX 78557
Tel (210) 843-9722, FAX (210) 843-7480

Houston

Houston Customhouse Brokers & Freight Forwarders Association
President: Alexander Arroyos, Sr.
Houston Customhouse Brokers & Freight Forwarders Association
P.O. Box 53538, Houston, TX 77052
Tel (713) 672-0515, FAX (713) 672-0786

NAC Member: Diana L. Bynum
D.L. Bynum & Company, Inc.
P.O. Box 60044 AMF, Houston, TX 77205
Tel (713) 821-2011, FAX (713) 821-0739

Executive Vice President: John O. Burke
Houston Customhouse Brokers & Freight Forwarders Association
P.O. Box 53359, Houston, TX 77052
Tel (713) 678-4300, FAX (713) 678-4236

JFK Airport, New York

JFK Airport Customs Brokers Association Inc.
President: Gary Scibelli
Overton & Co.
150 Broadway, New York, NY 10038
Tel (212) 233-3493, FAX (212) 267-5689

NAC Member: Michelle Maslow
Martin Strauss Air Freight
147-31 176th St., Jamaica, NY 11430
Tel (718) 656-5505, FAX (718) 656-4298

Administrative Assistant: Penny Dunklee
JFK Airport Customs Brokers Association, Inc.
P. O. Box 432, JFK Int'l Airport, Jamaica, NY 11430
Tel (718) 528-4117, FAX (718) 949-1286

Laredo

Laredo Customhouse Brokers Association
President: Hector Farias, Jr.
Farias & Farias, Inc.
U.S. Customhouse Broker
International Trade Center at La Posada
1000 Zaragosa St., Ste. 100, Laredo, TX 78040
Tel (210) 723-1583, FAX (210) 727-7627

NAC Member: Federico C. Zuniga
F. Zuniga, Inc., P.O. Box 692, Laredo, TX 78042-0692
Tel (210) 722-0745, FAX (210) 722-4928

Los Angeles

Los Angeles Customs & Freight Brokers Association, Inc.
President and NAC Member: Brenda Stringfield
William M. Stringfield
249 E. Ocean Blvd., Suite 1008, Long Beach, CA 90802
Tel (310) 436-5229, FAX (310) 437-2793

NAC Member: Enrico Salvo
Carmichael International
533 Glendale Blvd., Los Angeles, CA 90026
Tel (213) 250-0186, FAX (213) 250-1710

Executive Director: Monika Wegener
The Los Angeles Customs & Freight Brokers Association., Inc.
P. O. Box 4250, Sunland, CA 91040
Tel (818) 951-2842, FAX (818) 353-5976

Mobile

Association of Forwarding Agents & Foreign Freight Brokers of Mobile, Inc.
President: Michael Lee
Page & Jones, Inc.
P.O. Drawer "J", Mobile, AL 36601
Tel (205) 432-1646, FAX (205) 433-1402

NAC Member: Lila Davis
M.G. Maher & Company, Inc.
P.O. Box 2242, Mobile, AL 36601
Tel (205) 433-8474, FAX (205) 438-3103

New Orleans

International Freight Forwarders & Customs Brokers Association of New Orleans, Inc.
President and NAC Member: William App, Jr.
J. W. Allen & Company, Inc.
442 Canal Street, Ste. 206, New Orleans, LA 70130
Tel (504) 561-0181, FAX (504) 561-0191

Executive Secretary: Claire Maitre
International Freight Forwarders & Customs Brokers Association of New Orleans, Inc.
1132 World Trade Ctr., 2 Canal Street, New Orleans, LA 70130
Tel (504) 525-7201, FAX (504) 523-7201

New York

New York Foreign Freight Forwarders & Brokers Association
President: Stewart Hauser
D. Hauser, Inc.
182-23 150th Ave., Springfield Gardens, NY 11413
Tel (718) 656-7767, FAX (718) 656-4710

NAC Member: James A. Burghart
A. Burghart Shipping Co., Inc.
Rte. 1 & International Way, Newark, NJ 07114
Tel (201) 824-5201, FAX (201) 824-9741

Executive Director: Barbara Spector Yeninas
New York Freight Forwarders & Brokers Association
185 Fairfield Ave., Ste. 2D, West Caldwell, NJ 07006
Tel (201) 268-6960, FAX (201) 226-6685

Nogales

Nogales U.S. Customs Brokers Association, Inc.
President and NAC Member: Guillermo Valencia
Valencia International, Inc.
P.O. Box 2770, Nogales, AZ 85728-2770
Tel (602) 281-0672, FAX (602) 281-4506

North Texas

North Texas Customs Brokers & Foreign Freight Forwarders Association
President: Margaret Kelcey
Panalpina, Inc.
P.O. Box 610014, Dallas/Ft. Worth Airport, TX 75261
Tel (214) 456-0880, FAX (214) 456-0884

NAC Member: Ruby Wood
Evans and Wood & Co., Inc.
1722 Minters Chapel, Ste. 300, Grapevine, TX 76051
Tel (817) 481-2028, FAX (817) 481-4716

Northern Border

Customs Brokers Association Northern U. S. Border
President: Burtram W. Anderson
Tower Group International, C.J. Tower Division
128 Dearborn St., Buffalo, NY 14207
Tel (716) 874-1300, FAX (716) 874-4396

NAC Member: Arthur S. Spiegel
Trans-Border Customs Services
P.O. Box 800, Champlain, NY 12919
Tel (518) 298-8000, FAX (518) 298-3346

Northern California

Customs Brokers & Forwarders Association of Northern California
President: Dianne Weldon
Columbia Shipping Inc.
1164 Cherry Ave., San Bruno, CA 94066
Tel (415) 588-0468, FAX (415) 588-3279

NAC Member: Tim Hannon
R.S. Express, Inc.
300 Swift Ave., South San Francisco, CA 94080
Tel (415) 583-9122, FAX (415) 588-9598

Executive Director: Jeremy W. Potash
San Francisco Customs Brokers & Freight Forwarders Association
P.O. Box 26269, San Francisco, CA 94126-6269
Tel (415) 510) 536-2233, FAX (510) 261-9598

Philadelphia

Philadelphia Customs Broker & Forwarders Association
President: Francis A. Keegan
Philadelphia Customs Brokers & Forwarders Association
Cargo Building #2, Philadelphia International Airport
Philadelphia, PA 19153
Tel (215) 365-3307, FAX (215) 365-0390

NAC Member: David Weiss
Wolf D. Barth Company
721 Chestnut Street, Philadelphia, PA 19106
Tel (215) 238-8600, FAX (215) 592-1254

San Diego District

San Diego District Brokers Association
President and NAC Member: Barbara J. Camacho
Camacho Brokers Inc.
9465 Customhouse Plaza, Ste. B, San Ysidro, CA 92173-0205
Tel (619) 661-6311, FAX (619) 661-6315

Savannah

Independent Freight Forwarders & Customs Brokers Association of Savannah, Inc.
President and NAC Member: Jan Fields
John S. James Company
P.O. Box 2166, Savannah, GA 31498
Tel (912) 233-0211, FAX (912) 233-2150

Southern Border

Southern Border Customhouse Brokers Association
President and NAC Member: William F. Joffroy, Jr.
William F. Joffroy Customs Brokers Inc.
P.O. Box 698, Nogales, AZ 85628-0698
Tel (602) 287-1500, FAX (602) 287-1524

Virginia

Customs Brokers and International Freight Forwarders Association of Virginia, Inc.
President and NAC Member: Catherine M. Carney
The Harper Group
201 E. City Hall Ave., Norfolk, VA 23514
Tel (804) 622-3373, FAX (804) 627-0005

Washington State

Customhouse Brokers & International Freight Forwarders Association of Washington State
President and NAC Member: Crystal Osborne
Alfred H. Marzolf Inc.
157 Yesler Way, Seattle, WA 98104
Tel (206) 623-4284, FAX (206) 623-4139

Washington DC

Washington Custom Brokers & Freight Forwarders Association
President and NAC Member: Shirley Laing
Laing International, Inc.
P.O. Box 18144, Dulles International Airport
Washington, DC 20041
Tel (703) 471-9279, FAX (703) 471-8436

Wilmington

Customs Brokers & Freight Forwarders Association of Wilmington, NC, Inc.
President: Elsa Stokes
Wilmington Shipping Co., d/b/a Southern Overseas Corp.
P.O. Box 2110, Wilmington, NC 28402
Tel (919) 392-8200, FAX (919) 392-4251

NAC Member: Janice Wilson
A.J. Fritz & Co.
P.O. Box 1208, Wilmington, NC 28402
Tel (919) 791-5061, FAX (919) 392-4251

Wisconsin

Wisconsin Customs Brokers & Forwarders Association
President: Robert L. Gardenier
M.E. Dey & Co
P.O. Box 37165, Milwaukee, WI 53237-0165
Tel (414) 747-7000, FAX (414) 747-7010

InfoList #58

Role of the Customs Attorney

The Customs attorney advises and provides a varied group of services to his or her client. These include advising the client in connection with ongoing transactions to ensure that the correct rate of duty is being assessed, as well as providing advice and representation in various matters before the Customs Service or in litigation before the Court of International Trade.

The Customs attorney is active in counseling and representing importers on administrative matters before the United States Customs Service, at the local, regional and national levels. Areas of representation typically include advising importers on how to structure transactions to take full advantage of lower or free duty rates provided by the classification and valuation laws of the United States; representing importers who have had merchandise detained or seized, or against whom penalties or claims for liquidated damages have been asserted; representing importers involved in U.S. trademark, patent, or copyright issues; and representing importers in issues involving laws or quota restrictions for textiles and apparel. The Customs attorney also conducts compliance reviews for importers, and actively represents and assists importers in preparation for, during, or subsequent to, audits by the Customs Service. Other areas of emphasis include utilizing foreign trade zones for duty exemptions, drawbacks, the Generalized System of Preferences, U.S. goods returned exemptions, and marking requirements.

Activities before the administrative agency include settlement of disputes relating to possible classification and valuation of imported products as well as potential penalty assessments. Specific activities which a Customs attorney should consider in his or her review of import transactions include the following:

1. Correct classification of imported products under Headquarters rulings or pertinent court decisions.
2. Review of the status of pending issues or legislation regarding classification which could be of significance to the client.
3. Examination of the buyer/seller relationships, assists, the price paid or payable, and related and accounting procedures to verify that the proper import values are being reported to the Customs Service, and the appropriate duties paid thereon.
4. Review of the correctness of the marking of imported products and other agency laws which might affect the imported products.
5. Verification that there are no potential antidumping duties or countervailing duties applicable to the imported products or other relevant actions before the International Trade Commission or Office of the Special Trade Representative.
6. Verification that potential drawback is being properly captured and that the appropriate types of claims are being filed with the Customs Service.
7. Verification that the client has in effect appropriate recordkeeping procedures in compliance with the Customs laws and regulations and that the company will maintain these records over a five-year period of time.

   These record requirements relate to all documents concerning the company's import transactions. (Under the Modernization Act, the importer may be assessed penalties if appropriate records are not maintained.)

A Customs attorney provides advice, consultation, and representation to Customs brokers, bonded warehouse owners, foreign trade zone operators, freight forwarders, and other law firms in such diverse, specialized areas as electronics, textiles, steel, general merchandise, automotive, and food products.

The Customs attorney must have a substantial litigation background with the skills and support staff necessary to fully pursue clients' rights in what is one of the most complex and least understood areas of the law. The Customs attorney must be admitted to practice before the United States Court of International Trade and the Court of Appeals for the Federal Circuit, as well as various other federal and state courts.

A Customs attorney's litigation practice encompasses a broad spectrum of customs cases, including classification and value, special duty exemption, seized or prohibited merchandise, and penalty actions.

The Customs attorney often has expertise in the related field of international trade practice, which may include antidumping and Section 301 law concerning unfair trade practices. Additionally, the Customs attorney may assist clients in the area of export licensing by offering consultation and representation to chemical, electronic, and high-technology clients in penalty proceedings for violation of the Export Administration Regulations or the International Traffic and Arms Regulations, and before the Department of Commerce and the Department of State with regard to export licensing issues. Representation may include establishing corporate procedures for controlling exports; determining controlled commodities; obtaining emergency export licenses, and special licenses, such as distribution and protect licenses; and assisting exporters prepare for systems reviews by the Office of Export Licensing.

Courtesy of:

The Law Offices of George R. Tuttle, Customs Lawyers
3 Embarcadero Center, Suite 1160
San Francisco, California 94111
Tel (415) 986-8780

InfoList #59

The American Association of Exporters and Importers

The American Association of Exporters and Importers (AAEI) is a professional trade association representing U.S. businesses engaged in foreign trade. Founded in 1921, the AAEI promotes fair and open trade among nations. Its staff has developed strong expertise in numerous areas of trade and represents the foreign trade constituency before official bodies in Washington and around the country.

This voluntary association has more than 1,200 member firms covering a wide range of specific industries. The AAEI also includes members representing others involved in international trade, such as customs brokers, freight forwarders, trading companies, financial institutions, and attorneys, adding the perspective and support of even more parties with immediate interests in international trade. This broad base gives the association added heft as a voice for the concerns of its membership. This breadth has enabled the AAEI to deliver its pro-trade message without becoming bogged down in the particular problems of individual industries.

Services

The AAEI serves as a contact point with the executive and legislative branches and with government regulatory agencies. Its Weekly Trade Alert covers recent developments affecting international business and reports on deliberations and actions of various government bodies, including the Department of Commerce, the U.S. Trade Representative, the Department of the Treasury, the U.S. Customs Service, the Food and Drug Administration, the Federal Trade Commission, and the Consumer Product Safety Commission, among others. Regular features cover Customs decisions, judicial rulings relevant to trade, reports on export trading firms, countertrade, a Pacific Rim trade report, and product standards developments. It also has a section for opportunities and a countertrade clearing house. A digest of special information is offered through the association's weekly ALERTFAX.

The AAEI publishes a series of topical special reports, the Special Information Bulletins and Reference Manuals, which have covered such issues as the Harmonized Tariff Schedule, U.S. export controls, the Generalized System of Preferences, the Caribbean Basin Initiative, countertrade, the Foreign Sales Corporation Act, the U.S.-Israel Free Trade Agreement, the U.S.-Canada Free Trade Agreement, East-West trade, and related issues.

The Weekly Textile Quota Alert is a computer-based service available to members that allows them to keep abreast of the latest developments in the areas of textile quotas, embargoes, visas, and bilateral agreements. The GSP Subscription Service covers changes in eligibility, petitions to add and delete products in specific countries, legislative and executive activity, and publishes key documents. The Export Controls Progress Reports reports on changes in export controls policy and specific rulings; legislative, executive, and regulatory actions and initiatives; judicial decisions; and current news from the field. The association's International Trade Quarterly offers in-depth features on current issues in international trade, a Washington round-up, and sections on trade briefs and trade opportunities.

Programs

The AAEI actively monitors legislation and regulatory deliberations. It testifies before government bodies and intervenes in regulatory and legal proceedings in support of trade interests. Its staff offers advice, research capabilities, and support to members with specific trade concerns. Its One-Stop Hotline information and referral service can help with procedures and directions to the appropriate agencies, and it maintains a reference center for the use of members.

The association operates a network of active regional and national committees dealing with issues of interest to its members to share expertise and help set policy. Special committees are convened as needed to deal with specific areas of interest, such as automation, the Harmonized Tariff Schedule conversion, NAFTA, environmental and consumer issues, countervailing duties and antidumping issues, international finance, insurance, customs policy and enforcement, transportation, and trade legislation. Standing committees deal with general trade policy and regulation, formulating proactive policy positions to attempt to convey the opinions of international traders to government. The AAEI also helps organize industry-based associations to pool the expertise of members in a particular field for action on critical issues. For example, the association's Textile and Apparel Group has become the largest such interest group in the nation and is highly influential in lobbying for freer trade in these areas.

The AAEI sponsors an annual meeting held during World Trade Week in May which regularly attracts cabinet-level speakers for a series of briefing sessions to which all members are invited. AAEI conferences and seminars cover such topics as foreign exchange, international codes, transportation cost management, and trade legislation. The association's annual two-day Importing Techniques and Strategies conference is supplemented by trade basics seminars for small and medium-sized operators. This educational program includes more than 20 annual workshops dealing with operational level issues (members are entitled to attend one workshop free annually).

The AAEI maintains an exchange program with the U.S. Customs Service through which members and Customs personnel can meet to discuss operational and policy issues. These briefings are scheduled at major ports nationwide and are available to members.

The association, headquartered in New York, maintains regional offices in Chicago, Los Angeles, San Francisco, and Portland, OR, with a representative office in Washington, DC.

For more information, contact:

Director of Member Services
American Association of Exporters and Importers
11 West 42nd Street
New York, NY 10036
Tel (212) 944-230, FAX (212) 382-2606

InfoList #60

12 Ways to Sell Imported Merchandise

1. Sell Wholesale to Retail Outlets

Almost any consumer product imaginable—jewelry, wearing apparel, toys, art, utensils, and more—can be sold directly to retail outlets by an individual importer/sales person or a large-scale import/sales organization. One consideration is that the cost of traveling and making sales presentations makes selling a single product inefficient unless the product is in great demand or has a substantial margin of profit. Generally, you will be more effective if you have a whole product line of related goods to sell.

2. Sell to Distributors

An alternative to selling wholesale to retailers is to sell in bulk to distributors who have an established client base within a given geographic area and/or a specific industry group. They can often get wide coverage in a short time. Recognize that the discount you need to give them may eat up a substantial portion of your profit margin.

3. Sell Wholesale to Manufacturers

Most small- and medium-sized manufacturers don't have the time or inclination to travel the world, seeking raw materials and component parts for their manufacturing operations. They will often prefer to purchase from a steady local supplier.

4. Wholesale Direct Mail

Some small and less expensive products may lend themselves to wholesale direct-mail marketing, especially those which you can send a free sample of to the prospective client. The advantage of this marketing is that you can get large-scale distribution in a short time and avoid the discounts a distributor demands.

5. Retail Direct Mail

Some importers have cut out the middleman entirely by going direct to the consumer via direct mail sales. Beware: some products lend themselves to direct mail more than others. You will need a well-defined market niche, a high margin of profit, a superbly targeted mail campaign, and a highly effective—well-designed and written—marketing piece.

6. Catalog Sales

Some importers deal in items that they can sell to catalog houses while others seek to develop their own catalog company. The former opportunity generally means a lower margin of profit, lower risk, and lower required capitalization, while the latter generally offers the promise of a higher margin, greater risk, and the need for more capital. One of the key factors in a catalog business is the development of a mailing list of people or companies who will buy a particular type or style of product over and over again.

7. Retail

If you have an established retail business you are in an excellent position to gauge the market for products for your existing clientele. You will also have familiarity with wholesale and retail pricing structures and, if you buy right, the opportunity to take an additional slice of the profits by importing products yourself.

Start by importing goods you are familiar with before branching out into new products.

Starting your own retail store at the same time you start your import business is much riskier. You likely will not have the necessary feel for the market for products you are importing, and you will be juggling too many responsibilities to handles all of them well.

8. Television Shopping Shows

Television shopping programs are an interesting and nontraditional means of selling imported products. However, they have an interest in the unusual and are always looking for new, offbeat merchandise. Consider that the pricing has to be just right and that there has to be an immediately available supply.

9. Contract Manufacturing

Submit proposals to existing wholesalers, distributors, or retailers of products similar to yours to manufacture products to their specification on a contract basis. Be prepared to be able to satisfy them that you are capable of following through on your proposal.

10. Act as an Agent

If you have good contacts with overseas sources of supply, and with U.S. distributors, wholesalers, or manufacturers who need those products, consider acting as an agent for the U.S. buyers and/or for the overseas sellers. This is a good route to follow if your contacts and expertise are better than your ability to finance a transaction.

Refer to "The Transferable Letter of Credit" under "Special Documentary Credits" on page 134 for information on how to structure payment for such deals.

11. The "Show and Tell and Sell" Party

Many importers get their start by importing small quantities of a wide range of products that they know will be of interest to their friends and relatives. Upon their return from the buying trip they invite them over for a "show and tell and sell" party.

Some enterprising importers expanded on the theme by giving 10% commission to friends to host a theme import party (e.g. "Bali Imports Party").

12. "Flea" Markets

A big business has developed selling product lines of imported merchandise at large-scale flea markets across the country. Some importers have established distributorships in multi-state regions supplying quantities of merchandise to sellers who are paid a percentage of the profits. This method generally requires excellent direct-to-the-consumer pricing.

InfoList #61

Import Goods Duty-Free!

Preferential Trade Status

Through special trade agreements, the U.S. has established favorable—and in some cases, extremely favorable—trade conditions with specific countries and associations of countries. In a number of cases you can enter goods duty free as long as you satisfy the conditions of the specific program, usually having to do with origination of the products in the signatory country. Importers who take advantage of these programs are often able to undercut the competition by offering lower prices based on the more favorable duty rates they obtain on the products they import through these programs. Here is a review of trade categories and programs:

Generalized System of Preferences (GSP)

This is a program providing for duty-free entry of eligible merchandise into the United States from 117 countries, 26 nonindependent countries and territories, three associations of countries (the Cartagena Group in South America, ASEAN in Southeast Asia and the Pacific, and CARICOM in the Caribbean), and 36 least-developed countries which receive additional special preferential treatment. Refer to "Generalized System of Preferences (GSP)" on page 199.

Caribbean Basin Initiative (CBI)

Established by the Caribbean Basin Economic Recovery Act (CBERA), this is another program providing for duty-free entry of eligible merchandise into the United States from 24 developing countries of the Caribbean Basin. Refer to "Caribbean Basin Initiative (CBI)" on page 201.

North American Free Trade Agreement (NAFTA)

At the end of 1993 the United States, Canada, and Mexico signed a broad agreement to eliminate restrictions on the flow of goods, services, and investment among the three countries. This includes the phasing out of tariffs over a period of years, elimination of non-tariff barriers and full protection of intellectual property rights. The agreement also includes special treatment for the partners with regard to quotas and establishes a trilateral commission to adjudicate trade disputes. NAFTA supersedes the existing U.S.-Canada Free Trade Agreement, although the provisions governing trade with Canada remain essentially the same as under the earlier agreement and are incorporated into the new document. Refer to "The North American Free Trade Agreement (NAFTA)" on page 197 and to "Update on NAFTA" on page 60.

U.S.-Israel Free Trade Area Agreement

Israel is the beneficiary of a program providing for free or reduced rates of duty for eligible merchandise imported from Israel into the United States. "U.S.-Israel Free Trade Area Agreement" on page 203 for a fuller discussion of this program.

Compact of the Freely Associated States

The Compact of the Associated States provides for duty-free entry of eligible products manufactured in the Marshall Islands and the Federated States of Micronesia. Refer to General Note 9 of the Harmonized Tariff Schedule of the United States (HTSUS) and to "Compact of the Freely Associated States" on page 204.

Product Specific Preferences

The Automotive Products Trade Act provides for duty-free import of automotive parts to registered U.S. manufacturers. Refer to General Note 5 of the Harmonized Tariff Schedule of the United States (HTSUS).

The Articles for Duty-Free Treatment to the Agreement on Trade in Civil Aircraft provides for duty-free import of approved aircraft components for the manufacture of civil aircraft by U.S. firms. Refer to General Note 6 of the HTSUS.

Temporary Free Importation

An ATA carnet is an international customs document which may be used for the temporary duty-free importation of certain goods into a country (U.S.) in lieu of the usual customs documents required. Refer to "Temporary Free Importations" on page 195.

The Andean Trade Preference Act (ATPA)

Under the Andean Trade Preference Act (ATPA), eligible products from Bolivia, Colombia, Ecuador, and Peru may be imported duty free. Refer to Commodity Index Andean Trade Preference Act (ATPA), beginning on page 202, and to General Note 11 of the Harmonized Trade Schedule of the United States (HTSUS).

U.S. Foreign Trade Zones

U.S. Foreign Trade Zones are places in the U.S. which, for Customs purposes, are considered outside the Customs Territory of the U.S. There are many operations you can perform on goods to enable you to import them duty-free, or at reduced duty rates. Refer to "Foreign Trade Zones" on page 232.

Duty-Free Products and Commodities

There are thousands of products and commodities which are already duty-free. Refer to the Commodity Index, Sample Duty Rates subhead in this manual for examples of products which may be imported duty-free.

InfoList #62

Update on GATT and the WTO

What Is GATT?

The General Agreement on Tariffs and Trade (GATT) consists of a set of rules to govern international trade. It began in 1947 as a response to predatory and protectionist trade in the 1930s. Since its beginning, GATT has gained a total of 123 members and lowered average global tariffs from an average of roughly 40% to the current 5%. Under the latest amendments to the agreement, overall tariffs are expected to fall to about 3.75%. The latest agreement, the culmination of the Uruguay Round of GATT negotiations, was signed by 117 nations on December 15, 1993. Once the treaty is formally ratified by the signatories it is scheduled to go into effect on July 1, 1995.

What Is the WTO?

The World Trade Organization (WTO) is the successor to GATT. The agreement creates an international body to administer the new provisions, the majority of which are designed to reduce tariff and nontariff barriers to international trade.

Key provisions

- **Import tariffs:** Eventual overall reduction of 33% in tariffs worldwide, with elimination by the U.S., European, and other industrial nations of all tariffs on pharmaceuticals, construction equipment, agricultural equipment, medical equipment, paper, steel, furniture, and some liquors. Substantial cuts will also be made for chemicals, wood, aluminum, scientific instruments, and toys.
- **Textiles:** A 10-year phase-out of all quotas under the Multi-Fiber Arrangement that protects industrialized countries from cheaper overseas imports. U.S. tariffs on textile imports are scheduled to fall by about 25%.
- **Agriculture:** Phased in cut of 36% on agricultural tariffs and crop export subsidies by industrialized nations and 24% by developing countries.
- **Intellectual property:** Strengthens enforcement for copyright, patent, and trademark infringement.
- **Procurement:** Federal, state, and local preferential "Buy America" rules will be outlawed, opening more markets to imported goods.
- **Dumping:** Tougher restrictions on the export of goods at below-cost and below home market prices.
- **Limits on local content rules:** The agreement would bar excessive local content requirements as well as requirements for net export of production.

How Will GATT Affect U.S. Importers?

The primary benefits will accrue to exporters as tariffs fall on U.S. products sold abroad. Because the U.S. already has one of the lowest tariff structures in the world, importers are not expected to realize many immediate benefits. Nevertheless, increased world trade activity—economists estimate a $200 billion annual gain in world trade by 2005—should promote imports as well as facilitate exports. The creation of an estimated 2 million new jobs in the U.S. should also serve to increase domestic demand for many imported products.

The planned phaseout of textile quotas should be a boon to importers of textiles and apparel as it opens U.S. markets to lower priced foreign goods that had been kept out by restrictive quotas. More stringent rules on dumping could hurt imports of steel, automotive products, and ships. Agricultural products should become easier to import, although producers operating with large government subsidies are expected to find their goods less competitive as they lose this support. In particular, import quotas on such tightly controlled commodities as sugar, cotton, peanuts, and dairy products will be phased out and tariffs eventually lowered on these products. The U.S. retains the right to initiate antidumping actions against foreign manufacturers of semiconductors, which could prevent any windfalls in growth of imports of electronic components.

Administrative and Dispute Settlement System

The WTO will become the newly organized and empowered administrative arm of the agreement. Final details of its structure have yet to be worked out. However, the new agreement drops the rule allowing an individual member to block committee findings and prevent sanctions from being imposed on a country ruled to be practicing unfair trade. This removes the existing power of any nation thus charged to veto such sanctions, by requiring a minimum of one third of the members—more than 40—to vote to overturn a ruling. This has given rise to fears of loss of sovereignty. For example, opponents argue that countries with less stringent environmental regulations could override the more comprehensive rules of another country on the grounds of restraint of trade. Provisions in the agreement state that regulations with an objective scientific basis may not be upset in such tribunals, but the standards to be used to decide are as yet unclear. Review committees are also scheduled to meet and vote in closed session. Such committees can authorize penalties against violators, including offsetting and punitive tariffs on their goods to be collected by other member countries.

Implementing the WTO

The U.S. ratified the agreement in December 1994, and the European industrialized countries and Japan were expected to follow suit shortly thereafter. The agreement was slated to go into effect on January 1, 1995, but it is expected to take a period of some months for its provisions to be implemented.

InfoList #63

Update on NAFTA

What Is NAFTA?

The North American Free Trade Agreement (NAFTA) creates a preferred trade zone consisting of the U.S., Canada, and Mexico. Tariffs, quotas, and other trade barriers—such as licensing, local content, investment, and customs fee restrictions—are scheduled to be reduced or eliminated on transactions among the three countries. Some of the agreement's provisions were put in place on January 1, 1994 when the agreement went into effect, while others are scheduled to become operative over five or ten years. Restrictions on a few sensitive products—such as some manufactured, agricultural, and processed food products—are scheduled to take as long as 15 years to be phased out.

The U.S. and Canada were already participants in a free trade agreement that allowed a great deal of the trade between the two countries to be conducted on a streamlined basis with reduced or no tariffs on the products involved. NAFTA extends and reorganizes these preferences to include similar provisions for Mexico, while Mexico in turn has agreed to open its markets to U.S. and Canadian products.

Key Provisions

- **Import tariffs:** At the time of signing, import tariffs averaged roughly 10% on goods entered into Mexico and 3% on those entered into the U.S. Many of these tariffs were eliminated or lowered on January 1, 1994, while most of the rest are to be gradually reduced and eventually eliminated over the scheduled life of the agreement.
- **Local content and origin rules:** Specific national local content requirements will be removed. However, NAFTA will impose rules of origin designed to restrict the agreement's benefits to products actually produced in the member countries. Compliance rules are complex and stringent, requiring a minimum of 60% (62.5% for automotive products) of the product's customs assessed value to originate in North America or a minimum of 50% of net cost to represent North American value added.
- **Quotas:** NAFTA calls for quotas to be liberalized and eventually eliminated on imports from its members. During this transition, goods imported under quota from Mexico will not count against the total entry threshold amounts established for these products, so that absolute quotas are effectively raised for affected items imported from Mexico. The implementing regulations specify a schedule for specific products, including milk, cheese, and other dairy products; tomatoes and other fruit and vegetable products; sugars, syrups, and products containing them; orange juice; and some textile products.
- **Textiles and apparel:** Under NAFTA, the U.S. will immediately remove quotas on textiles and apparel wholly Mexican in origin. Quotas on other textile products imported from Mexico but failing to meet NAFTA origin rules will be phased out over 10 years. The U.S. will phase out tariffs on apparel imported from its NAFTA partners over 10 years and on textiles over eight.
- **Agricultural products:** All U.S. and Mexican nontariff barriers are to be converted into either tariff-rate quotas—allowing in unlimited quantities but charging higher rates once a threshold of imports has been reached—or ordinary tariffs with a set rate regardless of the amount of the product entered. These changes will be phased in over as long as 15 years for certain sensitive products.
- **Automotive industry:** Adjustments to the U.S. Corporate Fuel Economy rules will allow Mexican-produced parts and vehicles to be classified as domestic products, easing their import into the U.S. Relaxed Mexican tariff and nontariff barriers to foreign imports will allow greater and more economical flows of outside components into Mexico, which will in turn upgrade and increase the export production of the country's plants.
- **Trilateral Trade Commission:** NAFTA provides for the creation of a trilateral commission to adjudicate disputes under the agreement. This body is organized in an attempt to avoid national bias and is required to act on complaints within eight months. It will deal with antidumping and subsidy issues, as well as the implementation of the provisions of the agreement.

How Will NAFTA Affect U.S. Importers?

The immediate benefits of NAFTA will accrue to U.S. exporters because they will have increased access to previously protected Mexican markets. Because the U.S. already has one of the lowest tariff structures in the world, the lowering of tariffs will not have as dramatic an effect on those importing into the U.S. However, the easing of nontariff barriers, such as quotas and procedures, will have a positive effect on trade. Overall increased trade activity among the three parties to the agreement will also serve to promote imports, especially as the freer flow of capital goods to Mexico enables that country to make more competitive products for the U.S., its primary export market.

NAFTA and GATT

NAFTA is not really a "free" trade agreement because trade remains highly regulated among the three countries. However, the agreement does create a special preferential status for goods and services traded among the U.S., Canada, and Mexico relative to the rest of the world. Because it creates such a regional special interest trade bloc with provisions that favor participants while excluding outsiders from its benefits, NAFTA runs counter to the intent of the General Agreement on Tariffs and Trade (GATT), which is designed to open up trade on a worldwide basis. Nevertheless, NAFTA does represent a further opening of trade, and most observers expect it to promote wider inclusion of Latin and Caribbean countries and eventually to result in a near global agreement which lowers trade barriers on most international trade.

InfoList #64

23 Advantages and Uses of Foreign Trade Zones

U.S. Foreign Trade Zones (FTZs) are areas that are considered for Customs purposes to be outside U.S. Customs territory. FTZs therefore offer outstanding advantages to the importer (and exporter): merchandise can be landed and stored (and more) in a zone without being subject to U.S. Customs entry and clearance requirements.

1. Goods may remain in an FTZ for an unlimited amount of time. Thus, you can release your goods according to market demand, waiting for a favorable time and then make immediate deliveries, while avoiding possible cancellations of orders due to shipping delays. You can even wait for a favorable change in duty rates. However, you should realize that storage charges can eat into or offset these advantages.
2. You can save on transport costs by shipping goods to the FTZ in bulk and repacking them. Also, unassembled or disassembled goods, such as furniture or machinery, can be shipped for assembly it the zone.
3. Goods shipped in bulk can be dried in an FTZ to save duty which would have to be paid on the pre-evaporation or shrinkage amount; cleaned to save duty on dirt or culls; inspected and sorted to save duty on goods damaged by breakage, leaking, or seepage, or impure goods, on missing articles, and on waste, which can be destroyed or entered with duty being paid at a lower rate as recoverable waste.
4. Substandard goods may be processed and upgraded to meet requirements of federal regulatory agencies.
5. You may mark or label goods to meet U.S. Customs-enforced requirements, thus avoiding the fines that are assessed on improperly marked goods.
6. You can save on insurance by insuring goods only for cost plus transportation, rather than cost plus transportation plus duty and taxes.
7. FTZs do not require bonds for storage, manipulation, or manufacture. Nor are bonds are required for missing licenses, permits, or other documents; you may keep your merchandise in the zone until documents or copies are obtained. No bonding is required for exhibition within the FTZ.
8. Goods in excess of quotas may be held in the zone until the next quota period. The date of entry of the merchandise into Customs territory is the effective date applied for quota purposes, regardless of its status is, and whether or not it has been changed in form by manipulation or manufacture.
9. Goods subject to a quota may, under certain circumstances, be changed or manufactured into an item not subject to a quota, and entered into Customs territory. Proposed operations involving quota merchandise in such zones must obtain specific clearance from the FTZ's Executive Secretary. Basically, the Board will not approve operations which have the effect of directly circumventing a quota.
10. You can save money in duties by converting a product into an article which has a lower duty rate.
11. A sample of your product can be withdrawn from the zone and forwarded to Customs for a classification ruling, thus avoiding possible disputes over the classification of the product.
12. You can borrow on the goods stored in the zone using negotiable warehouse receipts as collateral.
13. Goods under $250.00 in value may be removed from a zone as an informal entry with duties paid to the Customs collector at the zone without affecting the status of the remaining goods.
14. Goods may be sold or auctioned in the zone, transferring duty and excise tax liability to the purchaser.
15. You may exhibit goods for an unlimiterd period without bond. Thus, you can display them where they are stored, establish showrooms of your own, or join with other importers in displaying merchandise in a permanent exhibit in the zone. You are not limited to a display of samples, but may sell from your stock in wholesale quantities.
16. Your goods are under federal protection—it is a federal offense to steal from a FTZ.
17. All foreign and domestic merchandise may be brought into the zone, so that you may combine them, use one to process the other, save by using domestic materials for packaging, etc., gaining a price advantage over wholly foreign or wholly domestic produced items, and avoiding sending domestic materials abroad for processing.
18. You can avoid hiring a special employee to receive, store, and then release your merchandise to your forwarding agent or broker.
19. Ship stores, aircraft supplies, and ground maintenance and repair equipment may be stockpiled at and withdrawn from a zone tax- and duty-free.
20. Goods in an FTZ may be exported without your having ever paid duty on them, and thus without having money tied up until drawback. Domestic goods are considered exported upon entering the zone for rebates of duty and Internal Revenue Service excise taxes. Thus an importer does not have to wait until he or she finds a foreign buyer, or to actually export the goods, to benefit by using the FTZ.
21. You do not have to complete your invoices until your goods are sold, so that you do not have to show the sale in your books until it is actually made. Thus, you may be able to postpone taxes to another period that is more to your advantage.
22. Merchandise may be withdrawn from a zone for exhibition at a trade fair without payment of duty or taxes. It must, however, be entered for consumption, exported, abandoned to the government, or destroyed within three months of the closing of the fair. Return of the goods to the FTZ for export satisfies this requirement.
23. You may transfer merchandise in Customs bonded warehouses to a zone for exportation or destruction before the term expires, cancelling the bond and removing a time limit for reexportation. This also applies to internal revenue bonded warehouses, with taxes paid recoverable by drawback once the goods are in a zone.

InfoList #65

U.S. Customs District Offices

Alabama
150 N. Royal St.
Mobile, AL 36602
(205) 441-5106

Alaska
605 West 4th St.
Anchorage, AK 99501
(907) 271-2675

Arizona
International & Terrace Sts.
Nogales, AZ 85621
(602) 761-2010

California
880 Front St., Room 5-S-9
San Diego, CA 92101
(619) 557-5360

555 Battery St
P.O. Box 2450
San Francisco, CA 94126
(415) 705-4340

300 S. Ferry St.
Terminal Island
San Pedro, CA 90731
(310) 514-6001

Florida
6601 NW 25th St.
Miami, FL 33102
(305) 876-6803

4430 East Adamo Dr., Suite 301
Tampa, FL 33605
(813) 228-2381

Georgia
1 East Bay St.
Savannah, GA 31401
(912) 652-4256

Hawaii
335 Merchant St.
P.O. Box 1641
Honolulu, HI 96806
(808) 541-1725

Illinois
610 S. Canal St
Chicago, IL 60607
(312) 353-6100

Louisiana
423 Canal St.
New Orleans, LA 70130
(504) 589-6353

Maine
312 Fore St.
P.O. Box 4688
Portland, ME 97209
(207) 780-3326

Maryland
200 St. Paul Place
Baltimore, MD 21202
(410) 962-2666

Massachusetts
10 Causeway St., Room 603
Boston, MA 02222
(617) 565-6147

Michigan
477 Michigan Ave.
Patrick V. McNamara Bldg., Room 200
Detroit, MI 48226-2568
(313) 226-3177

Minnesota
515 W. First St. #209
Duluth, MO 55802-1390
(218) 720-5201

110 S. Fourth St.
Minneapolis, MN 55401
(612) 348-1690

Missouri
7911 Forsyth Blvd. Suite 625
St. Louis, MO 63134-3716
(314) 428-2662

Montana
300 Second Ave. S
P.O. Box 789
Great Falls, MO 59405
(406) 453-7631

New Jersey
Hemisphere Center
Newark, NJ 07114
(201) 645-3760

New York
111 W. Huron St., Room 603
Buffalo, NY 14202
(716) 846-4373

Building 77, JFK Airport
Jamaica, NY 11430
(718) 553-1542

Customhouse
6 World Trade Center
New York, NY 10048
(212) 466-5817

127 N. Water St.
Ogdensburg, NY 13669
(315) 393-0660

North Carolina
1801-K Crossbeam Dr.
Charlotte, NC 28219
(704) 329-0770

North Dakota
Federal Bldg.
P.O. Box 610
Pembina, ND 58271
(701) 825-6201

Ohio
Plaza Nine Bldg., 6th Fl.
55 Erieview Plaza
Cleveland, OH 44114
(216) 891-3800

Oregon
511 NW Broadway
Portland, OR 97209
(503) 326-2865

Pennsylvania
2nd & Chestnut Sts.
Philadelphia, PA 19106
(215) 597-4605

Puerto Rico
Number One La Puntilla
Old San Juan, PR 00901
(809) 729-6950

Rhode Island
49 Pavilion Ave.
Providence, RI 02905
(401) 528-5080

South Carolina
200 E Bay St.
Charleston, SC
(803) 727-4312

Texas
1215 Royal Lane
P.O. Box 619050
Dallas, TX 75261
(214) 574-2170

9400 Viscount St.
P.O. Box 9516
El Paso, TX 79925
(915) 540-5800

Portway Plaza, Suite 400
1717 East Loop
Houston, TX 77029
(713) 671-1000

Lincoln Juarez Bridge
P.O. Box 3130
Laredo, TX 78041
(210) 726-2267

4550 75th St.
Port Arthur, TX 77642
(409) 724-0087

Vermont
Main & Stebbins Sts
Post Office Bldg.
P.O. Box 1490
St. Albans, VT
(802) 524-6527

Virginia
101 E Main St.
Norfolk, VA 23510
(804) 441-6546

44845 Falcon Pl.
Suite 101-A
Sterling, VA 20166
(703) 318-5900

Washington
1000 2nd Ave. Suite 2200
Seattle, VA 98104
(206) 553-0554

Wisconsin
6269 Ace Industrial Dr.
P.O. Box 37260
Milwaukee, WI 53237-0260
(414) 297-3925

U.S. Customs Service Reorganization

In September, 1994, the U.S. Customs Service announced that it would undergo a major reorganization. The plan is projected to take 18 to 36 months to fully implement. The restructuring will abolish management functions of seven current regional headquarters and forty-five district and area offices across the country while assigning their employees to nearby ports of entry or other Customs facilities.

Twenty Customs Management Centers (CMC) will then be established to oversee the internal management functions of the Customs Service. Five Strategic Trade Centers (STC) will also be created to enhance Customs capacity to address major international trade issues, such as textile fraud, anti-dumping, and protection of U.S. intellectual property rights.

The reorganization of the Washington headquarters is already underway. The staff of roughly 1,800 will be trimmed by one-third. Those 600 employees will be reassigned to field offices nationwide to provide better service direct to customers.

At press time the aforementioned U.S. Customs District Offices were still operating at the addresses and telephone numbers noted. During the reorganization process, offices which are in cities *not* on the following Customs Management Center list will be closing.

Customs Management Center Locations

Management Area	City
North Atlantic	Boston
New York	New York
Mid Atlantic	Baltimore
South Atlantic	Atlanta
North Florida	Tampa
South Florida	Miami
Puerto Rico/Virgin Islands	San Juan
Gulf	New Orleans
East Texas	Houston
South Texas	Laredo
West Texas/New Mexico	El Paso
Arizona	Tucson
Southern California	San Diego
South Pacific	Los Angeles
Mid Pacific	San Francisco
North Pacific	Seattle
Great Plains	Denver
Mid America	Chicago
West Great Lakes	Detroit
East Great Lakes	Buffalo

Strategic Trade Center Locations

Trade Area	City
Pacific Rim	Los Angeles
Mexico/Central America	Dallas/Ft. Worth
Canada	Chicago
Caribbean/South America	Miami
Europe/Africa/Middle East	New York

InfoList #66

U.S. Regulatory Agencies

These are some of the most important and useful U.S. government addresses for the importer, including many of the main regulatory agencies.

Centers for Disease Control (CDC)
Office of Biosafety
1600 Clifton Rd. NE
Atlanta, GA 30333
(404) 639-3883

Consumer Product Safety Commission (CPSC)
Office of Compliance
Division of Regulatory Management
5401 Westbard Avenue
Bethesda, MD 20207
(301) 504-0400

Customs Service
1301 Constitution Ave. NW
Washington, DC 20229
(202) 927-6724 (Information)
(202) 927-1000 (General)

Customs Service
Quota Branch
1301 Constitution Ave. NW, Rm. 2379-ICC
Washington, DC 20229
(202) 927-5850

Environmental Protection Agency (EPA)
TSCA System Information
EPA 7408, OPPT
401 M Street SW
Washington, DC 20460
(202) 554-1404 (TSCA Information Hotline)

Environmental Protection Agency (EPA)
Office of Pesticide Programs
401 M Street SW (7501-C)
Washington, DC 20460
(703) 305-7090 (General)
(703) 305-7102 (Import/export requirements)

Federal Communications Commission (FCC)
Enforcement Division, Investigations Branch
1919 M Street NW, Rm. 744
Washington, DC 20554
(202) 418-1170

Federal Trade Commission (FTC)
Division of Enforcement
601 Pennsylvania Ave. NW
Washington, DC 20580
(202) 326-2996 (General)
(202) 326-2841 (Textile and wool products labeling)

Fish and Wildlife Service (FWS)
Office of Management Authority
4401 N. Fairfax Drive, Rm. 432
Arlington, VA 22203
(703) 703-2095
(800) 358-2104, (703) 358-2104 (Permits office)

Food and Drug Administration (FDA)
Center for Drug Evaluation and Research (HFD-8)
5600 Fishers Lane
Rockville, MD 20857
(301) 594-1012

Food and Drug Administration (FDA)
Center for Devices and Radiological Health
Division of Small Manufactures Assistance
5600 Fishers Lane
Rockville, MD 20857
(800) 638-2041, (301) 638-2041

Food and Drug Administration (FDA)
Center for Food Safety and Applied Nutrition
200 C Street SW
Washington, DC 20204
(202) 205-5241, 205-5042

Food and Drug Administration (FDA)
Division of Enforcement, Imports Branch
200 C Street SW
Washington, DC 20204
(202) 205-4726

Food and Drug Administration (FDA)
Center for Veterinary Medicine
7500 Standish Place (HFV-12)
Rockville, MD 20855
(301) 594-5909

National Highway Traffic Safety Administration
Office of Vehicle Safety Compliance
400 7th St. SW
Washington, DC 20590
(202) 366-5311, 366-2830

U.S. Department of Agriculture (USDA)
Animal and Plant Health Inspection Service (APHIS)
Plant Protection and Quarantine (PPQ)
Federal Building, Rm. 631
6505 Belcrest Road
Hyattsville, MD 20782
(301) 436-8645

U.S. Department of Agriculture (USDA)
Animal and Plant Health Inspection Service (APHIS)
Veterinary Services (VS)
Import-Export Products Staff
Federal Building, Rm. 756
6505 Belcrest Road
Hyattsville, MD 20782
(301) 436-7885

U.S. Department of Agriculture (USDA)
Food Safety and Inspection Service (FSIS)
Import Inspection Division
Rm. 3715, Franklin Ct.
Suite 3700-W
Washington, DC 20250-3700
(202) 501-7515

U.S. Department of Transportation (DOT)
Research and Special Programs Administration
Office of Hazardous Materials Standards
400 7th St. SW
Washington, DC 20590
(202) 366-4488

U.S. Treasury Department
Office of Foreign Assets Control
Treasury Bldg.
Washington, DC 20220
(202) 622-2510

InfoList #67

U.S. Government Bookstores

The Government Printing Office (GPO) operates a number of U.S. Government bookstores around the country which carry many of the most popular GPO titles. You can also order any of the 12,000 GPO titles by mail order by calling (202) 512-2250. For a list of some of the most useful titles, ask for the catalog of "U.S. Government Information for Business" by writing to: Superintendent of Documents, Stop SM, Washington, DC 20402.

Alabama
O'Neill Building
2021 Third Ave. North
Birmingham, AL 35203
(205) 731-1056, FAX (205) 731-3444

California
ARCO Plaza, C-Level
505 South Flower Street
Los Angeles, CA 90071
(213) 239-9844, FAX (213) 239-9848

Marathon Plaza, Rm. 141-S
303 Second St.
San Francisco, CA 94107
(415) 512-2770, FAX (415) 512-2776

Colorado
Room 117, Federal Building
1961 Stout Street
Denver, CO 80294
(303) 844-3964, FAX (303) 844-4000

Norwest Banks Building
201 West 8th Street
Pueblo, CO 81003
(719) 544-3142, FAX (719) 544-6719

District of Colombia
U.S. Government Printing Office
710 N. Capitol Street, NW
Washington, DC 20401
(202) 512-0132, FAX (202) 512-1355

1510 H Street, NW
Washington, DC 20005
(202) 653-5075, FAX (202) 376-5055

Florida
100 West Bay Street, Suite 100
Jacksonville, FL 32202
(904) 353-0569, FAX (904) 353-1280

Georgia
First Union Plaza
999 Peachtree Street NE, Suite 120
Atlanta, GA 30309-1900
(404) 347-1900, FAX (404) 347-1897

Illinois
One Congress Center
401 South State St., Suite 124
Chicago, IL 60605
(312) 353-5133, FAX (312) 353-1590

Maryland
Warehouse Sales Outlet
8660 Cherry Lane
Laurel, MD 20707
(301) 953-7974, 792-0262, FAX (301) 498-8995

Massachusetts
Thomas P. O'Neill Building, Rm. 169
100 Causeway Street
Boston, MA 02222
(617) 720-4180, FAX (617) 720-5753

Michigan
Suite 160, Federal Building
477 Michigan Avenue
Detroit, MI 48226
(313) 226-7816, FAX (313) 226-4698

Missouri
120 Bannister Mall
5600 E. Bannister Road
Kansas City, MO 64137
(816) 765-2256, FAX (816) 767-8233

New York
Room 110, Federal Building
26 Federal Plaza
New York, NY 10278
(212) 264-3825, FAX (212) 264-9318

Ohio
Room 1653, Federal Building
1240 E. 9th Street
Cleveland, OH 44199
(216) 522-4922, FAX (216) 522-4714

Room 207, Federal Building
200 N. High Street
Columbus, OH 43215
(614) 469-6956, FAX (614) 469-5374

Oregon
1305 SW First Avenue
Portland, OR 97201-5801
(503) 221-6217, FAX (503) 225-0563

Pennsylvania
Robert Morris Building
100 North 17th Street
Philadelphia, PA 19103
(215) 636-1900, FAX (215) 636-1903

Room 118, Federal Building
1000 Liberty Avenue
Pittsburgh, PA 15222
(412) 644-2721, FAX (412) 644-4547

Texas
Room IC50, Federal Building
1100 Commerce Street
Dallas, TX 75242
(214) 767-0076, FAX (214) 767-3239

Texas Crude Building
801 Travis Street, Suite 120
Houston, TX 77002
(713) 228-1187, FAX (713) 228-1186

Washington
Room 194, Federal Building
915 Second Avenue
Seattle, WA 98174
(206) 553-4270, FAX (206) 553-6717

Wisconsin
Suite 150, Reuss Federal Plaza
310 W. Wisconsin Avenue
Milwaukee, WI 53203
(414) 297-1304, FAX (414) 297-1300

InfoList #68

Top Publications for the U.S. Importer

Books, Guides, and Reference Manuals

Container Specification
Hapag-Lloyd
1 Edgewater Plaza
Staten Island, NY 10305
(718) 442-9300

Croner's Reference Book for World Traders
Croner Publications, Inc.
211-03 Jamaica Avenue
Queens Village, NY 11428
(718) 464-0866

Customs Law and Administration
Textile Quota Report
American Association of Exporters and Importers
11 West 42nd Street
New York, New York 10036
(212) 944-2230

Dictionary of International Trade
World Trade Press
1505 Fifth Avenue
San Rafael, CA 94901
(415) 454-9934

Do's and Taboos Around the World: A Guide to International Behavior
By Roger E. Axtell
John Wiley & Sons, Inc.
605 Third Avenue
New York, NY 10518
(212) 850-6000

Documentary Credits, A Practical Guide
Foreign Exchange and Money Market Operations
Swiss Bank Corporation
Swiss Bank Tower
10 East 50th Street
New York, NY 10022
(212) 574-3000

Documentary Credits: UP 500 and 400 Compared
Funds Transfer in International Banking
Guide to Incoterms
Key Words in International Trade (3rd edition)
The New ICC Guide to Documentary Credit Operations
ICC Publishing, Inc.
156 Fifth Ave.
New York, NY 10010
(212) 206-1150

Harmonized Tariff Schedule of the United States
Superintendent of Documents
U.S. Government Printing Office
Washington, DC 20402
(202) 783-3238

Importers Manual USA
World Trade Press
1505 Fifth Avenue
San Rafael, CA 94901
(415) 454-9934

Import Reference Manual
Bureau of National Affairs, Inc.
1231 25th Street., N.W.
Washington, DC 20037
(202) 452-4200

Intercultural Interacting
By V. Lynn Tyler
David M. Kennedy Center for International Studies
Publication Services
Brigham Young University, 280 HRCB
Provo, UT 84602
(801) 378-3377

International Business Transactions, Third Edition
By Ralph H. Folsom, Michael Wallace, John Spanogle, Jr.
West Publishing Company
PO Box 64526
St. Paul, MN 55164
(612) 687-7000

OAG Air Cargo Guide
Official Airline Guides, Inc.
Transportation Guides Division
2000 Clearwater Drive
Oakbrook, IL 60521
(800) 323-3537

World Trade Resources Guide
Trade Shows Worldwide
Gale Research Inc.
835 Penobscot Building
Detroit, MI 48226-4094
(800) 877-GALE

Periodicals

American Import/Export Management Magazine
Global Trade
North American Publishing Company
401 N. Broad Street
Philadelphia, PA 19108
(215) 238-5300

Foreign Trade Magazine
Defense and Diplomacy, Inc.
6849 Old Dominion Drive, Suite 200
McLean, VA 22101
(703) 448-1338

Import Bulletin
Journal of Commerce
Journal of Commerce
110 Wall Street
New York, NY 10005
(212) 425-1616

International Business Magazine
American International Publishing Corporation
500 Mamaroneck Avenue, Suite 314
Harrison, NY 10528
(914) 381-7700

Trade and Culture
PO Box 10988
Baltimore, MD 21234-9871
(410) 426-2906

Wall Street Journal
Dow Jones and Co., Inc.
200 Liberty Street
New York, NY 10281
(212) 416-2000

World Trade
PO Box 3000
Denville, NJ 07834-9815
(714) 640-7070

Directories

Air Freight Directory
Air Cargo, Inc.
1819 Bay Ridge Ave.
Annapolis, MD 21403
(301) 263-8054

Directory of United States Importers
Journal of Commerce
110 Wall Street
New York, NY 10005
(212) 425-1616

Global Trade Directory of Major American Banks Doing Business Overseas
Global Trade FMC-Licensed Foreign Freight Forwarders
North American Publishing Co.
401 N. Broad Street
Philadelphia, PA 19108
(215) 238-5300

Global Trade White Pages: The One Source for International Trade Contact
Carroll Publishing Co.
1058 Thomas Jefferson St. NW
Washington, DC 20007
(202) 333-8620

International Directory of Importers
Croner Publications, Inc.
211-03 Jamaica Avenue
Queens Village, NY 11428
(718) 464-0866

Kompass Directories
Croner Publications, Inc.
211-03 Jamaica Avenue
Queens Village, NY 11428
(718) 464-0866

Maritime Guide
Lloyd's Register of Shipping
71 Fenchurch Street
London EC3 M4BS, UK
[44](71) 709-9166

Rand McNally Banker Directory, International Edition
Thomson Financial Publishing
P.O. Box 668
Skokie, IL 60076
(800) 321-3373

Trade Directories of the World
Croner Publications, Inc.
211-03 Jamaica Avenue
Queens Village, NY 11428
Tel (718) 464-0866

U.S. Customs House Guide
North American Publishing Co.
401 N. Broad Street
Philadelphia, PA 19108
(215) 238-5300

Worldwide Government Directory
Belmont Publications
7979 Old Georgetown Road, 9th Floor
Bethesda, MD 20814
(800) 332-3535

Country-Specific Information Series

Europa World Yearbook
Europa Publications Ltd.
18 Bedford Square
London WC1B 3JN, UK

Martindale-Hubbell International Law Digest
Martindale-Hubbell
PO Box 1001
Summit, NJ 07902-1001
(908) 464-6800

Business Profile Series
Hongkong Bank Group
PO Box 3140, Church Street Station
New York, NY 10008
(212) 658-2888

Country Business Guides
World Trade Press
1505 Fifth Avenue
San Rafael, CA 94901
(415) 454-9934

Culture Shock: A Guide to Customs and Etiquette
Graphic Arts Center Publishing Company
3019 NW Yeon
Portland, OR 97210
(503) 226-2402

Doing Business in...
Price Waterhouse
1251 Avenue of the Americas
New York, NY 10020
(212) 819-5000

Doing Business in...
Ernst and Young International
787 Seventh Avenue
New York, NY 10019
(212) 773-3000

U.S. Government Publications

19 CFR, Parts 1 to 199, Code of Federal Regulations *(Customs Duties)*
Background Notes *(U.S. State Dept.)*
Customs Regulations of the United States
Foreign Economic Trends *(U.S. Dept. of Commerce)*
Foreign Labor Trends *(U.S. Dept. of Labor)*
Harmonized Tariff Schedule of the United States (HTSUS)
Overseas Business Reports (Int'l Trade Administration)
Superintendent of Documents
U.S. Government Printing Office
Washington, DC 20402
(202) 783-3238

National Trade Data Bank (NTDB)
(CD-ROM publication)
U.S. Department of Commerce
Office of Business Analysis, HCHB Room 4885
Washington DC 20230
(202) 482-1986

International Law

Contents

Introduction

The greatest source of problems for U.S. residents doing business abroad is the erroneous assumption that they can operate according to U.S. laws and practices. When you trade internationally, you are subject not only to U.S. laws, but also to the laws of every country where you do business, even if you do not physically enter the other country.

The more complex your transactions, the more you travel overseas, the more you deal in high-risk or politically sensitive products, the more you obtain and extend credit, the more you trust others to perform their end of the bargain, the greater chance you will have of encountering legal difficulties in your international transactions.

This section reviews potential legal problems that you should keep in mind while traveling and doing business internationally. It addresses issues related to international travel, trading relationships, contracts, and world legal systems. The information is interrelated, and each section is equally important. Even if part of it does not seem relevant at the moment, you should review all of it so that, when legal issues arise (and they will), you can recognize them and can assert your legal rights.

Travel

The international travel issues covered include requirements for passports, visas, and work permits; registration with U.S. embassies overseas; ramifications of dual nationality; special customs considerations when traveling with commercial samples, protected items, negotiable instruments, and personal articles; compliance with foreign laws; and concerns related to driving abroad.

Trading Relationships

The international trading sections discuss the anti-bribery provisions of the Foreign Corrupt Practices Act, ramifications of agency and employment relationships abroad, types of relationships commonly formed with foreign suppliers, the role of domestic and foreign legal counsel, the need for insurance, the use of powers of attorney and notaries public, and import and export laws.

Contracts and Conflict Resolution

This part of the chapter concentrates on issues that arise when drafting and performing an international sales or purchase contract, including conflict resolution. Although you will most likely rely on the services of an attorney to draft and enforce the contract, you will need this knowledge to work in partnership with your attorney to your best advantage.

World Legal Systems

This section gives an overview of the world's major legal systems and the different requirements imposed on domestic and foreign business relationships.

Additional Resources

Other sources on commercial law include Martindale-Hubbell's *International Law Digest,* available at major public libraries and *International Business Practices,* available from the U.S. Government Printing Office.

Passports

Your U.S. passport is your most important travel document. It identifies you as an individual and as a U.S. citizen. International travel without a passport can be impossible. As you travel you will need your passport to:

- board international flights
- cross national borders
- register at foreign hotels
- cash traveler's checks
- pay by credit card

The U.S. Passport Agency of the Department of State issues passports.

Loss or Theft of a US Passport

Safeguard your passport. Its loss could cause you unnecessary travel complications as well as significant expense.

If your passport is lost or stolen in the U.S., report the loss or theft immediately to Passport Services, 1425 K Street, N.W., Department of State, Washington, DC 20522-1705, or to the nearest passport agency. Should your passport be lost or stolen abroad, report the loss immediately to the local police and to the nearest U.S. embassy or consulate.

As a contingency in the event that your passport is lost or stolen, you should carry several duplicate passport photos and a photocopy of your passport in a separate and safe place while traveling. For full information on passports refer to "Passports" on page 24.

Warning! Even if you are not required to have a passport to visit a country, U.S. Immigration requires you to prove your U.S. citizenship and identity when you reenter the U.S. Make certain that you take with you adequate documentation (original birth certificate and photo ID) to pass through U.S. Immigration on your return.

Tip: Although not required by law, hotels in some countries may insist that you leave your passport with hotel management to be checked by local police, or as a guarantee that you will pay your hotel bill. Always ask either your travel agent or the local U.S. embassy or consulate before you give your passport to a hotel.

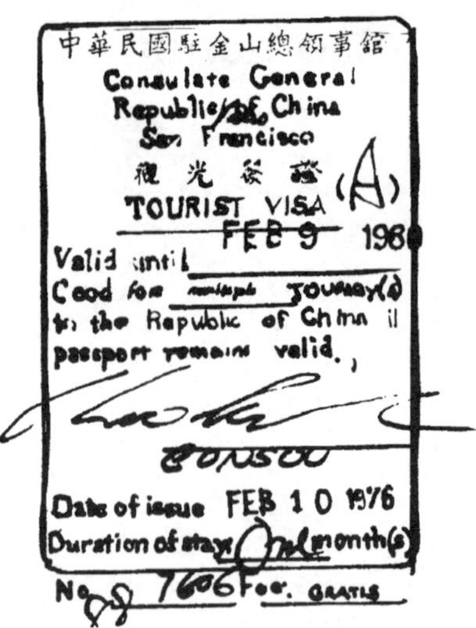

Visas and Work Permits

A visa is a certificate or stamp placed in your passport by a foreign government's embassy, consular office, or other representative. It permits you to either visit (tourist visa), conduct business (business visa) in, work (work permit or visa) in, or immigrate (residency visa or immigration visa) to the issuing country for a specified time. Most countries require foreigners working in their country to have a valid work permit in addition to a visa. Work permits are more difficult to obtain than business visas.

Before leaving the U.S., you should learn the entry requirements of each country you will visit and obtain all necessary visas. Each country has its own requirements: some insist that you obtain a visa in advance, some grant a visa at the border, some allow entry without a visa for particular purposes—such as tourism. Visa fees vary from country to country and for different types of visas. Passport photographs are often required. It can take from ten minutes to several weeks to obtain a visa. You should check with the embassy or consulate of the countries you plan to visit well in advance of your expected departure date.

Tip: In many countries, if you travel on a tourist visa, and once there decide to turn your pleasure trip into a buying trip, you won't have a problem. However you should be aware that business transactions are authorized under a business visa, and lack of a business visa could put you in a difficult position. For example, a foreign company with whom you make a contract could break the agreement on the grounds that you were doing business on a tourist and not a business visa. Though the argument might not hold up in a court of law, foreign countries tend to give preferential treatment to their own nationals, not to foreign nationals. By adhering carefully to visa requirements, you protect your own interests. To avoid problems, you can apply for a change of entry status and a new visa at a local immigration office while in the country. These offices also handle visa extensions, should you decide to stay after your visa expires.

Dual Nationality

Dual nationality means that an individual is a citizen of more than one country. It can result from being born in one country and then becoming a naturalized citizen of another, or from being the child of foreign nationals born in a country other than the parents' country of citizenship.

Are You a Dual National?

If any of the following conditions apply to you, dual nationality might be an issue:

- You were born in a foreign country and have since become a naturalized U.S. citizen;
- You were once a citizen of a foreign country, but have since become a naturalized U.S. citizen;
- Either of your parents is a citizen of a country other than your country of citizenship;
- You are married to a citizen of a country other than your country of citizenship.

Advantages and Disadvantages of Dual Nationality

Dual nationality has both advantages and disadvantages. Citizenship in a country may provide you with certain rights and business opportunities, such as tax or export credits, unavailable to foreigners. However a country claiming you as a citizen could detain you, could conscript you into its military, or could jail you and treat you under its own laws, without regard to the protections of your other country of nationality.

Research Dual Nationality Issues Before Foreign Travel

If you are in any of the categories listed above, *before* you depart the U.S., check your status (including military obligations) with the embassy or consulate of the country that might claim you as a citizen.

Tip: Countries with totalitarian regimes, torn by civil strife, or at war are more likely to regard you as one of their citizens. In some cases of dual nationality, foreign countries have refused to recognize the U.S. citizenship of persons arrested and have not allowed U.S. officials access to arrested U.S. citizens.

Registration with the U.S. Embassy or Consulate

The U.S. State Department recommends that in each country you visit you inform the U.S. Embassy of your travel plans. Although less of a consideration if you travel in Western Europe and stay in first class hotels, registration is highly recommended if you intend to travel the back roads of less developed and unstable countries.

When to Register

Register with the U.S. embassy or consulate if you are:

- Traveling to a country or area with civil unrest or an unstable political climate.
- Going to a country where there are no U.S. official offices (Lebanon, Iran, or Macedonia, for example). Register in an adjacent country, leave an itinerary, ask about conditions in the country you plan to visit, and find out which third country may represent U.S. interests.
- Going to a country or area that heavily restricts foreign travel. If you are on an escorted tour, make sure registration is made for you. If it is not, or if you are traveling on your own, leave a copy of your itinerary at the nearest U.S. embassy or consulate soon after arrival. Registration allows consular employees to help you more easily should you encounter difficulties.
- Planning to stay in another country for more than one month. Registration will facilitate replacement of a passport, and consular officials will be able to locate you should you need assistance or evacuation in an emergency.

U.S. consular officers can tell you about local conditions, customs and health issues. Refer to "Health Regulations for International Travel" on page 29 for discussion of vaccination certificates.

Tip: Though this safeguard may seem trivial to a U.S. citizen accustomed to unrestricted travel, it is not. U.S. citizens are often portrayed negatively. If you enter a region uninformed, you could become a pawn in a conflict you know nothing about. You also need to be aware of areas where there are significant health hazards. Refer to "Help from U.S. Consuls Abroad" on page 43 for additional information on consular assistance.

Traveling with Commercial Samples

Samples, advertising material, or equipment can often be temporarily brought into a country duty-free. Many countries issue and recognize a bond or document, such as an ATA Carnet, for the temporary entry of these articles without payment of customs duties. Some permit duty-free entry without documentation, provided specific restrictions are met. In some cases, you may have to request an exemption, a slow process of several months if the application is made to a central government agency.

ATA Carnets

ATA stands for "Admission Temporaire-Temporary Admission." An ATA carnet is an international customs document issued and recognized by member countries to the Customs Convention on the ATA Carnet. It authorizes the temporary duty-free importation of certain goods into a country. The carnet serves as both a customs entry document and as a guarantee against the payment of customs duties in the event that the items are in fact not reexported. Certain types of merchandise, such as textiles, are subject to quotas even when imported under an ATA carnet. The U.S. currently allows ATA carnets for temporary admission of professional equipment, commercial samples, and advertising material. Most ATA member countries also allow the use of carnets for temporary admission of these goods. ATA carnets can also be used for transit (in-bond movement of goods) in the U.S. under the applicable regulations, 19 CFR Part 114.

An ATA carnet is valid for one year. During that year the carnet holder may make as many trips as desired, provided the carnet has sufficient pages for each stop.

Local Chambers of Commerce, as affiliates of the Paris based International Chamber of Commerce, issue carnets to their residents. These associations guarantee the payment of duties to local customs for goods not reexported. In the U.S., the U.S. Council of the International Chamber of Commerce, located at 1212 Avenue of the Americas, New York, NY 10036, Tel (212) 354-4480, issues ATA carnets for a fee. Refer to "Temporary Free Importations" on page 195 for more information.

Traveling with Expensive Personal Possessions

Unless it is your business to wear your wealth, don't do so while you are abroad. People in other countries tend to be more conservative with demonstrations of wealth than those in the U.S. To prevent the loss or theft of valuables such as jewelry, family photographs, or objects of sentimental value, you should leave them home when you travel. If jewelry is brought, it should be worn discreetly to prevent grab-and-run theft.

U.S. Customs Pre-Registration

Foreign-made products that have already been imported to the U.S. are subject to duty when reimported unless you can prove you owned them before you left.

You can avoid repaying this import duty by carrying a copy of the U.S. sales invoice with your travel documents to present to Customs when you reenter the U.S.

You can also register foreign-made products—especially items identified with serial numbers, such as watches, cameras, camcorders, and binoculars—with U.S. Customs before you leave the U.S. Carry the registration with you and present it to Customs when you reenter the U.S.

Hotel Safe-Deposit Boxes

Most hotels have safe-deposit boxes you can use for your valuables. Be careful, though: there have been reports of abuses involving hotel staff with access to both keys to the safe-deposit box.

Endangered Species Laws

Do not take products of endangered species (such as leopard furs or elephant ivory jewelry) through signatory countries to the international Convention on Trade in Endangered Species of Wild Fauna and Flora (CITES). Incidentally, the U.S. is a signatory to CITES, so theoretically you should not own, let alone import, any products made from these species in the first place.

Traveling with Negotiables

Both U.S. and foreign laws regulate the transfer of personal and corporate assets. Assets may include cash, checks, stocks, bonds, or any negotiable instrument, as well as equipment, products, and other tangible property.

U.S. Regulations

The U.S. does not limit the amount of funds or assets imported or exported. Also, negotiable instruments, in current circulation in any country and imported into the U.S. for monetary purposes, are admitted duty free and without formal Customs entry.

All imports of currency, coin, and negotiable instruments are subject to the Currency and Foreign Transactions Reporting Act (CFTR), 31 USC 5311 et seq. Pursuant to CFTR, you must file a transaction report, Customs **Form 4790**, with U.S. Customs when you transport more than $10,000 in monetary instruments, by any means, on any occasion, into or out of the U. S. Monetary instruments include U.S. or foreign coin, currency, traveler's checks, money orders, and negotiable instruments or investment securities in bearer form. Bank checks, traveler's checks or money orders made payable to the order of a named person, but bearing a restrictive endorsement or not endorsed at all, are not considered monetary instruments.

Foreign Country Requirements

Foreign governments usually do not limit the amount of cash you bring into the country, but they often strictly limit how much you take out. These limits may apply both to local currency and any U.S. currency the U.S. citizen brought into the country. Before you take large sums of currency or assets into a country, research any restrictions with their consulate or embassy in the U.S., or a banker.

Tip: If you import assets of any kind that result from a profit-making enterprise overseas, interest on invested monies, or any other form of income, you must declare the sums to the U.S. Internal Revenue Service (IRS) as income.

Refer also to "Foreign Assets Control Restrictions" on page 226 and "Monetary Instruments" on page 223.

Both U.S. and foreign laws regulate the transfer of personal and corporate assets. Assets may include cash, checks, stocks, bonds, or any negotiable instrument.

Police Registration

Surname ....

Given Name ....

Nationality ....

Passport Number ....

Traveled From..

Traveling To ....

Local Registration

In many foreign countries individuals are required to register with the police on arrival in a city or town. Typical police registration cards ask for your name, passport number, local address, home address, destination, place from which you last came, place where you are going next, and your reason for traveling.

If you register at a hotel, the hotel will ask that you fill out the police registration card or will handle the formality for you. If you are staying with friends, or in an apartment, you will probably need to go to a police station to register in person.

To determine registration requirements for a particular country, you should call the U.S. Embassy in that country.

Obey Foreign Laws

When you are in a foreign country, you are subject to its laws. This means that not only must you comply with the laws of that country, but those laws will be applied to you in the same manner as to any citizen of that country. Foreign laws tend to be more stringent than U.S. laws. If you get into trouble, you will not be able to invoke the protection of U.S. laws.

Use common sense. Avoid areas of unrest and disturbance. Deal only with authorized outlets when you exchange money or buy airline tickets and traveler's checks. Do not deliver packages for anyone unless you are certain they do not contain drugs or other contraband. Do not carry concealed defensive canisters—pepper sprays, mace, etc.—even with a license, because in some countries mere possession is illegal and cause for arrest. Become familiar with local regulations before you sell personal effects, such as clothing, cameras, and jewelry. Strictly adhere to local laws. The penalties you risk can be severe.

Some countries—particularly those with totalitarian regimes, rampant civil strife, or warring factions—are sensitive about photographs. In such countries, you should refrain from photographing police and military installations and personnel; industrial structures including harbor, rail, and airport facilities; border areas; and scenes of civil disorder or other public disturbances, should you witness them during your stay. For taking such photographs, you may be detained and fined and your camera and all films may be confiscated.

For more information about prohibited and restricted activities, U.S. citizens should check with the U.S. embassy or consulate in the country concerned or with the Citizens Emergency Center before departing.

Drug Arrests

Despite repeated warnings, drug arrests and convictions of U.S. citizens abroad are still common. If you are caught with any drugs overseas, you are subject to local—not U.S.—laws. A number of countries impose stiffer penalties for drug violations and enforce existing drug laws more strictly. If you are arrested, you will find that:

- Few countries provide a jury trial.
- Most countries do not accept bail.
- Pretrial detention, often in solitary confinement, may last months.
- Prisons may lack even minimal comforts—bed, toilet, wash basin.
- Officials may not speak English.
- Physical abuse, confiscation of personal property, degrading or inhumane treatment, and extortion are possible.

If you are convicted, you face a sentence of:

- From 2 to 10 years in most countries.
- A minimum of 6 years' hard labor and a stiff fine in some countries.
- The death penalty in some countries.

Do not get involved with illegal drugs overseas. It can ruin more than your trip. It can ruin your life!

Tip: Some pharmaceutical products that are restricted or contraband in the U.S. are sold over the counter in foreign countries, where their use is perfectly legal. If you transport those products into the U.S., however, you will be breaking U.S. drug laws.

Legal Aid

Remember, you are subject to local laws. If you encounter difficulties with foreign authorities, U.S. consular officials can provide little assistance. Their ability to help is limited by both foreign and U.S. laws. The U.S. Government has no funds for your legal fees or related expenses.

If you find yourself in a dispute that could lead to legal or police action, consult a consular officer. Although U.S. consular officers cannot serve as attorneys or give legal advice, they can provide lists of local attorneys and can help you find adequate legal representation. These lists of attorneys, although carefully prepared, are compiled from local bar association lists and responses to questionnaires. Neither the Department of State nor U.S. embassies or consulates can assume responsibility for the professional caliber, competence, or integrity of the attorneys listed. Consular officers will attempt to protect your legitimate interests and to ensure that you are not discriminated against under local law. But they cannot get you out of jail. If you are arrested, ask the authorities to notify the consular officer at the nearest U.S. embassy or consulate. Under international agreement and practice, you have the right to talk to the U.S. consul. If you are denied this right, be persistent and try to have someone get in touch for you.

When alerted, U.S. officials will visit you, advise you of your rights according to local laws, and contact your family and friends if you so desire. Consuls can transfer money, food, and clothing to the prison authorities from your family or friends. If you are held under inhumane or unhealthful conditions or treated less favorably than others in the same situation, they will try to get you some relief.

Tip: When you are in a foreign country, you should be aware of the country's law. You will be held to the same standards. Until you are sure you know the rules, be circumspect in your personal and business dealings. Contact the U.S. Embassy in each country you visit. Tell them what you plan to do and where you plan to go in the country, and ask about unusual or strict laws that might affect you while visiting there.

Driving

Driver's License

If you intend to drive overseas, check with the embassy or consulate of the countries you will visit to learn their driver's license, road permit, and insurance requirements.

Some countries will recognize your U.S. state driver's license while others will not. Most, however, will accept an international driver's permit. Your local auto association will be able to issue an international driver's permit. You must be at least age 18, and you will need two passport size photographs and your valid U.S. license. Certain restrictions apply to international licenses. They are issued for specified periods of time, are not necessarily valid in every country, and must be presented with a valid U.S. state driver's license.

Auto Insurance

Many foreign countries require valid auto insurance and are far stricter than the U.S. in enforcing their requirements. Even a country that does not require insurance of its own citizens may require it of foreign drivers.

Car rental agencies overseas usually provide auto insurance, but in some countries, the required coverage is minimal. A good rule of thumb when renting a car overseas is to purchase insurance coverage that is at least equivalent to that which you carry at home.

Tip: Never assume that your U.S. auto insurance policy covers your driving abroad!

Accidents

Avoid accidents while driving abroad. Unfamiliarity with driving conditions and habits abroad leads many U.S. citizens into traffic accidents. Drive carefully, courteously and defensively. If you are involved in a driving accident in some countries, you will be considered guilty until proven innocent! For example, the police in Mexico usually detain all parties to a traffic accident until they determine who is at fault. You may be personally liable for any damage you cause while driving. The penalties can be devastating, such as providing financial support for a family whose breadwinner dies in the accident. Or you could be detained in a country until "things are straightened out," which could become a lengthy period.

Refer also to "What to Do in Case of . . ." on page 42.

Foreign Corrupt Practices Act

General Provisions

U.S. business owners are subject to the Foreign Corrupt Practices Act (FCPA). The FCPA makes it unlawful for any U.S. citizen or firm (or any person who acts on behalf of a U.S. citizen or firm) to use a means of U.S. interstate commerce—examples: mail, telephone, telegram, or electronic mail—to offer, pay, transfer, promise to pay or transfer, or authorize a payment, transfer, or promise of money or anything of value to any foreign appointed or elected official, foreign political party, or candidate for a foreign political office for a corrupt purpose (that is, to influence a discretionary act or decision of the official) for the purpose of obtaining or retaining business.

It is also unlawful for a U.S. business owner to make such an offer, promise, payment, or transfer to any person if the U.S. business owner knows, or has reason to know, that the person will give, offer, or promise directly or indirectly all or part of the payment to a foreign government official, political party, or candidate. For purposes of the FCPA, the term "knowledge" means both "actual knowledge"—the business owner in fact knew that the offer, payment, or transfer was included in the transaction—and "implied knowledge"—the business owner should have known from the facts and circumstances of a transaction that the agent paid a bribe, but failed to carry out a reasonable investigation into the transaction.

Tip: A business owner should make a reasonable investigation into the transaction if, for example, the sales representative requests a higher commission on a particular deal for no apparent reason, the buyer is a foreign government, the product has a military use, or the buyer's country is one where bribes are considered customary in business relationships.

The FCPA also contains provisions applicable to U.S. publicly held companies concerning financial recordkeeping and internal accounting controls.

Legal Payments

The provisions of the FCPA do not prohibit payments made to facilitate routine government action; a "facilitating payment" is one made in connection with an action that a foreign official must perform as part of the job. In comparison, a corrupt payment is made to influence an official's discretionary decision.

A person charged with violating FCPA provisions may assert as a defense that the payment was lawful under the written laws and regulations of the foreign country and therefore was not for a corrupt purpose. Alternatively, a person may contend that the payment was associated with demonstrating a product or performing a previously existing contractual obligation and therefore was not for obtaining or retaining business.

Tip: Corrupt payments are distinct from grease or "facilitating" payments made to an agent or official of a foreign government to expedite an action that the official would have taken anyway. For example, payments would not generally be considered corrupt if made to cover an official's overtime required to process export documentation for a legal shipment of merchandise or to cover the expense of additional crew to handle a shipment. Be careful, though. The distinction between a corrupt and a facilitating payment is not always obvious.

Enforcing Agencies; Criminal Penalties

The U.S. Department of Justice prosecutes criminal proceedings for FCPA violations. Firms are subject to a fine of up to US$2 million. Officers, directors, employees, agents, and stockholders are subject to fines of up to US$100,000, imprisonment for up to five years, or both.

A U.S. business owner may also be charged under other federal criminal laws. On conviction, the owner may be liable for one of the following: (1) a fine of up to US$250,000; or (2) if the owner derived pecuniary gain from the offense or caused a pecuniary loss to another person, a fine of up to twice the amount of the gross gain or loss.

Enforcing Agencies; Civil Penalties

Two agencies are responsible for enforcing civil provisions of the FCPA: the Department of Justice handles actions against domestic concerns, and the Securities and Exchange Commission (SEC) files actions against issuers. Civil fines of up to US$100,000 (but only up to US$10,000 in SEC actions) may be imposed on a firm, or on any officer, director, employee, agent, or stockholder acting for a firm. In addition, the appropriate government agency may seek an injunction against a person or firm that has violated or is about to violate FCPA provisions.

Conduct that constitutes a violation of FCPA provisions may also give rise to a cause of action under the federal Racketeer-Influenced and Corrupt Organizations Act (RICO), as well as under similar state statutes if such exist in a state with jurisdiction over the U.S. business.

Administrative Penalties

A person or firm held to have violated any FCPA provisions may be barred from doing business with the U.S. government. Indictment alone may result in suspension of the right to do business with the government.

Department of Justice Opinion Procedure

An issuer or domestic business concern may submit a written request to the Department of Justice to issue a written statement of opinion on whether specific proposed business conduct would be considered a violation of the FCPA. The person requesting the opinion must be a party to the transaction that is the subject of the request. The opinion procedure is detailed in 28 CFR Part 80. If the Department of Justice issues an opinion stating that certain conduct conforms with current enforcement policy, conduct in accordance with that opinion is presumed to comply with FCPA provisions.

Dilemmas Posed by the FCPA

The examples that follow illustrate two ways in which the Foreign Corrupt Practices Act poses dilemmas for U.S. citizens engaged in international business.

Example 1. If you have a partnership with foreign nationals, you may become liable under U.S. law for actions your foreign partners take that cause them no problems under their local law. For instance, if you own 49% of a foreign corporation with 51% local (foreign) ownership, and the local owners decide to bribe a local official, you may be liable under U.S. law if you benefit from the transaction. Even if bribery is illegal in both countries, U.S. penalties may be more stringent.

Example 2. You could become liable for a corrupt payment made by your foreign employee. For example, if you use a local purchasing agent who, in keeping with local custom, makes payments to government officials for export permits or preferential pricing from governmental entities, under FCPA the payments could be considered corrupt payments. You, the U.S. citizen, are subject to the FCPA. Your foreign employee is not. You will be the one to suffer the legal penalties.

Tip: The law requires that you monitor and evaluate the amount of money you pay your overseas agent or supplier. Always ask "Are we paying too much? Is this percentage too high? Who is getting that extra money?" If your agent is making corrupt payments, you may be subject to criminal liability.

Because of your liability under FCPA, you should insist that your written agreements with a foreign employee or agent expressly cover FCPA situations. To prevent problems, whenever you establish a relationship with someone in a foreign country to act as your purchasing or other business agent, insert a provision in the contract stating that any corrupt payment is cause for termination of the contract. As an employer, you must take a strong stand on this issue for your own protection. Unfortunately, protecting yourself can sometimes mean losing business.

Foreign Labor, Employment, and "Nationalist" Laws

Foreign Labor and Employment Laws

Both the U.S. and foreign governments have laws that, to varying degrees, regulate employment, including employee hiring, firing, benefits, workplace safety, etc. Foreign labor and employment laws, especially in socialist countries, are often stricter and more preferential to the employee than are U.S. laws. When you hire a national in a foreign country where you intend to do business, you must comply with that country's employment standards. Those standards are rarely if ever the same as those of the U.S.

Tip: The fact that you do not establish a manufacturing facility or set up an office in a foreign country where you have business dealings does not exempt you from its labor laws. In fact, you may find that, under the foreign country's labor laws, when you contract with a buyer's agent, you are entering into an employment relationship in which your responsibilities far surpass those you might have for a U.S. employee. In some countries, you may be able to structure your agreement as one for an independent contractor, and thus avoid some of the labor and employment law requirements. Such agreements must be carefully drafted and government approval may be necessary.

Responsibility of the Employer

In foreign countries, hiring an employee can be equivalent to adopting a child into a family. Your responsibility to your foreign employee may last years beyond his or her usefulness to your operation. Your company and you may be subject to significant requirements regarding insurance, vacations, working conditions, ability to fire, and severance pay. Employers in many European countries are required to give their employees a minimum of one month paid vacation each year and they have no authority to dictate when the vacation may be taken. Foreign employees get many more paid days off than those in the U.S.: in some countries as many as 12 legal holidays.

Employee Severance

Employee severance comes as perhaps the greatest shock to U.S. employers of foreign personnel. Termination benefits range from nothing to several or more years of salary paid over time or in a lump sum. In some instances, it may actually be more cost-effective to keep an unproductive employee on the payroll through the end of the contract than it would be to terminate. Some countries have dealer protective laws under which a person who employs a marketing agent is allowed to terminate the contract only for just cause, on payment of a substantial amount of termination compensation, and after lengthy advance notice of termination. Your contract with a dealer should include protective provisions, including clauses that define just cause for termination, specify the period required for advance notice, and provide for a finite employment term, such as one year, with an option to renew.

Tip: Your involvement in a corporate entity in some countries will incur a legal obligation to share a percentage of your profits with employees. Unless you are careful, this may also be read to mean that X percent of all your corporate profits must be shared with all your employees. So be careful about how you set up an overseas corporation to serve as a purchasing agent.

Nationalist Laws

Nationalist laws give special benefits to local employees of foreign-owned business organizations. They are designed to protect the domestic work force. For example, in some countries termination, even for cause, of an employee who works exclusively for you, can obligate you for as much as seven years severance pay, based on a formula that includes the last four years of his or her highest salary. You should fully research nationalist laws of any foreign country where you plan to establish employment or agency agreements with nationals.

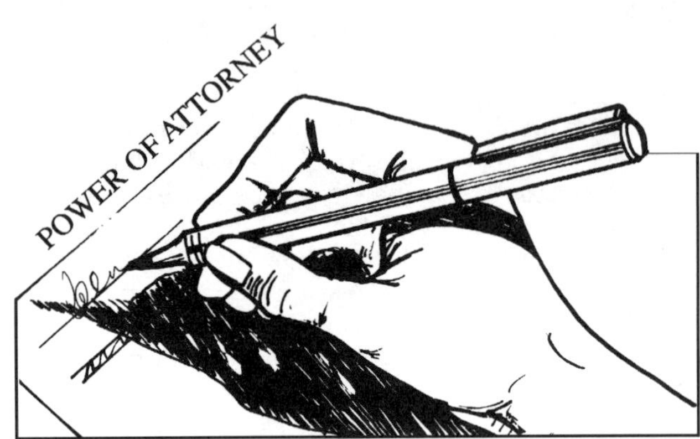

Power of Attorney

A power of attorney is a legal document authorizing one person to act on behalf of another: to enter into contracts, to sign documents, to sign checks and spend money, etc. If you intend to travel overseas a great deal, you should consider giving a power of attorney, or a limited power of attorney, to someone in the U.S. to handle specific business and personal transactions for you. You will also need to give a power of attorney to any Customs broker whose services you use in order for them to handle your customs transactions. This is true whether you are out of the country or not. You may also need to give a power of attorney to someone overseas who can then conduct business transactions in your absence.

Tip: When you set up a power of attorney, make it broad enough in its language to cover the types of situations likely to arise while you are away. It should not be so broad, however, that it gives more power to that individual than you intend. Powers of attorney fall under "agency" laws, which vary from country to country. Before giving someone power of attorney in a foreign country, be sure you understand the legal ramifications.

For U.S. Customs related issues refer also to "Power of Attorney" on page 186 and, for a sample power of attorney form to page 251.

Notary

In the U.S., a notary provides legal verification of an individual's signature in business and legal transactions. In foreign countries, a notary does the same, but often has broader powers. Many countries require notaries to be trained in law, some require notaries to be lawyers also, and some have different types of notaries whose authority to certify certain documents depends on their training. For example, a foreign notary might prepare legal documents, do a title search, certify title, translate documents, certify translations, and file and register documents with government authorities. Foreign notarial fees are commonly higher than those in the U.S. because of the extended services provided.

Agency

The widely misunderstood term "agent" means a representative who normally has authority, perhaps even power of attorney, to make commitments on behalf of the firm he or she represents. Firms in the U.S. and other developed countries have stopped using the term and instead rely on the term "representative," since "agent" can imply more than intended. Any contract should state whether the representative or agent does or does not have legal authority to obligate the firm. You will generally be subject to employment and labor laws in countries in which you employ an agent.

Legal Questions to Consider

In the drafting of an agreement that establishes an agency relationship, you should pay special attention to safeguarding your interests in the event that the agent proves less than satisfactory. An escape clause is vital; it will allow you to end the relationship safely and cleanly if the agent does not work out. Some contracts specify that either party may terminate the agreement with written notice 30, 60, or 90 days in advance. The contract may also spell out exactly what constitutes just cause for ending the agreement. Other contracts specify a certain term for the agreement (usually one year) but arrange for annual renewal options unless either party gives advance written notice of its intention not to renew.

In all cases, the laws of the country where the agent is located may limit the contents of escape clauses and other provisions. For this reason, a U.S. firm should learn as much as it can about the legal requirements of the agent's country and should obtain qualified legal counsel in preparing the contract. Some of the legal questions to consider include:

- How far in advance must the agent be notified of the importer's intention to terminate the agreement? Three months satisfies the requirements of most countries, but a verifiable means of conveyance (e.g., registered mail) may be advisable to establish when the notice was sent and received.
- What is just cause for terminating a relationship? A written contract clause that specifies the reasons for termination usually strength-

ens the importer's position.

- Which country's laws (or which international convention) govern a contract dispute? Laws in the agent's country may forbid the agent to waive that nation's legal jurisdiction.
- What compensation is due the agent on dismissal? Depending on the length of the relationship and whether termination is for just cause as defined by the foreign country, the U.S. importer may be required to compensate the agent for losses.
- What must the agent give up if dismissed? The contract should specify the return of patents, trademarks, name registrations, customer records, and other such property.
- Should the agent be referred to as an "agent?" In some countries, the word "agent" implies power of attorney. The contract may need to specify that the agreement does not confer power of attorney.
- In what language should the contract be drafted? An English-language text should be the official language of the contract in most cases.

Tip: The agency or representative relationship is defined in each country according to that country's domestic law. If you are considering a working relationship with someone in a foreign country, be sure you understand the local agency laws and their ramifications for your agreement. You may clearly intend that you are engaging someone's services as an "independent contractor" (thereby avoiding employer-employee responsibility), but the foreign government may have a different interpretation of your agreement.

Research Agency Laws

A good place to begin gathering information about the employment and agency laws of the country in which you plan to do business is Martindale-Hubbell's *International Law Digest* available in the reference section of most larger public or law libraries. You could also contact an international law firm specializing in employment law, or a major international accounting firm. The following major international accounting firms have offices in nearly every country of the world:

- Arthur Andersen
- Coopers & Lybrand
- Deloitte Touche Ross
- Ernst & Young
- KPMG Peat Marwick
- Price Waterhouse

Banks, chambers of commerce, commercial consulates, and economic development organizations in the foreign country may also be of help.

Relationship with Foreign Supplier

At some point you will have to establish what kind of business relationship you want to have with your foreign supplier. Here are some options:

- Simple buyer/seller
- Exclusive buyer/seller
- Regional/country/industry distributorship
- Joint venture

Simple Buyer/Seller

The most common relationship is that of simple buyer and seller. The seller manufactures or represents one or more products and has a number of buyers. You become one of these buyers and are not given any special or out-of-the-ordinary terms. The seller sells on a first-come first-serve basis. At the beginning of the relationship, you will be expected either to prepay, or to pay with a Documentary Letter of Credit or Documents Against Payment. (Refer to "Methods of International Payment" on page 116 for explanation of these banking terms.) As the relationship matures you may be offered, or negotiate for, credit terms of 30, 60, or 90 days or more. As the buyer in a simple buyer-seller relationship, you will have no special or exclusive rights to merchandise or to territory. Sales agreements in these relationships can range from simple invoices to full-blown sales contracts. Refer to "Drafting the International Sales Contract" on page 88 and "International Sales Contract Checklist" on page 91 for more information.

Exclusive Buyer/Seller

In this relationship, the buyer successfully negotiates for exclusive rights to a manufacturer's product, product line, or entire production. Exclusive right can apply to an existing product, or, through a contract provision, to the custom manufacture of a buyer-designed product. The seller will generally negotiate for certain minimum purchases per unit time by the buyer. For example, 100 units per month at $X per unit for two years.

Regional/Country/Industry Distributorships

A distributorship agreement is essentially just a sophisticated sales agreement. It leaves certain terms open and assumes an ongoing relationship. In this relationship, the buyer negotiates and obtains rights for exclusive distribution of a product or product line within a specified geographic area or industry. Industry distributorships might be established for automotive, banking and financial services, chemicals, textiles and clothing, etc. Geographic distributorships can cover a metropolitan area, state, group of states, or an entire country. For example, if you want to import a product, and you already have an existing distribution network in the eleven western states of the U.S., you could negotiate for an exclusive distributorship for those states.

Tip: If the manufacturer or supplier already has distributors in the states for which you seek exclusive rights, don't give up. If you can demonstrate the advantages of working with you, the supplier can allow the other distributorship agreements to lapse or can buy them out to do business with you.

Joint Ventures

Joint ventures are often established between two or more entities having products, resources, or expertise that, when combined, will produce greater benefits for all parties. A joint venture usually involves the joining of parties either for a particular project or for an ongoing relationship with growth potential. For example, you may have a distribution network in the U.S. for a product manufactured and distributed only in Europe. The manufacturer is convinced that your organization is the best to distribute it but recognizes that you do not have the capital to do so. The foreign manufacturer/supplier might either invest money in your distributorship and obtain interest on the investment, purchase stock in your corporation, or even extend excellent credit terms to help you get started. You may also set up a separate agreement for this transaction alone, agreeing to a percentage split of profits from the venture.

Tip: Before becoming involved in joint ventures with foreign suppliers you should consider potential tax ramifications. Complex rules affect U.S. citizens, nonresident aliens, and aliens in these situations. Before engaging in a venture with a nonresident alien, consult an attorney or skilled international accounting firm with applicable expertise. Some joint ventures have sought to circumvent full payment of customs duties by artificially reducing the sale price of the imported product, then transferring back to the overseas supplier amounts that are actually product cost disguised as profit. If you remit such monies to your foreign supplier, you may be liable for additional duties to U.S. Customs.

Legal Counsel

The role of the attorney in business dealings varies from legal system to legal system. Attorneys are used more in the U.S. than in many foreign countries. In very complex agreements, they structure and negotiate the deal for the client, and they commonly take an active role in enforcing contracts from the time problems first arise. In other countries, attorneys usually draft the contract after the parties have negotiated the terms on their own, and their services are sought as a last resort in contract disputes.

Fees

Lawyers work either on a job, time, or retainer basis. For a single task, such as the drafting of a contract, your attorney will probably charge a fixed fee or an hourly rate. If you have a larger volume of business, you hire a lawyer on retainer, meaning the attorney will charge a set fee per month to handle most or all of your legal requirements. The tasks performed on a retainer basis are often limited by the retainer agreement. You should ask your attorney to clarify in advance which tasks are covered.

Tip: Always discuss fees with your lawyer in advance. In many jurisdictions, your lawyer is required to discuss fees with you before accepting your case. Nobody likes end-of-the-month billing surprises. If you address fees at the beginning, you will avoid misunderstandings.

Domestic Counsel

The best way to select counsel in the U.S. is through existing relationships. Ask other importers or your banker to recommend an attorney helpful in international transactions. When getting referrals, probe for specifics: What is the specific expertise of the attorney? Has the attorney done a good job for the recommender? Does the attorney give personal attention, or are problems delegated to someone in the firm less familiar with the client's needs?

Tip: A U.S. attorney with international business law expertise, along with a customs broker, freight forwarder, and banker, is an important member of your planning team. Personal rapport with your attorney is essential. You must feel at ease with your lawyer and be able to communicate openly. Your lawyer should be available on short notice to discuss problems that arise. In the course of a long-term association, you will most likely need to consult your attorney about questionable, embarrassing, and even illegal actions. The attorney you share them with should be someone competent and someone you like and trust.

When to Consult an Attorney

Call in counsel before you agree to any agreement that is out of the ordinary for you, such as your first international contract. If you have any intimation, even just a hunch, that something about a transaction is questionable, call your attorney. Get legal advice on any transaction involving substantial sums of money relative to your operations generally. For some transactions, do a cost-benefit analysis before deciding whether to call in counsel. Spending $500 to have your attorney review a file and draft a contract could save thousands of dollars in mistakes.

Tip: Be prepared when you call your lawyer. Always have the file, documents, or other pertinent information, and a list of specific questions, in front of you before you call. Preliminary planning will reduce wasted time, keep hourly fee charges to a minimum, and maximize the quality of services your attorney can provide.

Overseas Local Counsel

International business dealings will sometimes require that you have not only a U.S. attorney, but also competent foreign counsel at the overseas business site.

Tip: Be sure that any foreign attorney you select is fluent in English. This requirement is essential. Your ability to say hello, order food, and get directions in a foreign language is not sufficient fluency to negotiate contracts. You hire a foreign lawyer to do that for you. Make sure that lawyer is fluent in both languages. Many people engaging in international business overlook the language barrier. It hurts their business. Don't be one of them.

Though locating a reliable attorney overseas can be difficult if you are unfamiliar with the local area, there are many sources of help. Your international bank is a good place to begin inquiries. Ask your banker to give you some names of trustworthy, effective attorneys situated near your foreign business site. Major international accounting firms such as Ernst & Young, Touche Ross, and Coopers and Lybrand may have offices in the country and may be able to refer reliable attorneys. A number of U.S. legal firms have overseas offices or joint ventures with foreign firms and will provide referrals to local counsel. Although the commercial attaché of the U.S. embassy or consulate in the foreign country is not be permitted, for diplomatic reasons, to recommend a specific attorney, he or she may give you a short list of attorneys in the area.

Tip: If you plan to do business in the Middle East, you are strongly advised to have local legal counsel. Be especially careful about your local referral sources. Middle Eastern countries do not have the equivalent of U.S. conflict of law considerations. A government employee's recommendation of a local attorney may in fact be based on family ties or obligations, not on any special talent or proven reliability on the attorney's part. Find someone whom you can trust to be disinterested when seeking referrals to local counsel particularly in the Middle East.

Insurance

General Business Insurance

General insurance on yourself, your business, and your products, including product liability insurance, is an absolute necessity. Your insurance broker will be able to advise you regarding how much insurance to carry. If your operation is large, you should talk to a lawyer and to a broker, both of whom are familiar with product liability Assess the risks involved in your business. High-risk situations require greater coverage. One million dollars is the absolute minimum coverage for even a small, one-person import business. Overseas purchasing involves particular insurance problems. When your purchasing and reselling is limited to the continental U.S., your supplier will generally have insurance. This may not be the case with your foreign supplier. You need to carry enough insurance to cover any settlements, including those that reach into the millions of dollars.

Tip: If you have an ongoing relationship with an overseas supplier, you should consider including an indemnification provision in your contract. The provision should require your supplier to tender the defense in the event of a lawsuit, and to reimburse any losses you incur by selling his or her products.

Insurance Clause in Purchase Contracts

You should also consider including a provision about insurance in your purchase contracts. If your contract requires your supplier to have insurance as part of the business agreement, include a provision requiring the insured to provide proof, within 10 days of execution of the contract, that the insurance has been paid for. Require that your supplier's insurance company send you a letter verifying the supplier's insurance coverage, and stating that you will be notified directly if there is any lapse in the policy. Refer to "International Sales Contract Checklist" on page 91 for further information.

Tip: Reliance on your supplier's insurance coverage can be a mistake. You should request advice from legal counsel, freight forwarders, and insurers on whether to obtain your own coverage. You should also consider such factors as the nature and length of your relationship with your supplier in deciding whether to trust your supplier to obtain adequate coverage.

Product Liability Insurance

Under U.S. product liability laws, both manufacturer and merchant who sell and resell in commerce are liable for damages that arise because of the defect. Thus, if you are the U.S. seller for a defective item manufactured in Hong Kong, you can be held responsible for distributing that defective item, provided you knew or should have known of the defect. Though the foreign seller is equally responsible, you are the U.S. distributor or seller, and therefore you are the most available and most likely target for a product liability suit.

For a U.S. supplier, some products are more risky than others and may involve liability far in excess of the value of the product. Examples of particularly risky products include:

- Food
- Drugs
- Cosmetics
- Toys
- Machinery
- Flammable fabrics

If you sell products with high risk factors, carry product liability insurance in an amount adequate to the risk involved. This type of insurance guards against loss if you are sued for selling someone else's defective product, especially if it causes bodily harm. The insurance company agrees to indemnify (reimburse) you for any resulting financial loss up to the policy's limit, and provides your legal defense. Legal defense coverage includes court costs and attorney's fees.

Export Restrictions

The export of the following essential commodities has been banned. Exceptions to this ban are also noted: 1) Live animals - exceptions include breeding buffaloes, cows, goats, camels, some horses, fillies/mares, poultry, fish, shrimps, lobsters, crab and frogs; 2) Beef and mutton except cooked and canned beef and meat and 50% of the total production of commercial feed lot units, livestock farms and bilateral joint ventures; 3) Animal fat; 4) Milk and milk products except infant formula foods, weaning foods and food for invalids; 5) Vegetables all sorts including dehydrated vegetables and potato seeds - exceptions include (a) Dried methi leaves packed in small airtight containers or packets, onions, potatoes, garlic, zira, large chillies, asparagus, beans, artichokes, celery, broccoli and brussel sprouts; (b) Turmeric, tomatoes, lady fingers, turnips, carrots, radish, cauliflower, pumpkins, karela, green chillies, tinda, tori, karripatta, chichinda, arvi, petha, corriander leaves, spinach; 6) Grains, all sorts with the exception of maize and barley (subject to quota); 7) Pepper; 8) Pulses and beans, all sorts; 9) Blood meals, meat meals, corn gluton meals, corn gluton feed and sesame oil cakes; 10) Bran and fodder, all sorts except oil cakes, rice bran, wheat bran (subject to quota and special procedure); 11) Sann hemp and arte-misia seeds; 12) Edible oils, all sorts, including butter oil and vegetable ghee and oilseeds except castor seeds, poppy seeds, kapok seeds and sesame seeds; 13) Gur Khandsari and jaggery powder; 14) Intoxicants and intoxicating liquors as defined in the Prohibition (Enforcement of Hadd) Order, 1979; 15) Hides and skins, all sorts except lamb skins (grades I to V); 16) Wet blue leather made from cow hides and cow calf-hides; 17) Wild animal skins and garments

Export Laws

Every country in the world has laws governing which goods may be exported, and under what circumstances. Many U.S. business people put themselves in embarrassing and tough legal situations by unknowingly breaking local export laws. Countries generally monitor and restrict exports in the following categories:

- National security
- National treasures/artifacts
- Export tax
- Raw materials

If your products fall into any of these categories, call the U.S. based consulate or embassy of the exporting country.

National Security

Most countries restrict the export of raw materials or products that could have an adverse effect on national and international security. Some examples are: strategic materials such as radioactive materials; arms and armaments; and computers or computer chips that could be used in weapons.

National Treasures/Artifacts

Most countries have laws which restrict or ban the export of what are considered "national treasures," or "cultural property." These may include items of artistic, zoological, botanical, mineralogical, anatomical, historical, archaeological, paleontological, ethnographic, or numismatic interest. Items considered to be part of the "national treasure," are sometimes listed. For example, there is a privately owned firearms collection in Spain that cannot be exported. For more information refer to "Cultural Property" on pages 800 and 801.

Export Tax

Most countries are so export promotion oriented that they do not impose taxes on exported merchandise. A few, however, do charge taxes (usually small) on exports.

Export of Raw Materials

Some countries ban the export of unfinished raw materials to promote the development of local manufacturing operations using those materials. For instance, Thailand restricts the export of raw teak logs, resulting in increased employment of Thai nationals in sawmills and in the wood products industry.

U.S. Import Laws, U.S. Customs

The U.S. government monitors, regulates, and collects import duties on merchandise entering the country. The agency with primary responsibility for this effort is the U.S. Customs Service, which is part of the U.S. Department of the Treasury.

U.S. Customs Service

The major responsibility of the U.S. Customs Service is to administer the Tariff Act of 1930, as amended. Primary functions include the assessment and collection of all duties, taxes, and fees on imported merchandise; the enforcement of customs and related laws; and the administration of certain navigation laws and treaties. As a major enforcement organization, Customs combats smuggling and revenue fraud and enforces the regulations of numerous other federal agencies at ports of entry and along the land and sea borders of the U.S.

Restricted and Prohibited Merchandise

While many products are straightforward to import, requiring only simple paperwork, many others are heavily regulated and require significant knowledge of the process. Compliance with Customs and other governmental regulations is vital for a successful import operation. Refer to "17 Difficult-to-Import Products" on page 5 for a summary of products that are subject to heavy import regulations.

If you plan to import restricted products, refer to the listing(s) in the Commodity Index in this manual for information on those specific products. Then obtain the advice of a customs broker and a U.S. Customs "commodity specialist" at the proposed port of entry. Also speak with administrators at the agencies that regulate your products. Getting information from several sources is prudent.

Liability for Duties

There is no provision under which U.S. duties or taxes may be prepaid in a foreign country before exportation to the U.S. This is true even in the case of gifts sent through the mail.

In the usual case, liability for the payment of duty becomes fixed at the time an entry for consumption or for warehouse is filed with Customs. The obligation for payment is on the person or firm in whose name the entry is filed. If goods are entered for warehouse, the liability for the payment of duties may be transferred to any person who purchases the goods and desires to withdraw them in his or her own name.

Payment to a Customs broker will not relieve an importer of record of liability for Customs charges (duties, taxes, and other debts owed Customs) if the charges are not paid by the broker. Therefore, if the importer pays by check, Customs charges may be paid with a separate check payable to "U.S. Customs Service," which will be delivered to Customs by the broker.

If an entry is made in the name of a Customs broker, the broker may obtain relief from statutory liability for the payment of increased or additional duties found due if (1) the actual owner of goods is named, and (2) within 90 days of the date of entry, the broker files with the district director a bond secured by the owner and a declaration by the owner agreeing to pay any additional amount.

Frequent Errors in Invoicing

If difficulties, delays, and possible penal sanctions affecting the importer are to be avoided, care must be exercised by foreign sellers and shippers in the preparation of invoices and other documents to be used in the entry of goods into the commerce of the U.S. Each document must contain all information required by law or regulations, and every statement of fact contained in the documents must be true and accurate.

Any inaccurate or misleading statement of fact in a document presented to a Customs officer in connection with an entry, or the omission from the document of required information, may result in delays in merchandise release, the detention of the goods, or a claim against the importer for forfeiture value. Even if the inaccuracy or omission is unintentional, the importer may have to establish that he or she exercised due diligence and was not negligent in order to avoid sanctions, with consequent delay in obtaining possession of goods and closing the transaction.

In particular, all statements relating to the merchandise description, price, or value—plus the amounts of discounts, charges, and commissions—must be accurately set forth. Equally important, for purchased goods, the invoice must designate the true names of the seller and purchaser. For goods shipped other than for purchase, the invoice must state the true names of the consignor and consignee. The invoice must reflect the real nature of the transaction pursuant to which the goods were shipped to the U.S.

The fundamental rule is that the shipper and importer must furnish Customs with all pertinent information for each import transaction to assist the Custom officers in determining the tariff status of the goods. Examples of omissions and inaccuracies to be avoided are:

- The shipper assumes that a commission, royalty, or other charge against the goods is a so-called "nondutiable" item and omits it from the invoice.
- A foreign shipper who purchases goods and sells them to a U.S. importer at a delivered price

shows on the invoice the cost of the goods to the shipper instead of the delivered price.

- A foreign shipper manufactures goods partly with the use of materials supplied by the U.S. importer, but invoices the goods at the actual cost to the manufacturer, without including the value of the materials supplied by the importer.
- The foreign manufacturer ships replacement goods to a U.S. customer and invoices the goods at the net price without stating the full price less the allowance for defective goods previously shipped and returned.
- A foreign shipper who sells goods at list price less a discount invoices them at the net price and fails to show the discount.
- A foreign shipper sells goods at a delivered price but invoices them at a price f.o.b. the place of shipment and omits the subsequent charges.
- A foreign shipper indicates in the invoice that the importer is the purchaser, but in fact the person listed is either an agent who is receiving a commission for selling the goods or a party who will receive part of the proceeds of the sale of the goods sold for the joint account of the shipper and consignee.
- The foreign shipper identifies the goods by vague invoice descriptions, such as by listing part numbers or truncated or coded descriptions only, or by lumping various distinct items together as one article.

Antidumping and Countervailing Duties

Antidumping duties (ADs) are assessed on imported merchandise of a class or kind that is sold to purchasers in the U.S. at a price less than the fair market value. Fair market value of merchandise is the price at which it is normally sold in the manufacturer's home market.

Countervailing duties (CVDs) are assessed to counter the effects of subsidies provided by foreign governments, to merchandise that is exported to the U.S. These subsidies cause the price of such merchandise to be artificially low, which causes economic "injury" to U.S. manufacturers.

Investigation and Enforcement. The Department of Commerce (DOC), the International Trade Commission (ITC), and U.S. Customs all play a part in enforcing antidumping and countervailing duty laws. The DOC is responsible for the overall administration of AD and CVD laws and for investigating allegations of dumping or foreign subsidization of imports. If warranted by the investigation, the DOC also establishes the duty to be imposed on the merchandise. The ITC determines whether injury to industry has occurred or is likely to occur and whether an industry may be hampered in its start-up efforts because of alleged dumping or subsidies. Customs assesses ADs and CVDs once the rates have been established and the ITC has made the necessary determinations.

Both types of duties are established and assessed through the following process:

Investigation. AD or CVD investigations are typically initiated when a domestic industry files a petition with the DOC or when another interested party—an industry association, for example—alleges unfair competition by foreign manufacturers. On receipt of the petition, the DOC investigates the merits of the allegations to determine whether dumping or unfair subsidization has indeed occurred. The ITC, meanwhile, investigates whether there is reasonable indication that U.S. industries are, or are likely to be, harmed by the alleged dumping or subsidies. Results of these investigations are published in the Federal Register.

The DOC then calculates the difference between prices at which the merchandise in question is being sold in the U.S. and its fair market value. On the basis of this calculation, Commerce directs the Customs Service to: (1) assess cash deposits or require bonds on imports of the merchandise to cover possible AD or CVD duty liability, and (2) suspend liquidation of the entries until the DOC has determined whether dumping or subsidization has occurred and has calculated the proper dumping or countervailing margins.

Completion of Investigation. When the DOC and, if applicable, the ITC have completed their investigations and determined that dumping or subsidization has occurred, the DOC will publish an Antidumping or Countervailing Duty Order, which will be announced in the Federal Register. At this point, DOC will generally direct Customs to collect only cash deposits, bonding being no longer permitted.

Administrative Review/Final Settlement. Each year, on the anniversary of the final determination of dumping or subsidization, the DOC must, by law, perform an administrative review of the AD or CVD case if requested by interested parties to determine whether duty rates in effect for that first-year period are correct. The DOC publishes the results of this review in the Federal Register. At the one-year anniversary or completion of the administrative review, the DOC will direct Customs to liquidate the entries for the affected period. Customs will then review the entries and, if called for, make refunds to the importer or assess whatever additional duties may be owed.

Marking: False Impression or Origin

Section 42 of the Trademark Act of 1946 (15 USC 1124) prohibits the importation into the U.S. of any article of foreign origin that bears a name or mark that (1) copies or simulates the name of a manufacturer or trader afforded protection under U.S. law—including foreigners protected through treaty, convention, or U.S. law; or (2) is calculated to induce the public to believe that the article was manufactured in the U.S., or in any foreign country or locality other than the country or locality of actual manufacture.

An imported article bearing a name or mark prohibited by Section 42 of the Trademark Act is subject to seizure and forfeiture. However, on the filing of a petition by the importer before final disposition of the article, Customs may release it on condition that the prohibited marking is removed or obliterated or that the article and containers are properly marked. Alternatively, Customs may permit the article to be exported or destroyed under Customs supervision and without expense to the Government.

Section 43 of the Trademark Act of 1946 (15 USC 1125) prohibits the entry of goods marked or labeled with a false designation of origin or with any false description or representation, including words or other symbols tending to falsely describe or represent the same.

In many cases, the words "United States," the letters "U.S.A.," or the name of any city or locality in the U.S. appearing on an imported article of foreign origin, or on its container, are considered to be calculated to induce the public to believe that the article was manufactured in the U.S., unless the name showing the country of origin appears in close proximity to the name that suggests a domestic origin.

Deliberate removal, obliteration, covering, or altering of required country of origin markings after release from Customs is a crime punishable by fines and imprisonment (19 USC 1304(h)).

Civil and Criminal Fraud Laws

Section 592 of the 1930 Tariff Act, as amended (19 USC 1592), imposes a monetary penalty on any person who by fraud, gross negligence, or negligence enters or introduces, tries to enter or introduce, or aids or abets another person to enter or introduce merchandise into U.S. commerce by means of any material and false written or oral statement, document, or act, or any material omission. In some situations, the imported merchandise may be seized to secure payment of the penalty and forfeited for failure to pay. This civil fraud statute has been applied by the Customs Service to individuals and companies in the U.S. and abroad that have negligently or intentionally provided false information about importations into the U.S.

Another criminal fraud statute sanctions persons who present false information to Customs officers (18 USC 542), and yet another penalizes those who obtain the entry of products by giving less than the true weight or measure of the imported articles, by stating a false classification as to quality or value, or by paying less than the duty due (18 USC 541). These statutes provide for imprisonment, a hefty fine, or both, for each violation involving an importation or attempted importation.

Federal laws that prohibit money laundering and illegal drug transactions authorize the government to seize and cause the forfeit of property involved—or assets traceable to property involved—in violations of these laws. The Money Laundering Control Act expressly identifies importation fraud violations as unlawful activities. Penalties include imprisonment for up to 20 years for each offense and fines of up to $500,000. These statutes were enacted by Congress to discourage persons from evading the payment of lawful duties owed to the U.S., although these laws now apply regardless of whether the U.S. is deprived of lawful duties. They are enforced by special agents assigned to the Office of Enforcement who operate throughout the U.S. and in major trading centers worldwide. Suspected or known violations of any law involved with the importation of merchandise into the U.S. can be reported toll free and anonymously by calling 1-800 BE-ALERT (232-5378). Rewards are applicable in many instances associated with the reporting of fraud.

Laws Restricting Imports

Copyrights. The Copyright Act (17 USC 101 et seq.) restricts importation into the U.S. of any copies of a work that is protected by copyright and that is acquired outside of the U.S. Such works may be imported only with the copyright owner's authorization. To ensure that pirated versions of copyrighted materials do not enter the U.S., Customs' Intellectual Property Rights Branch enforces this law. Articles imported in violation of the Copyright Act are subject to seizure and forfeiture. Forfeited articles are destroyed or, if Customs is satisfied that the violation was unintentional, may be returned to the country of export. A test of substantial similarity is applied to determine if a work has been copied.

Copyright owners who seek import protection must register their claim to copyright protection with the U.S. Copyright Office and must record their registration with U.S. Customs. Procedures and regulations for recordation are found in 37 CFR 201.8 and 19 CFR 133.31 et seq. Articles imported by mail, marked for copyright, and addressed to the Copyright Office of the Library of Congress or to the Register of Copyrights, Washington, DC, pass Customs duty-free without issuing an entry. For questions about Customs enforcement of copyright requirements, contact the district or port director of Customs for your area or:

Intellectual Property Rights Branch
Office of Regulations and Rulings
U.S. Customs Service
1301 Constitution Avenue, NW
Washington, DC 20227
(202) 566-6956

Trademarks and Trade Names. U.S. Customs affords import protection for U.S. owners of registered trademarks and trade names that have been filed with the Commissioner of Customs and recorded pursuant to regulations in 19 CFR 133. Under this protection, articles of foreign or domestic manufacture that bear a mark or name copying or simulating a recorded trademark or trade name will be refused entry. It is also unlawful to import articles bearing genuine trademarks owned by a U.S. citizen or corporation without permission of the U.S. trademark owner. If the foreign and domestic trademark owners are parent and subsidiary companies or otherwise under common ownership and control, entry will be permitted.

The Customs Reform and Simplification Act of 1978 strengthened the protection afforded trademark owners against the importation of articles bearing a counterfeit mark. A "counterfeit trademark" is a spurious trademark identical with, or substantially indistinguishable from, a registered trademark. Articles bearing a counterfeit trademark seized by customs and forfeited to the government may be 1) given to any federal, state, or local government agency that has established a need for the article; 2) given to a charitable institution; or 3) sold at public auction if more than one year has passed since forfeiture and no eligible organization has established a need for the article. The counterfeit marks must be removed before the forfeited articles may be given away or sold. If removal of marking is not feasible, the articles are destroyed.

The law also provides an exemption from all restrictions on trademarked articles (limited to one of each type) that accompany a person arriving in the U.S., provided the articles are for personal use and not for sale.

Obscene, Immoral, or Seditious Materials. The import of articles considered obscene, immoral, or seditious are strictly prohibted under the Tariff Act (18 USC 552, 1462, 1465, 2251 et seq.). These laws specifically prohibit the importation of any book, writing, advertisement, circular, or picture containing any matter advocating or urging treason or insurrection against the U.S. or forcible resistance to any U.S. law. Any such materials that contain a threat to take the life of or inflict bodily harm on any person in the U.S. must be refused entry.

The law also prohibits importation of any obscene book, writing, advertisement, circular, picture, or other representation, figure, or image on or of paper or other material, or any instrument, or other obscene or immoral article. Shipments of material relating to sexual exploitation of minors are prohibited. Any drug or medicine for causing unlawful abortion is also prohibited under the Tariff Act. The mailing of pandering and sexually oriented advertisements that fail to comply strictly with legal requirements for such mailing is prohibited, and the U.S. Postal Service is authorized to order any sender to refrain from sending such materials.

Disobedience is punishable by contempt of court, which may involve imposition of fines and imprisonment. See 18 USC 3008, 3010.

Books. If you import a book that is seized by U.S. Customs as being obscene, and you decline to execute an assent to forfeiture on the grounds that the book is a classic, or is of recognized and established literary or scientific merit, you may file a petition for release of the book, addressed to the Secretary of the Treasury. You will have to supply evidence to support your claim, along with your petition. Unsupported statements or allegations will not be considered. If the ruling is favorable, your book will be released to the ultimate consignee.

Films. If you are importing films, you must certify on Customs **Form 3291** that your films contain no prohibited material as defined in Section 305 of the Tariff Act. If you claim your imported films as duty-free U.S. goods returned, you may instead make this certification on Customs **Form 3311**, in the space designated "Remarks".

A qualified Customs employee will preview films exposed abroad before release from Customs custody. Films imported as undeveloped negatives exposed abroad will be viewed after development in the U.S. Before developing and printing, such films must be weighed and an approximation of their length in feet must be given to Customs. Any objectional film will be detained pending instructions from U.S. Customs headquarters or a decision of the court as to its final disposition.

Detention Procedures. Customs seizes prohibited items at entry and sends notice of seizure to the consignee. If the articles are of small value and no criminal intent is apparent, Customs includes a blank assent to forfeiture, Customs **Form 4607**, with the notice. If the articles are not needed for official use, they are destroyed when Customs receives the completed **Form 4607**. The case is then closed. However, for a repeat offender or for a situation in which the importation was deliberately made with intent to evade the law, Customs submits the facts and evidence (i.e. the prohibited article) to the U.S. attorney, who initiates prosecution.

Products of Convict or Forced Labor. The Tariff Act (18 USC 1761) prohibits the importation of merchandise produced, mined, or manufactured through convict, forced, or indentured-under-penal-sanctions labor. Customs enforces these provisions (19 CFR 12.45). Under Customs regulations (19 CFR 42), if a potential violation of this law is brought to the attention of U.S. Customs and is found to be reasonably substantiated by accompanying evidence, all such shipments will be temporarily detained. If, on investigation, the Commissioner of Customs determines that the products are the result of prohibited labor, the finding will be published in the Federal Register. All detained shipments will then be either reexported or destroyed.

If you import a shipment of merchandise detained as a product of prohibited forms of labor, you may petition the Commissioner of Customs for a redetermination of admissibility. To do so, you will have to submit a certificate of origin (19 CFR 43) signed by the foreign seller or owner of the article. The ultimate consignee must also provide a statement detailing every reasonable effort to ascertain the character of the labor used in producing the article and showing the results of the research. All relevant paperwork must be submitted to Customs within three months after the original importation. If Customs finds that the products are admissible, your shipment will be released, subject to normal entry requirements. If Customs decides your proof does not establish admissibility, you will be notified in writing that your merchandise is excluded from entry. After such notification, the merchandise will be destroyed within 60 days, unless you reexport it or file a further protest.

Unfair Competition or Business Practices. Section 337 of the Tariff Act of 1930 prohibits unfair methods of competition and unfair practices in the importation or sale of merchandise when the effect or tendency is 1) to destroy, injure substantially, or prevent the establishment of an efficiently and economically operated U.S. industry; or 2) to restrain or monopolize trade and commerce in the U.S. The International Trade Commission (ITC) conducts investigations of alleged Section 337 violations. If the ITC determines that a violation has occurred, or that there is reason to believe a violation has occurred, with respect to the importation of certain merchandise, it will issue an import exclusion order for all such merchandise. The order is published in the *Federal Register* and goes into effect on the date of its publication. The order becomes final after 60 days, unless revoked by the U.S. President. Customs refuses admission to all shipments of merchandise under import exclusion order. Until the order becomes final, however, the shipments may be provisionally imported under Customs bond (Customs **Form 301**). If the order is not revoked by presidential action, Customs recalls all provisional shipments when the order becomes final, provided the order requires a recall. If the President determines that entry of the merchandise is not in violation of Section 337, the bond is cancelled and the merchandise is not recalled.

Patent Protections. Section 337 of the Tariff Act of 1930 is most commonly invoked in the case of patent violations. The owner of a U.S.-registered patent who believes that merchandise being imported into the U.S. infringes the patent may apply for a Customs survey. The survey provides the patent owner with names and addresses of importers whose merchandise appears to infringe the registered patent. The application may be made by letter addressed to the Commissioner of Customs. It must give 1) the name and address of the patent owner; 2) if available, a description of the merchandise believed to infringe the registered patent; and 3) the country of manufacture. The patent owner must also submit a certified copy, plus three copies for Customs files, of the U.S. Patent and Trademark Office patent registration, and a check or money order to cover the fee for the survey. The applicant may request surveys for periods of 2, 4, or 6 months. If patent violation is confirmed, questionable merchandise is prohibited entry for the term of the patent. In some cases, a different term may be specified.

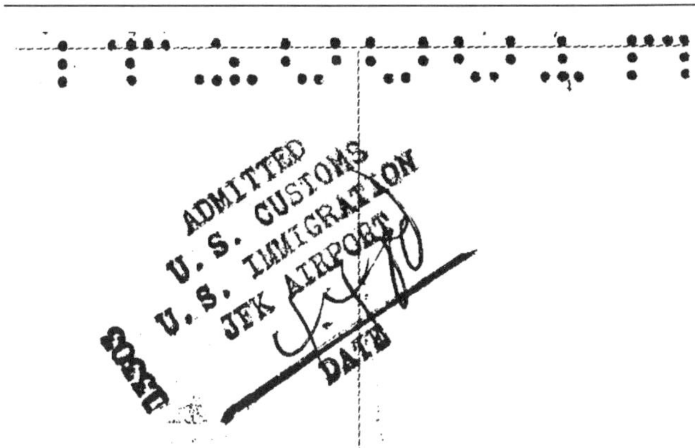

Reentry to the United States

All who reenter the U.S. from abroad must pass through immigration control. The U.S. Immigration and Naturalization Service (INS) works closely with U.S. Customs.

Nonresident Entry

If you are a U.S. resident alien and not a U.S. citizen, you will need a valid residency "green" card to gain entry to the U.S. A nonresident alien will require a U.S. visa or work permit to regain entry. U.S. Immigration may deny entry to foreign nationals for various reasons including:

- Those suspected of terrorist activities
- Those considered to be health risks
- Those convicted in a foreign court of law of certain felonies

Nonresident Customs Exemptions

The following articles may be brought in free of duty and internal revenue tax, provided they are for personal use, not for others, and not for sale.

- Personal effects (e.g., wearing apparel; articles of personal adornment; toilet articles; hunting, fishing, and photographic equipment; equipment for physically challenged persons)
- One U.S. quart (one liter) of alcoholic beverages (e.g., wine, beer, or liquor), if you are an adult nonresident
- 200 cigarettes, 50 cigars, or 4.5 pounds (2 kg) of smoking tobacco, or proportionate amounts of each
- Vehicles (e.g., automobiles, trailers, airplanes, motorcycles, boats), if imported in connection with your arrival

Gift Exemption. In addition to the above exemptions, articles of up to $100 in total value for use as bona fide gifts to other persons may be brought in free of duty and tax, as long as you will be in the U.S. for at least 72 hours and have not claimed this gift exemption in the past 6 months. You may include in this exemption up to 100 cigars, but not alcohol or cigarettes in any amount.

Note: Some states limit the amount of liquor that can be brought into the state. Customs cannot release alcoholic beverages in excess of restrictions of the state where you arrive.

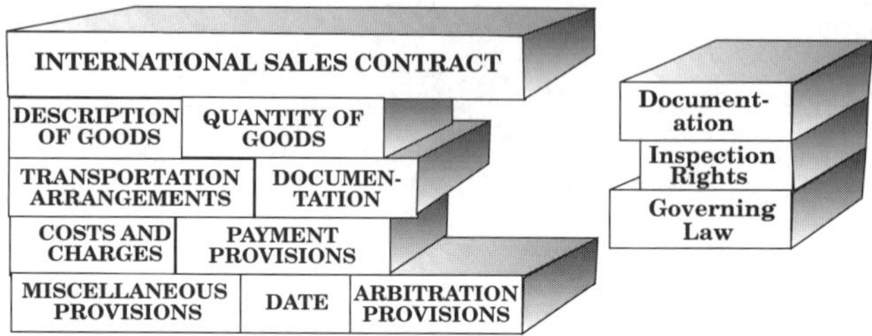

Drafting the International Sales Contract

Nature of a Contract

Contracts are simply agreements, usually between a buyer and a seller. For example, when you say that you agree to purchase a quantity of product at a certain price from a supplier, you have entered into an oral contract. Whether you will be able to enforce your contract is another question. As you move from the domestic to the international setting, enforcement issues increase in complexity.

Importance of Having a Written Contract

Formalities of contract formation—such as whether a contract must be written, whether oral terms can modify written ones, and whether the parties must authenticate their signatures or certify to their authority—vary according to local practices. In general, keep in mind that a precisely drafted, written contract will help to eliminate misunderstandings between your supplier and you. It will also serve as proof of your agreement, should enforcement prove necessary.

The laws of some jurisdictions require certain contracts to be written in order to be enforceable. For example, the U.S. Uniform Commercial Code (UCC) provides that every contract for the sale of goods with an aggregate value exceeding $500 must be in writing to be enforceable. The foreign jurisdiction where you are doing business may or may not have a similar requirement. Some jurisdictions also require written contracts for the transfer of certain types of property, such as immovable property or lease-to-buy items. Observation of other formalities—such as notarization or signatures of witnesses—may be required. In some countries, an individual who works for a corporation may not be allowed to bind that company in a contract without a corporate resolution.

At the very least, you should have a written contract whenever you pay for, but do not take possession of, goods. If you are simply paying c.o.d. for goods, get a bill of sale or invoice for tax and customs purposes. Make sure that you have documentation of the sale, even if it is just a simple description of goods, quantity, and price. This is usually sufficient for general merchandise if you take physical delivery and ship the goods yourself, rather than having the seller handle packaging, shipping, and other transfer arrangements.

For a contract that will be performed over time—that is, a series of transactions—you should anticipate potential problems at the outset. Most people enter into an agreement to purchase and sell with the expectation that all will go smoothly and both parties will gain from the transaction. These positive expectations can be realized if your supplier and you provide for contingencies. Even with a simple sales contract, you must think about possible downstream problems. The first rule of successful international business is also the last rule: *decide how to resolve problems and disputes before they occur.*

Tip: The best time to agree on how downstream problems will be handled is when you have reached an initial agreement to do business together and all parties are feeling positive. If you can't agree to a means of dispute resolution when your contract is drafted, you are unlikely to reach agreement once a problem does arise. Remember: whenever title to goods is not transferred at the time you make the agreement, you should have at least a simple written contract. The complexity of your written contract should reflect the complexity of your transaction. All foreseeable problems should be addressed and resolved in express contractual terms.

Domestic and Foreign Contract Laws

International business transactions are complicated by the movement of goods and services between foreign jurisdictions with different legal systems. The drafting of a contract, performance or modification of contractual obligations, resolution of disputes, and enforcement of judgments or orders are relatively straightforward in domestic U.S. transactions, but they can be arduous tasks when you face international transactions subject to foreign laws and legal systems with which you are unfamiliar.

The U.S. System: Cross-State Recognition. The U.S. has 52 different legal systems: a federal one, one in each state, and one in the District of Columbia. The U.S. is a common law country. Its law is based on a division of powers between federal and state governments. On the federal level, various district and circuit courts interpret federal law in different regions of the country, with conflicts eventually resolved by the U.S. Supreme Court. All powers that are neither expressly delegated to the federal government nor specifically prohibited to the states are reserved to the states. Under this system, each state is free to enact its own laws, and its local courts are free to develop their own judicial interpretations of those laws. As a result, two states can have conflicting laws. Even if two states enact exactly the same statute, their courts may develop distinct—if not contrary—interpretations of that law.

Nevertheless, the U.S. Constitution requires local state courts to give "full faith and credit" to judgments and orders validly entered by a court in another state. For example, if your business is located in California and you have a supplier in Nevada who fails to deliver goods as required by your contract, you may sue for breach of contract in California and may get a judgment in your favor. You can then take your California judgment to Nevada, where the Nevada courts will most likely than not recognize and enforce it.

State courts also recognize the rights of parties to choose which state's laws will apply to a transaction, and the courts will usually uphold such an agreement. For example, a California buyer may agree to have Nevada law applied to a contract with a Nevada supplier. If suit for breach of the contract is brought in California, the court in California will interpret and apply Nevada laws.

Other Countries: Discretionary Recognition. Although in the U.S. your transactions can cross state lines with relative ease, this is not always the case in the international business setting. Courts in countries with common law systems—such as the U.S. and the United Kingdom—will usually recognize foreign country laws and judgments through a doctrine known as "comity." Many U.S. states and some foreign countries have laws for registration and recognition of foreign country judgments, although enforcement is usually still discretionary with the local court. In countries that are members of international trade conventions, such as the U.N. Convention on Contracts for the International Sale of Goods (CISG) or the Convention on the Recognition and Enforcement of Foreign Arbitral Awards, cross-border enforcement may be available, but the ease with which enforcement can be accomplished depends on the legal system of the member country and the extent to which it has developed methods of enforcement. Before you commit to an international sales contract, you must consider all ramifications of crossing international legal and cultural boundaries relevant to the particular transaction proposed. A contract that is impossible to enforce is worthless.

Uniform Contract Laws

The U.S.: Uniform Commercial Code (UCC). All of the states have adopted some form of the Uniform Commercial Code (UCC). The UCC was drafted by a national commission, primarily made up of lawyers, to serve as a model law on commercial sales. Each U.S. state has discretion to adopt the UCC intact or with modifications, and they may also amend it from time to time. Because it works well, the UCC has had a great impact both on domestic U.S. transactions and on international sales. U.S. commercial law is so well-developed that it has become a model for commercial law in many foreign countries.

Internationally: The United Nations Sales Convention. On January 1,1988, the U.S. ratified the U.N. Convention on Contracts for the International Sale of Goods (CISG). This Convention establishes uniform legal rules to govern the formation of international sales contracts and the rights and obligations of the contracting parties. The CISG is designed to facilitate and stimulate international trade. When the U.S. became a signatory, it made a reservation to the effect that the CISG will apply only when the other party to the transaction also has its place of business in a country that applies the CISG.

The CISG applies automatically to all contracts for the sale of goods between traders from two different countries that have both ratified the Convention. To avoid application of the CISG, the contracting parties must expressly state that all or part of the CISG does not apply or must expressly stipulate to law other than the CISG. Parties can also expressly choose to apply the CISG to transactions not otherwise subject to this Convention.

The nations that have ratified the CISG include the following: Argentina, Australia, Austria, Bulgaria, Chile, China, Belarus, Denmark, Egypt, Finland, France, Germany, Guinea, Hungary, Iraq, Italy, Lesotho, Mexico, Netherlands, Norway, Spain, Sweden, Switzerland, Syria, Russia, U.S., and Zambia.

Convention Provisions. The provisions and scope of the CISG are similar to Article 2 of the Uniform Commercial Code (effective in the U.S.). The CISG comprises four parts:

- Part I, Sphere of Application and General Provisions (Arts. 1-13), provides that the CISG covers the international sale of most commercial goods.
- Part II, Formation of the Contract (Arts. 1-24), provides rules on offer and acceptance.
- Part III, Sale of Goods (Arts. 25-88), covers obligations and remedies of the seller and buyer and rules on the passing of risk and damages.
- Part IV, Final Provisions (Arts. 89-101), covers the right of a country to disclaim certain parts of the convention.

Applying (or Excluding) the CISG. U.S. businesses can avoid the difficulties of reaching agreement with foreign parties on choice-of-law issues through the use of the CISG, which may serve as a compromise in negotiating sale contract terms. Use of the CISG may decrease the time and legal costs otherwise involved in research of various unfamiliar foreign laws. Furthermore, the CISG may reduce problems of proof and recognition of foreign law in domestic and foreign courts. Application of the CISG may especially make sense for smaller firms—and for U.S. firms contracting with smaller companies—in countries where the legal systems are obscure, unfamiliar, undeveloped, or otherwise unsuited for international sales transactions.

Some larger, more experienced firms may prefer to continue their current practices, at least with regard to parties with whom they have been doing business regularly. A firm that chooses to exclude the CISG *cannot* do so by merely adding a choice of law clause—e.g., "the laws of XYZ shall apply"—to the contract, because the CISG may also be the law of the jurisdiction selected. Rather, the exclusion must be specific: "The provisions of the Uniform Commercial Code as adopted by the State of XYZ, and not the U.N. Convention on Contracts for the International Sale of Goods, shall govern this contract."

The CISG can be found in 15 USC app. To obtain an up-to-date listing of ratifying or acceding countries and their reservations call the U.N. Treaties Section at (212) 963-3918. For further information, contact the Office of the Assistant Legal Adviser for Private International Law, U.S. Department of State, at (202) 647-6575, or the Office of the Chief Counsel for International Commerce, U.S. Department of Commerce at (202) 482-0937.

Bilateral and Free Trade Agreements. The U.S., Canada, and Mexico have concluded the North American Free

Trade Agreement (NAFTA). In addition to eliminating and reducing tariffs and similar trade barriers among these countries, this Agreement mandates the establishment of enforcement and dispute resolution systems for cross-border transactions that are covered under the Agreement. It also provides for substantial industrial and intellectual property right protection.

Bilateral trade agreements have been made between the U.S. and several Eastern European countries, Russia, and Mongolia. These congressionally approved agreements are required by the Trade Act of 1974 for these countries to receive Most Favored Nation (MFN) treatment. These agreements provide for reciprocal MFN status and contain guarantees on intellectual property rights and business facilitation—such as the right to establish commercial representation offices in a country through at most a simple registration process; the right to serve as, and to hire, agents; the right to deal directly with customers and end users of products and services; and the right to hire employees of a company's choice. The intellectual property right provisions include protection for computer software and trade secrets.

Important Contract Terms

When dealing internationally, you must consider the business practices and legal requirements of the country where the buyer or seller is located. Parties generally have the freedom to agree to any contract terms that they desire, but the laws of your country or the foreign country may require a written contract. In some transactions, the laws may even specify all or some of the contract terms. Whether a contract term is valid in a particular country is mainly of concern if you have to seek enforcement. Otherwise, you have fairly broad flexibility in negotiating contract provisions. However, you should always be certain to come to a definite understanding with the other party on four basic issues: the goods (quantity, type, and quality); the time of delivery; the price; and the time and means of payment.

Conflict of law problems occur when you leave terms out of your contract because the gaps will be filled in by application of the law. The result will vary depending on which law is chosen. If terms are vague and open to interpretation, or if any aspect is left to implication or custom, you will have to rely on the law to determine your rights and obligations should a dispute arise. Disputes will be resolved according to the laws of the country with jurisdiction (for example, the country designated in your contract or the country where both parties have the most significant contacts).

Accordingly, the best way to control the results of your contract is to clarify each party's responsibility in the agreement by paying close attention to each contract term. Always be specific. For instance, you may have an agreement that you will buy a certain quantity of a specific product, but how are you going to pick up the goods? Is someone going to box them? Do you want the entire order at once? When do you want them?

Tip: Even if you specify your choice of law and method of dispute resolution in the contract, you may find that you are doing business with a national of a country that does not recognize such stipulations. In that case, the foreign country may not enforce a U.S. judgment. Before concluding an agreement, do your homework: find out about the country's policy on choice of law and conflict resolution for international contracts. Martindale-Hubbell's *International Law Digest*, available at the reference desk of most larger public and law libraries, is a good place to start.

After you have determined whether the CISG or another law applies to a particular transaction, you should review the related documentation to ensure consistency with the CISG or other governing law. For agreements about to expire, companies should make sure renewals take into account the applicability (or nonapplicability) of the CISG.

Payment Term. In international business transactions, you will use different methods of payment, and possibly different currency, than you do in domestic transactions. You will have to become familiar with different currencies, currency restrictions, and exchange rates, and you will need to consider these issues each time you draft a contract. Contact your international banker for information about foreign exchange and currency restrictions.

Transport and Delivery Terms. In any sales agreement, definitions of transport and delivery terms are essential. The terms commonly used in international business transactions often sound similar to those used in domestic contracts, but they frequently have different meanings in global transactions. Confusion over these terms can result in a lost sale or a financial loss on a sale. For this reason, you must know the meaning of these terms before completing your agreement.

A full list of important terms and definitions is contained in *Incoterms 1990*, a book issued by ICC Publications, Inc., 156 Fifth Avenue, New York, NY 10010; Tel (212) 206-1150; FAX (212) 633-6025. *Guide to Incoterms*—also available from ICC—uses illustrations and commentary to explain how a buyer and seller divide risks and obligations, and therefore costs, in specific kinds of international transactions. The 1990 update of *Incoterms 1990* resulted in several new terms and abbreviations; you should, therefore, take care to use the most recent edition of these terms to avoid confusion.

The following are a few of the more common terms used in international trade:

- **CIF** (cost, insurance, freight) to a named overseas port of import. Under this term, the seller quotes a price for the goods (including insurance), all transportation, and miscellaneous charges to the point of debarkation from the vessel. (Typically used for ocean shipments only.)
- **CFR** (cost and freight) to a named overseas port of import. Under this term, the seller quotes a price for the goods that includes the costs of transportation to the named point of debarkation. The buyer is responsible for the cost of insurance. (Typically used for ocean shipments only.)
- **CPT** (carriage paid to) and **CIP** (carriage and insurance paid to) a named place of destination. This term is used in place of CFR and CIF

respectively, for shipment by modes other than water.

- **EXW** (ex works) at a named point of origin (e.g., ex factory, ex mill, ex warehouse). Under this term, the price quoted applies only at the point of origin. The seller agrees to place the goods at the disposal of the buyer at the specified place on the date or within the period fixed in the contract. All other charges are the buyer's responsibility.
- **FCA** (free carrier) to a named place. This term replaces the former "FOB named inland port" to designate the seller's responsibility for the cost of loading goods at the named shipping point. It may be used for multimodal transport, container stations, and any mode of transport, including air.
- **FOB** (free on board) at a named port of export. The seller quotes the buyer a price that covers all costs up to and including delivery of goods aboard an overseas vessel.

International Sales Contract Checklist

The following items are elements of a complete contract. While all items may not apply to every contract, referring to a checklist like this when considering a contract will help ensure that you have provided for as many contingencies as possible. Though you may not always be in a position to dictate the terms of your contract, you should be aware of key elements. You can be flexible regarding some contract terms, but there are terms that you should insist on to protect your interests.

1. Contract date
2. Identification of parties
3. Goods
   a. Description
   b. Quantity
   c. Price
4. Packaging arrangements
5. Transportation arrangements
   a. Carrier
   b. Storage
   c. Notice provisions
   d. Shipping time
6. Costs and charges
   a. Duties and taxes
   b. Insurance costs
   c. Handling and transport
   d. Terms defined
7. Insurance or risk of loss protection
8. Payment provisions
   a. Method of payment
   b. Medium of exchange
   c. Exchange rate
9. Import documentation
10. Inspection rights
11. Warranty provisions
12. Indemnity
13. Enforcement and Remedies
    a. Time is of the essence
    b. Modification
    c. Cancellation
    d. Contingencies
    e. Governing law
    f. Choice of forum
    g. Arbitration provisions
    h. Severability

Contract Provisions Explained

For a small, one-time sale, an invoice or a simple contract may be acceptable. For a more involved business transaction or an ongoing relationship, a formal written contract is preferable to define clearly the rights, responsibilities, and remedies of all parties. Contracts that involve capital goods, high credit risks, or industrial or intellectual property rights will require special protective clauses. In preparing such contracts, it is essential to obtain legal advice from a professional who is familiar with the laws and practices of both countries.

Tip: In drafting international contracts, it is extremely wise to have each party go through each contract provision and ask for express comprehension—such as: "Do you understand that you are assuming the responsibility for packing these goods according to our shipper's instructions?" You may also want to have the other party initial certain paragraphs if you are concerned that misunderstandings over performance are likely. Some multinational contracts have every paragraph initialed after the parties have spent weeks negotiating the contract through interpreters.

For a simple, one-time deal you need to consider at least the following clauses:

1. **Contract Date.** Specify the date when the contract is signed. This date is particularly important if payment or delivery times are fixed in reference to it for example, "shipment within 30 days of the contract date."

2. **Identification of Parties.** Name the parties, describe their relation to each other and designate the persons who are authorized to act for each party. The persons designated should also be the ones who sign the contract.

   Tip: If performance of the agreement extends beyond a single transaction, the person's authority to act for the foreign company should be established additionally by a copy of a statement of capacity certified by a government official in that country. If the foreign company is a corporation or similar entity, authority to act should also be established by a corporate resolution of the company's governing body, such as its board of directors. The foreign company may require similar certified proof of authority from you. Your contract should describe documents that will be considered satisfactory evidence of authority.

3. **Goods.** The provisions related to goods are essential to the contract. If these provisions are missing or are not sufficiently specific, enforcement of the contract may be impossible because the goods cannot be identified.

   a. **Description.** Describe the type and quality of the goods. You may simply indicate a model number or you may have to attach detailed lists, plans, drawings, or other specifications. This clause should be clear enough that both parties fully understand the specifications and have no discretion in interpreting them.

   Tip: For certain transactions, you may have to state performance specifications. For example: "Under conditions x, y, and z, the product will a, b, and c."

   b. **Quantity.** Specify the number of units, or other measure of quantity, of the goods. If the goods are measured by weight, you should specify net weight, dry weight, or drained weight.

   Tip: If the goods are prepackaged and are subject to weight restrictions for sale in the U.S., you may want to ensure that the seller will provide goods packaged to comply with those restrictions.

   c. **Price.** Indicate the price per unit or other measure, such as per pound or ton, and the extended price.

4. **Packaging Arrangements.** Set forth packaging specifications, especially for goods that can be damaged in transit. At a minimum, this provision should require the seller to package the goods in such a way as to withstand transportation. If special packaging requirements are necessary to meet consumer and product liability standards and expectations in the U.S., you should specify them also. Refer to "Marking: Country of Origin" on page 215, "Special Marking Requirements" on page 217, and the marking and labeling portions of the Commodity Index chapters relevant to the specific products you intend to import.

5. **Transportation Arrangements.** This provision may simply state the name of the carrier you want to handle the freight shipment and who is to pay for transportation from point A to point B. However, if more than two or three carriers are involved or your goods require special treatment, you will have to add extra details to this provision.

   Tip: Use very precise language. Also, look for the weak link in the handling of your shipment. Ask: "If something will go wrong, where will it go wrong?"

   a. **Carrier.** Name a preferred carrier for transporting the goods. You should designate a particular carrier if, for example, a carrier offers you special pricing or is better able than others to transport the product.

   b. **Storage.** Specify any particular requirements for storage of the goods before or during shipment, such as security arrangements, special climate demands, and weather protection needs.

   c. **Notice Provisions.** Require the seller to notify you when the goods are ready for delivery or pickup, particularly if the goods are perishable or fluctuate in value. If your transaction is time-sensitive, you could even provide for several notices, which will allow you to track the goods and to take steps to minimize damages if delivery is delayed.

   d. **Shipping Time.** State the exact date for shipping or provide for shipment within a reasonable time from the contract date. If this clause is included and the seller fails to ship on time, you may claim a right to cancel the contract, even if the goods have been shipped, provided that you do not accept delivery.

   Tip: You may want to provide that you have the right to terminate the contract if the goods are not shipped by a specific date. An express statement of your termination right can avoid misunderstandings with the foreign supplier should you reject goods that are shipped later than the specified date, but still within a reasonable time from the contract date.

6. **Costs and Charges.** Specify which party is to pay any additional costs and charges related to the sale.

   a. **Duties and Taxes.** Designate the party that will be responsible for import, export, and other fees and taxes and for obtaining all required licenses. For example, each party may be made responsible for paying the duties, taxes, and charges imposed by that party's own country, because a party is best situated to know the legal requirements of his or her own country.

   Tip: You may request a "package deal," under which your supplier will be responsible for all costs of entry through U.S. Customs. If this proves impractical, you should at a minimum require your supplier to be responsible for export duties, taxes, or charges on your product or commodity, since your supplier is in the best position to know the requirements of his or her own country. Protect yourself with a provision that states: "Seller is responsible for paying all export duties and taxes and for obtaining any necessary export licenses."

   b. **Insurance Costs.** Identify the party that will pay the costs of insuring the goods in transit. This is a critical provision because, if the goods are lost during transit, the party responsible bears the risk. A seller is typically responsible for insurance until title to the goods passes to the buyer, at which time the buyer becomes responsible for insurance or becomes the named beneficiary under the seller's insurance policy. It is crucial, then, to provide for the time at which the title of the goods will change hands. Refer to "Ownership Situations: Terms of Sale" on page 298 for an explanation of responsibilities under different trade terms.

   c. **Handling and Transport.** Specify the party that will pay shipping, handling, packaging, security, and any other costs related to transportation, all of which should be specified.

   d. **Terms Defined.** Contracts for the sale of goods most commonly use international trade terms—usually Incoterms as defined by the International Chamber of Commerce in Paris—to assign responsibility for the risks and cost of transport. Although international trade terms have been standardized, in practice their meanings can vary. Precise definitions of these terms are important to your contract because these terms can determine such items as the party responsible for insuring the goods at any one time, the time at which title to the goods will transfer from seller to buyer, and the party responsible for paying certain transportation costs. Refer to "Glossary of Technical Terms" on page 167 for explanations of the Incoterms. Refer to "Ownership Situations: Terms of Sale" on page 298 for a more complete discussion of trade terms.

   Tip: If you use trade terms, be certain to establish your own definition or to specify the standard that you are using (e.g., FOB Incoterms 1990). For example, FOB (Free On Board) usually means that the risk of loss shifts to the purchaser once the goods have physically passed over the rail of the ship, regardless of whether they have been secured, or even set down, on the deck or in a cargo hold. If the goods are suspended from a crane mid-air on the deck side of the ship's rail, the risk of loss has passed to the buyer. However, in some trading circles, FOB also includes the costs of securing the shipment on board and means that title is transferred only after the goods are fastened for transport. By defining your own terms, you will gain the most control in avoiding misunderstandings with foreign suppliers whose trading practices are different than your customs.

   Tip: When establishing trade terms for your contract be sure to fully establish your own definition, or specify which standard you are using (e.g. FOB Incoterms 1990).

6. **Insurance or Risk of Loss Protection.** Specify the insurance required, the beneficiary of the policy, the party who will obtain the insurance and who will pay for it, and the date by which it must be obtained. You should also agree on which documents will be considered satisfactory evidence of insurance.

7. **Payment Provisions.** In a one-time transaction, the seller will typically seek the most secure form of payment before committing to shipment, while a buyer will want the goods cleared through customs and delivered in satisfactory condition before remitting payment. If payments cannot be made in advance, parties most often agree to use documentary credits. (Refer to the "International Banking" section, beginning on page 113 for an explanation of such payments.)

   a. **Method of Payment.** State the means by which payment will be tendered—for example, delivery of a documentary letter of credit or documents against payment; prepayment in cash or traveler's checks; or credit for a specified number of days. Refer to "Methods of International Payment" on page 116 for a complete discussion of payment methods.

   b. **Medium of Exchange.** Designate the currency to be used—for example, U.S. currency, currency of the country of origin, or currency of a third country.

   Tip: If you think the value of the U.S. dollar will decrease between the signing of the contract and the payment, specify U.S. dollars. If you believe that the currency of the country of origin will decrease relative to the U.S. dollar, specify that currency.

   c. **Exchange Rate.** Specify a fixed exchange rate for the price stated in the contract. You may use this clause to lock in a specific price and ensure against fluctuating currency values. Refer to "An Introduction to Foreign Exchange" on page 122 for a detailed discussion of exchange rates and foreign exchange.

8. **Import Documentation.** Designate the documents for exporting and importing that each party will be responsible for obtaining, completing, and presenting to customs. Shipment of the goods, and even the contract itself, may be made contingent on a party's having obtained in advance the proper licenses, in-

spection certificates, and other authorizations. For a discussion of general documentation requirements, read the U.S. Customs "Entry Process" on page 182 and consult the Commodity Index for documentation requirements specific to your product or commodity. For information specific to documentation in a banking/documentary credit context, refer to the "International Banking" section, beginning on page 113.

Tip: Always make complete documentation—that is, documentation that is satisfactory for U.S. Customs entry—a requirement of any contract for the purchase of products or commodities.

9. **Inspection Rights.** Provide that you have a right to inspect goods before taking delivery to determine whether the goods meet the contract specifications. This clause should specify the person who will do the inspection—for example, you, your agent, a neutral third party, or a licensed inspector; the location where the inspection will occur—for example, at the seller's plant, your warehouse, or a receiving dock; the time at which the inspection will occur; the presentation of a certified document of inspection, if needed; and any requirements related to the return of nonconforming goods, such as payment of return freight by the seller. You may not need this clause if you have an established relationship with your supplier.

   Tip: Your supplier may reject a provision that allows you to conduct your own inspection, particularly if the site of inspection is in the U.S. and the supplier is paying freight to the U.S. In this case, inspection by a third party may be justified, but for your protection, you should insist that the inspector certify his or her findings in writing: "Signed/certified by licensed inspector, finding 1, 2, and 3."

   Tip: A contract provision stating that the seller pays for return freight for any nonconforming goods will protect you in the event that you have to refuse a shipment.

10. **Warranty Provisions.** Limit or extend any implied warranties, and define any express warranties on property fitness and quality. The contract may, for example, state that the seller warrants that the goods are of merchantable quality, are fit for any purpose for which they would ordinarily be used, or are fit for a particular purpose requested by the buyer. The seller may also warrant that the goods will be of the same quality as any sample or model that the seller has furnished as representative of the goods. Finally, the seller may warrant that the goods will be packaged in a specific way or in a way that will adequately preserve and protect the goods.

11. **Indemnity.** Agree that one party will hold the other harmless from damages that arise from specific causes, such as a design flaw or manufacturing defect.

12. **Enforcement and Remedies**

    a. **Time Is of the Essence.** Stipulate that timely performance of the contract is essential. In the U.S., inclusion of this clause allows a party to claim breach merely because the other party fails to perform within the time prescribed in the contract. Although common in U.S. contracts, a clause of this type is considered less important in other countries, where contracting parties often waive or renegotiate terms, rather than sue for damages on breach of the contract.

    b. **Modification.** Require the parties to make all changes to the contract in advance and in a signed written modification.

    Tip: You should insist on this clause in contracts with foreign suppliers to avoid misunderstandings that can arise from oral modifications—when its your word against that of your supplier.

    c. **Cancellation.** State the reasons for which either party may cancel the contract and the advance notice required for cancellation.

    d. **Contingencies.** Specify any events that must occur before a party is obligated to perform the contract. For example, you may agree that the seller has no duty to ship goods until the buyer forwards documents that secure the payment for the goods.

    e. **Governing Law.** Choose the law of a specific jurisdiction to control any interpretation of the contract terms. The law that you choose will usually affect where you can sue or enforce a judgment and what laws, rules, and procedures will be applied. If you file suit in the U.S., where domestic counsel and commercial laws are familiar to you, your experience will be different than if you litigate in a foreign country, where you will be subject to unfamiliar laws, rules, and procedures and will have to rely on foreign counsel. Refer also to "Solving Contract Disputes" on page 95.

    Tip: Dealing with the legal systems of foreign countries can be a lengthy, costly, and frustrating process. In some countries, bringing a lawsuit can ruin your business and personal reputation because such action is considered extremely offensive. For these reasons, you should consider alternative methods of dispute resolution—negotiation, mediation, or arbitration—for settling international commercial conflicts before resorting to the courts.

    f. **Choice of Forum.** Identify the place where a dispute may be settled—for example, the country of origin of the goods, the country of destination, or a third country that is convenient to both parties. Refer also to "Solving Contract Disputes" on page 95.

    g. **Arbitration Provisions.** Provide for arbitration as an alternative to litigation for resolving contract disputes. Arbitration is less formal procedurally than a court trial, but still allows the parties to present their claims before a neutral person or panel for an objective decision. This remedy is increasing in popularity in commercial disputes, largely because it is less adversarial, less costly, and faster than litigation. An arbitration clause should specify whether arbitration is binding or nonbinding on the parties; the country where arbitration will be conducted; the procedure for enforcement of an award; the rules governing the arbitration—such as the U.N. Commission on International Trade Law Model Rules; the institute that will administer the arbitration—such as the International Chamber of Commerce (Paris); the law that will govern procedural issues or the merits of the dispute; any limitations on the selection of arbitrators (for example, a national of a disputing party may be excluded from being an arbitrator); the qualifications or expertise of the arbitrators; the language in which the arbitration will be conducted; and the availability of translations and translators if needed. Refer also to "Solving Contract Disputes" on page 95.

Tip: You should agree to arbitrate only if you seriously intend to settle disputes in this way. If you agree to arbitrate but later file suit, the court is likely to uphold the arbitration clause and force you to settle your dispute as you agreed under the contract.

Tip: Arbitration is not used in all countries. For example, disputes in Mexico are rarely settled by arbitration. Moreover, some countries do not recognize arbitration awards from other jurisdictions. You should consult an attorney familiar with the law of the country of your supplier before assuming that you will be able to arbitrate potential contract disputes.

h. **Severability.** Provide that individual clauses can be removed from the contract without affecting the validity of the contract as a whole. This clause is important because it provides that, if one clause is declared invalid and unenforceable for any reason, the rest of the contract remains in force.

Solving Contract Disputes

It is entirely likely that you will have to resort to legal measures from time to time to enforce a contract. In most countries, litigation is expensive, time consuming, and frustrating. In some countries, a lawsuit is viewed as a personal affront. Even with a solid case, the chances of successfully enforcing your contract through legal action are unpredictable. Problems may arise in communicating and prosecuting your case. You may encounter differing legal notions regarding contractual rights. Your case could suffer because of local prejudices against foreign business operators.

Disputes

There are essentially two types of disputes that can arise between your supplier and you: those in which you have a claim against your supplier and those in which your supplier has a claim against you.

The circumstances in which you find that you have a claim against your supplier are many and varied. The goods may not be delivered, or delivery may be delayed. The wrong goods, or goods of a different quantity or quality may be delivered. Proper documentation might not accompany the goods. The goods might turn out to be defective after you have resold them. In all these cases, you will have a claim against the supplier in which you seek either performance or damages, or a combination of the two.

A supplier's claim against you will almost always be for nonpayment of all or part of the purchase price. For example, if you refuse to pay the supplier because the goods are not delivered, the quantity received is less than ordered, or the goods received are nonconforming, the supplier may seek a legal remedy.

Immediate and Temporary Relief

Communication with your supplier is essential to keeping the relationship smooth. For minor discrepancies, or even major calamities, your business relationships and reputation will benefit if you approach the problem with understanding and a view toward finding a resolution that will satisfy both your supplier and you. Negotiation, followed by a written confirmation of any modified contract terms, is the most effective means of resolution in terms of cost and time. A good rule to remember: create a working relationship with your suppliers, not an adversarial one.

If a dispute continues despite your informal attempts to resolve it, you should take steps to protect your rights. Your most imminent concern will probably be to recover your own property quickly or to find an immediate replacement supplier so that you can honor your own commitments to third parties. Your contract should expressly authorize either party to take steps to mitigate damages should the other party breach. For example, you can insist on a provision that allows you to take immediate possession or repossession of goods, provided you post a bond that will cover the amount of the other party's claim. You may also expressly reserve your right to pursue legal remedies available in your supplier's country, such as attachment or lien rights.

Arbitration

The parties to a commercial transaction may provide in their contract that any disputes over interpretation or performance of the agreement will be resolved through arbitration. In the domestic context, arbitration may be appealing for a variety of reasons. Frequently cited advantages over conventional courtroom litigation include potential savings in time and expense, confidentiality of the proceedings, and expertise of the arbitrators.

For transactions in which the parties to the agreement are from different countries, additional advantages are neutrality (international arbitration allows each party to avoid the domestic courts of the other) and ease of enforcement (foreign arbitral awards can be easier to enforce than foreign court decisions). In many international commercial transactions, arbitration makes good sense.

However, approach arbitration in an international setting with caution. In many countries, arbitration is unavailable or is just being developed. Although less adversarial than a court trial, arbitration is still viewed in many cultures with suspicion, if not abhorrence. A request for arbitration may be viewed as a personal insult to your supplier, and instead of being a means of dispute resolution, it may destroy the potential for settlement through private negotiation. Because of the complexity of the subject, legal advice should be obtained for specific transactions.

Advantages of Arbitration. The following are advantages of using arbitration as a means of dispute resolution:

1) An arbitration award may be more enforceable in a foreign country than a U.S. court judgment.

2) Other societies are not as litigious as the U.S. A foreigner who is sued is likely to be insulted. Arbitration may be a less offensive means of resolving a dispute.

3) You can choose arbitrators who are experts in your particular industry, which may be particularly important if your contracts cover technically advanced goods. Arbitrators with technical expertise can evaluate whether a shipment meets your specifications more knowledgeably than a court judge who does not have the same training.

4) Arbitration is usually an informal proceeding, less expensive and less time consuming than litigation.

5 Evidence given in arbitration and the arbitration decision itself are confidential, unless all of the parties agree to release all or some of this information.

Disadvantages of Arbitration. The following are reasons to avoid or be cautious in using arbitration for resolving disputes:

1) Arbitrators will not necessarily try to resolve the conflict based on clearly defined legal obligations and precedents. In court, if one party is guilty of a breach of contract, a judgment is entered in favor of the other party. In arbitration, even if evidence of breach is absolute, compromise is usually the end result. Thus, if your supplier has not fulfilled the contract and you choose to arbitrate the dispute, you could end up bearing part of the loss if the arbitrators believe that would be more equitable to all parties concerned, whereas if you had sued, the court might have awarded you full damages.

2) Even arbitration has an adversarial aspect. If you want to keep an ongoing relationship with your supplier, you will better serve your interests through immediate and diligent negotiation with your supplier than a lengthier and more costly process involving various third parties—attorneys, witnesses, arbitrators, investigators, etc.

3) Arbitration is more costly and will cause further delay. Although the delay will usually not be as long as the time required for litigation, the parties will need to choose arbitrators, set up the arbitration hearing, compile evidence and information for the arbitrator, prepare a presentation, and wait for a decision. These activities are more costly and time-consuming than simply negotiating a resolution.

International Arbitration Organizations. Many organizations around the world provide arbitration services. The most well-known U.S. organization is the American Arbitration Association (AAA). The International Chamber of Commerce (ICC) in Paris is the most prominent international organization. Other international arbitration organizations include the London Court of Arbitration, the Japan Commercial Arbitration Association, the U.N. Commission on International Trade Law (UNCITRAL), the U.N. Economic Commission for Europe, the U.N. Economic and Social Commission for Asia and the Pacific (formerly ACAPE), and the Inter-American Arbitration Commission. National and international trade associations often maintain arbitration panels and have their own rules that cover specific trades or industries—such as shipping and construction—or commodities—such as coffee, sugar, oils and fats, grains, cocoa, and cotton, wool, and other textiles.

Each arbitration association has its own rules of practice and procedure, but most are similar. For example, most arbitration rules provide that each party to a dispute may choose one arbitrator, and that the two appointed arbitrators will then elect a third "neutral" arbitrator.

Arbitration Terms. In an agreement to arbitrate (commonly inserted as a term in the contract for the transaction), the parties have broad power to agree on many significant aspects of the arbitration. The arbitration clause should contain at least these elements:

- An agreement to arbitrate.
- The name of an arbitration organization to administer the arbitration. The International Chamber of Commerce based in Paris, the American Arbitration Association in New York, and the Arbitration Institute of the Stockholm Chamber of Commerce in Sweden are three such prominent institutions.
- The rules that will govern the arbitration, usually incorporating a set of existing arbitration rules such as the U.N. Commission on International Trade Law (UNCITRAL) Model Rules. The location where the arbitration will be conducted, which may be a "neutral site." You should select a country that has adopted the U.N. Convention on Recognition and Enforcement of Foreign Arbitral Awards or another convention providing for the enforcement of arbitral awards.
- The law that will govern procedural issues or the merits of the dispute, for example, the law of the State of New York. Before you choose the governing law, you should find out whether it will be disadvantageous to your interests. Instead of specifying the law of a particular country or jurisdiction, you may take a neutral position. For example, you may stipulate that "the arbitrators shall apply equitable principles, without regard to the laws of any country. The arbitrators may tend toward application of this equitable approach even if you don't specifically request it. However, an express provision ensures that, if the laws of your supplier's country are especially unfavorable or undeveloped, they won't be applied. It is best to choose governing law with which you are reasonably familiar and comfortable.
- Any limitations you may prefer on the selection of arbitrators, for example, the exclusion of nationals from the countries of the disputing parties.
- Any particular qualifications or expertise that the arbitrators must have.
- The language in which the proceedings will be conducted.
- The effect of the arbitration decision—binding or nonbinding on the parties.

The typical arbitration clause looks like this:

> "Any dispute between the parties that arises out of or in connection with this contract and that is not amicably settled shall be finally resolved by binding arbitration, conducted in the English language, in _______(location)_______ by ____(e.g., three)____ arbitrators in accordance with the _____(e.g., UN Commission on International Trade Law Model Rules)_____ of _____(e.g., the International Chamber of Commerce)_____ in effect at the time the dispute arises. Judgment on the award rendered may be entered in any court with jurisdiction."

Recognition and Enforcement of Award. For international arbitration to work effectively, the national courts in the countries of both parties to the dispute must recognize and support arbitration as a legitimate alternative means for resolving disputes. This support is particularly crucial at two stages of the arbitration process. First, if one party attempts to avoid arbitration after a dispute has arisen, the other party must be able to rely on the judicial system in either country to enforce the agreement to arbitrate by compelling arbitration. Second, the party that wins in the arbitration proceeding must be confident that the national courts will enforce the decision of the arbitrators. This will ensure that the arbitration process is not ultimately frustrated at the enforcement stage if the losing party refuses to pay or otherwise to satisfy the arbitral award.

The strong policy of U.S. federal law is to approve and support resolution of disputes by arbitration, a policy that is being adopted in many countries throughout the world. Most countries are now recognizing and enforcing arbitration awards made domestically, and many will allow cross-border enforcement of arbitration awards made in other countries. More than 80 countries, including the U.S., have ratified the U.N. Convention on the Recognition and Enforcement of Foreign Arbitral Awards (popularly known as the New York Convention). While several other arbitration treaties have been concluded, the New York Convention is by far the most important international agreement on commercial arbitration and may be credited for much of the explosive growth of arbitration of international disputes in recent decades.

Enforcement of arbitration awards is more common than enforcement of court judgments because arbitration is viewed as an outcome of an agreement between the parties. Most arbitration awards are not reviewed by foreign courts, unlike court judgments from other countries, which are usually carefully scrutinized. However, a foreign arbitral award that violates a country's laws or public policy is not likely to be recognized or enforced. For example, in Greece, where a summons and complaint must be served in person, an arbitral award resulting from a summons and complaint served by mail would not be honored. When you choose a procedure to follow in arbitrating, be aware of the rules governing such matters in both your and your supplier's countries.

Tip: If you are considering alternatives to litigation for resolving disputes, keep in mind the following.

1) It is always a nasty business to arbitrate or to battle it out in court. These should always be your very last resort. Try to negotiate disputes if at all possible. In many countries, especially in Asia and the Middle East, taking someone to court or to arbitration is regarded as an act of outright hostility. In China, for example, even the suggestion that disputes might not be amicably resolved raises eyebrows. If you initiate legal or arbitration proceedings, you can find that your relationship with the supplier has been irreparably damaged. The word can spread quickly that you do not do business as a "gentleman" and should be avoided. Protect yourself by provisions in the contract, but use that protection only as a last resort. Always try to negotiate an amicable settlement if

possible. A victory in court may be a Pyrrhic victory. Sometimes your business will be better served in the long run if you accept a breach of contract gracefully.

2) You have many options regarding contractual provision for the settlement of contract disputes. We recommend that you put an arbitration clause in every contract. Failure to do so exposes you to lawsuits in foreign courts, which should be avoided. The type of arbitration you choose will depend on your unique circumstances. The International Chamber of Commerce is, in most cases, a fairly safe choice.
3) Though the location for arbitration proceedings is negotiable, do not expect your foreign supplier to readily agree to arbitrate in the U.S. If the local country-of-origin Chamber of Commerce is sufficiently established in the supplier's locale, consider agreeing to arbitrate before it, unless your travel costs would be significant. Selecting a "neutral" country acceptable to both of you is a viable alternative.
4) Always stipulate that arbitration be conducted in the English language.
5) Before agreeing to arbitrate in a country other than that of the supplier, make sure that courts or another authority in the supplier's country will recognize and enforce an arbitration award rendered in the other country.

Litigation

If you have to resort to a lawsuit, the first hurdle you will face will be to find a court that can exercise its authority over your supplier and you. Even if you succeed in getting a favorable judgment, the biggest problem remains: collecting on it. Although the supplier will probably be able to get jurisdiction over you in the courts of the supplier's country, if you are neither present in that country nor have assets there, it will be difficult for your supplier to collect on a judgment against you. On the other hand, unless the supplier is present or has assets in the U.S., it is unlikely that you will be able to get jurisdiction in a U.S. court. You may have to seek legal recourse in the supplier's country.

To the extent possible, you would be wise to establish the best possible conditions for potential litigation when you first make your contract. The way to do this is to include clauses for choice of governing law and forum.

Forum. Forum refers to the place where any dispute will be settled. It is really a matter of convenience, and is usually negotiable. When it is infeasible for you to go to the supplier's country, or vice versa, to settle a dispute, you can jointly designate a third party country that would be more convenient.

Governing Law. The choice of law is critical. It determines not just where you can bring a suit or enforce a judgment, but what rules and procedures will govern the dispute settlement. Where and under what law you file suit will make a difference to you. If you file in the U.S., with domestic counsel familiar with commercial law and court procedures, your experience will be different than if you litigate your case in a foreign country, where you are subject to unfamiliar rules and must rely on foreign counsel.

Because of such complications, arbitration is a widely used means of settling international commercial disputes.

Measure of Damages in Breach of Contract Action. The measure of damages in a breach of contract action varies from country to country and among legal systems. In the U.S., damages are most commonly measured by the "lost benefit of the bargain rule." For example, if you contract to buy goods for $10 a unit when the market value of the goods is $12 a unit, and if your supplier fails to deliver, you are entitled to the $2 difference for the number of units you contracted to buy.

U.S. courts will also award consequential damages in certain circumstances. "Consequential damages" are losses that arise from a breach of contract and that, at the time you made the agreement, you made clear would result from breach. For example, you might tell a supplier that delivery at by a certain date is essential because you are reselling the product to someone who will incur substantial losses if you fail to perform timely. The supplier may then assure you that the goods will be delivered by that date. If the seller fails to deliver on time, causing you to incur damages for breach your resale contract, you can argue that your resulting financial losses are consequential damages. For this argument to hold up in court, you would have to show that your supplier knew or should have known at the time of contracting that you would become liable to a third party as a consequence of the seller's breach. To ensure that the seller has notice of the effect of a breach, you may describe in your written contract the consequential damages that can be expected to result in the event of breach.

Specific Performance. "Specific performance" is an alternative remedy to monetary damages. You can request a court to compel the breaching supplier to fulfill the contract agreement. If you have a contract to buy goods, you can demand those specific goods, and you may well get them. In civil law European countries, it is much easier to get specific performance than it is in the U.S. In the U.S., specific performance is usually not granted unless unique goods are involved. If you have a contract to purchase an item that cannot be duplicated—such as a Rembrandt—you may demand specific performance and get the actual painting. But if it is coal of #9 grade, which you can purchase elsewhere with relative ease, U.S. courts will probably grant you damages instead of specific performance.

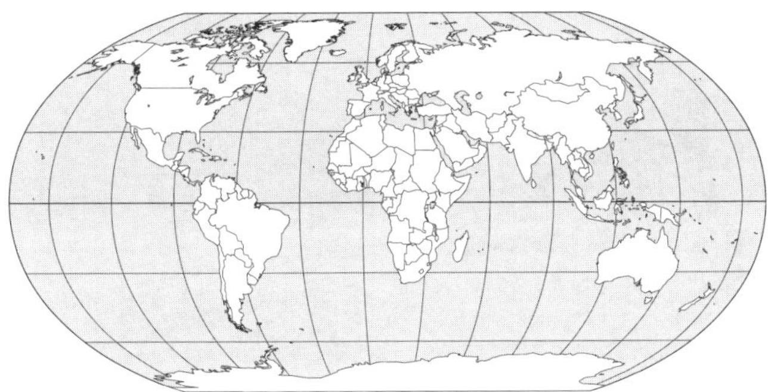

World Legal Systems

Introduction

Before you start trading in a foreign country, you should become familiar with its legal system, commercial laws, and export regulations. Gaining an overview of the law that will affect your relationship and transaction can be as important as running a background check on your supplier. You need to be aware of the major differences between the U.S. legal system and that of your supplier's country. These laws will influence your choices from the initial negotiation through enforcement of a contract. For example:

- You need to know which terms of your agreement are controlled by law and which are negotiable (if you negotiate a point already set by law, you've wasted your time, your negotiated term will be enforceable only to the extent allowed by the law, and by insisting on terms already fixed by law, you've given away your negotiating edge).
- You need to know whether the agreement you have in mind will be valid (if void, it will be unenforceable).
- You need to make an informed choice of which law will govern your agreement.
- You need to know to what extent the law will protect your interests beyond the terms of your agreement (you had better insist on protective contract terms if the law is inadequate or totally silent).
- You need to know what liabilities you might incur because of your supplier's actions or omissions—civil lawsuits, government-imposed fines, or other penalties—so that you can protect yourself by contract terms, such as for indemnity, proof of authority, or proof of compliance.
- You need to know the procedures that are available to enforce the contract or to recover for losses should your supplier breach and the extent to which these procedures will be an effective remedy.
- You need to know what your liability will be to your supplier, just in case you cannot perform the contract.

Laws vary from country to country, even among countries with the same basic legal system. To get a brief overview of the law of the particular country where you intend to do business, we suggest that you consult the *Digest of Commercial Laws of the World* (Ocean Publications, published for National Association of Credit Management) or Martindale-Hubbell's *International Law Digest*. These sources are available in the reference section of most larger public and law libraries.

Essentially, there are four major types of legal systems in the world that provide for commercial law. These are common law, civil law, Islamic or Shari'ah law, and communist or socialist law. However, many countries have adopted various combinations of these in response to the influences of different cultures throughout their history. In Asia, Africa, and South America, the legal system of each country is usually that of its former colonial master. For instance, Hong Kong follows common law, and Brazil applies the civil law system. However, the laws of these countries have also been adapted in some areas to reflect their original heritage. Japan took most of its law from Germany and thus follows the civil law system, although the commercial code shows U.S. influence. The civil law system developed in Egypt combines Islamic principles with French codes, and some common law principles are also applied because of lingering British influence.

Common Law System

The U.S., the United Kingdom, and Canada are under the common law system, distinctive for its reliance on precedents established by judges in earlier cases. The courts in common law countries apply and interpret statutes by following the principles developed in earlier decisions or by extrapolating new principles from the old ones to apply when new situations arise. Trials are typically before one judge, and the parties may request a jury. Complex rules and procedures aimed at ensuring a fair trial have been developed. Evidence presented to the court can be in the form of oral testimony and documents. Each party has the right to cross-examine witnesses and each other.

Refer to the main entry "Common Law" on page 104 and to "Canadian Common Law" on page 104 for a specific example of common law.

Civil Law System

Except for the common law countries and those countries heavily influenced by them, most of the other countries of the free world have civil law systems. Civil law systems are characterized by comprehensive and systematic compilations of statutes, or codes of law, governing most aspects of human endeavor. The codes set forth legal principles on which judicial decisions are based. The civil law system uses non-jury trials (except in criminal cases), and civil law courts at trial and appellate levels are typically composed of a panel of judges. In contrast to the common law system, there are few well-defined rules of evidence and relatively little oral testimony or argument. Most evidence and arguments are presented to the court in writing. Legal decisions usually are not based on precedents set in prior cases, but rather on abstract legal interpretations of the codified laws. For these reasons, the result of any particular lawsuit is somewhat less predictable than it might be in a common law court, which tries to adhere to interpretations established by precedents.

Refer also to the main entry "Civil Law" on page 100, and to "French Civil Law" on page 101 for a specific example of civil law.

Islamic Law

In Moslem or Islamic countries, the Law of Islam as set forth in the Koran, is applied in cases involving crimes, family matters (e.g., divorce or inheritance), or personal injury. Commercial cases are usually handled in commercial law courts that apply civil law concepts. Most Middle Eastern countries follow the French (Napoleonic) commercial code. In some of these countries—such as Saudi Arabia—commercial cases are handled by administrative tribunals rather than by the courts.

Refer also to the main entry "Islamic (Shari'ah) Law" on page 107 and for an example of Islamic Law to "Saudi Arabian Islamic Law" on page 108.

Communist Commercial Law

Communist commercial law is the system used in China (PRC), Cuba, North Korea, and Vietnam. It is similar to the socialist law system that was in effect in the Soviet bloc until recent years. Under communist commercial law, foreign trade is primarily operated by the state.

Disputes with suppliers in communist countries should be settled by negotiation. These cultures take particular pride in honoring commitments. A communist enterprise is more than likely to follow contract terms scrupulously, unless a sudden shift in government policy affects the contract. In many of these countries, the initiation of an adversarial or adjudicative proceeding is considered a personal insult. Parties are expected to resolve their conflicts privately. Therefore, few avenues of effective legal recourse have developed. If you must resolve a conflict through a more formal process, insist on arbitration if possible. In most cases, communist countries will recognize and uphold arbitration awards. Keep in mind, though, that few cases ever reach arbitration.

Avoid seeking legal recourse in a communist court. Communist laws have a strong ideological content unsuitable for interpreting commercial relations. Your supplier, as defendant, will be an agency of the same government that operates the courts and will hold essentially similar ideological views. Communist court proceedings are open, direct, and heavily reliant on oral testimony and examination. There are few rules of evidence. Legal precedents are of little weight. The court will consider all the evidence, decide what facts it believes are of relative value or importance, and determine the issues based on general principles of law and the dictates of communist ideology.

Refer also to the main entry "Communist Law" on page 110 and for an example of communist law to "Chinese Communist Law" on page 111.

Civil Law

Civil law is a combination of the Roman and Germanic legal systems. It is rooted in the legal system of ancient Rome, eventually codified as the *Corpus Juris Civilis*. Roman law governed broad areas of personal, business, and government relationships. Germanic law developed from individual tribal customs among the nomadic peoples of Europe. It primarily fixed specific rules for the resolution of particular problems, rather than established broad moral precepts. Eventually, as various political forces unified the countries of Europe, an amalgamation of these two legal systems was developed, resulting in modern Civil Law.

Comparison with Common Law

If you are trading with a country that follows a civil law system, you will probably find a well-developed court system. However, you may find that the civil law of that country is less developed or less favorable to your interests than the U.S. common law. You will also discover a number of significant differences:

A court in a civil law country may be authorized by law to accept jurisdiction over any suit brought by a national of the country, regardless of whether the suit involves a foreigner or a transaction in that country. A court may take jurisdiction even if the foreigner is absent. Thus, even if your only contact with a supplier's country is a faxed order for goods, your supplier could still sue you overseas. Under U.S. common law, the concept of jurisdiction is more limited. U.S. courts generally require a closer connection, or nexus, between the place where suit is brought and the defendant.

- The civil law system did not originally establish specific rules for calculating damages in breach of contract cases, and many civil law countries have not yet clearly defined standards for this purpose. The amount of damages that a court may award can therefore be difficult to predict. As a result, plaintiffs in civil law countries commonly sue for actual or specific performance of the contract. This remedy requires the seller to deliver the goods and the buyer to remit payment as required by their contract. If the seller cannot deliver the goods, the buyer is awarded the greater of the contract price or the cost of replacement. Jurisdictions vary over whether replacement cost means actual or market cost of the goods.

- Commercial contracts—those between business persons or merchants—usually do not need to be in writing. However, oral contracts may be difficult to enforce in practice. Civil law courts typically accept written evidence, not oral testimony. The terms of an oral agreement are more difficult to prove than those of a written contract.
- Contract clauses stating "time is of the essence" are uncommon because of the preference in civil law countries to negotiate rather than litigate when a party cannot perform to the exact letter of the agreement. In common law countries, a breach of a contract containing such a clause will give rise to an immediate legal action for damages.

French and German Codes

Most modern civil law countries have modeled their laws on one of two civil law codifications: the French Code Civil (Napoleonic Code), or the German Code. Two separate Codes have arisen because of nationalistic and political influences.

French Code Civil. The French Code Civil was created during the French Revolutionary period and has survived since 1804, with modifications to reflect advances in society since that time. Its drafters attempted to set forth general rules in clear language that could be easily understood by every citizen. They created a concise, yet flexible Code in the form of a series of short articles that were not intended to limit judicial interpretation or application. If no single article applied to a situation, a court could combine articles and extrapolate a general rule consistent with the intent of the Code, although not specified in its text.

Property Law. The Code Civil classifies goods as either movable or immovable. Ownership of property is absolute, with a few restrictions related to public safety issues. A bona fide purchaser of movable property becomes its owner immediately. That is, title passes when the contract is made or at the time the goods being sold are specifically identified.

Contract Law. Parties governed by the Code Civil have freedom to contract, limited only by a few public policy considerations. If parties enter into an agreement lawfully, a court will uphold the terms of the contract.

German Code. The German Code, finalized in 1900, is more orderly and precise than the French Code Civil. It expresses more exacting principles for its use. The system consists of generally formulated rules that are meant to be applied to individual cases.

Property Law. Under the German Code, property ownership entails responsibilities to the community. Title to property passes on physical delivery of the goods or title documents to the buyer.

Contract Law. Parties are free to enter into contracts, within the limits set by good morals and statutory prohibitions intended to eliminate fraudulent practices by contracting parties. The Code emphasizes such ethical imperatives as good faith and fair dealings. Transactions involving transgressions of moral standards, abuses of the rights of others, or shady dealings do not have the protection of law.

French Civil Law

The French system of civil law is based on five original Napoleonic Codes and two more recently adopted codes. Of the Napoleonic, the Code Civil and the Code de Commerce are the most pertinent to commercial transactions. The Code Civil creates the fundamental legal framework for French society and includes general provisions on contracts, civil status, and property. The Code de Commerce covers commercial transactions and procedure, bills and notes, maritime law, bankruptcy, and jurisdiction of commercial courts. Other codes govern civil court organization, jurisdiction, and procedure; criminal law and procedure; and tax and labor law.

Governmental Structure. France is a democratic and social republic. The French Constitution provides for a president, who is elected for a seven-year term, and a Prime Minister. A National Assembly and a Senate comprise the French Parliament. Separate judicial and administrative court systems operate independently of each other.

Traders. Under French law, persons whose regular occupation is to be engaged in commercial transactions are considered "traders." They must register with the Register of Commerce and must fulfill a variety of record keeping and reporting requirements. Commercial courts, not civil courts, hear disputes between traders. Traders have the option to designate arbitration in contracts as the preferred means of dispute settlement.

Aliens. In general, the civil rights accorded a foreigner in France are the same as those given to French citizens, usually as agreed on under international treaty. Foreigners are permitted to own real property in France, but such property remains subject to French law. An obligation entered into between a foreigner and a French national is automatically under the jurisdiction of French courts, unless the French national chooses to waive this right. In most cases, foreigners may sue in French courts. Under the 1959 Franco-American Establishment Treaty, U.S. citizens in France have the same rights as French nationals as regards freedom of the press, legal aid, industrial property rights, commercial activity, access to French courts, and taxation.

A foreigner who intends to stay in France more than three months must obtain a residence permit. A foreigner who plans to start a business in France must also obtain a "trader's card" from local police. To obtain a trader's card, a foreigner must already have the proper long-term visa.

Exchange Control. Transfers of cash between France and foreign countries must be made through licensed intermediary credit or financial institutions. With some exceptions, annual reporting to the Bank of France is required for transfers of funds between France and abroad, or within France between residents and nonresidents. Reporting is also required for direct financial operations abroad and for trading of currency or interest. Individuals must make customs declarations when they make cross-border transfers of cash, stocks, or securities equal to or exceeding 50,000 francs. Customs declaration must also be made when individuals make cross-border transfers of cash, stocks, or securities by mail in excess of 10,000 francs.

Foreign Corporations. A number of legal formalities are required of foreign corporations before establishing a branch to do business in France. The corporation must first obtain Ministry of Finance authorization and must register with the French Register of Commerce. The company must designate an authorized representative in France, and the representative must obtain a trader's card, unless he or she is a citizen of an EEC nation. Various papers, including two certified copies of the corporation's charter and bylaws legalized by the French Consul, must be filed with the Registrar of Tribunal of Commerce. Complete French translations of all the required documents must be included. To receive authorization to do business, the corporate branch must be able to prove that it has an office address in France by presenting a commercial lease. Once these legal formalities have been fulfilled, French law treats the foreign corporation in the same manner as a French one.

Foreign Investments. No general prohibition is imposed against foreign ownership or control of businesses in France, but there are some limitations. For the most part, firms and individuals that plan to make a direct investment in France must first declare that intention to the French Ministry of Economy, which must approve the proposed investment. Unless allowed by international treaty, state-owned economic sectors—such as communications and electricity—are not open to foreign investment. Certain enterprises—such as transportation, petroleum extraction, banking, and insurance—are either entirely prohibited to foreign investment or are available only with special authorization. By treaty, U.S. citizens may acquire majority interests in existing companies and may control or manage enterprises in the fields of communications, air, or water transport, banking, natural resources, and electricity. U.S. citizens may also acquire and dispose of any interest in real or personal property, except ships. All foreign investments in France are subject to currency exchange and other regulation.

Import-Export Regulations. Importers and exporters must handle all import or export related financial transactions through agents authorized by the French Ministry of Economy and Finance or Post Office Departments. Although most French exports are unrestricted, there are exceptions. Occasionally certain export commodities will be prohibited, requiring export licensing. Others may be restricted as to final destination or country of origin.

Arbitration and Foreign Judgments. France has formal and informal bilateral agreements with many countries providing for enforcement of foreign judgments and arbitral decisions. In the absence of a treaty, the French government decides the enforceability of a foreign judgment based on a review of the documents in the case. To be enforceable in France, a judgment must issue from a court deemed by French law to have jurisdiction in the matter. The foreign judicial procedure and decision must also coincide with French international public policy and right to defense. When a French court grants enforcement of a foreign judgment, the foreign judgment becomes, in legal effect, a French judgment.

France recognizes arbitration for the settlement of commercial disputes only. Arbitral awards are not reviewed except for claims of procedural error, bias by the arbitrator, failure to observe due process, or conflict with French public or international policy.

Courts. France has two separate and independent tri-level court systems: judicial and administrative. A case is assigned to one of the five lower-level judicial courts depending on its nature and severity, whether it is criminal or civil, and the amount of money involved. Administrative courts hear cases involving the government in areas of contract, tort, and tax law, as well as appeals from administrative decisions.

Negotiable Instruments. France's formal requirements for bills of exchange differ from those of U.S. law only in that the words "Bill of Exchange" must appear on the document. Under French law, a bill of exchange can be rendered null by the absence of these words. It can also be nullified if the parties' names, the date and place of issuance and payment, or the order or amount to pay are missing. France is a signatory to the Geneva Agreements on promissory notes and bills of exchange. Parties to any bill of exchange fulfilling Geneva Agreement requirements come within the jurisdiction of commercial law regardless of whether they are traders and whether the bill had commercial purposes. For this reason, lawsuits pertaining to these bills of exchange are tried in commercial courts.

It is a criminal offense to write a check on insufficient funds, to withdraw the funds after having written a check, or to instruct the bank not to pay a check. The only lawful grounds for making a stop-payment order are bankruptcy and a lost or stolen check. France has strict time limits for presenting checks for payment. Checks written and payable in France must be presented for payment within eight days. Those written outside France for payment in France must be submitted within 20 or 70 days, depending on where the check was written.

Consumer Protection. In France, consumer protection is a matter of civil and criminal law and procedure, as well as of administrative and tax laws. French law protects the consumer in the use of goods, and in receipt of services intended to satisfy individual or family needs, including public services. Representative organizations of both private and public law handle consumer protection issues. Associations of Consumers are the most important private consumer protection organizations.

Contracts. Commercial and civil law in France are governed by separate codes. For this reason, French contract law has different rules for commercial and noncommercial contracts. A contract entered into by a trader for business purposes is commercial, regulated by the commercial code, and enforceable in commercial courts. Contracts between nontraders are civil, regulated under the civil code and enforceable in civil courts. The separation is so complete that a contract between a trader and a nontrader may be considered commercial inasmuch as it pertains to the trader but civil inasmuch as it pertains to the nontrader.

Civil contracts may be either oral or written. No special formality is required to render an oral contract valid. However, contracts with value of 5,000 francs or more must be in writing. An oral contract in this category cannot be validated simply by the presence of witnesses. Written contracts may be either privately or formally made. There must be as many originals of a private contract as there are parties to the agreement with differing interests, and that number must be specified on the document. Witnesses are not required. Civil contracts cannot stipulate that disputes be resolved by arbitration. The parties must file suit in court, but once a suit has been initiated, they can request arbitration.

To be valid, a commercial contract in France must have the consent of parties who are legally allowed to contract, a specific object not contrary to public policy, and some kind of consideration. Written evidence must be submitted to prove contracts between corporations, on maritime rights, for sale of businesses. Bills of exchange and promissory notes must also be shown by written evidence. A written contract can be established simply by exchange of correspondence. Some contracts, such as those pertaining to partnerships or corporations, must be registered with French fiscal authorities, at which time contract-registration taxes must be paid.

France is a party to the U.N. Convention on Contracts for the International Sale of Goods. Liability arising from such contracts is determined by the U.N. Convention, not French law. If choice of law is not specified in the contract, French courts determine the governing law by considering such factors as the character of parties, the place where the contract was offered and accepted, the location for performance, and its form and purpose. Unless the parties expressly stipulate otherwise, a contract should be in the form required by the law of the place where it is executed. Contracts executed in foreign countries are proved according to the law of that country.

Interest. The French government establishes the legal interest rate each year by Decree. An interest rate agreed on by contract must be in writing and can exceed the legal rate, if not usurious. If an interest rate is 33.33% higher than the ordinary rate that banks charged during the preceding quarter for a similar transaction, it is considered usurious. Charging a usurious interest rate is a crime.

Labor Relations. French employment and labor relation policies are extensive. The following discussion outlines only a few requirements as examples. Every employee must have a pre-employment medical examination, with annual physicals if hired. There are specific conditions and procedures for termination after an initial trial period, violations of which can result in fines to the employer and damages awarded to the employee. For most types of employment, the work week may not exceed 39 hours, with a maximum workday of 10 hours. Employers must provide an annual 30-workday paid vacation and leaves of absence for certain family events. France has a national minimum wage. Other wages are a matter of negotiation between employees or labor unions and the individual company. Employers must pay payroll tax and mandatory social benefits for each employee. Firms employing 50 or more persons are required to provide profit sharing and must have labor-management committees. Firms of more than 10 employees must have employee-elected personnel representatives, who are accorded special employment protection under the law during their one-year term of service.

Notaries Public. A French notary is a high official appointed by the Minister of Justice. A notary must pass qualifying examinations and must possess at least a specified minimum professional experience. The number of notaries is limited, and all of them can practice anywhere in France. Notaries are exclusively authorized to prepare legal documents related to real estate, such as deeds of sale and mortgages, as well as deeds of gift and marriage contracts. Notaries verify and keep on file or record documents required by law to be notarized and any that parties want notarized. A notary can be sued for giving unsound advice on matters within his or her competence.

Principal and Agent. An agent can be authorized informally by a private writing—such as an agreement or letter—or formally by a notarized document. No form is prescribed for an agency agreement, but some situations require notarization. If the agency authorization is not in French, a legal translation must be presented before it can be used in any legal procedure. No matter what language it is in, the agreement should end with the words "bon pour pouvoir" (good for authority) in the principal's handwriting, appearing immediately before his or her signature. Although French law does not require a foreign agency authorization or power of attorney to be notarized and legalized by the French consulate, these legal precautions are advisable when initiating an agency relationship in France.

French law distinguishes between agencies that are general and specific, commercial and noncommercial. General agency gives management and administrative authority to handle all the principal's affairs except for the disposal of property, which must be specifically authorized in the agreement. Under specific agency, only limited functions are given to the agent, and those are expressly listed in the agreement. A commercial agent is a professional who buys and sells in the principal's name and must register as such with the Tribunal de Commerce. Foreign commercial agents are also required to register, but must first possess a valid trader's card. A written agreement is required to establish commercial agency. The legal requirements for commercial agents in France are stringent. They must scrupulously carry out the tasks for which they were engaged and are required to report regularly to the principal. A commercial agent is liable for his or her own mistakes, and those of any subagent, made while serving as an agent. The principal is absolved of this liability.

Records. All individuals or companies engaged in commercial activity in France must register their principal office in the Register of Commerce. Applications are made to the Tribunal of Commerce. This requirement applies to foreign or domestic commercial and noncommercial companies, whether doing business directly or indirectly through an agent, as well as to individuals. Traders must apply for registration within two weeks of beginning business activitiés, but companies are not subject to a time limit.

Sales. In a sales transaction, the seller's primary obligation is to deliver the goods, at his or her own expense unless the contract states otherwise, and to give certain warranties. Unless the contract otherwise stipulates, the buyer becomes the owner as soon as the parties agree on the goods and the price. Title changes regardless of whether delivery has occurred or money has changed hands. However, risk of loss for goods sold by weight, number, or measure passes to the buyer only after the goods have been weighed, counted, or measured. Sales contracts can be made as private agreements or by notarized deed, either of which will be satisfactory proof of the contract. Commercial contracts can also be proved by an accepted invoice, a signed broker's note or order, the parties' account books, correspondence, and even oral testimony.

Taxation. France levies a 42% tax on income from French sources on companies from foreign countries that have no international tax treaty with France. This tax applies equally to firms having permanent establishment in France, engaging in complete commercial cycle in France, or having an agent in France with authority to bind the company. The U.S. treaty limits the tax liability of U.S. firms to the taxes charged to companies with permanent establishment in France.

Common Law

Common law developed in England out of Norman customs and practices after the successful conquest of England in 1066. The conquerors established a court system to declare the common law for the entire country. As aresult, the English court system was already strongly centralized, with a powerful interest group of law experts and practitioners, before any statutes were adopted in this country. By the time statutes were drafted, a massive body of unwritten common law was well-entrenched. The statutes served to codify, clarify, limit, and supplement the common law. English laws have changed significantly over the past two centuries, particularly in areas of labor, consumer protection, commercial, and property law. Statutory law has grown alongside common law, with judges free to interpret the statutes to accord with common law except when a statute contains an express limitation.

Comparison of US and Other Common Law Systems

If you are trading internationally with a supplier in a common law country, do not assume that country's laws are the same as those in the U.S. It is true that English common law has served as the foundation for legal systems in the U.S. and other countries and that these systems will have many similarities. However, they will also have major differences because of a characteristic unique to the common law: flexibility. They can be easily adapted to fill the needs of different cultures and changed to reflect advances within a single society. Thus, U.S. statutes and legal procedures are unique to the needs of U.S. citizens. Similarly, the common law system of Singapore has been modified to allow for that country's own cultural and societal demands.

Canadian Common Law

Governmental Structure. Canada was created by Royal Proclamation on May 22, 1867, as part of the Commonwealth of the United Kingdom. Its constitution is similar to that of England. Until the passage of the Canada Act in 1982, Canada was subject to laws enacted by the British Parliament, as well as those enacted by its own. The Canada Act achieved Canada's legislative independence from England, though the British Sovereign remains the Sovereign of Canada.

Canada has a Federal Parliament, which consists of the British Sovereign, Canadian Senate, and House of Commons. This Parliament has exclusive legislative jurisdiction over issues that affect the country as a whole. Each province also has a legislature with jurisdiction over subjects specifically affecting that province. Each category discussed below may be solely under federal jurisdiction, controlled by local laws only, or governed by both. As an example of provincial regulations, we have chosen some from Ontario because that province has a substantial commercial relationship with the U.S. Laws specific to that province are identified by the subhead "Ontario."

Court System. Canada's court system includes provincial and Dominion courts. The Supreme Court of Canada is the highest court and exercises appellate jurisdiction in civil and criminal cases. At the federal level, the Tax Court adjudicates tax, pension, and unemployment insurance issues. The Federal Court of Canada is the law, equity, and admiralty court for the entire country and has Appeal and Trial Divisions. The Trial Division handles such issues as actions involving the Crown or federal entities, conflicts between provinces or between the federal government and a provincial government, as well as suits pertaining to citizenship disputes, industrial property, estate tax issues, and any issues not under the jurisdiction of other courts. The Appeal Division hears appeals from the Trial and Tax Courts, and determines questions of law, jurisdiction, or practice, including review of federal decisions.

Aliens. Noncitizens in Canada are subject to all Canadian laws. As part of the British Commonwealth, Canada recognizes both Canadian and Commonwealth citizenship. Although citizens of other Commonwealth nations are not also Canadian citizens, they do have certain rights in Canada as Commonwealth citizens, most notably with regard to property ownership and succession. Canadian law restricts certain types of property ownership for noncitizens; for example, a noncitizen cannot own a Canadian ship.

With some regulatory exceptions, such as for persons who enter for short-term business purposes, all noncitizens seeking employment in Canada must obtain work visas validated by the Canadian Employment Commission. U.S. citizens entering Canada for business purposes have preferential treatment under the Canada/U.S. Free Trade Agreement.

Ontario. A noncitizens may own property in Ontario in keeping with Canadian law, but any holdings of agricultural land by noncitizens must be registered with the provincial government.

Arbitration and Judgment. Canada is a signatory to the U.N. Foreign Arbitral Awards Convention Act.

Ontario. Ontario honors written agreements specifying arbitration as the means of dispute settlement. If parties designate in writing that they prefer to resolve a dispute by arbitration, this method must be used, unless Ontario's Supreme Court rules otherwise. Ontario adopted an amended version of the Model Law on International Commercial Arbitration in 1988. Both Supreme and District Courts may recognize a foreign arbitral award, which is then enforceable as if it were a judgment or order of that court.

Ontario has statutory provisions for reciprocal recognition and enforcement of civil and commercial judgments of the U.S., individual U.S. states, the U.K., other Canadian provinces, and other countries. To be enforced, a judgment must be the result of a civil court proceeding or arbitration and must involve an award of money. Suit must be brought where Ontario law gives the foreign court jurisdiction over the matter in question, or in the Supreme Court of Ontario. There is a six-year time limit, beginning at the date of judgment, after which a foreign judgment is no longer enforceable in Ontario.

Negotiable Instruments. Bills of exchange, promissory notes, and checks are regulated under the Canadian Bills of Exchange Act and applicable English common law rules. The Canadian law resembles the negotiable instruments provisions of the U.S. Uniform Commercial Code. When the Canadian Act and the English common law rules diverge, the provisions of the Act are enforced. Specific regulations and practices govern nonpayment of financial obligations entered into between Canadians and foreigners. To enforce legal proceedings for the nonacceptance or dishonor of a foreign bill, certain notarial procedures must be followed.

Contracts. Unless otherwise stipulated by the parties to a contract, the uniform rules of Canada's International Sale of Goods Contract Convention Act govern sales contracts made between Canadian and foreign business entities. Agreement formation, breach of contract, buyers' and sellers' obligations, and third-party claims are some of the issues covered by the Convention.

Ontario. Ontario's Frustrated Contracts Act applies to nearly all types of contract under Ontario law. It allows for cancellation of payment owed when a contract cannot be fulfilled, as well as for recovery of any money already paid under the agreement. Under the Act, a contract that has been partially fulfilled can be upheld to that extent, with the unfulfilled segment being frustrated. Contracts for overseas transport of goods, insurance contracts, and contracts under which the goods to be sold have perished before the contract is performed but without the seller's fault are not covered under the Act.

Foreign Corporations. As long as a foreign corporation intends to conduct business covered under the Canada Corporation Act, there are no federal licensing requirements. However some types of businesses are subject to other statutes that may require licensing, such as the Canadian and British Insurance Companies Act. In any case, all foreign companies conducting business in Canada must obtain a license in each Province where business will be conducted. Fees are charged for provincial business licenses.

Ontario. Ontario requires all foreign corporations wishing to conduct business in the Province to obtain a license first. The Ontario Minister of Consumer and Commercial Relations may impose restrictions, conditions, or other limitations on any license. Firms that neglect to obtain licenses, or that allow their agents or representatives to conduct business in the province before the license has been issued, risk fines of up to $25,000. Foreign companies doing business in Ontario must fulfill substantially the same reporting requirements and must pay substantially the same taxes on corporate income as domestic Ontario companies.

Exchange Controls. At present, no restrictions are imposed on currency entering or leaving Canada.

Foreign Investment in Canada. Canada welcomes beneficial foreign investments. Depending on the nature and dollar amount of the investment, governmental review to determine the benefit to Canada may be required. Whether an acquisition is subject to review depends on "acquisition thresholds" established by regulation. The review process is not required for investments falling below these regulatory thresholds, but all non-Canadians making Canadian investments must file notice with the Investment Canada Agency. The Agency determines the proposed investment's review status and informs the foreign investor. The Canadian federal government reviews proposed investments specifically related to Canada's cultural heritage or national identity on a case-by-case basis. Foreigners wishing to make a reviewable investment must apply to the Investment Canada Agency in advance.

Foreign Trade Regulations. Canada is a party to GATT. For U.S. importers, the most significant of Canada's many trade agreements is the North American Free Trade Agreement (NAFTA). Under this treaty, tariffs and other trade barriers between the U.S. and Canada have been progressively eliminated, and government procurement policies liberalized. U.S. acquisitions of Canadian businesses are currently reviewable at a higher dollar threshold than acquisitions by other nations, and U.S. business visitors to Canada enjoy simplified admission procedures and better access to financial services markets. In addition to many other general provisions regarding business relationships between the U.S. and Canada, the Agreement specifically provides for trade in automotive goods, alcoholic beverages, energy, and agricultural products.

Insurance Law. Canadian insurance law resembles that of both the U.K. and the U.S. Federal and provincial statutes regulate the insurance business, with Parliamentary jurisdiction based on its constitutional power to regulate trade and commerce.

Interest. Interest rates of 60% and above are prohibited by the Canadian Criminal Code. Any noncriminal rate of interest may be charged or contracted for, with the exception that Parliament reserves the right to restrict interest rates.

Environmental Protection. Canada has extensive federal and provincial environmental protection regulations. For example, interprovincial and transborder shipments of regulated dangerous goods, including hazardous waste, are subject to Transportation of Dangerous Goods Act requirements for labeling, shipping, registration, and notification. The Canadian Environmental Protection Act of 1988 regulates information disclosure, import and export, spill cleanup, nutrients, international air pollution, and ocean dumping issues pertaining to toxic substances. The Canada Labour Code requires worker information and training for handling hazardous materials.

Ontario. Ontario's environmental protection regulations are extensive and stringent, setting limits on discharge and covering all types of pollution. There are heavy penalties for violations. Common law doctrines of nuisance, negligence, strict liability, and riparian rights still apply. Ontario law interprets adverse environmental effect resulting from discharges and spills broadly. Individuals violating pollution-control regulations risk prison terms for actual pollution, and fines as high as $10,000 per day on first conviction. Corporate directors are required to exercise reasonable care to ensure that the corporation does not cause or permit damage to the environment, and the directors can be sued for damages for breach of that duty. Corporations face fines of up to $50,000 per day for violating environmental protection laws. For discharges resulting in actual pollution, corporate fines can go as high as $200,000 per day, absolute liability for the cost of spill clean-up and environmental restoration, and strict liability for other costs.

Employment. Enterprises that benefit more than one Province, such as banks, broadcasting, and the various types of transport industries are subject to federal jurisdiction. For these industries, Canadian law regulates industrial relations, standard hours of work, minimum and overtime wages, holidays and vacations, termination policies, employee safety, unemployment insurance, and equity in the workplace for minorities, women, disabled persons, and others. Employment policies in nonfederal enterprises are primarily a matter of provincial jurisdiction.

Ontario. Common law employment contract rules govern the employer-employee relationship in Ontario, along with extensive statutory regulation. The Ontario Labour Relations Board is instrumental in Ontario labor relations policy, its administrative decisions having spawned extensive case law on the subject. Under the Labour Relations Act, labor conflict resolution must be achieved by binding third-party arbitration rather than by strikes. In addition to stipulating a variety of minimum employment standards, Ontario statutes prohibit various types of discrimination in the workplace, promote protection of workers from workplace health and safety hazards, regulate the establishment of employee pension plans, mandate workers' compensation, and establish an employer health tax.

Restricted Trade Practices. Canadian law prohibits trade practices by both Canadian and foreign firms that attempt to establish a monopoly in Canada. Bid-rigging, misleading advertising, refusal to deal, exclusive dealing and tied selling, consignment selling intended to control prices or discriminate against other dealers, market restrictions likely to substantially lessen competition, and setting resale prices by means of resale price maintenance agreements are some of the trade practices prohibited by Canadian law.

Ontario. The following sections are all provincial law specific to Ontario.

Licensing. Ontario requires licensing by the provincial government for the following kinds of business: collection agencies, itinerant sellers, dealers in livestock and livestock products, motor vehicle dealers, and sellers of liquor.

Notaries Public. Ontario notaries are authorized to perform all of the usual functions associated with that office. Ontario law distinguishes between notaries who are lawyers and those who are not. Notaries who are not also lawyers have three-year commissions, which may be renewed and which are sometimes subject to territorial limitations on their practice. Although it is customary in Ontario for a notary to affix a seal to an affidavit, oath, or declaration, absence of the seal does not invalidate a notarized document of that type.

Principal and Agent. In Ontario, common law rules apply to principal-agent relationships. The Powers of Attorney Amendment Act of 1983 governs powers of attorney.

Sales. Ontario's Sale of Goods Act, similar to the English Act, codifies the law pertaining to sales. Ontario statutes govern such issues as product liability, bills of sale, transfer of title, conditions and warranties, delivery and stoppage in transit, and remedies for breach of contract for buyer and seller. If a seller fails to deliver the goods, the buyer may sue for damages or specific performance. If the goods have changed hands, the seller may sue for the price. The seller may sue for nonacceptance if the buyer refuses the shipment. Damages are based on estimated loss. Product liability for defective goods is based on case law precedent.

Islamic (Shari'ah) Law

Shari'ah law was originally derived from the Koran, believed by Muslims to be the revelations of Allah to the Prophet Mohammed. The Prophet's supplemental teachings and actions were recorded and later gathered in documents called the "Sunna." The Koran and the Sunna are the two primary sources for Shari'ah law. They do not contain extensive detailed codes, but principles and precepts. Muslims believe that after Mohammed's death, the direct revelations of God ceased, and therefore the law can no longer be modified.

Traditional Legal System. The principles of Shari'ah law have been interpreted and applied in individual cases by judicial decisions. Conflicts were resolved in "quadi" courts by individual judges. To reach a judgment, a quadi resorted first to the Koran, then to the Sunna. If neither document provided a basis for judgment, the quadi had authority to employ certain principles of Islamic judicial reasoning, which involved analogy, fairness, and the public interest.

An individual quadi's judgment was final for the single case to which it applied, but was not considered an authoritative interpretation of Shari'ah law until and unless all qualified scholars of that time agreed unanimously with the interpretation. Once such an agreement was reached, a given interpretation was incorporated into the text of the law, and had the same immutable, irreversible, unchallengeable status as the Koran and Sunna texts. These judicial interpretations were gathered over the years into legal texts on which subsequent decisions were reached. Compilation of these texts ceased after the 10th century, and the body of traditional Shari'ah law has not changed since.

Modern Legal System. With the exception of Muslim countries on the Arabian peninsula, most Muslim countries no longer adhere to the strict traditional form of Shari'ah law. In all other Muslim countries and jurisdictions, Shari'ah law tends to be limited to family and succession law. Even these laws are now codified, so that reference to the traditional authoritative law texts is rarely made, except when existing statutes and codes are not relevant to a specific decision.

To accommodate the changes in modern societies, most Muslim countries have abandoned Shari'ah criminal, civil and commercial laws and have adopted modified codes based on European legal models. For example, Pakistan uses a case law system, with Shari'ah laws codified into statutes. Judicial decisions have replaced the traditional legal manuals as the ultimate authority in these countries. The single-court system of quadis has been widely replaced with systems of appellate courts. Most countries that practice Shari'ah law in limited ways relegate issues such as family law to separate Shari'ah courts, handling all other legal conflicts in national courts. Some countries—such as Egypt and Tunisia—no longer have separate Shari'ah courts, but Shari'ah law is administered in a system of national courts. Many countries have abandoned the traditional Shari'ah procedures of evidence. Instead of accepting oaths as valid evidence, they have adopted Western procedures and philosophies. Many countries that still practice traditional Shari'ah law have found it necessary to institute significant procedural and other reforms to reflect the changing needs of their societies.

Comparison of Islamic Law to Common Law

Islamic law differs from Western legal systems in that it is religiously derived and constituted. Its precepts encompass not only civil, commercial, criminal, and family law, but also matters of religious observance and personal conscience. Islamic law is an ethical system, not a codified set of rules. Muslims consider it the direct revelation of the immutable, infallible will of God. It is therefore not open to question or modification. As can be imagined, this poses some problem in the changing and complex world of the 20th century. If you do business with a supplier in an Islamic country, be aware of the following:

- The terms of a contract are less likely to enforceable if they modify standard legal precepts and practices, particularly those that are part of the religious tradition of Shari'ah law.
- If traditional Shari'ah law applies, parties cannot choose any other law to govern their agreement instead.
- Competency to contract *rashid* is a key concept in the law of transactions. A person who is not considered *rashid* is forbidden to conduct any kind of transaction. All of their business must be conducted by a guardian. This applies to persons who are minors, mentally incompetent, or immoral.
- There are four elements of Shari'ah transaction law: sale, hire, gift, and loan. Virtually all commercial transactions fall under one or a combination of these elements.
- Shari'ah law forbids usury and speculation, which normally means any transaction involving interest.
- Procedures before a quadi are determined by the single judge who is presiding. The judge decides which party has the burden of proof. Evidence is usually taken in the form of testamentary declaration by the party with the burden of proof or by witnesses. An oath by a party to the suit can be considered adequate evidence for a decision.

Saudi Arabian Islamic Law

An interesting example of a country that continues to practice Shari'ah law unadulterated by reform or westernization is Saudi Arabia. The following discussion outlines some basic areas of Shari'ah law, as practiced in Saudi Arabia, that pertain to international business. It should give you a sense of how Shari'ah law may affect your business prospects and procedures in nations that continue to adhere to the traditional law.

Governmental Structure. Saudi Arabia is a monarchy without a constitution. Governmental structure is determined according to royal decree. In Saudi Arabia, the word "law" means Shari'ah law. All regulations, secular or otherwise, are subordinate to and interpreted by principles set forth in the authoritative documents of Shari'ah law: the Koran, the Sunna, and the legal manuals comprising scholarly interpretations compiled through the 10th century.

Official Language. Saudi Arabia's official language is Arabic. All business records, transactions, and dealings must be in Arabic. Documents submitted to the Saudi government and courts must be either in Arabic or translated by a licensed translator. All judicial proceedings, including arbitration, must be in Arabic. Clauses in contracts stipulating to use of a foreign language, such as for legal proceedings or business paperwork, are unenforceable.

Aliens. Foreigners in Saudi Arabia are subject to the jurisdiction of Saudi courts and tribunals and have the same rights as Saudi nationals. Except for citizens of parties to the Gulf Co-Operation Council (GCC), foreigners are not allowed to own real estate, to engage in commercial trading activities (see Agency below), or to own publicly traded shares of Saudi joint stock companies. Non-GCC aliens must obtain entry visas, and if they wish to establish residence in Saudi Arabia, residence permits before arriving in Saudi Arabia. No visas or permits are issued to foreigners on arrival in Saudi Arabia, and no foreigners are permitted entry without properly approved documentation. Visa and permit requirements are burdensome, strictly observed by Saudi officials, and can change without notice.

Agency. In principle, persons not Saudi citizens are not permitted to conduct business in Saudi Arabia. In practical terms, this tends to apply to business transactions related to sales of foreign goods in Saudi Arabia. To accommodate this restriction, persons and firms with business dealings in Saudi Arabia contract with Saudi nationals in some form of agency relationship, such as power of attorney. Agency relationship can be terminated by either party without legal repercussion, but in practice most contractual arrangements are strictly enforced.

Courts. A variety of courts are available for adjudication, depending on the area of conflict. Civil actions, including those related to family, real estate, and leasing concerns, are generally handled in Shari'ah courts. Other matters—disputes with the public sector, private sector commercial disputes, enforcement of foreign judgments—are handled by Boards of Grievances. There are also separate judicial bodies that handle conflicts related to banking, negotiable instruments, and labor relations. Saudi court and tribunal rulings are not subject to any form of public disclosure. Judicial decisions are not based on precedent; prior decisions are not binding on subsequent cases of similar nature.

Law of Choice. Shari'ah law is considered immutable and divinely ordained, and therefore no other legal system is recognized. Even if a contract in Saudi Arabia stipulates that the law of a foreign country will be the deciding law in the case of dispute, no Saudi tribunal will uphold that contractual agreement. All disputes are settled according to the Saudi version of Shari'ah law. There are no exceptions.

Arbitration and Foreign Judgments. Arbitration is a viable option for most private-sector commercial disputes in Saudi Arabia. Both the arbitration agreement and the final award must pass through Saudi governmental approval processes in the court that would handle the suit if arbitration had not been preferred. No arbitration award not subjected to the ratification process or prior agreement approval can be enforced in Saudi Arabia. It is unlikely that judgments of foreign courts can be enforced in Saudi Arabia, though this is an area in transition. Historically, Saudi Arabia enforces foreign judgments only by explicit treaty with a foreign nation. At present, Saudi Arabia has such a treaty (the Arab League Treaty) with Lebanon, Jordan, Egypt, Iraq, Syria, and Yemen.

Contracts. Saudi contract law is not codified. It is a matter of adherence to Shari'ah law precepts, and within the limitations of Shari'ah law, it affords considerable freedom. Shari'ah law deems contracts with persons not *rashid* to be invalid. Contracts involving speculation and interest are entirely prohibited and unenforceable. Although written contracts are preferred, oral contracts supported by a witness or other proofs are enforceable. If contracts are breached, Saudi courts will award only proven direct damages. No damages will be awarded for lost opportunity or lost profit because these damages are speculative, and speculation is forbidden under Shari'ah law. Saudi courts will accept as a valid reason for a breach of contract events or effects beyond the breaching party's control or ability to anticipate (force majeure), undue hardship, and impossibility.

Sales Agreements. There is no comprehensive Saudi law pertaining to sales and sales contracts. Any contract for sale executed in Saudi Arabia or with a Saudi entity should explicitly spell out every single term. Even so, the foreigner doing business in Saudi Arabia should be aware that some terms enforceable in Western countries will not be enforceable under Shari'ah law. Examples: terms relating to title retention, repossession, remedies, disclaimers, and limitations on liability. Warranties are implicit in Shari'ah precepts; nevertheless each contract should spell out warranty terms specifically.

Interest. Interest is a gray area in Saudi Arabia: there is a discrepancy between business practice and official stance. Though Shari'ah law expressly forbids the charging and collecting of any form of interest, banks, and other commercial enterprises do regularly charge and collect interest with impunity. However, should a legal conflict arise involving such a transaction, no Saudi court will uphold a claim for payment of interest owed. Charging interest is commercially viable and is practiced in Saudi Arabia, but it is not enforceable in the courts.

Exchange Control. There are no restrictions on the transmittal of money or other means of exchange across Saudi borders. You can take money in and you can remove it without limitation. This applies both to foreign and Saudi currency.

Foreign Investment. A "foreign capital investment license" is required to invest in Saudi Arabia. By "foreign capital" the Saudis mean currency and other means of exchange, as well as such items as machinery and hardware, and intangibles such as trademarks or patents. The Saudi Ministry of Industry and Electricity determines whether a commercial venture is open for foreign investment and limits such opportunities to "economic development projects." Licenses are not granted simply because an application is made. To obtain a foreign capital investment license, a foreign firm must substantiate its expertise in the relevant area. Once granted, a license limits the licensee's area of involvement, including corporate objects, shareholders, and share capital. No modifications may be made to any covered area of corporate activity without prior approval of the Ministry of Industry and Electricity.

Foreign Corporations in Saudi Arabia. The activities of foreign corporations in Saudi Arabia are limited and tend to require foreign capital investment licenses. This applies to participation in joint ventures with national companies, as well as to the opening of branch offices by wholly foreign-owned companies. Special licenses are required for foreign companies engaging in technical and scientific services, market research, or product research. Companies so licensed are not permitted to engage in commercial transactions. Corporations entering into public-sector contracts, if not otherwise licensed, must register with the Ministry of Commerce. This is known as temporary commercial registry and applies to each contract, even if a company is involved in multiple concurrent contracts.

Commercial Registry. Saudi law requires every business entity of any form or nature to register with the Ministry of Commerce in each place where it conducts business. Parent and subsidiary companies, and main and branch offices must register separately. The Ministry of Commerce issues a registration number to each registrant, which must then be used without fail on all written correspondence. Firms requiring foreign capital investment licenses will have to provide evidence of license before they will be permitted to register.

Notaries Public. Notaries public are high public officials, on a par with judges, appointed and supervised by the Minister of Justice and the Supreme Judicial Council. They are experts in Shari'ah Law. There are extensive and burdensome requirements, which are subject to change without notice, pertaining to form and content of documents submitted to a notary in Saudi Arabia.

Employment. In Saudi Arabia, written and unwritten labor contracts are enforceable, with written contracts being the most common. There are stringent requirements for employers. These include such benefits as mandatory annual 15-day paid vacations for employees after the first year of employment, increasing to 21-day vacations after 10 continuous years. Terminated employees must be awarded "end-of-service" remuneration amounting to a half month's pay for each of the first five years of continuous service, and one month's pay for each subsequent year. This remuneration is calculated on the employee's most recent rate of pay, and is payable to employees terminated by the employer as well as those conscripted into military service, or leaving for circumstances beyond their control. Female employees leaving jobs for marriage or childbirth are also awarded end-of-service payment. If employment is terminated on the instigation of the employee and the employee observes the mandatory 30-day notice, he or she is due a modified version of the standard end-of-service payment. Employees and employers can terminate the employment relationship at will, and are expected to give 30 days' notice in the case of monthly employees and 15 days' notice for all others. When an employment relationship is contracted for a specified length of time and is terminated by the employer for no valid reason, the employee is entitled to damages, which tend to amount to between three and five months' salary.

Shipping. Maritime transport activities fall under the jurisdiction of the Ministry of Communications. Use of Saudi Arabian seaports is regulated under GCC Rules and Regulations. These are available in English translation.

Taxation. The central Saudi government levies taxes according to royal decree. At present there are no regional, local, or sales taxes. However, foreigners can be subject to income tax on investments in capital of Saudi businesses. Corporations are taxed on net income, with no distinction between types of businesses.

Communist Law

The originating text for communist law was the Communist Manifesto of Karl Marx and Friedrich Engels. The Manifesto did not provide a systematic code of laws, but a general, philosophical mandate from which codes were developed gradually after the successful Russian Bolshevik Revolution in 1917. By depriving the middle class of its ownership of the means of production, and thus its economic power, and by educating citizens to a way of life that would make the new social order attainable, the Communist Manifesto hoped to transform society into first a socialist and then a communist society. The laws were intended to implement that transformation and then cease to exist, once the new society was functioning smoothly without the need for rules and regulations.

Comparison with Common and Civil Law

There are many parallels between communist and civil law systems in the area of civil and criminal court procedures, but socialist law differs from common and civil law in that it is a state-centered, state-motivated system. Communism assumes that the good of the citizen inheres in the goals of the state, and therefore its mandate is to further the aims of the state, not to protect the rights of the individual citizen. The concept of checks and balances does not pertain.

In dealing with suppliers located in communist countries, you should keep in mind the following:

- Communist law does not distinguish between private law and public law. Changing policies of the state—such as for national economic planning—can expand or eliminate private, individual rights, even if already accrued.
- Contracts with communist government agencies are heavily influenced by state policy and by the need to implement a planned economy. For example, escalation clauses are not used because of the need to know the exact price and its effect on the government's economic plan.
- Commercial contracts may only be entered into with government agencies. Negotiating these contracts can be extremely difficult. Government agencies are directed to purchase

only at the lowest price existing in the world market for the particular product, and to sell at highly competitive world market prices.

- The Communist party plays a dominant role in the society.
- Generally, the foreigner must deal with agencies called "Foreign Trade Organizations" (FTO's) or state trading corporations. Each FTO or state trading corporation has jurisdiction over a particular commodity or type of commodity and each must follow explicit directives from higher governmental echelon. Each FTO is treated as a separate juridical entity, has its own budget, and can be sued individually.

Chinese Communist Law

Governmental Structure. China's constitution declares that Chinese Communist ideology controls in all matters. The highest government body with legislative powers is the National People's Congress. The Congress appoints the State Council, which exercises administrative powers. China's highest judicial body is the Supreme People's Court, which is responsible to the Congress. The Supreme People's Procuratorate, an independent body, enforces the constitution and laws.

Aliens. To enter, exit, transit, reside in, or travel about China, foreigners must have prior permission from the Ministry of Public Security and Foreign Affairs. Visas are required, and for residential stays, a foreigner must usually register with local public security agencies. Areas of China are classified into unrestricted, restricted, and nonopen areas for foreigners who travel within the country.

Agency. Principals can generally be represented by agents in China. An agent will not be liable on a contract signed on behalf of the principal, provide the agent's capacity is clear. An agent can be appointed by a written power of attorney that specifies the matter, scope, and time for which the authority granted. If the principal is a foreigner not residing in China, the power of attorney must be notarized in the foreigner's country and attested by a local Chinese embassy or consulate.

Law of Choice. International contracts that designate a particular law to govern the transaction are enforceable, except when Chinese law mandates its application to a transaction. Unless otherwise expressly provided, Chinese law will apply.

Arbitration and Foreign Judgments. Arbitration is available before Chinese Arbitration Commissions. These are local arbitration boards established to handle economic contract disputes. Arbitration is initiated by petition. An arbitration panel is then chosen, usually consisting of one arbitrator chosen by each party and a third neutral arbitrator. The panel has authority to investigate, collect and hear evidence, and secure goods and proceeds until their final decision. Arbitration decisions may be appealed to the people's court. Parties may also agree to arbitrate under internationally recognized arbitration rules. China has acceded to the U.N. Convention on the Recognition and Enforcement of Foreign Arbitral Awards.

Contracts. Economic contracts must be written and must comply with Chinese law, national policy, and plans. Parties have freedom to contract, but contracts are void if they violate law, national policy, national plans, or public interests. They are also void if executed by an agent without proper authority or if executed under fraud or coercion. For some contracts, specific provisions are mandated by law. Contract remedies for breach are provided by statute, including the right to keep an advance deposit, payment of consequential damages, return of property, and compensation for actual losses. Mitigation of damages is required when possible. Parties may cancel or modify their contracts by mutual written agreement for any reason, including force majeure.

Sales Agreements. No particular form is required for the purchase of personal property in China. Firms engaged in international sales usually use standard printed form agreements that follow international practices. China has ratified the U.N. Convention on Contracts for the International Sale of Goods, with the reservation that it will not agree to apply the Convention beyond the member states and it will not give effect to oral sales contracts. Prices for goods are often established pursuant to regulations adopted by the national or local governments. Some prices are not negotiable. Prices that are fixed and free typically fluctuate within a certain range.

Foreign Exchange. Strict controls are imposed on the allocation of foreign exchange. Profits must be remitted, imported components or raw materials must be purchased, and foreign personnel must be compensated in foreign currency, not China's domestic currency.

Foreign Investment. China's central government held a virtual monopoly over the country's foreign trade until the early 1980's. Little foreign investment was permitted, and then only for highly specialized purposes—acquiring new technology, assuring capital and raw material supplies, or promoting exports. However, foreign investment is being encouraged in oil drilling and refining, coal mining, property development, and labor-intensive manufacturing and assembly plants.

Import/Export Controls. All commodities exported from or imported to China must be channeled through licensed trading companies. Local and provincial governments often have their own regulations and restrictions on importing and exporting, as well. China is encouraging exports, and therefore has substantially reduced the number of commodities that require export licenses. However, licenses are still required to export corn, soybeans, tea, coal, and crude and refined oil.

Notaries Public. Notaries public have legal education or training. The signature of a notary evidences the legality of a document or act.

Taxation. Foreign investment enterprises and foreign enterprises with establishments in China are subject to an income tax at the rate of 33%. Some industries are subject to additional business taxes, and a 17% value-added tax (VAT) is levied.

Glossary of Common Legal Terms

acceptance An unconditional assent to an offer, or one conditioned on minor changes that do not affect material terms of the offer. *See* counteroffer, offer.

acknowledgment *See* authentication.

agency The relationship between an agent and a principal. The agent represents and acts on behalf of the principal, who instructs and authorizes the agent to so act. Refer to "Agency" on page 78.

after sight A term in a financial instrument making the instrument payable a specified number of days after presentation or demand. Example: a bill of exchange payable 30 days after sight matures and becomes payable 30 days after the person for whom the bill is drawn (the drawee) presents it to a bank (the payee).

at sight A term in a financial instrument under which the instrument is payable on presentation or demand. Example: a bill of exchange that is payable at sight is payable at the time the person for whom the bill is drawn (the drawee) presents it to a bank (the payee).

attachment The legal process for seizing property before a judgment to secure the payment of damages if awarded. Attachment may be sought before commencing a court action or during the action. This process is also referred to as sequestration. Example: a party who claims damages for breach of contract may request a court to issue an order freezing all transfers of specific property owned by the breaching party pending resolution of the dispute.

authentication The act of conferring legal authenticity on a written document, typically made by a notary public, who attests and certifies that the document is in proper legal form and that it is executed by a person identified as having authority to do so. Authentication is also referred to as acknowledgment.

bill of exchange A written instrument signed by a person (the drawer) and addressed to another person (the drawee), typically a bank, ordering the drawee to pay unconditionally a stated sum of money to yet another person (the payee) on demand or at a future time.

bona fide In or with good faith, honesty, and sincerity. Example: A bona fide purchaser is one who buys goods for value and without knowledge of fraud or unfair dealing in the transaction. Knowledge of fraud or unfair dealing may be implied if the facts are such that the purchaser should have reasonably known that the transaction involved deceit, such as when goods that are susceptible to piracy are provided without documentation of their origin.

counteroffer A reply to an offer that materially alters the terms of the offer. Example: a seller who accepts a buyer's offer on condition that the goods will be made of a different material has made a counteroffer. *See* acceptance, offer.

crossed check A check that bears on its face two parallel transverse lines, indicating that it cannot be presented for cash. A bank that accepts such a check will pay the proceeds only to another bank, which will credit the money to the account of the payee of the check.

execution The legal process for enforcing a judgment for damages, usually by seizure and sale of the debtor's personal property. Example: if a court awards damages in a breach of contract action and the breaching party fails to remit them, the party awarded damages may request the court to order seizure and sale of the breaching party's inventory to satisfy the award.

force majeure clause A contract clause that excuses a party who breaches the contract when performance is prevented by the occurrence of an event—such as a natural disaster, war, or labor strike—that is beyond the party's reasonable control.

juridical (juristic) act An action intended to have, and capable of having, a legal effect, such as the creation, termination, or modification of a legal right. Example: The signing of a power of attorney is a juridical act because it gives legal authority to an agent.

juridical (juristic) person An individual or entity recognized under law as having legal rights and obligations. Example: limited liability companies, corporations, and partnerships are entities recognized as juridical persons.

negotiable instrument A written document transferable merely by endorsement or delivery. Example: a check or bill of exchange is a negotiable instrument.

offer A proposal that is made to a specific individual or entity to enter into a contract. The proposal must contain definite terms and must indicate the offeror's intent to be bound by an acceptance. Example: a buyer's order to purchase designated goods on certain delivery and payment terms is an offer. *See* acceptance, counteroffer.

power of attorney A written document by which one individual or entity (the principal) authorizes another individual or entity (the agent) to perform stated acts on the principal's behalf. Example: a principal may execute a special power of attorney (authorizing an agent to sign a specific contract) or a general power of attorney (authorizing the agent to sign all contracts for the principal). *See* agency. Refer to "Power of Attorney" on page 78.

promoter of corporation The individual or entity that organizes a corporation.

rescind A contracting party's right to cancel the contract. Example: a contract may allow one party to rescind if the other party fails to perform within a reasonable time.

sequestration *See* attachment.

statute of frauds A law that requires designated documents to be in writing in order to be enforced by a court. Example: contracting parties may orally agree to transfer ownership of immovable property, but a court might not enforce that contract, and might not award damages for breach, unless the contract was written.

ultra vires An act performed without the authority to do so. Example: If a contract provision requires both parties to approve an assignment of the contract but one party agrees to an assignment without obtaining the other's consent, the assignment is ultra vires.

Looking for international trade service providers in the USA?

Let your fingers do the walking.

Do you need:

- **An English–Korean translator?**
- **A freight forwarder in Miami?**
- **A customs broker in Seattle?**
- **An international banker in Chicago?**
- **A customs attorney in New York?**
- **A freight consolidator in Boston?**
- **A shipping line to Taiwan?**
- **A courier service to Cambodia?**
- **A Foreign Trade Zone in Brooklyn?**

Time to panic? Not if you have the new *World Trade Yellow Pages*, coming in June 1995 from World Trade Press.

The *World Trade Yellow Pages* contains listings for 46 categories of service providers to the US international trade community. Because the listings are free to service providers, you get lots of options to choose from, not just those who advertise. From freight forwarders to custom brokers, trade finance firms to translators, it's all here in one easy to use volume.

Bottom line: the *World Trade Yellow Pages* provides quick solutions for almost any service need imaginable, and at the low-price of only $24.95.

The *World Trade Yellow Pages* includes:

- 11,000 service providers to the US international trade community, organized into 46 categories,
- Alphabetical and categorical listings,
- Company names, contact person, addresses, telephone, and fax numbers.

Locating information about international trade has never been this easy — nor this inexpensive. Call toll–free 1–800–833–8586 to order your copy today.

World Trade Yellow Pages, 1995 Edition
820 pages, 8.5" x 11"
ISBN 0–885073–09–7
Softcover, US$24.95

Professional Books for International Trade

1505 Fifth Avenue
San Rafael, CA 94901 • USA
(415) 454-9934
FAX (415) 453-7980
Order Line: (800) 833-8586

International Banking
Contents

International Banking Overview

Introduction

Major domestic, foreign, and international banks provide a wide range of services to their customers involved in import and export operations. These services fall into four main categories: connections and information, movement of funds and financing, other banking services, and foreign exchange operations.

This introduction to international banking is designed to provide an overview of these services. The following section—"Documentary Credits (Letters of Credit)," beginning on page 126—gives more detailed information concerning international payments.

If you are planning to operate in international trade, it is important to cultivate your banking relationships early and often. All business is ultimately conducted person to person, and nowhere is this more important than in the international arena. Begin by establishing a strong personal relationship with the bankers whose support you will need as your enterprise progresses. Importers who view a professional service provider—such as a banker, a customs broker, or an attorney—as a partner in their business tend to be significantly more successful than those who fail to utilize these resources to the fullest.

In many cases the quality of your ongoing relationship with your bank and banker will determine the availability of certain of the services listed below. Also, be aware that not all banks or bankers will be able to provide every service listed. This is especially true of limited local banking institutions with little exposure to the international field.

Types of Banking Organizations

As many as 13,000 state- and federally-chartered banking institutions operate in the U.S. These are extremely varied, ranging from small, special purpose local operations to giant international outfits. Of all these, about 50 can be classed as truly international in scope and operations. However, even the smallest local bank will have connections—known as correspondents—among larger institutions and can begin to set you on the road to hooking up with the expertise you need.

In addition, about 300 foreign banks maintain a presence in the U.S. Some of these maintain only a representative office, which cannot offer services, but which can provide information and direct you to the appropriate people in their home country. Other foreign banks run agencies in the U.S. These specially licensed offices can lend, handle trade bills, issue letters of credit, act as an intermediary for parent company business, and offer payment services, but may not accept deposits. Others have branches, which can offer any service that fully licensed domestic banks are allowed to offer. Still others are subsidiaries: locally incorporated, licensed banks owned by overseas parent firms. Any of these foreign owned operations may be a good place to start when looking for information about doing business in their home countries.

The U.S. also has offshore banks, known as Edge Act and Agreement banks. These are separately incorporated banks physically located in the U.S., but legally separate and designed to service international business for both U.S. residents and foreigners. These entities are restricted from offering certain domestic banking services, but are relieved of some regulatory and other requirements (for example, they are not required to maintain reserve deposits with the Federal Reserve system) to enable them to compete with foreign operations. Edge Act banks are federally chartered, while Agreement banks operate under state licenses.

Investment banks and venture capital firms may also be interested in helping larger growing internationally-oriented firms secure additional financing. If you are big enough to interest them, you already know about their services. If not, there's always the future.

Most of these same types of financial institutions exist in other countries, although the specifics vary widely depending on the local system. Consult the U.S. office of the main bank in the country you are interested in, or a U.S. bank with offices in that country.

Connections and Information

Connections

Through its branch and correspondent bank relationships throughout the world, your bank may be able to provide you with names and references for country-of-origin suppliers of the commodities or products you wish to import. At the very least your banker should be able to supply you with a letter of introduction to an officer of a local bank in the country of origin. Do not take these letters of introduction lightly. To successfully find a good source of supply you may need to follow up on a number of leads and this is a good one. Unless you represent an already well known, internationally renowned firm, such a reference from a bank could play a crucial role in establishing your credibility.

Tip: If you are certain of the country of origin of the product(s) you propose to import, make it a top priority to get in touch with the U.S. branch of the major foreign bank from that country as soon as possible. Call to establish who you should be speaking with. Then make the connection by phone and tell them exactly what type of contact you are looking for in their country. If they are in a position to help, make an appointment to see them in person.

Supplier Information

International banks are also in a position to assist in securing current information on the reputation, capabilities, and creditworthiness of firms and individuals with whom business may be contemplated. Because you have made your banker an unofficial "partner" in your operation, he or she has a stake in seeing that you do not end up doing business with unreliable firms. Ask your bankers if they can provide a financial or other report on the supplier firms in the country of origin.

Securing Overseas Credit

Two of the most underutilized sources of credit for importers are suppliers and export trade promotion services in the country of origin. In the U.S. most official and quasi-official trade facilitating organizations—such as the U.S. Department of Commerce (DOC), the Export-Import Bank of the United States (Eximbank) and the Private Export Funding Corporation (PEFCO)—are concerned almost exclusively with promoting and financing exports from the U.S. rather than two-way trade or imports into the country. The same is often true of the agencies abroad, but there it can work to your benefit because you are buying what they have to sell. With your approval, your bank can furnish your credit history and written references to these sources to assist you in obtaining credit and other services from such entities. An endorsement from your banker may also help in securing more favorable terms.

Tip: Don't be bashful about proposing imaginative financing alternatives to your supplier. One small-time importer making regular buying trips to the Orient was able to get favorable terms based on his presentation of himself as an ultra-reliable business partner. He paid cash, using traveler's checks, on the first trip; by personal check on the second trip; by post-dated personal check on the third trip; and was able to get 60-day credit terms on the fourth trip. Eventually several of his suppliers fronted large quantities of merchandise for him to establish a distribution network in the U.S. without his having to finance the operation himself. It is okay to wheel and deal, but be sure you can deliver.

Domestic Market Information

Remember that importing merely involves getting the goods from one place (which happens to be overseas) to another (which happens to be in the U.S.), with an intermediate stop at U.S. Customs. This is a big task, but you aren't home free yet. You still have to know what you are doing in order to move the goods once you get them to their destination. Larger banks often conduct market studies and publish information on many types of commodities and domestic markets. This information can be a great help in marketing and distribution efforts. These reports are usually produced as studies organized by industry, commodity, or region.

Overseas Financial, Business, Economic, and Political Reports

Many of the larger banks produce reports on overseas financial, business, economic, and political conditions. These reports range from single page briefing sheets to thousand-page monsters with weekly updates. The smaller ones will often be provided free of charge, but the large-scale ones can be quite costly. Look to the major international banks for this sort of information.

Exchange Regulations

Many countries have complex and stringent currency regulations. Internationally-oriented banks deal with currency issues every day and are the obvious places to look for expertise on these matters. Although virtually any bank can hook you into the network, remember that there are no more than 50 institutions nationwide which can be considered players in international and foreign exchange business and choose accordingly.

Many importers get into trouble with country-of-origin currency regulations. Avoid this problem by asking your banker to check out any unusual potential problems in dealing with businesses in the country of origin.

Tip: If you are unsure of the expertise of your banker, ask for an officer in the foreign exchange department.

Country-of-Origin Export Regulations

While banks are not the prime source of this information, international banks can often assist U.S. importers in learning about country-of-origin export regulations for specific commodities.

Tip: Go to the U.S. office of an international bank headquartered or located in the country of origin for this information.

Joint Venture Partners

Your international banker may be in a position to introduce you to potential partners for a joint venture. In some instances banks have assisted in introducing an overseas manufacturer to a U.S. distributor. In other cases, the connection was made between overseas commodity suppliers and U.S. manufacturing companies which subsequently established plants both in the U.S. and the country of origin.

Tip: Even if you do not make the initial connection for your joint venture partner through your bank, try to arrange for a complete credit history of the potential partner through the bank. Also plan on using your bank as a reference to establish your *bona fides*.

Overseas Investment Information

You may wish to invest overseas to leverage your import operation. For example, some importers end up purchasing the company providing the goods they import into the U.S. in order to ensure a steady source of supply. Or you may wish to invest in the commodities from which your products are made, either by buying options on a commodities futures market in the country of origin, or by purchasing a share in an operation which produces these commodities. International banks often serve as the means of effecting such investments and thus may be able to assist you in finding and evaluating opportunities.

Letters of Introduction

Even if your business is well established, well regarded, and well recognized at home, it is unlikely that potential overseas suppliers will have any knowledge of you or any information on your creditworthiness or integrity. A well-written letter of introduction from your banker on bank letterhead may help break down some of these barriers. With an appropriate letter of introduction, overseas branches of your bank or its correspondent banks may be able to provide you with a wide range of excellent information on local suppliers and political and economic conditions.

Countertrade Connections

Trade with former Socialist countries and other nations lacking adequate hard currency reserves may require countertrade deals. In countertrade arrangements, a U.S. exporter trades U.S. goods for goods produced in another country and then sells those goods in the U.S. So why bring this up to importers? Because the U.S. exporter may have no real interest in marketing the products received and may be willing to cut a good deal on the very goods you need. A bank with good connections in the country of origin of the items you wish to import to the U.S. may be able to assist you in finding partners abroad for such countertrade deals.

Referrals to Local Professionals

International banks are often in an excellent position to recommend names of local attorneys, accountants, freight forwarders, and other professional people who can assist your overseas efforts.

High-Level Introductions. Larger banks can sometimes provide introductions to prominent local businesspeople, local bankers, potential investor groups, and government officials in foreign countries. Introductions to such movers and shakers can make all the difference in getting your deal going.

Movement of Funds and Financing

The following section serves as a review of the issues involved in and the primary methods used for making international trade payments.

A major factor determining the method of payment used is the degree of trust the seller/exporter has in the buyer/importer's ability and willingness to pay. In domestic situations, if the buyer has good credit, purchases are usually made on an open account (credit) basis. Open account terms may eventually be made available to you for purchases made abroad, but it is far more likely that another, more secure method of payment will be required. Foreign sellers always seek the most secure payment method from their perspective, while you, as the buyer, will seek the method of payment most advantageous to you.

Evaluation of Risks

International transactions pose risks for both seller and buyer. Exporters want to ensure timely and full payment for their goods, while importers want to be certain that they receive the goods they contract for as well as the documentation that is required for Customs clearance. One of the most important factors in reducing the risks is knowing what risks exist. For that reason, importers and exporters are both advised to consult with their professional partners (customs broker, banker, attorney) to determine an acceptable method of payment for each transaction.

In this discussion it is assumed that buyer and seller have agreed upon the substantive terms of a transaction, including:

- Merchandise, including quality, quantity, and specifications;
- Price to be paid per unit and total amount including the currency to be used in the transaction;
- Who will pay freight charges to the port of export as well as to the port of destination;
- Who will pay insurance during each leg of the journey;
- Shipment deadline(s);
- Required documentation and format; and
- Other special instructions or relevant matters affecting the transaction.

It is assumed that buyer and seller will draft and sign a formal commercial contract establishing these terms as conditions of the transaction. The next consideration is how the buyer will effect payment for the goods.

Methods of International Payment

Ranked from most secure for the exporter to the most desirable for the importer, the basic methods of payment are:

1. Prepayment (cash payment with order),
2. Documentary letter of credit,
3. Documentary collection or draft (documents against payment),
4. Open account or other credit terms.

In addition to these methods there are a number of less traditional methods including payment by personal or business check or credit card and the use of consignment sales. Each method of payment has its own set of advantages and disadvantages for both buyer and seller.

Prepayment or Cash with Order

Prepayment, or cash-in-advance, terms are the most favorable from the seller's point of view. For the seller, risk is substantially eliminated. Virtually all risk lies with the buyer who entrusts his money to the seller prior to the shipment of goods. Advance payment can create a cash flow problem for the importer and adds to the level of his or her risk.

Risks to the Importer/Buyer

Goods not shipped. The merchandise may not be shipped at all. The seller may, if unable or unwilling to ship the goods, retain the buyer's money and either refund it at a much later date, or not at all, in which case the importer usually has little recourse except to pursue a claim in the country of origin.

Goods shipped not goods ordered. The goods shipped may not be those contracted for, or the quality or quantity of goods shipped may be deficient.

Documents not forwarded. Documents necessary for exportation, shipment, and U.S. Customs entry and clearance may not be available when needed, or not available at all. These documents become more difficult to obtain as time goes on. Some documents may be virtually impossible to obtain after the fact.

Delay in shipment. Once the seller has possession of the funds, he or she may not be as concerned with moving the goods as when payment is tied to a shipping date. Prepayment, in many instances, removes the incentive on the part of the seller to deliver on time, whereas payment for goods on delivery invariably promotes a more expeditious availability of merchandise.

There is virtually no risk to the seller when orders are prepaid. Importers using this form of payment should know well and have boundless trust in their supplier. However, buyers should also remember that in many parts of the world, suppliers rely on prepayments or deposits to finance their production or acquisition of the goods to be sold and may be unable to conduct business without the implied credit from the buyer that such methods provide.

An alternative that is somewhat more palatable to the buyer is to pay with cash at the time of delivery. The buyer must be able to physically take possession of the goods and all necessary documentation at time of payment. This scenario gives the buyer some control, because he or she can reject the goods if they are not according to the terms agreed upon. However, this method still places the primary onus on the buyer who is operating away from home and may be confronted with a take-it-or-leave-it offer in a make-or-break situation.

Open Account or Credit Terms

At the other end of the spectrum, credit terms are most favorable to the importer/purchaser, with all risks accruing to the seller. The exporter/seller may consider open account transactions to be satisfactory, if not desirable, provided the buyer is well established, has demonstrated a long and favorable payment record, or has been thoroughly vetted for creditworthiness by an acceptably authoritative source. In open account arrangements, the exporter simply hands over the goods, billing the customer, who is expected to pay under agreed upon terms at a specified future date. Some of the largest firms abroad will make purchases only on an open account basis. Open account terms may also occur when the seller has excess inventory to move or when the seller has a very high profit margin built into the price structure to allow for potential losses.

Risks to the Exporter/Seller

By offering open credit terms to the buyer, the seller is exposing himself or herself to significant commercial risk. The seller passes title and physical control over the goods to the buyer prior to receiving payment. In most instances, full title passes to the buyer and the seller has no recourse to the goods, but only to the buyer for payment. The buyer may be unwilling or unable to pay the seller because of a lack of funds, a dispute over the goods delivered, or a basic unwillingness to pay.

In addition, the absence of external documents and the lack of direct involvement by banking intermediaries may make it difficult to pursue legal or other remedies. The exporter may be forced to pursue collection abroad, which can be difficult and costly. Also, receivables may be harder to finance, since drafts or other evidence of indebtedness are unavailable. On the other hand, the buyer may on occasion need to turn the goods over in order to finance the deal, although the importing business may not be the best place for someone who lives that close to the financial edge. It is little wonder that overseas suppliers are reluctant to deal on such terms.

Documentary Letters of Credit and Drafts

To protect the interests of both buyer and seller, documentary letters of credit or drafts are often used. Under both of these methods, outside intermediaries are involved and documents are required to be presented in order for payment to be made.

Both letters of credit and drafts may be paid immediately—that is, at sight—or at a later date. Drafts to be paid when presented are called sight drafts, while drafts that are to be paid at a later date—often well after the buyer receives the goods—are called time drafts or date drafts.

Since payment under these two methods is made on the basis of documents, all terms of sale need to be agreed to and clearly specified. For example, "net 30 days" should be specified as "net 30 days from acceptance" or "net 30 days from date of bill of lading," or some other similarly explicit event to avoid confusion and delay of payment. Likewise, the currency to be used in paying for the goods should be specified as "US$XXX" if payment is to be made in U.S. dollars or other currency or special arrangements. International bankers can explain local and bank requirements, as well as offer other helpful suggestions in how to structure such arrangements.

Banks charge fees—usually a (small) percentage of the amount of the payment—for handling letters of credit and generally lesser flat fees for handling drafts.

Documentary Collections

In a documentary collection the exporter forwards the goods to the importer, but forwards the documents (including all title and entry documents) necessary to take title and possession to his own bank for transmission to the buyer's bank. Under this arrangement—a form of international "cash on delivery"—the buyer's bank may not transfer the documents to the buyer until payment has been made or until the buyer's bank has guaranteed that payment will be made within a stated period of time.

Documentary collections function in the following manner:

1) Buyer and seller agree to the terms of the sale (as noted above);
2) Seller prepares goods and documentation for shipment;
3) Seller ships goods to buyer and then presents full documentation to his bank for transmission to the buyer's bank;
4) The buyer's bank receives the documents and notifies the buyer of their arrival;
5) Buyer inspects the documentation to ascertain its accuracy and completeness;
6) Buyer pays his bank for the documentation (including payment of the bank's fees);
7) In exchange for this payment, the bank turns the documentation over to the buyer;

8-9) Buyer then uses the documentation to take possession of and enter the goods;

8-9) Buyer's bank forwards payment to the seller's bank for the account of seller;

10) Seller's bank then credits the payment for the goods to the seller's account.

In this situation both the seller and the buyer experience only moderate risk.

Risks to the Seller

The buyer may not pay for the documents (and goods) which the seller has shipped. The buyer may not have actual funds or credit available when needed; the buyer may have lost the market for the goods; or simply have changed his or her mind about doing business with the seller.

In such cases, the seller may become liable for full freight charges, storage fees, cartage, legal and collection fees, spoilage, and other similar costs. The seller will have to ship the goods back to the port of origin, find a new buyer, or have the goods destroyed. In such a situation, the seller may be placed in a very compromising position.

However, there are several advantages to the buyer in this arrangement. First, the buyer has a period of time to secure financing (or sale) of the goods between the time the goods are ordered and the time he or she must actually pay for them. The buyer saves carrying charges during this time. In this type of arrangement, it is best for the seller to have a good association with the buyer.

Risks to the Buyer

Conversely, the buyer does not exercise any control over the date of shipment of the goods or the quality or quantity of goods shipped. The buyer may be desperately in need of the merchandise, whereas the seller might have changed the price, quantity, or the quality of the merchandise being forwarded. The buyer would then have the option to reject and not pay for the shipment. However, he might expose himself either to a greater loss or to a foregone profit by not accepting the shipment. In this case it is wise for the buyer to know the seller well enough to avoid these problems.

Import Letters of Credit

A letter of credit adds a bank's promise to pay the exporter to that of the importer once the exporter has complied with all the terms and conditions of the letter of credit. The importer applies for issuance of a letter of credit to the exporter and therefore is called the applicant; the exporter is referred to as the beneficiary.

Payment under a documentary letter of credit is based solely on the documents involved, not on the terms of sale or the condition of the goods sold. The documents essentially become the product, and the goods become largely irrelevant. Before payment, the bank responsible for making the payment verifies that all documents conform exactly to the terms in the letter of credit. If they do not match exactly, a discrepancy exists which must be resolved before payment can be made. Thus, the actual documents must comply with those specified in the letter of credit in every particular or detail.

A letter of credit issued by a U.S. bank is often confirmed by a foreign bank. This means that the foreign bank—the confirming bank—adds its promise to pay to that of the U.S.—or issuing—bank. An international banker can help importers determine what terms and level of bank involvement might be appropriate for a specific import transaction.

A letter of credit may be either irrevocable (that is, its terms cannot be altered unless both the importer and the exporter agree to the specific changes) or revocable (that is, either party may unilaterally make changes). A revocable letter of credit is inadvisable for the exporter, while it may offer some benefits to the importer. A letter of credit may be "at sight," requiring immediate payment upon presentation of the documents, or it may be a time or date letter of credit with payment to be made at a specified time in the future.

Any change made to a letter of credit after it has been issued is called an amendment. The fees charged by the banks involved in amending the letter of credit may be paid by either the exporter or the importer, but who is to pay which charges should be specified in the letter of credit in advance. Since changes can be time-consuming and expensive, every effort should be made to get the letter of credit right the first time.

The exporter is usually not paid until the advising or confirming bank receives the funds from the issuing bank, that is the advising bank does not advance funds before the transaction is fully completed. To expedite the receipt of funds, wire transfers may be used. However, individual bank practices vary, and the exporter may be able to obtain funds more rapidly by discounting the letter of credit at the bank. This does involve paying a service fee to the bank, as well as taking less than the face value.

A Typical Letter of Credit Transaction

Here is what typically happens when payment is made using an irrevocable letter of credit:

1. After the buyer and seller agree on the terms of a sale, the buyer arranges for his or her bank to open (issue) a letter of credit.
2. The buyer's bank prepares an irrevocable letter of credit, including all instructions to the seller concerning the shipment.
3. The buyer's bank sends the irrevocable letter of credit to a correspondent bank in the seller's country, requesting confirmation. The seller may request that a particular bank serve as the confirming bank. If not, the U.S. bank selects a foreign correspondent bank of its choice.
4. The foreign bank prepares a letter of confirmation to forward to the seller along with the irrevocable letter of credit.
5. The seller carefully reviews all conditions in the letter of credit. If the seller cannot comply with one or more of the conditions, the buyer is alerted, in which case the parties must negotiate an amendment to the letter of credit.
6. The seller arranges with his or her freight forwarder to deliver the goods to the appropriate port or airport.
7. When the goods are loaded, the forwarder completes the necessary documents.
8. The seller (or the forwarder) presents to the foreign correspondent bank all the specified documents indicating full compliance with the terms of the letter of credit.
9. The foreign correspondent bank reviews the documents. If they are in order, the documents are airmailed or sent by courier to the buyer's bank for review. If the documents are deemed satisfactory, the buyer's bank forwards the documents to the buyer.
10. The buyer (or agent) gets the documents needed to claim the goods.
11. A draft, which often accompanies the letter of credit, is paid by the seller's bank to the seller at the time specified; the draft may also be discounted at an earlier date.

Drafts

A draft, sometimes called a bill of exchange, is analogous to a foreign buyer's check. Like checks used in domestic commerce, drafts carry the risk that they may be dishonored.

Sight Drafts

A sight draft is used when the exporter/seller wishes to retain title to the shipment until it reaches its destination and is paid for. Before the cargo can be released, the original ocean bill of lading forwarded by the seller to the buyer through the agent banks must be properly endorsed by the importer/buyer and surrendered to the carrier, allowing the buyer to take title.

Air waybills of lading, on the other hand, need not be presented in order for the importer/buyer to claim the goods. Hence, there is an element of increased risk to the exporter/seller when a sight draft is used with an air shipment.

In actual practice, the bill of lading or air waybill is endorsed by the exporter/shipper and sent via the exporter's bank to the importer's bank or to another intermediary along with a sight draft, invoices, and other supporting documents specified by either the importer/buyer or the authorities in the buyer's country (for example, packing lists, consular invoices, or insurance certificates). The bank notifies the importer when it has received these documents. As soon as the draft is paid, the bank releases the bill of lading, enabling the buyer to obtain the shipment.

When a sight draft is being used to control the transfer of title of a shipment, some risk remains for the exporter because the importer's ability or willingness to pay may change between the time the goods are shipped and the time the drafts are presented for payment. If the buyer cannot or will not pay for and claim the goods, returning or disposing of them becomes the problem of the exporter.

Time Drafts and Date Drafts

If the exporter is willing to extend credit to the buyer, a time draft can be used to state that payment is due within a certain time after the buyer accepts the draft and receives the goods, for example, 30 days after acceptance. By signing and writing "accepted" on the draft, the buyer becomes formally obligated to pay within the stated time. Once this is done the draft is called a trade acceptance and can either be retained by the exporter until payable in full at maturity or sold to a bank at a discount for immediate payment.

A date draft differs slightly from a time draft in that it specifies a date on which payment is due, for example, December 1, 1995, rather than simply a number of days after the draft is accepted. When a sight draft or time draft is used, the importer/buyer can delay making payment by delaying acceptance of the draft. A date draft can prevent this delay in payment but still must be accepted by the importer.

When a bank accepts a draft, it becomes an obligation of the bank, creating a negotiable instrument known as a banker's acceptance. A banker's acceptance can also be sold to a bank at a discount for immediate payment or by the bank to a third party.

Other Payment Mechanisms

Credit Cards

The use of credit cards as a payment mechanism has increased dramatically in recent years. It is not at all uncommon for an individual to have half a dozen or more credit cards with a $5,000 to $10,000 limit on each. Many U.S. importers of low dollar value products purchased directly from the supplier can pay using credit cards. There are numerous stories of U.S. importers of jewelry, art, folk art, and handicrafts who got their start by using credit card payment to get an effective 25 to 40 days free financing between the purchase and the due date.

In some instances the exporter/seller will want to add a surcharge or lessen the discount on the goods sold to offset the charges that banks assess to the seller on the credit card transaction. You should also realize that merchants are particularly resistant to accepting credit card payments in countries experiencing high inflation, which can heighten their risk between the time of the transaction and the time they actually get paid by the bank (regardless of when the buyer pays off the charges). The several percentage points that the seller demands may make it inadvisable to use your card unless you really need the credit, or know you can turn the goods over quickly at a good margin upon your return to the U.S.

Tip: Get one of the "mileage" affinity credit cards, such as the "Mileage Plus" card tied to United, or the "Advantage Card" tied to American Airlines and get credit for airline flight coupons when you charge items (including your overseas airline tickets) on the credit card. Some of these cards do have a maximum of $10,000 of purchases per month which can be credited to the mileage program. Get a gold card for each program to rack up miles as you spend.

Tip: Be aware that a charge in a foreign currency on your domestic U.S. credit card will often subject you to disadvantageous foreign exchange rates. One solution: agree on the amount of the charge in U.S. dollars and have the credit card slip made out in U.S. dollars. (This ploy may not work in countries that have strict exchange controls, but it is worth a try.)

Consignment Sales

In international consignment sales, the same basic procedure is followed as in the U.S. The goods are shipped to a U.S. distributor to be sold on behalf of the foreign exporter/supplier. The foreign exporter/seller retains title to the goods until they are sold by the distributor. After the goods are sold, payment is forwarded to the exporter. Under the terms of this method, the exporter has the greatest risk and least control over the goods and may have to wait for an extended period before getting paid.

The U.S. importer/distributor can promote this sort of transaction with the foreign supplier by proposing and perhaps paying for some form of risk insurance or offering a particularly good discount or terms.

Countertrade and Barter

International countertrade is a trade practice whereby a supplier commits contractually, as a condition of the sale, to undertake specified initiatives that compensate and benefit the other party. It implies a set of linked quid pro quo transactions. The resulting trade gets around existing difficulties, such as financial (usually a lack of foreign exchange), marketing, or public policy concerns, while fulfilling the objectives of the trading parties. Not all suppliers consider countertrade to be objectionable, although perhaps the majority of U.S. exporters grudgingly view countertrade as a necessary evil that barely enables them to do business in markets that would otherwise be closed to them.

Simple barter is the direct exchange of goods or services between two parties; no money changes hands, although the parties must still impute values to their products. Pure barter arrangements in international commerce are rare, because the parties' needs for the goods of the other seldom coincide and because arriving at a mutually agreeable valuation of the goods may pose problems.

The most common form of compensatory trade practiced today involves contractually linked, parallel trade transactions each of which involves a separate financial settlement. For example, a countertrade contract may provide that the U.S. exporter will be paid in a convertible currency as long as the U.S. exporter (or another entity designated by the exporter) agrees to import a related quantity of goods from the foreign country in return.

U.S. exporters can take advantage of countertrade opportunities by trading through an intermediary with countertrade expertise, such as an international broker, an international bank, or an export management company. Some export management companies offer specialized countertrade services. Exporters should bear in mind that countertrade often involves higher transaction costs and greater risks than more straightforward export transactions.

The U.S. Department of Commerce can advise and assist U.S. exporters faced with countertrade requirements. The Office of Countertrade and Finance monitors countertrade trends, disseminates information (including lists of potentially beneficial countertrade opportunities), and provides general assistance to enterprises seeking barter and countertrade opportunities. For information, contact the Office of Countertrade and Finance, U.S. Department of Commerce, 14th and Constitution N.W., Rm. 1104, Washington, DC 20230; tel. (202) 482-4434.

The International Trade Administration publishes *International Countertrade: A Guide for Managers and Executives* and *International Countertrade: Individual Country Practices*, which give more information on countertrade and its use worldwide. These publications are available from:

U.S. Government Printing Office (USGPO)
Superintendent of Documents
Washington, DC 20402
(202) 512-1800 (Order line)
(202) 512-0000 (General)

The USGPO accepts phone orders paid by credit card as well as mail orders paid by credit card, a check drawn on a U.S. bank, or an international money order.

General Banking Services

Home Country Services for Importers

Banks provide the primary source of funding, not only for smaller export-import operations, but for larger operations as well. Most extend short-term credit—due in less than one year—on the basis of a line of credit which allows the customer to draw down amounts as needed up to the maximum specified. U.S. banks usually offer two kinds of lines of credit: straight advances and acceptances. Advances supply loans of fixed maturities on demand. The borrower usually must pay down outstanding balances at a specified time (often semiannually). Under acceptance credit, the bank will accept (pay) drafts on behalf of the customer, such as for approved import transactions. The customers themselves do not receive the funds, which are only disbursed to third party payees to cover specific eligible expenses. Borrowers usually must pay down their outstanding balances within six months.

For longer term credit—usually for periods up to three years' duration—most banks offer a revolving credit facility. Similar to a line of credit, revolving credit allows the borrower to use as much as he or she desires up to an agreed upon ceiling, paying off the outstanding balance at will. Interest is charged only on the amounts used, although there may be an annual commitment fee on the unused portion of the loan.

Loans for a period longer than three years—often called term loans because they are for a set time period, or term—generally involve a set payment schedule. This may include features such as amortization, grace period, balloon payment, or any number of other repayment scenarios. Amortization requires that each periodic payment be apportioned between interest and principal, so that the loan is largely self-canceling during its life. A grace period waives repayment of principal (and sometimes of interest as well) for a specified length of time. A balloon payment requires full repayment of remaining principal at the end of the loan period with only interest or relatively small principal payments being required prior to the actual closeout. Such intermediate credit facilities are often rolled over at the expiration of the term.

U.S. banks usually charge interest rates based on the prime rate—the rate charged to "prime," or average, business customers. The rate paid fluctuates with the prime rate, and the base may be prime-plus or prime-less, depending on the bank, the relationship with the borrower, and the circumstances and risk assessment of the particular deal.

Local currency financing source. Your bank may also be able to assist you in locating financing for your import operation in local currency in the country of origin. Terms, conditions, and costs for such financing vary literally all over the map.

Deposit and Payment Services

Most banks usually accept deposits and offer payment services, such as checks. If you have regular—or even temporary—cash balances, you may be able to take advantage of a cash management or other type of account paying interest on these balances.

Your international banker should be able to assist you in moving funds overseas via bank wire transfer, drafts issued in U.S. dollars, drafts issued in foreign currencies, international money orders, and letters of credit.

Few businesspeople operating overseas will be able to use personal checks or even business checks drawn on a U.S. bank. However, anything may be possible. It also helps if your bank has a branch in the country in which you are doing business.

U.S. banks can also arrange to transfer funds and conduct other transactions, often using advanced computer systems. The Clearing House Interbank Payment System (CHIPS), which links 90 New York financial institutions, handles about 90% of foreign exchange transactions and essentially all Eurodollar transactions (*see* "An Introduction to Foreign Exchange" below). The Society for Worldwide Interbank Financial Telecommunications (SWIFT) links U.S. banks to an international network designed to transmit messages regarding foreign exchange, bank wire transfers, and other financial advisories.

Domestic Foreign Exchange

Banks can often provide you with a supply of major foreign currencies with which to pay expenses abroad. This domestic purchase of foreign currency will generally be limited to the small amounts required for incidentals upon arrival in a foreign country. More favorable exchange rates will be available in the country of destination, but it is nice to have some local currency available when you land.

Trust receipts

Trust receipts are used when you want goods released to you for purposes of inspection, assembly, or Customs clearance. This often occurs when goods arrive ahead of documentation. The bank guarantees your performance to the shipping company. Banks also call these "ship-side bonds."

Credit Cards

Your bank can probably issue MasterCard and Visa credit cards to assist you in dealing with your general travel expenses. You may even be able to use such instruments to make some overseas purchases of goods (*see* above). You may also be able to use your credit card to get a cash advance or travelers checks from a member bank overseas. Depending on the charges and exchange rates applied to such transactions by your home bank, the host country bank, and local regulations, this may not be a particularly cheap way to transfer or access funds abroad. However, it beats getting stuck overseas without funds, and for smaller transactions is often much simpler and quicker than trying to have funds transferred through the banking system.

Tip: American Express allows its cardholders to obtain traveler's checks (and in some instances cash) overseas from its offices on presentation of their card and a personal check. You can also arrange for cash advances on your card. There are daily limits based on whether you hold a green, gold, or platinum American Express card.

Traveler's Checks

Traveler's checks are generally safer than cash because they can be replaced. They are usually easy to cash and convert in all but the most difficult venues. You can obtain them in U.S. dollars as well as in most other major currencies, allowing you to keep your funds in a stable currency until you need to use them. Many banks will issue traveler's checks to their established customers at no extra charge.

An Introduction to Foreign Exchange

One of the added uncertainties of conducting trade on an international basis is the fluctuation in exchange rates among currencies. The relative value between the U.S. dollar and the seller's currency may change between the time the deal is made and the time payment is received. A devaluation or rise in the foreign currency against the dollar causes either a windfall or a loss to one party or the other involved in the transaction.

For example, if the buyer has agreed to pay 200,000 French francs (F) for a shipment and the franc is valued at US$0.19 (its approximate value in Fall 1994), the buyer would expect to pay US$38,000. If the franc later rose in value to 19.5 cents—an increase of just over 2.5%, a not unlikely occurrence in the volatile short-term foreign exchange market—payment at the new rate would require US$39,000, for an added cost of US$1,000 to the importer. On the other hand, if the foreign currency fell in value to 18.5 cents, the importer would have to pay only US$37,000, saving US$1,000. Most exporters and importers prefer to avoid such risk rather than speculate on fluctuations in foreign exchange markets.

One of the simplest ways for a U.S. importer to avoid this type of risk is to quote prices and establish payment in U.S. dollars which places the burden and risk on the seller. Fortunately, the U.S. dollar is widely accepted as an international trading currency, and U.S. firms can often arrange to execute contracts and payments in dollars.

If the exporter/seller asks to receive payment in a foreign currency, the importer should consult an international banker before negotiating the purchase contract. Banks can offer advice on foreign exchange trends and risks. Many international banks can also help the importer hedge against such a risk if necessary.

Terms and Concepts

International trade and other transactions involving cross-border flows of funds require the participants to enter the world of foreign exchange. Foreign exchange is defined as claims payable in a foreign country in a foreign currency. (Foreign exchange is often referred to as forex or simply abbreviated as FX.) As a rule, businesses and individuals operate using their own national currencies—money recognized and legally acceptable for transactions (legal tender) within the particular currency zone (the territorial area in which a given currency is recognized, usually coinciding with national boundaries).

For example, the seller in Japan usually wants to be paid in his or her own currency—the yen (¥)—rather than in that of the importer, who in this case operates using U.S. dollars (US$). However, the seller may on occasion prefer to be paid in deutschemarks (DM) in order to pay off obligations due to a German firm in that currency. And the French business traveler going to Montreal to negotiate a deal needs to pay expenses in Canadian dollars (Can$) rather than in French francs (F). A British investor may need to convert English pounds sterling (£) into Dutch guilders (G) to put funds into a venture in that country.

All of these scenarios require the participants to convert a home currency into one or more foreign currencies or vice versa.

Currencies

A currency which can be readily exchanged for another is known as a convertible currency. If it can be fully, readily, and legally converted under virtually all circumstances, a currency is referred to as being unrestricted. Many countries maintain restricted convertibility on their currencies, often allowing full convertibility only for nonresidents while limiting the ability of residents to exchange domestic for foreign currencies. Other countries have inconvertible currencies, which cannot legally be taken out of the country or exchanged for foreign currencies at all. Yet other countries distinguish between foreign exchange involving current transactions (for goods and services) and those involving capital investments, with freedom of convertibility being restricted to some degree for one category or the other. This situation often results in what is known as a two-tier market, in which access to restricted currency is rationed and those who need it must obtain special authorization to acquire it. Such exchange controls ration the availability of foreign currency, which can block imports into the country. These limitations often result in a thriving illicit black market trade in currencies and commodities.

Hard currencies are those of large, strong economies which have few if any restrictions on the use and exchange of their currencies, while soft currencies are those for which there is little or no demand due to restrictions on free exchange (this is usually also a function of a limited or weak economy). International financial operations are usually transacted using key currencies, that is those which are relatively strong, broadly convertible, and generally accepted. Such currencies, sometimes referred to as reserve currencies, are used as a store of liquid wealth by other countries, which keep their international reserves in these hard currencies. The US$, ¥, £, DM, F, Can$, G (also abbreviated as "f," for Dutch florin), and Swiss franc (SwF) are generally considered to be key or reserve currencies, and most international business is transacted using—or at least with reference to—these currencies.

Rates of Exchange

The exchange rate is simply the amount of a nation's currency that can be bought at a given time for a specified amount of the currency of another country. For example, as of September 30, 1994, $/¥=98.48, meaning that one U.S. dollar was equal to 98.48 Japanese yen. The exchange rate is given either as a direct quote—expressed as the number of units of a foreign currency per US$ (1.547DM/$), or as an indirect quote, expressed as the number of US$ per unit of foreign currency (.646$/DM), which is the reciprocal of the first quote. Because the US$ is the most commonly traded currency, international foreign exchange transactions are usually quoted directly using the US$ as the reference point. Thus an inquiry from a Swiss bank to a German bank about their rates would be quoted not in SwF/DM but in DM/US$, even though both parties understand that the Swiss bank is interested in the rate of the DM against the SwF, not the US$.

This necessitates the use of cross-rates, in which currencies are not compared directly with each other but in terms of a reference currency which serves as a common denominator. For example, in order to find the rate for the SwF/DM, you must first have quotes on both currencies in US$ (1.2845SwF/US$ and 1.547DM/US$), then use them to calculate the rate for SwF/DM with reference to the common dollar rates of each (1.2845/1.547=.83SwF/DM).

Forex traders quote bid and ask price ranges, with the first figure always that at which they stand ready to buy currencies and the second (always higher) figure that at which they are willing to sell. This difference is conceptually similar to buying wholesale and selling retail, and constitutes the spread, or base profit margin for the institution. Professional traders deal not in full quotes but in a shorthand, referred to as pips or ticks. These are the last decimal places in a quote, usually 1/100th, or .001, of a percent (professionals are assumed to know the base rates and deal only in the marginal fluctuations).

The necessary series of conversions allows for the possibility of arbitrage, which involves taking advantage of temporal and spatial anomalies in pricing in the international currency markets. If, as in the example above, the German bank's price on SwF is less than the Swiss bank can get for them in Hong Kong, it will buy SwF from the German bank and immediately sell them to the Hong Kong bank to make a profit on the price differential. However, because virtually all international currency transactions are quoted against the US$ and because instant communications and 24-hour trading compensate for distance and time differences, the opportunities for such arbitrage are few. Professional traders now generally use the term to refer to trading for the institution's own account rather than for that of a client.

The actual amount received in a conversion, or the effective exchange rate, usually differs from the stated rate because it takes into account all taxes, commissions, and other costs that the public must pay to complete the transaction and actually receive the foreign funds.

Setting Exchange Rates

The relative value of one currency against another depends on a variety of economic and political factors, but ultimately it boils down to supply and demand. The main economic factor is the equilibrium rate, or purchasing power parity, at which goods would cost the same in each country. This ignores many important factors, such as quality, exportability, and long-term capital flow issues, but serves as a useful approximation of the relative strength of currencies against each other. If the same amount of currency in country A buys the same goods as an equivalent amount of currency in country B, the currencies are at parity. If the same amount of currency buys more goods in country A than in country B, then the currency of country A is undervalued and/or that of country B is overvalued.

A nation's current account balance (the sum of the value of goods and services it has exported during a given period netted against the value of those imported during the same period plus any transfer payments remitted abroad) can be used as a barometer of a country's economic strength. If the economy is consistently in a surplus position, that is it has received more than it has paid out, its currency can be expected to strengthen, or appreciate (rise in value) over time. Conversely, in a deficit position—one in which it spends more than it takes in—its currency will be expected to weaken, or depreciate (lose value) with respect to that of trading partners maintaining a surplus. Most countries keep foreign currency reserves to pay for current needs and serve as a cushion for fluctuations in the international income and outgo of funds.

Nations generally try to manage their currencies to maintain stable exchange rates against those of their trading partners. This can be done in a number of ways. The authorities may attempt to maintain a fixed exchange rate in which the value of their currency is linked to a commodity, such as gold, or to another strong currency, such as the US$. When a currency is linked directly to that of a stronger country (usually its main trading partner), it is said to be pegged to that of the stronger country whose lead it follows. The nations of the world have generally been unable to maintain such fixed rates in the volatile and increasingly integrated global economy of the 20th century, leading to the use of floating rates. Since the 1970s, most national currencies have floated, allowing their value to be determined through fluctuations against a variety of other currencies.

Floats can be clean, that is, determined solely by market forces without official interference (a situation that never really occurs in the real world), or dirty—managed to a greater or lesser extent by government authorities. Although some governments arbitrarily set exchange rates and policies to enforce them, such management usually involves intervention, or attempts to influence markets. This is accomplished primarily through open market operations in which the government buys or sells large quantities of its own or another country's currency or securities in an attempt to influence the relationship between the two by altering supply and demand factors. Because foreign exchange markets are so large and active, it has become virtually impossible for any government or international agency to effectively exercise control over exchange rates.

In practice, floating exchange systems rely on a variety of mechanisms to set actual prices. The main ones involve trade-weighted rates which hinge on the degree of importance of a given country's trade with the nation. A variation of this is to use a basket of currencies in which the exchange rate is figured in proportion to the value of the various currencies among the designated countries. This has been implemented by such schemes as the snake, a system in which northern European countries agreed to keep their currencies within a certain proportional relationship to each other (because adjustments occurred serially rather than simultaneously, the effect of such changes as they worked through the system was thought to resemble the undulations of a snake). The crawling peg—in which a country with a subsidiary currency commits to adjust by incremental stages to maintain its agreed upon level with respect to the stronger currency that it tracks—represents a further variation on this theme. Often the pegged currency will have a daily or weekly limit on how much it can rise or fall to adapt to the target currency. The fixed band within which a currency is allowed to fluctuate is called the grid.

On occasion a currency cannot move either rapidly or far enough by using such mechanisms to reach an equilibrium point. The authorities must then realign, or change the official value of, the currency. Such realignments may require officials to devalue—officially reduce its value relative to that of the currency of another country—or revalue—officially raise its value relative to that of another country. In devaluation, the country's currency buys less, hurting imports (but also perhaps boosting sales of its now-cheaper exports). Upward revaluation allows the country to buy more abroad with its more valuable currency, but usually cuts into overseas sales of its now more expensive exports.

The Mechanics of Foreign Exchange Operations

Most foreign exchange trading stems from the need to acquire foreign currency for a specific transaction. If the conversion is for use in a current transaction, it occurs in the spot market at the current price, or spot rate, for immediate delivery (actually within two business days). If the foreign exchange is required for a future transaction, it occurs in the forward market for future delivery. The basic difference between the prices in the spot and forward markets is due to the relative levels of interest rates in the two countries. If a currency is actually held by the party, it can earn interest between now and when it is needed at prevailing money market rates. Or, conversely, it must be borrowed at a cost commensurate with the value of the interest earnings foregone by the lender. So the forward price will include the amount of interest which could be earned during the period, usually making forward rates higher than spot rates due to this premium.

However, there are instances in which other economic or political factors cause a currency to depreciate so that it can be bought more cheaply in the future than in the present. When such a discount or markdown exists, it is profitable to buy the currency forward rather than at spot prices.

Hedging Risks

The ability to buy forward foreign exchange allows businesses to hedge their risks by counterbalancing a current transaction through a similar future transaction to offset the effects of price changes during the interim. In currency trading this is often accomplished through a swap—the spot purchase (or sale) of foreign exchange and a simultaneous forward sale (or purchase) of the same currency. A spot purchase coupled with a future sale is known as an outward swap, while a spot sale linked to a forward purchase is an inward swap. A forward purchase or sale not covered by an offsetting spot transaction is known an outright transaction. Actual holdings of a currency are known as long positions, while those with uncovered future positions, that is with net indebtedness, are said to be short of exchange.

It is possible to buy forward (or futures) contracts for set amounts of major currency deliverable at a specified future date. These can vary from short-term spot/next swaps (in which the spot side is the current price and the offsetting closeout position is the price on the next business day) and tom/next swaps (in which the current price is that for the next business day and the offsetting position is valued at the price for the next business day after that) to positions as far out as one year.

Standard futures contracts are for two, three, six, and 12 months, but coverage can be achieved for intermediate periods through contracts that specify broken dates—those which fall between two standard contracts. In this case the rates are interpolated between those of the standard contracts. Most entities hedge long-term risks by rolling over a series of short-term contracts.

Options

While futures—contracts to buy or sell a specified quantity of foreign currency at a stated date in the future, the basis of forward transactions—are useful for hedging risks, options are largely speculative instruments. Options contracts allow foreign exchange traders the right to buy (call) or sell (put) specified quantities of currencies at a point in the future. If an option is in the money—that is the actual price is above the exercise price and therefore the option is profitable—it can be exercised. If it is out of the money (the exercise price being below the actual price and therefore unprofitable to exercise), it can be allowed to expire. Options traders seldom if ever take delivery of the actual currencies but simply close out the profitable contracts for the amount of the profit. Contracts known as American options can be exercised at any time during the life of the contract, while European options can only be exercised on the expiration date.

Markets

Despite the growth of trade and an increasingly interdependent global economy, most foreign exchange trading involves financial institutions trading for their own accounts rather than straight business transactions on behalf of clients. Such activity serves to add depth and liquidity to the forex market. Because of the high turnover in self- liquidating transactions—many of which are highly leveraged—the nominal dollar value of the volume of such trade far outstrips that of the underlying economic and monetary base that supports it. Major foreign exchange markets are run out of New York, London, Frankfurt, Amsterdam, Zurich, Singapore, Hong Kong, and Tokyo, but traders can operate anywhere thanks to modern communications links. Trading is most active during the business hours in these respective locations, but can occur 24-hours a day.

Euromarkets—consisting of informal markets to deal in transactions involving a currency outside of its country of origin—provide offshore international access to funds unencumbered by governmental regulation. London, Frankfurt, Zurich, and Amsterdam are the main centers of this trade. The US$ accounts for about two-thirds of the Euromarket, with the DM, SwF, and ¥ collectively making up as much as one-quarter of the remainder. The Asian dollar market, operating primarily out of Singapore, is also growing rapidly. Again the US$ is the primary currency, but use of the ¥ is increasing. By some accounts, more US$ are traded in such markets than in the domestic market. For example, the average daily turnover in the Singapore Asian dollar market was nearly US$75 billion in 1990.

Within the U.S., futures contracts are handled through the International Monetary Market of the Chicago Mercantile Exchange. Standard foreign exchange options are traded through the Philadelphia Stock Exchange and the Chicago Board Options Exchange. Many large, internationally-oriented banks will write specific nonstandard futures contracts to cover the needs of clients.

Documentary Credits (Letters of Credit)

General Section

The following material has been provided by Swiss Bank Corporation. World Trade Press gratefully acknowledges Swiss Bank Corporation for their contribution.

Growing economic interdependence and new transport possibilities have now made it feasible to do business with even the remotest corners of our planet. For many transactions, both prepayment and supply of the goods on a credit basis are out of the question. Besides, many countries have sunk deeply into debt in recent years. These trends have increased the desire for security on the part of both sellers and buyers.

If the purchase contract or similar agreement provides for payment against a documentary credit, it is up to the buyer to instruct his bank to open a documentary credit in favour of the seller.

The documentary credit is a

commitment on the bank's part to place an agreed sum at the seller's disposal on behalf of the buyer under precisely defined conditions.

When the seller receives such a documentary credit, he knows that a party independent of the buyer will make payment as soon as he has delivered the goods and the bank has handed over the prescribed documents and fulfilled the other conditions of the documentary credit. The buyer, on the other hand, is sure that the documentary credit amount will be released only against receipt of the documents he has specified.

So it is nothing more than a typical cash-on-delivery transaction requiring simultaneous performance. The documentary credit makes it possible to bridge both distance and time.

The Bank as Fiduciary

The bank assumes an extremely important fiduciary function between the parties. On the one hand, it must make certain on behalf of the issuing bank that the guaranteed sum is released only when the credit conditions have been complied with to the letter. On the other hand, the bank should do everything possible to safeguard the interests of the beneficiary (seller)—usually a customer of the advising, confirming bank—vis-à-vis the buyer should the documents fail to meet the credit conditions in any respect.

The "Uniform Customs and Practice for Documentary Credits"

In the course of time, a number of practices, expressions and terms have evolved between banks dealing with documentary credits. To ensure uniformity of interpretation in international trade, the International Chamber of Commerce in Paris has worked out the "Uniform Customs and Practice for Documentary Credits." These have been revised and brought up to date several times in the past. They are now applied by the banks in nearly all countries.

For the sake of simplicity, we shall refer to these rules in this publication with the abbreviation

UCPDC

(**U**niform **C**ustoms and **P**ractice for **D**ocumentary **C**redits).

The UCPDC states that it should be applied for all transactions where a bank is instructed by a customer to make a payment or to accept bills of exchange against receipt of certain documents.

The Term "Documentary Credit"

For the sake of simplicity, the expression "credit" will be used in this publication.

In actual practice, however, a number of different expressions have emerged for this type of business, all of which basically mean the same thing. People speak of "documentary letter of credit," "commercial letter of credit," "letter of credit" (L/C, elcee, LoC) or "Lettre de Crédit." In its forms, Swiss Bank Corporation uses the expression "documentary credit."

Different Terms

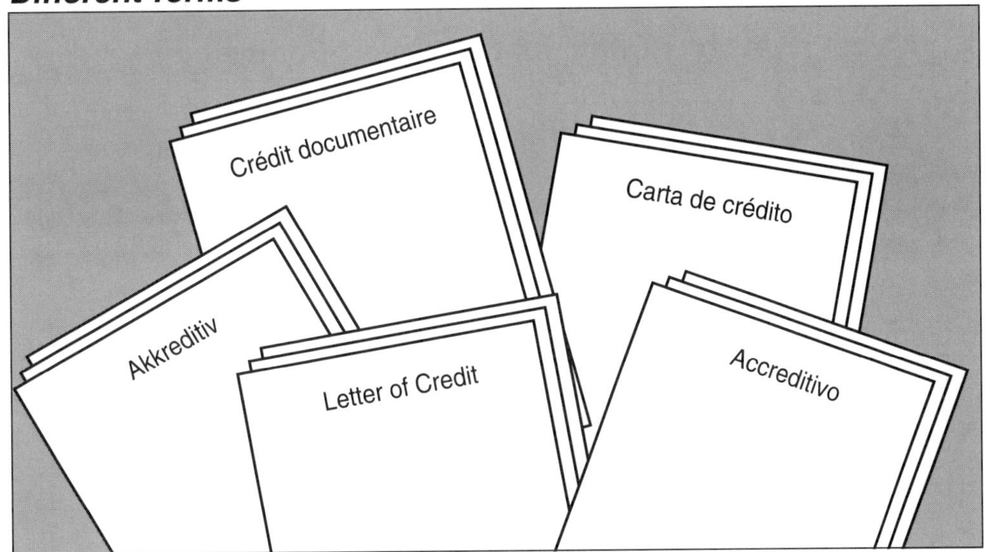

Some Important Principles

- Credits are separate transactions from the purchase contracts or other contracts on which they are based.

  Only the wording of the credit is binding on the bank.

As far as customers are concerned, this means that the banks act only on the basis of the credit's text in carrying out the transaction, and cannot take into account any contract provisions that differ from the credit wording. The same applies to contracts modified at a later date without the credit text being changed accordingly. In this case, too, the bank will act exclusively in accordance with the valid credit wording when receiving and checking the documents.

- **Banks deal exclusively with the documents and not with goods (or services, etc.).**

All the banks do is check, on the basis of documents presented to them, whether the conditions of the credit are fulfilled. They are not able to verify whether the goods supplied actually agree with those specified in the credit. The banks cannot be held liable for discrepancies between the goods invoiced and those actually delivered. It is up to the buyer and seller to settle questions of this nature between themselves.

Buyers' complaints are settled directly between buyer and seller.

- **Banks assume no responsibility for the authenticity, form or validity of the documents.**

The banks examine the documents they receive under a credit with due care. They check whether the documents appear on their face to comply with the specified terms and conditions.

- **Banks assume no responsibility for the acts of third parties taking any part in the credit transaction.**

  Banks assume no liability for

- delays, through no fault of their own, in the transmission of messages
- consequences of Acts of God
- acts of correspondent banks or other third parties whom they have instructed to carry out the transaction.

The Main Parties to a Documentary Credit Transaction

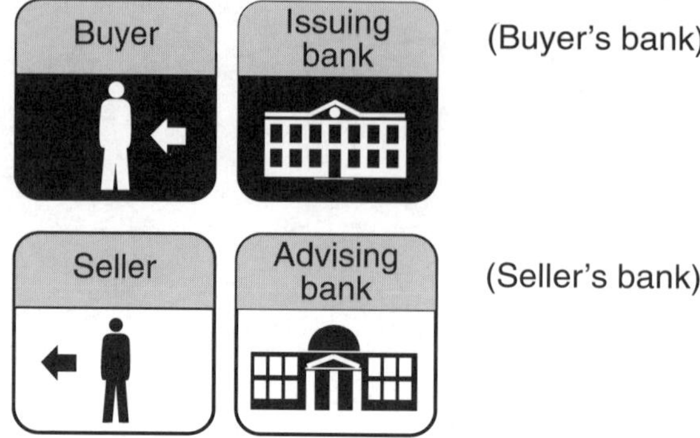

How a Documentary Credit Functions

Acting in accordance with the agreements between seller and buyer, the buyer instructs his bank to open a credit.

Before the bank acts on the instructions, it checks whether the customer's balances or credit facilities will permit the payment to be made under the documentary credit.

If the bank is asked to open a documentary credit in favour of a foreign seller, it generally utilizes the services of a correspondent bank, if possible at the same location as the seller. This second bank is referred to as the advising bank. It forwards the credit of the issuing bank to the beneficiary.

Following receipt, the beneficiary checks whether he can meet the conditions mentioned in the credit and whether they agree with those stated in the purchase contract or other agreements.

If this is not the case, he asks the buyer directly to modify the credit conditions.

If the credit agrees with the purchase contract and the stipulated conditions can be met, the exporter will start manufacturing the goods or deliver them from stock. Following shipment, the beneficiary will assemble the required documents and present them to the advising bank.

The advising bank checks whether the documents received agree with the conditions of the credit in all respects. Afterwards it makes payment in the manner prescribed in the credit and transmits the documents to the issuing bank. The latter reimburses the advising bank the amount specified by the documents.

Issuance

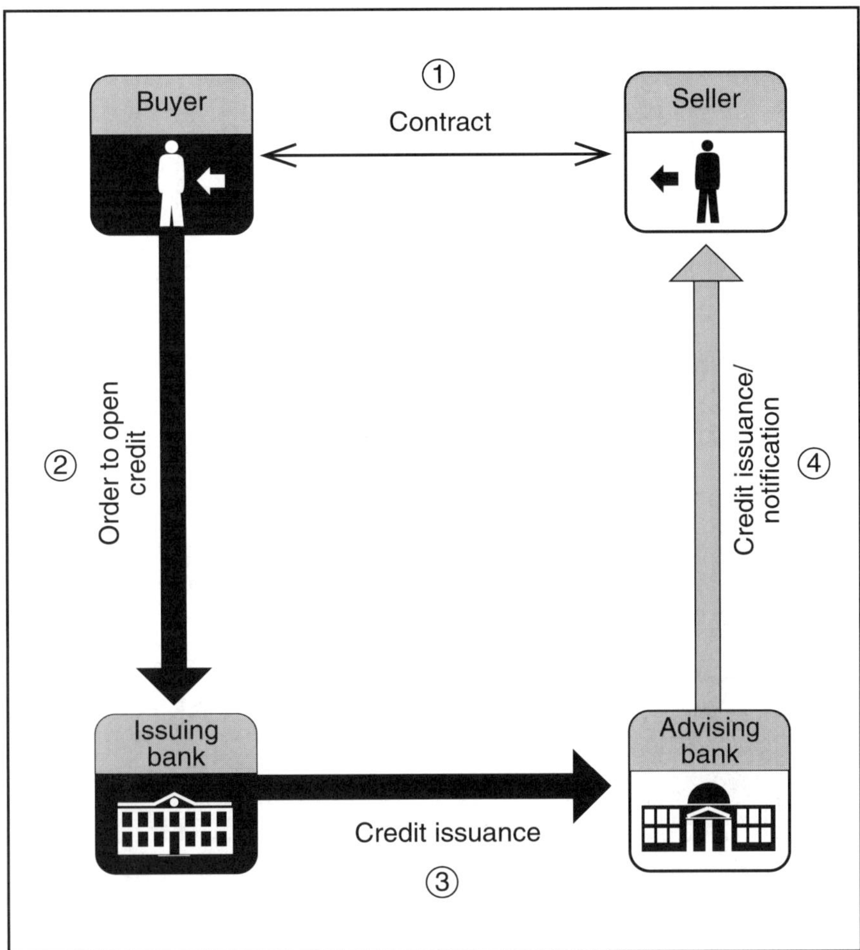

Issuance of a Letter of Credit

① **Buyer and seller agree on purchase contract.**

② **Buyer applies for and opens a letter of credit with issuing ("buyer's") bank.**

③ **Issuing bank issues the letter of credit, forwarding it to advising ("seller's") bank.**

④ **Advising bank notifies seller of letter of credit.**

Amendment

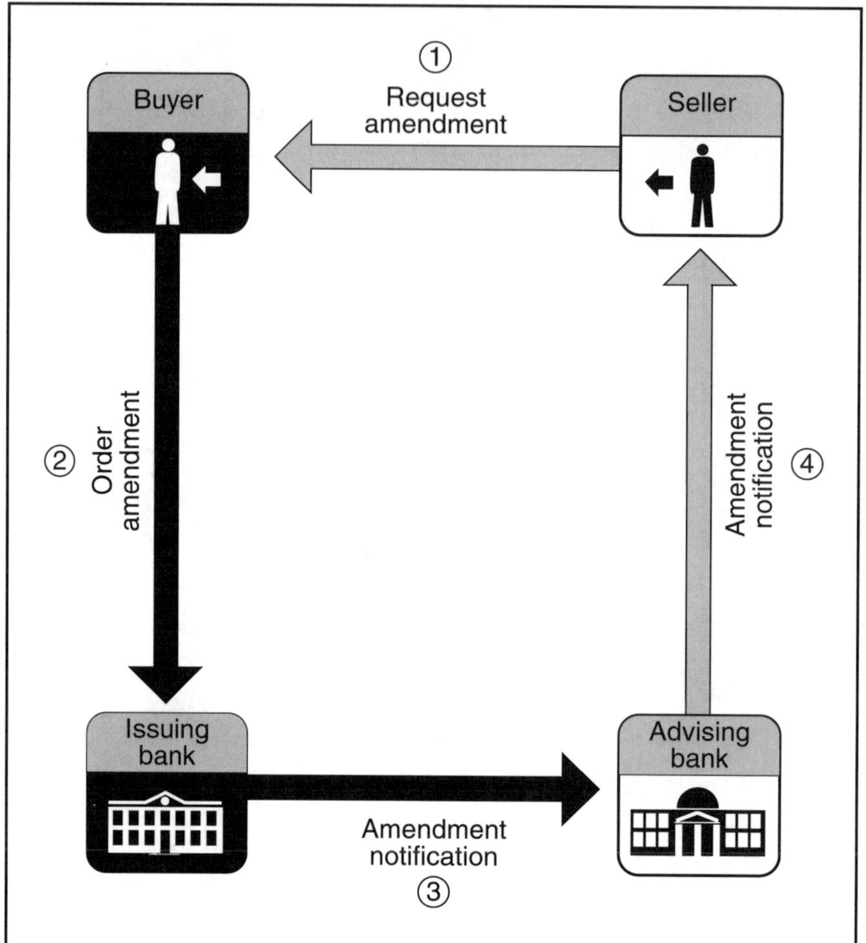

Amendment of a Letter of Credit

① **Seller requests (of the buyer) a modification (amendment) of the terms of the letter of credit. Once new terms are agreed upon:**

② **Buyer issues order to issuing ("buyer's") bank to make an amendment to the terms of the letter of credit.**

③ **Issuing bank notifies advising ("seller's") bank of amendment.**

④ **Advising bank notifies seller of amendment.**

Utilization

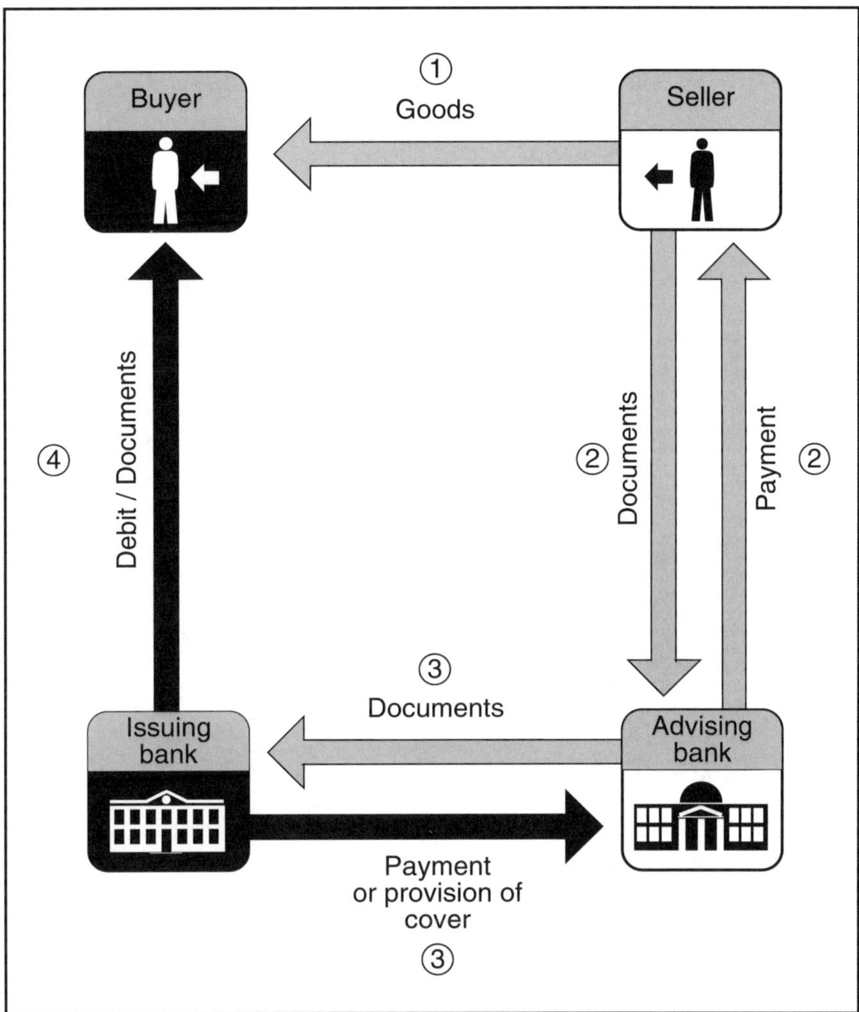

Utilization of a Letter of Credit

① **Seller ships goods to buyer.**

② **Seller forwards all documents (as stipulated in the letter of credit) to advising bank. Once documents are reviewed and accepted, advising bank pays seller for goods.**

③ **Advising bank forwards documents to issuing bank. Once documents are reviewed and accepted, issuing bank pays advising bank.**

④ **Issuing bank forwards documents to buyer. Seller's letter of credit, or account is debited.**

Forms of Documentary Credits

1. The revocable credit

The revocable credit can be modified or cancelled at any time. Because it offers little security, this form is hardly ever used.

2. The irrevocable credit

The issuing bank (buyer's bank) commits itself irrevocably to honour its obligation under the credit, provided that the beneficiary complies with all conditions.

Thus the beneficiary receives a firm undertaking of the issuing bank, giving him the security he desires.

There are two types of irrevocable credits:

a) The irrevocable credit not confirmed by the advising bank

Irrevocable documentary credits always involve a commitment on the part of the issuing bank to pay. In this case, the advising bank does not make any payment commitment. It merely acts on behalf of the issuing bank.

The Irrevocable Credit not Confirmed by the Advising Bank

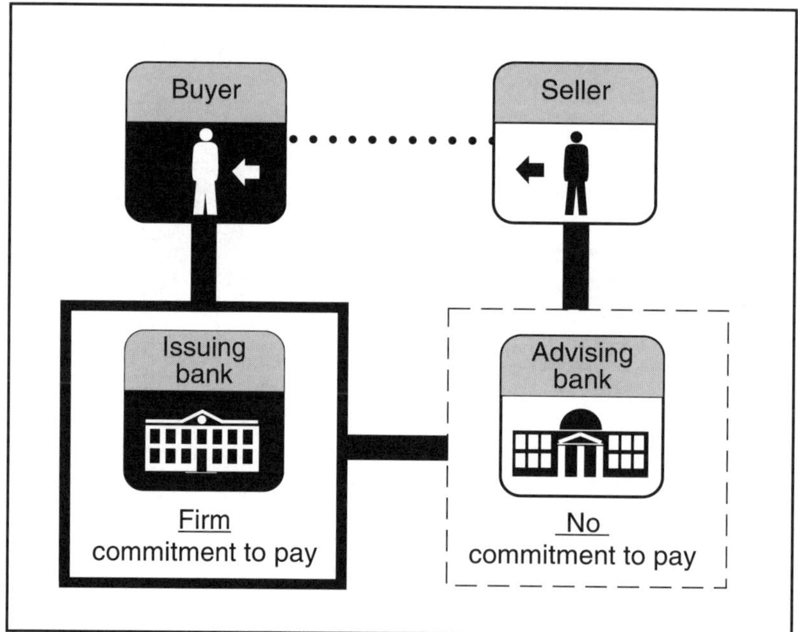

b) The irrevocable, confirmed credit

By confirming the credit, the advising bank enters into a commitment to pay that is independent of, and in addition to, the issuing bank's commitment. The confirming bank undertakes to honour its commitment regardless of whether or not the issuing bank is in a position to reimburse it.

The Irrevocable Confirmed Credit

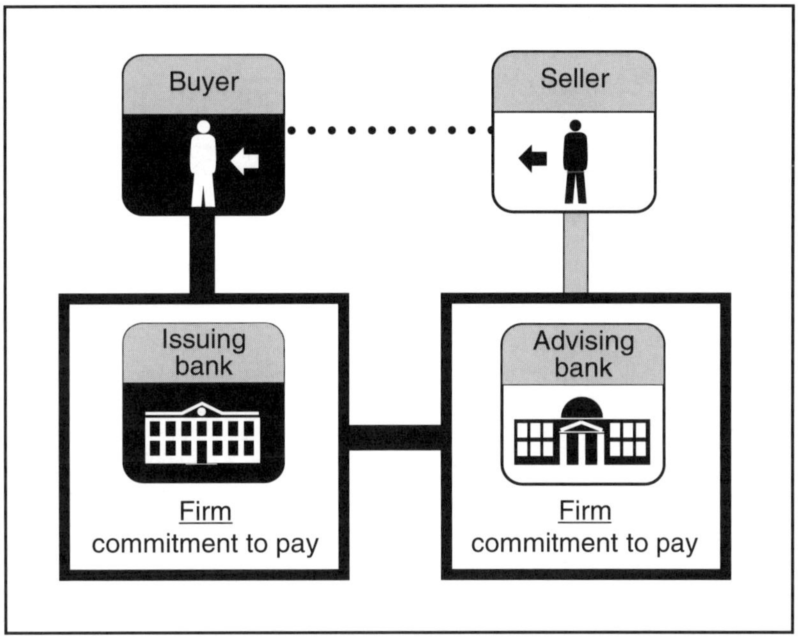

The documentary credit that affords an exporter the most security is one issued irrevocably by a foreign bank and confirmed by a domestic bank.

Availability

1. The sight credit

The amount is payable as soon as the prescribed documents have been presented and the bank has checked them. So the proceeds are normally at the immediate disposal of the beneficiary.

In some cases (e.g., foreign currencies) a few days may pass between presentation of the documents and actual transfer of the funds. As a rule it is the time required by the banks to remit the amount of the credit.

In the case of unconfirmed credits, situations can arise where the advising bank delays payment to the beneficiary until it has received the amount specified by the documents from the issuing bank.

2. The credit available against time drafts (usance credit)

In addition to presenting the documents, the beneficiary is required to draw a time draft on a specific bank (issuing, advising, or a third bank). After the documents have been found to be in order, the exporter receives the draft back after it has been accepted by the drawee bank, if he so wishes.

It is possible to discount this bank acceptance. So the draft can be cashed in immediately by the seller, while the buyer will be charged with the draft amount only upon maturity.

3. The deferred payment credit

The payment is not initiated immediately upon presentation of the documents, but only after a period of time specified in the credit.

A deferred payment credit allows the buyer a grace period, and ensures the seller that payment will be made on the due date.

Special Documentary Credits

1. Stand-by letter of credit

The stand-by letter of credit is a guarantee declaration in the broadest sense. It is used mainly in the USA, because American banks are prevented from giving guarantees by the regulations in that country.

Stand-by letters of credit can be used, for example, to guarantee the following types of payment and performance:

- repayment of loans
- fulfillment of subcontracts
- securing the payment of goods deliveries by third parties independent of the recipient

2. The revolving credit

The revolving credit is a commitment on the part of the issuing bank to restore the credit to the original amount after it has been utilized. The number of utilizations and the period of time within which these must take place are specified in the credit. It is either cumulative or non-cumulative. Cumulative means that unutilized sums can be added to the next instalment. In the case of non-cumulative credits, partial amounts not utilized in time expire.

The revolving credit is used in cases where a buyer wishes to have certain partial quantities of the ordered goods delivered at specified intervals (multiple delivery contract).

3. The transferable letter of credit

The beneficiary specified in the transferable letter of credit has the option of instructing his bank to transfer the credit fully or in part to another beneficiary.

4. The back-to-back credit

The "back-to-back" credit is a new credit opened on the basis of an already existing, *nontransferable* credit (original credit) in favour of another beneficiary (i.e., back-to-back).

The Documentary Credit and the Exporter

What benefits does the credit provide?

- The bank pays as specified in the credit independent of the buyer.
- The buyer cannot withhold the payment under any pretence.
- If the buyer wishes to complain about the goods, he must do this separately from the documentary credit, which gives the exporter a stronger negotiating position.
- The sort of delays that can occur in transmitting bank transfers are avoided to a large extent.
- Payments under documentary credits are generally made faster.

The exporter enjoys these advantages only if he adheres precisely to the conditions of the credit.

It should be noted that, in the case of credits in foreign currencies, the exchange risk can be eliminated by means of a forward sale of foreign exchange.

Which type of credit should the exporter demand?

Whether, for a particular transaction, it is better to open an irrevocable credit not confirmed by the advising bank or one confirmed by it depends on the circumstances of the particular case and the degree of security the exporter feels he needs.

- An irrevocable, unconfirmed credit:

  if the buyer's country has stable political conditions and an efficient banking system, and if the goods supplied are a product that could easily be sold to someone else if necessary.

- An irrevocable, confirmed credit:

  if any of the aforementioned points are not the case.

The longer the delivery period, the more difficult it becomes to evaluate how the risk will develop with regard to the buyer's country and the banks there. If the goods to be delivered are the type that have very few potential customers or are made to order, substantial losses can be suffered if the documents are refused.

The exporter can restrict these risks by requesting an irrevocable credit confirmed by the advising bank.

The exporter should also prescribe that a credit be opened which requires the documents to be presented in his country and is also payable there. Otherwise, he would have to bear the possible consequences of loss of the documents in the mail or delayed transmission of them to the issuing bank. As a rule, it is impossible to confirm a credit payable in other countries.

What does the exporter do before the contract is closed?

- Makes enquiries about the creditworthiness and business practices of the buyer. The bank will generally be prepared to assist the exporter in obtaining this sort of information.
- Finds out which bank the buyer works with. The credit is normally issued by the bank with which the buyer maintains his account.
- Enquires about the regulations and experience of others in dealing with the buyer's country. Foreign currency restrictions and other rules in the buyer's country can delay the issuance of the credit. Chambers of commerce and the banks will be happy to provide the exporter with this information.
- If the exporter is prepared to supply the goods against an irrevocable credit not confirmed by the other bank, he enquires about the standing of the credit-issuing bank in the buyer's country.
- If he desires an irrevocable credit that is confirmed by his bank, he asks the bank whether it is ready and willing to confirm credits emanating from the buyer's country and the bank in question.

The supply contract should be formulated in such a way that no difficulties arise later with regard to the credit's nature, conditions or procedure.

- For example, one should not readily accept contract provisions that specify credit documents such as acceptance reports, progress reports, etc., that have to be signed by the buyer.

  By refusing to sign such documents, the buyer can block the credit's availability.

It is therefore advisable to demand a "no later than" clause as a credit condition, which provides for utilization of the credit without presentation of any papers countersigned by the buyer. For instance:

x% of the credit sum is payable against presentation of an acceptance report, signed by... (Buyer), but no later than... months after shipment, against the Seller's declaration that the contract conditions have been fulfilled and the object supplied is operating properly.

In this case, it is not necessary to present the acceptance report.

What does the exporter do at contract closure?

The supply contract should contain the main data of the credit to be provided by the buyer, e.g.:

- Issuing bank
- Confirmation by the exporter's bank
- Time allowed for payment
- Validity period
- Bearer of the documentary credit expenses

Sample Supply Contract

Contract

xxx
xx
xxxxx

xxx
xxxxx
xxxx

xxxxx
xx

To secure payment, the buyer shall have bank x open an irrevocable credit (which is to be confirmed by bank y). The credit must remain valid for x months (corresponding to the delivery period) after issuance and be available at sight against presentation of the following documents:

. . . .
. . . .
. . . .

The cost of the credit shall be borne in full by the buyer.

The documents prescribed can vary considerably depending upon the import regulations in the buyer's country and the buyer's wishes.

The validity period of the credit should be set long enough to provide a reasonable amount of latitude and should include the time required for submission of the documents.

If the exporter is required by the contract to bear expenses arising in Switzerland, he should ask the bank for an estimate of the charges.

What does the exporter do when the credit arrives?

- Immediately upon receipt of the credit, the exporter checks whether its conditions agree with those of the supply contract and whether he is capable of complying with the clauses of the credit to the letter.
- If individual conditions of the credit have to be amended, which can be very time-consuming, the exporter should contact the buyer immediately so that the latter can instruct the issuing bank to make the required modifications.
- The modification becomes effective only when the exporter has received notification of the amendment from the advising/confirming bank.
- In the case of credits in foreign currency, the exporter decides whether to accept the concomitant risks himself or enter into a forward exchange transaction with the bank.
- Now the exporter should read the relevant Articles of the UCPDC and act in accordance with them.

If the exporter fails to comply with even one of the credit's stipulations, the security afforded by the credit is lost, because it is possible to refuse acceptance of the documents in such cases.

Checklist (Upon Receipt of the Credit)

1. Are my name and address correct?	☐
2. Is the amount correct?	☐
3. Are the terms of delivery correct? (CIF, FOB, etc.)	☐
4. Is the validity period sufficiently long?	☐
5. Does the credit's availability form agree with the contract conditions?	☐
6. Can the goods be shipped by the prescribed transport route?	☐
7. Can the provisions relating to partial shipments and transhipment be met?	☐
8. Can I meet the shipping date?	☐
9. Certain goods are accepted by shipping companies for deck stowage only. If this is the case, is "on deck" stowage authorized?	☐
10. Can the insurance company provide the coverage specified?	☐
11. Are the goods correctly described?	☐
12. Is the credit confirmed?	☐
13. Can I present the documents with all of the clauses stipulated in the credit within the prescribed period?	☐
14. Does the forwarding agent have a copy of the credit?	☐

What does the exporter have to bear in mind when preparing the documents?

Documents that agree with the credit conditions in all respects make it possible for the credit to function without any snags.

The exporter should observe the following points when preparing the documents:

The invoice

- Is generally made out to the buyer specified in the credit.
- Is made out in the same currency as the credit amount.
- Contains exactly the same description of the goods as the credit.
- Value of the goods, individual prices and delivery terms agree with those specified in the credit.
- Any special notations, confirmations and attestations specified in the credit should be included on the invoice and—if required—signed.

The bill of exchange (draft)

- It should be drawn in the language of the credit. The bill of exchange form should carry any prescribed notations and clauses.

The insurance document

The insurance document specified in the credit must be submitted.

- It should be made out in the currency of the credit.
- In the absence of a stipulation to the contrary in the credit, it must be made out for the CIF value of the goods + 10%.

If the banks cannot determine the CIF value from the documents on their face, however, they will accept a minimum insurance amount that equals either the amount for which payment is requested under the credit or the amount of the commercial invoice, whichever is greater.

- The insurance document should list those risks for which the credit requires coverage.
- The insurance document must state expressly that the goods are insured starting no later than the shipping date.
- All insurance policies/certificates issued by the insurance company should be submitted to the bank and endorsed if necessary.

Sample Bill of Exchange

① Place/Date Basle, 10th October 19.. ② US$ 23'400.--

③ At 120 days' sight please pay against this sole BILL of EXCHANGE (④ .... being unpaid)

⑤ to the order of Swiss Bank Corporation, Basle the amount of

② US Dollars twentythreethousandfourhundred ------------------------

⑥ Drawn under L/C No. 26784 dated 15th September 19..

of Universal Bank Inc., New York

⑦ Universal Bank Inc.
Park Street
New York, N.Y. 10005

MUELLER AG BASEL
Muller Reg ⑧

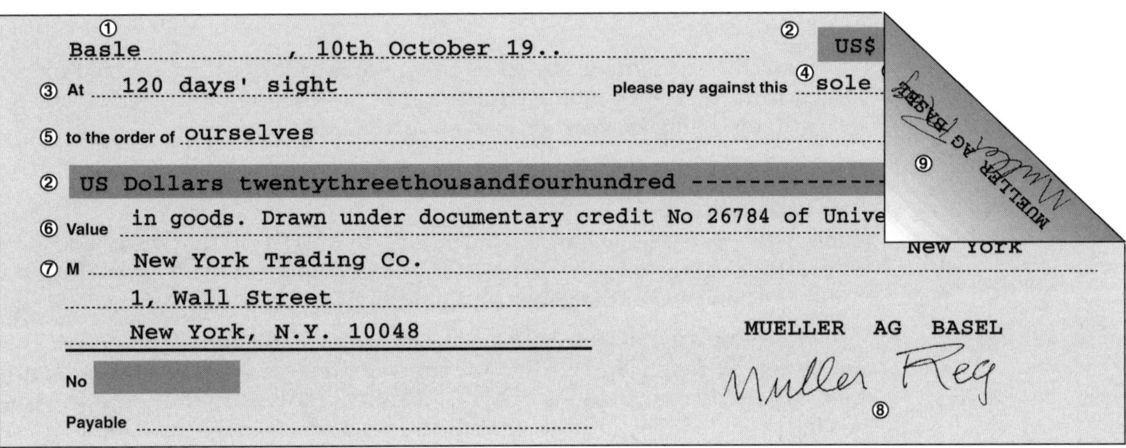

① Basle, 10th October 19.. ② US$

③ At 120 days' sight please pay against this ④ sole

⑤ to the order of ourselves

② US Dollars twentythreethousandfourhundred ------------

⑥ Value in goods. Drawn under documentary credit No 26784 of Unive

New York

⑦ M New York Trading Co.
1, Wall Street
New York, N.Y. 10048

No

Payable

MUELLER AG BASEL
Muller Reg ⑧

- ① Place drawn and date
- ② Bill of exchange currency and amount in numbers and words
- ③ Validity period
- ④ Number of originals (sole or first/second)
- ⑤ If issued to own order: endorsement required
- ⑥ Reference to credit
- ⑦ Drawee
- ⑧ Drawer (handwritten signature)
- ⑨ Endorsement

The transport documents

1. The ocean bill of lading

The banks will accept the following documents under this title:

- ocean bill of lading
- combined transport bill of lading
- short form bill of lading
- "received for shipment bill of lading," provided it carries the notation "on board."

Unless expressly permitted in the credit, the banks will reject the following bills of lading:

- charter party bills of lading
- bills of lading issued by a freight forwarder, if the forwarder does not act as carrier or as the agent of a named carrier.

2. Other marine transport documents

If the credit does not call specifically for an ocean bill of lading, the banks will accept a transport document that appears on its face to have been issued by a named carrier or his agent, and which indicates taking in charge of the goods, loading on board, or dispatch, and meets all other stipulations of the credit.

If the full set of transport documents consists of several identical originals, all of the originals should be submitted to the bank.

If these documents are drawn up to the order of the exporter or "to order," they must be endorsed.

Transport documents issued by freight forwarders will be rejected unless the document is the FIATA Combined Transport Bill of Lading (approved by the ICC) or the forwarder is acting as a carrier or agent of a named carrier.

3. The air waybill

The carrier or its agent confirms in the air waybill (AWB) that the goods have been received for carriage to the destination. This document contains information on the air route, the handling of the goods and their delivery to the consignee.

House air waybills (HAWB) are also common in the transport business today. They are issued by freight forwarders for consolidated air freight shipments. In the documentary credit transactions HAWBs are treated exactly the same as conventional AWBs, provided they indicate that the issuer itself assumes the liability as carrier or is acting as the agent of a named carrier, or if the credit expressly permits the acceptance of an HAWB.

4. Other transport documents

This heading includes, for instance:

- the postal receipt
- the rail waybill (duplicate)
- the forwarder's received bill of lading
- the road waybill

As a rule, none of these documents represents a negotiable instrument. They evidence the closure of the carriage contract between seller and carrier, and are documents in proof.

5. Additional documents

Any additional documents called for by the credit, such as certificates of origin, consular invoices, weight certificates, analysis certificates, etc., should be prepared by the parties prescribed in the credit.

In some cases, the certification and legalization of certain documents can take a considerable amount of time.

Sample Ocean Bill of Lading

BILL OF LADING FOR MULTIMODAL TRANSPORT OR PORT-TO-PORT SHIPMENT

1. SHIPPER
SWISS EXPORT LTD
INDUSTRIESTRASSE 200
8050 ZUERICH - OERLIKON

BOOKING No 55 | B/L No 2
REFERENCE No ABC/22/66 bu

2. CONSIGNEE: ORDER OF
TO ORDER

3. NOTIFY ADDRESS (carrier not responsible for failure to notify see clause 21 hereof)
TA PING CO. LTD
YACHT BUILDING
18-5, HARBOR STREET
TAIPEI / TAIWAN

Shipping company
Schiffahrtsgesellschaft
Société de transport maritime

4. Pre-carriage by (*)	5. Place of receipt (*) ANTWERP CFS
6. OCEAN VESSEL "HOLLANDIA"	7. PORT OF LOADING ROTTERDAM
8. PORT OF DISCHARGE KEELUNG	9. Place of delivery (**) KEELUNG CFS if goods to be transhipped by carrier at port of discharge.

Particulars furnished by shipper of the goods

10. Marks & Nos.	11. Number and kind of packages, description of goods	13. Gross weight kilos	14. Measurement m3
	ON BOARD - FREIGHT PREPAID		
ABC 1930-1934 VIA KEELUNG TA PING	5 CASES CIF KEELUNG "HARMLESS CHEMICALS"	kos 1050	
	IRREVOCABLE CREDIT No 25AB/26008/01		
	IMPORT LICENSE No 75 DGL - 01111		

Shipper's declaration of a value higher than the carrier's limit of liability - See clause 19:

Freight and charges
(particulars for calculation of freight only)

Freight: to be prepaid/to be collected

All agreements or freight engagements for the shipment of the goods are superseded by this Bill of Lading, except the conditions of the applicable tariff which are available from the carrier and which are deemed to be incorporated in this Bill of Lading. In case of inconsistency of any conditions of the applicable tariff with the terms stated on page 1 and 2 of this Bill of Lading the latter shall prevail unless otherwise expressly provided for herein. All the terms of this Bill of Lading, whether written, typed, stamped, or printed, are accepted and agreed by the merchant to be binding as fully as if signed by the merchant any local customs or privileges to the contrary notwithstanding. IN WITNESS WHEREOF the number of original Bills of Lading stated below all of this tenor and date has been signed, one of which being accomplished the others to stand void.

15. Freight payable at	16. Place and date of issue
ANTWERP	15.7.19
17. Number of original Bs/L 3/3	18 For the carrier FORWARDING LTD

(*) Applicable only when document used for transhipment (see clause 2 b)
(**) Applicable only when document used for INTERMODAL transportation (see clause 2 c)

Page 2

Sample Forwarder's Received Bill of Lading

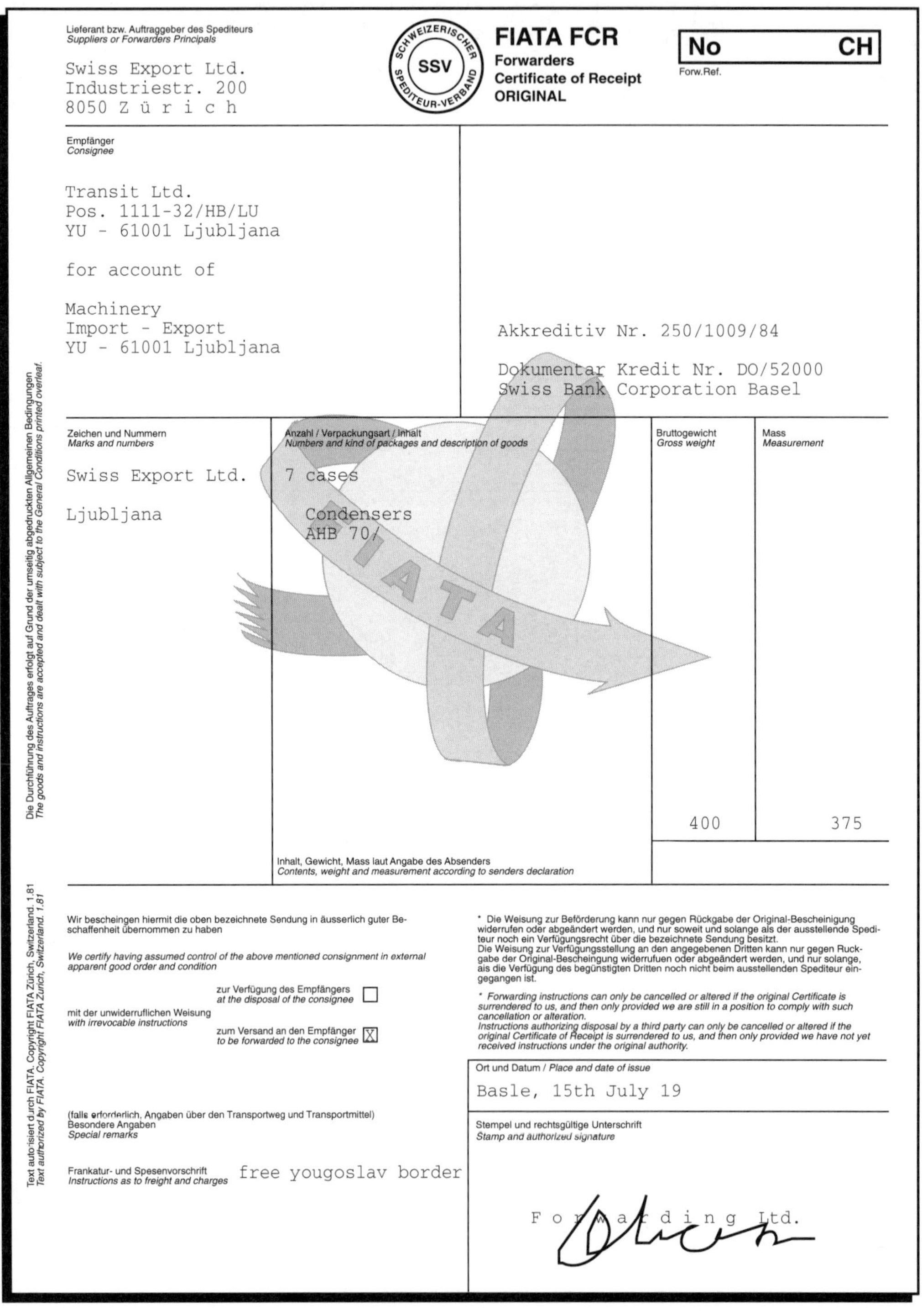

Lieferant bzw. Auftraggeber des Spediteurs
Suppliers or Forwarders Principals

Swiss Export Ltd.
Industriestr. 200
8050 Z ü r i c h

SCHWEIZERISCHER SPEDITEUR-VERBAND SSV

FIATA FCR
Forwarders Certificate of Receipt
ORIGINAL

No CH
Forw.Ref.

Empfänger
Consignee

Transit Ltd.
Pos. 1111-32/HB/LU
YU - 61001 Ljubljana

for account of

Machinery
Import - Export
YU - 61001 Ljubljana

Akkreditiv Nr. 250/1009/84

Dokumentar Kredit Nr. DO/52000
Swiss Bank Corporation Basel

Zeichen und Nummern *Marks and numbers*	Anzahl / Verpackungsart / Inhalt *Numbers and kind of packages and description of goods*	Bruttogewicht *Gross weight*	Mass *Measurement*
Swiss Export Ltd. Ljubljana	7 cases Condensers AHB 70/	400	375

Inhalt, Gewicht, Mass laut Angabe des Absenders
Contents, weight and measurement according to senders declaration

Die Durchführung des Auftrages erfolgt auf Grund der umseitig abgedruckten Allgemeinen Bedingungen
The goods and instructions are accepted and dealt with subject to the General Conditions printed overleaf.

Wir bescheingen hiermit die oben bezeichnete Sendung in äusserlich guter Beschaffenheit übernommen zu haben

We certify having assumed control of the above mentioned consignment in external apparent good order and condition

mit der unwiderruflichen Weisung
with irrevocable instructions

zur Verfügung des Empfängers
at the disposal of the consignee ☐

zum Versand an den Empfänger
to be forwarded to the consignee ☒

* Die Weisung zur Beförderung kann nur gegen Rückgabe der Original-Bescheinigung widerrufen oder abgeändert werden, und nur soweit und solange als der ausstellende Spediteur noch ein Verfügungsrecht über die bezeichnete Sendung besitzt.
Die Weisung zur Verfügungsstellung an den angegebenen Dritten kann nur gegen Ruckgabe der Original-Bescheingung widerrufuen oder abgeändert werden, und nur solange, ais die Verfügung des begünstigten Dritten noch nicht beim ausstellenden Spediteur eingegangen ist.

* *Forwarding instructions can only be cancelled or altered if the original Certificate is surrendered to us, and then only provided we are still in a position to comply with such cancellation or alteration.*
Instructions authorizing disposal by a third party can only be cancelled or altered if the original Certificate of Receipt is surrendered to us, and then only provided we have not yet received instructions under the original authority.

Ort und Datum / *Place and date of issue*

Basle, 15th July 19

(falls erforderlich, Angaben über den Transportweg und Transportmittel)
Besondere Angaben
Special remarks

Frankatur- und Spesenvorschrift
Instructions as to freight and charges free yougoslav border

Stempel und rechtsgültige Unterschrift
Stamp and authorized signature

F o r w a r d i n g Ltd.

Text autorisiert durch FIATA. Copyright FIATA Zürich, Switzerland. 1.81
Text authorized by FIATA. Copyright FIATA Zurich, Switzerland. 1.81

Sample Air Waybill

085 | BSL | 7260 2751 085-7260-2751

Shipper's Name and Address: SWISS EXPORT LTD, AIRFREIGHT DIVISION, ZUERICH

Shipper's account Number:

NOT NEGOTIABLE
AIR WAYBILL
AIR CONSIGNMENT NOTE

swissair
Issued by: Swiss Air Transport Co., Ltd., Zurich, Switzerland
Member of IATA (International Air Transport Association)

Copies 1, 2 and 3 of this Air Waybill are originals and have the same validity

Consignee's Name and Address: IMPORT KONTOR, VIENNA, Phone: 633 7876

Consignee's account Number:

It is agreed that the goods described herein are accepted in apparent good order and condition (except as noted) for carriage SUBJECT TO THE CONDITIONS OF CONTRACT ON THE REVERSE HEREOF. THE SHIPPER'S ATTENTION IS DRAWN TO THE NOTICE CONCERNING CARRIERS' LIMITATION OF LIABILITY. Shipper may increase such limitation of liability by declaring a higher value for carriage and paying a supplemental charge if required.

Issuing Carrier's Agent Name and City: FORWARDING LTD, BASLE

Accounting information

Agent's IATA Code: 81-4 0000 | Account No.:

Airport of Departure (Addr. of the Carrier) and requested Routing: BSL-VIE

to	By first Carrier (Routing and Destination)	to	by	to	by	Currency	CHGS Code	WT/VAL PPD	WT/VAL COLL	Other PPD	Other COLL	Declared Value for Carriage	Declared Value for Customs
VIE	SWISSAIR					SFR			CC	PP		NVD	

Airport of Destination	Flight/Date	For Carrier Use only	Flight/Date	Amount of Insurance
VIENNA	SR436/8.7.			

INSURANCE - If carrier offers insurance and such insurance is requested in accordance with conditions on reverse hereof, indicate amount to be insured in figures in box marked amount of insurance.

Handling Information

No of Pieces RCP	Gross Weight	kg lb	Rate Class	Commodity Item No.	Chargeable Weight	Rate / Charge	Total	Nature and Quantity of Goods (incl. Dimensions or Volume)
8	200,6	K	C	6750	201	1.90	381.90	CHEMICALS NOT RESTRICTED CONTRACT No 100-15-2
8	200,6							

Prepaid	Weight Charge	Collect
		381.90

Other Charges: AWA 15.00

Valuation Charge

Tax

Total other Charges Due Agent: 15.00

Total other Charges Due Carrier

Shipper certifies that the particulars on the face hereof are correct and that insofar as any part of the consignment contains dangerous goods, such part is properly described by name and is in proper condition for carriage by air according to the applicable Dangerous Goods Regulations.

SWISS EXPORT LTD / p.p. Forwarding LTD

Signature of Shipper or his Agent

Total Prepaid	Total Collect
15.00	381.90

Currency Conversion Rates	cc charges in Dest. Currency

07.07. BASLE Forwarding LTD

Executed on (Date) at (Place) Signature of Issuing Carrier or its Agent

For Carrier's Use only at Destination | Charges at Destination | Total collect Charges

085-7260 2751

No. 3 - ORIGINAL for SHIPPER

Form 30.301
Printed in the Fed. Rep. Germany - Bartsch Verlag, Munich-Ottobrunn 600j (III)

Sample International Road Waybill

INTERNATIONALER FRACHTBRIEF
LETTRE DE VOITURE INTERNATIONAL

Diese Beförderung unterliegt trotz einer gegenteiligen Abmachung den Bestimmungen des Übereinkommens über den Beförderungsvertrag im internat. Straßengüterverkehr (CMR)

Ce transport est soumis, nonobstant toute clause contraire, à la Convention relative au contrat de transport international de marchandises par route (CMR)

1 Absender (Name, Anschrift, Land) / Expéditeur (nom, adresse, pays)
METALLWAREN AG
CH-8904 AESCH

2 Empfänger (Name, Anschrift, Land) / Destinataire (nom, adresse, pays)
CIE PORTUGAISE D'ALUMINIUM
P-PORTO

16 Frachtführer (Name, Anschrift, Land) / Transporteur (nom, adresse, pays)
TRANSPORT AG
CH-4002 BASEL

3 Auslieferungsort des Gutes / Lieu prévu pour la livraison de la marchandise
Ort/Lieu: PORTO
Land/Pays: PORTUGAL

17 Nachfolgende Frachtführer (Name Anschrift, Land) / Transporteurs successifs (nom, adresse, pays)

4 Ort und Tag der Übernahme des Gutes / Lieu et date de la prise en charge de la marchandise
Ort/Lieu: 8904 AESCH
Land/Pays: SCHWEIZ
Datum/Date: 18.8.19..

18 Vorbehalte und Bemerkungen der Frachtführer / Réserves et observations des transporteurs

5 Beigefügte Dokumente / Documents annexés

6 Kennzeichen u. Nr / Marques et numéros	7 Anzahl d. Packstücke / Nombre des colis	8 Art der Verpackung / Mode d'emballage	9 Bezeichnung des Gutes* / Nature de la marchandise*	10 Statistik-Nr. / No statistique	11 Bruttogew. i. kg / Poids brut, kg	12 Umfang in m³ / Cubage m³
95140/1-2	2	CAISSES	FITA DE ALPACA PARA O FABRICO DE COMPONENTES 0,6 x 350 x 700 (AS PER CONFIRMATION 1182 dd. 15.6.19..)		985.-	

Klasse / Classe — Ziffer / Chiffre — Buchstabe / Lettre — (ADR)

13 Anweisungen des Absenders (Zoll- und sonstige amtliche Behandlung) / Instructions de l'expéditeur (formalités douanières et autres)
BANK REFERENZ CA 11-8804

19 Zu zahlen vom / A payer par	Absender / L'expéditeur	Währung / Monnaie	Empfänger / Le Destinataire
Fracht / Prix de transport			
Ermäßigungen / Réductions			
Zwischensumme / Solde			
Zuschläge / Suppléments			
Nebengebühren / Frais accessoires			
Sonstiges + / Divers			
Zu zahl. Gesamtsum. / Total à payer			

14 Rückerstattung / Remboursement

15 Frachtzahlungsanweisungen / Prescription d'affranchissement
Frei / Franco: FREIGHT PREPAID
Unfrei / Non franco

20 Besondere Vereinbarungen / Conventions particulières

21 Ausgefertigt in / Etablie à BASEL am / le 18.8. 19..

24 Gut empfangen / Réception des marchandises — Datum / Date — am / le .... 19 ....

22 TRANSPORT AG
Unterschrift und Stempel des Absenders (Signature et timbre de l'expéditeur)

23 Unterschrift und Stempel des Frachtführers (Signature et timbre du transporteur)

Unterschrift und Stempel des Empfängers (Signature et timbre du destinataire)

25 Angaben zur Ermittlung der Tarifentfernung mit Grenzübergängen

von	bis	km

28 Berechnung des Beförderungsentgelts

frachtpfl. Gewicht in kg	Tarifstelle: Sonderabmachung	Güterarten	Währung	Frachtsatz	Beförderungsentgelt

26 Vertragspartner des Frachtführers ist - kein - Hilfsgewerbetreibender im Sinne des ansuwendenden Tarifs

27 Amtl. Kennzeichen — Nutzlast in kg
Kfz
Anhänger
Summe

Benutzte Gen. Nr. .... National, Bilateral, EG, CEMT

Ausfüllen unter der Verantwortung des Absenders / A remplir sous las responsabilité de l'expéditeur 1 – 15 einschließlich y compris et 21 + 22

Die mit fett gedruckten Linien eingerahmten Rubriken müssen vom Frachtführer ausgefüllt werden.

Les parties encadrées de lignes grasses doivent être remplies par le transporteur.

weißes Exemplar für Tarifkontrolle • blanc exemplaire pour contrôle tarifaire • wit exemplaar voor tariefcontrole • blanco esemplare per controllo tarifario • white copy for tariffcontrol • hvid exemplar for tarifkontrolen
rosa Exemplar für Absender • rose exemplaire de l'expéditeur • rose exemplaar voor afzender • rosa esemplare per mittente • pink copy for sender • rosa exemplar for afsender
blaues Exemplar für Empfänger • bleu exemplaire du destinataire • blauw exemplaar voor geadresseerde • azzur esemplare per destinatario • blue copy for consignee • blå exemplar for modtager
grünes Exemplar für Frachtführer • vert exemplaire du transporteur • groen exemplaar voor vervoerder • verde esemplare per trasportone • green copy for carrier • grøn exemplar for befordrer

Checklist (Prior to Submission of the Documents)

1. Do all documents refer to the same order and the same credit?	☐
2. Are all the documents present in the prescribed number and in complete sets?	☐
3. Do all of the dimensions, weights, number of packing units, and markings agree on all the documents?	☐
4. If necessary, have all documents been certified and/or legalized?	☐
5. Is the invoice addressed exactly as prescribed in the credit?	☐
6. Do the goods description, unit price and goods value in the invoice agree exactly with the text of the credit?	☐
7. Does the amount of the invoice not exceed the available credit sum?	☐
8. Is the bill of exchange legally signed?	☐
9. Does the bill of exchange have to be endorsed?	☐
10. Does the insurance document cover all of the risks specified?	☐
11. Is the insurance document endorsed?	☐
12. Has the delivery period been maintained?	☐
13. Does the freight notation on the transport document agree with the supply conditions?	☐
14. Is the consignee in the transport document or the order in the bill of lading correct?	☐
15. Is the bill of lading clean?	☐
16. Are "on deck" bills of lading allowed under the terms of the credit?	☐
17. Are charter party bills of lading allowed under the terms of the credit?	☐
18. Is the notify address in the bill of lading correct?	☐
19. Is the bill of lading endorsed?	☐
20. Are corrections on the transport and insurance documents initialled by the originator?	☐

What does the bank do upon receipt of the documents?

It checks whether the documents agree with the credit conditions and the UCPDC in all respects. Because this check must be carried out painstakingly, the bank requires a reasonable period of time for it.

If the documents are found to be in order, the bank proceeds as follows:

- **In the case of a confirmed credit**

Depending on the type of availability specified in the credit, it either pays the value of the documents, or it accepts a bill of exchange for that value and places it at the disposal of the beneficiary, or, in the case of a deferred payment credit, it issues the beneficiary an irrevocable promise to pay.

- **In the case of an unconfirmed credit**

The advising bank has no commitment to pay, to accept, or to issue a promise to pay. If adequate credit balances are available or special arrangements have been made, however, the bank will pay immediately or accept the prescribed draft. If this is not the case, the bank sends the documents to the issuing bank and demands respective cover.

If it wishes to do so, the advising bank can credit the beneficiary's account with the value of the documents even before the requested cover is received, but with the notation "under usual reserves" (u.u.r.).

The notation "u.u.r." means that the beneficiary is obliged to repay the credited amount plus interest, charges and exchange rate difference if the issuing bank fails to provide the cover for one reason or another.

Discrepancies in the Documents

If the documents are found to be *not* in order, the bank's commitment to pay is invalidated. Thus the exporter loses the surety he had obtained with the credit.

The bank and the exporter then work together to arrive at solutions to restore the credit's surety:

- If possible, the exporter can correct the documents or have them rectified in order to be able to present them within the periods specified in the credit.
- The advising bank can ask the issuing bank for authorization to accept the documents despite the discrepancies found.

If the exporter agrees, the advising bank can send the documents to the issuing bank for collection.

In the case of a sight credit, the advising/confirming bank has the prerogative of deciding whether it wishes to credit the exporter's account under proviso despite the discrepancies in the documents.

Provisional Payment

By making a provisional payment, the advising/confirming bank accommodates the exporter even though it has no commitment nor is authorized by the credit terms to do so. If the documents are not accepted by those ordering the credit or the issuing bank, the advising bank will demand repayment of the credited amount plus accrued interest, charges and exchange rate differences (if any).

The Documentary Credit and the Export Risk Guarantee (ERG)

- For the fulfilling of export orders involving special payment risks, it is often possible to apply for the Swiss government's Export Risk Guarantee. [For Swiss exporters.] Information on the detailed requirements and conditions can be obtained from the Export Risk Guarantee Office.*
- Under certain circumstances, the advising bank may be prepared to confirm a credit only if the exporter is granted the ERG and agrees to assign the ERG claims, together with the original claim, to the confirming bank. In this case the exporter mentions expressly in his application to the ERG that the bank is prepared to confirm the credit only if the ERG is granted for this transaction.

---

*Swiss Export Risk Guarantee Office (GERG), P.O. Box, 8032 Zurich

The Documentary Credit and the Importer

What benefits does the documentary credit provide?

- By opening a credit, the importer confirms his financial soundness and may be able to obtain more favourable payment terms.
- The goods will be delivered in accordance with the delivery conditions stated in the credit.
- The buyer receives the documents he has demanded reasonably quickly.
- The buyer can be certain that he only has to pay if the documents comply with the credit terms in all respects.

Incidentally it should be borne in mind that the exchange risk involved with import credits in foreign currencies can be eliminated by purchasing forward foreign exchange.

Which type of credit should the importer provide?

As a rule, the foreign seller will demand an irrevocable credit. In this case, the backing of a first-class Swiss bank should satisfy him. The issuing bank assumes the commitment to pay on behalf of the importer. This commitment should be covered by a credit agreement between the issuing bank and the importer. But if the foreign seller insists on having the credit confirmed additionally by his own bank, he should bear the additional cost of this.

If the importer and seller have agreed upon an extended payment period, it is necessary to open a deferred payment credit. This documentary credit form increases the importer's expenses because of the prolonged commitment on the part of the issuing bank.

The banks are pleased to supply their customers with free application forms for opening documentary credits.

All documentary credits opened by banks in Switzerland are subject to the UCP-DC. Consequently, these guidelines also apply to the instructions the importer gives his bank.

When filling out the individual items of the credit application form, observe the following points:

Sample Application Form for Opening Documentary Credit

Instructions to open a Documentary Credit

Sender
Müller Ltd.
Tellstrasse 26
4053 Basle
Our reference AB/02

Basle, 30th September 19..
Place / Date

Please open the following
[X] irrevocable [ ] revocable documentary credit

Swiss Bank Corporation
Documentary Credits
P.O. Box
4002 Basle

Beneficiary
(1) Adilma Trading Corporation
27, Nihonbashi, Chiyoda-ku
Tokyo 125 / Japan

Beneficiary's bank (if known)
(4) Japanese Commercial Bank
Ginza Branch
Tokyo 37 / Japan

Amount
(2) US$ 70'200.--

Date and place of expiry
(3) 25th November 19.. in Basle

Please advise this bank
[ ] by letter
[X] by letter, cabling main details in advance
[ ] by telex / telegram with full text of credit

Partial shipments [X] allowed [ ] not allowed
Transhipment [ ] allowed [X] not allowed
Terms of shipment (FOB, C & F, CIF): CIF Rotterdam

Despatch from / Taking in charge at: Japan
For transportation to: Rotterdam
Latest date of shipment: 10th Nov. 19..
Documents must be presented not later than (3) 15 days after date of despatch

Beneficiary may dispose of the credit amount as follows
[X] at sight upon presentation of documents (5)
[ ] after ....days, calculated from date of ....
[ ] by a draft due ....
drawn on [ ] you [ ] your correspondents
which you / your correspondents will please accept

against surrender of the following documents (6)
[X] invoice (...3...copies)
Shipping document
[X] sea: bill of lading, to order, endorsed in blank
[ ] rail: dublicate waybill
[ ] air: air consignment note
[ ]

[X] insurance policy, certificte (.......... copies)
covering the following risks:
"all risks" including war up to final destination in Switzerland
[ ] Additional documents
[X] Confirmation of the carrier that the ship is not more than 15 years old
[X] packing list (3 copies)

Notify address in bill of lading / goods addressed to
Müller AG, Tellstrasse 26, (7)
4053 Basle

Goods insured by [ ] us [X] seller

Goods (8)
1'000 "Record players ANC 83 as per proforma invoice no. 74/1853 dd 10th September 19.."
at US$ 70.20 per item

Your correspondents to advise beneficiary [ ] adding their confirmation [X] without adding their confirmation (9)
Payments to be debited to our Swiss Francs account no 10-326'791.0

NB. The applicable text is marked by [X]

E 6801 N 1/2 3.81 5000

Signature MÜLLER AG BASEL

For mailing please see overleaf

This credit is subject to the «Uniform customs and practice for documentary credits» fixed by the International Chamber of Commerce. It is understood that you do not assume any responsibility neither for the correctness, validity or genuineness of the documents which will be remitted to you nor for the description, quality, quantity and weight of the goods thereby represented.

① **Beneficiary**

The company name and address should be written completely and correctly. Incomplete or incorrect information results in delays and unnecessary additional cost.

② **Amount**

Is the figure a maximum amount or an approximate amount?

If words like "circa," "ca.," "about," etc., are used in connection with the amount of the credit, it means that a difference as high as 10% upwards or downwards is permitted. In such a case, the same word should also be used in connection with the quantity.

③ **Validity period**

The validity and period for presentation of the documents following shipment of the goods should be sufficiently long to allow the exporter time to prepare his documents and submit them to the bank.

Under place of validity, state the domicile of either the advising or the issuing bank.

④ **Beneficiary's bank**

If no bank is named, the issuing bank is free to select the correspondent bank.

⑤ **Type of availability**

The various types of availability are discussed in the general section of this publication.

⑥ **Desired documents**

Here the importer specifies precisely which documents he requires. To obtain effective protection against the supply of poor quality goods, for instance, he can demand the submission of analysis or quality certificates. These are generally issued by specialized inspection companies or laboratories.

⑦ **Notify address**

Advice is given to the notify address of the imminent arrival of the ship at the port of destination or of the arrival of the goods at the airport. Notification is also given of damage during shipment, if any.

⑧ **Description of the goods**

To avoid errors and misunderstandings, it is advisable to keep the goods description and quantity information brief and precise.

If the credit amount carries the notation "ca.," the same notation should appear with the quantity.

⑨ **Confirmation order**

It may happen that the foreign beneficiary insists on having the credit confirmed by the bank in his country.

Clear formulations speed up handling.

When checking compliance with the credit terms, banks are concerned exclusively with the documents presented and not with contract clauses. So it is very important to demand documents in the credit that clearly reflect the agreements reached between importer and exporter.

Instead of:	*Specify:*
The beneficiary must notify the buyer by cable when the goods are shipped.	Copy of the cable to the buyer with shipping information.
The ship may not be more than 15 years old.	Confirmation of the shipping company or its agent that the ship is not more than 15 years old.
The beneficiary must send duplicate documents to the buyer.	Confirmation of the seller that he has sent duplicates of the following documents to the buyer: ... ...
The certificate of origin must accompany the goods.	Confirmation of the carrier/forwarding agent that the goods are accompanied by a certificate of origin.

Amendment of the Credit Terms

An amendment of the credit terms ordered by the importer becomes effective only if all parties, i.e. the issuing bank, the exporter, and possibly also the foreign confirming bank, agree to the amendment.

Other Important Points for the Importer

Upon receiving the documents, the issuing bank checks whether they agree on their face with the wording of the credit and with the stipulations of the UCPDC, and charges the importer's account.

Documents in conformity with the credit cannot be rejected on grounds that the goods were not delivered as specified by the contract.

The question of liability and responsibility of the bank is spelled out in the UCPDC.

The Documentary Credit and the Intermediary

For the handling of documentary credit transactions in international transit trade, the banks offer the following possibilities:

The Transferable Letter of Credit

Allows the intermediary to have a credit opened in his favour transferred to his own supplier. The intermediary has to commit only a very limited amount of his own funds.

It must be clearly designated as "transferable."

A transfer of partial quantities to various sellers is possible only if the original credit permits partial deliveries.

Under the transferable credit, the documents should be demanded in such a way that they can also be utilized for the original credit.

Of course the intermediary has the right to replace the invoice from the transferred credit with his own.

The insurance amount should be established for the transfer in such a way that it at least covers the insurance amount prescribed in the original credit.

The credit can be transferred only under the terms stated in the original credit. However, the following exceptions are permitted:

- Unit prices and credit amount can be reduced.
- Delivery period and validity period can be shortened.

If the intermediary wishes that discretion be exercised regarding the identity of the ultimate buyer and the seller, he should make sure that the original credit only specifies documents that make no mention of the names of the ultimate buyer and the seller.

The intermediary should do everything in his power to see that the party ordering the original credit has it opened in the simplest possible form.

The fewer the documents specified and the simpler the terms stipulated in the original credit, the smoother the transaction can be handled.

Transferable credits call for exceptional care and knowledge. The bank will be pleased to place its long experience at the disposal of customers in the search for solutions to particular problems.

Transferable Credit

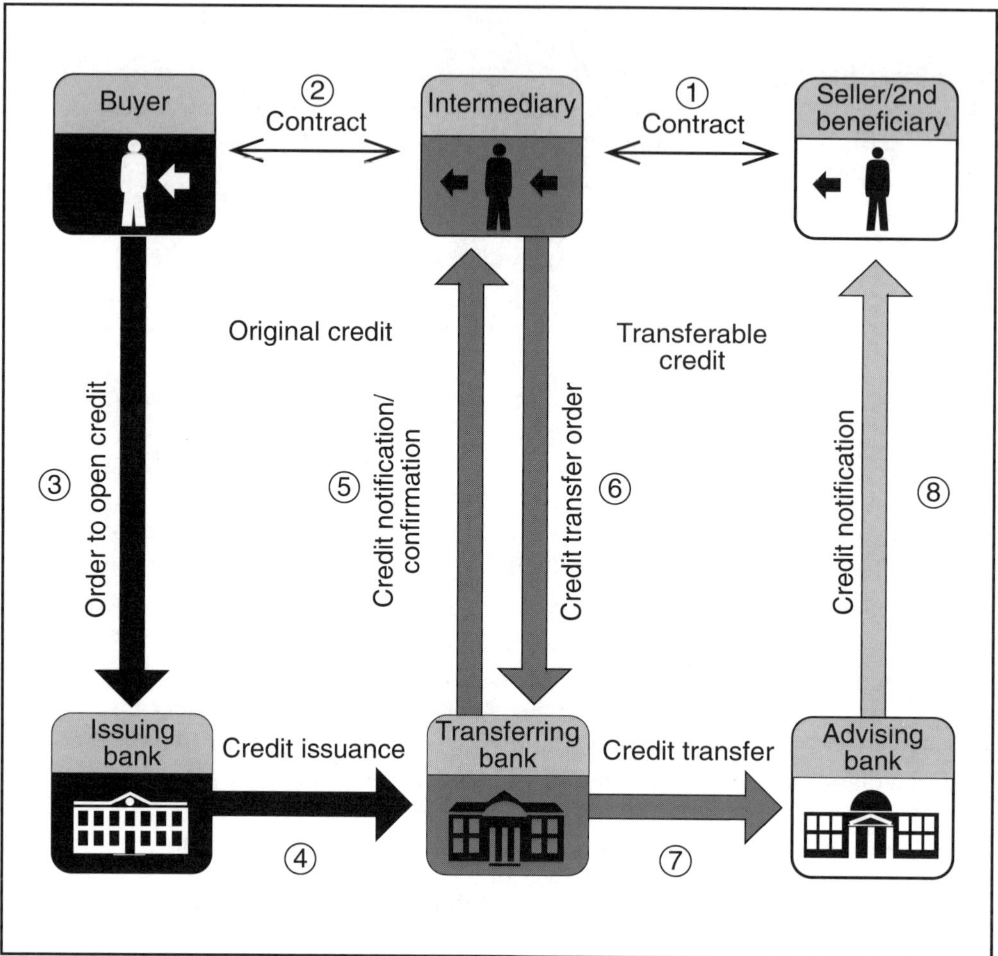

Transferable Credit

① **Intermediary contracts with seller/2nd beneficiary to purchase goods.**

② **Intermediary contracts to sell goods to buyer.**

③ **Buyer applies for and opens a letter of credit with issuing ("buyer's") bank.**

④ **Issuing bank issues the letter of credit, forwarding it to transferring bank.**

⑤ **Transferring bank notifies intermediary of letter of credit.**

⑥ **Intermediary orders transfer of letter of credit to seller/2nd beneficiary.**

⑦ **Transferring bank transfers credit in care of advising ("seller's") bank.**

⑧ **Advising bank notifies seller/2nd beneficiary of letter of credit.**

Sample Transferable, Confirmed Letter of Credit

Swiss Bank Corporation
Schweizerischer Bankverein
Société de Banque Suisse
Società di Banca Svizzera

Notre / Unsere / Our **Doc. Credit No** 173'896 /

4002 Basle, 20th October 19..
Lieu/Date Ort/Datum Luogo/Data

Nous vous informons de l'ouverture du crédit documentaire irrévocable suivant en votre faveur:

Wir benachrichtigen Sie von der Eröffnung des folgenden unwiderruflichen Dokumentarkredites zu Ihren Gunsten:

We inform you of the opening of the following irrevocable documentary credit in your favour:

REGISTERED
TRANSITO LTD.
Rheinallee 183

4002 B a s e l

Montant / Betrag / Amount	Banque émettrice / Eröffnende Bank / Issuing bank
max. DM 386'000.--	Bank for Trade and Industry P.O. Box 1283 D-6000 Frankfurt 30
Validité / Gültigkeit / Validity 15th January 19..	
Donneur d'ordre / Auftraggeber / Applicant Schmitt & Co. Ltd. Hinterlindenstrasse 47 Frankfurt 34	No de réf. de notre correspondant / Ref.-Nr. unseres Korrespondenten / Ref. no of our correspondent: LC/539284 Ordre du / Auftrag vom / Order dated: 19.10.19..

Utilisable contre remise des documents suivants:
Benützbar gegen Einreichung folgender Dokumente:
Available against surrender of the following documents:

- invoice, 3 copies
- inspection certificate, evidencing that the goods are in accordance with the specifications mentioned below
- full set of clean shipped on board ocean bills of lading, made out to order and endorsed in blank

covering: 1'000 metric tons steel sheets DIN 456/243 at DM 386.-- per mt, C & F Rotterdam

to be shipped from a Japanese seaport to Rotterdam not later than 1st January 19..
Partial deliveries are permitted. Transhipment not allowed.
Documents to be presented not later than 15 days after date of shipment.

This documentary credit is transferable.

We confirm this documentary credit to you as irrevocably valid until 15th January 19..

Yours faithfully

Swiss Bank Corporation

Ce crédit est soumis aux • Règles et usances uniformes relatives aux crédits documentaires • approuvées par la Chambre de Commerce Internationale.
Dieser Kredit unterliegt den • Einheitlichen Richtlinien und Gebräuchen für Dokumenten-Akkreditive • wie sie von der Internationalen Handelskammer gutgeheissen worden sind.
This credit is subject to the • Uniform customs and practice for documentary credits • fixed by the International Chamber of Commerce.

F 6804N 1/8 2.82 10000

Sample Transferable Letter of Credit Order

TRANSITO AG
Import - Export - Kommission
Rheinallee 183, 4087 Basel
Telefon: (061) 251 87 87

Basle, 21st October 19..

Swiss Bank Corporation
Documentary Credits
P.O. Box

4002 Basle

Documentary credit no. 173896 - DM 386'000.--, opened by Handels- und Industriebank, Frankfurt, by order of Schmitt & Co. KG, Frankfurt, confirmed by yourselves

Dear Sirs,

Would you please transfer the above-mentioned documentary credit as follows:

New beneficiaries :	Handels GmbH Sendlauerstrasse 28 Vienna 28
to be advised by :	Overseas Bank Ltd., Vienna
amount :	DM 350'000.--
validity :	5th January 19..,
price :	DM 350.-- per mt C & F Rotterdam

All other conditions remain unchanged. Please credit the balance of funds in our favour to our DM account with yourselves.

We appreciate your assistance in this matter and look forward to receiving your advice of execution.

Yours faithfully

TRANSITO LTD.

Baumann

The Back-to-Back Credit

If a credit is not transferable for one reason or another, the bank may be prepared, under certain circumstances and assuming that the main risks can be covered satisfactorily, to open a credit on a back-to-back basis at the request of the intermediary. In this case, the bank's main surety is the original credit.

The more the specifications of the original and the back-to-back credit differ from each other, the more difficult it becomes to carry out the transaction.

Therefore it is advisable for the intermediary to contact his bank at an early stage. On the basis of its experience, the bank will help him look for solutions to his particular problem.

Assignment of the Credit Proceeds

If a relationship of sufficient trust exists between the intermediary and his supplier, the latter may sometimes be prepared to accept the assignment of a certain sum in place of a new documentary credit. In this case, the bank will consent to pay the supplier, on behalf of the credit beneficiary, the assigned sum from the amounts becoming available under the credit.

The security resulting from the assignment cannot be equated with that from a back-to-back or even a transferable credit, because the beneficiary from the assignment has no control over the presentation of documents in conformity with the credit by the intermediary (credit beneficiary).

When the supplier receives notification of the assignment, he has the assurance that the partial amounts cannot be used for any other purpose as they become available.

Sample Order of Assignment

MÜLLER AG

Postfach 10283, 4087 Basel
Telefon: (061) 247 86 86
Telex: 247 86 86 mulag ch

Basle, 20th October 19..

Swiss Bank Corporation
Documentary Credits
P.O. Box

4002 B a s l e

Documentary credit no. 204356 in our favour,
for SFr. 65'000.--, covering 200 tons of fertilizer

Dear Sirs,

In accordance with article 164 et seq. of the Swiss Law of Contract we hereby assign from the above documentary credit an amount of SFr. 300.-- per delivered ton of fertilizer, total SFr. 60'000.--, to Dünger Ltd., Feldmeilenstrasse 21, 8002 Zurich.

Would you kindly inform Dünger Ltd., Zurich, that you have taken note of this assignment and that the amount due will be transferred to them once the credit has been negotiated and the funds are freely available.

Yours faithfully

M ü l l e r Ltd.

Müller Frey

Sample Forwarding of Assignment by the Bank

Swiss Bank Corporation
Schweizerischer Bankverein
Société de Banque Suisse
Società di Banca Svizzera

Dünger Ltd.
Feldmeilenstrasse 21

8002 Zurich

Your ref. Our dept./ref. DOK/BU Through dialing (061) 20 20 20 **4002 Basle,** 21st October 19..

Documentary credit no. 204356 in favour
Müller AG, Basel

Dear Sirs,

By order of Müller AG, Basle, we received the following assignment:

In accordance with article 164 et seq. of the Swiss Law of Contract we hereby assign from the above documentary credit an amount of SFr. 300.-- per delivered ton of fertilizer, total SFr. 60'000.-- to Dünger Ltd., Feldmeilenstrasse 21, 8002 Zurich.

At the request of Müller AG, Basle, we confirm that we have duly taken note of this assignment. We undertake to hold at your disposal an amount up to SFr. 60'000.--. The amount due will be transferred to you as soon as the credit has been negotiated and the funds are freely available.

Yours faithfully,

Swiss Bank Corporation

E 90001 S

The Back-to-Back Credit

Procedure for assignment of credit proceeds (Stage 1 - Issuance)

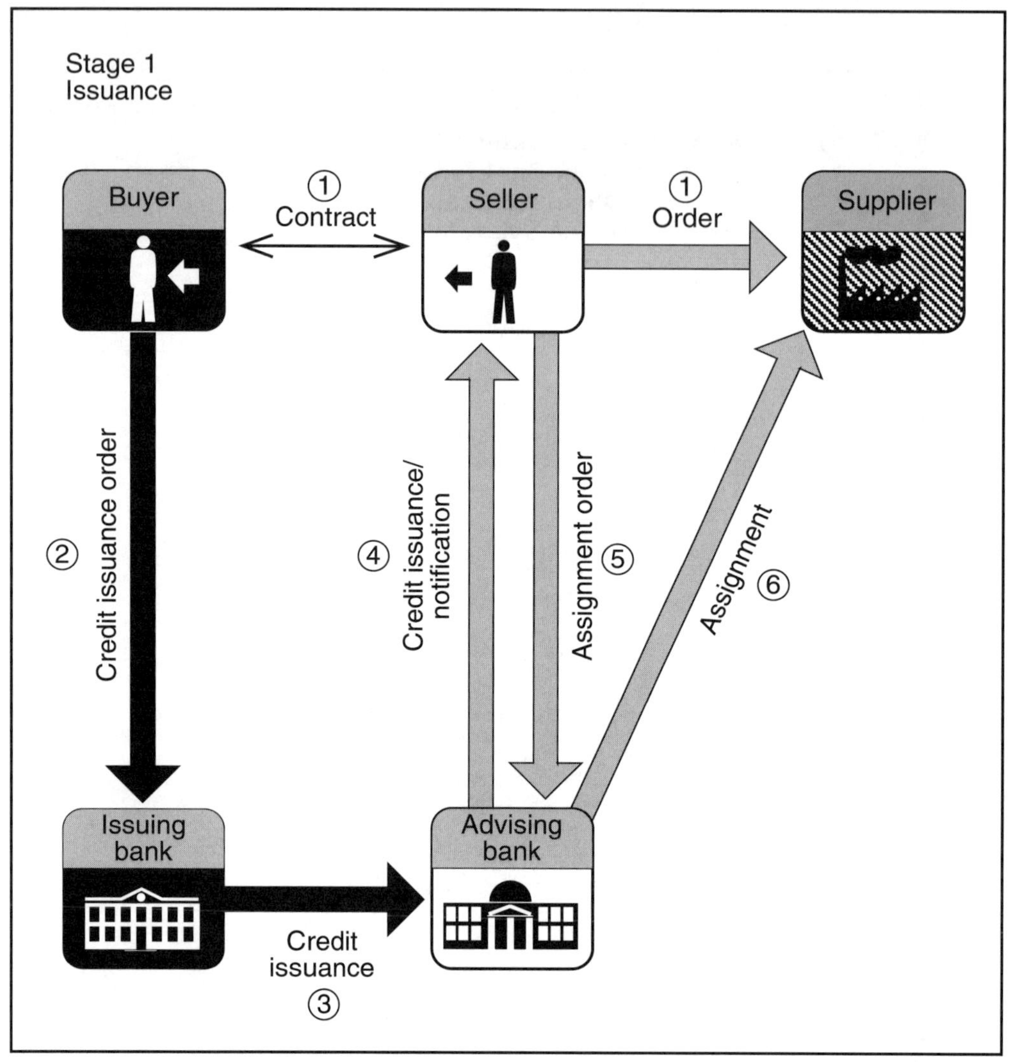

① **Buyer and seller negotiate a contract. Seller issues order to supplier.**

② **Buyer applies for and opens a letter of credit with issuing ("buyer's") bank.**

③ **Issuing bank issues the letter of credit, forwarding it to advising ("seller's") bank.**

④ **Advising bank notifies seller of letter of credit.**

⑤ **Seller orders assignment of letter of credit to supplier.**

⑥ **Advising bank assigns letter of credit to supplier.**

The Back-to-Back Credit

Procedure for assignment of credit proceeds (Stage 2 - Utilization)

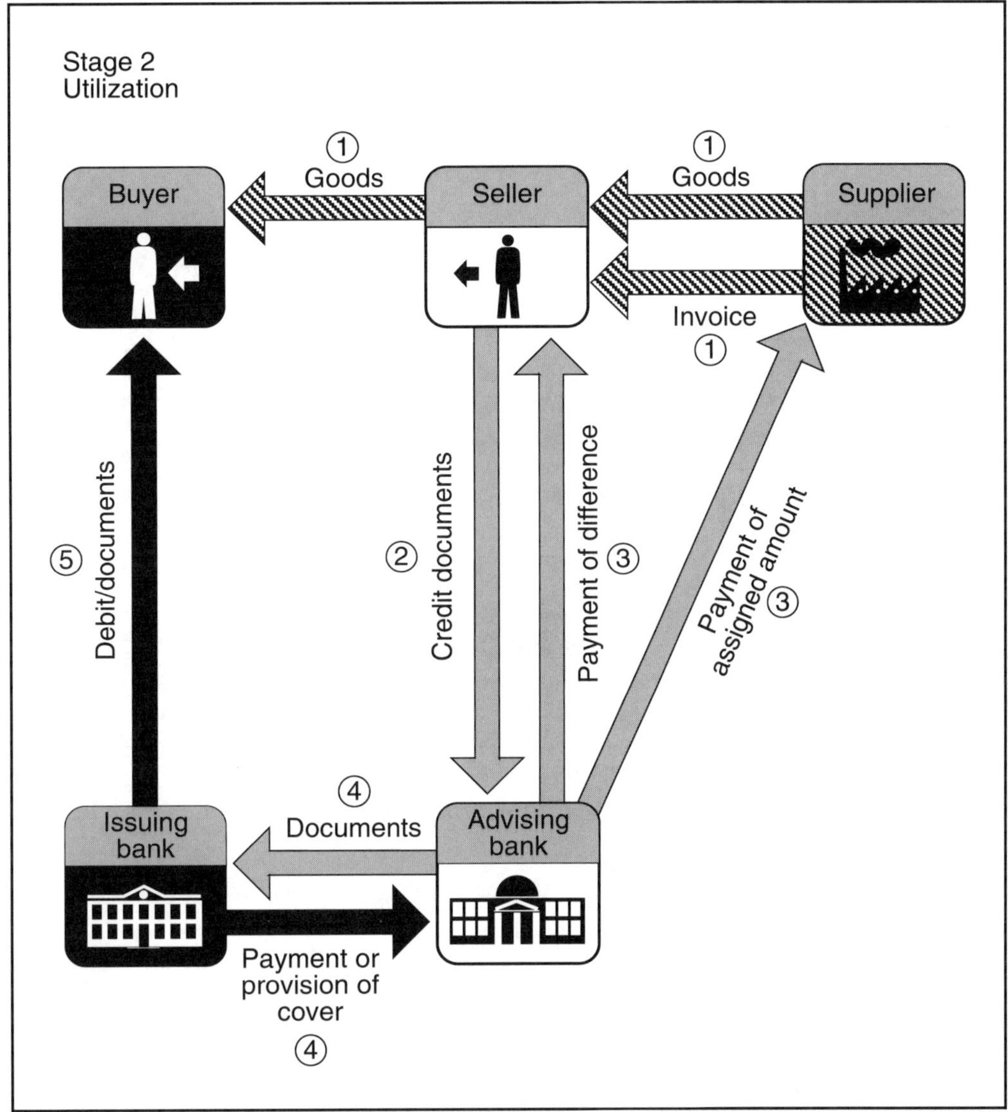

① **Supplier ships goods and invoice to seller who in turn ships goods to buyer.**

② **Seller forwards credit documents to advising ("seller's") bank.**

③ **Advising bank pays supplier amount assigned in seller's assignment order. Advising bank pays seller the difference between the letter of credit amount and the amount assigned to the supplier.**

④ **Advising bank forwards documents to issuing ("buyer's") bank. Issuing bank pays advising bank.**

⑤ **Issuing bank forwards documents to buyer and debits buyer's account.**

DOCUMENTARY COLLECTIONS

General Section

Documentary collection is a practical way of handling trade transactions for which the parties to the contract are prepared to forgo the security offered by documentary credits, but still do not wish to make deliveries on open account.

The documentary collection is an order by the seller to his bank to collect a certain sum from the buyer against transfer of the shipping documents. Payment may be made by cash or by acceptance of a bill of exchange.

The documentary collection is mainly appropriate in cases where

- the buyer's ability and willingness to pay are not doubted
- the political, economic and legal conditions in the importing country are considered to be regular
- no import restrictions, such as foreign exchange controls, exist in the import country, or else all of the necessary licences have already been obtained
- the goods being supplied are not made to order

The Bank as Fiduciary

In the case of documentary collections, the banks agree to execute the seller's collection order. While doing everything in their power to collect the payment due, they do not assume any liability in this regard.

The "Uniform Rules for Collections"

In the course of time, various formulations, expressions and terms have arisen among banks in connection with documentary collection business. In order to ensure uniform interpretations in international trade, the International Chamber of Commerce in Paris has prepared "Uniform Rules for Collections."

For the sake of simplicity, we shall use the abbreviation

URC

(**U**niform **R**ules for **C**ollections)

when referring to this publication.

Some Important Principles

1. The banks act only upon instructions given in the collection order. So the party issuing the order should be sure to give the bank clear and complete instructions.

2. The banks check whether the documents received appear on their face to agree with the collection order. The bank is under no obligation to make any further check of the documents.

3. The banks are not liable for the acts of third parties (such as forwarding agents, insurance companies, customs authorities, or even other banks) which are involved in the collection procedure. The banks assume no responsibility for

- delays through no fault of their own in the transmission of messages
- consequences of Acts of God
- acts or omissions by third parties

4. Any discrepancies arising with respect to quality or quantity of the goods delivered are to be settled directly between the drawee and the principal.

Parties to the Documentary Collection Operation

The principal (remitter, seller, exporter)
- Usually the seller, who prepares the collection documents and submits them to the bank with the collection order.

The remitting bank
- Receives the documents from the remitter (seller) and forwards them to the collecting bank in accordance with the instructions received.

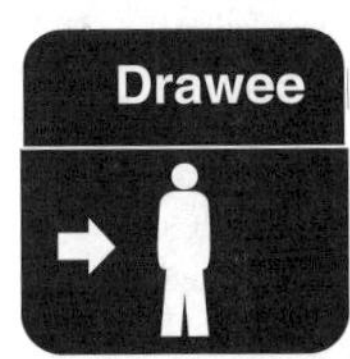

The buyer (drawee, importer)
- The collection papers are presented to him.

The collecting bank (presenting bank)
- Collects the cash payment or obtains the acceptance from the drawee in accordance with the instructions received from the remitting bank.

Documentary Collection Procedure

According to the arrangements between the buyer and the seller, the latter remits the agreed documents to the bank with instructions to present them to the buyer. As a rule, the remitting bank sends the documents to a correspondent bank (collecting or presenting bank), if possible at the same location as the buyer, with instructions to present them to the drawee.

On the basis of the collection order received, the collecting bank then notifies the buyer and informs him about the conditions under which he can take possession of the documents.

If the buyer draws the documents against payment, the collecting bank transfers the proceeds to the remitting bank for crediting to the remitter.

If the buyer draws the documents against acceptance of a bill of exchange, the collecting bank sends the acceptance back to the remitting bank or retains it on a fiduciary basis up to maturity. On maturity, the collecting bank collects the bill and transfers the proceeds to the remitting bank for crediting to the seller.

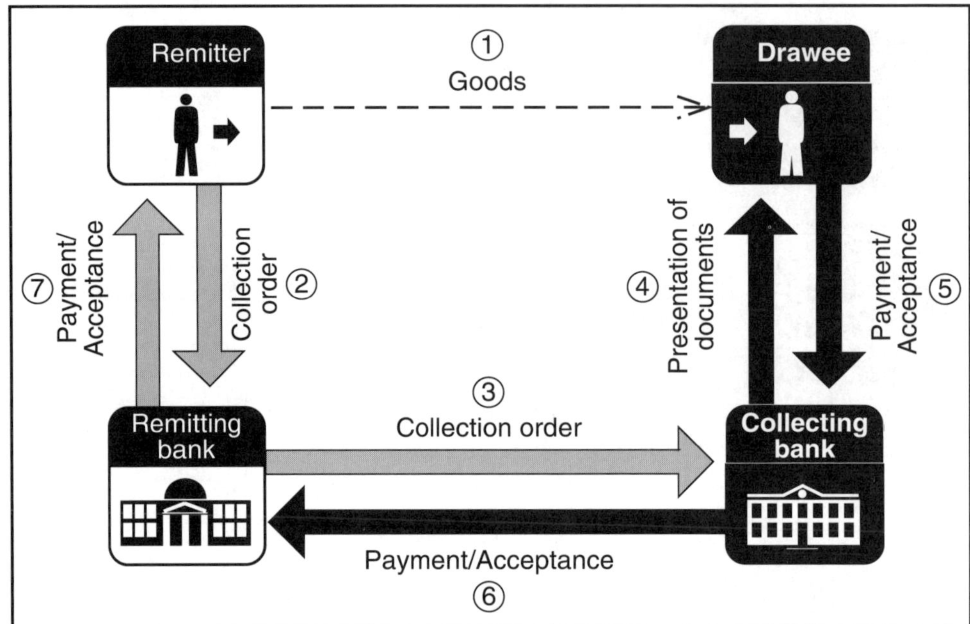

The Various Types of Collection

There are three types of collection:

1. Release of the documents against payment (D/P)

The collecting bank is allowed to release the documents to the buyer only against cash payment in the prescribed currency.

In this case, the URC prescribes that the documents may be released by the collecting bank only if the amount paid is freely available immediately, unless this is contrary to the provisions of local laws or regulations which cannot be avoided.

2. Release of the documents against acceptance (D/A)

The collecting bank is allowed to release the documents to the buyer only against acceptance of a bill of exchange. The seller must be aware that the bill of exchange represents his only security after the documents have been released. He will sell on this basis only if he is sure that the buyer will meet the bill at maturity.

Not all countries are familiar with Switzerland's strict Bills of Exchange Law.

3. Collection with acceptance—release of documents only against payment (Acceptance D/P)

The collecting bank presents a bill of exchange to the buyer for acceptance. The accepted bill remains at the collecting bank together with the documents up to maturity. Only then will the documents be released to the buyer.

The seller grants the buyer a certain payment term, but still wishes to be sure that the buyer can obtain the documents only after having made payment.

If the buyer refuses to accept the bill of exchange, the seller has early warning that he can expect trouble in completing the transaction. This gives him time to take appropriate precautions or possibly to look for another customer for the goods.

Although this type of collection is very seldom employed in actual practice, it is included here for the sake of completeness.

Special Services of the Bank

Shipment of the goods to the address of the collecting bank

If the goods are sent by rail, post, air freight or road to the buyer's address, the shipment will be surrendered to him without his first having to honour the collection documents presented to him by the bank.

If the seller wants to be sure that the buyer does not take possession of the goods before having paid, he can address them to the collecting bank or to a forwarding agent at the buyer's location with instructions to hold the consignment at the exclusive disposal of the bank. This should not be done, however, without first obtaining the consent of the collecting bank.

Monitoring

As far as possible, the banks monitor the proper processing of collection orders until the documents are redeemed. However, they cannot be held liable if the remitter receives no notification of delays for one reason or another and suffers inconvenience or damages as a result.

Without explicit instructions, the collecting bank takes no steps to store or insure the goods.

If a collection remains unpaid or a bill of exchange is not accepted and the presenting (collecting) bank receives no new instructions within 90 days, it is empowered to return the documents to the bank from which it received the collection order.

The Documentary Collection and the Exporter

What action does the exporter take?

The exporter carefully assembles the documents agreed between himself and the importer.

The exporter must bear in mind that regulations of the import countries often prescribe compulsory documents as well. The consulates of the import countries provide information on this.

The exporter makes certain that the documents are signed and endorsed where necessary.

In order to simplify collection transactions for the exporter, Swiss Bank Corporation is pleased to provide suitable forms and blank bill of exchange forms.

The remitting bank passes on the documents received from the exporter for collection without checking them.

In the case of documentary collection, the goods travel and are stored at the exporter's risk until payment/acceptance takes place. As a rule, the banks take no steps to protect the goods.

The banks cannot be held responsible if the goods are seized by customs in the consignee country and confiscated to cover the accrued storage costs.

① The payment period agreed upon with the buyer.

② Precise address of the buyer.

③ The buyer's bank (if known).

④ Instructions on what is to be done with the accepted bill of exchange.

⑤ The agreement with the buyer concerning charges.

The supply contract should specify which party is to pay which charges. If the buyer refuses to honour his agreement to pay certain charges, they will be invoiced to the remitter.

⑥ Instructions regarding the lodging of a protest in the event of non-acceptance or non-payment.

Protests cost money. So it is advisable to enquire about the consequences of protesting a bill in the buyer's country.

⑦ Address of the representative or agent in the buyer's country.

Without express authorization, the collecting bank does not accept any instructions from the representative or agent.

Sample Collection Letter

Sender:

Müller Ltd.
Tellstrase 26

4053 Basle

Documentary collection

Basle, 12th August 19..
Place / Date

Our Reference AK/83

We send you herewith the following documents for collection:

Registered

Swiss Bank Corporation
Schweizerischer Bankverein

Documentary collections
P.O. Box

4002 Basle

Amount	Maturity	Drawee (2)
US$ 14'300.--	90 days sight (1)	Maxwell Hammerton Inc. 12, Broadway New York, N.Y. 10014
		Drawee's bank: Commercial Credit Bank (3) New York

Draft/ Receipt	Invoice com-mercial	Invoice cust.-/ consul.	Insur.-Cert.	Certif. of Orig.	Weight/ Packing List	Bill of Lading	Waybill	Postal-/ Forw.-Receipt	other documents	
1		4	2		2	3/3			2	analysis certificates

Goods: 100 barrels "Chemical products - harmless"

by: s/s CAP SAN GIORGIO from: Le Havre to: New York on: 31.7.19..

Please follow the instructions marked «x»

	Documents/goods to be delivered against					Draft (4)		State the exact due-date		
	payment (1)	X	acceptance				to be sent back after acceptance		to be collected on due-date	
X	Your charges for drawee's account; if refused				X	waive charges			do not deliver documents	
X	Your correspondent's charges are for drawee's account; if refused					waive charges		X	do not deliver documents	
X	Protest in case of	X	non-payment		non-acceptance	X	Do not protest in case of		non-payment	X	non-acceptance
X	Advise	X	non-payment		non-acceptance		by airmail	X	by cable	X	giving reasons

(5) refers to the charges rows; (6) refers to the protest/advise rows.

Please credit the proceeds as follows:

☒ to our SFr account Nr. 10-326'791.0

☐ remit to

(7) Remarks:

In case of difficulties, the collecting bank is requested to inform our representatives: Messrs. Beach & Co. Inc., Broad Street 485, New York 34, who will be of assistance but who are not allowed to alter the above instructions.

Signature: Müller Ltd [signature]

Enclosures

E 6851 N 1/2 4.80 5000

The execution of this order is subject to the «Uniform rules for collections» issued by the International Chamber of Commerce

The Documentary Collection and the Importer

If the importer has purchased goods on a documentary collection basis, the collecting bank will notify him as soon as the documents are available for redemption.

The importer can inspect the documents at his bank. Once the importer has fulfilled the conditions required—acceptance or payment—the bank will release the documents and (if applicable) the goods.

What the Importer Should Know

- In the absence of authorization from the seller, the collecting bank is not empowered to allow the buyer to sample the goods or inspect their quality.
- The collecting bank may accept partial payments only if this is permitted by the collection order. In the absence of instructions to the contrary, it releases the documents only after having received full payment.
- As a special favour, the collecting bank can submit the collection documents to the importer in trust to allow him to inspect them at his leisure.

The decision whether to do so remains with the collecting bank, which bears responsibility for the documents vis-à-vis the remitting bank up to redemption and responsibility for their custody.

If the buyer is unable to honour the documents, he returns the complete set immediately to the collecting bank.

Closing Remarks

In the preceding sections we attempted to emphasize that, in the case of documentary credits, the seller receives the proceeds immediately upon presentation of his documents. In the case of documentary collection, on the other hand, the seller has to wait until the buyer has made payment or accepted a bill of exchange at the other end. In terms of security, the documentary credit is superior to collection, because the bank has committed itself to make payment upon presentation of proper documents. Sellers obtaining their proceeds by documentary collection must bear in mind that they are forced to rely on prompt redemption of the documents by the buyer.

The legal problems that can arise from disputes between the parties have been avoided deliberately, because different legal codes may apply depending on the circumstances.

We hope that this publication has helped to familiarize you with the rather complex subject of documentary operations. If some questions still remain unanswered, please have a talk with our specialists in the documentary operations departments of our branches. They will be pleased to work with you in solving your problems in this area.

Swiss Bank Corporation

Glossary of Technical Terms

acceptance credit — Refer to usance credit, page 133.

accepted draft — Bill of exchange accepted by the drawee (acceptor) by putting his signature (acceptance) on its face. In doing so, he commits himself to pay the bill upon presentation at maturity.

all risks — Extensive insurance cover, but usually excluding special risks (such as risks of war and strikes or perishing of the goods).

analysis certificate — Confirmation concerning the chemical analysis of the goods, issued by a competent organization.

aval — Joint and several guarantee on the draft of a person or firm, usually for the drawee, where the guarantor places his signature on the draft together with a notation indicating in whose favour his guarantee is given.

average — Damage to vessel or cargo.

AWB — Refer to air waybill, page 143.

back-to-back credit — Refer to page 134.

bid bond — Guarantee established in connection with international tenders. Guarantees fulfillment of the offer, i.e. that the contract will be signed if awarded.

bill of exchange — Document issued in a legal form, precisely defined, of which the two following versions are most common:
- draft, wherein the drawer instructs the drawee to pay a certain amount to a named person;
- promissory note, wherein the issuer promises to pay a certain amount.

bill of lading (B/L) — Document giving title to the goods, signed by the captain or his deputy or by the shipping company or its agent, containing the declaration regarding receipt of the goods (cargo), the conditions on which transportation is made, and the engagement to deliver goods at the prescribed port of destination to the lawful holder of the bill of lading. Refer to page 140.

certificate of manufacture — Confirmation of a producer that the goods have actually been produced by him in his factory.

c & f — Abbreviation for "cost and freight," which means that the price of the goods includes all costs for the shipment and the freight up to the port of destination. It is up to the buyer to cover insurance from the port of shipment. (*See* Incoterms.)

charter party — Contract according to which the owner leases the vessel to a charterer for a certain period or a certain voyage.

cif — Abbreviation for "cost, insurance and freight," which means that price of the goods includes all costs for the shipment and freight and insurance up to the port of destination. (*See* Incoterms.)

cifci	Abbreviation for "cost, insurance, freight, commission and interest." The same as "cif" plus commission and interest.
claused bill of lading	Bill of lading containing additional clauses limiting the responsibility of the shipping company.
clean bill of lading	Bill of lading which does not bear any superimposed clause or annotation expressly declaring the defective condition of the goods and/or the packaging.
clean letter of credit	Letter of credit available without presentation of shipping documents. Refer also to "stand-by letter of credit," page 134.
CMR	Abbreviation for "Convention relative au contrat de transport international de marchandises par route." *See* road waybill.
combined bill of lading	Bill of lading covering several modes of transport.
combined transport	Consignment sent by means of various modes of transport.
commercial letter of credit	Documentary credit. Refer to page 126.
consular invoice	Invoice with a certification of the consulate of the importing country usually issued on a special form. In use in only a few countries.
custody bill of lading	Bill of lading issued by American warehouses.
customs invoice	Invoice made out on a special form prescribed by the customs authorities of the importing country. Used only in a few countries.
D/A	Abbreviation for "documents against acceptance." Refer to page 163.
D/A draft	Documentary draft. Refer to page 163.
delivery order	Order to deliver specified packages out of a combined consignment covered by one single bill of lading.
deferred payment	Refer to page 133.
demurrage	Extra charge to be paid if a vessel is not loaded or unloaded within the time allowed.
dock receipt	Receipt issued by a warehouse supervisor or port officer certifying that goods have been received by the shipping company.
documentary draft	Draft drawn by seller on buyer accompanied by shipping documents. Refer to page 156.
D/P	Abbreviation for "documents against payment." Refer to page 163.
D/P draft	Documentary draft. Refer to page 163.
draft	Bill of exchange that has been drawn but not accepted.
endorsement	Written declaration on a document made out to order, usually written on the back, with which the owner (endorser) assigns his rights to the person named in the endorsement (endorsee).
ex warehouse	*See* "ex works."
ex works	Price of the goods including packing. (*See* Incoterms.)

fas — Abbreviation for "free alongside ship," which means the price of the goods covers transportation charges up to the port of shipment. Handling charges in the port of shipment, freight up to final destination and insurance are borne by the buyer. (*See* Incoterms.)

FCR — Abbreviation for "forwarder's certificate of receipt."

fio — Abbreviation for "free in and out." *See* "free in clause" and "free out clause."

foa — Abbreviation for "free on board airport."

fob — Abbreviation for "free on board," which means that the price of the goods covers transportation to the port of shipment and the usual loading charges. Freight and insurance from port of shipment are for the account of the buyer. (*See* Incoterms.)

for — Abbreviation for "free on rail" used in connection with transportation by rail, indicating that the price covers the goods loaded on the railcar.

forwarder's bill of lading — Bill of lading issued by a forwarding agent.

forwarding agent's bill of lading — Bill of lading issued by a forwarding agent.

forwarding agent's receipt — Receipt issued by a forwarding agent for goods received.

fot — Abbreviation for "free on truck" used in connection with road haulage, meaning that the price covers the goods loaded on the truck. (*See* Incoterms.)

fpa — *See* "free of particular average."

franco — Free from duties, transportation charges and other levies. Used also as delivery condition, e.g. franco ... (named place of delivery), which means that the seller must bear all transportation charges and duties up to the named place.

free of particular average (fpa) — Insurance cover that relates only to the consignment as a whole but does not cover the loss of single parcels or partial quantities.

free in clause — Clause in the bill of lading indicating that the loading charges are for the account of the supplier.

free out clause — Clause in the bill of lading indicating that unloading charges are for the account of the receiver.

full set — All originals of the bill of lading, the insurance document, etc.

HAWB — House air waybill. Refer to page 140.

house air waybill — Refer to page 140.

Incoterms — Publication of the International Chamber of Commerce regarding delivery terms currently in use. Refer to page 173.

inspection certificate — Confirmation that the goods have been inspected prior to shipment, issued by a neutral organization.

institute strike clause — Insurance clause internationally used regarding risks of strikes.

institute war clause — Insurance clause internationally used regarding risks of war.

in trust (goods/documents) — Refer to page 166.

letter of assignment — Document with which the assignor assigns his rights to a third party.

letter of guarantee
letter of indemnity — Declaration of indemnity on the part of a 3rd bank in the case of provisional negotiation. Refer to page 146.

mate's receipt — Declaration issued by an officer of the vessel in the name of the shipping company stating that certain goods have been received on board his vessel.

measurement list — List of the dimensions of the individual loaded cases.

merchant's credit — Letter of credit issued by the buyer himself. Contains no commitment whatever on the part of the bank.

negotiation — Action by which the advising bank buys the documents. Refer to page 146.

n.n. — "Not negotiable." Copy of the ocean bill of lading.

notify address — Address mentioned in a bill of lading or an air waybill, to which the carrier is to give notice when goods are due to arrive.

on board — Notation on the bill of lading indicating that the goods have actually been loaded onto ship named.

on deck bill of lading — Bill of lading containing the notation that goods have been shipped on deck.

option — Right to take up an offer. Also the right to choose from several different possibilities, e.g., in the bill of lading, to designate one or several ports of discharge.

packing credit — Advance granted by a bank in connection with shipments of storable goods guaranteed by the assignment of the payment expected later on under a documentary credit.

packing list — List showing details of the goods contained in each case.

performance bond — Guarantees proper fulfillment of the contract terms.

pro forma invoice — Invoice established pro forma, the payment of which is not intended. Used
- as preliminary invoice together with a quotation
- for customs purposes in connection with shipments of samples, advertising material, etc.

progress report — Declaration of the buyer in which he certifies the progress made by the seller up to a certain point of time. Refer to page 135.

promissory note — *See* bill of exchange.

protest — Legal procedure noting the refusal of the drawee to accept a bill of exchange (protest for non-acceptance) or to pay it (protest for non-payment). Essential in order to preserve the right of recourse on the endorser. Refer to page 138.

rail waybill — Duplicate of the freight document drawn up in rail traffic, which is given to the shipper of the goods.

received for shipment bill of lading	Bill of lading certifying only that goods have been received, but not evidencing that they have been loaded on board.
recourse	Right of claim against the joint and several guarantors (e.g., endorsers, drawers) of a bill of exchange or cheque. *See* protest.
red clause	Clause contained in a documentary credit authorizing the paying bank to make advances to the beneficiary on an unsecured basis even before the prescribed shipping documents have been presented.
reimbursing bank	Bank from which the advising bank requests cover on payment during negotiation.
remittance (documentary)	Forwarding of bills of exchange and/or documents.
restricted letter of credit	Letter of credit, the negotiation of which is restricted to a bank specially mentioned.
revolving credit	Documentary credit which, after utilization, is automatically reinstated for a further drawing. Refer to page 134.
road waybill	Transport document issued for road haulage (CMR = Convention relative au contrat de transport international de marchandises par route).
shipped on deck	Annotation in the bill of lading stating that the goods have been shipped on deck.
short form bill of lading	Bill of lading on which the detailed conditions of transportation are not listed in full.
s.r. & c.c.	Institute Strikes, Riots and Civil Commotions Clause. Internationally applied insurance clause regarding these risks.
straight bill of lading	Bill of lading issued to the name of a certain party and which cannot be transferred by endorsement.
survey report	Report of an expert, issued by an independent party. *See* inspection certificate.
through bill of lading, TBL	Bill of lading covering goods being transhipped en route. It covers the whole voyage from port of shipment to final destination.
TPND	Insurance clause covering theft, pilferage and non-delivery.
trust receipt	Under British and American law: declaration issued by a client towards the bank that ownership of the goods remains with the bank even after release of the goods documents to the customer, and thus that the client has received the goods in trust only.
transferable	Refer to page 134 and page 151.
T.T.	Abbreviation for "telegraphic transfer," indicating that cover is remitted by cable.
under reserve	Refer to page 146.
unrestricted letter of credit	Letter of credit which may be negotiated through any bank at the beneficiary's choice.
usance credit	Refer to page 133.

u.u.r. — Abbreviation for "credit under usual reserves." Refer to page 146.

warehouse to warehouse clause — Insurance clause indicating that the goods are insured from the warehouse of the seller up to the warehouse of the buyer.

warrant — Collateral certificate used for lending on goods. Not common in Switzerland, because Swiss law (Art. 1153 OR) prevents Swiss warehouses from issuing documents of title.

weight list — List of the weights of the individual parcels.

without recourse — Purchase of a bill of exchange without recourse.

with particular average — Insurance covering also the loss of single cases or partial quantities (as opposed to free from particular average, fpa).

Publications of the International Chamber of Commerce, Paris, France

The International Chamber of Commerce, as a world business organisation, has members in more than 80 countries. It acts to promote the greater freedom of world trade, to harmonize and facilitate business and trade practices, and to represent the business community at international levels.

Uniform Customs and Practice for Documentary Credits

(Publication No. 500) Rules unifying banking practice regarding documentary credits.

Uniform Rules for Collections

(Brochure No. 322) Codifies the main rules to be applied by the banks in connection with collection operations for drafts, their payment or non-payment, protest and for documentary collections.

The Problem of Clean Bills of Lading

(Brochure No. 283) An explanation of the problem arising out of the requirement for clean bills of lading together with a list of certain clauses often superimposed by carriers, for reference and optional use by parties to international sales contracts.

Incoterms

(Brochure No. 350) International rules for the uniform interpretation of trade terms (FOB, CIF, etc.).

Uniform Rules for a Combined Transport Document

(Brochure No. 298) Uniform rules in connection with transport documents covering several modes of transport.

Guide to Documentary Credit Operations

(Publication No. 305) Describes the basic steps required in financing an international credit transaction by means of a documentary credit operation.

These publications may be obtained from

International Chamber of Commerce
38, Cours Albert I-^{er}
F-75008 Paris

British National Committee of the ICC
Centre Point, 103 New Oxford Street
London WC1A 1QB

International Chamber of Commerce
Börsenstrasse 26
P.O. Box 4138
8022 Zürich

U.S. Council of the ICC
1212 Avenue of the Americas
New York, N.Y. 10036

Swiss Bank Corporation

Office of the Chairman and General Management:
4002 Basle, Aeschenplatz 6

General Management in Zurich:
8022 Zurich, Paradeplatz 6

OFFICES AND BRANCHES ABROAD

Atlanta: 235 Peachtree Street N.E. (S. 1700), Atlanta, GA 30303
Tel. (404) 522-1600, Telex 542356

Bahrain: Kanoo Commercial Centre II, Manama, Bahrain
Tel. 257221, Telex 8814

Chicago: Three First National Plaza, Suite 2100, Chicago IL 60602
Tel. (312) 346-0350, Telex WUD 25 4527

Hong Kong: One Exchange Square, 20th Floor, Central, Hong Kong
Tel. 5-842 1222, Telex 64127

Houston: One Allen Center (S. 600), Houston TX 77002
Tel. (713) 658-0561, Telex 275429

London: City Office, 99 Gresham Street, London EC2P 2BR
Swiss Centre Office, 6 Wardour Street, London W1V 4HA
Private Clients and Investment Office, 30A Charles II Street, London SW1Y 4AE
Tel. 71-606 4000, Telex 887 434

Miami: 701 Brickell Avenue, Suite 3250, Miami, FL 33131
Tel. (305) 375-0110, Telex 6812074

New York: Main Office U.S.A., Four World Trade Center, New York, NY 10048
Tel. (212) 574-3000, Telex ITT 420520
Swiss Center Office, 608 Fifth Avenue, New York, NY 10020
Tel. (212) 399-2400

San Francisco: 101 California Street, San Francisco, CA 94111-5884
Tel. (415) 774-3300, Telex WUD 34735

Singapore: 6 Battery Road, #35-01, Singapore 0104
Tel. 224-2200, Telex RS 24 140

Tokyo: Furukawa-Sogo Building, 6-1, Marunouchi 2-chome, Chiyoda-ku,
C.P.O. Box 513, Tokyo 100-91
Tel. 3-3214-1731, Telex J24842

Notes:

Notes:

U.S. Customs Entry and Clearance
Contents

The following section is adapted from the U.S. Department of the Treasury, U.S. Customs Service publication *Importing to the United States* (March 1993 edition). We have updated for 1993-1994 laws— including revisions required by NAFTA, GSP, and the Customs Modernization Act, among others—and we have included the most current address and contact information available at publication.

1
Customs Organization

Mission

The major responsibility of the U.S. Customs Service is to administer the Tariff Act of 1930, as amended. Primary duties include the assessment and collection of all duties, taxes, and fees on imported merchandise; the enforcement of customs and related laws; and the administration of certain navigation laws and treaties. As a major enforcement organization, the Customs Service combats smuggling and fraud and enforces the regulations of numerous other Federal agencies at ports of entry and along the land and sea borders of the U.S.

Organization

The customs territory of the U.S. consists of the 50 states, the District of Columbia, and Puerto Rico. The Customs Service, an agency under the Department of the Treasury, has its headquarters in Washington, DC, and is headed by a Commissioner of Customs. The field organization consists of seven geographical regions further divided into districts with ports of entry within each district. These organizational elements are headed respectively by regional commissioners, district directors (or area directors in the case of the New York region), and port directors. The Customs Service is also responsible for administering the customs laws of the Virgin Islands of the U.S.

Both an alphabetical list of all ports by State and a list of districts by region (including postal ZIP code) are provided. Whenever it is suggested that you write to the district or port director for information, the director referred to is the one at the district or port where your goods will be entered.

Ports of Entry by State

(Including Puerto Rico and the U.S. Virgin Islands)

Key: Districts shown in **boldface**
•Regional Headquarters
*Consolidated ports

ALABAMA
Birmingham, Huntsville, **Mobile**

ALASKA
Alcan, **Anchorage**, Dalton Cache, Fairbanks, Juneau, Ketchikan, Sitka, Skagway, Valdez, Wrangell

ARIZONA
Douglas, Lukeville, Naco, **Nogales**, Phoenix, San Luis, Sasabe, Tucson

ARKANSAS
Little Rock-North Little Rock

CALIFORNIA
Andrade, Calexico, Eureka, Fresno, • **L.A.-Long Beach**, Port San Luis, **San Diego**, **S.F.-Oakland**, Tecate, San Ysidro

COLORADO
Denver

CONNECTICUT
Bridgeport, Hartford, **New Haven**, **New London**

DELAWARE
Wilmington (See Philadelphia, PA)

DISTRICT OF COLUMBIA
Washington

FLORIDA
Boca Grande, Carrabelle, Fernandina Beach, Jacksonville, Key West, • **Miami**, Orlando, Panama City, Pensacola, Port Canaveral, Port Everglades, Port Manatee, St. Petersburg, **Tampa**, West Palm Beach

GEORGIA
Atlanta, Brunswick, **Savannah**

HAWAII
Honolulu, Hilo, Kahului, Nawiliwili-Pt. Allen

IDAHO
Eastport, Porthill, Boise

ILLINOIS
• Chicago, Peoria, Rock Island-Moline* (See Davenport, IA)

INDIANA
Evansville/Owensboro, KY, Indianapolis, Lawrenceburg/Cincinnati, OH

IOWA
Davenport-Rock Island-Moline*, Des Moines

KANSAS
Wichita

KENTUCKY
Louisville, Owensboro/Evansville, IN

LOUISIANA
Baton Rouge, Gramercy, Lake Charles, Morgan City, • **New Orleans**, Shreveport/Bossier City

MAINE
Bangor, Bar Harbor, Bath, Belfast, Bridgewater, Calais, Eastport, Fort Fairfield, Fort Kent, Houlton, Jackman, Jonesport, Limestone, Madawaska, **Portland**, Rockland, Van Buren, Vanceboro

MARYLAND
Annapolis, **Baltimore**, Cambridge

MASSACHUSETTS
• **Boston**, Fall River, Gloucester, Lawrence, New Bedford, Plymouth, Salem, Springfield, Worcester

MICHIGAN
Battle Creek, **Detroit**, Grand Rapids, Muskegon, Port Huron, Saginaw-Bay City/Flint, Sault Ste. Marie

MINNESOTA
Baudette, **Duluth/Superior, WI**, Grand Portage, Internationa Falls-Ranier, **Minneapolis-St. Paul**, Noyes, Pinecreek, Roseau, Warroad

MISSISSIPPI
Greenville, Gulfport, Pascagoula, Vicksburg

MISSOURI Kansas City St. Joseph
St. Louis Springfield (Temp.)

MONTANA Butte Del Bonita
Great Falls Morgan Opheim
Piegan Raymond Roosville
Scobey Sweetgrass Turner
Whitetail Whitlash

NEBRASKA Omaha

NEVADA Las Vegas Reno

NEW HAMPSHIRE Portsmouth

NEW JERSEY Perth Amboy (See N.Y./Newark)

NEW MEXICO Albuquerque Columbus

NEW YORK
Albany Alexandria Bay **Buffalo-Niagara**
Cape Vincent Champlain-Rouses Pt.
Chateaugay Clayton Fort Covington
Massena • **New York** **JFK Airport Area**
Newark Area **N.Y. Seaport** **Ogdensburg**
Oswego Rochester Sodus Point
Syracuse Trout River Utica

NORTH CAROLINA
Beaufort-Morehead CityCharlotte
Durham Reidsville **Wilmington**
Winston-Salem

NORTH DAKOTA Ambrose Antler
Carbury Duenseith Fortuna
Hannah Hansboro Maida
Neche Noonan Northgate
Pembina Portal Sarles
Sherwood St. John Walhalla
Westhope

OHIO
Akron Ashtabula/Conneaut
Cincinnati/Lawrenceburg, IN **Cleveland**
Columbus Dayton Toledo/Sandusky

OKLAHOMA Oklahoma City Tulsa

OREGON Astoria Coos Bay
Newport **Portland***

PENNSYLVANIA Chester (See Phil.) Erie
Harrisburg **Philadelphia/Chester/Wilmington**
Pittsburgh Wilkes-Barre/Scranton

PUERTO RICO Aguadilla Fajardo
Guanica HumacaoJobos
Mayaguez Ponce **San Juan**

RHODE ISLAND Newport **Providence**

SOUTH CAROLINA **Charleston** Columbia
Georgetown **Greenville-Spartanburg**

TENNESSEE Chattanooga Knoxville
Memphis Nashville

TEXAS Amarillo Austin
Beaumont* Brownsville Corpus Christi
Dallas/Ft. Worth Del Rio Eagle Pass
El Paso Fabens Freeport
Hidalgo • **Houston/Galveston**
Laredo Lubbock Orange*
Port Arthur* Pt. Lavaca-Pt. Comfort
Presidio Progreso Rio Grande City
Roma Sabine* San Antonio

UTAH Salt Lake City

VERMONT Beecher Falls Burlington
Derby Line Highgate Springs/Alburg
Norton Richford **St. Albans**

VIRGIN ISLANDS **Charlotte Amalie, St. Thomas**
Christiansted Coral Bay Cruz Bay
Frederiksted

VIRGINIA Alexandria
Norfolk-Newport News Richmond-Petersburg

WASHINGTON Aberdeen Anacortes*
Bellingham* Blaine Boundary
Danville Everett* Ferry
Friday Harbor* Frontier Laurier
Longview* Lynden Metaline Falls
Neah Bay* Nighthawk Olympia*
Oroville Point Roberts Port Angeles*
Port Townsend* **Seattle*** Spokane
Sumas Tacoma*

WEST VIRGINIA Charleston

WISCONSIN Ashland Green Bay
Manitowoc Marinette **Milwaukee**
Racine Sheboygan

Consolidated Ports:
Columbia River port of entry includes Longview, Washington, and Portland, OR.
Beaumont, Orange, Port Arthur, Sabine port of entry includes ports of the same name.
Port of Puget Sound includes Tacoma, Seattle, Port Angeles, Port Townsend, Neah Bay, Friday Harbor, Everette, Bellingham, Anacortes, and Olympia in the State of Washington.
Port of Philadelphia includes Wilmington and Chester.
Port of Rock Island includes Moline and Davenport, IA.
Port of Shreveport includes Bossier City, LA.

Designated User-fee Airports: Allentown-Bethlehem-Easton, PA; Casper, WY; Columbus, OH; Dona Ana County, NM; Fargo, ND; Ft. Myers, FL; Ft. Wayne, IN; Jackson, MS; Klamath County, OR; Lebanon, NH; Lexington, KY; Midland, TX; Morristown, NJ; Oakland-Pontiac, MI; Rockford, IL; Sanford, FL; St. Paul, AK; Waukegan, IL; Wilmington, OH; Yakima, WA.

Customs Regions and Districts

Headquarters
U.S. Customs Service
1301 Constitution Ave., NW
Washington, DC 20229

Northeast Region—
Boston, Mass. 02222-1056
Districts:
Portland, ME 04112
St. Albans, VT 05478
Boston, MA 02222-1059
Providence, RI 02905
Buffalo, NY 14202
Ogdensburg, NY 13669
Philadelphia, PA 19106
Baltimore, MD 21202

New York Region
New York, NY 10048
New York Seaport Area
New York, NY 10048
Kennedy Airport Area
Jamaica, NY 11430
Newark Area
Newark, NJ 07114

Southeast Region—
Miami, Fla. 33131
Districts:
Charlotte, NC 28219
Old San Juan, PR 00901
Charleston, SC 29401
Savannah, GA 31401
Tampa, FL 33605
Miami, FL 33102
St. Thomas, VI 00801
Norfolk, VA 23510
Washington, DC 20166

South Central Region—
New Orleans, La. 70130
Districts:
Mobile, AL 36602
New Orleans, LA 70130

Southwest Region—
Houston, TX 77057
Districts:
Port Arthur, TX 77642
Houston, TX 77029
Laredo, TX 78041-3130
El Paso, TX 79925
Dallas/Fort Worth, TX 75261
Nogales, AZ 85621

Pacific Region—
Los Angeles, Calif. 90831-0700
Districts:
San Diego, CA 92188
Los Angeles/Long Beach, CA 90731
San Francisco, CA 94126
Honolulu, HI 96806
Portland, OR 97209
Seattle, WA 98104
Anchorage, AK 99501

North Central Region—
Chicago, Ill. 60603-5790
Districts:
Chicago, IL 60607
Pembina, ND 58271
Minneapolis, MN 55401
Duluth, MN 55802-1390
Milwaukee, WI 53237-0260
Cleveland, OH 44114
St. Louis, MO 63105
Detroit, MI 48226-2568
Great Falls, MT 59405

U.S. Customs Officers in Foreign Countries

Austria
Customs Attaché
American Embassy
Boltzmanngasse 16
A-1091 Vienna
Tel: [43](1) 310-5896

Belgium
Customs Attaché
American Embassy
27 Boulevard du Regent
B-1000 Brussels
Tel: [32](2) 502-3300

Canada
Customs Attaché
American Embassy
100 Wellington St.
Ottawa, ON K1P 5T1
Tel: (613) 238-5335 Ext. 322

Dominican Republic
Customs Attaché
American Embassy
Calle Leopold a Navarro #1
Cazcue
Santo Domingo
Tel: (809) 221-6909

France
Customs Attaché
American Embassy
58 bis Rue la Boetie
Room 317
76008 Paris
Tel: [33](1) 42-96-12-02 Ext. 2392/2393

Germany
Customs Attaché
American Embassy
Deichmanns Ave. 29
5300 Bonn 2
Tel: [49](228) 3392207, 3312853

Hong Kong
Senior Customs Representative
American Consulate General
St. John's Building-11th Floor
33 Garden Road
Hong Kong
Tel: [852] 523-9011 Ext. 244

Italy
Customs Attaché
American Embassy
Via Veneto 119
Rome
Tel: [39](6) 467-42475

Senior Customs Representative
American Consulate General
Via Principe Amedeo 2/10
20121 Milano
Tel: [39](2) 2903-5218

Japan
Customs Attaché
American Embassy
10-5 Akasaka 1-Chome
Minato-ku
Tokyo 107
Tel: [81](3) 3224-5433

Korea
Customs Attaché
82 Sejong-ro
Chongro-ku
Seoul 110-050
Tel: [82](2) 397-4644

Mexico
Customs Attaché
American Embassy
Paseo de la Reforma 305
Colonia Cuauhtémoc
Mexico City
Tel: [52](5) 211-042, Ext. 3687

Senior Customs Representative
American Consulate
Paseo Montejo 453
97000 Merida, Yucatan
Tel: [52](99) 25-8235

Senior Customs Representative
American Consulate General
Avenida Constitucion
411 Poniente
Monterrey, N.L.
Tel: [52](83) 42-7972

The Netherlands
Customs Attaché
American Embassy
Lange Voorhout 102
2514EJ The Hague
Tel: [31](70) 392-4651

Panama
Customs Attaché
Calle 38 & Avenida Balboa
Panama
Tel: [507] 271777, Ext. 2445

Singapore
Customs Attaché
American Embassy
30 Hill Road
Singapore 0617
Tel: [65] 388-0251

Thailand
Customs Attaché
American Embassy
95 Wireless Road
Bangkok
Tel: [66](2) 252-5040 Ext. 2539

United Kingdom
Customs Attaché
American Embassy
24/31 Grosvenor Square
London, W1A 1AE
Tel: [44](71) 493-4599

Uruguay
Customs Attaché
American Embassy
1776 Lauro Muller
Montevideo
Tel: [598](2) 23-6061

Venezuela
Customs Attaché
American Embassy
Avenida Francisco de Miranda y Avenida Principal
De la Floresta
Caracas
Tel: [58](2) 285-2222

Suggestions to the Exporter

FOR FASTER CUSTOMS CLEARANCE:

1. Include all information required on your customs invoices.
2. Prepare your invoices carefully. Type them clearly. Allow sufficient space between lines. Keep the data within each column.
3. Make sure that your invoices contain the information that would be shown on a well-prepared packing list.
4. Mark and number each package so that it can be identified with the corresponding marks and numbers appearing on your invoice.
5. Show on your invoice a detailed description of each item of goods contained in each individual package.
6. Mark your goods legibly and conspicuously with the name of the country of origin, unless they are specifically exempted from the country of origin marking requirements, and with such other marking as required by the marking laws of the U.S. Exemptions and general marking requirements are detailed in Chapters 24 and 25.
7. Comply with the provisions of any special laws of the U.S. that may apply to your goods, such as the laws relating to foods, drugs, cosmetics, alcoholic beverages, and radioactive materials.
8. Observe closely the instructions with respect to invoicing, packaging, marking, labeling, etc., sent to you by your customer in the U.S. The customer has probably made a careful check of the requirements that will have to be met when your goods arrive.
9. Work with U.S. Customs in developing packing standards for your commodities.
10. Establishing sound security procedures at your facility and while transporting your goods for shipment. Do not allow narcotic smugglers the opportunity to introduce narcotics into your shipment. The 1993 Cusoms Modernization Act has set $500 as the minimum penalty for importation of undeclared controlled substances found in your shipment.
11. Consider shipping on a carrier participating in the Automated Manifest System or otherwise transmitting your entry documentation and declarations electronically through the National Customs Automation Program (NCAP), as it becomes available.

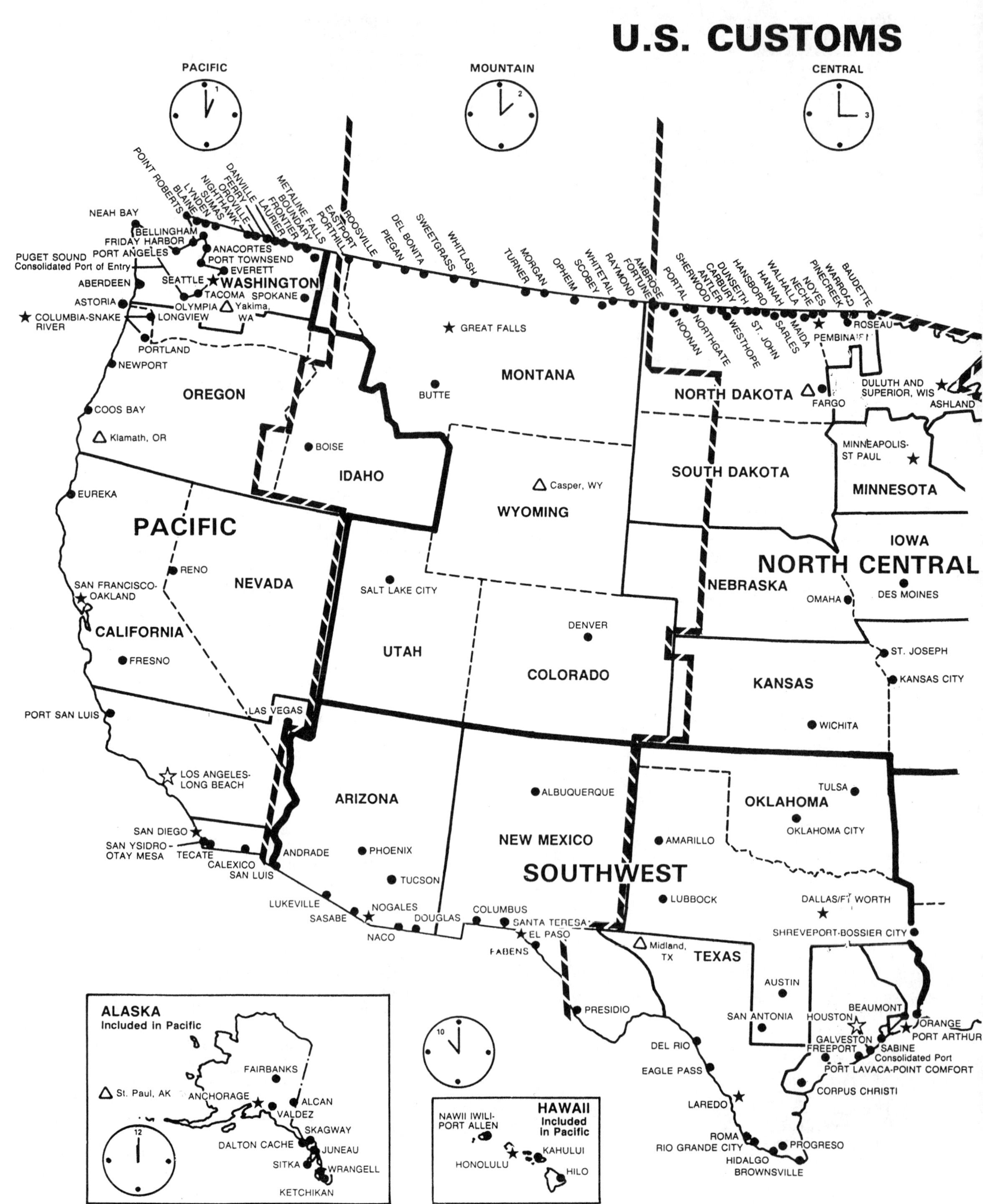
U.S. CUSTOMS
PACIFIC
MOUNTAIN
CENTRAL
PACIFIC
NORTH CENTRAL
SOUTHWEST
WASHINGTON
OREGON
IDAHO
MONTANA
WYOMING
NORTH DAKOTA
SOUTH DAKOTA
MINNESOTA
IOWA
NEBRASKA
NEVADA
CALIFORNIA
UTAH
COLORADO
KANSAS
ARIZONA
NEW MEXICO
OKLAHOMA
TEXAS
NEAH BAY
BELLINGHAM
FRIDAY HARBOR
PORT ANGELES
PUGET SOUND
Consolidated Port of Entry
ANACORTES
PORT TOWNSEND
EVERETT
SEATTLE
ABERDEEN
TACOMA
SPOKANE
ASTORIA
OLYMPIA
Yakima, WA
COLUMBIA-SNAKE RIVER
LONGVIEW
PORTLAND
NEWPORT
COOS BAY
Klamath, OR
EUREKA
RENO
SAN FRANCISCO-OAKLAND
FRESNO
PORT SAN LUIS
LAS VEGAS
LOS ANGELES-LONG BEACH
SAN DIEGO
SAN YSIDRO-OTAY MESA
TECATE
CALEXICO
SAN LUIS
ANDRADE
PHOENIX
TUCSON
LUKEVILLE
SASABE
NOGALES
NACO
DOUGLAS
COLUMBUS
SANTA TERESA
EL PASO
FABENS
PRESIDIO
POINT ROBERTS
BLAINE
LYNDEN
SUMAS
NIGHTHAWK
OROVILLE
FERRY
DANVILLE
LAURIER
FRONTIER
BOUNDARY
METALINE FALLS
PORTHILL
EASTPORT
ROOSVILLE
PIEGAN
DEL BONITA
SWEETGRASS
WHITLASH
TURNER
MORGAN
OPHEIM
SCOBEY
WHITETAIL
RAYMOND
FORTUNE
AMBROSE
PORTAL
NOONAN
SHERWOOD
NORTHGATE
ANTLER
CARBURY
WESTHOPE
DUNSEITH
HANSBORO
ST. JOHN
HANNAH
SARLES
WALHALLA
MAIDA
NECHE
NOYES
PINECREEK
WARROAD
BAUDETTE
ROSEAU
PEMBINA
GREAT FALLS
BUTTE
BOISE
Casper, WY
SALT LAKE CITY
DENVER
FARGO
DULUTH AND SUPERIOR, WIS
ASHLAND
MINNEAPOLIS-ST PAUL
OMAHA
DES MOINES
ST. JOSEPH
KANSAS CITY
WICHITA
TULSA
OKLAHOMA CITY
ALBUQUERQUE
AMARILLO
LUBBOCK
DALLAS/FT WORTH
SHREVEPORT-BOSSIER CITY
Midland, TX
AUSTIN
SAN ANTONIA
HOUSTON
BEAUMONT
ORANGE
PORT ARTHUR
GALVESTON
FREEPORT
SABINE
Consolidated Port
PORT LAVACA-POINT COMFORT
CORPUS CHRISTI
DEL RIO
EAGLE PASS
LAREDO
ROMA
RIO GRANDE CITY
PROGRESO
HIDALGO
BROWNSVILLE
ALASKA
Included in Pacific
FAIRBANKS
St. Paul, AK
ANCHORAGE
ALCAN
VALDEZ
SKAGWAY
DALTON CACHE
JUNEAU
SITKA
WRANGELL
KETCHIKAN
HAWAII
Included in Pacific
NAWII IWILI-PORT ALLEN
HONOLULU
KAHULUI
HILO

SERVICE

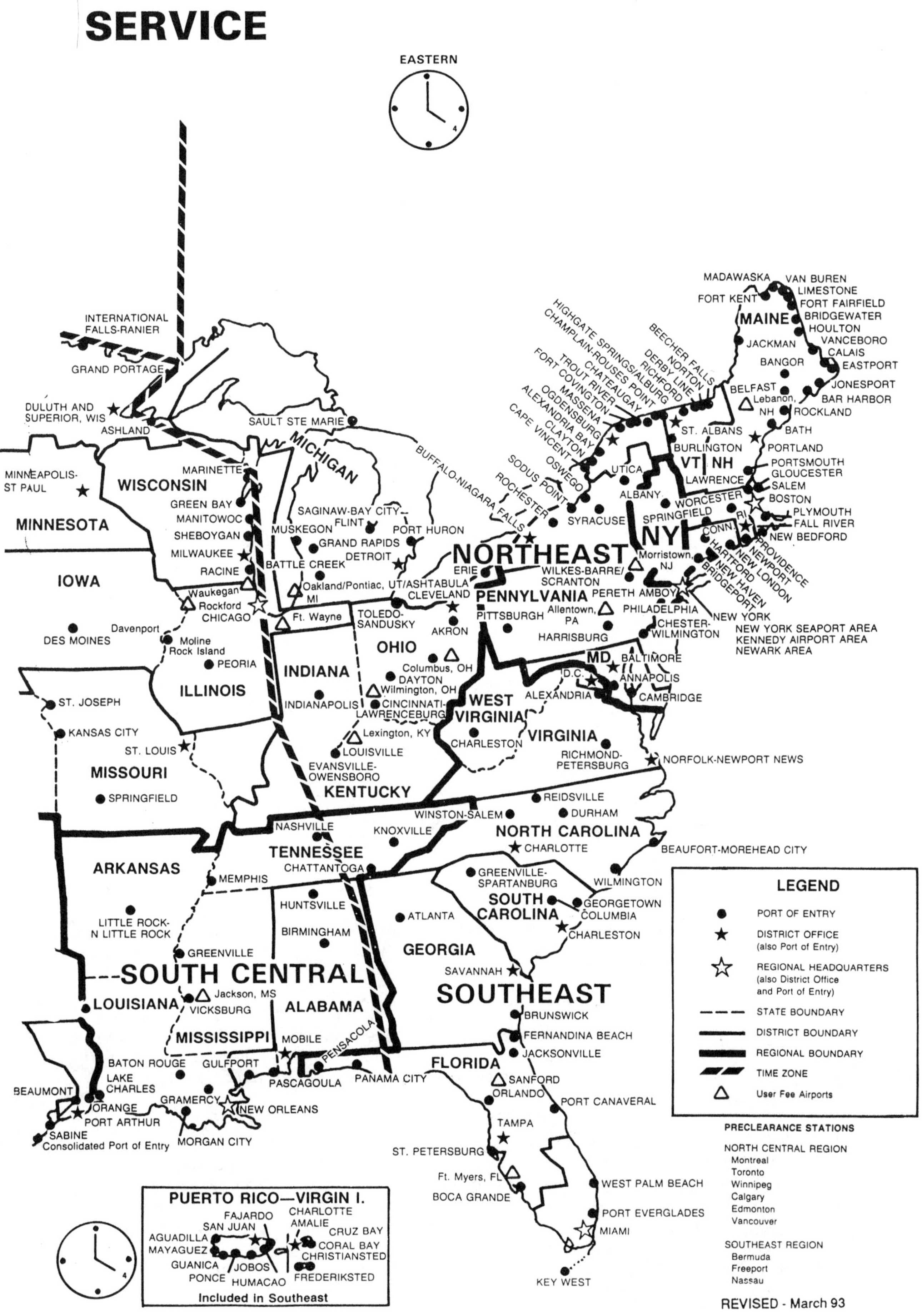
EASTERN
NORTHEAST
SOUTHEAST
SOUTH CENTRAL
LEGEND
PORT OF ENTRY
DISTRICT OFFICE (also Port of Entry)
REGIONAL HEADQUARTERS (also District Office and Port of Entry)
STATE BOUNDARY
DISTRICT BOUNDARY
REGIONAL BOUNDARY
TIME ZONE
User Fee Airports
PUERTO RICO—VIRGIN I.
Included in Southeast
PRECLEARANCE STATIONS
NORTH CENTRAL REGION
Montreal
Toronto
Winnipeg
Calgary
Edmonton
Vancouver
SOUTHEAST REGION
Bermuda
Freeport
Nassau
REVISED - March 93

2
Entry Process

When a shipment reaches the U.S., the importer of record (i.e., the owner, purchaser, or licensed customs broker designated by the owner, purchaser, or consignee) will file entry documents for the goods with the district or port director at the port of entry. Imported goods are not legally entered until after the shipment has arrived within the port of entry, delivery of the merchandise has been authorized by Customs and estimated duties have been paid. It is the responsibility of the importer to arrange for examination and release of the goods.

Note: In addition to the U.S. Customs Service, importers should contact other agencies when questions regarding particular commodities arise. For example, questions about products regulated by the Food and Drug Administration should be forwarded to the nearest FDA district office (check local phone book under "U.S. Government" listings) or to the Division of Enforcement, Imports Branch, FDA, 200 C Street SW, Washington, DC 20204, (202) 205-4726.

The same is true for alcohol, tobacco, firearms, wildlife products (furs, skins, shells), motor vehicles, and other products and merchandise regulated by the 60 federal agencies for which Customs enforces entry laws. Appropriate agencies are identified in this section and in the Commodity Index chapters covering specific products.

Goods may be entered for consumption, entered for warehouse at the port of arrival, or they may be transported in-bond to another port of entry and entered there under the same conditions as at the port of arrival. Arrangements for transporting the merchandise to an interior port in-bond may be made by the consignee, by a customs broker, or by any other person having a sufficient interest in the goods for that purpose. *Unless your merchandise arrives directly at the port where you wish to enter it, you may be charged additional fees by the carriers for transportation to the port of entry from the port of arrival unless other arrangements have been made.* Under some circumstances, your goods may be released through your local Customs port even though they arrive at another port from a foreign country. Arrangements must be made prior to arrival at the Customs port where you intend to file your duties and documentation.

Goods to be placed in a foreign trade zone are not entered at the customhouse. Refer to "Foreign Trade Zones" on page 232 for further information.

Evidence of Right to Make Entry

Goods may be entered only by the owner, purchaser, or a licensed customs broker. When the goods are consigned "to order," the bill of lading properly endorsed by the consignor may serve as evidence of the right to make entry. An air waybill may be used for merchandise arriving by air.

In most instances, entry is made by a person or firm certified by the carrier bringing the goods to the port of entry and is considered the "owner" of the goods for customs purposes. The document issued by the carrier is known as a "Carrier's Certificate." An example of the format is shown in the appendix. In certain circumstances, entry may be made by means of a duplicate bill of lading or a shipping receipt.

Entry for Consumption

The entry of merchandise is a two-part process consisting of (1) filing the documents necessary to determine whether merchandise may be released from Customs custody and (2) filing the documents that contain information for duty assessment and statistical purposes. Both of these processes can be accomplished electronically via the Automated Broker Interface program of the Automated Commercial Systems or through the National Customs Automation Program (NCAP), provided electronic filing is available. The NCAP was established by the 1993 Customs Modernization Act and is still in the implementation phase at many ports. To become a participant in one of these programs, importers or brokers should request information from Customs.

Entry Documents

Within five working days of the date of arrival of a shipment at a U.S. port of entry, entry documents must be filed at a location specified by the district or area director, unless an extension is granted. These documents consist of:

a. Entry Manifest, Customs **Form 7533**; or Application and Special Permit for Immediate Delivery, Customs **Form 3461**, or other form of merchandise release required by the district director.
b. Evidence of right to make entry.
c. Commercial invoice or a pro forma invoice when the commercial invoice cannot be produced.
d. Packing lists if appropriate.
e. Other documents necessary to determine merchandise admissibility.

If the goods are to be released from Customs custody on entry documents, an entry summary for consumption must be filed and estimated duties deposited at the port of entry within 10 working days of the time the goods are entered and released.

Surety

The entry must be accompanied by evidence that a bond is posted with Customs to cover any potential duties, taxes, and penalties that may accrue. Bonds may be secured through a resident U.S. surety company but may also be posted in the form of U.S. money or certain U.S. government obligations. They may also be posted electronically. In the event that a customhouse broker is employed for the purpose of making entry, the broker may permit the use of his bond to provide the required coverage.

Entry Summary Documentation

Following presentation of the entry, the shipment may be examined by Customs or examination may be waived. The shipment is then released, provided no legal or regulatory violations have been noted. Entry summary documentation is filed and estimated duties are deposited within 10 working days of the release of the merchandise at a designated customhouse. Entry summary documentation consists of:

a. The entry package returned to the importer, broker, or his authorized agent after merchandise is permitted release.

b. Entry summary (Customs **Form 7501**)

c. Other invoices and documents necessary for the assessment of duties, collection of statistics, or the determination that all import requirements have been satisfied. This paper documentation can be reduced or eliminated when utilizing features of the Automated Broker Interface or the National Customs Automation Program (NCAP).

Electronic Entry

The 1993 Customs Modernization Act created the National Customs Automation Program (NCAP) to allow for electronic entry filing. The phase-in of the NCAP is expected to be complete by 1999. This system will allow importers to file documentation and declarations, post bonds, and pay duties, fees, and taxes electronically. The NCAP will also provide for electronic batch filing of multiple entries, periodic reconciliation of entries, and payment of duties, taxes, and fees on a monthly account basis, rather than for each individual entry as in the present system.

An importer who uses NCAP may choose to transmit electronically by the entry/entry summary procedure or the entry/import activity summary statement. The first procedure is for filing individual entry summaries. The second procedure involves filing a single statement that covers all or some of the entries or warehouse withdrawals made during a calendar month. The statement is transmitted by the twentieth day following the end of the calendar month. In either procedure, reconciliation is available, allowing the importer to provide at a time after entry of the goods any information required for admission of the merchandise but undetermined at the time of entry. The importer must post a bond or security to cover reconciliation statements.

Immediate Delivery

An alternate procedure that provides for immediate release of a shipment may be used in some cases by making application for a Special Permit for Immediate Delivery on Customs **Form 3461** prior to the arrival of the merchandise. Carriers participating in the Automated Manifest System can receive conditional release authorizations after leaving the foreign country, and up to five days before the landing in the U.S. If the application is approved, the shipment is released expeditiously following arrival. An entry summary must then be filed in proper form, either on paper or electronically, and estimated duties deposited within 10 working days of release. Release using **Form 3461** is limited to the following merchandise:

a. Merchandise arriving from Canada or Mexico, if approved by the district director and an appropriate bond is on file.

b. Fresh fruits and vegetables for human consumption arriving from Canada and Mexico and removed from the area immediately contiguous to the border to the importer's premises within the port of importation.

c. Shipments consigned to or for the account of any agency or officer of the U.S. Government.

d. Articles for a trade fair.

e. Tariff-rate quota merchandise and under certain circumstances merchandise subject to an absolute quota. Absolute quota items require a formal entry at all times.

f. In very limited circumstances, merchandise released to a warehouse followed within 10 working days by a warehouse withdrawal for consumption.

g. Merchandise specifically authorized by Customs Headquarters to be entitled to release for immediate delivery.

Entry for Warehouse

If it is desirable to postpone the release of the goods, they may be placed in a Customs bonded warehouse under a warehouse entry. The goods may remain in the bonded warehouse up to five years from the date of importation. At any time during that period, warehoused goods may be reexported without the payment of duty or they may be withdrawn for consumption upon the payment of duty at the rate of duty in effect on the date of withdrawal. If the goods are destroyed under Customs supervision, no duty is payable.

While the goods are in the bonded warehouse, they may, under Customs supervision, be manipulated by cleaning, sorting, repacking, or otherwise changing their condition by processes that do not amount to manufacturing. After manipulation and within the warehousing period, the goods may be exported without the payment of duty or they may be withdrawn for consumption upon payment of duty at the rate applicable to the goods in their manipulated condition at the time of withdrawal. Perishable goods, explosive substances, or prohibited importations may not be placed in a bonded warehouse. Certain restricted articles, though not allowed release from custody, may be warehoused.

Information regarding bonded manufacturing warehouses is contained in section 311 of the Tariff Act. (19 USC 1311).

Unentered Goods

The 1993 Customs Modernization Act (Mod Act) has substantially amended the provisions for unentered goods. These amendments are intended to facilitate the automation of Customs procedures, reduce the costs of storing and processing unclaimed or abandoned merchandise, and authorize the conversion of such merchandise to official use. The changes are noted throughout the following discussion.

Goods that remain unentered for more than five working days after arrival at the port of entry, or the port of destination for in-bond shipments, are subject to the provisions for unclaimed or abandoned merchandise. The Mod Act has expanded application of these provisions to cover not only merchandise for which no entry is made at all, but also for which a complete entry is not made within five days after arrival.

Under the Mod Act, carriers of unentered goods must notify a bonded warehouse that the merchandise is unentered. The warehouse will arrange with a bonded carrier or licensed cartage firm to transport the merchandise to the warehouse at the risk and expense of the consignee of the goods. If the goods are not entered within six months from the date of importation, Customs can dispose of them. Perishable goods, goods liable to depreciation, and explosive substances, however, may be sold sooner. Immediate sale is also permitted if the storage expense of the seized merchandise is deemed disproportionate to its value.

The Mod Act has also created several options for disposal of unentered goods. Customs may elect to sell them at public auction or to notify all known interested parties that clear title to the merchandise will vest in the U.S. 30 days after notice in the absence of an entry for consumption. If title vests in the U.S. under the second option, the government may sell the goods, retain them for official use, or transfer them to any federal, state, or local agency. The government recipient must pay all transfer and storage charges on retained or transferred merchandise. A party can apply to the Secretary of the Treasury for relief from the forfeiture of unclaimed or abandoned goods, which relief is discretionary and depends on whether the party can establish that no notice was received of the imminent transfer of title to the U.S.

If the unclaimed or abandoned goods are sold, storage charges, expenses of sale, duties, taxes, fees, and amounts for the satisfaction of liens will be paid from the sale proceeds. Any surplus remaining after these deductions is deposited with the U.S. Treasury. This differs from previous policy under which any residuals from such liquidation went to the party holding title to the goods. If the goods are subject to internal revenue taxes and will not bring enough on sale at public auction to pay the taxes, they are subject to retention by the U.S. government, destruction, or other disposition at the discretion of Customs.

Mail Entries

Importers have found that in some cases it is to their advantage to use the mails to import merchandise into the U.S. Some benefits to be gained are:

a. Ease in clearing shipments through Customs. The duties on parcels valued at the regulatory amount or less are collected by the letter carrier delivering the parcel to the addressee (see note below).

b. Savings on shipping charges. Smaller, low-valued packages can often be sent less expensively through the mails.

c. No entry required on duty-free merchandise not exceeding the regulatory amount in value.

d. No need to clear shipments personally if they are valued at less than the regulatory amount.

Note: The exact amount is set by regulation, but the statutory cap has been raised from $1,250 to $2,500 by the 1993 Customs Modernization Act.

Joint Customs and postal regulations provide that all parcel post packages must have a Customs declaration securely attached giving an accurate description and valuation of the contents. This declaration may be obtained from post offices. Commercial shipments must also be accompanied by a commercial invoice enclosed with the parcel bearing the declaration.

Each mail article containing an invoice or statement of value should be marked on the address side "Invoice enclosed." If the invoice or statement cannot conveniently be enclosed within the sealed article, it may be securely attached to the article. Failure to comply with any of these requirements will delay clearance of the shipment through Customs.

Packages other than parcel post, such as letter-class mail, commercial papers, printed matter, and samples of merchandise, must bear on the address side a label, **Form C1**, provided by the Universal Postal Union, or the endorsement "May be opened for customs purposes before delivery" or similar words definitely waiving the privacy of the seal and indicating that Customs officers may open the parcel without recourse to the addressee. Parcels not labeled or endorsed in this manner and found to contain prohibited merchandise or merchandise subject to duty or tax are subject to forfeiture.

Customs prepares the customs entry for mail importations not exceeding the regulatory amount in value, and the letter carrier at the destination delivers the parcel to the addressee upon payment of the duty. If the value of a mail importation exceeds the regulatory amount, the addressee is notified to prepare and file a formal Customs entry (consumption entry) for it at the Customs port nearest to him. A commercial invoice is required with the entry. The informal entry amount is set by regulation, but the statutory cap has been raised from $1,250 to $2,500 by the 1993 Customs Modernization Act.

A Customs processing fee of $5.00 will be assessed on each item of dutiable mail for which Customs prepares documentation. This nominal charge on all dutiable or taxable mail, in addition to the duty, is collected from the addressee. This is a postal fee (in addition to prepaid postage) authorized by international postal conventions and agreements as partial reimbursement to the Postal Service for its work in clearing packages through Customs and delivering them.

Note: The following exceptions are made with respect to the regulatory amount for informal entry:

Articles classified in sub-chapters III and IV, HTSUS chapter 99 (temporary modifications of trade legislation and agricultural import restrictions)

Billfolds and other flat goods
Feathers and feather products
Flowers and foliage, artificial or preserved
Footwear
Fur, articles of
Gloves
Handbags
Headwear and hat braids
Leather, articles of
Luggage
Millinery ornaments
Pillows and cushions

Plastics, miscellaneous articles of
Rawhides and skins
Rubber, miscellaneous articles of
Textile fibers and products
Toys, games, and sports equipment
Trimmings

The limit for these articles is set at $250. However, almost all commercial shipments of textile fibers and products require formal entry regardless of value. Unaccompanied shipments of made-to-measure suits from Hong Kong require a formal entry regardless of value.

Shipment Detention

The 1993 Customs Modernization Act added new procedures for Customs to follow in detaining shipments. Pursuant to the Act, if Customs has authority to determine the admissibility of a shipment, that decision must be made within five working days (excluding weekends and holidays) following the date the merchandise is presented for customs examination. Any goods not released within that time are considered detained. No later than five days (excluding weekends and holidays) after deciding to detain the goods, Customs must issue a notice of detention to the importer or other party with an interest in the goods. The notice will include a description of what information would accelerate disposition if supplied to Customs by the importer.

If Customs fails to make a final determination on admissibility of detained merchandise within 30 days after it is presented for Customs examination, the merchandise is presumed to be excluded. The 30-day period may vary if specifically authorized by other laws.

Recordkeeping

Substantial recordkeeping is required for entries of imported merchandise, and Customs is authorized to make reasonable audits of records required for the entry of merchandise. Under the 1993 Customs Modernization Act (Mod Act), the recordkeeping and audit procedures have been amended to reduce paperwork demands on importers at the time of entry. Customs is being encouraged to waive the production of every relevant record at the time of entry. In this regard, the Act has extended the authority of Customs to demand production of such documents at a later date.

Customs may demand to examine the records of any of the following persons listed in the Act: owner of imported goods, importer, consignee, importer of record, entry filer, or other party who imports goods into U.S. customs territory, files a drawback claim, transports or stores merchandise carried or held under bond, or knowingly causes importation, transportation, or storage of merchandise under bond in U.S. customs territory. Records may also be demanded from agents acting for any of these parties, any person whose activities require filing a declaration, or both.

If you qualify as one of the above parties, the law requires you to keep specific records. A list of the records is available from Customs. Essentially, these include entry declarations, documents, and electronically generated or machine readable data that relate to entry activities and that are usually kept in the ordinary course of business. Records must be kept for the times prescribed by Customs regulations, but not exceeding five years from the entry or exportation date. An exception is made for records of drawback claims. Such records must be kept until the third anniversary of the date the claim was paid.

A party who fails to comply with Custom's lawful demand for records is subject to monetary fine at an amount determined by Customs based on the particular situation. For willful failure to maintain, store, or retrieve demanded information, the fine for each release of goods may not exceed the lesser of $100,000 or 75% of the appraised value of the goods. For failure because of negligence, the penalty for each release may not exceed the lesser of $10,000 or 40% of the appraised value of the goods. Customs also has discretion to raise duty rates against such goods. These penalties are not mandatory, and Customs may remit or mitigate them on consideration of the circumstances. They may also be avoided on proof that the demanded information was lost because of a disaster or other event beyond the party's fault, that the party substantially complied with the demand, or that the information had been presented to and retained by Customs.

Depending on the size, nature, and volume of an importer's business, the importer may request certification under the Customs Recordkeeping Compliance Program, created by the Mod Act. Program participants will be issued written warning notices instead of summarily fined for violations of recordkeeping requirements.

3
Right to Make Entry

Entry by Importer

Merchandise arriving in the U.S. by commercial carrier must be entered by the owner, purchaser, his authorized regular employee, or by the owner's licensed Customs broker designated by the owner, purchaser, or consignee. U.S. Customs officers and employees are not authorized to act as agents for importers or forwarders of imported merchandise, although they may give all reasonable advice and assistance to inexperienced importers.

The only persons who are authorized by the tariff laws of the U.S. to act as agents for importers in the transaction of their Customs business are Customs brokers who are private individuals or firms licensed by the Customs Service. Customs brokers will prepare and file the necessary Customs entries, arrange for the payment of the duties found due, take steps to effect the release of the goods in Customs custody, and otherwise represent their principals in customs matters. The fees charged for these services vary according to the Customs broker and the extent of services performed.

Every entry must be supported by one of the forms of evidence of the right to make entry outlined in this chapter. When entry is made by a Customs broker, a Customs power of attorney given by the person or firm for whom the Customs broker is acting as agent is made in the name of the Customs broker. Ordinarily, the authority of an employee to make entry for his employer is most satisfactorily established by a Customs power of attorney.

Entries Made by Others

Entry of goods may be made by a nonresident individual or partnership, or a foreign corporation through an agent or representative of the exporter in the U.S., a member of the partnership, or an officer of the corporation.

The surety firm guaranteeing any Customs bond required from a nonresident individual or organization must be incorporated in the U.S. In addition, a foreign corporation in whose name merchandise is entered must have a resident agent authorized to accept service of process on its behalf in the state where the port of entry is located.

A licensed Customs broker named in a Customs power of attorney may make entry on behalf of the exporter or the exporter's representative. The owner's declaration made by a nonresident individual or organization, which the Customs broker may request, must be supported by a surety bond providing for the payment of any increased or additional duties found due. Liability for duties is discussed in Chapter 9. An owner's declaration executed in a foreign country is acceptable, but it must be executed before a notary public and must bear the notary's seal. Notaries public are found in all U.S. embassies around the world and in most of the larger consulates.

Power of Attorney

A nonresident individual, partnership, or foreign corporation may issue a power of attorney to a regular employee, Customs broker, partner, or corporation officer to act for the nonresident employer in the U.S. Any person named in a power of attorney must be a resident of the U.S. who has been authorized to accept service of process on behalf of the person or organization issuing the power of attorney. The power of attorney to accept service of process becomes irrevocable with respect to Customs transactions duly undertaken. Either the applicable Customs form (see appendix) or a document using the same language as the form is acceptable. References to those acts that the issuer has not authorized his agent to perform may be deleted from the form or omitted from the document.

Power of Attorney

The X Corporation,____
(Address, city, and country)

organized under the laws of ______________________________ hereby authorizes

____
(Name or names of employee or officer in the United States

____
and address or addresses)

to perform on behalf of the said corporation any and all acts specified in Customs Form 5291, Power of Attorney: to accept service of process in the United States on behalf of the X Corporation; to issue powers of attorney on Customs Form 5291 authorizing a qualified resident or residents of the United States to perform on behalf of the X Corporation all acts specified in Customs Form 5291; and to empower such resident or residents to accept service of process in the United States on behalf of the said X Corporation.

A power of attorney from a foreign corporation must be supported by the following documents or their equivalent when foreign law or practice differs from that in the U.S.:

1. A certificate from the proper public officer of the country showing the legal existence of the corporation, unless the fact of incorporation is so generally known as to be a matter of common knowledge.
2. A copy of that part of the charter or articles of incorporation that shows the scope of business of the corporation and its governing body.
3. A copy of the document or part thereof by which the person signing the power of attorney derives his authority, such as a provision of the charter or articles of incorporation, a copy of the resolution, minutes of the meeting of the board of directors, or other document by which the governing body conferred the authority. In this case a copy of the bylaws or other document giving the governing board the authority to designate others to appoint agents or attorney is required.

A nonresident individual or partnership or a foreign corporation may issue a power of attorney to authorize the persons or firms named in the power of attorney to issue like powers of attorney to other qualified residents of the U.S. and to empower the residents to whom such powers of attorney are issued to accept service of process on behalf of the nonresident individual or organization.

A power of attorney issued by a partnership must be limited to a period not to exceed two years from the date of execution and shall state the names of all members of the partnership. One member of a partnership may execute a power of attorney for the transaction of the customs business of the partnership. When a new firm is formed by a change of membership, the power of attorney of the prior firm is no longer effective for any customs purpose. The new firm will be required to issue a power of attorney for the transaction of its custom business. All other powers of attorney may be granted for an unlimited period.

Customs **Form 5291** or a document using the same language as the form is also used to empower an agent other than an attorney-at-law or Customs broker to file protests on behalf of an importer under section 514 of the Tariff Act of 1930 as amended. (See 19 CFR 141.32.)

Foreign corporations may comply with Customs regulations by executing a power of attorney on the letterhead of the corporation. A form of power of attorney used for this purpose is given below. A nonresident individual or partner may use this same form.

Because the laws regarding incorporation, notion, and authentication of documents vary from country to country, the agent to be named in the power of attorney should consult the district director of Customs at the port of entry where proof of the document's existence may be required as to the proper form to be used and the formalities to be met.

4 Examination of Goods and Entry Documents

Prior to the release of the goods, the district or port director will designate representative quantities for examination by Customs officers under conditions properly safeguarding the goods. Some kinds of goods must be examined to determine whether they meet special requirements of the law. For example, food and beverages unfit for human consumption would not meet the requirements of the Food and Drug Administration.

Examination of goods and documents is necessary to determine, among other things:

a. The value of the goods for Customs purposes and their dutiable status.
b. Whether the goods must be marked with the country of their origin or require special marking or labeling. If so, whether they are marked in the manner required.
c. Whether the shipment contains prohibited articles.
d. Whether the goods are correctly invoiced.
e. Whether the goods are in excess of the invoiced quantities or a shortage exists.
f. Whether the shipment contains illegal narcotics.

One of the primary methods of smuggling narcotics into the U.S. is in cargo shipments. Drug smugglers will place narcotics into a legitimate cargo shipment or container to be retrieved upon arrival in the U.S. Because smugglers use any means possible to hide narcotics, all aspects of the shipment are examined, including: container, pallets, boxes, and product. Only through intensive inspection can narcotics be discovered. The 1993 Customs Modernization Act sets a minimum fine of $500 for importation of undeclared controlled substances.

Textiles and textile products are considered trade-sensitive and as such may be subject to a higher percentage of examinations than other commodities.

Customs officers will ascertain the quantity of goods imported, making allowances for shortages under specified conditions and assessing duty on any excess. The invoice may state the quantities in the weights and measures of the country from which the goods are shipped or in the weights and measures of the U.S., but the entry must state the quantities in metric terms. Any information that Customs requires for the release of examined goods must be provided electronically or in paper form at the port of examination. A lack of information will not limit the authority of Customs to examine the goods.

Examination may be made in a Customs Service laboratory or at a private laboratory accredited by Customs. The 1993 Customs Modernization Act provides for the development of an accreditation program. Customs will authorize the release of a representative sample of imported goods for testing at an accredited laboratory. The test results from such a laboratory will be accepted in the absence of results from a Customs Service laboratory. Test results will be given to an importer on request, unless the results reveal information proprietary to the Customs Service or a copyright or patent holder. Testing at a private laboratory is at the importer's expense.

Excess Goods and Shortages

Careful documentation and packing—including full descriptions and counts by package and clear marking and numbering of all packages in the shipment with all this information being provided on the invoice—allows Customs to assess the true value of the entry. It also enables both Customs and the interested parties to determine if any part of the shipment is missing or if the shipment includes excess goods.

If any package that has been designated for examination is found by the Customs officer to contain any article not specified in the invoice or entry, and if Customs has reason to believe the article was omitted from the invoice or entry with fraudulent intent, Customs may impose a fine or even seize the entire package in which the article is found. In the absence of fraudulent intent, the value of the article will simply be added to the entry, and Customs will assess duties, fees, and taxes accordingly. *See e.g.*, 19 USC 1592 and 1595 a(c).

When a deficiency in quantity, weight, or measure is found by the Customs officer in the examination of any package that has been selected for examination, an allowance in duty will be made for the deficiency. Allowance in duty is made for deficiencies in packages not designated for examination, provided that before liquidation of the entry becomes final, the importer notifies the district or port director of Customs of the shortage and establishes to the satisfaction of the district or port director that the missing goods were not delivered to him.

Damage or Deterioration

Goods that are found by the Customs officer to be entirely without commercial value at the time of arrival in the U.S. because of damage or deterioration are treated as a "nonimportation." No duties are assessed on these goods. When damage or deterioration is present with respect to part of the shipment only, allowance in duties is not made unless the importer segregates the damaged or deteriorated part from the remainder of the shipment under Customs supervision.

When the shipment consists of fruits, vegetables, or other perishable merchandise, allowance in duties cannot be made unless the importer files an application for an allowance with the district or port director within 96 hours after the unlading of the merchandise and before it has been removed from Customs custody.

On shipments consisting of any article partly or wholly manufactured of iron or steel, or any manufacture of iron or steel, allowance or reduction of duty for partial damage or loss as a result of discoloration or rust is precluded by law.

Tare and Draft

In ascertaining the quantity of goods dutiable on net weight, a deduction is made from the gross weight for just and reasonable tare, which is the allowance for a deficiency in the weight or quantity of the merchandise by reason of the weight of the box, cask, bag, or other receptacle that contains it and is weighed with it. The following schedule tares are provided for in the Customs Regulations:

Apple Boxes. 3.6 kg (8 lb) per box. This schedule tare includes the paper wrappers, if any, on the apples.

China Clay in So-called Half-ton Casks. 32.6 kg (72 lb) per cask.

Figs in Skeleton Cases. Actual tare for outer containers plus 13% of the gross weight of the inside wooden boxes and figs.

Fresh Tomatoes. 113 gm (4 oz) per 100 paper wrappings.

Lemons and Oranges. 283 gm (10 oz) per box and 142 gm (5 oz) per half-box for paper wrappings, and actual tare for outer containers.

Ocher, Dry, in Casks. 8% of the gross weight; in oil in casks, 12% of the gross weight.

Pimientos in Tins Imported from Spain.

Size can	*Drained weights*
3 k	13.6 kg (30 lb)-case of 6 tins
794 gm (28 oz)	16.7 kg (36.7 lb)-case of 24 tins
425 gm (15 oz)	8.0 kg (17.72 lb)-case of 24 tins
198 gm (7 oz)	3.9 kg (8.62 lb)-case of 24 tins
113 gm (4 oz)	2.4 kg (5.33 lb)-case of 24 tins

Tobacco, Leaf Not Stemmed. 59 kg (13 lb) per bale; Sumatra: actual tare for outside coverings, plus 1.9 kg (4 1/4 lb) for the inside matting and, if a certificate is attached to the invoice certifying that the bales contain paper wrappings and specifying whether light or heavy paper has been used, either 113 gm (4 oz) or 227 gm (8 oz) for the paper wrapping according to the thickness of paper used.

For other goods dutiable on the net weight an actual tare will be determined. An accurate tare stated on the invoice is acceptable for Customs purposes in certain circumstances.

If the importer of record files a timely application with the district or port director of Customs, an allowance may be made in any case for excessive moisture and impurities not usually found in or upon the particular kind of goods.

5
Packing of Goods—Commingling

Packing

Information on how to pack goods for transport may be obtained from shipping manuals, carriers, forwarding agents, and other sources. This chapter, therefore, deals with packing goods being exported in a way that will permit U.S. Customs officers to examine, weigh, measure, and release the goods promptly.

Orderly packing and proper invoicing go hand in hand. You will speed up the clearance of your goods through customs, if you:

Invoice your goods in a systematic manner.

Show the exact quantity of each item of goods in each box, bale, case, or other package.

Put marks and numbers on each package.

Show those marks or numbers on your invoice opposite the itemization of goods contained in the package that bears those marks and numbers.

When the packages contain goods of one kind only, or when the goods are imported in packages the contents and values of which are uniform, the designation of packages for examination and the examination for customs purposes is greatly facilitated. If the contents and values differ from package to package, the possibility of delay and confusion is increased. Sometimes, because of the kinds of goods or because of the unsystematic manner in which they are packed, the entire shipment must be examined.

Pack and invoice your goods in a manner that makes a speedy examination possible. Always bear in mind that it may not be possible to ascertain the contents of your packages without full examination unless your invoice clearly shows the marks and numbers on each package (whether box, case, or bale) and specifies the exact quantity of each item of adequately described goods in each marked and numbered package.

Also, be aware that Customs examines cargo for narcotics that may be hidden in cargo, unbeknownst to the shipper or the importer. This can be time-consuming and expensive for both the importer and the Customs Service. Narcotics inspections may require completely stripping a container in order to physically examine a large portion of the cargo. This labor-intensive handling of cargo, whether by Customs, labor organizations, or private individuals, results in added costs, increased delays, and possible damage to the product. Importers can expedite this inspection process by working with Customs to develop packing standards that will permit effective Customs examinations with a minimum of delay, damage, and cost.

A critical aspect in facilitating inspections is how the cargo is loaded. "Palletizing" cargo—loading it onto pallets or other consolidated units—is an effective way to expedite such examinations. Palletization allows for quick cargo removal, or "devanning" of containers, in minutes using a forklift, compared to the hours it takes manually. Another example is leaving enough space at the top of a container and an aisle down the center to allow access by a narcotic-detector dog.

Your cooperation in these respects will help the Customs officers to decide which packages must be opened and examined; how much weighing, counting, or measuring must be done; and whether the goods are properly marked. It will simplify the calculation of tare and reduce the number of samples to be taken for laboratory analysis or for any other customs purpose. It will facilitate the verification of the contents of the packages as well as the reporting by Customs officers of missing or excess goods. And it will minimize the possibility that the importer may be asked to redeliver for examination packages that were released to him on the theory that the packages designated for examination were sufficient for that purpose.

Packing that amounts to a confusion of different kinds of goods makes it impracticable for Customs officers to determine the quantity of each kind of product in an importation and leads to various complications. No problem arises from the orderly packing of several kinds of properly invoiced goods in one package-it is indiscriminate packing that causes difficulty.

Commingling

Except as mentioned hereafter, whenever articles subject to different rates of duty are so packed together or mingled such that the quantity or value of each class of articles cannot be readily ascertained by Customs officers (without physical segregation of the shipment or the contents of any package thereof) the commingled articles shall be subject to the highest rate of duty applicable to any part of the commingled lot, unless the consignee or his agent segregates them under Customs supervision.

The three methods of ready ascertainment specified by General Note 6, HTSUS, are (l) sampling, (2) verification of packing lists or other documents filed at the time of entry, or (3) evidence showing performance of commercial settlements tests generally accepted in the trade and filed in the time and manner as prescribed in the Customs Regulations.

The segregation is at the risk and expense of the consignee. It must be done within 30 days (unless a longer time is granted) after the date of personal delivery or the date of mailing of a notice to the consignee by the district or port director of Customs that the goods are commingled. The compensation and expenses of the Customs officers supervising the segregation must be paid for by the consignee.

Assessment of duty on the commingled lot at the highest applicable rate does not apply to any part of a shipment if the consignee or his agent furnishes satisfactory proof that (l) such part is commercially negligible, is not capable of segregation without excessive cost, and will not be segregated prior to its use in a manufacturing process or otherwise, and (2) the commingling was not intended to avoid the payment of lawful duties.

Any article for which such proof is furnished shall be considered for all Customs purposes as a part of the article, subject to the next lower rate of duty, with which it is commingled.

In addition, the highest rate rule mentioned does not apply to any part of a shipment if there is furnished satisfactory proof that (1) the value of the commingled articles is less than the aggregate value would be if the shipment were segregated, (2) the shipment is not capable of segregation without excessive cost and will not be segregated prior to its use in a manufacturing process or otherwise, and (3) the commingling was not intended to avoid the payment of lawful duties.

Any merchandise for which such proof is furnished shall be considered for all Customs purposes to be dutiable at the rate applicable to the material present in greater quantity than any other material.

The above rules do not apply if the tariff schedules provide a particular tariff treatment for commingled articles.

6
Commercial Invoice

A commercial invoice, signed by the seller or shipper, or his agent, is acceptable for customs purposes if it is prepared in accordance with Section 141.86, Customs Regulations, and in the manner customary for a commercial transaction involving goods of the kind covered by the invoice. Importers and brokers participating in the National Customs Automation Program (NCAP) or the Automated Broker Interface may elect to transmit invoice data electronically and eliminate the paper document.

The invoice must provide the following information, as required by the Tariff Act:

(1) The port of entry to which the merchandise is destined;

(2) If merchandise is sold or agreed to be sold, the time, place, and names of buyer and seller; if consigned, the time and origin of shipment, and names of shipper and receiver;

(3) A detailed description of the merchandise, including the commercial name by which each item is known, the grade or quality, and the marks, numbers, or symbols under which sold by the seller or manufacturer in the country of exportation, together with the marks and numbers of the packages in which the merchandise is packed;

(4) The quantities in weights and measures;

(5) If sold or agreed to be sold, the purchase price of each item in the currency of the sale;

(6) If the merchandise is shipped for consignment, the value for each item, in the currency in which the transactions are usually made or, in the absence of such value, the price in such currency that the manufacturer, seller, shipper, or owner would have received, or was willing to receive, for such merchandise if sold in the ordinary course of trade and in the usual wholesale quantities *in the country of exportation;*

(7) The kind of currency;

(8) All charges upon the merchandise, itemized by name and amount including freight, insurance, commission, cases, containers, coverings, and cost of packing; and if not included above, all charges, costs, and expenses incurred in bringing the merchandise from alongside the carrier at the first U.S. port of entry. The cost of packing, cases, containers, and inland freight to the port of exportation need not be itemized by amount if included in the invoice price and so identified. Where the required information does not appear on the invoice as originally prepared, it shall be shown on an attachment to the invoice;

(9) All rebates, drawbacks, and bounties, separately itemized, allowed upon the exportation of the merchandise;

(10) The country of origin; and

(11) All goods or services furnished for the production of the merchandise but not included in the invoice price.

If the merchandise on the documents is sold while in transit, the original invoice reflecting this transaction and the resale invoice or a statement of sale showing the price paid for each item by the purchaser shall be filed as part of the entry, entry summary, or withdrawal documentation.

The invoice and all attachments must be in the English language, or shall be accompanied by an accurate English translation.

Each invoice shall state in adequate detail what merchandise is contained in each individual package.

If the invoice or entry does not disclose the weight, gage, or measure of the merchandise necessary to ascertain duties, the importer of record shall pay expenses incurred to obtain this information prior to the release of the merchandise from Customs custody.

Each invoice shall set forth in detail, for each class or kind of merchandise, every discount from list or other base price that has been or may be allowed in fixing each purchaser price or value.

When more than one invoice is included in the same entry, each invoice with its attachments shall be numbered consecutively by the importer on the bottom of the face of each page, beginning with number 1. If invoice is more than two pages, begin with number 1 for the first page of the first invoice and continue in a single series of numbers through all the invoices and attachments included in one entry. If an entry covers one invoice of one page and a second invoice of two pages, the numbering at the bottom of the page shall be as follows: Inv. 1, p.1; Inv. 2, p.2; Inv. 2, p.3.

Any information required on an invoice may be set forth either on the invoice or on the attachment.

Specific Requirements

1. **Separate Invoice Required for Each Shipment.** Not more than one distinct shipment from one consignor to one consignee by one commercial carrier shall be included on the same invoice.
2. **Assembled Shipments.** Merchandise assembled for shipment to the same consignee by one commercial carrier may be included in one invoice. The original bills or invoices covering the merchandise, or extracts therefrom, showing the actual price paid or agreed to be paid, should be attached to the invoice.
3. **Installment Shipments.** Installments of a shipment covered by a single order or contract and shipped from one consignor to one consignee may be included in one invoice if the installments arrive at the port of entry by any means of transportation within a period not to exceed 10 consecutive days.

   The invoice should be prepared in the same manner as are invoices covering single shipments and should include any additional information that may be required for the particular class of goods concerned. If it is practical to do so, the invoice should show the quantities, values, and other invoice data with respect to each installment, and the identification of the importing conveyance in which each installment was shipped.
4. **Production "Assist."** The invoice should indicate whether the production of merchandise involved costs for "assists" (i.e., dies, molds, tooling, printing plates, artwork, engineering work, design and development, financial assistance, etc.) that are not included in the invoice price. If assists were involved, state their value, if known, and by whom supplied. Were they supplied without cost, or on a rental basis, or were they invoiced separately? If the latter, attach a copy of the invoice.

   Whenever U.S. Customs requires information on the cost of production of goods for customs valuation, the importer will be notified by the district director. Thereafter, invoices covering shipments of such goods must contain a statement on the cost of production by the manufacturer or producer.
5. **Additional Information Required.** Special information may be required on certain goods or classes of goods in addition to the information normally required on the invoice. Although the U.S. importer usually advises the exporter of these special situations, section 141.89 of the Customs Regulations, which covers the requirements for these goods, has been reproduced in "Additional Information" on page 237.
6. **Rates of Exchange.** In general, no rate(s) of exchange may be used to convert foreign currency for Customs purposes other than the rate(s) proclaimed or certified in 31 USC 5151. For merchandise imported from a country having a currency for which two or more rates of exchange have been certified by the Federal Reserve Bank of New York (section 522 of the Tariff Act of 1930), the invoice will show the exchange rate or rates used in converting the U.S. dollars received for the merchandise into the foreign currency and the percentage of each rate if two or more rates are used. If a rate or combination of rates used in payment of costs, charges, or expenses is different from those used in payment for the merchandise, state that rate or combination of rates separately. Where dollars have not been converted at the time the invoice is prepared, that fact is stated on the invoice, in which case the invoice shall also state the rate or combination of rates at which the dollars will be converted or that it is not known what rate or rates will be used. Rates of exchange are not required for merchandise unconditionally free of duty or subject only to a specific rate of duty not depending on value.

7
Other Invoices

Pro Forma Invoice

If the required commercial invoice is not filed at the time the merchandise is entered, a statement in the form of an invoice (a pro forma invoice) must be filed by the importer at the time of entry. A bond is given for production of the required invoice not later than 120 days from the date of entry. If the invoice is needed for statistical purposes, it must generally be produced within 50 days from the date the entry summary is required to be filed.

Exporters should bear in mind that unless they forward the required invoice in time, the U.S. importer will incur a liability under the bond for failure to file the invoice with the district or port director of Customs before the expiration of the 120-day period.

Although a pro forma invoice is not a document that is prepared by the exporter, it is of interest to exporters as it gives a general idea as to the kind of information needed for entry purposes and indicates what the importer may find necessary to furnish Customs officers at the time a formal entry is filed for a commercial shipment if a properly prepared customs or commercial invoice is not available at the time the goods are entered. An acceptable format for a pro forma invoice is reproduced in "Invoices" on page 235.

Some of the additional information specified for commodities under section 141.89 of the Customs Regulations may not be required when entry is made on a pro forma invoice. However, the pro forma invoice must contain sufficient data for examination, classification, and appraisal purposes.

Special Invoices

Special invoices are required for some merchandise. See 19 CFR 141.89 under "Additional Information" on page 237.

8
Frequent Errors in Invoicing

If difficulties, delays, and possible penal sanctions affecting the importer are to be avoided, due care must be exercised by foreign sellers and shippers in the preparation of invoices and other documents to be used in the entry of goods into the commerce of the U.S. Each document must contain all information required by law or regulations, and every statement of fact contained in the documents must be true and accurate. Any inaccurate or misleading statement of fact in a document presented to Customs in connection with an entry, or the omission from the document of required information, may result in delays in merchandise release, the detention of the goods or a claim against the importer for domestic value. Even if the inaccuracy or omission was unintentional, the importer may be required to establish the exercise of due diligence and the absence of negligence to avoid sanctions with consequent delays in obtaining possession of goods and closing the transaction.

It is particularly important that all statements relating to merchandise description, price, or value and to amounts of discounts, charges, and commissions be truthfully and accurately set forth. It is also important that the invoices set forth the true name of the actual seller and purchaser of the goods, in the case of purchased goods, or the true name of the actual consignor and consignee, when the goods are shipped otherwise than to secure a purchase. It is important, too, that the invoice shall otherwise reflect the real nature of the transaction for which the goods were shipped to the U.S.

The fundamental rule is that the shipper and importer must furnish the Custom officers with all pertinent information with respect to each import transaction to assist the Custom officers in determining the tariff status of the goods. Examples of omissions and inaccuracies to be avoided are:

- The shipper assumes that a commission, royalty, or other charge against the goods is a so-called "nondutiable" item and omits it from the invoice.
- A foreign shipper who purchases goods and sells them to a U.S. importer at a delivered price shows on the invoice the cost of the goods instead of the delivered price.
- A foreign shipper manufactures goods partly with the use of materials supplied by the U.S. importer, but invoices the goods at the actual cost to the manufacturer without including the value of the materials supplied by the importer.
- The foreign manufacturer ships replacement goods to a customer in the U.S. and invoices the goods at the net price without showing the full price less the allowance for defective goods previously shipped and returned.
- A foreign shipper who sells goods at list price, less a discount, invoices them at the net price, and fails to show the discount.

- A foreign shipper sells goods at a delivered price but invoices them at a price FOB the place of shipment and omits the subsequent charges.
- A foreign shipper indicates in the invoice that the importer is the purchaser, when in fact the importer is either an agent who is receiving a commission for selling the goods or a party who will receive part of the proceeds of the sale of the goods sold for the joint account of the shipper and consignee.

Invoice descriptions are vague if they list only part numbers, show truncated or coded descriptions, or lump various articles together as one when several distinct items are included.

9
Dutiable Status of Goods

Rates of Duty

All goods imported into the U.S. are subject to duty or duty-free entry in accordance with their classification under the applicable items in the Harmonized Tariff Schedule of the United States (HTSUS). An annotated, looseleaf edition of the tariff schedule may be purchased from the U.S. Government Printing Office, Washington, DC 20402. (See 19 USC 1202.)

When goods are dutiable, ad valorem, specific, or compound rates may be assessed. An ad valorem rate, which is the type of rate most often applied, is a percentage of value of the merchandise, such as 5% ad valorem. A specific rate is a specified amount per unit of weight or other quantity, such as 5.9 cents per dozen. A compound rate is a combination of both an ad valorem rate and a specific rate, such as 0.7 cents per pound plus 10% ad valorem.

Free of Duty or Dutiable

Rates of duty for imported merchandise may also vary depending upon the country of origin. Most merchandise is dutiable under the Most Favored Nation (MFN) rates in the General column under column 1 of the tariff schedule. Merchandise from countries to which the MFN rates have not been extended is dutiable at the full or "statutory" rates in column 2 of the tariff schedules.

Free rates are provided for many subheadings in columns 1 and 2 of the tariff schedule. Duty-free status is also available under various conditional exemptions that are reflected in the Special column under column 1 of the tariff schedule. It is the importer's burden to show eligibility for a conditional exemption from duty. One of the more frequently applied exemptions from duty occurs under the Generalized System of Preferences. GSP-eligible merchandise qualifies for duty-free entry when it is from a beneficiary developing country and meets other requirements as discussed in Chapter 13 below. Other exemptions are found under subheadings in HTSUS Chapter 98. These subheadings include, among other provisions, certain personal exemptions, exemptions for articles for scientific or other institutional purposes, and exemptions for returned U.S. goods. (Refer to the Commodity Index section, beginning on page 804.)

Rulings on Imports

The Customs Service makes its decision as to the dutiable status of merchandise when the entry is liquidated after the entry documents have been filed. When advance information is needed, do not depend on a small "trial" or "test" shipment since there is no guarantee that the next shipment will receive the same tariff treatment. Small importations may slip by, particularly if they are processed under informal procedures that apply to small shipments or in circumstances warranting application of a flat rate. An exporter, importer, or other interested party may get advance information on any matter affecting the dutiable status of merchandise by writing the district director where the merchandise will be entered or to the Regional

Commissioner of Customs, New York Region, New York, NY 10048 or to the U.S. Customs Service. Attention: Office of Regulations and Rulings, Washington, DC 20229. Detailed information on the procedures applicable to decisions on prospective importations is given in 19 CFR part 177.

Binding Decisions

While you will find that, for many purposes, the ports and districts are your best sources of information, informal information obtained on tariff classifications is not binding. Under 19 CFR part 177, The importing public may obtain a binding tariff classification ruling, which can be relied upon for placing or accepting orders or for making other business determinations, under Chapters 1 through 97 of the Harmonized Tariff Schedule (HTSUS) by writing to any Customs district director or to the Area Director of Customs, New York Seaport, 6 World Trade Center, New York, NY 10048. The rulings will be binding at all ports of entry unless revoked by the Customs Service's Office of Regulations and Rulings.

The following information is required in ruling requests:

1. The names, addresses, and other identifying information of all interested parties (if known) and the manufacturer ID code (if known).
2. The name(s) of the port(s) in which the merchandise will be entered (if known).
3. A description of the transaction, for example, a prospective importation of (merchandise) from (country).
4. A statement that there are, to the importer's knowledge, no issues on the commodity pending before the Customs Service or any court.
5. A statement as to whether classification advice had previously been sought from a Customs officer, and if so, from whom, and what advice was rendered, if any.

A request for a tariff classification should include the following information:

1. A complete description of the goods. Send samples, if practical, and sketches, diagrams, or other illustrative material that will be useful in supplementing the written description.
2. Cost breakdowns of component materials and their respective quantities shown in percentages, if possible.
3. A description of the principal use of the goods, as a class or kind of merchandise, in the U.S.
4. Information as to commercial, scientific, or common designations as may be applicable.
5. Any other information that may be pertinent or required for the purpose of tariff classification.

Any of the first four requirements above may be disregarded if you are certain the information will not be of use for tariff classification purposes. However, to avoid delays, your request should be as complete as possible. If you send a sample, do not rely on that to tell the whole story. Also, please note that samples may be subjected to laboratory analysis, which is done free of charge. However, if a sample is destroyed during laboratory analysis, it cannot be returned.

Information submitted and incorporated in the response to a request for a Customs decision may be disclosed or withheld in accordance with the provisions of the Freedom of Information Act, as amended (15 USC 552; 19 CFR 177.8(a)(3)).

Protests

The importer may disagree with the dutiable status after the entry has been liquidated. A decision at this stage of the entry transaction is requested by filing a protest and application for further review on Customs **Form 19** within 90 days after liquidation (see 19 CFR part 174). If the Customs Service denies a protest, dutiable status may then be determined through litigation against the Government.

Liability for Duties

No law or regulation provides for prepayment of U.S. duties or taxes in a foreign country before exportation to the U.S. This is true even for gifts sent through the mail.

Liability for the payment of duty usually becomes fixed at the time an entry for consumption or for warehouse is filed with Customs. The obligation for payment rests with the person or firm in whose name the entry is filed. When goods have been entered for warehouse, the liability for the payment of duties may be transferred to any person who purchases the goods and desires to withdraw them in his own name.

The 1993 Customs Modernization Act (Mod Act) authorizes periodic payment of duties. With advance permission from Customs, an importer may pay duties by filing a monthly import activity summary statement together with the payment. Interest is assessed against periodic payments from the first day of the month until the statement is filed.

Payments made to a Customs broker do not relieve an importer of record of liability for Customs charges (duties, taxes, and other debts owed to Customs) in the event the charges are not paid by the broker. Therefore, if the importer pays by check, Customs charges may be paid by separate check, payable to "U.S. Customs Service", which will be delivered to Customs by the broker.

If the entry is made in the name of a Customs broker, the broker may obtain relief from statutory liability for the payment of increased or additional duties found due if (1) the actual owner of the goods is named, and (2) the owner's declaration, by which the owner agrees to pay the additional amount of duty, and the owner's bond are filed by the broker with the district director within 90 days of the date of entry.

The Mod Act has created a five-year statute of limitations for collection of unpaid duties. The U.S. government must initiate suit or action to collect unpaid duties within five years after the date of the alleged violation, or in the case of fraud, after the date the fraud is discovered. This period is interrupted for any time during which the person is absent from the U.S. or the property is absent or concealed. See 15 USC 1621.

10
Containers or Holders

Lift vans, cargo vans, shipping tanks, pallets, and certain articles used in the shipment of goods in international traffic are designated as "instruments of international traffic" by the Customs Service. So long as this designation applies, they are not subject to entry or duty when they arrive, whether they are loaded or empty. Holders of merchandise of a different class may also be designated as instruments of international traffic upon application to the Commissioner of Customs. However, any article designated as an instrument of international traffic must be entered and duty paid, if applicable, if it is diverted to a domestic use.

Containers specially shaped or fitted to contain a specific article or set of articles, suitable for long-term use and entered with the articles for which they are intended, are classifiable with the accompanying articles if they are of a kind normally sold therewith. Examples of such containers are: camera cases, musical instrument cases, gun cases, drawing instrument cases, and necklace cases. This rule does not apply to containers that give the importation as a whole its essential character.

Subject to the above rule, packing materials and packing containers entered with goods packed in them are classified with these goods if they are of a kind normally used for packing such goods. However, this does not apply to packing materials or containers that are clearly suitable for repetitive use.

11
Temporary Free Importations

Temporary Importation Under Bond (TIB)

Goods of the types enumerated below when not imported for sale or for sale on approval may be admitted into the U.S. under bond without the payment of duty for exportation within one year from the date of importation. Generally, the amount of the bond is double the estimated duties. The one-year period for exportation may, upon application to the district or port director, be extended for one or more further periods that, when added to the initial one year period, shall not exceed a total of three years. There is an exception in the case of articles covered in item 15, for which the period of the bond may not exceed six months and may not be extended.

Merchandise entered under TIB must be exported before expiration of the bond period, or any extension, to avoid assessment of liquidated damages in the amount of the bond.

Classes of Goods

1. Merchandise to be repaired, altered, or processed (including processes that result in an article being manufactured or produced in the U.S.), provided that the following conditions are met:
   a. The merchandise will not be processed into an article manufactured or produced in the U.S. if the article is (1) potable grain alcohol, distilled spirits, wine, beer, or any dilution or mixture of these; (2) perfume or other commodity containing ethyl alcohol whether denatured or not; or (3) a product of wheat.
   b. If merchandise is processed and results in an article being manufactured or produced in the U.S. other than those described above, (1) a complete accounting will be made to the Customs Service for all articles, wastes, and irrecoverable losses resulting from the processing, and (2) all articles will be exported or destroyed under Customs supervision within the bonded period. Valuable waste must also be exported or so destroyed unless duty, if applicable, is paid.
2. Models of women's wearing apparel imported by manufacturers for use solely as models in their own establishments may require quota compliance.
3. Articles imported by illustrators and photographers for use solely as models in their own establishments to illustrate catalogs, pamphlets, or advertising matter.
4. Samples solely for use in taking orders for merchandise may require quota compliance.
5. Articles solely for examination with a view to reproduction or for examination and reproduction (except photoengraved printing plates for examination and reproduction); and motion picture advertising films.
6. Articles intended solely for testing, experimental, or review purposes, including plans, specifications, drawings, blueprints, photographs, and articles for

use in connection with experiments or for study. If articles under this category are destroyed in connection with the experiment or study, proof must be presented to satisfy the obligation under the bond to export the articles.

7. Automobiles, motorcycles, bicycles, airplanes, airships, balloons, boats, racing shells, and similar vehicles and craft, and the usual equipment of the foregoing, if brought temporarily into the U.S. by nonresidents for the purpose of taking part in races or other specific contests. District or port directors may defer the exaction of a bond for a period not to exceed 90 days after the date of importation for vehicles and craft to take part in races or other specific contests for other than money purposes. If the vehicle or craft is not exported or the bond is not given within the period of such deferment, the vehicle or craft shall be subject to forfeiture.
8. Locomotives and other railroad equipment brought temporarily into the U.S. for use in clearing obstructions, fighting fires, or making emergency repairs on railroads within the U.S., for use in transportation otherwise than in international traffic when the Secretary of the Treasury finds that the temporary use of foreign railroad equipment is necessary to meet an emergency.
9. Containers for compressed gases, filled or empty, and containers or other articles in use for covering or holding merchandise (including personal or household effects) during transportation and suitable for reuse for that purpose.
10. Professional equipment, tools of trade, repair components for equipment or tools admitted under this item, and camping equipment imported by or for nonresidents sojourning temporarily in the U.S. for the nonresident's use, or by an organization represented by the nonresident that is a legally established business in a foreign country.
11. Articles of special design for temporary use exclusively in connection with the manufacture or production of articles for export.
12. Animals and poultry brought into the U.S. for the purpose of breeding, exhibition, or competition for prizes, and the usual equipment therefor.
13. Theatrical scenery, properties, and apparel brought into the U.S. by proprietors or managers of theatrical exhibitions arriving from abroad for temporary use by them in such exhibitions.
14. Works of free fine arts, drawings, engravings, photographic pictures, and philosophical and scientific apparatus brought into the U.S. by professional artists, lecturers, or scientists arriving from abroad for use by them for exhibition and in illustration, promotion, and encouragement of art, science, or industry in the U.S.
15. Automobiles, automobile chassis, automobile bodies, cutaway portions of any of the foregoing, and parts for any of the foregoing, finished, unfinished, or cutaway, when intended solely for show purposes.

These articles may be admitted only on condition that the Secretary of the Treasury has found that the foreign country from which the articles were imported allows or will allow substantially reciprocal privileges with respect to similar imports to that country from the U.S. If the Secretary finds that a foreign country has discontinued or will discontinue the allowance of such privileges, the privileges under this item shall not apply thereafter to imports from that country.

Relief from Liability

Relief from liability under bond may be obtained in any case in which the articles are destroyed under Customs supervision, in lieu of exportation, within the original bond period. However, in the case of articles entered under item 6, destruction need not be under Customs supervision where articles are destroyed during the course of experiments or tests during the bond period or any lawful extension, but satisfactory proof of destruction shall be furnished to the district or port director with whom the customs entry is filed.

ATA Carnet

ATA stands for the combined French and English words "Admission Temporaire-Temporary Admission." ATA carnet is an international customs document that may be used for the temporary duty-free importation of certain goods into a country in lieu of the usual customs documents required. The carnet serves as a guarantee against the payment of customs duties that may become due on goods temporarily imported and not re-exported. Quota compliance may be required on certain types of merchandise. ATA textile carnets are subject to quota and visa requirements.

A carnet is valid for one year. The traveler or businessperson, however, may make as many trips as desired during the period the carnet is valid provided the carnet has sufficient pages for each stop.

The U.S. currently allows ATA carnets to be used for the temporary admission of professional equipment, commercial samples, and advertising material. Most other countries allow the use of carnets for the temporary admission of these goods and, in some cases, other uses of the ATA carnet are permitted. ATA carnets can also be used for transit (in-bond movement of goods) in the U.S. under the applicable regulations, 19 CFR Part 114.

Local country carnet associations, as members of the International Bureau of the Paris-based International Chamber of Commerce, issue carnets to their residents. These associations guarantee the payment of duties to local customs authorities should goods imported under cover of a foreign-issued carnet not be re-exported. In the U.S., the U.S. Council of the International Chamber of Commerce, located at 1212 Avenue of the Americas, New York, NY 10036, (212) 354-4480, has been designated by U.S. Customs as the U.S. issuing and guaranteeing organization. A fee is charged by the Council for its service.

ATA carnets can be used in the following countries:

Algeria	Hong Kong	New Zealand
Australia	Hungary	Norway
Austria	Iceland	Poland
Belgium	India	Portugal
Bulgaria	Iran*	Romania
Canada	Ireland	Senegal
Canary Islands	Israel	Singapore
China**	Italy	Slovakia
Cote d'Ivoire	Japan	Slovenia
Cyprus	Korea, Republic of	South Africa
Czech Republic	Luxembourg	Spain
Denmark	Malaysia	Sri Lanka
Finland	Malta	Sweden
France	Mauritius	Switzerland
French West Indies	Mexico**	Turkey
Germany	Netherlands	United Kingdom
Gibraltar	Netherlands Antilles	United States
Greece		

* Iran is an ATA member, but the U.S. embargo takes precedence over the issuance of ATA carnets for that country.

**China and Mexico are planning to implement the use of ATA carnets in 1995.

Egypt and certain other countries have accepted the ATA convention but have not implemented the use of carnets.

As countries are being continuously added to the carnet system, please check with the U.S. Council if a country you wish to visit is not included in the above list.

12 The North American Free Trade Agreement (NAFTA)

The North American Free Trade Agreement (NAFTA) was created on January 1, 1994, to form a preferred trade zone consisting of the U.S., Canada, and Mexico. Specifically, it was adopted according to the provisions of the North American Free Trade Agreement Implementation Act (107 Stat. 2057; this legislation also includes, as Title VI, the Customs Modernization Act, or Mod Act, referred to above). NAFTA supersedes the preexisting U.S.-Canada Free Trade Agreement (FTA), although the provisions of that earlier treaty remain essentially the same and are subsumed within the general framework of NAFTA. New provisions were negotiated to cover trade between the U.S. and Mexico, as well as between Mexico and Canada.

The agreement is divided into six titles dealing with general provisions, customs provisions, applications, dispute resolution, transitional provisions, and customs modifications. Parts of Title III further detail relief provisions and issues of agriculture, intellectual property, and standards. The parts of Title V cover transitional adjustment provisions, performance, customs user fees, internal revenue revisions, side agreements relating to labor and the environment, and the establishment of the North American Development Bank. Under the terms of NAFTA, tariffs, quotas, and nontariff barriers on most goods traded among the three countries are scheduled to be reduced, eased, or eliminated on transactions that are made among them. NAFTA provides for three classifications of goods affected by the agreement: products of Category A are allowed NAFTA benefits as of January 1, 1994; those of Category B, in 1998; and those of Category C, in 2003. The phase-out of restrictions on a few sensitive Category D products—such as textiles, automobiles, and certain food products—is scheduled to take as long as 15 years.

The U.S.-Canada FTA already allowed a great deal of the trade between these two countries to be conducted on a streamlined basis with reduced or no tariffs on the products involved and to a large degree mutual acceptance of the other's standards and procedures as equivalent. NAFTA extends and reorganizes these preferences to include many similar provisions for Mexico, while Mexico in turn has agreed to open its markets to U.S. and Canadian products. Goods eligible for special tariff treatment by the U.S. are denoted by a "CA" (Canadian) or an "MX" (Mexican) in the "Special Rates of Duty" column in the Harmonized Tariff Schedule of the United States (HTSUS).

NAFTA Origin and Eligibility

In an effort to eliminate tariffs on eligible goods and to preclude outside countries from obtaining tariff benefits by merely passing their goods through one of the three signatory countries, Rules of Origin were devised. These rules determine origin for purposes of NAFTA eligibility, not for country of origin determination in other areas such as marking, quotas, dumping, and countervailing duty assessment. Article 401 of NAFTA defines five categories of rules of origin eligibility:

a. Goods wholly obtained or produced in the U.S., Canada, or Mexico.

b. Goods not wholly obtained or produced within North America as defined by the agreement, but which have been transformed sufficiently to constitute a different product with a substantially different tariff classification (different HTSUS classification number). Compliance rules are complex and stringent, requiring a minimum of 60% (62.5% for automotive products) of the product's assessed customs value to originate in North America (transactions value) or a minimum of 50% of net cost to represent North American value added (net cost value), as calculated using the methods stipulated in the Act for determining eligibility of Regional Value Content (RVC).

c. Goods produced entirely in an eligible location from imported raw materials.

d. Goods produced in an eligible location from imported unassembled or disassembled parts and components.

A commodity specific rule takes precedence over a general rule (there exist special exceptions for many products, mainly certain consumer products and agricultural goods). Also, under the de minimis rule, a product for which no more than 7% of the value consists of nonregional inputs qualifies as an originating product under the definitions of NAFTA. Note that specific qualifying requirements are both complex and stringent. Refer to General Note 12 of the HTSUS for specifics.

Key Provisions

Import Tariffs. At the time of signing, import tariffs averaged roughly 10% on goods entered into Mexico and 3% on those entered into the U.S. Many of these tariffs were eliminated or lowered on January 1, 1994, while most of the rest are to be gradually reduced and eventually eliminated over the scheduled life of the agreement.

Local Content and Origin Rules. Specific national local content requirements are to be removed. However, NAFTA will impose rules of origin designed to restrict the agreement's benefits to products actually produced in the member countries (see above).

Quotas. NAFTA calls for quotas to be liberalized and eventually eliminated on imports from its members. During this transition, the amount of goods imported under quota from Mexico and Canada will be expanded. These imports will not count against the total entry threshold amounts established for these products, so that absolute quotas are effectively raised for specific items imported from Mexico and Canada. The implementing regulations specify a schedule for specific products, including milk, cheese, and other dairy products; tomatoes and other fruit and vegetable products; sugars, syrups, and products containing them; orange juice; and some textile products.

Textiles and Apparel. Under NAFTA, the U.S. will immediately remove quotas on textiles and apparel wholly Mexican in origin. Quotas on other textile products imported from Mexico but failing to meet NAFTA origin rules will be phased out over 10 years. The U.S. will phase out tariffs on apparel imported from its NAFTA partners over 10 years and on textiles over eight.

Agricultural Products. All U.S., Canadian, and Mexican nontariff barriers are to be converted into either tariff-rate quotas—allowing in unlimited quantities but charging higher rates once a threshold of level of imports has been reached—or ordinary tariffs with a set rate regardless of the amount of the product entered. These changes will be phased in over as long as 15 years for certain sensitive products.

Automotive Industry. Adjustments to the U.S. Corporate Fuel Economy rules will allow Mexican-produced parts and vehicles to be classified as domestic products, facilitating their import into the U.S. Relaxed Mexican tariff and nontariff barriers to foreign imports will allow greater and more economical flows of outside components into Mexico, which will in turn upgrade and increase the export production of the country's plants.

Drawback. NAFTA establishes new rules for drawbacks—refunds or waivers of duty on materials used in the production of products subsequently exported to a NAFTA partner. Existing drawback rules will expire for NAFTA parties in 2001. Upon expiration, changes will be implemented to avoid double taxation on such transactions. Under the new drawback arrangement, the amount of such waivers or refunds will be less than those on comparable nonoriginating materials.

Trilateral Trade Commission. NAFTA provides for the creation of a trilateral commission to adjudicate disputes under the agreement. This body is organized in an attempt to avoid national bias and is required to act on complaints within eight months. It will deal with antidumping and subsidy issues, as well as the implementation of the provisions of the agreement.

Entry Procedures

As with other trade preference programs, the importer must make a claim under NAFTA to receive the tariff treatment. An importer can make a claim by:

1. Prefixing either "CA" or "MX" to the tariff classification number
2. Submitting Customs **Form 434, NAFTA Certificate of Origin**
3. Submitting Customs **Form 7501, Entry Summary**

Sources of Additional Information

For additional information, refer to General Note 12 of the HTSUS, or contact:

NAFTA Help Desk
U.S. Customs Service
1301 Constitution Avenue, NW, Room 1325
Washington, DC 20229
Tel (202) 927-0066

13
Generalized System of Preferences (GSP)

The Generalized System of Preferences is a program providing for free rates of duty for merchandise from beneficiary developing independent countries and dependent countries and territories to encourage their economic growth (see below). This program was enacted by the U.S. in the Trade Act of 1974, became effective on January 1, 1976.

Eligible Items

The GSP eligibility list contains a wide range of products classifiable under more than 4,000 different subheadings in the Harmonized Tariff Schedule of the United States. These items are identified either by an "A" or "A*" in the "Special" column under column 1 of the tariff schedule. Merchandise classifiable under a subheading designated in this manner may qualify for duty-free entry if imported into the U.S. directly from any of the designated countries and territories. Merchandise from one or more of these countries, however, may be excluded from the exemption if there is an "A*" in the "Special" column. The list of countries and exclusions, as well as the list of GSP-eligible articles, will change from time to time over the life of the program. You should consult the latest edition of the Harmonized Tariff Schedules of the United States for the most up-to-date information.

If advance tariff classification information is needed to ascertain whether or not your commodity is eligible under the GSP, you may obtain this information under the procedures previously discussed in Chapter 9 relating to dutiable status.

Formal Entries

For commercial shipments requiring a formal entry, a claim for duty-free status is made under GSP by showing on the entry summary that the country of origin is a designated beneficiary developing country and by showing an "A" with the appropriate GSP-eligible subheading. Eligible merchandise will be entitled to duty-free treatment provided the following conditions are met:

1. The merchandise must be destined for the U.S. without contingency for diversion at the time of exportation from the beneficiary developing country.
2. The UNCTAD (United Nations Conference on Trade and Development) Certificate of Origin **Form A** must be properly prepared, signed by the exporter, and either filed with the entry or furnished before liquidation or other final action on the entry if requested by Customs.
3. The cost or value of materials produced in the beneficiary developing country and/or the direct cost of processing performed there must represent at least 35% of the appraised value of the goods.

The cost or value of materials imported into the beneficiary developing country may be included in calculating the 35% value-added requirement for an eligible article if the materials are first substantially transformed into new and different articles and are then used as constituent materials in the production of the eligible article. The phrase "direct costs of processing" includes costs directly incurred or reasonably allocated to the processing of the article, such as the cost of all actual labor, dies, molds, tooling, depreciation on machinery, research and development, and inspection and testing. Business overhead, administrative expenses, salaries, and profit, as well as general business expenses such as administrative salaries, casualty and liability insurance, advertising and salesperson's salaries may not be considered as direct costs of processing.

Certificate of Origin Form A

Normally, Customs will accept an entry at the free rate whether or not **Form A** is presented at the time of entry. **To receive GSP treatment, the importer must be prepared to produce Form A if requested to do so by Customs.**

The UNCTAD Certificate of Origin **Form A** is not available for sale in the U.S. The beneficiary developing countries and territories participating in the program are responsible for printing and supplying this form. Exporters may get this form from the appropriate government authority in their respective countries. If **Form A** is not available from the governmental certifying authority, the form may be purchased from any of the commercial printers listed below, or you may contact the Director, Technical Assistant Project/GSP, UNCTAD, 1211 Geneva 10, Switzerland, for further advice on obtaining the form.

Germany

Formular-Verlag Purschke & Hensel
Barbacher Strass 232
D-5300 Bonn

Wilhelm Kohler Verlag
495 Minden 2
Postfach 1530
Bruckenkopf 2a

Hong Kong

Che San & Company
10 Pottinger Street

Cheung Lee Printing Company
210 A Li Po Chun Chambers
185-195 Des Voeux Road, Central

Winson (HK) Printing Company
80-82 Wharf Road
North Point

Informal Entries

Although Certificates of Origin **Form A** are not required for merchandise covered by an informal entry, the district director of Customs may require such other evidence of the country of origin as he may deem necessary. The requirement of **Form A** for merchandise covered by a formal entry may be waived by the district director if determined to be appropriate, or if the imported articles are for household or personal use and are not intended for resale or brought in for the account of others, or if the district director is otherwise satisfied that the merchandise qualifies for duty-free treatment under GSP.

Sources of Additional Information

Customs rules and regulations on GSP are incorporated in sections 10.171-10.178 of the Customs Regulations. Address any question you may have as to the administrative or operational aspects of the GSP to the Director, Office of Trade Operations, U.S. Customs Service, Washington, DC 20229. Requests for information concerning additions to, or deletions from, the list of eligible merchandise under GSP, or the list of beneficiary development countries, should be directed to the Chairman, Trade Policy Staff Subcommittee, Office of U.S. Trade Representative, 600 17th St., NW, Washington, DC 20506.

Generalized System of Preferences (GSP) Independent Countries

Albania
Angola
Antigua & Barbuda***
Argentina
Bahamas***
Bahrain
Bangladesh
Barbados***
Belize***
Benin
Bhutan
Bolivia*
Botswana
Brazil
Bulgaria
Burkina Faso
Burundi
Cameroon
Cape Verde
Central African Republic
Chad
Chile
Colombia*
Comoros
Congo
Costa Rica
Cote d'Ivoire
Cyprus
Czech Republic
Djibouti
Dominica***
Dominican Republic
Ecuador*
Egypt
El Salvador
Equatorial Guinea
Estonia
Ethiopia
Fiji
Gambia, The
Ghana
Grenada***
Guatemala
Guinea
Guinea Bissau
Guyana***
Haiti
Honduras
Hungary
India
Indonesia**
Israel
Jamaica***
Jordan
Kenya
Kiribati
Kyrgyzstan
Latvia
Lebanon
Lesotho
Madagascar
Malawi
Malaysia**
Maldives
Mali
Malta
Mauritius
Morocco
Mozambique
Namibia
Nepal
Niger
Oman
Pakistan
Panama
Papua New Guinea
Paraguay
Peru*
Philippines**
Poland
Russia
Rwanda
Saint Kitts and Nevis***
Saint Lucia***
Saint Vincent and the Grenadines***
Sao Tome and Principe
Senegal
Seychelles
Sierra Leone
Solomon Islands
Somalia
Slovakia
Sri Lanka
Suriname
Swaziland
Tanzania
Thailand**
Togo
Tonga
Trinidad and Tobago***
Tunisia
Turkey
Tuvalu
Uganda
Uruguay
Vanuatu
Venezuela*
Western Samoa
Yemen Arab Republic (Sanaa)
Former Republics of Yugoslavia (except Serbia and Montenegro)
Zaire
Zambia
Zimbabwe

GSP Non-Independent Countries and Territories

Anguilla
Aruba
British Indian Ocean Territory
Cayman Islands
Christmas Island (Australia)
Cocos (Keeling) Islands
Cook Islands
Falkland Islands (Islas Malvinas)
French Polynesia
Gibraltar
Greenland
Heard Island and McDonald Islands
Macao
Montserrat***
Netherlands Antilles
New Caledonia
Niue
Norfolk Island
Pitcairn Islands
Saint Helena
Tokelau
Trust Territory of the Pacific Islands (Palau)
Turks and Caicos Islands
Virgin Islands, British
Wallis and Futuna
Western Sahara

* Member countries of the Cartagena Agreement—Andean Group (treated as one country).
** Association of South East Asian Nations—ASEAN (GSP-eligible countries only) treated as one country.
*** Member countries of the Caribbean Common Market—CARICOM (treated as one country).

14
Caribbean Basin Initiative (CBI)

The Caribbean Basin Initiative (CBI) is a program providing for the duty-free entry of merchandise from designated beneficiary countries or territories. This program was enacted by the U.S. as the Caribbean Basin Economic Recovery Act (CBERA), became effective on January 1, 1984, and has no expiration date.

Beneficiary Countries

The following countries and territories have been designated as beneficiary countries for purposes of the CBI:

Antigua and Barbuda	Honduras
Aruba	Jamaica
Bahamas	Montserrat
Barbados	Netherlands Antilles
Belize	Nicaragua
Costa Rica	Panama
Dominica	Saint Kitts and Nevis
Dominican Republic	Saint Lucia
El Salvador	Saint Vincent and the Grenadines
Grenada	Trinidad and Tobago
Guatemala	Virgin Islands, British
Guyana	
Haiti	

Eligible Items

The list of beneficiaries may change from time to time over the life of the program. Therefore, it is necessary to consult General Note 7 in the latest edition of the Harmonized Tariff Schedule of the United States (HTSUS), which will contain updated information.

Most products from designated beneficiaries may be eligible for CBI duty-free treatment. These items are identified by either an "E" or "E*" in the Special column under column 1 of the HTSUS. Merchandise classifiable under a subheading designated in this manner may qualify for duty-free entry if imported into the U.S. directly from any of the designated countries and territories. Merchandise from one or more of these countries, however, may be excluded from time to time over the life of the program. Therefore, the latest edition of the HTSUS will contain the most up-to-date information.

Special rules exist for certain goods, including beef and veal, some sugars, syrups, and molasses products, and some textile products and from specific locations. Refer to Note 7 of the HTSUS.

Rules of Origin

Merchandise will be eligible for CBI duty-free treatment only if the following conditions are met:

1. The merchandise must be imported directly from the beneficiary country into the customs territory of the U.S.
2. The merchandise must have been produced in a beneficiary country. This requirement is satisfied when (1) the goods are wholly the growth, product, or manufacture of a beneficiary country, or (2) the goods have been substantially transformed into a new and different article of commerce in a beneficiary country.
3. At least 35% of the appraised value of the article imported into the U.S. must consist of the cost or value of materials produced in one or more beneficiary countries and/or the direct costs of processing operations performed in one or more beneficiary countries. The Commonwealth of Puerto Rico and the U.S. Virgin Islands are defined as beneficiary countries for purposes of this requirement; therefore, value attributable to Puerto Rico or the Virgin Islands may also be counted. In addition, the cost or value of materials produced in the customs territory of the U.S. (other than Puerto Rico) may be counted toward the 35% value-added requirement, but only to a maximum of 15% of the appraised value of the imported article.

The cost or value of materials imported into a beneficiary country from a non-beneficiary country may be included in calculating the 35% value-added requirement for an eligible article if the materials are first substantially transformed into new and different articles of commerce and are then used as constituent materials in the production of the eligible article. The phrase "direct costs of processing operations" includes costs directly incurred or reasonably allocated to the production of the article, such as the cost of actual labor, dies, molds, tooling, depreciation of machinery, research and development, inspection, and testing. Business overhead, administrative expenses, and profit, as well as general business expenses such as casualty and liability insurance, advertising, and salesperson's salaries, may not be considered as direct costs of processing operations.

CBI II
Sections 215 & 222

In addition to the origin rules enumerated above, the Customs and Trade Act of 1990 added new criteria for duty-free eligibility under the Caribbean Basin Initiative. First, articles that are the growth product, or manufacture of Puerto Rico and that subsequently are processed in a CBI beneficiary country, may also receive duty-free treatment when entered, if the three following conditions are met:

1. They are imported directly from a beneficiary country into the customs territory of the U.S.
2. They are advanced in value or improved in condition by any means in a beneficiary country.
3. Any materials added to the article in a beneficiary country must be a product of a beneficiary country or the U.S.

Second, articles that are assembled or processed in whole from U.S. components or ingredients (other than water) in a beneficiary country may be entered free of duty. Duty-free treatment will apply if the components or ingredients are exported directly to the beneficiary country and the finished article is imported directly into the customs territory of the U.S.

If advance tariff classification information is needed to ascertain whether or not your merchandise would be eligible for CBI duty-free treatment, you may obtain this information under the procedures previously discussed in Chapter 9 relating to dutiable status.

Formal Entries—Evidence of Country of Origin

For commercial shipments requiring a formal entry, a claim for CBI duty-free treatment is made by showing on the entry summary that the country of origin is a designated beneficiary country and by adding the letter "E" as prefix to the applicable tariff schedule subheading. In addition, a properly completed Certificate of Origin **Form A**, as previously discussed in Chapter 13 relating to the Generalized System of Preferences, may be presented at the time of entry; however, the words "Generalized System of Preferences" appearing on the front of the **Form A** must be replaced by the words "Caribbean Basin Initiative" for purposes of a CBI entry.

Normally, the Customs Service will accept a CBI entry at the free rate whether or not the **Form A** is presented at the time of entry. The importer will need to be prepared to produce **Form A** in order to receive for CBI duty-free treatment, if requested to do so by Customs. In addition, where necessary value is added to an article in the U.S. or Puerto Rico after final exportation of the article from a beneficiary country, a detailed declaration, prepared by the party responsible for the addition of such value, shall be filed in lieu of the **Form A** as evidence of country of origin. All submitted evidence of country of origin may be subject to such verification as the district director deems necessary.

Informal Entries

Although Certificates of Origin **Form A** are not required for merchandise covered by informal entry, the district director may require such other evidence of the country of origin as may be deemed necessary.

Sources of Additional Information

Customs rules and regulations on the CBI are incorporated in sections 10.191-10.198 of the Customs Regulations. Address any question you may have as to the administrative or operational aspects of the CBI to the director of the port or district where the merchandise will be entered or to the Director, Office of Trade Operations, U.S. Customs Service, Washington, DC 20229.

15
Andean Trade Preference Act (ATPA)

The Andean Trade Preference Act (ATPA) is a program providing for the duty-free entry of merchandise from designated beneficiary countries. The ATPA was enacted into law by the U.S. on December 4, 1991 and is scheduled to expire on December 4, 2001.

Beneficiary Countries

The following countries have been designated as beneficiary countries for purposes of the ATPA:

Bolivia	Ecuador
Columbia	Peru

Eligible Items

Most products from designated beneficiaries may be eligible for ATPA duty-free treatment. Products that are statutorily excluded include: textile and apparel articles that are subject to textile agreements; some footwear; preserved tuna in airtight containers; petroleum products; watches and watch parts from countries subject to Column 2 rates of duty; various sugar products; rum and tafia. Eligible items are identified by either a "J" or "J*" in the Special subcolumn under column 1 of the Harmonized Tariff Schedule (HTSUS). Merchandise classifiable under a subheading designated in the manner may qualify for duty-free entry if imported into the U.S. directly from any designated ATPA beneficiary country. Merchandise from one or more of these countries, however, may be excluded from duty-free treatment if there is a "J*" in the Special subcolumn. Refer to General Note 11 of the HTSUS for specifics.

Rules of Origin

Merchandise will be eligible for ATPA duty-free treatment only if the following conditions are met:

1. The merchandise must be imported directly from any beneficiary country into the customs territory of the U.S.

2. The merchandise must have been produced in a beneficiary country. This requirement is satisfied when: (1) the goods are wholly the growth, product, or manufacture of a beneficiary country, or (2) the goods have been substantially transformed into a new and different article of commerce in a beneficiary country.

3. At least 35% of the appraised value of the article must consist of the cost or value of materials produced in one or more ATPA or CBI beneficiary countries and/or the direct costs of processing operations performed in one or more ATPA or CBI beneficiary countries. The Commonwealth of Puerto Rico and the U.S. Virgin Islands are defined as beneficiary countries for purposes of this requirement; therefore, value attributable to Puerto Rico or the Virgin Islands may also be counted. In addition, the cost or value of materials produced in the customs territory of the U.S. (other than Puerto Rico) may be counted toward the 35% value-added requirement, but only to a maximum of 15% of the appraised value of the imported article.

The cost or value of materials imported into ATPA or CBI beneficiary countries from non-beneficiary countries may be included in calculating the 35% value-added requirement for an eligible article if the materials are first substantially transformed into new and different articles of commerce and are then used as constituent materials in the production of the eligible article. The phrase "direct costs of processing operations" includes costs directly incurred or reasonably allocated to the production of the article, such as the cost of actual labor, dies, molds, tooling, depreciation of machinery, research and development, inspection and testing. Business overhead, administrative expenses and profit, as well as general business expenses such as casualty and liability insurance, advertising and salespersons' salaries may not be considered as direct costs of processing operations.

If advance tariff classification information is needed to ascertain whether your merchandise would be eligible for ATPA duty-free treatment, you may obtain this information under the procedures previously discusses in Chapter 9 relating to dutiable status.

Formal Entries—Evidence of Country of Origin

For commercial shipments requiring a formal entry, importers can claim ATPA duty-free treatment by showing on the entry summary that the country of origin is a designated beneficiary country and by using the letter "J" as a prefix to the applicable tariff schedule number. In addition, a properly completed Certificate of Origin **Form A**, as discussed in Chapter 13 relating to the Generalized System of Preferences, may be presented at the time of entry; however, the words "Generalized System of Preferences" appearing on the front of a **Form A** should be replaced by the words "Andean Trade Preference Act."

Normally, the Customs Service will accept an ATPA entry at the free rate whether or not the **Form A** is provided. To receive ATPA duty-free treatment, the importer will need to be prepared to produce **Form A** if requested to do so by Customs.

Informal Entries

Although Certificates of Origin **From A** are not required for merchandise covered by an informal entry, the district director may require such other evidence of the country of origin as may be deemed necessary.

Sources of Additional Information

Address questions you may have about the operational or administrative aspects of the ATPA to the Director, Office of Trade Operations, U.S. Customs Service, Washington, DC 20229.

16 U.S.-Israel Free Trade Area Agreement

The U.S.-Israel Free Trade Area agreement is a program providing for free or reduced rates of duty for merchandise from Israel to stimulate trade between the two countries. This program was authorized by the U.S. in the Trade and Tariff Act of 1984 and implemented by the U.S.-Israel Free Trade Area Implementation Act of 1985 and Presidential Proclamation 5365 of August 30, 1985. The program became effective September 1, 1985, and has no termination date. As of January 1, 1995, all currently eligible reduced rate importations from Israel were to be accorded duty-free treatment.

Eligible Items

The agreement relates to most tariff items listed in the Harmonized Tariff Schedule of the United States (HTSUS). These items are identified by "IL" in the "Special" column under column 1 of the Harmonized Tariff Schedule.

If a claim for duty-free or reduced-duty rates is being made for commercial shipments of Israeli goods covered by a formal entry, the HTSUS subheading must be prefixed with an "IL" on the Customs **Form 7501** (entry document) or Customs **Form 7505** (warehouse withdrawal document), as appropriate.

An article imported into the Customs territory of the U.S. is eligible for treatment as a "Product of Israel" only if:

- That article is the growth, product, or manufacture of Israel;
- That article is imported directly from Israel into the Customs territory of the U.S.;
- The sum of: (1) The cost or value of the materials produced in Israel, plus (2) the direct costs of processing operations performed in Israel is not less than 35% of the appraised value of such article at the time it is entered. If the cost or value of materials produced in the customs territory of the U.S. is included with respect to an eligible article, an amount not to exceed 15% of the appraised value of the article at the time it is entered that is attributable to such U.S. cost or value may be applied toward determining the 35%.
- The cost or value of materials imported into Israel from a third country may be included in calculating the 35% value-added requirement, provided they are first substantially transformed into new and different articles of commerce and are then used as constituent materials in the production of the eligible article.

No article may be considered to meet these requirements by virtue of having merely undergone:

- Simple combining or packaging operations; or
- Mere diluting with water or mere dilution with another substance that does not materially alter the characteristics of the article.

The phrase "direct costs of processing operations" includes, but is not limited to:

- All actual labor costs involved in the growth, production, manufacture, or assembly of the specific merchandise, including fringe benefits, on-the-job training, and the costs of engineering, supervisory, quality control, and similar personnel.
- Dies, molds, tooling, and depreciation on machinery and equipment that are allocable to the specific merchandise.

Direct costs of processing operations do not include costs that are not directly attributable to the merchandise concerned, or are not costs of manufacturing the product, such as (1) profit and (2) general expenses of doing business that are either not allocable to the specific merchandise or are not related to the growth, production, manufacture, or assembly of the merchandise, such as administrative salaries, casualty and liability insurance, advertising and sales staff's salaries, commissions, or expenses.

Certificate of Origin Form A

The United Nations Conference on Trade and Development (UNCTAD) Certificate of Origin **Form A** is used as documentary evidence to support duty-free and reduced rate claims for Israeli articles covered by a formal entry. It does not have to be produced at the time of entry, however, unless so requested by the Customs Service. The Form A can be obtained from the Israeli authorizing issuing authority, the commercial printers of this form listed or shown on page 199, or the UNCTAD address on the same page.

Informal Entries

The **Form A** is not required for commercial or non-commercial shipments covered by an informal entry. However, the district director may require such other evidence of the country of origin as deemed necessary. With regard to merchandise accompanying the traveler, it should be noted that in order to avoid delays to passengers, the inspecting Customs officer will extend Israeli duty-free or reduced rate treatment to all eligible articles when satisfied, from the facts available, that the merchandise concerned is a product of Israel.

Sources of Additional information

Address any questions you may have about the administrative or operational aspects of the agreement to the Director, Office of Trade Operations, U.S. Customs Service, Washington, DC 20229. Requests for information concerning policy issues related to the agreement should be directed to the Chairman, Trade Policy Staff Subcommittee, Office of U.S. Trade Representative, 600 17th St., NW, Washington, DC 20506.

17 Compact of the Freely Associated States

The Compact of the Freely Associated States (FAS) is a program providing for the duty-free entry of merchandise from designated freely associated states of the U.S. This program was established by Presidential Proclamation 60 30 of September 28, 1989, Section 242, became effective on October 18, 1989, and has no termination date.

Beneficiary Countries

The following freely associated states have been designated as beneficiary countries for purposes of the FAS:

Marshall Islands

Federated States of Micronesia

Eligible Items

The duty-free treatment is applied to most products from the designated beneficiaries. For commercial shipments requiring formal entry, a claim for duty-free status is made by placing the letter "Z" next to the eligible subheading. The following merchandise is excluded from the duty-free exemption:

1. Textile and apparel articles that are subject to textile agreements.
2. Footwear, handbags, luggage, flat goods, work gloves, and leather wearing apparel that were not eligible for GSP treatment, as discussed in Chapter 13, as of April 1, 1984.
3. Watches, clocks, and timing apparatus of Chapter 91 of the Harmonized Tariff Schedule (except such articles incorporating an optoelectronic display and no other type of display).
4. Buttons of subheading 9606.21.40 or 9606.29.20 of the Harmonized Tariff Schedule.
5. Tunas and skipjack, prepared or preserved, not in oil, in airtight containers weighing with their contents not more than 7 kg each, "in excess" of the consumption quota quantity allowed duty-free entry.

Duty-free treatment may be lost in a particular calendar year if the value of the quantity of articles exported to the U.S. by a freely associated state equals or exceeds certain amounts, as described in General Note 10(e) of the Harmonized Tariff Schedule of the United States (HTSUS). If in subsequent years exports to the U.S. from the country fall below the permissible limits, duty-free status may be reinstated.

Rules of Origin

Merchandise will be eligible for FAS duty-free treatment only if the following conditions are met:

1. It must be the growth, product, or manufacture of the freely associated state.
2. The merchandise must be imported directly from the freely associated state into the customs territory of the U.S.

3. At least 35% of the appraised value of the article imported into the U.S. must consist of the cost or value of materials produced in the beneficiary country and/or the direct costs of processing operations performed in the beneficiary country. In addition, the cost or value of materials produced in the customs territory of the U.S. may be counted toward the 35% value-added requirement, but only to a maximum of 15% of the appraised value of the imported article. The cost or value of the materials imported into the freely associated state from a non-beneficiary country may be included in calculating the 35% value-added requirement for an eligible article if the materials are first substantially transformed into new and different articles of commerce and are then used as constituent materials in the production of the eligible product.

Sources of Additional Information

Address any questions you may have about the administrative or operational aspects of the FAS to the director of the port or district where the merchandise will be entered or to the Director, Office of Trade Operations, U.S. Customs Service, Washington, DC 20229.

18 Antidumping and Countervailing Duties

Antidumping duties (ADs) are assessed on imported merchandise of a class or kind that is sold to purchasers in the U.S. at a price less than the fair market value. Fair market value of merchandise is the price at which it is normally sold in the manufacturer's home market.

Countervailing duties (CVDs) are assessed to counter the effects of subsidies provided by foreign governments to merchandise that is exported to the U.S. These subsidies cause the price of such merchandise to be artificially low, which causes economic "injury" to U.S. manufacturers.

The Department of Commerce, the International Trade Commission, and the U.S. Customs Service all play a part in enforcing antidumping and countervailing duty laws. The Department of Commerce is responsible for the overall administration of AD and CVD laws and for investigating allegations of dumping or foreign subsidization of imports. If warranted by the investigation, the Commerce Department also establishes the duty to be imposed on the merchandise. The ITC determines whether injury to industry has occurred, is likely to occur, or whether an industry may be hampered in its start-up efforts as a result of alleged dumping or subsidies. The Customs Service assesses ADs and CVDs once the rates have been established and the ITC has made the necessary determinations.

Investigation

AD or CVD investigations are typically initiated when a domestic industry files a petition with the Department of Commerce or when another interested party—an industry association, for example—alleges unfair competition by foreign manufacturers. Upon receipt of the petition, the Department of Commerce investigates the merits of the allegations to determine whether dumping or unfair subsidization has indeed occurred. The ITC, meanwhile, investigates whether there is reasonable indication that U.S. industries are, or are likely to be, harmed by the alleged dumping or subsidies. Results of these investigations are published in the Federal Register.

The Department of Commerce then calculates the difference between prices at which the merchandise in question is being sold in the U.S. and its fair market value. On the basis of such calculations, Commerce directs the Customs Service to: (1) assess cash deposits or require bonds on imports of the merchandise to cover possible AD or CVD duty liability, and (2) suspend liquidation of the entries until the Department has determined whether dumping or subsidization has occurred and has calculated the proper dumping or countervailing margins.

Completing the Investigation

When the Department of Commerce and, if applicable, the ITC have completed their investigations and determined that dumping or subsidization has occurred, Commerce will publish an Antidumping or Countervailing Duty Order, which will be announced in the Federal Register. At this point, Commerce will generally direct the Customs Service to collect only cash deposits. Bonding is no longer permitted for AD or CVD duty deposits.

Administrative Review/Final Settlement

Each year, on the anniversary of the final determination of dumping or subsidization, the Department of Commerce must, by law, perform an administrative review of the AD or CVD case if requested by interested parties to determine whether duty rates in effect for that first-year period are correct. Commerce publishes the results of this review in the Federal Register. At the one-year anniversary or completion of the administrative review, Commerce will direct Customs to liquidate the entries for the affected period. Customs will then review the entries and, if called for, make refunds to the importer or assess whatever additional duties may be owed.

19
Drawback—Refunds of Duties

Definition

Drawback is a refund of 99% of all ordinary Customs duties and internal revenue taxes. Drawback was initially authorized by the first tariff act of the U.S. in 1789. Since then it has been a part of the law, although from time to time the conditions under which it is payable have changed. For example, as a result of the Omnibus Trade & Competitiveness Act of 1988, antidumping and countervailing duties are not refundable on a drawback claim.

Purpose

The rationale for drawback has always been to encourage U.S. commerce or manufacturing, or both. It permits the U.S. manufacturer to compete in foreign markets without the handicap of including in his costs, and consequently in his sales price, the duty paid on imported merchandise. The types of drawback are authorized under 19 USC 1313, and implemented by 19 CFR Part 191.

Types of Drawback

There are three kinds of drawback provided for under the 1993 Customs Modernization Act.

Direct Identification Drawback. Direct identification drawback provides a refund of duties paid on imported merchandise that 1) is not used and is either exported or destroyed under Customs supervision; or 2) is partially or totally used in the manufacture of an exported article. Identification of the imported merchandise from import to export or destruction must be demonstrated through proper recordkeeping procedures. If the merchandise is not used in the U.S., drawback is available only if the articles are exported or destroyed within three years of the date of importation. If the imported merchandise is used in a manufacturing process, the articles must be exported within five years from the date of importation of the merchandise (19 USC 1313(a),(j)).

Substitution Drawback. Substitution drawback provides for a refund of duties paid on designated imported merchandise upon exportation or Customs-supervised destruction of articles manufactured or produced with the use of substituted domestic or imported merchandise that is of the same kind and quality as the designated imported merchandise. Same kind and quality means merchandise that is commercially interchangeable in a specific manufacturing process. Drawback is allowed if: 1) the imported materials are used in a manufacturing process within three years after receipt by the manufacturer; 2) the domestic materials, which are of the same kind and quality as the imported materials, are exported or destroyed before use in the U.S., or are used in a manufacturing process, within three years of receipt of the imported materials; and 3) if the materials are used in manufacturing, the articles are exported within five years of the date of importation of the designated material (19 USC 1313(b), (j)(2)).

Nonconforming Merchandise Drawback. Nonconforming merchandise drawback is a refund of duties on exportation or Custom-supervised destruction of merchandise rejected as nonconforming. This drawback is available for merchandise that does not conform to a sample or specifications, was shipped without the consignee's consent, or is determined to be defective as of the time of importation. Drawback may be claimed for such goods, provided that duties were paid, the goods were entered or withdrawn for consumption, and the goods are returned to Customs for exportation or destruction within three years after Customs released them (19 USC 1313(c)).

Procedure

The 1993 Customs Modernization Act permits an importer to claim drawback within three years after the articles are exported or destroyed. A claim is considered filed when the drawback entry and all documents necessary to complete the claim are submitted or requested by application to Customs. An exception is made for landing certificates, which must be filed in accordance with the time limits prescribed by specific regulation. The importer may accomplish a drawback filing electronically with permission of Customs. No extension of the time limit is allowed unless Customs is responsible for an untimely filing.

Questions relating to legal aspects of drawback should be addressed to: Chief, Drawback Section, Office of Trade Operations, U.S. Customs Service, 1301 Constitution Avenue, NW, Washington, DC 20229.

20 Classification—Liquidation

Classification

Classification and, when ad valorem rates of duty are applicable, appraisement are the two most important factors affecting dutiable status. Classifications and valuations, whether or not they are pertinent because an ad valorem rate of duty applies, must be provided by commercial importers when an entry is filed. In addition, classifications under the statistical suffixes of the tariff schedules must also be furnished even if this information is not pertinent to dutiable status. Accordingly, classification is initially the responsibility of an importer, customs broker, or other person preparing the entry papers.

Familiarity with the organization of the Harmonized Tariff Schedule of the United States (HTSUS) facilitates the classification process. (See Section 9 above relating to dutiable status.) The tariff schedule is divided into various sections and chapters dealing separately with merchandise in broad product categories. These categories, for example, separately cover animal products, vegetable products, products of various basic materials such as wood, textiles, plastics, rubber, and steel and other metal products in various stages of manufacture. Other sections encompass chemicals, machinery and electrical equipment, and other specified or non-enumerated products. The last section, Section XXII, covers certain exceptions from duty and special statutory provisions.

In Sections I through XXI, products are classifiable (1) under items or descriptions that name them, known as an *eo nomine* provision; (2) under provisions of general description; (3) under provisions that identify them by component material; or (4) under provisions that encompass merchandise in accordance with its actual or principal use. When two or more provisions seem to cover the same merchandise, the prevailing provision is determined in accordance with the legal notes and the General Rules of Interpretation for the tariff schedule. Also applicable are tariff classification principles contained in administrative precedents or in the case law of the U.S. Court of International Trade (formerly the U.S. Customs Court) or the U.S. Court of Appeals for the Federal Circuit (formerly the U.S. Court of Customs and Patent Appeals).

For product-specific information in HTSUS classifications, see the Commodity Index section, beginning on page 325.

Liquidation

Customs officers at the port of entry or other officials acting on behalf of the district director review the classifications and valuations, as well as other required import information, for correctness or as a proper basis for appraisement, as well as for agreement of the submitted data with the merchandise actually imported. The entry summary and documentation may be accepted as submitted without any changes. In this situation, the entry is liquidated as entered. Liquidation is the point at which the Customs Service's ascertainment of the rate of duty and amount of duty becomes final for most purposes.

Liquidation is accomplished by posting a notice on a public bulletin board at the customhouse. However, an importer may receive an advance notice on Customs **Form 4333A** "Courtesy Notice" stating when and in what amount duty will be liquidated. This form is not the liquidation, and protest rights do not accrue until the notice is posted. Time limits for protesting do not start to run until the date of posting, and a protest cannot be filed before liquidation is posted.

Once Customs implements electronic filing in accordance with the 1993 Customs Modernization Act (Mod Act), entries covered by an entry summary or import activity summary statement will be liquidated in accordance with normal Customs procedures or will be kept open at the importer's request. After liquidation of an entry, an importer may submit a reconciliation when information becomes available at a later time. Customs will compare the information provided at entry and in the reconciliation and make adjustments.

The Customs Service may determine that an entry cannot be liquidated as entered for one reason or another. For example, the tariff classification may not be correct or may not be acceptable because it is not consistent with an established and uniform classification practice. If the change required by this determination results in a rate of duty more favorable to an importer, the entry is liquidated accordingly and a refund of the applicable amount of the deposited estimated duties is authorized. On the other hand, a change may be necessary that imposes a higher rate of duty. For example, a claim for an exemption from duty under a free-rate provision or under a conditional exemption may be found to be insufficient for lack of the required supporting documentation. In this situation the importer may be given an advance notice of the proposed duty rate advancement and an opportunity to validate the claim for a free rate or more favorable rate of duty.

If the importer does not respond to the notice, or if the response is found to be without merit, duty is liquidated in accordance with the entry as corrected and the importer is billed for the additional duty. The port or district may find that the importer's response raises issues of such complexity that resolution by a Customs Headquarters decision through the internal advice procedure is warranted. Internal advice from Customs Headquarters may be requested by the local Customs officers on their own initiative or in response to a request by the importer.

The Mod Act takes a novel approach to liquidation by allowing reconciliation to occur after entry. An importer who wishes to submit reconciliation for a particular entry can specify the intent to provide relevant data when it becomes available at a later time. The Mod Act permits Customs to liquidate an entry before the unknown information has been transmitted to Customs. The Act further imposes a responsibility on importers to use reasonable care in making entry so that Customs can rely on the accuracy of information and can streamline the entry and liquidation procedures. If an importer fails to use reasonable care in classifying and valuing merchandise and presenting entry data, Customs may impose a penalty in an amount commensurate to the level of culpability. See 19 USC 1592.

Protests

After liquidation an importer may still pursue, on Customs **Form 19**, (19 CFR 174), any claims for an adjustment or refund by filing a protest within 90 days after liquidation. For protest, extension, and suspension purposes, the reconciliation of entries that have been liquidated is treated as if it were an entry summary. To apply for a Headquarters ruling, a request for further review must be filed with the protest. The same **Form 19** can be used for this purpose. If filed separately, application for further review must still be filed within 90 days of liquidation. Filing may be accomplished electronically.

If a ruling on the question has previously been issued in response to a request for a decision on a prospective transaction or a request for internal advice, further review will ordinarily be denied. If a protest is denied, an importer has the right to litigate the matter by filing a summons with the U.S. Court of International Trade within 180 days after denial of the protest. The rules of the court and other applicable statutes and precedents determine the course of customs litigation.

While the Customs ascertainment of dutiable status is final for most purposes at the time of liquidation, a liquidation is not final until any protest that has been filed against it has been decided. Similarly, the administrative decision issued on a protest is not final until any litigation filed against it has become final.

Entries must be liquidated within one year of the date of entry unless the liquidation needs to be extended for another one-year period (not to exceed a total of four years from the date of entry). The Customs Service will suspend liquidation of an entry when required by statute or court order. A suspension will remain in effect until the issue is resolved. When suspension is removed, the entry must be liquidated within six months from the date Customs is notified of the removal. Notifications of extensions and suspensions are given to importers, surety companies, and customs brokers who are parties to the transaction.

21
Conversion of Currency

The conversion of foreign currency for Customs purposes must be made in accordance with the provisions of 31 USC 5151. This section states that Customs is to use rates of exchange determined and certified by the Federal Reserve Bank of New York. These certified rates are based on the New York market buying rates for the foreign currencies involved.

In the case of widely used currencies, rates of exchange are certified each day. The rates certified on the first business day of each calendar quarter are used throughout the quarter except on days when fluctuations of 5% or more occur, in which case the actual certified rates for those days are used. For infrequently used currencies, the Federal Reserve Bank of New York certifies rates of exchange upon request by Customs. The rates certified are only for the currencies and dates requested.

For Customs purposes, the date of exportation of the goods is the date used to determine the applicable certified rate of exchange. This remains true even though a different rate may have been used in payment of the goods. Information as to the applicable rate of exchange in converting currency for customs purposes in the case of a given shipment may be obtained from a district or port director of Customs.

22
Transaction Value

U.S. Customs officers are required by law to determine the value for imported merchandise. The valuation provisions of the Tariff Act of 1930 are found in section 402, as amended by the Trade Agreements Act of 1979. Pertinent portions are reproduced in Appendix 3, "Customs Valuation" on page 244.

Generally, the customs value of all merchandise exported to the U.S. will be the transaction value for the goods. If the transaction value cannot be used, then certain secondary bases are considered. The secondary bases of value, listed in order of precedence for use, are:

Transaction value of identical merchandise,

Transaction value of similar merchandise,

Deductive value, and

Computed value.

The order of precedence of the last two values can be reversed if the importer so requests. These secondary bases are discussed in the next two chapters.

Transaction Value

The transaction value of imported merchandise is the price actually paid or payable for the merchandise when sold for exportation to the U.S., plus amounts for the following items if not included in the price:

1. The packing costs incurred by the buyer.
2. Any selling commission incurred by the buyer.
3. The value of any assist.
4. Any royalty or license fee that the buyer is required to pay as a condition of the sale.
5. The proceeds, accruing to the seller, of any subsequent resale, disposal, or use of the imported merchandise.

The amounts for these items are added only to the extent that each is not included in the price actually paid or payable and information is available to establish the accuracy of the specific amount. If sufficient information is not available, then the transaction value cannot be determined and the next basis of value, in order of precedence, must be considered for appraisement. A discussion of these added items follows:

Packing costs consist of the cost incurred by the buyer for all containers and coverings of whatever nature and for the labor and materials used in packing the imported merchandise to ready it for export.

Any selling commission incurred by the buyer with respect to the imported merchandise constitutes part of the transaction value. Buying commissions do not. A selling commission means any commission paid to the seller's agent, who is related to or controlled by, or works for or on behalf of, the manufacturer or the seller.

The apportioned value of any assist constitutes part of the transaction value of the imported merchandise. First the value of the assist is determined; then the value is prorated to the imported merchandise.

Assists. An assist is any of the items listed below that the buyer of imported merchandise provides directly or indirectly, free of charge or at a reduced cost, for use in the production or sale of merchandise for export to the U.S.

Materials, components, parts, and similar items incorporated in the imported merchandise.

Tools, dies, molds, and similar items used in producing the imported merchandise.

Merchandise consumed in producing the imported merchandise.

Engineering, development, artwork, design work, and plans and sketches that are undertaken outside the U.S. "Engineering...," will not be treated as an assist if the service or work is (1) performed by a person domiciled within the U.S., (2) performed while that person is acting as an employee or agent of the buyer of the imported merchandise, and (3) incidental to other engineering, development, artwork, design work, or plans or sketches undertaken within the U.S.

Value. In determining the value of an assist, the following rules apply:

1. The value is either (a) the cost of acquiring the assist, if acquired by the importer from an unrelated seller, or (b) the cost of the assist, if produced by the importer or a person related to the importer.
2. The value includes the cost of transporting the assist to the place of production.
3. The value of assists used in producing the imported merchandise is adjusted to reflect use, repairs, modifications, or other factors affecting the value of the assists. Assists of this type include such items as tools, dies, and molds.

   For example, if the importer previously used the assist, regardless of whether he acquired or produced it, the original cost of acquisition or of production must be decreased to reflect the use. Alternatively, repairs and modifications may result in the value of the assist having to be adjusted upward.
4. In the case of engineering, development, artwork, design work, and plans and sketches undertaken elsewhere than in the U.S., the value is (a) the cost of obtaining copies of the assist, if the assist is available in the public domain; (b) the cost of the purchase or lease, if the assist was bought or leased by the buyer from an unrelated person; (c) the value added outside the U.S., if the assist was produced in the U.S. and one or more foreign countries.

So far as possible, the buyer's commercial record system will be used to determine the value of an assist, especially such assists as engineering, development, artwork, design work, and plans and sketches undertaken elsewhere than in the U.S.

Apportionment. Having determined the value of an assist, the next step is to prorate that value to the imported merchandise. The apportionment is done reasonably and according to generally accepted accounting principles. By the latter is meant any generally recognized consensus or substantial authoritative support regarding the recording and measuring of assets and liabilities and changes, the disclosing of information, and the preparing of financial statements.

Royalty or license fees that a buyer must pay directly or indirectly, as a condition of the sale of the imported merchandise for exportation to the U.S. will be included in the transaction value. Ultimately, whether a royalty or license fee is dutiable will depend on whether the buyer had to pay it as a condition of the sale and to whom and under what circumstances it was paid. The dutiability status will have to be decided on a case-by-case basis.

Charges for the right to reproduce the imported goods in the U.S. are not dutiable. This right applies only to the following types of merchandise:

Originals or copies of artistic or scientific works.

Originals or copies of models and industrial drawings.

Model machines and prototypes.

Plant and animal species.

Any proceeds resulting from the subsequent resale, disposal, or use of the imported merchandise that accrue, directly or indirectly, to the seller are dutiable. These proceeds are added to the price actually paid or payable, if not otherwise included.

The price actually paid or payable for the imported merchandise is the total payment, excluding international freight, insurance, and other c.i.f. charges, that the buyer makes to the seller. This payment may be direct or indirect. Some examples of an indirect payment are when the buyer settles all or part of a debt owed by the seller, or when the seller reduces the price on a current importation to settle a debt he owes the buyer. Such indirect payments are part of the transaction value.

However, if a buyer performs an activity on his own account, other than those which may be included in the transaction value, then the activity is not considered an indirect payment to the seller and is not part of the transaction value. This applies even though the buyer's activity might be regarded as benefiting the seller—for example, advertising.

Exclusions

The amounts to be excluded from transaction value are as follows:

1. The cost, charges, or expenses incurred for transportation, insurance, and related services incident to the international shipment of the goods from the country of exportation to the place of importation in the U.S.
2. Any reasonable cost or charge incurred for:

   Constructing, erecting, assembling, maintaining, or providing technical assistance with respect to the goods after importation into the U.S., or

   Transporting the goods after importation.

3. The customs duties and other Federal taxes, including any Federal excise tax for which sellers in the U.S. are ordinarily liable.

Note: Foreign inland freight and related charges in item 1 (see part 152, Custom Regulations), as well as items 2 and 3 above, must be identified separately.

Limitations

The transaction value of imported merchandise is the appraised value of that merchandise, provided certain limitations do not exist. If any of these limitations are present, then transaction value cannot be used as the appraised value, and the next basis of value will be considered. The limitations can be divided into four groups:

1. Restrictions on the disposition or use of the merchandise.
2. Conditions for which a value cannot be determined.
3. Proceeds of any subsequent resale, disposal, or use of the merchandise, accruing to the seller, for which an appropriate adjustment to transaction value cannot be made.
4. Related-party transactions where the transaction value is not acceptable.

The term "acceptable" means that the relationship between the buyer and seller did not influence the price actually paid or payable. Examining the circumstances of the sale will help make this determination.

Alternatively, "acceptable" can also mean that the transaction value of the imported merchandise closely approximates one of the following test values, provided these values relate to merchandise exported to the U.S. at or about the same time as the imported merchandise:

1. The transaction value of identical merchandise or of similar merchandise in sales to unrelated buyers in the U.S.
2. The deductive value or computed value for identical merchandise or similar merchandise. The test values are used for comparison only; they do not form a substitute basis of valuation.

In determining if the transaction value is close to one of the foregoing test values, an adjustment is made if the sales involved differ in:

Commercial levels,

Quantity levels,

The costs, commission, values, fees, and proceeds added to the transaction value (price paid) if not included in the price, and

The costs incurred by the seller in sales in which he and the buyer are not related that are not incurred by the seller in sales in which he and the buyer are related.

As stated, the test values are alternatives to the relationship criterion. If one of the test values is met, it is not necessary to examine the question of whether the relationship influenced the price.

23
Transaction Value of Identical Merchandise or Similar Merchandise

When the transaction value cannot be determined, then the customs value of the imported goods being appraised is the transaction value of identical merchandise. If merchandise identical to the imported goods cannot be found or an acceptable transaction value for such merchandise does not exist, then the customs value is the transaction value of similar merchandise. The above value would be previously accepted customs values.

Besides the data common to all three transaction values, certain factors specifically apply to the transaction value of identical merchandise or similar merchandise. These factors concern (1) the exportation date, (2) the level and quantity of sales, (3) the meaning, and (4) the order of precedence of identical merchandise and of similar merchandise.

Exportation Date. The identical (similar) merchandise for which a value is being determined must have been sold for export to the U.S. and exported at or about the same time as the merchandise being appraised.

Sales Level/Quantity. The transaction value of identical (similar) merchandise must be based on sales of identical (similar) merchandise at the same commercial level and in substantially the same quantity as the sale of the merchandise being appraised. If no such sale exists, then sales at either a different commercial level or in different quantities, or both, can be used but must be adjusted to take account of any such difference. Any adjustment must be based on sufficient information, that is, information establishing the reasonableness and accuracy of the adjustment.

Meanings. The term "identical merchandise" means merchandise that is:

Identical in all respects to the merchandise being appraised.

Produced in the same country as the merchandise being appraised.

Produced by the same person as the merchandise being appraised.

If merchandise meeting all three criteria cannot be found, then identical merchandise is merchandise satisfying the first two criteria but produced by a different person than the producer of merchandise being appraised.

Note: Merchandise can be identical to the merchandise being appraised and still show minor differences in appearance.

Exclusion: Identical merchandise does not include merchandise that incorporates or reflects engineering, development, artwork, design work, and plans and sketches provided free or at reduced cost by the buyer and undertaken in the U.S.

The term "similar merchandise" means merchandise that is:

Produced in the same country and by the same person as the merchandise being appraised.

Like merchandise being appraised in characteristics and component materials.

Commercially interchangeable with the merchandise being appraised.

If merchandise meeting the foregoing criteria cannot be found, then similar merchandise is merchandise having the same country of production, like characteristics and component materials, and commercial interchangeability but produced by a different person.

In determining whether goods are similar, some of the factors to be considered are the quality of the goods, their reputation, and existence of a trademark.

Exclusion: Similar merchandise does not include merchandise that incorporates or reflects engineering, development, artwork, design work, and plans and sketches provided free or at reduced cost to the buyer and undertaken in the U.S.

Order of Precedence. It is possible that two or more transaction values for identical (similar) merchandise will be determined. In such a case the lowest value will be used as the appraised value of the imported merchandise.

24 Other Bases: Deductive and Computed Value

Deductive Value

If the transaction value of imported merchandise, of identical merchandise, or of similar merchandise cannot be determined, then deductive value is calculated for the merchandise being appraised. Deductive value is the next basis of appraisement at the time the entry summary is filed, to be used unless the importer designates computed value as the preferred method of appraisement. If computed value was chosen and subsequently determined not to exist for customs valuation purposes, then the basis of appraisement reverts to deductive value.

If an assist is involved in a sale, that sale cannot be used in determining deductive value. So any sale to a person who supplies an assist for use in connection with the production or sale for export of the merchandise concerned is disregarded for purposes of determining deductive value.

Basically, deductive value is the resale price in the U.S. after importation of the goods, with deductions for certain items. In discussing deductive value, the term "merchandise concerned" is used. The term means the merchandise being appraised, identical merchandise, or similar merchandise. Generally, the deductive value is calculated by starting with a unit price and making certain additions to and deductions from that price.

Unit Price. One of three prices constitutes the unit price in deductive value. The price used depends on when and in what condition the merchandise concerned is sold in the U.S.

1. Time and Condition: The merchandise is *sold in the condition* as imported *at or about the date of importation* of the merchandise being appraised.

   Price: The price used is the unit price at which the greatest aggregate quantity of the merchandise concerned is sold at or about date of importation.

2. Time and Condition: The merchandise concerned is *sold in the condition as imported but not sold at or about the date of importation* of the merchandise being appraised.

   Price: The price used is the unit price at which the greatest aggregate quantity of the merchandise concerned is sold after the date of importation of the merchandise being appraised but before the close of the 90th day after the date of importation.

3. Time and Condition: The merchandise concerned is *not sold in the condition* as imported and *not sold before the close of the 90th day* after the date of importation of the merchandise being appraised.

   Price: The price used is the unit price at which the greatest aggregate quantity of the merchandise being appraised, after further processing, is sold before the 180th day after the date of importation.

This third price is also known as the "further processing price" or "superdeductive."

Additions. Packing costs for the merchandise concerned are added to the price used for deductive value, provided these costs have not otherwise been included. These costs are added regardless of whether the importer or the buyer incurs the cost. Packing costs means the cost of:

1. All containers and coverings of whatever nature; and
2. Packing, whether for labor or materials, used in placing the merchandise in condition, packed ready for shipment to the U.S.

Deductions. Certain items are not part of deductive value and must be deducted from the unit price. These items are as follows:

1. Commissions or Profit and General Expenses. Any commission usually paid or agreed to be paid, or the addition usually made for profit and general expenses, applicable to sales in the U.S. of imported merchandise that is of the same class or kind as the merchandise concerned regardless of the country of exportation.
2. Transportation/Insurance Costs. The usual and associated costs of transporting and insuring the merchandise concerned from (a) the country of exportation to the place of importation in the U.S. and (b) the place of importation to the place of delivery in the U.S., provided these costs are not included as a general expense under the preceding item 1.
3. Customs Duties/Federal Taxes. The customs duties and other Federal taxes payable on the merchandise concerned because of its importation plus any Federal excise tax on, or measured by the value of, such merchandise for which sellers in the U.S. are ordinarily liable.
4. Value of Further Processing. The value added by the processing of the merchandise after importation, provided sufficient information exists concerning the cost of processing. The price determined for deductive value is reduced by the value of further processing only if the third unit price (the superdeductive) is used as deductive value.

Superdeductive. The importer has the option to ask that deductive value be based on the further- processing price. If the importer makes that choice, certain facts concerning valuing the further-processing method, termed "superdeductive," must be followed.

Under the superdeductive, the merchandise concerned is not sold in the condition as imported and not sold before the close of the 90th day after the date of importation, but is sold before the 180th day after the date of importation.

Under this method, an amount equal to the value of the further processing must be deducted from the unit price in determining deductive value. The amount so deducted must be based on objective and quantifiable data concerning the cost of such work as well as any spoilage, waste or scrap derived from that work. Items such as accepted industry formulas, methods of construction, and industry practices could be used as a basis for calculating the amount to be deducted.

Generally, the superdeductive method cannot be used if the further processing destroys the identity of the goods. Such situations will be decided on a case-by-case basis for the following reasons:

1. Sometimes, even though the identity of the goods is lost, the value added by the processing can be determined accurately without unreasonable difficulty for importers or for the Customs Service.
2. In some cases, the imported goods still keep their identity after processing but form only a minor part of the goods sold in the U.S. In such cases, using the superdeductive method to value the imported goods will not be justified.

The superdeductive method cannot be used if the merchandise concerned is sold in the condition as imported before the close of the 90th day after the date of importation of the merchandise being appraised.

Computed Value

The next basis of appraisement is computed value. If customs valuation cannot be based on any of the values previously discussed, then computed value is considered. This value is also the one the importer can select to precede deductive value as a basis of appraisement.

Computed value consists of the sum of the following items:

1. Materials, fabrication, and other processing used in producing the imported merchandise.
2. Profit and general expenses.
3. Any assist, if not included in items 1 and 2.
4. Packing costs.

Materials, Fabrication, and Other Processing. The cost or value of the materials, fabrication, and other processing of any kind used in producing the imported merchandise is based on (a) information provided by or on behalf of the producer and (b) the commercial accounts of the producer if the accounts are consistent with generally accepted accounting principles applied in the country of production of the goods.

Note: If the country of exportation imposes an internal tax on the materials or their disposition and refunds the tax when merchandise produced from the materials is exported, then the amount of the internal tax is not included as part of the cost or value of the materials.

Profit and General Expenses. The producer's profit and general expenses are used, provided they are consistent with the usual profit and general expenses reflected by producers in the country of exportation in sales of merchandise of the same class or kind as the imported merchandise. Some facts concerning the amount for profit and general expenses should be mentioned:

1. The amount is determined by information supplied by the producer and is based on his commercial accounts, provided such accounts are consistent with generally accepted accounting principles in the country of production.

   Note: As a point of contrast, for deductive value the generally accepted accounting principles used are those in the U.S., whereas in computed value the generally accepted accounting principles are those in the country of production.

2. The producer's profit and general expenses must be consistent with those usually reflected in sales of goods of the same class or kind as the imported merchandise that are made by producers in the country of exportation for export to the U.S. If they are not consistent, then the amount for profit and general expenses is based on the usual profit and general expenses of such producers.
3. The amount for profit and general expenses is taken as a whole. This is the same treatment as occurs in deductive value.

Basically, a producer's profit could be low and his general expenses high, so that the total amount is consistent with that usually reflected in sales of goods of the same class or kind. In such a situation, a producer's actual profit figures, even if low, will be used provided he has valid commercial reasons to justify them and his pricing policy reflects usual pricing policies in the industry concerned.

Assists. If the value of an assist used in producing the merchandise is not included as part of the producer's materials, fabrication, other processing, or general expenses, then the prorated value of the assist will be included in computed value. It is important that the value of the assist is not included elsewhere because no component of computed value should be counted more than once in determining computed value.

Note: The value of any engineering, development, artwork, design work, and plans and sketches undertaken in the U.S. is included in computed value only to the extent that such value has been charged to the producer.

Packing Costs. The cost of all containers and coverings of whatever nature, and of packing, whether for labor or material, used in placing merchandise in condition and packed ready for shipment to the U.S. is included in computed value.

Under computed value, "merchandise of the same class or kind" must be imported from the same country as the merchandise being appraised and must be within a group or range of goods produced by a particular industry or industry sector. Whether certain merchandise is of the same class or kind as other merchandise will be determined on a case-by-case basis.

In determining usual profit and general expenses, sales for export to the U.S. of the narrowest group or range of merchandise that includes the merchandise being appraised will be examined, providing the necessary information can be obtained.

Note: As a point of contrast, under deductive value, "merchandise of the same class or kind" includes merchandise imported from other countries besides the country from which the merchandise being appraised was imported. Under computed value, "Merchandise of the same class or kind" is limited to merchandise imported from the same country as the merchandise being appraised.

Value If Other Values Cannot Be Determined

If none of the previous five values can be used to appraise the imported merchandise, then the customs value must be based on a value derived from one of the five previous methods, reasonably adjusted as necessary. The value so determined should be based, to the greatest extent possible, on previously determined values. In order for Customs to consider an importer's argument regarding appraisement, the information upon which the argument is based must be made available to Customs, whether it was generated by a foreign or domestic source.

Some examples of how the other methods can be reasonably adjusted are:

1. Identical Merchandise (or Similar Merchandise):
   a. The requirement that the identical merchandise (or similar merchandise) should be exported at or about the same time as the merchandise being appraised could be flexibly interpreted.
   b. Identical imported merchandise (or similar imported merchandise) produced in a country other than the country of exportation of the merchandise being appraised could be the basis for customs valuation.
   c. Customs values of identical imported merchandise (or similar imported merchandise) already determined on the basis of deductive value and computed value could be used.
2. Deductive Method: The 90-day requirement could be administered flexibly (19 CFR 152.107(c)).

25
Marking: Country of Origin

The U.S. customs laws require each imported article produced abroad to be marked in a conspicuous place as legibly, indelibly, and permanently as the nature of the article permits, with the English name of the country of origin, to indicate to the ultimate purchaser in the U.S. the name of the country in which the article was manufactured or produced. Articles that are otherwise specifically exempted from individual marking are an exception to this rule. The exceptions are discussed below.

Marking Required

If the article (or the container when the container and not the article must be marked) is not properly marked at the time of importation, a marking duty equal to 10% of the customs value of the article will be assessed unless the article is exported, destroyed, or properly marked under Customs supervision before the liquidation of the entry concerned.

It is not feasible to state who will be the "ultimate purchaser" in every circumstance. Broadly stated, an "ultimate purchaser" may be defined as the last person in the U.S. who will receive the article in the form in which it was imported. Generally, if an imported article will be used in the U.S. in manufacture, which results in an article having a name, character, or usage different from that of the imported article, the manufacturer is the ultimate purchaser. If an article is to be sold at retail in its imported form, the purchaser at retail is the ultimate purchaser. A person who subjects an imported article to a process that results in a substantial transformation of the article is the ultimate purchaser, but if the process is merely a minor one that leaves the identity of the imported article intact, the processor of the article will not be regarded as the ultimate purchaser.

When an article (or its container) is required to be marked to indicate the country of origin of the article, the marking is sufficiently permanent if it will remain on the article (or its container) until it reaches the ultimate purchaser.

When an article is of a kind that is usually combined with another article subsequent to importation but before delivery to an ultimate purchaser, and the name indicating the country of origin of the article appears in a place on the article so that the name will be visible after such combining, the marking shall include, in addition to the name of the country of origin, words or symbols that clearly show that the origin indicated is that of the imported article only and not that of any other article with which the imported article may be combined after importation. For example, if marked bottles, drums, or other containers are imported empty, to be filled in the U.S., they shall be marked with such words as "Bottle (or drum or container) made in (name of country)." Labels and similar articles so marked that the name of the country of origin of the article is visible after it is affixed to another article in this country shall be marked with additional descriptive words such as "label made (or printed) in (name of country)" or words of similar import.

In any case in which the words "United States," or "American" or the letters "U.S.A.," any variation of such words or letters, or the name of any city or locality in the U.S., or the name of any foreign country or locality in which the article was manufactured or produced, appear on an imported article or container, there shall appear, legibly and permanently, in close proximity to such words, letters or name, the name of the country of origin preceded by "Made in," "Product of," or other words of similar meaning.

If marked articles are to be repacked in the U.S. after release from Customs custody, importers must certify on entry that they will not obscure the marking on properly marked articles if the article is repacked or that they will mark the repacked container. If the importers do not repack, but resell to repackers, importers must notify the repackers of the marking requirements. Failure to comply with the certification requirements may subject importers to penalties and/or additional duties.

Marking Not Required

The following articles and classes or kinds of articles are not required to be marked to indicate the country of their origin, i.e., the country in which they were grown, manufactured, or produced. However, the outermost containers in which these articles ordinarily reach the ultimate purchaser in the U.S. must be marked to indicate the English name of the country of origin of the articles.

Art, works of.
Articles classified subheads 9810.00.15, 9810.00.25, 9810.00.40, and 9810.00.45 of the HTSUS.
Articles entered in good faith as antiques and rejected as unauthentic.
Bagging, waste.
Bags, jute.
Bands, steel.
Beads, unstrung.
Bearings, ball, 5/8 inch or less in diameter.
Blanks, metal, to be plated.
Bodies, harvest hat.
Bolts, nuts, and washers.
Briarwood, in blocks.
Briquettes, coal or coke.
Buckles, 1 inch or less in greatest dimension.
Burlap.
Buttons.
Cards, playing.
Cellophane and celluloid in sheets, bands, or strips.
Chemicals, drugs, medicinal, and similar substances, when imported in capsules, pills, tablets, lozenges, or troches.
Cigars and cigarettes.
Covers, straw bottle.
Dies, diamond wire, unmounted.
Dowels, wooden.
Effects, theatrical.
Eggs.
Feathers.
Firewood.

Flooring, not further manufactured than planed, tongued and grooved.
Flowers, artificial, except bunches.
Flowers, cut.
Glass, cut to shape and size for use in clocks, hand pocket and purse mirrors, and other glass of similar shapes and sizes, not including lenses or watch crystals.
Glides, furniture, except glides with prongs.
Hairnets.
Hides, raw.
Hooks, fish (except snelled fish hooks).
Hoops (wood), barrel.
Laths.
Leather, except finished.
Livestock.
Lumber, sawed.
Metal bars except concrete reinforcement bars, billets, blocks, blooms, ingots, pigs, plates, sheets, except galvanized sheets, shafting, slabs, and metal in similar forms.
Mica not further manufactured than cut or stamped to dimensions, shape, or form.
Monuments.
Nails, spikes, and staples.
Natural products, such as vegetables, fruit, nuts, berries, and live or dead animals, fish, and birds; all the foregoing that are in their natural state or not advanced in any manner further than is necessary for their safe transportation.
Nets, bottle wire.
Paper, newsprint.
Paper, stencil.
Paper, stock.
Parchment and vellum.
Parts for machines imported from same country as parts.
Pickets (wood).
Pins, tuning.
Plants, shrubs, and other nursery stock.
Plugs, tie.
Poles, bamboo.
Posts (wood), fence.
Pulpwood.
Rags (including wiping rags).
Rails, joint bars, and tie plates of steel.
Ribbon.
Rivets.
Rope, including wire rope, cordage, cords, twines, threads, and yarns.
Scrap and waste.
Screws.
Shims, track.
Shingles (wood), bundles of, except bundles of red-cedar shingles.
Skins, fur, dressed or dyed.
Skins, raw fur.
Sponges.
Springs, watch.
Stamps, postage and revenue, and Government stamped envelopes and postal cards bearing no printing other than the official import thereon.
Staves (wood), barrel.
Steel, hoop.
Sugar, maple.
Ties (wood), railroad.
Tiles, not over 1 inch in greatest dimension.
Timbers, sawed.
Tips, penholder.
Trees, Christmas.
Weights, analytical and precision, in sets.
Wicking, candle.
Wire, except barbed.
Unless an article being shipped to the U.S. is specifically named in the foregoing list, it would be advisable for an exporter to obtain advice from U.S. Customs before concluding that it is exempted from marking.

If articles on the foregoing list are repackaged in the U.S., the new packages must be labeled to indicate the country of origin of the articles contained therein. Importers must certify on entry that, if they repackage, they will properly mark the repackaged containers; if they do not repackage, but resell to repackagers, notification of the marking requirements will be given to such repackagers. Failure to comply with the certification requirements may subject importers to penalties and marking duties.

Other Exceptions

The following classes of articles are excepted from the country of origin marking requirements. (The usual container in which one of these articles is imported will also be excepted.)

a. An article imported for use by the importer and not intended for sale in its imported or any other form.

b. An article that is to be processed in the U.S. by the importer or for his account otherwise than for the purpose of concealing the origin of the article and in such manner that any mark of origin would necessarily be obliterated, destroyed, or permanently concealed.

c. An article with respect to which an ultimate purchaser in the U.S., by reason of the character of the article, or by reason of the circumstances of its importation, must necessarily know the country of origin even though the article is not marked to indicate its origin. The clearest application of this exemption is when the contract between the ultimate purchaser in the U.S. and the supplier abroad insures that the order will be filled only with articles grown, manufactured, or produced in a named country.

The following classes of articles are also excepted from marking to indicate the country of their origin.

a. Articles that are incapable of being marked.

b. Articles that cannot be marked prior to shipment to the U.S. without injury.

c. Articles that cannot be marked prior to shipment to the U.S., except at an expense economically prohibitive of their importation.

d. Articles for which the marking of the containers will reasonably indicate the origin of the articles.

e. Crude substances.

f. Articles produced more than 20 years prior to their importation into the U.S.

g. Articles entered or withdrawn from warehouse for immediate exportation or for transportation and exportation.

Although such articles are exempted from marking to indicate the country of their origin, the outermost containers in which the articles will ordinarily reach the ultimate purchaser in the U.S. must be marked to show the country of origin of such articles.

When the marking of the container of an article will reasonably indicate the country of origin of the article, the article itself may be exempt from such marking. This exemption applies only when the articles will reach the ultimate purchaser in an unopened container. For example, articles that reach the retail purchaser in sealed containers marked clearly to indicate the country of origin come within this exception. Materials to be used in building or manufacture by the builder or manufacturer who will receive the materials in unopened cases likewise come within the exemption. The following articles, as well as their containers, are excepted from marking to indicate the country of their origin.

a. Products of U.S. fisheries that are free of duty.

b. Products of possessions of the U.S.

c. Products of the U.S. exported and returned.

d. Articles valued at not more than $5 that are passed without entry.

26 Special Marking Requirements

The Country of Origin marking requirements are separate and apart from any special marking or labeling required on specific products by other agencies. It is recommended that the specific agency be contacted for any special marking or labeling requirements.

Certain articles are subject to special country of origin marking requirements: Iron and steel pipe and pipe fittings, manhole rings, frames, or covers, and compressed gas cylinders, must generally be marked by one of four methods: die-stamped, cast-in-mold lettering, etching (acid or electrolytic) or engraving. In addition, none of the exceptions from marking discussed above are applicable to iron and steel pipe and pipe fittings.

The following articles, and parts thereof, shall be marked legibly and conspicuously to indicate their origin by die-stamping, cast-in-the-mold lettering, etching (acid or electrolytic), engraving, or by means of metal plates that bear the prescribed marking and that are securely attached to the article in a conspicuous place by welding, screws, or rivets:

Knives, clippers, shears, safety razors, surgical instruments, scientific, and laboratory instruments, pliers, pincers and vacuum containers.

Watch movements are required to be marked on one or more of the bridges or top plates to show (l) the name of the country of manufacture, (2) the name of the manufacturer or purchaser, and (3) in words, the number of jewels, if any, serving a mechanical purpose as frictional bearings.

Clock movements shall be marked on the most visible part of the front or back plate to show (1) the name of the country of manufacture, (2) the name of the manufacturer or purchaser, and (3) the number of jewels, if any.

Watch cases shall be marked on the inside or outside of the back cover to show (1) the name of the country of manufacture, and (2) the name of the manufacturer or purchaser.

Clock cases and other cases provided for in Chapter 91, HTSUS, are required to be marked on the most visible part of the outside of the back to show the name of the country of manufacture.

The terms "watch movement" and "clock movement" refer to devices regulated by a balance wheel and hairspring, quartz crystal, or any other system capable of determining intervals of time, with a display or system to which a mechanical display can be incorporated. "Watch movements" include those devices that do not exceed 12 mm in thickness and 50 mm in width, length, or diameter; "clock movements" include those devices that do not meet the watch movement dimensional specifications. The term "cases" embraces inner and outer cases, containers, and housings for movements, together with parts or pieces, such as, but not limited to, rings, feet, posts, bases, and outer frames, and any auxiliary or incidental features, that (with appropriate movements) serve to complete the watches, clocks, time switches, and other apparatus provided for in Chapter 91, HTSUS.

Articles required to be marked in accordance with the special marking requirements in Chapter 91 must be conspicuously and indelibly marked by cutting, die-sinking, engraving, or stamping. Articles required to be so marked shall be denied entry unless marked in exact conformity with these requirements.

Movements with opto-electronic display only and cases designed for their use, whether entered as separate articles or as components of assembled watches or clocks, are not subject to the special marking requirements. These items need only to be marked with the marking requirements of 19 USC 1304.

Parts of any of the foregoing not including those above mentioned.

In addition to the special marking requirements set forth above, all watches of foreign origin must comply with the usual country of origin marking requirements. Customs considers the country of origin of watches to be the country of manufacture of the watch movement. The name of this country should appear either on the outside back cover or on the face of the dial.

27
Marking—False Impression

Section 42 of the Trademark Act of 1946 (15 USC 1124) provides, among other things, that no imported article of foreign origin that bears a name or mark calculated to induce the public to believe that it was manufactured in the U.S., or in any foreign country or locality other than the country or locality in which it was in fact manufactured, shall be admitted to entry at any customhouse in the U.S.

In many cases, the words "United States," the letters "U.S.A.," or the name of any city or locality in the U.S. appearing on an imported article of foreign origin, or on the containers thereof, are considered to be calculated to induce the public to believe that the article was manufactured in the U.S. unless the name to indicate the country of origin appears in close proximity to the name that indicates a domestic origin. Merchandise discovered after conditional release to have been missing a required country of origin marking may be ordered redelivered to Customs custody. If such delivery is not promptly made, liquidated damages may be assessed against the Customs bond. (See 19 CFR 141.113(a), cf.; 19 CFR Part 172; and Customs **Form 4647**.)

An imported article bearing a name or mark prohibited by Section 42 of the Trademark Act is subject to seizure and forfeiture. However, upon the filing of a petition by the importer prior to final disposition of the article, the district or port director of Customs may release it upon the condition that the prohibited marking be removed or obliterated or that the article and containers be properly marked; or the district or port director may permit the article to be exported or destroyed under Customs supervision and without expense to the Government.

Section 43 of the Trademark Act of 1946 (15 USC 1125) prohibits the entry of goods marked or labeled with a false designation of origin or with any false description or representation, including words or other symbols tending to falsely describe or represent the same. Deliberate removal, obliteration, covering, or altering of required country of origin markings after release from Customs custody is also a crime punishable by fines and imprisonment (19 USC 1304(h)).

28 User Fees

Customs user fees were established by the Consolidated Omnibus Budget Reconciliation Act of 1985. This legislation was expanded in 1986 to include a merchandise processing fee. Also in 1986, Congress enacted the Water Resources Development Act, which authorized the Customs Service to collect a harbor maintenance fee for the Army Corps of Engineers. Further legislation has extended the User Fee Program until 1995.

The merchandise processing fee sets a fee schedule for formal entries (generally, those valued over $1,250) at a minimum of $21 per entry and a maximum of $400 per entry, with an ad valorem rate of 0.19%. The fee for informal entries (those valued under $1,250) is $2 for automated entries, $5 for manual entries not prepared by Customs, and $8 for manual entries prepared by Customs.

Note: The exact informal entry amount is set by regulation, but the statutory cap has been raised from $1,250 to $2,500 by the 1993 Customs Modernization Act.

The harbor maintenance fee is an ad valorem fee assessed on cargo imports and admissions into foreign trade zones. The fee is 0.125% of the value of the cargo and is paid quarterly, except for imports that are paid at the time of entry. Customs deposits the harbor maintenance fee collections into the Harbor Maintenance Trust Fund. The funds are made available, subject to appropriation, to the Army Corps of Engineers for the improvement and maintenance of U.S. ports and harbors.

29 Prohibitions, Restrictions, and Other Agency Requirements

The importation of certain classes of merchandise may be prohibited or restricted to protect the economy and security of the U.S., to safeguard consumer health and well-being, and to preserve domestic plant and animal life. Some commodities are also subject to an import quota or a restraint under bilateral trade agreements and arrangements.

Many of these prohibitions and restrictions on importations are subject, in addition to Customs requirements, to the laws and regulations administered by other U.S. Government agencies with which Customs cooperates in enforcement. These laws and regulations may, for example, prohibit entry; limit entry to certain ports; restrict routing, storage, or use; or require treatment, labeling, or processing as a condition of release. Customs clearance is given only if these various additional requirements are met. This applies to all types of importations, including those made by mail and those placed in foreign trade zones.

The foreign exporter should make certain that the U.S. importer has provided proper information to (1) permit the submission of necessary information concerning packing, labeling, etc., and (2) that necessary arrangements have been made by the importer for entry of the merchandise into the U.S.

It may be impracticable to list all articles specifically; however, various classes of articles are discussed below. Foreign exporters and U.S. importers should consult the agency mentioned for detailed information and guidance, as well as for any changes to the laws and regulations under which the commodities are controlled.

1. Cheese, Milk, and Dairy Products

Cheese and cheese products are subject to requirements of the Food and Drug Administration and the Department of Agriculture. Most importations of cheese require an import license and are subject to quotas administered by the Department of Agriculture, Foreign Agricultural Service, Washington, DC 20250.

The importation of milk and cream is subject to requirements of the Food, Drug, and Cosmetic Act and the Import Milk Act. These products may be imported only by holders of permits from the Department of Health and Human Services, Food and Drug Administration, Center for Food Safety and Applied Nutrition, Office of Food Labeling (HFS-156), 200 "C" Street, NW Washington, DC 20204; and the Department of Agriculture.

2. Fruits, Vegetables, and Nuts

Certain agricultural commodities (including fresh tomatoes, avocados, mangoes, limes, oranges, grapefruit, green peppers, Irish potatoes, cucumbers, eggplants, dry onions, walnuts and filberts, processed dates, prunes, raisins, and olives in tins) must meet U.S. import requirements relating to grade, size, quality, and maturity (7 USC 608(e)). These commodities are inspected and an inspection certificate must be issued by the Food Safety and Inspection Service (FSIS) of the Department of Agriculture to indicate import compliance. Inquiries on general requirements should be made to the Agricultural Marketing Service of the Department of Agriculture, Washington, DC 20250. Additional restrictions may be imposed by the Animal and Plant Health Inspection Service of that department, Washington, DC 20782, under the Plant Quarantine Act and by the Food and Drug Administration, Division of Import Operations and Policy (HFC-170), 5600 Fishers Lane, Rockville, MD 20857, under the Federal Food, Drug, and Cosmetic Act.

3. Insects

Insects in a live state that are injurious to cultivated crops (including vegetables, field crops, bush fruit, and orchard, forest, or shade trees) and the eggs, pupae, or larvae of such insects are prohibited importation, except for scientific purposes under regulations prescribed by the Secretary of Agriculture.

All packages containing live insects or their eggs, pupae, or larvae, that are not injurious to crops or trees, are permitted entry into the U.S. only if covered by a permit issued by the Animal and Plant Health Inspection Service of the Department of Agriculture and are not prohibited by the U.S. Fish and Wildlife Service.

4. Livestock and Animals

Inspection and quarantine requirements of the Animal and Plant Health Inspection Service must be met for the importation of (1) all cloven-hoofed animals (ruminants), such as cattle, sheep, deer, antelope, camels, giraffes; (2) swine including the various varieties of wild hogs and the meat from such animals; (3) horses, asses, mules, and zebras; (4) animal by-products, such as untanned hides, wool, hair, bones, bone meal, blood meal, animal casings, glands, organs, extracts or secretions of ruminants and swine; and (5) animal germ-plasm, including embryos and semen; and (6) hay and straw. A permit for importation must be obtained from that agency before shipping from the country of origin.

In addition, all animal imports must be accompanied by a health certificate. Entry procedures for livestock and animals from Mexico and Canada are not as rigorous as those for animals from other countries. Entry of animals is restricted to certain ports that are designated as quarantine stations. A special offshore, high-security facility, the Harry S. Truman Animal Import Center, has been established at Key West, Florida, so that livestock can be safely quarantined when imported from countries affected with foot and mouth disease (FMD) or other serious animal diseases that do not occur in the U.S.

5. Meat and Meat Products

All commercial shipments of meat and meat food products (derived from cattle, sheep, swine, goats, and horses) offered for entry into the U.S. are subject to the regulations of the Department of Agriculture and must be inspected by the Animal and Plant Health Inspection Service (APHIS) and the Food Safety and Inspection Service (FSIS) of that department prior to release by U.S. Customs. Meat products from other sources (including, but not limited to wild game) are subject to APHIS regulations and the provisions of the Federal Food, Drug, and Cosmetic Act, enforced by the Food and Drug Administration.

6. Plant and Plant Products

The importation of plants and plant products is subject to regulations of the Department of Agriculture and may be restricted or prohibited. Plants and plant products include fruits, vegetables, plants, nursery stock, bulbs, roots, seeds, certain fibers including cotton and broom- corn, cut flowers, sugarcane, certain cereals, and elm logs and elm lumber with bark attached. Import permits are required. Further information should be obtained from the Animal and Plant Health Inspection Service. Also certain endangered species of plants may be prohibited or require permits or certificates from the U.S. Fish and Wildlife Service (FWS), which enforces endangered species regulations. The Food and Drug Administration also regulates plant and plant products, particularly fruits and vegetables.

7. Poultry and Poultry Products

Poultry—live, dressed, or canned; eggs, including eggs for hatching; and egg products are subject to the requirements and regulations of the Animal and Plant Health Inspection Service (APHIS) and the Food Safety and Inspection Service (FSIS) of the Department of Agriculture.

Except for live poultry and poultry products entering through land ports from Canada, permits are required, as well as special marking and labeling, and, in some cases, foreign inspection certification. The term "poultry" is defined as any live or slaughtered domesticated bird, e.g. chickens, turkeys, ducks, geese, swans, partridges, guinea fowl, pea fowl, non-migratory ducks, pigeons, and doves. Other birds (e.g., commercial, domestic, or pen-raised grouse, pheasants, quail, and migratory birds) as well as certain egg products are subject to APHIS regulations and to the provisions of the Federal Food, Drug, and Cosmetic Act, enforced by the Food and Drug Administration. Inquiry should also be made to the Fish and Wildlife Service, Washington, DC 20240, about their requirements, restrictions, and prohibitions.

8. Seeds

The importation into the U.S. of agricultural and vegetable seeds and screenings is governed by the provisions of the Federal Seed Act of 1939 and regulations of the Agricultural Marketing Service, Department of Agriculture. Shipments are detained pending the drawing and testing of samples.

9. Arms, Ammunition, Explosives, and Implements of War

These items are prohibited importation except when a license is issued by the Bureau of Alcohol, Tobacco and Firearms of the Department of the Treasury, Washington, DC 20226, (202) 927-7920, or the importation is in compliance with the regulations of that department. The temporary importation, in-transit movement, and exportation of arms and ammunition is prohibited unless a license is issued by the Office of Defense Trade Control, Department of State, Washington, DC 20520.

10. Radioactive Materials and Nuclear Reactors

Many radioisotopes, all forms of uranium, thorium, and plutonium, and all nuclear reactors imported into the U.S. are subject to the regulations of the Nuclear Regulatory Commission (NRC), in addition to import regulations imposed by any other agency of the U.S. Authority to import these commodities or articles containing these commodities is granted by the Nuclear Regulatory Commission, Washington DC 20520.

Radioisotopes and radioactive sources intended for medical use are subject to the provisions of the Federal Food, Drug, and Cosmetic Act, enforced by the Food and Drug Administration.

In order to comply with the Nuclear Regulatory Commission requirements, the importer must be aware of the identity and amount of any NRC-controlled radioisotopes, or uranium, thorium, and plutonium, and of any nuclear reactor being imported into the U.S. To assure passage through Customs, the importer must demonstrate to U.S. Customs which NRC authority the controlled commodity is being imported under. The authority cited may be the number of a specific or general license, or the specific section of the NRC regulations that establishes a general license or grants an exemption to the regulations. The foreign exporter may save time for the prospective importer by furnishing him complete information concerning the presence of NRC-controlled commodities in U.S. importation.

11. Household Appliances

The Energy Policy and Conservation Act, as amended, calls for energy efficiency standards for household consumer appliances and for labeling them to indicate expected energy or secretions of consumption. The Department of Energy, Consumer Products Efficiency Branch, Washington, DC 20585, is responsible for test procedures and energy performance standards. The Federal Trade Commission, Division of Energy and Product Information, Washington, DC 20580, regulates the labeling of these appliances. The Act covers the following consumer products: (1) refrigerators and refrigerator-freezers; (2) freezers; (3) dishwashers; (4) clothes dryers; (5) water heaters; (6) room air conditioners; (7) home heating equipment, not including furnaces; (8) television sets; (9) kitchen ranges and ovens; (10) clothes washers; (11) humidifiers and dehumidifiers; (12) central air conditioners; (13) furnaces; (14) certain other types of household consumer appliances, as appropriate.

Importations of these products must comply with the applicable Department of Energy and Federal Trade Commission requirements. Importers should contact these agencies for requirements that will be in effect at the time of anticipated shipment. It should be noted that not all appliances are covered by requirements of both agencies.

Note: Any consumer product offered for importation will be refused admission if the product fails to comply with an applicable consumer product safety rule, specified labeling or certification requirements, or is determined to be a hazardous product or contain a product defect that constitutes a substantial product hazard.

12. Flammable Fabrics

Any article of wearing apparel or interior furnishing, or any fabric or related material that is intended for use or which may be used in wearing apparel or interior furnishings cannot be imported into the U.S. if it fails to conform to an applicable flammability standard issued under section 4 of the Flammable Fabrics Act. This Act is administered by the U.S. Consumer Product Safety Commission, Washington, DC 20207. Certain products can be imported into the U.S. as provided in Section 11(c) of the Act for the purpose of finishing or processing to render such products not so highly flammable as to be dangerous when worn by individuals, provided that the exporter states on the invoice or other paper relating to the shipment that the shipment is being made for that purpose. The provisions of the Flammable Fabrics Act apply to products manufactured in the U.S., as well as to imported products.

13. Radiation Producing Products, Including Sonic Radiation

Television receivers, cold-cathode gas discharge tubes, microwave ovens, cabinet and diagnostic X-ray equipment and devices, laser products, ultrasound generating equipment, sunlamps, and other electronic products for which there are radiation performance standards are subject to the Radiation Control for Health and Safety Act of 1968. An electronic product imported for sale or use in the U.S. for which there is a radiation performance standard may be imported only if there is filed with each importation an importer's entry notice (**Form FD 701**) and an electronic product declaration (**Form FD 2877**) both of which are issued by the Food and Drug Administration, National Center for Devices and Radiological Health, 1390 Piccard Dr., Rockville, MD 20850.

The declaration must describe the compliance status of the product. The importer must affirm that the product meets one of the following (1) manufactured prior to the effective date of the applicable Federal standard; (2) complies with the standard and has a label affixed by the manufacturer certifying compliance; (3) does not comply with the standard but is being imported only for purposes of research, investigation, study, demonstration, or training; or (4) does not now comply with the standard but will be brought into compliance. The provisions of the Radiation Control for Health and Safety Act apply to electronic products manufactured in the U.S., as well as to imported products.

14. Radio Frequency Devices

Radios, tape recorders, stereos, televisions, citizen band radios or combinations thereof, and other radio frequency devices are subject to radio emission standards of the Federal Communications Commission, Washington DC 20554, (202) 632-6345, under the Communications Act of 1934, as amended. Importations of such products may be accompanied by an FCC declaration (**FCC 740**) certifying that the imported model or device is in conformity with, will be brought into conformity, or is exempt from the Federal Communications Commission requirements.

15. Foods and Cosmetics

The importation into the U.S. of food, beverages, drugs, devices, and cosmetics is governed by the provisions of the Federal Food, Drug, and Cosmetic Act, which is administered by the Food and Drug Administration of the Department of Health and Human Services, Rockville, Md. 20857. That Act prohibits the importation of articles that are adulterated or misbranded including products that are defective, unsafe, filthy, or produced under unsanitary conditions. The term "misbranded" includes statements, designs, or pictures in labeling that are false or misleading and failure to provide required information in labeling.

Imported products regulated by the Food and Drug Administration are subject to inspection at the time of entry. Shipments found not to comply with the laws and regulations are subject to detention. They must be brought into compliance, destroyed, or re-exported. At the discretion of the Food and Drug Administration, an importer may be permitted to bring a nonconforming importation into compliance if it is possible to do so. Any sorting, reprocessing, or relabeling must be supervised by the Food and Drug Administration at the expense of the importer.

Various imported foods such as confectionery, dairy products, poultry, eggs and egg products, meats, fruit, nuts, and vegetables are also subject to requirements of other agencies. Seafoods are also subject to the requirements of the National Marine Fisheries Service of the National Oceanic and Atmosphere Administration of the Department of Commerce, 1335, East-West Highway, Silver Spring, MD 20910.

16. Biological Drugs

The manufacture and importation of biological products for human consumption are regulated under the Public Health Service Act. Domestic and foreign manufacturers of such products must obtain a license for both the manufacturing establishment and the product intended to be produced or imported. Additional information may be obtained from the Food and Drug Administration, Department of Health and Human Services, Rockville, MD 20857.

Biological drugs for animals are regulated under the Virus Serum Toxin Act administered by the Department of Agriculture. The importation of viruses, serums, toxins, and analogous products, and organisms and vectors for use in the treatment of domestic animals is prohibited unless the importer holds a permit from the Department of Agriculture covering the specific product. These importations are also subject to special labeling requirements.

17. Biological Materials and Vectors

The importation into the U.S. for sale, barter, or exchange of any virus, therapeutic serum, toxin, antitoxin, or analogous products, or arsphenamine or its derivatives (or any other trivalent organic arsenic compound), except materials to be used in research experiments, applicable to the prevention, treatment, or cure of diseases or injuries of man is prohibited unless these products have been propagated or prepared at any establishment holding an unsuspended and unrevoked license for such manufacturing issued by the Secretary, Department of Health and Human Services. Samples of the licensed product must accompany each importation for forwarding by the port director of Customs at the port of entry to the Director, National Center for Biologics Evaluation and Research, 5600 Fishers Lane, Rockville, MD 20857.

A permit from the U.S. Public Health Service, Centers for Disease Control (CDC), Atlanta, GA 30333, is required for shipments of any etiological agent or insect, animal, or plant vector of human disease or any exotic living insect, animal, or plant capable of being a vector of human disease.

18. Narcotic Drugs and Derivatives

The importation of controlled substances including narcotics, marijuana, and other dangerous drugs is prohibited except when imported in compliance with regulations of the Drug Enforcement Administration of the Department of Justice, Washington, DC 20537. Examples of some of the prohibited controlled substances are amphetamines; barbiturates; coca leaves and derivatives such as cocaine; hallucinogenic substances such as LSD, mescaline, peyote, marijuana, and other forms of *cannabis*; opiates including methadone; opium including opium derivatives, such as morphine and heroin; and synthetic substitutes for narcotic drugs.

19. Drug Paraphernalia

Items of drug paraphernalia are prohibited from importation or exportation under 21 USC 863. The term "drug paraphernalia" means any equipment, product, or material of any kind that is primarily intended or designed for use in manufacturing, compounding, converting, concealing, producing, processing, preparing, injecting, ingesting, inhaling, or otherwise introducing into the human body a controlled substance, possession of which is unlawful under the Controlled Substances Act (Title II of Public Law 91-513). Items of drug paraphernalia include, but are not limited to the following items:

a. Metal, wooden, acrylic, glass, stone, plastic, or ceramic pipes with or without screens, permanent screens, hashish heads, or punctured metal bowls;
b. Water pipes;
c. Carburetion tubes and devices;
d. Smoking and carburetion masks;
e. Roach clips: meaning objects used to hold burning material, such as a marijuana cigarette, that has become too small or too short to be held in the hand;
f. Miniature spoons with level capacities of one-tenth cubic centimeter or less;
g. Chamber pipes;
h. Carburetor pipes;
i. Electric pipes;
j. Air-driven pipes;
k. Chillums;
l. Bongs;
m. Ice pipes or chillers;
n. Wired cigarette papers; or
o. Cocaine freebase kits.

The penalty for violation of this section is imprisonment of not more than three years and a fine under 18 USC.

20. Gold and Silver

The provisions of the National Stamping Act, as amended (15 USC 291-300) are enforced by the Department of Justice, Washington, DC 20530. Articles made of gold or alloys thereof are prohibited importation into the U.S. if the gold content is one-half carat divergence below the indicated fineness. In the case of articles made of gold or gold alloys, including the solder and alloy of inferior fineness, a one-carat divergence below the indicated fineness is permitted. Articles marked "sterling" or "sterling silver" must assay at least 0.925 of pure silver with a 0.004 divergence allowed. Other articles of silver or silver alloys must assay not less than 0.004 part below the indicated fineness thereof. Articles marked "coin" or "coin silver" must contain at least 0.900 part pure silver with an allowable divergence therefrom of 0.004 part below.

A person placing articles of gold or silver bearing a fineness or quality mark such as 14K, sterling, etc., in the mail or in interstate commerce must place his name or registered trademark next to the fineness mark in letters the same size as the fineness mark. Because the trademark or name is not required at the time of importation, Customs has no direct responsibility for enforcement of the law. Persons making inquiry or seeking advice or interpretation of the law should consult the Department of Justice.

Articles bearing the words "United States Assay" are prohibited importations. Articles made wholly or in part of inferior metal and plated or filled with gold or silver or alloys thereof and that are marked with the degree of fineness must also be marked to indicate the plated or filled content, and in such cases, the use of the words "sterling" or "coin" is prohibited.

All restrictions on the purchase, holding, selling, or otherwise dealing with gold were removed effective December 31, 1974, and gold may be imported subject to the usual Customs entry requirements. Under the Hobby Protection Act, any imitation numismatic item must be plainly and permanently marked "copy"; those that do not comply are subject to seizure and forfeiture. Unofficial gold coin restrikes must be marked with the country of origin. It is advisable to obtain a copy of the legal proclamation under which the coins are issued or an affidavit of government sanction of coins should be secured from a responsible banking official if the proclamation is unavailable.

21. Counterfeit Articles

Articles bearing facsimiles or replicas of coins or securities of the U.S. or of any foreign country are prohibited importation. Counterfeits of coins in circulation in the U.S.; counterfeited, forged, or altered obligations or other securities of the U.S. or of any foreign government; and plates, dies, or other apparatus that may be used in making any of the foregoing are prohibited importations.

22. Monetary Instruments

Under the Currency and Foreign Transactions Reporting Act, 31 USC 5311 et seq., if a person knowingly transports, is about to transport, or has transported, more than $10,000 in monetary instruments at one time to, through, or from the U.S.; or if a person receives more than $10,000 at one time from or through a place outside the U.S., a report of the transportation (Customs **Form 4790**) must be filed with the U.S. Customs Service. Monetary instruments include U.S. or foreign coin, currency, traveler's checks in any form, personal and other checks, and money orders, either in bearer negotiable form or endorsed without restriction; and securities or stocks in bearer form. A bank check or money order made payable to a named person but not endorsed, or that bears a restrictive endorsement, is not considered to be a "monetary instrument." The Department of the Treasury regulations governing the report of monetary instruments are set forth at 31 CFR part 103.

23. Postage Stamps

Facsimiles of U.S. postage stamps are prohibited except those for philatelic, educational, historical, or newsworthy purposes. Further information should be obtained from the U.S. Secret Service, Department of the Treasury, Washington, DC 20223.

24. Pesticides

Section 17(c) of the Federal Insecticide, Fungicide, and Rodenticide Act (FIFRA) as amended, 1988, provides the statutory framework governing the importation of pesticides and devices into the U.S. Under this authority, the U.S. Customs Service regulations 19 CFR, Parts 12.112-.117, establish the requirements for importing pesticides and devices. Among the requirements, importers of pesticides and devices must submit a Notice of Arrival prior to importation. In addition, pesticides and devices may be refused entry, if they are: adulterated, misbranded, violate the provisions of FIFRA, or are injurious to health or the environment. For further information on importing pesticides or devices, you should contact the EPA Regional office serving the area where the pesticide or device will be imported.

25. Toxic Substances

The Toxic Substances Control Act (TSCA), effective January 1, 1977, regulates the manufacturing, importation, processing, distribution in commerce, use, or disposal of any chemical substance or mixture that are broadly defined in Section 3 of TSCA. Section 3 specifies that certain substances are excluded from the definition of "chemical substance" based upon their use. These substances include, but are not limited to, foods, drugs, cosmetics, and active ingredients in pesticides. Importations will not be released from Customs custody unless proper certification that the import "complies with" or "is not subject to" the requirements of the Toxic Substances Control Act is presented to Customs, or if it is already identified as a food, drug, or active pesticide ingredient. For further information from EPA, call the TSCA Information Hotline (202) 554-1404.

26. Hazardous Substances

The importation into the U.S. of dangerous caustic or corrosive substances in packages suitable for household use and of hazardous substances is regulated by the Hazardous Substance Act; the Caustic Poison Act; the Food, Drug, and Cosmetic Act; and the Consumer Product Safety Act. The marking, labeling, packaging, and transportation of hazardous materials, substances, wastes, and their containers is regulated by the Office of Hazardous Materials Transportation of the Department of Transportation, Washington, DC 20590. Hazardous waste is a special subcategory of hazardous substances and is regulated by the Resource Recovery and Conservation Act (RCRA), which requires a special EPA manifest for both imports and exports.

27. Textile Products

All textile fiber products imported into the U.S. shall be stamped, tagged, labeled, or otherwise marked with the following information as required by the Textile Fiber Products Identification Act, unless exempted from marking under section 12 of the Act:

a. The generic names and percentages by weight of the constituent fibers present in the textile fiber product, exclusive of permissive ornamentation, in amounts of more than 5% in order of predominance by weight, with any percentage of fiber or fibers required to be designated as "other fiber" or "other fibers" appearing last. Fibers present in amounts of 5% or less must be designated as "other fibers."

b. The name of the manufacturer or the name or registered identification number issued by the Federal Trade Commission of one or more persons marketing or handling the textile fiber product. A word trademark, used as a house mark, registered in the U.S. Patent Office, may be on labels in lieu of the name otherwise required if the owner of such trademark furnishes a copy of the registration to the Federal Trade Commission prior to use.

c. The name of the country where processed or manufactured.

For the purpose of the enforcement of the Textile Fiber Products Identification Act, a commercial invoice covering a shipment of textile fiber products exceeding $500 in value and subject to the labeling requirements of the Act is required to show the information noted in Chapter 6, above, in addition to that ordinarily required on the invoices.

Regulations and pamphlets containing the text of the Textile Fiber Products Identification Act may be obtained from the Federal Trade Commission, Washington, DC 20580.

28. Wool.

Any product containing woolen fiber imported into the U.S.—with the exception of carpets, rugs, mats, upholsteries—and articles made more than 20 years prior to importation, shall be tagged, labeled, or otherwise clearly marked with the following information as required by the Wool Products Labeling Act of 1939:

a. The percentage of the total fiber weight of the wool product, exclusive of ornamentation not exceeding 5% of the total fiber weight of (1) wool, (2) recycled wool, (3) each fiber other than wool if the percent by weight of such fiber is 5% or more, and (4) the aggregate of all other fibers.

b. The maximum percent of the total weight of the wool product, of any nonfibrous loading, filling, or adulterating matter.

c. The name of the manufacturer or person introducing the product in commerce in the U.S.; i.e., the importer. If the importer has a registered identification number issued by the Federal Trade Commission, that number may be used instead of the individual's name.

For the purpose of the enforcement of the Wool Products Labeling Act, a commercial invoice covering a shipment of wool products exceeding $500 in value and subject to the labeling requirements of the act is required to show the information noted in Chapter 6.

The provisions of the Wool Products Labeling Act apply to products manufactured in the U.S. as well as to imported products.

Pamphlets containing the text of the Wool Products Labeling Act and the regulations may be obtained from the Federal Trade Commission, Washington, DC 20580.

29. Fur

Any article of wearing apparel imported into the U.S. and made in whole or in part of fur or used fur, with the exception of articles that are made of new fur of which the cost or manufacturer's selling price does not exceed $7, imported into the U.S. shall be tagged, labeled, or otherwise clearly marked to show the following information as required by the Fur Products Labeling Act:

a. The name of the manufacturer or person introducing the product in commerce in the U.S.; i.e., the importer. If the importer has a registered identification number, that number may be used instead of the individual's name.

b. The name or names of the animal or animals that produced the fur as set forth in the Fur Products Name Guide and as permitted under the rules and regulations.

c. That the fur product contains used or damaged fur when such is the fact.

d. That the fur product is bleached, dyed, or otherwise artificially colored when such is the fact.

e. That the fur product is composed in whole or in substantial part of paws, tails, bellies, or waste fur when such is the fact.

f. The name of the country of origin of any imported furs contained in a fur product.

For the purpose of enforcement of the Fur Products Labeling Act, a commercial invoice covering a shipment exceeding $500 in value of furs or fur products is required to show the information noted in Chapter 6.

The provisions of the Fur Products Labeling Act apply to fur and fur products in the U.S. as well as to imported furs and fur products. Regulations and pamphlets containing the text of the Fur Products Labeling Act may be obtained from the Federal Trade Commission, Washington, DC 20580.

30. Trademarks and Trade Names

Articles bearing counterfeit trademarks or marks that copy or simulate a registered trademark of a U.S. or foreign corporation are prohibited importation, provided a copy of the U.S. trademark registration is filed with the Commissioner of Customs and recorded in the manner provided by regulations (19 CFR 133.1-133.7). The U.S. Customs Service also affords similar protection against unauthorized shipments bearing trade names that are recorded with Customs pursuant to regulations (19 CFR Part 133, Subpart B). It is also unlawful to import articles bearing genuine trademarks owned by a U.S. citizen or corporation without permission of the U.S. trademark owner, if the foreign and domestic trademark owners are not parent and subsidiary companies or otherwise under common ownership and control, provided the trademark has been recorded with Customs. (15 USC 1124; 19 USC 1526).

The Customs Reform and Simplification Act of 1978 strengthened the protection afforded trademark owners against the importation of articles bearing a counterfeit mark. A "counterfeit trademark" is defined as a spurious trademark that is identical with, or substantially indistinguishable from, a registered trademark. Articles bearing a counterfeit trademark that are seized by Customs and forfeited to the government may be (1) given to any Federal, state, or local government agency that has established a need for the article; (2) given to a charitable institution; or (3) sold at public auction if more than 90 days has passed since forfeiture and no eligible organization has established a need for the article. The counterfeit marks must be removed before the forfeited articles may be given away or sold. If this is not feasible, the articles are destroyed. The law also provides an exemption from all restrictions on trademarked articles (limited to one of each type) accompanying a person arriving in the U.S. when the articles are for personal use and not for sale.

31. Copyrights

Section 602(a) of the Copyright Revision Act of 1976 (17 USC 602(a)) provides that the importation into the U.S. of copies of a work acquired outside the U.S. without authorization of the copyright owner is an infringement of the copyright. Articles imported in violation of the import prohibitions are subject to seizure and forfeiture. Forfeited articles shall be destroyed; however, the articles may be returned to the country of export whenever Customs is satisfied that there was no intentional violation. The substantial similarity test is employed to determine if a design has been copied. Copyright owners seeking import protection from the U.S. Customs Service must register their claim to copyright with the U.S. Copyright Office and record their registration with Customs in accordance with applicable regulations (19 CFR Part 133, Subpart D).

32. Wildlife and Pets

The importation of live wildlife (i.e., game animals, birds, plants) or any part or product made therefrom, and the eggs of wild or game birds, is subject to certain prohibitions, restrictions, and permit and quarantine requirements of several Government agencies. Importations of wildlife, parts, or their products must be entered at certain designated U.S. Fish and Wildlife Service ports of entry unless an exception is granted by the U.S. Fish and Wildlife Service, Department of the Interior, Washington, DC 20240.

On or after January 1, 1981, most firms (with some significant exceptions) importing or exporting wildlife must obtain a license from the Fish and Wildlife Service. Applications and further information may be obtained from the U.S. Fish and Wildlife Service, Assistant Regional Director for Law Enforcement, for the state in which the importer or exporter is located.

Endangered species of wildlife and certain species of animals and birds are generally prohibited entry into the U.S. and may be imported only under a permit granted by the U.S. Fish and Wildlife Service. Specific information concerning import requirements should be obtained from that agency.

Antique articles that would otherwise be prohibited under the Endangered Species Act may be admitted provided certain conditions are met.

The taking and importation of marine mammals and their products are subject to the requirements of the Marine Mammal Protection Act of 1972 and cannot be imported without a permit from the National Marine Fisheries Service, Department of Commerce, Washington, DC 20235, or the U.S. Fish and Wildlife Service.

Regulations to implement the Convention on International Trade in Endangered Species of Wild Fauna and Flora became effective on May 23, 1977. Certain animals, mammals, birds, reptiles, amphibians, fish, snails, and clams, insects, crustaceans, mollusks, other invertebrates and plants may be prohibited or require permits or certification which may be obtained from the U.S. Fish and Wildlife Service.

The importation into the U.S. of any wild animal or bird is prohibited if the animal or bird was captured, taken, shipped, possessed, or exported contrary to the law of the foreign country or subdivision thereof. In addition, no wild animal or bird from any foreign country may be taken, purchased, sold, or possessed contrary to the laws of any State, territory, or possession of the U.S.

The importation of the feathers or skin of any wild bird, except for scientific and educational purposes, is prohibited, except for the species noted below. This prohibition does not apply to fully manufactured artificial flies used for fishing or to personally taken, noncommercial game birds. Feathers or skins of the following species are permitted entry: chicken, turkeys, guinea fowl, geese, ducks, pigeons, ostriches, rheas, English ring-necked pheasants, and pea fowl not taken from the wild.

Live birds protected under the Migratory Bird Treaty Act may be imported into the U.S. from foreign countries for scientific or propagating purposes only under permits issued by the U.S. Fish and Wildlife Service. These migratory birds and any game animals (e.g., antelope, mountain sheep, deer, bears, peccaries, squirrels, rabbits, and hares) imported from Mexico must be accompanied by Mexican export permits.

Importations in this class are also subject to the quarantine requirements of the Department of Agriculture and the U.S. Public Health Service. Appropriate inquiries in this respect should be directed to those agencies.

On June 9, 1989, the U.S. Fish and Wildlife Service announced a ban on the importation of most African elephant ivory and any products made from it. The ban covers all commercial and noncommercial shipments including household effects and personal baggage accompanying a tourist. There are limited exceptions for antiques, trophies, and personal household effects. For further information, contact the U.S. Fish and Wildlife Service, Washington, DC 20240.

The importation of birds, cats, dogs, monkeys, and turtles is subject to the requirements of the U.S. Public Health Service, Centers for Disease Control, Quarantine Division, Atlanta, GA 30333, and the Veterinary Services of the Animal and Plant Health Inspection Service, Department of Agriculture, Hyattsville, MD 20782.

The importation of turtles with a carapace length of less than four inches and of psittacine birds are subject to the requirements of the U.S. Department of Agriculture and the Fish and Wildlife Service.

Other Miscellaneous Prohibited or Restricted Merchandise

White or yellow phosphorus matches, fireworks banned under Federal or State restrictions, pepper shells, switchblade knives, and lottery tickets are prohibited.

33. Foreign Assets Control Restrictions

The Office of Foreign Assets Control administers regulations (31 CFR, Chapter V) that generally prohibit the importation of merchandise or goods that contain components from the following countries: Cuba, Iran, Iraq, Libya, North Korea, and the former republics of Yugoslavia (Serbia and Montenegro). These restrictions apply to the country of origin, regardless of where the item was purchased. For example, an Iranian rug purchased in England is still prohibited.

These proscriptions do not apply to informational materials such as pamphlets, books, tapes, films, or recordings, except for those from Yugoslavia or Iraq.

Specific licenses are required to bring prohibited merchandise into the U.S., but they are rarely granted. Foreign visitors to the U.S., however, may be permitted to bring in small articles for personal use as accompanied baggage, depending on the goods and the country of origin.

Travelers should be aware of certain travel restrictions that may apply to these countries. Because of the strict enforcement of these prohibitions, those anticipating foreign travel to any of the countries listed above would do well to write in advance to the Office of Foreign Assets Control, Department of the Treasury, Washington, DC 20220, or to call (202) 622-2500.

34. Obscene, Immoral, and Seditious Matter

Section 305, Tariff Act of 1930, as amended, prohibits the importation of any book, writing, advertisement, circular, or picture containing any matter advocating or urging treason or insurrection against the U.S., or forcible resistance to any law of the U.S., or containing any threat to take the life of or inflict bodily harm upon any person in the U.S., or any obscene book, writing, advertisement, circular, picture, or other representation, figure, or image on or of paper or other material, or any instrument, or other article that is obscene or immoral, or any drug or medicine for causing unlawful abortion.

35. Petroleum and Petroleum Products

Importations of petroleum and petroleum products are subject to the requirements of the Department of Energy. An import license is no longer required. These importations may be subject to an oil import license fee collected and administered by the Department of Energy. Inquiries should be directed to the Department of Energy, Washington, DC 20585.

36. Products of Convict or Forced Labor

Merchandise produced, mined, or manufactured by means of the use of convict labor, forced labor, or indentured labor under penal sanctions is prohibited importation, provided a finding has been published pursuant to section 12.42 of the Customs Regulations (19 CFR 12.42), that certain classes of merchandise from a particular country, produced by convict, forced, or indentured labor, were either being, or are likely to be, imported into the U.S. in violation of section 307 of the Tariff Act of 1930, as amended (19 USC 1307).

37. Unfair Competition

Section 337 of the Tariff Act, as amended, prohibits the importation of merchandise if the President finds that unfair methods of competition or unfair acts exist. This section is most commonly invoked in the case of patent violations, although a patent need not be at issue. Prohibition of entries of the merchandise in question generally is for the term of the patent, although a different term may by specified.

Following a section 337 investigation, the International Trade Commission may find that unfair methods of competition or unfair acts exist with respect to the importation of certain merchandise. After the International Trade Commission has issued an order, the President is allowed 60 days to take action; should the 60 days expire without Presidential action, the order becomes final. During the 60-day period or until the President acts, importation of the merchandise is allowed under a special bond but it must be recalled by Customs if appropriate under the conditions of the order when it becomes final. If the President determines that entry of the merchandise is not in violation of section 337, the bond is canceled.

38. Steel and Machine Tools

Certain types of machine tools from Japan and Taiwan are subject to Voluntary Restraint Agreements (VRAs) negotiated by the U.S. Trade Representative and the individual countries. These are agreements by which the level of exports of the covered products are voluntarily limited by the exporting country. The VRAs are administered by the Department of Commerce and presentation of an export certificate or license by the country of origin is a condition of entry.

30 Alcoholic Beverages

Any person or firm wishing to engage in the business of importing distilled spirits, wines, or malt beverages into the U.S. must first obtain an importer's basic permit from the Bureau of Alcohol, Tobacco and Firearms, Department of the Treasury, Washington, DC 20226, Tel. (202) 927-8110. That agency is responsible for administering the Federal Alcohol Administration Act.

Distilled spirits imported in bulk containers of a capacity of more than one gallon may be withdrawn from Customs custody only by persons to whom it is lawful to sell or otherwise dispose of distilled spirits in bulk. Bulk or bottled shipments of imported spirits or distilled or intoxicating liquors must at the time of importation be accompanied by a copy of a bill of lading or other documents, such as an invoice, showing the name of the consignee, the nature of its contents, and the quantity contained therein (18 USC 1263).

U.S. Customs will not release alcoholic beverages destined to any state for use in violation of its laws, and the importation of alcoholic beverages in the mails is prohibited.

The U.S. adopted the metric system of measure with the enactment of the Metric Conversion Act of 1975. In general, imported wine must conform with the metric standards of fill if bottled or packed on or after January 1, 1979. Imported distilled spirits, with some exceptions, must conform with the metric standards of fill if bottled or packed on or after January 1, 1980. Distilled spirits and wines bottled or packed prior to the respective dates must be accompanied by a statement to that effect signed by a duly authorized official of the appropriate foreign country. This statement may be a separate document or be shown on the invoice. Malt beverages including beer are not subject to metric standards of fill.

Marking

Imported wines in bottles and other containers are required to be packaged, marked, branded, and labeled in accordance with the regulations in 27 CFR Part 4. Imported malt beverages, including alcohol-free and nonalcoholic malt beverages, are also required to be labeled in conformance with the regulations in 27 CFR Part 7.

Each bottle, cask, or other immediate container of imported distilled spirits, wines, or malt beverages must be marked for customs purposes to indicate the country of origin of the alcoholic beverage contained therein, unless the shipment comes within one of the exceptions outlined in Chapter 28 of this booklet.

Certificate of Label Approval

Labels affixed to bottles of imported distilled spirits and wine must be covered by certificates of label approval issued to the importer by the Bureau of Alcohol, Tobacco and Firearms. Certificates of label approval or photostatic copies must be filed with Customs before the goods may be released for sale in the U.S. Certificate of label approval requirements must also be met for fermented malt beverages if similar to the Federal requirements (27 CFR Parts 4, 5, and 7).

Foreign Documentation

Importers of wines and distilled spirits should consult the Bureau of Alcohol, Tobacco and Firearms about foreign documentation required; for example, certificates of origin, age, etc.

Requirements of Other Agencies

In addition, importation of alcoholic beverages is subject to the specific requirements of the Food and Drug Administration. Certain plant materials when used for bottle jackets for wine or other liquids are subject to special restrictions under plant quarantine regulations of the Animal and Plant Health Inspection Service. All bottle jackets made of dried or unmanufactured plant materials are subject to inspection upon arrival and are referred to the Department of Agriculture.

Wines or other distilled spirits from certain countries require original certificates of origin as a condition of entry: Bulgaria, Canada, Chile, France, Germany, Republic of Ireland, Jamaica, Mexico, Portugal, Romania, Spain, and United Kingdom.

Public Law 100-690, codified under 27 USC 213-219A, requires that a health warning appear on the labels of containers of alcoholic beverages bottled on or after November 18, 1989:

> **Government Warning:** (1) According to the Surgeon General, women should not drink alcoholic beverages during pregnancy because of the risks of birth defects. (2) Consumption of alcoholic beverages impairs your ability to drive a car or operate machinery and may cause health problems.

31 Motor Vehicles and Boats

Vehicle Safety and Bumper Standards. As a general rule, all imported motor vehicles and items of motor vehicle equipment must comply with all applicable Federal Motor Vehicle Safety Standards in effect when these vehicles or items were manufactured. A Customs inspection at the time of entry will determine such compliance, which is verified by the original manufacturer's certification affixed to the vehicle or merchandise. A declaration, HS **Form 7**, must be filed when motor vehicles or items of motor vehicle equipment are entered. HS **Form 7** can be obtained from customs brokers or ports of entry.

If written approval is obtained from the U.S. Department of Transportation (DOT), certain temporary importations may be exempt from the requirements for certification and conformance, including vehicles brought in for research, investigation, studies, training, or demonstrations. Also, vehicles imported for temporary use by certain nonresidents or members of foreign delegations or armed forces may not be required to comply. Vehicles and motor vehicle equipment imported solely with the intention of exportation and so labeled are also exempt from these requirements.

A DOT bond in the amount of 150% of the dutiable value must be posted at the port of entry when a noncertified or nonconforming vehicle is imported for permanent use. This bond is intended to assure conformance of the vehicle within 120 days after entry. The importer must also sign a contract with a DOT-registered importer, who will modify the vehicle to conform with all applicable safety and bumper standards, and who can certify the modification(s). A copy of this contract must be furnished to the Customs Service at the port of entry. Furthermore, the vehicle model and model year must, prior to entry, be determined to be eligible for importation. Federal regulations 49 CFR, parts 593 and 594 specify the petitioning process and fees required to obtain such a determination of eligibility.

For additional information or details on these requirements, contact the U.S. Department of Transportation, National Highway Traffic Safety Administration, Director of the Office of Vehicle Safety Compliance (NEF-32), 400 Seventh Street, SW, Washington, DC 20590. Tel. (202) 366-5313.

Emission Requirements. The Clean Air Act, as amended, prohibits the importation into the U.S. of any motor vehicle or motor vehicle engine not in conformity with emission standards prescribed by the U.S. Environmental Protection Agency (EPA). This restriction applies whether the motor vehicle or motor vehicle engine is new or used, and whether it was originally produced for sale and use in a foreign country, or originally produced (or late modified) to conform to EPA requirements for sale or use in the U.S. In addition to passenger cars, all trucks, multipurpose vehicles, (e.g., all-terrain vehicles, campers), motorcycles, etc. that are capable of being registered by a state for use on public roads or that the EPA has deemed capable of being safely driven on public roads, are subject to these requirements. The term "vehicle" is used below to indicate all EPA-regulated vehicles and engines.

U.S. Version Vehicles. Any person may import U.S.-version vehicles. All such 1971 and later models are required to have a label in a readily visible position in the engine compartment stating that the vehicle conforms to U.S. requirements. This label will read "Vehicle Emission Control Information" and will have a statement by the manufacturer that the vehicle meets U.S. EPA emission requirements at the time of manufacture. If this label is not present, the importer should obtain a letter of conformity from the manufacturer's U.S. representative—not from a dealership—prior to importation.

The following U.S.-version (labeled) vehicles are not subject to EPA import restrictions and may be entered without bond under the applicable category on the EPA **Form 3520-1**:

- New vehicles driven less than 50 miles.
- Diesel-fueled vehicles.
- Gasoline- and methanol-fueled vehicles driven solely in the U.S., Canada, Mexico, Japan, Australia, Taiwan, and Grand Bahama Island (EPA **Form 3520-1** not required).

Qualifying U.S. version (labeled) vehicles participating in an overseas EPA-approved catalyst control program are not subject to additional EPA import restrictions and may be entered without bond under category "AA" on the EPA **Form 3520-1** if accompanied by appropriate documentation from the catalyst control program.

Non-U.S. Version Vehicles. Individuals are not permitted to import non-U.S. version vehicles (unless otherwise excluded or exempted). These vehicles must be imported (entered) by an Independent Commercial Importer (ICI) having a currently valid qualifying certificate of conformity for each vehicle being imported. The ICI will be responsible for performing all necessary modifications, testing, and labeling, as well as providing an emissions warranty identical to the emissions warranty required of new vehicles sold in the U.S.

Excluded Vehicles. Vehicles manufactured before EPA requirements took effect (e.g., gasoline-fueled passenger vehicles manufactured prior to 1968 and motorcycles manufactured prior to 1978) are excluded from import restrictions and may be imported by any person without bond under the applicable declaration category on the EPA **Form 3520-1**.

- Not all conforming vehicles are eligible for importation, and ICIs are not required to accept vehicles for which they have qualifying certificates of conformity.
- EPA certification of ICIs does not guarantee the actions or work of the ICIs, nor does it regulate contractual agreements and working relationships with vehicle owners.
- EPA strongly recommends that prospective importers buy only U.S. version (labeled) vehicles, because of the expense and potential difficulties involved with importing a non-U.S. version vehicle.

- EPA strongly recommends that current owners of non-U.S. version vehicles sell or otherwise dispose of those vehicles overseas rather than ship and import them into the U.S., because of the expense and potential difficulties involved with importing a non-U.S. version vehicle.
- Before shipping a non-conforming vehicle for importation, EPA strongly recommends that the importer either make final arrangements with an ICI for modifications and testing, or obtain EPA approval in writing for importation. Storage fees at the ports are costly, and the vehicle may not be eligible for importation.
- The EPA policy that permitted importers a one-time exemption for vehicles at least five years old has been eliminated.
- EPA considers a U.S.-version vehicle that has had modifications to its drive train or emission control system to be a non-U.S.-version vehicle, even though it may be labeled a U.S.-version vehicle.
- For U.S.-version vehicles driven in Europe, a bond will not be required upon return to the U.S. if the vehicle participates in one of the EPA-approved catalyst control programs operating in Europe.

For further information: Environmental Protection Agency, Investigation/Imports Section (6405-J), Washington, DC 20460, Tel (202) 233-9596, FAX (202) 233-9596.

Final Word of Caution. Modifications necessary to bring a nonconforming vehicle into conformity with the safety and bumper standards and/or emission standards may require extensive engineering, be impractical or even impossible, or the labor and materials may be unduly expensive. It is highly recommended that these modifications be investigated before a vehicle is purchased for importation.

Boat Safety Standards

Imported boats and associated equipment are subject to U.S. Coast Guard safety regulations or standards under the Federal Boat Safety Act of 1971. Products subject to standards must have a compliance certification label affixed. Certain hulls also require a hull identification number to be affixed. A U.S. Coast Guard import declaration is required to be filed with entries of nonconforming boats. Further information may be obtained from the Commandant, U.S. Coast Guard, Washington, DC 20593.

Dutiability

Vessels that are brought into the U.S. for use in trade or commerce are not dutiable. Yachts or pleasure boats brought into the U.S. by nonresidents for their own use in pleasure cruising are also not dutiable. Yachts or pleasure boats owned by a resident or brought into the U.S. for sale or charter to a resident are dutiable. Further information may be found in U.S. Customs pamphlet "Pleasure Boats."

Restrictions on Use

Vessels that are foreign-built or of foreign registry may be used in U.S. waters for pleasure purposes and in the foreign trade of the U.S. However, Federal law prohibits the use of such vessels in the coastwise trade, i.e. the transportation of passengers or merchandise between points in the U.S., including carrying fishing parties for hire. Questions concerning the use of foreign- built or foreign-flag vessels should be addressed to Chief, Carrier Rulings Branch, Office of Regulations and Rulings, U.S. Customs Service, 1301 Constitution Ave., NW, Washington, DC 20229.

32 Import Quotas

An import quota is a quantity control on merchandise imported during a certain period of time. Quotas are established by legislation, by directives, and by proclamations issued under the authority contained in specific legislation. The majority of import quotas are administered by the U.S. Customs Service. The Commissioner of Customs controls the importation of quota merchandise but has no authority to change or modify any quota. U.S. import quotas may be divided into two types: *absolute* and *tariff rate*.

Tariff-rate quotas provide for the entry of a specified quantity of the quota product at a reduced rate of duty during a given period. There is no limitation on the amount of the product that may be entered during the quota period, but quantities entered in excess of the quota for the period are subject to higher duty rates. In most cases, products of Communist-controlled areas are not entitled to the benefits of tariff-rate quotas.

Absolute quotas are quantitative; that is, no more than the amount specified may be permitted entry during a quota period. Some absolute quotas are global, while others are allocated to specified foreign countries. Imports in excess of a specified quota may be exported or warehoused for entry in a subsequent quota period.

The usual customs procedures generally applicable to other imports apply with respect to commodities subject to quota limitations.

The quota status of a commodity subject to a tariff-rate quota cannot be determined in advance of its entry. The quota rates of duty are ordinarily assessed on such commodities entered from the beginning of the quota period until such time in the period as it is determined that imports are nearing the quota level. District directors of Customs are then instructed to require the deposit of estimated duties at the over-quota duty rate and to report the time of official presentation of each entry. A final determination of the date and time when a quota is filled is made, and all district directors are advised accordingly.

Some of the absolute quotas are invariably filled at or shortly after the opening of the quota period. Each of these quotas is therefore officially opened at 12 noon E.S.T., or the equivalent in other time-zones, on the designated effective date. When the total quantity for which entries filed at the opening of the quota period exceeds the quota, the merchandise is released on a pro rata basis, the pro rata being the ratio between the quota quantity and the total quantity offered for entry. This assures an equitable distribution of the quota.

Merchandise is not regarded as presented for purposes of determining quota priority until an entry summary or withdrawal from warehouse for consumption has been submitted in proper form and the merchandise is located within the port limits.

Commodities Subject to Quotas Administered by Customs

As provided in the Harmonized Tariff Schedule of the United States (HTSUS), the commodities listed below are subject to quota limitations in effect as of the date of publication. Local Customs officers can be consulted about any changes. Information may also be obtained by contacting the Quota Branch, U.S. Customs Service, 1301 Constitution Avenue NW, Rm. 2379-ICC, Washington, DC 20229, (202) 927-5850.

Tariff-Rate Quotas

Milk and cream, not concentrated nor containing added sugar or other sweetening matter, of a fat content—by weight—exceeding 1% but not 6%.

Anchovies, in oil, in airtight containers.

Mandarins (Satsumas) in airtight containers.

Certain olives.

Tuna Fish.

Whiskbrooms wholly or in part of broom corn.

Other brooms wholly or in part of broom corn.

Certain textiles assembled in Guam.

Certain sugars, syrups, and molasses derived from sugarcane or sugar beets, except those entered pursuant to a license issued by the Secretary of Agriculture.

Certain textiles from Canada.

Absolute Quotas

Certain ethyl alcohol.

Milk and cream, condensed or evaporated.

Butter substitutes, containing over 45% of butterfat.

Animal feeds containing milk or milk derivatives.

Buttermix containing over 5.5% but not over 45% by weight of butterfat.

Chocolate, containing 5.5% or less by weight of butterfat.

Chocolate crumb and other related articles containing over 5.5% by weight of butterfat.

Dried milk containing 5.5% or less butterfat.

Ice cream.

Peanuts, shelled or not shelled, blanched, or otherwise prepared or preserved (except peanut butter).

Certain Cheddar cheese.

Cotton, not carded, combed, or otherwise processed:
Having a staple length under 28.575 mm; and
Having a staple length 28.575 mm or more but under 34.925 mm; and
Having a staple length 34.925 mm or more.

Cotton lap waste, sliver waste, and roving waste.

Fibers of cotton processed but not spun.

Upland cotton.

Certain sugar blends.

Fluid milk and sweet or sour cream of a fat content by weight exceeding 6% but not 45%.

Textile articles and wearing apparel from certain countries.

Textile Articles

The U.S. Customs Service administers import controls of certain cotton, wool, man-made fiber articles, silk blends and other vegetable fibers manufactured or produced in designated countries. These controls are imposed on the basis of directives issued to the Commissioner of Customs by the Chairman of the Committee for the Implementation of Textile Agreements.

Information concerning specific import controls in effect and visa requirements may be obtained from the Commissioner of Customs. Other information concerning the textile program may be obtained from the Chairman, Committee for the Implementation of Textile Agreements, U.S. Department of Commerce, Washington, DC 20230.

Quotas or Licenses Administered by Other Government Agencies

Watches and Watch Movements. There are no licensing requirements or quotas on watches and watch movements entering the U.S. unless the watches and watch movements are produced in the insular possessions (U.S. Virgin Islands, American Samoa, and Guam). The Departments of Commerce and the Interior administer a program that establishes an annual allocation for watches and watch movements assembled in the insular possessions to enter the U.S. free of duty under Note 5 to Chapter 91 of the Harmonized Tariff Schedule. Licenses are issued only to established insular producers. Further information on the insular watch program may be obtained from the Statutory Import Programs Staff, Import Administration, U.S. Department of Commerce, Washington, DC 20230.

Dairy Products. Certain dairy products listed below are subject to annual import quotas assigned by the Department of Agriculture and may be imported only under import licenses issued by that department. These quotas are administered through the U.S. Customs Service. Detailed information on the licensing of these products, or the conditions under which limited quantities may be imported without licenses, may be obtained from the Import Licensing Group, Foreign Agricultural Service, Room 5531-S, U.S. Department of Agriculture, Washington, DC 20250, Tel. (202) 720-1342.

Butter.

Dried cream.

Malted milk and compounds or mixtures of or substitutes for milk or cream.

Dried whole milk.

Dried skimmed milk.

Dried buttermilk and whey.

Cheddar cheese, and cheese and substitutes for cheese containing or processed from Cheddar cheese curd, and granular cheese and cheese substitutes for cheese containing or processed from such American-type cheese.

Cheese and substitutes for cheese containing, or processed from Edam and Gouda cheese.

Swiss or Emmenthaler cheese with eye formation; Gruyere-process cheese, and cheese and substitutes for cheese containing, or processed from, such cheese.

Edam and Gouda cheese.

Blue mold (except Stilton) cheese, and cheese and substitutes for cheese containing, or processed from, blue-mold cheese.

Italian-type cheeses, made from cow's milk, in original loaves (Romano made from cow's milk, Reggiano, Parmesano, Provolone, Provolette, and Sbrinz).

Italian-type cheese, not in original loaves.

American-type cheese, including Colby, washed curd and granular cheese and cheese substitutes for cheese containing, or processed from such American-type cheese.

Cheese and substitutes for cheese except cheese containing no butterfat or not over 0.5% by weight of butterfat

33
Civil and Criminal Fraud Laws

Section 592 of the Tariff Act of 1930, as amended (19 USC 1592), generally provides that any person who by fraud, gross negligence, or negligence, enters, introduces, or attempts to introduce, merchandise into the commerce of the U.S. by means of any material and false written document, oral statement, electronically transmitted data or information, or material act or omission will be subject to a monetary penalty. Penalties are usually not imposed for nonintentional repetitions of clerical errors through electronic systems. Under certain circumstances, the person's merchandise may be seized to ensure payment of the penalty and forfeited if the penalty is not paid.

Customs has applied the civil fraud statute in cases involving individuals and companies in the U. S. and abroad that have negligently or intentionally provided false information concerning imports into the U.S. In addition, a criminal fraud statute creates penalties against persons who present false information to Customs officers. A maximum of two years imprisonment, a $5,000 fine, or both, may be imposed for each violation involving an importation or attempted importation (18 USC 542). Additionally, the Money Laundering Control Act of 1986 and the Anti-Drug Abuse Act of 1988, created and amended Federal laws relating to criminal activities commonly known as "money laundering." The Acts created criminal and civil offenses that punishable by fines and imprisonment, enabling the government to prosecute and to seize and cause forfeiture of property involved in or traceable to property involved in Money Laundering or Bank Secrecy Act violations. Importation fraud violations are among the specified unlawful activities or predicate offenses within the Money Laundering Control Act. Penalties include imprisonment for up to 20 years for each offense and fines of up to $500,000.

The fraud statutes were enacted by Congress to discourage persons from evading the payment of lawful duties owed to the U.S. However, these laws apply whether or not the U.S. is deprived of lawful duties. They are enforced by special agents assigned to the Office of Enforcement who operate throughout the U.S. and in major trading centers worldwide. Suspected or known violations of any law involved with the importation of merchandise into the U.S. can be reported toll free and anonymously by calling 1-800 BE-ALERT (232-5378). Rewards are applicable in many instances associated with the reporting of fraud.

The 1993 Customs Modernization Act imposes additional criminal and civil penalties for presenting forged or altered documents at entry or for otherwise violating arrival, entry, clearance, or manifest requirements. These penalties also apply to electronic transmission of false or altered data or manifests to Customs (19 USC 1436). The Act also establishes monetary penalties for fraudulent submission of a false drawback claim, the amounts of which increase with repeated violations. These penalties become effective on implementation of the nationwide automated drawback selectivity program (19 USC 1593A).

34
Foreign Trade Zones

Foreign or "free" trade zones are secured areas considered to be legally outside a nation's customs territory, although physically located within it. Their purpose is to attract and promote international trade and commerce. The Foreign trade Zones Board authorizes operations based upon showing that the intended operations are not detrimental to the public interest. Subzones are special-purpose facilities for companies unable to operate effectively at public zone sites. Foreign trade zones are usually located in or near Customs ports of entry, at industrial parks, or terminal warehouse facilities. Foreign trade zones must be within 60 miles or 90 minutes' driving time from the Customs supervising office, while subzones have no limit and are located in the zone user's private facility. A Foreign Trade Zones Board, created by the Foreign Trade Zones Act of 1934, reviews and approves applications to establish, operate, and maintain foreign trade zones. It is important to note that although foreign trade zones are legally outside the Customs territory of the U.S., other federal laws, such as the Federal Food, Drug, and Cosmetic Act, are applicable to products and establishments with such zones.

Foreign exporters planning to expand or open up new U.S. outlets may forward their goods to a foreign trade zone in the U.S. to be held for an unlimited period while awaiting a favorable market in the U.S. or nearby countries without being subject to customs entry, payment of duty or tax, or bond.

Treatment of Goods

Merchandise lawfully brought into these zones may be stored, sold, exhibited, broken up, repacked, assembled, distributed, sorted, graded, cleaned, mixed with foreign or domestic merchandise, or otherwise manipulated or manufactured. However, imported merchandise for use in the zone, such as construction material and production equipment, must be entered for consumption before it is taken into a zone. The Foreign Trade Zones Board may determine, that an operation is not in the public interest. The resulting merchandise may thereafter be either exported or transferred into customs territory.

When foreign goods, in their condition at time of entry into the zone or after processing there, are transferred into customs territory of the U.S., the goods must be entered at the customhouse. If entered for consumption, duties and taxes will be assessed on the entered articles, according to the condition of the foreign merchandise at the time of entry into the zone. This occurs whether it has been placed in privileged foreign status or nonprivileged foreign status, merchandise prior to manipulation or manufacture, or on the basis of its condition at the time of entry for consumption, for foreign merchandise placed under nonprivileged status at the time of entry into the zone. Merchandise may be considered exported, for Customs or other purposes, upon its admission to a zone in zone-restricted status. However, the merchandise taken into a zone under zone-restricted status may be for the sole purpose of exportation, destruction (except destruction of distilled spirits, wines, and fermented malt liquors) or storage.

An important feature of foreign trade zones for foreign merchants entering the American market is that the goods may be brought to the threshold of the market, making immediate delivery certain and avoiding possible cancellation of orders due to shipping delays after a favorable market has closed.

Production of articles in zones by the combined use of domestic and foreign materials makes unnecessary either the sending of the domestic materials abroad for manufacture or the duty-paid or bonded importation of the foreign materials. Duties on the foreign goods involved in such processing or manufacture are payable only on the actual quantity of such foreign goods incorporated in merchandise transferred from a zone for entry into the commerce of the U.S. If there is any unrecoverable waste resulting from manufacture or manipulation, allowances are made for it, thereby eliminating payment of duty except on the articles that are actually entered. If there is any recoverable waste, it is dutiable only in its condition as such and in the quantity entered.

Another feature under the zone act is the authority to exhibit merchandise within a zone. Zone facilities may be utilized for the full exhibition of foreign merchandise without bond, for an unlimited length of time, and with no requirement of exportation or duty payment. Thus, the owner of goods in a zone may display his goods where they are stored, establish showrooms of his own, or join with other importers in displaying his merchandise in a permanent exhibition established in the zone. Because an importer may also store and process merchandise in a zone, the importer is not limited to mere display of samples but may also sell from stock in wholesale quantities. Retail trade is prohibited in such zones.

The owner of foreign merchandise that has not been manipulated or manufactured in any way that would effect a change in its U.S. tariff classification had it been taken into customs territory when first imported may, upon request to the district director of Customs, have its dutiable status fixed and liquidated. This dutiable status will apply irrespective of when the merchandise is entered into customs territory and even though its condition or form may have been changed by processing in the zone, as indicated above.

Domestic merchandise may be taken into a zone and, providing its identity is maintained in accordance with regulations, may be returned to customs territory free of quotas, duty, or tax, even though while in the zone it may have been combined with or made part of other articles. However, domestic distilled spirits, wine, and beer, and a limited number of other kinds of merchandise generally may not be processed while in the zone.

Advantages

Savings may result from manipulations and manufacture in a zone. For example, many products, shipped to the zone in bulk, can be dried, sorted, graded, or cleaned and bagged or otherwise packed, permitting savings of duties and taxes on moisture taken from content or on dirt removed and culls thrown out. Damaged packages or broken bottles can be removed from incoming shipments of packaged or bottled goods if evaporation results during shipment or while goods are stored in the zone, contents of barrels or other containers can be regauged and savings obtained, as no duties are payable on the portions lost or removed. In other words, barrels or other containers can be gauged at the time of transfer to customs territory to insure that duties will not be charged on any portion of their contents that has been lost due to evaporation, leakage, breakage, or otherwise. These operations may also be conducted in bonded warehouses.

Savings in shipping charges, duties, and taxes may result from such operations as shipping unassembled or disassembled furniture, machinery, etc., to the zone and assembling or reassembling it there.

Merchandise may be remarked or relabled in the zone (or in a bonded warehouse) to conform to requirements for entry into the commerce of the U.S. if otherwise up to standard. Remarking or relabeling that would be misleading is not permitted in the zone. Substandard foods and drugs may, in certain cases, be reconditioned to meet the requirements of the Food, Drug, and Cosmetics Act.

There is no time limit as to how long foreign merchandise may be stored in a zone, or when it must be entered into customs territory, reexported, or destroyed.

Transfer of Goods in Bonded Warehouses

Foreign merchandise in Customs bonded warehouses may be transferred to the zone at any time before the limitation on its retention in the bonded warehouse expires, but such a transfer to the zone may be made only for the purpose of eventual exportation, destruction, or permanent storage.

When foreign merchandise is transferred to the zone from Customs bonded warehouses, the bond is cancelled and all obligations in regard to duty payment, or as to the time when the merchandise is to be reexported, are terminated. Similarly, the owner of domestic merchandise stored in Internal Revenue bonded warehouses may transfer goods to a zone and obtain cancellation of bonds. In addition, domestic goods moved into a zone under zone restricted status are considered exported on entering the zone for purposes of excise and other internal revenue tax rebates. A manufacturer, operating in customs territory and using dutiable imported materials in products, may also obtain drawback of duties paid or cancellation of bond, upon transferring the product to the zone for export and complying with the appropriate regulations.

Location of, and general information on U.S. Foreign Trade Zones may be obtained from the Foreign Trade Zones Board, Department of Commerce, Washington, DC 20230. Questions relating to legal aspects of Customs Service responsibilities in regard to foreign trade zones should be addressed to: Chief, Entry Rulings Branch, U.S. Customs Service, 1301 Constitution Avenue, NW, Washington, DC 20229. Questions relating to operational aspects of such responsibilities should be addressed to the appropriate district or area director of Customs. The Foreign Trade Zones Manual for grantees, operators, users, and Customs brokers may be purchased from the Superintendent of Documents, U.S. Government Printing Office, Washington, DC 20402. When ordering refer to GPO Stock No. 048-002-00111-7 and Customs Publication No. 559. The cost is $13.00; $16.20 for foreign mailing.

Appendix

1 *Invoices*

Type of Invoices Required—Section 141.83, Customs Regulations

Pro Forma Invoice

2 *Additional Information*

Required for Certain Classes of Merchandise—Section 141.89, Customs Regulations

3 *Customs Valuation*

Tariff Act of 1930. Sec. 402 19 USC 1401a

4 *Other Forms*

Carrier's Certificate

CF 5291—Power of Attorney

CF 5297—Corporate Surety Power of Attorney

CF 301—Customs Bond

CF 7501—Entry Summary

1
Invoices

§ 141.83 Type of invoice required

(a) [Reserved]

(b) *Special summary invoice.*

A special summary invoice shall be presented for each shipment of merchandise described in § 141.89(b).

(c) *Commercial invoice*

(1) A commercial invoice shall be filed for each shipment of merchandise not exempted by paragraph (d) of this section. The commercial invoice shall be prepared in the manner customary in trade, contain the information required by Sections 141.86 through 141.89, and substantiate the statistical information required by Section 141.61(e) to be given on the entry, entry summary, or withdrawal documentation.

(2) The district director may accept a copy of a required commercial invoice in place of the original. A copy, other than a photostatic or photographic copy, shall contain a declaration by the foreign seller, the shipper, or the importer that it is a true copy.

(d) *Commercial invoice not required*

A commercial invoice shall not be required in connection with the filing of the entry, entry summary, or withdrawal documentation for merchandise listed in this paragraph. The importer, however, shall present any invoice, memorandum invoice, or bill pertaining to the merchandise that may be in his possession or available to him. If no invoice or bill is available, a pro forma (or substitute) invoice, as provided for in Section 141.85, shall be filed, and shall contain information adequate for the examination of merchandise and the determination of duties, and information and documentation which verify the information required for statistical purposes by Section 141.61(e). The merchandise subject to the foregoing requirements is as follows:

(1) Merchandise having an aggregate purchase price or value, as specified in paragraph (a) of this section, of $500 or less.

(2) Merchandise not intended for sale or any commercial use in its imported condition or any other form, and not brought in on commission for any person other than the importer.

(3) [Reserved.]

(4) [Reserved.]

(5) Merchandise returned to the United States after having been exported for repairs or alteration under subheadings 9802.00.04 or 9802.00.60, Harmonized Tariff Schedule of the United States (19 USC 1202).

(6) Merchandise shipped abroad, not delivered to the consignee, and returned to the United States.

(7) Merchandise exported from continuous Customs custody within 6 months after the date of entry.

(8) Merchandise consigned to, or entered in the name of, any agency of the U.S. Government.

(9) Merchandise for which an appraisement entry is accepted.

(10) Merchandise entered temporarily into the Customs territory of the United States under bond or for permanent exhibition under bond.

(11) Merchandise provided for in section 465 or 466, Tariff Act of 1930 (19 USC 1465 or 1466), which pertain to certain equipment, repair parts, and supplies for vessels.

(12) Merchandise imported as supplies, stores, and equipment of the importing carrier and subsequently made subject to entry pursuant to section 466, Tariff Act of 1930, as amended (19 USC 1446).

(13) Ballast (not including cargo used for ballast) landed from a vessel and delivered for consumption.

(14) Merchandise, whether privileged or nonprivileged, resulting from manipulation or manufacture in a foreign trade zone.

(15) Screenings contained in bulk importations of grain or seeds.

[T.D. 73-175, 38FR 17447, July 2, 1973, as amended by T.D. 78-53, 43 FR6069, Feb. 13, 1978: T.D. 79-221, 44 FR 46820, Aug. 9, 1979; T.D. 82-224, 47 FR 53728, Nov. 29, 1982; T.D. 84-213, 49 FR 41184, Oct. 19, 1984; T.D. 85-39, 50 FR 9612, Mar. 11, 1985; T.D. 89-1, 53 FR 51256, Dec. 21. 1988]

Note: *The requirement for a special Customs invoice was waived by the Customs Service on March 1, 1982. However, it may still be used. If a commercial invoice is used, it must be signed by the seller and shipper or their agents.*

PRO FORMA INVOICE

Importers Statement of Value or the Price Paid in the Form of an Invoice

Not being in possession of a special or commercial seller's or shipper's invoice I request that you accept the statement of value or the price paid in the form of an invoice submitted below:

Name of shipper ______________ address ______________
Name of seller ______________ address ______________
Name of consignee ______________ address ______________
Name of purchaser ______________ address ______________

The merchandise (has) (has not) been purchased or agreed to be purchased by me. The prices, or in the case of consigned goods the values, given below are true and correct to the best of my knowledge and belief, and are based upon (check basis with an "X"):

(a) The prices paid or agreed to be paid ( ) as per order dated ______________

(b) Advices from exporters by letter ( ) by cable ( ) dated ______________

(c) Comparative values of shipments previously received ( ) dated ______________

(d) Knowledge of the market in the country of exportation ( )

(e) Knowledge of the market in the United States (if U.S. value) ( )

(f) Advices of the District Director of Customs ( )

(g) Other ( )

A	B	C	D	E	F	G
Case marks numbers	Manufacturer's item number symbol or brand	Quantities and full description	Unit purchase price (currency)	Total purchase price (currency)	Unit foreign value	Total foreign value

Check which of the charges below are, and which are not, included in the prices listed in columns "D" and "E":

Amount Included Not Included

Packing ______________
Cartage ______________
Inland freight ______________
Wharfage and loading abroad ______________
Country of origin ______________

Lighterage ______________
Ocean freight ______________
U.S.duties ______________
Other charges (identify by name and amount ______________
Total ______________

If any other invoice is received, I will immediately file it with the District Director of Customs.

Date ______________ Signature of person making invoice ______________

Title and firm name ______________

2
Additional Information

§ 141.89 Additional information for certain classes of merchandise

Invoices for the following classes of merchandise, classifiable under the Harmonized Tariff Schedule of the United States (HTSUS), shall set forth the additional information specified: [75-42, 75-239, 78-53, 83-251, 84-149.]

Aluminum and alloys of aluminum classifiable under subheadings 7601.10.60, 7601.20.60, 7601.20.90, or 7602.00.00, HTSUS (T.D. 53092, 55977, 56143)—Statement of the percentages by weight of any metallic element contained in the article.

Articles manufactured of textile materials Coated or laminated with plastics or rubber, classifiable in Chapter(s) 39, 40, and 42—Include a description indicating whether the fabric is coated or laminated on both sides, on the exterior surface or on the interior surface.

Bags manufactured of plastic sheeting and not of a reinforced or laminated construction, classified in Chapter 39 or in heading 4202—Indicate the gauge of the plastic sheeting.

Ball or roller bearings classifiable under subheading 8482.10.50 through 8482.80.00, HTSUS (T.D. 68-306)—(1) Type of bearing (i.e. whether a ball or roller bearing); (2) If a roller bearing, whether a spherical, tapered, cylindrical, needled or other type; (3) Whether a combination bearing (i.e. a bearing containing both ball and roller bearings, etc.); and (4) If a ball bearing (not including ball bearing with integral shafts or parts of ball bearings), whether or not radial, the following: (a) outside diameter of each bearing; and (b) whether or not a radial bearing (the definition of radial bearing is, for Customs purposes, an antifriction bearing primarily designed to support a load perpendicular to shaft axis).

Beads (T.D. 50088, 55977)—(1) The length of the string, if strung; (2) The size of the beads expressed in millimeters; (3) The material of which the beads are composed, i.e. ivory, glass, imitation pearl, etc.

Bed linen and bedspreads Statement as to whether or not the article contains any embroidery, lace, braid, edging, trimming, piping or applique work.

Chemicals Furnish the use and Chemical Abstracts Service number of chemical compounds classified in Chapters 27, 28 and 29, HTSUS.

Colors, dyes, stains and related products provided for under heading 3204, HTSUS—The following information is required: (l) Invoice name of product; (2) Trade name of product; (3) Identity and percent by weight of each component; (4) Color Index number (if none, so state); (5) Color Index generic name (if none so state); (6) Chemical Abstracts Service number of the active ingredient; (7) Class of merchandise (state whether acid type dye, basic dye, disperse dye, fluorescent brightener, soluble dye, vat dye, toner or other (describe); (8) Material to which applied (name the material for which the color, dye, or toner is primarily designed).

Copper (T.D. 45878, 50158, 55977) articles classifiable under the provisions of Chapter 74, HTSUS—A statement of the weight of articles of copper, and a statement of percentage of copper content and all other elements—by weight—of articles classifiable according to copper content.

Copper ores and concentrates (T.D. 45878, 50158, 55977) classifiable in heading 2603, and subheadings 2620.19.60, 2620.20.00, 2620.30.00, and heading 7401—Statement of the percentage by weight of the copper content and any other metallic elements.

Cotton fabrics classifiable under the following HTSUS headings: 5208, 5209, 5210, 5211, and 5212—(1) Marks on shipping packages; (2) Numbers on shipping packages; (3) Customer's call number, if any; (4) Exact width of the merchandise; (5) Detailed description of the merchandise; trade name, if any; whether bleached, unbleached, printed, composed of yarns of different color, or dyed; if composed of cotton and other materials, state the percentage of each component material by weight; (6) Number of single threads per square centimeter (All ply yarns must be counted in accordance with the number of single threads contained in the yarn; to illustrate: a cloth containing 100 two-ply yarns in one square centimeter must be reported as 200 single threads); (7) Exact weight per square meter in grams; (8) Average yarn number use this formula:

$$\frac{100 \times (\text{Total Single Yarns Per Square Centimeter})}{(\text{Number of Grams Per Square Meter})}$$

(9) Yarn size or sizes in the warp; (10) Yarn size or sizes in the filling; (11) Specify whether the yarns are combed or carded; (12) Number of colors or kinds (different yarn sizes or materials) in the filling; (13) Specify whether the fabric is napped or not napped; and (14) Specify the type of weave, for example, plain, twill, sateen, oxford, etc., and (15) Specify the type of machine on which woven: if with Jacquard (Jacq), if with Swivel (Swiv), if with Lappet (Lpt.), if with Dobby (Dobby).

Cotton raw See §151.82 of this chapter for additional information required on invoices.

Cotton waste (T.D. 50044)—(1) The name by which the cotton waste is known, such as "cotton card strips"; "cotton comber waste"; "cotton lap waste"; "cotton silver waste"; "cotton roving waste"; "cotton fly waste"; etc.; (2) Whether the length of the cotton staple forming any cotton card strips covered by the invoice is less than 3.016 centimeters (1 3/16 inches) or is 3.016 centimeters (1 3/16 inches) or more.

Earthenware or crockeryware composed of a nonvitrified absorbent body (including white granite and semiporcelain earthenware and cream-colored ware, stoneware, and terra cotta, but not including common brown, gray, red, or yellow earthenware), embossed or plain; common salt-glazed stoneware; stoneware or earthenware crucibles; Rockingham earthenware; china, porcelain, or other vitrified wares, composed of a vitrified nonabsorbent body that, when broken, shows a vitrified, vitreous, semi-vitrified, or semivitreous fracture; and bisque or parian ware (T.D. 53236)—(l) If in sets, the kinds of articles in each set in the shipment and the quantity of each kind of article in each set in the shipment; (2) The exact maximum diameter, expressed in centimeters, of each size of all plates in the shipment; (3) The unit value for each style and size of plate, cup, saucer, or other separate piece in the shipment.

Fish or fish livers (T.D. 50724, 49640, 55977) imported in airtight containers classifiable under Chapter 3, HTSUS—(1) Statement whether the articles contain any oil, fat, or grease, (2) The name and quantity of any such oil, fat, or grease.

Footwear, classifiable in headings 6401 through 6405 of the HTSUS—

1. Manufacturer's style number.
2. Importer's style and/or stock number.
3. Percent by area of external surface area of upper (excluding reinforcements and accessories) that is:

Leather	a.	________%
Composition leather	b.	________%
Rubber and/or plastics	c.	________%
Textile materials	d.	________%
Other (give separate percent for each type	e.	________%
of material)	f.	________%

4. Percent by area of external surface area of outersole (excluding reinforcements and accessories) that is:

Leather	a.	________%
Composition leather	b.	________%
Rubber and/or plastics	c.	________%
Textile materials	d.	________%
Other (give separate	e.	________%
percent for each type of material)	f.	________%

You may skip this section if you choose to answer *all* questions A through Z below:

I. If 3(a) is larger than any other percent in 3 and if 4(a) is larger than any other percent in 4, answer questions F, G, L, M, O, Q, R, S, and X.

II. If 3(a) is larger than any other percent in 3 and if 4(c) is larger than any other percent in 4, answer questions F, G, L, M, N, O, Q, S and X.

III. If 3(a) plus 3(b) is larger than any single percent in 3 and 4(d), 4(e) or 4(f) is larger than any other percent in 4, stop.

IV. If 3(c) is larger than any other percent in 3 and if 4(a) or 4(b) is larger than any other percent in 4, stop.

V. If 3(c) is larger than any other percent in 3 and if 4(c) is larger than any other percent in 4, answer questions B, E, F, G, H, J, K, L, M, N, O, P, T and W.

VI. If 3(d) is larger than any other percent in 3 and if 4(a) plus 4(b) is greater than any single percent in 4, answer questions C and D.

VII. If 3(d) is larger than any other percent in 3 and if 4(c) is larger than any single percent in 4, answer questions A, C, J, K, M, N, P and T.

VIII. If 3(d) is larger than any other percent in 3 and if 4(d) is larger than any other percent in 4, answer questions U, Y and Z.

IX. If the article is made of paper, answer questions V and Z.

If the article does not meet any of the conditions I through IX above, answer all questions A through Z, below.

A. Percent of external surface area of upper (including leather reinforcements and accessories).
Which is leather ________%

B. Percent by area of external surface area of upper (including all reinforcements and accessories).
Which is rubber _______
and/or plastics) ________%

C. Percent by weight of rubber and/or plastics is ________%

D. Percent by weight of textile materials plus rubber and/or plastics is ________%

E. Is it waterproof?

F. Does it have a protective metal toe cap?

G. Will it cover the wearer's ankle bone?

H. Will it cover the wearer's knee cap?

I. [Reserved.]

J. Is it designed to be a protection against water, oil, grease, or chemicals or cold or inclement weather?

K. Is it a slip-on?

L. Is it a downhill or cross-country ski boot?

M. Is it serious sports footwear other than ski boots? (Chapter 64 subheading note defines sports footwear.)

N. Is it a tennis, basketball, gym, or training shoe or the like?

O. Is it made on a base or platform of wood?

P. Does it have open toes or open heels?

Q. Is it made by the (lipped insole) welt construction?

R. Is it made by the turned construction?

S. Is it worn exclusively by men, boys or youths?

T. Is it made by an exclusively adhesive construction?

U. Are the fibers of the upper, by weight, predominately vegetable fibers?

V. Is it disposable, i.e., intended for one-time use?

W. Is it a "Zori"?

X. Is the leather in the upper pigskin?

Y. Are the sole and upper made of wool felt

Z. Is there a line of demarcation between the outer sole and upper?

The information requested above may be furnished on CF 5523 or other appropriate format by the exporter, manufacturer or shipper.

Also, the following information must be furnished by the importer or his authorized agent if classification is claimed under one of the subheadings below, as follows:

If subheading 6401.99.80, 6402.19.10, 6402.30.30, 6402.91.40, 6402.99.15, 6402.99.30, 6404.11.40, 6404.11.60, 6404.19.35, 6404.19.40, or 6404.19.60 is claimed:

Does the shoe have a foxing or foxing-like band? If so, state its material(s).

Does the sole overlap the upper other than just at the front of the toe and/or at the back of the heel?

Definitions for some of the terms used in Question A to Z above: For the purpose of this section, the following terms have the approximate definitions below. If either a more complete definition or a decision as to its application to a particular article is needed, the maker or importer of record (or the agent of either) should contact Customs prior to entry of the article.

a. In an exclusively adhesive construction, all of the pieces of the bottom would separate from the upper or from each other if all adhesives, cements, and glues were dissolved. It includes shoes in which the pieces of the upper are stitched to each other, but not to any part of the bottom. Examples include:

1. Vulcanized construction footwear;
2. Simultaneous molded construction footwear;
3. Molded footwear in which the upper and the bottom is one piece of molded rubber or plastic, and
4. Footwear in which staples, rivets, stitching, or any of the methods above are either primary or even just extra or auxiliary, even though adhesive is a major part of the reason the bottom will not separate from the upper.

b. Composition leather is made by binding together leather fibers or small pieces of natural leather. It does not include imitation leathers not based on natural leather.

c. Leather is the tanned skin of any animal from which the fur or hair has been removed. Tanned skins coated or laminated with rubber and/or plastics are "leather" only if leather gives the material its essential character.

d. A Line of Demarcation exists if one can indicate where the sole ends and the upper begins. For example, knit booties do not normally have a line of demarcation.

e. Men's, boy's and youth's sizes cover footwear of American youths size 11 1/2 and larger for males, and does not include footwear commonly worn by both sexes. If more than 4% of the shoes sold in a given size will be worn by females, that size is "commonly worn by both sexes."

f. Footwear is designed to *protect* against water, oil or cold or inclement weather only if it is substantially more of a protection against those items than the usual shoes of that type. For example, a leather oxford will clearly keep your feet warmer and drier than going barefoot, but they are not a protection in this sense. On the other hand, the snow-jogger is the protective version of the non-protective jogging shoe.

g. Rubber and/or plastics includes any textile material visibly coated (or covered) externally with one or both of those materials.

h. Slip-on includes:

1. A boot that must be pulled on.
2. Footwear with elastic cores that must be stretched to get it on, but not a separate piece of elasticized fabric that forms a full circle around the foot or ankle.

i. Sports footwear includes only:

1. Footwear that is designed for a sporting activity and has, or has provision for, the attachment of spikes, sprigs, cleats, stops, clips, bars or the like;
2. Skating boots (without skates attached), ski boots and cross-country ski footwear, wrestling boots, boxing boots and cycling shoes.

j. Tennis shoes, basketball shoes, gym shoes, training shoes and the like cover athletic footwear other than sports footwear, whether or not principally used for such athletic games or purposes.

k. Textile materials are made from cotton, other vegetable fibers, wool, hair, silk or man-made fibers. Note: Cork, wood, cardboard and leather are not textile materials.

l. In turned construction, the upper is stitched to the leather sole wrong side out and the shoe is then turned right side out.

m. Vegetable fibers include cotton, flax and ramie, but does not include either rayon or plaiting materials such as rattan or wood strips.

n. Waterproof footwear includes footwear designed to protect against penetration by water or other liquids, whether or not such footwear is primarily designed for such purposes.

o. Welt footwear means footwear construction with a welt, that extends around the edge of the outer sole, and in which the welt and shoe upper are sewed to a lip on the surface of the insole, and the outer sole of which is sewed or cemented to the welt.

p. A zori has an upper consisting only of straps or thongs of molded rubber or plastic. This upper is assembled to a formed rubber or plastic sole by means of plugs.

Fur products and furs (T.D. 53064)—(1) Name or names (as set forth in the Fur Products Name Guide (16 CFR 301.0) of the animal or animals that produced the fur, and such qualifying statements as may be required pursuant to § 7(c) of the Fur Products Labeling Act (15 USC 69e(c));

(2) A statement that the fur product contains or is composed of used fur, when such is the fact; (3) A statement that the fur product contains or is composed of bleached, dyed, or otherwise artificially colored fur, when such is the fact; (4) A statement that the fur product is composed in whole or in substantial part of paws, tails, bellies, or waste fur, when such is the fact; (5) Name and address of the manufacturer of the fur product; (6) Name of the country of origin of the furs or those contained in the fur product.

Glassware and other glass products (T.D. 53079, 55977)—Classifiable under Chapter 70, HTSUS—Statement of the separate value of each component article in the set.

Gloves—classifiable in subheadings 6116.10.20 and 6216.00.20—Statement as to whether or not the article has been covered with plastics on both sides.

Grain or grain and screenings (T.D. 51284)—Statement on Customs invoices for cultivated grain or grain and screenings that no screenings are included with the grain, or, if there are screenings included, the percentage of the shipment that consists of screenings commingled with the principal grain.

Handkerchiefs—(1) State the exact dimensions (length and width) of the merchandise; (2) If of cotton indicate whether the handkerchief is hemmed and whether it contains lace or embroidery.

Hats or headgear—(1) If classifiable under subheading 6502.00.40 or 6502.00.60, HTSUS—Statement as to whether or not the article has been bleached or colored; (2) If classifiable under subheading 6502.00.20 through 6502.00.60 or 6504.00.30 through 6504.00.90, HTSUS—Statement as to whether or not the article is sewed or not sewed, exclusive of any ornamentation or trimming.

Hosiery—(1) Indicate whether a single yarn measures less than 67 decitex. (2) Indicate whether the hosiery is full length, knee length, or less than knee length. (3) Indicate whether it contains lace or net.

Iron or steel classifiable in Chapter 72 or headings 7301 to 7307, HTSUS (T.D. 53092, 55977)—Statement of the percentages by weight of carbon and any metallic elements contained in the articles, in the form of a mill analysis or mill test certificate.

Iron oxide (T.D. 49989, 50107)—For iron oxide to which a reduced rate of duty is applicable, a statement of the method of preparation of the oxide, together with the patent number, if any.

Machines, equipment and apparatus—Chapters 84 and 85, HTSUS—A statement as to the use or method of operation of each type of machine.

Machine parts (T.D. 51616)—Statement specifying the kind of machine for which the parts are intended, or if this is not known to the shipper, the kinds of machines for which the parts are suitable.

Machine tools: (1) Heading 8456 through 8462—machine tools covered by these headings equipped with a CNC (Computer Numerical Control) or the facings (electrical interface) for a CNC must state so; (2) heading 8458 through 8463—machine tools covered by these headings if used or rebuilt must state so; (3) subheading 8456.30.10—EDM: (Electrical Discharge Machines) if a Traveling Wire (Wire Cut) type must state so. Wire EDM's use a copper or brass wire for the electrode; (4) subheading 8457.10.0010 through 8457.10.0050—Machining Centers. Must state whether or not they have an ATC (Automatic Tool Changer). Vertical spindle machine centers with an ATC must also indicate the Y-travel; (5) subheadings 8458.11.0030 through 8458.11.0090—horizontal lathes: numerically controlled. Must indicate the rated HP (or KW rating) of the main spindle motor. Use the continuous rather than 30-minute rating.

Madeira embroideries (T.D. 49988)—(1) With respect to the materials used, furnish: (a) country of production; (b) width of the material in the piece; (c) name of the manufacturer; (d) kind of material, indicating manufacturer's quality number; (e) landed cost of the material used in each item; (f) date of the order; (g) date of the invoice; (h) invoice unit value in the currency of the purchase; (i) discount from purchase price allowed, if any; (2) With respect to the finished embroidered articles, furnish: (a) manufacturers' name, design number, and quality number; (b) importer's design number, if any; (c) finished size; (d) number of embroidery points per unit of quantity; (e) total for overhead and profit added in arriving at the price or value of the merchandise covered by the invoice.

Motion picture films—(1) Statement of footage, title, and subject matter of each film; (2) Declaration of shipper, cameraman, or other person with knowledge of the facts identifying the films with the invoice and stating that the basic films were to the best of his knowledge and belief exposed abroad and returned for use as newsreel; (3) Declaration of importer that he believes the films entered by him are the ones covered by the preceding declaration and that the films are intended for use as newsreel.

Paper classifiable in Chapter 48—Invoices covering paper shall contain the following information, or will be accompanied by specification sheets containing such information:

(1) Weight of paper in grams per square meter; (2) Thickness, in micrometers (microns); (3) If imported in rectangular sheets, length and width sheets, in cm; (4) If imported in strips, or rolls, the width, in cm. In the case of rolls, the diameter of rolls in cm; (5) Whether the paper is coated or impregnated, and with what materials; (6) Weight of coating, in grams per square meter; (7) Percentage by weight of the total fiber content consisting of wood fibers contained by a mechanical process, chemical sulfate or soda process, chemical sulfite process, or semi-chemical process, as appropriate; (8) Commercial designation, as "Writing," "Cover," "Drawing," "Bristol," "Newsprint," etc.; (9) Ash content; (10) Color; (11) Glaze, or finish; (12) Mullen bursting strength, and Mullen index; (13) Stretch factor, in machine direction and in cross direction; (14) Tear and tensile readings; in machine direction, in cross direction, and in machine direction plus cross direction; (15) Identification of fibers as "hardwood" where appropriate; (16) Crush resistance; (17) Brightness; (18) Smoothness; (19) If bleached, whether bleached uniform-

ly throughout the mass; (20) Whether embossed, perforated, creped or crinkled.

Plastic plates, sheets, film, foil, and strip of headings 3920 and 3921—(1) Statement as to whether the plastic is cellular or noncellular; (2) Specification of the type of plastic; (3) Indication of whether or not flexible and whether combined with textile or other material.

Printed matter classifiable in Chapter 49—Printed matter entered in the following headings shall have, on or with the invoices covering such matter, the following information: (1) *Heading 4901*—(a) Whether the books are: dictionaries, encyclopedias, textbooks, bound newspapers or journals or periodicals, directories, bibles or other prayer books, technical, scientific or professional books, art or pictorial books, or "other" books; (b) if "other" books, whether hardbound or paperbound; (c) if "other" books, paperbound, other than "rack size": number of pages (excluding covers). (2) *Heading 4902*—Whether the journal or periodical appears at least four times a week. If the journal or periodical appears other than at least four times a week, whether it is a newspaper supplement printed by a gravure process, is a newspaper, business or professional journal or periodical, or other than these; (3) *Heading 4904*—Whether the printed or manuscript music is sheet music, not bound (except by stapling or folding); (4) *Heading 4905*—(a) Whether globes, or not; (b) if not globes, whether in book form, or not; (c) in any case, whether or not in relief; (5) *Heading 4908*—Whether or not vitrifiable; (6) *Heading 4904*—Whether post cards, greeting cards, or other; (7) *Heading 4910*—(a) Whether or not printed on paper by a lithographic process; (b) if printed on paper by a lithographic process, the thickness of the paper, in mm; (8) *Subheading 4911.91*—(a) Whether or not printed over 20 years at time of importation; (b) if not printed over 20 years at time of importation, whether suitable for use in the production of articles of heading 4901; (c) if not printed over 20 years at time of importation, and not suitable for use in the production of articles of heading 4901, whether the merchandise is lithographs on paper or paperboard; (d) if lithographs on paper or paperboard, under the terms of the immediately preceding description, thickness of the paper or paperboard, and whether or not posters; (e) in any case, whether or not posters; (f) in any case, whether or not photographic negatives or positives on transparent bases; (g) *Subheading 4911.99*—If not carnets, or parts thereof, in English or French, whether or not printed on paper in whole or in part by a lithographic process.

Pulp classifiable in Chapter 47—(1) Invoices covering chemical wood pulp, dissolving grades, in Heading 4702 shall state the insoluble fraction (as a percentage) after 1 hour in a caustic soda solution containing 18% sodium hydroxide (NaOH) at 20° C; (2) *Subheading 4702.00.0020*—Pulp entered under this subheading shall in addition contain on or with the invoice the ash content as a percentage by weight.

Refrigeration equipment (1) Refrigerator-freezers classifiable under subheading 8418.10.00 and (2) refrigerators classifiable under 8418.21.00—(a) statement as to whether they are compression or absorption type; (b) statement of their refrigerated volume in liters; (3) freezers classifiable under subheading 8418.30.00 and 8418.40.00—statement as to whether they are chest or upright type; (4) liquid chilling refrigerating units classifiable under subheading 8418.69.0045 through 8418.69.0060 statement as to whether they are centrifugal open-type, centrifugal hermetic-type, absorption-type or reciprocating-type.

Rolling mills—Subheading 8455.30.0005 through 8455.30.0085. Rolls for rolling mills: Indicate the composition of the roll—gray iron, cast steel or other—and the weight of each roll.

Rubber Products of Chapter 40—(1) Statement as to whether combined with textile or other material; (2) statement whether the rubber is cellular or noncellular, unvulcanized or vulcanized, and if vulcanized, whether hard rubber or other than hard rubber.

Screenings or scalpings of grains or seeds (T.D. 51096)—(1) Whether the commodity is the product of a screening process; (2) If so, whether any cultivated grains have been added to such commodity; (3) If any such grains have been added, the kind and percentage of each.

Textile fiber products (T.D. 55095)—(1) The constituent fiber or combination of fibers in the textile fiber product, designating with equal prominence each natural or manufactured fiber in the textile fiber product by its generic name in the order of predominance by the weight thereof if the weight of such fiber is 5 per centum or more of the total fiber weight of the product; (2) The percentage of each fiber present, by weight, in the total fiber content of the textile fiber product; (3) The name, or other identification issued and registered by the Federal Trade Commission, of the manufacturer of the product or one or more persons subject to § 3 of the Textile Fiber Products Identification Act (15 USC 70a) with respect to such product; (4) The name of the country where processed or manufactured. *See also* "Wearing Apparel" below.

Tires and tubes for tires of rubber or plastics—(1) Specify the kind of vehicle for which the tire is intended, i.e. airplane, bicycle, passenger car, on-the-highway light or heavy truck or bus, motorcycle; (2) If designed for tractors provided for in subheading 8701.90.10, or for agricultural or horticultural machinery or implements provided for in Chapter 84 or in subheading 8716.80.10, designate whether the tire is new, recapped, or used; pneumatic or solid; (3) Indicate whether the tube is designed for tires provided for in subheading 4011.91.10, 4011.99.10, 4012.10.20, or 4012.20.20.

Tobacco (including tobacco in its natural state) (T.D. 44854, 45871)—(1) Specify in detail the character of the tobacco in each bale by giving (a) country and province of origin, (b) year of production, (c) grade or grades in each bale, (d) number of carrots or pounds of each grade if more than one grade is packed in a bale, (e) the time when, place where, and person from whom purchased, (f) price paid or to be paid for each bale or package, or price for the vega or lot if purchased in bulk, or if obtained otherwise than by purchase, state the actual market value per bale; (2) If an invoice covers or includes bales of tobacco that are part of a vega or lot purchased in bulk, the invoice must contain or be accompanied by a full description of the vega or lot purchased; or if such description has been furnished with a previous importation, the date and identity of such shipment; (3) Packages or bales containing only filler leaf shall be invoiced as filler; when containing filler and wrapper but not more than 35 percent of wrapper, they shall be invoiced as mixed; and when containing more than 35 percent of wrapper, they shall be invoiced as wrapper.

Watches and watch movements classifiable under Chapter 91 of the HTSUS—For all commercial shipments of such articles, there shall be required to be shown on the invoice, or on a separate sheet attached to and constituting a part of the invoice, such information as will reflect with respect to each group, type, or model, the following;

(A) For watches, a thorough description of the composition of the watch cases, the bracelets, bands or straps, the commercial description (ebauche caliber number, ligne size and number of jewels) of the movements contained in the watches, and the type of battery (manufacturer's name and reference number), if the watch is battery-operated;

(B) For watch movements, the commercial description (ebauche caliber number, ligne size and number of jewels). If battery operated, the type of battery (manufacturer's name and reference number);

(C) The name of the manufacturer of the exported watch movements and the name of the country in which the movements were manufactured.

Wearing apparel—(1) All invoices for textile wearing apparel should indicate a component material breakdown in percentages by weight for all component fibers present in the entire garment, as well as separate breakdowns of the fibers in the (outer) shell (exclusive of linings, cuffs, waistbands, collars and other trimmings) and in the lining; (2) for garments that are constructed of more than one component or material (combination of knits and not knit fabric or combinations of knit and/or not knit fabric with leather, fur, plastic including vinyl. etc.), the invoice must show a fiber breakdown in percentages by weight for each separate textile material in the garment and a breakdown in percentages by weight for each nontextile material for the entire garment; (3) For woven garments—Indicate whether the fabric is yarn dyed and whether there are "two or more colors in the warp and/or filling"; (4) For all-white T-shirts and singlets—Indicate whether or not the garment contains pockets, trim, or embroidery; (5) For mufflers—State the exact dimensions (length and width) of the merchandise.

Wood products—(1) Wood sawed or chipped lengthwise, sliced or peeled, whether or not planed, sanded, or finger-jointed, of a thickness exceeding 6 mm (lumber), classifiable under Chapter 44, heading 4407, HTSUS, and wood continuously shaped along any of its edges or faces, whether or not planed, sanded or finger-jointed; coniferous: Subheading 4409.10.90 and Nonconiferous: Subheading 4409.20.90, HTSUS, and dutiable on the basis of cubic meters—

Quantity in cubic meters (m) before dressing; (2) Fiberboard of wood or other ligneous materials whether or not bonded with resins or other organic substances, under Chapter 44, Heading 4411, HTSUS, and classifiable according to its density—Density in grams per cubic centimeter (cm); (3) Plywood consisting solely of sheets of wood, classifiable under Chapter 44, Subheading 4412.11, 4412.12, and 4412.19, HTSUS, and classifiable according to the thickness of the wood sheets—Thickness of each ply in millimeter (mm);

Wool and hair—See § 151.62 of this chapter for additional information required on invoices.

Wool products, except carpets, rugs, mats, and upholsteries, and wool products made more than 20 years before importation (T.D. 50388, 51019)—(1) The percentage of the total fiber weight of the wool product, exclusive of ornamentation not exceeding 5 per centum of said total fiber weight, of (a) wool; (b) reprocessed wool; (c) reused wool; (d) each fiber other than wool if said percentage by weight of such fiber is 5 per centum or more; and (e) the aggregate of all other fibers; (2) the maximum percentage of the total weight of the wool product, of any nonfibrous loading, filling, or adulterating matter; and (3) the name of the manufacturer of the wool product, except when such product consists of mixed wastes, residues, and similar merchandise obtained from several suppliers or unknown sources.

Woven fabric of man-made fibers in headings 5407, 5408, 5512, 5513, 5514, 5515, 5516—

(1) State the exact width of the fabric.

(2) Provide a detailed description of the merchandise, (trade name, if any).

(3) Indicate whether bleached, unbleached, dyed, of yarns of different colors and/or printed.

(4) If composed of more than one material, list percentage by weight in each.

(5) Identify the man-made fibers as artificial or synthetic, filament or staple, and state whether the yarns are high tenacity. Specify the number of turns per meter in each yarn.

(6) Specify yarn sizes in warp and filling.

(7) Specify how the fabric is woven (plain weave, twill, sateen, dobby, jacquard, swivel, lappet, etc.).

(8) Indicate the number of single threads per square centimeter in both warp and filling.

(9) Supply the weight per square meter in grams.

(10) Provide the average yarn number using this formula:

$$\frac{100 \text{ x number of single threads per square centimeter}}{\text{(number of grams per square meter)}}$$

(11) For spun yarns, specify whether combed or carded.

(12) For filament yarns, specify whether textured or not textured.

Yarns —(1) All yarn invoices should show: (a) Fiber content by weight; (b) whether single or plied; (c) whether or not put up for retail sale (*See* Section XI, Note 4, HTSUS); (d) whether or not intended for use as sewing thread.

(2) If chief weight of silk—show whether spun or filament.

(3) If chief weight of cotton—show:

(a) Whether combed or uncombed

(b) Metric number (mn)
(c) Whether bleached and/or mercerized.

(4) If chief weight of man-made fiber—show:
(a) Whether filament, or spun, or a combination of filament and spun
(b) If a combination of filament and spun—give percentage of filament and spun by weight.

(5) If chief weight of filament man-made fiber—show:
(a) Whether high tenacity (See Section XI, note 6 HTSUS)
(b) Whether monofilament, multifilament or strip
(c) Whether texturized
(d) Yarn number in decitex
(e) Number of turns per meter
(f) For monofilaments—show cross-sectional dimension in millimeters
(g) For strips—show the width of the strip in millimeters (measure in folded or twisted condition if so imported).

Items or classes of goods may be added to or removed from the list from time to time.

3
Customs Valuation

93 STAT. 194 et seq.

PUBLIC LAW 96-39—JULY 26, 1979

TARIFF ACT OF 1930

"SEC. 402, VALUE. [19 USC 1401a]

"(a) IN GENERAL.—(1) Except as otherwise specifically provided for in this Act, imported merchandise shall be appraised, for the purposes of this Act, on the basis of the following:

"(A) The transaction value provided for under subsection (b).

"(B) The transaction value of identical merchandise provided for under subsection (c), if the value referred to in subparagraph (A) cannot be determined, or can be determined but cannot be used by reason of subsection (b)(2).

"(C) The transaction value of similar merchandise provided for under subsection (c), if the value referred to in subparagraph (B) cannot be determined.

"(D) The deductive value provided for under subsection (d), if the value referred to in subparagraph (C) cannot be determined and if the importer does not request alternative valuation under Paragraph (2).

"(E) The computed value provided for under subsection (e), if the value referred to in subparagraph (D) cannot be determined.

"(F) The value provided for under subsection (f), if the value referred to in subparagraph (E) cannot be determined.

"(2) If the value referred to in paragraph (1)(C) cannot be determined with respect to imported merchandise, the merchandise shall be appraised on the basis of the computed value provided for under paragraph (1)(E), rather than the deductive value provided for under paragraph (1)(D), if the importer makes a request to that effect to the customs officer concerned within such time as the Secretary shall prescribe. If the computed value of the merchandise cannot subsequently be determined, the merchandise may not be appraised on the basis of the value referred to in paragraph (1)(F) unless the deductive value of the merchandise cannot be determined under paragraph (1)(D).

"(3) Upon written request therefor by the importer of merchandise, and subject to provisions of law regarding the disclosure of information, the customs officer concerned shall provide the importer with a written explanation of how the value of that merchandise was determined under this section.

"(b) TRANSACTION VALUE OF IMPORTED MERCHANDISE.—(1) The transaction value of imported merchandise is the price actually paid or payable for the merchandise when sold for exportation to the United States, plus amounts equal to—

"(A) the packing costs incurred by the buyer with respect to the imported merchandise;

"(B) any selling commission incurred by the buyer with respect to the imported merchandise;

"(C) the value, apportioned as appropriate, of any assist;

"(D) any royalty or license fee related to the imported merchandise that the buyer is required to pay, directly or indirectly, as a condition of the sale of the imported merchandise for exportation to the United States; and

"(E) the proceeds of any subsequent resale, disposal, or use of the imported merchandise that accrue, directly or indirectly, to the seller.

The price actually paid or payable for imported merchandise shall be increased by the amounts attributable to the items (and no others) described in subparagraphs (A) through (E) only to the extent that each such amount (i) is not otherwise included within the price actually paid or payable; and (ii) is based on sufficient information. If sufficient information is not available, for any reason, with respect to any amount referred to in the preceding sentence, the transaction value of the imported merchandise concerned shall be treated, for purposes of this section, as one that cannot be determined.

"(2)(A) The transaction value of imported merchandise determined under paragraph (1) shall be the appraised value of that merchandise for the purposes of this Act only if—

"(i) there are no restrictions on the disposition or use of the imported merchandise by the buyer other than restrictions that—

"(I) are imposed or required by law,

"(II) limit the geographical arm in which the merchandise may be resold, or

"(III) do not substantially affect the value of the merchandise;

"(ii) the sale of, or the price actually paid or payable for, the imported merchandise is not subject to any condition or consideration for which a value cannot be determined with respect to the imported merchandise;

"(iii) no part of the proceeds of any subsequent resale, disposal, or use of the imported merchandise by the buyer will accrue directly or indirectly to the seller, unless an appropriate adjustment therefor can be made under paragraph (1)(E); and

"(iv) the buyer and seller are not related, or the buyer and seller are related but the transaction value is acceptable, for purposes of this subsection, under subparagraph (B).

"(B) The transaction value between a related buyer and seller is acceptable for the purposes of this subsection if an examination of the circumstances of the sale of the imported merchandise indicates that the relationship between such buyer and seller did not influence the price actually paid or payable; or if the transaction value of the imported merchandise closely approximates—

"(i) the transaction value of identical merchandise, or of similar merchandise, in sales to unrelated buyers in the United States; or

Amended by P.L. 96-490, effective 1/1/81

"(ii) the deductive value or computed value for identical merchandise or similar merchandise;

but, only if each value referred to in clause (i) or (ii) that is used for comparison relates to merchandise that was exported to the United States at or about the same time as the imported merchandise.

"(C) In applying the values used for comparison purposes under subparagraph (B), there shall be taken into account differences with respect to the sales involved (if such differences are based on sufficient information whether supplied by the buyer or otherwise available to the customs officer concerned) in—

"(i) commercial levels;

"(ii) quantity levels;

"(iii) the costs, commissions, values, fees, and proceeds described in paragraph (1); and

"(iv) the costs incurred by the seller in sales in which he and the buyer are not related that are not incurred by the seller in sales in which he and the buyer are related.

"(3) The transaction value of imported merchandise does not include any of the following, if identified separately from the price actually paid or payable and from any cost or other item referred to in paragraph (1):

"(A) Any reasonable cost or charge that is incurred for—

"(i) the construction, erection, assembly, or maintenance of, or the technical assistance provided with respect to, the merchandise after its importation into the United States; or

"(ii) the transportation of the merchandise after such importation.

"(B) The customs duties and other Federal taxes currently payable on the imported merchandise by reason of its importation, and any Federal excise tax on, or measured by the value of, such merchandise for which vendors in the United States are ordinarily liable.

"(4) For purposes of this subsection—

"Price actually paid or payable."

"(A) The term 'price actually paid or payable' means the total payment (whether direct or indirect, and exclusive of any costs, charges, or expenses incurred for transportation, insurance, and related services incident to the international shipment of the merchandise from the country of exportation to the place of importation in the United States) made, or to be made, for imported merchandise by the buyer to, or for the benefit of, the seller.

"(B) Any rebate of, or other decrease in, the price actually paid or payable that is made or otherwise effected between the buyer and seller after the date of the importation of the merchandise into the United States shall be disregarded in determining the transaction value under paragraph (1).

"(c) TRANSACTION VALUE OF IDENTICAL MERCHANDISE AND SIMILAR MERCHANDISE.—(1) The transaction value of identical merchandise, or of similar merchandise, is the transaction value (acceptable as the appraised value for purposes of this Act under subsection (b) but adjusted under paragraph (2) of this subsection) of imported merchandise that is—

"(A) with respect to the merchandise being appraised, either identical merchandise or similar merchandise, as the case may be; and

"(B) exported to the United States at or about the time that the merchandise being appraised is exported to the United States.

"(2) Transaction values determined under this subsection shall be based on sales of identical merchandise or similar merchandise, as the case may be, at the same commercial level and in substantially the same quantity as the sales of the merchandise being appraised. If no such sale is found, sales of identical merchandise or similar merchandise at either a different commercial level or in different quantities, or both, shall be used, but adjusted to take account of any such difference. Any adjustment made under this paragraph shall be based on sufficient information. If in applying this paragraph with respect to any imported merchandise, two or more transaction values for identical merchandise, or for similar merchandise, are determined, such imported merchandise shall be appraised on the basis of the lower or lowest of such values.

"Merchandise concerned."

"(d) DEDUCTIVE VALVE.—(1) For purposes of this subsection, the term 'merchandise concerned' means the merchandise being appraised, identical merchandise, or similar merchandise.

"(2)(A) The deductive value of the merchandise being appraised is whichever of the following prices (as adjusted under paragraph (3)) is appropriate depending upon when and in what condition the merchandise concerned is sold in the United States:

"(i) If the merchandise concerned is sold in the condition as imported at or about the date of importation of the merchandise being appraised, the price is the unit price at which the merchandise concerned is sold in the greatest aggregate quantity at or about such date.

"(ii) If the merchandise concerned is sold in the condition as imported but not sold at or about the date of importation of the merchandise being appraised, the price is the unit price at which the merchandise concerned is sold in the greatest aggregate quantity after the date of importation of the merchandise being appraised but before the close of the 90th day after the date of such importation.

"(iii) If the merchandise concerned was not sold in the condition as imported and not sold before the close of the 90th day after the date of importation of the merchandise being appraised, the price is the unit price at which the merchandise being appraised, after further processing, is sold in the greatest aggregate quantity before the 180th day after the date of such importation. This clause shall apply to appraisement of merchandise only if the importer so elects and notifies the customs officer concerned of that election within such time as shall be prescribed by the Secretary.

"(B) For purposes of subparagraph (A), the unit price at which merchandise is sold in the greatest aggregate quantity is the unit price at which such merchandise is sold to unrelated persons, at the first commercial level after importation (in cases to which subparagraph (A)(i) or (ii) applies) or after further processing (in cases to which subparagraph (A)(iii) applies) at which such sales take place, in a total volume that is (i) greater than the total volume sold at any other unit price, and (ii) sufficient to establish the unit price. Unit Price.

"(3)(A) The price determined under paragraph (2) shall be reduced by an amount equal to—

"(i) any commission usually paid or agreed to be paid, or the addition usually made for profit and general expenses, in connection with sales in the United States of imported merchandise that is of the same class or kind, regardless of the country of exportation as the merchandise concerned;

"(ii) the actual costs and associated costs of transportation and insurance incurred with respect to international shipments of the merchandise concerned from the country of exportation to the United States;

"(iii) The usual costs and associated costs of transportation and insurance incurred with respect to shipments of such merchandise from the place of importation to the place of delivery in the United States, if such costs are not included as a general expense under clause (i);

"(iv) the customs duties and other Federal taxes currently payable on the merchandise concerned by reason of its importation, and any Federal excise tax on, or measured by the value of, such merchandise for which vendors in the United States are ordinarily liable; and

"(v) (but only in the case of a price determined under paragraph (2)(A)(iii)) the value added by the processing of the merchandise after importation to the extent that the value is based on sufficient information relating to cost of such processing.

"(B) For purposes of applying paragraph (A)—

"(i) the deduction made for profits and general expenses shall be based upon the importer's profits and general expenses, unless such profits and general expenses are inconsistent with those reflected in sales in the United States of imported merchandise of the same class or kind, in which case the deduction shall be based on the usual profit and general expenses reflected in such sales, as determined from sufficient information; and

"(ii) any State or local tax imposed on the importer with respect to the sale of imported merchandise shall be treated as a general expense.

"(C) The price determined under paragraph (2) shall be increased (but only to the extent that such costs are not otherwise included) by an amount equal to the packing costs incurred by the importer or the buyer, as the case may be, with respect to the merchandise concerned.

"(D) For purposes of determining the deductive value of imported merchandise, any sale to a person who supplies any assist for use in connection with the production or sale for export of the merchandise concerned shall be disregarded.

"(e) COMPUTED VALUE.—(1) The computed value of imported merchandise is the sum of—

"(A) the cost or value of the materials and the fabrication and other processing of any kind employed in the production of the imported merchandise;

"(B) an amount for profit and general expenses equal to that usually reflected in sales of merchandise of the same class or kind as the imported merchandise that are made by the producers in the country of exportation for export to the United States;

"(C) any assist, if its value is not included under subparagraph (A) or (B); and

"(D) the packing costs.

"(2) For purposes of paragraph (1)—

"(A) the cost or value of materials under paragraph (1)(A) shall not include the amount of any internal tax imposed by the country of exportation that is directly applicable to the materials or their disposition if the tax is remitted or refunded upon the exportation of the merchandise in the production of which the materials were used; and

"(B) the amount for profit and general expenses under paragraph (1)(B) shall be based upon the producer's profits and expenses, unless the producer's profits and expenses are inconsistent with those usually reflected in sales of merchandise of the same class or kind as the imported merchandise that are made by producers in the country of exportation for export to the United States, in which case the amount under paragraph (1)(B) shall be based on the usual profit and general expenses of such producers in such sales, as determined from sufficient information.

"(f) VALUE IF OTHER VALUES CANNOT BE DETERMINED OR USED.—

(1) If the value of imported merchandise cannot be determined, or otherwise used for the purposes of this Act, under subsections (b) through (e), the merchandise shall be appraised for the purposes of this Act on the basis of a value that is derived from the methods set forth in such subsections, with such methods being reasonably adjusted to the extent necessary to arrive at a value.

Imported merchandise appraisal

"(2) Imported merchandise may not be appraised, for the purposes of this Act, on the basis of—

"(A) the selling price in the United States of merchandise produced in the United States;

"(B) a system that provides for the appraisement of imported merchandise at the higher of two alternative values;

"(C) the price of merchandise in the domestic market of the country of exportation;

"(D) a cost of production, other than a value determined under subsection (e) for merchandise that is identical merchandise or similar merchandise to the merchandise being appraised;

"(E) the price of merchandise for export to a country other than the United States;

"(F) minimum values for appraisement; or

"(G) arbitrary or fictitious values.

This paragraph shall not apply with respect to the ascertainment, determination, or estimation of foreign market value or United States price under title VII.

Ante, p. 150.

"(g) SPECIAL RULES.—(1) For purposes of this section, the persons specified in any of the following subparagraphs shall be treated as persons who are related:

"(A) Members of the same family, including brothers and sisters (whether by whole or half blood), spouse, ancestors, and lineal descendants.

"(B) Any officer or director of an organization and such organization.

"(C) Any officer or director of an organization and an officer or director of another organization, if each such individual is also an officer or director in the other organization.

"(D) Partners.

"(E) Employer and employee.

"(F) Any person directly or indirectly owning, controlling, or holding with power to vote, 5% or more of the outstanding voting stock or shares of any organization and such organization.

"(G) Two or more persons directly or indirectly controlling, controlled by, or under common control with, any person.

"(2) For purposes of this section, merchandise (including, but not limited to, identical merchandise and similar merchandise) shall be treated as being of the same class or kind as other merchandise if it is within a group or range of merchandise produced by a particular industry or industry sector.

"(3) For purposes of this section, information that is submitted by an importer, buyer, or producer in regard to the appraisement of merchandise may not be rejected by the customs officer concerned on the basis of the accounting method by which that information was prepared, if the preparation was in accordance with generally accepted accounting principles. The term 'generally accepted accounting principles' refers to any generally recognized consensus or substantial authoritative support regarding—

Generally accepted accounting principles.

"(A) which economic resources and obligations should be recorded as assets and liabilities;

"(B) which changes in assets and liabilities should be recorded;

"(C) how the assets and liabilities and changes in them should be measured;

"(D) what information should be disclosed and how it should be disclosed; and

"(E) which financial statements should be prepared.

The applicability of a particular set of generally accepted accounting principles will depend upon the basis on which the value of the merchandise is sought to be established.

"(h) DEFINITIONS.—As used in this section—

"(1)(A) The term 'assist' means any of the following if supplied directly or indirectly, and free of charge or at reduced cost, by the buyer of imported merchandise for use in connection with the production or the sale for export to the United States of the merchandise:

"(i) Materials, components, parts and similar items incorporated in the imported merchandise.

"(ii) Tools, dies, molds, and similar items used in the production of the imported merchandise.

"(iii) Merchandise consumed in the production of the imported merchandise.

"(iv) Engineering, development, artwork, design work, and plans and sketches that are undertaken elsewhere than in the United States and are necessary for the production of the imported merchandise.

"(B) No service or work to which subparagraph (A)(iv) applies shall be treated as an assist for purposes of this section if such service or work—

"(i) is performed by an individual who is domiciled within the United

States;

"(ii) is performed by that individual while he is acting as an employee or agent of the buyer of the imported merchandise; and

"(iii) is incidental to other engineering, development, artwork, design work, or plans or sketches that are undertaken within the United States.

"(C) For purposes of this section, the following apply in determining the value of assists described in subparagraph (A)(iv):

"(i) The value of an assist that is available in the public domain is the cost of obtaining copies of the assist,

"(ii) If the production of an assist occurred in the United States and one or more foreign countries, the value of the assist is the value thereof that is added outside the United States.

"(2) The term 'identical merchandise' means—

"(A) merchandise that is identical in all respects to, and was produced in the same country and by the same person as, the merchandise being appraised; or

"(B) if merchandise meeting the requirements under subparagraph (A) cannot be found (or for purposes of applying subsection (b)(2)(B) (i), regardless of whether merchandise meeting such requirements can be found), merchandise that is identical in all respects to, and was produced in the same country as, but not produced by the same person as, the merchandise being appraised.

Such term does not include merchandise that incorporates or reflects any engineering, development, artwork, design work, or plan or sketch that—

"(I) was supplied free or at reduced cost by the buyer of the merchandise for use in connection with the production or the sale for export to the United States of the merchandise; and

"(II) is not an assist because undertaken within the United States.

"(3) The term 'packing costs' means the cost of all containers and coverings of whatever nature and of packing, whether for labor or materials, used in placing merchandise in condition, packed ready for shipment to the United States.

"(4) The term 'similar merchandise' means—

"(A) merchandise that—

"(i) was produced in the same country and by the same person as the merchandise being appraised,

"(ii) is like the merchandise being appraised in characteristics and component material, and

(iii) is commercially interchangeable with the merchandise being appraised; or

"(B) if merchandise meeting the requirements under subparagraph (A) cannot be found (or for purposes of applying subsection (b)(2)(B)(i), regardless of whether merchandise meeting such requirements can be found), merchandise that—

"(i) was produced in the same country as, but not produced by the same person as, the merchandise being appraised, and

"(ii) meets the requirement set forth in subparagraph (A)(ii) and (iii). Such term does not include merchandise that incorporates or reflects any engineering, development, art work, design work, or plan or sketch that—

"(I) was supplied free or at reduced cost by the buyer of the merchandise for use in connection with the production or the sale for export to the United States of the merchandise; and

"(II) is not an assist because undertaken within the United States.

"(5) The term 'sufficient information', when required under this section for determining—

"(A) any amount—

"(i) added under subsection (b)(1) to the price actually paid or payable,

"(ii) deducted under subsection (d)(3) as profit or general expense or value from further processing, or

"(iii) added under subsection (e)(2) as profit or general expense;

"(B) any difference taken into account for purposes of subsection (b)(2)(C); or

"(C) any adjustment made under susection(c)(2);

means information that establishes the accuracy of such amount, difference, or adjustment."

4 Other Forms

carriers certificate

To the District Director of Customs

______________ (Port of entry) ______________ (Date)

The undersigned carrier, to whom or upon whose order the articles described below or in the attached document must be released,* hereby certifies that ______________ of ______________ is the owner or consignee of such articles within the purview of section 484(h), Tariff Act of 1930.

Marks and number of packages	Description and quantity of merchandise—Number and kind of packages	Gross weight in pounds	Foreign port of landing and date of sailing	Bill of lading number

Carrier ______________ ______________ (Name of carrier)

Voyage No. ______________

Arrived ______________ (Date) ______________ (Agent)

*Under the tariff laws of the United States Customs officers do not deliver the goods to the consignee. The goods are released from Customs custody to or upon the order of the carrier by whom the goods are brought to the port at which they are entered for consumption. When the goods are entered for warehouse, they are released from Customs custody to or upon the order of the proprietor of the warehouse.

Department of the Treasury
U.S. Customs Service
141.32.C.R.

POWER OF ATTORNEY

Check appropriate box
- ☐ **Individual**
- ☐ **Partnership**
- ☐ **Corporation**
- ☐ **Sole Proprietorship**

KNOW ALL MEN BY THESE PRESENTS That ______________ **(Full Name of person, partnership, or corporation, or sole proprietorship (identify)**

a corporation doing business under the laws of the State of ______________ **or a** ______________

doing business as ______________ **residing at** ______________

having an office and place of business at ______________ **hereby constitues and appoints each of the following persons**

______________ **(Give full name of each agent designated)**

as a true and lawful agent and attorney of the grantor named above for and in the name, place and stead of said grantor from this date and in Customs District _____ and in no other name, to make, endorse, sign, declare, or swear to any entry, withdrawal, declaration, certificate, bill of lading, or other document required by law regulation in connection with the importation, transportation, or exportation of any merchandise shipped or consigned by or to said grantor to perform any act or condition which may be required by law or regulation in connection with such merchandise to receive any merchandise deliverable to said grantor.

To make endorsements on bills of lading conferring authority to make entry and collect drawback, and to make, sign, declare, or swear to any statement, supplemental statement, schedule, supplemental schedule, certificate of delivery, certificate of manufacture, certificate of manufacture and delivery, abstract of manufacuring records, declaration of proprietor on drawback entry, declaration of exporter on drawback entry or any other affidavit or document which may be required by law or regulation for drawback purposes, regardless of whether such bill of lading, sworn statement, schedule, certificate, abstract, declaration, or other affidavit or document is intended for filing in said district or in any other customs district.

To sign, seal, and deliver for and as the act of said grantor any bond required by law or regulation in connection with the entry or withdrawal of imported merchandise or merchandise exported with or without benefit of drawback, or in connection with the entry, clearance, lading, unlading or navigation of any vessel or other means of conveyance owned or operated by said grantor, and any and all bonds which may be voluntarily given and accepted under applicable laws and regulations, consignee's and owner's declarations provided for in section 485, Tariff Act of 1930, as amended, or affidavits in connection with the entry of merchandise.

To sign and swear to any document and to perform any act that may be necessary or required by law or regulation in connection with the entering, clearing, lading, unlading, or operation of any vessel or other means of conveyance owned or operated by said grantor.

And generally to transact at the customhouses in said district any and all customs business, including making, signing, and filing of protests under section 514 of the Tariff Act of 1930, in which said grantor is or may be concerned or interested and which may properly be transacted or performed by an agent and attorney, giving to said agent and attorney full power and authority to do anything whatever requisite and necessary to be done in the premises as fully as said grantor could do if present and acting, hereby ratifying and confirming all that the said agent and attorney shall lawfully do by virtue of these presents, the foregoing power of attorney to remain in full force and effect until the _______ day of ______________, 19 _____, or until notice of revocation in writing is duly given to and received by the District Director of Customs of the district aforesaid. If the donor of this power of attorney is a partnership, and said the power shall in no case have any force or effect after the expiration of 2 years from the date of its receipt in the office of the district director of customs of the said district.

IN WITNESS WHEREOF, the said ______________

has caused these presents to be sealed and signed (Signature) ______________

(Capacity) ______________ (Date) ______________

WITNESS ______________ ______________

______________ ______________

(Corporate seal) *(Optional)

Customs Form 5291 (10-07-80)

(SEE OVER)

INDIVIDUAL OR PARTNERSHIP CERTIFICATION *(Optional)

CITY ________ }
COUNTY ________ } ss:
STATE ________ }

On this ________ day of ________ , 19 ____, personally appeared before me ________ residing at ________ , personally known or sufficiently identified to me, who certifies that ________ (is) (are) the individual(s) who executed the foregoing instrument and acknowledge it to be ________ free act and deed.

(Notary Public)

CORPORATE CERTIFICATION *(Optional)

(To be made by an officer other than the one who executes the power of attorney)

I, ________ , certify that I am the ________ of ________ , organized under the laws of the State of ________ that ________ , who signed this power of attorney on behalf of the donor, is the ________ of said corporation; and that said power of attorney was duly signed, sealed, and attested for and behalf of said corporation by authority of its governing body as the name appears in a resolution of the Board of Directors passed at a regular meeting held on the ________ day of ________ , now in my possession or custody. I further certify that the resolution is in accordance with the articles of incorporation and bylaws of said corporation.

IN WITNESS WHEREOF, I have hereunto set my hand and affixed the seal of said corporation, at the City of ________ this ________ day of ________ , 19 ________

(Signature) (Date)

If the corporation has no corporate seal, the fact shall be stated, in which case a scroll or adhesive shall appear in the appropriate, designated place.

Customs powers of attorney of residents (including resident corporations) shall be without power of substitution except for the purpose of executing shipper's export declarations. However, a power of attorney executed in favor of a licensed customhouse broker may specify that the power of attorney is granted to the customhouse broker to act through any of its licensed officers or any employee specifically authorized to act for such customhouse broker by power of attorney.

*NOTE: The corporate seal may be omitted. Customs does not require completion of a certification. The grantor has the option of executing the certification or omitting it.

Note: Side two of CF5291, Power of Attorney, is optional. It is included here for the reader's clarification.

Approved through 4/30/87 OMB No. 1515-0144

1. THIS FORM MUST BE TYPED.
2. DO NOT ALTER THIS FORM.
3. ORIGINAL TO BE SUBMITTED TO CUSTOMS. (See Option explained in Instruction no. 2.)

DEPARTMENT OF THE TREASURY
UNITED STATES CUSTOMS SERVICE

CORPORATE SURETY POWER OF ATTORNEY

CUSTOMS USE ONLY
DATE RECEIVED

☐ GRANT (Instruction No. 3a.) ☐ CHANGE to Grant on file (Instruction No. 3b.) ☐ REVOCATION. The below-described powers previously granted are hereby revoked. (Instruction No. 3c.) | EFFECTIVE DATE

GRANTEE: NAME ☐ This is a name change | ADDRESS ☐ This is an address change
SOCIAL SECURITY NO.

GRANTOR: Surety Company's Corporate Name | Surety No. | State Under Whose laws organized as a surety

District Code(s) for Customs district(s) in which authorized to do business and limit on any single obligation -OR- district(s) being added to the original grant:

District	Limit	District	Limit	District	Limit	District	Limit	District	Limit	District	Limit

Grantor appoints the above-named person (Grantee) as its attorney in fact to sign its name as surety to, and to execute, seal, and acknowledge any bond so as to bind the surety corporation to the same extent as if done by a regularly elected officer, limited only to the extent shown above as to Customs district and amount on any single bond obligation. This grant, or change to a grant on file, or revocation, as specified, shall become active on the effective date shown provided the Customs Form 5297 is received at a district office 5 days before the effective date shown; otherwise the specified action will become active at the close of business 5 working days after the date of receipt at the district office.

In witness whereof, the said Grantor, by virtue of authority conferred by its Board of Directors, has caused these presents to be sealed with its corporate seal and attested by any two principal officers.	Date Attested Use a facsimile of corporate seal, and not impression seal.	Name and Title SIGNATURE	Name and Title SIGNATURE

Customs Form 5297 (113083)

Approved through 01/31/91
OMB No. 1515-0144

DEPARTMENT OF THE TREASURY
UNITED STATES CUSTOMS SERVICE

CUSTOMS BOND

19 CFR Part 113

CUSTOMS USE ONLY	BOND NUMBER[1] (Assigned by Customs)
	FILE REFERENCE

In order to secure payment of any duty, tax or charge and compliance with law or regulation as a result of activity covered by any condition referenced below, we, the below named principal(s) and surety(ies), bind ourselves to the United States in the amount or amounts, as set forth below.

Execution Date

SECTION I — Select Single Transaction **OR** Continuous Bond (not both) and fill in the applicable blank spaces.

☐ **SINGLE TRANSACTION BOND**	Identification of transaction secured by this bond (e.g., entry no., seizure no., etc.)	Date of transaction	Transaction district & port code
☐ **CONTINUOUS BOND**	Effective date	This bond remains in force for one year beginning with the effective date and for each succeeding annual period, or until terminated. This bond constitutes a separate bond for each period in the amounts listed below for liabilities that accrue in each period. The intention to terminate this bond must be conveyed within the time period and manner prescribed in the Customs Regulations.	

SECTION II — This bond includes the following agreements.[2] (Check one box only, except that, 1a may be checked independently or with 1, and 3a may be checked independently or with 3. Line out all other parts of this section that are not used.)

Activity Code	Activity Name and Customs Regulations in which conditions codified	Limit of Liability	Activity Code	Activity Name and Customs Regulations in which conditions codified	Limit of Liability
☐ 1	Importer or broker 113.62		☐ 5	Public Gauger 113.67	
☐ 1a	Drawback Payment Refunds 113.65		☐ 6	Wool & Fur Products Labeling Acts Importation (Single Entry Only) 113.68	
☐ 2	Custodian of bonded merchandise......113.63 (Includes bonded carriers, freight forwarders, cartmen and lightermne, all classes of warehouses, container station operators)		☐ 7	Bill of Lading (Single Entry Only).............113.69	
			☐ 8	Detention of Copyrighted Material (Single Entry Only) 113.70	
☐ 3	International Carrier.............................113.64		☐ 9	Neutrality (Single Entry Only)...................113.71	
☐ 3a	Instruments of International Traffic...113.66				
☐ 4	Foreign Trade Zone Operator 113.73		☐ 10	Court Costs for Condemned Goods (Single Entry Only)..................................113.72	

SECTION III — List below all tradenames or unincorporated divisions that will be permitted to obligate this bond in the principal's name including their Customs Identification Number(s).[3] (If more space is needed, use Section III(Continuation) on back of form.)

Importer Number	Importer Name	Importer Number	Importer Name

Total number of importer names listed in Section III:

Principal and surety agree that any charge against the bond under any of the listed names is as though it was made by the principal(s).

Principal and surety agree that they are bound to the same extent as if they executed a separate bond covering each set of conditions incorporated by reference to the Customs Regulations into this bond.

If the surety fails to appoint an agent under Title 6, United States Code, Section 7, surety consents to service on the Clerk of any United States District Court of the U.S. Court of International Trade, where suit is brought on this bond. That clerk is to send notice of the service to the surety at:

Mailing Address Requested by the Surety

PRINCIPAL[4]	Name and Address	Importer No.[3] / SIGNATURE[5]	SEAL
PRINCIPAL[4]	Name and Address	Importer No.[3] / SIGNATURE[5]	SEAL
SURETY[4, 6]	Name and Address[6]	Surety No.[7] / SIGNATURE[5]	SEAL
SURETY[4, 6]	Name and Address[6]	Surety No.[7] / SIGNATURE[5]	SEAL

SURETY AGENTS	Name[8]	Identification No.[9]	Name[8]	Identification No.[9]

PART 1—U.S. CUSTOMS

Customs Form 301 (092189)

Note: Turn carbons over before writing on back of form.

SECTION III (Continuation)

Importer Number	Importer Name	Importer Number	Importer Name

WITNESSES

Two witnesses are required to authenticate the signature of any person who signs as an individual or as a partner; however, a witness may authenticate the signatures of both such non-corporate principals and sureties. No witness is needed to authenticate the signature of a corporate official or agent who signs for the corporation.

SIGNED, SEALED, and DELIVERED in the PRESENCE OF:

Name and Address of Witness for the Principal	Name and Address of Witness for the Surety
SIGNATURE:	SIGNATURE:
Name and Address of Witness for the Principal	Name and Address of Witness for the Surety
SIGNATURE:	SIGNATURE:

EXPLANATIONS AND FOOTNOTES

1. The Customs Bond Number is a control number assigned by Customs to the bond contract when the bond is approved by an authorized Customs official.
2. For all bond coverage available and the language of the bond conditions refer to Part 113, subpart G, Customs Regulations.
3. The Importer Number is the Customs identification number filed pursuant to section 24.5, Customs Regulations. When the Internal Revenue Service employer identification number is used the two-digit suffix code must be shown.
4. If the principal or surety is a corporation, the name of the State in which incorporated must be shown.
5. See witness requirement above.
6. Surety Name, if a corporation, shall be the company's name as it is spelled in the Surety Companies Annual List published in the Federal Register by the Department of the Treasury (Treasury Department Circular 570).
7. Surety Number is the three digit identification code assigned by Customs to a surety company at the time the surety company initially gives notice to Customs that the company will be writing Customs bonds.
8. Surety Agent is the individual granted a Corporate Surety Power of Attorney, CF 5297, by the surety company executing the bond.
9. Agent Identification No. shall be the individual's Social Security number as shown on the Corporate Surety Power of Attorney, CF 5297, filed by the surety granting such power of attorney.

Paperwork Reduction Act Notice. The Paperwork Reduction Act of 1980 says we must tell you why we are collecting this information, how we will use it and whether you have to give it to us. We ask for this information to carry out the U.S. Customs Service laws of the United States. We need it to ensure that persons transacting business with Customs have the proper bond coverage to secure their transactions as required by law and regulation. Your response is required to enter into any transaction in which a bond is a prerequisite under the Tariff Act of 1930, as amended.

Privacy Act Statement: The following notice is given pursuant to section 7(b) of the Privacy Act of 1974 (5 U.S.C. 552a). Furnishing the information on this form, including the Social Security Number, is mandatory. The primary use of the Social Security Number is to verify, in the Customs Automated System, at the time an agent submits a Customs bond for approval that the individual was granted a Corporate Surety Power of Attorney by the surety company. Section 7 of Act of July 30, 1947, chapter 390, 61 Stat. 646, authorizes the collection of this information.

Statement Required by 5 CFR 1320.21: The estimated average burden associated with this collection of information is 0.25 hours per respondent or recordkeeper depending on individual circumstances. Comments concerning the accuracy of this burden estimate and suggestions for reducing this burden should be directed to U.S. Customs Service, Paperwork Management Branch, Washington DC 20229, and to the Office of Management and Budget, Paperwork Reduction Project (1515-0144), Washington, DC 20503.

Customs Form 301 (092189) (Back)

DEPARTMENT OF THE TREASURY
UNITED STATES CUSOMS SERVICE

ENTRY SUMMARY

Form Approved OMB No. 1515-0065

(1) Entry No.	(2) Entry Type Code	3. Entry Summary Date
4. Entry Date	(5) Port Code	
6. Bond No.	7. Bond Type Code	8. Broker / Importer File No.

9. Ultimate Consignee Name and Address	10. Consignee No.	(11) Importer of Record Name and Address	(12) Importer No.
		(13) Exporting Country	14. Export Date
		(15) Country of Origin	16. Missing Documents
	State	(17) I.T. No.	(18) I.T. Date
(19) B/L or AWB No.	20. Mode of Transportation	21. Manufacturer I.D.	22. Reference No.
(23) Importing Carrier	24. Foreign Port of Lading	25. Location of Goods / G.O. No.	
26. U.S. Port of Unlading	(27) Import Date		

(28) Line No.	(29) Description of Merchandise: 30. (A.) T.S.U.S.A. No. B. ADA/CVD Case No.	31. (A.) Gross Weight B. Manifest Qty.	(32) Net Quantity in T.S.U.S.A. Units	33. (A.) Entered Value B. CHGS C. Relationship	34. (A.) T.S.U.S.A. Rate B. ADA/CVD Rate (C.) I.R.C. Rate D. Visa No.	(35) Duty and I.R. Tax: Dollars	Cents

(36) Declaration of Importer of Record (Owner or Purchaser) or Authorized Agent

I declare that I am the
☐ importer of record and that the actual owner, purchaser, or consignee for customs purposes is as shown above. OR ☐ owner or purchaser or agnet thereof

I further declare that the merchandise
☐ was obtained pursuant to a purchase or agreement to purchase and that the prices set forth in the invoice are true. OR ☐ was not obtained pursuant to a purchase or agreement to purchase and the statements in the invoice as to value or pirce are true to the best of my knowledge and belief

I also declare that the statements in the documents herein filed fully disclose to the best of my knowledge and belief the true prices, values, quantities, rebates, drawbacks, fees, commissions, and royalties and are true and correct, and that all goods or services provided to the seller of the merchandise either free or at reduced cost are fully disclosed. I will immediately furnish to the appropriate customs officer any information showing a different state of facts.

Notice required by Paperwork Reduction Act of 1980: This information is needed to ensure that importers/exporters are complying with U.S. customs laws, to allow us to compute and collect the right amount of money, to enforce other agency requirements, and to collect accurate statistical information on imports. Your response is mandatory. (Continued on back of form.)

U.S. CUSTOMS USE		TOTALS	
A. Liq. Code	B. Ascertained Duty	(37) Duty	
	C. Ascertained Tax	(38) Tax	
	D. Ascertained Other	(39) Other	
	E. Ascertained Total	(40) Total	

(41) Signature of Declarant, Title, and Date

Customs Form 7501 (081790)

Notes:

Notes:

Packing, Shipping, Insurance Contents

Benefits and Opportunities of Efficient Container Packing

Material for this section on container packaging has been provided by Hapag-Lloyd AG. World Trade Press gratefully acknowledges this contribution.

You will really gain from taking extra care when stowing your products into a container:

- By saving yourself worry and expense, since your goods will reach your customer in good condition.
- By cutting transport costs for land transport and on commodity box rates, for instance, which are charged irrespective of utilization.
- By saving time and stowage material thanks to properly prepared and expert measures for ensuring safety of your goods.
- By preserving your good reputation for reliable deliveries of goods in perfect condition.

Smoothly executed container operations will ensure that you enjoy a competitive edge over your competitors. One important essential here is "correct" stowing, on which we aim to assist you with this brief manual. The facts conveyed in the manual are based on the experience and knowledge of cargo superintendents and stowage advisors as well as analysis of cargo damages.

However, this manual will not be able to answer all your questions. Whenever you need advice or information for your shipments, your Hapag-Lloyd Sales Office or your Hapag-Lloyd Agent in Europe or overseas will put you into immediate contact with an experienced stowage advisor.

Preparation for Container Transports

General Rules for Packing Containers

Goods of the following nature are not to be packed together

- Dusty goods not together with dust sensitive goods.
- Odor emitting goods not together with odor sensitive goods.
- Goods/packaging giving off moisture not together with moisture sensitive goods/packaging.
- Heavy parcels not to be placed on light parcels.
- Goods with protruding parts, sharp edges or corners not together with goods in comparatively soft packaging (e.g. sacks or bales).
- Wet goods not together with dry goods.
- If joint packing cannot be avoided, put the wet goods below the dry ones and separate them by dunnage. Place additional dunnage or sawdust under the wet goods.

As a general rule

Separate different types of packaging effectively from each other (e.g. cardboard boxes and wooden crates).

Do not ship goods with damaged packaging, but repair the packaging carefully before packing.

For especially sensitive goods, line the container with paper or foil.

When packing goods sensitive to odor, the container must be odorless. Should this not be the case, the container should be washed out. Any remaining odors can be neutralized by using an industrial deodorant.

When packing odorous cargo or cargo that might damage the container through leakage, you should line it with foil and add absorbent materials (such as peat moss, sawdust, silica gel). In this way you can avoid unnecessarily costly cleaning expenses.

Please inform us when shipping loose scrap metal or ore in containers. We will advise you about packing and unpacking methods that help you to avoid damage to the containers and thus save you trouble and expense.

Mixed stow of wet and dry commodities.

Weight Limits and Weight Distribution

The weight limits of the Hapag-Lloyd containers correspond to the norm ISO 668:

Permissible gross weights:

20' containers 24,000 kg (52,910 lbs)

40' containers 30,480 kg (67,200 lbs)

According to the 1985 change of the norm the permissible gross weight of most Hapag-Lloyd 20' containers is 30,480 kg (67,200 lbs).

The *technically maximum payload* results from the permissible gross weight minus tare of the container and can vary depending on the constructional series of the container. (You will find more precise details in our brochure "Container Specification.")

Apart from the constructionally defined load capacity of the container, the permissible weight limits of road and rail transport in the respective countries must be considered. Details about the possibilities of and restrictions on carrying out land transport overseas can be obtained from our Hapag-Lloyd Sales Offices and Hapag-Lloyd Agents.

If the permissible load is used to the full, all bottom cross member should be used for load support since the floors of containers are not suited for point loads. The bottom cross members are the load bearing elements taking the cargo pressure off the floor.

In order to avoid overloading when planning the packing of the container, the *line load* should be calculated by the following rule of thumb. The line load corresponds to the cargo weight in relation to the load transfer area of the cargo in longitudinal direction of the container. (Example: a load with a weight of 10 t with a load transfer length of 4 m (13'2") has a line load of 10 : 4 m (13'2") = 2.5 t/m (0.76 t/ft). The line load must not exceed the following limits:

for 20' containers: 4.5 t/m (1.37 t/ft)

for 40' containers: 3.0 t/m (0.91 t/ft).

Thus a relatively heavy piece of cargo or a cargo unit with a small load transfer area must be loaded in such a way that the load bearing area is increased in order to stay within the permissible floor loading limits. This may be done through dunnage (layered in alternate directions, the lowest layer lengthwise) or by using a "sled" the skids of which are orientated container lengthwise. When arranging the skids or the battens on the container floor, the following should be taken into account:

Timber dunnage used for load distribution must have a certain minimum width and lateral distance from the center-line of the container, because of the construction of a Standard Container's floors (above).

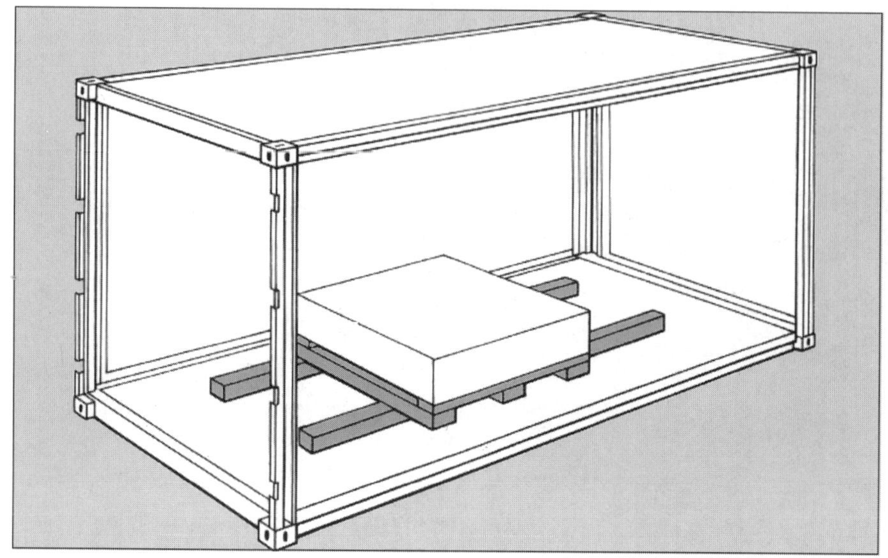

The load bearing area is increased with dunnage layered in alternate directions.

Type of container	20′	40′
A. width of timber-dunnage minimum	0.10 m (4")	0.15 m (6")
B. lateral distance of the timber-dunnage from the container center line minimum to each side	0.4 m (1'4")	0.4 m (1'4")

If a parcel exceeds this weight limit, please make use of our heavy duty Flats and Platforms; these are built with a special reinforced floor construction. (Platforms are in principle used only for ocean transport). Our stowage advisors are at your disposal at any time and can show you how to take advantage of container transport, even in borderline cases.

In order to enable containers to be packed by forklift truck, all Hapag-Lloyd containers meet the ISO-Recommendation 1496/1. This means that any forklift truck can drive into a container if the following limits are not exceeded:

Front axle load (payload + tare)	5,460 kg (12,000 lbs)
Contact area per wheel	142 cm^2 (22 sq. in)
Width of wheel	ca. 180 mm (7")
Width of track	ca. 760 mm (30")

Containers can be packed with forklift trucks, which do not exceed certain weights and are equipped with a suitable telescopic mast.

The cargo weight distribution within the container should be balanced, i.e. the cargo's centre of gravity should fall within the following limits:

Type of container	20'	40'
Longitudinal direction	maxim. + 0.60 m	maxim + 0.90 m
	from the centre of the container	
Transverse direction	in the center of the container	
Height	at or below the center of gravity of the container	

All Hapag-Lloyd containers meet the test requirements laid down in the ISO Norm 1496/1 for the load strength of side walls, front walls, doors and roof:

Construction element	Test load
Side walls	0.6 times the weight of the max. payload
Front wall and doors	0.4 times the weight of the max. payload
Roof	300 kg (660 lbs) for a surface of 600 x 300 mm (24" x 12")*

* This corresponds approximately to the weight of two persons working on the roof.

Asymmetrical weight distribution in a container requires special measures during transport and handling.

Stowage Plan

There are three main reasons for producing a stowage plan prior to packing a container:

- To achieve optimal utilization of the container's capacity.
- To simplify and increase the speed of packing and unpacking.
- To plan for necessary cargo securing aids well in advance.

For the stowage planning you require precise details of

- exact weights and measurements of the cargo to be loaded and its packaging,
- exact inside dimensions and permissible load limits of the containers. (Please ask for the Hapag-Lloyd brochure "Container-Specification.")

Prior to producing the stowage plan, you should select the container type which is best suited to your shipment. Your Hapag-Lloyd Sales Office or your Hapag-Lloyd Agent will gladly provide you with information about the broad range of Hapag-Lloyd special containers, as will our brochure "Container Specification." (You will find details of our worldwide sales network in our monthly schedule as well as in our "List of Agents.")

When selecting the type of container and producing the stowage plan, you should take account of

- the load limits of the container
- the load limits for inland transport in both the shipper's and consignee's country
- the weight distribution within the container
- the facilities available to the consignee to unpack the container.

Our sales offices and agents will gladly assist you in all these matters.

For the production of a stowage plan use a drawing of the container from the top and from the side (on draft paper), drawn to scale. Draw the pieces to be packed to scale or alternatively cut them out of the paper (again to scale) and lay them on the plan.

If this procedure seems too troublesome, you can also pre-stow your cargo in a rectangle which has been drawn in chalk or paint corresponding in size to the container.

Two further important items

Please note that the inside dimensions of door (and roof) openings are normally smaller than the inside dimensions of the container. You achieve an optimal utilization of the available space if the parcel sizes are divisible of the internal container dimensions given, e.g. for an inner width of the container of 2.31 m (7'7"), it is advantageous to put four cartons of 0.56 m (1'10") next to each other; 4 x 0.56 m (1'10") = 2.24 m (7'4"), i.e. only 0.08 m (3") unused.

Cartons of 0.61 m (2') width are highly disadvantageous since a lot of space is wasted; 3 x 0.61 m (2') = 1.83 m (6'), i.e. 0.48m (1'7") unused.

To prepare the packing of a container either a stowage plan can be drawn to scale... (upper photo)

... or the goods can be pre-stowed on an area of container size (lower photo).

Container Check Prior to Packing

Every container used on international routes must bear a valid CSC Safety Approval plate, as provided for in the International Convention on Safe Containers of December 2, 1972. All Hapag-Lloyd Containers are fitted with the plate.

In order to ensure that you receive only containers in sound conditions, we check all containers arriving or leaving port terminals or inland depots.

However, in addition to this inspection, we recommend that you always carry out a careful check of the container to prevent possible later damage to cargo.

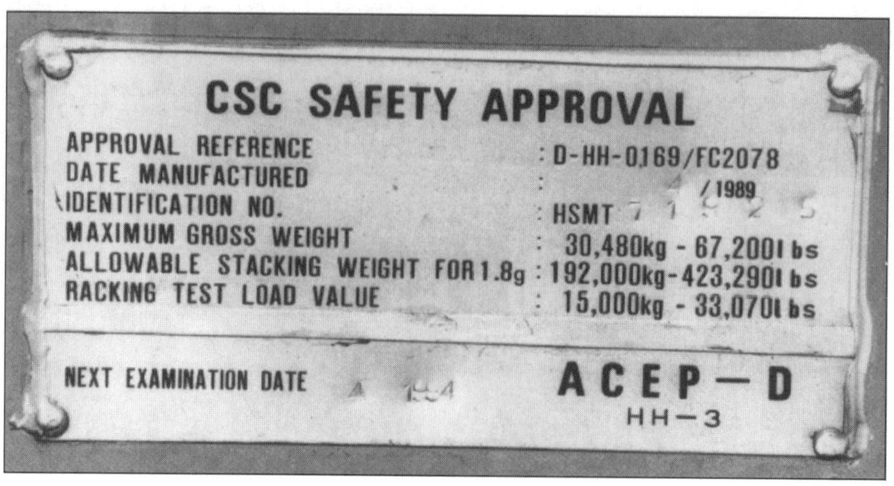

You will find this label on the inside of container doors.

Checklist (external)

1. No hole or cracks in walls and roof.
2. Doors can be easily operated.
3. Locking roods and handles function properly.
4. No placards/labels, e.g. IMO-placards, remain from the previous cargo.

Special containers

5. For Flats:

   Stanchions (if ordered) are complete and inserted properly.
6. For Open Top Containers:

   Roof bows are completed and inserted properly.
7. For Open Top Containers:

   Tarpaulins are undamaged and the right size, tarpaulin rope ends are undamaged.
8. For Hard Top Containers:

   The roof is undamaged, the roof fastening fits properly and is accessible.

Checklist (internal)

9. Container is waterproof

   Test method: stand inside the container, close both doors tightly and examine for any light coming through cracks, holes, door gaskets, etc.
10. Container is absolutely dry inside.

    Should there be any sweat water or hoar-frost, wipe this away so as to prevent any corrosion damage to cargo.
11. Container is clean, free of dirt and cargo residue and odorless.
12. No nails or other protruding objects that might damage cargo are present.

Please inform your Hapag-Lloyd Sales Office or Hapag-Lloyd Agent immediately of any defects so that they can ensure that you are provided with a sound container.

Attention!

Before loading the shipper must check the proper condition of the container. By accepting the container the shipper recognizes its suitability for the loading of the cargo to be carried

Furthermore, attention is drawn to the fact that the consignee is obliged to return the container after discharging clean and suitable for the transport of every kind of cargo.

This applies especially when poisonous, dangerous or obnoxious cargo has been transported.

All labels referring to cargo shall be removed.

In case of doubt please contact the next Hapag-Lloyd Representative.

Container Check After Packing

We recommend that after packing you verify, that the following checklist items have been fulfilled:

1. The container was loaded taking into account:
   - type of cargo
   - strains during transport
   - characteristics of the container.
2. A copy of the packing list is fixed at an easily visible position inside the container, for possible customs checks.
3. When shipping goods in wooden packaging to Australia or New Zealand:

   A copy of the certificate issued by the appropriate agricultural authority stating that the wood used has been treated according to the quarantine regulations must be displayed in a prominent position inside the container.
4. Doors and, in case of open top containers, hardtop or tarpaulin are carefully locked. (Strong steel wire, padlocks or High Security Seals offer protection against pilferage.)
5. The door handles are secured by seals to reduce the risk of pilferage (please note seal numbers!). Upon request we can supply you with Hapag-Lloyd seals.
6. For Open Top Containers:

   The tarpaulins and the tarpaulin ropes are correctly fixed (meeting customs requirements).
7. If cargo in special containers is covered with tarpaulins:

   Ensure the tarpaulins are securely fastened.
8. Old placards are removed.
9. For Reefer Containers with refrigeration unit and heatable Tank Containers ensure the correct temperature has been set. The temperature recorder of the Reefer Unit is running so that temperatures are constantly noted.

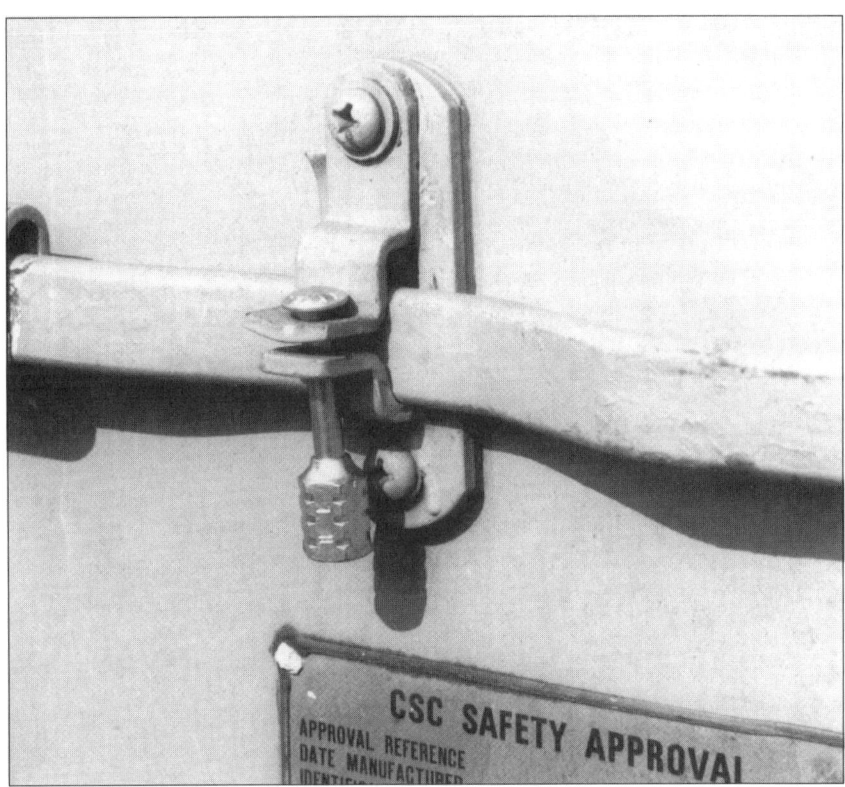

A properly sealed door reduces the risk of pilferage (above and below).

Strains Caused by Container Transports

Mechanical Strains

In order to enable you to judge which cargo securing measures are effective and will prevent possible damage, a summary of the mechanical strains to which your cargo may be exposed may be useful.

In door-to-door transport, the container is packed at the shipper's premises and is not unpacked until it arrives at the consignee's. In contrast to conventional break bulk transport, during the entire transport only the container itself is handled and not each package separately.

The cargo securing done by the shipper must withstand strains resulting from sea and land transport as well as from container handling. The sealed container rules out any visual inspection of the cargo within. No stowage corrections can be effected once packing has been done.

Basically, a distinction needs to be drawn between strains of two types:

Static strains are caused by storage and stacking. In the main, these arise from stacking pressure and the resultant bending and folding strains on the bottom layers of cargo. Stacking pressure depends on the dimensions and weights of the items stacked and the height of the stack.

Dynamic strains occur during loading of the container, during sea or land transport and during handling.

With dynamic strains, a distinction is made between jolts (accelerations) and vibrations.

Jolts (accelerations) occur during loading, when braking and on bends, when a container is set down, during shunting, during handling, and are also caused by the rolling, pitching, lurching and plunging of a ship at sea.

Vibrations occur in all forms of transport. These are caused by the engine, gearbox, transmission, suspension and road surface, etc.

So as to give you an outline of the strains involved in different means of transport, we have reprinted two tables from the brochure "Transport Chain 40" published by the Study Group for Combined Transport.

Type of transport	Vibrations up to max. Hz.	Normal vibration range Hz.	Max. Acceleration g.
Rail transport	800	16–350	1,0 *
Road transport	500		
– truck with conventional suspension		10– 20	4,0
– trailer with conventional suspention		10– 20	4,5
truck with pneumatic suspension		10– 20	0,4
trailer with pneumatic suspension		10– 20	1,5
saddle trailer with conventional suspension		10– 20	1,5
Air transport	3000	60–400	0,6
Seaborne transport	700	0,1– 10 **	1,3
Container handling	160	bis 5	0,4 ***

* 1,0 g with 16 Hz. filtering

** 0,05 – 0,1 Hz. during rolling and pitching

*** This rate declines with higher frequencies, so that at 160 Hz. it is no more than 0,05 g

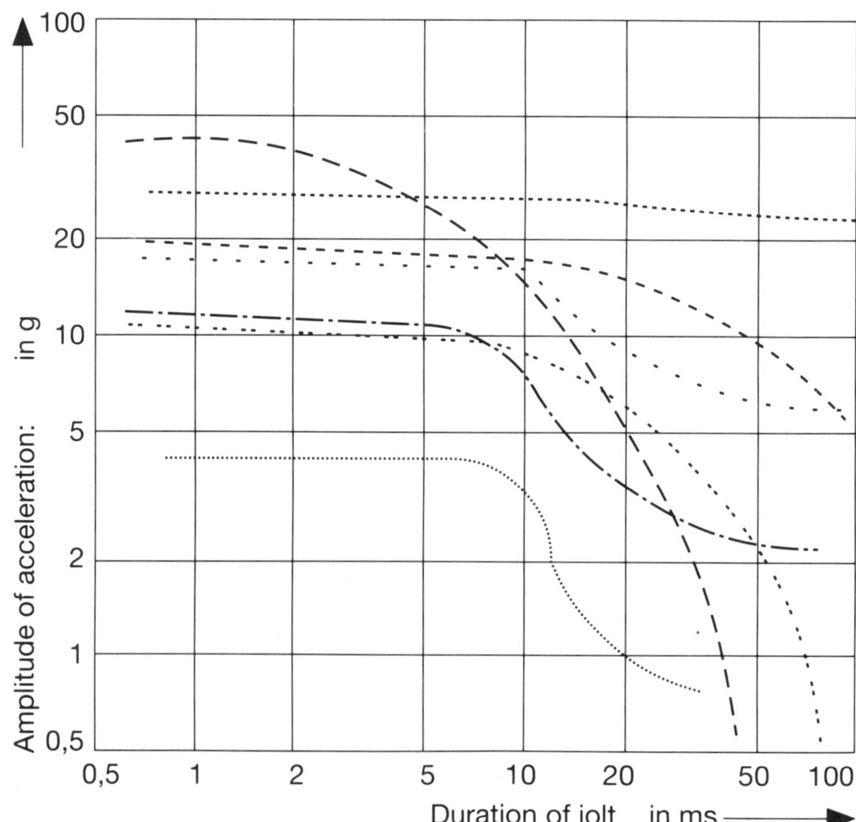

Jolt strain on load surfaces:

- -- -- -- -- rail wagon
- .... Boeing 707 F
- –·—·— truck, pneumatic suspension
- · – – – – – trailer, ditto
- · · · · · truck, conventional suspension
- .... trailer, ditto
- — — — container handling

Jolt strains
(no reliable, generally applicable data are available in respect of shipping)

Since it is normally not possible to know in advance the accelerations likely to affect a container during a forthcoming voyage, one can only work by rule of thumb. In this context, please see the figures to the right (gravitational acceleration g = 9.81 m/s^2).

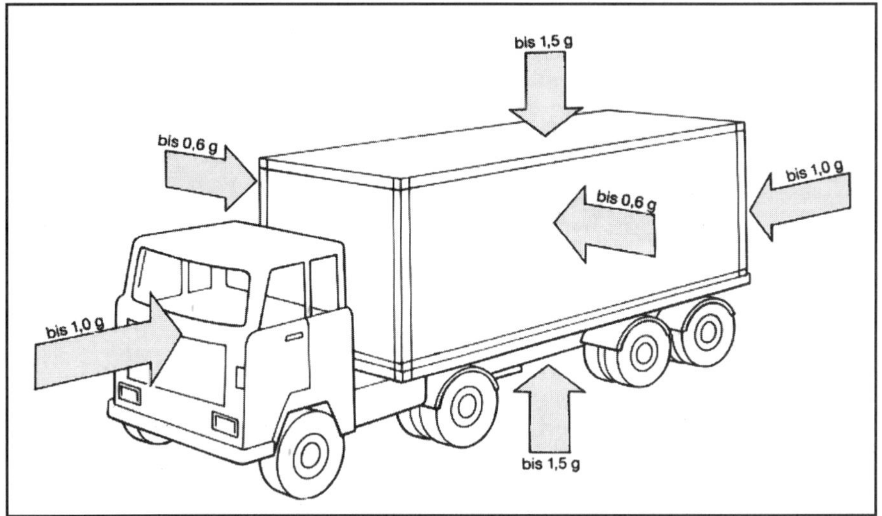

Potential jolting (acceleration) during truck transport.

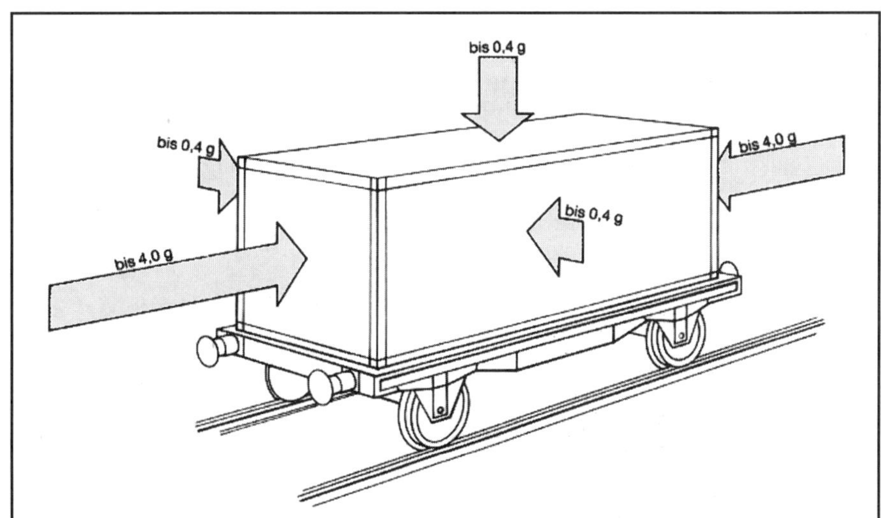

Potential jolting (acceleration) during rail transport.

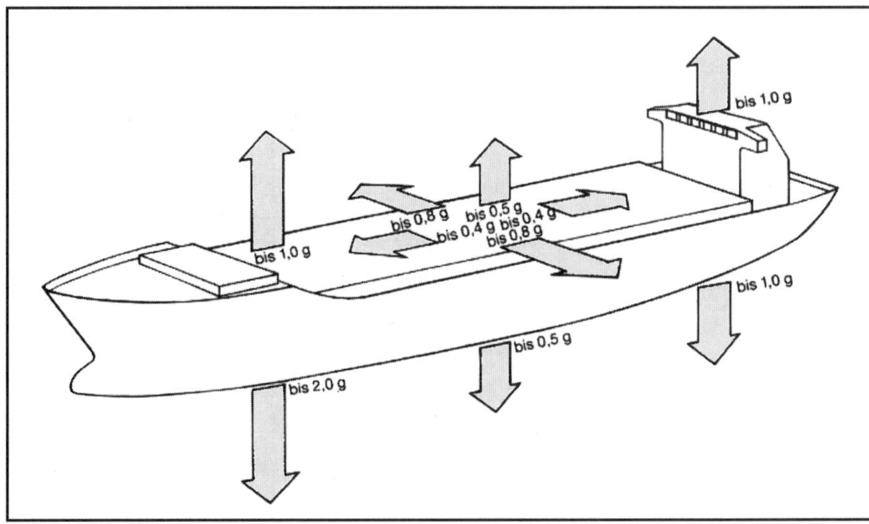

Potential jolting (acceleration) during sea transport.

Climatic Strains

Goods to be shipped are often subject to considerable climatic strains. These already commence during storage and continue during container packing. The strains are caused by being exposed to very disparate climatic zones during transport by truck, rail or barge; during loading, and most especially, during ocean transport. Extreme climatic strains are caused by shipment in winter at below-zero temperatures and transport into or through the tropics and also by transport from the latter into colder regions.

All closed containers protect the cargo from external climatic influences such as rain, snow, sea water, salt water spray, dust and sun radiation (heat and UV radiation).

Although the cargo is protected against external influences, condensation may occur inside the container. The containers are closed waterproof after packing. Thus the relative humidity inside the container is determined by the temperature and air humidity at the time of packing. Furthermore, it depends on the humidity of the cargo and its packaging. The relative humidity inside the container thus changes according to the changes in temperature.

Condensation may occur when a drop in temperature coincides with a source of humidity inside the container.

During a voyage to the Far East following results were obtained:

But even in port considerable differences between outside and inside temperature may occur!

The following differences to outside temperature are possible:

- in the temperate zone
  directly under the roof 20°C/68°F
  inside the container 10°C/50°F
- in the subtropical and tropical zone directly under the roof 30°C/86°F

Temperature variations may not only result from changing outside temperatures, but also through spontaneous heating of the cargo.

Sources of humidity may be:

- cargo itself
- dunnage
- packaging
- air entrapped during packing.

In particular, moisture condensing on the container walls, roof and on the packages or dripping from the roof onto the cargo may cause the following damage:

- rust
- mould
- stains and discolorations
- caking together of wet cartons
- removal of labels
- collapse of the stow.

Measuring point	Temperature in °C		Relative humidity in %	
	Max.	Min.	Max.	Min.
Outside atmosphere	31.5 89°F	1.5 35°F	99	45
Container				
– on deck	42.0 108°F	4.5 40°F	82	51
– under deck	33.0 91°F	15.5 60°F	75	38

Securing Cargo

General Rules for Securing Cargo

The contents of a container must be secured against shifts towards all sides, and especially towards the door.

Gaps between packages and/or container sides must be filled. To secure the cargo, the possibilities for lashing offered by the longitudinal rails on the floor and roof should be used.

Whenever packing a container or securing a cargo, attention should be paid to the Guidelines for Packing and Securing Cargoes in Containers for Transport by Land or by Sea (Container Packing Guidelines) issued by the International Maritime Organization (IMO) and the International Labour Organisation (ILO) on March 27, 1987.

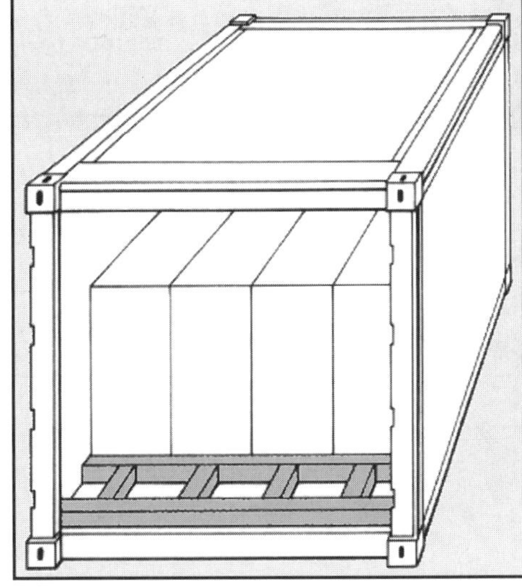

Securing of goods towards the door at the corner posts or in the corrugation of the side walls. For low profile corrugations the front ends of the square timbers must be adapted to the shape of the channels.

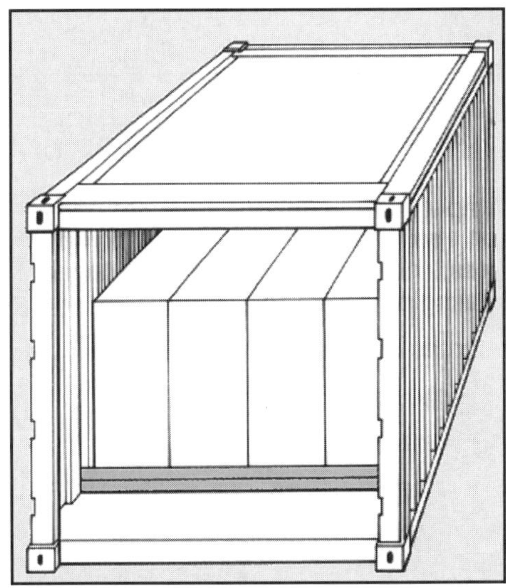

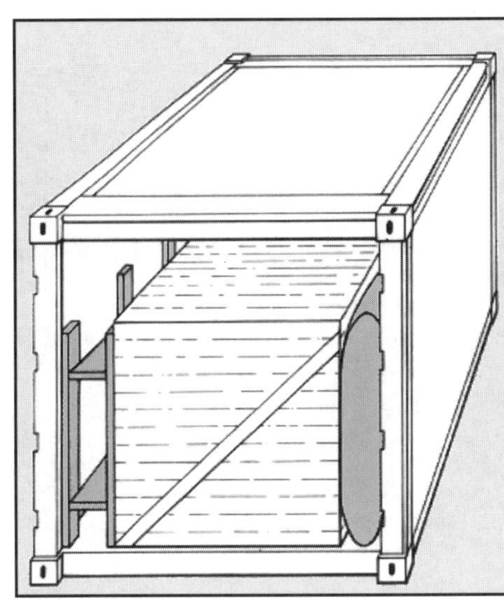

A crate is braced against the corner posts and with large bearing-surfaces against the side walls (either with dunnage—left side —or with air bags —right side).

Securing Facilities within the Container

You may use the following construction elements of a Hapag-Lloyd container for securing the cargo:

Construction element	Cargo securing
Lashing bars on corner posts, roof and floor longitudinal rails or bull rings in the floor	For the fastening of ropes, plastic ribbons, metal hoops, quick fasteners, etc.
Corrugated steel walls	For cargo securing in longitudinal direction transverse square timbers can be fitted into the recesses.
Corner posts	Suitable for the distribution of extreme point loads, e.g. by shoring.
Wooden container floor	Securing by timber connectors. Nailing.

Side and front walls as well as the doors can only take large surface loads, and are unsuited for point loads. For load limits of the walls see "Weight Limits and Weight Distribution" on page 260.

Cargo Securing Aids

Stowage aids / Utilization	Bracing and load distribution	Securing cargo in sections	Filling out gaps	Loading in several layers	Separating different goods	Securing cargo at lashing points	Fixing pallets and sledges with wooden blocks	Increasing friction
Wooden beams & planks Blocks Dunnage Stowage grids	■	■	■	■	■			
Empty pallets Air bags	■	■	■		■			
Empty packages	■		■		■			■
Intermediate decks and walls	■	■		■	■			
Nets		■				■		
Timber connectors							■	
Plastic foam/Corrugated cardboard			■					
Used tires			■					
Ropes						■		■
Wire Bands Steel straps Plastic straps Chains Nylon straps Hercules Span sets						■		
Plastic mats Sisal mats Sacks Rough paper Anti-slipping spray Gum mat								■

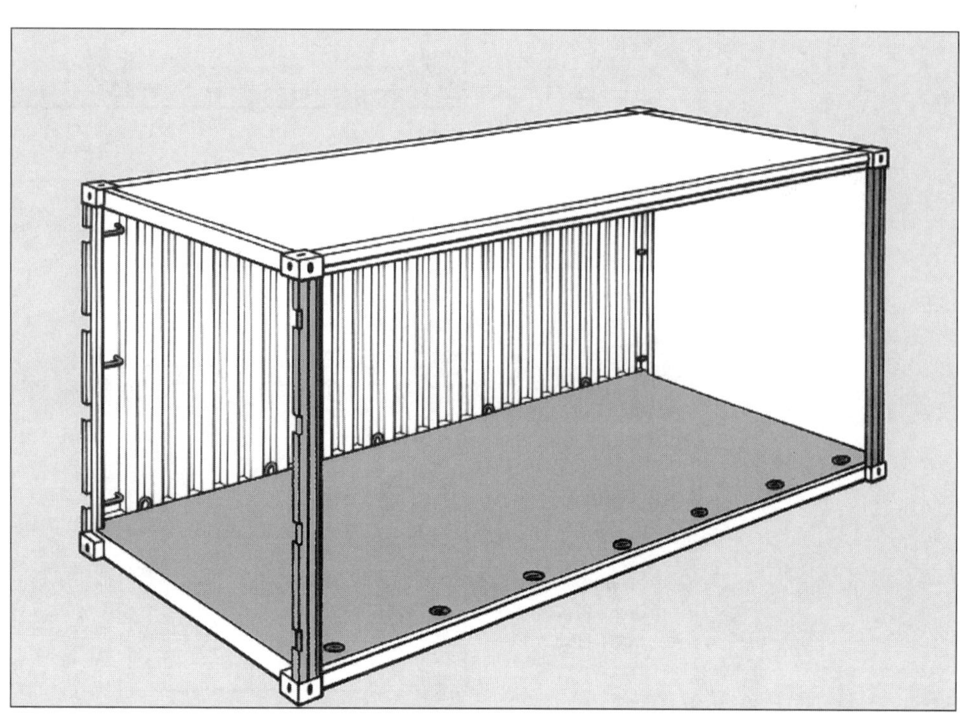

The containers are equipped with lashing bars and/or bull rings depending on constructional series.

Climatic Protection

Packaging of Goods

Export packaging has five functions:

- to protect the goods
- to keep them storable
- to make them transportable
- to ensure that they can be handled and
- to provide information on the cargo and its handling.

These functions must also be fulfilled when goods are transported in containers. Whether and to what extent packaging (and hence packaging costs) can be saved by transport in containers depends among other things on the cargo and the transport:

When packing a container with cargo in different types of packaging, the strains on these are greater than would be the case with cargo in uniform packaging.

If the container contains several layers on top of each other, the lowest layer must be capable of supporting the upper ones. The required stacking strength depends on the packaging material, transport duration and humidity conditions.

Door-to-door transport offers the greatest savings in packaging costs since the parcels remain in the protective container during the entire transport. They are directly affected only during packing and unpacking of the container. Under certain circumstances door-to-door transport enables cargo to be shipped without casing (e.g. for some types of machines and vehicles).

If during certain stages of the transport the cargo is handled "conventionally," i.e. unprotected by a container, its packaging must be able to withstand the strains of conventional handling.

Some special containers act in part as packaging and hence reduce packaging requirements (e.g. Reefer and Bulk Containers).

Loading of an unpacked engine for door-to-door transport (right).

Seaworthy packaging of machinery parts (below).

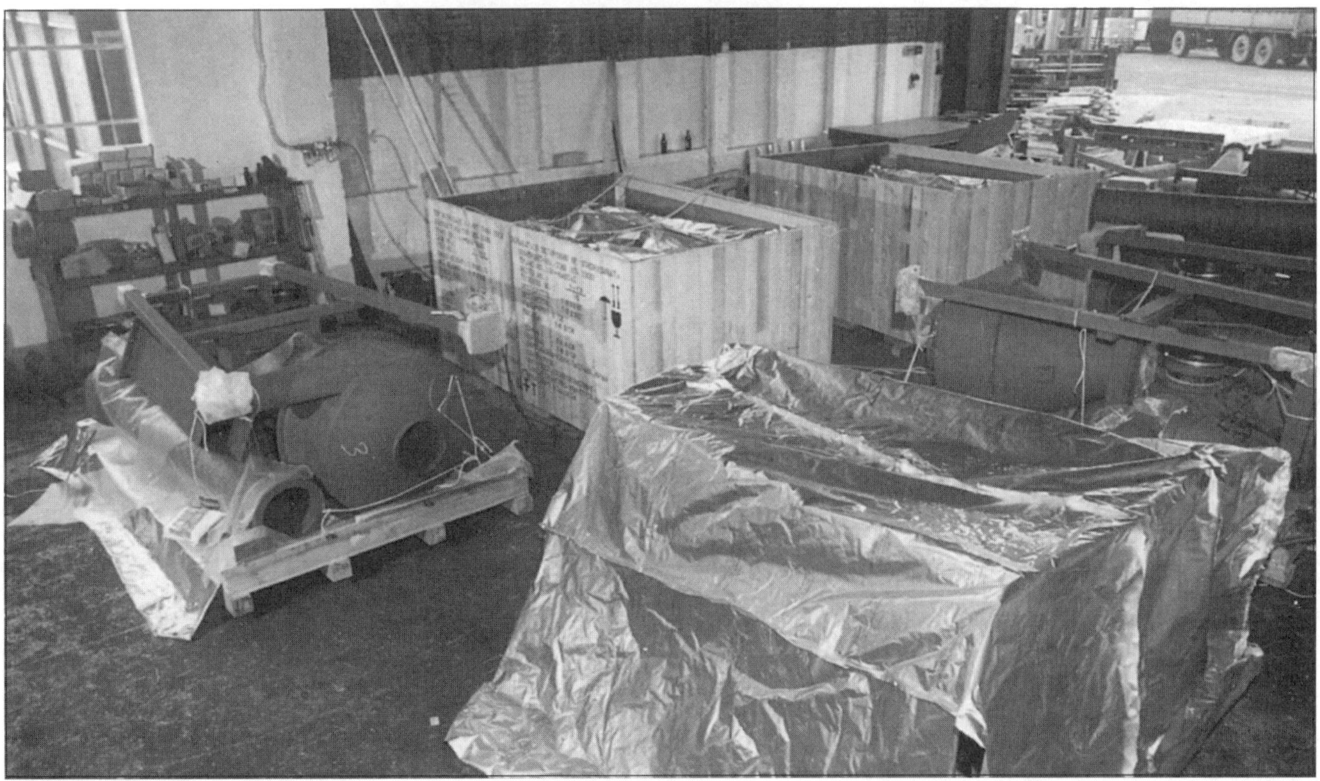

Protection against Humidity

Hapag-Lloyd ships and containers assist in protecting your cargo against condensation:

The double hull of the container vessels reduce the influence of air and water temperature on the hold.

The climatic conditions of the hold can be influenced by an electric ventilation system.

Special containers (e.g. Ventilated Containers or Flats with stanchions and stowage grids) permit the exchange of air between cargo hold and the interior of the container.

Furthermore, you have a range of alternatives as a precaution against cargo damage:

Do not pack moisture sensitive packages together with moisture exuding goods. Should this unavoidable, packages to be well separated and protected.

Put packages and dunnage as dry as possible into the container, i.e. store these in dry premises beforehand. If packages and dunnage are stored in open or damp space, they will absorb moisture from the surroundings. Wood should be of a humidity not exceeding 12-14%, and corrugated cardboard have a maximum water content of 8% (corresponding to DIN 53102).

Select those cargo securing means which cannot cause damage to the cargo as a result of climatic influences (e.g. rust).

When packing, ensure that air is allowed to circulate.

This can be achieved by stowage in blocks, interspersed with ventilation channels or by using separating material (dunnage). A space of 100 mm to 120 mm (4" to 5") between cargo and container roof should be left free.

When transporting moisture exuding goods, put paper or other moisture absorbing material onto the cargo. Plastic sheets are unsuitable for this purpose.

Moisture absorbing materials, e.g. silica gel, can prevent condensation. They are, however, only effective when used in absolutely air tight space, e.g. for shrink wrapped cargo. For 1 m^3 enclosed air, approximately 500 g absorbent material is required (recipe: 1/2 ounce per cu./ft).

Despite the use of absorption material, sweat water damage may occur since under extreme conditions these materials may exude the previously absorbed moisture.

Climatic Protecting Aids

In order to protect the cargo from climatic influences additional aids are available. The following table gives you a summary of various aids and their effects:

Effect / Aids	Humidity absorption	Humidity repellent	Humidity exclusion	Insulation	Slowing down of natural Ripening process
Drying agents (sachets) Silica Gel Pillo Dri Air Dri Bag Brano Gel	■				
Drying aids (sheets) Dew Catcher Cargo Dry System Preapre - Sheet Non-Sweat Paper Moisture Grip	■				
Paper	■				
VCI inhibitors		■			
Plastic foil			■		
Fats, oils		■			
Insulating foil				■	
Gases					■

Moisture emitting goods are to be covered with paper to avoid damage through dropping condensation

Cargo in Temperature Controlled Containers

For cargo that requires temperatures maintained at a constant level, Hapag-Lloyd supplies Insulated and Reefer Containers with or without their own cooling device.

Insulated containers do not have their own cooling facility. During ocean transport they are connected with the central cooling plant of the ship. The temperature range lies between -25°C and +40°C, (-14°F to 104°F), depending on type of ship and trade route. Since these containers lack a cooling unit, their pre- and on-carriage must be executed in the shortest possible time to prevent damage to cargo.

Reefer Containers have their own electrically operated cooling unit. Many of them have a diesel generator to provide power supply and are thus independent of external electricity supply during pre- and on-carriage. The maintainable temperature ranges from -25°C to +25°C, (-13°F to + 77°F).

These temperatures can be maintained if the difference to the outside temperature does not exceed the following limits:

- for heating maximum 42°C (76°F)
- for cooling maximum 60°C (108°F).

For the temperature ranges applicable to the different construction series, please refer to our brochure "Container Specification."

Thus it is easily possible to maintain a constant temperature of say -18°C (0°F) or +12°C (+54°F) during sea and land transport.

During storage at container terminals, the containers are exposed to severe conditional stresses (i.e. sun radiation). Thus storage should be kept as short as possible. When transporting Reefer Containers, which are run by diesel generators on land, ensure that they are equipped with sufficient fuel.

Please remember the Insulated and Reefer Containers are designed merely to maintain the temperature required by the particular cargo. They cannot cool down cargo to the required temperature. Consequently reefer cargo must be packed in a precooled state.

The temperature to be set will depend on the goods being shipped. When booking the cargo, please give us the appropriate cooling instructions.

There are certain types of cargo that "breathe," i.e. they not only give off heat, but due to a maturing process produce gas. In such cases it may be necessary to replace the air in the container by fresh air from the outside. All Hapag-Lloyd Reefer Containers have facilities for a controlled fresh-air supply. Please indicate such a requirement when booking.

Temperature controlled cargo may only be packed up to the "load line" to enable circulation of the cooling air.

Hold of a container vessel with couplings for Insulated Containers.

Packing a Reefer Container directly out of a cold-storage depot through an airlock.

Stowage in the container and packing of the cargo are crucial for maintaining a set temperature:

1. The entire floor grating must be evenly loaded with cargo. Should this be impossible, then all free spaces must be spread with cardboard or similar material so as to prevent a draft. This also applies to any gaps that could occur between pelletized cargoes.
2. A void space of at least 12 cm must be left between the cargo and the roof. Markings on the side walls indicate the maximum permissible cargo height.
3. Stowage should on the one hand be sufficiently loose to allow an air current to pass upwards between the separate packages, and on the other sufficiently tight to prevent the occurrence of any drafts. This is often ensured by the shape (bulges) of the packages, which should nevertheless be stacked—and special attention needs to be paid to this point—precisely on top of each other.
4. The packing must be sufficiently strong to bear the stack load and at the same time to protect the contents.
5. The packing must conform to the properties of the product: e.g. cartons with ventilation apertures permitting air circulation to the interior should be used for goods needing fresh air.

Cross-section of a loaded Reefer Container.

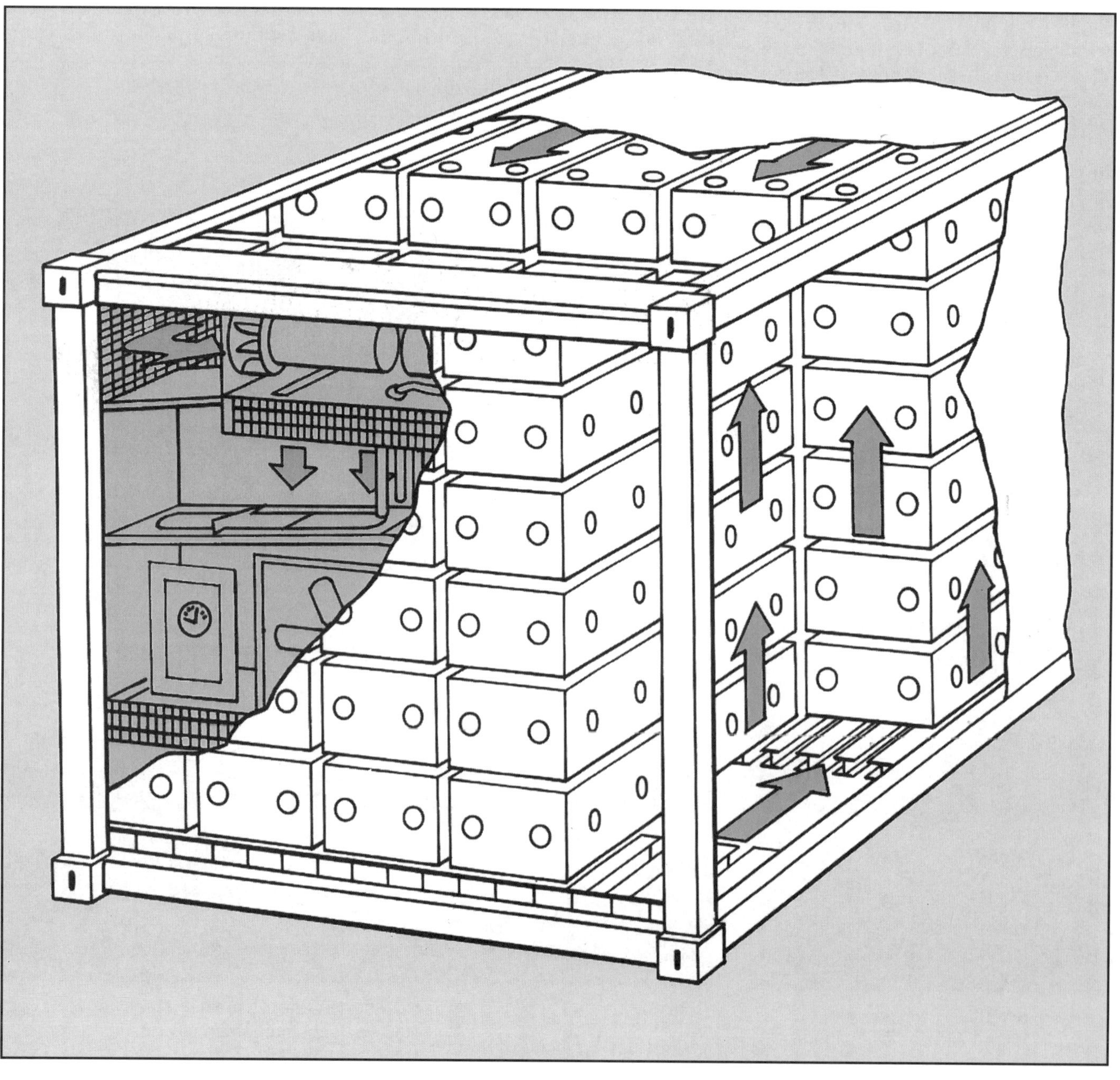

Advice on Packing and Securing Various Goods

Cartons, Cases, and Crates

When shipping cartons in containers you should bear two things in mind:

- With increasing humidity the stability of cartons decreases. (Countermeasures see "Protection against Humidity" on page 272).
- Cartons that move within the container are subject to crushing. A compact stow, the filling out of gaps and the bracing of cargo prevent this.

With regard to packing the following procedure is recommended:

- Check whether the cargo fills the entire volume of the container. If the entire container volume is not required for the cargo, pack the cargo in such a way that the entire floor area is covered to the same height. You thus achieve an equal weight distribution. Furthermore you save cargo securing material and save labor through lower stacking heights. Start the packing process at the front of the container (opposite of the doors), from the sides to the middle.
- Make full use of available space and do not leave gaps.
- You can achieve a particularly solid stow if you pack the units interlocking like bricks.

The parcels can be linked with each other and with the floor by timber connectors. This prevents the cargo from shifting.

- If gaps are unavoidable, brace the cargo row for row as packing progresses (suitable securing aids for load support and distribution see "Cargo Securing Aids" on page 270).
- Large and heavy crates should be put into the centre of the container and be braced against the corner posts. When bracing against the side walls ensure a large bearing surface.

Properly stowed cartons.

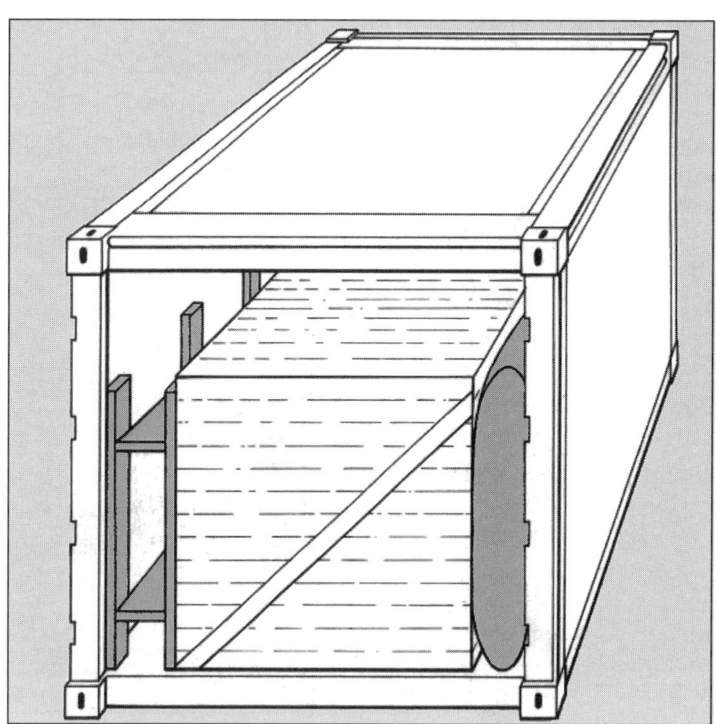

A crate is braced against the corner posts and with large bearing-surfaces against the side walls (either with dunnage—left side—or with air bags—right side).

Pallets, Forklift Adapted Unit Loads

The attainable utilization of the container is determined by the dimensions of the pallets:

The optimal size of the pallet depends on the internal dimensions of the container, the form and weight of the packages.

Fourway pallets (i.e. those that can be lifted from all four sides by a forklift truck), usually make best use of the floor area of a container.

The recommended packing patterns for standard pallet sizes are shown in the chart to the right.

Type of Container / Pallet size mm in	20′			40′		
	Recommended packing pattern	max. no.	Floor utilization %	Recommended packing pattern	max. no.	Floor utilization %
1000 x 800 40″ x 32″	1	14	83,2	1	28	81,2
1100 x 800 44″ x 32″	1	14	91,4	1	28	89,3
1100 x 900 44″ x 35 1/2″	1	12	88,1	1	26	93,3
1100 x 1100 44″ x 44″	1	10	99,7	1	20	87,7
1100 x 1400 44″ x 55″	1	8	91,3	1	16	89,3
1200 x 800 48″ x 32″	2/3	11	78,4	2/3	23	80,1
1200 x 1000 48″ x 40″	3	10	89	2/3	20	87,0

Packing pattern "1" for pallets.

Packing pattern "2" for pallets.

Packing pattern "3" for 4-way pallets only.

For the transport of pallets in containers it is important that cargo is well secured on the pallets, and that the pallets are well secured inside the container:

Fix the cargo by lashing, gluing or shrink wrapping it on to the pallet.

To secure the pallets (for single layered stowage) 2 to 4 timber connectors under each pallet should suffice.

If only one row of pallets fits into the container, place it in the middle.

Should the container be wide enough for two or more pallets, place the rows close to the container sides.

If gaps cannot be avoided, leave these in the centre of the container. This ensures an equal distribution of the load and requires less use of securing facilities.

The second layer of pallets is secured by stepwise packing.

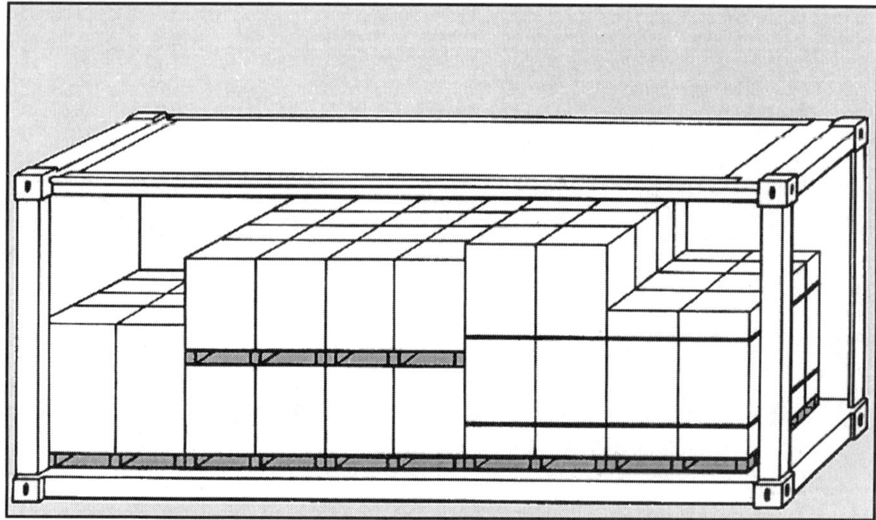

Drums, Barrels, and Plastic Cans

For the packing of drums, barrels and plastic cans the following procedure is recommended:

- Ensure that no leakage exists prior to packing; do not load leaking units.
- Place units with liquids on longitudinal wood dunnage. This prevents damage should leakage occur.
- Always stow drums and barrels with the drainage holes upwards.
- Drums are best stowed standing upright next to each other. The optimum arrangement of the units on the container floor can be determined by dividing the width of the container by the unit diameter:

If no remainder results: packing pattern "Full."

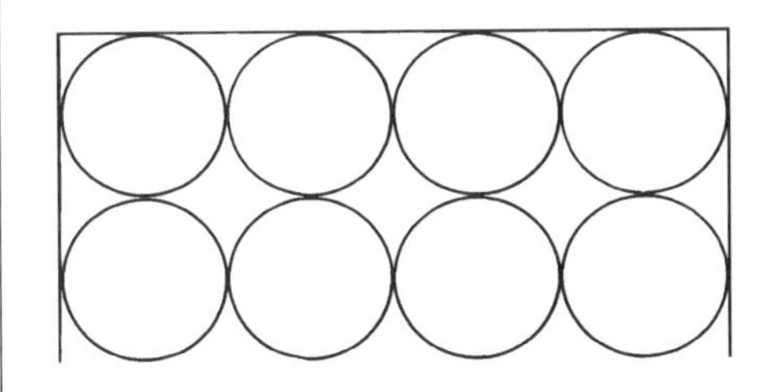

If a remainder of more than 73.2% of the unit diameter results, packing pattern "A."

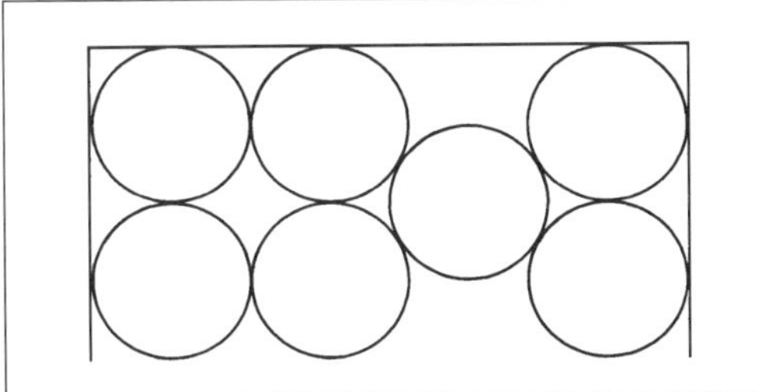

Should the remainder amount to 50 – 73.2% of the unit diameter: packing pattern "B."

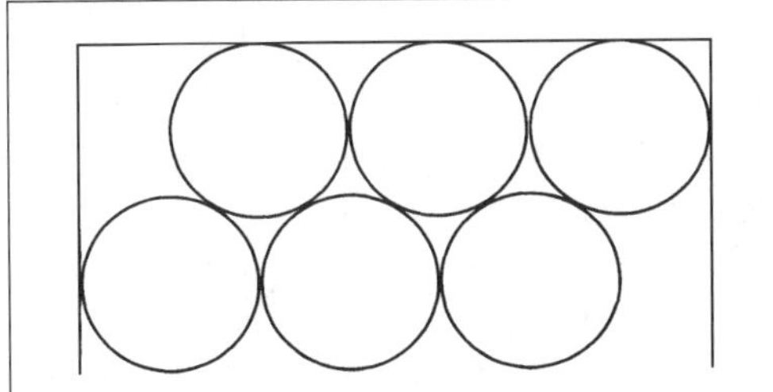

The number of units which you can place in a container is shown in the table at right.

Staggered packing of drums and securing towards the door.

Barrel diameter inch	cm	Packing pattern	Number per 20′ Container	Number per 40′ Container
10	25.4	Full	207	423
11	27.9	B	168	344
12	30.5	B	154	315
13	33.0	A	119	252
14	35.5	B	102	216
15	38.1	Full	90	186
16	40.6	B	80	165
17	43.2	B	65	140
18	45.7	Full	60	130
19	48.2	A	59	120
20	50.8	B	52	108
21	53.3	B	44	88
22	55.8	Full	40	84
22.5	57.1	Full	40	83
23	58.4	A	39	80
23.5	59.7	A	36	79
24	61.0	A	36	76
24.5	62.2	B	30	66
25	63.5	B	30	63
26	66.0	B	27	57
27	68.6	B	24	53
28	71.1	B	24	51
29	73.7	Full	23	48
30	76.2	Full	21	45
31	78.7	A	21	45
32	81.3	A	20	42
33	83.8	A	20	41
34	86.4	B	14	30
35	88.9	B	14	28
36	91.4	B	14	28
37	94.0	B	12	26
38	96.5	B	12	24
39	99.1	B	12	24
40	101.6	B	11	23

If you want to calculate the number of rows (from the front to the doors) please use the following formulae:

For "Full" and "A":

$$\frac{\text{Inner length of container}}{\text{Drum diameter}}$$

For "B":

$$1 + \frac{\text{Inner length of container less drum diameter}}{0.866 \times \text{drum diameter}}$$

Drums and barrels must be secured at the door end. For this several alternatives can be used:

- Bracing with wood.
- Securing with steel straps, preferably in "Olympic rings linkage."
- Staggered stowage (resulting from differing unit heights or using empty pallets) supports the top layer.

Wooden barrels are not built to withstand pressure around the middle. When packed horizontally, the following precautions should be taken:

Support the barrels at the ends with battens so the middle does not touch the container floor; prevent rolling by means of wedges.

When loading plastic cans in a container, two things should be observed:

- Check plastic cans for leakages, since one leaking unit endangers the stability of the entire stowage.
- Cover all layers with stowage gratings or dunnage to ensure stability of the stow. Jolts from below or vibration can otherwise easily cause a layer to "bulge" (bulging effect) and may dislodge individual cans.

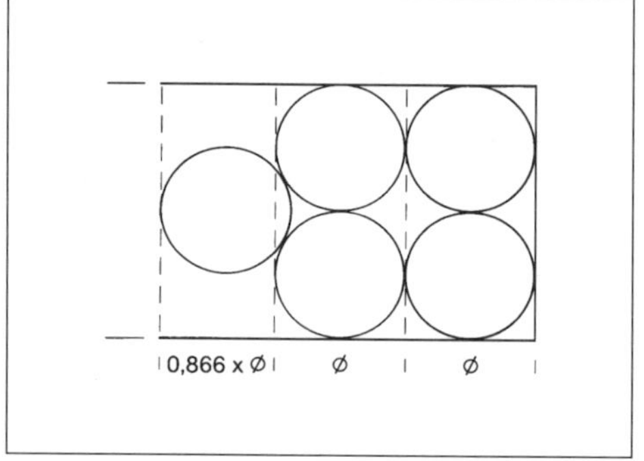

Number of rows for packing patterns "Full" and "A."

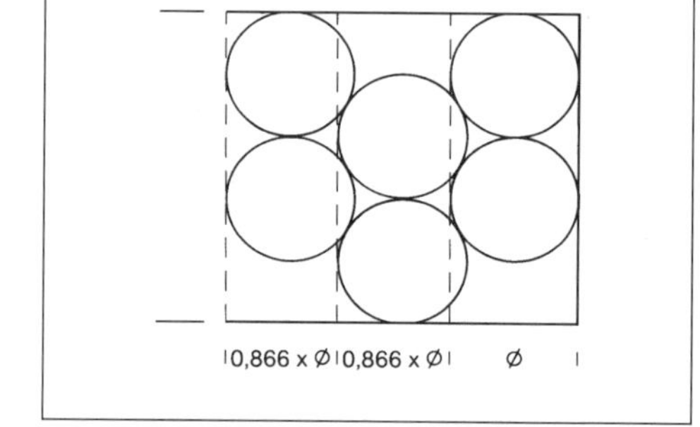

Number of rows for packing pattern "B."

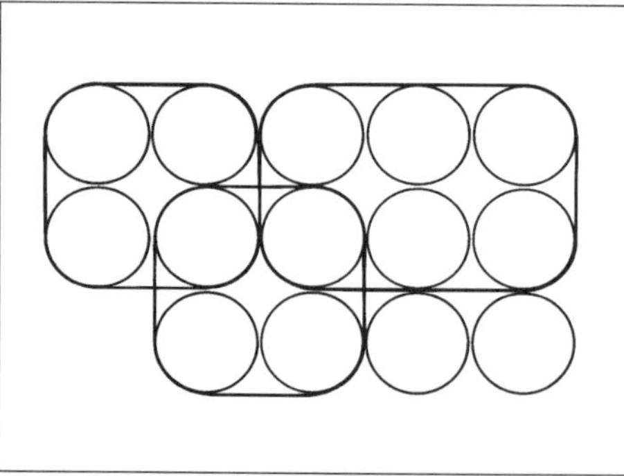

Drums are secured by means of steel straps in "Olympic-Rings" linkage.

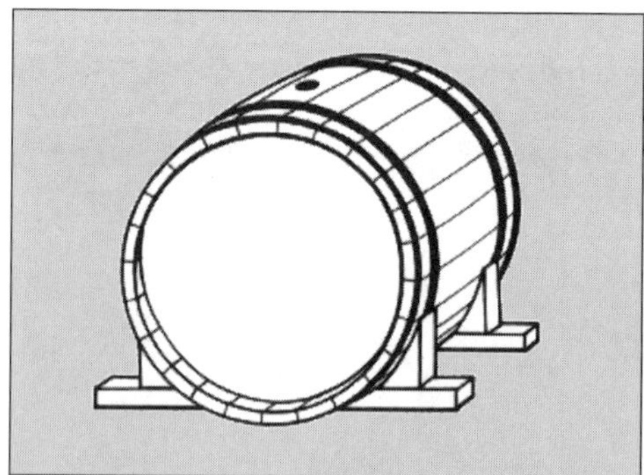

Wooden barrels are supported at the ends and secured against rolling by means of wedges.

Interim layer of dunnage timber or plywood sheets (above left and right).

Bagged Goods

Inexpert packing of bags in containers may cause the following damage:

When opening the doors of the container the bags slide out.

Denting of the container walls by excessive pressure may cause the container to get jammed in its slot and lead to damage during discharge.

To prevent damage you should pack the bags in such a way that they cannot shift as the ship rolls. For this you have two alternatives:

- *Stowage in alternate directions* so that each tier binds the tier above and below it (this, however, does not prevent plastic bags from shifting).
- *The palletizing of bags.* Under certain conditions the use of oneway pallets may even be more economical than the relatively time consuming packing (and unpacking) of the container with bagged cargo.

  The optimum size of a pallet is determined by the internal dimensions of the container, the shape of the bags and the weight put on each pallet.

  The bagged cargo is secured on the pallets through plastic straps or shrink wrapping (merely non-organic goods).

Bags shrinkwrapped on a pallet.

Bales

Most baled cargo is comparatively insensitive to mechanical transport strains, but can be easily damaged when packing or unpacking. Thus the following procedure is recommended:

- During packing, take care that the external covering of the bales is not damaged.
- To facilitate unpacking by forklift, place wooden planks lengthwise on the floor of the container and between each layer of bales while packing.
- If the bales are not flush with the doors, braces against the corner posts are usually sufficient for securing the cargo.

Bales can be stowed on their flat sides or in an upright position.

Rolls and Coils

Rolls and coils may be placed in the container upright (i.e. vertically, "eye to sky"), or on their side (i.e. horizontally). Different rules apply to the packing of paper and steel rolls.

Horizontal packing

Paper rolls may be packed on top of each other. Secure the bottom layer by wedges. Place suitable padding between layers to avoid movement. Fill out gaps at the sides. To avoid chafing place cardboard strips between side walls and paper rolls.

Heavy steel coils should be packed on heavy duty wooden cradles and have an underpinning of blocks or skids to increase the bearing surface. Use strong steel wire lashing with tensioning screws to secure each roll individually to the cradle and to each other. Lash these rolls to the container through their centre holes. Reinforce the front end of the container with cross bars positioned at the height of the centre of the rolls. Fill out empty spaces with wood.

Upright packing

Place paper rolls close to each other and fill out gaps. Secure at the door ends with nets or planks.

Steel coils should also be placed close to each other. For securing, link them with steel straps or brace them with wood.

Heavy steel coils which are shipped on skids or pallets should be securely fastened down.

For an optimum arrangement of the rolls please see "Drums, Barrels, and Plastic Cans" on page 277.

When packing more than one layer, stepwise stowage (different package heights, empty pallets) will secure the top layer (see chart in the section "Pallets, Forklift Adapted Unit Loads" on page 276).

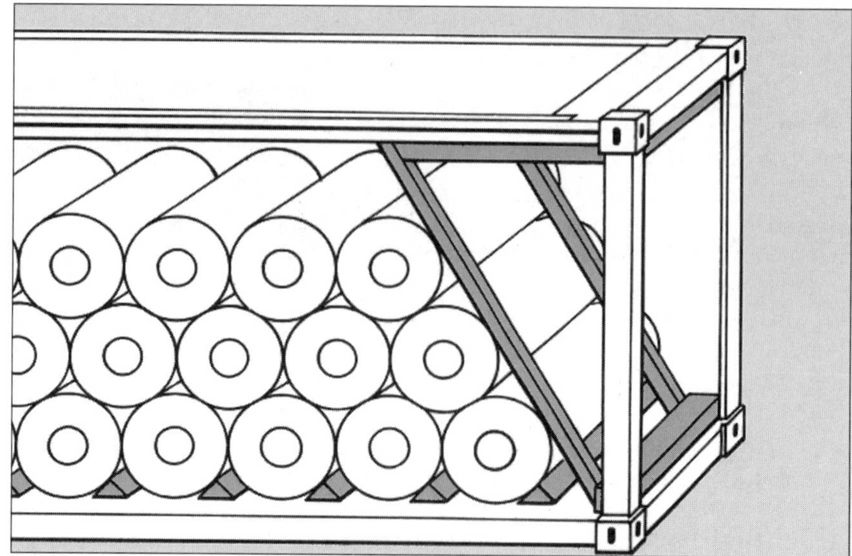

Securing of paper reels stowed in the roll.

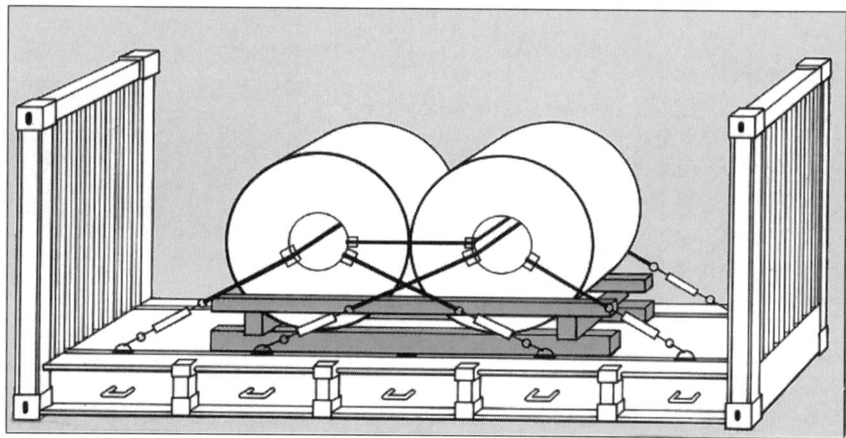

Securing of heavy steel coils.

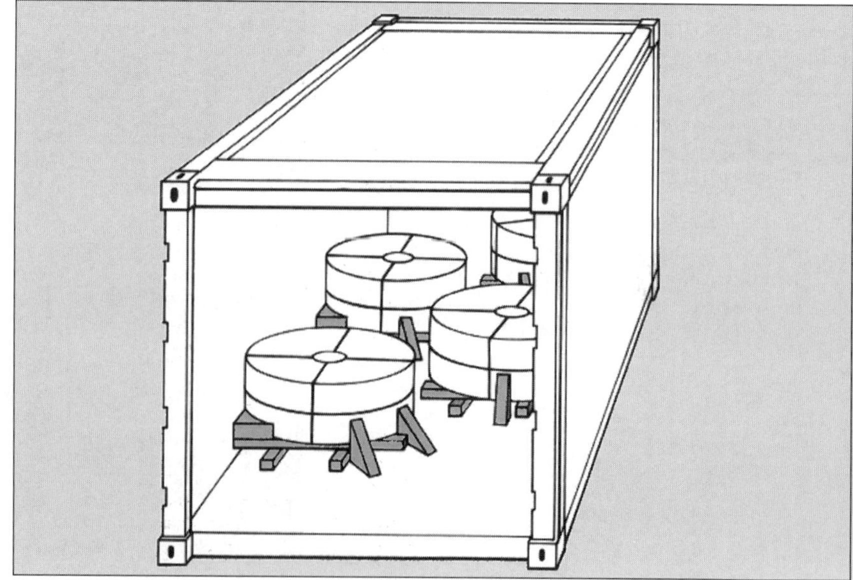

Securing of coils stowed "eye to sky."

Machinery, Heavy Lifts, and Oversized Items

These goods also can be transported by containers. This is especially advantageous in door-to-door transport as cargo needs to be secured only once.

The transport of heavy and oversized cargo requires particularly careful measures for cargo securing. Here are some rules which must be adhered to at all times:

- Check the regulations concerning weights and measures for inland transport both in the supplier's and the consignee's country.
- When packing the container, take into consideration whether the consignee has the mechanical and other facilities required for unpacking.
- All transport arrangements should be worked out well in advance. Our stowage advisors are at your disposal at all times; please contact your Hapag-Lloyd Sales Office or your Hapag-Lloyd Agent.

Machinery and heavy goods

Machines and heavy goods are often loaded into the container from the top. For this, Hapag-Lloyd will provide you with Open Top Containers, either with tarpaulin or hardtop, or Flats.

Heavy goods are usually transported on Flats or Platforms because of the higher load bearing capacity of the floor. Flats may be used for door-to-door transports, whereas Platforms are in principle only used for ocean transport. You will find detailed information about load limits in the Hapag-Lloyd brochure "Container Specification" or you can contact our stowage advisors.

For cargo securing we recommend the following procedure:

If only one item is loaded into the container, it should be placed in the middle of the container so that the centre of gravity of the cargo is as close as possible to the container's own centre of gravity, or better still below.

Heavy single items require load distribution supports since the point load of these items is too heavy for the container floor. Limits for the floor loading of Standard and Open Top Containers are

- 4.5 t/m (1.37 t/ft) inner length of a 20' container, and
- 3.0 t/m (0.91 t/ft) inner length of a 40' container.

"Flat" with oversized cargo for the door-to-door transport (above).

Sub-chassis and fastening for a single heavy lift (below).

If only two battens are used, they must be placed lengthwise and be at least 80 cm (2'8") from each other (see first chart in section "Weight Limits and Weight Distribution" on page 260).

Goods shipped on a wooden sled should be firmly bolted to it. The sled should be braced against the corner posts as well as against the bottom longitudinal rails and cross members; preferably not only on the floor but also at the height of the centre of gravity of the cargo against the corner posts. It is particularly important to brace top heavy goods at the level of their centre of gravity.

When using side walls for bracing ensure a large bearing surface.

Properly secured machinery.

The cargo is firmly bolted to the bedding and chocked against the side walls with a large bearing surface area (above).

Top-heavy goods are secured at the level of their center of gravity (below).

Oversized goods

For oversized goods, Open Top Containers, Flats or Platforms are suitable, depending on the direction in which the item exceeds the inner dimensions of the container. (Platforms are in principle used only for ocean transport.)

We will gladly advise you on the choice of the most suitable container. In our brochure "Container Specification" you will find information about the dimensions and load limits.

Even slightly overwidth goods can be stowed under deck if ample space is left for the cell guides. In these cases you can possibly save on premium freight by careful stowage on the container. Detailed information is available from our Sales Offices and Hapag-Lloyd Agents. In general, the same rules apply for securing of oversized cargo as for heavy goods. In case of doubt, please contact our experienced stowage advisors, who will gladly assist you.

If the goods are covered with special tarpaulins, stow the original tarpaulins and roof beams securely in the container.

Even overwidth goods can be stowed under deck, if ample space is left for the cell guides (above and below).

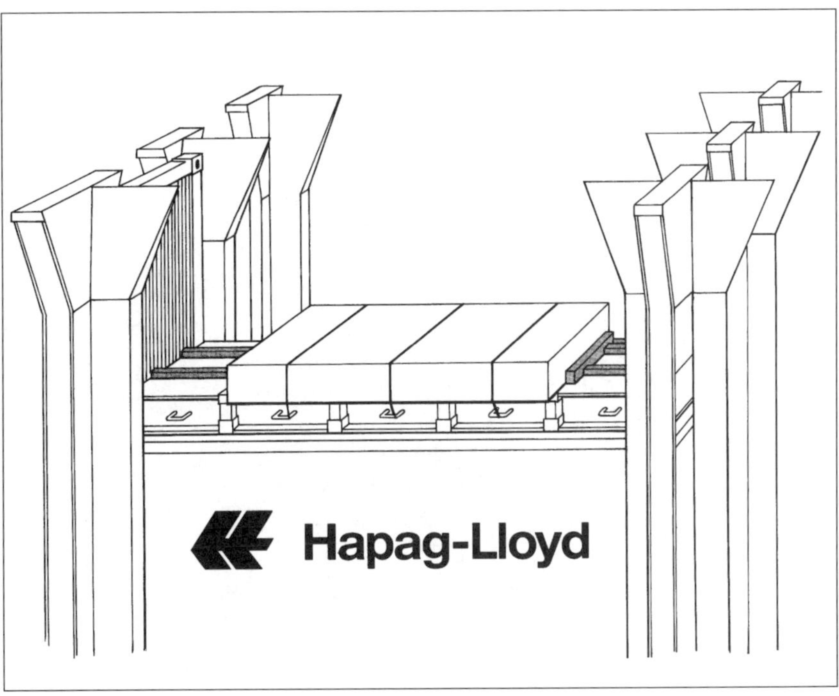

Uncontainerizable cargo can be transported by Hapag-Lloyd container vessels. If notified well in advance, large areas below deck as well as large free deck areas can be made available for transports of these items.

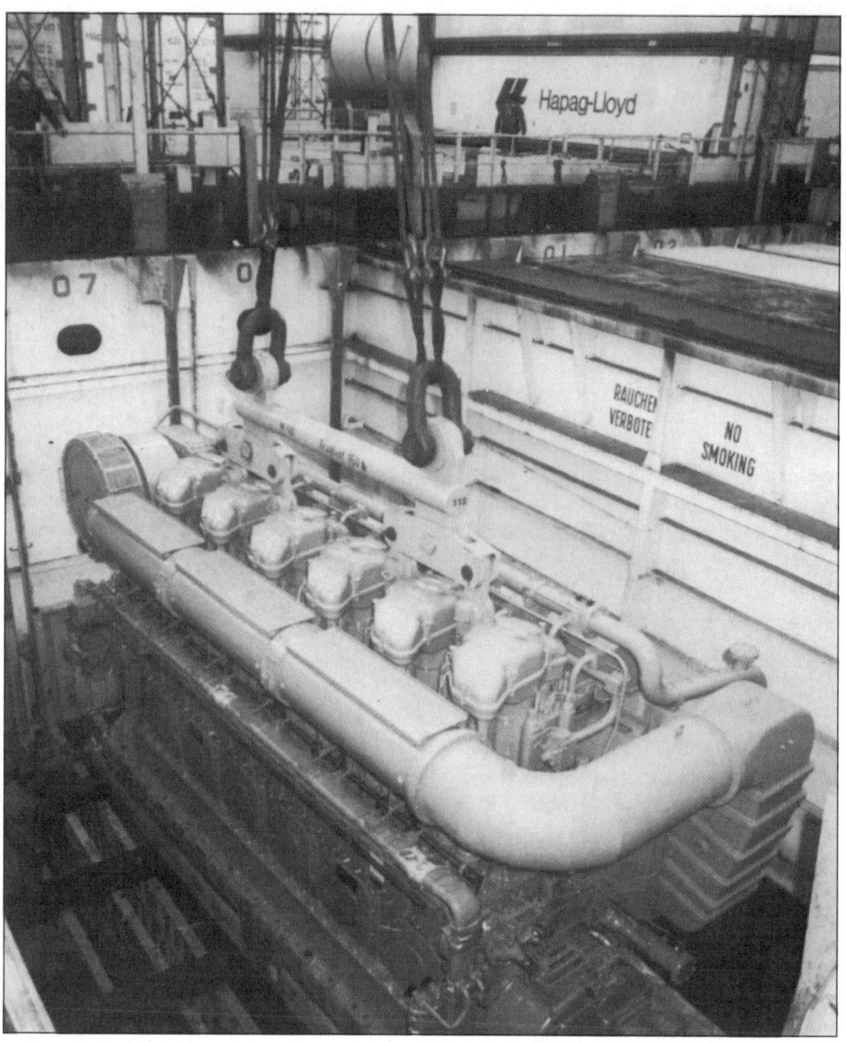

For this unit a complete bay under deck was made available.

Exceptionally bulky pieces can be stowed on large free deck areas.

Vehicles

All types of vehicles, ranging from motor cars to road building machinery, may be transported by container vessels.

In a few countries vehicles may be classified as dangerous goods and in some other countries there may be official recommendations regarding the carriage of vehicles by sea.

Please ensure vehicles are prepared in accordance with such instructions.

We recommend that batteries should be disconnected and fuel drained prior to loading the container.

Motor cars and small trucks

These vehicles can normally be wheeled into Standard Containers without difficulty (if necessary by using a small drive-on ramp). Load these vehicles absolutely dry. Leave a gap open in windows to facilitate air circulation.

Special span sets are available for lashing motor cars and small trucks.

Trucks, road construction, and farm machinery

These can be shipped in Open Top Containers with tarpaulin or hardtop, on Flats and Platforms (Platforms are in principle used only for ocean transport).

Use steel wire with tensioning screws to secure cargo.

Place additional wedges in front of and behind all wheels (the wedges should have a height of at least one sixth of the wheel diameter).

Securing of a tractor by means of wedges and steel wire with turnbuckles.

Cars can be driven into Standard Containers across a small drive-on ramp.

Glass Sheets

Due to its dimensions and weight, glass is best loaded into the container from the top. For this Hapag-Lloyd will provide you with Open Top Containers with a tarpaulin and hardtop.

Sheet glass in open top container.

In addition to careful packaging of sheets of glass in boxes, crates or A-frames, further cargo securing measures may be taken:

- Place the sheets, if possible, lengthwise in the container.
- When shipping several A-frames in a container, provide buffer zones between them.
- Provide additional covering for the glass as it is extremely moisture sensitive.

Bulk Liquids

Bulk liquids can be transported in our special Tank Containers. Please observe the following:

Tank Containers must be filled to at least 80% to avoid dangerous surge movements during transport.

Tank Containers must generally not be filled to more than 95% to allow for a possible heat expansion of the contents.

Please observe the working limits affixed to the Tank Containers.

You can find more information about Hapag-Lloyd Tank Containers in our brochure "Container Specification." Furthermore, our experienced stowage advisors are at your disposal at any time.

Non-hazardous liquids like wine, latex or ink can also be transported in "liquid bulk bags" in Standard, Open Top or Bulk Containers. We can advise you about purchasing opportunities. Lashing points to suspend these inlets in the aforementioned container types are available.

Bulk Solids

Loose bulk solids can be transported in our 20' Bulk Containers, and similarly in our Standard and Open Top Containers by using an inlet.

Bulk, Standard and Open Top Containers are all equipped with rings for suspension of the inlet.

The inlets currently in use are designed to match our more recent 20' Standard Containers.

Cargo has to be secured by a barrier on the door side, and indeed this is a strictly enforced mandatory requirement in many countries.

Apart from the four steel struts, our door barrier forms part of the inlet, is simple, and can be fitted rapidly and securely.

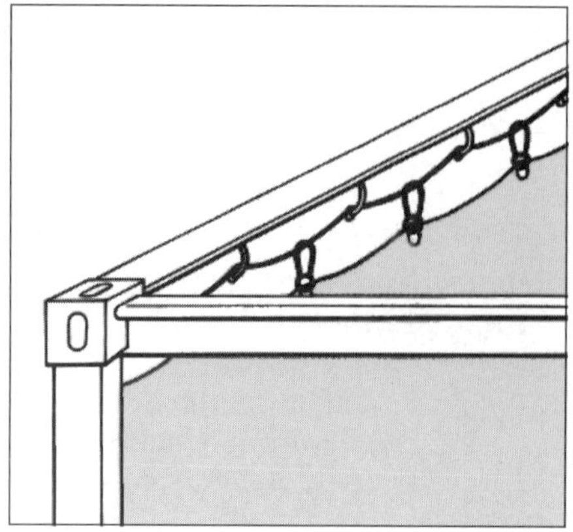

Suspending the inlet in a Bulk Container...

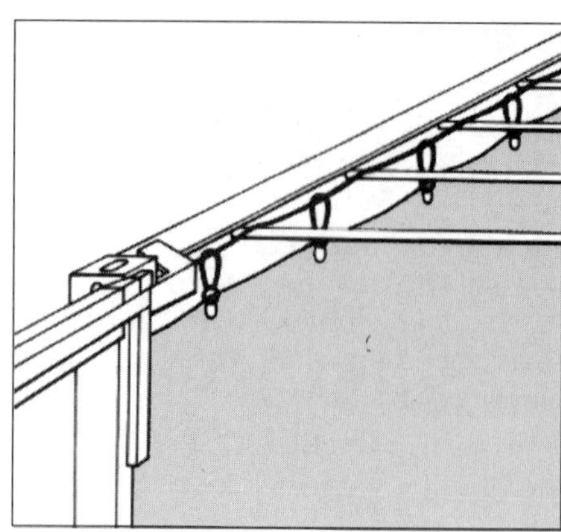

... and in an Open Top Container.

Further information may be found in our brochure Standard Containers with Inlets.

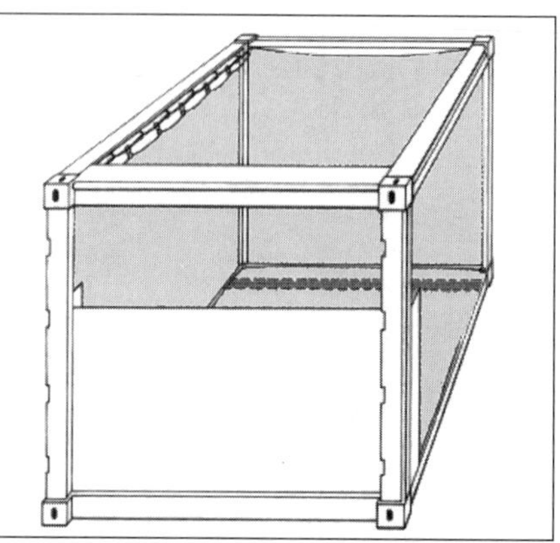

An inlet fitted in a Bulk/Open Top Container.

Suspension points and intervals for a standard container (below).

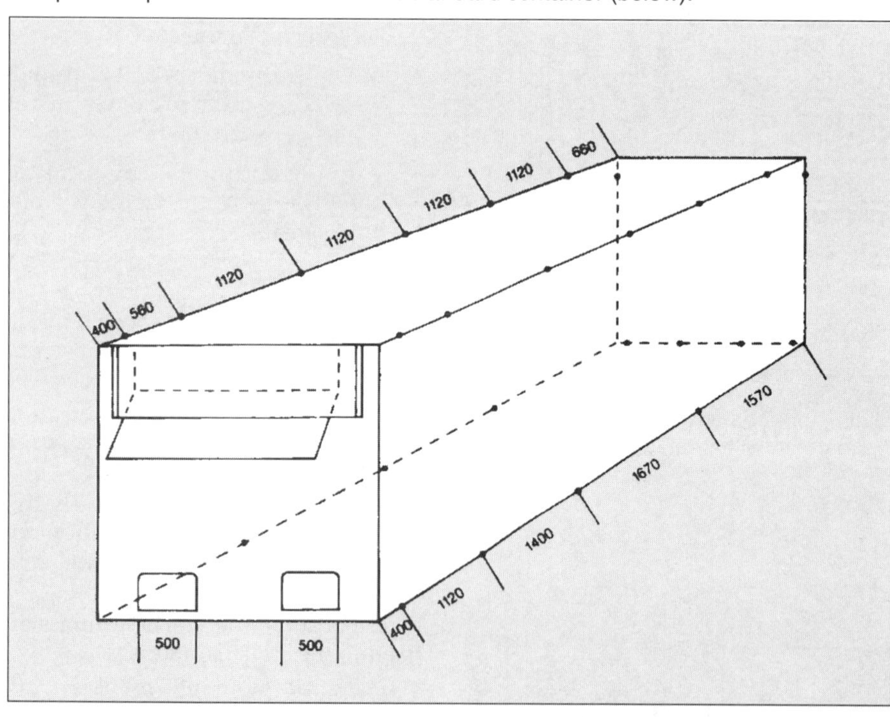

Securing the inlet.

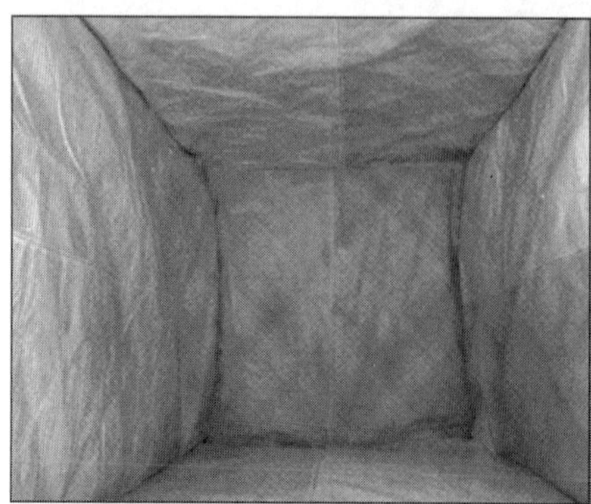

Interior view of an inlet after installation.

Door barrier.

Lengthy Goods

Due to their dimensions and weight, lengthy goods are best loaded into the container from the side or from the top. Hapag-Lloyd will provide you with flats or Open Top Containers with tarpaulin or hardtop.

Securing of lengthy goods in an Open Top Container...

For cargo securing we recommend the following procedure:

Strap the entire container load together with strong steel straps, which have been put into the container prior to packing.

This relieves pressure on the side walls. In case of using Flats place in the stanchions and tie them together above the load to keep them from splaying.

Material increasing friction should be placed between the individual layers of lengthy goods, since these goods have a tendency to slide lengthwise subjecting the end walls to stress.

Insert a vertical wooden bulkhead between cargo and front walls to distribute pressure caused by a possible shifting of the cargo on the corner posts and to avoid point loads.

...and on a Flat.

Livestock

Transport boxes for animals can be loaded on flats on deck for easy access at any time.

Personnel looking after the animals may travel on the ships.

Containers containing fodder can be stowed near the animals on deck.

Familiarize yourself with the quarantine regulations of the country of destination and of the transit ports.

Even livestock can be transported. Fodder can be stowed nearby. Keepers may travel on the ship.

Standard Specifications for Containers

Overall dimensions (see table) and corner castings are standardized for all types of containers (ISO 668, ISO 1161).

Standard Specification ISO 668	Length		Width	Height		
Overall Dimensions	20′ 6 058 mm	40′ 12 192 mm	8′ 2 438 mm	8′ 2 438 mm	8′6″ 2 591 mm	9′6″ 2 896 mm
Internal Dimensions Standard C.	5 867 mm 19′3″	11 998 mm 39′4 3/8″	2 330 mm 7′7 3/4″	2 197 mm 7′2 1/2″	2 350 mm 7′8 1/2″	2 655 mm 8′8 1/2″
Door Opening Standard Container	–	–	2 286 mm 7′6″	2 134 mm 7′	2 261 mm 7′5″	2 566 mm 8′5″

Minimum requirements are laid down for internal dimensions (see table), gross weight and the capacity of a container floor to carry a fork-lift truck during cargo handling.

According to ISO 668 containers may be utilized up to the following gross weights:

20′ containers:
24 000 kg (52 910 lbs) according to the latest issue of ISO 668, valid for most Hapag-Lloyd 20′ containers;

30 480 kg (67 200 lbs) valid for all new Hapag-Lloyd 20′ containers; exceeds ISO minimum standards;

20 320 kg (44 800 lbs)
only valid for some containers.

40′ containers:
30 480 kg (67 200 lbs).

A container floor is capable of carrying a fork-lift truck with a maximum axle load of 5 460 kg (12 040 lbs), if the contact area per wheel is at least 142 cm^2 (22 sq.ft) (ISO 1496/I).

Minimum Requirements for Hapag-Lloyd Containers

- All containers comply with the standards for overall dimensions and corner castings.
- All containers exceed the minimum requirements for internal dimensions.
- Exposed timber is treated according to Australian requirements (exceptions: 40′ flats and platforms).
- Container inside dimensions mentioned in the following pages are nominal figures. Because of production tolerances a difference in measurements is possible:

Tolerances	Length	Width	Height
Maximum Difference	10 mm 3/8″	10 mm 3/8″	10 mm 3/8″

Standard Container 40′ / 20′

- Suitable for any general cargo.
- 20′ containers may be equipped with liner bags suitable for bulk cargo, e.g. malt.
- Fork-lift pockets on a number of the 20′ containers (see footnote 1).
- All 40′ containers suitable for Gooseneck chassis.
- Various lashing devices on the top and bottom longitudinal rails and the corner posts (both 20′ + 40′) Lashing devices have a permissible load of 1 000 kg (2 205 lbs) each.
- **Note permissible weight limits for road and rail transport.**

High Cube Standard Container 40′

- Especially for light, voluminous cargo and overheight cargo up to max. 2,70 m (8′ 10¹/₄″) (see table).
- All containers suitable for Gooseneck chassis.
- Numerous lashing devices on the top and bottom longitudinal rails and the corner posts.
- Lashing devices have a permissible load of 1 000 kg (2 205 lbs) each.
- **Consider overheight for inland transportation.**
- **Note permissible weight limits for road and rail transport.**

Hardtop Container 40′

- This container type has been designed and developed by Hapag-Lloyd.
- The 40′ hardtop container has particularly been constructed for:
  - long loads which cannot be transported in the 20′ hardtop container
  - heavy loads
  - high and excessively high loads
  - loading, e. g. by crane, through roof opening and door side.
- The roof can be removed by using a forklift. The weight of the steel roof is approx. 450 kg (990 lbs) each section.
- With the roof removed and the door-header swung out, it is much easier to load cargo using a crane via the door side.
- In case your cargo has overheight the roof sections can be lashed to a sidewall inside the container using only some 13 cm (5 1/8″) of space.
- If required, we can provide disposable tarpaulins for the transport which can be fastened to the walls on the outside using lashing devices.
- The capacity of the container floor exceeds the ISO 1496/1 standard by 33 %, so that a forklift whose front axle weight does not exceed 7,280 kg (16,000 lbs) can be used inside.
- The hardtop container provides many lashing devices to fasten your goods.

- The lashing devices on the corner posts and on the longitudinal rails of the roof and floor are capable of bearing loads of up to 2,000 kg (4,410 lbs) each, and those in the middle of the side walls up to 500 kg (1,100 lbs) each. Lashing to the side walls can only be done after the roof has been closed.
- The roof can easily be raised by about 70 mm (2 3/4″), using the roof locking devices so that the door-header can be swung out without removing the roof.
- This container type has been designed for heavy loads. Whilst considering the technical data (including the permissible spreaded load limitations) please bear in mind the prevalent weight restrictions for land transport.
- For further information please see page 13 and our brochure "The 40′ Hardtop".

Note permissible weight limits for road and rail transport.

Hardtop Container 20′

- This container type has been designed and developed by Hapag-Lloyd.
- It has especially been constructed for
  - heavy loads
  - high, and excessively high loads
  - loading, e.g. by crane, through roof opening and door side.
- The steel roof of some series (please see footnote) is fitted with forklift rings so that it can be removed by using a forklift. The weight of the steel roof is approx. 450 kg (990 lbs).
- With the roof removed and the door-header swung out, it is much easier to load cargo using a crane via the door side.
- In case your cargo has overheight the roof sections can be lashed to a sidewall inside the container using only some 13 cm (5 1/8″) of space.
- If required, we can provide disposable tarpaulins for the transport which can be fastened to the walls on the outside using lashing devices.
- The capacity of the container floor exceeds the ISO 1496/1 standard by 33 %, so that a forklift whose front axle weight does not exceed 7,280 kg (16,000 lbs) can be used inside.
- The hardtop container provides many lashing devices to fasten your goods.

- The lashing devices on the corner posts and on the longitudinal rails of the roof and floor are capable of bearing loads of up to 2,000 kg (4,410 lbs) each, and those in the middle of the side walls up to 500 kg (1,100 lbs) each. Lashing to the side walls can only be done after the roof has been closed.
- This container type has been designed for heavy loads. Whilst considering the technical data (including the permissible spreaded load limitations) please bear in mind the prevalent weight restrictions for land transport.
- For further information please see page 15 and our brochure "The 20′ Hardtop".
- **Note permissible weight limits for road and rail transport.**

Open Top Container 40′

- Especially for
  - overheight cargo
  - loading from top side, e.g. by crane
  - loading from door side, e.g. with cargo hanging from overhead tackle.
- Door header can be swung out on all open top containers.
- If required, we can provide disposable tarpaulins. For fastening tarpaulins, lashing bars are available on the outside of the walls. Using one way tarpaulins requires the corner castings to be accessible.
- The capacity of the floor for use of forklift trucks exceeds the ISO standard by 33 % on all 40′ open top containers.
- Numerous lashing devices on the top and bottom longitudinal rails and the corner posts.

Lashing devices have a permissible load of 1 000 kg (2 205 lbs) each.

- **Dimensions of roof and door openings please see page 21.**
- **Note permissible weight limits for road and rail transport.**

Open Top Container 20′

- Especially for
  - overheight cargo
  - loading from top side, e.g. by crane
  - loading from door side, e.g. with cargo hanging from overhead tackle.
- Door header can be swung out on all open top containers.
- If required, we can provide disposable tarpaulins. For fastening tarpaulins, lashing bars are available on the outside of the walls. Using one way tarpaulins requires the corner castings to be accessible.
- Forklift pockets on a number of containers (please see footnote 1).
- The capacity of the floor for use of forklift trucks exceeds the ISO standard by 33% on all 20′ open top containers.
- Numerous lashing devices on the top and bottom longitudinal rails and the corner posts. Lashing devices have a permissible load of 1 000 kg (2 205 lbs) each.

- **Dimensions of roof and door openings please see page 25.**
- **Note permissible weight limits for road and rail transport.**

Flat 40′

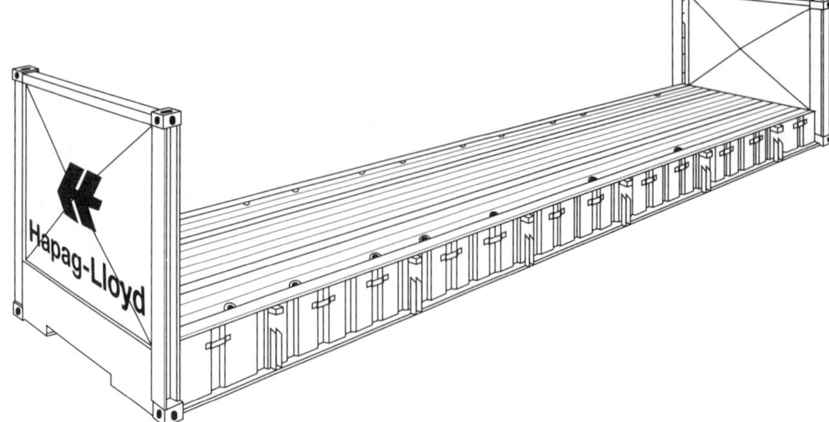

- Especially for heavy loads and overwidth cargo.
- Higher loadings possible if required (please see footnote 2).
- Strong bottom construction with fixed endwalls (which allow bracing and lashing of cargo as well as stacking).
- Gooseneck tunnel on both ends of all 40′ flats.
- Numerous very strong lashing devices on the corner posts, longitudinal rails and on the floor. Lashing devices on the longitudinal rails and on the floor of 40′ containers have a permissible load of 4 000 kg (8 820 lbs) each.
- Lashing winches with strong, 9 m (29′ 6½″) long synthetic lashing straps on some 40′ Flats (please see footnote 1). Straps have a permissible load of up to 2 000 kg (4 410 lbs) each.
- **Maximum payload can only be used if distributed over the total floor area of the flat.**

If concentration of heavy load on a small part of floor area is required please contact your Hapag-Lloyd partner office for stowage advice.

- **Flats are delivered without stanchions. If stanchions are required please inform us upon booking.**
- **Note permissible weight limits for road and rail transport.**

Flat 20′

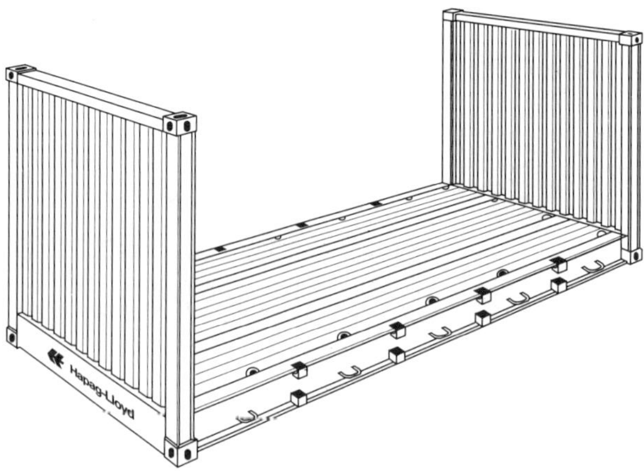

- Especially for heavy loads and overwidth cargo.
- Strong bottom construction with fixed endwalls (which allow bracing and lashing of cargo as well as stacking).
- Forklift pockets on a number of 20′ flats (please see footnote 1).
- Numerous very strong lashing devices on the corner posts, longitudinal rails and on the floor. Lashing devices on the longitudinal rails of 20′ containers have a permissible load of 2 000 kg or 4 000 kg respectively (4 410 lbs or 8 820 lbs respectively) each.
- **Maximum payload can only be used if distributed over the total floor area of flatrack.**
  If concentration of heavy load on a small part of floor area is required please contact your Hapag-Lloyd partner office for stowage advice.
- **Flats are delivered without stanchions. If stanchions are required please inform us upon booking.**
- **Note permissible weight limits for road and rail transport.**

Platform 40′ / 20′

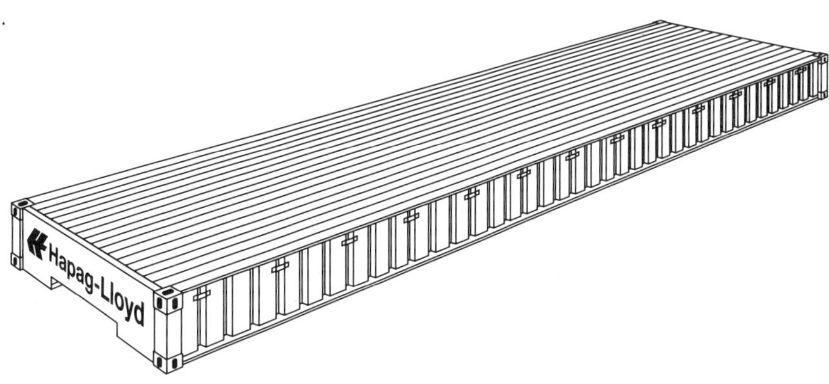

- Especially for heavy loads and oversized cargo.
- Strong bottom construction.
- Gooseneck tunnel on both ends of all 40′ Platforms.
- Numerous very strong lashing devices on the longitudinal rails. Lashing devices have a permissible load of 3 000 kg (6 615 lbs) each.
- **Transport of heavy loads concentrated on a small load transfer area is possible. Your Hapag-Lloyd partner will be pleased to advise you.**

Ventilated Container 20′

- Especially for cargo which needs ventilation.
- Natural ventilation is provided by openings in top and bottom longitudinal rails. The labyrinth construction of these ventilation openings ensures weatherproofness.
- Numerous lashing devices on the top and bottom longitudinal rails and the corner posts. Lashing devices have a permissible load of 1 000 kg (2 205 lbs) each.
- **Note permissible weight limits for road and rail transport.**

Insulated Container (Temperature Controlled Container) 40′ / 20′

- Especially for cargo which needs constant temperatures above or below freezing point.
- Walls in "sandwich-construction", with Polyurethane foam in or to provide maximum insulation.
- Temperature is controlled by ship's/terminal's cooling plant or "clip-on-unit".
- The air, delivered at the correct temperature, is circulated in the container through two apertures in the front wall (supply air via the lower aperture, return air via the upper aperture).
- Possible temperatures inside the 20′ containers, depending on specification of respective cooling device, from about + 12 °C to – 25 °C (+ 54 °F to – 14 °F).
- Please note maximum stowage height in below table and as indicated by red line inside container in order to ensure proper ventilation.
- Possible temperatures inside the 40′ containers, depending on specification of respective cooling device, from about + 13 °C to – 22 °C (+ 57 °F to – 8 °F).
- All 40′ containers suitable for Gooseneck chassis.
- **Note permissible weight limits for road and rail transport.**

Refrigerated Container (Temperature Controlled Container) 40′ / 20′

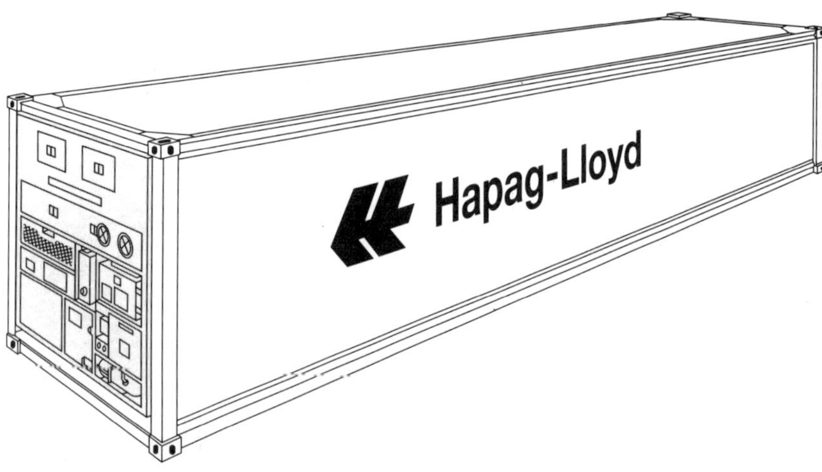

- Especially for cargo which needs constant temperatures above or below freezing point.
- Controlled fresh-air supply is possible. Containers are ATO-approved (formerly SPRENGER).
- Walls in "sandwich-construction", with Polyurethane foam in order to provide maximum insulation.
- The reefer unit is a compact-design compressor unit with aircooled condenser. It switches automatically from cooling to heating operation (and vice versa), if a change of the outside temperatures makes it necessary.
- Please note maximum stowage height in below table and as indicated by red line inside container in order to ensure proper ventilation.
- Possible voltages:
  - 380 V/50 Hz to 460 V/60 Hz (all refrigerated containers),
  - 200 V/50 Hz to 220 V/60 Hz **(exceptions footnote 2, see page 37-39).**
- Technical specification and illustration of electric plugs see page 46.
- **Note permissible weight limits for road and rail transport.**

Refrigerated High Cube Container 40′

(Temperature Controlled Container)

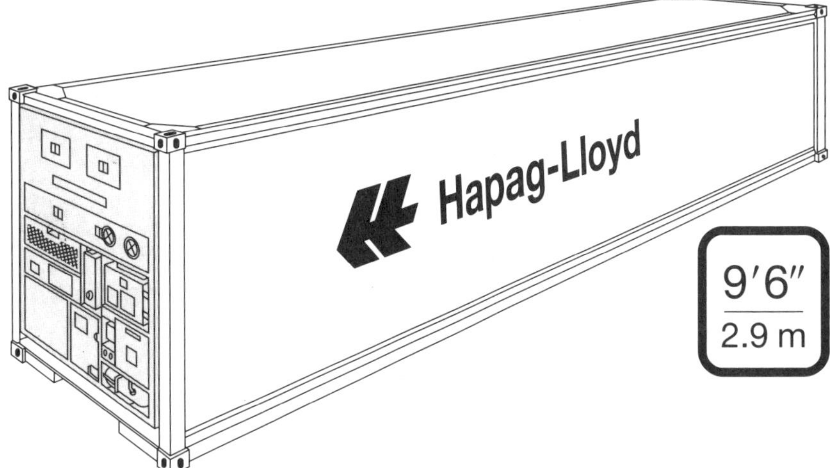

- Particularly suitable for voluminous, light-weight cargoes (e.g. fruit, flowers, ferns).
- Mainly made of aluminium in order to allow high payload.
- Especially for cargo which needs constant temperatures above or below freezing point.
- Controlled fresh-air supply is possible. Containers are ATO-approved (formerly SPRENGER)
- Walls in "sandwich-construction", with Polyurethane foam in oder to provide maximum insulation.
- The reefer unit is a compact-design compressor unit with aircooled condenser. It switches automatically from cooling to heating-operation (and vice versa), if a change of the outside temperatures makes it necessary.
- Possible voltages:
  – 380 V/50 Hz to 460 V/60 Hz
- Technical specification and illustration of electric plugs see page 46.
- **Note permissible weight limits for road and rail transport.**

Bulk Container 20′

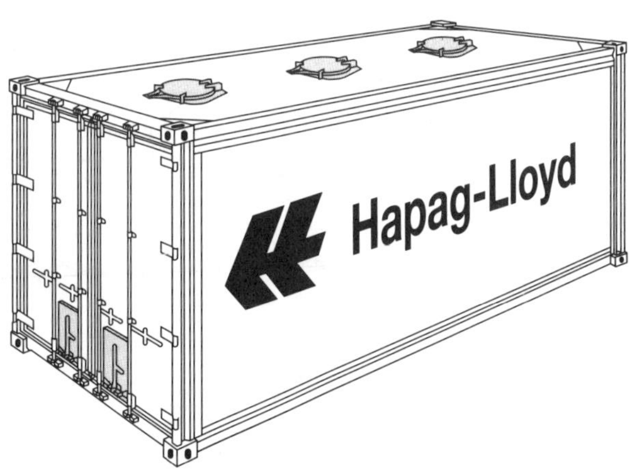

- Especially for dry bulk cargoes, e.g. malt.
- Three manholes for top loading of each container. Distance centerline to centerline manhole 1,83 m (6′).
- One discharge opening in each door wing. On demand short discharge tubes can be installed to move the cargo in desired directions.
- Fastening of linerbag possible.
- Fork-lift pockets on a number of the containers (please see footnote 1).
- Lashing devices on the top longitudinal rails.
- Roof openings ∅ 455 mm (1 3/4″), discharge door openings ∅ 340 x 380 mm (1 3/8″ x 1 1/2″).
- **Note permissible weight limits for road and rail transport.**

Tank Container 20′

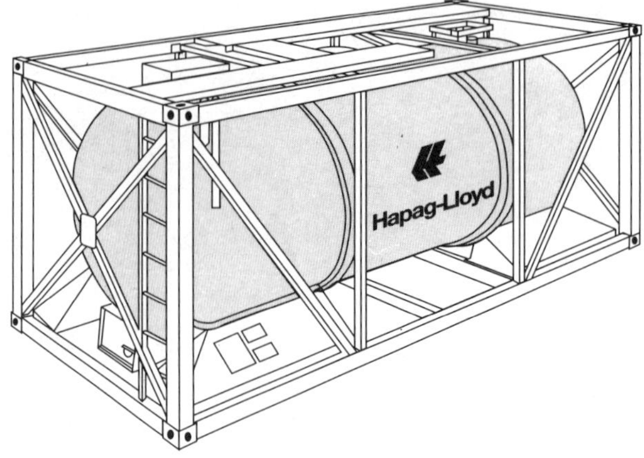

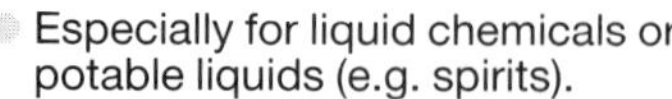

- Especially for liquid chemicals or potable liquids (e.g. spirits).
- All tank containers satisfy the requirements of the IMDG-Code for portable tanks of type 1 as well as the US-DOT specification for IM 101-tanks.
- All Tank Containers are designed for a working pressure of 3 bar (43.5 p.s.i.) (gauge pressure) the test pressure is 4.5 bar (65.3 p.s.i.) (gauge pressure).
- **For foodstuffs only certain containers are suitable (please see footnote 1). They are labeled "Potable Liquids only".**
- **Tank containers must be filled to at least 80 % to avoid dangerous surging-swell during transport (please see table).**
- **Generally tank containers must not be filled to more than 95 % to allow for possible heat expansion (please see table).**
- **Tank containers equipped for top discharge have no openings at bottom, therefore can only be used for pressure discharge (please see subheadings).**
- **Containers must be redelivered in clean condition.**
- **Note permissible weight limits for road and rail transport.**

Electric Plugs on Refrigerated Containers

- Depending on power sources refrigerated containers are equipped with 1 or 2 plugs 380V/50 Hz to 460V/60 Hz (32 A), 200V/50 Hz to 220V/60 Hz (60 A).
- There are fixed cables with a length of 15 m (49 ft).
- Couplings for adapters are available.
- **Adapters are subject to corresponding safety regulations.**

380/460 V plugs:

- 4poles according to CEE.
- According to ISO 1496/II annex O.
- **Earth contact in 3hr position according to socket.**

Earth Contact

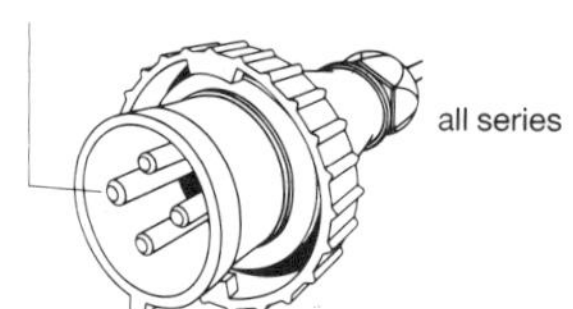

200/220 V plugs:

- 4poles
- According to ISO 1496/II annex M.
- **Position of earth contact according to illustration.**

Earth Contact

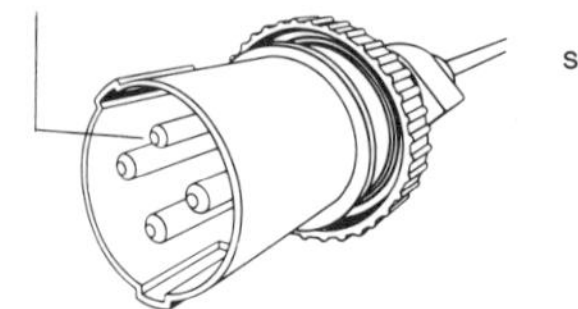

Marine Insurance

Notes and comments on ocean cargo insurance

Material for this section has been provided by the Insurance Company of North America (INA), a CIGNA Worldwide Company. World Trade Press gratefully acknowledges INA and CIGNA for this contribution.

Introduction

The Ever Present Need for Marine Insurance

In spite of all our modern developments in marine transportation, marine disasters are an ever present hazard for those engaged in the foreign trade and commerce of the world.

Here are only a few dispatches from various ports of the world, selected at random during a period of a few weeks.

M/T Bridgewater
(Cia. Atlantica Pacifica, S.A.)
Sydney, January 30: Rescue vessels are heading for the *Bridgewater*, reported to have broken in two off Australia. The two sections have drifted about 12 miles apart. The stern is still afloat but the bow is reported to be sinking. Some of her crew were seen aboard both sections.

SS President Fillmore
(American President Lines, Inc.)
Jacksonville, March 3: From Gulf ports for Mediterranean ports via New York, encountered severe weather on March 1 and/or 2 and put into Jacksonville at 2130 today in distress. Bulwarks on starboard side forecastle head carried away and two of four steel pontoons on number 1 hatch as well as the three tarpaulins were carried overboard. The remaining two pontoons are adrift on deck Number 1 hold filled with seas to the height of number 1 LTP. Number 2 hold, by soundings, is dry. Number 1 LH is stowed with 300 tons flour, cement and steel anchors, corn meal, steel buoys, electronic apparatus and radio equipment. Foredeck cargo consists of large cases of structural steel which externally appear sound.

SS Green Island
(Central Gulf S.S. Corp.)
Charleston, March 4: From Corpus Christi, Orange and Houston for Alexandria, Egypt and Middle East ports via Charleston, S.C. (for bunkers), encountered severe weather during the evening of March 2, and put into Charleston at 0140 this morning in distress. The anchor windlass was immobilized and the cement plugs in the chain pipe carried away. The chain locker and the forepeak flooded and soundings of number 1 hold indicated 25 inches of water in the bilges. The after steering station was also KO'ed.

M/T Gem
(Urania Transportation Co., Inc.)
New York, March 8: *Gem*, from Rio Haina for Baltimore, in Lat 33.33 North, Long 75.18 West at 0530 March 8, broken amidships. *Jytte Skou* was alongside but due to state of weather was unable to stand by, navy vessels proceeding to assist.

Portsmouth, Virginia: The Lib. *M/V Victoria* today rescued seven men from the bow section of the Gem, several hours after the tanker broke in two.

SS La Parnpa
(Buries Markes, Ltd.)
London, April 5: *Clan Buchanan*, Glasgow for Chittagong, and *La Parnpa*, Glasgow and Newport for Vancouver, have been in collision at Newport, England on April 4. The *La Pampa* is holed below the water line and the propeller of the *Clan Buchanan* is being examined.

MV Lys-Point
(Simonsen & Slang)
Boston, July 18: Ro-ro *MV Rolf-Buck*, outwards, and *MV Lys-Point*, inwards in collision. Rolf-Buck slightly damaged at bow, proceeding to Felixstowe as planned. *Lys-Point* sustained damage to upper bow railings on starboard side and one container on deck.

Marijeannie
(D.J. Chandris)
Rosario, July 18: M bulk carrier/container vessel *Marijeannie* left Rosario July 14 for Paranagua. Enroute, when heaving anchor, leakage was discovered in number 6 double bottom tank. Presently berthed at San Nicolas port and being inspected.

Rosario, July 21: Agents at Rosario advise damage located in number 6 double bottom hopper tank, consisting of two perforations in way of shell plating close to bildge keel. Divers installing cement box as temporary repair.

MV Kirsten Wesch
(Jonny Wesch)
London, July 19: *MV Kirsten Wesch* en route from Rotterdam to Warri sustained damage to auxiliary engine July 10. Called Las Palmas as port of refuge for temporary repairs.

MV Tolga
(Government of Algeria)
Bizerta, July 21: Ro-ro *MV Tolga* on fire early morning of July 20 off Les Fratelli Islands. Crew rescued. Vessel taken in tow by Tunisian and Algerian tugs and brought to Bizerta Roads. Extinguishing operations still underway as vessel continues to burn due to strong winds and bad weather.

Sumber Agang
Jakarta, July 24: Freighter *Sumber Agang* sank off an island in eastern Indonesia earlier this month and at least 80 passengers were reported missing. The vessel, carrying more than 90 passengers and crew, was traveling from port of Ambori to Kisar Island when she sank July 14. Ten survivors including seven crew members were rescued. The port authorities said the vessel was authorized to carry only 20 passengers and had been swamped by heavy seas near Buru Island.

Each of these marine disasters resulted in financial loss. If the owners of the ships and cargoes had insurance, those losses were covered to the extent of the insurance.

Marine insurance plays a vital part in international trade and economic progress. Through marine insurance, the financial losses resulting from perils of and on the sea are transferred to professional risk-takers known as underwriters, the marine insurance companies. They can absorb those losses because of their financial strength and their application of underwriting experience and principles.

Marine insurance has sometimes been regarded as mysterious and strange, as beyond the understanding of the uninitiated. Perhaps this feelings arises from the fact that marine insurance well antecedes the Middle Ages. Perhaps it arises from the fact that marine insurance touches so many different countries, languages, currencies and forms of commercial practice. Perhaps it arises from the flavor of the sea itself.

But marine insurance is not strange, not mysterious. It is as easily understood as any other type of insurance coverage. The growing importance of foreign trade increasingly focuses attention on marine insurance and requires a better understanding of it. The questionable stability and remittability of certain foreign currencies emphasizes the security and hence the advantage of marine insurance in United States dollars.

This article is designed to present, in a simple and non-technical manner, some of the basic facts of marine insurance practice and marine insurance coverage as they apply to cargo insurance.

It is intended to help the exporter, the importer, the freight forwarder and others in the broad field of foreign trade in their consideration of cargo insurance. Moreover, we hope that the insurance agent and the insurance broker will find it helpful in their service to their clients.

For simplicity we are taking up the subject of cargo insurance, from the standpoint of the insurance buyer, under six headings:

- When to Insure
- How to Insure
- How Much to Insure
- Terms and Conditions of Coverage
- Cost of Insurance
- Adjustment of Claims

This article is not an extended treatise. In the interest of brevity it treats only with simple fundamental considerations. For those who wish to go into the subject more deeply, refer to "Selected References" on page 313.

However, if this article gives you a better understanding of marine insurance as it applies to cargo insurance, it will have accomplished its purpose.

When to Insure

One of the most basic and fundamental principles of insurance is that of insurable interest. Insurable interest is a deciding factor in the question of when to insure.

Generally speaking, a person has an interest in a marine adventure when he will benefit from the safe arrival of the vessel or cargo, or when he will be prejudiced by its loss, damage or detention. It is immediately apparent that this covers a broad field. Not only do the owners of the vessel and cargo benefit from their safe arrival, or suffer from their loss or damage but so do a number of other people, who, in the operation of trade, will have an ultimate benefit or loss.

Insurable interest, then, falls into two broad categories, the insurable interest of owners and the insurable interest of non-owners.

Ownership Situations: Terms of Sale

At what point does the title to property actually pass from seller to buyer? Determination of the ownership of goods moving in foreign or domestic trade is not always a simple matter.

The terms of sale govern this relationship of property to owner. An understanding of the different types of terms of sale is essential if we are to know when insurance should be placed.

The most widely accepted terms of sale definitions may be referenced in "Incoterms" available from the International Chamber of Commerce in New York, New York (212) 206-1150. However, the National Foreign Trade Council's "Revised American Foreign Trade Definitions—1941" are also considered an acceptable guide to the six groups of terms of sale.

1. Ex Point of Origin

(as "Ex Factory, "Ex Warehouse," etc.)

These terms require the seller to place the goods at the disposal of the buyer at the specified point of origin on the date, and within the period fixed. The buyer must then take delivery at the agreed place and must bear all future costs and risks.

It should be emphasized that the goods are at the risk of the buyer from the time he is obligated to take delivery, even though he may not actually take delivery at that time. He acquires an insurable interest as of that time and should protect his interest accordingly, since he can no longer look to the seller to do so.

2. FOB

(Free on Board)

Here the seller is required to bear costs and charges and to assume risks until the good are loaded on board a named carrier at a named point. This might be on board a railroad car at an inland point of departure or on board an ocean vessel at a port of shipment.

Loss or damage to the shipment is borne by the seller until loaded at the point named and by the buyer after loading at that point, and insurance protection should be arranged accordingly. Actual transfer of interest is evidenced by the carrier furnishing a clean bill of lading or other transportation receipt.

It should be noted that FOB sales terms, specifying named points beyond the seller's premises (for example, FOB vessel), place upon the seller the risks of transit until the title passes to the buyer at the point specified. In actual practice, however, FOB terms are often so loosely specified that it is not easily resolved whether the seller or the buyer should bear the risk of physical loss or damage.

The seller is better advised in this case to provide his own insurance protection through the use of an FOB Sales Endorsement to his policy, rather than rely on the warehouse-to-warehouse coverage contained in the buyer's insurance policy. The suggested coverage protects the seller from transit risks from the point of origin to the point at which title passes to the buyer. (Refer also second half of "Non-Ownership Situations" on page 299.)

When sales are made under letters of credit, the letters of credit normally cannot be used until an on-board bill of lading has been issued. If a loss or damage occurs before goods are loaded on board the ocean vessel, a clean on-board bill of lading will not be available and letters of credit cannot be used. This places a financial risk on the seller since he may not then be able to get the benefit of any insurance that the buyer may have arranged. Here again the seller should arrange for insurance to give him full protection.

At times, and particularly in certain trades, the seller on FOB terms may provide marine insurance on behalf of the buyer. However, this involves a non-ownership situation and is discussed on page 299.

3. FAS

(Free Along Side) as "FAS Vessel, named port of shipment"

These sales terms require the seller to place goods along side the vessel or on the dock designated by the buyer and to be responsible for loss or damage up to that point. Insurance under these terms is ordinarily placed by the buyer, but the seller should protect himself with an FOB Sales Endorsement, as described above, for risks prior to the transfer of title. As in the FOB discussion the non-ownership situation is discussed in "Non-Ownership Situations" which follows.

4. C & F

(Cost & Freight) Named Point of Destination

Under these terms, the seller's price includes the cost of transportation to the named point but does not include the cost of insurance. Insurance under these terms is the responsibility of the buyer. The seller is responsible for loss or damage until the goods enter the custody of the ocean carrier or, if an on-board bill of lading is required, when the good are actually delivered on board. Here again the seller needs insurance protection to that point at which his responsibility for loss or damage ceases.

5. CIF

(Cost, Insurance and Freight) Named Point of Destination

Under these terms the selling price includes the cost of the goods, marine insurance and transportation charges to the named point of destination. The seller is responsible for loss or damage until the goods have been delivered into the custody of the ocean carrier or, when an "on board" bill of lading is required, until the goods have been delivered on board the vessel.

In CIF sales, the seller is obligated to provide and pay for marine insurance, and to provide war risk insurance as obtainable in his market at the time of shipment. War risk insurance is at the buyer's expense. The seller and buyer should be in clear agreement on this point since in time of war or crisis the cost of war risk insurance may change rapidly.

It is desirable that the goods be insured against both marine and war risk with the same underwriter so that there can be the least possibility of dispute arising as to the cause of loss, as in the case of missing vessels and, to a lesser degree, wartime collisions.

The character of the marine insurance should be agreed upon insofar as being WA (With Average) or FPA (Free of Particular Average), as well as any other special risks that are covered in specified trades, or against which the buyer may wish individual protection. Among the special risks that should be considered and agreed upon between seller and buyer, are theft, pilferage, leakage, breakage, sweat, contact with other cargoes and others peculiar to any particular trade. It is important that contingent or collect freight and customs duty should be insured to cover Free of Particular Average losses, as well as total loss after arrival and entry but before delivery.

In all cases, there should be a clear understanding as to the value for which the goods are to be insured. This may be of importance in case of assessment in general average (explained on page 311). Full insurance to value will avoid difficulty should a general average situation arise.

In CIF sales the seller must use ordinary care in selecting a financially sound underwriter. Should claims arise from a shipment, it is the buyer's responsibility to secure settlement. With the good will of the customer in mind, the exporter should select an underwriter providing fair, prompt and convenient loss service.

6. Ex Dock, Named Port of Importation

This term is more common to U.S. import than to export practice where it is seldom used. Under these terms the seller's price includes the cost of the goods and all additional charges necessary to put them on the dock at the named port of importation with import duty paid. The seller is then obligated to provide and pay for marine insurance and, in the absence of a specific agreement otherwise, war risk insurance.

The seller is responsible for any loss or damage, or both, until the expiration of the free time allowed on the dock at the named port of importation. Otherwise the comments under CIF terms above apply here as well.

Non-Ownership Situations

In many situations the seller has an insurable interest, even though title has passed to the buyer and he is therefore a non-owner. In these situations the seller should see that his interest is protected.

When the seller sells on terms FOB inland point, he transfers the title to the buyer before the commencement of the ocean voyage. In this case the obligation to place marine and war risk insurance rests, strictly speaking, with the buyer.

However, it is customary in many trades for the seller on FOB terms (or similar terms), by arrangement, to obtain insurance, as well as ocean freight space, for account of the buyer.

This is, in effect, an agency relationship. It can be provided for by a policy clause reading:

> "to cover all shipments made by or to the assured for their own account as principals, or as agents for others and in which they have an insurable interest, or for the account of others from which written instructions to insure them have been received prior to any known or reported loss, damage or accident or prior to sailing of vessel."

Moreover, the seller on FOB or other terms, under which the title passes to the buyer at some inland point of departure, will have a *financial* interest in the goods until payment has been received. This situation arises when the terms of payment call for sight draft against documents, or for acceptance at 30-60-90 days sight, or for open book account.

Under such circumstances, the seller will be well advised to place his own insurance to protect himself in the event that the loss or damage to the shipment impairs the buyer's desire to make payment as originally contemplated. For example, the buyer may be uninsured, or the buyer's coverage may be inadequate because of under-insurance or restricted conditions. The buyer's insurance company may be less liberal in loss adjustments than would the insurer of the seller or, because of currency restrictions, a foreign company may be hampered in its ability to transmit funds.

When claims are paid by a foreign insurance company, devaluation of foreign currencies may cause loss in exchange when the insurance is not expressed in United States dollars.

Insolvency of the foreign insurance carrier, while unlikely, could also occur to the embarrassment of the buyer.

In the event of the buyer's own insolvency, any claims collected under his own open policy might be recoverable in favor of his insolvent estate and not, in the first instance at least, in favor of the seller in this country.

At times the total loss of a shipment has prevented the payment for the goods. This has occurred in countries which would not allocate foreign exchange unless the goods are actually landed and cleared through customs.

While some of these contingencies may seem remote, others are not so remote. Certainly they all point up the fact that a seller does bear a financial risk until such time as payment from the foreign buyer is actually in hand.

The safe and simple way for the exporter to avoid these pitfalls is to merely stipulate in the sales terms that he will be responsible for providing the insurance as FOB Philadelphia, including Marine and War Risk insurance. This will enable him to place his own primary insurance coverage and deal throughout with his own insurance company in this country through his own agent or broker.

Whenever world currency dislocations exist this is a distinct advantage. In the event of a loss, the seller who has placed insurance in this country may be able to make replacement shipments without becoming involved in foreign exchange or import control difficulties. At the buyer's request, the seller can credit him with the insurance proceeds following the loss or damage to the original shipment and apply such credit to future shipments.

There are several countries whose laws require that marine insurance on shipments to those countries must be placed with local insurance companies. This has the effect of requiring the importer to furnish the insurance. However, the exporter can still protect himself by the purchase of "Contingency" or "Difference in Conditions" insurance which protects his own interests in the event the importer's insurance fails or falls short. While the cost of this is naturally less than the cost of primary insurance, it must be borne by the exporter.

In the situation facing the American importer the problems outlined above are reversed to some extent.

The American buyer on CIF terms must rely upon foreign underwriters, since the insurance will have been placed by the seller in the country of origin. Many of the insurance disadvantages already mentioned as applying to FOB export sales will apply to CIF purchases.

By purchasing on FOB, C & F or similar terms, the American importer can control his own insurance. He will then be able to deal with his own underwriters in case of loss or in case of demand for general average security.

In coastwise or intercoastal domestic shipments, sales are frequently made on an FOB dock basis, with or without instructions from the buyer as to the placing of marine insurance. However, a number of trade associations have adopted terms of sale under which the seller is required to effect insurance in the absence of instructions from the buyer to the contrary.

The terms of sale and terms of payment are all-important in the placing of marine insurance. The subject is a complex one, and needs will vary by trade and by commodity.

Both the foreign trader and the domestic trader will need to consult their insurance agents or brokers freely in working out the insurance protection best suited to his own requirements.

How to Insure

Formerly it was the practice to arrange specific marine insurance policies only when they were needed. This method is still used by those not regularly engaged in foreign trade—for example, by individuals shipping household goods or personal effects.

However, by far the greater volume of ocean marine insurance is now written under what is known as open policies. These are insurance contracts which remain in force until cancelled and under which individual successive shipments are reported or declared. The open policy saves time and expense for all concerned, whether underwriter, agent or assured.

The Open Policy

The shipper gains many advantages from the use of an open policy.

In the first place, he has automatic protection (up to the maximum limits stated in the policy) from the time shipments leave the warehouse at the place named in the policy for the commencement of transit. The policyholder warrants that shipments will be declared as soon as practicable, but unintentional failure to report will not void the insurance, since the goods are "held covered," subject to policy conditions. In effect, this is errors and omissions coverage, and it forestalls the possibility that, because of the press of business, goods may commence transit without being insured.

Second, the open policy provides a *convenient* way to report shipments. It also relieves the shipper from the necessity of arranging individual placings of insurance for each shipment.

Third, under an open policy the shipper has prior knowledge of the rate of premium that will be charged and thus can be *certain* of the cost. This in turn facilitates his quoting a landed sales price.

Finally, the use of the open policy creates a business relationship that may exist over a long period of time (CIGNA companies have more than one insured holding an open policy for over 100 years). This permits the insurer to learn the special requirements of its assureds and so to provide them with *individualized* protection, tailor-made to fit the specific situation. This may be an important factor in the case of loss adjustments at out-of-the-way ports around the world, or in overcoming problems peculiar to a given commodity.

From the underwriter's operating standpoint, the use of open policies represents a more *efficient* way of doing business. The ultimate benefits of this efficiency accrue to the policyholder through the reduction of the insurance company's expense.

Declarations, Bordereaus, Special Policies and Certificates

There are two methods of reporting shipments under open policies.

In the case of imports, a short form of declaration will usually be sufficient, since there is no need to furnish evidence of insurance to third parties. This form calls for the name of the vessel and sailing date, points of shipment and destination, nature of commodity, description of units comprising the shipment, the amount of insurance desired and the number of the open policy under which the declaration is made. The declaration forms are prepared by the assured and are forwarded daily, weekly, or as shipments are made. The forms are forwarded to the insurance agent or broker for transmission to the company. When full information is not available at the time a declaration is made, a *provisional* report may be sent in. The "provisional" is closed when value is finally known. The premium is billed monthly in accordance with the schedule of rates provided by the policy. The bordereau is similar to the declaration in that it is simple to complete and is non-negotiable. It provides for multiple shipments within a prescribed monthly reporting period.

The same short form of declaration may be used at times for exports, if claims are to be returned by foreign consignees for adjustment in this country, in which case no special marine policy is issued.

However, in most cases the exporter must furnish evidence of insurance to his customer, to banks or to other third parties in order to permit the collection of claims abroad. This calls for a special marine policy, occasionally referred to as a certificate.

The special marine policy contains information similar to that shown on the declaration. In addition, it calls for the marks and numbers of the shipment, the name of the party to whom loss shall be payable (usually the assured "or orders" thus making the instrument negotiable upon endorsement by the assured), and the applicable policy provisions. Some of these provisions are standard clauses and are incorporated by reference only, while others are specific and apply to the individual shipment in question.

The special marine policy is generally prepared in four or more copies. The original (and duplicate if necessary) is negotiable and is forwarded with the shipping documents to the consignee. The remaining documents serve as office copies for the assured and for the company.

A special marine policy may be prepared by the assured, by the freight forwarder, by the insurance agent or broker or by the company. It is important that it be made out with care. The shipment should be described in sufficient detail to make identification clear, especially if more than one shipment is going forward by the same vessel. The voyage should be explicitly stated, as "New Castle, Pa., by rail to Philadelphia, *SS John Doe* to Santiago, Chile." If the ultimate destination is an inland city, this should be made clear.

The terms "special marine policy" and "certificate" are both used. The practical effect of the two is the same, but a word as to their difference will be of interest.

In former years the use of "certificate" was customary. This, as the name implies, certifies that a shipment has been insured under a given open policy, and that the certificate represents and takes the place of such open policy, the provisions of which are controlling.

Because of the objections that an instrument of this kind did not constitute a "policy" within the requirements of letters of credit, it has become the practice to use a special marine policy. This makes no reference to the open policy and stands on its own feet as an obligation of the underwriting company.

In some cases, exporters insure through freight forwarders when arranging for forwarding, warehousing, documentation, ocean freight space and the other requirements of overseas trade. While this method may have the merit of simplicity, it should be emphasized that there are definite advantages in having one's own policy and that this need not entail burdensome clerical detail. These advantages are cited below.

In the first place, the exporter gets conditions of insurance suited to his own requirements, rather than coverage designed for general application over a wide diversity of commodities and trades.

Second, rates will be based upon the known hazards and experience of the exporter's business, rather than upon an average of which his business is only a part. There will thus be control of insurance costs rather than the reverse.

Third, the exporter will be able to call upon the services of his local insurance agent or brother, and through him upon the services of the company, in such matters as loss prevention service and packing advice, and in the adjustment of claims.

Fourth, in certain circumstances where the shipper desires coverage even after the goods reach the consignee, the open policy is able to provide extended coverage.

Fifth, the open policy attaches automatically and remains continuous until cancelled thus allowing the exporter freedom to ship.

The use of his own policy need not necessarily require the exporter to prepare special policies. Arrangements can be made allowing the freight forwarder to provide these special policies through the facilities of the exporter's insurance company.

How Much to Insure

Valuation Clauses

The question of how much to insure is closely related to the question of how to insure.

Unlike the fire insurance policy, and many others, the marine insurance policy is a "valued" one. That is, when the insurance is placed, a value is agreed upon. In the case of total loss, this amount is paid. In the case of partial loss, a percentage of the total insured value is recoverable. This will be discussed more fully in considering adjustment of claims (refer to "Particular Average" on page 309).

The purpose in taking out insurance on goods moving in foreign trade is to be made whole in case of loss. This "whole" clearly includes a number of factors. There are the basic invoice costs, additional charges in the invoice for export packing, inland freight, consular and other fees, ocean freight, insurance premiums and anticipated profit.

The amount of insurance must be governed accordingly, if the "whole" is to restored in case of loss. The profit item is customarily provided for by a percentage increase applied to the specific items. This increase is also useful in the event of assessment for general average contribution, which is based on the "sound arrival value" of the shipment. (Refer to "General Average" on page 310.) This value can well be larger than that contemplated at the time of shipment, because of an increase in market values while the shipment was in transit.

A valuation clause in common use reads:

> "valued premium included at amount of invoice, including all charges in the invoice and including prepaid and/or advanced and/or guaranteed freight, if any, plus _____%." (This is usually 10% on exports.)

This clause does not require the use of a formula to calculate the total premium, as is the case when the premium itself is included in the valuation as a specific item to which the increase also applies.

The "premium included" method is suitable when premium rates are low, as in normal times. However, when rates become higher, as for war risk in time of war, the premium should be calculated by separate item.

A clause may sometimes be used which provides that if insurance is declared prior to shipment or prior to known or reported loss, the valuation shall be in the amount of the declaration. This clause secures maximum flexibility, thus meeting the needs of letters of credit or other financial requirements. Shipments not so declared are valued as provided by the formula contained in the valuation clause.

At times of fluctuating values, importers dealing in such raw commodities as cotton, rubber, sugar, coffee, burlap, etc., may wish to be protected for an increase in value during the voyage. This can be accomplished by the use of an increased value clause. Under this, the premium is paid and losses are adjusted on the basis of the peak value reached while the shipment is in transit.

In certain trades special valuation classes may have become standardized by long usage and may be incorporated in the open policy accordingly.

Terms and Conditions of Coverage

More than a superficial knowledge of policy coverage is essential to a proper understanding of marine insurance. The study of an authoritative text is desirable, but it is hoped that this section will simplify an understanding of the more basic fundamentals of coverage.

Perils Insured Against

A current form of perils clause retains many quaint terms and may read as follows:

> "touching the adventures and perils which this company is contented to bear, and takes upon itself, they are of the seas, fires, assailing thieves, jettisons, barratry of the master and mariners and all other like perils, losses and misfortunes (illicit or contraband trade excepted in all cases) that have or shall come to the hurt, detriment or damage of the said goods and merchandise or any part thereof."

The terms in this clause might be explained.

"Perils of the sea" includes unusual action of wind and waves (often described as "stress of weather" or "heavy weather"), stranding, lightning, collision and damage by sea water when caused by insured perils such as opening of the seams of the vessel by stranding or collision.

"Fire" includes both direct fire damage and also consequential damage, as by smoke or steam, and loss resulting from efforts to extinguish a fire.

"Assailing thieves" refers to a forcible taking rather than clandestine theft or mere pilferage.

"Jettison" is the throwing of articles overboard, usually to lighten the ship in time of emergency.

"Barratry" is the willful misconduct of master or crew and would include theft, wrongful conversion, intentional casting away of vessel or any breach of trust with dishonest intent.

"All other perils" means perils like those already enumerated, i.e. perils of the sea. It does not mean "all risks" in the sense of today's use of that term.

Still other perils are included and represent extensions of coverage added from time to time to the basic protection of the sea perils.

Specific mention of explosion broadens the coverage to include explosion however caused, except by war perils. Explosion resulting from fire is covered under "fires."

The Inchmaree Clause (so-called for a celebrated legal decision involving a vessel of that name) extends the policy to cover loss resulting from a latent defect of the carrying vessel's hull or machinery. Defined as a defect that is not discoverable by due diligence, latent defect is not, by law, recoverable from the vessel owner, and the Inchmaree Clause thus plugs a gap that would otherwise exist in complete protection.

Loss resulting from errors of navigation or management of the vessel by the master or the crew, and for which the vessel owner is likewise relieved of liability by law, is also covered by the Inchmaree Clause.

A number of coverages refer to hazards to which goods are susceptible while on land. The shore clause extends the basic perils to include risks of collision, derailment, overturn, sprinkler leakage, windstorm, earthquake, flood and collapse of docks or wharves.

A third group of hazards may be specifically provided for and additional premium paid. The more common perils in this category are theft, pilferage, nondelivery, fresh water damage, oil damage, sweat damage (caused by condensation dripping from the skin or bulkheads of the vessel or forming on the cargo itself), contact with other cargo, breakage, leakage, hook hole damage and damage to refrigerated cargo resulting from the breakdown of refrigerating machinery.

Coverage is often provided upon an "all risks" basis. (*See* "Average Terms" which follows.)

"Average" Terms

The perils specified by the policy govern the *nature* of loss and damage recoverable under the insurance. The "average" terms govern the *extent* of coverage.

The word "average," in its insurance connotation, means "loss less than total." It comes from the French word *avarie*, which means "damage to ship or cargo," (and ultimately from the Arabic word *awarijah*, which means "merchandise damaged by sea water").

A "particular average" loss is one that affects specific interests only. A "general average" loss is one that affects all cargo interests on board the vessel as well as the ship herself. Particular average and general average losses will be discussed in the consideration of claims. (Refer to "Total Loss" on page 309, "Particular Average" on page 309, "General Average" on page 310, and "General Average: Illustration" on page 311.)

"Free of Particular Average" (FPA) coverage is the narrowest in common use. This clause provides that in addition to total losses, partial losses resulting from perils of the sea are recoverable, but only in the event that the carrying vessel has stranded, sunk, burnt, been on fire or been in collision.

Two forms of FPA coverage must be understood.

In the case of cargoes shipped underdeck, it is customary to use a modification of the English conditions form of FPA Clause (FPA-EC) reading:

> "Free of particular average (unless general) or *unless* the vessel or craft be stranded, sunk, burnt, on fire or in collision with another vessel..."

In the case of cargoes stowed on deck, it is more usual to find the American conditions form of FPA Clause (FPA-AC) reading:

> "Free of particular average (unless general) or *unless caused* by stranding, sinking, burning or collision with another vessel...."

It should be noted that under the English conditions, partial losses resulting from sea perils are recoverable, provided one of the enumerated disasters has taken place, without requiring that the damage actually be caused by such disaster. Under both the English and American forms of FPA Clause, both general average and salvage charges are recoverable.

"With Average" (WA) coverage is a more inclusive form of protection. In its standard form a typical clause may read:

> "Subject to particular average if amounting to 3%, unless general or the vessel and/or craft is stranded, sunk, burnt, on fire and/or in collision, each package separately insured or on the whole."

This coverage gives the assured protection for partial damage by sea perils, if the partial damage amounts to 3% (or other percentage as specified) or more of the value of the whole shipment or of a shipping package. If the vessel has stranded, sunk, been on fire or in collision, the percentage requirement is waived and losses from sea perils are recoverable in full.

Additional *named perils* may be added to the WA Clause. Theft, pilferage, nondelivery, fresh water damage, sweat damage, breakage and leakage are often covered. The combination of perils needed by a particular assured will naturally depend upon the commodity being shipped and the trade involved.

The "all risk" clause is a logical extension of the broader forms of "With Average" coverage. This clause reads:

> "To cover against all risks of physical loss or damage from any external cause irrespective of percentage, but excluding, nevertheless, the risk of war, strikes, riots, seizure, detention and other risks excluded by the F.C.&S. (Free of Capture and Seizure) Warranty and the S.R.&C.C. (Strikes, Riots and Civil Commotion) Warranty in this policy, excepting to the extent that such risk are specifically covered by endorsement."

Some types of loss are commonly excluded and others not recoverable, even under the "all risks" clauses.

Types of Loss Excluded

A careful reading of the so-called "all risk" clause will show that this coverage is not quite so all-inclusive as the name would indicate since it covers only physical loss or damage from external cause(s) and specifically affirms the exclusion of war risks and strikes and riots unless covered by endorsement. These losses are excluded, either by expressed exclusions, conditions or warranties written into the policy or by implied conditions or warranties that are read into every marine policy by legal interpretation.

An "all risks" policy may, of course, *expressly exclude* certain types of damage such as marring and scratching of unboxed automobiles or bending and twisting entirely or unless amounting to a specified percentage or amount.

Also, certain perils such as War and Strikes, Riots and Civil Commotions are commonly excluded, but these perils can be and usually are reinstated, at least in part, by special endorsement or by a separate policy for an additional premium. These perils are dealt with in this way to permit ready revision of terms, conditions and rates which may be required at short notice as world conditions change.

Another common exclusion is the "Delay Clause" which excludes claims for loss of market and for loss, damage or deterioration arising from delay. This exclusion appears in almost every cargo policy.

An underwriter is exceedingly reluctant, however, to assume any liability for loss of market, which is generally considered a "trade loss" and uninsurable. A market loss, furthermore, is an indirect or consequential damage. It is not a "physical loss or damage."

Legal decisions have established two important implied warranties in the marine policies, that of legality of the venture and that of seaworthiness. The latter is of little concern today since policies commonly waive the warranty of seaworthiness by stating that seaworthiness is admitted as between the assured and the insurer.

The insurer is not at liberty, however, to waive the implied warranty of legality. Such a waiver would be against public policy and the law of the land.

Certain implied conditions are not written into the policy but they are so basic to understanding between underwriter and assured that the law gives them much the same effect as if written. Thus, it is implied: (a) that the assured will exercise the utmost good faith in disclosing to his underwriter all facts material to the risk when applying for insurance; (b) that the generally established usages of trade applicable to the insured subject matter are followed; and (c) that the assured shall not contribute to loss through willful fault or negligence.

Furthermore, there is a rather broad class of losses, often described as arising from "inherent vice" whose exclusion is implied in every policy. This type of exclusion is reinforced by the words "from any external cause" in the "all risks" coverage. The word "risk" itself implies that only *fortuitous* losses are intended to be covered. Insurance protects against hazards, not certainties.

It is unreasonable to expect indemnity for damage which one can foresee is bound to occur during any normal transit, and which arises solely because of the nature or condition of the goods shipped. Such damage is said to arise from "inherent vice" which may be defined as an *internal* cause rather than an *external* cause of damage. An example of damage from inherent vice is deterioration of imperfectly cured skins.

Packing is an integral part of the thing shipped and damage caused by the original packing, or lack thereof, does not arise from an externality. It is excluded no matter when the damage itself may occur. For instance, nails may be driven by a careless packer into the contents of a package. Such damage occurring prior to attachment of the insurance is obviously not covered.

On the other hand, an underwriter may inspect a shipment and find that it is packed in an unusual and inferior manner, but may nevertheless accept the risk at a rate of premium which takes into account the hazard represented by the packing. In such a negotiation, the implied condition of utmost good faith, which is never waived, requires that the assured disclose fully all the facts bearing upon the special risk which he asks his insurer to assume.

Similarly, the underwriter is not liable for that ordinary and unavoidable loss of weight caused by evaporation as in ore shipments. Such loss of weight is a "trade loss," allowed for in the price quoted between traders and, from an insurance viewpoint, should not be regarded as a loss at all. In the United States it is not unusual to recognize this kind of exclusion, which would otherwise be implied, by stipulating the normal and expected shortage for which the underwriters will not respond.

When shortage, breakage or leakage is specifically insured "irrespective of percentage," the intent to so cover is clear.

Underwriters also have the ability to deal with small nuisance claims by introducing deductible averages and franchises into the policy. The deductible average is an amount that is subtracted from each loss whereby the assured always bears part of the loss. The franchise on the other hand rules out small claims. Franchises are usually stated as percentages, although occasionally a dollar amount is used. Claims equal to or in excess of the franchise will be paid in full.

It is thus seen that some exclusions can be modified by endorsement as a result of negotiation between assured and underwriter. Others such as the implied warranty of legality of the venture cannot be waived.

As the broadest form of coverage in common use, "all risks" insurance is also the most expensive, and it is not necessarily required by all types of cargo. A shipper whose goods are susceptible to many kinds of damage may need "all risks" insurance. But a shipper whose goods are not subject to various kinds of partial loss should not incur the expense of insurance protection that is broader than necessary.

Most exporters will wish to secure the most complete protection available to avoid controversy with customers, but a concern shipping to its own foreign branch may consider it unnecessary and uneconomical to insure against small losses as from breakage or pilferage. Similarly a large importer knowing by experience the range of losses from leakage or other causes may wish to treat this as a trade loss and insure only against those perils that entail the possibility of a large loss.

FPA coverage is ordinarily suitable for bulk cargoes such as oil, coal and ore.

In general, most manufactured goods will qualify for "all risks" protection. The policyholder's insurance agent or broker will be of help in arranging the coverage best suited to his needs. Letter of credit terms or other specific insurance instructions may determine the extent of coverage required by an exporter.

Damage resulting from negligence on the part of the vessel operators in loading, handling on board, stowing or discharging cargo is recoverable from the carrier under the provisions of the various "Carriage of Goods by Sea" Acts. However, prudent shippers will not rely on this to restrict their insurance coverage. By collecting such claims from underwriters, shippers need not concern themselves with seeking recovery from the carrier. They can leave this to the insurance company, confident that it will make every effort to secure all recoveries that may be due and to credit the assured's loss record with every possible deduction that will help him to merit lower rates.

Extensions of Coverage

Three specialized types of coverage are also provided by the open cargo policy.

The first covers *shipments by aircraft* on "all risks" conditions, irrespective of percentage, but excluding loss due to cold or changes in atmospheric pressure. While it is true that insurance on air express and air freight shipments can be obtained from the airlines, this has disadvantages over controlling the insurance of such shipments by declaring them under an open policy. The insurance purchased from the airlines may merely cover the shipment while it is in the possession of the carrier, without providing full warehouse-to-warehouse coverage. Moreover, the insurance perils may not be as broad as under the shipper's own policy. In addition, when insuring with the airlines, the shipper will be unable to deal with his own underwriters at the time of loss adjustment.

The second covers *mail shipments*, also upon "all risks" conditions, the insured warranting that all packages will be mailed in conformity with parcel post or foreign mail regulations in force at the time of shipment in the country of exportation. While mail insurance can be purchased through the post office, it has the same disadvantages as those given above for insurance purchased from airlines.

The third covers *U.S. import duties* in the case of shipments sustaining partial damage. A separate amount is declared on import shipments to cover the duty that will be due, and the assured agrees to make all reasonable efforts to secure refunds of duty on shipments arriving in damaged condition.

Currency (Term) of Insurance

Formerly, the marine policy covered only from the time the goods were actually loaded on board the ocean vessel at the port of shipment until they were "discharged and safely landed" at the port of destination. This was later extended by adding the words "including transit by craft, raft and/or lighter to and from the vessel."

More recently, warehouse-to-warehouse coverage was provided. Under this, the risks covered by the policy attach from the time goods leave the warehouse for commencement of transit and continue during ordinary course of transit until delivered to final warehouse at destination, or until the expiration of 15 days (30 if destination is outside the limits of the port), whichever shall first occur. In the case of delay in excess of the time limit specified, if it arises from circumstances beyond his control, the assured is "held covered" if he gives prompt notice and pays additional premium.

A growing demand for extension of coverage during World War II led underwriters to adopt the Marine Extension Clause 1943. This extension which supersedes the aforementioned Warehouse-to-Warehouse Clause, is found in practically all open cargo policies. The function of this clause is to broaden warehouse-to-warehouse coverage by eliminating the requirement that ordinary course of transit be maintained and the 15- or 30-day time limit at destination. Moreover, continuation of coverage is provided when certain conditions necessitate discharge of goods from vessel at a port other than the original destination. The most recent form of Marine Extension Clause was developed in 1952. It too provides for extensions as the 1943 version, and adds that the assured will act with reasonable dispatch.

The currency of insurance has thus been broadened from "waterborne" only to full warehouse-to-warehouse protection as extended. Underwriters must be notified and additional coverage secured only if interruption of transit under the assured's control is contemplated. Such situations will occur at times, and assureds should fully inform their insurance agents or brokers of their needs in this respect in order that coverage may be extended as necessary.

Strikes and War Risks

Strikes, riots and civil commotion coverage can be added to the open policy by endorsement. Usually referred to as the S.R.&C.C. Endorsement, it extends the policy to cover damage, theft, pilferage, breakage or destruction of the insured property directly caused by strikers, locked-out workmen or persons taking part in labor disturbances, riots or civil commotions.

Destruction of and damage to property caused by vandalism, sabotage and malicious acts of person(s) regardless of (political/ideological/terroristic) intent be it accidental or otherwise is also held covered under S.R.&C.C. unless so excluded in the F.C.&S. (free of capture and seizure) warranty in the policy.

The S.R.&C.C. Endorsement excludes coverage for any case damage or deterioration as a result of delay or loss of market, change in temperature/humidity, loss resulting from hostilities or warlike operations, absence/shortage/withholding power, fuel, labor during a strike (riot or civil commotion) weapons of war that employ atomic or nuclear fusion/fission.

The current form provides limited coverage within the United States, Commonwealth of Puerto Rico, Canal Zone, Virgin Islands and Canada for damage caused by any agent of any faction engaged in warlike hostilities/operations provided the agent is working secretly and is not in cohesion with the military forces where the described property is situated.

War coverage is customarily furnished in conjunction with marine insurance, even though it is written under a separate policy.

The older form of marine policies, in addition to insuring against the perils of the seas, insured against

> "men of war...enemies...letters of mart and countermart, arrests, restraint and detainments of all kings, princes and people of what nation, condition or quality soever..."

This ancient language granted war risks protection.

In order to eliminate the war cover from the marine policy it became customary to add a "free of capture and seizure" clause, stating that the policy did not cover warlike operations or its consequences, whether before or after the actual declaration of war. The current open policy omits war perils from its insuring conditions and in all cases will include a F.C.&S. clause. War coverage is customarily furnished in conjunction with an open cargo policy and is written under a separate, distinct policy—the War Risk Only Policy.

Not unlike its marine counterpart as respects the basic policy conditions, the war policy covers only against war risks as outlined in detail in some dozen rather specific paragraphs. The policy conditions must be read for complete understanding. In general, they cover risks of capture and seizure, destruction or damage by warlike operations in prosecution of hostilities, civil wars and insurrections or in the application of sanctions under international agreements. Delay or loss of market is excluded. Loss or expense arising from detainments, nationalization of the government to or from which the goods are insured or seizure under quarantine or customs regulations is also excluded.

War risk insurance attaches as goods are first loaded on board an overseas vessel at the port of shipment, and it ceases to attach as goods are landed at the intended port of discharge or on expiry of 15 days from arrival of the overseas vessel whichever first occurs. It includes transshipment and intermediate overland transit to an on-carrying overseas vessel, if any, but in no case for more than 15 days counting from midnight of the day of arrival of the overseas vessel at the intended port of discharge. If in transshipment, the 15-day period is exceeded, the insurance re-attaches as the interest is loaded on the on-carrying vessel. In case the voyage is terminated and the goods are discharged at a port or place other than the original port of discharge, such port or place shall be deemed the intended port of discharge.

The war risk policy is subject to 48 hours cancellation by either party. However, it cannot be cancelled on shipments upon which insurance has already attached. Since the cancellation provision is used at times for changing the conditions of insurance the current coverage should be studied for exact understanding of the war risk policy.

Is war risk insurance needed in ordinary times? Or should it be bought only when international relations become strained to the breaking point?

Loss from floating mines are still deemed to be war risks. More than five hundred mine casualties have been reported since the close of World War II. It is unhappily true that civil strife or other warlike operations have rarely been entirely absent from one quarter of the world or another during the past several decades. The possibility of full scale warfare can seldom be dismissed from our thinking.

It would seem that the prudent assured must continue, for many years to come, to carry war risks insurance for the protection of his overseas shipments.

Cost of Insurance

Considerations in Rating

Unlike most other types of insurance rates, the rates for marine insurance are not standardized. Rather, they are generally determined by the cargo, experience of the risk and the judgment of the underwriter.

In a broad sense, underwriters consider certain basic factors of experience. One is the *cost of loss from major casualties* in specific *voyage* classifications. This factor may be modified for certain commodities indicating variation in major casualty experience because of peculiarities of the trade. A second is *particular average* experience by *commodity*. A third factor is *particular average* experience by *individual accounts*, which differ from each other in varying degree and for innumerable reasons.

Underwriters usually give specific consideration to these factors:

1. Type of coverage
2. Characteristics of commodities involved
3. Origin, destination and routing
4. Carriers used
5. Storage or transshipment en route, if any
6. Effect of trade losses, such as shrinkage, normal loss in weight, etc.
7. Seasonal character of shipments
8. Packing
9. Value—as it affects packing, susceptibility to pilferage, etc.
10. Assured's experience as a foreign trader
11. Shipping and delivery practices
12. Attitude toward claims by assured or his consignees
13. Attitude toward third party recoveries
14. Salvage possibilities under the individual account

Any number of these factors may affect the experience

As experience under an open cargo policy develops, the premium and loss record will be reviewed at intervals, and rate adjustments will be made, if the record and existing circumstances justify such action in the opinion of the underwriter.

Loss Prevention

The primary function of insurance is to redistribute loss and so to manage risk. An equally important function of insurance, and one which is economically more creative, is the actual prevention of loss.

Loss and damage to overseas shipments may be attacked at point of origin through improved packing and marking. They may also be attacked by supervision of loading and discharge to minimize pilferage or by study of storage and handling in course of transit to limit breakage, leakage and other causes of loss. Knowledge of port conditions, both here and in foreign countries, and many other kinds of information of interest made available to the foreign trader are of assistance in preventing or reducing marine losses.

Underwriters have not been unmindful of the assistance that they can render in this connection. The extent and quality of the service which an insurance company is prepared to render in helping with loss prevention problems is one factor that a shipper should bear in mind in selecting his underwriter.

The theoretical goal of packaging engineers is to devise export packing that will be just strong enough to enable the shipment to reach destination in a sound condition. Too weak a package will fail in its purpose; too strong a package will add unnecessarily to the ultimate cost of the product. The marine loss control department of an insurance company makes available its long accumulated experience in this highly specialized and technical field to the overseas shipper.

There are many types of packing: the solid and corrugated fiber cartons; the nailed wood box; the wire bound or strapped box; the cleated fibre board or plywood box; the open wooden or sheathed crates; the drums of metal, fibre or plywood; textile and multiple-ply bags and bales; barrels of many types. The physical properties of the commodity being shipped, its value and the voyage it must undergo will all have a bearing on the optimum packaging that must be provided. Domestic packing is seldom suitable for export purposes, where increased handling, stowage pressures and a wide range of other hazards are likely to be encountered. The "loss prevention" representative of the insurance company will frequently be able to suggest improvements that will result in reduced costs and improved outturns.

Breakage will be reduced by packaging of sufficient strength and proper construction. Water damage and corrosion can be controlled by the use of liners, by the coating of metal parts with special preservatives and in other ways.

Pilferage, one of the most serous forms of marine loss, may be reduced through the use of clips and seals, the use of corrugated fasteners and the marking of packages in such a way as not to disclose the nature of the contents. By making theft physically more difficult, packing designed to prevent pilferage increases the likelihood that a thief will be caught in the act. At the same time, it makes pilferage activity more evident, and thus places greater responsibility on the carrier in whose custody the loss has occurred. This, in turn, facilitates the collection of recoveries and encourages greater care in handling future shipments of a similar nature.

Proper marking will indicate the requirement for any special handling or stowage. It will also make for easier identification at destination.

The use of intermodal containers and air freight carriers for the transport of a great variety of cargo has become increasingly popular in recent years. When loaded and sealed at assured's plant, carried overland to the port, stowed under deck aboard ship and discharged with care, the containers can be an efficient and protective means of shipping cargo. Equally, adequate packing and marking air cargo can effectively influence the sound arrival of goods. Loss prevention experts give important advice on how to load the container or air freight carrier to prevent damage and assist in routing to prevent hijack.

Also new and growing is the shipment of cargo by air freight.

Technical assistance in the loss control field should be available to all holders of open policies. However, attention must necessarily be concentrated where the volume of shipment, and the nature of the commodity, permits worthwhile savings to be effected.

Prevention and reduction of losses through better packing and handling will have these positive results: a more satisfied consignee; lower insurance costs; an economic saving to the commercial community.

Adjustment of Claims

In the adjustment of claims, exporters and their consignees will tend to rely largely upon foreign claims and settling agents. Importers and domestic shippers will avail themselves of the services of their insurance agents and brokers.

However, some knowledge of loss procedure is valuable to those engaged in foreign and domestic trade. It is helpful both in facilitating claim recoveries and in maintaining a closer control over loss experience.

Duties of the Assured

When loss or damage occurs, it is the responsibility of the insurance company to indemnify the assured in accordance with the policy terms and conditions. Nevertheless, the policyholder must meet certain obligations, and these should be clearly understood.

First, the assured must make every reasonable effort to minimize the loss, to "*sue and labor,*" in the language of marine insurance. Second he must *immediately notify* the nearest agent of his underwriters, arrange for a survey of the damage and supply the necessary commercial documents. Third, he must make *timely written claim* upon the carrier.

The *sue and labor* clause of the open cargo policy will read essentially as follows:

> "In case of any loss or misfortune it shall be lawful and necessary to and for the assured, his or their factors, servants and assigns to sue, labor, and travel, for, in and about the defense, safeguard and recovery of the goods and merchandise or any part thereof...to the charges whereof this company will contribute according to the rate and quantity of the sum herein insured."

In other words, the assured—shipper or consignee as the case may be—must act as a prudent uninsured owner would act in keeping his insured loss at a minimum. Reasonable charges incurred for this purpose are collectible under the policy.

Such steps should be taken promptly in order to prevent additional damage. For example, when a shipment of canned goods arrives with some leaking cans in each of several cartons, the leaking cans must be taken out if rusting and label damage are to be minimized. The expense insured in this operation may be recovered under the insurance.

Prompt notice of loss must be given to the nearest representative of the insurance company. In the United States and Canada, this will usually be given through the agent or broker to a claim and loss office of the insurance company. Abroad, underwriters are represented by claims or settling agents or, in some areas, by their own offices. Each special policy lists such loss representatives in the world's principal seaports. Representation at other ports will consist of the local correspondent of the Board of American Institute of Marine Underwriters, or, if none, the nearest Lloyd's Agent.

The claims agent or other representative should be asked to arrange survey and issue a certificate stating the cause and extent of loss or damage. Carrier's representative should be requested to attend the survey. Container and contents should be preserved in the condition in which received until survey has been completed, unless further damage would result by so doing. The survey fee is customarily paid by the consignee, but it is properly included in a valid claim under the insurance.

Claim upon the carrier (ocean or inland) should be made in writing in every instance, preferably before or at the time of taking delivery of the goods. In the case of concealed damage, claim should be made as soon as the damage is known. The form of claim is not important. It should identify the shipment by vessel and bill of lading and state that the carrier will be held responsible for damage thereto. A copy of this letter is necessary to support a claim on underwriters, who have a right to be subrogated to the assured's claim against the carrier.

If a shipment appears damaged or short weight at the time of taking delivery, the consignee or his agent should request an immediate survey by the carrier, and in receipting for the goods he should note the exact condition of the shipment as received. In the event that the carrier will not make delivery unless a clean receipt is given, he should immediately file written notice, describing the condition of the shipment as received and holding the carrier liable for any loss or damage that a subsequent survey may disclose.

Any reply from the carrier should be submitted with the other documents to the insurance company representative. However, the submission of the claim papers to the insurance company representative should not be held up for the carrier's acknowledgment.

The Adjustment

Should the survey confirm that loss or damage has occurred, the following documents will usually be needed in order that prompt adjustment may be carried out and payment secured.

1. Original and duplicate copies of the special marine policy or certificate of insurance.
2. Ocean bill of lading—also transshipment bill of lading and railway freight note when applicable.
3. Original shipper's invoice.
4. Packing list, weight certificates or other evidence of the nature and condition of the goods at the time of shipment.
5. Survey report of the underwriter's representative.
6. Copy of claim on ocean carrier and (if available) the reply thereto.
7. In special cases, other documents may be requested.

Total Loss

An *actual* total loss occurs when the goods are destroyed, when the assured is irretrievably deprived of their possession or when they arrive so damaged as to cease to be a thing of the kind insured. Examples of this last, which is spoken of as a "loss of Specie," are cement arriving as rock or textiles as rags.

Adjustment of actual total losses usually involves little difficulty. The policy being a valued one, payment for total loss is in the full amount of the policy. Disasters likely to give rise to total loss include fire, sinking or stranding of the vessel, collision and loss overboard in the course of loading or discharge.

A *constructive* total loss occurs when the expense of recovering or repairing the goods would exceed their value after this expenditure had been incurred.

In the adjustment of constructive total losses, the value of any remaining salvage abandoned to underwriters may at time, by agreement, be taken into consideration, with payment to the assured upon a net basis. Otherwise, underwriters pay full insured value and may then dispose of the salvage for their own account, provided they have elected to accept abandonment.

A survey report may not be practicable when a total loss has taken place, but the documents should include evidence that the shipment was actually loaded on board the ocean vessel in the full quantity claimed. If the loss was due to sea peril, a "master's protest" will usually be required. This certifies the fact that unusually heavy weather or other exceptional circumstance was encountered during the voyage and is extended to confirm the loss of the shipment in question. In claims for total loss, it is especially necessary that a full set of insurance certificates and bills of lading be submitted to the insurance company representative.

Particular Average

There are two kinds of particular average losses: the total loss of a part of the goods, and the arrival of goods at destination in a damaged condition.

In the first situation, it is necessary to determine how much of the total amount insured is applicable to the missing item. In homogeneous or fungible cargo that is, cargo which is capable of mutual substitution, like oil or coal—it is frequently a matter of simple arithmetic. The value of the unit of measurement of the cargo is found by dividing the amount of insurance by the total number of units in the shipment. This value multiplied by the number of missing units gives the value of the loss.

Where a normal or trade loss is to be expected, as in cargo subject to leakage, slackage or loss of moisture during the voyage, the method of calculation is slightly different. The value of the insurance is divided by the number of units in the "expected outturn," that is, the expected arrived quantity rather than the shipped quantity. This can be determined either by the normal percentage of trade loss for similar shipments or by examinations of sound arrived cargo forming part of the shipment in question. While this method will produce a somewhat higher insured value per unit, it naturally requires the normal or trade loss to be deducted in calculating the actual shortage sustained.

In the case of general cargo with the policy covering diverse articles as invoiced to the purchaser and insured in a lump sum, it will be necessary to apportion the total insurance over the specific item for which a claim is being made. The following example shows the usual method of doing this:

Total invoice	$1,000
Insured for	$1,100
Insurance ratio	110%
Invoice value of items lost	$50
Insured in proportion (110%)	$55

Adjustment of claims on goods arriving in a damaged condition requires a different method of approach. Here the consignee and the surveyor attempt to reach an agreed percentage of depreciation, and this is applied to the insured value of the damaged articles. At times the depreciation agreed upon may be in terms of units of goods (as yards of cloth, for example), and in such cases the insured value of such quantity is the loss recoverable. On the other hand, a flat dollar amount of depreciation may be assessed.

When the percentage of depreciation cannot be mutually agreed upon, the damaged goods must be sold in order to arrive at the extent of loss. When this method is used, the calculation is a comparison of the sound wholesale value of the goods with the damaged values at the time and place of sale. This percentage is then applied to the insured value of the damaged articles. Auction charges and other costs of sale are added to determine the total amount recoverable. The element of market fluctuation is thus eliminated.

It is sometimes incorrectly assumed that when damaged goods are sold to determine the extent of loss, the underwriter is obligated to pay the difference between the amount of insurance and the net proceeds of the sale. This method of adjustment, known as "salvage loss" is regularly used only if goods are justifiably sold short of destination.

If damaged goods can be advantageously repaired at destination, the underwriter will pay the actual cost of such repairs, not exceeding the insured value of the article. A specialized situation arises in the case of damage to *machinery.* Here the policy provides that either the company will be liable for the proportion of the insured value of the lost or damaged part, or it will be liable, at the assured's option, for the cost and expense (including labor and forwarding charges) of replacing or repairing the lost or damaged part. In no event, however, will the company's liability be greater than the insured value of the complete machine.

A somewhat similar situation arises in the case of damage to *labels or wrappers.* Here the policy ordinarily provides that the underwriter shall not be liable for more than an amount sufficient to pay the cost of new labels, together with the cost of reconditioning the goods, but in no event for more than the insured value of the damaged merchandise.

General Average

A general average loss may occur whether goods are insured or not. It is one that results from an intentional sacrifice (or expenditure) incurred by the master of a vessel in time of danger for the benefit of both ship and cargo. The classic example of this is jettison to lighten a stranded vessel. From the most ancient times, the maritime laws of all trading nations have held that such a sacrifice shall be borne by all for whose benefit the sacrifice was made, and not alone by the owner of the cargo thrown overboard.

The principles of general average have been refined over the years, and they have inevitably come to reflect the increasing complexity of present day commerce. A vessel owner may and does declare his vessel under general average whenever, *for the common good in time of danger* an intentional sacrifice of ship or cargo has been made, or an extraordinary expenditure has been incurred. In actual practice, general averages result mainly from strandings, fires, collisions and from engaging salvage assistance or putting into a port of refuge following a machinery breakdown or other peril.

The preparation of a general average adjustment is a complex accounting operation. It is entrusted to professionally trained *average adjusters* (not the insurance company) and frequently requires two or three years for completion.

While the shipper need not concern himself with the adjustment itself, he or his consignee must take action at three points. First, he must post *security* in order to obtain release of cargo at port of destination. Second, he must furnish certain *information* relating to the value of the shipment. Third, he must pay the general average *contribution* at such time as the assessment is finally levied.

Security is required by vessel agents before they release cargo under general average. Until this security has been provided, the ship owner has a lien on the goods and has the right to retain them in his possession.

The security is in two parts. First is the general average bond or agreement *signed by the cargo owner* himself (not the underwriter) by which he agrees to pay such general average contribution as may become due. This document should be signed and returned directly to the adjusters, to save valuable time. Second is a cash deposit or an underwriter's guarantee, which is held by the ship owner as security for the ultimate general average contribution.

An insured cargo owner will usually ask his underwriters or their agents to furnish the guarantee. The uninsured cargo owner will have to make a cash deposit or furnish equivalent security.

The general average deposit receipt is a negotiable instrument and should be carefully preserved. It must be tendered to the average adjusters upon completion of the adjustment for refund of any excess payment over and above the general average contribution as finally determined. (In practice, the required cash deposit or guarantee will slightly exceed the anticipated contribution in order to provide a margin of safety.) An assured who has not waited for an underwriter's guarantee and has posted a cash deposit should surrender his general average deposit receipt to his underwriters at the first opportunity. If fully insured, he will then be reimbursed in full.

The general average adjusters will also require of the cargo owner certain *information,* in order that they may calculate the landed value on which the contribution is to be based. This information will include a certified copy of the original shipper's invoice and a "statement of value" showing the gross wholesale market value at the port of discharge. It is desirable that these documents, together with copies of the bills of lading, be routed through the underwriter to the general average adjusters.

If the cargo owner is insured to value, his eventual payment of the general average *contribution* will be made by the underwriter who furnished the guarantee. If but partially insured, contributions and credits are shared *pro rata* by the assured and underwriter. In the case of the uninsured cargo owner, the contribution will be offset against his cash deposit plus any credit for sacrifices (*see* "General Average: Illustration" below), and the balance refunded to him.

The underwriters may not be liable for the full general average contribution of an assured unless the amount of insurance equals the landed value of the goods. The valuation clause in the open policy (which provides for declaring insurance in the amount of invoice, plus insurance, plus freight, plus 10%) provides a measure of leeway for just such a situation.

An insured cargo owner will collect his physical damage loss from his underwriters as in a particular average claim. Cargo interests that have had part or all of their goods sacrificed for the common safety will be entitled to receive an allowance in the general average. This appears as a credit entry in the adjustment and is offset against the contribution to determine the net amount to be paid or to receive. It is a fundamental principle of general average that contributions are assessed against credits allowed or "made good" for general average sacrifices. Otherwise the interests receiving allowances would be better off than those whose goods had not been sacrificed.

General Average: Illustration

A simplified illustration based upon an actual case, will help to make the application of general average more understandable.

A vessel carrying a bulk cargo of ore was stranded. In attempts to get free, part of the cargo was jettisoned, both the engines and the ship were damaged, and a salvage vessel was employed. The ship was refloated after 10 days and put into a port of refuge for repairs.

Adjustment of the general average will work out as follows:

Sound market value at destination of jettisoned cargo (less duty and handling charges)		$20,000
Cost of hull and engine repairs chargeable to general average, i.e., resulting from "intentional" damage in efforts to refloat	$50,000	
Services of salvage vessel	$70,000	
Disbursements at port of refuge and other charges	$35,000	
Total "vessel" sacrifice	$155,000	$155,000
Total to be allowed or "made good" in general average		$175,000
Value of cargo (including sacrifice)		$100,000
Value of vessel (including sacrifice)		$400,000
Total contributory values		$500,000
Rate of general average contribution	($175,000 / $500,000)	35%

The cargo and the vessel will each *contribute 35%* of their respective values, and they will *receive* their sacrifices and expenditures. The final reckoning will then be as follows:

	Pays contribution of	Receives	Balance
Cargo	$35,000 (35% of $100,000)	$20,000	$15,000 to pay
Vessel	$140,000 (35% of $400,000)	$155,000	$15,000 to receive

If the cargo owner was fully insured, he will have had his underwriters furnish a general average guarantee in order to secure possession of the balance of his ore at destination. He will have been reimbursed for the insured value of the ore jettisoned. He will then be relieved of any further participation in the general average.

If the cargo owner was uninsured, he will have had to give security in the amount of about $30,000 in order to gain custody of the balance of his shipment of ore. Eventually he will be credited with the allowance for the jettisoned ore, and this will reduce his balance to pay to $15,000, which will represent an out-of-pocket expense. In addition, of course, he will have had to stand the $20,000 loss of the ore jettisoned.

The example given above has assumed a single cargo owner. The same principle applies equally to general cargo vessels, and each individual shipper must personally sign a general average bond, and he or his underwriter must furnish further security and pay any balance due after receiving credit for allowances.

It is clear that liability for contribution in general average is far from an academic matter to the ocean shipper or consignee. His ownership of cargo entails certain personal obligations (such as signing the bond and furnishing information) which he cannot avoid. But by fully insuring his goods, the financial obligation can be transferred to his underwriters.

Subrogation: Recoveries from Carriers

It might be thought that the assured has no further interest in a claim, once it has been settled. This is not the case. It is basic in the law of insurance that the insurer, upon payment of a loss, is entitled to the benefit of any rights against third parties that may be held by the assured himself.

Recoveries from vessel owners and others play an important part in reducing the loss experience under an open policy. It is thus of very real value to the shipper to be insured by a company that vigorously pursues its rights of subrogation against inland and ocean carriers and other parties that may be held responsible for losses covered by the policy.

When goods arrive at destination in a damaged condition, the question arises as to the extent of the carrier's liability for such damage. Liability will depend in part upon the provisions of the bill of lading as the contract of carriage, in part upon common law modifications of the freedom of contract in this field, and in part upon statutory enactments, notably the Harter Act of 1893 and the Carriage of Goods by Sea Act of 1936 (known as COGSA).

The degree to which a steamship company can be held responsible for damaged sustained by a specific shipment is frequently difficult to determine. COGSA applies to import and export shipments and, by agreement, to much of our coastwise and intercoastal business a well. Where COGSA applies, general speaking, the vessel *is* responsible for damage resulting from negligence in the loading, stowing and discharge of cargo. It *is not* responsible for damage resulting from errors of navigation or management of the ship, from unseaworthiness of the vessel (unless caused by lack of due diligence to make it seaworthy), or from perils of the sea, fire, and a number of other listed causes. The burden of proof in establishing fault will rest at times upon the shipper and at times upon the carrier.

The intricacies of these situations cannot be dealt with at length here. The subject is complex and one that calls for expert handling, if maximum recoveries from carriers are to be secured. For many years, certain underwriters have found it expedient to utilize the service of a recovery agency devoted entirely to their own claims work. The results have amply justified this specialized attention.

In selecting a marine insurance company, shippers should not fail to satisfy themselves as to the competence of its recovery facilities. The subrogation efforts of insurance companies benefit the individual account by keeping down the insurance cost. They are also an important factor in securing improved cargo handling by ocean carriers.

The overall loss policy of his insurance company is important to the assured. The purpose of an insurance company is to pay losses. Loses covered by the policy should be adjusted fairly and paid without delay. In fairness to others, losses not covered by the policy cannot be accepted.

Borderline situations are bound to occur from time to time. For one reason or another, full information as to the cause and extent of damage cannot always be secured. At these times, the assured has a right to expect that his claim will be sympathetically considered and that he will be given every reasonable benefit of doubt that the circumstances permit.

Regardless of the type of claim, the assured is entitled to prompt, courteous and competent loss adjustment. Those marine underwriters who have a long established record of honorable dealing to maintain will make every effort to meet these exacting standards and to justify the continued confidence of policyholders in the trading community throughout the world.

Conclusion

The Agent or Broker

What is the function of the insurance agent and the insurance broker in marine insurance?

The insurance agent or broker will render valuable assistance in selecting reliable marine underwriters.

He will arrange the amount and kind of protection that the shipper's operations and the nature of the commodity require. If FPA only, or limited conditions is needed, the shipper should not pay for more. If "all risk" insurance is needed, he should not be provided with less.

He will be of help, moreover, in the presentation of losses, and he can facilitate the release of goods in general average situations. By keeping a watchful eye on the premium and loss record of an account, he should make certain that justifiable rate reductions are not overlooked by the underwriter. At times, he can make suggestions for loss prevention studies that will lead to improved experience and so justify reduced rates of premium.

In short, the insurance agent or broker is the policyholder's representative in all that concerns his ocean marine coverage.

The Insurance Company

What should the foreign and domestic trader look for in his insurance company?

Financial strength is the first consideration. Financial strength represented by the policyholder's surplus should be adequate to withstand the sudden shock of catastrophic loss or the slow attrition of business depression. This is the ultimate safeguard that an insurance company will meet its obligations.

Know-how is the second consideration. There is no substitute for judgment based upon experience, in underwriting, in loss prevention, in loss adjustment and in loss recovery. Know-how at the head office is of little value unless it can be brought to bear upon the needs of the policyholder in his office, in his shipping room and in the warehouses of his consignees throughout the world. A network of trained branch office personnel throughout the United States will insure that this know-how is available when it is needed in this country. A network of foreign underwriting and claims agents, supplemented by company branch offices, will insure that this know-how is available to shippers and consignees abroad.

Obligation is the third consideration. Just as the cash and securities behind the policyholder's surplus are the most tangible evidence of an insurance company's strength, so the sense of obligation underlying its operation is the most intangible, but nonetheless important, evidence of its strength. The obligation of an insurance company to fulfill both the letter and spirit of its contracts is basic. Beyond this, there is its further obligation to pioneer in new areas of usefulness to the insuring public and to be a leader, not a follower, in the insurance industry and in the larger business world.

The efforts of the insurance organization by which this booklet has been prepared have been directed toward these objectives every since its founding in 1792.

Selected References

Arnould, Sir Joseph
Arnould on the law of marine insurance and average. 16th ed. Sir Michael J. Mustill & Jonathan C.B. Giltman. Stevens & Sons, Ltd., 1981.

Dover, Victor
A handbook to marine insurance. London, 1962.

Gow, William
Marine insurance; a handbook. London, Macmillan, 1931.

Institute of London Underwriters.
Institute handbook on marine contracts. Rev. ed. London, Witherby & Co., 1964.

Lowndes, R. & Rudolf, G. R.
The law of general average and the York-Antwerp rules. 10th Edition. John Donaldson/C.S. Slaughton. London, Stevens & Sons, Ltd., 1975

Poole, Fred W.S.
The marine insurance of goods. 5th ed. London, Macdonald & Crans, 1981.

Turner, Harold A.
The principles of marine insurance, a primer. 6th ed. London, Stone & Co., Ltd., 1971.

Winter, William D.
Marine insurance, its principles and practice. 3rd ed. New York, McGraw Hill Book Co., Inc., 1952.

Marine Lines
Written by the Marine and Aviation Department of the CIGNA Property and Casualty companies.

Your Ocean Cargo Policy Guide

Material for this section has been provided by the Insurance Company of North America (INA), a CIGNA Worldwide Company. World Trade Press gratefully acknowledges INA and CIGNA for this contribution.

Introduction

Your Policy is called an "open" policy because it has no expiration date and automatically covers all shipments made on and after the inception date shown in Clause 6 which come within its scope. For your protection, it is important to report promptly each and every shipment which is to be insured. We call your attention to Clause 43 which deals with declaration requirements.

The purpose of this Guide is to provide you with a handy reference to be kept with your Open Policy which contains the information necessary to insure your overseas shipments properly. It is not a part of your Open Policy and in no way extends or restricts the coverage provided therein. Determining the value to be insured and completing the insurance document are two of the most difficult tasks for an Insured. It is our aim in the pages that follow to assist you in both these endeavors and to call your attention specifically to certain other clauses in your policy which are important to the proper functioning of our mutual contract.

Determining the Value to Be Insured

Because it is frequently impossible to determine at what point in an overseas transit loss or damage occurred, or if it can be determined, how much the merchandise was worth at the time, marine cargo insurance is always written on a **valued** basis. This means that in the event of an insured total loss, you are paid the face amount of insurance without quibbling, whether it occurred just after the truck pulled away from your warehouse or just prior to delivery to the customer overseas. If only a portion of the shipment is involved, the percentage of the total shipment lost or damaged is determined and this percentage is then applied to the sum insured to compute the amount of the claim (less any applicable deductible). Thus depreciation and/or fluctuations in the market value of the merchandise during the course of transit are not a factor in any settlement.

To be fully insured, it is necessary that **all costs** incurred in effecting the sale and transfer of the merchandise from the seller to be buyer be included. In addition it is customary to apply a percentage loading on top of the sum of the invoice cost and all other known expenses to allow for appreciation in the value of the property at destination. (See the Valuation Clause, No. 5, in your Open Policy.) In most instances this optional percentage is 10%.

The premium for cargo insurance is an element to be included in the cost of the goods, but which must be computed on the value of the goods to be insured after application of the percentage increase. To assist you in determining the proper amount of insurance if your policy provides for the usual 10% increase, we have developed a table of factors which will take the cost of the goods excluding the insurance premium and project it to include both the increase and insurance charge.

The following example illustrates how the insured Value should be computed, assuming a voyage for which the Marine and War risk rates are 0.55% and 0.0375% respectively:

Step 1.

Determine the Cost of the Merchandise except for the insurance charge.

Invoice Value of Merchandise	$10,000.
Inland Freight	100.
Ocean Freight	260.
Cost of Packaging	65.
Freight Forwarding Charges	100.
Consular & Other Fees	25.
Total Cost	$10,550.

Step 2.

Add Marine and War Risk rates, round off sum to nearest cent (even half cent takes next highest cent) and determine factor from Table of Factors on facing page for the applicable rate.

.55 + .0375 = .5875 which becomes .59. Factor is 1.1065.

Step 3.

Multiply Cost from Step 1 by factor from Step 2 to compute value to be insured. $10,550 x 1.1065 = $11,674.

Notes:

a. To compute the factor for a combined rate in excess of 2.00%, do the following:

1. Round off rate to nearest cent as in Step 1 and deduct 2.00 (Ex: 2.37 - 2.00 = .37)
2. Multiply difference by .011 (.37 x .011 = .0041)
3. Add result to factor for 2.00 and round off to four decimal places (1.1220 + .0041 = 1.1261)

b. A table of factors for other than a 10% increase will be provided upon request to the Company.

Table of factors for 10% increase in valuation clause

Rate	Factor	Rate	Factor	Rate	Factor	Rate	Factor	Rate	Factor
.01	1.1001	.41	1.1045	.81	1.1089	1.21	1.1133	1.61	1.1177
.02	1.1002	.42	1.1046	.82	1.1090	1.22	1.1134	1.62	1.1178
.03	1.1003	.43	1.1047	.83	1.1091	1.23	1.1135	1.63	1.1179
.04	1.1004	.44	1.1048	.84	1.1092	1.24	1.1136	1.64	1.1180
.05	1.1006	.45	1.1050	.85	1.1094	1.25	1.1138	1.65	1.1182
.06	1.1007	.46	1.1051	.86	1.1095	1.26	1.1139	1.66	1.1183
.07	1.1008	.47	1.1052	.87	1.1096	1.27	1.1140	1.67	1.1184
.08	1.1009	.48	1.1053	.88	1.1097	1.28	1.1141	1.68	1.1185
.09	1.1010	.49	1.1054	.89	1.1098	1.29	1.1142	1.69	1.1186
.10	1.1011	.50	1.1055	.90	1.1099	1.30	1.1143	1.70	1.1187
.11	1.1012	.51	1.1056	.91	1.1100	1.31	1.1144	1.71	1.1188
.12	1.1013	.52	1.1057	.92	1.1101	1.32	1.1145	1.72	1.1189
.13	1.1014	.53	1.1058	.93	1.1102	1.33	1.1146	1.73	1.1190
.14	1.1015	.54	1.1059	.94	1.1103	1.34	1.1147	1.74	1.1191
.15	1.1017	.55	1.1061	.95	1.1105	1.35	1.1149	1.75	1.1193
.16	1.1018	.56	1.1062	.96	1.1106	1.36	1.1150	1.76	1.1194
.17	1.1019	.57	1.1063	.97	1.1107	1.37	1.1151	1.77	1.1195
.18	1.1020	.58	1.1064	.98	1.1108	1.38	1.1152	1.78	1.1196
.19	1.1021	.59	1.1065	.99	1.1109	1.39	1.1153	1.79	1.1197
.20	1.1022	.60	1.1066	1.00	1.1110	1.40	1.1154	1.80	1.1198
.21	1.1023	.61	1.1067	1.01	1.1111	1.41	1.1155	1.81	1.1199
.22	1.1024	.62	1.1068	1.02	1.1112	1.42	1.1156	1.82	1.1200
.23	1.1025	.63	1.1069	1.03	1.1113	1.43	1.1157	1.83	1.1201
.24	1.1026	.64	1.1070	1.04	1.1114	1.44	1.1158	1.84	1.1202
.25	1.1028	.65	1.1072	1.05	1.1116	1.45	1.1160	1.85	1.1204
.26	1.1029	.66	1.1073	1.06	1.1117	1.46	1.1161	1.86	1.1205
.27	1.1030	.67	1.1074	1.07	1.1118	1.47	1.1162	1.87	1.1206
.28	1.1031	.68	1.1075	1.08	1.1119	1.48	1.1163	1.88	1.1207
.29	1.1032	.69	1.1076	1.09	1.1120	1.49	1.1164	1.89	1.1208
.30	1.1033	.70	1.1077	1.10	1.1121	1.50	1.1165	1.90	1.1209
.31	1.1034	.71	1.1078	1.11	1.1122	1.51	1.1166	1.91	1.1210
.32	1.1035	.72	1.1079	1.12	1.1123	1.52	1.1167	1.92	1.1211
.33	1.1036	.73	1.1080	1.13	1.1124	1.53	1.1168	1.93	1.1212
.34	1.1037	.74	1.1081	1.14	1.1125	1.54	1.1169	1.94	1.1213
.35	1.1039	.75	1.1083	1.15	1.1127	1.55	1.1171	1.95	1.1215
.36	1.1040	.76	1.1084	1.16	1.1128	1.56	1.1172	1.96	1.1216
.37	1.1041	.77	1.1085	1.17	1.1129	1.57	1.1173	1.97	1.1217
.38	1.1042	.78	1.1086	1.18	1.1130	1.58	1.1174	1.98	1.1218
.39	1.1043	.79	1.1087	1.19	1.1131	1.59	1.1175	1.99	1.1219
.40	1.1044	.80	1.1088	1.20	1.1132	1.60	1.1176	2.00	1.1220

Declaring Shipments to Be Insured

There are three methods by which shipments, either export or import, can be declared by the policyholder.

1. **The Special Marine Policy** is a negotiable document issued to cover a single shipment and a complete policy unto itself. This is usually utilized on export shipments when the sale is financed through a bank by letter of credit or otherwise and evidence of insurance is a part of the required documentation. (Sometimes a Special Marine Policy is erroneously called a "Certificate." This latter is more correctly applied to evidence of insurance in a non-negotiable form).
2. **The Declaration** is a simple form used for reporting a single shipment to the Insurer when there is no requirement for a Special Marine Policy. It is quite generally used to declare import shipments or for intra-company movements of goods.
3. **The Bordereau** is similar to the Declaration in that it is quite simple to complete and is not negotiable. It provides for the reporting of multiple shipments within a prescribed reporting period, usually a month.

Instructions for completion of these forms will be found in the pages that follow.

The Special Marine Policy (SMP)

Upon request, a supply of these forms will be provided you in quintuplicate in pads (with more copies if you need them). The "Original" and "Duplicate" copies are negotiable and will be transmitted with the rest of the shipping papers to the consignee. It is only upon presentation of one of these two documents as evidence of ownership that the Company will pay a claim to a third party.

The "Memorandum" copy is sent to this Company through your agent or broker. There are also two "Office Copies." One of these is for your records, and the other is for the agent or broker.

Following the numbers in the blank spaces on the specimen Special Marine Policy on the facing page, instructions for its completion are as follows:

1. Establish the insured value as determined in the previous section and insert in figures.
2. Enter your Open Policy number if it hasn't been pre-printed.
3. Enter the place of issuance (your city) and today's date.
4. Enter the name of your Company, if it hasn't been pre-printed.
5. Enter the name of the overseas vessel (or airline). If the shipment is strictly overland such as to Mexico, indicate whether by truck and/or rail.
6. Enter the name of the place where inland transportation commences. If it is not obvious by which route the shipment will move, please show the name of the seaport or coastal area. This is needed to determine the proper premium rate.

   Examples: Chicago via New York

   Chicago via Pacific Ports
7. Enter the name of the place of ultimate destination where the consignee takes delivery. As above, if it isn't obvious, please show name of port or area of arrival.
8. Enter the marks that appear on the outside of the package and if each is separately numbered, what they are. In the event of a potential claim, this enables the marine surveyor to identify the insured shipment and verify whether all packages have been delivered.
9. Enter a description of the merchandise and the total number of packages.
10. Show in script the amount that appears in figures in Step l.
11. This is almost without exception the same as the insured amount, so enter "sum insured." If for some reason the merchandise is to be insured for an amount different from its value, enter this latter amount in script. Bear in mind that in such cases loss settlement will be in proportion to the percentage that the sum insured bears to this value.
12. Enter "Assured" if any part of transit is at your risk. Policy can be endorsed when ownership transfers. Only if terms of sale call for "FOB, point of shipment" would you name the consignee. Endorsements are made on the revere side of the negotiable copies in the same manner as you would endorse a personal check.
13. Unless pre-printed, enter the applicable Average Terms as shown in Clause 12.
14. Enter your firm name and have a responsible official sign the original and duplicate.

SPECIAL MARINE POLICY

Insurance Company of North America
a CIGNA company

CIGNA

No. MA- 100000

Open Policy No. 999999 2 of SERVICE OFFICE: Pittsburg (512) **ORIGINAL** (ORIGINAL AND DUPLICATE ISSUED ONE OF WHICH BEING ACCOMPLISHED, THE OTHER TO BE NULL AND VOID)

$ 11,674. 1 (PLACE AND DATE) Philadelphia, Pa., September 4, 1988 3

This Company, in consideration of a premium as agreed, and subject to the Terms and Conditions printed or stamped hereon and/or attached hereto, does insure, lost or not lost THE CLUTCH CO. 4

For account of whom it may concern; to be shipped by the vessel SS "MARIA COSTA" 5

, and connecting conveyances.

From Woodwards Corner, Pa., via Philadelphia 6

To San Remo, Italy, via Levorno 7

Interest Industrial Clutches 9

, Number of Packages

Insured for 10 Eleven Thousand Six Hundred Seventy Four and no/100 Dollars

Valued at **Sum hereby insured** Sum Insured 11

Loss, if any, payable to **Assured** 12 or order.

MARKS AND NUMBERS

C-CL-C
Livorno
#1 - 4

8
VOID

TERMS AND CONDITIONS — SEE ALSO BACK HEREOF

WAREHOUSE TO WAREHOUSE: This insurance attaches from the time the goods leave the Warehouse and/or Store at the place named in the Policy for the commencement of the transit and continues during the ordinary course of transit, including customary transhipment if any, until the goods are discharged overside from the overseas vessel at the final port. Thereafter the insurance continues whilst the goods are in transit and/or awaiting transit until delivered to final warehouse at the destination named in the Policy or until the expiry of 15 days (or 30 days if the destination to which the goods are insured is outside the limits of the port) whichever shall first occur. The time limits referred to above to be reckoned from midnight of the day on which the discharge overside of the goods hereby insured from the overseas vessel is completed. Held covered at a premium to be arranged in the event of transhipment, if any, other than as above and/or in the event of delay in excess of the above time limits arising from circumstances beyond the control of the Assured.

NOTE—IT IS NECESSARY FOR THE ASSURED TO GIVE PROMPT NOTICE TO THESE ASSURERS WHEN THEY BECOME AWARE OF AN EVENT FOR WHICH THEY ARE "HELD COVERED" UNDER THIS POLICY AND THE RIGHT TO SUCH COVER IS DEPENDENT ON COMPLIANCE WITH THIS OBLIGATION.

SHORE CLAUSE: Where this insurance by its terms covers while on docks, wharves or elsewhere on shore, and/or during land transportation, it shall include the risks of collision, derailment, overturning or other accident to the conveyance, fire, lightning, sprinkler leakage, cyclones, hurricanes, earthquakes, floods (meaning the rising of navigable waters), and/or collapse or subsidence of docks or wharves, even though the insurance be otherwise F. P. A.

BOTH TO BLAME CLAUSE: Where goods are shipped under a Bill of Lading containing the so-called "Both to Blame Collision" Clause, these Assurers agree as to all losses covered by this insurance, to indemnify the Assured for this Policy's proportion of any amount (not exceeding the amount insured) which the Assured may be legally bound to pay to the shipowners under such clause. In the event that such liability is asserted the Assured agrees to notify these Assurers who shall have the right at their own cost and expense to defend the Assured against such claim.

MACHINERY CLAUSE: When the property insured under this Policy includes a machine consisting when complete for sale or use of several parts, then in case of loss or damage covered by this insurance to any part of such machine, these Assurers shall be liable only for the proportion of the insured value of the part lost or damaged, or at the Assured's option, for the cost and expense, including labor and forwarding charges, of replacing and repairing the lost or damaged part; but in no event shall these Assurers be liable for more than the insured value of the complete machine.

LABELS CLAUSE: In case of damage affecting labels, capsules or wrappers, these Assurers, if liable therefor under the terms of this policy, shall not be liable for more than an amount sufficient to pay the cost of new labels, capsules or wrappers, and the cost of reconditioning the goods, but in no event shall these Assurers be liable for more than the insured value of the damaged merchandise.

DELAY CLAUSE: Warranted free of claim for loss of market or for loss, damage or deterioration arising from delay, whether caused by a peril insured against or otherwise, unless expressly assumed in writing hereon.

AMERICAN INSTITUTE CLAUSES: This insurance, in addition to the foregoing, is also subject to the following **American Institute Cargo Clauses,** current forms:

1. CRAFT, ETC.
2. DEVIATION
3. WAREHOUSE & FORWARDING CHARGES, PACKAGES TOTALLY LOST LOADING, ETC.
4. GENERAL AVERAGE
5. EXPLOSION
6. BILL OF LADING, ETC.
7. INCHMAREE
8. CONSTRUCTIVE TOTAL LOSS
9. CARRIER

PERILS CLAUSE: Touching the adventures and perils which this Company is contented to bear, and takes upon itself, they are of the seas, fires, assailing thieves, jettisons, barratry of the master and mariners, and all other like perils, losses and misfortunes (illicit or contraband trade excepted in all cases), that have or shall come to the hurt, detriment or damage of the said goods and merchandise, or any part thereof.

AVERAGE TERMS: ON DECK AND SUBJECT TO AN "ON DECK" BILL OF LADING—(which must be so declared by the Assured): Free of Particular Average unless caused by the vessel being stranded, sunk, burnt, on fire or in collision, but including jettison and/or washing overboard irrespective of percentage.

EXCEPT WHILE SUBJECT TO AN "ON DECK" BILL OF LADING:

To cover against all risks of physical loss or damage from any external cause irrespective of percentage, but excluding, nevertheless, the risks of war, strikes, riots, seizure, detention and other risks excluded by the F. C. & S. (Free of Capture & Seizure) Warranty and the S. R. & C. C. (Strikes, Riots and Civil Commotions) Warranty in this policy, excepting to the extent that such risks are specifically covered by endorsement., but also excluding rust and oxidation.

13

This Policy is extended to include the provisions of the following clauses as if the current form of each were endorsed hereon:

American Institute Clauses—	Where Appropriate—
F. C. & S. Warranty	
Marine Extension Clauses	
S. R. & C. C. Endorsement	South America
War Risk Insurance	60-Day Clause

SPECIMEN

PARAMOUNT WARRANTIES: THE FOLLOWING WARRANTIES SHALL BE PARAMOUNT AND SHALL NOT BE MODIFIED OR SUPERSEDED BY ANY OTHER PROVISION INCLUDED HEREIN OR STAMPED OR ENDORSED HEREON UNLESS SUCH OTHER PROVISION REFERS SPECIFICALLY TO THE RISKS EXCLUDED BY THESE WARRANTIES AND EXPRESSLY ASSUMES THE SAID RISKS: F.C.&S. (a) NOTWITHSTANDING ANYTHING HEREIN CONTAINED TO THE CONTRARY THIS INSURANCE IS WARRANTED FREE FROM: (a) capture, seizure, arrest, restraint, detainment, confiscation, preemption, requisition or nationalization, and the consequences thereof or any attempt thereat, whether in time of peace or war and whether lawful or otherwise; (b) all loss, damage or expense, whether in time of peace or war, caused by (i) any weapon of war employing atomic or nuclear fission and/or fusion or other reaction or radioactive force or matter or (ii) any mine or torpedo; (c) all consequences of hostilities or warlike operations (whether there be a declaration of war or not), but this warranty shall not exclude collision or contact with aircraft, or with rockets or similar missiles (other than weapons of war) or with any fixed or floating object (other than a mine or torpedo), stranding, heavy weather, fire or explosion unless caused directly (and independently of the nature of the voyage or service which the vessel concerned or, in the case of a collision, any other vessel involved therein, is performing) by a hostile act by or against a belligerent power; and for the purposes of this warranty "power" includes any authority maintaining naval, military or air forces in association with a power; (d) the consequences of civil war, revolution, rebellion, insurrection, or civil strife arising therefrom; or from the consequences of the imposition of martial law, military or usurped power; or piracy. S.R.&C.C. (b) Notwithstanding anything herein contained to the contrary, this insurance is warranted free from loss, damage or expense caused by or resulting from: (1) strikes, lockouts, labor disturbances, riots, civil commotions, or the acts of any person or persons taking part in any such occurrences or disorders, (2) vandalism, sabotage or malicious act, which shall be deemed also to encompass the act or acts of one or more persons, whether or not agents of a sovereign power, carried out for political, terroristic or ideological purposes and whether any loss, damage or expense resulting therefrom is accidental or intentional.

Not transferable unless countersigned

Countersigned

14

INSTRUCTIONS TO CLAIMANTS ON REVERSE SIDE

MA-2098g Ptd. in U.S.A.

In Witness Whereof, this Company has caused these presents to be signed by its President and attested by its Secretary, in the City of Philadelphia.

Harry E. Hoyt
HARRY E. HOYT, Secretary

Caleb L. Fowler
CALEB L. FOWLER, President

The Declaration

This form is provided in pad form and can be made up in whatever number is required to meet your needs. Two copies are to be sent to your agent/broker.

Following the numbers in the blank spaces on the sample form on the facing page, instructions for completion are as follows:

1. Enter the name of your company.
2. Enter the number you have assigned to this declaration. This is for identification purposes only and is established to suit your needs. It can be from either a straight numerical sequence or with some identifying letter combination or year of issue prefix.
3. Enter today's date.
4. Enter the name of the overseas vessel (or airline). If the shipment is strictly overland, such as to Mexico, indicate whether by rail or truck.
5. Enter the number of your Open Policy.
6. Enter the name of the place where inland transportation commences. (*See* Step 6 of instructions for SMP for further clarification.)
7. Enter either the date of sailing or the date on the bill of lading and show which it is. In the event you ship merchandise on the same vessel on different sailings, this would enable us to identify the voyage in the event of a claim.
8. Enter a short description of the merchandise and how it is packed. (Example: Leaf Tobacco in bales.)
9. Enter the name of the ultimate destination. (*See* Step 7 of instructions for SMP for further clarification.)
10. Enter the number of packages.
11. Enter the name and address of your agent or broker.
12. Enter the amount of marine insurance computed as described in the previous section utilizing the blank for the invoice value, the sum of all other charges and their total. The applicable factor taken from the table is inserted in the blank "plus % advance."
13. If this is an import shipment and you wish to insure the U.S. duty separately, enter the amount of such duty here.
14. Computation of the premium by you is optional, using the rate schedule at the back of your Open Policy. It is not necessary since the Company will perform the same operation and send you an invoice for the premium due.

THE ACCEPTANCE OF THIS APPLICATION SHALL NOT COMMIT THE COMPANY IN THE EVENT OF CANCELLATION OF THE MARINE OR WAR RISK OPEN POLICIES, OR OF ANY ENDORSEMENT THEREON. IF SUCH CANCELLATION NOTICE BECOMES EFFECTIVE PRIOR TO ATTACHMENT OF THIS RISK UNDER THE INSURANCE SO CANCELLED.

Insurance Company of North America
a CIGNA company
CIGNA

ASSURED THE CLUTCH CO. **1**

DECLARATION NO. 74-95 **2**

NAME OF VESSEL OR CONVEYANCE SS "MARIA COSTA" **4**

DATE SEPTEMBER 4, 1988 **3**

VOYAGE: FROM Woodwards Corner, Pa., via Philadelphia **6**
(INITIAL POINT OF SHIPMENT)

OPEN POLICY NO. 999999 **5**

KIND OF MERCHANDISE Industrial Clutches in wooden cases **8**
(DESCRIBE FULLY—STATE WHETHER CASES, CRATES, CARTONS, ETC.)

SAILING OR B.L. DATE September 4, 1988 **7** NAME WHICH

AMOUNT INSURED (SEE POLICY VALUATION CLAUSE)

TO San Remo, Italy via Levorno **9**
(FINAL DESTINATION)

NO. OF PACKAGES 4 **10**

	$			
INVOICE VALUE	10,000.	AGENT OR BROKER: Marine Ins. Agency **11**		
FREIGHT & ALL OTHER CHARGES	550.	ADDRESS: 2410 Creek Road, Embreeville, Pa.		
TOTAL	10,500.	BROKER OR AGENT CODE		
PLUS % ADVANCE	1,1065		RATE OF PREMIUM	PREMIUM
AMOUNT OF MARINE INSURANCE	11,674. **12**	MARINE	.55	$64.21 **14**
		WAR & OR S&R	.0375	4.38
ACTUAL AMOUNT OF U.S. DUTY	**13**	DUTY		
		WAR & OR S&R		
		TOTAL PREMIUM		$68.59

MA-455a Printed in U.S.A.

The Bordereau

The form also comes in pads and the number of copies completed is up to you. Two copies are to be sent to your agent/broker. These should be sent to the Company at regular intervals, but at least monthly. Although there is no specific provision therefor, we ask that you indicate in the upper right hand corner either a consecutive numbering of this bordereaux or the month and year that it covers. This enables the Company to make certain all bordereaux are received and to identify it on the premium invoice.

Following the numbers in the blank spaces on the sample form on the facing page, instructions for completion are as follows:

1. Enter the number of your open policy.
2. Enter the name of your company.
3. Enter today's date.
4. Enter the name of the overseas vessel (or airline). If the shipment is strictly overland, such as to Mexico, indicate whether by rail or truck.
5. Enter either the date of sailing or the date on the bill of lading and show which it is. In the event you ship merchandise on the same vessel on different sailings, this would enable us to identify the voyage in the event of a claim.
6. Enter the name of the place where inland transportation commences. (*See* Step 6 of instructions for SMP for further clarification.)
7. Enter the name of the ultimate destination. (*See* Step 7 of instructions for SMP for further clarification.)
8. Enter a short description of the merchandise and how it is packed. (Example: Leaf Tobacco in bales.)
9. Enter the amount of marine insurance computed as described in the previous section utilizing the blank for the invoice value, the sum of all other charges and their total. When there is more than one coverage provided for a single shipment such as marine and war, please allow two lines per shipment. It will be understood that the first line will be for the marine coverage and the insertion of the word "War" in the "Amount Insured" column on the next line will provide for covering war risks without repeating all the information to the left. If duty or some other coverage is desired in a different amount of insurance, insert this in the "Amount Insured" column and identify it in the column to the left.
10. Computation of the premium by you is optional, using the rate schedule at the back of your open policy. It is not necessary since the Company will perform the same operation and send you an invoice for the premium due.
11. Enter the name and address of your agent or broker.

To the INSURANCE COMPANY OF NORTH AMERICA

Please enter the following shipments under Open Policy No. 999999 **1** issued to THE CLUTCH CO. **2**

DATE	VESSEL	SAILING OR DATE B/L	FROM	TO	MDSE	AMOUNT INSURED	RATE	PREMIUM			REMARKS
3 Sept. 4	"MARIA COSTA" **4**	**5** Sept. 4	Woodward Corner, Pa. **6**	San Remo, Italy **7**	Industrial Clutches **8**	11,674.00 **9**	.55	64.21 **10**			
						War	.0375	4.38			

TAX

THIS SPACE RESERVED FOR THE COMPANY

The acceptance of this application shall not commit the company in the event of cancellation of the marine or war risk open policies, or of any endorsement thereon, if such cancellation notice becomes effective prior to attachment of this risk under the insurance so cancelled. **11**

Broker ______

Approved for the Company ______ (If within the terms and conditions of the policy)

MA-779 Ptd. in U.S.A.

Other Important Policy Provisions

While all the clauses in your open policy have a purpose, and we urge you to familiarize yourself with them, there are certain ones that requires special amplification if your policy is to provide you with the full protection intended from the outset.

9. **Limit of Liability**—We have endeavored to set these amounts in excess of your maximum needs. However, should you have shipment in excess of the limits shown, please notify the Company immediately through your agent or broker. In most cases the additional coverage required can be arranged without difficulty. However, failure to do so could leave you underinsured, particularly on shipments reported on Declarations or Bordereaux where the terms of your Open Policy prevail.

12. **Average Terms**—If your policy provides for an option in average terms such as FPA or All Risks, make certain that the coverage applying to each shipment is clearly shown on the reporting document.

28. **Import Duty**—When goods imported into the United States are subject to Customs duty, you must pay this in order to take delivery. If you then find the merchandise has been damaged and is useless, you are either out of pocket for the amount of the duty or faced with much red tape to effect a recovery.

    You can insure this potential loss by indicating the amount of duty on the reporting document and identifying it as such. Because there is no duty payable if the goods are lost before reaching the U.S. port of discharge, you are charged a reduced rate for this coverage, usually a percentage of the marine rates. See the rate schedule at the back of your policy.

29. **General Average**—This clause provides coverage for a type of claim which is unique to marine insurance, even though your policy may be written on very limited terms otherwise. Moreover, it is the result of a fortuitous action completely beyond your control.

    As the name implies, general average claims affect all the interests which stand to suffer a financial loss if a particular voyage is not successfully completed. These include the owner of the hull and the owners of all the cargoes aboard for their respective values plus the owner or charterer who stands to earn a specific income from freight charges for the voyage.

    A General Average is usually incurred when in the face of an impending disaster, some sacrifice is made on the part of one of the interests described above which is successful and the venture is brought to safety. This can be in the form of the deliberate destruction of some physical property such as the tossing overboard of a part of the cargo to lighten ship in a storm or the flooding of a cargo hold to prevent the spread of fire. It can also include the expenditure of funds by the vessel own to hire tugs in the event of a lost propeller at sea or a stranding on the shore. In such circumstances, the owner or master will declare a General Average and eventually all those with a financial interest are asked to share the reimbursement for the values which have been sacrificed for the good of all. This can be compared to a boy hitting a baseball through a window in a backyard game. It is basically his financial loss to replace the glass, but all the players, including said batter, chip in to share the cost with him.

How does this affect you? If a General Average is declared, delivery of cargo by the vessel is predicated on the cargo owner posting some form of security as evidence that they will pay their share of the ultimate G.A. assessment. The amount of the deposit is based on an estimate. While this can be met by a cash deposit or bond, the simplest and least expensive solution is for CIGNA to file a General Average Guarantee on your behalf with the G.A. adjusters, and your cargo will be released. Thus if you are informed that your merchandise is involved in a General Average, contact the Company or the nearest claim or settling agent listed on the reverse side of the Special Marine Policy.

As a rule of thumb, cargo is valued at the invoice cost plus 10% for General Average estimating purposes. If you have not insured your cargo in accordance with the Valuation Clause No. 5, you could find yourself sharing in the General Average settlement.

The Rate Schedule—The rates shown for the various voyages are predicated on the assumption that shipments will be made on approved vessels as described at the top of the endorsement. Otherwise you may be charged an additional premium computed at a rate which varies with the age and net tonnage of the ship and the voyage involved. It is in your interest to ship by steamer lines offering regular service to your destinations whenever possible.

Note the other provisions at the bottom of your rate schedule, particularly the fact that there is a minimum premium per shipment, rates to or from places or for commodities not listed in the rate schedule can be obtained upon request, and that the Company may charge an additional rate for transshipment if your cargo is off-loaded from one vessel and re-loaded onto another at some intermediate port of call. This latter does not apply to lighterage or where a transshipment is a natural part of the voyage to the destination listed.

The rates shown on the schedule are for the marine risk only, and do not include war perils. Rates for this coverage are in addition, and the war premium is computed separately. Generally, these rates stay pretty constant to most parts of the World, but if hostilities break out somewhere, the War Risk Policy does provide for a shorter time period before a rate can be changed than does the Open Marine Policy. Such changes as may become necessary would apply only to voyages commencing on and after the date they become effective.

When Loss or Damage Occurs

If you are an exporter insuring your shipments under special marine policies, it is most likely that your overseas customer will first become aware of a potential claim. There is a listing on the reverse side of the special marine policy of the steps he should take including the names and addresses of CIGNA's claims and settling agents in major ports of the world. If there is none nearby, the claimant is directed to contact the nearest correspondent of the American Institute of Marine Underwriters or Lloyd's agent.

If you are an importer, there are certain instructions to be given those in your organization who receive or take delivery of your merchandise. It is most important that all packages be examined and counted before signing for the shipment. If there are any signs of potential loss or damage such as breakage or wetting of the shipping package or the number delivered does not match that shown on the bill of lading, an exception should be taken by noting the damage and/or shortage on the bill of lading or freight bill before accepting delivery.

Once damage is discovered, there are three things you must do without delay:

1. Make every effort to reduce the loss and/or prevent further loss as provided under the sue and labor clause (no. 19) of your Open Policy. This could include rebagging, recoopering barrels, separating wet cargo from dry, etc. Reasonable expenses incurred in taking such steps are reimbursable by the Company in addition to any payment of the claim itself. In short, we expect the Insured to do exactly what he would do if the shipment were uninsured.
2. Notify your agent or broker (or the nearest CIGNA office) so that a survey of the damage can be arranged as promptly as possible. The carrier or his agent should be notified of the time and place of the survey, so he can be represented. Insofar as possible, the damaged property and the containers in which it was delivered should be retained in the condition received until after the survey unless further damage will result by so doing.
3. It is essential that a claim be made in writing against the carrier (inland or ocean) as soon as the loss is known or upon taking delivery. This can be in any form, but must include the bill of lading number, the name of the carrying vessel, a description of the loss or damage, and should state that the carrier will be held responsible for the loss or damage.

The rates you are charged for your cargo insurance are influenced in the ultimate by the experience (premiums versus losses) of your account, so it is in your best interest to see that losses are reduced by putting the Company in a good position to take action against the carrier to recover all or at least a portion of the claims the Company pays you. This is called subrogation and amounts recovered are credited to your account. The bills of lading include a time limit following delivery in which a claim on the carrier will be accepted, so it is necessary to put them on notice immediately.

If your merchandise is of a fragile or delicate nature subject to breakage, etc., it is important that you unpack and check its condition as soon as possible even though there is no evidence of damage to or on the packing. You may have what is known as concealed damage.

Once the survey has confirmed that loss or damage has occurred which was caused by one of the insured perils, the following documents will be needed to substantiate your claim:

1. Whatever document was issued to substantiate the amount of insurance placed and the coverage provided. On an export shipment this would be the original and duplicate of the special marine policy. For imports, it would probably be a copy of the declaration or bordereau if this has been issued prior to your learning of a possible claim.
2. Ocean (or Air) bill of lading—also transshipment bill of lading and railway freight note when applicable.
3. Original shipper's invoice.
4. Packing list, weight certificates, or other evidence of the nature and condition of the goods at time of shipment.
5. The survey report if an outside surveyor was called in to represent your interest.
6. Copy of claim on carrier and (if available) the reply thereto.
7. In special cases, other documents may be requested.

If all the above papers are included in the submission of your claim, it will certainly speed up the adjustment and the payment thereof.

Commodity Index Contents

Introduction

This Commodity Index serves as a guide to the regulatory requirements relevant to imports into the U.S. It is organized according to the 99 chapters of the Harmonized Tariff Schedule of the United States (HTSUS). Each index chapter contains a broad range of information designed to assist you in being an educated importer. Listings are arranged according to the HTSUS. With a few exceptions, each chapter is designed to be a complete, stand-alone discussion, containing all the supplemental regulatory information of which you need to be aware when importing products assigned to the specific HTSUS chapter. Some chapters refer you to other pertinent material, either in the Commodity Index or elsewhere in this book. Be sure to read any such additional material, even if there is some duplication of information.

Each Commodity Index chapter is intended to give you an overview of the regulatory issues involved in importing a product. The purpose of this index is not to be an ultimate authority. Each chapter lists the government agencies with regulatory responsibility for the commodity. We strongly advise you to follow up on all references that direct you either to a U.S. government agency, a specific regulation, or other publications.

The section covering the commodity you wish to import may contain extensive and formidable details regarding restrictions, required forms, governmental agencies, procedures, etc. Don't be intimidated. Such details are a reflection of our conviction that knowledge is power: the more you know about importing a commodity, the less likely you are to experience problems. In practice, what looks complicated or even impossible may be as simple as having a customs broker fill out an extra form to go with your entry. On the other hand, some products are subject to stringent restrictions and are extremely difficult to import. Drugs and firearms are examples of such products.

Using the Commodity Index as a base, we recommend that you consult with your customs broker, U.S. Customs, and any relevant government agencies for clarification of your responsibilities before you make any financial commitments. In any activity as fast-paced as international trade, there are bound to be subtleties and changes relating to specific products and even whole classes of products. This index is not a substitute for the legwork necessary to confirm and clarify the material presented, but it will streamline that research and make it more effective.

Customs Brokers

Customs brokers are licensed by the U.S. Department of the Treasury to conduct business with U.S. Customs on behalf of importers. The primary function of a customs broker is to assist in clearing imports through Customs. Such individuals deal with Customs on a daily basis and are in a position to know both the theory and the practice of entering goods. Besides facilitating actual entry, customs brokers can often provide additional services to the importer. They can advise you in almost every aspect of the import process, including shipping, insurance, payment through draft or letter of credit, and delivery of cargo in the U.S.

We recommend the use of a licensed customs broker, especially if you are new to importing. A customs broker won't do everything for you—you still need to be closely involved with your own operation—but you won't need to reinvent the wheel. Brokers' fees are modest in comparison to the time and money you can save. Consult the yellow pages of a U.S. port city, under "Customs Brokers," for names and telephone numbers. You can also call the National Association of Customs Brokers and Freight Forwarders in New York at (212) 432-0050 for referrals to local affiliate brokers who are members of this national trade association. Refer also to "Selecting and Working with a Customs Broker" on page 50, and "Customs Brokers, Freight Forwarders, and Professional Associations" on page 51.

How to Use the Commodity Index

The Commodity Index is organized according to the HTSUS. To find the discussion relevant to your product, scan the Table of Contents of this Index for the 22 section headings of the HTSUS. These section headings represent broad classifications of goods. Refer to the specific chapters within the sections for more specific product types. If you still cannot find an appropriate listing for the product itself, look for a listing for the material the product is made of, such as Chapter 73, "Articles of Iron or Steel." The introductory part of each Commodity Index chapter explains the specific type of products it covers and also gives references to other chapters where some related products can be found. If no listing seems to cover the product you are interested in importing, consult the original HTSUS (with its more detailed index), a customs broker, or your nearest U.S. Customs office.

Commodity Index chapters are further divided into subsections containing the information you need to know to import the commodity. Some of these subsections are supplemental to general chapters in other parts of this manual dealing with the same topics. Each details the ways in which the general requirements apply to the specific commodity and lists special requirements. Requirements listed in these subsections should always be considered as being in addition to general import requirements. Each Commodity Index chapter is divided into the following subsections:

Key Factors

The "Key Factors" subsection is designed to alert the importer to any complicating factors associated with importing a product. While for many products importation is straightforward, requiring nothing more than standard Customs entry, many "straightforward" products have important exceptions, and some categories represent a regulatory minefield. In the Commodity Index, we have focused on the exceptions—not to scare you away, but to alert you to important issues that could present major problems. For example, importing jewelry is straightforward, with the important exception of jewelry made in whole or in part of any endangered species (such as elephant ivory, which is banned).

"Key Factors," found near the beginning of each chapter, is a highly abbreviated, selective version of this information. It is intended to provide an at-a-glance overview of what is to follow. If you stop reading after "Key Factors," you will have a schematic list of issues to be aware of, but you won't have much specific information. However, once you have read the chapter, a review of "Key Factors" should serve to help you remember the details. ("Key Factors" is omitted from Commodity Index chapters pertaining to commodities that have no special requirements.)

General Considerations

"General Considerations" provides a broad stroke background of information to give you an introduction to major issues associated with your commodity. It will tell you briefly whether importation of the commodity is complex or straightforward, which agencies regulate importations of the product, and what the regulations are. For example, if your product is regulated by an agency requiring port-of-entry documentation or inspection, that will be mentioned in "General Considerations." (More details follow, under "Prohibitions and Restrictions," "Marking and Labeling Requirements," etc., where relevant. As with "Key Factors," when a product is so straightforward that no special circumstances or regulations apply, you will not see a "General Considerations" segment in the Commodity Index chapter.)

Customs Classification

The "Customs Classification" of a commodity determines its duty rate. Products that appear to be similar can, for Customs purposes, have very different classifications, and thus be assessed radically different duties. Therefore, it is crucial that you understand how Customs classifies your product. It is also helpful to consult a customs broker with experience in your product area and who knows how things are actually done. Currently, a difference of opinion with Customs over how your product should be classified leads to little more than a delay, but under the "reasonable care" provisions of the 1993 Customs Modernization Act (Mod Act)—which is being implemented over the next several years as Customs automates its operations—unfounded, frivolous, or fraudulent misclassifications can lead to substantial fines and penalties. Therefore, you need to know precisely how Customs classifies your product, not just how you think it should be classified. Review "Classification—Liquidation" on page 207 for additional information.

Sample Import Duties

The HTSUS is a massive compilation containing all the duty rates for all defined import commodities. "Sample Import Duties" is an incomplete listing of all import duties for that commodity group. We list a representative range of duty rates for some items in each commodity category. You should not base your decision to import a product solely on these sample rates, but should consult the HTSUS, Customs, or your customs broker.

Entry and Documentation

An overview of the general U.S. Customs entry and documentation process appears in each Commodity Index chapter, with specific mention of any additional documentation required by U.S. Customs for that commodity. We recommend that you review the "U.S. Customs Entry and Clearance" section, beginning on page 175.

Prohibitions and Restrictions

This subsection details prohibitions and restrictions associated with the importation of a commodity into the U.S. In some cases, the restrictions and prohibitions are so detailed that they cannot be explained completely in this index. For example, the limitations on the importation and sale in the U.S. of Food and Drug Administration (FDA)-regulated drugs would itself require several volumes. In such cases, we give an overview of the scope of the restrictions and prohibitions, a sampling of pertinent rules, and references to more complete sources of information. For highly regulated commodities, we recommend that you obtain copies of the actual laws and regulations governing the commodity. Refer to "Laws and Regulations" below.

Country-Specific Import Restrictions

Product-specific country-of-origin restrictions are outlined in "Country-Specific Import Restrictions" in each Commodity Index chapter when relevant. For example, there is a Customs "Import Alert" on ceramics originating in the People's Republic of China (due to high levels of lead and cadmium).

Quotas

"Quotas" only appears when there are quotas on a commodity or commodity group. You should read the general entry on "Import Quotas" on page 230 as background for understanding the information you will find in the quota section for your commodity. If your commodity is subject to quota, the "Quota" subsection will give you information about the annual import limit, countries from which the product may be imported, and annual quantities allowed. The information is usually broken down by HTSUS classification number. Quotas are subject to change, and at any given point in time, the quota for your commodity may already be filled for the year. Some quota commodities require licensing and other forms of documentation. Never attempt to import a quota item without first consulting U.S. Customs or a customs broker regarding the product's current quota status.

Marking and Labeling Requirements

General U.S. Customs marking and labeling requirements pertain to most import commodities. These are covered in "Marking: Country of Origin" on page 215, and "Special Marking Requirements" on page 217. The "Marking and Labeling Requirements" portion of each Commodity Index chapter provides supplemental information specific to the product.

Relevant Government Agencies

Some commodities are regulated by many U.S. government agencies. For example, both the FDA and the U.S. Department of Agriculture (USDA) regulate the importation of dairy products. Each agency has its own area of regulatory responsibility. If you have a question about a commodity that is regulated by more than one agency, be sure to direct it to the appropriate agency. A USDA official will not be able to give you authoritative information on requirements for FDA permits for importing milk, and an FDA official will not be able to give you information about USDA-administered quotas on imported cheeses.

Each index section lists the headquarters, department, address, and phone number of the regulating agencies for the commodity covered. We recommend that you call these agencies for information. Many of these agencies have district offices in major U.S. cities. Such offices appear in the phone book under the "U.S. Government" listing. The headquarters can also direct you to the nearest district office or to the specific centralized office dealing with your issue. Note that it sometimes requires patience and several calls before you reach the person who can help you with your specific question. Persevere.

Laws and Regulations

This subsection lists the U.S. Government laws and regulations that are relevant to the importation of the commodity covered. Please note that this subsection does not cover state and local laws and regulations that may affect your commodity, although where such regulations exist for a general class of product, the Commodity Index section will alert you to this. You should always check with local authorities in the venue where you plan to do business.

Federal laws are contained in the United States Code (USC), which is generally available at larger public libraries and at law libraries. These laws form the basis of the regulatory actions that government agencies take with regard to the commodity. Specific regulations are published in the Code of Federal Regulations (CFR) to implement the laws. For example, The Federal Food, Drug, and Cosmetic Act (FDCA) is the foundation for regulatory activity for the listed product categories. It is found in Title 21 of the USC, and the supporting regulations are in 21 CFR. If you are dealing in a highly regulated commodity, obtain a copy of the relevant laws and regulations and study them. Copies of specific federal laws and regulations may be purchased from:

U.S. Government Printing Office (GPO)
Superintendent of Documents
Washington, DC 20402
(202) 512-1800 (Order line)
(202) 512-0000 (General)

Principal Exporting Countries

This subsection lists the major suppliers of products to the U.S. as compiled from Bureau of the Census statistics for customs value of entries for 1993, the most recent available. Countries are listed in descending rank order, beginning with the largest sources. The actual values are not given, and there can be huge differences between products and countries. The listing is organized by the major headings of the HTSUS chapters. Refer to the "Customs Classification" subsection for the key to the code numbers used.

The Harmonized Tariff Schedule of the United States (HTSUS)

This Commodity Index is organized according to the HTSUS, the document that Customs uses to classify and assign duty rates to all products imported into the U.S. It categorizes everything from ice and snow, to broccoli (*Brassica oleracea* var. *italica*), to 3-(N-Ethylanilino) propionic acid, to zippers, to skeet targets. As with any attempt at universal classification, it is complicated, and there are some idiosyncratic and questionable assignments, as well as some apparent contradictions, overlaps, and omissions. Omissions are often handled by "not elsewhere specified or included" (NESOI). The HTSUS can be obtained from the U.S. Government Printing Office (address listed earlier).

HTSUS Organization and Classification

The HTSUS consists of 22 sections, which contain 99 consecutively numbered chapters. Some sections contain a single chapter, while others have a dozen or more. The sections and the chapters they cover are as follows:

Section I—Live Animals and Animal Products (Chapters 1-5);

Section II—Vegetable Products (Chapters 6-14);

Section III—Animal and Vegetable Oils and Related Products (Chapter 15);

Section IV—Prepared Foods, Beverages, and Tobacco (Chapters 16-24);

Section V—Mineral Products (Chapters 25-27);

Section VI—Chemical and Allied Products (Chapters 28-38);

Section VII—Plastics and Rubber (Chapter 39-40);

Section VIII—Hides, Fur, Leather, and Leather Goods (Chapters 41-43);

Section IX—Wood, Cork, and Basketry (Chapters 44-46);

Section X—Pulp, Paper, and Paper Products (Chapters 47-49);

Section XI—Textiles (Chapters 50-63);

Section XII—Footwear, Headgear, Umbrellas, Prepared Feathers, and Artificial Flowers (Chapters 64-67);

Section XIII—Stone, Plaster, Cement, Ceramics, and Glassware (Chapters 68-70);

Section XIV—Gems and Jewelry (Chapter 71);

Section XV—Base Metals (Chapters 72-83);

Section XVI—Machinery and Electronics (Chapters 84-85);

Section XVII—Vehicles, Aircraft, Vessels, and Other Transportation Equipment (Chapter 86-89);

Section XVIII—Optical, Photographic, Scientific, Medical, Timekeeping, and Musical Instruments (Chapters 90-92);

Section XIX—Arms and Ammunition (Chapter 93);

Section XX—Miscellaneous Manufactures (Chapters 94-96);

Section XXI—Art and Antiques (Chapter 97);

Section XXII—Special and Temporary Classifications (Chapters 98-99).

There is no chapter 77—it is reserved for future use. Chapters 1 through 97 (77 excepted) represent the heart of the HTSUS, covering specific categories of products.

Below the chapter level, HTSUS is organized into nested categories beginning with major headings, such as the example "Other woven fabrics of cotton: Weighing not more than 200 g/m^2," which is major heading 12 of chapter 52. In the HTSUS this is referred to as major heading 5212. If the fabric is unbleached, it falls into subheading 5212.11 (bleached fabrics of this type fall within subheading 5212.12). If unbleached and "containing 36% or more by weight of wool or of fine animal hair," it falls into the next more specific level of classification, sub-subheading 5212.11.10. This eight-digit level of classification is the one on which duties are assigned. There are even finer classifications for many products, although some are not divided beyond the major heading level (such as 0509.00.00—"Natural sponges of animal origin"). For the unbleached cotton woven fabrics noted above, if the cotton is "not combed," the 10-digit classification would be 5212.11.10.10. Even though the 10-digit classification is used only for statistical reporting rather than for calculating tariffs owed, importers are nevertheless responsible for correctly classifying products to the 10-digit level of identification. Filing statistical data is part of the entry process.

In the illustration below, the first column of the HTSUS represents the "Heading/Subheading," containing up to the first eight digits of the classification number—all those necessary to assign duties. The next column represents the "Statistical Suffix,"

Heading/ Subheading	Stat. Suf- fix	Article Description	Units of Quantity	Rates of Duty 1 General	Rates of Duty 1 Special	Rates of Duty 2
5212		Other woven fabrics of cotton:				
		Weighing not more than 200 g/m^2:				
5212.11		Unbleached:				
5212.11.10		Containing 36 percent or more by weight of wool or fine animal hair.	. . . . .	33%	3.3% (IL) 13.2% (CA) 20% (MX)	68.5%
	10	Not combed. . . . . . (410)	m^2 v kg			
	20	Combed. . . . . (410)	m^2 v kg			
5212.11.60		Other.	. . . . .	7.8%	Free (IL) 3.1% (CA) 7.1% (MX)	40%
	10	Mixed mainly or solely with wool or fine animal hair. . (220)	m^2 v kg			

the ninth and tenth digits used for reporting statistics, but not for assessing duties. The next column—"Article Description"—contains the product description corresponding to the numbers listed in the first two columns. In the illustration, the number "(410)" following the product description "Not combed," refers to the quota category number for this category of textiles. The fourth column—"Units of Quantity"—consists of the units in which the imports are measured and reported, in this case square meters and kilograms.

Calculating Duty by the HTSUS

The next three subcolumns in the preceding illustration are all parts of the final major column heading, "Rates of Duty." The first subcolumn—"General"—contains the base duty payable on goods of the corresponding category. For imports of product category 5212.11.10, the duty charged—an ad valorem duty based on a percentage of the value of the entry—is 33%. This tariff applies to imports from all Most Favored Nations (MFNs), and represents the base level of duty payable.

The next duty subcolumn—"Special"—lists the duty charged in special circumstances, usually constituting lower duties for entries of the product from specific places under certain conditions established by trade agreements. These are labeled with letters: A or A*, B, C, CA, MX, E or E*, IL, and J or J*. "A" and "A*" designate those countries and commodities eligible for special reduced duty rates or duty-free entry under the terms of the Generalized System of Preferences (GSP) for less developed countries. "B" refers to the Automotive Products Trade Act, which covers eligible vehicle parts imported from Canada. "C" denotes the Agreement on Trade in Civil Aircraft, which covers eligible imports of aircraft and parts from countries certified by the Federal Aviation Administration.

"CA" refers to Canada and "MX" refers to Mexico, both of which are individually eligible to import certain products into the U.S. on favorable terms under the provisions of the North American Free Trade Agreement (NAFTA). "E" and "E*" denote the Caribbean Basin Initiative (CBI)—technically, the Caribbean Basin Economic Recovery Act (CBERA)—which allows favorable or duty free treatment of certain products imported from member entities of the CBI. "IL" refers to the United States-Israel Free Trade Area, which allows duty free entry for eligible products imported from Israel. "J" and "J*" refer to the Andean Trade Preference Act (ATPA), which covers eligible imports of duty free or reduced rate merchandise from the signatory nations of the ATPA. For additional information on these programs, refer to section 12 through 17 of "U.S. Customs and Clearance" beginning on page 197 or see the HTSUS General Notes 3-12.

The third and final subcolumn of "Rates of Duty" is labeled "2" for Column 2, which applies to countries that are assessed heavier duties than other countries on their imports into the U.S. In the past, most of the Column 2 countries have been Communist or former Communist states or other nations with which the U.S. allows trade to occur on restricted or unfavorable terms. The current edition of the HTSUS lists Afghanistan, Azerbaijan, Cuba, Kampuchea, Laos, North Korea, Tajikistan, Uzbekistan, and Vietnam as Column 2 countries. Those interested in trading with these countries should check with Customs regarding current Column 2 status, as diplomatic and trade initiatives can lead to alterations in this status.

Footnotes to the main HTSUS chapter headings usually refer the reader to an HTSUS chapter or section headnote, or to Chapter 99, which lists current quota and temporary tariff provisions. You should be sure to follow up on all such references, as they can contain significant information regarding your product.

Using the General Notes to the HTSUS

Time spent exploring the notes to the HTSUS can pay dividends to the importer. The introductory notes to the HTSUS—Supplement 1—which precede Section I, contain the latest information on trade issues covered in the HTSUS, as well as the basic rules for its use.

For example, the "General Rules of Interpretation" of these notes establish that the wording of the specific headings governs the assignments that can be made. If there is a disagreement over an assignment to a category based on apparent overlap or duplication, the category with the most specific description will prevail. Products consisting of mixtures of items will be classified under the category that gives the final product its essential character. Items—such as camera cases included with the camera (but not those imported separately)—and packing materials of a type customarily used with a product and not designed for reuse are classified with the primary product. In deciding between variant classifications, comparisons can be made only between subheadings of the same level of specificity (i.e., between subheadings, not between major headings and subheadings). The initial HTSUS notes set out general rules and procedures for making decisions on the these issues.

The "General Notes" provide information on basic definitions (Notes 1, 2, and 16), abbreviations used (Note 15), exemptions (Note 13), treatment of commingled goods (Note 14), and duty classifications and special provisions, primarily those established by treaty (Notes 3–12). "General Statistical Notes" (Notes 1–5) outline data required and procedures to be used in statistical reporting.

HTSUS Section and Chapter Notes

Some HTSUS sections and all individual HTSUS chapters have introductory notes, which give the ground rules for using those sections and chapters and often provide considerable additional information that can be of great use in navigating through HTSUS classifications. The amount of data varies by section and by chapter, but you should pay close attention to the information that can be gleaned from these often somewhat cryptic notes.

The introductory notes may include as many as four segments: "Notes," "Subheading Notes," "Additional U.S. Notes," and "Statistical Notes." The general notes usually outline the specific products and types of products that are not included in the section or chapter, and may redirect you to the appropriate chapter. "Subheading Notes" give specific information on definitions of products to be included in a particular subheading. The "Additional U.S. Notes" often give definitions or qualifications useful in classifying specific products. The "Statistical Notes" provide information for classifying products at the 10-digit level used for compiling import statistics.

Chapter 1: Live Animals*

This chapter relates to the importation of live animals, which are classified under Chapter 1 of the Harmonized Tariff Schedule of the United States (HTSUS). Specifically, it includes horses and related animals, cattle, pigs, sheep and goats, poultry, other birds, and virtually all other live animals, including pets and wildlife.

If you are interested in importing fish, crustaceans, molluscs, other aquatic animals, or cultures of microorganisms, refer to Commodity Index Chapter 3. Importation of live animals associated with traveling circuses, menageries, or similar exhibits is covered within Chapter 95.

Other special provisions affecting live animal imports include domesticated animals that stray or are driven across international boundaries for grazing purposes and are returned—along with their offspring—within eight months (HTSUS 9801.00.90); wild animals that are imported for use or for sale for scientific or educational purposes (HTSUS 9810.00.70); live animals, including poultry, that are imported for purposes of breeding, exhibition, or prize competition (HTSUS 9813.00.60); and live game animals that are imported for the purpose of stocking ranges (HTSUS 9817.00.70). No animals intended for use in fighting are allowed into the U.S.

Key Factors

The key factors in the importation of live animals are:

- Compliance with U.S. Department of Agriculture (USDA) Animal and Plant Health Inspection Service (APHIS) and U.S. Fish and Wildlife Service (FWS) import regulations, restrictions, and quarantine requirements
- Entry at USDA designated ports (at FWS designated ports for imports of wildlife)
- USDA, FWS, and Customs port of entry inspections—prior notification required
- Acquisition of appropriate permits—required for most importations
- Acquisition of required veterinary certificates
- Compliance with importer's declaration requirements
- Compliance with Centers for Disease Control (CDC) regulations, restrictions, and quarantine requirements for potential vectors of human disease
- Compliance with APHIS Plant Protection and Quarantine (PPQ) branch requirements for living organisms which affect plants or with APHIS Veterinary Service (VS) requirements for living organisms which affect animals
- Compliance with endangered species restrictions on living animals
- Compliance with FWS licenses and recordkeeping requirements for persons in the business of importing wildlife (licenses required with certain exceptions)
- Compliance with U.S. Food and Drug Administration (FDA) regulations, restrictions, and entry notification, which may be required under certain circumstances

Although most importers utilize the services of a licensed customs broker in making their entries, and we recommend this practice, you should be aware of the regulatory, entry, and documentation issues involved in importing your product. You, as importer, are ultimately responsible for the fulfillment of any legal requirements applicable to your shipment.

General Considerations

Regulatory Agencies. Importation of many live animals is highly restricted under several laws administered by Federal agencies. Any of a number of agencies may have a regulatory interest in your importation. USDA APHIS, PPQ branch regulates the importation and interstate movement of live plant pests and vectors—such as insects that potentially carry disease-producing viruses—and articles that may harbor them, under applicable provisions of the Plant Quarantine Act of 1912 (PQA) and the Federal Plant Pest Act of 1957 (FPPA). Imports of live animals are regulated by the USDA, and in some instances by the FDA. The FWS may impose restrictions on imports of live wildlife, pets, or endangered species. The U.S National Marine Fisheries Service enforces regulations pertinent to imports of marine mammals in conjunction with FWS. Imports of live organisms that may be vectors of human disease are controlled by the U.S. Department of Health and Human Services through its Centers for Disease Control (CDC).

If you wish to import any kind of live animal, you should contact the government agencies listed for complete details. See "Relevant Government Agencies" below. Customs plays a monitoring and enforcement role for the voluminous import provisions of the various agencies. If you are at all unsure as to the regulatory status of your intended import, contact Customs for a referral to the appropriate regulating agency.

Most individual states also have import requirements for live animals in addition to those of Federal agencies. When planning your importation, you should always contact not only the pertinent federal agencies, but also the appropriate state regulatory agencies at your shipment's U.S. destination. You should also check on any state regulations in jurisdictions through which your shipment is to pass en route to its final destination. Do this before you attempt to enter the animals into the U.S.

Health Certificates. All live animal imports must be accompanied by a health certificate. Entry procedures for live animals coming from Mexico or Canada are somewhat less rigorous than for those entering from other countries.

Quarantine Regulations. The importation of live animals is subject to quarantine regulations under 9 CFR Part 92, administered and enforced by the USDA APHIS. APHIS restricts the import of live animals primarily to safeguard U.S. animals from communicable disease. The following categories of livestock are subject to USDA regulation: 1) ruminants, that is all cloven-hoofed ani-

*IMPORTANT: Read the Commodity Index Introduction. It is the essential framework for understanding this section.

mals, such as cattle, sheep, deer, antelope, camels, and giraffes; 2) swine; 3) horses, asses, mules, and zebras; and 4) live poultry. The USDA also regulates the import of birds and dogs. Also subject to separate regulation are animal byproducts, such as untanned hides, wool, hair, bones, bone meal, blood meal, animal casings, glands, organs, extracts or secretions of ruminants and swine, as well as hay and straw and other articles accompanying livestock imports.

This entry provides an overview of rather than an exhaustive treatment of APHIS and other agency requirements. Most live animal shipments must comply with the general requirements outlined here, although there are exceptions, as well as more stringent requirements which may apply in specific cases. Importation of certain live animals from listed countries in which certain communicable diseases are considered to be endemic is prohibited entirely. If you are interested in importing live animals, you should contact the APHIS for full information (see addresses at end of this chapter).

Endangered Species. The U.S. Department of the Interior's Fish and Wildlife Service (FWS) regulates importation of live animals covered under the Endangered Species Act (ESA) and the Convention on International Trade in Endangered Species (CITES). Importation of wildlife and pets is highly regulated and restricted. This category includes—but is not limited to—game animals, wild animals, game and wild birds and their eggs, and extends to any parts or products of the above. Importation of marine wildlife is also restricted.

The FWS enforces regulations pursuant to a number of wildlife protection laws, which are listed in 50 CFR. FWS licensing, permits, import declarations, and port inspections are generally required for imports of the species covered under these regulations. Shipments of FWS-regulated species must enter at designated ports (see below) listed in 50 CFR 10. If you are interested in importing any exotic live animal, you should contact FWS with the scientific name of the species to ascertain whether or not it is protected. If it is, you will need a FWS permit to import it. You may also need country of origin export permits and documentation.

Animal or Insect Pests and Vectors. If you wish to import living organisms classified as plant pests, you will need an APHIS PPQ import permit. USDA APHIS VS regulates importation and movement of live animal pests and vectors, under provisions of 9 CFR 122. If you wish to import such an organism, you will need an APHIS VS import permit. The CDC of the Department of Health and Human Services regulates the import of vectors of human disease. If your shipment contains any etiological agent or insect, animal or plant vector of human disease or any exotic living insect, animal, or plant capable of serving as a vector of human disease, you will need a CDC import permit.

Customs Classification

For customs purposes, live animals are classified under Chapter 1 of the HTSUS. This chapter is broken into major headings, which are further divided into subheadings, and often into subsubheadings, each of which has its own HTSUS classification number. For example, the HTSUS number for cattle imported other than for dairy purposes is 0102.90.40, indicating that it is a subcategory of live cattle other than purebred breeding animals (0102.90.20), which is a subcategory of the major heading live bovine animals (0102.90.00). There are six major headings under Chapter 1.

0101—Live horses, asses, mules, and hinnies

0102—Live bovine animals

0103—Live swine

0104—Live sheep and goats

0105—Live poultry of the following kinds: chickens, ducks, geese, turkeys, and guineas

0106—Other live animals

For more details regarding classification of the specific animal you are interested in importing, consult a customs broker, the appropriate commodity specialist at your nearest customs port, or see HTSUS. HTSUS is available for purchase from the U.S. Government Printing Office (see addresses at end of this chapter), and may be found in larger public libraries. Refer to "Classification—Liquidation" on page 207 for a general discussion of customs classification.

Sample Import Duties

Import duties will vary depending on the HTSUS classification of your product. Therefore, to determine the correct amount of duties, your product must be properly classified under the HTSUS. The following sample duties are taken from the duty listings for HTSUS Chapter 1 products:

Purebred breeding horses (0101.11.00): free; asses other than purebred breeding animals (0101.20.20): 15%; cattle imported for dairy purposes (0102.90.20): free; cattle imported for other than dairy purposes (0102.90.40): 2.2 cents/kg; live swine (0103): free; chickens weighing less than 185 g (0105.11.00): 2 cents each; other poultry weighing more than 185 g (0105.9.00): 4.4 cents/kg; other live birds (0106.00.10): 4%; foxes (0106.00.30): 7.5%; other live animals (0106.00.50): free.

Entry and Documentation

The entry of merchandise is a two-part process consisting of 1) filing the documents necessary to determine whether merchandise may be released from Customs custody and 2) filing the documents which contain information for duty assessment and statistical purposes. In certain instances all documents must be filed and accepted by Customs prior to the release of the goods. Unless you have been granted an extension, you must file entry documents at a location specified by the district or area director within five working days of your shipment's date of arrival at a U.S. port of entry. These include a number of standard documents required by Customs for any entry, and, where applicable:

- USDA permits as required
- Veterinary certificate(s) from the country of origin
- Importer's declaration, two copies
- Valid APHIS PPQ Import Permit for living plant pests
- Valid APHIS VS Import Permit for living animal pests
- Valid CDC Import Permit for living organisms that may carry human disease
- FWS import permits required under CITES, ESA, and any other regulations applicable to the particular shipment; and any export certification from country of origin required under the specific laws governing endangered or threatened species
- FWS Wildlife Declaration **Form 3-177**—an original plus 3 copies—a copy of air waybill or bill of lading, and a copy of invoice (proforma invoice if shipment is noncommercial)
- FDA Importers Entry Notice **Form FD701,** as required

After you present the entry, Customs may examine your shipment, or may waive examination. The shipment is then released provided no legal or regulatory violations have been noted. You must then file entry summary documentation and deposit estimated duties at a designated customhouse within 10 working days of your shipment's release. For a detailed description of entry procedures, standard documentation, and informal entry, refer to "Entry Process" on page 182.

Prohibitions and Restrictions

Absolute Prohibitions. Animals to be used in fighting may not be imported.

USDA APHIS Entry and Permit Requirements. In general, all live animals must 1) enter at APHIS-designated quarantine ports (see listing below); 2) undergo APHIS port of entry inspection; 3) after passing entry must be immediately confined in an APHIS-operated or APHIS-approved privately-owned quarantine facility for a period of time which varies according to species. During quarantine, certain tests may be required to ascertain the health of the animals.

Import Permit. With a few exceptions, all live animals must be covered by an APHIS import permit, which must be presented to Customs at the first port of arrival. These permits must be obtained prior to the export of the animals from their country of origin. At the time you apply for a permit to import animals subject to quarantine requirements, you will need to make reservations for space in an appropriate quarantine facility. Fees for quarantine reservations vary according to species, and are due and payable at the time the reservation is requested.

Each shipment entering under an APHIS permit must comply with the permit's specifications in every particular. If your shipment is found not to conform in any way (such as entering at a port of entry other than the one specified in the permit), it will be refused entry.

Veterinary Certificate. A veterinary certificate, issued by a salaried veterinarian of the country of origin, stating that the animals are free of applicable livestock diseases must accompany each shipment. The specific information required on the certificate varies depending upon the species you are importing, as well as its country of origin. You must also present an importer's declaration that states: l) port of entry; 2) importer's name and address; 3) broker's name and address; 4) origin of the animal(s); 5) number, breed, species, and purpose of importation; and 6) consignee's name and location of intended delivery.

APHIS-designated Quarantine Ports. The following APHIS-designated ports generally have adequate quarantine facilities available for the import of live animals. With few exceptions, all shipments of live animals must enter at a designated port. Additional ports and any exceptions are listed under the heading pertaining to the particular type of livestock (such as ruminant, horse, etc.).

Air and ocean ports: Los Angeles, CA; Miami, FL; Honolulu, HI; and Newburgh, NY.

Land border ports with Canada: Eastport, ID; Houlton and Jackman, MN; Detroit, Port Huron, and Sault Ste. Marie, MI; Opheim, Raymond, and Sweetgrass, MT; Alexandria Bay, Buffalo, and Champlain, NY; Dunseith, Pembina, and Portal, ND; Derby Line and Highgate Springs, VT; Blaine, Lynden, Oroville, and Sumas, WA.

Land border ports with Mexico: Brownsville, Hidalgo, Laredo, Eagle Pass, Del Rio, Presidio, and El Paso, TX; Douglas, Naco, Nogales, Sasabe, and San Luis, AZ; Calexico and San Ysidro, CA; Antelope Wells and Columbus, NM.

Limited ports (ports with facilities for entry of live animals that do not appear to require restraint and holding inspection facilities): Anchorage and Fairbanks, AK; San Diego, CA; Denver, CO; Jacksonville, St. Petersburg, Clearwater, and Tampa, FL; Atlanta, GA; Chicago, IL; New Orleans, LA; Portland, MN; Baltimore, MD; Boston, MA; Minneapolis, MN; Great Falls, MT; Portland, OR; San Juan, PR; Galveston and Houston, TX; and Seattle, Spokane, and Tacoma, WA.

These listed ports have been designated as quarantine stations. The USDA Administrator has authority to designate other ports as quarantine stations as needed.

USDA Requirements for Poultry. Except for live poultry and products entering through land ports from Canada, APHIS permits are required for all entries of live poultry. Permits covering multiple poultry shipments transiting the port of Anchorage, AK are available, and if issued, are valid for the duration of the calendar year of issue. For more information on these permits, contact APHIS (see addresses at end of this chapter).

Poultry includes chickens, doves, ducks, geese, grouse, guinea fowl, partridges, pea fowl, pheasant, pigeons, quail, swans, and turkeys, and the fertilized eggs of these species. Import and quarantine restrictions on these birds are designed to prevent the introduction into the U.S. of communicable poultry diseases, such as European fowl pest (fowl plague) or viscerotropic velogenic Newcastle disease (VVND).

Veterinary Certificate. The veterinary certificate must show, among other things, that the flock was inspected and found to be free of disease immediately prior to export, and that the poultry was not exposed to disease common to poultry during the 90 days immediately preceding export.

Quarantine Requirements. Most poultry (exception is made for poultry from Canada) is quarantined for not less than 30 days, beginning with the date of arrival at the port of entry. During quarantine, poultry is subject to whatever inspections, disinfections, and tests that may be required by the USDA to determine the health of the animals. Most fertile eggs are quarantined until hatched, and the poultry must remain in quarantine not less than 30 days after hatching. The reservation fee for APHIS quarantine space is 100% of the cost of providing care, feed, and handling during quarantine, as estimated by the quarantine facility's veterinarian in charge.

USDA Requirements for Horses. Quarantine regulations governing the import of horses are extensive and complex. The ones mentioned here represent only a partial summary. If you are interested in importing horses, you should contact APHIS for specifics.

Horses (except those originating in or transited through countries where African horsesickness is known to exist) destined for quarantine facilities provided by the importer may be imported at any international customs port, provided all applicable provisions of the regulation have been met. If you wish to provide your own quarantine facilities, you must obtain prior APHIS approval. Reservation fees for APHIS quarantine facilities are 100% of the cost of providing care, feed, and handling during quarantine, and may be satisfied by a letter of credit. Quarantine requirements for horses vary depending upon country of origin, and generally last until negative results to tests conducted at the port of entry are obtained and the horses are certified by the port veterinarian to be free from clinical evidence of disease.

CEM Restrictions. The importation of horses from the following countries listed as affected with contagious equine metritis (CEM) is prohibited: Austria, Belgium, the Czech Republic, Denmark, France, Germany, Ireland, Italy, Japan, the Netherlands, Norway, Slovakia, Sweden, Switzerland, and the United Kingdom (including England, Northern Ireland, Scotland, Wales, and the Isle of Man). Exceptions to this blanket prohibition may be made for specific animals under APHIS permit. Such special case imports require stringent preexport veterinary examinations, which must be documented on the veterinary certificate necessary for entry.

The following horses meeting these conditions and originating in CEM countries may be imported: 1) horses imported under special provisions initiated by the USDA Administrator under 9 CFR 92.301(a); 2) geldings, weanlings, or yearlings whose age is certified on the import health certificate; 3) thoroughbred horses imported for permanent entry from Germany, the United Kingdom, Ireland, and France; 4) stallions over 731 days in age; 5) mares over 731 days in age; 5) horses over 731 days in age imported into the U.S. for no more than 60 days to compete in specified events; 6) horses temporarily exported from the U.S. to any listed country for a period not to exceed 60 days, not bred to any animal during that 60 days, and returned to the U.S. Each of these permissible importations are contingent on specific conditions as outlined in 9 CFR 92.301. For details, see that document, or contact APHIS (see addresses at end of this chapter).

You may import stallions over 731 days old originating in countries listed as affected with CEM only if destined for the following states: California, Colorado, Kentucky, Louisiana, Maryland, Montana, New York, North Carolina, Ohio, South Carolina, Tennessee, Virginia, and Wisconsin. Mares meeting the above specifications may be imported only if destined for: California, Colorado, Kentucky, Louisiana, Maryland, Montana, New York, Ohio, South Carolina, Tennessee, Virginia, and Wisconsin. Horses destined for these states must undergo state quarantine pursuant to regulations in 9 CFR 92 Subpart C.

In addition to the designated quarantine ports listed above, horses may be imported from Canada at International Falls, MN.

African Horsesickness Restrictions. Horses imported from countries considered to be affected with African horsesickness—Portugal, Spain, Yemen, and all countries on the continent of Africa—must enter the U.S. through the port of New York. Such horses will have to be quarantined at the New York Animal Import Center in Newburgh, New York, for at least 60 days. This restriction also applies to horses that have stopped in or transited a country considered affected with African horsesickness.

USDA Requirements for Ruminants. Permits are required for all ruminants. Veterinary certificates are also required for all ruminants offered for import, with extra information required for sheep and goats. APHIS is particularly concerned with brucellosis and tuberculosis in cattle and goats. In most cases, you will have to include test results concerning these diseases on the veterinary certificate. Quarantine reservation fees are 100% of the cost of providing care, feed, and handling during quarantine, and may be satisfied by a letter of credit.

The port of Los Angeles, CA is not approved for importation of ruminants.

Country-Specific Exceptions. Import permits are not required for ruminants imported from Canada through designated U.S.-Canadian border ports, as long as the animals are of either Canadian or U.S. origin, and have not been in any other country, or, if imported to Canada from a foreign country, have been unconditionally released in Canada for 60 days or longer. Cattle originating in Canada must be accompanied by specified health documentation (consult 9 CFR 92.418 for details). Special provisions and requirements also apply to ruminants from Central America, the West Indies, and Mexico (9 CFR 92.422-429). Special restrictions apply to cattle imported from the Republic of Ireland (9 CFR 92.432) and to sheep imported from New Zealand. For specific details, see 9 CFR 92 or contact APHIS.

USDA Requirements for Swine. Permits are required for all swine. APHIS is particularly concerned with rinderpest and foot-and-mouth disease in swine. Quarantine reservation fees are 100% of the cost of providing care, feed, and handling during quarantine, and may be satisfied by a letter of credit. You will not need an import permit for swine imported from Canada through designated U.S.-Canadian border ports, as long as your animals are of either Canadian or U.S. origin, and have not been in any other country, or, if imported to Canada from a foreign country, have been unconditionally released in Canada for 60 days or longer.

Harry S. Truman Animal Import Center (HSTAIC). It may be possible to import ruminants and swine originating in countries from which imports are otherwise prohibited because of the presence of disease. Such importations enter through HSTAIC, under cooperative agreement between APHIS and the importer. Application, accompanied by a $50,000 deposit, for this type of special import approval are made to APHIS. APHIS holds one lottery in October and another in April to choose which application will be approved. The applicant is responsible for all costs incurred in the HSTAIC quarantine process, as well as for fulfilling all of the requirements, such as providing a preexport quarantine site for the animals in the country of origin. For details, see 9 CFR 522 or contact APHIS.

USDA Requirements for Insects. It is impossible to list standard import requirements for all insects. Basically, insects that are in a live state and that are injurious to cultivated crops (including vegetables, field crops, bush fruit, and orchard, forest, or shade trees), and the eggs, pupae, or larvae of such insects, are prohibited entry. Exceptions are made for scientific purposes under regulations prescribed by the Secretary of Agriculture. Live insects—or their eggs, pupae, or larvae—that are not injurious to crops or trees, are permitted entry into the U.S. only if covered by an APHIS permit, which can be obtained only if the insects are not prohibited by the FWS.

The importation of certain species of insects does not require a permit. However, you must be very sure of such exemption before attempting unauthorized importation. We strongly advise that you provide all concerned federal agencies with specific biological information regarding any insect you intend to ship to the U.S., to be sure your bases are covered. Never assume that no permit is required. Let the agencies make that determination.

CDC Requirements for Insects. If you wish to import an insect that may be capable of being a vector of human disease, you will need a Centers for Disease Control (CDC) permit. You should complete and submit to CDC's Office of Biosafety (see addresses at end of this chapter), an original signed copy of CDC Application for Permit to Import or Transport Agents or Vectors of Human Disease. To qualify for a permit, you must reside in the U.S. You should only sign the application if you are actually the proposed permit holder. Permit applications signed by persons other than the proposed permit holder are invalid.

On the application, you will be expected to provide such information as: 1) person requesting permit, 2) source and description of material; 3) number of shipments; 4) method of transport; 5) quantity, i.e. volume and type of individual containers; 6) proposed use, including objectives, proposed plan of work, completion date, final disposition of materials; 7) description of available isolation and containment facilities; 8) qualifications and experience of technical personnel. If your approved permit stipulates additional restrictions and precautions, you must adhere to them.

FWS Regulations for Wild Animals and Pets. With some exceptions, persons engaged in the business of importing wildlife and wildlife products the value of which exceeds $25,000 per year must be licensed by FWS. Even if their annual importations are valued at less than $25,000, or they qualify for licensing exemption for other reasons, wildlife importers are still responsible for keeping thorough records of all wildlife transactions and of making these records available to officers of FWS as requested. For a full description of exemptions from licensing, and of recordkeeping requirements, contact the FWS or see 50 CFR 14.

FWS Designated Wildlife Ports. All wildlife shipments must enter and leave the U.S. through FWS designated ports, as listed in 50 CFR 14.12. Currently there are 10 such designated ports: New York, NY; Miami, FL; New Orleans, LA; Dallas/Ft. Worth, TX; Los Angeles, CA; San Francisco, CA; Chicago, IL; Seattle, WA; Honolulu, HI; and Portland, OR. If special circumstances prevent you from making your entry at a designated port, an Exception to Designated Port Permit is required and must be obtained from FWS (see addresses at end of this chapter).

FWS Entry Requirements. At least 72 hours before your shipment is due to arrive at the designated port, you should notify both U.S. Customs and FWS inspectors there of its expected arrival. The FWS and Customs will inspect your shipment to verify compliance with all of the legal requirements for entry. Importations may also be subject to the quarantine requirements of the USDA and the U.S. Public Health Service (see below). Questions on these requirements should be directed to those agencies.

You will need to furnish the officials with any documentation required by the laws under which your import is protected. Documents required by FWS at port of entry vary depending upon the nature of the shipment, but in general include: 1) all permits or certificates required under CITES, ESA, and any other regulations applicable to the particular shipment; 2) Wildlife Declaration **Form 3-177**, available at the port of entry (an original plus 3 copies); 3) copy of air waybill or bill of lading; 4) copy of invoice (proforma invoice if shipment is noncommercial). Invoices for wildlife shipments must specify the species covered and the quantity of each species.

In addition to this paperwork, importers of fish and wildlife must also present any appropriate foreign export permits and other acceptable foreign documentary evidence of the lawful taking, transportation, or sale of the wildlife. Appropriate U.S. consular certificates must be presented for importation of species subject to such documentation requirements in 50 CFR 17.4. A Mexican export permit is required for any game animals (e.g., antelope, mountain sheep, deer, bears, peccaries, squirrels, rabbits, and hares), including their parts or products, imported from Mexico.

Detention of Shipment. If Customs has any doubt about compliance of your FWS-regulated wildlife shipment, such as the endangered status of the wildlife, fulfillment of permit requirement particulars, or accurate identification of species, your importation will not be released. If your shipment is detained, you will be responsible for making arrangements acceptable to the FWS for proper handling, custody, and care of the specimens. All such arrangements are at the expense and risk of the importer. Customs will not dispose of the importation until FWS determines the true nature of the species. If you refuse to have the identity established, the FWS will determine final disposition of the importation.

Designated Injurious Species. Species listed as "injurious" in 50 CFR 13 are prohibited importation because they pose a threat of injury to human beings, or to U.S. agriculture, horticulture, forestry, wildlife, or wildlife resources. You may import certain injurious species as exceptions under FWS permit. If you attempt to enter a shipment of injurious species without appropriate FWS authorization, however, it will be immediately exported or destroyed. Keep abreast of listing changes in prohibited and restricted injurious species by consulting 50 CFR 13.

Currently listed are: 1) any species of the so-called "flying fox" or fruit bat of the genus *Pteropus*; 2) any species of mongoose or meerkat of the genera *Atilax, Cynictis, Helogale, Herpestes, Ichneumia, Mungos,* and *Suricata*; 3) any species of European rabbit of the genus *Oryctolagus*; 4) any species of Indian wild dog, red dog, or dhole of the genus *Cuon*; 5) any species of the multimammate rat or mouse of the genus *Mastomys*; 6) any live specimens or fertile eggs of the species of so-called "pink starling" or "rosy pastor," *Sturnus roseus*; 7) the species of dioch (including the subspecies black-fronted, red-billed, or Sudan dioch) *Quelea quelea*; 8) any species of Java sparrow, *Padda oryzivora*; 9) the species of red-whiskered bulbul, *Pycnonotus jocosus*; 10) any live fish or viable eggs of the family *Clariidae*.

Designated Endangered and Threatened Species. The FWS enforces a variety of laws protecting endangered species of animals and birds. Protected species are listed in 50 CFR 17. Listed species are generally prohibited entry into the U.S. However, specimens of some species may be imported under FWS permit. Under CITES, certain animals, mammals, birds, reptiles, amphibians, fish, snails, and clams may be prohibited or may require FWS permits or certification. You may import antique articles otherwise prohibited under the ESA, provided certain conditions are met. These articles must be entered at designated antique ports.

Marine Mammals. The taking and importation of marine mammals and their products are subject to the requirements of the Marine Mammal Protection Act of 1972 (MMPA). Importation is prohibited except under permit from the National Marine Fisheries Service or from FWS. For more information, contact either of those agencies (addresses below).

Birds. Live wild birds protected under the Migratory Bird Treaty Act (MBTA) may be imported into the U.S. from foreign countries for scientific or propagating purposes under FWS permit. State game departments, municipal game farms or parks; public museums, zoological parks, or societies; and scientific or educational institutions may import migratory birds without a permit. Mexican export permits are required for all such migratory birds, including their parts or products, imported from Mexico.

USDA Regulations for Wild Animals and Pets. Wild ruminants (all animals that chew their cud, such as cattle, buffaloes, sheep, goats, deer, antelopes, camels, llamas, and giraffes) and swine (various varieties of wild hogs), and ducks, geese, swans, turkeys, pigeons, doves, pheasant, grouse, partridges, quail, guinea fowl, and pea fowl may be imported only under USDA APHIS VS permit (see addresses at end of this chapter). You must obtain your APHIS permit before the animals are shipped from the country of exportation. All wild ruminants and swine are inspected at designated ports of entry by USDA veterinarians. USDA also regulates importation of hedgehogs, opossums, elephants, rhinoceros, hippopotamus, and tapirs, under 9 CFR. Permits are required.

CDC Regulations for Wild Animals and Pets. Importation of birds, cats, dogs, nonhuman primates, and turtles is subject to the requirements of the CDC, Quarantine Division (see addresses at end of this chapter).

Psittacine Birds. Psittacine birds include all birds commonly known as parrots: Amazons, African grays, cockatoos, macaws, parrotlets, beebees, parakeets, lovebirds, lories, lorikeets, and all other birds of the order *Psittaciformes*. If you wish to import birds destined for a zoological park or medical research institution, which have not had prior confinement and treatment abroad at an approved treatment center, you must obtain a CDC permit. Permits are also required for birds previously exported from the U.S. and returned under 19 CFR 12.26(b)(4)(c) without having been confined in the foreign country.

Psittacine Birds as Pets. Psittacine birds may be imported under prescribed conditions (42 CFR 71.164(e)) without permit and without prior confinement and treatment, to be kept as pets by the owner. Such importations may not exceed two such birds by members of a family comprising a single household in any 12-month period. If your import falls into this category, you must be sure to comply with all applicable CDC Foreign Quarantine Regulations. Birds taken out of the U.S. and returned may be admitted without permit, provided there is full compliance with prescribed conditions. If your import fits this category, you should be aware that your birds will not be released from Customs custody until you have complied with all applicable Public Health Service requirements. For more information, contact the CDC (see addresses at end of this chapter).

Nonhuman primates. Nonhuman primates include but are not limited to such animals commonly known as monkeys, chimpanzees, orangutans, gorillas, gibbons, apes, baboons, marmosets, tamarins, lemurs, lorises, and galagos. Importation of nonhuman primates as pets is prohibited. Nonhuman primates may only be imported for permitted purposes, i.e. bona fide research, education, or exhibition, and only by importers registered with CDC. Bona fide exhibition purposes include 1) display in an organized zoological exhibit regularly open to the general public, and 2) full-time use in a trained animal act open to the public. Display in a pet store or private home, or maintenance and training of a nonhuman primate primarily as a hobby, with occasional display to groups such as school children, does not constitute a bona fide exhibition.

If you import nonhuman primates, you must not sell, resell, or otherwise distribute the animals for exhibition purposes without clear evidence that they will be used as a bona fide exhibit. The intended recipient's possession of a USDA Animal Exhibitor's License is not sufficient documentation. Importation of nonhuman primates for use in breeding colonies is permitted, provided that all descendants of these animals will be solely used for the permitted purposes.

If you wish to register as an importer of nonhuman primates, you must comply with specific CDC transport and quarantine requirements. Guidelines are published in CDC's Morbidity and Mortality Weekly Report (MMWR) Vol. 39, No. 2, January 19, 1990: "Interim Guidelines for Handling Nonhuman Primates During Transit and Quarantine." A special CDC permit is required, in addition to registration, if you wish to import cynomolgus, African green, or rhesus monkeys. Special permit requirements were published in the Federal Register, April 20, 1990. For more information, see that publication or contact the CDC (see addresses at end of this chapter).

Nonhuman primates not meeting the import requirements of the current quarantine regulation will be refused entry. If your shipment is refused, you have the option to export, destroy, or give the animals to a scientific, educational, or exhibition facility under CDC-approved arrangements. Any such disposition will be at the importer's expense. Pending exportation or other disposition, the animals will be detained in Customs custody at the port of arrival, also at the importer's expense. Nonhuman primates must also meet FWS import requirements.

Dogs and Cats. Dogs and cats are subject to quarantine requirements under 42 CFR 71.51. All dogs and cats must be inspected by a CDC officer at port of entry. Only those animals which show no signs of communicable disease will be admitted entry. If your animals show signs of disease, or have been exposed to disease during transit, you must provide for confinement quarters, and must arrange for all necessary veterinary examinations and tests to ensure the animal's health prior to importation. Such confinement is at your expense. A valid rabies vaccination certificate is required for each dog unless the dog meets specific exemption qualifications (see 42 CFR 71.51). The carrier responsible for transit of dogs and cats must submit at port of entry a record of all diseases and/or deaths occurring during transit. Any dog or cat refused entry will be detained in Customs custody pending reexportation, at your expense.

Live Turtles and Viable Turtle Eggs. Live turtles with a carapace length of less than four inches, and viable turtle eggs are prohibited importation into the U.S. unless such importation is not in connection with a business, and the lot is limited to fewer than seven live turtles, seven viable turtle eggs, or any combination thereof totaling no more than seven. You may import shipments of more than seven, for bona fide scientific, educational, or exhibition purposes, but only under CDC permit. A CDC permit does not preclude the necessity for any other authorization from other governmental agency, as in the case of a turtle also protected under the Endangered Species Act, etc. For more information, contact CDC (see addresses at end of this chapter).

USDA Animal and Plant Health Inspection Service Veterinary Services also has a regulatory interest in these shipments. Contact that agency for more information.

FDA Regulations for Wild Animals and Pets. Importation of turtles with a carapace length of less than four inches, and of psittacine birds, is also subject to the requirements of the FDA. FDA Importer's Entry Notice **Form FD701** is required. For an annotated diagram of FDA entry procedures refer to the "Foods" appendix, beginning on page 808. For more information, contact FDA (see addresses at end of this chapter).

Country-Specific Import Restrictions

The USDA restricts the importation of domesticated animals based on country of origin and type of animal based on endemic disease among the types of animals in that geographic area. See the discussion above, or contact USDA APHIS (see addresses at end of this chapter) for more information. Endangered species restrictions under CITES are country-specific. Consult the FWS (see addresses at end of this chapter) for more information.

Live Animals from Canada, Mexico, Central America, and West Indies. There are special provisions for live animals originating in Canada, Mexico, Central America, and the West Indies. These provisions vary according to species, and include such elements as permit or quarantine waiver, special quarantine restrictions, and specific ports of entry for specific types of animals, as well as special provisions for animals imported for immediate slaughter or for transit across the U.S. only. For entries from these countries, only one copy of the import declaration must be presented to Customs. For more details, see the appropriate headings in 9 CFR 92, or contact APHIS.

Poultry from Canada, Virgin Islands, and Mexico. Poultry from Canada entering the U.S. at designated Canadian-U.S. land border ports do not require an APHIS permit, and are not subject to quarantine, provided all other requirements are met. APHIS may waive the permit requirement for poultry intended for immediate slaughter imported into the U.S. Virgin Islands from the British Virgin Islands. For poultry from Mexico, the importer must make application for inspection in writing, and submit it to the veterinary inspector at the port of entry. All poultry from Mexico must be imported through designated U.S.-Mexican land border ports. APHIS is particularly concerned with fever tick infestation in Mexican poultry. Any shipment of Mexican origin found to contain fever ticks will be refused entry and will be destroyed unless immediately removed.

Marking and Labeling Requirements

USDA APHIS Approved Imports. When APHIS PPQ issues a permit for a given shipment of insect, it also supplies a mailing label, which you must use on the package. The label provides specific instructions for packaging, marking, and labeling, which you must follow when preparing your package for transport.

Wildlife and Endangered Species. All wildlife shipments must be marked on the outside of the container with the names and addresses of the exporter and importer, an accurate identification of the species, and the numbers of each species in the container.

For a general discussion of U.S. Customs marking and labeling requirements, see "Marking: Country of Origin" on page 215 and "Special Marking Requirements" on page 217.

Shipping Considerations

You will need to ensure that animal imports are quartered and shipped with care so that they arrive in good condition and pass smoothly through Customs. You are responsible for ensuring that the shipment is in compliance with all applicable government regulations for shipping. In most instances, you should not leave these arrangements solely to the discretion of your supplier. Careful preparation of the shipment and selection of the mode of transport can be essential to a cost-effective, timely delivery of undamaged goods. We strongly advise you to consult your shipping representative, insurance agent, or freight broker for advice on packing and shipping. Refer also to the major tab section "Packing/Shipping/Insurance" for a general discussion of packing and shipping.

Import shipments of live animals are subject to stringent transport regulations intended to ensure the animals' health and safety en route. Regulations vary depending upon the species. You are responsible for fulfilling the transport requirements of all relevant government agencies. If you are interested in importing live animals, you should contact the appropriate government agency for shipping standards and instructions. In some cases, shipping requirements may be specified on the appropriate permit. If not, general safeguards apply.

Publications Available

The following publication gives brief, general guidelines on USDA regulated products. Although designed primarily for tourists, it contains a list of approved products that you may find helpful. It is published by USDA APHIS (see addresses at end of this chapter).

Travelers Tips On Bringing Food, Plant, and Animal Products into the United States

The *Harmonized Tariff Schedule of the United States* (HTSUS) is available from:

Government Printing Office (GPO)
Superintendent of Documents
Washington, DC 20402
(202) 512-1800 (Order line)
(202) 512-0000 (General)

The USGPO also has copies of specific laws available for purchase. The USGPO accepts credit card orders over the phone, as well as mail orders paid by credit card, a check drawn on a U.S. bank, or an international money order.

Relevant Government Agencies

Address your questions regarding USDA requirements for the importation of live animals to:

U.S. Department of Agriculture (USDA)
Animal and Plant Health Inspection Service (APHIS)
Veterinary Services (VS)
Import-Export Products Staff
Federal Building, Room 756
6505 Belcrest Road
Hyattsville, MD 20782
(301) 436-7885

Address your questions regarding the importation of wildlife, pets, or endangered species to:

U.S. Fish and Wildlife Service (FWS)
Office of Management Authority
4401 N. Fairfax Drive, Room 432
Arlington, VA 22203
(703) 358-2095
(800) 358-2104, (703) 358-2104 (Permits office)

National Marine Fisheries Service (NMFS)
Office of Marine Mammals and Endangered Species
1335 East West Highway
Silver Spring, MD 20910
(301) 713-2332

Address your questions regarding FDA requirements for the importation of live animals to:

Food and Drug Administration (FDA)
Center for Veterinary Medicine
7500 Standish Place (HFV-12)
Rockville, MD 20855
(301) 594-5909

Food and Drug Administration (FDA)
Division of Enforcement, Imports Branch
200 C Street SW
Washington, DC 20204
(202) 205-4726

Address your questions or requests for permit applications for import of live organisms that may be vectors of human disease to:

Centers for Disease Control (CDC)
Office of Biosafety
1600 Clifton Road, NE
Atlanta, GA 30333
(404) 639-3883

Address your questions regarding the importation of live animals to the district or port director of Customs for you area. For addresses see "U.S. Customs District Offices" on page 62 or contact:

U.S. Customs Service
1301 Constitution Ave. NW
Washington, DC 20229
(202) 927-6724 (Information)
(202) 927-1000 (General)

Laws and Regulations

The following laws and regulations may be relevant to the importation of live animals. The laws are contained in the U.S. Code (USC) and the regulations are published in the code of Federal Regulations (CFR), both of which may be available at larger public and law libraries. Copies of specific laws are also available from the United States Government Printing Office (address above).

7 USC 2156
Animal Fighting Venture Prohibition
This Act prohibits the transport in foreign commerce of animals to be used in an animal fighting venture and authorizes U.S. Customs to enforce the prohibition.

7 USC 4801 et seq.
Pork Promotion, Research, and Consumer Information Act
This Act provides that each importer of porcine animal, pork, or pork product shall remit an assessment to Customs at the time the product is imported. See 7 CFR 1230.71 and 1230.110.

18 USC 42 et seq.
Importation of Animals, Birds, Fish, and Plants
This Act governs the importation of mammals, birds, fish, amphibia, and reptiles into the U.S. and authorizes U.S. Customs to enforce the import requirements.

21 USC 101 et seq.
Importation of Cattle and Quarantine
This Act provides for suspension of importation of animals to prevent the spread of disease, and for the quarantine of prohibited classes of animals. Importation of all animals described by the Act is prohibited except at certain designated ports. All animals are to be inspected on import or export.

21 USC 113a
Foot-and-Mouth Memorandum of Understanding; Disease Research Act
This Act authorizes the study of animal disease and prohibits introduction of live foot-and-mouth disease virus into the United States except under certain defined circumstances. Customs enforces Agriculture restrictions and regulations.

42 USC 264 et seq.
Quarantine, Inspection, and Licensing
This Act restricts importations of dogs, cats, monkeys, psittacine birds, turtles, tortoises, and terrapins that do not comply with health standards. Customs enforces these restrictions. See 42 CFR 71.51 et seq.

19 CFR 12.24 and 12.26
Regulations for Animal and Animal Product Entry
These regulations provide for U.S. Customs entry declarations, documentation, and procedures for the animals and animal products subject to FWS and USDA regulations.

9 CFR Parts 91-96
Regulations on Animal Byproduct Quarantine Control
These regulations promulgated by the USDA prohibit the importation of animal products for use in industry unless the products meet certain processing standards and are not infected with certain diseases.

21 USC 135
Establishment of International Animal Quarantine Stations
This Act authorizes the establishment of international quarantine stations. Customs enforces laws regarding importation of livestock.

42 USC 264 et seq.
The Plant Quarantine Act
This Act gives the Plant Protection and Quarantine branch of the USDA authority to restrict or prohibit importation of plants or their seeds found to carry specific plant pests and pathogens.

7 USC 147a et seq.
Federal Plant Pest Act (FPPA)
This Act prohibits the importation into or movement through the U.S. of plant pests as defined in the Act, and provides for the inspection of any letter, box, parcel, or container that may carry a plant pest. Inspection is to be performed by U.S. Department of Agriculture in conjunction with Customs.

7 CFR Part 351
Regulations for Entry and Inspection of Plants by Mail
These regulations set forth the plant imports that are prohibited, the requirements for entering restricted plants by mail, and the inspection procedures followed by the USDA's Animal and Plant Health Inspection Service (APHIS).

19 CFR 12.10 et seq.
Regulations for Entry and Release of Restricted Plants
These regulations prescribe the procedures followed by U.S. Customs to enforce the USDA requirements for importation of plants.

Convention on International Trade in Endangered Species of Wild Fauna and Flora (CITES)
This comprehensive wildlife treaty signed by over 100 countries, including the United States, regulates and in many cases prohibits commercial imports and exports of wild animal and plant species threatened by trade.

16 USC 1531
Endangered Species Act
This Act prohibits the import and export of species listed as endangered and most species listed as threatened. It is the U.S. law that implements CITES.

16 USC 742a et seq.
Fish and Wildlife Act
This Act regulates and bars the import of certain wild animals or birds and authorizes U.S. Customs to enforce the restrictions.

16 USC 2401
Antarctic Conservation Act
This Act prohibits the importation, absent a special permit, of any flora or fauna native to Antarctica into the U.S.

16 USC 3371 et seq.
Lacey Act
This Act prohibits the import of species taken, possessed, transported, or sold in violation of the law of a foreign country.

16 USC 1361 et seq.
The Marine Mammal Protection Act
This Act prohibits the import of marine mammals and their parts and products. These species include whales, walruses, narwhals, seals, sea lions, sea otters, and polar bears.

16 USC 703 et seq.
The Migratory Bird Treaty Act
This Act protects designated wild migratory game birds and prohibits importation of them for commercial purposes.

16 USC 4201
The African Elephant Conservation Act
This Act prohibits imports of carved ivory products from any country and only permits imports of whole tusks from elephants legally hunted in certain African countries.

50 CFR Parts 10, 13, and 16
Regulations of FWS for Importing Wildlife and Fish
These regulations specify the animals and animal products subject to import prohibitions and restrictions.

Principal Exporting Countries

The following listing includes samples of the main supplier nations of the products of this chapter. It is organized by HTSUS major heading. (Refer to "Customs Classification" above for the product codes.) Countries are listed in rank order of the value of products imported to the U.S. Statistics represent customs value entries for 1993 from the Bureau of Census, U.S. Department of Commerce.

0101—Canada, United Kingdom, France, Ireland, Germany, Netherlands, Mexico, Argentina, New Zealand, Sweden

0102—Canada, Mexico, Japan, Turks and Caicos, United Kingdom, Australia

0103—Canada, United Kingdom, Denmark, Australia, Sweden, Ireland

0104—Canada, New Zealand, Australia

0105—Canada, France, Netherlands, Germany, United Kingdom

0106—Canada, Colombia, Netherlands, Indonesia, El Salvador, Peru, Philippines, Togo, Belgium, Australia

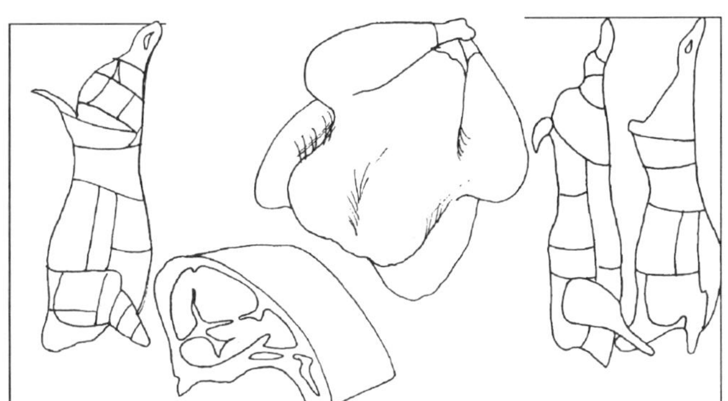

Chapter 2: Meat*

Full title: Meat and Edible Meat Offal

This chapter relates to the importation of meat and edible meat offal, which are classified under Chapter 2 of the Harmonized Tariff Schedule of the United States (HTSUS). Specifically, it includes fresh, chilled, or frozen carcasses or processed cuts of meat of beef, pork, sheep, goat, horses, poultry, and miscellaneous animals (such as frogs' legs, rabbit, etc.), as well as the edible internal parts of such animals (tongue, liver, etc.), and cured portions of such animals (such as hams), ground meat, edible meat flours and meals, and unrendered food grade pork and poultry fats. You should read this section in conjunction with the "Foods" appendix on page 808.

If you are interested in importing certain prepared meats and meat products, such as sausage or canned meats, you should refer to Commodity Index Chapter 16. Meat byproducts such as guts, bladders, and blood which are not fit for human consumption fall within Chapter 5 (some animal blood products for pharmaceutical uses are covered in Chapter 30). If you are interested in importing eggs or dairy products, you should refer to Chapter 4. Partially or fully processed animal fats are covered within Chapter 15. Fresh and frozen fish and related products are covered in Chapter 3. Non-edible flours and meals made of meat and intended primarily as animal feed or for industrial uses are covered in Chapter 23. The importation of live animals is covered in Chapter 1.

Key Factors

The key factors in the importation of meat and edible meat offal are:

- Compliance with U.S. Department of Agriculture (USDA) Food Safety and Inspection Service (FSIS) import restrictions, port inspections, and product certification
- Compliance with USDA Animal and Plant Health Inspection Service (APHIS) import restrictions, port inspections, and product certification
- APHIS permits are required for certain imports
- Compliance with U.S. Food and Drug Agency (FDA) requirements for certain imports

Although most importers utilize the services of a licensed customs broker in making their entries, and we recommend this practice, you should be aware of the regulatory, entry, and documentation issues involved in importing your product. You, as importer, are ultimately responsible for the fulfillment of any legal requirements applicable to your shipment.

General Considerations

Regulatory Agencies. Two agencies of the USDA, each having its own set of priorities, administer regulations regarding importation of meat and meat products. The APHIS Veterinary Service (VS) enforces the restrictions on importations of animals found in 9 CFR Chapter 1. The FSIS enforces the Federal Meat Inspection Act (FMIA) and the Poultry Products Inspection Act (PPIA) through regulations adopted as 9 CFR Chapter 3. These laws cover meat, poultry, and products derived from cattle, sheep, swine, goats, horses, and poultry.

Certain meat product imports are also controlled by the FDA under the Federal Food, Drug, and Cosmetic Act (FDCA). The FWS administers the provisions of the Endangered Species Act (ESA), the Convention on International Trade in Endangered Species of Wild Fauna and Flora (CITES), and the Marine Mammal Protection Act.

Entry Requirements. Meat and meat products are heavily regulated commodities. Relevant import regulation is extremely complex and specific. This discussion is in no way exhaustive. You should obtain further information from the USDA, the FDA, and U.S. Customs before attempting the importation of any meat or meat products into the U.S.

USDA Requirements. Import shipments of meat products must meet the inspection and certification requirements of both USDA departments. You must present foreign veterinary certification to the APHIS inspector at the port of entry for all shipments of meat and meat products. APHIS inspects every shipment to verify compliance with import regulations. Once APHIS passes a shipment, it then goes to FSIS personnel for further inspection prior to release. Your shipment will not be released until all USDA inspections have taken place, and Customs has received release clearances.

FDA Requirements. Although meat and meat products are primarily regulated by the USDA, imports of foods are also subject to the provisions of the FDCA, administered by the FDA. FDA regulations covering importation of foods of any kind are extensive and stringent. Meat products under USDA jurisdiction are not usually required to be entered using FDA personnel and procedures, but some products fall into a gray area and may be regulated by both agencies. Although the meats and meat products included in HTSUS Chapter 2 are usually handled by the USDA, certain food products containing meat—such as ravioli and other prepared food products containing meat, such as canned soups or stews—may be subject to primary FDA rather than USDA jurisdiction. If you have any doubt regarding your product, contact the FDA as well as the USDA for a determination.

Meats from wild game or domesticated varieties of wild game—such as rabbit—also fall within FDA jurisdiction. Imported products regulated by the FDA are subject to FDA port of entry inspection, and must comply with all FDCA requirements for those produced domestically. **Form FD701** is required for all FDA-regulated importations and may be obtained from your local FDA Import Operations office, from FDA headquarters (see addresses at end of this chapter) or from your customs broker. For an annotated diagram of required FDA import procedures refer to the "Foods" appendix on page 808.

Wildlife and Endangered Species. If you are interested in importing meat from exotic animals, including that of marine mammals, you should consult the U.S. Fish and Wildlife Service (FWS), which administers the provisions of the ESA, CITES, and the MMPA to be sure that your intended import is not covered

*IMPORTANT: Read the Commodity Index Introduction. It is the essential framework for understanding this section.

by these regulations. No animals or products derived from animals on any of these lists may be imported. There are many restrictions on the importation and sale of meat from wild animals. However, meat from animals grown in captivity is unlikely to fall within the purview of endangered species legislation.

Detention of Shipment. If your shipment is found to be noncomplying, it may be detained at the port of entry. In the case of products subject to FDA jurisdiction, the FDA may allow you to bring the shipment into compliance before making a final decision regarding admittance. However, any sorting, reprocessing, or relabeling must be supervised by FDA personnel and is done at the importer's expense. Such conditional release to allow the importer to bring a shipment into compliance is a privilege, not a right. The FDA may consider subsequent noncomplying shipments of the same type of product to constitute abuse of the privilege and require the importer to destroy or reexport the products. To ascertain what your legal responsibilities are, you should contact these agencies regarding the specific items to be imported.

Customs Classification

For customs purposes, meat and edible meat offal are classified under Chapter 2 of the HTSUS. This chapter is divided in to major headings, which are further divided into subheadings, and often into sub-subheadings, each of which has its own HTSUS classification number. For example, the HTSUS number for other cuts of lamb with the bone in is 0204.42.20, indicating that it is a subcategory of other cuts with bone in (0204.42.00), which is a subcategory of other meat of sheep, frozen: carcasses and half carcasses (0204.41.00), which in turn is a subcategory of the major heading meat of sheep or goats, fresh, chilled, or frozen (0204.00.00). There are 10 major headings in HTSUS Chapter 2.

0201—Meat of bovine animals, fresh or chilled

0202—Meat of bovine animals, frozen

0203—Meat of swine, fresh, chilled, or frozen

0204—Meat of sheep or goats, fresh, chilled, or frozen

0205—Meat of horses, asses, mules, or hinnies, fresh, chilled, or frozen

0206—Edible offal of bovine animals, swine, sheep, goats, horses, asses, mules, or hinnies, fresh, chilled, or frozen

0207—Meat and edible offal, of the poultry of heading 0105, fresh, chilled, or frozen

0208—Other meat and edible meat offal, fresh, chilled, or frozen

0209—Pig fat free of lean meat and poultry fat (not rendered), fresh, chilled, frozen, salted, in brine, dried, or smoked

0210—Meat and edible meat offal, salted, in brine, dried, or smoked; edible flours and meals of meat or meat offal

For more details regarding classification of the specific product you are interested in importing, consult a customs broker, the appropriate commodity specialist at your nearest Customs port, or see HTSUS. HTSUS is available for purchase from the U.S. Government Printing Office (see addresses at end of this chapter), and may be found in larger public libraries. Refer to "Classification—Liquidation" on page 207 for a general discussion of customs classification.

Sample Import Duties

Import duties will vary depending on the HTSUS classification of your product. Therefore, to determine the correct amount of duties, your product must be properly classified under the HTSUS. The following sample duties are taken from the duty listings for HTSUS Chapter 2 products.

Beef carcasses and half-carcasses, fresh or chilled (0201.10.00): 4.4 cents/kg; high quality beef cuts, bone-in (0201.20.20): 4%; other boneless, processed beef cuts (0201.30.40): 10%; swine carcasses and half-carcasses (0203.11.00): free; fresh or chilled hams or pork shoulders with bone in (0203.12.10): 2.2 cents/kg; boneless cuts of lamb, frozen (0204.43.20): 1.1 cents/kg; goat meat, fresh, chilled, or frozen (0204.50.00): free; horse meat, fresh, chilled, or frozen (0205.00.00): free; frozen beef tongue (0206.21.00): free; fresh or chilled pork offal (0206.30.00): free; whole fresh or chilled turkeys (0207.10.20): 18.7 cents/kg; fresh or chilled whole fryers or broilers (0207.10.40): 11 cents/kg; frozen poultry livers (0207.50.00): 22 cents/kg; fresh, chilled, or frozen rabbit (0208.10.00): 10%; frogs' legs, fresh, chilled, or frozen (0208.20.00): free; unrendered pig fat (0209.00.00): 5%; bone in cured hams and pork shoulders (0210.11.00): 2.2 cents/kg; bacon (0210.12.00): 2.2 cents/kg; preserved beef (0210.20.00): 10%; edible flours and meals of meat and meat offal (0210.90.00): 5%.

Special Provisions. Beef with bone in, fresh, chilled, or frozen of subheadings 0201.30.60 or 0202.30.60 originating in any of the countries of the European Community (Belgium, Denmark, France, Germany, Greece, Ireland, Italy, Luxembourg, the Netherlands, Portugal, Spain, and the United Kingdom) is currently subject to a 100% rate of duty.

Entry and Documentation

The entry of merchandise is a two-part process consisting of 1) filing the documents necessary to determine whether merchandise may be released from Customs custody and 2) filing the documents which contain information for duty assessment and statistical purposes. In certain instances all documents must be filed and accepted by Customs prior to release of the goods. Unless you have been granted an extension, you must file entry documents at a location specified by the district or area director within five working days of your shipment's date of arrival at a U.S. port of entry. These include a number of standard documents required by Customs for any entry, and:

- Foreign veterinary certification when required
- APHIS Import Permit when required
- FDA Importers Entry Notice, **Form FD701**, when required

After you present the entry, Customs may examine your shipment, or may waive examination. The shipment is then released provided no legal or regulatory violations have been noted. You must then file entry summary documentation and deposit estimated duties at a designated customhouse within 10 working days of your shipment's release. For a detailed description of entry procedures, standard documentation, and informal entry, refer to "Entry Process" on page 182.

Entry Document Certification for Beef. For imports of fresh, chilled, or frozen beef, entry documents must include a certification from an appropriate foreign official stating that: "I hereby certify to the best of my knowledge and belief that the herein described fresh, chilled, or frozen beef meets the specifications prescribed in regulations issued by the U.S. Department of Agriculture (7 CFR 2853.106 (a) and (b)."

Prohibitions and Restrictions

USDA APHIS Restrictions. APHIS regulates imports of meat, poultry, and their products to prevent the introduction of certain infectious animal diseases into the U.S. APHIS operates primarily under the authority of Subpart 94,which establishes import restrictions and procedures. It restricts imports from countries known to have incidence of a variety of listed diseases. For ruminants and swine: rinderpest and foot-and-mouth disease; for swine: African swine fever, swine vesicular disease, and hog cholera; for poultry: fowl pest, viscerotropic velogenic Newcastle disease (VVND), and *Salmonella enteritis* (phage-type 4). See "Country-Specific Import Restrictions" below.

Not only does APHIS restrict imports from countries known to have a specific disease, it also restricts imports from countries that do not have the disease, but that 1) are known to import and use animal products from countries that do; 2) have less stringent regulations regarding entry of such products or of potentially-infected live animals into their borders than those of the U.S.; or 3) border on countries known to have the disease. APHIS also restricts imports that originate from disease-free countries but that, in the course of transport, enter the territory of countries known to have the disease.

The importation of meat and meat products involves a very complicated set of qualifying factors. APHIS administers these restrictions primarily through product certification by qualified veterinarians of the country of origin. In some cases, permits are required. There are stringent cooking, processing, marking, packing, and shipping requirements for certain imports. The variables are too complex to cover exhaustively in this discussion, but the following examples will give you an idea of the issues that need to be addressed when importing these products.

Example 1. Importation of fresh, chilled, or frozen meat of ruminants or swine raised and slaughtered in a disease-free country but passing through a restricted country during transport. Sometimes a product originating in a noninfected country must pass through an infected country, or a port in an infected country, in the course of transport to the U.S. If this is the case for your shipment, you must see that a qualified country of origin official seals the product in a hold or compartment of the transport vessel prior to export. The seal must be APHIS-approved and serially-numbered. The sealed compartment must not be opened until the vessel reaches the U.S. port of entry. The seal's serial number must appear on the foreign inspection certificate accompanying the meat. At the U.S. port of entry, an APHIS official will inspect not only the product, but also the seal and the certificate, to ensure that your product was in no way exposed to any infectious disease while passing through the infected port or country.

Example 2. Importation of the cured or cooked meat of ruminants or swine originating in a country where rinderpest or foot-and-mouth disease exist. (This does not include meat that has been sterilized by heat in hermetically sealed containers.) If you are importing cured meats of HTSUS Chapter 2 (e.g. jerked, dried, or corned beef, Westphalia hams, etc.), the following conditions apply: 1) all bones must have been removed in the country of origin; 2) the meat must have been held in an unfrozen, fresh condition for at least 3 days immediately following slaughter of the animals from which it was derived; and 3) the meat must have been thoroughly cured and fully dried in such a manner that it may be stored and handled without refrigeration. If your product is deemed by the port of entry inspector to be in violation of the prescribed water-protein ratio for cured meat, it will be tested by APHIS, and the shipment will be held at the port of entry pending test results. Finally, the requisite country-of-origin foreign meat inspection certificate must be presented to the USDA inspector at the port of entry.

Example 3. Importations of fresh, chilled, or frozen (uncooked) meat of ruminants or swine from countries free of rinderpest and foot-and-mouth disease but which are under special restriction. Certain countries that are deemed to be free of rinderpest and foot-and-mouth disease nevertheless have less stringent regulations regarding import and use of products from infected countries than the U.S. Because of the danger of infection slipping into the U.S. through products imported from such countries, special restrictions apply. All uncooked meat and meat products from these restricted countries must have been prepared only in an inspected establishment eligible under the FMIA to export products to the U.S. Such product must be accompanied by a USDA-approved meat inspection certificate. (See FSIS requirements, below, for more details.) Note that these requirements apply whether you are importing the product for personal use or in commercial lots.

For shipments that fall into this category you must also provide additional certification by a full-time salaried veterinary official of the country-of-origin's national animal health agency. This veterinary certification must state the name and official establishment number of the slaughterhouse certifying that: 1) the slaughterhouse is not permitted to receive animals that have ever been in, or in a port of, a country listed as infected with rinderpest or foot-and-mouth disease; 2) the slaughterhouse is not permitted to receive meat originating in, or which has been transported through, infected countries. (The only exception to these rules covers meat in containers sealed with serially numbered seals of the noninfected country of origin's national government—see above); 3) the product covered by the certificate comes from animals born and raised in a country listed as free of rinderpest and foot-and-mouth disease and that have never been in any infected country; and 4) the product has been processed, stored, and transported in such a manner as to preclude its being commingled with any noncomplying products.

Pork Import Restrictions for African Swine Fever, Hog Cholera, or Swine Vesicular Disease. Imports of fresh, chilled, or frozen pork and edible pork offal are usually prohibited from countries in which these diseases exist, or from countries bordering countries in which they exist. Pork from such sources must usually be thoroughly heat-processed in an approved manner in an approved packing plant to render harmless any disease organisms before it is allowed to be imported into the U.S. (such importations fall within HTSUS Chapter 16). If you import from listed infected countries pork products that do not comply with requirements of Subpart 94, your shipment will be seized, quarantined, and disposed of as the USDA determines necessary to prevent introduction of such diseases into the U.S.

Small amounts of pork or pork products from countries where swine vesicular disease exists that are restricted under Subpart 94.12, may be imported in specific cases for examination, testing, or analysis. You must apply for and receive written APHIS approval for such importation.

Hams. APHIS enforces Subpart 94 covering the importation of ham. Ham—a cured meat covered under heading 0210—is allowed entry under the following conditions: 1) it came from a swine that was never out of the country in which the ham was processed; 2) it came from a country determined by the USDA to have and to enforce laws requiring the immediate reporting to the country's national veterinary services any premises found to have any animal infected with foot-and-mouth disease, rinderpest, African Swine fever, hog cholera, or swine vesicular disease; 3) it came from a swine that was not on any premises where the diseases mentioned above exist or had existed within 60 days prior to slaughter; 4) the ham was accompanied from the slaughterhouse to the processing establishment by a numbered certificate issued by a person authorized by the national government of the country of origin stating that the above provisions were met; and 5) the ham must have been processed according to regulations in 9 CFR Subpart 94.17 in a single establishment.

If you are interested in importing hams, you should be aware of the restrictions on foreign establishments eligible to export hams to the U.S. Be sure to purchase your product from a meatpacker that complies with all relevant regulations for the processing of hams, and which employs someone authorized by national veterinary officials to oversee and attest to that compliance. Hams from establishments which do not meet these criteria may not be imported. The only foreign hams eligible for import into the U.S. are those processed in APHIS-inspected establishments whose proprietor has signed a written agreement with the APHIS to the effect that all hams for import to the U.S. will be processed in accordance with standards established in Subpart 94. Foreign meatpackers must also meet APHIS recordkeeping and inspection access requirements. Foreign hams imported into the U.S. must bear certain markings (see "Marking and Labeling Requirements" below), and must be accompanied by a certificate issued by an authorized person stating that the ham was processed for at least 400 days and that all relevant provisions of Subpart 94 have been fulfilled.

Poultry. The law defines poultry as chickens, turkeys, swans, partridges, guinea fowl, pea fowl, nonmigratory ducks, geese, pigeons, and doves as well as commercial, domestic, or pen-raised grouse, pheasants, and quail. It restricts import of these products from countries known to have incidences of fowl pest, viscerotropic velogenic Newcastle disease (VVND), and *Salmonella enteritis* (phage-type 4).

Restrictions for VVND. You may import poultry, game birds, or other birds raised and slaughtered in any country where VVND is considered to exist only if they meet at least one of the conditions listed below. These restrictions also apply to products imported from, or moved into or through, any country where the disease is considered to exist, at any time before arrival in the U.S. In other words, if your product originates in a noninfected country, but passes through an infected country en route to the U.S., it becomes a restricted product and must meet the requirements for products originating in infected countries. Similarly, if your product is imported from an infected country into a noninfected country for processing prior to export to the U.S, it must meet the requirements for products originating in infected countries.

Poultry products in these categories may be entered into U.S. Customs territory only if:1) Game bird carcasses are eviscerated, with heads and feet removed. Viscera, heads, and feet removed from game birds are ineligible for entry into the U.S.; or 2) products are intended for consignment to a USDA-approved museum, educational institution, or other establishment. Such establishment must have provided the USDA with evidence that it has the equipment, facilities, and capabilities to store, handle, process, or disinfect such articles so as to prevent the introduction or dissemination of VVND into the U.S. (Names and addresses of approved establishments may be obtained from, and requests for approval may be made to, the USDA Administrator, c/o the Import-Export Products Staff—see addresses at end of this chapter.) Otherwise, poultry products must be fully heat-treated and prepared before they will be allowed to enter the U.S.

APHIS VS Permit Application. Requests for USDA APHIS VS permits authorizing importation of restricted products must be submitted on VS **Form 16-3**. You may obtain these forms from APHIS headquarters (see addresses at end of this chapter) or from any USDA port office. Application on a signed facsimile (copy) is acceptable, provided you send an original signed document as follow-up. If you need a supply of the forms on hand, you may photocopy the original **Form 16-3**.

Requested information on processing or production data and sources of meat products may often require more space than is provided on the application form. In such cases, you may attach extra sheets as necessary. You should include as much background information as possible in order for APHIS to properly evaluate the disease risk of the product you wish to import. Research papers intended as supporting information should not be sent by fax. It takes about two weeks for the APHIS to process an application and prepare a permit for return mail. If the application information is deemed insufficient, APHIS will contact you for clarification. The permit process can take longer in such cases. You should submit your requests for permit renewal or amendment in writing (fax is acceptable) to the USDA (see addresses at end of this chapter). You should note any changes from the original application and permit issued, such as addresses or production method, when making permit renewal requests.

Any importation for which a permit is issued must comply in all particulars with the permit's stipulations. You will facilitate the entry of your import shipments by making sure the permit number appears on the shipping documents—or simply include a copy of the permit with your entry documents. Meat products requiring permits will be subject to delay or refusal at the port of entry if an importation permit is not obtained before shipment to the U.S.

FSIS Requirements. The FMIA and the PPIA require countries exporting meat, poultry, and their products to the U.S. to impose domestic inspection requirements at least as stringent as those of the U.S. The FSIS reviews foreign inspection systems to ensure that they are equivalent to the U.S. system. Only those countries to which FSIS grants meat export eligibility may export these products to the U.S. See Country-Specific Import Restrictions below for list of currently eligible countries (by definition, imports from unlisted countries are prohibited).

An inspection certificate issued by the responsible official of the exporting country must accompany each shipment of meat or poultry products offered for entry into the U.S. Certificates identify products by country and packing plant of origin, destination, shipping marks, and amounts. They certify that the products have received ante-mortem and post-mortem inspection; that they are wholesome, unadulterated, and properly branded; and that they otherwise comply with U.S. requirements.

For imports of fresh, chilled, and frozen beef, entered under 0201.20.20, 0201.30.20, 0202.20.20, or 0202.30.20, 19 CFR 10.180 requires that the foreign official must attach an affidavit executed prior to export and to be filed with the entry documentation attesting that the beef in the shipment meets USDA specifications in 7 CFR 2853.106. Importers are urged to consult with the USDA prior to exportation of beef to be sure that their shipment will satisfy certification requirements.

In addition, the Pork Promotion, Research, and Consumer Information Act of 1985 (PPRCIA) requires that each importer of porcine animals, pork, or pork products shall remit an assessment to U.S. Customs at the time the product is imported.

Port-of-entry Inspection. The FSIS reinspects meat and meat products by sampling shipments as they enter the U.S. Your products may be checked for transportation damage, labeling compliance and accuracy, general condition, and proper certification. FSIS may also examine the product for accuracy of net weight, labeling requirements, and condition of the container, and make laboratory analyses of food chemistry (for example, fat, water, and nitrite levels) and test for drug and chemical residues. It may also test to confirm species. The actual inspection tasks and the scope of inspection are based on the nature of the product and on the performance history of the packing plant and country of origin.

If your shipment passes reinspection, FSIS will stamp the products "U.S. Inspected and Passed," and the shipment will be allowed entry. If the products fail this reinspection, they will be stamped "U.S. Refused Entry," in which case you must reexport or destroy the refused products. In some cases, such products may be converted to animal food. Once a shipment has been condemned, inspection is intensified for future shipments of that product from the same plant, and in some cases, for all meat shipments from the same country.

Residue Control. Chemical and drug residue control is one of the major features of an exporting country's inspection system that must be judged equal to the U.S. system. Exporting countries must be certified annually by FSIS as continuing to operate an equivalent residue control program. FSIS experts make sure that the country's residue program uses approved analytical methods, that officials are knowledgeable about the use of chemical compounds in their country, and that the country tests for those compounds which could potentially contaminate the food supply. Meat or meat products may not be imported from a country that fails to receive a FSIS annual residue certification.

As a further residue check, FSIS randomly samples products at the port of entry and analyzes them for drug and chemical residues. The FSIS annual import residue plan sets the initial sampling rate for each country based on the volume of product imported from that country. The plan includes the same chemical compounds as the domestic residue-monitoring program. Compounds are selected based on their likelihood of contaminating the food supply and their potential harm to the consuming public. The list can include chemical compounds not legal for use in the U.S. if they have the potential to contaminate a foreign country's meat supply.

If your shipment contains residues above the U.S. tolerance or action level, it will be considered adulterated and will be refused entry into the U.S. Shipments are not usually held pending laboratory test results unless FSIS has some reason to suspect contamination. If a laboratory reports a residue violation on a sample which has otherwise passed reinspection, as much as possible of the product must be recalled. Products so recovered may not be used for human food.

The occurrence of a residue violation at a port of entry raises concerns about the exporting country's ability to control residues. Port of entry sampling is then automatically increased for related products from the entire country, as well as on subsequent shipments from the specific plant where the noncomplying sample originated. From time to time, the FSIS will increase sampling for a specific country or for a specific compound. This can occur when there is an indication that a problem may exist or when there is a pattern of failed port of entry reinspections.

Country-Specific Import Restrictions

U.S.-Canada Free Trade Agreement. Canada has an inspection system that is virtually the same as that of the U.S. Under the U.S.-Canada Free Trade Agreement, FSIS has modified border reinspection requirements for Canadian products. Canadian plants may choose to follow the revised procedures or undergo traditional reinspection. Under the revised procedures, Agriculture Canada inspection officials provide information to be entered into the FSIS automated computer system before product destined for the U.S. leaves the Canadian plant. Unless the computer flags the shipment for reinspection at the border, the shipment automatically passes through U.S. Customs.

North American Free Trade Agreement (NAFTA). NAFTA reduces tariff and nontariff barriers to trade in meat and meat products between Mexico and the U.S. However, it does not specifically alter existing entry procedures for such trade. The existing provisions of the U.S.-Canada Free Trade Agreement continue in force to govern trade between those two countries.

Other FSIS-Certified Countries. The following countries are currently FSIS-certified for exportation of meat and poultry to the U.S.: Argentina, Australia, Belgium, Belize, Brazil, Canada, Costa Rica, the Czech Republic, Denmark, Dominican Republic, El Salvador, Finland, France, Guatemala, Honduras, Hong Kong, Hungary, Ireland, Israel, Italy, Mexico, Netherlands, New Zealand, Norway, Poland, Romania, the Slovak Republic, Sweden, Switzerland, United Kingdom, Uruguay, and the republics of the former Yugoslavia. Meat may not be imported from countries not on the list. The list is subject to change. For the most up-to-date information, contact FSIS (see addresses at end of this chapter).

APHIS-listed Countries. Countries certified free of rinderpest and foot-and-mouth disease from which ruminant and swine products may be imported: Australia, the Bahamas, Barbados, Belize, Bermuda, Canada, Channel Islands, Chile, Denmark, Costa Rica, Dominican Republic, El Salvador, Fiji, Finland, France, Great Britain (England, Scotland, Wales, and Isle of Man), Greenland, Guatemala, Haiti, Honduras, Iceland, Ireland, Jamaica, Japan, Mexico, Netherlands, New Caledonia, New Zealand, Nicaragua, Northern Ireland, Norway, Panama, Papua New Guinea, Poland, Spain, Sweden, Territory of St. Pierre and Miquelon, Trinidad and Tobago, and Trust Territory of the Pacific Islands.

African Swine Fever Prohibitions. African swine fever is believed to exist in the following countries, and pork imports are banned from them: Africa (all countries), Brazil, Cuba, Haiti, Italy, Malta, Portugal, and Spain.

Hog Cholera-free Countries. Countries deemed free of hog cholera and from which pork may be imported: Australia, Canada, Denmark, Dominican Republic, Fiji, Finland, Great Britain (England, Scotland, Wales, and Isle of Man), Iceland, New Zealand, Northern Ireland, Norway, the Republic of Ireland, Spain, Sweden, and Trust Territory of the Pacific Islands.

Swine Vesicular Disease Prohibitions: The following countries are deemed free of swine vesicular disease, and pork may be imported from them: Australia, the Bahamas, Bulgaria, Canada, Central American countries, Chile, Denmark, Dominican Republic, Fiji, Finland, Great Britain (England, Scotland, Wales, and the Isle of Man), Greenland, Haiti, Hungary, Iceland, Luxembourg, Mexico, New Zealand, Northern Ireland, Norway, Panama, Republic of Ireland, Rumania, Sweden, Switzerland, the Trust Territories of the Pacific Islands, and the republics of the former Yugoslavia.

Pork Import Restrictions. Imports from the following countries are subject to specific restrictions on the importation of pork products: the Bahamas, Bulgaria, Chile, Denmark, Great Britain (England, Scotland, Wales, and the Isle of Man), Hungary, Luxembourg, Northern Ireland, Republic of Ireland, Switzerland, and the republics of the former Yugoslavia.

Ruminant and Swine Import Restrictions. Countries subject to specific restrictions on the importation of ruminant and swine products: the Bahamas, Channel Islands, Denmark, Finland, Great Britain (England, Scotland, Wales, and Isle of Man), Japan, Northern Ireland, Norway, Papua New Guinea, and Sweden.

VVND-Free Countries. The following countries are certified free of viscerotropic velogenic Newcastle disease (VVND): Australia, Canada, Chile, Denmark, Fiji, Finland, Great Britain (England, Scotland, Wales, and the Isle of Man), Iceland, New Zealand, Northern Ireland, Norway, Republic of Ireland, Sweden.

***Salmonella enteritis* Free Countries.** The only country deemed free of *Salmonella enteritis* is Canada.

***Bovine Spongiform Encephalopathy* Prohibitions.** Imports of meat and meat products are banned or heavily restricted from the following countries where *bovine spongiform encephalopathy* is believed to exist: France, Great Britain, Northern Ireland, Republic of Ireland, Oman, Portugal, and Switzerland.

Quotas

Total meat imports are controlled by the Federal Meat Import Act (FMIA), which was designed to permit larger imports when the U.S. production is trending downward and to cut back on imports when U.S. production is rising. There is no licensing or absolute quota system in effect. However, P.L. 88-482, as amended, allows that certain meats may be made subject to absolute quota restriction by presidential proclamation.

The FMIA covers imports of fresh, chilled, or frozen beef, veal, mutton, and goat meat. It does not apply to beef that is prepared or preserved, nor does it cover pork, lamb, or poultry meat, or live animal imports. At the beginning of each year, the USDA announces the "trigger" import level at which quotas or restrictions may be applied. The law requires the USDA to estimate potential U.S. meat imports. If projected imports equal or exceed the trigger level, the U.S. Secretary of Agriculture is required to consider imposing import restrictions. The law specifies the actions that may be taken if the import estimate exceeds the trigger level. In addition to the option of imposing import quotas, the USDA may suspend potential import limitations or set them above the trigger level if it appears there will not be enough meat to supply U.S. demand at reasonable prices.

Quotas have been imposed only once since the FMIA became law. Generally, when it appears that meat imports will exceed the trigger level, the U.S. government negotiates agreements with exporting countries to voluntarily limit their exports to the U.S. in order to maintain imports slightly below the trigger level, while guaranteeing the supplier countries fair shares of the imports allowed under the law. As a result of the U.S.-Canada Free Trade Implementation Act of 1988, imports from Canada are excluded from the restrictions of the FMIA.

Marking and Labeling Requirements

FSIS Requirements. When meat and meat products are imported, the name of the country of origin must appear on the label. However, only imported products that reach consumers without further processing retain such labeling. For example, a can of ham or corned beef that goes directly to a retail outlet will name the country of origin on the label. However, if imported boneless beef is combined with U.S. beef and other ingredients in a U.S. plant to produce a can of beef stew, the label is not required to indicate the presence of imported beef.

The Farm Bill Amendments require foreign countries exporting products to the U.S. to impose controls equivalent to those administered by the FSIS to prevent species substitution. A product labeled "beef," for example, must be beef and cannot contain a less expensive or more readily available species. Exporting countries must maintain effective testing programs for species verification and adequate security measures to prevent species substitution.

APHIS Requirements. Imported hams must comply with all marking requirements of Subpart 94.17. Ham must bear a hot iron brand or an ink seal with the identifying number of the slaughterhouse. It must bear a button seal, approved by USDA to be tamper-proof, on the hock, stating the month and year the ham entered the processing establishment. It must bear a hot iron brand (with the identifying number of the processing establishment and the date salting began) executed at the processing establishment immediately prior to salting. All required branding must be performed under the direct supervision of a person authorized by the veterinary services of the country of origin's national government to supervise such activity.

FDA requirements. For basic FDA marking and labeling requirements, refer to the "Foods" appendix on page 808.

For a general discussion of U.S. Customs marking and labeling requirements, refer to "Marking: Country of Origin" on page 215 and "Special Marking Requirements" on page 217.

Shipping Considerations

You will need to ensure that your goods are packaged and shipped with care so that they arrive in good condition and pass smoothly through Customs. You are responsible for ensuring that the shipment is in compliance with all applicable government regulations for packaging and shipping. In most instances, you should not leave these arrangements solely to the discretion of your supplier. Careful preparation of the cargo and selection of the mode of transport can be essential to a cost-effective, timely delivery of undamaged goods. We strongly advise you to consult your shipping representative, insurance agent, or freight broker for advice on packing and shipping. Refer also to the major tab section "Packing/Shipping/Insurance" for a general discussion of packing and shipping.

Meat and meat products require expeditious and careful handling to avoid contamination and decomposition. They should always be moved under adequate refrigeration to ensure that they do not deteriorate into an unsalable condition during transit.

Publications Available

The following publication may be relevant to the importation of meat and edible offal:

Foreign Countries and Plants Certified to Export Meat and Poultry to the United States

This is a comprehensive listing of export-certified countries and plants, including previously certified plants that have been decertified. It is available from the FSIS (see addresses at end of this chapter).

The following publication explains the FDA requirements for importing meat and poultry. It is published by FDA and available on request from FDA headquarters (see addresses at end of this chapter).

Requirements of Laws and Regulations Enforced by the U.S. Food and Drug Administration

The following publication gives brief, general guidelines on USDA regulated products. Although designed primarily for tourists, it contains a list of approved products that you may find helpful. It is published by USDA APHIS (see addresses at end of this chapter).

Travelers Tips On Bringing Food, Plant, and Animal Products into the United States

The *Harmonized Tariff Schedule of the United States* (HTSUS) is available from:

Government Printing Office (GPO)
Superintendent of Documents
Washington, DC 20402
(202) 512-1800 (Order line)
(202) 512-0000 (General)

The USGPO also has copies of specific laws available for purchase. The USGPO accepts credit card orders over the phone, as well as mail orders paid by credit card, a check drawn on a U.S. bank, or an international money order.

Relevant Government Agencies

Address your questions regarding APHIS import requirements, port of entry inspections, permits, and approved establishments for the import of meat to:

U.S. Department of Agriculture (USDA)
Animal and Plant Health Inspection Service (APHIS)
Veterinary Services (VS)
Import-Export Products Staff
Federal Building, Room 756
6505 Belcrest Road
Hyattsville, MD 20782
(301) 436-7885

Address your questions regarding FSIS port of entry inspection or pre-import certification of meat, and meat products and establishments to:

U.S. Department of Agriculture (USDA)
Food Safety and Inspection Service (FSIS)
Import Inspection Service (FSIS)
Rm. 3715, Franklin Ct.
Suite 3700-W
Washington, DC 20250-3700
(202) 501-7515

Address your questions regarding FDA requirements for meat products to:

Food and Drug Administration (FDA)
Center for Food Safety and Applied Nutrition
200 C Street SW
Washington, DC 20204
(202) 205-5241, 205-5042

Food and Drug Administration (FDA)
Division of Enforcement, Imports Branch
200 C Street SW
Washington, DC 20204
(202) 205-4726

Address questions regarding any quota issues to:

U.S. Customs Service
Quota Branch
1301 Constitution Avenue NW, Rm. 2379-ICC
Washington, DC 20229
(202) 927-5850

Address your questions regarding importation of meats and edible offal to the district or port director of Customs for you area. For addresses see "U.S. Customs District Offices" on page 62 or contact:

U.S. Customs Service
1301 Constitution Ave. NW
Washington, DC 20229
(202) 927-6724 (Information)
(202) 927-1000 (General)

Laws and Regulations

The following laws and regulations may be relevant to the importation of meat and edible offal. The laws are contained in the U.S. Code (USC) and the regulations in the Code of Federal Regulations (CFR), both of which may be available at larger public and law libraries. Copies of specific laws are also available from the United States Government Printing Office (address above).

7 USC 1854
Delegations of Authority Concerning Certain Meats
EO 11539, as amended by EO 12188
These Executive Orders authorize Customs to enforce limitations on the importation and entry and withdrawal of meats from warehouses for consumption in the U.S.

7 CFR 16.1 et seq.
Regulations of USDA on Import and Entry of Meat and Meat Products
These regulations govern the importation and set forth the USDA inspection procedures for meat and meat products offered for entry into the U.S.

19 CFR 12.1 et seq.
Regulations on Customs Inspection and Release of Meat and Meat Products
These regulations set forth the conditions and bond under which U.S. Customs will release meat and meat products for entry into the U.S. and the penalties for breach of the bond.

7 USC 4801 et seq.
Pork Promotion, Research, and Consumer Information Act
This Act provides that each importer of porcine animal, pork, or pork product shall remit an assessment to Customs at the time the product is imported. See 7 CFR 1230.71 and 1230.110.

21 USC 601 et seq.
Federal Meat Inspection Act
This Act provides standards for inspection, packaging, and sale of meat and meat products and prohibits the importation of adulterated, misbranded, or improperly slaughtered meat.

19 USC 1306
Prohibited Meat Imports
This law prohibits the importation of cattle, sheep, swine, and meats from countries with rinderpest and foot-and-mouth disease, as determined in regulations adopted by the Secretary of Agriculture, and provides for enforcement by Customs.

9 CFR 327 et seq.
Regulations of USDA on Entry of Animal Food Products
These regulations prescribe certification and inspection procedures and marking and labeling requirements for products derived from cattle, sheep, swine, goats, horses, mules, and other equines.

19 CFR 4.71
Regulation on U.S. Customs Clearance of Vessels Carrying Cattle and Other Animals
This regulation requires submission of a USDA inspector's certificate to U.S. Customs before a vessel carrying cattle and other animals is cleared for entry.

21 USC 451 et seq.
Poultry Products Inspection Act
This Act provides standards for inspection, packaging, and sale of poultry and poultry products and prohibits the importation of slaughtered poultry not in compliance with prescribed standards and regulations.

9 CFR Part 381
Regulations for Inspection of Poultry Products
These regulations prescribe standards for sanitation and composition, inspection procedures, marking and labeling—including nutrition—requirements, exporting and importing certification procedures, and requirements.

21 USC 111 et seq.
Prevention of Introduction and Spread of Contagion
This statute authorizes the Secretary of Agriculture to prevent the introduction, and the Secretary of the Treasury to prevent the exportation, of diseased livestock and poultry.

9 CFR Part 50 et seq.
Regulations on Animal Byproduct Quarantine Control
These regulations promulgated by the USDA prohibit the importation of animal products for use in industry unless the products meet certain processing standards and are not infected with certain diseases.

21 USC 301 et seq.
Food, Drug, and Cosmetic Act
This Act prohibits deceptive practices and regulates the manufacture, sale and importation or exportation of food, drugs, cosmetics, and related products. See 21 USC 331, 381, 382.

19 CFR 12.1 et seq.; 21 CFR 1.83 et seq.
Regulations on Food, Drugs, and Cosmetics
These regulations of the Secretary of Health and Human Services and the Secretary of the Treasury govern the standards, labeling, marking, and importing of products used with food, drugs, and cosmetics.

Convention on International Trade in Endangered Species of Wild Fauna and Flora (CITES)
This comprehensive wildlife treaty signed by over 100 countries, including the United States, regulates and in many cases prohibits commercial imports and exports of wild animal and plant species threatened by trade.

16 USC 1531
Endangered Species Act
This Act prohibits the import and export of species listed as endangered and most species listed as threatened. It is the U.S. law that implements CITES.

16 USC 1361 et seq.
The Marine Mammal Protection Act
This Act prohibits the import of marine mammals and their parts and products. These species include whales, walruses, narwhals, seals, sea lions, sea otters, and polar bears.

19 CFR 12.26 et seq.
Regulations on Importation of Wild Animals
These regulations list the wild animals that are prohibited from importation or that require import permits.

50 CFR Parts 10, 13, and 16
Regulations of FWS for Importing Wildlife and Fish
These regulations specify the animals and animal products subject to import prohibitions and restrictions.

Principal Exporting Countries

The following listing includes samples of the main supplier nations of the products of this chapter. It is organized by HTSUS major heading. (Refer to "Customs Classification" above for the product codes.) Countries are listed in rank order of the value of products imported to the U.S. Statistics represent customs value entries for 1993 from the Bureau of Census, U.S. Department of Commerce.

0201—Canada, Costa Rica, Nicaragua, Honduras, Guatemala, Dominican Rep., New Zealand, Australia, Japan, Mexico

0202—Australia, New Zealand, Costa Rica, Nicaragua, Canada, Honduras, Guatemala, Dominican Rep., Sweden, Mexico

0203—Canada, Denmark, Sweden, Ireland, Australia, Finland, New Zealand, Italy, Switzerland, Netherlands

0204—Australia, New Zealand, Canada, Iceland, Denmark

0205—No listing

0206—Canada, Australia, New Zealand, Costa Rica, Iceland, Honduras, Nicaragua, Denmark

0207—Canada, Israel, Australia, Thailand, United Kingdom, Sweden

0208—New Zealand, Indonesia, Canada, Taiwan, China, Sweden, Australia, Belgium, Mexico, United Kingdom

0209—Canada, Japan

0210—Canada, Italy, Uruguay, Argentina, Ireland, Brazil, Switzerland, Germany, Venezuela, Belgium

Chapter 3: Fish*

Full title: Fish and Crustaceans, Molluscs, and Other Aquatic Invertebrates

This chapter relates to the importation of fish, crustaceans, molluscs, and other aquatic invertebrates, which are classified under Chapter 3 of the Harmonized Tariff Schedule of the United States (HTSUS). Specifically, it includes live fish, whole harvested fresh or chilled fish, frozen fish, fish fillets and other meat, fish preserved other than by freezing and its edible products, all crustaceans, and all molluscs and related aquatic invertebrates, such as squid, octopus, and sea urchins. You should read this section in conjunction with the "Foods" appendix on page 808.

If you are interested in importing preparations of fish, including canned fish or caviar, refer to Commodity Index Chapter 16. The importation of live marine mammals is covered in Chapter 1 (importation in connection with traveling circuses, menageries, or similar exhibits comes under Chapter 95), while the heavily restricted importation of meat of marine mammals is included in Chapter 2. Fish, crustaceans, molluscs, and other aquatic animals considered unfit for human consumption by reason of their species or condition are covered in Chapter 5. Fish oils are included in chapter 15. Edible products which contain a small portion of fish or seafood, such as seafood-filled pasta, are covered in Chapter 19, while soups with a fish or seafood base are included in Chapter 21. Inedible flours, meals, or pellets of fish and other aquatic species—largely imported for the preparation of animal feeds—are covered in Chapter 23.

Other special provisions that potentially affect fish and related aquatic species include those for wild, live specimens imported for use or sale for scientific or educational purposes (HTSUS 9801.00.00); live specimens imported for breeding, exhibition, or prize competition (HTSUS 9813.00.60); and live game specimens imported for the purpose of stocking ranges (HTSUS 9817.00.70).

Subchapter XV of Chapter 98 (major heading 9815) pertains explicitly to products of U.S. fisheries, which are defined as fishing enterprises conducted legally under treaty provisions or by international law under U.S. flag by U.S. vessels on the high seas or in foreign waters, whether or not they include operation of a shore station as part of the same enterprise. The heading excludes any marine products produced in a foreign country or its territorial waters involving the use of non-U.S. labor. Eligible marine products of such fisheries include those which have never been landed in a foreign country or which have been landed

*IMPORTANT: Read the Commodity Index Introduction. It is the essential framework for understanding this section.

solely for transshipment without change in condition of the products; fish—except cod, cusk, haddock, hake, mackerel, pollock, and swordfish—which have been so landed for partial processing, such as evisceration, chilling, or freezing; and those which have been landed for processing on the treaty coasts of Labrador, the Magdalen Islands, or Newfoundland as per the 1818 convention between Great Britain and the U.S. All such eligible products are admitted duty free.

Key Factors

The key factors in the importation of fish, crustaceans, molluscs, and other aquatic species are:

- Compliance with Food and Drug Administration (FDA) purity, identity, manufacturing, and other standards
- Compliance with FDA entry notification and procedures
- Special duty status for products of U.S. fisheries
- Compliance with U.S. Department of Agriculture (USDA) Animal and Plant Health Inspection Service (APHIS) and U.S. Fish and Wildlife Service (FWS) import regulations and quarantine requirements for live specimens

Although most importers utilize the services of a licensed customs broker in making their entries, and we recommend this practice, you should be aware of the regulatory, entry, and documentation issues involved in importing your product. You, as importer, are ultimately responsible for the fulfillment of any legal requirements applicable to your shipment.

General Considerations

Regulatory Agencies. Importation of fish and seafood products falls primarily under the jurisdiction of the FDA, which enforces the requirements of the Federal Food, Drug, and Cosmetic Act (FDCA). The importation of live specimens is subject to quarantine regulations under 9 CFR Part 92, administered and enforced by the USDA APHIS. The U.S. Department of the Interior's FWS regulates importation of animals and animal parts and products covered under the Endangered Species Act (ESA), the Convention on International Trade in Endangered Species (CITES), and the Marine Mammal Protection Act (MMPA). Seafoods are also subject to the requirements of the U.S. Department of Commerce's National Marine Fisheries Service (NMFS) (see addresses at end of this chapter).

Foods Subject to FDCA. The FDA regulations on the importation of foods of any kind are extensive and stringent. Seafoods and fishery products imported into the U.S. must comply with all FDCA requirements for those produced domestically. Imported products regulated by FDA are subject to FDA port of entry inspection. **Form FD701** is required for all FDA-regulated importations and may be obtained from your local FDA Import Operations office, from FDA headquarters (see addresses at end of this chapter), or from your customs broker. For an annotated diagram of required FDA import procedures refer to the "Foods" appendix on page 808.

Live Animals. APHIS restricts the import of live animals primarily in order to safeguard U.S. animals from communicable diseases. This entry provides an overview of rather than an exhaustive treatment of APHIS and other agency requirements. Actual requirements vary depending on the circumstances and the species involved. If you are interested in importing live aquatic animals, you should contact APHIS for full information (see addresses at end of this chapter).

Wildlife and Endangered Species. If you are interested in importing any exotic live animal, you should contact FWS with the scientific name of the species to ascertain whether it is protected. If it is, you will need a FWS permit to import it. You may also need country of origin export permits and documentation.

Detention of Shipment. If your shipment is found to be noncomplying, it may be detained at the port of entry. For products subject to FDA jurisdiction, the FDA may allow you to bring such a shipment into compliance before making a final decision regarding admittance. However, any sorting, reprocessing, or relabeling must be supervised by FDA personnel and is done at the importer's expense. Such conditional release to allow the importer to bring a shipment into compliance is a privilege, not a right. The FDA may consider subsequent noncomplying shipments of the same type of product to constitute abuse of the privilege and require the importer to destroy or reexport the products. To ascertain what your legal responsibilities are, you should contact these agencies regarding the specific items to be imported.

Customs Classification

For customs purposes, fish, crustaceans, molluscs, and related aquatic species are classified under Chapter 3 of the HTSUS. This chapter is divided into major headings, which are further divided into subheadings, and often into sub-subheadings, each of which has its own HTSUS classification number. For example, the HTSUS number for smelts, cusk, pollock, shad, sturgeon, swordfish, and freshwater fish is 0303.79.20, indicating that it is a subcategory of fish other than cod (0303.71.00), which is a subcategory of the major heading fish, frozen, excluding fish fillets and other fish meat of heading 0304 (0303.00.00). There are seven major headings in HTSUS Chapter 3.

0301—Live fish

0302—Fish, fresh or chilled, excluding fish fillets and other fish meat of heading 0304

0303—Fish, frozen, excluding fish fillets and other fish meat of heading 0304

0304—Fish fillets and other fish meat (whether or not minced), fresh, chilled, or frozen

0305—Fish, dried, salted, or in brine; smoked fish, whether or not cooked before or during the smoking process; flours, meals, or pellets of fish, fit for human consumption

0306—Crustaceans, whether in shell or not, live, fresh, chilled, frozen, dried, salted, or in brine; crustaceans, in shell, cooked by steaming or by boiling in water, whether or not chilled, frozen, dried, salted, or in brine; flours, meals, or pellets of crustaceans, fit for human consumption

0307—Molluscs, whether in shell or not, live, fresh, chilled, frozen, dried, salted, or in brine; aquatic invertebrates other than crustaceans and molluscs, live, fresh, chilled, frozen, dried, salted, or in brine; flours, meals, or pellets of aquatic invertebrates other than crustaceans, fit for human consumption

For more details regarding classification of the specific product you are interested in importing, consult a customs broker, the appropriate commodity specialist at your nearest customs port, or see HTSUS. HTSUS is available for purchase from the U.S. Government Printing Office (see addresses at end of this chapter), and may be found in larger public libraries. Refer to "Classification—Liquidation" on page 207 for a general discussion of customs classification.

Sample Import Duties

Import duties will vary depending on the HTSUS classification of your product. Therefore, to determine the correct amount of duties, your product must be properly classified under the HTSUS. The following sample duties are taken from the duty listings for HTSUS Chapter 3 products.

Sole (*Solea spp.*) (0302.23.00): 1.1 cents/kg; fish other than listed species in containers with a gross weight of less than 6.8 kg (0302.69.10): 6%; sturgeon roe (0302.70.20): 15%; dogfish and other sharks (0303.75.00): 1.1 cents/kg; fish of heading 0304, fresh, frozen, or chilled, fillet or meat (0304.20.30 and 0304.20.50): 4.134 cents/kg; fillets and fish meat of other than listed species (0304.90.90): 6%; herring fillets, dried, salted, or in brine, but not smoked, in containers with a gross weight of less than 6.8 kg (0305.30.20): 4%; smoked mackerel (0305.49.20): 2.5%; dried cod, whether or not salted, but nor smoked (0305.51.00): 0.2 cents/kg; dried shark fins (0305.59.20): 0.4 cents/kg; preserved fish other than listed species in containers with a gross weight of less than 6.8 kg (0305.69.50): 10%; crabmeat (0306.14.20): 7.5%; and snails, other than sea snails (0307.60.00): 5%.

Special Provisions. Much fresh, chilled, and frozen fish of headings 0301-0303 enters duty free. All fish and seafood products defined in heading 9815 as products of U.S. fisheries enter duty free.

Entry and Documentation

The entry of merchandise is a two-part process consisting of 1) filing the documents necessary to determine whether merchandise may be released from Customs custody and 2) filing the documents which contain information for duty assessment and statistical purposes. In certain instances all documents must be filed and accepted by Customs prior to release of the goods. Unless you have been granted an extension, you must file entry documents at a location specified by the district or area director within five working days of your shipment's date of arrival at a U.S. port of entry. These include a number of standard documents required by Customs for any entry, and:

- FDA Importers Entry Notice, **Form FD701**
- USDA quarantine requirements
- Importer's declaration, two copies
- FWS import permits required under CITES, ESA, and any other regulations applicable to then particular shipment; and any export certification from country of origin required under the specific laws governing endangered or threatened species
- FWS Wildlife Declaration **Form 3-177**—an original plus 3 copies—a copy of air waybill or bill of lading, and a copy of invoice (proforma invoice if shipment is noncommercial)

After you present the entry, Customs may examine your shipment, or may waive examination. The shipment is then released provided no legal or regulatory violations have been noted. You must then file entry summary documentation and deposit estimated duties at a designated customhouse within 10 working days of your shipment's release. For a detailed description of entry procedures, standard documentation, and informal entry, refer to "Entry Process" on page 182.

Entry Invoice. Invoices for fish or fish livers imported in airtight containers classifiable under HTSUS Chapter 3 must include the following information: 1) statement of whether the articles contain any oil, fat, or grease; and 2) the name and quantity of any such oil, fat, or grease.

Prohibitions and Restrictions

Fresh and Prepared Fish and Seafood. The FDA regulates importation of fresh, frozen, pickled, canned, salted, dried, and smoked fish and seafood under the Food, Drug, and Cosmetic Act (FDCA) (21 CFR 161). Raw seafood is extremely perishable. You must take care that your product is handled expeditiously and carefully and that it is kept under adequate refrigeration to avoid contamination and decomposition. You may use only FDA-approved preservatives to prevent or retard spoilage. The use of artificial coloring to conceal damage or to improve the appearance of an inferior product is prohibited by provisions of the FDCA. For a more detailed discussion of FDCA food additive regulations and labeling requirements, refer to the "Foods" appendix on page 808.

Species-specific Restrictions. Regulations covering fish and seafood products are extensive, complex, and specific, and the current discussion is far from exhaustive. Identity standards are particularly stringent. For example, regulations limit products represented as anchovies to fish of the family *Engraulidae.* Other small fish which may superficially resemble anchovies—such as small herring and herring-like fish—may not be labeled or sold as anchovies. The use of the term "sardines" is permitted for small clupeoid fish. Sea herring (*Clupea harengus*), European pilchards (*Sardina pilchardus* or *Clupea pilchardus*), and brisling or sprat (*Clupea sprattus*) are commonly called sardines, especially when packed. Large herring may not be labeled sardines. Only species listed as tuna in the FDCA standards of identity may be imported as such. Species resembling tuna, such as bonito (*Sarda chilenis*) and yellowtail (*Seriola dorsalis*), may not be imported or sold as tuna. Standards of identity have been set for shrimp and oysters, as have standards for size, and prescribed methods of washing and draining to prevent adulteration by excess water. The sea crayfish, *Palinurus vulgaris,* is frequently imported into the U.S. in the form of frozen tails. Common trade names used for these products include "rock lobster" and "spiny lobster." If you are importing this product, be sure that your labeling includes the modifying words "rock" or "spiny" in direct connection with the word "lobster," in type of equal size and prominence.

Contaminated and Decomposed Fish. Chapter 3 products are highly perishable and require extraordinary care if decomposition is to be avoided. You should exercise extreme care in selecting raw materials to remove any unfit, decomposed material, and to maintain the product in a sound, wholesome condition. A common cause of detention at the port of entry is the presence of "feedy, belly-blown" fish in a shipment. "Feedy fish" are those with stomachs full of feed when caught. They deteriorate rapidly, and the viscera and thin belly walls disintegrate, producing a characteristic ragged appearance called "belly-blown." If your shipment contains such fish, it is in violation of the FDCA and is subject to detention at the port of entry.

You should be aware that certain species of fish are likely to contain chemical contamination from lakes, rivers, and oceans or excessive residues of pesticides, mercury, and other heavy metals. Presence of such substances in food violates the FDCA, and such products are subject to detention at the U.S. port of entry.

Shellfish. If you are interested in importing raw shellfish (clams, mussels, and oysters), be sure they are obtained from unpolluted waters and produced, handled, and distributed in a rapid, sanitary manner. Because they may transmit intestinal diseases such as typhoid fever, or may be carriers of natural or chemical toxins, shellfish are subject to special FDA controls and licensing. Foreign shellfish intended for sale in the U.S. are subject to controls equivalent to those applied to domestic products.

All shellfish must comply with the general requirements of the FDCA as well as those of state health agencies cooperating in both the FDA-administered National Shellfish Sanitation Program (NSSP) and Interstate Shellfish Sanitation Conference (ISSC). Shellfish harvesting is prohibited in areas contaminated by sewage or industrial wastes. State inspectors issue approval certificates to facilities that pass inspection. These certificates are equivalent to a state license to operate. The state-approved plant's certification number must appear on each container or package of shellfish shipped. In addition, shippers are required to keep records showing the origin and disposition of all shellfish handled and to make these records available to the control authorities.

Imported fresh and fresh frozen oysters, clams, and mussels are similarly certified under the auspices of the NSSP through bilateral agreements with the country of origin. Canada, Japan, Korea, Iceland, Mexico, the United Kingdom, Australia, and New Zealand have such joint agreements with the U.S. For further information on NSSP requirements, contact FDA's Sanitation Branch.

Salmon. Fish and eggs of salmonids of the fish family *Salmonidae* are prohibited entry into the U.S. for any purpose, unless such importations are by direct shipment and accompanied by the signed certification of a qualified fish pathologist in substantially the form as prescribed in 50 CFR 13.7. The following are exempted from certification requirements: 1) salmon landed in North America and brought into the U.S. for processing or sale; 2) any salmonid caught in the wild in North America under a valid sport or a commercial fishing license; and 3) fish or eggs of the family *Salmonidae* when processed or prepared in accordance with 50 CFR 13.7(c) or otherwise exempted from certification requirement.

Marking and Labeling Requirements

Substitution of one kind of seafood for another is prohibited. Whether or not identity standards apply, your seafood labels must identify the product by its common or usual U.S. name (i.e. pollock, cod, shrimp). You may not replace the common U.S. name of a seafood either with a name common in the country of origin but unfamiliar in the U.S., or with a coined name. If you are importing a seafood product not previously marketed in the U.S., its name must reflect proper biological classification and must not duplicate, or risk being confused with, the common or usual U.S. name of any other species. In addition, any seafood product for which standards of identity have been promulgated must conform precisely to the applicable standards. It is illegal to use the name of a standardized seafood on the label of a product which deviates from that standard. Refer to the "Foods" appendix on page 808 for other labeling requirements pertinent to foods in general.

For a general discussion of U.S. Customs marking and labeling requirements, refer to "Marking: Country of Origin" on page 215 and"Special Marking Requirements" on page 217.

Shipping Considerations

You will need to ensure that fish and seafood product imports are packed and shipped with care so that they arrive in good condition and pass smoothly through Customs. You are responsible for ensuring that the shipment is in compliance with all applicable government regulations for shipping. In most instances, you should not leave these arrangements solely to the discretion of your supplier. Careful preparation of the shipment and selection of the mode of transport can be essential to a cost-effective, timely delivery of undamaged goods. We strongly advise you to consult your shipping representatives, insurance agent, or freight broker for advice on packing and shipping. Refer to the "Foods" appendix on page 808 and to the major tab section "Packing/Shipping/Insurance" for a general discussion of packing and shipping.

Publications Available

The following publication explains the FDA requirements for importing fish and seafood. It is published by the FDA and is available on request from FDA headquarters (see addresses at end of this chapter).

Requirements of Laws and Regulations Enforced by the U.S. Food and Drug Administration

The *Harmonized Tariff Schedule of the United States* (HTSUS) is available from:

Government Printing Office (GPO)
Superintendent of Documents
Washington, DC 20402
(202) 512-1800 (Order line)
(202) 512-0000 (General)

The USGPO also has copies of specific laws available for purchase. The USGPO accepts credit card orders over the phone, as well as mail orders paid by credit card, a check drawn on a U.S. bank, or an international money order.

Relevant Government Agencies

Address your questions regarding FDA requirements for the importation of fish and seafood products and regarding the National Shellfish Sanitation Program to:

Food and Drug Administration (FDA)
Center for Food Safety and Applied Nutrition
200 C Street SW
Washington, DC 20204
(202) 205-5241, 205-5042

Food and Drug Administration (FDA)
Division of Enforcement, Imports Branch
200 C Street SW
Washington, DC 20204
(202) 205-4726

Address your questions regarding National Marine Fisheries Service requirements to:

National Marine Fisheries Service (NMFS)
Office of Marine Mammals and Endangered Species
1335 East West Highway
Silver Spring, MD 20910
(301) 713-2370, 713-2239

Address your questions regarding endangered species issues to:

U.S. Fish and Wildlife Service (FWS)
Office of Management Activity
4401 N. Fairfax Drive, Room 432
Arlington, VA 22203
(703) 358-2095
(800) 358-2104, (703) 358-2104 (Permits office)

Address your questions regarding importation of fish and seafood products to the district or port director of Customs for you area. For addresses refer to"U.S. Customs District Offices" on page 62 or contact:

U.S. Customs Service
1301 Constitution Ave. NW
Washington, DC 20229
(202) 927-6724 (Information)
(202) 927-1000 (General)

Laws and Regulations

The following laws and regulations may be relevant to the importation of fish and seafood products. The laws are contained in the U.S. Code (USC) and the regulations are found in the Code of Federal Regulations (CFR), both of which may be available at larger public and law libraries. Copies of specific laws are also available from the United States Government Printing Office (address above).

21 USC 301 et seq.
Food, Drug, and Cosmetic Act
This Act prohibits deceptive practices and regulates the manufacture, sale and importation or exportation of food, drugs, cosmetics, and related products. See 21 USC 331, 381, 382.

19 CFR 12.1 et seq.; 21 CFR 1.83 et seq.
Regulations on Food, Drugs, and Cosmetics
These regulations of the Secretary of Health and Human Services and the Secretary of the Treasury govern the standards, labeling, marking, and importing of products used with food, drugs, and cosmetics.

18 USC 42 et seq.
Importation of Animals, Birds, Fish, and Plants
This Act governs the importation of mammals, birds, fish, amphibia, and reptiles into the U.S. and authorizes U.S. Customs to enforce the import requirements.

19 CFR 10.78
Regulations on Entry of American Fishery Products
This regulation allows for the free entry of fish and fish products taken on the high seas by U.S. vessels.

Convention on International Trade in Endangered Species of Wild Fauna and Flora (CITES)
This comprehensive wildlife treaty signed by over 100 countries, including the United States, regulates and in many cases prohibits commercial imports and exports of wild animal and plant species threatened by trade.

16 USC 1531
Endangered Species Act
This Act prohibits the import and export of species listed as endangered and most species listed as threatened. It is the U.S. law that implements CITES.

16 USC 742a et seq.
Fish and Wildlife Act
This Act regulates and bars the import of certain wild animals or birds and authorizes U.S. Customs to enforce the restrictions.

16 USC 2401
Antarctic Conservation Act
This Act prohibits the importation, absent a special permit, of any flora or fauna native to Antarctica into the U.S.

16 USC 1361 et seq.
The Marine Mammal Protection Act
This Act prohibits the import of marine mammals and their parts and products. These species include whales, walruses, narwhals, seals, sea lions, sea otters, and polar bears.

50 CFR Parts 10, 13, and 16
Regulations of FWS for Importing Wildlife and Fish
These regulations specify the animals and animal products subject to import prohibitions and restrictions.

19 CFR 12.26, 12.28, 12.30
Regulations of Customs on Importation of Fish
These regulations list the fish that are prohibited from importation into the U.S., require licenses for certain imports, and set forth procedures for entry.

Principal Exporting Countries

The following listing includes samples of the main supplier nations of the products of this chapter. It is organized by HTSUS major heading. (Refer to "Customs Classification" above for the product codes.) Countries are listed in rank order of the value of products imported to the U.S. Statistics represent customs value entries for 1993 from the Bureau of Census, U.S. Department of Commerce.

0301—Thailand, Singapore, Indonesia, Hong Kong, Philippines, Colombia, Peru, Brazil, Canada, Japan

0302—Canada, Chile, Ecuador, Mexico, Costa Rica, Panama, Taiwan, Venezuela, Philippines, Iceland

0303—Taiwan, Japan, Canada, France, South Africa, India, Norway, Chile, Portugal, China

0304—Canada, Iceland, New Zealand, China, Russia, Thailand, Argentina, Norway, Chile, South Korea

0305—Canada, Norway, Japan, United Kingdom, Iceland, Spain, Hong Kong, South Korea, Costa Rica, China

0306—Thailand, Ecuador, Mexico, Canada, China, Indonesia, Honduras, Brazil, Bangladesh, India

0307—Canada, China, Japan, Philippines, South Korea, Mexico, Taiwan, Australia, Chile, New Zealand

Chapter 4: Dairy Products*

Full title: Dairy Products; Birds' Eggs; Natural Honey; Edible Products of Animal Origin, Not Elsewhere Specified or Included

This chapter relates to the importation of dairy products, eggs, honey, and other edible products of animal origin not specified elsewhere, which are classified under Chapter 4 of the Harmonized Tariff Schedule of the United States (HTSUS). Specifically, it includes milk and cream, with or without sweetening; buttermilk, yogurt, and sour cream; whey; butter; cheese and curd; birds' eggs in the shell, shelled, and yolks; natural honey; and other edible products of animal origin. The key to the other products mentioned is that they must be edible. You should read this section in conjunction with the "Foods" appendix on page 808.

If you are interested in importing live dairy animals or poultry (or viable, fertile eggs), you should refer to Commodity Index Chapter 1. Meat of cattle and poultry is covered in Chapter 2. Other inedible animal products and byproducts, such as feathers, are covered in Chapter 5. If you are interested in importing animal fats other than butter, refer to Chapter 15. Food preparations containing dairy products are included in Chapters 17, 18, and 19. Albumins and globulins derived from eggs are covered in Chapter 35.

Key Factors

The key factors in the importation of these products are:

- Compliance with the U.S. Food and Drug Administration (FDA) purity, identity, manufacturing, and other standards
- Compliance with FDA entry notifications and procedures
- For milk and cream, FDA dairy import permit required
- Compliance with the U.S. Department of Agriculture (USDA) Animal and Plant Health Inspection Service (APHIS) Veterinary Service (VS) livestock disease-prevention requirements and restrictions; permits required in some cases
- Compliance with USDA Food Safety and Inspection Service (FSIS) import restrictions, port inspections, and product certification
- Compliance with quotas and licensing for certain products

*IMPORTANT: Read the Commodity Index Introduction. It is the essential framework for understanding this section.

Although most importers utilize the services of a licensed customs broker in making their entries, and we recommend this practice, you should be aware of the regulatory, entry and documentation issues involved in importing your product. You, as importer, are ultimately responsible for the fulfillment of any legal requirements applicable to your shipment.

General Considerations

Regulatory Agencies. Importation of dairy products into the U.S. is regulated by the USDA and the FDA. The following discussion will be divided into sections that deal with the requirements of each separate agency. In reality, these requirements, restrictions, permits, licenses, quotas, and other requirements are not so neatly divided. If, for example, under the USDA heading we say you may import a product that meets certain criteria, in no sense should you construe that statement to mean that the product thereby automatically meets criteria of all the other agencies, or that only the USDA is concerned in that product's import. Agency requirements for dairy imports overlap in ways that are not always evident. For example, a product that is permitted under APHIS country-of-origin disease prevention restrictions may be restricted under the Import Milk Act (IMA), as well as be subject to Section 22 dairy quotas. You may meet all those criteria, but if your product does not also meet an applicable FDA standard under the Food, Drug, and Cosmetic Act (FDCA)—such as standards of quality, identity, and manufacturing practices—you do not yet have an admissible product. It is the importer's responsibility to satisfy all of the U.S agencies with a regulatory interest in dairy products.

FDA Requirements. The FDA enforces applicable provisions of the FDCA. The FDA regulations regarding foods of any kind are extensive and stringent, and dairy products imported into the U.S. must comply with all FDCA requirements for those produced domestically.

Port of Entry Requirements. Imported products regulated by the FDA are subject to port of entry inspection. **Form FD701** is required for all FDA-regulated importations and may be obtained from your local FDA Import Operations office, from FDA headquarters, or from your customs broker. FDA also enforces the IMA. Under IMA, an FDA import permit is required in order to import milk, cream, or products containing significant amounts of milk and cream. For an annotated diagram of required FDA import procedures refer to the "Foods" appendix on page 808.

Detention of Shipment. If your shipment is found to be noncomplying, it may be detained at the port of entry. In the case of products subject to FDA jurisdiction, the FDA may allow you to bring such a shipment into compliance before making a final decision regarding admittance. However, any sorting, reprocessing, or relabeling must be supervised by FDA personnel and is done at the importer's expense. Such conditional release to allow the importer to bring a shipment into compliance is a privilege, not a right. The FDA may consider subsequent noncomplying shipments of the same type of product to constitute abuse of the privilege and require the importer to destroy or reexport the products. To ascertain what your legal responsibilities are, you should contact these agencies regarding the specific items to be imported.

USDA Requirements. USDA APHIS VS enforces restrictions on importation of certain milk and milk products found in 9 CFR Chapter 1 Subpart 94. Importation of some of these products requires a USDA APHIS VS import permit. The USDA only grants dairy import permits when the Administrator is satisfied that the product will not introduce or disseminate contagious livestock diseases into the U.S. Under Section 22 of the Agricultural Adjustment Act (AAA), USDA assigns annual import quotas to many dairy products, mainly cheeses. You must have a USDA import license in order to import these items. The importation of poultry products and eggs is also regulated by the USDA FSIS, which enforces the Wholesome Poultry Act (WPA) and Federal Poultry Inspection Act (FPIA).

Import Advisory

Importing dairy products is complicated. You will have to satisfy more than one branch of more than one U.S. government agency, and there are a wide variety of factors to stay on top of at every phase. Each agency is very good source of information about what you need to do, and the standards and procedures your product needs to comply with. However, do not expect an employee or official of one agency to be an accurate source of information about the requirements of another agency. Do not expect a government expert in a department regulating one aspect of dairy imports to be equally expert on the regulatory issues governed by a different department. This is true even though you are asking for information pertaining to a single commodity that is subject to regulation by both. For the most part, they simply do not know, and for good reason. Dairy regulations are complicated. Ask all relevant agencies about their requirements and only about their requirements.

Customs Classification

For customs purposes, dairy products are classified under Chapter 4 of the HTSUS. This chapter is divided into major headings, which are further divided into subheadings, and often into sub-subheadings, each of which has its own HTSUS classification number. For example, the HTSUS number for milk or cream of a fat content by weight not exceeding 45% is 0401.30.10, indicating that it is a subcategory of milk and cream of a fat content by weight exceeding 6% (0401.30.00), which is a subcategory of milk and cream not concentrated nor containing added sugar or other sweetening matter (0401.00.00). There are 10 major headings in HTSUS Chapter 4.

0401—Milk and cream, not concentrated nor containing added sugar or other sweetening matter

0402—Milk or cream, concentrated or containing added sugar or other sweetening matter

0403—Buttermilk, curdled milk and cream, yogurt, kephir, and other fermented or acidified milk and cream, whether or not concentrated or containing added sugar or other sweetening matter or flavored or containing added fruit, nuts, or cocoa

0404—Whey, whether or not concentrated or containing added sugar or other sweetening matter; products consisting of natural milk constituents, whether or not containing added sugar or other sweetening matter, not elsewhere specified or included

0405—Butter and other fats and oils derived from milk

0406—Cheese and curd

0407—Birds' eggs, in shell, fresh, preserved, or cooked

0408—Birds' eggs, not in shell, and egg yolks, fresh, dried, cooked by steaming or by boiling in water, molded, frozen, or otherwise preserved, whether or not containing added sugar or sweetening matter

0409—Natural honey

0410—Edible products of animal origin, not elsewhere specified or included

For more details regarding classification of the specific product you are interested in importing, consult a customs broker, the appropriate commodity specialist at your nearest customs port, or see HTSUS. HTSUS is available for purchase from the U.S. Government Printing Office (see addresses at end of this chapter), and may be found in larger public libraries. Refer to "Classification—Liquidation" on page 207 for a general discussion of customs classification.

Sample Import Duties

Import duties will vary depending on the HTSUS classification of your product. Therefore, to determine the correct amount of duties, your product must be properly classified under the HTSUS. The following sample duties are taken from the duty listings for HTSUS Chapter 4 products.

Milk and cream, of a fat content by weight not exceeding 1% (0401.10.00): 0.4 cents/liter; milk and cream of a fat content by weight of between 1% and 6% for calendar year entries of up to 11,356,236 liters (0401.20.20): 0.5 cents/liter; of quantities exceeding 11,356,236 liters per calendar year (0401.20.40): 1.7 cents/liter; milk and cream in powder, granules, or other solid forms, of a fat content, by weight, not exceeding 1.5% (0402.10.00): 3.3 cents/kg; not containing added sugar, of a fat content, by weight, exceeding 3% but not exceeding 35% (0402.21.40): 6.8 cents/kg; condensed milk in airtight containers (0402.99.20): 3.9 cents/kg; yogurt (0403.10.00): 20%; fluid buttermilk (0403.90.20): 0.4 cents/liter; sour cream containing over 45% by weight of butterfat (0403.90.70): 12.3 cents/kg; whey protein concentrates (0404.10.05): 10%; fluid whey (0404.10.20): 0.4 cents/liter; articles of milk or cream (0404.90.20): 17.5%; butter (0405.00.70): 12.3 cents/kg; fresh, unripened, uncured cheese (0406.10.00): 10%; grated or powdered Cheddar cheese (0406.20.30): 16%; grated or powdered Parmesan, Romano, Reggiano, Provolone, Proveletti, Sbrinz, and Goya cheese (0406.20.50): 15%; processed blue-veined cheese other than Roquefort (0406.30.10): 20%; Gruyere process cheese (0406.30.50): 6.4%; Cheddar cheese (0406.90.10): 12%; Edam and Gouda cheeses (0406.90.15): 15%; Swiss or Emmenthaler cheese with eye formation (0406.90.45): 6.4%; other cheeses and substitutes including mixtures (0406.90.80): 10%; birds' eggs, in the shell (0407.00.00): 3.5 cents/doz.; dried egg yolks (0408.11.00): 59.5 cents/kg; natural honey (0409.00.00): 2.2 cents/kg; edible products of animal origin not elsewhere specified or included (0410.00.00): 2.5%.

Entry and Documentation

The entry of merchandise is a two-part process consisting of 1) filing the documents necessary to determine whether merchandise may be released from Customs custody and 2) filing the documents that contain information for duty assessment and statistical purposes. In certain instances, such as the entry of merchandise subject to quotas, all documents must be filed and accepted by Customs prior to the release of the goods. Unless you have been granted an extension, you must file entry documents at a location specified by the district or area director within five working days of your shipment's date of arrival at a U.S. port of entry. These include a number of standard documents required by Customs for any entry, and:

- FDA Importers Entry Notice **Form FD701**
- For milk and cream and certain products containing large amounts of milk and cream: FDA Dairy Import Permit
- For certain products restricted by USDA: USDA APHIS Import Permit
- For cheeses imported from the European Community, an affidavit stating that the cheeses will not receive any restitution payments as per EO 11851 of April 5, 1975 and, if imported into Puerto Rico, will not be reexported into the U.S.; affidavits are not required on direct shipments to the U.S. on a through bill of lading

After you present the entry, Customs may examine your shipment, or may waive examination. The shipment is then released provided no legal or regulatory violations have been noted. You must then file entry summary documentation and deposit estimated duties at a designated customhouse within 10 working days of your shipment's release. For a detailed description of entry procedures, standard documentation, and informal entry, see "Entry Process" on page 182.

Prohibitions and Restrictions

FDA Requirements—*Milk Safety.* Milk, cream, and the dairy products made from them offer ideal conditions for the propagation of microorganisms. Therefore, you should be sure that any milk and cream in the products you wish to import are obtained from disease-free animals. You should be sure that all materials used in manufactured dairy products have been handled at all times under sanitary conditions to prevent contamination with organisms that produce disease or cause spoilage. Pasteurization offers a considerable safeguard against disease transmission. Nevertheless, contamination by workers suffering from disease, by rodents, by unclean equipment, or by the addition of unpasteurized ingredients after pasteurization, can create a serious health hazard. Unsanitary handling can introduce spoilage organisms, such as undesirable bacteria, yeasts, and molds, into otherwise pure raw materials or finished products, causing decomposition. If your imported dairy products were prepared from decomposed raw materials, are undergoing active spoilage, or are contaminated with disease-producing organisms, the FDA considers them adulterated. Not only will they not be admitted, but you may also be subject to legal action.

Mandatory pasteurization for all milk and milk products in final packaged form intended for direct human consumption after distribution in interstate commerce became a Federal requirement as of August 10, 1987. The regulation (21 CFR 1240) defines pasteurization as heating and holding every particle of milk or milk product in properly designed and operated equipment at times and temperatures specified in the regulation. Exemptions are provided for acceptable alternative methods, such as aging procedures for certain cheeses.

Nonfat Dry Milk. Imported nonfat dry milk and nonfat dry milk fortified with vitamins A and D must comply with FDCA identity standards for these products. Nonfat dry milk is defined in a standard provided by Act of Congress on July 2, 1956, as follows: "nonfat dry milk is the product resulting from the removal of fat and water from milk and contains the lactose, milk proteins, and milk minerals in the same relative proportions as in the fresh milk from which it is made. It contains not over 5 per centum by weight of moisture. The fat content is not over 1 1/2 per centum by weight unless otherwise indicated. The term 'milk,' when used herein, means sweetmilk of cows."

Butter. Butter is defined in the standard provided by Act of Congress of March 4, 1923, as follows: "butter shall be understood to mean the food product usually known as butter, and which is made exclusively from milk or cream or both, with or without common salt, and with or without additional coloring matter, and containing not less than 80 per centum by weight of milk fat, all tolerances having been allowed for." The FDA examines butter shipments for evidence of the use of dirty cream or milk, and for mold indicating the use of decomposed cream. You may not import butter containing chemical additives or artificial flavor.

Cheese. Imports of cheese are highly regulated. Standards of identity have been promulgated for most natural cheeses, process cheeses, cheese foods, and cheese spreads (21 CFR 133). If you are importing a particular variety of cheese for which a standard has been adopted, you should be aware that all cheeses belonging to that variety must comply with that standard. Cheeses must be labeled with the name prescribed in the applicable standard. Most of the standards prescribe limits for moisture and for fat. A few natural cheeses are required to be made from pasteurized milk. However, most may be made from either raw or pasteurized milk. To ensure that the cheese is safe to eat, those made from raw milk must be aged for 60 days or longer. Requirements for longer aging apply to cheeses that need additional aging to develop the characteristics of the variety. If you are considering importing cheese and foods made of cheese, you should consult the FDA standards before making your purchase. The FDA will not permit entry of cheese that does not comply with applicable standards.

Basically, a narrow range of problems accounts for the majority of FDA detentions of cheese at the port of entry. By avoiding these problems—through exercising care in your foreign purchases and in subsequent handling of cheeses—you are likely to assure your shipment's entry into the U.S. Be sure that your cheese has not been contaminated with insect and rodent filth during the handling of the milk, manufacture of the cheese, or during transport or storage. Pesticides are also an issue. If you buy cheese from a foreign producer whose cows are exposed to pesticides, either from careless use in barns, or in feed, you may find that yours is among the large number of shipments that FDA detains for that particular violation.

Evaporated Milk, Sweetened Condensed Milk. There are standards of identity for both evaporated milk and sweetened condensed milk (21 CFR 131). Evaporated milk must contain not less than 7.5% milk fat and not less than 25.5% total milk solids. Sweetened condensed milk must contain not less than 28% total milk solids, and not less than 8.5% milk fat. If you are considering importing sweetened condensed milk, you will need a FDA Dairy Import Permit under IMA. Evaporated milk is not subject to IMA because it has been sterilized by heat.

FDA Import Permits. Under IMA, you must hold an FDA Dairy Import Permit in order to import milk, cream, or products containing significant amounts of milk or cream. Cheese and heat-sterilized, hermetically sealed products are exempt from this requirement. The application for an FDA dairy permit is not a simple matter. You will have to provide many types of health and sanitation verifications as part of the application process. The description that follows is not at all exhaustive, but is intended to convey a rough sense of what is involved.

Each cow from which an import shipment of milk or cream is to be derived must be physically examined and tested for tuberculosis by a government veterinarian of the country of origin. The dairy farm must be inspected for compliance with FDA sanitary and processing requirements. The plant where the milk is processed must be inspected and receive an FDA sanitary rating. The state and country in which the processing plant and dairy are located must certify that all requisite inspections have been carried out, within one year of your permit application, by a regulatory official of the country of origin. Your permit application must include documentation for each aspect of this process. You will need as many as twenty or thirty different FDA forms to apply for a permit for a single shipment of milk or cream. If you are interested in obtaining a Dairy Import Permit, you should contact FDA's Center for Food Safety for detailed instructions (see addresses at end of this chapter).

USDA Requirements—*APHIS VS Restrictions.* Under 9 CFR Subpart 94, APHIS restricts the importation of milk and milk products from countries that are known to be infected with rinderpest or foot-and-mouth disease (see Country-Specific Import Restrictions below). The following products are exempt from these restrictions: 1) cheese that does not contain liquid or other articles restricted under Subpart 94; 2) butter; and 3) butter oil.

Milk or Milk Products. For USDA purposes, you may import other milk or a milk product originating in countries known to be infected with rinderpest or foot-and-mouth disease, provided the product meets one of the following criteria:

1) It has been heat-processed and hermetically sealed. You may import products in a concentrated liquid form which have been

processed by heat by a commercial method in a container hermetically sealed promptly after such heating, so as to be shelf-stable without refrigeration.

2) It is dry milk or a dry milk product. This includes dry whole milk, nonfat dry milk, dried whey, dried buttermilk, and formulations that contain any such dry milk products. You may import these products, but you must consign them directly to a USDA—approved establishment for further processing. With prior USDA permission, you may temporarily store your products in an approved warehouse under the supervision of an APHIS inspector, pending movement to an approved establishment. In any case, you must transport your product from the U.S. port of first arrival to either its destination (and, if temporarily stored, from the warehouse to the establishment) only under USDA or U.S. Customs Service seals. These seals may only be broken by an APHIS inspector or other USDA-authorized person. If you wish to remove your products from the warehouse or establishment, you must obtain special permission from the USDA Administrator, and comply with all the conditions and requirements specified for the move.

3) It is a milk product brought in under permit. If you wish to import milk products that are not covered by either of the two conditions listed above, you will need prior written permission from the USDA Administrator. Products requiring USDA import permits include—but are not limited to—condensed milk, long-life milks such as sterilized milk, casein and caseinates, lactose, and lactalbumin. For permit application procedures, see APHIS VS Permit Application below.

4) It is a milk product brought in under permit for testing. In specific cases USDA allows importation of small amounts of restricted milk products for examination, testing, or analysis. If your intended importation fits this description, you will need to obtain an APHIS VS permit prior to shipping the product to the U.S. For permit application procedures, see APHIS VS Permit Application below.

If your milk and milk products originate in and are shipped from countries listed as free of rinderpest and foot-and-mouth disease, but have entered a port or otherwise transited a country where the infection is present, they must meet the following conditions for import into the U.S. The product must be transported under serially numbered official seals, applied at the shipment's point of origin by an authorized representative of the country of origin. The numbers of the seals must be either listed directly on or attached to, the bill of lading or similar document accompanying the shipment. Upon arrival of the carrier at the U.S. port of entry, an APHIS inspector must determine that the seals on your shipment are intact and that the numbers match the numbers appearing on the accompanying document.

Poultry and Eggs. Subpart 94 details poultry and egg import restrictions and the procedures necessary to qualify a product for import. APHIS administers these restrictions primarily through import permits and product certification by qualified government veterinarians of the country of origin. (In the following information, "government veterinarian" always means full-time veterinary officer salaried by the national government of the country of origin.) The law defines poultry as chickens, turkeys, swans, partridges, guinea fowl, pea fowl; nonmigratory ducks, geese, pigeons, and doves; and commercial, domestic, or pen-raised grouse, pheasants, and quail. It restricts import of these products from countries known to have incidence of the following diseases: fowl pest, viscerotropic velogenic Newcastle Disease (VVND), and *Salmonella enteritidis*, phage-type 4. (See below, Country-Specific Import Restrictions, APHIS, for a list of countries currently under restriction because of the presence of these diseases.)

Subpart 94 restricts importation of eggs laid by poultry, game birds, or other birds raised in, imported from, or moved into or through any country where VVND or *S. enteritidis* is considered to exist at any time prior to importation to, or during shipment to, the U.S. *S. enteritidis* is considered to exist in all countries of the world except for Canada, and VVND in all but a few. For all practical purposes, the following restrictions apply to all importation of eggs into the U.S. You have four options for importing such eggs.

Option 1: Eggs brought in under certificate. If you bring eggs into the U.S. under this option, they must be imported in cases marked with the flock of origin's identity and sealed with the seal of the country of origin's national government. A certificate signed by a government veterinarian must accompany each shipment, which you must present to a USDA official at the U.S. port of entry. The certificate must identify: 1) flock of origin, 2) country of origin, 3) port of embarkation, 4) port of arrival, 5) names and addresses of exporter and importer, 6) total number of eggs and cases of eggs shipped with the certificate, 7) date the certificate was signed. In addition, the certificate must state that the eggs qualify for importation in accordance with all applicable requirements of Subpart 94.6.

No more than 90 days before the certificate is signed, a government veterinarian must inspect the flock of origin, finding no evidence of communicable poultry disease. Prior to export, the following processing must take place, all on the premises of origin: eggs must be 1) washed to remove foreign material from the shell surface; 2) sanitized with a hypochlorate solution of from 100 ppm to 200 ppm available chlorine; 3) packed in previously unused cases; and 4) the same government veterinarian who signs the certificate must seal the cases with a seal of the country of origin's national government.

If the eggs were laid in any country where VVND is considered to exist, the following restrictions also apply. There must be no evidence that the flock of origin was exposed to VVND during the 90 days before the certificate was signed, and no VVND occurred on the premises of origin during that time. The eggs must be from a flock of origin found free of VVND according to the specific veterinary testing and observation procedures outlined in 94.6 (ix)(C)(1,2). These procedures involve the use of "sentinel birds." These are chickens that 1) have been raised in an environment free of the pathogens that cause communicable poultry diseases, and 2) have not been infected with, exposed to, or immunized with any strain of virus that causes VVND. For information on sources of sentinel birds, contact APHIS VS (see addresses at end of this chapter).

If the eggs were laid in any country where *S. enteritidis*, phage type 4 is considered to exist, the flock of origin must similarly be found free of the disease by a government veterinarian, according to specific veterinary observation and testing procedures outlined in 94.6 (x)(C)(1-3).

Option 2: Eggs imported and moved to a USDA approved establishment for breaking and pasteurization. If you import eggs under this option, the shipment must be immediately moved under USDA seal from the U.S. port of arrival to an approved establishment for breaking and pasteurization. The USDA approves only those establishments it determines to have pasteurization and sanitation procedures for handling the eggs and for disposing of egg shells, cases, and packing materials adequate to prevent the introduction of communicable poultry disease into the U.S. The names and addresses of approved establishments may be obtained from USDA Import-Export Products staff (see addresses at end of this chapter). If you wish to request approval for an establishment, contact the USDA Administrator at the same address.

Option 3: Eggs entered under permit: those imported for scientific, educational, or research purposes. Eggs may be imported if they are imported for scientific, educational, or research purposes, and USDA has determined that the importation can be made under conditions that will prevent the introduction of VVND or *S. enteritidis* into the U.S. If your import fits this category, you will need to obtain an APHIS permit prior to importation. Your eggs must be moved and handled as specified on your permit. See APHIS VS Permit Application below for an outline of procedures and requirements for obtaining an APHIS permit.

Option 4: Eggs entered under permit: *those determined by USDA to have been cooked or processed or otherwise handled in a manner that will prevent introduction of disease into the U.S.* You may bring eggs in under APHIS permit when the Administrator determines that they have been cooked or processed or will be handled in a manner that will prevent the introduction of VVND or *S. enteritidis* into the U.S. You must obtain your permit prior to importation. Your eggs must be moved and handled as specified on the permit. See APHIS VS Permit Application below for an outline of procedures and requirements for obtaining an APHIS permit.

APHIS VS Permit Application Procedures. Requests for USDA APHIS VS permits authorizing importation of restricted products must be submitted on VS **Form 16-3.** You may obtain forms from APHIS headquarters (see addresses at end of this chapter) or any USDA port office. You may submit signed facsimiles, provided you send an original signed document as follow-up. If you intend multiple imports and need a supply of forms on hand, you may photocopy the original **Form 16-3.** Processing or production information and sources of milk products may often require more space than is allowed on the application form. In such cases, attach extra sheets as necessary. You should include as much background information as possible to allow APHIS to properly evaluate the disease risk associated with your import. You can send research papers as supporting evidence, but do not send them by fax.

It takes about two weeks for APHIS to process an application and prepare a permit for return mail. If your application information is insufficient, APHIS will contact you for clarification, and the permit process may take longer. Submit your requests for renewal or amendment of permits, in writing—submission by fax is acceptable—to USDA headquarters (see addresses at end of this chapter). Your renewal request should note any changes in particulars from the original application and permit issued. Once a permit has been issued, imports under that permit must comply in every detail with all of the permit's stipulations. Entry will be facilitated if your permit number appears on the shipping documents, or if a copy of the permit is attached. If you attempt to import products requiring permits without obtaining a permit prior to shipment, your import will be subject to delay or refusal at the port of entry.

FSIS Requirements. The Poultry Products Inspection Act (PPIA) requires countries exporting poultry to the U.S. to impose domestic inspection requirements at least equal to inspection requirements in the U.S. The FSIS reviews foreign inspection systems to ensure that they are equal to the U.S. system. Only those countries to which FSIS grants poultry export eligibility may export these products to the U.S. See Country-Specific Import Restrictions below for list of eligible countries.

An inspection certificate issued by the responsible official of the exporting country must accompany each import shipment of poultry and poultry products. Certificates identify products by country and plant of origin, destination, shipping marks, and amounts. They certify that the products have received ante-mortem and post-mortem inspection; that they are wholesome, not adulterated or misbranded, and that they otherwise comply with U.S. requirements.

Port of Entry Inspection. The FSIS reinspects poultry and poultry products on a sample basis as they enter the U.S. Your product will be checked for transportation damage, labeling, general condition, and proper certification. Additional inspection tasks that may be scheduled include: product examination; accuracy of net weight; condition of the container; laboratory analyses for food chemistry (such as fat, water, and nitrite levels) and drug and chemical residues; species testing; and monitoring of product labels. The actual inspection tasks and the scope of inspection are based on the nature of the product and on the performance history of the plant and country.

If your poultry or poultry products pass reinspection, FSIS will stamp them U.S. Inspected and Passed, and they will be allowed to enter U.S. commerce. If the products do not pass reinspection, they will be stamped U.S. Refused Entry. You must export, or destroy refused products. In some cases they may be converted to animal food. When condemnation occurs, inspection is intensified for future shipments of that product from the same plant, and in some cases, for all poultry shipments from the same country.

Residue Control. Chemical and drug residue control is one of the major features of an exporting country's inspection system that must be judged equal to the U.S. system. Each year, countries must be certified by the FSIS as continuing to operate an equivalent residue control program. FSIS experts make sure that the country's residue program uses approved analytical methods, that officials are knowledgeable about the use of chemical compounds in their country, and that the country tests for those compounds that could potentially contaminate the food supply. You cannot import poultry or eggs from a country that fails to receive an FSIS annual residue certification.

As a further residue check, the FSIS randomly samples products at the port of entry and analyzes them for drug and chemical residues. The FSIS annual import residue plan sets the initial sampling rate for each country based on the volume of product imported from that country. The plan includes the same chemical compounds as the domestic residue-monitoring program. Compounds are selected based on their likelihood of contaminating the food supply and their potential harm to the consuming public. The list can include chemical compounds not legal in the U.S. if they have the potential to contaminate a foreign country's poultry supply.

If your shipment contains residues above the U.S. tolerance or action level, it will be considered adulterated and will be refused entry into the U.S. Your shipment will not be held pending laboratory test results, however, unless FSIS has some reason to suspect contamination. If a laboratory reports a residue violation on a sample that has otherwise passed reinspection, as much as possible of the product must be recalled. Products so recovered may not be used for human food.

The occurrence of a residue violation at a port of entry raises concerns about the exporting country's ability to control residues. Port of entry sampling is then automatically increased for related products from the entire country, as well as on subsequent shipments from the specific plant where the violative sample originated.

From time to time, the FSIS will increase sampling for a specific country or for a specific compound. This can occur when there is an indication that a problem may exist or when a pattern develops of failed port-of-entry reinspections.

U.S.-Canada Free Trade Agreement. Canada has an inspection system that is virtually the same as that found in the US. Under the U.S.-Canada Free Trade Agreement, FSIS has modified border reinspection requirements for Canadian products. Canadian plants may choose to follow the revised procedures or go through traditional reinspection. Under the revised procedures, before a product destined for the U.S. leaves the Canadian plant, Agriculture Canada inspection officials provide information to be entered into the FSIS automated computer system. If the computer does not generate an assignment for reinspection at the border, the shipment automatically proceeds through U.S. Customs.

Entry of specific products can be difficult because many product categories affected by quota restrictions overlap, especially where milk and sugar products are concerned. Even when a product is not the target of a quota itself, it may be restricted because of other policy driven limitations. It is important to consult with the Quota Branch of the U.S. Customs Service (see addresses at end of this chapter) to determine whether quota restrictions apply to your specific product.

Section 22 Dairy Quotas and Import Licensing System

Presidential Proclamation 4708 of December 11, 1979, limited imports of quota cheese entering the U.S. during any calendar year to an aggregate 111,000 metric tons. Any increase in the 111,000-ton limit for dairy products subject to quota restrictions involves hearings and investigations by the International Trade Commission (ITC).

Import Regulation. Under Import Regulation 7 CFR 6.20-6.34, importers of certain dairy products must be licensed by the USDA. The Import Regulation licensing system is designed to allocate quotas in a fair and equitable manner among importers and users. Since the beginning of the import system, the major portion of each quota has been allocated to historical licensees (persons who were actually in the business of importing during the representative period chosen for the particular quota in question). A small portion of each quota was allocated among eligible nonhistorical licensees. This system continues to apply to quota quantities in effect prior to January 1, 1980.

Beginning January 1, 1980, as a result of the Trade Agreements Act of 1979 and Presidential Proclamation 4708, new cheese import allocations increased the total quota and extended coverage to most cheese types that were not previously included in the quota, primarily those free of quota by virtue of their high price. These new quota shares are allocated so that no more than 50% goes to new historical licenses and at least 50% is allocated in the form of supplementary licenses to eligible applicants on a first-come, first-served basis.

Eligibility Standards for Historical Licenses. For continued eligibility for historical licenses, importers must submit a certification each year at least 60 days prior to the beginning of the quota year for which application is made. Licensees must certify that they have not used any other firm's license or permitted another firm to use their license.

Nonhistorical Licenses. Nonhistorical license eligibility criteria limit eligibility to those persons or firms operating viable businesses importing or manufacturing cheese or cheese products. To be considered as being in the cheese importing business, you must show evidence of importation of at least 10,000 pounds during the 12-month period ending August 1 of each year. You can also gain eligibility by showing proof of the manufacture of at least 100,000 pounds of cheese or cheese products in your own certified plant during the same 12-month period. Your plant must be listed in the most current issue of "Dairy Plants Surveyed and Approved for USDA Grading Services." To qualify for a nonhistorical license, you must also complete Customs **Forms 7501** and **7505**, showing yourself as the importer of record or importer of account.

Supplementary Licenses. Supplementary licenses are granted for items listed in Appendix 2 of the Import Regulation. In order to be eligible for one of these licenses you must: 1) meet the same eligibility criteria as those for nonhistorical licenses; or 2) have historical eligibility under Appendix 2 for articles from the same country of origin for which you are seeking a supplementary license; or, 3) be endorsed in writing by the government of the supplying country as a "preferred" importer, in addition to and meeting one or both of requirements (1) and (2) above.

Application Period. The application period begins August 1 each year and is open for 90 days. Your application must be made in writing to the Head, Import Licensing Group (see addresses at end of this chapter), and must be canceled by the U.S. Postal Service, certifying the date. Licenses are issued during the last week of December for use during the coming year and are valid for the 12-month period beginning January 1 and ending December 31.

Issuance of Licenses. If you have an established record of importing cheese (quota or nonquota), or are actively engaged in the cheese manufacturing business, you should have no difficulty in meeting the qualifications for license eligibility. However, because quotas are often fully subscribed, eligibility alone will not guarantee that you will receive a license. Even if you do receive a license, there is no guarantee that it will be for the full allotment you have requested. Because of the limited shares available for each quota and the strong demand for certain quota products, it is quite possible that in any given year the nonhistorical quota shares for a specific quota will be fully subscribed by applicants who held shares for such quotas in the previous year. While supplementary licenses are granted on a first-come, first-served basis, established minima for such licenses may mean that some eligible applicants will not receive licenses despite having been granted licenses in previous years.

Cost of Licenses. The USDA charges an annual fee for licenses actually issued to cover the administrative costs of the licensing program. The fee is calculated each quota year for that year's license, and is announced in the Federal Register. License fees have consisted of relatively nominal amounts, primarily to cover processing costs.

Penalties. Licenses carry with them certain conditions and responsibilities. You may incur penalties if the Licensing Authority has reasonable cause to believe that you have 1) violated the provisions of the Import Regulation, or 2) furnished false or incomplete information in connection with your applications for or use of your license. In such cases the Authority may, after official notification, 1) revoke your historical eligibility and 2) bar you or your firm from receiving supplementary or nonhistorical licenses for a period of as long as three years. If your eligibility is revoked, you may appeal the determination to the Director of the Dairy, Livestock, and Poultry Division, Foreign Agricultural Service, Import Licensing Group (see addresses at end of this chapter), within 30 days from the date of notification.

Cancellation of Licenses. Licenses may also be canceled for the following reasons:

1) Historical licensees: If you fail to enter the article for which you hold the license during either a) two consecutive quota years or b) three nonconsecutive quota years within any five-year period, your eligibility for a historical license for that article will be suspended for the following quota year. Suspension may be lifted if you provide the Licensing Authority with documentary evidence that you did in fact enter the article during at least one of those years. If the you can provide an acceptable reason for failure to enter the article, the Licensing Authority may lift the suspension at its discretion. However, you will have to submit an application to the Licensing Authority, and that application will have to be approved three months after the beginning of the quota year for which your eligibility was suspended. 2) There is an 85% quota usage requirement per year. Failure to meet this requirement may result in the cancellation or reduction of your license. 3) Failure to pay the annual license fee is also cause for cancellation.

Licenses

Appendix 1: Old Historical. Old historical licenses (issued prior to 1979) and nonhistorical licenses are derived from Appendix 1 of the Import Regulation. Historical licenses were granted to firms that were in the business of importing certain articles that subsequently became subject to quota and licensing requirements. A representative period was used to determine the firm's quota base, which was used to calculate the basic annual allocations and license amount. For most Appendix 1 quotas, approximately 90% of the original quota was set aside for historical licenses. All old historical licenses have been applied for and issued, and no new licenses can be issued in this category.

Nonhistorical. These licenses are issued from Appendix 1 of the Import Regulation. Approximately 10% of the quotas were set aside so that new importers would have access to the licensing system. The amount available for nonhistorical licenses has subsequently been increased due to the cancellation of some historical licenses.

Appendix 2: New Historical. New historical licenses were issued as a result of the MTN of 1979. The MTN established several new quotas and expanded others. The basis for the establishment of these licenses was similar to the old historical licenses, with a representative period being used to calculate the firm's base quota. Some 50% of these quotas were set aside for new historical licenses. These licenses are listed together with supplementary licenses under Appendix 2 quotas of the Import Regulation. It should be noted that when a historical license is canceled, the license amount is moved to the portion of the quotas issued to either nonhistorical or supplementary licenses, whichever is appropriate. All new historical licenses have been applied for and issued, and none are available.

Supplementary. These licenses were established as a result of the 1979 MTN which established several new quotas and expanded others. Some 50% of these quotas were originally set aside for newcomers. These applicants may also apply for quota shares designated as "other countries." All countries with specific quotas, except the European Economic Community (EC), have the option to name "preferred importers" from the quotas in Appendix 2. Preferred importers are firms designated by the governments of supplier countries that have specific quotas. The quotas for the EC are issued as supplementary licenses on a first-come, first-served basis each year.

For more information on quota cheese import licensing, or for information on conditions under which limited quantities of quota cheeses may be imported without licenses, contact USDA's Import Licensing Group (see addresses at end of this chapter). See Quotas below for a listing of products that currently fall under import licensing regulations.

Quotas

The dairy products listed below are subject to annual import quotas assigned by the USDA and may be imported only under import licenses issued by that department (See USDA Requirements above). These quotas are administered through the U.S. Customs Service.

Butter; dried cream; malted milk and compounds or mixtures of or substitutes for milk or cream; dried whole milk, dried skimmed milk, dried buttermilk and whey; cheddar cheese, and cheese and substitutes for cheese containing or processed from Cheddar cheese curd, and granular cheese and cheese substitutes for cheese containing or processed from such American-type cheese; cheese and substitutes for cheese containing, or processed from Edam and Gouda cheese; Swiss or Emmenthaler cheese with eye formation; Gruyere-process cheese, and cheese and substitutes for cheese containing, or processed from, such cheese; Edam and Gouda cheese; blue mold (except Stilton) cheese, and cheese and substitutes for cheese containing, or processed from, blue-mold cheese; Italian-type cheeses, made from cow's milk, in original loaves (Romano made from cow's milk, Reggiano, Parmesano, Provolone, Provoletti and Sbrinz); Italian-type cheese, not in original loaves; American-type cheese, including Colby, washed curd and granular cheese and cheese substitutes for cheese containing, or processed from such American-type cheese; cheese and substitutes for cheese; cheese and substitutes for cheese, containing 0.5% or less by weight of butterfat.

In addition, there are tariff-rate quotas on milk and cream, not concentrated nor containing added sugar or other sweetening matter, of a fat content that exceeds 1% but not 6%, as measured by weight.

Absolute Quotas. There are absolute quotas on the following products: milk and cream, condensed or evaporated; butter substitutes, containing more than 45% butterfat; animal feeds containing milk or milk derivatives; buttermix containing more than 5.5% but less than 45% butterfat by weight; chocolate crumb and other related articles containing more than 5.5% butterfat by weight; ice cream; certain cheddar cheese; fluid milk and sweet or sour cream of a fat content by weight exceeding 6% but not 45%.

Country-specific Quotas. The following country-specific quota amounts are found in HTSUS Chapter 99:

Whenever in any 12-month period beginning January 1 in any year, the respective aggregate quantity specified below for one of the numbered classes of articles has been entered, no article in such class may be entered during the remainder of such period.

9904.10.03 Milk and cream, fluid or frozen, fresh or sour, containing over 6% but not over 45% by weight of butterfat: New Zealand: 5,678,117 liters, Other: 0 liters.

9904.10.06 Milk and cream, condensed or evaporated, in airtight containers, classifiable for tariff purposes under subheadings 0402.91.20, 0402.91.40, 0402.99.20, and 0402.99.40: Netherlands: evaporated: 548,393 kg, condensed: 153,314 kg; Canada: evaporated: 31,751 kg, condensed: 994,274 kg; Denmark: 4,989 kg, condensed: 605,092 kg; Germany: evaporated 9,979 kg, condensed: 0 kg; Australia: evaporated: 0 kg, condensed: 91,625 kg; Other: evaporated: 0 kg; condensed: 3,628 kg; evaporated in other than airtight containers: Netherlands, Canada, Denmark, Germany, Australia, and Other: none; condensed in other than airtight containers: Canada 2,267kg; Netherlands, Denmark; Germany; Australia, and Others: 0 kg.

9904.10.09, 12, 15, and 18 Dried milk, dried cream, and dried whey provided for in HTSUS Chapter 4: described in subheadings 0402.10 and 0402.21.20: 819,641 kg; described in subheadings 0402.21.40 and 0403.90.50: 3,175 kg; described in subheadings 0402.21.60 and 0403.90.60: 226 kg; described in subheadings 0403.90.40 and 0404.10.40: 224,981 kg.

9904.10.21 Butter, and fresh or sour cream containing over 45% by weight of butterfat, provided for in HTSUS Chapter 4: 320,689 kg.

9904.10.24 Butter substitutes containing over 45% by weight of butterfat provided for in subheading 0405.00.80 or 2106.90.15, and butter oil however provided for in the tariff schedule: 544,310 kg.

Cheeses and substitutes for cheese provided for in HTSUS Chapter 4:

9904.10.27 Blue-mold cheese (except Stilton produced in the United Kingdom) and cheese and substitutes for cheese containing, or processed from, blue-mold cheese (provided for in subheading 0406.10, 0406.20.20, 0406.20.60, 0406.30.10, 0406.30.60, 0406.40.60, 0406.40.80, or 0406.90.80: European Economic Community: 2,479,000 kg; Argentina: 2,000 kg; Other: 1 kg.

9904.10.30 Cheddar cheese, and cheese and substitutes for cheese containing, or processed from, cheddar cheese provided for in subheading 0406.10, 0406.20.30, 0406.20.60, 0406.30.20, 0406.30.60, 0406.90.10, or 0406.90.80: European Economic Community: 263,000 kg; Australia: 1,200,000 kg; New Zealand: 3,100,000 kg; Canada: 833,417 kg; Other: 139,889 kg.

9904.10.33 American-type cheese, including Colby, washed curd and granular cheese (but not including Cheddar) and cheese and substitutes for cheese containing, or processed from, such American-type cheese (provided for in subheading 0406.10, 0406.20.35, 0406.20.60, 0406.30.30, 0406.30.60, 0406.90.65, or 0406.90.80: European Economic Community: 254,000 kg; Australia: 1,000,000 kg; New Zealand: 2,000,000 kg; Other: 168,556 kg.

9904.10.36 Edam and Gouda cheeses (provided for in subheading 0406.10, 0406.20.40, or 0406.90.15): European Economic Community: 4,011,000; Sweden: 41,000 kg; Argentina: 125,000 kg; Other: 1 kg.

9904.10.39 Cheese and substitutes for cheese containing, or processed from, Edam and Gouda cheese (provided for in subheading 0406.10, 0406.20.40, 0406.20.60, 0406.30.40, 0406.30.60, or 0406.90.80): European Economic Community: 1,237,000 kg; Norway: 167,000 kg; Other: 25,401 kg.

9904.10.42 Italian-type cheeses, made from cow's milk, in original loaves (Romano made from cow's milk, Reggiano, Parmesan, Provolone, Provoletti, and Sbrinz) (provided for in subheading 0406.10, 0406.90.35, or 0406.90.40): European Economic Community: 3,335,000 kg; Argentina: 3,850,000 kg; Uruguay: 428,000 kg; Other: 1 kg.

9904.10.45 Italian-type cheeses, made from cow's milk, not in original loaves (Romano made from cow's milk, Reggiano, Parmesan, Provolone, Provoletti, Sbrinz, and Goya) and cheese and substitutes for cheese containing, or processed from, such Italian-type cheeses, whether or not in original loaves (provided for in subheading 0406.10, 0406.20.50, 0406.20.60, 0406.30.60, 0406.90.30, 0406.90.35, 0406.90.40, 0406.90.70 or 0406.90.80): European Economic Community: 47,000 kg; Argentina: 643,000 kg; Other: 13,063 kg.

9904.10.48 Swiss or Emmenthaler cheese with eye formation (provided for in subheading 0406.90.45): European Economic Community: 6,000,000 kg; Austria: 6,280,000 kg; Finland: 8,200,000 kg; Norway: 6,883,000 kg; Switzerland: 3,430,000 kg; Israel: 27,000 kg; Australia: 500,000 kg; Canada: 70,000 kg; Iceland: 300,000 kg; Argentina: 80,000 kg; Other: 85,276 kg.

9904.10.51 Swiss or Emmenthaler cheese other than with eye formation, Gruyere-process cheese and cheese and substitutes for cheese containing, or processed from, such cheeses (provided for in subheading 0406.10, 0406.20.60, 0406.30.50, 0406.30.60, or 0406.90.80): European Economic Community: 3,625,000 kg; Austria: 920,000 kg; Finland: 1,000,000 kg; Switzerland: 1,850,000 kg; Other: 79,833 kg.

9904.10.54 Cheeses and substitutes for cheese provided for in subheading 0406.10, 0406.20.60, 0406.30.60, or 0406.90.80 (except cheese not containing cow's milk and soft ripened cow's milk cheese, cheese (except cottage cheese) containing 0.5% or less by weight of butterfat and articles within the scope of other import quotas provided for in HTSUS Chapter 99): European Economic Community: 20,456,000 kg of which 353,000 kg are reserved for Portugal; Finland: 1,300,000 kg; Iceland: 323,000 kg; Norway: 150,000 kg; Poland: 936,224 kg; Sweden: 1,059,000 kg; Switzerland: 1,220,000 kg; New Zealand: 11,322,000 kg; Canada: 1,141,000 kg; Austria: 650,000 kg; Israel: 673,000 kg, not more than 160,000 kg of which shall contain more than 3% by weight of butterfat; Argentina: 100,000 kg; Australia: 1,050,000 kg; Other: 201,635 kg.

9904.10.57 Cheese, and substitutes for cheese, containing 0.5% or less by weight of butterfat, provided for in subheading 0406.10, 0406.20.60, 0406.30.60, or 0406.90.80 (except articles within the scope of other import quotas provided for in HTSUS Chapter 99): European Economic Community 4,000,000 kg; Poland: 174,907 kg; Australia: 250,000 kg; New Zealand: 1,000,000 kg; Sweden: 250,000 kg; Israel: 50,000 kg; Other: 1 kg.

9904.10.60 Malted milk, and articles of milk or cream (except (a) yogurt that is not in dry form, (b) fermented milk other than dried fermented milk or other than dried milk with added lactic ferments, (c) mixtures of nonfat dry milk and anhydrous butterfat containing over 5.5% but not over 45% by weight of butterfat, and (d) ice cream), all the foregoing provided for in subheadings 0401.29, 0402.99.60, 0403.10.00, 0403.90.80, 0404.90.20, 1901.10.00, 1901.90.30, 2105.00.00 and 2202.90.20: 2,721 kg.

9904.10.72 Ice cream, as provided for in heading 2105.00: Belgium: 922,315 liters; New Zealand: 589,312 liters; Denmark: 13,059 liters; Netherlands: 104,477 liters; Jamaica: 3,596 liters; Other: 0 liters.

9904.10.75 Dried milk, whey, and buttermilk (described in subheading 0402.10, 0402.21.20, 0402.21.40, 0403.90.40 or 0404.10.40) which contains not over 5.5% by weight of butterfat and which is mixed with other ingredients, including but not limited to sugar, if such mixtures contain over 16% milk solids by weight, are capable of being further processed or mixed with similar or other ingredients and are not prepared for marketing to the retail consumers in the identical form and package in which imported; all the foregoing mixtures provided for in subheadings 0402.10, 0404.10.40, 0404.10.09, 0404.90.65, 1517.90.40, 1704.90.40, 1704.90.60, 1806.20.80, 1806.32.40, 1806.90, 1901.20, 1901.90.81, 1901.90.89, and 2106.90.05, except articles within the scope of other import restrictions provided for in HTSUS Chapter 94.

Articles containing over 5.5% by weight of butterfat, the butterfat of which is commercially extractable, or which are capable of being used for any edible purpose (except (a) articles provided for in headings 0401, 0402, 0405, or 0406 or subheadings 1901.10, 1901.90.31, or 1901.90.39 other than mixtures of nonfat dry milk and anhydrous butterfat containing not over 45% by weight of butterfat classifiable for tariff purposes under subheading 1901.90.31 or 1901.90.39; (b) dried mixtures containing less than 31% by weight of butterfat and consisting of not less than 17.5% by weight each of sodium caseinate, butterfat, whey solids containing over 5.5% by weight of butterfat, and dried whole milk, but not containing dried milk, dried whey, or dried buttermilk any of which contains 5.5% or less by weight of butterfat; and (c) articles that are not suitable for use as ingredients in a commercial production of edible articles):

9904.10.78 Over 45% by weight of butterfat: 0 kg.

9904.10.81 Over 5.5% but not over 45% by weight of butterfat including mixtures of nonfat dry milk and anhydrous butterfat classifiable for tariff purposes under subheading 1901.90.31 or 1901.90.39 and other articles classifiable for tariff purposes under subheading 0404.10.07, 0404.10.09, 0404.90.45, 0404.90.65, 1517.90.40, 1704.90.40, 1704.90.60, 1806.20.80, 1806.32.40, 1806.90, 1901.20, 1901.90.41, 1901.90.49, 1901.90.81, 1901.90.89, 2105.00, 2106.901.41, 2106.90.49, 2106.90.51, or 2106.90.59: Australia: 1,016,046 kg; Belgium and Denmark aggregate: 154,221 kg; Other: 0 kg.

For a general discussion of quotas see"Import Quotas" on page 230.

Country-Specific Import Restrictions

Countries Free of Rinderpest and Foot-and-mouth Disease. The following countries are listed by APHIS as free of rinderpest and foot-and-mouth disease, meaning that dairy products are eligible to be imported from them: Australia, the Bahamas, Barbados, Bermuda, Belize, Canada, Channel Islands, Denmark, Finland, Great Britain (England, Scotland, Wales, and Isle of Man), Greenland, Guatemala, Haiti, Honduras, Iceland, Ireland, Jamaica, Japan, Costa Rica, Dominican Republic, El Salvador,

Fiji, Mexico, New Zealand, Nicaragua, Northern Ireland, Norway, Panama, Panama Canal Zone, Papua New Guinea, Territory of St. Pierre and Miquelon, Sweden, Trinidad and Tobago, and Trust Territory of the Pacific Islands.

Countries Free of Viscerotropic Velogenic Newcastle Disease (VVND). The following countries are listed by APHIS as being free of viscerotropic velogenic Newcastle disease (VVND), meaning that egg products can be imported from them: Australia, Canada, Denmark, Fiji, Finland, Great Britain (England, Scotland, Wales, and the Isle of Man), Iceland, Ireland, New Zealand, Northern Ireland, Norway, and Sweden.

FSIS-certified Countries. The following are the countries that are currently FSIS-certified for exportation of poultry to the U.S.: Argentina, Australia, Belgium, Belize, Brazil, Canada, Costa Rica, the Czech Republic, Denmark, Dominican Republic, El Salvador, Finland, France, Guatemala, Honduras, Hong Kong, Hungary, Ireland, Israel, Italy, Mexico, Netherlands, New Zealand, Norway, Poland, Romania, the Slovak Republic, Sweden, Switzerland, United Kingdom, Uruguay, the republics of the former Yugoslavia. This list is subject to change. For the most up-to-date information, contact FSIS (see addresses at end of this chapter).

Countries Free of *Salmonella Enteritis*. The only country listed as free of *Salmonella enteritis* is Canada.

Marking and Labeling Requirements

Milk and cream. The Import Milk Act requires that a tag be firmly attached to each container of permit milk or cream imported into the U.S. This tag must show, in clear and legible type, the following information: the product (raw milk, pasteurized milk, raw cream, or pasteurized cream), the permit number, and the name and address of the shipper. For unit shipments consisting of milk only or cream only, under one permit number, each container need not be tagged if the vehicle of transportation is sealed, and tagged as described above. In that case the tag must show, in addition to the other required information, the number of containers and the contents of each. Customs officers will not permit the importation of any milk or cream that is not tagged in accordance with the regulations.

FSIS Requirements. The name of the country of origin of all poultry and egg products must appear on the label. However, only imported products that reach consumers without further processing retain such labeling. The Farm Bill Amendments also require foreign countries exporting products to the U.S. to impose controls equivalent to those of FSIS to prevent species substitution. Exporting countries must have effective testing programs for species verification and adequate security measures to prevent species substitution.

APHIS Requirements. Cases of eggs imported under certificate (see above) must be marked with the identity of the flock of origin and sealed with the seal of the national government of the country of origin.

For marking and labeling requirements common to all food importations, refer to the "Foods" appendix on page 808. For a general discussion of U.S. Customs marking and labeling requirements, see "Marking: Country of Origin" on page 215 and "Special Marking Requirements" on page 217.

Shipping Considerations

You will need to ensure that your goods are packaged and shipped with care so that they arrive in good condition and pass smoothly through Customs. You are responsible for ensuring that the shipment is in compliance with all applicable government regulations for packaging and shipping. In most instances, you should not leave these arrangements solely to the discretion of your supplier. Careful preparation of the cargo and selection of the mode of transport can be essential to a cost-effective, timely delivery of undamaged gods. We strongly advise you to consult your shipping representative, insurance agent, or freight broker for advice on packing and shipping. Refer also to the the major tab section "Packing/Shipping/Insurance" for a general discussion of packing and shipping.

Rapidity of transport and protection from contamination and spoilage are of critical importance when packing and shipping dairy products, many of which have a short shelf life.

Publications Available

The following publication explains the FDA requirements for importing dairy products. It is published by the FDA and is available on request from FDA headquarters (see addresses at end of this chapter).

Requirements of Laws and Regulations Enforced by the U.S. Food and Drug Administration

The following publication may be relevant to the importation of dairy products:

Foreign Countries and Plants Certified to Export Meat and Poultry to the United States

This is a comprehensive listing of export-certified countries and plants, including previously certified plants that have been decertified. It is available from the FSIS (see addresses at end of this chapter).

The following publication gives brief, general guidelines on USDA regulated products. Although designed primarily for tourists, it contains a list of approved products that you may find helpful. It is published by USDA APHIS (see addresses at end of this chapter).

Travelers Tips On Bringing Food, Plant, and Animal Products into the United States

The *Harmonized Tariff Schedule of the United States* (HTSUS) is available from:

Government Printing Office (GPO)
Superintendent of Documents
Washington, DC 20402
(202) 512-1800 (Order line)
(202) 512-0000 (General)

The USGPO also has copies of specific laws available for purchase. The USGPO accepts credit card orders over the phone, as well as mail orders paid by credit card, a check drawn on a U.S. bank, or an international money order.

Relevant Government Agencies

Address your questions regarding FDA requirements for importation of dairy products to:

Food and Drug Administration (FDA)
Center for Food Safety and Applied Nutrition
200 C Street SW
Washington, DC 20204
(202) 205-5241, 205-5042

Food and Drug Administration (FDA)
Division of Enforcement, Imports Branch
200 C Street SW
Washington, DC 20204
(202) 205-4726

Address your questions regarding APHIS requirements and requests for APHIS import permit applications to:

U.S. Department of Agriculture (USDA)
Animal and Plant Health Inspection Service (APHIS)
Veterinary Services (VS)
Import-Export Products Staff
Federal Building, Room 756
6505 Belcrest Road
Hyattsville, MD 20782
(301) 436-7885

Address your questions regarding FSIS port of entry inspection or pre-import certification of poultry and poultry products and establishments to:

U.S. Department of Agriculture (USDA)
Food Safety and Inspection Service (FSIS)
Import Inspection Service (FSIS)
Rm. 3715, Franklin Ct.
Suite 3700-W
Washington, DC 20250-3700
(202) 501-7515

Address your questions regarding safe pesticide residue tolerances to:

Environmental Protection Agency (EPA)
Office of Pesticide Programs
401 M Street SW (7501-C)
Washington, DC 20460
(703) 305-7090 (General)
(703) 305-7102 (Import/export requirements)

Address your questions regarding dairy quotas to:

U.S. Customs Service
Quota Branch
1301 Constitution Avenue NW, Rm. 2379-ICC
Washington, DC 20229
(202) 927-5850

Agricultural Marketing Service
Dairy Division
P.O. Box 96456
Washington, DC 20090-6456
(202) 720-4392

Address your general questions regarding importation of dairy products to the district or port director of Customs for you area. For addresses refer to"U.S. Customs District Offices" on page 62 or contact:

U.S. Customs Service
1301 Constitution Ave. NW
Washington, DC 20229
(202) 927-6724 (Information)
(202) 927-1000 (General)

Laws and Regulations

The following laws and regulations may be relevant to the importation of dairy products. The laws are contained in the U.S. Code (USC) and the regulations are published in the Code of Federal Regulations (CFR), both of which may be available at larger public and law libraries. Copies of specific laws are also available from the United States Government Printing Office (address above).

21 USC 301 et seq.
Food, Drug, and Cosmetic Act
This Act prohibits deceptive practices and regulates the manufacture, sale and importation or exportation of food, drugs, cosmetics, and related products. See 21 USC 331, 381, 382.

19 CFR 12.1 et seq.; 21 CFR 1.83 et seq.
Regulations on Food, Drugs, and Cosmetics
These regulations of the Secretary of Health and Human Services and the Secretary of the Treasury govern the standards, labeling, marking, bonding, and importing of products used with food, drugs, and cosmetics.

21 USC 141 et seq.
Import Milk Act
This Act sets purity, sanitary, inspection, and permit requirements on milk imported into the U.S.

7 USC 601 et seq.
Agricultural Adjustment Act (AAA)
This Act authorizes the Secretary of Agriculture to establish and maintain orderly market conditions for agricultural products, including cotton.

19 CFR Part 132
Regulations for Enforcement of AAA Quotas
These regulations provide for Customs enforcement of AAA quotas and higher duty rates imposed on imported agricultural products, whenever investigation reveals that orderly market conditions require such action.

9 CFR Part 94
Regulations on Country-Specific Import Restrictions
These regulations prescribe health inspection requirements and procedures in order to prevent the introduction of livestock diseases into the U.S.

9 CFR 95.13 et seq.
Regulations on Animal Byproduct Quarantine Control
These regulations prohibit the importation of animal products for use in industry unless the products meet certain processing standards and are not infected with certain diseases.

21 USC 1031 et seq.
Egg Product Inspection Act
This Act requires the inspection of edible and nonconsumable egg products, including imports, and sets labeling and processing standards.

7 CFR 59.900 et seq.
Regulations of USDA on Importing Eggs
These regulations govern the inspection, import, transport, labeling, and processing of consumable and nonconsumable eggs and egg products.

7 CFR 56.1
Regulations for U.S. Egg Shell Standards
These regulations control the processing of domestic or imported eggs and egg products to ensure that they meet certain standards for sale to consumers.

Principal Exporting Countries

The following listing includes samples of the main supplier nations of the products of this chapter. It is organized by HTSUS major heading. (Refer to "Customs Classification" above for the product codes.) Countries are listed in rank order of the value of products imported to the U.S. Statistics represent customs value entries for 1993 from the Bureau of Census, U.S. Department of Commerce.

0401—New Zealand, United Kingdom, Denmark, Colombia, Germany, Canada, Venezuela

0402—Canada, United Kingdom, Poland, New Zealand, Netherlands, Australia, Mexico, Switzerland, Denmark, Germany

0403—Canada, New Zealand, Lebanon

0404—Sweden, Germany, Netherlands, Canada, Poland, Australia, Austria, New Zealand, France, Norway

0405—New Zealand, Canada, Denmark, Ireland, France, United Kingdom, Germany, Israel, Australia, Portugal

0406—Italy, France, Denmark, New Zealand, Netherlands, Norway, United Kingdom, Switzerland, Austria, Finland

0407—Canada, Namibia, United Kingdom, Israel, China, Botswana, Taiwan, South Africa, Netherlands, Portugal

0408—Canada, Thailand, China, Japan, Taiwan, France, Malaysia, Sweden, Hong Kong, Singapore

0409—China, Argentina, Canada, Mexico, Australia, Germany, Dominican Rep., New Zealand, Hong Kong, Switzerland

0410—China, Hong Kong, New Zealand, Germany, Indonesia, Taiwan, United Kingdom, Japan, Canada, Spain

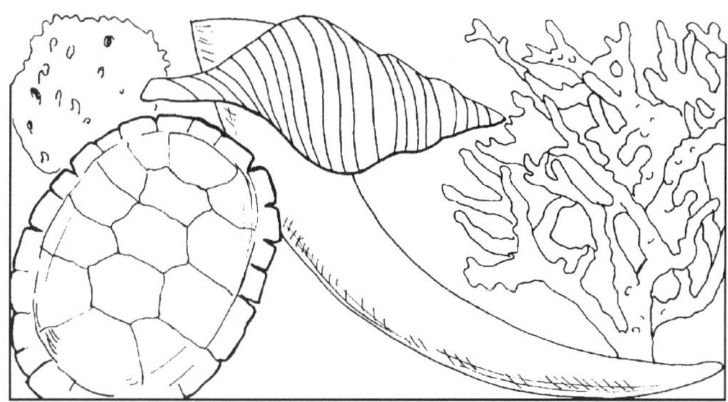

Chapter 5: Other Animal Products*

Full title: Products of Animal Origin, Not Elsewhere Specified or Included

This chapter relates to the importation of miscellaneous animal products not included elsewhere, which are classified under Chapter 5 of the Harmonized Tariff Schedule of the United States (HTSUS). Specifically, it includes human hair, horsehair, boar bristles, and other animal hair; birdskins with attached feathers, feathers and down (for stuffing), and feather meal; bone, horn, ivory, and tortoise-shell; coral and marine shell; natural sponges; guts, bladders, and stomachs; glands, organs, and animal secretions; dead animals not fit for human consumption; and miscellaneous animal products not otherwise classified.

Edible animal products are not covered within Commodity Index Chapter 5; if you are interested in importing edible animal products, refer to Chapter 2 for meat and meat products, Chapter 3 for fish and seafood products, and Chapter 16 for prepared animal food products. Live animal imports are covered in Chapter 1. Imports of hides, skins, furskins, and leather are covered in Chapters 41 through 43 (however, hide wastes are included in Chapter 5). Textile products made of animal hair are covered in Chapter 51, and intermediate products of animal bristles are found in Chapter 96. Although most imports of animal glands and substances for pharmaceutical manufacture are covered in Chapter 5, some imports of animal blood are reserved for Chapter 30—Pharmaceutical Products. If you are interested in importing prepared down or feathers, refer to Chapter 67; if you are interested in importing feather—or down—filled articles or apparel, refer to Chapter 62. Although Chapter 5 includes some raw and intermediate products used as animal feed and in the manufacture of animal feed, those interested in importing animal feeds as such should refer to Chapter 23.

Key Factors

The key factors in the importation of animal products of HTSUS Chapter 5 are:

- Compliance with U.S. Food and Drug Administration (FDA) purity, identity, manufacturing, and other standards
- Compliance with FDA notification and entry procedures
- Compliance with U.S. Department of Agriculture (USDA) and U.S. Fish and Wildlife Service (FWS) import regulations
- Feathers derived from wild migratory birds are subject to FWS restrictions and permit requirements; certain feathers are subject to quota restriction, FWS licenses and permits required; entry at FWS-designated ports for wildlife feathers; endangered species regulations may apply to certain feathers
- For raw down, down-feather ratio rating certification; if raw down is not derived from domesticated birds, compliance with any relevant wildlife and endangered species restrictions

Although most importers utilize the services of a licensed customs broker in making their entries, and we recommend this practice, you should be aware of the regulatory, entry, and documentation issues involved in importing your product. You, as importer, are ultimately responsible for the fulfillment of any legal requirements applicable to your shipment.

General Considerations

Regulatory Agencies. The FDA enforces the requirements of the Federal Food, Drug, and Cosmetic Act (FDCA), which governs all imports of goods intended for use as or in the manufacture of food, drugs, or cosmetics. The USDA regulates and inspects animal and animal—derived products presented for entry into the U.S. The Animal and Plant Health Inspection Service (APHIS) of the USDA is generally responsible for passing products derived from domesticated animals. The FWS controls the importation of products of animals classified as exotic wildlife or endangered species. U.S. Customs enforces USDA, FDA, and FWS requirements through entry documentation and restrictions. Because of the wide range of products covered within HTSUS Chapter 5 and the potentially complex regulations and overlapping jurisdictions covering them, you should contact these agencies to verify the specific requirements for your product. The following discussion covers only some of the major points involved in importing some of the prominent miscellaneous animal products of Chapter 5.

Feathers. Importation of certain feathers is highly restricted. Feathers taken from domesticated birds are not subject to FWS regulation and may be entered without authorization. The skins and feathers of certain game birds are subject to quota restrictions (see below), for which permits are required. Feathers or skins of the following species are permitted entry: chickens, turkeys, guinea fowl, geese, ducks, pigeons, ostriches, rheas, English ring-necked pheasants, and pea fowl not taken from the wild. Other feathers are usually prohibited. However, you may bring in fully manufactured fishing flies and personally taken, noncommercial game birds.

Feathers of certain species of birds as well as other animal products are restricted or prohibited importation because of status under the Endangered Species Act (ESA), or the Convention on International Trade in Endangered Species of Wild Fauna and Flora (CITES). If you are unsure whether the products you wish to import are derived from listed species, contact FWS with detailed species information.

If you are interested in importing feathers, you should become familiar with 50 CFR Parts 10, 13, 14, 15, and 21. Contact the regional FWS office nearest your intended port of entry for clarification of regulations, instructions, and import authorizations required.

Wildlife Products. Certain animal raw materials and products made of them, including ivory, coral, and sea turtle products, are banned from import into the U.S. under most circumstances. Many foreign countries have also established strict permit requirements for the export of such materials and articles. Most af-

*IMPORTANT: Read the Commodity Index Introduction. It is the essential framework for understanding this section.

fected African countries have prohibited the export of elephant ivory, and many countries in the Pacific, Southeast Asia, and the Caribbean have banned the harvest and export of coral, making the import of such items into the U.S.—which requires compliance with country of origin export permits and documentation when applicable—even more difficult and problematical.

If you are importing wildlife products, you must enter them only at FWS-designated U.S. ports of entry (see Designated Ports below). You must present a FWS Wildlife Import Declaration **Form 3-177** to the FWS agent at the U.S. port of entry for each shipment. The FWS conducts port of entry inspections on a case-by-case basis, as determined by the inspection agent after examining the entry paperwork. Your shipment will not be released from Customs custody until your FWS import declaration has been signed off by an FWS agent.

Down. Importation of raw down is also regulated by FWS. The exporter is required to test the down for percentage of feathers to down, with the down being given a rating based on that percentage. A certification of rating must accompany all import shipments of raw down. If your raw down is derived from domesticated raised birds, you need only fulfill normal customs entry requirements. However, the entry of down from wild migratory game birds is highly restricted and subject to FWS permit procedures under the Migratory Bird Treaty Act. If you are considering importing such products, you should contact the regional office of FWS closest to the intended port of entry for authorization. Do not attempt to import such products without FWS authorization.

Customs Classification

For customs purposes, miscellaneous animal products not elsewhere specified are classified under Chapter 5 of the HTSUS. This chapter is divided into major headings, which are further divided into subheadings, and often into sub-subheadings, each of which has its own HTSUS classification number. For example, the HTSUS number for other feathers is 0505.90.00, indicating that it is a subcategory of the major heading of skins and other parts of birds with their feathers or down, feathers and parts of feathers, not further worked; powder and waste of feathers or parts of feathers (0505.00.00). There are 11 major headings in HTSUS Chapter 5.

0501—Human hair, unworked, whether or not washed or scoured; waste of human hair

0502—Pigs', hogs', or boars' bristles and hair; badger hair and other brushmaking hair; waste of such bristles or hair

0503—Horsehair or horsehair waste, whether or not put up as a layer with or without supporting material

0504—Guts, bladders, and stomach of animals (other than fish), whole and pieces thereof

0505—Skins and other parts of birds, with their feathers or down, feathers and parts of feathers (whether or not with trimmed edges) and down, not further worked than cleaned, disinfected, or treated for preservation; powder and waste of feathers or parts of feathers; powder and waste of feathers or parts of feathers

0506—Bones and horn-cores, unworked, defatted, simply prepared (but not cut into shape), treated with acid or degeletanized; powder and waste of these products

0507—Ivory, tortoise-shell, whalebone, and whalebone hair, horns, antlers, hooves, nails, claws, and beaks, unworked or simply prepared but not cut to shape; powder and waste of these products

0508—Coral and similar materials, unworked or simply prepared but not otherwise worked; shells of molluscs, crustaceans, or echinoderms and cuttlebone, unworked or simply prepared but not cut to shape, powder and waste thereof

0509—Natural sponges of animal origin

0510—Ambergris, castoreum, civet, and musk; cantharides; bile, whether or not dried; glands and other animal products used in the preparation of pharmaceutical products, fresh, chilled, frozen, or otherwise provisionally preserved

0511—Animal products not elsewhere specified or included; dead animals of chapter 1 or 3, unfit for human consumption

For more details regarding classification of the specific product you are interested in importing, consult a customs broker, the appropriate commodity specialist at your nearest Customs port, or see HTSUS. HTSUS is available for purchase from the U.S. Government Printing Office (see addresses at end of this chapter), and may be found in larger public libraries. Refer to "Classification—Liquidation" on page 207 for a general discussion of customs classification.

Sample Import Duties

Import duties will vary depending on the HTSUS classification of your product. Therefore, to determine the correct amount of duties, you must classify your product under the HTSUS. The following sample duties are taken from the duty listings for HTSUS Chapter 2 products.

Unworked human hair (0501.00.00): 3.1%; pigs', hogs', or boar bristles, or waste thereof (0502.10.00): 1.7 cents/kg; horsehair and horsehair waste (0503.00.00): free; guts, bladders, and stomachs prepared as sausage casings (0504.00.00): free; feathers or down of a kind used for stuffing (0505.10.00): 7.5%; other feathers, such as feather meal (0505.90.00): 5% [note that products of 0505.10.00 and 0505.90.00 were entered duty free prior to December 31, 1992, when the present tariffs were instituted]; bones, crude, steamed, or ground (0506.90.00): free; ivory; ivory powder or waste (0507.00.00): free; unworked coral or shell (0508.00.00): free; natural sponges (0509.00.00): 3%; ambergris, castoreum, civet, and musk (0510.00.20): 8%; animal secretions, glands, and organs used in pharmaceutical preparation (0510.00.40): free; dead aquatic animals of chapter 3 unfit for human consumption (0511.91.00): free; parings and similar waste of raw hides or skins and glue stock not elsewhere specified or included (0511.9.20): free; other animal products, such as diary cattle embryos and dried animal blood (0511.99.40): 2.5%.

Entry and Documentation

The entry of merchandise is a two-part process consisting of 1) filing the documents necessary to determine whether merchandise may be released from Customs custody and 2) filing the documents that contain information for duty assessment and statistical purposes. In certain instances all documents must be filed and accepted by Customs prior to release of the goods. Unless you have been granted an extension, you must file entry documents at a location specified by the district or area director within five working days of your shipment's date of arrival at a U.S. port of entry. These include a number of standard documents required by Customs for any entry, and:

- FDA Importer's Entry Notice **Form FD701** for food, drug, and cosmetic-related products
- FWS Wildlife Declaration **Form 3-177** for feathers derived from wild birds
- FWS Permit when required
- If raw down: exporter's down-feather ratio rating certification of exporter
- If down is derived from wild migratory birds or other protected species, FWS authorization and any documentation required under relevant endangered species legislation

After you present the entry, Customs may examine your shipment, or may waive examination. The shipment is then released provided no legal or regulatory violations have been noted. You must then file entry summary documentation and deposit estimated duties at a designated customhouse within 10 working days of your shipment's release. For a detailed description of entry procedures, standard documentation, and informal entry, see "Entry Process" on page 182.

Prohibitions and Restrictions

Skins and feathers taken from wild migratory game birds listed in the Migratory Bird Treaty Act (16 USC 703) cannot be imported for commercial purposes. Plumage may be imported for scientific or educational purposes, as may fully manufactured artificial flies used for fishing made of such plumage. Plumage on game birds killed in foreign countries by hunters who are U.S. residents may also be imported as long as the plumage is not imported for sale or other commercial purposes.

Designated Ports. All wildlife shipments must enter and leave the U.S. through FWS designated ports, as listed in 50 CFR 14.12. Currently there are ten designated ports: New York, NY; Miami, FL; New Orleans, LA; Dallas/Ft. Worth, TX; Los Angeles, CA; San Francisco, CA; Chicago, IL; Seattle, WA; Honolulu, HI; and Portland, OR. If special circumstances preclude making entry at a designated port, an Exception to Designated Port Permit is required from FWS (see addresses at end of this chapter).

Quotas. Feathers of certain birds may be imported for use in the manufacture of artificial flies used for fishing, or for millinery purposes. These imports are restricted by annual quota allotments. You must have a permit and quota allotment issued by the FWS in order to import feathers subject to such quotas. Quota feathers are as follows: Mandarin ducks for use in manufacture of artificial flies used for fishing: 1,000 skins; Lady Amherst Pheasant, Golden Pheasant, Silver Pheasant, Reeves Pheasant, Blue-eared Pheasant, for use in manufacturing of artificial flies used for fishing, or for use in millinery products: aggregate 45,000. Quotas for these products can be reduced or eliminated at the discretion of the U.S. Secretary of the Interior upon a finding of serious reduction in the wild of the affected species.

Permit Application. If you wish to import quota feathers, you must submit your application for feather quota allocations and permits to FWS on the standard Federal Fish and Wildlife License/Permit Application **Form 3-200.** The annual quota period begins on January 1 of each year, and runs through December 31. Your application for initial allocations must reach FWS between September 1 and September 30 of the calendar year preceding the quota year for which you are requesting allotment. Any portions of established annual quotas not used by July 1 become available for reallocation. Applications for reallocations must be received by FWS between July 1 and July 31 of the current quota year.

Permit/quota allocation requests must include not only the standard information required for any permit, but also 1) species quantity; 2) port of entry, or port of entry and amount in storage (see exceptions, below); 3) statement of intended use; 4) nature of request, i.e. initial allocation or reallocation. After making the initial allocations, the FWS will furnish you with a tabulation of quantities of each species you requested, plus quantities FWS proposes to allocate to you. You must then report your acceptance, by a letter addressed to the FWS Director and postmarked not later than 30 days after the date you receive your notice. Your letter must contain satisfactory proof (e.g. a copy of a currently confirmed order) that you have already placed your feather orders. FWS will interpret your failure to respond as withdrawal of your application. You should respond by certified mail.

Permits. Permits for feather quota imports are issued in two segments. Permits authorizing calendar year initial allocations are issued as of January 1 of that quota year, and remain in effect through June 30 of the year of issue. You must import all feathers and/or skins authorized under this permit no later than June 30. Once your initial permit has expired, any portion of your allotment that you have not used will be subject to reallocation. No exceptions or extensions are granted. Permits authorizing reallocations are issued as promptly as possible after July 31 of the current quota year, and remain in effect through December 31. Once your reallocation permit expires, any unused portion of the quota is forfeited. Again, no exceptions or extensions are granted.

Exceptions to Requirements. There are certain exceptions to the permit requirements for quota feathers. However, even when a permit is not necessary, you must still file an FWS Wildlife Declaration at the port of entry. Permit exceptions are as follows: 1) you may import quota skins/feathers for storage in a warehouse under customs bond without permit. (This exception only applies to birds that are subject to quota. In such cases you must obtain a valid FWS permit before you remove the articles from the warehouse for use in the U.S.); 2) articles imported for scientific or educational purposes; 3) fully manufactured artificial flies for fishing; 4) game birds killed by U.S. hunters abroad and imported by such person for noncommercial purposes; 5) live birds (there are other stringent FWS requirements for live birds—refer to HTSUS Chapter 1); 6) import of any of the following birds, whether or not such bird was raised in captivity: chickens (including hens and roosters), turkeys, guinea fowl, geese, ducks, pigeons, ostriches, rheas, English ring-necked pheasants, and pea fowl.

Marking and Labeling Requirements

Marking and labeling requirements will vary depending upon the nature of your product. All wildlife shipments must be marked on the outside of the container with the names and addresses of the exporter and importer, an accurate identification of the species, and the numbers of each species in the container.

For a general discussion of U.S. Customs marking and labeling requirements, see "Marking: Country of Origin" on page 215 and "Special Marking Requirements" on page 217.

Shipping Considerations

You will need to ensure that your goods are packaged and shipped with care so that they arrive in good condition and pass smoothly through Customs. You are responsible for ensuring that the shipment is in compliance with all applicable government regulations for packaging and shipping. In most instances, you should not leave these arrangements solely to the discretion of your supplier. Careful preparation of the cargo and selection of the mode of transport can be essential to a cost-effective, timely delivery of undamaged goods. We strongly advise you to consult your shipping representative, insurance agent, or freight broker for advice on packing and shipping. Refer also to the major tab section "Packing/Shipping/Insurance" for a general discussion of packing and shipping.

Many of the products covered in HTSUS Chapter 5 must be packed so as to prevent contamination or decomposition. Some—such as shells—may require careful packing to avoid breakage.

Publications Available

The following publication explains the FDA requirements for importing miscellaneous animal products. It is published by the FDA and is available on request from FDA headquarters (see addresses at end of this chapter).

Requirements of Laws and Regulations Enforced by the U.S. Food and Drug Administration

The following publication gives brief, general guidelines on USDA regulated products. Although designed primarily for tourists, it contains a list of approved products that you may find helpful. It is published by USDA APHIS (see addresses at end of this chapter).

Travelers Tips On Bringing Food, Plant, and Animal Products into the United States

Buyer Beware is a pamphlet published by the World Wildlife Fund. The pamphlet discusses the products that may not be imported into the U.S. because of endangered species considerations. To order *Buyer Beware*, or to request a catalog of related publications, contact:

World Wildlife Fund
1250 24th Street NW
Washington, DC 20037
(202) 293-4800

The *Harmonized Tariff Schedule of the United States* (HTSUS) is available from:

Government Printing Office (GPO)
Superintendent of Documents
Washington, DC 20402
(202) 512-1800 (Order line)
(202) 512-0000 (General)

The USGPO also has copies of specific laws available for purchase. The USGPO accepts credit card orders over the phone, as well as mail orders paid by credit card, a check drawn on a U.S. bank, or an international money order.

Relevant Government Agencies

Address your questions regarding FDA requirements for the importation of miscellaneous animal products covered in HTSUS Chapter 5 to:

Food and Drug Administration (FDA)
Center for Food Safety and Applied Nutrition
200 C Street SW
Washington, DC 20204
(202) 205-5241, 205-5042

Food and Drug Administration (FDA)
Division of Enforcement, Imports Branch
200 C Street SW
Washington, DC 20204
(202) 205-4726

Address your questions regarding the importation of miscellaneous animal products of domesticated species to:

U.S. Department of Agriculture (USDA)
Animal and Plant Health Inspection Service (APHIS)
6505 Belcrest Road
Hyattsville, MD 20782
(301) 436-8645

Address your questions regarding the importation of raw feathers and down of wild animals and products of endangered or threatened species to:

U.S. Fish and Wildlife Service (FWS)
Office of Management Authority
4401 N. Fairfax Drive, Room 432
Arlington, VA 22203
(703) 358-2095
(800) 358-2104, (703) 358-2104 (Permits office)

Send your applications for quota feather allotments and permits to:

U.S. Fish and Wildlife Service (FWS)
Federal Wildlife Permit Office
P.O. Box 3654
Arlington VA 22203

Address your questions regarding importation of miscellaneous animal products of Chapter 5 to the district or port director of Customs for you area. For addresses refer to"U.S. Customs District Offices" on page 62 or contact:

U.S. Customs Service
1301 Constitution Ave. NW
Washington, DC 20229
(202) 927-6724 (Information)
(202) 927-1000 (General)

Laws and Regulations

The following laws and regulations may be relevant to the importation of miscellaneous animal products of Chapter 5. The laws are contained in the U.S. Code (USC) and the regulations are published in the Code of Federal Regulations (CFR), both of which may be available at larger public and law libraries. Copies of specific laws are also available from the United States Government Printing Office (address above).

21 USC 301 et seq.
Food, Drug, and Cosmetic Act (FDCA)
This Act prohibits deceptive practices and regulates the manufacture, sale and importation or exportation of food, drugs, cosmetics, and related products. See 21 USC 331, 381, 382.

19 CFR 12.1 et seq.; 21 CFR 1.83 et seq.
Regulations on Food, Drugs, and Cosmetics
These regulations of the Secretary of Health and Human Services and the Secretary of the Treasury govern the standards, labeling, marking, bonding, and importing of products used with food, drugs, and cosmetics.

Convention on International Trade in Endangered Species of Wild Fauna and Flora (CITES)
This comprehensive wildlife treaty signed by over 100 countries, including the United States, regulates and in many cases prohibits commercial imports and exports of wild animal and plant species threatened by trade.

16 USC 1531
Endangered Species Act
This Act prohibits the import and export of species listed as endangered and most species listed as threatened. It is the U.S. law that implements CITES.

16 USC 742a et seq.
Fish and Wildlife Act
This Act regulates and bars the import of certain wild animals or birds and authorizes U.S. Customs to enforce the restrictions.

16 USC 2401
Antarctic Conservation Act
This Act prohibits the importation, absent a special permit, of any flora or fauna native to Antarctica into the U.S.

16 USC 3371 et seq.
Lacey Act
This Act prohibits the import of species taken, possessed, transported, or sold in violation of the law of a foreign country.

16 USC 1361 et seq.
The Marine Mammal Protection Act
This Act prohibits the import of marine mammals and their parts and products. These species include whales, walruses, narwhals, seals, sea lions, sea otters, and polar bears.

16 USC 4201
The African Elephant Conservation Act
This Act prohibits imports of carved ivory products from any country and only permits imports of whole tusks from elephants legally hunted in certain African countries.

16 USC 703
The Migratory Bird Treaty Act

This Act protects designated wild migratory game birds and prohibits importation of them for commercial purposes.

18 USC 42 et seq.
Importation of Animals, Birds, Fish, and Plants
This Act governs the importation of mammals, birds, fish, amphibia, and reptiles into the U.S. and authorizes U.S. Customs to enforce the import requirements.

50 CFR Parts 10, 13, and 16
Regulations of FWS for Importing Wildlife and Fish
These regulations specify the animals and animal products subject to import prohibitions and restrictions.

19 CFR 12.26 et seq.
Regulations of Customs on Importing Wild Animals
These regulations list the wild animals that are prohibited from importation or that require import permits.

Principal Exporting Countries

The following listing includes samples of the main supplier nations of the products of this chapter. It is organized by HTSUS major heading. (Refer to "Customs Classification" above for the product codes.) Countries are listed in rank order of the value of products imported to the U.S. Statistics represent customs value entries for 1993 from the Bureau of Census, U.S. Department of Commerce.

0501—China, Italy, Switzerland, India, Hong Kong, Indonesia, Turkey, Spain, Bangladesh

0502—China, Germany, United Kingdom, Mexico, Argentina, South Korea, Japan, Uruguay, Taiwan, Australia

0503—China, Mexico, Uruguay, Germany, Hong Kong, Brazil, Argentina, Japan, South Korea, Canada

0504—New Zealand, Mexico, China, Denmark, Germany, Australia, Netherlands, Canada, Brazil, Sweden

0505—China, Taiwan, France, Hong Kong, Hungary, Germany, South Africa, Canada, Poland, United Kingdom

0506—Costa Rica, Australia, Canada, United Kingdom, New Zealand, Brazil, Russia, Belgium, Japan, Chile

0507—Russia, New Zealand, Brazil, Germany, Canada, Argentina, Mexico, Australia, Nigeria, South Korea

0508—Philippines, Indonesia, Mexico, Marshall Islands, Chile, Japan, Thailand, India, Taiwan, France

0509—Bahamas, Japan, France, Greece, Canada, Italy, China, Taiwan, Philippines, United Kingdom

0510—Canada, Brazil, Denmark, New Zealand, Argentina, Germany, Australia, France, Guatemala, Hungary

0511—Thailand, Canada, Colombia, New Zealand, South Korea, Australia, Mexico, Ecuador, Brazil, Japan

Chapter 6: Live Plants*

Full title: Live Trees and Other Plants; Bulbs, Roots, and the Like; Cut Flowers and Ornamental Foliage

This chapter relates to the importation of live plants, bulbs and roots, and cut flowers and ornamental foliage, which are classified under Chapter 6 of the Harmonized Tariff Schedule of the United States (HTSUS). Specifically, it includes most live plants and plant parts designed for propagation—including live seedlings, bulbs, rhizomes, germ, shoots, and other similar products—and specimens plants and related items, as well as cut flowers and other plant parts intended for decorative uses, including finished floral arrangements.

If you are interested in importing sets or seedlings of edible plants such as onions, garlic, or shallots, you should refer to Commodity Index Chapter 7. Seeds of most agricultural products are covered under Chapter 12, while those of cereal grains are included in Chapter 10. Although baskets and other containers and materials incidental to decorative arrangements of plant materials are included in Chapter 6, those interested in importing baskets for such arrangements or for other uses should refer to Chapter 46. Some collages and decorative plaques incorporating plant materials may be classified as works of art in Chapter 97.

Key Factors

The key factors in the importation of live plants, roots, and cut flowers are:

- Compliance with U.S. Department of Agriculture (USDA) restrictions and requirements (permits may be required)
- Compliance with any restrictions under endangered species legislation

Although most importers utilize the services of a licensed customs broker in making their entries, and we recommend this practice, you should be aware of the regulatory, entry, and documentation issues involved in importing your product. You, as importer, are ultimately responsible for the fulfillment of any legal requirements applicable to your shipment.

General Considerations

Regulatory Agencies. Importation of live plants, roots, and cut flowers is regulated by the USDA Animal and Plant Health In-

*IMPORTANT: Read the Commodity Index Introduction. It is the essential framework for understanding this section.

spection Service (APHIS) Plant Protection and Quarantine (PPQ) branch, primarily under provisions of the Plant Quarantine Act (PQA).

Flowers. The entry of cut flowers from all foreign countries except Canada is regulated under 7 CFR 319.74. No restrictions are imposed on cut flowers of Canadian origin, although these imports must be accompanied by a phytosanitary document stating that they originated in Canada. PPQ import permits are required for certain flowers (see Prohibitions and Restrictions below). You must submit duplicate copies of a PPQ Notice of Arrival to Customs at the U.S. port of entry for each commercial shipment of cut flowers entering under permit. When small quantities of flowers normally requiring formal permit are offered for entry without such permit, the APHIS port inspector may give oral entry authorization.

All admissible cut flowers, whether entering under permit or not, are subject to inspection at the first U.S. port of entry. If pests of quarantine significance are found in your shipment, the APHIS inspector will prescribe treatment in accordance with administratively authorized procedures known to be effective under similar conditions. Required treatments are at the importer's risk and expense and must be performed under the supervision of an APHIS inspector. If your products are found upon inspection to be infested with injurious insects, or infected with plant diseases that cannot be eliminated by treatment, they will be denied entry. In such cases, you have the option of abandoning the rejected shipment for destruction, or immediately shipping it to a point outside the U.S.

Certain flowers from specific countries are subject to antidumping actions and countervailing duties. These items are entered at additional rates of duty. For a general discussion of these extra duties, read "Antidumping and Countervailing Duties" on page 205.

Customs Classification

For customs purposes, live plants, roots, and cut flowers are classified under Chapter 6 of the HTSUS. This chapter is broken down into major headings, which are further divided into subheadings, and often sub-subheadings, each with its own HTSUS classification number. For example, the HTSUS number for Narcissus bulbs is 0601.10.60, indicating that it is a subcategory of bulbs, tubers, tuberous roots, corms, crowns, and rhizomes, dormant (0601.10.00), which is a subcategory of the major heading, bulbs, tubers, tuberous roots, corms, crowns, and rhizomes, dormant, in growth, or in flower (0601.00.00). There are four major headings within Chapter 6:

0601—Bulbs, tubers, tuberous roots, corms, crowns, and rhizomes, dormant, in growth, or in flower; chickory plants and roots other than roots of heading 1212

0602—Other live plants (including their roots), cuttings, and slips; mushroom spawn

0603—Cut flowers and flower buds of a kind suitable for bouquets or for ornamental purposes, fresh, dried, dyed, bleached, impregnated, or otherwise prepared

0604—Foliage, branches, and other parts of plants, without flowers or flower buds, and grasses, mosses, and lichens, being goods of a kind suitable for bouquets or for ornamental purposes, fresh, dried, dyed, bleached, impregnated, or otherwise prepared

For more details regarding classification of the specific product you are interested in importing, consult a customs broker, the appropriate commodity specialist at your nearest customs port, or see HTSUS. HTSUS is available for purchase from the U.S. Government Printing Office (see addresses at end of this chapter), and may be found in larger public libraries. Refer to "Classification—Liquidation" on page 207 for a general discussion of customs classification.

Sample Import Duties

Import duties will vary depending on the HTSUS classification of your product. Therefore, to determine the correct amount of duties, your product must be properly classified under the HTSUS. The following sample duties are taken from the duty listings for HTSUS Chapter 6 products.

Tulip bulbs (0601.10.15): $1.40/thousand; Iris bulbs (0601.10.90): 5.5%; trees, shrubs, and bushes, grafted or not (0602.20.00): free; roses, grafted or not (0602,40.00): free; chrysanthemums with soil attached to the roots (0602.99.30): 1.7% through December 31, 1994, 2.2% thereafter; poinsettias with soil attached to the roots (0602.99.60): 2.3% through December 31, 1994, 7.5% thereafter; miniature carnations (0603.10.30): 4%; roses (0603.10.60): 8%; chrysanthemums, standard carnations, anthuriums, and orchids (0603.10.70): 8%; mosses and lichens (0604.10.00): free; fresh evergreen Christmas trees (0604.91.00): free; other ornamental plant parts, dried or bleached (0604.99.30): free; other ornamental plant parts, other than dried or bleached (0604.99.60): 11%.

Entry and Documentation

The entry of merchandise is a two-part process consisting of 1) filing the documents necessary to determine whether merchandise may be released from Customs custody and 2) filing the documents that contain information for duty assessment and statistical purposes. In certain instances all documents must be filed and accepted by Customs prior to release of the goods. Unless you have been granted an extension, you must file entry documents at a location specified by the district or area director within five working days of your shipment's date of arrival at a U.S. port of entry. These include a number of standard documents required by Customs for any entry, and:

- PPQ Notice of Arrival
- PPQ permit, when required
- Phyto-sanitary certificate of origin (for Canadian cut flowers).

After you present the entry, Customs may examine your shipment, or may waive examination. The shipment is then released provided no legal or regulatory violations have been noted. You must then file entry summary documentation and deposit estimated duties at a designated customhouse within 10 working days of your shipment's release. For a detailed description of entry procedures, standard documentation, and informal entry, see "Entry Process" on page 182.

Prohibitions and Restrictions

Written APHIS PPQ permits are required for importation of cut flowers of the genus *Azalea, Camellia, Gardenia, Rhododendron, Rosa* (rose), and *Syringa* (lilac). No other admissible cut flowers require formal permits for entry. Permits are granted only to U.S. importers, upon receipt in the PPQ permit unit office (see addresses at end of this chapter) of a completed PPQ **Form 587.** APHIS will accept a letter or telegram stating the required information in lieu of an application on PPQ **Form 587**. You should submit your application for a permit in advance of your proposed importation. Your permit will be issued when PPQ approves your application. Permits authorize the specific importation, specify the port of entry, and prescribe any conditions necessary to safeguard against the entry of pests. You are responsible for fulfilling all permit conditions.

Your applications for a permit should name the cut flower you wish to import, using its botanical or scientific name. You will also need to supply the following information: your shipment's country of origin; means of shipment; first U.S. port of arrival; and your name, address (both street and P.O. box, if any), and telephone number (during regular business hours).

Imports from Drug-producing Countries. There have been instances of narcotic substances being concealed in importations of fresh flowers from certain drug-producing countries and, consequently, Customs' examination of shipments of fresh flowers is quite thorough and delays may be encountered in obtaining release of fresh flowers shipped from certain drug-producing countries.

Camellias and Gardenias. Cut camellias and gardenias are prohibited entry when consigned to destinations in Florida. Shipments of cut camellias and gardenias may enter through Florida ports for transit to points outside the state, provided they are securely wrapped in polyethylene or an equivalent material. Cut gardenias must be given a precautionary fumigation when entering at California ports, regardless of destination.

Other Plants. Cut branches of *Chaenomeles* (flowering quince), *Cydonia* (quince), *Malus* (apple), *Prunus* (plums, peach, cherry, etc.), *Pyrus* (pear), *Eucalyptus*, and *Salix* (willow) are prohibited unless they meet the entry conditions established in 7 CFR 319.37, including post-entry growing conditions.

All botanical fruits, such as the fresh fruits of *Capsicum spp.* or *Ananas spp.* on dry stems intended for decorative purposes that fail to meet standards regarding the country of origin or other requirements established in 7 CFR 319.56, will be refused entry.

Flowers for Propagation. A cut flower permit does not authorize the importation of cut flowers for propagation. All cut flowers imported for the purpose of propagation must enter the U.S. under the requirements of the Nursery Stock Regulations, and other appropriate regulations in 7 CFR 319.37.

Endangered Species Restrictions. Certain plants and their products are protected under a variety of endangered species laws and regulations. The U.S. Fish and Wildlife Service (FWS) is the agency with general responsibility for administering these laws, although the USDA enforces those relevant to plant materials. You must also generally have documentation from the country of origin allowing export from that country before such materials can become eligible for admission into the U.S. If you are unsure of the protected status of a plant or plant product that you wish to import, contact USDA APHIS (see addresses at end of this chapter).

Country-Specific Import Restrictions

No cut flowers of the plant family *Proteaceae* may be imported from South Africa and Swaziland because port-of-entry inspections of these articles have revealed a high rate of significant agricultural pests requiring treatment, destruction, or reexportation of the cut flowers.

Chrysanthemum spp., including cut flowers, from Venezuela are prohibited entry because of white rust disease of chrysanthemums, *Puccinia horiana P. Henn.*

Marking and Labeling

For a general discussion of U.S. Customs marking and labeling requirements, see "Marking: Country of Origin" on page 215 and "Special Marking Requirements" on page 217.

Shipping Considerations

You will need to ensure that your goods are packaged and shipped with care so that they arrive in good condition and pass smoothly through Customs. You are responsible for ensuring that the shipment is in compliance with all applicable government regulations for packaging and shipping. In most instances, you should not leave these arrangements solely to the discretion of your supplier. Careful preparation of the cargo and selection of the mode of transport can be essential to a cost-effective, timely delivery of undamaged goods. We strongly advise you to consult your shipping representative, insurance agent, or freight broker for advice on packing and shipping. Refer also to the major tab section "Packing/Shipping/Insurance" for a general discussion of packing and shipping.

Shipping live plants and such perishable commodities as cut flowers requires great care, special handling, and a short throughput period to ensure that the products arrive in a timely fashion and in marketable condition. Speed and ambient conditions are less critical for dormant live plant products—such as cuttings or bulbs—and for partially processed plant parts for arrangements. Nevertheless, packing, maintenance of environmental conditions (often of refrigeration for perishable cut flowers), and time are of the essence in transporting live or even no longer living but somewhat fragile plant materials.

Publications Available

The following publication gives brief, general guidelines on USDA regulated products. Although designed primarily for tourists, it contains a list of approved products that you may find helpful. It is published by USDA APHIS (see addresses at end of this chapter).

Travelers Tips On Bringing Food, Plant, and Animal Products into the United States

The *Harmonized Tariff Schedule of the United States* (HTSUS) is available from:

Government Printing Office (GPO)
Superintendent of Documents
Washington, DC 20402
(202) 512-1800 (Order line)
(202) 512-0000 (General)

The USGPO also has copies of specific laws available for purchase. The USGPO accepts credit card orders over the phone, as well as mail orders paid by credit card, a check drawn on a U.S. bank, or an international money order.

Relevant Government Agencies

Address questions regarding the importation of live plants, roots, and cut flowers, or requests for permit applications, to:

U.S. Department of Agriculture (USDA)
Animal and Plant Health Inspection Service (APHIS)
Plant Protection and Quarantine (PPQ)
Federal Building, Rm. 631
6505 Belcrest Road
Hyattsville, MD 20782
(301) 436-8645

Address your questions regarding endangered species restrictions to:

U.S. Fish and Wildlife Service (FWS)
Office of Management Authority
4401 N. Fairfax Drive
Arlington, VA 22203
(703) 358-2095
(800) 358-2104, (703) 358-2104 (Permits office)

Address questions regarding the importation of live plants, roots, and cut flowers, especially those regarding antidumping and countervailing duty rates on cut flowers to the district or port director of Customs for you area. For addresses refer to"U.S. Customs District Offices" on page 62 or contact:

U.S. Customs Service
1301 Constitution Ave. NW
Washington, DC 20229
(202) 927-6724 (Information)
(202) 927-1000 (General)

Laws and Regulations

The following laws and regulations may be relevant to the importation of live plants, roots, and cut flowers. The laws are contained in the U.S. Code (USC) and the regulations are published in the Code of Federal Regulations (CFR), both of which may be available at larger public and law libraries. Copies of specific laws are also available from the United States Government Printing Office (address above).

42 USC 264 et seq.
The Plant Quarantine Act
This Act gives the Plant Protection and Quarantine branch of the USDA authority to restrict or prohibit importation of plants or their seeds found to carry specific plant pests and pathogens.

7 USC 147a et seq.
Federal Plant Pest Act (FPPA)
This Act prohibits the importation into or movement through the U.S. of plant pests as defined in the Act, and provides for the inspection of any letter, box, parcel, or container that may carry a plant pest. Inspection is to be performed by U.S. Department of Agriculture in conjunction with Customs.

7 CFR Part 351
Regulations for Entry and Inspection of Plants by Mail
These regulations set forth the plant imports that are prohibited, the requirements for entering restricted plants by mail, and the inspection procedures followed by the USDA's Animal and Plant Health Inspection Service (APHIS).

19 CFR 12.10 et seq.
Regulations for Entry and Release of Restricted Plants
These regulations prescribe the procedures followed by U.S. Customs to enforce the USDA requirements for importation of plants.

Convention on International Trade in Endangered Species of Wild Fauna and Flora (CITES)
This comprehensive wildlife treaty signed by over 100 countries, including the United States, regulates and in many cases prohibits commercial imports and exports of wild animal and plant species threatened by trade.

16 USC 1531
Endangered Species Act
This Act prohibits the import and export of species listed as endangered and most species listed as threatened. It is the U.S. law that implements CITES.

Principal Exporting Countries

The following listing includes samples of the main supplier nations of the products of this chapter. It is organized by HTSUS major heading. (Refer to "Customs Classification" above for the product codes.) Countries are listed in rank order of the value of products imported to the U.S. Statistics represent customs value entries for 1993 from the Bureau of Census, U.S. Department of Commerce.

0601—Netherlands, Israel, Canada, United Kingdom, South Africa, Belgium, Japan, New Zealand, Panama, Turkey

0602—Canada, Costa Rica, Netherlands, Guatemala, Mexico, Taiwan, Thailand, Honduras, India, Dominican Rep.

0603—Colombia, Netherlands, Ecuador, Mexico, Costa Rica, Guatemala, Canada, Thailand, Australia, France

0604—Canada, Mexico, China, Italy, Costa Rica, Philippines, India, Netherlands, Guatemala, Australia

Chapter 7: Vegetables and Related Products*

Full title: Edible Vegetables and Certain Roots and Tubers

This chapter relates to the importation of edible vegetables and certain edible roots and tubers, which are classified under Chapter 7 of the Harmonized Tariff Schedule of the United States (HTSUS). Specifically, it includes fresh, dried, chilled, steamed or boiled, frozen, or otherwise provisionally preserved, whole, cut, or otherwise processed—but not prepared—vegetables as well as seeds and other means of propagating them. The category of vegetables includes not only those products understood in the standard sense of a herbaceous plant product grown for food use, but also such products as potatoes, tomatoes, mushrooms, olives, capers, pumpkins, eggplants, sweet corn, peppers, legumes, and herbs, which may be distinguished botanically as roots, tubers, fruits, or other forms distinct from vegetables. This section is supplemental to the "Foods" appendix on page 808. If you are interested in importing vegetable products, you should read that section in conjunction with this one.

If you are interested in importing fruit or nuts, you should refer to Commodity Index Chapter 8. Prepared foods made from the vegetable products included in Chapter 7 are classified within Chapter 20. If you are interested in importing cereal grains, consult Chapter 10. Juices or extracts of products covered in Chapter 7 for use in beverages are found in Chapter 22. If you are interested in importing vegetable oils, refer to Chapter 15. Seeds of vegetables as well as related plant products, such as fodder, as covered in Chapter 12. Flour, meal, flakes, granules, or pellets of potatoes or dried leguminous vegetables are covered in Chapter 11, while dried crushed peppers and allspice—which when fresh are classified as vegetables within Chapter 7—are covered in chapter 9.

Key Factors

The key factors in the importation of vegetables and roots are:

- Compliance with U.S. Food and Drug Administration (FDA) purity, identity, manufacturing, and other standards
- Compliance with FDA entry notification requirements and procedures
- Compliance with U.S. Department of Agriculture (USDA) plant quarantine restrictions—permits may be required

*IMPORTANT: Read the Commodity Index Introduction. It is the essential framework for understanding this section.

- Compliance with U.S. Department of Agriculture (USDA) Food Safety and Inspection Service (FSIS) import restrictions, port inspections, and product certification for grade, size, quality, etc.
- Observance of quotas on certain Chapter 7 agricultural products
- Compliance with U.S. Environmental Protection Agency (EPA) regulations on pesticide residues on imported agricultural products

Although most importers utilize the services of a licensed customs broker in making their entries, and we recommend this practice, you should be aware of the regulatory, entry, and documentation issues involved in importing your product. You, as importer, are ultimately responsible for the fulfillment of any legal requirements applicable to your shipment.

General Considerations

Regulatory Agencies. Importation into the U.S. of vegetables and edible roots is subject to regulation under several laws enforced by a number of U.S. governmental agencies. The USDA enforces provisions of the Agricultural Marketing Agreement Act (AMAA) and the Plant Quarantine Act (PQA). Plant standards under the Agricultural Adjustment Act are enforced by the FSIS of the USDA. The FDA enforces the Food, Drug, and Cosmetic Act (FDCA). The U.S. Environmental Protection Agency (EPA) enforces the Federal Insecticide, Fungicide, and Rodenticide Act (FIFRA).

USDA Regulations on Vegetables and Roots. Vegetables and roots may require USDA Animal and Plant Health Inspection Service (APHIS) Plant Protection and Quarantine (PPQ) branch import permits, depending on the nature of the product, its point of origin, and its destination. You should contact APHIS PPQ (see addresses at end of this chapter) to find out if a permit is required for the specific product you wish to import. APHIS inspects all fruits and vegetables at the U.S. port of entry.

FDA Requirements on Foods. The FDA regulations regarding importation of foods of any kind are extensive and stringent. For example, 21 CFR 158 establishes extensive regulations governing frozen vegetables. Vegetables and roots imported into the U.S. must comply with all FDCA requirements for those produced domestically. Imported products regulated by the FDA are subject to port-of-entry inspection. **Form FD701** is required for all FDA-regulated importations and may be obtained from your local FDA Import Operations office, from FDA headquarters (see addresses at end of this chapter), or from your customs broker. For an annotated diagram of required FDA import procedures refer to the "Foods" appendix on page 808.

EPA Requirements on Pesticide Residues. The EPA, under authority of the FIFRA, establishes and enforces regulatory limits on pesticide residues on edible plant products. For more information, contact the EPA (see addresses at end of this chapter).

Mexican and Canadian Vegetables. Fresh vegetables for human consumption arriving from Mexico or Canada are eligible for immediate release. Importers must apply for a Special Permit for Immediate Delivery (Customs **Form 3416**). Shipments must be removed from the area immediately contiguous to the border to the importer's premises within the port of importation.

Detention of Shipment. If your shipment is found to be noncomplying, it may be detained at the port of entry. The inspecting agency may permit you to bring such a shipment into compliance before making a final decision regarding admittance. However, any sorting, reprocessing, or relabeling must usually be supervised by the agency's personnel and is done at the importer's expense. A conditional release to allow the importer to bring a shipment into compliance is a privilege, not a right. The inspecting agency may consider subsequent noncomplying shipments of the same type of product to constitute abuse of the privilege and may require the importer to destroy or reexport the products. To ascertain what your legal responsibilities are, you should contact these agencies regarding the specific items to be imported.

Customs Classification

For customs purposes, vegetables and roots are classified under Chapter 7 of the HTSUS. This chapter is broken into major headings, which are further divided into subheadings, and often subsubheadings, each of which has its own HTSUS classification number. For example, the HTSUS number for head lettuce entered in the period from June 1 to October 31, inclusive, is 0705.11.20, indicating that it is a sub-subcategory of head lettuce (0705.11.00), which is a subcategory of the major heading, lettuce (*Lactuca sativa*) and chickory (*Cichorium spp.*), fresh or chilled (0705.00.00). There are 14 major headings within Chapter 7.

0701—Potatoes, fresh or chilled

0702—Tomatoes, fresh or chilled

0703—Onions, shallots, garlic, leeks, and other allied vegetables, fresh or chilled

0704—Cabbages, cauliflower, kohlrabi, kale, and similar edible brassicas, fresh or chilled

0705—Lettuce (*Lactuca sativa*) and chickory (*Cichorium spp.*), fresh or chilled

0706—Carrots, turnips, salad beets (salad beetroot), salsify, celeriac, radishes, and similar edible roots, fresh or chilled

0707—Cucumbers, including gherkins, fresh or chilled

0708—Leguminous vegetables, shelled or unshelled, fresh or chilled

0709—Other vegetables, fresh or chilled

0710—Vegetables (uncooked or cooked by steaming or boiling in water), frozen

0711—Vegetables provisionally preserved (for example, by sulfur dioxide gas, in brine, in sulfur water, or in other preservative solutions), but unsuitable in that state for immediate consumption

0712—Dried vegetables, whole, cut, sliced, broken, or in powder, but not further prepared

0713—Dried leguminous vegetables, shelled, whether or not skinned or split

0714—Cassava (manioc), arrowroot, salep, Jerusalem artichokes, sweet potatoes, and similar roots and tubers with high starch or inulin content, fresh or dried, whether or not sliced, or in the form of pellets; sago pith

For more details regarding classification of the specific product you are interested in importing, consult a customs broker, the appropriate commodity specialist at your nearest customs port, or see HTSUS. HTSUS is available for purchase from the U.S. Government Printing Office (see addresses at end of this chapter), and may be found in larger public libraries. Refer to "Classification—Liquidation" on page 207 for a general discussion of customs classification.

Sample Import Duties

Import duties will vary depending on the HTSUS classification of your product. Therefore, to determine the correct amount of duties, your product must be properly classified under the HTSUS. The following sample duties are taken from the duty listings for HTSUS Chapter 7 products.

Potatoes (0701.90.00): 0.77cents/kg; tomatoes, if entered from July 15 through August 31 (0702.00.40): 3.3 cents/kg; garlic (0703.20.00): 1.7 cents/kg; cauliflower and broccoli, if entered from June 5 through October 15 (0704.10.20): 5.5%; entered at other times, not reduced in size (0704.10.40): 12.5%, cut, sliced, or otherwise reduced in size: (0704.10.60): 17.5%; lettuce, if entered from June 1 through October 31 (0705.19.20): 0.88 cents/kg; carrots under 10cm in length (0706.10.10): 2.2 cents/kg; cucumbers, if entered from December 1 through the end of February (0707.00.20): 4.9 cents/kg; lima beans, if entered from November 1 through May 31 (0708.20.10): 5.2 cents/kg; mushrooms (0709.51.00): 11 cents/kg + 25%; spinach (0709.70.00): 25%; sweet corn (1709.90.4070): 25%; frozen string beans (0710.22.25): 7.7 cents/kg; frozen Brussels sprouts (0710.80.85): 17.5%; olives, pitted or stuffed (0711.20.40): 10.8 cents/kg drained weight; dried fennel, marjoram, parsley, savory, and tarragon (0712.90.40): free; dried kidney beans, if entered from May 1 through August 31 (0713.33.20): 2.2 cents/kg; sweet potatoes (0714.20.00): 10%.

Entry and Documentation

The entry of merchandise is a two-part process consisting of 1) filing the documents necessary to determine whether merchandise may be released from Customs custody and 2) filing the documents that contain information for duty assessment and statistical purposes. In certain instances, such as entry of products under quota, all documents must be filed and accepted by Customs prior to the release of the goods. Unless you have been granted an extension, you must file entry documents at a location specified by the district or area director within five working days of your shipment's date of arrival at a U.S. port of entry. These include a number of standard documents required by Customs for any entry, and:

- FDA Importers Entry Notice, **Form FD701**
- USDA Import Permit (when required)
- Special Permit for Immediate Delivery, **Form 3461** (immediate release of Mexican or Canadian vegetables)

After you present the entry, Customs may examine your shipment, or may waive examination (food items are almost always inspected). The shipment is then released provided no legal or regulatory violations have been noted. You must then file entry summary documentation and deposit estimated duties at a designated customhouse within 10 working days of your shipment's release. For a detailed description of entry procedures, standard documentation, and informal entry, see "Entry Process" on page 182.

Prohibitions and Restrictions

USDA FSIS Product Standards. Section 8e of the AMAA requires that whenever the U.S. Secretary of Agriculture issues grade, size, quality, or maturity regulations for commodities produced domestically, the same or comparable regulations must apply to imports of those commodities. Such import regulations apply only during periods when domestic marketing order regulations are in effect. Vegetables that may be subject to these import regulations include olives in tins (other than Spanish-style olives), dry onions, Irish potatoes, avocados, fresh tomatoes, green peppers, cucumbers, and eggplants.

If you import products subject to marketing orders, USDA's FSIS will inspect your shipment at the U.S. port of entry for compliance. If your shipment meets with the applicable standards, the USDA officer will issue an inspection certificate. If your shipment is found to be noncomplying, it will be refused entry. For additional information regarding requirements for regulated commodities contact USDA's Agricultural Marketing Service (see addresses at end of this chapter).

USDA Permit Requirements. USDA plant quarantine regulations under the PQA are divided into two classes: prohibitory and restrictive. Prohibitory orders forbid entirely the entry of designated plants and plant products subject to attack by plant pests for which no treatment is available that would insure complete freedom from such pests (special arrangements may be made for importation for research purposes, although commercial imports are banned). Restrictive orders allow the entry of plants or plant products with either a treatment or an inspection requirement. To import vegetables under restrictive orders, you must obtain an APHIS import permit. To qualify for a permit, you must be a U.S. resident. You will be held responsible for carrying out all conditions of entry specified in your permit. Address your questions regarding entry requirements for your product to USDA APHIS PPQ branch (see addresses at end of this chapter).

EPA Restrictions. If you are importing fresh vegetables, you should beware of products bearing excessive residues from insecticide sprays or dusts These items are considered to be adulterated under Federal law, as established by the EPA. If your shipment falls into this category, it will be refused entry.

FDA Restrictions. The FDA issues specific product alerts. In particular, importers should be aware of the following problems. For other products, the importer should check with the FDA for the most current tips and restrictions.

Dried Vegetables. You should take extreme care to prevent contamination of dried vegetables you intend to import. These products are particularly vulnerable to attack by insects or animals, or to deterioration resulting in moldiness or other forms of decomposition.

Dried Mushrooms. If you are offering dried mushrooms for import, you must be certain that they are edible species. Inedible species of dried mushrooms are prohibited imports. The most common bar to entry, however, is insect infestation, usually by flies or maggots. You can prevent mushroom contamination by insects, rodent, and bird filth, or other objectionable material by taking protective measures during drying and storage. Don't buy mushrooms from heavily insect-infested areas to import into the U.S. They will be refused entry.

Olives. Pitted and stuffed olives containing more than an unavoidable minimum of pits or pit fragments are in violation of the FDCA. While it may not be possible to completely eliminate this problem, dealers have been put on notice that they must take steps to reduce it to the extent that is reasonable.

Country-Specific Import Restrictions

APHIS PPQ may restrict importation of plant products from certain countries. The variables are often so complex that determinations must be made effectively on a case-by-case basis. As an example, PPQ may restrict the import of a specific product from a specific country that is known to carry a specific pest for a specific period of time. However, the restriction may only apply to areas in the U.S. with a climate in which the particular pest can thrive. A product that is refused import into California may be allowed in if its destination is New York State, or vice versa. The importer of agricultural products should ascertain from APHIS PPQ whether or not a product is subject to any such restrictions.

Quotas

Olives of subheadings 0711.20.15 and 2005.70.13, green and not pitted, in saline solution, in containers each holding more than 8 kg drained weight, certified by the importer to be used for repacking or sale as green olives as subject to tariff-rate quotas (that is, unlimited quantities may be imported, but tariff rates rise once a baseline level has been imported). A duty rate of 3.7 cents/kg on drained weight applies to the first 4,400 metric tons imported under both subheadings combined in any calendar year. After the first 4,400 metric tons, the duty rises to 7.4 cents/kg.

Quotas—both the commodities affected and rates charged—can change on short notice. For up-to-the minute information, or further details on quotas, contact the district director of Customs nearest you, or the U.S. Customs Quota Branch (address below.) For a general discussion of quotas refer to "Import Quotas" on page 230.

Marking and Labeling Requirements

For a general discussion of U.S. Customs marking and labeling requirements, see "Marking: Country of Origin" on page 215 and "Special Marking Requirements" on page 217. Refer also to the "Foods" appendix on page 808.

Shipping Considerations

You will need to ensure that your goods are packaged and shipped with care so that they arrive in good condition and pass smoothly through Customs. You are responsible for ensuring that the shipment is in compliance with all applicable government regulations for packaging and shipping. In most instances, you should not leave these arrangements solely to the discretion of your supplier. Careful preparation of the cargo and selection of the mode of transport can be essential to a cost-effective, timely delivery of undamaged goods. We strongly advise you to consult your shipping representative, insurance agent, or freight broker for advice on packing and shipping. Refer also to the major tab section "Packing/Shipping/Insurance" for a general discussion of packing and shipping and the "Foods" appendix on page 808.

Vegetables and edible root crops often require special handling to ensure that they reach their destination in marketable condition. It is also of critical importance that infestation by insects and other forms of contamination are avoided, or the shipment will be denied admission.

Publications Available

The following publication explains the FDA requirements for importing vegetables and edible roots. It is published by the FDA and is available on request from FDA headquarters (see addresses at end of this chapter).

Requirements of Laws and Regulations Enforced by the U.S. Food and Drug Administration

The following publication gives brief, general guidelines on USDA regulated products. Although designed primarily for tourists, it contains a list of approved products that you may find helpful. It is published by USDA APHIS (see addresses at end of this chapter).

Travelers Tips On Bringing Food, Plant, and Animal Products into the United States

The *Harmonized Tariff Schedule of the United States* (HTSUS) is available from:

Government Printing Office (GPO)
Superintendent of Documents
Washington, DC 20402
(202) 512-1800 (Order line)
(202) 512-0000 (General)

The USGPO also has copies of specific laws available for purchase. The USGPO accepts credit card orders over the phone, as well as mail orders paid by credit card, a check drawn on a U.S. bank, or an international money order.

Relevant Government Agencies

Address your questions regarding FDA requirements for the importation of vegetables and edible roots to:

Food and Drug Administration (FDA)
Center for Food Safety and Applied Nutrition
200 C Street SW
Washington, DC 20204
(202) 205-5241, 205-5042

Food and Drug Administration (FDA)
Division of Enforcement, Imports Branch
200 C Street SW
Washington, DC 20204
(202) 205-4726

Address your questions regarding USDA domestic marketing orders (AMAA) to:

Agricultural Marketing Service
Fruit and Vegetable Division
P.O. Box 96456
Washington, DC 20090-6456
(202) 720-4722

Address your questions regarding USDA prohibitory and restrictive orders and permits to import restricted plant products to:

U.S. Department of Agriculture (USDA)
Animal and Plant Health Inspection Service (APHIS)
Plant Protection and Quarantine (PPQ)
Federal Building, Rm. 631
6505 Belcrest Road
Hyattsville, MD 20782
(301) 436-8645

Address questions regarding allowable pesticide residues on vegetables and root crops to:

Environmental Protection Agency (EPA)
Office of Pesticide Programs
401 M Street SW (7501-C)
Washington, DC 20460
(703) 305-7090 (General)
(703) 305-7102 (Import/export requirements)

Address your questions regarding quotas to:

U.S. Customs Service
Quota Branch
1301 Constitution Avenue NW, Rm. 2379-ICC
Washington, DC 20229
(202) 927-5850

Address your questions regarding the importation of vegetables and root crops to the district or port director of Customs for you area. For addresses refer to"U.S. Customs District Offices" on page 62 or contact:

U.S. Customs Service
1301 Constitution Ave. NW
Washington, DC 20229
(202) 927-6724 (Information)
(202) 927-1000 (General)

Laws and Regulations

The following laws and regulations may be relevant to the importation of vegetables and root crops. The laws are contained in the U.S. Code (USC) and the regulations are published in the Code of Federal Regulations (CFR), both of which may be available at larger public and law libraries. Copies of specific laws are also available from the United States Government Printing Office (address above).

21 USC 301 et seq.
Food, Drug, and Cosmetic Act
This Act prohibits deceptive practices and regulates the manufacture, sale and importation or exportation of food, drugs, cosmetics, and related products. See 21 USC 331, 381, 382.

19 CFR 12.1 et seq.; 21 CFR 1.83 et seq.
Regulations on Food, Drugs, and Cosmetics
These regulations of the Secretary of Health and Human Services and the Secretary of the Treasury govern the standards, labeling, marking, and importing of products used with food, drugs, and cosmetics.

7 USC 601 et seq.
Agricultural Adjustment Act (AAA)
This Act authorizes the Secretary of Agriculture to establish and maintain orderly market conditions for agricultural products—including tomatoes, olives, green peppers, Irish potatoes, cucumbers, onions, or eggplant—and to impose quotas or higher duty rates on imported agricultural products whenever investigation reveals that orderly market conditions require such action.

19 CFR Part 132
Regulations for Enforcement of AAA Quotas
These regulations provide for Customs enforcement of AAA quotas and higher duty rates imposed on imported agricultural products.

7 USC 135 et seq.
Federal Insecticide, Fungicide, and Rodenticide Act (FIFRA)
This Act prohibits the importation of pesticides or devices that are adulterated, misbranded, or otherwise violative of the Act, provides for registration of pesticides and devices, and establishes standards for labeling and classifying pesticides.

19 CFR 12; 40 CFR 162
Regulations on Pesticides
These regulations set forth the procedures and guidelines for importing products exposed to pesticides.

42 USC 264 et seq.
The Plant Quarantine Act
This Act gives the Plant Protection and Quarantine branch of the USDA authority to restrict or prohibit importation of plants or their seeds found to carry specific plant pests and pathogens.

7 USC 147a et seq.
Federal Plant Pest Act (FPPA)
This Act prohibits the importation into or movement through the U.S. of plant pests as defined in the Act, and provides for the inspection of any letter, box, parcel, or container that may carry a plant pest. Inspection is to be performed by U.S. Department of Agriculture in conjunction with Customs.

7 CFR Part 351
Regulations of USDA for Entry of Plants
These regulations set forth the plant imports that are prohibited, the requirements for entering restricted plants by mail, and the inspection procedures followed by the USDA's Animal and Plant Health Inspection Service (APHIS).

19 CFR 12.10 et seq.
Regulations of Customs for Entry of Restricted Plants
These regulations prescribe the procedures followed by U.S. Customs to enforce the USDA requirements for importation of plants.

Principal Exporting Countries

The following listing includes samples of the main supplier nations of the products of this chapter. It is organized by HTSUS major heading. (Refer to "Customs Classification" above for the product codes.) Countries are listed in rank order of the value of products imported to the U.S. Statistics represent customs value entries for 1993 from the Bureau of Census, U.S. Department of Commerce.

0701—Canada, China, Hong Kong, Mexico, Colombia, Belize

0702—Mexico, Netherlands, Canada, Belgium, Israel, Bahamas, Dominican Rep., France, Italy, Chile

0703—Mexico, China, Canada, Chile, France, Argentina, Netherlands, New Zealand, Guatemala, Hong Kong

0704—Mexico, Canada, Netherlands, Guatemala, Chile, France, Costa Rica, Belgium, Italy, China

0705—Belgium, Mexico, Italy, Canada, Netherlands, Chile, Peru, Guatemala, India, Spain

0706—Mexico, Canada, Japan, China, Israel, Belgium, United Kingdom, Hong Kong, Netherlands, Taiwan

0707—Mexico, Canada, Honduras, Bahamas, Netherlands, Spain, Jamaica, Guatemala, Belgium, Ecuador

0708—Mexico, Guatemala, Canada, Dominican Rep., Turkey, China, India, Denmark, El Salvador, Peru

0709—Mexico, Netherlands, Canada, Costa Rica, Peru, Chile, Belgium, Italy, Honduras, Jamaica

0710—Mexico, Canada, Guatemala, China, Taiwan, Dominican Rep., Costa Rica, El Salvador, Israel, Peru

0711—Mexico, Greece, Turkey, Sri Lanka, China, Spain, Chile, Thailand, Honduras, Canada

0712—China, Chile, Spain, Mexico, Japan, Morocco, France, Israel, Switzerland, Germany

0713—Canada, Mexico, China, Thailand, India, Turkey, Peru, Australia, Chile, France

0714—Costa Rica, Jamaica, Dominican Rep., Japan, Colombia, Western Samoa, Ghana, Brazil, China, Tonga

Chapter 8: Fruit and Nuts*

Full title: Edible Fruit and Nuts; Peel of Citrus Fruit or Melons

This chapter relates to the importation of edible fruit and nuts and of the peel of citrus fruit or melons, which are classified under Chapter 8 of the Harmonized Tariff Schedule of the United States (HTSUS). Specifically, it includes fresh, dried, chilled, steamed or boiled, frozen, or otherwise provisionally preserved, shelled or in the shell nuts and whole or otherwise processed—but not prepared—fruits. The category includes all tree fruits, including citrus fruits, and vine or bush fruits—such as grapes, berries, and melons—as well as tree nuts and fruit peels. Products may be processed or provisionally preserved, but not prepared into other forms. This section is supplemental to the "Foods" appendix on page 808. If you are interested in importing fruit or nuts, you should read that section in conjunction with this one.

If you are interested in importing vegetables or edible root crops, you should refer to Commodity Index Chapter 7. Peanuts are covered in Chapter 12. Prepared foods made from the products included in Chapter 8 are classified within Chapter 20. Juices or extracts of products covered in Chapter 8 for use in beverages are found in Chapters 20 and 22. If you are interested in importing fruit and nut oils, refer to Chapter 15. Imports of fruit and nut trees falls within Chapter 6, while imports of seed for fruit and nuts as well as imports of oleaginous fruits come within Chapter 12. Inedible fruit and nuts intended for industrial uses are also classified elsewhere.

Key Factors

The key factors in the importation of fruit and nuts are:

- Compliance with U.S. Food and Drug Administration (FDA) purity, identity, manufacturing, and other standards
- Compliance with FDA entry notification requirements and procedures
- Compliance with U.S. Department of Agriculture (USDA) plant quarantine restrictions—permits may be required
- Compliance where applicable with USDA marketing orders for grade, size, quality, etc.
- Observation of quotas on certain Chapter 8 agricultural products
- Compliance with U.S. Environmental Protection Agency (EPA) regulations on pesticide residues on imported agricultural products

Although most importers utilize the services of a licensed customs broker in making their entries, and we recommend this practice, you should be aware of the regulatory, entry, and documentation issues involved in importing your product. You, as importer, are ultimately responsible for the fulfillment of any legal requirements applicable to your shipment.

General Considerations

Regulatory Agencies. Importation into the U.S. of fruit and nuts is subject to regulation under several laws enforced by a number of U.S. governmental agencies. The USDA enforces provisions of the Agricultural Marketing Agreement Act (AMAA) and the Plant Quarantine Act (PQA). The FDA enforces the Food, Drug, and Cosmetic Act (FDCA), and the EPA enforces the Federal Insecticide, Fungicide, and Rodenticide Act (FIFRA).

USDA Import and Quarantine Requirements. Fruit and nut products may require USDA Animal and Plant Health Inspection Service (APHIS) Plant Protection and Quarantine (PPQ) import permits, depending on the nature of the product, its point of origin, and its destination. You should contact APHIS PPQ (see addresses at end of this chapter) to find out if a permit is required for the specific product you wish to import. APHIS inspects all fruit and nuts at the U.S. port of entry.

FDA Food Regulations. FDA regulations on the importation of foods of any kind are extensive and stringent. For example, 21 CFR 164 establishes detailed regulations governing tree nut and peanut products. Fruit and nuts imported into the U.S. must comply with all FDCA requirements for those produced domestically. Imported products regulated by the FDA are subject to port-of-entry inspection. **Form FD701** is required for all FDA-regulated importations and may be obtained from your local FDA Import Operations office, from FDA headquarters (see addresses at end of this chapter), or from your customs broker. For an annotated diagram of required FDA import procedures refer to the "Foods" appendix on page 808.

EPA Pesticide Requirements. The EPA, under authority of FIFRA, establishes regulatory limits on pesticide residues on edible plant products. For more information, contact the EPA (see addresses at end of this chapter).

Mexican and Canadian Fruit. Fresh fruit for human consumption arriving from Mexico or Canada are eligible for immediate release. Importers must apply for a Special Permit for Immediate Delivery (Customs **Form 3416**). Shipments must be removed from the area immediately contiguous to the border to the importer's premises within the port of importation.

Detention of Shipment. If your shipment is found to be noncomplying, it may be detained at the port of entry. The inspecting agency may permit you to bring such a shipment into compliance before making a final decision regarding admittance. However, any sorting, reprocessing, or relabeling must usually be supervised by agency personnel and is done at the importer's expense. A conditional release to allow the importer to bring a shipment into compliance is a privilege, not a right. The inspecting agency may consider subsequent noncomplying shipments of the same type of product to constitute abuse of the privilege and may require the importer to destroy or reexport the products. To ascertain what your legal responsibilities are, you should contact these agencies regarding the specific items to be imported.

Customs Classification

For customs purposes, fruit and nuts are classified under Chapter 8 of the HTSUS. This chapter is broken into major headings,

*IMPORTANT: Read the Commodity Index Introduction. It is the essential framework for understanding this section.

which are further divided into subheadings, and often sub-sub-headings, each of which has its own HTSUS classification number. For example, the HTSUS number for pineapples not reduced in size in crates or other packages is 0804.30.40, indicating that it is a sub-subcategory of pineapples (0804.30.00), which is a subcategory of the major heading, Dates, figs, pineapples, avocados, guavas, mangos, and mangosteens, fresh and dried (0804.00.00). There are 14 major headings within Chapter 8.

0801—Coconuts, Brazil nuts, and cashew nuts, fresh or dried, whether or not shelled or peeled

0802—Other nuts, fresh or dried, whether or not shelled or peeled

0803—Bananas and plantains, fresh or dried

0804—Dates, figs, pineapples, avocados, guavas, mangoes, and mangosteens, fresh or dried

0805—Citrus fruit, fresh or dried

0806—Grapes, fresh or dried

0807—Melons (including watermelons) and papayas (papaws), fresh

0808—Apples, pears, and quinces, fresh

0809—Apricots, cherries, peaches, (including nectarines), plums (including prune plums), and sloes, fresh

0810—Other fruit, fresh

0811—Fruit and nuts, uncooked or cooked by steaming or boiling in water, frozen, whether or not containing added sugar or other sweetening matter

0812—Fruit and nuts, provisionally preserved (for example, by sulfur dioxide gas, in brine, in sulfur water, or in other preservative solutions), but unsuitable in that state for immediate consumption

0813—Fruit, dried, other than that of heading 0801 to 0806; mixtures of nuts or dried fruits of this chapter

0814—Peel of citrus fruit or melons (including watermelons), fresh, frozen, dried, or provisionally preserved in brine, sulfur water, or in other preservative solutions

For more details regarding classification of the specific product you are interested in importing, consult a customs broker, the appropriate commodity specialist at your nearest customs port, or see HTSUS. HTSUS is available for purchase from the U.S. Government Printing Office (see addresses at end of this chapter), and may be found in larger public libraries. Refer to "Classification—Liquidation" on page 207 for a general discussion of customs classification.

Sample Import Duties

Import duties will vary depending on the HTSUS classification of your product. Therefore, to determine the correct amount of duties, your product must be properly classified under the HTSUS. The following sample duties are taken from the duty listings for HTSUS Chapter 8 products.

Coconuts, in shell (0801.10.00): free; cashew nuts (0801.30.00): free; filberts, shelled (0802.21.00): 17.6 cents/kg; pistachios, in shell (0802.50.10): 1 cent/kg; Bananas, fresh (0803.00.20): free; whole dates, packed in containers of less than 4.6kg (0804.10.20): 16.5 cents/kg; pineapples, in bulk (0804.30.20): 0.64 cents/kg; fresh mangoes, if entered other than between September 1 and May 31 (0804.50.60): 8.27 cents/kg; lemons (0805.30.20): 2.75 cents/kg; raisins made from seedless grapes (0806.20.10): 2.2 cents/kg; cantaloupes entered from August through September 15 (0807.10.10): 20%; apples (0808.10.00): free; cherries (0809.20.00): free; cranberries (0810.40.00): free; frozen raspberries (0811.20.00): 7%; frozen boysenberries (0811.90.22): 14%; mixtures of two or more fruits, provisionally preserved (0812.90.10): 17.5%; dried apricots (0813.10.00): 2.2 cents/kg; mixtures of nuts or dried fruits (0813.50.00): 17.5%; lime peel (0814.00.40): 2 cents/kg.

Entry and Documentation

The entry of merchandise is a two-part process consisting of 1) filing the documents necessary to determine whether merchandise may be released from Customs custody and 2) filing the documents that contain information for duty assessment and statistical purposes. In certain instances, such as entry of products under quota, all documents must be filed and accepted by Customs prior to the release of the goods. Unless you have been granted an extension, you must file entry documents at a location specified by the district or area director within five working days of your shipment's date of arrival at a U.S. port of entry. These include a number of standard documents required by Customs for any entry, and:

- FDA Importers Entry Notice, **Form FD701**
- USDA Import Permit (when required)
- Special Permit for Immediate Delivery, **Form 3461** (immediate release of Mexican or Canadian vegetables)

After you present the entry, Customs may examine your shipment, or may waive examination (food items are almost always inspected). The shipment is then released provided no legal or regulatory violations have been noted. You must then file entry summary documentation and deposit estimated duties at a designated customhouse within 10 working days of your shipment's release. For a detailed description of entry procedures, standard documentation, and informal entry, see "Entry Process" on page 182.

Prohibitions and Restrictions

USDA Restrictions. Section 8e of AMAA requires that whenever the U.S. Secretary of Agriculture issues grade, size, quality, or maturity regulations for commodities produced domestically, the same or comparable regulations must apply to imports of those commodities. Such import regulations apply only during periods when domestic marketing order regulations are in effect. Fruit and nuts that may be subject to import regulations include raisins, mangoes, prunes, limes, avocados, grapefruit, oranges, walnuts, processed dates, and filberts.

If you import products subject to marketing orders, USDA's Food Safety and Quality Service Department will inspect your shipment at the U.S. port of entry for compliance. If your shipment meets with the applicable standards, the USDA officer will issue an inspection certificate. If your shipment is found to be noncomplying, it will be refused entry. For additional information regarding requirements for regulated commodities contact USDA's Agricultural Marketing Service (see addresses at end of this chapter).

USDA Permit Requirements. USDA plant quarantine regulations under the PQA are divided into two classes: prohibitory and restrictive. Prohibitory orders forbid entirely the entry of designated plants and plant products subject to attack by plant pests for which no treatment is available that would insure complete freedom from such pests (special arrangements may be made for importation for research purposes, although commercial imports are banned). Restrictive orders allow the entry of plants or plant products with either a treatment or an inspection requirement. To import fruit or nuts under restrictive orders, you must obtain an APHIS import permit. To qualify for a permit, you must be a U.S. resident. You will be held responsible for carrying out all conditions of entry specified in your permit. Address your questions regarding entry requirements for your product to USDA APHIS PPQ branch (see addresses at end of this chapter).

EPA Restrictions. If you are importing fresh fruit or nuts, you should beware of products bearing excessive residues from insecticide sprays or dusts These items are considered to be adulterated under federal law, as established by the EPA. If your shipment falls into this category, it will be refused entry.

FDA Restrictions. You should take extreme care to prevent contamination of dried fruit and nuts you intend for import. These products are particularly vulnerable to attack by insects or animals, or to deterioration resulting in moldiness or other forms of decomposition. The FDA issues specific product alerts. For other products, the importer should check with the FDA for the most current tips and restrictions.

Fresh Fruit. If you are importing fresh fruits, you should be aware of the following potential problems. If you are importing pineapples, be sure they are not showing or likely to show the internal condition known as "brown heart," or "black heart." Such pineapples will be refused entry. Blueberries and huckleberries sometimes contain small larvae, which render them unfit for consumption. Take care to avoid importing these berries from infested areas. If you are importing fresh blueberries, you should make sure they are held and transported under conditions that will prevent mold or other types of spoilage.

Dried Fruit. You should take extreme care to prevent contamination of dried fruit you intend for import. These products are particularly vulnerable to attack by insects or animals, or to deterioration resulting in moldiness or other forms of decomposition. Dried figs are susceptible to insect infestation both during growth and when improperly stored, and may become moldy if not properly stored and handled. The FDA refuses entry to dried figs and fig paste because of insect or rodent contamination, mold, sourness, or fermentation. Dried dates have been refused entry for insect infestation, presence of filth, mold, decomposition, and the presence of broken pieces of pits. You may avoid these problems by taking the necessary precautions during storage and transit.

Nuts and Nut Products. If you wish to import nut products, you should be aware of the FDA standards for mixed tree nuts, shelled nuts, and peanut butter (21 CFR 164). The standards establish such factors as proportions of various kinds of nuts and label designations for "mixed nuts," fill of container for shelled nuts, and ingredients and labeling for peanut butter. Nuts and nut meats must be prepared and stored under sanitary conditions to prevent contamination by insects, rodents, or other animals. Nuts imported for pressing for edible oil must be just as clean and sound as nuts intended to be eaten as such or to be used in manufactured foods.

If you wish to import nuts and nut products into the U.S., you should take care to prevent the following adulterating conditions: 1) Insect infestation. Nuts are insect-infected if they contain live or dead insects—larvae, pupae, or adults; if they show definite evidence of insect feeding or cutting; or if insect excreta pellets are present. 2) Dirt. Nut meats may become dirty because of lack of cleanliness in cracking, sorting, and packaging. 3) Mold. Nut meats are occasionally moldy in the shell and bear fruiting mold or mold hyphae. 4) Rancidity. Rancid nuts are frequently soft. They have a yellow, dark, or oily appearance and an abnormal flavor characterized by rancidity. 5) Extraneous material. Stems, shells, stones, or excreta should not be present.

FDA defect action levels have been established for tree nuts. You may not deliberately mix good and bad lots to result in defects below these levels, even though the percentage of defects in the mixed lots is thus rendered lower than the defect action level.

Aflatoxins. Aflatoxins are a group of chemically related substances produced naturally as the byproduct of the growth of certain common molds. Aflatoxins, especially aflatoxin B1, are highly toxic, causing acute liver damage in exposed animals. Aflatoxin B1 also exhibits highly potent carcinogenic properties in certain species of experimental animals. Studies of certain population groups reveal that the consumption of aflatoxin-containing foods is associated with liver cancer in humans. Excess aflatoxin levels in nuts and other products is a significant public health problem and is a basis for seizing or refusing imports of products containing it.

Bitter Almonds. Because of their toxicity, bitter almonds may not be marketed in the U.S. for unrestricted use. Shipments of sweet almonds may not contain more than 5% of bitter almonds. Almond paste and pastes made from other kernels should contain less than 25 parts per million of hydrocyanic acid (HCN), a compound that occurs naturally in the kernels.

Country-Specific Import Restrictions

APHIS PPQ may restrict importation of plant products from certain countries. The variables are often so complex that determinations must be made effectively on a case-by-case basis. As an example, PPQ may restrict the import of a specific product from a specific country that is known to carry a specific pest for a specific period of time. However, the restriction may only apply to areas in the U.S. in whose climate that particular pest can thrive. A product that is refused entry into California may be allowed in if its destination is New York State, or vice versa. The importer of agricultural products should ascertain from APHIS PPQ whether or not a product is subject to any such restrictions.

Quotas

Quotas—both the commodities affected and the rates charged—can change on short notice. For up-to-the minute information, or further details on quotas, contact the district director of Customs nearest you, or U.S. Customs Quota Branch (see addresses at end of this chapter). For a general discussion of quotas refer to "Import Quotas" on page 230.

Mandarins (satsumas) in airtight containers are subject to tariff rate quotas (that is, any quantity may be imported, although tariff rates are higher once the base-level quantity has been entered). Apple or pear juices, not mixed and not containing over 1.0% of ethyl alcohol by volume are subject to an annual absolute quota limit of 531,240 liters, after which no more of these products may be admitted during the calendar year.

Marking and Labeling Requirements

For a general discussion of U.S. Customs marking and labeling requirements, refer to "Marking: Country of Origin" on page 215 and "Special Marking Requirements" on page 217. Refer also to the "Foods" appendix on page 808.

Shipping Considerations

You will need to ensure that your goods are packaged and shipped with care so that they arrive in good condition and pass smoothly through Customs. You are responsible for ensuring that the shipment is in compliance with all applicable government regulations for packaging and shipping. In most instances, you should not leave these arrangements solely to the discretion of your supplier. Careful preparation of the cargo and selection of the mode of transport can be essential to a cost-effective, timely delivery of undamaged goods. We strongly advise you to consult your shipping representative, insurance agent, or freight broker for advice on packing and shipping. Refer also to the major tab section "Packing/Shipping/Insurance" for a general discussion of packing and shipping and the "Foods" appendix on page 808.

Nuts and in particular fresh fruit often require special handling to ensure that they reach their destination in marketable condition. It is also of critical importance that infestation by insects and other forms of contamination are avoided, or the shipment will be denied admission.

Publications Available

The following publication explains the FDA requirements for importing fruit and nuts. It is published by the FDA and is available on request from FDA headquarters (see addresses at end of this chapter).

Requirements of Laws and Regulations Enforced by the U.S. Food and Drug Administration

The following publication gives brief, general guidelines on USDA regulated products. Although designed primarily for tourists, it contains a list of approved products that you may find helpful. It is published by USDA APHIS (see addresses at end of this chapter).

Travelers Tips On Bringing Food, Plant, and Animal Products into the United States

The *Harmonized Tariff Schedule of the United States* (HTSUS) is available from:

Government Printing Office (GPO)
Superintendent of Documents
Washington, DC 20402
(202) 512-1800 (Order line)
(202) 512-0000 (General)

The USGPO also has copies of specific laws available for purchase. The USGPO accepts credit card orders over the phone, as well as mail orders paid by credit card, a check drawn on a U.S. bank, or an international money order.

Relevant Government Agencies

Address your questions regarding FDA requirements for the importation of fruit and nuts to:

Food and Drug Administration (FDA)
Center for Food Safety and Applied Nutrition
200 C Street SW
Washington, DC 20204
(202) 205-5241, 205-5042

Food and Drug Administration (FDA)
Division of Enforcement, Imports Branch
200 C Street SW
Washington, DC 20204
(202) 205-4726

Address your questions regarding USDA domestic marketing orders (AMAA) to:

Agricultural Marketing Service
Fruit and Vegetable Division
P.O. Box 96456
Washington, DC 20090-6456
(202) 720-4722

Address your questions regarding USDA prohibitory and restrictive orders and permits to import restricted plant products to:

U.S. Department of Agriculture (USDA)
Animal and Plant Health Inspection Service (APHIS)
Plant Protection and Quarantine (PPQ)
Federal Building, Rm. 631
6505 Belcrest Road
Hyattsville, MD 20782
(301) 436-8645

Address questions regarding allowable pesticide residues on fruit and nuts to:

Environmental Protection Agency (EPA)
Office of Pesticide Programs
401 M Street SW (7501-C)
Washington, DC 20460
(703) 305-7090 (General)
(703) 305-7102 (Import/export requirements)

Address your questions regarding quotas to:

U.S. Customs Service
Quota Branch
1301 Constitution Avenue NW, Rm. 2379-ICC
Washington, DC 20229
(202) 927-5850

Address your questions regarding the importation of fruit and nuts to the district or port director of Customs for you area. For addresses refer to"U.S. Customs District Offices" on page 62 or contact:

U.S. Customs Service
1301 Constitution Ave. NW
Washington, DC 20229
(202) 927-6724 (Information)
(202) 927-1000 (General)

Laws and Regulations

The following laws and regulations may be relevant to the importation of fruit and nuts. The laws are contained in the U.S. Code (USC) and the regulations are published in the Code of Federal Regulations (CFR), both of which may be available at larger public and law libraries. Copies of specific laws are also available from the United States Government Printing Office (address above).

21 USC 301 et seq.
Food, Drug, and Cosmetic Act
This Act prohibits deceptive practices and regulates the manufacture, sale and importation or exportation of food, drugs, cosmetics, and related products. See 21 USC 331, 381, 382.

19 CFR 12.1 et seq.; 21 CFR 1.83 et seq.
Regulations on Food, Drugs, and Cosmetics
These regulations of the Secretary of Health and Human Services and the Secretary of the Treasury govern the standards, labeling, marking, and importing of products used with food, drugs, and cosmetics.

7 USC 601 et seq.
Agricultural Adjustment Act (AAA)
This Act authorizes the Secretary of Agriculture to establish and maintain orderly market conditions for agricultural products—including raisins, prunes, avocados, mangoes, limes, grapefruit, oranges, walnuts, processed dates, and filberts—and to impose quotas or higher duty rates on imported agricultural products, whenever investigation reveals that orderly market conditions require such action.

19 CFR Part 132
Regulations for Enforcement of AAA Quotas
These regulations provide for Customs enforcement of AAA quotas and higher duty rates imposed on imported agricultural products, whenever investigation reveals that orderly market conditions require such action.

42 USC 264 et seq.
The Plant Quarantine Act
This Act gives the Plant Protection and Quarantine branch of the USDA authority to restrict or prohibit importation of plants or their seeds found to carry specific plant pests and pathogens.

7 USC 147a et seq.
Federal Plant Pest Act (FPPA)
This Act prohibits the importation into or movement through the U.S. of plant pests as defined in the Act, and provides for the inspection of any letter, box, parcel, or container that may carry a plant pest. Inspection is to be performed by U.S. Department of Agriculture in conjunction with Customs.

7 CFR Part 351
Regulations for Entry and Inspection of Plants by Mail
These regulations set forth the plant imports that are prohibited, the requirements for entering restricted plants by mail, and the inspection procedures followed by the USDA's Animal and Plant Health Inspection Service (APHIS).

19 CFR 12.10 et seq.
Regulations for Entry and Release of Restricted Plants
These regulations prescribe the procedures followed by U.S. Customs to enforce the USDA requirements for importation of plants.

7 USC 135 et seq.
Federal Insecticide, Fungicide, and Rodenticide Act (FIFRA)
This Act prohibits the importation of pesticides or devices that are adulterated, misbranded, or otherwise violative of the Act, provides for registration of pesticides and devices, and establishes standards for labeling and classifying pesticides.

19 CFR 12; 40 CFR Part 162
Regulations on Pesticides
These regulations set forth the procedures and guidelines for importing products exposed to pesticides.

Principal Exporting Countries

The following listing includes samples of the main supplier nations of the products of this chapter. It is organized by HTSUS major heading. (Refer to "Customs Classification" above for the product codes.) Countries are listed in rank order of the value of products imported to the U.S. Statistics represent customs value entries for 1993 from the Bureau of Census, U.S. Department of Commerce.

0801—India, Brazil, Philippines, Mozambique, Bolivia, Indonesia, Dominican Rep., Peru, Chile, Mexico

0802—Mexico, China, Australia, Turkey, Italy, Cote d'Ivoire, Hong Kong, India, Costa Rica, Guatemala

0803—Costa Rica, Ecuador, Colombia, Guatemala, Honduras, Mexico, Panama, Venezuela, Philippines, Dominican Rep.

0804—Mexico, Costa Rica, Honduras, Dominican Rep., Brazil, Thailand, Turkey, Pakistan, Haiti, Spain

0805—Mexico, Spain, Australia, Morocco, Chile, Bahamas, Japan, Israel, Dominican Rep., Jamaica

0806—Chile, Mexico, Turkey, Italy, St. Lucia, Canada, Argentina, Tokelau, Greece, Pakistan

0807—Mexico, Costa Rica, Honduras, Guatemala, Panama, El Salvador, Jamaica, Nicaragua, Ecuador, Dominican Rep.

0808—New Zealand, Chile, Canada, Argentina, South Africa, Brazil, South Korea, Japan, Australia, St. Lucia

0809—Chile, New Zealand, Canada, Mexico, Turkey, Australia, St. Lucia, Swaziland, France, Israel

0810—Mexico, Canada, New Zealand, Chile, Colombia, Thailand, Italy, Israel, Guatemala, Costa Rica

0811—Mexico, Canada, Philippines, Costa Rica, Chile, Guatemala, Thailand, Honduras, Dominican Rep., Haiti

0812—Mexico, Italy, Greece, Taiwan, Chile, China, Spain, Japan, Thailand, Germany

0813—Turkey, Argentina, Chile, Thailand, China, Taiwan, France, South Africa, Italy, Bulgaria

0814—Mexico, Israel, Germany, Spain, Haiti, Switzerland, China, Hong Kong, Dominican Rep., Turkey

Chapter 9: Coffee, Tea, and Spices*

Full title: Coffee, Tea, Maté, and Spices

This chapter relates to the importation of coffee, tea, maté, and spices, which are classified under Chapter 9 of the Harmonized Tariff Schedule of the United States (HTSUS). Specifically, it includes all forms of coffee or products containing coffee; green, black, and flavored teas; maté; pepper; vanilla, cinnamon, cloves, nutmegs, various spice seeds, ginger, various aromatic leaves, and mixtures or blends of spices, such as curry powder. This section is supplemental to the "Foods" appendix on page 808. If you are interested in importing coffee, tea, or spices, you should read that section in conjunction with this one.

If you are interested in importing seasoning and flavoring preparations or condiments—such as prepared mustard—or edible extracts of coffee or tea as beverages, you should refer to Commodity Index Chapter 21; for citrus peel for use in infusions or flavorings, see Chapter 8. For the importation of vegetables and vegetable products used for flavoring—such as onions, garlic, and capers—or herbs—such as tarragon, fennel, marjoram, and savory—and for fresh peppers, see Chapter 7. Those interested in importing herb teas, cubeb pepper, or aromatic or other leaves from which infusions or preparations having medicinal properties can be made should refer to Chapter 12. If products are represented as having therapeutic properties or are listed in the U.S. Pharmacopoeia or the National Formulary, you should refer to Chapter 30.

Key Factors

The key factors in the importation of coffee, tea, maté, and spices are:

- Compliance with U.S. Food and Drug Administration (FDA) purity, identity, manufacturing, and other standards
- Compliance with FDA entry notification and procedures
- If therapeutic claims are made for the product, compliance with the drug provisions of the Food, Drug, and Cosmetic Act (FDCA)

Although most importers utilize the services of a licensed customs broker in making their entries, and we recommend this practice, you should be aware of the regulatory, entry, and documentation issues involved in importing your product. You, as importer, are ultimately responsible for the fulfillment of any legal requirements applicable to your shipment.

*IMPORTANT: Read the Commodity Index Introduction. It is the essential framework for understanding this section.

General Considerations

Regulatory Agencies. Importation of coffee, tea, maté, and spices is regulated by the FDA, which enforces the Federal Food, Drug, and Cosmetic Act (FDCA). All products derived from plants may also be subject to U.S. Department of Agriculture (USDA) regulations and inspection.

USDA Regulations. In general, USDA does not restrict coffee, tea, maté, or spices, although products derived from plants are often subject to USDA-enforced quarantines, standards, and quotas. If you are in any doubt as to the regulatory status of your product, you should check with the USDA Animal and Plant Health Inspection Service (APHIS) (see addresses at end of this chapter). Information regarding USDA restrictions on edible plant products can be found in the "Foods" appendix on page 808.

FDA Inspections. FDA regulations regarding importation of foods of any kind are extensive and stringent. All imported food products must meet all FDCA standards for food produced domestically. An exception is made for tea, which is not produced anywhere in the U.S., but which is subject to the standards of the Tea Importation Act (TIA). Imported products regulated by the FDA are subject to port-of-entry inspection. **Form FD701** is required for all FDA-regulated importations and may be obtained from your local FDA Import Operations office, from FDA headquarters (see addresses at end of this chapter), or from your customs broker. For an annotated diagram of required FDA import procedures refer to the "Foods" appendix on page 808.

If your shipment is found to be noncomplying, it may be detained at the port of entry. The FDA may permit you to bring such a shipment into compliance before making a final decision regarding admittance. However, any sorting, reprocessing, or relabeling must be supervised by FDA personnel, and is done at the importer's expense. A conditional release to allow the importer to bring a shipment into compliance is a privilege, not a right. The FDA may consider subsequent noncomplying shipments of the same type of product to constitute abuse of the privilege and require the importer to destroy or reexport the products. To ascertain what your legal responsibilities are, you should contact the FDA about the specific items to be imported.

Customs Classification

For customs purposes, coffee, tea, maté, and spices are classified under Chapter 9 of the HTSUS. This chapter is broken into major headings, which are further divided into subheadings, each of which has its own HTSUS classification number. For example, the HTSUS number for flavored green tea is 0902.20.10, indicating that it is a sub-subcategory of other green tea (0902.20.00), which is a subcategory of the major heading tea, whether or not flavored (0902.00.00). There are 10 major headings within Chapter 9.

0901—Coffee, whether or not roasted or decaffeinated; coffee husks and skins; coffee substitutes containing coffee in any proportion

0902—Tea, whether or not flavored

0903—Maté

0904—Pepper of the genus *Piper*; dried or crushed or ground fruits of the genus *Capsicum* or of the genus *Pimenta*

0905—Vanilla beans

0906—Cinnamon and cinnamon tree flowers

0907—Cloves

0908—Nutmeg, mace, and cardamoms

0909—Seeds of anise, badian, fennel, coriander, cumin, or caraway; juniper berries

0910—Ginger, saffron, turmeric, thyme, bay leaves, curry, and other spices

For more details regarding classification of the specific product you are interested in importing, consult a customs broker, the appropriate commodity specialist at your nearest customs port, or see HTSUS. HTSUS is available for purchase from the U.S. Government Printing Office (see addresses at end of this chapter), and may be found in larger public libraries. Refer to "Classification—Liquidation" on page 207 for a general discussion of customs classification.

Sample Import Duties

Import duties will vary depending on the HTSUS classification of your product. Therefore, to determine the correct amount of duties, your product must be properly classified under the HTSUS. The following sample duties are taken from the duty listings for HTSUS Chapter 9 products.

Unroasted, undecaffeinated Arabica coffee (0901.11.00): free; decaffeinated coffee (0901.22.00): free; coffee substitutes containing coffee (0901.30.00): 3.3 cents/kg; flavored green tea in packages not exceeding 3 kg (0902.10.10): 10%; unflavored green tea in packages not exceeding 3 kg (0902.10.90): free; black tea, regardless of packaging (0902.30.00): free; maté (0903.00.00): free; whole pepper of the genus *Piper* (0904.11.00): free; dried, crushed, or ground pepper of the genus *Capsicum*—including cayenne, paprika, and red pepper (0904.20.20): 3 cents/kg; of anaheim or ancho (0904.20.40): 11 cents/kg; of other Capsicum peppers—bell, jalapeño, and others—not ground (0904.20.60): 5.5 cents/kg; vanilla beans (0905.00.00): free; crushed or ground cinnamon (0906.20.00): free; cloves (0907.00.00): free; nutmeg (0908.10.00): free; cumin seed (0909.30.00): free; ground ginger (0910.40): 2.2 cents/kg; saffron (0910.20.00): free; processed thyme (0910.40.30): 5.6% through December 31, 1994, 7.5% thereafter; mixtures of spices from different headings (0910.91.00): 3%; dill (0910.99.50): free.

Special Provisions. The weight of retail packaging for teas (0902) is dutiable at the separate weight of such packaging as if it were imported empty, except when originating from either Canada or Mexico. Imports of teas (0902) are also subject to an examination fee of 3.5 cents/hundredweight or fraction thereof (21 USC 46a).

Entry and Documentation

The entry of merchandise is a two-part process consisting of 1) filing the documents necessary to determine whether merchandise may be released from Customs custody and 2) filing the documents that contain information for duty assessment and statistical purposes. In certain instances all documents must be filed and accepted by Customs prior to release of the goods. Unless you have been granted an extension, you must file entry documents at a location specified by the district or area director within five working days of your shipment's date of arrival at a U.S. port of entry. These include a number of standard documents required by Customs for any entry, and:

- FDA Importers Entry Notice, **Form FD701**

After you present the entry, Customs may examine your shipment, or may waive examination (food items are almost always inspected). The shipment is then released, provided no legal or regulatory violations have been noted. You must then file entry summary documentation and deposit estimated duties at a designated customhouse within 10 working days of your shipment's release. For a detailed description of entry procedures, standard documentation, and informal entry, see "Entry Process" on page 182.

Prohibitions and Restrictions

Coffee. If you are importing green coffee of the genus *Coffea*, you should be sure that your product is held at all times under sanitary conditions to prevent contamination by insects, rats, and mice. If you aware of conditions the FDA sees as grounds for detention of a coffee berry shipment, you will not be able to do much to avoid having your shipment turned away at the U.S. port of entry. The following conditions class coffee berries as objectionable and subject to detention: 1) any black coloration; 2) moldy; 3) water-damaged; 4) evidence of insect infestation; 5) any brown coloration ("sour"); 6) immature berries ("Quakers"); 7) shriveled berries; 8) presence of foreign material e.g. pods, sticks, or stones; 9) "sweepings" of spilled coffee recovered from ships' holds or docks; 10) contamination by ores and other poisonous materials in the vessel's cargo.

Tea and Maté. Tea offered for entry must meet all requirements of the FDCA as well as those of purity, quality, and fitness for consumption established by the Tea Importation Act (TIA). Teas of other than the species *Thea sinensis* must be so labelled to avoid confusing them with the standard, regulated product.

Spices. Spices and spice seeds are particularly vulnerable to contamination by insects, rodents, birds, and mold or decomposition. You should take every precaution to be sure that your product has been harvested, stored, handled, packed, and shipped under sanitary conditions. Insect control is particularly difficult for these items. Once a spice lot becomes insect-infested it is beyond hope of compliance with FDCA requirements. The FDA will not permit entry of spices or spice seeds containing either live or dead insects. Fumigation of an insect-infested lot of herbs or spices does not constitute bringing the product into compliance, since no consumer would willingly season food with dead insects and pesticides.

Thorough pre-storage cleaning and fumigation of premises in which herbs are to be stored is a good preventive measure. However, there are stringent EPA regulations regarding pesticide residues on products intended for human ingestion. You should be cognizant of any pesticide or fumigant that has been used on the product or its premises before purchase. Presence of illegal pesticide residues is grounds for refusal of entry. See the "Foods" appendix on page 808 for a discussion of pesticide residues on agricultural products.

Many spices once thought to have medicinal value continue to be marketed for various other purposes. If no therapeutic claims are made or implied in their labeling or promotional material, such products are regarded as foods and subject only to the food provisions of the law. FDA regulations are intended to prevent the marketing and use of such products for medicinal purposes unless they have been determined safe and effective for their intended uses. Spices that are presented as having therapeutic qualities, or that may be used for drug purposes, are subject to the drug provisions of the FDCA. In addition, any spices or spice oils that are listed in the U.S. Pharmacopoeia or the National Formulary are subject to the standards set forth in these compendia when sold for drug purposes. If the herbs or spices you intend to import fall into either of these categories, you should become familiar with the regulatory requirements for drugs under FDCA.

Standards of identity have been established for spices and herbs, based on botanical name. Common spice names on container labels must accurately reflect what is in the container according to this system. You may not, for example, label a product "dried thyme" if it is not entirely made up of the dried leaves and flowering tops of *Thymus vulgaris*. Under FDCA spices obtained from—or mixed with—material from other plants are both adulterated and misbranded. Such products will not be permitted into U.S., and if they slip by Customs and enter domestic trade, will be subject to seizure or—at minimum—recall. The FDA uses the following definitions for common spices:

Aromatic vegetable substances used for the seasoning of food. They are true to name, and from them no portion of any volatile oil or other flavoring principle has been removed. Onions, garlic, and celery are regarded as foods, not spices, even if dried.

Allspice. The dried nearly ripe fruit of *Pimentia officinalis*, Lind.

Anise. The dried fruit of *Pimpinella anisum* L.

Bay leaves. The dried leaves of *Laurus nobilis* L.

Caraway seed. The dried fruit of *Carum carvi* L.

Cardamom. The dried, nearly ripe fruit of *Elettaria cardamomum* Maton.

Cinnamon. The dried bark of cultivated varieties of *Cinnamomum zeylanicum* Nees (Ceylon cinnamon) or of *C. cassia* (L.) Blume (Saigon cinnamon or cassia), from which the outer layers may or may not have been removed.

Cloves. The dried flower buds of *Caryophyllus aromaticus* L.

Coriander. The dried fruit of *Coriandrum sativum* L.

Cumin Seed. The dried fruit of *Cuminum cyminum* L.

Ginger. The washed and dried, or decorticated and dried, rhizome of *Zingiber officinale* Roscoe.

Mace. The dried arillus of *Myristica fragrans* Houtt.

Macassar Mace, Papua Mace. The dried arillus of *Myristica argentea* Warb.

Nutmeg. The dried seed of *Myristica fragrans* Houtt, deprived of its testa, with or without a thin coating of lime (CaO).

Macassar Nutmeg, Papua Nutmeg, Male Nutmeg, Long Nutmeg. The dried seed of *Myristica argentea* Jarb, deprived of its testa.

Paprika. The dried, ripe fruit of *Capsicum annuum* L.

Black Pepper. The dried, immature berry of *Piper nigrum* L.

White Pepper. The dried mature berry of *Piper nigrum* L. from which the outer coating or the outer and inner coatings have been removed.

Saffron. The dried stigma of *Crocus sativus* L.

Thyme. The dried leaves and flowering tops of *Thymus vulgaris*.

As with any agricultural commodity, no product may contain either residues of pesticides illegal for use in the U.S., or illegal levels of legal pesticides. Nor may any products of Chapter 9 be represented directly or indirectly as being capable of producing health, energy, endurance, or other physiological side effects. For a full discussion of pesticide residue on agricultural products, refer to the "Foods" appendix on page 808.

Marking and Labeling Requirements

Products must be clearly labeled to avoid misrepresentation of contents. Nor may products of Chapter 9 be marked to state or imply that they possess medicinal properties. For a general discussion of U.S. Customs marking and labeling requirements, see "Marking: Country of Origin" on page 215 and "Special Marking Requirements" on page 217.

Shipping Considerations

You will need to ensure that your goods are packaged and shipped with care so that they arrive in good condition and pass smoothly through Customs. You are responsible for ensuring that the shipment is in compliance with all applicable government regulations for packaging and shipping. In most instances, you should not leave these arrangements to the discretion of your supplier. Careful preparation of the cargo and selection of the mode of transport can be essential to a cost-effective, timely delivery of undamaged goods. We strongly advise you to consult your shipping representative, insurance agent, or freight broker for advice on packing and shipping. Refer to the "Foods" appendix on page 808 and also to the section "Packing/Shipping/Insurance" for a general discussion of packing and shipping.

Publications Available

The following publication explains the FDA requirements for importing coffee. It is published by the FDA and is available on request from FDA headquarters (see addresses at end of this chapter).

Requirements of Laws and Regulations Enforced by the U.S. Food and Drug Administration

The following publication gives brief, general guidelines on USDA regulated products. Although designed primarily for tourists, it contains a list of approved products that you may find helpful. It is published by USDA APHIS (see addresses at end of this chapter).

Travelers Tips On Bringing Food, Plant, and Animal Products into the United States

The *Harmonized Tariff Schedule of the United States* (HTSUS) is available from:

Government Printing Office (GPO)
Superintendent of Documents
Washington, DC 20402
(202) 512-1800 (Order line)
(202) 512-0000 (General)

The USGPO also has copies of specific laws available for purchase. The USGPO accepts credit card orders over the phone, as well as mail orders paid by credit card, a check drawn on a U.S. bank, or an international money order.

Relevant Government Agencies

Address your questions regarding FDA import requirements for coffee to:

Food and Drug Administration (FDA)
Center for Food Safety and Applied Nutrition
200 C Street SW
Washington, DC 20204
(202) 205-5241, 205-5042

Food and Drug Administration (FDA)
Division of Enforcement, Imports Branch
200 C Street SW
Washington, DC 20204
(202) 205-4726

Address your questions regarding USDA import requirements for coffee to:

U.S. Department of Agriculture (USDA)
Animal and Plant Health Inspection Service (APHIS)
Plant Protection and Quarantine (PPQ)
Federal Building, Rm. 631
6505 Belcrest Road
Hyattsville, MD 20782
(301) 436-8645

Address questions regarding allowable pesticide residues on coffee, tea, maté, and spices to:

Environmental Protection Agency (EPA)
Office of Pesticide Programs
401 M Street SW (7501-C)
Washington, DC 20460
(703) 305-7090 (General)
(703) 305-7102 (Import/export requirements)

Address your questions regarding importation of coffee to the district or port director of Customs for you area. For addresses refer to "U.S. Customs District Offices" on page 62 or contact:

U.S. Customs Service
1301 Constitution Ave. NW
Washington, DC 20229
(202) 927-6724 (Information)
(202) 927-1000 (General)

Laws and Regulations

The following laws and regulations may be relevant to the importation of coffee, tea, maté, and spices. The laws are contained in the U. S. Code (USC) and the regulations are found in the Code of Federal Regulations (CFR), both of which may be available at larger public and law libraries. Copies of specific laws are also available from the United States Government Printing Office (address above).

21 USC 301 et seq.
Food, Drug, and Cosmetic Act
This Act prohibits deceptive practices and regulates the manufacture, sale and importation or exportation of food, drugs, cosmetics, and related products. See 21 USC 331, 381, 382.

19 CFR 12.1 et seq.; 21 CFR 1.83 et seq.
Regulations on Food, Drugs, and Cosmetics
These regulations of the Secretary of Health and Human Services and the Secretary of the Treasury govern the standards, labeling, marking, and importing of products used with food, drugs, and cosmetics.

21 USC 41 et seq.
Tea Importation Act
This Act prohibits the import of tea that is inferior to the standards promulgated by the Secretary of Health and Human Services and the Secretary of the Treasury and allows imports of tea only as permitted by the Harmonized Tariff Schedule.

19 CFR 12.33; 21 CFR Part 1220
Regulations on Importing Tea
These regulations set the standards for imported tea and govern the entry and inspection procedures.

7 USC 135 et seq.
Federal Insecticide, Fungicide, and Rodenticide Act (FIFRA)
This Act prohibits the importation of pesticides or devices that are adulterated, misbranded, or otherwise violative of the Act, provides for registration of pesticides and devices, and establishes standards for labeling and classifying pesticides.

19 CFR 12; 40 CFR 162
Regulations on Pesticides
These regulations set forth the procedures and guidelines for importing products exposed to pesticides.

42 USC 264 et seq.
The Plant Quarantine Act
This Act gives the Plant Protection and Quarantine branch of the USDA authority to restrict or prohibit importation of plants or their seeds found to carry specific plant pests and pathogens.

7 CFR Part 351
Regulations for Entry and Inspection of Plants by Mail
These regulations set forth the plant imports that are prohibited, the requirements for entering restricted plants by mail, and the inspection procedures followed by the USDA's Animal and Plant Health Inspection Service (APHIS).

19 CFR 12.10 et seq.
Regulations for Entry and Release of Restricted Plants
These regulations prescribe the procedures followed by U.S. Customs to enforce the USDA requirements for importation of plants.

Principal Exporting Countries

The following listing includes samples of the main supplier nations of the products of this chapter. It is organized by HTSUS major heading. (Refer to "Customs Classification" above for the product codes.) Countries are listed in rank order of the value of products imported to the U.S. Statistics represent customs value entries for 1993 from the Bureau of Census, U.S. Department of Commerce.

0901—Colombia, Mexico, Brazil, Guatemala, El Salvador, Thailand, Ecuador, Germany, Indonesia, Costa Rica

0902—China, Argentina, Germany, Indonesia, Sri Lanka, Kenya, India, Malawi, Brazil, United Kingdom

0903—Argentina, Brazil, China, Paraguay, Taiwan, Mexico, Thailand

0904—India, Indonesia, Mexico, Chile, China, Brazil, Spain, Hong Kong, Thailand, Morocco

0905—Madagascar, Indonesia, Comoros, Tonga, Mexico, French Polynesia, Costa Rica, Jamaica

0906—Indonesia, Sri Lanka, China, India, Singapore, Germany, Malaysia, Taiwan, Hong Kong, Portugal

0907—Madagascar, Malaysia, Tanzania, Sri Lanka, Singapore, Indonesia, France, Brazil, Germany, Thailand

0908—Indonesia, Guatemala, Singapore, Grenada, Netherlands, India, Antigua And Barbuda, Colombia, Sri Lanka, Germany

0909—Turkey, Pakistan, Netherlands, Egypt, India, Syria, China, United Arab Emirates, Canada, Denmark

0910—Turkey, Spain, India, Mexico, Indonesia, Brazil, China, Costa Rica, Japan, Israel

Chapter 10: Cereals*

This chapter relates to the importation of cereals as raw agricultural products, either as grain or seed, which are classified under Chapter 10 of the Harmonized Tariff Schedule of the United States (HTSUS). Specifically, it includes wheat, corn, sorghum, rye, barley, oats, rice, and other grains—such as millet and buckwheat—as well as their seed (with the exception of rice). This section is supplemental to the "Foods" appendix on page 808. If you are interested in importing cereals, you should read that section in conjunction with this one.

If you are interested in importing intermediate processed products such as flour, worked grain, starches, gluten, and similar products, you should refer to Commodity Index Chapter 11, while cereal preparations that are either finished or at an advanced stage of processing and baked goods are covered in Chapter 19. The importation of sweet corn—which is considered a vegetable rather than a cereal—is covered in Chapter 7. If you are interested in importing oil seeds—such as soybeans or flax seed—or fodder crops, refer to Chapter 12.

Key Factors

The key factors in the importation of cereals are:

- Compliance with U.S. Food and Drug Administration (FDA) purity, identity, manufacturing, and other standards
- Compliance with FDA entry notification requirements and procedures
- Compliance with United States Department of Agriculture (USDA) plant quarantine restrictions—permits may be required
- Compliance with USDA import restrictions—permits may be required in some cases
- Compliance with USDA country-specific prohibitions on corn, wheat, and rice grain or seed
- Compliance with U.S. Environmental Protection Agency (EPA) regulations on pesticide residues on imported agricultural products

Although most importers use the services of a licensed customs broker in making their entries, and we recommend this practice, you should be aware of the regulatory, entry, and documentation issues involved in importing your product. You, as importer, are ultimately responsible for the fulfillment of any legal requirements applicable to your shipment.

*IMPORTANT: Read the Commodity Index Introduction. It is the essential framework for understanding this section.

General Considerations

Regulatory Agencies. The importation of cereal grains and seeds is regulated by a variety of U.S. government agencies. The USDA Animal and Plant Health Inspection Service (APHIS) Plant Protection and Quarantine Branch (PPQ) enforces the Plant Quarantine Act (PQA), while the FDA administers the provisions of the Food, Drug, and Cosmetic Act (FDCA). Other relevant regulations include the Federal Seed Act (FSA) and the Federal Noxious Weed Act (FNWA), also enforced by the USDA. The EPA enforces the Federal Insecticide, Fungicide, and Rodenticide Act (FIFRA), which establishes regulatory limits on pesticide residues on edible plant products. For more information contact the EPA (see addresses at end of this chapter).

FDA Inspection Requirements. Cereals imported into the U.S. must comply with all requirements for those produced domestically. Imported products regulated by FDA regulations are subject to port of entry inspection. **Form FD701** is required for all FDA-regulated importations and may be obtained from your local FDA Import Operations office, from FDA headquarters (see addresses at end of this chapter), or through your customs broker. For an annotated diagram of required FDA import procedures, refer to the "Foods" appendix on page 808.

Sampling. U.S. Customs is responsible for sampling cereal shipments imported from Canada. At all other border crossings, the Plant Protection and Quarantine unit of APHIS performs this sampling. The Federal Seed Act prescribes methods to be used in sampling. Quantities of cereals may be designated as a single lot for sampling purposes only if the shipment is uniform within established tolerances with respect to pure grain (that is, of a single kind, not of mixed varieties), percentage of weeds, and occurrence of noxious weed seed. When a shipment consists of more than a single lot, each lot is sampled separately. When importation is across the Canadian border, Customs will notify you that sampling has occurred and that the shipment is being held pending APHIS determination. Sampling done by APHIS PPQ officers is carried out at the port of entry. Shipments are usually released unless a suspected noxious weed is found.

Detention of Shipment. If your shipment is found to be noncomplying, it may be detained at the port of entry. The inspecting agency may allow you to bring such a shipment into compliance before making a final decision regarding admittance. However, any sorting, reprocessing, or relabeling must usually be supervised by agency personnel and is done at the importer's expense. A conditional release to allow the importer to bring a shipment into compliance is a privilege, not a right. The inspecting agency may consider subsequent noncomplying shipments of the same type of product to constitute abuse of the privilege and require the importer to destroy or reexport the products. To ascertain what your legal responsibilities are, you should contact these agencies regarding the specific items to be imported.

Customs Classification

For customs purposes, cereals are classified under Chapter 10 of the HTSUS. This chapter is broken into major headings, which are further divided into subheadings, and often sub-subheadings, each of which has its own HTSUS classification number. For example, the HTSUS number for red spring wheat is 1001.90.20, indicating it is a sub-subcategory of wheat other than durum wheat (1001.90.00), which is a subcategory of the major heading, wheat and meslin (1001.00.00). There are eight major headings within Chapter 10.

1001—Wheat and meslin

1002—Rye

1003—Barley

1004—Oats

1005—Corn (maize)

1006—Rice

1007—Grain sorghum (milo)

1008—Other cereals

For more details regarding classification of the specific product you are interested in importing, consult a customs broker, the appropriate commodity specialist at your nearest customs port, or see HTSUS. HTSUS is available for purchase from the US Government Printing Office (see addresses at end of this chapter), and may be found in larger public libraries. Refer to "Classification—Liquidation" on page 207 or a general discussion of customs classification.

Sample Import Duties

Import duties will vary depending on the HTSUS classification of your product. Therefore, to determine the correct amount of duties, your product must be properly classified under the HTSUS. The following sample duties are taken from the duty listings for HTSUS Chapter 10 products.

Red spring wheat (1001.90.20): 0.77 cents/kg; malting barley (1003.00.20): 0.23 cents/kg; oats (1004.00.00): free; yellow dent corn (1005.90.20): 0.2 cents/kg; rice in the husk (1006.10.00): 2.8 cents/kg; semi-milled or wholly milled rice, whether polished or glazed, parboiled (1006.30.10): 17.5%; grain sorghum (1007.00.00) 0.88 cents/kg; millet (1008.20.00): 0.7 cents/kg.

Entry and Documentation

The entry of merchandise is a two-part process consisting of 1) filing the documentation necessary to determine whether merchandise may be released from Customs custody and 2) filing the documents that contain information for duty assessment and statistical purposes. In certain instances all documents must be filed and accepted by Customs prior to release of the goods. Unless you have been granted an extension, you must file entry documents at a location specified by the district or area director within five working days of your shipment's date of arrival at a US port of entry. These include a number of standard documents required by Customs for any entry, and:

- FDA Entry Notification **Form FD701**
- USDA APHIS Import Permit when required

After you present the entry, Customs may examine your shipment, or may waive examination. The shipment is then released provided no legal or regulatory violations have been noted. You must then file entry summary documentation and deposit estimated duties at a designated customhouse within 10 working days of your shipment's release. For a detailed description of entry procedures, standard documentation, and informal entry, see "Entry Process" on page 182.

Entry Invoice—Grain or Grain and Screenings. Customs requires the following specific information on invoices for cultivated grain or grain and screenings: 1) a statement that no screenings are included with the grain; or 2) if screenings are included, the percentage of the shipment that consists of screenings commingled with the principal grain.

Entry Invoice—Screenings or Scalpings. Customs requires special information on the entry invoice for grain screenings or scalpings of grain or cereal seeds: 1) whether the commodity is the product of a screening process; 2) if so, whether any cultivated grains have been added to such commodity; and 3) if any such grains have been added, the kind and percentage of each.

Prohibitions and Restrictions

The USDA establishes "temporary" restrictions on the importation of specific cereal grains and seeds originating in specific countries to protect U.S. agriculture or public health from the proliferation of pests or weeds. Importation of the grain or seed of wheat and of corn and plants considered to be closely related (such as millet and sorghum) is currently subject to country-specific prohibitions. Wheat from countries not on the prohibited list is eligible for import without advance authorization. However, imports of corn, even from countries not on the prohibited list, require import permits from the USDA. Other grains generally may be imported with advance permission. No rice seed may be imported into the U.S. from any country in the world. All rice imports must be processed so that propagation cannot occur.

Inspection. All shipments of cereals are subject to USDA inspection and sampling at the port of entry, although imports of cereal grain for uses other than as seed may be treated somewhat more leniently. If you are importing cereals for use as seed in small lots (that is, up to 100 lbs.), your shipment is unlikely to be sampled. For a more complete discussion of lot and sampling levels, see the Federal Seed Act, Regulation Parts 201-202 and Table 6.

Detention of Shipment. If your shipment is sampled and found to contain evidence of noxious weeds, insect infestation, disease, or other contamination, it will be detained pending a USDA ruling on whether to allow entry. If the contaminant is one which is rare or nonexistent in the U.S., the shipment will be refused admission. If your shipment is found to be adulterated or unfit for seeding purposes according to FSA requirements, you may be allowed to have it cleaned or processed under USDA supervision, at your expense. Once grain has been cleaned or processed, any portion of it shown by test, analysis, or examination to meet FSA requirements can be admitted. The USDA APHIS makes the decision to allow such cleaning or processing on a case-by-case basis.

In most instances, cereal grain imports that fail to meet the more stringent requirements for importation as seed may be admitted for use as animal feed or for industrial purposes. This practice does not apply to grain found to contain weeds prohibited under the Federal Noxious Weed Act (FNWA), which allows zero tolerance for the presence of such harmful plants. Seeds of plants listed in the FNWA which may be present in lots of cereal grains, are subject to the restrictions defined in the act. You can get up-to-date-information on current FNWA restrictions from USDA APHIS (see addresses at end of this chapter).

Screenings. Screenings of most seeds are banned from importation, although screenings of cereal grains including wheat, oats, rye, barley, buckwheat, field corn, sorghum, broomcorn, and proso millet may be imported as long as they are not from prohibited sources and are not intended for use as seed. The words "screenings for processing, not for seeding" must appear on the invoice or other paperwork for such imports.

Imports for Research Purposes. The USDA may permit small amounts of cereal seed of prohibited varieties or from prohibited countries into the U.S. under permit for research purposes on a case-by-case basis. Such research imports are closely monitored by APHIS, and are subject to stringent quarantine and handling requirements. If you are interested in importing small amounts of cereal seed for research purposes, contact the USDA APHIS Permit Unit for further information. Commercial lot amounts of prohibited seed will not be permitted to enter the U.S. For a listing of current prohibitions, refer to "Country-Specific Import Restrictions" below.

Country-Specific Import Restrictions

The following cereal grains and their seeds are banned from importation into the U.S. by the USDA if they originate from the countries listed.

Corn and closely related plants and their parts (including those of the genus *Chionachne, Coix, Echinochloa, Eleusina, Euchleana, Miscanthus, Panicum, Pennisetum, Polytoca, Sclerachne, Setaria, Sorghum, Trilobachne,* and *Tripsicum*) [Note: these restrictions are under review, but no changes are anticipated in the near term]: Africa (all countries), Australia, Bangladesh, Bhutan, Brunei, Bulgaria, Burma (Myanmar), Cambodia (Kampuchea), Hong Kong, India, Indonesia, Japan and adjacent islands, Laos, Malaysia, Nepal, New Zealand [shelled corn may be imported from New Zealand under permit], North Korea, Oceania, Pakistan, Papua New Guinea, People's Republic of China, Philippines, Russia and the other republics of the former Soviet Union, Singapore, South Korea, Sri Lanka, Taiwan, Thailand, and Vietnam.

Wheat—Prohibited because of flag smut: Algeria, Australia, Bangladesh, Bulgaria, Chile, China, Cyprus, Egypt, Falkland Islands/Malvinas, Greece, Guatemala, Hungary, Iran, Israel, Italy, Japan, Korea, Libya, Morocco, Oman, Portugal, Romania, Russia and the other republics of the former Soviet Union, South Africa, Spain, Tanzania, Tunisia, Turkey, and Venezuela.

Wheat—Prohibited because of Karnal burnt: Mexico.

Wheat—Prohibited because of flag smut and Karnal burnt: Afghanistan, India, Iraq, Nepal, and Pakistan.

Rice from Thailand. As of mid-1994, a countervailing duties case had been filed regarding imports of rice from Thailand and imports of such products were being held up at Customs pending resolution. Those interested in importing this item may experience delays in clearing Customs or be subject to additional duties and should check with U.S. Customs to verify the current status of imports of this product from Thailand.

Marking and Labeling Requirements

All food imports must be labeled with the country of origin of the product. Imports of cereal grains must bear a statement by the importer as to the intended use of the product. If the shipment is denied admission for use as seed but subsequently allowed in for other purposes, the importer may withdraw the original statement and submit an amended declaration stating that the shipment is intended for feed or industrial purposes and that no part is intended to be used as seed.

Seed imports are required to be packaged in separate containers and labeled with the certification of the appropriate official agency of the exporting country to the effect that the product was grown in that country and has been approved for use as seed. Containers must also bear a record number demonstrating inspection of the lot by agricultural officials in the exporting country.

The invoice and any other labeling shall bear the lot identification, the kind of product present, and note any treatment given to the product.

For a general discussion of U.S. Customs marking and labeling requirements, see "Marking: Country of Origin" on page 215 and the following sections.

Shipping Considerations

You will need to ensure that your goods are packaged and shipped with care so that they arrive in good condition and pass smoothly through Customs. You are responsible for ensuring that the shipment is in compliance with all applicable government regulations for packaging and shipping. In most instances, you should not leave these arrangements solely to the discretion of your supplier. Careful preparation of the cargo and selection of the mode of transport can be essential to a cost-effective, timely delivery of undamaged goods. We strongly advise you to consult your shipping representative, insurance agent, or freight broker for advice on packing and shipping. Refer also to the major tab section "Packing/Shipping/Insurance" for a general discussion of packing and shipping.

Cereal grains are usually transported in bulk, although in some instances they may be shipped in bags or other types of containers (seeds must be packaged separately). General considerations include protection from contamination by dirt, pests, or other foreign matter, as well as the effects of heat and dampness on the goods shipped.

Publications Available

The following publication explains the FDA requirements for importing cereal grains. It is published by the FDA and is available on request from FDA headquarters (see addresses at end of this chapter).

Requirements of Laws and Regulations Enforced by the U.S. Food and Drug Administration

The *Harmonized Tariff Schedule of the United States* (HTSUS) is available from:

Government Printing Office (GPO)
Superintendent of Documents
Washington, DC 20402
(202) 512-1800 (Order line)
(202) 512-0000 (General)

The USGPO also has copies of specific laws available for purchase. The USGPO accepts credit card orders over the phone, as well as mail orders paid by credit card, a check drawn on a U.S. bank, or an international money order.

Relevant Government Agencies

Address your inquiries regarding requirements for importation of cereal grains and any necessary permits to:

Food and Drug Administration (FDA)
Center for Food Safety and Applied Nutrition
200 C Street SW
Washington, DC 20204
(202) 205-5241, 205-5042

Food and Drug Administration (FDA)
Division of Enforcement, Imports Branch
200 C Street SW
Washington, DC 20204
(202) 205-4726

U.S. Department of Agriculture (USDA)
Animal and Plant Health Inspection Service (APHIS)
Plant Protection and Quarantine (PPQ)
Federal Building, Rm. 631
6505 Belcrest Road
Hyattsville, MD 20782
(301) 436-8645

Address questions regarding allowable pesticide residues on grain to:

Environmental Protection Agency (EPA)
Office of Pesticide Programs
401 M Street SW (7501-C)
Washington, DC 20460
(703) 305-7090 (General)
(703) 305-7102 (Import/export requirements)

Address your questions regarding importation of cereal grains to the district or port director of Customs for you area. For addresses refer to "U.S. Customs District Offices" on page 62 or contact:

U.S. Customs Service
1301 Constitution Ave. NW
Washington, DC 20229
(202) 927-6724 (Information)
(202) 927-1000 (General)

Laws and Regulations

The following laws and regulations may be relevant to the importation of cereals. The laws are contained in the U.S. Code (USC) and the regulations are published in the Code of Federal Regulations (CFR), both of which may be available at larger public and law libraries. Copies of specific laws are also available from the United States Government Printing Office (address above).

21 USC 301 et seq.
Food, Drug, and Cosmetic Act
This Act prohibits deceptive practices and regulates the manufacture, sale and importation or exportation of food, drugs, cosmetics, and related products. See 21 USC 331, 381, 382.

19 CFR 12.1 et seq.; 21 CFR 1.83 et seq.
Regulations on Food, Drugs, and Cosmetics
These regulations of the Secretary of Health and Human Services and the Secretary of the Treasury govern the standards, labeling, marking, and importing of products used with food, drugs, and cosmetics.

7 USC 135 et seq.
Federal Insecticide, Fungicide, and Rodenticide Act (FIFRA)
This Act prohibits the importation of pesticides or devices that are adulterated, misbranded, or otherwise in violation of the Act, provides for registration of pesticides and devices, and establishes standards for labeling and classifying pesticides.

19 CFR 12; 21 CFR 180 and 193; 40 CFR 162
Regulations on Pesticides
These regulations set forth the procedures and guidelines for importing products exposed to pesticides.

7 USC 1551 et seq.
Federal Seed Act
This Act restricts the entry of agricultural seed to ensure that the seed is what its label says it is and is free from any noxious weed as identified in the Federal Seed Act (not the same as the noxious weeds listed in the Federal Noxious Weed Act). Purity and germination standards are no longer covered by this act. Weeds specifically restricted under the act include: quack grass, Canada thistle, perennial sow thistle, dodder, whitetop, Johnsongrass, Russian knapweed, bindweed, and leafy spurge. A tolerance of two of these is allowed per given amount of seed.

42 USC 264 et seq.
The Plant Quarantine Act
This Act gives the Plant Protection and Quarantine branch of the USDA authority to restrict or prohibit importation of plants or their seeds found to carry specific plant pests and pathogens.

7 USC 147a et seq.
Federal Plant Pest Act (FPPA)
This Act prohibits the importation into or movement through the U.S. of plant pests as defined in the Act, and provides for the inspection of any letter, box, parcel, or container that may carry a plant pest. Inspection is to be performed by U.S. Department of Agriculture in conjunction with Customs.

7 CFR Part 351
Regulations for Entry and Inspection of Plants by Mail
These regulations set forth the plant imports that are prohibited, the requirements for entering restricted plants by mail, and the inspection procedures followed by the USDA's Animal and Plant Health Inspection Service (APHIS).

19 CFR 12.10 et seq.
Regulations for Entry and Release of Restricted Plants
These regulations prescribe the procedures followed by U.S. Customs to enforce the USDA requirements for importation of plants.

7 USC 2801
Federal Noxious Weed Act
This Act defines, delineates, and restricts weeds and their seeds found to be harmful to agricultural crops, livestock, irrigation, navigation, fish and wildlife resources, or public health. No tolerances are allowed.

Principal Exporting Countries

The following listing includes samples of the main supplier nations of the products of this chapter. It is organized by HTSUS major heading. (Refer to "Customs Classification" above for the product codes.) Countries are listed in rank order of the value of products imported to the U.S. Statistics represent customs value entries for 1993 from the Bureau of Census, U.S. Department of Commerce.

1001—Canada, Venezuela, United Kingdom, Germany, Turkey, Mauritania, Egypt, Peru, Austria, South Korea

1002—Canada, Mexico, Poland

1003—Canada, China, Thailand, France, South Korea, Italy, Spain, Germany, Japan, El Salvador

1004—Canada, Finland, Sweden, Fiji, Poland, Colombia, New Zealand, Jamaica

1005—Canada, Chile, Argentina, Romania, France, Mexico, Hungary, Thailand, Turkey, Brazil

1006—Thailand, India, Pakistan, Italy, United Kingdom, Canada, Brazil, Denmark, Taiwan, Hong Kong

1007—Argentina, Venezuela, Mexico, France, Canada

1008—Canada, Germany, France, South Africa, Bolivia, Poland, China, Japan, United Kingdom, Netherlands

Chapter 11: Milling Products*

Full title: Products of the Milling Industry; Malt; Starches; Inulin; Wheat Gluten

This chapter relates to the importation of milled cereals and related intermediate processed products, which are classified under Chapter 11 of the Harmonized Tariff Schedule of the United States (HTSUS). Specifically it includes such products as flour, worked grains, starches, and gluten. This section is supplemental to the "Foods" appendix on page 808. If you are interested in importing milled products, you should read that section in conjunction with this one.

If you are interested in importing cereal grains as a raw agricultural product, you should refer to Commodity Index Chapter 10. If you are interested in importing finished products, more highly processed cereal-based preparations, or baked goods you should consult Chapter 19. Flours and meals of oil seeds or oleaginous fruits are classified under Chapter 12. Cereal products are classified within Chapter 11 if they have been partially processed and—specifically—if they have a starch content generally greater than 45 percent and an ash content of less than from 1.6 to 5 percent of dry weight, depending on the particular type of grain. Products are intended primarily to be further prepared for human or animal consumption and for industrial uses.

Key Factors

The key factors in the importation of milled products are:

- Compliance with U.S. Food and Drug Administration (FDA) purity, identity, manufacturing, and other standards
- Compliance with FDA entry notification requirements and procedures
- Compliance with U.S. Department of Agriculture (USDA) plant quarantine restrictions—permits may be required
- Compliance with USDA import restrictions—permits may be required in some cases
- Compliance with USDA country-specific prohibitions on certain wheat and corn and related products
- Compliance with U.S. Environmental Protection Agency (EPA) restrictions on pesticide residues on agricultural products

*__IMPORTANT__: Read the Commodity Index Introduction. It is the essential framework for understanding this section.

Although most importers use the services of a licensed customs broker in making their entries, and we recommend this practice, you should be aware of the regulatory, entry, and documentation issues involved in importing your product. You, as the importer, are ultimately responsible for the fulfillment of any legal requirements applicable to your shipment.

General Considerations

Regulatory Agencies. The importation of milled products is regulated by a variety of U.S. government agencies. The USDA Animal and Plant Health Inspection Service (APHIS), Plant Protection and Quarantine Branch (PPQ) enforces the Plant Quarantine Act (PQA), while the FDA administers the provisions of the Food, Drug, and Cosmetic Act (FDCA). The EPA enforces the Federal Insecticide, Fungicide, and Rodenticide Act (FIFRA), which establishes regulatory limits on pesticide residues in edible plant products. Note also that any chemicals that leave detectable traces must be approved for use in the U.S. For more information, contact the EPA (see addresses at end of this chapter).

FDA Inspections. Milled products imported into the U.S. must comply with all requirements for those produced domestically. These include standards for nomenclature, levels of nutritional elements, and allowable additives as prescribed in detail in 21 CFR 137. Imported products regulated by FDA regulations are subject to port of entry inspection. **Form FD701** is required for all FDA-regulated importations and may be obtained from your local FDA Import Operations office, from FDA headquarters (see addresses at end of this chapter), or through your customs broker. For an annotated diagram of required FDA import procedures, refer to the "Foods" appendix on page 808.

Detention of Shipment. If your shipment is found to be noncomplying, it may be detained at the port of entry. The FDA may permit you to bring such a shipment into compliance before a final decision is made regarding admittance. However, any sorting, reprocessing, or relabeling must be supervised by FDA personnel and is done at the importer's expense. Such conditional release to allow the importer to bring a shipment into compliance is a privilege, not a right. The FDA may consider any subsequent noncomplying shipments of the same type of product to constitute abuse of the privilege and require the importer to destroy or reexport the products. To ascertain what your legal responsibilities are, you should contact this agency regarding the specific items to be imported.

USDA APHIS Sampling. U.S. Customs is responsible for sampling milled product shipments imported from Canada. At other border crossings, the Plant Protection and Quarantine (PPQ) Branch of APHIS performs this sampling directly. Quantities of milled products may be designated as a single lot for sampling purposes only if the shipment is uniform within established tolerances with respect to the variety of product involved, percentage of weeds and other foreign matter, and size uniformity within the shipment. When a shipment consists of more than a single lot, each lot is sampled separately. When importation is across the Canadian border, Customs will notify you that sampling has occurred and that the shipment is being held pending APHIS determination. Sampling done by PPQ officers is carried out at the port of entry.

Customs Classification

For customs purposes, milled products are classified under Chapter 11 of the HTSUS. This chapter is broken into major headings, which are further divided into subheadings, and often sub-subheadings, each of which has its own HTSUS classification number. For example, the HTSUS number for cornmeal is 1103.13.00, indicating that it is a sub-subcategory of groats and meals (1103.11.00), which is a subcategory of the major heading cereal groats, meal, and pellets (1103.00.00). There are nine major headings within Chapter 11.

1101—Wheat or meslin flour

1102—Cereal flours other than of wheat or meslin

1103—Cereal groats, meal, and pellets

1104—Cereal grains otherwise worked

1105—Flour, meal, flakes, granules, and pellets of potatoes

1106—Flour and meal of dried leguminous vegetables, sago, roots, tubers, or products of Chapter 8

1107—Malt

1108—Starches and inulin

1109—Wheat gluten

For more details regarding classification of the specific product you are interested in importing, consult a customs broker, the appropriate commodity specialist at your nearest customs port, or see HTSUS. HTSUS is available for purchase from the US Government Printing Office (see addresses at end of this chapter), and may be found in larger public libraries. For a general discussion of customs classification, see "Classification—Liquidation" on page 207.

Sample Import Duties

Import duties will vary depending on the HTSUS classification of your product. Therefore, to determine the correct amount of duties, your product must be properly classified under the HTSUS. The following sample duties are taken from duty listings for HTSUS Chapter 11 products.

Durum wheat flour (1101.00.20): 1.1 cents/kg; corn flour (1102.20.00) 0.66 cents/kg; rice flour (1102.30.00): 0.2 cents/kg; groats of wheat (1103.11.00): 1.1 cents/kg; pellets of other cereals (1103.29.00): free; rolled or flaked oats (1104.12.00): 1.8 cents/kg; pearled barley (1104.21.00): 2.7%; germ of cereals—whole, rolled, flaked, or ground (1104.30.00): 10%; potato flour and meal (1105.10.00): 2.6 cents/kg; flour and meal of sago, roots, or tubers of heading 0714 (1106.20.00): free; malt, whether or not roasted (1107.00.00): 0.66 cents/kg; corn starch (1108.12.00): 1.2 cents/kg; inulin (1108.20.00): 5.8 percent; wheat gluten—to be used as animal feed (1109.00.10): 4%.

Special Provisions. Mixtures of products in headings 1101 through 1104 are dutiable at 20% unless otherwise provided for or covered by a specific treaty (for example, US-Israel Free Trade Agreement: free; US-Canada Free Trade Agreement: 8%).

Entry and Documentation

The entry of merchandise is a two-part process consisting of 1) filing the documentation necessary to determine whether merchandise may be released from Customs custody and 2) filing the documents that contain information for duty assessment and statistical purposes. In certain instances all documents must be filed and accepted by Customs prior to release of the goods. Unless you have been granted an extension, you must file entry documents at a location specified by the district or area director within five working days of your shipment's date of arrival at a U.S. port of entry. These include a number of standard documents required by Customs for any entry, and:

- FDA Entry Notification **Form FD701**
- USDA APHIS Import Permit when required (contact USDA APHIS regarding permit requirements)

After you present the entry, Customs may examine your shipment, or may waive examination (food items are almost always inspected). The shipment is then released provided no legal or regulatory violations have been noted. You must then file entry summary documentation and deposit estimated duties at a designated customhouse within 10 working days of your shipment's release. For a detailed description of entry procedures, standard documentation, and informal entry, see "Entry Process" on page 182.

Prohibitions and Restrictions

The USDA establishes "temporary" restrictions on the importation of specific cereal grains and some intermediate products originating in specific countries to protect U.S. agriculture or public health from the proliferation of pests or weeds. Importation of wheat as well as of corn and closely related plants (such as millet and sorghum) is currently subject to country-specific prohibitions. For a listing of current prohibitions, see Country-Specific Import Restrictions below.

Imports of products made from corn and related plants (including millet and sorghum) require USDA permits. Intermediate milled products, such as meals (but not flours), made from wheat that originates in countries from which wheat imports are prohibited from entering the U.S. Milled products of wheat from other countries and those made from other grains require no special entry permits. All shipments of cereal products are subject to USDA quarantine, inspection, and sampling at the port of entry.

Country-Specific Import Restrictions

The following cereal grains are banned by the USDA from importation into the U.S. if they originate from the countries listed.

Corn and closely related plants, their parts, and intermediate products (including plants of the genus *Chionachne, Coix, Echinochloa, Eleusina, Euchleana, Miscanthus, Panicum, Pennisetum, Polytoca, Sclerachne, Setaria, Sorghum, Trilobachne,* and *Tripsicum*) [Note: regulations governing corn are under review, but no changes are anticipated in the near term]: Africa (all countries), Australia, Bangladesh, Bhutan, Brunei, Bulgaria, Burma (Myanmar), Cambodia (Kampuchea), Hong Kong, India, Indonesia, Japan and adjacent islands, Laos, Malaysia, Nepal, New Zealand [raw shelled corn may be imported from New Zealand], North Korea, Oceania, Pakistan, Papua New Guinea, People's Republic of China, Philippines, Russia and the other republics of the former Soviet Union, Singapore, South Korea, Sri Lanka, Taiwan, Thailand, and Vietnam.

Wheat—Prohibited because of flag smut: Algeria, Australia, Bangladesh, Bulgaria, Chile, China, Cyprus, Egypt, Falkland Islands/Malvinas, Greece, Guatemala, Hungary, Iran, Israel, Italy, Japan, Korea, Libya, Morocco, Oman, Portugal, Romania, Russia and the other republics of the former Soviet Union, South Africa, Spain, Tanzania, Tunisia, Turkey, and Venezuela.

Wheat—Prohibited because of Karnal burnt: Mexico.

Wheat—Prohibited because of flag smut and Karnal burnt: Afghanistan, India, Iraq, Nepal, and Pakistan.

Marking and Labeling Requirements

Imports of milled products must declare the country of origin for all imported products. The invoice and any other labeling shall bear the lot identification, the kind of product present, and note any treatment given to the product.

For a general discussion of U.S. Customs marking and labeling requirements, see "Marking: Country of Origin" on page 215 and the following sections.

Shipping Considerations

You will need to ensure that your goods are packaged and shipped with care so that they arrive in good condition and pass smoothly through Customs. You are responsible for ensuring that the shipment is in compliance with all applicable government regulations for packaging and shipping. In most instances, you should not leave these arrangements solely to the discretion of your supplier. Careful preparation of the cargo and selection of the mode of transport can be essential to a cost-effective, timely delivery of undamaged goods. We strongly advise you to consult your shipping representative, insurance agent, or freight broker for advice on packing and shipping. Refer also to the major tab section "Packing/Shipping/Insurance" for a general discussion of packing and shipping.

Milled products are usually transported in bulk, although in some instances they are shipped in bags or other types of containers. General considerations include protection from contamination by dirt, pests, or other foreign matter, as well as the effects of heat and dampness on the goods shipped.

Publications Available

The following publication explains the FDA requirements for importing milled cereal. It is published by the FDA and is available on request from FDA headquarters (see addresses at end of this chapter).

Requirements of Laws and Regulations Enforced by the U.S. Food and Drug Administration

The *Harmonized Tariff Schedule of the United States* (HTSUS) is available from:

Government Printing Office (GPO)
Superintendent of Documents
Washington, DC 20402
(202) 512-1800 (Order line)
(202) 512-0000 (General)

The USGPO also has copies of specific laws available for purchase. The USGPO accepts credit card orders over the phone, as well as mail orders paid by credit card, a check drawn on a U.S. bank, or an international money order.

Relevant Government Agencies

Address your inquiries regarding requirements for importation of milled cereal products and requests for permits to:

Food and Drug Administration (FDA)
Center for Food Safety and Applied Nutrition
200 C Street SW
Washington, DC 20204
(202) 205-5241, 205-5042

Food and Drug Administration (FDA)
Division of Enforcement, Imports Branch
200 C Street SW
Washington, DC 20204
(202) 205-4726

U.S. Department of Agriculture (USDA)
Animal and Plant Health Inspection Service (APHIS)
Plant Protection and Quarantine (PPQ)
Federal Building, Rm. 631
6505 Belcrest Road
Hyattsville, MD 20782
(301) 436-8645

Address questions regarding allowable pesticide residues on milled products to:

Environmental Protection Agency (EPA)
Office of Pesticide Programs
401 M Street SW (7501-C)
Washington, DC 20460
(703) 305-7090 (General)
(703) 305-7102 (Import/export requirements)

Address your questions regarding importation of cereal grains to the district or port director of Customs for you area. For addresses refer to "U.S. Customs District Offices" on page 62 or contact:

U.S. Customs Service
1301 Constitution Ave. NW
Washington, DC 20229
(202) 927-6724 (Information)
(202) 927-1000 (General)

Laws and Regulations

The following laws and regulations may be relevant to the importation of milled products. The laws are contained in the U.S. Code (USC) and the regulations are published in the Code of Federal Regulations (CFR), both of which may be available at larger public and law libraries. Copies of specific laws are also available from the United States Government Printing Office (address above).

21 USC 301 et seq.
Food, Drug, and Cosmetic Act
This Act prohibits deceptive practices and regulates the manufacture, sale and importation or exportation of food, drugs, cosmetics, and related products. See 21 USC 331, 381, 382.

19 CFR 12.1 et seq.; 21 CFR 1.83 et seq.
Regulations on Food, Drugs, and Cosmetics
These regulations of the Secretary of Health and Human Services and the Secretary of the Treasury govern the standards, labeling, marking, and importing of products used with food, drugs, and cosmetics. See Part 137, which establishes nomenclature and technical standards for cereal flours and related products.

7 USC 135 et seq.
Federal Insecticide, Fungicide, and Rodenticide Act (FIFRA)
This Act prohibits the importation of pesticides or devices that are adulterated, misbranded, or otherwise in violation of the Act, provides for registration of pesticides and devices, and establishes standards for labeling and classifying pesticides.

19 CFR 12; 40 CFR 162
Regulations on Pesticides
These regulations set forth the procedures and guidelines for importing products—including grains and other raw agricultural products—exposed to pesticides.

42 USC 264 et seq.
The Plant Quarantine Act
This Act gives the Plant Protection and Quarantine branch of the USDA authority to restrict or prohibit importation of plants or their seeds found to carry specific plant pests and pathogens.

7 USC 147a et seq.
Federal Plant Pest Act (FPPA)
This Act prohibits the importation into or movement through the U.S. of plant pests as defined in the Act, and provides for the inspection of any letter, box, parcel, or container that may carry a plant pest. Inspection is to be performed by U.S. Department of Agriculture in conjunction with Customs.

7 CFR Part 351
Regulations for Entry and Inspection of Plants by Mail
These regulations set forth the plant imports that are prohibited, the requirements for entering restricted plants by mail, and the inspection procedures followed by the USDA's Animal and Plant Health Inspection Service (APHIS).

19 CFR 12.10 et seq.
Regulations for Entry and Release of Restricted Plants
These regulations prescribe the procedures followed by U.S. Customs to enforce the USDA requirements for importation of plants.

Principal Exporting Countries

The following listing includes samples of the main supplier nations of the products of this chapter. It is organized by HTSUS major heading. (Refer to "Customs Classification" above for the product codes.) Countries are listed in rank order of the value of products imported to the U.S. Statistics represent customs value entries for 1993 from the Bureau of Census, U.S. Department of Commerce.

1101—Canada, Japan, South Korea, Switzerland, Hong Kong, Mexico, Sweden, France, Italy, Portugal

1102—Thailand, Canada, Colombia, Venezuela, Mexico, Israel, Italy, El Salvador, South Korea, India

1103—Canada, Australia, United Kingdom, Italy, Ireland, Mexico, France, Venezuela, Ecuador, Jamaica

1104—Canada, United Kingdom, Ireland, Peru, South Korea, Germany, Thailand, Poland, Ecuador, Japan

1105—Canada, Netherlands, Taiwan, Italy, Germany, China, Japan, Hungary, New Zealand, India

1106—Canada, Thailand, Japan, United Kingdom, Switzerland, Spain, Ecuador, China, Jamaica, Malaysia

1107—Canada, United Kingdom, Belgium, Australia, Germany, South Korea, France, Netherlands

1108—Canada, Netherlands, Germany, Denmark, Thailand, Mexico, Belgium, France, Japan, China

1109—Australia, Canada, Germany, Netherlands, France, China, Sweden, Czech Rep., Belgium, Slovakia

Chapter 12: Oil Seeds and Related Products*

Full title: Oil Seeds and Oleaginous Fruits; Miscellaneous Grains, Seeds, and Fruit; Industrial or Medicinal Plants; Straw and Fodder

This chapter relates to the importation of oil seeds and oily fruits; miscellaneous grains, seeds, and fruits; industrial and medicinal plants; and fodder crops, which are classified under Chapter 12 of the Harmonized Tariff Schedule of the United States (HTSUS). This chapter is somewhat of a catch-all, including such varied plant products as soybeans, peanuts, copra, linseed, rapeseed, sunflower seed, and sesame seed; seed for cultivation of fodder crops, vegetables, trees, shrubs, and fruits; straw and fodder crops, including those consisting of roots, grasses, or herbs; plants used for perfume or pharmaceuticals, and as insecticides or fungicides, including herb teas; as well as plant products not elsewhere specified, such as locust beans, sugar cane, algae, fruit pits, etc. Note that coca leaves—the source of cocaine and a controlled substance—are included in Chapter 12. Most agricultural and horticultural seeds are classified within this chapter, although coverage is not universal, and those interested in importing seed should verify whether their product is included. If you are interested in importing products of Chapter 12 for use in food preparations, you should read this section in conjunction with the "Foods" appendix on page 808.

If you are interested in importing leguminous vegetable seeds, seed potatoes, or sweet corn seeds, refer to Commodity Index Chapter 7. The importation of spice seeds is covered under Chapter 9, while importation of cereal grains and their seeds are covered in Chapter 10. If you are interested in importing olives for the extraction of oil, refer to Chapters 7 and 20. If you are interested in importing prepared animal feeds or residues of other products used as animal feed, refer to Chapter 23. Although herb teas are covered under Chapter 12, if you are interested in importing regular tea products, you need to refer to Chapter 9. If products are represented as having therapeutic value or are listed in the U.S. Pharmacopoeia or the National Formulary, you should refer to Chapter 30. For products imported specifically for cosmetic purposes, refer to Chapter 33; insecticides, fungicides, herbicides, and disinfectants are covered under Chapter 38.

*IMPORTANT: Read the Commodity Index Introduction. It is the essential framework for understanding this section.

Key Factors

The key factors in the importation of oil seeds, miscellaneous plant products, and fodder crops are:

- Compliance with U.S. Department of Agriculture (USDA) plant quarantine restrictions—permits may be required
- Compliance with USDA import restrictions—permits may be required
- Compliance with U.S. Food and Drug Administration (FDA) purity, identity, manufacturing, and other standards for products imported for human consumption
- Compliance with FDA entry notification requirements and procedures for products imported for use as food or drugs
- Compliance with U.S. Environmental Protection Agency (EPA) on pesticide residues on imported agricultural products
- Compliance with restrictions under endangered species regulation
- Compliance with Drug Enforcement Administration (DEA) requirements for permitting, importer registration, recordkeeping, and distribution (for importation of controlled substances)

Although most importers utilize the services of a licensed customs broker in making their entries, and we recommend this practice, you should be aware of the regulatory, entry, and documentation issues involved in importing your product. You, as importer, are ultimately responsible for the fulfillment of any legal requirements applicable to your shipment.

General Considerations

Regulatory Agencies. The importation of plant products of Chapter 12 is regulated primarily by the USDA Animal and Plant Health Inspection Service (APHIS), Plant Protection and Quarantine branch (PPQ). This agency acts primarily under the authorization of the Plant Quarantine Act (PQA). It specifically monitors the importation of seed under provisions of the Federal Seed Act of 1939 and the Federal Noxious Weed Act (FNWA). The USDA also enforces the provisions of the Agricultural Marketing Agreement Act of 1937 (AMAA), which limits the importation of certain commodities. The FDA enforces the Food, Drug, and Cosmetic Act (FDCA).

The U.S. Environmental Protection Agency (EPA) enforces the Federal Insecticide, Fungicide, and Rodenticide Act (FIFRA), which establishes regulatory limits on pesticide residues on edible plant products. Restrictions under the Endangered Species Act (ESA) and the Convention on International Trade in Endangered Species (CITES) apply to seeds of listed plant species, and are enforced by the U.S. Fish and Wildlife Service (FWS), usually in consultation with and often through the USDA.

FDA Inspection Requirements. The FDA regulations regarding importation of foods and drugs of any kind are extensive and stringent. Plant products intended for human consumption or as medicaments must comply with all the FDCA requirements for those produced domestically. Imported products regulated by the FDA are subject to port of entry inspection. **Form FD701** is required for all FDA-regulated importations and may be obtained from your local FDA Import Operations office, from FDA headquarters (see addresses at end of this chapter), or from your customs broker. For an annotated diagram of FDA import procedures, see the "Foods" appendix on page 808.

Detention of Shipment. If your shipment is found to be noncomplying, it may be detained at the port of entry. In the case of products subject to FDA jurisdiction, the FDA may allow you to bring such a shipment into compliance before making a final decision regarding admittance. However, any sorting, reprocessing, or relabeling must be supervised by FDA personnel and is done at the importer's expense. Such conditional release to allow the importer to bring a shipment into compliance is a privilege, not a right. The FDA may consider subsequent noncomplying shipments of the same type of product to constitute abuse of the privilege and require the importer to destroy or reexport the products. To ascertain what your legal responsibilities are, you should contact this agency regarding the specific items to be imported.

Coca Leaves. The DEA, a unit of the U.S. Department of Justice, licenses and controls the importation of coca leaves—which are considered Schedule II items with high potential for abuse—under the provisions of the Controlled Substances Act (CSA). If you are interested in importing this product, contact the DEA (see addresses at end of this chapter).

USDA Quarantines and Sampling. All shipments of plant materials, especially of seed, are subject to USDA inspection and sampling at the port of entry. If you are importing seed in small lots (that is, lots of between 25 and as much as 100 lbs., depending on the type of plant), your shipment is unlikely to be sampled. For a more complete listing of seed lot and sampling levels, see the Federal Seed Act, Regulation Parts 201-202, Table 6.

U.S. Customs is responsible for sampling grain and seed shipments imported from Canada. At all other border crossings, the USDA's PPQ branch performs this sampling. The FSA prescribes methods to be used in sampling. Quantities of products may be designated as a single lot for sampling purposes only if the shipment is uniform within established tolerances with respect to pure product (that is, of a single kind, not of mixed varieties), percentage of weeds, and occurrence of noxious weed seed. When a shipment consists of more than a single lot, each lot is sampled separately. When importation is across the Canadian border, Customs will notify you that sampling has occurred and that the shipment is being held pending APHIS determination. Sampling done by APHIS PPQ officers is carried out at the port of entry. Shipments are usually released unless a specific problem—such as a suspected noxious weed—is found.

Detention of Shipment. If your seed shipment is sampled and found to contain contaminants of any kind—noxious weed, insect, disease, or other contaminant—it will be detained pending USDA decision whether to allow entry. If the contaminant is one which is rare or nonexistent in the U.S., it will be refused admission. If a shipment of seed is found to be adulterated or unfit for seeding purposes according to FSA requirements, you may have it cleaned or processed under USDA supervision, at your expense. Once the seed has been cleaned or processed, any portion of it that is shown by analysis, test, or examination to meet FSA requirements will be admitted. Although this practice is allowed for seed contaminated under Federal Seed Act standards, it is not allowed for seed containing weeds prohibited under the Federal Noxious Weed Act. In those cases, the decision to allow cleaning or processing is made by USDA APHIS on a case-by-case basis.

Import Advisory

Regulations governing the importation of plant products, especially seed, are complex, and can change rapidly. APHIS permits are required for certain plant product imports, and FWS permits or CITES documentation may also be required. To ascertain what your legal responsibilities are, you should contact these agencies with specific identification of the materials you wish to import.

Customs Classification

For customs purposes, oil seeds and fruits; miscellaneous grains, seeds, and fruits; industrial and medicinal plants; and fodder crops are classified under Chapter 12 of the HTSUS. This chapter is broken into major headings, which are further divided into subheadings, and often into sub-subheadings, each of which has its own HTSUS classification number. For example, the HTSUS number for red clover seed is 1209.22.40, indicating that it is a subcategory of clover seed other than white or ladino clover (1209.22.20), which is a subcategory of the subheading, seeds of forage plants other than beet seed (1209.21.00), itself a subheading of the major heading, seeds, fruits, and spores of a kind used for sowing (1209.00.00). There are 14 major headings in Chapter 12.

1201—Soybeans, whether or not broken

1202—Peanuts (ground nuts), not roasted or otherwise cooked, whether or not shelled or broken

1203—Copra

1204—Flaxseed (linseed), whether or not broken

1205—Rape or colza seeds, whether or not broken

1206—Sunflower seeds, whether or not broken

1207—Other oil seeds and oleaginous fruits, whether or not broken

1208—Flours and meals of oil seeds or oleaginous fruits, other than those of mustard

1209—Seeds, fruits, and spores, of a kind for sowing

1210—Hop cones, fresh or dried, whether or not ground, powdered, or in the form of pellets; lupulin

1211—Plants and parts of plants (including seeds and fruits), of a kind used primarily in perfumery, in pharmacy, or for insecticidal, fungicidal, or similar purposes, fresh or dried, whether or not cut, crushed, or powdered

1212—Locust beans, seaweeds and other algae, sugar beet and sugar cane, fresh or dried, whether or not ground; fruit stones and kernels and other vegetable products (including unroasted chicory roots of the variety *Cichorium intybus sativum*) of a kind used primarily for human consumption, not elsewhere specified or included

1213—Cereal straw and husks, unprepared, whether or not chopped, ground, pressed, or in the form of pellets

1214—Rutabagas (swedes), mangolds, fodder roots, hay, alfalfa (lucerne), clover, sainfoin, forage kale, lupines, vetches, and similar forage products, whether or not in the form of pellets

For more details regarding classification of the specific product you are interested in importing, consult a customs broker, the appropriate commodity specialist at your nearest customs port, or see HTSUS. HTSUS is available for purchase from the U.S. Government Printing Office (see addresses at end of this chapter), and may be found in larger public libraries. Refer to "Classification—Liquidation" on page 207 for a general discussion of customs classification.

Sample Import Duties

Import duties will vary depending on the HTSUS classification of your product. Therefore, to determine the correct amount of duties, your product must be properly classified under the HTSUS. The following sample duties are taken from the duty listings for HTSUS Chapter 12 products.

Soybean seeds of a kind used as oil stock (1201.00.00): free; peanuts in the shell, up to the maximum amount allowed by quota (1202.10.00): 9.35 cents/kg; copra (1203.00.00): free; flaxseed for sowing (1204.00.00): 0.86 cents/kg; rape seed (1205.00.00): 0.9 cents/kg; sunflower seed for human consumption (1206.00.00): free; palm nuts and kernels (1207.10.00): free; poppy seeds (1207.91.00): 0.13 cents/kg; soybean flour or meal (1208.10.00): 3%; sugar beet seed (1209.11.00): free; alfalfa seed (1209.21.00):

3.3 cents/kg; fescue seed (1209.23.00): free; timothy grass seed (1209.26.00): free; cauliflower seed (1209.91.10): 13.2 cents/kg; onion seed (1209.91.40): free; spinach seed (1209.91.80): 3.3 cents/kg; tree and shrub seed (1209.99.20): free; melon seed (1209.99.40): 3.3 cents/kg; hop cones in pellets (1210.20.00): 16.5 cents/kg; ginseng root (1211.20.00): free; herbal teas (1211.90.40): 5.6% through December 31, 1994, 7.5% thereafter; coca leaves (1211.90.80): free; sage (1211.90.80): free; seaweed and algae (1212.20.00): free; sugar cane (1212.92.00): $2.76/ton; cereal straw (1213.00.00): free; hay (1214.90.00): free.

Entry and Documentation

The entry of merchandise is a two-part process consisting of 1) filing the documents necessary to determine whether merchandise may be released from Customs custody and 2) filing the documents that contain information for duty assessment and statistical purposes. In certain instances all documents must be filed and accepted by Customs prior to release of the goods. Unless you have been granted an extension, you must file entry documents at a location specified by the district or area director within five working days of your shipment's date of arrival at a U.S. port of entry. These include a number of standard documents required by Customs for any entry, and:

- USDA APHIS Import Permit when required (contact USDA, APHIS regarding permit requirements)
- FDA Entry and Notification **Form FD701**, when required
- DEA permits when required (contact DEA regarding permit requirements for importation of controlled substances)

After you present the entry, Customs may examine your shipment, or may waive examination. The shipment is then released provided no legal or regulatory violations have been noted. You must then file entry summary documentation and deposit estimated duties at a designated customhouse within 10 working days of your shipment's release. For a detailed description of entry procedures, standard documentation, and informal entry, see "Entry Process" on page 182.

Entry Invoice. Customs requires special information on the entry invoice for screenings or scalpings of grains or seeds: 1) whether the commodity is the product of a screening process; 2) if so, whether any cultivated grains have been added to such commodity; and 3) if any such grains have been added, the kind and percentage of each.

Prohibitions and Restrictions

The USDA establishes temporary restrictions on specific types of seeds originating in specific countries, as necessary to protect U.S. agriculture or public health from the proliferation of pests or weeds, although there are currently no prohibitions in effect with respect to plants or seeds of plants covered within Chapter 12. All seed imports must comply with the provisions of the Federal Noxious Weed Act (FNWA), which bans the importation of a variety of such weed seeds or plant parts directly or indirectly as contaminants within shipments of other plant materials. Seeds of plants listed in the FNWA, the Endangered Species Act, and in the Convention on International Trade in Endangered Species of Fauna and Flora (CITES) are subject to the restrictions defined in those acts. You can get up-to-date information on current FNWA restrictions from USDA APHIS (see addresses at end of this chapter). For information on seed restricted under CITES or other endangered species regulation, contact the Fish and Wildlife Service (see addresses at end of this chapter).

Screenings. With the following exceptions, screenings of all seed subject to the FSA are prohibited entry into the U.S. Screenings consisting of most edible grains as well as those of flax, soybeans, cowpeas, field peas, and field beans may be imported, as long as they are not imported for seeding purposes. The words "screening for processing, not for seeding" must appear on the invoice or other entry paperwork for these types of imports.

Certificate or Declaration of Origin. Customs requires documentation as to the origin of alfalfa and red clover seed, or any mixture of either or both. A certificate of origin from a properly authorized official of the foreign country in which the seed was grown, or a declaration of origin by the shipper can serve as documentation of the country of origin. In the absence of such documentation, Customs may accept other evidence as to the shipment's origin, or the seed may be permitted entry after being stained. Such seed, when its origin is other than Canada or South America, must be stained 10% red. When the seed's origin is South America, it must be stained 10% red or 10% orange.

Exemptions. Imported seed may be exempt from FSA import requirements under certain conditions:

1) Seed grown in the United States, exported, and returned from a foreign country is not subject to the prohibition against the importation of seed that is adulterated or unfit for seeding purposes. If your import falls in this category, you will have to provide statements or other documents with entry papers, establishing that the seed was grown in the U.S. and exported, that it was not admitted into the commerce of a foreign country, and that it was not commingled with other seed after being exported. You will have to include the quantity of seed, number of containers, date of exportation from the U.S., distinguishing marks on the containers at the time of exportation, and the name and address of the U.S. exporter in this documentation. The documentation verifying that the seed was not admitted into foreign commerce or commingled with other seed after being exported from the U.S. must come from a Customs officer or other appropriate government official of the country from which the seed is being reimported into the U.S.

2) Seed shipped in bond through the U.S. is not subject to the import requirements of the FSA.

3) Seed imported for sowing for seed production only, by or for the importer or consignee, and not to be sold within the U.S., is not subject to the prohibition against the importation of seed that is adulterated, nor is it required to be stained. If your import falls into this category, you will be required to present a declaration with entry papers, identifying the port of entry, and stating the noncommercial purpose of the importation.

For information on country-specific restrictions under endangered species regulations, contact FWS (see addresses at end of this chapter).

Quotas

9904.20.00 Whenever in any 12-month period beginning August 1 in any year, the aggregate quantity specified below of peanuts (ground nuts), shelled or not shelled, blanched or otherwise prepared or preserved (except as peanut butter) of headings 1202.10, 1202.20, or 2008.11, has been entered, no such products may be entered during the remainder of such period: 775,189 kg, provided that peanuts in the shell shall be charged against this quota on the basis of 75 kg for each 100 kg of peanuts in the shell.

Quotas—both the commodities affected and the rates charged—can change on short notice. For up-to-the minute information, or further details on quotas, contact the district director of Customs nearest you, or the U.S. Customs Quota Branch (see addresses at end of this chapter). For a general discussion of quotas refer to "Import Quotas" on page 230.

Marking and Labeling Requirements

Seed Labeling Requirements. For seed lots containing alfalfa or red clover, a declaration of origin is required. Imports of seeds or other plant material protected under endangered species regulations must be accompanied by any appropriate permits or export documentation established by the country from which the material originates.

All shipments of seed must be accompanied by a declaration of labeling, which must include the following information: 1) kind and variety of seed (if agricultural seed, just kind; if vegetable, variety); 2) lot numbers and weight of each lot; 3) country of origin; 4) for treated seed: chemical name of treatment substance and warning statement. The sales invoice and labeling tags on the seed container usually suffice for this declaration. In addition, each shipping container should be stenciled or otherwise labeled to show the lot designation and the name of the kind, or kind and variety appearing on the invoice and other entry papers. For information on specific labeling requirements for the type of seed you are interested in importing, contact APHIS (see addresses at end of this chapter).

For a general discussion of U.S. Customs marking and labeling requirements, see "Marking: Country of Origin" on page 215 and "Special Marking Requirements" on page 217.

Shipping Considerations

You will need to ensure that your goods are packaged and shipped with care so that they arrive in good condition and pass smoothly through Customs. You are responsible for ensuring that the shipment is in compliance with all applicable government regulations for packaging and shipping. In most instances, you should not leave these arrangements solely to the discretion of your supplier. Careful preparation of the cargo and selection of the mode of transport can be essential to a cost-effective, timely delivery of undamaged goods. We strongly advise you to consult your shipping representative, insurance agent, or freight broker for advice on packing and shipping. Refer also to the major tab section "Packing/Shipping/Insurance" for a general discussion of packing and shipping.

Products of Chapter 12 vary widely in their mode of shipping and specific considerations. Some are transported in bulk, while others are packaged in much smaller lots. Seeds in particular must be packaged separately. General considerations include protection from contamination by dirt, pests, or other foreign matter, as well as the effects of heat and dampness on the goods shipped. Timeliness is an additional consideration for some products that require relatively quick transit time in order to arrive in good and marketable condition.

Publications Available

The *Harmonized Tariff Schedule of the United States* (HTSUS) is available from:

Government Printing Office (GPO)
Superintendent of Documents
Washington, DC 20402
(202) 512-1800 (Order line)
(202) 512-0000 (General)

The USGPO also has copies of specific laws available for purchase. The USGPO accepts credit card orders over the phone, as well as mail orders paid by credit card, a check drawn on a U.S. bank, or an international money order.

Relevant Government Agencies

Address your questions regarding USDA requirements for importation of seeds and other Chapter 12 products as well as your requests for permits to:

U.S. Department of Agriculture (USDA)
Animal and Plant Health Inspection Service (APHIS)
Plant Protection and Quarantine (PPQ)
Federal Building, Rm. 631
6505 Belcrest Road
Hyattsville, MD 20782
(301) 436-8645

You may also address questions on importation of agricultural and vegetable seed to:

Agricultural Marketing Service
Seed Regulatory and Testing Division
Bldg. 506, BARC East
Soil Conservation Road
Beltsville, MD 20705
(301) 504-9237

Address questions regarding FDA requirements for the importation of plant products intended for human consumption or as medicaments to:

Food and Drug Administration (FDA)
Center for Food Safety and Applied Nutrition
200 C Street SW
Washington, DC 20204
(202) 205-5241, 205-5042

Food and Drug Administration (FDA)
Center for Drug Evaluation and Research (HFD-8)
5600 Fishers Lane
Rockville, MD 20857
(301) 594-1012

Food and Drug Administration (FDA)
Division of Enforcement, Imports Branch
200 C Street SW
Washington, DC 20204
(202) 205-4726

Address your questions regarding endangered species restrictions for seed to:

U.S. Fish and Wildlife Service (FWS)
Office of Management Authority
4401 N. Fairfax Drive, Room 432
Arlington, VA 22203
(703) 358-2095
(800) 358-2104, (703) 358-2104 (Permits office)

Address questions regarding allowable pesticide residues on plant products to:

Environmental Protection Agency (EPA)
Office of Pesticide Programs
401 M Street SW (7501-C)
Washington, DC 20460
(703) 305-7090 (General)
(703) 305-7102 (Import/export requirements)

Address questions regarding the importation of controlled substances (coca leaves) to:

Drug Enforcement Administration (DEA)
Public Information Office
700 Army-Navy Drive
Arlington, VA 22202
(202) 307-7977

Address your questions regarding quotas to:

U.S. Customs Service
Quota Branch
1301 Constitution Avenue NW, Rm. 2379-ICC
Washington, DC 20229
(202) 927-5850

Address your questions regarding importation of seed to the district or port director of Customs for you area. For addresses refer to"U.S. Customs District Offices" on page 62 or contact:

U.S. Customs Service
1301 Constitution Ave. NW
Washington, DC 20229
(202) 927-6724 (Information)
(202) 927-1000 (General)

Laws and Regulations

The following laws and regulations may be relevant to the importation of plant products of Chapter 12. The laws are contained in the U.S. Code (USC) and the regulations are published in the Cope of Federal Regulations (CFR), both of which may be available at larger public and law libraries. Copies of specific laws are also available from the United States Government Printing Office (address above).

7 USC 1551 et seq.
Federal Seed Act
This Act restricts the entry of agricultural seed to ensure that the seed is what its label says it is and is free from any noxious weed as identified in the Federal Seed Act (not the same as the noxious weeds listed in the Federal Noxious Weed Act). Purity and germination standards are no longer covered by this Act. Weeds specifically restricted under the act include: quack grass, Canada thistle, perennial sow thistle, dodder, whitetop, Johnsongrass, Russian knapweed, bindweed, and leafy spurge. A tolerance of two of these is allowed per given amount of seed.

42 USC 264 et seq.
The Plant Quarantine Act
This Act gives the Plant Protection and Quarantine branch of the USDA authority to restrict or prohibit importation of plants or their seeds found to carry specific plant pests and pathogens.

7 USC 147a et seq.
Federal Plant Pest Act (FPPA)
This Act defines, and prohibits the import of, seeds of parasitic plants as defined in the Act, and provides for the inspection of any letter, box, parcel, or container that may carry a plant pest. Inspection is to be performed by U.S. Department of Agriculture in conjunction with Customs.

7 CFR Part 351
Regulations for Entry and Inspection of Plants by Mail
These regulations set forth the plant imports that are prohibited, the requirements for entering restricted plants by mail, and the inspection procedures followed by the USDA's Animal and Plant Health Inspection Service (APHIS).

19 CFR 12.10 et seq.
Regulations for Entry and Release of Restricted Plants
These regulations prescribe the procedures followed by U.S. Customs to enforce the USDA requirements for importation of plants.

7 USC 2801
Federal Noxious Weed Act
This Act defines, delineates, and restricts weeds and their seeds found to be harmful to agricultural crops, livestock, irrigation, navigation, fish and wildlife resources, or public health. No tolerances are allowed.

7 USC 601 et seq.
Agricultural Adjustment Act (AAA)
This Act authorizes the Secretary of Agriculture to establish and maintain orderly market conditions for agricultural products, including cotton.

19 CFR Part 132
Regulations for Enforcement of AAA Quotas
These regulations provide for Customs enforcement of AAA quotas and higher duty rates imposed on imported agricultural products, whenever investigation reveals that orderly market conditions require such action.

7 USC 516 et seq.
Tobacco Seed and Plant Exportation Act
This Act requires exporters of tobacco seeds or plants to obtain written permits from the Secretary of Agriculture.

7 CFR Part 34
Regulations of USDA on Tobacco Products Permits
These regulations describe the permitting process and the tobacco products requiring permits for exportation.

21 USC 801 et seq.
Controlled Substances Act
This Act gives the Drug Enforcement Administration of the Justice Department authority to restrict or prohibit importation of products defined as controlled substances under the Act and authorizes stringent controls on permitting, registration, recordkeeping, and distribution of such substances.

Convention on International Trade in Endangered Species of Wild Fauna and Flora (CITES)
This comprehensive wildlife treaty signed by over 100 countries, including the United States, regulates and in many cases prohibits commercial imports and exports of wild animal and plant species threatened by trade.

16 USC 1531
Endangered Species Act
This Act prohibits the import and export of plant and seed species listed as endangered and most species listed as threatened. Seeds labeled as "of cultivated origin" may be traded. It is the U.S. law that implements CITES.

21 USC 301 et seq.
Food, Drug, and Cosmetic Act
This Act prohibits deceptive practices and regulates the manufacture, sale and importation or exportation of food, drugs, cosmetics, and related products. See 21 USC 331, 381, 382.

19 CFR 12.1 et seq.; 21 CFR 1.83 et seq.
Regulations on Food, Drugs, and Cosmetics
These regulations of the Secretary of Health and Human Services and the Secretary of the Treasury govern the standards, labeling, marking, and importing of products used with food, drugs, and cosmetics.

7 USC 135 et seq.
Federal Insecticide, Fungicide, and Rodenticide Act (FIFRA)
This Act prohibits the importation of pesticides or devices that are adulterated, misbranded, or otherwise violative of the Act, provides for registration of pesticides and devices, and establishes standards for labeling and classifying pesticides.

19 CFR 12; 21 CFR 180 and 193; 40 CFR 162
Regulations on Pesticides
These regulations set forth the procedures and guidelines for importing products exposed to pesticides.

Principal Exporting Countries

The following listing includes samples of the main supplier nations of the products of this chapter. It is organized by HTSUS major heading. (Refer to "Customs Classification" above for the product codes.) Countries are listed in rank order of the value of products imported to the U.S. Statistics represent customs value entries for 1993 from the Bureau of Census, U.S. Department of Commerce.

1201—Canada, Japan, Taiwan, Chile, China, Mexico, France, South Korea, Argentina, Hong Kong

1202—Canada, Colombia

1203—Marshall Islands, Dominican Rep., Thailand, Netherlands

1204—Canada, Belgium, Mexico, China, Vatican City, Netherlands

1205—Canada

1206—Canada, Israel, Argentina, France, Chile, Switzerland, Taiwan, Philippines, Netherlands, United Kingdom

1207—Mexico, Canada, Guatemala, India, El Salvador, Nepal, Australia, Costa Rica, Nicaragua, Netherlands

1208—Canada, China, Lebanon, Germany, South Korea, United Kingdom, Hong Kong, Taiwan, Japan, Jamaica

1209—Canada, Netherlands, Japan, Chile, China, Mexico, Guatemala, New Zealand, Thailand, Germany

1210—Germany, Czech Rep., France, Poland, United Kingdom, Canada, New Zealand, Australia, Slovenia, Dominica

1211—China, India, Hong Kong, Italy, Germany, South Korea, Egypt, Albania, Mexico, Syria

1212—Japan, China, South Korea, Philippines, Chile, Canada, Mexico, Ireland, Indonesia, Taiwan

1213—Canada, Mexico, India, Italy

1214—Canada, France, Mexico, Australia, Chile, Morocco, United Kingdom

Chapter 13: Gums and Resins*

Full title: Lac; Gums; Resins and Other Vegetable Saps and Extracts

This chapter relates to the importation of naturally occurring substances that are gelatinous when moist but harden when dry and are classified under Chapter 13 of the Harmonized Tariff Schedule of the United States (HTSUS). These products are usually imported to be used in producing a variety of other items, from varnishes to plastics to medicines to food additives, primarily as thickeners. They may be derived from insects (lac), plants (gums, resins, and saps), algae (agar-agar), or other organic sources. Note that opium and its derivatives such as morphine—controlled substances obtained from the sap of the opium poppy—are included in Chapter 13. If you are interested in importing products of Chapter 13 for use in food preparations, you should read this section in conjunction with the "Foods" appendix on page 808.

Commodity Index Chapter 13 does not cover a variety of related specific products such as organic extracts of licorice for confectionery (heading 1704); inulin (1108); malt extract (1901); extracts of coffee or tea (2101); extracts for the preparation of alcoholic beverages (Chapter 22); camphor and related products (2914 and 2938); medicaments (3003 and 3004); blood grouping reagents (3006); tanning and dyeing extracts (3201 and 3203); essential oils (Chapter 33); or natural rubber, chicle, and related gum products (4001).

Key Factors

The key factors in the importation of lac, gums, resins, and related products are:

- Compliance with U.S. Food and Drug Administration (FDA) purity, identity, manufacturing, and other standards
- Compliance with FDA entry and notification requirements and procedures
- Compliance with the requirements of the Toxic Substances Control Act (TSCA) for products not covered by FDA entry notifications
- Compliance with Drug Enforcement Administration (DEA) requirements for permitting, importer registration, recordkeeping, and distribution (for importation of controlled substances)

*IMPORTANT: Read the Commodity Index Introduction. It is the essential framework for understanding this section.

Although most importers use the services of a licensed customs broker in making their entries, and we recommend this practice, you should be aware of the regulatory, entry, and documentation issues involved in importing your product. You, as importer, are ultimately responsible for the fulfillment of any legal requirements applicable to your shipment.

General Considerations

The importation of lacs, gums, resins, and related products is regulated by a variety of U.S. government agencies, the primary one being the FDA, which administers the provisions of the Food, Drug, and Cosmetic Act (FDCA). All commodities imported for uses governed by the FDCA—those involved in the manufacture of food, drug, and related products—require FDA entry notification (**Form FD701**—for an annotated diagram of FDA entry procedures, refer to the "Foods" appendix on page 808). All plant and animal products entering the U.S. are subject to port of entry inspection by the Animal and Plant Health Inspection Service (APHIS) of the U.S. Department of Agriculture (USDA). Products that are imported for uses other than those covered in the FDCA (that is, those not covered by an FD701 submission) must comply with the requirements of the TSCA, administered through the U.S. Customs Service by the U.S. Environmental Protection Agency (EPA). The DEA, a unit of the U.S. Department of Justice, licenses and controls the importation of opium and opium products—which are considered Schedule II items with a high potential for abuse—under the provisions of the Controlled Substances Act (CSA). If you are interested in importing opium products, contact the DEA (see addresses at end of this chapter).

Customs Classification

For customs purposes, lac, gums, resins, and other vegetable extracts are classified under Chapter 13 of the HTSUS. This chapter is broken into major headings, which are further divided into subheadings, and often sub-subheadings, each of which has its own HTSUS classification number. For example, the HTSUS number for balsam is 1301.90.90, indicating that it is a subcategory of other gum-resins, which is a subcategory of products other than lac or gum arabic (1301.90.0), which is a subcategory of the major heading lac; natural gums, resins, gum-resins, and balsams (1301.00.00). There are two major headings within Chapter 13.

1301—Lac; natural gums, resins, gum-resins, and balsams

1302—Vegetable saps and extracts; pectic substances, pectinates, and pectates; agar-agar and other mucilages and thickeners derived from vegetable products

For more details regarding classification of the specific product you are interested in importing, consult a customs broker, the appropriate commodity specialist at your nearest customs port, or see HTSUS. HTSUS is available for purchase from the U.S. Government Printing Office (see addresses at end of this chapter), and may be found in larger public libraries. Refer to "Classification—Liquidation" on page 207 for a general discussion of customs classification.

Sample Import Duties

Import duties will vary depending on the HTSUS classification of your product. Therefore, to determine the correct amount of duties, your product must be properly classified under the HTSUS. The following sample duties are taken from duty listings for HTSUS Chapter 13:

Lac (1301.10.00): free; turpentine gum (1301.90.40): 5%; opium (1302.11.00): free; extract of hops (1302.13.00): $1.98/kg; ginseng extract (1302.19.40): 1.5%; pectic substances, pectinates, and pectates (1302.20.00): 5%; agar-agar (1302.31.00): 3%; mucilages derived from locust beans or seeds or guar seeds (1302.32.00): free.

Entry and Documentation

The entry of merchandise is a two-part process consisting of 1) filing the documentation necessary to determine whether merchandise may be released from Customs custody and 2) filing the documents that contain information for duty assessment and statistical purposes. In certain instances all documents must be filed and accepted by Customs prior to release of the goods. Unless you have been granted an extension, you must file entry documents at a location specified by the district or area director within five working days of your shipment's date of arrival at a U.S. port of entry. These include a number of standard documents required by Customs for any entry, and:

- FDA Entry Notification **Form FD701**
- TSCA certification for products destined for uses other than those covered by FD701 notification
- DEA permits when required (contact DEA regarding permit requirements for importation of controlled substances)

After you present the entry, Customs may examine your shipment, or may waive examination. The shipment is then released provided no legal or regulatory violations have been noted. You must then file entry summary documentation and deposit estimated duties at a designated customhouse within 10 working days of your shipment's release. For a detailed description of entry procedures, standard documentation, and informal entry, see "Entry Process" on page 182.

Prohibitions and Restrictions

Specific requirements for importation of products covered under Chapter 13 generally depend on their intended use, and some products that may be allowed entry for a particular use may be subject to controls if imported for an alternative use.

Marking and Labeling Requirements

Specific labeling requirements depend on the use for which a particular product is intended. For a general discussion of U.S. Customs marking and labeling requirements, see "Marking: Country of Origin" on page 215 and "Special Marking Requirements" on page 217.

Shipping Considerations

You will need to ensure that your goods are packaged and shipped with care so that they arrive in good condition and pass smoothly through Customs. You are responsible for ensuring that the shipment is in compliance with all applicable government regulations for packaging and shipping. In most instances, you should not leave these arrangements solely to the discretion of your supplier. Careful preparation of the cargo and selection of the mode of transport can be essential to a cost-effective, timely delivery of undamaged goods. We strongly advise you to consult your shipping representative, insurance agent, or freight broker for advice on packing and shipping. Refer also to the major tab section "Packing/Shipping/Insurance" for a general discussion of packing and shipping.

Because lac, gums, resins, and related products are soluble in water or other solvents, care should be taken to protect shipments from moisture. Also because of the intended use of many of these products as food additives or in medicinal preparations, and the fact that many can serve as a growth media for microorganisms, care must be taken that the products are packaged and handled so as to avoid contamination.

Publications Available

The following publication explains the FDA requirements for importing lacs, gums, resins, and related products. It is published by the FDA and is available on request from FDA headquarters (see addresses at end of this chapter).

Requirements of Laws and Regulations Enforced by the U.S. Food and Drug Administration

The *Harmonized Tariff Schedule of the United States* (HTSUS) is available from:

Government Printing Office (GPO)
Superintendent of Documents
Washington, DC 20402
(202) 512-1800 (Order line)
(202) 512-0000 (General)

The USGPO also has copies of specific laws available for purchase. The USGPO accepts credit card orders over the phone, as well as mail orders paid by credit card, a check drawn on a U.S. bank, or an international money order.

Relevant Government Agencies

Address your inquiries regarding FDA requirements for importation of lacs, gums, resins, and related products for uses covered by the Food, Drug, and Cosmetic Act (FDCA) to:

Food and Drug Administration (FDA)
Center for Food Safety and Applied Nutrition
200 C Street SW
Washington, DC 20204
(202) 205-5241, 205-5042

Food and Drug Administration (FDA)
Division of Enforcement, Imports Branch
200 C Street SW
Washington, DC 20204
(202) 205-4726

Address your inquiries regarding USDA requirements for importation of lacs, gums, resins, and related products to:

U.S. Department of Agriculture
Animal and Plant Health Inspection Service (APHIS)
Plant Protection and Quarantine (PPQ)
Federal Building, Rm. 631
6505 Belcrest Road
Hyattsville, MD 20782
(301) 436-8645

Address your inquiries regarding EPA requirements with respect to the TSCA for the importation of lac, gums, resins, and related products not intended for FDCA-approved uses to:

Environmental Protection Agency (EPA)
TSCA System Information
EPA 7408, OPPT
401 M Street SW
Washington, DC 20460
(202) 554-1404 (TSCA Information Hotline)

Address questions regarding the importation of controlled substances (opium and its derivatives) to:

Drug Enforcement Administration (DEA)
Public Information Office
700 Army-Navy Drive
Arlington, VA 22202
(202) 307-7977

Address your questions regarding importation of lacs, gums, resins, and related products to the district or port director of Customs for you area. For addresses refer to"U.S. Customs District Offices" on page 62 or contact:

U.S. Customs Service
1301 Constitution Ave. NW
Washington, DC 20229
(202) 927-6724 (Information)
(202) 927-1000 (General)

Laws and Regulations

The following laws and regulations may be relevant to the importation of lacs, gums, resins, and related products. The laws are contained in the U.S. Code (USC) and the regulations are published in the Code of Federal Regulations (CFR), both of which may be available at larger public and law libraries. Copies of specific laws are also available from the United States Government Printing Office (address above).

21 USC 301 et seq.
Food, Drug, and Cosmetic Act
This Act prohibits deceptive practices and regulates the manufacture, sale and importation or exportation of food, drugs, cosmetics, and related products. See 21 USC 331, 381, 382.

19 CFR 12.1 et seq.; 21 CFR 1.83 et seq.
Regulations on Food, Drugs, and Cosmetics
These regulations of the Secretary of Health and Human Services and the Secretary of the Treasury govern the standards, labeling, marking, and importing of products used with food, drugs, and cosmetics.

42 USC 264 et seq.
The Plant Quarantine Act
This Act gives the Plant Protection and Quarantine branch of the USDA authority to restrict or prohibit importation of plants or their seeds found to carry specific plant pests and pathogens.

7 CFR Part 351
Regulations for Entry and Inspection of Plants by Mail
These regulations set forth the plant imports that are prohibited, the requirements for entering restricted plants by mail, and the inspection procedures followed by the USDA's Animal and Plant Health Inspection Service (APHIS).

19 CFR 12.10 et seq.
Regulations for Entry and Release of Restricted Plants
These regulations prescribe the procedures followed by U.S. Customs to enforce the USDA requirements for importation of plants.

15 USC 2601 et seq.
Toxic Substances Control Act
This Act authorizes the EPA to determine whether a substance is harmful and to restrict importation, sale, and use of such substances.

19 CFR 12.118 et seq.
Regulations of Customs on Toxic Substances Control
These regulations require importers of chemical substances imported in bulk or as part of a mixture to certify to Customs that the shipment complies with the TSCA or is not subject to that Act.

21 USC 801 et seq.
Controlled Substances Act
This Act gives the Drug Enforcement Administration of the Justice Department authority to restrict or prohibit importation of products defined as controlled substances under the Act and authorizes stringent controls on permitting, registration, recordkeeping, and distribution of such substances.

Principal Exporting Countries

The following listing includes samples of the main supplier nations of the products of this chapter. It is organized by HTSUS major heading. (Refer to "Customs Classification" above for the product codes.) Countries are listed in rank order of the value of products imported to the U.S. Statistics represent customs value entries for 1993 from the Bureau of Census, U.S. Department of Commerce.

1301—India, France, Sudan, Thailand, United Kingdom, Germany, Canada, Dominican Rep., El Salvador, Honduras

1302—India, Denmark, Germany, Spain, China, Kenya, France, Pakistan, Morocco, Ireland

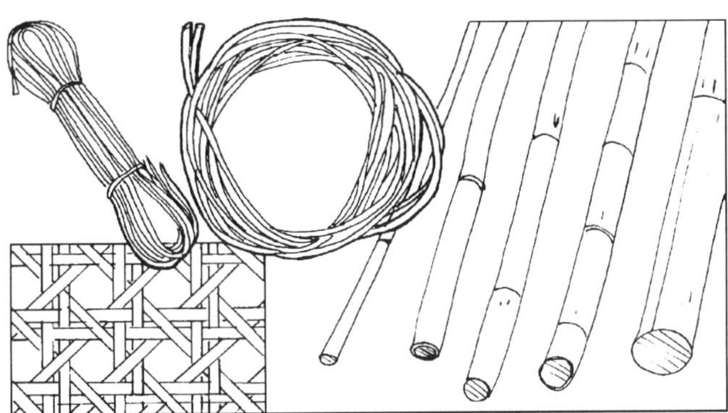

Chapter 14: Vegetable Plaiting Materials*

Full title: Vegetable Plaiting Materials; Vegetable Products Not Elsewhere Specified or Included

This section pertains to the importation of plaiting materials; vegetable materials used primarily as stuffing; vegetable materials used primarily for the manufacture of brushes and brooms; and miscellaneous vegetable materials, which are classified within Chapter 14 of the Harmonized Tariff Schedule of the United States (HTSUS). Specifically, it includes materials such as bamboo, rattan, reed, rush, osier, raffia, and prepared cereal straw; kapok; broomcorn and istle; and vegetable materials used primarily in dyeing and tanning.

If you are interested in importing finished products made of these materials, such as baskets, you should refer to Commodity Index Chapter 46. If you are interested in importing brooms and brushes—or intermediate products, such as prepared knots and tufts for the manufacture of these products—refer to Chapter 96. If you are interested in importing miscellaneous vegetable materials for use in the manufacture of textiles, refer to Chapter 53. Wood wool and chipwood made from plaiting materials are covered in Chapter 44. If you are interested in importing unprocessed cereal straw, refer to Chapter 12.

Key Factors

The key factors in the importation of vegetable plaiting and related miscellaneous materials are:

- Random U.S. Department of Agriculture (USDA) port-of-entry inspections
- Import restrictions on certain plant materials
- Endangered species restrictions on certain plant materials

Although most importers utilize the services of a licensed customs broker in making their entries, and we recommend this practice, you should be aware of the regulatory, entry and documentation issues involved in importing your product. You, as importer, are ultimately responsible for the fulfillment of any legal requirements applicable to your shipment.

General Considerations

Importation of vegetable plaiting material and related miscellaneous plant products is regulated by the USDA under the Plant Quarantine Act (PQA). The USDA Animal Plant Health Inspection Service (APHIS) Plant Protection and Quarantine (PPQ) branch inspects shipments of plaiting and related materials on a random basis, depending upon the port of entry, the risk factor involved in the type of material being offered for entry, etc. You do not generally need permits or licenses to import these products, but the type of plant material is pertinent (see Prohibitions and Restrictions, below). For most shipments of plaiting materials entering under Chapter 14, importation is straightforward. If you are importing related articles classified under different HTSUS chapters, there may be additional requirements administered by other governmental agencies. This depends entirely upon the specific article you are importing.

Restrictions under the Endangered Species Act (ESA) and the Convention on International Trade in Endangered Species (CITES) apply to plant materials of listed plants species, and are enforced by the U.S. Fish and Wildlife Service (FWS), usually in consultation with and often through the USDA. Regulations governing the importation of plant products are complex, and FWS permits or CITES documentation may be required. To ascertain what your legal responsibilities are, you should contact these agencies with specific identification of the materials you wish to import.

Customs Classification

For customs purposes, vegetable plaiting and related materials are classified under Chapter 14 of the HTSUS. This chapter is broken into major headings, which are further divided into subheadings, and often into sub-subheadings, each of which has its own HTSUS classification number. For example, the HTSUS number for willow (osier) is 1401.90.20, indicating that it is a subcategory of other vegetable materials (1401.90.00), which is a subcategory of the major heading, vegetable materials of a kind used primarily for plaiting (1401.00.00). There are four major headings in Chapter 14.

1401—Vegetable materials of a kind used primarily for plaiting (for example, bamboos, rattans, reeds, rushes, osier, raffia, cleaned, bleached, or dyed cereal straw, and lime bark)

1402—Vegetable materials of a kind used primarily as stuffing or as padding (for example, kapok, vegetable hair, and eel-grass), whether or not put up as a layer with or without supporting material

1403—Vegetable materials of a kind used primarily in brooms or in brushes (for example, broomcorn, piassava, couch grass, and istle), whether or not in hanks or bundles

1404—Vegetable products not elsewhere specified or included

For more details regarding classification of the specific product you are interested in importing, consult a customs broker, the appropriate commodity specialist at your nearest Customs port, or see HTSUS. HTSUS is available for purchase from the U.S. Government Printing Office (see addresses at end of this chapter), and may be found in larger public libraries. Refer to "Classification—Liquidation" on page 207 for a general discussion of customs classification.

Sample Import Duties

Import duties will vary depending on the HTSUS classification of your product. Therefore, to determine the correct amount of duties, your product must be properly classified according to the HTSUS. The following sample duties are taken from the duty listings for HTSUS Chapter 14 products.

Bamboos (1401.10.00): free; rattans, in the rough or cut transversely into sections (1401.20.20): free; willow (osier) (1401.90.20): 6.8%; kapok (1402.10.00): free; vegetable hair (1402.91.00): 0.8 cents/kg through December 31, 1994, 1.1 cents/kg thereafter; broomcorn (*Sorghum vulgare* var. *technicum*) (1403.10.00): $11/ton; istle (1403.90.20): free; gall nuts (1404.10.00): free; oak tanbark (1404.10.00): free; cotton linters (1404.20.00): free.

*IMPORTANT: Read the Commodity Index Introduction. It is the essential framework for understanding this section.

Entry and Documentation

The entry of merchandise is a two-part process consisting of 1) filing the documents necessary to determine whether merchandise may be released from Customs custody and 2) filing the documents that contain information for duty assessment and statistical purposes. In certain instances all documents must be filed and accepted by Customs prior to the release of the goods. Unless you have been granted an extension, you must file entry documents at a location specified by the district or area director within five working days of your shipment's date of arrival at a U.S. port of entry. These include a number of standard documents required by Customs for any entry, and:

- If applicable, USDA permits
- If applicable, FWS permits and/or export certification from the country of origin required under endangered species regulations

After you present the entry, Customs may examine your shipment, or may waive examination. The shipment is then released provided no legal or regulatory violations have been noted. You must then file entry summary documentation and deposit estimated duties at a designated customhouse within 10 working days of your shipment's release. For a detailed description of entry procedures, standard documentation, and informal entry, see "Entry Process" on page 182

Prohibitions and Restrictions

USDA Restrictions. In general, any shipment of vegetable plaiting material is subject to random port-of-entry inspection by USDA. If the inspector finds evidence of the presence of insects, you may be required to submit your shipment to USDA-prescribed fumigation procedures. If the insect is of a kind for which there is no viable U.S. treatment, your shipment will be refused. Our source at USDA assured us that most shipments that are found to be infested can be treated to allow entry.

The following USDA restrictions apply to the importation of vegetable plaiting and related materials. Shipments of the following plant materials will be inspected at the port of entry.

Grapevines. Shipments of grapevines must be accompanied by a Phytosanitary Certificate issued by the Plant Protection Service of the exporting country, attesting that the grapevines have been heat-treated to 135 degrees Fahrenheit (or the equivalent Celsius) for 2 hours. If your grapevines are dry (not green or fresh) and you have no certification to present to USDA at the port of entry, your shipment will be detained and samples will be taken and forwarded to the nearest USDA inspection station, where they will be examined under a microscope for viable or live buds. If the procedure reveals live buds, your shipment will be refused entry.

Rice straw. Rice straw must be accompanied by a Phytosanitary Certificate issued by the Plant Protection Service of the country of origin, attesting that the material has been fumigated with methyl bromide. The USDA may still refuse entry. Check with the USDA for conditions for admission of rice straw.

Tree Ferns. The importation of tree ferns is restricted under the Convention on International Trade in Endangered Species (CITES). Any such materials must meet applicable CITES requirements. The FWS is the regulatory agency generally responsible for monitoring compliance under endangered species regulation, but USDA enforces regulations applicable to plants and plant materials. If you are interested in importing this type of material, you should contact USDA PPQ branch (see addresses at end of this chapter) for instructions.

Willow. Green or fresh willow imported from Europe will be refused entry. Dry willow material from Europe is admissible, as are green or fresh willow from non-European countries.

Country-Specific Import Restrictions

Willows from Europe. Fresh or green willow materials from European countries are banned. Dry willow materials may be admitted. Fresh or green willow from other countries will be admitted.

Corn and Related Plants. Corn and closely related plants and their parts (including those of the genus *Chionachne, Coix, Echinochloa, Eleusina, Euchleana, Miscanthus, Panicum, Pennisetum, Polytoca, Sclerachne, Setaria, Sorghum, Trilobachne,* and *Tripsicum*), including materials used in plaiting and the manufacture of brooms and brushes—specifically broomcorn—are banned form importation into the U.S. if they originate from the following countries: Africa (all countries), Australia, Bangladesh, Bhutan, Brunei, Bulgaria, Burma (Myanmar), Cambodia (Kampuchea), Hong Kong, India, Nepal, New Zealand, North Korea, Oceania, Pakistan, Papua New Guinea, People's Republic of China, Philippines, Russia, and the other republics of the former Soviet Union, Singapore, South Korea, Sri Lanka, Taiwan, Thailand, and Vietnam. The import of corn-related products from other countries requires prior USDA approval.

Marking and Labeling Requirements

For a general discussion of U.S. Customs marking and labeling requirements, see "Marking: Country of Origin" on page 215 and "Special Marking Requirements" on page 217.

Shipping Considerations

You will need to ensure that your goods are packaged and shipped with care so that they arrive in good condition and pass smoothly through Customs. You are responsible for ensuring that the shipment is in compliance with all applicable government regulations for packaging and shipping. In most instances, you should not leave these arrangements solely to the discretion of your supplier. Careful preparation of the cargo and selection of the mode of transport can be essential to a cost-effective, timely delivery of undamaged goods. We strongly advise you to consult your shipping representative, insurance agent, or freight broker for advice on packing and shipping. Refer also to the major tab section "Packing/Shipping/Insurance" for a general discussion of packing and shipping.

Vegetable plaiting and related materials may be transported in bulk or in other forms, such as in bales or bundles. General considerations include protection from infestation by insects or contamination by dirt or other foreign matter, as well as the effects of dampness on the materials.

Publications Available

The *Harmonized Tariff Schedule of the United States* (HTSUS) is available from:

Government Printing Office (GPO)
Superintendent of Documents
Washington, DC 20402
(202) 512-1800 (Order line)
(202) 512-0000 (General)

The USGPO also has copies of specific laws available for purchase. The USGPO accepts credit card orders over the phone, as well as mail orders paid by credit card, a check drawn on a U.S. bank, or an international money order.

Relevant Government Agencies

Address your questions regarding USDA requirements for imported basketry to:

U.S. Department of Agriculture (USDA)
Animal and Plant Health Inspection Service (APHIS)
Plant Protection and Quarantine (PPQ)
Federal Building, Rm. 631
6505 Belcrest Road
Hyattsville, MD 20782
(301) 436-8645

Address your questions regarding endangered species restrictions to:

U.S. Fish and Wildlife Service (FWS)
Office of Management Authority
4401 N. Fairfax Drive, Room 432
Arlington, VA 22203
(703) 358-2095
(800) 358-2104, (703) 358-2104 (Permits office)

Address your questions regarding the importation of vegetable plaiting and related materials to the district or port director of Customs for you area. For addresses refer to"U.S. Customs District Offices" on page 62 or contact:

U.S. Customs Service
1301 Constitution Ave. NW
Washington, DC 20229
(202) 927-6724 (Information)
(202) 927-1000 (General)

Laws and Regulations

The following laws and regulations may be relevant to the importation of vegetable plaiting and related materials. The laws are contained in the U.S. Code (USC) and the regulations are published in the code of Federal Regulations (CFR), both of which may be available at larger public and law libraries. Copies of specific laws are also available from the United States Government Printing Office (address above).

42 USC 264 et seq.
The Plant Quarantine Act
This Act gives the Plant Protection and Quarantine branch of the USDA authority to restrict or prohibit importation of plants or their seeds found to carry specific plant pests and pathogens.

7 CFR Part 351
Regulations for Entry and Inspection of Plants by Mail
These regulations set forth the plant imports that are prohibited, the requirements for entering restricted plants by mail, and the inspection procedures followed by the USDA's Animal and Plant Health Inspection Service (APHIS).

19 CFR 12.10 et seq.
Regulations for Entry and Release of Restricted Plants
These regulations prescribe the procedures followed by U.S. Customs to enforce the USDA requirements for importation of plants.

Convention on International Trade in Endangered Species of Wild Fauna and Flora (CITES)
This comprehensive wildlife treaty signed by over 100 countries, including the United States, regulates and in many cases prohibits commercial imports and exports of wild animal and plant species threatened by trade.

16 USC 1531
Endangered Species Act
This Act prohibits the import and export of plant and seed species listed as endangered and most species listed as threatened. It is the U.S. law that implements CITES.

21 USC 301 et seq.
Food, Drug, and Cosmetic Act
This Act prohibits deceptive practices and regulates the manufacture, sale and importation or exportation of food, drugs, cosmetics, and related products. See 21 USC 331, 381, 382.

19 CFR 12.1 et seq.; 21 CFR 1.83 et seq.
Regulations on Food, Drugs, and Cosmetics
These regulations of the Secretary of Health and Human Services and the Secretary of the Treasury govern the standards, labeling, marking, and importing of products used with food, drugs, and cosmetics.

Principal Exporting Countries

The following listing includes samples of the main supplier nations of the products of this chapter. It is organized by HTSUS major heading. (Refer to "Customs Classification" above for the product codes.) Countries are listed in rank order of the value of products imported to the U.S. Statistics represent customs value entries for 1993 from the Bureau of Census, U.S. Department of Commerce.

1401—China, France, Singapore, Hong Kong, Philippines, Thailand, Japan, Taiwan, Netherlands, Madagascar

1402—Thailand, Sri Lanka, South Korea, Taiwan, Germany, Mexico

1403—Mexico, India, Netherlands, Sierra Leone, Colombia, Ethiopia, Sri Lanka, Romania, Thailand, China

1404—Mexico, China, United Kingdom, Chile, Hong Kong, Madagascar, Kenya, Philippines, Malaysia, Cyprus

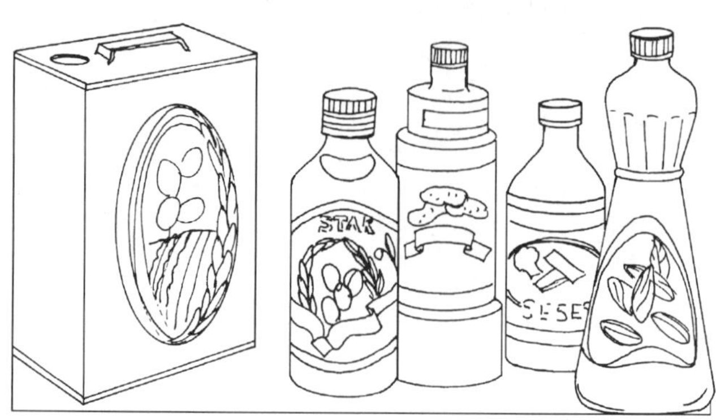

Chapter 15: Animal or Vegetable Fats and Oils*

Full title: Animal or Vegetable Fats and Oils and their Cleavage Products; Prepared Edible Fats; Animal or Vegetable Waxes

This chapter relates to the importation of animal or vegetable fats or oils and related products; prepared edible oils; and organic waxes, which are classified under Chapter 15 of the Harmonized Tariff Schedule of the United States (HTSUS). Specifically, it includes rendered lard; tallow; stearins and related products; fish and other marine oils; wool grease and lanolin; other animal fats; soybean, peanut, olive oil, and related blends; palm oil; sunflower, cottonseed, and safflower oils; coconut oil; rapeseed and related oils; linseed oil, corn oil, and other vegetable oils; hydrogenated and partially hydrogenated animal and vegetable fats and oils; margarine and other cooking and edible oils; chemically-modified industrial animal or vegetable oils; industrial fatty acids; glycerol; vegetable and animal waxes; and degras and related products. If you are interested in importing products of Chapter 15 for use as foods or in food preparations, you should read this section in conjunction with the "Foods" appendix on page 808.

If you are interested in importing raw, unrendered pig or poultry fat, refer to Commodity Index Chapter 2. Importation of butter and products with butterfat content of up to 45 percent as well as related dairy products is covered under Chapter 4. If you are interested in importing cocoa butter, fat, or oil, refer to Chapter 18. Edible products containing more than 45 percent by weight of dairy fats and oils are classified under Chapter 21. Oilcake destined for processing into animal feed is classified within Chapter 23. Cod liver oil and related products are covered within Chapter 30 when put up as medicaments. In general, fatty acids and related products intended for use in the manufacture of other products, including waxes, medicaments, paints, varnishes, perfumes, or soaps and toilet articles are classified and treated under the specific headings for those products.

Key Factors

The key factors in the importation of animal or vegetable fats or oils and related products are:

- Compliance with U.S. Food and Drug Administration (FDA) purity, identity, manufacturing, and other standards
- Compliance with FDA entry notification requirements and other procedures
- Compliance with U.S. Environmental Protection Agency (EPA) regulations on pesticide residues in imported agriculture products

Although most importers utilize the services of a licensed customs broker in making their entries, and we recommend this practice, you should be aware of the regulatory, entry, and documentation issues involved in importing your product. You, as importer, are ultimately responsible for the fulfillment of any legal requirements applicable to your shipment.

General Considerations

The importation of animal or vegetable fats or oils and related products falls primarily under the jurisdiction of the FDA, which enforces the provisions of the Federal Food, Drug, and Cosmetic Act (FDCA). FDA regulations regarding importation of food items of any kind are extensive and stringent. Such products imported into the U.S. must comply with all requirements for those produced domestically.

Imported products regulated by the FDA are subject to FDA port of entry inspection. **Form FD701** is required of all FDA-regulated importations and may be obtained from your local FDA Import Operations office, from FDA headquarters (see addresses at end of this chapter), or from your customs broker. For an annotated diagram of required FDA import procedures, refer to the "Foods" appendix on page 808.

The EPA enforces the Federal Insecticide, Fungicide, and Rodenticide Act (FIFRA), which establishes regulatory limits on pesticide residues in edible plant products. For more information, contact EPA (see addresses at end of this chapter).

Detention of Shipment. If your shipment is found to be noncomplying, it may be detained at the port of entry. In the case of products subject to FDA jurisdiction, the FDA may allow you to bring such a shipment into compliance before making a final decision regarding admittance. However, any sorting, reprocessing, or relabeling must be supervised by FDA personnel and is done at the importer's expense. Such conditional release to allow the importer to bring a shipment into compliance is a privilege, not a right. The FDA may consider subsequent noncomplying shipments of the same type of product to constitute abuse of the privilege and require the importer to destroy or reexport the products. To ascertain what your legal responsibilities are, you should contact these agencies regarding the specific items to be imported.

Customs Classification

For customs purposes, animal and vegetable fats and oils and related products are classified under Chapter 15 of the HTSUS. This chapter is broken into major headings, which are further divided into subheadings, and often into sub-subheadings, each of which has its own HTSUS classification number. For example, the HTSUS number for denatured rape or colza seed oil is 1514.90.50, indicating that it is a subcategory of other oil (1514.90.00), which is a subcategory of the major heading Rapeseed, colza, or mustard oil, and fractions thereof, whether or not refined, but not chemically modified (1514.00.00). There are 22 major headings in Chapter 15.

1501—Lard; other pig fat and poultry fat, rendered, whether or not pressed or solvent-extracted

1502—Fats of bovine animals, sheep, or goats, raw or rendered, whether or not pressed or solvent-extracted

1503—Lard stearin, lard oil, oleostearin, oleo-oil, and tallow oil, not emulsified or mixed or otherwise prepared

1504—Fats and oils and their fractions, of fish or marine mammals, whether or not refined, but not chemically modified

*IMPORTANT: Read the Commodity Index Introduction. It is the essential framework for understanding this section.

1505—Wool grease and fatty substances derived therefrom (including lanolin)

1506—Other animal fats and oils and their fractions, whether or not refined, but not chemically modified

1507—Soybean oil and its fractions, whether or not refined, but not chemically processed

1508—Peanut (ground-nut) oil and its fractions, whether or not refined, but not chemically modified

1509—Olive oil and its fractions, whether or not refined, but not chemically modified

1510—Other oils and their fractions, obtained solely from olives, whether or not refined, but not chemically modified, including blends of these oils and fractions with oils and fractions of heading 1509

1511—Palm oil and its fractions, whether or not refined, but nor chemically modified

1512—Sun-flower seed, safflower, or cottonseed oil, and fractions thereof, whether or not refined, but not chemically modified

1513—Coconut (copra), palm kernel, or babassu oil, and fractions thereof, whether or not refined, but not chemically modified

1514—Rapeseed, colza, or mustard oil, and fractions thereof, whether or not refined, but not chemically modified

1515—Other fixed vegetable fats and oils (including jojoba oil) and their fractions, whether or not refined, but not chemically modified

1516—Animal and vegetable fats and oils and their fractions, partly or wholly hydrogenated, inter-esterified, reesterified or elaidinized, whether or not refined, but not further prepared

1517—Margarine; edible mixtures or preparations of animal or vegetable fats or oils or of fractions of different fats or oils of this chapter, other than edible fats or oils or their fractions of heading 1516

1518—Animal or vegetable fats or oils and their fractions, boiled, oxidized, dehydrated, sulfurized, blown, polymerized by heat in vacuum or in inert gas or otherwise chemically modified, excluding those of heading 1516; inedible mixtures of preparations of animal or vegetable fats or oils or of fractions of different fats or oils this chapter not elsewhere specified or included

1519—Industrial monocarboxylic fatty acids; acid oils from refining; industrial fatty alcohols

1520—Glycerol (glycerine), whether or not pure; glycerol waters and glycerol lyes

1521—Vegetable waxes (other than triglycerides), beeswax, other insect waxes and spermaceti, whether or not refined or colored

1522—Degras; residues resulting from the treatment of fatty substances or animal or vegetable waxes

For more details regarding classification of the specific product you are interested in importing, consult a customs broker, the appropriate commodity specialist at your nearest customs port, or see HTSUS. HTSUS is available for purchase from the U.S. Government Printing Office (see addresses at end of this chapter), and may be found in larger public libraries. Refer to "Classification—Liquidation" on page 207 for a general discussion of customs classification.

Sample Import Duties

Import duties will vary depending on the HTSUS classification of your product. Therefore, to determine the correct amount of duties, your product must be properly classified under the HTSUS. The following sample duties are taken from the duty listings for HTSUS Chapter 15 products.

Lard (1501.00.00): 6.6 cents/kg; tallow (1502.00.00): 0.95 cents/kg; lard stearin (1503.00.00): 4.4 cents/kg; cod liver oil (1504.10.20): free; menhaden oil (1504.20.60): 1.5 cents/kg + 5%; crude wool grease (1505.10.00): 2.9 cents/kg; other animal fats not otherwise classified (1506.00.00): 5%; crude soybean oil (1507.10.00): 22.5%; pharmaceutical grade soybean oil valued at over $5/kg (1507.90.20): 1.5%; crude peanut oil (1508.10.00): 8.8 cents/kg; virgin olive oil weighing with the immediate container under 18 kg (1509.10.20): 5 cents/kg on contents and container; other olive oil, rendered unfit for use as food (1510.00.20): free; crude palm oil (1511.10.00): free; safflower oil (1512.11.00): 2 cents/kg + 4%; once-refined cottonseed oil (1512.29.00): 6.6 cents/kg; coconut oil (1513.11.00): free; denatured rape, colza, or mustard oils (1514.90.50): 1.5 cents/kg; crude corn oil (1515.21.00): 4%; tung oil (1515.40.00): free; sesame oil (1515.50.00): 1.5 cents/kg; animal fats or oils, partly or wholly hydrogenated (1516.10.00): 11 cents/kg; margarine (1517.10.00): 15.4 cents/kg; edible mixtures or preparations of salad or cooking oils other than soybean oil (1517.90.20): 10%; processed linseed oil (1518.00.20): 9.9 cents/kg; oleic acid (1519.12.00): 3.3 cents/kg + 5%; oleyl (1519.20.20): 7.9%; crude glycerol (1520.10.00): 0.3 cents/kg through December 31, 1994, 0.4 cents/kg thereafter; carnauba vegetable wax (1521.10.0): free; bleached beeswax (1521.90.20): 7.5%; residues from the treatment of fatty substances (1522.00.00): 6%.

Entry and Documentation

The entry of merchandise is a two-part process consisting of 1) filing the documents necessary to determine whether merchandise may be released from Customs custody and 2) filing the documents that contain information for duty assessment and statistical purposes. In certain instances all documents must be filed and accepted by Customs prior to release of the goods. Unless you have been granted an extension, you must file entry documents at a location specified by the district or area director within five working days of your shipment's date of arrival at a U.S. port of entry. These include a number of standard documents required by Customs for any entry, and:

- FDA Import Notice **Form FD701**

After you present the entry, Customs may examine your shipment, or may waive examination. The shipment is then released provided no legal or regulatory violations have been noted. You must then file entry summary documentation and deposit estimated duties at a designated customhouse within 10 working days of your shipment's release. For a detailed description of entry procedures, standard documentation, and informal entry, see "Entry Process" on page 182.

Prohibitions and Restrictions

Edible Oils. Margarine is subject to extensive regulation and standards found in 21 CFR 166, to which all imported products must conform. If you are importing olive oil, you must be sure your product complies with the established standard: olive oil is the edible oil expressed from the sound, mature fruit of the olive tree. Refined or extracted oil is not entitled to the unqualified name "olive oil." Other vegetable oils should be labeled by their common or usual name, such as cottonseed, sunflower, peanut, and sesame. If you import mixtures of edible oils, be sure they are labeled to show all the oils present, with names listed in descending order of prominence in the product. If the terms "vegetable oil" or "shortening" are used in food labeling, the plant and animal source of each oil or fat used in the product must be identified on the label (31 CFR 101).

Inedible Oils. Olive, palm kernel, rapeseed, sunflower, and sesame oils may be imported outside FDCA regulations and duty free for industrial or mechanical use, provided that they have been denatured and rendered unfit for food use. To qualify for this provision, such oils must bear certification from their country of origin that their method of production has rendered them unfit for consumption, or they must undergo prescribed processes under Customs supervision prior to release at the expense of the importer rendering them unfit. Customs will sample all lots of oils for which denatured status is claimed (19 CFR 10.56).

Cod Liver Oil. Cod liver oil is recognized as a drug in the U.S. Pharmacopoeia (USP). It is therefore both a food and a drug, and subject to both the food and drug provisions of the FDCA. If you are interested in importing cod liver oil, you should refer to Commodities Index Chapter 30. Any shipment you import into the U.S. as cod liver oil must conform to the USP identity standard for cod liver oil, as well as any other USP specifications for the product.

Quotas

Artificial mixtures of two or more of the products provided for in headings 1501 to 1515, inclusive (1517.90.40) are subject to the following quotas: 1) entry of products enumerated in 9904.10.75 is prohibited; 2) entry of products enumerated in 9904.10.81 is limited to 1,016,046 kg from Australia, 154,221 kg from Belgium and Denmark (aggregate), and none from other countries.

Quotas—both the commodities affected and rates charged—can change on short notice. For up-to-the-minute information, or further details on quotas, contact the U.S. Customs Service Quota Branch (see addresses at end of this chapter). For a general discussion of quotas, refer to "Import Quotas" on page 230.

Marking and Labeling

Refer to the "Foods" appendix on page 808. For a general discussion of U.S. Customs marking and labeling requirements, see "Marking: Country of Origin" on page 215 and "Special Marking Requirements" on page 217.

Shipping Considerations

You will need to ensure that your goods are packaged and shipped with care so that they arrive in good condition and pass smoothly through Customs. You are responsible for ensuring that the shipment is in compliance with all applicable government regulations for packaging and shipping. In most instances, you should not leave these arrangements solely to the discretion of your supplier. Careful preparation of the cargo and selection of the mode of transport can be essential to a cost-effective, timely delivery of undamaged goods. We strongly advise you to consult your shipping representative, insurance agent, or freight broker for advice on packing and shipping. Refer also to the major tab section "Packing/Shipping/Insurance" for a general discussion of packing and shipping.

Products of Chapter 15 vary in their mode of shipping, packaging, and special considerations. Some are transported in bulk, while others are packaged in much smaller lots. General considerations include protection from contamination by dirt, insects, or other foreign matter, as well as the effects of heat and dampness on the goods shipped. Timeliness is an additional consideration for some products that require relatively quick transit time in order to arrive in good and marketable condition.

Publications Available

The following publication explains the FDA requirements for importing fats and oils. It is published by the FDA and is available on request from FDA headquarters (see addresses at end of this chapter).

Requirements of Laws and Regulations Enforced by the U.S. Food and Drug Administration

The *Harmonized Tariff Schedule of the United States* (HTSUS) is available from:

Government Printing Office (GPO)
Superintendent of Documents
Washington, DC 20402
(202) 512-1800 (Order line)
(202) 512-0000 (General)

The USGPO also has copies of specific laws available for purchase. The USGPO accepts credit card orders over the phone, as well as mail orders paid by credit card, a check drawn on a U.S. bank, or an international money order.

Relevant Government Agencies

Address your questions regarding FDA requirements for the importation of fats and oils of Chapter 15 to:

Food and Drug Administration (FDA)
Center for Food Safety and Applied Nutrition
200 C Street SW
Washington, DC 20204
(202) 205-5241, 205-5042

Food and Drug Administration (FDA)
Division of Enforcement, Imports Branch
200 C Street SW
Washington, DC 20204
(202) 205-4726

Address your questions regarding allowable pesticide residues in fats and oils to:

Environmental Protection Agency (EPA)
Office of Pesticide Programs
401 M Street SW (7501-C)
Washington, DC 20460
(703) 305-7090 (General)
(703) 305-7102 (Import/export requirements)

Address your questions regarding quotas to:

U.S. Customs Service
Quota Branch
1301 Constitution Avenue NW, Rm. 2379-ICC
Washington, DC 20229
(202) 927-5850

Address your questions regarding importation of fats and oils of Chapter 15 to the district or port director of Customs for you area. For addresses refer to "U.S. Customs District Offices" on page 62 or contact:

U.S. Customs Service
1301 Constitution Ave. NW
Washington, DC 20229
(202) 927-6724 (Information)
(202) 927-1000 (General)

Laws and Regulations

The following laws and regulations may be relevant to the importation of fats and oils of Chapter 15. The laws are contained in the U.S. Code (USC) and the regulations are published in the Code of Federal Regulations (CFR), both of which may be available at larger public and law libraries. Copies of specific laws are also available from the United States Government Printing Office (address above).

21 USC 301 et seq.
Food, Drug, and Cosmetic Act
This Act prohibits deceptive practices and regulates the manufacture, sale and importation or exportation of food, drugs, cosmetics, and related products. See 21 USC 331, 381, 382.

19 CFR 12.1 et seq.; 21 CFR 1.83 et seq.
Regulations on Food, Drugs, and Cosmetics
These regulations of the Secretary of Health and Human Services and the Secretary of the Treasury govern the standards, labeling, marking, and importing of products used with food, drugs, and cosmetics.

7 USC 135 et seq.
Federal Insecticide, Fungicide, and Rodenticide Act (FIFRA)
This Act prohibits the importation of pesticides or devic-

es that are adulterated, misbranded, or otherwise violative of the Act, provides for registration of pesticides and devices, and establishes standards for labeling and classifying pesticides.

19 CFR 12; 40 CFR 162
Regulations on Pesticides
These regulations set forth the procedures and guidelines for importing products exposed to pesticides.

Principal Exporting Countries

The following listing includes samples of the main supplier nations of the products of this chapter. It is organized by HTSUS major heading. (Refer to "Customs Classification" above for the product codes.) Countries are listed in rank order of the value of products imported to the U.S. Statistics represent customs value entries for 1993 from the Bureau of Census, U.S. Department of Commerce.

1501—Canada, Jordan, Mexico

1502—Canada, Netherlands, Mexico, Germany, Sweden, France, Australia

1503—Canada

1504—Norway, Canada, Japan, Chile, Netherlands, United Kingdom, Iceland, Denmark, South Korea, Colombia

1505—Singapore, Germany, Japan, United Kingdom, Mexico, France, Australia, Netherlands, Taiwan, Italy

1506—Canada, Germany, Australia, Netherlands, Colombia, Egypt, United Kingdom

1507—Argentina, Sweden, Canada, Jamaica, Germany, Japan

1508—Argentina, Hong Kong, Germany, Netherlands, Taiwan, Canada, United Kingdom, Malawi

1509—Italy, Spain, Greece, Tunisia, Turkey, Portugal, Morocco, France, Lebanon, Argentina

1510—Italy, Greece, Spain, Morocco

1511—Malaysia, Indonesia, Philippines, Singapore, Netherlands, China, Japan, Cote d'Ivoire, Ghana, Thailand

1512—Argentina, Mexico, Brazil, Panama, United Kingdom, Canada, Australia, Turkey, Portugal, France

1513—Philippines, Malaysia, Indonesia, Dominican Rep., Marshall Islands, Canada, Singapore, China, Sweden, Chile

1514—Canada, Germany, United Kingdom, Netherlands, Denmark, Belgium, India, Hong Kong

1515—India, Japan, Argentina, Brazil, Canada, Mexico, Paraguay, Taiwan, Ecuador, United Kingdom

1516—Canada, Brazil, Germany, Sweden, Denmark, China, Thailand, Malaysia, Italy, Singapore

1517—Canada, Denmark, Trinidad and Tobago, Hong Kong, Germany, Japan, Netherlands, China, Norway, United Kingdom

1518—Mexico, India, Netherlands, Canada, Brazil, France, Switzerland, United Kingdom, Belgium, Pakistan

1519—Malaysia, Netherlands, Germany, Canada, Indonesia, Philippines, Brazil, Japan, India, United Kingdom

1520—Malaysia, Germany, Mexico, Canada, Indonesia, Brazil, Philippines, Colombia, India, Egypt

1521—Brazil, Mexico, China, Japan, Thailand, Chile, Canada, Dominican Rep., Australia, Tanzania

1522—Canada

Chapter 16: Meat and Fish Preparations*

Full title: Preparations of Meat, of Fish, or of Crustaceans, Molluscs, or Other Aquatic Invertebrates

This chapter relates to the importation of edible preparations of meat and fish and related animals, which are classified under Chapter 16 of the Harmonized Tariff Schedule of the United States (HTSUS). Specifically, it includes meat sausage, homogenized preparations of meat or poultry (primarily baby foods), prepared and canned meats (such as canned hams and corned beef), extracts and juices of fish, prepared or preserved fish (including caviar and canned tuna and salmon), fish sticks, fish paste, packed crabmeat, shrimp, lobster, and oysters, and other similar products. In general, any product that by weight includes 20% prepared meat, poultry, fish, or other seafood is included in Chapter 16. You should read this section in conjunction with the "Foods" appendix on page 808.

If you are interested in importing fresh or provisionally preserved meat, including smoked and cured meats such as some hams, refer to Commodity Index Chapter 2. Fresh or provisionally preserved fish, crustaceans, molluscs, and similar aquatic invertebrates are covered in Chapter 3. Live animals—meat on the hoof—are dealt with in Chapter 1. If you are interested in importing prepared foods made predominately of flour that have an incidental component of prepared meat, poultry, or fish—such as filled pasta products—refer to Chapter 19. Prepared foods that do not contain meat or fish—those made primarily of fruit, vegetables, and nuts—are covered in Chapter 20. Products of animal origin not fit or intended for human consumption are classified in Chapters 5 and 23.

Key Factors

The key factors in the importation of these products are:

- Compliance with U.S. Food and Drug Administration (FDA) purity, identity, manufacturing, and other standards
- Compliance with FDA entry notification and other procedures
- Compliance with U.S. Department of Agriculture (USDA) Animal and Plant Health Inspection Services (APHIS) and the Food Safety and Inspection Service (FSIS) requirements; permits may be required

*IMPORTANT: Read the Commodity Index Introduction. It is the essential framework for understanding this section.

Although most importers utilize the services of a licensed customs broker in making their entries, and we recommend this practice, you should be aware of the regulatory, entry, and documentary issues involved in importing your product. You, as importer, are ultimately responsible for the fulfillment of any legal requirements applicable to your shipment.

General Considerations

Regulatory Agencies. Importation of prepared meat and fish products falls primarily under the jurisdiction of the FDA, which enforces the requirements of the Federal Food, Drug, and Cosmetic Act (FDCA). The USDA controls imports of meat, poultry, fish, and seafood products to prevent contamination of U.S. food sources. The FWS regulates importation of products prepared from endangered species and wildlife.

FDA Requirements. FDA regulations regarding importation of foods of any kind are extensive and stringent. Meat and fish products prepared from wild game and domesticated varieties of wild animals also fall within the FDA's purview. Prepared foods imported into the U.S. must comply with all requirements for those produced domestically.

FDA Inspections. Imported products regulated by the FDA are subject to port of entry inspection. **Form FD701** is required for all FDA-regulated imports and may be obtained from your local FDA Import Operations office, from FDA headquarters (see addresses at end of this chapter), or from your customs broker. For an annotated diagram of required FDA importing procedures refer to the "Foods" appendix on page 808.

Detention of Shipment. If your shipment is found to be noncomplying, the FDA inspector may detain it at the port of entry. The FDA may allow you to bring the shipment into compliance before making a final decision regarding admittance. However, any sorting, reprocessing, or relabeling must be supervised by FDA personnel and is done at the importer's expense. Such conditional release to allow the importer to bring a shipment into compliance is a privilege, not a right. The FDA may consider subsequent noncomplying shipments of the same type of product to constitute abuse of the privilege and require the importer to destroy or reexport the products. To ascertain what your legal responsibilities are, you should contact the FDA regarding the specific items to be imported.

USDA Requirements. APHIS and FSIS are the main USDA agencies responsible for enforcement of the regulations on the import of meat, poultry, fish, and seafood. You should check with these agencies to ascertain what your USDA responsibilities are with respect to imports of HTSUS Chapter 16 products.

Wildlife Products. If you are interested in importing products prepared from exotic animals, you should consult the U.S. Fish and Wildlife Service (FWS), which administers the provisions of the Endangered Species Act (ESA) and the Convention on International Trade in Endangered Species of Wild Fauna and Flora (CITES), to be sure that your intended import is not covered by these regulations. No animal products derived from animals on these lists may be imported. There are many restrictions on the importation and sale of any products derived from wild animals. However, products made from the meat of animals raised in captivity is unlikely to fall within the jurisdiction of endangered species legislation.

Customs Classification

For customs purposes, preparations of meat and fish are classified under Chapter 16 of the HTSUS. This chapter is divided into major headings, which are further divided into subheadings, and often into sub-subheadings, each of which has its own HTSUS classification number. For example, the HTSUS number for beef other than in airtight containers is 1601.00.60, indicating that it is a subcategory of meat preparations other than pork (1601.00.40), which is a subcategory of sausages and similar products of meat, meat offal, or blood; food preparations based on these products (1601.00.00). There are five major headings in HTSUS Chapter 16.

1601—Sausages and similar products, of meat, meat offal, or blood; food preparations based on these products

1602—Other preparations of preserved meat, meat offal, or blood

1603—Extracts and juices of meat, fish, or crustaceans, molluscs, or other aquatic invertebrates

1604—Prepared or preserved fish; caviar and caviar substitutes prepared from fish eggs

1605—Crustaceans, molluscs, and other aquatic invertebrates, prepared or preserved

For more details regarding classification of then specific product you are interested in importing, consult a customs broker, the appropriate commodity specialist at your nearest customs port, or se HTSUS. HTSUS is available for purchase from the U.S. Government Printing Office (see addresses at end of this chapter), and may be found in larger public libraries. Refer to "Classification—Liquidation" on page 207 for a general discussion of customs classification.

Sample Import Duties

Import duties will vary depending on the HTSUS classification of your product. Therefore, to determine the correct amount of duties, your product must be properly classified under the HTSUS. The following sample duties are taken from the duty listings for HTSUS Chapter 16 products.

Pork sausage and preparations made from pork (1601.00.20): 1.3 cents/kg; canned beef (1601.00.40): 7.5%; beef sausage and other preparations made from beef (1601.00.60): 5%; homogenized preparations (baby foods) (1602.10.00): 3%; preparations of goose liver (1602.20.20): 7.7 cents/kg; hams and cuts thereof containing cereals or vegetables (1602.41.10): 10%; pork shoulders and cuts thereof boned and cooked and packed in airtight containers (1602.42.20): 6.6 cents/kg; other prepared meats, including mixtures and offal (1602.49.10): 5%; corned beef in containers holding less than 1 kg (1602.50.10): 7.5% [prior to December 31, 1992, this product was duty free]; prepared meals of other meats (1602.50.90): 10%; clam juice (1603.00.10): 8.5%; meat extract (1603.00.90): free; salmon canned in oil (1604.11.20): 12.5%; other canned salmon (1604.11.40): 3%; sardines packed in oil (1604.13.10): 4%; other sardines, skinned or boned (1604.13.30): 20%; tuna packed in oil (1604.14.10): 35%; anchovies packed in oil, up to 3,000 metric tons per calendar year (1604.16.10): 3%; anchovies packed in oil exceeding 3,000 metric tons per calendar year (1604.16.30): 6%; fish sticks and similar products of any size or shape, fish fillets or other portions of fish, if breaded, coated with batter, or similarly prepared, neither cooked nor in oil (1604.19.30): 10%; if cooked or in oil (1604.19.50): 15%; shrimp paste (1604.20.10): free; balls, cakes, or puddings made of crustaceans, molluscs, or similar aquatic invertebrates, in oil (1604.20.15): 6.6%; caviar (1604.30.20): 15%; caviar substitutes (1604.30.30): 2.5%; canned crabmeat (1605.10.20): 11%; frozen crabmeat (1605.10.40): 5%; prepared meals of shrimp or prawns (1605.20.05): 10%; other frozen shrimp products, such as breaded, butterflied shrimp (1605.20.10): free; canned lobster meat (1605.30.05): 10%; lobster meat cooked by steaming or boiling in water and out of the shell, whether or not frozen but not further prepared or preserved (1605.30.10): free; smoked oysters (1605.90.40): free; snails, other than sea snails (1605.90.55): 5%.

Entry and Documentation

The entry of merchandise is a two-part process consisting of 1) filing the documents necessary to determine whether merchandise may be released from Customs custody and 2) filing the documents that contain information for duty assessment and statistical purposes. In certain instances all documents must be filed and accepted by Customs prior to release of the goods. Unless you have been granted an extension, you must file entry documents at a location specified by the district or area director within five working days of your shipment's date of arrival at a U.S. port of entry. These include a number of standard documents required by Customs for any entry, and:

- FDA Importers Entry Notice, **Form FD701**
- APHIS Import Permit where required
- Foreign veterinary certification where required

After you present the entry, Customs may examine your shipment, or may waive examination. The shipment is then released provided no legal or regulatory violations have been noted. You must then file entry summary documentation and deposit estimated duties at a designated customhouse within 10 working days of your shipment's release. For a detailed description of entry procedures, standard documentation, and informal entry, see "Entry Process" on page 182.

Prohibitions and Restrictions

FSIS Requirements. The FSIS enforces the provisions of the Federal Meat Inspection Act (FMIA) and the Poultry Products Inspection Act (PPIA), which require countries exporting meat, poultry, and their products to the U.S. to impose domestic inspection requirements at least as stringent as those of the U.S. The FSIS reviews foreign inspection systems to ensure that they are equivalent to the U.S. system. Only those countries to which FSIS grants meat export eligibility may export these products to the U.S. See Country-Specific Import Restrictions below for list of currently eligible countries (by definition, imports from unlisted countries are prohibited).

An inspection certificate issued by the responsible official of the exporting country must accompany each shipment of meat or poultry products offered for entry into the U.S. Certificates identify products by country and packing plant of origin, destination, shipping marks, and amounts. They certify that the products have received ante-mortem and post-mortem inspection; that they are wholesome, unadulterated, and properly branded; and that they otherwise comply with U.S. requirements.

In addition, the Pork Promotion, Research, and Consumer Information Act of 1985 (PPRCIA) requires that each importer of porcine animals, pork, or pork products shall remit an assessment to U.S. Customs at the time the product is imported.

Port of Entry Inspection. The FSIS reinspects meat and meat products by sampling shipments as they enter the U.S. Your products may be checked for transportation damage, labeling compliance and accuracy, general condition, and proper certification. FSIS may also examine the product for accuracy of net weight, labeling requirements, and condition of the container, and make laboratory analyses of food chemistry (for example, fat, water, and nitrite levels) and test for drug and chemical residues. It may also test to confirm species. The actual inspection tasks and the scope of inspection are based on the nature of the product and on the performance history of the packing plant and country of origination.

If your shipment passes reinspection, FSIS will stamp the products "U.S. Inspected and Passed," and they will be allowed entry. If the products fail this reinspection, they will be stamped "U.S. Refused Entry," in which case you must reexport or destroy the refused products. In some cases, such products may be converted to animal food. Once a shipment has been condemned, inspection is intensified for future shipments of that product from the same plant, and in some cases, for all meat shipments from the same country.

Residue Control. Chemical and drug residue control is one of the major features of an exporting country's inspection system that must be judged equal to the U.S. system. Exporting countries must be certified annually by FSIS as continuing to operate an equivalent residue control program. FSIS experts make sure that the country's residue program uses approved analytical methods, that officials are knowledgeable about the use of chemical compounds in their country, and that the country tests for those compounds that could potentially contaminate the food supply. Meat or meat products may not be imported from a country that fails to receive a FSIS annual residue certification.

As a further residue check, FSIS randomly samples products at the port of entry and analyzes them for drug and chemical residues. The FSIS annual import residue plan sets the initial sampling rate for each country based on the volume of product imported from that country. The plan includes the same chemical compounds as the domestic residue-monitoring program. Compounds are selected based on their likelihood of contaminating the food supply and their potential harm to the consuming public. The list can include chemical compounds not legal for use in the U.S. if they have the potential to contaminate a foreign country's meat supply.

If your shipment contains residues above the U.S. tolerance or action level, it will be considered adulterated and will be refused entry into the U.S. Shipments are not usually held pending laboratory test results unless FSIS has some reason to suspect contamination. If a laboratory reports a residue violation on a sample that has otherwise passed reinspection, as much as possible of the product must be recalled. Products so recovered may not be used for human food.

The occurrence of a residue violation at a port of entry raises concerns about the exporting country's ability to control residues. Port of entry sampling is then automatically increased for related products from the entire country, as well as on subsequent shipments from the specific plant where the noncomplying sample originated. From time to time, the FSIS will increase sampling for a specific country or for a specific compound. This can occur when there is an indication that a problem may exist or when there is a pattern of failed port of entry reinspections.

USDA APHIS Requirements. APHIS regulates meat and meat product imports in order to prevent the introduction of certain infectious diseases into the U.S., operating primarily under the authority of Subpart 94 which establishes import restrictions and procedures. APHIS restricts imports from countries known to have incidence of a variety of listed diseases. For ruminants and swine: rinderpest and foot-and-mouth disease; for swine: African swine fever, swine vesicular disease, and hog cholera; for poultry: fowl pest, viscerotropic velogenic Newcastle disease (VVND), and *Salmonella enteritis* (phage-type 4).(see "Country-Specific Import Restrictions" below).

Not only does APHIS restrict imports from countries known to have a specific disease, it also restricts imports from countries that do not have the disease, but that 1) are known to import and use animal products from countries that do; 2) whose regulations regarding entry of such products or of potentially-infected live animals into their borders are less stringent than those of the U.S.; or 3) that border on countries known to have the disease. APHIS also restricts imports originating from disease-free countries but which, in the course of transport, enter the territory of countries known to have the disease. Meat products may be allowed entry provided they are processed in such a fashion as to kill the disease organisms and prevent the transmission of the diseases in question.

The importation of prepared meat and fish products involves a very complicated set of qualifying factors. APHIS administers these restrictions primarily through product certification by qualified veterinarians of the country of origin. In some cases, permits are required. There are stringent cooking, processing, marking, packing, and shipping requirements for certain imports. The variables are too complex to cover exhaustively in this discussion, but the following examples will give you an idea of the issues that need to be addressed in importing these products.

Importation of Cured or Cooked Meat of Ruminants or Swine Originating in Country Where Rinderpest or Foot-and-Mouth Disease Exist. If you are importing cured meats—such as jerked or dried beef, corned beef, or Westphalia hams, but not including meat that has been sterilized by heat in hermetically sealed containers—of HTSUS Chapter 2, the following conditions apply: 1) all bones must have been removed in the country of origin; 2) the meat must have been held in an unfrozen, fresh condition for at least 3 days immediately following slaughter of the animals from which it was derived; and 3) the meat must have been thoroughly cured and fully dried in such a manner that it may be stored and handled without refrigeration. If your product is deemed by the port of entry inspector to be in violation of the prescribed water-protein ratio for cured meat, it will be tested by APHIS, and the shipment will be held at port of entry pending test results. Finally, the requisite country-of-origin foreign meat inspection certificate must be presented to the USDA inspector at port of entry.

Pork Products From Countries Where African Swine Fever Exists. If you are importing pork products that either originate in or were processed in a country identified as one in which African swine fever exists, you must be sure your products comply with the following requirements: 1) be a fully sterilized product that is shelf-stable without refrigeration because it was fully cooked by commercial method and packaged in a container hermetically sealed promptly after filling but prior to such cooking; or 2) is not otherwise prohibited and is consigned directly to a USDA-approved, federally inspected meat-processing establishment for further heat processing. You must convey the product under U.S. Customs or APHIS seals, which may not be broken except by USDA-authorized officials; and 3) if your product originated in a disease-free country, but was processed in an infected country, or transported through one, you must provide certification that it was sealed and inspected in accordance with the regulations governing such cases. Furthermore, all processing must have been accomplished in a single establishment in the infected country, which must meet both FSIS certification requirements and APHIS requirements for pork-processing plants (9 CFR 1 Subpart 94.8). After having all bones removed, the product must have been thoroughly heated according to regulations. Certification must be presented to the FDA inspector at U.S. port of entry.

If you would like the names and address of approved establishments, or if you wish to request approval to use an establishment, contact APHIS Import-Export Products Staff (see addresses at end of this chapter). If you import pork products from listed infected countries, which do not comply with requirements of Subpart 94, your shipment will be seized, quarantined, and disposed of as the USDA determines necessary to prevent introduction of African swine fever into the U.S.

Hog Cholera and Swine Vesicular Disease. Regulations covering importation of pork from countries where hog cholera and vesicular swine fever exist are similar in nature (but not in specifics) to those covering African swine fever. Regulations similar to those covering products from countries that either border on or allow entry of products from infected countries also apply to hog cholera and vesicular swine fever countries. These regulations vary depending upon what is necessary to ensure that the product does not carry contaminating disease organisms into the U.S. Pork products originating in countries infected with these diseases must comply with specific processing and preparation provisions of Subpart 94. They must be offered for entry under government veterinary certification additional to that normally required by FMIA. The additional certification may be placed on the foreign meat inspection certificate or may be contained in a separate document. What must appear on the additional certificate varies depending upon the nature of the import.

Hams. APHIS enforces Subpart 94 covering the importation of ham and similar cured pork products. Ham products are allowed entry under the following conditions: 1) they came from a swine that was never out of the country in which the ham was processed; 2) they came from a country determined by the USDA to have and to enforce laws requiring the immediate reporting to the country's national veterinary services any premises found to have any animal infected with foot-and-mouth disease, rinderpest, African Swine fever, hog cholera, or swine vesicular disease; 3) they came from a swine that was not on any premises where the diseases mentioned above exist or had existed within 60 days prior to slaughter; 4) the hams were accompanied from the slaughterhouse to the processing establishment by a numbered certificate issued by a person authorized by the national government of the country of origin stating that the above provisions were met; and 5) the hams must have been processed according to regulations in 9 CFR 1 Subpart 94.17 in a single establishment.

If you are interested in importing hams, you should be aware of the restrictions on foreign establishments eligible to export hams to the U.S. Be sure to purchase your product from an meatpacker that complies with all relevant regulations for the processing of hams, and that employs someone authorized by national veterinary officials to oversee and attest to that compliance. Hams from establishments that do not meet these criteria may not be imported. The only foreign hams eligible for import into the U.S. are those processed in APHIS-inspected establishments whose proprietor has signed a written agreement with the APHIS to the effect that all hams for import to the U.S. will be processed in accordance with standards established in Subpart 94. Foreign meatpackers must also meet APHIS recordkeeping and inspection access requirements. Foreign hams imported into the U.S. must bear certain markings (see "Marking and Labeling Requirements" below), and must be accompanied by a certificate issued by an authorized person stating that the ham was processed for at least 400 days and that all relevant provisions of Subpart 94 have been fulfilled.

Poultry Products. The law defines poultry as chickens, turkeys, swans, partridges, guinea fowl, pea fowl, nonmigratory ducks, geese, pigeons, and doves as well as commercial, domestic, or pen-raised grouse, pheasants, and quail. It restricts import of these products from countries known to have incidences of fowl pest, viscerotropic velogenic Newcastle disease (VVND), and *Salmonella enteritis* (phage-type 4). Poultry products that have been fully processed into food preparations by methods that serve to kill the disease organisms are allowed entry, provided that compliance can be demonstrated. For example, poultry products originating, or passing through a country where VVND is considered endemic may be imported into the U.S. if 1) they are packed in hermetically sealed containers and cooked by a commercial method after such packing to produce articles that are shelf-stable without refrigeration; or 2) they are determined by a USDA inspector at the port of entry to have a thoroughly cooked appearance throughout (Subpart 94 defines "thoroughly cooked" as heated so that the flesh and juices have lost all red or pink color).

APHIS VS Permit Application. Requests for USDA APHIS VS permits authorizing importation of restricted products must be submitted on a completed VS **Form 16-3.** You may obtain these forms from APHIS headquarters (see addresses at end of this chapter) or from any USDA port office. Application on a signed facsimile (copy) is acceptable, provided you send an original signed document as follow-up. If you need a supply of the forms on hand, you may photocopy the original **Form 16-3**.

Requested information on processing or production data and sources of meat products may often require more space than is provided on the application form. In such cases, you may attach extra sheets as necessary. You should include as much background information as possible in order for APHIS to properly evaluate the disease risk of the product you wish to import. Research papers intended as supporting information should not be sent by fax. It takes about two weeks for the APHIS to process an application and prepare a permit for return mail. If the application information is deemed insufficient, APHIS will contact you for clarification. The permit process can take longer in such cases. You should submit your requests for permit renewal or amendment in writing (fax is acceptable) to the USDA (see addresses at end of this chapter). You should note any changes from the original application and permit issued, such as addresses or production method, when making permit renewal requests.

Any importation for which a permit is issued must comply in all particulars with the permit's stipulations. You will facilitate the entry of your import shipments by making sure the permit number appears on the shipping documents—or simply include a copy of the permit with your entry documents. Meat products requiring permits will be subject to delay or refusal at the port of entry if an importation permit is not obtained before shipment to the U.S.

FDA Requirements. The FDA regulates importation of all food products, including fresh, frozen, pickled, canned, salted, dried, and smoked meat, poultry, fish, and shellfish and preparations thereof under the Food, Drug, and Cosmetic Act (21 CFR 161). You may use only FDA-approved preservatives to prevent or retard spoilage. Artificial coloring that conceals damage or inferiority, or makes the product appear better or of greater value than it really is, is prohibited under FDCA. For more detailed discussion of FDCA food additive regulations and labeling requirements, refer to the "Foods" appendix on page 808.

You should be aware that certain species of animals, especially of fish and seafood, may contain chemical contamination from lakes, rivers, and oceans, and/or excessive residues of pesticides, mercury, and other heavy metals. Presence of such substances in food is a violation of the FDCA, and renders the product subject to detention at the U.S. port of entry.

Canned Meat, Poultry, Fish, and Seafood. Many canned animal products are low-acid canned foods and as such must comply with applicable FDCA regulations. Packers are subject to registration requirements for low-acid canned food manufacturers. Low acid canned foods are heat-processed foods other than alcoholic beverages that have an acidity greater than pH 4.6, a water activity greater than 0.85, and that are packaged in hermetically sealed containers. "Water activity" is a measure of the water available for microbial growth. "Hermetically sealed containers" include any package, regardless of composition, capable of maintaining the commercial sterility of contents after processing. Acidified foods are those to which acid(s) or acid food(s) are added to reduce the pH to 4.6 or lower (increase the acidity), and with a water activity greater than 0.85. If you are unsure whether your canned product fits one of these categories, contact the FDA's Industry Guidelines Branch for clarification (see addresses at end of this chapter).

You should be sure that your canned products are properly and adequately labeled. If they are not, they will not be permitted entry into U.S. Customs territory. The FDA has denied entry of canned products because labeling did not accurately declare: 1) presence of added salt; 2) nature of packing medium, e.g. type of oil; or 3) presence of artificial colors or chemical preservatives. Other violations for which shipments of canned products have been detained are: 1) excessive amounts of packing medium (e.g. oil), or 2) excessive headspace (the space between the lid of the can and the surface of the food). Canned foods must meet certain FDA standards of fill, including minimum drained weight and minimum total volume of product relative to that of the container. If you are importing a product for which no formal fill-of-container standards have been promulgated, you should be sure that containers are well filled with only enough packing medium to fill the interstitial spaces. There may also be regulations covering whether or not water may be added to a product and how it must be labeled if water is added.

Identity standards are relatively straightforward for meat products. They are somewhat more elaborate for fish and seafood products involving a variety of species. For example, there are standards of identity and fill-of-container for canned pacific salmon. The standards establish species, names required on labels, and permitted styles of pack. If you are importing these products, you should be sure they comply with any established standards in every respect.

Anchovies. Regulations limit products represented as anchovies to fish of the family *Engraulidae*. If you are importing anchovies, they must be of that family. You may not label other small fish that may superficially resemble anchovies, such as small herring and herring-like fish, as anchovies.

Sardines. The term "sardines" is permitted in the labeling of the canned products prepared from small clupeoid fish. Sea herring (*Clupea harengus*), European pilchards (*Sardina pilchardus* or *Clupea pilchardus*), and brisling or sprat (*Clupea sprattus*) are commonly packed in small cans and labeled as sardines. The terms "brisling sardines" and "sild sardines" are permissible in the labeling of canned small brisling and herring, respectively. Large herring may not be labeled sardines. If you are importing canned sardines, be sure they are adequately processed to prevent active spoilage by microorganisms. They must be free from all forms of decomposition. A common cause of detention is the presence of "feedy, belly-blown" fish in a shipment. "Feedy fish" are those whose stomachs are full of feed when they are caught. They deteriorate rapidly. Viscera and thin belly wall disintegrate, producing a characteristic ragged appearance called "belly-blown." If your shipment contains such fish it is in violation of FDCA and subject to detention at port of entry.

Tuna. If you are importing canned tuna, you should be aware of FDCA standards of identity and standards of fill, and make sure that your product complies. The standards provide for various styles of pack, including solid, chunk or chunk style, flakes, and grated. Provision is also made for various types of packing media, certain specified seasonings and flavorings, color designations, and methods for determining proper fill of containers. Fill-of-container standards for canned tuna specify minimum values for pressed cake weight, depending on tuna ingredient style (chunk, flake, etc.) and can size. Species of fish that resemble tuna, such as bonito (*Sarda chilenis*) and yellowtail (*Seriola dorsalis*) are sometimes canned and labeled as tuna. This is misbranding, and is cause for legal action if you attempt to import such products into the U.S. You may label as tuna only those species listed in FDCA tuna standards of identity.

Shellfish Certification and Imports. Standards of identity have been set for canned oysters. The standards define sizes of oysters, and prescribe methods of washing and draining to prevent adulteration with excess water. Fill-of-container standard for canned oysters fixes the drained weight at not less than 59% of the container's water capacity.

If you are interested in importing shellfish (clams, mussels, and oysters), be sure they are obtained from unpolluted waters and produced, handled, and distributed in a sanitary manner. Because they may transmit intestinal diseases such as typhoid fever, or be carriers of natural or chemical toxins, shellfish are subject to special FDA controls and licensing. Foreign shellfish products intended for sale in the U.S. are subject to controls equivalent to those applied to domestic products. All shellfish must comply with the general requirements of the FDCA plus those of state health agencies cooperating in both the FDA-administered National Shellfish Sanitation Program (NSSP) and Interstate Shellfish Sanitation Conference (ISSC). Shellfish harvesting is prohibited in areas contaminated by sewage or industrial wastes. State inspectors issue approval certificates to facilities that pass inspection. These certificates are equivalent to a state license to operate. The state-approved plant's certification number must appear on each container or package of shellfish shipped. In addition, shippers are required to keep records showing the origin and disposition of all shellfish handled and to make these records available to the control authorities.

Rock Lobster, Spiny Lobster, Sea Crayfish. The sea crayfish, *Palinurus vulgaris,* is frequently imported into the U.S. in the form of frozen tails, frozen cooked meat, or canned meat. Common or usual names for these products are "rock lobster" and "spiny lobster." If you are importing this product, be sure that your labeling shows the modifying words "rock" or "spiny" in direct connection with the word "lobster," in type of equal size and prominence.

Shrimp. There are standards of identity for shrimp in the following forms: 1) canned wet-and dry-pack, 2) frozen raw breaded, and 3) frozen raw lightly breaded.

Caviar and Fish Roe. The unqualified name "caviar" may be applied only to sturgeon eggs prepared by a process unique to caviar. If roe is prepared by caviar process, but from eggs of fish other than sturgeon, the label name must include the identity of that fish, e.g. "whitefish caviar."

The following violations are common reasons for detention of these products at port of entry: 1) decomposition of canned product due to the packing of decomposed raw material; 2) decomposition of canned product due to active bacterial spoilage; 3) presence in frozen cooked product of microorganisms indicative of contamination with human or animal filth; 4) decomposition of frozen cooked product.

Country-Specific Import Restrictions

Countries currently FSIS-certified for exportation of meat and poultry to the U.S.: Argentina, Australia, Belgium, Belize, Brazil, Canada, Costa Rica, the Czech Republic, Denmark, Dominican Republic, El Salvador, Finland, France, Guatemala, Honduras, Hong Kong, Hungary, Ireland, Israel, Italy, Mexico, Netherlands, New Zealand, Norway, Poland, Romania, the Slovak Republic, Sweden, Switzerland, United Kingdom, Uruguay, and the republics of the former Yugoslavia. Meat may not be imported from countries not on the list. The list is subject to change. For the most up-to-date information, contact FSIS (see addresses at end of this chapter).

APHIS-listed Countries. The following countries are listed by APHIS as being free of, or as having, the diseases indicated below. Imports of certain meat products are banned from countries where animal diseases are deemed to exist.

Countries certified free of rinderpest and foot-and-mouth disease, from which ruminant and swine products may be imported: Australia, the Bahamas, Barbados, Belize, Bermuda, Canada, Channel Islands, Denmark, Finland, Great Britain (England, Scotland, Wales, and Isle of Man), Greenland, Guatemala, Haiti, Honduras, Iceland, Ireland, Jamaica, Japan, Costa Rica, Dominican Republic, El Salvador, Fiji, Mexico, New Zealand, Nicaragua, Northern Ireland, Norway, Panama, Panama Canal Zone, Papua New Guinea, Territory of St. Pierre and Miquelon, Sweden, Trinidad and Tobago, and Trust Territory of the Pacific Islands.

Countries where African swine fever is believed to exist and from which pork imports are banned: Africa (all countries), Brazil, Cuba, Haiti, Italy, Malta, Portugal, and Spain.

Countries deemed free of hog cholera and from which pork may be imported: Australia, Canada, Denmark, Dominican Republic, Fiji, Finland, Great Britain (England, Scotland, Wales, and Isle of Man), Iceland, New Zealand, Northern Ireland, Norway, the Republic of Ireland, Sweden, Trust Territory of the Pacific Islands.

Countries deemed free of swine vesicular disease and from which pork may be imported: Australia, the Bahamas, Bulgaria, Canada, Central American countries, Denmark, Dominican Republic, Fiji, Finland, Great Britain (England, Scotland, Wales, and the Isle of Man), Greenland, Haiti, Hungary, Iceland, Luxembourg, Mexico, New Zealand, Northern Ireland, Norway, Panama, Republic of Ireland, Rumania, Sweden, Switzerland, Trust Territories of the Pacific Islands, and the republics of the former Yugoslavia.

Countries subject to specific restrictions on the importation of pork products: the Bahamas, Bulgaria, Great Britain (England, Scotland, Wales, and the Isle of Man), Hungary, Luxembourg, Switzerland, and the republics of the former Yugoslavia.

Countries subject to specific restrictions on the importation of ruminant and swine products: the Bahamas, Channel Islands, Denmark, Finland, Great Britain (England, Scotland, Wales, and Isle of Man), Japan, Northern Ireland, Norway, Papua New Guinea, and Sweden.

Countries certified free of viscerotropic velogenic Newcastle disease (VVND): Australia, Canada, Denmark, Fiji, Finland, Great Britain (England, Scotland, Wales, and the Isle of Man), Iceland, New Zealand, Northern Ireland, Norway, Republic of Ireland, Sweden.

Countries free of **Salmonella enteritis***:* Canada.

Marking and Labeling Requirements

FSIS Requirements. When meat and meat products are imported, the name of the country of origin must appear on the label. However, only imported products that reach consumers without further processing retain such labeling. For example, a can of ham or corned beef that goes directly to a retail outlet will name the country of origin on the label. However, if imported boneless beef is combined with U.S. beef and other ingredients in a U.S. plant to produce a can of beef stew, the label is not required to indicate the presence of imported beef.

The Farm Bill Amendments require foreign countries exporting products to the U.S. to impose controls, equivalent to those administered by the FSIS, to prevent species substitution. A product labeled "beef," for example, must be beef and cannot contain a less expensive or more readily available species. Exporting countries must maintain effective testing programs for species verification, and adequate security measures to prevent species substitution.

APHIS Requirements. Imported hams must comply with all marking requirements of Subpart 94.17. Ham must bear a hot iron brand or an ink seal with the identifying number of the slaughterhouse. It must bear a button seal, approved by USDA to be tamper-proof, on the hock, stating the month and year the ham entered the processing establishment. It must bear a hot iron brand (with the identifying number of the processing establishment and the date salting began) executed at the processing establishment immediately prior to salting. All required branding must be performed under the direct supervision of a person authorized by the veterinary services of the country of origin's national government to supervise such activity.

FDA Requirements. Substitution of one kind of species for another is prohibited. Whether or not identity standards apply, labels must identify the product by its common or usual U.S. name. You may not replace the common U.S. name of a product either with a name common in the country of origin but unfamiliar in the U.S. or with a coined name. If you are importing a product not previously marketed in the U.S., its name must reflect proper biological classification and must not duplicate, or risk being confused with, the common or usual U.S. name of any other species or product. Any product for which identity standards exist must conform precisely to those standards. It is illegal to use the name of a standard product on a product that deviates from that standard. For basic FDA marking and labeling requirements, refer to the "Foods" appendix on page 808.

For a general discussion of U.S. Customs marking and labeling requirements, see "Marking: Country of Origin" on page 215 and "Special Marking Requirements" on page 217.

Shipping Considerations

You will need to ensure that your goods are packaged and shipped with care so that they arrive in good condition and pass smoothly through Customs. You are responsible for ensuring that the shipment is in compliance with all applicable government regulations for packaging and shipping. In most instances, you should not leave these arrangements solely to the discretion of your supplier. Careful preparation of the cargo and selection of the mode of transport can be essential to a cost-effective, timely delivery of undamaged goods. We strongly advise you to consult your shipping representative, insurance agent, or freight broker for advice on packing and shipping. Refer also to the major tab section "Packing/Shipping/Insurance" for a general discussion of packing and shipping.

Publications Available

The following publications may be relevant to the importation of meat:

Foreign Countries and Plants Certified to Export Meat and Poultry to the United States

This is a comprehensive listing of export-certified countries and plants, including previously certified plants that have been decertified. It is available from the FSIS (see addresses at end of this chapter).

The following publication explains the FDA requirements for importing meat and fish. It is published by the FDA and is available on request from FDA headquarters (see addresses at end of this chapter).

Requirements of Laws and Regulations Enforced by the U.S. Food and Drug Administration

The following publication gives brief, general guidelines on USDA regulated products. Although designed primarily for tourists, it contains a list of approved products that you may find helpful. It is published by USDA APHIS (see addresses at end of this chapter).

Travelers Tips On Bringing Food, Plant, and Animal Products into the United States

The *Harmonized Tariff Schedule of the United States* (HTSUS) is available from:

Government Printing Office (GPO)
Superintendent of Documents
Washington, DC 20402
(202) 512-1800 (Order line)
(202) 512-0000 (General)

The USGPO also has copies of specific laws available for purchase. The USGPO accepts credit card orders over the phone, as well as mail orders paid by credit card, a check drawn on a U.S. bank, or an international money order.

Relevant Government Agencies

Address your questions regarding APHIS import requirements, port of entry inspections, permits, and approved establishments for the import of meat to:

U.S. Department of Agriculture (USDA)
Animal and Plant Health Inspection Service (APHIS)
Veterinary Services (VS)
Import-Export Products Staff
Federal Building, Room 756
6505 Belcrest Road
Hyattsville, MD 20782
(301) 436-7885

Address your questions regarding FSIS port of entry inspection or pre-import certification of meat, fish, and related products and establishments to:

U.S. Department of Agriculture (USDA)
Food Safety and Inspection Service (FSIS)
Import Inspection Service (FSIS)
Rm. 3715, Franklin Ct.
Suite 3700-W
Washington, DC 20250-3700
(202) 501-7515

Address your questions regarding FDA requirements for meat products and canned products to:

Food and Drug Administration (FDA)
Center for Food Safety and Applied Nutrition
200 C Street SW
Washington, DC 20204
(202) 205-5241, 205-5042

Food and Drug Administration (FDA)
Division of Enforcement, Imports Branch
200 C Street SW
Washington, DC 20204
(202) 205-4726

Address your questions regarding importation of meats and edible offal to the district or port director of Customs for you area. For addresses refer to"U.S. Customs District Offices" on page 62 or contact:

U.S. Customs Service
1301 Constitution Ave. NW
Washington, DC 20229
(202) 927-6724 (Information)
(202) 927-1000 (General)

Laws and Regulations

The following laws and regulations may be relevant to the importation of meat and edible offal. The laws are contained in the U.S. Code (USC) and the regulations in the Code of Federal Regulations (CFR), both of which may be available at larger public and law libraries. Copies of specific laws are also available from the United States Government Printing Office (address above).

7 USC 1854
Delegations of Authority Concerning Certain Meats
EO 11539, as amended by EO 12188
These Executive Orders authorize Customs to enforce limitations on the importation and entry and withdrawal of meats from warehouses for consumption in the U.S.

7 CFR 16.1 et seq.
Regulations of USDA on Import and Entry of Meat and Meat Products
These regulations govern the importation and set forth the USDA inspection procedures for meat and meat products offered for entry into the U.S.

19 CFR 12.1 et seq.
Regulations on Customs Inspection and Release of

Meat and Meat Products
These regulations set forth the conditions and bond under which U.S. Customs will release meat and meat products for entry into the U.S. and the penalties for breach of the bond.

7 USC 4801 et seq.
Pork Promotion, Research, and Consumer Information Act
This Act provides that each importer of porcine animal, pork, or pork product shall remit an assessment to Customs at the time the product is imported. See 7 CFR 1230.71 and 1230.110.

21 USC 601 et seq.
Federal Meat Inspection Act
This act provides standards for inspection, packaging, and sale of meat and meat products and prohibits the importation of adulterated, misbranded, or improperly slaughtered meat.

21 USC 451 et seq.
Poultry Products Inspection Act
This Act provides standards for inspection, packaging, and sale of poultry and poultry products and prohibits the importation of slaughtered poultry not in compliance with prescribed standards and regulations.

9 CFR Part 381
Regulations for Inspection of Poultry Products
These regulations prescribe standards for sanitation and composition, inspection procedures, marking and labeling—including nutrition—requirements, exporting and importing certification procedures, and requirements.

9 CFR Part 50 et seq.
Regulations on Animal Byproduct Quarantine Control
These regulations promulgated by the USDA prohibit the importation of animal products for use in industry unless the products meet certain processing standards and are not infected with certain diseases.

21 USC 301 et seq.
Food, Drug, and Cosmetic Act
This Act prohibits deceptive practices and regulates the manufacture, sale and importation or exportation of food, drugs, cosmetics, and related products. See 21 USC 331, 381, 382.

19 CFR 12.1 et seq.; 21 CFR 1.83 et seq.
Regulations on Food, Drugs, and Cosmetics
These regulations of the Secretary of Health and Human Services and the Secretary of the Treasury govern the standards, labeling, marking, and importing of products used with food, drugs, and cosmetics.

Convention on International Trade in Endangered Species of Wild Fauna and Flora (CITES)
This comprehensive wildlife treaty signed by over 100 countries, including the United States, regulates and in many cases prohibits commercial imports and exports of wild animal and plant species threatened by trade.

16 USC 1531
Endangered Species Act
This Act prohibits the import and export of species listed as endangered and most species listed as threatened. It is the U.S. law that implements CITES.

19 CFR 12.26 et seq.
Regulations on Importation of Wild Animals
These regulations list the wild animals that are prohibited from importation or that require import permits.

50 CFR Parts 10, 13, and 16
Regulations of FWS for Importing Wildlife and Fish
These regulations specify the animals and animal products subject to import prohibitions and restrictions.

Principal Exporting Countries

The following listing includes samples of the main supplier nations of the products of this chapter. It is organized by HTSUS major heading. (Refer to "Customs Classification" above for the product codes.) Countries are listed in rank order of the value of products imported to the U.S. Statistics represent customs value entries for 1993 from the Bureau of Census, U.S. Department of Commerce.

1601—Canada, Denmark, Hungary, Ireland, Poland, Dominican Rep., Spain, Netherlands, Germany, Argentina

1602—Argentina, Denmark, Brazil, Canada, Hungary, Netherlands, Poland, Belgium, Uruguay, Croatia

1603—Japan, Argentina, Brazil, Uruguay, France, Mexico, Netherlands, Denmark, Hong Kong, South Korea

1604—Thailand, Philippines, Indonesia, Canada, Taiwan, Ecuador, Morocco, Japan, Norway, Chile

1605—Thailand, Canada, South Korea, Mexico, Indonesia, Japan, Venezuela, China, Spain, India

Chapter 17: Sugars and Sugar Confectionery*

This chapter relates to the importation of sugars and sugar confectionery, which are classified within Chapter 17 of the Harmonized Tariff Schedule of the United States (HTSUS). Specifically, it includes cane and beet sugar; lactose, maltose, glucose, and fructose; maple sugar; molasses; candies not including chocolate; and chemically pure sugars for food and beverage uses. If you are interested in importing sugars for food purposes or candy, should read this section in conjunction with the "Foods" appendix on page 808.

If you are interested in importing candies containing cocoa, you should refer to Commodity Index Chapter 18. Chemically pure sugars other than lactose, maltose, sucrose, glucose, and fructose destined for industrial uses are included in Chapter 29, while sugars for medical or pharmaceutical purposes or used in the manufacture of such products are covered in Chapter 30.

Key Factors

The key factors in the importation of sugars and candy are:

- Compliance with U.S. Food and Drug Administration (FDA) purity, identity, manufacturing, and other standards
- Compliance with FDA entry notifications and procedures
- Quotas on certain sugar products derived from sugar beets and sugar cane as well as on confectionery

For dutiable sugars imported in bulk, U.S. Customs requires a description of the unloading facilities in advance of the shipment.

Although most importers utilize the services of a licensed customs broker in making their entries, and we recommend this practice, you should be aware of the regulatory, entry, and documentation issues involved in importing your product. You, as importer, are ultimately responsible for the fulfillment of any legal requirements applicable to your shipment.

General Considerations

Certain sugars and sugar products derived from sugar cane or sugar beets are subject to quotas or additional duties levied pursuant to Section 22 of the Agricultural Adjustment Act (AAA). For specifics regarding the nature and extent of these quotas and fees, refer to HTSUS Chapter 99, Subchapter V. Sugars subject to additional duties under HTSUS headings 9904.40.20 through .60 and intended for use in the production (other than distillation) of polyhydric alcohols (except for polyhydric alcohols intended as a substitute for sugar in human food products) may be entered free of the extra fees under a license issued by the Secretary of Agriculture. For more information concerning such licensing contact the USDA International Trade Policy Staff (see addresses at end of this chapter).

Chapter 17 products are subject to regulation under the Federal Food, Drug, and Cosmetic Act (FDCA), administered by the FDA. FDA entry notification, **Form FD701,** is required for all FDA-regulated imports. For a more detailed discussion of FDA requirements, and an annotated diagram of FDA entry procedures refer to the "Foods" appendix on page 808. For more information concerning FDA requirements for imported sugar, contact the nearest regional FDA import operations office, or FDA headquarters (see addresses at end of this chapter).

Under 19 CFR 151, Subpart B, importers of dutiable sugar in bulk must submit a full description of the unloading facilities to the Commissioner of Customs as far in advance of the dates of importation as possible. Customs will then issue special weighing and sampling instructions to you. Any weighing or sampling required for your shipment must be done when the shipment is unloaded. When both weighing and sampling are required, you must have these operations performed simultaneously.

When importing molasses in tank cars, you must file a certificate with the district director of the port of entry showing whether there is any substantial difference either in the total sugars or the character of the molasses in the different cars. When you import syrup or molasses that is to be pumped or discharged into storage tanks in bulk in tank vessels, you must file a certified copy of the plans of the storage tanks and the gauge table with the port district director before discharging. The plans must accurately state tank capacity and show all inlets and outlets. After discharge and prior to gauging, all tank inlets must be carefully sealed and the syrup or molasses left undisturbed for a period not to exceed 20 days to allow for settling. Immediate gauging will be allowed if you so request in writing. No expense incidental to the unloading, transporting, or handling of sugar, syrup, or molasses for convenient weighing, gauging, measuring, sampling, or marking will be borne by the U.S. Government.

The U.S. Environmental Protection Agency (EPA) enforces the Federal Insecticide, Fungicide, and Rodenticide Act (FIFRA), which establishes regulatory limits on pesticide and other chemical residues found in edible plant products. For more information, contact EPA (see addresses at end of this chapter).

Compliance. If your shipment is found to be noncomplying, it may be detained at the port of entry. In the case of products subject to FDA jurisdiction, the FDA may allow you to bring such a shipment into compliance before making a final decision regarding admittance. However, any sorting, reprocessing, or relabeling must be supervised by FDA personnel and is done at the importer's expense. Such conditional release to allow the importer to bring a shipment into compliance is a privilege, not a right. The FDA may consider subsequent noncomplying shipments of the same type of product to constitute abuse of the privilege and require the importer to destroy or reexport the products. To ascertain what your legal responsibilities are, you should contact these agencies regarding the specific items to be imported.

Customs Classification

For customs purposes, sugars and candy are classified under Chapter 17 of the HTSUS. This chapter is divided into major headings, which are further divided into subheadings, and often

*IMPORTANT: Read the Commodity Index Introduction. It is the essential framework for understanding this section.

into subheadings, each of which has its own HTSUS classification number. For example, the HTSUS number for invert molasses is 1702.90.35, indicating that it is a subcategory of invert sugars derived from sugar cane or sugar beets (1702.90.00), which is a subcategory of other sugars (1702.00.00). There are four major headings in HTSUS Chapter 17.

1701—Cane or beet sugar and chemically pure sucrose, in solid form

1702—Other sugars, including chemically pure lactose, maltose, glucose, and fructose, in solid form; sugar syrups not containing added flavoring or coloring matter; artificial honey, whether or not mixed with natural honey; caramel

1703—Molasses, resulting from the extraction or refining of sugar

1704—Sugar confectionery (including white chocolate) not containing cocoa

For more details regarding classification of the specific product you are interested in importing, consult a customs broker, the appropriate commodity specialist at your nearest customs port, or see HTSUS. HTSUS is available for purchase from the U.S. Government Printing Office (see addresses at end of this chapter), and may be found in larger public libraries. Refer to "Classification—Liquidation" on page 207 for a general discussion of customs classification.

Sample Import Duties

Import duties will vary depending on the HTSUS classification of your product. Therefore, to determine the correct amount of duties, your product must be properly classified under the HTSUS. The following sample duties are taken from the duty listings for HTSUS Chapter 17.

Cane or beet sugar in solid form, raw sugar not containing added flavoring or coloring matter (1701.11.01): 1.4606 cents/kg, less 0.020668 cents/kg for each degree under 100 degrees (and fractions of a degree in proportion) but not less than 0.943854 cents/kg; other cane sugar not to be refined further (1701.11.03): 37.386 cents/kg for each degree under 100 degrees (and fractions of a degree in proportion) but not less than 24.161 cents/kg; other cane or beet sugar containing added flavoring matter whether or not containing added coloring (1701.91.40): 6%; lactose and lactose syrup (1702.10.00): 10%; maple sugar and maple syrup, blended with other sugars (1702.20.20): 6%; other (pure) maple syrup or maple sugar (1702.20.40): free; other (pure) glucose syrup (1702.30.40): 3.5 cents/kg; chemically pure fructose (1702.50.00): 15%; invert sugar derived from sugar cane or sugar beets (1702.90.31): 1.4605 cents/kg of total sugars; sugarcane molasses imported for the commercial extraction or refining of sugar, or for human consumption (1703.10.30): 0.77 cents/liter; chewing gum (1704.10.00): 5%; other sugar confections put up for retail sale (1704.90.20): 7%; articles of milk or cream (1704.90.40): 17.5%.

Special Provisions. The following provisions apply with respect to the duty rates on the products indicated below:

9904.40.20 Sugars, syrups, and molasses derived from sugar cane or beets, except those entered pursuant to a license issued by the Secretary of Agriculture (see note below) principally of crystalline structure or in dry amorphous form, provided for in subheading 1701.11, 1701.12, 1701.91.21, 1709.91.22, or 1701.99, not to be further refined or improved in quality: 2.2 cents/kg, but not in excess of 50%.

9904.40.60 Products of the same origin as above, but not principally of crystalline structure and not in dry amorphous form, containing soluble non-sugar solids (excluding any foreign substance that may have been added or developed in the product) equal to 6% or less by weight of the total soluble solids, provided for in heading 1702 or in subheadings 2106.90.11 or 2106.90.12: 2.2 cents/kg of total sugars, but not in excess of 50%.

9904.40.40 Products of 9904.40.20 to be further refined or improved. This provision has been suspended.

Exemptions. Licenses may be issued by the Secretary of Agriculture or his designee authorizing the entry of articles exempt from the fees provided for in these headings on the condition that such articles will be used only for the production of polyhydric alcohols other than for use as a sugar substitute in foods for human consumption.

Entry and Documentation

The entry of merchandise is a two-part process consisting of 1) filing the documents necessary to determine whether merchandise may be released from Customs custody and 2) filing the documents that contain information for duty assessment and statistical purposes. In certain instances all documents must be filed and accepted by Customs prior to release of the goods. Unless you have been granted an extension, you must file entry documents at a location specified by the district or area director within five working days of your shipment's date of arrival at a U.S. port of entry. These include a number of standard documents required by Customs for any entry, and:

- FDA Importers Entry Notice, **Form FD701**
- For molasses imported in tank cars, certificates showing any substantial difference in total sugars or character of the molasses from car to car

After you present the entry, Customs may examine your shipment, or may waive examination. The shipment is then released provided no legal or regulatory violations have been noted. You must then file entry summary documentation and deposit estimated duties at a designated customhouse within 10 working days of your shipment's release. For a detailed description of entry procedures, standard documentation, and informal entry, refer to "Entry Process" on page 182.

Prohibitions and Restrictions

If you are considering importing confectionery, you should ascertain before making your purchase that the utmost in cleanliness and sanitation have governed the product's manufacture. Both the raw materials and finished products tend to attract rodents and insects. Your stored materials should be inspected frequently and carefully. Any equipment you use in relation to your product, or that the manufacturer uses, should be washed thoroughly and kept free from accumulation of materials that would attract vermin.

The following FDA requirements pertain to confectionery products. The only non-nutritive substances allowed in confectionery are those that are: 1) not harmful to health, and 2) of practical functional value to the product. Only such alcohol as is contained in flavoring extracts may be present in confectionery, with a ceiling of 0.5 percent by weight. Color additives must fulfill all pertinent requirements of the FDCA. Only colors authorized for use in the U.S. are permitted in imported confectionery. Some colors require FDA certification. If these are used in your products, you should be sure that they are from a certified batch and are identified on the product labeling (refer to the "Foods" appendix on page 808 for details). If your shipment is in violation of these requirements (21 CFR 101), it may be detained at the U.S. port of entry.

Other common causes of confectionery shipment detention at U.S. ports of entry are: 1) incorrect label listing of ingredients (misbranding); 2) evidence of vermin or insect contamination; or 3) improper labeling of fruit-type candies using artificial flavorings (these must be identified on the label).

Quotas

The importation of sugars is strictly controlled to protect the domestic industry. This is accomplished through the use and administration of extremely complex quota mechanisms, including quotas and duties on finished products containing sugars that could potentially be processed to extract their sugar content for other uses in order to get around the primary controls. Entry of specific products can be difficult because many product categories affected by quota restrictions overlap, especially where sugar and dairy products are concerned. A wide variety of products containing sugar may be restricted because of policy-driven limitations. It is important to consult the Quota Branch of the U.S. Customs Service (see addresses at end of this chapter) to determine whether quota restrictions apply to your specific product.

The following quotas apply to certain types of sugars and confectionery products:

9904.50.20 Blended syrups provided for in subheadings 1702.20.20, 1702.30.20, 1702.40, 1702.60 1702.90.50, 1806.20.80, 1806.90, 2101.10.40, 2101.20.40, 2106.90.51, or 2106.90.59 containing sugars derived from sugar cane or sugar beets, capable of being further processed or mixed with similar or other ingredients and not prepared for marketing to the retail consumers in the identical form and package in which imported: 0 metric tons. Exclusion: blended syrups of 9904.50.20 entered from a foreign trade zone by a foreign trade zone user whose facilities were in operation on June 1, 1990, to the extent that the annual quantity entered into the customs territory from the zone does not contain an amount of sugar of nondomestic origin greater than that authorized by the Foreign Trade Zone Board for processing in the zone during calendar year 1985.

9904.50.40 Articles containing over 65% by dry weight of sugar derived from sugar cane or sugar beets, whether or not mixed with other ingredients, capable of being further processed or mixed with similar or other ingredients, and not prepared for marketing to retail consumers in the identical form and package in which imported; all the foregoing articles provided for in subheading 1701.91.40, 1702.90.50, 1704.90.60, 1806.10.30, 1806.20.70, 1806.90, 1901.20, 1901.90.81, 1901.90.89, 2101.10.40, 2101.20.40, 2103.90.60, 2106.90.51, or 2106.90.59, except articles within the scope of other import restrictions provided for in Subchapter IV of Chapter 99: 0 metric tons.

9904.60 Whenever, in any 12-month period beginning October 1 in any year, the respective aggregate quantity specified below for one of the numbered classes of articles has been entered, no article in such class may be entered during the remainder of such period: Articles containing over 10% by dry weight of sugar derived from sugar cane or sugar beets, whether or not mixed with other ingredients, except (a) articles not principally of crystalline structure or not in dry amorphous form that are prepared for marketing to the retail consumer in the identical form and package in which imported, or (b) articles within the scope of headings 9904.50.20, 9904.50.40 or other import restrictions provided for in this subchapter.

9904.60.20 Provided for in subheading 1806.10.20 or 1806.10.30: 2,313 metric tons.

9904.60.40 Provided for in subheading 1901.20: 5,398 metric tons.

9904.60.60 Provided for in subheading 1704.90.60, 1806.20.70, 1806.20.80, 1806.90, 1901.90.81, 1901.90.89, 2101.10.40, 2101.20.40, 2103.90.60, 2106.90.51, or 2106.90.59, except cake decorations and similar products to be used in the same condition as imported without any further processing other than the direct application to individual pastries or confections; finely ground or masticated coconut meat or juice thereof mixed with those sugars; and sauces and preparations therefore: 64,773 metric tons.

9904.10.75 Whenever, in any 12-month period beginning January 1 in any year, the respective aggregate quantity specified below for one of the numbered classes of articles has been entered, no article in such class may be entered during the remainder of such period:

Dried milk, whey, and buttermilk that contains not more than 5.5% by weight of butterfat and that is mixed with other ingredients, including but not limited to sugar, if such mixtures contain over 16% milk solids by weight, are capable of being further processed or mixed with similar or other ingredients, and are not prepared marketing to retail consumers in the identical form and package in which imported; all of the foregoing mixtures provided for in subheadings 0402.10, 0404.10.40, 0404.10.09, 0404.90.65, 1517.90.40, 1704.90.40, 1704.90.60, 1806.20.80, 1806.32.40, 1806.90, 1901.20, 1901.90.81, 1901.90.89, and 2106.90.05, except articles within the scope of other import restrictions provided for in this subchapter: 0 metric tons.

9904.10.81 Whenever in any 12-month period beginning January 1 in any year, the respective aggregate quantity specified below for one of the numbered classes of articles has been entered, no article in such class may be entered during the remainder of such period:

Articles containing over 5.5% by weight of butterfat, the butterfat of which is commercially extractable, or that are capable of being used for any edible purpose (except (a) articles provided for in headings 0401, 0402, 0405, or 0406 or subheadings 1901.10, 1901.90.31, or 1901.90.39 other than mixtures of nonfat dry milk and anhydrous butterfat containing not over 45% by weight of butterfat classifiable for tariff purposes under subheading 1901.90.31 or 1901.90.39; (b) dried mixtures containing less than 31% by weight of butterfat and consisting of not less than 17.5% by weight of each of sodium caseinate, butterfat, whey solids containing over 5.5% by weight of butterfat, and dried whole milk, but not containing dried milk, dried whey, or dried buttermilk any of which contains 5.5% or less by weight of butterfat; and (c) articles that are not suitable for use as ingredients in the commercial production of edible articles):

Over 5.5% but not over 45% by weight of butterfat including mixtures of nonfat dry milk and anhydrous butterfat classifiable for tariff purposes under subheading 1901.90.31 or 1901.90.39 and other articles classifiable for tariff purposes under subheading 0404.10.07, 0404.10.09, 0404.90.45, 0404.90.65, 1517.90.40, 1704.90.40, 1704.90.60, 1806.20.80, 1806.32.40, 1806.90, 1901.20, 1901.90.41, 1901.90.49, 1901.90.81, 1901.90.89, 2105.00, 2106.90.41, 2106.90.49, 2106.90.51, or 2106.90.59: Australia: 1,016,046 kg; Belgium and Denmark (aggregate): 154,221 kg; Other: 0 kg.

North American Free Trade Agreement (NAFTA) Provisions for Import of Chapter 17 Products From Mexico. The aggregate quantity of sugars, syrups, and molasses entered under subheadings 9906.17.01, 9906.17.16, 9906.18.11, and 906.21.29 that are qualifying goods is the quantity determined by the Secretary of Agriculture in accordance with paragraphs 13 through 15 of Section A, Annex 703.2, Chapter Seven of NAFTA. The Secretary of Agriculture shall inform the Secretary of the Treasury of any determination made under such provisions and shall publish a notice of such determination in the Federal Register. Beginning October 1, 2008, quantitative limitations shall cease to apply to such qualifying goods.

Raw and Refined Sugar. Notwithstanding the quota provided for in this note, effective on or about October 1, 1994, raw sugar that is a qualifying good and that is entered for refining in the U.S. and reexported to Mexico, and refined sugar that is a qualifying good and that is entered after refining in Mexico from raw sugar produced in and exported from the U.S., in accordance with paragraph 22 of the Section A, Annex 703.2, Chapter Seven of NAFTA shall not be subject to duty. Such sugar shall be entered only under such terms, conditions, bonds, or other requirements as the Secretary of Agriculture may determine are necessary to ensure compliance with the provisions of paragraph 22.

Sugars from Cane or Beets and Not Prepared for Retail. The aggregate quantity of articles containing over 65% by dry weight of sugars derived from sugar cane or sugar beets, whether or not mixed with other ingredients, capable of being further processed or mixed with similar or other ingredients, and not prepared for marketing to retail consumers in the identical form and package in which imported, that are qualifying goods entered under subheadings 9906.17.03, 906.17.32, 9906.18.04, 9906.18.17, 9906.18.41, 906.19.08, 9906.19.31, 9906.21.01, 906.21.11, and 9906.21.44 in any calendar year shall not exceed the quantity specified below for that year: 1994: 1,500,000 kg; 1995: 1,545,000 kg; 1996: 1,591,000 kg; 1997: 1.639,000 kg; 1998: 1,688,000 kg; 1999: 1,739,000 kg; 2000: 1,791,000 kg; 2001: 1,845,000 kg; 2002: 1,900,000 kg Beginning in calendar year 2003, quantitative limitations shall cease to apply on such qualifying goods.

Blended Syrups of Sugars from Cane or Beets and Not Prepared for Retail. The aggregate quantity of blended syrups containing sugars derived from sugar cane and sugar beets capable of being further processed or mixed with similar or other ingredients and not prepared for marketing to retail consumers in the identical form and package in which imported that are qualifying goods entered under subheadings 9906.17.07, 9906.17.12, 9906.17.21, 9906.18.27, 9906.18.44, 9906.21.04, and 9906.21.47 in any calendar year shall not exceed the quantity specified below for that year: 1994: 1,500,000 kg; 1995: 1,545,000 kg; 1996: 1,591,000 kg; 1997: 1,639,000 kg; 1998: 1,688,000 kg; 1999: 1,739,000 kg; 2000: 1,791,000 kg; 2001: 1,845,000 kg; 2002: 1,900,000 kg. Beginning in calendar year 2003, quantitative limitations shall cease to apply to such qualifying goods.

Other Articles of Sugars from Cane or Beets. The aggregate quantity of articles containing over 10% by dry weight of sugars derived from sugar cane or sugar beets whether or not mixed with other ingredients except (a) articles not principally of crystalline structure or not in dry amorphous form that are prepared for marketing to retail consumers in the identical form and package in which imported, (b) blended syrups containing sugars derived from sugar cane or sugar beets capable of being further processed or mixed with similar or other ingredients and not prepared for marketing to retail consumers in the identical form and package in which imported, (c) articles containing over 65% by dry weight of sugars derived from sugar cane or sugar beets whether or not mixed with other ingredients capable of being further processed or mixed with similar or other ingredients and not prepared for marketing to retail consumers in the identical form or package in which imported, or (d) cake decorations and similar products to be used in the same condition as imported without any further processing other than the direct application to individual pastries or confections; finely ground or masticated coconut meat or juice thereof mixed with those sugars; and sauces and preparations thereof that are qualifying goods entered under subheadings 9906.17.35, 9906.18.01, 9906.18.07, 9906.18.20, 9906.18.30, 9906.18.47, 9906.19.11, 9906.19.34, 9906.21.07, 9906.21.14, and 9906.21.50 in any calendar year shall not exceed the quantity specified below for that year: 1994: 12,791,000 kg; 1995: 13,175,000 kg; 1995: 13,570,000 kg; 1997: 13,977,000 kg; 1998: 14,396,000 kg; 1999: 14,828,000 kg; 2000: 15,273,000 kg; 2001: 15,731,000 kg; 2002: 16,203,000 kg; beginning in calendar year 2003 quantitative limitations shall cease to apply on such qualifying goods.

For a general discussion of quotas, refer to "Import Quotas" on page 230.

Marking and Labeling Requirements

For a general discussion of U.S. Customs marking and labeling requirements, see "Marking: Country of Origin" on page 215 and "Special Marking Requirements" on page 217.

Shipping Considerations

You will need to ensure that your goods are packaged and shipped with care so that they arrive in good condition and pass smoothly through Customs. You are responsible for ensuring that the shipment is in compliance with all applicable government regulations for packaging and shipping. In most instances, you should not leave these arrangements solely to the discretion of your supplier. Careful preparation of the cargo and selection of the mode of transport can be essential to a cost-effective, timely delivery of undamaged goods. We strongly advise you to consult your shipping representative, insurance agent, or freight broker for advice on packing and shipping. Refer also to the major tab section "Packing/Shipping/Insurance" for a general discussion of packing and shipping.

Sugar and sugar products require careful handling during transit. Although most sugars are not subject to spoilage, care must be taken to prevent contamination during storage, packing, and transport. Sugar confectionery products are often considerably more fragile and perishable, and require greater care to protect them from damage, spoilage, or contamination en route.

Publications Available

The following publication explains the FDA requirements for importing sugars and sugar confectionery. It is published by the FDA and is available on request from FDA headquarters (see addresses at end of this chapter).

Requirements of Laws and Regulations Enforced by the U.S. Food and Drug Administration

The *Harmonized Tariff Schedule of the United States* (HTSUS) is available from:

Government Printing Office (GPO)
Superintendent of Documents
Washington, DC 20402
(202) 512-1800 (Order line)
(202) 512-0000 (General)

The USGPO also has copies of specific laws available for purchase. The USGPO accepts credit card orders over the phone, as well as mail orders paid by credit card, a check drawn on a U.S. bank, or an international money order.

Relevant Government Agencies

Address your questions regarding USDA licensing to:

U.S. Department of Agriculture (USDA)
Foreign Agriculture Division
International Trade Policy Staff
14th Street and Independence Ave. SW
Washington, DC 20250
(202) 690-1823, 720-7115

Address your questions regarding requirements for FDA-regulated products to:

Food and Drug Administration (FDA)
Center for Food Safety and Applied Nutrition
200 C Street SW
Washington, DC 20204
(202) 205-5241, 205-5042

Food and Drug Administration (FDA)
Division of Enforcement, Imports Branch
200 C Street SW
Washington, DC 20204
(202) 205-4726

Address questions regarding allowable chemical residues in sugar and confectionery products to:

Environmental Protection Agency (EPA)
Office of Pesticide Programs
401 M Street SW (7501-C)
Washington, DC 20460
(703) 305-7090 (General)
(703) 305-7102 (Import/export requirements)

Address questions regarding quotas to:

U.S. Customs Service
Quota Branch
1301 Constitution Avenue NW, Rm. 2379-ICC
Washington, DC 20229
(202) 927-5850

Address your questions regarding Customs requirements, quotas and duties for sugars and candies to the district or port director of Customs for you area. For addresses refer to"U.S. Customs District Offices" on page 62 or contact:

U.S. Customs Service
1301 Constitution Ave. NW
Washington, DC 20229
(202) 927-6724 (Information)
(202) 927-1000 (General)

Laws and Regulations

The following laws and regulations may be relevant to the importation of sugars and sugar confectionery. The laws are contained in the U.S. Code (USC) and the regulations are published in the Code of Federal Regulations (CFR), both of which may be available at larger public and law libraries. Copies of specific laws are also available from the United States Government Printing Office (address above).

7 USC 3601 et seq.
International Sugar Agreement of 1977
This Agreement authorizes Customs to regulate the entry of sugar into the U.S.

7 CFR 6.50
Regulations of USDA Exempting Certain Sugars from Import Fees
These regulations allow importers to secure licenses to import sugar and related products free of import fees if the sugar products are used solely for production—other than by distillation—of polyhydric alcohols not used as sugar substitutes in human food.

15 CFR 2011.1
Regulations Allocating Tariff-Rate Quotas on Imported Sugars, Syrups, and Molasses
These regulations specify the terms and conditions under which certificates of quota eligibility will be issued to foreign countries that have been allocated shares of the US sugar tariff-rate quota.

7 USC 601 et seq.
Agricultural Adjustment Act (AAA)
This Act authorizes the Secretary of Agriculture to establish and maintain orderly market conditions for agricultural products and to impose quotas or higher duty rates on imported agricultural products whenever investigation reveals that orderly market conditions require such action.

19 CFR Part 132
Regulations for Enforcement of AAA Quotas
These regulations provide for Customs enforcement of AAA quotas and higher duty rates imposed on imported agricultural products.

21 USC 301 et seq.
Food, Drug, and Cosmetic Act
This Act prohibits deceptive practices and regulates the manufacture, sale and importation or exportation of food, drugs, cosmetics, and related products. See 21 USC 331, 381, 382.

19 CFR 12.1 et seq.; 21 CFR 1.83 et seq.
Regulations on Food, Drugs, and Cosmetics
These regulations of the Secretary of Health and Human Services and the Secretary of the Treasury govern the standards, labeling, marking, and importing of products used with food, drugs, and cosmetics.

7 USC 135 et seq.
Federal Insecticide, Fungicide, and Rodenticide Act (FIFRA)
This Act prohibits the importation of pesticides or devices that are adulterated, misbranded, or otherwise violative of the Act, provides for registration of pesticides and devices, and establishes standards for labeling and classifying pesticides.

19 CFR 12; 40 CFR 162
Regulations on Pesticides
These regulations set forth the procedures and guidelines for importing products exposed to pesticides.

Principal Exporting Countries

The following listing includes samples of the main supplier nations of the products of this chapter. It is organized by HTSUS major heading. (Refer to "Customs Classification" above for the product codes.) Countries are listed in rank order of the value of products imported to the U.S. Statistics represent customs value entries for 1993 from the Bureau of Census, U.S. Department of Commerce.

1701—Dominican Rep., Guatemala, Brazil, Philippines, Australia, Canada, Colombia, Costa Rica, El Salvador, Peru

1702—Canada, Dominican Rep., Belize, Mexico, France, Sweden, Germany, Japan, Netherlands, Finland

1703—Dominican Rep., Australia, Colombia, Poland, Guatemala, Venezuela, Mexico, El Salvador, Nicaragua, Mauritius

1704—Canada, Germany, Mexico, United Kingdom, Brazil, Netherlands, Italy, Spain, Argentina, Taiwan

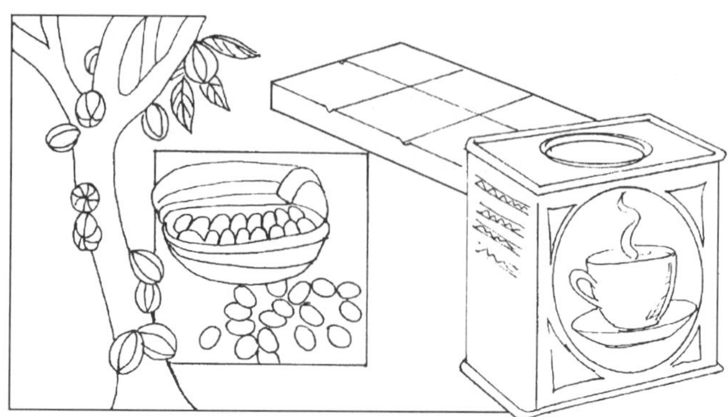

Chapter 18: Cocoa and Cocoa Preparations*

This chapter relates to the importation of cocoa (cacao), chocolate, and other products derived primarily from the cacao plant, which are classified within Chapter 18 of the Harmonized Tariff Schedule of the United States (HTSUS). Specifically, it includes cocoa beans and parts of cocoa beans; cocoa paste, butter, fat, and oil; unsweetened cocoa powder; and chocolate in whatever form and products containing chocolate as a major constituent. This section is supplemental to the "Foods" appendix on page 808 and should be read in conjunction with it.

If you are interested in importing confectionery that does not contain chocolate (including white chocolate), refer to Commodity Index Chapter 17 (heading 1704). Dairy products, such as yogurt, that contain chocolate flavoring are covered in heading 0403 of Chapter 4. Products containing cocoa or chocolate that are covered in Chapter 19 include malt extract (heading 1901), breakfast cereals and related products (heading 1904), and baked goods, such as cakes (heading 1905). If you are interested in importing ice cream containing chocolate flavoring, refer to Chapter 21 (heading 2105). Beverages containing chocolate, such as chocolate milk, are covered in Chapter 22 (heading 2202), while alcoholic beverages containing chocolate, such as liqueurs, are found in heading 2208 of that chapter. Pharmaceuticals that contain cocoa are covered in Chapter 30 (headings 3003 and 3004).

Key Factors

The key factors in the importation of cocoa and cocoa products are:

- Compliance with U.S. Food and Drug Administration (FDA) purity, identity, manufacturing, and other standards
- Compliance with FDA entry notifications and procedures
- Import quotas on certain types of chocolate

Although most importers utilize the services of a licensed customs broker in making their entries, and we recommend this practice, you should be aware of the regulatory, entry, and documentation issues involved in importing your product. You, as importer, are ultimately responsible for the fulfillment of any legal requirements applicable to your shipment.

*IMPORTANT: Read the Commodity Index Introduction. It is the essential framework for understanding this section.

General Considerations

Regulatory Agencies. Importation of cocoa and products containing chocolate falls primarily under the jurisdiction of the FDA, which enforces the requirements of the Federal Food, Drug, and Cosmetic Act (FDCA). The USDA controls imports of plant products to prevent contamination of U.S. food sources. The EPA inspects imported edible plant products for pesticide residues.

FDA Requirements. FDA regulations regarding importation of foods of any kind are extensive and stringent. Cocoa products imported into the U.S. must comply with all FDCA requirements for those produced domestically.

Entry Requirements. Imported products regulated by the FDA are subject to FDA port-of-entry inspection. **Form FD701** is required for all FDA-regulated importations and may be obtained from your local FDA Import Operations office, from FDA headquarters (see addresses at end of this chapter), or from your customs broker. For an annotated diagram of required FDA import procedures refer to the "Foods" appendix on page 808.

Detention of Shipment. If your shipment is found to be noncomplying, it may be detained at the port of entry. The FDA may allow you to bring such a shipment into compliance before making a final decision regarding admittance. However, any sorting, reprocessing, or relabeling must be supervised by FDA personnel, and is done at the importer's expense. Such conditional release to allow an importer to bring a shipment into compliance is a privilege, not a right. The FDA may consider subsequent noncomplying shipments of the same type of product to constitute abuse of the privilege and require the importer to destroy or reexport the products. To ascertain what your legal responsibilities are, you should contact this agencies regarding the specific items to be imported.

USDA Requirements. All products derived from plants are also subject to U.S. Department of Agriculture (USDA) regulations. In general, USDA does not restrict processed cacao products. If you are in any doubt as to the regulatory status of your product, you should check with USDA Animal and Plant Health Inspection Service (APHIS) (see addresses at end of this chapter).

EPA Requirements. The U.S. Environmental Protection Agency (EPA) enforces the Federal Insecticide, Fungicide, and Rodenticide Act (FIFRA), which establishes regulatory limits on pesticide and other chemical residues found in edible plant products. For more information, contact EPA (see addresses at end of this chapter).

Quotas. Some cocoa products from certain countries are subject to quotas under Section 22 of the Agricultural Adjustment Act (AAA) as amended.

Customs Classification

For customs purposes, cocoa and cocoa products are classified under Chapter 18 of the HTSUS. This chapter is broken into major headings, which are further divided into subheadings, and often sub-subheadings, each of which has its own HTSUS classification number. For example, the HTSUS number for cocoa powder containing less than 65% by weight of sugar is 1806.10.20, indicating that it is a sub-subcategory of cocoa powder containing added sugar or other sweetening matter (1806.10.00), which is a subcategory of the major heading Chocolate and other food preparations containing cocoa (1806.00.00). There are six major headings in HTSUS Chapter 18.

1801—Cocoa beans, whole or broken, raw or roasted

1802—Cocoa shells, husks, skins, and other cocoa waste

1803—Cocoa paste, whether or not defatted

1804—Cocoa butter, fat, or oil

1805—Cocoa powder, not containing added sugar or other sweetening matter

1806—Chocolate and other food preparations containing cocoa

For more details regarding classification of the specific product you are interested in importing, consult a customs broker, the appropriate commodity specialist at your nearest customs port, or see HTSUS. HTSUS is available for purchase from the U.S. Government Printing Office (see addresses at end of this chapter), and may be found in larger public libraries. Refer to "Classification—Liquidation" on page 207 for a general discussion of customs classification.

Sample Import Duties

Import duties vary depending on the HTSUS classification of your product. Therefore, to determine the correct amount of duties, your product must be properly classified under the HTSUS. The following sample duties are taken from the duty listings for HTSUS Chapter 18 products.

Cocoa beans, whether whole or broken, raw or roasted (1801.00.00): free; cocoa shells, husks, skins, and other cocoa waste (1802.00.00): free; cocoa paste, not defatted (1803.10.00): free; cocoa paste, wholly or partially defatted (1803.20.00): 0.62 cents/kg through December 31, 1994, thereafter 0.82 cents/kg; cocoa butter, fat, or oil (1804.00.00): free; unsweetened cocoa powder (1805.00.00): 0.62 cents/kg through December 31, 1994, thereafter 0.82 cents/kg; cocoa powder containing less than 65% sugar by weight (1806.10.20): free; cocoa powder containing more than 65% sugar by weight (1806.10.30): 10%; chocolate containing not more than 32% butterfat by weight and not more than 60% sugar by weight in blocks or slabs weighing 4.5 kg or more (1806.20.20): free; other chocolate (1806.20.40): 5%; confectioners' coatings containing by weight not less than 6.8% non-fat cocoa bean solids and not less than 15% vegetable fats other than cocoa butter (1806.20.60): 2.5%; chocolate products subject to quotas in 9904.10.66, 9904.10.75, 9904.10.81, 9904.50.20, and 9904.60.60 (1806.20.80): 10%; filled chocolate confectionery in blocks, slabs, or bars (1806.31.00): 7%; unfilled chocolate containing not more than 32% butterfat by weight and not more than 60% sugar by weight (1806.32.20): 5%; other chocolate products (1806.90.00): 7%.

Entry and Documentation

The entry of merchandise is a two-part process consisting of 1) filing the documents necessary to determine whether merchandise may be released from Customs custody and 2) filing the documents that contain information for duty assessment and statistical purposes. In certain instances, such as the entry of merchandise subject to quotas, all documents must be filed and accepted by Customs prior to the release of the goods. Unless you have been granted an extension, you must file entry documents at a location specified by the district or area director within five working days of your shipment's date of arrival at a U.S. port of entry. These include a number of standard documents required by Customs for any entry, and:

- FDA Importers Entry Notice **Form FD701**

After you present the entry, Customs may examine your shipment, or may waive examination. The shipment is then released provided no legal or regulatory violations have been noted. You must then file entry summary documentation and deposit estimated duties at a designated customhouse within 10 working days of your shipment's release. For a detailed description of entry procedures, standard documentation, and informal entry, see "Entry Process" on page 182.

Prohibitions and Restrictions

Standards of identity have been promulgated under the FDCA for approximately 40 cocoa products. If your cocoa product is labeled as one of the standardized products listed in the regulations, it must conform to the standard for that product (21 CFR 163). There are some frequent problems with cocoa shipments that you would be wise to guard against.

Excess shell is a frequent cause for port of entry detention of various standardized cocoa products. The presence of the following types of contamination often form the basis for detention of cocoa bean imports: 1) mold, 2) worms, 3) live or dead insects, their excreta, or webbing, 4) animal excreta. Precautions taken prior to shipping cocoa beans can eliminate many of these problems. Remove any moldy and insect-infested beans before and during shipping, and store the good beans in such a way as to prevent contamination. Such actions will materially lessen the chance of having a shipment detained at the U.S. port of entry.

Quotas

Entry of specific products can be difficult because many product categories affected by quota restrictions overlap, especially if the product contains sugar or milk—both of which are major components of prepared cocoa products. Even if cocoa itself is not the target of a quota, products containing cocoa, whether listed within Chapter 18 or elsewhere in the HTSUS, may be restricted because of other policy driven limitations. It is important to consult with the Quota Branch of the U.S. Customs Service (see addresses at end of this chapter) to determine whether quota restrictions apply to your specific product.

Quotas on chocolate and other food preparations containing cocoa include:

1806.20 Other preparations in blocks or slabs weighing more than 2 kg or in liquid, paste, powder, granular, or other bulk form in containers or immediate packings, of a content exceeding 2 kg: Preparations consisting wholly of ground cocoa beans, with or without added cocoa fat, flavoring, or emulsifying agents, and containing not more than 32% by weight of butterfat or other milk solids and not more than 60% by weight of sugar: In blocks or slabs weighing 4.5 kg or more each, containing butterfat or other milk solids: 6,408,000 kg, not containing butterfat or other milk solids: 6,408,000 kg.

9904.10 Whenever, in any 12-month period beginning January 1 in any year, the respective aggregate quantity specified below for one of the numbered classes of articles has been entered, no article in such class may be entered during the remainder of such period:

9904.10.63 Chocolate provided for in subheading 1806.20.40, 1806.32.20, or 1806.90 containing over 5.5% by weight of butterfat (except articles for consumption at retail as candy or confection): Ireland: 4,286,491 kg; United Kingdom: 3,379,297 kg; Netherlands: 45,359 kg; Australia: 2,000,000 kg; New Zealand: 1 kg; Other: 0 kg.

9904.10.66 Chocolate, provided for in subheadings 1806.20.40, 1806.32.20, and 1806.90, and low fat chocolate crumb, provided for in subheadings 1806.20.80 and 1806.90, containing 5.5% or less by weight of butterfat (except articles for consumption at retail as candy or confection): United Kingdom: 421,845 kg; Ireland: 1,700,988 kg; New Zealand: 1 kg; Other: 0 kg.

9904.10.75 Dried milk, whey, and buttermilk (described in subheading 0402.10, 0402.21.20, 0402.21.40, 0403.90.40, or 0404.10.40) that contains not over 5.5% by weight of butterfat and that is mixed with other ingredients, including but not limited to sugar, if such mixtures contain over 16% milk solids by weight, are capable of being further processed or mixed with similar or other ingredients, and are not prepared for marketing to retail consumers in the identical form and package in which imported; all the foregoing mixtures provided for in subheadings 0402.10, 0404.10.40, 0404.10.09, 0404.90.65, 1517.90.40, 1704.90.40, 1704.90.60, 1806.20.80, 1806.32.40, 1806.90, 1901.20, 1901.90.81, 1901.90.89, and 2106.90.05, except articles within the scope of other import restrictions provided for in this subchapter: none.

9904.10.81 Articles containing over 5.5% by weight of butterfat, the butterfat of which is commercially extractable, or that are capable of being used for any edible purpose (except (a) articles provided for in headings 0401, 0402, 0405, or 0406 or subheadings 1901.10, 1901.90.31, or 1901.90.39 other than mixtures of nonfat dry milk and anhydrous butterfat containing not over 45% by weight classifiable for tariff purposes under subheading 1901.90.31 or 1901.90.39; (b) dried mixtures containing less than 31% by weight of butterfat and consisting of not less than 17.5% by weight each of sodium caseinate, butterfat, whey solids containing over 5.5% by weight of butterfat, and dried whole milk, but not containing dried milk, dried whey, or dried buttermilk any of which contains 5.5% or less by weight of butterfat; and (c) articles that are not suitable for use as ingredients in the commercial production of edible articles):

Over 5.5% but not over 45% by weight of butterfat, including mixtures of nonfat dry milk and anhydrous butterfat classifiable for tariff purposes under subheading 1901.90.31 or 1901.90.39 and other articles classifiable for tariff purposes under subheading 0404.10.07, 0404.10.09, 0404.90.45, 0404.90.65, 1517.90.40, 1704.90.40, 1704.90.60, 1806.20.80, 1806.32.40, 1806.90, 1901.20, 1901.90.41, 1901.90.49, 1901.90.81, 1901.90.89, 2105.00, 2106.90.41, 2106.90.49, 2106.90.51, or 2106.90.59: Australia: 1,016,046 kg; Belgium and Denmark (aggregate): 154,221 kg; Other: 0 kg.

9904.50.20 Blended syrups provided for in subheading 1702.20.20, 1702.30.20, 1702.40, 1702.60, 1702.90.50, 1806.20.80, 1806.90, 2101.10.40, 2101.20.40, 2106.90.51, or 2106.90.59, containing sugars derived from sugar cane or sugar beets, capable of being further processed or mixed with similar or other ingredients and not prepared for marketing to retail consumers in the identical form and package in which imported: 0 metric tons.

9904.50.40 Articles containing over 65% by dry weight of sugars derived from sugar cane or sugar beets, whether or not mixed with other ingredients, capable of being further processed or mixed with similar or other ingredients, and not prepared for marketing to retail consumers in the identical form and package in which imported; all the foregoing articles provided for in subheading 1701.91.40, 1702.90.50, 1704.90.60, 1806.10.30, 1806.20.70, 2101.10.40, 2101.20.40, 2103.90.60, 2106.90.51, or 2106.90.59, except articles within the scope of other import restrictions provided for in subchapter IV of this chapter: 0 metric tons.

9904.60 Whenever in any 12-month period beginning October 1 in any year, the respective aggregate quantity specified below for one of the numbered classes of articles has been entered, no article in such class may be entered during the remainder of the such period:

Articles containing over 10% by dry weight of sugars derived from sugar cane or sugar beets, whether or not mixed with other ingredients, except (a) articles not principally of crystalline structure or not in dry amorphous form that are prepared for marketing to the retail consumer in the identical form and package in which imported, or (b) articles within the scope of headings 9904.50.20, 9904.50.40, or other import restrictions provided for in this subchapter:

9904.60.20 Provided for in subheadings 1806.10.20 or 1806.10.30: 2,313 metric tons.

9904.60.60 Provided for in subheading 1704.90.60, 1806.20.70, 1806.20.80, 1806.90, 1901.90.81, 1901.90.89, 2101.10.40, 2101.20.40, 2103.90.60, 2106.90.51, or 2106.90.59, except cake decorations and similar products to be used in the same condition as imported without any further processing other than the direct application to individual pastries or confections; finely ground or masticated coconut meat or juice thereof mixed with those sugars; and sauces and preparations thereof: 64,773 metric tons.

For a general discussion of quotas, refer to "Import Quotas" on page 230.

Marking and Labeling Requirements

For basic FDA marking and labeling requirements, refer to the "Foods" appendix on page 808. For a general discussion of U.S. Customs marking and labeling requirements, see "Marking: Country of Origin" on page 215 and "Special Marking Requirements" on page 217.

Shipping Considerations

You will need to ensure that your goods are packaged and shipped with care so that they arrive in good condition and pass smoothly through Customs. You are responsible for ensuring that the shipment is in compliance with all applicable government regulations for packaging and shipping. In most instances, you should not leave these arrangements solely to the discretion of your supplier. Careful preparation of the cargo and selection of the mode of transport can be essential to a cost-effective, timely delivery of undamaged goods. We strongly advise you to consult your shipping representative, insurance agent, or freight broker for advice on packing and shipping. Refer also to the major tab section "Packing/Shipping/Insurance" for a general discussion of packing and shipping.

As with any edible product, careful packing is necessary to prevent contamination and spoilage en route. Protection from insect and animal contamination is especially important for cocoa and cocoa products. Heat and moisture control are also important. Because cocoa contains oils that can become rancid and is subject to the growth of mold if kept in a hot, moist environment, packing and the avoidance of delays in transit are important to ensuring the delivery of a salable product.

Publications Available

The following publication explains the FDA requirements for importing cocoa and cocoa products. It is published by the FDA and is available on request from FDA headquarters (see addresses at end of this chapter).

Requirements of Laws and Regulations Enforced by the U.S. Food and Drug Administration

The following publication gives brief, general guidelines on USDA regulated products. Although designed primarily for tourists, it contains a list of approved products that you may find helpful. It is published by USDA APHIS (see addresses at end of this chapter).

Travelers Tips On Bringing Food, Plant, and Animal Products into the United States

The *Harmonized Tariff Schedule of the United States* (HTSUS) is available from:

Government Printing Office (GPO)
Superintendent of Documents
Washington, DC 20402
(202) 512-1800 (Order line)
(202) 512-0000 (General)

The USGPO also has copies of specific laws available for purchase. The USGPO accepts credit card orders over the phone, as well as mail orders paid by credit card, a check drawn on a U.S. bank, or an international money order.

Relevant Government Agencies

Address your questions regarding FDA requirements for the importation of cocoa and cocoa products to:

Food and Drug Administration (FDA)
Center for Food Safety and Applied Nutrition
200 C Street SW
Washington, DC 20204
(202) 205-5241, 205-5042

Food and Drug Administration (FDA)
Division of Enforcement, Imports Branch
200 C Street SW
Washington, DC 20204
(202) 205-4726

Address your questions regarding USDA requirements for the importation of cocoa and cocoa products to:

U.S. Department of Agriculture (USDA)
Animal and Plant Health Inspection Service (APHIS)
Plant Protection and Quarantine (PPQ)
Federal Building, Rm. 631
6505 Belcrest Road
Hyattsville, MD 20782
(301) 436-8645

Address questions regarding allowable chemical residues in cocoa and cocoa products to:

Environmental Protection Agency (EPA)
Office of Pesticide Programs
401 M Street SW (7501-C)
Washington, DC 20460
(703) 305-7090 (General)
(703) 305-7102 (Import/export requirements)

Address your questions regarding quotas to:

U.S. Customs Service
Quota Branch
1301 Constitution Avenue NW, Rm. 2379-ICC
Washington, DC 20229
(202) 927-5850

Address your questions regarding importation of cocoa and cocoa products to the district or port director of Customs for you area. For addresses refer to"U.S. Customs District Offices" on page 62 or contact:

U.S. Customs Service
1301 Constitution Ave. NW
Washington, DC 20229
(202) 927-6724 (Information)
(202) 927-1000 (General)

Laws and Regulations

The following laws and regulations may be relevant to the importation of cocoa and cocoa products. The laws are contained in the U.S. Code (USC) and the regulations are published in the Code of Federal Regulations (CFR), both of which may be available at larger public and law libraries. Copies of specific laws are also available from the United States Government Printing Office (address above).

7 USC 601 et seq.
Agricultural Adjustment Act (AAA)
This Act authorizes the Secretary of Agriculture to establish and maintain orderly market conditions for agricultural products and to impose quotas or higher duty rates on imported agricultural products whenever investigation reveals that orderly market conditions require such action.

19 CFR Part 132
Regulations for Enforcement of AAA Quotas
These regulations provide for Customs enforcement of AAA quotas and higher duty rates imposed on imported agricultural products.

21 USC 301 et seq.
Food, Drug, and Cosmetic Act
This Act prohibits deceptive practices and regulates the manufacture, sale and importation or exportation of food, drugs, cosmetics, and related products. See 21 USC 331, 381, 382.

19 CFR 12.1 et seq.; 21 CFR 1.83 et seq.
Regulations on Food, Drugs, and Cosmetics
These regulations of the Secretary of Health and Human Services and the Secretary of the Treasury govern the standards, labeling, marking, and importing of products used with food, drugs, and cosmetics.

7 USC 135 et seq.
Federal Insecticide, Fungicide, and Rodenticide Act (FIFRA)
This Act prohibits the importation of pesticides or devices that are adulterated, misbranded, or otherwise violative of the Act, provides for registration of pesticides and devices, and establishes standards for labeling and classifying pesticides.

19 CFR 12; 40 CFR 162
Regulations on Pesticides
These regulations set forth the procedures and guidelines for importing products exposed to pesticides.

Principal Exporting Countries

The following listing includes samples of the main supplier nations of the products of this chapter. It is organized by HTSUS major heading. (Refer to "Customs Classification" above for the product codes.) Countries are listed in rank order of the value of products imported to the U.S. Statistics represent customs value entries for 1993 from the Bureau of Census, U.S. Department of Commerce.

1801—Cote d'Ivoire, Indonesia, Ghana, Brazil, Dominican Rep., Nigeria, Ecuador, Malaysia, Papua New Guinea, Mexico

1802—Brazil, Canada

1803—Brazil, Cote d'Ivoire, Ecuador, Canada, United Kingdom, Malaysia, Indonesia, France, Ghana, Cameroon

1804—Brazil, China, Malaysia, Indonesia, Ecuador, Cote d'Ivoire, Mexico, Singapore, Peru, Philippines

1805—Netherlands, Singapore, Brazil, Germany, Spain, Canada, France, China, Belgium, Costa Rica

1806—Canada, Belgium, Germany, United Kingdom, Switzerland, Italy, Mexico, France, Brazil, Ireland

Chapter 19: Baked Goods*

Full title: Preparations of Cereals, Flour, Starch, or Milk; Bakers' Wares

This chapter relates to the importation of processed foods consisting primarily of cereals essentially as finished products, which are classified under Chapter 19 of the Harmonized Tariff Schedule of the United States (HTSUS). Specifically, it includes preparations of flour, such as dough, mixes, and finished baked goods—bread, pasta, cakes, pastries, puddings, prepared pizzas, breakfast foods, and corn chips—as well as tapioca and related products, some products containing milk—such as malted milk and some infant formulas—some products containing cocoa—other than confections—and some products with meat fillings, such as ravioli. This section is supplemental to the "Foods" appendix on page 808. If you are interested in importing cereal preparations, bakers' wares, or related products, you should read that section in conjunction with this one.

If you are interested in importing intermediate, partially processed cereal products—such as flour, worked grains, starches, and gluten—you should refer to Commodity Index Chapter 11. Those interested in importing fabricated cereal-based products intended for use as animal feed should refer to Chapter 23. For importation of any cereal-based medicated products for which the preparation is intended either primarily as a vehicle to deliver the medication or to have some inherent medicinal property, refer to Chapter 30. Those interested in importing prepared foods with a meat content of more than 20% by weight should refer to Chapter 16, while those interested in importing prepared foods with a cocoa content greater than 8% should refer to Chapter 18. Chapter 19 uses the same definitions—such as for "flour" and "meal"—as Chapter 11, but pertains to products that have been processed to an extent beyond that provided for in Chapter 11.

Key Factors

The key factors in the importation of cereal preparations and related products are:

- Compliance with U.S. Food and Drug Administration (FDA) purity, identity, manufacturing, and other standards
- Compliance with FDA entry notification procedures
- Compliance with Environmental Protection Agency (EPA) pesticide residue requirements

*IMPORTANT: Read the Commodity Index Introduction. It is the essential framework for understanding this section.

Although most importers use the services of a licensed customs broker in making their entries, and we recommend this practice, you should be aware of the regulatory, entry, and documentation issues involved in importing your product. You, as importer, are ultimately responsible for the fulfillment of any legal requirements applicable to your shipment.

General Considerations

The importation of cereal preparations is regulated primarily by the FDA, which administers the provisions of the Food, Drug, and Cosmetic Act (FDCA). The EPA also exercises jurisdiction over pesticide residues in foodstuffs through the Federal Insecticide, Fungicide, and Rodenticide Act (FIFRA), which establishes allowable levels for the presence of such residues. Not only must any chemical residues found on foodstuffs fall within the designated levels, but residues must also be from approved chemicals—the presence of chemicals not approved for use on U.S. food crops is grounds for refusing entry regardless of the status of the chemical in its country of origin.

Cereal preparations imported into the U.S. must comply with all requirements for those produced domestically. These include standards of nomenclature, levels of nutritional elements, and allowable additives as prescribed in detail in 21 CFR, particularly Parts 107 (Infant Formula), 136 (Bakery Products), and 139 (Macaroni and Noodle Products). Imported products regulated by the FDA are subject to port of entry inspection, and all such importations must file **Form FD701,** which may be obtained from your local FDA Import Operations office, from FDA headquarters (see addresses at end of this chapter), or through your customs broker. For an annotated diagram of required FDA import procedures, refer to the "Foods" appendix on page 808.

Detention of Shipment. If your shipment is found to be noncomplying, it may be detained at the port of entry. The FDA may permit you to bring such a shipment into compliance before making a final decision regarding admittance. However, any sorting, reprocessing, or relabeling must be supervised by FDA personnel and is done at the importer's expense. Such conditional release to allow the importer to bring a shipment into compliance is a privilege, not a right. The FDA may consider subsequent noncomplying shipments of the same type of product to constitute abuse of the privilege and require the importer to destroy or reexport the products. To ascertain what your legal responsibilities are, you should contact these agencies regarding the specific items to be imported.

Customs Classifications

For customs purposes, cereal preparations are classified under Chapter 19 of the HTSUS. This chapter is broken into major headings, which are further divided into subheadings, and often sub-subheadings, each of which has its own HTSUS classification number. For example, the HTSUS number for pasta packaged with sauce preparations is 1902.11.40, indicating that it is a sub-subcategory of uncooked pasta containing eggs (1902.11.00), which is a subcategory of the major heading pasta whether or not cooked or stuffed or otherwise prepared (1902.00.00). There are five major headings within Chapter 19.

1901—Malt extract; food preparations of flour, meal, starch, or malt extract, not containing cocoa powder in a proportion by weight of less than 50%, not elsewhere specified or included; food preparations of goods of headings 0401 to 0404, not containing cocoa powder in a proportion by weight of less than 10%, not elsewhere specified or included

1902—Pasta, whether or not cooked or stuffed or otherwise prepared, such as spaghetti, macaroni, noodles, lasagna, gnocchi, ravioli, canneloni; couscous, whether or not prepared

1903—Tapioca and substitutes therefor prepared from starch, in the form of flakes, grains, pearls, siftings, or in similar forms

1904—Prepared foods obtained by the swelling or roasting of cereals or cereal products; cereals other than corn in grain form, precooked or otherwise prepared

1905—Bread, pastry, cakes, biscuits, and other bakers' wares, whether or not containing cocoa; communion wafers, empty capsules of a kind suitable for pharmaceutical use, sealing wafers, rice paper, and similar products

For more details regarding classification of the specific product you are interested in importing, consult a customs broker, the appropriate commodity specialist at your nearest customs port, or see HTSUS. HTSUS is available for purchase from the U.S. Government Printing Office (see addresses at end of this chapter), and may be found in larger public libraries. Refer to "Classification—Liquidation" on page 207 for a general discussion of customs classification.

Sample Import Duties

Import duties will vary depending on the HTSUS classification of your product. Therefore, to determine the correct amount of duties, your product must be properly classified under the HTSUS. The following sample duties are taken from the duty listings for HTSUS Chapter 19 products.

Preparations for infant use, put up for retail sale, containing over 10 percent milk solids by weight (1901.10.10): 17.5%; mixes and doughs for the preparation of bakers' wares of heading 1905 containing over 25% butterfat by weight, not put up for retail sale (1901.20.10): 10%; malt extract (1901.90.10): 5 cents/liter; dairy preparations containing over 10% milk solids by weight (1901.90.81): 10%; uncooked pasta, not stuffed or otherwise prepared, containing eggs (1902.1.00): free; stuffed pasta, not otherwise cooked or prepared (1902.20.00): 10%; tapioca and substitutes prepared from starch of arrowroot, cassava, or sago (1903.00.20): free; prepared foods obtained by the swelling or roasting of cereals or cereal products (1904.10.00): 2.5%; rusks, toasted bread, or similar toasted products (1905.40.00): free; corn chips and similar crisp snack foods (1905.90.90): 10%.

Entry and Documentation

The entry of merchandise is a two-part process consisting of 1) filing the documentation necessary to determine whether merchandise may be released from Customs custody and 2) filing the documents that contain the information for duty assessment and statistical purposes. In certain instances all documents must be filed and accepted by Customs prior to release of the goods. Unless you have been granted an extension, you must file entry documents at a location specified by the district or area director within five working days of your shipment's arrival at a U.S. port of entry. These include a number of standard documents required by Customs for entry and:

- FDA Entry Notification **Form FD701**

After you present the entry, Customs may examine your shipment, or may waive examination (food items are almost always inspected). The shipment is then released provided no legal or regulatory violations have been noted. You must then file entry summary documentation and deposit estimated duties at a designated customhouse within 10 working days of your shipment's release. For a detailed description of entry procedures, standard documentation, and informal entry, see "Entry Process" on page 182.

Prohibitions and Restrictions

Prepared cereal products falling within Chapter 19 are generally allowed into the U.S. without the need for prior authorization regardless of country of origin, provided they meet all domestic standards set for such products (some intermediate and raw cereal products are prohibited under USDA restrictions). Note that passage of a shipment by Customs does not relieve the importer from future responsibility should a discrepancy or violation come to light at a later time.

Quotas

Entry of specific products can be difficult because many product categories affected by quota restrictions overlap, especially where sugar, milk, and cocoa products—all of which are major components in many baked goods—are concerned. Although baked goods themselves are not the target of a quota, they contain products that may be restricted because of other policy driven limitations. It is important to consult with the Quota Branch of the U.S. Customs Service (see addresses at end of this chapter) to determine whether quota restrictions apply to your specific product.

Quotas applying to baked goods include:

9904.10 Whenever in any 12-month period beginning January 1 in any year, the respective aggregate quantity specified below for one of the numbered classes of articles has been entered, no article in such class may be entered during the remainder of such period:

9904.10.57 Cheese and substitutes for cheese, containing 0.5% or less by weight of butterfat, provided for in subheading 0406.10, 0406.20.60, 0406.30.60 or 0406.90.80 (except articles within the scope of other import quotas provided for in this subchapter), and margarine cheese, provided for in subheading for in subheading 1901.31 or 1901.90.39: European Economic Community, 4,000,000 kg; Poland, 174,907 kg; Australia, 250,000 kg; New Zealand, 1,000,000 kg; Sweden, 250,000 kg; Israel, 50,000 kg; and Others, 0 kg.

9904.10.60 Malted milk, and articles of milk or cream (except (a) yogurt that is not in dry form, (b) fermented milk other than dried milk with added lactic ferments, (c) mixtures of nonfat dry milk and anhydrous butterfat containing over 5.5% but not over 45% by weight of butterfat, (d) ice cream, (e) cajeta not made from cow's milk, (f) inedible dried milk powders certified to be used for calibrating infrared milk analyzers, and (g) margarine cheese), all the foregoing provided for in subheadings 0402.29, 0402.99.60, 0403.10.00, 0403.90.80, 0404.90.20, 1901.10, 1901.90.31, 1901.90.39, 2105.00.00, and 2202.90.20: 2,721 kg.

9904.10.75 Dried milk, whey, buttermilk (described in subheading 0402.10, 0402.21.20, 0402.21.40, 0403.90.40, or 0404.10.40) which contains not over 5.5% by weight of butterfat and which is mixed with other ingredients, including but nor limited to sugar, if such mixtures contain over 16% milk solids by weight, are capable of being further processed or mixed with similar or other ingredients and are not prepared for marketing to retail consumers in the identical form and package in which imported; all the foregoing mixtures provided for in subheadings 0402.10, 0404.10.40, 0404.10.09, 0404.90.65, 1517.90.40, 1704.90.40, 1704.90.60, 1806.20.80, 1806.32.40, 1806.90, 1901.20, 1901.90.81, 1901.90.89, and 2106.90.05, except articles within the scope of other import restrictions provided for in this subchapter: none.

9904.10.81 Articles containing over 5.5% by weight of butterfat, the butterfat of which is commercially extractable, or which are capable of being used for any edible purpose (except (a) articles provided for in headings 0401, 0402, 0405, or 0406 of subheadings 1901.10, 1901.90.31, or 1901.90.39 other than mixtures of nonfat dry milk and anhydrous butterfat containing not over 45% by weight of butterfat classifiable for tariff purposes under subheading 1901.90.31 or 1901.90.39; (b) dried mixtures containing less than 31% by weight of butterfat and consisting of not less than 17.5% by weight each of sodium caseinate, butterfat, whey solids containing over 5.5% by weight of butterfat, and dried whole milk, but not containing dried milk, dried whey, or dried buttermilk any of which contains 5.5% or less by weight of butterfat; and (c) articles which are not suitable for use as ingredients in the commercial production of edible articles):

Over 5.5% but not over 45% by weight of butterfat, including mixtures of nonfat dry milk and anhydrous butterfat classifiable for tariff purposes under subheading 0404.10.07, 0404.10.09, 0404.90.45, 0404.90.65, 1517.90.40, 1704.90.40, 1704.90.60, 1806.20.80, 1806.32.40, 1806.90, 1901.20, 1901.90.41, 1901.90.49, 1901.90.81, 1901.90.89, 2105.00, 2106.90.41, 2106.90.49, 2106.90.51, or 2106.90.59: Australia, 1,016,046 kg; Belgium and Denmark (aggregate), 154,221 kg; and Other, none.

For a general discussion of quotas, refer to "Import Quotas" on page 230.

Marking and Labeling Requirements

Imports of cereal preparations must declare the country of origin for all imported products. The invoice and any other labeling shall bear the lot identification, the kind of product present, note any treatment given to the product, and comply with all nutritional labeling requirements.

For a general discussion of U.S. Customs marking and labeling requirements, see "Marking: Country of Origin" on page 215 and the following sections.

Shipping Considerations

You will ned to ensure that your goods are packaged and shipped with care so that they arrive in good condition and pass smoothly through Customs. You are responsible for ensuring that the shipment is in compliance with all applicable government regulations for packaging and shipping. In most instances, you should not leave these arrangements solely to the discretion of your supplier. Careful preparation of the cargo and selection of the mode of transport can be essential to a cost-effective, timely delivery of undamaged goods. We strongly advise you to consult your shipping representative, insurance agent, or freight broker for advice on packing and shipping. Refer to the section "Packing/Shipping/Insurance" for a general discussion of packing and shipping.

Cereal preparations may be transported in bulk, although in most instances they are shipped in various types of containers designed to prevent damage during transit, and may be packaged by units for retail sale. General considerations include protection from contamination by dirt, pests, or other foreign matter, as well as the effects of heat and dampness on the goods shipped. Many cereal preparations—especially bakers' wares—have a limited shelf life and care must be taken that they arrive at their destination in a timely fashion as well as in marketable condition.

Publications Available

The following publication explains the FDA requirements for importing cereal preparations. It is published by the FDA and is available on request from FDA headquarters (see addresses at end of this chapter).

Requirements of Laws and Regulations Enforced by the U.S. Food and Drug Administration

The *Harmonized Tariff Schedule of the United States* (HTSUS) is available from:

Government Printing Office (GPO)
Superintendent of Documents
Washington, DC 20402
(202) 512-1800 (Order line)
(202) 512-0000 (General)

The USGPO also has copies of specific laws available for purchase. The USGPO accepts credit card orders over the phone, as well as mail orders paid by credit card, a check drawn on a U.S. bank, or an international money order.

Relevant Government Agencies

Address your inquiries regarding USDA requirements for importation of cereal preparations to:

Food and Drug Administration (FDA)
Center for Food Safety and Applied Nutrition
200 C Street SW
Washington, DC 20204
(202) 205-5241, 205-5042

Food and Drug Administration (FDA)
Division of Enforcement, Imports Branch
200 C Street SW
Washington, DC 20204
(202) 205-4726

Address questions regarding allowable pesticide residues on cereal preparations to:

Environmental Protection Agency (EPA)
Office of Pesticide Programs
401 M Street SW (7501-C)
Washington, DC 20460
(703) 305-7090 (General)
(703) 305-7102 (Import/export requirements)

Address your questions regarding importation of cereal preparations to the district or port director of Customs for you area. For addresses refer to"U.S. Customs District Offices" on page 62 or contact:

U.S. Customs Service
1301 Constitution Ave. NW
Washington, DC 20229
(202) 927-6724 (Information)
(202) 927-1000 (General)

Laws and Regulations

The following laws and regulations may be relevant to the importation of cereal preparations. The laws are contained in the U.S. Code (USC) and the regulations are published in the Code of Federal Regulations (CFR), both of which may be available at larger public and law libraries. Copies of specific laws are also available from the United States Government Printing Office (address above).

21 USC 301 et seq.
Food, Drug, and Cosmetic Act
This Act prohibits deceptive practices and regulates the manufacture, sale and importation or exportation of food, drugs, cosmetics, and related products. See 21 USC 331, 381, 382.

19 CFR 12.1 et seq.; 21 CFR 1.83 et seq.
Regulations on Food, Drugs, and Cosmetics
These regulations of the Secretary of Health and Human Services and the Secretary of the Treasury govern the standards, labeling, marking, and importing of products used with food, drugs, and cosmetics.

21 CFR Parts 107, 136, and 139
Regulations of FDA on Infant Formula (Part 107), Bakery Products (Part 136), Macaroni and Noodle Products (Part 139)
These regulations establish nomenclatural and technical standards and requirements for many of the major products covered in Chapter 19.

7 USC 135 et seq.
Federal Insecticide, Fungicide, and Rodenticide Act (FIFRA)
This Act prohibits the importation of pesticides or devices that are adulterated, misbranded, or otherwise violative of the Act, provides for registration of pesticides and devices, and establishes standards for labeling and classifying pesticides.

19 CFR 12; 21 CFR 180, 193; 40 CFR 162
Regulations on Pesticides
These regulations set forth the procedures and guidelines for importing products exposed to pesticides.

Principal Exporting Countries

The following listing includes samples of the main supplier nations of the products of this chapter. It is organized by HTSUS major heading. (Refer to "Customs Classification" above for the product codes.) Countries are listed in rank order of the value of products imported to the U.S. Statistics represent customs value entries for 1993 from the Bureau of Census, U.S. Department of Commerce.

1901—Canada, United Kingdom, Hong Kong, France, Mexico, Germany, Japan, Taiwan, Brazil, Jamaica

1902—Italy, Canada, South Korea, Japan, Thailand, Taiwan, Turkey, China, Hong Kong, Mexico

1903—Thailand, France, Brazil, China, Taiwan, Malaysia, Philippines, Singapore, Japan, Hong Kong

1904—Canada, Mexico, Colombia, Switzerland, Trinidad and Tobago, Costa Rica, Germany, India, United Kingdom, Belgium

1905—Canada, Denmark, Mexico, United Kingdom, Belgium, Japan, Germany, Italy, France, Netherlands

Chapter 20: Vegetable, Fruit, and Nut Preparations*

Full title: Preparations of Vegetables, Fruit, Nuts, and Other Parts of Plants

This section pertains to the importation of edible preparations of vegetables, fruit, nuts, and other plant products, which are classified under Chapter 20 of the Harmonized Tariff Schedule of the United States (HTSUS). Specifically, it includes pickled and canned vegetables; fruit and nuts prepared and preserved using sugar; jams, jellies, and pastes; fruit and nut preparations, including canned and otherwise preserved; and natural (that is, unfortified) fruit and vegetable juices. You should read this section in conjunction with the "Foods" appendix on page 808.

If you are interested in importing fresh or provisionally preserved but not prepared, fruit, vegetables, or nuts, refer to Commodity Index Chapters 7 and 8. Seeds and live plants are included in Chapter 6. Edible vegetable fats and oils are covered in Chapter 15. Confectionery of fruit and nuts without chocolate is covered in Chapter 17 (with chocolate in Chapter 18). Preparations of flour and baked goods with an incidental component of vegetables, fruit, or nuts are covered in Chapter 19. Miscellaneous food preparations—such as extracts, sauces, condiments, soups, and various other preparations—are included in Chapter 21. Foods in which meat or fish make up a significant portion—greater than 20% by weight—are classified in Chapter 16, no matter what their other contents. Fortified fruit and vegetable juices are treated as beverages in Chapter 22.

Key Factors

The key factors in the importation of prepared vegetables, fruit, and nuts are:

- Compliance with U.S. Food and Drug Administration (FDA) purity, identity, manufacturing, and other standards
- Compliance with FDA entry notifications and procedures

Although most importers utilize the services of a licensed customs broker in making their entries, and we recommend this practice, you should be aware of the regulatory, entry, and documentation issues involved in importing your product. You, as importer, are ultimately responsible for the fulfillment of any legal requirements applicable to your shipment.

*__IMPORTANT__: Read the Commodity Index Introduction. It is the essential framework for understanding this section.

General Considerations

Importation of prepared vegetable, fruit, and nut products falls primarily under the jurisdiction of the FDA, which enforces the requirements of the Federal Food, Drug, and Cosmetic Act (FDCA). FDA regulations regarding importation of foods of any kind are extensive and stringent. Prepared vegetable, fruit, and nut food products imported into the U.S. must comply with all FDCA requirements for those produced domestically.

Imported products regulated by the FDA are subject to FDA port of entry inspection. **Form FD701** is required for all FDA-regulated importations and may be obtained from your local FDA Import Operations office, from FDA headquarters (see addresses at end of this chapter), or from your customs broker. For an annotated diagram of required FDA importing procedures refer to the "Foods" appendix on page 808.

Food products imported into the U.S. must also comply with established tolerances for pesticide and other chemical residues. The U.S. Environmental Protection Agency (EPA) enforces the provisions of the Federal Insecticide, Fungicide, and Rodenticide Act (FIFRA), which establishes regulatory limits on pesticide residues on edible plant products. For more information, contact EPA (see addresses at end of this chapter).

Detention of Shipment. If your shipment is found to be noncomplying, it may be detained at the port of entry. In the case of products subject to FDA jurisdiction, the FDA may allow you to bring such a shipment into compliance before making a final decision regarding admittance. However, any sorting, reprocessing, or relabeling must be supervised by FDA personnel, and is done at the importer's expense. Such conditional release to allow the importer to bring a shipment into compliance is a privilege, not a right. The FDA may consider subsequent noncomplying shipments of the same type of product to constitute abuse of the privilege and require the importer to destroy or reexport the products. To ascertain what your legal responsibilities are, you should contact the agencies involved in advance regarding the specific items to be imported.

Customs Classification

For customs purposes, prepared vegetable, fruit, or nut products are classified within Chapter 20 of the HTSUS. This chapter is divided into major headings, which are further divided into subheadings, and often into sub-subheadings, each of which has its own HTSUS classification number. For example, the HTSUS number for artichokes is 2001.90.25, which is a subcategory of other vegetables (2001.90.20), indicating that it is a subcategory of vegetables other than cucumbers and onions (2001.90.00), which is a subcategory of the major heading vegetables, fruit, and nuts and other edible parts of plants, prepared or preserved by vinegar or acetic acid (2001.00.00). There are nine major headings in HTSUS Chapter 20.

2001—Vegetables, fruit, nuts, and other edible parts of plants, prepared or preserved by vinegar or acetic acid

2002—Tomatoes prepared or preserved otherwise than by vinegar or acetic acid

2003—Mushrooms or truffles, prepared or preserved otherwise than by vinegar or acetic acid

2004—Other vegetables prepared or preserved otherwise than by vinegar or acetic acid, frozen

2005—Other vegetables prepared or preserved otherwise than by vinegar or acetic acid, not frozen.

2006—Fruit, nuts, fruit peel, and other parts of plants, preserved by sugar (drained, glacé, or crystallized)

2007—Jams, fruit jellies, marmalades, fruit or nut puree, and fruit or nut pastes, being cooked preparations, whether or not containing added sugar or other sweetening matter

2008—Fruit, nuts, and other edible parts of plants, otherwise prepared or preserved, whether or not containing added sugar or other sweetening matter or spirit, not elsewhere specified or included

2009—Fruit juices (including grape must) and vegetable juices, not fortified with vitamins or minerals, unfermented and not containing added spirit, whether or not containing added sugar or other sweetening matter

For more details regarding classification of the specific product you are interested in importing, consult a customs broker, the appropriate commodity specialist at your nearest customs port, or see HTSUS. HTSUS is available for purchase from the U.S. Government Printing Office (see addresses at end of this chapter), and may be found in larger public libraries. Refer to "Classification—Liquidation" on page 207 for a general discussion of customs classification.

Sample Import Duties

Import duties will vary depending on the HTSUS classification of your product. Therefore, to determine the correct amount of duties, your product must be properly classified under the HTSUS. The following sample duties are taken from the duty listings for HTSUS Chapter 20 products.

Cucumber pickles (2001.10.00): 12%; capers, other than in immediate containers holding more than 3.4 kg (2001.90.20): 8%; pickled beans (2001.90.30): 9%; whole tomatoes (2002.10.00): 14.7%; tomato paste in containers holding less than 1.4 kg (2002.90.00): 13.6%; canned mushrooms (2003.10.00): 7.1 cents/kg on drained weight + 10%; frozen potatoes (2004.10.809): 10%; frozen mixed vegetables (2004.90.90): 17.5%; frozen peas (2004.90.90): 17.5%; homogenized vegetables (baby food) (2005.10.00): 17.5%; canned beans (005.51.40): 3.3 cents/kg on entire contents of container; canned corn (2005.80.00): 12.5%; canned water chestnuts (2005.90.40): free; canned pimentos (2005.90.50): 9.5%; canned chickpeas (2005.90.87): 1.7 cents/kg on entire weight of container; preserved ginger (2006.00.30): 5.4%; candied citrus peel (2006.00.60): 7.5 cents/kg; orange marmalade (2007.91.40): 5.5%; strawberry jam (2007.99.10): 4.9%; currant or other berry jam (2007.99.15): 3%; guava or mango paste (2007.99.50): 2.8%; fruit jellies other than currant or berry (2007.99.75): 7%; peanut butter (2008.11.10): 6.6 cents/kg; pecans (2008.19.25): 22 cents/kg; almonds (2008.19.40): 40.8 cents/kg; mixed nuts (2008.19.85): 28%; orange pulp (2008.30.35): 17.5%; canned pears (2008.40.00): 18%; maraschino cherries (2008.60.00): 15.4 cents/kg + 10%; canned peaches (2008.70.00): 20%; canned blueberries (2008.99.18): 3.5%; canned plums (2008.99.60): 17.5%; bean curd (2008.99.90): 7%; frozen natural orange juice (2009.11.00): 9.25 cents/liter; grapefruit juice not concentrated and not made from a juice having a degree of concentration of 1.5 or more (2009.20.20): 5.3 cents/liter; lime juice unfit for beverage purposes (2009.30.10): 2.76 cents/liter; tomato juice (2009.50.10): 0.3 cents/liter; grape juice (2009.60.00): 6.6 cents/liter; apple juice (2009.70.00): free; juices of any other single fruit not specially provided for (2009.80.60): 0.8 cents/liter; mixtures of vegetable juices (2009.90.20): 0.3 cents/liter.

Special Provisions. The duties for certain products are increased as follows:

Tomatoes. Tomatoes prepared or preserved (other than paste) by process other than those specified in Chapters 7 or 11 or in heading 2001 or subheading 2002.10.00 are subject to a 100% duty.

Fruit Juices. Fruit juices not specifically provided for, concentrated or not, whether or not sweetened, not mixed, and not containing more than 0.5% of ethyl alcohol by volume (provided for in subheading 2009.80.60) are subject to a 100% duty under 9903.23.30.

Excise Taxes on Alcohol. In addition to any duties levied on them, products of heading 2008 that contain alcohol are subject to federal excise taxes based on the type and content of alcohol. Excise taxes range from $1.07 per gallon on still wines containing not more than 14% alcohol to $3.40 per gallon on champagne and other sparkling wine; $18.00 per standard 31-gallon barrel of beer; and $13.50 per proof gallon of distilled spirits. A proof gallon is one gallon of product at 100 proof (50% alcohol); actual duty rates are calculated based on the proportion of actual alcohol content less than or more than 100 proof.

Entry and Documentation

The entry of merchandise is a two-part process consisting of 1) filing the documents necessary to determine whether merchandise may be released from Customs custody and 2) filing the documents that contain information for duty assessment and statistical purposes. In certain instances all documents must be filed and accepted by Customs prior to the release of the goods. Unless you have been granted an extension, you must file entry documents at a location specified by the district or area director within five working days of your shipment's date of arrival at a U.S. port of entry. These include a number of standard documents required by Customs for any entry, and:

- FDA Importers Entry Notice, **Form FD701**

After you present the entry, Customs may examine your shipment, or may waive examination. The shipment is then released provided no legal or regulatory violations have been noted. You must then file entry summary documentation and deposit estimated duties at a designated customhouse within 10 working days of your shipment's release. For a detailed description of entry procedures, standard documentation, and informal entry, see "Entry Process" on page 182.

Restrictions and Prohibitions

All food products whether produced domestically or imported must comply with a variety of established standards, guidelines, and procedures. These include specific for premarket testing and approval of products, testing and certification on food additives and colors, regulations for interstate transport, and nutritional and other product labeling. For a discussion of these aspects, refer to the "Foods" appendix on page 808.

Low-Acid Canned Foods and Acidified Foods. Low-acid canned foods are heat-processed foods other than alcoholic beverages that have an acidity greater than pH 4.6 and a water activity greater than 0.85 and that are packaged in hermetically sealed containers. "Water activity" is a measure of the water available for microbial growth. Hermetically sealed containers are any packages, regardless of composition, that are capable of maintaining the commercial sterility of their contents after processing. Acidified foods are low-acid foods to which acid(s) or acid food(s) have been added to reduce the pH to 4.6 or below (increase the acidity), and with a water activity greater than 0.85. Pimientos, artichokes, some puddings, and some sauces are examples of acidified foods. If you are unsure whether your food product falls within these categories, contact FDA's Industry Guidance Branch for clarification (see addresses at end of this chapter).

Registration Requirements. The FDA requires all commercial processors of low-acid canned foods and acidified foods intended for sale in the U.S. to register their establishments and file processing information for each product. This applies both to U.S. and foreign firms. If you are purchasing canned foods for import, you should be sure that the company from which you buy is FDA-registered. For more information, or for registration and processing forms, contact FDA's Industry Guidance Branch (see addresses at end of this chapter).

Canned Fruits and Fruit Juices. If you are importing canned fruit and fruit juices, you are responsible for seeing that your product meets all FDA standards of identity, quality, and fill-of-container. You can find these standards detailed in 21 CFR 145 and 146. What follows is a brief overview of the standards for such products; it is not intended to be exhaustive and importers should consult the agencies involved and the governing regulations.

Fill-of-Container Standards for Fruit. The standards of fill for canned peaches, pears, apricots, and cherries require that the fill of the solid food component be the maximum practicable quantity that can be sealed in the container and processed by heat without crushing or breaking the individual fruit. Standards for canned fruit cocktail, grapefruit, and plums specify minimum drained weights for the solid food component, expressed as a percentage of the water capacity of the container. The drained weight requirements are as follows: fruit cocktail 65%; grapefruit and whole plums 50%; plum halves 55%. Plums and applesauce in metal containers, crushed pineapple, and pineapple in juice have an additional 90% fill requirement, based on total container capacity for both the solid and liquid components. A similar 85% fill applies to applesauce in glass containers. Crushed pineapple may be labeled as "heavy pack" or "solid pack," as long as the fruit component has a minimum drained weight of 63% of the net weight.

If you are importing canned fruit for which no standards have been officially set, you must be sure that the containers are well filled with fruit. Only as much packing medium as is needed to fill the interstitial spaces may be added. If your products deviate from this guideline, they may be considered deceptive, and prohibited by FDCA. Deceptive fill is grounds for shipment refusal at the U.S. port of entry.

Canned Vegetables. There are FDA standards of identity, quality, and fill-of-container for many canned vegetables. FDA identity standards require that "the food is processed by heat, in an appropriate manner, before or after being sealed in a container so as to prevent spoilage." The special regulations for low-acid canned foods emphasize the importance of adequate heat-processing for canned vegetables, particularly the nonacid types that are more prone to the growth of bacteria if inadequately processed. If you are importing canned vegetables, you should be sure that your product complies with all applicable standards and guidelines.

Standards of Quality. Quality standards provide for special labeling of any product that is not up to the usual expectations of the consumer but is nevertheless a wholesome food. FDA standards of quality for canned vegetables establish minimum specifications for tenderness, color, freedom from defects, etc. The fact that your food does not measure up to these standards does not necessarily mean that you may not import it. However, if this is the case you must make sure your cans are labeled in bold type "Below Standard in Quality" followed by the statement "Good Food-Not High Grade," or a clear statement explaining in what respect the product fails to meet the standard, such as "excessively broken," or "excessive peel" (21 CFR 130).

Fill-of-Container Standards for Vegetables. Your canned vegetables must meet certain FDA standards of fill. Canned tomatoes and canned corn must be in the container such that solid and liquid together occupy not less than 90% of total container capacity. Minimum drained weight of the actual corn in canned corn must be no less than 61% of the container's water capacity. Minimum drained weight for solid tomatoes in canned tomatoes is 50% of the container's water capacity. Canned mushrooms must meet minimum drained weight requirements, stated in ounces, for various can sizes. Under volumetric fill requirements for canned green and field peas, the peas must completely fill the container before the addition of liquid packing medium.

If you are importing a canned vegetable for which no fill-of-container standard has been promulgated, you should be sure that the container is well filled with the vegetable, with only enough packing medium to fill the interstitial spaces. You are not permitted to add water to canned tomatoes.

Tomato Products. If you are importing tomato products (canned tomatoes, tomato juice, paste, puree, and catsup), you should consult the standards of identity for these items in 21 CFR 155. No artificial colors or preservatives are permitted in tomato products. Tomato juice may not be concentrated. Tomato puree must contain not less than 8%, and tomato paste not less than 24%, of salt free tomato solids.

Canned tomato products are occasionally contaminated with rot, flies, and worms resulting from improper processing. You should be very careful about the conditions under which your product was processed. If your shipment contains contaminated product, it is adulterated under FDCA rules and will be refused entry. The FDA uses the Howard mold-count test to determine whether tomato products have been properly prepared. If your shipment contains mold filaments in excess of amounts stated in the Food Defect Action Levels, it will be refused entry, as will any food products in which the cans have become swollen or otherwise abnormal.

Fruit Jams (Preserves), Jellies, Fruit Butters, and Marmalade. If you are importing fruit jams, jellies, butters, or marmalades, you need to be aware of the following FDA standards of identity for these products. Jams and jellies must be prepared by mixing not less than 45 parts by weight of certain specified fruits (or fruit juice in the case of jelly), and 47 parts by weight of other designated fruits, to each 55 parts by weight of sugar or other optional nutritive carbohydrate sweetening ingredient. Pectin may be added to jams and jellies only in quantities sufficient to compensate for a deficiency, if any, of the particular fruit's natural pectin content. As finished product, both jams (preserves) and jellies must be concentrated to not less than 65% soluble solids. Standards of identity for artificially sweetened jams and jellies require the fruit ingredient to be not less than 55% by weight of the finished food product.

Fruit butters must be smooth, semisolid foods made from not less than five parts by weight of fruit ingredient to each two parts by weight of sweetening ingredient. Only enough pectin may be added to compensate for a deficiency, if any, of the particular fruit's natural pectin content. Your finished fruit butter must be concentrated to not less than 43% soluble solids.

There is no formal standard of identity for citrus marmalade. However, the FDA expects a product labeled "sweet orange marmalade" to be prepared by mixing at least 30 pounds of fruit (peel and juice) to each 70 pounds of sweetening ingredients. Sour or bitter (Seville) orange marmalade, lemon marmalade, and lime marmalade would be prepared by mixing at least 25 pounds of fruit (peel and juice) to each 75 pounds of sweetening ingredient. Peel should not exceed amounts normally associated with the raw fruit. The product should be concentrated to not less than 65% soluble solids. If your imported citrus marmalade product follows these guidelines, FDA would not regard it as misbranded.

Mushrooms. If you are offering mushrooms for import, you must be sure that they are edible species. Inedible species may not be imported. However, the most common bar to entry is insect infestation, usually by flies or maggots. You can prevent mushroom contamination with insects, rodent and bird filth, or other objectionable material by taking protective measures during processing. Don't buy mushrooms from heavily insect-infested areas to import into the U.S. They will be refused entry.

Nuts and Nut Products. Nuts and nut meats must be prepared and stored under sanitary conditions to prevent contamination by insects, rodents, or other animals. If you wish to import nuts and nut products into the U.S., you should take care to prevent the following adulterating conditions: 1) Insect infestation. Nuts are insect-infected if they contain live or dead insects, whether larvae, pupae, or adults, or if they show definite evidence of insect feeding or cutting, or if insect excreta pellets are present. 2) Dirt. Nut meats may become dirty because of lack of cleanliness in cracking, sorting, and packaging. 3) Mold. Nut meats are occasionally moldy in the shell and bear fruiting mold or mold hyphae. 4) Rancidity. Rancid nuts are frequently soft. They have a yellow, dark, or oily appearance and an abnormal flavor characterized by rancidity. 5) Extraneous material. Stems, shells, stones, excreta or other foreign material should not be present.

FDA defect action levels have been established for tree nuts. You may not deliberately mix good and bad lots to result in defects below these levels, even though the percentage of defects in the mixed lots is thus rendered lower than the defect action level.

Aflatoxins. Aflatoxins are a group of chemically related substances produced naturally by the growth of certain common molds. Aflatoxins, especially aflatoxin B1, are highly toxic, primarily causing acute liver damage in exposed animals. Alfatoxin B1 also exhibits cancer-producing properties in certain species of experimental animals. Studies of certain population groups reveal that the consumption of aflatoxin-containing foods is associated with liver cancer in humans. Excess aflatoxin levels in nuts and other products is a significant public health problem and is a basis for seizing or refusing imports of products containing it.

Bitter Almonds. Because of their toxicity, bitter almonds may not be marketed in the U.S. for unrestricted use. Shipments of sweet almonds may not contain more than 5% of bitter almonds. Almond paste and pastes made from other kernels should contain less than 25 parts per million of hydrocyanic acid (HCN) naturally occurring in the kernels.

Standards for Nut Products. If you wish to import nut products, you should be aware of the FDA standards for mixed tree nuts, shelled nuts, and peanut butter (21 CFR 164). The standards establish such factors as proportions of various kinds of nuts and label designations for "mixed nuts," fill of container for shelled nuts, and ingredients and labeling for peanut butter.

Olives. Pitted and stuffed olives containing more than an unavoidable minimum of pits or pit fragments are in violation of FDCA provisions. While it may not be possible to completely eliminate this problem, dealers have been put on notice that they must take steps to reduce it to the extent that is reasonably feasible.

Quotas

Tariff-rate Quotas. The following commodities are subject to tariff-rate quotas:

0711.20.15; 2005.70.13 Olives, green and not pitted, in saline solution, in containers each holding more than 8 kg drained weight, certified by the importer to be used for repacking or sale as green olives, for an aggregate quantity entered in any calendar year not to exceed 4,400 metric tons: 3.7 cents/kg on drained weight; exceeding 4,400 metric tons: 7.4 cents/kg on drained weight.

2005.70.21 Olives, green, pitted or stuffed, place packed, stuffed in containers each holding not more than 1 kg, drained weight, in an aggregate quantity not to exceed 2,700 metric tons in any calendar year: 5.4 cents/kg on drained weight; exceeding 2,700 metric tons: 10.8 cents/kg on drained weight.

2005.70.81 Olives, green, otherwise prepared or preserved, in containers holding less than 13 kg, drained weight, in an aggregate quantity not to exceed 550 metric tons in any calendar year: 5.5 cents/kg on drained weight; exceeding 550 metric tons: 11 cents/kg on drained weight

2008.30.52 Mandarins (satsumas) in airtight containers, for an aggregate quantity entered in any calendar year not to exceed 40,000 metric tons: free; exceeding 40,000 metric tons: 0.4 cents/kg.

Absolute Quotas. The following commodities are currently subject to absolute quotas:

2005.70.11 Olives, green and not pitted, in saline solution, in containers each holding less than 13 kg drained weight in an aggregate quantity not to exceed 730 metric tons entered in any calendar year: 5.4 cents/kg on drained weight

22008.11.20, 2008.11.90 Whenever in any 12-month period beginning August 1 in any year, the aggregate quantity specified below of peanuts (ground nuts), shelled or not shelled, blanched or otherwise prepared or preserved (except peanut butter) provided for in subheadings 1202.10, 1202.20, and 2008.11, has been entered, no such products may be entered during the remainder of such period: 775,189 kg; provided that peanuts in the shell shall be charged against this quota on the basis of 75 kg for each 100 kg of peanuts in the shell

For current information, or further details on quotas, contact the district director of Customs nearest you, or U.S. Customs Quota Branch (see addresses at end of this chapter). For a general discussion of quotas see "Import Quotas" on page 230.

Marking and Labeling Requirements

Refer to the "Foods" appendix on page 808 for nutritional labeling requirements. For a general discussion of U.S. Customs marking and labeling requirements, see "Marking: Country of Origin" on page 215 and "Special Marking Requirements" on page 217.

Shipping Considerations

You will need to ensure that your goods are packaged and shipped with care to ensure that they arrive in good condition and pass smoothly through Customs. You are responsible for ensuring that the shipment is in compliance with all applicable government regulations for packaging and shipping. In most instances, you should not leave these arrangements solely to the discretion of your supplier. Careful preparation of the cargo and selection of the mode of transport can be essential to a cost-effective, timely delivery of undamaged goods. We strongly advise you to consult your shipping representative, insurance agent, or freight broker for advice on packing and shipping. Refer also to the major tab section "Packing/Shipping/Insurance" for a general discussion of packing and shipping.

As with all edible products, careful attention to packing and shipping conditions are necessary to prevent contamination and spoilage en route. Although prepared foods of Chapter 20 are generally required to be shelf-stable and not require refrigeration—some products may be dated and require both expeditious and refrigerated transport—they nevertheless must be properly handled to maintain their integrity and salability. Protection from insect or animal contamination is especially important, as contamination from filth is a major cause of the rejection of entry of food products.

Publications Available

The following publication explains the FDA requirements for importing prepared vegetable, fruit, or nut products. It is published by the FDA and is available on request from FDA headquarters (see addresses at end of this chapter).

Requirements of Laws and Regulations Enforced by the U.S. Food and Drug Administration

The following publication gives brief, general guidelines on USDA regulated products. Although designed primarily for tourists, it contains a list of approved products that you may find helpful. It is published by USDA APHIS (see addresses at end of this chapter).

Travelers Tips On Bringing Food, Plant, and Animal Products into the United States

The *Harmonized Tariff Schedule of the United States* (HTSUS) is available from:

Government Printing Office (GPO)
Superintendent of Documents
Washington, DC 20402
(202) 512-1800 (Order line)
(202) 512-0000 (General)

The USGPO also has copies of specific laws available for purchase. The USGPO accepts credit card orders over the phone, as well as mail orders paid by credit card, a check drawn on a U.S. bank, or an international money order.

Relevant Government Agencies

Address general inquiries regarding importation of foods to:

Food and Drug Administration (FDA)
Center for Food Safety and Applied Nutrition
200 C Street SW
Washington, DC 20204
(202) 205-5241, 205-5042

Food and Drug Administration (FDA)
Division of Enforcement, Imports Branch
200 C Street SW
Washington, DC 20204
(202) 205-4726

Address your questions regarding safe pesticide residue tolerances to:

Environmental Protection Agency (EPA)
Office of Pesticide Programs
401 M Street SW (7501-C)
Washington, DC 20460
(703) 305-7090 (General)
(703) 305-7102 (Import/export requirements)

Address your questions regarding quotas to:

U.S. Customs Service
Quota Branch
1301 Constitution Avenue NW, Rm. 2379-ICC
Washington, DC 20229
(202) 927-5850

Address questions regarding the importation of prepared vegetable, fruit, and nut products to the district or port director of Customs for you area. For addresses refer to"U.S. Customs District Offices" on page 62 or contact:

U.S. Customs Service
1301 Constitution Ave. NW
Washington, DC 20229
(202) 927-6724 (Information)
(202) 927-1000 (General)

Laws and Regulations

The following laws and regulations may be relevant to the importation of prepared vegetable, fruit, or nut products. The laws are contained in the U.S. Code (USC) and the regulations are published in the Code of Federal Regulations (CFR), both of which may be available at larger public and law libraries. Copies of specific laws are also available from the United States Government Printing Office (address above).

21 USC 301 et seq.
Food, Drug, and Cosmetic Act
This Act prohibits deceptive practices and regulates the manufacture, sale and importation or exportation of food, drugs, cosmetics, and related products. See 21 USC 331, 381, 382.

19 CFR 12.1 et seq.; 21 CFR 1.83 et seq.
Regulations on Food, Drugs, and Cosmetics
These regulations of the Secretary of Health and Human Services and the Secretary of the Treasury govern the standards, labeling, marking, and importing of products used with food, drugs, and cosmetics.

7 USC 135 et seq.
Federal Insecticide, Fungicide, and Rodenticide Act (FIFRA)
This Act prohibits the importation of pesticides or devices that are adulterated, misbranded, or otherwise violative of the Act, provides for registration of pesticides and devices, and establishes standards for labeling and classifying pesticides.

19 CFR 12; 21 CFR 180, 193; 40 CFR 162
Regulations on Pesticides
These regulations set forth the procedures and guidelines for importing products exposed to pesticides.

Principal Exporting Countries

The following listing includes samples of the main supplier nations of the products of this chapter. It is organized by HTSUS major heading. (Refer to "Customs Classification" above for the product codes.) Countries are listed in rank order of the value of products imported to the U.S. Statistics represent customs value entries for 1993 from the Bureau of Census, U.S. Department of Commerce.

2001—Mexico, Spain, Greece, Thailand, Israel, Canada, Japan, Turkey, Germany, Morocco

2002—Mexico, Chile, Italy, Israel, Canada, Turkey, Hungary, Spain, Portugal, Brazil

2003—Indonesia, China, Hong Kong, Mexico, Chile, Taiwan, Thailand, India, France, Netherlands

2004—Canada, Mexico, Dominican Rep., Guatemala, Japan, France, Israel, Honduras, Thailand, Netherlands

2005—Spain, Thailand, China, Mexico, Greece, Japan, Taiwan, Dominican Rep., Morocco, Canada

2006—Thailand, Australia, Costa Rica, Israel, Philippines, Taiwan, France, China, Canada, Dominican Rep.

2007—France, Denmark, Canada, United Kingdom, Croatia, Switzerland, Philippines, Costa Rica, Brazil, Germany

2008—Thailand, Philippines, Canada, Mexico, China, Spain, Japan, Israel, Indonesia, Greece

2009—Brazil, Argentina, Germany, Philippines, Chile, Thailand, Mexico, Austria, Sweden, South Africa

Chapter 21: Miscellaneous Edible Preparations*

This section pertains to the importation of miscellaneous edible preparations, which are classified within Chapter 21 of the Harmonized Tariff Schedule of the United States (HTSUS). Specifically, it includes extracts and essences of tea or coffee; yeast and other similar baking products; sauces and condiments; soups; ice cream; and miscellaneous protein and dairy substitutes, juices, and related products. This section is supplemental to the "Foods" appendix on page 808. If you are interested in importing products of Chapter 21, you should read that section in conjunction with this one.

If you are interested in importing prepared products of vegetables, fruit, or nuts for which identity standards exist or that are recognizable as identifiable products, refer to Commodity Index Chapter 20. Prepared products of meat, fish, and other aquatic products containing more than 20% of such ingredients are covered in Chapter 16, with the exception of some sauces, condiments, and soups covered in subheadings 2103 and 2104. Coffee and tea, including flavored teas and coffee substitutes, and spices, are covered in Chapter 9 (although essences and extracts are covered in Chapter 21). With the exception of ice cream and some condiments that contain or are based on milk products, dairy products are covered in Chapter 4. Many Chapter 21 products contain oils and fats, however these products are primarily covered as such in Chapter 15, while sugars are covered in Chapter 17 and preparations of flour and baked goods in Chapter 19. Ethyl alcohol may be a component of products in Chapter 21, but alcoholic beverages and beverage components are covered in Chapter 22, as are other products designed specifically as beverages. Yeasts for medicinal use or as part of a medicament are classified within Chapter 30. Prepared enzyme products are covered by Chapter 35.

Key Factors

The key factors in the importation of miscellaneous edible preparations are:

- Compliance with U.S. Food and Drug Administration (FDA) purity, identity, manufacturing, and other standards
- Compliance with FDA entry notifications and procedures

*IMPORTANT: Read the Commodity Index Introduction. It is the essential framework for understanding this section.

Although most importers utilize the services of a licensed customs broker in making their entries, and we recommend this practice, you should be aware of the regulatory, entry, and documentation issues involved in importing your product. You, as importer, are ultimately responsible for the fulfillment of any legal requirements applicable to your shipment.

General Considerations

Importation of miscellaneous edible products falls primarily under the jurisdiction of the FDA, which enforces requirements of the Federal Food, Drug, and Cosmetic Act (FDCA). FDA regulations regarding importation of foods of any kind are extensive and stringent. All Chapter 21 food products imported into the U.S. must comply with all FDCA requirements for those produced domestically. Imported products regulated by the FDA are subject to FDA port of entry inspection. **Form FD701** is required for all FDA-regulated importations and may be obtained from your local FDA Import Operations office, from FDA headquarters (see addresses at end of this chapter), or from your customs broker. For an annotated diagram of required FDA import procedures refer to the "Foods" appendix on page 808.

The U.S. Environmental Protection Agency (EPA) enforces the Federal Insecticide, Fungicide, and Rodenticide Act (FIFRA). FIFRA establishes regulatory limits on pesticide residues on edible plant products. For more information, contact the EPA (see addresses at end of this chapter).

Compliance. If your shipment is found to be noncomplying, it may be detained at the port of entry. In the case of products subject to FDA jurisdiction, the FDA may allow you to bring such a shipment into compliance before making a final decision regarding admittance. However, any sorting, reprocessing, or relabeling must be supervised by FDA personnel, and is done at the importer's expense. Such conditional release to allow the importer to bring a shipment into compliance is a privilege, not a right. The FDA may consider subsequent noncomplying shipments of the same type of product to constitute an abuse of the privilege and require you to destroy or reexport the products. To ascertain what your legal responsibilities are, you should contact the agencies involved in advance regarding the specific items to be imported.

Customs Classification

For customs purpose, miscellaneous edible preparations are classified within Chapter 21 of the HTSUS. This chapter is divided into major headings, which are further divided into subheadings, and often into sub-subheadings, each of which has its own HTSUS classification number. For example, the HTSUS number for mayonnaise is 2103.90.60, indicating that it is a subcategory of other preparations (2103.90.00), which is a subcategory of the major heading sauces and preparations; mixed condiments and seasonings; mustard flour, meal, and prepared mustard (2103.00.00). There are six major headings in HTSUS Chapter 21.

2101—Extracts, essences, and concentrates of coffee, tea, or maté and preparations with a base of these products or with a basis of coffee, tea, or maté; roasted chicory and other roasted coffee substitutes, and extracts, essences, and concentrates thereof

2102—Yeasts (active and inactive); other single-celled microorganisms, dead (but not including vaccines of heading 3002); prepared baking powders

2103—Sauces and preparations therefor; mixed condiments and mixed seasonings; mustard flour and meal and prepared mustard

2104—Soups and broths and preparations therefor; homogenized composite food preparations

2105—Ice cream and other edible ice, whether or not containing cocoa

2106—Food preparations not elsewhere specified or included

For more details regarding classification of the specific product you are interested in importing, consult a customs broker, the appropriate commodity specialist at your nearest customs port, or see HTSUS. HTSUS is available for purchase from the U.S. Government Printing Office (see addresses at end of this chapter), and may be found in larger public libraries. Refer to "Classification—Liquidation" on page 207 for a general discussion of customs classification.

Sample Import Duties

Import duties will vary depending on the HTSUS classification of your product. Therefore, to determine the correct amount of duties, your product must be properly classified under the HTSUS. The following sample duties are taken from the duty listings for HTSUS Chapter 21 products.

Instant coffee, not flavored (2101.10.21): free; other preparations with a base of coffee (2101.10.40): 10%; roasted chicory and other roasted coffee substitutes and extracts, essences, and concentrates thereof (2101.30.00): 3.3 cents/kg; active yeast (2102.10.00): 10%; dried brewers' yeast (2102.20.40): free; prepared baking powder (2102.30.00): free; soy sauce (2103.10.00): 3%; tomato ketchup (2103.20.20): 7.5%; mustard flour (2103.30.20): free; prepared mustard (2103.30.40): 4.4 cents/kg; fish sauce (2103.90.20): free; mayonnaise and other salad dressings (2103.90.60): 7.5%; soups and broths (2104.10.00): 7%; mixed baby foods (2104.20.00): 10%; ice cream (2105.00.00): 20%; protein concentrates and textured protein (2106.10.00): 10%; products derived from dried milk, buttermilk, or dried whey (2106.90.05): 2.9 cents/kg; other colored sugar syrups (2106.90.10): 1.4606 cents/kg of total sugars; butter substitutes (2106.90.13): 15.4 cents/kg; fortified orange juice (2106.90.16): 9.25 cents/liter; other juice of any single fruit or vegetable (2106.90.17): the rate applicable to the natural juice in heading 2009; gelatin put up for retail sale (2106.90.20): 6%; non-dairy coffee whiteners containing over 10% by weight of milk solids (2106.90.61): 10%; herbal teas and herbal infusions comprising mixed herbs without milk solids 2106.90.69): 10%

Special Provisions. The following provisions of the HTSUS change the duties on certain products as indicated below:

9903.23.20 Soluble or instant coffee (containing no admixture of sugar, cereal, or other additive) (provided for in subheading 2101.10.21): 100%

9904.40.60 Sugars, syrups, and molasses derived from sugar cane or sugar beets, except those entered pursuant to a license issued by the secretary of Agriculture in accordance with U.S. note 4(a) of this subchapter not principally of crystalline structure and not in dry amorphous form, containing soluble non-sugar solids (excluding any foreign substance that may have been added or developed in the product) equal to 6% or less by weight of the total soluble solids, provided for in the heading 1702 or in subheading 2106.90.11 or 2106.90.12: 2.2 cents/kg of total sugars, but not in excess of 50%

Entry and Documentation

The entry of merchandise is a two-part process consisting of 1) filing the documents necessary to determine whether merchandise may be released from Customs custody and 2) filing the documents that contain information for duty assessment and statistical purposes. In certain instances all documents must be filed and accepted by Customs prior to the release of the goods. Unless you have been granted an extension, you must file entry documents at a location specified by the district or area director within five working days of your shipment's date of arrival at a U.S. port of entry. These include a number of standard documents required by Customs for any entry, and:

- FDA Importers Entry Notice, **Form FD701**

After you present the entry, Customs may examine your shipment, or may waive examination. The shipment is then released, provided no legal or regulatory violations have been noted. You must then file entry summary documentation and deposit estimated duties at a designated customhouse within 10 working days of your shipment's release. For a detailed description of entry procedures, standard documentation, and informal entry, see "Entry Process" on page 182.

Prohibitions and Restrictions

Dressings. Standards of identity have been established for mayonnaise, French dressing, and salad dressing (21 CFR 169). If you intend to import these products, you should be sure that they comply in every way with those standards. Dressings for which no standards have been established should be labeled according to general FDCA food labeling requirements. Mineral oil is not a permitted ingredient in any of these foods (21 CFR 169).

Low-Acid Canned Foods and Acidified Foods. Low-acid canned foods are heat-processed foods other than alcoholic beverages that have an acidity greater than pH 4.6 and a water activity greater than 0.85 and that are packaged in hermetically sealed containers. "Water activity" is a measure of the water available for microbial growth. Hermetically sealed containers are any packages, regardless of composition, that are capable of maintaining the commercial sterility of their contents after processing. Acidified foods are low-acid foods to which acid(s) or acid food(s) are added to reduce the pH to 4.6 or below (increase the acidity), and with a water activity greater than 0.85. Some sauces are classified as acidified foods. If you are unsure whether your canned food fits one of these categories, you may contact FDA's Industry Guidance Branch for clarification (see addresses at end of this chapter).

Registration Requirements. The FDA requires all commercial processors of low-acid canned foods and acidified foods intended for sale in the U.S. to register their establishments and file processing information for each product. This applies both to U.S. and foreign firms. If you are purchasing canned foods for import, you should be sure that the company from which you buy is FDA-registered. For more information, or for registration and processing forms, contact FDA's Industry Guidance Branch (see addresses at end of this chapter).

Canned Fruit and/or Vegetable Juices and Other Products. If you are importing canned fruit or vegetable juices or other fruit- or vegetable-based preparations, you are responsible for seeing that your product meets FDA standards of identity, quality, and fill-of-container. You can find these standards detailed in 21 CFR 145, 146.

Fill-of-container. Your canned food preparations must meet certain FDA standards of fill. If you are importing products for which no fill-of-container standard has been promulgated, you should be sure that the container is well filled with the product, with only enough packing medium to fill the interstitial spaces.

Tomato Products. If you are importing tomato products (including ketchup), you should consult the standards of identity for these items in 21 CFR 155. Neither artificial color nor preservatives are permitted in tomato products. Tomato juice is unconcentrated. Tomato products are occasionally contaminated with rot, flies. and worms resulting from improper processing. You should be very careful about the conditions under which your product was processed. If your shipment contains contaminated product, it is adulterated under the FDCA and will be refused entry. The FDA uses the Howard mold-count test to determine whether tomato products have been properly prepared. If your shipment contains mold filaments in excess of amounts stated in the Food Defect Action Levels, it will be refused entry, as will cans of food that have become swollen or otherwise abnormal.

Quotas

Entry of specific products can be difficult because many product categories affected by quota restrictions overlap, especially where dairy products and sugars are concerned. It is important to consult the U.S. Customs Service Quota Branch (see addresses at end of this chapter) to determine whether quota restrictions apply to your specific product.

Quotas affecting miscellaneous edible products of HTSUS Chapter 21 include the following:

Whenever, in any 12-month period beginning January 1 in any year, the respective aggregate quantity specified below for one of the numbered classes of articles has been entered, no article in such class may be entered during the remainder of such period:

9904.10.24 Butter substitutes containing over 45% butterfat by weight of butterfat provided for in subheading 0405.00.80, 2106.90.13, or 2106.90.14 and butteroil however provided for in the schedule: 544,310 kg.

9904.10.60 Malted milk and articles of milk or cream (except (a) yogurt that is not in dry form, (b) fermented milk other than dried fermented milk or other dried milk with added lactic ferments, (c) mixtures of nonfat dry milk and anhydrous butterfat containing over 5.5% but not over 45% by weight of butterfat, (d) ice cream, (e) cajeta not made from cow's milk, (f) inedible dried milk powders certified to be used for calibrating infrared milk analyzers, and (g) margarine cheese), all the foregoing provided for in subheadings 0402.29, 0402.99.60, 0403.10.00, 0403.90.80, 0404.90.20, 1901.10, 1901.90.31, 1901.90.39, 2105.00.00, and 2202.90.20: 2,721 kg.

9904.10.72 Ice cream, as provided for in heading 2105.00: Belgium: 922,315 liters; New Zealand: 589,312 liters; Denmark: 13,059 liters; Netherlands: 104,477 liters; Jamaica: 3,596 liters; Other: 0 liters

9904.10.75 Dried milk, whey, and buttermilk (described in subheading 0402.10, 0402.21.20, 0402.21.40, 0403.90.40, or 0404.10.40) that contains not over 5.5% by weight of butterfat and that is mixed with other ingredients, including but not limited to sugar, if such mixtures contain over 16% milk solids by weight, are capable of being further processed or mixed with similar or other ingredients and are not prepared for marketing to retail consumers in the identical form or package in which imported; all the foregoing mixtures provided for in subheadings 0402.10, 0404.10.40, 0404.10.09, 0404.90.65, 1517.90.40, 1704.90.40, 1704.90.60, 1806.20.80, 1806.32.40, 1806.90, 1901.20, 1901.90.81, 1901.90.89, and 2106.90.05, except articles within the scope of other import restrictions provided for in this subchapter: 0 liters

9904.10.78 Articles over 45% by weight of butterfat: 0 kg.

9904.10.81 Over 5.5% but not over 45% by weight of butterfat, including mixtures of nonfat dry milk and anhydrous butterfat classifiable for tariff purposes under subheading 1901.90.31 or 1901.90.39 and other articles classifiable for tariff purposes under subheading 0404.10.07, 04043.10.09, 0404.90.45, 0404.90.65, 1517.90.40, 1704.90.40, 1704.90.60, 1806.20.80, 1806.32.40, 1806.90, 1901.20, 1901.90.41, 1901.90.49, 1901.90.81, 1901.90.89, 2105.00, 2106.90.41, 2106.90.49, 2106.90.51, or 2106.90.59: Australia: 1,016,046 kg; Belgium and Denmark (aggregate): 154,221 kg; Other: 0 kg.

9904.50.20 Blended syrups provided for in subheading 1702.20.20, 1702.30.20, 1702.40, 1702.60, 1702.90.50, 1806.20.80, 1806.90, 2101.10.40, 2101.20.40, 2106.90.51, or 2106.90.59, containing sugars derived from sugar cane or sugar beets, capable of being further processed or mixed with similar or other ingredients and not prepared for marketing to retail consumers in the identical form and package in which imported: 0 metric tons

9904.50.40 Articles containing over 65% by dry weight of sugars derived from sugar cane or sugar beets, whether or not mixed with other ingredients, capable of being further processed or mixed with similar or other ingredients and not prepared for marketing to retail consumers in the identical form and package in which imported; all the foregoing articles provided for in subheading 1701.91.40, 1702.90.50, 1704.90.60, 1806.10.30, 1806.20.70, 1806.90, 1901.20, 1901.90.81, 1901.90.89, 2101.10.40, 2101.20.40, 2103.90.60, 2106.90.51, or 2106.90.59 except articles within the scope of other import restrictions provided for in subchapter IV of this chapter: 0 metric tons

9904.60.60 Whenever in any 12-month period beginning October 1 in any year, the respective aggregate quantity specified below for one of the numbered classes of articles has been entered during the remainder of such period: Articles containing over 10% by dry weight of sugars derived from sugar cane or sugar beets, whether or not mixed with other ingredients, except (a) articles not principally of crystalline structure or not in dry amorphous form that are prepared for marketing to retail consumers in the identical form and package in which imported, or (b) articles within the scope of headings 9904.50.20, 9904.50.40, or other import restrictions provided for in this subchapter: Provided for in subheading 1704.90.60, 1806.20.70, 1806.20.80, 1806.90, 1901.90.81, 1901.90.89, 2101.10.40, 2101.20.40, 2103.90.60, 2106.90.51, or 2106.90.59, except cake decorations and similar products to be used in the same condition as imported without any further processing other than the direct application to individual pastries or confections; finely ground or masticated coconut meat or juice thereof mixed with those sugars; and sauces and preparations therefore: 64,773 metric tons.

For a general discussion of quotas, refer to "Import Quotas" on page 230.

Marking and Labeling Requirements

Refer to the "Foods" appendix on page 808. For a general discussion of U.S. Customs marking and labeling requirements, see "Marking: Country of Origin" on page 215 and "Special Marking Requirements" on page 217.

Shipping Considerations

You will need to ensure that your goods are packaged and shipped with care to ensure that they arrive in good condition and pass smoothly through Customs. You are responsible for ensuring that the shipment is in compliance with all applicable government regulations for packaging and shipping. In most instances, you should not leave these arrangements solely to the discretion of your supplier. Careful preparation of the cargo and selection of the mode of transport can be essential to a cost-effective, timely delivery of undamaged goods. We strongly advise you to consult your shipping representative, insurance broker, or freight broker for advice on packing and shipping. Refer also to the major tab section "Packing/Shipping/Insurance" for a general discussion of packing and shipping.

As with all edible products, careful attention to packing and shipping conditions are necessary to prevent contamination and spoilage en route. Although many miscellaneous edible preparations are required to be shelf-stable, some products—especially ice cream—may be dated and require expeditious and climate controlled transport. All products must be handled properly to maintain their integrity and salability. Protection from insect or animal contamination is especially important, as contamination from filth is a major cause of the rejection of entry of food products.

Publications Available

The following publication explains the FDA requirements for importing miscellaneous edible preparations. It is published by the FDA and is available on request from FDA headquarters (see addresses at end of this chapter).

Requirements of Laws and Regulations Enforced by the U.S. Food and Drug Administration

The *Harmonized Tariff Schedule of the United States* (HTSUS) is available from:

Government Printing Office (GPO)
Superintendent of Documents
Washington, DC 20402
(202) 512-1800 (Order line)
(202) 512-0000 (General)

The USGPO also has copies of specific laws available for purchase. The USGPO accepts credit card orders over the phone, as well as mail orders paid by credit card, a check drawn on a U.S. bank, or an international money order.

Relevant Government Agencies

Address questions regarding FDA requirements for the importation of miscellaneous edible preparations to:

Food and Drug Administration (FDA)
Center for Food Safety and Applied Nutrition
200 C Street SW
Washington, DC 20204
(202) 205-5241, 205-5042

Food and Drug Administration (FDA)
Division of Enforcement, Imports Branch
200 C Street SW
Washington, DC 20204
(202) 205-4726

Address your questions regarding safe pesticide residue tolerances to:

Environmental Protection Agency (EPA)
Office of Pesticide Programs
401 M Street SW (7501-C)
Washington, DC 20460
(703) 305-7090 (General)
(703) 305-7102 (Import/export requirements)

Address questions regarding quotas to:

U.S. Customs Service
Quota Branch
1301 Constitution Avenue NW, Rm. 2379-ICC
Washington, DC 20229
(202) 927-5850

Address questions regarding importation of miscellaneous edible preparations to the district or port director of Customs for you area. For addresses refer to"U.S. Customs District Offices" on page 62 or contact:

U.S. Customs Service
1301 Constitution Ave. NW
Washington, DC 20229
(202) 927-6724 (Information)
(202) 927-1000 (General)

Laws and Regulations

The following laws may be relevant to the importation of miscellaneous edible preparations. The laws are contained in the U.S. Code (USC) and the regulations are published in the Code of Federal Regulations (CFR), both of which may be available at larger public and law libraries. Copies of specific laws are also available from the United States Government Printing Office (address above).

21 USC 301 et seq.
Food, Drug, and Cosmetic Act
This Act prohibits deceptive practices and regulates the manufacture, sale and importation or exportation of food, drugs, cosmetics, and related products. See 21 USC 331, 381, 382.

19 CFR 12.1 et seq.; 21 CFR 1.83 et seq.
Regulations on Food, Drugs, and Cosmetics
These regulations of the Secretary of Health and Human Services and the Secretary of the Treasury govern the standards, labeling, marking, and importing of products used with food, drugs, and cosmetics.

7 USC 135 et seq.
Federal Insecticide, Fungicide, and Rodenticide Act (FIFRA)
This Act prohibits the importation of pesticides or devices that are adulterated, misbranded, or otherwise violative of the Act, provides for registration of pesticides and devices, and establishes standards for labeling and classifying pesticides.

19 CFR 12; 21 CFR 180, 193; 40 CFR 162
Regulations on Pesticides
These regulations set forth the procedures and guidelines for importing products exposed to pesticides.

Principal Exporting Countries

The following listing includes samples of the main supplier nations of the products of this chapter. It is organized by HTSUS major heading. (Refer to "Customs Classification" above for the product codes.) Countries are listed in rank order of the value of products imported to the U.S. Statistics represent customs value entries for 1993 from the Bureau of Census, U.S. Department of Commerce.

2101—Canada, Brazil, Netherlands, India, Germany, Colombia, Mexico, Ecuador, Australia, Switzerland

2102—Canada, Mexico, United Kingdom, France, Switzerland, Japan, Germany, Belgium, Denmark, Colombia

2103—Hong Kong, Japan, Canada, Thailand, Mexico, Taiwan, China, France, Australia, Philippines

2104—Japan, Argentina, Canada, Mexico, Switzerland, South Korea, Philippines, Germany, Israel, Venezuela

2105—Italy, Spain, South Korea, Taiwan, Japan, France, Canada

2106—Canada, France, Netherlands, Germany, Thailand, Taiwan, Japan, China, Dominican Rep., South Korea

Chapter 22: Beverages, Spirits, and Vinegar*

This section pertains to the importation of beverages, spirits, and vinegar, which are classified within Chapter 22 of the Harmonized Tariff Schedule of the United States (HTSUS). Specifically, it covers all beverages, including bottled water, fruit and vegetable juices prepared and fortified with vitamins, carbonated or uncarbonated soft drinks, milk-based drinks, beer, wine, other fermented beverages, ethyl alcohol suitable for both beverage and industrial uses, liquors, liqueurs, and vinegar for culinary purposes. Generally, it includes all preparations designed to be drunk.

If you are interested in importing food preparations containing beverages or alcohol but not designed to be drunk, refer to Commodity Index Chapter 21. Plain fruit and vegetable juices—that is, natural juices unfortified with vitamins or minerals—and tomato juice with a tomato content of greater than 7% are classified within Chapter 20. Dairy beverages—milk other than prepared milk-based drinks such as chocolate milk—are found in Chapter 4. Other liquid products covered elsewhere include sea water (Chapter 25); distilled, conductivity, or other pure water for industrial uses (Chapter 28); acetic acid of a concentration of greater than 10% by weight for industrial purposes (Chapter 29); medicaments in beverage form or containing beverage products, including alcohol (Chapter 30); and perfumes or toilet articles (Chapter 33). Some commercial samples of beverages that may be imported duty free are covered in Chapter 98, under heading 9811.00.20.

Key Factors

The key factors in the importation of nonalcoholic beverages are:

- Compliance with U.S. Food and Drug Administration (FDA) purity, identity, manufacturing, and other standards
- Compliance with FDA entry notifications and procedures

The key factors in the importation of alcoholic beverages are:

- U.S. Treasury Bureau of Alcohol, Tobacco, and Firearms (BATF) permits for importation of alcoholic beverages
- Compliance with federal, state, and municipal alcohol regulations

*__IMPORTANT__: Read the Commodity Index Introduction. It is the essential framework for understanding this section.

- Federal excise taxes payable at entry; red strip stamps required for distilled spirits
- Standards of fill and standards of identity
- Certificates of various standards required at entry
- Extensive labeling requirements, including BATF pre-approval of all labels

Although most importers utilize the services of a licensed customs broker in making their entries, and we recommend this practice, you should be aware of the regulatory, entry, and documentation issues involved in importing your product. You, as importer, are ultimately responsible for the fulfillment of any legal requirements applicable to your shipment.

General Considerations

Nonalcoholic Beverages. The importation of nonalcoholic beverages falls primarily under the jurisdiction of the FDA, which enforces requirements of the Federal Food, Drug, and Cosmetic Act (FDCA). FDA regulations regarding the importation of products of any kind designed to be ingested are extensive and stringent. Nonalcoholic beverages imported into the U.S. must comply with all FDCA requirements for those produced domestically.

Alcoholic Beverages. The importation of alcoholic beverages is a complex business, requiring lots of specialized knowledge, not only of federal, state, and municipal regulations, but of the products themselves. It is an enterprise not to be entered into without extensive preparation.

The term "alcoholic beverage" includes any beverage in liquid form intended for human consumption that contains not less than one-half of one percent (0.5%) of alcohol by volume. For customs purposes, any beverage that contains more than 0.5% alcohol is an alcoholic beverage. However, for Internal Revenue Service (IRS) or Treasury Department BATF purposes, such products may not be considered alcoholic beverages unless they contain more than 7% alcohol. In addition, there may be separate FDA standards that apply to products, such as cooking wines, hard ciders, wine coolers, or similar products, that contain between 0.5% and 7% alcohol. U.S. Customs does not consider cooking wine a beverage, but a preparation that falls within HTSUS Chapter 20.

Alcoholic beverages are divided into three major categories: distilled spirits, wines, and malt beverages. Importation of alcoholic beverages is strictly regulated by U.S. Customs and by the BATF, primarily under the provisions of the Federal Alcohol Administration Act (FAAA). If you wish to engage in the business of importing distilled spirits, wines, or malt beverages into the U.S., you must first obtain an Importer's Basic Permit from the BATF (see addresses at end of this chapter). You must also comply with the separate licensing requirements of any state in which you expect to sell your product. Individual cities or other local jurisdictions sometimes have specific regulations as well. You will have to fulfill stringent federal and state requirements for recordkeeping and reporting. Distilled spirits imported in bulk containers of a capacity of more than one gallon may be withdrawn from customs custody only by persons to whom it is lawful to sell or otherwise dispose of distilled spirits in bulk. Customs will not release alcoholic beverages destined to any U.S. state for use in violation of that state's laws. Importation of alcoholic beverages by mail is prohibited.

Although most alcoholic beverages fall under BATF jurisdiction, there are certain exceptions. Beverages and other products containing less than 7% alcohol by volume are solely within the jurisdiction of the FDA, under the FDCA. The FDA also regulates the presence of deleterious substances in any alcoholic beverage (including those covered primarily by the BATF), such as excess fusel oil and excess aldehydes in whisky; the presence of methyl alcohol in brandy; glass splinters from defective bottles; and toxic ingredients, such as arsenic, lead, or fluorine, resulting from spraying of fruit used to make wine or of the manufacturing process, as well as residues of toxic clarifying substances. The appendix entitled "Foods" on page 808 is an overview of general FDA import requirements. If you are interested in importing alcoholic beverages that fall under FDA regulation, you should read that section in conjunction with this one. For further information on applicable FDA standards, contact the regional FDA Import Operations office nearest you, or FDA headquarters (see addresses at end of this chapter).

FDA Requirements. Imported products regulated by the FDA are subject to FDA port of entry inspection. **Form FD701** is required for all FDA-regulated importations. **Form FD701** may be obtained from your local FDA Import Operations office, from FDA headquarters (see addresses at end of this chapter), or from your customs broker.

Detention of Shipment. If your shipment is found to be noncomplying, it may be detained at the port of entry. The FDA may permit you to bring such a shipment into compliance before making a final decision regarding admittance. However, any sorting, reprocessing, or relabeling must be supervised by FDA personnel, and is done at the importer's expense. Such conditional release to allow an importer to bring a shipment into compliance is a privilege, not a right. The FDA may consider subsequent noncomplying shipments of the same type of product to constitute abuse of the privilege and require the importer to destroy or reexport the products. To ascertain what your legal responsibilities are, you should contact the FDA regarding the specific items to be imported.

Bottle Jackets of Plant Materials. Certain plant materials used for bottle jackets—such as the raffia covers of traditional bottles of Chianti wine—are subject to special restrictions under the plant quarantine regulations of the U.S. Department of Agriculture's (USDA) Animal and Plant Health Inspection Service (APHIS). All bottle jackets made of dried or unmanufactured plant materials are subject to APHIS port of entry inspection.

Customs Classification

For customs purposes, beverages, spirits, and vinegar products are classified under Chapter 22 of the HTSUS. This chapter is broken into major headings, which are further divided into subheadings, and often sub-subheadings, each of which has its own HTSUS classification number. For example, the HTSUS number for vodka valued at over $2.05/liter is 2208.90.65, indicating that it is a subcategory of vodka in containers each holding not over 4 liters (2208.90.60), which is a subcategory of other spirits (2208.90.00), itself a subcategory of the major heading undenatured ethyl alcohol of an alcoholic strength by volume of less than 80%; spirits, liqueurs, and other spirituous beverages; and compound alcoholic preparations of a kind used for the manufacture of beverages (2208.00.00). There are nine major headings in Chapter 22.

2201—Waters, including natural or artificial mineral waters and aerated waters, not containing added sugar or other sweetening matter not flavored; snow and ice

2201—Waters, including mineral waters and aerated waters, containing added sugar or other sweetening matter or flavored, and other nonalcoholic beverages, not including fruit or vegetable juices of heading 2009

2203—Beer made from malt

2204—Wine of fresh grapes, including fortified wines; grape must other than of heading 2009

2205—Vermouth and other wine of fresh grapes flavored with plants or aromatic substances

2206—Other fermented beverages (for example, cider, perry, mead); mixtures of fermented beverages and nonalcoholic beverages not elsewhere specified or included

2207—Undenatured ethyl alcohol of an alcoholic strength by volume of 80% or higher; ethyl alcohol and other spirits, denatured, of any strength

2208—Undenatured ethyl alcohol of an alcoholic strength by volume of less than 80%; spirits, liqueurs, and other spirituous beverages; compound alcoholic preparations of a kind used for the manufacture of beverages

2209—Vinegar and substitutes for vinegar obtained from acetic acid

For more details regarding classification of the specific product you are interested in importing, consult a customs broker, the appropriate commodity specialist at your nearest customs port, or see HTSUS. HTSUS is available for purchase from the U.S. Government Printing Office (see addresses at end of this chapter), and may be found in larger public libraries. Refer to "Classification—Liquidation" on page 207 for a general discussion of customs classification.

Sample Import Duties

Import duties vary depending on the HTSUS classification of your product. Therefore, to determine the correct amount of duties, your product must be properly classified under the HTSUS. The following sample duties are taken from the duty listings for HTSUS Chapter 22 products.

Mineral waters and aerated waters (2201.10.00): 0.4 cents/liter; sweetened and/or flavored mineral and aerated waters (2202.10.00): 0.3 cents/liter; carbonated soft drinks (2202.10.00): 0.3 cents/liter; chocolate milk (2202.90.10): 20%; orange juice not made from juice having a concentration of 1.5 or more (2202.90.30): 5.3 cents/liter; juice of any single fruit or vegetable (2202.90.36): the rate applicable to the natural juice in heading 2009; nonalcoholic beer (2202.90.90): 0.3 cents/liter; beer (2203.00.00): 1.6 cents/liter; sparkling grape wine (2204.10.00): 30.9 cents/liter; fortified wine not over 14% alcohol and entitled to a type designation, such as Tokay (2204.21.30): 9.9 cents/liter; fortified wine over 14% alcohol and entitled to a type designation such as Marsala (2204.21.60): 8.3 cents/liter; other fortified grape wine, such as sherry (2204.21.80): 26.4 cents/liter; other grape wine in containers of between two and four liters, not over 14% alcohol (2204.29.20): 9.9 cents/liter; other grape wine in containers of between two and four liters, more than 14% alcohol (2204.29.80): 26.4 cents/liter; other grape must (2204.30.00): 6.9 cents/liter + 49 cents/proof liter; vermouth in containers holding two liters or less (2205.10.30): 5.5 cents/liter; still or sparkling cider (2206.00.15): 0.4 cents/liter; sake (2206.00.45): 6.6 cents/liter; undenatured ethyl alcohol for beverage purposes (2207.10.30): 29.6 cents/liter; undenatured ethyl alcohol for other than beverage purposes (2207.10.60): 3%; denatured ethyl alcohol (2207.20.00): 3%; compound alcoholic preparations of a kind used for the manufacture of beverages, between 20% and 50% alcohol (2208.10.60): 13.2 cents/liter + 3%; brandy in containers of not more than four liters valued at not over $2.38/liter (2208.20.20): 89.8 cents/proof liter; Scotch whiskey (2208.30.30): 5.3 cents/proof liter; bourbon (2208.30.60): 6.6 cents/proof liter; rum (2208.40.00): 37 cents/proof liter; gin (2208.50.00): 13.2 cents/proof liter; bitters for beverage use (2208.90.10): 10 cents/proof liter; liqueurs (2208.90.45): 13.2 cents/proof liter; tequila in containers holding not more than four liters (208.90.50): 60 cents/proof liter; vodka in containers holding not over four liters and valued at less than $2.05/liter (2208.90.60): 67.6 cents/proof liter; imitation brandy (2208.90.72): $1.52/proof liter; vinegar (2209.00.0): 0.8 cents/proof liter.

Special Provisions. Under the provisions of heading 9901.00.50, ethyl alcohol of subheading 2207.10.60 and 2207.20 are subject to an addition of duty of 14.2 cents/liter. Special tariff levies are also in effect under 9903.23.25 for other fermented alcoholic beverages containing less than 7% alcohol by volume (provided for in subheading 2206.00.90): 100%.

Excise Taxes. All alcoholic beverages, whether produced domestically or imported, are subject to a federal excise tax in addition to any duties levied on them. Excise taxes range from $1.07 per gallon on still wines containing not more than 14% alcohol to $3.40 per gallon on champagne and other sparkling wines; $18.00 per standard 31 gallon barrel of beer; and $13.50 per proof gallon of distilled spirits. A proof gallon is one gallon of product at 100 proof strength (50% alcohol); actual duty rates are calculated based on the proportion of actual alcohol content less than or more than 100 proof (most liquors are bottled at 80 proof).

Entry and Documentation

The entry of merchandise is a two-part process consisting of 1) filing the documents necessary to determine whether merchandise may be released from Customs custody and 2) filing the documents that contain information for duty assessment and statistical purposes. In certain instances all documents must be filed and accepted by Customs prior to the release of the goods. Unless you have been granted an extension, you must file entry documents at a location specified by the district or area director within five working days of your shipment's date of arrival at a U.S. port of entry. These include a number of standard documents required by Customs for any entry, and:

- FDA Importer's Notice **Form FD701**
- Certificate of Label Approval
- For wines: Certificate of Origin
- For distilled spirits: Certificates of Age and Origin
- For certain non-standard fill items: Certificates of Non-Standard Fill

After you present the entry, Customs may examine your shipment, or may waive examination. The shipment is then released provided no legal or regulatory violations have been noted. You must then file entry summary documentation and deposit estimated duties at a designated customhouse within 10 working days of your shipment's release. For a detailed description of entry procedures, standard documentation, and informal entry, see "Entry Process" on page 182.

Prohibitions and Restrictions

Fruit Juices. Products sold as fruit juices may be sweetened provided the label states the presence of the added sugar or some other approved wholesome, nutritive sweetening agent. If you add water, the product is no longer considered "fruit juice." Added water is prohibited for products presented as fruit juice. Fruit juice beverages containing added water are subject to all the requirements for nonstandard foods, particularly the use of a common or usual name. If your product fits this category, you should be sure that its labeling includes a declaration of the percent of any characterizing ingredient that has a material bearing on the price, or on consumer acceptance of the product. Labels on diluted orange juice beverages, for example, are specifically required to show the percentage of juice, expressed in increments of 5% (21 CFR 102).

Noncarbonated Beverages. Noncarbonated beverages containing no fruit or vegetable juice must be named as required by the regulation (21 CFR 102). If your label in any way suggests that fruit or vegetable juice is present in your product, you must be sure the label includes an added statement such as "contains no juice." You should include the name of the fruit or vegetable indicated by the flavor, color, or labeling of the product.

Carbonated Beverages. Nonalcoholic carbonated beverages are subject to the standards established for "soda water" (21 CFR

165). Caffeine from kola nut extract or other natural caffeine-containing extracts may be used in any soda water but may not exceed 0.02% by weight of the finished food. All optional ingredients must be declared on the label.

Bottled Waters. The FDA has established standards of quality for bottled drinking water (21 CFR 103). All bottled waters other than mineral waters must comply with these standards. The FDA assumes that natural mineral waters, by their very nature, would exceed physical and chemical limits prescribed in the Bottled Drinking Water Standard. Therefore mineral waters are exempt from the standard. However, in no case will the FDA permit the presence of any substance in bottled mineral water at any level deemed toxic. The FDA has also established Current Good Manufacturing Practice Regulations for processing and bottling waters (21 CFR 129), with which your product must comply.

It is misleading to list on the label of mineral water products minerals that are only present in the product in insignificant amounts. Such a listing may be deemed an attempt to imply that your product has nutritional and/or therapeutic benefit that it cannot actually be shown to possess. Furthermore, if you make any nutritional or health claims in your product's labeling, then you must comply in full with all nutritional labeling requirements. You should be sure that all bottled waters you offer for import are: 1) obtained from sources free from pollution; 2) bottled or otherwise prepared for the market under sanitary conditions, with special reference to the condition of the bottles or other containers and of their stoppers; 3) free from microorganisms of the coliform group; 4) of good sanitary quality when judged by the result of a bacteriological examination to determine the numbers of bacteria growing on gelatin at 20°C and on agar at 37°C; and 5) of good sanitary quality when judged by the results of a sanitary chemical analysis.

Customs will refuse misbranded shipments of mineral waters. Furthermore, if you offer misbranded shipments for import, you are subject to legal action. The following are some frequently assessed examples of misbranding on mineral water labels: 1) objectionable therapeutic claims; 2) false and misleading statements other than therapeutic claims; 3) inaccurate or otherwise misleading label statement of analysis; 4) undeclared addition of salts, carbon dioxide, etc.; and 5) labeling of artificially prepared waters as "mineral water."

Alcoholic Beverages. Regulations governing the importation of alcoholic beverages are complex and vary depending upon the category of alcohol in question. They cover such issues as documentation, storage, labeling, content, and bottling. This section is in no way exhaustive. If you are interested in importing alcoholic beverages, you should contact the BATF for an importer's information packet, and consult with any pertinent state regulatory agencies for details regarding their requirements.

Classification and standards of identity (distilled spirits, wine, and malt beverages). Wines and distilled spirits are divided into separate classifications under which customs duties are calculated. Malt liquors are divided into separate classifications for labeling purposes only.

Distilled Spirits. Distilled spirits classifications are as follows: 1) neutral spirits of alcohol; 2) whisky; 3) gin; 4) brandy; 5) blended applejack; 6) rum; 7) tequila; 8) cordials and liqueurs; 9) flavored brandy, gin, rum, vodka, and whiskey; 10) imitations; 11) distinctive types known by geographical designation; and 12) types distinctive of a particular place but without geographical designation.

Wines. Wines are classified as follows: 1) grape wine; 2) sparkling grape wine; 3) carbonated grape wine; 4) citrus wine; 5) fruit wine; 6) wine from other agricultural products; 7) aperitif wine; 8) imitation and substandard wine; and 9) retsina wine. These classifications are further complicated by three factors: 1) alteration: if a wine is altered by a process such as blending or carbonation, it must be reclassified. If there is no known trade classification for such a wine, its label must give a truthful and adequate description of the wine's composition; 2) varietal designation: if the wine derives its predominant taste, aroma, characteristics, and at least 51% of its volume from a particular variety of grape, the variety can be used in its type designation; e.g. Cabernet Sauvignon or Chenin Blanc; 3) geographical or place of origin designations: the BATF has a number of rules regarding the naming of wines, mainly to ensure that consumers get the product from the location specified on the label. In some cases these rules are not specifically defined in the law except by example; the final decision as to the proper identity of the wine is up to the BATF specialist.

Wines named with a geographic term that relates to a whole group of wines, such as vermouth, are called "generic" wines. Those named with a geographic term specific to a region of origin and distinguishable from all others are called "nongeneric" wines. Nongeneric names cannot be said to be the distinctive name of a specific wine from a particular place or region distinguishable from all others, unless the BATF director finds that it is known to consumers and to the trade as such. Examples of nongeneric wines are Bordeaux Rouge and Liebfraumilch. Examples of distinctive nongeneric wines are St. Emilion and Chateauneuf-du-Pape.

Malt Beverages. The system of classification and standards of identity for malt beverages is used only to label the product correctly, there being no elaborate classification for determining duty as there is for wine and distilled spirits. Several types of malt beverages are mentioned in the BATF regulations, although they are not precisely defined. Categories include: 1) beer; 2) lager beer; 3) lager; 4) ale; 5) porter; 6) stout; 7) half and half; and 8) types distinguished by geographical name, such as Pilsner and Dortmunder.

Customs will inspect your shipment to ensure proper classification for duty and federal excise tax purposes.

Standards of Fill and Bottles Per Case (Distilled Liquor and Wine Only). Standards of fill are specifications established by the law standardizing bottle size and headroom. Size of liquor and wine bottle, the amount of liquid allowed in a bottle of a given size, and the number of bottles that may be shipped in a case are strictly regulated, varying with the category of alcohol. If you are importing distilled spirits bottled or packed on or after January 1, 1980, and imported wines bottled or packed on or after January 1, 1979, your product must comply with metric standards of fill. If the products were packed or bottled prior to these respective dates, you must include with your entry a Certificate of Non-Standard Fill, signed by a duly authorized country-of-origin government official, stating that such is the case. This statement may be a separate document or may be included on the invoice. If you wish to import wines or distilled liquors that were bottled or packed after the respective dates and that do not comply with the standards, you may petition the BATF on a case-by-case basis for an exemption. Your petition must show cause for the noncompliance. For details on standards of fill, contact the BATF or see 27 CFR.

Red Strip Stamps (Distilled Liquors Only). All distilled liquors are subject to federal excise taxes, which must be paid at entry. BATF Red Strip Stamps, which show that IRS excise taxes have been paid, are affixed to all individual bottles of distilled liquor of one-gallon size or less. Red strip stamps are not required on bulk containers. You may obtain red strip stamps in quantity from the BATF at no charge. They must be imprinted with your basic permit number, and affixed to each individual bottle so that when the bottle is opened the number is still identifiable on the remaining stamp. Stamps may be affixed 1) by the foreign bottler;

2) while the shipment is being stored in a foreign trade zone or Customs bonded warehouse; 3) at the U.S. bottler's warehouse (for liquor imported in bulk); or 4) in some cases, if you can document prior payment of the IRS excise tax, Customs will release the shipment to your custody, allowing you to apply the stamps at any time before the bottles enter the commercial market.

Certificate of Age and Origin (Distilled Spirits Only). Scotch, Irish, and Canadian whiskies, brandy, cognac, rum, tequila, and all Class 2 whiskies and blends require special documentation of age and origin. Many specific rules apply to these Certificates of Age and Origin, which are issued by a duly authorized country of origin official. Because these certificates are issued by foreign governments, their form and content varies. However, they must at least state that the products are what they purport to be, have been manufactured in compliance with the applicable laws of that government, and are of the specified age. You must present the certificate to Customs before your shipment will be released. For complete details regarding Certificates of Age and Origin, see BATF Industry Circular #89-1 available from BATF (see addresses at end of this chapter).

Certificate of Origin (Wine Only). A Certificate of Origin signed by an authorized country of origin government official must confirm the identity of the wine, and its production in compliance with that government's laws regulating the production of wines manufactured for home consumption. You must present the certificate to Customs before your shipment will be released. For complete details regarding Certificates of Origin, see BATF Industry Circular #89-1 available from BATF (see addresses at end of this chapter).

Original certificates of origin are required for wines and distilled spirits from Bulgaria, Canada, Chile, France, Germany, Ireland, Jamaica, Mexico, Portugal, Romania, Spain, and the United Kingdom.

Invoices (Distilled Spirits, Wines, and Malt Beverages). You must present a copy of the shipping invoice or bill of lading for each shipment of alcoholic beverages in order to obtain release from Customs. This documentation must show the nature and quantity of the contents and the name of the consignee.

Excise Taxes and Duty Payments (Distilled Spirits, Wines, and Malt Beverages). Federal excise tax on wine and distilled spirits is a set fee per gallon (by category) levied by the IRS but collected by U.S. Customs. For malt beverages it is levied on a per barrel basis. The customs duty per gallon varies according to type of alcohol. All federal excise taxes and all customs duties are payable at the time of entry.

Customs Bonded Warehouses. Since payment of duties and taxes is not required until goods are withdrawn from Customs custody, you may wish to store shipments in a Customs bonded warehouse until you are ready to deliver the goods to your buyers. Goods may be stored for a period of up to three years, after which time extensions are possible. You can either pay a fee to store products in a bonded warehouse operated by someone else, or you can apply to the BATF to establish your own bonded warehouse. For more information on Customs bonded warehouse options, consult your local district director of Customs.

Quotas

9904.10.60 Some milk-based beverage products (heading 2202.90.20) may be affected by the provisions of this subheading: Malted milk, and articles of milk or cream (except (a) yogurt that is not in dry form, (b) fermented milk other than dried fermented milk or other than dried milk with added lactic ferments, (c) mixtures of nonfat dry milk and anhydrous butterfat containing over 5.5% but not over 45% by weight of butterfat, (d) ice cream, (e) cajeta not made from cow's milk, (f) inedible dried milk powders certified to be used for calibrating infrared milk analyzers (g) margarine cheese), all the foregoing provided for in subheadings 0402.29, 0402.99.60, 0403.10.00, 0403.90.80, 0404.90.02, 1901.10, 1901.90.31, 1901.90.39, 2105.00.00, and 2202.90.20: 2,721 kg.

For a general discussion of quotas, refer to "Import Quotas" on page 230.

Marking and Labeling Requirements

Certificate of Label Approval. The following discussion of labeling requirements is meant to serve only as a general guidelines. The BATF regulations regarding labeling of alcoholic beverage containers are specific and extensive. For complete details, see 27 CFR or contact the BATF (see addresses at end of this chapter).

Approval Procedures. The BATF has specific regulations governing labeling of all final packaging of alcoholic beverages. The label requirements vary depending on the category of alcohol, i.e. distilled spirits, wines, or malt beverages. You must submit samples of your printed labels for pre-approval, using **Form BATF-F-1649**. If the label is approved, the BATF director will endorse the form and return it to you as a Certificate of Label Approval. You must present the certificate to Customs before your shipment will be released. BATF recommends that importers submit mock-ups of proposed labels for informal feedback prior to printing. You should send these with a letter, not with **Form 1649**.

Distilled Spirit Labels. In general, labels for distilled spirits must contain the following information: brand name, class and type, alcoholic contents, net contents, name and address of the importer, country of origin, coloring or flavoring where applicable, percentage of neutral spirits where applicable, and statement of age, if required.

Wine Labels. In general, labels for wines must show: brand name; class, type, or other lawful designation; statement of the exact percentage of foreign wine if the bottle contains a blend of foreign and domestic; net contents; alcoholic content—or the term "table" or "light" wine if the alcoholic content is less than 14%—name and business address of the importer. As discussed in the paragraph on classification, wine designation and classification is strictly regulated and must be accurately reflected on the label.

Malt Beverage Labels. In general, labels for malt beverages must show: brand name, class and type, net contents, name and address of importer, name of bottler or packer—if required by state or foreign law—and alcoholic content—when required by state law.

Warning and Content Labels. All alcoholic beverages containing 10 parts per million or more of sulfites must bear warning labels to that effect. The presence of FD&C Yellow #5—tartrazine—in any alcoholic beverage, must be stated on the label.

The use of the word "light" or "lite" on alcoholic beverage labels must be accompanied by statement of calorie, carbohydrate, fat, and protein content. The statement will not be required when "light" is used as authorized in other regulations (e.g. "light sherry") or when the term is used to describe a characteristic of the product ("light taste"), versus an imputation regarding caloric content.

All alcoholic beverages bottled on or after November 18, 1989 must include, in a conspicuous place on the label, the following warning statement: "GOVERNMENT WARNING: (1) According to the Surgeon General, women should not drink alcoholic beverages during pregnancy because of the risks of birth defects. (2) Consumption of alcoholic beverages impairs your ability to drive a car or operate machinery and may cause health problems." The BATF strictly regulates wording, type size, number of words per inch, and other variables relating to the presentation of the warning. Noncompliance with this labeling regulation can result in huge fines, levied on a daily basis during the period of noncompliance, and the revocation of your import permit. For complete information regarding warning statements on alcohol labels see BATF Industry Circular #90-1, available from the BATF (see addresses at end of this chapter).

Prohibited Labels. The BATF not only regulates what must appear on bottle labels, but also what must not appear on bottle labels. For example, labels of alcoholic beverages may not contain any statements that are false or misleading, disparaging to a competitor's product, obscene or indecent, that relate to scientific tests or standards that may be misleading, or specific reference other than permit number to the product's compliance with state or government regulations. For complete details regarding label requirements, contact the BATF or see 27 CFR.

Bottle and Container Labels. If distilled spirits are bottled abroad in containers having a capacity of 200 milliliters or more, these containers must be legibly and permanently marked with 1) the words "Liquor Bottle" and 2) the city or country address of the manufacturer of the spirits or of the exporter abroad, or the city of address of the U.S. importer. Empty liquor bottles imported to be filled in the U.S. shall be marked with the words "Liquor Bottle" and the location of the bottle manufacturer. You may import empty or filled distinctive liquor bottles not bearing such indicia only with prior BATF approval.

Each bottle, cask, or other immediate container of imported distilled spirits, wines, or malt beverages must be marked for customs purposes to indicate the country of origin of the alcoholic beverage contained therein.

For a general discussion of U.S. Customs marking and labeling requirements, see "Marking: Country of Origin" on page 215 and "Special Marking Requirements" on page 217.

Shipping Considerations

You will need to ensure that your goods are packaged and shipped with care so that they arrive in good condition and pass smoothly through Customs. You are responsible for ensuring that the shipment is in compliance with all applicable government regulations for packing and shipping. In most instances, you should not leave these arrangements solely to the discretion of your supplier. Careful preparation of the cargo and selection of the mode of transport can be essential to a cost-effective, timely delivery of undamaged goods. We strongly advise you to consult your shipping representative, insurance agent, or freight broker for advice on packing and shipping. Refer also to the major tab section "Packing/Shipping/Insurance" for a general discussion of packing and shipping.

Shipping procedures are an important factor in the importation of malt beverages and of fine wines, since both products can be ruined by too much movement and sharp shifts in temperature. It is best to pack them in container sizes which reduce the amount of individual handling, and to store them below decks and as close to the ship's center of gravity as possible. You should be familiar with your particular product's requirements before arranging for shipping. Security against pilferage is also a concern.

Publications Available

The following publication explains the FDA requirements for importing beverages. It is published by the FDA and is available on request from FDA headquarters.

Requirements of Laws and Regulations Enforced by the U.S. Food and Drug Administration

The *Harmonized Tariff Schedule of the United States* (HTSUS) is available from:

Government Printing Office (GPO)
Superintendent of Documents
Washington, DC 20402
(202) 512-1800 (Order line)
(202) 512-0000 (General)

The USGPO also has copies of specific laws available for purchase. The USGPO accepts credit card orders over the phone, as well as mail orders paid by credit card, a check drawn on a U.S. bank, or an international money order.

Relevant Government Agencies

Address your questions regarding BATF requirements for importation of alcoholic beverages to:

Bureau of Alcohol, Tobacco and Firearms (BATF)
Alcohol Import Export Branch
650 Massachusetts Avenue
Washington, DC 20226
(202) 927-8100

Address your questions regarding FDA import requirements for all beverages containing less than 7% alcohol by volume to:

Food and Drug Administration (FDA)
Center for Food Safety and Applied Nutrition
200 C Street SW
Washington, DC 20204
(202) 205-5241, 205-5042

Food and Drug Administration (FDA)
Division of Enforcement, Imports Branch
200 C Street SW
Washington, DC 20204
(202) 205-4726

Address your questions regarding importation of beverages to the district or port director of Customs for you area. For addresses refer to"U.S. Customs District Offices" on page 62 or contact:

U.S. Customs Service
1301 Constitution Ave. NW
Washington, DC 20229
(202) 927-6724 (Information)
(202) 927-1000 (General)

Laws and Regulations

The following laws and regulations may be relevant to the importation of beverages. The laws are contained in the U.S. Code (USC) and the regulations in the Code of Federal Regulations (CFR), both of which may be available at larger public and law libraries. Copies of specific laws are also available from the United States Government Printing Office (address above).

21 USC 301 et seq.
Food, Drug, and Cosmetic Act
This Act prohibits deceptive practices and regulates the manufacture, sale and importation or exportation of food, drugs, cosmetics, and related products. See 21 USC 331, 381, 382.

19 CFR 12.1 et seq.; 21 CFR 1.83 et seq.
Regulations on Food, Drugs, and Cosmetics
These regulations of the Secretary of Health and Human Services and the Secretary of the Treasury govern the standards, labeling, marking, and importing of products used with food, drugs, and cosmetics.

18 USC 960 et seq.
Exportation of Armed Vessels, Arms, Liquor, and Narcotics
Customs enforces the provisions of law regulating the prerequisites to a vessel's departure and the prohibitions against exportation of armed vessels, arms, liquor, and narcotics.

18 USC 1263
Marks and Labels on Packages of Liquor
This Act provides for imposition of a fine or imprisonment on persons who knowingly ship into the U.S. any unmarked or unlabeled package of liquor, and the seizure and forfeiture of any such liquor. See also 18 USC 3615; 21 USC 342(d); 27 USC 201 et seq.

19 CFR 12.37, 12.38; 27 CFR 251, Parts 1, 3-5, 7
Regulations on Labeling Alcoholic Beverages
These regulations describe the required labeling for alcoholic beverages and set forth the procedures for approval of labels and enforcement of the label requirements.

26 USC 5001 et seq.
Excise Tax on Alcohol
This law imposes a tax on distilled spirits, wines, and beers.

27 CFR 251.48, 251.173
Regulations on Collection of Alcohol Excise Taxes
These regulations authorize Customs to collect excise taxes imposed on distilled spirits, wines, and beer, including taxes paid by electronic funds transfer (EFT). Customs further assists in the enforcement of the tax laws through its inspection powers. A Customs officer must not release distilled spirits until he or she inspects them, with particular emphasis on losses in transit, and makes certain that various documentary requirements are met.

27 USC 122
Webb-Kenyon Act
This Act authorizes Customs to enforce prohibitions against the importation of alcoholic beverages contrary to the laws of individual states.

27 USC 201 et seq.
Federal Alcohol Administration Act (FAAA)
This Act prohibits the importation of distilled spirits, wine, or malt beverages into the U.S. without a permit issued by the Secretary of the Treasury and authorizes Customs to enforce this prohibition and any labeling requirements.

19 CFR 12.37
Regulations of Customs for Entry of Alcohol
This regulation sets forth the procedures by which Customs will enforce compliance with the FAAA.

40 USC 304(h), (j), and (k)
Liquor Law Repeal and Enforcement Act
This law provides for the disposition of property forfeited to the U.S., the payment of liens and other charges on such property, and the retention or delivery of abandoned or forfeited property.

Principal Exporting Countries

The following listing includes samples of the main supplier nations of the products of this chapter. It is organized by HTSUS major heading. (Refer to "Customs Classification" above for the product codes.) Countries are listed in rank order of the value of products imported to the U.S. Statistics represent customs value entries for 1993 from the Bureau of Census, U.S. Department of Commerce.

2201—France, Canada, Italy, Mexico, Belgium, United Kingdom, Iceland, Switzerland, Germany, Portugal

2202—Canada, Mexico, Germany, Hong Kong, France, Thailand, Japan, Taiwan, South Korea, Ireland

2203—Netherlands, Mexico, Canada, Germany, United Kingdom, Ireland, Japan, China, New Zealand, Denmark

2204—France, Italy, Spain, Australia, Chile, Germany, Portugal, Brazil, Argentina, Slovenia

2205—Italy, France, Denmark, Spain, Netherlands, Germany, Greece, Japan

2206—Japan, Canada, United Kingdom, Spain, Italy, South Korea, China, Taiwan, Denmark, France

2207—Saudi Arabia, Jamaica, Costa Rica, United Kingdom, El Salvador, Brazil, Argentina, Switzerland, France, Germany

2208—United Kingdom, Canada, France, Ireland, Mexico, Sweden, Italy, Russia, Germany, Finland

2209—Italy, Japan, France, Spain, Philippines, Hong Kong, China, Taiwan, South Korea, Germany

Chapter 23: Prepared Animal Feed*

Full title: Residues and Waste from the Food Industry; Animal Feeds

This section pertains to the importation of prepared animal feeds and byproducts of the food industry generally unfit for human consumption and used for industrial purposes, which are classified within Chapter 23 of the Harmonized Tariff Schedule of the United States (HTSUS). Specifically, it includes meat and fish meals, cereal and starch residues, oilcake residues from oil seed extraction, other vegetable processing residues, and prepared pet and animal feeds. This section is supplemental to the "Foods" appendix on page 808. If you are interested in importing products of Chapter 23, you should read that section in conjunction with this one.

If you are interested in importing medicated feeds or medicated feed premixes, refer to Commodity Index Chapter 30. Primary products producing the residues covered in Chapter 23 are covered in Chapter 2, 3, 7, 8, 10, and 12.

Key Factors

The key factors in the importation of animal feeds are:

- Compliance with U.S. Food and Drug Administration (FDA) purity, safety, manufacturing, and other standards
- FDA import entry notification
- Compliance with U.S. Environmental Protection Agency (EPA) pesticide regulations, including pesticide residue monitoring for feeds that could affect U.S. food supplies
- Import quotas on animal feeds containing milk or milk derivatives, licensing required

Although most importers utilize the services of a licensed customs broker in making their entries, and we recommend this practice, you should be aware of the regulatory, entry, and documentation issues involved in importing your product. You, as importer, are ultimately responsible for the fulfillment of any legal requirements applicable to your shipment.

General Considerations

Regulations governing certain products intended for animal use are stringent and complex. Importation of these products is reg-

*IMPORTANT: Read the Commodity Index Introduction. It is the essential framework for understanding this section.

ulated by the FDA under applicable provisions of the Federal Food, Drug, and Cosmetic Act (FDCA). Products designed for use by animals imported into the U.S. must comply with all FDCA requirements for those produced domestically. Animal feeds and pet foods, including color and food additives, are generally subject to the same FDCA requirements for similar products intended for human use.

Imported products regulated by the FDA are subject to FDA port of entry inspection. **Form FD701** is required for all FDA-regulated importations. **Form FD701** may be obtained from your local FDA Import Operations office, from FDA headquarters (see addresses at end of this chapter), or from your customs broker. For an annotated diagram of required FDA import procedures refer to the "Foods" appendix on page 808.

Detention of Shipment. If your shipment is found to be noncomplying, it may be detained at the port of entry. The FDA may permit you to bring such a shipment into compliance before making a final decision regarding admittance. However, any sorting, reprocessing, or relabeling must be supervised by FDA personnel, and will be done at the importer's expense. Such conditional release to allow an importer to bring a shipment into compliance is a privilege, not a right. The FDA may consider subsequent noncomplying shipments of the same type of product to constitute abuse of the privilege and require the importer to destroy or reexport the products. To ascertain what your legal responsibilities are, you should contact the FDA regarding the specific items to be imported.

Customs Classification

For customs purposes, animal feeds and food residues are classified under Chapter 23 of the HTSUS. This chapter is broken into major headings, which are further divided into subheadings, and often sub-subheadings, each of which has its own HTSUS classification number. For example, the HTSUS number for animal feeds containing egg is 2309.90.60, indicating that it is a subcategory of feeds other than prepared dog and cat food put up for retail sale (2309.90.00), itself a subcategory of the major heading preparations of a kind used in animal feeding (2309.00.00). There are nine major headings in HTSUS Chapter 23.

2301—Flour, meals, and pellets, of meat or meat offal, of fish or of crustaceans, molluscs, or other aquatic invertebrates; unfit for human consumption; greaves (cracklings)

2302—Bran, sharps (middlings), and other residues, whether or not in the form of pellets, derived from the sifting, milling, or other working of cereals or of leguminous plants

2303—Residues of starch manufacture and similar residues, beetpulp, bagasse, and other waste of sugar manufacture, brewing, or distillation of dregs and waste, whether or not in the form of pellets

2304—Oilcake and other solid residues, whether or not ground or in the form of pellets, resulting from the extraction of soybean oil

2305—Oilcake and other solid residues, whether or not ground or in the form of pellets, resulting from the extraction of peanut (ground-nut) oil

2306—Oilcake and other solid residues, whether or not ground or in the form of pellets, resulting from the extraction of vegetable fats or oils, other than those of heading 2304 or 2305

2307—Wine lees; argol

2308—Vegetable materials and vegetable waste, vegetable residues and byproducts, whether or not in the form of pellets, of a kind used for animal feeding, not elsewhere specified or included

2309—Preparations of a kind used in animal feeding

For more details regarding classification of the specific product you are interested in importing, consult a customs broker, the appropriate commodity specialist at your nearest Customs port, or see HTSUS. HTSUS is available for purchase from the U.S. Government Printing Office (see addresses at end of this chapter), and may be found in larger public libraries. Refer to "Classification—Liquidation" on page 207 for a general discussion of customs classification.

Sample Import Duties

Import duties vary depending on the HTSUS classification of your product. Therefore, to determine the correct amount of duties, your product must be properly classified under the HTSUS. The following sample duties are taken from the duty listings for HTSUS Chapter 23 products.

Flours, meals, and pellets of meat or meat offal, greaves (cracklings) (2301.10.00): free; herring meal (2301.20.00): free; bran, sharps, or other residues of corn (2302.10.00): free; of cereals other than corn, rice, or wheat (2302.40.00): free; of leguminous plants (2302.50.00): 3%; corn gluten meal (2303.10.00): 3%; brewing or distilling dregs or waste (2303.30.00): free; soybean oilcake (2304.00.00): 0.7 cents/kg; peanut oilcake (2305.00.00): 0.7 cents/kg; linseed oilcake (2306.20.00): 0.26 cents/kg; palm nut or kernel oilcake (2306.60.00): 0.5 cents/kg through December 31, 1994, 0.7 cents/kg thereafter; wine lees (2307.00.00): free; flaxseed screenings (2308.90.30): free; citrus pulp pellets (2308.90.80): 3%; dog or cat food put up for retail sale (2309.10.00): free; bird seed (2309.90.10):free; swine feed (2309.90.10): free; animal feed containing over 10% by weight of milk solids (2309.90.31): 7.5% [some products subject to quota restrictions; see "Quotas" below]; animal feeds containing egg (2309.90.50): 3%.

Special Provisions. Under heading 9903.23.35, duty on certain products is changed as follows: Pet food packaged for retail sale, of byproducts obtained from the milling of grains, mixed feeds, and mixed-feed ingredients (provided for in subheading 2309.10): 100%.

Entry and Documentation

The entry of merchandise is a two-part process consisting of 1) filing the documents necessary to determine whether merchandise may be released from Customs custody and 2) filing the documents that contain information for duty assessment and statistical purposes. In certain instances all documents must be filed and accepted by Customs prior to the release of the goods. Unless you have been granted an extension, you must file entry documents at a location specified by the district or area director within five working days of your shipment's date of arrival at a U.S. port of entry. These include a number of standard documents required by Customs for any entry, and:

- FDA Entry Notification, **Form FD701**

After you present the entry, Customs may examine your shipment, or may waive examination. The shipment is then released provided no legal or regulatory violations have been noted. You must then file entry summary documentation and deposit estimated duties at a designated customhouse within 10 working days of your shipment's release. For a detailed description of entry procedures, standard documentation, and informal entry, see "Entry Process" on page 182.

Prohibitions and Restrictions

Although the FDCA defines food and drugs as articles intended "for man and other animals," you should be aware of some important distinctions between the law's provisions for products intended for human use and those intended for animal use. For example, drugs, food additives, and color additives for use in food-producing animals are evaluated for safety in meat, milk, and eggs, as well as safety and effectiveness for the animal itself. The FDCA requires approval of applications for use of new animal drugs in the manufacture of animal feed.

Animal Feeds and Pet Foods. Commercial animal feeds are commonly sold in bags or in bulk through feed stores and mills, while pet foods are commonly sold through the same distribution channels as human food. Both commercial feed and pet food must meet the requirements of the FDCA and those of individual state's laws (see "Marking and Labeling Requirements" below). As with human food, animal feeds and pet food may not be adulterated or misbranded. For example, animal feeds may not contain any 1) poisonous or deleterious substances; 2) residues of pesticides in excess of established tolerances; 3) unsafe food or color additives; or 4) filthy, putrid, or decomposed material.

You may not import or sell animal feed or pet food in which damage or inferiority has been concealed in any manner; under the name of any other food; or that has any valuable constituents omitted or extracted. You should be sure that canned pet food is manufactured and registered in accordance with the regulations for low-acid canned foods (21 CFR 507, 508).

Food Additives. Substances that by their intended use may become components of animal feed or pet food either directly or indirectly, or that may otherwise affect the characteristics of the animal feed or pet food are defined as "food additives" (21 CFR 570, 571, 573). Food additives are illegal in the absence of prior FDA approval (sanction) or regulation for their safe use. The FDA promulgates food additive regulations based on data submitted in a formal Food Additive Petition. If you wish to initiate the FDA approval process for an additive for animal feed ingredient, submit a Food Additive Petition to FDA's Center for Veterinary Medicine, Division of Animal Feeds (see addresses at end of this chapter).

Food additives that have been found to induce cancer, or whose metabolites have been found to induce cancer, may be used in feed for food-producing animals if no harm comes to the animal and there is no residue of the substance or its metabolites in edible tissues or other products reaching the consumer (21 CFR Sec. 409). However, such substances may not be added to other animal or pet foods.

Quotas

Entry of specific products can be difficult because many product categories affected by quota restrictions overlap, especially where dairy products—which may be components of animal feeds—are concerned. It is important to consult the USDA Import Licensing Group or the U.S. Customs Service Quota Branch (addresses below) to determine whether quota restrictions apply to your specific product.

Quotas exist for animal feeds containing milk or milk derivatives:

Whenever, in any 12-month period beginning January 1 in any year, the respective aggregate quantity specified below for one of the numbered classes of articles has been entered, no article in such class may be entered during the remainder of such period:

9904.10.69 Animal feeds containing milk or milk derivatives, classified under subheading 2309.90.31 or 2309.39: Ireland: 5,470,323 kg; United Kingdom: 83,914 kg; New Zealand: 1,782,618 kg; Australia: 56,699 kg; Other: 0 kg.

These quotas are administered by the Department of Agriculture under license and may not be imported unless the importer holds a license issued by the Department of Agriculture.

For a general discussion of quotas, refer to "Import Quotas" on page 230.

Marking and Labeling Requirements

Animal feed and pet food labeling may not be false or misleading in any particular. U.S. state laws require that animal feed labels bear, in addition to the information required by federal law, a label statement of "Guaranteed Analysis" for minimum protein and fat content, maximum fiber content, and, in some instances, maximum moisture content. You may obtain additional information concerning state registration and labeling requirements from the U.S. state(s) in which you intend to sell your products, or from the Official Publication of the Association of American Feed Control Officials, Inc. (see addresses at end of this chapter).

In addition to the labeling requirements specified by the FDCA and the individual states, pet foods are subject to labeling requirements of the Fair Packaging and Labeling Act (FPLA). Commercial feeds are not. For further details regarding labeling requirements contact FDA (see addresses at end of this chapter).

For a general discussion of U.S. Customs marking and labeling requirements, see "Marking: Country of Origin" on page 215.

Shipping Considerations

You will need to ensure that your goods are packaged and shipped with care to ensure that they arrive in good condition and pass smoothly through Customs. You are responsible for ensuring that the shipment is in compliance with all applicable government regulations for packaging and shipping. In most instances, you should not leave these arrangements solely to the discretion of your supplier. Careful preparation of the cargo and selection of the mode of transport can be essential to a cost-effective, timely delivery of undamaged goods. We strongly advise you to consult your shipping representative, insurance agent, or freight broker for advice on packing and shipping. Refer also to the major tab section "Packing/Shipping/Insurance" for a general discussion of packing and shipping.

As with any edible product, careful packing is necessary to prevent contamination and spoilage en route. Protection from insect and animal contamination is especially important for such products, as contamination with filth is cause for a shipment to be rejected by Customs. Heat and moisture control is also important. Because many food residues contain oils that can become rancid and are subject to the growth of mold if kept in a hot, moist environment, packing and avoidance of delays in transit are important to ensuring the delivery of a salable product.

Publications Available

The following publication explains the FDA requirements for importing animal feed products. It is published by the FDA and is available on request from FDA headquarters (see addresses at end of this chapter).

Requirements of Laws and Regulations Enforced by the U.S. Food and Drug Administration

The *Harmonized Tariff Schedule of the United States* (HTSUS) is available from:

Government Printing Office (GPO)
Superintendent of Documents
Washington, DC 20402
(202) 512-1800 (Order line)
(202) 512-0000 (General)

The USGPO also has copies of specific laws available for purchase. The USGPO accepts credit card orders over the phone, as well as mail orders paid by credit card, a check drawn on a U.S. bank, or an international money order.

Relevant Government Agencies

Address general questions regarding FDA import requirements for products intended for animal use and questions regarding registration and compliance status of animal products to:

Food and Drug Administration (FDA)
Center for Veterinary Medicine
7500 Standish Place (HFV-12)
Rockville, MD 20855
(301) 594-5909

Food and Drug Administration (FDA)
Division of Enforcement, Imports Branch
200 C Street SW
Washington, DC 20204
(202) 205-4726

Address questions regarding import licensing of quota animal feeds to:

Agricultural Marketing Service
Livestock and Feed Division
P.O. Box 96456
Washington, DC 20090-6456
(202) 720-5705

Address questions regarding regulation of pesticide residues to:

Environmental Protection Agency (EPA)
Office of Pesticide Programs
401 M Street SW (7501-C)
Washington, DC 20460
(703) 305-7090 (General)
(703) 305-7102 (Import/export requirements)

Address questions regarding quotas to:

U.S. Customs Service
Quota Branch
1301 Constitution Avenue NW, Rm. 2379-ICC
Washington, DC 20229
(202) 927-5850

Address general questions regarding importation of animal feeds to the district or port director of Customs for you area. For addresses refer to"U.S. Customs District Offices" on page 62 or contact:

U.S. Customs Service
1301 Constitution Ave. NW
Washington, DC 20229
(202) 927-6724 (Information)
(202) 927-1000 (General)

Laws and Regulations

The following laws and regulations may be relevant to the importation of animal feeds and pet foods of HTSUS Chapter 23. The laws are contained in the U.S. Code (USC) and the regulations are published in the Code of Federal Regulations (CFR), both of which may be available at larger public and law libraries. Copies of specific laws are also available from the United States Government Printing Office (address above).

21 USC 301 et seq.
Food, Drug, and Cosmetic Act
This Act prohibits deceptive practices and regulates the manufacture, sale and importation or exportation of food, drugs, cosmetics, and related products. See 21 USC 331, 381, 382.

19 CFR 12.1 et seq.; 21 CFR 1.83 et seq.
Regulations on Food, Drugs, and Cosmetics
These regulations of the Secretary of Health and Human Services and the Secretary of the Treasury govern the standards, labeling, marking, and importing of products used with food, drugs, and cosmetics.

7 USC 135 et seq.
Federal Insecticide, Fungicide, and Rodenticide Act (FIFRA)
This Act prohibits the importation of pesticides or devices that are adulterated, misbranded, or otherwise violative of the Act, provides for registration of pesticides and devices, and establishes standards for labeling and classifying pesticides.

19 CFR 12; 21 CFR 180 and 193; 40 CFR 162
Regulations on Pesticides
These regulations set forth the procedures and guidelines for importing products exposed to pesticides.

Sources of Additional Information

You may obtain state registration and labeling requirements for animal feeds and pet foods from the Official Publication of the:

Association of American Feed Control Officials, Inc.
Capitol Complex
Guthrie Center
Charleston, WV 25305.

Principal Exporting Countries

The following listing includes samples of the main supplier nations of the products of this chapter. It is organized by HTSUS major heading. (Refer to "Customs Classification" above for the product codes.) Countries are listed in rank order of the value of products imported to the U.S. Statistics represent customs value entries for 1993 from the Bureau of Census, U.S. Department of Commerce.

2301—Peru, Canada, Chile, Panama, Norway, Taiwan, France, Mexico, Argentina, United Kingdom

2302—Canada, Argentina, Zaire, Nigeria, Cote d'Ivoire, Sierra Leone, Cameroon, Jamaica, Guadeloupe, Togo

2303—Canada, Pakistan, United Kingdom, Thailand, Italy, France, Denmark

2304—Canada, Trinidad and Tobago, Japan

2305—Netherlands

2306—Canada, Marshall Islands, Lebanon, France, Mexico, Peru

2307—Australia, Canada

2308—Canada, Thailand, Mexico, Taiwan, China, El Salvador, Belgium, United Kingdom

2309—Canada, Germany, Thailand, Slovakia, Ireland, Japan, Italy, New Zealand, Croatia, United Kingdom

Chapter 24: Tobacco Products*

Full title: Tobacco and Manufactured Tobacco Substitutes

This section pertains to the importation of tobacco and tobacco products, which are classified within Chapter 24 of the Harmonized Tariff Schedule of the United States (HTSUS). Specifically, it includes all recognized varieties of unmanufactured tobacco for wrappers and filler as well as tobacco waste; cigars, cheroots, cigarillos, and cigarettes of tobacco or of tobacco substitutes; other tobacco products, including pipe tobacco and snuff; and reconstituted tobacco products. All tobacco products are included in this chapter with the exception of some medicinal cigarettes, which are covered in Commodity Index Chapter 30. Certain tobacco products brought in as samples may be entered duty free (refer to Chapter 98).

Key Factors

The key factors in the importation of tobacco products are:

- U.S. Treasury Department Bureau of Alcohol, Tobacco, and Firearms (BATF) excise tax, collected by Customs
- BATF labeling requirements
- Federal Trade Commission (FTC) labeling and ingredient-reporting requirements

Although most importers utilize the services of a licensed customs broker in making their entries, and we recommend this practice, you should be aware of the regulatory, entry, and documentation issues involved in importing your product. You, as importer, are ultimately responsible for the fulfillment of any legal requirements applicable to your shipment.

General Considerations

Importation of processed tobacco products into the U.S. is straightforward. No permits, prior licensing, or special entry paperwork are required. However, there are several regulatory issues you should be aware of if you are considering importing these commodities.

BATF Requirements. The U.S. Treasury Bureau of Alcohol, Tobacco, and Firearms (BATF) administers certain marking and labeling requirements under 27 CFR 270. BATF also levies excise taxes on tobacco products. Customs collects the BATF tax on each shipment at port of entry. Tobacco imported from beneficiary countries under the Caribbean Basin Initiative (CBI) enters duty-free. (For a general discussion of the CBI see "Caribbean Basin Initiative (CBI)" on page 201.)

USDA Requirements. As with any plant product, tobacco falls under the jurisdiction of the U.S. Department of Agriculture (USDA) as authorized by the Plant Quarantine Act of 1912 (PQA). Because no raw or fresh tobacco enters the U.S.—only cured or processed tobacco is allowed into the country—there are no prohibitions or restrictions under PQA. USDA's Animal and Plant Health Inspection Service (APHIS) may inspect your tobacco shipment at the port of entry, but most shipments of tobacco enter without such inspection.

FTC Requirements. The Federal Trade Commission (FTC) administers the Federal Cigarette Labeling and Advertising Act (FCLAA) as amended by the Public Health Cigarette Smoking Act of 1969 (PHCSA) and the Comprehensive Smoking Education Act (CSEA). FCLAA as amended requires that specific health warnings appear on cigarette and small cigar packages. These requirements apply equally to domestic and imported products. The importer is responsible for complying with any applicable labeling regulations for any tobacco products. For more details, see "Marking and Labeling Requirements" below.

Although the importation of tobacco products is straightforward in the sense that there are no licensing or permit requirements, and no out-of-the-ordinary entry paperwork, you should take the requirements of FCLAA seriously. The law specifically states that importers are responsible for making sure that any foreign-made cigarettes they offer for entry into the U.S. comply with all of its provisions. Noncompliance is a federal offense and may result in a misdemeanor conviction, with fines of up to $10,000.

If you are importing cigarettes for commercial purposes, you must provide the FTC annually with a list of ingredients added to the tobacco during the manufacture of the cigarettes. Your list should not identify the company that uses the ingredients, or the brand of cigarettes in which they are contained. The purpose of the annual listing is not to restrict added ingredients, but to provide FTC with information to conduct ongoing research into the health hazards of cigarettes, and to enable the FTC to make periodic reports to Congress based on the information provided. The FTC considers these ingredient lists to be confidential trade secrets, to be provided only to authorized Congressional committee or subcommittee. Recent leaks of such information resulted in the unattributed release of some such data.

Customs Classification

For customs purposes, tobacco and tobacco products are classified under Chapter 24 of the HTSUS. This chapter is broken into major headings, which are further divided into subheadings, and often sub-subheadings, each of which has its own HTSUS classification number. For example, the HTSUS number for cigarette leaf, not containing wrapper tobacco, or not containing over 35% wrapper tobacco is 2401.20.30, indicating that it is a subcategory of tobacco, partly or wholly stemmed /stripped (2401.20.00), which is a subcategory of the major heading unmanufactured tobacco (whether or not threshed or similarly processed) (2401.00.00). There are three major headings in HTSUS Chapter 24.

2401—Unmanufactured tobacco (whether or not threshed or similarly processed); tobacco refuse

2402—Cigars, cheroots, cigarillos, and cigarettes, of tobacco or of tobacco substitutes

2403—Other manufactured tobacco and manufactured tobacco substitutes; "homogenized" or "reconstituted" tobacco; tobacco extracts and essences

For more details regarding classification of the specific product you are interested in importing, consult a customs broker, the appropriate commodity specialist at your nearest Customs port, or

*IMPORTANT: Read the Commodity Index Introduction. It is the essential framework for understanding this section.

see HTSUS. HTSUS is available for purchase from the U.S. Government Printing Office (see addresses at end of this chapter), and may be found in larger public libraries. Refer to "Classification—Liquidation" on page 207 for a general discussion of customs classification.

Sample Import Duties

Import duties vary depending on the HTSUS classification of your product. Therefore, to determine the correct amount of duties, your product must be properly classified under the HTSUS. The following sample duties are taken from the duty listings for HTSUS Chapter 24 products.

Unmanufactured wrapper tobacco (2401.10.21): 79.4 cents/kg; oriental or Turkish type cigarette leaf not over 21.6 cm in length (2401.10.40): 25.4 cents/kg; other cigarette leaf (2401.10.60): 28.1 cents/kg; other leaf, including cigar leaf (2401.10.80): 35.5 cents/kg + 43.9 cents/kg on wrapper content; partially processed leaf tobacco mixed from two or more countries (2401.20.05): $6.45.kg; partially processed cigarette leaf (2401.20.30): 44.1 cents/kg + 92.9 cents/kg on wrapper content; tobacco stems, not cut, ground, or pulverized (2401.30.30): free; other tobacco refuse (2401.30.90): 35.5 cents/kg; cigars, cheroots, or cigarillos each valued at less than 15 cents (2402.10.30): $4.21/kg + 10.5%; cigars, cheroots, or cigarillos each valued at between 15 cents and 23 cents (2402.10.60): $1.26/kg + 3%; cigars, cheroots, or cigarillos each valued at 23 cents or more (2402.10.80): $1.26/kg + 3% [cigars subject to federal excise tax of 1) $1.125 per 1,000 on cigars weighing not more than 3 pounds per 1,000; and 2) 12.75% of the price for which sold but not more than $30 per 1,000]; clove cigarettes (2402.20.10): 92.6 cents/kg + 2%; paper-wrapped cigarettes (2402.20.80): $2.34/kg + 5% [cigarettes subject to federal excise tax of 1) $12.00 per 1,000 on cigarettes weighing not more than 3 pounds per 1,000; 2) $25.20 per 1,000 on cigarettes weighing not more than 3 pounds per 1,000; however, if more than 6 1/2 inches in length they shall be taxable at the rate for cigarettes weighing not more than 3 pounds per 1,000 counting each 2 3/4 inches of length or fraction thereof as one cigarette]; smoking (pipe) tobacco (2403.10.00): 38.6 cents/kg; homogenized or reconstituted tobacco suitable for use as wrapper (2403.91.20): $1.37/kg chewing tobacco or snuff (2403.99.00): 38.6 cents/kg.

Entry and Documentation

The entry of merchandise is a two-part process consisting of 1) filing the documents necessary to determine whether merchandise may be released from Customs custody and 2) filing the documents that contain information for duty assessment and statistical purposes. In certain instances all documents must be filed and accepted by Customs prior to the release of the goods. Unless you have been granted an extension, you must file entry documents at a location specified by the district or area director within five working days of your shipment's date of arrival at a U.S. port of entry. These include a number of standard documents required by Customs for any entry.

After you present the entry, Customs may examine your shipment, or may waive examination. The shipment is then released provided no legal or regulatory violations have been noted. You must then file entry summary documentation and deposit estimated duties at a designated customhouse within 10 working days of your shipment's release. For a detailed description of entry procedures, standard documentation, and informal entry, see "Entry Process" on page 182.

Entry Invoice. You must provide the following information for all shipments of unmanufactured tobacco on the entry invoice: 1) Specify in detail the character of the tobacco in each bale by giving a) country and province of origin, b) year of production, c) grade or grades in each bale, d) number of carrots or pounds of each grade if more than one grade is packed in a bale, e) the time when, place where, and person from whom purchased, f) price paid or to be paid for each bale or package, or price for the vega or lot if purchased in bulk—if obtained otherwise than by purchase, state the actual market value per bale; 2) if an invoice covers or includes bales of tobacco that are part of a vega or lot purchased in bulk, the invoice must contain or be accompanied by a full description of the complete vega or lot purchased; or if such description has been furnished with a previous importation, the reference to such entry, including date and identity of such shipment; 3) packages or bales containing only filler leaf must be invoiced as filler; when containing filler and wrapper but not more than 35% wrapper, they must be invoiced as mixed; and when containing more than 35% wrapper, they must be invoiced as wrapper.

Country-Specific Import Restrictions

Cuban Tobacco Products. An embargo exists on all products, including cigars and unmanufactured tobacco, from Cuba.

Marking and Labeling Requirements

BATF Requirements. The BATF enforces specific requirements for tobacco product package labeling. The manufacturer's name or Tobacco Products Permit number must appear on the package label. (Note: Tobacco Products Permits are not required. They simply offer the manufacturer an alternative method of company identification on the label.) The product's tax class must be stated (i.e. cigar, cigarette, chewing tobacco, snuff, etc.). If there are subclasses within a given class, e.g. large and small cigarettes, the subclass must also be identified. The words "Class A" may be substituted for "large" and the words "Class B" may be substituted for "small." The labeling must show the number of individual product units contained in the package, e.g. "20 cigarettes," or "5 cigars." Bulk products such as loose pipe tobacco must show content in terms of net weight, using the U.S. (English) system of avoirdupois pounds and ounces. No statement that U.S. tax has been paid may be made on tobacco product labeling. Labeling may contain no depiction or display that is deemed immoral. Tobacco products may not be associated in any way with lottery material. For more information, contact BATF (see addresses at end of this chapter).

FTC Requirements. The Federal Cigarette Labeling and Advertising Act, as amended, is designed to inform the public about the health risks associated with smoking in a consistent and clear manner. To that end, a specifically worded warning must appear on each package, print advertisement, and outdoor billboard advertisement. The Act specifies such aspects of the warning statement as: 1) placement on package; 2) type size and style; 3) size of the border rectangle enclosing the statement; 4) width of the rule bordering the rectangle; and 5) distance of statement from outer edge of the advertisement or package, among other specific requirements.

Four separate health warnings required by law:

SURGEON GENERAL'S WARNING: Smoking Causes Lung Cancer, Heart Disease, and Emphysema.

SURGEON GENERAL'S WARNING: Quitting Smoking Now Greatly Reduces Serious Health Risks.

SURGEON GENERAL'S WARNING: Pregnant Women Who Smoke Risk Fetal Injury and Premature Birth.

SURGEON GENERAL'S WARNING: Cigarette Smoke Contains Carbon Monoxide.

All four warnings must appear on cigarette packaging, advertisements, and outdoor billboards during any one-year period. Companies must rotate the warnings quarterly, in alternating sequence, for each brand or brand style of cigarettes. If you are importing these products, you must submit a rotation plan for FTC approval. The proposed rotation plan must be such that the printed warning will be the same on packaging, advertising, and billboards during a given quarter. The FTC-approved rotation plan becomes effective for the one-year period beginning on the date of application approval. During this period each warning statement must appear an equal number of times. For more information, contact the FTC (see addresses at end of this chapter).

For a general discussion of U.S. Customs marking and labeling requirements, see "Marking: Country of Origin" on page 215 and "Special Marking Requirements" on page 217.

Shipping Considerations

You will need to ensure that your goods are packaged and shipped with care so that they arrive in good condition and pass smoothly through Customs. You are responsible for ensuring that the shipment is in compliance with all applicable government regulations for packaging and shipping. In most instances, you should not leave these arrangements solely to the discretion of your supplier. Careful preparation of the cargo and selection of the mode of transport can be essential to a cost-effective, timely delivery of undamaged goods. We strongly advise you to consult your shipping representative, insurance agent, or freight broker for advice on packing and shipping. Refer to the section "Packing/Shipping/Insurance" for a general discussion of packing and shipping.

Heat, humidity, and moisture can affect the quality of tobacco and tobacco products. Shipments must be packed and transported so as to minimize any damage from these sources. Care must also be taken to avoid contamination by insects, animals, or other sources.

Publications Available

The *Harmonized Tariff Schedule of the United States* (HTSUS) is available from:

Government Printing Office (GPO)
Superintendent of Documents
Washington, DC 20402
(202) 512-1800 (Order line)
(202) 512-0000 (General)

The USGPO also has copies of specific laws available for purchase. The USGPO accepts credit card orders over the phone, as well as mail orders paid by credit card, a check drawn on a U.S. bank, or an international money order.

Relevant Government Agencies

Address questions regarding the importation of partially processed and cured unmanufactured tobacco to:

U.S. Department of Agriculture (USDA)
Animal and Plant Health Inspection Service (APHIS)
Plant Protection and Quarantine (PPQ)
Federal Building, Rm. 631
6505 Belcrest Road
Hyattsville, MD 20782
(301) 436-8645

Address your questions regarding labeling requirements for imported tobacco products to:

Federal Trade Commission (FTC)
Division of Advertising Practices
601 Pennsylvania Ave. NW
Washington, DC 20580
(202) 326-3150

Address your questions regarding importation of tobacco products to:

Bureau of Alcohol, Tobacco, and Firearms (BATF)
Office of Compliance Operations
Washington, DC 20226
(202) 927-7777

Agricultural Marketing Service
Tobacco Division
P.O. Box 96456
Washington, DC 20090-6456
(202) 205-0567

U.S. Department of Agriculture
Foreign Agricultural Service
Tobacco, Cotton & Seeds Division
14th and Independence Avenue SW, Room 5932
Washington, DC 20250
(202) 702-7115

Address your questions regarding importation of tobacco products to the district or port director of Customs for you area. For addresses refer to"U.S. Customs District Offices" on page 62 or contact:

U.S. Customs Service
1301 Constitution Ave. NW
Washington, DC 20229
(202) 927-6724 (Information)
(202) 927-1000 (General)

Laws and Regulations

The following laws and regulations may be relevant to the importation of tobacco and tobacco products. The laws are contained in the U.S. Code (USC) and the regulations are published in the Code of Federal Regulations (CFR), both of which may be available at larger public and law libraries. Copies of specific laws are also available from the United States Government Printing Office (address above).

7 USC 511 et seq.
Tobacco Inspection Act
This Act prohibits the importation of tobacco unless the shipment is accompanied by a certificate as prescribed by the Secretary of Agriculture.

7 CFR Part 29
Regulations on Tobacco Certificates
These regulations prescribe the form of the certificate required by the USDA for importation of tobacco and the procedure for obtaining a certificate.

15 USC 1331 et seq.
Federal Cigarette Labeling and Advertising Act
This Act prohibits the manufacture, importation, or packaging for sale within the U.S. of any cigarettes that fail to bear the Surgeon General's warning label. Cigarettes for export are exempt from the labeling requirement.

15 USC 4401 et seq.
Comprehensive Smokeless Tobacco Health Education Act
This Act prohibits the manufacture, importation, or package for sale within the U.S. of any smokeless tobacco product that fails to bear the Surgeon General's warning label.

16 CFR 307 et seq.
Regulations on Tobacco Warning Labels
These regulations set forth the labels required for tobacco products sold within the U.S.

26 USC 5701 et seq.
Tax on Tobacco
This law imposes an excise tax on tobacco products and cigarette papers and tubes imported or brought into the U.S. The taxes are to be collected, accounted for, and deposited as internal revenue collections by the District Director of Customs.

27 CFR 275.62, 275.63
Regulations on Collection of Tobacco Excise Tax
These regulations provide for the collection of the tobacco excise tax by Customs, including by means of electronic funds transfer (EFT).

27 CFR 175.117
Regulations on Entry of Puerto Rican Tobacco
These regulations set forth the procedures followed for inspection of Puerto Rican tobacco products and cigarette papers and tubes at the U.S. port of entry. This inspection is conducted by U.S. Customs.

Principal Exporting Countries

The following listing includes samples of the main supplier nations of the products of this chapter. It is organized by HTSUS major heading. (Refer to "Customs Classification" above for the product codes.) Countries are listed in rank order of the value of products imported to the U.S. Statistics represent customs value entries for 1993 from the Bureau of Census, U.S. Department of Commerce.

2401—Brazil, Turkey, Greece, Zimbabwe, Bulgaria, Argentina, Malawi, Guatemala, Macedonia, Thailand

2402—Canada, Dominican Rep., United Kingdom, Honduras, Jamaica, Japan, Mexico, Germany, Panama, Indonesia

2403—Canada, Sweden, Netherlands, Denmark, Belgium, United Kingdom, Switzerland, India, Ireland, Germany

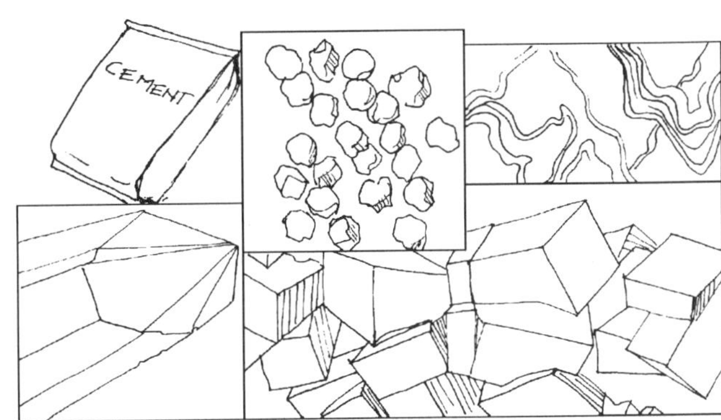

Chapter 25: Quarry Products*

Full title: Salt; Sulfur; Earths and Stone; Plastering Materials, Lime, and Cement

This chapter relates to the importation of minerals and mineral products, which are classified under Chapter 25 of the Harmonized Tariff Schedule of the United States (HTSUS). Specifically, it includes salt and salt solutions; unroasted iron pyrites; sulfur; natural graphite, sand, barium, calcium, magnesium, steatite, cryolite, chiolite, and borate substances, quartz, feldspar, and mica; kaolin, other clays, and earth substances, chalk; pumice, emery, and other natural abrasive; slate; granite, marble, and calcareous stones for monuments or buildings; pebbles, gravel, and crushed stones; dolomite; gypsum, limestone, and lime products; cements; asbestos; and a few miscellaneous minerals.

If you are interested in importing sublimed, precipitated, or colloidal sulfur, you should refer to Commodity Index Chapter 28, which also covers separately defined organic chemicals, including certain earth colors. Products that are intended for use as medicaments should be imported in accordance with the requirements discussed in Chapter 30. If you are interested in importing perfumery, cosmetics, or toilet preparations, refer to Chapter 33. Prepared stones, such as setts, curbstones, flagstones, mosaic cubes, and roofing, facing, or damp course slates are found in Chapter 68. For precious or semiprecious stones, refer to Chapter 71. The importation of cultured crystals and optical elements is covered in Chapter 90, billiard chalks in Chapter 95, and writing, drawing, and tailors' chalks in Chapter 96. You should also consult the related chapters on ores (Chapter 26) and mineral fuels (Chapter 27).

Key Factors

The key factors in the importation of minerals and mineral products are:

- Compliance with U.S. Food and Drug Administration (FDA) regulations and entry notification (if the product can be used in foods, pharmaceuticals, or cosmetics)
- Compliance with U.S. Environmental Protection Agency (EPA) requirements under Toxic Substances Control Act (TSCA) (if the product contains asbestos or other hazardous substances)
- Compliance with U.S. Department of Transportation (DOT) regulations for transport of hazardous cargo (if the product is a hazardous substance)

*IMPORTANT: Read the Commodity Index Introduction. It is the essential framework for understanding this chapter.

Although most importers use the services of a licensed customs broker in making their entries, and we recommend this practice, you should be aware of the regulatory, entry, and documentation issues involved in importing your product. You, as importer, are ultimately responsible for the fulfillment of any legal requirements applicable to your shipment.

General Considerations

Regulatory Agencies. As a general category, minerals are straightforward importations. The FDA regulates the importation of minerals used in foodstuffs, cosmetics, and pharmaceuticals. The EPA, under authority of the TSCA, imposes certain controls on the importation of asbestos and any other minerals that contain toxic substances. The TSCA defines a toxic substance as any substance determined to present the possibility of an unreasonable risk of injury to health and the environment. The DOT enforces regulations for transporting hazardous cargo. Materials are deemed hazardous if listed in DOT transport regulations (49 CFR 172 appendix).

FDA-Regulated Minerals. The products of HTSUS Chapter 25 that are subject to regulation by the FDA are as follows: salt and pure sodium chloride, sea water; kaolin and other kaolinic clays; bentonite; pumice; calcined dolomite; plasters consisting of calcined gypsum or calcium sulfate; and epsom salts. For all of these products, you must submit FDA entry notification, **Form FD701**, to U.S. Customs. For an annotated diagram of FDA import procedures refer to the "Foods" appendix on page 808. If you are interested in importing one of these products, you should ascertain its regulatory status by contacting FDA (see addresses at end of this chapter).

Toxic or Hazardous Substances. Products containing asbestos and other mineral products listed as hazardous or toxic substances and imported in bulk, as articles, or as part of a mixture must be in compliance with toxic and hazardous substance regulations of the EPA and DOT. These include packaging, shipping, marking, and labeling requirements. Refer to listing of laws and regulations below. For more information on Environmental Protection Agency requirements and TSCA certification as it pertains to asbestos, contact EPA's Office of Toxic Substances (see addresses at end of this chapter).

You must file a TSCA certification of compliance or exemption at the time you make the entry at Customs. The certification may be in the form of a typed or stamped statement on an appropriate entry document or commercial invoice or a preprinted attachment to such entry document or invoice. You may sign the certificate by means of an authorized facsimile signature. If your entry is electronically processed, the certification will be in the form of a Certification Code, which is part of the Automated Broker Interface (ABI) transmission. Customs will not release your shipment without proper certification.

If you will be importing several or regular shipments, you should ask the appropriate Customs district director to authorize your use of a blanket certification. If you receive such authorization, you must include on the commercial invoice or entry document for each shipment a statement that the blanket certification is on file and that it is incorporated by reference. This statement need not be signed. The blanket certification is valid for one calendar year, is subject to renewal, and may be revoked at any time for cause.

Articles Exclusion. If you are importing products that are classified as hazardous substances but are part of articles, you are subject to TSCA certification requirements only if certification for your product is specifically required by a rule or order promulgated under the TSCA. No specific rules have been adopted at this time. An "article" is a manufactured item 1) that is formed into a specific shape or design during manufacture, 2) that has end-use functions dependent on the shape or design during end use, and 3) that during the end use, does not change in its chemical composition or that changes only for a noncommercial purpose separate from the article and only as allowed by law (19 CFR 12.120(2)). Fluids and particles are not articles, regardless of shape or design.

Shipment Detention. A shipment containing inorganic chemicals will be detained at the U.S. port of arrival (or entry if same), at your risk and expense, if: 1) it contains banned substances (15 USC 2604, 2605); or 2) it contains substances ordered seized because of imminent hazards (15 USC 2606). Further detention will occur at the port of entry, again at your risk and expense, if: 1) the EPA administrator or Customs district director has reasonable grounds to believe the shipment is not in compliance with the TSCA; or 2) you do not provide proper TSCA certification.

If your shipment is detained, it will be held by Customs for no more than 48 hours. It will then be turned over to the EPA administrator, unless you have arranged to release it in bond. You must either bring it into TSCA compliance or reexport it within the earlier of 90 days after notice of detention or 30 days of demand for redelivery. Customs may grant an extension if failure to comply or reexport is the result of delays in EPA or Customs procedures. If you fail to comply or reexport within the time allowed, the EPA administrator is authorized to have the shipment stored or disposed of at your expense.

Customs Classification

For customs purposes, minerals and mineral products are classified under Chapter 25 of the HTSUS. This chapter is broken into major headings, which are further divided into subheadings, and often sub-subheadings, each of which has its own HTSUS classification number. For example, the HTSUS number for cut blocks of marble is 2515.12.10, indicating it is a sub-subcategory of cut marble and travertine (2515.12.00), which is a subcategory of the major heading, marble, travertine, and other calcareous monumental or building stone, etc. (2515.00.00). There are 28 major headings within Chapter 25.

2501—Salt (including table salt and denatured salt) and pure sodium chloride, whether or not in aqueous solution or containing added anticaking or free-flowing agents; sea water

2502—Unroasted iron pyrites

2503—Sulfur of all kinds, other than sublimed sulfur, precipitated sulfur, and colloidal sulfur

2504—Natural graphite

2505—Natural sands of all kinds, whether or not colored, other than metal-bearing sands of Chapter 26

2506—Quartz (other than natural sands); quartzite, whether or not roughly trimmed or merely cut, by sawing or otherwise, into blocks or slabs of a rectangular (including square) shape

2507—Kaolin and other kaolinic clays, whether or not calcined

2508—Other clays (not including expanded clays of heading 6806) andalusite, kyanite, and sillimanite, whether or not calcined; mullite; chamotte or dinas earths

2509—Chalk

2510—Natural calcium phosphates, natural aluminum calcium phosphates and phosphatic chalk

2511—Natural barium sulfate (barytes); natural barium carbonate (witherite), whether or not calcined, other than barium oxide of heading 2816

2512—Siliceous fossil meals (for example, kieselguhr, tripolite, and diatomite) and similar siliceous earths, whether or not calcined, of an apparent specific gravity of 1 or less

2513—Pumice; emery; natural corundum, natural garnet, and other natural abrasives, whether or not heat-treated

2514—Slate, whether or not roughly trimmed or merely cut, by sawing or otherwise, into blocks or slabs of a rectangular (including square) shape

2515—Marble, travertine, and other calcareous monumental or building stone of an apparent specific gravity of 2.5 or more, and alabaster, whether or not roughly trimmed or merely cut, by sawing or otherwise, into blocks or slabs of a rectangular (including square) shape

2516—Granite, porphyry, basalt, sandstone, and other monumental or building stone, whether or not roughly trimmed or merely cut, by sawing or otherwise, into blocks or slabs of rectangular (including square) shape

2517—Pebbles, gravel, broken, or crushed stone, of a kind commonly used for concrete aggregates, for road metalling, or for railway or other ballast; shingle and flint, whether or not heat-treated; macadam of slag, dross, or similar industrial waste, whether or not incorporating the materials cited in the first part of the heading; tarred macadam; granules, chippings, and powder, of stones of heading 2515 or 2516, whether or not heat-treated

2518—Dolomite, whether or not calcined; dolomite roughly trimmed or merely cut, by sawing or otherwise, into blocks or slabs of rectangular (including square) shape; agglomerated dolomite (including tarred dolomite)

2519—Natural magnesium carbonate (magnesite); fused magnesia; dead-burned (sintered) magnesia, whether or not containing small quantities of other oxides added before sintering; other magnesium oxide, whether or not pure

2520—Gypsum; anhydrite; plasters (consisting of calcined gypsum or calcium sulfate) whether or not colored, with or without small quantities of accelerators or retarders

2521—Limestone flux; limestone and other calcareous stone, of a kind used for the manufacture of lime or cement

2522—Quicklime, slaked lime, and hydraulic lime, other than calcium oxide and hydroxide of heading 2825

2523—Portland cement, aluminous cement, slag cement, supersulfate cement, and similar hydraulic cements, whether or not colored or in the form of clinkers

2524—Asbestos

2525—Mica, including splittings; mica waste

2526—Natural steatite, roughly trimmed or merely cut, by sawing or otherwise into blocks or slabs of a rectangular (including square) shape; talc

2527—Natural cryolite; natural chiolite

2528—Natural borates and concentrates thereof (calcined or not), but not including borates separated from natural brine; natural boric acid containing not more than 85%of H_3Bo_3 calculated on the dry weight

2529—Feldspar; leucite; nepheline and nepheline syenite; fluorspar

2530—Mineral substances not elsewhere specified or included

For more details regarding classifications of the specific product you are interested in importing, consult a customs broker, the appropriate commodity specialist at your nearest customs port, or the HTSUS. HTSUS is available for purchase from the U.S. Government Printing Office (see addresses at end of this chapter), and may be found in larger public libraries. Refer to "Classification—Liquidation" on page 207 for a general discussion of customs classification.

Sample Import Duties

Import duties will vary depending on the HTSUS classification of your product. Therefore, to determine the correct amount of duties, your product must be properly classified under the HTSUS. The following sample duties are taken from the duty listings for HTSUS Chapter 25 products.

Salt (2501.00.00): free; natural graphite in crystalline flake (2504.10.10): 0.7 cents/kg; quartz (2506.10.00): free; kaolin and other kaolinic clays (2507.00.00): 32.5 cents/metric ton; pumice, crude or in irregular pieces, including crushed pumice (2513.11.00): free; slate (2514.00.00): 3.7%; cut blocks of marble (2515.11.00): 2.1%; alabaster (2515.20.00): 6%; calcined dolomite (2518.20.00): 6%; limestones (2521.00.00): free; white Portland cement (2523.21.00): 22 cents/ton, including container weight; mica powder (2525.20.00): 2.4%; epsom salts (2530.20.20): 3.7%.

Entry and Documentation

The entry of merchandise is a two-part process consisting of 1) filing the documentation necessary to determine whether merchandise may be released from Customs custody, and 2) filing the documents that contain information for duty assessment and statistical purposes. In certain instances, all documents must be filed and accepted by Customs prior to release of the goods. Unless you have been granted an extension, you must file entry documents at a location specified by the district or area director within five working days of your shipment's date of arrival at a U.S. port of entry. These include a number of standard documents required by Customs for any entry, and:

- FDA entry notification, **Form FD701** (if product is FDA-regulated)
- U.S. Customs TSCA Certification (hazardous materials)

After you present the entry, Customs may examine your shipment or may waive examination. The shipment is then released provided no legal or regulatory violations have been noted. You must then file entry summary documentation and deposit estimated duties at a designated customhouse within 10 working days of your shipment's release. For a detailed description of entry procedures, standard documentation, and informal entry, refer to "Entry Process" on page 182.

Marking and Labeling Requirements

A shipment of any products containing substances that are classified as hazardous (49 CFR 172) must comply with the marking and labeling regulations adopted by the EPA (46 CFR 147.30) and the DOT (49 CFR 171 et seq.).

For a general discussion of U.S. Customs marking and labeling requirements, refer to "Marking: Country of Origin" on page 215 and "Special Marking Requirements" on page 217.

Shipping Considerations

You will need to ensure that your goods are packaged and shipped with care so that they pass smoothly through Customs and arrive in good condition. You are responsible for ensuring that the shipment is in compliance with all applicable government regulations for packaging and shipping. In most instances, you should not leave these arrangements solely to the discretion of your supplier. Careful preparation of the cargo and selection of the mode of transport can be essential to a cost-effective, timely delivery of undamaged goods. We strongly advise you to consult your shipping representative, insurance agent, or freight broker for advice on packing and shipping. Refer also to the major tab section "Packing/Shipping/Insurance" for a general discussion of packing and shipping.

Minerals and mineral products may be shipped in bulk, bags, crates, or other types of containers, depending on the type of product and whether it is prepackaged. General considerations include protection from contamination, weather, and pests. If a product must be kept in a sanitary environment, all tables, utensils, platforms, and devices used for moving or handling the product, the compartments in which it is stowed while being transported will need to be maintained in a sanitary condition. For liquid shipments, venting and vapor collection systems may be required. Safety precautions should also be implemented as required to protect against breakage, spillage, corrosion of containers, and combustion. Containers should be constructed so as to be safe for handling during transport.

Mineral products. Mineral products in particular may have to be shipped in pressurized, ventilated, and temperature-and vapor-controlled enclosures. Solid products that are listed as hazardous substances (49 CFR 172 appendix) may be transported in bulk only on compliance with Coast Guard notification procedures, shipping permit requirements, and complex transportation regulations (46 CFR 148). All hazardous substances must be packaged and transported in accordance with DOT regulations (49 CFR 171 et seq.).

Publications Available

The following publication explains the FDA requirements for importing minerals and mineral products. It is published by the FDA and is available on request from FDA headquarters (see addresses at end of this chapter).

Requirements of Laws and Regulations Enforced by the U.S. Food and Drug Administration

The following publications may be relevant to the importation of toxic or hazardous minerals and mineral products:

Toxic Substances Control Act: A Guide for Chemical Importers/ Exporters (published by EPA).

TSCA Chemical Substance Inventory (1985 edition) (Doc. Code S/N 055-000-00254-1) $161.00 U.S. and Canada; $201.21 all other countries.

Supplement to TSCA Chemical Substances Inventory (1990) (Doc. Code S/N 055-000-00361-1) $15.00 U.S.; $18.75 Canada and all other countries.

The above publications and the *Harmonized Tariff Schedule of the United States* (HTSUS) are available from:

Government Printing Office (GPO)
Superintendent of Documents
Washington, DC 20402
(202) 512-1800 (Order line)
(202) 512-0000 (General)

The USGPO also has copies of specific laws available for purchase. The USGPO accepts credit card orders over the phone, as well as mail orders paid by credit card, a check drawn on a U.S. bank, or an international money order.

Relevant Government Agencies

Address your questions regarding TSCA requirements for asbestos products to:

Environmental Protection Agency (EPA)
TSCA System Information
EPA 7408, OPPT
401 M Street SW
Washington, DC 20460
(202) 554-1404 (TSCA Information Hotline)

Address your questions regarding FDA requirements to:

Food and Drug Administration (FDA)
Center for Drug Evaluation and Research (HFD-8)
5600 Fishers Lane
Rockville, MD 20857
(301) 594-1012

Food and Drug Administration (FDA)
Center for Food Safety and Applied Nutrition
200 C Street SW
Washington, DC 20204
(202) 205-5241, 205-5042

Food and Drug Administration (FDA)
Division of Enforcement, Imports Branch
200 C Street SW
Washington, DC 20204
(202) 205-4726

Address your questions regarding transportation of hazardous substances to:

U.S. Department of Transportation (DOT)
Research and Special Programs Administration
Office of Hazardous Materials Standards
400 7th St. SW
Washington, DC 20590
(202) 366-4488

Address your questions regarding the importation of minerals and mineral products to the district or port director of Customs for you area. For addresses refer to"U.S. Customs District Offices" on page 62 or contact:

U.S. Customs Service
1301 Constitution Ave. NW
Washington, DC 20229
(202) 927-6724 (Information)
(202) 927-1000 (General)

Laws and Regulations

The following laws and regulations may be relevant to the importation of minerals and mineral products. The laws are contained in the United States Code (USC), and the regulations are published in the Code of Federal Regulations (CFR), both of which are available at larger public and law libraries. Copies of specific laws and regulations may be purchased from the United States Government Printing Office (address above).

21 USC 301 et seq.
Food, Drug, and Cosmetic Act
This Act prohibits deceptive practices and regulates the manufacture, sale and importation or exportation of food, drugs, cosmetics, and related products. See 21 USC 331, 381, 382.

19 CFR 12.1 et seq.; 21 CFR 1.83 et seq.
Regulations on Food, Drugs, and Cosmetics
These regulations of the Secretary of Health and Human Services and the Secretary of the Treasury govern the standards, labeling, marking, and importing of products used with food, drugs, and cosmetics.

15 USC 2601 et seq.
Toxic Substances Control Act
This Act authorizes the EPA to determine whether a substance is harmful and to restrict importation, sale, and use of such substances.

19 CFR 12.118 et seq.
Regulations on Toxic Substances Control
These regulations require importers of chemical substances imported in bulk or as part of a mixture to certify to Customs that the shipment complies with the TSCA or is not subject to that Act.

15 USC 1261
Federal Hazardous Substances Act
This Act controls the importation of hazardous substances, sets forth prohibited imports, and authorizes various agencies to promulgate labeling, marking, and transport requirements.

49 CFR 170 et seq.
Regulations on Hazardous Materials
These regulations list all substances deemed hazardous and provide transport, marking, labeling, safety, and emergency response rules.

46 CFR 147.30
Regulations on Labeling of Hazardous Materials
This regulation requires the labeling of containers of hazardous substances and specifies the label contents.

46 CFR 148 et seq.
Regulations on Carriage of Solid Hazardous Materials in Bulk
These regulations govern the transport of solid hazardous substances in bulk, including reporting, permitting, loading, stowing, and shipping requirements.

Principal Exporting Countries

The following listing includes samples of the main supplier nations of the products of this chapter. It is organized by HTSUS major heading. (Refer to "Customs Classification" above for the product codes.) Countries are listed in rank order of the value of products imported to the U.S. Statistics represent customs value entries for 1993 from the Bureau of Census, U.S. Department of Commerce.

2501—Canada, Mexico, Bahamas, Chile, Netherlands, Netherlands Antilles, Brazil, Spain, France, South Korea

2502—Canada, Peru, Germany, Spain, Italy, United Kingdom, France, Hong Kong

2503—Canada, Mexico, France, Japan, Netherlands Antilles, Germany, United Kingdom, Chile, Netherlands

2504—Canada, Brazil, China, Madagascar, Mexico, Germany, Japan, Zimbabwe, France, Sri Lanka

2505—Germany, Australia, Canada, Japan, Bahamas, United Kingdom, Sweden, Malaysia, Antigua and Barbuda, Norway

2506—Japan, Canada, Brazil, Germany, Netherlands, Russia, Colombia, Belgium, Taiwan, China

2507—United Kingdom, New Zealand, Canada, China, Germany, Japan, Italy, Netherlands, Belgium, Norway

2508—South Africa, United Kingdom, China, Canada, Germany, France, Italy, Japan, Mexico, Thailand

2509—Norway, France, Canada, Denmark, Taiwan, Italy, Switzerland, China, Germany, United Kingdom

2510—Morocco, Israel, Japan, France, Canada, India, Netherlands, Taiwan

2511—China, India, Mexico, Canada, Switzerland, Germany, Japan, Netherlands, Denmark

2512—France, Mexico, Peru, Germany, Belgium, Canada, Japan, China, Hong Kong, United Kingdom

2513—Turkey, Greece, Canada, Ecuador, Italy, Australia, Spain, France, Mexico, Germany

2514—Italy, South Africa, India, Spain, France, China, United Kingdom, Argentina, Hong Kong, Belgium

2515—Italy, France, Spain, Mexico, Germany, Greece, China, Turkey, India, United Kingdom

2516—Canada, South Africa, India, Italy, Zimbabwe, Norway, Brazil, Portugal, Switzerland, Mexico

2517—Mexico, Canada, Bahamas, France, Jamaica, United Kingdom, Italy, Philippines, Japan, Germany

2518—Canada, Austria, United Kingdom, China, Mexico, Taiwan, Germany, Hong Kong

2519—China, Canada, Mexico, Israel, Japan, Austria, Greece, Ireland, Germany, Australia

2520—Canada, Mexico, Spain, Jamaica, Bahamas, Australia, China, Germany, United Kingdom, Japan

2521—Canada, Bahamas, Mexico, United Kingdom, France, Bulgaria, Sweden, Dominican Rep., Japan

2522—Canada, Mexico, Sweden, Japan, Thailand, France

2523—Canada, Mexico, Spain, Colombia, France, China, Venezuela, Greece, Denmark, Australia

2524—Canada, Zimbabwe

2525—Canada, India, Japan, China, Germany, Norway, Brazil, France, Indonesia, Madagascar

2526—Canada, China, Japan, Australia, France, Italy, Netherlands, United Kingdom, Mexico, Brazil,

2527—Denmark, Germany

2528—Turkey, Chile, Italy, Netherlands, Canada, Peru, Germany, Russia, Switzerland, China

2529—China, Canada, South Africa, Mexico, Italy, Germany, United Kingdom, France

2530—Turkey, Morocco, Canada, South Africa, Mexico, Greece, Bahamas, Germany, Italy, Norway

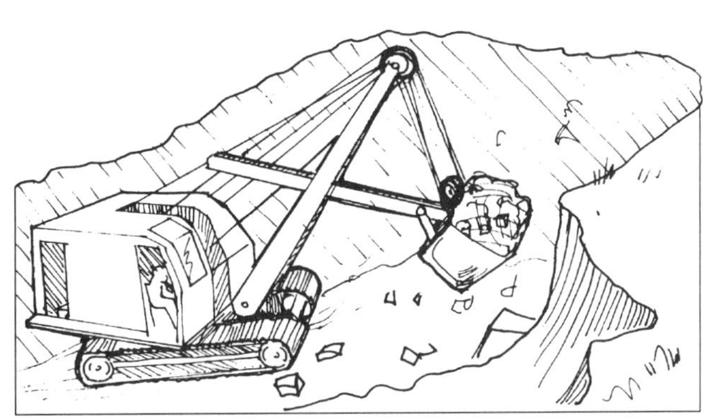

Chapter 26: Ores, Slag, and Ash*

This chapter relates to the importation of ores, slag, and ash, which are classified under Chapter 26 of the Harmonized Tariff Schedule of the United States (HTSUS). Specifically, it includes ores of iron, manganese, nickel, cobalt, aluminum, lead, zinc, tin, chromium, tungsten, uranium, molybdenum, titanium, niobium, tantalum, vanadium, zirconium, precious metals, antimony, beryllium, and others. It also covers slag, dross, other waste from manufacture of iron or steel, and ash and ash residues.

If you are interested in importing minerals, you should read Commodity Index Chapter 25, which covers such related products as slag prepared as macadam and natural magnesium carbonate. Slag wool, rock wool, and other mineral wools are found in Chapter 68, and basic slag is in Chapter 31. For importing precious metal waste or scrap or metal clad with precious metal, refer to Chapter 71. The importation of base metal products is covered in Chapters 72 through 81.

Key Factors

The key factors in the importation of ores, slag, and ash are:

- Port-of-entry sampling (if product is a copper-bearing or metal-bearing ore)

Although most importers use the services of a licensed customs broker in making their entries, and we recommend this practice, you should be aware of the regulatory, entry, and documentation issues involved in importing your product. You, as importer, are ultimately responsible for the fulfillment of any legal requirements applicable to your shipment.

General Considerations

The importation of ores, slag, and ash is generally straightforward. The primary regulation of these products is by U.S. Customs, which requires sampling of copper-bearing and metal-bearing ores at the time of entry.

Copper-Bearing Fluxing Material. If you are importing ores that contain copper (2603.00.00) and that are usable as flux or sulphur reagent, you must submit a declaration to U.S. Customs stating that the material is to be used for fluxing purposes only. If the entry is for consumption, you must deposit the estimated tax at the time of the entry. Entry will be delayed until you provide this declaration or other proof of use for fluxing purposes.

*IMPORTANT: Read the Commodity Index Introduction. It is the essential framework for understanding this chapter.

There is a sampling requirement for this type of ore. Customs will take samples of the ore in a shipment to be tested for copper content by a government chemist.

If you are importing this type of ore for a smelting or converting plant, the plant management must file with Customs at all appropriate ports of entry a detailed statement about plant operations for each quarter. This statement must be based on the plant's records of operation, showing for each furnace or converter the quantities of material charged, materials used for fluxing, and imported materials used for fluxing and claimed for free entry. It must also specify the copper content of the imported ores, as computed by the government assay. If at any time during the quarterly period, the quantity of ores used for fluxing in any furnace or converter exceeds 25% of the charge, the quarterly statement must also explain the reason for the excess usage.

Metal-bearing Ores: Sampling Requirements. When metal-bearing ores and other metal-bearing materials are offered for entry, they must be sampled for assay and moisture purposes (19 CFR 151.51). If proper weighing or sampling facilities are not available at the port of entry, your merchandise will have to be transported under bond to an appropriate facility. If your products are sampled at any place other than the port of entry, you will be required to bear the expense.

The district director of the port of entry may allow exceptions to the sampling requirement for low-metal-content ores if the director is satisfied, based on invoice information, the nature of available samples, knowledge of prior importations of similar materials, and other data, that the ores have been accurately classified. Sampling procedures are described in 19 CFR 151.52. If you have questions regarding metal-ore sampling, contact your nearest U.S. Customs port office.

Customs Classification

For customs purposes, ores, slag, and ash are classified under Chapter 26 of the HTSUS. This chapter is broken into major headings, which are further divided into subheadings, and often sub-subheadings, each of which has its own HTSUS classification number. For example, the HTSUS number for zinc dross is 2620.19.30, indicating it is a sub-subcategory of other zinc-containing ash and residues (2620.19.00), which is a subcategory of the major heading ash and residues containing metals or metal compounds (2620.00.00). There are 21 major headings within Chapter 26.

2601—Iron ores and concentrates, including roasted iron pyrites

2602—Manganese ores and concentrates including manganiferous iron ores and concentrates with a manganese content of 20%or more, calculated on the dry weight

2603—Copper ores and concentrates

2604—Nickel ores and concentrates

2605—Cobalt ores and concentrates

2606—Aluminum ores and concentrates

2607—Lead ores and concentrates

2608—Zinc ores and concentrates

2609—Tin ores and concentrates

2610—Chromium ores and concentrates

2611—Tungsten ores and concentrates

2612—Uranium or thorium ores and concentrates

2613—Molybdenum ores and concentrates

2614—Titanium ores and concentrates

2615—Niobium (columbium), tantalum, vanadium, or zirconium ores and concentrates

2616—Precious metal ores and concentrates

2617—Other ores and concentrates

2618—Granulated slag (slag sand) from the manufacture of iron or steel

2619—Slag, dross (other than granulated slag), scalings, and other waste from the manufacture of iron or steel

2620—Ash and residues (other than from the manufacture of iron or steel) containing metals or metal compounds

2621—Other slag and ash, including seaweed ash (kelp)

For more details regarding classifications of the specific product you are interested in importing, consult a customs broker, the appropriate commodity specialist at your nearest customs port, or the HTSUS. HTSUS is available for purchase from the U.S. Government Printing Office (see addresses at end of this chapter), and may be found in larger public libraries. Refer to "Classification—Liquidation" on page 207 for a general discussion of customs classification.

Sample Import Duties

Import duties will vary depending on the HTSUS classification of your product. Therefore, to determine the correct amount of duties, your product must be properly classified under the HTSUS. The following sample duties are taken from the duty listings for HTSUS Chapter 26 products.

Roasted iron pyrites (2601.20.00): free; copper ores and concentrates (2603.00.00): 1.7 cents/kg on lead content; aluminum ores and concentrates (2606.00.00): free; lead ores and concentrates (2607.00.00): 1.7 cents/kg on lead content; tungsten ores and concentrates (2611.00.00): 37.5 cents/kg on tungsten content; roasted molybdenum ores and concentrates (2613.10.00): 13.2 cents/kg on molybdenum content plus 1.9%; silver ores and concentrates (2616.10.00): 1.7 cents/kg on lead content; granulated slag from iron or steel manufacture (2618.00.00): free; ferrous scale (2619.00.30): 29.5 cents/ton; seaweed ash (2621.00.00): free.

Entry and Documentation

The entry of merchandise is a two-part process consisting of 1) filing the documentation necessary to determine whether merchandise may be released from Customs custody, and 2) filing the documents that contain information for duty assessment and statistical purposes. In certain instances, all documents must be filed and accepted by Customs prior to release of the goods. Unless you have been granted an extension, you must file entry documents at a location specified by the district or area director within five working days of your shipment's date of arrival at a U.S. port of entry. These include a number of standard documents required by Customs for any entry, and:

- Customs declaration on usage of copper-bearing fluxing materials (if product is copper ore or concentrate)

After you present the entry, Customs may examine your shipment or may waive examination. The shipment is then released provided no legal or regulatory violations have been noted. You must then file entry summary documentation and deposit estimated duties at a designated customhouse within 10 working days of your shipment's release. For a detailed description of entry procedures, standard documentation, and informal entry, refer to "Entry Process" on page 182.

Entry Invoice. For copper ores and concentrates classifiable under heading 2603 and subheadings 2620.19.60, 2620.20.00, 2620.30.00, and heading 7401, the invoice must include a statement of the percentage by weight of copper content and any other metallic element.

Marking and Labeling Requirements

For a general discussion of U.S. Customs marking and labeling requirements, refer to "Marking: Country of Origin" on page 215 and "Special Marking Requirements" on page 217.

Shipping Considerations

You will need to ensure that your goods are packaged and shipped with care so that they pass smoothly through Customs and arrive in good condition. You are responsible for ensuring that the shipment is in compliance with all applicable government regulations for packaging and shipping. In most instances, you should not leave these arrangements solely to the discretion of your supplier. Careful preparation of the cargo and selection of the mode of transport can be essential to a cost-effective, timely delivery of undamaged goods. We strongly advise you to consult your shipping representative, insurance agent, or freight broker for advice on packing and shipping. Refer also to the major tab section "Packing/Shipping/Insurance" for a general discussion of packing and shipping.

Ores, slag, and ash may be shipped in bulk, bags, crates, or other types of containers, depending on the type of product and whether it is prepackaged. General considerations include protection from contamination, weather, and pests. If a product must be kept in a sanitary environment, all tables, utensils, platforms, and devices used for moving or handling the product, the compartments in which it is stowed while being transported will need to be maintained in a sanitary condition. Safety precautions should also be implemented as required to protect against breakage, spillage, corrosion of containers, and combustion. Containers should be constructed so as to be safe for handling during transport.

Publications Available

The *Harmonized Tariff Schedule of the United States* (HTSUS) is available from:

Government Printing Office (GPO)
Superintendent of Documents
Washington, DC 20402
(202) 512-1800 (Order line)
(202) 512-0000 (General)

The USGPO also has copies of specific laws available for purchase. The USGPO accepts credit card orders over the phone, as well as mail orders paid by credit card, a check drawn on a U.S. bank, or an international money order.

Relevant Government Agencies

Address your questions regarding the importation of minerals and mineral products to the district or port director of Customs for you area. For addresses refer to"U.S. Customs District Offices" on page 62 or contact:

U.S. Customs Service
1301 Constitution Ave. NW
Washington, DC 20229
(202) 927-6724 (Information)
(202) 927-1000 (General)

Laws and Regulations

The following laws and regulations may be relevant to the importation of ores, slag, and ash. The laws are contained in the United States Code (USC), and the regulations are published in the Code of Federal Regulations (CFR), both of which are available at larger public and law libraries. Copies of specific laws are also available from the United States Government Printing Office (address above).

26 USC 4611 et seq.
Environmental Taxes
This law imposes an excise tax on a number of imported petroleum products, chemicals, and "taxable substances" if the Secretary of the Treasury determines, after consulting with Customs and the EPA, that taxable chemicals constitute more than 50% of the weight. Customs is authorized to collect this excise tax.

19 CFR 10.98
Regulations on Sampling of Copper-Bearing Flux Materials
These regulations set forth the procedures for Customs entry declarations and sampling of copper-bearing flux materials.

19 CFR 151.51 et seq.
Regulations on Sampling of Metal-Bearing Ores
These regulations set forth the procedures for Customs entry declarations and sampling of copper-bearing flux materials.

Principal Exporting Countries

The following listing includes samples of the main supplier nations of the products of this chapter. It is organized by HTSUS major heading. (Refer to "Customs Classification" above for the product codes.) Countries are listed in rank order of the value of products imported to the U.S. Statistics represent customs value entries for 1993 from the Bureau of Census, U.S. Department of Commerce.

2601—Canada, Venezuela, Brazil, Mauritania, Australia, Sweden, Chile, Finland, Norway, Peru

2602—Gabon, Australia, Mexico, South Africa, Brazil, Morocco

2603—Indonesia, Chile, Portugal, Canada, New Guinea

2604—New Caledonia

2605—No listing

2606—Jamaica, Guinea, Brazil, Guyana, China, Indonesia, Greece, Australia, Cyprus, Canada

2607—Peru, Canada, South Korea, Bolivia, Brazil, Ecuador, Mexico

2608—Canada, Mexico, Peru

2609—No listing

2610—South Africa, Philippines

2611—Bolivia, Portugal, Peru, Rwanda, Burma, Uganda, Thailand, Netherlands, Japan, Mexico

2612—No listing

2613—Canada, Chile, China, Belgium, United Kingdom, Japan

2614—Australia, South Africa, Sierra Leone, Malaysia, Canada, India, United Kingdom, Japan, Russia, France

2615—Australia, Canada, Germany, South Africa, Brazil, Japan, Rwanda, Burundi, Zaire, Thailand, Mexico, Canada, Peru, Germany, Netherlands, Denmark

2617—Canada, Australia, China, France, Guatemala, Mexico, Austria

2618—Canada, South Africa, Mexico

2619—Canada, South Africa, Brazil, Belgium, Zaire, Taiwan, Spain, Mexico, United Kingdom

2620—South Africa, Canada, United Kingdom, Finland, Saudi Arabia, Belgium, Mexico, Argentina, Norway, Germany

2621—Canada, United Kingdom, Germany, Philippines, Brazil, Spain, France, Australia, Netherlands, Taiwan

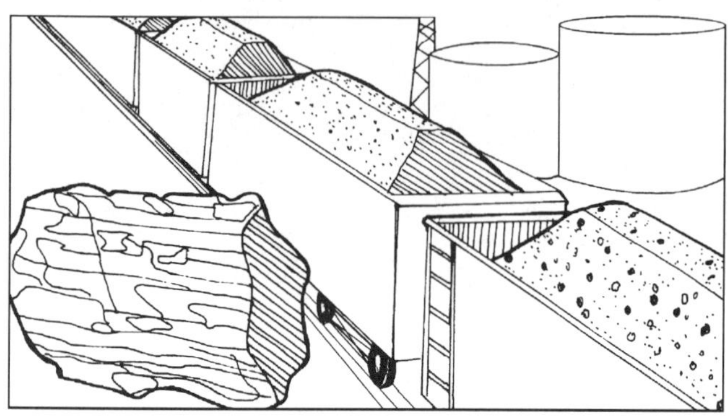

Chapter 27: Mineral Fuels, Oils, and Waxes*

Full title: Mineral Fuels, Mineral Oils and Products of Their Distillation; Bituminous Substances; Mineral Waxes

This chapter relates to the importation of mineral fuels, oils, and waxes and bituminous substances, which are classified under Chapter 27 of the Harmonized Tariff Schedule of the United States (HTSUS). Specifically, it includes coal; lignite; peat; coke; coal, water, and producer gases; mineral tars; mineral oils; pitch and pitch coke; petroleum oils and gases; hydrocarbon gases; petroleum jelly, paraffin and other mineral waxes; petroleum oil residues; bitumen, asphalt, and derivatives; bituminous mixtures; and electrical energy.

If you are interested in importing separately defined organic compounds, you should refer to Commodity Index Chapter 29. Products that are intended as medicaments will probably be classified under Chapter 30. For the importation requirements related to essential oils and perfume oils, refer to Chapter 33. Terpenic oils are covered in Chapter 38. Review of the related Chapter 25, "Minerals and Mineral Products," may also be useful.

Key Factors

The key factors in the importation of mineral fuels, oils, and waxes and bituminous substances, are:

- Compliance with U.S. Federal Trade Commission (FTC) and Consumer Product Safety Commission (CPSC) standards (if a consumer product)
- Compliance with U.S. Food and Drug Administration (FDA) entry notification and standards requirements (petroleum jelly, white mineral oil, and paraffin wax)
- Compliance with U.S. Customs port-of-entry sampling and metering requirements (petroleum products)
- Compliance with U.S. Environmental Protection Agency (EPA) requirements under Toxic Substances Control Act (TSCA) (if the product is a hazardous material)
- Compliance with U.S. Department of Transportation (DOT) regulations for transport of hazardous cargo (if the product is a hazardous material)
- Authorization of U.S. Department of Energy (DOE) (natural gas) and compliance with regulations of Federal Energy Regulatory Commission (FERC)

*IMPORTANT: Read the Commodity Index Introduction. It is the essential framework for understanding this chapter.

Although most importers use the services of a licensed customs broker in making their entries, and we recommend this practice, you should be aware of the regulatory, entry, and documentation issues involved in importing your product. You, as importer, are ultimately responsible for the fulfillment of any legal requirements applicable to your shipment.

General Considerations

Regulatory Agencies. The EPA, under authority of the TSCA, imposes certain controls on the importation of mineral fuels, oils, waxes, and bituminous materials that contain toxic substances. The TSCA defines a toxic substance as any substance determined to present the possibility of an unreasonable risk of injury to health and the environment. The DOT enforces regulations for transporting hazardous cargo. Materials are deemed hazardous if listed in DOT transport regulations (49 CFR 172 appendix). Import of natural gas requires DOE authorization and compliance with the FERC requirements. The FDA, under the Federal Food, Drug, and Cosmetic Act (FDCA) and the Public Health Service Act (PHSA), regulates the importation of petroleum jelly, white mineral oil, and paraffin wax. The FTC sets standards for processing and labeling products that are sold to consumers.

Natural Gas. Importation of natural gas is subject to regulation by both the DOE and the FERC. Depending on the nature of the import, authorization is required from one or both of these agencies. The DOE enforces regulations in 10 CFR 590 for importing natural gas through existing facilities. If you wish to import natural gas through existing facilities, you should contact the DOE Office of Fossil Energy, FE-14GTN (see addresses at end of this chapter) for Section 3 Authorization. The FERC administers regulations in 18 CFR 153 regarding importation of natural gas through newly constructed facilities. If you are intending this type of import, you should contact the FERC Office of Pipeline and Producer Regulation (see addresses at end of this chapter). In addition to federal requirements, you have the responsibility for obtaining any licenses required by the country of export. For more information, contact the relevant agency.

Petroleum Products. Customs regulations regarding import of petroleum and petroleum products are found in 19 CFR 151, Subpart C. This subpart details the information required on each petroleum entry summary, Customs controls on unloading and measuring bulk petroleum shipments, requirements for storage tanks, and options for using storage tanks bonded as warehouses for bulk shipments. The U.S. Department of Energy (DOE) also regulates petroleum importation and may require an oil import license fee. In general, import licensing is no longer required for these commodities, except for Canadian crude oils entered under a bilateral trade agreement (see Canadian crude oil below). For more information, contact DOE (see addresses at end of this chapter).

Entry Summary. On the entry summary for petroleum or petroleum products in bulk, you must show the API gravity at 600F, in accordance with the current edition of the ASTM-IP Petroleum Measurement Tables (American Edition), approved by the American Society for Testing and Materials. The appropriate unabridged table must be used in the reduction of volume to 600F. If the exact volumetric quantity cannot be determined in advance, the entry summary may be made for "___ barrels, more or less," but in no case may the estimate vary by more than 3% from the gross quantity unladen. The term "barrels" is defined in Chapter 27, Additional U.S. Note 7, HTSUS. You must also show the required information on your entry summary permit if the entry summary is filed at the time of entry, and on each entry summary continuation sheet regardless of when your entry summary is filed.

Sampling and Metering. Each district director of Customs establishes checks and controls on the unlading and measurement of petroleum and petroleum products imported in bulk by any means. One of the following methods will be used: 1) Customs-approved metering and sampling installations provided by the importer; 2) shore tank gauging; or 3) weighing for trucks and railroad cars. Importer-provided metering and sampling installations are approved by Customs on a case-by-case basis. If you wish to seek approval for a metering and sampling installation, you must send a complete description of the installation to the district director of the intended port of entry. Approved installations are subject to periodic verification by Customs. Once Customs has approved your installation, you may not modify it without first obtaining Customs approval.

Canadian Crude Oil. Crude petroleum oils, crude bituminous mineral oils, and reconstituted crude petroleum produced in Canada may be admitted free of duty. For duty-free treatment of Canadian crude oils, you must submit with your entry a certificate establishing that 1) the oil is imported pursuant to a commercial exchange agreement between U.S. and Canadian refiners that has been approved by the U.S. Secretary of Energy; 2) the oil is imported under import license issued by the Secretary of Energy; 3) an equivalent amount of domestic or duty-paid foreign crude oil, on which you have executed a written waiver of drawback, has been exported to Canada under an export license and previously has not been used to effect the duty-free entry of like Canadian products; and 4) an export license has been issued by the Secretary of Commerce for the oil exported to Canada.

The provisions above may be applied to: 1) liquidated or reliquidated entries if the required certification is filed with the district director at the port where the original entry was made on or before the 180th day after the date of entry; and 2) articles entered or withdrawn from storage for consumption pursuant to a commercial exchange agreement. Verification of the quantities of crude oil exported to or imported from Canada under such a commercial exchange agreement must be made in accordance with import verification provided in 19 CFR 151, Subpart C. Details are in 19 CFR 10.179. For more information on importation of Canadian crude, contact U.S. Customs or the DOE.

Coal. Customs distinguishes between two types of coal: anthracite and bituminous. Anthracite (HTSUS 2701.11) is coal having a volatile matter limit on a dry mineral-matter-free basis not exceeding 14%. Bituminous coal (HTSUS 2701.12) is coal having a volatile matter limit on a dry mineral-matter-free basis exceeding 14% and a calorific value limit on a moist, mineral-matter-free basis equal to or greater than 5,833 kcal/kg.

Electrical Energy. Electrical energy is subject to regulations prescribed by the Secretary of the Treasury, instead of the entry requirements for imported merchandise under the Tariff Act (19 USC 1484). An exclusion is made for electrical energy transmitted as a medium of communication.

FDA-Regulated Products. Imports of petroleum jelly, white mineral oil, and paraffin wax are regulated by the FDA. For all of these products, you must submit FDA entry notification, **Form FD701**, to U.S. Customs. For an annotated diagram of FDA import procedures refer to the "Foods" appendix on page 808. If you are interested in importing one of these products, you should ascertain its regulatory status by contacting the FDA (see addresses at end of this chapter).

Toxic or Hazardous Substances. Mineral fuels, oils, and waxes and bituminous substances listed as hazardous or toxic substances and imported in bulk, as articles, or as part of a mixture must be in compliance with toxic and hazardous substance regulations of the EPA and DOT. These include packaging, shipping, marking, and labeling requirements.

You must file a TSCA certification of compliance or exemption at the time you make the entry at Customs. The certification may be in the form of a typed or stamped statement on an appropriate entry document or commercial invoice or a preprinted attachment to such entry document or invoice. You may sign the certificate by means of an authorized facsimile signature. If your entry is electronically processed, the certification will be in the form of a Certification Code, which is part of the Automated Broker Interface (ABI) transmission. Customs will not release your shipment without proper certification.

If you will be importing several or regular shipments, you should ask the appropriate Customs district director to authorize your use of a blanket certification. If you receive such authorization, you must include on the commercial invoice or entry document for each shipment a statement that the blanket certification is on file and that it is incorporated by reference. This statement need not be signed. The blanket certification is valid for one calendar year, is subject to renewal, and may be revoked at any time for cause.

Articles Exclusion. If you are importing products that are classified as hazardous substances but are part of articles, you are subject to TSCA certification requirements only if certification for your product is specifically required by a rule or order promulgated under the TSCA. No specific rules have been adopted at this time. An "article" is a manufactured item 1) that is formed into a specific shape or design during manufacture, 2) that has end-use functions dependent on the shape or design during end use, and 3) that during the end use, does not change in its chemical composition or that changes only for a noncommercial purpose separate from the article and only as allowed by law (19 CFR 12.120(2)). Fluids and particles are not articles, regardless of shape or design.

Shipment Detention. A shipment containing inorganic chemicals will be detained at the U.S. port of arrival (or entry if same), at your risk and expense, if: 1) it contains banned substances (15 USC 2604, 2605); or 2) it contains substances ordered seized because of imminent hazard (15 USC 2606). Further detention will occur at the port of entry, again at your risk and expense, if: 1) the EPA administrator or Customs district director has reasonable grounds to believe the shipment is not in compliance with the TSCA; or 2) you do not provide proper TSCA certification.

If your shipment is detained, it will be held by Customs for no more than 48 hours. It will then be turned over to the EPA administrator, unless you have arranged to release it in bond. You must either bring it into TSCA compliance or reexport it within the earlier of 90 days after notice of detention or 30 days of demand for redelivery. Customs may grant an extension if failure to comply or reexport is the result of delays in EPA or Customs procedures. If you fail to comply or reexport within the time allowed, the EPA administrator is authorized to have the shipment stored or disposed of at your expense.

Hazardous Consumer Products. Under the FHSA, a mineral fuel, oil, wax, or bituminous substance intended for the consumer market is a hazardous substance if it is flammable, combustible, or has the potential to cause substantial personal injury during, or as a proximate result of, any customary or reasonably foreseeable handling or use. The CPSC does not require permits, special invoicing, limited entry, licenses, or any special approval process for importing hazardous consumer products into the U.S. However, if you are importing these types of products, you are responsible for ensuring that they meet all applicable FHSA and CPSA requirements. There are detailed regulations regarding testing and labeling of hazardous products. The Commission's enforcement posture regarding compliance with labeling and product safety standards changes as new facts become available. Contact the CPSC (see addresses at end of this chapter) for specific requirements on the consumer product you are considering importing.

Substantial Product Hazard Reports. Defect-reporting is required for products covered under the CPSA. The law requires every manufacturer, distributor, or retailer of such products, who obtains information that reasonably supports the conclusion that such products fail to comply with an applicable consumer product safety rule, or contain a defect that could create a substantial product hazard, to immediately inform the CPSC of the potential violation or defect. A firm's willful failure to make a Substantial Product Hazard Report can result in litigation by the CPSC.

Customs Classification

For customs purposes, mineral fuels, oils, and waxes and bituminous substances, are classified under Chapter 27 of the HTSUS. This chapter is broken into major headings, which are further divided into subheadings, and often sub-subheadings, each of which has its own HTSUS classification number. For example, the HTSUS number for montan wax is 2712.90.10, indicating it is a sub-subcategory of other mineral waxes (2712.90.00), which is a subcategory of the major heading, petroleum jelly, paraffin wax, etc. (2712.00.00). There are 16 major headings within Chapter 27.

2701—Coal; briquettes, ovoids, and similar solid fuels manufactured from coal

2702—Lignite, whether or not agglomerated, excluding jet

2703—Peat (including peat litter), whether or not agglomerated

2704—Coke and semicoke of coal, if lignite or of peat, whether or not agglomerated; retort carbon

2705—Coal gas, water gas, producer gas, and similar gases, other than petroleum gases and other gaseous hydrocarbons

2706—Tars distilled from coal, from lignite, or from peat, and other mineral tars, whether or not dehydrated or partially distilled, including reconstituted tars

2707—Oils and other products of the distillation of high temperature coal tar; similar products in which the weight of the aromatic constituents exceeds that of the nonaromatic constituents

2708—Pitch and pitch coke, obtained from coal tar or other mineral tars

2709—Petroleum oils and oils obtained from bituminous minerals, crude

2710—Petroleum oils and oils obtained from bituminous minerals, other than crude; preparations not otherwise specified or included, containing by weight 70% or more of petroleum oils or of oils obtained from bituminous minerals, these oils being the basic constituents of the preparations

2711—Petroleum gases and other gaseous hydrocarbons

2712—Petroleum jelly; paraffin wax, microcrystalline petroleum wax, slack wax, ozokerite, lignite wax, peat wax, other mineral waxes, and similar products obtained by synthesis or by other processes, whether or not colored

2713—Petroleum coke, petroleum bitumen, and other residues of petroleum oils or of oils obtained from bituminous minerals

2714—Bitumen and asphalt, natural; bituminous or oil shale and tar sands; asphaltites and asphaltic rocks

2715—Bituminous mixtures based on natural asphalt, on natural bitumen, on petroleum bitumen, on mineral tar, or on mineral tar pitch (for example, bituminous mastics, cut-backs)

2716—Electrical energy

For more details regarding classifications of the specific product you are interested in importing, consult a customs broker, the appropriate commodity specialist at your nearest customs port, or the HTSUS. HTSUS is available for purchase from the U.S. Government Printing Office (see addresses at end of this chapter), and may be found in larger public libraries. Refer to "Classification—Liquidation" on page 207 for a general discussion of customs classification.

Sample Import Duties

Import duties will vary depending on the HTSUS classification of your product. Therefore, to determine the correct amount of duties, your product must be properly classified under the HTSUS. The following sample duties are taken from the duty listings for HTSUS Chapter 27 products.

Coal (2701.00.00): free; phenols (2707.60.00): 2.9 cents/kg plus 12.5%; crude petroleum oils and oils from bituminous minerals testing under 25 degrees API (2709.00.10): 5.25 cents/barrel; natural gas, propane, butanes, and other petroleum and hydrocarbon gases (2711): free; petroleum jelly, paraffin wax, and other mineral waxes (2712): free; petroleum coke, not calcined (2713.11.00): free; petroleum coke, calcined (2713.12.00): 3%; electrical energy (2716.00.00): free.

Special Provisions. Additional duties may be imposed on motor fuels (HTSUS 2710.00.15) and motor fuel blending stock (HTSUS 2710.00.18). Refer to HTSUS 9901.00.50 (ethyl alcohol as fuel or for producing fuel), 9901.00.52 (ethyl tertiary-butyl ether).

Entry and Documentation

The entry of merchandise is a two-part process consisting of 1) filing the documentation necessary to determine whether merchandise may be released from Customs custody, and 2) filing the documents that contain information for duty assessment and statistical purposes. In certain instances, all documents must be filed and accepted by Customs prior to release of the goods. Unless you have been granted an extension, you must file entry documents at a location specified by the district or area director within five working days of your shipment's date of arrival at a U.S. port of entry. These include a number of standard documents required by Customs for any entry, and:

- Import certificate (duty-free classification of Canadian crude oils)
- U.S. Customs TSCA Certification (hazardous materials)
- DOE or FERC authorization (natural gas)
- FDA Importers Entry Notice, **Form FD701**, as required

After you present the entry, Customs may examine your shipment or may waive examination. The shipment is then released provided no legal or regulatory violations have been noted. You must then file entry summary documentation and deposit estimated duties at a designated customhouse within 10 working days of your shipment's release. For a detailed description of entry procedures, standard documentation, and informal entry, refer to "Entry Process" on page 182.

Entry Invoice. The entry invoice should specify the use and the Chemical Abstracts Service (CAS) number of the chemical compounds in your shipment.

Prohibitions and Restrictions

Hazardous Consumer Products. Importation of any consumer product that has been declared a banned hazardous substance by a rule under the CPSA is prohibited. Any product considered hazardous and not labeled according to provisions of the FHSA is a misbranded hazardous substance and is an illegal import. Certain hazardous substances listed in the FHSA and in regulations promulgated by the CPSC are completely banned from importation. A shipment of consumer products cannot be imported if it poses an imminent hazard. See 15 USC 1261, 2604-2606; 16 CFR 1500.265-1500.272.

The CPSC may detain your shipment of hazardous substances and take samples for testing to determine compliance with the FHSA. If your shipment is found to contain banned hazardous substances, it will be refused admission and will be destroyed if not exported within 90 days of the date of refusal notice. If it is found to contain misbranded hazardous substances, you may make arrangements to bring it into conformance through relabeling. For complete details regarding testing, labeling, and safety regulations for hazardous products, contact the CPSC (see addresses at end of this chapter).

Marking and Labeling Requirements

Hazardous Substances. A shipment of products containing substances classified as hazardous (49 CFR 172) must comply with the marking and labeling regulations adopted by the EPA (46 CFR 147.30) and the DOT (49 CFR 171 et seq.).

Flammable Products. Any flammable product must be conspicuously and appropriately labeled according to regulations under FHSA. The labeling must distinguish between "extremely flammable," "flammable," and "combustible," and must accurately reflect the form of the product (liquid, solid, or other) or the contents of a self-pressurized container. The label must appear on the immediate container intended for the end user. If the product is being shipped in bulk, the labeling must be affixed to the bulk container in a conspicuous place. Any accompanying printed material that has instructions for use must also bear the same warning in a conspicuous place.

Labeling for a flammable product must contain the following information: 1) name and place of business of the manufacturer, packer, distributor, or seller; 2) common or usual name (or chemical name if there is no common name) of the hazardous substance, or of each component that contributes substantially to its hazard; 3) the word "DANGER" on extremely flammable substances; 4) the word "CAUTION" or "WARNING" on flammable or combustible substances; 5) an affirmative statement of the principle hazard or hazards (i.e. "flammable," "extremely flammable," or "combustible"); 6) precautionary measures describing the action to be followed or avoided; 7) instruction, if necessary, for first-aid treatment; 8) instructions for handling and storage of packages that require special care in handling and storage; 9) the statement "Keep Out of Reach of Children" or its practical equivalent. For more information, contact the CPSC (see addresses at end of this chapter).

For a general discussion of U.S. Customs marking and labeling requirements, refer to "Marking: Country of Origin" on page 215 and "Special Marking Requirements" on page 217.

Shipping Considerations

You will need to ensure that your goods are packaged and shipped with care so that they pass smoothly through Customs and arrive in good condition. You are responsible for ensuring that the shipment is in compliance with all applicable government regulations for packaging and shipping. In most instances, you should not leave these arrangements solely to the discretion of your supplier. Careful preparation of the cargo and selection of the mode of transport can be essential to a cost-effective, timely delivery of undamaged goods. We strongly advise you to consult your shipping representative, insurance agent, or freight broker for advice on packing and shipping. Refer also to the major tab section "Packing/Shipping/Insurance" for a general discussion of packing and shipping.

Mineral fuels, oils, and waxes and bituminous substances, may be shipped in bulk, bags, tanks, bottles, or other types of containers, depending on the type of product and whether it is prepackaged. General considerations include protection from contamination, weather, and pests. If a product must be kept in a sanitary environment, all tables, utensils, platforms, and devices used for moving or handling the product, the compartments in which it is stowed while being transported will need to be maintained in a sanitary condition. For liquid shipments, venting and vapor collection systems may be required. Safety precautions should also be implemented as required to protect against breakage, spillage, corrosion of containers, and combustion. Containers should be constructed so as to be safe for handling during transport.

Mineral and chemical products. Mineral products in particular may have to be shipped in pressurized, ventilated, and temperature-and vapor-controlled enclosures. Solid mineral and chemical products that are listed as hazardous substances (49 CFR 172 appendix) may be transported in bulk only on compliance with Coast Guard notification procedures, shipping permit requirements, and complex transportation regulations (46 CFR 148). All hazardous substances must be packaged and transported in accordance with DOT regulations (49 CFR 171 et seq.).

Publications Available

The following publication explains the FDA requirements for importing mineral fuels, oils, and waxes. It is published by the FDA and is available on request from FDA headquarters (see addresses at end of this chapter).

Requirements of Laws and Regulations Enforced by the U.S. Food and Drug Administration

The following publications may be relevant to the importation of toxic or hazardous mineral fuels, oils, and waxes:

Toxic Substances Control Act: A Guide for Chemical Importers/Exporters (published by EPA).

TSCA Chemical Substance Inventory (1985 edition) (Doc. Code S/N 055-000-00254-1) $161.00 U.S. and Canada; $201.21 all other countries.

Supplement to TSCA Chemical Substances Inventory (1990) (Doc. Code S/N 055-000-00361-1) $15.00 U.S.; $18.75 Canada and all other countries.

These publications and the *Harmonized Tariff Schedule of the United States* (HTSUS) are available from:

Government Printing Office (GPO)
Superintendent of Documents
Washington, DC 20402
(202) 512-1800 (Order line)
(202) 512-0000 (General)

The USGPO also has copies of specific laws available for purchase. The USGPO accepts credit card orders over the phone, as well as mail orders paid by credit card, a check drawn on a U.S. bank, or an international money order.

Relevant Government Agencies

Address your questions regarding CPSC requirements for mineral fuels, oils, and waxes and bituminous substances to:

U.S. Consumer Product Safety Commission (CPSC)
Office of Compliance
Division of Regulatory Management
5401 Westbard Avenue
Bethesda, MD 20207
(301) 504-0400

Address your inquiries regarding TSCA and EPA requirements for importation of mineral fuels, oils, and waxes and bituminous substances to:

Environmental Protection Agency (EPA)
TSCA System Information
EPA 7408, OPPT
401 M Street SW
Washington, DC 20460
(202) 554-1404 (TSCA Information Hotline)

Address your questions regarding transportation of hazardous substances to:

U.S. Department of Transportation (DOT)
Research and Special Programs Administration
Office of Hazardous Materials Standards
400 7th St. SW
Washington, DC 20590
(202) 366-4488

Address your questions regarding importation of natural gas through existing facilities to:

Department of Energy
Fuels Program
1000 Independence Ave. SW
Washington, DC 20585
(202) 586-9482

Address your questions regarding importation of natural gas involving the construction of new facilities to:

Federal Energy Regulatory Commission (FERC)
Office of Pipeline and Producer Regulation
825 North Capitol Street, NE
Washington, DC 20426
(202) 208-0700

Address your questions regarding the importation of mineral fuels, oils, and waxes and bituminous substances to the district or port director of Customs for you area. For addresses refer to"U.S. Customs District Offices" on page 62 or contact:

U.S. Customs Service
1301 Constitution Ave. NW
Washington, DC 20229
(202) 927-6724 (Information)
(202) 927-1000 (General)

Laws and Regulations

The following laws and regulations may be relevant to the importation of mineral fuels, oils, and waxes and bituminous substances. The laws are contained in the United States Code (USC), and the regulations are published in the Code of Federal Regulations (CFR), both of which are available at larger public and law libraries. Copies of specific laws and regulations may be purchased from the U.S. Government Printing Office (address above).

15 USC 717 et seq.
The Natural Gas Act
This Act regulates the transport and sale of natural gas in interstate and foreign commerce. Section 717b prohibits the exportation or importation of natural gas without authorization from the Federal Energy Regulatory Commission (FERC).

18 CFR 152, 153
Regulations of FERC on Natural Gas
These regulations specify the requirements and procedures for obtaining authorization for the import or export of natural gas. Customs enforces these provisions.

15 USC 784
Federal Energy Administration Act
Customs ensures that petroleum imports comply with licensing requirements.

33 USC 1321, 1901 et seq.
Act to Prevent Pollution From Ships
This Act prohibits the discharge of oil or hazardous substances into or on the navigable waters of the U.S. and authorizes Customs to withhold clearance of any vessel not in compliance.

19 CFR 4.66b, 4.66c, 33 CFR 153.105
Regulations on Vessel Clearance
These regulations require vessels to be in compliance with the oil and hazardous substance discharge laws before Customs will grant clearance from the port.

15 USC 1263
Consumer Product Safety Act (CPSA)
This Act sets standards for the manufacturing, processing, and labeling of products sold to U.S. consumers.

15 USC 2601 et seq.
Toxic Substances Control Act (TSCA)
This Act authorizes the EPA to determine whether a substance is harmful and to restrict importation, sale, and use of such substances.

19 CFR 12.118 et seq.
Regulations on Toxic Substances Control
These regulations require importers of chemical substances imported in bulk or as part of a mixture to certify to Customs that the shipment complies with the TSCA or is not subject to that Act.

15 USC 1261
Federal Hazardous Substances Act (FHSA)
This Act controls the importation of hazardous substances, sets forth prohibited imports, and authorizes various agencies to promulgate labeling, marking, and transport requirements.

49 CFR 170 et seq.
Regulations on Hazardous Materials
These regulations list all substances deemed hazardous and provide transport, marking, labeling, safety, and emergency response rules.

46 CFR 147.30
Regulations on Labeling of Hazardous Materials
This regulation requires the labeling of containers of hazardous substances and specifies the label contents.

46 CFR 148 et seq.
Regulations on Carriage of Solid Hazardous Materials in Bulk
These regulations govern the transport of solid hazardous substances in bulk, including reporting, permitting, loading, stowing, and shipping requirements.

16 CFR 1500 et seq.
Regulations on Hazardous Substances Safety Standards
These regulations set standards for processing, manufacturing, importing, and labeling all substances classified as hazardous that are to be sold to U.S. consumers.

Principal Exporting Countries

The following listing includes samples of the main supplier nations of the products of this chapter. It is organized by HTSUS major heading. (Refer to "Customs Classification" above for the product codes.) Countries are listed in rank order of the value of products imported to the U.S. Statistics represent customs value entries for 1993 from the Bureau of Census, U.S. Department of Commerce.

2701—Colombia, Venezuela, Indonesia, Canada, Australia, South Africa, New Zealand, Swaziland, China, Mexico

2702—Canada

2703—Canada, Finland, Ireland, Germany, Norway, New Zealand, Vatican City

2704—Japan, Australia, Canada, South Africa, Venezuela, China

2705—Canada

2706—Mexico, Canada, Poland, Ukraine, Finland, Sweden, France, Taiwan, Netherlands

2707—Brazil, Canada, Mexico, South Africa, Netherlands, United Kingdom, Spain, Germany, South Korea, France

2708—Japan, South Korea, China, Germany, South Africa, Canada, Switzerland, Russia, Belgium, Netherlands

2709—Saudi Arabia, Canada, Nigeria, Venezuela, Mexico, United Kingdom, Angola, Kuwait, Colombia, Gabon

2710—Venezuela, Canada, Algeria, Mexico, Aruba, Saudi Arabia, Brazil, Italy, Netherlands Antilles, United Kingdom

2711—Canada, Algeria, Saudi Arabia, Mexico, United Kingdom, South Korea, Kuwait, Venezuela, Turkey, Australia

2712—Canada, Germany, Japan, South Africa, China, Netherlands, Hungary, Mexico, Brazil, Egypt

2713—Canada, Argentina, Japan, Brazil, China, Venezuela, Germany, France, Spain, Aruba

2714—Venezuela, Spain, Netherlands Antilles, Canada, Mexico, Aruba, Trinidad and Tobago, Vatican City, United Kingdom, Switzerland

2715—Canada, Venezuela, United Kingdom, France, Germany, Mexico, Trinidad and Tobago, Belgium, Taiwan, Japan

2716—Canada

Chapter 28: Inorganic Chemicals*

Full title: Inorganic Chemicals; Organic or Inorganic Compounds of Precious Metals, of Rare-Earth Metals, of Radioactive Elements, or of Isotopes

This chapter relates to the importation of separate inorganic chemical elements and chemically defined compounds, which are classified under Chapter 28 of the Harmonized Tariff Schedule of the United States (HTSUS). Specifically, it includes inorganic chemical elements; inorganic acids; nonmetal oxygen, halogen, and sulfur compounds; metal oxides, hydroxides, and peroxides; colloidal and other compounds of precious metal; certain radioactive chemicals; and phosphides, carbides, hydrides, nitrides, azides, silicides, and borides.

The importation of organic chemical substances is covered in related Commodity Index Chapter 29. If you are interested in importing a product that is not in the form of a bulk chemical, you should read the chapters that pertain to the specific type of product. For importing requirements related to mineral products, see Chapters 25 through 27. The importation of chemical fertilizers is covered in Chapter 31, and inorganic products used as luminophores are in Chapter 32. Chapter 38 discusses artificial graphite, fire-extinguishing grenades and charges, ink removers, and non-optical cultured crystals of halides of alkali or alkaline-earth metals. Chapter 71 covers the importation of precious and semiprecious stones, metals, and metal alloys. Refer to Chapters 72 through 83 if you are importing base metals and related products. Nuclear reactors and related equipment are classified within Chapter 84. Requirements for importing optical elements are in Chapter 90.

Key Factors

The key factors in the importation of inorganic chemical substances are:

- Compliance with U.S. Environmental Protection Agency (EPA) requirements under the Toxic Substances Control Act (TSCA) (if the product is a hazardous substance)
- Compliance with U.S. Department of Transportation (DOT) regulations for transport of hazardous cargo (if the product is a hazardous substance)
- Compliance with Nuclear Regulatory Commission (NRC) requirements, including NRC import authorization (if the product is radioactive)

*IMPORTANT: Read the Commodity Index Introduction. It is the essential framework for understanding this chapter.

Although most importers use the services of a licensed customs broker in making their entries, and we recommend this practice, you should be aware of the regulatory, entry, and documentation issues involved in importing your product. You, as importer, are ultimately responsible for the fulfillment of any legal requirements applicable to your shipment.

General Considerations

Regulatory Agencies. The EPA, under authority of the TSCA, imposes certain controls on the importation of inorganic chemicals that contain toxic substances. The TSCA defines a toxic substance as any substance determined to present the possibility of an unreasonable risk of injury to health and the environment. The DOT enforces regulations for transporting hazardous cargo. Substances are deemed hazardous if listed in DOT transport regulations (49 CFR 172 appendix).

Toxic and Hazardous Substances. Inorganic chemicals imported in bulk, as articles, or as part of a mixture must be in compliance with toxic and hazardous substance regulations of the EPA and DOT. These include packaging, shipping, marking, and labeling requirements. Refer to "Laws and Regulations" below.

In addition, all inorganic chemical products are subject to the U.S. Customs Service TSCA Import Certification Rule (19 CFR 12.118 et seq.). If you import these products, you must sign one of the following statements: "I certify that all chemical substances in this shipment comply with all applicable rules or orders under TSCA and that I am not offering a chemical substance for entry in violation of TSCA or any applicable rule or order thereunder" or "I certify that all chemicals in this shipment are not subject to TSCA."

You must file this TSCA certification of compliance or exemption at the time you make the entry at Customs. The certification may be in the form of a typed or stamped statement on an appropriate entry document or commercial invoice or a preprinted attachment to such entry document or invoice. You may sign the certificate by means of an authorized facsimile signature. If your entry is electronically processed, the certification will be in the form of a Certification Code, which is part of the Automated Broker Interface (ABI) transmission. Customs will not release your shipment without proper certification.

If you will be importing several or regular shipments, you should ask the appropriate Customs district director to authorize your use of a blanket certification. If you receive such authorization, you must include on the commercial invoice or entry document for each shipment a statement that the blanket certification is on file and that it is incorporated by reference. This statement need not be signed. The blanket certification is valid for one calendar year, is subject to renewal, and may be revoked at any time for cause.

In filling out TSCA forms and Customs entry documents, you should provide the Chemical Abstracts Service (CAS) number for each chemical in the shipment. These CAS numbers are given in the appendix to the HTSUS. You are not required to include the CAS number, but Customs will be able to process your shipment more quickly if you give this number.

Articles Exclusion. If you are importing products that are classified as hazardous substances but are part of articles, you are subject to TSCA certification requirements only if certification for your product is specifically required by a rule or order promulgated under the TSCA. No specific rules have been adopted at this time. An "article" is a manufactured item 1) that is formed into a specific shape or design during manufacture, 2) that has end-use functions dependent on the shape or design during end use, and 3) that during the end use, does not change in its chemical composition or that changes only for a noncommercial purpose separate from the article and only as allowed by law (19 CFR 12.120(2)). Fluids and particles are not articles, regardless of shape or design.

Shipment Detention. A shipment containing inorganic chemicals will be detained at the U.S. port of arrival (or entry if same), at your risk and expense, if: 1) it contains banned chemical substances (15 USC 2604, 2605); or 2) it contains chemical substances ordered seized because of imminent hazard (15 USC 2606). Further detention will occur at the port of entry, again at your risk and expense, if: 1) the EPA administrator or Customs district director has reasonable grounds to believe the shipment is not in compliance with the TSCA; or 2) you do not provide proper TSCA certification.

If your shipment is detained, it will be held by Customs for no more than 48 hours. It will then be turned over to the EPA administrator, unless you have arranged to release it in bond. You must either bring it into TSCA compliance or reexport it within the earlier of 90 days after notice of detention or 30 days of demand for redelivery. Customs may grant an extension if failure to comply or reexport is the result of delays in EPA or Customs procedures. If you fail to comply or reexport within the time allowed, the EPA administrator is authorized to have the shipment stored or disposed of at your expense.

Radioactive Compounds. Many radioisotopes and all forms of uranium, thorium, and plutonium imported into the U.S. are subject to the regulations of the NRC in addition to import regulations imposed by any other U.S. agency. Authority to import these commodities, or articles containing these commodities, is granted by the NRC.

To comply with NRC requirements, the importer must be aware of the identity and amount of all NRC-controlled radioisotopes or uranium, thorium, and plutonium being imported into the U.S. To assure passage through Customs, the importer must demonstrate to U.S. Customs that the NRC has authorized import of the controlled commodity. The authority cited may be the number of a specific or general license, or the specific section of an NRC regulation that allows a general license or an exemption to the regulations. A foreign exporter may save time for a prospective importer by furnishing complete information about the presence of NRC-controlled commodities in the imported shipment.

Customs Classification

For customs purposes, inorganic chemical substances are classified under Chapter 28 of the HTSUS. This chapter is broken into major headings, which are further divided into subheadings, and often sub-subheadings, each of which has its own HTSUS classification number. For example, the HTSUS number for fluorine is 2801.30.10, indicating it is a sub-subcategory of fluorine and bromine (2801.30.00), which is a subcategory of the major heading, fluorine, chlorine, bromine, and iodine (2801.00.00). There are 51 major headings within Chapter 28.

2801—Fluorine, chlorine, bromine, and iodine

2802—Sulfur, sublimed or precipitated; colloidal sulfur

2803—Carbon (carbon blacks and other forms of carbon not elsewhere specified or included)

2804—Hydrogen, rare gases, and other nonmetals

2805—Alkali or alkaline-earth metals; rare-earth metals, scandium, and yttrium, whether or not intermixed or interalloyed; mercury

2806—Hydrogen chloride (Hydrochloric acid); chlorosulfuric acid

2807—Sulfuric acid; oleum

2808—Nitric acid; sulfonitric acids

2809—Diphosphorus pentaoxide; phosphoric acid and polyphosphoric acids

2810—Oxides of boron; boric acids

2811—Other inorganic acids and oxygen compounds of nonmetals

2812—Halides and halide oxides of nonmetals

2813—Sulfides of nonmetals; and commercial phosphorus trisulfide

2814—Ammonia, anhydrous or in aqueous solution

2815—Sodium hydroxide (Caustic soda); potassium hydroxide (Caustic potash); peroxides of sodium or potassium

2816—Hydroxide and peroxide of magnesium; oxides, hydroxides, and peroxides of strontium and barium

2817—Zinc oxide; zinc peroxide

2818—Artificial corundum, whether or not chemically defined; aluminum oxide; aluminum hydroxide

2819—Chromium oxides and hydroxides

2820—Manganese oxides

2821—Iron oxides and hydroxides; earth colors containing 70% or more by weight of combined iron evaluated as Fe_2O_3

2822—Cobalt oxides and hydroxides; commercial cobalt oxides

2823—Titanium oxides

2824—Lead oxides; red lead and orange lead

2825—Hydrazine and hydroxylamine and their inorganic salts; other inorganic bases; other metal oxides, hydroxides and peroxides

2826—Fluorides; fluorosilicates, fluoroaluminates, and other complex fluorine salts

2827—Chlorides, chloride oxides, and chloride hydroxides; bromides and bromide oxides; iodides and iodide oxides

2828—Hypochlorites; commercial calcium hypochlorite; chlorites; hypobromites

2829—Chlorates and perchlorates; bromates and perbromates; iodates and periodates

2830—Sulfides; polysulfides

2831—Dithionites and sulfoxylates

2832—Sulfites; thiosulfates

2833—Sulfates; alums; peroxosulfates (persulfates)

2834—Nitrites; nitrates

2835—Phosphinates (hypophosphites), phosphonates (phosphites), phosphates, and polyphosphates

2836—Carbonates; peroxocarbonates (percarbonates); commercial ammonium carbonate containing ammonium carbamate

2837—Cyanides, cyanide oxides, and complex cyanides

2838—Fulminates, cyanates, and thiocyanates

2839—Silicates; commercial alkali metal silicates

2840—Borates; peroxoborates (perborates)

2841—Salts of oxometallic or peroxometallic acids

2842—Other salts of inorganic acids or peroxoacids, excluding azides

2843—Colloidal precious metals; inorganic or organic compounds of precious metals, whether or not chemically defined; amalgams of precious metals

2844—Radioactive chemical elements and radioactive isotopes (including the fissile or fertile chemical elements and isotopes) and their compounds; mixtures and residues containing these products

2845—Isotopes other than those of heading 2844; compounds, inorganic or organic, of such isotopes, whether or not chemically defined

2846—Compounds, inorganic or organic, of rare-earth metals, of yttrium or of scandium, or of mixtures of these metals

2847—Hydrogen peroxide, whether or not solidified with urea

2848—Phosphides, whether or not chemically defined, excluding ferrophosphorus

2849—Carbides, whether or not chemically defined

2850—Hydrides, nitrides, azides, silicides, and borides, whether or not chemically defined, other than compounds which are also carbides of heading 2849

2851—Other inorganic compounds (including distilled or conductivity water and water of similar purity); liquid air (whether or not rare gases have been removed); compressed air; amalgams, other than amalgams of precious metals

For more details regarding classifications of the specific product you are interested in importing, consult a customs broker, the appropriate commodity specialist at your nearest customs port, or the HTSUS. HTSUS is available for purchase from the U.S. Government Printing Office (see addresses at end of this chapter), and may be found in larger public libraries. Refer to "Classification—Liquidation" on page 207 for a general discussion of customs classification.

Sample Import Duties

Import duties will vary depending on the HTSUS classification of your product. Therefore, to determine the correct amount of duties, your product must be properly classified under the HTSUS. The following sample duties are taken from the duty listings for HTSUS Chapter 28 products.

Chlorine (2801.10.00): free; iodine (2801.20.00): free; fluorine (2801.30.10): 3.7%; sulfur (2802.00.00): free; carbon black (2803.00.00): free; sodium (2805.11.00): 5.3%; calcium (2805.21.00): 3%; mercury (2805.40.00): 16.5 cents/kg; nitric acid (2808.00.00): free; synthetic silica gel (2811.22.10): 3.7%; phosphorus pentachloride (2812.10.10): free; iron oxides (2821.10.00): 3.7%; tungsten oxides (2825.90.30): 10%; sodium nitrates (2834.10.10): 8.6%; uranium metal (2844.10.10): 5%; uranium compounds (2844.10.20): free; hydrogen peroxide (2847.00.00): 3.7%; calcium carbide (2849.10.00): 1.8%.

Entry and Documentation

The entry of merchandise is a two-part process consisting of 1) filing the documents necessary to determine whether merchandise may be released from Customs custody and 2) filing the documents that contain information for duty assessment and statistical purposes. In certain instances, all documents must be filed and accepted by Customs prior to release of the goods. Unless you have been granted an extension, you must file entry documents at a location specified by the district or area director within five working days of your shipment's date of arrival at a U.S. port of entry. These include a number of standard documents required by Customs for any entry, and:

- U.S. Customs TSCA Certification when required
- Documentation of NRC import authorization, if required

After you present the entry, Customs may examine your shipment, or may waive examination. The shipment is then released, provided no legal or regulatory violations have been noted. You must then file entry summary documentation and deposit estimated duties at a designated customhouse within 10 working days of your shipment's release. For a detailed description of entry procedures, standard documentation, and informal entry, refer to "Entry Process" on page 182.

Entry Invoice. Specify the use and Chemical Abstracts Service (CAS) number of the inorganic chemical compounds included in the shipment.

Prohibitions and Restrictions

Importation of inorganic chemicals that are considered hazardous substances is prohibited if the chemicals are misbranded. Certain hazardous substances listed in the FHSA and in regulations promulgated by the Consumer Product Safety Commission (CPSC) are completely banned from importation. A shipment of an inorganic chemical cannot be imported if it poses an imminent hazard. See 15 USC 1261, 2604-2606; 16 CFR 1500.265-1500.272.

Marking and Labeling Requirements

A shipment of any products containing inorganic chemicals that are classified as hazardous substances (49 CFR 172) must comply with the marking and labeling regulations adopted by the EPA (46 CFR 147.30) and the DOT (49 CFR 171 et seq.).

For a general discussion of U.S. Customs marking and labeling requirements, see "Marking: Country of Origin" on page 215 and "Special Marking Requirements" on page 217.

Shipping Considerations

You will need to ensure that your goods are packaged and shipped with care so that they pass smoothly through Customs and arrive in good condition. You are responsible for ensuring that the shipment is in compliance with all applicable government regulations for packaging and shipping. In most instances, you should not leave these arrangements solely to the discretion of your supplier. Careful preparation of the cargo and selection of the mode of transport can be essential to a cost-effective, timely delivery of undamaged goods. We strongly advise you to consult your shipping representative, insurance agent, or freight broker for advice on packing and shipping. Refer also to the major tab section "Packing/Shipping/Insurance" for a general discussion of packing and shipping.

Inorganic chemicals may be shipped in bulk, bags, bottles, crates, or other types of containers, depending on the type of product and whether it is prepackaged. General considerations include protection from contamination, weather, and pests. For liquid shipments, venting and vapor collection systems may be required. Safety precautions should also be implemented as required to protect against breakage, spillage, corrosion of containers, combustion, and explosion. Containers should be constructed so as to be safe for handling during transport.

Chemical products in particular may have to be shipped in pressurized, ventilated, and temperature-and vapor-controlled enclosures. Solid chemical products that are listed as hazardous substances (49 CFR 172 appendix) may be transported in bulk only on compliance with Coast Guard notification procedures, shipping permit requirements, and complex transportation regulations (46 CFR 148). All hazardous substances must be packaged and transported in accordance with DOT regulations (49 CFR 171 et seq.).

Publications Available

The following publications may be relevant to the importation of toxic or hazardous inorganic chemicals:

Toxic Substances Control Act: A Guide for Chemical Importers/Exporters (published by EPA).

TSCA Chemical Substance Inventory (1985 edition) (Doc. Code S/N 055-000-00254-1) $161.00 U.S. and Canada; $201.21 all other countries.

Supplement to TSCA Chemical Substances Inventory (1990) (Doc. Code S/N 055-000-00361-1) $15.00 U.S.; $18.75 Canada and all other countries.

The above publications and the *Harmonized Tariff Schedule of the United States* (HTSUS) are available from:

Government Printing Office (GPO)
Superintendent of Documents
Washington, DC 20402
(202) 512-1800 (Order line)
(202) 512-0000 (General)

The USGPO also has copies of specific laws available for purchase. The USGPO accepts credit card orders over the phone, as well as mail orders paid by credit card, a check drawn on a U.S. bank, or an international money order.

Relevant Government Agencies

Address your inquiries regarding TSCA and EPA requirements for importation of inorganic chemical substances to:

Environmental Protection Agency (EPA)
TSCA System Information
EPA 7408, OPPT
401 M Street SW
Washington, DC 20460
(202) 554-1404 (TSCA Information Hotline)

Address your questions regarding transportation of hazardous substances to:

U.S. Department of Transportation (DOT)
Research and Special Programs Administration
Office of Hazardous Materials Standards
400 7th St. SW
Washington, DC 20590
(202) 366-4488

Address your questions regarding importation of inorganic chemical substances generally to the district or port director of customs for you area. For addresses, refer to "U.S. Customs District Offices" on page 62 or contact:

U.S. Customs Service
1301 Constitution Ave. NW
Washington, DC 20229
(202) 927-6724 (Information)
(202) 927-1000 (General)

Laws and Regulations

The following laws and regulations may be relevant to the importation of inorganic chemical substances. The laws are contained in the United States Code (USC), and the regulations are published in the Code of Federal Regulations (CFR), both of which are available at larger public and law libraries. Specific laws and regulations may also be purchased from the U.S. Government Printing Office (address above).

18 USC 831 et seq.
Dangerous Cargo Act
This Act restricts the import of nuclear substances into the U.S. and authorizes Customs to enforce the restrictions.

42 USC 2077, 2111, 2122, 2131, 2155
Atomic Energy Act
This Act restricts the importation of certain nuclear substance, atomic weapons, and byproduct material into the U.S.

46 USC 870)
Nuclear Materials Act
This Act restricts the import of nuclear substances.

10 CFR 30, 40, 50, 70, 110
Regulations on Nuclear Materials, Weapons, and Byproducts
These regulations implement the laws restricting importation of special nuclear substance, atomic weapons, and byproduct material and authorize enforcement by Customs.

15 USC 2601 et seq.
Toxic Substances Control Act
This Act authorizes the EPA to determine whether a substance is harmful and to restrict importation, sale, and use of such substances.

19 CFR 12.118 et seq.
Regulations on Toxic Substances Control
These regulations require importers of chemical substances imported in bulk or as part of a mixture to certify to Customs that the shipment complies with the TSCA or is not subject to that Act.

15 USC 1261
Federal Hazardous Substances Act
This Act controls the importation of hazardous substances, sets forth prohibited imports, and authorizes various agencies to promulgate labeling, marking, and transport requirements.

49 CFR 170 et seq.
Regulations on Hazardous Materials
These regulations list all substances deemed hazardous and provide transport, marking, labeling, safety, and emergency response rules.

46 CFR 147.30
Regulations on Labeling of Hazardous Materials
This regulation requires the labeling of containers of hazardous substances and specifies the label contents.

46 CFR 148 et seq.
Regulations on Carriage of Solid Hazardous Materials in Bulk
These regulations govern the transport of solid hazardous substances in bulk, including reporting, permitting, loading, stowing, and shipping requirements.

Sources of Additional Information

The TSCA Chemical Substance Inventory in computerized form is available from:

National Technical Information Service (NTIS)
U.S. Department of Commerce
5285 Port Royal Road
Springfield, VA 22161
(703) 487-4650

Access to the computerized TSCA Chemical Substance Inventory through a commercial database is available at:

Scientific and Technical Network International
Chemical Abstracts Service (CAS)
File: CAS ONLINE
(800) 848-6533
Dialog Information Services
TSCA Chemical Substances Inventory
File: Number 52
(800) 334-2564

Principal Exporting Countries

The following listing includes samples of the main supplier nations of the products of this chapter. It is organized by HTSUS major heading. (Refer to "Customs Classification" above for the product codes.) Countries are listed in rank order of the value of products imported to the U.S. Statistics represent customs value entries for 1993 from the Bureau of Census, U.S. Department of Commerce.

2801—Canada, Japan, Chile, Israel, Germany, Mexico, Belgium, United Kingdom, South Africa, France

2802—Chile, Japan, Netherlands, Germany, Mexico, Canada

2803—Canada, Germany, Japan, Mexico, Belgium, United Kingdom, Russia, Finland, Czech Rep., Bahamas

2804—Canada, Russia, Italy, Germany, Japan, Argentina, Macedonia, South Africa, Australia, China

2805—Canada, France, China, United Kingdom, Japan, Russia, Germany, Brazil, Italy, Belgium

2806—Canada, Germany, Mexico, Belgium, Japan, Norway, United Kingdom, Netherlands, South Africa, Switzerland

2807—Canada, Japan, Germany, Mexico, Spain, Netherlands, Sweden, United Kingdom, Italy, Belgium

2808—Canada, Japan, Sweden, Mexico, Germany, Netherlands, France

2809—Israel, France, Italy, Japan, Germany, United Kingdom, Canada, Netherlands, Belgium, South Africa

2810—Italy, Chile, Mexico, Turkey, Russia, United Kingdom, Japan, Bolivia, Netherlands, Canada

2811—Mexico, Germany, Japan, Canada, United Kingdom, China, Taiwan, France, Chile, Hungary

2812—Japan, Switzerland, Germany, Italy, Canada, France, United Kingdom, South Korea, India

2813—Japan, Canada, Austria, United Kingdom, India, France, Argentina, Netherlands, Russia

2814—Canada, Trinidad and Tobago, Ukraine, Mexico, Russia, Venezuela, Qatar, Algeria, Saudi Arabia, Bahrain

2815—Canada, France, Sweden, United Kingdom, Belgium, Brazil, Germany, Japan, Mexico, Italy

2816—Germany, Italy, Japan, China, Brazil, Israel, Australia, Ireland, Hong Kong, Canada

2817—Canada, Mexico, Japan, China, Peru, Germany, United Kingdom, Belgium, India, Hong Kong

2818—Australia, Canada, Jamaica, Suriname, Germany, Japan, India, France, Venezuela, Switzerland

2819—Germany, Japan, China, Kazakhstan, Canada, United Kingdom, Netherlands, Russia, Mexico, Brazil

2820—Australia, Ireland, Belgium, Brazil, Japan, United Kingdom, South Africa, Mexico, Germany, Russia

2821—Japan, Germany, China, Canada, United Kingdom, Mexico, Netherlands, Brazil, Italy, Sweden

2822—Finland, Belgium, United Kingdom, Zaire, Canada, France, Japan, Russia, China, Switzerland

2823—Canada, France, Germany, Belgium, Japan, Norway, United Kingdom, Czech Rep., South Korea, Poland

2824—Mexico, Canada, Japan, Philippines

2825—Germany, China, Japan, United Kingdom, Canada, Australia, Bolivia, Mexico, Russia, Belgium

2826—Germany, Mexico, Japan, China, Canada, Norway, Italy, United Kingdom, Belgium, Switzerland

2827—Canada, Germany, Israel, Mexico, Japan, Chile, Netherlands, France, China, United Kingdom

2828—Canada, Japan, France, Italy, Denmark, Brazil, Mexico, Israel, Netherlands

2829—Canada, United Kingdom, Spain, Israel, Sweden, China, Switzerland, Italy, Germany, Japan

2830—Germany, Japan, Canada, United Kingdom, Mexico, China, Netherlands, Sweden, Hong Kong, Austria

2831—Germany, Italy, China, United Kingdom, Japan, Taiwan, Belgium, Mexico, Switzerland, India

2832—Germany, United Kingdom, Italy, Taiwan, China, Switzerland, Argentina, Canada, Japan, Chile

2833—Canada, Mexico, Germany, Finland, Japan, South Africa, Belgium, China, Italy, United Kingdom

2834—Norway, Chile, Israel, Mexico, Finland, China, Germany, Denmark, Japan, United Kingdom

2835—Canada, Germany, United Kingdom, Japan, Israel, Mexico, France, China, Sweden, Netherlands

2836—Mexico, Canada, Chile, Japan, Finland, Germany, France, Sweden, China, United Kingdom

2837—Germany, United Kingdom, South Korea, China, Italy, Brazil, Japan, Canada, Malaysia, Netherlands

2838—Germany, Japan, United Kingdom, India, Switzerland

2839—Netherlands, Canada, Germany, United Kingdom, Japan, Switzerland, Mexico, South Africa, Venezuela, Sweden

2840—Germany, Belgium, Turkey, China, Spain, Italy, United Kingdom, Japan, Hong Kong, Canada

2841—Japan, China, United Kingdom, Germany, France, Canada, Czech Rep., Netherlands, Kazakhstan, Sweden

2842—Canada, Japan, Germany, South Africa, Belgium, United Kingdom, Zaire, Netherlands, Taiwan, India

2843—Canada, Chile, Japan, Ireland, United Kingdom, South Africa, Netherlands, Germany, Argentina, Switzerland

2844—Canada, United Kingdom, France, Netherlands, Russia, China, Australia, Germany, South Africa, Kazakhstan

2845—Canada, France, Netherlands, Russia, China, Switzerland, Israel, United Kingdom, Germany, Denmark

2846—France, Japan, China, India, United Kingdom, Germany, Hong Kong, Austria, Russia, Sweden

2847—Canada, Japan, Germany, United Kingdom, Austria, Italy, France

2848—India, United Kingdom, Canada, Japan, Germany, Greece, Chile, China

2849—Canada, China, Germany, Norway, Japan, Brazil, United Kingdom, Venezuela, Mexico, Austria

2850—Japan, Canada, Brazil, Germany, India, Ireland, United Kingdom, China, France, Belgium

Chapter 29: Organic Chemicals*

This chapter pertains to the importation of separate organic chemical elements and chemically defined compounds, which are classified under Chapter 29 of the Harmonized Tariff Schedule of the United States (HTSUS). Specifically, it includes hydrocarbons; alcohols, phenols, and phenol-alcohols; ethers; peroxides and epoxides; acetals; aldehyde-, ketone-, quinone-, and nitrogen-function compounds; organo-inorganic compounds; carboxylic acids; heterocyclic compounds; nucleic acids; sulfonamides; provitamins, vitamins, and hormones; glycosides, vegetable alkaloids, and certain sugars; and antibiotics.

The importation of inorganic chemical substances is covered in related Commodity Index Chapter 28, which includes certain forms of carbon. If you are interested in importing a product that is not in the form of a bulk chemical, you should read the chapters that pertain to the specific type of product. Fat and oil substances are covered in Chapter 15. For ethyl alcohol products, refer to Chapter 22. The importation requirements for methane and propane are found in Chapter 27, for urea in Chapter 31, and for enzymes in Chapter 35. If you are interested in importing dyes, tannins, and other coloring agents, refer to Chapter 32. Chemicals put up in forms for use as fuels are covered in Chapter 36, for fertilizers are in Chapter 31, for ink removers and fire extinguishers in Chapter 38. Optical elements are classified in Chapter 90.

Key Factors

The key factors in the importation of organic chemical substances are:

- Compliance with U.S. Environmental Protection Agency (EPA) requirements under the Toxic Substances Control Act (TSCA) (if the product is a hazardous substance)
- Compliance with U.S. Department of Transportation (DOT) regulations for transport of hazardous cargo (if the product is a hazardous substance)

Although most importers use the services of a licensed customs broker in making their entries, and we recommend this practice, you should be aware of the regulatory, entry, and documentation issues involved in importing your product. You, as importer, are ultimately responsible for the fulfillment of any legal requirements applicable to your shipment.

*IMPORTANT: Read the Commodity Index Introduction. It is the essential framework for understanding this chapter.

General Considerations

Regulatory Agencies. The EPA, under authority of the TSCA, imposes certain controls on the importation of organic chemicals that contain toxic substances. The TSCA defines a toxic substance as any substance determined to present the possibility of an unreasonable risk of injury to health and the environment. The DOT enforces regulations for transporting hazardous cargo. Substances are deemed hazardous if listed in DOT transport regulations (49 CFR 172 appendix).

Toxic and Hazardous Substances. Organic chemicals imported in bulk, as articles, or as part of a mixture must be in compliance with toxic and hazardous substance regulations of the EPA and DOT. These include packaging, shipping, marking, and labeling requirements. In addition, all organic chemical products are subject to the U.S. Customs Service TSCA Import Certification Rule (19 CFR 12.118 et seq.). If you import these products, you must sign one of the following statements: "I certify that all chemical substances in this shipment comply with all applicable rules or orders under TSCA and that I am not offering a chemical substance for entry in violation of TSCA or any applicable rule or order thereunder" or "I certify that all chemicals in this shipment are not subject to TSCA."

You must file this TSCA certification of compliance or exemption at the time you make the entry at Customs. The certification may be in the form of a typed or stamped statement on an appropriate entry document or commercial invoice or a preprinted attachment to such entry document or invoice. You may sign the certificate by means of an authorized facsimile signature. If your entry is electronically processed, the certification will be in the form of a Certification Code, which is part of the Automated Broker Interface (ABI) transmission. Customs will not release your shipment without proper certification.

If you will be importing several or regular shipments, you should ask the appropriate Customs district director to authorize your use of a blanket certification. If you receive such authorization, you must include on the commercial invoice or entry document for each shipment a statement that the blanket certification is on file and that it is incorporated by reference. This statement need not be signed. The blanket certification is valid for one calendar year, is subject to renewal, and is may be revoked at any time for cause.

In filling out TSCA forms and Customs entry documents, you should provide the Chemical Abstracts Service (CAS) number for each chemical in the shipment. These CAS numbers are given in the appendix to the HTSUS. You are not required to include the CAS number, but Customs will be able to process your shipment more quickly if you give this number.

Articles Exclusion. If you are importing organic chemicals that are classified as hazardous substances but are part of articles, you are subject to TSCA certification requirements only if certification for your product is specifically required by a rule or order promulgated under the TSCA. No specific rules have been adopted at this time. An "article" is a manufactured item 1) that is formed into a specific shape or design during manufacture, 2) that has end-use functions dependent on the shape or design during end use, and 3) that during the end use, does not change in its chemical composition or that changes only for a noncommercial purpose separate from the article and only as allowed by law (19 CFR 12.120(2)). Fluids and particles are not articles, regardless of shape or design.

Shipment Detention. A shipment containing organic chemicals will be detained at the U.S. port of arrival (or entry if same), at your risk and expense, if: 1) it contains banned chemical substances (15 USC 2604, 2605); or 2) it contains chemical substances ordered seized because of imminent hazards (15 USC 2606). Further detention will occur at the port of entry, again at your risk and expense, if: 1) the EPA administrator or Customs district director has reasonable grounds to believe the shipment is not in compliance with the TSCA; or 2) you do not provide proper TSCA certification.

If your shipment is detained, it will be held by Customs for no more than 48 hours. It will then be turned over to the EPA administrator, unless you have arranged to release it in bond. You must either bring it into TSCA compliance or reexport it within the earlier of 90 days after notice of detention or 30 days of demand for redelivery. Customs may grant an extension if failure to comply or reexport is the result of delays in EPA or Customs procedures. If you fail to comply or reexport within the time allowed, the EPA administrator is authorized to have the shipment stored or disposed of at your expense.

Customs Classification

For customs purposes, organic chemical substances are classified under Chapter 29 of the HTSUS. This chapter is broken into major headings, which are further divided into subheadings, and often sub-subheadings, each of which has its own HTSUS classification number. For example, the HTSUS number for nitrated benzene is 2904.20.35, indicating it is a sub-subcategory of derivatives containing only nitro or nitroso groups (2904.20.00), which is a subcategory of the major heading, sulfonated, nitrated, or nitrosated derivatives of hydrocarbons (2904.00.00). There are 41 major headings within Chapter 29.

2901—Acyclic hydrocarbons

2902—Cyclic hydrocarbons

2903—Halogenated derivatives of hydrocarbons

2904—Sulfonated, nitrated, or nitrosated derivatives of hydrocarbons, whether or not halogenated

2905—Acyclic alcohols and their halogenated, sulfonated, nitrated, or nitrosated derivatives

2906—Cyclic alcohols and their halogenated, sulfonated, nitrated, or nitrosated derivatives

2907—Phenol, phenol-alcohols

2908—Halogenated, sulfonated, nitrated, or nitrosated derivatives of phenols or phenol-alcohols

2909—Ethers, ether-alcohols, ether-phenols, ether-alcohol-phenols, alcohol peroxides, ether peroxides, ketone peroxides (whether or not chemically defined), and their halogenated, sulfonated, nitrated, or nitrosated derivatives

2910—Epoxides, epoxyalcohols, epoxyphenols, and epoxyethers, with a three-membered ring, and their halogenated, sulfonated, nitrated, or nitrosated derivatives

2911—Acetals and hemiacetals, whether or not with other oxygen function, and their halogenated, sulfonated, nitrated, or nitrosated derivatives

2912—Aldehydes, whether or not with other oxygen function; cyclic polymers of aldehydes; paraformaldehyde

2913—Halogenated, sulfonated, nitrated, or nitrosated derivatives of products of heading 2912

2914—Ketones and quinones, whether or not with other oxygen function, and their halogenated, sulfonated, nitrated, or nitrosated derivatives

2915—Saturated acyclic monocarboxylic acids and their anhydrides, halides, peroxides, and peroxyacids; their halogenated, sulfonated, nitrated, or nitrosated derivatives

2916—Unsaturated acyclic monocarboxylic acids, cyclic monocarboxylic acids, their anhydrides, halides, peroxides, and peroxyacids; their halogenated, sulfonated, nitrated, or nitrosated derivatives

2917—Polycarboxylic acids, their anhydrides, halides, peroxides, and peroxyacids; their halogenated, sulfonated, nitrated, or nitrosated derivatives

2918—Carboxylic acid with additional oxygen function and their anhydrides, halides, peroxides, and peroxyacids; their halogenated, sulfonated, nitrated, or nitrosated derivatives

2919—Phosphoric esters and salts, including lactophosphates; their halogenated, sulfonated, nitrated, or nitrosated derivatives

2920—Esters of other inorganic acids (excluding esters of hydrogen halides) and their salts; their halogenated, sulfonated, nitrated, or nitrosated derivatives

2921—Amine-function compounds

2922—Oxygen-function amino-compounds

2923—Quaternary ammonium salts and hydroxides; lecithins and other phosphoaminolipids

2924—Carboxyamide-function compounds; amide-function compounds of carbonic acid

2925—Carboxyimide-function compounds (including saccharin and its salts) and imine-function compounds

2926—Nitrile-function compounds

2927—Diazo-, azo-, or azoxy-compounds

2928—Organic derivatives of hydrazine or of hydroxylamine

2930—Organo-sulfur compounds

2932—Heterocyclic compounds with oxygen hetero-atom(s) only

2933—Heterocyclic compounds with nitrogen hetero-atom(s) only; nucleic acids and their salts

2935—Sulfonamides

2936—Provitamins and vitamins, natural or reproduced by synthesis (including natural concentrates), derivatives thereof used primarily as vitamins, and intermixtures of the foregoing, whether or not in any solvent

2937—Hormones, natural or reproduced by synthesis; derivatives thereof, used primarily as hormones; other steroids used primarily as hormones

2938—Glycosides, natural or reproduced by synthesis, and their salts, ethers, esters, and other derivatives

2939—Vegetable alkaloids, natural or reproduced by synthesis, and their salts, ethers, esters, and other derivatives

2940—Sugars, chemically pure, other than sucrose, lactose, maltose, glucose, and fructose; sugar ethers and sugar esters, and their salts, other than products of heading 2937, 2938 or 2939

2941—Antibiotics

For more details regarding classifications of the specific product you are interested in importing, consult a customs broker, the appropriate commodity specialist at your nearest customs port, or the HTSUS. HTSUS is available for purchase from the U.S. Government Printing Office (see addresses at end of this chapter), and may be found in larger public libraries. Refer to "Classification—Liquidation" on page 207 for a general discussion of customs classification.

Sample Import Duties

Import duties will vary depending on the HTSUS classification of your product. Therefore, to determine the correct amount of duties, your product must be properly classified under the HTSUS. The following sample duties are taken from the duty listings for HTSUS Chapter 28 products.

Butane (2901.10.10): free; cyclohexane (2902.11.00): 2 cents/kg plus 12.5%; benzene (2902.20.00): free; styrene (2902.50.00): 7.4%; chloromethane (2903.11.00): 20%; chloroform (2903.13.00): 15.9%; vinyl chloride (2903.21.00): 12%; nitrated naphthalene (2904.20.35): 2.9 cents/kg plus 12.5%; methanol for producing synthetic natural gas or as fuel directly (2905.11.10): free; ethylene glycol (2905.31.00): 12%; menthol (2906.11.00): 37.5 cents/kg; tartaric acid (2918.12.00) 4.3%; citric acid (2918.14.00): 6%; ampicillin (2941.10.10): 6.9%; tetracyclines (2941.30.00): 3.7%.

Special Provisions. Additional duties may apply to ethyl tertiary-butyl ether and any mixture containing this chemical, which is classified under 2909.19.10.

Entry and Documentation

The entry of merchandise is a two-part process consisting of 1) filing the documents necessary to determine whether merchandise may be released from Customs custody and 2) filing the documents that contain information for duty assessment and statistical purposes. In certain instances, all documents must be filed and accepted by Customs prior to release of the goods. Unless you have been granted an extension, you must file entry documents at a location specified by the district or area director within five working days of your shipment's date of arrival at a U.S. port of entry. These include a number of standard documents required by Customs for any entry, and:

- U.S. Customs TSCA Certification when required

After you present the entry, Customs may examine your shipment, or may waive examination. The shipment is then released, provided no legal or regulatory violations have been noted. You must then file entry summary documentation and deposit estimated duties at a designated customhouse within 10 working days of your shipment's release. For a detailed description of entry procedures, standard documentation, and informal entry, refer to "Entry Process" on page 182.

Entry Invoice. Specify the use and Chemical Abstracts Service (CAS) number of the organic chemical compounds included in the shipment.

Prohibitions and Restrictions

Importation of organic chemicals that are considered hazardous substances is prohibited if the chemicals are misbranded. Certain hazardous substances listed in the FHSA and in regulations promulgated by the Consumer Product Safety Commission (CPSC) are completely banned from importation. A shipment of an organic chemical cannot be imported if it poses an imminent hazard. See 15 USC 1261, 2604-2606; 16 CFR 1500.265-1500.272.

Marking and Labeling Requirements

A shipment of any products containing organic chemicals that are classified as hazardous substance (49 CFR 172) must comply with the marking and labeling regulations adopted by the EPA (46 CFR 147.30) and the DOT (49 CFR 171 et seq.).

For a general discussion of U.S. Customs marking and labeling requirements, see "Marking: Country of Origin" on page 215 and "Special Marking Requirements" on page 217.

Shipping Considerations

You will need to ensure that your goods are packaged and shipped with care so that they pass smoothly through Customs and arrive in good condition. You are responsible for ensuring that the shipment is in compliance with all applicable government regulations for packaging and shipping. In most instances, you should not leave these arrangements solely to the discretion of your supplier. Careful preparation of the cargo and selection of the mode of transport can be essential to a cost-effective, timely delivery of undamaged goods. We strongly advise you to consult your shipping representative, insurance agent, or freight broker for advice on packing and shipping. Refer also to the major tab section "Packing/Shipping/Insurance" for a general discussion of packing and shipping.

Organic chemicals may be shipped in bulk, bags, bottles, crates, or other types of containers, depending on the type of product and whether it is prepackaged. General considerations include protection from contamination, weather, and pests. For liquid shipments, venting and vapor collection systems may be required. Safety precautions should also be implemented as required to protect against breakage, spillage, corrosion of containers, combustion, and explosion. Containers should be constructed so as to be safe for handling during transport.

Organic chemical products in particular may have to be shipped in pressurized, ventilated, and temperature-and vapor-controlled enclosures. Solid organic chemical products that are listed as hazardous substances (49 CFR 172 appendix) may be transported in bulk only on compliance with Coast Guard notification procedures, shipping permit requirements, and complex transportation regulations (46 CFR 148). All hazardous substances must be packaged and transported in accordance with DOT regulations (49 CFR 171 et seq.).

Publications Available

The following publications may be relevant to the importation of toxic or hazardous organic chemicals:

Toxic Substances Control Act: A Guide for Chemical Importers/Exporters (published by EPA).

TSCA Chemical Substance Inventory (1985 edition) (Doc. Code S/N 055-000-00254-1) $161.00 U.S. and Canada; $201.21 all other countries.

Supplement to TSCA Chemical Substances Inventory (1990) (Doc. Code S/N 055-000-00361-1) $15.00 U.S.; $18.75 Canada and all other countries.

The above publications and the *Harmonized Tariff Schedule of the United States* (HTSUS) are available from:

Government Printing Office (GPO)
Superintendent of Documents
Washington, DC 20402
(202) 512-1800 (Order line)
(202) 512-0000 (General)

The USGPO also has copies of specific laws available for purchase. The USGPO accepts credit card orders over the phone, as well as mail orders paid by credit card, a check drawn on a U.S. bank, or an international money order.

Relevant Government Agencies

Address your inquiries regarding TSCA and EPA requirements for importation of organic chemical substances to:

Environmental Protection Agency (EPA)
TSCA System Information
EPA 7408, OPPT
401 M Street SW
Washington, DC 20460
(202) 554-1404 (TSCA Information Hotline)

Address your questions regarding transportation of organic chemicals that are classified as hazardous substances to:

U.S. Department of Transportation (DOT)
Research and Special Programs Administration
Office of Hazardous Materials Standards
400 7th St. SW
Washington, DC 20590
(202) 366-4488

Address your questions regarding importation of organic chemical substances generally to the district or port director of customs for you area. For addresses, refer to "U.S. Customs District Offices" on page 62 or contact:

U.S. Customs Service
1301 Constitution Ave. NW
Washington, DC 20229
(202) 927-6724 (Information)
(202) 927-1000 (General)

Laws and Regulations

The following laws and regulations may be relevant to the importation of organic chemicals. The laws are contained in the United States Code (USC), and the regulations are published in the Code of Federal Regulations (CFR), both of which are available at larger public and law libraries. Specific laws and regulations may also be purchased from the U.S. Government Printing Office (address above).

15 USC 2601 et seq.
Toxic Substances Control Act
This Act authorizes the EPA to determine whether a substance is harmful and to restrict importation, sale, and use of such substances.

19 CFR 12.118 et seq.
Regulations on Toxic Substances Control
These regulations require importers of chemical substances imported in bulk or as part of a mixture to certify to Customs that the shipment complies with the TSCA or is not subject to that Act.

15 USC 1261
Federal Hazardous Substances Act
This Act controls the importation of hazardous substances, sets forth prohibited imports, and authorizes various agencies to promulgate labeling, marking, and transport requirements.

49 CFR 170 et seq.
Regulations on Hazardous Materials
These regulations list all substances deemed hazardous and provide transport, marking, labeling, safety, and emergency response rules.

46 CFR 147.30
Regulations on Labeling of Hazardous Materials
This regulation requires the labeling of containers of hazardous substances and specifies the label contents.

46 CFR 148 et seq.
Regulations on Carriage of Solid Hazardous Materials in Bulk
These regulations govern the transport of solid hazardous substances in bulk, including reporting, permitting, loading, stowing, and shipping requirements.

Sources of Additional Information

The TSCA Chemical Substance Inventory in computerized form is available from:

National Technical Information Service (NTIS)
U.S. Department of Commerce
5285 Port Royal Road
Springfield, VA 22161
(703) 487-4650

Access to the computerized TSCA Chemical Substance Inventory through a commercial database is available at:

Scientific and Technical Network International
Chemical Abstracts Service (CAS)
File: CAS ONLINE
(800) 848-6533
Dialog Information Services
TSCA Chemical Substances Inventory
File: Number 52
(800) 334-2564

Principal Exporting Countries

The following listing includes samples of the main supplier nations of the products of this chapter. It is organized by HTSUS major heading. (Refer to "Customs Classification" above for the product codes.) Countries are listed in rank order of the value of products imported to the U.S. Statistics represent customs value

entries for 1993 from the Bureau of Census, U.S. Department of Commerce.

2901—Canada, Netherlands, Japan, South Korea, Spain, Belgium, Italy, Brazil, Portugal, France

2902—Canada, Netherlands, Brazil, South Korea, Japan, Mexico, France, Russia, Germany, Spain

2903—Japan, United Kingdom, Canada, France, Germany, Brazil, Netherlands, Belgium, Greece, Italy

2904—Germany, Japan, Switzerland, Canada, China, India, United Kingdom, Netherlands, France, Israel

2905—Canada, Germany, Japan, Chile, Mexico, Switzerland, Trinidad and Tobago, France, Bahrain, Saudi Arabia

2906—China, Germany, Japan, India, France, Paraguay, Netherlands, Italy, Singapore, Belgium

2907—Japan, Germany, France, United Kingdom, Switzerland, Mexico, Italy, Brazil, Canada, China

2908—Japan, United Kingdom, Germany, Mexico, France, Italy, China, Switzerland, South Korea, India

2909—Canada, Venezuela, Saudi Arabia, United Kingdom, Japan, Netherlands, Taiwan, Brazil, Mexico, France

2910—Canada, Japan, Italy, Germany, Brazil, Switzerland, Belgium, Netherlands, Russia, France

2911—Germany, Japan, France, Switzerland, United Kingdom, Netherlands, Belgium, Spain, Austria, Israel

2912—Japan, Germany, France, Canada, Switzerland, Taiwan, China, United Kingdom, Netherlands, Israel

2913—Japan, Germany, France, Switzerland, Hungary, Brazil, Italy, United Kingdom, China, Austria

2914—United Kingdom, Germany, Japan, France, Netherlands, Switzerland, Italy, China, Mexico, South Africa

2915—Mexico, Canada, Germany, United Kingdom, France, Netherlands, Japan, Malaysia, Denmark, Switzerland

2916—Japan, United Kingdom, Germany, France, Mexico, Netherlands, India, Switzerland, South Korea, Sweden

2917—Canada, Japan, Mexico, Italy, France, China, Germany, Belgium, United Kingdom, Venezuela

2918—Bahamas, Japan, Austria, United Kingdom, Netherlands, Israel, Mexico, Italy, France, China

2919—Germany, United Kingdom, Japan, Belgium, France, Switzerland, Italy, Netherlands, Canada, Austria

2920—Israel, Denmark, France, Germany, Canada, Netherlands, Italy, Belgium, Mexico, United Kingdom

2921—Germany, Japan, Canada, Israel, Italy, Switzerland, United Kingdom, France, Netherlands, China

2922—United Kingdom, Japan, France, Germany, South Korea, Switzerland, Brazil, Italy, Taiwan, India

2923—Canada, Japan, Switzerland, Germany, United Kingdom, Sweden, Italy, France, Mexico, Venezuela

2924—Switzerland, Italy, Japan, Norway, Ireland, Germany, United Kingdom, France, Israel, Brazil

2925—Japan, Germany, United Kingdom, France, Austria, South Korea, Switzerland, India, Spain, China

2926—United Kingdom, Switzerland, France, Italy, Germany, Belgium, Japan, Norway, Netherlands, China

2927—Japan, Germany, United Kingdom, South Korea, Switzerland, France, Mexico, Canada, China, Indonesia

2928—United Kingdom, Japan, France, Netherlands, Israel, Germany, Italy, Spain, Switzerland, Colombia

2929—Germany, France, Japan, United Kingdom, Netherlands, Switzerland, Brazil, Finland, Italy, Russia

2930—Japan, France, Germany, Belgium, Denmark, Switzerland, United Kingdom, Italy, Israel, India

2931—Germany, Japan, Sweden, United Kingdom, Belgium, Israel, Canada, France, Mexico, Italy

2932—Singapore, Japan, United Kingdom, China, France, Switzerland, Germany, Netherlands, Dominican Rep., Italy

2933—Germany, United Kingdom, Japan, Ireland, Switzerland, Italy, France, Israel, Belgium, Netherlands

2934—Japan, United Kingdom, Switzerland, Germany, Ireland, Italy, Netherlands, Belgium, France, Austria

2935—Ireland, United Kingdom, Germany, Italy, Japan, Croatia, China, South Korea, South Africa, Sweden

2936—Japan, Switzerland, Germany, China, Denmark, France, United Kingdom, Belgium, Italy, Croatia

2937—France, Germany, Switzerland, Mexico, Netherlands, United Kingdom, Bahamas, Ireland, Italy, Denmark

2938—Switzerland, Japan, Italy, France, United Kingdom, Germany, Brazil, China, Israel, Spain

2939—Germany, Switzerland, China, Brazil, Japan, Netherlands, Italy, India, Indonesia, France

2940—Japan, Italy, Netherlands, Germany, United Kingdom, Switzerland, Spain, Brazil, Israel, Belgium

2941—Italy, Japan, United Kingdom, Switzerland, Singapore, Netherlands, Austria, Spain, China, Croatia

2942—Ireland, Japan, Germany, United Kingdom, India, Italy, France, Canada, Switzerland, Spain

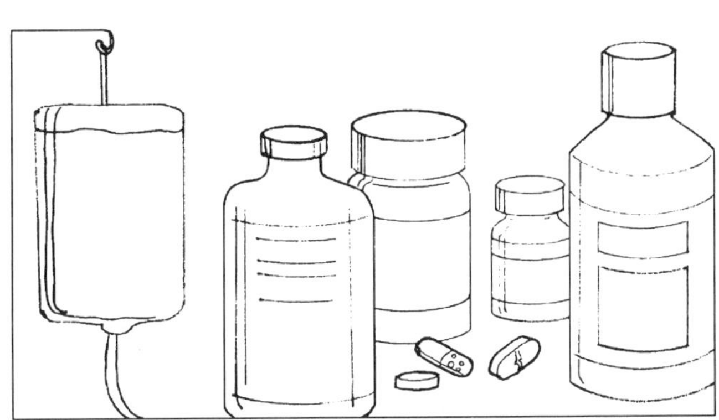

Chapter 30: Pharmaceutical Products*

This chapter relates to the importation of pharmaceutical products, which are classified under Chapter 30 of the Harmonized Tariff Schedule of the United States (HTSUS). Specifically, it includes human and animal substances prepared for therapeutic or prophylactic uses; medicaments; wadding, gauze, and bandages; and miscellaneous related items. It includes pharmaceuticals for both human and animal use.

If you are interested in importing food or beverage products for special diets—such as dietetic foods or mineral waters—refer to Commodity Index Chapters 16 through 24. For plasters used in dentistry, refer to Chapter 25. The importing requirements for cosmetics, perfume, and essential oil products are covered in Chapter 33. Soap and similar products that contain medicaments are classified under Chapter 34, which also covers the importation of dental preparations with a plaster base. Refer to Chapter 35 for importing requirements related to blood albumin not prepared for therapeutic or prophylactic uses. For importing separately defined chemicals, refer to Chapters 28 (inorganic) and 29 (organic).

Key Factors

The key factors in the importation of pharmaceuticals are:

- Compliance with Food and Drug Administration (FDA) safety, purity, identity, manufacturing, labeling, packaging, recordkeeping, reporting, and other standards
- Compliance with FDA pharmaceutical registration, testing, approval, and listing procedures
- Compliance with FDA import entry notification and procedures
- Compliance with U.S. Federal Trade Commission (FTC) and Consumer Product Safety Commission (CPSC) standards
- Compliance with U.S. Department of Agriculture (USDA) permit requirements (if the product is biological derivative intended for veterinary use)
- Compliance with Environmental Protection Agency (EPA) pesticide regulations, including pesticide residue monitoring for animal feeds that could affect U.S. food supplies
- Compliance with EPA requirements under Toxic Substances Control Act (TSCA) (if the product is a hazardous substance)
- Compliance with U.S. Department of Transportation (DOT) regulations for transport of hazardous cargo (if the product contains a hazardous substance)
- Compliance with U.S. Public Health Service Centers for Disease Control (CDC) permit requirements (if the product is a vector of human disease)

Although most importers use the services of a licensed customs broker in making their entries, and we recommend this practice, you should be aware of the regulatory, entry, and documentation issues involved in importing your product. You, as importer, are ultimately responsible for the fulfillment of any legal requirements applicable to your shipment.

General Considerations

Regulatory Agencies. Regulations governing pharmaceutical products are stringent and complex. The FDA, under the Federal Food, Drug, and Cosmetic Act (FDCA) and the Public Health Service Act (PHSA), regulates the importation of pharmaceuticals for human and animal use. The USDA, pursuant to the Virus Serum Toxin Act (VSTA), licenses importers who ship veterinary biologic drugs. The EPA, under authority of the TSCA, imposes certain controls on the importation of toxic substances. The TSCA defines a toxic substance as any substance determined to present possibility of an unreasonable risk of injury to health and the environment. The FTC, CPSC, and DOT enforce regulations for transporting hazardous cargo. Materials are deemed hazardous if listed in DOT transport regulations (49 CFR 172 appendix). Pharmaceutical products consisting of vectors of human disease may be shipped only under permit issued by the CDC. This discussion is in no way exhaustive. If you are interested in importing pharmaceuticals, you should contact relevant federal agencies at the addresses below.

The intended use of a pharmaceutical determines whether an item is a drug. Foods and cosmetics may be subject to the drug provisions of the FDCA if therapeutic claims are made for them. To arrange for entry of a pharmaceutical preparation or component, you must determine which regulatory category applies to your product and make sure that all requirements for that category have been met. The general discussion of pharmaceutical regulation that follows is not exhaustive. You should be sure to contact FDA with your specific questions.

FDA Regulations. All drugs imported into the U.S. must comply with the FDCA requirements that apply to domestically produced pharmaceuticals. Manufacturing firms must be registered, and the drugs those firms produce must be listed with the FDA. The FDCA defines drugs as "articles intended for use in the diagnosis, cure, mitigation, treatment, or prevention of disease in man or other animals" and "articles (other than food) intended to affect the structure or any function of the body of man or other animals" (for example, articles intended for weight reduction). This definition encompasses homeopathic substances and biological derivatives.

Biological Products. A biological product is any virus, therapeutic serum, toxin, antitoxin, vaccine, blood, blood component or derivative, allergenic product, or analogous product applicable to the prevention, treatment, or cure of diseases or injuries of man. Biologics include such products as polio and measles vaccines, diphtheria and tetanus toxoids, skin test substances, whole blood, and blood components for transfusion. Samples of the licensed product must accompany each importation for forwarding by the port-of-entry Customs port director to the Director, National Center for Biologics Evaluation and Research (see addresses at end of this chapter).

*IMPORTANT: Read the Commodity Index Introduction. It is the essential framework for understanding this chapter.

Homeopathic Pharmaceuticals. The Homeopathic Pharmacopoeia of the United States (HP) is designated as the official compendium for homeopathic medicines. All medicines named in HP are required by law to meet the standards of strength, quality, or purity set forth therein, and to conform to all packaging and labeling requirements. If your medicine differs in strength, quality, or purity under or above the limits specified in HP, you should be sure that the nature and extent of that difference is plainly stated on the label.

Animal Pharmaceuticals. For importing purposes, the law makes several significant distinctions between products and pharmaceuticals intended for human use and those intended for animal use. For example, drugs for use in food-producing animals are evaluated for safety in products derived from those animals—meat, milk, and eggs—as well as safety and effectiveness for the animal. The FDCA requires approval of applications for use of new animal drugs in the manufacture of animal feed. Animal biological products are subject to the provisions of the VSTA administered by USDA's Veterinary Biologics staff (see addresses at end of this chapter).

To import viruses, serums, toxins and analogous products, and organisms and vectors for use in the treatment of domestic animals, you must hold a USDA import permit covering the specific product. These importations are subject to special labeling requirements. If you wish to import any etiological agent or insect, animal, or plant vector of human disease or any exotic living insect, animal, or plant capable of serving as a vector of human disease, you must first obtain a permit from the CDC (see addresses at end of this chapter).

Medical devices for animals, while subject to the same prohibitions against misbranding and adulteration as human medical devices, are not subject to premarket approval. FDCA regulates cosmetics for human use only. Similar products for animal use are termed "grooming aids" and are not subject to FDCA, provided no therapeutic claims are made.

Inspection. Imported products regulated by the FDA are subject to port-of-entry inspection. **Form FD701** is required for all FDA-regulated importations and may be obtained from your local FDA Import Operations office, from FDA headquarters (see addresses at end of this chapter), or from your customs broker. For an annotated diagram of required FDA import procedures, refer to the "Foods" appendix on page 808.

Shipment Detention. If your shipment is found to be noncomplying, it may be detained at the port of entry. FDA may permit you to bring an illegal importation into compliance with the law before a final decision is made regarding admittance. However, any sorting, reprocessing, or relabeling must be supervised by an FDA investigator, and will be done at your expense. Conditional release of an illegal importation to allow an importer to bring it into compliance is not a right but a privilege. If you repeat noncomplying shipments of the same article, the FDA may interpret this as abuse of the privilege and may require you to destroy or reexport subsequent shipments.

Hazardous or Toxic Substances. Shipments of products containing chemicals must be in compliance with toxic and hazardous substance regulations of the EPA and DOT. These include packaging, shipping, marking, and labeling requirements. In addition, all products containing chemicals are subject to the U.S. Customs Service TSCA Import Certification Rule (19 CFR 12.118 et seq.). If you import these products, you must sign one of the following statements: "I certify that all chemical substances in this shipment comply with all applicable rules or orders under TSCA and that I am not offering a chemical substance for entry in violation of TSCA or any applicable rule or order thereunder" or "I certify that all chemicals in this shipment are not subject to TSCA."

You must file this TSCA certification of compliance or exemption at the time you make the entry at Customs. The certification may be in the form of a typed or stamped statement on an appropriate entry document or commercial invoice or a preprinted attachment to such entry document or invoice. You may sign the certificate by means of an authorized facsimile signature. If your entry is electronically processed, the certification will be in the form of a Certification Code, which is part of the Automated Broker Interface (ABI) transmission. Customs will not release your shipment without proper certification.

If you will be importing several or regular shipments, you should ask the appropriate Customs district director to authorize your use of a blanket certification. If you receive such authorization, you must include on the commercial invoice or entry document for each shipment a statement that the blanket certification is on file and that it is incorporated by reference. This statement need not be signed. The blanket certification is valid for one calendar year, is subject to renewal, and may be revoked at any time for cause.

In filling out TSCA forms and Customs entry documents, you should provide the Chemical Abstracts Service (CAS) number for each chemical in the shipment. These CAS numbers are given in the appendix to the HTSUS. You are not required to include the CAS number, but Customs will be able to process your shipment more quickly if you include this number.

Articles Exclusion. If you are importing items that are classified as hazardous substances but are part of articles, you are subject to TSCA certification requirements only if certification for your product is specifically required by a rule or order promulgated under the TSCA. No specific rules have been adopted at this time. An "article" is a manufactured item 1) that is formed into a specific shape or design during manufacture, 2) that has end-use functions dependent on the shape or design during end use, and 3) that during the end use, does not change in its chemical composition or that changes only for a noncommercial purpose separate from the article and only as allowed by law (19 CFR 12.120(2)). Fluids and particles are not articles, regardless of shape or design.

Shipment Detention. A shipment containing chemicals will be detained at the U.S. port of arrival (or entry if same), at your risk and expense, if: 1) it contains banned chemical substances (15 USC 2604, 2605); or 2) it contains chemical substances ordered seized because of imminent hazards (15 USC 2606). Further detention will occur at the port of entry, again at your risk and expense, if: 1) the EPA administrator or Customs district director has reasonable grounds to believe the shipment is not in compliance with the TSCA; or 2) you do not provide proper TSCA certification.

If your shipment is detained, it will be held by Customs for no more than 48 hours. It will then be turned over to the EPA administrator, unless you have arranged to release it in bond. You must either bring it into TSCA compliance or reexport it within the earlier of 90 days after notice of detention or 30 days of demand for redelivery. Customs may grant an extension if failure to comply or reexport is the result of delays in EPA or Customs procedures. If you fail to comply or reexport within the time allowed, the EPA administrator is authorized to have the shipment stored or disposed of at your expense.

Customs Classification

For customs purposes, pharmaceuticals are classified under Chapter 30 of the HTSUS. This chapter is broken into major headings, which are further divided into subheadings, and often sub-subheadings, each of which has its own HTSUS classification number. For example, the HTSUS number for cough drops is 3004.90.30, indicating it is a sub-subcategory of other medicants (3004.90.00), which is a subcategory of the major heading medicaments put up for retail (3004.00.00). There are six major headings within Chapter 30.

3001—Glands and other organs for organotherapeutic uses, dried, whether or not powdered; extracts of glands or other organs or of their secretions for organotherapeutic uses; heparin and its salts; other human or animal substances prepared for therapeutic or prophylactic uses, not elsewhere specified or included

3002—Human blood; animal blood prepared for therapeutic, prophylactic or diagnostic uses; antisera and other blood fractions; vaccines, toxins, cultures of micro-organisms (excluding yeasts), and similar products

3003—Medicaments (excluding goods of heading 3002, 3005, or 3006) consisting of two or more constituents which have been mixed together for therapeutic or prophylactic uses, not put up in measured doses or in forms or packings for retail sale

3004—Medicaments (excluding goods of heading 3002, 3005, or 3006) consisting of mixed or unmixed products for therapeutic or prophylactic uses, put up in measured doses or in forms or packings for retail sale

3005—Wadding, gauze, bandages, and similar articles (for example, dressings, adhesive plasters, poultices), impregnated or coated with pharmaceutical substances or put up in forms or packings for retail sale for medical, surgical, dental, or veterinary purposes

3006—Pharmaceutical goods specified in HTSUS note 3 to Chapter 30

For more details regarding classifications of the specific product you are interested in importing, consult a customs broker, the appropriate commodity specialist at your nearest customs port, or the HTSUS. HTSUS is available for purchase from the U.S. Government Printing Office (see addresses at end of this chapter), and may be found in larger public libraries. Refer to "Classification—Liquidation" on page 207 for a general discussion of customs classification.

Sample Import Duties

Import duties will vary depending on the HTSUS classification of your product. Therefore, to determine the correct amount of duties, your product must be properly classified under the HTSUS. The following sample duties are taken from the duty listings for HTSUS Chapter 30 products.

Antisera and other blood fractions (3002.10.00): free; vaccines for human medicine (3002.20.00): free; vaccines against foot-and-mouth disease (3002.31.00): free; medicaments mixed of two or more constituents, containing penicillins, for therapeutic or prophylactic uses, and not put up in measured doses or for retail (3003.10.00): 6.9%; medicaments containing antibiotics, for therapeutic or prophylactic uses, and put up in measured doses or for retail (3004.20.00): 3.7%; cough drops (3004.90.30): 3.9%; adhesive dressings coated or impregnated with pharmaceutical substances (3005.10.10): 2.4%; laparotomy sponges (3005.90.50): 7%; sterile suture materials (3006.10.00): 3.5%; dental cements and filings (3006.40.00): 5.8%.

Entry and Documentation

The entry of merchandise is a two-part process consisting of 1) filing the documentation necessary to determine whether merchandise may be released from Customs custody, and 2) filing the documents that contain information for duty assessment and statistical purposes. In certain instances, all documents must be filed and accepted by Customs prior to release of the goods. Unless you have been granted an extension, you must file entry documents at a location specified by the district or area director within five working days of your shipment's date of arrival at a U.S. port of entry. These include a number of standard documents required by Customs for any entry, and:

- FDA Importers Entry Notice, **Form FD701**
- U.S. Customs TSCA Certification (hazardous substances)
- USDA permit (veterinary biologics)
- CDC permit (agents or vectors of human disease)

After you present the entry, Customs may examine your shipment or may waive examination. The shipment is then released provided no legal or regulatory violations have occurred. You must then file entry summary documentation and deposit estimated duties at a designated customhouse within 10 working days of your shipment's release. For a detailed description of entry procedures, standard documentation, and informal entry, refer to "Entry Process" on page 182.

Prohibitions and Restrictions

FDCA prohibits the misbranding or adulteration of any drug and requires that "new drugs" be reviewed and approved by the FDA before they go on the market. A drug that has been used outside the U.S. and that may be regarded as safe and effective by experts in other countries, but that has not been marketed in the U.S., is likely to be regarded as a new drug under U.S. law. The Prescription Drug Marketing Act (PDMA) generally prohibits the reimportation of U.S.-made drugs by anyone other than the original manufacturer.

For purposes of regulation, drugs are divided into several major categories, each subject to particular requirements as follows:

New Drugs. This is the largest regulatory category of drugs. A drug may be categorized as new for many reasons. For example, a drug is new if: 1) it contains a newly developed chemical; 2) it contains a chemical or substance not previously used in medicine; 3) it has previously been used in medicine but not in the dosages or conditions for which the sponsor now recommends its use; or 4) as a result of investigational studies it has become recognized by qualified experts as safe and effective for its intended uses, but it has not otherwise been used to a material extent or for a material time.

A new drug may not be imported into, commercially marketed in, or exported from the U.S., unless it has been approved as safe and effective by the FDA. Such approval is based on a New Drug Application (NDA) (21 CFR 314) submitted to FDA by the sponsor of the drug (usually, but not always, its manufacturer). An NDA must contain acceptable scientific data, results of specific tests to evaluate safety, and substantial evidence of effectiveness for the conditions for which the drug is to be offered.

Once a drug is approved, its formula, manufacturing process, labeling, packaging, dosage, methods of testing, etc., generally may not be changed from those stated in its approved NDA. Supplemental applicationS may be filed by sponsors wishing to make such change. A change may be made only with FDA approval (21 CFR 314). However, changes to increase assurance of safety and effectiveness should be put into effect at the earliest possible time, without waiting for approval. Detailed instructions are given in the regulations. Antibiotics are treated as new drugs and must have the equivalent of an approved NDA before being offered on the U.S. market.

Drugs that are not "new" are not subject to the new drug procedure, but must comply with all other drug requirements, including registration, labeling, and manufacturing practices. Obviously, you should ascertain the status of any drug you intend to import, and be sure that the product complies with applicable regulation. For further information regarding NDAs, contact the FDA (see addresses at end of this chapter).

Investigational Drugs. These are new drugs intended solely for investigational use by qualified scientific experts. If your import falls into this category, you may bring it into the U.S. and distribute it without an approved NDA. However, the drug and the plans for research must comply with FDA's Investigational New Drug (IND) regulations (21 CFR 312). Investigational drugs may not be distributed or imported for trial on humans unless the sponsor has filed a Notice of Claimed Investigational Exemption for a New Drug and has received FDA approval.

Insulin. Section 506 requires FDA batch-testing and certification for both insulin crystal and finished dosage forms. An NDA for the product must be approved before FDA will accept samples for certification. FDA tests samples for conformance to standards published in the insulin regulations, and charges testing fees to defray costs of the insulin certification program.

Biological Products. Since most biological products are derived from living organisms, they are by their nature potentially dangerous if improperly prepared or tested. FDA's Center for Biologics Evaluation and Research (CBER) monitors biologics production closely, does batch testing, and conducts research toward improving the quality of biologics. CBER's research provides standards for these products, as well as proper control procedures.

In addition to the traditional biological products described in the Public Health Service Act, the Federal Food, Drug, and Cosmetic Act gives CBER jurisdiction over selected medical devices and drug products. The devices are primarily articles used in blood banks or plasmapheresis centers, such as containers for collecting and processing blood components, blood storage refrigeration, and blood bank supplies.

Licensing. Under PHSA, a manufacturer wishing to ship a biological product for sale in U.S. commerce or for import or export must obtain a U.S. license for both the manufacturing establishment and the product intended for shipment. These licenses are granted if the manufacturer shows that the establishment and product meet specific standards that insure continued safety, purity, potency, and effectiveness (21 CFR 600-680,211). To apply for licensing, the manufacturer must submit protocols detailing affirmative proof that the manufactured product meets PHSA standards. The manufacturer must pass a prelicensing inspection by FDA inspectors. Once licensed, most establishments are inspected annually by FDA.

Lot-release Procedures: Samples and Protocols. Certain licensed products are subject to special pre-release procedures. The manufacturer must submit specified materials to the CBER for clearance. These materials include: 1) a sample of the product in the size specified in the regulations; 2) detailed records (protocols) of the manufacture of each lot; and 3) all results of each test required by CBER for that particular product. CBER reviews the protocols and may conduct its own safety, purity, and potency tests on the samples before issuing a release for that product lot. A product subject to these lot-release procedures cannot be issued by the manufacturer until notification of official release is received from the FDA.

Standard Preparations. CBER supplies standard reference preparations for potency tests of certain licensed products, including antitoxins, bacterial and viral vaccines, and skin tests. Manufacturers are required to obtain and use these preparations in their testing of licensed products.

Blood Banks. Interstate shipment of blood and blood components requires the issuance of U.S. product and establishment licenses in accordance with PHSA. A licensed blood bank must comply with appropriate federal standards in preparing and testing the products being shipped. In accordance with FDA regulations (21 CFR 607), every blood bank collecting units of blood must register with the FDA within five days after commencing operations and submit a list of blood products prepared. All blood banks must operate in compliance with FDA current Good Manufacturing Practice Regulations for Blood and Blood Components (21 CFR 606), and are by law subject to FDA inspection every two years.

Blood bank establishment registration and product listing must be submitted on **Form FD 2830**. Only those blood banks that have complied with the necessary establishment registration and product listing and also hold valid U.S. establishment and product licenses may ship blood or blood components in U.S. interstate commerce.

Investigational New Drugs (INDs). The requirements for filing an IND application for a biological product are essentially the same as for drugs, except that it should be sent to the Director, Office of Biological Product Review (see addresses at end of this chapter).

Veterinary Biologics (USDA-regulated). Biologics intended for use with animals are subject to licensing provisions of the VSTA enforced by the USDA Animal and Plant Health Inspection Service's (APHIS) Veterinary Biologics Staff. Technically, biologics are also drugs under FDCA, but are not subject to the new animal drug provisions of the Act when in full compliance with the VSTA.

You must have a USDA permit for each shipment and each separate product of any veterinary biologic you wish to import. Only persons residing in the U.S., or operating a business establishment in the U.S., who hold a valid USDA Veterinary Services (VS) permit, may import a veterinary biologic. USDA VS issues three types of permits for import of biological products: Permit for Research and Evaluation; Permit for Distribution and Sale; Permit for Transit Shipment Only. Each type of permit has its own general requirements and conditions, to which specific conditions may be added for any given shipment at the discretion of the USDA Biologics Staff.

The USDA will not issue permits for products originating from any country known to have exotic diseases of livestock, if such products may endanger U.S. livestock or poultry. For a complete listing of countries listed by USDA as having such diseases, refer to Commodity Index Chapter 2, beginning on page 339 and Chapter 1, beginning on page 331. USDA inspection of producer and applicant equipment and facilities is a prerequisite to permit approval. Permits will not be issued for biologic products prepared in the U.S., exported, and presented for re-entry, except in cases where a small quantity of product is required for in vitro research and evaluation. In these cases, your product will be admitted only if USDA has determined that it poses no threat to U.S. livestock or poultry.

If you wish to import a veterinary biological product, you should contact Veterinary Services (see addresses at end of this chapter) for application forms. Your application should specify the type of permit you need, the intended port of entry, the estimated quantity of product, and the anticipated date of your importation. In addition, certain specific requirements apply, depending upon the type of permit requested.

Permit for Research and Evaluation. On your application for this type of permit, VS requires a brief description of your product, methods of propagating antigens (including composition of the medium), species of animals or cell cultures involved, degree of inactivation or attenuation, recommendations for use, and the proposed plan of evaluation in addition to general permit application information. The USDA may also ask you to supply information necessary to assess your product's impact on the environment. Special restrictions or tests may be specified as part of the permit when deemed necessary or advisable by USDA. The product under permit must comply with all applicable provisions of the law, and must be packaged and labeled in accordance with 9 CFR 112.

Permit for Distribution and Sale. In addition to general information required on the permit application, you must provide the

USDA with supporting materials necessary to satisfy the following requirements: 1) The product must be prepared in such a way as to insure its purity, safety, potency, and effectiveness. Three copies of blueprints of the producing foreign establishment must accompany the application, unless satisfactory plans are already on file with Veterinary Services. Production facilities to be used for each product prepared at the establishment must be designated. The manufacturer must submit written authorization for USDA inspectors to inspect the premises without previous notification. You must provide written assurance that the product under permit will be prepared under supervision of a person with requisite education and experience and in accordance with any applicable regulation. Methods of production must be written into an approved Outline of Production, four copies of which must be submitted to USDA and approved before the permit will be issued. You will also have to furnish data that establishes that the product complies with the law. In some cases, VS may require product testing under field conditions before issuing a permit.

As a permit holder, you will be required to provide the following: 1) adequate facilities for storing biologics; 2) information regarding all claims to be made on labels and advertising matter relating to the product; 3) mounted copies of final container and carton labels and enclosures to be used with the product; and 4) samples of each serial from each shipment of biological product. The product being sampled may not be distributed until released by Veterinary Services.

Permit for Transit Shipment Only. This type of permit is only required when a biological product is being shipped from one foreign country to another by way of the U.S. Such a shipment may only move under permit, subject to the following restrictions: 1) When the shipment is to transit the U.S. on the same carrier on which it arrived, it must be confined to that carrier at all times. If it is to transit the U.S. on a carrier other than that on which it arrived, a schedule of arrival and departure of each shipment must be furnished by the permit holder to Veterinary Services prior to arrival in the U.S. 2) The permit holder is responsible to VS for handling, storing, and forwarding of the biological product. VS must be notified of all shipments received and forwarded by the permit holder, and an accurate accounting must be made.

Illegal Shipments. If you present veterinary biologics for importation without a permit, your products will be returned to the country of origin at your own expense, or else destroyed by USDA personnel. If you present biological products for importation under permit for distribution and sale, and they are found to be worthless, contaminated, dangerous, or harmful, either you will have to return them to the country of origin at your own expense, or they will be destroyed by USDA personnel. This remedial action must be accomplished within 30 days after such finding. If your product is returned to the country of origin, it must not bear a U.S. permit number on the label. For more information, or to request permit application, contact APHIS VS (see addresses at end of this chapter).

APHIS VS Permits for Controlled Material, Organisms, and Vectors. The USDA APHIS's VS regulates the importation of all animal-origin materials that could represent a disease risk to U.S. livestock. This includes not only animal products and byproducts, but also biological materials that contain or have been in contact with animal material (including all cell cultures). You should submit your request for USDA APHIS VS permit authorizing the importation of such controlled materials on a completed VS **Form 16-3.** Cell cultures and their products need a VS **Form 16-7** in addition. You may obtain forms from the Veterinary Services Import-Export office (see addresses at end of this chapter) or from any USDA port office.

When applying for an import permit, you should include as much background information on the material as you feel might be necessary for the VS to evaluate the disease risk. You may include research papers if you think they will be helpful in the evaluation process, but don't send them by fax.

For shipments of cell lines, including human cell lines and cell culture deriviates such as monoclonal antibodies, you should complete both the basic permit application and the supplemental **Form 16-7.** This form requests such information as cell line history, country of origin, and source of nutrient supplement used in the media. If you do not provide the information in full, APHIS will not issue you a permit.

It takes about two weeks for APHIS to process the application and have a permit ready for return mail. If the information on your application is incomplete, there will be a delay while VS contacts you for the missing information. You can make your application on a signed facsimile, as long as you send an original signed document as a follow-up. If you will need more than one application form, you are free to make copies. Once your permit is issued, you are responsible to comply with all of its stipulations. For more information, or to request a permit application, contact APHIS VS (see addresses at end of this chapter).

CDC Permit Requirements. An original signed copy of the Centers for Disease Control Application for Permit to Import or Transport Agents or Vectors of Human Disease must be completed and submitted to CDC's Office of Biosafety (see addresses at end of this chapter). The person signing the permit application must reside in the U.S. and must be the proposed permit holder. The application requires such information as: 1) person requesting permit; 2) source and description of material; 3) number of shipments; 4) method of transport; 5) quantity, i.e. volume and type of individual containers; 6) proposed use, including objectives, proposed plan of work, completion date, and final disposition of materials; 7) description of available isolation and containment facilities; and 8) qualifications and experience of technical personnel. Your approved permit may stipulate additional restrictions and precautions that you must strictly adhere to. There are specific packaging and labeling requirements for etiologic agents and biomedical materials specified in 42 CFR Part 72. (See "Marking and Labeling Requirements" and "Shipping Considerations" below.)

Dispensing Requirements. Prescription drugs may be dispensed only by or on the prescription of a licensed practitioner, such as a physician, dentist, or veterinarian. They must be labeled: "Caution: Federal law prohibits dispensing without prescription." In general, a drug is restricted to the prescription class if it is not safe for use except under professional supervision. Under the law, this includes habit-forming drugs and any drug that is unsafe because of its toxicity or other potential for harmful effect, or the method of its use, or the collateral measures necessary to its use. Most prescription drugs are new drugs under the FDCA.

You may legally ship prescription drugs only to persons and firms who are regularly and lawfully engaged in the wholesale or retail distribution of prescription drugs, and to hospitals, clinics, physicians, and others licensed to prescribe such drugs.

Nonprescription drugs are those generally regarded as safe for the consumer to use when following the required label directions and warnings. These are commonly called "over-the-counter" (OTC) drugs because they may be purchased without a prescription. Nonprescription OTC drugs must comply with the requirements of the Fair Packaging and Labeling Act (FPLA) (21 CFR 201).

Registration Requirements. Owners or operators of all establishments that manufacture or process drugs and devices in the U.S. must register their establishments and list their products with the FDA. All drugs marketed within the U.S., including imported drugs, must be listed with the FDA. Establishments required to register include facilities to repackage or otherwise change the container, wrapper, or labeling of any drug or device package for distribution from the original place of manufacture to the person who makes final delivery or sale to the ultimate consumer. The law applies to both bulk and finished-dosage-form drugs, finished devices, products exported to the U.S. by foreign firms, and products exported by domestic firms.

Foreign establishments offering drugs or devices for import into the U.S. must comply with the listing requirements. Bulk drug substances being brought in by a domestic firm, even when imported from a foreign subsidiary, must also be listed. Drug and device distributors not required to register their establishments may submit listing information directly to FDA for products they distribute under their own label or trade name.

All registration and product listing submissions must be in English, except for labeling in a foreign language, which should be the actual labeling on the product and accompanied by an English translation.

Establishment registration must be updated annually. Product listing submissions must be updated each June and December if certain material changes have occurred. Changes requiring updated listings include: 1) newly introduced drugs; 2) discontinued drugs; 3) changes in information previously submitted (i.e. change in product name, quantity or identity of active ingredients, etc.); or 4) significant change in labeling.

No registration or listing fees are required. Failure to register and list is a violation of the FDCA.

The National Drug Code (NDC) provides index numbers to specifically identify drug products. The labeler code portion of the number is assigned by the FDA, and product and package portions are assigned by the vendor. The NDC number may be printed on the label, but such printing is not required at the present time.

Wholesale Drug Distributors. FDCA requires wholesale drug distributors to be licensed by the state where they do business. State licensing laws must meet minimum federally prescribed standards, including requirements for storage, handling, and recordkeeping. Wholesale drug distributors who are not authorized distributors-of-record for a particular drug are required to provide wholesale purchasers with a statement identifying each prior sale.

Reporting Requirements. The FDCA requires drug sponsors to keep the FDA apprised of developments that may affect the safety and effectiveness of their products. This applies both to drugs under clinical study and those that have received FDA approval for marketing. 21 CFR 310, 312, 314, 343 and 431 detail required records and reports. The most significant of these are **adverse reaction reports**. These notify the FDA of "any adverse experience associated with the use of a drug, whether or not considered drug-related, and includes any side effect, injury, toxicity, or sensitivity reaction, or significant failure of expected pharmacological action." Such reports originate largely as voluntary communications from physicians, pharmacists, or other health professionals to the manufacturer. The drug firm must transmit such information to FDA within 15 working days from its receipt, or in the periodic reports required on approved new drugs. Forms, instructions, and additional information regarding reporting may be obtained from FDA's Division of Epidemiology and Surveillance (see addresses at end of this chapter).

Sales Restrictions. The FDCA prohibits selling, purchasing, or trading of drug samples and drug coupons. Resale of drugs purchased by hospitals or health care entities is prohibited, with exceptions for group purchasing organizations, nonprofit affiliates, and entities under common control.

Drug Samples. Manufacturers or distributors are permitted to distribute samples to a licensed practitioner or health care entity by common carrier or through marketing representatives, upon written request. Certain drug sample records must be maintained and made available to government officials on request. Manufacturers and distributors must maintain their products in a manner that will prevent contamination, deterioration, or adulteration of their samples; they must provide the FDA with the name and phone number of an employee or agent in charge of drug samples; and they must maintain lists of representatives and drug sample storage sites. Manufacturers and distributors must notify the FDA of losses, thefts, and in the event that representatives are convicted for illegal trafficking in drug samples.

Drug Manufacturing Controls. The FDCA requires that drug manufacturers operate in conformity with current Good Manufacturing Practice regulations (21 CFR 210, 211). These include adequately equipped manufacturing facilities, adequately trained personnel, stringent controls over the manufacturing processes, reliable and secure computerized operations, and appropriate finished product examination and testing. Each manufacturing plant must have a quality assurance unit or person with responsibility and authority to accept or reject all drugs and raw materials. The FDA also publishes guidelines for acceptable methods and procedures for compliance. For more information, contact the FDA's Center for Biologics Evaluation and Research (see addresses at end of this chapter).

Sanitary Safeguards. A drug must not consist in whole or in part of any filthy, putrid, or decomposed substance. A drug must not be prepared, packed, or held under insanitary conditions whereby it may be contaminated with filth, or whereby it may be rendered injurious to health.

Containers. Drug containers must not be composed, in whole or in part, of any poisonous or deleterious substance that may render the contents injurious to health. They must not be made, formed, or filled so as to be misleading as to content amount. Containers and their components, such as caps, cap liners, etc. must not be reactive, additive, or absorptive so as to alter the safety, identity, strength, quality, or purity of the contents beyond official or established requirements. They must provide adequate protection against external factors that can cause deterioration or contamination of the product (21 CFR 211).

Tamper-resistant packaging is required for certain drugs, cosmetics, and medical devices sold through retail outlets. Tamper-resistant packaging is defined as packaging in such a manner that any product tampering will be visibly evident to the consumer-purchaser. Oral OTC drug products (except dentifrices, dermatologics, and insulin); nasal, optic, ophthalmic, rectal, and vaginal drugs; cosmetics used orally, such as mouth washes, gargles, breath fresheners, etc.; and vaginal cosmetics all requires this type of packaging. Address questions regarding compliance of a particular package to the FDA's Division of Manufacturing and Product Quality. Contact FDA headquarters for address.

Imitations. A drug must not imitate another drug or be offered for sale under the name of another drug. A drug or its container or labeling must not bear the trademark, tradename, or other identifying mark, imprint, device, or any likeness thereof, of another drug manufacturer, processor, packer, or distributor.

Germicides and Antiseptics. A product represented as a germicide should be capable, in the dilutions mentioned in its labeling, of meeting the criteria and standards set in official references for killing microorganisms. A product represented as an antiseptic should be germicidal when used as its labeling directs. However, if the recommended conditions of use provide for prolonged contact with the body (wet dressing, ointment, dusting powder, etc.), capability of inhibiting bacterial growth is sufficient.

Official Drugs. The law designates the United States Pharmacopoeia (USP), the Homeopathic Pharmacopoeia of the United States (HP), and the National Formulary (NF) as official compendia. All drugs named therein are required by law to meet the standards of strength, quality, or purity set forth in such compendia. They must be packaged and labeled in the manner prescribed therein. If a drug differs in strength, quality, or purity under or above the limits specified in an official compendium, the nature and extent of that difference must be plainly stated on the label.

A drug not recognized in an official compendium is adulterated if its strength differs from, or its purity or quality falls below, that which it purports to have or is represented to posses. For example, any drug intended for use by injection, and any ophthalmic ointment or solution, must be sterile.

A drug is adulterated under the law if any substance has been mixed or packed therewith so as to reduce the quality or strength of the article or to constitute a substitute. For example, the addition of exhausted belladonna leaves to unexhausted leaves not only reduces quality and strength, but also constitutes substitution.

Danger to Health. A drug must not be dangerous to health when used in the dosage or with the frequency or duration prescribed, recommended, or suggested in its labeling.

Drugs of Abuse. There are severe criminal penalties for the distribution of anabolic steroids and human growth hormones without a doctor's prescription. Butylnitrate and its isomers are banned from sale except for commercial purposes that may not result in its misuse for euphoric effects, and uses approved by the FDA. At this time, there are no FDA-approved uses for this drug.

Animal Dosage-form Drugs. Veterinary drugs are divided into the same major classes as other drugs, each being subject to additional requirements.

Animal prescription drugs may be dispensed only by a licensed veterinarian, or on the prescription or other order of a licensed veterinarian. In general, a drug is restricted to the prescription class if it is only safe for use under professional supervision (21 CFR 201). The label must state: "Caution: Federal law restricts this drug to use by or on the order of a licensed veterinarian."

Animal nonprescription drugs are those for which adequate directions for safe and effective lay use can be written.

New Animal Drugs (NADs) are drugs not generally recognized as safe and effective for use in the animal species for which they are intended (21 CFR. 201). You may not import an NAD for commercial marketing unless it has been FDA-approved as safe and effective for use in the United States. To request approval, you should file a New Animal Drug Application **FDA 356V** with FDA's Center for Veterinary Medicine (see addresses at end of this chapter). **Form FDA 356V** must contain substantial evidence supporting the drug's effectiveness, including results of adequate tests to establish safety (21 CFR Sec. 512). The data you provide must be specific for each species of animal for which your drug is intended. For food-producing animals, the data must include evidence of safety from residues of both the drug and its metabolites. This includes acceptable methods for recovery, and measurement of such residues from edible tissues of any food-producing animal for which the drug is intended. The FDA may approve an NAD or metabolites thereof found to induce cancer, if no harm comes to the animal and if there is no residue of drug or metabolites in any edible product reaching the consumer. Such a drug, however, may not be approved for pets. You must also submit technical data regarding manufacturing methods and controls, and the environmental impact of the manufacture and use of the drug.

Investigational New Animal Drugs (INADs) may only be distributed for investigational use by qualified scientific experts, for a particular purpose (21 CFR Sec. 512). If you fit this category, you may import an INAD for distribution in the U.S. without an approved New Animal Drug Application. However, your INAD and plans for research must comply with the INAD regulations (21 CFR 511). Before shipping an INAD for clinical tests in animals, you must submit a Notice of Claimed Investigational Exemption for New Animal Drug to the Center for Veterinary Medicine (see addresses at end of this chapter) (21 CFR 511).

Antibiotic Drugs. The law provides for FDA testing and certification of each batch of animal drugs composed in whole or in part of any kind of penicillin, streptomycin, chlortetracycline, chloramphenicol, or bacitracin, or any derivative thereof except where exempted by regulation. These antibiotic drugs for animal use are also NAD's under the law (Sec. 201) The regulations now exempt all antibiotic drugs from the requirements of batch certification, though not from meeting specified quality characteristics.

Pesticidal Drugs. Animal products that are pesticidal preparations such as rodenticides, fungicides, and insecticides, are subject to the Federal Insecticide, Fungicide, and Rodenticide Act (FIFRA) administered by the Pesticide Registration Division of the Environmental Protection Agency (EPA) (see addresses at end of this chapter). Depending upon the claims made, such products may be subject both to FIFRA and the FDCA. A Memorandum of Understanding between the two agencies specifies which agency will process petitions for products under dual jurisdiction. Petitions may be submitted to either agency and will be referred if necessary.

Medicated Feeds. If you are importing medicated feeds and medicated feed premixes (Type A articles), you should be sure that they are manufactured, processed, packaged, or held under methods, facilities, and controls that conform to the requirements of FDA Good Manufacturing Practice Regulations (21 CFR 225-6). In order to import NADs for commercial distribution, you must submit a Medicated Feed Application **Form FDA-1900** to FDA, unless you have been granted a waiver by the regulations (21 CFR 558). You should submit **Form FDA-1900** to the Center for Veterinary Medicine (see addresses at end of this chapter). The information you submit with the application must include the NAD approval regulation on which you base your expectation of FDA's approval.

Animal Grooming Aids. Products intended for cleansing or promoting attractiveness of animals are not subject to FDA control. You are not required to submit **Form FD701** for these items. However, if you represent your products as having any therapeutic purpose or as containing an active drug ingredient, they are subject to FDCA as animal drugs or possibly as animal devices. In this case, you must comply with any applicable part of the regulation and you must submit **Form FD701** at Customs entry.

Animal Devices. Veterinary medical devices and diagnostic aids are subject to general FDCA misbranding and adulteration provisions (21 CFR Secs. 501 and 502). Though FDA approval of devices intended for animal use is not required, you should be sure that your device's labeling is not false or misleading in any particular, and that the device is not otherwise misbranded or adulterated. If your device is dangerous to animal health when used in the manner prescribed, recommended, or suggested in its labeling, it is a prohibited import.

Animal prescription devices may be dispensed only by a licensed veterinarian or on the prescription or other order of a licensed veterinarian. In general, a device is restricted to the prescription class if it is not safe for use except under professional supervision (21 CFR 801). The label must state: "Caution: Federal law restricts this device to sale by or on the order of a veterinarian."

Animal Drug Registration and Listing. The FDCA requires all U.S. manufacturers of animal drugs and certain medicated feeds to register annually. This includes manufacturers of 1) dosage form drugs; 2) type A medicated articles (premixes); 3) medicated feeds that require approved **Form FDA-1 900.** Foreign manufacturers are permitted to register (21 CFR Sec. 510). All registered establishments, except medicated feed manufacturers, must file a listing of all drugs manufactured, prepared, propagated, compounded, or processed for commercial distribution. Dosage-form drugs and medicated feed premixes must be listed. Foreign products imported into the U.S. must be listed. Listing is not required for medicated feeds.

You may obtain additional information concerning registration and status of animal products under FDCA from FDA's Division of Compliance, Center for Veterinary Medicine (see addresses at end of this chapter). When making inquiries, you should provide full information concerning the product identity, including, insofar as possible, a quantitative formula and a draft label.

Marking and Labeling Requirements

How your drug must be labeled is determined by its regulatory category; i.e., whether it is an investigational drug, a new drug, a prescription-only drug, or an OTC drug. The law defines "label" to mean the written, printed, or graphic matter on the immediate container. Any information required in the label must also appear on the outer carton or wrapper of the package. "Labeling" includes all labels and other written, printed, or graphic matter accompanying the product. The word "accompanying" is interpreted very broadly, so that "labeling" may include material that does not physically accompany the product if it serves to identify the article, tell its uses, give directions, etc.

The following discussion is an overview of drug labeling requirements. You should contact FDA for specific details pertinent to the product you wish to import. For a general discussion of U.S. Customs marking and labeling requirements, refer to "Marking: Country of Origin" on page 215 and "Special Marking Requirements" on page 217.

Chemical Products. A shipment of any products containing chemicals that are classified as hazardous substance (49 CFR 172) must comply with the marking and labeling regulations adopted by the EPA (46 CFR 147.30) and the DOT (49 CFR 171 et seq.).

All Drugs. All labeling information required by the FDCA must be in English and must appear conspicuously on the label and in the labeling so that such information will be read and understood by the ordinary individual under customary conditions of purchase and use. Labeling information may also be given in a foreign language, but if any statement is made in a foreign language, all of the labeling information required by FDCA must appear in the foreign language as well as in English.

The label must bear: 1) name and address of manufacturer, packer, or distributor; 2) accurate statement of dosage strength; 3) quantity of contents in terms of weight, measure, or numerical count (prescription drugs may show quantity either in "English" or metric units. OTC drugs must show quantity in the "English" system of measure, but may also have a separate metric declaration); 4) list of active ingredients, using the established name for each such active ingredient; 5) an expiration date (applies to all prescription drugs and most OTC drugs); 6) name and quantity or proportions of any habit-forming substance or derivative, with the statement "Warning—May be habit-forming"; 7) established name and quantity or proportion of the following, if present (or if any derivative or preparation of such is present) in the drug: alcohol, bromides, ether, chloroform, acetanilide, acetophenetidin, amidopyrine, antipyrine atropine, hyoscine, hyoscyamine, arsenic, digitalis, digitalis glucosides, mercury, ouabain, strophanthin, strychnine, or thyroid; 8) If the drug has an established name, it must be displayed with the trade name. For prescription drugs, the established name must appear in type that is at least half as large as the type used for the trade name.

Prescription Drugs. The label must bear: 1) the legend "Caution: Federal law prohibits dispensing without prescription"; 2) quantity or portion of each active ingredient, and, if the drug is intended for any use other than oral, the names of all other ingredients; 3) if the drug is intended for injection, the label must state the names and quantities of all ingredients; 4) a statement of recommended or usual dosage; 5) package labeling (such as booklet or circular) should ordinarily contain information in substantially the following format and order and with section headings as follows: Descriptions, Actions, Indications, Warnings, Precautions, Adverse Reactions, Dosage and Administration, Overdosage (where applicable), and How Supplied.

OTC Drugs. The principal display panel must bear: 1) an identity statement followed by general pharmacological category or principal intended actions, and 2) quantity of contents declaration. The requirements for the latter are the same as those for foods except that in the case of a drug that is in tablet, capsule, ampule or other unit form, the quantity must be expressed in terms of numerical count, augmented, when necessary, with the strength, e.g. "100 tablets, 5 grains each."

Outer Wrapper or Carton. If the immediate container has an outer wrapper or carton, it must also bear all required label information, unless such wording is legible through the outer wrapper or carton.

Adequate Directions for Use. The package labeling must bear adequate directions for use. Omission (in whole or in part) of the following information on products distributed to the public, constitute inadequate directions. 1) Statements of all conditions, purposes, or uses for which the drug is intended, including conditions, purposes, or uses for which it is prescribed, recommended, or suggested in its oral, written, printed, or graphic advertising and conditions, purposes, or uses for which the drug is commonly used. Such statements shall not refer to conditions, uses, or purposes for which the drug can be safely used only under the supervision of a practitioner licensed by law and for which it is advertised solely to such practitioners; 2) quantity of dose, including usual quantities for each of the uses for which it is intended and usual quantities for persons of different ages and different physical conditions; 3) frequency, duration, route or method, and time (in relation to time of meals, time of onset of symptoms, or other time factors) of administration or application; 4) preparation for use (shaking, dilution, adjustment of temperature, or other manipulation or process).

Adequate Warnings. The package labeling must bear adequate warnings, when necessary, for the protection of users. Label warnings may be needed because of the nature of the ingredients. For example, antacids are required to be labeled with specific warnings, depending upon product composition. For example: "GENERAL WARNING--Do not take more than maximum recommended daily dosage"; for aluminum-containing antacids: "Drug interaction precaution—do not take this product if you are taking a prescription antibiotic drug containing any form of tetracycline."

A warning may be needed because of the nature of the intended use. For example, one type of cough syrup should bear a warning such as: "WARNING—Keep out of the reach of children. Do not administer to children under 2 years of age unless directed by physician. Persistent cough may indicate the presence of a serious condition. Persons with a high fever or persistent cough should not use this preparation unless directed by physician."

False and Misleading Statements. Labeling must not contain any statement that is false or misleading in any particular. A drug should be recommended for use only for those conditions for which it has been shown by scientific tests to be effective treatment. Serious disease conditions that cannot be diagnosed or successfully treated by consumers should not be referred to in labeling of OTC drugs. User testimonials that imply that a preparation is effective for a certain condition for which it is in fact ineffective or has not been demonstrated to be effective, constitutes misbranding.

Biologics for Human Use. The Public Health Service Act specifies that biologics be plainly labeled with the proper name of the article, the name, address, and license number of the manufacturer, and the appropriate expiration date of the product. The Center for Biologics Evaluation and Research reviews and approves all labeling for biologics prior to their licensing. In addition, all important changes in approved labeling must be submitted for approval. For prescription biological drugs, the manufacturer must also comply with FDA regulations pertaining to the package insert (21 CFR 201).

Biologics for Animal Use. The USDA requires each separate container in a shipment of biologics for animal use to bear the true name of the product, the permit number assigned by the USDA, the serial number affixed by the manufacturer to identify the product with the records of its preparation, and the return date of the product.

CDC-regulated Biomedical Materials. Any etiologic agent regulated by the Centers for Disease Control must be labeled precisely as illustrated and described in 42 CFR 72.

Shipping Considerations

You will need to ensure that your goods are packaged and shipped with care so that they pass smoothly through Customs and arrive in good condition. You are responsible for ensuring that the shipment is in compliance with all applicable government regulations for packaging and shipping. In most instances, you should not leave these arrangements solely to the discretion of your supplier. Careful preparation of the cargo and selection of the mode of transport can be essential to a cost-effective, timely delivery of undamaged goods. We strongly advise you to consult your shipping representative, insurance agent, or freight broker for advice on packing and shipping. Refer also to the major tab section "Packing/Shipping/Insurance" for a general discussion of packing and shipping.

Pharmaceutical products may be shipped in bulk, bags, bottles, or other types of containers, depending on the type of product and whether it is prepackaged. General considerations include protection from contamination, weather, and pests. If a product must be kept in a sanitary environment, all tables, utensils, platforms, and devices used for moving or handling the product, the compartments in which it is stowed while being transported will need to be maintained in a sanitary condition. For liquid shipments, venting and vapor collection systems may be required. Safety precautions should also be implemented as required to protect against breakage, spillage, corrosion of containers, and combustion. Containers should be constructed so as to be safe for handling during transport.

Chemical Products. Chemical products in particular may have to be shipped in pressurized, ventilated, and temperature-and vapor-controlled enclosures. Solid chemical products that are listed as hazardous substances (49 CFR 172 appendix) may be transported in bulk only on compliance with Coast Guard notification procedures, shipping permit requirements, and complex transportation regulations (46 CFR 148). All hazardous substances must also be packaged and transported in accordance with DOT regulations (49 CFR 171 et seq.).

CDC-regulated Etiologic and Biologic Agents. If you are importing diagnostic specimens and biological products that may contain an etiologic agent you should see that they are packaged to withstand leakage of contents, shocks, pressure changes, and other conditions incident to ordinary handling in transportation. 45 CFR 72 lists specific bacterial and fungal agents and details minimum packaging requirements for these substances. Your biological materials must be placed in a securely closed, watertight container (primary container) such as test tube or vial. You should then enclose this primary container in a second, durable watertight container (secondary container). You may enclose more than one primary container in the secondary container. The space surrounding the primary container must be filled with enough absorbent material to absorb its entire contents in case of breakage or leakage. Paper towel will suffice. You should enclose the secondary container in an outer shipping container constructed of corrugated fiberboard, cardboard, wood, or other material of equivalent strength.

When the volume of the substance to be transported exceeds 50 ml., a shock-absorbent material in volume at least equal to that of the absorbent material between the primary and secondary containers must surround the secondary container, filling the space between it and the outer shipping container. The maximum amount of etiologic agent enclosed within a single outer shipping container must not exceed 4,000 ml. If you use dry ice as a refrigerant, you must place it outside the secondary container(s). In such cases, the shock absorbent material between secondary and outer containers must be placed so that the secondary container does not become loose inside the outer shipping container as the dry ice sublimates.

Certain etiologic agents may only be shipped by registered mail or by an equivalent system that requires or provides for sending notification of receipt to the sender immediately upon delivery. In such cases, if notice of delivery is not received by the sender within 5 days following anticipated delivery, CDC must be notified.

Publications Available

The following publication explains the FDA requirements for importing pharmaceuticals. It is published by the FDA and is available on request from FDA headquarters (see addresses at end of this chapter).

Requirements of Laws and Regulations Enforced by the U.S. Food and Drug Administration

The following publications may be relevant to the importation of toxic or hazardous pharmaceutical products:

Toxic Substances Control Act: A Guide for Chemical Importers/Exporters (published by EPA).

TSCA Chemical Substance Inventory (1985 edition) (Doc. Code S/N 055-000-00254-1) $161.00 U.S. and Canada; $201.21 all other countries.

Supplement to TSCA Chemical Substances Inventory (1990) (Doc. Code S/N 055-000-00361-1) $15.00 U.S.; $18.75 Canada and all other countries.

The above publications and the *Harmonized Tariff Schedule of the United States* (HTSUS) are available from:

Government Printing Office (GPO)
Superintendent of Documents
Washington, DC 20402
(202) 512-1800 (Order line)
(202) 512-0000 (General)

The USGPO also has copies of specific laws available for purchase. The USGPO accepts credit card orders over the phone, as well as mail orders paid by credit card, a check drawn on a U.S. bank, or an international money order.

Relevant Government Agencies

Note: It is not a simple matter to import biological products and vectors. Never assume that a material you wish to import is regulated only by one of the federal agencies mentioned in this chapter. Contact each agency with specific details regarding your product, and let agency personnel determine your need for a permit.

Address your questions regarding FDA requirements for the importation of pharmaceuticals to:

Food and Drug Administration (FDA)
Center for Drug Evaluation and Research (HFD-8)
5600 Fishers Lane
Rockville, MD 20857
(301) 594-1012

Food and Drug Administration (FDA)
Division of Enforcement, Imports Branch
200 C Street SW
Washington, DC 20204
(202) 205-4726

Address your requests for information, instruction booklets, forms, etc. regarding establishment registration or product listing to:

U.S. Food and Drug Administration (FDA)
Drug Listing Branch (HFD-058)
5600 Fishers Lane
Rockville, MD 20857
(301) 443-1086

Address your questions for information regarding compliance with Good Manufacturing Practice to:

U.S. Food and Drug Administration (FDA)
Center for Biologics Evaluation and Research
8800 Rockville Pike
Bethesda, MD 20892
(301) 443-3285, 496-3556

Address your requests for information, license applications, or registration forms regarding biologics for human consumption to:

U.S. Food and Drug Administration (FDA)
Center for Biologics Evaluation and Research
8800 Rockville Pike
Bethesda, MD 20892
(301) 443-3285, 496-3556

Address your requests for permit applications or information regarding importation of veterinary biologics, organisms, and vectors to:

U.S. Department of Agriculture (USDA)
Animal and Plant Health Inspection Service (APHIS)
Veterinary Services (VS)
Import-Export Products Staff
Federal Building, Room 756
6505 Belcrest Road
Hyattsville, MD 20782
(301) 436-7885

Address your requests for information or permit applications for importation of etiologic agents or insects to:

Centers for Disease Control (CDC)
Office of Biosafety
1600 Clifton Road, NE
Atlanta, GA 30333
(404) 639-3883

Address your questions regarding registration and compliance status of animal products to:

U.S. Food and Drug Administration (FDA)
Center for Veterinary Medicine
Division of Compliance (HFV-230)
5600 Fishers Lane
Rockville, MD 20857
(301) 442-1544

Address your questions regarding regulation of pesticide residues to:

Environmental Protection Agency (EPA)
Office of Pesticide Programs
401 M Street SW (7501-C)
Washington, DC 20460
(703) 305-7090 (General)
(703) 305-7102 (Import/export requirements)

Address your inquiries regarding TSCA and EPA requirements for importation of chemical products to:

Environmental Protection Agency (EPA)
TSCA System Information
EPA 7408, OPPT
401 M Street SW
Washington, DC 20460
(202) 554-1404 (TSCA Information Hotline)

Address your questions regarding transportation of hazardous substances to:

U.S. Department of Transportation (DOT)
Research and Special Programs Administration
Office of Hazardous Materials Standards
400 7th St. SW
Washington, DC 20590
(202) 366-4488

Address your questions regarding importation of pharmaceutical products generally to the district or port director of customs for you area. For addresses, refer to"U.S. Customs District Offices" on page 62 or contact:

U.S. Customs Service
1301 Constitution Ave. NW
Washington, DC 20229
(202) 927-6724 (Information)
(202) 927-1000 (General)

Laws and Regulations

The following laws and regulations may be relevant to the importation of pharmaceuticals. The laws are contained in the United States Code (USC), and the regulations are published in the Code of Federal Regulations (CFR), both of which are available at larger public and law libraries. Specific laws and regulations may also be purchased from the U.S. Government Printing Office (address above).

15 USC 1261
Federal Hazardous Substances Act
This Act controls the importation of hazardous substances, sets forth prohibited imports, and authorizes various agencies to promulgate labeling, marking, and transport requirements.

49 CFR 170 et seq.
Hazardous Materials Regulations
These regulations list all substances deemed hazardous and provide transport, marking, labeling, safety, and emergency response rules.

46 CFR 147.30
Labeling of Hazardous Materials
This regulation requires the labeling of containers of hazardous substances and specifies the label contents.

46 CFR 148 et seq.
Carriage of Solid Hazardous Materials in Bulk
These regulations govern the transport of solid hazardous substances in bulk, including reporting, permitting, loading, stowing, and shipping requirements.

15 USC 2601 et seq.
Toxic Substances Control Act
This Act authorizes the EPA to determine whether a substance is harmful and to restrict importation, sale, and use of such substances.

19 CFR 12.118 et seq.
Toxic Substances Control Regulations
These regulations require importers of chemical substances imported in bulk or as part of a mixture to certify to Customs that the shipment complies with the TSCA or is not subject to that Act.

21 USC 301 et seq.
Food, Drug, and Cosmetic Act
This Act prohibits deceptive practices and regulates the manufacture, sale and importation or exportation of food, drugs, cosmetics, and related products. See 21 USC 331, 381, 382.

19 CFR 12.1 et seq.; 21 CFR 1.83 et seq.
Regulations on Food, Drugs, and Cosmetics
These regulations of the Secretary of Health and Human Services and the Secretary of the Treasury govern the standards, labeling, marking, and importing of pharmaceutical products.

21 USC 151 et seq.
Virus Serum Toxin Act
This Act prohibits the preparation, sale and importation of any worthless or harmful virus, serum, toxin, or analogous product for use in the treatment of domestic animals without a permit. Special rules apply to such importations from Canada. See 21 USC 152.

42 USC 262
Licensing of Biological Products
This Act requires persons dealing in biological products, including importers and exporters, to adhere to specific standards and to be licensed.

9 CFR 101 et seq.; 19 CFR 12.17 et seq.; 45 CFR 204; 21 CFR 5, 7, 25, 50, 58, 433 and 510
Regulations on Biological Products
These regulations include procedures and requirements for importing, exporting, labeling, and transporting biological products.

42 USC 201 et seq.
Public Health Service Act
This Act provides regulatory mechanism for premarket controls of biological products to protect the U.S. consumer from health dangers associated with improperly prepared or tested substances.

7 USC 135 et seq.
Federal Insecticide, Fungicide, and Rodenticide Act (FIFRA)
This Act prohibits the importation of products exposed to certain pesticides or devices that are adulterated, misbranded, or otherwise in violation of the Act, provides for registration of pesticides and devices, and establishes standards for labeling and classifying pesticides.

19 CFR 12; 40 CFR 162
Regulations on Pesticides
These regulations set forth the procedures and guidelines for importing products exposed to pesticides.

Sources of Additional Information

The TSCA Chemical Substance Inventory in computerized form is available from:

National Technical Information Service (NTIS)
U.S. Department of Commerce
5285 Port Royal Road
Springfield, VA 22161
(703) 487-4650

Access to the computerized TSCA Chemical Substance Inventory through commercial database is available at:

Scientific and Technical Network International
Chemical Abstracts Service (CAS)
File: CAS ONLINE
(800) 848-6533
Dialog Information Services
TSCA Chemical Substances Inventory
File: Number 52
(800) 334-2564

Principal Exporting Countries

The following listing includes samples of the main supplier nations of the products of this chapter. It is organized by HTSUS major heading. (Refer to "Customs Classification" above for the product codes.) Countries are listed in rank order of the value of products imported to the U.S. Statistics represent customs value entries for 1993 from the Bureau of Census, U.S. Department of Commerce.

3001—Canada, Germany, China, Netherlands, France, Argentina, Denmark, Sweden, Switzerland, Japan

3002—Belgium, Ireland, Switzerland, United Kingdom, France, Canada, Austria, Germany, Japan, Spain

3003—United Kingdom, France, Japan, Canada, Germany, Belgium, Ireland, Argentina, Switzerland, Norway

3004—United Kingdom, Switzerland, Sweden, Germany, Japan, Canada, Belgium, Italy, Ireland, Israel

3005—China, Germany, Canada, United Kingdom, Japan, Ireland, Mexico, Sweden, France, Denmark

3006—Germany, United Kingdom, France, Finland, Japan, Australia, Netherlands, Norway, Canada, New Zealand

Chapter 31: Fertilizers*

This chapter relates to the importation of fertilizers, which are classified under Chapter 31 of the Harmonized Tariff Schedule of the United States (HTSUS). Specifically, it includes solid and liquid forms of fertilizers derived from animal, vegetable, mineral, and chemical substances.

If you are interested in importing separate chemical compounds that are not intended for use as fertilizer, you should refer to Commodity Index Chapters 28 (inorganic) and 29 (organic). This chapter includes animal blood products imported as components of fertilizer, but not animal blood products covered in Chapter 5. Refer to Chapter 90 for importation requirements related to optical elements of potassium chloride. Cultured potassium chloride crystals, other than optical elements, that weigh no less than 2.5 grams each are covered in Chapter 38.

Key Factors

The key factors in the importation of fertilizers are:

- Compliance with U.S. Department of Agriculture (USDA) requirements (if the product is derived from an animal or vegetable substance)
- Compliance with Federal Plant Pest Act (if the product is derived from a vegetable, soil, or quarry substance)
- Compliance with Plant Quarantine Act (if the product is derived from a vegetable, soil, or quarry substance)
- Compliance with U.S. Federal Trade Commission (FTC) and Consumer Product Safety Commission (CPSC) standards (if the product will be marketed to consumers)
- Compliance with U.S. Environmental Protection Agency (EPA) requirements under Toxic Substances Control Act (TSCA) (if the product contains a hazardous substance)
- Compliance with U.S. Department of Transportation (DOT) regulations for transport of hazardous cargo

Although most importers use the services of a licensed customs broker in making their entries, and we recommend this practice, you should be aware of the regulatory, entry, and documentation issues involved in importing your product. You, as importer, are ultimately responsible for the fulfillment of any legal requirements applicable to your shipment.

*IMPORTANT: Read the Commodity Index Introduction. It is the essential framework for understanding this chapter.

General Considerations

Regulatory Agencies. The USDA regulates animal and vegetable fertilizers and fertilizers containing soil or quarry products. The EPA, under authority of the TSCA., imposes certain controls on the importation of chemical fertilizers. The TSCA defines a toxic substance as any substance determined to present the possibility of an unreasonable risk of injury to health and the environment. The DOT enforces regulations for transporting hazardous cargo. Materials are deemed hazardous if listed in DOT transport regulations (49 CFR 172 appendix).

Animal Byproduct Fertilizers. Byproducts of animals intended for use as fertilizer, including blood meal, bone meal, hoof meal, and animal organs, secretions, or similar items, are subject to quarantine regulations, marking requirements, and processing standards. Shipments of these products are inspected at the port of arrival by the Animal and Plant Health Inspection Service (APHIS) of the USDA. Unless the shipment is in compliance with all applicable laws and regulations, it will be denied entry into the U.S. Some shipments may be restricted or prohibited completely.

Vegetable, Soil, and Quarry Fertilizers. Shipments of fertilizers containing vegetable, soil, or quarry products will be inspected at the port of arrival by APHIS. Entry may be denied for noncompliance with the regulations, and the shipment could be seized, quarantined, destroyed, treated, or otherwise dealt with at the discretion of the inspector. Some shipments may be restricted or prohibited completely.

Chemical fertilizers. All chemical fertilizers are subject to the U.S. Customs Service TSCA Import Certification Rule (19 CFR 12.118 et seq.). If you import these products, you must sign one of the following statements: "I certify that all chemical substances in this shipment comply with all applicable rules or orders under TSCA and that I am not offering a chemical substance for entry in violation of TSCA or any applicable rule or order thereunder" or "I certify that all chemicals in this shipment are not subject to TSCA."

You must file this TSCA certification of compliance or exemption at the time you make the entry at Customs. The certification may be in the form of a typed or stamped statement on an appropriate entry document or commercial invoice or a preprinted attachment to such entry document or invoice. You may sign the certificate by means of an authorized facsimile signature. If your entry is electronically processed, the certification will be in the form of a Certification Code, which is part of the Automated Broker Interface (ABI) transmission. Customs will not release your shipment of chemical fertilizer without proper certification.

If you will be importing several or regular shipments of chemical fertilizer, you should ask the appropriate Customs district director to authorize your use of a blanket certification. If you receive such authorization, you must include on the commercial invoice or entry document for each shipment a statement that the blanket certification is on file and that it is incorporated by reference. This statement need not be signed. The blanket certification is valid for one calendar year, is subject to renewal, and may be revoked at any time for cause.

In filling out TSCA forms and Customs entry documents, you should provide the Chemical Abstracts Service (CAS) number for each chemical in the shipment. These CAS numbers are given in the appendix to the HTSUS. You are not required to include the CAS number, but Customs will be able to process your shipment more quickly if you include this number.

Shipments of chemical fertilizers must additionally be in compliance with toxic and hazardous substance regulations of the EPA and DOT. These include packaging, shipping, marking, and labeling requirements.

Articles Exclusion. If you are importing products that are classified as hazardous substances but are part of articles, you are subject to TSCA certification requirements only if certification for your product is specifically required by a rule or order promulgated under the TSCA. No specific rules have been adopted at this time. An "article" is a manufactured item 1) that is formed into a specific shape or design during manufacture, 2) that has end-use functions dependent on the shape or design during end use, and 3) that during the end use, does not change in its chemical composition or that changes only for a noncommercial purpose separate from the article and only as allowed by law (19 CFR 12.120(2)). Fluids and particles are not articles, regardless of shape or design.

Shipment Detention. A shipment of chemical fertilizer will be detained at the U.S. port of arrival (or entry if same), at your risk and expense, if: 1) it contains banned chemical substances (15 USC 2604, 2605); or 2) it contains chemical substances ordered seized because of imminent hazards (15 USC 2606). Further detention will occur at the port of entry, again at your risk and expense, if: 1) the EPA administrator or Customs district director has reasonable grounds to believe the shipment is not in compliance with the TSCA; or 2) you do not provide proper TSCA certification.

If your shipment is detained, it will be held by Customs for no more than 48 hours. It will then be turned over to the EPA administrator, unless you have arranged to release it in bond. You must either bring it into TSCA compliance or reexport it within the earlier of 90 days after notice of detention or 30 days of demand for redelivery. Customs may grant an extension if failure to comply or reexport is the result of delays in EPA or Customs procedures. If you fail to comply or reexport within the time allowed, the EPA administrator is authorized to have the shipment stored or disposed of at your expense.

Hazardous Consumer Products. Under the Federal Hazardous Substances Act (FHSA), a fertilizer intended for the consumer market is a hazardous substance if it is flammable, combustible, or has the potential to cause substantial personal injury during, or as a proximate result of, any customary or reasonably foreseeable handling or use. The CPSC does not require permits, special invoicing, limited entry, licenses, or any special approval process for importing hazardous consumer products into the U.S. However, if you are importing these types of products, you are responsible for ensuring that they meet all applicable FHSA and Consumer Product Safety Act (CPSA) requirements. There are detailed regulations regarding testing and labeling of hazardous products. The Commission's enforcement posture regarding compliance with labeling and product safety standards changes as new facts become available. Contact the CPSC (see addresses at end of this chapter) for specific requirements on the consumer product you are considering importing.

Substantial Product Hazard Reports. Defect-reporting is required for products covered under the CPSA. The law requires every manufacturer, distributor, or retailer of such products, who obtains information that reasonably supports the conclusion that such products fail to comply with an applicable consumer product safety rule, or contain a defect that could create a substantial product hazard, to immediately inform the CPSC of the potential violation or defect. A firm's willful failure to make a Substantial Product Hazard Report can result in litigation by the CPSC.

Customs Classification

For customs purposes, fertilizers are classified under Chapter 31 of the HTSUS. This chapter is broken into major headings, which are further divided into subheadings, and often sub-subheadings, each of which has its own HTSUS classification number. For example, the HTSUS number for potassium chloride fertilizer is 3104.20.00, indicating it is a subcategory of potassic mineral or chemical fertilizers (3104.00.00). There are five major headings within Chapter 31.

3101—Animal or vegetable fertilizers, whether or not mixed together or chemically treated; fertilizers produced by the mixing or chemical treatment of animal or vegetable products

3102—Mineral or chemical fertilizers, nitrogenous

3103—Mineral or chemical fertilizers, phosphatic

3104—Mineral or chemical fertilizers, potassic

3105—Mineral or chemical fertilizers containing two or three of the fertilizing elements nitrogen, phosphorus, and potassium; other fertilizers; goods of this chapter in tablets or similar forms or in packages of a gross weight not exceeding 10 kg

For more details regarding classifications of the specific product you are interested in importing, consult a customs broker, the appropriate commodity specialist at your nearest customs port, or the HTSUS. HTSUS is available for purchase from the U.S. Government Printing Office (see addresses at end of this chapter), and may be found in larger public libraries. Refer to "Classification—Liquidation" on page 207 for a general discussion of customs classification.

Sample Import Duties

No duties are levied on fertilizers.

Entry and Documentation

The entry of merchandise is a two-part process consisting of 1) filing the documentation necessary to determine whether merchandise may be released from Customs custody, and 2) filing the documents that contain information for duty assessment and statistical purposes. In certain instances, all documents must be filed and accepted by Customs prior to release of the goods. Unless you have been granted an extension, you must file entry documents at a location specified by the district or area director within five working days of your shipment's date of arrival at a U.S. port of entry. These include a number of standard documents required by Customs for any entry, and:

- U.S. Customs TSCA Certification (for chemical fertilizers)

After you present the entry, Customs may examine your shipment or may waive examination. The shipment is then released provided no legal or regulatory violations have been noted. You must then file entry summary documentation and deposit estimated duties at a designated customhouse within 10 working days of your shipment's release. For a detailed description of entry procedures, standard documentation, and informal entry, refer to "Entry Process" on page 182.

Prohibitions and Restrictions

Animal Byproduct Fertilizers. Animal byproduct fertilizers are subject to quarantine if they arrive from certain countries that are known to have specific infectious diseases. These countries are listed in 9 CFR 94. If a USDA inspector determines that a shipment is infected with anthrax, foot-and-mouth disease, rinderpest, or bovine spongiform encephalopathy, entry will be denied.

Bone meal may be imported without restriction, provided it has been processed in compliance with USDA regulations; is free of pieces of bone, hide, flesh, and sinew; and contains no more than traces of hair or wool (9 CFR 95.13). Entry is denied for shipments that are not in compliance.

Dried blood, blood meal, animal organs, tankage, meat meal, wool waste, wool manure, and similar animal byproducts for use as fertilizer cannot be imported unless: 1) the product originated in and was shipped from a country that is not on the quarantine list for foot-and-mouth disease or rinderpest; 2) the USDA inspector finds that the product has been fully processed by tanking under live steam or by dry rendering; or 3) the products are handled through quarantine procedures at the port of arrival and are found to be in compliance with USDA conditions (9 CFR 95.14, 95.16).

Manure of horses, cattle, sheep, other ruminants, and swine cannot be imported without permission of the Deputy Administrator, Veterinary Services.

Vegetable, Soil, or Quarry Fertilizers. At the port of entry, the USDA inspector will examine fertilizers with plant, soil, or quarry components for pest infestation. If an infestation is found or reasonably suspected, the inspector has authority to deny entry and to dispose of the shipment by the least drastic means available that will protect against spread of the infestation. Disposal will be at the expense of the owner of the shipment.

Hazardous Substances. Importation of fertilizers that contain chemicals considered hazardous is prohibited if the chemicals are misbranded. Certain hazardous substances listed in the FHSA and in regulations promulgated by the Consumer Product Safety Commission (CPSC) are completely banned from importation. A shipment of chemical fertilizer cannot be imported if it poses an imminent hazard. See 15 USC 1261, 2604-2606; 16 CFR 1500.265-1500.272.

Marking and Labeling Requirements

Animal Byproduct Fertilizers. Containers of fertilizers composed of animal byproducts must be marked with the country of origin—that is, the country where the animal was located. If fertilizers are quarantined at the port of arrival, marks and signs are required on shipping documents and any mode of transport used to move the product while under restrictions (9 CFR 95.25).

Chemical Fertilizers. A shipment of any chemical fertilizer that contains a hazardous substance must comply with the marking and labeling regulations adopted by the EPA (46 CFR 147.30) and the DOT (49 CFR 171 et seq.)

For a general discussion of U.S. Customs marking and labeling requirements, refer to "Marking: Country of Origin" on page 215 and "Special Marking Requirements" on page 217.

Shipping Considerations

You will need to ensure that your goods are packaged and shipped with care so that they pass smoothly through Customs and arrive in good condition. You are responsible for ensuring that the shipment is in compliance with all applicable government regulations for packaging and shipping. In most instances, you should not leave these arrangements solely to the discretion of your supplier. Careful preparation of the cargo and selection of the mode of transport can be essential to a cost-effective, timely delivery of undamaged goods. We strongly advise you to consult your shipping representative, insurance agent, or freight broker for advice on packing and shipping. Refer also to the major tab section "Packing/Shipping/Insurance" for a general discussion of packing and shipping.

Fertilizers may be shipped in bulk, bags, bottles, or other types of containers, depending on the type of fertilizer and whether it is prepackaged. General considerations include protection from contamination, weather, and pests. Venting and vapor collection systems may be required. Safety precautions should also be implemented as required to protect against spillage, air pollution, corrosion of containers, and combustion. Containers should be constructed so as to be safe for handling during transport.

Chemical Fertilizers. Chemical fertilizers in particular may have to be shipped in pressurized, ventilated, and temperature-and vapor-controlled enclosures. Solid chemical fertilizers that are listed as hazardous substances (49 CFR 172 appendix) may be transported in bulk only on compliance with Coast Guard notification procedures, shipping permit requirements, and complex transportation regulations (46 CFR 148). All hazardous substances must also be packaged and transported in accordance with DOT regulations (49 CFR 171 et seq.).

Publications Available

The following publications may be relevant to the importation of toxic or hazardous fertilizers:

Toxic Substances Control Act: A Guide for Chemical Importers/Exporters (published by EPA).

TSCA Chemical Substance Inventory (1985 edition) (Doc. Code S/N 055-000-00254-1) $161.00 U.S. and Canada; $201.21 all other countries.

Supplement to TSCA Chemical Substances Inventory (1990) (Doc. Code S/N 055-000-00361-1) $15.00 U.S.; $18.75 Canada and all other countries.

The above publications and the *Harmonized Tariff Schedule of the United States* (HTSUS) are available from:

Government Printing Office (GPO)
Superintendent of Documents
Washington, DC 20402
(202) 512-1800 (Order line)
(202) 512-0000 (General)

The USGPO also has copies of specific laws available for purchase. The USGPO accepts credit card orders over the phone, as well as mail orders paid by credit card, a check drawn on a U.S. bank, or an international money order.

Relevant Government Agencies

Address your inquiries regarding USDA requirements for importation of animal or vegetable byproduct fertilizers to:

U.S. Department of Agriculture (USDA)
Animal and Plant Health Inspection Service (APHIS)
Veterinary Services (VS)
Import-Export Products Staff
Federal Building, Rm. 756
6505 Belcrest Road
Hyattsville, MD 20782
(301) 436-7885

U.S. Department of Agriculture
Animal and Plant Health Inspection Service (APHIS)
Plant Protection and Quarantine (PPQ)
Federal Building, Rm. 631
6505 Belcrest Road
Hyattsville, MD 20782
(301) 436-8645

Address your inquiries regarding TSCA and EPA requirements for importation of chemical fertilizers to:

Environmental Protection Agency (EPA)
TSCA System Information
EPA 7408, OPPT
401 M Street SW
Washington, DC 20460
(202) 554-1404 (TSCA Information Hotline)

Address your questions regarding transportation of hazardous substances to:

U.S. Department of Transportation (DOT)
Research and Special Programs Administration
Office of Hazardous Materials Standards
400 7th St. SW
Washington, DC 20590
(202) 366-4488

Address your questions regarding CPSC requirements for fertilizers marketed to consumers to:

U.S. Consumer Product Safety Commission (CPSC)
Office of Compliance
Division of Regulatory Management
5401 Westbard Avenue
Bethesda, MD 20207
(301) 504-0400

Address your questions regarding importation of fertilizers generally to the district or port director of customs for you area. For addresses, refer to"U.S. Customs District Offices" on page 62 or contact:

U.S. Customs Service
1301 Constitution Ave. NW
Washington, DC 20229
(202) 927-6724 (Information)
(202) 927-1000 (General)

Laws and Regulations

The following laws and regulations may be relevant to the importation of fertilizers. The laws are contained in the United States Code (USC), and the regulations are published in the Code of Federal Regulations (CFR), both of which are available at larger public and law libraries. Specific laws and regulations may also be purchased from the U.S. Government Printing Office (address above).

15 USC 2601 et seq.
Toxic Substances Control Act
This Act authorizes the EPA to determine whether a substance is harmful and to restrict importation, sale, and use of such substances.

19 CFR 12.118 et seq.
Regulations on Toxic Substances Control
These regulations require importers of chemical substances imported in bulk or as part of a mixture to certify to Customs that the shipment complies with the TSCA or is not subject to that Act.

15 USC 1261
Federal Hazardous Substances Act
This Act controls the importation of hazardous substances, sets forth prohibited imports, and authorizes various agencies to promulgate labeling, marking, and transport requirements.

49 CFR 170 et seq.
Regulations of Hazardous Materials
These regulations list all substances deemed hazardous and provide transport, marking, labeling, safety, and emergency response rules.

46 CFR 147.30
Regulations on Labeling on Hazardous Materials
This regulation requires the labeling of containers of hazardous substances and specifies the label contents.

46 CFR 148 et seq.
Regulations of Carriage of Solid Hazardous Materials in Bulk
These regulations govern the transport of solid hazardous substances in bulk, including reporting, permitting, loading, stowing, and shipping requirements.

15 USC 1263
Consumer Product Safety Act (CPSA)
This Act gives the Consumer Product Safety Commission authority to set safety standards, testing procedures, and reporting requirements to ensure that consumer products not already covered under other regulations are not harmful.

9 CFR 95.13 et seq.
Regulations on Animal Byproduct Quarantine Control
These regulations prohibit the importation of animal byproducts for use in fertilizer unless the byproducts meet certain processing standards and are not infected with certain diseases.

Sources of Additional Information

The TSCA Chemical Substance Inventory in computerized form is available from:

National Technical Information Service (NTIS)
U.S. Department of Commerce
5285 Port Royal Road
Springfield, VA 22161
(703) 487-4650

Access to the computerized TSCA Chemical Substance Inventory through commercial database is available at:

Scientific and Technical Network International
Chemical Abstracts Service (CAS)
File: CAS ONLINE
(800) 848-6533
Dialog Information Services
TSCA Chemical Substances Inventory
File: Number 52
(800) 334-2564

Principal Exporting Countries

The following listing includes samples of the main supplier nations of the products of this chapter. It is organized by HTSUS major heading. (Refer to "Customs Classification" above for the product codes.) Countries are listed in rank order of the value of products imported to the U.S. Statistics represent customs value entries for 1993 from the Bureau of Census, U.S. Department of Commerce.

3101—Canada, France, Iceland, Austria, Norway, South Africa, Japan, Mexico, United Kingdom, Jamaica

3102—Canada, Trinidad and Tobago, Bulgaria, Netherlands, Chile, Venezuela, Brazil, Mexico, Nigeria, Italy

3103—Canada, United Kingdom, Germany, Spain, Australia, Taiwan, Belgium, Mexico, Finland

3104—Canada, Israel, Belarus, Germany, Russia, Chile, Belgium, Latvia, Jordan, Netherlands

3105—Canada, Russia, Norway, Belgium, Japan, Poland, Chile, Netherlands, Israel, Mexico

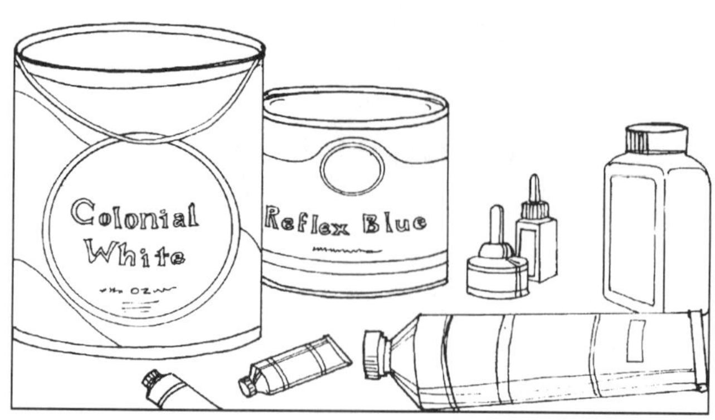

Chapter 32: Paints and Related Products*

Full title: Tanning or Dyeing Extracts; Tannins and Their Derivatives; Dyes, Pigments, and Other Coloring Matter; Paints and Varnishes; Putty and Other Mastics; Inks

This chapter relates to the importation of dyes, tannins, paints, mastics, and inks, which are classified under Chapter 32 of the Harmonized Tariff Schedule of the United States (HTSUS). Specifically, it includes vegetable and synthetic tannins and tanning extracts; vegetable, animal, and synthetic coloring extracts; color lakes, prepared pigments, opacifiers, enamels, glazes, paints, varnishes, prepared driers, putties, resin cements, mastics, and inks.

If you are interested in importing separate chemical compounds, you should refer to Commodity Index Chapters 28 (inorganic) or 29 (organic). The importing requirements for specific types of dyed fabrics are covered in Chapters 50 through 63. Leather products are found in Chapters 41 (raw leather) and 42 (leather goods). If you are interested in importing separately defined organic chemicals or tannates or tannin derivatives, you should refer to Chapters 29 or 35, respectively. Mastics of asphalt and other bituminous mastics are covered in Chapter 27. You should also refer to Chapter 38 for a number of related products, including ink removers, turpentines, graphite, animal black and activated carbons, and various rosin and resin products. Importation of glues and other adhesives is discussed in Chapter 35.

Key Factors

The key factors in the importation of flammable household products are:

- Compliance with U.S. Federal Trade Commission (FTC) and Consumer Product Safety Commission (CPSC) standards (if the product will be marketed to consumers)
- Compliance with U.S. Environmental Protection Agency (EPA) requirements under Toxic Substances Control Act (TSCA) (if the product is a hazardous substance)
- Compliance with U.S. Department of Transportation (DOT) regulations for transport of hazardous cargo (if the product is a hazardous substance)

*IMPORTANT: Read the Commodity Index Introduction. It is the essential framework for understanding this chapter.

Although most importers use the services of a licensed customs broker in making their entries, and we recommend this practice, you should be aware of the regulatory, entry, and documentation issues involved in importing your product. You, as importer, are ultimately responsible for the fulfillment of any legal requirements applicable to your shipment.

General Considerations

Regulatory Agencies. The CPSC, under the Federal Hazardous Substances Act (FHSA) and the Consumer Product Safety Act (CPSA) regulates the importation of products considered hazardous. The EPA, under authority of the TSCA, regulates the importation of combustible materials that contain toxic substances The TSCA defines a toxic substance as any substance determined to present the possibility of an unreasonable risk of injury to health and the environment. The DOT enforces regulations for transporting hazardous cargo. Materials are deemed hazardous if listed in DOT transport regulations (49 CFR 172 appendix).

Hazardous Consumer Products. Under the FHSA, a product intended for the consumer market is a hazardous substance if it is flammable, combustible, or could potentially cause substantial personal injury during, or as a proximate result of, any customary or reasonably foreseeable handling or use. The CPSC does not require permits, special invoicing, limited entry, licenses, or any special approval process for importing hazardous consumer products into the U.S. However, if you are importing these types of products, you are responsible for ensuring that they meet all applicable FHSA and CPSA requirements. There are detailed regulations regarding testing and labeling of hazardous products. The Commission's enforcement posture regarding compliance with labeling and product safety standards changes as new facts become available. Contact the CPSC (see addresses at end of this chapter) for specific requirements on the consumer product you are considering importing.

Substantial Product Hazard Reports. Defect-reporting is required for products covered under the CPSA. The law requires every manufacturer, distributor, or retailer of such products, who obtains information that reasonably supports the conclusion that such products fail to comply with an applicable consumer product safety rule, or contain a defect that could create a substantial product hazard, to immediately inform the CPSC of the potential violation or defect. A firm's willful failure to make a Substantial Product Hazard Report can result in litigation by the CPSC.

Toxic and Hazardous Substances. Shipments of products containing chemical substances must be in compliance with toxic and hazardous substance regulations of the EPA and DOT. These include packaging, shipping, marking, and labeling requirements. In addition, all products containing chemicals are subject to the U.S. Customs Service TSCA Import Certification Rule (19 CFR 12.118 et seq.). If you import these products, you must sign one of the following statements: "I certify that all chemical substances in this shipment comply with all applicable rules or orders under TSCA and that I am not offering a chemical substance for entry in violation of TSCA or any applicable rule or order thereunder" or "I certify that all chemicals in this shipment are not subject to TSCA."

You must file this TSCA certification of compliance or exemption at the time you make the entry at Customs. The certification may be in the form of a typed or stamped statement on an appropriate entry document or commercial invoice or a preprinted attachment to such entry document or invoice. You may sign the certificate by means of an authorized facsimile signature. If your entry is electronically processed, the certification will be in the form of a Certification Code, which is part of the Automated Broker Interface (ABI) transmission. Customs will not release your shipment without proper certification.

If you will be importing several or regular shipments, you should ask the appropriate Customs district director to authorize your use of a blanket certification. If you receive such authorization, you must include on the commercial invoice or entry document for each shipment a statement that the blanket certification is on file and that it is incorporated by reference. This statement need not be signed. The blanket certification is valid for one calendar year, is subject to renewal, and may be revoked at any time for cause.

In filling out TSCA forms and Customs entry documents, you should provide the Chemical Abstracts Service (CAS) number for each chemical in the shipment. These CAS numbers are given in the appendix to the HTSUS. You are not required to include the CAS number, but Customs will be able to process your shipment more quickly if you include this number.

Articles Exclusion. If you are importing items that are classified as hazardous substances but are part of articles, you are subject to TSCA certification requirements only if certification for your product is specifically required by a rule or order promulgated under the TSCA. No specific rules have been adopted at this time. An "article" is a manufactured item 1) that is formed into a specific shape or design during manufacture, 2) that has end-use functions dependent on the shape or design during end use, and 3) that during the end use, does not change in its chemical composition or that changes only for a noncommercial purpose separate from the article and only as allowed by law (19 CFR 12.120(2)). Fluids and particles are not articles, regardless of shape or design.

Shipment Detention. A shipment containing chemicals will be detained at the U.S. port of arrival (or entry if same), at your risk and expense, if: 1) it contains banned chemical substances (15 USC 2604, 2605); or 2) it contains chemical substances ordered seized because of imminent hazards (15 USC 2606). Further detention will occur at the port of entry, again at your risk and expense, if: 1) the EPA administrator or Customs district director has reasonable grounds to believe the shipment is not in compliance with the TSCA; or 2) you do not provide proper TSCA certification.

If your shipment is detained, it will be held by Customs for no more than 48 hours. It will then be turned over to the EPA administrator, unless you have arranged to release it in bond. You must either bring it into TSCA compliance or reexport it within the earlier of 90 days after notice of detention or 30 days of demand for redelivery. Customs may grant an extension if failure to comply or reexport is the result of delays in EPA or Customs procedures. If you fail to comply or reexport within the time allowed, the EPA administrator is authorized to have the shipment stored or disposed of at your expense.

Customs Classification

For customs purposes, dyes, tannins, paints, mastics, and inks are classified under Chapter 32 of the HTSUS. This chapter is broken into major headings, which are further divided into subheadings, and often sub-subheadings, each of which has its own HTSUS classification number. For example, the HTSUS number for drawing ink is 3215.90.10, indicating it is a sub-subcategory of non-printing inks (3215.90.00), which is a subcategory of the major heading printing, writing, drawing, and other inks (3215.00.00). There are 15 major headings within Chapter 32.

3201—Tanning extracts of vegetable origin; tannins and their salts, ethers, esters, and other derivatives

3202—Synthetic organic tanning substances; inorganic tanning substances; tanning preparations, whether or not containing natural tanning substances; enzymatic preparations for pretanning

3203—Coloring matter of vegetable or animal origin (including dyeing extracts but excluding animal black), whether or not chemically defined; preparations as specified in note 3 to this chapter based on coloring matter of vegetable or animal origin

3204—Synthetic organic coloring matter, whether or not chemically defined; preparations as specified in note 3 to this chapter based on synthetic organic coloring matter; synthetic organic products of a kind used as fluorescent brightening agents or as luminophores, whether or not chemically defined

3205—Color lakes; preparations as specified in note 3 to this chapter based on color lakes

3206—Other coloring matter; preparations as specified in note 3 to this chapter, other than those of heading 3203, 3204 or 3205; inorganic products of a kind used as luminophores, whether or not chemically defined

3207—Prepared pigments, prepared opacifiers, and prepared colors, vitrifiable enamels and glazes, engobes (slips), liquid lustres, and similar preparations, of a kind used in the ceramic, enamelling, or glass industry; glass frit and other glass, in the form of powder, granules, or flakes

3208—Paints and varnishes (including enamels and lacquers) based on synthetic polymers or chemically modified natural polymers, dispersed or dissolved in a nonaqueous medium; solutions as defined in note 4 to this chapter

3209—Paints and varnishes (including enamels and lacquers) based on synthetic polymers or chemically modified natural polymers, dispersed or dissolved in an aqueous medium

3210—Other paints and varnishes (including enamels, lacquers, and distempers); prepared water pigments of a kind used for finishing leather

3211—Prepared driers

3212—Pigments (including metallic powders and flakes) dispersed in nonaqueous media, in liquid or paste form, of a kind used in the manufacture of paints (including enamels); stamping foils; dyes and other coloring matter put up in forms or packings for retail sale

3213—Artists', students', or signboard painters' colors, modifying tints, amusement colors, and the like, in tablets, tubes, jars, bottles, pans, or in similar forms or packings

3214—Glaziers' putty, grafting putty, resin cements, caulking compounds, and other mastics; painters' filings; nonrefractory surfacing preparations for facades, indoor walls, floors, ceilings, or the like

3215—Printing ink, writing or drawing ink, and other inks, whether or not concentrated or solid

For more details regarding classifications of the specific product you are interested in importing, consult a customs broker, the appropriate commodity specialist at your nearest customs port, or the HTSUS. HTSUS is available for purchase from the U.S. Government Printing Office (see addresses at end of this chapter), and may be found in larger public libraries. Refer to "Classification—Liquidation" on page 207 for a general discussion of customs classification.

Sample Import Duties

Import duties will vary depending on the HTSUS classification of your product. Therefore, to determine the correct amount of duties, your product must be properly classified under the HTSUS. The following sample duties are taken from the duty listings for HTSUS Chapter 32 products.

Oak or chestnut tanning extract (3201.30.00): free; disperse blue 30 dye (3204.11.15): 14.2%; carmine (3205.00.20): 15%; titanium dioxide pigments (3206.10.00): 6%; cadmium pigments (3206.30.00): 3.1%; vitrifiable enamels and glazes (3207.20.00): 4.9%; acrylic paints in nonaqueous medium (3208.20.00): 3.6%;

acrylic paints in aqueous medium (3209.10.00): 5.1%; prepared driers (3211.00.00): 3.7%; stamping foils for retail (3212.10.00): 4.7%; artists' and students' colors in sets for retail (3213.10.00): 6.5% on entire set; mastics (3214.10.00): 3.7%; black printing ink (3215.11.00): 1.8%; drawing ink (3215.90.10): 3.1%.

Entry and Documentation

The entry of merchandise is a two-part process consisting of 1) filing the documentation necessary to determine whether merchandise may be released from Customs custody, and 2) filing the documents that contain information for duty assessment and statistical purposes. In certain instances, all documents must be filed and accepted by Customs prior to release of the goods. Unless you have been granted an extension, you must file entry documents at a location specified by the district or area director within five working days of your shipment's date of arrival at a U.S. port of entry. These include a number of standard documents required by Customs for any entry, and:

- U.S. Customs TSCA Certification (for hazardous substances)

After you present the entry, Customs may examine your shipment or may waive examination. The shipment is then released provided no legal or regulatory violations have been noted. You must then file entry summary documentation and deposit estimated duties at a designated customhouse within 10 working days of your shipment's release. For a detailed description of entry procedures, standard documentation, and informal entry, refer to "Entry Process" on page 182.

Invoices—Colors, Dyes, Stains, and Related Products. Invoices for colors, dyes, stains, and related products provided for under HTSUS heading 3204 must show the following information: 1) invoice name of products; 2) trade name of products; 3) identity and percent by weight of each component; 4) color index number or a statement that there is none; 5) color index generic name or a statement that there is none; 6) Chemical Abstracts Service (CAS) number of the active ingredient; 7) class of merchandise as acid type dye, basic dye, disperse dye, fluorescent brightener, soluble dye, vat dye, toner, or other described substance; 8) material to which the color dye or toner is primarily designed to be applied.

Prohibitions and Restrictions

Importation of any consumer product that has been declared a banned hazardous substance by a rule under the CPSA is prohibited. Any product considered hazardous and not labeled according to provisions of the FHSA is a misbranded hazardous substance and is an illegal import. Certain hazardous substances listed in the FHSA and in regulations promulgated by the CPSC are completely banned from importation. A shipment of consumer products cannot be imported if it poses an imminent hazard. See 15 USC 1261, 2604-2606; 16 CFR 1500.265-1500.272.

The CPSC may detain your shipment of hazardous substances and take samples for testing to determine compliance with the FHSA. If your shipment is found to contain banned hazardous substances, it will be refused admission and will be destroyed if not exported within 90 days of the date of refusal notice. If it is found to contain misbranded hazardous substances, you may make arrangements to bring it into conformance through relabeling. For complete details regarding testing, labeling, and safety regulations for hazardous products, contact the CPSC (see addresses at end of this chapter).

Marking and Labeling Requirements

Chemical Products. A shipment of any products containing chemicals that are classified as hazardous substance (49 CFR 172) must comply with the marking and labeling regulations adopted by the EPA (46 CFR 147.30) and the DOT (49 CFR 171 et seq.).

Flammable Products. Any flammable product must be conspicuously and appropriately labeled according to regulations under FHSA. The labeling must distinguish between "extremely flammable," "flammable," and "combustible," and must accurately reflect the form of the product (liquid, solid, or other) or the contents of a self-pressurized container. The label must appear on the immediate container intended for the end user. If the product is being shipped in bulk, the labeling must be affixed to the bulk container in a conspicuous place. Any accompanying printed material that has instructions for use must also bear the same warning in a conspicuous place. Labeling for a flammable product must contain the following information: 1) name and place of business of the manufacturer, packer, distributor, or seller; 2) common or usual name (or chemical name if there is no common name) of the hazardous substance, or of each component that contributes substantially to its hazard; 3) the word "DANGER" on extremely flammable substances; 4) the word "CAUTION" or "WARNING" on flammable or combustible substances; 5) an affirmative statement of the principle hazard or hazards (i.e. "flammable," "extremely flammable," or "combustible"); 6) precautionary measures describing the action to be followed or avoided; 7) instruction, if necessary, for first-aid treatment; 8) instructions for handling and storage of packages that require special care in handling and storage; 9) the statement "Keep Out of Reach of Children" or its practical equivalent. For more information, contact the CPSC (see addresses at end of this chapter).

For a general discussion of U.S. Customs marking and labeling requirements, refer to "Marking: Country of Origin" on page 215 and "Special Marking Requirements" on page 217.

Shipping Considerations

You will need to ensure that your goods are packaged and shipped with care so that they pass smoothly through Customs and arrive in good condition. You are responsible for ensuring that the shipment is in compliance with all applicable government regulations for packaging and shipping. In most instances, you should not leave these arrangements solely to the discretion of your supplier. Careful preparation of the cargo and selection of the mode of transport can be essential to a cost-effective, timely delivery of undamaged goods. We strongly advise you to consult your shipping representative, insurance agent, or freight broker for advice on packing and shipping. Refer also to the major tab section "Packing/Shipping/Insurance" for a general discussion of packing and shipping.

Dyes, tannins, paints, mastics, and inks may be shipped in bulk, bags, bottles, crates, or other types of containers, depending on the type of product and whether it is prepackaged. General considerations include protection from contamination, weather, and pests. For liquid shipments, venting and vapor collection systems may be required. Safety precautions should also be implemented as required to protect against breakage, spillage, corrosion of containers, combustion, and explosion. Containers should be constructed so as to be safe for handling during transport.

Chemical Products. Chemical products in particular may have to be shipped in pressurized, ventilated, and temperature-and vapor-controlled enclosures. Solid chemical products that are listed as hazardous substances (49 CFR 172 appendix) may be transported in bulk only on compliance with Coast Guard notification procedures, shipping permit requirements, and complex transportation regulations (46 CFR 148). All hazardous substances must also be packaged and transported in accordance with DOT regulations (49 CFR 171 et seq.).

Publications Available

The following publications may be relevant to the importation of toxic or hazardous dyes, tannins, paints, mastics, and inks:

Toxic Substances Control Act: A Guide for Chemical Importers/ Exporters (published by EPA).

TSCA Chemical Substance Inventory (1985 edition) (Doc. Code S/N 055-000-00254-1) $161.00 U.S. and Canada; $201.21 all other countries.

Supplement to TSCA Chemical Substances Inventory (1990) (Doc. Code S/N 055-000-00361-1) $15.00 U.S.; $18.75 Canada and all other countries.

The above publications and the *Harmonized Tariff Schedule of the United States* (HTSUS) are available from:

Government Printing Office (GPO)
Superintendent of Documents
Washington, DC 20402
(202) 512-1800 (Order line)
(202) 512-0000 (General)

The USGPO also has copies of specific laws available for purchase. The USGPO accepts credit card orders over the phone, as well as mail orders paid by credit card, a check drawn on a U.S. bank, or an international money order.

Relevant Government Agencies

Address your questions regarding CPSC requirements for dyes, tannins, paints, mastics, and inks to:

U.S. Consumer Product Safety Commission (CPSC)
Office of Compliance
Division of Regulatory Management
5401 Westbard Avenue
Bethesda, MD 20207
(301) 504-0400

Address your inquiries regarding TSCA and EPA requirements for importation of dyes, tannins, paints, mastics, and inks to:

Environmental Protection Agency (EPA)
TSCA System Information
EPA 7408, OPPT
401 M Street SW
Washington, DC 20460
(202) 554-1404 (TSCA Information Hotline)

Address your questions regarding transportation of hazardous substances to:

U.S. Department of Transportation (DOT)
Research and Special Programs Administration
Office of Hazardous Materials Standards
400 7th St. SW
Washington, DC 20590
(202) 366-4488

Address your questions regarding importation of dyes, tannins, paints, mastics, and inks to the district or port director of Customs for you area. For addresses refer to"U.S. Customs District Offices" on page 62 or contact:

U.S. Customs Service
1301 Constitution Ave. NW
Washington, DC 20229
(202) 927-6724 (Information)
(202) 927-1000 (General)

Laws and Regulations

The following laws and regulations may be relevant to the importation of dyes, tannins, paints, mastics, and inks. The laws are contained in the United States Code (USC), and the regulations are published in the Code of Federal Regulations (CFR), both of which are available at larger public and law libraries. Specific laws and regulations may also be purchased from the U.S. Government Printing Office (address above).

15 USC 1263
Consumer Product Safety Act (CPSA)
This Act gives the Consumer Product Safety Commission authority to set safety standards, testing procedures, and reporting requirements to ensure that consumer products not already covered under other regulations are not harmful.

16 CFR 1500 et seq.
Regulations on Hazardous Substances Safety Standards
These regulations set standards for processing, manufacturing, importing, and labeling all substances classified as hazardous that are to be sold to U.S. consumers.

15 USC 2601 et seq.
Toxic Substances Control Act
This Act authorizes the EPA to determine whether a substance is harmful and to restrict importation, sale, and use of such substances.

19 CFR 12.118 et seq.
Regulations on Toxic Substances Control
These regulations require importers of chemical substances imported in bulk or as part of a mixture to certify to Customs that the shipment complies with the TSCA or is not subject to that Act.

15 USC 1261
Federal Hazardous Substances Act
This Act controls the importation of hazardous substances, sets forth prohibited imports, and authorizes various agencies to promulgate labeling, marking, and transport requirements.

49 CFR 170 et seq.
Regulations on Hazardous Materials
These regulations list all substances deemed hazardous and provide transport, marking, labeling, safety, and emergency response rules.

46 CFR 147.30
Regulations on Labeling of Hazardous Materials
This regulation requires the labeling of containers of hazardous substances and specifies the label contents.

46 CFR 148 et seq.
Regulations on Carriage of Solid Hazardous Materials in Bulk
These regulations govern the transport of solid hazardous substances in bulk, including reporting, permitting, loading, stowing, and shipping requirements.

Sources of Additional Information

The TSCA Chemical Substance Inventory in computerized form is available from:

National Technical Information Service (NTIS)
U.S. Department of Commerce
5285 Port Royal Road
Springfield, VA 22161
(703) 487-4650

Access to the computerized TSCA Chemical Substance Inventory through a commercial database is available at:

Scientific and Technical Network International
Chemical Abstracts Service (CAS)
File: CAS ONLINE
(800) 848-6533
Dialog Information Services
TSCA Chemical Substances Inventory
File: Number 52
(800) 334-2564

Principal Exporting Countries

The following listing includes samples of the main supplier nations of the products of this chapter. It is organized by HTSUS major heading. (Refer to "Customs Classification" above for the product codes.) Countries are listed in rank order of the value of products imported to the U.S. Statistics represent customs value entries for 1993 from the Bureau of Census, U.S. Department of Commerce.

3201—Japan, Argentina, South Africa, Brazil, France, Peru, Belgium, Italy, Paraguay, Germany

3202—Germany, United Kingdom, Italy, Spain, Chile, France, Switzerland, Brazil, South Africa, India

3203—Mexico, Chile, Peru, Italy, Germany, Ecuador, Costa Rica, Belgium, Japan, Netherlands

3204—Germany, Japan, Switzerland, United Kingdom, India, China, France, Taiwan, South Korea, Canada

3205—Germany, Peru, Taiwan, Japan, United Kingdom, Denmark, Mexico, South Korea, Belgium, Canada

3206—Canada, Germany, United Kingdom, Japan, France, Spain, South Africa, Norway, Singapore, Finland

3207—Mexico, Germany, Japan, United Kingdom, Italy, France, Spain, Netherlands, Canada, Belgium

3208—Canada, Germany, Japan, Netherlands, United Kingdom, Belgium, Italy, France, Switzerland, Denmark

3209—Canada, Japan, Sweden, Germany, France, Argentina, United Kingdom, Spain, Netherlands, Italy

3210—Canada, United Kingdom, Italy, Japan, Germany, Netherlands, Switzerland, France, Austria, Mexico

3211—Canada, Italy, France, South Korea, India, United Kingdom, Belgium, Germany, Netherlands, Mexico

3212—Japan, Germany, Canada, United Kingdom, Sweden, Slovenia, South Korea, Spain, France, Italy

3213—United Kingdom, Taiwan, China, Japan, Netherlands, Canada, France, Germany, Australia, Mexico

3214—Canada, Germany, Switzerland, United Kingdom, France, Belgium, Japan, Netherlands, Liechtenstein, Mexico

3215—Japan, Germany, Canada, United Kingdom, Netherlands, Mexico, Switzerland, Sweden, France, Italy

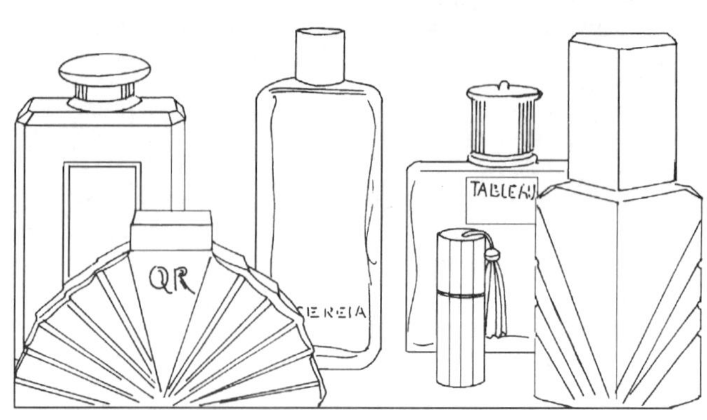

Chapter 33: Perfumes and Cosmetics*

Full title: Essential Oils and Resinoids; Perfumery, Cosmetic, or Toilet Preparations

This chapter relates to the importation of essential oils, perfumes, and cosmetics, which are classified under Chapter 33 of the Harmonized Tariff Schedule of the United States (HTSUS). Specifically, it includes essential oils in various solid and liquid forms, resinoids, perfumes, toilet waters, mixtures of such substances used as raw materials, animal toilet products, make-up, sun lotions, deodorants and antiperspirants, room deodorizers, and hair, dental hygiene, shaving, and bath products.

If you are importing cosmetics that have therapeutic or medicinal value, you should also read Commodity Index Chapter 30, "Pharmaceuticals." For the importation of separately defined chemicals, refer to Chapters 28 (inorganic) and 29 (organic). If you are importing soap products, refer to Chapter 34. Alcohol preparations used for the manufacture of beverages are covered in Chapter 22.

Key Factors

The key factors in the importation of essential oils, perfumes, and cosmetics are:

- Compliance with U.S. Food and Drug Administration (FDA) purity, identity, manufacturing, and other standards
- Compliance with FDA entry notification and procedures
- Compliance with U.S. Environmental Protection Agency (EPA) requirements under Toxic Substances Control Act (TSCA) (if the product is a hazardous substance)
- Compliance with U.S. Department of Transportation (DOT) regulations for transport of hazardous cargo (if the product is a hazardous substance)

Although most importers use the services of a licensed customs broker in making their entries, and we recommend this practice, you should be aware of the regulatory, entry, and documentation issues involved in importing your product. You, as importer, are ultimately responsible for the fulfillment of any legal requirements applicable to your shipment.

*IMPORTANT: Read the Commodity Index Introduction. It is the essential framework for understanding this chapter.

General Considerations

Regulatory Agencies. The FDA, under the Federal Food, Drug, and Cosmetic Act (FDCA), regulates the importation of essential oils, perfumes, and cosmetics. Cosmetics imported into the United States must comply with all FDCA requirements for those produced domestically. Cosmetics are also subject to the Fair Packaging and Labeling Act (FPLA). The EPA, under authority of the TSCA, imposes certain controls on the importation of any of these products that contain toxic substances. The TSCA defines a toxic substance as any substance determined to present the possibility of an unreasonable risk of injury to health and the environment. The DOT enforces regulations for transporting hazardous cargo. Materials are deemed hazardous if listed in DOT transport regulations (49 CFR 172 appendix).

Essential Oils, Perfumes, and Cosmetics. Imported cosmetics regulated by the FDA are subject to port-of-entry inspection. The FDCA defines cosmetics as articles intended to be applied to the human body for cleansing, beautifying, promoting attractiveness, or altering the appearance, without affecting the body's structure or functions. Included in this definition are products such as skin creams, lotions, perfumes, lipsticks, fingernail polishes, eye and facial make-up preparations, shampoos, permanent waves, hair colors, toothpastes, deodorants, and any ingredient intended for use as a component of a cosmetic product. Soap products consisting primarily of an alkali salt of fatty acid and making no label claim other than cleansing of the human body are not considered cosmetics under the law.

You must submit to Customs **Form FD701** for all FDA-regulated importations. It may be obtained from your local FDA Import Operations office, from FDA headquarters (see addresses at end of this chapter), or from your customs broker. For an annotated diagram of required FDA import procedures refer to the "Foods" appendix on page 808.

Shipment Detention. If your shipment fails to comply with applicable laws and regulations, it may be detained at the port of entry. The FDA may permit you to bring an illegal importation into compliance with the law before a final decision is made regarding admittance. However, any sorting, reprocessing, or relabeling must be supervised by an FDA investigator, and will be done at your expense. Conditional release of an illegal importation to allow an importer to bring it into compliance is not a right but a privilege. If you repeat noncomplying shipments of the same article, the FDA may interpret this as abuse of the privilege and require you to destroy or reexport subsequent shipments.

Hazardous Chemicals. All products containing hazardous chemicals are subject to the U.S. Customs Service TSCA Import Certification Rule (19 CFR 12.118 et seq.). If you import these products, you must sign one of the following statements: "I certify that all chemical substances in this shipment comply with all applicable rules or orders under TSCA and that I am not offering a chemical substance for entry in violation of TSCA or any applicable rule or order thereunder" or "I certify that all chemicals in this shipment are not subject to TSCA."

You must file this TSCA certification of compliance or exemption at the time you make the entry at Customs. The certification may be in the form of a typed or stamped statement on an appropriate entry document or commercial invoice or a preprinted attachment to such entry document or invoice. You may sign the certificate by means of an authorized facsimile signature. If your entry is electronically processed, the certification will be in the form of a Certification Code, which is part of the Automated Broker Interface (ABI) transmission. Customs will not release your shipment without proper certification.

If you will be importing several or regular shipments of the same product, you should ask the appropriate Customs district director to authorize your use of a blanket certification. If you receive such authorization, you must include on the commercial invoice or entry document for each shipment a statement that the blanket certification is on file and that it is incorporated by reference. This statement need not be signed. The blanket certification is valid for one calendar year, is subject to renewal, and may be revoked at any time for cause.

In filling out TSCA forms and Customs entry documents, you should provide the Chemical Abstracts Service (CAS) number for each chemical in the shipment. These CAS numbers are given in the appendix to the HTSUS. You are not required to include the CAS number, but Customs will be able to process your shipment more quickly if you include this number.

Shipments of products containing hazardous chemicals must additionally be in compliance with toxic and hazardous substance regulations of the EPA and DOT. These include packaging, shipping, marking, and labeling requirements.

Articles Exclusion. If you are importing products that are classified as hazardous substances but are part of articles, you are subject to TSCA certification requirements only if certification for your product is specifically required by a rule or order promulgated under the TSCA. No specific rules have been adopted at this time. An "article" is a manufactured item 1) that is formed into a specific shape or design during manufacture, 2) that has end-use functions dependent on the shape or design during end use, and 3) that during the end use, does not change in its chemical composition or that changes only for a noncommercial purpose separate from the article and only as allowed by law (19 CFR 12.120(2)). Fluids and particles are not articles, regardless of shape or design.

Shipment Detention. A shipment of a chemical product will be detained at the U.S. port of arrival (or entry if same), at your risk and expense, if: 1) it contains banned chemical substances (15 USC 2604, 2605); or 2) it contains chemical substances ordered seized because of imminent hazards (15 USC 2606). Further detention will occur at the port of entry, again at your risk and expense, if: 1) the EPA administrator or Customs district director has reasonable grounds to believe the shipment is not in compliance with the TSCA; or 2) you do not provide proper TSCA certification.

If your shipment is detained, it will be held by Customs for no more than 48 hours. It will then be turned over to the EPA administrator, unless you have arranged to release it in bond. You must either bring it into TSCA compliance or reexport it within the earlier of 90 days after notice of detention or 30 days of demand for redelivery. Customs may grant an extension if failure to comply or reexport is the result of delays in EPA or Customs procedures. If you fail to comply or reexport within the time allowed, the EPA administrator is authorized to have the shipment stored or disposed of at your expense.

Customs Classification

For customs purposes, essential oils, perfumes, and cosmetics are classified under Chapter 33 of the HTSUS. This chapter is broken into major headings, which are further divided into subheadings, and often sub-subheadings, each of which has its own HTSUS classification number. For example, the HTSUS number for bath salts is 3307.30.10, indicating it is a sub-subcategory of perfumed bath salts and other bath preparations (3307.30.00), which is a subcategory of the major heading, shaving, deodorant, and bath preparations, etc. (3307.00.00). There are seven major headings within Chapter 33.

3301—Essential oils (terpeneless or not), including concretes and absolutes; resinoids; concentrates of essential oils in fats, in fixed oils, in waxes, or the like, obtained by enfleurage or maceration; terpenic byproducts of the deterpenation of essential oils; aqueous distillates and aqueous solutions of essential oils

3302—Mixtures of odoriferous substances and mixtures (including alcoholic solutions) with a basis of one or more of these substances, of a kind used as raw materials in industry

3303—Perfumes and toilet waters

3304—Beauty or make-up preparations and preparations for the care of the skin (other than medicaments), including sunscreen or suntan preparations; manicure or pedicure preparations

3305—Preparations for use on the hair

3306—Preparations for oral or dental hygiene, including denture fixative pastes and powders

3307—Pre-shave, shaving, or after-shave preparations, personal deodorants, bath preparations, depilatories and other perfumery, cosmetic, or toilet preparations, not elsewhere specified or included; prepared room deodorizers, whether or not perfumed or having disinfectant properties

For more details regarding classifications of the specific product you are interested in importing, consult a customs broker, the appropriate commodity specialist at your nearest customs port, or the HTSUS. HTSUS is available for purchase from the U.S. Government Printing Office (see addresses at end of this chapter), and may be found in larger public libraries. Refer to "Classification—Liquidation" on page 207 for a general discussion of customs classification.

Sample Import Duties

Import duties will vary depending on the HTSUS classification of your product. Therefore, to determine the correct amount of duties, your product must be properly classified under the HTSUS. The following sample duties are taken from the duty listings for HTSUS Chapter 33 products.

Essential oil of lemon (3301.13.00): 8.5%; attar of roses (3301.29.50): free; perfumes and toilet waters containing alcohol (3303.00.30): 5%; resinoids (3301.30.00): free; lip make-up preparations (3304.10.00): 4.9%; eye make-up preparations (3304.20.00): 4.9%; dentifrices (3306.10.00): 4.9%; manicure or pedicure preparations (3304.30.00): 4.9%; shampoos (3305.10.00): 4.9%; bath salts (3307.30.10): 5.8%.

Certain cosmetic items containing alcohol are subject to a federal excise tax (26 USC 5001) of $13.50 per proof gallon, and a proportionate tax at the like rate on all fractional parts. For some products, the amount of this tax varies depending on alcohol content. Customs collects the federal excise tax on alcohol-containing products.

Entry and Documentation

The entry of merchandise is a two-part process consisting of 1) filing the documentation necessary to determine whether merchandise may be released from Customs custody, and 2) filing the documents that contain information for duty assessment and statistical purposes. In certain instances, all documents must be filed and accepted by Customs prior to release of the goods. Unless you have been granted an extension, you must file entry documents at a location specified by the district or area director within five working days of your shipment's date of arrival at a U.S. port of entry. These include a number of standard documents required by Customs for any entry, and:

- FDA Importers Entry Notice, **Form FD701**
- U.S. Customs TSCA Certification (for hazardous substances)

After you present the entry, Customs may examine your shipment or may waive examination. The shipment is then released provided no legal or regulatory violations have been noted. You must then file entry summary documentation and deposit estimated duties at a designated customhouse within 10 working days of your shipment's release. For a detailed description of entry procedures, standard documentation, and informal entry, refer to "Entry Process" on page 182.

Prohibitions and Restrictions

Cosmetics Containing Drugs. Cosmetic products that contain elements for treating or preventing disease, or affecting the structure or functions of a human body, must comply with the drug, as well as the cosmetic, provisions of the law. Examples include "fluoride" toothpaste, hormone creams, suntan preparations with skin protective components, antiperspirants mixed with deodorants, and anti-dandruff shampoos. Most of these cosmetics contain over-the-counter drugs. The regulations for importing and retailing drugs are more extensive than those for cosmetics. If you are interested in importing cosmetics that may fall under this category, you should also read "Pharmaceuticals," beginning on page 467.

Adulterated or Misbranded Cosmetics. The FDCA prohibits the importation and distribution of cosmetics that are adulterated. Your cosmetic product is considered adulterated if it meets any of the following conditions: 1) it contains a substance that may make it harmful to consumers under customary conditions of use; 2) it contains a filthy, putrid, or decomposed substance; 3) its container is composed of a harmful substance; 4) it is manufactured or held in insanitary conditions under which it may have become contaminated with filth or harmful to consumers; or 5) it contains an impermissible color and is not a hair dye. Coal-tar hair dyes labeled with the caution statement prescribed by law (21 CFR Sec. 601) and "patch-test" instructions are exempt from the adulteration provision, even if they are irritating to the skin or otherwise harmful. This exemption does not apply to eyelash and eyebrow dyes, which must be approved by the FDA for such use.

The FDCA also prohibits the importation and distribution of cosmetics that are misbranded. If your cosmetic meets any of the following conditions, it is misbranded: 1) its labeling is false or misleading; 2) it does not bear the required labeling information; or 3) the container is made or filled in a deceptive manner (21 CFR Sec. 602).

Cosmetic Safety. The FDCA does not require cosmetic manufacturers or marketers to test their products for safety. However, the FDA strongly urges cosmetic manufacturers to conduct all toxicological or other tests appropriate to substantiate the safety of the cosmetics. A product whose safety is not adequately substantiated may be considered misbranded and may be subject to regulatory action unless the label bears the following statement: "Warning: The safety of this product has not been determined" (21 CFR 740).

With the exception of color additives and a few prohibited ingredients, a cosmetic manufacturer may, at his or her own risk, use any raw material as a cosmetic ingredient and market the product without FDA approval. The law requires that every color additives used in food, drugs, and cosmetics be tested for safety and approved by the FDA for its intended use. A cosmetic containing an unlisted color additive (i.e., one not approved by the FDA) is considered adulterated and its use is subject to regulatory action. The colors approved for use in cosmetics are listed in 21 CFR 73, 74, 81 and 82.

Restricted Ingredients. The use of the following ingredients in cosmetics is restricted or prohibited: bithionol, mercury compounds, vinyl chloride, halogenated salicylanilides, zirconium complexes in aerosol cosmetics, chloroform, chlorofluorocarbon propellants, and hexachlorophene (21 CFR 700, 250). Cosmetic nail products containing methyl methacrylate monomer or those containing more than 5% formaldehyde are considered adulterated under the FDCA.

Voluntary Registration. The FDCA does not require cosmetic firms to register their establishments or formulas with the FDA, or to make available safety data or other information before a product is marketed in the U.S. However, manufacturers or distributors may submit their information voluntarily. Voluntary registration and assignment of a registration number by the FDA does not denote approval of a firm, raw material, or product. If you are registered with the FDA and you use your registration number in labeling, you must include on the label a conspicuous disclaimer phrase as prescribed by regulation (21 CFR 710, 720, and 730).

Tamper-resistant Packaging. Liquid oral hygiene products (e.g., mouthwashes, fresheners) and all cosmetic vaginal products (e.g., douches, tablets) must be packaged in tamper-resistant packages when sold at retail. A package is considered tamper-resistant if it has an indicator or barrier to entry (e.g., shrink or tape seal, sealed carton, tube, or pouch, or aerosol container) that, if breached or missing, alerts a consumer that tampering has occurred. The indicator must be distinctive by design (breakable cap or blister) or appearance (logo, vignette, or other illustration) to preclude substitution. The tamper-resistant feature may involve the immediate or outer container, or both. The package must also bear a prominently placed statement alerting the consumer to the tamper-resistant feature. This statement must remain unaffected if the tamper-resistant feature is breached or missing (21 CFR 700).

Enforcement Authority. For enforcement of the law, the FDA may conduct examinations and investigations of products, inspect establishments where products are manufactured or held, and seize adulterated or misbranded cosmetics. If you attempt to import adulterated or misbranded foreign products, your shipment may be refused entry into the U.S. To prevent further shipment of an adulterated or misbranded product, the FDA may request a Federal district court to issue a restraining order against the U.S. manufacturer or distributor of the cosmetic in question. The FDA may also initiate criminal action against you for violating the law. Examples of products seized in recent years are nail preparations containing methyl methacrylate and formaldehyde, various eyebrow and eyelash dye products containing prohibited coal-tar dyes, and products contaminated with harmful microorganisms.

If you have questions regarding regulatory requirements for cosmetics, contact FDA's Division of Colors and Cosmetics (see addresses at end of this chapter). If you have questions regarding requirements for products that are also drugs, contact FDA's Division of Drug Labeling Compliance (see addresses at end of this chapter).

Marking and Labeling Requirements

Cosmetic Labeling. Cosmetics distributed in the U.S. must comply with the labeling regulations published by the FDA under the FDCA and the Fair Packaging and Labeling Act (FPLA). "Labeling" means all labels and other written, printed, or graphic matter on or accompanying a product. The label statements required by FDCA must appear on the inside as well as any outside container or wrapper. FPLA requirements (e.g., ingredient labeling) only apply to the label of the outer container. The labeling requirements are detailed at 21 CFR 701 and 740. Cosmetics bearing false or misleading label statements, or otherwise not labeled in accordance with these requirements, may be considered misbranded and may be subject to regulatory action. All label statements required by regulation must be in the English language and must be placed conspicuously on the label or labeling with such prominence that they are readily noticed and understood by consumers under customary conditions of purchase (21 CFR 701).

Display and Informational Panels. The principal display panel must state the product name, identify by descriptive name or illustration the product's nature or use, and bear an accurate statement of the net quantity of contents in terms of weight, measure, numerical count, or a combination of numerical count and weight or measure. The declaration must be distinct. It must be placed in the bottom area of the panel, in a line generally parallel to the base on which the package rests, and in a type size commensurate with the size of the container as prescribed by regulation. The net quantity of contents of a solid, semisolid, or viscous cosmetic must be stated in terms of the avoirdupois pound and ounce. A statement of liquid measure must be in terms of the U.S. gallon of 321 cubic inches and the quart, pint, and fluid ounce subdivisions thereof. If the net quantity of contents is one pound or one pint or more, it must be expressed in ounces, followed in parenthesis by a declaration of the largest whole units (i.e., pounds and ounces or quarts and pints and ounces). The net quantity of contents may also be stated in terms of the U.S. system and the metric system of weights or measures.

The name and place of business of the firm marketing the product must be stated on an information panel of the label (21 CFR 701). The address must state the street address, city, state, and zip code. If a domestic firm is listed in a current city or telephone directory, the street address may be omitted. If the distributor is not the manufacturer or packer, this fact must be stated on the label by the qualifying phrase "Manufactured for ___" or "Distributed by ___" or similar, appropriate wording. A firm located outside the U.S. may omit the zip code.

Declaration of Ingredients. Cosmetics produced or distributed for retail sale to consumers for their personal care are required to bear an ingredient declaration (21 CFR 701). Cosmetics not customarily distributed for retail sale, e.g. hair preparations or make-up products used by professionals on customers at their establishments and skin cleansing or emollient creams used by persons at their places of work, are exempt from the requirement. However, if professional establishments or workplaces sell these products to consumers for home use, the requirements apply.

The ingredient declaration must be conspicuous so that it is likely to be read at the time of purchase. It may appear on any information panel of the package including a firmly affixed tag, tape, or card. The letters must not be less than 1/16 of an inch in height. If the total package surface available to bear labeling is less than 12 square inches, the letters must not be less than half an inch in height. Off-package ingredient labeling is permitted if the cosmetic is held in tightly compartmented trays or racks, is not enclosed in a folding carton, and the package surface area is less than 12 square inches.

The ingredients must be declared in descending order of predominance. Color additives and ingredients present at 1% or less may be declared without regard for predominance. The ingredients must be identified by the names established or adopted by regulation; those accepted by the FDA as exempt from public disclosure may be stated as "and other ingredients."

Label Warnings. Cosmetics that may be hazardous to consumers when misused must bear appropriate label warnings and adequate directions for safe use. The statements must be prominent and conspicuous. Some cosmetics (e.g. aerosol products, feminine deodorant sprays, children's bubble bath products) must bear label warnings or cautions prescribed by regulation (21 CFR 740).

Hazardous Chemicals. A shipment of any products containing chemicals that are classified as hazardous substance (49 CFR 172) must comply with the marking and labeling regulations adopted by the EPA (46 CFR 147.30) and the DOT (49 CFR 171 et seq.).

For a general discussion of U.S. Customs marking and labeling requirements, refer to "Marking: Country of Origin" on page 215 and "Special Marking Requirements" on page 217.

Shipping Considerations

You will need to ensure that your goods are packaged and shipped with care so that they pass smoothly through Customs and arrive in good condition. You are responsible for ensuring that the shipment is in compliance with all applicable government regulations for packaging and shipping. In most instances, you should not leave these arrangements solely to the discretion of your supplier. Careful preparation of the cargo and selection of the mode of transport can be essential to a cost-effective, timely delivery of undamaged goods. We strongly advise you to consult your shipping representative, insurance agent, or freight broker for advice on packing and shipping. Refer also to the major tab section "Packing/Shipping/Insurance" for a general discussion of packing and shipping.

Cosmetic products may be shipped in bulk, bags, bottles, or other types of containers, depending on the type of product and whether it is prepackaged. General considerations include protection from contamination, weather, and pests. If a product must be kept in a sanitary environment, all tables, utensils, platforms, and devices used for moving or handling the product, the compartments in which it is stowed while being transported will need to be maintained in a sanitary condition. For liquid shipments, venting and vapor collection systems may be required. Safety precautions should also be implemented as required to protect against breakage, spillage, corrosion of containers, and combustion. Containers should be constructed so as to be safe for handling during transport.

Chemical Products. Chemical products in particular may have to be shipped in pressurized, ventilated, and temperature-and vapor-controlled enclosures. Solid chemical products that are listed as hazardous substances (49 CFR 172 appendix) may be transported in bulk only on compliance with Coast Guard notification procedures, shipping permit requirements, and complex transportation regulations (46 CFR 148). All hazardous substances must also be packaged and transported in accordance with DOT regulations (49 CFR 171 et seq.).

Publications Available

The following publication explains the FDA requirements for importing cosmetics. It is published by the FDA and is available on request from FDA headquarters (see addresses at end of this chapter).

Requirements of Laws and Regulations Enforced by the U.S. Food and Drug Administration

The following publications may be relevant to the importation of toxic or hazardous cosmetic ingredients:

Toxic Substances Control Act: A Guide for Chemical Importers/Exporters (published by EPA).

TSCA Chemical Substance Inventory (1985 edition) (Doc. Code S/N 055-000-00254-1) $161.00 U.S. and Canada; $201.21 all other countries.

Supplement to TSCA Chemical Substances Inventory (1990) (Doc. Code S/N 055-000-00361-1) $15.00 U.S.; $18.75 Canada and all other countries.

The above publications and the *Harmonized Tariff Schedule of the United States* (HTSUS) are available from:

Government Printing Office (GPO)
Superintendent of Documents
Washington, DC 20402
(202) 512-1800 (Order line)
(202) 512-0000 (General)

The USGPO also has copies of specific laws available for purchase. The USGPO accepts credit card orders over the phone, as well as mail orders paid by credit card, a check drawn on a U.S. bank, or an international money order.

Relevant Government Agencies

Address your questions regarding FDA requirements for cosmetics to:

Food and Drug Administration (FDA)
Division of Enforcement, Imports Branch
200 C Street SW
Washington, DC 20204
(202) 205-4726

Address your questions regarding FDA requirements for products that are also drugs to:

Food and Drug Administration (FDA)
Center for Drug Evaluation and Research (HFD-8)
5600 Fishers Lane
Rockville, MD 20857
(301) 594-1012

Address your questions regarding CPSC requirements for cosmetics and other products under chapter 33 to:

Consumer Product Safety Commission (CPSC)
Office of Compliance
Division of Regulatory Management
5401 Westbard Avenue
Bethesda, MD 20207
(301) 504-0400

Address your inquiries regarding TSCA and EPA requirements for importation of chemical products to:

Environmental Protection Agency (EPA)
TSCA System Information
EPA 7408, OPPT
401 M Street SW
Washington, DC 20460
(202) 554-1404 (TSCA Information Hotline)

Address your questions regarding transportation of hazardous substances to:

U.S. Department of Transportation (DOT)
Research and Special Programs Administration
Office of Hazardous Materials Standards
400 7th St. SW
Washington, DC 20590
(202) 366-4488

Address your questions regarding importation of cosmetics to the district or port director of Customs for you area. For addresses refer to"U.S. Customs District Offices" on page 62 or contact:

U.S. Customs Service
1301 Constitution Ave. NW
Washington, DC 20229
(202) 927-6724 (Information)
(202) 927-1000 (General)

Laws and Regulations

The following laws and regulations may be relevant to the importation of cosmetics. The laws are contained in the United States Code (USC), and the regulations are published in the Code of Federal Regulations (CFR), both of which are available at larger public and law libraries. Specific laws and regulations may also be purchased from the U.S. Government Printing Office (address above).

21 USC 301 et seq.
Food, Drug, and Cosmetic Act
This Act prohibits deceptive practices and regulates the manufacture, sale and importation or exportation of food, drugs, cosmetics, and related products. See 21 USC 331, 381, 382.

19 CFR 12.1 et seq.; 21 CFR 1.83 et seq.
Regulations on Food, Drugs, and Cosmetics
These regulations of the Secretary of Health and Human Services and the Secretary of the Treasury govern the

standards, labeling, marking, and importing of products used with food, drugs, and cosmetics.

15 USC 2601 et seq.
Toxic Substances Control Act
This Act authorizes the EPA to determine whether a substance is harmful and to restrict importation, sale, and use of such substances.

19 CFR 12.118 et seq.
Regulations on Toxic Substances Control
These regulations require importers of chemical substances imported in bulk or as part of a mixture to certify to Customs that the shipment complies with the TSCA or is not subject to that Act.

15 USC 1261
Federal Hazardous Substances Act
This Act controls the importation of hazardous substances, sets forth prohibited imports, and authorizes various agencies to promulgate labeling, marking, and transport requirements.

49 CFR 170 et seq.
Regulations on Hazardous Materials
These regulations list all substances deemed hazardous and provide transport, marking, labeling, safety, and emergency response rules.

46 CFR 147.30
Regulations on Labeling of Hazardous Materials
This regulation requires the labeling of containers of hazardous substances and specifies the label contents.

46 CFR 148 et seq.
Regulations on Carriage of Solid Hazardous Materials in Bulk
These regulations govern the transport of solid hazardous substances in bulk, including reporting, permitting, loading, stowing, and shipping requirements.

Sources of Additional Information

The TSCA Chemical Substance Inventory in computerized form is available from:

National Technical Information Service (NTIS)
U.S. Department of Commerce
5285 Port Royal Road
Springfield, VA 22161
(703) 487-4650

Access to the computerized TSCA Chemical Substance Inventory through a commercial database is available at:

Scientific and Technical Network International
Chemical Abstracts Service (CAS)
File: CAS ONLINE
(800) 848-6533
Dialog Information Services
TSCA Chemical Substances Inventory
File: Number 52
(800) 334-2564

Principal Exporting Countries

The following listing includes samples of the main supplier nations of the products of this chapter. It is organized by HTSUS major heading. (Refer to "Customs Classification" above for the product codes.) Countries are listed in rank order of the value of products imported to the U.S. Statistics represent customs value entries for 1993 from the Bureau of Census, U.S. Department of Commerce.

3301—France, China, Brazil, Argentina, India, Indonesia, Spain, United Kingdom, Switzerland, Mexico

3302—Switzerland, France, Canada, Germany, Japan, Netherlands, Brazil, United Kingdom, Spain, Ireland

3303—France, Spain, Germany, Italy, Canada, United Kingdom, Switzerland, Netherlands, Panama, Brazil

3304—France, Canada, Germany, Taiwan, Japan, United Kingdom, Italy, Switzerland, Monaco, China

3305—Canada, Italy, Germany, Belgium, United Kingdom, Japan, France, Mexico, China, Spain

3306—Canada, South Korea, Brazil, Mexico, Malaysia, Chile, China, Germany, Japan, India

3307—Canada, France, United Kingdom, Mexico, Germany, China, Japan, Taiwan, Belgium, Italy

Chapter 34: Soaps and Waxes*

Full title: Soap, Organic Surface-active Agents, Washing Preparations, Lubricating Preparations, Artificial Waxes, Prepared Waxes, Polishing or Scouring Preparations, Candles and Similar Articles, Modeling Pastes, "Dental Waxes" and Dental Preparations With a Basis of Plaster

This chapter relates to the importation of soaps, washing and lubricating products, and wax articles, which are classified under Chapter 34 of the Harmonized Tariff Schedule of the United States (HTSUS). Specifically, it includes soap, organic products used as soap, items impregnated, coated, or covered with soap or detergent, and washing and cleaning products. It also covers lubricating preparations, preparations for oiling or greasing textiles, leather, furskins, or other materials, and polishes and creams. This chapter additionally contains artificial and prepared waxes, candles, tapers, modeling pastes, dental wax and impression compounds, and dentistry preparations with a plaster base.

If you are interested in importing edible mixtures or preparations of animal or vegetable fats or oils used as mold release preparations, you should refer to Commodity Index Chapter 15. Separate chemically defined compounds are found in Chapters 28 (inorganic) or 29 (organic). Refer to Chapter 33 for the importation requirements for shampoos, dentifrices, shaving creams and foams, or bath preparations that contain soap or other organic surface-active agents.

Key Factors

The key factors in the importation of soaps, washing and lubricating products, and wax articles are:

- Compliance with U.S. Federal Trade Commission (FTC) and Consumer Product Safety Commission (CPSC) standards (if the product will be marketed to consumers)
- Compliance with U.S. Environmental Protection Agency (EPA) requirements under Toxic Substances Control Act (TSCA) (if the product is a hazardous substance)
- Compliance with U.S. Department of Transportation (DOT) regulations for transport of hazardous cargo (if the product is a hazardous substance)

*IMPORTANT: Read the Commodity Index Introduction. It is the essential framework for understanding this chapter.

Although most importers use the services of a licensed customs broker in making their entries, and we recommend this practice, you should be aware of the regulatory, entry, and documentation issues involved in importing your product. You, as importer, are ultimately responsible for the fulfillment of any legal requirements applicable to your shipment.

General Considerations

Regulatory Agencies. The EPA, under authority of the TSCA, regulates the importation of soap, washing, lubricating, or wax products that contain toxic substances. The TSCA defines a toxic substance as any substance determined to present the possibility of an unreasonable risk of injury to health and the environment. The DOT enforces regulations for transporting hazardous cargo. Materials are deemed hazardous if listed in DOT transport regulations (49 CFR 172 appendix).

Hazardous Consumer Products. Under the Federal Hazardous Substances Act (FHSA), soap, washing, lubricating, or wax products intended for the consumer market are hazardous substances if they are flammable, combustible, or have the potential to cause substantial personal injury during, or as a proximate result of, any customary or reasonably foreseeable handling or use. The CPSC does not require permits, special invoicing, limited entry, licenses, or any special approval process for importing hazardous consumer products into the U.S. However, if you are importing these types of products, you are responsible for ensuring that they meet all applicable FHSA and Consumer Product Safety Act (CPSA) requirements. There are detailed regulations regarding testing and labeling of hazardous products. The Commission's enforcement posture regarding compliance with labeling and product safety standards changes as new facts become available. Contact the CPSC (see addresses at end of this chapter) for specific requirements on the consumer product you are considering importing.

Substantial Product Hazard Reports. Defect-reporting is required for products covered under the CPSA. The law requires every manufacturer, distributor, or retailer of such products, who obtains information that reasonably supports the conclusion that such products fail to comply with an applicable consumer product safety rule, or contain a defect that could create a substantial product hazard, to immediately inform the CPSC of the potential violation or defect. A firm's willful failure to make a Substantial Product Hazard Report can result in litigation by the CPSC.

Hazardous Substances. Shipments of products containing toxic or hazardous chemicals must be in compliance with regulations of the EPA and DOT. These include packaging, shipping, marking, and labeling requirements. In addition, all products containing chemicals are subject to the U.S. Customs Service TSCA Import Certification Rule (19 CFR 12.118 et seq.). If you import these products, you must sign one of the following statements: "I certify that all chemical substances in this shipment comply with all applicable rules or orders under TSCA and that I am not offering a chemical substance for entry in violation of TSCA or any applicable rule or order thereunder" or "I certify that all chemicals in this shipment are not subject to TSCA."

You must file this TSCA certification of compliance or exemption at the time you make the entry at Customs. The certification may be in the form of a typed or stamped statement on an appropriate entry document or commercial invoice or a preprinted attachment to such entry document or invoice. You may sign the certificate by means of an authorized facsimile signature. If your entry is electronically processed, the certification will be in the form of a Certification Code, which is part of the Automated Broker Interface (ABI) transmission. Customs will not release your shipment without proper certification.

If you will be importing several or regular shipments, you should ask the appropriate Customs district director to authorize your use of a blanket certification. If you receive such authorization, you must include on the commercial invoice or entry document for each shipment a statement that the blanket certification is on file and that it is incorporated by reference. This statement need not be signed. The blanket certification is valid for one calendar year, is subject to renewal, and may be revoked at any time for cause.

In filling out TSCA forms and Customs entry documents, you should provide the Chemical Abstracts Service (CAS) number for each chemical in the shipment. These CAS numbers are given in the appendix to the HTSUS. You are not required to include the CAS number, but Customs will be able to process your shipment more quickly if you include this number.

Articles Exclusion. If you are importing items that are classified as hazardous substances but are part of articles, you are subject to TSCA certification requirements only if certification for your product is specifically required by a rule or order promulgated under the TSCA. No specific rules have been adopted at this time. An "article" is a manufactured item 1) that is formed into a specific shape or design during manufacture, 2) that has end-use functions dependent on the shape or design during end use, and 3) that during the end use, does not change in its chemical composition or that changes only for a noncommercial purpose separate from the article and only as allowed by law (19 CFR 12.120(2)). Fluids and particles are not articles, regardless of shape or design.

Shipment Detention. A shipment containing chemicals will be detained at the U.S. port of arrival (or entry if same), at your risk and expense, if: 1) it contains banned chemical substances (15 USC 2604, 2605); or 2) it contains chemical substances ordered seized because of imminent hazards (15 USC 2606). Further detention will occur at the port of entry, again at your risk and expense, if: 1) the EPA administrator or Customs district director has reasonable grounds to believe the shipment is not in compliance with the TSCA; or 2) you do not provide proper TSCA certification.

If your shipment is detained, it will be held by Customs for no more than 48 hours. It will then be turned over to the EPA administrator, unless you have arranged to release it in bond. You must either bring it into TSCA compliance or reexport it within the earlier of 90 days after notice of detention or 30 days of demand for redelivery. Customs may grant an extension if failure to comply or reexport is the result of delays in EPA or Customs procedures. If you fail to comply or reexport within the time allowed, the EPA administrator is authorized to have the shipment stored or disposed of at your expense.

Customs Classification

For customs purposes, soaps, washing and lubricating products, and wax articles are classified under Chapter 34 of the HTSUS. This chapter is broken into major headings, which are further divided into subheadings, and often sub-subheadings, each of which has its own HTSUS classification number. For example, the HTSUS number for castile soap is 3401.11.10, indicating it is a sub-subcategory of soap for toilet use (3401.11.00), which is a subcategory of the major heading, soap and other soap products (3401.00.00). There are seven major headings within Chapter 34.

3401—Soap; organic surface-active products and preparations for use as soap, in the form of bars, cakes, molded pieces, or shapes, whether or not containing soap; paper, wadding, felt, and other nonwovens impregnated, coated, or covered with soap or detergent

3402—Organic surface-active agents (other than soap); surface-active preparations, washing preparations (including auxiliary washing preparations) and cleaning preparations, whether or not containing soap, other than those of heading 3401

3403—Lubricating preparations (including cutting-oil preparations, bolt or nut release preparations, antirust or anticorrosion preparations, and mold release preparations, based on lubricants) and preparations of a kind used for the oil or grease treatment of textile materials, leather, furskins, or other materials, but excluding preparations containing, as basic constituents, 70% or more, by weight, of petroleum oils or oils obtained from bituminous minerals

3404—Artificial waxes and prepared waxes

3405—Polishes and creams, for footwear, furniture, floors, coachwork, glass or metal, scouring pastes and powders, and similar preparations (whether or not in the form of paper, wadding, felt, nonwovens, cellular plastics, or cellular rubber, impregnated, coated, or covered with such preparations), excluding waxes of heading 3404

3406—Candles, tapers, and the like

3407—Modeling pastes, including those put up for children's amusement; preparations known as "dental wax" or as "dental impression compounds", put up in sets, in packings for retail sale, or in plates, horseshoe shapes, sticks, or similar forms; other preparations for use in dentistry, with a basis of plaster (of calcined gypsum or calcium sulfate)

For more details regarding classifications of the specific product you are interested in importing, consult a customs broker, the appropriate commodity specialist at your nearest customs port, or the HTSUS. HTSUS is available for purchase from the U.S. Government Printing Office (see addresses at end of this chapter), and may be found in larger public libraries. Refer to "Classification—Liquidation" on page 207 for a general discussion of customs classification.

Sample Import Duties

Import duties will vary depending on the HTSUS classification of your product. Therefore, to determine the correct amount of duties, your product must be properly classified under the HTSUS. The following sample duties are taken from the duty listings for HTSUS Chapter 34 products.

Castille soap for toilet use (3401.11.10): 3.1%; bar, cake, or molded soaps for nontoilet uses (3401.19.00): 0. 9 cents/kg plus 2.9%; surface-active preparations for retail sale containing aromatic or modified aromatic surface-active agents (3402.20.10): 6.6%; synthetic detergents (3402.90.10): 3.8%; chemically modified lignite wax (3404.10.00): free; artificial or prepared wax containing bleached beeswax (3404.90.10): 7.5%; polishes or creams for footwear and leather (3405.10.00): 2.5%; scouring pastes and powders (3405.40.00): 0.9 cents/kg plus 2.9%; candles, tapers, and the like (3406.00.00): 5.8%; modeling pastes (3407.00.20): 10%; dentistry preparations (3407.00.40): 10%.

Entry and Documentation

The entry of merchandise is a two-part process consisting of 1) filing the documentation necessary to determine whether merchandise may be released from Customs custody, and 2) filing the documents that contain information for duty assessment and statistical purposes. In certain instances, all documents must be filed and accepted by customs prior to release of the goods. Unless you have been granted an extension, you must file entry documents at a location specified by the district or area director within five working days of your shipment's date of arrival at a U.S. port of entry. These include a number of standard documents required by Customs for any entry, and:

- U.S. Customs TSCA Certification (for hazardous substances)

After you present the entry, Customs may examine your shipment or may waive examination. The shipment is then released provided no legal or regulatory violations have been noted. You must then file entry summary documentation and deposit estimated duties at a designated customhouse within 10 working days of your shipment's release. For a detailed description of entry procedures, standard documentation, and informal entry, see "Entry Process" on page 182.

Prohibitions and Restrictions

Importation of any consumer product that has been declared a banned hazardous substance by a rule under the CPSA is prohibited. Any product considered hazardous and not labeled according to provisions of the FHSA is a misbranded hazardous substance and is an illegal import. Certain hazardous substances listed in the FHSA and in regulations promulgated by the CPSC are completely banned from importation. A shipment of consumer products cannot be imported if it poses an imminent hazard. See 15 USC 1261, 2604-2606; 16 CFR 1500.265-1500.272.

The CPSC may detain your shipment of hazardous substances and take samples for testing to determine compliance with the FHSA. If your shipment is found to contain banned hazardous substances, it will be refused admission and will be destroyed if not exported within 90 days of the date of refusal notice. If it is found to contain misbranded hazardous substances, you may make arrangements to bring it into conformance through relabeling. For complete details regarding testing, labeling, and safety regulations for hazardous products, contact the CPSC (see addresses at end of this chapter).

Marking and Labeling Requirements

Chemical Products. A shipment of any products containing chemicals that are classified as hazardous substance (49 CFR 172) must comply with the marking and labeling regulations adopted by the EPA (46 CFR 147.30) and the DOT (49 CFR 171 et seq.).

For a general discussion of U.S. Customs marking and labeling requirements, refer to "Marking: Country of Origin" on page 215 and "Special Marking Requirements" on page 217.

Shipping Considerations

You will need to ensure that your goods are packaged and shipped with care so that they pass smoothly through Customs and arrive in good condition. You are responsible for ensuring that the shipment is in compliance with all applicable government regulations for packaging and shipping. In most instances, you should not leave these arrangements solely to the discretion of your supplier. Careful preparation of the cargo and selection of the mode of transport can be essential to a cost-effective, timely delivery of undamaged goods. We strongly advise you to consult your shipping representative, insurance agent, or freight broker for advice on packing and shipping. Refer also to the major tab section "Packing/Shipping/Insurance" for a general discussion of packing and shipping.

Soaps, washing and lubricating products, and wax articles may be shipped in bulk, bags, bottles, crates, or other types of containers, depending on the type of product and whether it is prepackaged. General considerations include protection from contamination, weather, and pests. For liquid shipments, venting and vapor collection systems may be required. Safety precautions should also be implemented as required to protect against breakage, spillage, corrosion of containers, and combustion. Containers should be constructed so as to be safe for handling during transport.

Chemical Products. Chemical products in particular may have to be shipped in pressurized, ventilated, and temperature-and vapor-controlled enclosures. Solid chemical products that are listed as hazardous substances (49 CFR 172 appendix) may be transported in bulk only on compliance with Coast Guard notification procedures, shipping permit requirements, and complex transportation regulations (46 CFR 148). All hazardous substances must also be packaged and transported in accordance with DOT regulations (49 CFR 171 et seq.).

Publications Available

The following publications may be relevant to the importation of toxic or hazardous ingredients for soaps, washing and lubricating products, and wax articles:

Toxic Substances Control Act: A Guide for Chemical Importers/ Exporters (published by EPA).

TSCA Chemical Substance Inventory (1985 edition) (Doc. Code S/N 055-000-00254-1) $161.00 U.S. and Canada; $201.21 all other countries.

Supplement to TSCA Chemical Substances Inventory (1990) (Doc. Code S/N 055-000-00361-1) $15.00 U.S.; $18.75 Canada and all other countries.

The above publications and the *Harmonized Tariff Schedule of the United States* (HTSUS) are available from:

Government Printing Office (GPO)
Superintendent of Documents
Washington, DC 20402
(202) 512-1800 (Order line)
(202) 512-0000 (General)

The USGPO also has copies of specific laws available for purchase. The USGPO accepts credit card orders over the phone, as well as mail orders paid by credit card, a check drawn on a U.S. bank, or an international money order.

Relevant Government Agencies

Address your questions regarding CPSC requirements for soaps, washing and lubricating products, and wax articles to:

U.S. Consumer Product Safety Commission (CPSC)
Office of Compliance
Division of Regulatory Management
5401 Westbard Avenue
Bethesda, MD 20207
(301) 504-0400

Address your inquiries regarding TSCA and EPA requirements for importation of chemical products to:

Environmental Protection Agency (EPA)
TSCA System Information
EPA 7408, OPPT
401 M Street SW
Washington, DC 20460
(202) 554-1404 (TSCA Information Hotline)

Address your questions regarding transportation of hazardous substances to:

U.S. Department of Transportation (DOT)
Research and Special Programs Administration
Office of Hazardous Materials Standards
400 7th St. SW
Washington, DC 20590
(202) 366-4488

Address your questions regarding importation of soaps, washing and lubricating products, and wax articles generally to the district or port director of customs for you area. For addresses, refer to "U.S. Customs District Offices" on page 62 or contact:

U.S. Customs Service
1301 Constitution Ave. NW
Washington, DC 20229
(202) 927-6724 (Information)
(202) 927-1000 (General)

Laws and Regulations

The following laws and regulations may be relevant to the importation of soaps, washing and lubricating products, and wax articles. The laws are contained in the United States Code (USC), and the regulations are published in the Code of Federal Regulations (CFR), both of which are available at larger public and law libraries. Specific laws and regulations may also be purchased from the U.S. Government Printing Office (address above).

21 USC 301 et seq.
Food, Drug, and Cosmetic Act
This Act prohibits deceptive practices and regulates the manufacture, sale and importation or exportation of food, drugs, cosmetics, and related products. See 21 USC 331, 381, 382.

19 CFR 12.1 et seq.; 21 CFR 1.83 et seq.
Regulations on Food, Drugs, and Cosmetics
These regulations of the Secretary of Health and Human Services and the Secretary of the Treasury govern the standards, labeling, marking, and importing of products used with food, drugs, and cosmetics.

15 USC 1263
Consumer Product Safety Act (CPSA)
This Act gives the Consumer Product Safety Commission authority to set safety standards, testing procedures, and reporting requirements to ensure that consumer products not already covered under other regulations are not harmful.

16 CFR 1500 et seq.
Regulations on Hazardous Substances Safety Standards
These regulations set standards for processing, manufacturing, importing, and labeling all substances classified as hazardous that are to be sold to U.S. consumers.

15 USC 2601 et seq.
Toxic Substances Control Act
This Act authorizes the EPA to determine whether a substance is harmful and to restrict importation, sale, and use of such substances.

19 CFR 12.118 et seq.
Regulations on Toxic Substances Control
These regulations require importers of chemical substances imported in bulk or as part of a mixture to certify to Customs that the shipment complies with the TSCA or is not subject to that Act.

15 USC 1261
Federal Hazardous Substances Act
This Act controls the importation of hazardous substances, sets forth prohibited imports, and authorizes various agencies to promulgate labeling, marking, and transport requirements.

49 CFR 170 et seq.
Regulations on Hazardous Materials
These regulations list all substances deemed hazardous and provide transport, marking, labeling, safety, and emergency response rules.

46 CFR 147.30
Regulations on Labeling of Hazardous Materials
This regulation requires the labeling of containers of hazardous substances and specifies the label contents.

46 CFR 148 et seq.
Regulations on Carriage of Solid Hazardous Materials in Bulk
These regulations govern the transport of solid hazardous substances in bulk, including reporting, permitting, loading, stowing, and shipping requirements.

Sources of Additional Information

The TSCA Chemical Substance Inventory in computerized form is available from:

National Technical Information Service (NTIS)
U.S. Department of Commerce
5285 Port Royal Road
Springfield, VA 22161
(703) 487-4650

Access to the computerized TSCA Chemical Substance Inventory through commercial database is available at:

Scientific and Technical Network International
Chemical Abstracts Service (CAS)
File: CAS ONLINE
(800) 848-6533
Dialog Information Services
TSCA Chemical Substances Inventory
File: Number 52
(800) 334-2564

Principal Exporting Countries

The following listing includes samples of the main supplier nations of the products of this chapter. It is organized by HTSUS major heading. (Refer to "Customs Classification" above for the product codes.) Countries are listed in rank order of the value of products imported to the U.S. Statistics represent customs value entries for 1993 from the Bureau of Census, U.S. Department of Commerce.

3401—Canada, United Kingdom, Mexico, Germany, France, South Korea, Turkey, China, Guatemala, Switzerland

3402—Canada, Mexico, Germany, Japan, United Kingdom, France, Netherlands, Switzerland, Norway, Brazil

3403—Japan, Germany, France, Canada, United Kingdom, Austria, Sweden, Belgium, Argentina, Switzerland

3404—Germany, United Kingdom, Japan, Mexico, France, Belgium, Israel, Brazil, Malaysia, Canada

3405—Japan, Canada, Germany, United Kingdom, Denmark, Netherlands, Mexico, Switzerland, France, China

3406—China, Hong Kong, Israel, Italy, Macao, Mexico, Germany, South Korea, France, Denmark

3407—Germany, Switzerland, Italy, France, Taiwan, Thailand, China, Belgium, Mexico, United Kingdom

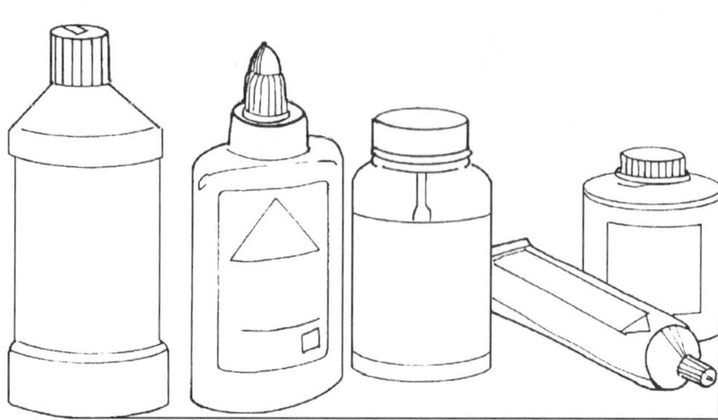

Chapter 35: Albumins, Glues, and Enzymes*

Full title: Albuminoidal Substances; Modified Starches; Glues; Enzymes

This chapter relates to the importation of albuminoidal substances, modified starches, glues, and enzymes, which are classified under Chapter 35 of the Harmonized Tariff Schedule of the United States (HTSUS). Specifically, it includes caseins, albumins, gelatins, peptones, other protein substances, hide powder, dextrins, other modified starches, and animal, fish, and synthetic glues and adhesives.

If you are interested in importing yeasts, you should refer to Commodity Index Chapter 21. Blood fractions (except blood albumin not for therapeutic or prophylactic uses), medicaments, or other products are classified under Chapter 30. Enzymatic preparations for pretanning are found in Chapter 32, and other enzymatic preparations, such as for soaking or washing, are in Chapter 34. This chapter also does not apply to hardened proteins, which are in Chapter 39. Gelatin products of the printing industry fall under Chapter 49.

Key Factors

The key factors in the importation of albuminoidal substances, modified starches, glues, and enzymes are:

- Compliance with U.S. Department of Agriculture (USDA) requirements (if an animal or fish product)
- Compliance with U.S. Federal Trade Commission (FTC) and Consumer Product Safety Commission (CPSC) standards (if a consumer product)
- Compliance with U.S. Environmental Protection Agency (EPA) requirements under Toxic Substances Control Act (TSCA) (if the product is a hazardous substance)
- Compliance with U.S. Department of Transportation (DOT) regulations for transport of hazardous cargo (if the product is a hazardous substance)

Although most importers use the services of a licensed customs broker in making their entries, and we recommend this practice, you should be aware of the regulatory, entry, and documentation issues involved in importing your product. You, as importer, are ultimately responsible for the fulfillment of any legal requirements applicable to your shipment.

*IMPORTANT: Read the Commodity Index Introduction. It is the essential framework for understanding this chapter.

General Considerations

Regulatory Agencies. The USDA regulates the importation of products derived from animals. The FTC sets standards for processing and labeling products that are sold to consumers. The EPA, under authority of the TSCA, imposes certain controls on the importation of albuminoidal substances, modified starches, glues, and enzymes that contain toxic substances. The TSCA defines a toxic substance as any substance determined to present the possibility of an unreasonable risk of injury to health and the environment. The DOT enforces regulations for transporting hazardous cargo. Materials are deemed hazardous if listed in DOT transport regulations (49 CFR 172 appendix).

Animal Products. Products derived from animals are subject to quarantine regulations, marking requirements, and processing standards. Shipments of these products are inspected at the port of arrival by the Animal and Plant Health Inspection Service (APHIS) of the USDA. Unless the shipment is in compliance with all applicable laws and regulations, it will be denied entry into the U.S. Some shipments may be restricted or prohibited completely.

The USDA heavily regulates eggs and egg products, including dried egg substances. An importer of egg products must apply for inspection on PY **Form 222**-Import Request, Eggs and Egg Products. The application should be made as far in advance before arrival at a U.S. port as possible. It may be submitted to the Poultry Division of the Poultry Grading Branch office at the port of importation (7 CFR 59.920). Each shipment of egg products must also be accompanied by a foreign egg products inspection certificate (7 CFR 59.915) and a warning sign or special import seal must be affixed to the packages or means of conveyance for the products. Before admittance into the U.S., the shipment will be inspected at the port of arrival for compliance with product and labeling standards. For small shipments, an importer may be required to transport the product to the inspector's location. Importers may also be required to supply an inspector with a sample. Egg products may be released in bond prior to inspection. Exemptions from these requirements are allowed for small importations (up to 30 pounds of liquid or frozen, or 50 pounds of dried, egg products) for laboratory analysis or personal use.

To be sold in the U.S., dried and frozen egg albumin and other products must be processed and labeled in compliance with FTC regulations.

Hazardous Consumer Products. Under the Federal Hazardous Substances Act (FHSA), albuminoidal substances, modified starches, glues, and enzymes intended for the consumer market are hazardous substances if they are flammable, combustible, or have the potential to cause substantial personal injury during, or as a proximate result of, any customary or reasonably foreseeable handling or use. The CPSC does not require permits, special invoicing, limited entry, licenses, or any special approval process for importing hazardous consumer products into the U.S. However, if you are importing these types of products, you are responsible for ensuring that they meet all applicable FHSA and CPSA requirements. There are detailed regulations regarding testing and labeling of hazardous products. The Commission's enforcement posture regarding compliance with labeling and product safety standards changes as new facts become available. Contact the CPSC (see addresses at end of this chapter) for specific requirements on the consumer product you are considering importing.

Substantial Product Hazard Reports. Defect-reporting is required for products covered under the Consumer Product Safety Act (CPSA). The law requires every manufacturer, distributor, or retailer of such products, who obtains information that reasonably supports the conclusion that such products fail to comply with an applicable consumer product safety rule, or contain a defect that could create a substantial product hazard, to immediately inform the CPSC of the potential violation or defect. A firm's willful failure to make a Substantial Product Hazard Report can result in litigation by the CPSC.

Chemical Products. Shipments of products containing chemicals must be in compliance with toxic and hazardous substance regulations of the EPA and DOT. These include packaging, shipping, marking, and labeling requirements. In addition, all products containing chemicals are subject to the U.S. Customs Service TSCA Import Certification Rule (19 CFR 12.118 et seq.). If you import these products, you must sign one of the following statements: "I certify that all chemical substances in this shipment comply with all applicable rules or orders under TSCA and that I am not offering a chemical substance for entry in violation of TSCA or any applicable rule or order thereunder" or "I certify that all chemicals in this shipment are not subject to TSCA."

You must file this TSCA certification of compliance or exemption at the time you make the entry at Customs. The certification may be in the form of a typed or stamped statement on an appropriate entry document or commercial invoice or a preprinted attachment to such entry document or invoice. You may sign the certificate by means of an authorized facsimile signature. If your entry is electronically processed, the certification will be in the form of a Certification Code, which is part of the Automated Broker Interface (ABI) transmission. Customs will not release your shipment without proper certification.

If you will be importing several or regular shipments, you should ask the appropriate Customs district director to authorize your use of a blanket certification. If you receive such authorization, you must include on the commercial invoice or entry document for each shipment a statement that the blanket certification is on file and that it is incorporated by reference. This statement need not be signed. The blanket certification is valid for one calendar year, is subject to renewal, and may be revoked at any time for cause.

In filling out TSCA forms and Customs entry documents, you should provide the Chemical Abstracts Service (CAS) number for each chemical in the shipment. These CAS numbers are given in the appendix to the HTSUS. You are not required to include the CAS number, but Customs will be able to process your shipment more quickly if you include this number.

Articles Exclusion. If you are importing items that are classified as hazardous substances but are part of articles, you are subject to TSCA certification requirements only if certification for your product is specifically required by a rule or order promulgated under the TSCA. No specific rules have been adopted at this time. An "article" is a manufactured item 1) that is formed into a specific shape or design during manufacture, 2) that has end-use functions dependent on the shape or design during end use, and 3) that during the end use, does not change in its chemical composition or that changes only for a noncommercial purpose separate from the article and only as allowed by law (19 CFR 12.120(2)). Fluids and particles are not articles, regardless of shape or design.

Shipment Detention. A shipment containing chemicals will be detained at the U.S. port of arrival (or entry if same), at your risk and expense, if: 1) it contains banned chemical substances (15 USC 2604, 2605); or 2) it contains chemical substances ordered seized because of imminent hazards (15 USC 2606). Further detention will occur at the port of entry, again at your risk and expense, if: 1) the EPA administrator or Customs district director has reasonable grounds to believe the shipment is not in compliance with the TSCA; or 2) you do not provide proper TSCA certification.

If your shipment is detained, it will be held by Customs for no more than 48 hours. It will then be turned over to the EPA administrator, unless you have arranged to release it in bond. You must either bring it into TSCA compliance or reexport it within the earlier of 90 days after notice of detention or 30 days of demand for redelivery. Customs may grant an extension if failure to comply or reexport is the result of delays in EPA or Customs procedures. If you fail to comply or reexport within the time allowed, the EPA administrator is authorized to have the shipment stored or disposed of at your expense.

Customs Classification

For customs purposes, albuminoidal substances, modified starches, glues, and enzymes are classified under Chapter 35 of the HTSUS. This chapter is broken into major headings, which are further divided into subheadings, and often sub-subheadings, each of which has its own HTSUS classification number. For example, the HTSUS number for milk protein concentrate is 3501.10.10, indicating it is a sub-subcategory of casein (3501.10.00), which is a subcategory of the major heading, casein and related products (3501.00.00). There are seven major headings within Chapter 35.

3501—Casein, caseinates, and other casein derivatives; casein glues

3502—Albumins (including concentrates of two or more whey proteins, containing by weight more than 80% whey proteins, calculated on the dry matter), albuminates, and other albumin derivatives

3503—Gelatin (including gelatin in rectangular (including square) sheets, whether or not surface-worked or colored) and gelatin derivatives; isinglass; other glues of animal origin, excluding casein glues of heading 3501

3504—Peptones and their derivatives; other protein substances and their derivatives, not elsewhere specified or included; hide powder, whether or not chromed

3505—Dextrins and other modified starches (for example, pregelatinized or esterified starches); glues based on starches, or on dextrins or other modified starches

3506—Prepared glues and other prepared adhesives, not elsewhere specified or included; products suitable for use as glues or adhesives, put up for retail sale as glues or adhesives, not exceeding a net weight of 1 kg

3507—Enzymes; prepared enzymes not elsewhere specified or included

For more details regarding classifications of the specific product you are interested in importing, consult a customs broker, the appropriate commodity specialist at your nearest customs port, or the HTSUS. HTSUS is available for purchase from the U.S. Government Printing Office (see addresses at end of this chapter), and may be found in larger public libraries. Refer to "Classification—Liquidation" on page 207 for a general discussion of customs classification.

Sample Import Duties

Import duties will vary depending on the HTSUS classification of your product. Therefore, to determine the correct amount of duties, your product must be properly classified under the HTSUS. The following sample duties are taken from the duty listings for HTSUS Chapter 35 products.

Milk protein concentrate (3501.10.10): 0.44 cents/kg; casein glue (3501.90.20): 7.5%; dried egg albumin (3502.10.10): 59.5 cents/kg; fish glue (3503.00.10): 1.8 cents/kg plus 2.4%; inedible gelatin valued under 88 cents/kg (3503.00.20): 1.8 cents/kg plus 5%; edible or photographic gelatin (3503.00.55): 4.4 cents/kg plus 6%; protein isolates (3504.00.10): 10%; dextrins (3505.10.00): 1.1 cents/kg; glues based on dextrin or starches (3505.20.00): 2.6 cents/kg plus 3.6%; adhesives based on rubber or plastics (3506.91.00): 2.1%; rennet (3507.10.00): free; other enzymes (3507.90.00): 5%.

Entry and Documentation

The entry of merchandise is a two-part process consisting of 1) filing the documentation necessary to determine whether merchandise may be released from Customs custody, and 2) filing the documents that contain information for duty assessment and statistical purposes. In certain instances, all documents must be filed and accepted by Customs prior to release of the goods. Unless you have been granted an extension, you must file entry documents at a location specified by the district or area director within five working days of your shipment's date of arrival at a U.S. port of entry. These include a number of standard documents required by Customs for any entry, and:

- PY **Form 222**-Import Request (for egg products)
- Foreign inspection certificate (for egg products)
- U.S. Customs TSCA Certification (for hazardous substances)

After you present the entry, Customs may examine your shipment or may waive examination. The shipment is then released provided no legal or regulatory violations have been noted. You must then file entry summary documentation and deposit estimated duties at a designated customhouse within 10 working days of your shipment's release. For a detailed description of entry procedures, standard documentation, and informal entry, refer to "Entry Process" on page 182.

Prohibitions and Restrictions

Animal Products. Animal products are subject to quarantine if they arrive from certain countries that are known to have specific infectious diseases. These countries are listed in 9 CFR 94. If a USDA inspector determines that a shipment is infected with anthrax, foot-and-mouth disease, rinderpest, or bovine spongiform encephalopathy, entry will be denied.

Bone meal may be imported without restriction, provided it has been processed in compliance with USDA regulations; is free of pieces of bone, hide, flesh, and sinew; and contains no more than traces of hair or wool (9 CFR 95.13). Entry is denied for shipments that are not in compliance.

Dried blood, blood meal, animal organs, tankage, meat meal, wool waste, wool manure, and similar animal byproducts for industrial use cannot be imported unless 1) the product originated in and was shipped from a country that is not on the quarantine list for foot-and-mouth disease or rinderpest; or 2) the products are handled through quarantine procedures at the port of arrival and are found to be in compliance with USDA conditions (9 CFR 95.15, 95.16).

Hazardous Consumer Products. Importation of any consumer product that has been declared a banned hazardous substance by a rule under the CPSA is prohibited. Any product considered hazardous and not labeled according to provisions of the FHSA is a misbranded hazardous substance and is an illegal import. Certain hazardous substances listed in the FHSA and in regulations promulgated by the CPSC are completely banned from importation. A shipment of consumer products cannot be imported if it poses an imminent hazard. See 15 USC 1261, 2604-2606; 16 CFR 1500.265-1500.272.

The CPSC may detain your shipment of hazardous substances and take samples for testing to determine compliance with the FHSA. If your shipment is found to contain banned hazardous substances, it will be refused admission and will be destroyed if not exported within 90 days of the date of refusal notice. If it is found to contain misbranded hazardous substances, you may make arrangements to bring it into conformance through relabeling. For complete details regarding testing, labeling, and safety regulations for hazardous products, contact the CPSC (see addresses at end of this chapter).

Country-Specific Restrictions

Egg products can be imported only from Canada and the Netherlands. Importation from all other countries is prohibited except for small importations (up to 30 pounds of liquid or frozen, or 50 pounds of dried egg products) for laboratory analysis or personal use.

Marking and Labeling Requirements

Animal Products. Containers in which animal products are packaged and shipped must be marked with the country of origin—that is, the country where the animal was located. If the products are quarantined at the port of arrival, marks and signs are required on shipping documents and any mode of transport used to move the product while under restrictions (9 CFR 95.25).

Special labeling requirements are required for immediate containers of egg products and for the containers in which they are shipped (7 CFR 59.950, 59.955). A USDA inspector can deny these products entry if the labeling is false or misleading.

Chemical Products. A shipment of any products containing chemicals that are classified as hazardous substance (49 CFR 172) must comply with the marking and labeling regulations adopted by the EPA (46 CFR 147.30) and the DOT (49 CFR 171 et seq.).

For a general discussion of U.S. Customs marking and labeling requirements, refer to "Marking: Country of Origin" on page 215 and "Special Marking Requirements" on page 217.

Shipping Considerations

You will need to ensure that your goods are packaged and shipped with care so that they pass smoothly through Customs and arrive in good condition. You are responsible for ensuring that the shipment is in compliance with all applicable government regulations for packaging and shipping. In most instances, you should not leave these arrangements solely to the discretion of your supplier. Careful preparation of the cargo and selection of the mode of transport can be essential to a cost-effective, timely delivery of undamaged goods. We strongly advise you to consult your shipping representative, insurance agent, or freight broker for advice on packing and shipping. Refer also to the major tab section "Packing/Shipping/Insurance" for a general discussion of packing and shipping.

Albuminoidal substances, modified starches, glues, and enzymes may be shipped in bulk, bags, bottles, or other types of containers, depending on the type of product and whether it is prepackaged. General considerations include protection from contamination, weather, and pests. If a product must be kept in a sanitary environment, all tables, utensils, platforms, and devices used for moving or handling the product, the compartments in which it is stowed while being transported will need to be maintained in a sanitary condition. For liquid shipments, venting and vapor collection systems may be required. Safety precautions should also be implemented as required to protect against breakage, spillage, corrosion of containers, and combustion. Containers should be constructed so as to be safe for handling during transport.

Chemical Products. Chemical products in particular may have to be shipped in pressurized, ventilated, and temperature-and vapor-controlled enclosures. Solid chemical products that are listed as hazardous substances (49 CFR 172 appendix) may be transported in bulk only on compliance with Coast Guard notification procedures, shipping permit requirements, and complex transportation regulations (46 CFR 148). All hazardous substances must also be packaged and transported in accordance with DOT regulations (49 CFR 171 et seq.).

Publications Available

The following publication explains the FDA requirements for importing albuminoidal substances, modified starches, glues, and enzymes. It is published by the FDA and is available on request from FDA headquarters (see addresses at end of this chapter).

Requirements of Laws and Regulations Enforced by the U.S. Food and Drug Administration

The following publications may be relevant to the importation of toxic or hazardous albuminoidal substances, modified starches, glues, and enzymes:

Toxic Substances Control Act: A Guide for Chemical Importers/Exporters (published by EPA).

TSCA Chemical Substance Inventory (1985 edition) (Doc. Code S/N 055-000-00254-1) $161.00 U.S. and Canada; $201.21 all other countries.

Supplement to TSCA Chemical Substances Inventory (1990) (Doc. Code S/N 055-000-00361-1) $15.00 U.S.; $18.75 Canada and all other countries.

These publications and the *Harmonized Tariff Schedule of the United States* (HTSUS) are available from:

Government Printing Office (GPO)
Superintendent of Documents
Washington, DC 20402
(202) 512-1800 (Order line)
(202) 512-0000 (General)

The USGPO also has copies of specific laws available for purchase. The USGPO accepts credit card orders over the phone, as well as mail orders paid by credit card, a check drawn on a U.S. bank, or an international money order.

Relevant Government Agencies

Address your inquiries regarding USDA requirements for importation of animal products to:

U.S. Department of Agriculture (USDA)
Animal and Plant Health Inspection Service (APHIS)
Plant Protection and Quarantine (PPQ)
Federal Building, Rm. 631
6505 Belcrest Road
Hyattsville, MD 20782
(301) 436-8645

Address your inquiries regarding importation of egg products to:

Agricultural Marketing Service
Poultry Division
P.O. Box 96456
Washington, DC 20090-6456
(202) 720-4476

Address your questions regarding CPSC requirements for albuminoidal substances, modified starches, glues, and enzymes to:

U.S. Consumer Product Safety Commission (CPSC)
Office of Compliance
Division of Regulatory Management
5401 Westbard Avenue
Bethesda, MD 20207
(301) 504-0400

Address your inquiries regarding TSCA and EPA requirements for importation of chemical products to:

Environmental Protection Agency (EPA)
TSCA System Information
EPA 7408, OPPT
401 M Street SW
Washington, DC 20460
(202) 554-1404 (TSCA Information Hotline)

Address your questions regarding transportation of hazardous substances to:

U.S. Department of Transportation (DOT)
Research and Special Programs Administration
Office of Hazardous Materials Standards
400 7th St. SW
Washington, DC 20590
(202) 366-4488

Address your questions regarding importation of albuminoidal substances, modified starches, glues, and enzymes generally to the district or port director of customs for you area. For addresses, refer to"U.S. Customs District Offices" on page 62 or contact:

U.S. Customs Service
1301 Constitution Ave. NW
Washington, DC 20229
(202) 927-6724 (Information)
(202) 927-1000 (General)

Laws and Regulations

The following laws and regulations may be relevant to the importation of albuminoidal substances, modified starches, glues, and enzymes. The laws are contained in the United States Code (USC), and the regulations are published in the Code of Federal Regulations (CFR), both of which are available at larger public and law libraries. Specific laws and regulations may also be purchased from the U.S. Government Printing Office (address above).

21 USC 301 et seq.
Food, Drug, and Cosmetic Act
This Act prohibits deceptive practices and regulates the manufacture, sale and importation or exportation of food, drugs, cosmetics, and related products. See 21 USC 331, 381, 382.

19 CFR 12.1 et seq.; 21 CFR 1.83 et seq.
Regulations on Food, Drugs, and Cosmetics
These regulations of the Secretary of Health and Human Services and the Secretary of the Treasury govern the standards, labeling, marking, and importing of products used with food, drugs, and cosmetics.

15 USC 1263
Consumer Product Safety Act (CPSA)
This Act gives the Consumer Product Safety Commission authority to set safety standards, testing procedures, and reporting requirements to ensure that consumer products not already covered under other regulations are not harmful.

16 CFR 1500 et seq.
Regulations on Hazardous Substances Safety Standards
These regulations set standards for processing, manufacturing, importing, and labeling all substances classified as hazardous that are to be sold to U.S. consumers.

16 CFR 235
Regulations on Epoxy Adhesive Labeling
This regulation requires that an adhesive contain certain chemicals in order to be labeled epoxy.

21 USC 1031 et seq.
Egg Product Inspection Act
This Act requires the inspection of edible and nonconsumable egg products, including imports, and sets labeling and processing standards.

7 CFR 59
Regulations on Egg and Egg Product Inspection
These regulations govern the inspection, import, transport, labeling, and processing of consumable and nonconsumable eggs and egg products.

16 CFR 160
Regulations on Egg Product Standards
These regulations control the processing of domestic or imported eggs and egg products to ensure that they meet certain standards for sale to consumers.

9 CFR 95.13 et seq.
Regulations on Animal Byproduct Quarantine Control
These regulations prohibit the importation of animal products for use in industry unless the products meet certain processing standards and are not infected with certain diseases.

15 USC 2601 et seq.
Toxic Substances Control Act
This Act authorizes the EPA to determine whether a substance is harmful and to restrict importation, sale, and use of such substances.

19 CFR 12.118 et seq.
Regulations on Toxic Substances Control
These regulations require importers of chemical substances imported in bulk or as part of a mixture to certify to Customs that the shipment complies with the TSCA or is not subject to that Act.

15 USC 1261
Federal Hazardous Substances Act
This Act controls the importation of hazardous substances, sets forth prohibited imports, and authorizes various agencies to promulgate labeling, marking, and transport requirements.

49 CFR 170 et seq.
Regulations on Hazardous Materials
These regulations list all substances deemed hazardous and provide transport, marking, labeling, safety, and emergency response rules.

46 CFR 147.30
Regulations on Labeling of Hazardous Materials
This regulation requires the labeling of containers of hazardous substances and specifies the label contents.

46 CFR 148 et seq.
Regulations on Carriage of Solid Hazardous Materials in Bulk
These regulations govern the transport of solid hazardous substances in bulk, including reporting, permitting, loading, stowing, and shipping requirements.

Sources of Additional Information

The TSCA Chemical Substance Inventory in computerized form is available from:

National Technical Information Service (NTIS)
U.S. Department of Commerce
5285 Port Royal Road
Springfield, VA 22161
(703) 487-4650

Access to the computerized TSCA Chemical Substance Inventory through commercial database is available at:

Scientific and Technical Network International
Chemical Abstracts Service (CAS)
File: CAS ONLINE
(800) 848-6533
Dialog Information Services
TSCA Chemical Substances Inventory
File: Number 52
(800) 334-2564

Principal Exporting Countries

The following listing includes samples of the main supplier nations of the products of this chapter. It is organized by HTSUS major heading. (Refer to "Customs Classification" above for the product codes.) Countries are listed in rank order of the value of products imported to the U.S. Statistics represent customs value entries for 1993 from the Bureau of Census, U.S. Department of Commerce.

3501—Ireland, New Zealand, France, Netherlands, Russia, Australia, Poland, Germany, Denmark, Norway

3502—New Zealand, Canada, Denmark, Australia, Germany, Ireland, France, Lithuania, Israel, Russia

3503—France, Brazil, Japan, Germany, United Kingdom, Sweden, Colombia, Netherlands, Canada, Belgium

3504—United Kingdom, France, Canada, Germany, Argentina, Israel, Japan, Switzerland, Denmark, Netherlands

3505—Netherlands, Thailand, Germany, France, Canada, Belgium, Mexico, Sweden, Taiwan, Brazil

3506—Japan, Germany, Canada, France, Taiwan, Belgium, United Kingdom, South Korea, Ireland, Switzerland

3507—Denmark, Germany, Japan, Canada, United Kingdom, Ireland, France, Finland, Belgium, Italy

Chapter 36: Explosives, Fireworks, and Other Combustibles*

Full title: Explosives; Pyrotechnic Products; Matches; Pyrophoric Alloys; Certain Combustible Preparations

This chapter relates to the importation of explosives, fireworks, and other combustible materials, which are classified under Chapter 36 of the Harmonized Tariff Schedule of the United States (HTSUS). Specifically, it includes propellant powders, other prepared explosives, fuses, detonators, igniters, fireworks, flares, rain rockets, matches, ferrocerium, other pyrophoric alloys, and lighter fuels.

If you are interested in importing separate chemical compounds, you should refer to Commodity Index Chapters 28 (inorganic) or 29 (organic). Refer to Chapter 22 for a discussion of the importation of ethyl alcohol for fuel or other purposes. The importation of arms and ammunition is covered in Chapter 93.

Key Factors

The key factors in the importation of explosives, fireworks, and other combustible materials are:

- Compliance with U.S. Federal Trade Commission (FTC) and Consumer Product Safety Commission (CPSC) standards (for matches, lighter fluids, and hazardous substances)
- Compliance with U.S. Mine Safety and Health Administration (MSHA) standards (for explosives and detonators for use in underground mines)
- Compliance with U.S. Bureau of Alcohol, Tobacco, and Firearms (BATF) regulations, including license and permit requirements
- Compliance with U.S. Environmental Protection Agency (EPA) requirements under Toxic Substances Control Act (TSCA) (if the product is a hazardous substance)
- Compliance with U.S. Department of Transportation (DOT) regulations for transport of hazardous cargo (if the product is a hazardous substance)

Although most importers use the services of a licensed customs broker in making their entries, and we recommend this practice, you should be aware of the regulatory, entry, and documentation issues involved in importing your product. You, as importer, are ultimately responsible for the fulfillment of any legal requirements applicable to your shipment.

General Considerations

Regulatory Agencies. The BATF controls commerce in all explosives, including those listed in the regulations (27 CFR 55.23). The MSHA approves explosives and detonators used in underground mines. The FTC and CPSC enforce standards for consumer products that contain hazardous substances, as well as specific requirements for matchbooks and lighter fluids. The EPA, under authority of the TSCA, regulates the importation of explosives, fireworks, and other combustible materials that contain toxic substances The TSCA defines a toxic substance as any substance determined to present the possibility of an unreasonable risk of injury to health and the environment. The DOT enforces regulations for transporting hazardous cargo. Materials are deemed hazardous if listed in DOT transport regulations (49 CFR 172 appendix).

Explosives. If you intend to engage in business as an importer of explosives you must first obtain a license from the BATF. The term "explosives" includes any chemical compound, mixture, or device that has a primary or common purpose to function by an explosion. With few exceptions, you must have a license for each business premises at which you import or distribute these substances. The application for a license is **Form BATF F 5400.13.** If you want to acquire for use explosive materials from a foreign supplier, you must obtain a permit from the BATF. You will also need a permit to transport explosives in interstate or foreign commerce. The application for a permit is **Form BATF F 5400.16.** These application forms are available from the BATF. Most original licenses and permits are valid for one year and may then be renewed for three-year periods.

There are a number of exemptions from the BATF explosive regulations, such as for small arms ammunition, common fireworks regulated by the DOT, products delivered to a government agency or military installation, products used as medicines and medicinal agents, gasoline, fertilizers, propellant-actuated devices or industrial tools, and industrial or laboratory chemicals intended for use as reagents. The BATF regulations also exclude commercially manufactured black powder in quantities not exceeding 50 pounds or contained in percussion caps, safety and pyrotechnic fuses, quills, quick and slow matches, and friction primers, provided it intended use is for sporting, recreational, or cultural purposes in antique firearms or devices.

Matches. At the time of filing an entry for imported matches, the importer must make a declaration that to the best of the importer's knowledge and belief no matches included in the invoice and entry are white phosphorus matches.

With two exceptions, the invoice covering a shipment of matches imported to the U.S. must be accompanied by a certificate of official inspection from the government of the country of manufacture. That certificate must be signed by a person who conducts a chemical analysis of the matches, stating that the analysis shows no white or yellow phosphorus in the matches. It must also list the cases of matches tested and, for each case, a description of the matches, the manufacturer, the consignee, and information on shipping. Customs will detain any shipment of matches until this certificate is produced.

The certificate need not be produced if the importer submits other satisfactory evidence that the matches were not manufactured with the use of poisonous white or yellow phosphorus or if the matches were manufactured in a country that prohibits the use of such phosphorus in the manufacture of matches.

*IMPORTANT: Read the Commodity Index Introduction. It is the essential framework for understanding this chapter.

Hazardous Consumer Products. The Federal Hazardous Substances Act (FHSA) imposes special controls on hazardous consumer products, which are defined as substances that are flammable, combustible, or have the potential to cause substantial personal injury during, or as a proximate result of, any customary or reasonably foreseeable handling or use. The CPSC does not require permits, special invoicing, limited entry, licenses, or any special approval process for importing hazardous consumer products into the U.S. However, if you are importing these types of products, you are responsible for ensuring that they meet all applicable FHSA and Consumer Product Safety Act (CPSA) requirements. There are detailed regulations regarding testing and labeling of hazardous products. The Commission's enforcement posture regarding compliance with labeling and product safety standards changes as new facts become available. Contact the CPSC (see addresses at end of this chapter) for specific requirements on the consumer product you are considering importing.

Substantial Product Hazard Reports. Defect-reporting is required for products covered under the CPSA. The law requires every manufacturer, distributor, or retailer of such products, who obtains information that reasonably supports the conclusion that such products fail to comply with an applicable consumer product safety rule, or contain a defect that could create a substantial product hazard, to immediately inform the CPSC of the potential violation or defect. A firm's willful failure to make a Substantial Product Hazard Report can result in litigation by the CPSC.

Toxic and Hazardous Substances. Shipments of products containing chemicals must be in compliance with toxic and hazardous substance regulations of the EPA and DOT. These include packaging, shipping, marking, and labeling requirements. In addition, all products containing chemicals are subject to the U.S. Customs Service TSCA Import Certification Rule (19 CFR 12.118 et seq.). If you import these products, you must sign one of the following statements: "I certify that all chemical substances in this shipment comply with all applicable rules or orders under TSCA and that I am not offering a chemical substance for entry in violation of TSCA or any applicable rule or order thereunder" or "I certify that all chemicals in this shipment are not subject to TSCA."

You must file this TSCA certification of compliance or exemption at the time you make the entry at Customs. The certification may be in the form of a typed or stamped statement on an appropriate entry document or commercial invoice or a preprinted attachment to such entry document or invoice. You may sign the certificate by means of an authorized facsimile signature. If your entry is electronically processed, the certification will be in the form of a Certification Code, which is part of the Automated Broker Interface (ABI) transmission. Customs will not release your shipment without proper certification.

If you will be importing several or regular shipments, you should ask the appropriate Customs district director to authorize your use of a blanket certification. If you receive such authorization, you must include on the commercial invoice or entry document for each shipment a statement that the blanket certification is on file and that it is incorporated by reference. This statement need not be signed. The blanket certification is valid for one calendar year, is subject to renewal, and may be revoked at any time for cause.

In filling out TSCA forms and Customs entry documents, you should provide the Chemical Abstracts Service (CAS) number for each chemical in the shipment. These CAS numbers are given in the appendix to the HTSUS. You are not required to include the CAS number, but Customs will be able to process your shipment more quickly if you include this number.

Articles Exclusion. If you are importing items that are classified as hazardous substances but are part of articles, you are subject to TSCA certification requirements only if certification for your product is specifically required by a rule or order promulgated under the TSCA. No specific rules have been adopted at this time. An "article" is a manufactured item 1) that is formed into a specific shape or design during manufacture, 2) that has end-use functions dependent on the shape or design during end use, and 3) that during the end use, does not change in its chemical composition or that changes only for a noncommercial purpose separate from the article and only as allowed by law (19 CFR 12.120(2)). Fluids and particles are not articles, regardless of shape or design.

Shipment Detention. A shipment containing chemicals will be detained at the U.S. port of arrival (or entry if same), at your risk and expense, if: 1) it contains banned chemical substances (15 USC 2604, 2605); or 2) it contains chemical substances ordered seized because of imminent hazards (15 USC 2606). Further detention will occur at the port of entry, again at your risk and expense, if: 1) the EPA administrator or Customs district director has reasonable grounds to believe the shipment is not in compliance with the TSCA; or 2) you do not provide proper TSCA certification.

If your shipment is detained, it will be held by Customs for no more than 48 hours. It will then be turned over to the EPA administrator, unless you have arranged to release it in bond. You must either bring it into TSCA compliance or reexport it within the earlier of 90 days after notice of detention or 30 days of demand for redelivery. Customs may grant an extension if failure to comply or reexport is the result of delays in EPA or Customs procedures. If you fail to comply or reexport within the time allowed, the EPA administrator is authorized to have the shipment stored or disposed of at your expense.

Customs Classification

For customs purposes, explosives, fireworks, and other combustible materials are classified under Chapter 36 of the HTSUS. This chapter is broken into major headings, which are further divided into subheadings, and often sub-subheadings, each of which has its own HTSUS classification number. For example, the HTSUS number for ferrocerium is 3606.90.30, indicating it is a sub-subcategory of other liquid fuels (3606.90.00), which is a subcategory of the major heading, ferrocerium, other pyrophoric alloys, and lighter fuels (3606.00.00). There are six major headings within Chapter 36.

3601—Propellant powders

3602—Prepared explosives, other than propellant powders

3603—Safety fuses, detonating fuses; percussion or detonating caps; igniters; electric detonators

3604—Fireworks, signaling flares, rain rockets, fog signals, and other pyrotechnic articles

3605—Matches, other than pyrotechnic articles of heading 3604

3606—Ferrocerium and other pyrophoric alloys in all forms; articles of combustible materials as specified in note 2 to this chapter

For more details regarding classifications of the specific product you are interested in importing, consult a customs broker, the appropriate commodity specialist at your nearest customs port, or the HTSUS. HTSUS is available for purchase from the U.S. Government Printing Office (see addresses at end of this chapter), and may be found in larger public libraries. Refer to "Classification—Liquidation" on page 207 for a general discussion of customs classification.

Sample Import Duties

Import duties will vary depending on the HTSUS classification of your product. Therefore, to determine the correct amount of duties, your product must be properly classified under the HTSUS. The following sample duties are taken from the duty listings for HTSUS Chapter 36 products.

Propellant powders (3601.00.00): 7.2%; dynamite in form suitable for blasting (3602.00.00): free; safety or detonating fuses (3603.00.30): $1.18/1000 m; percussion caps (3603.00.60): 4.2%; electric detonators (3603.00.90) 0.14 cent each; fireworks (3604.10.00): 11 cents/kg, including weight of coverings, packing material, and wrappings; matches (3605.00.00): free; liquid fuel for cigarette lighters (3606.10.00): free.

Entry and Documentation

The entry of merchandise is a two-part process consisting of 1) filing the documentation necessary to determine whether merchandise may be released from Customs custody, and 2) filing the documents that contain information for duty assessment and statistical purposes. In certain instances, all documents must be filed and accepted by Customs prior to release of the goods. Unless you have been granted an extension, you must file entry documents at a location specified by the district or area director within five working days of your shipment's date of arrival at a U.S. port of entry. These include a number of standard documents required by Customs for any entry, and:

- Importer's license or permit from the BATF (for explosives)
- U.S. Customs TSCA Certification (for hazardous substances)

After you present the entry, Customs may examine your shipment or may waive examination. The shipment is then released provided no legal or regulatory violations have been noted. You must then file entry summary documentation and deposit estimated duties at a designated customhouse within 10 working days of your shipment's release. For a detailed description of entry procedures, standard documentation, and informal entry, refer to "Entry Process" on page 182.

Prohibitions and Restrictions

Matches. The importation of white phosphorus matches is prohibited.

Hazardous Consumer Products. Importation of any consumer product that has been declared a banned hazardous substance by a rule under the CPSA is prohibited. Any product considered hazardous and not labeled according to provisions of the FHSA is a misbranded hazardous substance and is an illegal import. Certain hazardous substances listed in the FHSA and in regulations promulgated by the CPSC are completely banned from importation. A shipment of consumer products cannot be imported if it poses an imminent hazard. See 15 USC 1261, 2604-2606; 16 CFR 1500.265-1500.272.

The CPSC may detain your shipment of hazardous substances and take samples for testing to determine compliance with the FHSA. If your shipment is found to contain banned hazardous substances, it will be refused admission and will be destroyed if not exported within 90 days of the date of refusal notice. If it is found to contain misbranded hazardous substances, you may make arrangements to bring it into conformance through relabeling. For complete details regarding testing, labeling, and safety regulations for hazardous products, contact the CPSC (see addresses at end of this chapter).

Marking and Labeling Requirements

Chemical Products. A shipment of any products containing chemicals that are classified as hazardous substance (49 CFR 172) must comply with the marking and labeling regulations adopted by the EPA (46 CFR 147.30) and the DOT (49 CFR 171 et seq.).

Explosives. A shipment of explosive substances must comply with marking and labeling regulations adopted by the BATF (46 CFR 55) and the DOT (49 CFR 171 et seq.).

For a general discussion of U.S. Customs marking and labeling requirements, refer to "Marking: Country of Origin" on page 215 and "Special Marking Requirements" on page 217.

Shipping Considerations

You will need to ensure that your goods are packaged and shipped with care so that they pass smoothly through Customs and arrive in good condition. You are responsible for ensuring that the shipment is in compliance with all applicable government regulations for packaging and shipping. In most instances, you should not leave these arrangements solely to the discretion of your supplier. Careful preparation of the cargo and selection of the mode of transport can be essential to a cost-effective, timely delivery of undamaged goods. We strongly advise you to consult your shipping representative, insurance agent, or freight broker for advice on packing and shipping. Refer also to the major tab section "Packing/Shipping/Insurance" for a general discussion of packing and shipping.

Explosives, fireworks, and other combustible materials may be shipped in bulk, bags, bottles, crates, or other types of containers, depending on the type of product and whether it is prepackaged. General considerations include protection from contamination, weather, and pests. For liquid shipments, venting and vapor collection systems may be required. Safety precautions should also be implemented as required to protect against breakage, spillage, corrosion of containers, combustion, and explosion. Containers should be constructed so as to be safe for handling during transport.

Chemical Products. Chemical products in particular may have to be shipped in pressurized, ventilated, and temperature-and vapor-controlled enclosures. Solid chemical products that are listed as hazardous substances (49 CFR 172 appendix) may be transported in bulk only on compliance with Coast Guard notification procedures, shipping permit requirements, and complex transportation regulations (46 CFR 148). All hazardous substances must also be packaged and transported in accordance with DOT regulations (49 CFR 171 et seq.).

Publications Available

The following publications may be relevant to the importation of toxic or hazardous explosives, fireworks, and other combustible materials:

Toxic Substances Control Act: A Guide for Chemical Importers/Exporters (published by EPA).

TSCA Chemical Substance Inventory (1985 edition) (Doc. Code S/N 055-000-00254-1) $161.00 U.S. and Canada; $201.21 all other countries.

Supplement to TSCA Chemical Substances Inventory (1990) (Doc. Code S/N 055-000-00361-1) $15.00 U.S.; $18.75 Canada and all other countries.

The above publications and the *Harmonized Tariff Schedule of the United States* (HTSUS) are available from:

Government Printing Office (GPO)
Superintendent of Documents
Washington, DC 20402
(202) 512-1800 (Order line)
(202) 512-0000 (General)

The USGPO also has copies of specific laws available for purchase. The USGPO accepts credit card orders over the phone, as well as mail orders paid by credit card, a check drawn on a U.S. bank, or an international money order.

Relevant Government Agencies

Address your inquiries regarding TSCA and EPA requirements for importation of chemical products to:

Environmental Protection Agency (EPA)
TSCA System Information
EPA 7408, OPPT
401 M Street SW
Washington, DC 20460
(202) 554-1404 (TSCA Information Hotline)

Address your questions regarding import licenses and permits for explosives to a local BATF office or to:

Bureau of Alcohol, Tobacco and Firearms (BATF)
Firearms and Explosives Import Export Branch
650 Massachusetts Avenue
Washington, DC 20226
(202) 927-8300

Address your questions regarding standards for mining explosives to:

Mine Safety and Health Administration (MSHA)
Approval and Certification Center
RR #1, Box 251
Triadelphia, West Virginia 26059
(304) 547-0400

Address your questions regarding CPSC requirements for explosives, fireworks, and consumer combustible materials to:

U.S. Consumer Product Safety Commission (CPSC)
Office of Compliance
Division of Regulatory Management
5401 Westbard Avenue
Bethesda, MD 20207
(301) 504-0400

Address your questions regarding transportation of hazardous substances to:

U.S. Department of Transportation (DOT)
Research and Special Programs Administration
Office of Hazardous Materials Standards
400 7th St. SW
Washington, DC 20590
(202) 366-4488

Address your questions regarding importation of explosives, fireworks, and other combustible materials generally to the district or port director of customs for you area. For addresses, refer to"U.S. Customs District Offices" on page 62 or contact:

U.S. Customs Service
1301 Constitution Ave. NW
Washington, DC 20229
(202) 927-6724 (Information)
(202) 927-1000 (General)

Laws and Regulations

The following laws may be relevant to the importation of explosives, fireworks, and other combustible materials. They are contained in the United States Code (USC), which is available at larger public and law libraries. Specific laws and regulations may also be purchased from the U.S. Government Printing Office (address above).

18 USC 40 et seq.
Organized Crime Control Act
This chapter of this Act regulates commerce in explosives by requiring the licensing of importers, manufacturers, and dealers and by authorizing the BATF to implement standards for business operations involving explosives.

27 CFR 55
Regulations on Explosives in Interstate and Foreign Commerce
These regulations require licenses and permits for importing and transporting explosives, set forth standards for recordkeeping, business operations, storage, labeling, and transport, and establish procedures for inspection and seizure of noncomplying goods.

15 USC 1263
Consumer Product Safety Act (CPSA)
This Act gives the Consumer Product Safety Commission authority to set safety standards, testing procedures, and reporting requirements to ensure that consumer products not already covered under other regulations are not harmful.

16 CFR 1202
Matchbook Safety Standards
These regulations set standards for processing, manufacturing, importing, and labeling matchbooks to be sold to U.S. consumers.

16 CFR 1210 et seq.
Cigarette Lighter Safety Standards
These regulations set standards for processing, manufacturing, and labeling cigarette lighters to be sold in the U.S. and require importers to certify that their products meet these standards.

16 CFR 1500 et seq.
Regulations on Hazardous Substances Safety Standards
These regulations set standards for processing, manufacturing, importing, and labeling all substances classified as hazardous that are to be sold to U.S. consumers.

15 USC 2601 et seq.
Toxic Substances Control Act
This Act authorizes the EPA to determine whether a substance is harmful and to restrict importation, sale, and use of such substances.

19 CFR 12.118 et seq.
Regulations on Toxic Substances Control
These regulations require importers of chemical substances imported in bulk or as part of a mixture to certify to Customs that the shipment complies with the TSCA or is not subject to that Act.

15 USC 1261
Federal Hazardous Substances Act
This Act controls the importation of hazardous substances, sets forth prohibited imports, and authorizes various agencies to promulgate labeling, marking, and transport requirements.

49 CFR 170 et seq.
Regulations on Hazardous Materials
These regulations list all substances deemed hazardous and provide transport, marking, labeling, safety, and emergency response rules.

46 CFR 147.30
Regulations on Labeling of Hazardous Materials
This regulation requires the labeling of containers of hazardous substances and specifies the label contents.

46 CFR 148 et seq.
Regulations on Carriage of Solid Hazardous Materials in Bulk
These regulations govern the transport of solid hazardous substances in bulk, including reporting, permitting, loading, stowing, and shipping requirements.

Sources of Additional Information

The TSCA Chemical Substance Inventory in computerized form is available from:

National Technical Information Service (NTIS)
U.S. Department of Commerce
5285 Port Royal Road
Springfield, VA 22161
(703) 487-4650

Access to the computerized TSCA Chemical Substance Inventory through commercial database is available at:

Scientific and Technical Network International
Chemical Abstracts Service (CAS)
File: CAS ONLINE
(800) 848-6533
Dialog Information Services
TSCA Chemical Substances Inventory
File: Number 52
(800) 334-2564

Principal Exporting Countries

The following listing includes samples of the main supplier nations of the products of this chapter. It is organized by HTSUS major heading. (Refer to "Customs Classification" above for the product codes.) Countries are listed in rank order of the value of products imported to the U.S. Statistics represent customs value entries for 1993 from the Bureau of Census, U.S. Department of Commerce.

3601—Canada, Australia, Sweden, Finland, China, United Kingdom, Czech Rep., Israel, Brazil

3602—Canada, China, Sweden, Chile, United Kingdom, Germany, Norway, France, Finland, Argentina

3603—Canada, France, Mexico, Germany, Austria, Czech Rep., United Kingdom, Brazil, Italy, Japan

3604—China, Taiwan, Hong Kong, Japan, United Kingdom, Macao, Italy, Canada, France, Germany

3605—Canada, Sweden, Japan, Taiwan, Chile, China, South Korea, Indonesia, Portugal, United Kingdom

3606—France, United Kingdom, Brazil, South Korea, Austria, Ireland, Belgium, Netherlands, Hong Kong, Germany

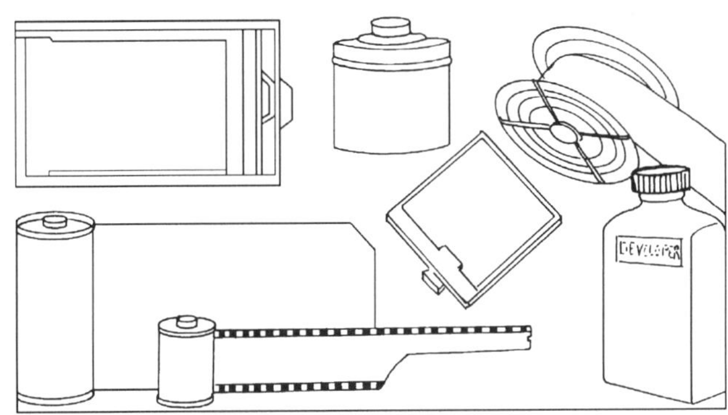

Chapter 37: Photographic or Cinematographic Goods*

This chapter relates to the importation of photographic and cinematographic goods, which are classified under Chapter 37 of the Harmonized Tariff Schedule of the United States (HTSUS). Specifically, it includes photographic film, paper, plates, and other media, motion picture film, and chemical preparations for photographic uses.

If you are interested in importing separately defined chemicals, you should refer to Commodity Index Chapters 28 (inorganic) and 29 (organic). Cameras and photographic equipment are covered in Chapter 90. Import requirements for works of art are covered in Chapter 97.

Key Factors

The key factors in the importation of photographic or cinematographic goods are:

- Compliance with U.S. Environmental Protection Agency (EPA) requirements under Toxic Substances Control Act (TSCA) (if the product is a hazardous substance)
- Compliance with U.S. Department of Transportation (DOT) regulations for transport of hazardous cargo (if the product is a hazardous substance)
- Compliance with U.S. Federal Trade Commission (FTC) and Consumer Product Safety Commission (CPSC) standards (if a consumer product)

Although most importers use the services of a licensed customs broker in making their entries, and we recommend this practice, you should be aware of the regulatory, entry, and documentation issues involved in importing your product. You, as importer, are ultimately responsible for the fulfillment of any legal requirements applicable to your shipment.

General Considerations

Regulatory Agencies. Importation of photographic and cinematographic goods, other than chemicals, is straightforward. For many products, no permits, licenses, or special entry paperwork are required. The FTC sets standards for processing and labeling products that are sold to consumers. The EPA, under authority of the TSCA, imposes certain controls on the importation of photographic or cinematographic supplies that contain toxic substances. The TSCA defines a toxic substance as any substance

*IMPORTANT: Read the Commodity Index Introduction. It is the essential framework for understanding this chapter.

determined to present the possibility of an unreasonable risk of injury to health and the environment. The DOT enforces regulations for transporting hazardous cargo. Materials are deemed hazardous if listed in DOT transport regulations (49 CFR 172 appendix).

Hazardous Consumer Products. The Federal Hazardous Substances Act (FHSA) imposes special controls on hazardous consumer products, which are defined as substances that are flammable, combustible, or have the potential to cause substantial personal injury during, or as a proximate result of, any customary or reasonably foreseeable handling or use. The CPSC does not require permits, special invoicing, limited entry, licenses, or any special approval process for importing hazardous consumer products into the U.S. However, if you are importing these types of products, you are responsible for ensuring that they meet all applicable FHSA and Consumer Product Safety Act (CPSA) requirements. There are detailed regulations regarding testing and labeling of hazardous products. The Commission's enforcement posture regarding compliance with labeling and product safety standards changes as new facts become available. Contact the CPSC (see addresses at end of this chapter) for specific requirements on the consumer product you are considering importing.

Substantial Product Hazard Reports. Defect-reporting is required for products covered under the CPSA. The law requires every manufacturer, distributor, or retailer of such products, who obtains information that reasonably supports the conclusion that such products fail to comply with an applicable consumer product safety rule, or contain a defect that could create a substantial product hazard, to immediately inform the CPSC of the potential violation or defect. A firm's willful failure to make a Substantial Product Hazard Report can result in litigation by the CPSC.

Toxic and Hazardous Substances. Shipments of photochemical products—such as developer, fixer, and toner—must be in compliance with toxic and hazardous substance regulations of the EPA and DOT. These include packaging, shipping, marking, and labeling requirements. In addition, all products containing chemicals are subject to the U.S. Customs Service TSCA Import Certification Rule (19 CFR 12.118 et seq.). If you import these products, you must sign one of the following statements: "I certify that all chemical substances in this shipment comply with all applicable rules or orders under TSCA and that I am not offering a chemical substance for entry in violation of TSCA or any applicable rule or order thereunder" or "I certify that all chemicals in this shipment are not subject to TSCA."

You must file this TSCA certification of compliance or exemption at the time you make the entry at Customs. The certification may be in the form of a typed or stamped statement on an appropriate entry document or commercial invoice or a preprinted attachment to such entry document or invoice. You may sign the certificate by means of an authorized facsimile signature. If your entry is electronically processed, the certification will be in the form of a Certification Code, which is part of the Automated Broker Interface (ABI) transmission. Customs will not release your shipment without proper certification.

If you will be importing several or regular shipments, you should ask the appropriate Customs district director to authorize your use of a blanket certification. If you receive such authorization, you must include on the commercial invoice or entry document for each shipment a statement that the blanket certification is on file and that it is incorporated by reference. This statement need not be signed. The blanket certification is valid for one calendar year, is subject to renewal, and may be revoked at any time for cause.

In filling out TSCA forms and Customs entry documents, you should provide the Chemical Abstracts Service (CAS) number for each chemical in the shipment. These CAS numbers are given in the appendix to the HTSUS. You are not required to include the CAS number, but Customs will be able to process your shipment more quickly if you include this number.

Articles Exclusion. If you are importing items that are classified as hazardous substances but are part of articles, you are subject to TSCA certification requirements only if certification for your product is specifically required by a rule or order promulgated under the TSCA. No specific rules have been adopted at this time. An "article" is a manufactured item 1) that is formed into a specific shape or design during manufacture, 2) that has end-use functions dependent on the shape or design during end use, and 3) that during the end use, does not change in its chemical composition or that changes only for a noncommercial purpose separate from the article and only as allowed by law (19 CFR 12.120(2)). Fluids and particles are not articles, regardless of shape or design.

Shipment Detention. A shipment containing chemicals will be detained at the U.S. port of arrival (or entry if same), at your risk and expense, if: 1) it contains banned chemical substances (15 USC 2604, 2605); or 2) it contains chemical substances ordered seized because of imminent hazards (15 USC 2606). Further detention will occur at the port of entry, again at your risk and expense, if: 1) the EPA administrator or Customs district director has reasonable grounds to believe the shipment is not in compliance with the TSCA; or 2) you do not provide proper TSCA certification.

If your shipment is detained, it will be held by Customs for no more than 48 hours. It will then be turned over to the EPA administrator, unless you have arranged to release it in bond. You must either bring it into TSCA compliance or reexport it within the earlier of 90 days after notice of detention or 30 days of demand for redelivery. Customs may grant an extension if failure to comply or reexport is the result of delays in EPA or Customs procedures. If you fail to comply or reexport within the time allowed, the EPA administrator is authorized to have the shipment stored or disposed of at your expense.

Customs Classification

For customs purposes, photographic and cinematographic goods are classified under Chapter 37 of the HTSUS. This chapter is broken into major headings, which are further divided into subheadings, and often sub-subheadings, each of which has its own HTSUS classification number. For example, the HTSUS number for sound recordings on motion picture film suitable for exhibits is 3706.10.30, indicating it is a sub-subcategory of film that is 35 mm or wider (3706.10.00), which is a subcategory of the major heading, motion picture film (3706.00.00). There are seven major headings within Chapter 37.

3701—Photographic plates and film in the flat, sensitized, unexposed, of any material other than paper, paperboard, or textiles; instant print film in the flat, sensitized, unexposed, whether or not in packs

3702—Photographic film in rolls, sensitized, unexposed, of any material other than paper, paperboard, or textiles; instant print film in rolls, sensitized, unexposed

3703—Photographic paper, paperboard, and textiles, sensitized, unexposed

3704—Photographic plates, film, paper, paperboard, and textiles, exposed but not developed

3705—Photographic plates and film, exposed and developed, other than motion picture film

3706—Motion picture film, exposed and developed, whether or not incorporating sound track or consisting only of sound track

3707—Chemical preparations for photographic uses (other than varnishes, glues, adhesives, and similar preparations); unmixed products for photographic uses, put up in measured portions or put up for retail sale in a form ready for use

For more details regarding classifications of the specific product you are interested in importing, consult a customs broker, the appropriate commodity specialist at your nearest customs port, or the HTSUS. HTSUS is available for purchase from the U.S. Government Printing Office (see addresses at end of this chapter), and may be found in larger public libraries. Refer to "Classification—Liquidation" on page 207 for a general discussion of customs classification.

Sample Import Duties

Import duties will vary depending on the HTSUS classification of your product. Therefore, to determine the correct amount of duties, your product must be properly classified under the HTSUS. The following sample duties are taken from the duty listings for HTSUS Chapter 37 products.

Instant print film (3701.20.00): 3.7%; silver halide photographic paper, sensitized, unexposed, and rolled (3703.10.30): 3.7%; photographic plates, film, paper, paperboard, and textiles, exposed but not developed (3704.00.00): free; sound recordings on motion picture film at least 35 mm wide and suitable for motion picture exhibits (3706.10.30): 0.66 cents/m; all other types of motion picture film (3706.10.60, 3706.90.00): free; sensitizing emulsions (3707.10.00): 3%; photochemicals (3707.90.30): 8.5%.

Entry and Documentation

The entry of merchandise is a two-part process consisting of 1) filing the documentation necessary to determine whether merchandise may be released from Customs custody, and 2) filing the documents that contain information for duty assessment and statistical purposes. In certain instances, all documents must be filed and accepted by Customs prior to release of the goods. Unless you have been granted an extension, you must file entry documents at a location specified by the district or area director within five working days of your shipment's date of arrival at a U.S. port of entry. These include a number of standard documents required by Customs for any entry, and:

- U.S. Customs TSCA Certification (for hazardous substances)

After you present the entry, Customs may examine your shipment or may waive examination. The shipment is then released provided no legal or regulatory violations have been noted. You must then file entry summary documentation and deposit estimated duties at a designated customhouse within 10 working days of your shipment's release. For a detailed description of entry procedures, standard documentation, and informal entry, refer to "Entry Process" on page 182.

Entry Invoice. An invoice for a shipment of motion picture film must include the following: 1) a statement of the footage, title, and subject matter of each film; 2) a declaration of the shipper, cameraman, or other person with knowledge of the facts identifying the films with the invoice and stating that the basic films were to the best of that person's knowledge and belief exposed abroad and returned for use as newsreel; and 3) a declaration of the importer that the importer believes the films entered are the ones covered by the preceding declaration and that the films are intended for use as newsreel.

Prohibitions and Restrictions

Hazardous Consumer Products. Importation of any consumer product that has been declared a banned hazardous substance by a rule under the CPSA is prohibited. Any product considered hazardous and not labeled according to provisions of the FHSA is a misbranded hazardous substance and is an illegal import. Certain hazardous substances listed in the FHSA and in regulations promulgated by the CPSC are completely banned from importation. A shipment of consumer products cannot be imported if it poses an imminent hazard. See 15 USC 1261, 2604-2606; 16 CFR 1500.265-1500.272.

The CPSC may detain your shipment of hazardous substances and take samples for testing to determine compliance with the FHSA. If your shipment is found to contain banned hazardous substances, it will be refused admission and will be destroyed if not exported within 90 days of the date of refusal notice. If it is found to contain misbranded hazardous substances, you may make arrangements to bring it into conformance through relabeling. For complete details regarding testing, labeling, and safety regulations for hazardous products, contact the CPSC (see addresses at end of this chapter).

Marking and Labeling Requirements

Chemical Products. A shipment of any chemical product that contains a hazardous substance must comply with the marking and labeling regulations adopted by the EPA (46 CFR 147.30) and the DOT (49 CFR 171 et seq.)

For a general discussion of U.S. Customs marking and labeling requirements, refer to "Marking: Country of Origin" on page 215 and "Special Marking Requirements" on page 217.

Shipping Considerations

You will need to ensure that your goods are packaged and shipped with care so that they pass smoothly through Customs and arrive in good condition. You are responsible for ensuring that the shipment is in compliance with all applicable government regulations for packaging and shipping. In most instances, you should not leave these arrangements solely to the discretion of your supplier. Careful preparation of the cargo and selection of the mode of transport can be essential to a cost-effective, timely delivery of undamaged goods. We strongly advise you to consult your shipping representative, insurance agent, or freight broker for advice on packing and shipping. Refer also to the major tab section "Packing/Shipping/Insurance" for a general discussion of packing and shipping.

Photographic and cinematographic goods may be shipped in bulk, bags, bottles, or other types of containers, depending on the type of product and whether it is prepackaged. General considerations include protection from contamination, weather, and pests. For liquid shipments, venting and vapor collection systems may be required. Safety precautions should also be implemented as required to protect against breakage, spillage, corrosion of containers, and combustion. Containers should be constructed so as to be safe for handling during transport.

Chemical Products. Chemical products in particular may have to be shipped in pressurized, ventilated, and temperature-and vapor-controlled enclosures. Solid chemical products that are listed as hazardous substances (49 CFR 172 appendix) may be transported in bulk only on compliance with Coast Guard notification procedures, shipping permit requirements, and complex transportation regulations (46 CFR 148). All hazardous substances must also be packaged and transported in accordance with DOT regulations (49 CFR 171 et seq.).

Publications Available

The following publications may be relevant to the importation of toxic or hazardous photographic and cinematographic goods:

Toxic Substances Control Act: A Guide for Chemical Importers/Exporters (published by EPA).

TSCA Chemical Substance Inventory (1985 edition) (Doc. Code S/N 055-000-00254-1) $161.00 U.S. and Canada; $201.21 all other countries.

Supplement to TSCA Chemical Substances Inventory (1990) (Doc. Code S/N 055-000-00361-1) $15.00 U.S.; $18.75 Canada and all other countries.

The above publications and the *Harmonized Tariff Schedule of the United States* (HTSUS) are available from:

Government Printing Office (GPO)
Superintendent of Documents
Washington, DC 20402
(202) 512-1800 (Order line)
(202) 512-0000 (General)

The USGPO also has copies of specific laws available for purchase. The USGPO accepts credit card orders over the phone, as well as mail orders paid by credit card, a check drawn on a U.S. bank, or an international money order.

Relevant Government Agencies

Address your inquiries regarding EPA regulation of imported photochemicals to:

Environmental Protection Agency (EPA)
TSCA System Information
EPA 7408, OPPT
401 M Street SW
Washington, DC 20460
(202) 554-1404 (TSCA Information Hotline)

Address your questions regarding transportation of hazardous substances to:

U.S. Department of Transportation (DOT)
Research and Special Programs Administration
Office of Hazardous Materials Standards
400 7th St. SW
Washington, DC 20590
(202) 366-4488

Address your questions regarding CPSC requirements for photographic and cinematographic goods to:

U.S. Consumer Product Safety Commission (CPSC)
Office of Compliance
Division of Regulatory Management
5401 Westbard Avenue
Bethesda, MD 20207
(301) 504-0400

Address questions regarding the importation of photographic and cinematographic goods to the district or port director of Customs for you area. For addresses refer to"U.S. Customs District Offices" on page 62 or contact:

U.S. Customs Service
1301 Constitution Ave. NW
Washington, DC 20229
(202) 927-6724 (Information)
(202) 927-1000 (General)

Laws and Regulations

The following laws and regulations may be relevant to the importation of photographic and cinematographic goods. The laws are contained in the United States Code (USC), and the regulations are published in the Code of Federal Regulations (CFR), both of which are available at larger public and law libraries. Specific laws and regulations may also be purchased from the U.S. Government Printing Office (address above).

15 USC 1263
Consumer Product Safety Act (CPSA)
This Act gives the Consumer Product Safety Commission authority to set safety standards, testing procedures, and reporting requirements to ensure that consumer products not already covered under other regulations are not harmful.

15 USC 2601 et seq.
Toxic Substances Control Act
This Act authorizes the EPA to determine whether a substance is harmful and to restrict importation, sale, and use of such substances.

19 CFR 12.118 et seq.
Regulations on Toxic Substances Control
These regulations require importers of chemical substances imported in bulk or as part of a mixture to certify to Customs that the shipment complies with the TSCA or is not subject to that Act.

15 USC 1261
Federal Hazardous Substances Act
This Act controls the importation of hazardous substances, sets forth prohibited imports, and authorizes various agencies to promulgate labeling, marking, and transport requirements.

49 CFR 170 et seq.
Regulations on Hazardous Materials
These regulations list all substances deemed hazardous and provide transport, marking, labeling, safety, and emergency response rules.

46 CFR 147.30
Regulations on Labeling of Hazardous Materials
This regulation requires the labeling of containers of hazardous substances and specifies the label contents.

46 CFR 148 et seq.
Regulations on Carriage of Solid Hazardous Materials in Bulk
These regulations govern the transport of solid hazardous substances in bulk, including reporting, permitting, loading, stowing, and shipping requirements.

Sources of Additional Information

The TSCA Chemical Substance Inventory in computerized form is available from:

National Technical Information Service (NTIS)
U.S. Department of Commerce
5285 Port Royal Road
Springfield, VA 22161
(703) 487-4650

Access to the computerized TSCA Chemical Substance Inventory through a commercial database is available at:

Scientific and Technical Network International
Chemical Abstracts Service (CAS)
File: CAS ONLINE
(800) 848-6533
Dialog Information Services
TSCA Chemical Substances Inventory
File: Number 52
(800) 334-2564

Principal Exporting Countries

The following listing includes samples of the main supplier nations of the products of this chapter. It is organized by HTSUS major heading. (Refer to "Customs Classification" above for the product codes.) Countries are listed in rank order of the value of products imported to the U.S. Statistics represent customs value entries for 1993 from the Bureau of Census, U.S. Department of Commerce.

3701—Japan, Netherlands, Belgium, United Kingdom, Germany, Mexico, France, Argentina, Brazil, Italy

3702—Japan, Canada, United Kingdom, Germany, Belgium, Italy, Mexico, France, Switzerland, Australia

3703—Japan, Canada, Germany, Netherlands, France, United Kingdom, Belgium, Switzerland, Taiwan, Italy

3704—Japan, Canada, Germany, United Kingdom, Netherlands, Chile, France, Belgium, Switzerland, Mexico

3705—Japan, United Kingdom, Germany, Canada, Mexico, France, Malaysia, Taiwan, Switzerland, Hong Kong

3706—Canada, South Korea, Philippines, United Kingdom, Japan, Italy, Thailand, France, Taiwan, Germany

3707—Japan, Canada, Netherlands, Germany, United Kingdom, Brazil, Italy, France, South Korea, Switzerland

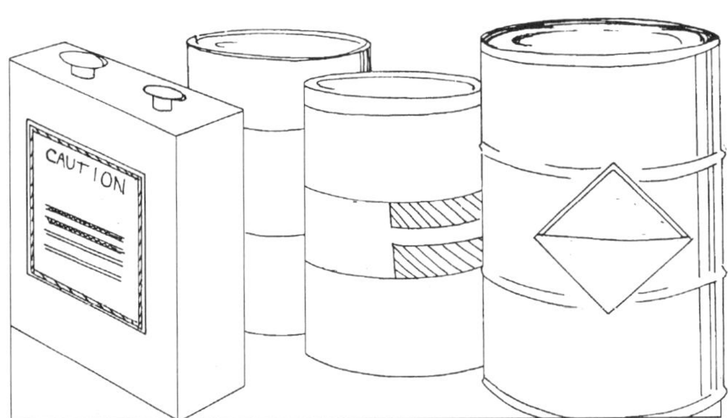

Chapter 38: Miscellaneous Chemical Products*

This chapter relates to the importation of miscellaneous chemical substances, which are classified under Chapter 38 of the Harmonized Tariff Schedule of the United States (HTSUS). Specifically, it includes organic and inorganic chemical products and preparations that are not otherwise specified or included in any other chapter of the HTSUS. A few of these items are artificial graphite, activated carbon, mineral, and animal products; tall oil, residual lyes from wood pulp, turpentines, wood tars, creosote, and naptha; insecticides, pesticides, disinfectants, finishing agents, metal pickling preparations, antiknock and other additives for lubricating oils, rubber or plastics additives, fire-extinguisher preparations and charges, hydraulic fluids, and anitfreezing preparations and fluids. For a more detailed listing, refer to "Customs Classification" in this chapter.

If you are interested in importing a separate chemically defined chemical substance, you should read this chapter in conjunction with Commodity Index Chapter 28 (inorganic) or 29 (organic) to determine which of these chapters covers that particular chemical substance. Chapter 21 covers mixtures of chemicals with foodstuffs and other substances having nutritive value and used in preparation of human foodstuffs. For products that are medicaments, refer to Chapter 30.

Key Factors

The key factors in the importation of chemical substances are:

- Compliance with U.S. Federal Trade Commission (FTC) and Consumer Product Safety Commission (CPSC) standards (if a consumer product)
- Compliance with U.S. Environmental Protection Agency (EPA) registration, safety, import, and recordkeeping requirements for the import of poisons (if the product is insecticide, pesticide, or other poisonous substance)
- Compliance with EPA requirements under Toxic Substances Control Act (TSCA) (if the product is a hazardous substance)
- Compliance with U.S. Department of Transportation (DOT) regulations for transport of hazardous cargo (if the product is a hazardous substance)

*IMPORTANT: Read the Commodity Index Introduction. It is the essential framework for understanding this chapter.

Although most importers use the services of a licensed customs broker in making their entries, and we recommend this practice, you should be aware of the regulatory, entry, and documentation issues involved in importing your product. You, as importer, are ultimately responsible for the fulfillment of any legal requirements applicable to your shipment.

General Considerations

Regulatory Agencies. The FTC sets standards for processing and labeling products that are sold to consumers. The EPA, under authority of the Federal Insecticide, Fungicide, and Rodenticide Act of 1947 (FIFRA), regulates the import of poisons, including insecticides, Paris greens, lead arsenates, fungicides, herbicides, and rodenticides. Under authority of the TSCA, the EPA also imposes certain controls on the importation of chemicals that contain toxic substances. The TSCA defines a toxic substance as any substance determined to present the possibility of an unreasonable risk of injury to health and the environment. The DOT enforces regulations for transporting hazardous cargo. Materials are deemed hazardous if listed in DOT transport regulations (49 CFR 172 appendix).

Toxic and Hazardous Substances. Chemicals imported in bulk, as articles, or as part of a mixture must be in compliance with toxic and hazardous substance regulations of the EPA and DOT. These include packaging, shipping, marking, and labeling requirements. In addition, all chemical products are subject to the U.S. Customs Service TSCA Import Certification Rule (19 CFR 12.118 et seq.). If you import these products, you must sign one of the following statements: "I certify that all chemical substances in this shipment comply with all applicable rules or orders under TSCA and that I am not offering a chemical substance for entry in violation of TSCA or any applicable rule or order thereunder" or "I certify that all chemicals in this shipment are not subject to TSCA."

You must file this TSCA certification of compliance or exemption at the time you make the entry at Customs. The certification may be in the form of a typed or stamped statement on an appropriate entry document or commercial invoice or a preprinted attachment to such entry document or invoice. You may sign the certificate by means of an authorized facsimile signature. If your entry is electronically processed, the certification will be in the form of a Certification Code, which is part of the Automated Broker Interface (ABI) transmission. Customs will not release your shipment without proper certification.

If you will be importing several or regular shipments, you should ask the appropriate Customs district director to authorize your use of a blanket certification. If you receive such authorization, you must include on the commercial invoice or entry document for each shipment a statement that the blanket certification is on file and that it is incorporated by reference. This statement need not be signed. The blanket certification is valid for one calendar year, is subject to renewal, and may be revoked at any time for cause.

In filling out TSCA forms and Customs entry documents, you should provide the Chemical Abstracts Service (CAS) number for each chemical in the shipment. These CAS numbers are given in the appendix to the HTSUS. You are not required to include the CAS number, but Customs will be able to process your shipment more quickly if you include this number.

Articles Exclusion. If you are importing products that are classified as hazardous substances but are part of articles, you are subject to TSCA certification requirements only if certification for your product is specifically required by a rule or order promulgated under the TSCA. No specific rules have been adopted at this time. An "article" is a manufactured item 1) that is formed into a specific shape or design during manufacture, 2) that has end-use functions dependent on the shape or design during end use, and 3) that during the end use, does not change in its chemical composition or that changes only for a noncommercial purpose separate from the article and only as allowed by law (19 CFR 12.120(2)). Fluids and particles are not articles, regardless of shape or design.

Shipment Detention. A shipment containing chemicals will be detained at the U.S. port of arrival (or entry if same), at your risk and expense, if: 1) it contains banned chemical substances (15 USC 2604, 2605); or 2) it contains chemical substances ordered seized because of imminent hazards (15 USC 2606). Further detention will occur at the port of entry, again at your risk and expense, if: 1) the EPA administrator or Customs district director has reasonable grounds to believe the shipment is not in compliance with the TSCA; or 2) you do not provide proper TSCA certification.

If your shipment is detained, it will be held by Customs for no more than 48 hours. It will then be turned over to the EPA administrator, unless you have arranged to release it in bond. You must either bring it into TSCA compliance or reexport it within the earlier of 90 days after notice of detention or 30 days of demand for redelivery. Customs may grant an extension if failure to comply or reexport is the result of delays in EPA or Customs procedures. If you fail to comply or reexport within the time allowed, the EPA administrator is authorized to have the shipment stored or disposed of at your expense.

Hazardous Consumer Products. The Federal Hazardous Substances Act (FHSA) imposes special controls on hazardous consumer products, which are defined as substances that are flammable, combustible, or have the potential to cause substantial personal injury during, or as a proximate result of, any customary or reasonably foreseeable handling or use. The CPSC does not require permits, special invoicing, limited entry, licenses, or any special approval process for importing hazardous consumer products into the U.S. However, if you are importing these types of products, you are responsible for ensuring that they meet all applicable FHSA and Consumer Product Safety Act (CPSA) requirements. There are detailed regulations regarding testing and labeling of hazardous products. The Commission's enforcement posture regarding compliance with labeling and product safety standards changes as new facts become available. Contact the CPSC (see addresses at end of this chapter) for specific requirements on the consumer product you are considering importing.

Substantial Product Hazard Reports. Defect-reporting is required for products covered under the CPSA. The law requires every manufacturer, distributor, or retailer of such products, who obtains information that reasonably supports the conclusion that such products fail to comply with an applicable consumer product safety rule, or contain a defect that could create a substantial product hazard, to immediately inform the CPSC of the potential violation or defect. A firm's willful failure to make a Substantial Product Hazard Report can result in litigation by the CPSC.

Insecticides and Pesticides. Before importation, all insecticides and pesticides must be registered in accordance with the criteria established by the EPA's Office of Pesticides Programs (OPP) (see addresses at end of this chapter). For each import shipment, an EPA Notice of Arrival of Pesticides or Devices **Form 3540-1** must be presented to Customs at the U.S. port of entry. You should obtain this form from either an EPA regional office or the EPA's Office of Compliance Monitoring. You need to fill out the applicable part of the form and submit it to the appropriate EPA office for completion. The EPA regional office completes the form, indicating how the shipment is to be handled when it arrives at the U.S. port, and returns it to you. When your shipment arrives at the port, it may be released immediately if the product and all the papers are in order.

Shipment Detention. Your shipment may be detained at the port of entry if: 1) the Notice of Arrival is incomplete; 2) the Notice refuses entry of the shipment; 3) the Notice orders that the shipment be examined or analyzed to determine if it is in compliance with FIFRA. If your shipment is detained, you can avoid storage charges at the port by posting a delivery bond approximately equal to the shipment's value. You may not sell or distribute your insecticide or pesticide without EPA release. If you do, your delivery bond may be forfeited.

Customs Classification

For customs purposes, miscellaneous chemical substances are classified under Chapter 38 of the HTSUS. This chapter is broken into major headings, which are further divided into subheadings, and often sub-subheadings, each of which has its own HTSUS classification number. For example, the HTSUS number for ribbon fly catchers is 3808.10.20, indicating it is a sub-subcategory of insecticides (3808.10.00), which is a subcategory of the major heading, insecticides, rodenticides, fungicides, etc. (3808.00.00). There are 23 major headings within Chapter 38.

3801—Artificial graphite; colloidal or semi-colloidal graphite; preparations based on graphite or other carbon in the form of pastes, blocks, plates, or other semimanufactures

3802—Activated carbon; activated natural mineral products; animal black, including spent animal black

3803—Tall oil, whether or not refined

3804—Residual lyes from the manufacture of wood pulp, whether or not concentrated, desugared or chemically treated, including lignin sulfonates, but excluding tall oil of heading 3803

3805—Gum, wood, or sulfate turpentine and other terpenic oils produced by the distillation or other treatment of coniferous woods; crude dipentene; sulfite turpentine and other crude para-cymene; pine oil containing alpha-terpineol as the main constituent

3806—Rosin and resin acids, and derivatives thereof; rosin spirit and rosin oils; run gums

3807—Wood tar; wood tar oils; wood creosote; wood naphtha; vegetable pitch; brewers' pitch and similar preparations based on rosin, resin acids, or on vegetable pitch

3808—Insecticides, rodenticides, fungicides, herbicides, antisprouting products, and plant-growth regulators, disinfectants, and similar products, put up in forms or packages for retail sale or as preparations or articles (for example, sulfur-treated bands, wicks and candles, and flypapers)

3809—Finishing agents, dye carriers to accelerate the dyeing or fixing of dyestuffs, and other products and preparations (for example, dressings and mordants), of a kind used in the textile, paper, leather, or like industries, not elsewhere specified or included

3810—Pickling preparations for metal surfaces; fluxes and other auxiliary preparations for soldering, brazing, or welding; soldering, brazing, or welding powders and pastes consisting of metal and other materials; preparations of a kind used as cores or coatings for welding electrodes or rods

3811—Antiknock preparations, oxidation inhibitors, gum inhibitors, viscosity improvers, anti-corrosive preparations, and other prepared additives, for mineral oils (including gasoline) or for other liquids used for the same purposes as mineral oils

3812—Prepared rubber accelerators; compound plasticizers for rubber or plastics, not elsewhere specified or included; antioxidizing preparations and other compound stabilizers for rubber or plastics

3813—Preparations and charges for fire extinguishers; charged fire-extinguishing grenades

3814—Organic composite solvents and thinners, not elsewhere specified or included; prepared paint or varnish removers

3815—Reaction initiators, reaction accelerators, and catalytic preparations, not elsewhere specified or included

3816—Refractory cements, mortars, concretes, and similar compositions, other than products of heading 3801

3817—Mixed alkylbenzenes & mixed alkylnaphthalenes, other than those of heading 2707 or 2902

3818—Chemical elements doped for use in electronics, in the form of discs, wafers, or similar forms; chemical compounds doped for use in electronics

3819—Hydraulic brake fluids and other prepared liquids for hydraulic transmission, not containing or containing less than 70% by weight of petroleum oils or oils obtained from bituminous minerals

3820—Antifreezing preparations and prepared de-icing fluids

3821—Prepared culture media for development of microorganisms

3822—Composite diagnostic or laboratory reagents, other than those of heading 3002 or 3006

3823—Prepared binders for foundry molds or cores; chemical products and preparations of the chemical or allied industries (including those consisting of mixtures of natural products), not elsewhere specified or included; residual products of the chemical or allied industries, not elsewhere specified or included

For more details regarding classifications of the specific product you are interested in importing, consult a customs broker, the appropriate commodity specialist at your nearest customs port, or the HTSUS. HTSUS is available for purchase from the U.S. Government Printing Office (see addresses at end of this chapter), and may be found in larger public libraries. Refer to "Classification—Liquidation" on page 207 for a general discussion of customs classification.

Sample Import Duties

Import duties will vary depending on the HTSUS classification of your product. Therefore, to determine the correct amount of duties, your product must be properly classified under the HTSUS. The following sample duties are taken from the duty listings for HTSUS Chapter 38 products.

Artificial graphite to be manufactured into brushes for electric generators, motors, and other machines and appliances (3801.10.10): 3.7%; activated carbon (3802.10.00): 4.8%; tall oil (3803.00.00): free; pine oil (3805.20.00): free; gum, wood, and sulfate turpentine oils (3805.10.00): 5%; gum rosin (3806.10.00): 5%; wood tar (3807.00.00): 0.9 cents/kg; fly-catching ribbons (3808.10.10): 2.8%; aromatic or modified aromatic fungicides (3808.20.10): 1.8 cents/kg plus 9.7%; lubricating oil additive containing petroleum oil (3811.21.00): 12%; hydraulic brake fluids (3819.00.00): 3.7 cents/kg plus 13.6%; antifreezing preparations (3820.00.00): 12%; fatty substances derived from animals or vegetables (3823.90.40): 4.6%.

Special Provisions. Under 9901.00.50, any mixture of ethyl alcohol, such as in heading 3823, is subject to an additional duty of 14.27 cents/liter.

Entry and Documentation

The entry of merchandise is a two-part process consisting of 1) filing the documentation necessary to determine whether merchandise may be released from Customs custody, and 2) filing the documents that contain information for duty assessment and statistical purposes. In certain instances, all documents must be filed and accepted by Customs prior to release of the goods. Unless you have been granted an extension, you must file entry documents at a location specified by the district or area director within five working days of your shipment's date of arrival at a U.S. port of entry. These include a number of standard documents required by Customs for any entry, and:

- U.S. Customs TSCA Certification (hazardous substances)
- EPA Notice of Arrival of Pesticides or Devices **Form 3540-1**

After you present the entry, Customs may examine your shipment or may waive examination. The shipment is then released provided no legal or regulatory violations have been noted. You must then file entry summary documentation and deposit estimated duties at a designated customhouse within 10 working days of your shipment's release. For a detailed description of entry procedures, standard documentation, and informal entry, refer to "Entry Process" on page 182.

Entry Invoice. Furnish the use and Chemical Abstracts Service (CAS) number of the chemical compounds.

Prohibitions and Restrictions

Hazardous Consumer Products. Importation of any consumer product that has been declared a banned hazardous substance by a rule under the CPSA is prohibited. Any product considered hazardous and not labeled according to provisions of the FHSA is a misbranded hazardous substance and is an illegal import. Certain hazardous substances listed in the FHSA and in regulations promulgated by the CPSC are completely banned from importation. A shipment of consumer products cannot be imported if it poses an imminent hazard. See 15 USC 1261, 2604-2606; 16 CFR 1500.265-1500.272.

The CPSC may detain your shipment of hazardous substances and take samples for testing to determine compliance with the FHSA. If your shipment is found to contain banned hazardous substances, it will be refused admission and will be destroyed if not exported within 90 days of the date of refusal notice. If it is found to contain misbranded hazardous substances, you may make arrangements to bring it into conformance through relabeling. For complete details regarding testing, labeling, and safety regulations for hazardous products, contact the CPSC (see addresses at end of this chapter).

Insecticides and Pesticides. Insecticides or pesticides not cleared through the EPA's stringent product-and establishment-registration procedures cannot be imported into the U.S. EPA registration is designed to ensure, among other things, that an insecticide or pesticide entering the U.S., when used as directed: 1) is effective against the pests listed on the label; 2) is neither injurious to human, animals, and crops, nor damaging to the environment; and 3) will not result in illegal residues on food or feed. All imported insecticides and pesticides must meet FIFRA requirements before they can enter the U.S.

A single exception is made for chemicals imported in small amounts to test for pesticidal value. If your importation fits this category, and you have no intention of receiving any direct pest control benefits from your chemicals, the only requirement you must fulfill for importation is to be sure that the products carry instructions for proper handling during transport.

Inspections. All other shipments must comply with EPA import procedures, and are subject to port-of-entry inspections. EPA may examine your incoming shipment at the port of entry to determine if it is properly labeled. If you are importing products never previously sampled, or products of firms with histories of violations, the EPA may take samples of your shipment for testing. If your products were previously in violation of FIFRA, they will be inspected, and samples will be analyzed to determine current compliance. After the inspection, the EPA may: 1) release the shipment if it is in compliance; 2) order changes to bring the shipment into compliance; or 3) refuse entry, in which case you must return it to the country of origin or destroy it.

Product Registration. All insecticides and pesticides intended for sale in the U.S.—including imported products—must be registered with the EPA. Application for registration is a complex procedure requiring specific types of product data and documentation. Registration must be completed for each type of pesticide being imported. If you need to seek registration for the product you wish to import, contact the EPA (see addresses at end of this chapter). The agency publishes an information manual designed to help importers and producers complete the application process.

Establishment Registration. The Federal Insecticide, Fungicide, and Rodenticide Act requires both domestic and foreign producers of pesticides and devices to register the establishments in which they these products are produced. Producers should obtain EPA **Form 3540-8,** Application for the Registration of Pesticide-Producing Establishments from the EPA's Office of Compliance Monitoring (EN-342) (see addresses at end of this chapter) or from any regional EPA office. Completed forms should be submitted to the EPA headquarters office.

If the application is approved, the establishment will be assigned an EPA Establishment Number (EPA Est.). This number must appear on the label or container of each pesticide product. The foreign producer must submit annual reports to the EPA on all types and amounts of pesticides shipped to the U.S.

Recordkeeping Requirements. All registered establishments must maintain detailed books and records of production and distribution of insecticides and pesticides. For any materials shipped to the U.S., a foreign producer must keep the following records: 1) brand names, registration numbers, batch numbers, and amounts per batch; 2) brand names and quantities of devices; 3) brand names and quantities of receipts and shipments, as well as the name of the originating or delivering carrier, the name and address of the shipper, name and address of the consignee, and the dates of receipt or shipment. Such records are required even for transfers between plants of the same company; 4) inventories covering the brand names and quantities in stock; 5) all tests conducted on human beings and any adverse effects on the environment.

Production and shipment records must be retained for two years. Other records must be retained for various periods as specified by federal regulations. All records are subject to inspection and reproduction by authorized EPA representatives.

Marking and Labeling Requirements

Chemicals. A shipment of any products containing chemicals that are classified as hazardous substance (49 CFR 172) must comply with the marking and labeling regulations adopted by the EPA (46 CFR 147.30) and the DOT (49 CFR 171 et seq.).

Insecticides and Pesticides. Registered insecticide and pesticide products must meet all FIFRA labeling requirements. Your product's label must include the EPA product registration number, EPA Establishment Number, an ingredient statement, the name and address of the producer or the registrant, the necessary cautionary statements, and directions for use. Required label information must also be included on any printed materials that accompany the product to the end user. Statements or graphic representations on the label may not be false or misleading. If the product is to be used on a food or feed crop, a tolerance level for residues must be established by the EPA. Products failing to comply with registration or labeling requirements will be denied entry into the U.S. For more details on marking and labeling requirements, see FIFRA and implementing regulations, and contact the EPA (see addresses at end of this chapter).

For a general discussion of U.S. Customs marking and labeling requirements, refer to "Marking: Country of Origin" on page 215 and "Special Marking Requirements" on page 217.

Shipping Considerations

You will need to ensure that your goods are packaged and shipped with care so that they pass smoothly through Customs and arrive in good condition. You are responsible for ensuring that the shipment is in compliance with all applicable government regulations for packaging and shipping. In most instances, you should not leave these arrangements solely to the discretion of your supplier. Careful preparation of the cargo and selection of the mode of transport can be essential to a cost-effective, timely delivery of undamaged goods. We strongly advise you to consult your shipping representative, insurance agent, or freight broker for advice on packing and shipping. Refer also to the major tab section "Packing/Shipping/Insurance" for a general discussion of packing and shipping.

Chemical products may be shipped in bulk, bags, bottles, or other types of containers, depending on the type of product and whether it is prepackaged. General considerations include protection from contamination, weather, and pests. If a product must be kept in a sanitary environment, all tables, utensils, platforms, and devices used for moving or handling the product, the compartments in which it is stowed while being transported will need to be maintained in a sanitary condition. For liquid shipments, venting and vapor collection systems may be required. Safety precautions should also be implemented as required to protect against breakage, spillage, corrosion of containers, and combustion. Containers should be constructed so as to be safe for handling during transport.

Chemical products in particular may have to be shipped in pressurized, ventilated, and temperature-and vapor-controlled enclosures. Solid chemical products that are listed as hazardous substances (49 CFR 172 appendix) may be transported in bulk only on compliance with Coast Guard notification procedures, shipping permit requirements, and complex transportation regulations (46 CFR 148). All hazardous substances must be packaged and transported in accordance with DOT regulations (49 CFR 171 et seq.).

Publications Available

The following publications may be relevant to the importation of toxic or hazardous chemicals:

Toxic Substances Control Act: A Guide for Chemical Importers/Exporters (published by EPA).

TSCA Chemical Substance Inventory (1985 edition) (Doc. Code S/N 055-000-00254-1) $161.00 U.S. and Canada; $201.21 all other countries.

Supplement to TSCA Chemical Substances Inventory (1990) (Doc. Code S/N 055-000-00361-1) $15.00 U.S.; $18.75 Canada and all other countries.

The above publications and the *Harmonized Tariff Schedule of the United States* (HTSUS) are available from:

Government Printing Office (GPO)
Superintendent of Documents
Washington, DC 20402
(202) 512-1800 (Order line)
(202) 512-0000 (General)

The USGPO also has copies of specific laws available for purchase. The USGPO accepts credit card orders over the phone, as well as mail orders paid by credit card, a check drawn on a U.S. bank, or an international money order.

The following publications are relevant to the importation of pesticides:

General Information on Applying for Registration of Pesticides in the United States (published by EPA Office of Pesticide Programs Registration Division) (see addresses at end of this chapter)

Availability of OPP Publication Listings
(Lists all the available publications of the Office of Pesticide Programs, their EPA Document Numbers, and costs.)

These publications are available from:

Document Management Section (H7502C)
Information Services Branch, PMSD
EPA
(Washington DC address below)
(703) 557-4474

Relevant Government Agencies

Address your inquiries regarding TSCA and EPA requirements for importation of chemical substances to:

Environmental Protection Agency (EPA)
TSCA System Information
EPA 7408, OPPT
401 M Street SW
Washington, DC 20460
(202) 554-1404 (TSCA Information Hotline)

Address your questions regarding EPA requirements for the importation of insecticides and pesticides to:

Environmental Protection Agency (EPA)
Office of Pesticide Programs
401 M Street SW (7501-C)
Washington, DC 20460
(703) 305-7090 (General)
(703) 305-7102 (Import/export requirements)

To obtain EPA Forms 3540-1 and 3540-8, add to the above address: Office of Compliance Monitoring (EN-342).

To obtain Environmental Protection Agency forms relating to the registration of products, call (703) 557-7700 or add to the main address: Registration Support Branch, Registration Division (H5704C).

Address your questions regarding transportation of hazardous substances to:

U.S. Department of Transportation (DOT)
Research and Special Programs Administration
Office of Hazardous Materials Standards
400 7th St. SW
Washington, DC 20590
(202) 366-4488

Address your questions regarding CPSC requirements for miscellaneous chemical products to:

U.S. Consumer Product Safety Commission (CPSC)
Office of Compliance
Division of Regulatory Management
5401 Westbard Avenue
Bethesda, MD 20207
(301) 504-0400

Address your questions regarding importation of chemical substances generally to the district or port director of customs for you area. For addresses, refer to "U.S. Customs District Offices" on page 62 or contact:

U.S. Customs Service
1301 Constitution Ave. NW
Washington, DC 20229
(202) 927-6724 (Information)
(202) 927-1000 (General)

Laws and Regulations

The following laws and regulations may be relevant to the importation of chemical substances. The laws are contained in the United States Code (USC), and the regulations are published in the Code of Federal Regulations (CFR), both of which are available at larger public and law libraries. Specific laws and regulations may also be purchased from the U.S. Government Printing Office (address above).

15 USC 1263
Consumer Product Safety Act (CPSA)
This Act gives the Consumer Product Safety Commission authority to set safety standards, testing procedures, and reporting requirements to ensure that consumer products not already covered under other regulations are not harmful.

7 USC 135 et seq.
Federal Insecticide, Fungicide, and Rodenticide Act (FIFRA)
This Act prohibits the importation of pesticides or devices that are adulterated, misbranded, or otherwise in violation of the Act, provides for registration of pesticides and devices, and establishes standards for labeling and classifying pesticides.

19 CFR 12; 40 CFR 162
Regulations on Pesticides
These regulations set forth the procedures and guidelines for importing products exposed to pesticides.

15 USC 2601 et seq.
Toxic Substances Control Act
This Act authorizes the EPA to determine whether a substance is harmful and to restrict importation, sale, and use of such substances.

19 CFR 12.118 et seq.
Regulations on Toxic Substances Control
These regulations require importers of chemical substances imported in bulk or as part of a mixture to certify to Customs that the shipment complies with the TSCA or is not subject to that Act.

15 USC 1261
Federal Hazardous Substances Act
This Act controls the importation of hazardous substances, sets forth prohibited imports, and authorizes various agencies to promulgate labeling, marking, and transport requirements.

49 CFR 170 et seq.
Regulations on Hazardous Materials
These regulations list all substances deemed hazardous and provide transport, marking, labeling, safety, and emergency response rules.

46 CFR 147.30
Regulations on Labeling of Hazardous Materials
This regulation requires the labeling of containers of hazardous substances and specifies the label contents.

46 CFR 148 et seq.
Regulations on Carriage of Solid Hazardous Materials in Bulk
These regulations govern the transport of solid hazardous substances in bulk, including reporting, permitting, loading, stowing, and shipping requirements.

Sources of Additional Information

The TSCA Chemical Substance Inventory in computerized form is available from:

National Technical Information Service (NTIS)
U.S. Department of Commerce
5285 Port Royal Road
Springfield, VA 22161
(703) 487-4650

Access to the computerized TSCA Chemical Substance Inventory through a commercial database is available at:

Scientific and Technical Network International
Chemical Abstracts Service (CAS)
File: CAS ONLINE
(800) 848-6533
Dialog Information Services
TSCA Chemical Substances Inventory
File: Number 52
(800) 334-2564

Principal Exporting Countries

The following listing includes samples of the main supplier nations of the products of this chapter. It is organized by HTSUS major heading. (Refer to "Customs Classification" above for the product codes.) Countries are listed in rank order of the value of products imported to the U.S. Statistics represent customs value entries for 1993 from the Bureau of Census, U.S. Department of Commerce.

3801—Switzerland, Japan, Germany, France, China, Canada, United Kingdom, Netherlands, Russia, Norway

3802—Philippines, Sri Lanka, United Kingdom, Germany, Netherlands, Mexico, China, Japan, France, Indonesia

3803—Brazil, Canada, Mexico, New Zealand, Finland

3804—Norway, Finland, Canada, Iceland, Netherlands, Japan, Sweden, Germany, China

3805—Canada, Mexico, Finland, Brazil, Japan, Honduras, Germany, United Kingdom, Indonesia, Switzerland

3806—Canada, Brazil, Argentina, Portugal, China, Indonesia, Finland, Mexico, Japan, United Kingdom

3807—Canada, Sweden, Norway, Germany, Taiwan

3808—United Kingdom, Germany, Canada, Japan, France, Netherlands, Brazil, Israel, Switzerland, Colombia

3809—Japan, Canada, Germany, United Kingdom, Israel, Switzerland, France, Belgium, China, Mexico

3810—Japan, Germany, France, Netherlands, Switzerland, Canada, China, United Kingdom, Belgium, Sweden

3811—Canada, France, United Kingdom, Mexico, Germany, Italy, Japan, Netherlands, Belgium, Singapore

3812—Germany, Switzerland, Italy, United Kingdom, Canada, Japan, Mexico, Bahamas, Brazil, France

3813—Mexico, Germany, Canada, France, United Kingdom, Italy, Japan, Norway, Netherlands, Taiwan

3814—Canada, United Kingdom, Japan, Germany, Brazil, Norway, Netherlands, Mexico, Australia, Sweden

3815—Japan, Germany, Canada, United Kingdom, Netherlands, Denmark, Australia, Italy, Belgium, France

3816—Canada, Germany, United Kingdom, Austria, Japan, France, Australia, Spain, Mexico, Norway

3817—France, Spain, Indonesia, Japan, Italy, Philippines, Netherlands, Venezuela, Germany, Belgium

3818—Japan, Germany, Malaysia, Italy, South Korea, Canada, Denmark, United Kingdom, France, Israel

3819—Canada, United Kingdom, Germany, Japan, Netherlands, Venezuela, France, Denmark, Mexico, Switzerland

3820—Canada, United Kingdom, Japan, Germany, Norway, Belgium, Netherlands

3821—United Kingdom, Germany, Canada, Switzerland, Ireland, France, Finland, New Zealand, Spain, Norway

3822—United Kingdom, Japan, Germany, Ireland, Denmark, Canada, France, Italy, Switzerland, Australia

3823—Germany, Japan, Canada, United Kingdom, Mexico, Ireland, France, Switzerland, Netherlands, Italy

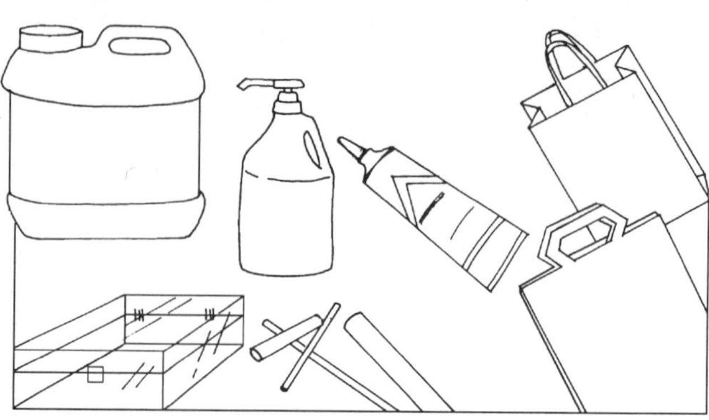

Chapter 39: Plastics and Articles Thereof*

This chapter relates to the importation of plastics and plastic products, which are classified under Chapter 39 of the Harmonized Tariff Schedule of the United States (HTSUS). Specifically, it includes 1) primary forms of plastics—such as polymers of ethylene, olefins, styrene, halogenated olefins, vinyl esters, and acrylic; polyethers, polyesters, and polyamides; amino-resins, phenolic resins, and polyurethanes; silicones; petroleum resin; cellulose and its derivatives; natural polymers; and ion-exchangers; 2) plastic articles—such as tubes, piping, adhesives, bath and sanitary ware, containers, housewares, gloves, and statutes; and 3) semimanufactures, waste, parings, and scrap of plastics.

If you are interested in importing separate chemically defined organic compounds, refer to Commodity Index Chapter 29. If you are interested in importing a specific plastic product, such as toys or lighting fixtures, you should also look for a relevant chapter in this index pertaining to that particular product. For example, importing requirements for textiles with plastic fibers are found in Chapters 50 through 63, plastic footwear in Chapter 64, umbrellas in Chapter 66, headgear in Chapter 65, imitation jewelry in Chapter 71, and wall coverings in Chapter 48. Mineral waxes are covered in Chapter 27 and prepared waxes are in Chapter 34. For importing plastics and plastic products printed with motifs, characters, or pictures not merely incidental to the use of the product, refer to Chapter 49 on printed articles.

Key Factors

The key factors in the importation of plastics and plastic products are:

- Compliance with U.S. Federal Trade Commission (FTC) and Consumer Product Safety Commission (CPSC) standards (if a consumer product)
- Compliance with U.S. Food and Drug Administration (FDA) entry notification and standards requirements (for products used with food, for sanitation, and for medical or similar purposes)
- Compliance with U.S. Environmental Protection Agency (EPA) requirements under Toxic Substances Control Act (TSCA) (if the product is a hazardous material)
- Compliance with U.S. Department of Transportation (DOT) regulations for transport of hazardous cargo (if the product is a hazardous material)

*IMPORTANT: Read the Commodity Index Introduction. It is the essential framework for understanding this chapter.

Although most importers use the services of a licensed customs broker in making their entries, and we recommend this practice, you should be aware of the regulatory, entry, and documentation issues involved in importing your product. You, as importer, are ultimately responsible for the fulfillment of any legal requirements applicable to your shipment.

General Considerations

Regulatory Agencies. The agency that regulates your imported shipment of plastics depends on whether the products are in primary form or in the form of articles, semimanufactures, waste, parings, or scrap. The EPA, under authority of the TSCA, imposes certain controls on the importation of plastics, mainly in primary form, that contain toxic substances. The TSCA defines a toxic substance as any substance determined to present the possibility of an unreasonable risk of injury to health and the environment. The DOT enforces regulations for transporting hazardous cargo. Materials are deemed hazardous if listed in DOT transport regulations (49 CFR 172 appendix). Articles of plastic that are intended for use with food, for sanitation, and for medicinal or similar purposes are regulated by the FDA, under the Federal Food, Drug, and Cosmetic Act (FDCA) and the Public Health Service Act (PHSA). The FTC sets standards for processing and labeling products sold to consumers.

Hazardous or Toxic Substances. Plastics in primary form are chemical mixtures. If listed as hazardous or toxic substances and imported in bulk, as articles, or as part of a mixture, these plastics must be in compliance with toxic and hazardous substance regulations of the EPA and DOT. These include packaging, shipping, marking, and labeling requirements.

In addition, all chemical products are subject to the U.S. Customs Service TSCA Import Certification Rule (19 CFR 12.118 et seq.). If you import these products, you must sign one of the following statements: "I certify that all chemical substances in this shipment comply with all applicable rules or orders under TSCA and that I am not offering a chemical substance for entry in violation of TSCA or any applicable rule or order thereunder" or "I certify that all chemicals in this shipment are not subject to TSCA."

You must file a TSCA certification of compliance or exemption at the time you make the entry at Customs. The certification may be in the form of a typed or stamped statement on an appropriate entry document or commercial invoice or a preprinted attachment to such entry document or invoice. You may sign the certificate by means of an authorized facsimile signature. If your entry is electronically processed, the certification will be in the form of a Certification Code, which is part of the Automated Broker Interface (ABI) transmission. Customs will not release your shipment without proper certification.

If you will be importing several or regular shipments, you should ask the appropriate Customs district director to authorize your use of a blanket certification. If you receive such authorization, you must include on the commercial invoice or entry document for each shipment a statement that the blanket certification is on file and that it is incorporated by reference. This statement need not be signed. The blanket certification is valid for one calendar year, is subject to renewal, and may be revoked at any time for cause.

Articles Exclusion. If you are importing products that are classified as hazardous substances but are part of articles, you are subject to TSCA certification requirements only if certification for your product is specifically required by a rule or order promulgated under the TSCA. No specific rules have been adopted at this time. An "article" is a manufactured item 1) that is formed into a specific shape or design during manufacture, 2) that has end-use functions dependent on the shape or design during end use, and 3) that during the end use, does not change in its chemical composition or that changes only for a noncommercial purpose separate from the article and only as allowed by law (19 CFR 12.120(2)). Fluids and particles are not articles, regardless of shape or design.

Shipment Detention. A shipment containing chemicals will be detained at the U.S. port of arrival (or entry if same), at your risk and expense, if: 1) it contains banned substances (15 USC 2604, 2605); or 2) it contains substances ordered seized because of imminent hazards (15 USC 2606). Further detention will occur at the port of entry, again at your risk and expense, if: 1) the EPA administrator or Customs district director has reasonable grounds to believe the shipment is not in compliance with the TSCA; or 2) you do not provide proper TSCA certification.

If your shipment is detained, it will be held by Customs for no more than 48 hours. It will then be turned over to the EPA administrator, unless you have arranged to release it in bond. You must either bring it into TSCA compliance or reexport it within the earlier of 90 days after notice of detention or 30 days of demand for redelivery. Customs may grant an extension if failure to comply or reexport is the result of delays in EPA or Customs procedures. If you fail to comply or reexport within the time allowed, the EPA administrator is authorized to have the shipment stored or disposed of at your expense.

FDA-Regulated Products. Imports of plastic products intended for use with food, for sanitation, or for medicinal or similar purposes are regulated by the FDA. These articles are currently exempt from required FDA entry notification (**Form FD701**). However, if routine Customs examinations of applicable shipments reveal problems that could have adverse effects on public health, the FDA will reconsider the exempt status. Selectivity criteria and entry notification may be reinstituted at any time, at the discretion of the FDA. If you are interested in importing plastic articles intended for these purposes, you should be familiar with FDA import entry procedures and the requirements of the governing laws, the FDCA and the PHSA. For an annotated diagram of FDA import procedures see the "Foods" appendix on page 808. If you are interested in importing one of these products, you should ascertain its regulatory status by contacting the FDA (see addresses at end of this chapter).

Hazardous Consumer Products. Under the Federal Hazardous Substances Act (FHSA), a plastic product intended for the consumer market is a hazardous substance if it is flammable, combustible, or has the potential to cause substantial personal injury during, or as a proximate result of, any customary or reasonably foreseeable handling or use. The CPSC does not require permits, special invoicing, limited entry, licenses, or any special approval process for importing hazardous consumer products into the U.S. However, if you are importing these types of products, you are responsible to ensure that they meet all applicable FHSA and CPSA requirements. There are detailed regulations regarding testing and labeling of hazardous products. The Commission's enforcement posture regarding compliance with labeling and product safety standards changes as new facts become available. Contact the CPSC (see addresses at end of this chapter) for specific requirements on the consumer product you are considering importing.

Substantial Product Hazard Reports. Defect-reporting is required for products covered under the CPSA. The law requires every manufacturer, distributor, or retailer of such products, who obtains information that reasonably supports the conclusion that such products fail to comply with an applicable consumer product safety rule, or contain a defect that could create a substantial product hazard, to immediately inform the CPSC of the potential violation or defect. A firm's willful failure to make a Substantial Product Hazard Report can result in litigation by the CPSC.

Customs Classification

For customs purposes, plastics and plastic products are classified under Chapter 39 of the HTSUS. This chapter is broken into major headings, which are further divided into subheadings, and often sub-subheadings, each of which has its own HTSUS classification number. For example, the HTSUS number for plastic trays is 3924.10.30, indicating it is a sub-subcategory of tableware and kitchenware (3924.10.00), which is a subcategory of the major heading, tableware, kitchenware, other household articles and toilet articles of plastics (3924.00.00). There are 26 major headings within Chapter 39.

3901—Polymers of ethylene, in primary forms

3902—Polymers of propylene or of other olefins, in primary forms

3903—Polymers of styrene, in primary forms

3904—Polymers of vinyl chloride or of other halogenated olefins, in primary forms

3905—Polymers of vinyl acetate or of other vinyl esters, in primary forms; other vinyl polymers in primary forms

3906—Acrylic polymers in primary forms

3907—Polyacetals, other polyethers and expoxide resins, in primary forms; polycarbonates, alkyd resins, polyallyl esters, and other polyesters, in primary forms

3908—Polyamides in primary forms

3909—Amino-resins, phenolic resins, and polyurethanes, in primary forms

3910—Silicones in primary forms

3911—Petroleum resins, coumarone-indene resins, polyterpenes, polysulfides, polysulfones, and other products specified in note 3 to this chapter, not elsewhere specified or included, in primary forms

3912—Cellulose and its chemical derivatives, not elsewhere specified or included, in primary forms

3913—Natural polymers (for example, alginic acid) and modified natural polymers (for example, hardened proteins, chemical derivatives of natural rubber), not elsewhere specified or included, in primary forms

3914—Ion-exchangers based on polymers of headings 3901 to 3913, in primary forms

3915—Waste, parings, and scrap of plastics

3916—Monofilament of which any cross-sectional dimension exceeds 1 mm, rods, sticks, and profile shapes, whether or not surface-worked but not otherwise worked, of plastics

3917—Tubes, pipes, and hoses and fittings therefor (for example, joints, elbows, flanges), of plastics

3918—Floor coverings of plastics, whether or not self-adhesive, in rolls or in the form of tiles; wall or ceiling coverings of plastics, as defined in note 9 to this chapter

3919—Self-adhesive plates, sheets, film, foil, tape, strip, and other flat shapes, of plastics, whether or not in rolls

3920—Other plates, sheets, film, foil, and strip, of plastics, noncellular and not reinforced, laminated, supported, or similarly combined with other materials

3921—Other plates, sheets, film, foil, and strip, of plastics

3922—Baths, shower baths, washbasins, bidets, lavatory pans, seats and covers, flushing cisterns, and similar sanitary ware, of plastics

3923—Articles for the conveyance or packing of goods of plastics; stoppers, lids, caps, and other closures, of plastics

3924—Tableware, kitchenware, other household articles, and toilet articles, of plastics

3925—Builders' ware of plastics, not elsewhere specified or included

3926—Other articles of plastics and articles of other materials of headings 3901 to 3914

For more details regarding classifications of the specific product you are interested in importing, consult a customs broker, the appropriate commodity specialist at your nearest customs port, or the HTSUS. HTSUS is available for purchase from the U.S. Government Printing Office (see addresses at end of this chapter), and may be found in larger public libraries. Refer to "Classification—Liquidation" on page 207 for a general discussion of customs classification.

Sample Import Duties

Import duties will vary depending on the HTSUS classification of your product. Therefore, to determine the correct amount of duties, your product must be properly classified under the HTSUS. The following sample duties are taken from the duty listings for HTSUS Chapter 39 products.

Polyethylene having a specific gravity of less than 0.94 (3901.10.00): 12.5%; polyvinyl chloride not mixed with other substances (3904.10.00): 10.1%; expandable polystyrene (3903.11.00): 0.9 cents/kg plus 9.2%; silicones in primary forms (3910.00.00): 3%; vinyl chloride tubes, pipes, and hoses (3917.23.00): 3.1%; vinyl tile floor coverings (3918.10.10): 5.3%; vinyl chloride wall coverings with a backing of man-made textile fibers and over 70% by weight of plastics (3918.10.31): 4.2%; electrical tape (3919.10.20): 5.8%; baths, shower baths, and washbasins (3922.10.00): 6.3%; plastic bottles (3923.30.00): 3%; plates, cups, saucers, soup bowls, cereal bowls, sugar bowls, creamers, gravy boats, serving dishes and platters (3924.10.20): 7%; plastic trays (3924.10.30): 5.3%; plastic picture frames (3924.90.20): 3.4%; venetian and other blinds (3925.30.10): 3.36%; seamless surgical and medical plastic gloves (3926.20.10): 3.7%.

Entry and Documentation

The entry of merchandise is a two-part process consisting of 1) filing the documentation necessary to determine whether merchandise may be released from Customs custody, and 2) filing the documents that contain information for duty assessment and statistical purposes. In certain instances, all documents must be filed and accepted by Customs prior to release of the goods. Unless you have been granted an extension, you must file entry documents at a location specified by the district or area director within five working days of your shipment's date of arrival at a U.S. port of entry. These include a number of standard documents required by Customs for any entry, and:

- U.S. Customs TSCA Certification (for plastics in primary form that are toxic or hazardous substances)

After you present the entry, Customs may examine your shipment or may waive examination. The shipment is then released provided no legal or regulatory violations have been noted. You must then file entry summary documentation and deposit estimated duties at a designated customhouse within 10 working days of your shipment's release. For a detailed description of entry procedures, standard documentation, and informal entry, refer to "Entry Process" on page 182.

Entry Invoice for Plates, Sheets, Film, Foil, and Strip. The following additional information is required on entry invoices for plastic plates, sheets, film, foil, and strip of HTSUS headings 3920 and 3921: 1) statement as to whether the plastic is cellular or noncellular; 2) specification of the type of plastic; 3) indication of whether the plastic is flexible or inflexible and whether it is combined with a textile or other material.

Entry Invoice for Plastic-Coated or -Laminated Textiles. For articles manufactured of textile materials and coated or laminated with plastics, include a description indicating whether the fabric is coated or laminated on both sides, on the exterior surface, or on the interior surface.

Entry Invoice for Bags. The entry invoice for bags manufactured of plastic sheeting and not of a reinforced or laminated construction must indicate the gauge of the plastic sheeting.

Entry Invoice for Plastic Beads. For beads of plastic, specify: 1) the length of the string, if strung; 2) the size of the beads in mm; and 3) the material of which the beads are composed.

Prohibitions and Restrictions

Hazardous Consumer Products. Importation of any consumer product that has been declared a banned hazardous substance by a rule under the CPSA is prohibited. Any product considered hazardous and not labeled according to provisions of the FHSA is a misbranded hazardous substance and is an illegal import. Certain hazardous substances listed in the FHSA and in regulations promulgated by the CPSC are completely banned from importation. A shipment of consumer products cannot be imported if it poses an imminent hazard. See 15 USC 1261, 2604-2606; 16 CFR 1500.265-1500.272.

The CPSC may detain your shipment of hazardous substances and take samples for testing to determine compliance with the FHSA. If your shipment is found to contain banned hazardous substances, it will be refused admission and will be destroyed if not exported within 90 days of the date of refusal notice. If it is found to contain misbranded hazardous substances, you may arrange to bring it into conformance through relabeling. For complete details on testing, labeling, and safety regulations for hazardous products, contact the CPSC (see addresses at end of this chapter).

Marking and Labeling Requirements

Hazardous or Toxic Substances. A shipment of products containing substances classified as toxic or hazardous (49 CFR 172) must comply with the marking and labeling regulations adopted by the EPA (46 CFR 147.30) and the DOT (49 CFR 171 et seq.).

Consumer Products. A specific type of consumer product may have marking or labeling requirements, such as children's articles or electronic musical instruments. For further details, refer to the Commodity Index chapter applicable to the specific product in question.

For a general discussion of U.S. Customs marking and labeling requirements, refer to "Marking: Country of Origin" on page 215 and "Special Marking Requirements" on page 217.

Shipping Considerations

You will need to ensure that your goods are packaged and shipped with care so that they pass smoothly through Customs and arrive in good condition. You are responsible for ensuring that the shipment is in compliance with all applicable government regulations for packaging and shipping. In most instances, you should not leave these arrangements solely to the discretion of your supplier. Careful preparation of the cargo and selection of the mode of transport can be essential to a cost-effective, timely delivery of undamaged goods. We strongly advise you to consult your shipping representative, insurance agent, or freight broker for advice on packing and shipping. Refer also to the major tab section "Packing/Shipping/Insurance" for a general discussion of packing and shipping.

Plastics and plastic products may be shipped in bulk, bags, tanks, bottles, or other types of containers, depending on the type of product and whether it is prepackaged. General considerations include protection from contamination, weather, and pests. If a product must be kept in a sanitary environment, all tables, utensils, platforms, and devices used for moving or handling the product, the compartments in which it is stowed while being transported will need to be maintained in a sanitary condition. For liquid shipments, venting and vapor collection systems may be required. Safety precautions should also be implemented as required to protect against breakage, spillage, corrosion of containers, and combustion. Containers should be constructed so as to be safe for handling during transport.

Plastics in Primary Form. A plastic that is shipped in its primary liquid form may have to be enclosed in pressurized, ventilated, and temperature-and vapor-controlled containers. Solid plastics in primary form that are listed as hazardous substances (49 CFR 172 appendix) may be transported in bulk only on compliance with Coast Guard notification procedures, shipping permit requirements, and complex transportation regulations (46 CFR 148). All hazardous substances must be packaged and transported in accordance with DOT regulations (49 CFR 171 et seq.).

Publications Available

The following publication explains the FDA requirements related to importing plastics and plastic products for sanitary use. It is published by the FDA and is available on request from FDA headquarters (see addresses at end of this chapter).

Requirements of Laws and Regulations Enforced by the U.S. Food and Drug Administration

The following publications may be relevant to the importation of toxic or hazardous plastics and plastic products:

Toxic Substances Control Act: A Guide for Chemical Importers/ Exporters (published by EPA).
TSCA Chemical Substance Inventory (1985 edition) (Doc. Code S/N 055-000-00254-1) $161.00 U.S. and Canada; $201.21 all other countries.
Supplement to TSCA Chemical Substances Inventory (1990) (Doc. Code S/N 055-000-00361-1) $15.00 U.S.; $18.75 Canada and all other countries.

The above publications and the *Harmonized Tariff Schedule of the United States* (HTSUS) are available from:

Government Printing Office (GPO)
Superintendent of Documents
Washington, DC 20402
(202) 512-1800 (Order line)
(202) 512-0000 (General)

The USGPO also has copies of specific laws available for purchase. The USGPO accepts credit card orders over the phone, as well as mail orders paid by credit card, a check drawn on a U.S. bank, or an international money order.

Relevant Government Agencies

Address your questions regarding CPSC requirements for plastic products to:

U.S. Consumer Product Safety Commission (CPSC)
Office of Compliance
Division of Regulatory Management
5401 Westbard Avenue
Bethesda, MD 20207
(301) 504-0400

Address your questions regarding FDA regulation or requirements for plastic products to:

Food and Drug Administration (FDA)
Center for Food Safety and Applied Nutrition
200 C Street SW
Washington, DC 20204
(202) 205-5241, 205-5042

Address your questions regarding TSCA and EPA requirements for importation of plastic products in primary form to:

Environmental Protection Agency (EPA)
TSCA System Information
EPA 7408, OPPT
401 M Street SW
Washington, DC 20460
(202) 554-1404 (TSCA Information Hotline)

Address your questions regarding transportation of hazardous substances to:

U.S. Department of Transportation (DOT)
Research and Special Programs Administration
Office of Hazardous Materials Standards
400 7th St. SW
Washington, DC 20590
(202) 366-4488

Address your questions regarding the importation of plastics and plastic products to the district or port director of Customs for you area. For addresses refer to "U.S. Customs District Offices" on page 62 or contact:

U.S. Customs Service
1301 Constitution Ave. NW
Washington, DC 20229
(202) 927-6724 (Information)
(202) 927-1000 (General)

Laws and Regulations

The following laws and regulations may be relevant to the importation of plastics and plastic products. The laws are contained in the United States Code (USC), and the regulations are published in the Code of Federal Regulations (CFR), both of which are available at larger public and law libraries. Copies of specific laws and regulations may be purchased from the U.S. Government Printing Office (address above).

15 USC 1263
Consumer Product Safety Act (CPSA)
This Act gives the Consumer Product Safety Commission authority to set safety standards, testing procedures, and reporting requirements to ensure that consumer products not already covered under other regulations are not harmful.

21 USC 301 et seq.
Food, Drug, and Cosmetic Act
This Act prohibits deceptive practices and regulates the manufacture, sale and importation or exportation of food, drugs, cosmetics, and related products. See 21 USC 331, 381, 382.

19 CFR 12.1 et seq.; 21 CFR 1.83 et seq.
Regulations on Food, Drugs, and Cosmetics
These regulations of the Secretary of Health and Human Services and the Secretary of the Treasury govern the standards, labeling, marking, and importing of products used with food, drugs, and cosmetics.

15 USC 2601 et seq.
Toxic Substances Control Act
This Act authorizes the EPA to determine whether a substance is harmful and to restrict importation, sale, and use of such substances.

19 CFR 12.118 et seq.
Regulations on Toxic Substances Control
These regulations require importers of chemical substances imported in bulk or as part of a mixture to certify to Customs that the shipment complies with the TSCA or is not subject to that Act.

15 USC 1261
Federal Hazardous Substances Act
This Act controls the importation of hazardous substances, sets forth prohibited imports, and authorizes various agencies to promulgate labeling, marking, and transport requirements.

49 CFR 170 et seq.
Regulations on Hazardous Materials
These regulations list all substances deemed hazardous and provide transport, marking, labeling, safety, and emergency response rules.

46 CFR 147.30
Regulations on Labeling of Hazardous Materials
This regulation requires the labeling of containers of hazardous substances and specifies the label contents.

46 CFR 148 et seq.
Regulations on Carriage of Solid Hazardous Materials in Bulk
These regulations govern the transport of solid hazardous substances in bulk, including reporting, permitting, loading, stowing, and shipping requirements.

Principal Exporting Countries

The following listing includes samples of the main supplier nations of the products of this chapter. It is organized by HTSUS major heading. (Refer to "Customs Classification" above for the product codes.) Countries are listed in rank order of the value of products imported to the U.S. Statistics represent customs value entries for 1993 from the Bureau of Census, U.S. Department of Commerce.

3901—Canada, Japan, Italy, Germany, Belgium, France, South Korea, Saudi Arabia, United Kingdom, Brazil

3902—Canada, Japan, Germany, Belgium, Brazil, Argentina, Netherlands, Mexico, France, Hungary

3903—Canada, Mexico, Japan, Germany, Taiwan, South Korea, Netherlands, Brazil, Belgium, Italy

3904—Canada, Japan, Netherlands, Germany, Italy, Brazil, United Kingdom, France, Belgium, Mexico

3905—Japan, Germany, Taiwan, China, United Kingdom, Canada, France, Switzerland, Mexico, Spain

3906—Japan, United Kingdom, Canada, Germany, France, Sweden, South Korea, Netherlands, Taiwan, Belgium

3907—Canada, Japan, Germany, Switzerland, Mexico, Netherlands, Italy, Taiwan, Belgium, United Kingdom

3908—Canada, Germany, Japan, France, Netherlands, Switzerland, Mexico, Italy, United Kingdom, Brazil

3909—Germany, Canada, Japan, Belgium, United Kingdom, Spain, France, Argentina, Italy, Netherlands

3910—Germany, Japan, France, Canada, United Kingdom, Belgium, Mexico, Italy, Spain, Netherlands

3911—France, Germany, Japan, Italy, United Kingdom, Canada, Switzerland, Netherlands, South Korea, Taiwan

3912—Japan, Germany, Netherlands, France, United Kingdom, Sweden, Brazil, Mexico, Taiwan, Italy

3913—Ireland, France, United Kingdom, Austria, Canada, Japan, Germany, Norway, Denmark, Taiwan

3914—Sweden, France, United Kingdom, Germany, Japan, Canada, India, Italy, Mexico, Finland

3915—Germany, Canada, Mexico, Italy, Netherlands, United Kingdom, France, Belgium, Taiwan, Spain

3916—Canada, Japan, Germany, Taiwan, Italy, United Kingdom, Israel, Switzerland, France, Belgium

3917—Canada, Germany, Japan, Mexico, United Kingdom, Taiwan, Finland, Israel, Belgium, Switzerland

3918—Canada, Taiwan, China, United Kingdom, Sweden, Mexico, Japan, France, Philippines, Germany

3919—Canada, Japan, Taiwan, Germany, Mexico, United Kingdom, Italy, Belgium, Philippines, Singapore

3920—Japan, Canada, Germany, Taiwan, South Korea, United Kingdom, Mexico, Italy, France, Israel

3921—Canada, Japan, Taiwan, Germany, South Korea, Colombia, United Kingdom, France, Italy, Brazil

3922—Canada, Israel, Germany, Mexico, Taiwan, China, United Kingdom, Hong Kong, Portugal, Italy

3923—Canada, China, Taiwan, Japan, France, Mexico, Hong Kong, Germany, Thailand, United Kingdom

3924—China, Taiwan, Canada, Japan, Hong Kong, Thailand, Mexico, Malaysia, South Korea, Philippines

3925—Taiwan, Canada, China, Mexico, Thailand, Germany, Hong Kong, Indonesia, United Kingdom, Italy

3926—China, Taiwan, Canada, Japan, Mexico, Germany, South Korea, Hong Kong, United Kingdom, France

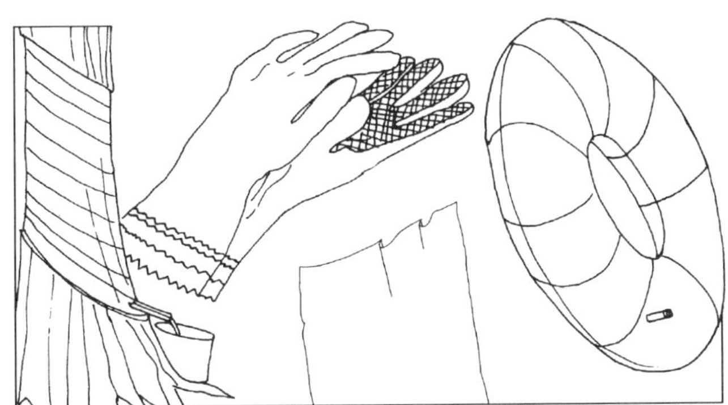

Chapter 40: Rubber and Articles Thereof*

This chapter relates to the importation of rubber and rubber articles, which are classified under Chapter 40 of the Harmonized Tariff Schedule of the United States (HTSUS). Specifically, it includes natural rubber and other gums, synthetic rubber and similar products derived from oils; reclaimed rubber; rubber waste, parings, and scrap; vulcanized and unvulcanized rubber in various forms; conveyor or transmission belts; new, retreaded, or used tires; inner tubes; hygienic or pharmaceutical rubber articles; rubber apparel and accessories; and a variety of soft vulcanized rubber articles.

If you are interested in importing specific rubber products, you should check this index for the chapter that relates to that particular item. For example, footwear is covered in Commodity Index Chapter 64, headgear in Chapter 65, mechanical and electrical appliances in Chapters 84 and 85, watches in Chapter 91, furniture in Chapter 94, and toys in Chapter 95. If you are interested in importing separate chemically defined organic substances, you should refer to Chapter 29. For textiles that may contain rubber substances, refer to Chapters 50 through 63.

Key Factors

The key factors in the importation of rubber and rubber products are:

- Compliance with U.S. Food and Drug Administration (FDA) regulations and entry notification (if the product is chicle, hygienic or pharmaceutical articles, or gloves)
- Compliance with U.S. Federal Trade Commission (FTC) and Consumer Product Safety Commission (CPSC) labeling and safety standards (for consumer products, such as bicycle tires)
- Compliance with U.S. Environmental Protection Agency (EPA) requirements under Toxic Substances Control Act (TSCA) (if the product is a hazardous material)
- Compliance with U.S. Department of Transportation (DOT) regulations for transport of hazardous cargo (if the product is a hazardous material)
- Compliance with DOT, National Highway Traffic Safety Administration (NHTSA), safety standards and regulations (for motor vehicle tires)

*IMPORTANT: Read the Commodity Index Introduction. It is the essential framework for understanding this chapter.

Although most importers use the services of a licensed customs broker in making their entries, and we recommend this practice, you should be aware of the regulatory, entry, and documentation issues involved in importing your product. You, as importer, are ultimately responsible for the fulfillment of any legal requirements applicable to your shipment.

General Considerations

Regulatory Agencies. The agency that regulates your imported shipment of rubber depends on whether the products are in primary form or in a manufactured form. The EPA, under authority of the TSCA, imposes certain controls on the importation of rubber products, mainly in primary form, classified as toxic substances. The TSCA defines a toxic substance as any substance determined to present the possibility of an unreasonable risk of injury to health and the environment. The DOT enforces regulations for transporting hazardous cargo. Materials are deemed hazardous if listed in DOT transport regulations (49 CFR 172 appendix). The import of chicle, hygienic articles, pharmaceuticals, and gloves made of rubber are regulated by the FDA, under the Federal Food, Drug, and Cosmetic Act (FDCA) and the Public Health Service Act (PHSA). The FTC sets standards for processing and labeling products sold to consumers.

Primary Forms of Rubber. Importation of rubber in its premanufactured state is straightforward. Unless the product is listed as hazardous or toxic, there are no restrictions or prohibitions. No permits or licenses are required. You must provide additional information on the entry invoice for your shipments of rubber and rubber products (see "Entry and Documentation," below).

Hazardous or Toxic Substances. Rubber substances in primary form are chemical mixtures. If listed as hazardous or toxic substances and imported in bulk, as articles, or as part of a mixture, rubber products must be in compliance with toxic and hazardous substance regulations of the EPA and DOT. These include packaging, shipping, marking, and labeling requirements.

In addition, all chemical products are subject to the U.S. Customs Service TSCA Import Certification Rule (19 CFR 12.118 et seq.). If you import these products, you must sign one of the following statements: "I certify that all chemical substances in this shipment comply with all applicable rules or orders under TSCA and that I am not offering a chemical substance for entry in violation of TSCA or any applicable rule or order thereunder" or "I certify that all chemicals in this shipment are not subject to TSCA."

You must file a TSCA certification of compliance or exemption at the time you make the entry at Customs. The certification may be in the form of a typed or stamped statement on an appropriate entry document or commercial invoice or a preprinted attachment to such entry document or invoice. You may sign the certificate by means of an authorized facsimile signature. If your entry is electronically processed, the certification will be in the form of a Certification Code, which is part of the Automated Broker Interface (ABI) transmission. Customs will not release your shipment without proper certification.

If you will be importing several or regular shipments, you should ask the appropriate Customs district director to authorize your use of a blanket certification. If you receive such authorization, you must include on the commercial invoice or entry document for each shipment a statement that the blanket certification is on file and that it is incorporated by reference. This statement need not be signed. The blanket certification is valid for one calendar year, is subject to renewal, and may be revoked at any time for cause.

Articles Exclusion. If you are importing products that are classified as hazardous substances but are part of articles, you are subject to TSCA certification requirements only if certification for your product is specifically required by a rule or order promulgated under the TSCA. No specific rules have been adopted at this time. An "article" is a manufactured item 1) that is formed into a specific shape or design during manufacture, 2) that has end-use functions dependent on the shape or design during end use, and 3) that during the end use, does not change in its chemical composition or that changes only for a noncommercial purpose separate from the article and only as allowed by law (19 CFR 12.120(2)). Fluids and particles are not articles, regardless of shape or design.

Shipment Detention. A shipment containing chemicals will be detained at the U.S. port of arrival (or entry if same), at your risk and expense, if: 1) it contains banned substances (15 USC 2604, 2605); or 2) it contains substances ordered seized because of imminent hazards (15 USC 2606). Further detention will occur at the port of entry, again at your risk and expense, if: 1) the EPA administrator or Customs district director has reasonable grounds to believe the shipment is not in compliance with the TSCA; or 2) you do not provide proper TSCA certification.

If your shipment is detained, it will be held by Customs for no more than 48 hours. It will then be turned over to the EPA administrator, unless you have arranged to release it in bond. You must either bring it into TSCA compliance or reexport it within the earlier of 90 days after notice of detention or 30 days of demand for redelivery. Customs may grant an extension if failure to comply or reexport is the result of delays in EPA or Customs procedures. If you fail to comply or reexport within the time allowed, the EPA administrator is authorized to have the shipment stored or disposed of at your expense.

FDA-Regulated Products. The following Chapter 40 products are subject to regulation under the Federal Food, Drug, and Cosmetic Act (FDCA), enforced by the FDA: 1) chicle (natural gum); 2) hygienic or pharmaceutical articles, including sheath contraceptives and nursing nipples; and 3) surgical, medical, and other rubber gloves. All FDA-regulated imports require an FDA entry notice **Form FD701**. If you are interested in importing these articles, you should be familiar with the FDA import entry procedures and requirements under the FDCA. For an annotated diagram of FDA entry refer to the "Foods" appendix on page 808. For more information on FDA requirements, contact the regional FDA office nearest you, or FDA headquarters (see addresses at end of this chapter).

Motor Vehicle Tires. Importation of motor vehicle tires for resale is highly regulated. The DOT, through the NHTSA administers the National Traffic and Motor Vehicle Safety Act (NTMVSA). Regulations pertaining to motor vehicle equipment are found in 49 CFR 591. For regulatory purposes under this law, importers of motor vehicle tires for resale are considered manufacturers. As such, the importer is responsible for compliance with all pertinent regulations.

As a general rule, all tires manufactured on or after the date on which any applicable Federal Motor Vehicle Safety Standard (FMVSS) takes effect must conform to that standard to be imported into the U.S. When you import tires, you must provide the original manufacturer's certification of compliance with the applicable standard. Unless otherwise specified in the applicable standard, this certification must be in the form of a label or tag directly on the tire or on the outside of the container in which the tire is delivered. If you attempt to import tires for which there is an applicable standard without certification by the original manufacturer, your shipment will be refused entry. In addition, before offering tires for importation into the U.S., a foreign manufacturer is required to register as an "Agent-for-Service" of process, as set forth in 49 CFR 551.45.

In addition to the manufacturer's certification, the importer must submit DOT Declaration **HS-7** in duplicate to U.S. Customs at the time of the entry of the shipment. In this declaration, the importer must affirm 1) whether the imported tires are subject to a FMVSS; 2) whether the tires are in compliance or will be brought into compliance within the period allowed by the regulations; and 3) whether the tires are within one of the exceptions to compliance. The contents of the declaration are detailed in 19 CFR 12.80.

If you are interested in importing motor vehicle tires, you should contact the DOT (see addresses at end of this chapter). On request, a DOT compliance specialist will send you a packet of instructional and informational materials enumerating the responsibilities you will incur on bringing tires into the U.S. for resale. For a list of the materials, refer to "Publications Available" below.

Bicycle Tires. If you are interested in importing bicycle tires, no special permits, licenses, or entry paperwork is required. However, the tires must be in compliance with stringent bicycle safety standards promulgated under the Consumer Product Safety Act (CPSA), and enforced by the CPSC (16 CFR 1512). To ascertain compliance, the CPSC randomly inspects shipments of bicycles at the port of entry. Contact CPSC (see addresses at end of this chapter) with your questions.

Customs Classification

For customs purposes, rubber and rubber products are classified under Chapter 40 of the HTSUS. This chapter is broken into major headings, which are further divided into subheadings, and often sub-subheadings, each of which has its own HTSUS classification number. For example, the HTSUS number for retreaded tractor tires is 4012.10.20, indicating it is a sub-subcategory of retreaded tires (4012.10.00), which is a subcategory of the major heading, retreaded or used pneumatic rubber tires, etc. (4012.00.00). There are 17 major headings within Chapter 40.

4001—Natural rubber, balata, gutta-percha, guayule, chicle, and similar natural gums, in primary forms or in plates, sheets, or strip

4002—Synthetic rubber and factice derived from oils, in primary forms or in plates, sheets, or strip; mixtures of any product of heading 4001 with any product of this heading, in primary forms or in plates, sheets, or strip

4003—Reclaimed rubber in primary forms or in plates, sheets, or strips

4004—Waste, parings, and scrap of rubber (other than hard rubber) and powders and granules obtained therefrom

4005—Compounded rubber, unvulcanized, in primary forms or in plates, sheets, or strip

4006—Other forms (for example, rods, tubes, and profile shapes) and articles (for example, discs and rings), of unvulcanized rubber

4007—Vulcanized rubber thread and cord

4008—Plates, sheets, strip, rods, and profile shapes, of vulcanized rubber other than hard rubber

4009—Tubes, pipes, and hoses, of vulcanized rubber other than hard rubber, with or without their fittings (for example, joints, elbows, flanges)

4010—Conveyor or transmission belts or belting, of vulcanized rubber

4011—New pneumatic tires, of rubber

4012—Retreaded or used pneumatic tires of rubber; solid or cushion tires, interchangeable tire treads and tire flaps, of rubber

4013—Inner tubes, of rubber

4014—Hygienic or pharmaceutical articles (including nursing nipples), of vulcanized rubber other than hard rubber, with or without fittings of hard rubber

4015—Articles of apparel and clothing accessories (including gloves), for all purposes, of vulcanized rubber other than hard rubber

4016—Other articles of vulcanized rubber other than hard rubber

4017—Hard rubber (for example, ebonite) in all forms, including waste and scrap; articles of hard rubber

For more details regarding classifications of the specific product you are interested in importing, consult a customs broker, the appropriate commodity specialist at your nearest customs port, or the HTSUS. HTSUS is available for purchase from the U.S. Government Printing Office (see addresses at end of this chapter), and may be found in larger public libraries. Refer to "Classification—Liquidation" on page 207 for a general discussion of customs classification.

Sample Import Duties

Import duties will vary depending on the HTSUS classification of your product. Therefore, to determine the correct amount of duties, your product must be properly classified under the HTSUS. The following sample duties are taken from the duty listings for HTSUS Chapter 40 products.

Rubber in primary forms (4001-4005): free; other forms, e.g., rods, tubes, and profile shapes, of natural rubber (4006.90.10): 4.2%, of other (4006.90.50): 5.3%; plates, sheets, and strips of noncellular rubber (4008.21.00): 3.4%; new pneumatic rubber radial car tires (4011.10.00): 4%; rubber inner tubes for motor vehicles (4013.10.00): 3.7%, for bicycles (4013.20.00): 15%; nursing nipples (4014.90.10): 3.1%; sheath contraceptives (4014.10.00): 4.2%; surgical gloves (4015.11.00): 3.7%; vulcanized rubber erasers (4016.92.00): 4.2%, pet toys (4016.99.20): 8.5%.

Entry and Documentation

The entry of merchandise is a two-part process consisting of 1) filing the documentation necessary to determine whether merchandise may be released from Customs custody, and 2) filing the documents that contain information for duty assessment and statistical purposes. In certain instances, all documents must be filed and accepted by Customs prior to release of the goods. Unless you have been granted an extension, you must file entry documents at a location specified by the district or area director within five working days of your shipment's date of arrival at a U.S. port of entry. These include a number of standard documents required by Customs for any entry, and:

- FDA Importers Entry Notice, **Form FD701** (for chicle, hygienic or pharmaceutical article, or gloves)
- DOT Declaration **HS-7**, in duplicate (for motor vehicle tires)
- U.S. Customs TSCA Certification (for rubber in primary form classified as a hazardous or toxic substance)

After you present the entry, Customs may examine your shipment or may waive examination. The shipment is then released provided no legal or regulatory violations have been noted. You must then file entry summary documentation and deposit estimated duties at a designated customhouse within 10 working days of your shipment's release. For a detailed description of entry procedures, standard documentation, and informal entry, refer to "Entry Process" on page 182.

Entry Invoice for Rubber and Rubber Products. Entry invoices for Chapter 40 rubber and rubber products must state the following: 1) whether the rubber is combined with textile or other material; 2) whether the rubber is cellular or noncellular, vulcanized or unvulcanized; and 3) if vulcanized, whether the rubber is or is not hard.

Entry Invoice for Tires and Inner Tubes. When you import tires or inner tubes for tires, you must include the following information on your entry invoice: 1) specify the kind of vehicle for which the tire is intended—i.e., airplane, bicycle, passenger car, on-the-highway light or heavy truck or bus, motorcycle; 2) if designed for tractors (HTSUS 8601.90.10), or for agricultural or horticultural machinery or implements (HTSUS Chapter 84 or 8716.80.10), designate whether the tire is new, recapped, or used and whether it is pneumatic or solid; and 3) indicate whether the tube is designed for tires classified in HTSUS 4011.91.10, 4011.99.10, 4012.10.20, or 4012.20.20.

Entry Invoice for Rubber-Coated or -Laminated Textiles. For articles manufactured of textile materials and coated or laminated with rubber, include a description indicating whether the fabric is coated or laminated on both sides, on the exterior surface, or on the interior surface.

Prohibitions and Restrictions

Tires. Motor vehicle tires covered by a Federal Motor Vehicle Safety Standards (FMVSS) must conform to that standard to be imported into the U.S. If you attempt to import tires covered by an applicable standard without the vehicle equipment DOT Declaration **HS-7** or a certification of compliance by the original manufacturer, your shipment will be refused entry.

Bicycle tires must be in compliance with the CPSC safety and labeling regulations. The CPSC enforces these restrictions through random border inspections, and if your tires are found to be noncomplying, the shipment will be refused entry. If your shipment passes through Customs without inspection, but is later found to be noncomplying, you are liable for a product recall. The CPSC has authority to take legal action for noncompliance as part of its responsibility to protect consumers.

Substantial Product Hazard Reports. Defect-reporting is required for products covered under the CPSA. The law requires every manufacturer, distributor, or retailer of such products, who obtains information that reasonably supports the conclusion that such products fail to comply with an applicable consumer product safety rule, or contain a defect that could create a substantial product hazard, to immediately inform the CPSC of the potential violation or defect. A firm's willful failure to make a Substantial Product Hazard Report can result in litigation by the CPSC.

Marking and Labeling Requirements

Motor Vehicle Tires. There are specific DOT marking requirements for motor vehicle tires. You can obtain a copy of these requirements by contacting the DOT Office of Vehicle Safety Compliance (see addresses at end of this chapter) and requesting the importers' information packet.

Hazardous or Toxic Substances. A shipment of products containing substances classified as toxic or hazardous (49 CFR 172) must comply with the marking and labeling regulations adopted by the EPA (46 CFR 147.30) and the DOT (49 CFR 171 et seq.).

Consumer Products. A specific type of consumer product may have marking or labeling requirements, such as pharmaceuticals and rubber inflatable articles. For further details, refer to the Commodity Index chapter applicable to the specific product in question.

For a general discussion of U.S. Customs marking and labeling requirements, refer to "Marking: Country of Origin" on page 215 and "Special Marking Requirements" on page 217.

Shipping Considerations

You will need to ensure that your goods are packaged and shipped with care so that they pass smoothly through Customs and arrive in good condition. You are responsible for ensuring that the shipment is in compliance with all applicable government regulations for packaging and shipping. In most instances, you should not leave these arrangements solely to the discretion of your supplier. Careful preparation of the cargo and selection of the mode of transport can be essential to a cost-effective, time-

ly delivery of undamaged goods. We strongly advise you to consult your shipping representative, insurance agent, or freight broker for advice on packing and shipping. Refer also to the major tab section "Packing/Shipping/Insurance" for a general discussion of packing and shipping.

Rubber and rubber products may be shipped in bulk, bags, bales, tanks, or other types of containers, depending on the type of product and whether it is prepackaged. General considerations include protection from contamination, weather, and pests. If a product must be kept in a sanitary environment, all tables, utensils, platforms, and devices used for moving or handling the product, the compartments in which it is stowed while being transported will need to be maintained in a sanitary condition. For liquid shipments, venting and vapor collection systems may be required. Safety precautions should also be implemented as required to protect against breakage, spillage, corrosion of containers, and combustion. Containers should be constructed so as to be safe for handling during transport.

Rubber in Primary Form. Rubber that is shipped in its primary form may have to be enclosed in pressurized, ventilated, and temperature-and vapor-controlled containers. Solid rubber in primary form that is listed as a hazardous substance (49 CFR 172 appendix) may be transported in bulk only on compliance with Coast Guard notification procedures, shipping permit requirements, and complex transportation regulations (46 CFR 148). All hazardous substances must be packaged and transported in accordance with DOT regulations (49 CFR 171 et seq.).

Publications Available

The following informational materials are available from the DOT as an importer's packet, free of charge and on request:

1) The National Traffic and Motor Vehicle Safety Act of 1966; 2) 49 CFR 551: Procedural Rules; 3) 49 CFR 574: Tire Identification and Recordkeeping; 4) 49 CFR 575.104: Uniform Tire Quality Grading Standards; 5) 49 CFR 591: Importation of Vehicles & Equipment Subject to Federal Motor Vehicle Safety Standards; 6) Where to Obtain Motor Vehicle Safety Standards and Regulations; 7) Information for New Manufacturers of Motor Vehicles and Motor Vehicle Equipment; 8) FMVSS No. 109: New Pneumatic Tires—Passenger Cars; 9) FMVSS No. 117: Retreaded Pneumatic Tires; 10) FMVSS No. 119: New Pneumatic Tires for Vehicles Other Than Passenger Cars; 11) FMVSS No. 129: New Non Pneumatic Tires for Passenger Cars; 12) Application for a tire manufacturers identification number.

If you wish to obtain a packet, contact the Safety Compliance Specialist of DOT's **Office of Vehicle Safety Compliance** (see addresses at end of this chapter).

The following publication explains the FDA requirements for importing rubber and rubber products for sanitary use. It is published by the FDA and is available on request from FDA headquarters (see addresses at end of this chapter).

Requirements of Laws and Regulations Enforced by the U.S. Food and Drug Administration

The following publications may be relevant to the importation of toxic or hazardous rubber and rubber products:

Toxic Substances Control Act: A Guide for Chemical Importers/Exporters (published by EPA).

TSCA Chemical Substance Inventory (1985 edition) (Doc. Code S/N 055-000-00254-1) $161.00 U.S. and Canada; $201.21 all other countries.

Supplement to TSCA Chemical Substances Inventory (1990) (Doc. Code S/N 055-000-00361-1) $15.00 U.S.; $18.75 Canada and all other countries.

The above publications and the *Harmonized Tariff Schedule of the United States* (HTSUS) are available from:

Superintendent of Documents
Government Printing Office (GPO)
Superintendent of Documents
Washington, DC 20402
(202) 512-1800 (Order line)
(202) 512-0000 (General)

The USGPO also has copies of specific laws available for purchase. The USGPO accepts credit card orders over the phone, as well as mail orders paid by credit card, a check drawn on a U.S. bank, or an international money order.

Relevant Government Agencies

Address your questions regarding requirements for FDA-regulated rubber products to:

Food and Drug Administration (FDA)
Center for Food Safety and Applied Nutrition
200 C Street SW
Washington, DC 20204
(202) 205-5241, 205-5042

Address your questions regarding the importation of motor vehicle tires to:

National Highway Traffic Safety Administration
Office of Vehicle Safety Compliance
400 7th St. SW
Washington, DC 20590
(202) 366-5311, 366-2830

Address your questions regarding CPSC requirements for bicycle tires and other consumer products to:

Consumer Product Safety Commission (CPSC)
5401 Westbard Avenue
Bethesda, MD 20207
(301) 492-6580

Address your inquiries regarding TSCA and EPA requirements for importation of rubber products in primary form to:

Environmental Protection Agency (EPA)
TSCA System Information
EPA 7408, OPPT
401 M Street SW
Washington, DC 20460
(202) 554-1404 (TSCA Information Hotline)

Address your questions regarding transportation of hazardous substances to:

U.S. Department of Transportation (DOT)
Research and Special Programs Administration
Office of Hazardous Materials Standards
400 7th St. SW
Washington, DC 20590
(202) 366-4488

Address your questions regarding the importation of rubber and rubber products to the district or port director of Customs for you area. For addresses refer to "U.S. Customs District Offices" on page 62 or contact:

U.S. Customs Service
1301 Constitution Ave. NW
Washington, DC 20229
(202) 927-6724 (Information)
(202) 927-1000 (General)

Laws and Regulations

The following laws and regulations may be relevant to the importation of rubber and rubber products. The laws are contained in the United States Code (USC), and the regulations are published in the Code of Federal Regulations (CFR), both of which are available at larger public and law libraries. Copies of specific laws and regulations may be purchased from the U.S. Government Printing Office (address above).

21 USC 301 et seq.
Food, Drug, and Cosmetic Act
This Act prohibits deceptive practices and regulates the manufacture, sale and importation or exportation of food, drugs, cosmetics, and related products. See 21 USC 331, 381, 382.

19 CFR 12.1 et seq.; 21 CFR 1.83 et seq.
Regulations on Food, Drugs, and Cosmetics
These regulations of the Secretary of Health and Human Services and the Secretary of the Treasury govern the standards, labeling, marking, and importing of products used with food, drugs, and cosmetics.

15 USC 1263
Consumer Product Safety Act (CPSA)
This Act gives the Consumer Product Safety Commission authority to set safety standards, testing procedures, and reporting requirements to ensure that consumer products not already covered under other regulations are not harmful.

15 USC 1390 et seq.
National Traffic and Motor Vehicle Safety Act of 1966 (NTMVSA)
This Act authorizes the National Highway Traffic Safety Administration (NHTSA) to set motor vehicle safety standards and prohibits the manufacture, sale, delivery, or importation of substandard vehicles.

49 CFR 571
Regulations on Motor Vehicle Safety Standards
These regulations are safety standards prescribed by the Secretary of Transportation pursuant to the NTMVSA to regulate the quality of motor vehicles and motor vehicle equipment imported into the U.S., as well as offered for sale in, introduced into, or delivered for introduction into interstate commerce.

19 CFR 12.80
Regulations on Motor Vehicle Entry Declaration
These regulations govern the import of motor vehicles and motor vehicle equipment through U.S. Customs, require the importer to submit a specific detailed declaration, and authorize Customs to deny entry in the absence of a declaration.

15 USC 2601 et seq.
Toxic Substances Control Act
This Act authorizes the EPA to determine whether a substance is harmful and to restrict importation, sale, and use of such substances.

19 CFR 12.118 et seq.
Regulations on Toxic Substances Control
These regulations require importers of chemical substances imported in bulk or as part of a mixture to certify to Customs that the shipment complies with the TSCA or is not subject to that Act.

15 USC 1261
Federal Hazardous Substances Act
This Act controls the importation of hazardous substances, sets forth prohibited imports, and authorizes various agencies to promulgate labeling, marking, and transport requirements.

49 CFR 170 et seq.
Regulations on Hazardous Materials
These regulations list all substances deemed hazardous and provide transport, marking, labeling, safety, and emergency response rules.

16 CFR 1500 et seq.
Regulations on Hazardous Substances Safety Standards
These regulations set standards for processing, manufacturing, importing, and labeling all substances classified as hazardous that are to be sold to U.S. consumers.

46 CFR 147.30
Regulations on Labeling of Hazardous Materials
This regulation requires the labeling of containers of hazardous substances and specifies the label contents.

46 CFR 148 et seq.
Regulations on Carriage of Solid Hazardous Materials in Bulk
These regulations govern the transport of solid hazardous substances in bulk, including reporting, permitting, loading, stowing, and shipping requirements.

Principal Exporting Countries

The following listing includes samples of the main supplier nations of the products of this chapter. It is organized by HTSUS major heading. (Refer to "Customs Classification" above for the product codes.) Countries are listed in rank order of the value of products imported to the U.S. Statistics represent customs value entries for 1993 from the Bureau of Census, U.S. Department of Commerce.

4001—Indonesia, Thailand, Malaysia, Nigeria, Sri Lanka, Cote d'Ivoire, Singapore, Cameroon, Guatemala, India

4002—Canada, Japan, France, Germany, Belgium, Mexico, Italy, United Kingdom, Netherlands, South Korea

4003—Canada, Germany, Malaysia, Netherlands, Romania, France, Hungary, Japan, Belgium, Brazil

4004—Netherlands, Germany, Canada, Mexico, South Korea, Belgium, United Kingdom, Russia, Japan, Switzerland

4005—Canada, Japan, France, Germany, Italy, United Kingdom, Cote d'Ivoire, Malaysia, Spain, Netherlands

4006—Canada, Germany, United Kingdom, Taiwan, Thailand, Japan, Sweden, Israel, Italy, Hong Kong

4007—Malaysia, Indonesia, Thailand, Brazil, Taiwan, Canada, China, Hong Kong, Turkey, Israel

4008—Germany, Canada, Mexico, Italy, Japan, South Korea, United Kingdom, France, Taiwan, Sweden

4009—Japan, Canada, Mexico, Italy, Germany, United Kingdom, France, Taiwan, Malaysia, South Korea

4010—Japan, Canada, Germany, Switzerland, South Korea, Taiwan, United Kingdom, Italy, France, Netherlands

4011—Canada, Japan, South Korea, France, Brazil, Taiwan, Spain, Germany, India, United Kingdom

4012—Japan, Canada, Sri Lanka, South Korea, France, Guatemala, United Kingdom, Belgium, Mexico, Taiwan

4013—Taiwan, South Korea, Mexico, Thailand, Japan, Canada, Italy, Brazil, Indonesia, China

4014—Japan, South Korea, United Kingdom, Malaysia, Germany, China, Thailand, Mexico, France, India

4015—Malaysia, Thailand, Mexico, Indonesia, China, Sri Lanka, India, Taiwan, France, Guatemala

4016—Japan, Canada, Germany, Taiwan, United Kingdom, Thailand, France, China, Costa Rica, Mexico

4017—Japan, Germany, Italy, Taiwan, United Kingdom, Netherlands, Canada, China, Malaysia, France

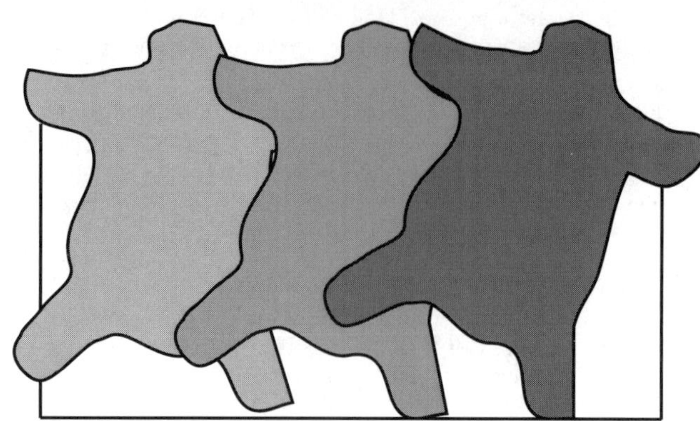

Chapter 41: Raw Hides, Skins, and Leather*

Full title: Raw Hides and Skins (Other than Furskins) and Leather.

This chapter relates to the importation of raw hides, skins, and leather, which are classified under Chapter 41 of the Harmonized Tariff Schedule of the United States (HTSUS). Specifically, it includes raw and prepared animal and reptile hides and skins; chamois leather; patent leather; leather parings and waste not suitable for making articles; leather dust, powder, and flour; and composition leather.

If you are interested in importing leather articles, you should read Commodity Index Chapter 41. Furskins are covered in Chapter 43. Import requirements for bird skins, feathers, and down are found in Chapters 5 and 67. The importation of live animals is covered in Chapter 1.

Key Factors

The key factors in the importation of raw hides, skins, and leather are:

- Compliance with Fish and Wildlife Service (FWS) license, permit, country-of-origin permit, import documentation, and recordkeeping requirements (if the products are derived from exotic wildlife or endangered species)
- Entry at FWS-designated ports, and compliance with FWS and Customs advance notification and port-of-entry inspection requirements (if the products are derived from exotic wildlife or endangered species)
- Compliance with U.S. Department of Agriculture (USDA) APHIS import, quarantine, permit, and certification requirements (if the products are derived from domesticated animals)
- Entry at USDA-designated ports (if the products are derived from domesticated animals)

Although most importers use the services of a licensed customs broker in making their entries, and we recommend this practice, you should be aware of the regulatory, entry, and documentation issues involved in importing your product. You, as importer, are ultimately responsible for the fulfillment of any legal requirements applicable to your shipment.

*IMPORTANT: Read the Commodity Index Introduction. It is the essential framework for understanding this chapter.

General Considerations

Regulatory Agencies. The USDA regulates and inspects the importation of all products derived from animals. The FWS, primarily under provisions of the U.S. Endangered Species Act (ESA) and the Convention on International Trade in Endangered Species of Wild Fauna and Flora (CITES), controls the importation of products derived from animals that are classified as exotic wildlife or endangered or threatened species. U.S. Customs enforces USDA and FWS requirements through entry documentation and restrictions.

Domesticated Animal Hides, Skins, and Leathers. Importation of hides, skins, and leathers of domesticated animals—such as cattle, pigs, sheep, and goats—is generally straightforward. Products derived from such animals are subject to quarantine regulations, marking requirements, and processing standards. Shipments of these products are inspected at the port of arrival by USDA'S Animal and Plant Health Inspection Service (APHIS). Unless the shipment is in compliance with all applicable laws and regulations, it will be denied entry into the U.S. Some shipments may be restricted or prohibited completely.

Quarantine and Inspection. At the time of applying for a permit to import animal products subject to quarantine requirements, you will have to make reservations for space in an appropriate quarantine facility. Fees for quarantine reservations vary according to species, and are due and payable when the reservation is requested. Each shipment entering under APHIS permit must comply in every detail with the permit's specifications. If your shipment is found to be aberrant in any way (such as entering at a port of entry other than the one specified in the permit), it will be refused entry.

Veterinary Certificates. A veterinary certificate, issued by a salaried veterinarian of the country of origin, stating that the animal products are free of applicable livestock diseases, must accompany each shipment. The specific information required on the certificate varies depending on the species you are importing, and its country of origin. You must also present an importer's declaration, which states: 1) port of entry; 2) importer's name and address; 3) broker's name and address; 4) livestock origin; 5) number, breed, species, and purpose of importation; 6) consignee's name, and location of intended delivery.

APHIS-designated Quarantine Ports. The following listings are APHIS-designated ports with adequate quarantine facilities available for the import of livestock and livestock products. With very few exceptions, all shipments of livestock and livestock products must enter at one of these designated ports:

Air and Ocean Ports: Los Angeles, CA; Miami, FL; Honolulu, HI; and Newburgh, NY.

Canadian Border Land Ports: Eastport, ID; Houlton and Jackman, MN; Detroit, Port Huron, and Sault Ste. Marie, MI; Opheim, Raymond, and Sweetgrass, MT; Alexandria Bay, Buffalo, and Champlain, NY; Dunseith, Pembina, and Portal, ND; Derby Line and Highgate Springs, VT; Blaine, Lynden, Oroville, and Sumas, WA.

Mexican Border Land Ports: Brownsville, Hidalgo, Laredo, Eagle Pass, Del Rio, Presidio, and El Paso, TX; Douglas, Naco, Nogales, Sasabe, and San Luis, AZ; Calexico and San Ysidro, CA; Antelope Wells and Columbus, NM.

Limited Ports. These ports have facilities for the entry of livestock or livestock products that do not appear to require restraint and holding inspection facilities: Anchorage and Fairbanks, AK; San Diego, CA; Denver, CO; Jacksonville, St. Petersburg, Clearwater, and Tampa, FL; Atlanta, GA; Chicago, IL; New Orleans, LA; Portland, MN; Baltimore, MD; Boston, MA; Minneapolis, MN; Great Falls, MT; Portland, OR; San Juan, PR; Galveston and Houston, TX; and Seattle, Spokane, and Tacoma, WA.

The ports listed above have been designated as quarantine stations. The USDA Administrator has authority to designate other ports as quarantine stations as needed.

Exotic and Endangered Species. The FWS enforces a complex set of laws and regulations (see 50 CFR 1 et seq.) pertaining to wildlife and wildlife product importation. These laws include the international Convention on International Trade in Endangered Species of Wild Fauna and Flora (CITES), the Endangered Species Act (ESA), and a number of other U.S. laws, such as the African Elephant Conservation Act (AECA), Marine Mammal Protection Act (MMPA), Migratory Bird Treaty Act (MBTA), Eagle Protection Act (EPA), and the Lacey Act (LA). Most foreign countries also have their own domestic measures, and you will need to meet the requirements of the country of export in addition to U.S. requirements. For more information, contact the FWS Office of Management Authority (OMA) (see addresses at end of this chapter).

Certain types of hides, skins, and leathers are entirely prohibited, others are allowed entry only under permit and/or license, and still others are allowed entry only for specific noncommercial purposes. When applying for a permit, you must satisfy the requirements of all laws under which the species is protected. The following briefly describes the two major laws governing importation of protected wildlife products into the U.S. This discussion is not comprehensive or exhaustive. If you wish to import hides, skins, or leathers of exotic or endangered animals, you should always contact the FWS (see addresses at end of this chapter) with species information before making any transactions.

CITES. Over 100 nations participate in the Convention on International Trade in Endangered Species of Wild Fauna and Flora (CITES) treaty, which took effect in May 1977. The degree of protection afforded to a species depends on which of the three CITES appendices contains the name of that species. Documentation required for import varies depending on the species, and the CITES section where it is listed. The CITES export documentation from the country of origin is always required. If you are importing a CITES-listed species from a country that does not participate in the treaty, you must still obtain from that nation documents that contain all the information normally required in CITES export permits.

Appendix I. This appendix lists species deemed presently threatened with extinction (e.g., orangutan, chinchilla, gray whale). Importation of Appendix I species for commercial purposes is prohibited. You must have two permits to import these species: one from the U.S., which must be obtained first, and one from the exporting country. If you are importing Appendix I species taken in the marine environment and outside the jurisdiction of any country or state, you must have an Introduction from the Sea Permit.

Appendix II. This appendix lists species that are not presently threatened with extinction but may become threatened if their trade is not regulated (e.g., brown bear, musk deer, elephant seal). There are no restrictions on the purpose of import, provided it is not detrimental to the survival of the species. You will need an export permit or reexport certificate from the exporting country. If you are importing Appendix II species taken in the marine environment and outside the jurisdiction of any country or state, you will need an Introduction from the Sea Permit.

Appendix III. This appendix lists species for which any CITES member country has domestic regulations "for the purpose of preventing or restricting exploitation, and as needing the cooperation of other Parties in control of trade." For example, Canada lists the walrus, and Nepal lists the blackbuck antelope. Three different types of documents are issued for Appendix III species: 1) Export Permit: Issued for specimens that originated in a country that listed the species on Appendix III; 2) Certificate of Origin: Issued by any country other than the listing country if the wildlife in question originated in that country; 3) Reexport Certificate: Issued for the export of Appendix III specimens that were previously imported into the U.S.

Exemptions. Under certain conditions, Certificates of Exemption may be issued for the importation of wildlife products listed under CITES. Exceptions are allowed for shipments of wildlife transiting a country under Customs bond, shipments between U.S. states or territories, and certain personal or household effects. For information, contact FWS (see addresses at end of this chapter).

Permit Applications. Applications for CITES permits and certificates are available from the FWS Office of Management Authority (see addresses at end of this chapter). You will need to fill out the FWS Standard Permit Application **(Form 3-200)** and provide certain information specifically required under CITES. You should submit your application at least 60 days before the date you wish the permit to take effect. FWS charges processing fees for CITES applications.

ESA. The U.S. Endangered Species Act (ESA) was passed on December 28, 1973, to prevent the extinction of many species of animals and plants and to protect their habitats. By definition, an "endangered species" is any animal or plant listed by regulation as being in danger of extinction. A "threatened species" is any animal or plant likely to become endangered within the foreseeable future. The U.S. List of Endangered and Threatened Wildlife and Plants includes native and foreign species.

Permits. ESA's import provisions prohibit the import or export of any endangered or threatened species or products derived from them without one of the following permits from the FWS Federal Wildlife Permit Office (FWPO):

> *Endangered Species Permits:* This permit is issued for importation for purposes of 1) scientific research; 2) enhancement of propagation or survival of the species; or 3) incidental taking.
>
> *Threatened Species Permits:* This permit is issued for importation for purposes of 1) scientific research; 2) enhancement of propagation or survival of the species; 3) zoological, horticultural, or botanical exhibition; 4) education purposes; 5) special purposes consistent with ESA purposes and policy; or 6) incidental taking.

Permit Exemptions. A few imports of endangered species products are exempt from the ESA permit requirements. For example, if a species is listed as threatened or as an experimental population, special rules may allow otherwise prohibited activities. Some species covered by special rules include certain kangaroos, several primates, the grizzly bear, gray wolf, African elephant, American alligator, and leopard. If you are unsure as to the exemption status of your import, contact FWS (see addresses at end of this chapter).

FWS Import Licenses. With some exceptions, persons engaged in the business of importing wildlife products valued in excess of $25,000 per year must be licensed by the FWS. If your annual importations are valued at less than $25,000, or if you qualify for another exemption from licensing, you are still responsible for keeping thorough records of all wildlife transactions and of making these records available to FWS officers if necessary. For a full description of exemptions from licensing, and of recordkeeping requirements, contact the Fish and Wildlife Service (see addresses at end of this chapter) or see 50 CFR 14.

Procedures at Port of Entry. At least 72 hours before your shipment is due to arrive at a designated port, you should notify U.S. Customs and the FWS inspectors of its expected arrival. The FWS conducts port-of-entry shipment inspections on a case-by-case basis, as determined by the inspection agent after looking at the entry paperwork. Both FWS and Customs may inspect your shipment to verify compliance with all of the legal requirements for entry. Any documentation required by the laws governing your import must be submitted by the time of entry. You must present an FWS Wildlife Declaration **Form 3-177**, available at the port of entry, with every shipment, regardless of any other paperwork required. Customs will not release your shipment until the import declaration has been signed off by an FWS agent.

Designated Ports. Shipments of wildlife products are restricted to designated U.S. ports of entry. All wildlife shipments must enter and leave through one of the ports listed in 50 CFR 14.12. Currently, 10 ports are designated: New York, NY; Miami, FL; New Orleans, LA; Dallas/Ft. Worth, TX; Los Angeles, CA; San Francisco, CA; Chicago, IL; Seattle, WA; Honolulu, HI; and Portland, OR. If special circumstances prevent you from making your entry at a designated port, you will need to obtain an Exception to Designated Port Permit from the FWS Divisions of Law Enforcement (see addresses at end of this chapter).

Country-Specific Import Regulations

There are special provisions for livestock products originating in Canada, Mexico, Central America, and the West Indies. These provisions vary according to species, and include such things as permit or quarantine waivers, special quarantine restrictions, specific ports of entry for specific types of livestock products, and provisions for transit across the U.S. only. One general requirement applicable across the board is that two import declarations (see above) must be presented, instead of only one. For more details see appropriate headings in 9 CFR 92, or contact the Animal and Plant Health Inspection Service.

Import Advisory

Always be prepared to provide the Fish and Wildlife Service or U.S. Customs with both common and scientific names of any species you have questions about or are planning to import. When you are unsure of the regulations governing the export or import of a wildlife product, check with the FWS or TRAFFIC (USA) World Wildlife Fund (see addresses at end of this chapter) well in advance of going abroad, or once there, with the local authorities or the U.S. Embassy before making a purchase. When in doubt, don't buy! Products made from parts of endangered species will be seized and in some cases an importer may be subject to substantial fines.

Wildlife Products [reprinted with permission by World Wildlife Fund from its brochure: "Buyer Beware"]:

> Ensuring that your wildlife product is legal to import is not simple. Wildlife may be "laundered" to conceal its true country of origin. It is often illegally killed or collected in one country, smuggled into another, and then exported with false permits to a third, making its origins hard to trace. If you are considering the purchase of any wildlife or wildlife product while abroad, you should first try to determine its origin and any U.S. restrictions on its import.

Customs Classification

For customs purposes, raw hides, skins, and leather are classified under Chapter 41 of the HTSUS. This chapter is broken into major headings, which are further divided into subheadings, and often sub-subheadings, each of which has its own HTSUS classification number. For example, the HTSUS number for lining leather is 4104.10.40, indicating it is a sub-subcategory of whole bovine skin leather, etc. (4104.10.00), which is a subcategory of the major heading, leather of bovine or equine animals, without hair, etc. (4104.00.00). There are 11 major headings within Chapter 41.

4101—Raw hides and skins of bovine or equine animals (fresh, or salted, dried, limed, pickled, or otherwise preserved, but not tanned, parchment-dressed, or further prepared), whether or not dehaired or split

4102—Raw skins of sheep or lambs (fresh, salted, dried, limed, pickled, or otherwise preserved, but not tanned, parchment-dressed, or further prepared), whether or not with wool on or split, other than those excluded by note 1(c) to this chapter

4103—Other raw hides and skins (fresh, salted, dried, limed, pickled, or otherwise preserved, but not tanned, parchment-dressed, or further prepared), whether or not dehaired or split, other than those excluded by note 1(b) or 1(c) to this chapter

4104—Leather of bovine or equine animals, without hair on, other than leather of heading 4108 or 4109

4105—Sheep or lamb skin leather, without wool on, other than leather of heading 4108 or 4109

4106—Goat or kidskin leather, without hair on, other than leather of heading 4108 or 4109

4107—Leather of other animals, without hair on, other than leather of heading 4108 or 4109

4108—Chamois (including combination chamois) leather

4109—Patent leather and patent laminated leather; metallized leather

4110—Parings and other waste of leather or of composition leather, not suitable for the manufacture of leather articles; leather dust, powder, and flour

4111—Composition leather with a basis of leather or leather fiber, in slabs, sheets, or strip, whether or not in rolls

For more details regarding classifications of the specific product you are interested in importing, consult a customs broker, the appropriate commodity specialist at your nearest customs port, or the HTSUS. HTSUS is available for purchase from the U.S. Government Printing Office (see addresses at end of this chapter), and may be found in larger public libraries. Refer to "Classification—Liquidation" on page 207 for a general discussion of customs classification.

Sample Import Duties

Import duties will vary depending on the HTSUS classification of your product. Therefore, to determine the correct amount of duties, your product must be properly classified under the HTSUS. The following sample duties are taken from the duty listings for HTSUS Chapter 41 products.

Raw hides and skins (4101-4103): free; whole bovine skin leather, of a unit surface area not exceeding 28 square feet, upper leather (4104.10.20): 5.5%, lining leather (4104.10.40): 3.1%; other, not fancy (4104.10.60): 3.7%; other, fancy (4104.10.80): 5.5%; vegetable pretanned sheep or lamb skin leather without wool (4105.11.00): 2.4%; parchment-dressed fancy goat or kidskin leather without hair (4106.20.60): 4.2%; vegetable pretanned reptile leather (4107.21.00): 5%; chamois (including combination chamois) leather (4108.00.00): 4.9%; patent leather (4109.00.30): 3.5%; composition leather (4111.00.00): 2.8%.

Special Provisions. Duty on certain leathers from Japan is temporarily increased: (9903.41.05): Bovine (including buffalo) and equine leather (provided for in heading 4014); goat, kid, sheep and lamb leather, the foregoing dyed, colored, stamped, or embossed (provided for in heading 4105 or 4106): 40%.

Entry and Documentation

The entry of merchandise is a two-part process consisting of 1) filing the documentation necessary to determine whether merchandise may be released from Customs custody, and 2) filing the documents that contain information for duty assessment and statistical purposes. In certain instances, all documents must be filed and accepted by Customs prior to release of the goods. Unless you have been granted an extension, you must file entry documents at a location specified by the district or area director within five working days of your shipment's date of arrival at a

U.S. port of entry. These include a number of standard documents required by Customs for any entry, and:

- FWS Import Declaration **Form 3-177**, original and 3 copies (if the products are derived from exotic wildlife or endangered species)
- FWS permit or import documentation (if the products are derived from exotic wildlife or endangered species)
- Permits or certificates required under CITES, ESA, and any other regulations applicable to the particular shipment (if the products are derived from exotic wildlife or endangered species)
- Certificates of export, origin, sanitation, veterinary inspection, and other conditions from the country of origin or export, as required by Customs, FWS, or USDA
- Copy of air waybill or bill of lading
- Copy of invoice (pro forma invoice if the shipment is noncommercial)

After you present the entry, Customs may examine your shipment or may waive examination. The shipment is then released provided no legal or regulatory violations have been noted. You must then file entry summary documentation and deposit estimated duties at a designated customhouse within 10 working days of your shipment's release. For a detailed description of entry procedures, standard documentation, and informal entry, refer to "Entry Process" on page 182.

Prohibitions and Restrictions

Animal Products. Animal products are subject to quarantine if they arrive from certain countries that are known to have specific infectious diseases. These countries are listed in 9 CFR 94. If a USDA inspector determines that a shipment is infected with anthrax, foot-and-mouth disease, rinderpest, or bovine spongiform encephalopathy, entry will be denied.

Exotic and Endangered Species. Hides of certain animals are restricted or prohibited from importation because of species status under the CITES, ESA, or another U.S. law. For example, importation of species listed in CITES Appendix I for commercial purposes is prohibited. Prohibitions and restrictions may additionally be imposed by the law of the exporting country. You are legally responsible for fulfilling the requirements of all of them, as well as any laws of the country of export. If you import, or attempt to import, a product in violation of a wildlife or endangered species law, even if you are not aware of the violation, your product may be seized, you may be charged substantial fines, and you could be imprisoned.

Importers should be particularly cautious in importing the following wildlife products, which are prohibited from import into the U.S. [reprinted with permission by World Wildlife Fund from its brochure: "Buyer Beware"]:

> ***Reptile Skins and Leathers.*** Products made from most crocodile skins, including black caiman, American crocodile, Orinoco crocodile, and, in many cases, the common caiman from Latin America and the Caribbean; Philippine crocodile, Chinese alligator, and Nile crocodile. Most lizard skin products originating in Brazil, Colombia, Costa Rica, Ecuador, Paraguay, Peru, Venezuela, and a number of Asian countries, including India, Nepal, and Pakistan. Many snakeskin products originating in Latin America—Argentina, Brazil, Colombia, Costa Rica, Ecuador, Guatemala, Mexico, Paraguay, and Venezuela, for example—and certain Asian countries, such as India. All sea turtle products, including [leather].
>
> ***Other Leather Products.*** Made from pangolin (sometimes labeled "anteater") skin originating in Thailand, Malaysia, and Indonesia.

Country-Specific Restrictions

Duty on certain leathers from Japan is temporarily increased. Refer to "Sample Import Duties" above.

Marking and Labeling Requirements

Animal Products. Containers of animal hides, skins, and leathers must be marked with the country of origin—that is, the country where the animal was located. If hides, skins, or leathers are quarantined at the port of arrival, marks and signs are required on shipping documents and any mode of transport used to move the product while under restrictions (9 CFR 95.25).

Wildlife Hides, Skins, and Leather. All wildlife shipments must be marked on the outside of the container with the names and addresses of the exporter and importer, an accurate identification of the species, and the numbers of each species in the container.

For a general discussion of U.S. Customs marking and labeling requirements, refer to "Marking: Country of Origin" on page 215 and "Special Marking Requirements" on page 217.

Shipping Considerations

You will need to ensure that your goods are packaged and shipped with care so that they pass smoothly through Customs and arrive in good condition. You are responsible for ensuring that the shipment is in compliance with all applicable government regulations for packaging and shipping. In most instances, you should not leave these arrangements solely to the discretion of your supplier. Careful preparation of the cargo and selection of the mode of transport can be essential to a cost-effective, timely delivery of undamaged goods. We strongly advise you to consult your shipping representative, insurance agent, or freight broker for advice on packing and shipping. Refer also to the major tab section "Packing/Shipping/Insurance" for a general discussion of packing and shipping.

Hides, skins, and leathers may be shipped in bulk, sacks, crates, or other types of containers, depending on the type of product. General considerations include protection from contamination, weather, and pests. Containers should be constructed so as to be safe for handling during transport.

Publications Available

The following books are especially pertinent to endangered species regulations and wildlife trade. They are published by and available from World Wildlife Fund at the address below.

> *International Wildlife Trade: Whose Business Is It?* by Sarah Fitzgerald. Paperback $25.00; cloth $40.00, 459 pp, ISBN 0-942635-10-8.
>
> *The Wildlife Trade Laws of Asia and Oceania* by David Nichols, Kathryn Fuller, Erica McShane-Caluzi and Eva Eckinrode. 1991. Loose-leaf binder. Order Code NIAO. $50.00.
>
> *Latin American Wildlife Trade Laws* (2d ed.) Kathryn S. Fuller, Byron Swift, Amanda Jorgenson, and Amie Brautigam. 1985. 418 pp. Loose-leaf binder. Order Code FULA (English language). #35.00.

To order these publications, or to request a catalog of related publications, contact:

> **World Wildlife Fund**
> 1250 24th Street NW
> Washington, DC 20037
> (202) 293-4800

The *Harmonized Tariff Schedule of the United States* (HTSUS) is available from:

Government Printing Office (GPO)
Superintendent of Documents
Washington, DC 20402
(202) 512-1800 (Order line)
(202) 512-0000 (General)

The USGPO also has copies of specific laws available for purchase. The USGPO accepts credit card orders over the phone, as well as mail orders paid by credit card, a check drawn on a U.S. bank, or an international money order.

Relevant Government Agencies

Address your questions regarding USDA requirements for the importation of domesticated animal products to:

U.S. Department of Agriculture (USDA)
Animal and Plant Health Inspection Service (APHIS)
Veterinary Services (VS)
Import-Export Products Staff
Federal Building, Room 756
6505 Belcrest Road
Hyattsville, MD 20782
(301) 436-7885

Address your questions regarding the importation of exotic or endangered animal hides, skins, and leathers to:

U.S. Fish and Wildlife Service (FWS)
Office of Management Authority
4401 N. Fairfax Drive, Room 432
Arlington, VA 22203
(703) 358-2095
(800) 358-2104, (703) 358-2104 (Permits office)

National Marine Fisheries Service (NMFS)
Office of Marine Mammals and Endangered Species
1335 East West Highway
Silver Spring, MD 20910
(301) 713-2332

Address your questions regarding importation of hides, skins and leathers to the district or port director of Customs for you area. For addresses refer to"U.S. Customs District Offices" on page 62 or contact:

U.S. Customs Service
1301 Constitution Ave. NW
Washington, DC 20229
(202) 927-6724 (Information)
(202) 927-1000 (General)

Laws and Regulations

The following laws and regulations may be relevant to the importation of hides, skins, and leathers. The laws are contained in the United States Code (USC), and the regulations are published in the Code of Federal Regulations (CFR), both of which are available at larger public and law libraries. Copies of specific laws and regulations are also available from the USGPO (address above.

7 USC 4801 et seq.
Pork Promotion, Research, and Consumer Information Act
This Act provides that each importer of porcine animal, pork, or pork product shall remit an assessment to Customs at the time the product is imported. See 7 CFR 1230.71 and 1230.110.

18 USC 42 et seq.
Importation of Animals, Birds, Fish, and Plants
This Act governs the importation of mammals, birds, fish, amphibia, and reptiles into the U.S. and authorizes U.S. Customs to enforce the import requirements.

21 USC 101 et seq.
Importation of Cattle and Quarantine
This Act provides for suspension of importation of animals to prevent the spread of disease, and for the quarantine of prohibited classes of animals. Importation of all animals described by the Act is prohibited except at certain designated ports. All animals are to be inspected on import or export.

21 USC 113a
Foot-and-Mouth Disease Memorandum of Understanding; Disease Research Act
This Act authorizes the study of animal disease and prohibits introduction of live foot-and-mouth disease virus into the U.S. except under certain defined circumstances. Customs enforces Agriculture restrictions and regulations.

21 USC 135
Establishment of International Animal Quarantine Stations
This Act authorizes the establishment of international quarantine stations. Customs enforces laws regarding importation of livestock.

42 USC 264 et seq.
Quarantine, Inspection, and Licensing
This Act restricts importations of dogs, cats, monkeys, psittacine birds, turtles, tortoises, and terrapins that do not comply with health standards. Customs enforces these restrictions. See 42 CFR 71.51 et seq.

19 CFR 12.24 and 12.26
Regulations for Animal and Animal Product Entry
These regulations provide for U.S. Customs entry declarations, documentation, and procedures for the animals and animal products subject to FWS and USDA regulations.

9 CFR Parts 91-96
Regulations on Animal Byproduct Quarantine Control
These regulations promulgated by the USDA prohibit the importation of animal products for use in industry unless the products meet certain processing standards and are not infected with certain diseases.

Convention on International Trade in Endangered Species of Wild Fauna and Flora (CITES)
This comprehensive wildlife treaty signed by over 100 countries, including the United States, regulates and in many cases prohibits commercial imports and exports of wild animal and plant species threatened by trade.

16 USC 1531
Endangered Species Act
This Act prohibits the import and export of species listed as endangered and most species listed as threatened. It is the U.S. law that implements CITES.

16 USC 742a et seq.
Fish and Wildlife Act
This Act regulates and bars the import of certain wild animals or birds and authorizes U.S. Customs to enforce the restrictions.

50 CFR Parts 10, 13, and 16
Regulations of FWS for Importing Wildlife and Fish
These regulations specify the animals and animal products subject to import prohibitions and restrictions.

16 USC 2401
Antarctic Conservation Act
This Act prohibits the importation, absent a special permit, of any flora or fauna native to Antarctica into the U.S.

16 USC 3371 et seq.
Lacey Act
This Act prohibits the import of species taken, possessed, transported, or sold in violation of the law of a foreign country.

16 USC 1361 et seq.
The Marine Mammal Protection Act
This Act prohibits the import of marine mammals and their parts and products. These species include whales, walruses, narwhals, seals, sea lions, sea otters, and polar bears.

16 USC 4201
The African Elephant Conservation Act
This Act prohibits imports of carved ivory products from any country and only permits imports of whole tusks from elephants legally hunted in certain African countries.

Principal Exporting Countries

The following listing includes samples of the main supplier nations of the products of this chapter. It is organized by HTSUS major heading. (Refer to "Customs Classification" above for the product codes.) Countries are listed in rank order of the value of products imported to the U.S. Statistics represent customs value entries for 1993 from the Bureau of Census, U.S. Department of Commerce.

4101—Canada, Mexico, United Kingdom, Ireland, Belgium, Brazil, Sweden, Argentina, Thailand, Finland

4102—United Kingdom, New Zealand, Ethiopia, Sudan, Mexico, Ethiopia, Nigeria, Kenya, Australia, Canada

4103—Canada, Thailand, Sweden, New Zealand, Colombia, Australia, Nicaragua, Taiwan, Greece, China

4104—Argentina, Italy, Brazil, United Kingdom, Uruguay, Thailand, Mexico, Norway, Germany, Canada

4105—Italy, United Kingdom, Spain, France, New Zealand, Sudan, South Korea, Kenya, Mexico, Haiti

4106—Pakistan, India, Haiti, United Kingdom, Italy, Greece, Mexico, Bangladesh, Kenya, Sudan

4107—South Africa, Taiwan, Indonesia, Japan, Slovenia, Italy, United Kingdom, China, Argentina, France

4108—United Kingdom, Mexico, Belgium, Netherlands, Italy, South Africa, Canada, India, El Salvador, Portugal

4109—Italy, Brazil, India, Argentina, Mexico, China, United Kingdom, South Korea, Japan, Taiwan

4110—Mexico, Canada, Czech Rep., Germany, Sweden, Italy, Argentina, Uruguay, Thailand

4111—Germany, Italy, Spain, Brazil, Taiwan, Costa Rica, Canada, Mexico, India, Dominican Rep.

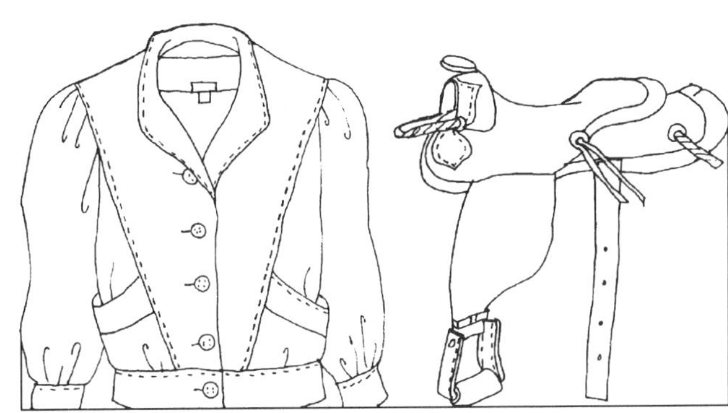

Chapter 42: Leather Articles*

Full title: Articles of Leather; Saddlery, and Harness; Travel Goods, Handbags, and Similar Containers; Articles of Animal Gut (Other Than Silkworm Gut)

This chapter relates to the importation of articles of leather and animal gut, which are classified under Chapter 42 of the Harmonized Tariff Schedule of the United States (HTSUS). Specifically, it includes leather and composition leather saddlery, harness equipment, cases, bags, other containers, apparel, clothing accessories; leather and composition leather articles for machinery, mechanical applications, and technical uses; shoelaces, straps, and other leather articles; and articles made from animal gut, bladders, or tendons.

If you are interested in importing raw hides, skins, or leathers, you should refer to Commodity Index Chapter 41. The importation requirements for articles of apparel or clothing accessories, except gloves, lined or covered with furskins, are covered in Chapter 43. The requirements for importing fittings or trimmings for harnesses are covered in Chapters 72 through 83. For importing specific products that contain leather or composition leather, you should refer to the Commodity Index chapters that cover the particular item of interest. For example, footwear is covered in Chapter 64, headgear in Chapter 65, plaiting materials in Chapter 46, whips and riding crops in Chapter 66, imitation jewelry in Chapter 71, and furniture in Chapter 94. If you are interested in importing articles of netting, refer to Chapter 56. The importation of sterile surgical catgut or other suture materials is discussed in Chapter 30; strings, drum skins, and other parts of musical instruments in Chapter 92; and toys, games, and sports equipment in Chapter 95.

Key Factors

The key factors in the importation of articles of leather and animal gut goods:

- Compliance with U.S. Fish and Wildlife Service (FWS) requirements (if the product is derived from endangered species or wildlife)
- Entry at FWS-designated ports, and compliance with FWS and Customs advance notification and port-of-entry inspection requirements (if the products are derived from exotic wildlife or endangered species)

*IMPORTANT: Read the Commodity Index Introduction. It is the essential framework for understanding this section.

- Compliance with U.S. Department of Agriculture (USDA) APHIS import, quarantine, permit, and certification requirements (if the products are derived from domesticated animals)
- Entry at USDA-designated ports (if the products are derived from domesticated animals)
- Compliance with U.S. Customs and U.S. Department of Commerce (DOC) textile import regulations and procedures (if the product includes textiles)
- Compliance with U.S. Federal Trade Commission (FTC) and Consumer Product Safety Commission (CPSC) standards (if the product includes textiles)

Although most importers use the services of a licensed customs broker in making their entries, and we recommend this practice, you should be aware of the regulatory, entry, and documentation issues involved in importing your product. You, as importer, are ultimately responsible for the fulfillment of any legal requirements applicable to your shipment.

General Considerations

Regulatory Agencies. The USDA regulates the importation of products derived from animals. The FWS, primarily under provisions of the U.S. Endangered Species Act (ESA) and the Convention on International Trade in Endangered Species of Wild Fauna and Flora (CITES), controls the importation of products derived from animals that are classified as exotic wildlife or endangered or threatened species. U.S. Customs enforces USDA and FWS requirements through entry documentation and restrictions. Customs also administers the import of textile luggage under the U.S. Customs Textile Import Program.

Domesticated Animal Products. Importation of articles made of leather or animal gut derived from domesticated animals—such as cattle, pigs, sheep, and goats—is generally straightforward. Products derived from such animals are subject to quarantine regulations, marking requirements, and processing standards. Shipments of these products are inspected at the port of arrival by the Animal and Plant Health Inspection Service (APHIS) of the USDA. Unless the shipment is in compliance with all applicable laws and regulations, it will be denied entry into the U.S. Some shipments may be restricted or prohibited completely.

Quarantine and Inspection. At the time of applying for a permit to import animal products subject to quarantine requirements, you will have to make reservations for space in an appropriate quarantine facility. Fees for quarantine reservations vary according to species, and are due and payable when the reservation is requested. Each shipment entering under USDA APHIS permit must comply in every detail with the permit's specifications. If your shipment is found to be aberrant in any way (such as entering at a port of entry other than the one specified in the permit), it will be refused entry.

Veterinary Certificates. A veterinary certificate, issued by a salaried veterinarian of the country of origin, stating that the animal products are free of applicable livestock diseases, must accompany each shipment. The specific information required on the certificate varies depending on the species you are importing and its country of origin. You must also present an importer's declaration, which states: 1) port of entry; 2) importer's name and address; 3) broker's name and address; 4) livestock origin; 5) number, breed, species, and purpose of importation; 6) consignee's name and location of intended delivery.

APHIS-designated Quarantine Ports. The following listings are APHIS-designated ports with adequate quarantine facilities available for the import of livestock and livestock products. With very few exceptions, all shipments of livestock and livestock products must enter at one of these designated ports:

Air and Ocean Ports: Los Angeles, CA; Miami, FL; Honolulu, HI; and Newburgh, NY.

Canadian Border Land Ports: Eastport, ID; Houlton and Jackman, MN; Detroit, Port Huron, and Sault Ste. Marie, MI; Opheim, Raymond, and Sweetgrass, MT; Alexandria Bay, Buffalo, and Champlain, NY; Dunseith, Pembina, and Portal, ND; Derby Line and Highgate Springs, VT; Blaine, Lynden, Oroville, and Sumas, WA.

Mexican Border Land Ports: Brownsville, Hidalgo, Laredo, Eagle Pass, Del Rio, Presidio, and El Paso, TX; Douglas, Naco, Nogales, Sasabe, and San Luis, AZ; Calexico and San Ysidro, CA; Antelope Wells and Columbus, NM.

Limited Ports. These ports have facilities for the entry of livestock or livestock products that do not appear to require restraint and holding inspection facilities: Anchorage and Fairbanks, AK; San Diego, CA; Denver, CO; Jacksonville, St. Petersburg, Clearwater, and Tampa, FL; Atlanta, GA; Chicago, IL; New Orleans, LA; Portland, MN; Baltimore, MD; Boston, MA; Minneapolis, MN; Great Falls, MT; Portland, OR; San Juan, PR; Galveston and Houston, TX; and Seattle, Spokane, and Tacoma, WA.

The ports listed above have been designated as quarantine stations. The USDA Administrator has authority to designate other ports as quarantine stations as needed.

Exotic and Endangered Species. The FWS enforces a complex set of laws and regulations (see 50 CFR 1 et seq.) pertaining to wildlife and wildlife product importation. These laws include the international Convention on International Trade in Endangered Species of Wild Fauna and Flora (CITES), the Endangered Species Act (ESA), and a number of other U.S. laws, such as the African Elephant Conservation Act (AECA), Marine Mammal Protection Act (MMPA), Migratory Bird Treaty Act (MBTA), Eagle Protection Act (EPA), and the Lacey Act (LA). Most foreign countries also have their own domestic measures, and you will need to meet the requirements of the country of export in addition to U.S. requirements. For more information, contact the FWS Office of Management Authority (OMA) (see addresses at end of this chapter).

Certain articles of leather and animal gut are entirely prohibited, others are allowed entry only under permit and/or license, and still others are allowed entry only for specific noncommercial purposes. When applying for a permit, you must satisfy the requirements of all laws under which the species is protected. The following briefly describes the two major laws governing importation of protected wildlife products into the U.S. This discussion is not comprehensive or exhaustive. If you wish to import hides, skins, or leathers of exotic or endangered animals, you should always contact the FWS (see addresses at end of this chapter) with species information before making any transactions.

CITES. Over 100 nations participate in the Convention on International Trade in Endangered Species of Wild Fauna and Flora (CITES) treaty, which took effect in May 1977. The degree of protection afforded to a species depends on which of the three CITES appendices contains the name of that species. Documentation required for import varies depending on the species, and the CITES section where it is listed. The CITES export documentation from the country of origin is always required. If you are importing a CITES-listed species from a country that does not participate in the treaty, you must still obtain from that nation documents that contain all the information normally required in CITES export permits.

Appendix I. This appendix lists species deemed presently threatened with extinction (e.g., orangutan, chinchilla, gray whale). Importation of Appendix I species for commercial purposes is prohibited. You must have two permits to import these species: one from the U.S., which must be obtained first, and one from the exporting country. If you are importing Appendix I species taken in the marine environment and outside the jurisdiction of any country or state, you must have an Introduction from the Sea Permit.

Appendix II. This appendix lists species that are not presently threatened with extinction but may become threatened if their trade is not regulated (e.g., brown bear, musk deer, elephant seal). There are no restrictions on the purpose of import, provided it is not detrimental to the survival of the species. You will need an export permit or reexport certificate from the exporting country. If you are importing Appendix II species taken in the marine environment and outside the jurisdiction of any country or state, you will need an Introduction from the Sea Permit.

Appendix III. This appendix lists species for which any CITES member country has domestic regulations "for the purpose of preventing or restricting exploitation, and as needing the cooperation of other Parties in control of trade." For example, Canada lists the walrus, and Nepal lists the blackbuck antelope. Three different types of documents are issued for Appendix III species: 1) Export Permit: Issued for specimens that originated in a country that listed the species on Appendix III; 2) Certificate of Origin: Issued by any country other than the listing country if the wildlife in question originated in that country; 3) Reexport Certificate: Issued for the export of Appendix III specimens that were previously imported into the U.S.

Exemptions. Under certain conditions, Certificates of Exemption may be issued for the importation of wildlife products listed under CITES. Exceptions are allowed for shipments of wildlife transiting a country under Customs bond, shipments between U.S. states or territories, and certain personal or household effects. For information, contact FWS (see addresses at end of this chapter).

Permit Applications. Applications for CITES permits and certificates are available from the FWS Office of Management Authority (see addresses at end of this chapter). You will need to fill out the FWS Standard Permit Application **(Form 3-200)** and provide certain information specifically required under CITES. You should submit your application at least 60 days before the date you wish the permit to take effect. FWS charges processing fees for CITES applications.

ESA. The U.S. Endangered Species Act (ESA) was passed on December 28, 1973, to prevent the extinction of many species of animals and plants and to protect their habitats. By definition, an "endangered species" is any animal or plant listed by regulation as being in danger of extinction. A "threatened species" is any animal or plant likely to become endangered within the foreseeable future. The U.S. List of Endangered and Threatened Wildlife and Plants includes native and foreign species.

Permits. ESA's import provisions prohibit the import or export of any endangered or threatened species or products derived from them without one of the following permits from the FWS Federal Wildlife Permit Office (FWPO):

> *Endangered Species Permits:* This permit is issued for importation for purposes of 1) scientific research; 2) enhancement of propagation or survival of the species; or 3) incidental taking.
>
> *Threatened Species Permits:* This permit is issued for importation for purposes of 1) scientific research; 2) enhancement of propagation or survival of the species; 3) zoological, horticultural, or botanical exhibition; 4) education purposes; 5) special purposes consistent with ESA purposes and policy; or 6) incidental taking.

Permit Exemptions. A few imports of endangered species products are exempt from the ESA permit requirements. For example, if a species is listed as threatened or as an experimental population, special rules may allow otherwise prohibited activities. Some species covered by special rules include certain kangaroos, several primates, the grizzly bear, gray wolf, African elephant, American alligator, and leopard. If you are unsure as to the exemption status of your import, contact FWS (see addresses at end of this chapter).

FWS Import Licenses. With some exceptions, persons engaged in the business of importing wildlife products valued in excess of $25,000 per year must be licensed by the FWS. If your annual importations are valued at less than $25,000, or if you qualify for another exemption from licensing, you are still responsible for keeping thorough records of all wildlife transactions and of making these records available to FWS officers if necessary. For a full description of exemptions from licensing, and of recordkeeping requirements, contact the Fish and Wildlife Service (see addresses at end of this chapter) or see 50 CFR 14.

Procedures at Port of Entry. At least 72 hours before your shipment is due to arrive at a designated port, you should notify U.S. Customs and the FWS inspectors of its expected arrival. The FWS conducts port-of-entry shipment inspections on a case-by-case basis, as determined by the inspection agent after looking at the entry paperwork. Both FWS and Customs may inspect your shipment to verify compliance with all of the legal requirements for entry. Any documentation required by the laws governing your import must be submitted by the time of entry. You must present an FWS Wildlife Declaration **Form 3-177**, available at the port of entry, with every shipment, regardless of any other paperwork required. Customs will not release your shipment until the import declaration has been signed off by an FWS agent.

Designated Ports. Shipments of wildlife products are restricted to designated U.S. ports of entry. All wildlife shipments must enter and leave through one of the ports listed in 50 CFR 14.12. Currently, 10 ports are designated: New York, NY; Miami, FL; New Orleans, LA; Dallas/Ft. Worth, TX; Los Angeles, CA; San Francisco, CA; Chicago, IL; Seattle, WA; Honolulu, HI; and Portland, OR. If special circumstances prevent you from making your entry at a designated port, you will need to obtain an Exception to Designated Port Permit from the FWS Divisions of Law Enforcement (see addresses at end of this chapter).

Textile Luggage. Regulation of textile product imports is complex, and luggage that includes textiles is subject to stringent textile import regulations. If your luggage imports contain textile fibers, you should read the Commodity Index chapter (Chapters 50 through 63) that pertains to that particular textile. The following discussion outlines the basic requirements.

U.S. Customs administers import controls on certain cotton, wool, man-made fiber, silk blend, and other vegetable fiber articles manufactured or produced in designated countries. When considering importation of textile luggage, you should first ascertain if the product is subject to textile restrictions or quotas. The DOC Office of Textile and Apparel should be able to advise you on the regulatory status of specific products. Textile luggage must be entered under regulations of the U.S. Customs Textile Import Program. Customs requires a U.S. Customs Country-of-Origin Declaration to be submitted at the port of entry with each shipment of any textile or textile product. You are also responsible for your textile luggage's compliance with the Textile Fiber Products Identification Act (TFPIA), administered by the FTC. Entry invoices for articles subject to TFPIA must show certain additional information.

Specific Country Import Regulations

There are special provisions for livestock products originating in Canada, Mexico, Central America, and the West Indies. These provisions vary according to species, and include such things as permit or quarantine waivers, special quarantine restrictions, specific ports of entry for specific types of livestock products, and provisions for transit across the U.S. only. One general requirement applicable across the board is that two import declarations (see above) must be presented, instead of only one. For more details see appropriate headings in 9 CFR 92, or contact the Animal and Plant Health Inspection Service.

Import Advisory

Always be prepared to provide the Fish and Wildlife Service or U.S. Customs with both common and scientific names of any species you have questions about or are planning to import. When you are unsure of the regulations governing the export or import of a wildlife product, check with the FWS or TRAFFIC (USA) World Wildlife Fund (see addresses at end of this chapter) well in advance of going abroad, or once there, with the local authorities or the U.S. Embassy before making a purchase. When in doubt, don't buy! Products made from parts of endangered species will be seized and in some cases the importer will be subject to substantial fines.

Wildlife Products [reprinted with permission by World Wildlife Fund from its brochure: "Buyer Beware"]:

> Ensuring that your wildlife product is legal to import is not simple. Wildlife may be "laundered" to conceal its true country of origin. It is often illegally killed or collected in one country, smuggled into another, and then exported with false permits to a third, making its origins hard to trace. If you are considering the purchase of any wildlife or wildlife product while abroad, you should first try to determine its origin and any U.S. restrictions on its import.

Customs Classification

For customs purposes, articles of leather and animal gut are classified under Chapter 42 of the HTSUS. This chapter is broken into major headings, which are further divided into subheadings, and often sub-subheadings, each of which has its own HTSUS classification number. For example, the HTSUS number for reptile leather handbags is 4202.21.30, indicating it is a sub-subcategory of handbags with outer surface of leather, etc. (4202.21.00), which is a subcategory of the major heading, trunks, suitcases, etc. (4202.00.00). There are six major headings within Chapter 42.

4201—Saddlery and harness for any animal (including traces, leads, knee pads, muzzles, saddle cloths, saddle bags, dog coats, and the like), of any material

4202—Trunks, suitcases, vanity cases, attache cases, briefcases, school satchels, spectacle cases, binocular cases, camera cases, musical instrument cases, gun cases, holsters, and similar containers; traveling bags, toiletry bags, knapsacks and backpacks, handbags, shopping bags, wallets, purses, map cases, cigarette cases, tobacco pouches, tool bags, sports bags, bottle cases, jewelry boxes, powder cases, cutlery cases, and similar containers, of leather or of composition leather, of sheeting of plastics, of textile materials, of vulcanized fiber, or of paperboard, or wholly or mainly covered with such materials or with paper

4203—Articles of apparel and clothing accessories, of leather or of composition leather

4204—Articles of leather or of composition leather used in machinery or mechanical appliances of for other technical uses

4205—Other articles of leather or of composition leather

4206—Articles of gut (other than silkworm gut), of goldbeater's skin, of bladders, or of tendons

For more details regarding classifications of the specific product you are interested in importing, consult a customs broker, the appropriate commodity specialist at your nearest customs port, or the HTSUS. HTSUS is available for purchase from the U.S. Government Printing Office (see addresses at end of this chapter), and may be found in larger public libraries. Refer to "Classification—Liquidation" on page 207 for a general discussion of customs classification.

Sample Import Duties

Import duties will vary depending on the HTSUS classification of your product. Therefore, to determine the correct amount of duties, your product must be properly classified under the HTSUS. The following sample duties are taken from the duty listings for HTSUS Chapter 42 products.

Dog leashes, collars, muzzles, harnesses, and similar dog equipment (4201.00.30): 2.4%; handbags of reptile leather (4202.21.30): 5.3%; handbags of other leathers valued not over $20 each (4202.21.60): 10%; valued over $20 each (4202.21.90): 9%; golf bags (4202.91.00): 6.8%; apparel of reptile leather (4203.10.20): 4.7%; apparel of other leathers (4203.10.40): 6%; batting gloves (4203.21.20): 3%; belts and bandoliers with or without buckles (4203.30.00): 5.3%; shoelaces (4205.00.20): free; racquet strings (4206.10.90): 7.7%.

Entry and Documentation

The entry of merchandise is a two-part process consisting of 1) filing the documentation necessary to determine whether merchandise may be released from Customs custody, and 2) filing the documents that contain information for duty assessment and statistical purposes. In certain instances, all documents must be filed and accepted by Customs prior to release of the goods. Unless you have been granted an extension, you must file entry documents at a location specified by the district or area director within five working days of your shipment's date of arrival at a U.S. port of entry. These include a number of standard documents required by Customs for any entry, and:

- FWS Import Declaration **Form 3-177**, original and 3 copies (if the products are derived from exotic wildlife or endangered species)
- FWS permit or import documentation (if the products are derived from exotic wildlife or endangered species)
- Permits or certificates required under CITES, ESA, and any other regulations applicable to the particular shipment (if the products are derived from exotic wildlife or endangered species)
- Certificates of export, origin, sanitation, veterinary inspection, and other conditions from the country of origin or export, as required by Customs, FWS, or USDA
- USDA importer's declaration (if the products are derived from domesticated animals).
- U.S. Customs Textile Entry Declaration (if textile luggage is imported)
- Export visa or other documentation (textile luggage subject to Multi-Fiber Arrangement)
- Copy of air waybill or bill of lading
- Copy of invoice (pro forma invoice if shipment is noncommercial)

After you present the entry, Customs may examine your shipment or may waive examination. The shipment is then released provided no legal or regulatory violations have been noted. You must then file entry summary documentation and deposit estimated duties at a designated customhouse within 10 working days of your shipment's release. For a detailed description of entry procedures, standard documentation, and informal entry, refer to "Entry Process" on page 182.

Entry Invoice for Textile Luggage. The invoice presented at the port of entry for luggage composed of textiles must be in compliance with the requirements of the Textile Fiber Products Identification Act (TFPIA), as enforced by U.S. Customs (19 CFR 11.12b).

Prohibitions and Restrictions

Animal Products. Animal products are subject to quarantine if they arrive from certain countries that are known to have specific infectious diseases. These countries are listed in 9 CFR 94. If a USDA inspector determines that a shipment is infected with anthrax, foot-and-mouth disease, rinderpest, or bovine spongiform encephalopathy, entry will be denied.

Exotic and Endangered Species. Products derived from certain animals are restricted or prohibited from importation because of species status under the CITES, ESA, or another U.S. law. For example, importation of species listed in CITES Appendix I for commercial purposes is prohibited. Prohibitions and restrictions may additionally be imposed by the law of the exporting country. You are legally responsible for fulfilling the requirements of all of them, as well as any laws of the country of export. If you import, or attempt to import, a product in violation of a wildlife or endangered species law, even if you are not aware of the violation, your product may be seized, you may be charged substantial fines, and you could be imprisoned.

Importers should be particularly cautious in importing the following wildlife products, which are prohibited from import into the U.S. [reprinted with permission by World Wildlife Fund from its brochure: "Buyer Beware"]:

> ***Reptile Skins and Leathers.*** Products made from most crocodile skins, including black caiman, American crocodile, Orinoco crocodile, and, in many cases, the common caiman from Latin America and the Caribbean; Philippine crocodile, Chinese alligator, and Nile crocodile. Most lizard skin products originating in Brazil, Colombia, Costa Rica, Ecuador, Paraguay, Peru, Venezuela, and a number of Asian countries, including India, Nepal, and Pakistan. Many snakeskin products originating in Latin America—Argentina, Brazil, Colombia, Costa Rica, Ecuador, Guatemala, Mexico, Paraguay, and Venezuela, for example—and certain Asian countries, such as India. All sea turtle products, including [leather].
>
> ***Other Leather Products.*** Made from pangolin (sometimes labeled "anteater") skin originating in Thailand, Malaysia, and Indonesia.

Textile Luggage. The import of certain textiles is restricted under the U.S. Department of Commerce Multi-Fiber Arrangements. The Department of Commerce Office of Textile and Apparel (see addresses at end of this chapter) can advise you on the regulatory status of specific products originating in certain countries.

Quotas

Textile Luggage. Textile product import quotas are issued on a per country basis. A product may be under quota if it originates from one country but not from another. To find out if a particular type of luggage from a particular country is subject to textile quota, contact the Department of Commerce textile team (see addresses at end of this chapter). For details regarding quotas on luggage made from textile products, see the Commodity Index chapter (Chapters 50 through 63) that covers the particular type of fabric used in the luggage you are interested in importing

Marking and Labeling Requirements

Animal Products. Containers of animal products must be marked with the country of origin—that is, the country where the animal was located. If leather or animal gut products are quarantined at the port of arrival, marks and signs are required on shipping documents and any mode of transport used to move the product while under restrictions (9 CFR 95.25).

Wildlife Hides, Skins, and Leather. All wildlife shipments must be marked on the outside of the container with the names and addresses of the exporter and importer, an accurate identification of the species, and the numbers of each species in the container.

Textile Luggage. With certain exceptions, textile products must be labeled in accordance with the Textile Fiber Products Identification Act (TFPIA). For details on marking and labeling requirements, refer to the Commodity Index chapter (Chapters 50 through 63) that covers the particular type of fabric used in the luggage you are interested in importing.

For a general discussion of U.S. Customs marking and labeling requirements, refer to "Marking: Country of Origin" on page 215 and "Special Marking Requirements" on page 217.

Shipping Considerations

You will need to ensure that your goods are packaged and shipped with care so that they pass smoothly through Customs and arrive in good condition. You are responsible for ensuring that the shipment is in compliance with all applicable government regulations for packaging and shipping. In most instances, you should not leave these arrangements solely to the discretion of your supplier. Careful preparation of the cargo and selection of the mode of transport can be essential to a cost-effective, timely delivery of undamaged goods. We strongly advise you to consult your shipping representative, insurance agent, or freight broker for advice on packing and shipping. Refer also to the major tab section "Packing/Shipping/Insurance" for a general discussion of packing and shipping.

Articles of leather or animal gut may be shipped in bulk, sacks, crates, packages, or other types of containers, depending on the type of product and whether it is prepackaged for consumers. General considerations include protection from contamination, weather, and pests. Containers should be constructed so as to be safe for handling during transport.

Publications Available

The following books are especially pertinent to Endangered Species regulations and wildlife trade. They are published by and available from World Wildlife Fund at the address below.

> *International Wildlife Trade: Whose Business Is It?* by Sarah Fitzgerald. Paperback $25.00; cloth $40.00, 459 pp, ISBN 0-942635-10-8.
>
> *The Wildlife Trade Laws of Asia and Oceania* by David Nichols, Kathryn Fuller, Erica McShane-Caluzi and Eva Eckinrode. 1991. Loose-leaf binder. Order Code NIAO. $50.00.
>
> *Latin American Wildlife Trade Laws* (2d ed.) Kathryn S. Fuller, Byron Swift, Amanda Jorgenson, and Amie Brautigam. 1985. 418 pp. Loose-leaf binder. Order Code FULA (English language). #35.00.

To order these publications, or to request a catalog of related publications, contact:

> **World Wildlife Fund**
> 1250 24th Street NW
> Washington, DC 20037
> (202) 293-4800

The *Harmonized Tariff Schedule of the United States* (HTSUS) is available from:

> **Government Printing Office (GPO)**
> **Superintendent of Documents**
> Washington, DC 20402
> (202) 512-1800 (Order line)
> (202) 512-0000 (General)

The USGPO also has copies of specific laws available for purchase. The USGPO accepts credit card orders over the phone, as well as mail orders paid by credit card, a check drawn on a U.S. bank, or an international money order.

Relevant Government Agencies

Address your questions regarding USDA requirements for the importation of domesticated animal products to:

U.S. Department of Agriculture (USDA)
Animal and Plant Health Inspection Service (APHIS)
Veterinary Services (VS)
Import-Export Products Staff
Federal Building, Room 756
6505 Belcrest Road
Hyattsville, MD 20782
(301) 436-7885

Address your questions regarding the importation of products of exotic or endangered animals to:

U.S. Fish and Wildlife Service (FWS)
Office of Management Authority
4401 N. Fairfax Drive, Room 432
Arlington, VA 22203
(703) 358-2095
(800) 358-2104, (703) 358-2104 (Permits office)

National Marine Fisheries Service (NMFS)
Office of Marine Mammals and Endangered Species
1335 East West Highway
Silver Spring, MD 20910
(301) 713-2332

Address your questions regarding textile import regulations to:

International Trade Administration
Office of Textile and Apparel
14th and Constitution Ave. NW, Rm. 3100
Washington, DC 20230
(202) 482-5078, 482-3737

Address your questions regarding TFPIA to:

Federal Trade Commission (FTC)
Division of Enforcement
601 Pennsylvania Ave. NW
Washington, DC 20580
(202) 326-2996 (General)
(202) 326-2841 (Textile and wool products labeling)

Address your questions regarding textile quotas to:

Commissioner of Customs
Washington, DC 20229
(202) 566-8195

The following information numbers for U.S. Customs in Washington, DC provide recorded information. The Quota Branch numbers listed by country provide updated status reports on textile quotas from those countries. All area codes are (202).
General information: 927-5850

Quota Branch: China 927-6703; India 927-6705; Indonesia 927-6704; Japan 927-6706; Korea 927-6707; Macao 927-6709; Malaysia 927-6712; Mexico 927-6711; Pakistan 927-6714; Philippines 927-6713; Romania 927-6715; Singapore 927-6716; Sri Lanka 927-6708; Taiwan 927-6719; Thailand 927-6717; Turkey 927-6718; All others 927-5850.

Address your questions regarding importation of leather or animal gut products generally to the district or port director of Customs for you area. For addresses refer to"U.S. Customs District Offices" on page 62 or contact:

U.S. Customs Service
1301 Constitution Ave. NW
Washington, DC 20229
(202) 927-6724 (Information)
(202) 927-1000 (General)

Laws and Regulations

The following laws and regulations may be relevant to the importation of articles of leather or animal gut. The laws are contained in the United States Code (USC), and the regulations are published in the Code of Federal Regulations (CFR), both of which are available at larger public and law libraries. Copies of specific laws are also available from the United States Government Printing Office (address above).

7 USC 4801 et seq.
Pork Promotion, Research, and Consumer Information Act
This Act provides that each importer of porcine animal, pork, or pork product shall remit an assessment to Customs at the time the product is imported. See 7 CFR 1230.71 and 1230.110.

18 USC 42 et seq.
Importation of Animals, Birds, Fish, and Plants
This Act governs the importation of mammals, birds, fish, amphibia, and reptiles into the U.S. and authorizes U.S. Customs to enforce the import requirements.

21 USC 101 et seq.
Importation of Cattle and Quarantine
This Act provides for suspension of importation of animals to prevent the spread of disease, and for the quarantine of prohibited classes of animals. Importation of all animals described by the Act is prohibited except at certain designated ports. All animals are to be inspected on import or export.

21 USC 113a
Foot-and-Mouth Disease Memorandum of Understanding; Disease Research Act
This Act authorizes the study of animal disease and prohibits introduction of live foot-and-mouth disease virus into the U.S. except under certain defined circumstances. Customs enforces Agriculture restrictions and regulations.

21 USC 135
Establishment of International Animal Quarantine Stations
This Act authorizes the establishment of international quarantine stations. Customs enforces laws regarding importation of livestock.

42 USC 264 et seq.
Quarantine, Inspection, and Licensing
This Act restricts importations of dogs, cats, monkeys, psittacine birds, turtles, tortoises, and terrapins that do not comply with health standards. Customs enforces these restrictions. See 42 CFR 71.51 et seq.

19 CFR 12.24 and 12.26
Regulations for Animal and Animal Product Entry
These regulations provide for U.S. Customs entry declarations, documentation, and procedures for the animals and animal products subject to FWS and USDA regulations.

9 CFR Parts 91-96
Regulations on Animal Byproduct Quarantine Control
These regulations promulgated by the USDA prohibit the importation of animal products for use in industry unless the products meet certain processing standards and are not infected with certain diseases.

Convention on International Trade in Endangered Species of Wild Fauna and Flora (CITES)
This comprehensive wildlife treaty signed by over 100 countries, including the United States, regulates and in many cases prohibits commercial imports and exports of wild animal and plant species threatened by trade.

16 USC 1531
Endangered Species Act
This Act prohibits the import and export of species listed as endangered and most species listed as threatened. It is the U.S. law that implements CITES.

16 USC 742a et seq.
Fish and Wildlife Act
This Act regulates and bars the import of certain wild animals or birds and authorizes U.S. Customs to enforce the restrictions.

50 CFR Parts 10, 13, and 16
Regulations of FWS for Importing Wildlife and Fish
These regulations specify the animals and animal products subject to import prohibitions and restrictions.

16 USC 2401
Antarctic Conservation Act
This Act prohibits the importation, absent a special permit, of any flora or fauna native to Antarctica into the U.S.

16 USC 3371 et seq.
Lacey Act
This Act prohibits the import of species taken, possessed, transported, or sold in violation of the law of a foreign country.

16 USC 1361 et seq.
The Marine Mammal Protection Act
This Act prohibits the import of marine mammals and their parts and products. These species include whales, walruses, narwhals, seals, sea lions, sea otters, and polar bears.

16 USC 4201
The African Elephant Conservation Act
This Act prohibits imports of carved ivory products from any country and only permits imports of whole tusks from elephants legally hunted in certain African countries.

7 USC 1854
Textile Trade Agreements and Import Program Implementation
This Act limits the importation of textiles and textile products to the U.S. and their introduction to U.S. consumer.

19 CFR 12.130, 12.131
Regulations of Customs on Country of Origin and Import Entry
These Regulations define the country of origin to be specified on import documents and set forth the mandatory declarations to be submitted at the port of entry for each shipment of textile products.

15 USC 70 et seq.
Textile Fiber Products Identification Act
This Act prohibits false or deceptive labeling and advertising of textile products, requires the labeling of these products, and authorizes enforcement of labeling standards by Customs.

19 CFR 11.12b
Regulations of Customs on TFPIA Entry Labeling
These regulations set forth procedures, including invoice requirements, that U.S. Customs follows to enforce the Textile Fiber Products Identification Act with regard to the labeling of imported textile products.

16 CFR 303
Regulations of FTC on Textile Marking and Labeling
These regulations are promulgated and enforced by the FTC to ensure compliance with the Textile Fiber Products Identification Act.

15 USC 1191-1204
Flammable Fabrics Act
This Act authorizes the Consumer Product Safety Commission (CPSC) to set flammability standards for fabric sold to U.S. consumers.

16 CFR 1610 et seq.
Regulations and Standards for Flammable Fabrics
These regulations fix the textile flammability standards and allow for Customs to prohibit the importation of any products that fail to conform to the standards.

Principal Exporting Countries

The following listing includes samples of the main supplier nations of the products of this chapter. It is organized by HTSUS major heading. (Refer to "Customs Classification" above for the product codes.) Countries are listed in rank order of the value of products imported to the U.S. Statistics represent customs value entries for 1993 from the Bureau of Census, U.S. Department of Commerce.

4201—Taiwan, Mexico, United Kingdom, Germany, China, India, Japan, South Korea, France, Argentina

4202—China, South Korea, Taiwan, Italy, Thailand, France, India, Mexico, Philippines, Hong Kong

4203—China, South Korea, Indonesia, India, Philippines, Pakistan, Taiwan, Italy, Hong Kong, Mexico

4204—Thailand, United Kingdom, Switzerland, Japan, Slovenia, Italy, Taiwan, Australia, Germany, India

4205—Mexico, Thailand, Argentina, China, Canada, Brazil, Colombia, India, South Korea, Italy

4206—Australia, Dominican Rep., France, Mexico, Brazil, Japan, United Kingdom, Taiwan, Italy, Thailand

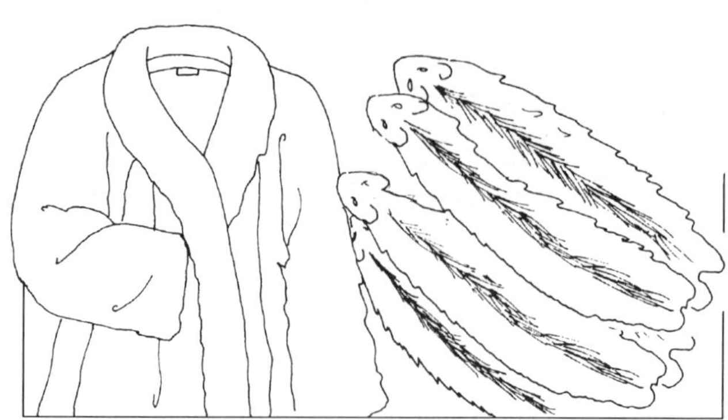

Chapter 43: Fur and Fur Products*

Full title: Furskins and Artificial Fur; Manufactures Thereof

This chapter relates to the importation of animal furs, artificial furs, and fur products, which are classified within Chapter 43 of the Harmonized Tariff Schedule of the United States (HTSUS). Specifically, it includes raw, tanned, and dressed furskins, articles made of furskins, artificial fur, and articles of artificial fur.

If you are interested in importing bird skins with feathers or down, refer to Commodity Index Chapters 5 or 67. The import requirements for most raw hides or skins covered with hair are discussed in Chapter 41. If you are interested in importing gloves of leather and furskin or artificial fur, you should read Chapter 42, which also covers leather articles. If you want to import wool or shorn animal hair, refer to Chapter 51. Requirements for importing fur footwear are in Chapter 64, fur headgear in Chapter 65, and parts for toys, games, and sports equipment in Chapter 95. Imitation furskins that are derived from weaving or knitting, instead of wool, hair, or other fibers attached to leather, are covered under Chapters 58 or 60.

Key Factors

The key factors in the importation of furskins and fur products are:

- Compliance with U.S. Fish and Wildlife Service (FWS) requirements (if the product is derived from endangered species or wildlife
- Entry at FWS-designated ports, and compliance with FWS and Customs advance notification and port-of-entry inspection requirements (if the products are derived from exotic wildlife or endangered species)
- Compliance with Federal Trade Commission (FTC) labeling requirements under the Fur Products Labeling Act (FPLA)
- Compliance with U.S. Department of Agriculture (USDA) APHIS import, quarantine, permit, and certification requirements (if the products are derived from domesticated animals)
- Entry at USDA-designated ports (if the products are derived from domesticated animals)

*IMPORTANT: Read the Commodity Index Introduction. It is the essential framework for understanding this section.

Although most importers use the services of a licensed customs broker in making their entries, and we recommend this practice, you should be aware of the regulatory, entry, and documentation issues involved in importing your product. You, as importer, are ultimately responsible for the fulfillment of any legal requirements applicable to your shipment.

General Considerations

Regulatory Agencies. The USDA regulates and inspects the importation of all products derived from animals, including furskins. The FWS, primarily under provisions of the U.S. Endangered Species Act (ESA) and the Convention on International Trade in Endangered Species of Wild Fauna and Flora (CITES), controls the importation of products derived from animals that are classified as exotic wildlife or endangered species. U.S. Customs enforces USDA and FWS requirements through entry documentation and restrictions.

Domesticated Animal Furskins and Fur Products. Importation of furskins and fur products of domesticated animals—such as sheep and lambs—and of animals bred in captivity for the purpose of providing furskins for commercial uses is generally straightforward. Products derived from such animals are subject to quarantine regulations, marking requirements, and processing standards. Shipments of these products are inspected at the port of arrival by the Animal and Plant Health Inspection Service (APHIS) of the USDA. Unless the shipment is in compliance with all applicable laws and regulations, it will be denied entry into the U.S. Some shipments may be restricted or prohibited completely.

Quarantine and Inspection. At the time of applying for a permit to import animals products subject to quarantine requirements, you will have to make reservations for space in an appropriate quarantine facility. Fees for quarantine reservations vary according to species, and are due and payable when the reservation is requested. Each shipment entering under USDA APHIS permit must comply in every detail with the permit's specifications. If your shipment is found to be aberrant in any way (such as entering at a port of entry other than the one specified in the permit), it will be refused entry.

Veterinary Certificates. A veterinary certificate, issued by a salaried veterinarian of the country of origin, stating that the animal products are free of applicable livestock diseases, must accompany each shipment. The specific information required on the certificate varies depending on the species you are importing and its country of origin. You must also present an importer's declaration, which states: l) port of entry; 2) importer's name and address; 3) broker's name and address; 4) livestock origin; 5) number, breed, species, and purpose of importation; 6) consignee's name and location of intended delivery.

APHIS-designated Quarantine Ports. The following listings are APHIS-designated ports with adequate quarantine facilities available for the import of livestock and livestock products. With very few exceptions, all shipments of livestock and livestock products must enter at one of these designated ports:

Air and Ocean Ports: Los Angeles, CA; Miami, FL; Honolulu, HI; and Newburgh, NY.

Canadian Border Land Ports: Eastport, ID; Houlton and Jackman, MN; Detroit, Port Huron, and Sault Ste. Marie, MI; Opheim, Raymond, and Sweetgrass, MT; Alexandria Bay, Buffalo, and Champlain, NY; Dunseith, Pembina, and Portal, ND; Derby Line and Highgate Springs, VT; Blaine, Lynden, Oroville, and Sumas, WA.

Mexican Border Land Ports: Brownsville, Hidalgo, Laredo, Eagle Pass, Del Rio, Presidio, and El Paso, TX; Douglas, Naco, Nogales, Sasabe, and San Luis, AZ; Calexico and San Ysidro, CA; Antelope Wells and Columbus, NM.

Limited Ports. These ports have facilities for the entry of livestock or livestock products that do not appear to require restraint and holding inspection facilities: Anchorage and Fairbanks, AK; San Diego, CA; Denver, CO; Jacksonville, St. Petersburg, Clearwater, and Tampa, FL; Atlanta, GA; Chicago, IL; New Orleans, LA; Portland, MN; Baltimore, MD; Boston, MA; Minneapolis, MN; Great Falls, MT; Portland, OR; San Juan, PR; Galveston and Houston, TX; and Seattle, Spokane, and Tacoma, WA.

The ports listed above have been designated as quarantine stations. The USDA Administrator has authority to designate other ports as quarantine stations as needed.

Exotic and Endangered Species. The FWS enforces a complex set of laws and regulations (see 50 CFR 1 et seq.) pertaining to wildlife and wildlife product importation. These laws include the international Convention on International Trade in Endangered Species of Wild Fauna and Flora (CITES), the Endangered Species Act (ESA), and a number of other U.S. laws, such as the African Elephant Conservation Act (AECA), Marine Mammal Protection Act (MMPA), Migratory Bird Treaty Act (MBTA), Eagle Protection Act (EPA), and the Lacey Act (LA). Most foreign countries also have their own domestic measures, and you will need to meet the requirements of the country of export in addition to U.S. requirements. For more information, contact the FWS Office of Management Authority (OMA) (see addresses at end of this chapter).

Certain types of furskins and fur products are entirely prohibited, others are allowed entry only under permit and/or license, and still others are allowed entry only for specific noncommercial purposes. When applying for a permit, you must satisfy the requirements of all laws under which the species is protected. The following briefly describes the two major laws governing importation of protected wildlife products into the U.S. This discussion is not comprehensive or exhaustive. If you wish to import furskins or fur products of exotic or endangered animals, you should always contact the FWS (see addresses at end of this chapter) with species information before making any transactions.

CITES. Over 100 nations participate in the Convention on International Trade in Endangered Species of Wild Fauna and Flora (CITES) treaty, which took effect in May 1977. The degree of protection afforded to a species depends on which of the three CITES appendices contains the name of that species. Documentation required for import varies depending on the species, and the CITES section where it is listed. The CITES export documentation from the country of origin is always required. If you are importing a CITES-listed species from a country that does not participate in the treaty, you must still obtain from that nation documents that contain all the information normally required in CITES export permits.

Appendix I. This appendix lists species deemed presently threatened with extinction (e.g., orangutan, chinchilla, gray whale). Importation of Appendix I species for commercial purposes is prohibited. You must have two permits to import these species: one from the U.S., which must be obtained first, and one from the exporting country. If you are importing Appendix I species taken in the marine environment and outside the jurisdiction of any country or state, you must have an Introduction from the Sea Permit.

Appendix II. This appendix lists species that are not presently threatened with extinction but may become threatened if their trade is not regulated (e.g., brown bear, musk deer, elephant seal). There are no restrictions on the purpose of import, provided it is not detrimental to the survival of the species. You will need an export permit or reexport certificate from the exporting country. If you are importing Appendix II species taken in the marine environment and outside the jurisdiction of any country or state, you will need an Introduction from the Sea Permit.

Appendix III. This appendix lists species for which any CITES member country has domestic regulations "for the purpose of preventing or restricting exploitation, and as needing the cooperation of other Parties in control of trade." For example, Canada lists the walrus, and Nepal lists the blackbuck antelope. Three different types of documents are issued for Appendix III species: 1) Export Permit: Issued for specimens that originated in a country that listed the species on Appendix III; 2) Certificate of Origin: Issued by any country other than the listing country if the wildlife in question originated in that country; 3) Reexport Certificate: Issued for the export of Appendix III specimens that were previously imported into the U.S.

Exemptions. Under certain conditions, Certificates of Exemption may be issued for the importation of wildlife products listed under CITES. Exceptions are allowed for shipmentS of wildlife transiting a country under Customs bond, shipments between U.S. states or territories, and certain personal or household effects. For information, contact FWS (see addresses at end of this chapter).

Permit Applications. Applications for CITES permits and certificates are available from the FWS Office of Management Authority (see addresses at end of this chapter). You will need to fill out the FWS Standard Permit Application **(Form 3-200)** and provide certain information specifically required under CITES. You should submit your application at least 60 days before the date you wish the permit to take effect. FWS charges processing fees for CITES applications.

ESA. The U.S. Endangered Species Act (ESA) was passed on December 28, 1973, to prevent the extinction of many species of animals and plants and to protect their habitats. By definition, an "endangered species" is any animal or plant listed by regulation as being in danger of extinction. A "threatened species" is any animal or plant likely to become endangered within the foreseeable future. The U.S. List of Endangered and Threatened Wildlife and Plants includes native and foreign species.

Permits. ESA's import provisions prohibit the import or export of any endangered or threatened species or products derived from them without one of the following permits from the FWS Federal Wildlife Permit Office (FWPO):

> *Endangered Species Permits:* This permit is issued for importation for purposes of 1) scientific research; 2) enhancement of propagation or survival of the species; or 3) incidental taking.
>
> *Threatened Species Permits:* This permit is issued for importation for purposes of 1) scientific research; 2) enhancement of propagation or survival of the species; 3) zoological, horticultural, or botanical exhibition; 4) education purposes; 5) special purposes consistent with ESA purposes and policy; or 6) incidental taking.

Permit Exemptions. A few imports of endangered species products are exempt from the ESA permit requirements. For example, if a species is listed as threatened or as an experimental population, special rules may allow otherwise prohibited activities. Some species covered by special rules include certain kangaroos, several primates, the grizzly bear, gray wolf, and leopard. If you are unsure as to the exemption status of your import, contact FWS (see addresses at end of this chapter).

FWS Import Licenses. With some exceptions, persons engaged in the business of importing wildlife products valued in excess of $25,000 per year must be licensed by the FWS. If your annual importations are valued at less than $25,000, or if you qualify for another exemption from licensing, you are still responsible for keeping thorough records of all wildlife transactions and of making these records available to FWS officers if necessary. For a full description of exemptions from licensing, and of recordkeeping requirements, contact the Fish and Wildlife Service (see addresses at end of this chapter) or see 50 CFR 14.

Procedures at Port of Entry. At least 72 hours before your shipment is due to arrive at a designated port, you should notify U.S. Customs and the FWS inspectors of its expected arrival. The FWS conducts port-of-entry shipment inspections on a case-by-case basis, as determined by the inspection agent after looking at the entry paperwork. Both FWS and Customs may inspect your shipment to verify compliance with all of the legal requirements for entry. Any documentation required by the laws governing your import must be submitted by the time of entry. You must present an FWS Wildlife Declaration **Form 3-177**, available at the port of entry, with every shipment, regardless of any other paperwork required. Customs will not release your shipment until the import declaration has been signed off by an FWS agent.

Designated Ports. Shipments of wildlife products are restricted to designated U.S. ports of entry. All wildlife shipments must enter and leave through one of the ports listed in 50 CFR 14.12. Currently, ten ports are designated: New York, NY; Miami, FL; New Orleans, LA; Dallas/Ft. Worth, TX; Los Angeles, CA; San Francisco, CA; Chicago, IL; Seattle, WA; Honolulu, HI; and Portland, OR. If special circumstances prevent you from making your entry at a designated port, you will need to obtain an Exception to Designated Port Permit from the FWS Divisions of Law Enforcement (see addresses at end of this chapter).

You may import fur and fur products derived from animals bred in captivity for the purpose of providing furskins for commercial uses, without permit or special paperwork. These products are not restricted to FWS-designated ports. Certain fur products are subject to the requirements of the Fur Products Labeling Act (FPLA), administered by the Federal Trade Commission (FTC), and enforced by U.S. Customs at the port of entry. It is your responsibility as importer to make sure that your shipment complies in every detail with FPLA requirements. Customs entry is contingent upon proper labeling.

If Customs finds your import shipment to be mislabeled, you will be allowed to relabel the products under Customs supervision, as long as the district director is satisfied that your labeling error or omission did not involve fraud or willful neglect. If your shipment is discovered after entry to have been mislabeled, it will be recalled to Customs custody at your expense, unless you can satisfy the district director that your products have since been brought into compliance. You will be held responsible for all expenses incurred in bringing your shipment into compliance, including compensation and expenses related to Customs supervision.

Fraudulent violations of FPLA will result in seizure of the shipment. Shipments already released from Customs custody and later found to be in fraudulent violation of FPLA will be ordered to be redelivered to Customs. Customs reports all cases of fraudulent violation to the FTC in Washington, DC.

Specific-Country Import Regulations

There are special provisions for livestock products originating in Canada, Mexico, Central America, and the West Indies. These provisions vary according to species, and include such things as permit or quarantine waivers, special quarantine restrictions, specific ports of entry for specific types of livestock products, and provisions for transit across the U.S. only. One general requirement applicable across the board is that two import declarations (see above) must be presented, instead of only one. For more details see appropriate headings in 9 CFR 92, or contact the Animal and Plant Health Inspection Service.

Customs Classification

For customs purposes, animal furs, artificial furs, and fur products are classified under Chapter 43 of the HTSUS. This chapter is broken into major headings, which are further divided into subheadings, and often sub-subheadings, each of which has its own HTSUS classification number. For example, the HTSUS number for whole silver, black, or platinum fox skins is 4301.60.30, indicating it is a sub-subcategory of fox, whole, with or without head, tail, or paws (4301.60.00), which is a subcategory of the major heading, raw furskins (4301.00.00). There are 43 major headings within Chapter 43.

4301—Raw furskins (including heads, tails, paws, and other pieces or cuttings, suitable for furriers' use), other than raw hides and skins of heading 4101, 4102, or 4103

4302—Tanned or dressed furskins (including heads, tails, paws, and other pieces or cuttings), unassembled, or assembled (without the addition of other materials) other than those of heading 4303

4303—Articles of apparel, clothing accessories, and other articles of furskin

4304—Artificial fur and articles thereof

For more details regarding classifications of the specific product you are interested in importing, consult a customs broker, the appropriate commodity specialist at your nearest customs port, or the HTSUS. HTSUS is available for purchase from the U.S. Government Printing Office (see addresses at end of this chapter), and may be found in larger public libraries. Refer to "Classification—Liquidation" on page 207 for a general discussion of customs classification.

Sample Import Duties

Import duties will vary depending on the HTSUS classification of your product. Therefore, to determine the correct amount of duties, your product must be properly classified under the HTSUS. The following sample duties are taken from the duty listings for HTSUS Chapter 43 products.

Raw furskins (4301): free, except for raw fur skins of silver, black or platinum fox (4301.60.30): 8%; tanned or dressed furskins of mink (4302.11.00): 2.1%; of rabbit (4302.12.00): 3.7%; of lamb (4302.13.00): 3.1%; articles of apparel and clothing accessories (4303.10.00): 5.8%; artificial fur and articles thereof (4304.00.00): 11%.

Entry and Documentation

The entry of merchandise is a two-part process consisting of 1) filing the documentation necessary to determine whether merchandise may be released from Customs custody, and 2) filing the documents that contain information for duty assessment and statistical purposes. In certain instances, all documents must be filed and accepted by Customs prior to release of the goods. Unless you have been granted an extension, you must file entry documents at a location specified by the district or area director within five working days of your shipment's date of arrival at a U.S. port of entry. These include a number of standard documents required by Customs for any entry, and:

- FWS Import Declaration **Form 3-177**, original and 3 copies (if the products are derived from exotic wildlife or endangered species)
- FWS permit or import documentation (if the products are derived from exotic wildlife or endangered species)
- Permits or certificates required under CITES, ESA, and any other regulations applicable to the particular shipment (if the products are derived from exotic wildlife or endangered species)

- Certificates of export, origin, sanitation, veterinary inspection, and other conditions from the country of origin or export, as required by Customs, FWS, or USDA
- USDA importer's declaration (if the products are derived from domesticated animals)
- Copy of air waybill or bill of lading
- Copy of invoice (pro forma invoice if shipment is noncommercial)

After you present the entry, Customs may examine your shipment or may waive examination. The shipment is then released provided no legal or regulatory violations have been noted. You must then file entry summary documentation and deposit estimated duties at a designated customhouse within 10 working days of your shipment's release. For a detailed description of entry procedures, standard documentation, and informal entry, refer to "Entry Process" on page 182.

Entry Invoice. The entry invoice for a shipment of fur or fur products must specify the following: 1) name or names (as set forth in the Fur Products Name Guide (16 CFR 301.0)) of the animal or animals that produced the fur, and such qualifying statements as may be required pursuant to section 7(c) of the Fur Products Labeling Act (15 USC 69e(c)); 2) a statement that the fur product contains or is composed of used fur, when such is the fact; 3) a statement that the fur product contains or is composed of bleached, dyed, or otherwise artificially colored fur, when such is the fact; 4) a statement that the fur product is composed in whole or in substantial part of paws, tails, bellies, or waste fur, when such is the fact; 5) name and address of the manufacturer of the fur product; 6) name of the country of origin of the furs or those contained in the fur product.

If a fur product shipment valued at over $500 and subject to the FPLA is offered for entry, special information must appear on the entry invoice. This information is intended to facilitate Customs monitoring and enforcement of the FPLA. It is identical to that required by the FPLA on labeling (see "Marking and Labeling Requirements" below).

Prohibitions and Restrictions

Animal Products. Animal products are subject to quarantine if they arrive from certain countries that are known to have specific infectious diseases. These countries are listed in 9 CFR 94. If a USDA inspector determines that a shipment is infected with anthrax, foot-and-mouth disease, rinderpest, or bovine spongiform encephalopathy, entry will be denied.

Exotic and Endangered Species. Hides of certain animals are restricted or prohibited from importation because of species status under the CITES, ESA, or another U.S. law. For example, importation of species listed in CITES Appendix I for commercial purposes is prohibited. Prohibitions and restrictions may additionally be imposed by the law of the exporting country. You are legally responsible for fulfilling the requirements of all of them, as well as any laws of the country of export. If you import, or attempt to import, a product in violation of a wildlife or endangered species law, even if you are not aware of the violation, your product may be seized, you may be charged substantial fines, and you could be imprisoned.

Importers should be particularly cautious in importing the following wildlife products, which are prohibited from import into the U.S. [reprinted with permission by World Wildlife Fund from its brochure: "Buyer Beware"]:

> Furs from the larger spotted cats, such as jaguar, leopard, snow leopard, and tiger, and from most smaller cats, such as ocelot, margay, and tiger cat, cannot enter the United States legally, nor can furs of marine mammals like seals and polar bears.

Marking and Labeling Requirements

Animal Products. Containers of animal furskins and fur products must be marked with the country of origin—that is, the country where the animal was located. If these items are quarantined at the port of arrival, marks and signs are required on shipping documents and any mode of transport used to move the product while under restrictions (9 CFR 95.25).

Wildlife Furskins and Fur Products. All wildlife shipments must be marked on the outside of the container with the names and addresses of the exporter and importer, an accurate identification of the species, and the numbers of each species in the container.

Fur Products Labeling Act (FPLA). You should be sure that any article of wearing apparel made in whole or in part of fur that you are importing into the U.S. is tagged, labeled, or otherwise clearly marked to show the following FPLA-required information: 1) name of the manufacturer or importer. If you have an FTC-issued registered identification number, you may use that number instead of your name.; 2) the name or names of the animal or animals that produced the fur, as set forth in the Fur Products Name Guide, and as permitted under the rules and regulations; 3) that the fur product contains used or damaged fur when such is the fact; 4) that the fur product is bleached, dyed, or otherwise artificially colored when such is the fact; 5) that the fur product is composed in whole or in substantial part of paws, tails, bellies, or waste fur when such is the fact; 6) the name of the country of origin of any imported furs contained in a fur product.

This discussion does not include all FPLA requirements. The regulations are extensive and detailed. They specify such things as arrangement of required information; allowable wording and punctuation on required labels; size; means of attachment and position of labeling; requirements for labeling articles made of more than one type of fur, or of fur and other materials; labeling of multi-unit garments; labeling of samples; invoicing; recordkeeping, etc. If you are interested in importing fur garments, you should contact the Federal Trade Commission (address above) for the booklet entitled *Rules and Regulations under the Fur Products Labeling Act*, available from that agency free of charge.

If Customs finds your import shipment to be mislabeled, you will be allowed to relabel the products under Customs supervision, as long as the district director is satisfied that your labeling error or omission did not involve fraud or willful neglect. If your shipment is discovered after entry to have been mislabeled, it will be recalled to Customs custody at your expense, unless you can satisfy the district director that your products have since been brought into compliance. You will be held responsible for all expenses incurred in bringing your shipment into compliance, including compensation and expenses related to Customs supervision.

Fraudulent violations of FPLA will result in seizure of the shipment. Shipments already released from Customs custody and later found to be in fraudulent violation of FPLA will be ordered to be redelivered to Customs. Customs reports all cases of fraudulent violation to the FTC in Washington, DC.

Exemptions. Articles made of new fur of which the cost or manufacturer's selling price does not exceed $7 are not subject to FPLA.

For a general discussion of U.S. Customs marking and labeling requirements, refer to "Marking: Country of Origin" on page 215 and "Special Marking Requirements" on page 217.

Shipping Considerations

You will need to ensure that your goods are packaged and shipped with care so that they pass smoothly through Customs and arrive in good condition. You are responsible for ensuring that the shipment is in compliance with all applicable government regulations for packaging and shipping. In most instances, you should not leave these arrangements solely to the discretion of your supplier. Careful preparation of the cargo and selection of the mode of transport can be essential to a cost-effective, timely delivery of undamaged goods. We strongly advise you to consult your shipping representative, insurance agent, or freight broker for advice on packing and shipping. Refer also to the major tab section "Packing/Shipping/Insurance" for a general discussion of packing and shipping.

Animal furs, artificial furs, and fur products may be shipped in bulk, bags, cartons, or other types of containers, depending on the type of product. General considerations include protection from contamination, weather, and pests. Containers should be constructed so as to be safe for handling during transport.

Publications Available

The following publication is an excellent source of information on labeling requirements for fur products.

Rules and Regulations under the Fur Products Labeling Act

This publication is available free of charge on request from the FTC. We recommend that anyone interested in importing fur products who is not familiar with the regulation obtain a copy of this booklet.

The following books are especially pertinent to Endangered Species regulations and wildlife trade. They are published by and available from World Wildlife Fund at the address below.

International Wildlife Trade: Whose Business Is It? by Sarah Fitzgerald. Paperback $25.00; cloth $40.00, 459 pp, ISBN 0-942635-10-8.

The Wildlife Trade Laws of Asia and Oceania by David Nichols, Kathryn Fuller, Erica McShane-Caluzi and Eva Eckinrode. 1991. Loose-leaf binder. Order Code NIAO. $50.00.

Latin American Wildlife Trade Laws (2d ed.) Kathryn S. Fuller, Byron Swift, Amanda Jorgenson, and Amie Brautigam. 1985. 418 pp. Loose-leaf binder. Order Code FULA (English language). #35.00.

To order these publications, or to request a catalog of related publications, contact:

World Wildlife Fund
1250 24th Street NW
Washington, DC 20037
(202) 293-4800

The *Harmonized Tariff Schedule of the United States* (HTSUS) is available from:

Government Printing Office (GPO)
Superintendent of Documents
Washington, DC 20402
(202) 512-1800 (Order line)
(202) 512-0000 (General)

The USGPO also has copies of specific laws available for purchase. The USGPO accepts credit card orders over the phone, as well as mail orders paid by credit card, a check drawn on a U.S. bank, or an international money order.

Relevant Government Agencies

Address your questions regarding USDA requirements for the importation of domesticated animal products to:

U.S. Department of Agriculture (USDA)
Animal and Plant Health Inspection Service (APHIS)
Veterinary Services (VS)
Import-Export Products Staff
Federal Building, Room 756
6505 Belcrest Road
Hyattsville, MD 20782
(301) 436-7885

Address your questions regarding the importation of products of exotic or endangered animals to:

U.S. Fish and Wildlife Service (FWS)
Office of Management Authority
4401 N. Fairfax Drive, Room 432
Arlington, VA 22203
(703) 358-2095
(800) 358-2104, (703) 358-2104 (Permits office)

National Marine Fisheries Service (NMFS)
Office of Marine Mammals and Endangered Species
1335 East West Highway
Silver Spring, MD 20910
(301) 713-2332

Address your questions regarding FPLA requirements to:

Federal Trade Commission (FTC)
Division of Enforcement
601 Pennsylvania Ave. NW
Washington, DC 20580
(202) 326-2996 (General)
(202) 326-2841 (Textile and wool products labeling)

Address your questions regarding importation of furskins, artificial furs, and fur products generally to the district or port director of Customs for you area. For addresses refer to"U.S. Customs District Offices" on page 62 or contact:

U.S. Customs Service
1301 Constitution Ave. NW
Washington, DC 20229
(202) 927-6724 (Information)
(202) 927-1000 (General)

Laws and Regulations

The following laws and regulations may be relevant to the importation of furskins, artificial furs, and fur products. The laws are contained in the United States Code (USC), and the regulations are published in the Code of Federal Regulations (CFR), both of which are available at larger public and law libraries. Copies of specific laws are also available from the United States Government Printing Office (address above).

15 USC 69-69j
Fur Products Labeling Act
This Act prohibits false or deceptive labeling (misbranding) and false advertising of fur products. It also requires the labeling of fur products to indicate composition and specific information that must be included on the invoices provided at the time of importation.

16 CFR 301 et seq.; 19 CFR 11.12.a
Labeling of Fur Products Regulations
These regulations contain the FTC rules and procedures for labeling fur products and the procedures for Customs to enforce the labeling requirements.

18 USC 42 et seq.
Importation of Animals, Birds, Fish, and Plants
This Act governs the importation of mammals, birds, fish, amphibia, and reptiles into the U.S. and authorizes U.S. Customs to enforce the import requirements.

21 USC 135
Establishment of International Animal Quarantine Stations
This Act authorizes the establishment of international quarantine stations. Customs enforces laws regarding importation of livestock.

42 USC 264 et seq.
Quarantine, Inspection, and Licensing
This Act restricts importations of dogs, cats, monkeys, psittacine birds, turtles, tortoises, and terrapins that do not comply with health standards. Customs enforces these restrictions. See 42 CFR 71.51 et seq.

19 CFR 12.24 and 12.26
Regulations for Animal and Animal Product Entry
These regulations provide for U.S. Customs entry declarations, documentation, and procedures for the animals and animal products subject to FWS and USDA regulations.

9 CFR Parts 91-96
Regulations on Animal Byproduct Quarantine Control
These regulations promulgated by the USDA prohibit the importation of animal products for use in industry unless the products meet certain processing standards and are not infected with certain diseases.

Convention on International Trade in Endangered Species of Wild Fauna and Flora (CITES)
This comprehensive wildlife treaty signed by over 100 countries, including the United States, regulates and in many cases prohibits commercial imports and exports of wild animal and plant species threatened by trade.

16 USC 1531
Endangered Species Act
This Act prohibits the import and export of species listed as endangered and most species listed as threatened. It is the U.S. law that implements CITES.

16 USC 742a et seq.
Fish and Wildlife Act
This Act regulates and bars the import of certain wild animals or birds and authorizes U.S. Customs to enforce the restrictions.

50 CFR Parts 10, 13, and 16
Regulations of FWS for Importing Wildlife and Fish
These regulations specify the animals and animal products subject to import prohibitions and restrictions.

16 USC 2401
Antarctic Conservation Act
This Act prohibits the importation, absent a special permit, of any flora or fauna native to Antarctica into the U.S.

16 USC 3371 et seq.
Lacey Act
This Act prohibits the import of species taken, possessed, transported, or sold in violation of the law of a foreign country.

16 USC 1361 et seq.
The Marine Mammal Protection Act
This Act prohibits the import of marine mammals and their parts and products. These species include whales, walruses, narwhals, seals, sea lions, sea otters, and polar bears.

Principal Exporting Countries

The following listing includes samples of the main supplier nations of the products of this chapter. It is organized by HTSUS major heading. (Refer to "Customs Classification" above for the product codes.) Countries are listed in rank order of the value of products imported to the U.S. Statistics represent customs value entries for 1993 from the Bureau of Census, U.S. Department of Commerce.

4301—Canada, Denmark, Finland, Russia, Netherlands, Germany, Belgium, Argentina, Norway, Sweden

4302—New Zealand, Canada, France, Spain, Australia, Portugal, Argentina, Iceland, Brazil, Greece

4303—Canada, Hong Kong, China, Greece, Italy, South Korea, Uruguay, Argentina, Brazil, Finland

4304—Germany, France, Canada, China, South Korea, United Kingdom, Italy, Taiwan, Australia, Mexico

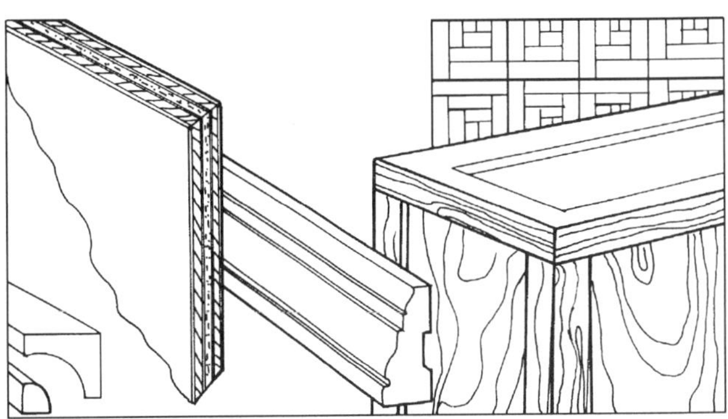

Chapter 44: Wood and Wood Products*

Full tile: Wood and Articles of Wood; Wood Charcoal

This chapter relates to the importation of wood and wood products, which are classified under Chapter 44 of the Harmonized Tariff Schedule of the United States (HTSUS). Specifically, it includes fuel wood; wood charcoal; rough wood; hoopwood; poles and stakes; wood wool and flour; railway and tramway ties; wood sawn, chipped, sliced, and peeled; veneers, plywoods, particle boards, fiberboards, and laminates; densified wood; wooden frames; wooden packing materials; coopers' products; tool and tool parts; carpentry and builders' joinery items; tableware and kitchenware; wood marquetry and inlaid articles; and small wooden articles (e.g., clothes hangers, clothespins, canoe paddles, wooden blind slats, and toothpicks).

If you are interested in importing wood pieces for perfumery, pharmaceutical, insecticidal, fungicidal, or similar purposes, you should refer to Commodity Index Chapter 12. The importing of bamboo and plaiting materials is covered in Chapter 14, which also includes chipped, shaved, ground, or powdered wood used for dyeing or tanning. For import requirements related to activated charcoal, refer to Chapter 38. If you are interested in importing a particular manufactured wood product, you should refer to the Commodity Index chapter that covers that product. For example, import requirements for baskets and wickerware are in Chapter 46, footwear parts are in Chapter 64, umbrellas and walking canes are in Chapter 66, imitation jewelry is in Chapter 71, wood cases, covers, and other parts used in machinery are in Chapters 84 through 89, clock cases are in Chapter 91, musical instruments are in Chapter 92, firearm parts are in Chapter 93, furniture is in Chapter 94, toys, games, and sports equipment are in Chapter 95, and works of art are in Chapter 97.

Key Factors

The key factors in the importation of wood and wood products are:

- Compliance with U.S. Department of Agriculture (USDA) port-of-entry inspections and other requirements
- Compliance with Federal Plant Pest Act
- Compliance with Plant Quarantine Act
- Compliance with U.S. Federal Trade Commission (FTC) and Consumer Product Safety Commission (CPSC) standards (if the product will be marketed to consumers)

*IMPORTANT: Read the Commodity Index Introduction. It is the essential framework for understanding this chapter.

- Submission of Canadian Government Export Notice (if importing softwood lumber from Canada)
- Compliance with invoice requirements (if importing certain types of lumber)
- Compliance with Fish and Wildlife Service (FWS) license, permit, country-of-origin permit, import documentation, and recordkeeping requirements (if the products are derived from endangered species)
- Entry at FWS-designated ports, and compliance with FWS and Customs advance notification and port-of-entry inspection requirements (if the products are derived from endangered species)

Although most importers use the services of a licensed customs broker in making their entries, and we recommend this practice, you should be aware of the regulatory, entry, and documentation issues involved in importing your product. You, as importer, are ultimately responsible for the fulfillment of any legal requirements applicable to your shipment.

General Considerations

Regulatory Agencies. The USDA administers applicable provisions of the Plant Quarantine Act (PQA), which are designed to prevent the introduction into the U.S. of any plant pest or disease potentially harmful to U.S. agriculture. The FWS, primarily under provisions of the U.S. Endangered Species Act (ESA) and the Convention on International Trade in Endangered Species of Wild Fauna and Flora (CITES), controls the importation of products derived from plants that are classified as endangered species. The FTC and CPSC sets standards for products being sold to U.S. consumers. U.S. Customs enforces USDA and FWS requirements through entry documentation and restrictions.

Lumber and Other Raw Wood. Shipments of lumber and raw wood are inspected at the port of arrival by the USDA's Animal and Plant Health Inspection Service (APHIS). Entry may be denied for noncompliance with the regulations, and the shipment could be seized, quarantined, destroyed, treated, or otherwise dealt with at the discretion of the inspector. Some shipments may be restricted or prohibited completely. APHIS inspectors also enforce FWS requirements under the ESA and the CITES. Lumber derived from an endangered species may be prohibited, or may require export and/or import permits (see below). You are responsible for ensuring that your shipment is either not derived from listed species, or if it is, that you have the appropriate import authorization.

Elm Logs and Lumber. The import of elm logs and elm lumber with bark attached requires a permit from AHPIS.

Wood Products. If you wish to import wood products, for the most part you will not need permits or other special paperwork. However, goods classified as hazardous consumer products must comply with consumer standards to be sold in the U.S. (see below) and goods derived from endangered tree species are subject to complex import restrictions (see below).

Hazardous Consumer Products. Under the Federal Hazardous Substances Act (FHSA) and the Consumer Products Safety Act (CPSA), a wood product that is flammable or combustible and that is intended for the consumer market is a hazardous substance. To be sold in the U.S., the product must be in compliance with FTC and CPSC standards. The CPSC does not require permits, special invoicing, limited entry, licenses, or any special approval process for importing hazardous consumer products into the U.S. However, if you are importing these types of products, you are responsible for making sure that they meet all applicable FHSA and CPSA requirements. There are detailed regulations regarding testing and labeling of hazardous products. The Commission's enforcement posture regarding compliance with labeling and product safety standards changes as new facts become available. Contact the CPSC (see addresses at end of this chapter) for specific requirements on the consumer product you are considering importing.

Substantial Product Hazard Reports. Defect-reporting is required for products covered under the CPSA. The law requires every manufacturer, distributor, or retailer of such products, who obtains information that reasonably supports the conclusion that such products fail to comply with an applicable consumer product safety rule, or contain a defect that could create a substantial product hazard, to immediately inform the CPSC of the potential violation or defect. A firm's willful failure to make a Substantial Product Hazard Report can result in litigation by the CPSC.

Exotic and Endangered Species. The FWS enforces a complex set of laws and regulations (see 50 CFR 1 et seq.) pertaining to endangered species product importation. These laws include the CITES, ESA, and a number of other U.S. laws, such as the Lacey Act (LA). Most foreign countries also have their own domestic measures, and you will need to meet the requirements of the country of export in addition to U.S. requirements. For more information, contact the FWS Office of Management Authority (OMA) (see addresses at end of this chapter).

Certain types of woods are entirely prohibited, others are allowed entry only under permit and/or license, and still others are allowed entry only for specific noncommercial purposes. When applying for a permit, you must satisfy the requirements of all laws under which the species is protected. The following briefly describes the two major laws governing importation of protected products into the U.S. This discussion is not comprehensive or exhaustive. If you wish to import endangered species, you should always contact the FWS (see addresses at end of this chapter) with species information before making any transactions.

CITES. Over 100 nations participate in CITES, which took effect in May 1977. The degree of protection afforded to a species depends on which of the three CITES appendices contains the name of that species. Documentation required for import varies depending on the species, and the CITES section where it is listed. The CITES export documentation from the country of origin is always required. If you are importing a CITES-listed species from a country that does not participate in the treaty, you must still obtain from that nation documents that contain all the information normally required in CITES export permits.

Appendix I. This appendix lists species deemed presently threatened with extinction. Importation of Appendix I species for commercial purposes is prohibited. You must have two permits to import these species: one from the U.S., which must be obtained first, and one from the exporting country.

Appendix II. This appendix lists species that are not presently threatened with extinction but may become threatened if their trade is not regulated (e.g., boojum tree). There are no restrictions on the purpose of import, provided it is not detrimental to the survival of the species. You will need an export permit or reexport certificate from the exporting country.

Appendix III. This appendix lists species for which any CITES member country has domestic regulations "for the purpose of preventing or restricting exploitation, and as needing the cooperation of other Parties in control of trade." For example, Nepal lists several varieties of magnolia. Three different types of documents are issued for Appendix III species: 1) Export Permit: Issued for specimens that originated in a country that listed the species on Appendix III; 2) Certificate of Origin: Issued by any country other than the listing country if the species in question originated in that country; 3) Reexport Certificate: Issued for the export of Appendix III specimens that were previously imported into the U.S.

Exemptions. Under certain conditions, Certificates of Exemption may be issued for the importation of endangered species products listed under CITES. Exceptions are allowed for shipments of products transiting a country under Customs bond, shipments between U.S. states or territories, and certain personal or household effects. For information, contact FWS (see addresses at end of this chapter).

Permit Applications. Applications for CITES permits and certificates are available from the FWS Office of Management Authority (see addresses at end of this chapter). You will need to fill out the FWS Standard Permit Application **(Form 3-200)** and provide certain information specifically required under CITES. You should submit your application at least 60 days before the date you wish the permit to take effect. FWS charges processing fees for CITES applications.

ESA. The U.S. Endangered Species Act (ESA) was passed on December 28, 1973, to prevent the extinction of many species of animals and plants and to protect their habitats. By definition, an "endangered species" is any animal or plant listed by regulation as being in danger of extinction. A "threatened species" is any animal or plant likely to become endangered within the foreseeable future. The U.S. List of Endangered and Threatened Wildlife and Plants includes native and foreign species.

Permits. ESA's import provisions prohibit the import or export of any endangered or threatened species or products derived from them without one of the following permits from the FWS Federal Wildlife Permit Office (FWPO):

> *Endangered Species Permits:* This permit is issued for importation for purposes of 1) scientific research; 2) enhancement of propagation or survival of the species; or 3) incidental taking.
>
> *Threatened Species Permits:* This permit is issued for importation for purposes of 1) scientific research; 2) enhancement of propagation or survival of the species; 3) zoological, horticultural, or botanical exhibition; 4) education purposes; 5) special purposes consistent with ESA purposes and policy; or 6) incidental taking.

Permit Exemptions. A few imports of endangered species products are exempt from the ESA permit requirements. For example, if a species is listed as threatened or as an experimental population, special rules may allow otherwise prohibited activities. If you are unsure as to the exemption status of your import, contact FWS (see addresses at end of this chapter).

FWS Import Licenses. With some exceptions, persons engaged in the business of importing endangered species products valued in excess of $25,000 per year must be licensed by the FWS. If your annual importations are valued at less than $25,000, or if you qualify for another exemption from licensing, you are still responsible for keeping thorough records of all transactions and of making these records available to FWS officers if necessary. For a full description of exemptions from licensing, and of recordkeeping requirements, contact the FWS (see addresses at end of this chapter) or see 50 CFR 14.

Procedures at Port of Entry. At least 72 hours before your shipment is due to arrive at a designated port, you should notify U.S. Customs and the FWS inspectors of its expected arrival. The FWS conducts port-of-entry shipment inspections on a case-by-case basis, as determined by the inspection agent after looking at the entry paperwork. Both FWS and Customs may inspect your shipment to verify compliance with all of the legal requirements for entry. Any documentation required by the laws governing your import must be submitted by the time of entry. You must present an FWS Wildlife Declaration **Form 3-177**, available at the port of entry, with every shipment, regardless of any other paperwork required. Customs will not release your shipment until the import declaration has been signed off by an FWS agent.

Designated Ports. Shipments of endangered species products are restricted to designated U.S. ports of entry. All shipments must enter and leave through one of the ports listed in 50 CFR 14.12. Currently, 10 ports are designated: New York, NY; Miami, FL; New Orleans, LA; Dallas/Ft. Worth, TX; Los Angeles, CA; San Francisco, CA; Chicago, IL; Seattle, WA; Honolulu, HI; and Portland, OR. If special circumstances prevent you from making your entry at a designated port, you will need to obtain an Exception to Designated Port Permit from the FWS Divisions of Law Enforcement (see addresses at end of this chapter).

Import Advisory

The endangered species issue is particularly important. As the list of endangered trees expands, the likelihood that your lumber or timber is of a protected species increases. It is your responsibility as importer to be aware of the regulatory status of your commodity. If you have any doubts as to the compliance status of your product under the PQA, CITES, or the ESA, you should check with APHIS, the FWS, or U.S. Customs. Always be prepared to provide the common and scientific names of any species you have questions about or are planning to import. When you are unsure of the regulations governing the export or import of a product, check with the FWS before making a purchase. When in doubt, don't buy! The importation of products made from endangered species can be seized and in some cases the importer can be subject to substantial fines.

Customs Classification

For customs purposes, wood and wood products are classified under Chapter 44 of the HTSUS. This chapter is broken into major headings, which are further divided into subheadings, and often sub-subheadings, each of which has its own HTSUS classification number. For example, the HTSUS number for pine wood molding is 4409.10.40, indicating it is a sub-subcategory of coniferous (4409.10.00), which is a subcategory of the major heading, wood continuously shaped along any of its edges or faces (4409.00.00). There are 21 major headings within Chapter 44.

4401—Fuel wood, in logs, in billets, in twigs, in faggots, or in similar forms; wood in chips or particles; sawdust and wood waste and scrap, whether or not agglomerated in logs, briquettes, pellets, or similar forms

4402—Wood charcoal (including shell or nut charcoal), whether or not agglomerated

4403—Wood in the rough, whether or not stripped of bark or sapwood, or roughly squared

4404—Hoopwood; split poles; piles, pickets, and stakes of wood, pointed but not sawn lengthwise; wooden sticks, roughly trimmed but not turned, bent, or otherwise worked, suitable for the manufacture of walking-sticks, umbrellas, tool handles, or the like; chipwood and the like

4405—Wood wool (excelsior); wood flour

4406—Railway or tramway sleepers (cross-ties) of wood

4407—Wood sawn or chipped lengthwise, sliced or peeled, whether or not planed, sanded, or finger-jointed, of a thickness exceeding 6 mm

4408—Veneer sheets and sheets for plywood (whether or not spliced) and other wood sawn lengthwise, sliced, or peeled, whether or not planed, sanded, or finger-jointed, of a thickness not exceeding 6 mm

4409—Wood (including strips and friezes for parquet flooring, not assembled) continuously shaped (tongued, grooved, rebated, chamfered, V-jointed, beaded, molded, rounded, or the like) along any of its edges or faces, whether or not planed, sanded, or finger-jointed

4410—Particle board and similar board of wood or other ligneous materials, whether or not agglomerated with resins or other organic binding substances.

4411—Fiberboard of wood or other ligneous materials, whether or not bonded with resins or other organic substances

4412—Plywood, veneered panels, and similar laminated wood

4413—Densified wood, in blocks, plates, strips, or profile shapes

4414—Wooden frames for paintings, photographs, mirrors, or similar objects

4415—Packing cases, boxes, crates, drums, and similar packings, of wood; cable-drums, of wood; pallets, box-pallets, and other load boards, of wood

4416—Casks, barrels, vats, tubs, and other coopers' products and parts thereof, of wood, including staves

4417—Tools, tool bodies, tool handles, broom or brush bodies, and handles, of wood; boot or shoe lasts and trees, of wood

4418—Builders' joinery and carpentry of wood, including cellular wood panels and assembled parquet panels; shingles and shakes

4419—Tableware and kitchenware, of wood

4420—Wood marquetry and inlaid wood; caskets and cases for jewelry or cutlery and similar articles, of wood; statuettes and other ornaments, of wood; wooden articles of furniture not falling within chapter 94

4421—Other articles of wood

For more details regarding classifications of the specific product you are interested in importing, consult a customs broker, the appropriate commodity specialist at your nearest customs port, or the HTSUS. HTSUS is available for purchase from the U.S. Government Printing Office (see addresses at end of this chapter), and may be found in larger public libraries. Refer to "Classification—Liquidation" on page 207 for a general discussion of customs classification.

Sample Import Duties

Import duties will vary depending on the HTSUS classification of your product. Therefore, to determine the correct amount of duties, your product must be properly classified under the HTSUS. The following sample duties are taken from the duty listings for HTSUS Chapter 44 products.

Artificial fire logs of wax and sawdust (4401.30.40): 2.5%; wood charcoal (4402.00.00): free; wood in rough (4403.00.00): free; wood wool and flour (4405.00.00): 5.1%; veneer sheets and sheets for plywood (4408.00.00): free; coniferous wood flooring (4409.10.20): 3.2%; nonconiferous wood flooring (4409.20.25): free; wood particle board (4410.10.00): 4%; plywood with at least one outer ply of tropical wood and with a face ply of birch (4412.11.10): 3%, of spanish cedar, walnut, sen or mahogany (4412.11.20): 8%; wooden frames for painting, photographs, mirrors, or similar objects (4414.00.00): 6%; casks, barrels, and hogsheads (4416.00.30): 2.8%; doors and their frames and thresholds (4418.20.00): 7.5%; parquet panels (4418.30.00): 3.2%; wooden forks and spoons (4419.00.40): 5.3%; wood statuettes and other ornaments (4420.10.00): 5.1%; clothes hangers (4421.10.00): 5.1%; toothpicks (4421.90.50): 4.2%; spring-type clothespins (4421.90.80): 10 cents/gross.

Entry and Documentation

The entry of merchandise is a two-part process consisting of 1) filing the documentation necessary to determine whether merchandise may be released from Customs custody, and 2) filing the documents that contain information for duty assessment and statistical purposes. In certain instances, all documents must be filed and accepted by Customs prior to release of the goods. Unless you have been granted an extension, you must file entry documents at a location specified by the district or area director within five working days of your shipment's date of arrival at a U.S. port of entry. These include a number of standard documents required by Customs for any entry, and:

- FWS Import Declaration **Form 3-177**, original and 3 copies (if the products are derived from endangered species)
- FWS permit or import documentation (if the products are derived from endangered species)
- Permits or certificates required under CITES, ESA, and any other regulations applicable to the particular shipment (if the products are derived from endangered species)
- Certificates of export, origin, sanitation, inspection, and other conditions from the country of origin or export, as required by Customs, FWS, or USDA
- USDA importer's declaration (if importing lumber or raw wood)
- USDA APHIS permit for import of logs or lumber with bark attached (if required by USDA, such as for importing elm logs or lumber)
- Canadian Government Export Notice (if importing softwood originating in Canada)
- Copy of air waybill or bill of lading
- Copy of invoice (pro forma invoice if shipment is noncommercial)

After you present the entry, Customs may examine your shipment or may waive examination. The shipment is then released provided no legal or regulatory violations have been noted. You must then file entry summary documentation and deposit estimated duties at a designated customhouse within 10 working days of your shipment's release. For a detailed description of entry procedures, standard documentation, and informal entry, refer to "Entry Process" on page 182.

Entry Invoice. If you are importing wood classified under the following headings, the entry invoice must additionally include the information noted below:

1) The quantity of the wood in cubic meters (m^3) before dressing, if importing the following: Wood sawed or chipped lengthwise, sliced or peeled, whether or not planed, sanded, or finger-jointed, of a thickness exceeding 6 mm (lumber) (HTSUS heading 4407), and wood continuously shaped along any of its edges or faces, whether or not planed, sanded, or fingerjointed—coniferous (HTSUS subheading 4409.10.90) and nonconiferous (HTSUS subheading 4409.20.90)—and dutiable on the basis of cubic meters.

2) The density in grams per cubic cm (cm^3) if importing the following: Fiberboard of wood or other ligneous materials whether or not bonded with resins or other organic substances (HTSUS subheadings 4412.11, 4412.12, and 4412.19) and classifiable according to its density.

3) The thickness of each ply in mm, if importing the following: Plywood consisting solely of sheets of wood (HTSUS subheading 4412.11, 4412.12, and 4412.19) and classifiable according to the thickness of the wood sheets.

Prohibitions and Restrictions

Lumber and Raw Wood. At the port of entry, the USDA inspector will examine lumber and raw wood for pest infestation. If an infestation is found or reasonably suspected, the inspector has authority to deny entry and to dispose of the shipment by the least drastic means available that will protect against spread of the infestation. Disposition will be at the expense of the owner of the shipment.

Elm Logs and Lumber. The import of elm logs and elm lumber with bark attached requires a permit from AHPIS.

Plants and Plant Products. When plants and plant products are particularly vulnerable to plant pests for which the U.S. has no reliable method of extermination, USDA designates those items as being subject to prohibitory orders. Prohibitory orders forbid completely the entry of designated plants and plant products. Restrictive orders allow the entry of plants or plant products either under a treatment or an inspection requirement. If the plant product you wish to import is under restrictive orders, you will need an APHIS import permit, issued only to resident importers in the U.S. Once a permit has been issued to you, you will be held responsible for carrying out any conditions of entry specified in the permit. Questions on entry requirements for plants and plant products should be addressed to USDA APHIS PPQ (see addresses at end of this chapter).

Endangered Species. If you are importing exotic woods or articles derived from exotic woods, you should ascertain whether the tree from which the wood is derived is a protected species. The import of certain woods is restricted or prohibited because of species status under the CITES, ESA, or another U.S. law. For example, importation of species listed in CITES Appendix I for commercial purposes is prohibited. Prohibitions and restrictions may additionally be imposed by the law of the exporting country. You are legally responsible for fulfilling the requirements of all of them, as well as any laws of your country of export. If you import, or attempt to import, a product in violation of a wildlife or endangered species law, even if you are not aware of the violation, your product may be seized, you may be charged substantial fines, and you could be imprisoned.

Country-Specific Import Restrictions

Canadian Softwood Lumber. If you are importing softwood lumber from Canada, you must obtain an Export Notice from the Canadian Government. This requirement is enforced and administered on the U.S. side by the U.S. Department of Commerce (DOC). The notice requires much the same information found on the normal invoice, but also includes the Canadian province of origination and the amount of Canadian tax levied before entry into the U.S. Your Export Notice must be filled out in full, and you must present it to U.S. Customs officials at the U.S. port of entry. For more information, contact the DOC (see addresses at end of this chapter).

Siberian Logs. APHIS has issued PQA-authorized administrative quarantines on raw lumber from Siberia. These products are considered to constitute a substantial risk to U.S. agriculture. The agency is in process of developing new regulations that will specify conditions of entry for these products. Until such regulations are promulgated, all raw logs from Siberia are prohibited. Any such shipment will be refused entry.

Marking and Labeling Requirements

Endangered Tree Species. All shipments of wood and wood products derived from endangered tree species must be marked on the outside of the container with the names and addresses of the exporter and importer, an accurate identification of the species, and the numbers of each species in the container.

For a general discussion of U.S. Customs marking and labeling requirements, refer to "Marking: Country of Origin" on page 215 and "Special Marking Requirements" on page 217.

Shipping Considerations

You will need to ensure that your goods are packaged and shipped with care so that they pass smoothly through Customs and arrive in good condition. You are responsible for ensuring that the shipment is in compliance with all applicable government regulations for packaging and shipping. In most instances, you should not leave these arrangements solely to the discretion of your supplier. Careful preparation of the cargo and selection of the mode of transport can be essential to a cost-effective, timely delivery of undamaged goods. We strongly advise you to consult your shipping representative, insurance agent, or freight broker for advice on packing and shipping. Refer also to the major tab section "Packing/Shipping/Insurance" for a general discussion of packing and shipping.

Wood and wood products may be shipped in bulk, bags, crates, or other types of containers, depending on the type of product and whether it is prepackaged. General considerations include protection from contamination, weather, and pests. Containers should be constructed so as to be safe for handling during transport. If a product must be kept in a sanitary environment, all tables, utensils, platforms, and devices used for moving or handling the product, the compartments in which it is stowed while being transported will need to be maintained in a sanitary condition. Safety precautions should also be implemented as required to protect against breakage and combustion. Containers should be constructed so as to be safe for handling during transport.

Publications Available

The following books are especially pertinent to endangered species regulations and trade. They are published by and available from World Wildlife Fund at the address below.

International Wildlife Trade: Whose Business Is It? by Sarah Fitzgerald. Paperback $25.00; cloth $40.00, 459 pp, ISBN 0-942635-10-8.

The Wildlife Trade Laws of Asia and Oceania by David Nichols, Kathryn Fuller, Erica McShane-Caluzi and Eva Eckinrode. 1991. Loose-leaf binder. Order Code NIAO. $50.00.

Latin American Wildlife Trade Laws (2d ed.) Kathryn S. Fuller, Byron Swift, Amanda Jorgenson, and Amie Brautigam. 1985. 418 pp. Loose-leaf binder. Order Code FULA (English language). #35.00.

To order these publications, or to request a catalog of related publications, contact:

World Wildlife Fund
1250 24th Street NW
Washington, DC 20037
(202) 293-4800

The *Harmonized Tariff Schedule of the United States* (HTSUS) is available from:

Government Printing Office (GPO)
Superintendent of Documents
Washington, DC 20402
(202) 512-1800 (Order line)
(202) 512-0000 (General)

The USGPO also has copies of specific laws available for purchase. The USGPO accepts credit card orders over the phone, as well as mail orders paid by credit card, a check drawn on a U.S. bank, or an international money order.

Relevant Government Agencies

Address your inquiries regarding USDA requirements for importation of lumber or raw wood to:

U.S. Department of Agriculture (USDA)
Animal and Plant Health Inspection Service (APHIS)
Plant Protection and Quarantine (PPQ)
Federal Building, Rm. 631
6505 Belcrest Road
Hyattsville, MD 20782
(301) 436-8645

Address your questions regarding endangered species regulation to:

U.S. Fish and Wildlife Service (FWS)
Office of Management Authority
4401 N. Fairfax Drive, Room 432
Arlington, VA 22203
(703) 358-2095
(800) 358-2104, (703) 358-2104 (Permits office)

Address your questions regarding importation of wood and wood products to the district or port director of Customs for you area. For addresses refer to"U.S. Customs District Offices" on page 62 or contact:

U.S. Customs Service
1301 Constitution Ave. NW
Washington, DC 20229
(202) 927-6724 (Information)
(202) 927-1000 (General)

Laws and Regulations

The following laws and regulations may be relevant to the importation of woods and wood products. The laws are contained in the United States Code (USC), and the regulations are published in the Code of Federal Regulations (CFR), both of which are available at larger public and law libraries. Copies of specific laws are also available from the United States Government Printing Office (address above).

15 USC 1263
Consumer Product Safety Act
This Act gives the Consumer Product Safety Commission authority to set safety standards, testing procedures, and reporting requirements to ensure that consumer products not already covered under other regulations are not harmful.

18 USC 42 et seq.
Importation of Animals, Birds, Fish, and Plants
This Act governs the importation of plants, mammals, birds, fish, amphibia, and reptiles into the U.S. and authorizes U.S. Customs to enforce the import requirements.

42 USC 264 et seq.
The Plant Quarantine Act
This Act gives the Plant Protection and Quarantine branch of the USDA authority to restrict or prohibit importation of plants or their seeds found to carry specific plant pests and pathogens.

7 CFR Part 351
Regulations of USDA on Plant Inspection
These regulations set forth the plant imports that are prohibited, the requirements for entering restricted plants by mail, and the inspection procedures followed by the USDA's Animal and Plant Health Inspection Service (APHIS).

19 CFR 12.10 et seq.
Regulations of Customs on Plant Inspection and Entry
These regulations specify the procedure for importing plants and plant products into the U.S, including USDA inspection requirements, submission of notices of arrival for products requiring quarantine permits, release under bond, disposition of unclaimed or detained shipments.

Convention on International Trade in Endangered Species of Wild Fauna and Flora (CITES)
This comprehensive wildlife treaty signed by over 100 countries, including the United States, regulates and in many cases prohibits commercial imports and exports of wild animal and plant species threatened by trade.

16 USC 1531
Endangered Species Act
This Act prohibits the import and export of species listed as endangered and most species listed as threatened. It is the U.S. law that implements CITES.

16 USC 3371 et seq.
Lacey Act
This Act prohibits the import of species taken, possessed, transported, or sold in violation of the law of a foreign country.

Principal Exporting Countries

The following listing includes samples of the main supplier nations of the products of this chapter. It is organized by HTSUS major heading. (Refer to "Customs Classification" above for the product codes.) Countries are listed in rank order of the value of products imported to the U.S. Statistics represent customs value entries for 1993 from the Bureau of Census, U.S. Department of Commerce.

4401—Canada, Mexico, Brazil, China, Honduras, Ecuador, Jamaica, United Kingdom, Nigeria, France

4402—Mexico, Colombia, Canada, Netherlands, China, Japan, Taiwan, United Kingdom, Guatemala, Greece

4403—Canada, New Zealand, Brazil, Malaysia, Germany, Chile, France, Cameroon, Australia, Cote d'Ivoire

4404—Canada, Honduras, Malaysia, Indonesia, Brazil, Taiwan, Guyana, Madagascar, Chile, China

4405—Canada, Taiwan, United Kingdom, Germany

4406—Canada, Nigeria, Cameroon

4407—Canada, Brazil, Chile, New Zealand, Mexico, Bolivia, Malaysia, Singapore, Philippines, Indonesia

4408—Canada, Brazil, Paraguay, Germany, Italy, Malaysia, Cote d'Ivoire, Singapore, France, United Kingdom

4409—Canada, Mexico, Indonesia, Malaysia, Chile, New Zealand, Taiwan, Brazil, Singapore, Philippines

4410—Canada, Germany, Mexico, Indonesia, South Africa, Taiwan, Brazil, Sweden, Portugal, New Zealand

4411—Canada, Brazil, Spain, Poland, Mexico, Argentina, Chile, Norway, Australia, Russia

4412—Indonesia, Brazil, Malaysia, Canada, Taiwan, Finland, Russia, China, Ecuador, Italy

4413—Germany, Ecuador, Chile, Denmark, Malaysia, Canada, New Zealand, Italy, Taiwan, Mexico

4414—Thailand, Mexico, Taiwan, China, Indonesia, Italy, Hong Kong, Philippines, United Kingdom, France

4415—Canada, Mexico, Japan, Germany, France, Sweden, Taiwan, Brazil, Thailand, China

4416—France, Canada, Mexico, New Zealand, Czech Rep., Japan, Taiwan, Slovakia, Hungary, Finland

4417—Indonesia, Honduras, Brazil, Italy, Canada, Taiwan, Chile, China, Finland, Malaysia

4418—Canada, Malaysia, Mexico, Brazil, Indonesia, Sweden, Taiwan, Philippines, Costa Rica, Chile

4419—Thailand, Taiwan, China, Philippines, Indonesia, Malaysia, United Kingdom, Japan, Brazil, India

4420—Taiwan, China, Mexico, Philippines, Indonesia, Thailand, Italy, India, Hong Kong, Malaysia

4421—Canada, Taiwan, China, Italy, Malaysia, Mexico, Indonesia, Brazil, Ecuador, Thailand

Chapter 45: Cork and Articles of Cork*

This chapter relates to the importation of cork and cork articles, which are classified under Chapter 45 of the Harmonized Tariff Schedule of the United States (HTSUS). Specifically, it includes natural raw cork, waste cork, and crushed, granulated or ground cork; debacked or squared cork pieces; cork stoppers, disks, wafers, washers, wall coverings, and other cork articles; and items made of agglomerated cork, such as vulcanized sheets, insulation, floor and wall coverings, and stoppers, disks, wafers, washers, gaskets, and other cork seals.

If you are interested in importing cork parts for footwear, you should refer to Commodity Index Chapter 64. Requirements for importing headgear and headgear parts made of cork are covered in chapter 65. If you are interested in importing toys, games, or sports equipment that contain cork pieces, refer to Chapter 95.

Key Factors

Although most importers use the services of a licensed customs broker in making their entries, and we recommend this practice, you should be aware of the regulatory, entry, and documentation issues involved in importing your product. You, as importer, are ultimately responsible for the fulfillment of any legal requirements applicable to your shipment.

General Considerations

Importation of cork is straightforward. There are no restrictions or prohibitions. You need no permits or licenses, nor is special entry paperwork required.

Customs Classification

For customs purposes, cork and cork articles are classified under Chapter 45 of the HTSUS. This chapter is broken into major headings, which are further divided into subheadings, and often sub-subheadings, each of which has its own HTSUS classification number. For example, the HTSUS number for compressed cork insulation is 4504.10.20, indicating it is a sub-subcategory of blocks, plates, sheets, and strip, etc. (4504.10.00), which is a subcategory of the major heading, agglomerated cork (4504.00.00). There are four major headings within Chapter 45.

4501—Natural cork, raw or simply prepared; waste cork; crushed, granulated, or ground cork

4502—Natural cork, debacked or roughly squared, or in rectangular (including square) blocks, plates, sheets, or strip (including sharp-edged blanks for corks or stoppers)

4503—Articles of natural cork

4504—Agglomerated cork (with or without a binding substance) and articles of agglomerated cork

For more details regarding classifications of the specific product you are interested in importing, consult a customs broker, the appropriate commodity specialist at your nearest customs port, or the HTSUS. HTSUS is available for purchase from the U.S. Government Printing Office (see addresses at end of this chapter), and may be found in larger public libraries. Refer to "Classification—Liquidation" on page 207 for a general discussion of customs classification.

Sample Import Duties

Import duties will vary depending on the HTSUS classification of your product. Therefore, to determine the correct amount of duties, your product must be properly classified under the HTSUS. The following sample duties are taken from the duty listings for HTSUS Chapter 45 products.

Natural cork, raw or simply prepared (4501.10.00): free; crushed, granulated, or ground natural cork (4501.90.40): 2.2 cents/kg; natural cork, debacked, roughly squared, or in rectangular (including square) blocks, plates, sheets, or strip (4502.00.00): 5.5 cents/kg; corks and stoppers of natural cork, tapered and of a thickness (or length) greater than the maximum diameter with maximum diameter not over 19 mm (4503.10.20): 18.7 cents/kg; agglomerated cork, vulcanized sheets and slabs wholly of ground or pulverized cork or rubber (4504.10.10): 3.7%; floor coverings (4504.10.30): free.

Entry and Documentation

The entry of merchandise is a two-part process consisting of 1) filing the documentation necessary to determine whether merchandise may be released from Customs custody, and 2) filing the documents that contain information for duty assessment and statistical purposes. In certain instances, all documents must be filed and accepted by Customs prior to release of the goods. Unless you have been granted an extension, you must file entry documents at a location specified by the district or area director within five working days of your shipment's date of arrival at a U.S. port of entry. These include a number of standard documents required by Customs for any entry.

After you present the entry, Customs may examine your shipment or may waive examination. The shipment is then released provided no legal or regulatory violations have been noted. You must then file entry summary documentation and deposit estimated duties at a designated customhouse within 10 working days of your shipment's release. For a detailed description of entry procedures, standard documentation, and informal entry, refer to "Entry Process" on page 182.

Marking and Labeling Requirements

For a general discussion of U.S. Customs marking and labeling requirements, refer to "Marking: Country of Origin" on page 215 and "Special Marking Requirements" on page 217.

Shipping Considerations

You will need to ensure that your goods are packaged and shipped with care so that they pass smoothly through Customs and arrive in good condition. You are responsible for ensuring that the shipment is in compliance with all applicable government regulations for packaging and shipping. In most instances, you should not leave these arrangements solely to the discretion of your supplier. Careful preparation of the cargo and selection of the mode of transport can be essential to a cost-effective, timely delivery of undamaged goods. We strongly advise you to consult your shipping representative, insurance agent, or freight

*IMPORTANT: Read the Commodity Index Introduction. It is the essential framework for understanding this section.

broker for advice on packing and shipping. Refer also to the major tab section "Packing/Shipping/Insurance" for a general discussion of packing and shipping.

Cork and cork articles may be shipped in bulk, bags, crates, or other types of containers, depending on the type of product and whether it is prepackaged. General considerations include protection from contamination, weather, and pests. If a product must be kept in a sanitary environment, all tables, utensils, platforms, and devices used for moving or handling the product, the compartments in which it is stowed while being transported will need to be maintained in a sanitary condition. Containers should be constructed so as to be safe for handling during transport.

Publications Available

The *Harmonized Tariff Schedule of the United States* (HTSUS) is available from:

Government Printing Office (GPO)
Superintendent of Documents
Washington, DC 20402
(202) 512-1800 (Order line)
(202) 512-0000 (General)

The USGPO also has copies of specific laws available for purchase. The USGPO accepts credit card orders over the phone, as well as mail orders paid by credit card, a check drawn on a U.S. bank, or an international money order.

Relevant Government Agencies

Address your questions regarding the importation of cork to the district or port director of Customs for you area. For addresses refer to "U.S. Customs District Offices" on page 62.

Principal Exporting Countries

The following listing includes samples of the main supplier nations of the products of this chapter. It is organized by HTSUS major heading. (Refer to "Customs Classification" above for the product codes.) Countries are listed in rank order of the value of products imported to the U.S. Statistics represent customs value entries for 1993 from the Bureau of Census, U.S. Department of Commerce.

4501—Portugal, Morocco, Spain, Netherlands, Canada

4502—Portugal, United Kingdom, China, Germany, Canada, Spain

4503—Portugal, Germany, France, China, United Kingdom, Spain, Italy, Mexico, Taiwan, Canada

4504—Portugal, Spain, France, Ireland, Canada, Taiwan, United Kingdom, China, Japan, Netherlands

Chapter 46: Baskets and Wickerware*

Full title: Manufactures of Straw, of Esparto, or of Other Plaiting Materials; Basketware and Wickerwork

This chapter relates to the importation of baskets and wickerware, which are classified under Chapter 46 of the Harmonized Tariff Schedule of the United States (HTSUS). Specifically, it includes plaited articles in sheets—such as mats, matting, and screens; and basketwork, wickerwork, and other shaped plaited articles—such as bags, handbags, and luggage. Articles covered in this chapter are those plaited from straw, osier, willow, bamboos, rushes, reeds, strips of wood, raffia, strips of other vegetable matter, bark, unspun natural textile fibers, and monofilament, strip, and similar forms of plastics and paper strips.

The importing of plaiting materials in unfinished form is covered in Commodity Index Chapter 14. If you are interested in importing articles plaited from strips of leather, composition leather, felt or other nonwoven fabrics, human hair, horsehair, textile rovings, yarn, or monofilament, strip, and the like, refer to Chapter 54. For the importing requirements related to twine, ropes, cables, and cordage, regardless of whether plaited, refer to Chapter 56. If you are interested in importing furniture, lamps, and lighting fixtures, you should read Chapter 94. Basketware for vehicles and bodies of vehicles is covered in Chapter 87, footwear in Chapter 64, headgear in Chapter 65, and wall coverings in Chapter 48.

Key Factors

The key factors in the importation of baskets and wickerware are:

- Compliance with U.S. Department of Agriculture (USDA) random port-of-entry inspections, import restrictions and quarantines, and other entry requirements
- Compliance with Federal Plant Pest Act
- Compliance with Plant Quarantine Act
- Compliance with Fish and Wildlife Service (FWS) license, permit, country-of-origin permit, import documentation, and recordkeeping requirements (if the products are derived from endangered species)
- Entry at FWS-designated ports, and compliance with FWS and Customs advance notification and port-of-entry inspection requirements (if the products are derived from endangered species)

*IMPORTANT: Read the Commodity Index Introduction. It is the essential framework for understanding this section.

Although most importers use the services of a licensed customs broker in making their entries, and we recommend this practice, you should be aware of the regulatory, entry, and documentation issues involved in importing your product. You, as importer, are ultimately responsible for the fulfillment of any legal requirements applicable to your shipment.

General Considerations

Regulatory Agencies. The USDA administers applicable provisions of the Plant Quarantine Act (PQA), which are designed to prevent the introduction into the U.S. of any plant pest or disease potentially harmful to U.S. agriculture. The FWS, primarily under provisions of the U.S. Endangered Species Act (ESA) and the Convention on International Trade in Endangered Species of Wild Fauna and Flora (CITES), controls the importation of products derived from plants that are classified as endangered species. U.S. Customs enforces USDA and FWS requirements through entry documentation and restrictions.

Baskets and Wickerware. For most shipments of baskets and wickerware, importation is straightforward. With some exceptions, you do not need permits or licenses to import these products (see "Prohibitions and Restrictions" below). The USDA's Animal and Plant Health Inspection Service (APHIS) inspects shipments of baskets and wickerware on a random basis, depending on such factors as the port of entry, the country of origin, and the risk of contamination involved in the type of material being imported.

Entry may be denied for noncompliance with the regulations, and the shipment could be seized, quarantined, destroyed, treated, or otherwise dealt with at the discretion of the inspector. APHIS inspectors also enforce FWS requirements for plaited products derived from endangered plant species, the import of which may be prohibited or may require export and/or import permits (see below). You are responsible to be sure that your shipment is either not derived from listed species, or if it is, that you have the appropriate import authorization.

Exotic and Endangered Species. The FWS enforces a complex set of laws and regulations (see 50 CFR 1 et seq.) pertaining to endangered species product importation. These laws include CITES, the ESA, and a number of other U.S. laws, such as the Lacey Act (LA). Most foreign countries also have their own domestic measures, and you will need to meet the requirements of the country of export in addition to U.S. requirements. For more information, contact the FWS Office of Management Authority (OMA) (see addresses at end of this chapter).

Certain types of vegetable plaiting materials and products made from them are entirely prohibited, others are allowed entry only under permit and/or license, and still others are allowed entry only for specific noncommercial purposes. When applying for a permit, you must satisfy the requirements of all laws under which the species is protected. The following briefly describes the two major laws governing importation of protected products into the U.S. This discussion is not comprehensive or exhaustive. If you wish to import endangered species, you should always contact the FWS (see addresses at end of this chapter) with specific species information before making any transactions.

CITES. Over 100 nations participate in CITES, which took effect in May 1977. The degree of protection afforded to a species depends on which of the three CITES appendices contains the name of that species. Documentation required for import varies depending on the species, and the CITES section where it is listed. The CITES export documentation from the country of origin is always required. If you are importing a CITES-listed species from a country that does not participate in the treaty, you must still obtain from that nation documents that contain all the information normally required in CITES export permits.

Appendix I. This appendix lists species deemed presently threatened with extinction. Importation of Appendix I species for commercial purposes is prohibited. You must have two permits to import these species: one from the U.S., which must be obtained first, and one from the exporting country.

Appendix II. This appendix lists species that are not presently threatened with extinction but may become threatened if their trade is not regulated (e.g., boojum tree). There are no restrictions on the purpose of import, provided it is not detrimental to the survival of the species. You will need an export permit or reexport certificate from the exporting country.

Appendix III. This appendix lists species for which any CITES member country has domestic regulations "for the purpose of preventing or restricting exploitation, and as needing the cooperation of other Parties in control of trade." For example, Nepal lists several varieties of magnolia. Three different types of documents are issued for Appendix III species: 1) Export Permit: Issued for specimens that originated in a country that listed the species on Appendix III; 2) Certificate of Origin: Issued by any country other than the listing country if the species in question originated in that country; 3) Reexport Certificate: Issued for the export of Appendix III specimens that were previously imported into the U.S.

Exemptions. Under certain conditions, Certificates of Exemption may be issued for the importation of endangered species products listed under CITES. Exceptions are allowed for shipments of products transiting a country under Customs bond, shipments between U.S. states or territories, and certain personal or household effects. For information, contact FWS (see addresses at end of this chapter).

Permit Applications. Applications for CITES permits and certificates are available from the FWS Office of Management Authority (see addresses at end of this chapter). You will need to fill out the FWS Standard Permit Application **(Form 3-200)** and provide certain information specifically required under CITES. You should submit your application at least 60 days before the date you wish the permit to take effect. FWS charges processing fees for CITES applications.

ESA. The U.S. Endangered Species Act (ESA) was passed on December 28, 1973, to prevent the extinction of many species of animals and plants and to protect their habitats. By definition, an "endangered species" is any animal or plant listed by regulation as being in danger of extinction. A "threatened species" is any animal or plant likely to become endangered within the foreseeable future. The U.S. List of Endangered and Threatened Wildlife and Plants includes native and foreign species.

Permits. ESA's import provisions prohibit the import or export of any endangered or threatened species or products derived from them without one of the following permits from the FWS Federal Wildlife Permit Office (FWPO):

> *Endangered Species Permits:* This permit is issued for importation for purposes of 1) scientific research; 2) enhancement of propagation or survival of the species; or 3) incidental taking.
>
> *Threatened Species Permits:* This permit is issued for importation for purposes of 1) scientific research; 2) enhancement of propagation or survival of the species; 3) zoological, horticultural, or botanical exhibition; 4) education purposes; 5) special purposes consistent with ESA purposes and policy; or 6) incidental taking.

Permit Exemptions. A few imports of endangered species products are exempt from the ESA permit requirements. For example, if a species is listed as threatened or as an experimental population, special rules may allow otherwise prohibited activities. If you are unsure as to the exemption status of your import, contact FWS (see addresses at end of this chapter).

FWS Import Licenses. With some exceptions, persons engaged in the business of importing endangered species products valued in excess of $25,000 per year must be licensed by the FWS. If your annual importations are valued at less than $25,000, or if you qualify for another exemption from licensing, you are still responsible for keeping thorough records of all transactions and of making these records available to FWS officers if necessary. For a full description of exemptions from licensing, and of recordkeeping requirements, contact the FWS (see addresses at end of this chapter) or see 50 CFR 14.

Procedures at Port of Entry. At least 72 hours before your shipment is due to arrive at a designated port, you should notify U.S. Customs and the FWS inspectors of its expected arrival. The FWS conducts port-of-entry shipment inspections on a case-by-case basis, as determined by the inspection agent after looking at the entry paperwork. Both FWS and Customs may inspect your shipment to verify compliance with all of the legal requirements for entry. Any documentation required by the laws governing your import must be submitted by the time of entry. You must present an FWS Wildlife Declaration **Form 3-177**, available at the port of entry, with every shipment, regardless of any other paperwork required. Customs will not release your shipment until the import declaration has been signed off by an FWS agent.

Designated Ports. Shipments of endangered species products are restricted to designated U.S. ports of entry. All shipments must enter and leave through one of the ports listed in 50 CFR 14.12. Currently, 10 ports are designated: New York, NY; Miami, FL; New Orleans, LA; Dallas/Ft. Worth, TX; Los Angeles, CA; San Francisco, CA; Chicago, IL; Seattle, WA; Honolulu, HI; and Portland, OR. If special circumstances prevent you from making your entry at a designated port, you will need to obtain an Exception to Designated Port Permit from the FWS Divisions of Law Enforcement (see addresses at end of this chapter).

Import Advisory

The endangered species issue is particularly important. As the list of endangered plants expands, the likelihood that your plaited article import is derived from a protected plant species increases. It is your responsibility as importer to be aware of the regulatory status of your commodity. If you have any doubts as to the compliance status of your product under the PQA, CITES, or the ESA, you should check with APHIS, the FWS, or U.S. Customs. Always be prepared to provide the common and scientific names of any species you have questions about or are planning to import. When you are unsure of the regulations governing the export or import of a product, check with the FWS before making a purchase. When in doubt, don't buy! The importation of products made from endangered species can be seized and in some cases the importer can be subject to substantial fines.

Customs Classification

For customs purposes, baskets and wickerware are classified under Chapter 46 of the HTSUS. This chapter is broken into major headings, which are further divided into subheadings, and often sub-subheadings, each of which has its own HTSUS classification number. For example, the HTSUS number for rattan webbing is 4601.20.20, indicating it is a sub-subcategory of mats, matting and screens of vegetable materials (4601.20.00), which is a subcategory of the major heading, plaits and similar products of plaiting materials, etc. (4601.00.00). There are two major headings within Chapter 46.

4601—Plaits and similar products of plaiting materials, whether or not assembled into strips; plaiting materials, plaits, and similar products of plaiting materials, bound together in parallel strands or woven, in sheet form, whether or not being finished articles (for example, mats, matting, screens)

4602—Basketwork, wickerwork, and other articles, made directly to shape from plaiting materials or made up from articles of heading 4601; articles of loofah

For more details regarding classifications of the specific product you are interested in importing, consult a customs broker, the appropriate commodity specialist at your nearest customs port, or the HTSUS. HTSUS is available for purchase from the U.S. Government Printing Office (see addresses at end of this chapter), and may be found in larger public libraries. Refer to "Classification—Liquidation" on page 207 for a general discussion of customs classification.

Sample Import Duties

Import duties will vary depending on the HTSUS classification of your product. Therefore, to determine the correct amount of duties, your product must be properly classified under the HTSUS. The following sample duties are taken from the duty listings for HTSUS Chapter 46 products.

Rattan webbing (4601.20.20): 3.1%; fishing baskets or creels (4602.10.05): 5%; other baskets and bags, whether or not lined: of bamboo (4602.10.11): 10%; of willow (4602.10.12): 5.8%, of rattan or palm leaf (4602.10.13): 10%; luggage, handbags, and flat goods, whether or not lined, of bamboo (4602.10.21): 12.5%; rattan or palm leaf articles carried in a pocket or handbag (4602.10.23): 18%.

Special Provisions. Duties have been temporarily reduced for the following products: rattan webbing (4601.20.20): 2.3%; rattan or palm leaf baskets or bags, whether or not lined (4602.10.13): 7.5%; baskets, wickerwork, and other articles made up from plaited materials or products of plaited materials (4602.10.50): 2.3%.

Entry and Documentation

The entry of merchandise is a two-part process consisting of 1) filing the documents necessary to determine whether merchandise may be released from Customs custody and 2) filing the documents that contain information for duty assessment and statistical purposes. In certain instances all documents must be filed and accepted by Customs prior to the release of the goods. Unless you have been granted an extension, you must file entry documents at a location specified by the district or area director within five working days of your shipment's date of arrival at a U.S. port of entry. These include a number of standard documents required by Customs for any entry, and

- Phytosanitary certificate (if importing rice straw baskets originating in North Korea or grapevine baskets)
- FWS Import Declaration **Form 3-177**, original and 3 copies (if the products are derived from endangered species)
- FWS permit or import documentation (if the products are derived from endangered species)
- Permits or certificates required under CITES, ESA, and any other regulations applicable to the particular shipment (if the products are derived from endangered species)
- Certificates of export, origin, sanitation, inspection, and other conditions from the country of origin or export, as required by Customs, FWS, or USDA
- Copy of air waybill or bill of lading
- Copy of invoice (pro forma invoice if shipment is noncommercial)

After you present the entry, Customs may examine your shipment or may waive examination. The shipment is then released provided no legal or regulatory violations have been noted. You must then file entry summary documentation and deposit estimated duties at a designated customhouse within 10 working days of your shipment's release. For a detailed description of entry procedures, standard documentation, and informal entry, refer to "Entry Process" on page 182.

Prohibitions and Restrictions

In general, any shipment of basketry is subject to random port-of-entry inspection by the USDA. If the inspector finds evidence of the presence of insects in your basketry, you may be required to submit your shipment to USDA-prescribed fumigation procedures. If the insect is of a kind for which there is no viable U.S. treatment, your shipment will be refused. Our source at USDA assured us that most shipments that are found to have insects in them can be treated to afford entry.

Baskets of Grapevines. Baskets made from grapevines must be accompanied by a Phytosanitary Certificate issued by the Plant Protection Service of the exporting country. The certificate must show evidence that the grapevines have been heat-treated to 135 degrees Fahrenheit (or the equivalent Celsius) for 2 hours. If your grapevine baskets are dry (not green or fresh) and you have no certification to present to the USDA at the port of entry, your shipment will be detained and samples will be taken and forwarded to the nearest USDA inspection station. If the examination procedure reveals live buds, your shipment will be refused entry.

Baskets of Rice Straw. Baskets made of rice straw that are intended for outdoor use will be refused entry. Those intended for indoor use will be permitted. If your baskets could be construed as being both for indoor and outdoor use, the USDA is likely to refuse entry.

Baskets of Endangered Plant Species. The import of baskets made from endangered plant species—such as tree ferns—are restricted under CITES. Any such baskets offered for import must meet applicable CITES requirements, as enforced by the FWS and the USDA. If you are interested in importing this type of basketry, you should contact USDA's APHIS PPQ office (see addresses at end of this chapter).

Country-Specific Import Restrictions

Korean Rice Straw Baskets. Baskets made of rice straw and originating in North Korea must be accompanied by a Phytosanitary Certificate issued by the North Korean Plant Protection Service. The certificate must show that the shipment has been fumigated with methyl bromide. A shipment without certification will be denied entry into the U.S.

European Willow Baskets. If willow baskets imported from Europe are found, on inspection at the port of entry, to be green or fresh will be refused entry. Baskets of dry willow from Europe are admissible, as are baskets of green or fresh willow from non-European countries.

Corn Baskets and Wickerware. Corn and closely related plants and their parts (including those of the genus *Chionachne, Coix, Echinochloa, Eleusina, Euchleana, Miscanthus, Panicum, Pennisetum, Polytoca, Sclerachne, Setaria, Sorghum, Trilobachne,* and *Tripsicum*), including materials used in plaited articles, are banned from importation into the U.S. if they originate from the countries listed: Africa (all countries), Australia, Bangladesh, Bhutan, Brunei, Bulgaria, Burma (Myanmar), Cambodia (Kampuchea), Hong Kong, India, Nepal, New Zealand, North Korea, Oceania, Pakistan, Papua New Guinea, People's Republic of China, Philippines, Russia, and the other republics of the former Soviet Union, Singapore, South Korea, Sri Lanka, Taiwan, Thailand, and Vietnam. Corn-related products from other countries require prior USDA approval.

Marking and Labeling Requirements

Endangered Plant Species. All shipments of baskets and wickerware derived from endangered plant species must be marked on the outside of the container with the names and addresses of the exporter and importer, an accurate identification of the species, and the numbers of each species in the container.

For a general discussion of U.S. Customs marking and labeling requirements, see "Marking: Country of Origin" on page 215 and "Special Marking Requirements" on page 217.

Shipping Considerations

You will need to ensure that your goods are packaged and shipped with care so that they arrive in good condition and pass smoothly through Customs. You are responsible for ensuring that the shipment is in compliance with all applicable government regulations for packaging and shipping. In most instances, you should not leave these arrangements solely to the discretion of your supplier. Careful preparation of the cargo and selection of the mode of transport can be essential to a cost-effective, timely delivery of undamaged goods. We strongly advise you to consult your shipping representative, insurance agent, or freight broker for advice on packing and shipping. Refer also to the major tab section "Packing/Shipping/Insurance" for a general discussion of packing and shipping.

Baskets and wickerware may be transported in bulk, boxes, crates, or other forms of packaging. General considerations include protection from infestation by insects, contamination by dirt or other foreign matter, and damage from exposure to dampness or other weather conditions.

Publications Available

The following books are especially pertinent to endangered species regulations and trade. They are published by and available from World Wildlife Fund at the address below.

International Wildlife Trade: Whose Business Is It? by Sarah Fitzgerald. Paperback $25.00; cloth $40.00, 459 pp, ISBN 0-942635-10-8.

The Wildlife Trade Laws of Asia and Oceania by David Nichols, Kathryn Fuller, Erica McShane-Caluzi and Eva Eckinrode. 1991. Loose-leaf binder. Order Code NIAO. $50.00.

Latin American Wildlife Trade Laws (2d ed.) Kathryn S. Fuller, Byron Swift, Amanda Jorgenson, and Amie Brautigam. 1985. 418 pp. Loose-leaf binder. Order Code FULA (English language). $35.00.

To order these publications, or to request a catalog of related publications, contact:

World Wildlife Fund
1250 24th Street NW
Washington, DC 20037
(202) 293-4800

The *Harmonized Tariff Schedule of the United States* (HTSUS) is available from:

Government Printing Office (GPO)
Superintendent of Documents
Washington, DC 20402
(202) 512-1800 (Order line)
(202) 512-0000 (General)

The USGPO also has copies of specific laws available for purchase. The USGPO accepts credit card orders over the phone, as well as mail orders paid by credit card, a check drawn on a U.S. bank, or an international money order.

Relevant Government Agencies

Address your questions regarding USDA requirements for imported baskets and wickerware to:

U.S. Department of Agriculture (USDA)
Animal and Plant Health Inspection Service (APHIS)
Plant Protection and Quarantine (PPQ)
Federal Building, Rm. 631
6505 Belcrest Road
Hyattsville, MD 20782
(301) 436-8645

Address your questions regarding endangered species regulation to:

U.S. Fish and Wildlife Service (FWS)
Office of Management Authority
4401 N. Fairfax Drive, Room 432
Arlington, VA 22203
(703) 358-2095
(800) 358-2104, (703) 358-2104 (Permits office)

Address your questions regarding the importation of baskets and wickerware to the district or port director of Customs for you area. For addresses refer to"U.S. Customs District Offices" on page 62 or contact:

U.S. Customs Service
1301 Constitution Ave. NW
Washington, DC 20229
(202) 927-6724 (Information)
(202) 927-1000 (General)

Laws and Regulations

The following laws and regulations may be relevant to the importation of woods and wood products. The laws are contained in the United States Code (USC), and the regulations are published in the Code of Federal Regulations (CFR), both of which are available at larger public and law libraries. Copies of specific laws are also available from the United States Government Printing Office (address above).

18 USC 42 et seq.
Importation of Animals, Birds, Fish, and Plants
This Act governs the importation of plants, mammals, birds, fish, amphibia, and reptiles into the U.S. and authorizes U.S. Customs to enforce the import requirements.

42 USC 264 et seq.
The Plant Quarantine Act
This Act gives the Plant Protection and Quarantine branch of the USDA authority to restrict or prohibit importation of plants or their seeds found to carry specific plant pests and pathogens.

7 CFR Part 351
Regulations of USDA on Plant Inspection
These regulations set forth the plant imports that are prohibited, the requirements for entering restricted plants by mail, and the inspection procedures followed by the USDA's Animal and Plant Health Inspection Service (APHIS).

19 CFR 12.10 et seq.
Regulations of Customs on Plant Inspection and Entry
These regulations specify the procedure for importing plants and plant products into the U.S, including USDA inspection requirements, submission of notices of arrival for products requiring quarantine permits, release under bond, disposition of unclaimed or detained shipments.

Convention on International Trade in Endangered Species of Wild Fauna and Flora (CITES)
This comprehensive wildlife treaty signed by over 100 countries, including the United States, regulates and in many cases prohibits commercial imports and exports of wild animal and plant species threatened by trade.

16 USC 1531
Endangered Species Act
This Act prohibits the import and export of species listed as endangered and most species listed as threatened. It is the U.S. law that implements CITES.

16 USC 3371 et seq.
Lacey Act
This Act prohibits the import of species taken, possessed, transported, or sold in violation of the law of a foreign country.

Principal Exporting Countries

The following listing includes samples of the main supplier nations of the products of this chapter. It is organized by HTSUS major heading. (Refer to "Customs Classification" above for the product codes.) Countries are listed in rank order of the value of products imported to the U.S. Statistics represent customs value entries for 1993 from the Bureau of Census, U.S. Department of Commerce.

4601—China, India, Philippines, Mexico, South Korea, Hong Kong, Taiwan, Japan, United Kingdom, Canada

4602—China, Philippines, Indonesia, Hong Kong, Taiwan, Mexico, Thailand, South Korea, Italy, El Salvador

Chapter 47: Wood Pulp and Paper Waste*

Full title: Pulp of Wood or of Other Fibrous Cellulosic Material; Waste and Scrap of Paper or Paperboard

This chapter relates to the importation of wood pulp and paper waste, which are classified under Chapter 47 of the Harmonized Tariff Schedule of the United States (HTSUS). Specifically, it includes mechanical, chemical, and semichemical wood pulps; fibrous cellulosic pulps; and waste and scrap.

If you are interested in importing paper and paperboard products, you should refer to Commodity Index Chapter 48. The import requirements for wood and wood products are covered in Chapter 44.

Key Factors

The key factors in the importation of wood pulp and paper waste are:

- Compliance with U.S. Customs documentation
- Compliance with invoice requirements (if importing chemical wood pulp, dissolving grades)

Although most importers use the services of a licensed customs broker in making their entries, and we recommend this practice, you should be aware of the regulatory, entry, and documentation issues involved in importing your product. You, as importer, are ultimately responsible for the fulfillment of any legal requirements applicable to your shipment.

General Considerations

Importation of wood pulp and paper waste is straightforward. There are no restrictions or prohibitions. You do not need permits or licenses, nor is special entry paperwork required. If you are importing chemical wood pulp of dissolving grades (HTSUS heading 4702), your entry invoice must show certain additional information.

Customs Classification

For customs purposes, wood pulp and paper waste are classified under Chapter 47 of the HTSUS. This chapter is broken into major headings, which are further divided into subheadings, and often sub-subheadings, each of which has its own HTSUS classification number. For example, the HTSUS number for cotton linters pulp is 4706.10.00, indicating it is a subcategory of the major heading, pulps of other fibrous cellulosic material (4706.00.00). There are seven major headings within Chapter 47.

4701—Mechanical wood pulp

4702—Chemical wood pulp, dissolving grades

4703—Chemical wood pulp, soda or sulfate, other than dissolving grades

4704—Chemical wood pulp, sulfite, other than dissolving grades

4705—Semichemical wood pulp

4706—Pulps of other fibrous cellulosic material

4707—Waste and scrap of paper or paperboard

For more details regarding classifications of the specific product you are interested in importing, consult a customs broker, the appropriate commodity specialist at your nearest customs port, or the HTSUS. HTSUS is available for purchase from the U.S. Government Printing Office (see addresses at end of this chapter), and may be found in larger public libraries. Refer to "Classification—Liquidation" on page 207 for a general discussion of customs classification.

Sample Import Duties

No import duties are levied on wood pulp and paper waste.

Entry and Documentation

The entry of merchandise is a two-part process consisting of 1) filing the documentation necessary to determine whether merchandise may be released from Customs custody, and 2) filing the documents that contain information for duty assessment and statistical purposes. In certain instances, all documents must be filed and accepted by Customs prior to release of the goods. Unless you have been granted an extension, you must file entry documents at a location specified by the district or area director within five working days of your shipment's date of arrival at a U.S. port of entry. These include a number of standard documents required by Customs for any entry.

After you present the entry, Customs may examine your shipment or may waive examination. The shipment is then released provided no legal or regulatory violations have been noted. You must then file entry summary documentation and deposit estimated duties at a designated customhouse within 10 working days of your shipment's release. For a detailed description of entry procedures, standard documentation, and informal entry, refer to "Entry Process" on page 182.

Entry Invoice. Invoices covering chemical wood pulp, dissolving grades, (HTSUS heading 4702) must state the insoluble fraction (as a percentage) after 1 hour in a caustic soda solution containing 18% sodium hydroxide at 20 degrees Centigrade. Invoices for sulfate or soda chemical wood pulp, dissolving grades (HTSUS subheading 4702.00.00.40) must additionally contain, on or with the invoice, a notation of the ash content as a percentage by weight.

Marking and Labeling Requirements

For a general discussion of U.S. Customs marking and labeling requirements, refer to "Marking: Country of Origin" on page 215 and "Special Marking Requirements" on page 217.

Shipping Considerations

You will need to ensure that your goods are packaged and shipped with care so that they pass smoothly through Customs and arrive in good condition. You are responsible for ensuring that the shipment is in compliance with all applicable government regulations for packaging and shipping. In most instances, you should not leave these arrangements solely to the discretion of your supplier. Careful preparation of the cargo and selection of the mode of transport can be essential to a cost-effective, time-

*IMPORTANT: Read the Commodity Index Introduction. It is the essential framework for understanding this chapter.

ly delivery of undamaged goods. We strongly advise you to consult your shipping representative, insurance agent, or freight broker for advice on packing and shipping. Refer also to the major tab section "Packing/Shipping/Insurance" for a general discussion of packing and shipping.

Wood pulp and paper waste may be shipped in bulk, bags, barrels, or other types of containers, depending on the type of product. General considerations include protection from contamination, weather, and pests. For liquid shipments, venting and vapor collection systems may be required. Safety precautions should also be implemented as required to protect against spillage and corrosion of containers. Containers should be constructed so as to be safe for handling during transport.

Publications Available

The *Harmonized Tariff Schedule of the United States* (HTSUS) is available from:

Government Printing Office (GPO)
Superintendent of Documents
Washington, DC 20402
(202) 512-1800 (Order line)
(202) 512-0000 (General)

The USGPO also has copies of specific laws available for purchase. The USGPO accepts credit card orders over the phone, as well as mail orders paid by credit card, a check drawn on a U.S. bank, or an international money order.

Relevant Government Agencies

Address your questions regarding importation of wood pulp and paper waste generally to the district or port director of customs for you area. For addresses, refer to"U.S. Customs District Offices" on page 62.

Principal Exporting Countries

The following listing includes samples of the main supplier nations of the products of this chapter. It is organized by HTSUS major heading. (Refer to "Customs Classification" above for the product codes.) Countries are listed in rank order of the value of products imported to the U.S. Statistics represent customs value entries for 1993 from the Bureau of Census, U.S. Department of Commerce.

4701—Canada, Sweden, United Kingdom

4702—South Africa, Canada, United Kingdom, Norway, Germany

4703—Canada, Brazil, Chile, Portugal, Sweden, Finland, New Zealand, Taiwan, Belgium, Norway

4704—Canada, Sweden, Germany, Swaziland, Brazil, South Africa, Netherlands, Norway, France, United Kingdom

4705—Canada, Finland, Italy

4706—Philippines, Germany, Spain, Tunisia, Italy, Canada, Taiwan, Japan

4707—Canada, Mexico, Finland, United Kingdom, Japan, Taiwan, Estonia, France, Netherlands, Thailand

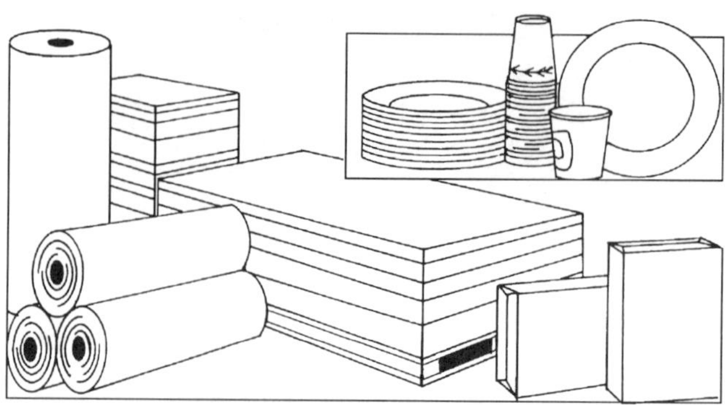

Chapter 48: Paper and Paperboard*

Full title: Paper and Paperboard; Articles of Paper Pulp, of Paper, or of Paperboard

This chapter relates to the importation of paper and paperboard products, which are classified under Chapter 48 of the Harmonized Tariff Schedule of the United States (HTSUS). Specifically, it includes newsprint; writing and drawing papers; personal hygiene paper products; paper articles for household use and food service; ledgers, notebooks, and paper pads; composite, corrugated, creped, crinkled, embossed, or perforated papers and paperboards; parchment, transparent, and translucent papers; carbon and other transfer papers; filters composed of paper pulp; cigarette paper; paper wallcoverings and floor coverings; paper packaging materials; paper and paperboard labels; and paper or paperboard bobbins, spools, and similar supports.

If you are interested in importing printed paper materials, you should refer to Commodity Index Chapter 49. For articles made of paper or paperboard products, refer to the Chapter that covers the particular article. For example, papers used with pharmaceutical products are in Chapter 30, papers for photographic purposes in Chapter 37, plaited articles in Chapter 46, footwear in Chapter 64, and headgear in Chapter 65. For papers that have been impregnated, coated, or covered for a particular use, you should refer to the Commodity Index Chapter that deals with products for that intended use. For example, papers treated with perfume or cosmetics are classified in Chapter 33, soap, detergent, polishes, or creams in Chapter 34, plastics in Chapter 39. Stamping foils are covered in Chapter 32, paper-backed metal foils are in Chapters 72 through 83, and abrasive papers are in Chapter 68. If you are interested in importing wood pulp or paper waste, you should refer to Chapter 47. The importing requirements for articles made from a combination of textiles and paper are covered in Chapters 50 through 63. Vinyl wallcoverings must be imported in accordance with the requirements explained in Chapter 39, and textile wallcoverings in compliance with the requirements noted in Chapters 50 through 63.

Key Factors

The key factors in the importation of paper and paperboard products are:

- Compliance with U.S. Food and Drug Administration (FDA) inspection and entry requirements (if the products are intended for use with food or for medical or sanitary purposes)

*IMPORTANT: Read the Commodity Index Introduction. It is the essential framework for understanding this section.

- Compliance with U.S. Customs regulations on invoicing (for imports of paper stock)

Although most importers use the services of a licensed customs broker in making their entries, and we recommend this practice, you should be aware of the regulatory, entry, and documentation issues involved in importing your product. You, as importer, are ultimately responsible for the fulfillment of any legal requirements applicable to your shipment.

General Considerations

Regulatory Agencies. The FDA, under authority of the Federal Food, Drug, and Cosmetic Act (FDCA), regulates the importation of products intended for use with food or for medical or sanitary purposes. U.S. Customs enforces entry requirements for the importation of paper stock and inspects products subject to FDCA requirements for compliance.

Paper and Paperboard Products. In general, importation of paper and paper products is straightforward. There are no restrictions or prohibitions. You do not need permits or licenses. For most products, no special entry paperwork is required. However, if you are importing paper stock, you will need to provide extra information on the entry invoice (see below).

Paper Products Used With Food. The importation of paper products intended for use with food—such as food and beverage containers, dishes, trays, and coffee filters—is regulated by the FDA. Usually, if you import FDA-regulated articles, you must follow certain import procedures prescribed by that agency, and you must file FDA entry notification, **Form FD701**. If you are importing these articles at present, however, you are not required to follow normal FDA entry procedures because these articles are exempt. If routine Customs examinations of applicable shipments reveal problems that could have adverse effects on public health, the FDA will reconsider this exempt status. Selectivity criteria and entry notification may be reinstituted at any time, at the discretion of FDA. Therefore, if your products fall into this category, you should be familiar with FDA import entry procedures and requirements under FDCA. For an annotated diagram of FDA import procedures refer to the "Foods" appendix on page 808. If you are interested in importing a food-related paper product, you should ascertain its regulatory status by contacting the FDA (see addresses at end of this chapter).

Customs Classification

For customs purposes, paper and paperboard products are classified under Chapter 48 of the HTSUS. This chapter is broken into major headings, which are further divided into subheadings, and often sub-subheadings, each of which has its own HTSUS classification number. For example, the HTSUS number for record sleeves is 4819.50.30, indicating it is a sub-subcategory of other packing containers (4819.50.00), which is a subcategory of the major heading, cartons, boxes, cases, bags, and other packing containers, etc. (4819.50.00). There are 23 major headings within Chapter 48.

4801—Newsprint, in rolls or sheets

4802—Uncoated paper and paperboard, of a kind used for writing, printing or other graphic purposes, and punch card stock and punch tape paper, in rolls or sheets, other than paper of heading 4801 or 4803; handmade paper and paperboard

4803—Toilet or facial tissue stock, towel or napkin stock, and similar paper of a kind used for household or sanitary purposes, cellulose wadding and webs of cellulose fibers, whether or not creped, crinkled, embossed, perforated, surface-colored, surface-decorated, or printed, in rolls of a width exceeding 36 cm or in rectangular (including square) sheets with at least one side exceeding 36 cm in unfolded state

4804—Uncoated kraft paper and paperboard, in rolls or sheets, other than that of heading 4802 or 4803

4805—Other uncoated paper and paperboard, in rolls or sheets

4806—Vegetable parchment, greaseproof papers, tracing papers, and glassine and other glazed transparent or translucent papers, in rolls or sheets

4807—Composite paper and paperboard (made by sticking flat layers of paper or paperboard together with an adhesive), not surface-coated or impregnated, whether or not internally reinforced, in rolls or sheets

4808—Paper and paperboard, corrugated (with or without glued flat surface sheets), creped, crinkled, embossed, or perforated, in rolls or sheets, other than that of heading 4803 or 4818

4809—Carbon paper, self-copy paper, and other coated or impregnated copying or transfer papers (including coated or impregnated paper for duplicator stencils or offset plates) whether or not printed, in rolls of a width exceeding 36 cm or in rectangular (including square) sheets with at least one side exceeding 36 cm in unfolded state

4810—Paper and paperboard, coated on one or both sides with kaolin (China clay) or other inorganic substances, with or without a binder, and with no other coating, whether or not surface-colored, surface-decorated, or printed, in rolls or sheets

4811—Paper, paperboard, cellulose wadding, and webs of cellulose fibers, coated, impregnated, covered, surface-colored, surface-decorated, or printed, in rolls or sheets, other than goods of heading 4803, 4809, 4810, or 4818

4812—Filter blocks, slabs, and plates, of paper pulp

4813—Cigarette paper, whether or not cut to size or in the form of booklets or tubes

4814—Wallpaper and similar wallcoverings; window transparencies of paper

4815—Floor coverings on a base of paper or of paperboard, whether or not cut to size

4816—Carbon paper, self-copy paper, and other copying or transfer papers (other than those of heading 4809), duplicator stencils and offset plates, of paper, whether or not put up in boxes

4817—Envelopes, letter cards, plain postcards, and correspondence cards, of paper or paperboard; boxes, pouches, wallets, and writing compendiums, of paper or paperboard, containing an assortment of paper stationery;

4818—Toilet paper, handkerchiefs, cleansing tissues, towels, tablecloths, table napkins, diapers, tampons, bed sheets, and similar household, sanitary or hospital articles, articles of apparel and clothing accessories, or paper pulp, paper, cellulose wadding or webs of cellulose fibers

4819—Cartons, boxes, cases, bags, and other packing containers, of paper, paperboard, cellulose, wadding, or webs of cellulose fibers; box files, letter trays, and similar articles, of paper or paperboard of a kind used in offices, shops, or the like

4820—Registers, account books, notebooks, order books, receipt books, letter pads, memorandum pads, diaries, and similar articles, exercise books, blotting pads, binders (looseleaf or other), folders, file covers, manifold business forms, interleaved carbon sets, and other articles of stationery, of paper or paperboard; albums for samples or for collections and book covers (including cover boards and book jackets) of paper or paperboard

4821—Paper and paperboard labels of all kinds, whether or not printed

4822—Bobbins, spools, cops, and similar supports of paper pulp, paper, or paperboard (whether or not perforated or hardened)

4823—Other paper, paperboard, cellulose wadding and webs of cellulose fibers, cut to size or shape; other articles of paper pulp, paper, paperboard, cellulose wadding, or webs of cellulose fibers

For more details regarding classifications of the specific product you are interested in importing, consult a customs broker, the appropriate commodity specialist at your nearest customs port, or the HTSUS. HTSUS is available for purchase from the U.S. Government Printing Office (see addresses at end of this chapter), and may be found in larger public libraries. Refer to "Classification—Liquidation" on page 207 for a general discussion of customs classification.

Sample Import Duties

Import duties will vary depending on the HTSUS classification of your product. Therefore, to determine the correct amount of duties, your product must be properly classified under the HTSUS. The following sample duties are taken from the duty listings for HTSUS Chapter 48 products.

Newsprint (4801.00.00): free; uncoated handmade paper and paperboard (4802.10.00): 2.4%; uncoated kraftliner (4804.11.00, 4804.19.00) and sack kraft paper (4804.21.00, 4804.29.00): free; uncoated filter paper and paperboard (4805.40.00): 4.2%; vegetable parchment and greaseproof, tracing, transparent, and translucent papers (4806.00.00): free; corrugated paper and paperboard (4808.10.00): 4%; self-copy writing paper (4809.20.20):4.4%; filters of paper pulp (4812.00.00): 3.7%; cigarette papers (4813.00.00): 4.9%; wallcoverings (4814.00.00): free; floor coverings (4815.00.00): 3.7%; carbon or similar copying papers (4816.10.00): 3%; envelopes (4817.10.00): 4%; toilet paper (4818.10.00): 5.3%; handkerchiefs, cleansing, or facial tissues and towels (4818.20.00): 5.3%; tablecloths and table napkins (4818.30.00): 5.3%; corrugated cartons, boxes, and cases (4819.10.00): 2.8%; noncorrugated folding cartons, boxes, and cases (4819.20.00): 2.8%; record sleeves (4819.50.30): 4.4 cents/kg; diaries, address books, memo pads, etc. (4820.10.20): 4%; trays, dishes, cups, etc. (4823.60.00): 4.3%; photographic slide frames or mounts (4823.90.40): 3.8%; hand fans (4823.90.50): 17%.

Excise Tax. Imports of cigarette papers are subject to a federal excise tax as follows: 0.625 cents/50 papers or 1.25 cents/50 tubes (26 USC 5701).

Entry and Documentation

The entry of merchandise is a two-part process consisting of 1) filing the documentation necessary to determine whether merchandise may be released from Customs custody, and 2) filing the documents that contain information for duty assessment and statistical purposes. In certain instances, all documents must be filed and accepted by Customs prior to release of the goods. Unless you have been granted an extension, you must file entry documents at a location specified by the district or area director within five working days of your shipment's date of arrival at a U.S. port of entry. These include a number of standard documents required by Customs for any entry.

After you present the entry, Customs may examine your shipment or may waive examination. The shipment is then released provided no legal or regulatory violations have been noted. You must then file entry summary documentation and deposit estimated duties at a designated customhouse within 10 working days of your shipment's release. For a detailed description of entry procedures, standard documentation, and informal entry, refer to "Entry Process" on page 182.

Entry Invoice. To facilitate classification of your paper shipment, Customs requires certain additional information on the invoice. You should be sure the information is either included on the invoice or on additional specification sheets submitted with it. Your invoice must show: 1) weight of paper in grams per square meter; 2) thickness, in micrometers (microns); 3) if imported in rectangular sheets, length and width sheets, in cm; 4) if imported in strips or rolls, the width in cm. In the case of rolls, the diameter of rolls in cm; 5) whether the paper is coated or impregnated, and with what materials; 6) weight of coating, in grams per square meter; 7) percentage by weight of the total fiber content consisting of wood fibers contained by a mechanical process, chemical sulfate or soda process, chemical sulfite process, or semichemical process, as appropriate; 8) commercial designation, as "writing," "cover," "drawing," "Bristol," "newsprint," etc.; 9) ash content; 10) color; 11) glaze or finish; 12) Mullen bursting strength, and Mullen index; 13) stretch factor, in machine direction and in cross direction; 14) tear and tensile readings; in machine direction, in cross direction, and in machine direction plus cross direction; 15) identification of fibers as "hardwood" where appropriate; 16) crush resistance; 17) brightness; 18) smoothness; 19) if bleached, whether bleached uniformly throughout the mass; and 20) whether embossed, perforated, creped, or crinkled.

Marking and Labeling Requirements

For a general discussion of U.S. Customs marking and labeling requirements, refer to "Marking: Country of Origin" on page 215 and "Special Marking Requirements" on page 217.

Shipping Considerations

You will need to ensure that your goods are packaged and shipped with care so that they pass smoothly through Customs and arrive in good condition. You are responsible for ensuring that the shipment is in compliance with all applicable government regulations for packaging and shipping. In most instances, you should not leave these arrangements solely to the discretion of your supplier. Careful preparation of the cargo and selection of the mode of transport can be essential to a cost-effective, timely delivery of undamaged goods. We strongly advise you to consult your shipping representative, insurance agent, or freight broker for advice on packing and shipping. Refer also to the major tab section "Packing/Shipping/Insurance" for a general discussion of packing and shipping.

Paper and paperboard products may be shipped in bulk, bags, crates, or other types of containers, depending on the type of product and whether it is prepackaged. General considerations include protection from contamination, weather, and pests. If a product must be kept in a sanitary environment, all tables, utensils, platforms, and devices used for moving or handling the product, and the compartments in which it is stowed while being transported will need to be maintained in a sanitary condition. Containers should be constructed so as to be safe for handling during transport.

Publications Available

The following publication explains the FDA requirements for importing paper and paperboard products for sanitary use. It is published by the FDA and is available on request from FDA headquarters (see addresses at end of this chapter).

Requirements of Laws and Regulations Enforced by the U.S. Food and Drug Administration

The *Harmonized Tariff Schedule of the United States* (HTSUS) is available from:

Government Printing Office (GPO)
Superintendent of Documents
Washington, DC 20402
(202) 512-1800 (Order line)
(202) 512-0000 (General)

The USGPO also has copies of specific laws available for purchase. The USGPO accepts credit card orders over the phone, as well as mail orders paid by credit card, a check drawn on a U.S. bank, or an international money order.

Relevant Government Agencies

Address your questions regarding FDA regulation or requirements for paper products intended for use with food to:

Food and Drug Administration (FDA)

Center for Food Safety and Applied Nutrition
200 C Street SW
Washington, DC 20204
(202) 205-5241, 205-5042

Address your questions regarding the importation of paper and paperboard products to the district or port director of customs for you area. For addresses, refer to"U.S. Customs District Offices" on page 62 or contact:

U.S. Customs Service
1301 Constitution Ave. NW
Washington, DC 20229
(202) 927-6724 (Information)
(202) 927-1000 (General)

Laws and Regulations

The following laws and regulations may be relevant to the importation of paper and paperboard products. The laws are contained in the United States Code (USC), and the regulations are published in the Code of Federal Regulations (CFR), both of which are available at larger public and law libraries. Copies of specific laws are also available from the United States Government Printing Office (address above).

21 USC 301 et seq.
Food, Drug, and Cosmetic Act
This Act prohibits deceptive practices and regulates the manufacture, sale and importation or exportation of food, drugs, cosmetics, and related products. See 21 USC 331, 381, 382.

19 CFR 12.1 et seq.; 21 CFR 1.83 et seq.
Regulations on Food, Drugs, and Cosmetics
These regulations of the Secretary of Health and Human Services and the Secretary of the Treasury govern the standards, labeling, marking, and importing of pharmaceutical products.

Principal Exporting Countries

The following listing includes samples of the main supplier nations of the products of this chapter. It is organized by HTSUS major heading. (Refer to "Customs Classification" above for the product codes.) Countries are listed in rank order of the value of products imported to the U.S. Statistics represent customs value entries for 1993 from the Bureau of Census, U.S. Department of Commerce.

4801—Canada, Sweden, Norway, Finland, Russia, United Kingdom, Switzerland, Germany, Venezuela, Mexico

4802—Canada, Finland, Norway, Brazil, Sweden, Belgium, Germany, Austria, Mexico, United Kingdom

4803—Canada, Mexico, Sweden, China, New Zealand, Colombia, Denmark, United Kingdom, France, Austria

4804—Canada, Germany, Japan, Sweden, Finland, Venezuela, Netherlands, France, United Kingdom, China

4805—Canada, France, Mexico, Netherlands, United Kingdom, Germany, Japan, Finland, Sweden, Brazil

4806—Norway, Sweden, France, United Kingdom, Canada, Finland, Germany, Argentina, Switzerland, Japan

4807—Germany, Canada, Netherlands, France, South Korea, Japan, Switzerland, Sweden, China, Taiwan

4808—Canada, France, Switzerland, Germany, South Korea, United Kingdom, Taiwan, Japan, Mexico, Italy

4809—Switzerland, Germany, United Kingdom, Japan, France, Taiwan, Canada, Brazil, Italy, China

4810—Canada, Finland, Germany, France, United Kingdom, Belgium, Italy, Sweden, Japan, Netherlands

4811—Canada, Japan, Germany, United Kingdom, Finland, Sweden, Switzerland, France, Brazil, South Korea

4812—Germany, United Kingdom, France, Switzerland, Canada, Japan, Hong Kong, Finland, Taiwan, Austria

4813—France, Spain, Austria, United Kingdom, Canada, Belgium, Australia, Germany, Italy, Netherlands

4814—Canada, United Kingdom, Germany, Italy, France, Japan, South Korea, Netherlands, Belgium, Sweden

4815—Finland, United Kingdom, Canada

4816—Japan, Germany, United Kingdom, South Korea, Canada, Switzerland, Netherlands, Hong Kong, Finland, Colombia

4817—Canada, China, United Kingdom, Taiwan, Hong Kong, Germany, Italy, France, India, Mexico

4818—Canada, Mexico, Germany, Costa Rica, Trinidad and Tobago, Colombia, Belgium, Netherlands, China, Japan

4819—Canada, China, South Korea, Mexico, Taiwan, Hong Kong, Japan, Germany, France, Denmark

4820—China, Taiwan, Mexico, Canada, South Korea, United Kingdom, Singapore, Japan, Malaysia, Hong Kong

4821—Canada, Japan, Germany, Taiwan, France, Dominican Rep., United Kingdom, Hong Kong, Italy, South Korea

4822—Canada, Japan, Taiwan, Mexico, Italy, Germany, United Kingdom, Costa Rica, China, Belgium

4823—Canada, Japan, Germany, United Kingdom, China, Mexico, Brazil, Singapore, France, Taiwan

Chapter 49: Printed Materials*

Full title: Printed Books, Newspapers, Pictures, and Other Products of the Printing Industry; Manuscripts, Typescripts, and Plans

This chapter relates to the importation of printed materials, which are classified under Chapter 49 of the Harmonized Tariff Schedule of the United States (HTSUS). Specifically, it includes printed books, brochures, leaflets, newspapers, periodicals, children's books, printed and manuscript music, maps, charts, plans, drawings, unused stamps, banknotes and other financial instruments, printed or illustrated postcards, greeting cards, calendars, trade and commercial advertising materials, tourist and similar literature, and printed forms.

If you are interested in importing photographic negatives or positives on transparent bases, refer to Commodity Index Chapter 37. The import requirements for maps, plans, or globes in relief are explained in Chapter 90. Playing cards and printed materials for toys, games, and sports equipment are imported in accordance with the requirements in Chapter 95. If you are interested in importing original engravings, prints, lithographs, postage or revenue stamps, stamp-postmarks, first-day covers, postal stationery, or antique printed materials, refer to Chapter 97.

Key Factors

The key factors in the importation of printed materials are:

- Compliance with copyright laws and regulations
- Compliance with trademark laws and regulations
- Compliance with counterfeit laws and regulations
- Compliance with restrictions pertaining to seditious, obscene, or threatening subject matter
- Compliance with restrictions on the importation of facsimiles (if importing postage stamps)
- Submission of Customs **Form 4790** (if importing currencies or negotiable instruments valued at more than $10,000)

Although most importers use the services of a licensed customs broker in making their entries, and we recommend this practice, you should be aware of the regulatory, entry, and documentation issues involved in importing your product. You, as importer, are ultimately responsible for the fulfillment of any legal requirements applicable to your shipment.

*IMPORTANT: Read the Commodity Index Introduction. It is the essential framework for understanding this section.

General Considerations

Regulatory Agencies. The U.S. Customs Intellectual Property Rights branch enforces pertinent copyright laws and regulations to ensure that pirated versions of copyrighted materials do not enter the U.S. The principle laws include Section 305 of the Tariff Act of 1930, as amended, Section 602(a) of the Copyright Revision Act of 1976 (CRA), and Section 42 of the Trademark Act (TMA). These laws and regulations are designed to protect the general consumer, the holders of copyrights, and the national security of the U.S.

Books, Newspapers, and Periodicals. The importation of books, magazines, newspapers, and periodicals into the U.S. is relatively straightforward. There are no quotas, no duties, and no special licensing or permit requirements. However, you need to be concerned about three major issues pertinent to these printed materials: marking, copyrights, and content. If your shipments of books, newspapers, or periodicals are found to violate any of the U.S. copyright or trademark laws, they are subject to seizure by Customs. Such shipments may be destroyed, auctioned, or reexported, depending on the nature of the item and the nature of the violation (see "Prohibitions and Restrictions" below).

Currency and Negotiable Instruments. All imports of currency and negotiable instruments are subject to the Currency and Foreign Transactions Reporting Act, 31 U.S. 1101 et seq. (CFTR). Under CFTR, you must file a transaction report, Customs **Form 4790**, with U.S. Customs when you transport more than $10,000 in monetary instruments, by any means, on any occasion, into or out of the U.S. Monetary instruments include U.S. or foreign currency, traveler's checks, money orders, and negotiable instruments or investment securities in bearer form. Bank checks, travelers checks, or money orders made payable to the order of a named person but that have not been endorsed, or that bear restrictive endorsement, are not considered monetary instruments.

Postage Stamps. Importation of foreign postage stamps into the U.S. is straightforward. You do not need permits or licenses, nor is special paperwork required. Importation of facsimiles of U.S. postage stamps is regulated by the U.S. Secret Service (see "Prohibitions and Restrictions" below).

Articles Exempt from Formal Customs Entry. The following articles pass Customs without issuing an entry: 1) Articles imported by mail, marked for copyright, and addressed to the Library of Congress, to the Copyright Office, or to the Register of Copyrights, Washington, DC; 2) negotiable instruments in current circulation in any country and imported into the U.S. for monetary purposes; and 3) postage stamps in current use.

Customs Classification

For customs purposes, printed materials are classified under Chapter 49 of the HTSUS. This chapter is broken into major headings, which are further divided into subheadings, and often sub-subheadings, each of which has its own HTSUS classification number. For example, the HTSUS number for newspaper supplements printed by a gravure process is 4902.90.10, indicating it is a sub-subcategory of other materials (4902.90.00), which is a subcategory of the major heading, newspapers, journals, and periodicals, etc. (4902.00.00). There are 11 major headings within Chapter 49.

4901—Printed books, brochures, leaflets, and similar printed matter, whether or not in single sheets

4902—Newspapers, journals, and periodicals, whether or not illustrated or containing advertising material

4903—Children's picture, drawing, or coloring books

4904—Music, printed or in manuscript, whether or not bound or illustrated

4905—Maps and hydrographic or similar charts of all kinds, including atlases, wall maps, topographical plans, and globes, printed

4906—Plans and drawings for architectural, engineering, industrial, commercial, topographical, or similar purposes, being originals drawn by hand; handwritten texts; photographic reproductions on sensitized paper and carbon copies of the foregoing

4907—Unused postage, revenue or similar stamps of current or new issue in the country to which they are destined; stamp-impressed paper; banknotes; check forms; stock, share, or bond certificates and similar documents of title

4908—Transfers (decalcomanias)

4909—Printed or illustrated post cards; printed cards bearing personal greetings, messages or announcements, whether or not illustrated, with or without envelopes or trimmings

4910—Calendars of any kind, printed, including calendar blocks

4911—Other printed matter, including printed pictures and photographs

For more details regarding classifications of the specific product you are interested in importing, consult a customs broker, the appropriate commodity specialist at your nearest customs port, or the HTSUS. HTSUS is available for purchase from the U.S. Government Printing Office (see addresses at end of this chapter), and may be found in larger public libraries. Refer to "Classification—Liquidation" on page 207 for a general discussion of customs classification.

Sample Import Duties

Import duties will vary depending on the HTSUS classification of your product. Therefore, to determine the correct amount of duties, your product must be properly classified under the HTSUS. The following sample duties are taken from the duty listings for HTSUS Chapter 49 products.

Printed books, brochures, leaflets, and similar printed matter, whether or not in single sheets (4901.00.00): free; newspaper supplements printed by a gravure process (4902.90.10): 1.8%; other newspapers, journals, and periodicals (4902.00.00): free; children's books (4903.00.00): free; music (4904.00.00): free; printed globes (4905.10.00): 5.3%; unused stamps, banknotes, checks, stock, share, and bond certificates, and title documents (4907.00.00): free; vitrifiable transfers (decalcomanias): 13.2 cents/kg plus 3.5%; printed or illustrated postcards (4909.00.20) 4%; greeting cards (4909.00.40): 4.9%; commercial catalogs (4911.10.00): free.

Special Provisions. Articles imported by mail, marked for copyright, and addressed to the Library of Congress, to the Copyright Office, or to the Register of Copyrights, Washington, DC, pass Customs duty-free without a formal entry. Negotiable instruments in current circulation in any country and imported into the U.S. for monetary purposes are admitted duty-free without formal Customs entry.

Entry and Documentation

The entry of merchandise is a two-part process consisting of 1) filing the documentation necessary to determine whether merchandise may be released from Customs custody, and 2) filing the documents that contain information for duty assessment and statistical purposes. In certain instances, all documents must be filed and accepted by Customs prior to release of the goods. Unless you have been granted an extension, you must file entry documents at a location specified by the district or area director within five working days of your shipment's date of arrival at a U.S. port of entry. These include a number of standard documents required by Customs for any entry, and:

- Customs **Form 4790** (if importing currencies or negotiable instruments valued at more than $10,000)

After you present the entry, Customs may examine your shipment or may waive examination. The shipment is then released provided no legal or regulatory violations have been noted. You must then file entry summary documentation and deposit estimated duties at a designated customhouse within 10 working days of your shipment's release. For a detailed description of entry procedures, standard documentation, and informal entry, refer to "Entry Process" on page 182.

Entry Invoice. If you seek entry for printed matter in the following headings, you must include on the invoice, or on a separate sheet submitted with the invoice, the following information:

HTSUS Heading 4901: 1) whether the books are dictionaries; encyclopedias; textbooks; bound newspapers, journals, or periodicals; directories; bibles or other prayer books; technical, scientific, or professional books; art or pictorial books; or "other" books; 2) if "other" books, whether hardbound or paperbound; 3) if "other" books and paperbound but not "rack size," number of pages (excluding covers).

HTSUS Heading 4902: 1) Whether they appear at least four times a week; 2) if they appear other than at least four times a week, whether they are newspaper supplements printed by a gravure process, newspapers, business or professional journals or periodicals, or other than these.

HTSUS Heading 4904: Whether the printed or manuscript music is sheet music, not bound (except by stapling or folding).

HTSUS Heading 4905: 1) Whether globes or not; 2) if not globes, whether in book form or not; and 3) in any case, whether or not in relief;

HTSUS Heading 4908: Whether or not vitrifiable.

HTSUS Heading 4909: Whether post cards, greeting cards, or other.

HTSUS Heading 4910: 1) Whether or not printed on paper by a lithographic process; 2) if printed on paper by a lithographic process, the thickness of the paper, in mm.

HTSUS Subheading 4911.91: 1) Whether or not printed over 20 years at time of importation; 2) if not printed over 20 years at time of importation, whether suitable for use in the production of articles of heading 4901; 3) if not printed over 20 years at time of importation, and not suitable for use in the production of articles of heading 4901, whether the merchandise is lithographs on paper or paperboard; 4) if lithographs on paper or paperboard, under the terms of the immediately preceding description, thickness of the paper or paperboard, and whether or not posters; 5) in any case, whether or not posters; and 6) in any case, whether or not photographic negatives or positives on transparent bases.

HTSUS Subheading 4911.99: If not carnets, or parts thereof, in English or French, whether or not printed on paper in whole or in part by a lithographic process.

Prohibitions and Restrictions

Content. Under Section 305 of the Tariff Act of 1930, as amended, you may not import any book, writing, advertisement, circular, or picture containing any matter advocating or urging the following unlawful acts: 1) treason or insurrection against the U.S.; or 2) forcible resistance to any U.S. law. You may not import any book, writing, advertisement, circular, or picture containing any threat to take the life of, or inflict bodily harm on, any person in the U.S. Importation of any obscene book, writing, advertisement, circular, picture or other representation, figure, or image on or of paper is also prohibited.

Copyright. Section 602(a) of the CRA makes it an infringement of copyright to import copies of a work acquired outside the U.S. without the copyright owner's authorization. If you import articles in violation of Section 602(a), your shipment will be subject to seizure and forfeiture. Customs destroys forfeited articles. If Customs is satisfied, however, that your violation was unintentional, you may have the option of returning the articles to the country of export. Customs employs the substantial similarity test to determine if a design has been copied. Copyright owners seeking import protection from U.S. Customs must register their claim to copyright with the U.S. Copyright Office and record their registration with Customs in accordance with applicable regulations (19 CFR Part 133, Subpart D).

Counterfeit Articles. Articles bearing facsimiles or replicas of U.S. or foreign securities are prohibited from importation. Also prohibited are counterfeited, forged, or altered obligations or other securities of the U.S. or of any foreign government.

Exceptions. Black and white illustrations of U.S. postage stamps are permitted entry under the following conditions. The illustrations must be for philatelic, numismatic, educational, historical or newsworthy purposes. They must be published in articles, books, journals, newspapers, or albums. If the illustrations are intended for advertising purposes, the advertising must be limited to legitimate philatelic or numismatic purposes.

Motion-picture films, microfilms, or slides of postage and revenue stamps and other obligations and securities of the U.S. and or foreign countries are permitted, provided they are intended for projection on a screen or for use in telecasting. Reproductions in printed matter that adheres to the requirements of 18 USC 504 are permitted entry. However, printed matter containing illustrations or reproductions not executed in accordance with Section 504 will be considered counterfeit and are subject to forfeiture.

Forfeiture. If no application for exportation or assent to forfeiture is received by the district director of Customs within 30 days from the date of notification to the importer that articles are prohibited, the articles will be reported to the U.S. attorney for forfeiture.

For more information regarding distinctions under the law between counterfeit and noncounterfeit representations, see 18 USC 504 and 19 CFR 12.48, or contact U.S. Customs.

Postage Stamps. Facsimiles of postage stamps are prohibited entry except those for philatelic, educational, historical, or newsworthy purposes. You may obtain further information from the U.S. Secret Service (see addresses at end of this chapter).

Country-Specific Import Restrictions

If you wish to import books, magazines, newspapers, or periodicals into the U.S. from countries that fall under Foreign Assets Control import bans, you may apply for a waiver from the U.S. Department of Treasury's Office of Foreign Assets Control (see addresses at end of this chapter).

The importation of monetary instruments from countries that are under economic sanctions by the U.S.—such as Iran, North Korea, Libya, and Cuba—is severely restricted. In some instances, importation is prohibited altogether. For more information, contact the Office of Foreign Assets Control (see addresses at end of this chapter) and read "Foreign Assets Control Restrictions" on page 226.

Marking and Labeling Requirements

Foreign Books. Section 42 of the TMA specifies marking requirements for foreign books imported into the U.S. The Section deems the words "United States," the letters "U.S.A.," or the name of any city or locality in the U.S. appearing on an item of foreign origin, as calculated to induce the public to believe that the item was manufactured in the U.S. In such cases, for your item to be considered properly marked, the name of the foreign country of origin must appear in close proximity to the name that implies a U.S. origin.

This regulation applies to imported, foreign-printed (bound or unbound) books that bear on the title page either 1) the name and address of the U.S. importer, consignee, or publisher; or 2) the name of any country or locality other than the one in which the book was actually printed. The ultimate purchaser could construe these names to mean that the book is a product of the U.S. Customs will accept the usual practice in the printing and publishing trade for meeting the requirements of TMA, which is to have the following wording in close proximity to the potentially misleading information: 1) the words "Printed in," followed by the name of the country of origin; or 2) the words "Printed by," followed by the name and address of the foreign printer and the name of the country of origin, or 3) words of similar significance. This wording must appear either 1) on the front or back of the title page, or 2) on the inside or outside of the cover (provided the marking is not covered by a dust cover or jacket), or 3) on a page near the front or back of your book.

Seizure and Forfeiture. An imported article bearing a name or mark prohibited by Section 42 of TMA is subject to seizure and forfeiture. A shipment that violates the Trademark Act may be reexported or destroyed at the importer's cost. If your shipment is seized by Customs for a TMA violation, you may file a petition prior to the final disposition, requesting the district or port director to release it on the condition that the prohibited marking will be removed or obliterated or that the article will be properly marked. The final decision regarding disposition of a mismarked shipment rests with Customs.

For a general discussion of U.S. Customs marking and labeling requirements, refer to "Marking: Country of Origin" on page 215 and "Special Marking Requirements" on page 217.

Shipping Considerations

You will need to ensure that your goods are packaged and shipped with care so that they pass smoothly through Customs and arrive in good condition. You are responsible for ensuring that the shipment is in compliance with all applicable government regulations for packaging and shipping. In most instances, you should not leave these arrangements solely to the discretion of your supplier. Careful preparation of the cargo and selection of the mode of transport can be essential to a cost-effective, timely delivery of undamaged goods. We strongly advise you to consult your shipping representative, insurance agent, or freight broker for advice on packing and shipping. Refer also to the major tab section "Packing/Shipping/Insurance" for a general discussion of packing and shipping.

Printed materials may be shipped in bulk, boxes, crates, or other types of containers, depending on the type of product and whether it is prepackaged. General considerations include protection from contamination, weather, and pests. Containers should be constructed so as to be safe for handling during transport.

Publications Available

The *Harmonized Tariff Schedule of the United States* (HTSUS) is available from:

Government Printing Office (GPO)
Superintendent of Documents
Washington, DC 20402
(202) 512-1800 (Order line)
(202) 512-0000 (General)

The USGPO also has copies of specific laws available for purchase. The USGPO accepts credit card orders over the phone, as well as mail orders paid by credit card, a check drawn on a U.S. bank, or an international money order.

Relevant Government Agencies

Address your questions regarding waiver of country-specific import restrictions under Foreign Assets Control to:

U.S. Treasury Department
Office of Foreign Assets Control
Treasury Bldg.
Washington, DC 20220
(202) 622-2510

Address your questions regarding Customs-enforced copyright regulations to:

U.S. Customs Service
Office of Intellectual Property Rights
1301 Constitution Avenue NW
Washington, DC 20229
(202) 482-6960

Address your questions regarding importation of facsimiles of U.S. postage stamps to:

U.S. Secret Service
Department of Public Affairs
1800 G St. NW
Washington, DC 20223
(202) 435-5708

Address your questions regarding importation of printed materials to the district or port director of customs for you area. For addresses, refer to"U.S. Customs District Offices" on page 62 or contact:

U.S. Customs Service
1301 Constitution Ave. NW
Washington, DC 20229
(202) 927-6724 (Information)
(202) 927-1000 (General)

Laws and Regulations

The following laws and regulations may be relevant to the importation of printed materials. The laws are contained in the United States Code (USC), and the regulations are published in the Code of Federal Regulations (CFR), both of which are available at larger public and law libraries. Copies of specific laws are also available from the United States Government Printing Office (address above).

15 USC 1124
Trademark Act
This Act provides, among other things, that no imported article of foreign origin that bears a name or mark calculated to induce the public to believe that it was manufactured in the United States, or in any foreign country or locality other than the country or locality where it was in fact manufactured, shall be admitted entry at any customhouse in the U.S.

17 USC 101 et seq., 602(a)
Copyright Revision Act
This law provides that the importation into the U.S. of copies of a work acquired outside the U.S. without authorization of the copyright owner is an infringement of the copyright.

8 USC 2319
Criminal Penalties for Copyright Violations
This law imposes criminal penalties on persons who are found to have violated U.S. Copyright laws.

19 CFR 133.31 et seq.
Regulations of Customs on Recordation of Copyrights, Trademarks, and Trade Names
These regulations provide procedures and requirements for registering a copyright, trademark, or trade name with U.S. Customs, as well as procedures for enforcement, forfeiture of merchandise, and assessment of monetary penalties.

31 USC 1101 et seq.
Currency and Foreign Transactions Reporting Act (CFTR)
This Act controls the import of currency and negotiable instruments and requires the filing of a transaction report, Customs **Form 4790**, with U.S. Customs when you transport more than $10,000 in monetary instruments into or out of the U.S.

18 USC 471 et seq.
Importation of Counterfeit or Forged Obligations or Securities Act
This law prohibits the import of counterfeit obligations, securities, coins, currency, Customs forms, ships' papers, and the plates or stones for counterfeiting the same.

18 USC 955
Foreign Securities Act
This Act prohibits importation of counterfeit coins, stamps, securities, and similar items.

18 USC 2318
Trafficking in Counterfeit Labels
This law forbids the importation of counterfeit phonorecord labels, copies of motion pictures, and other audiovisual works.

18 USC 2320
Trafficking in Counterfeit Goods or Services
This law prohibits trafficking of counterfeit goods or services.

19 CFR 12.48
Regulations of Customs on Enforcement of Counterfeit Laws
These regulations describe the printed material prohibited from importation under counterfeit restrictions and the exceptions allowed.

31 CFR Part 401
Seizure and Forfeiture of Vessels, Vehicles, and Aircraft Used to Transport Counterfeit Coins, Obligations, and Paraphernalia
These regulations authorize the District Director of Customs to hold in custody vessels, vehicles, and aircraft used to violate 49 USC 781 and seized by the U.S. Secret Service officers while enforcing counterfeit laws.

46 USC App. 98
Conveyance of Bullion, Coin, Notes, or Bonds for United States
This law governs the carriage and conveyance of U.S. securities on vessels between U.S. ports and between U.S. ports and foreign ports.

Principal Exporting Countries

The following listing includes samples of the main supplier nations of the products of this chapter. It is organized by HTSUS major heading. (Refer to "Customs Classification" above for the product codes.) Countries are listed in rank order of the value of products imported to the U.S. Statistics represent customs value entries for 1993 from the Bureau of Census, U.S. Department of Commerce.

4901—United Kingdom, Hong Kong, Canada, Japan, Germany, Italy, Singapore, Spain, South Korea, China

4902—Canada, United Kingdom, Germany, Mexico, Japan, France, Italy, Spain, Hong Kong, Netherlands

4903—Singapore, Hong Kong, Mexico, China, Canada, Italy, Colombia, Thailand, Taiwan, United Kingdom

4904—United Kingdom, Germany, Australia, Canada, Italy, France, China, Austria, Japan, South Korea

4905—United Kingdom, Hong Kong, Canada, Italy, Germany, France, Spain, Singapore, Switzerland, Denmark

4906—Canada, Japan, Germany, United Kingdom, South Korea, France, Italy, Sweden, Switzerland, Israel

4907—Germany, United Kingdom, Canada, Japan, Sri Lanka, Indonesia, France, Belgium, Switzerland, Italy

4908—Germany, France, United Kingdom, Japan, Italy, Taiwan, Canada, South Korea, Mexico, Denmark

4909—China, United Kingdom, Canada, Mexico, Hong Kong, South Korea, Sweden, Denmark, Japan, Italy

4910—South Korea, Hong Kong, Canada, Japan, Singapore, Germany, Taiwan, Italy, China, Mexico

4911—Canada, Japan, United Kingdom, Germany, France, Italy, Hong Kong, Taiwan, China, Mexico

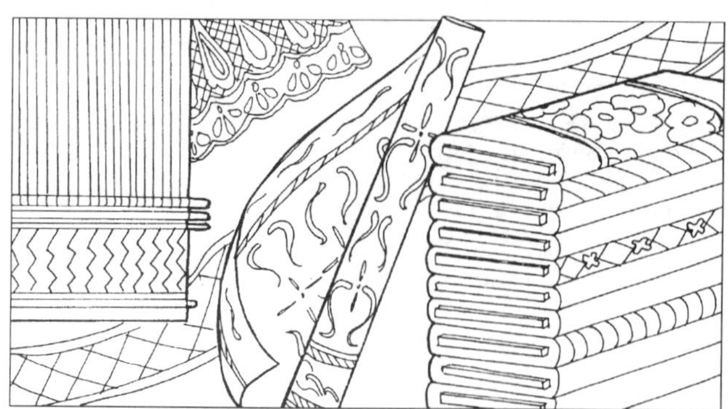

Chapter 50: Silk*

This chapter relates to the importation of silk products, which are classified under Chapter 50 of the Harmonized Tariff Schedule of the United States (HTSUS). Specifically, it includes silkworm cocoons for reeling, raw silk, silk waste, silk yarns, and fabrics woven of silk or silk waste.

If you are interested in importing silk apparel, you should refer to Commodity Index Chapter 62. If you are interested in importing footwear or leggings made of silk, you should refer to Chapter 64. For import requirements related to headgear made of silk, refer to Chapter 65.

Key Factors

The key factors in the importation of silk products are:

- Compliance with quota restraints and visa requirements under U.S. Department of Commerce (DOC) Multi-Fiber Arrangements
- Submission of U.S. Customs Country-of-Origin Declaration(s)
- Compliance with entry invoice requirements
- Compliance with labeling requirements under Textile Fiber Products Identification Act (TFPIA) and/ or the Wool Products Labeling Act (WPLA)
- Compliance with flammability standards adopted and enforced by the Consumer Product Safety Commission (CPSC) under the Flammable Fabrics Act (FFA)

Although most importers use the services of a licensed customs broker in making their entries, and we recommend this practice, you should be aware of the regulatory, entry, and documentation issues involved in importing your product. You, as importer, are ultimately responsible for the fulfillment of any legal requirements applicable to your shipment.

General Considerations

Regulatory Agencies. The DOC's Committee for Implementation of Textile Agreements (CITA) regulates certain textile imports under Section 204 of the Agricultural Adjustment Act. U.S. Customs enforces CITA textile and textile product entry quotas. Customs also enforces compliance with labeling and invoice requirements of the TFPIA and flammability standards under the FFA. The CPSC monitors imports and from time to time inspects textile shipments for compliance with FFA standards. If you are importing products that contain wool fibers, importation is subject to complex textile import regulations. The Federal Trade Commission (FTC) administers the WPLA requirements.

Quotas. If you are interested in importing silk products, the most important issue you need to be aware of is quotas. Under the Multi-Fiber Arrangement provisions of Section 204 of the Agricultural Adjustment Act, CITA initiates specific agreements with individual exporting countries. Section 204 of the Agricultural Adjustment Act covers textiles that: 1) are in chief value of cotton, wool, or man-made fibers, any textile fibers subject to the terms of any textile trade agreement, or any combination of such fibers; 2) contain 50% or more by weight of cotton or man-made fibers, or any textile fibers subject to the terms of any textile trade agreement; 3) contain 17% or more by weight of wool; or 4) if in chief value of textile fibers or textile materials, contain a blend of cotton, wool, or man-made fibers, any textile fibers subject to the terms of any textile trade agreement, or any combination of such fibers that, in total, amount to 50% or more by weight of all component fibers. For silk textile products, quotas currently apply to blends of silk and other fibers.

The U.S. has Multi-Fiber Arrangements with 40 countries. Each agreement with each country is unique, and may specify quotas for a type of textile or a specific article. Visas or export licenses may be required. Currently, certain silk blends are subject to some quota restraints, but these agreements often change. Therefore, if you are interested in importing any silk products, you should contact the International Trade Administration's Office of Textile and Apparel (see addresses at end of this chapter). Refer to "Prohibitions and Restrictions" below for further details.

Country-of-Origin Declarations. U.S. Customs enforces CITA textile and textile product entry quotas (see Prohibitions and Restrictions below). Requirements for entry include submission of Country-of-Origin Declarations with every silk textile shipment, regardless of whether it is subject to a specific multi-fiber arrangement (19 CFR 12.130, 12.131).

Country of Origin. Quota restrictions are country-specific and therefore are applied based on the country of origin for the textiles shipped. The last country from which a textile shipment was exported to the U.S. is not necessarily its country of origin. A textile or textile product imported into the U.S. is considered a product of the particular foreign territory or country, or a U.S. insular possession, where it is wholly grown, produced, or manufactured. For the following discussion, "country" means a foreign territory or country, or a U.S. insular possession.

Substantial transformation rules may affect the country-of-origin determination. For example, if a textile or textile product originates in Country A and is subject to quota, the quota restrictions apply at entry into the U.S. But if, prior to export to the U.S., you move the shipment to Country B where there are fewer restrictions, the shipment may nevertheless remain subject to quota and visa requirements under the Multi-Fiber Arrangement with Country A. Customs determines whether the quota restrictions apply based on the criteria of "substantial transformation." If your textiles do not undergo any major processing or manufacturing while in Country B, or if the manufacturing or processing is minor, your shipment will be deemed to originate in Country A. *You cannot claim substantial transformation on the basis of minor manufacturing procedures.*

In contrast, if your shipment undergoes major processing or manufacturing while in Country B, rendering the textiles "new and different articles of commerce," Customs will treat the shipment as the product of Country B. To qualify as having undergone substantial transformation, an article must evince a change in: 1) commercial designation or identity; b) fundamental character; or c) commercial use. If your shipment is processed in

*IMPORTANT: Read the Commodity Index Introduction. It is the essential framework for understanding this chapter.

more than one country, the country where it last underwent substantial transformation is the country of origin for Customs entry. In deciding whether the manufacturing or processing operation in a country is major, Customs considers the following factors: 1) the resultant physical change in the material or article; 2) the complexity, the level or degree of skill and/or technology required, and the amount of time involved in the operations; and 3) the value added to the article or material, compared to its value when imported into the U.S.

Validating Operations. The operations that Customs will usually acknowledge as validating a claim of substantial transformation are the following: 1) dyeing and printing, when accompanied by two or more of the following finishing operations: bleaching, shrinking, fulling, napping, decating, permanent stiffening, weighting, permanent embossing, or moireing; 2) spinning fibers into yarn; 3) weaving, knitting, or otherwise forming fabric; 4) cutting fabric into parts and assembling the parts into completed articles; or 5) substantial assembly, by sewing and/or tailoring into a completed garment all cut pieces of apparel articles that have been cut from fabric in another country —e.g., complete assembly and tailoring of all cut pieces of suit-type jackets, suits, and shirts.

Insubstantial Operations. Operations that usually will not support a claim of substantial transformation, even if more than one are performed, are the following: 1) simple operations of combining, labeling, pressing, cleaning, dry cleaning, or packaging; 2) cutting to length or width and hemming or overlocking fabrics that are readily identifiable as being intended for a particular commercial use; 3) trimming and/or joining together by sewing, looping, linking, or other means of attaching otherwise completed knit-to-shape component parts produced in a single country, even if accompanied by other processes—e.g., washing, drying, mending—normally incident to assembly; 4) one or more finishing operations on yarns, fabrics, or their textile articles—such as showerproofing, superwashing, bleaching, decating, fulling, shrinking, mercerizing, or similar operations; or 5) dyeing and/or printing fabrics or yarns.

Declarations. The country of origin of the silk textiles in a shipment must be stated on a declaration submitted to U.S. Customs at the time of entry. There are three Customs Country-of-Origin Declarations: single-country, multiple-country, and negative. The Declaration to be submitted with your shipment of silk textile products depends on the nature of the import.

- **Single-country declarations** are used for entries of textiles or textile products that clearly originate from only one country or that have been assembled in one country from fabricated components wholly produced in the U.S. or the foreign country of manufacture. Information required includes: marks of identification and numbers; description of article and quantity; country of origin; and date of exportation.
- **Multiple-country declarations** are used for entries of textiles or textile products that were manufactured or processed and/or that incorporate materials originating in more than one foreign country or territory. Information required includes: marks of identification and numbers; for articles, description, quantity, identification of manufacturing and/or processing operations, country, and date of exportation; for materials used to make articles, description of materials, country of production, and date of exportation.
- **Negative declarations** must accompany all textile imports that are not subject to FFA Section 204 restrictions. Information required includes: marks of identification and numbers; descriptions of article and quantity; and country of origin.

The date of exportation to be indicated on the above declarations is the date on which the carrier leaves the last port in the country of origin, as determined by Customs. Diversion to another country during transit does not affect the export date.

Procedure for Declarations. The manufacturer, producer, exporter, or importer may prepare the declaration. If more than one of these parties is involved in the importation, each party may prepare a separate declaration. You may file a separate declaration for each invoice presented with your entry. The declaration must be dated and signed by the responsible party, and must include the person's title and the company name and address. Your shipment's entry will be denied unless it is accompanied by a properly executed declaration. Customs will not treat a textile declaration as a missing document for which a bond may be filed.

Customs will base its country-of-origin determination on the information contained in each declaration, unless the information is insufficient. If the information on the declaration is insufficient, Customs will require that you submit such additional information as will enable the determination to be made. The shipment will not be released until the determination is made. Thus, if you want to clear Customs with minimal delay, be sure that the information on the declarations is as complete as possible for each shipment.

Textile Labeling and Invoice Requirements. You are responsible for your imported silk textile product's compliance with applicable provisions of the TFPIA. Silk textile products that require labeling under TFPIA must already be labeled at entry, or the shipment will be refused. (See "Marking and Labeling Requirements" below.) If you import shipments of silk textiles subject to TFPIA and valued at over $500, you must provide special information on the entry invoice (see "Entry and Documentation" below).

Flammability Standards. Silk textile products imported into the U.S. for use in consumer products must be in compliance with the FFA, a federal law that gives the CPSC the authority and responsibility for protecting the public from the hazards of dangerously flammable items of wearing apparel and interior furnishings. Under the FFA, standards have been established for flammability of clothing textiles. You cannot import any article of wearing apparel or interior furnishing, or any fabric or related material that is intended for use or that may be used in such items, if it fails to conform to an applicable flammability standard (FFA Section 4). Certain products may be imported into the U.S. (FFA Section 11c) for finishing or processing to render them less flammable so as to meet the standards. For these products, the exporter must state on the invoice or other paper relating to the shipment that the shipment is being made for that purpose.

The CPSC monitors imports of textiles under its Import Surveillance Program. From time to time, your textile shipments may be inspected to ascertain compliance with mandatory safety standards. Shipments may also be subject to testing by the CPSC to determine compliance. If the CPSC believes a product, fabric, or related material does not comply with a flammability standard, it is authorized to pursue a variety of legal sanctions (see "Prohibitions and Restrictions" below).

Substantial Product Hazard Reports. Any firm that obtains information that reasonably supports the conclusion that one of its products presents an unreasonable risk of serious injury or death must report that information to the CPSC's Division of Corrective Actions (CPSC address below). Importers must also report to the CPSC if 1) a type of product is the subject of at least three civil actions filed in U.S. federal or state courts, 2) each suit alleges the involvement of that product type in death or grievous bodily injury (as defined in FFA Section 37(3)1), and 3) at least three of the actions result in a final settlement with the manufacturer or in a judgment for the plaintiff within any one of the two-year periods specified in FFA Section 37(b).

Wool Product Entry Requirements. Depending on the nature of your wool fiber imports, as many as four different types of special entry documents may be required. First, for all imported textile fibers and yarns covered by the Agricultural Adjustment Act (AAA), including wool, you must file a U.S. Customs Textile Entry Declaration (see "Country-of-Origin Declarations" below). Second, with each wool shipment's entry summary, you must file Customs **Form 6451**, Notice of Percentage of Clean Yield and Grade of Wool or Hair, in duplicate, showing your name and address. Third, for all wool products subject to the WPLA, special information is required on the entry invoices (see "Entry and Documentation" below). Finally, certain wool articles manufactured or produced in certain countries may be subject to quotas under U.S. Department of Commerce Multi-Fiber Arrangements. Such products require export certificates or visas issued by the appropriate country of origin, in addition to other requisite entry paperwork (see "Quotas" above).

Wool Products Labeling Act. The term "wool product" means any product or any portion of a product that contains, purports to contain, or in any way is represented as containing wool, reprocessed wool, or reused wool. All wool products imported into the U.S., except those made more than 20 years before importation, and except carpets, rugs, mats, and upholsteries, must have affixed a stamp, tag, label, or other means of identification as required by the WPLA. If you are importing wool products exempt from labeling under the WPLA, do not assume they are also exempt from labeling under the TFPIA. These are two distinct laws, with some overlapping requirements (see "Marking and Labeling Requirements" below).

Import Advisory

Importation of textiles is trade-sensitive and highly regulated. Shipments of textiles and textile products not complying with all government regulations, including quotas and visas, are subject to seizure and could result in the imposition of penalties as well as possible forfeiture of the goods. You should always verify the available quota for any textile product you plan to import before your shipment leaves the country of manufacture. Furthermore, Customs textile classification rulings change frequently, and prior administrative rulings are often modified and sometimes reversed.

Customs Classification

For customs purposes, silk products are classified under Chapter 50 of the HTSUS. This chapter is broken into major headings, which are further divided into subheadings, and often sub-subheadings, each of which has its own HTSUS classification number. For example, the HTSUS number for noil silk fabric with 85% or more by weight of silk or silk waste is 5007.10.30, indicating it is a sub-subcategory of noil silk fabric (5007.10.00), which is a subcategory of the major heading, woven fabrics of silk or silk waste (5007.00.00). There are seven major headings within Chapter 50.

5001—Silkworm cocoons suitable for reeling

5002—Raw silk (not thrown)

5003—Silk waste (including cocoons unsuitable for reeling, yarn waste, and garnetted stock)

5004—Silk yarn (other than yarn spun from silk waste) not put up for retail sale

5005—Yarn spun from silk waste, not put up for retail sale

5006—Silk yarn and yarn spun from silk waste, put up for retail sale; silkworm gut

5007—Woven fabrics of silk or silk waste

For more details regarding classifications of the specific product you are interested in importing, consult a customs broker, the appropriate commodity specialist at your nearest customs port, or the HTSUS. HTSUS is available for purchase from the U.S. Government Printing Office (see addresses at end of this chapter), and may be found in larger public libraries. Refer to "Classification—Liquidation" on page 207 for a general discussion of customs classification.

Sample Import Duties

Import duties will vary depending on the HTSUS classification of your product. Therefore, to determine the correct amount of duties, your product must be properly classified under the HTSUS. The following sample duties are taken from the duty listings for HTSUS Chapter 50 products.

Raw silk (5002.00.00): free; silk waste not carded or combed (5003.10.00): free; other silk waste (5003.90.00): 5.5%; silk yarn not for retail (5004.00.00): 5%; yarn spun from silk or silk waste and put up for retail sale (5006.00.00): 5%; noil silk, with 85% or more by weight of silk or silk waste (5007.10.30): 5%; other noil silk fabrics (5007.10.60): 7.8%; silk fabrics other than noil silk, with 85% or more by weight of silk or silk waste (5007.20.00): 5%.

Entry and Documentation

The entry of merchandise is a two-part process consisting of 1) filing the documentation necessary to determine whether merchandise may be released from Customs custody, and 2) filing the documents that contain information for duty assessment and statistical purposes. In certain instances, all documents must be filed and accepted by Customs prior to release of the goods. Unless you have been granted an extension, you must file entry documents at a location specified by the district or area director within five working days of your shipment's date of arrival at a U.S. port of entry. These include a number of standard documents required by Customs for any entry, and:

- U.S. Customs Country-of-Origin Declaration(s)
- Export documentation and/or visa for textiles subject to Multi-Fiber Arrangement
- Customs **Form 6451**, Notice of Percentage of Clean Yield and Grade of Wool or Hair, in duplicate, showing your name and address (for articles containing wool)

After you present the entry, Customs may examine your shipment or may waive examination. The shipment is then released provided no legal or regulatory violations have been noted. You must then file entry summary documentation and deposit estimated duties at a designated customhouse within 10 working days of your shipment's release. For a detailed description of entry procedures, standard documentation, and informal entry, refer to "Entry Process" on page 182.

NAFTA Certificates of Origin. An importer of textiles for which NAFTA treatment is sought need not file a separate NAFTA Certificate of Origin in addition to the Customs Country-of-Origin Declaration. The declaration is sufficient. However, the importer must take care to submit a declaration from each U.S., Canadian, or Mexican producer or manufacturer. Thus, for multiple producers or manufacturers, a separate declaration must be filed for each. If a Customs district director cannot determine the country of origin because the declaration is absent or incomplete, the shipment is not entitled to preferential NAFTA tariff treatment or other NAFTA benefits. See 12 CFR 132.

Entry Invoices. You must provide certain additional information on the entry invoice for silk and silk products. The specific information varies depending on the nature of your product, as noted below.

TFPIA Requirements. For the purpose of TFPIA enforcement, a commercial shipment of textile products exceeding $500 in value and subject to TFPIA labeling requirements must show the following information: 1) The constituent fiber or combination of fibers, designating with equal prominence each natural or manufactured fiber by its generic name, in order of predominance by weight if the weight of such fiber is 5% or more of the total fiber weight of the product; 2) percentage of each fiber present, by weight, in the total fiber content; 3) the name or other identification issued and registered by the FTC of the manufacturer of the product or one or more persons subject to Section 3 of the TFPIA with respect to such product; 4) the name of the country where processed or manufactured.

Wool Products Subject to WPLA. When you offer for entry a wool product shipment valued at over $500 and subject to the WPLA, you must include certain information intended to facilitate Customs monitoring and enforcement of that Act. This extra information is identical to that required by WPLA on labeling (see "Marking and Labeling Requirements" below), with the addition of the manufacturer's name. If your product consists of mixed waste, residues, and similar merchandise obtained from several suppliers or unknown sources, you may omit the manufacturer's name from the entry invoice.

Yarn. All entry invoices for yarn should show: 1) Fiber content by weight; 2) whether the yarn is single or plied; 3) whether or not the yarn is put up for retail sale (as defined in HTSUS Section XI, Note 4); and 4) whether or not the yarn is intended for use as sewing thread.

In addition, if the yarn's chief weight is of silk, the entry invoice must show whether the silk is spun or filament.

Prohibitions and Restrictions

Quotas. Textile import restrictions are primarily a matter of quotas and the way in which these quotas are administered and monitored. Under the Multi-Fiber Arrangement provisions of Section 204 of the Agricultural Adjustment Act, CITA has negotiated Multi-Fiber Arrangements with 40 countries. These Agreements may impose quotas for a type of textile or a specific article, and they are country-specific. Currently, certain silk blends are subject to some quota restraints, but these agreements often change. Therefore, if you are interested in importing any silk products, you should contact the International Trade Administration's Office of Textile and Apparel (see addresses at end of this chapter). The Office of Textile and Apparel has a team of country specialists who can inform you of the latest developments and inform you about a product's quota or restriction status.

U.S. Customs enforces CITA textile and textile product entry quotas. If formal entry procedures are not followed, Customs will usually refuse entry for textiles that are subject to Section 204. Formal entry requires submission of a Country-of-Origin Declaration (see "General Considerations" above). U.S. Customs maintains a current textile quota status report, available for perusal at any Customs port. In addition, U.S. Customs in Washington, DC, operates a telephone service to provide quota status reports, which are updated weekly (see "Relevant Government Agencies" below).

Flammable Fabrics. U.S. Customs may refuse entry for any article of wearing apparel or interior furnishing, or any fabric or related material that is intended for use or that may be used in wearing apparel or interior furnishings, if it fails to conform to an applicable flammability standard issued under Section 4 of the FFA. An exception is allowed for certain products (FFA Section 11c) that are imported for finishing or processing to bring them within the legal standard. For these products, the exporter must state on the invoice or other paper relating to the shipment that the shipment is being made for that purpose.

The CPSC, as the primary enforcement agency of flammability standards, inspects products for compliance with the FFA. If the CPSC believes a product, fabric, or related material does not comply with a flammability standard, it is authorized to pursue a variety of legal sanctions, including: 1) seizure, condemnation, and forfeiture of the noncomplying products; 2) administrative cease-and-desist order requiring an individual or firm to stop sale and distribution of the noncomplying products or; 3) temporary injunction requiring the individual or firm to stop sale and distribution of the noncomplying products, pending final disposition of an administrative cease-and-desist proceeding. The CPSC also has authority to seek civil penalties against any person who knowingly violates a regulation or standard issued under Section 4 of the FFA.

Country-Specific Restrictions.

Restrictions under Multi-Fiber Arrangements are country-specific. A product originating in one country may be subject to quota and to export license or visa requirements, while the same product originating in a different country may not. At present, the U.S. has Multi-Fiber Arrangements with 40 countries. Many different categories of products are covered under these Arrangements; it is beyond the scope of this book to list each country and its restricted commodities. If you are interested in importing textiles and textile products, you should contact the International Trade Administration's Office of Textile and Apparel (see addresses at end of this chapter) or U.S. Customs to ascertain your product's restraint status.

The U.S. Customs Quota Branch phone numbers provide recorded status reports, by quota category number, for current charges against the quotas for that country. For convenience, the HTSUS shows the 3-digit category number in parentheses to the right of each listed commodity that is subject to textile restraints. For example, under Chapter 50, heading 5007.90.60, woven silk fabrics, other than fabrics containing 85% or more by weight of silk or silk waste, that are subject to wool restraints, is followed by the number "(410)." If you know the category number for your product, you can find out to what extent that quota is filled simply by calling the number for the appropriate country. A word of caution, though: if you do not know for sure that your article is subject to quota from a particular country, and you call the number for that country, you may not be any more enlightened after the phone call. Many of the recordings give status reports only when a certain percentage of the quota has been filled. Thus, if 410 for Indonesia is among the categories for which not enough quantity has entered the U.S. to warrant specific mention, it will be lumped under "all other categories" and you will be none the wiser. To find out if your product is subject to textile restraints, call the DOC or a local Customs port office. Then you can find out the current charges against that quota by calling the country number listed below. For a complete listing of Customs Quota Branch information numbers, see "Relevant Government Agencies" below.

Marking and Labeling Requirements

TFPIA Requirements. All textile fiber products imported into the U.S. must be stamped, tagged, labeled, or otherwise marked with the following information as required by the TFPIA, unless exempt from marking (see TFPIA, Section 12): 1) the generic names and percentages by weight of the constituent fibers present in the textile fiber product, exclusive of permissible ornamentation, in amounts of more than 5% in order of predominance by weight, with any percentage of fiber or fibers required to be designated as "other fiber" or "other fibers" (including those present in amounts of 5% or less) appearing last; and 2) the name of the manufacturer or the name or registered identification number issued by the FTC of one or more persons marketing or handling the textile fiber product; and 3) the name of the country where processed. A word trademark, used as a house mark and registered with the U.S. Patent Office, may appear on labels instead of the name otherwise required, provided the owner of the trademark furnishes a copy of the registration to the FTC prior to use (see "Registered Identification Numbers" below).

The information listed above is not exhaustive. TFPIA requirements are extensive. The Act specifies such details as types of labels, means of attachment, label position on the article, package labeling, unit labeling for two-piece garments, and arrangement of information on the label; allowable fiber designations; country-of-origin indications; requirements for trim and ornamentation, linings and interlinings, and pile fabrics; sectional disclosure; use of trade names and trademarks; and requirements for swatches and samples. The FTC publishes a booklet intended to clarify TFPIA requirements to facilitate voluntary compliance in the industry (see "Publications Available" below). It is available on request, at no charge, from the FTC (see addresses at end of this chapter).

Wool Products Labeling Act (WPLA). Wool product labeling requirements for foreign products are the responsibility of the importer. The WPLA requires the following information to appear on wool products subject to the Act: 1) percentage of the wool product's total fiber weight (exclusive of ornamentation) not exceeding 5% of the total fiber weight of a) wool, b) recycled wool, c) each fiber other than wool if the percent by weight of such fiber is 5% or more, and d) the aggregate of all other fibers; 2) the maximum percent of the wool product's total weight, of any nonfibrous loading, filling, or adulterating matter; and 3) the importer's name. If you, as importer, have a registered identification number issued by the FTC, that number may be used instead of your name (see "Registered Identification Numbers" below).

Customs entry is contingent on proper labeling. If your shipment is found to be mislabeled at entry, you will be given the option of relabelling the products under Customs supervision, as long as the district director is satisfied that your labeling error or omission did not involve fraud or willful neglect. If your shipment is discovered after entry to have been noncomplying with WPLA, it will be recalled to Customs custody at your expense, unless you can satisfy the district director that the products have since been brought into compliance. You will be held responsible for all expenses incurred in bringing a shipment into compliance, including compensation of personnel and other expenses related to Customs supervision.

Fraudulent violations of WPLA will result in seizure of the shipment. Shipments already released from Customs custody will be ordered to be redelivered to Customs. Customs reports all cases of fraudulent violation to the FTC in Washington, DC.

The information listed above is not intended to be exhaustive. WPLA requirements are extensive. The Act specifies such details as types of labels, means of attachment, label position on the article, package labeling, unit labeling (as in the case of a two-piece garment), arrangement of information on the label, allowable fiber designations, country-of-origin indications, trim and ornamentation, pile fabrics, sectional disclosure, use of trade names and trademarks, requirements for swatches and samples, etc. The FTC publishes a booklet intended to clarify WPLA requirements in order to facilitate voluntary compliance within the industry (see "Publications Available" below). It is available on request, at no charge, from the FTC (see addresses at end of this chapter).

Registered Identification Numbers. Any domestic firm or person residing in the U.S. and engaged in the manufacture or marketing of textile products covered under the TFPIA may obtain an FTC-registered identification number for use on required tags and labels instead of the name of a firm or person. For applications, contact the FTC (address below.)

For a general discussion of U.S. Customs marking and labeling requirements, refer to "Marking: Country of Origin" on page 215 and "Special Marking Requirements" on page 217.

Shipping Considerations

You will need to ensure that your goods are packaged and shipped with care so that they pass smoothly through Customs and arrive in good condition. You are responsible for ensuring that the shipment is in compliance with all applicable government regulations for packaging and shipping. In most instances, you should not leave these arrangements solely to the discretion of your supplier. Careful preparation of the cargo and selection of the mode of transport can be essential to a cost-effective, timely delivery of undamaged goods. We strongly advise you to consult your shipping representative, insurance agent, or freight broker for advice on packing and shipping. Refer also to the major tab section "Packing/Shipping/Insurance" for a general discussion of packing and shipping.

Silk products may be shipped in bulk, bolts, cartons, or other types of containers, depending on the type of product and whether it is prepackaged. General considerations include protection from contamination, weather, and pests. Containers should be constructed so as to be safe for handling during transport.

Publications Available

The following publications may be relevant to the importation of silk textiles, silk articles, and silk-wool blends:

Questions and Answers Relating to the Textile Fiber Products Identification Act and Regulations

Questions and Answers Relating to the Wool Products Labeling Act and Regulations

Available free of charge on request from the Federal Trade Commission, these publications are excellent sources of information written in clear lay language. We recommend that anyone interested in importing textile fiber products but unfamiliar with the regulations obtain a copy of each of these booklets.

The *Harmonized Tariff Schedule of the United States* (HTSUS) is available from:

Government Printing Office (GPO)
Superintendent of Documents
Washington, DC 20402
(202) 512-1800 (Order line)
(202) 512-0000 (General)

The USGPO also has copies of specific laws available for purchase. The USGPO accepts credit card orders over the phone, as well as mail orders paid by credit card, a check drawn on a U.S. bank, or an international money order.

Relevant Government Agencies

Address your questions regarding textile Multi-Fiber Arrangements to:

International Trade Administration
Office of Textile and Apparel
14th and Constitution Ave. NW, Rm. 3100
Washington, DC 20230
(202) 482-5078, 482-3737

Address your questions regarding the Flammable Fabrics Act (FFA) to:

Consumer Product Safety Commission (CPSC)
5401 Westbard Avenue
Bethesda, MD 20207
(301) 492-6580

Address your questions regarding requirements under the Textile Fiber Products Identification Act (TFPIA) or the Wool Products Labeling Act (WPLA) to:

Federal Trade Commission (FTC)
Division of Enforcement
601 Pennsylvania Ave. NW
Washington, DC 20580
(202) 326-2996 (General)
(202) 326-2841 (Textile and wool products labeling)

Address your questions regarding silk textile imports to the district or port director of Customs for you area. For addresses, refer to"U.S. Customs District Offices" on page 62 or contact:

U.S. Customs Service
1301 Constitution Ave. NW
Washington, DC 20229
(202) 927-6724 (Information)
(202) 927-1000 (General)

The following information numbers for U.S. Customs in Washington, DC, provide recorded information. The Quota Branch numbers listed by country provide updated status reports on textile quotas from those countries. All area codes are (202).
General information: 927-5850

Quota Branch: China 927-6703; India 927-6705; Indonesia 927-6704; Japan 927-6706; Korea 927-6707; Macao 927-6709; Malaysia 927-6712; Mexico 927-6711; Pakistan 927-6714; Philippines 927-6713; Romania 927-6715; Singapore 927-6716; Sri Lanka 927-6708; Taiwan 927-6719; Thailand 927-6717; Turkey 927-6718; All others 927-5850.

Laws and Regulations

The following laws and regulations may be relevant to the importation of silk products. The laws are contained in the United States Code (USC), and the regulations are published in the Code of Federal Regulations (CFR), both of which are available at larger public and law libraries. Copies of specific laws are also available from the United States Government Printing Office (address above).

7 USC 1854
Textile Trade Agreements
(EO 11651, as amended by EO 11951 and 12188, and supplemented by EO 12475)
This Act authorizes the CITA of the DOC to enter into Multi-Fiber Agreements with other countries to control trade in textiles and establishes the Textile Import Program, which is enforced by U.S. Customs.

19 CFR 12.130 et seq.
Regulations on Entry of Textiles
These regulations provide the requirements and procedures followed by Customs in enforcing limitations on the importation and entry and withdrawal of textiles and textile products from warehouses for consumption in the U.S.

19 CFR 141.89
Regulation on Additional Invoice Requirements
This regulation specifies the additional information for certain classes of merchandise, including footwear and textile products, being imported into the U.S.

15 USC 70-77
Textile Fiber Products Identification Act (TFPIA)
This Act prohibits false or deceptive labeling (misbranding) and false advertising of any textile fiber products and requires all textile fiber products imported into the U.S. to be labeled in accordance with the requirements set forth in the law.

19 CFR 11.12b; 16 CFR 303 et seq.
Regulations on Labeling and Marking
These regulations detail the labeling and marking requirements for textiles as specified by the CPSC and the invoice contents required by U.S. Customs for purpose of enforcing the labeling and marking rules.

15 USC 68-68j
Wool Products Labeling Act (WPLA)
This Act prohibits the false or deceptive labeling (misbranding) of wool products and requires all wool products imported into the U.S. to be labeled in accordance with requirements set forth in the law.

19 CFR 11.12; 16 CFR 300 et seq.
Regulations on WPLA Labeling and Marking
These regulations set forth the wool labeling and marking requirements adopted by the FTC to administer the requirements of the WPLA and provide the procedures followed by U.S. Customs in enforcing the WPLA and the FTC regulations, including entry invoice requirements.

15 USC 1191-1204
Flammable Fabrics Act (FFA)
This Act provides for the setting of flammability standards for fabric by the Consumer Product Safety Commission (CPSC) and for enforcement by U.S. Customs.

16 CFR 1610, 1611, 1615, 1616, 1630-1632
Regulations on Flammable Fabric Standards
These regulations specify the flammability standards adopted by the CPSC under the FFA for various types of textiles.

Principal Exporting Countries

The following listing includes samples of the main supplier nations of the products of this chapter. It is organized by HTSUS major heading. (Refer to "Customs Classification" above for the product codes.) Countries are listed in rank order of the value of products imported to the U.S. Statistics represent customs value entries for 1993 from the Bureau of Census, U.S. Department of Commerce.

5001—Canada

5002—Brazil, China, Hong Kong, Germany, United Kingdom, Italy, Egypt, India, Australia

5003—China, India, Thailand, Japan, United Kingdom, Belgium, Germany, Colombia, Italy, Netherlands

5004—China, Brazil, Italy, France, Switzerland, Hong Kong, Japan, Austria, United Kingdom, Dominican Rep.

5005—China, Thailand, France, Switzerland, Germany, Italy, Japan, Brazil, Hong Kong, Dominica

5006—China, Japan, France, Switzerland, Germany, United Kingdom, India, Italy, Australia, Spain

5007—Italy, South Korea, China, India, United Kingdom, Japan, Thailand, France, Hong Kong, Switzerland

Chapter 51: Wool and Animal Hair*

Full title: Wool, Fine or Coarse Animal Hair; Horsehair Yarn and Woven Fabric

This chapter relates to the importation of wool and animal hair products, which are classified under Chapter 51 of the Harmonized Tariff Schedule of the United States (HTSUS). Specifically, it includes uncarded and uncombed wool, uncarded and uncombed fine or coarse animal hair, yarn waste and other waste of wool or animal hair, wool or animal hair yarns, and woven fabrics of wool or animal hair. Animal hair includes the hair of alpaca, llama, vicuna, camel, yak, goat, rabbit, beaver, nutria, muskrat, and horse.

If you are interested in importing horsehair, human hair, brushmaking hair, and bristles, you should refer to Commodity Index Chapter 5. If you are interested in importing hides and skins with hair or wool attached, read Chapters 41 and 43. For importing a particular product made of wool or animal hair, you should refer to the Commodity Index chapter for that product. For example, wigs are covered in Chapter 67, footwear and leggings in Chapter 64, headgear in Chapter 65, carpets in Chapter 57, needlework sets and other textile art products in Chapter 63, and apparel in Chapters 60 through 62.

Key Factors

The key factors in the importation of wool and animal hair products are:

- Compliance with quota restraints and visa requirements under U.S. Department of Commerce (DOC) Multi-Fiber Arrangement
- Determination of grade and/or purpose of wool products being imported to ascertain dutiable status.
- Submission of U.S. Customs Country-of-Origin Declaration(s)
- Compliance with entry invoice requirements.
- Compliance with Wool Products Labeling Act (WPLA) or the Textile Fiber Products Identification Act (TFPIA)
- Compliance with flammability standards adopted and enforced by the Consumer Product Safety Commission (CPSC) under the Flammable Fabrics Act (FFA) (if importing fabrics and other textile products)

*IMPORTANT: Read the Commodity Index Introduction. It is the essential framework for understanding this section.

Although most importers use the services of a licensed customs broker in making their entries, and we recommend this practice, you should be aware of the regulatory, entry, and documentation issues involved in importing your product. You, as importer, are ultimately responsible for the fulfillment of any legal requirements applicable to your shipment.

General Considerations

Regulatory Agencies. Importation of wool and wool products is subject to complex textile import regulations. The Federal Trade Commission (FTC) administers the WPLA requirements. The DOC's Committee for Implementation of Textile Agreements (CITA) regulates certain textile imports under Section 204 of the Agricultural Adjustment Act. U.S. Customs enforces CITA textile and textile product entry quotas. Customs also enforces compliance with labeling and invoice requirements of the WPLA and the TFPIA, as well as flammability standards under the FFA. The CPSC monitors imports and from time to time inspects textile shipments for compliance with FFA standards.

Entry Requirements. Depending on the nature of your wool product imports, as many as five different types of special entry documents may be required. First, for all imported textile fibers, yarns, and fabrics covered by the Agricultural Adjustment Act (AAA), including wool, you must file a U.S. Customs Textile Entry Declaration (see "Country-of-Origin Declarations" below). Second, with each wool shipment's entry summary, you must file Customs **Form 6451**, Notice of Percentage of Clean Yield and Grade of Wool or Hair, in duplicate, showing your name and address. Third, for all wool products subject to the WPLA and all raw wool dutiable at a rate per clean kilogram, special information is required on the entry invoices (see "Entry and Documentation" below). Fourth, for shipments of wool dutiable at a rate per clean kilogram, you must also file one extra copy of the standard entry summary in addition to the copies otherwise required. Finally, certain wool articles manufactured or produced in certain countries may be subject to quotas under U.S. Department of Commerce Multi-Fiber Arrangements. Such products require export certificates or visas issued by the appropriate country of origin, in addition to other requisite entry paperwork (see "Quotas" below).

Wool Products Labeling Act. The term "wool product" means any product or any portion of a product that contains, purports to contain, or in any way is represented as containing wool, reprocessed wool, or reused wool. All wool products imported into the U.S., except those made more than 20 years before importation, and except carpets, rugs, mats, and upholsteries, must have affixed a stamp, tag, label, or other means of identification as required by the WPLA. If you are importing wool products exempt from labeling under the WPLA, do not assume they are also exempt from labeling under the TFPIA. These are two distinct laws, with some overlapping requirements (see "Marking and Labeling Requirements" below).

Quotas. If you are interested in importing wool and animal hair products, the most important issue you need to be aware of is quotas. Under the Multi-Fiber Arrangement provisions of Section 204 of the Agricultural Adjustment Act, CITA initiates specific agreements with individual exporting countries. Section 204 of the Agricultural Adjustment Act covers textiles that: 1) are in chief value of cotton, wool, or man-made fibers, any textile fibers subject to the terms of any textile trade agreement, or any combination of such fibers; 2) contain 50% or more by weight of cotton or man-made fibers, or any textile fibers subject to the terms of any textile trade agreement; 3) contain 17% or more by weight of wool; or 4) if in chief value of textile fibers or textile materials, contain a blend of cotton, wool, or man-made fibers, any textile fibers subject to the terms of any textile trade agreement, or any combination of such fibers that, in total, amount to 50% or more by weight of all component fibers.

The U.S. has Multi-Fiber Arrangements with 40 countries. Each agreement with each country is unique, and may specify quotas for a type of textile or a specific article. Visas or export licenses may be required. These agreements, however, often change. Therefore, if you are interested in importing any wool or animal hair products, you should contact the International Trade Administration's Office of Textile and Apparel (see addresses at end of this chapter). Refer to "Prohibitions and Restrictions" below for further details.

Country-of-Origin Declarations. U.S. Customs enforces CITA textile and textile product entry quotas (see "Prohibitions and Restrictions" below). Requirements for entry include submission of Country-of-Origin Declarations with every wool or animal hair textile shipment, regardless of whether it is subject to a specific multi-fiber arrangement (19 CFR 12.130, 12.131).

Country of Origin. Quota restrictions are country-specific and therefore are applied based on the country of origin for the textiles shipped. The last country from which a textile shipment was exported to the U.S. is not necessarily its country of origin. A textile or textile product imported into the U.S. is considered a product of the particular foreign territory or country, or a U.S. insular possession, where it is wholly grown, produced, or manufactured. For the following discussion, "country" means a foreign territory or country, or a U.S. insular possession.

Substantial transformation rules may affect the country-of-origin determination. For example, if a textile or textile product originates in Country A and is subject to quota, the quota restrictions apply at entry into the U.S. But if, prior to export to the U.S., you move the shipment to Country B where there are fewer restrictions, the shipment may nevertheless remain subject to quota and visa requirements under the Multi-Fiber Arrangement with Country A. Customs determines whether the quota restrictions apply based on the criteria of "substantial transformation." If your textiles do not undergo any major processing or manufacturing while in Country B, or if the manufacturing or processing is minor, your shipment will be deemed to originate in Country A. *You cannot claim substantial transformation on the basis of minor manufacturing procedures.*

In contrast, if your shipment undergoes major processing or manufacturing while in Country B, rendering the textiles "new and different articles of commerce," Customs will treat the shipment as the product of Country B. To qualify as having undergone substantial transformation, an article must evince a change in: 1) commercial designation or identity; b) fundamental character; or c) commercial use. If your shipment is processed in more than one country, the country where it last underwent substantial transformation is the country of origin for Customs entry. In deciding whether the manufacturing or processing operation in a country is major, Customs considers the following factors: 1) the resultant physical change in the material or article; 2) the complexity, the level or degree of skill and/or technology required, and the amount of time involved in the operations; and 3) the value added to the article or material, compared to its value when imported into the U.S.

Validating Operations. Operations that Customs will usually acknowledge as validating a claim of substantial transformation are the following: 1) dyeing and printing, when accompanied by two or more of the following finishing operations: bleaching, shrinking, fulling, napping, decating, permanent stiffening, weighting, permanent embossing, or moireing; 2) spinning fibers into yarn; 3) weaving, knitting, or otherwise forming fabric; 4) cutting fabric into parts and assembling the parts into completed articles; or 5) substantial assembly, by sewing and/or tailoring into a completed garment all cut pieces of apparel articles that have been cut from fabric in another country—e.g., complete assembly and tailoring of all cut pieces of suit-type jackets, suits, and shirts.

Insubstantial Operations. Operations that usually will not support a claim of substantial transformation, even if more than one are performed, are the following: 1) simple operations of combining, labeling, pressing, cleaning, dry cleaning, or packaging; 2) cutting to length or width and hemming or overlocking fabrics that are readily identifiable as being intended for a particular commercial use; 3) trimming and/or joining together by sewing, looping, linking, or other means of attaching otherwise completed knit-to-shape component parts produced in a single country, even if accompanied by other processes—e.g., washing, drying, mending—normally incident to assembly; 4) one or more finishing operations on yarns, fabrics, or their textile articles—such as showerproofing, superwashing, bleaching, decating, fulling, shrinking, mercerizing, or similar operations; or 5) dyeing and/or printing fabrics or yarns.

Declarations. The country of origin of the wool or animal hair textile products in a shipment must be stated on a declaration submitted to U.S. Customs at the time of entry. There are three Customs Country-of-Origin Declarations: single-country, multiple-country, and negative. The Declaration to be submitted with your shipment of wool or animal hair textile products depends on the nature of the import.

- **Single-country declarations** are used for entries of textiles or textile products that clearly originate from only one country or that have been assembled in one country from fabricated components wholly produced in the U.S. or the foreign country of manufacture. Information required includes: marks of identification and numbers; description of article and quantity; country of origin; and date of exportation.
- **Multiple-country declarations** are used for entries of textiles or textile products that were manufactured or processed and/or that incorporate materials originating in more than one foreign country or territory. Information required includes: marks of identification and numbers; for articles, description, quantity, identification of manufacturing and/or processing operations, country, and date of exportation; for materials used to make articles, description of materials, country of production, and date of exportation.
- **Negative declarations** must accompany all textile imports that are not subject to FFA Section 204 restrictions. Information required includes: marks of identification and numbers; descriptions of article and quantity; and country of origin.

The date of exportation to be indicated on the above declarations is the date on which the carrier leaves the last port in the country of origin, as determined by Customs. Diversion to another country during transit does not affect the export date.

Procedure for Declarations. The manufacturer, producer, exporter, or importer may prepare the declaration. If more than one of these parties is involved in the importation, each party may prepare a separate declaration. You may file a separate declaration for each invoice presented with your entry. The declaration must be dated and signed by the responsible party, and must include the person's title and the company name and address. Your shipment's entry will be denied unless it is accompanied by a properly executed declaration. Customs will not treat a textile declaration as a missing document for which a bond may be filed.

Customs will base its country-of-origin determination on the information contained in each declaration, unless the information is insufficient. If the information on the declaration is insufficient, Customs will require that you submit such additional information as will enable the determination to be made. The shipment will not be released until the determination is made. Thus, if you want to clear Customs with minimal delay, be sure that the information on the declarations is as complete as possible for each shipment.

Flammability Standards. Wool and animal hair textile products imported into the U.S. for use in consumer products must be in compliance with the FFA, a federal law that gives the CPSC the authority and responsibility for protecting the public from the hazards of dangerously flammable items of wearing apparel and interior furnishings. Under the FFA, standards have been established for flammability of clothing textiles. You cannot import any article of wearing apparel or interior furnishing, or any fabric or related material that is intended for use or that may be used in such items, if it fails to conform to an applicable flammability standard (FFA Section 4). Certain products may be imported into the U.S. (FFA Section 11c) for finishing or processing to render them less flammable so as to meet the standards. For these products, the exporter must state on the invoice or other paper relating to the shipment that the shipment is being made for that purpose.

The CPSC monitors imports of textiles under its Import Surveillance Program. From time to time, your textile shipments may be inspected to ascertain compliance with mandatory safety standards. Shipments may also be subject to testing by the CPSC to determine compliance. If the CPSC believes a product, fabric, or related material does not comply with a flammability standard, it is authorized to pursue a variety of legal sanctions (see "Prohibitions and Restrictions" below).

Substantial Product Hazard Reports. Any firm that obtains information that reasonably supports the conclusion that one of its products presents an unreasonable risk of serious injury or death must report that information to the CPSC's Division of Corrective Actions (CPSC address below). Importers must also report to the CPSC if 1) a type of product is the subject of at least three civil actions filed in U.S. federal or state courts, 2) each suit alleges the involvement of that product type in death or grievous bodily injury (as defined in FFA Section 37(3)1), and 3) at least three of the actions result in a final settlement with the manufacturer or in a judgment for the plaintiff within any one of the two-year periods specified in FFA Section 37(b).

Import Advisory

Importation of textiles is trade-sensitive and highly regulated. Shipments of textiles and textile products not complying with all government regulations, including quotas and visas, are subject to seizure and could result in the imposition of penalties as well as possible forfeiture of the goods. You should always verify the available quota for any textile product you plan to import before your shipment leaves the country of manufacture. Furthermore, Customs textile classification rulings change frequently, and prior administrative rulings are often modified and sometimes reversed.

Customs Classification

For customs purposes, wool and animal hair products are classified under Chapter 51 of the HTSUS. This chapter is broken into major headings, which are further divided into subheadings, and often sub-subheadings, each of which has its own HTSUS classification number. For example, the HTSUS number for carded Angora rabbit hair yarn is 5108.10.30, indicating it is a sub-subcategory of carded yarn (5108.10.00), which is a subcategory of the major heading, yarn of fine animal hair, etc., not for retail sale (5108.00.00). There are 13 major headings within Chapter 51.

5101—Wool, not carded or combed

5102—Fine or coarse animal hair, not carded or combed

5103—Waste of wool or of fine or coarse animal hair, including yarn waste but excluding garnetted stock

5104—Garnetted stock of wool or of fine or coarse animal hair

5105—Wool and fine or coarse animal hair, carded or combed (including combed wool in fragments)

5106—Yarn of carded wool, not put up for retail sale

5107—Yarn of combed wool, not put up for retail sale

5108—Yarn of fine animal hair (carded or combed), not put up for retail sale

5109—Yarn of wool or fine animal hair, put up for retail sale

5110—Yarn of coarse animal hair or of horsehair (including gimped horsehair yarn), whether or not put up for retail sale

5111—Woven fabrics of carded wool or of carded fine animal hair

5112—Woven fabrics of combed wool or of combed fine animal hair

5113—Woven fabrics of coarse animal hair or of horsehair

Classification of Wool. Customs makes several basic distinctions among wools for duty classification purposes. Duty rates vary depending on the degree to which the wool is processed (i.e. sheared and degreased only versus in finished fabric form), whether the wool is rated as unimproved, and whether the wool is brought in "for special uses."

Processed and Unprocessed Wool. In general, wool not carded or combed and not processed other than degreased enters free under bond. Most other "raw" wool is dutiable per clean kilogram, with rates rising as the grade of wool becomes finer. All shipments of wool are examined to determine grade based on the standards established by the Secretary of Agriculture and in effect on the date of importation. Roughly defined, clean yield means absolute clean content (i.e. all that portion of the merchandise that consists exclusively of wool and is free from all vegetable and other foreign material). There are allowances for moisture content and other factors. If you need more technical details, see Additional U.S. Note 2 to HTSUS Chapter 51. For information on duty determination procedures, see 19 CFR 151.65 et seq.

Unimproved and Improved Wool. Unimproved wool includes Aleppo, Arabian, Bagdad, Black Spanish, Chinese, Cordova, Cyprus, Donskoi, East Indian, Ecuadorian, Egyptian, Georgian, Has lock, Iceland, Karakul, Kerry, Manchurian, Mongolian, Oporto, Persian, Pyrenean, Sardinian, Scotch Blackface, Sistan, Smyrna, Sudan, Syrian, Tibetan Turkestan, Valparaiso, or Welsh Mountain wool, and similar wool not improved by an admixture of merino or English blood.

Wool for Special Uses. Unimproved wool and other wool of any blood or origin not finer than 46s may be entered duty-free under the category "for special uses" by a dealer, manufacturer, or processor. It must be certified for use only in the manufacture of the following: 1) felt or knit boots; 2) floor coverings; 3) heavy filled lumbermen's socks; 3) press cloth; 4) papermakers' felts; or 5) pressed felt for polishing plate and mirror glass.

If you enter wool for special purposes, you must file a bond with the Customs port of entry which insures that the wool will be used only for the allowed purposes. Your shipment will be released when the bond is filed. As original importer, you are liable for the use limitations of the bond, until or unless you transfer the shipment under similar bond to a different dealer, manufacturer, or processor.

If the wool is used, or transferred for use, outside permitted uses under the bond, the current bondholder will be liable for any duties applicable because of tariff reclassification. Furthermore, every bondholder is required to report any such transfer or use of merchandise within 30 days to the district director of Customs in whose district the bond is filed. Failure to report will result in a penalty—in addition to duties—equal to the value of the merchandise in question.

Sampling for Classification. Customs determines clean yield for classification purposes by testing samples taken from all raw wool shipments. Testing is done in a Customs laboratory, pursuant to regulations in 19 CFR 151.71. If sampling is not feasible for your shipment, Customs will estimate the percentage clean yield of each lot by examination. For either means of clean-yield determination, Customs will report the percentage clean yield of each lot to you by mail.

If, as a result of Customs examination, the wool is classified at a higher grade than the grade you stated at entry, thus incurring a higher rate of duty, the district director will notify you by mail. You have the option to contest the assessment by filing within 14 days of the date on which Customs mails your clean-yield notification a request, in duplicate, for redetermination of grade. You will have to state reasons for requesting this reexamination, and you will need to make a second general sample available for such retesting, or an adequate number of the packages represented by the general sample must be available in their original imported condition. All costs of this retesting or re-examination, except for compensation of Customs employees, will be charged to you. Customs will mail a notice of reexamination results to you.

If you are not satisfied with the results of the second test or examination, you may request testing in a commercial lab. Again, this request must be filed with the appropriate district director within 14 days of the date on which Customs mails you the second test results. The district director chooses the commercial lab. All costs associated with such testing, including any travel-related expenses for Customs officers, are your responsibility.

Preliminary duties may be estimated when you file the entry summary, on the basis of the clean yield shown on it. However, liquidated duties are based on the district director's final determination of clean yield. If more than one examination or test has been performed on your shipment, the district director will take the findings from all applicable tests or examinations into consideration in making the final duty determination. For more details regarding sampling, testing, and contesting procedures, see 19 CFR 151.68-75.

For more details regarding classifications of the specific product you are interested in importing, consult a customs broker, the appropriate commodity specialist at your nearest customs port, or the HTSUS. HTSUS is available for purchase from the U.S. Government Printing Office (see addresses at end of this chapter), and may be found in larger public libraries. Refer to "Classification—Liquidation" on page 207 for a general discussion of customs classification.

Sample Import Duties

Import duties will vary depending on the HTSUS classification of your product. Therefore, to determine the correct amount of duties, your product must be properly classified under the HTSUS. The following sample duties are taken from the duty listings for HTSUS Chapter 51 products.

Shorn wool, not carded or combed, greasy, not for special uses, and unimproved or not finer than 40s (5101.11.20): 5.5 cents/clean kg; finer than 40s but not finer than 44s (5101.11.40): 6.6 cents/clean kg; finer than 44s (5101.11.50): 22 cents/clean kg; camel hair, not processed beyond degreased or carbonized condition (5102.10.20): 11 cents/clean kg; cashmere goat hair, not processed beyond degreased or carbonized condition (5102.10.40): 8 cents/clean kg; coarse animal hair not carded or combed (5102.20.00): free; noils of wool or fine animal hair (5103.10.00): 4 cents/kg; garnetted stock of wool or animal hair (5104.00.00): 5.5 cents/kg; carded wool (5105.10.00): 7.7 cents/kg plus 6.25%; yarn of carded or combed wool, not for retail sale (5106, 5107): 9%; yarn of carded Angora rabbit hair, not for retail sale (5108.10.30) 5%; yarn with 85% or more by weight of wool, for retail sale, colored, and cut into uniform lengths of not over 8 cm (5109.10.20): free; yarn of coarse animal hair or horsehair (5110.00.00): 3.7%; woven tapestry or upholstery fabrics with 85% or more by weight of carded wool or fine animal hair and of a weight not exceeding 140 g/m^2 (5111.11.20): 7%; woven fabrics of carded wool or fine animal hair with 30% or more by weight of silk or silk waste, valued at over $33/kg (5111.90.30): 7.8%; woven fabrics of coarse animal hair or horsehair (5113.00.00): 5.3%

Entry and Documentation

The entry of merchandise is a two-part process consisting of 1) filing the documentation necessary to determine whether merchandise may be released from Customs custody, and 2) filing the documents that contain information for duty assessment and statistical purposes. In certain instances, all documents must be filed and accepted by Customs prior to release of the goods. Unless you have been granted an extension, you must file entry documents at a location specified by the district or area director within five working days of your shipment's date of arrival at a U.S. port of entry. These include a number of standard documents required by Customs for any entry, and:

- U.S. Customs Country-of-Origin Declaration(s)
- Customs **Form 6451**, Notice of Percentage of Clean Yield and Grade of Wool or Hair, in duplicate
- Export documentation and/or visa for textiles subject to Multi-Fiber Arrangement
- One extra copy of the standard entry summary (for shipments of wool dutiable at a rate per clean kg)

After you present the entry, Customs may examine your shipment or may waive examination. The shipment is then released provided no legal or regulatory violations have been noted. You must then file entry summary documentation and deposit estimated duties at a designated customhouse within 10 working days of your shipment's release. For a detailed description of entry procedures, standard documentation, and informal entry, refer to "Entry Process" on page 182.

NAFTA Certificates of Origin. An importer of textiles for which NAFTA treatment is sought need not file a separate NAFTA Certificate of Origin in addition to the Customs Country-of-Origin Declaration. The declaration is sufficient. However, the importer must take care to submit a declaration from each U.S., Canadian, or Mexican producer or manufacturer. Thus, for multiple producers or manufacturers, a separate declaration must be filed for each. If a Customs district director cannot determine the country of origin because the declaration is absent or incomplete, the shipment is not entitled to preferential NAFTA tariff treatment or other NAFTA benefits. See 12 CFR 132.

Entry Invoices. You must provide certain additional information on the entry invoice for wool and wool products. The specific information varies depending on the nature of your product, as noted below.

Wool Products Subject to WPLA. When you offer for entry a wool product shipment valued at over $500 and subject to the WPLA, you must include certain information intended to facilitate Customs monitoring and enforcement of that Act. This extra information is identical to that required by WPLA on labeling (see "Marking and Labeling Requirements" below), with the addition of the manufacturer's name. If your product consists of mixed waste, residues, and similar merchandise obtained from several suppliers or unknown sources, you may omit the manufacturer's name from the entry invoice.

Raw Wool. Invoices of wool subject to duty at a rate per clean kilogram under HTSUS Chapter 51 must show the following detailed information in addition to other information required: 1) Condition—that is, whether greasy, washed, pulled, on the skin, scoured, carbonized, burrpicked, willowed, handshaken, or beaten; 2) whether free of vegetable matter, practically free, slightly burry, medium burry, or heavy burry; 3) whether in fleece, skirted, matchings, or sorted; 4) length—that is, whether super combing, ordinary combing, clothing, or filling; 5) country of origin, and, if possible, the province, section, or locality of production; 6) the type symbol by which the wool is bought and sold in the country of origin, and the grade of each lot, specifying the standard or basis used—that is, U.S. Official Standards or the country of shipment's commercial grade designation terms; and 7) net weight of each lot covered by the invoice in the condition in which it is shipped, and the shipper's estimate of the clean yield of each lot by weight or by percentage.

Wool Products Subject to TFPIA. For the purpose of TFPIA enforcement, a commercial shipment of textile products exceeding $500 in value and subject to TFPIA labeling requirements must show the following information: 1) the constituent fiber or combination of fibers, designating with equal prominence each natural or manufactured fiber by its generic name, in order of predominance by weight if the weight of such fiber is 5% or more of the total fiber weight of the product; 2) percentage of each fiber present, by weight, in the total fiber content; 3) the name or other identification issued and registered by the FTC of the manufacturer of the product or one or more persons subject to Section 3 of the TFPIA with respect to such product; and 4) the name of the country where processed or manufactured.

Yarn. All entry invoices for yarn should show: 1) fiber content by weight; 2) whether the yarn is single or plied; 3) whether or not the yarn is put up for retail sale (as defined in HTSUS Section XI, Note 4); and 4) whether or not the yarn is intended for use as sewing thread.

Prohibitions and Restrictions

Quotas. Textile import restrictions are primarily a matter of quotas and the way in which these quotas are administered and monitored. Under the Multi-Fiber Arrangement provisions of Section 204 of the Agricultural Adjustment Act, CITA has negotiated Multi-Fiber Arrangements with 40 countries. These Agreements may impose quotas for a type of textile or a specific article, and they are country-specific. These agreements, however, often change. Therefore, if you are interested in importing any wool products, you should contact the International Trade Administration's Office of Textile and Apparel (see addresses at end of this chapter). The Office of Textile and Apparel has a team of country specialists who can inform you of the latest developments and inform you about a product's quota or restriction status.

U.S. Customs enforces CITA textile and textile product entry quotas. If formal entry procedures are not followed, Customs will usually refuse entry for textiles that are subject to Section 204. Formal entry requires submission of a Country-of-Origin Declaration (see "General Considerations" above). U.S. Customs maintains a current textile quota status report, available for perusal at any Customs port. In addition, U.S. Customs in Washington, DC, operates a telephone service to provide quota status reports, which are updated weekly (see "Relevant Government Agencies" below).

Flammable Fabrics. U.S. Customs may refuse entry for any article of wearing apparel or interior furnishing, or any fabric or related material that is intended for use or that may be used in wearing apparel or interior furnishings, if it fails to conform to an applicable flammability standard issued under Section 4 of the FFA. An exception is allowed for certain products (FFA Section 11c) that are imported for finishing or processing to bring them within the legal standard. For these products, the exporter must state on the invoice or other paper relating to the shipment that the shipment is being made for that purpose.

The CPSC, as the primary enforcement agency of flammability standards, inspects products for compliance with the FFA. If the CPSC believes a product, fabric, or related material does not comply with a flammability standard, it is authorized to pursue a variety of legal sanctions, including: 1) seizure, condemnation, and forfeiture of the noncomplying products; 2) administrative cease-and-desist order requiring an individual or firm to stop sale and distribution of the noncomplying products or; 3) temporary injunction requiring the individual or firm to stop sale and distribution of the noncomplying products, pending final disposition of an administrative cease-and-desist proceeding. The CPSC also has authority to seek civil penalties against any person who knowingly violates a regulation or standard issued under Section 4 of the FFA.

Country-Specific Restrictions.

Restrictions under Multi-Fiber Arrangements are country-specific. A product originating in one country may be subject to quota and to export license or visa requirements, while the same product originating in a different country may not. At present, the U.S. has Multi-Fiber Arrangements with 40 countries. Many different categories of products are covered under these Arrangements; it is beyond the scope of this book to list each country and its restricted commodities. If you are interested in importing textiles and textile products, you should contact the International Trade Administration's Office of Textile and Apparel (see addresses at end of this chapter) or U.S. Customs to ascertain your product's restraint status.

The U.S. Customs Quota Branch phone numbers provide recorded status reports, by quota category number, for current charges against the quotas for that country. For convenience, the HTSUS shows the 3-digit category number in parentheses to the right of each listed commodity that is subject to textile restraints. For example, under Chapter 51, heading 5111.11.20, tapestry and upholstery fabrics with 85% or more by weight of carded wool or fine animal hair and of a weight not exceeding 140 g/m^2, is followed by the number "(414)." If you know the category number for your product, you can find out to what extent that quota is filled simply by calling the number for the appropriate country. A word of caution, though: if you do not know for sure that your article is subject to quota from a particular country, and you call the number for that country, you may not be any more enlightened after the phone call. Many of the recordings give status reports only when a certain percentage of the quota has been filled. Thus, if 414 for Korea is among the categories for which not enough quantity has entered the U.S. to warrant specific mention, it will be lumped under "all other categories" and you will be none the wiser. To find out if your product is subject to textile restraints, call the DOC or a local Customs port office. Then you can find out the current charges against that quota by calling the country number listed below. For a complete listing of Customs Quota Branch information numbers, see "Relevant Government Agencies" below.

Marking and Labeling Requirements

Wool Products Labeling Act (WPLA). Wool product labeling requirements for foreign products are the responsibility of the importer. The WPLA requires the following information to appear on wool products subject to the Act: 1) percentage of the wool product's total fiber weight (exclusive of ornamentation) not exceeding 5% of the total fiber weight of a) wool, b) reprocessed wool, c) reused wool, d) each fiber other than wool if the percentage by weight of such fiber is 5% or more, and e) the aggregate of all other fibers; 2) the maximum percentage of the wool product's total weight, of any nonfibrous loading, filling, or adulterating matter; and 3) the importer's name. If you, as importer, have a registered identification number issued by the FTC, that number may be used instead of your name (see Registered Identification Numbers below).

Customs entry is contingent on proper labeling. If your shipment is found to be mislabeled at entry, you will be given the option of relabelling the products under Customs supervision, as long as the district director is satisfied that your labeling error or omission did not involve fraud or willful neglect. If your shipment is discovered after entry to have been noncomplying with WPLA, it will be recalled to Customs custody at your expense, unless you can satisfy the district director that the products have since been brought into compliance. You will be held responsible for all expenses incurred in bringing a shipment into compliance, including compensation of personnel and other expenses related to Customs supervision.

Fraudulent violations of WPLA will result in seizure of the shipment. Shipments already released from Customs custody will be ordered to be redelivered to Customs. Customs reports all cases of fraudulent violation to the FTC in Washington, DC.

The information listed above is not intended to be exhaustive. WPLA requirements are extensive. The Act specifies such details as types of labels, means of attachment, label position on the article, package labeling, unit labeling (as in the case of a two-piece garment), arrangement of information on the label, allowable fiber designations, country-of-origin indications, trim and ornamentation, pile fabrics, sectional disclosure, use of trade names and trademarks, requirements for swatches and samples, etc. The FTC publishes a booklet intended to clarify WPLA requirements in order to facilitate voluntary compliance within the industry (see "Publications Available" below). It is available on request, at no charge, from the FTC (see addresses at end of this chapter).

Wool Products Subject to TFPIA. All textile fiber products imported into the U.S. must be stamped, tagged, labeled, or otherwise marked with the following information as required by the TFPIA, unless exempt from marking (see TFPIA, Section 12): 1) the generic names and percentages by weight of the constituent fibers present in the textile fiber product, exclusive of permissible ornamentation, in amounts of more than 5% in order of predominance by weight, with any percentage of fiber or fibers required to be designated as "other fiber" or "other fibers" (including those present in amounts of 5% or less) appearing last; and 2) the name of the manufacturer or the name or registered identification number issued by the FTC of one or more persons marketing or handling the textile fiber product; and 3) the name of the country where processed. A word trademark, used as a house mark and registered with the U.S. Patent Office, may appear on labels instead of the name otherwise required, provided the owner of the trademark furnishes a copy of the registration to the FTC prior to use (see "Registered Identification Numbers" below).

The information listed above is not exhaustive. TFPIA requirements are extensive. The Act specifies such details as types of labels, means of attachment, label position on the article, package labeling, unit labeling for two-piece garments, and arrangement of information on the label; allowable fiber designations; country-of-origin indications; requirements for trim and ornamentation, linings and interlinings, and pile fabrics; sectional disclosure; use of trade names and trademarks; and requirements for swatches and samples. The FTC publishes a booklet intended to clarify TFPIA requirements to facilitate voluntary compliance in the industry (see "Publications Available" below). It is available on request, at no charge, from the FTC (see addresses at end of this chapter).

Registered Identification Numbers. Any domestic firm or person residing in the U.S. and engaged in the manufacture or marketing of textile products covered under the WPLA or the TFPIA may obtain an FTC-registered identification number for use on required tags and labels instead of the name of a firm or person. For applications, contact the FTC (address below.)

For a general discussion of U.S. Customs marking and labeling requirements, refer to "Marking: Country of Origin" on page 215 and "Special Marking Requirements" on page 217.

Shipping Considerations

You will need to ensure that your goods are packaged and shipped with care so that they pass smoothly through Customs and arrive in good condition. You are responsible for ensuring that the shipment is in compliance with all applicable government regulations for packaging and shipping. In most instances, you should not leave these arrangements solely to the discretion of your supplier. Careful preparation of the cargo and selection of the mode of transport can be essential to a cost-effective, timely delivery of undamaged goods. We strongly advise you to consult your shipping representative, insurance agent, or freight broker for advice on packing and shipping. Refer also to the major tab section "Packing/Shipping/Insurance" for a general discussion of packing and shipping.

Wool products may be shipped in bulk, bolts, cartons, or other types of containers, depending on the type of product and whether it is prepackaged. General considerations include protection from contamination, weather, and pests. Containers should be constructed so as to be safe for handling during transport.

Publications Available

The following publications may be relevant to the importation of wool products.

Questions and Answers Relating to the Wool Products Labeling Act and Regulations

Questions and Answers Relating to the Textile Fiber Products Identification Act and Regulations

Available free of charge on request from the Federal Trade Commission, these publications are excellent sources of information written in clear lay language. We recommend that anyone interested in importing wool products but unfamiliar with the regulations obtain a copy of each of these booklets.

The *Harmonized Tariff Schedule of the United States* (HTSUS) is available from:

Government Printing Office (GPO)
Superintendent of Documents
Washington, DC 20402
(202) 512-1800 (Order line)
(202) 512-0000 (General)

The USGPO also has copies of specific laws available for purchase. The USGPO accepts credit card orders over the phone, as well as mail orders paid by credit card, a check drawn on a U.S. bank, or an international money order.

Relevant Government Agencies

Address your questions regarding FTC wool labeling requirements and requirements under the Textile Fiber Products Identification Act (TFPIA) to:

Federal Trade Commission (FTC)
Division of Enforcement
601 Pennsylvania Ave. NW

Washington, DC 20580
(202) 326-2996 (General)
(202) 326-2841 (Textile and wool products labeling)

Address your questions regarding textile Multi-Fiber Arrangements to:

International Trade Administration
Office of Textile and Apparel
14th and Constitution Ave. NW, Rm. 3100
Washington, DC 20230
(202) 482-5078, 482-3737

Address your questions regarding the Flammable Fabrics Act (FFA) to:

Consumer Product Safety Commission (CPSC)
5401 Westbard Avenue
Bethesda, MD 20207
(301) 492-6580

Address your questions regarding wool product imports to the district or port director of Customs for you area. For addresses, refer to"U.S. Customs District Offices" on page 62 or contact:

U.S. Customs Service
1301 Constitution Ave. NW
Washington, DC 20229
(202) 927-6724 (Information)
(202) 927-1000 (General)

The following information numbers for U.S. Customs in Washington, DC, provide recorded information. The Quota Branch numbers listed by country provide updated status reports on textile quotas from those countries. All area codes are (202).
General information: 927-5850

Quota Branch: China 927-6703; India 927-6705; Indonesia 927-6704; Japan 927-6706; Korea 927-6707; Macao 927-6709; Malaysia 927-6712; Mexico 927-6711; Pakistan 927-6714; Philippines 927-6713; Romania 927-6715; Singapore 927-6716; Sri Lanka 927-6708; Taiwan 927-6719; Thailand 927-6717; Turkey 927-6718; All others 927-5850.

Laws and Regulations

The following laws and regulations may be relevant to the importation of wool products. The laws are contained in the United States Code (USC), and the regulations are published in the Code of Federal Regulations (CFR), both of which are available at larger public and law libraries. Copies of specific laws are also available from the United States Government Printing Office (address above).

15 USC 68-68j
Wool Products Labeling Act (WPLA)
This Act prohibits the false or deceptive labeling (misbranding) of wool products and requires all wool products imported into the U.S. to be labeled in accordance with requirements set forth in the law.

19 CFR 11.12; 16 CFR 300 et seq.
Regulations on WPLA Labeling and Marking
These regulations set forth the wool labeling and marking requirements adopted by the FTC to administer the requirements of the WPLA and provide the procedures followed by U.S. Customs in enforcing the WPLA and the FTC regulations, including entry invoice requirements.

7 USC 1854
Textile Trade Agreements
(EO 11651, as amended by EO 11951 and 12188, and supplemented by EO 12475)
This Act authorizes the CITA of the DOC to enter into Multi-Fiber Agreements with other countries to control trade in textiles and establishes the Textile Import Program, which is enforced by U.S. Customs.

19 CFR 12.130 et seq.
Regulations on Entry of Textiles
These regulations provide the requirements and procedures followed by Customs in enforcing limitations on the importation and entry and withdrawal of textiles and textile products from warehouses for consumption in the U.S.

19 CFR 141.89
Regulation on Additional Invoice Requirements
This regulation specifies the additional information for certain classes of merchandise, including footwear and textile products, being imported into the U.S.

15 USC 70-77
Textile Fiber Products Identification Act
This Act prohibits false or deceptive labeling (misbranding) and false advertising of any textile fiber products and requires all textile fiber products imported into the U.S. to be labeled in accordance with the requirements set forth in the law.

19 CFR 11.12b; 16 CFR 303 et seq.
Regulations on TFPIA Labeling and Marking
These regulations detail the labeling and marking requirements for textiles as specified by the CPSC and the invoice contents required by U.S. Customs for purpose of enforcing the labeling and marking rules.

15 USC 1191-1204
Flammable Fabrics Act (FFA)
This Act provides for the setting of flammability standards for fabric by the Consumer Product Safety Commission (CPSC) and for enforcement by U.S. Customs.

16 CFR 1610, 1611, 1615, 1616, 1630-1632
Regulations on Flammable Fabric Standards
These regulations specify the flammability standards adopted by the CPSC under the FFA for various types of textiles.

Principal Exporting Countries

The following listing includes samples of the main supplier nations of the products of this chapter. It is organized by HTSUS major heading. (Refer to "Customs Classification" above for the product codes.) Countries are listed in rank order of the value of products imported to the U.S. Statistics represent customs value entries for 1993 from the Bureau of Census, U.S. Department of Commerce.

5101—Australia, New Zealand, Uruguay, United Kingdom, South Africa, Canada, Argentina, Mexico, Chile, Ireland

5102—China, Mongolia, Bulgaria, United Kingdom, Belgium, France, Afghanistan, Pakistan, Netherlands, Brazil

5103—United Kingdom, Uruguay, Germany, Australia, South Africa, Belgium, France, Brazil, China, Canada

5104—United Kingdom

5105—Australia, Germany, Israel, Mexico, United Kingdom, South Africa, Netherlands, Chile, France, India

5106—New Zealand, United Kingdom, Canada, Italy, Germany, Poland, Switzerland, Malaysia, Australia, Ireland

5107—Italy, United Kingdom, Canada, Germany, Malaysia, Peru, Japan, Switzerland, France, Mexico

5108—United Kingdom, Italy, France, Peru, China, Switzerland, Spain, Norway, New Zealand, Japan

5109—Italy, New Zealand, France, United Kingdom, Canada, Switzerland, Germany, Malaysia, Peru, Ireland

5110—United Kingdom, Italy, Belgium

5111—Italy, Canada, United Kingdom, Mexico, Switzerland, Netherlands, Czech Rep., Germany, France, Japan

5112—Italy, United Kingdom, Israel, South Korea, Brazil, Japan, China, Uruguay, Chile, Canada

5113—Italy, United Kingdom, France, Netherlands, Germany, Mexico, China

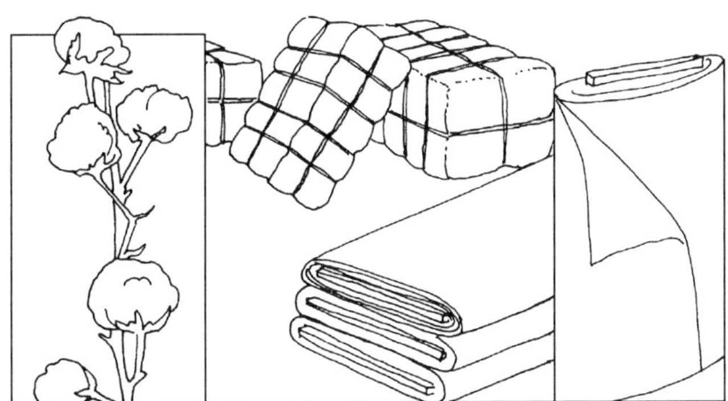

Chapter 52: Cotton*

This chapter relates to the importation of cotton products, which are classified under Chapter 52 of the Harmonized Tariff Schedule of the United States (HTSUS). Specifically, it includes unprocessed cotton, cotton waste, carded and combed cotton, cotton sewing thread and yarn, and cotton fabrics.

If you are interested in importing cotton apparel, you should refer to Commodity Index Chapters 61 through 63. For importation of cotton-blend fibers and fabrics, you should consider whether your product might be classified under the Commodity Index chapter that covers the specific blended fiber. For example, silk blends are covered in Chapter 50, blends with man-made filaments are in Chapter 54, and those with man-made staple fibers are in Chapter 55. If you are interested in importing footwear or leggings made of cotton, you should refer to Chapter 64. For import requirements related to headgear made of cotton, refer to Chapter 65. Cotton linters are covered in Chapter 14, cotton rugs and carpets are in Chapter 57, and cotton wadding and cordage may be under Chapter 56.

Key Factors

The key factors in the importation of cotton products are:

- Compliance with absolute quota restraints.
- Compliance with quota restraints and visa requirements under U.S. Department of Commerce (DOC) Multi-Fiber Arrangements
- Compliance with import quotas on certain raw and semi-processed cottons
- Submission of U.S. Customs Country-of-Origin Declaration(s)
- Compliance with entry invoice requirements
- Compliance with labeling requirements under the Textile Fiber Products Identification Act (TFPIA) and the Wool Products Labeling Act (WPLA)
- Compliance with flammability standards adopted and enforced by the Consumer Product Safety Commission (CPSC) under the Flammable Fabrics Act (FFA) (if importing fabrics and other textile products)

Although most importers use the services of a licensed customs broker in making their entries, and we recommend this practice, you should be aware of the regulatory, entry, and documentation issues involved in importing your product. You, as importer, are ultimately responsible for the fulfillment of any legal requirements applicable to your shipment.

General Considerations

Regulatory Agencies. The DOC's Committee for Implementation of Textile Agreements (CITA) regulates certain textile imports under Section 204 of the Agricultural Adjustment Act. U.S. Customs enforces CITA textile and textile product entry quotas. Customs also enforces compliance with labeling and invoice requirements of the TFPIA and flammability standards under the FFA. The CPSC monitors imports and from time to time inspects textile shipments for compliance with FFA standards. If you are importing textiles containing wool, importation is subject to complex textile import regulations. The Federal Trade Commission (FTC) administers the WPLA requirements.

Entry of Cotton. Cotton enters the U.S. in various conditions, including raw uncombed and uncarded, raw combed and carded, waste, yarn, thread, and woven fabric of various types. Different types of special entry documents may be required, depending on which type of cotton you are importing. You must provide additional information on the entry invoice for certain cotton imports (see "Entry and Documentation" below). If you are importing textiles, you must file a U.S. Customs Textile Entry Declaration at the U.S port of entry. This declaration is required for all textiles (see "Textile Country-of-Origin Declarations" below). Some cotton products are subject to absolute quotas (see "Absolute Quotas" below). In addition, certain cotton and cotton articles manufactured or produced in certain countries are subject to quota and other restraints under U.S. Department of Commerce Multi-Fiber Arrangements pursuant to Section 204 of the Agricultural Adjustment Act (AAA) (see "Quotas" below). Such products may require export certificates or visas issued by the appropriate country of origin, in addition to other entry documents for cotton. Cotton-wool blends may be subject to further requirements and restrictions placed on the import of wool (see "Wool Product Entry Requirements" below).

Absolute Quotas. The Agricultural Adjustment Act, Section 22, establishes absolute quotas on raw cotton from certain countries. Do not confuse these quotas with DOC Multi-Fiber Arrangement quotas for textiles and manufactured textile products. They are different. For details, see "Country-Specific Prohibitions" below.

Multi-Fiber Arrangement Quotas. If you are interested in importing cotton products, the most important issue you need to be aware of is quotas. Under the Multi-Fiber Arrangement provisions of Section 204 of the Agricultural Adjustment Act, CITA initiates specific agreements with individual exporting countries. Section 204 of the Agricultural Adjustment Act covers textiles that: 1) are in chief value of cotton, wool, or man-made fibers, any textile fibers subject to the terms of any textile trade agreement, or any combination of such fibers; 2) contain 50% or more by weight of cotton or man-made fibers, or any textile fibers subject to the terms of any textile trade agreement; 3) contain 17% or more by weight of wool; or 4) if in chief value of textile fibers or textile materials, contain a blend of cotton, wool, or man-made fibers, any textile fibers subject to the terms of any textile trade agreement, or any combination of such fibers that, in total, amount to 50% or more by weight of all component fibers.

The U.S. has Multi-Fiber Arrangements with 40 countries. Each agreement with each country is unique, and may specify quotas for a type of textile or a specific article. Visas or export licenses may be required These agreements, however, often change. Therefore, if you are interested in importing any cotton products, you should contact the International Trade Administration's Office of Textile and Apparel (see addresses at end of this chapter). Refer to "Prohibitions and Restrictions" below for further details.

*IMPORTANT: Read the Commodity Index Introduction. It is the essential framework for understanding this section.

Textile Country-of-Origin Declarations. U.S. Customs enforces CITA textile and textile product entry quotas (see "Prohibitions and Restrictions" below). Requirements for entry include submission of Country-of-Origin Declarations with every cotton shipment, regardless of whether it is subject to a specific multi-fiber arrangement (19 CFR 12.130, 12.131).

Country of Origin. Quota restrictions are country-specific and therefore are applied based on the country of origin for the textiles shipped. The last country from which a textile shipment was exported to the U.S. is not necessarily its country of origin. A textile or textile product imported into the U.S. is considered a product of the particular foreign territory or country, or a U.S. insular possession, where it is wholly grown, produced, or manufactured. For the following discussion, "country" means a foreign territory or country, or a U.S. insular possession.

Substantial transformation rules may affect the country-of-origin determination. For example, if a textile or textile product originates in Country A and is subject to quota, the quota restrictions apply at entry into the U.S. But if, prior to export to the U.S., you move the shipment to Country B where there are fewer restrictions, the shipment may nevertheless remain subject to quota and visa requirements under the Multi-Fiber Arrangement with Country A. Customs determines whether the quota restrictions apply based on the criteria of "substantial transformation." If your textiles do not undergo any major processing or manufacturing while in Country B, or if the manufacturing or processing is minor, your shipment will be deemed to originate in Country A. *You cannot claim substantial transformation on the basis of minor manufacturing procedures.*

In contrast, if your shipment undergoes major processing or manufacturing while in Country B, rendering the textiles "new and different articles of commerce," Customs will treat the shipment as the product of Country B. To qualify as having undergone substantial transformation, an article must evince a change in: 1) commercial designation or identity; b) fundamental character; or c) commercial use. If your shipment is processed in more than one country, the country where it last underwent substantial transformation is the country of origin for Customs entry. In deciding whether the manufacturing or processing operation in a country is major, Customs considers the following factors: 1) the resultant physical change in the material or article; 2) the complexity, the level or degree of skill and/or technology required, and the amount of time involved in the operations; and 3) the value added to the article or material, compared to its value when imported into the U.S.

Validating Operations. Operations that Customs will usually acknowledge as validating a claim of substantial transformation are the following: 1) dyeing and printing, when accompanied by two or more of the following finishing operations: bleaching, shrinking, fulling, napping, decating, permanent stiffening, weighting, permanent embossing, or moireing; 2) spinning fibers into yarn; 3) weaving, knitting, or otherwise forming fabric; 4) cutting fabric into parts and assembling the parts into completed articles; or 5) substantial assembly, by sewing and/or tailoring into a completed garment cut pieces of apparel articles that have been cut from fabric in another country—e.g., complete assembly and tailoring of all cut pieces of suit-type jackets, suits, and shirts.

Insubstantial Operations. Operations that usually will not support a claim of substantial transformation, even if more than one are performed, are the following: 1) simple operations of combining, labeling, pressing, cleaning, dry cleaning, or packaging; 2) cutting to length or width and hemming or overlocking fabrics that are readily identifiable as being intended for a particular commercial use; 3) trimming and/or joining together by sewing, looping, linking, or other means of attaching otherwise completed knit-to-shape component parts produced in a single country, even if accompanied by other processes—e.g., washing, drying, mending—normally incident to assembly; 4) one or more finishing operations on yarns, fabrics, or their textile articles—such as showerproofing, superwashing, bleaching, decating, fulling, shrinking, mercerizing, or similar operations; or 5) dyeing and/or printing fabrics or yarns.

Declarations. The country of origin of the cotton fabrics in a shipment must be stated on a declaration submitted to U.S. Customs at the time of entry. There are three Customs Country-of-Origin Declarations: single-country, multiple-country, and negative. The Declaration to be submitted with your shipment of cotton fabrics depends on the nature of the import.

- **Single-country declarations** are used for entries of textiles or textile products that clearly originate from only one country or that have been assembled in one country from fabricated components wholly produced in the U.S. or the foreign country of manufacture. Information required includes: marks of identification and numbers; description of article and quantity; country of origin; and date of exportation.
- **Multiple-country declarations** are used for entries of textiles or textile products that were manufactured or processed and/or that incorporate materials originating in more than one foreign country or territory. Information required includes: marks of identification and numbers; for articles, description, quantity, identification of manufacturing and/or processing operations, country, and date of exportation; for materials used to make articles, description of materials, country of production, and date of exportation.
- **Negative declarations** must accompany all textile imports that are not subject to FFA Section 204 restrictions. Information required includes: marks of identification and numbers; descriptions of article and quantity; and country of origin.

The date of exportation to be indicated on the above declarations is the date on which the carrier leaves the last port in the country of origin, as determined by Customs. Diversion to another country during transit does not affect the export date.

Procedure for Declarations. The manufacturer, producer, exporter, or importer may prepare the declaration. If more than one of these parties is involved in the importation, each party may prepare a separate declaration. You may file a separate declaration for each invoice presented with your entry. The declaration must be dated and signed by the responsible party, and must include the person's title and the company name and address. Your shipment's entry will be denied unless it is accompanied by a properly executed declaration. Customs will not treat a textile declaration as a missing document for which a bond may be filed.

Customs will base its country-of-origin determination on the information contained in each declaration, unless the information is insufficient. If the information on the declaration is insufficient, Customs will require that you submit such additional information as will enable the determination to be made. The shipment will not be released until the determination is made. Thus, if you want to clear Customs with minimal delay, be sure that the information on the declarations is as complete as possible for each shipment.

Textile Labeling and Invoice Requirements. You are responsible for your imported cotton fabric's compliance with applicable provisions of the TFPIA. Cotton fabrics that require labeling under TFPIA must already be labeled at entry, or the shipment will be refused. (See "Marking and Labeling Requirements" below.) If you import shipments of cotton fabrics subject to TFPIA and valued at over $500, you must provide special information on the entry invoice (see "Entry and Documentation" below).

Flammability Standards. Cotton fabrics imported into the U.S. for use in consumer products must be in compliance with the FFA, a federal law that gives the CPSC the authority and responsibility for protecting the public from the hazards of dangerously flammable items of wearing apparel and interior furnishings. Under the FFA, standards have been established for flammability of clothing textiles. You cannot import any article of wearing apparel or interior furnishing, or any fabric or related material that is intended for use or that may be used in such items, if it fails to conform to an applicable flammability standard (FFA Section 4). Certain products may be imported into the U.S. (FFA Section 11c) for finishing or processing to render them less flammable so as to meet the standards. For these products, the exporter must state on the invoice or other paper relating to the shipment that the shipment is being made for that purpose.

The CPSC monitors imports of textiles under its Import Surveillance Program. From time to time, your textile shipments may be inspected to ascertain compliance with mandatory safety standards. Shipments may also be subject to testing by the CPSC to determine compliance. If the CPSC believes a product, fabric, or related material does not comply with a flammability standard, it is authorized to pursue a variety of legal sanctions (see "Prohibitions and Restrictions" below).

Substantial Product Hazard Reports. Any firm that obtains information that reasonably supports the conclusion that one of its products presents an unreasonable risk of serious injury or death must report that information to the CPSC's Division of Corrective Actions (CPSC address below). Importers must also report to the CPSC if 1) a type of product is the subject of at least three civil actions filed in U.S. federal or state courts, 2) each suit alleges the involvement of that product type in death or grievous bodily injury (as defined in FFA Section 37(3)1), and 3) at least three of the actions result in a final settlement with the manufacturer or in a judgment for the plaintiff within any one of the two-year periods specified in FFA Section 37(b).

Wool Product Entry Requirements. If you are importing cotton-wool blends, depending on the nature of your wool fiber imports, as many as four different types of special entry documents may be required. First, for all imported textile fibers and yarns covered by the Agricultural Adjustment Act (AAA), including wool, you must file a U.S. Customs Textile Entry Declaration (see "Textile Country-of-Origin Declarations" above). Second, with each wool shipment's entry summary, you must file Customs **Form 6451**, Notice of Percentage of Clean Yield and Grade of Wool or Hair, in duplicate, showing your name and address. Third, for all wool products subject to the WPLA, special information is required on the entry invoices (see "Entry and Documentation" below). Finally, certain wool articles manufactured or produced in certain countries may be subject to quotas under U.S. Department of Commerce Multi-Fiber Arrangements. Such products require export certificates or visas issued by the appropriate country of origin, in addition to other requisite entry paperwork (see "Quotas" above).

Certified Hand-Loomed Fabric. Foreign fabrics made on a hand loom—that is, a nonpower-driven loom—by cottage industry producers may be entered under a special tariff category. Textile restraints may not apply to such products when exported from developing countries. If you import a shipment of these fabrics, you must have them certified by a government official of the country-of-origin before exporting them to the U.S. To enter a cotton fabric as a certified hand-loomed fabric, you must present the appropriate certification to Customs at the port of entry. You should mark your entry summary or withdrawal forms with the symbol "F" as a prefix to the appropriate 10-digit statistical reporting number.

Wool Products Labeling Act. The term "wool product" means any product or any portion of a product that contains, purports to contain, or in any way is represented as containing wool, reprocessed wool, or reused wool. All wool products imported into the U.S., except those made more than 20 years before importation, and except carpets, rugs, mats, and upholsteries, must have affixed a stamp, tag, label, or other means of identification as required by the WPLA. If you are importing wool products exempt from labeling under the WPLA, do not assume they are also exempt from labeling under the TFPIA. These are two distinct laws, with some overlapping requirements (see "Marking and Labeling Requirements" below).

Import Advisory

Importation of textiles is trade-sensitive and highly regulated. Shipments of textiles and textile products not complying with all government regulations, including quotas and visas, are subject to seizure and could result in the imposition of penalties as well as possible forfeiture of the goods. You should always verify the available quota for any textile product you plan to import before your shipment leaves the country of manufacture. Furthermore, Customs textile classification rulings change frequently, and prior administrative rulings are often modified and sometimes reversed.

Customs Classification

For customs purposes, cotton products are classified under Chapter 52 of the HTSUS. This chapter is broken into major headings, which are further divided into subheadings, and often sub-subheadings, each of which has its own HTSUS classification number. For example, the HTSUS number for satin weave or twill weave of cotton is 5208.19.20, indicating it is a sub-subcategory of other fabrics (5208.19.00), which is a subcategory of the major heading, unbleached woven fabrics of cotton, with 85% or more by weight of cotton, etc. (5208.00.00). There are 12 major headings within Chapter 52.

5201—Cotton, not carded or combed

5202—Cotton waste (including yarn waste and garnetted stock)

5203—Cotton, carded or combed

5204—Cotton sewing thread, whether or not put up for retail sale

5205—Cotton yarn (other than sewing thread), containing 85% or more by weight of cotton, not put up for retail sale

5206—Cotton yarn (other than sewing thread), containing less than 85% by weight of cotton, not put up for retail sale

5207—Cotton yarn (other than sewing thread) put up for retail sale

5208—Woven fabrics of cotton, containing 85% or more by weight of cotton, weighing not more than 200 g/m2

5209—Woven fabrics of cotton, containing 85% or more by weight of cotton, weighing more than 200 g/m2

5210—Woven fabrics of cotton, containing less than 85% by weight of cotton, mixed mainly or solely with man-made fibers, weighing not more than 200 g/m2

5211—Woven fabrics of cotton, containing less than 85% by weight of cotton, mixed mainly or solely with man-made fibers, weighing more than 200 g/m2

5212—Other woven fabrics of cotton

For more details regarding classifications of the specific product you are interested in importing, consult a customs broker, the appropriate commodity specialist at your nearest customs port, or the HTSUS. HTSUS is available for purchase from the U.S. Government Printing Office (see addresses at end of this chapter), and may be found in larger public libraries. Refer to "Classification—Liquidation" on page 207 for a general discussion of customs classification.

Sample Import Duties

Import duties will vary depending on the HTSUS classification of your product. Therefore, to determine the correct amount of duties, your product must be properly classified under the HTSUS. The following sample duties are taken from the duty listings for HTSUS Chapter 52 products.

Cotton not carded or combed with a staple length under 28.575 mn (5201.00.10): free; with a staple length of 28.575 mn or more but under 42.8625 mn (5201.00.20): 4.4 cents/kg, with a staple length of 42.8625 mn or more (5201.00.50): 1.5 cents/kg; cotton yarn waste (5202.10.00): free; garnetted stock of cotton waste (5202.91.00): 5%; carded or combed cotton (5203.00.00): 5%; cotton sewing thread (5204): 5%; multiple or cabled yarn of combed cotton fibers with 85% or more by weight of cotton, not for retail, and with fibers not exceeding 14 mn per single yarn (5205.41.00): 5.8%, exceeding 43 mn but not exceeding 52 mn per single yarn (5205.43.00): 8.6%, exceeding 80 mn per single yarn (5205.45.00): 12%; unbleached cotton poplin, broadcloth, sheeting, or cheesecloth, with 85% or more by weight of cotton, weighing not more than 200 g/m^2 of number 42 or less (5208.11.20): 7%; printed cotton poplin, broadcloth, sheeting, or cheesecloth, with 85% or more by weight of cotton, weighing not more than 100 g/m^2 of number 42 or less (5208.51.40): 9.6%; dyed woven fabrics of cotton weighing not more than 200 g/m^2, with 36% or more by weight of wool or fine animal hair (5212.13.10): 33%.

Cotton Fabrics. Duty rates vary depending on the percentage of cotton in the fabric, weave type, weight of textile, and number of threads used to create the textile. Cotton fabrics containing 85% or more by weight of cotton tend to enter at lower duties than those containing less than 85% cotton and mixed with man-made fabrics. Unbleached cotton enters at a lower duty rate than dyed. Duty rates get higher as thread count gets higher.

Nonwoven Cotton. Rates for nonwoven cottons vary depending on degree of processing and staple length. Duty rates for yarns vary depending on the weight of the yarn, whether it is of combed or of uncombed fibers, and whether it is put up for retail sales.

Sample Testing. Customs will use the Official Cotton Standards of the United States, as established by the Secretary of Agriculture, to determine the staple length of the cotton in your shipment. Staple length is the length of the fibers in a particular quantity of cotton and is pertinent in determining duty rates as well as quota status. To determine the staple length of any lot of cotton, Customs takes samples of the lot in accordance with commercial practice. These samples are then stapled, or measured, either by a qualified Customs officer, or by a qualified U.S. Department of Agriculture (USDA) employee. Customs will mail you a notice of its results.

If you are dissatisfied with Customs' staple length determination for your shipment, you may file an appeal with the responsible district director. To do this, you must file a written request, in duplicate, within 14 calendar days after the Customs notice was mailed to you. In your request for staple-length redetermination, you must clearly state 1) your claimed staple length for the cotton in question, and 2) the basis for your claim. The district director grants all such requests that appear to be made in good faith. He or she may deem it necessary to consult a USDA board of cotton examiners in making the redetermination. You will be held responsible for all relevant costs, other than compensation of Customs personnel, in the redetermination process.

Entry and Documentation

The entry of merchandise is a two-part process consisting of 1) filing the documentation necessary to determine whether merchandise may be released from Customs custody, and 2) filing the documents that contain information for duty assessment and statistical purposes. In certain instances, all documents must be filed and accepted by Customs prior to release of the goods. Unless you have been granted an extension, you must file entry documents at a location specified by the district or area director within five working days of your shipment's date of arrival at a U.S. port of entry. These include a number of standard documents required by Customs for any entry, and:

- U.S. Customs Country-of-Origin Declaration(s)
- Export documentation and/or visa for textiles subject to Multi-Fiber Arrangement
- Customs **Form 6451**, Notice of Percentage of Clean Yield and Grade of Wool or Hair, in duplicate, showing your name and address (if importing cotton-wool blends)

After you present the entry, Customs may examine your shipment or may waive examination. The shipment is then released provided no legal or regulatory violations have been noted. You must then file entry summary documentation and deposit estimated duties at a designated customhouse within 10 working days of your shipment's release. For a detailed description of entry procedures, standard documentation, and informal entry, refer to "Entry Process" on page 182.

NAFTA Certificates of Origin. An importer of textiles for which NAFTA treatment is sought need not file a separate NAFTA Certificate of Origin in addition to the Customs Country-of-Origin Declaration. The declaration is sufficient. However, the importer must take care to submit a declaration from each U.S., Canadian, or Mexican producer or manufacturer. Thus, for multiple producers or manufacturers, a separate declaration must be filed for each. If a Customs district director cannot determine the country of origin because the declaration is absent or incomplete, the shipment is not entitled to preferential NAFTA tariff treatment or other NAFTA benefits. See 12 CFR 132.

Entry Invoices. You must provide certain additional information on the entry invoice for cotton and cotton products. The specific information varies depending on the nature of your product, as noted below.

TFPIA Requirements. For the purpose of TFPIA enforcement, a commercial shipment of textile products exceeding $500 in value and subject to TFPIA labeling requirements must show the following information: 1) the constituent fiber or combination of fibers, designating with equal prominence each natural or manufactured fiber by its generic name, in order of predominance by weight if the weight of such fiber is 5% or more of the total fiber weight of the product; 2) percentage of each fiber present, by weight, in the total fiber content; 3) the name or other identification issued and registered by the FTCof the manufacturer of the product or one or more persons subject to Section 3 of the TFPIA with respect to such product; 4) the name of the country where processed or manufactured.

Cotton Products. The following headings describe the invoice information required for different types of cotton shipments. If your shipment fits one or more of these categories, you will need to supply this information on your entry invoice, in addition to what is normally expected.

Raw Cotton. If you are importing raw cotton, your invoice must identify: 1) quota category, in terms of staple length and type of cotton; 2) country of origin, and, if practicable, province or other country subdivision where grown; 3) cotton variety, e.g. Karnak, Gisha, Pima, Tanguis, etc.

Cotton Waste. If you are importing cotton waste, your invoice must state: 1) name by which the cotton waste is known (e.g. cotton card strips; cotton comber waste; cotton lap waste; cotton sliver waste; cotton roving waste; cotton fly waste; etc.; 2) cotton staple length, identified in the following terms: either a) less than 3.016 cm (1 3/16 inches), or b) 3.016 cm or more.

Cotton Fabrics. If you are importing cotton fabrics (HTSUS headings 5208, 5209, 5210, 5211, and 5212), your invoice must show the following information: 1) marks on shipping packages; 2) numbers on shipping packages; 3) customer's call number, if any; 4) exact width of your merchandise; 5) detailed description of your merchandise: trade name, if any; whether bleached, unbleached, printed, composed of yarns of different color, or dyed; if composed of cotton plus other materials, percentage of each component material by weight; 6) number of single threads per cm^2 (ply yarns must be counted in terms of single threads comprising the yarn); 7) exact weight per m^2, in grams; 8) average yarn number; 9) warp yarn size or sizes; 10) filling yarn size or sizes; 11) statement of whether the yarns are combed or carded; 12) number of colors or kinds (different yarn sizes or materials) in the filling; 13) statement of whether the fabric is napped or not; 14) type of weave; and 15) type of machine on which your fabric was woven.

Yarn. All entry invoices for yarn should show: 1) fiber content by weight; 2) whether the yarn is single or plied; 3) whether or not the yarn is put up for retail sale (as defined in HTSUS Section XI, Note 4); and 4) whether or not the yarn is intended for use as sewing thread.

In addition, if the yarn's chief weight is of cotton, the entry invoice must show: 1) Whether the cotton is combed or uncombed; 2) the metric number (mn); and 3) whether it is bleached and or mercerized.

Wool Products Subject to WPLA. When you offer for entry a shipment of cotton-wool blend fibers or fabrics valued at over $500 and subject to WPLA, you must include certain information intended to facilitate Customs monitoring and enforcement of that Act. This extra information is identical to that required by WPLA on labeling (see "Marking and Labeling Requirements" below), with the addition of the manufacturer's name. If your product consists of mixed waste, residues, and similar merchandise obtained from several suppliers or unknown sources, you may omit the manufacturer's name from the entry invoice.

Prohibitions and Restrictions

Textile Quotas. Textile import restrictions are primarily a matter of quotas and the way in which these quotas are administered and monitored. Under the Multi-Fiber Arrangement provisions of Section 204 of the Agricultural Adjustment Act, CITA has negotiated Multi-Fiber Arrangements with 40 countries. These Agreements may impose quotas for a type of textile or a specific article, and they are country-specific. The agreements, however, often change. Therefore, if you are interested in importing any special woven fabric products, you should contact the International Trade Administration's Office of Textile and Apparel (see addresses at end of this chapter). The Office of Textile and Apparel has a team of country specialists who can inform you of the latest developments and inform you about a product's quota or restriction status.

U.S. Customs enforces CITA textile and textile product entry quotas. If formal entry procedures are not followed, Customs will usually refuse entry for textiles that are subject to Section 204. Formal entry requires submission of a Country-of-Origin Declaration (see "General Considerations" above). U.S. Customs maintains a current textile quota status report, available for perusal at any Customs port. In addition, U.S. Customs in Washington, DC, operates a telephone service to provide quota status reports, which are updated weekly (see "Relevant Government Agencies" below).

Flammable Fabrics. U.S. Customs may refuse entry for any article of wearing apparel or interior furnishing, or any fabric or related material that is intended for use or that may be used in wearing apparel or interior furnishings, if it fails to conform to an applicable flammability standard issued under Section 4 of the FFA. An exception is allowed for certain products (FFA Section 11c) that are imported for finishing or processing to bring them within the legal standard. For these products, the exporter must state on the invoice or other paper relating to the shipment that the shipment is being made for that purpose.

The CPSC, as the primary enforcement agency of flammability standards, inspects products for compliance with the FFA. If the CPSC believes a product, fabric, or related material does not comply with a flammability standard, it is authorized to pursue a variety of legal sanctions, including: 1) seizure, condemnation, and forfeiture of the noncomplying products; 2) administrative cease-and-desist order requiring an individual or firm to stop sale and distribution of the noncomplying products or; 3) temporary injunction requiring the individual or firm to stop sale and distribution of the noncomplying products, pending final disposition of an administrative cease-and-desist proceeding. The CPSC also has authority to seek civil penalties against any person who knowingly violates a regulation or standard issued under Section 4 of the FFA.

Quotas

Absolute Raw Cotton Quotas. The Agricultural Adjustment Act, Section 22, establishes quotas on raw cotton from certain countries. Do not confuse these quotas with Department of Commerce Multi-Fiber Arrangement quotas for textiles and manufactured textile products. They are different. Raw cotton quotas are as follows, stated in kilograms:

9904.30.10-9904.30.40 Cotton, not carded, not combed, and not otherwise processed, the product of any country or area including the U.S.:

9904.30.10 Having a staple length under 28.575 mm (1-1/8 inches), except harsh or rough cotton having a staple length under 19.05 mm (3/4 inch). Quota year begins September 20. Maximum quantities per country:

Egypt and Sudan (aggregate): 355,532; Peru: 112,469; India and Pakistan (aggregate): 908,764; China: 621,780; Brazil: 280,648; former Soviet Socialist Republics: 215,512; Argentina: 2,360; Haiti: 107; Ecuador: 4,233; Honduras: 341; Paraguay: 395; Colombia: 56; Iraq: 88; British East Africa: 1,016; Indonesia and Netherlands New Guinea (aggregate): 32,381; British West Indies (except Barbados, Bermuda, Jamaica, Trinidad, Tobago) 9,671; Nigeria: 2,438; British West Africa (except Nigeria and Ghana): 7,259.

Cotton, not carded, not combed, staple length 28.575 mm (1-1/8 inches) or more but under 34.925—(1-3/8 inches). Quota year begins August 1. This quota applies to any area including the U.S.

9904.30.20-9904.30.30 Having a staple length 28.575 mm (1-1/8 inches) or more but under 34.925 mm (1-3/8 inches). Quota year begins August 1:

9904.30.20 Harsh or rough cotton (except cotton of perished staple, grabbots, and cotton pickings), white in color and having a staple length of 29.36875 mm (1-5/32 inches) or more: 680,388

9904.30.30 Other cotton: 2,070,940.

9904.30.40 Staple length 34.925 mm (1-3/8 inches) or more. Quota year begins August 1: 17,958,074.

9904.30.50 Cotton wastes (lap, sliver, and roving), except comber waste, the product of any country or area including the U.S. Quota year begins September 20.

United Kingdom: 653,695; Canada: 108,721; France: 34,385; India and Pakistan (aggregate): 31,582; Netherlands: 10,317; Switzerland: 6,711; Belgium: 5,830; Japan: 154,917; China: 7,857; Egypt: 3,689; Cuba: 2,968; Germany: 11,540; Italy: 3,215.

9904.30.60 Fibers of cotton, processed but not spun. Quota year begins September 11: 453.

Exemptions. There are exemptions from quota restrictions, as follows: 1) Commercial samples of cotton or cotton waste, of any origin, in uncompressed packages each weighing not more than 22.65 kilograms gross weight, imported as samples for taking orders, for the personal use of the importer, or for research. 2) Articles entered for exhibition, display, or sampling at a trade fair or for research. If your import falls under this category, you must receive written approval for your import from the Secretary of Agriculture or his designated representative and present it to U.S. Customs at time of entry. You may also enter your shipment under bond, as long as Customs receives the written approval for the import within six months from the date of provisional entry. In any case, you will have to pay duties at time of entry.

Global Import Quota on *Gossypium hirsutum*. Notwithstanding any other quantitative limits on upland cotton imports, varieties of *Gossypium hirsutum* cotton certified by agents of the country of origin may be entered according to established procedures and in the amounts specified in the Secretary of Agriculture's Special Limited Global Import Quota Announcements and Special Cotton Quota Announcements.

Multi-Fiber Arrangement Quotas. Restrictions under Multi-Fiber Arrangements are country-specific. A product originating in one country may be subject to quota and to export license or visa requirements, while the same product originating in a different country may not. At present, the U.S. has Multi-Fiber Arrangements with 40 countries. Many different categories of products are covered under these Arrangements; it is beyond the scope of this book to list each country and its restricted commodities. If you are interested in importing textiles and textile products, you should contact the International Trade Administration's Office of Textile and Apparel (see addresses at end of this chapter) or U.S. Customs to ascertain your product's restraint status.

The U.S. Customs Quota Branch phone numbers provide recorded status reports, by quota category number, for current charges against the quotas for that country. For convenience, the HTSUS shows the 3-digit category number in parentheses to the right of each listed commodity that is subject to textile restraints. For example, under Chapter 52, heading 5204.20.00, cotton sewing thread for retail sale, is followed by the number "(200)." If you know the category number for your product, you can find out to what extent that quota is filled simply by calling the number for the appropriate country. A word of caution, though: if you do not know for sure that your article is subject to quota from a particular country, and you call the number for that country, you may not be any more enlightened after the phone call. Many of the recordings give status reports only when a certain percentage of the quota has been filled. Thus, if 200 for Indonesia is among the categories for which not enough quantity has entered the U.S. to warrant specific mention, it will be lumped under "all other categories" and you will be none the wiser. To find out if your product is subject to textile restraints, call the DOC or a local Customs port office. Then you can find out the current charges against that quota by calling the country number listed below. For a complete listing of Customs Quota Branch information numbers, see "Relevant Government Agencies" below.

Marking and Labeling Requirements

TFPIA Requirements. All textile fiber products imported into the U.S. must be stamped, tagged, labeled, or otherwise marked with the following information as required by the TFPIA, unless exempt from marking (see TFPIA, Section 12): 1) the generic names and percentages by weight of the constituent fibers present in the textile fiber product, exclusive of permissible ornamentation, in amounts of more than 5% in order of predominance by weight, with any percentage of fiber or fibers required to be designated as "other fiber" or "other fibers" (including those present in amounts of 5% or less) appearing last; and 2) the name of the manufacturer or the name or registered identification number issued by the FTC of one or more persons marketing or handling the textile fiber product; and 3) the name of the country where processed. A word trademark, used as a house mark and registered with the U.S. Patent Office, may appear on labels instead of the name otherwise required, provided the owner of the trademark furnishes a copy of the registration to the FTC prior to use (see "Registered Identification Numbers" below).

The information listed above is not exhaustive. TFPIA requirements are extensive. The Act specifies such details as types of labels, means of attachment, label position on the article, package labeling, unit labeling for two-piece garments, and arrangement of information on the label; allowable fiber designations; country-of-origin indications; requirements for trim and ornamentation, linings and interlinings, and pile fabrics; sectional disclosure; use of trade names and trademarks; and requirements for swatches and samples. The FTC publishes a booklet intended to clarify TFPIA requirements to facilitate voluntary compliance in the industry (see "Publications Available" below). It is available on request, at no charge, from the FTC (see addresses at end of this chapter).

Wool Products Labeling Act (WPLA). Wool product labeling requirements for foreign products are the responsibility of the importer. The WPLA requires the following information to appear on wool products subject to the Act: 1) percentage of the wool product's total fiber weight (exclusive of ornamentation) not exceeding 5% of the total fiber weight of a) wool, b) recycled wool, c) each fiber other than wool if the percent by weight of such fiber is 5% or more, and d) the aggregate of all other fibers; 2) the maximum percent of the wool product's total weight, of any nonfibrous loading, filling, or adulterating matter; and 3) the importer's name. If you, as importer, have a registered identification number issued by the FTC, that number may be used instead of your name (see "Registered Identification Numbers" below).

Customs entry is contingent on proper labeling. If your shipment is found to be mislabeled at entry, you will be given the option of relabeling the products under Customs supervision, as long as the district director is satisfied that your labeling error or omission did not involve fraud or willful neglect. If your shipment is discovered after entry to have been noncomplying with WPLA, it will be recalled to Customs custody at your expense, unless you can satisfy the district director that the products have since been brought into compliance. You will be held responsible for all expenses incurred in bringing a shipment into compliance, including compensation of personnel and other expenses related to Customs supervision.

Fraudulent violations of WPLA will result in seizure of the shipment. Shipments already released from Customs custody will be ordered to be redelivered to Customs. Customs reports all cases of fraudulent violation to the FTC in Washington, DC.

The information listed above is not intended to be exhaustive. WPLA requirements are extensive. The Act specifies such details as types of labels, means of attachment, label position on the article, package labeling, unit labeling (as in the case of a two-piece garment), arrangement of information on the label, allowable fiber designations, country-of-origin indications, trim and ornamentation, pile fabrics, sectional disclosure, use of trade names and trademarks, requirements for swatches and samples, etc. The FTC publishes a booklet intended to clarify WPLA requirements in order to facilitate voluntary compliance within the industry (see "Publications Available" below). It is available on request, at no charge, from the FTC (see addresses at end of this chapter).

Registered Identification Numbers. Any domestic firm or person residing in the U.S. and engaged in the manufacture or marketing of textile products covered under the TFPIA may obtain an FTC-registered identification number for use on required tags and labels instead of the name of a firm or person. For applications, contact the FTC (see addresses at end of this chapter).

For a general discussion of U.S. Customs marking and labeling requirements, refer to "Marking: Country of Origin" on page 215 and "Special Marking Requirements" on page 217.

Shipping Considerations

You will need to ensure that your goods are packaged and shipped with care so that they pass smoothly through Customs and arrive in good condition. You are responsible for ensuring that the shipment is in compliance with all applicable government regulations for packaging and shipping. In most instances, you should not leave these arrangements solely to the discretion of your supplier. Careful preparation of the cargo and selection of the mode of transport can be essential to a cost-effective, timely delivery of undamaged goods. We strongly advise you to consult your shipping representative, insurance agent, or freight broker for advice on packing and shipping. Refer also to the major tab section "Packing/Shipping/Insurance" for a general discussion of packing and shipping.

Cotton fabrics may be shipped in bulk, bolts, rolls, or other types of containers, depending on the type of product and whether it is prepackaged. General considerations include protection from contamination, weather, and pests. Containers should be constructed so as to be safe for handling during transport.

Publications Available

The following publications may be relevant to the importation of cotton fabrics and cotton-wool blend fabrics:

Questions and Answers Relating to the Textile Fiber Products Identification Act and Regulations

Questions and Answers Relating to the Wool Products Labeling Act and Regulations

Available free of charge on request from the Federal Trade Commission, these publications are excellent sources of information written in clear lay language. We recommend that anyone interested in importing textile fiber products but unfamiliar with the regulations obtain a copy of each of these booklets.

The *Harmonized Tariff Schedule of the United States* (HTSUS) is available from:

Government Printing Office (GPO)
Superintendent of Documents
Washington, DC 20402
(202) 512-1800 (Order line)
(202) 512-0000 (General)

The USGPO also has copies of specific laws available for purchase. The USGPO accepts credit card orders over the phone, as well as mail orders paid by credit card, a check drawn on a U.S. bank, or an international money order.

Relevant Government Agencies

Address your questions regarding absolute raw cotton quotas to:

U.S. Department of Agriculture
Foreign Agricultural Service
Tobacco, Cotton & Seeds Division
14th and Independence Avenue SW, Room 5932
Washington, DC 20250
(202) 702-7115
Agricultural Marketing Service
Cotton Division
P.O. Box 96456
Washington, DC 20090
(202) 720-3193

Address your questions regarding textile Multi-Fiber Arrangements to:

International Trade Administration
Office of Textile and Apparel
14th and Constitution Ave. NW, Rm. 3100
Washington, DC 20230
(202) 482-5078, 482-3737

Address your questions regarding the Flammable Fabrics Act (FFA) to:

Consumer Product Safety Commission (CPSC)
5401 Westbard Avenue
Bethesda, MD 20207
(301) 492-6580

Address your questions regarding labeling requirements under the Textile Fiber Products Identification Act (TFPIA) or the Wool Products Labeling Act (WPLA) to:

Federal Trade Commission (FTC)
Division of Enforcement
601 Pennsylvania Ave. NW
Washington, DC 20580
(202) 326-2996 (General)
(202) 326-2841 (Textile and wool products labeling)

Address your questions regarding cotton product imports to the district or port director of Customs for you area. For addresses, refer to"U.S. Customs District Offices" on page 62 or contact:

U.S. Customs Service
1301 Constitution Ave. NW
Washington, DC 20229
(202) 927-6724 (Information)
(202) 927-1000 (General)

The following information numbers for U.S. Customs in Washington, DC, provide recorded information. The Quota Branch numbers listed by country provide updated status reports on textile quotas from those countries. All area codes are (202).

General information: 927-5850

Quota Branch: China 927-6703; India 927-6705; Indonesia 927-6704; Japan 927-6706; Korea 927-6707; Macao 927-6709; Malaysia 927-6712; Mexico 927-6711; Pakistan 927-6714; Philippines 927-6713; Romania 927-6715; Singapore 927-6716; Sri Lanka 927-6708; Taiwan 927-6719; Thailand 927-6717; Turkey 927-6718; All others 927-5850.

Laws and Regulations

The following laws and regulations may be relevant to the importation of special woven fabrics. The laws are contained in the United States Code (USC), and the regulations are published in the Code of Federal Regulations (CFR), both of which are available at larger public and law libraries. Copies of specific laws are also available from the United States Government Printing Office (address above).

7 USC 601 et seq.
Agricultural Adjustment Act (AAA)
This Act authorizes the Secretary of Agriculture to establish and maintain orderly market conditions for agricultural products, including cotton.

19 CFR Part 132
Regulations for Enforcement of AAA Quotas
These regulations provide for Customs enforcement of AAA quotas and higher duty rates imposed on imported agricultural products, whenever investigation reveals that orderly market conditions require such action.

7 USC 1854
Textile Trade Agreements
(EO 11651, as amended by EO 11951 and 12188, and supplemented by EO 12475)
This Act authorizes the CITA of the DOC to enter into

Multi-Fiber Agreements with other countries to control trade in textiles and establishes the Textile Import Program, which is enforced by U.S. Customs.

19 CFR 12.130 et seq.
Regulations on Entry of Textiles
These regulations provide the requirements and procedures followed by Customs in enforcing limitations on the importation and entry and withdrawal of textiles and textile products from warehouses for consumption in the U.S.

15 USC 70-77
Textile Fiber Products Identification Act (TFPIA)
This Act prohibits false or deceptive labeling (misbranding) and false advertising of any textile fiber products and requires all textile fiber products imported into the U.S. to be labeled in accordance with the requirements set forth in the law.

19 CFR 11.12b; 16 CFR 303 et seq.
Regulations on Labeling and Marking
These regulations detail the labeling and marking requirements for textiles as specified by the CPSC and the invoice contents required by U.S. Customs for purpose of enforcing the labeling and marking rules.

15 USC 68-68j
Wool Products Labeling Act (WPLA)
This Act prohibits the false or deceptive labeling (misbranding) of wool products and requires all wool products imported into the U.S. to be labeled in accordance with requirements set forth in the law.

19 CFR 11.12; 16 CFR 300 et seq.
Regulations on WPLA Labeling and Marking
These regulations set forth the wool labeling and marking requirements adopted by the FTC to administer the requirements of the WPLA and provide the procedures followed by U.S. Customs in enforcing the WPLA and the FTC regulations, including entry invoice requirements.

15 USC 1191-1204
Flammable Fabrics Act (FFA)
This Act provides for the setting of flammability standards for fabric by the Consumer Product Safety Commission (CPSC) and for enforcement by U.S. Customs.

16 CFR 1610, 1611, 1615, 1616, 1630-1632
Regulations on Flammable Fabric Standards
These regulations specify the flammability standards adopted by the CPSC under the FFA for various types of textiles.

Principal Exporting Countries

The following listing includes samples of the main supplier nations of the products of this chapter. It is organized by HTSUS major heading. (Refer to "Customs Classification" above for the product codes.) Countries are listed in rank order of the value of products imported to the U.S. Statistics represent customs value entries for 1993 from the Bureau of Census, U.S. Department of Commerce.

5201—India, Pakistan, Mexico, Turkmenistan, United Kingdom, Uzbekistan, Japan, Egypt, Italy

5202—Canada, United Kingdom, Pakistan, South Korea, Hong Kong, Spain, Russia, Germany, Turkey, Colombia

5203—France, Switzerland, Colombia, Italy, Canada

5204—Pakistan, China, Hungary, Switzerland, France, Germany, Colombia, Portugal, Canada, Spain

5205—Egypt, Thailand, Indonesia, Brazil, Australia, El Salvador, China, Peru, Canada, Turkey

5206—Thailand, Mexico, Taiwan, South Korea, Spain, Canada, South Africa, Japan, China, France

5207—France, Mexico, Brazil, Italy, Germany, United Kingdom, Canada, Greece, Thailand, Portugal

5208—China, Japan, India, Pakistan, South Korea, Taiwan, Portugal, Brazil, Indonesia, Thailand

5209—Hong Kong, India, Taiwan, China, Brazil, Canada, United Arab Emirates, Turkey, Germany, Pakistan

5210—China, Thailand, South Korea, Indonesia, Taiwan, Malaysia, Pakistan, Japan, Sri Lanka, Italy

5211—Italy, Germany, Taiwan, Canada, Netherlands, France, Belgium, Japan, Mexico, Austria

5212—Italy, France, United Kingdom, Portugal, Japan, Pakistan, Canada, Germany, Belgium, Poland

Chapter 53: Other Vegetable Textile Fibers*

Full title: Other Vegetable Textile Fibers; Paper Yarn and Woven Fabrics of Paper Yarn

This chapter relates to the importation of vegetable textile fibers, yarns, and fabrics, which are classified under Chapter 53 of the Harmonized Tariff Schedule of the United States (HTSUS). Specifically, it includes raw or processed unspun flax, true hemp, jute, sisal, coconut, abaca, and ramie; flax, jute, paper, and other vegetable textile fiber yarns; and woven fabrics of flax, jute, paper, and other vegetable yarns.

If you are interested in importing cotton textiles and products, you should refer to Commodity Index Chapter 52. The import requirements for vegetable plaiting materials are covered in Chapter 14. For importing paper products, including cellulose wadding, you should read Chapter 48. If you are interested in importing apparel, refer to Chapters 60 through 63.

Key Factors

The key factors in the importation of other vegetable textile fibers, yarns, and fabrics are:

- Compliance with quota restraints and visa requirements under U.S. Department of Commerce (DOC) Multi-Fiber Arrangements
- Submission of U.S. Customs Country-of-Origin Declaration(s)
- Compliance with entry invoice requirements
- Compliance with labeling requirements under Textile Fiber Products Identification Act (TFPIA) and the Wool Products Labeling Act (WPLA)
- Compliance with flammability standards adopted and enforced by the Consumer Product Safety Commission (CPSC) under the Flammable Fabrics Act (FFA)

Although most importers use the services of a licensed customs broker in making their entries, and we recommend this practice, you should be aware of the regulatory, entry, and documentation issues involved in importing your product. You, as importer, are ultimately responsible for the fulfillment of any legal requirements applicable to your shipment.

*IMPORTANT: Read the Commodity Index Introduction. It is the essential framework for understanding this section.

General Considerations

Regulatory Agencies. The DOC's Committee for Implementation of Textile Agreements (CITA) regulates certain textile imports under Section 204 of the Agricultural Adjustment Act. U.S. Customs enforces CITA textile and textile product entry quotas. Customs also enforces compliance with labeling and invoice requirements of the TFPIA and flammability standards under the FFA. The CPSC monitors imports and from time to time inspects textile shipments for compliance with FFA standards. If you are importing products that contain wool fibers, importation is subject to complex textile import regulations. The Federal Trade Commission (FTC) administers the WPLA requirements.

Textile Quotas. If you are interested in importing vegetable textile products, the most important issue you need to be aware of is quotas. Under the Multi-Fiber Arrangement provisions of Section 204 of the Agricultural Adjustment Act, CITA initiates specific agreements with individual exporting countries. Section 204 of the Agricultural Adjustment Act covers textiles that: 1) are in chief value of cotton, wool, or man-made fibers, any textile fibers subject to the terms of any textile trade agreement, or any combination of such fibers; 2) contain 50% or more by weight of cotton or man-made fibers, or any textile fibers subject to the terms of any textile trade agreement; 3) contain 17% or more by weight of wool; or 4) if in chief value of textile fibers or textile materials, contain a blend of cotton, wool, or man-made fibers, any textile fibers subject to the terms of any textile trade agreement, or any combination of such fibers that, in total, amount to 50% or more by weight of all component fibers. For vegetable textile products, quotas currently apply to blends with other fibers.

The U.S. has Multi-Fiber Arrangements with 40 countries. Each agreement with each country is unique, and may specify quotas for a type of textile or a specific article. Visas or export licenses may be required. Currently, certain vegetable textile blends are subject to some quota restraints, but these agreements often change. Therefore, if you are interested in importing any vegetable textile products, you should contact the International Trade Administration's Office of Textile and Apparel (see addresses at end of this chapter). Refer to "Prohibitions and Restrictions" below for further details.

Country-of-Origin Declarations. U.S. Customs enforces CITA textile and textile product entry quotas (see "Prohibitions and Restrictions" below). Requirements for entry include submission of Country-of-Origin Declarations with every textile shipment, regardless of whether it is subject to a specific multi-fiber arrangement (19 CFR 12.130, 12.131).

Country of Origin. Quota restrictions are country-specific and therefore are applied based on the country of origin for the textiles shipped. The last country from which a textile shipment was exported to the U.S. is not necessarily its country of origin. A textile or textile product imported into the U.S. is considered a product of the particular foreign territory or country, or a U.S. insular possession, where it is wholly grown, produced, or manufactured. For the following discussion, "country" means a foreign territory or country, or a U.S. insular possession.

Substantial Transformation. Substantial transformation rules may affect the country-of-origin determination. For example, if a textile or textile product originates in Country A and is subject to quota, the quota restrictions apply at entry into the U.S. But if, prior to export to the U.S., you move the shipment to Country B where there are fewer restrictions, the shipment may nevertheless remain subject to quota and visa requirements under the Multi-Fiber Arrangement with Country A. Customs determines whether the quota restrictions apply based on the criteria of "substantial transformation." If your textiles do not undergo any major processing or manufacturing while in Country B, or if the manufacturing or processing is minor, your shipment will be deemed to originate in Country A. *You cannot claim substantial transformation on the basis of minor manufacturing procedures.*

In contrast, if your shipment undergoes major processing or manufacturing while in Country B, rendering the textiles "new and different articles of commerce," Customs will treat the shipment as the product of Country B. To qualify as having undergone substantial transformation, an article must evince a change in: 1) commercial designation or identity; b) fundamental character; or c) commercial use. If your shipment is processed in more than one country, the country where it last underwent substantial transformation is the country of origin for Customs entry. In deciding whether the manufacturing or processing operation in a country is major, Customs considers the following factors: 1) the resultant physical change in the material or article; 2) the complexity, the level or degree of skill and/or technology required, and the amount of time involved in the operations; and 3) the value added to the article or material, compared to its value when imported into the U.S.

Validating Operations. Operations that Customs will usually acknowledge as validating a claim of substantial transformation are the following: 1) dyeing and printing, when accompanied by two or more of the following finishing operations: bleaching, shrinking, fulling, napping, decating, permanent stiffening, weighting, permanent embossing, or moireing; 2) spinning fibers into yarn; 3) weaving, knitting, or otherwise forming fabric; 4) cutting fabric into parts and assembling the parts into completed articles; or 5) substantial assembly, by sewing and/or tailoring into a completed garment cut pieces of apparel articles that have been cut from fabric in another country—e.g., complete assembly and tailoring of all cut pieces of suit-type jackets, suits, and shirts.

Insubstantial Operations. Operations that usually will not support a claim of substantial transformation, even if more than one are performed, are the following: 1) simple operations of combining, labeling, pressing, cleaning, dry cleaning, or packaging; 2) cutting to length or width and hemming or overlocking fabrics that are readily identifiable as being intended for a particular commercial use; 3) trimming and/or joining together by sewing, looping, linking, or other means of attaching otherwise completed knit-to-shape component parts produced in a single country, even if accompanied by other processes—e.g., washing, drying, mending—normally incident to assembly; 4) one or more finishing operations on yarns, fabrics, or their textile articles—such as showerproofing, superwashing, bleaching, decating, fulling, shrinking, mercerizing, or similar operations; or 5) dyeing and/or printing fabrics or yarns.

Declarations. The country of origin of the silk textiles in a shipment must be stated on a declaration submitted to U.S. Customs at the time of entry. There are three Customs Country-of-Origin Declarations: single-country, multiple-country, and negative. The Declaration to be submitted with your shipment of vegetable textile products depends on the nature of the import.

- **Single-country declarations** are used for entries of textiles or textile products that clearly originate from only one country or that have been assembled in one country from fabricated components wholly produced in the U.S. or the foreign country of manufacture. Information required includes: marks of identification and numbers; description of article and quantity; country of origin; and date of exportation.
- **Multiple-country declarations** are used for entries of textiles or textile products that were manufactured or processed and/or that incorporate materials originating in more than one foreign country or territory. Information required includes: marks of identification and numbers; for articles, description, quantity, identification of manufacturing and/or processing operations, country, and date of exportation; for materials used to make articles, description of materials, country of production, and date of exportation.
- **Negative declarations** must accompany all textile imports that are not subject to FFA Section 204 restrictions. Information required includes: marks of identification and numbers; descriptions of article and quantity; and country of origin.

The date of exportation to be indicated on the above declarations is the date on which the carrier leaves the last port in the country of origin, as determined by Customs. Diversion to another country during transit does not affect the export date.

Procedure for Declarations. The manufacturer, producer, exporter, or importer may prepare the declaration. If more than one of these parties is involved in the importation, each party may prepare a separate declaration. You may file a separate declaration for each invoice presented with your entry. The declaration must be dated and signed by the responsible party, and must include the person's title and the company name and address. Your shipment's entry will be denied unless it is accompanied by a properly executed declaration. Customs will not treat a textile declaration as a missing document for which a bond may be filed.

Customs will base its country-of-origin determination on the information contained in each declaration, unless the information is insufficient. If the information on the declaration is insufficient, Customs will require that you submit such additional information as will enable the determination to be made. The shipment will not be released until the determination is made. Thus, if you want to clear Customs with minimal delay, be sure that the information on the declarations is as complete as possible for each shipment.

Textile Labeling and Invoice Requirements. You are responsible for your imported vegetable textile product's compliance with applicable provisions of the TFPIA. Vegetable textile products that require labeling under TFPIA must already be labeled at entry, or the shipment will be refused. (See "Marking and Labeling Requirements" below.) If you import shipments of vegetable textiles subject to TFPIA and valued at over $500, you must provide special information on the entry invoice (see "Entry and Documentation" below).

Flammability Standards. Vegetable textile products imported into the U.S. for use in consumer products must be in compliance with the FFA, a federal law that gives the CPSC the authority and responsibility for protecting the public from the hazards of dangerously flammable items of wearing apparel and interior furnishings. Under the FFA, standards have been established for flammability of clothing textiles. You cannot import any article of wearing apparel or interior furnishing, or any fabric or related material that is intended for use or that may be used in such items, if it fails to conform to an applicable flammability standard (FFA Section 4). Certain products may be imported into the U.S. (FFA Section 11c) for finishing or processing to render them less flammable so as to meet the standards. For these products, the exporter must state on the invoice or other paper relating to the shipment that the shipment is being made for that purpose.

The CPSC monitors imports of textiles under its Import Surveillance Program. From time to time, your textile shipments may be inspected to ascertain compliance with mandatory safety standards. Shipments may also be subject to testing by the CPSC to determine compliance. If the CPSC believes a product, fabric, or related material does not comply with a flammability standard, it is authorized to pursue a variety of legal sanctions (see "Prohibitions and Restrictions" below).

Substantial Product Hazard Reports. Any firm that obtains information that reasonably supports the conclusion that one of its products presents an unreasonable risk of serious injury or death must report that information to the CPSC's Division of Corrective Actions (CPSC address below). Importers must also report to the CPSC if 1) a type of product is the subject of at least three civil actions filed in U.S. federal or state courts, 2) each suit alleges the involvement of that product type in death or grievous bodily injury (as defined in FFA Section 37(3)1), and 3) at least three of the actions result in a final settlement with the manufacturer or in a judgment for the plaintiff within any one of the two-year periods specified in FFA Section 37(b).

Wool Product Entry Requirements. Depending on the nature of your wool fiber imports, as many as four different types of special entry documents may be required. First, for all imported textile fibers and yarns covered by the Agricultural Adjustment Act (AAA), including wool, you must file a U.S. Customs Textile Entry Declaration (see "Country-of-Origin Declarations" above). Second, with each wool shipment's entry summary, you must file Customs Form 6451, Notice of Percentage of Clean Yield and Grade of Wool or Hair, in duplicate, showing your name and address. Third, for all wool products subject to the WPLA, special information is required on the entry invoices (see "Entry and Documentation" below). Finally, certain wool articles manufactured or produced in certain countries may be subject to quotas under U.S. Department of Commerce Multi-Fiber Arrangements. Such products require export certificates or visas issued by the appropriate country of origin, in addition to other requisite entry paperwork (see "Quotas" above).

Wool Products Labeling Act. The term "wool product" means any product or any portion of a product that contains, purports to contain, or in any way is represented as containing wool, reprocessed wool, or reused wool. All wool products imported into the U.S., except those made more than 20 years before importation, and except carpets, rugs, mats, and upholsteries, must have affixed a stamp, tag, label, or other means of identification as required by the WPLA. If you are importing wool products exempt from labeling under the WPLA, do not assume they are also exempt from labeling under the TFPIA. These are two distinct laws, with some overlapping requirements (see "Marking and Labeling Requirements" below).

Import Advisory

Importation of textiles is trade-sensitive and highly regulated. Shipments of textiles and textile products not complying with all government regulations, including quotas and visas, are subject to seizure and could result in the imposition of penalties as well as possible forfeiture of the goods. You should always verify the available quota for any textile product you plan to import before your shipment leaves the country of manufacture. Furthermore, Customs textile classification rulings change frequently, and prior administrative rulings are often modified and sometimes reversed.

Customs Classification

For customs purposes, other vegetable textile fibers, yarns, and fabrics are classified under Chapter 53 of the HTSUS. This chapter is broken into major headings, which are further divided into subheadings, and often sub-subheadings, each of which has its own HTSUS classification number. For example, the HTSUS number for woven fabrics of flax, bleached or unbleached, containing less than 85% by weight of flax and more than 17 percent by weight of wool or fine animal hair is 5309.21.20, indicating it is a sub-subcategory of unbleached or bleached with less than 85% by weight of flax (5309.21.00), which is a subcategory of the major heading, woven fabrics of flax (5309.00.00). There are 11 major headings within Chapter 53.

5301—Flax, raw or processed but not spun; flax tow and waste (including yarn waste and garnetted stock)

5302—True hemp (*Cannabis sativa* L.), raw or processed but not spun; tow and waste of true hemp (including yarn waste and garnetted stock)

5303—Jute and other textile bast fibers (excluding flax, true hemp, and ramie), raw or processed but not spun; tow and waste of these fibers (including yarn waste and garnetted stock)

5304—Sisal and other textile fibers of the genus *Agave*, raw or processed but not spun; tow and waste of these fibers (including yarn waste and garnetted stock)

5305—Coconut, abaca (Manila hemp or *Musa textiles* Nee), ramie, and other vegetable textile fibers, not elsewhere specified or included, raw or processed but not spun; tow, noils, and waste of these fibers (including yarn waste and garnetted stock)

5306—Flax yarn

5307—Yarn of jute or of other textile bast fibers of heading 5303

5308—Yarn of other vegetable textile fibers; paper yarn

5309—Woven fabrics of flax

5310—Woven fabrics of jute or of other textile bast fibers of heading 5303

5311—Woven fabric of other vegetable textile fibers; woven fabrics of paper yarn

For more details regarding classifications of the specific product you are interested in importing, consult a customs broker, the appropriate commodity specialist at your nearest customs port, or the HTSUS. HTSUS is available for purchase from the U.S. Government Printing Office (see addresses at end of this chapter), and may be found in larger public libraries. Refer to "Classification—Liquidation" on page 207 for a general discussion of customs classification.

Sample Import Duties

Import duties will vary depending on the HTSUS classification of your product. Therefore, to determine the correct amount of duties, your product must be properly classified under the HTSUS. The following sample duties are taken from the duty listings for HTSUS Chapter 53 products.

Flax, raw or retted (5301.10.00): free; flax, broken or scutched (5301.21.00): 0.4 cents/kg; flax, otherwise processed but not spun (5301.29.00): 6%; true hemp, raw or processed but not spun (5302): free; jute, raw or processed but not spun (5303): free; sisal, raw or processed but not spun (5304): free; coconut, abaca, ramie, etc., raw or processed but not spun (5305): free; single flax yarn (5306.10.00): 6.6%; multiple or cabled jute yarn (5307.20.00): 4%; paper yarn (5308.30.00): 5.3%; unbleached or bleached woven flax fabric with 85% or more by weight of flax (5309.11.00): 3%; unbleached or bleached woven flax fabric with less than 85% by weight of flax and more than 17% by weight of wool or fine animal hair (5309.21.20): 25%; woven fabrics of paper yarn (5311.00.60): 5.3%

Special Provisions. The duties on products made from jute and other textile bast fibers are reduced temporarily as follows: Single yarn of these fibers (5307.10.00): 2.3%; multiple (folded) or cabled yarn of these fibers (5307.20.00): 3%; and woven fabrics of these fibers (5310.90.00): 0.8%. The reduced duties are set to expire as of December 31, 1994.

Entry and Documentation

The entry of merchandise is a two-part process consisting of 1) filing the documentation necessary to determine whether merchandise may be released from Customs custody, and 2) filing the documents that contain information for duty assessment and statistical purposes. In certain instances, all documents must be filed and accepted by Customs prior to release of the goods. Unless you have been granted an extension, you must file entry documents at a location specified by the district or area director within five working days of your shipment's date of arrival at a U.S. port of entry. These include a number of standard documents required by Customs for any entry, and:

- U.S. Customs Country-of-Origin Declaration(s)
- Export documentation and/or visa for textiles subject to Multi-Fiber Arrangement
- Customs **Form 6451**, Notice of Percentage of Clean Yield and Grade of Wool or Hair, in duplicate, showing your name and address (if importing articles containing wool)

After you present the entry, Customs may examine your shipment or may waive examination. The shipment is then released provided no legal or regulatory violations have been noted. You must then file entry summary documentation and deposit estimated duties at a designated customhouse within 10 working days of your shipment's release. For a detailed description of entry procedures, standard documentation, and informal entry, refer to "Entry Process" on page 182.

NAFTA Certificates of Origin. An importer of textiles for which NAFTA treatment is sought need not file a separate NAFTA Certificate of Origin in addition to the Customs Country-of-Origin Declaration. The declaration is sufficient. However, the importer must take care to submit a declaration from each U.S., Canadian, or Mexican producer or manufacturer. Thus, for multiple producers or manufacturers, a separate declaration must be filed for each. If a Customs district director cannot determine the country of origin because the declaration is absent or incomplete, the shipment is not entitled to preferential NAFTA tariff treatment or other NAFTA benefits. See 12 CFR 132.

Entry Invoices. You must provide certain additional information on the entry invoice for vegetable textile products. The specific information varies depending on the nature of your product, as noted below.

TFPIA Requirements. For the purpose of TFPIA enforcement, a commercial shipment of textile products exceeding $500 in value and subject to TFPIA labeling requirements must show the following information: 1) the constituent fiber or combination of fibers, designating with equal prominence each natural or manufactured fiber by its generic name, in order of predominance by weight if the weight of such fiber is 5% or more of the total fiber weight of the product; 2) percentage of each fiber present, by weight, in the total fiber content; 3) the name or other identification issued and registered by the FTC of the manufacturer of the product or one or more persons subject to Section 3 of the TFPIA with respect to such product; 4) the name of the country where processed or manufactured.

Wool Products Subject to WPLA. When you offer for entry a wool product shipment valued at over $500 and subject to WPLA, you must include certain information intended to facilitate Customs monitoring and enforcement of that Act. This extra information is identical to that required by WPLA on labeling (see "Marking and Labeling Requirements" below), with the addition of the manufacturer's name. If your product consists of mixed waste, residues, and similar merchandise obtained from several suppliers or unknown sources, you may omit the manufacturer's name from the entry invoice.

Yarn. All entry invoices for yarn should show: 1) fiber content by weight; 2) whether the yarn is single or plied; 3) whether or not the yarn is put up for retail sale (as defined in HTSUS Section XI, Note 4); and 4) whether or not the yarn is intended for use as sewing thread.

Prohibitions and Restrictions

Quotas. Textile import restrictions are primarily a matter of quotas and the way in which these quotas are administered and monitored. Under the Multi-Fiber Arrangement provisions of Section 204 of the Agricultural Adjustment Act, CITA has negotiated Multi-Fiber Arrangements with 40 countries. These Agreements may impose quotas for a type of textile or a specific article, and they are country-specific. Currently, certain vegetable textiles blended with other fibers are subject to quota restraints, but these agreements often change. Therefore, if you are interested in importing any vegetable textiles fiber, yarns, or fabrics, you should contact the International Trade Administration's Office of Textile and Apparel (see addresses at end of this chapter). The Office of Textile and Apparel has a team of country specialists who can inform you of the latest developments and inform you about a product's quota or restriction status.

U.S. Customs enforces CITA textile and textile product entry quotas. If formal entry procedures are not followed, Customs will usually refuse entry for textiles that are subject to Section 204. Formal entry requires submission of a Country-of-Origin Declaration (see "General Considerations" above). U.S. Customs maintains a current textile quota status report, available for perusal at any Customs port. In addition, U.S. Customs in Washington, DC, operates a telephone service to provide quota status reports, which are updated weekly (see "Relevant Government Agencies" below).

Flammable Fabrics. U.S. Customs may refuse entry for any article of wearing apparel or interior furnishing, or any fabric or related material that is intended for use or that may be used in wearing apparel or interior furnishings, if it fails to conform to an applicable flammability standard issued under Section 4 of the FFA. An exception is allowed for certain products (FFA Section 11c) that are imported for finishing or processing to bring them within the legal standard. For these products, the exporter must state on the invoice or other paper relating to the shipment that the shipment is being made for that purpose.

The CPSC, as the primary enforcement agency of flammability standards, inspects products for compliance with the FFA. If the CPSC believes a product, fabric, or related material does not comply with a flammability standard, it is authorized to pursue a variety of legal sanctions, including: 1) seizure, condemnation, and forfeiture of the noncomplying products; 2) administrative cease-and-desist order requiring an individual or firm to stop sale and distribution of the noncomplying products or; 3) temporary injunction requiring the individual or firm to stop sale and distribution of the noncomplying products, pending final disposition of an administrative cease-and-desist proceeding. The CPSC also has authority to seek civil penalties against any person who knowingly violates a regulation or standard issued under Section 4 of the FFA.

Country-Specific Restrictions

Restrictions under Multi-Fiber Arrangements are country-specific. A product originating in one country may be subject to quota and to export license or visa requirements, while the same product originating in a different country may not. At present, the U.S. has Multi-Fiber Arrangements with 40 countries. Many different categories of products are covered under these Arrangements; it is beyond the scope of this book to list each country and its restricted commodities. If you are interested in importing textiles and textile products, you should contact the International Trade Administration's Office of Textile and Apparel (see addresses at end of this chapter) or U.S. Customs to ascertain your product's restraint status.

The U.S. Customs Quota Branch phone numbers provide recorded status reports, by quota category number, for current charges against the quotas for that country. For convenience, the HTSUS shows the 3-digit category number in parentheses to the right of each listed commodity that is subject to textile restraints. For example, under Chapter 53, heading 5306.10.00, single flax yarn, is followed by the number "(800)." If you know the category number for your product, you can find out to what extent that quota is filled simply by calling the number for the appropriate country. A word of caution, though: if you do not know for sure that your article is subject to quota from a particular country, and you call the number for that country, you may not be any more enlightened after the phone call. Many of the recordings give status reports only when a certain percentage of the quota has been filled. Thus, if 800 for Indonesia is among the categories for which not enough quantity has entered the U.S. to warrant specific mention, it will be lumped under "all other categories" and you will be none the wiser. To find out if your product is subject to textile restraints, call the DOC or a local Customs port office. Then you can find out the current charges against that quota by calling the country number listed below. For a complete listing of Customs Quota Branch information numbers, see "Relevant Government Agencies" below.

Marking and Labeling Requirements

TFPIA Requirements. All textile fiber products imported into the U.S. must be stamped, tagged, labeled, or otherwise marked with the following information as required by the TFPIA, unless exempt from marking (see TFPIA, Section 12): 1) the generic names and percentages by weight of the constituent fibers present in the textile fiber product, exclusive of permissible ornamentation, in amounts of more than 5% in order of predominance by weight, with any percentage of fiber or fibers required to be designated as "other fiber" or "other fibers" (including those present in amounts of 5% or less) appearing last; and 2) the name of the manufacturer or the name or registered identification number issued by the FTC of one or more persons marketing or handling the textile fiber product; and 3) the name of the country where processed. A word trademark, used as a house mark and registered with the U.S. Patent Office, may appear on labels instead of the name otherwise required, provided the owner of the trademark furnishes a copy of the registration to the FTC prior to use (see "Registered Identification Numbers" below).

The information listed above is not exhaustive. TFPIA requirements are extensive. The Act specifies such details as types of labels, means of attachment, label position on the article, package labeling, unit labeling for two-piece garments, and arrangement of information on the label; allowable fiber designations; country-of-origin indications; requirements for trim and ornamentation, linings and interlinings, and pile fabrics; sectional disclosure; use of trade names and trademarks; and requirements for swatches and samples. The FTC publishes a booklet intended to clarify TFPIA requirements to facilitate voluntary compliance in the industry (see "Publications Available" below). It is available on request, at no charge, from the FTC (see addresses at end of this chapter).

Wool Products Labeling Act (WPLA). Wool product labeling requirements for foreign products are the responsibility of the importer. The WPLA requires the following information to appear on wool products subject to the Act: 1) percentage of the wool product's total fiber weight (exclusive of ornamentation) not exceeding 5% of the total fiber weight of a) wool, b) recycled wool, c) each fiber other than wool if the percent by weight of such fiber is 5% or more, and d) the aggregate of all other fibers; 2) the maximum percent of the wool product's total weight, of any nonfibrous loading, filling, or adulterating matter; and 3) the importer's name. If you, as importer, have a registered identification number issued by the FTC, that number may be used instead of your name (see "Registered Identification Numbers" below).

Customs entry is contingent on proper labeling. If your shipment is found to be mislabeled at entry, you will be given the option of relabeling the products under Customs supervision, as long as the district director is satisfied that your labeling error or omission did not involve fraud or willful neglect. If your shipment is discovered after entry to have been noncomplying with WPLA, it will be recalled to Customs custody at your expense, unless you can satisfy the district director that the products have since been brought into compliance. You will be held responsible for all expenses incurred in bringing a shipment into compliance, including compensation of personnel and other expenses related to Customs supervision.

Fraudulent violations of WPLA will result in seizure of the shipment. Shipments already released from Customs custody will be ordered to be redelivered to Customs. Customs reports all cases of fraudulent violation to the FTC in Washington, DC.

The information listed above is not intended to be exhaustive. WPLA requirements are extensive. The Act specifies such details as types of labels, means of attachment, label position on the article, package labeling, unit labeling (as in the case of a two-piece garment), arrangement of information on the label, allowable fiber designations, country-of-origin indications, trim and ornamentation, pile fabrics, sectional disclosure, use of trade names and trademarks, requirements for swatches and samples, etc. The FTC publishes a booklet intended to clarify WPLA requirements in order to facilitate voluntary compliance within the industry (see "Publications Available" below). It is available on request, at no charge, from the FTC (see addresses at end of this chapter).

Registered Identification Numbers. Any domestic firm or person residing in the U.S. and engaged in the manufacture or marketing of textile products covered under the TFPIA may obtain an FTC-registered identification number for use on required tags and labels instead of the name of a firm or person. For applications, contact the FTC (address below.)

For a general discussion of U.S. Customs marking and labeling requirements, refer to "Marking: Country of Origin" on page 215 and "Special Marking Requirements" on page 217.

Shipping Considerations

You will need to ensure that your goods are packaged and shipped with care so that they pass smoothly through Customs and arrive in good condition. You are responsible for ensuring that the shipment is in compliance with all applicable government regulations for packaging and shipping. In most instances, you should not leave these arrangements solely to the discretion of your supplier. Careful preparation of the cargo and selection of the mode of transport can be essential to a cost-effective, timely delivery of undamaged goods. We strongly advise you to consult your shipping representative, insurance agent, or freight broker for advice on packing and shipping. Refer also to the major tab section "Packing/Shipping/Insurance" for a general discussion of packing and shipping.

Vegetable textile fibers, yarns, and fabrics may be shipped in bulk, bolts, cartons, or other types of containers, depending on the type of product and whether it is prepackaged. General considerations include protection from contamination, weather, and pests. Containers should be constructed so as to be safe for handling during transport.

Publications Available

The following publications may be relevant to the importation of vegetable textile fiber, yarn, and fabric:

Questions and Answers Relating to the Textile Fiber Products Identification Act and Regulations

Questions and Answers Relating to the Wool Products Labeling Act and Regulations

Available free of charge on request from the Federal Trade Commission, these publications are excellent sources of information written in clear lay language. We recommend that anyone interested in importing textile fiber products but unfamiliar with the regulations obtain a copy of each of these booklets.

The *Harmonized Tariff Schedule of the United States* (HTSUS) is available from:

Government Printing Office (GPO)
Superintendent of Documents
Washington, DC 20402
(202) 512-1800 (Order line)
(202) 512-0000 (General)

The USGPO also has copies of specific laws available for purchase. The USGPO accepts credit card orders over the phone, as well as mail orders paid by credit card, a check drawn on a U.S. bank, or an international money order.

Relevant Government Agencies

Address your questions regarding textile Multi-Fiber Arrangements to:

International Trade Administration
Office of Textile and Apparel
14th and Constitution Ave. NW, Rm. 3100
Washington, DC 20230
(202) 482-5078, 482-3737

Address your questions regarding the Flammable Fabrics Act (FFA) to:

Consumer Product Safety Commission (CPSC)
5401 Westbard Avenue
Bethesda, MD 20207
(301) 492-6580

Address your questions regarding requirements under the Textile Fiber Products Identification Act (TFPIA) or the Wool Products Labeling Act (WPLA) to:

Federal Trade Commission (FTC)
Division of Enforcement
601 Pennsylvania Ave. NW
Washington, DC 20580
(202) 326-2996 (General)
(202) 326-2841 (Textile and wool products labeling)

Address your questions regarding vegetable textile fiber, yarn, and fabric imports to the district or port director of Customs for you area. For addresses, refer to"U.S. Customs District Offices" on page 62 or contact:

U.S. Customs Service
1301 Constitution Ave. NW
Washington, DC 20229
(202) 927-6724 (Information)
(202) 927-1000 (General)

The following information numbers for U.S. Customs in Washington, DC, provide recorded information. The Quota Branch numbers listed by country provide updated status reports on textile quotas from those countries. All area codes are (202).

General information: 927-5850

Quota Branch: China 927-6703; India 927-6705; Indonesia 927-6704; Japan 927-6706; Korea 927-6707; Macao 927-6709; Malaysia 927-6712; Mexico 927-6711; Pakistan 927-6714; Philippines 927-6713; Romania 927-6715; Singapore 927-6716; Sri Lanka 927-6708; Taiwan 927-6719; Thailand 927-6717; Turkey 927-6718; All others 927-5850.

Laws and Regulations

The following laws and regulations may be relevant to the importation of vegetable textile fiber, yarn, and fabric products. The laws are contained in the United States Code (USC), and the regulations are published in the Code of Federal Regulations (CFR), both of which are available at larger public and law libraries. Copies of specific laws are also available from the United States Government Printing Office (address above).

7 USC 1854
Textile Trade Agreements
(EO 11651, as amended by EO 11951 and 12188, and supplemented by EO 12475)
This Act authorizes the CITA of the DOC to enter into Multi-Fiber Agreements with other countries to control trade in textiles and establishes the Textile Import Program, which is enforced by U.S. Customs.

19 CFR 12.130 et seq.
Regulations on Entry of Textiles
These regulations provide the requirements and procedures followed by Customs in enforcing limitations on the importation and entry and withdrawal of textiles and textile products from warehouses for consumption in the U.S.

15 USC 70-77
Textile Fiber Products Identification Act (TFPIA)
This Act prohibits false or deceptive labeling (misbranding) and false advertising of any textile fiber products and requires all textile fiber products imported into the U.S. to be labeled in accordance with the requirements set forth in the law.

19 CFR 11.12b; 16 CFR 303 et seq.
Regulations on Labeling and Marking
These regulations detail the labeling and marking requirements for textiles as specified by the CPSC and the invoice contents required by U.S. Customs for purpose of enforcing the labeling and marking rules.

15 USC 68-68j
Wool Products Labeling Act (WPLA)
This Act prohibits the false or deceptive labeling (misbranding) of wool products and requires all wool products imported into the U.S. to be labeled in accordance with requirements set forth in the law.

19 CFR 11.12; 16 CFR 300 et seq.
Regulations on WPLA Labeling and Marking
These regulations set forth the wool labeling and marking requirements adopted by the FTC to administer the requirements of the WPLA and provide the procedures followed by U.S. Customs in enforcing the WPLA and the FTC regulations, including entry invoice requirements.

15 USC 1191-1204
Flammable Fabrics Act (FFA)
This Act provides for the setting of flammability standards for fabric by the Consumer Product Safety Commission (CPSC) and for enforcement by U.S. Customs.

16 CFR 1610, 1611, 1615, 1616, 1630-1632
Regulations on Flammable Fabric Standards
These regulations specify the flammability standards adopted by the CPSC under the FFA for various types of textiles.

Principal Exporting Countries

The following listing includes samples of the main supplier nations of the products of this chapter. It is organized by HTSUS major heading. (Refer to "Customs Classification" above for the product codes.) Countries are listed in rank order of the value of products imported to the U.S. Statistics represent customs value

entries for 1993 from the Bureau of Census, U.S. Department of Commerce.

5301—Canada, Belgium, Egypt, France, United Kingdom, Germany, Italy

5302—Italy, Germany

5303—India, Bangladesh, China, Canada, Taiwan, United Kingdom, Hungary, Belgium, Italy

5304—Kenya, Mexico, India, Philippines, Canada, Taiwan, Brazil, Italy

5305—Philippines, Ecuador, Sri Lanka, Mexico, India, Portugal, Hungary, United Kingdom, Hong Kong, China

5306—Ireland, United Kingdom, China, Austria, France, Belgium, Hungary, Italy, Canada, Chile

5307—Bangladesh, India, United Kingdom, Thailand, Canada, Australia, Bosnia and Herzegovina, Belgium, South Korea, Ireland

5308—Sri Lanka, India, Brazil, Hungary, Taiwan, Mexico, United Kingdom, Italy, Denmark, China

5309—Italy, China, United Kingdom, Poland, Belgium, Czech Rep., France, South Korea, Ireland, Slovenia

5310—India, Bangladesh, Italy, United Kingdom, Netherlands, Germany, Philippines, Belgium, China, Indonesia

5311—China, Italy, South Korea, Mexico, Brazil, Japan, United Kingdom, Hungary, France, Spain

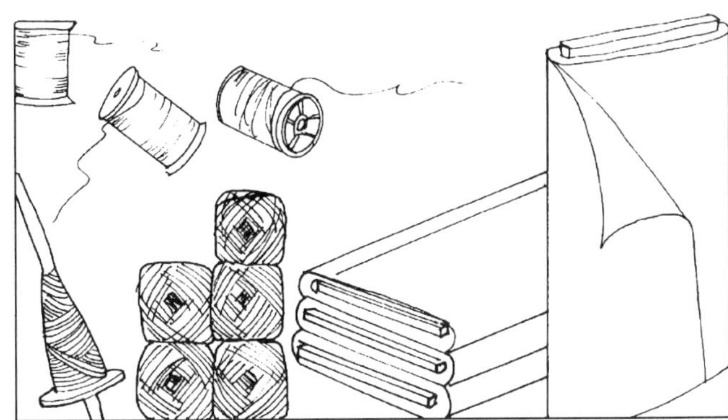

Chapter 54: Man-made Filaments*

This chapter relates to the importation of man-made filament products, which are classified under Chapter 54 of the Harmonized Tariff Schedule of the United States (HTSUS). Specifically, it includes sewing threads of synthetic—such as nylon or polyester—or artificial—such as viscose rayon or cellulose acetate—filaments, synthetic and artificial filament yarns, and woven fabrics of synthetic or artificial filament yarns.

If you are interested in importing cotton textiles and products, you should refer to Commodity Index Chapter 52. The import requirements for wool textile products are covered in Chapter 53. For importing monofilaments of plastics, you should also read Chapter 39. If you are interested in importing apparel, refer to Chapters 60 through 63. Hairnets and headgear of man-made filaments are covered in Chapter 65.

Key Factors

The key factors in the importation of man-made filament products are:

- Compliance with quota restraints and visa requirements under U.S. Department of Commerce (DOC) Multi-Fiber Arrangements
- Submission of U.S. Customs Country-of-Origin Declaration(s)
- Compliance with entry invoice requirements
- Compliance with labeling requirements under Textile Fiber Products Identification Act (TFPIA) and the Wool Products Labeling Act (WPLA)
- Compliance with flammability standards adopted and enforced by the Consumer Product Safety Commission (CPSC) under the Flammable Fabrics Act (FFA)

Although most importers use the services of a licensed customs broker in making their entries, and we recommend this practice, you should be aware of the regulatory, entry, and documentation issues involved in importing your product. You, as importer, are ultimately responsible for the fulfillment of any legal requirements applicable to your shipment.

General Considerations

Regulatory Agencies. The DOC's Committee for Implementation of Textile Agreements (CITA) regulates certain textile im-

*IMPORTANT: Read the Commodity Index Introduction. It is the essential framework for understanding this section.

ports under Section 204 of the Agricultural Adjustment Act. U.S. Customs enforces CITA textile and textile product entry quotas. Customs also enforces compliance with labeling and invoice requirements of the TFPIA and flammability standards under the FFA. The CPSC monitors imports and from time to time inspects textile shipments for compliance with FFA standards. If you are importing products that contain wool fibers, importation is subject to complex textile import regulations. The Federal Trade Commission (FTC) administers the WPLA requirements.

Quotas. If you are interested in importing man-made filament products, the most important issue you need to be aware of is quotas. Under the Multi-Fiber Arrangement provisions of Section 204 of the Agricultural Adjustment Act, CITA initiates specific agreements with individual exporting countries. Section 204 of the Agricultural Adjustment Act covers textiles that: 1) are in chief value of cotton, wool, or man-made fibers, any textile fibers subject to the terms of any textile trade agreement, or any combination of such fibers; 2) contain 50% or more by weight of cotton or man-made fibers, or any textile fibers subject to the terms of any textile trade agreement; 3) contain 17% or more by weight of wool; or 4) if in chief value of textile fibers or textile materials, contain a blend of cotton, wool, or man-made fibers, any textile fibers subject to the terms of any textile trade agreement, or any combination of such fibers that, in total, amount to 50% or more by weight of all component fibers.

The U.S. has Multi-Fiber Arrangements with 40 countries. Each agreement with each country is unique, and may specify quotas for a type of textile or a specific article. Visas or export licenses may be required. These agreements, however, often change. Therefore, if you are interested in importing any man-made filament products, you should contact the International Trade Administration's Office of Textile and Apparel (see addresses at end of this chapter). Refer to "Prohibitions and Restrictions" below for further details.

Country-of-Origin Declarations. U.S. Customs enforces CITA textile and textile product entry quotas (see "Prohibitions and Restrictions" below). Requirements for entry include submission of Country-of-Origin Declarations with every textile shipment, regardless of whether it is subject to a specific multi-fiber arrangement (19 CFR 12.130, 12.131).

Country of Origin. Quota restrictions are country-specific and therefore are applied based on the country of origin for the textiles shipped. The last country from which a textile shipment was exported to the U.S. is not necessarily its country of origin. A textile or textile product imported into the U.S. is considered a product of the particular foreign territory or country, or a U.S. insular possession, where it is wholly grown, produced, or manufactured. For the following discussion, "country" means a foreign territory or country, or a U.S. insular possession.

Substantial transformation rules may affect the country-of-origin determination. For example, if a textile or textile product originates in Country A and is subject to quota, the quota restrictions apply at entry into the U.S. But if, prior to export to the U.S., you move the shipment to Country B where there are fewer restrictions, the shipment may nevertheless remain subject to quota and visa requirements under the Multi-Fiber Arrangement with Country A. Customs determines whether the quota restrictions apply based on the criteria of "substantial transformation." If your textiles do not undergo any major processing or manufacturing while in Country B, or if the manufacturing or processing is minor, your shipment will be deemed to originate in Country A. *You cannot claim substantial transformation on the basis of minor manufacturing procedures.*

In contrast, if your shipment undergoes major processing or manufacturing while in Country B, rendering the textiles "new and different articles of commerce," Customs will treat the shipment as the product of Country B. To qualify as having undergone substantial transformation, an article must evince a change in: 1) commercial designation or identity; b) fundamental character; or c) commercial use. If your shipment is processed in more than one country, the country where it last underwent substantial transformation is the country of origin for Customs entry. In deciding whether the manufacturing or processing operation in a country is major, Customs considers the following factors: 1) the resultant physical change in the material or article; 2) the complexity, the level or degree of skill and/or technology required, and the amount of time involved in the operations; and 3) the value added to the article or material, compared to its value when imported into the U.S.

Validating Operations. Operations that Customs will usually acknowledge as validating a claim of substantial transformation are the following: 1) dyeing and printing, when accompanied by two or more of the following finishing operations: bleaching, shrinking, fulling, napping, decating, permanent stiffening, weighting, permanent embossing, or moireing; 2) spinning fibers into yarn; 3) weaving, knitting, or otherwise forming fabric; 4) cutting fabric into parts and assembling the parts into completed articles; or 5) substantial assembly, by sewing and/or tailoring into a completed garment cut pieces of apparel articles that have been cut from fabric in another country—e.g., complete assembly and tailoring of all cut pieces of suit-type jackets, suits, and shirts.

Insubstantial Operations. Operations that usually will not support a claim of substantial transformation, even if more than one are performed, are the following: 1) simple operations of combining, labeling, pressing, cleaning, dry cleaning, or packaging; 2) cutting to length or width and hemming or overlocking fabrics that are readily identifiable as being intended for a particular commercial use; 3) trimming and/or joining together by sewing, looping, linking, or other means of attaching otherwise completed knit-to-shape component parts produced in a single country, even if accompanied by other processes—e.g., washing, drying, mending—normally incident to assembly; 4) one or more finishing operations on yarns, fabrics, or their textile articles—such as showerproofing, superwashing, bleaching, decating, fulling, shrinking, mercerizing, or similar operations; or 5) dyeing and/or printing fabrics or yarns.

Declarations. The country of origin of the man-made filament products in a shipment must be stated on a declaration submitted to U.S. Customs at the time of entry. There are three Customs Country-of-Origin Declarations: single-country, multiple-country, and negative. The Declaration to be submitted with your shipment of man-made filament products depends on the nature of the import.

- **Single-country declarations** are used for entries of textiles or textile products that clearly originate from only one country or that have been assembled in one country from fabricated components wholly produced in the U.S. or the foreign country of manufacture. Information required includes: marks of identification and numbers; description of article and quantity; country of origin; and date of exportation.
- **Multiple-country declarations** are used for entries of textiles or textile products that were manufactured or processed and/or that incorporate materials originating in more than one foreign country or territory. Information required includes: marks of identification and numbers; for articles, description, quantity, identification of manufacturing and/or processing operations, country, and date of exportation; for materials used to make articles, description of materials, country of production, and date of exportation.

- **Negative declarations** must accompany all textile imports that are not subject to FFA Section 204 restrictions. Information required includes: marks of identification and numbers; descriptions of article and quantity; and country of origin.

The date of exportation to be indicated on the above declarations is the date on which the carrier leaves the last port in the country of origin, as determined by Customs. Diversion to another country during transit does not affect the export date.

Procedure for Declarations. The manufacturer, producer, exporter, or importer may prepare the declaration. If more than one of these parties is involved in the importation, each party may prepare a separate declaration. You may file a separate declaration for each invoice presented with your entry. The declaration must be dated and signed by the responsible party, and must include the person's title and the company name and address. Your shipment's entry will be denied unless it is accompanied by a properly executed declaration. Customs will not treat a textile declaration as a missing document for which a bond may be filed.

Customs will base its country-of-origin determination on the information contained in each declaration, unless the information is insufficient. If the information on the declaration is insufficient, Customs will require that you submit such additional information as will enable the determination to be made. The shipment will not be released until the determination is made. Thus, if you want to clear Customs with minimal delay, be sure that the information on the declarations is as complete as possible for each shipment.

Textile Labeling and Invoice Requirements. You are responsible for your imported man-made filament product's compliance with applicable provisions of the TFPIA. Man-made filament products that require labeling under TFPIA must already be labeled at entry, or the shipment will be refused. (See "Marking and Labeling Requirements" below.) If you import shipments of man-made filaments subject to TFPIA and valued at over $500, you must provide special information on the entry invoice (see "Entry and Documentation" below).

Flammability Standards. Man-made filament products imported into the U.S. for use in consumer products must be in compliance with the FFA, a federal law that gives the CPSC the authority and responsibility for protecting the public from the hazards of dangerously flammable items of wearing apparel and interior furnishings. Under the FFA, standards have been established for flammability of clothing textiles. You cannot import any article of wearing apparel or interior furnishing, or any fabric or related material that is intended for use or that may be used in such items, if it fails to conform to an applicable flammability standard (FFA Section 4). Certain products may be imported into the U.S. (FFA Section 11c) for finishing or processing to render them less flammable so as to meet the standards. For these products, the exporter must state on the invoice or other paper relating to the shipment that the shipment is being made for that purpose.

The CPSC monitors imports of textiles under its Import Surveillance Program. From time to time, your textile shipments may be inspected to ascertain compliance with mandatory safety standards. Shipments may also be subject to testing by the CPSC to determine compliance. If the CPSC believes a product, fabric, or related material does not comply with a flammability standard, it is authorized to pursue a variety of legal sanctions (see "Prohibitions and Restrictions" below).

Substantial Product Hazard Reports. Any firm that obtains information that reasonably supports the conclusion that one of its products presents an unreasonable risk of serious injury or death must report that information to the CPSC's Division of Corrective Actions (CPSC address below). Importers must also report to the CPSC if 1) a type of product is the subject of at least three civil actions filed in U.S. federal or state courts, 2) each suit alleges the involvement of that product type in death or grievous bodily injury (as defined in FFA Section 37(3)1), and 3) at least three of the actions result in a final settlement with the manufacturer or in a judgment for the plaintiff within any one of the two-year periods specified in FFA Section 37(b).

Wool Product Entry Requirements. Depending on the nature of your wool fiber imports, as many as four different types of special entry documents may be required. First, for all imported textile fibers and yarns covered by the Agricultural Adjustment Act (AAA), including wool, you must file a U.S. Customs Textile Entry Declaration (see "Country-of-Origin Declarations" above). Second, with each wool shipment's entry summary, you must file Customs **Form 6451**, Notice of Percentage of Clean Yield and Grade of Wool or Hair, in duplicate, showing your name and address. Third, for all wool products subject to the WPLA, special information is required on the entry invoices (see "Entry and Documentation" below). Finally, certain wool articles manufactured or produced in certain countries may be subject to quotas under U.S. Department of Commerce Multi-Fiber Arrangements. Such products require export certificates or visas issued by the appropriate country of origin, in addition to other requisite entry paperwork (see "Quotas" above).

Wool Products Labeling Act. The term "wool product" means any product or any portion of a product that contains, purports to contain, or in any way is represented as containing wool, reprocessed wool, or reused wool. All wool products imported into the U.S., except those made more than 20 years before importation, and except carpets, rugs, mats, and upholsteries, must have affixed a stamp, tag, label, or other means of identification as required by the WPLA. If you are importing wool products exempt from labeling under the WPLA, do not assume they are also exempt from labeling under the TFPIA. These are two distinct laws, with some overlapping requirements (see "Marking and Labeling Requirements" below).

Import Advisory

Importation of textiles is trade-sensitive and highly regulated. Shipments of textiles and textile products not complying with all government regulations, including quotas and visas, are subject to seizure and could result in the imposition of penalties as well as possible forfeiture of the goods. You should always verify the available quota for any textile product you plan to import before your shipment leaves the country of manufacture. Furthermore, Customs textile classification rulings change frequently, and prior administrative rulings are often modified and sometimes reversed.

Customs Classification

For customs purposes, man-made filament product's are classified under Chapter 54 of the HTSUS. This chapter is broken into major headings, which are further divided into subheadings, and often sub-subheadings, each of which has its own HTSUS classification number. For example, the HTSUS number for single high tenacity polyester yarns is 5402.20.30, indicating it is a sub-subcategory of high tenacity yarn of polyesters (5402.20.00), which is a subcategory of the major heading, synthetic filament yarn, etc. (5402.00.00). There are eight major headings within Chapter 54.

5401—Sewing thread of man-made filaments, whether or not put up for retail sale

5402—Synthetic filament yarn (other than sewing thread), not put up for retail sale, including synthetic monofilament of less than 67 decitex

5403—Artificial filament yarn (other than sewing thread), not put up for retail sale, including artificial monofilament of less than 67 decitex

5404—Synthetic monofilament of 67 decitex or more and of which no cross-sectional dimension exceeds 1 mm; strip and the like (or example, artificial straw) of synthetic textile materials of an apparent width not exceeding 5 mm

5405—Artificial monofilament of 67 decitex or more and of which no cross-sectional dimension exceeds 1 mm; strip and the like (for example, artificial straw) of artificial textile materials of an apparent width not exceeding 5 mm

5406—Manmade filament yarn (other than sewing thread), put up for retail sale

5407—Woven fabrics of synthetic filament yarn, including woven fabrics obtained from materials of heading 5404

5408—Woven fabrics of artificial filament yarn, including woven fabrics obtained from materials of heading 5405

For more details regarding classifications of the specific product you are interested in importing, consult a customs broker, the appropriate commodity specialist at your nearest customs port, or the HTSUS. HTSUS is available for purchase from the U.S. Government Printing Office (see addresses at end of this chapter), and may be found in larger public libraries. Refer to "Classification—Liquidation" on page 207 for a general discussion of customs classification.

Sample Import Duties

Import duties will vary depending on the HTSUS classification of your product. Therefore, to determine the correct amount of duties, your product must be properly classified under the HTSUS. The following sample duties are taken from the duty listings for HTSUS Chapter 54 products.

Sewing thread of man-made filaments (5401): 13%; synthetic filament, single high tenacity yarn, not for sewing or retail, of nylon or other polyamides (5402.10.30): 10%; of polyesters (5402.20.30): 10%; artificial filament, single high tenacity yarn, not for sewing or retail, or vicose rayon (5403.10.30): 10%; racket strings (5404.10.10): 3.1%; man-made filament yarn for retail (5406): 13%; woven fabrics of high tenacity yarn of nylon or other polyamides or of polyesters (5407.10.00): 17%; woven fabrics of high tenacity yarn of viscose rayon (5408.10.00): 17%

Entry and Documentation

The entry of merchandise is a two-part process consisting of 1) filing the documentation necessary to determine whether merchandise may be released from Customs custody, and 2) filing the documents that contain information for duty assessment and statistical purposes. In certain instances, all documents must be filed and accepted by Customs prior to release of the goods. Unless you have been granted an extension, you must file entry documents at a location specified by the district or area director within five working days of your shipment's date of arrival at a U.S. port of entry. These include a number of standard documents required by Customs for any entry, and:

- U.S. Customs Country-of-Origin Declaration(s)
- Export documentation and/or visa for textiles subject to Multi-Fiber Arrangement
- Customs **Form 6451**, Notice of Percentage of Clean Yield and Grade of Wool or Hair, in duplicate, showing your name and address (if importing articles containing wool)

After you present the entry, Customs may examine your shipment or may waive examination. The shipment is then released provided no legal or regulatory violations have been noted. You must then file entry summary documentation and deposit estimated duties at a designated customhouse within 10 working days of your shipment's release. For a detailed description of entry procedures, standard documentation, and informal entry, refer to "Entry Process" on page 182.

NAFTA Certificates of Origin. An importer of textiles for which NAFTA treatment is sought need not file a separate NAFTA Certificate of Origin in addition to the Customs Country-of-Origin Declaration. The declaration is sufficient. However, the importer must take care to submit a declaration from each U.S., Canadian, or Mexican producer or manufacturer. Thus, for multiple producers or manufacturers, a separate declaration must be filed for each. If a Customs district director cannot determine the country of origin because the declaration is absent or incomplete, the shipment is not entitled to preferential NAFTA tariff treatment or other NAFTA benefits. See 12 CFR 132.

Entry Invoices. You must provide certain additional information on the entry invoice for man-made filament products. The specific information varies depending on the nature of your product, as noted below.

TFPIA Requirements. For the purpose of TFPIA enforcement, a commercial shipment of textile products exceeding $500 in value and subject to TFPIA labeling requirements must show the following information: 1) the constituent fiber or combination of fibers, designating with equal prominence each natural or manufactured fiber by its generic name, in order of predominance by weight if the weight of such fiber is 5% or more of the total fiber weight of the product; 2) percentage of each fiber present, by weight, in the total fiber content; 3) the name or other identification issued and registered by the Federal Trade Commission of the manufacturer of the product or one or more persons subject to Section 3 of the TFPIA with respect to such product; 4) the name of the country where processed or manufactured.

Woven Fabrics. The invoice for woven fabric of man-made fibers in HTSUS headings 5407 and 5408 must include the following information: 1) exact width of fabric; 2) detailed description of the merchandise; 3) any trade name; 4) indication of whether bleached, unbleached, dyed, of yarns of different colors, and/or printed; 5) if composed of more than one material, percentage by weight of each; 6) identification of the man-made fibers as artificial or synthetic, filament or staple, and high tenacity or other; 7) number of turns per meter in each yarn; 8) yarn sizes in warp and filling; 9) type of weave—such as plain weave, twill, sateen, dobby, jacquard, swivel, lappet; 10) number of single threads per cm^2 in both warp and filling; 11) weight per m^2 in grams; 12) average yarn number; 13) for spun or filament yarns, indication of whether textured.

Yarn. All entry invoices for yarn should show: 1) fiber content by weight; 2) whether the yarn is single or plied; 3) whether or not the yarn is put up for retail sale (as defined in HTSUS Section XI, Note 4); and 4) whether or not the yarn is intended for use as sewing thread.

In addition, if the yarn's chief weight is of filament man-made fiber, the entry invoice must show: 1) whether the filament is high tenacity (as defined in HTSUS Section XI, Note 6); 2) whether it is monofilament, multifilament, or strip; 3) whether it is texturized; 4) the yarn number in decitex; 5) the number of turns per meter; 5) for monofilaments, the cross-sectional dimension in millimeters; and 6) for strips, the width of the strip in mm (measure in folded or twisted condition if so imported).

Wool Products Subject to WPLA. When you offer for entry a wool product shipment valued at over $500 and subject to WPLA, you must include certain information intended to facilitate Customs monitoring and enforcement of that Act. This extra information is identical to that required by WPLA on labeling (see "Marking and Labeling Requirements" below), with the addition of the manufacturer's name. If your product consists of mixed waste, residues, and similar merchandise obtained from several suppliers or unknown sources, you may omit the manufacturer's name from the entry invoice.

Prohibitions and Restrictions

Quotas. Textile import restrictions are primarily a matter of quotas and the way in which these quotas are administered and monitored. Under the Multi-Fiber Arrangement provisions of Section 204 of the Agricultural Adjustment Act, CITA has negotiated Multi-Fiber Arrangements with 40 countries. These Agreements may impose quotas for a type of textile or a specific article, and they are country-specific. The agreements, however, often change. Therefore, if you are interested in importing any manmade filament products, you should contact the International Trade Administration's Office of Textile and Apparel (see addresses at end of this chapter). The Office of Textile and Apparel has a team of country specialists who can inform you of the latest developments and inform you about a product's quota or restriction status.

U.S. Customs enforces CITA textile and textile product entry quotas. If formal entry procedures are not followed, Customs will usually refuse entry for textiles that are subject to Section 204. Formal entry requires submission of a Country-of-Origin Declaration (see "General Considerations" above). U.S. Customs maintains a current textile quota status report, available for perusal at any Customs port. In addition, U.S. Customs in Washington, DC, operates a telephone service to provide quota status reports, which are updated weekly (see "Relevant Government Agencies" below).

Flammable Fabrics. U.S. Customs may refuse entry for any article of wearing apparel or interior furnishing, or any fabric or related material that is intended for use or that may be used in wearing apparel or interior furnishings, if it fails to conform to an applicable flammability standard issued under Section 4 of the FFA. An exception is allowed for certain products (FFA Section 11c) that are imported for finishing or processing to bring them within the legal standard. For these products, the exporter must state on the invoice or other paper relating to the shipment that the shipment is being made for that purpose.

The CPSC, as the primary enforcement agency of flammability standards, inspects products for compliance with the FFA. If the CPSC believes a product, fabric, or related material does not comply with a flammability standard, it is authorized to pursue a variety of legal sanctions, including: 1) seizure, condemnation, and forfeiture of the noncomplying products; 2) administrative cease-and-desist order requiring an individual or firm to stop sale and distribution of the noncomplying products or; 3) temporary injunction requiring the individual or firm to stop sale and distribution of the noncomplying products, pending final disposition of an administrative cease-and-desist proceeding. The CPSC also has authority to seek civil penalties against any person who knowingly violates a regulation or standard issued under Section 4 of the FFA.

Country-Specific Restrictions

Restrictions under Multi-Fiber Arrangements are country-specific. A product originating in one country may be subject to quota and to export license or visa requirements, while the same product originating in a different country may not. At present, the U.S. has Multi-Fiber Arrangements with 40 countries. Many different categories of products are covered under these Arrangements; it is beyond the scope of this book to list each country and its restricted commodities. If you are interested in importing textiles and textile products, you should contact the International Trade Administration's Office of Textile and Apparel (see addresses at end of this chapter) or U.S. Customs to ascertain your product's restraint status.

The U.S. Customs Quota Branch phone numbers provide recorded status reports, by quota category number, for current charges against the quotas for that country. For convenience, the HTSUS shows the 3-digit category number in parentheses to the right of each listed commodity that is subject to textile restraints. For example, under Chapter 54, heading 5401.10.00, sewing thread of synthetic filaments, is followed by the number "(200)." If you know the category number for your product, you can find out to what extent that quota is filled simply by calling the number for the appropriate country. A word of caution, though: if you do not know for sure that your article is subject to quota from a particular country, and you call the number for that country, you may not be any more enlightened after the phone call. Many of the recordings give status reports only when a certain percentage of the quota has been filled. Thus, if 200 for the Philippines is among the categories for which not enough quantity has entered the U.S. to warrant specific mention, it will be lumped under "all other categories" and you will be none the wiser. To find out if your product is subject to textile restraints, call the DOC or a local Customs port office. Then you can find out the current charges against that quota by calling the country number listed below. For a complete listing of Customs Quota Branch information numbers, see "Relevant Government Agencies" below.

Marking and Labeling Requirements

TFPIA Requirements. All textile fiber products imported into the U.S. must be stamped, tagged, labeled, or otherwise marked with the following information as required by the TFPIA, unless exempt from marking (see TFPIA, Section 12): 1) the generic names and percentages by weight of the constituent fibers present in the textile fiber product, exclusive of permissible ornamentation, in amounts of more than 5% in order of predominance by weight, with any percentage of fiber or fibers required to be designated as "other fiber" or "other fibers" (including those present in amounts of 5% or less) appearing last; and 2) the name of the manufacturer or the name or registered identification number issued by the FTC of one or more persons marketing or handling the textile fiber product; and 3) the name of the country where processed. A word trademark, used as a house mark and registered with the U.S. Patent Office, may appear on labels instead of the name otherwise required, provided the owner of the trademark furnishes a copy of the registration to the FTC prior to use (see "Registered Identification Numbers" below).

The information listed above is not exhaustive. TFPIA requirements are extensive. The Act specifies such details as types of labels, means of attachment, label position on the article, package labeling, unit labeling for two-piece garments, and arrangement of information on the label; allowable fiber designations; country-of-origin indications; requirements for trim and ornamentation, linings and interlinings, and pile fabrics; sectional disclosure; use of trade names and trademarks; and requirements for swatches and samples. The FTC publishes a booklet intended to clarify TFPIA requirements to facilitate voluntary compliance in the industry (see "Publications Available" below). It is available on request, at no charge, from the FTC (see addresses at end of this chapter).

Wool Products Labeling Act (WPLA). Wool product labeling requirements for foreign products are the responsibility of the importer. The WPLA requires the following information to appear on wool products subject to the Act: 1) percentage of the wool product's total fiber weight (exclusive of ornamentation) not exceeding 5% of the total fiber weight of a) wool, b) recycled wool, c) each fiber other than wool if the percent by weight of such fiber is 5% or more, and d) the aggregate of all other fibers; 2) the maximum percent of the wool product's total weight, of any nonfibrous loading, filling, or adulterating matter; and 3) the importer's name. If you, as importer, have a registered identification number issued by the FTC, that number may be used instead of your name (see "Registered Identification Numbers" below).

Customs entry is contingent on proper labeling. If your shipment is found to be mislabeled at entry, you will be given the option of relabeling the products under Customs supervision, as long as the district director is satisfied that your labeling error or omission did not involve fraud or willful neglect. If your shipment is discovered after entry to have been noncomplying with WPLA, it will be recalled to Customs custody at your expense, unless you can satisfy the district director that the products have since been brought into compliance. You will be held responsible for all expenses incurred in bringing a shipment into compliance, including compensation of personnel and other expenses related to Customs supervision.

Fraudulent violations of WPLA will result in seizure of the shipment. Shipments already released from Customs custody will be ordered to be redelivered to Customs. Customs reports all cases of fraudulent violation to the FTC in Washington, DC.

The information listed above is not intended to be exhaustive. WPLA requirements are extensive. The Act specifies such details as types of labels, means of attachment, label position on the article, package labeling, unit labeling (as in the case of a two-piece garment), arrangement of information on the label, allowable fiber designations, country-of-origin indications, trim and ornamentation, pile fabrics, sectional disclosure, use of trade names and trademarks, requirements for swatches and samples, etc. The FTC publishes a booklet intended to clarify WPLA requirements in order to facilitate voluntary compliance within the industry (see "Publications Available" below). It is available on request, at no charge, from the FTC (see addresses at end of this chapter).

Registered Identification Numbers. Any domestic firm or person residing in the U.S. and engaged in the manufacture or marketing of textile products covered under the TFPIA may obtain an FTC-registered identification number for use on required tags and labels instead of the name of a firm or person. For applications, contact the FTC (address below.)

For a general discussion of U.S. Customs marking and labeling requirements, refer to "Marking: Country of Origin" on page 215 and "Special Marking Requirements" on page 217.

Shipping Considerations

You will need to ensure that your goods are packaged and shipped with care so that they pass smoothly through Customs and arrive in good condition. You are responsible for ensuring that the shipment is in compliance with all applicable government regulations for packaging and shipping. In most instances, you should not leave these arrangements solely to the discretion of your supplier. Careful preparation of the cargo and selection of the mode of transport can be essential to a cost-effective, timely delivery of undamaged goods. We strongly advise you to consult your shipping representative, insurance agent, or freight broker for advice on packing and shipping. Refer also to the major tab section "Packing/Shipping/Insurance" for a general discussion of packing and shipping.

Man-made filament products may be shipped in bulk, spools, cartons, or other types of containers, depending on the type of product and whether it is prepackaged. General considerations include protection from contamination, weather, and pests. Containers should be constructed so as to be safe for handling during transport.

Publications Available

The following publications may be relevant to the importation of man-made fibers:

Questions and Answers Relating to the Textile Fiber Products Identification Act and Regulations

Questions and Answers Relating to the Wool Products Labeling Act and Regulations

Available free of charge on request from the Federal Trade Commission, these publications are excellent sources of information written in clear lay language. We recommend that anyone interested in importing textile fiber products but unfamiliar with the regulations obtain a copy of each of these booklets.

The *Harmonized Tariff Schedule of the United States* (HTSUS) is available from:

Government Printing Office (GPO)
Superintendent of Documents
Washington, DC 20402
(202) 512-1800 (Order line)
(202) 512-0000 (General)

The USGPO also has copies of specific laws available for purchase. The USGPO accepts credit card orders over the phone, as well as mail orders paid by credit card, a check drawn on a U.S. bank, or an international money order.

Relevant Government Agencies

Address your questions regarding textile Multi-Fiber Arrangements to:

International Trade Administration
Office of Textile and Apparel
14th and Constitution Ave. NW, Rm. 3100
Washington, DC 20230
(202) 482-5078, 482-3737

Address your questions regarding the Flammable Fabrics Act (FFA) to:

Consumer Product Safety Commission (CPSC)
5401 Westbard Avenue
Bethesda, MD 20207
(301) 492-6580

Address your questions regarding requirements under the Textile Fiber Products Identification Act (TFPIA) or the Wool Products Labeling Act (WPLA) to:

Federal Trade Commission (FTC)
Division of Enforcement
601 Pennsylvania Ave. NW
Washington, DC 20580
(202) 326-2996 (General)
(202) 326-2841 (Textile and wool products labeling)

Address your questions regarding man-made filament imports to the district or port director of Customs for you area. For addresses, refer to"U.S. Customs District Offices" on page 62 or contact:

U.S. Customs Service
1301 Constitution Ave. NW
Washington, DC 20229
(202) 927-6724 (Information)
(202) 927-1000 (General)

The following information numbers for U.S. Customs in Washington, DC, provide recorded information. The Quota Branch numbers listed by country provide updated status reports on textile quotas from those countries. All area codes are (202).
General information: 927-5850

Quota Branch: China 927-6703; India 927-6705; Indonesia 927-6704; Japan 927-6706; Korea 927-6707; Macao 927-6709; Malaysia 927-6712; Mexico 927-6711; Pakistan 927-6714; Philippines 927-6713; Romania 927-6715; Singapore 927-6716; Sri Lanka 927-6708; Taiwan 927-6719; Thailand 927-6717; Turkey 927-6718; All others 927-5850.

Laws and Regulations

The following laws and regulations may be relevant to the importation of man-made filament products. The laws are contained in the United States Code (USC), and the regulations are published in the Code of Federal Regulations (CFR), both of which are available at larger public and law libraries. Copies of specific laws are also available from the United States Government Printing Office (address above).

7 USC 1854
Textile Trade Agreements
(EO 11651, as amended by EO 11951 and 12188, and supplemented by EO 12475)
This Act authorizes the CITA of the DOC to enter into Multi-Fiber Agreements with other countries to control trade in textiles and establishes the Textile Import Program, which is enforced by U.S. Customs.

19 CFR 12.130 et seq.
Regulations on Entry of Textiles
These regulations provide the requirements and procedures followed by Customs in enforcing limitations on the importation and entry and withdrawal of textiles and textile products from warehouses for consumption in the U.S.

15 USC 70-77
Textile Fiber Products Identification Act (TFPIA)
This Act prohibits false or deceptive labeling (misbranding) and false advertising of any textile fiber products and requires all textile fiber products imported into the U.S. to be labeled in accordance with the requirements set forth in the law.

19 CFR 11.12b; 16 CFR 303 et seq.
Regulations on Labeling and Marking
These regulations detail the labeling and marking requirements for textiles as specified by the CPSC and the invoice contents required by U.S. Customs for purpose of enforcing the labeling and marking rules.

15 USC 68-68j
Wool Products Labeling Act (WPLA)
This Act prohibits the false or deceptive labeling (misbranding) of wool products and requires all wool products imported into the U.S. to be labeled in accordance with requirements set forth in the law.

19 CFR 11.12; 16 CFR 300 et seq.
Regulations on WPLA Labeling and Marking
These regulations set forth the wool labeling and marking requirements adopted by the FTC to administer the requirements of the WPLA and provide the procedures followed by U.S. Customs in enforcing the WPLA and the FTC regulations, including entry invoice requirements.

15 USC 1191-1204
Flammable Fabrics Act (FFA)
This Act provides for the setting of flammability standards for fabric by the Consumer Product Safety Commission (CPSC) and for enforcement by U.S. Customs.

16 CFR 1610, 1611, 1615, 1616, 1630-1632
Regulations on Flammable Fabric Standards
These regulations specify the flammability standards adopted by the CPSC under the FFA for various types of textiles.

Principal Exporting Countries

The following listing includes samples of the main supplier nations of the products of this chapter. It is organized by HTSUS major heading. (Refer to "Customs Classification" above for the product codes.) Countries are listed in rank order of the value of products imported to the U.S. Statistics represent customs value entries for 1993 from the Bureau of Census, U.S. Department of Commerce.

5401—Germany, Switzerland, Japan, Taiwan, Canada, France, South Korea, Israel, Thailand, United Kingdom

5402—Canada, Germany, United Kingdom, Japan, Mexico, Netherlands, France, South Korea, Costa Rica, Israel

5403—Canada, Germany, Netherlands, Japan, Brazil, Mexico, Italy, Belgium, United Kingdom, France

5404—Canada, Germany, Japan, Netherlands, Mexico, United Kingdom, Italy, France, Brazil, Taiwan

5405—Japan, Colombia, Germany, Italy, Dominican Rep., Taiwan, Honduras

5406—Canada, Turkey, France, Mexico, Italy, United Kingdom, Taiwan, Germany, Japan, Ireland

5407—South Korea, Japan, Canada, Italy, Taiwan, Indonesia, Pakistan, France, Switzerland, Germany

5408—Japan, Germany, South Korea, Italy, Thailand, Indonesia, Canada, Taiwan, Slovenia, China

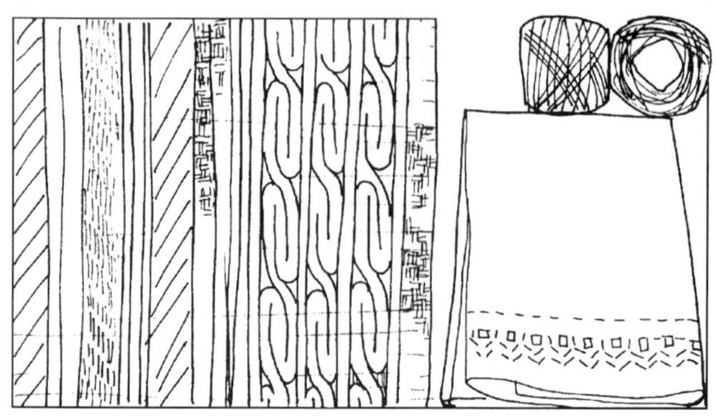

Chapter 55: Man-made Staple Fibers*

This chapter relates to the importation of man-made staple fiber products, which are classified under Chapter 55 of the Harmonized Tariff Schedule of the United States (HTSUS). Specifically, it includes synthetic (such as nylon or polyester) or artificial (such as viscose rayon or cellulose acetate) stable fibers combed, carded, otherwise processed, or not processed; filament tow; waste from such fibers; and sewing thread, yarn, and woven fabrics made of such fibers.

If you are interested in importing products derived from man-made filaments, you should read Commodity Index Chapter 54. The import requirements for cotton textiles and products are covered in Chapter 52, and for wool textile products in Chapter 53. For importing monofilaments of plastics, you should also read Chapter 39. If you are interested in importing apparel, refer to Chapters 60 through 63. Hairnets and headgear of man-made filaments are covered in Chapter 65, and footwear in Chapter 64. Import requirements for specific types of fibers are found in related chapters, such as glass fibers in Chapter 70.

Key Factors

The key factors in the importation of man-made staple fiber products are:

- Compliance with quota restraints and visa requirements under U.S. Department of Commerce (DOC) Multi-Fiber Arrangements
- Submission of U.S. Customs Country-of-Origin Declaration(s)
- Compliance with entry invoice requirements
- Compliance with labeling requirements under Textile Fiber Products Identification Act (TFPIA) and the Wool Products Labeling Act (WPLA)
- Compliance with flammability standards adopted and enforced by the Consumer Product Safety Commission (CPSC) under the Flammable Fabrics Act (FFA).

Although most importers use the services of a licensed customs broker in making their entries, and we recommend this practice, you should be aware of the regulatory, entry, and documentation issues involved in importing your product. You, as importer, are ultimately responsible for the fulfillment of any legal requirements applicable to your shipment.

*IMPORTANT: Read the Commodity Index Introduction. It is the essential framework for understanding this section.

General Considerations

Regulatory Agencies. The DOC's Committee for Implementation of Textile Agreements (CITA) regulates certain textile imports under Section 204 of the Agricultural Adjustment Act. U.S. Customs enforces CITA textile and textile product entry quotas. Customs also enforces compliance with labeling and invoice requirements of the TFPIA and flammability standards under the FFA. The CPSC monitors imports and from time to time inspects textile shipments for compliance with FFA standards. If you are importing products that contain wool fibers, importation is subject to complex textile import regulations. The Federal Trade Commission (FTC) administers the WPLA requirements.

Textile Quotas. If you are interested in importing man-made staple fiber products, the most important issue you need to be aware of is quotas. Under the Multi-Fiber Arrangement provisions of Section 204 of the Agricultural Adjustment Act, CITA initiates specific agreements with individual exporting countries. Section 204 of the Agricultural Adjustment Act covers textiles that: 1) Are in chief value of cotton, wool, or man-made fibers, any textile fibers subject to the terms of any textile trade agreement, or any combination of such fibers; 2) contain 50% or more by weight of cotton or man-made fibers, or any textile fibers subject to the terms of any textile trade agreement; 3) contain 17% or more by weight of wool; or 4) if in chief value of textile fibers or textile materials, contain a blend of cotton, wool, or man-made fibers, any textile fibers subject to the terms of any textile trade agreement, or any combination of such fibers that, in total, amount to 50% or more by weight of all component fibers.

The U.S. has Multi-Fiber Arrangements with 40 countries. Each agreement with each country is unique, and may specify quotas for a type of textile or a specific article. Visas or export licenses may be required. These agreements, however, often change. Therefore, if you are interested in importing any man-made staple fiber products, you should contact the International Trade Administration's Office of Textile and Apparel (see addresses at end of this chapter). Refer to "Prohibitions and Restrictions" below for further details.

Country-of-Origin Declarations. U.S. Customs enforces CITA textile and textile product entry quotas (see "Prohibitions and Restrictions" below). Requirements for entry include submission of Country-of-Origin Declarations with every textile shipment, regardless of whether it is subject to a specific multi-fiber arrangement (19 CFR 12.130, 12.131).

Country of Origin. Quota restrictions are country-specific and therefore are applied based on the country of origin for the textiles shipped. The last country from which a textile shipment was exported to the U.S. is not necessarily its country of origin. A textile or textile product imported into the U.S. is considered a product of the particular foreign territory or country, or a U.S. insular possession, where it is wholly grown, produced, or manufactured. For the following discussion, "country" means a foreign territory or country, or a U.S. insular possession.

Substantial transformation rules may affect the country-of-origin determination. For example, if a textile or textile product originates in Country A and is subject to quota, the quota restrictions apply at entry into the U.S. But if, prior to export to the U.S., you move the shipment to Country B where there are fewer restrictions, the shipment may nevertheless remain subject to quota and visa requirements under the Multi-Fiber Arrangement with Country A. Customs determines whether the quota restrictions apply based on the criteria of "substantial transformation." If your textiles do not undergo any major processing or manufacturing while in Country B, or if the manufacturing or processing is minor, your shipment will be deemed to originate in Country

A. *You cannot claim substantial transformation on the basis of minor manufacturing procedures.*

In contrast, if your shipment undergoes major processing or manufacturing while in Country B, rendering the textiles "new and different articles of commerce," Customs will treat the shipment as the product of Country B. To qualify as having undergone substantial transformation, an article must evince a change in: 1) commercial designation or identity; b) fundamental character; or c) commercial use. If your shipment is processed in more than one country, the country where it last underwent substantial transformation is the country of origin for Customs entry. In deciding whether the manufacturing or processing operation in a country is major, Customs considers the following factors: 1) the resultant physical change in the material or article; 2) the complexity, the level or degree of skill and/or technology required, and the amount of time involved in the operations; and 3) the value added to the article or material, compared to its value when imported into the U.S.

Validating Operations. Operations that Customs will usually acknowledge as validating a claim of substantial transformation are the following: 1) dyeing and printing, when accompanied by two or more of the following finishing operations: bleaching, shrinking, fulling, napping, decating, permanent stiffening, weighting, permanent embossing, or moireing; 2) spinning fibers into yarn; 3) weaving, knitting, or otherwise forming fabric; 4) cutting fabric into parts and assembling the parts into completed articles; or 5) substantial assembly, by sewing and/or tailoring into a completed garment cut pieces of apparel articles that have been cut from fabric in another country—e.g., complete assembly and tailoring of all cut pieces of suit-type jackets, suits, and shirts.

Insubstantial Operations. Operations that usually will not support a claim of substantial transformation, even if more than one are performed, are the following: 1) simple operations of combining, labeling, pressing, cleaning, dry cleaning, or packaging; 2) cutting to length or width and hemming or overlocking fabrics that are readily identifiable as being intended for a particular commercial use; 3) trimming and/or joining together by sewing, looping, linking, or other means of attaching otherwise completed knit-to-shape component parts produced in a single country, even if accompanied by other processes—e.g., washing, drying, mending—normally incident to assembly; 4) one or more finishing operations on yarns, fabrics, or their textile articles—such as showerproofing, superwashing, bleaching, decating, fulling, shrinking, mercerizing, or similar operations; or 5) dyeing and/or printing fabrics or yarns.

Declarations. The country of origin of the man-made staple fiber products in a shipment must be stated on a declaration submitted to U.S. Customs at the time of entry. There are three Customs Country-of-Origin Declarations: single-country, multiple-country, and negative. The Declaration to be submitted with your shipment of man-made staple fiber products depends on the nature of the import.

- **Single-country declarations** are used for entries of textiles or textile products that clearly originate from only one country or that have been assembled in one country from fabricated components wholly produced in the U.S. or the foreign country of manufacture. Information required includes: marks of identification and numbers; description of article and quantity; country of origin; and date of exportation.
- **Multiple-country declarations** are used for entries of textiles or textile products that were manufactured or processed and/or that incorporate materials originating in more than one foreign country or territory. Information required includes: marks of identification and numbers; for articles, description, quantity, identification of manufacturing and/or processing operations, country, and date of exportation; for materials used to make articles, description of materials, country of production, and date of exportation.
- **Negative declarations** must accompany all textile imports that are not subject to FFA Section 204 restrictions. Information required includes: marks of identification and numbers; descriptions of article and quantity; and country of origin.

The date of exportation to be indicated on the above declarations is the date on which the carrier leaves the last port in the country of origin, as determined by Customs. Diversion to another country during transit does not affect the export date.

Procedure for Declarations. The manufacturer, producer, exporter, or importer may prepare the declaration. If more than one of these parties is involved in the importation, each party may prepare a separate declaration. You may file a separate declaration for each invoice presented with your entry. The declaration must be dated and signed by the responsible party, and must include the person's title and the company name and address. Your shipment's entry will be denied unless it is accompanied by a properly executed declaration. Customs will not treat a textile declaration as a missing document for which a bond may be filed.

Customs will base its country-of-origin determination on the information contained in each declaration, unless the information is insufficient. If the information on the declaration is insufficient, Customs will require that you submit such additional information as will enable the determination to be made. The shipment will not be released until the determination is made. Thus, if you want to clear Customs with minimal delay, be sure that the information on the declarations is as complete as possible for each shipment.

Textile Labeling and Invoice Requirements. You are responsible for your imported man-made staple fiber product's compliance with applicable provisions of the TFPIA. Man-made staple fiber products that require labeling under TFPIA must already be labeled at entry, or the shipment will be refused. (See "Marking and Labeling Requirements" below.) If you import shipments of man-made staple fiber textiles subject to TFPIA and valued at over $500, you must provide special information on the entry invoice (see "Entry and Documentation" below).

Flammability Standards. Man-made staple fiber products imported into the U.S. for use in consumer products must be in compliance with the FFA, a federal law that gives the CPSC the authority and responsibility for protecting the public from the hazards of dangerously flammable items of wearing apparel and interior furnishings. Under the FFA, standards have been established for flammability of clothing textiles. You cannot import any article of wearing apparel or interior furnishing, or any fabric or related material that is intended for use or that may be used in such items, if it fails to conform to an applicable flammability standard (FFA Section 4). Certain products may be imported into the U.S. (FFA Section 11c) for finishing or processing to render them less flammable so as to meet the standards. For these products, the exporter must state on the invoice or other paper relating to the shipment that the shipment is being made for that purpose.

The CPSC monitors imports of textiles under its Import Surveillance Program. From time to time, your textile shipments may be inspected to ascertain compliance with mandatory safety standards. Shipments may also be subject to testing by the CPSC to determine compliance. If the CPSC believes a product, fabric, or related material does not comply with a flammability standard, it is authorized to pursue a variety of legal sanctions (see "Prohibitions and Restrictions" below).

Substantial Product Hazard Reports. Any firm that obtains information that reasonably supports the conclusion that one of its products presents an unreasonable risk of serious injury or death must report that information to the CPSC's Division of Corrective Actions (CPSC address below). Importers must also report to the CPSC if 1) a type of product is the subject of at least three civil actions filed in U.S. federal or state courts, 2) each suit alleges the involvement of that product type in death or grievous bodily injury (as defined in FFA Section 37(3)1), and 3) at least three of the actions result in a final settlement with the manufacturer or in a judgment for the plaintiff within any one of the two-year periods specified in FFA Section 37(b).

Wool Product Entry Requirements. Depending on the nature of your wool fiber imports, as many as four different types of special entry documents may be required. First, for all imported textile fibers and yarns covered by the Agricultural Adjustment Act (AAA), including wool, you must file a U.S. Customs Textile Entry Declaration (see "Country-of-Origin Declarations" above). Second, with each wool shipment's entry summary, you must file Customs **Form 6451**, Notice of Percentage of Clean Yield and Grade of Wool or Hair, in duplicate, showing your name and address. Third, for all wool products subject to the WPLA, special information is required on the entry invoices (see "Entry and Documentation" below). Finally, certain wool articles manufactured or produced in certain countries may be subject to quotas under U.S. Department of Commerce Multi-Fiber Arrangements. Such products require export certificates or visas issued by the appropriate country of origin, in addition to other requisite entry paperwork (see "Quotas" above).

Wool Products Labeling Act. The term "wool product" means any product or any portion of a product that contains, purports to contain, or in any way is represented as containing wool, reprocessed wool, or reused wool. All wool products imported into the U.S., except those made more than 20 years before importation, and except carpets, rugs, mats, and upholsteries, must have affixed a stamp, tag, label, or other means of identification as required by the WPLA. If you are importing wool products exempt from labeling under the WPLA, do not assume they are also exempt from labeling under the TFPIA. These are two distinct laws, with some overlapping requirements (see "Marking and Labeling Requirements" below).

Import Advisory

Importation of textiles is trade-sensitive and highly regulated. Shipments of textiles and textile products not complying with all government regulations, including quotas and visas, are subject to seizure and could result in the imposition of penalties as well as possible forfeiture of the goods. You should always verify the available quota for any textile product you plan to import before your shipment leaves the country of manufacture. Furthermore, Customs textile classification rulings change frequently, and prior administrative rulings are often modified and sometimes reversed.

Customs Classification

For customs purposes, man-made staple fiber product's are classified under Chapter 55 of the HTSUS. This chapter is broken into major headings, which are further divided into subheadings, and often sub-subheadings, each of which has its own HTSUS classification number. For example, the HTSUS number for dyed woven fabrics with 85% by weight of artificial staple fibers mixed with 36% or more by weight of wool or fine animal hair is 5516.32.05, indicating it is a sub-subcategory of dyed woven fabrics with less than 85% by weight of artificial staple fibers mixed wool or fine animal hair (5516.32.00), which is a subcategory of the major heading, woven fabrics of artificial staple fibers (5516.00.00). There are 16 major headings within Chapter 55.

5501—Synthetic filament tow

5502—Artificial filament tow

5503—Synthetic staple fibers, not carded, combed, or otherwise processed for spinning

5504—Artificial staple fibers, not carded, combed, or otherwise processed for spinning

5505—Waste (including noils, yarn waste, and garnetted stock) of man-made fibers

5506—Synthetic staple fibers, carded, combed, or otherwise processed for spinning

5507—Artificial staple fibers, carded, combed, or otherwise processed for spinning

5508—Sewing thread of man-made staple fibers, whether or not put up for retail sale

5509—Yarn (other than sewing thread) of synthetic staple fibers, not put up for retail sale

5510—Yarn (other than sewing thread) of artificial staple fibers, not put up for retail sale

5511—Yarn (other than sewing thread) of man-made staple fibers, put up for retail sale

5512—Woven fabrics of synthetic staple fibers, containing 85% or more by weight of synthetic staple fibers

5513—Woven fabrics of synthetic staple fibers, containing less than 85% by weight of such fibers, mixed with cotton, of a weight not exceeding 170 g/m^2

5514—Woven fabrics of synthetic staple fibers, containing less than 85% by weight of such fibers, mixed mainly or solely with cotton, of a weight exceeding 170 g/m^2

5515—Other woven fabrics of synthetic staple fibers

5516—Woven fabrics of artificial staple fibers

For more details regarding classifications of the specific product you are interested in importing, consult a customs broker, the appropriate commodity specialist at your nearest customs port, or the HTSUS. HTSUS is available for purchase from the U.S. Government Printing Office (see addresses at end of this chapter), and may be found in larger public libraries. Refer to "Classification—Liquidation" on page 207 for a general discussion of customs classification.

Sample Import Duties

Import duties will vary depending on the HTSUS classification of your product. Therefore, to determine the correct amount of duties, your product must be properly classified under the HTSUS. The following sample duties are taken from the duty listings for HTSUS Chapter 55 products.

Synthetic or artificial filament tow (5501.00.00, 5502.00.00): 10%; synthetic or artificial staple fibers not carded, combed, or otherwise processed for spinning (5503.00.00, 5504.00.00): 4.9%, carded, combed, or otherwise processed for spinning (5506.00.00, 5507.00.00): 6.5%; waste of man-made staple fibers (5505.00.00): 2.1%; sewing thread of man-made staple fibers (5508.00.00): 13%; multiple (folded) or cabled yarn of synthetic staple fibers with 85% or more by weight of staple fibers of nylon or other polyamides not for retail sale (5509.12.00): 12%; yarn of man-made staple fibers for retail sale (5511.00.00): 13%; poplin or broadcloth with 85% or more by weight of polyester staple fibers (5512.11.00): 17%; blue denim with 85% or more by weight of polyester staple fibers (5512.19.00): 17%.

Entry and Documentation

The entry of merchandise is a two-part process consisting of 1) filing the documentation necessary to determine whether merchandise may be released from Customs custody, and 2) filing the documents that contain information for duty assessment and statistical purposes. In certain instances, all documents must be filed and accepted by Customs prior to release of the goods. Unless you have been granted an extension, you must file entry documents at a location specified by the district or area director within five working days of your shipment's date of arrival at a U.S. port of entry. These include a number of standard documents required by Customs for any entry, and:

- U.S. Customs Country-of-Origin Declaration(s)
- Export documentation and/or visa for textiles subject to Multi-Fiber Arrangement
- Customs **Form 6451**, Notice of Percentage of Clean Yield and Grade of Wool or Hair, in duplicate, showing your name and address (if importing articles containing wool)

After you present the entry, Customs may examine your shipment or may waive examination. The shipment is then released provided no legal or regulatory violations have been noted. You must then file entry summary documentation and deposit estimated duties at a designated customhouse within 10 working days of your shipment's release. For a detailed description of entry procedures, standard documentation, and informal entry, refer to "Entry Process" on page 182.

NAFTA Certificates of Origin. An importer of textiles for which NAFTA treatment is sought need not file a separate NAFTA Certificate of Origin in addition to the Customs Country-of-Origin Declaration. The declaration is sufficient. However, the importer must take care to submit a declaration from each U.S., Canadian, or Mexican producer or manufacturer. Thus, for multiple producers or manufacturers, a separate declaration must be filed for each. If a Customs district director cannot determine the country of origin because the declaration is absent or incomplete, the shipment is not entitled to preferential NAFTA tariff treatment or other NAFTA benefits. See 12 CFR 132.

Entry Invoices. You must provide certain additional information on the entry invoice for man-made stable fiber products. The specific information varies depending on the nature of your product, as noted below.

TFPIA Requirements. For the purpose of TFPIA enforcement, a commercial shipment of textile products exceeding $500 in value and subject to TFPIA labeling requirements must show the following information: 1) the constituent fiber or combination of fibers, designating with equal prominence each natural or manufactured fiber by its generic name, in order of predominance by weight if the weight of such fiber is 5% or more of the total fiber weight of the product; 2) percentage of each fiber present, by weight, in the total fiber content; 3) the name or other identification issued and registered by the Federal Trade Commission of the manufacturer of the product or one or more persons subject to Section 3 of the TFPIA with respect to such product; 4) the name of the country where processed or manufactured.

Woven Fabrics. The invoice for woven fabric of man-made fibers in HTSUS headings 5512 through 5516 must include the following information: 1) exact width of fabric; 2) detailed description of the merchandise; 3) any trade name; 4) indication of whether bleached, unbleached, dyed, of yarns of different colors, and/or printed; 5) if composed of more than one material, percentage by weight of each; 6) identification of the man-made fibers as artificial or synthetic, filament or staple, and high tenacity or other; 7) number of turns per meter in each yarn; 8) yarn sizes in warp and filling; 9) type of weave—such as plain weave, twill, sateen, dobby, jacquard, swivel, lappet; 10) number of single threads per cm^2 in both warp and filling; 11) weight per m^2 in grams; 12) average yarn number; 13) for spun or filament yarns, indication of whether textured.

Yarn. All entry invoices for yarn should show: 1) fiber content by weight; 2) whether the yarn is single or plied; 3) whether or not the yarn is put up for retail sale (as defined in HTSUS Section XI, Note 4); and 4) whether or not the yarn is intended for use as sewing thread.

In addition, if the yarn's chief weight is of man-made fibers, the entry invoice must show:1) whether the fibers are filament, spun, or a combination of filament and spun; and 2) if a combination, the percentage of filament and spun by weight.

Wool Products Subject to WPLA. When you offer for entry a wool product shipment valued at over $500 and subject to WPLA, you must include certain information intended to facilitate Customs monitoring and enforcement of that Act. This extra information is identical to that required by WPLA on labeling (see "Marking and Labeling Requirements" below), with the addition of the manufacturer's name. If your product consists of mixed waste, residues, and similar merchandise obtained from several suppliers or unknown sources, you may omit the manufacturer's name from the entry invoice.

Prohibitions and Restrictions

Quotas. Textile import restrictions are primarily a matter of quotas and the way in which these quotas are administered and monitored. Under the Multi-Fiber Arrangement provisions of Section 204 of the Agricultural Adjustment Act, CITA has negotiated Multi-Fiber Arrangements with 40 countries. These Agreements may impose quotas for a type of textile or a specific article, and they are country-specific. The agreements, however, often change. Therefore, if you are interested in importing any man-made staple fiber products, you should contact the International Trade Administration's Office of Textile and Apparel (see addresses at end of this chapter). The Office of Textile and Apparel has a team of country specialists who can inform you of the latest developments and inform you about a product's quota or restriction status.

U.S. Customs enforces CITA textile and textile product entry quotas. If formal entry procedures are not followed, Customs will usually refuse entry for textiles that are subject to Section 204. Formal entry requires submission of a Country-of-Origin Declaration (see "General Considerations" above). U.S. Customs maintains a current textile quota status report, available for perusal at any Customs port. In addition, U.S. Customs in Washington, DC, operates a telephone service to provide quota status reports, which are updated weekly (see "Relevant Government Agencies" below).

Flammable Fabrics. U.S. Customs may refuse entry for any article of wearing apparel or interior furnishing, or any fabric or related material that is intended for use or that may be used in wearing apparel or interior furnishings, if it fails to conform to an applicable flammability standard issued under Section 4 of the FFA. An exception is allowed for certain products (FFA Section 11c) that are imported for finishing or processing to bring them within the legal standard. For these products, the exporter must state on the invoice or other paper relating to the shipment that the shipment is being made for that purpose.

The CPSC, as the primary enforcement agency of flammability standards, inspects products for compliance with the FFA. If the CPSC believes a product, fabric, or related material does not comply with a flammability standard, it is authorized to pursue a variety of legal sanctions, including: 1) seizure, condemnation, and forfeiture of the noncomplying products; 2) administrative cease-and-desist order requiring an individual or firm to stop sale and distribution of the noncomplying products or; 3) temporary injunction requiring the individual or firm to stop sale and distribution of the noncomplying products, pending final disposition of an administrative cease-and-desist proceeding. The CPSC also has authority to seek civil penalties against any person who knowingly violates a regulation or standard issued under Section 4 of the FFA.

Country-Specific Restrictions

Restrictions under Multi-Fiber Arrangements are country-specific. A product originating in one country may be subject to quota and to export license or visa requirements, while the same product originating in a different country may not. At present, the U.S. has Multi-Fiber Arrangements with 40 countries. Many different categories of products are covered under these Arrangements; it is beyond the scope of this book to list each country and its restricted commodities. If you are interested in importing textiles and textile products, you should contact the International Trade Administration's Office of Textile and Apparel (see addresses at end of this chapter) or U.S. Customs to ascertain your product's restraint status.

The U.S. Customs Quota Branch phone numbers provide recorded status reports, by quota category number, for current charges against the quotas for that country. For convenience, the HTSUS shows the 3-digit category number in parentheses to the right of each listed commodity that is subject to textile restraints. For example, under Chapter 55, heading 5512.11.00, unbleached or bleached poplin or broadcloth, is followed by the number "(614)." If you know the category number for your product, you can find out to what extent that quota is filled simply by calling the number for the appropriate country. A word of caution, though: if you do not know for sure that your article is subject to quota from a particular country, and you call the number for that country, you may not be any more enlightened after the phone call. Many of the recordings give status reports only when a certain percentage of the quota has been filled. Thus, if 614 for Taiwan is among the categories for which not enough quantity has entered the U.S. to warrant specific mention, it will be lumped under "all other categories" and you will be none the wiser. To find out if your product is subject to textile restraints, call the DOC or a local Customs port office. Then you can find out the current charges against that quota by calling the country number listed below. For a complete listing of Customs Quota Branch information numbers, see "Relevant Government Agencies" below.

Marking and Labeling Requirements

TFPIA Requirements. All textile fiber products imported into the U.S. must be stamped, tagged, labeled, or otherwise marked with the following information as required by the TFPIA, unless exempt from marking (see TFPIA, Section 12): 1) the generic names and percentages by weight of the constituent fibers present in the textile fiber product, exclusive of permissible ornamentation, in amounts of more than 5% in order of predominance by weight, with any percentage of fiber or fibers required to be designated as "other fiber" or "other fibers" (including those present in amounts of 5% or less) appearing last; and 2) the name of the manufacturer or the name or registered identification number issued by the FTC of one or more persons marketing or handling the textile fiber product; and 3) the name of the country where processed. A word trademark, used as a house mark and registered with the U.S. Patent Office, may appear on labels instead of the name otherwise required, provided the owner of the trademark furnishes a copy of the registration to the FTC prior to use (see "Registered Identification Numbers" below).

The information listed above is not exhaustive. TFPIA requirements are extensive. The Act specifies such details as types of labels, means of attachment, label position on the article, package labeling, unit labeling for two-piece garments, and arrangement of information on the label; allowable fiber designations; country-of-origin indications; requirements for trim and ornamentation, linings and interlinings, and pile fabrics; sectional disclosure; use of trade names and trademarks; and requirements for swatches and samples. The FTC publishes a booklet intended to clarify TFPIA requirements to facilitate voluntary compliance in the industry (see "Publications Available" below). It is available on request, at no charge, from the FTC (see addresses at end of this chapter).

Wool Products Labeling Act (WPLA). Wool product labeling requirements for foreign products are the responsibility of the importer. The WPLA requires the following information to appear on wool products subject to the Act: 1) percentage of the wool product's total fiber weight (exclusive of ornamentation) not exceeding 5% of the total fiber weight of a) wool, b) recycled wool, c) each fiber other than wool if the percent by weight of such fiber is 5% or more, and d) the aggregate of all other fibers; 2) the maximum percent of the wool product's total weight, of any nonfibrous loading, filling, or adulterating matter; and 3) the importer's name. If you, as importer, have a registered identification number issued by the FTC, that number may be used instead of your name (see "Registered Identification Numbers" below).

Customs entry is contingent on proper labeling. If your shipment is found to be mislabeled at entry, you will be given the option of relabeling the products under Customs supervision, as long as the district director is satisfied that your labeling error or omission did not involve fraud or willful neglect. If your shipment is discovered after entry to have been noncomplying with WPLA, it will be recalled to Customs custody at your expense, unless you can satisfy the district director that the products have since been brought into compliance. You will be held responsible for all expenses incurred in bringing a shipment into compliance, including compensation of personnel and other expenses related to Customs supervision.

Fraudulent violations of WPLA will result in seizure of the shipment. Shipments already released from Customs custody will be ordered to be redelivered to Customs. Customs reports all cases of fraudulent violation to the FTC in Washington, DC.

The information listed above is not intended to be exhaustive. WPLA requirements are extensive. The Act specifies such details as types of labels, means of attachment, label position on the article, package labeling, unit labeling (as in the case of a two-piece garment), arrangement of information on the label, allowable fiber designations, country-of-origin indications, trim and ornamentation, pile fabrics, sectional disclosure, use of trade names and trademarks, requirements for swatches and samples, etc. The FTC publishes a booklet intended to clarify WPLA requirements in order to facilitate voluntary compliance within the industry (see "Publications Available" below). It is available on request, at no charge, from the FTC (see addresses at end of this chapter).

Registered Identification Numbers. Any domestic firm or person residing in the U.S. and engaged in the manufacture or marketing of textile products covered under the TFPIA may obtain an FTC-registered identification number for use on required tags and labels instead of the name of a firm or person. For applications, contact the FTC (address below.)

For a general discussion of U.S. Customs marking and labeling requirements, refer to "Marking: Country of Origin" on page 215 and "Special Marking Requirements" on page 217.

Shipping Considerations

You will need to ensure that your goods are packaged and shipped with care so that they pass smoothly through Customs and arrive in good condition. You are responsible for ensuring that the shipment is in compliance with all applicable government regulations for packaging and shipping. In most instances, you should not leave these arrangements solely to the discretion of your supplier. Careful preparation of the cargo and selection of the mode of transport can be essential to a cost-effective, timely delivery of undamaged goods. We strongly advise you to consult your shipping representative, insurance agent, or freight broker for advice on packing and shipping. Refer also to the major tab section "Packing/Shipping/Insurance" for a general discussion of packing and shipping.

Man-made staple fiber products may be shipped in bulk, spools, cartons, or other types of containers, depending on the type of product and whether it is prepackaged. General considerations include protection from contamination, weather, and pests. Containers should be constructed so as to be safe for handling during transport.

Publications Available

The following publications may be relevant to the importation of man-made staple fibers:

Questions and Answers Relating to the Textile Fiber Products Identification Act and Regulations

Questions and Answers Relating to the Wool Products Labeling Act and Regulations

Available free of charge on request from the Federal Trade Commission, these publications are excellent sources of information written in clear lay language. We recommend that anyone interested in importing textile fiber products but unfamiliar with the regulations obtain a copy of each of these booklets.

The *Harmonized Tariff Schedule of the United States* (HTSUS) is available from:

Government Printing Office (GPO)
Superintendent of Documents
Washington, DC 20402
(202) 512-1800 (Order line)
(202) 512-0000 (General)

The USGPO also has copies of specific laws available for purchase. The USGPO accepts credit card orders over the phone, as well as mail orders paid by credit card, a check drawn on a U.S. bank, or an international money order.

Relevant Government Agencies

Address your questions regarding textile Multi-Fiber Arrangements to:

International Trade Administration
Office of Textile and Apparel
14th and Constitution Ave. NW, Rm. 3100
Washington, DC 20230
(202) 482-5078, 482-3737

Address your questions regarding the Flammable Fabrics Act (FFA) to:

Consumer Product Safety Commission (CPSC)
5401 Westbard Avenue
Bethesda, MD 20207
(301) 492-6580

Address your questions regarding requirements under the Textile Fiber Products Identification Act (TFPIA) or the Wool Products Labeling Act (WPLA) to:

Federal Trade Commission (FTC)
Division of Enforcement
601 Pennsylvania Ave. NW
Washington, DC 20580
(202) 326-2996 (General)
(202) 326-2841 (Textile and wool products labeling)

Address your questions regarding man-made staple fiber imports to the district or port director of Customs for you area. For addresses, refer to"U.S. Customs District Offices" on page 62 or contact:

U.S. Customs Service
1301 Constitution Ave. NW
Washington, DC 20229
(202) 927-6724 (Information)
(202) 927-1000 (General)

The following information numbers for U.S. Customs in Washington, DC, provide recorded information. The Quota Branch numbers listed by country provide updated status reports on textile quotas from those countries. All area codes are (202).

General information: 927-5850

Quota Branch: China 927-6703; India 927-6705; Indonesia 927-6704; Japan 927-6706; Korea 927-6707; Macao 927-6709; Malaysia 927-6712; Mexico 927-6711; Pakistan 927-6714; Philippines 927-6713; Romania 927-6715; Singapore 927-6716; Sri Lanka 927-6708; Taiwan 927-6719; Thailand 927-6717; Turkey 927-6718; All others 927-5850.

Laws and Regulations

The following laws and regulations may be relevant to the importation of man-made staple fiber products. The laws are contained in the United States Code (USC), and the regulations are published in the Code of Federal Regulations (CFR), both of which are available at larger public and law libraries. Copies of specific laws are also available from the United States Government Printing Office (address above).

7 USC 1854
Textile Trade Agreements
(EO 11651, as amended by EO 11951 and 12188, and supplemented by EO 12475)
This Act authorizes the CITA of the DOC to enter into Multi-Fiber Agreements with other countries to control trade in textiles and establishes the Textile Import Program, which is enforced by U.S. Customs.

19 CFR 12.130 et seq.
Regulations on Entry of Textiles
These regulations provide the requirements and procedures followed by Customs in enforcing limitations on the importation and entry and withdrawal of textiles and textile products from warehouses for consumption in the U.S.

15 USC 70-77
Textile Fiber Products Identification Act (TFPIA)
This Act prohibits false or deceptive labeling (misbranding) and false advertising of any textile fiber products and requires all textile fiber products imported into the U.S. to be labeled in accordance with the requirements set forth in the law.

19 CFR 11.12b; 16 CFR 303 et seq.
Regulations on Labeling and Marking
These regulations detail the labeling and marking requirements for textiles as specified by the CPSC and the invoice contents required by U.S. Customs for purpose of enforcing the labeling and marking rules.

15 USC 68-68j
Wool Products Labeling Act (WPLA)
This Act prohibits the false or deceptive labeling (misbranding) of wool products and requires all wool products imported into the U.S. to be labeled in accordance with requirements set forth in the law.

19 CFR 11.12; 16 CFR 300 et seq.
Regulations on WPLA Labeling and Marking
These regulations set forth the wool labeling and marking requirements adopted by the FTC to administer the

requirements of the WPLA and provide the procedures followed by U.S. Customs in enforcing the WPLA and the FTC regulations, including entry invoice requirements.

15 USC 1191-1204
Flammable Fabrics Act (FFA)
This Act provides for the setting of flammability standards for fabric by the Consumer Product Safety Commission (CPSC) and for enforcement by U.S. Customs.

16 CFR 1610, 1611, 1615, 1616, 1630-1632
Regulations on Flammable Fabric Standards
These regulations specify the flammability standards adopted by the CPSC under the FFA for various types of textiles.

Principal Exporting Countries

The following listing includes samples of the main supplier nations of the products of this chapter. It is organized by HTSUS major heading. (Refer to "Customs Classification" above for the product codes.) Countries are listed in rank order of the value of products imported to the U.S. Statistics represent customs value entries for 1993 from the Bureau of Census, U.S. Department of Commerce.

5501—United Kingdom, France, Japan, Germany, Spain, South Korea, Italy, Turkey, Israel, Australia

5502—United Kingdom, Canada, Sweden, Russia, Belgium, Belarus, Switzerland, Japan, Germany, Mexico

5503—South Korea, Taiwan, Canada, Japan, Germany, Mexico, Switzerland, United Kingdom, Ireland, Italy

5504—Austria, United Kingdom, Finland, Taiwan, Thailand, Sweden, Japan, Czech Rep., Germany, Canada

5505—Mexico, Canada, Germany, United Kingdom, Japan, South Korea, Indonesia, Argentina, Australia, Israel

5506—Germany, Russia, Italy, Austria, United Kingdom, Canada, Mexico, Japan, France, Turkey

5507—France, Germany, Spain, China

5508—Thailand, South Korea, Taiwan, Hong Kong, Israel, Germany, China, United Kingdom, Indonesia, Singapore

5509—Canada, Mexico, Germany, Thailand, Malaysia, Turkey, Singapore, Saudi Arabia, China, Italy

5510—Austria, Germany, Finland, Belgium, Thailand, Indonesia, Japan, Canada, Italy, India

5511—Canada, United Kingdom, Mexico, Italy, France, Belgium, Turkey, Brazil, Spain, Germany

5512—South Korea, Canada, Japan, France, China, Germany, Italy, Austria, Switzerland, United Kingdom

5513—Thailand, Malaysia, China, Pakistan, Indonesia, Taiwan, Sri Lanka, Costa Rica, South Korea, Israel

5514—Taiwan, Pakistan, China, Canada, Indonesia, Thailand, Italy, Japan, Malaysia, Germany

5515—Italy, Taiwan, South Korea, Japan, Russia, Canada, Czech Rep., Slovenia, Brazil, Thailand

5516—Germany, Italy, Taiwan, Japan, Canada, Thailand, South Korea, Belgium, France, Turkey

Chapter 56: Nonwovens and Cordage*

Full title: Wadding, Felt, and Nonwovens; Special Yarns; Twine, Cordage, Ropes, and Cables and Articles Thereof

This chapter relates to the importation of nonwoven fabrics and cordage, which are classified under Chapter 56 of the Harmonized Tariff Schedule of the United States (HTSUS). Specifically, it includes sanitary articles of wadding; felt, nonwoven fabrics, textile-covered rubber thread and cord, textile yarn with rubber or plastic components, metalized and gimped yarn, twine, cordage, ropes, cables, and netting.

If you are interested in importing sewing thread, yarns, and other fibers or filaments, you should refer to Commodity Index Chapters 50 through 55. For importing nonwoven fabrics that are impregnated, coated, or covered with substances or preparations, you should read the Commodity Index chapter that covers that particular substance or preparation. For example, articles containing perfumes and cosmetics are in Chapter 33, soaps, detergents, polishes, and creams are in Chapter 34, and fabric softeners are in Chapter 38. If your product has plastic or rubber components, it may be classified under Chapter 39 or 40, respectively. If you are interested in importing metal foil on a backing of felt or nonwovens, refer to Chapters 72 through 81. Import requirements for articles consisting of mica or abrasive powder or grain on felt or nonwoven backing are covered in Chapter 68

Imports of cellulose and other paper wadding products are covered in Chapter 48. If you are interested in importing wadding, gauze, bandages, suture materials, and other articles for medical or surgical purposes, read Chapter 30. The import requirements for asbestos products are covered in Chapters 25 and 68. Hairnets are classified as headgear under Chapter 65. For importing nonwovens or cordage incorporated into toys, games, or sports equipment, refer to Chapter 95. If your product could be used as plaiting material, you should read Chapters 14 and 46. You should also review Chapter 58 to determine whether your import is classified as a special woven product.

Key Factors

The key factors in the importation of nonwoven fabrics and cordage are:

- Compliance with quota restraints and visa requirements under U.S. Department of Commerce (DOC) Multi-Fiber Arrangements (if importing fabrics and other textile products)

*IMPORTANT: Read the Commodity Index Introduction. It is the essential framework for understanding this section.

- Submission of U.S. Customs Country-of-Origin Declaration(s)
- Compliance with entry invoice requirements
- Compliance with labeling requirements under Textile Fiber Products Identification Act (TFPIA) and the Wool Products Labeling Act (WPLA)
- Compliance with flammability standards adopted and enforced by the Consumer Product Safety Commission (CPSC) under the Flammable Fabrics Act (FFA) (if importing fabrics and other textile products)
- Compliance with U.S. Food and Drug Administration (FDA) inspection and entry requirements (if importing products intended for sanitary purposes for which there is no exemption)
- Compliance with Federal Plant Pest Act (FPPA) and Plant Quarantine Act (PQA) requirements, and with U.S. Department of Agriculture (USDA) random port-of-entry inspections, import restrictions and quarantines, and other entry requirements (if importing cordage composed of vegetable materials)

Although most importers use the services of a licensed customs broker in making their entries, and we recommend this practice, you should be aware of the regulatory, entry, and documentation issues involved in importing your product. You, as importer, are ultimately responsible for the fulfillment of any legal requirements applicable to your shipment.

General Considerations

Regulatory Agencies. The DOC's Committee for Implementation of Textile Agreements (CITA) regulates certain textile imports under Section 204 of the Agricultural Adjustment Act. U.S. Customs enforces CITA textile and textile product entry quotas. Customs also enforces compliance with labeling and invoice requirements of the TFPIA and flammability standards under the FFA. The CPSC monitors imports and from time to time inspects textile shipments for compliance with FFA standards. If you are importing products that contain wool fibers, importation is subject to complex textile import regulations. The Federal Trade Commission (FTC) administers the WPLA requirements.

The USDA administers applicable provisions of the Plant Quarantine Act (PQA) and the Federal Plant Pest Act (FPPA), which are designed to prevent introduction into the U.S. of any plant pest or disease potentially harmful to U.S. agriculture. Shipments of cordage made of vegetable materials—e.g., jute or sisal—must be in compliance with PQA, FPPA, and USDA requirements. The FDA, under authority of the Federal Food, Drug, and Cosmetic Act (FDCA), regulates the importation of products intended for medical or sanitary purposes. U.S. Customs enforces entry requirements for products subject to FDCA requirements for compliance.

Cordage of Vegetable Materials. For most shipments of cordage made of vegetable materials, importation is straightforward. With some exceptions, you do not need permits or licenses to import these products (see "Prohibitions and Restrictions" below). The USDA's Animal and Plant Health Inspection Service (APHIS) inspects shipments of cordage made of vegetable materials on a random basis, depending on such factors as the port of entry, the country of origin, and the risk of contamination involved in the type of material being imported. Entry may be denied for noncompliance with the regulations, and the shipment could be seized, quarantined, destroyed, treated, or otherwise dealt with at the discretion of the inspector.

Wadding and Nonwoven Products for Sanitary Purposes. The importation of wadding and nonwoven products intended for sanitary uses—diapers, sanitary napkins, and similar items—is regulated by the FDA. Usually, if you import FDA-regulated articles, you must follow certain import procedures prescribed by that agency, and you must file FDA entry notification, **Form FD701**. If you are importing these articles at present, however, you are not required to follow normal FDA entry procedures because these articles are exempt. If routine Customs examinations of applicable shipments reveal problems that could have adverse effects on public health, the FDA will reconsider this exempt status. Selectivity criteria and entry notification may be reinstituted at any time at the discretion of FDA. Therefore, if your products fall into this category, you should be familiar with FDA import entry procedures and requirements under the FDCA. For an annotated diagram of FDA import procedures refer to the "Foods" appendix on page 808. If you are interested in importing a food-related product, you should ascertain its regulatory status by contacting the FDA (see addresses at end of this chapter).

Textile Quotas. If you are interested in importing nonwoven fabrics, the most important issue you need to be aware of is quotas. Under the Multi-Fiber Arrangement provisions of Section 204 of the Agricultural Adjustment Act, CITA initiates specific agreements with individual exporting countries. Section 204 of the Agricultural Adjustment Act covers textiles that: 1) are in chief value of cotton, wool, or man-made fibers, any textile fibers subject to the terms of any textile trade agreement, or any combination of such fibers; 2) contain 50% or more by weight of cotton or man-made fibers, or any textile fibers subject to the terms of any textile trade agreement; 3) contain 17% or more by weight of wool; or 4) if in chief value of textile fibers or textile materials, contain a blend of cotton, wool, or man-made fibers, any textile fibers subject to the terms of any textile trade agreement, or any combination of such fibers that, in total, amount to 50% or more by weight of all component fibers.

The U.S. has Multi-Fiber Arrangements with 40 countries. Each agreement with each country is unique, and may specify quotas for a type of textile or a specific article. Visas or export licenses may be required. These agreements, however, often change. Therefore, if you are interested in importing any nonwoven fabrics, you should contact the International Trade Administration's Office of Textile and Apparel (see addresses at end of this chapter). Refer to "Prohibitions and Restrictions" below for further details.

Textile Country-of-Origin Declarations. U.S. Customs enforces CITA textile and textile product entry quotas (see "Prohibitions and Restrictions" below). Requirements for entry include submission of Country-of-Origin Declarations with every nonwoven fabric shipment, regardless of whether it is subject to a specific multi-fiber arrangement (19 CFR 12.130, 12.131).

Country of Origin. Quota restrictions are country-specific and therefore are applied based on the country of origin for the textiles shipped. The last country from which a textile shipment was exported to the U.S. is not necessarily its country of origin. A textile or textile product imported into the U.S. is considered a product of the particular foreign territory or country, or a U.S. insular possession, where it is wholly grown, produced, or manufactured. For the following discussion, "country" means a foreign territory or country, or a U.S. insular possession.

Substantial transformation rules may affect the country-of-origin determination. For example, if a textile or textile product originates in Country A and is subject to quota, the quota restrictions apply at entry into the U.S. But if, prior to export to the U.S., you move the shipment to Country B where there are fewer restrictions, the shipment may nevertheless remain subject to quota and visa requirements under the Multi-Fiber Arrangement with Country A. Customs determines whether the quota restrictions apply based on the criteria of "substantial transformation." If your textiles do not undergo any major processing or manufacturing while in Country B, or if the manufacturing or processing is minor, your shipment will be deemed to originate in Country A. *You cannot claim substantial transformation on the basis of minor manufacturing procedures.*

In contrast, if your shipment undergoes major processing or manufacturing while in Country B, rendering the textiles "new and different articles of commerce," Customs will treat the shipment as the product of Country B. To qualify as having undergone substantial transformation, an article must evince a change in: 1) commercial designation or identity; b) fundamental character; or c) commercial use. If your shipment is processed in more than one country, the country where it last underwent substantial transformation is the country of origin for Customs entry. In deciding whether the manufacturing or processing operation in a country is major, Customs considers the following factors: 1) the resultant physical change in the material or article; 2) the complexity, the level or degree of skill and/or technology required, and the amount of time involved in the operations; and 3) the value added to the article or material, compared to its value when imported into the U.S.

Validating Operations. Operations that Customs will usually acknowledge as validating a claim of substantial transformation are the following: 1) dyeing and printing, when accompanied by two or more of the following finishing operations: bleaching, shrinking, fulling, napping, decating, permanent stiffening, weighting, permanent embossing, or moireing; 2) spinning fibers into yarn; 3) weaving, knitting, or otherwise forming fabric; 4) cutting fabric into parts and assembling the parts into completed articles; or 5) substantial assembly, by sewing and/or tailoring into a completed garment cut pieces of apparel articles that have been cut from fabric in another country—e.g., complete assembly and tailoring of all cut pieces of suit-type jackets, suits, and shirts.

Insubstantial Operations. Operations that usually will not support a claim of substantial transformation, even if more than one are performed, are the following: 1) simple operations of combining, labeling, pressing, cleaning, dry cleaning, or packaging; 2) cutting to length or width and hemming or overlocking fabrics that are readily identifiable as being intended for a particular commercial use; 3) trimming and/or joining together by sewing, looping, linking, or other means of attaching otherwise completed knit-to-shape component parts produced in a single country, even if accompanied by other processes—e.g., washing, drying, mending—normally incident to assembly; 4) one or more finishing operations on yarns, fabrics, or their textile articles—such as showerproofing, superwashing, bleaching, decating, fulling, shrinking, mercerizing, or similar operations; or 5) dyeing and/or printing fabrics or yarns.

Declarations. The country of origin of the nonwoven fabrics products in a shipment must be stated on a declaration submitted to U.S. Customs at the time of entry. There are three Customs Country-of-Origin Declarations: single-country, multiple-country, and negative. The Declaration to be submitted with your shipment of nonwoven fabric products depends on the nature of the import.

- **Single-country declarations** are used for entries of textiles or textile products that clearly originate from only one country or that have been assembled in one country from fabricated components wholly produced in the U.S. or the foreign country of manufacture. Information required includes: marks of identification and numbers; description of article and quantity; country of origin; and date of exportation.
- **Multiple-country declarations** are used for entries of textiles or textile products that were manufactured or processed and/or that incorporate materials originating in more than one foreign country or territory. Information required includes: marks of identification and numbers; for articles, description, quantity, identification of manufacturing and/or processing operations, country, and date of exportation; for materials used to make articles, description of materials, country of production, and date of exportation.
- **Negative declarations** must accompany all textile imports that are not subject to FFA Section 204 restrictions. Information required includes: marks of identification and numbers; descriptions of article and quantity; and country of origin.

The date of exportation to be indicated on the above declarations is the date on which the carrier leaves the last port in the country of origin, as determined by Customs. Diversion to another country during transit does not affect the export date.

Procedure for Declarations. The manufacturer, producer, exporter, or importer may prepare the declaration. If more than one of these parties is involved in the importation, each party may prepare a separate declaration. You may file a separate declaration for each invoice presented with your entry. The declaration must be dated and signed by the responsible party, and must include the person's title and the company name and address. Your shipment's entry will be denied unless it is accompanied by a properly executed declaration. Customs will not treat a textile declaration as a missing document for which a bond may be filed.

Customs will base its country-of-origin determination on the information contained in each declaration, unless the information is insufficient. If the information on the declaration is insufficient, Customs will require that you submit such additional information as will enable the determination to be made. The shipment will not be released until the determination is made. Thus, if you want to clear Customs with minimal delay, be sure that the information on the declarations is as complete as possible for each shipment.

Textile Labeling and Invoice Requirements. You are responsible for your imported nonwoven fabric product's compliance with applicable provisions of the TFPIA. Nonwoven fabric products that require labeling under TFPIA must already be labeled at entry, or the shipment will be refused. (See "Marking and Labeling Requirements" below.) If you import shipments of nonwoven fabrics subject to TFPIA and valued at over $500, you must provide special information on the entry invoice (see "Entry and Documentation" below).

Flammability Standards. Nonwoven fabric products imported into the U.S. for use in consumer products must be in compliance with the FFA, a federal law that gives the CPSC the authority and responsibility for protecting the public from the hazards of dangerously flammable items of wearing apparel and interior furnishings. Under the FFA, standards have been established for flammability of clothing textiles. You cannot import any article of wearing apparel or interior furnishing, or any fabric or related material that is intended for use or that may be used in such items, if it fails to conform to an applicable flammability standard (FFA Section 4). Certain products may be imported into the U.S. (FFA Section 11c) for finishing or processing to render them less flammable so as to meet the standards. For these products, the exporter must state on the invoice or other paper relating to the shipment that the shipment is being made for that purpose.

The CPSC monitors imports of textiles under its Import Surveillance Program. From time to time, your textile shipments may be inspected to ascertain compliance with mandatory safety standards. Shipments may also be subject to testing by the CPSC to determine compliance. If the CPSC believes a product, fabric, or related material does not comply with a flammability standard, it is authorized to pursue a variety of legal sanctions (see "Prohibitions and Restrictions" below).

Substantial Product Hazard Reports. Any firm that obtains information that reasonably supports the conclusion that one of its products presents an unreasonable risk of serious injury or death must report that information to the CPSC's Division of Corrective Actions (CPSC address below). Importers must also report to the CPSC if 1) a type of product is the subject of at least three civil actions filed in U.S. federal or state courts, 2) each suit alleges the involvement of that product type in death or grievous bodily injury (as defined in FFA Section 37(3)1), and 3) at least three of the actions result in a final settlement with the manufacturer or in a judgment for the plaintiff within any one of the two-year periods specified in FFA Section 37(b).

Wool Product Entry Requirements. Depending on the nature of your wool fiber imports, as many as four different types of special entry documents may be required. First, for all imported textile fibers and yarns covered by the Agricultural Adjustment Act (AAA), including wool, you must file a U.S. Customs Textile Entry Declaration (see "Textile Country-of-Origin Declarations" above). Second, with each wool shipment's entry summary, you must file Customs **Form 6451**, Notice of Percentage of Clean Yield and Grade of Wool or Hair, in duplicate, showing your name and address. Third, for all wool products subject to the WPLA, special information is required on the entry invoices (see "Entry and Documentation" below). Finally, certain wool articles manufactured or produced in certain countries may be subject to quotas under U.S. Department of Commerce Multi-Fiber Arrangements. Such products require export certificates or visas issued by the appropriate country of origin, in addition to other requisite entry paperwork (see "Quotas" above).

Wool Products Labeling Act. The term "wool product" means any product or any portion of a product that contains, purports to contain, or in any way is represented as containing wool, reprocessed wool, or reused wool. All wool products imported into the U.S., except those made more than 20 years before importation, and except carpets, rugs, mats, and upholsteries, must have affixed a stamp, tag, label, or other means of identification as required by the WPLA. If you are importing wool products exempt from labeling under the WPLA, do not assume they are also exempt from labeling under the TFPIA. These are two distinct laws, with some overlapping requirements (see "Marking and Labeling Requirements" below).

Import Advisory

Importation of textiles is trade-sensitive and highly regulated. Shipments of textiles and textile products not complying with all government regulations, including quotas and visas, are subject to seizure and could result in the imposition of penalties as well as possible forfeiture of the goods. You should always verify the available quota for any textile product you plan to import before your shipment leaves the country of manufacture. Furthermore, Customs textile classification rulings change frequently, and prior administrative rulings are often modified and sometimes reversed.

Customs Classification

For customs purposes, nonwoven fabrics and cordage are classified under Chapter 56 of the HTSUS. This chapter is broken into major headings, which are further divided into subheadings, and often sub-subheadings, each of which has its own HTSUS classification number. For example, the HTSUS number for laminated needleloom felt fabrics is 5602.10.10, indicating it is a subsubcategory of needleloom felt and stitch-bonded fiber fabrics (5602.10.00), which is a subcategory of the major heading, felt, whether or not impregnated, coated, covered, or laminated (5602.00.00). There are nine major headings within Chapter 56.

5601—Wadding of textile materials and articles thereof; textile fibers, not exceeding 5 mm in length (flock), textile dust, and mill neps

5602—Felt, whether or not impregnated, coated, covered, or laminated

5603—Nonwovens, whether or not impregnated, coated, covered, or laminated

5604—Rubber thread and cord, textile covered; textile yarn, strip, and the like of heading 5404 or 5405, impregnated, coated, covered, or sheathed with rubber or plastics

5605—Metalized yarn, whether or not gimped, being textile yarn, or strip or the like of heading 5404 or 5405, combined with metal in the form of thread, strip, or powder or covered with metal

5606—Gimped yarn, strip, and the like of heading 5404 or 5405, gimped (other than those of heading 5605 and gimped horsehair yarn); chenille yarn (including flock chenille yarn); loop wale-yarn

5607—Twine, cordage, rope, and cables, whether or not plaited or braided and whether or not impregnated, coated, covered, or sheathed with rubber or plastics

5608—Knotted netting of twine, cordage, or rope; made up fishing nets and other made up nets, of textile materials

5609—Articles of yarn, strip, or the like of heading 5404 or 5405, twine, cordage, rope, or cables, not elsewhere specified or included

For more details regarding classifications of the specific product you are interested in importing, consult a customs broker, the appropriate commodity specialist at your nearest customs port, or the HTSUS. HTSUS is available for purchase from the U.S. Government Printing Office (see addresses at end of this chapter), and may be found in larger public libraries. Refer to "Classification—Liquidation" on page 207 for a general discussion of customs classification.

Sample Import Duties

Import duties will vary depending on the HTSUS classification of your product. Therefore, to determine the correct amount of duties, your product must be properly classified under the HTSUS. The following sample duties are taken from the duty listings for HTSUS Chapter 56 products.

Sanitary articles of cotton wadding (5601.10.10): 7.2%; laminated needleloom felt and stitch-bonded fiber fabrics (5602.10.10): 16%; felt of wool or fine animal hair untreated (6602.21.00): 66.1 cents/kg plus 10%; felt of other textile materials untreated (5602.29.00): 12.5%; nonwoven floor covering underlays (5603.00.10): 3.4%; textile-covered rubber thread and cord (5604.10.00): 7.2%; metalized yarn (5605.00.00): 15%; gimped yarn (5606.00.00): 11.5%; twine, cordage, rope, or cables of jute (5607.10.00): 4%; made-up fishing nets of man-made textile materials (5608.11.00): 17%, of other materials (5608.90.10):17%; cotton hammocks (5608.90.23):16%.

Entry and Documentation

The entry of merchandise is a two-part process consisting of 1) filing the documentation necessary to determine whether merchandise may be released from Customs custody, and 2) filing the documents that contain information for duty assessment and statistical purposes. In certain instances, all documents must be filed and accepted by Customs prior to release of the goods. Unless you have been granted an extension, you must file entry documents at a location specified by the district or area director within five working days of your shipment's date of arrival at a U.S. port of entry. These include a number of standard documents required by Customs for any entry, and:

- U.S. Customs Country-of-Origin Declaration(s)

- Export documentation and/or visa for textiles subject to Multi-Fiber Arrangement
- Customs **Form 6451**, Notice of Percentage of Clean Yield and Grade of Wool or Hair, in duplicate, showing your name and address (if importing articles containing wool)
- Phytosanitary certificate (if importing cordage made of vegetable material)

After you present the entry, Customs may examine your shipment or may waive examination. The shipment is then released provided no legal or regulatory violations have been noted. You must then file entry summary documentation and deposit estimated duties at a designated customhouse within 10 working days of your shipment's release. For a detailed description of entry procedures, standard documentation, and informal entry, refer to "Entry Process" on page 182.

NAFTA Certificates of Origin. An importer of textiles for which NAFTA treatment is sought need not file a separate NAFTA Certificate of Origin in addition to the Customs Country-of-Origin Declaration. The declaration is sufficient. However, the importer must take care to submit a declaration from each U.S., Canadian, or Mexican producer or manufacturer. Thus, for multiple producers or manufacturers, a separate declaration must be filed for each. If a Customs district director cannot determine the country of origin because the declaration is absent or incomplete, the shipment is not entitled to preferential NAFTA tariff treatment or other NAFTA benefits. See 12 CFR 132.

Entry Invoices. You must provide certain additional information on the entry invoice for nonwoven and cordage products. The specific information varies depending on the nature of your product, as noted below.

TFPIA Requirements. For the purpose of TFPIA enforcement, a commercial shipment of textile products exceeding $500 in value and subject to TFPIA labeling requirements must show the following information: 1) the constituent fiber or combination of fibers, designating with equal prominence each natural or manufactured fiber by its generic name, in order of predominance by weight if the weight of such fiber is 5% or more of the total fiber weight of the product; 2) percentage of each fiber present, by weight, in the total fiber content; 3) the name or other identification issued and registered by the Federal Trade Commission of the manufacturer of the product or one or more persons subject to Section 3 of the TFPIA with respect to such product; 4) the name of the country where processed or manufactured.

Wool Products Subject to WPLA. When you offer for entry a wool product shipment valued at over $500 and subject to WPLA, you must include certain information intended to facilitate Customs monitoring and enforcement of that Act. This extra information is identical to that required by WPLA on labeling (see "Marking and Labeling Requirements" below), with the addition of the manufacturer's name. If your product consists of mixed waste, residues, and similar merchandise obtained from several suppliers or unknown sources, you may omit the manufacturer's name from the entry invoice.

Yarn. All entry invoices for yarn should show: 1) fiber content by weight; 2) whether the yarn is single or plied; 3) whether or not the yarn is put up for retail sale (as defined in HTSUS Section XI, Note 4); and 4) whether or not the yarn is intended for use as sewing thread.

Prohibitions and Restrictions

Cordage of Vegetable Materials. In general, any shipment of cordage made of vegetable materials is subject to random port-of-entry inspection by the USDA. If the inspector finds evidence of the presence of insects in your shipment, you may be required to submit your shipment to USDA-prescribed fumigation procedures. If the insect is of a kind for which there is no viable U.S. treatment, your shipment will be refused. Our source at USDA assured us that most shipments that are found to have insects in them can be treated to afford entry.

Textile Quotas. Textile import restrictions are primarily a matter of quotas and the way in which these quotas are administered and monitored. Under the Multi-Fiber Arrangement provisions of Section 204 of the Agricultural Adjustment Act, CITA has negotiated Multi-Fiber Arrangements with 40 countries. These Agreements may impose quotas for a type of textile or a specific article, and they are country-specific. The agreements, however, often change. Therefore, if you are interested in importing any nonwoven fabric products, you should contact the International Trade Administration's Office of Textile and Apparel (see addresses at end of this chapter). The Office of Textile and Apparel has a team of country specialists who can inform you of the latest developments and inform you about a product's quota or restriction status.

U.S. Customs enforces CITA textile and textile product entry quotas. If formal entry procedures are not followed, Customs will usually refuse entry for textiles that are subject to Section 204. Formal entry requires submission of a Country-of-Origin Declaration (see General Considerations above). U.S. Customs maintains a current textile quota status report, available for perusal at any Customs port. In addition, U.S. Customs in Washington, DC, operates a telephone service to provide quota status reports, which are updated weekly (see "Relevant Government Agencies" below).

Flammable Fabrics. U.S. Customs may refuse entry for any article of wearing apparel or interior furnishing, or any fabric or related material that is intended for use or that may be used in wearing apparel or interior furnishings, if it fails to conform to an applicable flammability standard issued under Section 4 of the FFA. An exception is allowed for certain products (FFA Section 11c) that are imported for finishing or processing to bring them within the legal standard. For these products, the exporter must state on the invoice or other paper relating to the shipment that the shipment is being made for that purpose.

The CPSC, as the primary enforcement agency of flammability standards, inspects products for compliance with the FFA. If the CPSC believes a product, fabric, or related material does not comply with a flammability standard, it is authorized to pursue a variety of legal sanctions, including: 1) seizure, condemnation, and forfeiture of the noncomplying products; 2) administrative cease-and-desist order requiring an individual or firm to stop sale and distribution of the noncomplying products or; 3) temporary injunction requiring the individual or firm to stop sale and distribution of the noncomplying products, pending final disposition of an administrative cease-and-desist proceeding. The CPSC also has authority to seek civil penalties against any person who knowingly violates a regulation or standard issued under Section 4 of the FFA.

Country-Specific Restrictions

Restrictions under Multi-Fiber Arrangements are country-specific. A product originating in one country may be subject to quota and to export license or visa requirements, while the same product originating in a different country may not. At present, the U.S. has Multi-Fiber Arrangements with 40 countries. Many different categories of products are covered under these Arrangements; it is beyond the scope of this book to list each country and its restricted commodities. If you are interested in importing textiles and textile products, you should contact the International Trade Administration's Office of Textile and Apparel (see addresses at end of this chapter) or U.S. Customs to ascertain your product's restraint status.

The U.S. Customs Quota Branch phone numbers provide recorded status reports, by quota category number, for current charges against the quotas for that country. For convenience, the HTSUS shows the 3-digit category number in parentheses to the right of each listed commodity that is subject to textile restraints. For example, under Chapter 56, heading 5604.10.00, textile-covered rubber thread and cord, is followed by the number "(201)." If you know the category number for your product, you can find out to what extent that quota is filled simply by calling the number for the appropriate country. A word of caution, though: if you do not know for sure that your article is subject to quota from a particular country, and you call the number for that country, you may not be any more enlightened after the phone call. Many of the recordings give status reports only when a certain percentage of the quota has been filled. Thus, if 201for South Korea is among the categories for which not enough quantity has entered the U.S. to warrant specific mention, it will be lumped under "all other categories" and you will be none the wiser. To find out if your product is subject to textile restraints, call the DOC or a local Customs port office. Then you can find out the current charges against that quota by calling the country number listed below. For a complete listing of Customs Quota Branch information numbers, see "Relevant Government Agencies" below.

Marking and Labeling Requirements

TFPIA Requirements. All textile fiber products imported into the U.S. must be stamped, tagged, labeled, or otherwise marked with the following information as required by the TFPIA, unless exempt from marking (see TFPIA, Section 12): 1) the generic names and percentages by weight of the constituent fibers present in the textile fiber product, exclusive of permissible ornamentation, in amounts of more than 5% in order of predominance by weight, with any percentage of fiber or fibers required to be designated as "other fiber" or "other fibers" (including those present in amounts of 5% or less) appearing last; and 2) the name of the manufacturer or the name or registered identification number issued by the FTC of one or more persons marketing or handling the textile fiber product; and 3) the name of the country where processed. A word trademark, used as a house mark and registered with the U.S. Patent Office, may appear on labels instead of the name otherwise required, provided the owner of the trademark furnishes a copy of the registration to the FTC prior to use (see "Registered Identification Numbers" below).

The information listed above is not exhaustive. TFPIA requirements are extensive. The Act specifies such details as types of labels, means of attachment, label position on the article, package labeling, unit labeling for two-piece garments, and arrangement of information on the label; allowable fiber designations; country-of-origin indications; requirements for trim and ornamentation, linings and interlinings, and pile fabrics; sectional disclosure; use of trade names and trademarks; and requirements for swatches and samples. The FTC publishes a booklet intended to clarify TFPIA requirements to facilitate voluntary compliance in the industry (see "Publications Available" below). It is available on request, at no charge, from the FTC (see addresses at end of this chapter).

Wool Products Labeling Act (WPLA). Wool product labeling requirements for foreign products are the responsibility of the importer. The WPLA requires the following information to appear on wool products subject to the Act: 1) percentage of the wool product's total fiber weight (exclusive of ornamentation) not exceeding 5% of the total fiber weight of a) wool, b) recycled wool, c) each fiber other than wool if the percent by weight of such fiber is 5% or more, and d) the aggregate of all other fibers; 2) the maximum percent of the wool product's total weight, of any nonfibrous loading, filling, or adulterating matter; and 3) the importer's name. If you, as importer, have a registered identification number issued by the FTC, that number may be used instead of your name (see "Registered Identification Numbers" below).

Customs entry is contingent on proper labeling. If your shipment is found to be mislabeled at entry, you will be given the option of relabeling the products under Customs supervision, as long as the district director is satisfied that your labeling error or omission did not involve fraud or willful neglect. If your shipment is discovered after entry to have been noncomplying with WPLA, it will be recalled to Customs custody at your expense, unless you can satisfy the district director that the products have since been brought into compliance. You will be held responsible for all expenses incurred in bringing a shipment into compliance, including compensation of personnel and other expenses related to Customs supervision.

Fraudulent violations of WPLA will result in seizure of the shipment. Shipments already released from Customs custody will be ordered to be redelivered to Customs. Customs reports all cases of fraudulent violation to the FTC in Washington, DC.

The information listed above is not intended to be exhaustive. WPLA requirements are extensive. The Act specifies such details as types of labels, means of attachment, label position on the article, package labeling, unit labeling (as in the case of a two-piece garment), arrangement of information on the label, allowable fiber designations, country-of-origin indications, trim and ornamentation, pile fabrics, sectional disclosure, use of trade names and trademarks, requirements for swatches and samples, etc. The FTC publishes a booklet intended to clarify WPLA requirements in order to facilitate voluntary compliance within the industry (see "Publications Available" below). It is available on request, at no charge, from the FTC (see addresses at end of this chapter).

Registered Identification Numbers. Any domestic firm or person residing in the U.S. and engaged in the manufacture or marketing of textile products covered under the TFPIA may obtain an FTC-registered identification number for use on required tags and labels instead of the name of a firm or person. For applications, contact the FTC (address below.)

For a general discussion of U.S. Customs marking and labeling requirements, refer to "Marking: Country of Origin" on page 215 and "Special Marking Requirements" on page 217.

Shipping Considerations

You will need to ensure that your goods are packaged and shipped with care so that they pass smoothly through Customs and arrive in good condition. You are responsible for ensuring that the shipment is in compliance with all applicable government regulations for packaging and shipping. In most instances, you should not leave these arrangements solely to the discretion of your supplier. Careful preparation of the cargo and selection of the mode of transport can be essential to a cost-effective, timely delivery of undamaged goods. We strongly advise you to consult your shipping representative, insurance agent, or freight broker for advice on packing and shipping. Refer also to the major tab section "Packing/Shipping/Insurance" for a general discussion of packing and shipping.

Nonwoven fabrics and cordage may be shipped in bulk, bolts, rolls, or other types of containers, depending on the type of product and whether it is prepackaged. General considerations include protection from contamination, weather, and pests. If a product must be kept in a sanitary environment, all tables, utensils, platforms, and devices used for moving or handling the product, the compartments in which it is stowed while being transported will need to be maintained in a sanitary condition.

Safety precautions should also be implemented as required to protect against breakage, spillage, corrosion of containers, and combustion. Containers should be constructed so as to be safe for handling during transport.

Publications Available

The following publication explains the FDA requirements for importing textile wadding products for sanitary use. It is published by the FDA and is available on request from FDA headquarters (see addresses at end of this chapter).

Requirements of Laws and Regulations Enforced by the U.S. Food and Drug Administration

The following publication may be relevant to the importation of nonwoven fabric products:

Questions and Answers Relating to the Textile Fiber Products Identification Act and Regulations

Available free of charge on request from the Federal Trade Commission, this publication is an excellent source of information written in clear lay language. We recommend that anyone interested in importing textile fiber products but unfamiliar with the regulations obtain a copy of this booklet.

The *Harmonized Tariff Schedule of the United States* (HTSUS) is available from:

Government Printing Office (GPO)
Superintendent of Documents
Washington, DC 20402
(202) 512-1800 (Order line)
(202) 512-0000 (General)

The USGPO also has copies of specific laws available for purchase. The USGPO accepts credit card orders over the phone, as well as mail orders paid by credit card, a check drawn on a U.S. bank, or an international money order.

Relevant Government Agencies

Address your questions regarding FDA regulation or requirements for textile wadding products intended for sanitary uses to:

U.S. Food and Drug Administration (FDA)
5600 Fishers Lane
Rockville, MD 20857
(301) 443-1544

Address your questions regarding USDA requirements for imported cordage made of vegetable materials to:

U.S. Department of Agriculture (USDA)
Animal and Plant Health Inspection Service (APHIS)
Plant Protection and Quarantine (PPQ)
Federal Building, Rm. 631
6505 Belcrest Road
Hyattsville, MD 20782
(301) 436-8645

Address your questions regarding textile Multi-Fiber Arrangements to:

International Trade Administration
Office of Textile and Apparel
14th and Constitution Ave. NW, Rm. 3100
Washington, DC 20230
(202) 482-5078, 482-3737

Address your questions regarding the Flammable Fabrics Act (FFA) to:

Consumer Product Safety Commission (CPSC)
5401 Westbard Avenue
Bethesda, MD 20207
(301) 492-6580

Address your questions regarding requirements under the Textile Fiber Products Identification Act (TFPIA) or the Wool Products Labeling Act (WPLA) to:

Federal Trade Commission (FTC)
Division of Enforcement
601 Pennsylvania Ave. NW
Washington, DC 20580
(202) 326-2996 (General)
(202) 326-2841 (Textile and wool products labeling)

Address your questions regarding cordage and nonwoven fabric imports to the district or port director of Customs for you area. For addresses, refer to"U.S. Customs District Offices" on page 62 or contact:

U.S. Customs Service
1301 Constitution Ave. NW
Washington, DC 20229
(202) 927-6724 (Information)
(202) 927-1000 (General)

The following information numbers for U.S. Customs in Washington, DC, provide recorded information. The Quota Branch numbers listed by country provide updated status reports on textile quotas from those countries. All area codes are (202).
General information: 927-5850

Quota Branch: China 927-6703; India 927-6705; Indonesia 927-6704; Japan 927-6706; Korea 927-6707; Macao 927-6709; Malaysia 927-6712; Mexico 927-6711; Pakistan 927-6714; Philippines 927-6713; Romania 927-6715; Singapore 927-6716; Sri Lanka 927-6708; Taiwan 927-6719; Thailand 927-6717; Turkey 927-6718; All others 927-5850.

Laws and Regulations

The following laws and regulations may be relevant to the importation of cordage and nonwoven fabrics. The laws are contained in the United States Code (USC), and the regulations are published in the Code of Federal Regulations (CFR), both of which are available at larger public and law libraries. Copies of specific laws are also available from the United States Government Printing Office (address above).

7 USC 1854
Textile Trade Agreements
(EO 11651, as amended by EO 11951 and 12188, and supplemented by EO 12475)
This Act authorizes the CITA of the DOC to enter into Multi-Fiber Agreements with other countries to control trade in textiles and establishes the Textile Import Program, which is enforced by U.S. Customs.

19 CFR 12.130 et seq.
Regulations on Entry of Textiles
These regulations provide the requirements and procedures followed by Customs in enforcing limitations on the importation and entry and withdrawal of textiles and textile products from warehouses for consumption in the U.S.

15 USC 70-77
Textile Fiber Products Identification Act (TFPIA)
This Act prohibits false or deceptive labeling (misbranding) and false advertising of any textile fiber products and requires all textile fiber products imported into the U.S. to be labeled in accordance with the requirements set forth in the law.

19 CFR 11.12b; 16 CFR 303 et seq.
Regulations on Labeling and Marking
These regulations detail the labeling and marking requirements for textiles as specified by the CPSC and the invoice contents required by U.S. Customs for purpose of enforcing the labeling and marking rules.

15 USC 68-68j
Wool Products Labeling Act (WPLA)

This Act prohibits the false or deceptive labeling (misbranding) of wool products and requires all wool products imported into the U.S. to be labeled in accordance with requirements set forth in the law.

19 CFR 11.12; 16 CFR 300 et seq.
Regulations on WPLA Labeling and Marking
These regulations set forth the wool labeling and marking requirements adopted by the FTC to administer the requirements of the WPLA and provide the procedures followed by U.S. Customs in enforcing the WPLA and the FTC regulations, including entry invoice requirements.

15 USC 1191-1204
Flammable Fabrics Act (FFA)
This Act provides for the setting of flammability standards for fabric by the Consumer Product Safety Commission (CPSC) and for enforcement by U.S. Customs.

16 CFR 1610, 1611, 1615, 1616, 1630-1632
Regulations on Flammable Fabric Standards
These regulations specify the flammability standards adopted by the CPSC under the FFA for various types of textiles.

21 USC 301 et seq.
Food, Drug, and Cosmetic Act
This Act prohibits deceptive practices and regulates the manufacture, sale and importation or exportation of food, drugs, cosmetics, and related products. See 21 USC 331, 381, 382.

19 CFR 12.1 et seq.; 21 CFR 1.83 et seq.
Regulations on Food, Drugs, and Cosmetics
These regulations of the Secretary of Health and Human Services and the Secretary of the Treasury govern the standards, labeling, marking, and importing of products used with food, drugs, and cosmetics.

Principal Exporting Countries

The following listing includes samples of the main supplier nations of the products of this chapter. It is organized by HTSUS major heading. (Refer to "Customs Classification" above for the product codes.) Countries are listed in rank order of the value of products imported to the U.S. Statistics represent customs value entries for 1993 from the Bureau of Census, U.S. Department of Commerce.

5601—United Kingdom, Netherlands, Japan, Canada, Mexico, South Korea, Switzerland, France, Italy, Spain

5602—Canada, Germany, Mexico, Spain, Japan, Italy, Brazil, United Kingdom, France, South Africa

5603—Luxembourg, Japan, Canada, Germany, Israel, Mexico, Belgium, United Kingdom, Netherlands, Italy

5604—Japan, Canada, Singapore, Germany, Netherlands, Taiwan, China, France, Malaysia, South Korea

5605—Japan, France, Germany, Mexico, South Korea, United Kingdom, Italy, Taiwan, Canada, China

5606—Germany, Mexico, Canada, Italy, Austria, Netherlands, Japan, Taiwan, Belgium, Indonesia

5607—Brazil, Mexico, Philippines, South Korea, Portugal, Bangladesh, Canada, Taiwan, Japan, Tanzania

5608—Japan, Canada, Taiwan, Thailand, Norway, South Korea, Ireland, Mexico, China, Portugal

5609—Taiwan, China, Dominican Rep., South Korea, Malaysia, Mexico, France, St. Lucia, Canada, Philippines

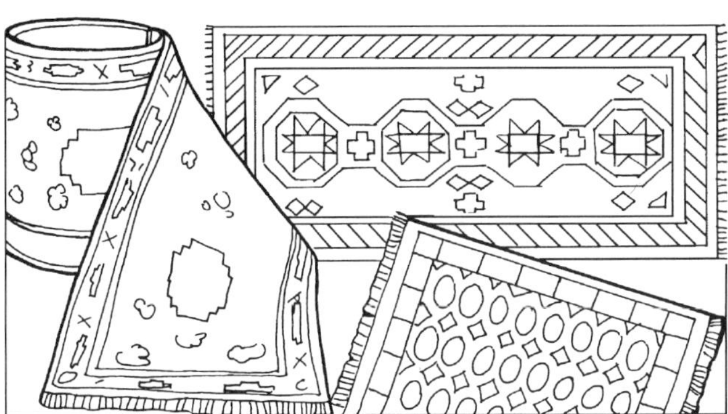

Chapter 57: Carpets and Other Textile Floor Coverings*

This chapter relates to the importation of carpets and other textile floor coverings, which are classified under Chapter 57 of the Harmonized Tariff Schedule of the United States (HTSUS). Specifically, it includes knotted, hand-woven, and machine-woven textile floor coverings. Articles are classified in this chapter only if the textile materials are exposed on the surface when the item is in use. This chapter also includes articles with characteristics of textile floor coverings but intended for other uses.

If you are interested in importing floor covering underlays, you should refer to Commodity Index Chapter 56. The import requirements for vinyl and other plastic floor coverings are in Chapter 39. If you are interested in importing rubber floor coverings and mats, read Chapter 40. Textile floor coverings that are more than 100 years old are classified under Chapter 97.

Key Factors

The key factors in the importation of carpets and other textile floor coverings are:

- Compliance with quota restraints and visa requirements under U.S. Department of Commerce (DOC) Multi-Fiber Arrangements
- Submission of U.S. Customs Country-of-Origin Declaration(s)
- Compliance with entry invoice requirements
- Compliance with labeling requirements under Textile Fiber Products Identification Act (TFPIA)
- Compliance with flammability standards adopted and enforced by the Consumer Product Safety Commission (CPSC) under the Flammable Fabrics Act (FFA)
- Prohibition and license requirements for Iranian carpets and rugs

Although most importers use the services of a licensed customs broker in making their entries, and we recommend this practice, you should be aware of the regulatory, entry, and documentation issues involved in importing your product. You, as importer, are ultimately responsible for the fulfillment of any legal requirements applicable to your shipment.

*IMPORTANT: Read the Commodity Index Introduction. It is the essential framework for understanding this chapter.

General Considerations

Regulatory Agencies. The DOC's Committee for Implementation of Textile Agreements (CITA) regulates certain textile imports under Section 204 of the Agricultural Adjustment Act. U.S. Customs enforces CITA textile and textile product entry quotas. Customs also enforces compliance with labeling and invoice requirements of the TFPIA and flammability standards under the FFA. The CPSC monitors imports and from time to time inspects textile shipments for compliance with FFA standards.

Wool Carpets and Flooring Coverings. Carpets, rugs, and mats made of wool are specifically exempted from the requirements of the Wool Products Labeling Act (WPLA). These articles must, however, be labeled in accordance with the TFPIA.

Textile Quotas. If you are interested in importing carpets, rugs, and other textile floor coverings, the most important issue you need to be aware of is quotas. Under the Multi-Fiber Arrangement provisions of Section 204 of the Agricultural Adjustment Act, CITA initiates specific agreements with individual exporting countries. Section 204 of the Agricultural Adjustment Act covers textiles that: 1) are in chief value of cotton, wool, or man-made fibers, any textile fibers subject to the terms of any textile trade agreement, or any combination of such fibers; 2) contain 50% or more by weight of cotton or man-made fibers, or any textile fibers subject to the terms of any textile trade agreement; 3) contain 17% or more by weight of wool; or 4) if in chief value of textile fibers or textile materials, contain a blend of cotton, wool, or man-made fibers, any textile fibers subject to the terms of any textile trade agreement, or any combination of such fibers that, in total, amount to 50% or more by weight of all component fibers.

The U.S. has Multi-Fiber Arrangements with 40 countries. Each agreement with each country is unique, and may specify quotas for a type of textile or a specific article. Visas or export licenses may be required. These agreements, however, often change. Therefore, if you are interested in importing any carpets, rugs, or other textile floor coverings, you should contact the International Trade Administration's Office of Textile and Apparel (see addresses at end of this chapter). Refer to "Prohibitions and Restrictions" below for further details.

Textile Country-of-Origin Declarations. U.S. Customs enforces CITA textile and textile product entry quotas (see "Prohibitions and Restrictions" below). Requirements for entry include submission of Country-of-Origin Declarations with every carpet, rug, and other textile floor covering shipment, regardless of whether it is subject to a specific multi-fiber arrangement (19 CFR 12.130, 12.131).

Country of Origin. Quota restrictions are country-specific and therefore are applied based on the country of origin for the textiles shipped. The last country from which a textile shipment was exported to the U.S. is not necessarily its country of origin. A textile or textile product imported into the U.S. is considered a product of the particular foreign territory or country, or a U.S. insular possession, where it is wholly grown, produced, or manufactured. For the following discussion, "country" means a foreign territory or country, or a U.S. insular possession.

Substantial transformation rules may affect the country-of-origin determination. For example, if a textile or textile product originates in Country A and is subject to quota, the quota restrictions apply at entry into the U.S. But if, prior to export to the U.S., you move the shipment to Country B where there are fewer restrictions, the shipment may nevertheless remain subject to quota and visa requirements under the Multi-Fiber Arrangement with Country A. Customs determines whether the quota restrictions apply based on the criteria of "substantial transformation." If your textiles do not undergo any major processing or manufacturing while in Country B, or if the manufacturing or processing is minor, your shipment will be deemed to originate in Country A. *You cannot claim substantial transformation on the basis of minor manufacturing procedures.*

In contrast, if your shipment undergoes major processing or manufacturing while in Country B, rendering the textiles "new and different articles of commerce," Customs will treat the shipment as the product of Country B. To qualify as having undergone substantial transformation, an article must evince a change in: 1) commercial designation or identity; b) fundamental character; or c) commercial use. If your shipment is processed in more than one country, the country where it last underwent substantial transformation is the country of origin for Customs entry. In deciding whether the manufacturing or processing operation in a country is major, Customs considers the following factors: 1) the resultant physical change in the material or article; 2) the complexity, the level or degree of skill and/or technology required, and the amount of time involved in the operations; and 3) the value added to the article or material, compared to its value when imported into the U.S.

Validating Operations. Operations that Customs will usually acknowledge as validating a claim of substantial transformation are the following: 1) dyeing and printing, when accompanied by two or more of the following finishing operations: bleaching, shrinking, fulling, napping, decating, permanent stiffening, weighting, permanent embossing, or moireing; 2) spinning fibers into yarn; 3) weaving, knitting, or otherwise forming fabric; 4) cutting fabric into parts and assembling the parts into completed articles; or 5) substantial assembly, by sewing and/or tailoring into a completed garment cut pieces of apparel articles that have been cut from fabric in another country—e.g., complete assembly and tailoring of all cut pieces of suit-type jackets, suits, and shirts.

Insubstantial Operations. Operations that usually will not support a claim of substantial transformation, even if more than one are performed, are the following: 1) simple operations of combining, labeling, pressing, cleaning, dry cleaning, or packaging; 2) cutting to length or width and hemming or overlocking fabrics that are readily identifiable as being intended for a particular commercial use; 3) trimming and/or joining together by sewing, looping, linking, or other means of attaching otherwise completed knit-to-shape component parts produced in a single country, even if accompanied by other processes—e.g., washing, drying, mending—normally incident to assembly; 4) one or more finishing operations on yarns, fabrics, or their textile articles—such as showerproofing, superwashing, bleaching, decating, fulling, shrinking, mercerizing, or similar operations; or 5) dyeing and/or printing fabrics or yarns.

Declarations. The country of origin of carpets, rugs, or other textile floor coverings in a shipment must be stated on a declaration submitted to U.S. Customs at the time of entry. There are three Customs Country-of-Origin Declarations: single-country, multiple-country, and negative. The Declaration to be submitted with your shipment of carpets, rugs, or other textile floor coverings depends on the nature of the import.

- **Single-country declarations** are used for entries of textiles or textile products that clearly originate from only one country or that have been assembled in one country from fabricated components wholly produced in the U.S. or the foreign country of manufacture. Information required includes: marks of identification and numbers; description of article and quantity; country of origin; and date of exportation.
- **Multiple-country declarations** are used for entries of textiles or textile products that were manufactured or processed and/or that incorporate materials originating in more than one foreign country or

territory. Information required includes: marks of identification and numbers; for articles, description, quantity, identification of manufacturing and/or processing operations, country, and date of exportation; for materials used to make articles, description of materials, country of production, and date of exportation.

- **Negative declarations** must accompany all textile imports that are not subject to FFA Section 204 restrictions. Information required includes: marks of identification and numbers; descriptions of article and quantity; and country of origin.

The date of exportation to be indicated on the above declarations is the date on which the carrier leaves the last port in the country of origin, as determined by Customs. Diversion to another country during transit does not affect the export date.

Procedure for Declarations. The manufacturer, producer, exporter, or importer may prepare the declaration. If more than one of these parties is involved in the importation, each party may prepare a separate declaration. You may file a separate declaration for each invoice presented with your entry. The declaration must be dated and signed by the responsible party, and must include the person's title and the company name and address. Your shipment's entry will be denied unless it is accompanied by a properly executed declaration. Customs will not treat a textile declaration as a missing document for which a bond may be filed.

Customs will base its country-of-origin determination on the information contained in each declaration, unless the information is insufficient. If the information on the declaration is insufficient, Customs will require that you submit such additional information as will enable the determination to be made. The shipment will not be released until the determination is made. Thus, if you want to clear Customs with minimal delay, be sure that the information on the declarations is as complete as possible for each shipment.

Textile Labeling and Invoice Requirements. You are responsible for your imported textile floor covering product's compliance with applicable provisions of the TFPIA. Textile floor coverings that require labeling under TFPIA must already be labeled at entry, or the shipment will be refused. (See "Marking and Labeling Requirements" below.) If you import shipments of textile floor coverings subject to TFPIA and valued at over $500, you must provide special information on the entry invoice (see "Entry and Documentation" below).

Flammability Standards. Textile floor coverings imported into the U.S. for use in consumer products must be in compliance with the FFA, a federal law that gives the CPSC the authority and responsibility for protecting the public from the hazards of dangerously flammable items of wearing apparel and interior furnishings. Under the FFA, standards have been established for flammability of such textiles. You cannot import any textile floor covering if it fails to conform to an applicable flammability standard (FFA Section 4). Certain products may be imported into the U.S. (FFA Section 11c) for finishing or processing to render them less flammable so as to meet the standards. For these products, the exporter must state on the invoice or other paper relating to the shipment that the shipment is being made for that purpose.

The CPSC monitors imports of textiles under its Import Surveillance Program. From time to time, your textile shipments may be inspected to ascertain compliance with mandatory safety standards. Shipments may also be subject to testing by the CPSC to determine compliance. If the CPSC believes a product, fabric, or related material does not comply with a flammability standard, it is authorized to pursue a variety of legal sanctions (see "Prohibitions and Restrictions" below)

Substantial Product Hazard Reports. Any firm that obtains information that reasonably supports the conclusion that one of its products presents an unreasonable risk of serious injury or death must report that information to the CPSC's Division of Corrective Actions (CPSC address below). Importers must also report to the CPSC if 1) a type of product is the subject of at least three civil actions filed in U.S. federal or state courts, 2) each suit alleges the involvement of that product type in death or grievous bodily injury (as defined in FFA Section 37(3)1), and 3) at least three of the actions result in a final settlement with the manufacturer or in a judgment for the plaintiff within any one of the two-year periods specified in FFA Section 37(b).

Certified Hand-loomed Products. Foreign rugs made on a hand loom—that is, a nonpower-driven loom—by cottage industry producers may be entered under a special tariff category. Textile restraints may not apply to such products when exported from developing countries. A country-of-origin government official must certify your products before exportation. To enter a rug as a certified hand-loomed product, you must present the certification at the port of entry. You should mark your entry summary or withdrawal forms with the symbol "F" as a prefix to the appropriate 10-digit statistical reporting number.

Import Advisory

Importation of textiles is trade-sensitive and highly regulated. Shipments of textiles and textile products not complying with all government regulations, including quotas and visas, are subject to seizure and could result in the imposition of penalties as well as possible forfeiture of the goods. You should always verify the available quota for any textile product you plan to import before your shipment leaves the country of manufacture. Furthermore, Customs textile classification rulings change frequently, and prior administrative rulings are often modified and sometimes reversed.

Customs Classification

For customs purposes, carpets and other textile flooring coverings are classified under Chapter 57 of the HTSUS. This chapter is broken into major headings, which are further divided into subheadings, and often sub-subheadings, each of which has its own HTSUS classification number. For example, the HTSUS number for woven, certified hand-loomed and folklore rugs is 5702.10.10, indicating it is a sub-subcategory of "Kelem", "Schumacks", "Karamanie" and similar hand-woven rugs (5702.10.00), which is a subcategory of the major heading, carpets and other textile floor coverings, woven, etc. (5702.00.00). There are five major headings within Chapter 57.

5701—Carpets and other textile floor coverings, knotted, whether or not made up

5702—Carpets and other textile floor coverings, woven, not tufted or flocked, whether or not made up, including "Kelem", "Schumacks", "Karamanie," and similar hand-woven rugs

5703—Carpets and other textile floor coverings, tufted, whether or not made up

5704—Carpets and other textile floor coverings, of felt, not tufted or flocked, whether or not made up

5705—Other carpets and other textile floor coverings, whether or not made up

For more details regarding classifications of the specific product you are interested in importing, consult a customs broker, the appropriate commodity specialist at your nearest customs port, or the HTSUS. HTSUS is available for purchase from the U.S. Government Printing Office (see addresses at end of this chapter), and may be found in larger public libraries. Refer to "Classification—Liquidation" on page 207 for a general discussion of customs classification.

Sample Import Duties

Import duties will vary depending on the HTSUS classification of your product. Therefore, to determine the correct amount of duties, your product must be properly classified under the HTSUS. The following sample duties are taken from the duty listings for HTSUS Chapter 57 products.

Certified hand-loomed and folklore products, woven (5702.10.10): 4.9%; Wilton and velvet floor coverings of pile construction made of wool or fine animal hair, not made up (5702.31.10): 10%, of man-made textile materials (5702.32.10): 10%; carpets and other textile floor coverings, tufted and made of wool or fine animal hair (5703.10.00): 7%; of nylon or other polyamides and not hand-hooked (5703.20.20): 7.6%; of other man-made textiles (5703.30.00):7.6%; tiles of carpet and other textile floor coverings of felt, not tufted or flocked (5704.10.00): 5.3%.

Entry and Documentation

The entry of merchandise is a two-part process consisting of 1) filing the documentation necessary to determine whether merchandise may be released from Customs custody, and 2) filing the documents that contain information for duty assessment and statistical purposes. In certain instances, all documents must be filed and accepted by Customs prior to release of the goods. Unless you have been granted an extension, you must file entry documents at a location specified by the district or area director within five working days of your shipment's date of arrival at a U.S. port of entry. These include a number of standard documents required by Customs for any entry, and:

- U.S. Customs Country-of-Origin Declaration(s)
- Export documentation and/or visa for textiles subject to Multi-Fiber Arrangement
- Certification for products entered as Certified Hand-loomed Products

After you present the entry, Customs may examine your shipment or may waive examination. The shipment is then released provided no legal or regulatory violations have been noted. You must then file entry summary documentation and deposit estimated duties at a designated customhouse within 10 working days of your shipment's release. For a detailed description of entry procedures, standard documentation, and informal entry, refer to "Entry Process" on page 182.

NAFTA Certificates of Origin. An importer of textiles for which NAFTA treatment is sought need not file a separate NAFTA Certificate of Origin in addition to the Customs Country-of-Origin Declaration. The declaration is sufficient. However, the importer must take care to submit a declaration from each U.S., Canadian, or Mexican producer or manufacturer. Thus, for multiple producers or manufacturers, a separate declaration must be filed for each. If a Customs district director cannot determine the country of origin because the declaration is absent or incomplete, the shipment is not entitled to preferential NAFTA tariff treatment or other NAFTA benefits. See 12 CFR 132.

Entry Invoice TFPIA Requirements. For the purpose of TFPIA enforcement, a commercial shipment of textile products exceeding $500 in value and subject to TFPIA labeling requirements must show the following information: 1) The constituent fiber or combination of fibers, designating with equal prominence each natural or manufactured fiber by its generic name, in order of predominance by weight if the weight of such fiber is 5% or more of the total fiber weight of the product; 2) percentage of each fiber present, by weight, in the total fiber content; 3) the name or other identification issued and registered by the FTC of the manufacturer of the product or one or more persons subject to Section 3 of the TFPIA with respect to such product; and 4) the name of the country where processed or manufactured.

Prohibitions and Restrictions

Textile Quotas. Textile import restrictions are primarily a matter of quotas and the way in which these quotas are administered and monitored. Under the Multi-Fiber Arrangement provisions of Section 204 of the Agricultural Adjustment Act, CITA has negotiated Multi-Fiber Arrangements with 40 countries. These Agreements may impose quotas for a type of textile or a specific article, and they are country-specific. The agreements, however, often change. Therefore, if you are interested in importing any textile floor coverings, you should contact the International Trade Administration's Office of Textile and Apparel (see addresses at end of this chapter). The Office of Textile and Apparel has a team of country specialists who can inform you of the latest developments and inform you about a product's quota or restriction status.

U.S. Customs enforces CITA textile and textile product entry quotas. If formal entry procedures are not followed, Customs will usually refuse entry for textiles that are subject to Section 204. Formal entry requires submission of a Country-of-Origin Declaration (see General Considerations above). U.S. Customs maintains a current textile quota status report, available for perusal at any Customs port. In addition, U.S. Customs in Washington, DC, operates a telephone service to provide quota status reports, which are updated weekly (see "Relevant Government Agencies" below).

Flammable Fabrics. U.S. Customs may refuse entry for any article of wearing apparel or interior furnishing, or any fabric or related material that is intended for use or that may be used in wearing apparel or interior furnishings, if it fails to conform to an applicable flammability standard issued under Section 4 of the FFA. An exception is allowed for certain products (FFA Section 11c) that are imported for finishing or processing to bring them within the legal standard. For these products, the exporter must state on the invoice or other paper relating to the shipment that the shipment is being made for that purpose.

The CPSC, as the primary enforcement agency of flammability standards, inspects products for compliance with the FFA. If the CPSC believes a product, fabric, or related material does not comply with a flammability standard, it is authorized to pursue a variety of legal sanctions, including: 1) seizure, condemnation, and forfeiture of the noncomplying products; 2) administrative cease-and-desist order requiring an individual or firm to stop sale and distribution of the noncomplying products or; 3) temporary injunction requiring the individual or firm to stop sale and distribution of the noncomplying products, pending final disposition of an administrative cease-and-desist proceeding. The CPSC also has authority to seek civil penalties against any person who knowingly violates a regulation or standard issued under Section 4 of the FFA.

Country-Specific Restrictions

Multi-Fiber Arrangements. Restrictions under Multi-Fiber Arrangements are country-specific. A product originating in one country may be subject to quota and to export license or visa requirements, while the same product originating in a different country may not. At present, the U.S. has Multi-Fiber Arrangements with 40 countries. Many different categories of products are covered under these Arrangements; it is beyond the scope of this book to list each country and its restricted commodities. If you are interested in importing textiles and textile products, you should contact the International Trade Administration's Office of Textile and Apparel (see addresses at end of this chapter) or U.S. Customs to ascertain your product's restraint status.

The U.S. Customs Quota Branch phone numbers provide recorded status reports, by quota category number, for current charges against the quotas for that country. For convenience, the HTSUS shows the 3-digit category number in parentheses to the right of each listed commodity that is subject to textile restraints. For example, under Chapter 57, heading 5703.10.10, tufted textile floor coverings of wool or fine animal hair, is followed by the number "(465)." If you know the category number for your product, you can find out to what extent that quota is filled simply by calling the number for the appropriate country. A word of caution, though: if you do not know for sure that your article is subject to quota from a particular country, and you call the number for that country, you may not be any more enlightened after the phone call. Many of the recordings give status reports only when a certain percentage of the quota has been filled. Thus, if 465 for India is among the categories for which not enough quantity has entered the U.S. to warrant specific mention, it will be lumped under "all other categories" and you will be none the wiser. To find out if your product is subject to textile restraints, call the DOC or a local Customs port office. Then you can find out the current charges against that quota by calling the country number listed below. For a complete listing of Customs Quota Branch information numbers, see "Relevant Government Agencies" below.

Iranian Carpets. Iranian carpets and rugs that were still in Iran as of October 29, 1987, may not be imported into the United States. There are some exceptions for carpets imported together with household goods by the owner. If it can be established that they left Iran before that date, they may then be commercially imported, but only after a license has been obtained from the Office of Foreign Assets Control (see addresses at end of this chapter).

Marking and Labeling Requirements

TFPIA Requirements. All textile fiber products imported into the U.S. must be stamped, tagged, labeled, or otherwise marked with the following information as required by the TFPIA, unless exempt from marking (see TFPIA, Section 12): 1) the generic names and percentages by weight of the constituent fibers present in the textile fiber product, exclusive of permissible ornamentation, in amounts of more than 5% in order of predominance by weight, with any percentage of fiber or fibers required to be designated as "other fiber" or "other fibers" (including those present in amounts of 5% or less) appearing last; and 2) the name of the manufacturer or the name or registered identification number issued by the FTC of one or more persons marketing or handling the textile fiber product; and 3) the name of the country where processed. A word trademark, used as a house mark and registered with the U.S. Patent Office, may appear on labels instead of the name otherwise required, provided the owner of the trademark furnishes a copy of the registration to the FTC prior to use. (See "Registered Identification Numbers" below.)

The information listed above is not exhaustive. TFPIA requirements are extensive. The Act specifies such details as types of labels, means of attachment, label position on the article, package labeling, unit labeling for two-piece garments, and arrangement of information on the label; allowable fiber designations; country-of-origin indications; requirements for trim and ornamentation, linings and interlinings, and pile fabrics; sectional disclosure; use of trade names and trademarks; and requirements for swatches and samples. The FTC publishes a booklet intended to clarify TFPIA requirements to facilitate voluntary compliance in the industry (see "Publications Available" below). It is available on request, at no charge, from the FTC (see addresses at end of this chapter).

Registered Identification Numbers. Any domestic firm or person residing in the U.S. and engaged in the manufacture or marketing of textile products covered under the TFPIA may obtain an FTC-registered identification number for use on required tags and labels instead of the name of a firm or person. For applications, contact the FTC (address below.)

For a general discussion of U.S. Customs marking and labeling requirements, refer to "Marking: Country of Origin" on page 215 and "Special Marking Requirements" on page 217.

Shipping Considerations

You will need to ensure that your goods are packaged and shipped with care so that they pass smoothly through Customs and arrive in good condition. You are responsible for ensuring that the shipment is in compliance with all applicable government regulations for packaging and shipping. In most instances, you should not leave these arrangements solely to the discretion of your supplier. Careful preparation of the cargo and selection of the mode of transport can be essential to a cost-effective, timely delivery of undamaged goods. We strongly advise you to consult your shipping representative, insurance agent, or freight broker for advice on packing and shipping. Refer also to the major tab section "Packing/Shipping/Insurance" for a general discussion of packing and shipping.

Textile floor coverings may be shipped in bulk, bolts, rolls, or other types of containers, depending on the type of product and whether it is prepackaged. General considerations include protection from contamination, weather, and pests. Safety precautions should also be implemented as required to protect against breakage, spillage, corrosion of containers, and combustion. Containers should be constructed so as to be safe for handling during transport.

Publications Available

The following publication may be relevant to the importation of textile floor coverings:

Questions and Answers Relating to the Textile Fiber Products Identification Act and Regulations

Available free of charge on request from the Federal Trade Commission, this publication is an excellent source of information written in clear lay language. We recommend that anyone interested in importing textile fiber products but unfamiliar with the regulations obtain a copy of this booklet.

The *Harmonized Tariff Schedule of the United States* (HTSUS) is available from:

Government Printing Office (GPO)
Superintendent of Documents
Washington, DC 20402
(202) 512-1800 (Order line)
(202) 512-0000 (General)

The USGPO also has copies of specific laws available for purchase. The USGPO accepts credit card orders over the phone, as well as mail orders paid by credit card, a check drawn on a U.S. bank, or an international money order.

Relevant Government Agencies

Address your questions regarding textile Multi-Fiber Arrangements to:

International Trade Administration
Office of Textile and Apparel
14th and Constitution Ave. NW, Rm. 3100
Washington, DC 20230
(202) 482-5078, 482-3737

Address your questions regarding the Flammable Fabrics Act (FFA) to:

Consumer Product Safety Commission (CPSC)
5401 Westbard Avenue
Bethesda, MD 20207
(301) 492-6580

Address your questions regarding requirements under the Textile Fiber Products Identification Act (TFPIA) to:

Federal Trade Commission (FTC)
Division of Enforcement
601 Pennsylvania Ave. NW
Washington, DC 20580
(202) 326-2996 (General)
(202) 326-2841 (Textile and wool products labeling)

Address your questions regarding licenses for Iranian carpets and rugs to:

U.S. Treasury Department
Office of Foreign Assets Control
Treasury Bldg.
Washington, DC 20220
(202) 622-2510

Address your questions regarding textile floor covering imports to the district or port director of Customs for you area. For addresses, refer to"U.S. Customs District Offices" on page 62 or contact:

U.S. Customs Service
1301 Constitution Ave. NW
Washington, DC 20229
(202) 927-6724 (Information)
(202) 927-1000 (General)

The following information numbers for U.S. Customs in Washington, DC, provide recorded information. The Quota Branch numbers listed by country provide updated status reports on textile quotas from those countries. All area codes are (202).
General information: 927-5850

Quota Branch: China 927-6703; India 927-6705; Indonesia 927-6704; Japan 927-6706; Korea 927-6707; Macao 927-6709; Malaysia 927-6712; Mexico 927-6711; Pakistan 927-6714; Philippines 927-6713; Romania 927-6715; Singapore 927-6716; Sri Lanka 927-6708; Taiwan 927-6719; Thailand 927-6717; Turkey 927-6718; All others 927-5850.

Laws and Regulations

The following laws and regulations may be relevant to the importation of textile floor coverings. The laws are contained in the United States Code (USC), and the regulations are published in the Code of Federal Regulations (CFR), both of which are available at larger public and law libraries. Copies of specific laws are also available from the United States Government Printing Office (address above).

7 USC 1854
Textile Trade Agreements
(EO 11651, as amended by EO 11951 and 12188, and supplemented by EO 12475)
This Act authorizes the CITA of the DOC to enter into Multi-Fiber Agreements with other countries to control trade in textiles and establishes the Textile Import Program, which is enforced by U.S. Customs.

19 CFR 12.130 et seq.
Regulations on Entry of Textiles
These regulations provide the requirements and procedures followed by Customs in enforcing limitations on the importation and entry and withdrawal of textiles and textile products from warehouses for consumption in the U.S.

15 USC 70-77
Textile Fiber Products Identification Act (TFPIA)
This Act prohibits false or deceptive labeling (misbranding) and false advertising of any textile fiber products and requires all textile fiber products imported into the U.S. to be labeled in accordance with the requirements set forth in the law.

19 CFR 11.12b; 16 CFR 303 et seq.
Regulations on Labeling and Marking
These regulations detail the labeling and marking requirements for textiles as specified by the CPSC and the invoice contents required by U.S. Customs for purpose of enforcing the labeling and marking rules.

15 USC 1191-1204
Flammable Fabrics Act (FFA)
This Act provides for the setting of flammability standards for fabric by the Consumer Product Safety Commission (CPSC) and for enforcement by U.S. Customs.

16 CFR 1610, 1611, 1615, 1616, 1630-1632
Regulations on Flammable Fabric Standards
These regulations specify the flammability standards adopted by the CPSC under the FFA for various types of textiles.

Principal Exporting Countries

The following listing includes samples of the main supplier nations of the products of this chapter. It is organized by HTSUS major heading. (Refer to "Customs Classification" above for the product codes.) Countries are listed in rank order of the value of products imported to the U.S. Statistics represent customs value entries for 1993 from the Bureau of Census, U.S. Department of Commerce.

5701—India, China, Pakistan, Turkey, Nepal, Egypt, Romania, Germany, Portugal, Afghanistan

5702—India, Belgium, United Kingdom, Turkey, China, Spain, Ireland, Egypt, Netherlands, France

5703—Canada, China, Belgium, India, Thailand, Japan, Philippines, United Kingdom, Australia, Netherlands

5704—Netherlands, Belgium, Germany, United Kingdom, Mexico, Sweden, Japan, Spain, Canada, France

5705—China, India, Canada, Japan, United Kingdom, Ireland, Taiwan, France, Germany, Mexico

Chapter 58: Special Woven Fabrics*

Full title: Special Woven Fabrics; Tufted Textile Fabrics; Lace; Tapestries; Trimmings; Embroidery

This chapter relates to the importation of special woven fabrics, which are classified under Chapter 58 of the Harmonized Tariff Schedule of the United States (HTSUS). Specifically, it includes woven pile and chenille fabrics, terry cloth and tufted textile fabrics, gauze, tulles and other net fabric, lace, hand-woven and needle-work tapestries, labels and similar articles of textile materials, braids, pompons, tassels, and other ornamental trimmings, woven fabrics of metal thread and metalized yarn, embroidery articles, and quilted textile products.

If you are interested in importing sewing thread, yarns, and other fibers or filaments, you should refer to Commodity Index Chapters 50 through 55. Articles of cordage are covered in Chapter 56, hair-nets are classified as headgear under Chapter 65, and special woven fabrics incorporated into footwear are covered under Chapter 64. If you are interested in importing articles created from glass fibers, read Chapter 58. For importing special woven fabrics as part of toys, games, or sports equipment, refer to Chapter 95. The import requirements for impregnated, coated, covered, or laminated textile fabrics and textile articles suitable for industrial use are found in Chapter 59.

Key Factors

The key factors in the importation of special woven fabrics are:

- Compliance with quota restraints and visa requirements under U.S. Department of Commerce (DOC) Multi-Fiber Arrangements)
- Submission of U.S. Customs Country-of-Origin Declaration(s)
- Compliance with entry invoice requirements
- Compliance with labeling requirements under the Textile Fiber Products Identification Act (TFPIA) and the Wool Products Labeling Act (WPLA)
- Compliance with flammability standards adopted and enforced by the Consumer Product Safety Commission (CPSC) under the Flammable Fabrics Act (FFA)

Although most importers use the services of a licensed customs broker in making their entries, and we recommend this practice, you should be aware of the regulatory, entry, and documentation issues involved in importing your product. You, as importer, are ultimately responsible for the fulfillment of any legal requirements applicable to your shipment.

General Considerations

Regulatory Agencies. The DOC's Committee for Implementation of Textile Agreements (CITA) regulates certain textile imports under Section 204 of the Agricultural Adjustment Act. U.S. Customs enforces CITA textile and textile product entry quotas. Customs also enforces compliance with labeling and invoice requirements of the TFPIA and flammability standards under the FFA. The CPSC monitors imports and from time to time inspects textile shipments for compliance with FFA standards. If you are importing wool textiles, importation is subject to complex textile import regulations. The Federal Trade Commission (FTC) administers the WPLA requirements.

Wool Product Entry Requirements. Depending on the nature of your wool fabric imports, as many as four different types of special entry documents may be required. First, for all imported textile fibers, yarns, and fabrics covered by the Agricultural Adjustment Act (AAA), including wool, you must file a U.S. Customs Textile Entry Declaration (see "Textile Country-of-Origin Declarations" below). Second, with each wool shipment's entry summary, you must file Customs **Form 6451**, Notice of Percentage of Clean Yield and Grade of Wool or Hair, in duplicate, showing your name and address. Third, for all wool products subject to the WPLA, special information is required on the entry invoices (see "Entry and Documentation" below). Finally, certain wool articles manufactured or produced in certain countries may be subject to quotas under U.S. Department of Commerce Multi-Fiber Arrangements. Such products require export certificates or visas issued by the appropriate country of origin, in addition to other requisite entry paperwork (see "Quotas" below).

Wool Products Labeling Act. The term "wool product" means any product or any portion of a product that contains, purports to contain, or in any way is represented as containing wool, reprocessed wool, or reused wool. All wool products imported into the U.S., except those made more than 20 years before importation, and except carpets, rugs, mats, and upholsteries, must have affixed a stamp, tag, label, or other means of identification as required by the WPLA. If you are importing wool products exempt from labeling under the WPLA, do not assume they are also exempt from labeling under the TFPIA. These are two distinct laws, with some overlapping requirements (see "Marking and Labeling Requirements" below).

Textile Quotas. If you are interested in importing special woven fabrics, the most important issue you need to be aware of is quotas. Under the Multi-Fiber Arrangement provisions of Section 204 of the Agricultural Adjustment Act, CITA initiates specific agreements with individual exporting countries. Section 204 of the Agricultural Adjustment Act covers textiles that: 1) are in chief value of cotton, wool, or man-made fibers, any textile fibers subject to the terms of any textile trade agreement, or any combination of such fibers; 2) contain 50% or more by weight of cotton or man-made fibers, or any textile fibers subject to the terms of any textile trade agreement; 3) contain 17% or more by weight of wool; or 4) if in chief value of textile fibers or textile materials, contain a blend of cotton, wool, or man-made fibers, any textile fibers subject to the terms of any textile trade agreement, or any combination of such fibers that, in total, amount to 50% or more by weight of all component fibers.

The U.S. has Multi-Fiber Arrangements with 40 countries. Each agreement with each country is unique, and may specify quotas for a type of textile or a specific article. Visas or export licenses may be required. These agreements, however, often change.

*IMPORTANT: Read the Commodity Index Introduction. It is the essential framework for understanding this chapter.

Therefore, if you are interested in importing any special woven fabrics, you should contact the International Trade Administration's Office of Textile and Apparel (see addresses at end of this chapter). Refer to "Prohibitions and Restrictions" below for further details.

Textile Country-of-Origin Declarations. U.S. Customs enforces CITA textile and textile product entry quotas (see "Prohibitions and Restrictions" below). Requirements for entry include submission of Country-of-Origin Declarations with every special woven fabric shipment, regardless of whether it is subject to a specific multi-fiber arrangement (19 CFR 12.130, 12.131).

Country of Origin. Quota restrictions are country-specific and therefore are applied based on the country of origin for the textiles shipped. The last country from which a textile shipment was exported to the U.S. is not necessarily its country of origin. A textile or textile product imported into the U.S. is considered a product of the particular foreign territory or country, or a U.S. insular possession, where it is wholly grown, produced, or manufactured. For the following discussion, "country" means a foreign territory or country, or a U.S. insular possession.

Substantial transformation rules may affect the country-of-origin determination. For example, if a textile or textile product originates in Country A and is subject to quota, the quota restrictions apply at entry into the U.S. But if, prior to export to the U.S., you move the shipment to Country B where there are fewer restrictions, the shipment may nevertheless remain subject to quota and visa requirements under the Multi-Fiber Arrangement with Country A. Customs determines whether the quota restrictions apply based on the criteria of "substantial transformation." If your textiles do not undergo any major processing or manufacturing while in Country B, or if the manufacturing or processing is minor, your shipment will be deemed to originate in Country A. *You cannot claim substantial transformation on the basis of minor manufacturing procedures.*

In contrast, if your shipment undergoes major processing or manufacturing while in Country B, rendering the textiles "new and different articles of commerce," Customs will treat the shipment as the product of Country B. To qualify as having undergone substantial transformation, an article must evince a change in: 1) commercial designation or identity; b) fundamental character; or c) commercial use. If your shipment is processed in more than one country, the country where it last underwent substantial transformation is the country of origin for Customs entry. In deciding whether the manufacturing or processing operation in a country is major, Customs considers the following factors: 1) the resultant physical change in the material or article; 2) the complexity, the level or degree of skill and/or technology required, and the amount of time involved in the operations; and 3) the value added to the article or material, compared to its value when imported into the U.S.

Validating Operations. Operations that Customs will usually acknowledge as validating a claim of substantial transformation are the following: 1) dyeing and printing, when accompanied by two or more of the following finishing operations: bleaching, shrinking, fulling, napping, decating, permanent stiffening, weighting, permanent embossing, or moireing; 2) spinning fibers into yarn; 3) weaving, knitting, or otherwise forming fabric; 4) cutting fabric into parts and assembling the parts into completed articles; or 5) substantial assembly, by sewing and/or tailoring into a completed garment cut pieces of apparel articles that have been cut from fabric in another country—e.g., complete assembly and tailoring of all cut pieces of suit-type jackets, suits, and shirts.

Insubstantial Operations. Operations that usually will not support a claim of substantial transformation, even if more than one are performed, are the following: 1) simple operations of combining, labeling, pressing, cleaning, dry cleaning, or packaging; 2) cutting to length or width and hemming or overlocking fabrics that are readily identifiable as being intended for a particular commercial use; 3) trimming and/or joining together by sewing, looping, linking, or other means of attaching otherwise completed knit-to-shape component parts produced in a single country, even if accompanied by other processes—e.g., washing, drying, mending—normally incident to assembly; 4) one or more finishing operations on yarns, fabrics, or their textile articles—such as showerproofing, superwashing, bleaching, decating, fulling, shrinking, mercerizing, or similar operations; or 5) dyeing and/or printing fabrics or yarns.

Declarations. The country of origin of the special woven fabrics products in a shipment must be stated on a declaration submitted to U.S. Customs at the time of entry. There are three Customs Country-of-Origin Declarations: single-country, multiple-country, and negative. The Declaration to be submitted with your shipment of special woven fabric products depends on the nature of the import.

- **Single-country declarations** are used for entries of textiles or textile products that clearly originate from only one country or that have been assembled in one country from fabricated components wholly produced in the U.S. or the foreign country of manufacture. Information required includes: marks of identification and numbers; description of article and quantity; country of origin; and date of exportation.
- **Multiple-country declarations** are used for entries of textiles or textile products that were manufactured or processed and/or that incorporate materials originating in more than one foreign country or territory. Information required includes: marks of identification and numbers; for articles, description, quantity, identification of manufacturing and/or processing operations, country, and date of exportation; for materials used to make articles, description of materials, country of production, and date of exportation.
- **Negative declarations** must accompany all textile imports that are not subject to FFA Section 204 restrictions. Information required includes: marks of identification and numbers; descriptions of article and quantity; and country of origin.

The date of exportation to be indicated on the above declarations is the date on which the carrier leaves the last port in the country of origin, as determined by Customs. Diversion to another country during transit does not affect the export date.

Procedure for Declarations. The manufacturer, producer, exporter, or importer may prepare the declaration. If more than one of these parties is involved in the importation, each party may prepare a separate declaration. You may file a separate declaration for each invoice presented with your entry. The declaration must be dated and signed by the responsible party, and must include the person's title and the company name and address. Your shipment's entry will be denied unless it is accompanied by a properly executed declaration. Customs will not treat a textile declaration as a missing document for which a bond may be filed.

Customs will base its country-of-origin determination on the information contained in each declaration, unless the information is insufficient. If the information on the declaration is insufficient, Customs will require that you submit such additional information as will enable the determination to be made. The shipment will not be released until the determination is made. Thus, if you want to clear Customs with minimal delay, be sure that the information on the declarations is as complete as possible for each shipment.

Textile Labeling and Invoice Requirements. You are responsible for your imported special woven fabric product's compliance with applicable provisions of the TFPIA. Special woven fabrics that require labeling under TFPIA must already be labeled at entry, or the shipment will be refused. (See "Marking and Labeling Requirements" below.) If you import shipments of special woven fabrics subject to TFPIA and valued at over $500, you must provide special information on the entry invoice (see "Entry and Documentation" below).

Flammability Standards. Special woven fabric products imported into the U.S. for use in consumer products must be in compliance with the FFA, a federal law that gives the CPSC the authority and responsibility for protecting the public from the hazards of dangerously flammable items of wearing apparel and interior furnishings. Under the FFA, standards have been established for flammability of clothing textiles. You cannot import any article of wearing apparel or interior furnishing, or any fabric or related material that is intended for use or that may be used in such items, if it fails to conform to an applicable flammability standard (FFA Section 4). Certain products may be imported into the U.S. (FFA Section 11c) for finishing or processing to render them less flammable so as to meet the standards. For these products, the exporter must state on the invoice or other paper relating to the shipment that the shipment is being made for that purpose.

The CPSC monitors imports of textiles under its Import Surveillance Program. From time to time, your textile shipments may be inspected to ascertain compliance with mandatory safety standards. Shipments may also be subject to testing by the CPSC to determine compliance. If the CPSC believes a product, fabric, or related material does not comply with a flammability standard, it is authorized to pursue a variety of legal sanctions (see "Prohibitions and Restrictions" below).

Substantial Product Hazard Reports. Any firm that obtains information that reasonably supports the conclusion that one of its products presents an unreasonable risk of serious injury or death must report that information to the CPSC's Division of Corrective Actions (CPSC address below). Importers must also report to the CPSC if 1) a type of product is the subject of at least three civil actions filed in U.S. federal or state courts, 2) each suit alleges the involvement of that product type in death or grievous bodily injury (as defined in FFA Section 37(3)1), and 3) at least three of the actions result in a final settlement with the manufacturer or in a judgment for the plaintiff within any one of the two-year periods specified in FFA Section 37(b).

Import Advisory

Importation of textiles is trade-sensitive and highly regulated. Shipments of textiles and textile products not complying with all government regulations, including quotas and visas, are subject to seizure and could result in the imposition of penalties as well as possible forfeiture of the goods. You should always verify the available quota for any textile product you plan to import before your shipment leaves the country of manufacture. Furthermore, Customs textile classification rulings change frequently, and prior administrative rulings are often modified and sometimes reversed.

Customs Classification

For customs purposes, special woven fabrics are classified under Chapter 58 of the HTSUS. This chapter is broken into major headings, which are further divided into subheadings, and often sub-subheadings, each of which has its own HTSUS classification number. For example, the HTSUS number for gauze made of man-made fibers is 5803.90.30, indicating it is a sub-subcategory of gauze of other textile materials (5803.90.00), which is a subcategory of the major heading gauze, other than narrow fabrics of heading 5806 (5803.00.00). There are 11 major headings within Chapter 56.

5801—Woven pile fabrics and chenille fabrics, other than fabrics of heading 5802 or 5806

5802—Terry toweling and similar woven terry fabrics, other than narrow fabrics of heading 5806; tufted textile fabrics, other than products of heading 5703

5803—Gauze, other than narrow fabrics of heading 5806

5804—Tulles and other net fabrics, not including woven, knitted, and crocheted fabrics; lace in the piece, in strips, or in motifs

5805—Hand-woven tapestries of the type Gobelins, Flanders, Aubusson, Beauvais, and the like, and needle-worked tapestries (for example, petit point, cross stitch), whether or not made up

5806—Narrow woven fabrics, other than goods of heading 5807; narrow fabrics consisting of warp without weft assembled by means of an adhesive (bolducs)

5807—Labels, badges, and similar articles of textile materials, in the piece, in strips, or cut to shape or size, not embroidered

5808—Braids in the piece; ornamental trimmings in the piece, without embroidery, other than knitted or crocheted; tassels, pompons, and similar articles

5809—Woven fabrics of metal thread and woven fabrics of metalized yarn of heading 5605, of a kind used in apparel, as furnishing fabrics, or for similar purposes, not elsewhere specified or included

5810—Embroidery in the piece, in strips, or in motifs

5811—Quilted textile products in the piece, composed of one or more layers of textile materials assembled with padding by stitching or otherwise, other than embroidery of heading 5810

For more details regarding classifications of the specific product you are interested in importing, consult a customs broker, the appropriate commodity specialist at your nearest customs port, or the HTSUS. HTSUS is available for purchase from the U.S. Government Printing Office (see addresses at end of this chapter), and may be found in larger public libraries. Refer to "Classification—Liquidation" on page 207 for a general discussion of customs classification.

Sample Import Duties

Import duties will vary depending on the HTSUS classification of your product. Therefore, to determine the correct amount of duties, your product must be properly classified under the HTSUS. The following sample duties are taken from the duty listings for HTSUS Chapter 58 products.

Woven pile fabrics and chenille fabrics of wool or animal hair (5801.10.00): 5.4%, of cotton, uncut weft pile fabrics (5801.21.00): 23%, of cotton, chenille fabrics (5801.26.00): 12.6%, of man-made fibers, uncut weft pile fabrics (5801.31.00): 19.5%, of man-made fibers, chenille fabrics (5801.36.00): 19.5%; cotton gauze (5803.10.00): 11.3%; gauze of man-made fibers (5803.90.30): 17%; tulles and other net fabrics (5804.10.00): 12%; mechanically made lace of man-made fibers (5804.21.00): 16%; hand-made lace (5804.30.00): 15%; hand-woven tapestries fit only for use as wall hangings and valued over $215 per square meter (5805.00.10): free; ribbons of man-made fibers (5806.32.10): 9%; woven fabrics of metal thread or metalized yarn of heading 5605 (5809.00.00): 17%; embroidery without visible ground (5810.10.00): 16%; quilted textile products in the piece, of man-made fibers (5811.00.30): 16%.

Entry and Documentation

The entry of merchandise is a two-part process consisting of 1) filing the documentation necessary to determine whether merchandise may be released from Customs custody, and 2) filing the documents that contain information for duty assessment and statistical purposes. In certain instances, all documents must be filed and accepted by Customs prior to release of the goods. Unless you have been granted an extension, you must file entry documents at a location specified by the district or area director within five working days of your shipment's date of arrival at a U.S. port of entry. These include a number of standard documents required by Customs for any entry, and:

- U.S. Customs Country-of-Origin Declaration(s)
- Export documentation and/or visa for textiles subject to Multi-Fiber Arrangement
- Customs **Form 6451**, Notice of Percentage of Clean Yield and Grade of Wool or Hair, in duplicate, showing your name and address (if importing articles containing wool)

After you present the entry, Customs may examine your shipment or may waive examination. The shipment is then released provided no legal or regulatory violations have been noted. You must then file entry summary documentation and deposit estimated duties at a designated customhouse within 10 working days of your shipment's release. For a detailed description of entry procedures, standard documentation, and informal entry, refer to "Entry Process" on page 182.

NAFTA Certificates of Origin. An importer of textiles for which NAFTA treatment is sought need not file a separate NAFTA Certificate of Origin in addition to the Customs Country-of-Origin Declaration. The declaration is sufficient. However, the importer must take care to submit a declaration from each U.S., Canadian, or Mexican producer or manufacturer. Thus, for multiple producers or manufacturers, a separate declaration must be filed for each. If a Customs district director cannot determine the country of origin because the declaration is absent or incomplete, the shipment is not entitled to preferential NAFTA tariff treatment or other NAFTA benefits. See 12 CFR 132.

Entry Invoices. You must provide certain additional information on the entry invoice for special woven fabric products. The specific information varies depending on the nature of your product, as noted below.

TFPIA Requirements. For the purpose of TFPIA enforcement, a commercial shipment of textile products exceeding $500 in value and subject to TFPIA labeling requirements must show the following information: 1) the constituent fiber or combination of fibers, designating with equal prominence each natural or manufactured fiber by its generic name, in order of predominance by weight if the weight of such fiber is 5% or more of the total fiber weight of the product; 2) percentage of each fiber present, by weight, in the total fiber content; 3) the name or other identification issued and registered by the Federal Trade Commission of the manufacturer of the product or one or more persons subject to Section 3 of the TFPIA with respect to such product; 4) the name of the country where processed or manufactured.

Wool Products Subject to WPLA. When you offer for entry a wool product shipment valued at over $500 and subject to WPLA, you must include certain information intended to facilitate Customs monitoring and enforcement of that Act. This extra information is identical to that required by WPLA on labeling (see "Marking and Labeling Requirements" below), with the addition of the manufacturer's name. If your product consists of mixed waste, residues, and similar merchandise obtained from several suppliers or unknown sources, you may omit the manufacturer's name from the entry invoice.

Invoice for Madeira Embroideries. The entry invoice for Madeira embroideries must show the following information: 1) about the materials used: a) country of production; b) width of the material in the piece; c) name of the manufacturer; d) kind of material (indicating manufacturer's quality number); e) landed cost of the material used in each item; f) date of the order; g) date of the invoice; h) invoice unit value in the currency of the purchase; i) discount from purchase price allowed, if any; 2) about the finished embroidered articles: a) manufacturer's name, design number, and quality number; b) importer's design number, if any; c) finished size; d) number of embroidery points per unit of quantity; and e) total for overhead and profit added in arriving at the price or value of the merchandise covered by the invoice.

Prohibitions and Restrictions

Textile Quotas. Textile import restrictions are primarily a matter of quotas and the way in which these quotas are administered and monitored. Under the Multi-Fiber Arrangement provisions of Section 204 of the Agricultural Adjustment Act, CITA has negotiated Multi-Fiber Arrangements with 40 countries. These Agreements may impose quotas for a type of textile or a specific article, and they are country-specific. The agreements, however, often change. Therefore, if you are interested in importing any special woven fabric products, you should contact the International Trade Administration's Office of Textile and Apparel (see addresses at end of this chapter). The Office of Textile and Apparel has a team of country specialists who can inform you of the latest developments and inform you about a product's quota or restriction status.

U.S. Customs enforces CITA textile and textile product entry quotas. If formal entry procedures are not followed, Customs will usually refuse entry for textiles that are subject to Section 204. Formal entry requires submission of a Country-of-Origin Declaration (see "General Considerations" above). U.S. Customs maintains a current textile quota status report, available for perusal at any Customs port. In addition, U.S. Customs in Washington, DC, operates a telephone service to provide quota status reports, which are updated weekly (see "Relevant Government Agencies" below).

Flammable Fabrics. U.S. Customs may refuse entry for any article of wearing apparel or interior furnishing, or any fabric or related material that is intended for use or that may be used in wearing apparel or interior furnishings, if it fails to conform to an applicable flammability standard issued under Section 4 of the FFA. An exception is allowed for certain products (FFA Section 11c) that are imported for finishing or processing to bring them within the legal standard. For these products, the exporter must state on the invoice or other paper relating to the shipment that the shipment is being made for that purpose.

The CPSC, as the primary enforcement agency of flammability Standards, inspects products for compliance with the FFA. If the CPSC believes a product, fabric, or related material does not comply with a flammability standard, it is authorized to pursue a variety of legal sanctions, including: 1) seizure, condemnation, and forfeiture of the noncomplying products; 2) administrative cease-and-desist order requiring an individual or firm to stop sale and distribution of the noncomplying products or; 3) temporary injunction requiring the individual or firm to stop sale and distribution of the noncomplying products, pending final disposition of an administrative cease-and-desist proceeding. The CPSC also has authority to seek civil penalties against any person who knowingly violates a regulation or standard issued under Section 4 of the FFA.

Country-Specific Restrictions

Restrictions under Multi-Fiber Arrangements are country-specific. A product originating in one country may be subject to quota and to export license or visa requirements, while the same product originating in a different country may not. At present, the U.S. has Multi-Fiber Arrangements with 40 countries. Many different categories of products are covered under these Arrangements; it is beyond the scope of this book to list each country and its restricted commodities. If you are interested in importing textiles and textile products, you should contact the International Trade Administration's Office of Textile and Apparel (see addresses at end of this chapter) or U.S. Customs to ascertain your product's restraint status.

The U.S. Customs Quota Branch phone numbers provide recorded status reports, by quota category number, for current charges against the quotas for that country. For convenience, the HTSUS shows the 3-digit category number in parentheses to the right of each listed commodity that is subject to textile restraints. For example, under Chapter 58, heading 5804.21.00, mechanically made lace of man-made fibers, is followed by the number "(229)." If you know the category number for your product, you can find out to what extent that quota is filled simply by calling the number for the appropriate country. A word of caution, though: if you do not know for sure that your article is subject to quota from a particular country, and you call the number for that country, you may not be any more enlightened after the phone call. Many of the recordings give status reports only when a certain percentage of the quota has been filled. Thus, if 229 for Indonesia is among the categories for which not enough quantity has entered the U.S. to warrant specific mention, it will be lumped under "all other categories" and you will be none the wiser. To find out if your product is subject to textile restraints, call the DOC or a local Customs port office. Then you can find out the current charges against that quota by calling the country number listed below. For a complete listing of Customs Quota Branch information numbers, see "Relevant Government Agencies" below.

Marking and Labeling Requirements

TFPIA Requirements. All textile fiber products imported into the U.S. must be stamped, tagged, labeled, or otherwise marked with the following information as required by the TFPIA, unless exempt from marking (see TFPIA, Section 12): 1) the generic names and percentages by weight of the constituent fibers present in the textile fiber product, exclusive of permissible ornamentation, in amounts of more than 5% in order of predominance by weight, with any percentage of fiber or fibers required to be designated as "other fiber" or "other fibers" (including those present in amounts of 5% or less) appearing last; and 2) the name of the manufacturer or the name or registered identification number issued by the FTC of one or more persons marketing or handling the textile fiber product; and 3) the name of the country where processed. A word trademark, used as a house mark and registered with the U.S. Patent Office, may appear on labels instead of the name otherwise required, provided the owner of the trademark furnishes a copy of the registration to the FTC prior to use (see "Registered Identification Numbers" below).

The information listed above is not exhaustive. TFPIA requirements are extensive. The Act specifies such details as types of labels, means of attachment, label position on the article, package labeling, unit labeling for two-piece garments, and arrangement of information on the label; allowable fiber designations; country-of-origin indications; requirements for trim and ornamentation, linings and interlinings, and pile fabrics; sectional disclosure; use of trade names and trademarks; and requirements for swatches and samples. The FTC publishes a booklet intended to clarify TFPIA requirements to facilitate voluntary compliance in the industry (see "Publications Available" below). It is available on request, at no charge, from the FTC (see addresses at end of this chapter).

Wool Products Labeling Act (WPLA). Wool product labeling requirements for foreign products are the responsibility of the importer. The WPLA requires the following information to appear on wool products subject to the Act: 1) percentage of the wool product's total fiber weight (exclusive of ornamentation) not exceeding 5% of the total fiber weight of a) wool, b) recycled wool, c) each fiber other than wool if the percent by weight of such fiber is 5% or more, and d) the aggregate of all other fibers; 2) the maximum percent of the wool product's total weight, of any nonfibrous loading, filling, or adulterating matter; and 3) the importer's name. If you, as importer, have a registered identification number issued by the FTC, that number may be used instead of your name (see "Registered Identification Numbers" below).

Customs entry is contingent on proper labeling. If your shipment is found to be mislabeled at entry, you will be given the option of relabeling the products under Customs supervision, as long as the district director is satisfied that your labeling error or omission did not involve fraud or willful neglect. If your shipment is discovered after entry to have been noncomplying with WPLA, it will be recalled to Customs custody at your expense, unless you can satisfy the district director that the products have since been brought into compliance. You will be held responsible for all expenses incurred in bringing a shipment into compliance, including compensation of personnel and other expenses related to Customs supervision.

Fraudulent violations of WPLA will result in seizure of the shipment. Shipments already released from Customs custody will be ordered to be redelivered to Customs. Customs reports all cases of fraudulent violation to the FTC in Washington, DC.

The information listed above is not intended to be exhaustive. WPLA requirements are extensive. The Act specifies such details as types of labels, means of attachment, label position on the article, package labeling, unit labeling (as in the case of a two-piece garment), arrangement of information on the label, allowable fiber designations, country-of-origin indications, trim and ornamentation, pile fabrics, sectional disclosure, use of trade names and trademarks, requirements for swatches and samples, etc. The FTC publishes a booklet intended to clarify WPLA requirements in order to facilitate voluntary compliance within the industry (see "Publications Available" below). It is available on request, at no charge, from the FTC (see addresses at end of this chapter).

Registered Identification Numbers. Any domestic firm or person residing in the U.S. and engaged in the manufacture or marketing of textile products covered under the TFPIA may obtain an FTC-registered identification number for use on required tags and labels instead of the name of a firm or person. For applications, contact the FTC (see addresses at end of this chapter).

For a general discussion of U.S. Customs marking and labeling requirements, refer to "Marking: Country of Origin" on page 215 and "Special Marking Requirements" on page 217.

Shipping Considerations

You will need to ensure that your goods are packaged and shipped with care so that they pass smoothly through Customs and arrive in good condition. You are responsible for ensuring that the shipment is in compliance with all applicable government regulations for packaging and shipping. In most instances, you should not leave these arrangements solely to the discretion of your supplier. Careful preparation of the cargo and selection of the mode of transport can be essential to a cost-effective, time-

ly delivery of undamaged goods. We strongly advise you to consult your shipping representative, insurance agent, or freight broker for advice on packing and shipping. Refer also to the major tab section "Packing/Shipping/Insurance" for a general discussion of packing and shipping.

Special woven fabrics may be shipped in bulk, bolts, rolls, or other types of containers, depending on the type of product and whether it is prepackaged. General considerations include protection from contamination, weather, and pests. Safety precautions should also be implemented as required to protect against breakage, spillage, corrosion of containers, and combustion. Containers should be constructed so as to be safe for handling during transport.

Publications Available

The following publications may be relevant to the importation of special woven fabrics and wool fabrics:

Questions and Answers Relating to the Textile Fiber Products Identification Act and Regulations

Questions and Answers Relating to the Wool Products Labeling Act and Regulations

Available free of charge on request from the Federal Trade Commission, these publications are excellent sources of information written in clear lay language. We recommend that anyone interested in importing textile fiber products but unfamiliar with the regulations obtain a copy of each of these booklets.

The *Harmonized Tariff Schedule of the United States* (HTSUS) is available from:

Government Printing Office (GPO)
Superintendent of Documents
Washington, DC 20402
(202) 512-1800 (Order line)
(202) 512-0000 (General)

The USGPO also has copies of specific laws available for purchase. The USGPO accepts credit card orders over the phone, as well as mail orders paid by credit card, a check drawn on a U.S. bank, or an international money order.

Relevant Government Agencies

Address your questions regarding textile Multi-Fiber Arrangements to:

International Trade Administration
Office of Textile and Apparel
14th and Constitution Ave. NW, Rm. 3100
Washington, DC 20230
(202) 482-5078, 482-3737

Address your questions regarding the Flammable Fabrics Act (FFA) to:

Consumer Product Safety Commission (CPSC)
5401 Westbard Avenue
Bethesda, MD 20207
(301) 492-6580

Address your questions regarding labeling requirements under the Textile Fiber Products Identification Act (TFPIA) or the Wool Products Labeling Act (WPLA) to:

Federal Trade Commission (FTC)
Division of Enforcement
601 Pennsylvania Ave. NW
Washington, DC 20580
(202) 326-2996 (General)
(202) 326-2841 (Textile and wool products labeling)

Address your questions regarding special woven fabric imports to the district or port director of Customs for you area. For addresses, refer to"U.S. Customs District Offices" on page 62 or contact:

U.S. Customs Service
1301 Constitution Ave. NW
Washington, DC 20229
(202) 927-6724 (Information)
(202) 927-1000 (General)

The following information numbers for U.S. Customs in Washington, DC, provide recorded information. The Quota Branch numbers listed by country provide updated status reports on textile quotas from those countries. All area codes are (202).
General information: 927-5850

Quota Branch: China 927-6703; India 927-6705; Indonesia 927-6704; Japan 927-6706; Korea 927-6707; Macao 927-6709; Malaysia 927-6712; Mexico 927-6711; Pakistan 927-6714; Philippines 927-6713; Romania 927-6715; Singapore 927-6716; Sri Lanka 927-6708; Taiwan 927-6719; Thailand 927-6717; Turkey 927-6718; All others 927-5850.

Laws and Regulations

The following laws and regulations may be relevant to the importation of special woven fabrics. The laws are contained in the United States Code (USC), and the regulations are published in the Code of Federal Regulations (CFR), both of which are available at larger public and law libraries. Copies of specific laws are also available from the United States Government Printing Office (address above).

7 USC 1854
Textile Trade Agreements
(EO 11651, as amended by EO 11951 and 12188, and supplemented by EO 12475)
This Act authorizes the CITA of the DOC to enter into Multi-Fiber Agreements with other countries to control trade in textiles and establishes the Textile Import Program, which is enforced by U.S. Customs.

19 CFR 12.130 et seq.
Regulations on Entry of Textiles
These regulations provide the requirements and procedures followed by Customs in enforcing limitations on the importation and entry and withdrawal of textiles and textile products from warehouses for consumption in the U.S.

15 USC 70-77
Textile Fiber Products Identification Act (TFPIA)
This Act prohibits false or deceptive labeling (misbranding) and false advertising of any textile fiber products and requires all textile fiber products imported into the U.S. to be labeled in accordance with the requirements set forth in the law.

19 CFR 11.12b; 16 CFR 303 et seq.
Regulations on Labeling and Marking
These regulations detail the labeling and marking requirements for textiles as specified by the CPSC and the invoice contents required by U.S. Customs for purpose of enforcing the labeling and marking rules.

15 USC 1191-1204
Flammable Fabrics Act (FFA)
This Act provides for the setting of flammability standards for fabric by the Consumer Product Safety Commission (CPSC) and for enforcement by U.S. Customs.

16 CFR 1610, 1611, 1615, 1616, 1630-1632
Regulations on Flammable Fabric Standards
These regulations specify the flammability standards adopted by the CPSC under the FFA for various types of textiles.

15 USC 68-68j
Wool Products Labeling Act (WPLA)
This Act prohibits the false or deceptive labeling (misbranding) of wool products and requires all wool products imported into the U.S. to be labeled in accordance with requirements set forth in the law.

19 CFR 11.12; 16 CFR 300 et seq.
Regulations on WPLA Labeling and Marking
These regulations set forth the wool labeling and marking requirements adopted by the FTC to administer the requirements of the WPLA and provide the procedures followed by U.S. Customs in enforcing the WPLA and the FTC regulations, including entry invoice requirements.

Principal Exporting Countries

The following listing includes samples of the main supplier nations of the products of this chapter. It is organized by HTSUS major heading. (Refer to "Customs Classification" above for the product codes.) Countries are listed in rank order of the value of products imported to the U.S. Statistics represent customs value entries for 1993 from the Bureau of Census, U.S. Department of Commerce.

5801—South Korea, Canada, China, Japan, Germany, United Kingdom, Italy, France, Netherlands, Belgium

5802—Guatemala, Pakistan, Brazil, Mexico, Canada, Germany, Turkey, United Kingdom, Netherlands, France

5803—United Kingdom, Canada, Mexico, Germany, Switzerland, Ireland, India, Taiwan, Italy, Hong Kong

5804—France, Liechtenstein, United Kingdom, South Korea, Colombia, Taiwan, China, Germany, Philippines, Haiti

5805—France, Belgium, Israel, Portugal, New Zealand, China, Canada, Italy, Turkey, United Kingdom

5806—Taiwan, France, Japan, Canada, Switzerland, Germany, Italy, Mexico, United Kingdom, South Korea

5807—Taiwan, Canada, South Korea, Hong Kong, Germany, United Kingdom, Japan, Thailand, Italy, Brazil

5808—France, Taiwan, South Africa, Japan, Italy, Jamaica, China, Germany, Mexico, United Kingdom

5809—Japan, India, Switzerland, South Korea, France, Taiwan, Bangladesh, Germany, Spain, Italy

5810—Taiwan, China, South Korea, France, Thailand, India, Philippines, Haiti, Hong Kong, Canada

5811—Canada, United Kingdom, South Korea, Italy, France, Germany, India, Thailand, Japan, Belgium

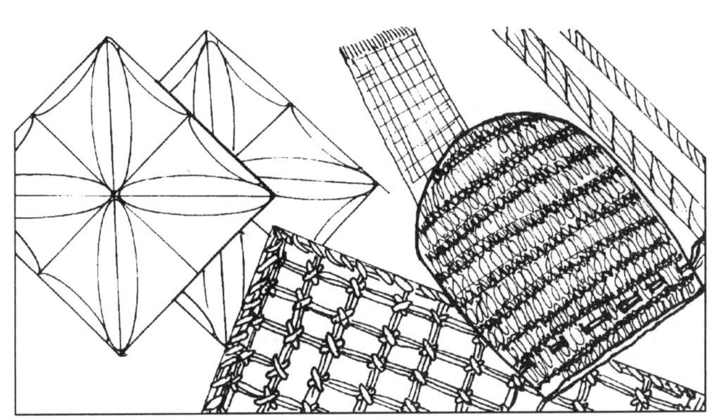

Chapter 59: Coated Textiles*

Full title: Impregnated, Coated, Covered, or Laminated Textile Fabrics; Textile Articles of a Kind Suitable for Industrial Use

This chapter relates to the importation of coated textiles, which are classified under Chapter 59 of the Harmonized Tariff Schedule of the United States (HTSUS). Specifically, it includes textile fabrics stiffened with a coating of gum, amylaceous substances, or other coatings for book covers, tracing cloth, painting canvas, hat foundations, theatrical scenery, and studio back-cloths; tire cord fabric and other rubberized textile fabrics; textile fabrics coated with plastics; linoleum or other floor coverings on textile backing; textile wall coverings; textile wicks, textile hosepiping and tubing; textile transmission or conveyor belts or belting; and textile products for technical uses.

The term "textile fabrics" refers to woven fabrics of Commodity Index Chapters 50 through 55, gauze (HTSUS heading 5803), narrow woven fabrics (HTSUS heading 5806), braids and ornamental trimmings (HTSUS heading 5808), and knitted or crocheted fabrics (HTSUS heading 6002).

If you are interested in importing textile products that are combined with plastic or rubber substances, you should also read Commodity Index Chapters 39 (plastics) or 40 (rubber). Fabrics that are partially covered with plastics, that bear designs resulting from such treatments, or that are combined with rubber are also covered in Chapters 50 through 55, 58, and 60. For importing sensitized textiles, refer to Chapter 37. The import requirements for abrasive-coated textile material are covered in Chapter 68. Wall coverings consisting of textile flock or dust fixed on paper backing are classified under Chapter 48. If you are interested in importing wood veneer on a textile fabric backing, refer to Chapter 44. Metal foils with a textile fabric backing is covered in Chapter 72 through 81. The import requirements for certain types of transmission and conveyor belts are dealt with in Chapter 40.

Key Factors

The key factors in the importation of coated textiles are:

- Compliance with quota restraints and visa requirements under U.S. Department of Commerce (DOC) Multi-Fiber Arrangements
- Submission of U.S. Customs Country-of-Origin Declaration(s)

*IMPORTANT: Read the Commodity Index Introduction. It is the essential framework for understanding this chapter.

- Compliance with entry invoice requirements
- Compliance with labeling requirements under Textile Fiber Products Identification Act (TFPIA) and the Wool Products Labeling Act (WPLA)
- Compliance with flammability standards adopted and enforced by the Consumer Product Safety Commission (CPSC) under the Flammable Fabrics Act (FFA)

Although most importers use the services of a licensed customs broker in making their entries, and we recommend this practice, you should be aware of the regulatory, entry, and documentation issues involved in importing your product. You, as importer, are ultimately responsible for the fulfillment of any legal requirements applicable to your shipment.

General Considerations

Regulatory Agencies. The DOC's Committee for Implementation of Textile Agreements (CITA) regulates certain textile imports under Section 204 of the Agricultural Adjustment Act. U.S. Customs enforces CITA textile and textile product entry quotas. Customs also enforces compliance with labeling and invoice requirements of the TFPIA and flammability standards under the FFA. The CPSC monitors imports and from time to time inspects textile shipments for compliance with FFA standards. If you are importing products that contain wool fibers, importation is subject to complex textile import regulations. The Federal Trade Commission (FTC) administers the WPLA requirements.

Textile Quotas. If you are interested in importing coated textiles, the most important issue you need to be aware of is quotas. Under the Multi-Fiber Arrangement provisions of Section 204 of the Agricultural Adjustment Act, CITA initiates specific agreements with individual exporting countries. Section 204 of the Agricultural Adjustment Act covers textiles that: 1) are in chief value of cotton, wool, or man-made fibers, any textile fibers subject to the terms of any textile trade agreement, or any combination of such fibers; 2) contain 50% or more by weight of cotton or man-made fibers, or any textile fibers subject to the terms of any textile trade agreement; 3) contain 17% or more by weight of wool; or 4) if in chief value of textile fibers or textile materials, contain a blend of cotton, wool, or man-made fibers, any textile fibers subject to the terms of any textile trade agreement, or any combination of such fibers that, in total, amount to 50% or more by weight of all component fibers.

The U.S. has Multi-Fiber Arrangements with 40 countries. Each agreement with each country is unique, and may specify quotas for a type of textile or a specific article. Visas or export licenses may be required. These agreements, however, often change. Therefore, if you are interested in importing any coated textiles, you should contact the International Trade Administration's Office of Textile and Apparel (see addresses at end of this chapter). Refer to "Prohibitions and Restrictions" below for further details.

Textile Country-of-Origin Declarations. U.S. Customs enforces CITA textile and textile product entry quotas (see "Prohibitions and Restrictions" below). Requirements for entry include submission of Country-of-Origin Declarations with every coated textile shipment, regardless of whether it is subject to a specific multi-fiber arrangement (19 CFR 12.130, 12.131).

Country of Origin. Quota restrictions are country-specific and therefore are applied based on the country of origin for the textiles shipped. The last country from which a textile shipment was exported to the U.S. is not necessarily its country of origin. A textile or textile product imported into the U.S. is considered a product of the particular foreign territory or country, or a U.S. insular possession, where it is wholly grown, produced, or manufactured. For the following discussion, "country" means a foreign territory or country, or a U.S. insular possession.

Substantial transformation rules may affect the country-of-origin determination. For example, if a textile or textile product originates in Country A and is subject to quota, the quota restrictions apply at entry into the U.S. But if, prior to export to the U.S., you move the shipment to Country B where there are fewer restrictions, the shipment may nevertheless remain subject to quota and visa requirements under the Multi-Fiber Arrangement with Country A. Customs determines whether the quota restrictions apply based on the criteria of "substantial transformation." If your textiles do not undergo any major processing or manufacturing while in Country B, or if the manufacturing or processing is minor, your shipment will be deemed to originate in Country A. *You cannot claim substantial transformation on the basis of minor manufacturing procedures.*

In contrast, if your shipment undergoes major processing or manufacturing while in Country B, rendering the textiles "new and different articles of commerce," Customs will treat the shipment as the product of Country B. To qualify as having undergone substantial transformation, an article must evince a change in: 1) commercial designation or identity; b) fundamental character; or c) commercial use. If your shipment is processed in more than one country, the country where it last underwent substantial transformation is the country of origin for Customs entry. In deciding whether the manufacturing or processing operation in a country is major, Customs considers the following factors: 1) the resultant physical change in the material or article; 2) the complexity, the level or degree of skill and/or technology required, and the amount of time involved in the operations; and 3) the value added to the article or material, compared to its value when imported into the U.S.

Validating Operations. Operations that Customs will usually acknowledge as validating a claim of substantial transformation are the following: 1) dyeing and printing, when accompanied by two or more of the following finishing operations: bleaching, shrinking, fulling, napping, decating, permanent stiffening, weighting, permanent embossing, or moireing; 2) spinning fibers into yarn; 3) weaving, knitting, or otherwise forming fabric; 4) cutting fabric into parts and assembling the parts into completed articles; or 5) substantial assembly, by sewing and/or tailoring into a completed garment cut pieces of apparel articles that have been cut from fabric in another country—e.g., complete assembly and tailoring of all cut pieces of suit-type jackets, suits, and shirts.

Insubstantial Operations. Operations that usually will not support a claim of substantial transformation, even if more than one are performed, are the following: 1) simple operations of combining, labeling, pressing, cleaning, dry cleaning, or packaging; 2) cutting to length or width and hemming or overlocking fabrics that are readily identifiable as being intended for a particular commercial use; 3) trimming and/or joining together by sewing, looping, linking, or other means of attaching otherwise completed knit-to-shape component parts produced in a single country, even if accompanied by other processes—e.g., washing, drying, mending—normally incident to assembly; 4) one or more finishing operations on yarns, fabrics, or their textile articles—such as showerproofing, superwashing, bleaching, decating, fulling, shrinking, mercerizing, or similar operations; or 5) dyeing and/or printing fabrics or yarns.

Declarations. The country of origin of the coated textile products in a shipment must be stated on a declaration submitted to U.S. Customs at the time of entry. There are three Customs Country-of-Origin Declarations: single-country, multiple-country, and negative. The Declaration to be submitted with your shipment of coated textile products depends on the nature of the import.

- **Single-country declarations** are used for entries of textiles or textile products that clearly originate from only one country or that have been assembled in one country from fabricated components wholly produced in the U.S. or the foreign country of manufacture. Information required includes: marks of identification and numbers; description of article and quantity; country of origin; and date of exportation.
- **Multiple-country declarations** are used for entries of textiles or textile products that were manufactured or processed and/or that incorporate materials originating in more than one foreign country or territory. Information required includes: marks of identification and numbers; for articles, description, quantity, identification of manufacturing and/or processing operations, country, and date of exportation; for materials used to make articles, description of materials, country of production, and date of exportation.
- **Negative declarations** must accompany all textile imports that are not subject to FFA Section 204 restrictions. Information required includes: marks of identification and numbers; descriptions of article and quantity; and country of origin.

The date of exportation to be indicated on the above declarations is the date on which the carrier leaves the last port in the country of origin, as determined by Customs. Diversion to another country during transit does not affect the export date.

Procedure for Declarations. The manufacturer, producer, exporter, or importer may prepare the declaration. If more than one of these parties is involved in the importation, each party may prepare a separate declaration. You may file a separate declaration for each invoice presented with your entry. The declaration must be dated and signed by the responsible party, and must include the person's title and the company name and address. Your shipment's entry will be denied unless it is accompanied by a properly executed declaration. Customs will not treat a textile declaration as a missing document for which a bond may be filed.

Customs will base its country-of-origin determination on the information contained in each declaration, unless the information is insufficient. If the information on the declaration is insufficient, Customs will require that you submit such additional information as will enable the determination to be made. The shipment will not be released until the determination is made. Thus, if you want to clear Customs with minimal delay, be sure that the information on the declarations is as complete as possible for each shipment.

Textile Labeling and Invoice Requirements. You are responsible for your imported coated textile product's compliance with applicable provisions of the TFPIA. Coated textile products that require labeling under TFPIA must already be labeled at entry, or the shipment will be refused. (See "Marking and Labeling Requirements" below.) If you import shipments of coated textiles subject to TFPIA and valued at over $500, you must provide special information on the entry invoice (see "Entry and Documentation" below).

Flammability Standards. Coated textile products imported into the U.S. for use in consumer products must be in compliance with the FFA, a federal law that gives the CPSC the authority and responsibility for protecting the public from the hazards of dangerously flammable items of wearing apparel and interior furnishings. Under the FFA, standards have been established for flammability of clothing textiles. You cannot import any article of wearing apparel or interior furnishing, or any fabric or related material that is intended for use or that may be used in such items, if it fails to conform to an applicable flammability standard (FFA Section 4). Certain products may be imported into the U.S. (FFA Section 11c) for finishing or processing to render them less flammable so as to meet the standards. For these products, the exporter must state on the invoice or other paper relating to the shipment that the shipment is being made for that purpose.

The CPSC monitors imports of textiles under its Import Surveillance Program. From time to time, your textile shipments may be inspected to ascertain compliance with mandatory safety standards. Shipments may also be subject to testing by the CPSC to determine compliance. If the CPSC believes a product, fabric, or related material does not comply with a flammability standard, it is authorized to pursue a variety of legal sanctions (see "Prohibitions and Restrictions" below).

Substantial Product Hazard Reports. Any firm that obtains information that reasonably supports the conclusion that one of its products presents an unreasonable risk of serious injury or death must report that information to the CPSC's Division of Corrective Actions (CPSC address below). Importers must also report to the CPSC if 1) a type of product is the subject of at least three civil actions filed in U.S. federal or state courts, 2) each suit alleges the involvement of that product type in death or grievous bodily injury (as defined in FFA Section 37(3)1), and 3) at least three of the actions result in a final settlement with the manufacturer or in a judgment for the plaintiff within any one of the two-year periods specified in FFA Section 37(b).

Wool Product Entry Requirements. Depending on the nature of your wool fiber imports, as many as four different types of special entry documents may be required. First, for all imported textile fibers and yarns covered by the Agricultural Adjustment Act (AAA), including wool, you must file a U.S. Customs Textile Entry Declaration (see "Textile Country-of-Origin Declarations" above). Second, with each wool shipment's entry summary, you must file Customs **Form 6451**, Notice of Percentage of Clean Yield and Grade of Wool or Hair, in duplicate, showing your name and address. Third, for all wool products subject to the WPLA, special information is required on the entry invoices (see "Entry and Documentation" below). Finally, certain wool articles manufactured or produced in certain countries may be subject to quotas under U.S. Department of Commerce Multi-Fiber Arrangements. Such products require export certificates or visas issued by the appropriate country of origin, in addition to other requisite entry paperwork (see "Quotas" above).

Wool Products Labeling Act. The term "wool product" means any product or any portion of a product that contains, purports to contain, or in any way is represented as containing wool, reprocessed wool, or reused wool. All wool products imported into the U.S., except those made more than 20 years before importation, and except carpets, rugs, mats, and upholsteries, must have affixed a stamp, tag, label, or other means of identification as required by the WPLA. If you are importing wool products exempt from labeling under the WPLA, do not assume they are also exempt from labeling under the TFPIA. These are two distinct laws, with some overlapping requirements (see "Marking and Labeling Requirements" below).

Import Advisory

Importation of textiles is trade-sensitive and highly regulated. Shipments of textiles and textile products not complying with all government regulations, including quotas and visas, are subject to seizure and could result in the imposition of penalties as well as possible forfeiture of the goods. You should always verify the available quota for any textile product you plan to import before your shipment leaves the country of manufacture. Furthermore, Customs textile classification rulings change frequently, and prior administrative rulings are often modified and sometimes reversed.

Customs Classification

For customs purposes, coated textiles are classified under Chapter 59 of the HTSUS. This chapter is broken into major headings, which are further divided into subheadings, and often sub-subheadings, each of which has its own HTSUS classification number. For example, the HTSUS number for textile fabrics of man-made fibers is 5901.10.10, indicating it is a sub-subcategory of textile fabrics coated with gum or amylaceous substances for book covers (5901.10.00), which is a subcategory of the major heading, textile fabrics coated with coated with gum or amylaceous substances, etc. (5901.00.00). There are 11 major headings within Chapter 59.

5901—Textile fabrics coated with gum or amylaceous substances, of a kind used for the outer covers of books or the like; tracing cloth; prepared painting canvas; buckram and similar stiffened textile fabrics of a kind used for hat foundations

5902—Tire cord fabric of high tenacity yarn of nylon or other polyamides, polyesters, or viscose rayon

5903—Textile fabrics impregnated, coated, covered, or laminated with plastics, other than those of heading 5902

5904—Linoleum, whether or not cut to shape; floor coverings consisting of a coating or covering applied on a textile backing, whether or not cut to shape

5905—Textile wall coverings

5906—Rubberized textile fabrics, other than those of heading 5902

5907—Textile fabrics otherwise impregnated, coated, or covered; painted canvas being theatrical scenery, studio back-cloths, or the like

5908—Textile wicks, woven, plaited, or knitted for lamps, stoves, lighters, candles, or the like; incandescent gas mantles and tubular knitted gas mantle fabric therefor, whether or not impregnated

5910—Transmission or conveyor belts or belting, of textile material, whether or not reinforced with metal or other material

5911—Textile products and articles, for technical uses, specified in note 7 to this chapter

For more details regarding classifications of the specific product you are interested in importing, consult a customs broker, the appropriate commodity specialist at your nearest customs port, or the HTSUS. HTSUS is available for purchase from the U.S. Government Printing Office (see addresses at end of this chapter), and may be found in larger public libraries. Refer to "Classification—Liquidation" on page 207 for a general discussion of customs classification.

Sample Import Duties

Import duties will vary depending on the HTSUS classification of your product. Therefore, to determine the correct amount of duties, your product must be properly classified under the HTSUS. The following sample duties are taken from the duty listings for HTSUS Chapter 59 products.

Textile fabrics of man-made fibers coated with gum or amylaceous substances for book covers (5901.10.10): 8%; tire cord fabrics (5902): 6.6%; cotton fabrics impregnated, coated, covered, or laminated with polyvinyl chloride (5903.10.10): 5.3%; linoleum (5904.10.00): 4.2%; textile wall coverings backed with permanently affixed paper (5905.00.10): free, other (5905.00.90): 12.5%; adhesive tape of rubberized textile fabrics, not exceeding 20 cm in width (5906.10.00): 5.8%; textile wicks (5908.00.00): 6.8%; textile hosepiping of vegetable fibers (5909.00.10): 4.5%; transmission or conveyor belts or belting of man-made fibers (5910.00.10): 8%; press and dryer felts (5911.31.00, 591.32.00): 7.5%.

Entry and Documentation

The entry of merchandise is a two-part process consisting of 1) filing the documentation necessary to determine whether merchandise may be released from Customs custody, and 2) filing the documents that contain information for duty assessment and statistical purposes. In certain instances, all documents must be filed and accepted by Customs prior to release of the goods. Unless you have been granted an extension, you must file entry documents at a location specified by the district or area director within five working days of your shipment's date of arrival at a U.S. port of entry. These include a number of standard documents required by Customs for any entry, and:

- U.S. Customs Country-of-Origin Declaration(s)
- Export documentation and/or visa for textiles subject to Multi-Fiber Arrangement
- Customs **Form 6451,** Notice of Percentage of Clean Yield and Grade of Wool or Hair, in duplicate, showing your name and address (if importing articles containing wool)

After you present the entry, Customs may examine your shipment or may waive examination. The shipment is then released provided no legal or regulatory violations have been noted. You must then file entry summary documentation and deposit estimated duties at a designated customhouse within 10 working days of your shipment's release. For a detailed description of entry procedures, standard documentation, and informal entry, refer to "Entry Process" on page 182.

NAFTA Certificates of Origin. An importer of textiles for which NAFTA treatment is sought need not file a separate NAFTA Certificate of Origin in addition to the Customs Country-of-Origin Declaration. The declaration is sufficient. However, the importer must take care to submit a declaration from each U.S., Canadian, or Mexican producer or manufacturer. Thus, for multiple producers or manufacturers, a separate declaration must be filed for each. If a Customs district director cannot determine the country of origin because the declaration is absent or incomplete, the shipment is not entitled to preferential NAFTA tariff treatment or other NAFTA benefits. See 12 CFR 132.

Entry Invoices. You must provide additional information on the entry invoice for certain coated textiles. The specific information varies with the nature of your product, as noted below.

TFPIA Requirements. For the purpose of TFPIA enforcement, a commercial shipment of textile products exceeding $500 in value and subject to TFPIA labeling requirements must show the following information: 1) the constituent fiber or combination of fibers, designating with equal prominence each natural or manufactured fiber by its generic name, in order of predominance by weight if the weight of such fiber is 5% or more of the total fiber weight of the product; 2) percentage of each fiber present, by weight, in the total fiber content; 3) the name or other identification issued and registered by the Federal Trade Commission of the manufacturer of the product or one or more persons subject to Section 3 of the TFPIA with respect to such product; 4) the name of the country where processed or manufactured.

Wool Products Subject to WPLA. When you offer for entry a wool product shipment valued at over $500 and subject to WPLA, you must include certain information intended to facilitate Customs monitoring and enforcement of that Act. This extra information is identical to that required by WPLA on labeling (see "Marking and Labeling Requirements" below), with the addition of the manufacturer's name. If your product consists of mixed waste, residues, and similar merchandise obtained from several suppliers or unknown sources, you may omit the manufacturer's name from the entry invoice.

Prohibitions and Restrictions

Textile Quotas. Textile import restrictions are primarily a matter of quotas and the way in which these quotas are administered and monitored. Under the Multi-Fiber Arrangement provisions of Section 204 of the Agricultural Adjustment Act, CITA has negotiated Multi-Fiber Arrangements with 40 countries. These Agreements may impose quotas for a type of textile or a specific article, and they are country-specific. The agreements, however, often change. Therefore, if you are interested in importing any coated textile products, you should contact the International Trade Administration's Office of Textile and Apparel (see addresses at end of this chapter). The Office of Textile and Apparel has a team of country specialists who can inform you of the latest developments and inform you about a product's quota or restriction status.

U.S. Customs enforces CITA textile and textile product entry quotas. If formal entry procedures are not followed, Customs will usually refuse entry for textiles that are subject to Section 204. Formal entry requires submission of a Country-of-Origin Declaration (see "General Considerations" above). U.S. Customs maintains a current textile quota status report, available for perusal at any Customs port. In addition, U.S. Customs in Washington, DC, operates a telephone service to provide quota status reports, which are updated weekly (see "Relevant Government Agencies" below).

Flammable Fabrics. U.S. Customs may refuse entry for any article of wearing apparel or interior furnishing, or any fabric or related material that is intended for use or that may be used in wearing apparel or interior furnishings, if it fails to conform to an applicable flammability standard issued under Section 4 of the FFA. An exception is allowed for certain products (FFA Section 11c) that are imported for finishing or processing to bring them within the legal standard. For these products, the exporter must state on the invoice or other paper relating to the shipment that the shipment is being made for that purpose.

The CPSC, as the primary enforcement agency of flammability standards, inspects products for compliance with the FFA. If the CPSC believes a product, fabric, or related material does not comply with a flammability standard, it is authorized to pursue a variety of legal sanctions, including: 1) seizure, condemnation, and forfeiture of the noncomplying products; 2) administrative cease-and-desist order requiring an individual or firm to stop sale and distribution of the noncomplying products or; 3) temporary injunction requiring the individual or firm to stop sale and distribution of the noncomplying products, pending final disposition of an administrative cease-and-desist proceeding. The CPSC also has authority to seek civil penalties against any person who knowingly violates a regulation or standard issued under Section 4 of the FFA.

Country-Specific Restrictions

Restrictions under Multi-Fiber Arrangements are country-specific. A product originating in one country may be subject to quota and to export license or visa requirements, while the same product originating in a different country may not. At present, the U.S. has Multi-Fiber Arrangements with 40 countries. Many different categories of products are covered under these Arrangements; it is beyond the scope of this book to list each country and its restricted commodities. If you are interested in importing textiles and textile products, you should contact the International Trade Administration's Office of Textile and Apparel (see addresses at end of this chapter) or U.S. Customs to ascertain your product's restraint status.

The U.S. Customs Quota Branch phone numbers provide recorded status reports, by quota category number, for current charges against the quotas for that country. For convenience, the HTSUS shows the 3-digit category number in parentheses to the right of each listed commodity that is subject to textile restraints. For example, under Chapter 59, heading 5901.10.10, textile fabrics of man-made fibers coated with gum or amylaceous substances for book covers, etc., is followed by the number "(229)." If you know the category number for your product, you can find out to what extent that quota is filled simply by calling the number for the appropriate country. A word of caution, though: if you do not know for sure that your article is subject to quota from a particular country, and you call the number for that country, you may not be any more enlightened after the phone call. Many of the recordings give status reports only when a certain percentage of the quota has been filled. Thus, if 229 for South Korea is among the categories for which not enough quantity has entered the U.S. to warrant specific mention, it will be lumped under "all other categories" and you will be none the wiser. To find out if your product is subject to textile restraints, call the DOC or a local Customs port office. Then you can find out the current charges against that quota by calling the country number listed below. For a complete listing of Customs Quota Branch information numbers, see "Relevant Government Agencies" below.

Marking and Labeling Requirements

TFPIA Requirements. All textile fiber products imported into the U.S. must be stamped, tagged, labeled, or otherwise marked with the following information as required by the TFPIA, unless exempt from marking (see TFPIA, Section 12): 1) the generic names and percentages by weight of the constituent fibers present in the textile fiber product, exclusive of permissible ornamentation, in amounts of more than 5% in order of predominance by weight, with any percentage of fiber or fibers required to be designated as "other fiber" or "other fibers" (including those present in amounts of 5% or less) appearing last; and 2) the name of the manufacturer or the name or registered identification number issued by the FTC of one or more persons marketing or handling the textile fiber product; and 3) the name of the country where processed. A word trademark, used as a house mark and registered with the U.S. Patent Office, may appear on labels instead of the name otherwise required, provided the owner of the trademark furnishes a copy of the registration to the FTC prior to use (see "Registered Identification Numbers" below).

The information listed above is not exhaustive. TFPIA requirements are extensive. The Act specifies such details as types of labels, means of attachment, label position on the article, package labeling, unit labeling for two-piece garments, and arrangement of information on the label; allowable fiber designations; country-of-origin indications; requirements for trim and ornamentation, linings and interlinings, and pile fabrics; sectional disclosure; use of trade names and trademarks; and requirements for swatches and samples. The FTC publishes a booklet intended to clarify TFPIA requirements to facilitate voluntary compliance in the industry (see "Publications Available" below). It is available on request, at no charge, from the FTC (see addresses at end of this chapter).

Wool Products Labeling Act (WPLA). Wool product labeling requirements for foreign products are the responsibility of the importer. The WPLA requires the following information to appear on wool products subject to the Act: 1) percentage of the wool product's total fiber weight (exclusive of ornamentation) not exceeding 5% of the total fiber weight of a) wool, b) recycled wool, c) each fiber other than wool if the percent by weight of such fiber is 5% or more, and d) the aggregate of all other fibers; 2) the maximum percent of the wool product's total weight, of any nonfibrous loading, filling, or adulterating matter; and 3) the importer's name. If you, as importer, have a registered identification number issued by the FTC, that number may be used instead of your name (see "Registered Identification Numbers" below).

Customs entry is contingent on proper labeling. If your shipment is found to be mislabeled at entry, you will be given the option of relabeling the products under Customs supervision, as long as the district director is satisfied that your labeling error or omission did not involve fraud or willful neglect. If your shipment is discovered after entry to have been noncomplying with WPLA, it will be recalled to Customs custody at your expense, unless you can satisfy the district director that the products have since been brought into compliance. You will be held responsible for all expenses incurred in bringing a shipment into compliance, including compensation of personnel and other expenses related to Customs supervision.

Fraudulent violations of WPLA will result in seizure of the shipment. Shipments already released from Customs custody will be ordered to be redelivered to Customs. Customs reports all cases of fraudulent violation to the FTC in Washington, DC.

The information listed above is not intended to be exhaustive. WPLA requirements are extensive. The Act specifies such details as types of labels, means of attachment, label position on the article, package labeling, unit labeling (as in the case of a two-piece garment), arrangement of information on the label, allowable fiber designations, country-of-origin indications, trim and ornamentation, pile fabrics, sectional disclosure, use of trade names and trademarks, requirements for swatches and samples, etc. The FTC publishes a booklet intended to clarify WPLA requirements in order to facilitate voluntary compliance within the industry (see "Publications Available" below). It is available on request, at no charge, from the FTC (see addresses at end of this chapter).

Registered Identification Numbers. Any domestic firm or person residing in the U.S. and engaged in the manufacture or marketing of textile products covered under the TFPIA may obtain an FTC-registered identification number for use on required tags and labels instead of the name of a firm or person. For applications, contact the FTC (address below.)

For a general discussion of U.S. Customs marking and labeling requirements, refer to "Marking: Country of Origin" on page 215 and "Special Marking Requirements" on page 217.

Shipping Considerations

You will need to ensure that your goods are packaged and shipped with care so that they pass smoothly through Customs and arrive in good condition. You are responsible for ensuring that the shipment is in compliance with all applicable government regulations for packaging and shipping. In most instances, you should not leave these arrangements solely to the discretion of your supplier. Careful preparation of the cargo and selection of the mode of transport can be essential to a cost-effective, timely delivery of undamaged goods. We strongly advise you to consult your shipping representative, insurance agent, or freight broker for advice on packing and shipping. Refer also to the major tab section "Packing/Shipping/Insurance" for a general discussion of packing and shipping.

Coated textiles may be shipped in bulk, bolts, rolls, or other types of containers, depending on the type of product and whether it is prepackaged. General considerations include protection from contamination, weather, and pests. For textiles coated or impregnated with combustible substances, safety precautions should be taken to allow for ventilation and to prevent combustion. Containers should be constructed so as to be safe for handling during transport.

Publications Available

The following publications may be relevant to the importation of coated textiles:

Questions and Answers Relating to the Textile Fiber Products Identification Act and Regulations

Questions and Answers Relating to the Wool Products Labeling Act and Regulations

Available free of charge on request from the Federal Trade Commission, these publications are excellent sources of information written in clear lay language. We recommend that anyone interested in importing textile fiber products but unfamiliar with the regulations obtain a copy of each of these booklets.

The *Harmonized Tariff Schedule of the United States* (HTSUS) is available from:

Government Printing Office (GPO)
Superintendent of Documents
Washington, DC 20402
(202) 512-1800 (Order line)
(202) 512-0000 (General)

The USGPO also has copies of specific laws available for purchase. The USGPO accepts credit card orders over the phone, as well as mail orders paid by credit card, a check drawn on a U.S. bank, or an international money order.

Relevant Government Agencies

Address your questions regarding textile Multi-Fiber Arrangements to:

International Trade Administration
Office of Textile and Apparel
14th and Constitution Ave. NW, Rm. 3100
Washington, DC 20230
(202) 482-5078, 482-3737

Address your questions regarding requirements under the Textile Fiber Products Identification Act (TFPIA) or the Wool Products Labeling Act (WPLA)to:

Federal Trade Commission (FTC)
Division of Enforcement
601 Pennsylvania Ave. NW
Washington, DC 20580
(202) 326-2996 (General)
(202) 326-2841 (Textile and wool products labeling)

Address your questions regarding the Flammable Fabrics Act (FFA) to:

Consumer Product Safety Commission (CPSC)
5401 Westbard Avenue
Bethesda, MD 20207
(301) 492-6580

Address your questions regarding cordage and nonwoven fabric imports to the district or port director of Customs for you area. For addresses, refer to"U.S. Customs District Offices" on page 62 or contact:

U.S. Customs Service
1301 Constitution Ave. NW
Washington, DC 20229
(202) 927-6724 (Information)
(202) 927-1000 (General)

The following information numbers for U.S. Customs in Washington, DC, provide recorded information. The Quota Branch numbers listed by country provide updated status reports on textile quotas from those countries. All area codes are (202).
General information: 927-5850

Quota Branch: China 927-6703; India 927-6705; Indonesia 927-6704; Japan 927-6706; Korea 927-6707; Macao 927-6709; Malaysia 927-6712; Mexico 927-6711; Pakistan 927-6714; Philippines 927-6713; Romania 927-6715; Singapore 927-6716; Sri Lanka 927-6708; Taiwan 927-6719; Thailand 927-6717; Turkey 927-6718; All others 927-5850.

Laws and Regulations

The following laws and regulations may be relevant to the importation of cordage and nonwoven fabrics. The laws are contained in the United States Code (USC), and the regulations are published in the Code of Federal Regulations (CFR), both of which are available at larger public and law libraries. Copies of specific laws are also available from the United States Government Printing Office (address above).

7 USC 1854
Textile Trade Agreements
(EO 11651, as amended by EO 11951 and 12188, and supplemented by EO 12475)
This Act authorizes the CITA of the DOC to enter into Multi-Fiber Agreements with other countries to control trade in textiles and establishes the Textile Import Program, which is enforced by U.S. Customs.

19 CFR 12.130 et seq.
Regulations on Entry of Textiles
These regulations provide the requirements and procedures followed by Customs in enforcing limitations on the importation and entry and withdrawal of textiles and textile products from warehouses for consumption in the U.S.

15 USC 70-77
Textile Fiber Products Identification Act (TFPIA)
This Act prohibits false or deceptive labeling (misbranding) and false advertising of any textile fiber products and requires all textile fiber products imported into the U.S. to be labeled in accordance with the requirements set forth in the law.

19 CFR 11.12b; 16 CFR 303 et seq.
Regulations on Labeling and Marking
These regulations detail the labeling and marking requirements for textiles as specified by the CPSC and the invoice contents required by U.S. Customs for purpose of enforcing the labeling and marking rules.

15 USC 68-68j
Wool Products Labeling Act (WPLA)
This Act prohibits the false or deceptive labeling (misbranding) of wool products and requires all wool products imported into the U.S. to be labeled in accordance with requirements set forth in the law.

19 CFR 11.12; 16 CFR 300 et seq.
Regulations on WPLA Labeling and Marking
These regulations set forth the wool labeling and marking requirements adopted by the FTC to administer the requirements of the WPLA and provide the procedures followed by U.S. Customs in enforcing the WPLA and the FTC regulations, including entry invoice requirements.

15 USC 1191-1204
Flammable Fabrics Act (FFA)
This Act provides for the setting of flammability standards for fabric by the Consumer Product Safety Commission (CPSC) and for enforcement by U.S. Customs.

16 CFR 1610, 1611, 1615, 1616, 1630-1632
Regulations on Flammable Fabric Standards
These regulations specify the flammability standards adopted by the CPSC under the FFA for various types of textiles.

Principal Exporting Countries

The following listing includes samples of the main supplier nations of the products of this chapter. It is organized by HTSUS major heading. (Refer to "Customs Classification" above for the product codes.) Countries are listed in rank order of the value of products imported to the U.S. Statistics represent customs value entries for 1993 from the Bureau of Census, U.S. Department of Commerce.

5901—Netherlands, Russia, France, Belgium, Czech Rep., United Kingdom, Japan, Canada, Italy, Germany

5902—Canada, Japan, Luxembourg, Germany, United Kingdom, Belgium, France, Thailand, Austria, Netherlands

5903—Canada, Italy, Taiwan, Germany, Japan, South Korea, France, Thailand, Spain, United Kingdom

5904—Netherlands, United Kingdom, Germany, Italy, Sweden, Belgium, Canada, Singapore

5905—Belgium, Netherlands, Japan, Denmark, South Korea, Italy, Germany, Switzerland, United Kingdom, France

5906—Germany, Taiwan, Japan, United Kingdom, Canada, Austria, France, Italy, China, South Korea

5907—Canada, Germany, United Kingdom, Switzerland, Japan, Italy, Turkey, Spain, Taiwan, France

5908—United Kingdom, Japan, South Korea, Malta, Germany, Brazil, India, Israel, Chile, China

5909—Canada, Japan, Germany, United Kingdom, China, Denmark, Taiwan, Israel, Switzerland, Norway

5910—Germany, United Kingdom, Switzerland, Italy, Japan, Netherlands, Spain, Canada, South Africa, France

5911—Japan, Switzerland, Canada, Mexico, Germany, Italy, France, United Kingdom, Belgium, Finland

Chapter 60: Knitted or Crocheted Fabrics*

This chapter relates to the importation of knitted or crocheted fabrics, which are classified under Chapter 60 of the Harmonized Tariff Schedule of the United States (HTSUS). Specifically, it includes knitted or crocheted pile and terry fabrics, fabrics containing elastomeric yarn or rubber thread, and warp knit fabrics—such as open-work, circular, and double or interlock knitted fabrics. The term "knitted goods" includes stitch-bonded goods in which the chain stitches are formed of textile yarns.

If you are interested in importing sewing thread, yarns, and other fibers or filaments, you should refer to Commodity Index Chapters 50 through 55. For importing knitted apparel, review Chapter 61. The import requirements for particular articles made of knitted or crocheted fabrics are covered in the Commodity Index chapters related to that article. For example, knitted or crocheted headgear is in Chapter 65 and footwear is in Chapter 64. Fabrics that are impregnated, coated, or covered with substances or preparations—with the exception of knitted or crocheted pile fabrics—are classified in Chapter 59 or in the Commodity Index chapter that covers the particular substance or preparation. For example, items impregnated with perfumes and cosmetics are in Chapter 33, soaps, detergents, polishes, and creams are in Chapter 34, and fabric softeners are in Chapter 38. If your product has plastic or rubber components, it may come under Chapter 39 or 40, respectively. If you are interested in importing knitted or crocheted lace, labels, badges, and similar items, you should refer to Chapter 58.

Key Factors

The key factors in the importation of knitted or crocheted fabrics are:

- Compliance with quota restraints and visa requirements under U.S. Department of Commerce (DOC) Multi-Fiber Arrangements (if importing fabrics and other textile products)
- Submission of U.S. Customs Country-of-Origin Declaration(s)
- Compliance with entry invoice requirements
- Compliance with labeling requirements under Textile Fiber Products Identification Act (TFPIA)
- Compliance with flammability standards adopted and enforced by the Consumer Product Safety Commission (CPSC) under the Flammable Fabrics Act (FFA)

*IMPORTANT: Read the Commodity Index Introduction. It is the essential framework for understanding this chapter.

Although most importers use the services of a licensed customs broker in making their entries, and we recommend this practice, you should be aware of the regulatory, entry, and documentation issues involved in importing your product. You, as importer, are ultimately responsible for the fulfillment of any legal requirements applicable to your shipment.

General Considerations

Regulatory Agencies. The DOC's Committee for Implementation of Textile Agreements (CITA) regulates certain textile imports under Section 204 of the Agricultural Adjustment Act. U.S. Customs enforces CITA textile and textile product entry quotas. Customs also enforces compliance with labeling and invoice requirements of the TFPIA and flammability standards under the FFA. The CPSC monitors imports and from time to time inspects textile shipments for compliance with FFA standards. If you are importing wool textiles, importation is subject to complex textile import regulations. The Federal Trade Commission (FTC) administers the WPLA requirements.

Wool Product Entry Requirements. Depending on the nature of your wool fabric imports, as many as four different types of special entry documents may be required. First, for all imported textile fibers, yarns, and fabrics covered by the Agricultural Adjustment Act (AAA), including wool, you must file a U.S. Customs Textile Entry Declaration (see "Textile Country-of-Origin Declarations" below). Second, with each wool shipment's entry summary, you must file Customs **Form 6451**, Notice of Percentage of Clean Yield and Grade of Wool or Hair, in duplicate, showing your name and address. Third, for all wool products subject to the WPLA, special information is required on the entry invoices (see "Entry and Documentation" below). Finally, certain wool articles manufactured or produced in certain countries may be subject to quotas under U.S. Department of Commerce Multi-Fiber Arrangements. Such products require export certificates or visas issued by the appropriate country of origin, in addition to other requisite entry paperwork (see "Quotas" below).

Wool Products Labeling Act. The term "wool product" means any product or any portion of a product that contains, purports to contain, or in any way is represented as containing wool, reprocessed wool, or reused wool. All wool products imported into the U.S., except those made more than 20 years before importation, and except carpets, rugs, mats, and upholsteries, must have affixed a stamp, tag, label, or other means of identification as required by the WPLA. If you are importing wool products exempt from labeling under the WPLA, do not assume they are also exempt from labeling under the TFPIA. These are two distinct laws, with some overlapping requirements (see "Marking and Labeling Requirements" below).

Textile Quotas. If you are interested in importing knitted or crocheted fabrics, the most important issue you need to be aware of is quotas. Under the Multi-Fiber Arrangement provisions of Section 204 of the Agricultural Adjustment Act, CITA initiates specific agreements with individual exporting countries. Section 204 of the Agricultural Adjustment Act covers textiles that: 1) are in chief value of cotton, wool, or man-made fibers, any textile fibers subject to the terms of any textile trade agreement, or any combination of such fibers; 2) contain 50% or more by weight of cotton or man-made fibers, or any textile fibers subject to the terms of any textile trade agreement; 3) contain 17% or more by weight of wool; or 4) if in chief value of textile fibers or textile materials, contain a blend of cotton, wool, or man-made fibers, any textile fibers subject to the terms of any textile trade agreement, or any combination of such fibers that, in total, amount to 50% or more by weight of all component fibers.

The U.S. has Multi-Fiber Arrangements with 40 countries. Each agreement with each country is unique, and may specify quotas for a type of textile or a specific article. Visas or export licenses may be required. These agreements, however, often change. Therefore, if you are interested in importing any knitted or crocheted fabrics, you should contact the International Trade Administration's Office of Textile and Apparel (see addresses at end of this chapter). Refer to "Prohibitions and Restrictions" below for further details.

Textile Country-of-Origin Declarations. U.S. Customs enforces CITA textile and textile product entry quotas (see "Prohibitions and Restrictions" below). Requirements for entry include submission of Country-of-Origin Declarations with every knitted or crocheted fabric shipment, regardless of whether it is subject to a specific multi-fiber arrangement (19 CFR 12.130, 12.131).

Country of Origin. Quota restrictions are country-specific and therefore are applied based on the country of origin for the textiles shipped. The last country from which a textile shipment was exported to the U.S. is not necessarily its country of origin. A textile or textile product imported into the U.S. is considered a product of the particular foreign territory or country, or a U.S. insular possession, where it is wholly grown, produced, or manufactured. For the following discussion, "country" means a foreign territory or country, or a U.S. insular possession.

Substantial transformation rules may affect the country-of-origin determination. For example, if a textile or textile product originates in Country A and is subject to quota, the quota restrictions apply at entry into the U.S. But if, prior to export to the U.S., you move the shipment to Country B where there are fewer restrictions, the shipment may nevertheless remain subject to quota and visa requirements under the Multi-Fiber Arrangement with Country A. Customs determines whether the quota restrictions apply based on the criteria of "substantial transformation." If your textiles do not undergo any major processing or manufacturing while in Country B, or if the manufacturing or processing is minor, your shipment will be deemed to originate in Country A. *You cannot claim substantial transformation on the basis of minor manufacturing procedures.*

In contrast, if your shipment undergoes major processing or manufacturing while in Country B, rendering the textiles "new and different articles of commerce," Customs will treat the shipment as the product of Country B. To qualify as having undergone substantial transformation, an article must evince a change in: 1) commercial designation or identity; b) fundamental character; or c) commercial use. If your shipment is processed in more than one country, the country where it last underwent substantial transformation is the country of origin for Customs entry. In deciding whether the manufacturing or processing operation in a country is major, Customs considers the following factors: 1) the resultant physical change in the material or article; 2) the complexity, the level or degree of skill and/or technology required, and the amount of time involved in the operations; and 3) the value added to the article or material, compared to its value when imported into the U.S.

Validating Operations. Operations that Customs will usually acknowledge as validating a claim of substantial transformation are the following: 1) dyeing and printing, when accompanied by two or more of the following finishing operations: bleaching, shrinking, fulling, napping, decating, permanent stiffening, weighting, permanent embossing, or moireing; 2) spinning fibers into yarn; 3) weaving, knitting, or otherwise forming fabric; 4) cutting fabric into parts and assembling the parts into completed articles; or 5) substantial assembly, by sewing and/or tailoring into a completed garment cut pieces of apparel articles that have been cut from fabric in another country—e.g., complete assembly and tailoring of all cut pieces of suit-type jackets, suits, and shirts.

Insubstantial Operations. Operations that usually will not support a claim of substantial transformation, even if more than one are performed, are the following: 1) simple operations of combining, labeling, pressing, cleaning, dry cleaning, or packaging; 2) cutting to length or width and hemming or overlocking fabrics that are readily identifiable as being intended for a particular commercial use; 3) trimming and/or joining together by sewing, looping, linking, or other means of attaching otherwise completed knit-to-shape component parts produced in a single country, even if accompanied by other processes—e.g., washing, drying, mending—normally incident to assembly; 4) one or more finishing operations on yarns, fabrics, or their textile articles—such as showerproofing, superwashing, bleaching, decating, fulling, shrinking, mercerizing, or similar operations; or 5) dyeing and/or printing fabrics or yarns.

Declarations. The country of origin of the knitted or crocheted fabrics in a shipment must be stated on a declaration submitted to U.S. Customs at the time of entry. There are three Customs Country-of-Origin Declarations: single-country, multiple-country, and negative. The Declaration to be submitted with your shipment of knitted or crocheted fabrics depends on the nature of the import.

- **Single-country declarations** are used for entries of textiles or textile products that clearly originate from only one country or that have been assembled in one country from fabricated components wholly produced in the U.S. or the foreign country of manufacture. Information required includes: marks of identification and numbers; description of article and quantity; country of origin; and date of exportation.
- **Multiple-country declarations** are used for entries of textiles or textile products that were manufactured or processed and/or that incorporate materials originating in more than one foreign country or territory. Information required includes: marks of identification and numbers; for articles, description, quantity, identification of manufacturing and/or processing operations, country, and date of exportation; for materials used to make articles, description of materials, country of production, and date of exportation.
- **Negative declarations** must accompany all textile imports that are not subject to FFA Section 204 restrictions. Information required includes: marks of identification and numbers; descriptions of article and quantity; and country of origin.

The date of exportation to be indicated on the above declarations is the date on which the carrier leaves the last port in the country of origin, as determined by Customs. Diversion to another country during transit does not affect the export date.

Procedure for Declarations. The manufacturer, producer, exporter, or importer may prepare the declaration. If more than one of these parties is involved in the importation, each party may prepare a separate declaration. You may file a separate declaration for each invoice presented with your entry. The declaration must be dated and signed by the responsible party, and must include the person's title and the company name and address. Your shipment's entry will be denied unless it is accompanied by a properly executed declaration. Customs will not treat a textile declaration as a missing document for which a bond may be filed.

Customs will base its country-of-origin determination on the information contained in each declaration, unless the information is insufficient. If the information on the declaration is insufficient, Customs will require that you submit such additional information as will enable the determination to be made. The shipment will not be released until the determination is made. Thus, if you want to clear Customs with minimal delay, be sure that the information on the declarations is as complete as possible for each shipment.

Textile Labeling and Invoice Requirements. You are responsible for your imported knitted or crocheted fabric's compliance with applicable provisions of the TFPIA. Knitted or crocheted fabrics that require labeling under TFPIA must already be labeled at entry, or the shipment will be refused. (See "Marking and Labeling Requirements" below.) If you import shipments of special woven fabrics subject to TFPIA and valued at over $500, you must provide special information on the entry invoice (see "Entry and Documentation" below).

Flammability Standards. Knitted or crocheted fabrics imported into the U.S. for use in consumer products must be in compliance with the FFA, a federal law that gives the CPSC the authority and responsibility for protecting the public from the hazards of dangerously flammable items of wearing apparel and interior furnishings. Under the FFA, standards have been established for flammability of clothing textiles. You cannot import any article of wearing apparel or interior furnishing, or any fabric or related material that is intended for use or that may be used in such items, if it fails to conform to an applicable flammability standard (FFA Section 4). Certain products may be imported into the U.S. (FFA Section 11c) for finishing or processing to render them less flammable so as to meet the standards. For these products, the exporter must state on the invoice or other paper relating to the shipment that the shipment is being made for that purpose.

The CPSC monitors imports of textiles under its Import Surveillance Program. From time to time, your textile shipments may be inspected to ascertain compliance with mandatory safety standards. Shipments may also be subject to testing by the CPSC to determine compliance. If the CPSC believes a product, fabric, or related material does not comply with a flammability standard, it is authorized to pursue a variety of legal sanctions (see "Prohibitions and Restrictions" below).

Substantial Product Hazard Reports. Any firm that obtains information that reasonably supports the conclusion that one of its products presents an unreasonable risk of serious injury or death must report that information to the CPSC's Division of Corrective Actions (CPSC address below). Importers must also report to the CPSC if 1) a type of product is the subject of at least three civil actions filed in U.S. federal or state courts, 2) each suit alleges the involvement of that product type in death or grievous bodily injury (as defined in FFA Section 37(3)1), and 3) at least three of the actions result in a final settlement with the manufacturer or in a judgment for the plaintiff within any one of the two-year periods specified in FFA Section 37(b).

Import Advisory

Importation of textiles is trade-sensitive and highly regulated. Shipments of textiles and textile products not complying with all government regulations, including quotas and visas, are subject to seizure and could result in the imposition of penalties as well as possible forfeiture of the goods. You should always verify the available quota for any textile product you plan to import before your shipment leaves the country of manufacture. Furthermore, Customs textile classification rulings change frequently, and prior administrative rulings are often modified and sometimes reversed.

Customs Classification

For customs purposes, knitted or crocheted fabrics are classified under Chapter 60 of the HTSUS. This chapter is broken into major headings, which are further divided into subheadings, and often sub-subheadings, each of which has its own HTSUS classification number. For example, the HTSUS number for long pile fabrics of man-made fibers is 6001.10.20, indicating it is a sub-subcategory of long-pile fabrics (6001.10.00), which is a subcategory of the major heading pile fabrics, etc. (6001.00.00). There are two major headings within Chapter 60.

6001—Pile fabrics, including "long pile" fabrics and terry fabrics, knitted or crocheted

6002—Other knitted or crocheted fabrics

For more details regarding classifications of the specific product you are interested in importing, consult a customs broker, the appropriate commodity specialist at your nearest customs port, or the HTSUS. HTSUS is available for purchase from the U.S. Government Printing Office (see addresses at end of this chapter), and may be found in larger public libraries. Refer to "Classification—Liquidation" on page 207 for a general discussion of customs classification.

Sample Import Duties

Import duties will vary depending on the HTSUS classification of your product. Therefore, to determine the correct amount of duties, your product must be properly classified under the HTSUS. The following sample duties are taken from the duty listings for HTSUS Chapter 60 products.

Long pile fabrics of man-made fibers (6001.10.20): 19.5%; looped pile fabrics of cotton (6001.21.00): 11.1%; open-work fabrics, warp knit, of a width not exceeding 30 cm (6002.20.10): 16%; warp knit fabrics of wool or fine animal hair (6002.41.00): 19%; of cotton (6002.42.00): 14%; of manmade fibers (6002.43.00): 14%.

Entry and Documentation

The entry of merchandise is a two-part process consisting of 1) filing the documentation necessary to determine whether merchandise may be released from Customs custody, and 2) filing the documents that contain information for duty assessment and statistical purposes. In certain instances, all documents must be filed and accepted by Customs prior to release of the goods. Unless you have been granted an extension, you must file entry documents at a location specified by the district or area director within five working days of your shipment's date of arrival at a U.S. port of entry. These include a number of standard documents required by Customs for any entry, and:

- U.S. Customs Country-of-Origin Declaration(s)
- Export documentation and/or visa for textiles subject to Multi-Fiber Arrangement
- Customs **Form 6451**, Notice of Percentage of Clean Yield and Grade of Wool or Hair, in duplicate, showing your name and address (if importing articles containing wool)

After you present the entry, Customs may examine your shipment or may waive examination. The shipment is then released provided no legal or regulatory violations have been noted. You must then file entry summary documentation and deposit estimated duties at a designated customhouse within 10 working days of your shipment's release. For a detailed description of entry procedures, standard documentation, and informal entry, refer to "Entry Process" on page 182.

NAFTA Certificates of Origin. An importer of textiles for which NAFTA treatment is sought need not file a separate NAFTA Certificate of Origin in addition to the Customs Country-of-Origin Declaration. The declaration is sufficient. However, the importer must take care to submit a declaration from each U.S., Canadian, or Mexican producer or manufacturer. Thus, for multiple producers or manufacturers, a separate declaration must be filed for each. If a Customs district director cannot determine the country of origin because the declaration is absent or incomplete, the shipment is not entitled to preferential NAFTA tariff treatment or other NAFTA benefits. See 12 CFR 132.

Entry Invoice TFPIA Requirements. For the purpose of TFPIA enforcement, a commercial shipment of textile products exceeding $500 in value and subject to TFPIA labeling requirements must show the following information: 1) the constituent fiber or combination of fibers, designating with equal prominence each natural or manufactured fiber by its generic name, in order of predominance by weight if the weight of such fiber is 5% or more of the total fiber weight of the product; 2) percentage of each fiber present, by weight, in the total fiber content; 3) the name or other identification issued and registered by the Federal Trade Commission of the manufacturer of the product or one or more persons subject to Section 3 of the TFPIA with respect to such product; 4) the name of the country where processed or manufactured.

Wool Products Subject to WPLA. When you offer for entry a wool product shipment valued at over $500 and subject to WPLA, you must include certain information intended to facilitate Customs monitoring and enforcement of that Act. This extra information is identical to that required by WPLA on labeling (see "Marking and Labeling Requirements" below), with the addition of the manufacturer's name. If your product consists of mixed waste, residues, and similar merchandise obtained from several suppliers or unknown sources, you may omit the manufacturer's name from the entry invoice.

Prohibitions and Restrictions

Textile Quotas. Textile import restrictions are primarily a matter of quotas and the way in which these quotas are administered and monitored. Under the Multi-Fiber Arrangement provisions of Section 204 of the Agricultural Adjustment Act, CITA has negotiated Multi-Fiber Arrangements with 40 countries. These Agreements may impose quotas for a type of textile or a specific article, and they are country-specific. The agreements, however, often change. Therefore, if you are interested in importing any knitted or crocheted fabrics, you should contact the International Trade Administration's Office of Textile and Apparel (see addresses at end of this chapter). The Office of Textile and Apparel has a team of country specialists who can inform you of the latest developments and inform you about a product's quota or restriction status.

U.S. Customs enforces CITA textile and textile product entry quotas. If formal entry procedures are not followed, Customs will usually refuse entry for textiles that are subject to Section 204. Formal entry requires submission of a Country-of-Origin Declaration (see General Considerations above). U.S. Customs maintains a current textile quota status report, available for perusal at any Customs port. In addition, U.S. Customs in Washington, DC, operates a telephone service to provide quota status reports, which are updated weekly (see "Relevant Government Agencies" below).

Flammable Fabrics. U.S. Customs may refuse entry for any article of wearing apparel or interior furnishing, or any fabric or related material that is intended for use or that may be used in wearing apparel or interior furnishings, if it fails to conform to an applicable flammability standard issued under Section 4 of the FFA. An exception is allowed for certain products (FFA Section 11c) that are imported for finishing or processing to bring them within the legal standard. For these products, the exporter must state on the invoice or other paper relating to the shipment that the shipment is being made for that purpose.

The CPSC, as the primary enforcement agency of flammability standards, inspects products for compliance with the FFA. If the CPSC believes a product, fabric, or related material does not comply with a flammability standard, it is authorized to pursue a variety of legal sanctions, including: 1) seizure, condemnation, and forfeiture of the noncomplying products; 2) administrative cease-and-desist order requiring an individual or firm to stop sale and distribution of the noncomplying products or; 3) temporary injunction requiring the individual or firm to stop sale and distribution of the noncomplying products, pending final disposition of an administrative cease-and-desist proceeding. The CPSC also has authority to seek civil penalties against any person who knowingly violates a regulation or standard issued under Section 4 of the FFA.

Country-Specific Restrictions

Restrictions under Multi-Fiber Arrangements are country-specific. A product originating in one country may be subject to quota and to export license or visa requirements, while the same product originating in a different country may not. At present, the U.S. has Multi-Fiber Arrangements with 40 countries. Many different categories of products are covered under these Arrangements; it is beyond the scope of this book to list each country and its restricted commodities. If you are interested in importing textiles and textile products, you should contact the International Trade Administration's Office of Textile and Apparel (see addresses at end of this chapter) or U.S. Customs to ascertain your product's restraint status.

The U.S. Customs Quota Branch phone numbers provide recorded status reports, by quota category number, for current charges against the quotas for that country. For convenience, the HTSUS shows the 3-digit category number in parentheses to the right of each listed commodity that is subject to textile restraints. For example, under Chapter 60, heading 6001.21.00, looped pile fabrics of cotton, is followed by the number "(224)." If you know the category number for your product, you can find out to what extent that quota is filled simply by calling the number for the appropriate country. A word of caution, though: if you do not know for sure that your article is subject to quota from a particular country, and you call the number for that country, you may not be any more enlightened after the phone call. Many of the recordings give status reports only when a certain percentage of the quota has been filled. Thus, if 224 for Indonesia is among the categories for which not enough quantity has entered the U.S. to warrant specific mention, it will be lumped under "all other categories" and you will be none the wiser. To find out if your product is subject to textile restraints, call the DOC or a local Customs port office. Then you can find out the current charges against that quota by calling the country number listed below. For a complete listing of Customs Quota Branch information numbers, see "Relevant Government Agencies" below.

Marking and Labeling Requirements

TFPIA Requirements. All textile fiber products imported into the U.S. must be stamped, tagged, labeled, or otherwise marked with the following information as required by the TFPIA, unless exempt from marking (see TFPIA, Section 12): 1) the generic names and percentages by weight of the constituent fibers present in the textile fiber product, exclusive of permissible ornamentation, in amounts of more than 5% in order of predominance by weight, with any percentage of fiber or fibers required to be designated as "other fiber" or "other fibers" (including those present in amounts of 5% or less) appearing last; and 2) the name of the manufacturer or the name or registered identification number issued by the FTC of one or more persons marketing or handling the textile fiber product; and 3) the name of the country where processed. A word trademark, used as a house mark and registered with the U.S. Patent Office, may appear on labels instead of the name otherwise required, provided the owner of the trademark furnishes a copy of the registration to the FTC prior to use (see "Registered Identification Numbers" below).

The information listed above is not exhaustive. TFPIA requirements are extensive. The Act specifies such details as types of labels, means of attachment, label position on the article, package labeling, unit labeling for two-piece garments, and arrangement of information on the label; allowable fiber designations; country-of-origin indications; requirements for trim and ornamentation, linings and interlinings, and pile fabrics; sectional disclosure; use of trade names and trademarks; and requirements for swatches and samples. The Federal Trade Commission publishes a booklet intended to clarify TFPIA requirements to facilitate voluntary compliance in the industry (see "Publications Available" below). It is available on request, at no charge, from the FTC (see addresses at end of this chapter).

Wool Products Labeling Act (WPLA). Wool product labeling requirements for foreign products are the responsibility of the importer. The WPLA requires the following information to appear on wool products subject to the Act: 1) percentage of the wool product's total fiber weight (exclusive of ornamentation) not exceeding 5% of the total fiber weight of a) wool, b) recycled wool, c) each fiber other than wool if the percent by weight of such fiber is 5% or more, and d) the aggregate of all other fibers; 2) the maximum percent of the wool product's total weight, of any nonfibrous loading, filling, or adulterating matter; and 3) the importer's name. If you, as importer, have a registered identification number issued by the FTC, that number may be used instead of your name (see "Registered Identification Numbers" below).

Customs entry is contingent on proper labeling. If your shipment is found to be mislabeled at entry, you will be given the option of relabeling the products under Customs supervision, as long as the district director is satisfied that your labeling error or omission did not involve fraud or willful neglect. If your shipment is discovered after entry to have been noncomplying with WPLA, it will be recalled to Customs custody at your expense, unless you can satisfy the district director that the products have since been brought into compliance. You will be held responsible for all expenses incurred in bringing a shipment into compliance, including compensation of personnel and other expenses related to Customs supervision.

Fraudulent violations of WPLA will result in seizure of the shipment. Shipments already released from Customs custody will be ordered to be redelivered to Customs. Customs reports all cases of fraudulent violation to the FTC in Washington, DC.

The information listed above is not intended to be exhaustive. WPLA requirements are extensive. The Act specifies such details as types of labels, means of attachment, label position on the article, package labeling, unit labeling (as in the case of a two-piece garment), arrangement of information on the label, allowable fiber designations, country-of-origin indications, trim and ornamentation, pile fabrics, sectional disclosure, use of trade names and trademarks, requirements for swatches and samples, etc. The FTC publishes a booklet intended to clarify WPLA requirements in order to facilitate voluntary compliance within the industry (see "Publications Available" below). It is available on request, at no charge, from the FTC (see addresses at end of this chapter).

Registered Identification Numbers. Any domestic firm or person residing in the U.S. and engaged in the manufacture or marketing of textile products covered under the TFPIA may obtain an FTC-registered identification number for use on required tags and labels instead of the name of a firm or person. For applications, contact the FTC (see addresses at end of this chapter).

For a general discussion of U.S. Customs marking and labeling requirements, refer to "Marking: Country of Origin" on page 215 and "Special Marking Requirements" on page 217.

Shipping Considerations

You will need to ensure that your goods are packaged and shipped with care so that they pass smoothly through Customs and arrive in good condition. You are responsible for ensuring that the shipment is in compliance with all applicable government regulations for packaging and shipping. In most instances, you should not leave these arrangements solely to the discretion of your supplier. Careful preparation of the cargo and selection of the mode of transport can be essential to a cost-effective, timely delivery of undamaged goods. We strongly advise you to consult your shipping representative, insurance agent, or freight broker for advice on packing and shipping. Refer also to the major tab section "Packing/Shipping/Insurance" for a general discussion of packing and shipping.

Knitted or crocheted fabrics may be shipped in bulk, bolts, rolls, or other types of containers, depending on the type of product and whether it is prepackaged. General considerations include protection from contamination, weather, and pests. Safety precautions should also be implemented as required to protect against breakage, spillage, corrosion of containers, and combustion. Containers should be constructed so as to be safe for handling during transport.

Publications Available

The following publications may be relevant to the importation of knitted or crocheted fabrics and wool fabrics:

Questions and Answers Relating to the Textile Fiber Products Identification Act and Regulations

Questions and Answers Relating to the Wool Products Labeling Act and Regulations

Available free of charge on request from the Federal Trade Commission, these publications are excellent sources of information written in clear lay language. We recommend that anyone interested in importing textile fiber products but unfamiliar with the regulations obtain a copy of these booklets.

The *Harmonized Tariff Schedule of the United States* (HTSUS) is available from:

Government Printing Office (GPO)
Superintendent of Documents
Washington, DC 20402
(202) 512-1800 (Order line)
(202) 512-0000 (General)

The USGPO also has copies of specific laws available for purchase. The USGPO accepts credit card orders over the phone, as well as mail orders paid by credit card, a check drawn on a U.S. bank, or an international money order.

Relevant Government Agencies

Address your questions regarding textile Multi-Fiber Arrangements to:

International Trade Administration
Office of Textile and Apparel
14th and Constitution Ave. NW, Rm. 3100
Washington, DC 20230
(202) 482-5078, 482-3737

Address your questions regarding the Flammable Fabrics Act (FFA) to:

Consumer Product Safety Commission (CPSC)
5401 Westbard Avenue
Bethesda, MD 20207
(301) 492-6580

Address your questions regarding labeling requirements under the Textile Fiber Products Identification Act (TFPIA) or the Wool Products Labeling Act (WPLA) to:

Federal Trade Commission (FTC)
Division of Enforcement

601 Pennsylvania Ave. NW
Washington, DC 20580
(202) 326-2996 (General)
(202) 326-2841 (Textile and wool products labeling)

Address your questions regarding knitted or crocheted fabric imports to the district or port director of Customs for you area. For addresses, refer to"U.S. Customs District Offices" on page 62 or contact:

U.S. Customs Service
1301 Constitution Ave. NW
Washington, DC 20229
(202) 927-6724 (Information)
(202) 927-1000 (General)

The following information numbers for U.S. Customs in Washington, DC, provide recorded information. The Quota Branch numbers listed by country provide updated status reports on textile quotas from those countries. All area codes are (202).
General information: 927-5850

Quota Branch: China 927-6703; India 927-6705; Indonesia 927-6704; Japan 927-6706; Korea 927-6707; Macao 927-6709; Malaysia 927-6712; Mexico 927-6711; Pakistan 927-6714; Philippines 927-6713; Romania 927-6715; Singapore 927-6716; Sri Lanka 927-6708; Taiwan 927-6719; Thailand 927-6717; Turkey 927-6718; All others 927-5850.

Laws and Regulations

The following laws and regulations may be relevant to the importation of knitted or crocheted fabrics. The laws are contained in the United States Code (USC), and the regulations are published in the Code of Federal Regulations (CFR), both of which are available at larger public and law libraries. Copies of specific laws are also available from the United States Government Printing Office (address above).

7 USC 1854
Textile Trade Agreements
(EO 11651, as amended by EO 11951 and 12188, and supplemented by EO 12475)
This Act authorizes the CITA of the DOC to enter into Multi-Fiber Agreements with other countries to control trade in textiles and establishes the Textile Import Program, which is enforced by U.S. Customs.

19 CFR 12.130 et seq.
Regulations on Entry of Textiles
These regulations provide the requirements and procedures followed by Customs in enforcing limitations on the importation and entry and withdrawal of textiles and textile products from warehouses for consumption in the U.S.

15 USC 70-77
Textile Fiber Products Identification Act (TFPIA)
This Act prohibits false or deceptive labeling (misbranding) and false advertising of any textile fiber products and requires all textile fiber products imported into the U.S. to be labeled in accordance with the requirements set forth in the law.

19 CFR 11.12b; 16 CFR 303 et seq.
Regulations on Labeling and Marking
These regulations detail the labeling and marking requirements for textiles as specified by the CPSC and the invoice contents required by U.S. Customs for purpose of enforcing the labeling and marking rules.

15 USC 68-68j
Wool Products Labeling Act (WPLA)
This Act prohibits the false or deceptive labeling (misbranding) of wool products and requires all wool products imported into the U.S. to be labeled in accordance with requirements set forth in the law.

19 CFR 11.12; 16 CFR 300 et seq.
Regulations on WPLA Labeling and Marking
These regulations set forth the wool labeling and marking requirements adopted by the FTC to administer the requirements of the WPLA and provide the procedures followed by U.S. Customs in enforcing the WPLA and the FTC regulations, including entry invoice requirements.

15 USC 1191-1204
Flammable Fabrics Act (FFA)
This Act provides for the setting of flammability standards for fabric by the Consumer Product Safety Commission (CPSC) and for enforcement by U.S. Customs.

16 CFR 1610, 1611, 1615, 1616, 1630-1632
Regulations on Flammable Fabric Standards
These regulations specify the flammability standards adopted by the CPSC under the FFA for various types of textiles.

Principal Exporting Countries

The following listing includes samples of the main supplier nations of the products of this chapter. It is organized by HTSUS major heading. (Refer to "Customs Classification" above for the product codes.) Countries are listed in rank order of the value of products imported to the U.S. Statistics represent customs value entries for 1993 from the Bureau of Census, U.S. Department of Commerce.

6001—Taiwan, South Korea, China, Canada, Germany, Hong Kong, United Kingdom, Japan, Italy, France

6002—Taiwan, Canada, Hong Kong, Pakistan, South Korea, Germany, Italy, Israel, Guatemala, Japan

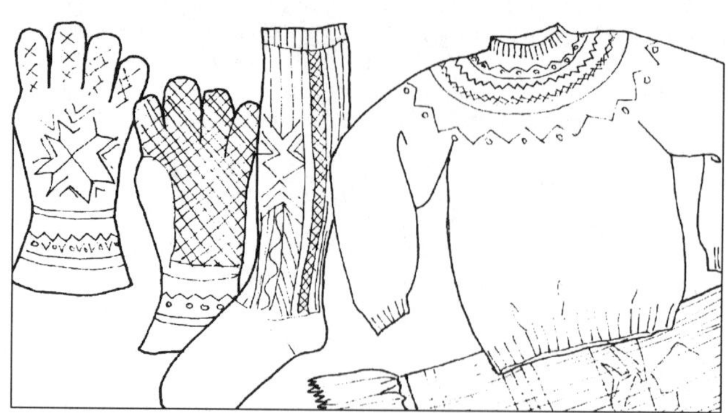

Chapter 61: Knitted or Crocheted Articles*

Full title: Articles of Apparel and Clothing Accessories, Knitted or Crocheted

This chapter relates to the importation of knitted or crocheted articles, which are classified under Chapter 61 of the Harmonized Tariff Schedule of the United States (HTSUS). Specifically, it covers knitted or crocheted garments for adults and children, including coats and jackets; suits, blazers, trousers, overalls, shorts, dresses, skirts, shirts, and blouses; undergarments and night clothes; t-shirts, tank tops, and singlets; sweaters, sweatshirts, and vests; track suits, ski suits, and swimwear; stockings and hosiery; footwear without applied soles; gloves, mittens, and mitts; and shawls, scarves, and similar clothing accessories.

If you are interested in importing articles of apparel that are not knitted or crocheted, you should read Commodity Index Chapter 62. Worn articles of apparel are covered in Chapter 63, and surgical belts and orthopedic items are classified in Chapter 90. If you are interested in importing footwear or headgear, you should refer to Chapter 64 or 65, respectively. Textiles, garment parts, thread, yarns, and other similar materials are covered in Chapters 50 through 58. Articles of apparel that contain leather parts may be imported in accordance with the requirements explained in Chapter 42.

Key Factors

The key factors in the importation of knitted or crocheted articles are:

- Compliance with quota restraints and visa requirements under U.S. Department of Commerce (DOC) Multi-Fiber Arrangements
- Submission of U.S. Customs Country-of-Origin Declaration(s)
- Compliance with entry invoice requirements
- Compliance with labeling requirements under the Textile Fiber Products Identification Act (TFPIA) and the Wool Products Labeling Act (WPLA)
- Compliance with flammability standards adopted and enforced by the Consumer Product Safety Commission (CPSC) under the Flammable Fabrics Act (FFA)
- Compliance with export licence requirements (if importing made-to-measure suits from Hong Kong)
- Compliance with Special Access or Regime entry requirements (if importing garments assembled and bleached, dyed, or perma-pressed abroad from components formed and cut in the US)

Although most importers use the services of a licensed customs broker in making their entries, and we recommend this practice, you should be aware of the regulatory, entry, and documentation issues involved in importing your product. You, as importer, are ultimately responsible for the fulfillment of any legal requirements applicable to your shipment.

General Considerations

Regulatory Agencies. The DOC's Committee for Implementation of Textile Agreements (CITA) regulates certain textile imports under Section 204 of the Agricultural Adjustment Act. U.S. Customs enforces CITA textile and textile product entry quotas. Customs also enforces compliance with labeling and invoice requirements of the TFPIA and flammability standards under the FFA. The CPSC monitors imports and from time to time inspects textile shipments for compliance with FFA standards. If you are importing wool textiles, importation is subject to complex textile import regulations. The Federal Trade Commission (FTC) administers the WPLA requirements.

Wool Product Entry Requirements. Depending on the nature of your wool article imports, as many as four different types of special entry documents may be required. First, for all imported articles that contain textile fibers, yarns, and fabrics covered by the Agricultural Adjustment Act (AAA), including wool, you must file a U.S. Customs Textile Entry Declaration (see "Textile Country-of-Origin Declarations" below). Second, with the entry summary for each shipment of wool articles, you must file Customs **Form 6451,** Notice of Percentage of Clean Yield and Grade of Wool or Hair, in duplicate, showing your name and address. Third, for all wool products subject to the WPLA, special information is required on the entry invoices (see "Wool Products Labeling Act" below). Finally, certain articles of apparel manufactured or produced in certain countries may be subject to quotas and other restraints under U.S. DOC Multi-Fiber Arrangements. Such products require export licenses, certificates, or visas issued by the appropriate country of origin, in addition to other requisite entry paperwork (see "Textile Quotas" below).

Wool Products Labeling Act. The term "wool product" means any product or any portion of a product that contains, purports to contain, or in any way is represented as containing wool, reprocessed wool, or reused wool. All wool products imported into the U.S., except those made more than 20 years before importation, and except carpets, rugs, mats, and upholsteries, must have affixed a stamp, tag, label, or other means of identification as required by the WPLA. If you are importing wool products exempt from labeling under the WPLA, do not assume they are also exempt from labeling under the TFPIA. These are two distinct laws, with some overlapping requirements (see "Marking and Labeling Requirements" below).

Textile Quotas. If you are interested in importing knitted or crocheted articles, the most important issue you need to be aware of is quotas. Under the Multi-Fiber Arrangement provisions of Section 204 of the Agricultural Adjustment Act, CITA initiates specific agreements with individual exporting countries. Section 204 of the Agricultural Adjustment Act covers textiles articles that: 1) are in chief value of cotton, wool, or man-made fibers, any textile fibers subject to the terms of any textile trade agreement, or any combination of such fibers; 2) contain 50% or more by weight of cotton or man-made fibers, or any textile fibers subject to the terms of any textile trade agreement; 3) contain 17% or more by weight of wool; or 4) if in chief value of textile fibers or textile materials, contain a blend of cotton, wool, or man-made fibers, any textile fibers subject to the terms of any textile trade agree-

*IMPORTANT: Read the Commodity Index Introduction. It is the essential framework for understanding this chapter.

ment, or any combination of such fibers that, in total, amount to 50% or more by weight of all component fibers.

The U.S. has Multi-Fiber Arrangements with 40 countries. Each agreement with each country is unique, and may specify quotas for a type of textile or a specific article. Visas or export licenses may be required. These agreements, however, often change. Therefore, if you are interested in importing any knitted or crocheted articles of apparel, you should contact the International Trade Administration's Office of Textile and Apparel (see addresses at end of this chapter). Refer to "Prohibitions and Restrictions" below for further details.

Textile Country-of-Origin Declarations. U.S. Customs enforces CITA textile and textile product entry quotas (see "Prohibitions and Restrictions" below). Requirements for entry include submission of Country-of-Origin Declarations with every shipment of knitted or crocheted apparel articles, regardless of whether it is subject to a specific multi-fiber arrangement (19 CFR 12.130, 12.131).

Country of Origin. Quota restrictions are country-specific and therefore are applied based on the country of origin for the textiles shipped. The last country from which a textile shipment was exported to the U.S. is not necessarily its country of origin. A textile or textile product imported into the U.S. is considered a product of the particular foreign territory or country, or a U.S. insular possession, where it is wholly grown, produced, or manufactured. For the following discussion, "country" means a foreign territory or country, or a U.S. insular possession.

Substantial transformation rules may affect the country-of-origin determination. For example, if a textile or textile product originates in Country A and is subject to quota, the quota restrictions apply at entry into the U.S. But if, prior to export to the U.S., you move the shipment to Country B where there are fewer restrictions, the shipment may nevertheless remain subject to quota and visa requirements under the Multi-Fiber Arrangement with Country A. Customs determines whether the quota restrictions apply based on the criteria of "substantial transformation." If your textiles do not undergo any major processing or manufacturing while in Country B, or if the manufacturing or processing is minor, your shipment will be deemed to originate in Country A. *You cannot claim substantial transformation on the basis of minor manufacturing procedures.*

In contrast, if your shipment undergoes major processing or manufacturing while in Country B, rendering the textiles "new and different articles of commerce," Customs will treat the shipment as the product of Country B. To qualify as having undergone substantial transformation, an article must evince a change in: 1) commercial designation or identity; b) fundamental character; or c) commercial use. If your shipment is processed in more than one country, the country where it last underwent substantial transformation is the country of origin for Customs entry. In deciding whether the manufacturing or processing operation in a country is major, Customs considers the following factors: 1) the resultant physical change in the material or article; 2) the complexity, the level or degree of skill and/or technology required, and the amount of time involved in the operations; and 3) the value added to the article or material, compared to its value when imported into the U.S.

Validating Operations. Operations that Customs will usually acknowledge as validating a claim of substantial transformation are the following: 1) dyeing and printing, when accompanied by two or more of the following finishing operations: bleaching, shrinking, fulling, napping, decating, permanent stiffening, weighting, permanent embossing, or moireing; 2) spinning fibers into yarn; 3) weaving, knitting, or otherwise forming fabric; 4) cutting fabric into parts and assembling the parts into completed articles; or 5) substantial assembly, by sewing and/or tailoring into a completed garment cut pieces of apparel articles that have been cut from fabric in another country—e.g., complete assembly and tailoring of all cut pieces of suit-type jackets, suits, and shirts.

Insubstantial Operations. Operations that usually will not support a claim of substantial transformation, even if more than one are performed, are the following: 1) simple operations of combining, labeling, pressing, cleaning, dry cleaning, or packaging; 2) cutting to length or width and hemming or overlocking fabrics that are readily identifiable as being intended for a particular commercial use; 3) trimming and/or joining together by sewing, looping, linking, or other means of attaching otherwise completed knit-to-shape component parts produced in a single country, even if accompanied by other processes—e.g., washing, drying, mending—normally incident to assembly; 4) one or more finishing operations on yarns, fabrics, or their textile articles—such as showerproofing, superwashing, bleaching, decating, fulling, shrinking, mercerizing, or similar operations; or 5) dyeing and/ or printing fabrics or yarns.

Declarations. The country of origin of the knitted or crocheted apparel articles in a shipment must be stated on a declaration submitted to U.S. Customs at the time of entry. There are three Customs Country-of-Origin Declarations: single-country, multiple-country, and negative. The Declaration to be submitted with your shipment of knitted or crocheted apparel articles depends on the nature of the import.

- **Single-country declarations** are used for entries of textiles or textile products that clearly originate from only one country or that have been assembled in one country from fabricated components wholly produced in the U.S. or the foreign country of manufacture. Information required includes: marks of identification and numbers; description of article and quantity; country of origin; and date of exportation.
- **Multiple-country declarations** are used for entries of textiles or textile products that were manufactured or processed and/or that incorporate materials originating in more than one foreign country or territory. Information required includes: marks of identification and numbers; for articles, description, quantity, identification of manufacturing and/or processing operations, country, and date of exportation; for materials used to make articles, description of materials, country of production, and date of exportation.
- **Negative declarations** must accompany all textile imports that are not subject to FFA Section 204 restrictions. Information required includes: marks of identification and numbers; descriptions of article and quantity; and country of origin.

The date of exportation to be indicated on the above declarations is the date on which the carrier leaves the last port in the country of origin, as determined by Customs. Diversion to another country during transit does not affect the export date.

Procedure for Declarations. The manufacturer, producer, exporter, or importer may prepare the declaration. If more than one of these parties is involved in the importation, each party may prepare a separate declaration. You may file a separate declaration for each invoice presented with your entry. The declaration must be dated and signed by the responsible party, and must include the person's title and the company name and address. Your shipment's entry will be denied unless it is accompanied by a properly executed declaration. Customs will not treat a textile declaration as a missing document for which a bond may be filed.

Customs will base its country-of-origin determination on the information contained in each declaration, unless the information is insufficient. If the information on the declaration is insufficient, Customs will require that you submit such additional information as will enable the determination to be made. The shipment will not be released until the determination is made. Thus, if you want to clear Customs with minimal delay, be sure that the information on the declarations is as complete as possible for each shipment.

Textile Labeling and Invoice Requirements. You are responsible for your imported product's compliance with applicable provisions of the TFPIA. Knitted or crocheted apparel articles that require labeling under TFPIA must already be labeled at entry, or the shipment will be refused. (See "Marking and Labeling Requirements" below.) If you import shipments of knitted or crocheted articles subject to TFPIA and valued at over $500, you must provide special information on the entry invoice (see "Entry and Documentation" below).

Flammability Standards. Knitted or crocheted apparel articles imported into the U.S. for use in consumer products must be in compliance with the FFA, a federal law that gives the CPSC the authority and responsibility for protecting the public from the hazards of dangerously flammable items of wearing apparel and interior furnishings. Under the FFA, standards have been established for flammability of clothing textiles. You cannot import any article of wearing apparel or interior furnishing, or any fabric or related material that is intended for use or that may be used in such items, if it fails to conform to an applicable flammability standard (FFA Section 4). Certain products may be imported into the U.S. (FFA Section 11c) for finishing or processing to render them less flammable so as to meet the standards. For these products, the exporter must state on the invoice or other paper relating to the shipment that the shipment is being made for that purpose.

The CPSC monitors imports of textiles under its Import Surveillance Program. From time to time, your textile shipments may be inspected to ascertain compliance with mandatory safety standards. Shipments may also be subject to testing by the CPSC to determine compliance. If the CPSC believes a product, fabric, or related material does not comply with a flammability standard, it is authorized to pursue a variety of legal sanctions (see "Prohibitions and Restrictions" below).

Substantial Product Hazard Reports. Any firm that obtains information that reasonably supports the conclusion that one of its products presents an unreasonable risk of serious injury or death must report that information to the CPSC's Division of Corrective Actions (CPSC address below). Importers must also report to the CPSC if 1) a type of product is the subject of at least three civil actions filed in U.S. federal or state courts, 2) each suit alleges the involvement of that product type in death or grievous bodily injury (as defined in FFA Section 37(3)1), and 3) at least three of the actions result in a final settlement with the manufacturer or in a judgment for the plaintiff within any one of the two-year periods specified in FFA Section 37(b).

Import Advisory

Importation of textile products is trade-sensitive and highly regulated. Shipments of textile products not complying with all government regulations, including quotas and visas, are subject to seizure and could result in the imposition of penalties as well as possible forfeiture of the goods. You should always verify the available quota for any textile product you plan to import before your shipment leaves the country of manufacture. Furthermore, Customs textile classification rulings change frequently, and prior administrative rulings are often modified and sometimes reversed.

Customs Classification

For customs purposes, knitted or crocheted articles are classified under Chapter 61 of the HTSUS. This chapter is broken into major headings, which are further divided into subheadings, and often sub-subheadings, each of which has its own HTSUS classification number. For example, the HTSUS number for men's wool trousers, breeches, and shorts is 6103.41.10, indicating it is a sub-subcategory of trousers, etc., of wool or fine animal hair (6103.41.00), which is a subcategory of the major heading men's and boys' suits, ensembles, etc. (6103.00.00). There are 17 major headings within Chapter 61.

6101—Men's or boys' overcoats, carcoats, capes, cloaks, anoraks (including ski-jackets), windbreakers, and similar articles, knitted or crocheted, other than those of heading 6103

6102—Women's or girls' overcoats, carcoats, capes cloaks, anoraks (including ski-jackets), windbreakers, and similar articles, knitted or crocheted, other than those of heading 6104

6103—Men's or boys' suits, ensembles, suit-type jackets, blazers, trousers, bib and brace overalls

6104—Women's or girl's suits, ensembles, suit-type jackets, blazers, dresses, skirts, divided skirts, trousers, bib and brace overalls, breeches and shorts (other than swimwear), knitted or crocheted

6105—Men's or boys' shirts, knitted or crocheted

6106—Women's or girls' blouses and shirts, knitted or crocheted

6107—Men's or boys' underpants, briefs, nightshirts, pajamas, bathrobes, dressing gowns, and similar articles, knitted or crocheted

6108—Women's or girls' slips, petticoats, briefs, panties, nightdresses, pajamas, negligees, bathrobes, dressing gowns, and similar articles, knitted or crocheted

6109—T-shirts, singlets, tank tops, and similar garments, knitted or crocheted

6110—Sweaters, pullovers, sweatshirts, waistcoats (vests), and similar articles, knitted or crocheted

6111—Babies' garments and clothing accessories, knitted or crocheted

6112—Track suits, ski suits, and swimwear, knitted or crocheted

6113—Garments, made up of knitted or crocheted fabrics of heading 5903, 5906, or 5907

6114—Other garments, knitted or crocheted

6115—Panty hose, tights, stockings, socks, and other hosiery, including stockings for varicose veins, and footwear without applied soles, knitted or crocheted

6116—Gloves, mittens and mitts, knitted or crocheted

6117—Other made up clothing accessories, knitted or crocheted; knitted or crocheted parts of garments or of clothing accessories

Definitions. For duty purposes, Customs defines suits, ensembles, and ski suits as follows.

Suits. The term "suit" means a set of garments composed of two or three pieces made up in identical fabric and comprising: 1) one garment designed to cover the lower part of the body and consisting of trousers, breeches, or shorts, (other than swimwear), or a skirt or a divided skirt, having neither braces nor bibs; and 2) one suit coat or jacket, with the outer shell, exclusive of sleeves, made of four or more panels, designed to cover the upper part of the body, possibly with a tailored waistcoat in addition. if several separate components to cover the lower part of the body are entered together—such as trousers and shorts—the trousers, or for women's or girl's suits, the skirt or divided skirt will be considered part of the suit, and the other garments will be considered separately. All components of a suit must be of the same fabric construction, style, color, and composition. They must also be of corresponding or compatible size.

The following sets of garments are considered suits, whether or not they fulfill all the above conditions: l) morning dress, comprising a plain jacket (cutaway) with rounded tails hanging well down at the back and striped trousers; 2) evening dress (tailcoat), generally made of black fabric, the jacket of which is relatively short at the front, does not close and has narrow skirts cut in at the hips and hanging down behind; or 3) dinner jacket suits, in which the jacket is similar in style to an ordinary jacket (though perhaps revealing more of the shirt front), but has shiny silk or imitation silk lapels.

Ensembles. The term "ensemble" means a set of garments (other than suits and articles of HTSUS heading 6107, 6108, or 6109) composed of several pieces made up in identical fabric, put up for retail sale, and comprising: 1) one garment designed to cover the upper part of the body, (with the exception of pullovers, which may form a second upper garment in the sole context of twin sets, and of waistcoats, which may also form a second upper garment), and 2) one or two different garments, designed to cover the lower part of the body and consisting of trousers, bib and brace overalls, breeches, shorts (other than swimwear), a skirt, or a divided skirt. All of the components must be of the same fabric construction, style, color, and composition and must be of corresponding or compatible sizes. Track suits and ski suits are not classified as ensembles.

Ski Suits. The term "ski suit" means garments or sets of garments that, by their general appearance and texture, are identifiable as intended to be worn principally for skiing (cross-country or alpine). They consist either of: 1) a ski overall—that is, a one-piece garment that is designed to cover the upper and the lower parts of the body and that may have sleeves, a collar, pockets, and/or footstraps; or 2) a ski ensemble—that is a set of garments composed of two or three pieces, put up for retail sale and comprising: a) one garment, such as an anorak, windbreaker, or similar article, closed by a slide fastener (zipper), possibly with a waistcoat in addition; and b) one pair of trousers whether or not extending above waist level, one pair of breeches, or one bib and brace overall. A ski ensemble may also consist of an overall similar to the one mentioned in paragraph (a) above and a type of padded, sleeveless jacket worn over the overall. All components of a ski ensemble must be made up in a fabric of the same texture, style, and composition, whether or not of the same color. They also must be of corresponding or compatible size.

Sample Import Duties

Import duties will vary depending on the HTSUS classification of your product. Therefore, to determine the correct amount of duties, your product must be properly classified under the HTSUS. The following sample duties are taken from the duty listings for HTSUS Chapter 61 products.

Men's or boys' overcoats, carcoats, capes, cloaks, anoraks, windbreakers, and similar articles of wool or fine animal hair (6101.10.00): 77.2 cents/kg, plus 20%, of cotton (6101.20.00): 16.9%, of man-made fibers with 25% or more by weight of leather (6101.30.10): 6%; women's or girls' overcoats, carcoats, capes, cloaks, anoraks, windbreakers, and similar articles of wool or fine animal hair (6102.10.00): 68.3 cents/kg, plus 20%, of cotton (6102.20.00): 16.9%, of man-made fibers with 25% or more by weight of leather (6102.30.05): 6%; men's or boys' suits of wool or fine animal hair (6103.11.00): 77.2 cents/kg, plus 20%, of cotton (6103.19.20): 18.7%; women's or girls' suits of wool or fine animal hair (6104.11.00): 17%, of cotton (6104.12.00): 17%, of man-made fibers with 25% or more by weight of leather (6102.30.05): 6%; men's or boys' shirts of cotton (6105.10.00): 21%; women's and girls' blouses and shirts of silk (6106.90.20): 6%; men's or boys' pajamas of cotton (6107.21.00): 9.5%; sweaters wholly of cashmere (6110.10.10): 7.5%; babies' blouses and shirts, except those imported as part of sets, of cotton (6111.20.10): 21%; track suits of synthetic fibers (6112.12.00): 30%; wool gloves (6116.91.00): 33.1 cents/kg, plus 7.4%; shawls, scarves, veils, etc., of man-made fibers (6117.10.20): 12%; ties, bows, and cravats (6117.20.00): 8.2%.

Guam Sweaters. Under 9902.61.00, sweaters assembled in Guam from specified foreign components enter duty-free to the extent that they are entered before the annual aggregate quantity of such sweaters is reached on or before October 31, 1996.

Entry and Documentation

The entry of merchandise is a two-part process consisting of 1) filing the documentation necessary to determine whether merchandise may be released from Customs custody, and 2) filing the documents that contain information for duty assessment and statistical purposes. In certain instances, all documents must be filed and accepted by Customs prior to release of the goods. Unless you have been granted an extension, you must file entry documents at a location specified by the district or area director within five working days of your shipment's date of arrival at a U.S. port of entry. These include a number of standard documents required by Customs for any entry, and:

- U.S. Customs Country-of-Origin Declaration(s)
- Export documentation and/or visa for textiles subject to Multi-Fiber Arrangement
- Customs **Form 6451**, Notice of Percentage of Clean Yield and Grade of Wool or Hair, in duplicate, showing your name and address (if importing articles containing wool)
- Hong Kong government export license (if importing made-to-measure suits from Hong Kong)

After you present the entry, Customs may examine your shipment or may waive examination. The shipment is then released provided no legal or regulatory violations have been noted. You must then file entry summary documentation and deposit estimated duties at a designated customhouse within 10 working days of your shipment's release. For a detailed description of entry procedures, standard documentation, and informal entry, refer to "Entry Process" on page 182.

NAFTA Certificates of Origin. An importer of textiles for which NAFTA treatment is sought need not file a separate NAFTA Certificate of Origin in addition to the Customs Country-of-Origin Declaration. The declaration is sufficient. However, the importer must take care to submit a declaration from each U.S., Canadian, or Mexican producer or manufacturer. Thus, for multiple producers or manufacturers, a separate declaration must be filed for each. If a Customs district director cannot determine the country of origin because the declaration is absent or incomplete, the shipment is not entitled to preferential NAFTA tariff treatment or other NAFTA benefits. See 12 CFR 132.

Entry Invoices. You must provide certain additional information on the entry invoice for knitted or crocheted articles. The specific information varies depending on the nature of your product, as noted below.

TFPIA Requirements. All invoices for textile wearing apparel should indicate: 1) a component material breakdown in percentages by weight for all component fibers present in the entire garment, as well as separate breakdowns of the fibers in the (outer) shell (exclusive of linings, cuffs, waistbands, collars and other trimmings) and in the lining; 2) for garments that are constructed of more than one component or material (combination of knit and not-knit fabric or combinations of knit and/or not-knit fabric with leather, fur, plastic—including vinyl, etc.) the invoice must show a fiber breakdown in percentages by weight for each separate textile material in the garment and a breakdown in percentages by weight for each nontextile material of the entire garment; 3) for woven garments: indicate whether the fabric is yarn-dyed and whether there are "two or more colors in the warp and/or filling;" 4) for all-white T-shirts and singlets: indicate whether or not the garment contains pockets, trim, or embroidery; 5) for mufflers: state the exact dimensions, length, and width of the merchandise.

Wool Products Subject to WPLA. When you offer for entry a wool product shipment valued at over $500 and subject to WPLA, you must include certain information intended to facilitate Customs monitoring and enforcement of that Act. This extra information is identical to that required by WPLA on labeling (see "Marking and Labeling Requirements" below), with the addition of the manufacturer's name. If your product consists of mixed waste, residues, and similar merchandise obtained from several suppliers or unknown sources, you may omit the manufacturer's name from the entry invoice.

Invoices for Gloves. For any gloves classifiable under HTSUS subheading 6116.10.20, the entry invoice must state whether the gloves have been covered with plastics on both sides.

Invoices for Hosiery. The entry invoice for items of hosiery must indicate 1) whether a single yarn measures less than 67 decitex; 2) whether the hosiery is full length, knee length, or less than knee length; and 3) whether it contains lace or net.

Invoices for Hong Kong Made-to-Measure Suits. Imports from Hong Kong of "made-to-measure" suits that do not accompany a returning traveler are subject to a special agreement. Suits made to the specific measurements of a particular person require a "made-to-measure" export license from the Hong Kong government. You must identify "made-to-measure" suits of Hong Kong origin on your entry summary by placing the symbol "G" as a prefix to the appropriate tariff number. The importer is responsible for the payment of any Customs duties at the time of importation, even if the suits are made to measure for an individual person. For more information, contact your nearest U.S. Customs port office.

Special Access or Regime Entries. Certain garments assembled abroad from components formed and cut in the U.S. that, after assembly have been subject to bleaching, garment dyeing, or perma-pressing abroad, may be eligible for entry under the Special Access Program. Eligibility must be established under a bilateral agreement, and entry must be in compliance with procedures established by the Committee for the Implementation of Textile Agreements. You must identify such garments on the entry summary or withdrawal forms by placing the symbol "H" as a prefix to the appropriate tariff number.

Prohibitions and Restrictions

Textile Quotas. Textile import restrictions are primarily a matter of quotas and the way in which these quotas are administered and monitored. Under the Multi-Fiber Arrangement provisions of Section 204 of the Agricultural Adjustment Act, CITA has negotiated Multi-Fiber Arrangements with 40 countries. These Agreements may impose quotas for a type of textile or a specific article, and they are country-specific. The agreements, however, often change. Therefore, if you are interested in importing any knitted or crocheted apparel articles, you should contact the International Trade Administration's Office of Textile and Apparel (see addresses at end of this chapter). The Office of Textile and Apparel has a team of country specialists who can inform you of the latest developments and inform you about a product's quota or restriction status.

U.S. Customs enforces CITA textile and textile product entry quotas. If formal entry procedures are not followed, Customs will usually refuse entry for textiles that are subject to Section 204. Formal entry requires submission of a Country-of-Origin Declaration (see "General Considerations" above). U.S. Customs maintains a current textile quota status report, available for perusal at any Customs port. In addition, U.S. Customs in Washington, DC, operates a telephone service to provide quota status reports, which are updated weekly (see "Relevant Government Agencies" below).

Flammable Fabrics. U.S. Customs may refuse entry for any article of wearing apparel or interior furnishing, or any fabric or related material that is intended for use or that may be used in wearing apparel or interior furnishings, if it fails to conform to an applicable flammability standard issued under Section 4 of the FFA. An exception is allowed for certain products (FFA Section 11c) that are imported for finishing or processing to bring them within the legal standard. For these products, the exporter must state on the invoice or other paper relating to the shipment that the shipment is being made for that purpose.

The CPSC, as the primary enforcement agency of flammability standards, inspects products for compliance with the FFA. If the CPSC believes a product, fabric, or related material does not comply with a flammability standard, it is authorized to pursue a variety of legal sanctions, including: 1) seizure, condemnation, and forfeiture of the noncomplying products; 2) administrative cease-and-desist order requiring an individual or firm to stop sale and distribution of the noncomplying products or; 3) temporary injunction requiring the individual or firm to stop sale and distribution of the noncomplying products, pending final disposition of an administrative cease-and-desist proceeding. The CPSC also has authority to seek civil penalties against any person who knowingly violates a regulation or standard issued under Section 4 of the FFA.

Country-Specific Restrictions

Restrictions under Multi-Fiber Arrangements are country-specific. A product originating in one country may be subject to quota and to export license or visa requirements, while the same product originating in a different country may not. At present, the U.S. has Multi-Fiber Arrangements with 40 countries. Many different categories of products are covered under these Arrangements; it is beyond the scope of this book to list each country and its restricted commodities. If you are interested in importing textiles and textile products, you should contact the International Trade Administration's Office of Textile and Apparel (see addresses at end of this chapter) or U.S. Customs to ascertain your product's restraint status.

The U.S. Customs Quota Branch phone numbers provide recorded status reports, by quota category number, for current charges against the quotas for that country. For convenience, the HTSUS shows the 3-digit category number in parentheses to the right of each listed commodity that is subject to textile restraints. For example, under Chapter 61, heading 6104, Women's or Girl's Cotton Trousers, is followed by the number "(348)". If you know the category number for your product, you can find out to what extent that quota is filled simply by calling the number for the appropriate country. A word of caution, though: if you do not know for sure that your article is subject to quota from a particular country, and you call the number for that country, you may not be any more enlightened after the phone call. Many of the recordings give status reports only when a certain percentage of the quota has been filled. Thus, if 348 for Indonesia is among the categories for which not enough quantity has entered the U.S. to warrant specific mention, it will be lumped under "all other categories" and you will be none the wiser. To find out if your product is subject to textile restraints, call the DOC or a local Customs port office. Then you can find out the current charges against that quota by calling the country number listed below. For a complete listing of Customs Quota Branch information numbers, see "Relevant Government Agencies" below.

Marking and Labeling Requirements

TFPIA Requirements. All textile products imported into the U.S. must be stamped, tagged, labeled, or otherwise marked with the following information as required by the TFPIA, unless exempt from marking (see TFPIA, Section 12): 1) the generic names and percentages by weight of the constituent fibers present in the textile fiber product, exclusive of permissible ornamentation, in amounts of more than 5% in order of predominance by weight, with any percentage of fiber or fibers required to be designated as "other fiber" or "other fibers" (including those present in amounts of 5% or less) appearing last; and 2) the name of the manufacturer or the name or registered identification number issued by the FTC of one or more persons marketing or handling the textile fiber product; and 3) the name of the country where processed. A word trademark, used as a house mark and registered with the U.S. Patent Office, may appear on labels instead of the name otherwise required, provided the owner of the trademark furnishes a copy of the registration to the FTC prior to use (see "Registered Identification Numbers" below).

The information listed above is not exhaustive. TFPIA requirements are extensive. The Act specifies such details as types of labels, means of attachment, label position on the article, package labeling, unit labeling for two-piece garments, and arrangement of information on the label; allowable fiber designations; country-of-origin indications; requirements for trim and ornamentation, linings and interlinings, and pile fabrics; sectional disclosure; use of trade names and trademarks; and requirements for swatches and samples. The FTC publishes a booklet intended to clarify TFPIA requirements to facilitate voluntary compliance in the industry (see "Publications Available" below). It is available on request, at no charge, from the FTC (see addresses at end of this chapter).

Wool Products Labeling Act (WPLA). Wool product labeling requirements for foreign products are the responsibility of the importer. The WPLA requires the following information to appear on wool products subject to the Act: 1) percentage of the wool product's total fiber weight (exclusive of ornamentation) not exceeding 5% of the total fiber weight of a) wool, b) recycled wool, c) each fiber other than wool if the percent by weight of such fiber is 5% or more, and d) the aggregate of all other fibers; 2) the maximum percent of the wool product's total weight, of any nonfibrous loading, filling, or adulterating matter; and 3) the importer's name. If you, as importer, have a registered identification number issued by the FTC, that number may be used instead of your name (see "Registered Identification Numbers" below).

Customs entry is contingent on proper labeling. If your shipment is found to be mislabeled at entry, you will be given the option of relabeling the products under Customs supervision, as long as the district director is satisfied that your labeling error or omission did not involve fraud or willful neglect. If your shipment is discovered after entry to have been noncomplying with WPLA, it will be recalled to Customs custody at your expense, unless you can satisfy the district director that the products have since been brought into compliance. You will be held responsible for all expenses incurred in bringing a shipment into compliance, including compensation of personnel and other expenses related to Customs supervision.

Fraudulent violations of WPLA will result in seizure of the shipment. Shipments already released from Customs custody will be ordered to be redelivered to Customs. Customs reports all cases of fraudulent violation to the FTC in Washington, DC.

The information listed above is not intended to be exhaustive. WPLA requirements are extensive. The Act specifies such details as types of labels, means of attachment, label position on the article, package labeling, unit labeling (as in the case of a two-piece garment), arrangement of information on the label, allowable fiber designations, country-of-origin indications, trim and ornamentation, pile fabrics, sectional disclosure, use of trade names and trademarks, requirements for swatches and samples, etc. The FTC publishes a booklet intended to clarify WPLA requirements in order to facilitate voluntary compliance within the industry (see "Publications Available" below). It is available on request, at no charge, from the FTC (see addresses at end of this chapter).

Registered Identification Numbers. Any domestic firm or person residing in the U.S. and engaged in the manufacture or marketing of textile products covered under the TFPIA may obtain an FTC-registered identification number for use on required tags and labels instead of the name of a firm or person. For applications, contact the FTC (see addresses at end of this chapter).

For a general discussion of U.S. Customs marking and labeling requirements, refer to "Marking: Country of Origin" on page 215 and "Special Marking Requirements" on page 217.

Shipping Considerations

You will need to ensure that your goods are packaged and shipped with care so that they pass smoothly through Customs and arrive in good condition. You are responsible for ensuring that the shipment is in compliance with all applicable government regulations for packaging and shipping. In most instances, you should not leave these arrangements solely to the discretion of your supplier. Careful preparation of the cargo and selection of the mode of transport can be essential to a cost-effective, timely delivery of undamaged goods. We strongly advise you to consult your shipping representative, insurance agent, or freight broker for advice on packing and shipping. Refer also to the major tab section "Packing/Shipping/Insurance" for a general discussion of packing and shipping.

Knitted or crocheted apparel articles may be shipped in bulk, cartons, or other types of containers, depending on the type of product and whether it is prepackaged. General considerations include protection from contamination, weather, and pests. Containers should be constructed so as to be safe for handling during transport.

Publications Available

The following publications may be relevant to the importation of knitted or crocheted apparel articles:

Questions and Answers Relating to the Textile Fiber Products Identification Act and Regulations

Questions and Answers Relating to the Wool Products Labeling Act and Regulations

Available free of charge on request from the Federal Trade Commission, these publications are excellent sources of information written in clear lay language. We recommend that anyone interested in importing textile fiber products but unfamiliar with the regulations obtain a copy of each of these booklets.

The *Harmonized Tariff Schedule of the United States* (HTSUS) is available from:

Government Printing Office (GPO)
Superintendent of Documents
Washington, DC 20402
(202) 512-1800 (Order line)
(202) 512-0000 (General)

The USGPO also has copies of specific laws available for purchase. The USGPO accepts credit card orders over the phone, as well as mail orders paid by credit card, a check drawn on a U.S. bank, or an international money order.

Relevant Government Agencies

Address your questions regarding textile Multi-Fiber Arrangements to:

International Trade Administration
Office of Textile and Apparel
14th and Constitution Ave. NW, Rm. 3100
Washington, DC 20230
(202) 482-5078, 482-3737

Address your questions regarding the Flammable Fabrics Act (FFA) to:

Consumer Product Safety Commission (CPSC)
5401 Westbard Avenue
Bethesda, MD 20207
(301) 492-6580

Address your questions regarding labeling requirements under the Textile Fiber Products Identification Act (TFPIA) or the Wool Products Labeling Act (WPLA) to:

Federal Trade Commission (FTC)
Division of Enforcement
601 Pennsylvania Ave. NW
Washington, DC 20580
(202) 326-2996 (General)
(202) 326-2841 (Textile and wool products labeling)

Address your questions regarding knitted or crocheted apparel article imports to the district or port director of Customs for you area. For addresses, refer to"U.S. Customs District Offices" on page 62 or contact:

U.S. Customs Service
1301 Constitution Ave. NW
Washington, DC 20229
(202) 927-6724 (Information)
(202) 927-1000 (General)

The following information numbers for U.S. Customs in Washington, DC, provide recorded information. The Quota Branch numbers listed by country provide updated status reports on textile quotas from those countries. All area codes are (202).
General information: 927-5850

Quota Branch: China 927-6703; India 927-6705; Indonesia 927-6704; Japan 927-6706; Korea 927-6707; Macao 927-6709; Malaysia 927-6712; Mexico 927-6711; Pakistan 927-6714; Philippines 927-6713; Romania 927-6715; Singapore 927-6716; Sri Lanka 927-6708; Taiwan 927-6719; Thailand 927-6717; Turkey 927-6718; All others 927-5850.

Laws and Regulations

The following laws and regulations may be relevant to the importation of knitted or crocheted apparel articles. The laws are contained in the United States Code (USC), and the regulations are published in the Code of Federal Regulations (CFR), both of which are available at larger public and law libraries. Copies of specific laws are also available from the United States Government Printing Office (address above).

7 USC 1854
Textile Trade Agreements
(EO 11651, as amended by EO 11951 and 12188, and supplemented by EO 12475)
This Act authorizes the CITA of the DOC to enter into Multi-Fiber Agreements with other countries to control trade in textiles and establishes the Textile Import Program, which is enforced by U.S. Customs.

19 CFR 12.130 et seq.
Regulations on Entry of Textiles
These regulations provide the requirements and procedures followed by Customs in enforcing limitations on the importation and entry and withdrawal of textiles and textile products from warehouses for consumption in the U.S.

15 USC 70-77
Textile Fiber Products Identification Act (TFPIA)
This Act prohibits false or deceptive labeling (misbranding) and false advertising of any textile fiber products and requires all textile fiber products imported into the U.S. to be labeled in accordance with the requirements set forth in the law.

19 CFR 11.12b; 16 CFR 303 et seq.
Regulations on Labeling and Marking
These regulations detail the labeling and marking requirements for textiles as specified by the CPSC and the invoice contents required by U.S. Customs for purpose of enforcing the labeling and marking rules.

15 USC 68-68j
Wool Products Labeling Act (WPLA)
This Act prohibits the false or deceptive labeling (misbranding) of wool products and requires all wool products imported into the U.S. to be labeled in accordance with requirements set forth in the law.

19 CFR 11.12; 16 CFR 300 et seq.
Regulations on WPLA Labeling and Marking
These regulations set forth the wool labeling and marking requirements adopted by the FTC to administer the requirements of the WPLA and provide the procedures followed by U.S. Customs in enforcing the WPLA and the FTC regulations, including entry invoice requirements.

15 USC 1191-1204
Flammable Fabrics Act (FFA)
This Act provides for the setting of flammability standards for fabric by the Consumer Product Safety Commission (CPSC) and for enforcement by U.S. Customs.

16 CFR 1610, 1611, 1615, 1616, 1630-1632
Regulations on Flammable Fabric Standards
These regulations specify the flammability standards adopted by the CPSC under the FFA for various types of textiles.

Principal Exporting Countries

The following listing includes samples of the main supplier nations of the products of this chapter. It is organized by HTSUS major heading. (Refer to "Customs Classification" above for the product codes.) Countries are listed in rank order of the value of products imported to the U.S. Statistics represent customs value entries for 1993 from the Bureau of Census, U.S. Department of Commerce.

6101—China, Pakistan, Taiwan, United Arab Emirates, Romania, Singapore, Philippines, Hong Kong, Malaysia, Mauritius

6102—Hong Kong, Taiwan, Singapore, Malaysia, Macao, Thailand, China, Mexico, Sri Lanka, South Korea

6103—Dominican Rep., Taiwan, Costa Rica, Singapore, El Salvador, Hong Kong, China, South Korea, Honduras, Jamaica

6104—Taiwan, Hong Kong, South Korea, China, Singapore, Macao, Israel, Malaysia, Canada, Turkey

6105—Hong Kong, Philippines, China, South Korea, Pakistan, Thailand, Indonesia, Taiwan, Dominican Rep., Singapore

6106—Hong Kong, China, Macao, Taiwan, Singapore, South Korea, Thailand, Sri Lanka, Mexico, Turkey

6107—Dominican Rep., Hong Kong, Taiwan, Costa Rica, Mexico, Honduras, Thailand, Israel, Bangladesh, China

6108—Hong Kong, Costa Rica, Dominican Rep., Mexico, Turkey, Jamaica, Taiwan, Bangladesh, Israel, China

6109—Jamaica, Mexico, Dominican Rep., Hong Kong, China, Honduras, Pakistan, India, Turkey, El Salvador

6110—China, Hong Kong, Taiwan, South Korea, Macao, Indonesia, Thailand, Singapore, Philippines, Italy

6111—Philippines, Taiwan, Hong Kong, Thailand, China, Costa Rica, South Korea, Dominican Rep., Mexico, Sri Lanka

6112—Taiwan, China, Canada, Israel, Hong Kong, Dominican Rep., Singapore, Malaysia, Colombia, Philippines

6113—Taiwan, Thailand, Mexico, China, Canada, South Korea, Hong Kong, Sweden, Australia, United Kingdom

6114—Hong Kong, Taiwan, China, South Korea, Thailand, Sri Lanka, Malaysia, Philippines, Mexico, Italy

6115—Jamaica, Taiwan, South Korea, Colombia, Japan, Canada, United Kingdom, Turkey, Italy, Israel

6116—China, Taiwan, Philippines, Hong Kong, Sri Lanka, Thailand, South Korea, Haiti, Pakistan, Malaysia

6117—Taiwan, South Korea, Canada, Italy, China, Philippines, Hong Kong, Dominican Rep., Thailand, United Kingdom

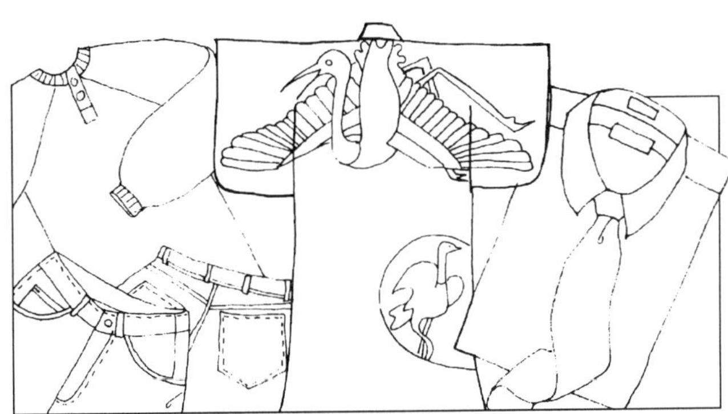

Chapter 62: Apparel Not Knitted or Crocheted*

Full title: Articles of Apparel and Clothing Accessories, Not Knitted or Crocheted

This chapter relates to the importation of textile apparel articles and clothing accessories other than knitted or crocheted items, which are classified under Chapter 62 of the Harmonized Tariff Schedule of the United States (HTSUS). Specifically, it covers textile garments, not knitted or crocheted, for adults and children, including coats and jackets; suits, blazers, trousers, overalls, shorts, dresses, skirts, shirts, and blouses; undergarments and night clothes; track suits, ski suits, and swimwear; handkerchiefs; shawls, scarves, and similar clothing accessories; ties, bows, and cravats; and gloves, mittens, and mitts.

If you are interested in importing articles of apparel that are knitted or crocheted, you should read Commodity Index Chapter 61. Articles made of textile wadding are covered in Chapter 56, worn articles of apparel are covered in Chapter 63, and surgical belts and orthopedic items are classified in Chapter 90. If you are interested in importing footwear or headgear, you should refer to Chapter 64 or 65, respectively. Textiles, garment parts, thread, yarns, and other similar materials are covered in Chapters 50 through 58. Articles of apparel that contain leather parts may be imported in accordance with the requirements explained in Chapter 42.

Key Factors

The key factors in the importation of articles not knitted or crocheted are:

- Compliance with quota restraints and visa requirements under U.S. Department of Commerce (DOC) Multi-Fiber Arrangements
- Submission of U.S. Customs Country-of-Origin Declaration(s)
- Compliance with entry invoice requirements
- Compliance with labeling requirements under the Textile Fiber Products Identification Act (TFPIA) and the Wool Products Labeling Act (WPLA)
- Compliance with flammability standards adopted and enforced by the Consumer Product Safety Commission (CPSC) under the Flammable Fabrics Act (FFA)

*__IMPORTANT__: Read the Commodity Index Introduction. It is the essential framework for understanding this chapter.

- Compliance with export licence requirements (if importing made-to-measure suits from Hong Kong)
- Compliance with Special Access or Regime entry requirements (if importing garments assembled and bleached, dyed, stone-washed, acid-washed, or perma-pressed abroad from components formed and cut in the US)

Although most importers use the services of a licensed customs broker in making their entries, and we recommend this practice, you should be aware of the regulatory, entry, and documentation issues involved in importing your product. You, as importer, are ultimately responsible for the fulfillment of any legal requirements applicable to your shipment.

General Considerations

Regulatory Agencies. The DOC's Committee for Implementation of Textile Agreements (CITA) regulates certain textile imports under Section 204 of the Agricultural Adjustment Act. U.S. Customs enforces CITA textile and textile product entry quotas. Customs also enforces compliance with labeling and invoice requirements of the TFPIA and flammability standards under the FFA. The CPSC monitors imports and from time to time inspects textile shipments for compliance with FFA standards. If you are importing wool textiles, importation is subject to complex textile import regulations. The Federal Trade Commission (FTC) administers the WPLA requirements.

Wool Product Entry Requirements. Depending on the nature of your wool article imports, as many as four different types of special entry documents may be required. First, for all imported articles that contain textile fibers, yarns, and fabrics covered by the Agricultural Adjustment Act (AAA), including wool, you must file a U.S. Customs Textile Entry Declaration (see "Textile Country-of-Origin Declarations" below). Second, with the entry summary for each shipment of wool articles, you must file Customs **Form 6451**, Notice of Percentage of Clean Yield and Grade of Wool or Hair, in duplicate, showing your name and address. Third, for all wool products subject to the WPLA, special information is required on the entry invoices (see "Wool Products Labeling Act" below). Finally, certain articles of apparel manufactured or produced in certain countries may be subject to quotas and other restraints under U.S. DOC Multi-Fiber Arrangements. Such products require export licenses, certificates, or visas issued by the appropriate country of origin, in addition to other requisite entry paperwork (see "Textile Quotas" below).

Wool Products Labeling Act. The term "wool product" means any product or any portion of a product that contains, purports to contain, or in any way is represented as containing wool, reprocessed wool, or reused wool. All wool products imported into the U.S., except those made more than 20 years before importation, and except carpets, rugs, mats, and upholsteries, must have affixed a stamp, tag, label, or other means of identification as required by the WPLA. If you are importing wool products exempt from labeling under the WPLA, do not assume they are also exempt from labeling under the TFPIA. These are two distinct laws, with some overlapping requirements (see "Marking and Labeling Requirements" below).

Textile Quotas. If you are interested in importing textile apparel articles or clothing accessories, the most important issue you need to be aware of is quotas. Under the Multi-Fiber Arrangement provisions of Section 204 of the Agricultural Adjustment Act, CITA initiates specific agreements with individual exporting countries. Section 204 of the Agricultural Adjustment Act covers textiles articles that: 1) are in chief value of cotton, wool, or man-made fibers, any textile fibers subject to the terms of any textile trade agreement, or any combination of such fibers; 2) contain 50% or more by weight of cotton or man-made fibers, or any textile fibers subject to the terms of any textile trade agreement; 3) contain 17% or more by weight of wool; or 4) if in chief value of textile fibers or textile materials, contain a blend of cotton, wool, or man-made fibers, any textile fibers subject to the terms of any textile trade agreement, or any combination of such fibers that, in total, amount to 50% or more by weight of all component fibers.

The U.S. has Multi-Fiber Arrangements with 40 countries. Each agreement with each country is unique, and may specify quotas for a type of textile or a specific article. Visas or export licenses may be required. These agreements, however, often change. Therefore, if you are interested in importing any textile apparel articles or clothing accessories, you should contact the International Trade Administration's Office of Textile and Apparel (see addresses at end of this chapter). Refer to "Prohibitions and Restrictions" below for further details.

Textile Country-of-Origin Declarations. U.S. Customs enforces CITA textile and textile product entry quotas (see "Prohibitions and Restrictions" below). Requirements for entry include submission of Country-of-Origin Declarations with every shipment of woven textile apparel articles or clothing accessories, regardless of whether it is subject to a specific multi-fiber arrangement (19 CFR 12.130, 12.131).

Country of Origin. Quota restrictions are country-specific and therefore are applied based on the country of origin for the textiles shipped. The last country from which a textile shipment was exported to the U.S. is not necessarily its country of origin. A textile or textile product imported into the U.S. is considered a product of the particular foreign territory or country, or a U.S. insular possession, where it is wholly grown, produced, or manufactured. For the following discussion, "country" means a foreign territory or country, or a U.S. insular possession.

Substantial transformation rules may affect the country-of-origin determination. For example, if a textile or textile product originates in Country A and is subject to quota, the quota restrictions apply at entry into the U.S. But if, prior to export to the U.S., you move the shipment to Country B where there are fewer restrictions, the shipment may nevertheless remain subject to quota and visa requirements under the Multi-Fiber Arrangement with Country A. Customs determines whether the quota restrictions apply based on the criteria of "substantial transformation." If your textiles do not undergo any major processing or manufacturing while in Country B, or if the manufacturing or processing is minor, your shipment will be deemed to originate in Country A. *You cannot claim substantial transformation on the basis of minor manufacturing procedures.*

In contrast, if your shipment undergoes major processing or manufacturing while in Country B, rendering the textiles "new and different articles of commerce," Customs will treat the shipment as the product of Country B. To qualify as having undergone substantial transformation, an article must evince a change in: 1) commercial designation or identity; b) fundamental character; or c) commercial use. If your shipment is processed in more than one country, the country where it last underwent substantial transformation is the country of origin for Customs entry. In deciding whether the manufacturing or processing operation in a country is major, Customs considers the following factors: 1) the resultant physical change in the material or article; 2) the complexity, the level or degree of skill and/or technology required, and the amount of time involved in the operations; and 3) the value added to the article or material, compared to its value when imported into the U.S.

Validating Operations. Operations that Customs will usually acknowledge as validating a claim of substantial transformation are the following: 1) dyeing and printing, when accompanied by two or more of the following finishing operations: bleaching, shrinking, fulling, napping, decating, permanent stiffening, weighting, permanent embossing, or moireing; 2) spinning fibers into yarn; 3) weaving, knitting, or otherwise forming fabric; 4) cutting fabric into parts and assembling the parts into completed articles; or 5) substantial assembly, by sewing and/or tailoring into a completed garment cut pieces of apparel articles that have been cut from fabric in another country—e.g., complete assembly and tailoring of all cut pieces of suit-type jackets, suits, and shirts.

Insubstantial Operations. Operations that usually will not support a claim of substantial transformation, even if more than one are performed, are the following: 1) simple operations of combining, labeling, pressing, cleaning, dry cleaning, or packaging; 2) cutting to length or width and hemming or overlocking fabrics that are readily identifiable as being intended for a particular commercial use; 3) trimming and/or joining together by sewing, looping, linking, or other means of attaching otherwise completed knit-to-shape component parts produced in a single country, even if accompanied by other processes—e.g., washing, drying, mending—normally incident to assembly; 4) one or more finishing operations on yarns, fabrics, or their textile articles—such as showerproofing, superwashing, bleaching, decating, fulling, shrinking, mercerizing, or similar operations; or 5) dyeing and/or printing fabrics or yarns.

Declarations. The country of origin of the textile apparel articles or clothing accessories in a shipment must be stated on a declaration submitted to U.S. Customs at the time of entry. There are three Customs Country-of-Origin Declarations: single-country, multiple-country, and negative. The Declaration to be submitted with your shipment of textile apparel articles or clothing accessories depends on the nature of the import.

- **Single-country declarations** are used for entries of textiles or textile products that clearly originate from only one country or that have been assembled in one country from fabricated components wholly produced in the U.S. or the foreign country of manufacture. Information required includes: marks of identification and numbers; description of article and quantity; country of origin; and date of exportation.
- **Multiple-country declarations** are used for entries of textiles or textile products that were manufactured or processed and/or that incorporate materials originating in more than one foreign country or territory. Information required includes: marks of identification and numbers; for articles, description, quantity, identification of manufacturing and/or processing operations, country, and date of exportation; for materials used to make articles, description of materials, country of production, and date of exportation.
- **Negative declarations** must accompany all textile imports that are not subject to FFA Section 204 restrictions. Information required includes: marks of identification and numbers; descriptions of article and quantity; and country of origin.

The date of exportation to be indicated on the above declarations is the date on which the carrier leaves the last port in the country of origin, as determined by Customs. Diversion to another country during transit does not affect the export date.

Procedure for Declarations. The manufacturer, producer, exporter, or importer may prepare the declaration. If more than one of these parties is involved in the importation, each party may prepare a separate declaration. You may file a separate declaration for each invoice presented with your entry. The declaration must be dated and signed by the responsible party, and must include the person's title and the company name and address. Your shipment's entry will be denied unless it is accompanied by a properly executed declaration. Customs will not treat a textile declaration as a missing document for which a bond may be filed.

Customs will base its country-of-origin determination on the information contained in each declaration, unless the information is insufficient. If the information on the declaration is insufficient, Customs will require that you submit such additional information as will enable the determination to be made. The shipment will not be released until the determination is made. Thus, if you want to clear Customs with minimal delay, be sure that the information on the declarations is as complete as possible for each shipment.

Textile Labeling and Invoice Requirements. You are responsible for your imported product's compliance with applicable provisions of the TFPIA. Textile apparel articles or clothing accessories that require labeling under TFPIA must already be labeled at entry, or the shipment will be refused. (See "Marking and Labeling Requirements" below.) If you import shipments of textile apparel articles or clothing accessories subject to TFPIA and valued at over $500, you must provide special information on the entry invoice (see "Entry and Documentation" below).

Flammability Standards. Textile apparel articles or clothing accessories imported into the U.S. for use in consumer products must be in compliance with the FFA, a federal law that gives the CPSC the authority and responsibility for protecting the public from the hazards of dangerously flammable items of wearing apparel and interior furnishings. Under the FFA, standards have been established for flammability of clothing textiles. You cannot import any article of wearing apparel or interior furnishing, or any fabric or related material that is intended for use or that may be used in such items, if it fails to conform to an applicable flammability standard (FFA Section 4). Certain products may be imported into the U.S. (FFA Section 11c) for finishing or processing to render them less flammable so as to meet the standards. For these products, the exporter must state on the invoice or other paper relating to the shipment that the shipment is being made for that purpose.

The CPSC monitors imports of textiles under its Import Surveillance Program. From time to time, your textile shipments may be inspected to ascertain compliance with mandatory safety standards. Shipments may also be subject to testing by the CPSC to determine compliance. If the CPSC believes a product, fabric, or related material does not comply with a flammability standard, it is authorized to pursue a variety of legal sanctions (see "Prohibitions and Restrictions" below).

Substantial Product Hazard Reports. Any firm that obtains information that reasonably supports the conclusion that one of its products presents an unreasonable risk of serious injury or death must report that information to the CPSC's Division of Corrective Actions (CPSC address below). Importers must also report to the CPSC if 1) a type of product is the subject of at least three civil actions filed in U.S. federal or state courts, 2) each suit alleges the involvement of that product type in death or grievous bodily injury (as defined in FFA Section 37(3)1), and 3) at least three of the actions result in a final settlement with the manufacturer or in a judgment for the plaintiff within any one of the two-year periods specified in FFA Section 37(b).

Import Advisory

Importation of textile products is trade-sensitive and highly regulated. Shipments of textile products not complying with all government regulations, including quotas and visas, are subject to seizure and could result in the imposition of penalties as well as possible forfeiture of the goods. You should always verify the available quota for any textile product you plan to import before your shipment leaves the country of manufacture. Furthermore, Customs textile classification rulings change frequently, and prior administrative rulings are often modified and sometimes reversed.

Customs Classification

For customs purposes, textile apparel articles or clothing accessories are classified under Chapter 62 of the HTSUS. This chapter is broken into major headings, which are further divided into subheadings, and often sub-subheadings, each of which has its own HTSUS classification number. For example, the HTSUS number for babies' cotton dresses is 6209.20.10, indicating it is a sub-subcategory of garments of cotton (6209.20.00), which is a subcategory of the major heading babies' garments and clothing accessories (6209.00.00). There are 17 major headings within Chapter 62.

6201—Men's or boys' overcoats, carcoats, capes, cloaks, anoraks (including ski-jackets), windbreakers, and similar articles (including padded, sleeveless jackets), other than those of heading 6203

6202—Women's or girls' overcoats, carcoats, capes cloaks, anoraks (including ski-jackets), windbreakers, and similar articles (including padded, sleeveless jackets), other than those of heading 6204

6203—Men's or boys' suits, ensembles, suit-type jackets, blazers, trousers, bib and brace overalls, breeches, and shorts (other than swimwear)

6204—Women's or girls' suits, ensembles, suit-type jackets, blazers, dresses, skirts, divided skirts, trousers, bib and brace overalls, breeches, and shorts (other than swimwear)

6205—Men's or boys' shirts

6206—Women's or girls' blouses, shirts, and shirt-blouses

6207—Men's or boys' singlets and other undershirts, underpants, briefs, nightshirts, pajamas, bathrobes, dressing gowns, and similar articles

6208—Women's or girls' singlets, and other undershirts, slips, petticoats, briefs, panties, nightdresses, pajamas, negligees, bathrobes, dressing gowns, and similar articles

6209—Babies' garments and clothing accessories

6210—Garments, made up of fabrics of heading 5602, 5603, 5903, 5906, or 5907

6211—Track suits, ski suits, and swimwear; other garments

6212—Brassieres, girdles, corsets, braces, suspenders, garters, and similar articles and parts thereof, whether or not knitted or crocheted

6213—Handkerchiefs

6214—Shawls, scarves, mufflers, mantillas, veils, and the like

6215—Ties, bow ties, and cravats

6216—Gloves, mittens, and mitts

6217—Other made up clothing accessories; parts of garments or of clothing accessories, other than those of heading 6212

Definitions. For classification for duty purposes, Customs defines suits, ensembles, and ski suits as follows.

Suits. The term "suit" means a set of garments composed of two or three pieces made up in identical fabric and comprising: 1) one garment designed to cover the lower part of the body and consisting of trousers, breeches, or shorts (other than swimwear), or a skirt or divided skirt, having neither braces nor bibs; and 2) one suit coat or jacket, with the outer shell, exclusive of sleeves, made of four or more panels, designed to cover the upper part of the body, possibly with a tailored waistcoat in addition. If several separate components to cover the lower part of the body are entered together—such as trousers and shorts—the trousers, or for women's or girl's suits, the skirt or divided skirt, will be considered part of the suit, and the other garments will be considered separately. All components of a suit must be of the same fabric construction, style, color, and composition. They must also be of corresponding or compatible size.

The following sets of garments are considered suits, whether or not they fulfill all the above conditions: l) morning dress, comprising a plain jacket (cutaway) with rounded tails hanging well down at the back and striped trousers; 2) evening dress (tailcoat), generally made of black fabric, the jacket of which is relatively short at the front, does not close and has narrow skirts cut in at the hips and hanging down behind; or 3) dinner jacket suits, in which the jacket is similar in style to an ordinary jacket (though perhaps revealing more of the shirt front), but has shiny silk or imitation silk lapels.

Ensembles. The term "ensemble" means a set of garments (other than suits and articles of HTSUS heading 6207 or 6208) composed of several pieces made up in identical fabric, put up for retail sale, and comprising: 1) one garment designed to cover the upper part of the body, (with the exception of waistcoats, which may form a second upper garment), and 2) one or two different garments, designed to cover the lower part of the body, and consisting of trousers, bib and brace overalls, breeches, shorts (other than swimwear), a skirt, or a divided skirt. All of the components must be of the same fabric construction, style, color, and composition and must be of corresponding or compatible sizes. Track suits and ski suits are not classified as ensembles.

Ski Suits. The term "ski suit" means garments or sets of garments that, by their general appearance and texture, are identifiable as intended to be worn principally for skiing (cross-country or alpine). They consist either of: 1) a ski overall—that is, a one-piece garment that is designed to cover the upper and the lower parts of the body and that may have sleeves, a collar, pockets, and/or footstraps; or 2) a ski ensemble—that is a set of garments composed of two or three pieces, put up for retail sale and comprising: a) one garment, such as an anorak, windbreaker, or similar article, closed by a slide fastener (zipper), possibly with a waistcoat in addition; and b) one pair of trousers whether or not extending above waist level, one pair of breeches, or one bib and brace overall. A ski ensemble may also consist of an overall similar to the one mentioned in paragraph (a) above and a type of padded, sleeveless jacket worn over the overall. All components of a ski ensemble must be made up in a fabric of the same texture, style, and composition, whether or not of the same color. They also must be of corresponding or compatible size.

Sample Import Duties

Import duties will vary depending on the HTSUS classification of your product. Therefore, to determine the correct amount of duties, your product must be properly classified under the HTSUS. The following sample duties are taken from the duty listings for HTSUS Chapter 62 products.

Men's or boys' overcoats, carcoats, capes, cloaks, and similar articles of wool or fine animal hair (6201.11.00): 55.9 cents/kg, plus 21%, of cotton without any down or other plumage (6201.12.20): 10%, of man-made fibers without any down or plumage or wool content (6201.13.40): 29.5%; women's or girls' overcoats, carcoats, capes, cloaks, and similar articles of wool or fine animal hair (6202.11.00): 46.3cents/kg, plus 21%, of cotton without any down or other plumage (6202.12.20): 9.5%, of man-made fibers without any down or other plumage or wool content (6202.13.30): 29.5%; men's or boys' suits of wool or fine animal hair without silk (6203.11.20): 52.9 cents/kg, plus 21%, of cotton (6203.19.10): 16.5%; women's or girls' suits of wool or fine animal hair (6204.11.00): 17%, of cotton (6204.12.00): 17.1%, of synthetic fibers with 36% or more by weight of wool or fine animal hair (6204.13.10): 17%; men's or boys' shirts of cotton, not handloomed or folklore products (6205.20.20): 21%; women's and girls' blouses and shirts of silk (6206.10.00): 7.5%; men's or boys' pajamas of cotton (6207.21.00): 9.5%; babies' dresses of cotton

(6209.20.10): 12.6%; men's or boys' swimwear of man-made fibers (6211.11.10): 29.6%; women's or girls' swimwear of man-made fibers (6211.12.10): 23.5%; handkerchiefs of silk (6213.10.00): 17%; of cotton, hemmed, without lace or embroidery (6213.20.10): 14%; shawls, scarves, veils, etc., of synthetic or artificial fibers (6214.30.00, 6214.40.00): 10.6%; ties, bows, and cravats of silk or silk waste (6215.10.00): 8%.

Special Provisions. Under 9902.62.10, surgical gowns of 6210.10.40 originating in Canada are eligible for import duty-free through December 31, 1988.

Entry and Documentation

The entry of merchandise is a two-part process consisting of 1) filing the documentation necessary to determine whether merchandise may be released from Customs custody, and 2) filing the documents that contain information for duty assessment and statistical purposes. In certain instances, all documents must be filed and accepted by Customs prior to release of the goods. Unless you have been granted an extension, you must file entry documents at a location specified by the district or area director within five working days of your shipment's date of arrival at a U.S. port of entry. These include a number of standard documents required by Customs for any entry, and:

- U.S. Customs Country-of-Origin Declaration(s)
- Export documentation and/or visa for textiles subject to Multi-Fiber Arrangement
- Customs **Form 6451,** Notice of Percentage of Clean Yield and Grade of Wool or Hair, in duplicate, showing your name and address (if importing articles containing wool)
- Hong Kong government export license (if importing made-to-measure suits from Hong Kong)

After you present the entry, Customs may examine your shipment or may waive examination. The shipment is then released provided no legal or regulatory violations have been noted. You must then file entry summary documentation and deposit estimated duties at a designated customhouse within 10 working days of your shipment's release. For a detailed description of entry procedures, standard documentation, and informal entry, refer to "Entry Process" on page 182.

NAFTA Certificates of Origin. An importer of textiles for which NAFTA treatment is sought need not file a separate NAFTA Certificate of Origin in addition to the Customs Country-of-Origin Declaration. The declaration is sufficient. However, the importer must take care to submit a declaration from each U.S., Canadian, or Mexican producer or manufacturer. Thus, for multiple producers or manufacturers, a separate declaration must be filed for each. If a Customs district director cannot determine the country of origin because the declaration is absent or incomplete, the shipment is not entitled to preferential NAFTA tariff treatment or other NAFTA benefits. See 12 CFR 132.

Entry Invoices. You must provide certain additional information on the entry invoice for apparel which is neither knitted nor crocheted. The specific information varies depending on the nature of your product, as noted below.

TFPIA Requirements. All invoices for textile wearing apparel should indicate: 1) a component material breakdown in percentages by weight for all component fibers present in the entire garment, as well as separate breakdowns of the fibers in the (outer) shell (exclusive of linings, cuffs, waistbands, collars and other trimmings) and in the lining; 2) for garments that are constructed of more than one component or material (combination of knit and not-knit fabric or combinations of knit and/or not-knit fabric with leather, fur, plastic—including vinyl, etc.) the invoice must show a fiber breakdown in percentages by weight for each separate textile material in the garment and a breakdown in percentages by weight for each nontextile material of the entire garment; 3) for woven garments: indicate whether the fabric is yarn-dyed and whether there are "two or more colors in the warp and/or filling;" 4) for all-white T-shirts and singlets: indicate whether or not the garment contains pockets, trim, or embroidery; 5) for mufflers: state the exact dimensions, length, and width of the merchandise.

Wool Products Subject to WPLA. When you offer for entry a wool product shipment valued at over $500 and subject to WPLA, you must include certain information intended to facilitate Customs monitoring and enforcement of that Act. This extra information is identical to that required by WPLA on labeling (see "Marking and Labeling Requirements" below), with the addition of the manufacturer's name. If your product consists of mixed waste, residues, and similar merchandise obtained from several suppliers or unknown sources, you may omit the manufacturer's name from the entry invoice.

Handkerchiefs. The entry invoice for a shipment of handkerchiefs must show: 1) the exact dimensions (length and width) of the merchandise, and 2) if made of cotton, whether hemmed and whether containing lace or embroidery.

Made-to-Measure Suits. Imports from Hong Kong of "made-to-measure" suits that do not accompany a returning traveler are subject to a special agreement. Suits made to the specific measurements of a particular person require a "made-to-measure" export license from the Hong Kong government. You must identify "made-to-measure" suits of Hong Kong origin on your entry summary by placing the symbol "G" as a prefix to the appropriate tariff number. The importer is responsible for the payment of any Customs duties at the time of importation, even if the suits are made to measure for an individual person. For more information, contact your nearest U.S. Customs port office.

Special Access or Regime Entries. Certain garments assembled abroad from components formed and cut in the U.S. that, after assembly have been subject to bleaching, garment dyeing, or perma-pressing abroad, may be eligible for entry under the Special Access Program. Eligibility must be established under a bilateral agreement, and entry must be in compliance with procedures established by the Committee for the Implementation of Textile Agreements. You must identify such garments on the entry summary or withdrawal forms by placing the symbol "H" as a prefix to the appropriate tariff number.

Prohibitions and Restrictions

Textile Quotas. Textile import restrictions are primarily a matter of quotas and the way in which these quotas are administered and monitored. Under the Multi-Fiber Arrangement provisions of Section 204 of the Agricultural Adjustment Act, CITA has negotiated Multi-Fiber Arrangements with 40 countries. These Agreements may impose quotas for a type of textile or a specific article, and they are country-specific. The agreements, however, often change. Therefore, if you are interested in importing any textile apparel articles or clothing accessories, you should contact the International Trade Administration's Office of Textile and Apparel (see addresses at end of this chapter). The Office of Textile and Apparel has a team of country specialists who can inform you of the latest developments and inform you about a product's quota or restriction status.

U.S. Customs enforces CITA textile and textile product entry quotas. If formal entry procedures are not followed, Customs will usually refuse entry for textiles that are subject to Section 204. Formal entry requires submission of a Country-of-Origin Declaration (see General Considerations above). U.S. Customs maintains a current textile quota status report, available for perusal at any Customs port. In addition, U.S. Customs in Washington, DC, operates a telephone service to provide quota status reports, which are updated weekly (see "Relevant Government Agencies" below).

Flammable Fabrics. U.S. Customs may refuse entry for any article of wearing apparel or interior furnishing, or any fabric or related material that is intended for use or that may be used in wearing apparel or interior furnishings, if it fails to conform to an applicable flammability standard issued under Section 4 of the FFA. An exception is allowed for certain products (FFA Section 11c) that are imported for finishing or processing to bring them within the legal standard. For these products, the exporter must state on the invoice or other paper relating to the shipment that the shipment is being made for that purpose.

The CPSC, as the primary enforcement agency of flammability standards, inspects products for compliance with the FFA. If the CPSC believes a product, fabric, or related material does not comply with a flammability standard, it is authorized to pursue a variety of legal sanctions, including: 1) seizure, condemnation, and forfeiture of the noncomplying products; 2) administrative cease-and-desist order requiring an individual or firm to stop sale and distribution of the noncomplying products or; 3) temporary injunction requiring the individual or firm to stop sale and distribution of the noncomplying products, pending final disposition of an administrative cease-and-desist proceeding. The CPSC also has authority to seek civil penalties against any person who knowingly violates a regulation or standard issued under Section 4 of the FFA.

Country-Specific Restrictions

Restrictions under Multi-Fiber Arrangements are country-specific. A product originating in one country may be subject to quota and to export license or visa requirements, while the same product originating in a different country may not. At present, the U.S. has Multi-Fiber Arrangements with 40 countries. Many different categories of products are covered under these Arrangements; it is beyond the scope of this book to list each country and its restricted commodities. If you are interested in importing textiles and textile products, you should contact the International Trade Administration's Office of Textile and Apparel (see addresses at end of this chapter) or U.S. Customs to ascertain your product's restraint status.

The U.S. Customs Quota Branch phone numbers provide recorded status reports, by quota category number, for current charges against the quotas for that country. For convenience, the HTSUS shows the 3-digit category number in parentheses to the right of each listed commodity that is subject to textile restraints. For example, under Chapter 62, heading 6209.20.10, Babies' Dresses of Cotton, is followed by the number "(239)". If you know the category number for your product, you can find out to what extent that quota is filled simply by calling the number for the appropriate country. A word of caution, though: if you do not know for sure that your article is subject to quota from a particular country, and you call the number for that country, you may not be any more enlightened after the phone call. Many of the recordings give status reports only when a certain percentage of the quota has been filled. Thus, if 239 for Indonesia is among the categories for which not enough quantity has entered the U.S. to warrant specific mention, it will be lumped under "all other categories" and you will be none the wiser. To find out if your product is subject to textile restraints, call the DOC or a local Customs port office. Then you can find out the current charges against that quota by calling the country number listed below. For a complete listing of Customs Quota Branch information numbers, see "Relevant Government Agencies" below.

Marking and Labeling Requirements

TFPIA Requirements. All textile products imported into the U.S. must be stamped, tagged, labeled, or otherwise marked with the following information as required by the TFPIA, unless exempt from marking (see TFPIA, Section 12): 1) the generic names and percentages by weight of the constituent fibers present in the textile fiber product, exclusive of permissible ornamentation, in amounts of more than 5% in order of predominance by weight, with any percentage of fiber or fibers required to be designated as "other fiber" or "other fibers" (including those present in amounts of 5% or less) appearing last; and 2) the name of the manufacturer or the name or registered identification number issued by the FTC of one or more persons marketing or handling the textile fiber product; and 3) the name of the country where processed. A word trademark, used as a house mark and registered with the U.S. Patent Office, may appear on labels instead of the name otherwise required, provided the owner of the trademark furnishes a copy of the registration to the FTC prior to use (see "Registered Identification Numbers" below).

The information listed above is not exhaustive. TFPIA requirements are extensive. The Act specifies such details as types of labels, means of attachment, label position on the article, package labeling, unit labeling for two-piece garments, and arrangement of information on the label; allowable fiber designations; country-of-origin indications; requirements for trim and ornamentation, linings and interlinings, and pile fabrics; sectional disclosure; use of trade names and trademarks; and requirements for swatches and samples. The FTC publishes a booklet intended to clarify TFPIA requirements to facilitate voluntary compliance in the industry (see "Publications Available" below). It is available on request, at no charge, from the FTC (see addresses at end of this chapter).

Wool Products Labeling Act (WPLA). Wool product labeling requirements for foreign products are the responsibility of the importer. The WPLA requires the following information to appear on wool products subject to the Act: 1) percentage of the wool product's total fiber weight (exclusive of ornamentation) not exceeding 5% of the total fiber weight of a) wool, b) recycled wool, c) each fiber other than wool if the percent by weight of such fiber is 5% or more, and d) the aggregate of all other fibers; 2) the maximum percent of the wool product's total weight, of any nonfibrous loading, filling, or adulterating matter; and 3) the importer's name. If you, as importer, have a registered identification number issued by the FTC, that number may be used instead of your name (see "Registered Identification Numbers" below).

Customs entry is contingent on proper labeling. If your shipment is found to be mislabeled at entry, you will be given the option of relabeling the products under Customs supervision, as long as the district director is satisfied that your labeling error or omission did not involve fraud or willful neglect. If your shipment is discovered after entry to have been noncomplying with WPLA, it will be recalled to Customs custody at your expense, unless you can satisfy the district director that the products have since been brought into compliance. You will be held responsible for all expenses incurred in bringing a shipment into compliance, including compensation of personnel and other expenses related to Customs supervision.

Fraudulent violations of WPLA will result in seizure of the shipment. Shipments already released from Customs custody will be ordered to be redelivered to Customs. Customs reports all cases of fraudulent violation to the FTC in Washington, DC.

The information listed above is not intended to be exhaustive. WPLA requirements are extensive. The Act specifies such details as types of labels, means of attachment, label position on the article, package labeling, unit labeling (as in the case of a two-piece garment), arrangement of information on the label, allowable fiber designations, country-of-origin indications, trim and ornamentation, pile fabrics, sectional disclosure, use of trade names and trademarks, requirements for swatches and samples, etc. The FTC publishes a booklet intended to clarify WPLA requirements in order to facilitate voluntary compliance within the industry (see "Publications Available" below). It is available on request, at no charge, from the FTC (see addresses at end of this chapter).

Registered Identification Numbers. Any domestic firm or person residing in the U.S. and engaged in the manufacture or marketing of textile products covered under the TFPIA may obtain an FTC-registered identification number for use on required tags and labels instead of the name of a firm or person. For applications, contact the FTC (see addresses at end of this chapter).

For a general discussion of U.S. Customs marking and labeling requirements, refer to "Marking: Country of Origin" on page 215 and "Special Marking Requirements" on page 217.

Shipping Considerations

You will need to ensure that your goods are packaged and shipped with care so that they pass smoothly through Customs and arrive in good condition. You are responsible for ensuring that the shipment is in compliance with all applicable government regulations for packaging and shipping. In most instances, you should not leave these arrangements solely to the discretion of your supplier. Careful preparation of the cargo and selection of the mode of transport can be essential to a cost-effective, timely delivery of undamaged goods. We strongly advise you to consult your shipping representative, insurance agent, or freight broker for advice on packing and shipping. Refer also to the major tab section "Packing/Shipping/Insurance" for a general discussion of packing and shipping.

Textile apparel articles or clothing accessories may be shipped in bulk, cartons, or other types of containers, depending on the type of product and whether it is prepackaged. General considerations include protection from contamination, weather, and pests. Containers should be constructed so as to be safe for handling during transport.

Publications Available

The following publications may be relevant to the importation of textile apparel articles or clothing accessories:

Questions and Answers Relating to the Textile Fiber Products Identification Act and Regulations

Questions and Answers Relating to the Wool Products Labeling Act and Regulations

Available free of charge on request from the Federal Trade Commission (see addresses at end of this chapter), these publications are excellent sources of information written in clear lay language. We recommend that anyone interested in importing textile fiber products but unfamiliar with the regulations obtain a copy of each of these booklets.

The *Harmonized Tariff Schedule of the United States* (HTSUS) is available from:

Government Printing Office (GPO)
Superintendent of Documents
Washington, DC 20402
(202) 512-1800 (Order line)
(202) 512-0000 (General)

The USGPO also has copies of specific laws available for purchase. The USGPO accepts credit card orders over the phone, as well as mail orders paid by credit card, a check drawn on a U.S. bank, or an international money order.

Relevant Government Agencies

Address your questions regarding textile Multi-Fiber Arrangements to:

International Trade Administration
Office of Textile and Apparel
14th and Constitution Ave. NW, Rm. 3100
Washington, DC 20230
(202) 482-5078, 482-3737

Address your questions regarding the Flammable Fabrics Act (FFA) to:

Consumer Product Safety Commission (CPSC)
5401 Westbard Avenue
Bethesda, MD 20207
(301) 492-6580

Address your questions regarding labeling requirements under the Textile Fiber Products Identification Act (TFPIA) or the Wool Products Labeling Act (WPLA) to:

Federal Trade Commission (FTC)
Division of Enforcement
601 Pennsylvania Ave. NW
Washington, DC 20580
(202) 326-2996 (General)
(202) 326-2841 (Textile and wool products labeling)

Address your questions regarding imports of textile apparel articles or clothing accessories to the district or port director of Customs for you area. For addresses, refer to"U.S. Customs District Offices" on page 62 or contact:

U.S. Customs Service
1301 Constitution Ave. NW
Washington, DC 20229
(202) 927-6724 (Information)
(202) 927-1000 (General)

The following information numbers for U.S. Customs in Washington, DC, provide recorded information. The Quota Branch numbers listed by country provide updated status reports on textile quotas from those countries. All area codes are (202).
General information: 927-5850

Quota Branch: China 927-6703; India 927-6705; Indonesia 927-6704; Japan 927-6706; Korea 927-6707; Macao 927-6709; Malaysia 927-6712; Mexico 927-6711; Pakistan 927-6714; Philippines 927-6713; Romania 927-6715; Singapore 927-6716; Sri Lanka 927-6708; Taiwan 927-6719; Thailand 927-6717; Turkey 927-6718; All others 927-5850.

Laws and Regulations

The following laws and regulations may be relevant to the importation of textile apparel articles or clothing accessories. The laws are contained in the United States Code (USC), and the regulations are published in the Code of Federal Regulations (CFR), both of which are available at larger public and law libraries. Copies of specific laws are also available from the United States Government Printing Office (address above).

7 USC 1854
Textile Trade Agreements
(EO 11651, as amended by EO 11951 and 12188, and supplemented by EO 12475)
This Act authorizes the CITA of the DOC to enter into Multi-Fiber Agreements with other countries to control trade in textiles and establishes the Textile Import Program, which is enforced by U.S. Customs.

19 CFR 12.130 et seq.
Regulations on Entry of Textiles
These regulations provide the requirements and procedures followed by Customs in enforcing limitations on the importation and entry and withdrawal of textiles and textile products from warehouses for consumption in the U.S.

15 USC 70-77
Textile Fiber Products Identification Act (TFPIA)
This Act prohibits false or deceptive labeling (misbranding) and false advertising of any textile fiber products and requires all textile fiber products imported into the U.S. to be labeled in accordance with the requirements set forth in the law.

19 CFR 11.12b; 16 CFR 303 et seq.
Regulations on Labeling and Marking
These regulations detail the labeling and marking requirements for textiles as specified by the CPSC and the invoice contents required by U.S. Customs for purpose of enforcing the labeling and marking rules.

15 USC 68-68j
Wool Products Labeling Act (WPLA)
This Act prohibits the false or deceptive labeling (misbranding) of wool products and requires all wool products imported into the U.S. to be labeled in accordance with requirements set forth in the law.

19 CFR 11.12; 16 CFR 300 et seq.
Regulations on WPLA Labeling and Marking
These regulations set forth the wool labeling and marking requirements adopted by the FTC to administer the requirements of the WPLA and provide the procedures followed by U.S. Customs in enforcing the WPLA and the FTC regulations, including entry invoice requirements.

15 USC 1191-1204
Flammable Fabrics Act (FFA)
This Act provides for the setting of flammability standards for fabric by the Consumer Product Safety Commission (CPSC) and for enforcement by U.S. Customs.

16 CFR 1610, 1611, 1615, 1616, 1630-1632
Regulations on Flammable Fabric Standards
These regulations specify the flammability standards adopted by the CPSC under the FFA for various types of textiles.

Principal Exporting Countries

The following listing includes samples of the main supplier nations of the products of this chapter. It is organized by HTSUS major heading. (Refer to "Customs Classification" above for the product codes.) Countries are listed in rank order of the value of products imported to the U.S. Statistics represent customs value entries for 1993 from the Bureau of Census, U.S. Department of Commerce.

6201—China, South Korea, Hong Kong, Taiwan, Thailand, Sri Lanka, Philippines, Macao, Malaysia, Bangladesh

6202—China, Hong Kong, South Korea, Sri Lanka, Thailand, Taiwan, Dominican Rep., Philippines, Bangladesh, Macao

6203—Dominican Rep., Mexico, China, Hong Kong, Costa Rica, Italy, Canada, Indonesia, Taiwan, Honduras

6204—China, Hong Kong, Dominican Rep., South Korea, Taiwan, India, Philippines, Mexico, Guatemala, Indonesia

6205—China, Hong Kong, South Korea, Taiwan, Malaysia, India, Bangladesh, Guatemala, Sri Lanka, Indonesia

6206—China, Hong Kong, India, Indonesia, Bangladesh, Sri Lanka, South Korea, Malaysia, Taiwan, Thailand

6207—China, Hong Kong, Dominican Rep., Taiwan, Brazil, Turkey, Honduras, Costa Rica, South Korea, Bangladesh

6208—China, Hong Kong, Philippines, Sri Lanka, Turkey, Indonesia, Taiwan, Bangladesh, Mexico, South Korea

6209—Philippines, China, Hong Kong, Bangladesh, Taiwan, Thailand, Sri Lanka, Indonesia, Colombia, South Korea

6210—Mexico, China, Taiwan, South Korea, Hong Kong, Thailand, Dominican Rep., Philippines, Bangladesh, Canada

6211—China, Taiwan, Hong Kong, India, Philippines, South Korea, Thailand, Indonesia, Sri Lanka, Bangladesh

6212—Dominican Rep., Mexico, Costa Rica, Philippines, China, Honduras, Thailand, Jamaica, Hong Kong, Indonesia

6213—China, Czech Rep., Italy, Taiwan, Philippines, South Korea, Malaysia, France, Switzerland, United Kingdom

6214—Italy, Japan, South Korea, France, India, China, United Kingdom, Germany, Taiwan, Hong Kong

6215—Italy, South Korea, France, Costa Rica, Dominican Rep., China, Canada, Japan, United Kingdom, Spain

6216—China, Sri Lanka, Hong Kong, Indonesia, South Korea, Philippines, Taiwan, Thailand, Pakistan, Guatemala

6217—Taiwan, China, Canada, South Korea, Mexico, Italy, Hong Kong, Guatemala, India, Dominican Rep.

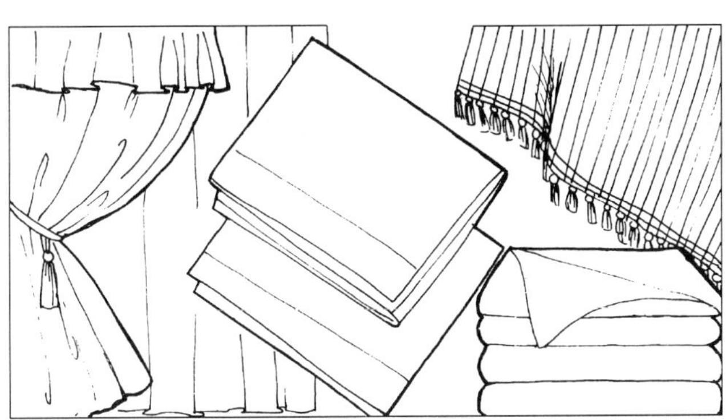

Chapter 63: Other Textile Articles*

Full title: Other Made-up Articles; Needlecraft Sets; Worn Clothing and Worn Textile Articles; Rags

This chapter relates to the importation of textile articles not covered elsewhere, which are classified under Chapter 63 of the Harmonized Tariff Schedule of the United States (HTSUS). Specifically, it covers blankets and traveling rugs; bed, table, bath, and kitchen linen; curtains, interior blinds, and valances, bedspreads not classified under HTSUS 9404, sacks and bags; tarpaulins, awning, sunblinds, tents, and camping goods; sails for boats, sailboards, or landcraft; cleaning cloths; lifejackets and life belts; dress patterns; footwear and other lacings; textile pet toys; wall banners; surgical towels; needlecraft sets; worn clothing and other articles; rags, scrap cordage, and worn out cordage. Articles are classified as worn only if the show signs of appreciable wear and are entered in bulk or in bales, sacks, or similar packings.

If you are interested in importing articles of apparel that are not worn, you should read Commodity Index Chapter 61 (knitted or crocheted) or Chapter 62 (not knitted or crocheted). Quilts and textile furnishings are found in Chapter 94, and surgical belts and orthopedic items are classified in Chapter 90. If you are interested in importing footwear or headgear, you should refer to Chapter 64 or 65, respectively. Textiles, garment parts, thread, yarns, and other similar materials are covered in Chapters 50 through 58. Articles of apparel that contain leather parts may be imported in accordance with the requirements explained in Chapter 42. Cordage that is not scrap or worn out must be imported in accordance with Chapter 56.

Key Factors

The key factors in the importation of other textile articles are:

- Compliance with quota restraints and visa requirements under U.S. Department of Commerce (DOC) Multi-Fiber Arrangements
- Submission of U.S. Customs Country-of-Origin Declaration(s)
- Compliance with entry invoice requirements
- Compliance with labeling requirements under the Textile Fiber Products Identification Act (TFPIA) and the Wool Products Labeling Act (WPLA)
- Compliance with flammability standards adopted and enforced by the Consumer Product Safety Commission (CPSC) under the Flammable Fabrics Act (FFA) (if importing fabrics and other textile products)
- Compliance with U.S. Food and Drug Administration (FDA) inspection and entry requirements (if importing products intended for sanitary purposes and no exemption applies)
- Compliance with Federal Plant Pest Act (FPPA) and Plant Quarantine Act (PQA) requirements, and with U.S. Department of Agriculture (USDA) random port-of-entry inspections, import restrictions and quarantines, and other entry requirements (if importing cordage of vegetable materials)

Although most importers use the services of a licensed customs broker in making their entries, and we recommend this practice, you should be aware of the regulatory, entry, and documentation issues involved in importing your product. You, as importer, are ultimately responsible for the fulfillment of any legal requirements applicable to your shipment.

General Considerations

Regulatory Agencies. The DOC's Committee for Implementation of Textile Agreements (CITA) regulates certain textile imports under Section 204 of the Agricultural Adjustment Act. U.S. Customs enforces CITA textile and textile product entry quotas. Customs also enforces compliance with labeling and invoice requirements of the TFPIA and flammability standards under the FFA. The CPSC monitors imports and from time to time inspects textile shipments for compliance with FFA standards. If you are importing wool articles, importation is subject to complex textile import regulations. The Federal Trade Commission (FTC) administers the WPLA requirements.

The USDA administers applicable provisions of the Plant Quarantine Act (PQA) and the Federal Plant Pest Act (FPPA), which are designed to prevent introduction into the U.S. of any plant pest or disease potentially harmful to U.S. agriculture. Shipments of cordage made of vegetable materials—e.g., jute—must be in compliance with PQA, FPPA, and USDA requirements. The FDA, under authority of the Federal Food, Drug, and Cosmetic Act (FDCA), regulates the importation of products intended for medical or sanitary purposes. U.S. Customs enforces compliance with entry requirements for products subject to the FDCA.

Wool Product Entry Requirements. Depending on the nature of your wool article imports, as many as four different types of special entry documents may be required. First, for all imported articles that contain textile fibers, yarns, and fabrics covered by the Agricultural Adjustment Act (AAA), including wool, you must file a U.S. Customs Textile Entry Declaration (see "Textile Country-of-Origin Declarations" below). Second, with the entry summary for each shipment of wool articles, you must file Customs **Form 6451,** Notice of Percentage of Clean Yield and Grade of Wool or Hair, in duplicate, showing your name and address. Third, for all wool products subject to the WPLA, special information is required on the entry invoices (see "Wool Products Labeling Act" below). Finally, certain articles of apparel manufactured or produced in certain countries may be subject to quotas and other restraints under U.S. DOC Multi-Fiber Arrangements. Such products require export licenses, certificates, or visas issued by the appropriate country of origin, in addition to other requisite entry paperwork (see "Textile Quotas" below).

Wool Products Labeling Act. The term "wool product" means any product or any portion of a product that contains, purports to contain, or in any way is represented as containing wool, reprocessed wool, or reused wool. All wool products imported into the U.S., except those made more than 20 years before importation, and except carpets, rugs, mats, and upholsteries, must

*IMPORTANT: Read the Commodity Index Introduction. It is the essential framework for understanding this chapter.

have affixed a stamp, tag, label, or other means of identification as required by the WPLA. If you are importing wool products exempt from labeling under the WPLA, do not assume they are also exempt from labeling under the TFPIA. These are two distinct laws, with some overlapping requirements (see "Marking and Labeling Requirements" below).

Cordage of Vegetable Materials. For most shipments of worn out cordage made of vegetable materials, importation is straightforward. With some exceptions, you do not need permits or licenses to import these products (see "Prohibitions and Restrictions", below). The USDA's Animal and Plant Health Inspection Service (APHIS) inspects shipments of cordage made of vegetable materials on a random basis, depending on such factors as the port of entry, the country of origin, and the risk of contamination involved in the type of material being imported. Entry may be denied for noncompliance with the regulations, and the shipment could be seized, quarantined, destroyed, treated, or otherwise dealt with at the discretion of the inspector.

Products for Sanitary Purposes. The importation of products intended for surgical, medical, or other sanitary uses are regulated by the FDA. Usually, if you import FDA-regulated articles, you must follow certain import procedures prescribed by that agency, and you must file FDA entry notification, **Form FD701.** For an annotated diagram of FDA import procedures, refer to the "Foods" appendix on page 808. If you are interested in importing such a product, you should ascertain its regulatory status by contacting the FDA (see addresses at end of this chapter).

Textile Quotas. If you are interested in importing other textile articles, the most important issue you need to be aware of is quotas. Under the Multi-Fiber Arrangement provisions of Section 204 of the Agricultural Adjustment Act, CITA initiates specific agreements with individual exporting countries. Section 204 of the Agricultural Adjustment Act covers textiles articles that: 1) are in chief value of cotton, wool, or man-made fibers, any textile fibers subject to the terms of any textile trade agreement, or any combination of such fibers; 2) contain 50% or more by weight of cotton or man-made fibers, or any textile fibers subject to the terms of any textile trade agreement; 3) contain 17% or more by weight of wool; or 4) if in chief value of textile fibers or textile materials, contain a blend of cotton, wool, or man-made fibers, any textile fibers subject to the terms of any textile trade agreement, or any combination of such fibers that, in total, amount to 50% or more by weight of all component fibers.

The U.S. has Multi-Fiber Arrangements with 40 countries. Each agreement with each country is unique, and may specify quotas for a type of textile or a specific article. Visas or export licenses may be required. These agreements, however, often change. Therefore, if you are interested in importing any other textile articles, you should contact the International Trade Administration's Office of Textile and Apparel (see addresses at end of this chapter). Refer to "Prohibitions and Restrictions" below for further details.

Textile Country-of-Origin Declarations. U.S. Customs enforces CITA textile and textile product entry quotas (see "Prohibitions and Restrictions" below). Requirements for entry include submission of Country-of-Origin Declarations with every shipment of other textile articles, regardless of whether it is subject to a specific multi-fiber arrangement (19 CFR 12.130, 12.131).

Country of Origin. Quota restrictions are country-specific and therefore are applied based on the country of origin for the textiles shipped. The last country from which a textile shipment was exported to the U.S. is not necessarily its country of origin. A textile or textile product imported into the U.S. is considered a product of the particular foreign territory or country, or a U.S. insular possession, where it is wholly grown, produced, or manufactured. For the following discussion, "country" means a foreign territory or country, or a U.S. insular possession.

Substantial transformation rules may affect the country-of-origin determination. For example, if a textile or textile product originates in Country A and is subject to quota, the quota restrictions apply at entry into the U.S. But if, prior to export to the U.S., you move the shipment to Country B where there are fewer restrictions, the shipment may nevertheless remain subject to quota and visa requirements under the Multi-Fiber Arrangement with Country A. Customs determines whether the quota restrictions apply based on the criteria of "substantial transformation." If your textiles do not undergo any major processing or manufacturing while in Country B, or if the manufacturing or processing is minor, your shipment will be deemed to originate in Country A. *You cannot claim substantial transformation on the basis of minor manufacturing procedures.*

In contrast, if your shipment undergoes major processing or manufacturing while in Country B, rendering the textiles "new and different articles of commerce," Customs will treat the shipment as the product of Country B. To qualify as having undergone substantial transformation, an article must evince a change in: 1) commercial designation or identity; b) fundamental character; or c) commercial use. If your shipment is processed in more than one country, the country where it last underwent substantial transformation is the country of origin for Customs entry. In deciding whether the manufacturing or processing operation in a country is major, Customs considers the following factors: 1) the resultant physical change in the material or article; 2) the complexity, the level or degree of skill and/or technology required, and the amount of time involved in the operations; and 3) the value added to the article or material, compared to its value when imported into the U.S.

Validating Operations. Operations that Customs will usually acknowledge as validating a claim of substantial transformation are the following: 1) dyeing and printing, when accompanied by two or more of the following finishing operations: bleaching, shrinking, fulling, napping, decating, permanent stiffening, weighting, permanent embossing, or moireing; 2) spinning fibers into yarn; 3) weaving, knitting, or otherwise forming fabric; 4) cutting fabric into parts and assembling the parts into completed articles; or 5) substantial assembly, by sewing and/or tailoring into a completed garment cut pieces of apparel articles that have been cut from fabric in another country—e.g., complete assembly and tailoring of all cut pieces of suit-type jackets, suits, and shirts.

Insubstantial Operations. Operations that usually will not support a claim of substantial transformation, even if more than one are performed, are the following: 1) simple operations of combining, labeling, pressing, cleaning, dry cleaning, or packaging; 2) cutting to length or width and hemming or overlocking fabrics that are readily identifiable as being intended for a particular commercial use; 3) trimming and/or joining together by sewing, looping, linking, or other means of attaching otherwise completed knit-to-shape component parts produced in a single country, even if accompanied by other processes—e.g., washing, drying, mending—normally incident to assembly; 4) one or more finishing operations on yarns, fabrics, or their textile articles—such as showerproofing, superwashing, bleaching, decating, fulling, shrinking, mercerizing, or similar operations; or 5) dyeing and/or printing fabrics or yarns.

Declarations. The country of origin of the other textile articles in a shipment must be stated on a declaration submitted to U.S. Customs at the time of entry. There are three Customs Country-of-Origin Declarations: single-country, multiple-country, and negative. The Declaration to be submitted with your shipment of knitted or crocheted apparel articles depends on the nature of the import.

- **Single-country declarations** are used for entries of textiles or textile products that clearly originate from only one country or that have been assembled in one country from fabricated components wholly produced in the U.S. or the foreign country of manufacture. Information required includes: marks of identification and numbers; description of article and quantity; country of origin; and date of exportation.
- **Multiple-country declarations** are used for entries of textiles or textile products that were manufactured or processed and/or that incorporate materials originating in more than one foreign country or territory. Information required includes: marks of identification and numbers; for articles, description, quantity, identification of manufacturing and/or processing operations, country, and date of exportation; for materials used to make articles, description of materials, country of production, and date of exportation.
- **Negative declarations** must accompany all textile imports that are not subject to FFA Section 204 restrictions. Information required includes: marks of identification and numbers; descriptions of article and quantity; and country of origin.

The date of exportation to be indicated on the above declarations is the date on which the carrier leaves the last port in the country of origin, as determined by Customs. Diversion to another country during transit does not affect the export date.

Procedure for Declarations. The manufacturer, producer, exporter, or importer may prepare the declaration. If more than one of these parties is involved in the importation, each party may prepare a separate declaration. You may file a separate declaration for each invoice presented with your entry. The declaration must be dated and signed by the responsible party, and must include the person's title and the company name and address. Your shipment's entry will be denied unless it is accompanied by a properly executed declaration. Customs will not treat a textile declaration as a missing document for which a bond may be filed.

Customs will base its country-of-origin determination on the information contained in each declaration, unless the information is insufficient. If the information on the declaration is insufficient, Customs will require that you submit such additional information as will enable the determination to be made. The shipment will not be released until the determination is made. Thus, if you want to clear Customs with minimal delay, be sure that the information on the declarations is as complete as possible for each shipment.

Textile Labeling and Invoice Requirements. You are responsible for your imported product's compliance with applicable provisions of the TFPIA. Other textile articles that require labeling under TFPIA must already be labeled at entry, or the shipment will be refused. (See "Marking and Labeling Requirements" below.) If you import shipments of other textile articles subject to TFPIA and valued at over $500, you must provide special information on the entry invoice (see "Entry and Documentation" below).

Flammability Standards. Other textile articles imported into the U.S. for use in consumer products must be in compliance with the FFA, a federal law that gives the CPSC the authority and responsibility for protecting the public from the hazards of dangerously flammable items of wearing apparel and interior furnishings. Under the FFA, standards have been established for flammability of clothing textiles. You cannot import any article of wearing apparel or interior furnishing, or any fabric or related material that is intended for use or that may be used in such items, if it fails to conform to an applicable flammability standard (FFA Section 4). Certain products may be imported into the U.S. (FFA Section 11c) for finishing or processing to render them less flammable so as to meet the standards. For these products, the exporter must state on the invoice or other paper relating to the shipment that the shipment is being made for that purpose.

The CPSC monitors imports of textiles under its Import Surveillance Program. From time to time, your textile shipments may be inspected to ascertain compliance with mandatory safety standards. Shipments may also be subject to testing by the CPSC to determine compliance. If the CPSC believes a product, fabric, or related material does not comply with a flammability standard, it is authorized to pursue a variety of legal sanctions (see "Prohibitions and Restrictions" below).

Substantial Product Hazard Reports. Any firm that obtains information that reasonably supports the conclusion that one of its products presents an unreasonable risk of serious injury or death must report that information to the CPSC's Division of Corrective Actions (CPSC address below). Importers must also report to the CPSC if 1) a type of product is the subject of at least three civil actions filed in U.S. federal or state courts, 2) each suit alleges the involvement of that product type in death or grievous bodily injury (as defined in FFA Section 37(3)1), and 3) at least three of the actions result in a final settlement with the manufacturer or in a judgment for the plaintiff within any one of the two-year periods specified in FFA Section 37(b).

Import Advisory

Importation of textile products is trade-sensitive and highly regulated. Shipments of textile products not complying with all government regulations, including quotas and visas, are subject to seizure and could result in the imposition of penalties as well as possible forfeiture of the goods. You should always verify the available quota for any textile product you plan to import before your shipment leaves the country of manufacture. Furthermore, Customs textile classification rulings change frequently, and prior administrative rulings are often modified and sometimes reversed.

Customs Classification

For customs purposes, other textile articles are classified under Chapter 63 of the HTSUS. This chapter is broken into major headings, which are further divided into subheadings, and often sub-subheadings, each of which has its own HTSUS classification number. For example, the HTSUS number for table linen, knitted or crocheted, of vegetable fiber other than cotton, is 6302.40.10, indicating it is a sub-subcategory of table linen, knitted or crocheted (6302.40.00), which is a subcategory of the major heading bed linen, table linen, etc. (6302.00.00). There are 10 major headings within Chapter 63.

6301—Blankets and traveling rugs

6302—Bed linen, table linen, toilet linen, and kitchen linen

6303—Curtains (including drapes) and interior blinds; curtain or bed valances

6304—Other furnishing articles, excluding those of heading 9404

6305—Sacks and bags, of a kind used for the packing of goods

6306—Tarpaulins, awnings, and sunblinds; tents; sails for boats, sailboards, or landcraft; camping goods

6307—Other made up articles, including dress patterns

6308—Needlecraft sets consisting of woven fabric and yarn, whether or not with accessories, for making up into rugs, tapestries, embroidered tablecloths or napkins, or similar textile articles, put up in packings for retail sale

6309—Worn clothing and other worn articles

6310—Used or new rags, scrap twine, cordage, rope, and cables, and worn out articles of twine, cordage, rope, or cables, of textile materials

Sample Import Duties

Import duties will vary depending on the HTSUS classification of your product. Therefore, to determine the correct amount of duties, your product must be properly classified under the HTSUS. The following sample duties are taken from the duty listings for HTSUS Chapter 63 products.

Electric blankets (6301.10.00): 13%; other blankets and traveling rugs of wool (6301.20.00): 4.4 cents/kg plus 15%, of cotton (6301.30.00): 9.5%, of synthetic fibers (6301.40.00): 13%; bed linen, knitted or crocheted (6302.10.00): 7.6%; other bed linen, printed, of cotton, trimmed, embroidered, etc. (6302.21.10): 23.8%; table linen, knitted or crocheted, of vegetable fibers except cotton (6302.40.10): 12.8%; Damask tablecloths and napkins (6302.51.10): 6.9%; bath and kitchen terry towels (6302.60.00): 10.3%; cotton curtains, knitted or crocheted (6303.11.00): 11.7%; bedspreads, knitted or crocheted, of cotton (6304.11.10): 13.6%; tarpaulins, awnings, and sunblinds of synthetic fibers (6306.12.00): 10%; cotton tents (6306.21.00): 16%; backpacking tents (6306.22.10): 4.64%; dust, mop, and polishing cloths, of cotton (6307.10.10): 4.7%; lifejackets and lifebelts (6307.20.00): 9%; lacings (6307.90.50): 7.9%; textile pet toys (6307.90.75): 8.5%; needlecraft sets (6308.00.00): 13%; worn clothing and other articles (6309.00.00): 1.8%.

Special Provisions. Under 9902.62.10, disposable surgical drapes of subheading 6307.90.70 are eligible to be imported duty-free from Canada through December 31, 1998.

Entry and Documentation

The entry of merchandise is a two-part process consisting of 1) filing the documentation necessary to determine whether merchandise may be released from Customs custody, and 2) filing the documents that contain information for duty assessment and statistical purposes. In certain instances, all documents must be filed and accepted by Customs prior to release of the goods. Unless you have been granted an extension, you must file entry documents at a location specified by the district or area director within five working days of your shipment's date of arrival at a U.S. port of entry. These include a number of standard documents required by Customs for any entry, and:

- U.S. Customs Country-of-Origin Declaration(s).
- Export documentation and/or visa for textiles subject to Multi-Fiber Arrangement
- Customs **Form 6451**, Notice of Percentage of Clean Yield and Grade of Wool or Hair, in duplicate, showing your name and address (if importing articles containing wool)
- Phytosanitary certificate (if importing cordage made of vegetable material)
- **Form FD701**, FDA entry notification (if importing sanitary items)

After you present the entry, Customs may examine your shipment or may waive examination. The shipment is then released provided no legal or regulatory violations have been noted. You must then file entry summary documentation and deposit estimated duties at a designated customhouse within 10 working days of your shipment's release. For a detailed description of entry procedures, standard documentation, and informal entry, refer to "Entry Process" on page 182.

NAFTA Certificates of Origin. An importer of textiles for which NAFTA treatment is sought need not file a separate NAFTA Certificate of Origin in addition to the Customs Country-of-Origin Declaration. The declaration is sufficient. However, the importer must take care to submit a declaration from each U.S., Canadian, or Mexican producer or manufacturer. Thus, for multiple producers or manufacturers, a separate declaration must be filed for each. If a Customs district director cannot determine the country of origin because the declaration is absent or incomplete, the shipment is not entitled to preferential NAFTA tariff treatment or other NAFTA benefits. See 12 CFR 132.

Entry Invoices. You must provide certain additional information on the entry invoice for other textile articles. The specific information varies depending on the nature of your product, as noted below.

TFPIA Requirements. All invoices for textile wearing apparel should indicate a component material breakdown in percentages by weight for all component fibers present in the entire garment, as well as separate breakdowns of the fibers in the (outer) shell (exclusive of linings, cuffs, waistbands, collars and other trimmings) and in the lining; 2) for garments that are constructed of more than one component or material (combination of knit and not-knit fabric or combinations of knit and/or not-knit fabric with leather, fur, plastic—including vinyl, etc.) the invoice must show a fiber breakdown in percentages by weight for each separate textile material in the garment and a breakdown in percentages by weight for each nontextile material of the entire garment; 3) for woven garments: indicate whether the fabric is yarn-dyed and whether there are "two or more colors in the warp and/or filling;" 4) for all-white T-shirts and singlets: indicate whether or not the garment contains pockets, trim, or embroidery; 5) for mufflers: state the exact dimensions, length, and width of the merchandise.

Wool Products Subject to WPLA. When you offer for entry a wool product shipment valued at over $500 and subject to WPLA, you must include certain information intended to facilitate Customs monitoring and enforcement of that Act. This extra information is identical to that required by WPLA on labeling (see "Marking and Labeling Requirements" below), with the addition of the manufacturer's name. If your product consists of mixed waste, residues, and similar merchandise obtained from several suppliers or unknown sources, you may omit the manufacturer's name from the entry invoice.

Bed Linens and Bedspreads. The entry invoice for a shipment of bed linens or bedspreads must state whether the article contains any embroidery, lace, braid, edging, trimming, piping, or applique work.

Prohibitions and Restrictions

Textile Quotas. Textile import restrictions are primarily a matter of quotas and the way in which these quotas are administered and monitored. Under the Multi-Fiber Arrangement provisions of Section 204 of the Agricultural Adjustment Act, CITA has negotiated Multi-Fiber Arrangements with 40 countries. These Agreements may impose quotas for a type of textile or a specific article, and they are country-specific. The agreements, however, often change. Therefore, if you are interested in importing other textile articles, you should contact the International Trade Administration's Office of Textile and Apparel (see addresses at end of this chapter). The Office of Textile and Apparel has a team of country specialists who can inform you of the latest developments and inform you about a product's quota or restriction status.

U.S. Customs enforces CITA textile and textile product entry quotas. If formal entry procedures are not followed, Customs will usually refuse entry for textiles that are subject to Section 204. Formal entry requires submission of a Country-of-Origin Declaration (see "General Considerations" above). U.S. Customs maintains a current textile quota status report, available for perusal at any Customs port. In addition, U.S. Customs in Washington, DC, operates a telephone service to provide quota status reports, which are updated weekly (see "Relevant Government Agencies" below).

Flammable Fabrics. U.S. Customs may refuse entry for any article of wearing apparel or interior furnishing, or any fabric or related material that is intended for use or that may be used in wearing apparel or interior furnishings, if it fails to conform to an applicable flammability standard issued under Section 4 of the FFA. An exception is allowed for certain products (FFA Section 11c) that are imported for finishing or processing to bring them within the legal standard. For these products, the exporter must state on the invoice or other paper relating to the shipment that the shipment is being made for that purpose.

The CPSC, as the primary enforcement agency of flammability standards, inspects products for compliance with the FFA. If the CPSC believes a product, fabric, or related material does not comply with a flammability standard, it is authorized to pursue a variety of legal sanctions, including: 1) seizure, condemnation, and forfeiture of the noncomplying products; 2) administrative cease-and-desist order requiring an individual or firm to stop sale and distribution of the noncomplying products or; 3) temporary injunction requiring the individual or firm to stop sale and distribution of the noncomplying products, pending final disposition of an administrative cease-and-desist proceeding. The CPSC also has authority to seek civil penalties against any person who knowingly violates a regulation or standard issued under Section 4 of the FFA.

Cordage of Vegetable Materials. In general, any shipment of cordage made of vegetable materials is subject to random port-of-entry inspection by the USDA. If the inspector finds evidence of the presence of insects in your shipment, you may be required to submit your shipment to USDA-prescribed fumigation procedures. If the insect is of a kind for which there is no viable U.S. treatment, your shipment will be refused. Our source at USDA assured us that most shipments that are found to have insects in them can be treated to afford entry.

Country-Specific Restrictions

Restrictions under Multi-Fiber Arrangements are country-specific. A product originating in one country may be subject to quota and to export license or visa requirements, while the same product originating in a different country may not. At present, the U.S. has Multi-Fiber Arrangements with 40 countries. Many different categories of products are covered under these Arrangements; it is beyond the scope of this book to list each country and its restricted commodities. If you are interested in importing textiles and textile products, you should contact the International Trade Administration's Office of Textile and Apparel (see addresses at end of this chapter) or U.S. Customs to ascertain your product's restraint status.

The U.S. Customs Quota Branch phone numbers provide recorded status reports, by quota category number, for current charges against the quotas for that country. For convenience, the HTSUS shows the 3-digit category number in parentheses to the right of each listed commodity that is subject to textile restraints. For example, under Chapter 63, heading 6303.11.00, Curtains, etc., Knitted or Crocheted, of Cotton, is followed by the number "(369)". If you know the category number for your product, you can find out to what extent that quota is filled simply by calling the number for the appropriate country. A word of caution, though: if you do not know for sure that your article is subject to quota from a particular country, and you call the number for that country, you may not be any more enlightened after the phone call. Many of the recordings give status reports only when a certain percentage of the quota has been filled. Thus, if 369 for China is among the categories for which not enough quantity has entered the U.S. to warrant specific mention, it will be lumped under "all other categories" and you will be none the wiser. To find out if your product is subject to textile restraints, call the DOC or a local Customs port office. Then you can find out the current charges against that quota by calling the country number listed below. For a complete listing of Customs Quota Branch information numbers, see "Relevant Government Agencies" below.

Marking and Labeling Requirements

TFPIA Requirements. All textile products imported into the U.S. must be stamped, tagged, labeled, or otherwise marked with the following information as required by the TFPIA, unless exempt from marking (see TFPIA, Section 12): 1) the generic names and percentages by weight of the constituent fibers present in the textile fiber product, exclusive of permissible ornamentation, in amounts of more than 5% in order of predominance by weight, with any percentage of fiber or fibers required to be designated as "other fiber" or "other fibers" (including those present in amounts of 5% or less) appearing last; and 2) the name of the manufacturer or the name or registered identification number issued by the FTC of one or more persons marketing or handling the textile fiber product; and 3) the name of the country where processed. A word trademark, used as a house mark and registered with the U.S. Patent Office, may appear on labels instead of the name otherwise required, provided the owner of the trademark furnishes a copy of the registration to the FTC prior to use (see "Registered Identification Numbers" below).

The information listed above is not exhaustive. TFPIA requirements are extensive. The Act specifies such details as types of labels, means of attachment, label position on the article, package labeling, unit labeling for two-piece garments, and arrangement of information on the label; allowable fiber designations; country-of-origin indications; requirements for trim and ornamentation, linings and interlinings, and pile fabrics; sectional disclosure; use of trade names and trademarks; and requirements for swatches and samples. The FTC n publishes a booklet intended to clarify TFPIA requirements to facilitate voluntary compliance in the industry (see "Publications Available" below). It is available on request, at no charge, from the FTC (see addresses at end of this chapter).

Wool Products Labeling Act (WPLA). Wool product labeling requirements for foreign products are the responsibility of the importer. The WPLA requires the following information to appear on wool products subject to the Act: 1) percentage of the wool product's total fiber weight (exclusive of ornamentation) not exceeding 5% of the total fiber weight of a) wool, b) recycled wool, c) each fiber other than wool if the percent by weight of such fiber is 5% or more, and d) the aggregate of all other fibers; 2) the maximum percent of the wool product's total weight, of any nonfibrous loading, filling, or adulterating matter; and 3) the importer's name. If you, as importer, have a registered identification number issued by the FTC, that number may be used instead of your name (see "Registered Identification Numbers" below).

Customs entry is contingent on proper labeling. If your shipment is found to be mislabeled at entry, you will be given the option of relabeling the products under Customs supervision, as long as the district director is satisfied that your labeling error or omission did not involve fraud or willful neglect. If your shipment is discovered after entry to have been noncomplying with WPLA, it will be recalled to Customs custody at your expense, unless you can satisfy the district director that the products have since been brought into compliance. You will be held responsible for all expenses incurred in bringing a shipment into compliance, including compensation of personnel and other expenses related to Customs supervision.

Fraudulent violations of WPLA will result in seizure of the shipment. Shipments already released from Customs custody will be ordered to be redelivered to Customs. Customs reports all cases of fraudulent violation to the FTC in Washington, DC.

The information listed above is not intended to be exhaustive. WPLA requirements are extensive. The Act specifies such details as types of labels, means of attachment, label position on the article, package labeling, unit labeling (as in the case of a two-piece garment), arrangement of information on the label, allowable fiber designations, country-of-origin indications, trim and ornamentation, pile fabrics, sectional disclosure, use of trade names and trademarks, requirements for swatches and samples, etc. The FTC publishes a booklet intended to clarify WPLA requirements in order to facilitate voluntary compliance within the industry (see "Publications Available" below). It is available on request, at no charge, from the FTC (see addresses at end of this chapter).

Registered Identification Numbers. Any domestic firm or person residing in the U.S. and engaged in the manufacture or marketing of textile products covered under the TFPIA may obtain an FTC-registered identification number for use on required tags and labels instead of the name of a firm or person. For applications, contact the FTC (see addresses at end of this chapter).

For a general discussion of U.S. Customs marking and labeling requirements, refer to "Marking: Country of Origin" on page 215 and "Special Marking Requirements" on page 217.

Shipping Considerations

You will need to ensure that your goods are packaged and shipped with care so that they pass smoothly through Customs and arrive in good condition. You are responsible for ensuring that the shipment is in compliance with all applicable government regulations for packaging and shipping. In most instances, you should not leave these arrangements solely to the discretion of your supplier. Careful preparation of the cargo and selection of the mode of transport can be essential to a cost-effective, timely delivery of undamaged goods. We strongly advise you to consult your shipping representative, insurance agent, or freight broker for advice on packing and shipping. Refer also to the major tab section "Packing/Shipping/Insurance" for a general discussion of packing and shipping.

Other textile articles may be shipped in bulk, cartons, sacks, bales, or other types of containers, depending on the type of product and whether it is prepackaged. General considerations include protection from contamination, weather, and pests. Containers should be constructed so as to be safe for handling during transport.

Publications Available

The following publications may be relevant to the importation of other textile articles:

Questions and Answers Relating to the Textile Fiber Products Identification Act and Regulations

Questions and Answers Relating to the Wool Products Labeling Act and Regulations

Available free of charge on request from the Federal Trade Commission (see addresses at end of this chapter), these publications are excellent sources of information written in clear lay language. We recommend that anyone interested in importing textile products but unfamiliar with the regulations obtain a copy of each of these booklets.

The following publication explains the FDA requirements for importing textile wadding products for sanitary use. It is published by the FDA and is available on request from FDA headquarters (see addresses at end of this chapter).

Requirements of Laws and Regulations Enforced by the U.S. Food and Drug Administration

The *Harmonized Tariff Schedule of the United States* (HTSUS) is available from:

Government Printing Office (GPO)
Superintendent of Documents
Washington, DC 20402
(202) 512-1800 (Order line)
(202) 512-0000 (General)

The USGPO also has copies of specific laws available for purchase. The USGPO accepts credit card orders over the phone, as well as mail orders paid by credit card, a check drawn on a U.S. bank, or an international money order.

Relevant Government Agencies

Address your questions regarding textile Multi-Fiber Arrangements to:

International Trade Administration
Office of Textile and Apparel
14th and Constitution Ave. NW, Rm. 3100
Washington, DC 20230
(202) 482-5078, 482-3737

Address your questions regarding the Flammable Fabrics Act (FFA) to:

Consumer Product Safety Commission (CPSC)
5401 Westbard Avenue
Bethesda, MD 20207
(301) 492-6580

Address your questions regarding labeling requirements under the Textile Fiber Products Identification Act (TFPIA) or the Wool Products Labeling Act (WPLA) to:

Federal Trade Commission (FTC)
Division of Enforcement
601 Pennsylvania Ave. NW
Washington, DC 20580
(202) 326-2996 (General)
(202) 326-2841 (Textile and wool products labeling)

Address your questions regarding FDA regulation or requirements for textile wadding products intended for sanitary uses to:

U.S. Food and Drug Administration (FDA)
5600 Fishers Lane
Rockville, MD 20857
(301) 443-1544

Address your questions regarding USDA requirements for imported cordage made of vegetable materials to:

U.S. Department of Agriculture (USDA)
Animal and Plant Health Inspection Service (APHIS)
Plant Protection and Quarantine (PPQ)
Federal Building, Rm. 631
6505 Belcrest Road
Hyattsville, MD 20782
(301) 436-8645

Address your questions regarding other textile article imports to the district or port director of Customs for you area. For addresses, refer to"U.S. Customs District Offices" on page 62 or contact:

U.S. Customs Service
1301 Constitution Ave. NW
Washington, DC 20229
(202) 927-6724 (Information)
(202) 927-1000 (General)

The following information numbers for U.S. Customs in Washington, DC, provide recorded information. The Quota Branch numbers listed by country provide updated status reports on textile quotas from those countries. All area codes are (202).
General information: 927-5850

Quota Branch: China 927-6703; India 927-6705; Indonesia 927-6704; Japan 927-6706; Korea 927-6707; Macao 927-6709; Malaysia 927-6712; Mexico 927-6711; Pakistan 927-6714; Philippines 927-

6713; Romania 927-6715; Singapore 927-6716; Sri Lanka 927-6708; Taiwan 927-6719; Thailand 927-6717; Turkey 927-6718; All others 927-5850.

Laws and Regulations

The following laws and regulations may be relevant to the importation of other textile articles. The laws are contained in the United States Code (USC), and the regulations are published in the Code of Federal Regulations (CFR), both of which are available at larger public and law libraries. Copies of specific laws are also available from the United States Government Printing Office (address above).

7 USC 1854
Textile Trade Agreements
(EO 11651, as amended by EO 11951 and 12188, and supplemented by EO 12475)
This Act authorizes the CITA of the DOC to enter into Multi-Fiber Agreements with other countries to control trade in textiles and establishes the Textile Import Program, which is enforced by U.S. Customs.

19 CFR 12.130 et seq.
Regulations on Entry of Textiles
These regulations provide the requirements and procedures followed by Customs in enforcing limitations on the importation and entry and withdrawal of textiles and textile products from warehouses for consumption in the U.S.

15 USC 70-77
Textile Fiber Products Identification Act (TFPIA)
This Act prohibits false or deceptive labeling (misbranding) and false advertising of any textile fiber products and requires all textile fiber products imported into the U.S. to be labeled in accordance with the requirements set forth in the law.

19 CFR 11.12b; 16 CFR 303 et seq.
Regulations on Labeling and Marking
These regulations detail the labeling and marking requirements for textiles as specified by the CPSC and the invoice contents required by U.S. Customs for purpose of enforcing the labeling and marking rules.

15 USC 68-68j
Wool Products Labeling Act (WPLA)
This Act prohibits the false or deceptive labeling (misbranding) of wool products and requires all wool products imported into the U.S. to be labeled in accordance with requirements set forth in the law.

19 CFR 11.12; 16 CFR 300 et seq.
Regulations on WPLA Labeling and Marking
These regulations set forth the wool labeling and marking requirements adopted by the FTC to administer the requirements of the WPLA and provide the procedures followed by U.S. Customs in enforcing the WPLA and the FTC regulations, including entry invoice requirements.

15 USC 1191-1204
Flammable Fabrics Act (FFA)
This Act provides for the setting of flammability standards for fabric by the Consumer Product Safety Commission (CPSC) and for enforcement by U.S. Customs.

16 CFR 1610, 1611, 1615, 1616, 1630-1632
Regulations on Flammable Fabric Standards
These regulations specify the flammability standards adopted by the CPSC under the FFA for various types of textiles.

21 USC 301 et seq.
Food, Drug, and Cosmetic Act
This Act prohibits deceptive practices and regulates the manufacture, sale and importation or exportation of food, drugs, cosmetics, and related products. See 21 USC 331, 381, 382.

19 CFR 12.1 et seq.; 21 CFR 1.83 et seq.
Regulations on Food, Drugs, and Cosmetics
These regulations of the Secretary of Health and Human Services and the Secretary of the Treasury govern the standards, labeling, marking, and importing of products used with food, drugs, and cosmetics.

Principal Exporting Countries

The following listing includes samples of the main supplier nations of the products of this chapter. It is organized by HTSUS major heading. (Refer to "Customs Classification" above for the product codes.) Countries are listed in rank order of the value of products imported to the U.S. Statistics represent customs value entries for 1993 from the Bureau of Census, U.S. Department of Commerce.

6301—Mexico, Spain, China, South Korea, United Kingdom, Germany, Taiwan, Italy, Turkey, Japan

6302—China, Pakistan, India, Portugal, Taiwan, Brazil, Israel, Spain, Thailand, Turkey

6303—China, Taiwan, United Kingdom, Turkey, Thailand, Colombia, India, Poland, Canada, Mexico

6304—China, India, Portugal, Italy, Taiwan, Mexico, Philippines, Israel, Turkey, Thailand

6305—Canada, India, Mexico, Thailand, China, Philippines, Brazil, Bangladesh, Indonesia, Israel

6306—South Korea, China, Dominican Rep., Taiwan, Bangladesh, Sri Lanka, Canada, Philippines, Hong Kong, Indonesia

6307—Mexico, China, Taiwan, Pakistan, Canada, Hong Kong, India, South Korea, Japan, Philippines

6308—United Kingdom, Taiwan, Denmark, Japan, Jamaica, Netherlands, China, Canada, France, Belgium

6309—Germany, Canada, France, Netherlands, Switzerland, United Kingdom, Japan, Mexico, Italy, Sweden

6310—Mexico, Pakistan, Canada, Netherlands, United Kingdom, Germany, France, Belgium, Japan, Italy

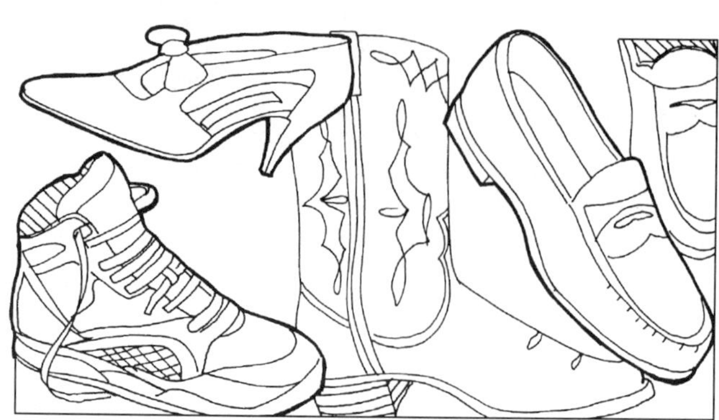

Chapter 64: Footwear*

Full title: Footwear, Gaiters, and the Like; Parts of Such Articles

This chapter relates to the importation of footwear, which are classified under Chapter 64 of the Harmonized Tariff Schedule of the United States (HTSUS). Specifically, it covers footwear for adults and children and made of rubber, plastic, leather, composition leather, pigskin, wood, cork, and textiles. Articles covered include footwear with metal toe-caps, ski boots, work boots and shoes, sandals, thongs, rain boots, house slippers, tennis shoes, sports shoes, and disposable footwear. This chapter also covers parts of footwear, gaiters, and leggings.

If you are interested in importing footwear without applied soles and made of textile material, you should read Commodity Index Chapter 61 (knitted or crocheted) or Chapter 62 (not knitted or crocheted). Worn footwear is covered in Chapter 63, and footwear containing asbestos is classified in Chapter 68. For importing orthopedic appliances and footwear, refer to Chapter 90. Toy footwear, ice or roller skating boots, shin-guards, and other protective sportswear are covered in Chapter 95. If you are interested in importing parts of footwear not covered in this chapter, you should read the Commodity Index chapter in which those parts are classified. For example, eyelets and buckles are covered in Chapter 96, and braid, lace, pompoms, and other textile trimmings are covered in Chapter 58.

Key Factors

The key factors in the importation of footwear are:

- Compliance with entry invoice requirements for footwear and component materials
- Compliance with textile quota restraints and visa requirements under U.S. Department of Commerce (DOC) Multi-Fiber Arrangements (if importing footwear with textile components)
- Submission of U.S. Customs Country-of-Origin Declaration(s) (if importing footwear with textile components)
- Compliance with labeling requirements under the Textile Fiber Products Identification Act (TFPIA) and the Wool Products Labeling Act (WPLA) (if importing footwear with textile components)
- Compliance with flammability standards adopted and enforced by the Consumer Product Safety Commission (CPSC) under the Flammable Fabrics Act (FFA) (if importing footwear with textile components)

Although most importers use the services of a licensed customs broker in making their entries, and we recommend this practice, you should be aware of the regulatory, entry, and documentation issues involved in importing your product. You, as importer, are ultimately responsible for the fulfillment of any legal requirements applicable to your shipment.

General Considerations

Regulatory Agencies. U.S. Customs determines the classification of footwear for purposes of import duties. The DOC's Committee for Implementation of Textile Agreements (CITA) regulates certain textile imports under Section 204 of the Agricultural Adjustment Act. U.S. Customs enforces CITA textile and textile product entry quotas. Customs also enforces compliance with labeling and invoice requirements of the TFPIA and flammability standards under the FFA. The CPSC monitors imports and from time to time inspects textile shipments for compliance with FFA standards. If you are importing wool textiles, importation is subject to complex textile import regulations. The Federal Trade Commission (FTC) administers the WPLA requirements.

Import Duties on Footwear. The main issue associated with the importation of footwear is determination of duty. Duty rates vary widely depending first on the material of the upper and outer sole, and then on construction and/or intended use of the footwear. The value of the footwear also affects the duty status. Because there are so many variables in determining duty status, extensive extra information is required on each invoice for an import shipment entering under HTSUS headings 6401 through 6405. You may furnish this information on Customs **Form 5523** or in another appropriate format. There are numerous definitions regarding footwear found in HTSUS Chapter 64 that are essential to the classification of imported footwear as well as providing the information called for on Customs **Form 5523**.

Footwear with Textile Components. A few articles of footwear are subject to textile restraints under Multi-Fiber Arrangements and to wool product entry requirements. These articles are generally within HTSUS headings 6405 and 6406, and include removable insoles, heel cushions, gaiters, and leggings of cotton, wool, fine animal hair, man-made, and other fibers. Footwear with uppers and soles made of wool felt are also subject to these requirements. The following is an overview of the textile importing requirements.

Wool Product Entry Requirements. Depending on the nature of your wool footwear imports, as many as four different types of special entry documents may be required. First, for all imported articles that contain textile fibers, yarns, and fabrics covered by the Agricultural Adjustment Act of 1924 (1956) (AAA), including wool, you must file a U.S. Customs Textile Entry Declaration (see "Textile Country-of-Origin Declarations" below). Second, with the entry summary for each shipment of wool articles, you must file Customs **Form 6451,** Notice of Percentage of Clean Yield and Grade of Wool or Hair, in duplicate, showing your name and address. Third, for all wool products subject to the WPLA, special information is required on the entry invoices (see "Wool Products Labeling Act" below). Finally, certain articles of apparel manufactured or produced in certain countries may be subject to quotas and other restraints under U.S. DOC Multi-Fiber Arrangements. Such products require export licenses, certificates, or visas issued by the appropriate country of origin, in addition to other requisite entry paperwork (see "Textile Quotas" below).

Wool Products Labeling Act. The term "wool product" means any product or any portion of a product that contains, purports to contain, or in any way is represented as containing wool, re-

*IMPORTANT: Read the Commodity Index Introduction. It is the essential framework for understanding this chapter.

processed wool, or reused wool. All wool products imported into the U.S., except those made more than 20 years before importation, and except carpets, rugs, mats, and upholsteries, must have affixed a stamp, tag, label, or other means of identification as required by the WPLA. If you are importing wool products exempt from labeling under the WPLA, do not assume they are also exempt from labeling under the TFPIA. These are two distinct laws, with some overlapping requirements (see "Marking and Labeling Requirements" below).

Textile Quotas. If you are interested in importing footwear with textile components, the most important issue you need to be aware of is quotas. Under the Multi-Fiber Arrangement provisions of Section 204 of the Agricultural Adjustment Act, CITA initiates specific agreements with individual exporting countries. Section 204 of the Agricultural Adjustment Act covers textiles articles that: 1) are in chief value of cotton, wool, or man-made fibers, any textile fibers subject to the terms of any textile trade agreement, or any combination of such fibers; 2) contain 50% or more by weight of cotton or man-made fibers, or any textile fibers subject to the terms of any textile trade agreement; 3) contain 17% or more by weight of wool; or 4) if in chief value of textile fibers or textile materials, contain a blend of cotton, wool, or man-made fibers, any textile fibers subject to the terms of any textile trade agreement, or any combination of such fibers that, in total, amount to 50% or more by weight of all component fibers.

The U.S. has Multi-Fiber Arrangements with 40 countries. Each agreement with each country is unique, and may specify quotas for a type of textile or a specific article. Visas or export licenses may be required. These agreements, however, often change. Therefore, if you are interested in importing any footwear with textile components, you should contact the International Trade Administration's Office of Textile and Apparel (see addresses at end of this chapter). Refer to "Prohibitions and Restrictions" below for further details.

Textile Country-of-Origin Declarations. U.S. Customs enforces CITA textile and textile product entry quotas (see "Prohibitions and Restrictions" below). Requirements for entry include submission of Country-of-Origin Declarations with every shipment of footwear with textile components, regardless of whether it is subject to a specific multi-fiber arrangement (19 CFR 12.130, 12.131).

Country of Origin. Quota restrictions are country-specific and therefore are applied based on the country of origin for the textiles shipped. The last country from which a textile shipment was exported to the U.S. is not necessarily its country of origin. A textile or textile product imported into the U.S. is considered a product of the particular foreign territory or country, or a U.S. insular possession, where it is wholly grown, produced, or manufactured. For the following discussion, "country" means a foreign territory or country, or a U.S. insular possession.

Substantial transformation rules may affect the country-of-origin determination. For example, if a textile or textile product originates in Country A and is subject to quota, the quota restrictions apply at entry into the U.S. But if, prior to export to the U.S., you move the shipment to Country B where there are fewer restrictions, the shipment may nevertheless remain subject to quota and visa requirements under the Multi-Fiber Arrangement with Country A. Customs determines whether the quota restrictions apply based on the criteria of "substantial transformation." If your textiles do not undergo any major processing or manufacturing while in Country B, or if the manufacturing or processing is minor, your shipment will be deemed to originate in Country A. *You cannot claim substantial transformation on the basis of minor manufacturing procedures.*

In contrast, if your shipment undergoes major processing or manufacturing while in Country B, rendering the textiles "new and different articles of commerce," Customs will treat the shipment as the product of Country B. To qualify as having undergone substantial transformation, an article must evince a change in: 1) commercial designation or identity; b) fundamental character; or c) commercial use. If your shipment is processed in more than one country, the country where it last underwent substantial transformation is the country of origin for Customs entry. In deciding whether the manufacturing or processing operation in a country is major, Customs considers the following factors: 1) the resultant physical change in the material or article; 2) the complexity, the level or degree of skill and/or technology required, and the amount of time involved in the operations; and 3) the value added to the article or material, compared to its value when imported into the U.S.

Validating Operations. Operations that Customs will usually acknowledge as validating a claim of substantial transformation are the following: 1) dyeing and printing, when accompanied by two or more of the following finishing operations: bleaching, shrinking, fulling, napping, decating, permanent stiffening, weighting, permanent embossing, or moireing; 2) spinning fibers into yarn; 3) weaving, knitting, or otherwise forming fabric; 4) cutting fabric into parts and assembling the parts into completed articles; or 5) substantial assembly, by sewing and/or tailoring into a completed garment cut pieces of apparel articles that have been cut from fabric in another country—e.g., complete assembly and tailoring of all cut pieces of suit-type jackets, suits, and shirts.

Insubstantial Operations. Operations that usually will not support a claim of substantial transformation, even if more than one are performed, are the following: 1) simple operations of combining, labeling, pressing, cleaning, dry cleaning, or packaging; 2) cutting to length or width and hemming or overlocking fabrics that are readily identifiable as being intended for a particular commercial use; 3) trimming and/or joining together by sewing, looping, linking, or other means of attaching otherwise completed knit-to-shape component parts produced in a single country, even if accompanied by other processes—e.g., washing, drying, mending—normally incident to assembly; 4) one or more finishing operations on yarns, fabrics, or their textile articles—such as showerproofing, superwashing, bleaching, decating, fulling, shrinking, mercerizing, or similar operations; or 5) dyeing and/or printing fabrics or yarns.

Declarations. The country of origin of the footwear with textile components in a shipment must be stated on a declaration submitted to U.S. Customs at the time of entry. There are three Customs Country-of-Origin Declarations: single-country, multiple-country, and negative. The Declaration to be submitted with your shipment of footwear with textile components depends on the nature of the import.

- **Single-country declarations** are used for entries of textiles or textile products that clearly originate from only one country or that have been assembled in one country from fabricated components wholly produced in the U.S. or the foreign country of manufacture. Information required includes: marks of identification and numbers; description of article and quantity; country of origin; and date of exportation.
- **Multiple-country declarations** are used for entries of textiles or textile products that were manufactured or processed and/or that incorporate materials originating in more than one foreign country or territory. Information required includes: marks of identification and numbers; for articles, description, quantity, identification of manufacturing and/or processing operations, country, and date of exportation; for materials used to make articles, description of materials, country of production, and date of exportation.

- **Negative declarations** must accompany all textile imports that are not subject to FFA Section 204 restrictions. Information required includes: marks of identification and numbers; descriptions of article and quantity; and country of origin.

The date of exportation to be indicated on the above declarations is the date on which the carrier leaves the last port in the country of origin, as determined by Customs. Diversion to another country during transit does not affect the export date.

Procedure for Declarations. The manufacturer, producer, exporter, or importer may prepare the declaration. If more than one of these parties is involved in the importation, each party may prepare a separate declaration. You may file a separate declaration for each invoice presented with your entry. The declaration must be dated and signed by the responsible party, and must include the person's title and the company name and address. Your shipment's entry will be denied unless it is accompanied by a properly executed declaration. Customs will not treat a textile declaration as a missing document for which a bond may be filed.

Customs will base its country-of-origin determination on the information contained in each declaration, unless the information is insufficient. If the information on the declaration is insufficient, Customs will require that you submit such additional information as will enable the determination to be made. The shipment will not be released until the determination is made. Thus, if you want to clear Customs with minimal delay, be sure that the information on the declarations is as complete as possible for each shipment.

Textile Labeling and Invoice Requirements. You are responsible for your imported product's compliance with applicable provisions of the TFPIA. Footwear with textile components that require labeling under TFPIA must already be labeled at entry, or the shipment will be refused. (See "Marking and Labeling Requirements" below.) If you import shipments of footwear with textile components subject to TFPIA and valued at over $500, you must provide special information on the entry invoice (see "Entry and Documentation" below).

Flammability Standards. Footwear with textile components imported into the U.S. for use in consumer products must be in compliance with the FFA, a federal law that gives the CPSC the authority and responsibility for protecting the public from the hazards of dangerously flammable items of wearing apparel and interior furnishings. Under the FFA, standards have been established for flammability of clothing textiles. You cannot import any article of wearing apparel or interior furnishing, or any fabric or related material that is intended for use or that may be used in such items, if it fails to conform to an applicable flammability standard (FFA Section 4). Certain products may be imported into the U.S. (FFA Section 11c) for finishing or processing to render them less flammable so as to meet the standards. For these products, the exporter must state on the invoice or other paper relating to the shipment that the shipment is being made for that purpose.

The CPSC monitors imports of textiles under its Import Surveillance Program. From time to time, your textile shipments may be inspected to ascertain compliance with mandatory safety standards. Shipments may also be subject to testing by the CPSC to determine compliance. If the CPSC believes a product, fabric, or related material does not comply with a flammability standard, it is authorized to pursue a variety of legal sanctions (see "Prohibitions and Restrictions" below).

Substantial Product Hazard Reports. Any firm that obtains information that reasonably supports the conclusion that one of its products presents an unreasonable risk of serious injury or death must report that information to the CPSC's Division of Corrective Actions (CPSC address below). Importers must also report to the CPSC if 1) a type of product is the subject of at least three civil actions filed in U.S. federal or state courts, 2) each suit alleges the involvement of that product type in death or grievous bodily injury (as defined in FFA Section 37(3)1), and 3) at least three of the actions result in a final settlement with the manufacturer or in a judgment for the plaintiff within any one of the two-year periods specified in FFA Section 37(b).

Import Advisory

Importation of textile products is trade-sensitive and highly regulated. Shipments of textile products not complying with all government regulations, including quotas and visas, are subject to seizure and could result in the imposition of penalties as well as possible forfeiture of the goods. You should always verify the available quota for any textile product you plan to import before your shipment leaves the country of manufacture. Furthermore, Customs textile classification rulings change frequently, and prior administrative rulings are often modified and sometimes reversed.

Customs Classification

For customs purposes, footwear with textile components are classified under Chapter 64 of the HTSUS. This chapter is broken into major headings, which are further divided into subheadings, and often sub-subheadings, each of which has its own HTSUS classification number. For example, the HTSUS number for plastic ski-boots is 6401.92.30, indicating it is a sub-subcategory of other footwear covering the ankle but not the knee (6401.92.00), which is a subcategory of the major heading waterproof footwear with outer soles and uppers of rubber or plastics, etc. (6401.00.00). There are six major headings within Chapter 64.

6401—Waterproof footwear with outer soles and uppers of rubber or plastics, the uppers of which are neither fixed to the sole nor assembled by stitching, riveting, nailing, screwing, plugging, or similar processes

6402—Other footwear with outer soles and uppers of rubber or plastics

6403—Footwear with outer soles of rubber, plastics, leather, or composition leather and uppers of leather

6404—Footwear with outer soles of rubber, plastics, leather, or composition leather and uppers of textile materials

6405—Other footwear

6406—Parts of footwear (including uppers whether or not attached to soles other than outer soles); removable insoles, heel cushions, and similar articles; gaiter, leggings, and similar articles, and parts thereof

Sample Import Duties

Import duties will vary depending on the HTSUS classification of your product. Therefore, to determine the correct amount of duties, your product must be properly classified under the HTSUS. The following sample duties are taken from the duty listings for HTSUS Chapter 64 products.

Waterproof footwear with outer soles and uppers of rubber or plastics, etc., with a protective metal toe-cap (6401.10.00): 37.5%; ski boots, waterproof, with outer soles and uppers of rubber or plastics, etc. (6401.92.30): 6%; footwear with upper straps or thongs assembled to the sole by plugs (zoris) (6402.20.00): 2.4%; footwear with outer soles of leather, and uppers of leather straps across the instep and around the big toe (6403.20.00): 10%; footwear on a wood base or platform, without an inner sole or protective metal toe-cap (6403.30.00): 8%; sports footwear, tennis shoes, basketball shoes, gym shoes, training shoes, and the like, with outer soles of rubber or plastics and uppers of which over 50% of the external surface area is leather (6404.11.20): 10.5%; disposable footwear for one-time use (6405.90.20): 7.5%; outer soles and heels, of rubber or plastics (6406.20.00): 5.3%; wood footwear parts (6406.91.00): 5.1%; leg warmers and textile footwear parts (6406.99.15): 17%.

Special Provisions for Japanese Footwear Imports. Imports of the following types of footwear from Japan are subject to a duty of 40%: footwear with outer soles of leather and uppers wholly or in part of leather, and footwear with outer soles of rubber or plastics and uppers having an exterior surface area predominantly of leather. This duty is not applied to a) slip-on footwear of a type not suitable for outdoor use, without backs or back straps, having outer soles with a thickness of less than 5 mm and with less than 20 mm difference between the thickness of the bottom at the ball of the foot and at the heel; and (b) footwear that is designed for a sporting activity and has, or has provision for, attached spikes, sprigs, stops, clips, bars or the like, and skating boots, ski-boots, cross-country ski footwear, wrestling boots, boxing boots, and cycling shoes.

Entry and Documentation

The entry of merchandise is a two-part process consisting of 1) filing the documentation necessary to determine whether merchandise may be released from Customs custody, and 2) filing the documents that contain information for duty assessment and statistical purposes. In certain instances, all documents must be filed and accepted by Customs prior to release of the goods. Unless you have been granted an extension, you must file entry documents at a location specified by the district or area director within five working days of your shipment's date of arrival at a U.S. port of entry. These include a number of standard documents required by Customs for any entry, and:

- Customs **Form 5523**, footwear entry invoice
- U.S. Customs Country-of-Origin Declaration(s) (if importing textile products)
- Export documentation and/or visa (if importing textiles products subject to Multi-Fiber Arrangements
- Customs **Form 6451**, Notice of Percentage of Clean Yield and Grade of Wool or Hair, in duplicate, showing your name and address (if importing articles containing wool)

After you present the entry, Customs may examine your shipment or may waive examination. The shipment is then released provided no legal or regulatory violations have been noted. You must then file entry summary documentation and deposit estimated duties at a designated customhouse within 10 working days of your shipment's release. For a detailed description of entry procedures, standard documentation, and informal entry, refer to "Entry Process" on page 182.

Entry Invoice for Footwear—Definitions. Customs will employ the following terms and definitions in assessing the duty status of your shipment of footwear:

1) Exclusively adhesive construction: all pieces of the bottom would separate from the upper or from each other if all adhesives, cements, and glues were dissolved. It includes shoes with pieces of the upper stitched to each other, but not to any part of the bottom. Examples include: a) vulcanized construction footwear; b) simultaneous molded construction footwear; c) molded footwear with the upper and the bottom made as one piece of molded rubber or plastic; and d) footwear in which staples, rivets, stitching, or any of the methods above are either primary or even just extra or auxiliary, even though adhesive is a major part of the reason the bottom will not separate from the upper.

2) Composition leather: made by binding together leather fibers or small pieces of natural leather. This does not include imitation leathers not based on natural leather.

3) Leather: the tanned skin of any animal from which the fur or hair has been removed. Tanned skins coated or laminated with rubber and/or plastics are "leather" only if leather gives the material its essential character.

4) Line of demarcation: exists if one can indicate where the sole ends and the upper begins. For example, knit booties do not normally have a line of demarcation.

5) Men's, boy's, and youth's sizes cover footwear of American youths size 11 1/2 and larger for males, and does not include footwear commonly worn by both sexes. If more than 4% of the shoes sold in a given size will be worn by females, that size is "commonly worn by both sexes."

6) Protective footwear: footwear is designed to protect against water, oil, or cold or inclement weather only if it is substantially more of a protection against those conditions than the usual shoes of that type. For example, though wearing leather oxfords will clearly keep your feet warmer and drier than going barefoot, they afford only a normal degree of protection. On the other hand, the snow-jogger is the protective version of the nonprotective jogging shoe.

7) Rubber and/or plastics includes any textile material visibly coated (or covered) externally with one or both of those materials.

8) Slip-on includes: a) a boot that must be pulled on; b) footwear with elastic cores that must be stretched to get it on, but not a separate piece of elasticized fabric that forms a full circle around the foot or ankle.

9) Sports footwear includes only a) footwear designed for a sporting activity and having, or having provision for, the attachment of spikes, sprigs, cleats, stops, clips, bars, or the like; b) skating boots (without skates attached), ski boots, and cross-country ski footwear, wrestling boots, boxing boots, and cycling shoes.

10) Tennis shoes, basketball shoes, gym shoes, training shoes, and the like cover athletic footwear other than sports footwear, whether or not principally used for such athletic games or purposes.

11) Textile materials are made from cotton, other vegetable fibers, wool, hair, silk, or man-made fibers. Note: cork, wood, cardboard, and leather are not textile materials.

12) Turned construction: the upper is stitched to the leather sole wrong side out, and the shoe is then turned right side out.

13) Vegetable fibers include cotton, flax, and ramie, but not rayon or plaiting materials, such as rattan or wood strips.

14) Waterproof footwear includes footwear designed to protect against penetration by water or other liquids, whether or not such footwear is primarily designed for such purposes.

15) Welt footwear means footwear construction with a welt, which extends around the edge of the outer sole, and in which the welt and shoe upper are sewed to a lip on the surface of the insole, and the outer sole of which is sewed or cemented to the welt.

16) A zori has an upper consisting only of straps or thongs of molded rubber or plastic. This upper is assembled to a formed rubber or plastic sole by means of plugs.

Entry Invoice for Footwear—Contents. The invoice or other entry documentation for footwear must show:

1) manufacturer's style number; 2) importer's style and/or stock number; 3) for the upper, the percent by area of external surface area (excluding reinforcements and accessories), that is a) leather, b) composition leather, c) rubber and/or plastics, d) textile materials, e) other, by percentage; and 4) for the outersole, the same percentage breakdown as required for uppers.

Depending on the percentages of component materials cited in items 3) and 4) above, a combination of additional questions must be answered. You may choose to answer all the questions, or only those required by your answers to items 3) and 4) above. The questions are as follows: a) What percent of external surface area of upper (including leather reinforcements and accessories) is leather? b) What percent by area of external surface area of upper (including all reinforcements and accessories) is rubber and/or plastics? c) What percent by weight is of rubber and/or plastics? d) What percent by weight is textile materials plus rubber and/or plastics? e) Is it waterproof? f) Does it have a protective metal toe cap? g) Will it cover the wearer's ankle bone? h) Will it cover the wearer's knee cap? i) [Reserved]; j) Is it designed to be a protection against water, oil, grease, or chemicals, or cold or inclement weather? k) Is it a slip-on? l) Is it a downhill or cross-country ski boot? m) Is it serious sports footwear other than ski boots? n) Is it a tennis, basketball, gym, or training shoe or the like? o) Is it made on a base or platform of wood? p) Does it have open toes or open heels? q) Is it made by the (lipped insole) welt construction? r) Is it made by the turned construction? s) Is it worn exclusively by men, boys, or youths? t) Is it made by an exclusively adhesive construction? u) Are the fibers of the upper, by weight, predominantly vegetable fibers? v) Is it disposable, i.e. intended for one-time use? w) Is it a "Zori"? x) Is the leather in the upper pigskin? y) Are the sole and upper made of wool felt? z) Is there a line of demarcation between the outer sole and upper?

If you claim duty classification under subheading 6401.99.80, 6402.19.10, 6402.30.30, 6402.91.40, 6402.99.15, 6402.99.30, 6404.11.40, 6404.11.60, 6404.19.35, 6404.19.40, or 6404.19.60, you must also provide the following information: Does the shoe have a foxing or foxing-like band? If so, state its material(s). Does the sole overlap the upper other than just at the front of the toe and/or at the back of the heel?

Entry Invoice—TFPIA Requirements. All invoices for textile wearing apparel should indicate: 1) a component material breakdown in percentages by weight for all component fibers present in the entire garment, as well as separate breakdowns of the fibers in the (outer) shell (exclusive of linings, cuffs, waistbands, collars and other trimmings) and in the lining; 2) for garments that are constructed of more than one component or material (combination of knit and not-knit fabric or combinations of knit and/or not-knit fabric with leather, fur, plastic—including vinyl, etc.) the invoice must show a fiber breakdown in percentages by weight for each separate textile material in the garment and a breakdown in percentages by weight for each nontextile material of the entire garment; 3) for woven garments: indicate whether the fabric is yarn-dyed and whether there are "two or more colors in the warp and/or filling;" 4) for all-white T-shirts and singlets: indicate whether or not the garment contains pockets, trim, or embroidery; 5) for mufflers: state the exact dimensions, length, and width of the merchandise.

Entry Invoice—Wool Products Subject to WPLA. When you offer for entry a wool product shipment valued at over $500 and subject to WPLA, you must include certain information intended to facilitate Customs monitoring and enforcement of that Act. This extra information is identical to that required by WPLA on labeling (see "Marking and Labeling Requirements" below), with the addition of the manufacturer's name. If your product consists of mixed waste, residues, and similar merchandise obtained from several suppliers or unknown sources, you may omit the manufacturer's name from the entry invoice.

Prohibitions and Restrictions

Textile Quotas. Textile import restrictions are primarily a matter of quotas and the way in which these quotas are administered and monitored. Under the Multi-Fiber Arrangement provisions of Section 204 of the Agricultural Adjustment Act, CITA has negotiated Multi-Fiber Arrangements with 40 countries. These Agreements may impose quotas for a type of textile or a specific article, and they are country-specific. The agreements, however, often change. Therefore, if you are interested in importing any knitted or crocheted apparel articles, you should contact the International Trade Administration's Office of Textile and Apparel (see addresses at end of this chapter). The Office of Textile and Apparel has a team of country specialists who can inform you of the latest developments and inform you about a product's quota or restriction status.

U.S. Customs enforces CITA textile and textile product entry quotas. If formal entry procedures are not followed, Customs will usually refuse entry for textiles that are subject to Section 204. Formal entry requires submission of a Country-of-Origin Declaration (see "General Considerations" above). U.S. Customs maintains a current textile quota status report, available for perusal at any Customs port. In addition, U.S. Customs in Washington, DC, operates a telephone service to provide quota status reports, which are updated weekly (see "Relevant Government Agencies" below).

Flammable Fabrics. U.S. Customs may refuse entry for any article of wearing apparel or interior furnishing, or any fabric or related material that is intended for use or that may be used in wearing apparel or interior furnishings, if it fails to conform to an applicable flammability standard issued under Section 4 of the FFA. An exception is allowed for certain products (FFA Section 11c) that are imported for finishing or processing to bring them within the legal standard. For these products, the exporter must state on the invoice or other paper relating to the shipment that the shipment is being made for that purpose.

The CPSC, as the primary enforcement agency of flammability standards, inspects products for compliance with the FFA. If the CPSC believes a product, fabric, or related material does not comply with a flammability standard, it is authorized to pursue a variety of legal sanctions, including: 1) seizure, condemnation, and forfeiture of the noncomplying products; 2) administrative cease-and-desist order requiring an individual or firm to stop sale and distribution of the noncomplying products or; 3) temporary injunction requiring the individual or firm to stop sale and distribution of the noncomplying products, pending final disposition of an administrative cease-and-desist proceeding. The CPSC also has authority to seek civil penalties against any person who knowingly violates a regulation or standard issued under Section 4 of the FFA.

Country-Specific Restrictions

Restrictions under Multi-Fiber Arrangements are country-specific. A product originating in one country may be subject to quota and to export license or visa requirements, while the same product originating in a different country may not. At present, the U.S. has Multi-Fiber Arrangements with 40 countries. Many different categories of products are covered under these Arrangements; it is beyond the scope of this book to list each country and its restricted commodities. If you are interested in importing textiles and textile products, you should contact the International Trade Administration's Office of Textile and Apparel (see addresses at end of this chapter) or U.S. Customs to ascertain your product's restraint status.

The U.S. Customs Quota Branch phone numbers provide recorded status reports, by quota category number, for current charges against the quotas for that country. For convenience, the HTSUS shows the 3-digit category number in parentheses to the right of each listed commodity that is subject to textile restraints. For example, under Chapter 64, heading 6406.99.15, Leg-Warmers of Cotton, is followed by the number "(359)". If you know the category number for your product, you can find out to what extent that quota is filled simply by calling the number for the appropriate country. A word of caution, though: if you do not know for sure that your article is subject to quota from a particular country, and you call the number for that country, you may not be any more enlightened after the phone call. Many of the recordings give status reports only when a certain percentage of the quota has been filled. Thus, if 359 for Taiwan is among the categories for which not enough quantity has entered the U.S. to warrant specific mention, it will be lumped under "all other categories" and you will be none the wiser. To find out if your product is subject to textile restraints, call the DOC or a local Customs port office. Then you can find out the current charges against that quota by calling the country number listed below. For a complete listing of Customs Quota Branch information numbers, see "Relevant Government Agencies" below.

Marking and Labeling Requirements

TFPIA Requirements. All textile products imported into the U.S. must be stamped, tagged, labeled, or otherwise marked with the following information as required by the TFPIA, unless exempt from marking (see TFPIA, Section 12): 1) the generic names and percentages by weight of the constituent fibers present in the textile fiber product, exclusive of permissible ornamentation, in amounts of more than 5% in order of predominance by weight, with any percentage of fiber or fibers required to be designated as "other fiber" or "other fibers" (including those present in amounts of 5% or less) appearing last; and 2) the name of the manufacturer or the name or registered identification number issued by the FTC of one or more persons marketing or handling the textile fiber product; and 3) the name of the country where processed. A word trademark, used as a house mark and registered with the U.S. Patent Office, may appear on labels instead of the name otherwise required, provided the owner of the trademark furnishes a copy of the registration to the FTC prior to use (see "Registered Identification Numbers" below).

The information listed above is not exhaustive. TFPIA requirements are extensive. The Act specifies such details as types of labels, means of attachment, label position on the article, package labeling, unit labeling for two-piece garments, and arrangement of information on the label; allowable fiber designations; country-of-origin indications; requirements for trim and ornamentation, linings and interlinings, and pile fabrics; sectional disclosure; use of trade names and trademarks; and requirements for swatches and samples. The FTC publishes a booklet intended to clarify TFPIA requirements to facilitate voluntary compliance in the industry (see "Publications Available" below). It is available on request, at no charge, from the FTC (see addresses at end of this chapter).

Wool Products Labeling Act (WPLA). Wool product labeling requirements for foreign products are the responsibility of the importer. The WPLA requires the following information to appear on wool products subject to the Act: 1) percentage of the wool product's total fiber weight (exclusive of ornamentation) not exceeding 5% of the total fiber weight of a) wool, b) recycled wool, c) each fiber other than wool if the percent by weight of such fiber is 5% or more, and d) the aggregate of all other fibers; 2) the maximum percent of the wool product's total weight, of any nonfibrous loading, filling, or adulterating matter; and 3) the importer's name. If you, as importer, have a registered identification number issued by the FTC, that number may be used instead of your name (see "Registered Identification Numbers" below).

Customs entry is contingent on proper labeling. If your shipment is found to be mislabeled at entry, you will be given the option of relabeling the products under Customs supervision, as long as the district director is satisfied that your labeling error or omission did not involve fraud or willful neglect. If your shipment is discovered after entry to have been noncomplying with WPLA, it will be recalled to Customs custody at your expense, unless you can satisfy the district director that the products have since been brought into compliance. You will be held responsible for all expenses incurred in bringing a shipment into compliance, including compensation of personnel and other expenses related to Customs supervision.

Fraudulent violations of WPLA will result in seizure of the shipment. Shipments already released from Customs custody will be ordered to be redelivered to Customs. Customs reports all cases of fraudulent violation to the FTC in Washington, DC.

The information listed above is not intended to be exhaustive. WPLA requirements are extensive. The Act specifies such details as types of labels, means of attachment, label position on the article, package labeling, unit labeling (as in the case of a two-piece garment), arrangement of information on the label, allowable fiber designations, country-of-origin indications, trim and ornamentation, pile fabrics, sectional disclosure, use of trade names and trademarks, requirements for swatches and samples, etc. The FTC publishes a booklet intended to clarify WPLA requirements in order to facilitate voluntary compliance within the industry (see "Publications Available" below). It is available on request, at no charge, from the FTC (see addresses at end of this chapter).

Registered Identification Numbers. Any domestic firm or person residing in the U.S. and engaged in the manufacture or marketing of textile products covered under the TFPIA or WPLA may obtain an FTC-registered identification number for use on required tags and labels instead of the name of a firm or person. For applications, contact the FTC (see addresses at end of this chapter).

For a general discussion of U.S. Customs marking and labeling requirements, refer to "Marking: Country of Origin" on page 215 and "Special Marking Requirements" on page 217.

Shipping Considerations

You will need to ensure that your goods are packaged and shipped with care so that they pass smoothly through Customs and arrive in good condition. You are responsible for ensuring that the shipment is in compliance with all applicable government regulations for packaging and shipping. In most instances, you should not leave these arrangements solely to the discretion of your supplier. Careful preparation of the cargo and selection of the mode of transport can be essential to a cost-effective, timely delivery of undamaged goods. We strongly advise you to consult your shipping representative, insurance agent, or freight broker for advice on packing and shipping. Refer also to the major tab section "Packing/Shipping/Insurance" for a general discussion of packing and shipping.

Footwear may be shipped in bulk, crates, boxes, or other types of containers, depending on the type of product and whether it is prepackaged. General considerations include protection from contamination, weather, and pests. Containers should be constructed so as to be safe for handling during transport.

Publications Available

The following publications may be relevant to the importation of footwear:

Questions and Answers Relating to the Textile Fiber Products Identification Act and Regulations

Questions and Answers Relating to the Wool Products Labeling Act and Regulations

Available free of charge on request from the Federal Trade Commission, these publications are excellent sources of information written in clear lay language. We recommend that anyone interested in importing textile products but unfamiliar with the regulations obtain a copy of each of these booklets.

The *Harmonized Tariff Schedule of the United States* (HTSUS) is available from:

Government Printing Office (GPO)
Superintendent of Documents
Washington, DC 20402
(202) 512-1800 (Order line)
(202) 512-0000 (General)

The USGPO also has copies of specific laws available for purchase. The USGPO accepts credit card orders over the phone, as well as mail orders paid by credit card, a check drawn on a U.S. bank, or an international money order.

Relevant Government Agencies

Address your questions regarding textile Multi-Fiber Arrangements to:

International Trade Administration
Office of Textile and Apparel
14th and Constitution Ave. NW, Rm. 3100
Washington, DC 20230
(202) 482-5078, 482-3737

Address your questions regarding the Flammable Fabrics Act (FFA) to:

Consumer Product Safety Commission (CPSC)
5401 Westbard Avenue
Bethesda, MD 20207
(301) 492-6580

Address your questions regarding labeling requirements under the Textile Fiber Products Identification Act (TFPIA) or the Wool Products Labeling Act (WPLA) to:

Federal Trade Commission (FTC)
Division of Enforcement
601 Pennsylvania Ave. NW
Washington, DC 20580
(202) 326-2996 (General)
(202) 326-2841 (Textile and wool products labeling)

Address your questions regarding footwear imports to the district or port director of Customs for you area. For addresses, refer to "U.S. Customs District Offices" on page 62 or contact:

U.S. Customs Service
1301 Constitution Ave. NW
Washington, DC 20229
(202) 927-6724 (Information)
(202) 927-1000 (General)

The following information numbers for U.S. Customs in Washington, DC, provide recorded information. The Quota Branch numbers listed by country provide updated status reports on textile quotas from those countries. All area codes are (202).
General information: 927-5850

Quota Branch: China 927-6703; India 927-6705; Indonesia 927-6704; Japan 927-6706; Korea 927-6707; Macao 927-6709; Malaysia 927-6712; Mexico 927-6711; Pakistan 927-6714; Philippines 927-6713; Romania 927-6715; Singapore 927-6716; Sri Lanka 927-6708; Taiwan 927-6719; Thailand 927-6717; Turkey 927-6718; All others 927-5850.

Laws and Regulations

The following laws and regulations may be relevant to the importation of footwear. The laws are contained in the United States Code (USC), and the regulations are published in the Code of Federal Regulations (CFR), both of which are available at larger public and law libraries. Copies of specific laws are also available from the United States Government Printing Office (address above).

7 USC 1854
Textile Trade Agreements
(EO 11651, as amended by EO 11951 and 12188, and supplemented by EO 12475 below)
This Act authorizes the CITA of the DOC to enter into Multi-Fiber Agreements with other countries to control trade in textiles and establishes the Textile Import Program, which is enforced by U.S. Customs.

19 CFR 12.130 et seq.
Regulations on Entry of Textiles
These regulations provide the requirements and procedures followed by Customs in enforcing limitations on the importation and entry and withdrawal of textiles and textile products from warehouses for consumption in the U.S.

19 CFR 141.89
Regulation on Additional Invoice Requirements
This regulation specifies the additional information for certain classes of merchandise, including footwear and textile products, being imported into the U.S.

15 USC 70-77
Textile Fiber Products Identification Act (TFPIA)
This Act prohibits false or deceptive labeling (misbranding) and false advertising of any textile fiber products and requires all textile fiber products imported into the U.S. to be labeled in accordance with the requirements set forth in the law.

19 CFR 11.12b; 16 CFR 303 et seq.
Regulations on Labeling and Marking
These regulations detail the labeling and marking requirements for textiles as specified by the CPSC and the invoice contents required by U.S. Customs for purpose of enforcing the labeling and marking rules.

15 USC 68-68j
Wool Products Labeling Act (WPLA)
This Act prohibits the false or deceptive labeling (misbranding) of wool products and requires all wool products imported into the U.S. to be labeled in accordance with requirements set forth in the law.

19 CFR 11.12; 16 CFR 300 et seq.
Regulations on WPLA Labeling and Marking
These regulations set forth the wool labeling and marking requirements adopted by the FTC to administer the requirements of the WPLA and provide the procedures followed by U.S. Customs in enforcing the WPLA and the FTC regulations, including entry invoice requirements.

15 USC 1191-1204
Flammable Fabrics Act (FFA)
This Act provides for the setting of flammability standards for fabric by the Consumer Product Safety Commission (CPSC) and for enforcement by U.S. Customs.

16 CFR 1610, 1611, 1615, 1616, 1630-1632
Regulations on Flammable Fabric Standards
These regulations specify the flammability standards adopted by the CPSC under the FFA for various types of textiles.

Principal Exporting Countries

The following listing includes samples of the main supplier nations of the products of this chapter. It is organized by HTSUS major heading. (Refer to "Customs Classification" above for the product codes.) Countries are listed in rank order of the value of products imported to the U.S. Statistics represent customs value entries for 1993 from the Bureau of Census, U.S. Department of Commerce.

6401—China, Canada, South Korea, Italy, Malaysia, Germany, Taiwan, Thailand, Austria, Hong Kong

6402—China, South Korea, Indonesia, Taiwan, Italy, Thailand, Hong Kong, France, Switzerland, Austria

6403—China, Brazil, Italy, South Korea, Indonesia, Taiwan, Thailand, Spain, Mexico, India

6404—China, South Korea, Indonesia, Thailand, Mexico, Taiwan, Italy, Philippines, Spain, Hong Kong

6405—China, Brazil, Hong Kong, Italy, Spain, Taiwan, Philippines, South Korea, France, Indonesia

6406—Dominican Rep., China, Mexico, Argentina, Thailand, India, South Korea, Taiwan, Canada, Italy

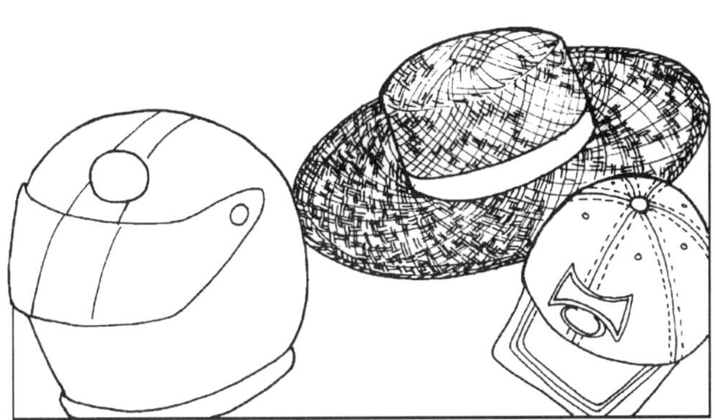

Chapter 65: Headgear*

Full title: Headgear and Parts Thereof

This chapter relates to the importation of headgear, which are classified under Chapter 65 of the Harmonized Tariff Schedule of the United States (HTSUS). Specifically, it covers hats and parts of hats of felt, and plaited, woven, and knitted materials; helmets and other headgear; and articles such as headbands, linings, covers, foundations, visors, chinstraps, and similar parts of headgear.

Materials for weaving straw hats are covered in Commodity Index Chapter 14. If you are interested in importing worn headgear, refer to Chapter 63. Headgear made from asbestos is covered in Chapter 68. Dolls' hats, party hats, and similar articles are found in Chapter 95. If you are interested in importing scarves, shawls, veils, and similar products, refer to Chapters 61 or 62.

Key Factors

The key factors in the importation of headgear are:

- Compliance with entry invoice requirements for headgear and component materials
- Compliance with textile quota restraints and visa requirements under U.S. Department of Commerce (DOC) Multi-Fiber Arrangements (if importing headgear with textile components)
- Submission of U.S. Customs Country-of-Origin Declaration(s) (if importing headgear with textile components)
- Compliance with labeling requirements under the Textile Fiber Products Identification Act (TFPIA) and the Wool Products Labeling Act (WPLA) (if importing headgear with textile components)
- Compliance with flammability standards adopted and enforced by the Consumer Product Safety Commission (CPSC) under the Flammable Fabrics Act (FFA) (if importing headgear with textile components)
- Motor vehicle helmets must meet U.S. Department of Transportation (DOT) safety, labeling, and entry documentation requirements
- Bicycle helmets must meet voluntary safety standards enforced by the CPSC
- Random U.S. Department of Agriculture (USDA) port-of-entry inspections on certain plant materials
- Import restrictions on certain plant materials
- Endangered species restrictions on certain plan materials

Although most importers use the services of a licensed customs broker in making their entries, and we recommend this practice, you should be aware of the regulatory, entry, and documentation issues involved in importing your product. You, as importer, are ultimately responsible for the fulfillment of any legal requirements applicable to your shipment.

General Considerations

Regulatory Agencies. U.S. Customs determines the classification of headgear for purposes of import duties. The DOC's Committee for Implementation of Textile Agreements (CITA) regulates certain textile imports under Section 204 of the Agricultural Adjustment Act. U.S. Customs enforces CITA textile and textile product entry quotas. Customs also enforces compliance with labeling and invoice requirements of the TFPIA and flammability standards under the FFA. The CPSC monitors imports and from time to time inspects textile shipments for compliance with FFA standards. If you are importing wool textiles, importation is subject to complex textile import regulations. The Federal Trade Commission (FTC) administers the WPLA requirements.

Wool Product Entry Requirements. Depending on the nature of your wool headgear imports, as many as four different types of special entry documents may be required. First, for all imported articles that contain textile fibers, yarns, and fabrics covered by the Agricultural Adjustment Act (AAA), including wool, you must file a U.S. Customs Textile Entry Declaration (see Textile Country-of-Origin Declarations below). Second, with the entry summary for each shipment of wool articles, you must file Customs **Form 6451**, Notice of Percentage of Clean Yield and Grade of Wool or Hair, in duplicate, showing your name and address. Third, for all wool products subject to the WPLA, special information is required on the entry invoices (see "Wool Products Labeling Act" below). Finally, certain articles of headgear manufactured or produced in certain countries may be subject to quotas and other restraints under U.S. DOC Multi-Fiber Arrangements. Such products require export licenses, certificates, or visas issued by the appropriate country of origin, in addition to other requisite entry paperwork (see "Textile Quotas" below).

Wool Products Labeling Act. The term "wool product" means any product or any portion of a product that contains, purports to contain, or in any way is represented as containing wool, reprocessed wool, or reused wool. All wool products imported into the U.S., except those made more than 20 years before importation, and except carpets, rugs, mats, and upholsteries, must have affixed a stamp, tag, label, or other means of identification as required by the WPLA. If you are importing wool products exempt from labeling under the WPLA, do not assume they are also exempt from labeling under the TFPIA. These are two distinct laws, with some overlapping requirements (see "Marking and Labeling Requirements" below).

Textile Quotas. If you are interested in importing headgear with textile components, the most important issue you need to be aware of is quotas. Under the Multi-Fiber Arrangement provisions of Section 204 of the Agricultural Adjustment Act, CITA initiates specific agreements with individual exporting countries. Section 204 of the Agricultural Adjustment Act covers textiles articles that: 1) are in chief value of cotton, wool, or man-made fibers, any textile fibers subject to the terms of any textile trade agreement, or any combination of such fibers; 2) contain 50% or more by weight of cotton or man-made fibers, or any textile fibers subject to the terms of any textile trade agreement; 3) contain 17% or more by weight of wool; or 4) if in chief value of textile fibers or textile materials, contain a blend of cotton, wool, or man-made fibers, any

*IMPORTANT: Read the Commodity Index Introduction. It is the essential framework for understanding this chapter.

textile fibers subject to the terms of any textile trade agreement, or any combination of such fibers that, in total, amount to 50% or more by weight of all component fibers.

The U.S. has Multi-Fiber Arrangements with 40 countries. Each agreement with each country is unique, and may specify quotas for a type of textile or a specific article. Visas or export licenses may be required. These agreements, however, often change. Therefore, if you are interested in importing any headgear with textile components, you should contact the International Trade Administration's Office of Textile and Apparel (see addresses at end of this chapter). Refer to "Prohibitions and Restrictions" below for further details.

Textile Country-of-Origin Declarations. U.S. Customs enforces CITA textile and textile product entry quotas (see "Prohibitions and Restrictions" below). Requirements for entry include submission of Country-of-Origin Declarations with every shipment of headgear with textile components, regardless of whether it is subject to a specific multi-fiber arrangement (19 CFR 12.130, 12.131).

Country of Origin. Quota restrictions are country-specific and therefore are applied based on the country of origin for the textiles shipped. The last country from which a textile shipment was exported to the U.S. is not necessarily its country of origin. A textile or textile product imported into the U.S. is considered a product of the particular foreign territory or country, or a U.S. insular possession, where it is wholly grown, produced, or manufactured. For the following discussion, "country" means a foreign territory or country, or a U.S. insular possession.

Substantial transformation rules may affect the country-of-origin determination. For example, if a textile or textile product originates in Country A and is subject to quota, the quota restrictions apply at entry into the U.S. But if, prior to export to the U.S., you move the shipment to Country B where there are fewer restrictions, the shipment may nevertheless remain subject to quota and visa requirements under the Multi-Fiber Arrangement with Country A. Customs determines whether the quota restrictions apply based on the criteria of "substantial transformation." If your textiles do not undergo any major processing or manufacturing while in Country B, or if the manufacturing or processing is minor, your shipment will be deemed to originate in Country A. *You cannot claim substantial transformation on the basis of minor manufacturing procedures.*

In contrast, if your shipment undergoes major processing or manufacturing while in Country B, rendering the textiles "new and different articles of commerce," Customs will treat the shipment as the product of Country B. To qualify as having undergone substantial transformation, an article must evince a change in: 1) commercial designation or identity; b) fundamental character; or c) commercial use. If your shipment is processed in more than one country, the country where it last underwent substantial transformation is the country of origin for Customs entry. In deciding whether the manufacturing or processing operation in a country is major, Customs considers the following factors: 1) the resultant physical change in the material or article; 2) the complexity, the level or degree of skill and/or technology required, and the amount of time involved in the operations; and 3) the value added to the article or material, compared to its value when imported into the U.S.

Validating Operations. Operations that Customs will usually acknowledge as validating a claim of substantial transformation are the following: 1) dyeing and printing, when accompanied by two or more of the following finishing operations: bleaching, shrinking, fulling, napping, decating, permanent stiffening, weighting, permanent embossing, or moireing; 2) spinning fibers into yarn; 3) weaving, knitting, or otherwise forming fabric; 4) cutting fabric into parts and assembling the parts into completed articles; or 5) substantial assembly, by sewing and/or tailoring, of all cut pieces of articles that have been cut from fabric in another country into a completed article—e.g., complete assembly of pre-cut pieces to form a hat.

Insubstantial Operations. Operations that usually will not support a claim of substantial transformation, even if more than one are performed, are the following: 1) simple operations of combining, labeling, pressing, cleaning, dry cleaning, or packaging; 2) cutting to length or width and edging or overlocking fabrics that are readily identifiable as being intended for a particular commercial use; 3) trimming and/or joining together by sewing, looping, linking, or other means of attaching otherwise completed knit-to-shape component parts produced in a single country, even if accompanied by other processes—e.g., washing, drying, mending—normally incident to assembly; 4) one or more finishing operations on yarns, fabrics, or their textile articles—such as showerproofing, superwashing, bleaching, decating, fulling, shrinking, mercerizing, or similar operations; or 5) dyeing and/or printing fabrics or yarns.

Declarations. The country of origin of the headgear with textile components in a shipment must be stated on a declaration submitted to U.S. Customs at the time of entry. There are three Customs Country-of-Origin Declarations: single-country, multiple-country, and negative. The Declaration to be submitted with your shipment of footwear with textile components depends on the nature of the import.

- **Single-country declarations** are used for entries of textiles or textile products that clearly originate from only one country or that have been assembled in one country from fabricated components wholly produced in the U.S. or the foreign country of manufacture. Information required includes: marks of identification and numbers; description of article and quantity; country of origin; and date of exportation.
- **Multiple-country declarations** are used for entries of textiles or textile products that were manufactured or processed and/or that incorporate materials originating in more than one foreign country or territory. Information required includes: marks of identification and numbers; for articles, description, quantity, identification of manufacturing and/or processing operations, country, and date of exportation; for materials used to make articles, description of materials, country of production, and date of exportation.
- **Negative declarations** must accompany all textile imports that are not subject to FFA Section 204 restrictions. Information required includes: marks of identification and numbers; descriptions of article and quantity; and country of origin.

The date of exportation to be indicated on the above declarations is the date on which the carrier leaves the last port in the country of origin, as determined by Customs. Diversion to another country during transit does not affect the export date.

Procedure for Declarations. The manufacturer, producer, exporter, or importer may prepare the declaration. If more than one of these parties is involved in the importation, each party may prepare a separate declaration. You may file a separate declaration for each invoice presented with your entry. The declaration must be dated and signed by the responsible party, and must include the person's title and the company name and address. Your shipment's entry will be denied unless it is accompanied by a properly executed declaration. Customs will not treat a textile declaration as a missing document for which a bond may be filed.

Customs bases its country-of-origin determination on the information contained in each declaration, unless the information is insufficient. If the information on the declaration is insufficient, Customs will require that you submit such additional information as will enable the determination to be made. The shipment will not be released until the determination is made. Thus, if you want to clear Customs with minimal delay, be sure that the information on the declarations is as complete as possible for each shipment.

Textile Labeling and Invoice Requirements. You are responsible for your imported product's compliance with applicable provisions of the TFPIA. Headgear with textile components that require labeling under TFPIA must already be labeled at entry, or the shipment will be refused. (See "Marking and Labeling Requirements" below.) If you import shipments of headgear with textile components subject to TFPIA and valued at over $500, you must provide special information on the entry invoice (see "Entry and Documentation" below).

Flammability Standards. Headgear with textile components imported into the U.S. for use in consumer products must be in compliance with the FFA, a federal law that gives the CPSC the authority and responsibility for protecting the public from the hazards of dangerously flammable items of wearing apparel and interior furnishings. Under the FFA, standards have been established for flammability of clothing textiles. You cannot import any article of wearing apparel or interior furnishing, or any fabric or related material that is intended for use or that may be used in such items, if it fails to conform to an applicable flammability standard (FFA Section 4). Certain products may be imported into the U.S. (FFA Section 11c) for finishing or processing to render them less flammable so as to meet the standards. For these products, the exporter must state on the invoice or other paper relating to the shipment that the shipment is being made for that purpose.

The CPSC monitors imports of textiles under its Import Surveillance Program. From time to time, your textile shipments may be inspected to ascertain compliance with mandatory safety standards. Shipments may also be subject to testing by the CPSC to determine compliance. If the CPSC believes a product, fabric, or related material does not comply with a flammability standard, it is authorized to pursue a variety of legal sanctions (see "Prohibitions and Restrictions" below).

Substantial Product Hazard Reports. Any firm that obtains information that reasonably supports the conclusion that one of its products presents an unreasonable risk of serious injury or death must report that information to the CPSC's Division of Corrective Actions (CPSC address below). Importers must also report to the CPSC if 1) a type of product is the subject of at least three civil actions filed in U.S. federal or state courts, 2) each suit alleges the involvement of that product type in death or grievous bodily injury (as defined in FFA Section 37(3)1), and 3) at least three of the actions result in a final settlement with the manufacturer or in a judgment for the plaintiff within any one of the two-year periods specified in FFA Section 37(b).

Motor Vehicle Helmets. Helmets for use with motor vehicles are considered motor vehicle equipment, and are regulated by U.S. Department of Transportation (DOT), National Highway Traffic Safety Administration (NHTSA), Office of Vehicle Safety Compliance (OVSC). Motor vehicle helmets must bear labeling certifying that they comply with provisions of Federal Motor Vehicle Safety Standard (FMVSS) Number 218 (see "Marking and Labeling Requirements" below). You must present a completed DOT **Declaration HS-7**, in duplicate, with each shipment at the U.S. port of entry. You can get Declaration HS-7 forms at any Customs port office or from your customs broker. No permits or licenses are required.

Bicycle Helmets. Helmets for use with bicycles are subject to voluntary standards published by the American National Standards Institute, Inc. (ANSI) (see addresses at end of this chapter). ANSI is a U.S. society whose members develop and coordinate both domestic and international voluntary consensus standards for more than 10,000 products. For the most part, the helmet industry itself is responsible for compliance enforcement. However, if you are importing foreign-made bicycle helmets, you should be cognizant of applicable ANSI standards. You are responsible for your shipment's compliance with these standards. Since compliance is voluntary, the CPSC will not inspect your shipments at the port of entry to ascertain compliance. But if, for example, your product is noncomplying, and is later found to be a causative factor in a head injury, CPSC would assume an enforcement role. CPSC is authorized to initiate various administrative and legal enforcement proceedings to prevent imports that pose a hazard to the ultimate consumer. So although standards for bicycle helmets are voluntary, compliance with those standards is nevertheless important. For further information, see "Publications Available" below.

Hats Woven from Vegetable Materials. Importation of vegetable plaiting material and related miscellaneous plant products is regulated by the USDA under the Plant Quarantine Act (PQA). The USDA Animal Plant Health Inspection Service (APHIS) Plant Protection and Quarantine (PPQ) branch inspects shipments of plaiting and related materials on a random basis, depending upon the port of entry, the risk factor involved in the type of material being offered for entry, etc. You do not generally need permits or licenses to import these products, but the type of plant material is pertinent (see "Prohibitions and Restrictions", below). For most shipments of plaiting materials, importation is straightforward. If you are importing related articles classified under different Commodity Index chapters, there may be additional requirements administered by other governmental agencies. This depends entirely upon the specific article you are importing.

Restrictions under the Endangered Species Act (ESA) and the Convention on International Trade in Endangered Species (CITES) apply to plant materials of listed plants species, and are enforced by the U.S. Fish and Wildlife Service (FWS), usually in consultation with and often through the USDA. Regulations governing the importation of plant products are complex, and FWS permits or CITES documentation may be required. To ascertain what your legal responsibilities are, you should contact these agencies with specific identification of the materials you wish to import.

Import Advisory

Importation of textile products is trade-sensitive and highly regulated. Shipments of textile products not complying with all government regulations, including quotas and visas, are subject to seizure and could result in the imposition of penalties as well as possible forfeiture of the goods. You should always verify the available quota for any textile product you plan to import before your shipment leaves the country of manufacture. Furthermore, Customs textile classification rulings change frequently, and prior administrative rulings are often modified and sometimes reversed.

Customs Classification

For customs purposes, headgear with textile components are classified under Chapter 65 of the HTSUS. This chapter is broken into major headings, which are further divided into subheadings, and often sub-subheadings, each of which has its own HTSUS classification number. For example, the HTSUS number for knitted hats of cotton for babies is 6505.90.15, indicating it is a sub-subcategory of other knitted headgear of cotton or flax other than hairnets (6505.90.00), which is a subcategory of the major heading hats and other headgear knitted or crocheted (6505.00.00). There are seven major headings in HTSUS chapter 65.

6501—Hat forms, hat bodies, and hoods of felt, neither blocked to shape nor with made brims; plateaux and manchons (including slit manchons), of felt

6502—Hat shapes, plaited or made by assembling strips of any material, neither blocked to shape, nor with made brims, not lined nor trimmed

6503—Felt hats and other felt headgear, made from the hat bodies or plateaux of heading 6501, whether or not lined or trimmed

6504—Hats and other headgear, plaited or made by assembling strips of any material, whether or not lined or trimmed

6505—Hats and other headgear, knitted or crocheted, or made up from lace, felt, or other textile fabric, in the piece (but not in strips), whether or not lined or trimmed; hair-nets of any material, whether or not lined or trimmed

6506—Other headgear, whether or not lined or trimmed

6507—Headbands, linings, covers, hat foundations, hat frames, peaks (visors), and chinstraps, for headgear

Sample Import Duties

Import duties will vary depending on the HTSUS classification of your product. Therefore, to determine the correct amount of duties, your product must be properly classified under the HTSUS. The following sample duties are taken from the duty listings for HTSUS Chapter 65 products.

Hat forms of fur felt for men or boys (6501.00.30): $1.10/dozen + 1.6%; sewed hat shapes (6502.00.20): 34 cents/dozen + 3.4%; not sewed, bleached or colored (6502.00.60): 2.4 cents/dozen + 2%; other fur felt hats made up but not lined or trimmed (6503.00.60): $1.92/dozen + 2.8%; sewed hats of vegetable fibers (6504.00.30): 6.4%; other hats of man-made fibers (6504.00.90): 7.2%; hair nets (6505.10.00): 10%; knitted or crocheted hats of cotton or flax (6505.90.15): 8.4%; knitted hats of wool (6505.90.30): 50.7 cents/kg + 15.4%; other knitted hats of man-made fibers not fashioned of braid (6505.90.60): 39.7 cents/kg + 14.1%; other knitted hats of silk or of fine animal hair (6505.90.90): 22 cents/kg + 8%; motorcycle helmets of reinforced or laminated plastics (6506.10.30): 8.8 cents/kg + 3.4%; other athletic headgear (6506.10.60): 2.4%; other headgear of rubber or plastics—bathing caps (6506.91.00): 2.4%; headbands, visors, and other parts (6507.00.00): 1.3%.

Entry and Documentation

The entry of merchandise is a two-part process consisting of 1) filing the documentation necessary to determine whether merchandise may be released from Customs custody, and 2) filing the documents that contain information for duty assessment and statistical purposes. In certain instances, all documents must be filed and accepted by Customs prior to release of the goods. Unless you have been granted an extension, you must file entry documents at a location specified by the district or area director within five working days of your shipment's date of arrival at a U.S. port of entry. These include a number of standard documents required by Customs for any entry, and:

- U.S. Customs Country-of-Origin Declaration(s) (if importing textile products)
- Export documentation and/or visa (if importing textiles products subject to Multi-Fiber Arrangements
- Customs **Form 6451**, Notice of Percentage of Clean Yield and Grade of Wool or Hair, in duplicate, showing your name and address (if importing articles containing wool)
- For motor vehicle helmets: DOT **Declaration HS-7**, in duplicate
- Where applicable for hats of woven vegetable materials, USDA permits
- Where applicable for hats of woven vegetable materials, FWS permits and/or export certification from the country of origin required under endangered species regulations

After you present the entry, Customs may examine your shipment or may waive examination. The shipment is then released provided no legal or regulatory violations have been noted. You must then file entry summary documentation and deposit estimated duties at a designated customhouse within 10 working days of your shipment's release. For a detailed description of entry procedures, standard documentation, and informal entry, refer to "Entry Process" on page 182.

Special Entry Invoices. Hats and headgear classified under subheading 6502.00.40 or 6502.00.60 require a statement as to whether or not the article has been bleached or colored. Articles classified subheading 6502.00.20 through 6502.00.60 or 6504.00.30 through 6504.00.90 require a statement as to whether or not the article is sewed or not, exclusive of any ornamentation or trimming.

Entry Invoice—TFPIA Requirements. All invoices for textile wearing apparel should indicate: 1) a component material breakdown in percentages by weight for all component fibers present in the entire garment, as well as separate breakdowns of the fibers in the (outer) shell (exclusive of linings, cuffs, waistbands, collars and other trimmings) and in the lining; 2) for garments which are constructed of more than one component or material (combination of knit and not-knit fabric or combinations of knit and/or not-knit fabric with leather, fur, plastic—including vinyl, etc.) the invoice must show a fiber breakdown in percentages by weight for each separate textile material in the garment and a breakdown in percentages by weight for each nontextile material of the entire garment; 3) for woven garments: indicate whether the fabric is yarn-dyed and whether there are "two or more colors in the warp and/or filling."

Entry Invoice—Wool Products Subject to WPLA. When you offer for entry a wool product shipment valued at more than $500 and subject to WPLA, you must include certain information intended to facilitate Customs monitoring and enforcement of that act. This extra information is identical to that required by WPLA on labeling (see "Marking and Labeling Requirements" below), with the addition of the manufacturer's name. If your product consists of mixed waste, residues, and similar merchandise obtained from several suppliers or unknown sources, you may omit the manufacturer's name from the entry invoice.

Prohibitions and Restrictions

Textile Quotas. Textile import restrictions are primarily a matter of quotas and the way in which these quotas are administered and monitored. Under the Multi-Fiber Arrangement provisions of Section 204 of the Agricultural Adjustment Act, CITA has negotiated Multi-Fiber Arrangements with 40 countries. These agreements may impose quotas for a type of textile or a specific article, and they are country-specific. However, the agreements often change. Therefore, if you are interested in importing any knitted or crocheted apparel articles, you should contact the International Trade Administration's Office of Textile and Apparel (see addresses at end of this chapter). The Office of Textile and Apparel has a team of country specialists who can inform you of the latest developments and inform you about a product's quota or restriction status.

U.S. Customs enforces CITA textile and textile product entry quotas. If formal entry procedures are not followed, Customs will usually refuse entry for textiles that are subject to Section 204. Formal entry requires submission of a Country-of-Origin Declaration (see "General Considerations" above). U.S. Customs maintains a current textile quota status report, available for perusal at any customs port. In addition, U.S. Customs in Washington, D.C., operates a telephone service to provide quota status reports, which are updated weekly (see "Relevant Government Agencies" below).

Flammable Fabrics. U.S. Customs may refuse entry for any article of wearing apparel or interior furnishing, or any fabric or related material that is intended for use or that may be used in wearing apparel or interior furnishings, if it fails to conform to an applicable flammability standard issued under Section 4 of the FFA. An exception is allowed for certain products (FFA Section 11c) that are imported for finishing or processing to bring them within the legal standard. For these products, the exporter must state on the invoice or other document relating to the shipment that the shipment is being made for that purpose.

The CPSC, as the primary enforcement agency of flammability standards, inspects products for compliance with the FFA. If the CPSC believes a product, fabric, or related material does not comply with a flammability standard, it is authorized to pursue a variety of legal sanctions, including: 1) seizure, condemnation, and forfeiture of the noncomplying products; 2) administrative cease-and-desist order requiring an individual or firm to stop sale and distribution of the noncomplying products or; 3) temporary injunction requiring the individual or firm to stop sale and distribution of the noncomplying products, pending final disposition of an administrative cease-and-desist proceeding. The CPSC also has authority to seek civil penalties against any person who knowingly violates a regulation or standard issued under Section 4 of the FFA.

Helmets. Motor vehicle helmets that do not comply with provisions of FMVSS Number 218 are prohibited. Unlike the voluntary standards for bicycle helmets, these standards are compulsory. You, as importer, are responsible for your product's compliance. The standard has been developed in order to reduce deaths and injuries to motorcyclists and other motor vehicle users resulting from head impacts. Each helmet must meet specific requirements when subjected to certain conditioning and testing procedures contained within the regulation. Components of the testing procedures include impact attenuation, penetration, and testing of retention systems (i.e. straps and assemblies that keep the helmet on the head). In addition to meeting testing requirements, helmets must meet configuration requirements that determine such things as peripheral vision clearance, brow opening, and continuous contour of the protective surface. Helmets may not have any rigid projections inside the shell, and those outside the shell must be limited to those required for operation of essential accessories. The regulation limits the size of such projections to 0.20 inch. Manufacturers must establish a positioning index for each helmet manufactured. If you make inquiry regarding that index for a helmet specified by manufacturer, model designation and size, the manufacturer is required by law to provide the information. For more details, contact DOT (see addresses at end of this chapter).

Hats and Components of Woven Vegetable Materials. In general, any shipment of vegetable plaiting material is subject to random port-of-entry inspection by USDA. If the inspector finds evidence of the presence of insects, you may be required to submit your shipment to USDA-prescribed fumigation procedures. If the insect is of a kind for which there is no viable U.S. treatment, your shipment will be refused. Our source at USDA assured us that most shipments that are found to be infested can be treated to afford entry.

Country-Specific Restrictions

Restrictions under Multi-Fiber Arrangements are country-specific. A product originating in one country may be subject to quota and to export license or visa requirements, while the same product originating in a different country may not. At present, the U.S. has Multi-Fiber Arrangements with 40 countries. Many different categories of products are covered under these arrangements; it is beyond the scope of this discussion to list each country and its restricted commodities. If you are interested in importing textiles and textile products, you should contact the International Trade Administration's Office of Textile and Apparel (see addresses at end of this chapter) or U.S. Customs to ascertain your product's restraint status.

The U.S. Customs Quota Branch phone numbers provide recorded status reports, by quota category number, for current charges against the quotas for that country. For convenience, the HTSUS shows the 3-digit category number in parentheses to the right of each listed commodity that is subject to textile restraints. For example, under Chapter 64, heading 6502.0.90, other hat shapes of man-made fibers, is followed by the number "(659)". If you know the category number for your product, you can find out to what extent that quota is filled simply by calling the number for the appropriate country. A word of caution, though: if you do not know for sure that your article is subject to quota from a particular country, and you call the number for that country, you may not be any more enlightened after the phone call. Many of the recordings give status reports only when a certain percentage of the quota has been filled. Thus, if 659 is among the categories for which not enough quantity has entered the U.S. to warrant specific mention, it will be lumped under "all other categories" and you will be none the wiser. To find out if your product is subject to textile restraints, call the DOC or a local Customs port office. Then you can find out the current charges against that quota by calling the country number listed below. For a complete listing of Customs Quota Branch information numbers, see "Relevant Government Agencies" below.

Marking and Labeling Requirements

TFPIA Requirements. All textile products imported into the U.S. must be stamped, tagged, labeled, or otherwise marked with the following information as required by the TFPIA, unless exempt from marking—such as sweatbands for the head—(see TFPIA, Section 12): 1) the generic names and percentages by weight of the constituent fibers present in the textile fiber product, exclusive of permissible ornamentation, in amounts of more than 5% in order of predominance by weight, with any percentage of fiber or fibers required to be designated as "other fiber" or "other fibers" (including those present in amounts of 5% or less) appearing last; and 2) the name of the manufacturer or the name or registered identification number issued by the FTC of one or more persons marketing or handling the textile fiber product; and 3) the name of the country where processed. A word trademark, used as a house mark and registered with the U.S. Patent Office, may appear on labels instead of the name otherwise required, provided the owner of the trademark furnishes a copy of the registration to FTC prior to use (see "Registered Identification Numbers" below).

The information listed above is not exhaustive. TFPIA requirements are extensive. The Act specifies such details as types of labels, means of attachment, label position on the article, package labeling, unit labeling for two-piece garments, and arrangement of information on the label; allowable fiber designations; country-of-origin indications; requirements for trim and ornamentation, linings and interlinings, and pile fabrics; sectional disclosure; use of trade names and trademarks; and requirements for swatches and samples. The FTC publishes a booklet intended to clarify TFPIA requirements to facilitate voluntary compliance in the industry (see "Publications Available" below). It is available on request, at no charge, from the FTC (see addresses at end of this chapter).

Wool Products Labeling Act (WPLA). Wool product labeling requirements for foreign products are the responsibility of the importer. The WPLA requires the following information to appear on wool products subject to the act: 1) percentage of the wool product's total fiber weight (exclusive of ornamentation) not exceeding 5% of the total fiber weight of a) wool, b) recycled wool, c) each fiber other than wool if the percent by weight of such fiber is 5% or more, and d) the aggregate of all other fibers; 2) the maximum percent of the wool product's total weight, of any nonfibrous loading, filling, or adulterating matter; and 3) the importer's name. If you, as importer, have a registered identification number issued by the FTC, that number may be used instead of your name (see "Registered Identification Numbers" below).

Customs entry is contingent on proper labeling. If your shipment is found to be mislabeled at entry, you will be given the option of relabeling the products under Customs supervision, as long as the district director is satisfied that your labeling error or omission did not involve fraud or willful neglect. If your shipment is discovered after entry to have been noncomplying with WPLA, it will be recalled to Customs custody at your expense, unless you can satisfy the district director that the products have since been brought into compliance. You will be held responsible for all expenses incurred in bringing a shipment into compliance, including compensation of personnel and other expenses related to Customs supervision.

Fraudulent violations of WPLA will result in seizure of the shipment. Shipments already released from Customs custody will be ordered to be redelivered to Customs. Customs reports all cases of fraudulent violation to the FTC in Washington, D.C.

The information listed above is not intended to be exhaustive. WPLA requirements are extensive. The act specifies such details as types of labels, means of attachment, label position on the article, package labeling, unit labeling (as in the case of a two-piece garment), arrangement of information on the label, allowable fiber designations, country-of-origin indications, trim and ornamentation, pile fabrics, sectional disclosure, use of trade names and trademarks, requirements for swatches and samples, etc. The FTC publishes a booklet intended to clarify WPLA requirements in order to facilitate voluntary compliance within the industry (see "Publications Available" below). It is available on request, at no charge, from the FTC (see addresses at end of this chapter).

Registered Identification Numbers. Any domestic firm or person residing in the U.S. and engaged in the manufacture or marketing of textile products covered under the TFPIA or WPLA may obtain an FTC-registered identification number for use on required tags and labels instead of the name of a firm or person. For applications, contact the FTC (see addresses at end of this chapter).

Helmets. Motor vehicle helmets must be labeled permanently and legibly, in such a manner that labels can be read easily without removing padding or any other permanent helmet part. Labeling must include the following information: 1) manufacturer's name or identification; 2) precise model designation; 3) size; 4) month and year of manufacture, either spelled out (e.g. June 1988) or expressed in numerals (e.g. 6/88); 5) the symbol "DOT," constituting the manufacturer's certification that the helmet conforms to the applicable FMVSS. This symbol must appear on the outer surface of the helmet, in a color that contrasts with the background, in letters at least 3/8 inch high, centered laterally with the horizontal center line of the symbol located a minimum of 1-1/8 inches and a maximum of 1-3/8 inches from the bottom edge of the posterior portion of the helmet. In addition, labeling must include the following instructions to purchasers: 1) "Shell and liner constructed of (identify types of materials);" 2) "Helmet can be seriously damaged by some common substances without damage being visible to the user. Apply only the following: (recommended cleaning agents, paints, adhesives, etc., as appropriate);" 3) "Make no modifications. Fasten helmet securely. If helmet experiences a severe blow, return it to the manufacturer for inspection, or destroy it and replace it." Any additional relevant safety information should be supplied at the time of purchase, by means of an attached tag, brochure, or other suitable means.

For a general discussion of U.S. Customs marking and labeling requirements, refer to "Marking: Country of Origin" on page 215 and "Special Marking Requirements" on page 217.

Shipping Considerations

You will need to ensure that your goods are packaged and shipped with care so that they pass smoothly through Customs and arrive in good condition. You are responsible for ensuring that the shipment is in compliance with all applicable government regulations for packaging and shipping. In most instances, you should not leave these arrangements solely to the discretion of your supplier. Careful preparation of the cargo and selection of the mode of transport can be essential to a cost-effective, timely delivery of undamaged goods. We strongly advise you to consult your shipping representative, insurance agent, or freight broker for advice on packing and shipping. Refer also to the major tab section "Packing/Shipping/Insurance" for a general discussion of packing and shipping.

Headgear may be shipped in bulk, crates, boxes, or other types of containers, depending on the type of product and whether it is prepackaged. General considerations include protection from contamination, weather, and pests. Containers should be constructed so as to be safe for handling during transport.

Publications Available

The following publications may be relevant to the importation of headgear:

Questions and Answers Relating to the Textile Fiber Products Identification Act and Regulations

Questions and Answers Relating to the Wool Products Labeling Act and Regulations

Available free of charge on request from the Federal Trade Commission (see addresses at end of this chapter), these publications are excellent sources of information written in clear lay language. We recommend that anyone interested in importing textile products but unfamiliar with the regulations obtain a copy of each of these booklets.

The American National Standards Institute, Inc. (ANSI) publishes domestic and international voluntary consensus standards for more than 10,000 commodities. For ANSI standards applicable to bicycle helmets, request: Document ANSI Z-90.4, 1984 Edition: *Protective Headgear for Bicyclists*; $20.00. Also available: ANSI General Catalog, 1995 Edition; $20.00. You may purchase documents outlining these standards from the Institute by mail. Prepayment in the form of personal check, company check, or money order is required of non-members. Address your inquiries to:

American National Sales Institute, Inc. (ANSI)
11 W. 42nd St.
New York, NY 10036
(212) 642-4900

The *Harmonized Tariff Schedule of the United States* (HTSUS) is available from:

Government Printing Office (GPO)
Superintendent of Documents
Washington, DC 20402
(202) 512-1800 (Order line)
(202) 512-0000 (General)

The USGPO also has copies of specific laws available for purchase. The USGPO accepts credit card orders over the phone, as well as mail orders paid by credit card, a check drawn on a U.S. bank, or an international money order.

Relevant Government Agencies

Address questions regarding textile Multi-Fiber Arrangements to:

International Trade Administration
Office of Textile and Apparel
14th and Constitution Ave. NW, Rm. 3100
Washington, DC 20230
(202) 482-5078, 482-3737

Address questions regarding the Flammable Fabrics Act (FFA) to:

Consumer Product Safety Commission (CPSC)
5401 Westbard Avenue
Bethesda, MD 20207
(301) 492-6580

Address questions regarding labeling requirements under the Textile Fiber Products Identification Act (TFPIA) or the Wool Products Labeling Act (WPLA) to:

Federal Trade Commission (FTC)
Division of Enforcement
601 Pennsylvania Ave. NW
Washington, DC 20580
(202) 326-2996 (General)
(202) 326-2841 (Textile and wool products labeling)

Address questions regarding DOT requirements for motor vehicle helmets to:

National Highway Traffic Safety Administration
Office of Vehicle Safety Compliance
400 7th St. SW
Washington, DC 20590
(202) 366-5311, 366-2830

Address questions regarding USDA requirements for importation of vegetable woven materials to:

U.S. Department of Agriculture (USDA)
Animal and Plant Health Inspection Service (APHIS)
Plant Protection and Quarantine (PPQ)
Federal Building, Rm. 631
6505 Belcrest Road
Hyattsville, MD 20782
(301) 436-8645

Address questions regarding endangered species restrictions to:

U.S. Fish and Wildlife Service (FWS)
Office of Management Authority
4401 N. Fairfax Drive, Room 432
Arlington, VA 22203
(703) 358-2095
(800) 358-2104, (703) 358-2104 (Permits office)

Address your questions regarding headgear imports to the district or port director of Customs for you area. For addresses, refer to"U.S. Customs District Offices" on page 62 or contact:

U.S. Customs Service
1301 Constitution Ave. NW
Washington, DC 20229
(202) 927-6724 (Information)
(202) 927-1000 (General)

The following information numbers for U.S. Customs in Washington, DC, provide recorded information. The Quota Branch numbers listed by country provide updated status reports on textile quotas from those countries. All area codes are (202).
General information: 927-5850

Quota Branch: China 927-6703; India 927-6705; Indonesia 927-6704; Japan 927-6706; Korea 927-6707; Macao 927-6709; Malaysia 927-6712; Mexico 927-6711; Pakistan 927-6714; Philippines 927-6713; Romania 927-6715; Singapore 927-6716; Sri Lanka 927-6708; Taiwan 927-6719; Thailand 927-6717; Turkey 927-6718; All others 927-5850.

Laws and Regulations

The following laws and regulations may be relevant to the importation of footwear. The laws are contained in the United States Code (USC), and the regulations are published in the Code of Federal Regulations (CFR), both of which are available at larger public and law libraries. Copies of specific laws are also available from the United States Government Printing Office (address above).

19 CFR 141.89
Regulation on Additional Invoice Requirements
This regulation specifies the additional information for certain classes of merchandise, including footwear and textile products, being imported into the U.S.

7 USC 1854
Textile Trade Agreements
(EO 11651, as amended by EO 11951 and 12188, and supplemented by EO 12475 below)
This Act authorizes the CITA of the DOC to enter into Multi-Fiber Agreements with other countries to control trade in textiles and establishes the Textile Import Program, which is enforced by U.S. Customs.

19 CFR 12.130 et seq.
Regulations on Entry of Textiles
These regulations provide the requirements and procedures followed by Customs in enforcing limitations on the importation and entry and withdrawal of textiles and textile products from warehouses for consumption in the U.S.

15 USC 70-77
Textile Fiber Products Identification Act (TFPIA)
This Act prohibits false or deceptive labeling (misbranding) and false advertising of any textile fiber products and requires all textile fiber products imported into the U.S. to be labeled in accordance with the requirements set forth in the law.

19 CFR 11.12b; 16 CFR 303 et seq.
Regulations on Labeling and Marking
These regulations detail the labeling and marking requirements for textiles as specified by the CPSC and the invoice contents required by U.S. Customs for purpose of enforcing the labeling and marking rules.

15 USC 68-68j
Wool Products Labeling Act (WPLA)
This Act prohibits the false or deceptive labeling (misbranding) of wool products and requires all wool products imported into the U.S. to be labeled in accordance with requirements set forth in the law.

19 CFR 11.12; 16 CFR 300 et seq.
Regulations on WPLA Labeling and Marking
These regulations set forth the wool labeling and marking requirements adopted by the FTC to administer the requirements of the WPLA and provide the procedures followed by U.S. Customs in enforcing the WPLA and the FTC regulations, including entry invoice requirements.

15 USC 1191-1204
Flammable Fabrics Act (FFA)
This Act provides for the setting of flammability standards for fabric by the Consumer Product Safety Commission (CPSC) and for enforcement by U.S. Customs.

16 CFR 1610, 1611, 1615, 1616, 1630-1632
Regulations on Flammable Fabric Standards
These regulations specify the flammability standards adopted by the CPSC under the FFA for various types of textiles.

15 USC 1391-1431
National Traffic and Motor Vehicle Safety Act of 1966
Customs assists in the enforcement of this Act which pro-

vides for the setting of motor vehicle safety standards by the National Highway Traffic Safety Administration (NHTSA), and prohibits the manufacture, sale, delivery or importation of substandard vehicles. Temporary importations may be permitted for the purpose of bringing substandard vehicles into conformity with the safety standards (Section 1397). See 19 CFR 12.80.

42 USC 264 et seq.
The Plant Quarantine Act
This Act gives the Plant Protection and Quarantine branch of the USDA authority to restrict or prohibit importation of plants or their seeds found to carry specific plant pests and pathogens.

Convention on International Trade in Endangered Species of Wild Fauna and Flora (CITES)
This comprehensive wildlife treaty signed by over 100 countries, including the United States, regulates and in many cases prohibits commercial imports and exports of wild animal and plant species threatened by trade.

16 USC 1531
Endangered Species Act
This Act prohibits the import and export of plant and seed species listed as endangered and most species listed as threatened. Seeds labeled as "of cultivated origin" may be traded. It is the U.S. law that implements CITES.

Principal Exporting Countries

The following listing includes samples of the main supplier nations of the products of this chapter. It is organized by HTSUS major heading. (Refer to "Customs Classification" above for the product codes.) Countries are listed in rank order of the value of products imported to the U.S. Statistics represent customs value entries for 1993 from the Bureau of Census, U.S. Department of Commerce.

6501—Brazil, Portugal, Czech Rep., China, Ecuador, Colombia, Poland, Slovenia, Russia, Germany

6502—China, Ecuador, Japan, Mexico, Hong Kong, Madagascar, Philippines, Taiwan, South Korea, Switzerland

6503—Australia, Italy, Colombia, Czech Rep., Canada, China, United Kingdom, Mexico, Spain, Greece

6504—Mexico, China, Taiwan, Italy, Philippines, Canada, Hong Kong, Ecuador, Madagascar, South Korea

6505—China, Taiwan, South Korea, Dominican Rep., Bangladesh, Philippines, Mexico, Sri Lanka, Hong Kong, Indonesia

6506—Japan, Italy, Canada, South Korea, Mexico, China, Taiwan, Australia, Belgium, Malaysia

6507—Taiwan, Canada, China, Mexico, Italy, Switzerland, Costa Rica, Sweden, Hong Kong, France

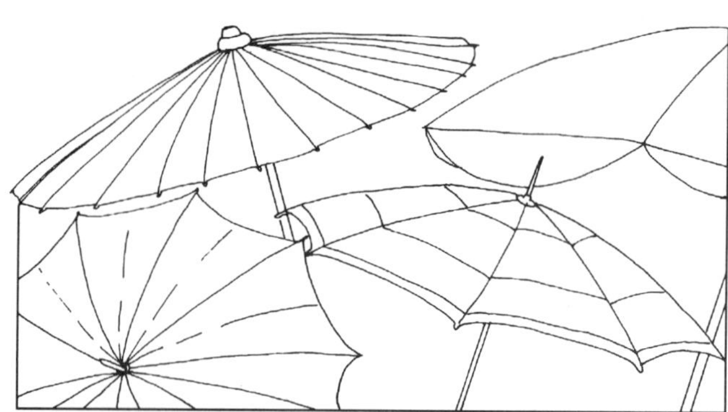

Chapter 66: Umbrellas and Related Items*

Full title: Umbrellas, Sun Umbrellas, Walking-Sticks, Seat-Sticks, Whips, Riding Crops, and Parts Thereof

This chapter relates to the importation of umbrellas, walking-sticks, whips, and related items, which are classified under Chapter 66 of the Harmonized Tariff Schedule of the United States (HTSUS). Specifically, it covers sun, garden, rain, walking-stick, and other umbrellas, walking-sticks, seat-sticks, whips, riding crops, and parts of these articles—such as handles, knobs, and umbrella frames and shafts.

If you are interested in importing measure walking-sticks and similar items, you should read Commodity Index Chapter 90. Toy umbrellas, sticks, and whips are covered in Chapter 95. The import requirements for sticks designed for use as weapons, such as firearm-sticks, sword-sticks, and loaded walking-sticks, are explained in Chapter 93. Trimmings or accessories of textile material, covers, tassels, thongs, cases, and similar items entered with but not fitted to articles imported under Chapter 66 are classified separately under the chapter applicable to the specific item.

Key Factors

Although most importers use the services of a licensed customs broker in making their entries, and we recommend this practice, you should be aware of the regulatory, entry, and documentation issues involved in importing your product. You, as importer, are ultimately responsible for the fulfillment of any legal requirements applicable to your shipment.

General Considerations

Importation of umbrellas, walking-sticks, whips, and related items is straightforward. There are no restrictions or prohibitions. You do not need permits or licenses, nor is special entry documentation required.

Customs Classification

For customs purposes, umbrellas, walking-sticks, whips, and related items are classified under Chapter 66 of the HTSUS. This chapter is broken into major headings, which are further divided into subheadings, and often sub-subheadings, each of which has its own HTSUS classification number. For example, the HTSUS number for frames for hand-held rain umbrellas is 6603.20.30, indicating it is a sub-subcategory of umbrella frames, etc. (6603.20.00), which is a subcategory of the major heading parts,

*IMPORTANT: Read the Commodity Index Introduction. It is the essential framework for understanding this chapter.

trimmings, and accessories, etc. (6603.00.00). There are three major headings within Chapter 64.

6601—Umbrellas and sun umbrellas (including walking-sticks, umbrellas, garden umbrellas, and similar umbrellas)

6602—Walking-sticks, seat-sticks, whips, riding-crops, and the like

6603—Parts, trimmings, and accessories of articles of heading 6601 or 6602

Sample Import Duties

Import duties will vary depending on the HTSUS classification of your product. Therefore, to determine the correct amount of duties, your product must be properly classified under the HTSUS. The following sample duties are taken from the duty listings for HTSUS Chapter 66 products.

Garden or similar umbrellas (6601.10.00): 8.2%; other umbrellas, having a telescopic shaft (6601.91.00): 8.2%, without telescopic shaft (6601.99.00): 8.2%; walking-sticks, seat-sticks, whips, riding-crops, and the like (6602.00.00): 5.8%; handles and knobs for articles of heading 6601 or 6602 (6603.00.00): 7.5%; umbrella frames, including frames mounted on shafts (6603.20.00): 12%; other parts (6603.90.00): 75%.

Entry and Documentation

The entry of merchandise is a two-part process consisting of 1) filing the documentation necessary to determine whether merchandise may be released from Customs custody, and 2) filing the documents that contain information for duty assessment and statistical purposes. In certain instances, all documents must be filed and accepted by Customs prior to release of the goods. Unless you have been granted an extension, you must file the standard entry documents at a location specified by the district or area director within five working days of your shipment's date of arrival at a U.S. port of entry.

After you present the entry, Customs may examine your shipment or may waive examination. The shipment is then released provided no legal or regulatory violations have been noted. You must then file entry summary documentation and deposit estimated duties at a designated customhouse within 10 working days of your shipment's release. For a detailed description of entry procedures, standard documentation, and informal entry, refer to "Entry Process" on page 182.

Marking and Labeling Requirements

For a general discussion of U.S. Customs marking and labeling requirements, refer to "Marking: Country of Origin" on page 215 and "Special Marking Requirements" on page 217.

Shipping Considerations

You will need to ensure that your goods are packaged and shipped with care so that they pass smoothly through Customs and arrive in good condition. You are responsible for ensuring that the shipment is in compliance with all applicable government regulations for packaging and shipping. In most instances, you should not leave these arrangements solely to the discretion of your supplier. Careful preparation of the cargo and selection of the mode of transport can be essential to a cost-effective, timely delivery of undamaged goods. We strongly advise you to consult your shipping representative, insurance agent, or freight broker for advice on packing and shipping. Refer also to the major tab section "Packing/Shipping/Insurance" for a general discussion of packing and shipping.

Umbrellas, walking-sticks, whips, and related items may be shipped in bulk, crates, boxes, bags, or other types of containers, depending on the type of product and whether it is prepackaged. General considerations include protection from contamination, weather, and pests. Containers should be constructed so as to be safe for handling during transport.

Publications Available

The *Harmonized Tariff Schedule of the United States* (HTSUS) is available from:

Government Printing Office (GPO)
Superintendent of Documents
Washington, DC 20402
(202) 512-1800 (Order line)
(202) 512-0000 (General)

The USGPO also has copies of specific laws available for purchase. The USGPO accepts credit card orders over the phone, as well as mail orders paid by credit card, a check drawn on a U.S. bank, or an international money order.

Relevant Government Agencies

Address your questions regarding umbrellas and related items to the district or port director of Customs for you area. For addresses, refer to "U.S. Customs District Offices" on page 62 or contact:

U.S. Customs Service
1301 Constitution Ave. NW
Washington, DC 20229
(202) 927-6724 (Information)
(202) 927-1000 (General)

Principal Exporting Countries

The following listing includes samples of the main supplier nations of the products of this chapter. It is organized by HTSUS major heading. (Refer to "Customs Classification" above for the product codes.) Countries are listed in rank order of the value of products imported to the U.S. Statistics represent customs value entries for 1993 from the Bureau of Census, U.S. Department of Commerce.

6601—China, Taiwan, Thailand, Hong Kong, Indonesia, Italy, South Korea, Chile, France, Malaysia

6602—Taiwan, United Kingdom, Italy, India, Mexico, Canada, South Korea, Philippines, China, Germany

6603—Taiwan, Canada, China, Thailand, Chile, Mexico, Indonesia, United Kingdom, Italy, South Korea

Chapter 67: Feathers, Down, Artificial Flowers, and Wigs*

Full title: Prepared Feathers and Down and Articles Made of Feathers or of Down; Artificial Flowers; Articles of Human Hair

This chapter relates to the importation of feathers, down, artificial flowers, and wigs and related items, which are classified under Chapter 67 of the Harmonized Tariff Schedule of the United States (HTSUS). Specifically, it covers feathers, down, articles of feathers or down, bird skins with feathers or down; artificial flowers, foliage, and fruit made of plastics, feathers, man-made fibers, or other materials; human or animal hair or other textile materials prepared for use in wigs; and wigs, false beards, eyebrows, eyelashes, and similar articles made of human or animal hair or textile materials.

If you are interested in importing straining cloth of human hair, you should read Commodity Index Chapter 59. Footwear and parts of footwear are covered in Chapter 63, and headgear and hair-nets are in Chapter 65. For importing worked quills and scapes, refer to Chapter 5. Toys, sports equipment, and carnival articles are covered in Chapter 95. If you are interested in importing feather dusters, powder-puffs, or hair sieves, you should read Chapter 96. Articles in which feathers or down are used only as filling or padding are covered in the specific Commodity Index chapters related to the particular article. For example, down or feather quilts are in Chapter 94, and down or feather jackets are in Chapter 62. Flowers made of glass are imported in accordance with Chapter 70.

Key Factors

The key factors in the importation of feathers, down, artificial flowers, and wigs and related items are:

- Compliance with down-feather ratio rating certification (if importing raw down)
- Compliance with Fish and Wildlife Service (FWS) license, permit, country-of-origin permit, import documentation, and recordkeeping requirements (if feathers or down are derived from exotic wildlife or endangered species)
- Entry at FWS-designated ports, and compliance with FWS and Customs advance notification and port-of-entry inspection requirements (if feathers or down are derived from exotic wildlife or endangered species)
- Compliance with U.S. Department of Agriculture (USDA) APHIS import, quarantine, permit, and certification requirements (if products are derived from domesticated animals)
- Entry at USDA-designated ports (if products are derived from domesticated animals)
- Compliance with textile quota restraints and visa requirements under U.S. Department of Commerce (DOC) Multi-Fiber Arrangements (if importing articles with textile components)
- Submission of U.S. Customs Country-of-Origin Declaration(s) (if importing articles with textile components)
- Compliance with labeling requirements under the Wool Products Labeling Act (WPLA) (if importing articles containing wool)
- Compliance with flammability standards adopted and enforced by the Consumer Product Safety Commission (CPSC) under the Flammable Fabrics Act (FFA) (if importing articles with textile components)

Although most importers use the services of a licensed customs broker in making their entries, and we recommend this practice, you should be aware of the regulatory, entry, and documentation issues involved in importing your product. You, as importer, are ultimately responsible for the fulfillment of any legal requirements applicable to your shipment.

General Considerations

Regulatory Agencies. The USDA regulates and inspects the importation of all products derived from animals, including down and feathers. The FWS, primarily under provisions of the U.S. Endangered Species Act (ESA) and the Convention on International Trade in Endangered Species of Wild Fauna and Flora (CITES), controls the importation of products derived from animals that are classified as exotic wildlife, endangered species, or threatened species. U.S. Customs enforces USDA and FWS requirements through entry documentation and restrictions.

If you are importing articles with textile components, you must be aware of the standards adopted by the CPSC under authority of the Flammable Fabrics Act (FFA). U.S. Customs enforces compliance with labeling requirements related to the flammability standards under the FFA. The CPSC monitors imports and from time to time inspects textile shipments for compliance with FFA standards. If you are importing articles containing wool, importation is subject to complex textile import regulations. The Federal Trade Commission (FTC) administers the WPLA requirements. Wigs and artificial flowers made of textiles are exempt from the labeling requirements of Textile Fiber Products Identification Act (TFPIA). However, these products may be subject to regulation by the DOC's Committee for Implementation of Textile Agreements (CITA) under Section 204 of the Agricultural Adjustment Act.

Down Products. Down products may or may not be regulated, depending on the nature of the product. For example, a down-filled sleeping bag might be a straightforward entry, requiring no special entry paperwork or labeling, etc. But a down-filled article of wearing apparel, depending on the textile used and the origin of the article, might be subject to textile quota regulations, and would probably be subject to labeling requirements under the TFPIA. This is a grey area. You need to be aware of any regulations pertinent to the specific product you are importing, and should read the Commodity Index chapter pertaining to the par-

*IMPORTANT: Read the Commodity Index Introduction. It is the essential framework for understanding this chapter.

ticular textile used in the product. If you are unsure as to the regulatory status of your product, contact the nearest U.S Customs port office or your customs broker.

Importation of raw down is regulated by the FWS. The exporter is required to test the down for percentage of feathers to down. The down is given a rating based on that percentage. A certification of rating must accompany all import shipments of raw down. If your raw down is derived from domesticated raised birds, there are no FWS regulatory issues. However, down from wild migratory game birds is highly restricted and subject to FWS permit procedures under the Migratory Bird Treaty Act. If you are considering such products, you should contact the regional office of FWS closest to the intended port of entry, for authorization. Do not attempt such importation without FWS authorization (see "Exotic and Endangered Species" below).

Domesticated Bird Skins. Products derived from skins and other parts of domesticated animals are subject to quarantine regulations, marking requirements, and processing standards. Shipments of these products are inspected at the port of arrival by the Animal and Plant Health Inspection Service (APHIS) of the USDA. Unless the shipment is in compliance with all applicable laws and regulations, it will be denied entry into the U.S. Some shipments may be restricted or prohibited completely.

Quarantine and Inspection. At the time of applying for a permit to import animals products subject to quarantine requirements, you will have to make reservations for space in an appropriate quarantine facility. Fees for quarantine reservations vary according to species, and are due and payable when the reservation is requested. Each shipment entering under APHIS permit must comply in every detail with the permit's specifications. If your shipment is found to be aberrant in any way (such as entering at a port of entry other than the one specified in the permit), it will be refused entry.

Veterinary Certificates. A veterinary certificate, issued by a salaried veterinarian of the country of origin, stating that the animal products are free of applicable livestock diseases, must accompany each shipment. The specific information required on the certificate varies depending on the species you are importing, and its country of origin. You must also present an importer's declaration, which states: l) port of entry; 2) importer's name and address; 3) broker's name and address; 4) livestock origin; 5) number, breed, species, and purpose of importation; AND 6) consignee's name and location of intended delivery.

Specific Country Import Regulations. There are special provisions for livestock products originating in Canada, Mexico, Central America, and the West Indies. These provisions vary according to species, and include such things as permit or quarantine waivers, special quarantine restrictions, specific ports of entry for specific types of products, and provisions for transit across the U.S. only. One general requirement applicable across the board is that two import declarations (see above) must be presented, instead of only one. For more details see appropriate headings in 9 CFR 92, or contact the APHIS.

APHIS-designated Quarantine Ports. The following listings are APHIS-designated ports with adequate quarantine facilities available for the import of animal products. With very few exceptions, all shipments of animal products must enter at one of these designated ports:

Air and Ocean Ports: Los Angeles, CA; Miami, FL; Honolulu, HI; and Newburgh, NY.

Canadian Border Land Ports: Eastport, ID; Houlton and Jackman, MN; Detroit, Port Huron, and Sault Ste. Marie, MI; Opheim, Raymond, and Sweetgrass, MT; Alexandria Bay, Buffalo, and Champlain, NY; Dunseith, Pembina, and Portal, ND; Derby Line and Highgate Springs, VT; Blaine, Lynden, Oroville, and Sumas, WA.

Mexican Border Land Ports: Brownsville, Hidalgo, Laredo, Eagle Pass, Del Rio, Presidio, and El Paso, TX; Douglas, Naco, Nogales, Sasabe, and San Luis, AZ; Calexico and San Ysidro, CA; Antelope Wells and Columbus, NM.

Limited Ports. These ports have facilities for the entry of livestock or livestock products that do not appear to require restraint and holding inspection facilities: Anchorage and Fairbanks, AK; San Diego, CA; Denver, CO; Jacksonville, St. Petersburg, Clearwater, and Tampa, FL; Atlanta, GA; Chicago, IL; New Orleans, LA; Portland, MN; Baltimore, MD; Boston, MA; Minneapolis, MN; Great Falls, MT; Portland, OR; San Juan, PR; Galveston and Houston, TX; and Seattle, Spokane, and Tacoma, WA.

The ports listed above have been designated as quarantine stations. The USDA Administrator has authority to designate other ports as quarantine stations as needed.

Exotic and Endangered Species. The FWS enforces a complex set of laws and regulations (see 50 CFR 1 et seq.) pertaining to wildlife and wildlife product importation. These laws include the international Convention on International Trade in Endangered Species of Wild Fauna and Flora (CITES), the Endangered Species Act (ESA), and a number of other U.S. laws, such as the Migratory Bird Treaty Act (MBTA), Eagle Protection Act (EPA), and the Lacey Act (LA). Most foreign countries also have their own domestic measures, and you will need to meet the requirements of the country of export in addition to U.S. requirements. For more information, contact the FWS Office of Management Authority (OMA) (see addresses at end of this chapter).

Certain types of bird skins are entirely prohibited; others are allowed entry only under permit and/or license; and still others are allowed entry only for specific noncommercial purposes. When applying for a permit, you must satisfy the requirements of all laws under which the species is protected. The following briefly describes the two major laws governing importation of protected wildlife products into the U.S. This discussion is not comprehensive or exhaustive. If you wish to import bird skins of exotic or endangered animals, you should always contact the FWS (see addresses at end of this chapter) with specific species information before making any transactions.

CITES. More than 100 nations participate in the CITES treaty, which took effect in May 1977. The degree of protection afforded to a species depends on which of the three CITES appendices contains the name of that species. Documentation required for import varies depending on the species, and the CITES section where it is listed. The CITES export documentation from the country of origin is always required. If you are importing a CITES-listed species from a country that does not participate in the treaty, you must still obtain from that nation documents that contain all the information normally required in CITES export permits.

Appendix I. This appendix lists species deemed presently threatened with extinction. Importation of Appendix I species for commercial purposes is prohibited. You must have two permits to import these species: one from the U.S., which must be obtained first, and one from the exporting country. If you are importing Appendix I species taken in the marine environment and outside the jurisdiction of any country or state, you must have an Introduction from the Sea Permit.

Appendix II. This appendix lists species that are not presently threatened with extinction but may become threatened if their trade is not regulated. There are no restrictions on the purpose of import, provided it is not detrimental to the survival of the species. You will need an export permit or reexport certificate from the exporting country. If you are importing Appendix II species taken in the marine environment and outside the jurisdiction of any country or state, you will need an Introduction from the Sea Permit.

Appendix III. This appendix lists species for which any CITES member country has domestic regulations "for the purpose of preventing or restricting exploitation, and as needing the cooperation of other Parties in control of trade." Three different types of documents are issued for Appendix III species: 1) Export Permit: Issued for specimens that originated in a country that listed the species on Appendix III; 2) Certificate of Origin: Issued by any country other than the listing country if the wildlife in question originated in that country; 3) Reexport Certificate: Issued for the export of Appendix III specimens that were previously imported into the U.S.

Exemptions. Under certain conditions, Certificates of Exemption may be issued for the importation of wildlife products listed under CITES. Exceptions are allowed for shipment of wildlife transiting a country under Customs bond, shipments between U.S. states or territories, and certain personal or household effects. For information, contact FWS (see addresses at end of this chapter).

Permit Applications. Applications for CITES permits and certificates are available from the FWS Office of Management Authority (see addresses at end of this chapter). You will need to fill out the FWS Standard Permit Application (**Form 3-200**) and provide certain information specifically required under CITES. You should submit your application at least 60 days before the date you wish the permit to take effect. FWS charges processing fees for CITES applications.

ESA. The U.S. Endangered Species Act (ESA) was passed on December 28, 1973, to prevent the extinction of many species of animals and plants and to protect their habitats. By definition, an "endangered species" is any animal or plant listed by regulation as being in danger of extinction. A "threatened species" is any animal or plant likely to become endangered within the foreseeable future. The U.S. List of Endangered and Threatened Wildlife and Plants includes native and foreign species.

Permits. ESA's import provisions prohibit the import or export of any endangered or threatened species or products derived from them without one of the following permits from the FWS Federal Wildlife Permit Office (FWPO):

Endangered Species Permits: This permit is issued for importation for purposes of 1) scientific research; 2) enhancement of propagation or survival of the species; or 3) incidental taking.

Threatened Species Permits: This permit is issued for importation for purposes of 1) scientific research; 2) enhancement of propagation or survival of the species; 3) zoological, horticultural, or botanical exhibition; 4) education purposes; 5) special purposes consistent with ESA purposes and policy; or 6) incidental taking.

Permit Exemptions. A few imports of endangered species products are exempt from the ESA permit requirements. For example, if a species is listed as threatened or as an experimental population, special rules may allow otherwise prohibited activities. If you are unsure as to the exemption status of your import, contact FWS (see addresses at end of this chapter).

FWS Import Licenses. With some exceptions, persons engaged in the business of importing wildlife products valued in excess of $25,000 per year must be licensed by the FWS. If your annual importations are valued at less than $25,000, or if you qualify for another exemption from licensing, you are still responsible for keeping thorough records of all wildlife transactions and of making these records available to FWS officers if necessary. For a full description of exemptions from licensing, and of recordkeeping requirements, contact the Fish and Wildlife Service (see addresses at end of this chapter) or see 50 CFR 14.

Procedures at Port of Entry. At least 72 hours before your shipment is due to arrive at a designated port, you should notify U.S. Customs and the FWS inspectors of its expected arrival. The FWS conducts port-of-entry shipment inspections on a case-by-case basis, as determined by the inspection agent after looking at the entry paperwork. Both FWS and Customs may inspect your shipment to verify compliance with all of the legal requirements for entry. Any documentation required by the laws governing your import must be submitted by the time of entry. You must present an FWS Wildlife Declaration **Form 3-177**, available at the port of entry, with every shipment, regardless of any other paperwork required. Customs will not release your shipment until the import declaration has been signed off by an FWS agent.

Designated Ports. Shipments of wildlife products are restricted to designated U.S. ports of entry. All wildlife shipments must enter and leave through one of the ports listed in 50 CFR 14.12. Currently, 10 ports are designated: New York, NY; Miami, FL; New Orleans, LA; Dallas/Ft. Worth, TX; Los Angeles, CA; San Francisco, CA; Chicago, IL; Seattle, WA; Honolulu, HI; and Portland, OR. If special circumstances prevent you from making your entry at a designated port, you will need to obtain an Exception to Designated Port Permit from the FWS Divisions of Law Enforcement (see addresses at end of this chapter).

Articles with Textile Components. Articles with textile components may be subject to absolute quotas, textile restraints under Multi-Fiber Arrangements, or wool product entry requirements. The following is an overview of the textile importing requirements.

Wool Product Entry Requirements. Depending on the nature of your wool imports, as many as four different types of special entry documents may be required. First, for all imported articles that contain textile fibers, yarns, and fabrics covered by the Agricultural Adjustment Act (AAA), including wool, you must file a U.S. Customs Textile Entry Declaration (see "Textile Country-of-Origin Declarations" below). Second, with the entry summary for each shipment of wool articles, you must file Customs **Form 6451**, Notice of Percentage of Clean Yield and Grade of Wool or Hair, in duplicate, showing your name and address. Third, for all wool products subject to the WPLA, special information is required on the entry invoices (see "Wool Products Labeling Act" below). Finally, certain articles of apparel manufactured or produced in certain countries may be subject to quotas and other restraints under U.S. DOC Multi-Fiber Arrangements. Such products require export licenses, certificates, or visas issued by the appropriate country of origin, in addition to other requisite entry paperwork (see "Textile Quotas" below).

Wool Products Labeling Act. The term "wool product" means any product or any portion of a product that contains, purports to contain, or in any way is represented as containing wool, reprocessed wool, or reused wool. All wool products imported into the U.S., except those made more than 20 years before importation, and except carpets, rugs, mats, and upholsteries, must have affixed a stamp, tag, label, or other means of identification as required by the WPLA. If you are importing wool products exempt from labeling under the WPLA, do not assume they are also exempt from labeling under the TFPIA. These are two distinct laws, with some overlapping requirements (see "Marking and Labeling Requirements" below).

Textile Quotas. If you are interested in importing articles with textile components, the most important issue you need to be aware of is quotas. Under the Multi-Fiber Arrangement provisions of Section 204 of the Agricultural Adjustment Act, CITA initiates specific agreements with individual exporting countries. Section 204 of the Agricultural Adjustment Act covers textiles articles that: 1) are in chief value of cotton, wool, or man-made fibers, any textile fibers subject to the terms of any textile trade agreement, or any combination of such fibers; 2) contain 50% or more by weight of cotton or man-made fibers, or any textile fibers subject to the terms of any textile trade agreement; 3) contain 17% or more by weight of wool; or 4) if in chief value of textile fibers or textile materials, contain a blend of cotton, wool, or man-made fibers, any textile fibers subject to the terms of any textile trade agreement, or any combination of such fibers that, in total, amount to 50% or more by weight of all component fibers.

The U.S. has Multi-Fiber Arrangements with 40 countries. Each agreement with each country is unique, and may specify quotas for a type of textile or a specific article. Visas or export licenses may be required. These agreements, however, often change. Therefore, if you are interested in importing any articles with textile components, you should contact the International Trade Administration's Office of Textile and Apparel (see addresses at end of this chapter). Refer to "Prohibitions and Restrictions" below for further details.

Textile Country-of-Origin Declarations. U.S. Customs enforces CITA textile and textile product entry quotas (see "Prohibitions and Restrictions" below). Requirements for entry include submission of Country-of-Origin Declarations with every shipment of articles with textile components, regardless of whether it is subject to a specific multi-fiber arrangement (19 CFR 12.130, 12.131).

Country of Origin. Quota restrictions are country-specific and therefore are applied based on the country of origin for the textiles shipped. The last country from which a textile shipment was exported to the U.S. is not necessarily its country of origin. A textile or textile product imported into the U.S. is considered a product of the particular foreign territory or country, or a U.S. insular possession, where it is wholly grown, produced, or manufactured. For the following discussion, "country" means a foreign territory or country, or a U.S. insular possession.

Substantial transformation rules may affect the country-of-origin determination. For example, if a textile or textile product originates in Country A and is subject to quota, the quota restrictions apply at entry into the U.S. But if, prior to export to the U.S., you move the shipment to Country B where there are fewer restrictions, the shipment may nevertheless remain subject to quota and visa requirements under the Multi-Fiber Arrangement with Country A. Customs determines whether the quota restrictions apply based on the criteria of "substantial transformation." If your textiles do not undergo any major processing or manufacturing while in Country B, or if the manufacturing or processing is minor, your shipment will be deemed to originate in Country A. *You cannot claim substantial transformation on the basis of minor manufacturing procedures.*

In contrast, if your shipment undergoes major processing or manufacturing while in Country B, rendering the textiles "new and different articles of commerce," Customs will treat the shipment as the product of Country B. To qualify as having undergone substantial transformation, an article must evince a change in: 1) commercial designation or identity; b) fundamental character; or c) commercial use. If your shipment is processed in more than one country, the country where it last underwent substantial transformation is the country of origin for Customs entry. In deciding whether the manufacturing or processing operation in a country is major, Customs considers the following factors: 1) the resultant physical change in the material or article; 2) the complexity, the level or degree of skill and/or technology required, and the amount of time involved in the operations; and 3) the value added to the article or material, compared to its value when imported into the U.S.

Validating Operations. Operations that Customs will usually acknowledge as validating a claim of substantial transformation are the following: 1) dyeing and printing, when accompanied by two or more of the following finishing operations: bleaching, shrinking, fulling, napping, decating, permanent stiffening, weighting, permanent embossing, or moireing; 2) spinning fibers into yarn; 3) weaving, knitting, or otherwise forming fabric; 4) cutting fabric into parts and assembling the parts into completed articles; or 5) substantial assembly, by sewing and/or tailoring into a completed garment cut pieces of apparel articles that have been cut from fabric in another country—e.g., complete assembly and tailoring of all cut pieces of suit-type jackets, suits, and shirts.

Insubstantial Operations. Operations that usually will not support a claim of substantial transformation, even if more than one are performed, are the following: 1) simple operations of combining, labeling, pressing, cleaning, dry cleaning, or packaging; 2) cutting to length or width and hemming or overlocking fabrics that are readily identifiable as being intended for a particular commercial use; 3) trimming and/or joining together by sewing, looping, linking, or other means of attaching otherwise completed knit-to-shape component parts produced in a single country, even if accompanied by other processes—e.g., washing, drying, mending—normally incident to assembly; 4) one or more finishing operations on yarns, fabrics, or their textile articles—such as showerproofing, superwashing, bleaching, decating, fulling, shrinking, mercerizing, or similar operations; or 5) dyeing and/or printing fabrics or yarns.

Declarations. The country of origin of the articles with textile components in a shipment must be stated on a declaration submitted to U.S. Customs at the time of entry. There are three Customs Country-of-Origin Declarations: single-country, multiple-country, and negative. The Declaration to be submitted with your shipment of articles with textile components depends on the nature of the import.

- **Single-country declarations** are used for entries of textiles or textile products that clearly originate from only one country or that have been assembled in one country from fabricated components wholly produced in the U.S. or the foreign country of manufacture. Information required includes: marks of identification and numbers; description of article and quantity; country of origin; and date of exportation.
- **Multiple-country declarations** are used for entries of textiles or textile products that were manufactured or processed and/or that incorporate materials originating in more than one foreign country or territory. Information required includes: marks of identification and numbers; for articles, description, quantity, identification of manufacturing and/or processing operations, country, and date of exportation; for materials used to make articles, description of materials, country of production, and date of exportation.
- **Negative declarations** must accompany all textile imports that are not subject to FFA Section 204 restrictions. Information required includes: marks of identification and numbers; descriptions of article and quantity; and country of origin.

The date of exportation to be indicated on the above declarations is the date on which the carrier leaves the last port in the country of origin, as determined by Customs. Diversion to another country during transit does not affect the export date.

Procedure for Declarations. The manufacturer, producer, exporter, or importer may prepare the declaration. If more than one of these parties is involved in the importation, each party may prepare a separate declaration. You may file a separate declaration for each invoice presented with your entry. The declaration must be dated and signed by the responsible party, and must include the person's title and the company name and address. Your shipment's entry will be denied unless it is accompanied by a properly executed declaration. Customs will not treat a textile declaration as a missing document for which a bond may be filed.

Customs will base its country-of-origin determination on the information contained in each declaration, unless the information is insufficient. If the information on the declaration is insufficient, Customs will require that you submit such additional information as will enable the determination to be made. The shipment will not be released until the determination is made. Thus, if you want to clear Customs with minimal delay, be sure that the information on the declarations is as complete as possible for each shipment.

Flammability Standards. Articles with textile components imported into the U.S. for use in consumer products must be in compliance with the FFA, a federal law that gives the CPSC the authority and responsibility for protecting the public from the hazards of dangerously flammable items of wearing apparel and interior furnishings. Under the FFA, standards have been established for flammability of clothing textiles. You cannot import any article of wearing apparel or interior furnishing, or any fabric or related material that is intended for use or that may be used in such items, if it fails to conform to an applicable flammability standard (FFA Section 4). Certain products may be imported into the U.S. (FFA Section 11c) for finishing or processing to render them less flammable so as to meet the standards. For these products, the exporter must state on the invoice or other paper relating to the shipment that the shipment is being made for that purpose.

The CPSC monitors imports of textiles under its Import Surveillance Program. From time to time, your textile shipments may be inspected to ascertain compliance with mandatory safety standards. Shipments may also be subject to testing by the CPSC to determine compliance. If the CPSC believes a product, fabric, or related material does not comply with a flammability standard, it is authorized to pursue a variety of legal sanctions (see "Prohibitions and Restrictions" below).

Substantial Product Hazard Reports. Any firm that obtains information that reasonably supports the conclusion that one of its products presents an unreasonable risk of serious injury or death must report that information to the CPSC's Division of Corrective Actions (CPSC address below). Importers must also report to the CPSC if 1) a type of product is the subject of at least three civil actions filed in U.S. federal or state courts, 2) each suit alleges the involvement of that product type in death or grievous bodily injury (as defined in FFA Section 37(3)1), and 3) at least three of the actions result in a final settlement with the manufacturer or in a judgment for the plaintiff within any one of the two-year periods specified in FFA Section 37(b).

Import Advisory

Feathers and Down. Always be prepared to provide the FWS or U.S. Customs with both common and scientific names of any species of bird skins that you have questions about or are planning to import. When you are unsure of the regulations governing the export or import of a wildlife product, check with the FWS or TRAFFIC (USA) World Wildlife Fund (see addresses at end of this chapter) well in advance of going abroad, or once there, with the local authorities or the U.S. Embassy before making a purchase. When in doubt, don't buy! Products made from parts of endangered species incur seizure and in some cases substantial fines.

Wildlife Products [reprinted with permission by World Wildlife Fund from its brochure: "Buyer Beware"].

> It's difficult to be sure what wildlife products may be brought into the United States. Regulations are complex, and wildlife may be "laundered" to conceal its true country of origin. Wildlife is often illegally killed or collected in one country, smuggled into another, and then exported with false permits to a third, making its origins hard to trace. If you're considering the purchase of any wildlife or wildlife product while abroad, you should first try to determine its origin and any U.S. restrictions on its import.

Articles with Textile Components. Importation of textile products is trade-sensitive and highly regulated. Shipments of textile products not complying with all government regulations, including quotas and visas, are subject to seizure and could result in the imposition of penalties as well as possible forfeiture of the goods. You should always verify the available quota for any textile product you plan to import before your shipment leaves the country of manufacture. Furthermore, Customs textile classification rulings change frequently, and prior administrative rulings are often modified and sometimes reversed.

Customs Classification

For customs purposes, feathers, down, artificial flowers, and wigs and related items are classified under Chapter 67 of the HTSUS. This chapter is broken into major headings, which are further divided into subheadings, and often sub-subheadings, each of which has its own HTSUS classification number. For example, the HTSUS number for artificial flowers made of feathers is 6702.90.10, indicating it is a sub-subcategory of artificial flowers, etc., of other materials (6702.90.00), which is a subcategory of the major heading artificial flowers, foliage, and fruit, etc. (6702.00.00). There are four major headings within Chapter 67.

6701—Skins and other parts of birds with their feathers or down, feathers, parts of feathers, down, and articles thereof (other than goods of heading 0505 and worked quills and scapes)

6702—Artificial flowers, foliage and fruit, and parts thereof; articles made of artificial flowers, foliage, or fruit

6703—Human hair, dressed, thinned, bleached, or otherwise worked; wool or other animal hair or other textile materials, prepared for use in making wigs or the like

6704—Wigs, false beards, eyebrows and eyelashes, switches, and the like, of human or animal hair or of textile materials; articles of human hair not elsewhere specified or included

Sample Import Duties

Import duties will vary depending on the HTSUS classification of your product. Therefore, to determine the correct amount of duties, your product must be properly classified under the HTSUS. The following sample duties are taken from the duty listings for HTSUS Chapter 67 products.

Articles of feathers or down (6701.00.30): 4.7%; other imports of feathers or down (6701.00.60): 4.7%; artificial flowers, foliage, fruit, and parts, of plastics, assembled by binding with flexible materials, by gluing, or by similar methods (6702.10.20): 8.4%; of feathers (6702.90.10): 4.7%; of man-made fibers (6702.90.35): 9%; of other materials (6702.90.65): 17%; human hair, dressed, thinned, bleached, or otherwise worked (6703.00.30): 3.1%; wool, other animal hair, or other textile materials prepared for use in making wigs or the like (6703.00.60): 4.7%; wigs, false beards, eyebrows, eyelashes, switches, and similar items of human or animal hair or of textile materials, and articles of human hair not elsewhere specified or included (6704): 2.8%,

Entry and Documentation

The entry of merchandise is a two-part process consisting of 1) filing the documentation necessary to determine whether merchandise may be released from Customs custody, and 2) filing the documents that contain information for duty assessment and statistical purposes. In certain instances, all documents must be filed and accepted by Customs prior to release of the goods. Unless you have been granted an extension, you must file entry documents at a location specified by the district or area director within five working days of your shipment's date of arrival at a U.S. port of entry. These include a number of standard documents required by Customs for any entry, and:

- Exporter's down-feather ratio rating certification (if importing raw down)
- FWS **Import Declaration Form 3-177**, original and 3 copies (if products are derived from exotic wildlife or endangered species)
- FWS permit or import documentation (if products are derived from exotic wildlife or endangered species)
- Permits or certificates required under CITES, ESA, and any other regulations applicable to the particular shipment (if products are derived from exotic wildlife or endangered species)
- Certificates of export, origin, sanitation, veterinary inspection, and other conditions from the country of origin or export, as required by Customs, FWS, or USDA (if importing feathers, down, bird skins, or parts thereof)
- USDA importer's declaration (if products are derived from domesticated birds)
- U.S. Customs Country-of-Origin Declaration(s) (if importing textile products)
- Export documentation and/or visa (if importing textiles products subject to Multi-Fiber Arrangements
- Customs **Form 6451**, Notice of Percentage of Clean Yield and Grade of Wool or Hair, in duplicate, showing your name and address (if importing articles containing wool)

After you present the entry, Customs may examine your shipment or may waive examination. The shipment is then released provided no legal or regulatory violations have been noted. You must then file entry summary documentation and deposit estimated duties at a designated customhouse within 10 working days of your shipment's release. For a detailed description of entry procedures, standard documentation, and informal entry, refer to "Entry Process" on page 182.

Wool Products Subject to WPLA. When you offer for entry a wool product shipment valued at over $500 and subject to WPLA, you must include certain information intended to facilitate Customs monitoring and enforcement of that Act. This extra information is identical to that required by WPLA on labeling (see "Marking and Labeling Requirements" below), with the addition of the manufacturer's name. If your product consists of mixed waste, residues, and similar merchandise obtained from several suppliers or unknown sources, you may omit the manufacturer's name from the entry invoice.

Prohibitions and Restrictions

Bird Products. Feathers and skins of the following species are permitted entry: chickens, turkeys, guinea fowl, geese, ducks, pigeons, ostriches, rheas, English ring-necked pheasants, and pea fowl not taken from the wild. Other feathers are usually prohibited. Skins and feathers taken from wild migratory game birds listed in the Migratory Bird Treaty Act (50 CFR 10) are prohibited imports. Bird products that can be imported are subject to quarantine if they arrive from certain countries that are known to have specific infectious diseases.

There are a number of exceptions: plumage imported for scientific or educational purposes, fully manufactured artificial flies used for fishing, and plumage on game birds killed in foreign countries by hunters who are U.S. residents as long as the plumage is not imported for sale or other commercial purposes.

Quota Birds. Feathers of certain birds may be imported for use in the manufacture of artificial flies used for fishing, and/or for millinery purposes. These imports are restricted by annual quota allotments. You must have a permit and quota allotment issued by the FWS to import quota feathers. Quota feathers are as follows: Mandarin ducks for use in the manufacture of artificial flies used for fishing: 1,000 skins; Lady Amherst Pheasant, Golden Pheasant, Silver Pheasant, Reeves Pheasant, and Blue-eared Pheasant, for use in the manufacture of artificial flies used for fishing, or for use in millinery products: aggregate 45,000.

Permit Application. If you wish to import quota feathers, submit your application for feather quota allocations and permits to FWS on the standard Federal Fish and Wildlife License/Permit Application **Form 3-200.** The annual quota begins on January 1 of each year, and runs through December 31. Your application for initial allocations must reach FWS between September 1 and September 30 of the calendar year preceding the quota year for which you are requesting allotment. Any portions of established annual quotas not used by July 1 become available for reallocation. Applications for reallocations must be received by FWS between July 1 and July 31 of the current quota year.

Your permit/quota allocation request must include not only the standard information required for any permit, but also 1) species quantity; 2) port of entry, or port of entry and amount in storage (see "Exceptions to Requirements" below); 3) statement of intended use; and 4) nature of request, i.e. initial allocation or reallocation.

After making the initial allocations, the FWS will furnish you with a tabulation of quantities of each species you requested, plus quantities FWS proposes to allocate to you. You must then report your acceptance, by a letter addressed to the FWS Director and postmarked not later than 30 days after the date you receive your notice. Your letter must contain satisfactory proof (e.g. a copy of a currently confirmed order) that you have already placed your feather orders. FWS will interpret your failure to respond as withdrawal of your application. You would be wise to make your response by certified mail.

Permits. Permits for feather quota imports are issued in two segments. Permits authorizing calendar year initial allocations are issued as of January 1 of that quota year, and remain in effect through June 30 of the year of issue. You must import all feathers and/or skins authorized under this permit no later than June 30. Once your initial permit has expired, any portion of your allotment that you have not used will be subject to reallocation. There are no exceptions, and no extensions are granted. Permits authorizing reallocations are issued as promptly as possible after July 31 of the current quota year, and remain in effect through December 31. Once your reallocation permit expires, any unused portion of the quota is forfeited. There are no exceptions, and no extensions are granted.

Exceptions to Requirements. There are certain exceptions to the permit requirements for quota feathers. However, even when a permit is not necessary, you must still file an FWS Wildlife Declaration at the port of entry. Permit exceptions are as follows: 1) you may import quota skins/feathers for storage in a warehouse under Customs bond without permit. This exception only applies to birds that are subject to quota. In such cases you must obtain a valid FWS permit before you remove the articles from the warehouse for use in the U.S.; 2) articles imported for scientific or educational purposes; 3) fully manufactured artificial flies for fishing; 4) game birds killed by U.S. hunters abroad and imported by such person for noncommercial purposes; 5) live birds (there are other FWS requirements for live birds); and 6) import of any of the following birds, whether or not such bird was raised in captivity: chickens (including hens and roosters), turkeys, guinea fowl, geese, ducks, pigeons, ostriches, rheas, English ring-necked pheasants, and pea fowl.

Exotic and Endangered Species. Hides of certain animals are restricted or prohibited from importation because of species status under the CITES, ESA, or another U.S. law. For example, importation of species listed in CITES Appendix I for commercial purposes is prohibited. Prohibitions and restrictions may additionally be imposed by the law of the exporting country. You are legally responsible to fulfill the requirements of all of them, as well as any laws of your country of export. If you import, or attempt to import, a product in violation of a wildlife or endangered species law, even if you are not aware of the violation, your product may be seized, you may be charged substantial fines, and you could be imprisoned.

Wildlife Products [reprinted with permission by World Wildlife Fund from its brochure: "Buyer Beware"].

> Birds and feathers may not be imported into the United States, except under certain conditions. The survival of many wild bird species is threatened by habitat destruction and trade. Alarming numbers of birds die during capture, transit, and the required 30-day quarantine period (for some species, as much as 70% of the shipment). Birds frequently are taken from countries that ban their export to neighboring countries where falsified documents can be obtained. Concerned consumers should be aware of the protected status of any wild bird before attempting to bring it into this country. Prohibited from import are: Most wild bird feathers, mounted birds, and skins.

Textile Quotas. Textile import restrictions are primarily a matter of quotas and the way in which these quotas are administered and monitored. Under the Multi-Fiber Arrangement provisions of Section 204 of the Agricultural Adjustment Act, CITA has developed Multi-Fiber Arrangements with 40 countries. These Agreements may impose quotas for a type of textile or a specific article, and they are country-specific. The agreements, however, often change. Therefore, if you are interested in importing any articles with textile components, you should contact the International Trade Administration's Office of Textile and Apparel (see addresses at end of this chapter). The Office of Textile and Apparel has a team of country specialists who can inform you of the latest developments and inform you about a product's quota or restriction status.

U.S. Customs enforces CITA textile and textile product entry quotas. If formal entry procedures are not followed, Customs will usually refuse entry for textiles that are subject to Section 204. Formal entry requires submission of a Country-of-Origin Declaration (see "General Considerations" above). U.S. Customs maintains a current textile quota status report, available for perusal at any Customs port. In addition, U.S. Customs in Washington, DC, operates a telephone service to provide quota status reports, which are updated weekly (see "Relevant Government Agencies" below).

Flammable Fabrics. U.S. Customs may refuse entry for any article of wearing apparel or interior furnishing, or any fabric or related material that is intended for use or that may be used in wearing apparel or interior furnishings, if it fails to conform to an applicable flammability standard issued under Section 4 of the FFA. An exception is allowed for certain products (FFA Section 11c) that are imported for finishing or processing to bring them within the legal standard. For these products, the exporter must state on the invoice or other paper relating to the shipment that the shipment is being made for that purpose.

The CPSC, as the primary enforcement agency of flammability standards, inspects products for compliance with the FFA. If the CPSC believes a product, fabric, or related material does not comply with a flammability standard, it is authorized to pursue a variety of legal sanctions, including: 1) seizure, condemnation, and forfeiture of the noncomplying products; 2) administrative cease-and-desist order requiring an individual or firm to stop sale and distribution of the noncomplying products or; 3) temporary injunction requiring the individual or firm to stop sale and distribution of the noncomplying products, pending final disposition of an administrative cease-and-desist proceeding. The CPSC also has authority to seek civil penalties against any person who knowingly violates a regulation or standard issued under Section 4 of the FFA.

Country-Specific Restrictions

Restrictions under Multi-Fiber Arrangements are country-specific. A product originating in one country may be subject to quota and to export license or visa requirements, while the same product originating in a different country may not. At present, the U.S. has Multi-Fiber Arrangements with 40 countries. Many different categories of products are covered under these Arrangements; it is beyond the scope of this book to list each country and its restricted commodities. If you are interested in importing textiles and textile products, you should contact the International Trade Administration's Office of Textile and Apparel (see addresses at end of this chapter) or U.S. Customs to ascertain your product's restraint status.

The U.S. Customs Quota Branch phone numbers provide recorded status reports, by quota category number, for current charges against the quotas for that country. To find out if your product is subject to textile restraints, call the DOC or a local Customs port office. Then you can find out the current charges against that quota by calling the country number listed below. For a complete listing of Customs Quota Branch information numbers, see "Relevant Government Agencies" below.

Marking and Labeling Requirements

Animal Products. Containers of animal skins must be marked with the country of origin—that is, the country where the animal was located. If skins are quarantined at the port of arrival, marks and signs are required on shipping documents and any mode of transport used to move the product while under restrictions (9 CFR 95.25).

Wildlife Skins. All wildlife shipments must be marked on the outside of the container with the names and addresses of the exporter and importer, an accurate identification of the species, and the numbers of each species in the container.

Wool Products Labeling Act (WPLA). Wool product labeling requirements for foreign products are the responsibility of the importer. The WPLA requires the following information to appear on wool products subject to the Act: 1) percentage of the wool product's total fiber weight (exclusive of ornamentation) not exceeding 5% of the total fiber weight of a) wool, b) recycled wool, c) each fiber other than wool if the percent by weight of such fiber is 5% or more, and d) the aggregate of all other fibers; 2) the maximum percent of the wool product's total weight, of any nonfibrous loading, filling, or adulterating matter; and 3) the importer's name. If you, as importer, have a registered identification number issued by the FTC, that number may be used instead of your name (see "Registered Identification Numbers" below).

Customs entry is contingent on proper labeling. If your shipment is found to be mislabeled at entry, you will be given the option to relabel the products under Customs supervision, as long as the district director is satisfied that your labeling error or omission did not involve fraud or willful neglect. If your shipment is discovered after entry to have been noncomplying with WPLA, it will be recalled to Customs custody at your expense, unless you can satisfy the district director that the products have since been brought into compliance. You will be held responsible for all expenses incurred in bringing a shipment into compliance, including compensation of personnel and other expenses related to Customs supervision.

Fraudulent violations of WPLA will result in seizure of the shipment. Shipments already released from Customs custody will be ordered to be redelivered to Customs. Customs reports all cases of fraudulent violation to the FTC in Washington, DC.

The information listed above is not intended to be exhaustive. WPLA requirements are extensive. The Act specifies such details as types of labels, means of attachment, label position on the article, package labeling, unit labeling (as in the case of a two-piece garment), arrangement of information on the label, allowable fiber designations, country-of-origin indications, trim and ornamentation, pile fabrics, sectional disclosure, use of trade names and trademarks, requirements for swatches and samples, etc. The FTC publishes a booklet intended to clarify WPLA requirements in order to facilitate voluntary compliance within the industry (see "Publications Available" below). It is available on request, at no charge, from the FTC (see addresses at end of this chapter).

Registered Identification Numbers. Any domestic firm or person residing in the U.S. and engaged in the manufacture or marketing of textile products covered under the WPLA may obtain an FTC-registered identification number for use on required tags and labels instead of the name of a firm or person. For applications, contact the FTC (see addresses at end of this chapter).

For a general discussion of U.S. Customs marking and labeling requirements, refer to "Marking: Country of Origin" on page 215 and "Special Marking Requirements" on page 217.

Shipping Considerations

You will need to ensure that your goods are packaged and shipped with care so that they pass smoothly through Customs and arrive in good condition. You are responsible for ensuring that the shipment is in compliance with all applicable government regulations for packaging and shipping. In most instances, you should not leave these arrangements solely to the discretion of your supplier. Careful preparation of the cargo and selection of the mode of transport can be essential to a cost-effective, timely delivery of undamaged goods. We strongly advise you to consult your shipping representative, insurance agent, or freight broker for advice on packing and shipping. Refer also to the major tab section "Packing/Shipping/Insurance" for a general discussion of packing and shipping.

Feathers, down, artificial flowers, and wigs and related items may be shipped in bulk, crates, boxes, bags, or other types of containers, depending on the type of product and whether it is prepackaged. General considerations include protection from contamination, weather, and pests. Containers should be constructed so as to be safe for handling during transport.

Publications Available

The following books are especially pertinent to Endangered Species regulations and wildlife trade. They are published by and available from World Wildlife Fund at the address below.

International Wildlife Trade: Whose Business Is It? by Sarah Fitzgerald. Paperback $25.00; cloth $40.00, 459 pp, ISBN 0-942635-10-8.

The Wildlife Trade Laws of Asia and Oceania by David Nichols, Kathryn Fuller, Erica McShane-Caluzi and Eva Eckinrode. 1991. Looseleaf binder. Order Code NIAO. $50.00.

Latin American Wildlife Trade Laws (2d ed.) Kathryn S. Fuller, Byron Swift, Amanda Jorgenson, and Amie Brautigam. 1985. 418 pp. Looseleaf binder. Order Code FULA (English language). #35.00.

To order these publications, or to request a catalog of related publications, contact:

World Wildlife Fund
1250 24th Street NW
Washington, DC 20037
(202) 293-4800

The following publication may be relevant to the importation of wigs and related items with wool components:

Questions and Answers Relating to the Wool Products Labeling Act and Regulations

Available free of charge on request from the Federal Trade Commission (see addresses at end of this chapter), this publication is an excellent source of information written in clear lay language. We recommend that anyone interested in importing textile products but unfamiliar with the regulations obtain a copy of each of these booklets.

The *Harmonized Tariff Schedule of the United States* (HTSUS) is available from:

Government Printing Office (GPO)
Superintendent of Documents
Washington, DC 20402
(202) 512-1800 (Order line)
(202) 512-0000 (General)

The USGPO also has copies of specific laws available for purchase. The USGPO accepts credit card orders over the phone, as well as mail orders paid by credit card, a check drawn on a U.S. bank, or an international money order.

Relevant Government Agencies

Address your questions regarding USDA requirements for the importation of domestic animal products to:

U.S. Department of Agriculture (USDA)
Animal and Plant Health Inspection Service (APHIS)
Veterinary Services (VS)
Import-Export Products Staff
Federal Building, Room 756
6505 Belcrest Road
Hyattsville, MD 20782
(301) 436-7885

Address your questions regarding the importation of raw down or exotic or endangered bird skins to:

U.S. Fish and Wildlife Service (FWS)
Office of Management Authority
4401 N. Fairfax Drive, Room 432
Arlington, VA 22203
(703) 358-2095
(800) 358-2104, (703) 358-2104 (Permits office)

Address your questions regarding textile Multi-Fiber Arrangements to:

International Trade Administration
Office of Textile and Apparel
14th and Constitution Ave. NW, Rm. 3100
Washington, DC 20230
(202) 482-5078, 482-3737

Address your questions regarding the Flammable Fabrics Act (FFA) to:

Consumer Product Safety Commission (CPSC)
5401 Westbard Avenue
Bethesda, MD 20207
(301) 492-6580

Address your questions regarding labeling requirements under the Wool Products Labeling Act (WPLA) to:

Federal Trade Commission (FTC)
Division of Enforcement
601 Pennsylvania Ave. NW
Washington, DC 20580
(202) 326-2996 (General)
(202) 326-2841 (Textile and wool products labeling)

Address your questions regarding imports of feathers, down, artificial flowers, and wigs and related items to the district or port director of Customs for you area. For addresses, refer to"U.S. Customs District Offices" on page 62 or contact:

U.S. Customs Service
1301 Constitution Ave. NW
Washington, DC 20229
(202) 927-6724 (Information)
(202) 927-1000 (General)

The following information numbers for U.S. Customs in Washington, DC, provide recorded information. The Quota Branch numbers listed by country provide updated status reports on textile quotas from those countries. All area codes are (202).
General information: 927-5850

Quota Branch: China 927-6703; India 927-6705; Indonesia 927-6704; Japan 927-6706; Korea 927-6707; Macao 927-6709; Malaysia 927-6712; Mexico 927-6711; Pakistan 927-6714; Philippines 927-6713; Romania 927-6715; Singapore 927-6716; Sri Lanka 927-6708; Taiwan 927-6719; Thailand 927-6717; Turkey 927-6718; All others 927-5850.

Laws and Regulations

The following laws and regulations may be relevant to the importation of feathers, down, artificial flowers, and wigs and related items. The laws are contained in the United States Code (USC), and the regulations are published in the Code of Federal Regulations (CFR), both of which are available at larger public and law libraries. Copies of specific laws are also available from the United States Government Printing Office (address above).

18 USC 42 et seq.
Importation of Animals, Birds, Fish, and Plants
This Act governs the importation of animals, including birds, into the U.S.

50 CFR Parts 10, 13 and 16
Regulations of FWS for Importing Wildlife and Fish
These Regulations specify the animals and animal products subject to import prohibitions and restrictions.

21 USC 135
Establishment of International Animal Quarantine Stations
This Act authorizes the establishment of international quarantine stations. Customs enforces laws regarding importation of livestock.

42 USC 264-271
Quarantine, Inspection, and Licensing
This Act restricts importations of many animals, including psittacine birds, that do not comply with health standards. Customs enforces these restrictions. See 19 CFR 12.26 and 42 CFR 71.51 et seq.

19 CFR 12.24, 12.26
U.S. Customs Animal and Animal Product Entry Regulations
These regulations provide for entry declarations, documentation, and procedures for the animals and animal products subject to FWS and USDA regulations.

9 CFR 95.13 et seq.
Animal Byproduct Quarantine Control Regulations
These regulations prohibit the importation of animal products for use in industry unless the products meet certain processing standards and are not infected with certain diseases.

Convention on International Trade in Endangered Species of Wild Fauna and Flora (CITES)
This comprehensive wildlife treaty signed by over 100 countries, including the United States, regulates and in many cases prohibits commercial imports and exports of wild animal and plant species threatened by trade.

16 USC 1531
Endangered Species Act
This Act prohibits the import and export of plant and seed species listed as endangered and most species listed as threatened. Seeds labeled as "of cultivated origin" may be traded. It is the U.S. law that implements CITES.

16 USC 3371-3378
Lacey Act
This Act prohibits the import of species taken, possessed, transported, or sold in violation of foreign law.

7 USC 1854
Textile Trade Agreements
(EO 11651, as amended by EO 11951 and 12188, and supplemented by EO 12475 below)
This Act authorizes the CITA of the DOC to enter into Multi-Fiber Agreements with other countries to control trade in textiles and establishes the Textile Import Program, which is enforced by U.S. Customs.

19 CFR 12.130 et seq.
Regulations on Entry of Textiles
These regulations provide the requirements and procedures followed by Customs in enforcing limitations on the importation and entry and withdrawal of textiles and textile products from warehouses for consumption in the U.S.

15 USC 68-68j
Wool Products Labeling Act (WPLA)
This Act prohibits the false or deceptive labeling (misbranding) of wool products and requires all wool products imported into the U.S. to be labeled in accordance with requirements set forth in the law.

19 CFR 11.12; 16 CFR 300 et seq.
Regulations on WPLA Labeling and Marking
These regulations set forth the wool labeling and marking requirements adopted by the FTC to administer the requirements of the WPLA and provide the procedures followed by U.S. Customs in enforcing the WPLA and the FTC regulations, including entry invoice requirements.

15 USC 1191-1204
Flammable Fabrics Act (FFA)
This Act provides for the setting of flammability standards for fabric by the Consumer Product Safety Commission (CPSC) and for enforcement by U.S. Customs.

16 CFR 1610, 1611, 1615, 1616, 1630-1632
Regulations on Flammable Fabric Standards
These regulations specify the flammability standards adopted by the CPSC under the FFA for various types of textiles.

Principal Exporting Countries

The following listing includes samples of the main supplier nations of the products of this chapter. It is organized by HTSUS major heading. (Refer to "Customs Classification" above for the product codes.) Countries are listed in rank order of the value of products imported to the U.S. Statistics represent customs value entries for 1993 from the Bureau of Census, U.S. Department of Commerce.

6701—China, Hong Kong, Dominican Rep., Taiwan, Macao, Belgium, France, Saudi Arabia, India, South Africa

6702—China, Thailand, Hong Kong, South Korea, Taiwan, Mexico, Sri Lanka, Canada, Philippines, Switzerland

6703—China, Indonesia, South Korea, United Kingdom, Hong Kong, Taiwan, Japan, Mexico, Lithuania, Philippines

6704—South Korea, China, Indonesia, Hong Kong, Canada, Philippines, Senegal, Thailand, Sri Lanka, Germany

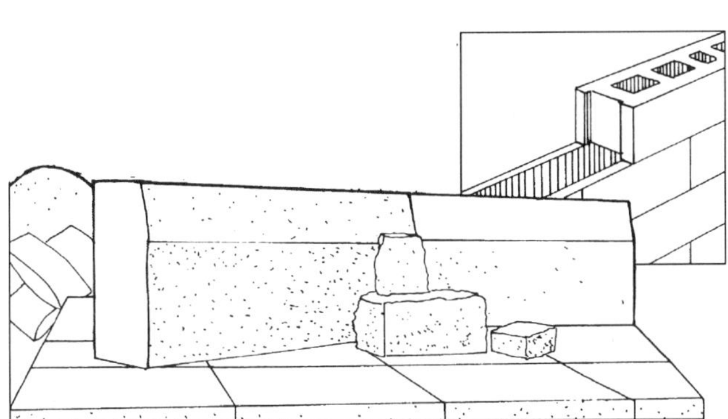

Chapter 68: Articles of Stone and Related Products*

Full title: Articles of Stone, Plaster, Cement, Asbestos, Mica, or Similar Materials

This section pertains to the importation of finished and semifinished stone and related items, which are classified within Chapter 68 of the Harmonized Tariff Schedule of the United States (HTSUS). Specifically, it includes such finished and semifinished products as stone flagstones; worked building stones, including marble, travertine, and granite; worked slate; grinding stones; abrasive powders and sandpapers; insulation materials; asphalt roofing; plasterboard and fabricated building materials; cement blocks, tiles, and pipes; and fabricated asbestos products, including brake liners and pads; worked mica; and various other products made of stone. Many building materials are included within this chapter.

If you are interested in importing raw stone or unfinished products of stone and related materials, refer to Commodity Index Chapter 25. Coated or impregnated papers are covered in Chapter 48, while coated or impregnated textiles are covered in Chapters 58 and 59. Gemstones related to the jewelry trade are included in Chapter 71. Tools for cutting and working stone and related products are found in Chapter 82. If you are interested in importing stones for lithographic printing, refer to Chapter 84. Stone products used as electrical insulators are covered in Chapter 85; dental grinding equipment is covered in Chapter 90; and works of art including worked stone—such as statuary—are found in Chapter 97. Stone and related materials which are incidental components of other products are covered in various other Commodity Index chapters: clocks (chapter 91), furniture (chapter 94), toys and games (chapter 95), and other items, such as drawing slates (chapter 96).

Key Factors

The key factors in importing finished and semifinished stone and related products of Chapter 68 are:

- Compliance with U.S. Environmental Protection Agency (EPA) requirements under the Toxic Substances Control Act (TSCA) if the product contains asbestos or other hazardous substances
- Compliance with U.S. Department of Transportation (DOT) regulations for transport of hazardous cargo (if the product contains a hazardous substance)

*IMPORTANT: Read the Commodity Index Introduction. It is the essential framework for understanding this chapter.

Although most importers utilize the services of a licensed customs broker in making their entries, and we recommend this practice, you should be aware of the regulatory, entry, and documentation issues involved in importing your product. You, as importer, are ultimately responsible for the fulfillment of any legal requirements applicable to your shipment.

General Considerations

Regulatory Agencies. As a general rule, finished stone and related products are straightforward importations. The EPA, under the authority of the TSCA, imposes certain controls on the importation of asbestos and any other products containing toxic substances. The TSCA defines toxic substances as those determined to present the possibility of an unreasonable risk of injury to health or the environment. The DOT enforces regulations for transportation of hazardous cargo. Products are deemed hazardous if listed in DOT transport regulations (49 CFR 172, appendix). The relevant regulations include packaging, shipping, marking, and labeling requirements. Refer to "Laws and Regulations" below. For additional information on EPA requirements and TSCA certification as it pertains to asbestos products, contact EPA's Office of Toxic Substances (see addresses at end of this chapter).

Hazardous Substances. If importing a hazardous substance, you must file a TSCA certification of compliance or exemption at the time you make a regulated entry at customs. This certification may be in the form of a typed or stamped statement on an appropriate entry document or commercial invoice. You may endorse the statement by means of an authorized facsimile signature. If your entry is electronically processed, the certification will be in the form of aCertification Code, which is part of the Automated Broker Interface (ABI) transmission. Customs will not release a shipment until proper certification has been obtained.

If you are importing several or regular shipments, you should ask the appropriate customs district director to authorize the use of a blanket certification. If you receive such authorization, you must include on the commercial invoice or entry document for each shipment a statement that the blanket certification is on file and that it is incorporated by specific reference. This statement need not be signed. The blanket certification is valid for one calendar year, is renewable, and may be revoked at any time for cause.

Articles Excluded. If you are bringing in articles that contain materials classified as hazardous substances, you are subject to TSCA certification requirements only if certification is specifically required by a rule or order promulgated under the TSCA. No specific rules have been adopted at this time. An "article" is a manufactured item 1) that is formed into a specific shape or design during manufacture, 2) that has end-use functions dependent on the shape or design, and 3) that during its intended end use does not change its chemical composition or changes it only into noncommercial byproducts as allowed by law (19 CFR 12.120(2)). Fluids and particles are not articles.

Shipment Detention. Detention can occur at a port of entry if the EPA administrator or customs district director has reasonable grounds to believe that it is not in compliance with the TSCA or if the importer fails to provide proper TSCA certification. If your shipment is detained, it will be held by customs for no more than 48 hours before it is turned over to the EPA administrator unless arrangements have been made by the importer to release it under bond. The importer must then bring it into compliance or re-export it within 90 days after notice of detention or 30 days after demand for redelivery. Customs may grant an extension if the importer can show that delays were due to inaction by the EPA or by customs. Failure by the importer to comply within the time allotted allows the EPA to order storage or disposal of the shipment at the importer's expense.

Customs Classification

For customs purposes, finished and semifinished stone and related products are classified under Chapter 68 of the HTSUS. This chapter is broken down into major headings, which are further divided into subheadings, and often sub-subheadings, each with its own HTSUS classification number. For example, the HTSUS number for dressed or polished but otherwise unworked travertine is 6802.91.20, indicating that it is a subcategory of other building stone (6802.91.00), which is a subcategory of the major heading worked monumental or building stone (except slate) and articles thereof (6802.00.00). There are 15 major headings in Chapter 68.

6801—Setts, curbstones, and flagstones, of natural stone (except slate)

6802—Worked monumental or building stone (except slate) and articles thereof, other than goods of heading 6801; mosaic cubes, and the like, of natural stone (including slate), whether or not on a backing; artificially colored granules, chippings, and powder, of natural stone (including slate)

6803—Worked slate and articles of slate or of agglomerated slate

6804—Millstones, grindstones, grinding wheels, and the like, without frameworks, for grinding, sharpening, polishing, trueing, or cutting; hand sharpening or polishing stones, and parts thereof, of natural stone, of agglomerated natural or artificial abrasives, or of ceramic, with or without parts of other materials

6805—Natural or artificial abrasive powder or grain, on a base of textile material, of paper, of paperboard, or of other materials, whether of not cut to shape or sewn or otherwise made up

6806—Slag wool, rock wool, and similar mineral wools; exfoliated vermiculite, expanded clays, foamed slag, and similar expanded mineral materials; mixtures and articles of heat-insulating, sound insulating, or sound-absorbing mineral materials, other than those of heading 6811 or 6812, or of chapter 69

6807—Articles of asphalt or of similar material (for example, petroleum bitumen or coal tar pitch)

6808—Panels, boards, tiles, blocks, and similar articles of vegetable fiber, of straw, or of shavings, chips, particles, sawdust, or other waste wood, agglomerated with cement, plaster, or other mineral binders

6809—Articles of plaster or of compositions based on plaster

6810—Articles of cement, of concrete, or of artificial stone, whether or not reinforced

6811—Articles of asbestos-cement; of cellulose fiber cement, or the like

6812—Fabricated asbestos fibers; mixtures with a basis of asbestos or with a basis of asbestos and magnesium carbonate; articles of such mixtures or of asbestos (for example, thread, woven fabric, clothing, headgear, footwear, gaskets), whether or not reinforced, other than goods of heading 6811 or 6813

6813—Friction material and articles thereof (for example, sheets, rolls, strips, segments, discs, washers, pads), not mounted, for brakes, for clutches, or the like, with a basis of asbestos, of other mineral substances or of cellulose, whether or not combined with textile or other materials

6814—Worked mica and articles of mica, including agglomerated or reconstituted mica, whether or not on a support of paper, paperboard, or other materials

6815—Articles of stone or of other mineral substances (including articles of peat), not elsewhere specified or included

For more details regarding classification of the specific product you are interested in importing, consult a customs broker, the appropriate commodity specialist at your nearest customs port, or see HTSUS. HTSUS is available for purchase from the U.S. Government Printing Office (see addresses at end of this chapter), and may be found in larger public libraries. Refer to "Classification—Liquidation" on page 207 for a general discussion of customs classification.

Sample Import Duties

Import duties will vary depending on the HTSUS classification of your product. Therefore, to determine the correct amount of duties, your product must be properly classified under the HTSUS. The following sample duties are taken from the duty listings for HTSUS Chapter 68 products.

Flagstones of natural stone (6801.00.00): 4.2%; natural or agglomerated stone tiles less than 7cm on a side (6802.10.00): 6.9%; sawn granite with a flat surface (6802.23.00): 4.2%; marble slabs (6802.91.05): 2.8%; other dressed stone (6802.99.00): 6.5%; roofing slate (6803.00.10): 6.6%; millstones (6804.10.00): free; grindstones of agglomerated abrasives or ceramics bonded with synthetic resins (6804.22.10): 9.9 cents/kg + 3.9%; hand sharpening stones (6804.30.00): free; abrasive powder on a base of paper or paperboard (6805.20.00): 2.5%; rock wool in bulk, sheets, or rolls (6806.10.00): 4.9%; asphalt roofing in rolls (6807.10.00): 4.9%; panels of sawdust agglomerated with plaster (6808.00.00): free; plasterboard reinforced with paper only (6809.11.00): 2,4%; concrete building blocks (6810.11.00): 4.9%; prefabricated structural concrete building components (6810.91.00): 4.9%; tubes or pipes of asbestos-cement (6811.30.00): 0.3 cents/kg; asbestos yarns (6812.20.00): free; asbestos footwear (6812.50.10): 12.5%; asbestos gaskets, packing, and seals for use in civil aircraft (6812.90.00): free; asbestos brake pads and lining for automotive use (6813.10.00): free; plates, sheets, and strips of agglomerated mica (6814.10.00): 5.3%; articles of nonelectric graphite or carbon (6815.10.00): 4.9%; articles of peat (6815.20.00): free; articles of talc, steatite, or soapstone (6815.9.20): free.

Entry and Documentation

The entry of merchandise is a two-part process consisting of 1) filing the documents necessary to determine whether merchandise may be released from Customs custody and 2) filing the documents that contain information for duty assessment and statistical purposes. In certain instances all documents must be filed and accepted by Customs prior to the release of the goods. Unless you have been granted an extension, you must file entry documents at a location specified by the district or area director within five working days of your shipment's date of arrival at a U.S. port of entry. These include a number of standard documents required by Customs for any entry and:

- TSCA certification for products containing asbestos or other hazardous substance

After you present the entry, Customs may examine your shipment, or may waive examination. The shipment is then released provided no legal or regulatory violations have been noted. You must then file entry summary documentation and deposit estimated duties at a designated customhouse within 10 working days of your shipment's release. For a detailed description of entry procedures, standard documentation, and informal entry, see "Entry Process" on page 182.

Marking and Labeling Requirements

A shipment of any products containing substances that are classified as hazardous (49 CFR 172) must comply with the marking and labeling regulations adopted by the EPA (46 CFR 147.30) and the DOT (49 CFR 171 et seq.).

For a general description of U.S. Customs marking and labeling requirements, refer to "Marking: Country of Origin" on page 215 and "Special Marking Requirements" on page 217.

Shipping Considerations

You will need to ensure that your goods are packaged and shipped with care to ensure that they arrive in good condition and pass smoothly through Customs. You are responsible for ensuring that the shipment is in compliance with all applicable government regulations for packaging and shipping. In most instances, you should not leave these arrangements solely to the discretion of your supplier. Careful preparation of the cargo and selection of the mode of transport can be essential to a cost-effective, timely delivery of undamaged goods. We strongly advise you to consult your shipping representative, insurance agent, or freight broker for advice on packing and shipping. Refer also to the major tab section "Packing/Shipping/Insurance" for a general discussion of packing and shipping.

Finished and semifinished stone and related products may be shipped in bulk, in crates, or in other types of containers and packages, depending on the nature of the products and whether or not they are prepackaged. General considerations include contamination, weather, and pests. Safety precautions should be taken to protect against breakage, spillage, corrosion, and combustion. Containers should be constructed to be safe during transport. Some products that are listed as hazardous substances (49 CFR 172 appendix) may be transported in bulk only in compliance with Coast Guard notification procedures, shipping permit requirements, and complex transportation regulations (46 CFR 148). All hazardous substances must be packaged and transported in accordance with DOT regulations (49 CFR 171 et seq.).

Publications Available

The following publication may be relevant to the importation of finished and semifinished stone and related products. It is published by the EPA (see addresses at end of this chapter) and discusses the various categories of toxic substances and specific procedures required for dealing with them:

Toxic Substances Control Act: A Guide for Chemical Importers/Exporters

The *Harmonized Tariff Schedule of the United States* (HTSUS) is available from:

Government Printing Office (GPO)
Superintendent of Documents
Washington, DC 20402
(202) 512-1800 (Order line)
(202) 512-0000 (General)

The USGPO also has copies of specific laws available for purchase. The USGPO accepts credit card orders over the phone, as well as mail orders paid by credit card, a check drawn on a U.S. bank, or an international money order.

Relevant Government Agencies

Address questions regarding TSCA requirements for asbestos products to:

Environmental Protection Agency (EPA)
TSCA System Information
EPA 7408, OPPT
401 M Street SW
Washington, DC 20460
(202) 554-1404 (TSCA Information Hotline)

Address questions regarding transportation of hazardous materials to:

U.S. Department of Transportation (DOT)
Research and Special Programs Administration
Office of Hazardous Materials Standards
400 7th St. SW
Washington, DC 20590
(202) 366-4488

Address your questions regarding the importation of finished and semifinished stone and related products to the district or port director of customs for you area. For addresses refer to"U.S. Customs District Offices" on page 62 or contact:

U.S. Customs Service
1301 Constitution Ave. NW
Washington, DC 20229
(202) 927-6724 (Information)
(202) 927-1000 (General)

Laws and Regulations

The following laws and regulations may be relevant to the importation of finished and semifinished stone and related products. The laws are contained in the U.S. Code (USC), and the regulations are published in the Code of Federal Regulations (CFR), both of which may be available at larger public and law libraries. Copies of specific laws are also available from the United States Government Printing Office (address above).

15 USC 2601 et seq.
Toxic Substances Control Act
This Act authorizes the EPA to determine whether a substance is harmful and to restrict importation, sale, and use of such substances.

19 CFR 12.118 et seq.
Regulations on Toxic Substances Control
These regulations require importers of chemical substances imported in bulk or as part of a mixture to certify to Customs that the shipment complies with the TSCA or is not subject to that Act.

15 USC 1261
Federal Hazardous Substances Act
This Act controls the importation of hazardous substances, sets forth prohibited imports, and authorizes various agencies to promulgate labeling, marking, and transport requirements.

49 CFR 170 et seq.
Regulations on Hazardous Materials
These regulations list all substances deemed hazardous and provide transport, marking, labeling, safety, and emergency response rules.

46 CFR 147.30
Regulations on Labeling of Hazardous Materials
This regulation requires the labeling of containers of hazardous substances and specifies the label contents.

46 CFR 148 et seq.
Regulations on Carriage of Solid Hazardous Materials in Bulk
These regulations govern the transport of solid hazardous substances in bulk, including reporting, permitting, loading, stowing, and shipping requirements.

Principal Exporting Countries

The following listing includes samples of the main supplier nations of the products of this chapter. It is organized by HTSUS major heading. (Refer to "Customs Classification" above for the product codes.) Countries are listed in rank order of the value of products imported to the U.S. Statistics represent customs value entries for 1993 from the Bureau of Census, U.S. Department of Commerce.

6801—India, Italy, Canada, Brazil, Japan, China, France, United Kingdom

6802—Italy, Spain, Taiwan, India, Canada, Greece, Mexico, Brazil, France, Turkey

6803—Italy, United Kingdom, Brazil, India, China, Spain, South Africa, Portugal, France, Canada

6804—Japan, Germany, Italy, Brazil, Mexico, Canada, Taiwan, United Kingdom, Israel, Austria

6805—Canada, Germany, Finland, Japan, United Kingdom, Italy, South Korea, Mexico, Sweden, France

6806—Canada, United Kingdom, Japan, Mexico, Denmark, Germany, France, Netherlands, Sweden, Austria

6807—Canada, Mexico, Venezuela, Italy, Netherlands, France, Saudi Arabia, Brazil, Japan, Germany

6808—Canada, United Kingdom, Finland, Germany, Italy, Jamaica, Mexico, Philippines, Japan, Australia

6809—Canada, United Kingdom, Mexico, China, Thailand, Spain, Italy, Taiwan, South Korea, Greece

6810—Canada, Mexico, China, Italy, Taiwan, Germany, United Kingdom, South Korea, Thailand, Hong Kong

6811—Mexico, Canada, Belgium, New Zealand, South Africa, United Kingdom, Costa Rica, Venezuela, Guatemala, Australia

6812—Germany, Japan, Canada, Mexico, Brazil, United Kingdom, South Africa, France, Zimbabwe, Taiwan

6813—Canada, Mexico, United Kingdom, France, Brazil, Japan, Germany, Colombia, Uruguay, Czech Rep.

6814—Belgium, Switzerland, India, Argentina, Germany, Brazil, Japan, China, France, South Korea

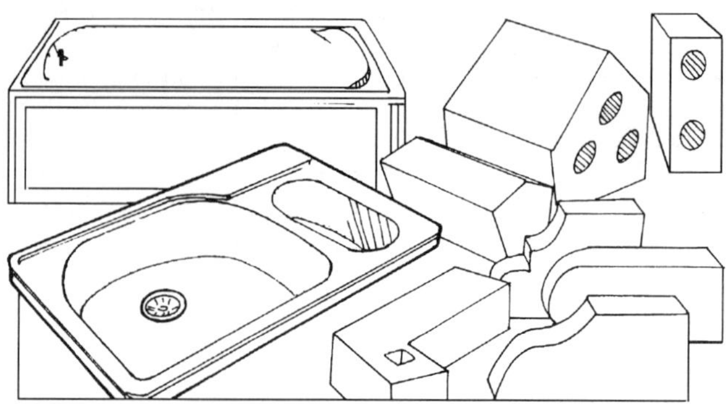

Chapter 69: Ceramic Products*

This section pertains to the importation of ceramic products, which are classified within Chapter 69 of the Harmonized Tariff Schedule of the United States (HTSUS). Specifically, it includes articles of siliceous fossil meals; refractory ceramic bricks and tiles; other refractory items, such as crucibles; ceramic architectural products, such as building blocks, roofing tiles, pipes, and glazed tiles; ceramic laboratory and agricultural fixtures; ceramic sinks, tubs, and bathroom fixtures; ceramic packaging; tableware, kitchenware, and other housewares of porcelain, china, earthenware, stoneware, and other types of ceramic materials; and ornamental and other ceramic items, all of which possess the characteristic of having been fired after shaping.

If you are interested in importing glass or glassware, refer to Commodity Index Chapter 70. Ceramic jewelry is covered under Chapter 71. Cermets—products of combined ceramics and metal, such as are used in turbine blades—are covered in Chapter 81. Tools with a ceramic component or used in working or making ceramics are found in Chapter 82. Ceramic electrical insulators and fittings are covered in Chapter 85. For dental ceramics, refer to Chapter 90. Articles for which ceramics are an incidental component are covered under other Commodity Index chapters: clocks (Chapter 91), furniture and lamps (Chapter 94), toys and games (Chapter 95), ceramic buttons or smoking pipes (Chapter 96), and works of art of ceramics or containing ceramic components (Chapter 97).

Key Factors

The key factors in the importation of ceramics and ceramic products are:

- For U.S. Food and Drug Administration (FDA) regulated ceramics, compliance with FDA standards
- For FDA-regulated ceramics, compliance with FDA entry notifications and procedures
- For articles intended for use with food, compliance with FDA regulatory limits for extractable lead and cadmium content
- For decorative items not intended for use with food, compliance with FDA marking and labeling requirements
- Restrictions on china from People's Republic of China (certificates required), and on china from or transshipped through Hong Kong

*IMPORTANT: Read the Commodity Index Introduction. It is the essential framework for understanding this chapter.

- Automatic port of entry sampling of products originating in, or transshipped through, countries other than the People's Republic of China and Hong Kong

Although most importers utilize the services of a licensed customs broker in making their entries, and we recommend this practice, you should be aware of the regulatory, entry, and documentation issues involved in importing your product. You, as importer, are ultimately responsible for the fulfillment of any legal requirements applicable to your shipment.

General Considerations

Regulatory Agencies. In general, no permits or licenses are required to import ceramic articles. However, some governmental agencies may have requirements that must be met when importing specific products. For example, ceramic products intended for use with food, or products that could be construed as being used with food, such as decorative ceramicware, are subject to regulations under the Federal Food, Drug, and Cosmetic Act (FDCA), enforced by the FDA. An Importer's Entry Notice—**Form FD701**—is required for all FDA-regulated shipments. For an annotated diagram of required FDA entry procedures and requirements refer to the "Foods" appendix on page 808.

Articles Used with Food. We cannot stress highly enough the importance of complying with FDA limits on extractable lead or cadmium levels in articles intended for use with food. Toxic levels result in chronic, essentially irreversible lead or cadmium poisoning. The FDA is both vigilant and stringent in administering its procedures to protect the consumer. The fact that your product is manufactured by a well-known overseas producer is no guarantee that it is in compliance. When a specific item or group of items offered for entry into the U.S. is found to be in violation, the FDA issues an Import Alert to all regional FDA Import Operations offices ordering detention of all related shipments at U.S. ports of entry. If an imported product previously released for resale in the U.S. is later found to be in violation, for example through sampling of a subsequent shipment, all of that product will be recalled. Any expenses incurred in recalling, relabeling, or reexporting noncomplying products accrue to the importer and distributor.

Clearly, you stand to lose significant amounts of money if your shipment contains higher than permitted lead or cadmium levels. It is in your best interest as well as the best interest of your customers, to ascertain your product's compliance prior to purchase. In the same way, Customs is not lenient in dealing with decorative plates that are not labeled according to FDA requirements. If such items are detected at entry, you could incur considerable expense in modifying them. If you are importing ceramic items not intended for food use, be sure your products are properly marked.

Tableware and Kitchenware. U.S. Customs makes the following distinctions among certain ceramic products designated as tableware or kitchenware: 1) porcelain, china, and chinaware: ceramicware other than stoneware, whether or not glazed or decorated, having a fired white body (unless artificially colored) that will absorb no more than 0.5% of its weight in water, and is translucent in thicknesses of several millimeters; 2) stoneware: ceramicware with clay as an essential ingredient, not commonly white, which will absorb no more than 3% of its weight of water, and is naturally opaque (except in very thin pieces) even when absorption is less than 0.1%; 3) bone chinaware: chinaware or porcelain, the body of which contains 25% or more of calcined bone or tricalcium phosphate; 4) earthenware: ceramicware, whether or not glazed or decorated, having a fired body with clay as an essential ingredient, which will absorb more than 3% of its weight of water. Customs also maintains special technical definitions for refractory ceramics that reflect the properties of these items. Ceramic tiles are also generally defined as being no more than 3.2 cm in thickness.

These definitions are based on technical specifications, which for dinnerware have to do with factors such as the nature of the clay body, thickness, water absorption, and opacity. In addition, there are provisions for classification of articles available in specified sets. For example, dinnerware offered as a set must contain specified numbers of pieces of specified sizes. You should be familiar with these definitions when contracting for certain ceramic products for import. A product fitting the definition of stoneware cannot be entered as porcelain or vice versa, and a set of dishes that does not contain the requisite size and number of pieces may not be entered.

Detention of Shipment. If your shipment is found to be noncomplying, it may be detained at the port of entry. In the case of products subject to FDA jurisdiction, the FDA may permit you to bring such a shipment into compliance before making a final decision regarding admittance. However, any sorting, reprocessing, or relabeling must be supervised by FDA personnel, and is done at the importer's expense. Such conditional release to allow an importer to bring a shipment into compliance is a privilege, not a right. The FDA may consider subsequent noncomplying shipments of the same type of product to constitute an abuse of the privilege and require you to destroy or reexport the products. Note that the FDA is particularly strict with noncomplying ceramic dinnerware shipments. To ascertain what your legal responsibilities are, you should contact the agencies involved in advance regarding the specific items to be imported.

Customs Classification

For customs purposes, ceramic products are classified within Chapter 69 of the HTSUS. This chapter is divided into major headings, which are further divided into subheadings, and often into sub-subheadings, each of which has its own HTSUS classification number. For example, the HTSUS number for bone chinaware is 6911.10.20, indicating that it is a subcategory of tableware and kitchenware (6911.10.00), which is a subcategory of the major heading tableware, kitchenware, other household articles and toilet articles, of porcelain or china (6911.00.00). There are 14 major headings in Chapter 69.

6901—Bricks, blocks, tiles, and other ceramic goods of siliceous fossil meals (for example, kieselguhr, tripolite, or diatomite) or of similar siliceous earths

6902—Refractory bricks, blocks, tiles, and similar refractory ceramic constructional goods, other than those of siliceous fossil meals or similar siliceous earths

6903—Other refractory ceramic goods (for example, retorts, crucibles, muffles, nozzles, plugs, supports, cupels, tubes, pipes, sheaths, and rods), other than those of siliceous fossil meals or of similar siliceous earths

6904—Ceramic building bricks, flooring blocks, support or filler tiles, and the like

6905—Roofing tiles, chimney pots, cowls, chimney liners, architectural ornaments, and other ceramic constructional goods

6906—Ceramic pipes, conduits, guttering, and pipe fittings

6907—Unglazed ceramic flags and paving, hearth or wall tiles; unglazed ceramic mosaic cubes and the like, whether or not with a backing

6908—Glazed ceramic flags and paving, hearth and wall tiles; glazed ceramic mosaic cubes and the like, whether or not on a backing

6909—Ceramic wares for laboratory, chemical, or other technical uses; ceramic troughs, tubs, and similar receptacles of a kind used in agriculture; ceramic pots, jars, and similar articles of a kind used for the conveyance or packing of goods

6910—Ceramic sinks, washbasins, washbasin pedestals, baths, bidets, water closet bowls, flush tanks, urinals, and similar sanitary fixtures

6911—Tableware, kitchenware, other household articles and toilet articles, of porcelain or china

6912—Ceramic tableware, kitchenware, other household articles and toilet articles, other than porcelain or china

6913—Statuettes and other ornamental ceramic articles

6914—Other ceramic articles

For more details regarding classification of the specific product you are interested in importing, consult a customs broker, the appropriate commodity specialist at your nearest customs port, or see HTSUS. HTSUS is available for purchase from the U.S. Government Printing Office (see addresses at end of this chapter), and may be found in larger public libraries. Refer to "Classification—Liquidation" on page 207 for a general discussion of customs classification.

Sample Import Duties

Import duties will vary depending on the HTSUS classification of your product. Therefore, to determine the correct amount of duties, your product must be properly classified under the HTSUS. The following sample duties are taken from the duty listings for HTSUS Chapter 69 products.

Blocks of siliceous fossil meals (6901.00.00): 4.9%; magnesite refractory bricks (6902.10.10): free; refractory bricks other than of alumina or silica (6902.20.50): 4.9%; clay refractory bricks (6902.90.10): free; other refractory ceramic products containing by weight more than 50% graphite or other carbon (6903.10.00): 4.9%; hollow insulating ceramic building bricks (6904.10.00): free; ceramic roofing tiles (6905.10.00): 13.5%; ceramic guttering (6906.00.00): 4.9%; unglazed ceramic tiles of less than 7 cm on a side (6907.10.00): 20%; glazed ceramic tiles of less than 7 cm on a side (6908.10.00): 20%; ceramic machinery parts for laboratory uses (6909.11.20): 4.7%; ferrite core memories (6909.19.10): 3.9%; ceramic bearings (6909.19.50): 8%; toilet bowls, sinks, and lavatories (6910.10.00): 7.2%; hotel and restaurant ware of porcelain or china (6911.10.10): 35%; tableware of bone china (6911.10.20): 8%; other tableware of porcelain or china, in sets valued at not more than $56 (6911.10.35): 26%; mugs of porcelain or china (6911.10.45): 17.5%; other products of porcelain or china suitable for food or drink contact (6911.10.80): 26%; toilet articles of porcelain or china (6911.90.00): 9%; earthenware or stoneware dinnerware (6912.00.10): 1.4%; dinnerware not of porcelain or china in sets valued at not more than $38 (6912.00.35): 11.5%; ceramic serviette rings not made of porcelain or china (6912.00.46): 11.5%; statuettes valued at over $2.50 each and made by professional sculptors or directly from molds (6913.10.10): 3.1%; other ceramic items of bone chinaware (6913.10.20): 6.6%; decorative items of ceramic tile (6913.90.20): 4.2%; other ceramic articles of porcelain or china (6914.10.00): 9%; other ceramic articles not of porcelain or china (6914.90.00): 8%.

Entry and Documentation

The entry of merchandise is a two-part process consisting of 1) filing the documents necessary to determine whether merchandise may be released from Customs custody and 2) filing the documents that contain information for duty assessment and statistical purposes. In certain instances all documents must be filed and accepted by Customs prior to the release of the goods. Unless you have been granted an extension, you must file entry documents at a location specified by the district or area director within five working days of your shipment's date of arrival at a U.S. port of entry. These include a number of standard documents required by Customs for any entry, and:

- For ceramic products regulated by FDA, FDA Importers Entry Notice, **Form FD701**
- For shipments of restricted products from the People's Republic of China, valid CCIB certificate

After you present the entry, Customs may examine your shipment, or may waive examination. The shipment is then released provided no legal or regulatory violations have been noted. You must then file entry summary documentation and deposit estimated duties at a designated customhouse within 10 working days of your shipment's release. For a detailed description of entry procedures, standard documentation, and informal entry, see "Entry Process" on page 182.

Entry Invoice for Ceramic Tile. Entry invoices for ceramic tile should state the shape and size of the individual tiles, quantity per case, and whether the tiles are glazed or unglazed.

Entry Invoice for Earthenware or Crockeryware. The entry invoice for articles composed of a nonvitrified absorbent body (including white granite and semiporcelain earthenware and cream-colored ware, stoneware, and terra cotta, but not including common brown, gray, red, or yellow earthenware), embossed or plain; common salt-glazed stoneware; stoneware or earthenware crucibles; Rockingham earthenware; china, porcelain, or other vitrified wares, composed of a vitrified nonabsorbent body that, when broken, shows a vitrified, vitreous, semivitrified, or semivitreous fracture; and bisque or parian ware (T.D. 53236) must show the following: 1) if in sets, the kinds of articles in each set in the shipment and the quantity of each kind of article in each set in the shipment; 2) the exact maximum diameter, expressed in cm, of each size of all plates in the shipment; and 3) the unit value for each style and size of plate, cup, saucer, or other separate piece in the shipment.

Prohibitions and Restrictions

Articles for Use with Food. FDA regulations regarding the importation of china, porcelain, and ceramic flatware and hollowware intended for use with food are designed to ensure that extractable lead and/or cadmium levels in the product are at a lower-than-toxic level, as defined by the FDCA. Your **Form FD701** attests to your shipment's compliance. At time of entry, the FDA may 1) accept the documentation as proof of compliance and release the shipment; 2) take a sample for testing and release the shipment provisionally, pending test results; 3) take a sample for testing and hold the shipment in customs custody pending test results. If your shipment is sample-audited and provisionally released, and test results show higher-than-permissible extractable lead or cadmium content, the FDA will issue a recall order and you will have to comply immediately. Noncomplying shipments will be detained in customs custody and must be either modified to effect compliance, immediately reexported, or destroyed. In addition, a shipment of goods that passes customs as in compliance, and that is identical to a later shipment found to be in violation, will be recalled.

Release of a Detained Shipment. If your shipment is detained due to toxic levels of extractable lead or cadmium, you may qualify the shipment for release by rendering the articles unsuitable for use with food. Articles so rendered are not required to meet FDA safety guidelines for dinnerware. There are two ways to do this: 1) render the articles unsuitable for food use by some artifice such as holes bored through the potential food contact surface; or 2) permanently affix a label, incapable of obliteration, to the article's potential food contact surface. If you choose the second option, your label must identify the article as "Not for Food Use" and state the specific hazard associated with its use for food service. When your china violation is due to toxic cadmium levels, your label must include the words "Article May Poison Food." The FDA releases modified shipments on a lot-by-lot basis, with checks by the district laboratory to verify compliance.

Exemptions. Articles manufactured solely for ornamental display, and not intended for use with food, are not subject to the regulations for dinnerware. These include, but are not limited to: commemorative plates, souvenir plates, hand-painted plates, and other highly decorated plates. If your shipment of these types of items comes in place settings for the table, it qualifies by definition as a dinnerware shipment, and you are liable for any lead and cadmium content. Articles imported solely as ornaments must be permanently labeled on the back of the plate as follows: "Not for Food Use-Plate May Poison Food. For Decorative Purposes Only."

Country-Specific Import Restrictions

Chinese Ceramicware. An Import Alert is in force for shipments of ceramicware coming directly from the People's Republic of China (PRC), or originating in the PRC but coming through Hong Kong. If your import fits this description, you must present for each shipment—along with the shipping manifest and packing list supplied by the manufacturer—a validated certificate issued by the Chinese government's Import and Export Commodity Inspection Bureau (CCIB). Your CCIB certificate must show production lot identification, name and address of the manufacturer, test methodology and results for lead and cadmium, number and types of ceramicware pieces in the production lot and those tested, date of certification, name of the authorizing official, and seal of the office. In addition, shipments of ceramicware originating in the Peoples Republic of China and shipped via Hong Kong must be sealed by the CCIB in such a way as to prevent opening during transit. Even if your shipment complies with these procedures, the FDA may choose to audit-sample it when it arrives at the U.S. port of entry. Any shipment of ceramicware from the PRC that is not accompanied by a valid CCIB certificate will be automatically detained in customs custody while you arrange for a private lab test of a sample of the product. Testing is done at your expense.

Shipments of ceramicware originating (manufactured) in Hong Kong, or transshipped through Hong Kong from countries other than the People's Republic of China, will be automatically detained at the U.S. port of entry for audit-sampling. Certain Hong Kong firms have been exempted from automatic detention. For details, contact the nearest regional FDA Import Operations office, or FDA headquarters (see addresses at end of this chapter).

Marking and Labeling Requirements

Articles Used with Food. FDA-regulated ceramic articles are subject to specific labeling requirements under the FDCA. There are marking and/or labeling requirements for noncomplying articles rendered unsuitable for use with food in order to qualify for entry, and for articles intended solely for decorative purposes. See "Prohibitions and Restrictions" above.

For a general discussion of U.S. Customs marking and labeling requirements, see "Marking: Country of Origin" on page 215 and "Special Marking Requirements" on page 217.

Shipping Considerations

You will need to ensure that your goods are packaged and shipped with care to ensure that they arrive in good condition and pass smoothly through Customs. You are responsible for ensuring that the shipment is in compliance with all applicable government regulations for packaging and shipping. In most instances, you should not leave these arrangements solely to the discretion of your supplier. Careful preparation of the cargo and selection of the mode of transport can be essential to a cost-effective, timely delivery of undamaged goods. We strongly advise you to consult your shipping representative, insurance agent, or freight broker for advice on packing and shipping. Refer also to the major tab section "Packing/Shipping/Insurance" for a general discussion of packing and shipping.

As with all fragile products, packing and shipping must take breakage into account. All shipments of ceramic products must be packaged to withstand the rigors of transport.

Publications Available

The *Harmonized Tariff Schedule of the United States* (HTSUS) is available from:

Government Printing Office (GPO)
Superintendent of Documents
Washington, DC 20402
(202) 512-1800 (Order line)
(202) 512-0000 (General)

The USGPO also has copies of specific laws available for purchase. The USGPO accepts credit card orders over the phone, as well as mail orders paid by credit card, a check drawn on a U.S. bank, or an international money order.

Relevant Government Agencies

Address questions regarding requirements for FDA-regulated products to:

Food and Drug Administration (FDA)
Center for Food Safety and Applied Nutrition
200 C Street SW
Washington, DC 20204
(202) 205-5241, 205-5042

Address questions regarding the importation of ceramics and ceramic products to the district or port director of customs for you area. For addresses refer to"U.S. Customs District Offices" on page 62 or contact:

U.S. Customs Service
1301 Constitution Ave. NW
Washington, DC 20229
(202) 927-6724 (Information)
(202) 927-1000 (General)

Laws and Regulations

The following laws and regulations may be relevant to the importation of ceramics and ceramic products. The laws are contained in the U.S. Code (USC) and the regulations are published in the Code of Federal Regulations (CFR), both of which may be available at larger public and law libraries. Copies of specific laws are also available from the United States Government Printing Office (address above).

21 USC 301 et seq.
Food, Drug, and Cosmetic Act
This Act prohibits deceptive practices and regulates the manufacture, sale and importation or exportation of food, drugs, cosmetics, and related products. See 21 USC 331, 381, 382.

19 CFR 12.1 et seq.; 21 CFR 1.83 et seq.
Regulations on Food, Drugs, and Cosmetics
These regulations of the Secretary of Health and Human Services and the Secretary of the Treasury govern the standards, labeling, marking, and importing of products used with food, drugs, and cosmetics.

Principal Exporting Countries

The following listing includes samples of the main supplier nations of the products of this chapter. It is organized by HTSUS major heading. (Refer to "Customs Classification" above for the product codes.) Countries are listed in rank order of the value of products imported to the U.S. Statistics represent customs value entries for 1993 from the Bureau of Census, U.S. Department of Commerce.

6901—Mexico, Germany, Japan, Spain, Canada, United Kingdom, Denmark, Italy, France, China

6902—Germany, Canada, Mexico, United Kingdom, Japan, France, Austria, China, Brazil, Venezuela

6903—Japan, Germany, United Kingdom, Canada, Mexico, Belgium, France, Brazil, Israel, China

6904—Canada, Italy, Mexico, Panama, Germany, Spain, United Kingdom, Venezuela, Denmark, India

6905—Venezuela, Mexico, Spain, Japan, Germany, Italy, France, United Kingdom, Colombia, El Salvador

6906—Germany, Canada, Japan, Switzerland, United Kingdom, Austria, Australia

6907—Italy, Mexico, Germany, Spain, France, Portugal, Dominican Rep., Colombia, Netherlands, Japan

6908—Italy, Spain, Mexico, Japan, Brazil, Venezuela, Thailand, Germany, Indonesia, Argentina

6909—Japan, France, Germany, United Kingdom, Australia, Taiwan, Italy, China, Mexico, Switzerland

6910—Mexico, Chile, Venezuela, Taiwan, Colombia, Thailand, Brazil, Canada, Dominican Rep., France

6911—Japan, China, United Kingdom, Germany, France, Thailand, Taiwan, Luxembourg, Sri Lanka, Spain

6912—China, Taiwan, Japan, United Kingdom, Thailand, Italy, Indonesia, Portugal, South Korea, Malaysia

6913—China, Taiwan, Spain, Thailand, Germany, Italy, Japan, Mexico, Malaysia, Philippines

6914—China, Japan, Italy, Taiwan, Germany, France, Mexico, Belgium, Thailand, Portugal

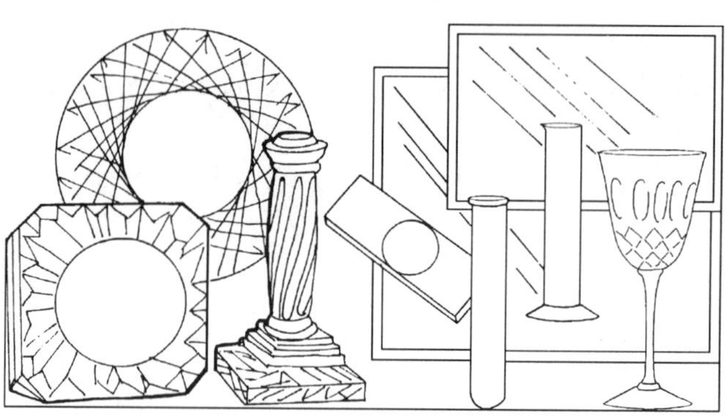

Chapter 70: Glass and Glassware*

This section pertains to the importation of glass and glassware, which are classified within Chapter 70 of the Harmonized Tariff Schedule of the United States (HTSUS). Specifically, it includes glass waste; balls, rods, or tubes for further manufacture; cast or rolled glass; drawn or blown glass; float or ground glass; edge-worked or similar intermediate glass products; safety glass; multilayered insulating glass; mirrors; carboys, bottles, jars, and similar products; glass envelopes, such as bulbs and tubes; glass liners for vacuum flasks; glass tableware, kitchenware, and items for toilet, office, or home use; optical glass; watch crystals; architectural elements of glass; laboratory or pharmaceutical glassware; glass fibers and fabrics; and other miscellaneous articles of glass.

Although Chapter 70 is generally comprehensive with respect to products made of or containing glass, certain specific glass products may be classified within other Commodity Index chapters. If you are interested in importing glazes and vitrifiable enamels, refer to Commodity Index Chapter 32. Jewelry made from glass is classified in Chapter 71, although some related products are found in heading 7018. Glass fiber optic cables, electrical insulators, and fittings are covered in Chapter 85.

Specific products, including optical fibers, worked optical elements, hypodermic syringes, artificial eyes, thermometers, barometers, hydrometers, and similar devices and scientific instruments are found in Chapter 90. Lamps, lighting fixtures, illuminated signs, and similar products having a fixed light source are covered in Chapter 94. Toys, games, and related products, including glass Christmas tree ornaments, are classified within Chapter 95. Such miscellaneous manufactured glass products as buttons, vacuum flasks, and scent and similar spray bottles are found in Chapter 96.

Key Factors

The key factors in the importation of glass and glass products are:

- For glass products intended for use with food, compliance with U.S. Food and Drug Administration (FDA) requirements
- For some FDA-regulated products subject to entry notification, compliance with FDA entry procedures and notification, as needed
- Compliance with FDA regulations regarding leachable lead and cadmium

*IMPORTANT: Read the Commodity Index Introduction. It is the essential framework for understanding this chapter.

- Special invoice information required
- Invoice documentation required for lead crystal

Although most importers utilize the services of a licensed customs broker in making their entries, and we recommend this practice, you should be aware of the regulatory, entry, and documentation issues involved in importing your product. You, as importer, are ultimately responsible for the fulfillment of any legal requirements applicable to your shipment.

General Considerations

Regulatory Agencies. Glass is for the most part a straightforward import commodity. No licenses or permits are required; nor, with certain exceptions, is any special entry documentation necessary. U.S. Customs does require certain specific information on the entry invoice for certain glass and glassware products. Special packing requirements apply to glass entering under HTSUS headings 7003 and 7004 (see "Packing Requirements" below). However, depending on the nature of your product, you may have to meet the requirements of other governmental agencies, particularly the U.S. Food and Drug Administration (FDA).

Articles Used with Food. All glass products intended for table or kitchen purposes, such as drinking glasses, bowls, and other containers, are subject to regulations under the Federal Food Drug, and Cosmetic Act (FDCA), enforced by the FDA. The following glass items are also subject to FDA regulation: 1) HTSUS heading 7010: carboys, bottles, flasks, jars, pots, vials, ampoules, and related products; 2) HTSUS heading 7012.00.00: glass liners for vacuum flasks or for other vacuum vessels; 3) HTSUS heading 7015.10.00: glasses for corrective spectacles; 4) HTSUS heading 7015.90.50: clock or watch crystals; and 5) HTSUS heading 7017: laboratory, hygienic, or pharmaceutical glassware.

Entry Procedures. An Importers Entry Notice—**Form FD701**—is normally required for all FDA-regulated shipments. However, at present the FDA is not requiring importers of glassware to follow normal FDA entry procedures, and these articles are currently exempt from standard required FDA entry notification. If routine customs examinations of shipments of these items reveal problems that could have adverse effects on public health, the FDA may reconsider their exempt status, reinstituting selectivity criteria and entry notification at any time. Therefore, if you are interested in importing any FDA-regulated glass product, you should be familiar with FDA import entry procedures and requirements under the FDCA, and be prepared to comply with all requirements. For more details regarding FDA import requirements and an annotated diagram of FDA entry procedures, refer to the "Foods" appendix on page 808.

Lead and Cadmium Restrictions. Although FDA entry notification is not currently required for glassware, all the FDA lead and cadmium restrictions pertinent to ceramic tableware also apply to glassware. Regulations are designed to ensure that extractable lead and/or cadmium levels in the product are at a-lower-than toxic level, as defined by the FDCA. At the time of entry, the FDA and/or U.S. Customs, acting on behalf of the FDA, may accept implicit compliance; retain a sample for testing while provisionally releasing the shipment pending test results; or detain the shipment pending test results. If your shipment is sampled-audited and provisionally released, and test results show higher-than-permissible levels of extractable lead or cadmium, the FDA will issue a recall order and you will have to comply immediately. Noncomplying shipments will be detained in customs, and must be modified, reexported, or destroyed. In addition, a shipment of goods that passes customs as in compliance, and that is identical to a later shipment found to be in violation, will be recalled. Toxic levels of these elements are rare in glassware, but they do occur occasionally. If your shipment is in violation of admissible levels, you will be held financially responsible for any necessary detention, modification, or product recall. Contact your regional FDA Import Operations office, or FDA headquarters (see addresses at end of this chapter) with specific questions.

Customs distinguishes between lead crystal glassware and that which is not lead crystal. Glassware entered as lead crystal is subject to a lower duty rate than other types. When you enter a shipment, you should be prepared to present documentation at the port of entry stating that the glassware contains not less than 24% lead monoxide by content to qualify as lead crystal. No special form or certificate is necessary: a statement of lead content on the invoice will suffice. However, if the customs official suspects that your glassware is not true lead crystal, a sample will be taken and tested for lead content. If your glassware is found to contain less than 24% lead, you will be charged the higher rate of duty.

Customs Classification

For customs purposes, glass and glassware products are classified within Chapter 70 of the HTSUS. This chapter is divided into major headings, which are further divided into subheadings, and often into sub-subheadings, each of which has its own HTSUS classification number. For example, the HTSUS number for glass measuring more than 2 mm but less than 3.5 mm in thickness is 7004.90.25, indicating that it is a subcategory of other glass, rectangular in shape (7004.90.00), which is a subcategory of drawn glass and blown glass, in sheets, whether of not having an absorbent or reflecting layer, but not otherwise worked (7004.00.00). There are 20 major headings within HTSUS Chapter 70.

7001—Cullet and other waste and scrap of glass; glass in mass

7002—Glass in balls (other than microspheres of heading 7018), rods, or tubes, unworked

7003—Cast glass and rolled glass, in sheets or profiles, whether or not having an absorbent or reflecting layer, but not otherwise worked

7004—Drawn glass and blown glass, in sheets, whether or not having an absorbent or reflecting layer, but not otherwise worked

7005—Float glass and surface ground or polished glass, in sheets, whether or not having an absorbent or reflecting layer, but not otherwise worked

7006—Glass of heading 7003, 7004, or 7005, bent, edge-worked, engraved, drilled, enameled, or otherwise worked, but not framed or fitted with other materials

7007—Safety glass, consisting of toughened (tempered) or laminated glass

7008—Multiple-walled insulating units of glass

7009—Glass mirrors, whether or not framed, including rear-view mirrors

7010—Carboys, bottles, flasks, jars, pots, vials, ampoules, and other containers, of glass, of a kind used for the conveyance or packing of goods; preserving jars of glass; stoppers, lids, and other closures, of glass

7011—Glass envelopes (including bulbs and tubes), open, and glass parts thereof, without fittings, for electric lamps, cathode-ray tubes, or the like

7012—Glass liners for vacuum flasks or for other vacuum vessels

7013—Glassware of a kind used for table, kitchen, toilet, office, indoor decoration, or a similar purpose (other than of heading 7010 or 7018)

7014—Signaling glassware and optical elements of glass (other than those of heading 7015), not optically worked

7015—Clock and watch glasses and similar glasses, glasses for noncorrective or corrective spectacles, curved, bent, hollowed, or the like, not optically worked; hollow glass spheres and their segments, for the manufacture of such glasses

7016—Paving blocks, slabs, bricks, squares, tiles, and other articles of pressed or molded glass, whether or not wired, of a kind used for building or construction purposes; glass cubes and other glass smallwares, whether or not on a backing, for mosaics or similar decorative purposes; leaded glass windows, and the like; multicellular or foam glass in blocks, panels, plates, shells, or similar forms

7017—Laboratory, hygienic, or pharmaceutical glassware, whether or not graduated or calibrated

7018—Glass beads, imitation pearls, imitation precious or semiprecious stones, and similar glass smallwares and articles thereof other than imitation jewelry; glass eyes other than prosthetic articles; statuettes and other ornaments of lamp-worked glass, other than imitation jewelry; glass microspheres not exceeding 1 mm in diameter

7019—Glass fibers (including glass wool) and articles thereof (for example, yarn, woven fabrics)

7020—Other articles of glass

For more details regarding classification of the specific product you are interested in importing, consult a customs broker, the appropriate commodity specialist at your nearest customs port, or see HTSUS. HTSUS is available for purchase from the U.S. Government Printing Office (see addresses at end of this chapter), and may be found in larger public libraries. Refer to "Classification—Liquidation" on page 207 for a general discussion of customs classification.

Sample Import Duties

Import duties will vary depending on the HTSUS classification of your product. Therefore, to determine the correct amount of duties, your product must be properly classified under the HTSUS. The following sample duties are taken from the duty listings for HTSUS Chapter 70 products.

Glass in the mass, of fused quartz or other fused silica (7001.00.10): 4.9%; other (scrap) (7001.00.50): free; glass in balls not over 6 mm in diameter (7002.10.10): 7.8%; glass tubes not longer than 200 mm (7002.39.00): 7.5%; cast or rolled glass in wired sheets (7003.20.00): 1.7%; drawn or blown glass, tinted throughout, in rectangular sheets (7004.10.20): 1.3 cents/kg + 2%; drawn or blown glass, in sheets, untinted, measuring over 0.26 m^2 in area (7004.90.10): 2 cents/kg; as above, measuring more than 3.5mm in thickness and less than 0.65 m^2 in area (7004.90.30): 1.1 cents/kg; other non-wired float and surface ground glass, tinted, measuring less than 10 mm in thickness (7005.21.10): 16.1 cents/kg + 0.4%; wired float or surface ground glass (7005.30.00): 32.3 cents/kg; glass strips not over 15.2 cm in width, more than 2 mm in thickness, and having all edges ground or otherwise processed (7006.10.00): 8.8%; tempered safety glass (7007.11.00): 6.2%; multiple-walled insulating units of glass (7008.00.00): 4.4%; rear-view mirrors for automobiles (7009.10.00): 7.8%; framed mirrors over 929 cm^2 in reflecting area (7009.92.50): 10%; glass ampoules (7010.10.00): 12.5 cents/gross; other containers with or without their closures (7010.90.50): free; glass envelopes for incandescent lamps (7011.10.10): 3.7%; cathode-ray tube cones (7011.20.10): 6.6%; glass liners for vacuum flasks (7012.00.00): 4 cents each + 8%; lead crystal drinking glasses valued at not over $1 each (7013.21.10): 20%; other as above valued at over $5 each (7013.29.60): 7.2%; drinking glasses other than lead crystal valued at over $3 but not over $5 (7013.39.50): 15%; glassware decorated with metal flecking (7013.99.10): 20%; lens blanks other than for spectacles (7014.00.10): 8.2%; lenses for corrective spectacles (7015.10.00): 4%; round watch crystals (7015.90.10): 4.9%; glass paving blocks (7016.90.10): 12%; laboratory, hygienic, or pharmaceutical glassware of fused quartz (7017.10.00): 5.8%; imitation glass pearls (7018.10.10): 8%; glass microspheres (7018.20.00): 17.5%; glass eyes, except prosthetic articles (7018.90.10): 8.4%; uncolored glass spun yarns (7019.10.10): 7.4%; narrow woven glass fabrics (7019.20.10): 6%; insulation products (fiberglass) (7019.39.10): 6.2%; other articles of glass (7020.00.00): 6.6%.

Entry and Documentation

The entry of merchandise is a two-part process consisting of 1) filing the documents necessary to determine whether merchandise may be released from Customs custody and 2) filing the documents that contain information for duty assessment and statistical purposes. In certain instances all documents must be filed and accepted by Customs prior to the release of the goods. Unless you have been granted an extension, you must file entry documents at a location specified by the district or area director within five working days of your shipment's date of arrival at a U.S. port of entry. These include a number of standard documents required by Customs for any entry.

After you present the entry, customs may examine your shipment, or may waive examination. The shipment is then released provided no legal or regulatory violations have been noted. You must then file entry summary documentation and deposit estimated duties at a designated customhouse within 10 working days of your shipment's release. For a detailed description of entry procedures, standard documentation, and informal entry, see "Entry Process" on page 182.

Entry Invoice for Glassware. Invoices for glassware and other glass products must show a statement of the separate value of each component article in the set.

Entry Invoice For Lead Crystal. Entry invoices for shipments entered as lead crystal must bear a verification statement that the glassware contains not less than 24% lead monoxide by content.

Entry Invoice for Beads. An entry invoice for glass beads must state: 1) The length of the string, if strung; 2) the size of the beads in mm; and 3) the material of which the beads are composed.

Restrictions and Prohibitions

Lead or Cadmium Content. Most shipments of glass products pass customs easily. However, once the FDA has identified a shipment of glassware as containing unlawful quantities of leachable lead or cadmium, it issues an Import Alert regarding either products of the responsible foreign manufacturer, or those brought in by the specific importer. In some instances, all glassware from a certain country will be named in an Import Alert. If you propose to enter a shipment covered by an FDA Import Alert, customs will certainly inspect and possibly detain it for testing. If it is found to be noncomplying, you will be required either to modify the product so that it does comply, or to destroy or reexport the shipment.

Release of Shipment. If your shipment is detained due to toxic levels of extractable lead or cadmium, you may be able to obtain its release by rendering the articles unsuitable for food or beverage uses. There are two ways to do this: 1) render the articles unsuitable for food use by a modification such as drilling holes through the potential food contact surface; or 2) permanently affix a label—incapable of obliteration or removal—to the article's potential food contact surface. If you choose the second option, your label must identify the article as "Not for Food Use" and state the specific hazard associated with its use for food or beverage service. When your product has toxic levels of cadmium, your label must include the words "Article May Poison Food." The FDA releases modified shipments on a lot-by-lot basis, with checks by the district laboratory to verify compliance. These procedures will be undertaken at the importer's expense.

Exemptions. Articles manufactured solely for ornamental display and not intended for food or beverage service are exempt from these requirements. Such articles must be permanently labeled as follows: "Not for Food Use-May Poison Food. For Decorative Purposes Only."

Import Advisory

Before purchasing foreign glassware for importation into the United States, check with the FDA or U.S. Customs to make sure that the manufacturer or pattern of glassware is not the subject of an FDA Import Alert. Although noncomplying glassware is much less common than noncomplying ceramicware, if your shipment is found to be toxic, you stand to lose large sums of money as a result of detention, testing, modifying, or even destruction of the products.

Marking and Labeling Requirements

Ceramic with Cadmium or Lead. The FDA requires noncomplying glassware containing toxic levels of cadmium or lead to be either 1) marked indelibly with the words "Not for Food Use" and a statement of the potential hazard, or 2) rendered unsuitable for food use by some artifice such as a hole bored through the potential food contact surface. Articles intended for decorative purposes must be so marked. Contact FDA's Import Operations office (see addresses at end of this chapter) for answers to specific questions.

For a general discussion of U.S. Customs marking and labeling requirements, see "Marking: Country of Origin" on page 215 and "Special Marking Requirements" on page 217.

Shipping Considerations

You will need to ensure that your goods are packaged and shipped with care to ensure that they arrive in good condition and pass smoothly through Customs. You are responsible for ensuring that the shipment is in compliance with all applicable government regulations for packaging and shipping. In most instances, you should not leave these arrangements solely to the discretion of your supplier. Careful preparation of the cargo and selection of the mode of transport can be essential to a cost-effective, timely delivery of undamaged goods. We strongly advise you to consult your shipping representative, insurance agent, or freight broker for advice on packing and shipping. Refer also to the major tab section "Packing/Shipping/Insurance" for a general discussion of packing and shipping.

Specific Packing Requirements. For the purposes of headings 7003 and 7004, glass of the same size and thickness imported in any shipment in quantities over 4.6 m^2 shall be denied entry unless it is: 1) packed in units containing, as nearly as the particular size permits, 4.6 m^2, or multiples thereof; or 2) packed in units containing multiples of the number of sheets of the same size and thickness that would be contained in a unit if packed to contain, as nearly as such size permits, 4.6 or 9.3 m^2; or 3) otherwise packed in a manner that conforms to the packing practices of the domestic glass industry as determined and published from time to time by the Secretary of the Treasury.

As with all fragile products, packing and shipping must take breakage into account. All shipments of glass products must be packaged to withstand the rigors of transport.

Publications Available

The *Harmonized Tariff Schedule of the United States* (HTSUS) is available from:

Government Printing Office (GPO)
Superintendent of Documents
Washington, DC 20402
(202) 512-1800 (Order line)
(202) 512-0000 (General)

The USGPO also has copies of specific laws available for purchase. The USGPO accepts credit card orders over the phone, as well as mail orders paid by credit card, a check drawn on a U.S. bank, or an international money order.

Relevant Government Agencies

Address questions regarding requirements for FDA-regulated products to:

Food and Drug Administration (FDA)
Center for Food Safety and Applied Nutrition
200 C Street SW
Washington, DC 20204
(202) 205-5241, 205-5042

Address questions regarding specific FDA requirements for importation of glassware to:

Food and Drug Administration (FDA)
Division of Enforcement, Imports Branch
200 C Street SW
Washington, DC 20204
(202) 205-4726

Address questions regarding the importation of glass and glass products to the district or port director of Customs for you area. For addresses refer to"U.S. Customs District Offices" on page 62 or contact:

U.S. Customs Service
1301 Constitution Ave. NW
Washington, DC 20229
(202) 927-6724 (Information)
(202) 927-1000 (General)

Laws and Regulations

The following laws and regulations may be relevant to the importation of glass and glass products. The laws are contained in the U.S. Code (USC) and the regulations are published in the Code of Federal Regulations (CFR), both of which may be available at larger public and law libraries. Copies of specific laws are also available from the United States Government Printing Office (address above).

21 USC 301 et seq.
Food, Drug, and Cosmetic Act
This Act prohibits deceptive practices and regulates the manufacture, sale and importation or exportation of food, drugs, cosmetics, and related products. See 21 USC 331, 381, 382.

19 CFR 12.1 et seq.; 21 CFR 1.83 et seq.
Regulations on Food, Drugs, and Cosmetics
These regulations of the Secretary of Health and Human Services and the Secretary of the Treasury govern the standards, labeling, marking, and importing of products used with food, drugs, and cosmetics.

Principal Exporting Countries

The following listing includes samples of the main supplier nations of the products of this chapter. It is organized by HTSUS major heading. (Refer to "Customs Classification" above for the product codes.) Countries are listed in rank order of the value of products imported to the U.S. Statistics represent customs value entries for 1993 from the Bureau of Census, U.S. Department of Commerce.

7001—Japan, Canada, United Kingdom, Russia, Mexico, Germany, Belgium, France, Italy, Malaysia

7002—Germany, Japan, Netherlands, France, United Kingdom, Brazil, Mexico, South Korea, Italy, Malaysia

7003—Germany, United Kingdom, Japan, Austria, Belgium, Russia, Canada, Czech Rep., Brazil, Australia

7004—Germany, Switzerland, United Kingdom, Czech Rep., France, Japan, Venezuela, China, Canada, South Korea

7005—Canada, Japan, United Kingdom, Mexico, Belgium, Germany, Venezuela, South Korea, Spain, Luxembourg

7006—Japan, Belgium, Mexico, Indonesia, Taiwan, China, Germany, United Kingdom, South Korea, Canada

7007—Canada, Mexico, Japan, South Africa, Germany, United Kingdom, New Zealand, Australia, France, South Korea

7008—Mexico, Canada, South Korea, Germany, France, United Kingdom, Italy, Switzerland, Taiwan, Netherlands

7009—Japan, Taiwan, China, Germany, Canada, Mexico, Australia, South Korea, Italy, France

7010—Mexico, France, Canada, Italy, Taiwan, Germany, Belgium, United Kingdom, Switzerland, Spain

7011—Japan, Taiwan, Germany, South Korea, France, Italy, Belgium, China, Poland, Netherlands

7012—India, Japan, China, United Kingdom, Brazil, Venezuela, Netherlands

7013—France, Germany, Ireland, Japan, Italy, Taiwan, Austria, Poland, Slovenia, Mexico

7014—Japan, Germany, Italy, United Kingdom, Taiwan, France, Austria, Canada, Sweden, China

7015—Germany, Switzerland, United Kingdom, France, Japan, Hong Kong, South Korea, Thailand, Canada, Mexico

7016—Germany, South Korea, Thailand, Italy, Canada, Czech Rep., China, Mexico, France, Indonesia

7017—Germany, Brazil, Switzerland, United Kingdom, Japan, France, Canada, Finland, Israel, Taiwan

7018—Austria, Czech Rep., Taiwan, China, Japan, Germany, United Kingdom, India, Italy, Canada

7019—Canada, United Kingdom, France, Japan, Mexico, Taiwan, Italy, Germany, Belgium, Brazil

7020—France, Austria, Japan, Germany, Taiwan, United Kingdom, Singapore, China, Italy, Canada

Chapter 71: Gems, Jewelry, and Related Products*

Full title: Natural or Cultured Pearls, Precious or Semiprecious Stones, Precious Metals, Metals Clad With Precious Metals, and Articles Thereof; Imitation Jewelry; Coin

This section pertains to the importation of pearls, precious and semiprecious stones, precious metals, jewelry, and coins, which are classified within Chapter 71 of the Harmonized Tariff Schedule of the United States (HTSUS). In general, articles or parts that are wholly made of or derive their primary value from precious stones, precious metals, or other products of this chapter are classified within Chapter 71.

Specifically, this chapter includes worked or unworked, but not strung or set natural or cultured pearls; worked or unworked industrial and gemstone diamonds, unmounted and not set; other precious and semiprecious stones, worked or unworked, but not mounted or set; synthetic or reconstructed stones; dust and powder of precious, semiprecious, or synthetic stones; silver, whether as powder, bullion, semimanufactured, or plated; base metals plated with silver; gold, whether as powder, bullion, semimanufactured, or as coins; base metals or silver plated with gold; platinum and related metals; base metals, silver, or gold plated with platinum; precious metal scrap; jewelry made of precious metals; other articles of goldsmiths' or silversmiths' wares; industrial products that include precious metals; articles of pearls or stones; imitation jewelry; and coins and medallions valued primarily for their precious metal content.

Although the tariff classification for precious metals includes certain products made from these metals, many products made from or containing precious metals are entered under different Commodity Index chapters. In general, articles containing precious metals but in which the precious metal component is minor and incidental to the nature and value of the article are entered under the classification of the primary article. For example, a gold-handled umbrella would be entered under Commodity Index Chapter 66, while a piece of original statuary made from a precious metal, would be entered under Chapter 97. Watch and clock cases are covered in Chapter 91.

If you are interested in importing amalgams of precious metal or colloidal precious metal, refer to Chapter 28. Precious metals used for medical purposes—such as sutures and dental fillings—

*IMPORTANT: Read the Commodity Index Introduction. It is the essential framework for understanding this chapter.

are covered in Chapter 30. Precious metal components of paints and dyes, such as lustres, are found in Chapter 32. Leather goods with precious metal fittings are found in Chapter 42, while ornamented fur products are covered in Chapter 43. Decorated textiles and textile products are covered in Commodity Index Chapters 50 through 63. Industrial abrasives containing precious or semiprecious stones or material from them are covered in Chapter 68, while such items contained as incidental parts of other apparatus are classified within Chapters 82, 84, or 85 (the latter includes precious stones used in record styli). Products of Chapter 71 may be found as components in the products of Chapters 90 through 97. Chapter 96 in particular includes items, such as hair ornaments, that may include precious stones, metals, or pearls, but that are classified there rather than as jewelry in Chapter 71.

Key Factors

The key factors in the importation of gems and jewelry and related products are:

- Requirements for accurate fineness marking on sterling silver and gold items
- Marking requirements and restrictions for certain articles
- Alloy classifications
- Compliance with marking requirements under the National Stamping Act
- Compliance with marking requirements under the Hobby Protection Act
- Compliance with endangered species prohibitions and restrictions on any wildlife components of jewelry
- Submission of Customs **Form 4790** for entries of monetary instruments valued at more than $10,000

Although most importers utilize the services of a licensed customs broker in making their entries, and we recommend this practice, you should be aware of the regulatory, entry, and documentation issues involved in importing your product. You, as importer, are ultimately responsible for the fulfillment of any legal requirements applicable to your shipment.

General Considerations

Gems, Jewelry, and Related Articles. Jewelry is defined as any small object of personal adornment or any article of personal use normally carried about the person. Examples of the category include rings, bracelets, necklaces, brooches, earrings, watch chains, tie pins, cufflinks, religious or other medals or insignia, cigarette cases, compacts, and pill boxes. Articles of the goldsmiths' or silversmiths' arts generally refer to items such as ornaments, silverware, toilet articles, smokers' articles, and other items used in the home or office, or for religious purposes.

The importation of gems, jewelry, and related products is relatively straightforward. No permits, licenses, or special entry paperwork are required. However, there are certain restrictions of which you should be aware. These are explained below.

Wildlife Products. If your jewelry contains components derived from wildlife, it is subject to extensive regulation, including laws that protect endangered and threatened species. The U.S. Fish and Wildlife Service (FWS) enforces, among many other laws, the U.S. Endangered Species Act (ESA) and the Convention on International Trade in Endangered Species of Wild Fauna and Flora (CITES). Jewelry containing items such as feathers, shell, horn, or ivory may be entirely prohibited, prohibited when originating from certain countries, or restricted in other ways. See "Prohibitions and Restrictions" below.

Pearls. Importation of pearls is straightforward. There are no restrictions or prohibitions. You do not need permits or licenses, nor is special entry paperwork required. Customs distinguishes between natural and cultured pearls for duty purposes, and all commercially grown pearls are considered cultured pearls. A truly "natural" pearl is rarely seen, and Customs considers all shipments of pearls to be de facto cultured pearls. If you attempt to enter a shipment of pearls as "natural," you must be prepared to show documentation that your pearls were not commercially grown, but were found in the wild.

Coins. Gold and silver coins must comply with provisions of the National Stamping Act (NSA) as amended, which is enforced by the Department of the Treasury (see "Prohibitions and Restrictions" below). If you are importing imitation numismatic items, you should be sure that they meet provisions of the Hobby Protection Act (HPA). You should be prepared to present documentation of government authorization for any coins, especially any nonstandard coins or medallions (see "Marking and Labeling Requirements" below). Coins currently in circulation in any country and imported as monetary instruments enter duty free. However, any entries made on a single occasion and valued at $10,000 or more must be declared.

Precious Metals. Importation of precious metals is relatively straightforward, with few prohibitions or restrictions, most of which have to do with accurate marking to identify the fineness of the metal. Marking requirements are found primarily in provisions of the NSA. No permits, licenses, or special entry paperwork are required. The term "precious metals" as defined in Chapter 71 of the Harmonized Tariff Schedule (HTSUS) means silver, gold, and platinum. "Platinum" is also defined to include platinum, iridium, omnium, palladium, rhodium, and ruthenium.

Alloys. Any alloy containing a precious metal is considered an alloy of precious metal if any one precious metal constitutes as much as 2% by weight of the alloy. Specifically, an alloy containing 2% or more by weight of platinum is considered an alloy of platinum. An alloy containing 2% or more by weight of gold but no platinum or with less than 2% by weight of platinum, is considered an alloy of gold. Other alloys containing 2% or more by weight of silver are considered alloys of silver. There are special requirements for accurate fineness marking on sterling silver and gold items. See "Marking and Labeling Requirements" below.

Form of Metal. For precious metals, "unwrought" refers to refined or unrefined metal in the form of ingots, pigs, sponge, pellets, or similar manufactured primary forms. "Semimanufactured" refers to processed, or wrought, products in the form of bars, plates, sheets, wires, tubes, and similar intermediate forms. "Scrap" refers to leftovers suited only for recovery of the metal content.

Customs Classification

For customs purposes, gems, jewelry, and related products are classified within Chapter 71 of the HTSUS. This chapter is divided into major headings, which are further divided into subheadings, and often into sub-subheadings, each of which has its own HTSUS classification number. For example, the HTSUS number for other gold containing by weight not less than 99.95% of gold is 7108.12.50, indicating that it is a subcategory of other unwrought forms of nonmonetary gold (7108.12.00), which is a subcategory of the major heading gold, unwrought or in semimanufactured forms (7108.00.00). There are 18 major headings in HTSUS Chapter 71.

7101—Pearls, natural or cultured, whether or not worked or graded but not strung, mounted, or set; ungraded pearls, natural or cultured, temporarily strung for convenience of transport

7102—Diamonds, whether or not worked, but not mounted or set

7103—Precious stones (other than diamonds) and semiprecious stones, whether or not worked or graded but not strung, mounted, or set; ungraded precious stones (other than diamonds) and semiprecious stones, temporarily strung for convenience of transport

7104—Synthetic or reconstructed precious or semiprecious stones, whether or not worked or graded but not strung, mounted, or set; ungraded synthetic or reconstructed precious or semiprecious stones, temporarily strung for convenience of transport

7105—Dust and powder of natural or synthetic precious or semiprecious stones

7106—Silver (including silver plated with gold or platinum), unwrought or in semimanufactured forms, or in powder form

7107—Base metals clad with silver, not further worked than semimanufactured

7108—Gold (including gold plated with platinum) unwrought or in semimanufactured forms, or in powder form

7109—Base metals or silver, clad with gold, not further worked than semimanufactured

7110—Platinum, unwrought or in semimanufactured forms, or in powder form

7111—Base metals, silver, or gold, clad with platinum, not further worked than semimanufactured

7112—Waste and scrap of precious metal or of metal clad with precious metal

7113—Articles of jewelry and parts thereof, of precious metal or of metal clad with precious metal

7114—Articles of goldsmiths' or silversmiths' wares and parts thereof, of precious metal or of metal clad with precious metal

7115—Other articles of precious metal or of metal clad with precious metal

7116—Articles of natural or cultured pearls, precious or semiprecious stones (natural, synthetic, or reconstructed)

7117—Imitation jewelry

7118—Coin

For more details regarding classification of the specific product you are interested in importing, consult a customs broker, the appropriate commodity specialist at your nearest customs port, or see HTSUS. HTSUS is available for purchase from the U.S. Government Printing Office (see addresses at end of this chapter), and may be found in larger public libraries. Refer to "Classification—Liquidation" on page 207 for a general discussion of customs classification.

Sample Import Duties

Import duties will vary depending on the HTSUS classification of your product. Therefor, to determine the correct amount of duties, your product must be properly classified under the HTSUS. The following sample duties are taken from the duty listings for HTSUS Chapter 71 products.

Natural pearls (7101.10.00): free; cultured pearls, worked or unworked (7101.21.00): 2.1%; unworked industrial diamonds (miners') (7102.21.10): free; other unworked industrial diamonds (7102.21.30): 4.9%; nonindustrial diamonds (7102.31.00): free; precious stones (other than diamonds) and semiprecious stones, unworked (7103.10.20): free; worked (7103.10.40): 21%; synthetic stones, piezo-electric quartz (7104.10.00): 6%; other synthetic stones of gem quality, cut but not set (7104.90.10): 3.1%; natural or synthetic diamond dust or powder (7105.10.00): free; natural or synthetic dust or powder of other stones (7105.90.00): 0.7 cents/kg; unwrought silver bullion (7106.91.10): free; semimanufactured silver (7106.92.00): 6%; base metal stock clad with silver (7107.00.00): 6.5%; nonmonetary gold bullion (7108.12.10): free; gold leaf (7108.13.10): 3.1%; monetary gold (7108.20.00): free; base metals or silver clad with gold (7109.00.00): 20%; unwrought or semimanufactured or powdered platinum (7110.11.00): free; base metals, silver, or gold clad with platinum (7111.00.00): 20%; waste or scrap of precious metals or of metal clad with precious metals (7112.00.00): free; articles of jewelry of silver, such as chains, in continuous lengths (7113.11.10): 7%; other silver jewelry valued at not over $18 per dozen pieces (7113.11.20): 27.5%; gold rope necklaces and chains (7113.19.21): 6.5%; articles of jewelry of base metal clad with a precious metal, such as chains, in continuous lengths (7113.20.10): 7%; knives with silver handles (7114.11.10): 5.5%; sterling silver tableware (7114.11.50): 6.6%; tableware and related items of precious metals other than silver (7114.19.00): 7.9%; platinum wire cloth catalysts (7115.10.00): 8%; finished articles of natural pearls (7116.10.10): 6.5%; of cultured pearls (7116.10.20): 1%; finished articles of jewelry of precious or semiprecious stones (7116.20.10): 6.5%; imitation jewelry of base metals in continuous lengths, such as chains, valued not over 33 cents per meter (7117.19.10): 8%; valued at more than 33 cents per meter (7117.19.20): 11%; imitation jewelry religious articles other than rosaries (7117.90.30): 5.8%; coins, not legal tender (7118.10.00): free; gold coins (7118.90.00): free.

Entry and Documentation

The entry of merchandise is a two-part process consisting of 1) filing the documents necessary to determine whether merchandise may be released from Customs custody and 2) filing the documents that contain information for duty assessment and statistical purposes. In certain instances all documents must be filed and accepted by Customs prior to the release of the goods. Unless you have been granted an extension, you must file entry documents at a location specified by the district or area director within five working days of your shipment's date of arrival at a U.S. port of entry. These include a number of standard documents required by Customs for any entry, and

- For unofficial gold coin restrikes: a copy of the legal proclamation under which the coin was issued, or official bank affidavit
- For jewelry that is admissible but comprised of components from protected species, any documentation required under applicable endangered species regulations

After you present the entry, Customs may examine your shipment, or may waive examination. The shipment is then released provided no legal or regulatory violations have been noted. You must then file entry summary documentation and deposit estimated duties at a designated customhouse within 10 working days of your shipment's release. For a detailed description of entry procedures, standard documentation, and informal entry, see "Entry Process" on page 182.

Prohibitions and Restrictions

Coins. Counterfeit coins or the means of counterfeiting them may not be imported into the U.S., nor may representations of such articles be imported. Penalties for such actions can be extreme, including criminal penalties (under the Importation of Counterfeit or Forged Obligations or Securities Act), seizure of the goods (under the Contraband Seizure Act), and even forfeiture of the means of transport involved in an attempt to import such items (under regulations governing the Seizure and Forfeiture of Vessels, Vehicles, and Aircraft).

Gold and Silver. Additional prohibitions and restrictions on importation of coins have to do with the composition of the coin. All restrictions on the purchase, holding, selling, or otherwise dealing with gold by U.S. citizens were removed effective December 31, 1974. However, legislation exists providing a framework for revoking or controlling the export or import of gold or silver coins or bullion in times of war or national emergency.

Nevertheless, you may freely import gold—or other precious metals—subject to the usual customs declaration and entry requirements.

Marking and Labeling Requirements. Articles or containers of articles that bear false designations of origin, or false descriptions or representations, are prohibited importation under 15 USC. This is especially pertinent to the importation of precious metals intended for commercial sale, because such articles are often marked with degree of fineness indicating value. Particular fineness marking requirements are detailed in "Marking and Labeling Requirements" below. If you import articles intended for resale in the U.S. that fail to meet these requirements, your shipment is subject to detention by U.S. Customs at the port of entry.

Detention of Shipments. Customs notifies the U.S. attorney when noncomplying shipments are discovered and detained. The U.S. attorney may or may not initiate litigation against the importer. If the U.S. attorney chooses not to prosecute, the mismarked shipment will be subject to normal Customs seizure and forfeiture. If your shipment is seized because of mismarking, you may petition the district director of the customs port of entry for release of the shipment on condition the noncompliance is redressed. If the district director releases your shipment you will be required either to remove or obliterate the prohibited marking, or to see that the articles and containers are properly marked to indicate their origin, contents, or condition. As an alternative to remarking, customs may permit you to export the articles or to destroy them under customs supervision. All remedial procedures resulting from mismarking will be undertaken at your expense.

Wildlife Products. Endangered species regulation is complex. The number of protected species grows every year. If you are considering importing jewelry that could contain wildlife components of any kind, you should be familiar with the various laws. Ivory, for example, is a prohibited import unless the importer presents documentary proof that the ivory is antique (more than 100 years old) and that it meets certain other requirements. Entry of wildlife products is restricted to FWS-designated ports. Contact FWS (see addresses at end of this chapter) with your specific questions.

It is difficult to overstress the importance of endangered species regulation. Ignorance of these laws can result in the loss of your shipment, and therefore your investment. In some cases a prohibited shipment can incur sizable additional fines. If you are importing items constructed using parts from protected species, such as ivory, certain types of shell, horn, feathers, etc., it is essential that you ascertain the status of those components before making your purchase. Country of origin is a tricky issue here, and it is crucial. Under CITES, some species are prohibited export for commercial purposes from certain countries, but not from others. Wildlife pirating is a common practice, and the country of origin of a jewelry component may not be the same as the country from which you purchased the final product. Many items are categorically prohibited, regardless of country of origin. Items only mildly restricted under CITES may be entirely prohibited under the ESA or one of the other more stringent regulations. If you inadvertently import products made from protected species, the fact that you were not aware of your shipment's violation will not protect you from the consequences.

Marking and Labeling Requirements

Goods that bear markings denoting value, such as carat markings for gold, or the designation "sterling" on silver, must be accurately marked. Gold or silver articles marked or labeled in a manner indicating a greater-than-actual degree of metal fineness, and imported for sale by manufacturers or dealers, are prohibited entry. This prohibition applies regardless of the actual amount of precious metal in the article, and also applies to alloys.

Under the National Stamping Act (NSA), articles made of gold or gold alloys may not be imported into the U.S. if the gold content is one-half carat below the indicated fineness. In the case of articles made of gold or gold alloys that include solder and alloy of inferior fineness, a one-carat divergence below the indicated fineness is permitted. Articles marked "sterling" or "sterling silver" must assay at least 0.925 of pure silver, with a 0.004 allowable divergence. Other articles of silver or silver alloys must assay not less than 0.004 part below the indicated fineness. Articles marked "coin" or "coin silver" must contain at least 0.900 part pure silver with an allowable divergence of 0.004 part.

It is unlawful to enter for import into the U.S. items of jewelry bearing inaccurate or misleading valuation markings. If your shipment is found to be inaccurately marked, it is subject to seizure by customs.

Articles bearing the words "United States Assay" are prohibited. Articles made wholly or in part of inferior metal and plated or filled with gold or silver or alloys thereof, and that are marked with the degree of fineness, must also be marked to indicate the plated or filled content. In such cases, the use of the words "sterling" or "coin" is prohibited.

If you deal via mail or operate in interstate commerce in articles of gold or silver that bear a fineness or quality mark such as 14K, sterling, or other mark, you must place your name or registered trademark next to the fineness mark, in letters the same size as the fineness mark. This trademark or name is not required at the time of importation; therefore, customs has no direct responsibility for enforcement of this law and shipments are not held up on this count. Address your questions regarding this requirement to the U.S. Department of Justice (see addresses at end of this chapter).

Under the Hobby Protection Act, any imitation numismatic item must be plainly and permanently marked "copy." Those that do not comply are subject to seizure and forfeiture. Unofficial gold coin restrikes must be marked with the country of origin. If you are importing these types of coins, you should obtain a copy of the legal proclamation under which the coins are issued. If you are unable to procure the proclamation, you should get an affidavit of government sanction of the coins from a responsible banking official.

For marking or labeling requirements applicable to specific products or types of products made from precious metals (e.g. watches), see the pertinent Commodity Index chapter.

For a general discussion of U.S. Customs marking and labeling requirements, see "Marking: Country of Origin" on page 215 and "Special Marking Requirements" on page 217.

Shipping Considerations

You will need to ensure that your goods are packaged and shipped with care to ensure that they arrive in good condition and pass smoothly through Customs. You are responsible for ensuring that the shipment is in compliance with all applicable government regulations for packaging and shipping. In most instances, you should not leave these arrangements solely to the discretion of your supplier. Careful preparation of the cargo and selection of the mode of transport can be essential to a cost-effective, timely delivery of undamaged goods. We strongly advise you to consult your shipping representative, insurance agent, or freight broker for advice on packaging and shipping. Refer also to the major tab section "Packing/Shipping/Insurance" for a general discussion of packing and shipping.

Although goods of Chapter 71 may be subject to damage during transport if improperly packaged, the major concern lies in ensuring adequate security en route for these high-value, often highly portable products. The weight factor relative to the bulk of many of these goods is also a consideration.

Publications Available

The *Harmonized Tariff Schedule of the United States* (HTSUS) is available from:

Government Printing Office (GPO)
Superintendent of Documents
Washington, DC 20402
(202) 512-1800 (Order line)
(202) 512-0000 (General)

The USGPO also has copies of specific laws available for purchase. The USGPO accepts credit card orders over the phone, as well as mail orders paid by credit card, a check drawn on a U.S. bank, or an international money order.

Relevant Government Agencies

Address questions regarding NSA, HPA, and the importation of coins, precious metals, or jewelry made thereof to:

U.S. Customs Service
Office of Regulations and Rulings
Metals and Machinery
1301 Constitution Ave. NW
Washington, DC 20229
(202) 482-7030

Address questions regarding the importation of jewelry involving protected species to:

U.S. Fish and Wildlife Service (FWS)
Office of Management Authority
4401 N. Fairfax Drive, Room 432
Arlington, VA 22203
(703) 358-2095
(800) 358-2104, (703) 358-2104 (Permits office)

Address questions regarding the importation of gems, jewelry, and related products to the district or port director of customs for you area. For addresses refer to"U.S. Customs District Offices" on page 62 or contact:

U.S. Customs Service
1301 Constitution Ave. NW
Washington, DC 20229
(202) 927-6724 (Information)
(202) 927-1000 (General)

Laws and Regulations

The following laws and regulations may be relevant to the importation of gems, jewelry, and related products. The laws are contained in the U.S. Code (USC) and the regulations are published in the code of Federal Regulations (CFR), both of which may be available at larger public and law libraries. Copies of specific laws are also available from the United States Government Printing Office (address above).

15 USC 2101
Hobby Protection Act (HPA)
This act prescribes marking requirements for imitation numismatic items and for unofficial gold coin restrikes.

15 USC 291-300
National Stamping Act (NSA)
This Act provides requirements for accurate fineness marking on articles of gold or gold alloy.

Convention on International Trade in Endangered Species of Wild Fauna and Flora (CITES)
This comprehensive wildlife treaty signed by over 100 countries, including the United States, regulates and in many cases prohibits commercial imports and exports of wild animal and plant species threatened by trade.

16 USC 1531
Endangered Species Act
This Act prohibits the import and export of plant and seed species listed as endangered and most species listed as threatened. Seeds labeled as "of cultivated origin" may be traded. It is the U.S. law that implements CITES.

12 USC 95a
Importation and Exportation of Gold and Silver
Customs enforces laws relating to the importation or exportation of gold and silver coins or bullion during times of war or national emergency.

15 USC 291-300
Gold Labeling Act of 1976
Customs enforces restrictions on the importation of gold or silver stamped with the words "United States Assay" or any words calculated to convey the impression that an official U.S. agency has certified the quality of such gold or silver. Section 294 prohibits the importation of falsely marked gold or silver See 19 CFR 11.12.

49 USC App. 781 et seq.
Contraband Seizure Act
Pursuant to this act which makes it unlawful to transport, conceal, or facilitate the transportation of "contraband articles" as defined in the statute (including certain narcotic drugs, firearms, and counterfeit coins) Customs assists in the seizures made by the U.S. Secret Service. See also 19 CFR 12.48.

18 USC 471 et seq.
Importation of Counterfeit or Forged Obligations or Securities Act
Customs enforces the law prohibiting the importation of counterfeit obligations, securities, coins, currency, customs forms, ships' papers, and the plates or other means for counterfeiting the same.

31 CFR Part 401
Seizure and Forfeiture of Vessels, Vehicles, and Aircraft used to transport Counterfeit Coins, Obligations, and Paraphernalia
These regulations authorize the district director of customs to hold in custody the means of transport used to violate 49 USC 781 and seized by the Secret Service in enforcing laws against counterfeiting.

Principal Exporting Countries

The following listing includes samples of the main supplier nations of the products of this chapter. It is organized by HTSUS major heading. (Refer to "Customs Classification" above for the product codes.) Countries are listed in rank order of the value of products imported to the U.S. Statistics represent customs value entries for 1993 from the Bureau of Census, U.S. Department of Commerce.

7101—Japan, Hong Kong, Australia, French Polynesia, Switzerland, India, China, Thailand, Taiwan, Cote d'Ivoire

7102—Israel, Belgium, India, United Kingdom, Switzerland, Ghana, Hong Kong, South Africa, Russia, Zaire

7103—Thailand, Colombia, Hong Kong, Switzerland, India, Israel, Brazil, Germany, Taiwan, Sri Lanka

7104—Thailand, Germany, Switzerland, Austria, Japan, Australia, South Korea, Hong Kong, France, China

7105—Ireland, Germany, United Kingdom, Belgium, Japan, Switzerland, Russia, China, South Korea, Ukraine

7106—Canada, Mexico, Chile, Peru, Dominican Rep., Japan, Germany, Argentina, Brazil, United Kingdom

7107—Canada, France, Mexico, Hong Kong

7108—Canada, Uruguay, South Africa, Chile, Switzerland, Bolivia, Peru, Ecuador, Mexico, United Kingdom

7109—Chile, Mexico, Netherlands, France

7110—South Africa, Russia, United Kingdom, Belgium, Switzerland, Germany, Colombia, Japan, Canada, Italy

7111—United Kingdom, Canada

7112—Canada, Dominican Rep., Mexico, United Kingdom, Malaysia, Estonia, Trinidad and Tobago, Taiwan, Hong Kong, Germany

7113—Italy, Thailand, Israel, Hong Kong, India, Dominican Rep., Peru, Mexico, Canada, Bolivia

7114—Chile, Italy, United Kingdom, Israel, Taiwan, China, India, Mexico, France, Germany

7115—Argentina, Chile, Japan, Canada, Italy, Israel, Switzerland, Sweden, France, Pakistan

7116—Japan, Hong Kong, Thailand, Taiwan, Brazil, China, India, Australia, Ireland, South Korea

7117—South Korea, China, Taiwan, Hong Kong, Thailand, India, Philippines, Japan, Canada, France

7118—South Africa, Canada, United Kingdom, Australia, Mexico, China, Uruguay, Austria, Chile, France

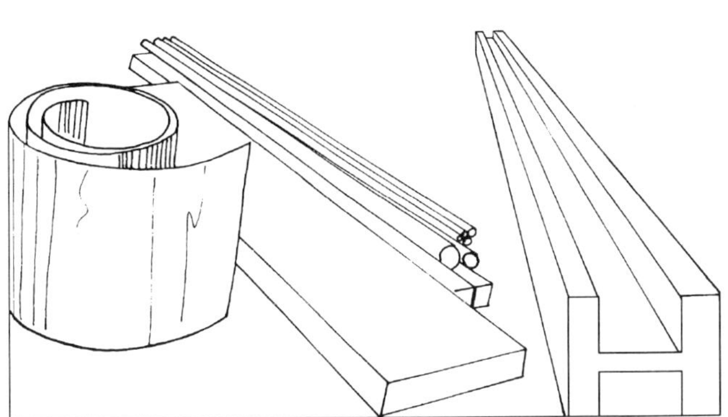

Chapter 72: Iron and Steel*

This chapter relates to the importation of iron and steel, which are classified within Chapter 72 of the Harmonized Tariff Schedule of the United States (HTSUS). Specifically, it includes primary materials, such as pig iron, ferroalloys, and waste and scrap; iron and nonalloy steel, including flat-rolled, bars, rods, and wire in rolls, coils, and basic intermediate shapes; stainless steel in the same forms as iron and nonalloy steel; and other alloy steel in the same forms as stainless steel, but including hollow drill bars and rods. Basically, Chapter 72 includes all primary and intermediate products of iron and steel.

If you are interested in importing finished goods of iron or steel, refer to Commodity Index Chapter 73. Goods of base metals in which metals other than iron or steel predominate are covered in other Commodity Index chapters, including copper and its alloys, such as brass, bronze, nickel-silver, and cupro-nickel (Chapter 74), nickel (Chapter 75), aluminum (Chapter 76), lead (Chapter 78), zinc (Chapter 79), tin (Chapter 80), and other base metals (Chapter 81). Tools, other implements, and cutlery are found in Chapter 82, while miscellaneous articles of base metals are contained in Chapter 83. Precious metals, alloys of precious metals, and articles containing the same are covered specifically in Chapter 71.

Other products for which metals are incidental—even if critical and major—components are found within a variety of Commodity Index chapters and headings. For example, if you are interested in importing metallic paints, refer to Chapter 36. For headgear with metal elements, see Chapter 65; for umbrella frames and related items, see Chapter 66. Finished and semifinished products classified as machinery, mechanical appliances, and electrical goods are found in Chapters 84 and 85. Assembled railway track and related equipment is covered in chapter 86, vehicles in Chapter 87, aircraft in Chapter 88, and boats in Chapter 89. Instruments and apparatus are covered in other Commodity Index chapters on the particular items, including optical, medical, and precision instruments (Chapter 90), clocks and watches (Chapter 91), and musical instruments (Chapter 92). Metal articles as parts of firearms, including ammunition, are found in Chapter 93. The Commodity Index chapters that cover miscellaneous manufactures include furniture (Chapter 94), toys, games, and sporting goods (Chapter 95), and miscellaneous manufactured articles (Chapter 96). Works of art in which iron and steel are components, even dominant components, are covered in Chapter 97 if the primary value derives from the artistry rather than from the metal content.

*IMPORTANT: Read the Commodity Index Introduction. It is the essential framework for understanding this chapter.

Key Factors

The key factors in the importation of iron and steel are:

- Compliance with U.S. Environmental Protection Agency (EPA) requirements under the Toxic Substances Control Act (TSCA) (if the product is classified as a hazardous substance)
- Compliance with U.S. Department of Transportation (DOT) regulations for transport of hazardous cargo (if the product is a hazardous substance)

Although most importers utilize the services of a licensed customs broker in making their entries, and we recommend this practice, you should be aware of the regulatory, entry, and documentation issues involved in importing your product. You, as importer, are ultimately responsible for the fulfillment of any legal requirements applicable to your shipment.

General Considerations

Regulatory Agencies. Importation of iron and steel is relatively straightforward, with few restrictions or special requirements. The Environmental Protection Agency (EPA), under authority of the Toxic Substances Control Act (TSCA), imposes certain controls on the importation of products that contain toxic substances. The Department of Transportation (DOT) enforces regulations for transporting hazardous cargo.

Definitions. Unlike alloys of precious metals, in which any alloy having as much as 2% of a precious metal is considered an alloy of that metal, alloys of base metals are classified according to the metal that predominates by weight over every other individual metal in the alloy. For customs purposes, alloys of a metal are included with the metal that they are an alloy of. Similarly, for customs purposes, iron and steel—which is processed iron—are considered to be the same metal.

Pig iron is defined for customs purposes as an iron-carbon alloy not usefully malleable that contains more than 2% by weight of carbon and less than the listed percentages of the any of the following materials: chromium, 10%; manganese, 6%; phosphorus, 3%; silicon, 8%; and other elements, 10%. Spiegeleisen is an iron-carbon alloy containing by weight between 6% and 30% of manganese but otherwise conforming to the definition of pig iron. Ferroalloys contain by weight more than 4% iron and more than the listed percentages of the following materials: chromium, 10%; manganese, 30%; phosphorus, 3%; silicon, 8%; and a total of more than 10% of other elements excluding carbon and with a maximum of 10% for copper. Steel is defined as a ferrous material that is usefully malleable and contains by weight no more than 2% of carbon (chromium steels may have a higher carbon content). Stainless steel consists of alloy steels containing by weight no more than 1.2% carbon and at least 10.5% chromium. Other alloy steels include specified varying percentages of elements such as aluminum, boron, chromium, cobalt, copper, lead, manganese, molybdenum, nickel, niobium, silicon, titanium, tungsten, vanadium, zirconium, and other elements—except sulfur, phosphorus, carbon, and nitrogen. HTSUS also gives specific definitions and ranges for such products as tool steel, chipper knife steel, heat-resisting steel, and ball-bearing steel. For details, see the notes to HTSUS Chapter 72.

Hazardous Substances Regulations. The EPA imposes certain controls on the importation of toxic substances. The TSCA defines a toxic substance as any substance determined to present the possibility of an unreasonable risk of injury to health and the environment. The DOT enforces regulations for transporting hazardous cargo. Substances are deemed hazardous if listed in DOT transport regulations (49 CFR 172 appendix). Unwrought primary metals, such as pigs, ingots, billets, blooms, and similar materials, are generally categorized as toxic substances within the definitions of the TSCA and thus are required to be in compliance with its provisions. These include packaging, shipping, marking, and labeling requirements. Refer to "Laws and Regulations" below.

Products defined as articles—that is, any manufactured item 1) that is formed into a specific shape or design during manufacture, 2) that has end-use functions dependent on the shape or design during end use, and 3) that during the end use, does not change in its chemical composition or that changes only for a noncommercial purpose separate from the article and only as allowed by law (19 CFR 12.120(2))—are not subject to the provisions of the TSCA. Metal products other than primary metals are generally considered to be articles even if they are to be further processed. For example, rolled steel is an article even if it is to be subsequently processed.

Certification. All products covered by the TSCA are subject to the U.S. Customs Service TSCA Import Certification Rule (19 CFR 12.118 et seq.). If you import these products, you must sign one of the following statements: "I certify that all materials in this shipment comply with all applicable rules or orders under TSCA and that I am not offering a chemical substance for entry in violation of TSCA or any applicable rule or order thereunder" or "I certify that all materials in this shipment are not subject to TSCA." You must file this TSCA certification of compliance or exemption at the time you make the entry at customs. Customs will not release your shipment without proper certification.

If you will be importing several or regular shipments, you should ask the appropriate Customs district director to authorize your use of a blanket certification. A blanket certification is valid for one calendar year, is renewable, and may be revoked at any time for cause.

Dumping or Countervailing Duty Actions. Actions to restrict importation of or impose punitive duties on imports of iron and steel products from countries that are alleged to be involved in selling these products in the U.S. at below cost or the prices charged in their home countries (dumping) are occasionally brought to protect the domestic steel industry. Although no such actions are currently in force, restrictions can be imposed on short notice. You should contact customs to verify the status of your proposed imports.

Customs Classification

For customs purposes, iron and steel are classified within Chapter 72 of the HTSUS. This chapter is divided into major headings, which are further divided into subheadings, and often into sub-subheadings, each of which has its own HTSUS classification number. For example, the HTSUS number for iron or nonalloy steel not coated or plated with metal and not clad is 7210.70.30, indicating that it is a subcategory of iron and nonalloy steel, painted, varnished, or coated with plastics (7210.70.00), which is a subcategory of the major heading flat-rolled products of iron or steel, of a width of 600 mm or more, clad, plated, or coated (7210.00.00). There are 29 major headings in HTSUS Chapter 72.

7201—Pig iron and spiegeleisen in pigs, blocks, or other primary forms

7202—Ferroalloys

7203—Ferrous products obtained by direct reduction of iron ore and other spongy ferrous products, in lumps, pellets, or similar forms; iron having a minimum purity by weight of 99.94%, in lumps, pellets, or similar forms

7204—Ferrous waste and scrap; remelting scrap ingots of iron or steel

7205—Granules or powders, of pig iron, spiegeleisen, iron, and steel

7206—Iron and nonalloy steel in ingots or other primary forms (excluding iron of heading 7203)

7207—Semifinished products of iron or nonalloy steel

7208—Flat-rolled products of iron and nonalloy steel, of a width of 600 mm or more, hot-rolled, not clad, plated, or coated

7209—Flat-rolled products of iron or nonalloy steel, of a width of 600 mm or more, cold-rolled (cold-reduced), not clad, plated, or coated

7210—Flat-rolled products of iron or nonalloy steel, of a width of 600 mm or more, clad, plated, or coated

7211—Flat-rolled products of iron or nonalloy steel, of a width of less than 600 mm, not clad, plated, or coated

7212—Flat-rolled products of iron or nonalloy steel, of a width of less than 600 mm, not clad, plated, or coated

7213—Bars and rods, hot-rolled, in irregularly wound coils, of iron or nonalloy steel

7214—Other bars and rods of iron or nonalloy steel, not further worked than forged, hot-rolled, hot-drawn, or hot-extruded, but including those twisted after rolling

7215—Other bars and rods of iron and nonalloy steel

7216—Angles, shapes, and sections of iron or nonalloy steel

7217—Wire of iron or nonalloy steel

7218—Stainless steel in ingots or other primary forms; semifinished products of stainless steel

7219—Flat-rolled products of stainless steel, of a width of 600 mm or more

7220—Flat-rolled products of stainless steel, of a width of less than 600 mm

7221—Bars and rods, hot-rolled, in irregularly wound coils, of stainless steel

7222—Other bars and rods of stainless steel; angles, shapes, and sections of stainless steel

7223—Wire of stainless steel

7224—Other alloy steel in ingots or other primary forms; semifinished products of other alloy steel

7225—Flat-rolled products of other alloy steel, of a width of 600 mm or more

7226—Flat-rolled products of other alloy steel, of a width of less than 600 mm

7227—Bars and rods, hot-rolled, in irregularly wound coils, of other alloy steel

7228—Other bars and rods of other alloy steel; angles, shapes, and sections, of other alloy steel; hollow drill bars and rods, of alloy or nonalloy steel

7229—Wire of other alloy steel

For more details regarding classification of the specific product you are interested in importing, consult a customs broker, the appropriate commodity specialist at your nearest customs port, or see HTSUS. HTSUS is available for purchase from the U.S. Government Printing Office (see addresses at end of this chapter), and may be found in larger public libraries. Refer to "Classification—Liquidation" on page 207 for a general discussion of customs classification.

Sample Import Duties

Import duties will vary depending on the HTSUS classification of your product. Therefore, to determine the correct amount of duties, your product must be properly classified under the HTSUS. The following sample duties are taken from the duty listings for HTSUS Chapter 72 products.

Nonalloy pig iron containing by weight less than 0.5% phosphorus (7201.10.0): free; spiegeleisen (7201.40.00): 0.2%; ferromanganese containing by weight more than 4% of carbon (7202.11.50): 1.5%; ferrosilicon containing by weight more than 90% silicon (7202.21.90): 5.8%; ferromolybdenum (7202.70.00): 4.5%; ferrous products obtained by direct reduction of iron ore (7203.10.00): free; waste and scrap of stainless steel (7204.21.00): free; powders of alloy steel (7205.21.00): 4%; ingots of iron or nonalloy steel other than iron of heading 7203 (7206.10.00): 4.2%; semifinished products of iron or nonalloy steel containing by weight 0,25% or more of carbon (7207.20.00): 4.2%; flat-rolled products of iron or nonalloy steel, of a width of 600 mm or more, hot-rolled of a thickness of 3 mm or more but not exceeding 10 mm (7208.12.00): 6%; flat-rolled products of iron or nonalloy steel of a width of 600 mm or more, cold-rolled, not clad, plated, or coated in coils, of a thickness exceeding 1 mm but less than 3 mm (7209.12.00): 5.1%; flat-rolled products of high-strength nonalloy steel of a width of 600 mm or more electrolytically plated or coated with zinc (7210.31.00): 6.5%; flat-rolled products of high strength nonalloy steel of a width of less than 600 mm not further worked than rolled in universal mill plate (7211.11.00): 6%; flat-rolled products of iron or nonalloy steel of a width of less than 600 mm plated or coated with tin (7212.10.00): 3.5%; concrete reinforcing bars and rods, hot-rolled in irregularly wound coils (7213.10.00): 4.9%; other forged bars or rods of iron or nonalloy steel not further worked (7214.10.00): 4.7%; other bars and rods of iron or nonalloy steel not further worked than cold-formed containing by weight 0.6% or more of carbon (7215.40.00): 7.5%; U, I, or H sections of iron or nonalloy steel not further worked than hot-rolled of a height less than 80 mm (7216.10.00): 0.9%; round wire of iron or nonalloy steel with a diameter of less than 1.5 mm (7217.11.50): 5.3%; round wire of iron or nonalloy steel plated or coated with zinc (7217.32.10): 5.3%; high nickel alloy steel in ingots (7218.90.00): 5.2%; flat-rolled products of stainless steel of a width of 600 mm or more not further worked than hot-rolled of a thickness exceeding 10 mm (7219.11.00): 10.1%; flat-rolled products of stainless steel of a width of less than 600 mm not further worked than hot rolled of a thickness of 4.75 mm or more (7220.20.10): 10.1%; hot-rolled bars and rods of stainless steel in irregularly wound coils (7221.00.00): 4.7%; angles of stainless steel, hot-rolled but not drilled (7222.40.30): 2.1%; stainless steel flat wire (7223.00.50): 3.3%; other alloy steel, not in ingots (7221.90.00): 5.1%; flat-rolled high speed alloy steel of a width of 600 mm or more (7225.20.00): 10.5%; flat-rolled products of chipper knife alloy steel of a width of less than 600 mm (7226.91.05): free; bars and rods of hot-rolled irregularly wound silico-manganese steel (7227.20.00): 4.5%; other bars and rods of tool steel (7228.50.00): 10.6%; wire of high-speed alloy steel (7229.10.00): 10%.

Entry and Documentation

The entry of merchandise is a two-part process consisting of 1) filing the documents necessary to determine whether merchandise may be released from Customs custody and 2) filing the documents that contain information for duty assessment and statistical purposes. In certain instances all documents must be filed and accepted by Customs prior to the release of the goods. Unless you have been granted an extension, you must file entry documents at a location specified by the district or area director within five working days of your shipment's date of arrival at a U.S. port of entry. These include a number of standard documents required by Customs for any entry, and:

- U.S. Customs TSCA Certification when required

After you present the entry, Customs may examine your shipment, or may waive examination. The shipment is then released provided no legal or regulatory violations have been noted. You must then file entry summary documentation and deposit estimated duties at a designated customhouse within 10 working days of your shipment's release. For a detailed description of entry procedures, standard documentation, and informal entry, see "Entry Process" on page 182.

Entry Invoice. For all products entered under HTSUS Chapter 72, a statement is required giving the percentages by weight of carbon and any other metallic elements contained in the articles. The statement must be in the form of a mill analysis or mill test certificate.

Summary Steel Invoice. The requirement that an importer submit a Special Summary Steel Invoice (Customs **Form 5520**) was removed effective April 26, 1993. No such invoice is needed.

Piping, Manhole Fittings, and Gas Cylinders. Special country of origin markings are required for iron and steel pipe and pipe fittings; manhole rings, frames, and covers; and compressed gas cylinders. These articles must be marked by die-stamping, cast-in-mold lettering, acid or electrolytic etching, or engraving.

Hazardous Substances. Shipments including any products that are classified as hazardous substances (49 CFR 172) must comply with the marking and labeling regulations adopted by the EPA (46 CFR 147.30) and the DOT (49 CFR 171 et seq.).

For a general discussion of U.S. Customs marking and labeling requirements, see "Marking: Country of Origin" on page 215 and "Special Marking Requirements" on page 217.

Shipping Considerations

You will need to ensure that your goods are packaged and shipped with care to ensure that they arrive in good condition and pass smoothly through Customs. You are responsible for ensuring that the shipment is in compliance with all applicable government regulations for packaging and shipping. In most instances, you should not leave these arrangements solely to the discretion of your supplier. Careful preparation of the cargo and selection of the mode of transport can be essential to a cost-effective, timely delivery of undamaged goods. We strongly advise you to consult your shipping representative, insurance agent, or freight broker for advice on packing and shipping. Refer also to the major tab section "Packing/Shipping/Insurance" for a general discussion of packing and shipping.

Solid chemical products that are listed as hazardous substances (49 CFR 172 appendix) may be transported in bulk only on compliance with Coast Guard notification procedures, shipping permit requirements, and complex transportation regulations (46 CFR 148). All hazardous substances must be packaged and transported in accordance with DOT regulations (49 CFR 171 et seq.).

Iron and steel products are often heavy and bulky, and should be securely stowed to avoid damage due to shifting en route. Ferrous products are subject to corrosion, which should be guarded against, especially as no allowance is made by customs for partial damage or loss due to discoloration or rusting.

Publications Available

The *Harmonized Tariff Schedule of the United States* (HTSUS) is available from:

Government Printing Office (GPO)
Superintendent of Documents
Washington, DC 20402
(202) 512-1800 (Order line)
(202) 512-0000 (General)

The USGPO also has copies of specific laws available for purchase. The USGPO accepts credit card orders over the phone, as well as mail orders paid by credit card, a check drawn on a U.S. bank, or an international money order.

Relevant Government Agencies

Address inquiries regarding TSCA and EPA requirements for importation of hazardous or toxic substances to:

Environmental Protection Agency (EPA)
TSCA System Information
EPA 7408, OPPT
401 M Street SW
Washington, DC 20460
(202) 554-1404 (TSCA Information Hotline)

Address questions regarding transportation of hazardous substances to:

U.S. Department of Transportation (DOT)
Research and Special Programs Administration
Office of Hazardous Materials Standards
400 7th St. SW
Washington, DC 20590
(202) 366-4488

Address questions regarding the importation of iron and steel to the district or port director of Customs for you area. For addresses refer to "U.S. Customs District Offices" on page 62 or contact:

U.S. Customs Service
1301 Constitution Ave. NW
Washington, DC 20229
(202) 927-6724 (Information)
(202) 927-1000 (General)

Laws and Regulations

The following laws and regulations may be relevant to the importation of iron and steel products. The laws are contained in the U.S. Code (USC) and the regulations are published in the code of federal Regulations (CFR), both of which may be available at larger public and law libraries. Copies of specific laws are also available from the United States Government Printing Office (address above).

15 USC 2601 et seq.
Toxic Substances Control Act
This Act authorizes the EPA to determine whether a substance is harmful and to restrict importation, sale, and use of such substances.

19 CFR 12.118 et seq.
Regulations on Toxic Substances Control
These regulations require importers of chemical substances imported in bulk or as part of a mixture to certify to Customs that the shipment complies with the TSCA or is not subject to that Act.

15 USC 1261
Federal Hazardous Substances Act
This Act controls the importation of hazardous substances, sets forth prohibited imports, and authorizes various agencies to promulgate labeling, marking, and transport requirements.

49 CFR 170 et seq.
Regulations on Hazardous Materials
These regulations list all substances deemed hazardous and provide transport, marking, labeling, safety, and emergency response rules.

46 CFR 147.30
Regulations on Labeling of Hazardous Materials
This regulation requires the labeling of containers of hazardous substances and specifies the label contents.

46 CFR 148 et seq.
Regulations of Carriage of Solid Hazardous Materials in Bulk
These regulations govern the transport of solid hazardous substances in bulk, including reporting, permitting, loading, stowing, and shipping requirements.

Principal Exporting Countries

The following listing includes samples of the main supplier nations of the products of this chapter. It is organized by HTSUS major heading. (Refer to "Customs Classification" above for the product codes.) Countries are listed in rank order of the value of products imported to the U.S. Statistics represent customs value entries for 1993 from the Bureau of Census, U.S. Department of Commerce.

7201—Brazil, Russia, Canada, South Africa, Latvia, Ukraine, Japan, Switzerland, Lithuania, Germany

7202—South Africa, Brazil, France, Norway, Turkey, Russia, China, Dominican Rep., Germany, Mexico

7203—Venezuela, Russia, Canada, Japan, Spain, Sweden, United Kingdom, France, Italy, Germany

7204—Canada, Venezuela, Mexico, Jamaica, Germany, Japan, Ukraine, Brazil, China, Netherlands

7205—Canada, Japan, Germany, Sweden, China, United Kingdom, Italy, France, Venezuela, Netherlands

7206—Germany, Japan, Australia, Canada, United Kingdom, France, Switzerland, Taiwan, China

7207—Brazil, Germany, Italy, France, Mexico, Belgium, Australia, Canada, United Kingdom, Netherlands

7208—Canada, South Korea, Netherlands, France, South Africa, Germany, Belgium, Italy, Ukraine, India

7209—Germany, Canada, Netherlands, Japan, Mexico, Belgium, South Africa, France, Greece, Australia

7210—Canada, Japan, Germany, South Korea, Italy, South Africa, Luxembourg, Venezuela, Taiwan, Mexico

7211—Canada, Germany, United Kingdom, Sweden, Japan, Italy, Taiwan, Brazil, France, Czech Rep.

7212—Canada, Japan, Germany, United Kingdom, South Korea, Australia, Belgium, Greece, Austria, Mexico

7213—Canada, Japan, Germany, France, United Kingdom, Trinidad & Tobago, Netherlands, Brazil, Belgium, Switzerland

7214—Canada, United Kingdom, Brazil, Turkey, Mexico, Australia, Japan, Trinidad & Tobago, Argentina, Venezuela

7215—Canada, United Kingdom, France, India, Brazil, Germany, Spain, Australia, Japan, China

7216—Canada, United Kingdom, Luxembourg, Germany, Spain, Mexico, Belgium, Japan, Brazil, Russia

7217—Canada, Belgium, Japan, France, United Kingdom, Germany, Sweden, Brazil, Taiwan, China

7218—Canada, United Kingdom, Sweden, South Africa, Germany, Italy, Japan, Belgium, Mexico, Spain

7219—Mexico, Japan, Spain, France, Germany, Italy, South Korea, Canada, United Kingdom, Belgium

7220—Japan, Sweden, France, United Kingdom, Canada, Italy, Germany, Belgium, South Korea, Austria

7221—France, Japan, Sweden, Spain, Taiwan, Italy, India, South Korea, United Kingdom, Brazil

7222—Japan, Spain, Italy, Canada, Brazil, France, India, South Korea, Sweden, Germany

7223—Sweden, Canada, Japan, France, Taiwan, Italy, United Kingdom, South Korea, Belgium, Germany

7224—Canada, United Kingdom, Germany, Australia, Brazil, Finland, Netherlands, Sweden, France, Mexico

7225—Japan, Canada, France, Germany, Sweden, Italy, United Kingdom, Brazil, Belgium, Finland

7226—Canada, Japan, France, Sweden, Italy, Germany, United Kingdom, Switzerland, Austria, Brazil

7227—Japan, Canada, Sweden, France, Netherlands, Germany, Italy, Brazil, South Korea, Belgium

7228—Canada, United Kingdom, France, Germany, Japan, Sweden, Brazil, Austria, Italy, Luxembourg

7229—Japan, Canada, Sweden, United Kingdom, South Korea, Germany, Austria, Netherlands, Taiwan, Thailand

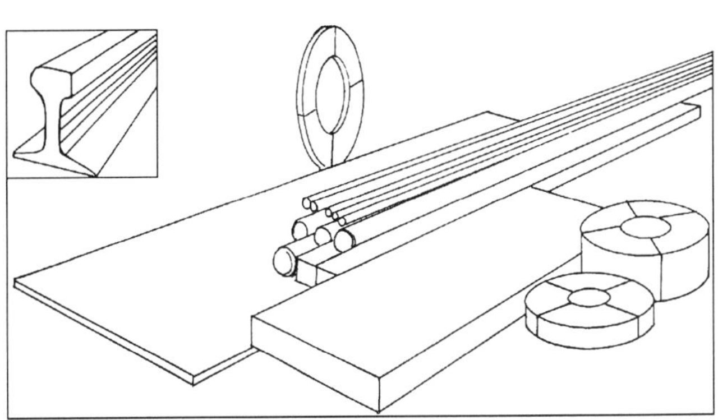

Chapter 73: Articles of Iron and Steel*

This chapter relates to the importation of articles of iron and steel, which are classified within Chapter 73 of the Harmonized Tariff Schedule of the United States (HTSUS). Specifically, it includes sheet pilings, welded angles, and similar products; railway track materials; cast iron and other steel pipes and casings, including drilling and pipeline sections; fittings; parts of architectural structures; tanks and reservoirs; containers, including those for compressed or liquefied gases; stranded wire, rope, and cable; barbed wire and other fencing wire; woven metal fabrics, including chain-link fencing and netting; chains; anchors and related items; nails, screws, nuts and bolts, and similar fasteners; needles; wound and leaf springs; stoves, ranges, and ovens—other than electric appliances; radiators and furnaces; table, kitchen, and household articles; sanitary wares, such as bathtubs and basins; and other miscellaneous articles—such as horseshoes—of iron and steel.

If you are interested in importing primary or intermediate products of iron or steel, refer to Commodity Index Chapter 72. Goods of base metals and their alloys in which metals other than iron or steel predominate in related chapters, including copper (Chapter 74), nickel (Chapter 75), aluminum (Chapter 76), lead (Chapter 78), zinc (Chapter 79), tin (Chapter 80), and other base metals (Chapter 81). Tools, other implements, and cutlery are found in Chapter 82, while miscellaneous articles of base metals—including hinges, fittings, and similar articles—are contained in Chapter 83. Precious metals, alloys of precious metals, and articles containing the same are covered specifically in Chapter 71.

Other products for which metals are incidental to use—even if critical and major components—are found within a variety of Commodity Index chapters and headings. For example, if you are interested in importing metallic paints, refer to Chapter 36. Under haberdashery, see Chapter 65 for headgear with metal elements, and Chapter 66 for umbrella frames and related items. Finished and semifinished products classified as machinery, mechanical appliances, and electrical goods are found in Chapters 84 and 85. Assembled railway track and related equipment is covered in chapter 86, vehicles in Chapter 87, aircraft in Chapter 88, and boats in Chapter 89. Instruments and apparatus are covered in Commodity Index chapters that cover the particular type of article, including optical, medical, and precision instruments (Chapter 90), clocks and watches (Chapter 91), and musical instruments (Chapter 92). Metal articles used as parts of firearms,

*IMPORTANT: Read the Commodity Index Introduction. It is the essential framework for understanding this chapter.

including ammunition, are found in Chapter 93. Other chapters cover miscellaneous manufactures, including furniture and prefabricated structures (Chapter 94), toys, games, and sporting goods (Chapter 95), and miscellaneous manufactured articles (Chapter 96). Works of art in which iron and steel are components, even dominant components, are covered in Chapter 97 if the primary value derives from the artistry rather than from the metal content.

Key Factors

The key factors in the importation of articles of iron and steel are:

- For items to be used with food, compliance with U.S. Food and Drug Administration (FDA) requirements for entry notification

Although most importers utilize the services of a licensed customs broker in making their entries, and we recommend this practice, you should be aware of the regulatory, entry, and documentation issues involved in importing your product. You, as importer, are ultimately responsible for the fulfillment of any legal requirements applicable to your shipment.

General Considerations

Regulatory Agencies. Importation of articles of iron and steel products is straightforward. There are no restrictions or prohibitions. You do not need a permit or license, nor is special entry paperwork required in most cases (see "Entry and Documentation" below). The Food and Drug Administration (FDA) controls the importation of items for use with food.

Definitions. Unlike alloys of precious metals, in which any alloy having as much as 2% of a precious metal is considered an alloy of that metal, alloys of base metals are classified according to the metal that predominates by weight over every other individual metal in the alloy. For customs purposes, alloys of a metal are included with the metal that they are an alloy of. Similarly, for customs purposes, articles of iron and steel—which is processed iron—are considered to be the same metal.

Cast iron refers to products obtained by casting in which iron predominates by weight over each of the remaining elements, and that does not qualify as steel. Steel is defined as a ferrous material that is usefully malleable and contains by weight no more than 2% of carbon (chromium steels may have a higher carbon content). Stainless steel consists of alloy steels containing by weight no more than 1.2% carbon and at least 10.5% chromium. Other alloy steels include specified varying percentages of elements such as aluminum, boron, chromium, cobalt, copper, lead, manganese, molybdenum, nickel, niobium, silicon, titanium, tungsten, vanadium, zirconium, and other elements—except sulfur, phosphorus, carbon, and nitrogen. HTSUS also gives specific definitions and ranges for such products as tool steel, chipper knife steel, heat-resisting steel, and ball-bearing steel. For details, see the notes to Chapter 72 in HTSUS.

HTSUS Chapter 73 covers a wide variety of products. Many articles included in the chapter, such as bolts, nuts, and screws, are frequently utilized as parts of machines or other products. To avoid the difficulties inherent in determining whether a particular piece is a part of a particular machine or not, there is a legal definition in the HTSUS (Note 2, Section XV), which provides that parts of general use—such as nuts, bolts, screws, and springs—are always classified in their own heading rather than as a part of a particular machine or other product.

Articles Used with Food. Kitchenware and tableware of iron and steel intended for use with food are subject to the provisions of the Federal Food, Drug, and Cosmetic Act (FDCA) enforced by the FDA. FDA entry notification is required for applicable items. Shipments of FDA-regulated products are subject to FDA port of entry inspection. You must file an FDA Importers Entry Notice, **Form FD701**, with each shipment. For more information, see the annotated diagram of FDA entry procedures and requirements in the "Foods" appendix on page 808. Contact your nearest regional FDA office or FDA headquarters with questions regarding the importation of food-related iron and steel products (see addresses at end of this chapter).

Dumping and Countervailing Duties Actions. Actions to restrict importation of or impose punitive duties on imports of certain iron and steel products from countries that are alleged to be involved in selling these products in the U.S. at below cost or the prices charged in their home country (dumping) are occasionally brought to protect the domestic steel industry. Although no such actions are currently pending, restrictions can be imposed on short notice. You should contact customs to verify the status of your proposed imports.

Customs Classification

For customs purposes, articles of iron and steel are classified within Chapter 73 of the HTSUS. This chapter is divided into major headings, which are further divided into subheadings, and often into sub-subheadings, each of which has its own HTSUS classification number. For example, the HTSUS number for threaded or coupled casings of iron or steel is 7314.20.10, indicating that it is a subcategory of casing, tubing, or drill pipe of a kind used in drilling for oil or gas (7304.20.00), which is a subcategory of the major heading tubes, pipes, and hollow profiles, seamless, other than cast iron or steel (7304.00.00). There are 26 major headings in HTSUS Chapter 73.

7301—Sheet piling of iron or steel, whether or not drilled, punched, or made from assembled elements; welded angles, shapes, and sections of iron or steel

7302—Railway or tramway track construction material of iron or steel, including the following: rails, check-rails, and rack rails, switch blades, crossing frogs, point rods, and other crossing pieces, sleepers (cross-ties), fish-plates, chairs, chair wedges, sole plates (base plates), rail clips, bedplates, ties, and other material specialized for jointing or fixing rails

7303—Tubes, pipes, and hollow profiles of cast iron

7304—Tubes, pipes, and hollow profiles of iron (other than cast iron) or steel

7305—Other tubes and pipes (for example, welded, riveted, or similarly closed), having internal and external circular cross sections, the external diameter of which exceeds 406.4 mm, of iron or steel

7306—Other tubes, pipes, and hollow profiles (for example, open seamed or welded, riveted, or simply closed), of iron or steel

7307—Tube or pipe fittings (for example, couplings, elbows, sleeves), of iron or steel

7308—Structures (excluding prefabricated buildings of heading 9406) and parts of structures (for example, bridges and bridge sections, lock gates, towers, lattice masts, roofs, roofing, frameworks, doors and windows, shutters, balustrades, pillars, and columns) of iron or steel; plates, rods, angles, shapes, sections, tubes, and the like, prepared for use in structures, of iron or steel

7309—Reservoirs, tanks, vats, and similar containers for any material (other than compressed or liquefied gas), of iron or steel, of a capacity exceeding 300 liters, whether or not lined or heat insulated, but not fitted with mechanical or thermal equipment

7310—Tanks, casks, drums, cans, boxes, and similar containers, for any material (other than compressed or liquefied gas), of iron or steel, of a capacity not exceeding 300 liters, whether or not lined or heat insulated, but not fitted with mechanical or thermal equipment

7311—Containers for compressed or liquefied gas, of iron or steel

7312—Stranded wire, ropes, cables, plaited bands, slings, and the like, of iron or steel, not electrically insulated

7313—Barbed wire of iron or steel; twisted hoop or single flat wire, barbed or not, and loosely twisted double wire, of a kind used for fencing, of iron or steel

7314—Cloth (including endless bands), grill, netting, and fencing, of iron or steel wire; expanded metal of iron or steel

7315—Chain and parts thereof, of iron or steel

7316—Anchors, grapnels, and parts thereof, of iron or steel

7317—Nails, tacks, drawing pins, corrugated nails, staples (other than those of heading 8305), and similar articles, of iron or steel, whether or not with heads of other material, but excluding such articles with heads of copper

7318—Screws, bolts, nuts, coach screws, screw hooks, rivets, cotters, cotter pins, washers, (including spring washers), and similar articles, of iron or steel

7319—Sewing needles, knitting needles, bodkins, crochet hooks, embroidery stilettos, and similar articles for use in the hand, of iron or steel; safety pins and other pins of iron or steel, not elsewhere specified or included

7320—Springs and leaves for springs, of iron or steel

7321—Stoves, ranges, grates, cookers (including those with subsidiary boilers for central heating), barbecues, braziers, gas rings, plate warmers, and similar nonelectric domestic appliances, and parts thereof, of iron or steel

7322—Radiators for central heating, not electrically heated, and parts thereof, of iron or steel; air heaters and hot air distributors (including distributors which can also distribute fresh or conditioned air), not electrically heated, incorporating a motor-driven fan or blower, and parts thereof, of iron or steel

7323—Table, kitchen, or other household articles and parts thereof, of iron or steel; iron or steel wool; pot scourers, and scouring or polishing pads, gloves, and the like, of iron or steel

7324—Sanitary ware and parts thereof, of iron or steel

7325—Other cast articles of iron or steel

7326—Others articles of iron or steel

For more details regarding classification of the specific product you are interested in importing, consult a customs broker, the appropriate commodity specialist at your nearest customs port, or see HTSUS. HTSUS is available for purchase from the U.S. Government Printing Office (see addresses at end of this chapter), and may be found in larger public libraries. Refer to "Classification—Liquidation" on page 207 for a general discussion of Customs classification.

Sample Import Duties

Import duties will vary depending on the HTSUS classification of your product. Therefore, to determine the correct amount of duties, your product must be properly classified under the HTSUS. The following sample duties are taken from the duty listings for HTSUS Chapter 73 products.

Steel pilings (7301.10.00): 0.8%; welded angles of iron or nonalloy steel (7301.20.10): 2.8%; rails of alloy steel (7302.10.50): 3.5%; cast iron soil pipes (7303.00.00): 6.5%; line pipe of iron or nonalloy steel of a type used for oil or gas pipelines (7304.10.10): 8%; casing of iron or nonalloy steel of a kind used for oil and gas drilling (7304.20.20): 0.5%; drill pipe of alloy steel (7304.20.80): 7.5%; tubes and pipes of other alloy steel suitable for use in the manufacture of ball or roller bearings (7304.59.10): 6.8%; line pipe of a kind used for oil or gas pipelines, longitudinally arc-welded, of iron or nonalloy steel (7304.05.10): 1.9%; casing of a kind used in drilling for oil or gas, of alloy steel, threaded and coupled (7305.20.60): 6.2%; open seamed line pipe of a kind used for oil and gas drilling, of iron or nonalloy steel (7306.10.10): 1.9%; other pipe, welded, of circular cross-section, of stainless steel, having a wall thickness of more than 1.65 mm (7306.40.50): 5%; cast fittings of cast iron (7307.11.00): 4.8%; threaded elbows, bends, and sleeves, of stainless steel (7307.22.10): 6.2%; bridges and bridge sections (7308.10.00): 5.7%; scaffolding (7308.40.00): 5.7%; steel tanks (7309.00.00): 2.6%; steel cans to be closed by soldering or crimping with a capacity of less than 50 liters (7310.21.00): free; containers for compressed or liquefied gas (7311.00.00): 5%; steel tire cord (7312.10.10): 5.8%; galvanized cable (7312.10.90): 4%; barbed wire (7313.00.00): free; chain link fencing coated with plastic (7314.41.00): 0.2 cents/kg; stud link chain (7315.81.00): free; chain with round links not over 8 mm in diameter (7315.89.10): 1.5%; anchors (7316.00.00): 4.2%; one piece nails made of round wire (7317.00.55): 0.5%; nails made of two or more pieces (7317.00.75): 2.3%; wood screws (7318.12.00): 12.5%; bolts and bolts with their washers exported in the same shipment (7318.15.20): 0.7%; rivets (7318.23.00): 0.4 cents/kg; safety pins (7319.20.00): 9%; leaf springs suitable for motor vehicles (7320.10.30): 4%; helical springs, other than for motor vehicles (7320.20.50): 5.7%; cooking stoves or ranges for gas fuel (7321.11.30): 4.2%; cast iron radiators (7322.11.00): 4.2%; scouring pads (7323.10.00): 2.2 cents/kg + 2.5%; stainless steel teakettles (7323.93.00): 3.4%; enameled steel cookware (7323.94.00): 2.7%; enameled bathtubs (7324.21.50): 3.1%; cast iron or steel manhole covers (7325.10.00): free; forged or stamped grinding balls (7326.11.00): 4.2%; horseshoes (7326.90.45): free.

Entry and Documentation

The entry of merchandise is a two-part process consisting of 1) filing the documents necessary to determine whether merchandise may be released from Customs custody and 2) filing the documents that contain information for duty assessment and statistical purposes. In certain instances all documents must be filed and accepted by Customs prior to the release of the goods. Unless you have been granted an extension, you must file entry documents at a location specified by the district or area director within five working days of your shipment's date of arrival at a U.S. port of entry. These include a number of standard documents required by Customs for any entry, and:

- For iron and steel products intended for use with food: FDA Importers Entry Notice: **Form FD701**

After you present the entry, Customs may examine your shipment, or may waive examination. The shipment is then released provided no legal or regulatory violations have been noted. You must then file entry summary documentation and deposit estimated duties at a designated customhouse within 10 working days of your shipment's release. For a detailed description of entry procedures, standard documentation, and informal entry, see "Entry Process" on page 182.

Entry Invoice for Articles of Iron or Steel. For articles entered under HTSUS headings 7301 through 7307, a statement is required giving the percentages by weight of carbon and any metallic elements contained in the articles. This must be in the form of a mill analysis or mill test certificate.

Summary Steel Invoice. The requirement that an importer submit a Special Summary Steel Invoice (Customs **Form 5520**) was removed effective April 26, 1993. No such invoice is needed.

Marking and Labeling Requirements

Piping, Manhole Fittings, and Gas Cylinders. Special country-of-origin marking requirements apply to certain iron and steel items covered under HTSUS Chapter 73. Iron and steel pipe and pipe fittings, manhole rings, frames or covers, and compressed gas cylinders must generally be marked by one of four methods: die-stamped, cast-in-mold lettering, etching (acid or electrolytic), or engraving. In general, the exemptions from required country-of-origin marking do not apply to iron and steel pipe and pipe fittings.

For a general discussion of U.S. Customs marking and labeling requirements, see "Marking: Country of Origin" on page 215 and "Special Marking Requirements" on page 217.

Shipping Considerations

You will need to ensure that your goods are packaged and shipped with care to ensure that they arrive in good condition and pass smoothly through Customs. You are responsible for ensuring that the shipment is in compliance with all applicable government regulations for packaging and shipping. In most instances, you should not leave these arrangements solely to the discretion of your supplier. Careful preparation of the cargo and selection of the mode of transport can be essential to a cost-effective, timely delivery of undamaged goods. We strongly advise you to consult your shipping representative, insurance agent, or freight broker for advice on packing and shipping. Refer also to the major tab section "Packing/Shipping/Insurance" for a general discussion of packing and shipping.

Articles of iron and steel are often bulky and heavy, and should be securely stowed to avoid damage due to shifting en route. Articles of iron and steel are also subject to corrosion, which should be guarded against, especially as no allowance is made by customs for partial loss due to discoloration or rusting or to damage during shipping.

Publications Available

The *Harmonized Tariff Schedule of the United States* (HTSUS) is available from:

Government Printing Office (GPO)
Superintendent of Documents
Washington, DC 20402
(202) 512-1800 (Order line)
(202) 512-0000 (General)

The USGPO also has copies of specific laws available for purchase. The USGPO accepts credit card orders over the phone, as well as mail orders paid by credit card, a check drawn on a U.S. bank, or an international money order.

Relevant Government Agencies

Address questions regarding FDA requirements for iron and steel products intended for use with foods to:

U.S. Food and Drug Administration
5600 Fishers Lane
Rockville, MD 20857

Address questions regarding the importation of articles of iron and steel to the district or port director of Customs for you area. For addresses refer to"U.S. Customs District Offices" on page 62 or contact:

U.S. Customs Service
1301 Constitution Ave. NW
Washington, DC 20229
(202) 927-6724 (Information)
(202) 927-1000 (General)

Laws and Regulations

Various laws and regulations may be relevant to importing. Laws are contained in the U.S. Code (USC) and regulations are published in the Code of Federal Regulations (CFR), both of which may be available in larger public and law libraries. Copies of specific laws are also available from the United States Government Printing Office (address above).

21 USC 301 et seq.
Food, Drug, and Cosmetic Act
This Act prohibits deceptive practices and regulates the manufacture, sale and importation or exportation of food, drugs, cosmetics, and related products. See 21 USC 331, 381, 382.

19 CFR 12.1 et seq.; 21 CFR 1.83 et seq.
Regulations on Food, Drugs, and Cosmetics
These regulations of the Secretary of Health and Human Services and the Secretary of the Treasury govern the standards, labeling, marking, and importing of products used with food, drugs, and cosmetics.

Principal Exporting Countries

The following listing includes samples of the main supplier nations of the products of this chapter. It is organized by HTSUS major heading. (Refer to "Customs Classification" above for the product codes.) Countries are listed in rank order of the value of products imported to the U.S. Statistics represent customs value entries for 1993 from the Bureau of Census, U.S. Department of Commerce.

7301—Luxembourg, Japan, Canada, Germany, France, United Kingdom, Belgium, Netherlands, Taiwan, Mexico

7302—Japan, Canada, Luxembourg, Germany, Austria, United Kingdom, Belgium, France, Australia, South Korea

7303—Canada, Venezuela, Israel, China, Switzerland, Belgium, Germany, Taiwan, Mexico, United Kingdom

7304—Japan, Germany, Italy, Argentina, France, Brazil, Spain, Mexico, United Kingdom, Canada

7305—Canada, Japan, Germany, Mexico, South Korea, United Kingdom, Denmark, Brazil, Austria, Czech Rep.

7306—Canada, South Korea, Japan, Mexico, South Africa, Thailand, Taiwan, Netherlands, Germany, Italy

7307—Taiwan, Japan, Italy, Canada, India, Germany, Thailand, Mexico, China, Brazil

7308—Canada, Mexico, Germany, Brazil, United Kingdom, Japan, Netherlands, Denmark, Israel, New Zealand

7309—Canada, Mexico, Japan, Germany, Italy, Finland, France, United Kingdom, Taiwan, South Korea

7310—Canada, United Kingdom, Mexico, Germany, China, Japan, Dominican Rep., Italy, Hong Kong, France

7311—Canada, Brazil, Mexico, United Kingdom, South Korea, China, Netherlands, Germany, Israel, Italy

7312—Japan, South Korea, Canada, Belgium, Italy, France, Spain, Germany, Brazil, Taiwan

7313—Brazil, Mexico, Chile, Canada, India, South Africa, France, Poland, New Zealand, Indonesia

7314—Japan, Germany, Mexico, Canada, China, South Korea, Taiwan, Switzerland, United Kingdom, Italy

7315—Japan, Taiwan, China, Germany, Canada, Italy, Sweden, France, United Kingdom, Switzerland

7316—Netherlands, Taiwan, United Kingdom, China, Belgium, Germany, Mexico, Argentina, Canada, South Korea

7317—South Korea, Canada, Taiwan, China, Japan, Switzerland, Indonesia, Spain, Germany, Mexico

7318—Taiwan, Japan, Canada, Germany, South Korea, China, Italy, United Kingdom, Switzerland, France

7319—China, Japan, Malaysia, Taiwan, Germany, United Kingdom, Hong Kong, India, South Korea, France

7320—Canada, Mexico, Japan, Germany, India, United Kingdom, China, Brazil, Switzerland, Singapore

7321—Mexico, Canada, Japan, Taiwan, China, United Kingdom, France, Spain, Austria, Brazil

7322—Canada, Japan, Mexico, Germany, China, Italy, France, United Kingdom, Sweden, Brazil

7323—Taiwan, China, South Korea, Indonesia, Mexico, Thailand, Japan, France, Hong Kong, India

7324—Taiwan, Canada, China, Italy, Mexico, Germany, South Korea, Switzerland, Sweden, Portugal

7325—India, Canada, Germany, Brazil, China, Taiwan, South Korea, United Kingdom, Austria, Mexico

7326—Canada, Taiwan, Japan, Germany, China, Mexico, South Korea, France, United Kingdom, Italy

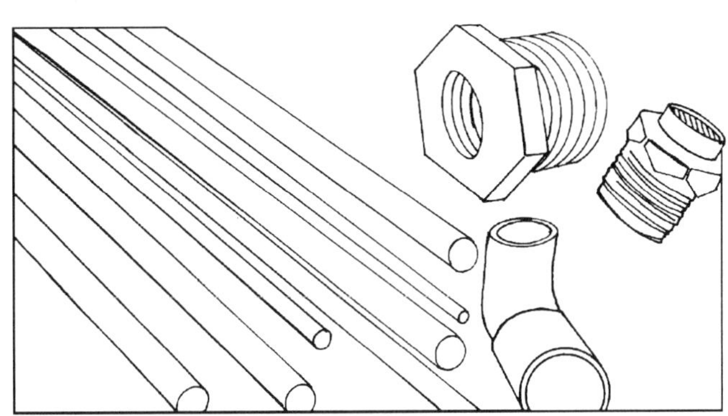

Chapter 74: Copper and Articles Thereof*

This section pertains to the importation of copper, copper alloys, and articles made from these products, which are classified within Chapter 74 of the Harmonized Tariff Schedule of the United States (HTSUS). Specifically, it includes copper mattes and other forms of unrefined copper; refined copper and copper alloys—including brass, bronze, cupro-nickel, and nickel-silver, among others; copper waste and scrap; master alloys of copper—including those of phosphorus and beryllium; powder and flakes; bars, rods, wire, plates, sheets, strips, and foil; copper tubes, pipes, and fittings; stranded wire cables; woven copper fabrics; nails and other fasteners; springs; heating apparatus; pots and other kitchen, table, and housewares; and miscellaneous articles of copper, such as chain, brass plumbing goods, and containers.

Goods of base metals in which metals other than copper predominate are covered in the Commodity Index chapters on the particular metal, including iron and steel (Chapter 72), nickel (Chapter 75), aluminum (Chapter 76), lead (Chapter 78), zinc (Chapter 79), tin (Chapter 80), and other base metals (Chapter 81). Tools, other implements, and cutlery are found in Chapter 82, while miscellaneous articles of base metals are contained in Chapter 83. Precious metals, alloys of precious metals, and articles containing the same are covered specifically in Chapter 71.

Other products for which metals are incidental—even if critical and major—components are found within a variety of Commodity Index chapters. For example, if you are interested in importing metallic paints, refer to Chapter 36. For headgear with metal elements, see Chapter 65; for umbrella frames and related items, see Chapter 66. Finished and semifinished products classified as machinery, mechanical appliances, and electrical goods are found in Chapters 84 and 85. Assembled railway track and related equipment is covered in Chapter 86, vehicles in Chapter 87, aircraft in Chapter 88, and boats in Chapter 89. Instruments and apparatus are covered in Commodity Index chapters specific to the type of article, including optical, medical, and precision instruments (Chapter 90), clocks and watches (Chapter 91), and musical instruments (Chapter 92). Metal articles as parts of firearms, including ammunition, are found in Chapter 93. Commodity Index chapters that cover miscellaneous manufactures include furniture (Chapter 94), toys, games, and sporting goods (Chapter 95), and miscellaneous manufactured articles (Chapter 96). Works of art in which copper or its alloys are components, even dominant components, are covered in Chapter 97 if the primary value derives from the artistry rather than from the metal content.

*IMPORTANT: Read the Commodity Index Introduction. It is the essential framework for understanding this chapter.

Key Factors

The key factors in importing copper and copper alloy products are:

- Compliance with U.S. Environmental Protection Agency (EPA) requirements under the Toxic Substances Control Act (TSCA) (if the product is classified as a hazardous substance)
- Compliance with U.S. Department of Transportation (DOT) regulations for transport of hazardous cargo (if the product is a hazardous substance)
- For items to be used with food, compliance with U.S. Food and Drug Administration (FDA) requirements and entry notification

Although most importers utilize the services of a licensed customs broker in making their entries, and we recommend this practice, you should be aware of the regulatory, entry, and documentation issues involved in importing your product. You, as importer, are ultimately responsible for the fulfillment of any legal requirements applicable to your shipment.

General Considerations

Regulatory Agencies. The importation of copper, copper alloys, and products made of them is relatively straightforward, with few restrictions or special requirements. The Food and Drug Administration (FDA) controls the importation of items for use with food. The Environmental Protection Agency (EPA), under authority of the Toxic Substances Control Act (TSCA), imposes certain controls on the importation of copper and copper articles that contain toxic substances. The Department of Transportation (DOT) enforces regulations for transporting hazardous cargo.

Definitions. Unlike alloys of precious metals, in which any alloy having as much as 2% of a precious metal is considered an alloy of that metal, alloys of base metals are classified according to the metal that predominates by weight over every other individual metal in the alloy. For customs purposes, alloys of a metal are included with the metal that they are an alloy of.

Chapter 74 of HTSUS covers copper and copper alloys. Refined copper is defined as metal containing at least 99.85% by weight of copper or metal containing at least 97.5% by weight of copper, provided that the content by weight of any other element does not exceed specified limits as set out in the notes to the chapter. Copper alloys are defined as being metallic substances other than unrefined copper in which copper predominates by weight over each of the other elements, provided that the content by weight of at least one of the other elements is greater than the limit specified in the notes to HTSUS Chapter 74 or the total content by weight of such other elements exceeds 2.5%. There are also specific definitions for copper-zinc base alloys (brass), copper-tin base alloys (bronze), copper-nickel-zinc base alloys (nickel silver) and copper-nickel (cupro-nickel) base alloys.

FDA Regulations. Kitchenware and tableware of copper and its alloys intended for use with food are subject to the provisions of the Federal Food, Drug, and Cosmetic Act (FDCA) enforced by the FDA. FDA entry notification is required for applicable items. Shipments of FDA-regulated products are subject to FDA port of entry inspection. You must file an FDA Importers Entry Notice, **Form FD701**, with each shipment. For more information, see the annotated diagram of FDA entry procedures and requirements in the "Foods" appendix on page 808. Contact your nearest regional FDA office or FDA headquarters with questions regarding the importation of food-related copper products (see addresses at end of this chapter).

Hazardous Substances Regulations. The EPA imposes certain controls on the importation of toxic substances. The TSCA defines a toxic substance as any substance determined to present the possibility of an unreasonable risk of injury to health and the environment. The DOT enforces regulations for transporting hazardous cargo. Substances are deemed hazardous if listed in DOT transport regulations (49 CFR 172 appendix). Unwrought primary metals, such as pigs, ingots, billets, blooms, and similar materials, are generally categorized as toxic substances within the definitions of the TSCA and thus are required to be in compliance with its provisions. These include packaging, shipping, marking, and labeling requirements. Refer to "Laws and Regulations" below.

Products defined as articles—that is, any manufactured item 1) that is formed into a specific shape or design during manufacture, 2) that has end-use functions dependent on the shape or design during end use, and 3) that during the end use, does not change in its chemical composition or that changes only for a noncommercial purpose separate from the article and only as allowed by law (19 CFR 12.120(2))—are not subject to the provisions of the TSCA. Metal products other than primary metals are generally considered to be articles even if they are to be further processed. For example, copper in sheets is an article even if it is to be subsequently fabricated into other products.

Certification. All products covered by the TSCA are subject to the U.S. Customs Service TSCA Import Certification Rule (19 CFR 12.118 et seq.). If you import these products, you must sign one of the following statements: "I certify that all materials in this shipment comply with all applicable rules or orders under TSCA and that I am not offering a chemical substance for entry in violation of TSCA or any applicable rule or order thereunder" or "I certify that all materials in this shipment are not subject to TSCA." You must file this TSCA certification of compliance or exemption at the time you make the entry at customs. Customs will not release your shipment without proper certification.

If you will be importing several or regular shipments, you should ask the appropriate Customs district director to authorize your use of a blanket certification. A blanket certification is valid for one calendar year, may be renewed, and may be revoked at any time for cause.

Customs Classification

For customs purposes, copper, copper alloys, and their products are classified within Chapter 74 of the HTSUS. This chapter is divided into headings, which are further divided into subheadings, and often into sub-subheadings, each of which has its own HTSUS classification number. For example, the HTSUS number for low fuming brazing rods of copper is 7407.21.50, indicating that it is a subcategory of rods of copper alloys (7407.21.00), which is a subsubcategory of the major heading copper bars, rods, and profiles (7407.00.00). There are 19 major headings in HTSUS Chapter 74.

7401—Copper mattes; cement copper (precipitated copper)

7402—Unrefined copper; copper anodes for electrolytic refining

7403—Refined copper and copper alloys, unwrought (other than master alloys of heading 7405)

7404—Copper waste and scrap

7405—Master alloys of copper

7406—Copper powders and flakes

7407—Copper bars, rods, and profiles

7408—Copper wire

7409—Copper plates, sheets, and strips, of a thickness exceeding 0.15 mm.

7410—Copper foil (whether or not printed or backed with paper, paperboard, plastics, or similar backing materials) of a thickness (excluding any backing) not exceeding 0.15 mm.

7411—Copper tubes and pipes

7412—Copper tube or pipe fittings (for example couplings, elbows, sleeves)

7413—Stranded wire cables, plaited bands, and the like, including slings and similar articles, of copper, not electrically insulated

7414—Cloth (including endless bands), grill, and netting, of copper wire; expanded metal of copper

7415—Nails, tacks, drawing pins, staples (other than those of heading 8305), and similar articles of copper or of iron or steel with heads of copper; screws, bolts, nuts, screw hooks, rivets, cotters, cotter pins, washers (including spring washers), and similar articles of copper

7416—Copper springs

7417—Cooking or heating apparatus of a kind used for domestic purposes, non-electric, and parts thereof, of copper

7418—Table, kitchen, or other household articles and parts thereof, of copper; pot scourers and scouring or polishing pads, gloves, and the like, of copper; sanitary ware and parts thereof, of copper

7419—Other articles of copper

For more details regarding classification of the specific product you are interested in importing, consult a customs broker, the appropriate commodity specialist at your nearest customs port, or see HTSUS. HTSUS is available for purchase from the U.S. Government Printing Office (see addresses at end of this chapter), and may be found in larger public libraries. Refer to "Classification—Liquidation" on page 207 for a general discussion of customs classification.

Sample Import Duties

Import duties will vary depending on the HTSUS classification of your product. Therefore, to determine the correct amount of duties, your product must be properly classified under the HTSUS. The following sample duties are taken from the duty listings for HTSUS Chapter 74 products.

Copper mattes (7401.10.00): 0.7 cents/kg on copper content + 0.7 cents/kg on lead content; precipitated copper (copper cement) (7401.20.00): 1.7% on the value of the copper content; copper anodes for electrolytic refining (7402.0.00): 1% on the value of the copper content; refined copper billets (7403.12.00): 1%; copper-zinc alloys (brass) (7403.21.00): 1%; copper-tin alloys (bronze) (7403.22.00): 1%; spent anodes and other copper waste and scrap of a copper content of less than 94% by weight (7404.00.30): free; master alloys of copper containing by weight 5% or more but not more than 15% of phosphorus (7405.00.10): 2.6%; powders of copper of lamellar structure or flakes (7406.20.00): 3%; copper bars and rods (7407.100.00): 1%; brass hollow profiles (7407.21.15): 3.2%; low fuming brazing rods (7407.21.50): 2.2%; other (not hollow) profiles of nickel-silver (copper-nickel-zinc alloy) (7407.22.30): 6.3%; refined copper wire of a diameter greater than 9.5 mm (7408.11.30): 1%; wire of cupro-nickel alloy, coated or plated (7408.22.10): 4.4%; copper plates of a thickness of 5 mm or more (7409.19.10): 4.7%; copper sheets of beryllium copper of a thickness of 5 mm or more (7409.90.10): 5.1%; unbacked refined copper foil (7410.11.00): 1%; seamless refined copper tubes (7411.10.10): 1.5%; copper alloy tube or pipe fittings (7412.20.00): 3.2%; stranded copper wire (7413.00.10): 4.9%; endless bands for machinery with 94 or more wires to the lineal centimeter (7414.10.30): free; nails and tacks (7415.10.00): 5.1%; wood screws (7415.31.00): 5.5%; copper springs (7416.00.00): 5.7%; copper cooking apparatus (7417.00.00): 4.2%; brass cookware (7418.10.20): 3.7%; other copper cookware (7418.10.20): 4.9%; brass cast, molded, and stamped plumbing goods (7419.91.00): 5%.

Entry and Documentation

The entry of merchandise is a two-part process consisting of 1) filing the documents necessary to determine whether merchandise may be released from Customs custody and 2) filing the documents that contain information for duty assessment and statistical purposes. In certain instances all documents must be filed and accepted by Customs prior to the release of the goods. Unless you have been granted an extension, you must file entry documents at a location specified by the district or area director within five working days of your shipment's date of arrival at a U.S. port of entry. These include a number of standard documents required by Customs for any entry, and

- For copper and copper alloy items intended for use with food: FDA Importers Entry Notice: **Form FD701**
- U.S. Customs TSCA Certification when required

After you present the entry, Customs may examine your shipment, or may waive examination. The shipment is then released provided no legal or regulatory violations have been noted. You must then file entry summary documentation and deposit estimated duties at a designated customhouse within 10 working days of your shipment's release. For a detailed description of entry procedures, standard documentation, and informal entry, see "Entry Process" on page 182.

Entry Invoice. For articles of copper entered under HTSUS Heading 7401, the entry invoice must state the percentage—by weight—of copper content and of any other metallic elements.

Marking and Labeling Requirements

For a general discussion of U.S. Customs marking and labeling requirements, see "Marking: Country of Origin" on page 215 and "Special Marking Requirements" on page 217.

Shipping Considerations

You will need to ensure that your goods are packaged and shipped with care to ensure that they arrive in good condition and pass smoothly through Customs. You are responsible for ensuring that the shipment is in compliance with all applicable government regulations for packaging and shipping. In most instances, you should not leave these arrangements solely to the discretion of your supplier. Careful preparation of the cargo and selection of the mode of transport can be essential to a cost-effective, timely delivery of undamaged goods. We strongly advise you to consult your shipping representative, insurance agent, or freight broker for advice on packing and shipping. Refer also to the major tab section "Packing/Shipping/Insurance" for a general discussion of packing and shipping.

Products that are listed as hazardous substances (49 CFR 172 appendix) may be transported in bulk only on compliance with Coast Guard notification procedures, shipping permit requirements, and complex transportation regulations (46 CFR 148). All hazardous substances must be packaged and transported in accordance with DOT regulations (49 CFR 171 et seq.).

Copper, copper alloys, and products made of them are often bulky and heavy, and should be securely stowed to avoid damage due to shifting en route. Copper and its products are also subject to tarnish and corrosion, which should be guarded against, especially as no allowance is made by customs for partial damage or loss due to such.

Publications Available

The *Harmonized Tariff Schedule of the United States* (HTSUS) is available from:

Government Printing Office (GPO)
Superintendent of Documents
Washington, DC 20402
(202) 512-1800 (Order line)
(202) 512-0000 (General)

The USGPO also has copies of specific laws available for purchase. The USGPO accepts credit card orders over the phone, as well as mail orders paid by credit card, a check drawn on a U.S. bank, or an international money order.

Relevant Government Agencies

Address inquiries regarding TSCA and EPA requirements for importation of hazardous or toxic substances to:

Environmental Protection Agency (EPA)
TSCA System Information
EPA 7408, OPPT
401 M Street SW
Washington, DC 20460
(202) 554-1404 (TSCA Information Hotline)

Address questions regarding transportation of hazardous substances to:

U.S. Department of Transportation (DOT)
Research and Special Programs Administration
Office of Hazardous Materials Standards
400 7th St. SW
Washington, DC 20590
(202) 366-4488

Address your questions regarding FDA requirements for copper products intended for use with food to:

Food and Drug Administration (FDA)
Center for Food Safety and Applied Nutrition
200 C Street SW
Washington, DC 20204
(202) 205-5241, 205-5042

Address questions regarding the importation of copper and copper products to the district or port director of Customs for you area. For addresses refer to "U.S. Customs District Offices" on page 62 or contact:

U.S. Customs Service
1301 Constitution Ave. NW
Washington, DC 20229
(202) 927-6724 (Information)
(202) 927-1000 (General)

Laws and Regulations

The following laws and regulations may be relevant to the importation of copper and copper products. The laws are contained in the U.S. Code (USC) and the regulations are published in the Code of Federal Regulations (CFR), both of which may be available at larger public and law libraries. Copies of specific laws are also available from the United States Government Printing Office (address above).

15 USC 2601 et seq.
Toxic Substances Control Act
This Act authorizes the EPA to determine whether a substance is harmful and to restrict importation, sale, and use of such substances.

19 CFR 12.118 et seq.
Regulations on Toxic Substances Control
These regulations require importers of chemical substances imported in bulk or as part of a mixture to certify to Customs that the shipment complies with the TSCA or is not subject to that Act.

15 USC 1261
Federal Hazardous Substances Act
This Act controls the importation of hazardous substances, sets forth prohibited imports, and authorizes various agencies to promulgate labeling, marking, and transport requirements.

49 CFR 170 et seq.
Regulations on Hazardous Materials
These regulations list all substances deemed hazardous and provide transport, marking, labeling, safety, and emergency response rules.

46 CFR 147.30
Regulations on Labeling of Hazardous Materials

This regulation requires the labeling of containers of hazardous substances and specifies the label contents.

46 CFR 148 et seq.
Regulations of Carriage of Solid Hazardous Materials in Bulk
These regulations govern the transport of solid hazardous substances in bulk, including reporting, permitting, loading, stowing, and shipping requirements.

21 USC 301 et seq.
Food, Drug, and Cosmetic Act
This Act prohibits deceptive practices and regulates the manufacture, sale and importation or exportation of food, drugs, cosmetics, and related products. See 21 USC 331, 381, 382.

19 CFR 12.1 et seq.; 21 CFR 1.83 et seq.
Regulations on Food, Drugs, and Cosmetics
These regulations of the Secretary of Health and Human Services and the Secretary of the Treasury govern the standards, labeling, marking, and importing of products used with food, drugs, and cosmetics.

Principal Exporting Countries

The following listing includes samples of the main supplier nations of the products of this chapter. It is organized by HTSUS major heading. (Refer to "Customs Classification" above for the product codes.) Countries are listed in rank order of the value of products imported to the U.S. Statistics represent customs value entries for 1993 from the Bureau of Census, U.S. Department of Commerce.

7401—Chile, Mexico, Bolivia, Japan

7402—Mexico, Chile, Peru, Bulgaria, Indonesia, Zaire, Russia, South Africa, Spain, Hong Kong

7403—Canada, Chile, Zaire, Peru, Germany, Mexico, Netherlands, Japan, United Kingdom, Kazakhstan

7404—Canada, Mexico, Spain, United Kingdom, Germany, Venezuela, Chile, Finland, Sweden, Dominican Rep.

7405—United Kingdom, China, Russia, Hong Kong, Belgium, South Africa, Mexico, Germany

7406—Germany, United Kingdom, France, Japan, Belgium, Brazil, Canada, Italy, Mexico, Israel

7407—Germany, Japan, Canada, France, Netherlands, Poland, Brazil, Switzerland, United Kingdom, Finland

7408—Canada, Germany, Japan, Mexico, Israel, Poland, France, Finland, Netherlands, United Kingdom

7409—Japan, Germany, Canada, Mexico, Switzerland, Hungary, Finland, Chile, Poland, Brazil

7410—Taiwan, Japan, Sweden, Netherlands, Canada, Luxembourg, United Kingdom, Germany, Singapore, Belgium

7411—Mexico, Germany, Canada, Japan, France, Malaysia, United Kingdom, Chile, Hungary, Brazil

7412—Canada, Thailand, Taiwan, United Kingdom, Italy, China, Mexico, Japan, Brazil, France

7413—Canada, Turkey, Japan, Italy, France, Mexico, Venezuela, Taiwan, Germany, United Kingdom

7414—Germany, Japan, China, France, Taiwan, Mexico, United Kingdom, Hong Kong, Netherlands, South Korea

7415—Taiwan, Japan, Switzerland, Germany, Hong Kong, Canada, United Kingdom, China, Italy, Poland

7416—Barbados, Italy, Germany, Portugal, Greece, Taiwan, Japan, France, Canada, Switzerland

7417—Japan, United Kingdom, Taiwan, France, South Korea, Spain, Belgium, Portugal, Germany, Hong Kong

7418—Taiwan, India, China, Thailand, South Korea, Germany, Italy, Mexico, Hong Kong, Indonesia

7419—Taiwan, India, China, Canada, Germany, Italy, Hong Kong, Japan, Thailand, South Korea

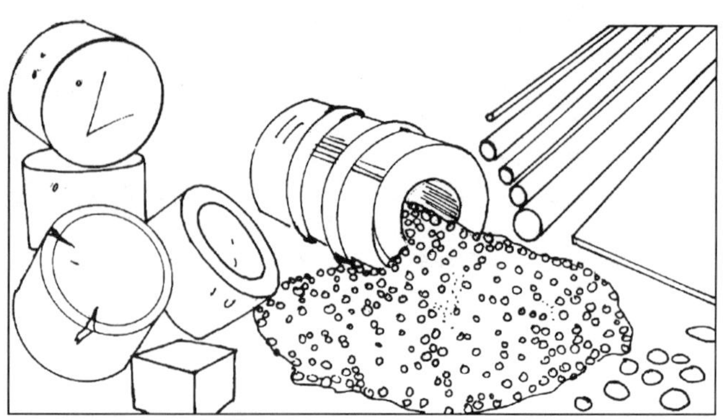

Chapter 75: Nickel and Articles Thereof*

This section pertains to the importation of nickel, nickel alloys, and articles made from these products, which are classified within Chapter 75 of the Harmonized Tariff Schedule of the United States (HTSUS). Specifically, it includes nickel mattes and other intermediate forms of nickel; unwrought nickel and nickel alloys; nickel waste and scrap; powder and flakes; bars, rods, profiles, wire, plates, sheets, strips, and foil; nickel tubes, pipes, and fittings; and other miscellaneous articles of nickel.

Goods of base metals and their alloys in which metals other than nickel predominate are covered in Commodity Index chapters on the specific metals, including iron and steel (Chapter 72), copper (Chapter 74), aluminum (Chapter 76), lead (Chapter 78), zinc (Chapter 79), tin (Chapter 80), and other base metals (Chapter 81). Tools, other implements, and cutlery are found in Chapter 82, while miscellaneous articles of base metals are contained in Chapter 83. Precious metals, alloys of precious metals, and articles containing the same are covered specifically in Chapter 71.

Other products for which metals are incidental—even if critical and major—components are found within a variety of Commodity Index chapters. For example, if you are interested in importing metallic paints, refer to Chapter 36. For headgear with metal elements, see Chapter 65; for umbrella frames and related items, see Chapter 66. Finished and semifinished products classified as machinery, mechanical appliances, and electrical goods are found in Chapters 84 and 85. Assembled railway track and related equipment is covered in chapter 86, vehicles in Chapter 87, aircraft in Chapter 88, and boats in Chapter 89. Instruments and apparatus are covered in Commodity Index chapters related to the specific articles, including optical, medical, and precision instruments (Chapter 90), clocks and watches (Chapter 91), and musical instruments (Chapter 92). Metal articles as parts of firearms, including ammunition, are found in Chapter 93. Commodity Index chapters that cover miscellaneous manufactures include furniture (Chapter 94), toys, games, and sporting goods (Chapter 95), and miscellaneous manufactured articles (Chapter 96). Works of art in which nickel or its alloys are components, even dominant components, are covered in Chapter 97 if the primary value derives from the artistry rather than from the metal content.

Key Factors

The key factors in importing nickel and nickel alloy products are:

- Compliance with U.S. Environmental Protection

*__IMPORTANT__: Read the Commodity Index Introduction. It is the essential framework for understanding this chapter.

Agency (EPA) requirements under the Toxic Substances Control Act (TSCA) (if the product is classified as a hazardous substance)

- Compliance with U.S. Department of Transportation (DOT) regulations for transport of hazardous cargo (if the product is a hazardous substance)

Although most importers utilize the services of a licensed customs broker in making their entries, and we recommend this practice, you should be aware of the regulatory, entry, and documentation issues involved in importing your product. You, as importer, are ultimately responsible for the fulfillment of any legal requirements applicable to your shipment.

General Considerations

Regulatory Agencies. The importation of nickel, nickel alloys, and products made of them is relatively straightforward, with few restrictions or special requirements. The Environmental Protection Agency (EPA), under authority of the Toxic Substances Control Act (TSCA), imposes certain controls on the importation of nickel and nickel articles that contain toxic substances. The Department of Transportation (DOT) enforces regulations for transporting hazardous cargo.

Definitions. Unlike alloys of precious metals, in which any alloy containing as much as 2% by weight of a precious metal is considered an alloy of that metal, alloys of base metals are classified according to the metal that predominates by weight over every other individual metal in the alloy. For customs purposes, alloys of a metal are included with the metal that they are an alloy of.

Chapter 75 of HTSUS covers nickel and nickel alloys. Nickel is defined as metal containing at least 99% by weight of nickel plus cobalt, provided the cobalt content does not exceed 1.5% by weight and the content by weight is less than 0.5% for iron, 0.4% for oxygen, and 0.3% individually for any other elements. Nickel alloys are defined as being metallic substances in which nickel predominates by weight, provided that the content by weight of cobalt exceeds 1.5%, the content of at least one of the other elements is greater than the limit specified above, or the total content by weight of such other elements other than nickel and cobalt exceeds 1%.

Hazardous Substances Regulations. The EPA imposes certain controls on the importation of toxic substances. The TSCA defines a toxic substance as any substance determined to present the possibility of an unreasonable risk of injury to health and the environment. The DOT enforces regulations for transporting hazardous cargo. Substances are deemed hazardous if listed in DOT transport regulations (49 CFR 172 appendix). Unwrought primary metals, such as pigs, ingots, billets, blooms, and similar materials, are generally categorized as toxic substances within the definitions of the TSCA and thus are required to be in compliance with its provisions. These include packaging, shipping, marking, and labeling requirements. Refer to "Laws and Regulations" below.

Products defined as articles—that is, any manufactured item 1) that is formed into a specific shape or design during manufacture, 2) that has end-use functions dependent on the shape or design during end use, and 3) that during the end use, does not change in its chemical composition or that changes only for a noncommercial purpose separate from the article and only as allowed by law (19 CFR 12.120(2))—are not subject to the provisions of the TSCA. Metal products other than primary metals are generally considered to be articles even if they are to be further processed. For example, nickel in bars is an article even if it is to be subsequently fabricated into other products.

Certification. All products covered by the TSCA are subject to the U.S. Customs Service TSCA Import Certification Rule (19 CFR 12.118 et seq.). If you import these products, you must sign one of the following statements: "I certify that all materials in this shipment comply with all applicable rules or orders under TSCA and that I am not offering a chemical substance for entry in violation of TSCA or any applicable rule or order thereunder" or "I certify that all materials in this shipment are not subject to TSCA." You must file this TSCA certification of compliance or exemption at the time you make the entry at customs. Customs will not release your shipment without proper certification.

If you will be importing several or regular shipments, you should ask the appropriate customs district director to authorize your use of a blanket certification. A blanket certification is valid for one calendar year, may be renewed, and may be revoked at any time for cause.

Customs Classification

For customs purposes, nickel, nickel alloys, and their products are classified within Chapter 75 of the HTSUS. This chapter is divided into headings, which are further divided into subheadings, and often into sub-subheadings, each of which has its own HTSUS classification number. For example, the HTSUS number for cold-formed bars is 7505.12.10, indicating that it is a subcategory of bars and rods of nickel alloy (7405.12.00), which is a subsubcategory of the major heading nickel bars, rods, profiles, and wire (7405.00.00). There are eight major headings in HTSUS Chapter 75.

7501—Nickel mattes, nickel oxide sinters, and other intermediate products of nickel metallurgy

7502—Unwrought nickel

7503—Nickel waste and scrap

7504—Nickel powders and waste

7505—Nickel bars, rods, profiles, and wire

7506—Nickel plates, sheets, strip, and foil

7507—Nickel tubes, pipes, and tube or pipe fittings

7508—Other

For more details regarding classification of the specific product you are interested in importing, consult a customs broker, the appropriate commodity specialist at your nearest customs port, or see HTSUS. HTSUS is available for purchase from the U.S. Government Printing Office (see addresses at end of this chapter), and may be found in larger public libraries. Refer to "Classification—Liquidation" on page 207 for a general discussion of customs classification.

Sample Import Duties

Import duties will vary depending on the HTSUS classification of your product. Therefore, to determine the correct amount of duties, your product must be properly classified under the HTSUS. The following sample duties are taken from the duty listings for HTSUS Chapter 75 products.

Nickel mattes (7501.10.00): free; unwrought nickel (7502.10.00): free; unwrought nickel alloys (7502.10.00): free; nickel waste and scrap (7503.00.00): free; nickel powders and flakes (7504.00.00): free; cold-formed bars and rods of unalloyed nickel (7505.11.10): 4.7%; profiles (7505.11.50): 5.5%; bars and rods of nickel alloy, not cold-formed (7505.12.30): 3.7%; cold-formed nickel alloy wire (7505.22.1): 4.7%; cold-formed unalloyed nickel plates, sheets, and strips (7506.10.10): 4.7%; nickel foil not over 1.5 mm in thickness (7506.10.45): 3.6%; nickel alloy tubes and pipes (7507.12.00): 3%; nickel tube or pipe fittings (7507.20.00): 3.6%; stranded nickel wire (7508.00.10): 4.7%.

Entry and Documentation

The entry of merchandise is a two-part process consisting of 1) filing the documents necessary to determine whether merchandise may be released from Customs custody and 2) filing the documents that contain information for duty assessment and statistical purposes. In certain instances all documents must be filed and accepted by Customs prior to the release of the goods. Unless you have been granted an extension, you must file entry documents at a location specified by the district/area director within five working days of your shipment's date of arrival at a U.S. port of entry. These include a number of standard documents required by Customs for any entry, and

- U.S. Customs TSCA Certification, if required

After you present the entry, Customs may examine your shipment, or may waive examination. The shipment is then released provided no legal or regulatory violations have been noted. You must then file entry summary documentation and deposit estimated duties at a designated customhouse within 10 working days of your shipment's release. For a detailed description of entry procedures, standard documentation, and informal entry, see "Entry Process" on page 182.

Marking and Labeling Requirements

For a general discussion of U.S. Customs marking and labeling requirements, see "Marking: Country of Origin" on page 215 and "Special Marking Requirements" on page 217.

Shipping Considerations

You will need to ensure that your goods are packaged and shipped with care to ensure that they arrive in good condition and pass smoothly through Customs. You are responsible for ensuring that the shipment is in compliance with all applicable government regulations for packaging and shipping. In most instances, you should not leave these arrangements solely to the discretion of your supplier. Careful preparation of the cargo and selection of the mode of transport can be essential to a cost-effective, timely delivery of undamaged goods. We strongly advise you to consult your shipping representative, insurance agent, or freight broker for advice on packing and shipping. Refer also to the major tab section "Packing/Shipping/Insurance" for a general discussion of packing and shipping.

Products that are listed as hazardous substances (49 CFR 172 appendix) may be transported in bulk only on compliance with Coast Guard notification procedures, shipping permit requirements, and complex transportation regulations (46 CFR 148). All hazardous substances must be packaged and transported in accordance with DOT regulations (49 CFR 171 et seq.).

Nickel, nickel alloy, and products made of them are often bulky and heavy, and should be securely stowed to avoid damage due to shifting en route. Nickel and its products are also subject to tarnish and corrosion, which should be guarded against, especially as no allowance is made by customs for partial damage or loss due to such.

Publications Available

The *Harmonized Tariff Schedule of the United States* (HTSUS) is available from:

Government Printing Office (GPO)
Superintendent of Documents
Washington, DC 20402
(202) 512-1800 (Order line)
(202) 512-0000 (General)

The USGPO also has copies of specific laws available for purchase. The USGPO accepts credit card orders over the phone, as well as mail orders paid by credit card, a check drawn on a U.S. bank, or an international money order.

Relevant Government Agencies

Address inquiries regarding TSCA and EPA requirements for importation of hazardous or toxic substances to:

Environmental Protection Agency (EPA)
TSCA System Information
EPA 7408, OPPT
401 M Street SW
Washington, DC 20460
(202) 554-1404 (TSCA Information Hotline)

Address questions regarding transportation of hazardous substances to:

U.S. Department of Transportation (DOT)
Research and Special Programs Administration
Office of Hazardous Materials Standards
400 7th St. SW
Washington, DC 20590
(202) 366-4488

Address questions regarding the importation of nickel and nickel products to the district or port director of Customs for you area. For addresses refer to "U.S. Customs District Offices" on page 62 or contact:

U.S. Customs Service
1301 Constitution Ave. NW
Washington, DC 20229
(202) 927-6724 (Information)
(202) 927-1000 (General)

Laws and Regulations

The following laws and regulations may be relevant to the importation of nickel and nickel products. The laws are contained in the U.S. Code (USC) and the regulations are published in the Code of Federal Regulations (CFR), both of which may be available at larger public and law libraries. Copies of specific laws are also available from the United States Government Printing Office (address above).

15 USC 2601 et seq.
Toxic Substances Control Act
This Act authorizes the EPA to determine whether a substance is harmful and to restrict importation, sale, and use of such substances.

19 CFR 12.118 et seq.
Regulations on Toxic Substances Control
These regulations require importers of chemical substances imported in bulk or as part of a mixture to certify to Customs that the shipment complies with the TSCA or is not subject to that Act.

15 USC 1261
Federal Hazardous Substances Act
This Act controls the importation of hazardous substances, sets forth prohibited imports, and authorizes various agencies to promulgate labeling, marking, and transport requirements.

49 CFR 170 et seq.
Regulations on Hazardous Materials
These regulations list all substances deemed hazardous and provide transport, marking, labeling, safety, and emergency response rules.

46 CFR 147.30
Regulations on Labeling of Hazardous Materials
This regulation requires the labeling of containers of hazardous substances and specifies the label contents.

46 CFR 148 et seq.
Regulations of Carriage of Solid Hazardous Materials in Bulk
These regulations govern the transport of solid hazardous substances in bulk, including reporting, permitting, loading, stowing, and shipping requirements.

Principal Exporting Countries

The following listing includes samples of the main supplier nations of the products of this chapter. It is organized by HTSUS major heading. (Refer to "Customs Classification" above for the product codes.) Countries are listed in rank order of the value of products imported to the U.S. Statistics represent customs value entries for 1993 from the Bureau of Census, U.S. Department of Commerce.

7501—Australia, Canada, United Kingdom, France, Germany

7502—Canada, Norway, Australia, Russia, South Africa, Finland, Zimbabwe, France, Brazil, United Kingdom

7503—Canada, United Kingdom, South Africa, France, Germany, Finland, Netherlands, Saudi Arabia, Trinidad and Tobago, Norway

7504—Canada, Australia, Austria, South Africa, United Kingdom, Israel, Germany, Sweden, Russia, Netherlands

7505—Germany, France, Sweden, United Kingdom, Italy, Brazil, Japan, China, Canada, Hong Kong

7506—Germany, Japan, Canada, United Kingdom, Sweden, France, Switzerland, Mexico, Israel, Singapore

7507—Sweden, Germany, Japan, Canada, United Kingdom, Finland, Italy, France, Switzerland, Ireland

7508—United Kingdom, Japan, Canada, France, Germany, Taiwan, Spain, Mexico, Netherlands, Indonesia

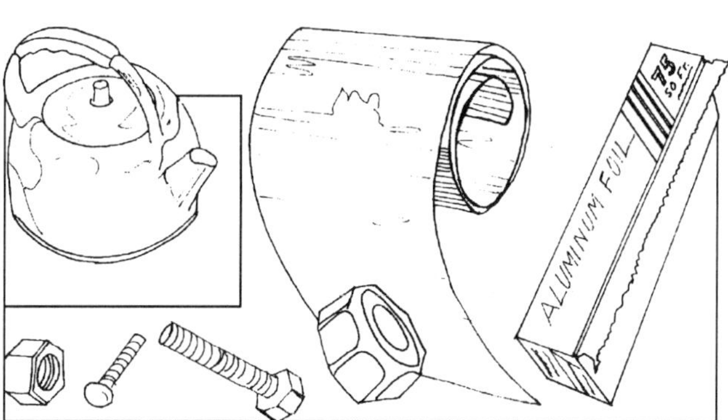

Chapter 76: Aluminium and Articles Thereof*

This section pertains to the importation of aluminum, aluminum alloys, and articles made from these products, which are classified within Chapter 76 of the Harmonized Tariff Schedule of the United States (HTSUS). Specifically, it includes unwrought aluminum; aluminum waste and scrap; powder and flakes; bars, rods, wire, plates, sheets, strips, and foil; aluminum tubes, pipes, and fittings; aluminum structural elements, reservoirs, and tanks; aluminum containers, including those for pressurized gases; stranded wire cables; tableware, kitchenware, and other household articles; aluminum hardware; and miscellaneous articles of aluminum, such as ladders, venetian blinds, pipe hangars, and castings.

Goods of base metals in which metals other than aluminum predominate are covered in Commodity Index chapters specific to the type of metal, including iron and steel (Chapter 72), copper (Chapter 74), nickel (Chapter 75), lead (Chapter 78), zinc (Chapter 79), tin (Chapter 80), and other base metals (Chapter 81). Tools, other implements, and cutlery are found in Chapter 82, while miscellaneous articles of base metals are contained in Chapter 83. Precious metals, alloys of precious metals, and articles containing the same are covered specifically in Chapter 71.

Other products for which metals are incidental—even if critical and major—components are found within a variety of Commodity Index chapters. For example, if you are interested in importing metallic paints, refer to Chapter 36. For headgear with metal elements, see Chapter 65; for umbrella frames and related items, see Chapter 66. Finished and semifinished products classified as machinery, mechanical appliances, and electrical goods are found in Chapters 84 and 85. Assembled railway track and related equipment is covered in Chapter 86, vehicles in Chapter 87, aircraft in Chapter 88, and boats in Chapter 89. Instruments and apparatus are covered in Commodity Index chapters covering specific items, including optical, medical, and precision instruments (Chapter 90), clocks and watches (Chapter 91), and musical instruments (Chapter 92). Metal articles as parts of firearms, including ammunition, are found in Chapter 93. Chapters that cover miscellaneous manufactures include furniture (Chapter 94), toys, games, and sporting goods (Chapter 95), and miscellaneous manufactured articles (Chapter 96). Works of art in which aluminum or its alloys are components, even dominant components, are covered in Chapter 97 if the primary value derives from the artistry rather than from the metal content.

*IMPORTANT: Read the Commodity Index Introduction. It is the essential framework for understanding this chapter.

Key Factors

The key factors in importing aluminum and aluminum alloy products are:

- Compliance with U.S. Environmental Protection Agency (EPA) requirements under the Toxic Substances Control Act (TSCA) (if the product is classified as a hazardous substance)
- Compliance with U.S. Department of Transportation (DOT) regulations for transport of hazardous cargo (if the product is a hazardous substance)
- Classification of alloy
- For items to be used with food, compliance with U.S. Food and Drug Administration (FDA) requirements and entry notification

Although most importers utilize the services of a licensed customs broker in making their entries, and we recommend this practice, you should be aware of the regulatory, entry, and documentation issues involved in importing your product. You, as importer, are ultimately responsible for the fulfillment of any legal requirements applicable to your shipment.

General Considerations

Regulatory Agencies. The importation of aluminum, aluminum alloys, and products made of them is relatively straightforward, with few restrictions or special requirements. The Food and Drug Administration (FDA) controls the importation of items for use with food. The Environmental Protection Agency (EPA), under authority of the Toxic Substances Control Act (TSCA), imposes certain controls on the importation of aluminum and aluminum articles that contain toxic substances. The Department of Transportation (DOT) enforces regulations for transporting hazardous cargo.

Definitions. Unlike alloys of precious metals, in which any alloy having as much as 2% of a precious metal is considered an alloy of that metal, alloys of base metals are classified according to the metal that predominates by weight over every other individual metal in the alloy. For customs purposes, alloys of a metal are included with the metal that they are an alloy of.

Chapter 76 of HTSUS covers aluminum and aluminum alloys. Aluminum is defined as metal containing at least 99% by weight of aluminum provided that the content by weight of iron plus silicon does not exceed 1%, and that the content of other elements is limited to no more than 0.1% for any given element. Copper is permitted at levels of between 0.1% and 0.2%, provided that neither the chromium nor the manganese content exceeds 0.05%. Aluminum alloys are defined as being metallic substances in which aluminum predominates by weight over each of the other elements, provided that the content by weight of at least one of the other elements is greater than the limit specified in the notes to HTSUS Chapter 76 or the total content by weight of such other elements exceeds 1%. Aluminum vanadium master alloy is also defined as an aluminum alloy that contains more than 20% vanadium by weight.

FDA Regulation. Kitchenware and tableware of aluminum and its alloys intended for use with food are subject to the provisions of the Federal Food, Drug, and Cosmetic Act (FDCA) enforced by the FDA. FDA entry notification is required for applicable items. Shipments of FDA-regulated products are subject to FDA port of entry inspection. You must file an FDA Importers Entry Notice, **Form FD701**, with each shipment. For more information, see the annotated diagram of FDA entry procedures and requirements in the "Foods" appendix on page 808. Contact your nearest regional FDA office or FDA headquarters with questions regarding the importation of aluminum products (see addresses at end of this chapter).

Hazardous Substances Regulations. The EPA imposes certain controls on the importation of toxic substances. The TSCA defines a toxic substance as any substance determined to present the possibility of an unreasonable risk of injury to health and the environment. The DOT enforces regulations for transporting hazardous cargo. Substances are deemed hazardous if listed in DOT transport regulations (49 CFR 172 appendix). Unwrought primary metals, such as pigs, ingots, billets, blooms, and similar materials, are generally categorized as toxic substances within the definitions of the TSCA and thus are required to be in compliance with its provisions. These include packaging, shipping, marking, and labeling requirements. Refer to "Laws and Regulations" below.

Products defined as articles—that is, any manufactured item 1) that is formed into a specific shape or design during manufacture, 2) that has end-use functions dependent on the shape or design during end use, and 3) that during the end use, does not change in its chemical composition or that changes only for a noncommercial purpose separate from the article and only as allowed by law (19 CFR 12.120(2))—are not subject to the provisions of the TSCA. Metal products other than primary metals are generally considered to be articles even if they are to be further processed. For example, copper in sheets is an article even if it is to be subsequently fabricated into other products.

Certification. All products covered by the TSCA are subject to the U.S. Customs Service TSCA Import Certification Rule (19 CFR 12.118 et seq.). If you import these products, you must sign one of the following statements: "I certify that all materials in this shipment comply with all applicable rules or orders under TSCA and that I am not offering a chemical substance for entry in violation of TSCA or any applicable rule or order thereunder" or "I certify that all materials in this shipment are not subject to TSCA." You must file this TSCA certification of compliance or exemption at the time you make the entry at customs. Customs will not release your shipment without proper certification.

If you will be importing several or regular shipments, you should ask the appropriate Customs district director to authorize your use of a blanket certification. A blanket certification is valid for one calendar year, may be renewed, and may be revoked at any time for cause.

Customs Classification

For customs purposes, aluminum and aluminum products are classified within Chapter 76 of the HTSUS. This chapter is divided into headings, which are further divided into subheadings, and often into sub-subheadings, each of which has its own HTSUS classification number. For example, the HTSUS number for aluminum alloy bars and rods other than with a round cross-section is 7604.29.50, indicating that it is a subcategory of aluminum alloys other than hollow profiles (7604.29.00), which is a subsubcategory of the major heading aluminum bars, rods, and profiles (7604.00.00). There are 16 major headings in HTSUS Chapter 76.

7601—Unwrought aluminum

7602—Aluminum waste and scrap

7603—Aluminum powders and flakes

7604—Aluminum bars, rods, and profiles

7605—Aluminum wire

7606—Aluminum plates, sheets, and strips, of a thickness exceeding 0.2 mm.

7607—Aluminum foil (whether or not printed or backed with paper, paperboard, plastics, or similar backing materials) of a thickness (excluding any backing) not exceeding 0.2 mm.

7608—Aluminum tubes and pipes

7609—Aluminum tube or pipe fittings (for example, couplings, elbows, sleeves)

7610—Aluminum structures (excluding prefabricated buildings of heading 9406) and parts of structures (for example, bridges and bridge sections, towers, lattice masts, roofs, roofing frameworks, doors and windows and their frames and thresholds for doors, balustrades, pillars, and columns); aluminum plates, rods, profiles, tubes, and the like, prepared for use in structures

7611—Aluminum reservoirs, tanks, vats, and similar containers, for any material (other than compressed or liquefied gas), of a capacity exceeding 300 liters, whether or not lined or heat insulated, but not fitted with mechanical or thermal equipment

7612—Aluminum casks, drums, cans, boxes, and similar containers (including rigid or collapsible tubular containers) for any material (other than compressed or liquefied gas), of a capacity not exceeding 300 liters, whether or not lined or heat insulated, but not fitted with mechanical or thermal equipment

7613—Aluminum containers for compressed or liquefied gas

7614—Stranded wire, cables, plaited bands, and the like, including slings and similar articles, of aluminum, not electrically insulated

7615—Table, kitchen, or other household articles and parts thereof, of aluminum; pot scourers and scouring or polishing pads, gloves, and the like, of aluminum,; sanitary ware and parts thereof, of aluminum

7616—Other articles of aluminum

For more details regarding classification of the specific product you are interested in importing, consult a customs broker, the appropriate commodity specialist at your nearest customs port, or see HTSUS. HTSUS is available for purchase from the U.S. Government Printing Office (see addresses at end of this chapter), and may be found in larger public libraries. Refer to "Classification—Liquidation" on page 207 for a general discussion of customs classification.

Sample Import Duties

Import duties will vary depending on the HTSUS classification of your product. Therefore, to determine the correct amount of duties, your product must be properly classified under the HTSUS. The following sample duties are taken from the duty listings for HTSUS Chapter 76 products.

Unalloyed aluminum of uniform cross-section the least dimension of which is not greater than 9.5 mm, in coils (7601.10.30): 2.6%; aluminum vanadium master alloy (7601.20.90): free; used aluminum beverage container scrap (7602.00.00): free; powders of lamellar structure or flakes (7603.20.00): 3.9%; unalloyed bars or rods with an outer diameter of less than 10 mm (7604.10.30): 2.6%; aluminum wire, not alloyed, of cross-section greater than 7 mm (7605.11.00): 2.6%; rectangular sheets of aluminum, not alloyed or clad, with a thickness of greater than 6.3 mm (7606.11.30): 3%; sheets of aluminum alloy, clad, with a thickness of more than 6.3 mm (7606.92.60): 6.5%; aluminum foil, not backed rolled but not further worked of a thickness exceeding 0.01 mm (7607.11.60): 5.3%; aluminum can stock (7607.11.90): 3%; seamless aluminum tubes or pipes (7608.10.00): 5.7%; aluminum pipe fittings (7609.00.00): 5.7%; aluminum doors, windows, and their frames (7610.10.00): 5.7%; aluminum sheet metal roofing or siding (7610.90.00): 5.7%; aluminum tanks (7611.00.00): 2.6%; aluminum cans of a capacity not exceeding 355 ml (7612.90.10): 5.7%; aluminum containers for compressed or liquefied gas (7613.00.00): 5%; stranded aluminum wire with a steel core without fittings (7614.10.10): 4.9%; aluminum cooking ware enameled, glazed, or with a nonstick interior finish, not cast (7615.10.30): 5.7%; sanitary ware (7615.20.00): 3.8%; nails, tacks, and staples (7616.10.10): 5.7%; venetian blinds (7616.90.00): 5.7%.

Entry and Documentation

The entry of merchandise is a two-part process consisting of 1) filing the documents necessary to determine whether merchandise may be released from Customs custody and 2) filing the documents that contain information for duty assessment and statistical purposes. In certain instances all documents must be filed and accepted by Customs prior to the release of the goods. Unless you have been granted an extension, you must file entry documents at a location specified by the district/area director within five working days of your shipment's date of arrival at a U.S. port of entry. These include a number of standard documents required by Customs for any entry, and

- For aluminum and aluminum alloy items intended for use with food: FDA Importers Entry Notice **Form FD701**
- U.S. Customs TSCA Certification when required

After you present the entry, Customs may examine your shipment, or may waive examination. The shipment is then released provided no legal or regulatory violations have been noted. You must then file entry summary documentation and deposit estimated duties at a designated customhouse within 10 working days of your shipment's release. For a detailed description of entry procedures, standard documentation, and informal entry, see "Entry Process" on page 182.

Entry Invoice. If you are importing aluminum and alloys of aluminum classifiable under subheadings 7601.10.60, 7601.20.60, 7601.20.90, or 7602.00.00, your invoice must include a statement of the percentages by weight of any metallic element contained in the article.

Marking and Labeling Requirements

For a general discussion of U.S. Customs marking and labeling requirements, see "Marking: Country of Origin" on page 215 and "Special Marking Requirements" on page 217.

Shipping Considerations

You will need to ensure that your goods are packaged and shipped with care to ensure that they arrive in good condition and pass smoothly through Customs. You are responsible for ensuring that the shipment is in compliance with all applicable government regulations for packaging and shipping. In most instances, you should not leave these arrangements solely to the discretion of your supplier. Careful preparation of the cargo and selection of the mode of transport can be essential to a cost-effective, timely delivery of undamaged goods. We strongly advise you to consult your shipping representative, insurance agent, or freight broker for advice on packing and shipping. Refer also to the major tab section "Packing/Shipping/Insurance" for a general discussion of packing and shipping.

Products that are listed as hazardous substances (49 CFR 172 appendix) may be transported in bulk only on compliance with Coast Guard notification procedures, shipping permit requirements, and complex transportation regulations (46 CFR 148). All hazardous substances must be packaged and transported in accordance with DOT regulations (49 CFR 171 et seq.).

Aluminum, aluminum alloy, and products made of them are often bulky, and should be securely stowed to avoid damage due to shifting en route. Aluminum and its products are also subject to tarnish and corrosion, which should be guarded against, especially as no allowance is made by customs for partial damage or loss due to such.

Publications Available

The *Harmonized Tariff Schedule of the United States* (HTSUS) is available from:

Government Printing Office (GPO)
Superintendent of Documents
Washington, DC 20402
(202) 512-1800 (Order line)
(202) 512-0000 (General)

The USGPO also has copies of specific laws available for purchase. The USGPO accepts credit card orders over the phone, as well as mail orders paid by credit card, a check drawn on a U.S. bank, or an international money order.

Relevant Government Agencies

Address inquiries regarding TSCA and EPA requirements for importation of hazardous or toxic substances to:

Environmental Protection Agency (EPA)
TSCA System Information
EPA 7408, OPPT
401 M Street SW
Washington, DC 20460
(202) 554-1404 (TSCA Information Hotline)

Address questions regarding transportation of hazardous substances to:

U.S. Department of Transportation (DOT)
Research and Special Programs Administration
Office of Hazardous Materials Standards
400 7th St. SW
Washington, DC 20590
(202) 366-4488

Address your questions regarding FDA requirements for aluminum products intended for use with food to:

Food and Drug Administration (FDA)
Center for Food Safety and Applied Nutrition
200 C Street SW
Washington, DC 20204
(202) 205-5241, 205-5042

Address questions regarding the importation of aluminum and aluminum products to the district or port director of Customs for you area. For addresses refer to"U.S. Customs District Offices" on page 62 or contact:

U.S. Customs Service
1301 Constitution Ave. NW
Washington, DC 20229
(202) 927-6724 (Information)
(202) 927-1000 (General)

Laws and Regulations

The following laws and regulations may be relevant to the importation of aluminum and aluminum products. The laws are contained in the U.S. Code (USC) and the regulations are published in the Code of Federal Regulations (CFR), both of which may be available at larger public and law libraries. Copies of specific laws are also available from the United States Government Printing Office (address above).

15 USC 2601 et seq.
Toxic Substances Control Act
This Act authorizes the EPA to determine whether a substance is harmful and to restrict importation, sale, and use of such substances.

19 CFR 12.118 et seq.
Regulations on Toxic Substances Control
These regulations require importers of chemical substances imported in bulk or as part of a mixture to certify to Customs that the shipment complies with the TSCA or is not subject to that Act.

15 USC 1261
Federal Hazardous Substances Act
This Act controls the importation of hazardous substances, sets forth prohibited imports, and authorizes various agencies to promulgate labeling, marking, and transport requirements.

49 CFR 170 et seq.
Regulations on Hazardous Materials
These regulations list all substances deemed hazardous and provide transport, marking, labeling, safety, and emergency response rules.

46 CFR 147.30
Regulations on Labeling of Hazardous Materials
This regulation requires the labeling of containers of hazardous substances and specifies the label contents.

46 CFR 148 et seq.
Regulations of Carriage of Solid Hazardous Materials in Bulk
These regulations govern the transport of solid hazardous substances in bulk, including reporting, permitting, loading, stowing, and shipping requirements.

21 USC 301 et seq.
Food, Drug, and Cosmetic Act
This Act prohibits deceptive practices and regulates the manufacture, sale and importation or exportation of food, drugs, cosmetics, and related products. See 21 USC 331, 381, 382.

19 CFR 12.1 et seq.; 21 CFR 1.83 et seq.
Regulations on Food, Drugs, and Cosmetics
These regulations of the Secretary of Health and Human Services and the Secretary of the Treasury govern the standards, labeling, marking, and importing of products used with food, drugs, and cosmetics.

Principal Exporting Countries

The following listing includes samples of the main supplier nations of the products of this chapter. It is organized by HTSUS major heading. (Refer to "Customs Classification" above for the product codes.) Countries are listed in rank order of the value of products imported to the U.S. Statistics represent customs value entries for 1993 from the Bureau of Census, U.S. Department of Commerce.

7601—Canada, Russia, Venezuela, Brazil, Switzerland, Tajikistan, Germany, Netherlands, United Kingdom, France

7602—Canada, Mexico, Russia, Venezuela, Israel, United Kingdom, Panama, France, Netherlands, Switzerland

7603—Germany, Bahrain, Canada, South Korea, Ireland, Japan, Brazil, Mexico, United Kingdom, Sweden

7604—Canada, Slovenia, Brazil, Germany, Russia, Belgium, Croatia, France, Spain, Italy

7605—Canada, United Kingdom, Japan, Venezuela, Argentina, Germany, France, Slovenia, Norway, Malaysia

7606—Canada, Germany, Japan, France, Spain, Venezuela, United Kingdom, Bahrain, Sweden, Belgium

7607—Germany, Canada, Japan, Sweden, France, Switzerland, Italy, South Africa, Brazil, United Kingdom

7608—Japan, Canada, Germany, France, United Kingdom, Taiwan, Ireland, Denmark, Switzerland, Venezuela

7609—Canada, Mexico, Taiwan, Japan, Israel, Germany, United Kingdom, Sweden, India, France

7610—Canada, Germany, Mexico, United Kingdom, Denmark, Sweden, Netherlands, France, Ireland, Italy

7611—Netherlands, Canada, United Kingdom, Ireland, Germany, Japan, Brazil, Mexico, Belize, Switzerland

7612—Canada, Venezuela, United Kingdom, France, Germany, Finland, Brazil, Switzerland, Israel, Mexico

7613—France, Venezuela, Italy, United Kingdom, Canada, Germany, Thailand, Peru, Mexico, Japan

7614—Venezuela, Brazil, Canada, Italy, Germany, Norway, Taiwan, Singapore, Japan, France

7615—France, Hong Kong, Taiwan, Thailand, Indonesia, Canada, South Korea, China, India, Colombia

RESERVED
FOR
FUTURE
USE

Chapter 77: Reserved

Chapter 77 is reserved for future use by the U.S. Customs Service.

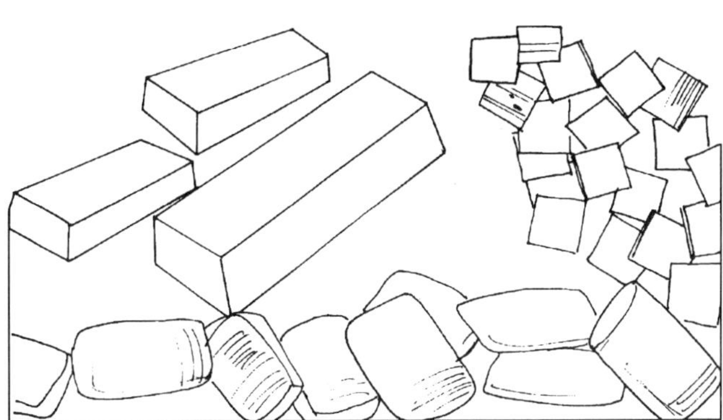

Chapter 78: Lead and Articles Thereof*

This section pertains to the importation of lead, lead alloys, and articles made from these products, which are classified within Chapter 78 of the Harmonized Tariff Schedule of the United States (HTSUS). Specifically, it includes unwrought lead and lead alloys; lead waste and scrap; powders and flakes; lead bars, rods, profiles, wire, plates, sheets, strips, and foil; lead tubes, pipes, and fittings; and other miscellaneous articles of lead.

Goods of base metals and their alloys in which metals other than lead predominate are covered in Commodity Index chapters related to the specific metals, including iron and steel (Chapter 72), copper (Chapter 74), nickel (Chapter 75), aluminum (Chapter 76), zinc (Chapter 79), tin (Chapter 80), and other base metals (Chapter 81). Tools, other implements, and cutlery are found in Chapter 82, while miscellaneous articles of base metals are contained in Chapter 83. Precious metals, alloys of precious metals, and articles containing the same are covered specifically in Chapter 71.

Other products for which metals are incidental components are found within a variety of Commodity Index chapters and headings. For example, if you are interested in importing metallic paints, refer to Chapter 36. For headgear with metal elements, see Chapter 65; for umbrella frames and related items, see Chapter 66. Finished and semifinished products classified as machinery, mechanical appliances, and electrical goods are found in Chapters 84 and 85. Assembled railway track and related equipment is covered in Chapter 86, vehicles in Chapter 87, aircraft in Chapter 88, and boats in Chapter 89. Instruments and apparatus are covered in Commodity Index chapters related to the particular articles, including optical, medical, and precision instruments (Chapter 90), clocks and watches (Chapter 91), and musical instruments (Chapter 92). Metal articles as parts of firearms, including ammunition, are found in Chapter 93. Commodity Index chapters that cover miscellaneous manufactures include furniture (Chapter 94), toys, games, and sporting goods (Chapter 95), and miscellaneous manufactured articles (Chapter 96). Works of art in which lead or its alloys are components, even dominant components, are covered in chapter 97 if the primary value derives from the artistry rather than from the metal content.

*IMPORTANT: Read the Commodity Index Introduction. It is the essential framework for understanding this chapter.

Key Factors

The key factors in importing lead and lead alloy products are:

- Compliance with U.S. Environmental Protection Agency (EPA) requirements under the Toxic Substances Control Act (TSCA) (if the product is classified as a hazardous substance)
- Compliance with U.S. Department of Transportation (DOT) regulations for transport of hazardous cargo (if the product is a hazardous substance)

Although most importers utilize the services of a licensed customs broker in making their entries, and we recommend this practice, you should be aware of the regulatory, entry, and documentation issues involved in importing your product. You, as importer, are ultimately responsible for the fulfillment of any legal requirements applicable to your shipment.

General Considerations

Regulatory Agencies. The importation of lead, lead alloys, and products made of them is relatively straightforward, with few restrictions or special requirements. The Environmental Protection Agency (EPA), under authority of the Toxic Substances Control Act (TSCA), imposes certain controls on the importation of lead and lead articles that constitute toxic substances. The Department of Transportation (DOT) enforces regulations for transporting hazardous cargo.

Definitions. Unlike alloys of precious metals, in which any alloy containing as much as 2% by weight of a precious metal is considered an alloy of that metal, alloys of base metals are classified according to the metal that predominates by weight over every other individual metal in the alloy. For customs purposes, alloys of a metal are included with the metal that they are an alloy of.

Chapter 78 of HTSUS covers lead and lead alloys. Refined lead is defined as metal containing at least 99.9% by weight provided that the content of any other element does not exceed, by weight, that noted in the table found in the notes to HTSUS Chapter 78, which ranges from a low of 0.001% for other elements and a high of 0.05% bismuth. Lead alloys are defined as being metallic substances in which lead is less than 99% by weight, but not less than any other metallic element.

Toxic Substances Regulations. The EPA imposes certain controls on the importation of toxic substances. The TSCA defines a toxic substance as any substance determined to present the possibility of an unreasonable risk of injury to health and the environment. Because of long-term deleterious effects on health caused by lead, regulators pay special heed to it. The DOT enforces regulations for transporting hazardous cargo. Substances are deemed hazardous if listed in DOT transport regulations (49 CFR 172 appendix). Unwrought primary metals, such as pigs, ingots, billets, blooms, and similar materials, are generally categorized as toxic substances within the definitions of the TSCA and thus are required to be in compliance with its provisions. These include packaging, shipping, marking, and labeling requirements. Refer to listing of laws and regulations below.

Products defined as articles—that is, any manufactured item 1) that is formed into a specific shape or design during manufacture, 2) that has end-use functions dependent on the shape or design during end use, and 3) that during the end use, does not change in its chemical composition or that changes only for a noncommercial purpose separate from the article and only as allowed by law (19 CFR 12.120(2))—are not subject to the provisions of the TSCA. Metal products other than primary metals are generally considered to be articles even if they are to be further processed. For example, lead in bars is an article even if it is to be subsequently fabricated into other products.

Certification. All products covered by the TSCA are subject to the U.S. Customs Service TSCA Import Certification Rule (19 CFR 12.118 et seq.). If you import these products, you must sign one of the following statements: "I certify that all materials in this shipment comply with all applicable rules or orders under TSCA and that I am not offering a chemical substance for entry in violation of TSCA or any applicable rule or order thereunder" or "I certify that all materials in this shipment are not subject to TSCA." You must file this TSCA certification of compliance or exemption at the time you make the entry at customs. Customs will not release your shipment without proper certification.

If you will be importing several or regular shipments, you should ask the appropriate Customs district director to authorize your use of a blanket certification. A blanket certification is valid for one calendar year, may be renewed, and may be revoked at any time for cause.

Customs Classification

For customs purposes, lead, lead alloys, and their products are classified within Chapter 78 of the HTSUS. This chapter is divided into headings, which are further divided into subheadings, and often into sub-subheadings, each of which has its own HTSUS classification number. For example, the HTSUS number for unwrought alloys of lead is 7801.99.90, indicating that it is a subcategory of lead other than refined lead (7801.99.00), which is a subsubcategory of the major heading unwrought lead (7801.00.00). There are six major headings in HTSUS Chapter 75.

7801—Unwrought lead

7802—Lead waste and scrap

7803—Lead bars, rods, profiles, and wire

7804—Lead plates, sheets, strip, and foil; lead powders and flakes

7805—Leads tubes, pipes, and tube or pipe fittings

7806—Other articles of lead

For more details regarding classification of the specific product you are interested in importing, consult a customs broker, the appropriate commodity specialist at your nearest customs port, or see HTSUS. HTSUS is available for purchase from the U.S. Government Printing Office (see addresses at end of this chapter), and may be found in larger public libraries. Refer to "Classification—Liquidation" on page 207 for a general discussion of customs classification.

Sample Import Duties

Import duties will vary depending on the HTSUS classification of your product. Therefore, to determine the correct amount of duties, your product must be properly classified under the HTSUS. The following sample duties are taken from the duty listings for HTSUS Chapter 78 products.

Refined lead (7801.10.00): 3.5% on the value of the lead content; alloys of lead (7801.9.90): 3.5% on the value of the lead content; lead waste and scrap obtained from lead-acid storage batteries (7802.00.00): 2.3% on the value of the lead content; lead bars (7803.00.00): 1.2%; lead sheets of an thickness, excluding any backing not exceeding 0.2 mm (7804.11.00): 2.2%; lead powders and flakes (7804.20.00): 11.25%; lead tube or pipe fittings (7805.00.00): 2%; other articles of lead (7806.00.00): 3.9%.

Entry and Documentation

The entry of merchandise is a two-part process consisting of 1) filing the documents necessary to determine whether merchandise may be released from Customs custody and 2) filing the documents that contain information for duty assessment and statistical purposes. In certain instances all documents must be filed and accepted by Customs prior to the release of the goods. Unless you have been granted an extension, you must file entry documents at a location specified by the district/area director within five working days of your shipment's date of arrival at a

U.S. port of entry. These include a number of standard documents required by Customs for any entry, and

- U.S. Customs TSCA Certification when required

After you present the entry, Customs may examine your shipment, or may waive examination. The shipment is then released provided no legal or regulatory violations have been noted. You must then file entry summary documentation and deposit estimated duties at a designated customhouse within 10 working days of your shipment's release. For a detailed description of entry procedures, standard documentation, and informal entry, see "Entry Process" on page 182.

Marking and Labeling Requirements

For a general discussion of U.S. Customs marking and labeling requirements, see "Marking: Country of Origin" on page 215 and "Special Marking Requirements" on page 217.

Shipping Considerations

You will need to ensure that your goods are packaged and shipped with care to ensure that they arrive in good condition and pass smoothly through Customs. You are responsible for ensuring that the shipment is in compliance with all applicable government regulations for packaging and shipping. In most instances, you should not leave these arrangements solely to the discretion of your supplier. Careful preparation of the cargo and selection of the mode of transport can be essential to a cost-effective, timely delivery of undamaged goods. We strongly advise you to consult your shipping representative, insurance agent, or freight broker for advice on packing and shipping. Refer also to the major tab section "Packing/Shipping/Insurance" for a general discussion of packing and shipping.

Products that are listed as hazardous substances (49 CFR 172 appendix) may be transported in bulk only on compliance with Coast Guard notification procedures, shipping permit requirements, and complex transportation regulations (46 CFR 148). All hazardous substances must be packaged and transported in accordance with DOT regulations (49 CFR 171 et seq.).

Lead, lead alloy, and products made of them are often bulky and heavy, and should be securely stowed to avoid damage due to shifting en route. Lead and its products are also subject to oxidation and corrosion, which should be guarded against, especially as no allowance is made by customs for partial damage or loss due to such.

Publications Available

The *Harmonized Tariff Schedule of the United States* (HTSUS) is available from:

Government Printing Office (GPO)
Superintendent of Documents
Washington, DC 20402
(202) 512-1800 (Order line)
(202) 512-0000 (General)

The USGPO also has copies of specific laws available for purchase. The USGPO accepts credit card orders over the phone, as well as mail orders paid by credit card, a check drawn on a U.S. bank, or an international money order.

Relevant Government Agencies

Address inquiries regarding TSCA and EPA requirements for importation of hazardous or toxic substances to:

Environmental Protection Agency (EPA)
TSCA System Information
EPA 7408, OPPT
401 M Street SW
Washington, DC 20460
(202) 554-1404 (TSCA Information Hotline)

Address questions regarding transportation of hazardous substances to:

U.S. Department of Transportation (DOT)
Research and Special Programs Administration
Office of Hazardous Materials Standards
400 7th St. SW
Washington, DC 20590
(202) 366-4488

Address questions regarding the importation of lead and lead products to the district or port director of Customs for you area. For addresses refer to "U.S. Customs District Offices" on page 62 or contact:

U.S. Customs Service
1301 Constitution Ave. NW
Washington, DC 20229
(202) 927-6724 (Information)
(202) 927-1000 (General)

Laws and Regulations

The following laws and regulations may be relevant to the importation of lead, lead alloys, and products made of them. The laws are contained in the U.S. Code (USC) and the regulations are published in the Code of Federal Regulations (CFR), both of which may be available at larger public and law libraries. Copies of specific laws are also available from the United States Government Printing Office (address above).

15 USC 2601 et seq.
Toxic Substances Control Act
This Act authorizes the EPA to determine whether a substance is harmful and to restrict importation, sale, and use of such substances.

19 CFR 12.118 et seq.
Regulations on Toxic Substances Control
These regulations require importers of chemical substances imported in bulk or as part of a mixture to certify to Customs that the shipment complies with the TSCA or is not subject to that Act.

15 USC 1261
Federal Hazardous Substances Act
This Act controls the importation of hazardous substances, sets forth prohibited imports, and authorizes various agencies to promulgate labeling, marking, and transport requirements.

49 CFR 170 et seq.
Regulations on Hazardous Materials
These regulations list all substances deemed hazardous and provide transport, marking, labeling, safety, and emergency response rules.

46 CFR 147.30
Regulations on Labeling of Hazardous Materials
This regulation requires the labeling of containers of hazardous substances and specifies the label contents.

46 CFR 148 et seq.
Regulations of Carriage of Solid Hazardous Materials in Bulk
These regulations govern the transport of solid hazardous substances in bulk, including reporting, permitting, loading, stowing, and shipping requirements.

Principal Exporting Countries

The following listing includes samples of the main supplier nations of the products of this chapter. It is organized by HTSUS major heading. (Refer to "Customs Classification" above for the product codes.) Countries are listed in rank order of the value of products imported to the U.S. Statistics represent customs value

entries for 1993 from the Bureau of Census, U.S. Department of Commerce.

7801—Canada, Mexico, Peru, United Arab Emirates, Germany, Australia, Belgium, France, South Korea, United Kingdom

7802—Canada, Mexico, Germany, United Kingdom, Venezuela, Finland, Belgium, Spain

7803—Canada, Namibia, Mexico, Germany, United Kingdom, Japan, Switzerland, France, United Arab Emirates, Taiwan

7804—Germany, Canada, Japan, United Kingdom, Italy, Chile, Peru, South Korea, Belgium

7805—Canada, Taiwan, Thailand, Japan

7806—Canada, Mexico, Hong Kong, South Africa, China, Italy, Taiwan, United Kingdom, Japan, Netherlands

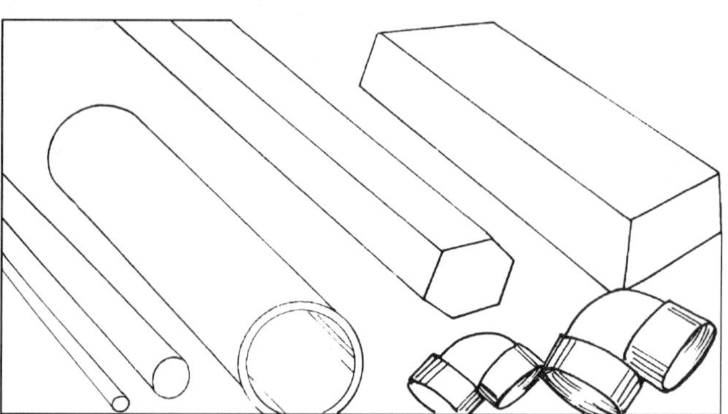

Chapter 79: Zinc and Articles Thereof*

This section pertains to the importation of zinc, zinc alloys, and articles made from these products, which are classified within Chapter 79 of the Harmonized Tariff Schedule of the United States (HTSUS). Specifically, it includes unwrought zinc; zinc waste and scrap; zinc dust, powders, and flakes; bars, rods, wire, plates, sheets, strips, and foil; zinc tubes, pipes, and fittings; and miscellaneous articles of zinc, such as gutters, skylight frames, and household articles.

Goods of base metals and their alloys in which metals other than zinc predominate are covered in Commodity Index chapters that relate to the specific metals, including iron and steel (Chapter 72), copper (Chapter 74), nickel (Chapter 75), aluminum (Chapter 76), lead (Chapter 78), tin (Chapter 80), and other base metals (Chapter 81). Tools, other implements, and cutlery are found in Chapter 82, while miscellaneous articles of base metals are contained in Chapter 83. Precious metals, alloys of precious metals, and articles containing the same are covered specifically in Chapter 71.

Other products for which metals are incidental—even if critical and major—components are found within a variety of Commodity Index chapters. For example, if you are interested in importing metallic paints, refer to Chapter 36. For headgear with metal elements, see Chapter 65; for umbrella frames and related items, see Chapter 66. Finished and semifinished products classified as machinery, mechanical appliances, and electrical goods are found in Chapters 84 and 85. Assembled railway track and related equipment is covered in Chapter 86, vehicles in Chapter 87, aircraft in Chapter 88, and boats in Chapter 89. Instruments and apparatus are covered in Commodity Index chapters that relate to the specific article, including optical, medical, and precision instruments (Chapter 90), clocks and watches (Chapter 91), and musical instruments (Chapter 92). Metal articles as parts of firearms, including ammunition, are found in Chapter 93. Commodity Index chapters that cover miscellaneous manufactures include furniture (Chapter 94), toys, games, and sporting goods (Chapter 95), and miscellaneous manufactured articles (Chapter 96). Works of art in which zinc or its alloys are components, even dominant components, are covered in Chapter 97 if the primary value derives from the artistry rather than from the metal content.

*IMPORTANT: Read the Commodity Index Introduction. It is the essential framework for understanding this chapter.

Key Factors

The key factors in importing zinc and zinc alloy products are:

- Compliance with U.S. Environmental Protection Agency (EPA) requirements under the Toxic Substances Control Act (TSCA) (if the product is classified as a hazardous substance)
- Compliance with U.S. Department of Transportation (DOT) regulations for transport of hazardous cargo (if the product is a hazardous substance)
- For items to be used with food, compliance with U.S. Food and Drug Administration (FDA) requirements and entry notification

Although most importers utilize the services of a licensed customs broker in making their entries, and we recommend this practice, you should be aware of the regulatory, entry, and documentation issues involved in importing your product. You, as importer, are ultimately responsible for the fulfillment of any legal requirements applicable to your shipment.

General Considerations

Regulatory Agencies. The importation of zinc, zinc alloys, and products made of them is relatively straightforward, with few restrictions or special requirements. The Food and Drug Administration (FDA) controls the importation of items for use with food. The Environmental Protection Agency (EPA), under authority of the Toxic Substances Control Act (TSCA), imposes certain controls on the importation of zinc and zinc articles that contain toxic substances. The Department of Transportation (DOT) enforces regulations for transporting hazardous cargo.

Definitions. Unlike alloys of precious metals, in which any alloy having as much as 2% of a precious metal is considered an alloy of that metal, alloys of base metals are classified according to the metal that predominates by weight over every other individual metal in the alloy. For customs purposes, alloys of a metal are included with the metal that they are an alloy of.

Chapter 79 of HTSUS covers zinc and zinc alloys. Zinc is defined as metal containing by weight at least 97.5% by weight of zinc. Zinc alloys are defined as being metallic substances in which zinc predominates by weight over each of the other elements, provided that the content by weight of at least one of the other elements exceeds 2.5%. Zinc dust is defined as the product obtained from condensation of vapor that is finer than zinc powder (generally finer than 63 micrometers and composed of at least 85% by weight of metallic zinc). Casting-grade zinc is defined as containing specified components of various other metals, such as 1.8% of cadmium, etc., as specified in the notes to HTSUS Chapter 79.

FDA Regulation. Kitchenware and tableware of zinc and its alloys intended for use with food are subject to the provisions of the Federal Food, Drug, and Cosmetic Act (FDCA) enforced by the FDA. FDA entry notification is required for applicable items. Shipments of FDA-regulated products are subject to FDA port of entry inspection. You must file an FDA Importers Entry Notice, **Form FD701**, with each shipment. For more information, see the annotated diagram of FDA entry procedures and requirements in the "Foods" appendix on page 808. Contact your nearest regional FDA office or FDA headquarters with questions regarding the importation of zinc products (see addresses at end of this chapter).

Toxic Substances Regulations. The EPA imposes certain controls on the importation of toxic substances. The TSCA defines a toxic substance as any substance determined to present the possibility of an unreasonable risk of injury to health and the environment. The DOT enforces regulations for transporting hazardous cargo. Substances are deemed hazardous if listed in DOT transport regulations (49 CFR 172 appendix). Unwrought primary metals, such as pigs, ingots, billets, blooms, and similar materials, are generally categorized as toxic substances within the definitions of the TSCA and thus are required to be in compliance with its provisions. These include packaging, shipping, marking, and labeling requirements. Refer to "Laws and Regulations" below.

Products defined as articles—that is, any manufactured item 1) that is formed into a specific shape or design during manufacture, 2) that has end-use functions dependent on the shape or design during end use, and 3) that during the end use, does not change in its chemical composition or that changes only for a noncommercial purpose separate from the article and only as allowed by law (19 CFR 12.120(2))—are not subject to the provisions of the TSCA. Metal products other than primary metals are generally considered to be articles even if they are to be further processed. For example, zinc in sheets is an article even if it is to be subsequently fabricated into other products.

Certification. All products covered by the TSCA are subject to the U.S. Customs Service TSCA Import Certification Rule (19 CFR 12.118 et seq.). If you import these products, you must sign one of the following statements: "I certify that all materials in this shipment comply with all applicable rules or orders under TSCA and that I am not offering a chemical substance for entry in violation of TSCA or any applicable rule or order thereunder" or "I certify that all materials in this shipment are not subject to TSCA." You must file this TSCA certification of compliance or exemption at the time you make the entry at customs.

If you will be importing several or regular shipments, you should ask the appropriate Customs district director to authorize your use of a blanket certification. A blanket certification is valid for one calendar year, may be renewed, and may be revoked at any time for cause.

Customs Classification

For customs purposes, zinc and zinc products are classified within Chapter 79 of the HTSUS. This chapter is divided into headings, which are further divided into subheadings, and often into sub-subheadings, each of which has its own HTSUS classification number. For example, the HTSUS number for zinc powders is 7903.90.30, indicating that it is a subcategory of zinc powders, dust, and flakes other than zinc dust (7903.90.00), which is a subsubcategory of the major heading zinc dust, powders, and flakes (7903.00.00). There are seven major headings in HTSUS Chapter 79.

7901—Unwrought zinc

7902—Zinc waste and scrap

7903—Zinc dust, powders, and flakes

7904—Zinc bars, rods, and profiles

7905—Zinc plates, sheets, strip, and foil

7906—Zinc tubes, pipes, and tube or pipe fittings

7907—Other articles of zinc

For more details regarding classification of the specific product you are interested in importing, consult a customs broker, the appropriate commodity specialist at your nearest customs port, or see HTSUS. HTSUS is available for purchase from the U.S. Government Printing Office (see addresses at end of this chapter), and may be found in larger public libraries. Refer to "Classification—Liquidation" on page 207 for a general discussion of customs classification.

Sample Import Duties

Import duties will vary depending on the HTSUS classification of your product. Therefore, to determine the correct amount of duties, your product must be properly classified under the HTSUS. The following sample duties are taken from the duty listings for HTSUS Chapter 79 products.

Unwrought zinc, not alloyed, containing by weight 99.99% or more of zinc (7901.11.00): 1.5%; unwrought casting zinc containing by weight less than 99.99% of zinc (7901.12.10): 19%; zinc alloys (7901.20.00): 19%; zinc waste and scrap (7902.00.00): 2.1%; zinc dust (7903.10.00): 0.7 cents/kg; zinc flakes (7903.90.60): 9.5%; zinc bars, rods, profiles, and wire (7904.00.00): 4.2%; zinc plates, sheets, strip, and foil (7905.00.00): 4.2%; zinc tubes, pipes, and tube or pipe fittings (7906.00.00): 3.8%; gutters and other fabricated building components (7907.10.00): 5.7%; household articles of zinc (7907.90.30): 3.4%.

Entry and Documentation

The entry of merchandise is a two-part process consisting of 1) filing the documents necessary to determine whether merchandise may be released from Customs custody and 2) filing the documents that contain information for duty assessment and statistical purposes. In certain instances all documents must be filed and accepted by Customs prior to the release of the goods. Unless you have been granted an extension, you must file entry documents at a location specified by the district or area director within five working days of your shipment's date of arrival at a U.S. port of entry. These include a number of standard documents required by Customs for any entry, and

- For zinc and zinc alloy items intended for use with food: FDA Importers Entry Notice: **Form FD701**
- U.S. Customs TSCA Certification when required

After you present the entry, Customs may examine your shipment, or may waive examination. The shipment is then released provided no legal or regulatory violations have been noted. You must then file entry summary documentation and deposit estimated duties at a designated customhouse within 10 working days of your shipment's release. For a detailed description of entry procedures, standard documentation, and informal entry, see "Entry Process" on page 182.

Marking and Labeling Requirements

For a general discussion of U.S. Customs marking and labeling requirements, see "Marking: Country of Origin" on page 215 and "Special Marking Requirements" on page 217.

Shipping Considerations

You will need to ensure that your goods are packaged and shipped with care to ensure that they arrive in good condition and pass smoothly through Customs. You are responsible for ensuring that the shipment is in compliance with all applicable government regulations for packaging and shipping. In most instances, you should not leave these arrangements solely to the discretion of your supplier. Careful preparation of the cargo and selection of the mode of transport can be essential to a cost-effective, timely delivery of undamaged goods. We strongly advise you to consult your shipping representative, insurance agent, or freight broker for advice on packing and shipping. Refer also to the major tab section "Packing/Shipping/Insurance" for a general discussion of packing and shipping.

Products that are listed as hazardous substances (49 CFR 172 appendix) may be transported in bulk only on compliance with Coast Guard notification procedures, shipping permit requirements, and complex transportation regulations (46 CFR 148). All hazardous substances must be packaged and transported in accordance with DOT regulations (49 CFR 171 et seq.).

Zinc, zinc alloy, and products made of them are often bulky, and should be securely stowed to avoid damage due to shifting en route. Zinc and its products are also subject to tarnish and corrosion, which should be guarded against, especially as no allowance is made by customs for partial damage or loss due to such.

Publications Available

The *Harmonized Tariff Schedule of the United States* (HTSUS) is available from:

Government Printing Office (GPO)
Superintendent of Documents
Washington, DC 20402
(202) 512-1800 (Order line)
(202) 512-0000 (General)

The USGPO also has copies of specific laws available for purchase. The USGPO accepts credit card orders over the phone, as well as mail orders paid by credit card, a check drawn on a U.S. bank, or an international money order.

Relevant Government Agencies

Address inquiries regarding TSCA and EPA requirements for importation of hazardous or toxic substances to:

Environmental Protection Agency (EPA)
TSCA System Information
EPA 7408, OPPT
401 M Street SW
Washington, DC 20460
(202) 554-1404 (TSCA Information Hotline)

Address questions regarding transportation of hazardous substances to:

U.S. Department of Transportation (DOT)
Research and Special Programs Administration
Office of Hazardous Materials Standards
400 7th St. SW
Washington, DC 20590
(202) 366-4488

Address your questions regarding FDA requirements for zinc products intended for use with food to:

Food and Drug Administration (FDA)
Center for Food Safety and Applied Nutrition
200 C Street SW
Washington, DC 20204
(202) 205-5241, 205-5042

Address questions regarding the importation of zinc and zinc products to the district or port director of Customs for you area. For addresses refer to "U.S. Customs District Offices" on page 62 or contact:

U.S. Customs Service
1301 Constitution Ave. NW
Washington, DC 20229
(202) 927-6724 (Information)
(202) 927-1000 (General)

Laws and Regulations

The following laws and regulations may be relevant to the importation of zinc and zinc products. The laws are contained in the U.S. Code (USC) and the regulations are published in the Code of Federal Regulations (CFR), both of which may be available at larger public and law libraries. Copies of specific laws are also available from the United States Government Printing Office (address above).

15 USC 2601 et seq.
Toxic Substances Control Act
This Act authorizes the EPA to determine whether a substance is harmful and to restrict importation, sale, and use of such substances.

19 CFR 12.118 et seq.
Regulations on Toxic Substances Control
These regulations require importers of chemical substances imported in bulk or as part of a mixture to certify to Customs that the shipment complies with the TSCA or is not subject to that Act.

15 USC 1261
Federal Hazardous Substances Act
This Act controls the importation of hazardous substances, sets forth prohibited imports, and authorizes various agencies to promulgate labeling, marking, and transport requirements.

49 CFR 170 et seq.
Regulations on Hazardous Materials
These regulations list all substances deemed hazardous and provide transport, marking, labeling, safety, and emergency response rules.

46 CFR 147.30
Regulations on Labeling of Hazardous Materials
This regulation requires the labeling of containers of hazardous substances and specifies the label contents.

46 CFR 148 et seq.
Regulations of Carriage of Solid Hazardous Materials in Bulk
These regulations govern the transport of solid hazardous substances in bulk, including reporting, permitting, loading, stowing, and shipping requirements.

21 USC 301 et seq.
Food, Drug, and Cosmetic Act
This Act prohibits deceptive practices and regulates the manufacture, sale and importation or exportation of food, drugs, cosmetics, and related products. See 21 USC 331, 381, 382.

19 CFR 12.1 et seq.; 21 CFR 1.83 et seq.
Regulations on Food, Drugs, and Cosmetics
These regulations of the Secretary of Health and Human Services and the Secretary of the Treasury govern the standards, labeling, marking, and importing of products used with food, drugs, and cosmetics.

Principal Exporting Countries

The following listing includes samples of the main supplier nations of the products of this chapter. It is organized by HTSUS major heading. (Refer to "Customs Classification" above for the product codes.) Countries are listed in rank order of the value of products imported to the U.S. Statistics represent customs value entries for 1993 from the Bureau of Census, U.S. Department of Commerce.

7901—Canada, Mexico, Spain, Peru, Australia, Brazil, Finland, Russia, Norway, South Korea

7902—Canada, Mexico, Dominican Rep., Nicaragua, Honduras, Jamaica, Sweden, Panama

7903—Canada, Japan, Belgium, Mexico, Austria, Taiwan, Venezuela, Germany, Australia, Italy

7904—Mexico, Poland, Canada, South Africa, Russia, Japan, Malaysia, Honduras, Taiwan, Netherlands

7905—Canada, France, South Africa, Germany, Japan, Mexico, Poland, United Kingdom

7906—Canada, Taiwan, Ireland, Mexico, China, United Kingdom, Japan, Germany, Sweden

7907—Taiwan, China, Canada, South Korea, Italy, Mexico, Hong Kong, Malaysia, Japan, United Kingdom

Chapter 80: Tin and Articles Thereof*

This section pertains to the importation of tin, tin alloys, and articles made from these products, which are classified within Chapter 80 of the Harmonized Tariff Schedule of the United States (HTSUS). Specifically, it includes unwrought tin; tin waste and scrap; tin bars, rods, wire, plates, sheets, strips, and foil; tin tubes, pipes, and fittings; and miscellaneous articles of tin, including household articles suitable for food and beverage service.

Goods of base metals and their alloys in which metals other than tin predominate are covered in Commodity Index chapters on the specific metals, including iron and steel (Chapter 72), copper (Chapter 74), nickel (Chapter 75), aluminum (Chapter 76), lead (Chapter 78), zinc (Chapter 79), and other base metals (Chapter 81). Tools, other implements, and cutlery are found in Chapter 82, while miscellaneous articles of base metals are contained in Chapter 83. Precious metals, alloys of precious metals, and articles containing the same are covered specifically in Chapter 71.

Other products for which metals are incidental—even if critical and major—components are found within a variety of Commodity Index chapters. For example, if you are interested in importing metallic paints, refer to Chapter 36. For headgear with metal elements, see Chapter 65; for umbrella frames and related items, see Chapter 66. Finished and semifinished products classified as machinery, mechanical appliances, and electrical goods are found in Chapters 84 and 85. Assembled railway track and related equipment is covered in Chapter 86, vehicles in Chapter 87, aircraft in Chapter 88, and boats in Chapter 89. Instruments and apparatus are covered in Commodity Index chapters that relate to the particular article, including optical, medical, and precision instruments (Chapter 90), clocks and watches (Chapter 91), and musical instruments (Chapter 92). Metal articles as parts of firearms, including ammunition, are found in Chapter 93. Commodity Index chapters that cover miscellaneous manufactures include furniture (Chapter 94), toys, games, and sporting goods (Chapter 95), and miscellaneous manufactured articles (Chapter 96). Works of art in which tin or its alloys are components, even dominant components, are covered in Chapter 97 if the primary value derives from the artistry rather than from the metal content.

Key Factors

The key factors in importing tin and tin alloy products are:

- Compliance with U.S. Environmental Protection

*IMPORTANT: Read the Commodity Index Introduction. It is the essential framework for understanding this chapter.

Agency (EPA) requirements under the Toxic Substances Control Act (TSCA) (if the product is classified as a hazardous substance)

- Compliance with U.S. Department of Transportation (DOT) regulations for transport of hazardous cargo (if the product is a hazardous substance)
- For items to be used with food, compliance with U.S. Food and Drug Administration (FDA) requirements and entry notification

Although most importers utilize the services of a licensed customs broker in making their entries, and we recommend this practice, you should be aware of the regulatory, entry, and documentation issues involved in importing your product. You, as importer, are ultimately responsible for the fulfillment of any legal requirements applicable to your shipment.

General Considerations

Regulatory Agencies. The importation of tin, tin alloys, and products made of them is relatively straightforward, with few restrictions or special requirements. The Food and Drug Administration (FDA) controls the importation of items for use with food. The Environmental Protection Agency (EPA), under authority of the Toxic Substances Control Act (TSCA), imposes certain controls on the importation of tin and tin articles that contain toxic substances. The Department of Transportation (DOT) enforces regulations for transporting hazardous cargo.

Definitions. Unlike alloys of precious metals, in which any alloy having as much as 2% of a precious metal is considered an alloy of that metal, alloys of base metals are classified according to the metal that predominates by weight over every other individual metal in the alloy. For customs purposes, alloys of a metal are included with the metal that they are an alloy of.

Chapter 80 of HTSUS covers tin and tin alloys. Tin is defined as metal containing by weight at least 99% by weight of tin with no more than 0.1% of bismuth or 0.4% of copper. Tin alloys are defined as being metallic substances in which tin predominates by weight over each of the other elements, provided that the total content by weight of the other elements exceeds 1%, with the total content of bismuth or copper being greater than that defined for unalloyed tin.

FDA Regulation. Kitchenware and tableware of tin and its alloys intended for use with food are subject to the provisions of the Federal Food, Drug, and Cosmetic Act (FDCA) enforced by the FDA. FDA entry notification is required for applicable items. Shipments of FDA-regulated products are subject to FDA port of entry inspection. You must file an FDA Importers Entry Notice, **Form FD701**, with each shipment. For more information, see the annotated diagram of FDA entry procedures and requirements in the "Foods" appendix on page 808. Contact your nearest regional FDA office or FDA headquarters with questions regarding the importation of tin products (see addresses at end of this chapter).

Toxic Substances Regulations. The EPA imposes certain controls on the importation of toxic substances. The TSCA defines a toxic substance as any substance determined to present the possibility of an unreasonable risk of injury to health and the environment. The DOT enforces regulations for transporting hazardous cargo. Substances are deemed hazardous if listed in DOT transport regulations (49 CFR 172 appendix). Unwrought primary metals, such as pigs, ingots, billets, blooms, and similar materials, are generally categorized as toxic substances within the definitions of the TSCA and thus are required to be in compliance with its provisions. These include packaging, shipping, marking, and labeling requirements. Refer to "Laws and Regulations" below.

Products defined as articles—that is, any manufactured item 1) that is formed into a specific shape or design during manufacture, 2) that has end-use functions dependent on the shape or design during end use, and 3) that during the end use, does not change in its chemical composition or that changes only for a noncommercial purpose separate from the article and only as allowed by law (19 CFR 12.120(2))—are not subject to the provisions of the TSCA. Metal products other than primary metals are generally considered to be articles even if they are to be further processed. For example, tin in sheets is an article even if it is to be subsequently fabricated into other products.

Certification. All products covered by the TSCA are subject to the U.S. Customs Service TSCA Import Certification Rule (19 CFR 12.118 et seq.). If you import these products, you must sign one of the following statements: "I certify that all materials in this shipment comply with all applicable rules or orders under TSCA and that I am not offering a chemical substance for entry in violation of TSCA or any applicable rule or order thereunder" or "I certify that all materials in this shipment are not subject to TSCA." You must file this TSCA certification of compliance or exemption at the time you make the entry at customs. Customs will not release your shipment without proper certification.

If you will be importing several or regular shipments, you should ask the appropriate Customs district director to authorize your use of a blanket certification. A blanket certification is valid for one calendar year, may be renewed, and may be revoked at any time for cause.

Customs Classification

For customs purposes, tin and tin products are classified within Chapter 80 of the HTSUS. This chapter is divided into headings, which are further divided into subheadings, and often into subsubheadings, each of which has its own HTSUS classification number. For example, the HTSUS number for tin alloys is 8001.20.00, indicating that it is a subcategory of the major heading unwrought tin (8001.00.00). There are seven major headings in HTSUS Chapter 80.

8001—Unwrought tin

8002—Tin waste and scrap

8003—Tin bars, rods, profiles, and wire

8004—Tin plates, sheets, and strip, of a thickness exceeding 0.2 mm.

8005—Tin foil (whether or not printed of backed with paper, paperboard, plastics, or similar backing materials), of a thickness (excluding any backing) not exceeding 0.2 mm; tin powders and flakes

8006—Tin tubes, pipes, and tube or pipe fittings (for examples, couplings, elbows, sleeves)

8007—Other articles of tin

For more details regarding classification of the specific product you are interested in importing, consult a customs broker, the appropriate commodity specialist at your nearest customs port, or see HTSUS. HTSUS is available for purchase from the U.S. Government Printing Office (see addresses at end of this chapter), and may be found in larger public libraries. Refer to "Classification—Liquidation" on page 207 for a general discussion of customs classification.

Sample Import Duties

Import duties will vary depending on the HTSUS classification of your product. Therefore, to determine the correct amount of duties, your product must be properly classified under the HTSUS. The following sample duties are taken from the duty listings for HTSUS Chapter 80 products.

Tin, not alloyed (8001.10.00): free; tin alloys (8001.20.00): free; tin waste and scrap (8002.00.00): free; tin bars and rods (8003.00.00):

4.2%; tin plates exceeding 0.2 mm in thickness (8004.00.00): 2.4%; tin foil not exceeding 0.2 mm in thickness (8005.10.00): 7%; tin powders and flakes (8005.20.00): 4.2%; tin pipes and fittings (8006.00.00): 2.4%; kitchenwares of tin (8007.00.10): 3.1%.

Entry and Documentation

The entry of merchandise is a two-part process consisting of 1) filing the documents necessary to determine whether merchandise may be released from Customs custody and 2) filing the documents that contain information for duty assessment and statistical purposes. In certain instances all documents must be filed and accepted by Customs prior to the release of the goods. Unless you have been granted an extension, you must file entry documents at a location specified by the district or area director within five working days of your shipment's date of arrival at a U.S. port of entry. These include a number of standard documents required by Customs for any entry, and

- For tin and tin alloy items intended for use with food: FDA Importers Entry Notice **Form FD701**
- U.S. Customs TSCA Certification when required

After you present the entry, Customs may examine your shipment, or may waive examination. The shipment is then released provided no legal or regulatory violations have been noted. You must then file entry summary documentation and deposit estimated duties at a designated customhouse within 10 working days of your shipment's release. For a detailed description of entry procedures, standard documentation, and informal entry, see "Entry Process" on page 182.

Marking and Labeling Requirements

For a general discussion of U.S. Customs marking and labeling requirements, see "Marking: Country of Origin" on page 215 and "Special Marking Requirements" on page 217.

Shipping Considerations

You will need to ensure that your goods are packaged and shipped with care to ensure that they arrive in good condition and pass smoothly through Customs. You are responsible for ensuring that the shipment is in compliance with all applicable government regulations for packaging and shipping. In most instances, you should not leave these arrangements solely to the discretion of your supplier. Careful preparation of the cargo and selection of the mode of transport can be essential to a cost-effective, timely delivery of undamaged goods. We strongly advise you to consult your shipping representative, insurance agent, or freight broker for advice on packing and shipping. Refer also to the major tab section "Packing/Shipping/Insurance" for a general discussion of packing and shipping.

Products that are listed as hazardous substances (49 CFR 172 appendix) may be transported in bulk only on compliance with Coast Guard notification procedures, shipping permit requirements, and complex transportation regulations (46 CFR 148). All hazardous substances must be packaged and transported in accordance with DOT regulations (49 CFR 171 et seq.).

Tin, tin alloys, and products made of them are often bulky, and should be securely stowed to avoid damage due to shifting en route. Tin and its products are also subject to tarnish and corrosion, which should be guarded against, especially as no allowance is made by customs for partial damage or loss due to such.

Publications Available

The *Harmonized Tariff Schedule of the United States* (HTSUS) is available from:

Government Printing Office (GPO)
Superintendent of Documents
Washington, DC 20402
(202) 512-1800 (Order line)
(202) 512-0000 (General)

The USGPO also has copies of specific laws available for purchase. The USGPO accepts credit card orders over the phone, as well as mail orders paid by credit card, a check drawn on a U.S. bank, or an international money order.

Relevant Government Agencies

Address inquiries regarding TSCA and EPA requirements for importation of hazardous or toxic substances to:

Environmental Protection Agency (EPA)
TSCA System Information
EPA 7408, OPPT
401 M Street SW
Washington, DC 20460
(202) 554-1404 (TSCA Information Hotline)

Address questions regarding transportation of hazardous substances to:

U.S. Department of Transportation (DOT)
Research and Special Programs Administration
Office of Hazardous Materials Standards
400 7th St. SW
Washington, DC 20590
(202) 366-4488

Address your questions regarding FDA requirements for tin products intended for use with food to:

Food and Drug Administration (FDA)
Center for Food Safety and Applied Nutrition
200 C Street SW
Washington, DC 20204
(202) 205-5241, 205-5042

Address questions regarding the importation of tin and tin products to the district or port director of Customs for you area. For addresses refer to"U.S. Customs District Offices" on page 62 or contact:

U.S. Customs Service
1301 Constitution Ave. NW
Washington, DC 20229
(202) 927-6724 (Information)
(202) 927-1000 (General)

Laws and Regulations

The following laws and regulations may be relevant to the importation of tin and tin products. The laws are contained in the U.S. Code (USC) and the regulations are published in the Code of Federal Regulations (CFR), both of which may be available at larger public and law libraries. Copies of specific laws are also available from the United States Government Printing Office (address above).

15 USC 2601 et seq.
Toxic Substances Control Act
This Act authorizes the EPA to determine whether a substance is harmful and to restrict importation, sale, and use of such substances.

19 CFR 12.118 et seq.
Regulations on Toxic Substances Control
These regulations require importers of chemical substances imported in bulk or as part of a mixture to certify to Customs that the shipment complies with the TSCA or is not subject to that Act.

15 USC 1261
Federal Hazardous Substances Act
This Act controls the importation of hazardous substances, sets forth prohibited imports, and authorizes various agencies to promulgate labeling, marking, and transport requirements.

49 CFR 170 et seq.
Regulations on Hazardous Materials

These regulations list all substances deemed hazardous and provide transport, marking, labeling, safety, and emergency response rules.

46 CFR 147.30
Regulations of Labeling of Hazardous Materials
This regulation requires the labeling of containers of hazardous substances and specifies the label contents.

46 CFR 148 et seq.
Regulations of Carriage of Solid Hazardous Materials in Bulk
These regulations govern the transport of solid hazardous substances in bulk, including reporting, permitting, loading, stowing, and shipping requirements.**21 USC 301 et seq.**
Food, Drug, and Cosmetic Act
This Act prohibits deceptive practices and regulates the manufacture, sale and importation or exportation of food, drugs, cosmetics, and related products. See 21 USC 331, 381, 382.

19 CFR 12.1 et seq.; 21 CFR 1.83 et seq.
Regulations on Food, Drugs, and Cosmetics
These regulations of the Secretary of Health and Human Services and the Secretary of the Treasury govern the standards, labeling, marking, and importing of products used with food, drugs, and cosmetics.

Principal Exporting Countries

The following listing includes samples of the main supplier nations of the products of this chapter. It is organized by HTSUS major heading. (Refer to "Customs Classification" above for the product codes.) Countries are listed in rank order of the value of products imported to the U.S. Statistics represent customs value entries for 1993 from the Bureau of Census, U.S. Department of Commerce.

8001—Brazil, Bolivia, Indonesia, China, Hong Kong, Malaysia, Chile, Canada, Germany, Mexico

8002—Mexico, Taiwan, Canada, Belgium, Japan, China, United Kingdom, Dominican Rep., Jamaica

8003—Canada, Japan, Brazil, Taiwan, Malaysia, China, United Kingdom, Germany, Mexico

8004—Taiwan, Canada, Netherlands, Japan, Singapore, China, Norway, France, United Kingdom, South Korea

8005—Germany, United Kingdom, Japan, Netherlands, Canada, Taiwan, Denmark, Australia

8006—Denmark, Norway, Taiwan

8007—China, Taiwan, Canada, United Kingdom, Thailand, Hong Kong, Germany, Mexico, Philippines, Brazil

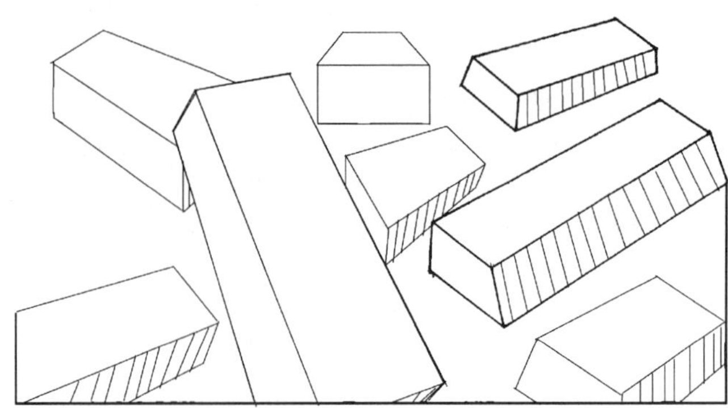

Chapter 81: Other Base Metals; Cermets; and Articles Thereof*

This section pertains to the importation of base metals not specified elsewhere, their alloys, materials of combined ceramics and metals (cermets), and articles made from these products, which are classified within Chapter 81 of the Harmonized Tariff Schedule of the United States (HTSUS). Specifically, it includes tungsten (wolfram), molybdenum, tantalum, magnesium, cobalt, bismuth, cadmium, titanium, zirconium, antimony, manganese, beryllium, chromium, germanium, vanadium, gallium, hafnium, indium, niobium, rhenium, and thallium and articles of these metals, as well as cermets and articles made of them. Chapter 81 represents a catch-all designation for relatively minor but highly specialized base metals.

Goods of base metals and their alloys in which metals other than those listed in Chapter 81 predominate are covered in Commodity Index chapters that relate to the specific metals, including iron and steel (Chapter 72), copper (Chapter 74), nickel (Chapter 75), aluminum (Chapter 76), lead (Chapter 78), zinc (Chapter 79), and tin (Chapter 80). Tools, other implements, and cutlery are found in Chapter 82, while miscellaneous articles of base metals are contained in Chapter 83. Precious metals, alloys of precious metals, and articles containing the same are covered specifically in Chapter 71.

Other products for which metals are incidental components are found within a variety of Commodity Index chapters. For example, if you are interested in importing metallic paints, refer to Chapter 36. For headgear with metal elements, see Chapter 65; for umbrella frames and related items, see Chapter 66. Finished and semifinished products classified as machinery, mechanical appliances, and electrical goods are found in Chapters 84 and 85. Assembled railway track and related equipment is covered in Chapter 86, vehicles in Chapter 87, aircraft in Chapter 88, and boats in Chapter 89. Instruments and apparatus are covered in Commodity Index chapters that relate to the specific articles, including optical, medical, and precision instruments (Chapter 90), clocks and watches (Chapter 91), and musical instruments (Chapter 92). Metal articles as parts of firearms, including ammunition, are found in Chapter 93. Commodity Index chapters that cover miscellaneous manufactures include furniture (Chapter 94), toys, games, and sporting goods (Chapter 95), and miscellaneous manufactured articles (Chapter 96). Works of art in which lead or its alloys are components, even dominant components, are covered in Chapter 97 if the primary value derives from the artistry rather than from the metal content.

*IMPORTANT: Read the Commodity Index Introduction. It is the essential framework for understanding this chapter.

Key Factors

The key factors in importing products of miscellaneous base metals are:

- Compliance with U.S. Environmental Protection Agency (EPA) requirements under the Toxic Substances Control Act (TSCA) (if the product is classified as a hazardous substance)
- Compliance with U.S. Department of Transportation (DOT) regulations for transport of hazardous cargo (if the product is a hazardous substance)

Although most importers utilize the services of a licensed customs broker in making their entries, and we recommend this practice, you should be aware of the regulatory, entry, and documentation issues involved in importing your product. You, as importer, are ultimately responsible for the fulfillment of any legal requirements applicable to your shipment.

General Considerations

Regulatory Agencies. The importation of specialized base metals, their alloys, and products made of them is relatively straightforward, with few restrictions or special requirements. The Environmental Protection Agency (EPA), under authority of the Toxic Substances Control Act (TSCA), imposes certain controls on the importation of base metals and articles that contain toxic substances. The Department of Transportation (DOT) enforces regulations for transporting hazardous cargo.

Definitions. Unlike alloys of precious metals, in which any alloy containing as much as 2% by weight of a precious metal is considered an alloy of that metal, alloys of base metals are classified according to the metal that predominates by weight over every other individual metal in the alloy. For customs purposes, alloys of a metal are included with the metal that they are an alloy of.

Chapter 81 of HTSUS covers other base metals and their alloys. The metals covered are defined as containing at least 99% by weight of the specified metal. Alloys are defined as being metallic substances in which the specified metal is less than 99% by weight, but not less than any other metallic element.

Toxic Substances Regulations. The EPA imposes certain controls on the importation of toxic substances. The TSCA defines a toxic substance as any substance determined to present the possibility of an unreasonable risk of injury to health and the environment. The DOT enforces regulations for transporting hazardous cargo. Substances are deemed hazardous if listed in DOT transport regulations (49 CFR 172 appendix). Unwrought primary metals, such as pigs, ingots, billets, blooms, and similar materials, are generally categorized as toxic substances within the definitions of the TSCA and thus are required to be in compliance with its provisions. These include packaging, shipping, marking, and labeling requirements. Refer to "Laws and Regulations" below.

Products defined as articles—that is, any manufactured item 1) that is formed into a specific shape or design during manufacture, 2) that has end-use functions dependent on the shape or design during end use, and 3) that during the end use, does not change in its chemical composition or that changes only for a noncommercial purpose separate from the article and only as allowed by law (19 CFR 12.120(2))—are not subject to the provisions of the TSCA. Metal products other than primary metals are generally considered to be articles even if they are to be further processed. For example, base metal products are articles even if they are to be subsequently fabricated into other products.

Certification. All products covered by the TSCA are subject to the U.S. Customs Service TSCA Import Certification Rule (19 CFR 12.118 et seq.). If you import these products, you must sign one of the following statements: "I certify that all materials in this shipment comply with all applicable rules or orders under TSCA and that I am not offering a chemical substance for entry in violation of TSCA or any applicable rule or order thereunder" or "I certify that all materials in this shipment are not subject to TSCA." You must file this TSCA certification of compliance or exemption at the time you make the entry at customs. Customs will not release your shipment without proper certification.

If you will be importing several or regular shipments, you should ask the appropriate customs district director to authorize your use of a blanket certification. A blanket certification is valid for one calendar year, may be renewed, and may be revoked at any time for cause.

Customs Classification

For customs purposes, specialized base metals, their alloys, and their products are classified within Chapter 81 of the HTSUS. This chapter is divided into headings, which are further divided into subheadings, and often into sub-subheadings, each of which has its own HTSUS classification number. For example, the HTSUS number for unwrought molybdenum is 8102.91.10, indicating that it is a subcategory of molybdenum other than powders (8102.91.00), which is a subsubcategory of the major heading molybdenum and articles thereof, including waste and scrap (8102.00.00). There are 13 major headings in HTSUS Chapter 81.

8101—Tungsten (wolfram) and articles thereof, including waste and scrap

8102—Molybdenum and articles thereof, including waste and scrap

8103—Tantalum and articles thereof, including waste and scrap

8104—Magnesium and articles thereof, including waste and scrap

8105—Cobalt mattes and other intermediate products of cobalt metallurgy; cobalt and articles thereof, including waste and scrap

8106—Bismuth and articles thereof, including waste and scrap

8107—Cadmium and articles thereof, including waste and scrap

8108—Titanium and articles thereof, including waste and scrap

8109—Zirconium and articles thereof, including waste and scrap

8110—Antimony and articles thereof, including waste and scrap

8111—Manganese and articles thereof, including waste and scrap

8112—Beryllium, chromium, germanium, vanadium, gallium, hafnium, indium, niobium (colombium), rhenium, and thallium, and articles of these metals, including waste and scrap

8113—Cermets and articles thereof, including waste and scrap

For more details regarding classification of the specific product you are interested in importing, consult a customs broker, the appropriate commodity specialist at your nearest customs port, or see HTSUS. HTSUS is available for purchase from the U.S. Government Printing Office (see addresses at end of this chapter), and may be found in larger public libraries. Refer to "Classification—Liquidation" on page 207 for a general discussion of customs classification.

Sample Import Duties

Import duties will vary depending on the HTSUS classification of your product. Therefore, to determine the correct amount of duties, your product must be properly classified under the HTSUS. The following sample duties are taken from the duty listings for HTSUS Chapter 81 products.

Tungsten waste and scrap (8101.91.10): 4.2%; tungsten plates and sheets (8101.92.00): 6.5%; molybdenum powders (8102.10.00): 13.9 cents/kg on molybdenum + 1.9%; molybdenum waste and scrap (8102.91.50): free; unwrought tantalum other than waste and scrap (8103.10.60): 3.7%; unwrought magnesium containing at least 99.8% by weight of magnesium (8104.11.00): 8%; magnesium turnings graded as to size (8104.30.00): 6.5%; unwrought cobalt alloys (8105.10.30): 5.5%; bismuth and articles thereof

(8106.00.00): free; cadmium other than unwrought cadmium, waste, scrap, or powders (8107.90.00): 5.5%; unwrought titanium sponge (8108.10.50): 15%; titanium castings (8108.90.30): 5.5%; tubes and pipes of titanium (8108.90.60): 15%; zirconium waste and scrap (8109.10.30): free; antimony and articles thereof (8110.00.00): free; unwrought manganese (8111.00.45): 14%; articles of beryllium (8112.19.00): 5.5%; chromium waste and scrap (8112.20.30): free; unwrought germanium (8112.30.60): 3.7%; articles of vanadium (8112.40.60): 3%; other listed metals of heading 8112, waste and scrap (8112.91.05): free; articles of other listed metals of heading 8112 (8112.99.00): 5.5%; cermets and articles thereof (813.00.00): 5.5%.

Entry and Documentation

The entry of merchandise is a two-part process consisting of 1) filing the documents necessary to determine whether merchandise may be released from Customs custody and 2) filing the documents that contain information for duty assessment and statistical purposes. In certain instances all documents must be filed and accepted by Customs prior to the release of the goods. Unless you have been granted an extension, you must file entry documents at a location specified by the district/area director within five working days of your shipment's date of arrival at a U.S. port of entry. These include a number of standard documents required by Customs for any entry, and

- U.S. Customs TSCA Certification when required

After you present the entry, Customs may examine your shipment, or may waive examination. The shipment is then released provided no legal or regulatory violations have been noted. You must then file entry summary documentation and deposit estimated duties at a designated customhouse within 10 working days of your shipment's release. For a detailed description of entry procedures, standard documentation, and informal entry, see "Entry Process" on page 182.

Marking and Labeling Requirements

For a general discussion of U.S. Customs marking and labeling requirements, see "Marking: Country of Origin" on page 215 and "Special Marking Requirements" on page 217.

Shipping Considerations

You will need to ensure that your goods are packaged and shipped with care to ensure that they arrive in good condition and pass smoothly through Customs. You are responsible for ensuring that the shipment is in compliance with all applicable government regulations for packaging and shipping. In most instances, you should not leave these arrangements solely to the discretion of your supplier. Careful preparation of the cargo and selection of the mode of transport can be essential to a cost-effective, timely delivery of undamaged goods. We strongly advise you to consult your shipping representative, insurance agent, or freight broker for advice on packing and shipping. Refer also to the major tab section "Packing/Shipping/Insurance" for a general discussion of packing and shipping.

Products that are listed as hazardous substances (49 CFR 172 appendix) may be transported in bulk only on compliance with Coast Guard notification procedures, shipping permit requirements, and complex transportation regulations (46 CFR 148). All hazardous substances must be packaged and transported in accordance with DOT regulations (49 CFR 171 et seq.).

Specialized base metals, their alloy, and products made of them are often bulky and heavy, and should be securely stowed to avoid damage due to shifting en route. Products made of these metals are also subject to oxidation and corrosion, which should be guarded against, especially as no allowance is made by customs for partial damage or loss due to such.

Publications Available

The *Harmonized Tariff Schedule of the United States* (HTSUS) is available from:

Government Printing Office (GPO)
Superintendent of Documents
Washington, DC 20402
(202) 512-1800 (Order line)
(202) 512-0000 (General)

The USGPO also has copies of specific laws available for purchase. The USGPO accepts credit card orders over the phone, as well as mail orders paid by credit card, a check drawn on a U.S. bank, or an international money order.

Relevant Government Agencies

Address inquiries regarding TSCA and EPA requirements for importation of hazardous or toxic substances to:

Environmental Protection Agency (EPA)
TSCA System Information
EPA 7408, OPPT
401 M Street SW
Washington, DC 20460
(202) 554-1404 (TSCA Information Hotline)

Address questions regarding transportation of hazardous substances to:

U.S. Department of Transportation (DOT)
Research and Special Programs Administration
Office of Hazardous Materials Standards
400 7th St. SW
Washington, DC 20590
(202) 366-4488

Address questions regarding the importation of specialized base metals and their products to the district or port director of Customs for you area. For addresses refer to"U.S. Customs District Offices" on page 62 or contact:

U.S. Customs Service
1301 Constitution Ave. NW
Washington, DC 20229
(202) 927-6724 (Information)
(202) 927-1000 (General)

Laws and Regulations

The following laws and regulations may be relevant to the importation of specialized base metals, their alloys, and products made of them. The laws are contained in the U.S. Code (USC) and the regulations are published in the Code of Federal Regulations (CFR), both of which may be available at larger public and law libraries. Copies of specific laws are also available from the United States Government Printing Office (address above).

15 USC 2601 et seq.
Toxic Substances Control Act
This Act authorizes the EPA to determine whether a substance is harmful and to restrict importation, sale, and use of such substances.

19 CFR 12.118 et seq.
Regulations on Toxic Substances Control
These regulations require importers of chemical substances imported in bulk or as part of a mixture to certify to Customs that the shipment complies with the TSCA or is not subject to that Act.

15 USC 1261
Federal Hazardous Substances Act
This Act controls the importation of hazardous substances, sets forth prohibited imports, and authorizes various agencies to promulgate labeling, marking, and transport requirements.

49 CFR 170 et seq.
Regulations on Hazardous Materials
These regulations list all substances deemed hazardous and provide transport, marking, labeling, safety, and emergency response rules.

46 CFR 147.30
Regulations on Labeling of Hazardous Materials
This regulation requires the labeling of containers of hazardous substances and specifies the label contents.

46 CFR 148 et seq.
Regulations of Carriage of Solid Hazardous Materials in Bulk
These regulations govern the transport of solid hazardous substances in bulk, including reporting, permitting, loading, stowing, and shipping requirements.

Principal Exporting Countries

The following listing includes samples of the main supplier nations of the products of this chapter. It is organized by HTSUS major heading. (Refer to "Customs Classification" above for the product codes.) Countries are listed in rank order of the value of products imported to the U.S. Statistics represent customs value entries for 1993 from the Bureau of Census, U.S. Department of Commerce.

8101—Japan, Germany, Austria, Israel, United Kingdom, Mexico, China, Netherlands, Belgium, Hungary

8102—Germany, Austria, Japan, China, United Kingdom, Netherlands, Hong Kong, Belgium, Russia, Uzbekistan

8103—Germany, Thailand, Japan, Mexico, Hong Kong, China, France, Kazakhstan, United Kingdom, Netherlands

8104—Russia, Canada, Ukraine, Mexico, China, Brazil, United Kingdom, Norway, Kazakhstan, Netherlands

8105—Zambia, Norway, Canada, Zaire, Finland, Russia, Germany, Belgium, United Kingdom, Japan

8106—Mexico, Belgium, China, Peru, United Kingdom, Kazakhstan, Canada, Spain, Germany, Taiwan

8107—Canada, Mexico, Russia, Belgium, Germany, Bulgaria, Norway, Finland, Spain, Netherlands

8108—Japan, United Kingdom, Russia, Germany, France, Canada, China, Italy, Sweden, Ukraine

8109—France, Germany, Japan, Canada, Belgium, United Kingdom, Italy, Australia, China, Hong Kong

8110—China, Japan, Kyrgyzstan, Hong Kong, United Kingdom, Canada, Bolivia, Germany, Thailand, Mexico

8111—South Africa, China, France, Saudi Arabia, Canada, Switzerland, United Kingdom, Germany, Belgium, Mexico

8112—China, Japan, France, United Kingdom, Canada, South Africa, Germany, Belgium, Russia, Italy

8113—Sweden, Canada, United Kingdom, Germany, Australia, Switzerland, Netherlands, Taiwan, France

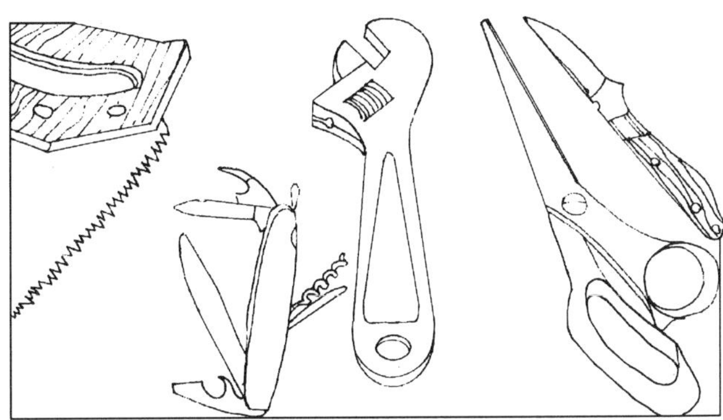

Chapter 82: Metal Tools and Implements*

Full title: Implements, Cutlery, Spoons, and Forks, of Base Metal; Parts Thereof of Base Metal

This section pertains to the importation of metal tools and implements, which are classified within Chapter 82 of the Harmonized Tariff Schedule of the United States (HTSUS). Specifically, it includes hand tools of a type involved primarily in gardening and agriculture; handsaws and blades; files, rasps, and cutting tools designed primarily to cut or work metal; wrenches; other hand tools, including torches, hammers, woodworking tools, screwdrivers, and other household tools, including sets of tools for retail sale; interchangeable parts and bits for hand tools—including pieces for power or machine tools but not the tools themselves; industrial knives; kitchen and table knives; razors and blades; scissors; other cutlery; and kitchen and table utensils. With the exception of blowtorches, portable forges, grinding wheels, and goods of heading 8209, articles covered in Chapter 82 basically represent implements with a blade, working edge or surface, or other similar part. Cutting tools of cermets (materials of ceramic and metal), and of precious and semiprecious stones, natural or synthetic, are also covered.

If you are interested in importing power tools, refer to Commodity Index Chapter 84. Other electrical machinery, including parts and working edges—such as blades or cutting plates for electric shavers or electric hair clippers—are covered in Chapter 85. Medical instruments are covered in Chapter 90. Intermediate products of base metals and their alloys are covered in various other Commodity Index chapters, including iron and steel (Chapter 73), copper (Chapter 74), nickel (Chapter 75), aluminum (Chapter 76), lead (Chapter 78), zinc (Chapter 79), tin (Chapter 80), and other base metals (Chapter 81). Articles of precious metals are found in Chapter 71.

Key Factors

The key factors in the importation of metal tools and implements are:

- Compliance with U.S. Federal Trade Commission (FTC) and Consumer Product Safety Commission (CPSC) standards for consumer products
- Compliance with U.S. Food and Drug Administration (FDA) regulations (for items to be used with food)
- For many edged tools, compliance with special marking requirements

*IMPORTANT: Read the Commodity Index Introduction. It is the essential framework for understanding this chapter.

Although most importers utilize the services of a licensed customs broker in making their entries, and we recommend this practice, you should be aware of the regulatory, entry, and documentation issues involved in importing your product. You, as importer, are ultimately responsible for the fulfillment of any legal requirements applicable to your shipment.

General Considerations

Regulatory Agencies. The importation of metal tools and implements is generally straightforward. There are few Customs restrictions or prohibitions. No permits, licenses, or special entry paperwork are required. However, regulations of other agencies may apply. For example, the Consumer Product Safety Commission (CPSC) regulates the import and sale of hazardous consumer products. The Food and Drug Administration (FDA) may control the import of products used with food.

Consumer Products. Many of the products found in this section are covered by the provisions of the Consumer Product Safety Act (CPSA), which establishes standards for the manufacturing and labeling of potentially hazardous consumer products. Imported consumer products for which such standards exist must comply with the full range of requirements prescribed for domestic products. In addition, the CPSA requires all manufacturers, distributors, retailers, and others involved in the commercial handling of such products to report immediately any potentially hazardous defects or failures to conform to established standards to the CPSC for investigation and potential action. Failure to submit such a Substantial Product Hazard Report can result in action by the CPSC. Contact the CPSC (see addresses at end of this chapter) with questions regarding specific products.

Articles Used with Foods. The importation of some metal tools and implements designed for use with food is regulated by the FDA under the provisions of the Federal Food, Drug, and Cosmetic Act (FDCA). Most commodities entering the U.S. under FDA jurisdiction require an FDA **Form 701**. However, tools, utensils, knives, and silverware are currently exempt from entry notification requirements and may be entered without the submission of **Form FD701**. The FDA's regulatory focus is on items that pose immediate and long-term public health hazards, such as lead-glaze dinnerware. Historically, imported implements of base metals have not posed threats of this nature. The FDA is authorized to institute entry notice requirements at any time should it rule that a problem exists. Therefore, if you are interested in importing these products, you should be familiar with FDA import entry procedures and requirements. For an annotated diagram of FDA entry procedures refer to the "Foods" appendix on page 808.

Cutting Tools. Importers should be aware of the special country of origin marking requirements for knives and some other cutting tools. For details, see "Marking and Labeling Requirements" below. If your shipment is ruled not to be in compliance with these requirements, it will be refused entry.

Tool Sets. If you are importing hand tools or other implements in sets—including sets of silverware—keep in mind that duties are levied on the basis of the highest rate applicable to any given piece contained in the set. To keep your duty rates as low as possible, choose the components of your sets carefully.

Customs Classification

For customs purposes, metal tools and implements are classified within Chapter 82 of the HTSUS. This chapter is divided into headings, which are further divided into subheadings, and often into sub-subheadings, each of which has its own HTSUS classification number. For example, the HTSUS number for slip joint pliers is 8203.20.40, indicating that it is a subcategory of pliers, pincers, tweezers, and similar tools (8203.20.00), which is a subcategory of the major heading files, rasps, pliers, pincers, tweezers, metal cutting shears, pipe-cutters, bolt cutters, perforating punches, and similar hand tools (8203.00.00). There are 15 major headings in HTSUS chapter 82.

8201—Hand tools of the following kinds and base metal parts thereof: spades, shovels, mattocks, picks, hoes, forks, and rakes; axes, bill hooks, and similar hewing tools; secateurs and pruners of any kind; scythes, sickles, hay knives, hedge shears, timber wedges, and other tools of a kind used in agriculture, horticulture, or forestry

8202—Handsaws and metal parts thereof; blades for saws of all kinds (including slitting, slotting, or toothless saw blades), and base metal parts thereof

8203—Files, rasps, pliers (including cutting pliers), pincers, tweezers, metal cutting shears, pipe-cutters, bolt cutters, perforating punches, and similar hand tools, and base metal parts thereof

8204—Hand-operated spanners and wrenches (including torque meter wrenches but not including tap wrenches); socket wrenches, with or without handles, drives, or extensions; base metal parts thereof

8205—Hand tools (including glass cutters) not elsewhere specified or included; blow torches and similar self-contained torches; vises, clamps, and the like, other than accessories for and parts of machine tools; anvils; portable forges; hand-or pedal-operated grinding wheels with frameworks; base metal parts thereof

8206—Tools of two or more headings 8202 to 8205, put up in sets for retail sale

8207—Interchangeable tools for hand tools, whether or not power-operated, or for machine tools (for example, for pressing, stamping, punching, tapping, threading, drilling, boring, broaching, milling, turning, or screwdriving), including dies for drawing or extruding metal, and rock drilling or earth boring tools; base metal parts thereof

8208—Knives and cutting blades, for machines or for mechanical appliances, and base metal parts thereof

8209—Plates, sticks, tips, and the like for tools, unmounted, of sintered metal carbides or cermets

8210—Hand-operated mechanical appliances, weighing 10 kg or less, used in preparation, conditioning, or serving of food or drink, and base metal parts thereof

8211—Knives and cutting blades, serrated or not (including pruning knives), other than knives of heading 8208, and blades and other base metal parts thereof

8212—Razors and razor blades (including razor blade blanks and strips), and base metal parts thereof

8213—Scissors, tailors' shears, and similar shears, and blades and other base metal parts thereof

8214—Other articles of cutlery (for example hair clippers, butchers' or kitchen cleavers, chopping or mincing knives, paper knives); manicure or pedicure sets and instruments (including nail files); base metal parts thereof

8215—Spoons, forks, ladles, skimmers, cake-servers, fish-knives, butter-knives, sugar tongs, and similar kitchen or tableware; base metal parts thereof

For more details regarding classification of the specific product you are interested in importing, consult a customs broker, the appropriate commodity specialist at your nearest Customs port, or see HTSUS. HTSUS is available for purchase from the U.S. Government Printing Office (see addresses at end of this chapter), and may be found in larger public libraries. Refer to "Classification—Liquidation" on page 207 for a general discussion of customs classification.

Sample Import Duties

Import duties will vary depending on the HTSUS classification of your product. Therefore, to determine the correct amount of duties, your product must be properly classified under the HTSUS. The following sample duties are taken from the duty listings for HTSUS Chapter 82 products.

Shovels (8201.10.00): 3%; axes (8201.1.40.60): 6.2%; pruning shears (8201.60.00): 1 cents each + 2.8%; handsaws (8202.10.00): free; hacksaw blades (8202.91.30): 3.7%; files and rasps over 11 cm but less than 17 cm in length (including tang) 12 cents/dozen; pliers (8203.20.60): 12 cents/dozen + 5.5%; bolt cutters (8203.40.30): 6%; nonadjustable hand-operated wrenches (8204.11.00): 9%; hammers with heads not over 1.5 kg each (8205.20.30): 6.2%; planes (8205.30.30): 7.2%; screwdrivers (8205.40.00): 6.2%; kitchen tools of aluminum (8205.51.60): 2.2 cents/kg + 5%; crowbars (8205.59.30): 0.4 cents/kg; caulking guns (8205.59.45): 5.3%; vises (8205.70.00): 5%; tools of two or more of headings 8202 to 8205, put up in sets for retail sale (8206.00.00): the rate of duty applicable to that article in the set subject to the highest rate of duty; carbide-tipped rock drilling bits (8207.11.00): 7.2%; dies for drawing or extruding metal (8207.20.00): 4.9%; tools for boring or broaching (8207.60.00): 7.2%; knives for metal-working (8208.10.00): 3.7%; knives for kitchen appliances or for machines used in the food industry (8208.30.00): 3.7%; plates, sticks, or tips of cermets (8209.00.00): 7%; table knives with fixed metal blades and silver-plated handles (8211.91.10): 0.6 cents each + 4.7%; other knives with stainless steel handles valued at under 25 cents each not over 25.9 cm in overall length (821.91.30): 1 cent each + 12.5%; hunting knives with wood handles (8211.92.60): 4.4%; pen knives, pocket knives, or other knives with folding blades (821.93.00): 3 cents each + 5.4%; safety razor blades (8212.20.00): 0.06 cents each +1.8%; scissors, valued not over $1.75/dozen (8213.00.30): 2 cents each + 5.1%; manicure or pedicure sets in leather cases (8214.20.60): 4%; cleavers (8214.90.30): 1 cents each + 4.9%; sets of assorted spoons, forks, and serving pieces (8215.20.00): the rate of duty applicable to that article in the set subject to the highest rate of duty; forks with rubber or plastic handles (8215.99.20): 0.5 cents each + 3.2%; spoons with stainless steel handles valued at under 25 cents each (8215.99.30): 17%.

Entry and Documentation

The entry of merchandise is a two-part process consisting of 1) filing the documents necessary to determine whether merchandise may be released from Customs custody and 2) filing the documents that contain information for duty assessment and statistical purposes. In certain instances all documents must be filed and accepted by Customs prior to the release of the goods. Unless you have been granted an extension, you must file entry documents at a location specified by the district or area director within five working days of your shipment's date of arrival at a U.S. port of entry. These include a number of standard documents required by Customs for any entry.

After you present the entry, Customs may examine your shipment, or may waive examination. The shipment is then released provided no legal or regulatory violations have been noted. You must then file entry summary documentation and deposit estimated duties at a designated customhouse within 10 working days of your shipment's release. For a detailed description of entry procedures, standard documentation, and informal entry, see "Entry Process" on page 182.

Prohibitions and Restrictions

The importation of switchblade knives is prohibited, with two exceptions: 1) the military may officially import switchblade knives, although individual military personnel may not; and 2) an individual who has only one arm may import, on his or her person, a switchblade knife the blade of which may not exceed three inches in length.

Marking and Labeling Requirements

Clippers, shears, safety razors, surgical instruments, scientific and laboratory instruments, pliers, pincers, knives, and other similar cutting tools must be marked legibly and conspicuously to indicate country of origin by one of the following methods: 1) die-stamping; 2) cast-in-the-mold lettering; 3) etching (acid or electrolytic); 4) engraving; 5) metal plates that bear the prescribed marking and that are securely attached to the article in a conspicuous place by welding, screws, or rivets.

For a general discussion of U.S. Customs marking and labeling requirements, see "Marking: Country of Origin" on page 215 and "Special Marking Requirements" on page 217.

Shipping Considerations

You will need to ensure that your goods are packaged and shipped with care to ensure that they arrive in good condition and pass smoothly through Customs. You are responsible for ensuring that the shipment is in compliance with all applicable government regulations for packaging and shipping. In most instances, you should not leave these arrangements solely to the discretion of your supplier. Careful preparation of the cargo and selection of the mode of transport can be essential to a cost-effective, timely delivery of undamaged goods. We strongly advise you to consult your shipping representative, insurance agent, or freight broker for advice on packing and shipping. Refer also to the major tab section "Packing/Shipping/Insurance" for a general discussion of packing and shipping.

Although most products of HTSUS Chapter 82 are neither perishable nor particularly fragile in nature, they must still be properly packaged and stowed to avoid damage during transit.

Publications Available

The *Harmonized Tariff Schedule of the United States* (HTSUS) is available from:

Government Printing Office (GPO)
Superintendent of Documents
Washington, DC 20402
(202) 512-1800 (Order line)
(202) 512-0000 (General)

The USGPO also has copies of specific laws available for purchase. The USGPO accepts credit card orders over the phone, as well as mail orders paid by credit card, a check drawn on a U.S. bank, or an international money order.

Relevant Government Agencies

Address questions regarding consumer product safety standards for hand tools and other implements to:

U.S. Consumer Product Safety Commission (CPSC)
Office of Compliance
Division of Regulatory Management
5401 Westbard Avenue
Bethesda, MD 20207
(301) 504-0400

Address your questions regarding FDA's involvement in importation of tools, utensils, cutlery, and silverware to:

Food and Drug Administration (FDA)
Center for Food Safety and Applied Nutrition
200 C Street SW
Washington, DC 20204
(202) 205-5241, 205-5042

Address your other questions regarding the importation of tools, utensils, cutlery, and silverware to the district or port director of Customs for you area. For addresses refer to "U.S. Customs District Offices" on page 62 or contact:

U.S. Customs Service
1301 Constitution Ave. NW
Washington, DC 20229
(202) 927-6724 (Information)
(202) 927-1000 (General)

Laws and Regulations

The following laws and regulations may be relevant to the importation of metal tools and implements. The laws are contained in the U.S. Code (USC) and the regulations are published in the Code of federal Regulations (CFR), both of which may be available at larger public and law libraries. Copies of specific laws are also available from the United States Government Printing Office (address above).

15 USC 1263
Consumer Product Safety Act
This Act sets standards for the manufacture, processing, and labeling of products sold to U.S. consumers.

21 USC 301 et seq.
Food, Drug, and Cosmetic Act
This Act prohibits deceptive practices and regulates the manufacture, sale and importation or exportation of food, drugs, cosmetics, and related products. See 21 USC 331, 381, 382.

19 CFR 12.1 et seq.; 21 CFR 1.83 et seq.
Regulations on Food, Drugs, and Cosmetics
These regulations of the Secretary of Health and Human Services and the Secretary of the Treasury govern the standards, labeling, marking, and importing of products used with food, drugs, and cosmetics.

Principal Exporting Countries

The following listing includes samples of the main supplier nations of the products of this chapter. It is organized by HTSUS major heading. (Refer to "Customs Classification" above for the product codes.) Countries are listed in rank order of the value of products imported to the U.S. Statistics represent customs value entries for 1993 from the Bureau of Census, U.S. Department of Commerce.

8201—Taiwan, China, Canada, Japan, Brazil, United Kingdom, Germany, Switzerland, Austria, France

8202—Japan, Switzerland, South Korea, United Kingdom, Germany, Italy, Canada, Sweden, Taiwan, New Zealand

8203—Taiwan, China, Japan, Switzerland, Germany, Ireland, India, Pakistan, United Kingdom, Italy

8204—Taiwan, China, Japan, India, Malaysia, Germany, Canada, United Kingdom, South Korea, Mexico

8205—Taiwan, China, Japan, Germany, United Kingdom, Switzerland, Mexico, Italy, Canada, France

8206—Taiwan, Japan, China, Turkey, France, Germany, Netherlands, South Korea

8207—Japan, Canada, Germany, Taiwan, Ireland, Sweden, United Kingdom, Italy, Mexico, Israel

8208—Germany, Japan, United Kingdom, Canada, Italy, Austria, Sweden, Switzerland, Taiwan, Slovenia

8209—Sweden, Japan, Israel, Germany, United Kingdom, Luxembourg, Canada, Austria, Mexico, Denmark

8210—Taiwan, China, Italy, Mexico, Hong Kong, France, Japan, South Korea, Germany, United Kingdom

8211—Japan, Taiwan, Switzerland, China, Germany, Brazil, South Korea, Pakistan, Hong Kong, France

8212—Greece, Mexico, United Kingdom, Hong Kong, Israel, Germany, India, South Korea, France, Canada

8213—Taiwan, South Korea, Germany, China, Japan, Italy, Brazil, Finland, Pakistan, Hong Kong

8214—South Korea, Germany, China, Taiwan, Brazil, Italy, Japan, Pakistan, Hong Kong, France

8215—China, Japan, South Korea, Taiwan, Indonesia, Mexico, Thailand, France, Malaysia, Germany

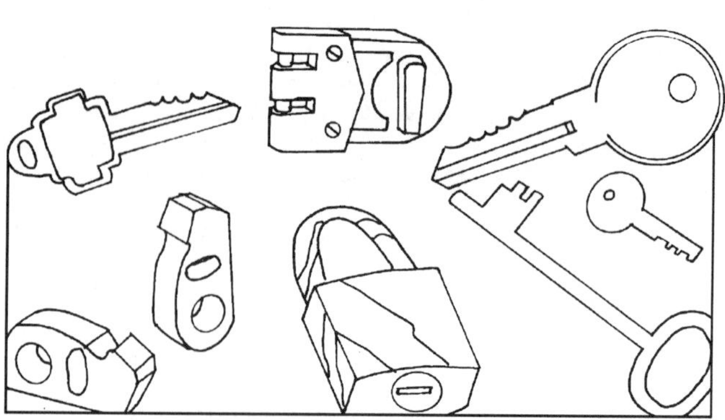

Chapter 83: Miscellaneous Articles of Base Metal*

This chapter relates to the importation of miscellaneous articles of base metals, which are classified within Chapter 83 of the Harmonized Tariff Schedule of the United States (HTSUS). Specifically, it includes locks, padlocks, keys, and lock hardware; mountings and fittings used for furniture, vehicles, architectural accents, leather goods, and window coverings, such as hinges, castors, harness fittings, drapery hardware, and hatracks; safes and strong-boxes; metal desk equipment; office accessories, such as ring binder hardware and paper clips; ornaments, picture frames, and mirrors of metal; flexible metal tubing; clasps, buckles, eyelets, grommets, and other metal fasteners; stoppers, caps, and lids; name plates and signs; and rods, such as for soldering. Chapter 83 represents something of a catch-all classification for a variety of products that are only tenuously related, often simply by the fact that they are made of metal and have not been classified elsewhere.

If you are interested in importing primary or intermediate products of iron or steel, refer to Commodity Index Chapter 72. Many other intermediate and finished goods of iron and steel are covered in Chapter 73. Other base metals, their alloys, and many products made from them in which specified base metals predominate are covered in Commodity Index chapters on the specific metal, including copper (Chapter 74), nickel (Chapter 75), aluminum (Chapter 76), lead (Chapter 78), zinc (Chapter 79), tin (Chapter 80), and other base metals (Chapter 81). Basic hardware items, such as nails and screws, are found in the chapter that covers the specific metal from which the articles are made. Hand tools, other implements, and cutlery are found in Chapter 82. Precious metals, alloys of precious metals, and articles containing the same are covered specifically in Chapter 71.

Other products for which metals are incidental—even if critical and major—components are found within a variety of Commodity Index chapters. For example, if you are interested in importing metallic paints, refer to Chapter 36. For haberdashery, see Chapter 65 for headgear with metal elements, and Chapter 66 for umbrella frames and related items. Finished and semifinished products classified as machinery, mechanical appliances, and electrical goods are found in Chapters 84 and 85. Assembled railway track and other equipment related to railways is covered in chapter 86; vehicles are covered in Chapter 87, aircraft in Chapter 88, and boats in Chapter 89. Instruments and apparatus are covered in Commodity Index chapters that relate to the specific articles, including optical, medical, and precision instruments (Chapter 90), clocks and watches (Chapter 91), and musical instruments (Chapter 92). Metal articles as parts of firearms, including ammunition,

*IMPORTANT: Read the Commodity Index Introduction. It is the essential framework for understanding this chapter.

are found in Chapter 93. Commodity Index chapters that cover miscellaneous manufactures include furniture and prefabricated structures (Chapter 94), toys, games, and sporting goods (Chapter 95), and miscellaneous manufactured articles (Chapter 96), all of which may contain metal components. Works of art that include metals, even as dominant components, are covered in Chapter 97 if the primary interest derives from the artistry rather than from the value of the metal content.

Although most importers utilize the services of a licensed customs broker in making their entries, and we recommend this practice, you should be aware of the regulatory, entry, and documentation issues involved in importing your product. You, as importer, are ultimately responsible for the fulfillment of any legal requirements applicable to your shipment.

General Considerations

Importation of articles of base metals of Chapter 83 is straightforward. There are no restrictions or prohibitions. You do not need permits or licenses, nor is special entry paperwork required.

HTSUS Chapter 83 covers a wide variety of products. Many articles included in this chapter are frequently utilized as parts of machines or other products. To avoid the difficulties inherent in determining whether a specific piece is a part of a particular machine or not, Note 2 of the introduction to HTSUS Section XV provides that parts of general use are always classified in their own heading rather than as a part of a particular machine or other product.

Consumer Products. Some of the products found in this section may be covered by the provisions of the Consumer Product Safety Act (CPSA), which establishes standards for the manufacturing and labeling of potentially hazardous consumer products. Imported consumer products for which such standards exist must comply with the full range of requirements prescribed for domestic products. In addition, the CPSA requires all manufacturers, distributors, retailers, and others involved in the commercial handling of such products to report immediately any potentially hazardous defects or failures to conform to established standards to the CPSC for investigation and potential action. Failure to submit such a Substantial Product Hazard Report can result in action by the CPSC. Contact the CPSC (see addresses at end of this chapter) with questions regarding specific products.

Dumping and Countervailing Duties Actions. Actions to restrict importation of or impose equalizing or punitive duties on imports of certain metal products from countries that are alleged to be involved in selling these products in the U.S. at below cost or their home country sale price (dumping) are occasionally brought, primarily to protect the domestic steel industry or other metalworking operations. Although no such actions are currently in force, restrictions can be imposed on short notice. You should contact U.S. Customs to verify the status of your proposed imports.

Customs Classification

For customs purposes, miscellaneous articles of base metals are classified within Chapter 83 of the HTSUS. This chapter is divided into major headings, which are further divided into subheadings, and often into sub-subheadings, each of which has its own HTSUS classification number. For example, the HTSUS number for base metal mountings or fittings for curtains, draperies, and window shades is 8302.49.80, indicating that it is a subcategory of other base metal mountings or fittings (8302.49.00), which is a subcategory of the major heading base metal mountings, fittings, and similar articles (8302.00.00). There are 11 major headings in HTSUS Chapter 83.

8301—Padlocks and locks (key, combination, or electronically operated), of base metal; clasps and frames with clasps, incorporating locks, of base metal; keys and parts of any of the foregoing articles of base metal

8302—Base metal mountings, fittings, and similar articles for furniture, doors, staircases, windows, blinds, coachwork, saddlery, trunks, chests, caskets, or the like; base metal hat racks, hat-pegs, brackets, and similar fixtures; castors with mountings of base metal; automatic door closers of base metal; and base metal parts thereof

8303—Armored or reinforced safes, strong-boxes, and doors and safe deposit lockers for strong-rooms, cash, or deed boxes and the like, and parts thereof

8304—Desk-top filing or card-index cabinets, paper trays, paper rests, pen trays, office-stamp stands, and similar office or desk equipment and parts thereof, of base metal, other than office furniture of heading 9403

8305—Fittings for looseleaf binders or files, letter clips, letter corners, paper clips, indexing tags, and similar office articles, and parts thereof, of base metal; staples in strips (for example, for office, upholstery, or packing), of base metal

8306—Bells, gongs, and the like, nonelectric, of base metal; statuettes and other ornaments, of base metal; photograph, picture, and similar frames, of base metal; mirrors of base metal; and base metal parts thereof

8307—Flexible tubing of base metal, with or without fittings

8308—Clasps, frames with clasps, buckles, buckle clasps, hooks, eyes, eyelets, and the like and parts thereof, of base metal, of a kind used for clothing, footwear, awnings, handbags, travel goods, or other madeup articles; tubular or bifurcated rivets of base metal; beads and spangles of base metal

8309—Stoppers, caps, and lids (including crown corks, screw caps, and pouring stoppers), capsules for bottles, threaded bungs, bung covers, seals, and other packing accessories, and parts thereof, of base metal

8310—Sign plates, name plates, address plates, and similar plates, numbers, letters, and other symbols, and parts thereof, of base metal, excluding those of heading 9405

8311—Wire, rods, tubes, plates, electrodes, and similar products of base metal or of metal carbides, coated or cored with flux material, of a kind used for soldering, brazing, welding, or deposition of metal or of metal carbides; wire and rods, of agglomerated base metal powder, used for metal spraying; base metal parts thereof

For more details regarding classification of the specific product you are interested in importing, consult a customs broker, the appropriate commodity specialist at your nearest customs port, or see HTSUS. HTSUS is available for purchase from the U.S. Government Printing Office (see addresses at end of this chapter), and may be found in larger public libraries. Refer to "Classification—Liquidation" on page 207 for a general discussion of customs classification.

Sample Import Duties

Import duties will vary depending on the HTSUS classification of your product. Therefore, to determine the correct amount of duties, your product must be properly classified under the HTSUS. The following sample duties are taken from the duty listings for HTSUS Chapter 83 products.

Padlocks not of cylinder or pin tumbler construction, not over 3.8 cm in width (8301.10.20): 2.3%; motor vehicle locks (8301.20.00): 5.7%; luggage locks (8301.40.50): 6.2%; keys (8301.70.00): 5.7%; iron, steel, aluminum, or zinc hinges, designed for motor vehicles (8302.10.30): 3.1%; other hinges suitable for interior or exterior doors (8302.10.90): 5.1%; other fittings and mountings suitable for furniture (8302.42.60): 5.1%; harness or saddlery hardware, coated or plated with precious metal (8302.49.20): 7.5%; other hardware for curtains, draperies, or window shades (8302.49.80): 5.1%; hat racks (8302.50.00): 3.4%; armored safes or strong-boxes (8303.00.00): 5.7%; desk-top file card boxes (8304.00.00): 5.7%; fittings for loose leaf binders (8305.10.00): 5.7%; staples in strips (8305.20.00): 0.9%; paper clips (8305.90.30):

3.8%; statuettes or ornaments of base metal, not plated with precious metal (8306.29.00): 5%; picture frames of base metal (8306.30.00): 5.3%; flexible tubing of iron or steel with fittings (8307.10.30): 5.8%; hooks, eyes, and eyelets (8308.10.00): 2.2 cents/kg + 5.8%; tubular or bifurcated rivets other than of iron or steel (8308.20.60): 4.7%; buckles and clasps (8308.90.60): 5.7%; crown corks (8309.10.00): 4.2%; name plates (8310.00.00): 3.8%; coated electrodes for arc-welding (8311.10.00): free.

Entry and Documentation

The entry of merchandise is a two-part process consisting of 1) filing the documents necessary to determine whether merchandise may be released from Customs custody and 2) filing the documents that contain information for duty assessment and statistical purposes. In certain instances all documents must be filed and accepted by Customs prior to the release of the goods. Unless you have been granted an extension, you must file entry documents at a location specified by the district or area director within five working days of your shipment's date of arrival at a U.S. port of entry. These include a number of standard documents required by Customs for any entry.

After you present the entry, Customs may examine your shipment, or may waive examination. The shipment is then released provided no legal or regulatory violations have been noted. You must then file entry summary documentation and deposit estimated duties at a designated customhouse within 10 working days of your shipment's release. For a detailed description of entry procedures, standard documentation, and informal entry, see "Entry Process" on page 182.

Entry Invoice for Metal Beads. If importing beads made of a base metal, the entry invoice must show: 1) the length of the string, if strung; 2) the size of the beads expressed in millimeters; and 3) the material of which the beads are composed.

Marking and Labeling Requirements

For a general discussion of U.S. Customs marking and labeling requirements, see "Marking: Country of Origin" on page 215 and "Special Marking Requirements" on page 217.

Shipping Considerations

You will need to ensure that your goods are packaged and shipped with care to ensure that they arrive in good condition and pass smoothly through Customs. You are responsible for ensuring that the shipment is in compliance with all applicable government regulations for packaging and shipping. In most instances, you should not leave these arrangements solely to the discretion of your supplier. Careful preparation of the cargo and selection of the mode of transport can be essential to a cost-effective, timely delivery of undamaged goods. We strongly advise you to consult your shipping representative, insurance agent, or freight broker for advice on packing and shipping. Refer also to the major tab section "Packing/Shipping/Insurance" for a general discussion of packing and shipping.

Articles of base metals are often bulky and heavy, and should be well packed and securely stowed to avoid damage due to shifting en route. Articles of base metals are also subject to oxidation and corrosion, which should be guarded against, especially as no allowance is made by customs for partial loss due to discoloration or rusting or to damage during shipping.

Publications Available

The *Harmonized Tariff Schedule of the United States* (HTSUS) is available from:

Government Printing Office (GPO)
Superintendent of Documents
Washington, DC 20402
(202) 512-1800 (Order line)
(202) 512-0000 (General)

The USGPO also has copies of specific laws available for purchase. The USGPO accepts credit card orders over the phone, as well as mail orders paid by credit card, a check drawn on a U.S. bank, or an international money order.

Relevant Government Agencies

Address questions regarding consumer product safety standards for articles of base metals to:

U.S. Consumer Product Safety Commission (CPSC)
Office of Compliance
Division of Regulatory Management
5401 Westbard Avenue
Bethesda, MD 20207
(301) 504-0400

Address questions regarding the importation of miscellaneous articles of base metals to the district or port director of Customs for you area. For addresses refer to "U.S. Customs District Offices" on page 62 or contact:

U.S. Customs Service
1301 Constitution Ave. NW
Washington, DC 20229
(202) 927-6724 (Information)
(202) 927-1000 (General)

Laws and Regulations

Various laws and regulations may be relevant to importing miscellaneous articles of base metals. Laws are contained in the U.S. Code (USC) and regulations are published in the Code of Federal Regulations (CFR), both of which may be available in larger public and law libraries. Copies of specific laws are also available from the United States Government Printing Office (address above).

15 USC 1263
Consumer Product Safety Act
This Act sets standards for the manufacture, processing, and labeling of products sold to U.S. consumers.

Principal Exporting Countries

The following listing includes samples of the main supplier nations of the products of this chapter. It is organized by HTSUS major heading. (Refer to "Customs Classification" above for the product codes.) Countries are listed in rank order of the value of products imported to the U.S. Statistics represent customs value entries for 1993 from the Bureau of Census, U.S. Department of Commerce.

8301—Taiwan, Mexico, Canada, Japan, China, Germany, United Kingdom, Malaysia, Spain, South Korea

8302—Japan, Taiwan, Canada, Germany, Austria, China, Mexico, Italy, United Kingdom, South Korea

8303—Taiwan, Thailand, South Korea, Brazil, Mexico, Canada, Israel, Norway, China, Japan

8304—Taiwan, China, Hong Kong, Japan, South Korea, France, Germany, India, Canada, Netherlands

8305—China, Malaysia, Hong Kong, Dominican Rep., Taiwan, Germany, Austria, Japan, South Korea, Singapore

8306—China, Taiwan, South Korea, India, Mexico, Thailand, Hong Kong, Malaysia, Canada, Indonesia

8307—Japan, South Korea, Canada, France, United Kingdom, Germany, Switzerland, Italy, Taiwan, Sweden

8308—Taiwan, Mexico, United Kingdom, Italy, China, Canada, Hong Kong, Germany, South Korea, Spain

8309—Canada, France, Spain, Japan, Germany, United Kingdom, Mexico, Italy, Taiwan, Dominican Rep.

8310—Japan, Taiwan, Germany, Canada, Israel, China, Switzerland, Hong Kong, Italy, Denmark

8311—Japan, Germany, Mexico, Canada, France, South Korea, United Kingdom, Taiwan, Israel, Ireland

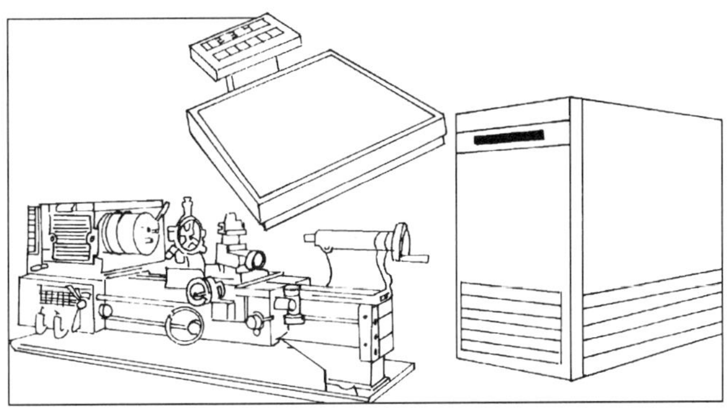

Chapter 84: Large Mechanical Appliances and Machines*

Full title: Nuclear Reactors, Boilers, Machinery, and Mechanical Appliances; Parts Thereof.

This chapter relates to the importation of large mechanical appliances and machines, which are classified within Chapter 84 of the Harmonized Tariff Schedule of the United States (HTSUS). Chapter 84 covers an extremely broad range of often highly specialized, generally large machinery, equipment, parts, and assemblies. The items in the chapter are those that are mechanical rather than electrical in function and power, although the primary function of the product determines its inclusion more than the nature of the power source. In general, items classified in Chapter 84 are those used to produce or prepare other goods rather than end-user products themselves.

Specifically, Chapter 84 includes power generating equipment; internal combustion engines, turbines, turbojets, and other types of engines; pumps; air conditioners; furnaces and industrial and laboratory ovens, refrigerators, and freezers; machinery designed to process materials by changing their temperature; rolling machines; centrifuges; washing and packing machinery; weighing machines; dispensers; cranes, forklifts, and other loading/unloading machinery; self-propelled heavy equipment, including construction and farm equipment; food processing machinery; pulp and paper-making machinery; printing equipment; textile spinning, weaving, knitting, and sewing machinery; laundry machinery; leatherworking machinery; metallurgical machinery; machine tools for working wood, metal, and other materials; hand power tools; soldering and welding machinery; calculators, adding machines, cash registers, postage meters, and similar office machines; computers; machinery for working minerals, electronics and electrical goods, rubber, plastics, and tobacco; molding apparatus; valves, bearings, transmissions, and other vehicle apparatus; miscellaneous machinery; and parts for all of the above.

Some machines, assemblies, components, and parts are covered elsewhere in the Commodity Index. For example, grindstones and milling stones are found in Commodity Index Chapter 68; machinery and parts made of ceramic materials are covered in Chapter 69; while industrial glassware and associated articles are covered in Chapter 70. Although parts of the machines covered in Chapter 84 are generally included with those machines, parts of general use—such as nuts and bolts, screws, and other general hardware—are found in Chapters 72-83 if made of a base metal, in Chapter 39 if made of plastic, and in Chapter 40 if made of rubber.

If you are interested in importing electronics products, refer to Chapter 85, which includes electric motors; transformers; batteries; some hand power tools; furnaces and heaters; communications devices; audio, video, and related systems; tapes and records; radio and television receivers and transmitters; radars; signaling devices; resistors, circuits, switches, tubes, and semiconductors; lightbulbs; and insulated wire and cable. Small hand tools, implements, and utensils are covered in Chapter 82, while finished products are found in Chapters 86-89 (transportation equipment), Chapters 90-92 (optical, precision, medical, and musical instruments and clocks), Chapter 93 (arms and ammunition), and Chapters 94-96 (miscellaneous manufactured articles).

Key Factors

The key factors in the importation of large appliances and machinery are:

- Compliance with Nuclear Regulatory Commission (NRC) requirements, including NRC import authorization, as needed for radioactive materials and equipment
- Compliance with U.S. Food and Drug Administration (FDA) requirements and FDA entry notification, as needed
- Compliance with U.S. Federal Communications Commission (FCC) requirements and FCC entry notification, as needed
- Compliance with U.S. Department of Energy (DOE) performance standards
- Compliance with Occupational Safety and Health Administration (OSHA) requirements for industrial products
- Compliance with Consumer Product Safety Commission (CPSC) and Federal Trade Commission (FTC) requirements for consumer products

Although most importers utilize the services of a licensed customs broker in making their entries, and we recommend this practice, you should be aware of the regulatory, entry, and documentation issues involved in importing your product. You, as importer, are ultimately responsible for the fulfillment of any legal requirements applicable to your shipment.

General Considerations

Regulatory Agencies. For the majority of items classified within HTSUS Chapter 84, no particular restrictions or prohibitions are imposed on importations into the U.S. and no permits, licenses, or special entry paperwork are required. For example, the importation of engines, machine tools, power tools, and most other forms of machinery included in the classification is straightforward.

However, some appliances or machines within Chapter 84 may be imported only on compliance with certain government regulations. For this reason, U.S. Customs requires special information on the entry invoice for machine tools (see below). All imports of industrial machinery and apparatus must comply with the appropriate regulations of the Occupational Safety and Health Administration (OSHA), while those intended for consumer use must comply with the appropriate regulations of the Consumer Product Safety Commission (CPSC) and Federal Trade Commission (FTC). Electronic products are subject to controls based on their compliance with standards for radioactive emissions, radio frequency limits, and performance standards,

*IMPORTANT: Read the Commodity Index Introduction. It is the essential framework for understanding this chapter.

which are enforced, respectively, by the Food and Drug Administration (FDA), the Federal Communications Commission (FCC), and the Department of Energy (DOE). Nuclear and radioactive products are licensed and controlled by the Nuclear Regulatory Commission (NRC). Because of the wide range of products and the variety of specialized requirements involved, it is necessary for importers to proceed with considerable care in ascertaining what agencies regulate the products they wish to import and what their legal responsibilities are early in the process.

FDA Regulations. Both domestic and imported electronic products are subject to federal radiation performance standards under the Radiation Control for Health and Safety Act of 1968 (RCHSA), enforced by the FDA. You will have to file two FDA forms with each import shipment of these products: an Importer's Entry Notice **Form FD701** and an Electronic Product Declaration **Form FD2877**. If you are interested in importing any products regulated by the FDA, you should be familiar with that agency's import requirements and procedures. For an annotated diagram of FDA import entry procedures, refer to the "Foods" appendix on page 808.

Radiation-producing devices are subject to relevant portions of the Federal Food, Drug, and Cosmetic Act (FDCA), enforced by the FDA. Radioisotopes and radioactive sources for medical use are also subject to provisions of the FDCA. Imported products regulated by the FDA are subject to port of entry inspection. **Form FD701** is required for FDA-regulated imports and may be obtained from your local FDA Import Operations office, from FDA headquarters (see addresses at end of this chapter), or from your customs broker.

Form FD2877 identifies your product's compliance status as one of the following: 1) manufactured prior to the effective date of the applicable federal standard; 2) complies with the standard, with manufacturer's certification label affixed; 3) noncomplying, imported only for purposes of research investigation, study, demonstration, or training; or 4) noncomplying, to be brought into compliance. Certain products subject to FDA regulation are also subject to FCC regulation.

Detention of Shipment. If your shipment is found to be noncomplying, it may be detained at the port of entry. In the case of products subject to FDA jurisdiction, the FDA may allow you to bring such a shipment into compliance before making a final decision regarding admittance. However, any sorting, reprocessing, or relabeling must be supervised by FDA personnel, and is done at the importer's expense. Such conditional release to allow an importer to bring a shipment into compliance is a privilege, not a right. The FDA may consider subsequent noncomplying shipments of the same type of product to constitute abuse of the privilege and require the importer to destroy or reexport the products. To ascertain what your legal responsibilities are, you should contact these agencies regarding the specific items to be imported.

FCC Regulations. Most items of computer hardware, such as cathode ray tube (CRT) screens/monitors, keyboards, floppy and flexible disk drives, hard drives, printers, central processing units, and peripherals, as well as other electronic devices such as computer machine controls, are radio frequency (rf) devices. RF devices are subject to FCC regulation under 47 CFR 2 and 15. You will have to file an FCC entry notification—**Form 740**—for each shipment. If your shipment includes a number of different items of computer hardware, a separate **Form 740** must be submitted for each type of item. Subassemblies that are essentially complete devices requiring only minor attachment or assembly prior to marketing and use—such as circuit boards and disk drives—are also subject to FCC regulation.

Form 740 must be filed with both the FCC and U.S. Customs prior to entry. You must certify on the form that the devices or subassemblies being entered comply with FCC technical regulations and thus can legally be imported. This requirement is intended to keep noncomplying devices from reaching the general public, thereby reducing the potential for harmful interference with authorized communications channels.

If you have questions regarding the regulatory status of an item such as computer hardware, how to fill out **Form 740**, or other questions, contact the regional FCC office nearest you, FCC headquarters (see addresses at end of this chapter), or your customs broker.

DOE Regulations. Both domestic and imported household consumer appliances must comply with applicable energy efficiency standards and labeling requirements under the Energy Policy and Conservation Act (EPCA). The DOE Consumer Products Efficiency Branch is responsible for test procedures and energy performance standards. The FTC Division of Energy and Product Information regulates labeling of such appliances. Importers should contact these agencies (addresses below) to find out about any requirements that may be in effect at the time they anticipate making their shipments.

EPCA covers 1) refrigerators, 2) freezers, 3) dishwashers, 4) clothes dryers, 5) water heaters, 6) room air conditioners, 7) home heating equipment, 8) television sets, 9) kitchen ranges and ovens, 10) clothes washers, 11) humidifiers, 12) central air conditioning, 13) furnaces, and 14) certain other types of household appliances. Not all appliances are covered by both agencies.

NRC Regulations. Many radioisotopes, all forms of uranium, thorium, and plutonium, and all nuclear reactors imported into the U.S. are subject to the regulations of the NRC, which are in addition to the import regulations that may be imposed by other U.S. agencies. Authority to import these items, or articles containing these items, is granted solely by the NRC.

To comply with NRC requirements, the importer must be aware of the identity and amount of any NRC-controlled radioisotopes, or uranium, thorium, and plutonium, and of any nuclear reactor being imported into the U.S. It is up to the importer to present to U.S. Customs satisfactory proof of the NRC authorization under which the controlled commodity is being imported. The authority cited may be the number of a specific or general license, or the specific section of NRC regulations that establishes a general license or grants a standing exemption for the specific type of product being entered. The foreign exporter may save time for the prospective importer by furnishing him or her complete information concerning the presence of NRC-controlled commodities in the importation.

OSHA Regulations. OSHA establishes and enforces regulations designed to ensure safety in the workplace, including standards for equipment and its use. Although most OSHA regulations deal with installation and use procedures, some equipment is subject to OSHA-imposed specifications. Imported machinery must comply with all OSHA standards and procedures, which are often specific and voluminous. Consult OSHA (see addresses at end of this chapter) for more information regarding specific products.

CPSC and FTC Regulations. Some of the products found in this section are covered by the provisions of the Consumer Product Safety Act (CPSA), which establishes standards for the manufacturing and labeling of potentially hazardous consumer products. Imported consumer products for which such standards exist must comply with the full range of requirements prescribed for domestic products. In addition, the CPSA requires all manufacturers, distributors, retailers, and others involved in the commercial handling of such products to report immediately any potentially hazardous defects or failures to conform to established standards to the CPSC for investigation and potential action. Failure to submit such a Substantial Product Hazard Report can result in action by the CPSC. Contact the CPSC (see addresses at end of this chapter) with questions regarding specific products.

Customs Classification

For customs purposes, large appliances and machinery are classified within Chapter 84 of the HTSUS. This chapter is divided into major headings, which are further divided into subheadings, and often into sub-subheadings, each of which has its own HTSUS classification number. For example, the HTSUS number for other (screw-type) compressors is 8414.30.80, indicating that it is a subcategory of compressors of a kind used in refrigerating equipment (8414.30.00), which is a subcategory of the major heading air or vacuum pumps, air or other gas compressors and fans (8414.00.00). There are 85 major headings in HTSUS Chapter 84.

8401—Nuclear reactors; fuel elements (cartridges), non-irradiated, for nuclear reactors; machinery and apparatus for isotopic separation; parts thereof

8402—Steam and other vapor generating boilers (other than central heating hot water boilers capable also of producing low pressure steam); super-heated water boiler; parts thereof

8403—Central heating boilers (other than those of heading 8402) and parts thereof

8404—Auxiliary plant for use with boilers of heading 8402 or 8403 (for example, economizers, superheaters, soot removers, gas recoverers); condensers for steam or other vapor power units; parts thereof

8405—Producer gas or water gas generators, with or without their purifiers; acetylene gas generators and similar water process gas generators, with or without their purifiers; parts thereof

8406—Steam turbines and other vapor turbines, and parts thereof

8407—Spark-ignition reciprocating or rotary internal combustion piston engines

8408—Compression-ignition internal combustion piston engines (diesel or semi-diesel engines)

8409—Parts suitable for use solely or principally with the engines of heading 8407 or 8408

8410—Hydraulic turbines, water wheels, and regulators therefore; parts thereof

8411—Turbojets, turbopropellers, and other turbines, and parts thereof

8412—Other engines and motors, and parts thereof

8413—Pumps for liquids, whether or not fitted with a measuring device; liquid elevators; parts thereof

8414—Air or vacuum pumps, air or other gas compressors and fans; ventilating or recycling hoods incorporating a fan, whether or not fitted with filters; parts thereof

8415—Air conditioning machines, comprising a motor-driven fan and elements for changing the temperature and humidity, including those machines in which the humidity cannot be separately regulated; parts thereof

8416—Furnace burners for liquid fuel, for pulverized solid fuel or for gas; mechanical stokers, including their mechanical grates, mechanical ash dischargers and similar appliances; parts thereof

8417—Industrial or laboratory furnaces and ovens, including incinerators, nonelectric, and parts thereof

8418—Refrigerators, freezers, and other refrigerating or freezing equipment, electric and other; heat pumps, other than the air conditioning machines of heading 8415; parts thereof

8419—Machinery, plant, or laboratory equipment, whether or not electrically heated, for the treatment of materials such as heating, cooking, roasting, distilling, rectifying, sterilizing, pasteurizing, steaming, drying, evaporating, vaporizing, condensing, or cooling, other than machinery or plant of a kind used for domestic purposes; instantaneous or storage water heaters, nonelectric; parts thereof

8420—Calendering or other rolling machines, other than for metals or glass, and cylinders therefor; parts thereof

8421—Centrifuges, including centrifugal dryers; filtering or purifying machinery and apparatus, for liquids or gases; parts thereof

8422—Dishwashing machines; machinery for cleaning or drying bottles or other containers; machinery for filling, closing, sealing, capsuling, or labeling bottles, cans, boxes, bags, or other containers; other packing or wrapping machinery; machinery for aerating beverages; parts thereof

8423—Weighing machinery (excluding balances of a sensitivity of 5 cg or better), including weight-operated counting or checking machines; weighing machine weights of all kinds; parts thereof

8424—Mechanical appliances (whether or not hand operated) for projecting, dispersing, or spraying liquids or powders; fire extinguishers, whether or not charged; spray guns and similar appliances; steam or sand blasting machines and similar jet projecting machines; parts thereof

8425—Pulley tackle and hoists other than skip hoists; winches and capstans; jacks

8426—Ships derricks; cranes, including cable cranes; mobile lifting frames, straddle carriers and works trucks fitted with a crane

8427—Fork-lift trucks; other works trucks fitted with lifting or handling equipment

8428—Other lifting, handling, loading, or unloading machinery (for example, elevators, escalators, conveyers, teleferics)

8429—Self-propelled bulldozers, angledozers, graders, levelers, scrapers, mechanical shovels, excavators, shovel loaders, tamping machines, and road rollers

8430—Other moving, grading, leveling, scraping, excavating, tamping, compacting, extracting, or boring machinery, for earth, minerals, or ores; pile-drivers and pile-extractors; snowplows and snowblowers

8431—Parts suitable for use solely or principally with the machinery of heading 8425 to 8430

8432—Agricultural, horticultural, or forestry machinery for soil preparation or cultivation; lawn or sports ground rollers; parts thereof

8433—Harvesting or threshing machinery, including straw or fodder balers; grass or hay mowers; machines for cleaning, sorting, or grading eggs, fruit, or other agricultural produce, other than machinery of heading 8437; parts thereof

8434—Milking machines and dairy machinery, and parts thereof

8435—Presses, crushers, and similar machinery, used in the manufacture of wine, cider, fruit juices, or similar beverages; parts thereof

8436—Other agricultural, horticultural, forestry, poultry-keeping or bee-keeping machinery, including germination plant fitted with mechanical or thermal equipment; poultry incubators and brooders; parts thereof

8437—Machines for cleaning, sorting, or grading seed, grain, or dried leguminous vegetables, and parts thereof; machinery used in the milling industry or for the working of cereals or dried leguminous vegetables, other than farm-type machinery; parts thereof

8438—Machinery, not specified or included elsewhere in this chapter, for the industrial preparation or manufacture of food or drink, other than machinery for the extraction or preparation of animal or vegetable fats or oils; parts thereof

8439—Machinery for making pulp of fibrous cellulosic material or for making or finishing paper or paperboard (other than machinery of heading 8419); parts thereof

8440—Bookbinding machinery, including book-sewing machines, and parts thereof

8441—Other machinery for making up paper pulp, paper, or paperboard, including cutting machines of all kinds, and parts thereof

8442—Machinery, apparatus, and equipment (other than the machine tools of heading 8456 to 8465), for type-founding or typesetting, for preparing or making printing blocks, plates, cylinders, or other printing components; blocks, plates, cylinders, and lithographic stones, prepared for printing purposes (for example, paned, grained, or polished); parts thereof

8443—Printing machinery; machines for uses ancillary to printing; parts thereof

8444—Machines for extruding, drawing, texturing, or cutting manmade textile materials

8445—Machines for preparing textile fibers; spinning, doubling, or twisting machines, and other machinery for producing textile yarns; textile reeling or winding (including weft winding) machines and machines for preparing textile yarns for use on the machines of heading 8446 or 8447

8446—Weaving machines (looms)

8447—Knitting machines, stitch-bonding machines, and machines for making gimped yarn, tulle, lace, embroidery, trimmings, braid, or net and machines for tufting

8448—Auxiliary machinery for use with machines of heading 8444, 8445, 8446, or 8447 (for example, dobbies, Jacquards, automatic stop motions, and shuttle changing mechanisms); parts and accessories suitable for use solely or principally with the machines of this heading or of heading 8444, 8445, 8446, or 8447 (for example, spindles and spindle flyers, card clothing, combs, extruding nipples, shuttles, healds and heald-frames, hosiery needles)

8449—Machinery for the manufacture or finishing of felt or nonwovens in the piece or in shapes, including machinery for making felt hats; blocks for making hats; parts thereof

8450—Household-or laundry-type washing machines, including machines which both wash and dry; parts thereof

8451—Machinery (other than machines of heading 8450) for washing, cleaning, wringing, drying, ironing, pressing (including fusing presses), bleaching, dyeing, dressing, finishing, coating or impregnating textile yarns, fabrics or made up textile articles and machines for applying the paste to the base fabric or other support used in the manufacture of floor coverings such as linoleum; machines for reeling, unreeling, folding, cutting, or pinking textile fabrics; parts thereof

8452—Sewing machines, other than book-sewing machines of heading 8440; furniture bases and covers specially designed for sewing machines; sewing machine needles; parts thereof

8453—Machinery for preparing, tanning, or working hides, skins, or leather or for making or repairing footwear or other articles of hides, skins, or leather, other than sewing machines; parts thereof

8454—Converters, ladles, ingot molds, and casting machines, of a kind used in metallurgy or in metal foundries, and parts thereof

8455—Metal-rolling mills and rolls therefore; parts thereof

8456—Machine tools for working any material by removal of material, by laser or other light or photon beam, ultrasonic, electro-discharge, electro-chemical, electron-beam, ionic beam, or plasma arc processes

8457—Machining centers, unit construction machines (single station) and multistation transfer machines, for working metal

8458—Lathes for removing metal

8459—Machine tools (including way-type unit head machines) for drilling, boring, milling, threading, or tapping by removing metal, other than lathes of heading 8458

8460—Machine tools for deburring, sharpening, grinding, honing, lapping, polishing, or otherwise finishing metal, sintered metal carbides or cermets by means of grinding stones, abrasives, or polishing products, other than gear cutting, gear grinding, or gear finishing machines of heading 8461

8461—Machine tools for planing, shaping, slotting, broaching, gear cutting, gear grinding, or gear finishing, sewing, cutting-off, and other machine tools working by removing metal, sintered metal carbides, or cermets, not elsewhere specified or included

8462—Machine tools (including presses) for working metal by forging, hammering, or die-stamping; machine tools (including presses) for working metal by bending, folding, straightening, flattening, shearing, punching, or notching; presses for working metal or metal carbides, not specified above

8463—Other machine tools for working metal, sintered metal carbides, or cermets, without removing material

8464—Machine tools for working stone, ceramics, concrete, asbestos-cement, or like mineral materials or for cold working glass

8465—Machine tools (including machines for nailing, stapling, gluing, or otherwise assembling) for working wood, cork, bone, hard rubber, hard plastics, or similar hard materials

8566—Parts and accessories suitable for use solely or principally with the machines of heading 8456 to 8465, including work or tool holders, self-opening dieheads, dividing heads, and other special attachments for machine tools; tool holders for any type of tool for working in the hand

8467—Tools for working in the hand, pneumatic or with self-contained nonelectric motor, and parts thereof

8468—Machinery and apparatus for soldering, brazing, or welding, whether of not capable of cutting, other than those of heading 8515; gas-operated surface tempering machines and appliances; parts thereof

8469—Typewriters and word processing machines

8470—Calculating machines; accounting machines, postage-franking machines, ticket-issuing machines, and similar machines, incorporating a calculating device; cash registers

8471—Automatic data processing machines and units thereof; magnetic or optical readers, machines for transcribing data onto data media in coded form and machines for processing such data, not elsewhere specified or included

8472—Other office machines (for example, hectograph or stencil duplicating machines, addressing machines, automatic banknote dispensers, coin-sorting machines, coin-counting or wrapping machines, pencil-sharpening machines, or stapling machines)

8473—Parts and accessories (other than covers, carrying cases, and the like) suitable for use solely or principally with machines of headings 8469 to 8472

8474—Machinery for sorting, screening, separating, washing, crushing, grinding, mixing, or kneading earth, stone, ores, or other mineral substances, in solid (including powder or paste) form; machinery for agglomerating, shaping, or molding solid mineral fuels, ceramic paste, unhardened cements, plastering materials, or other mineral products, in powder or paste form; machines for forming foundry molds of sand; parts thereof

8475—Machines for assembling electric or electronic lamps, tubes, or flashbulbs, in glass envelopes; machines for manufacturing or hot-working glass or glassware; parts thereof

8476—Automatic goods-vending machines (for example, postage stamp, cigarette, food, or beverage machines), including money-changing machines; parts thereof

8477—Machinery for working rubber or plastics or for the manufacture of products from these materials, not specified or included elsewhere in this chapter; parts thereof

8478—Machinery for preparing or making up tobacco, not specified or included elsewhere in this chapter; parts thereof

8479—Machines and mechanical appliances having individual functions, not specified or included elsewhere in this chapter; parts thereof

8480—Molding boxes for metal foundry; mold bases; molding patterns; molds for metal (other than ingot molds), metal carbides, glass, mineral materials, rubber, or plastics

8481—Taps, cocks, valves, and similar appliances, for pipes, boiler shells, tanks, vats, or the like, including pressure-reducing valves and thermostatically controlled valves; parts thereof

8482—Ball or roller bearings, and parts thereof

8483—Transmission shafts (including camshafts and crankshafts) and cranks; bearing housings, housed bearings, and plain shaft bearings; gears and gearing; ball screws; gear boxes and other speed changers, including torque converters; flywheels and pulleys, including pulley blocks; clutches and shaft couplings (including universal joints); parts thereof

8484—Gaskets and similar joints of metal sheeting combined with other material or of two or more layers of metal; sets of assortments of gaskets and similar joints, dissimilar in composition, put in pouches, envelopes, or similar packings

8485—Machinery parts, not containing electrical connectors, insulators, coils, contacts, or other electrical features, and not specified elsewhere in this chapter

For more details regarding classification of the specific product you are interested in importing, consult a customs broker, the appropriate commodity specialist at your nearest customs port, or see HTSUS. HTSUS is available for purchase from the U.S. Government Printing Office (see addresses at end of this chapter), and may be found in larger public libraries. Refer to "Classification—Liquidation" on page 207 for a general discussion of customs classification.

Sample Import Duties

Import duties will vary depending on the HTSUS classification of your product. Therefore, to determine the correct amount of duties, your product must be properly classified under the HTSUS. The following sample duties are taken from the duty listings for HTSUS Chapter 84 products.

Nuclear fuel elements (cartridges), non-irradiated, and parts thereof (8401.30.00): 6.5%; super-heated water boilers (8402.20.00): 6.4%; central heating boilers (8403.10.00): 4.2%; condensers for steam or other vapor power units (8404.20.00): 7%; producer gas or water generators (8405,10.00): 2.8%; other (non-marine) steam turbines (8406.19.10): 7.5%; reciprocating piston engines of a kind used for propulsion of vehicles of Chapter 87 (8407.31.00): free; compression-ignition marine propulsion engines (8408.10.00): 3.7%; cast-iron vehicle engine parts, cleaned but nor machined (8409.99.10): free; hydraulic turbines of a power not exceeding 1,000 kw (8410.11.00): 7.5%; aircraft turbines of a thrust not exceeding 25 kw (8411.11.40): 5%; hydraulic power engines and motors (8412.21.00): 3.4%; other reciprocating positive displacement pumps (oil well and oil field pumps) (8413.50.00): 3%; electric table fans (8914.51.00): 4.7%; window air conditioners (8415.10.00): 2.2%; gas burners (8416.20.00): 3.4%; bakery ovens (8417.20.00): 5.7%; household compression type refrigerators (8418.21.00): 2.9%; instantaneous gas water heaters (8419.11.00): 4%; cylinders for textile calendering and rolling machines (8420.91.10): 5.1%; catalytic converters (8421.39.40): 3.9%; can-sealing machines (8422.30.10): 4.5%; scales for continuous weighing of goods on conveyors (8423.20.00): 4.4%; fire extinguishers (8424.10.00): 3.7%; electric winches (8425.31.00): 2%; self-propelled electric rider forklift trucks (8427.10.40): free; belt-type conveyors (8438.33.00): 2%; wheeled front-end shovel loaders (8429.51.10): 2%; snowblowers (8430.20.00): 2.5%; parts for offshore oil and gas drilling platforms (8431.43.40): 5.7%; disc harrows (8432.10.00): free; lawn mowers (8433.11.00): 4%; milking machines (8434.10.00): free; wine presses (8435.10.00): 4.2%; parts for poultry incubators (8436.91.00): free; flour mill and grain mill machinery (8437.80.00): 3.5%; machinery for preparation of meat or poultry (8438.50.00): 3.5%; machinery for finishing paper or paperboard (8439.30.00): 2%; bookbinding machinery (8439.10.00): 3.7%; machines for making bags, sacks, or envelopes (8440.21.00): 2%; phototypesetting and composing machines (8442.10.00): free; gravure printing machinery (8443.40.00): 3.3%; textile spinning machines (8445.20.00): 4.2%; shuttleless machines for weaving fabrics of a width exceeding 30 cm (8445.30.00): 4.7%; embroidery machines (8447.90.50): 4.2%; loom parts and accessories—shuttles (8448.41.00): 4.7%; finishing machinery for felt (8449.00.10): 5.1%; fully automatic washing machines of a dry linen capacity not exceeding 10 kg (8450.11.00): 2.8%; dry-cleaning machines (8451.10.00): 3.9%; household sewing machines (8452.10.00): 3.7%; machinery for making or repairing footwear (8453.20.00): free; die casting machines (8454.30.00): free; laser-operated numerically controlled metalworking machines (8456.10.10): 4.4%; numerically controlled vertical turret metal working lathes (8458.91.10): 4.2%; used or rebuilt boring machines (8459.40.00): 4.2%; sharpening (tool or cutter grinding) machines (8460.31.00): 4.4%; gear cutting machines (8461.40.10): 5.8%; die-stamping machines (8462.10.00): 4.4%; glass-working machines (8464.90.00): 3%; woodworking sawing machines (8465.91.00): 3%; jigs and fixtures (8466.20.10): 5.8%; chain saws (8467.81.00): 2.5%; word processing machines (8469.10.40): 2.2%; cash registers (8470.50.00): free; digital automatic data processing machines containing a central processing unit and an input/output unit (8471.20.00): 3.9%; ink jet printers (8471.92.44): 3.7%; numbering, dating, and check-writing machines (8472.90.60): free; concrete mixers (8374.31.00): 2.9%; automatic goods-vending machines (8476.19.00): 3.9%; blow-molding machines (8477.30.00): 3.9%; presses for the manufacture of particle board (8479.30.00): 3.7%; parts of industrial robots (8479.90.95): 3.7%; glass molds (8480.50.00): 3.9%; pneumatic transmission valves (8481.20.00): 3.7%; ball bearings (8482.10.10): 4.2%; camshafts and crankshafts for automobile engines (8483.10.10): 3.1%; gaskets (8484.10.00): 3.7%; ships' propellers (8485.10.00): 4.2%.

Entry and Documentation

The entry of merchandise is a two-part process consisting of 1) filing the documents necessary to determine whether merchandise may be released from Customs custody and 2) filing the documents that contain information for duty assessment and statistical purposes. In certain instances all documents must be filed and accepted by Customs prior to the release of the goods. Unless you have been granted an extension, you must file entry documents at a location specified by the district or area director within five working days of your shipment's date of arrival at a U.S. port of entry. These include a number of standard documents required by Customs for any entry, and:

- For radio frequency devices, FCC Entry Notification, **Form 740**
- For radiation-producing devices, FDA Importers Entry Notice, **Form FD701** and FDA Electronic Product Declaration **Form FD2877**
- Documentation of NRC import authorization

After you present the entry, Customs may examine your shipment, or may waive examination. The shipment is then released provided no legal or regulatory violations have been noted. You must then file entry summary documentation and deposit estimated duties at a designated customhouse within 10 working days of your shipment's release. For a detailed description of entry procedures, standard documentation, and informal entry, see "Entry Process" on page 182.

Entry Invoice for Machinery, Equipment, and Apparatus. For all articles of machinery, equipment, and apparatus, a statement is required detailing the use or method of operation of each type of machine.

Entry Invoices for Machine Parts. For machine parts, a statement is required specifying the kind of machine for which the parts are intended, or—if it is not known to the shipper—the kinds of machines for which the parts are suitable.

Entry Invoices for Machine Tools. Special information is required on invoices of machine tools entered under the following HTSUS headings: 1) 8456—8462, if equipped with a Computer Numerical Control (CNC) or the facings (electrical interface) for a CNC, must so state; 2) 8458—8463, if rebuilt, must so state; 3) 8456.30.10 Electrical Discharge Machines (EDM), if a Traveling Wire (Wire Cut) type, must so state. Wire EDM's use a copper or brass wire for the electrode; 4) 8457.10.0010—8457.10.0050 Machining Centers: must state whether or not they have an Automatic Tool Changer (ATC); vertical spindle machine centers with an ATC must also indicate the Y-travel; 5) 8458.11.0030—8458.11.00.90, horizontal lathes, numerically controlled: must indicate the rated hp (or kw rating) of the main spindle motor. (Use the continuous rather than 30-minute rating.)

Entry Invoices for Refrigerator-Freezers. For refrigerator-freezers classifiable under subheading 8418.10.00 and refrigerators classifiable under subheading 8418.20.00, a statement is required as to 1) whether they are compression or absorption type; and 2) refrigerated volume in liters. For freezers classifiable under subheadings 8418.30.00 and 8418.40.00, a statement is required as to whether they are chest or upright type. Liquid chilling units classifiable under subheadings 8418.69.0045 through 8418.69.0060 must include a statement as to whether they are centrifugal open-type, centrifugal hermetic-type, absorption-type, or reciprocating-type.

Entry Invoices for Rolling Mills. For rolling mills classifiable under subheadings 8455.30.0005 through 8455.30.0085, a statement is required indicating the composition of the roll—gray iron, cast steel, or other—and the weight of each roll.

Entry Invoices for Bearings. For ball or roller bearings classified under headings 8482.10.50 through 8482.80.00, the invoice must state 1) the type of bearing (whether ball or roller); 2) if a roller bearing, whether spherical, tapered, cylindrical, needled, or other; 3) whether a combination bearing (one containing both ball and roller components); and 4) if a ball bearing (excluding bearings with integral shafts or parts of ball bearings) whether or not radial, the following additional information: a) outside diameter of each bearing; and b) whether or not a radial bearing (i.e., an antifriction bearing primarily designed to support a load perpendicular to the shaft axis).

Restrictions and Prohibitions

Radioactive Materials. Many radioisotopes, all forms of uranium, thorium, and plutonium, and all nuclear reactors imported into the U.S. are subject to the regulations of the NRC (see addresses at end of this chapter), in addition to any other regulations imposed by any other agency (for example, the FDA also exercises jurisdiction over radioactive materials imported for medical uses). Formal authority to import these commodities or articles containing these commodities must be granted by the NRC, which exercises very tight controls.

Machine Tools. Certain types of machine tools from Japan and Taiwan are subject to Voluntary Restraint Agreements (VRAs) negotiated by the U.S. Trade Representative with those countries. Under these agreements, the level of exports by these countries to the U.S. are kept below an agreed-upon level. These agreements are monitored by the Department of Commerce (DOC). Presentation of an export certificate or license issued by the country of origin is a condition of entry through Customs.

Marking and Labeling Requirements

Country of origin markings may not be required on certain whole engines or on engine parts that are imported in order to be further manufactured in the U.S. Customs makes this determination on a case-by-case basis. If you have questions, you should contact the nearest customs port office for more information.

All electronic devices subject to FCC regulation are required to bear special labeling.

The FTC has specific labeling requirements for electrical appliances.

All radiation-producing products for which federal standards have been determined must be certified for compliance. The manufacturer must affix a certification label to each product stating that it conforms to the applicable standard. If you attempt to import products that require certification but that are not labeled, your shipment will be refused entry.

For a general discussion of U.S. Customs marking and labeling requirements, see "Marking: Country of Origin" on page 215 and "Special Marking Requirements" on page 217.

Shipping Considerations

You will need to ensure that your goods are packaged and shipped with care to ensure that they arrive in good condition and pass smoothly through Customs. You are responsible for ensuring that the shipment is in compliance with all applicable government regulations for packaging and shipping. In most instances, you should not leave these arrangements solely to the discretion of your supplier. Careful preparation of the cargo and selection of the mode of transport can be essential to a cost-effective, timely delivery of undamaged goods. We strongly advise you to consult your shipping representative, insurance agent, or freight broker for advice on packing and shipping. Refer also to the major tab section "Packing/Shipping/Insurance" for a general discussion of packing and shipping.

Machinery and large appliances are often bulky and heavy, and should be securely stowed to avoid damage due to shifting en route. Many products of Chapter 84 are also subject to corrosion, which should be guarded against, especially as no allowance is made by customs for partial loss due to deterioration or to damage during shipping.

Publications Available

The *Harmonized Tariff Schedule of the United States* (HTSUS) is available from:

Government Printing Office (GPO)
Superintendent of Documents
Washington, DC 20402
(202) 512-1800 (Order line)
(202) 512-0000 (General)

The USGPO also has copies of specific laws available for purchase. The USGPO accepts credit card orders over the phone, as well as mail orders paid by credit card, a check drawn on a U.S. bank, or an international money order.

Relevant Government Agencies

Address questions concerning FCC requirements for the importation of radiation-producing devices and radio frequency devices to:

Federal Communications Commission (FCC)
Enforcement Division, Investigations Branch
1919 M Street NW, Rm. 744
Washington, DC 20554
(202) 418-1170

Address questions regarding FDA requirements for the importation of radiation-producing devices to:

Food and Drug Administration (FDA)
Center for Devices and Radiological Health
Division of Small Manufactures Assistance
5600 Fishers Lane
Rockville, MD 20857
(800) 638-2041, (301) 638-2041

To obtain addresses of regional FDA offices contact FDA headquarters at:

U.S. Food and Drug Administration (FDA)
5600 Fishers Lane
Rockville, MD 20857
(301) 443-1544

Address questions regarding energy labeling and consumer product safety issues on household appliances to:

Federal Trade Commission (FTC)
Division of Enforcement
601 Pennsylvania Ave. NW
Washington, DC 20580
(202) 326-3035, 326-2996

Address questions regarding energy performance and testing standards for household appliances to:

U.S. Department of Energy (DOE)
Building Technologies Branch
Office of Codes and Standards
1000 Independence Ave. SW
Washington, DC 20585
(202) 586-9127, 586-1510

Address questions regarding the NRC regulations pertinent to importation of radioactive materials and nuclear reactors to:

Nuclear Regulatory Commission (NRC)
Washington, DC 20555
(301) 504-3352

Address questions regarding consumer product safety standards for machinery and appliances to:

U.S. Consumer Product Safety Commission (CPSC)
Office of Compliance
Division of Regulatory Management
5401 Westbard Avenue
Bethesda, MD 20207
(301) 504-0400

Address questions regarding the importation of machinery and large appliances to the district or port director of customs for you area. For addresses refer to"U.S. Customs District Offices" on page 62 or contact:

U.S. Customs Service
1301 Constitution Ave. NW
Washington, DC 20229
(202) 927-6724 (Information)
(202) 927-1000 (General)

Laws and Regulations

The following laws and regulations may be relevant to the importation of computer hardware. The laws are contained in the U.S. Code (USC) and the regulations are published in the code of Federal Regulations (CFR), both of which may be available at larger public and law libraries. Copies of specific laws are also available from the United States Government Printing Office (address above).

42 USC 6201 et seq.
Energy Policy and Conservation Act (EPCA)
This Act authorizes adoption of standards for operating at maximum energy efficiency and prescribes labeling and testing requirements for compliance.

10 CFR Part 430
Regulations on EPCA
These regulations set test procedures and standards for measuring energy consumption of refrigerators, freezers, dishwashers, clothes washers and dryers, water heaters, air conditioners, heaters and furnaces, televisions, oven and cooking appliances, and fluorescent lamps.

29 USC 651 et seq.
Occupational Safety and Health Act
This Act authorizes the adoption of standards for safety of employees in the workplace, including safety requirements for machinery being operated, and provides incentives for compliance and penalties for noncompliance.

29 CFR Part 1926
Regulations of OSHA
These regulations specify safety and health standards and inspection procedures for certain equipment, including equipment used in shipbuilding and repairing, protective equipment, hand and power tools, welding tools, cranes, derricks, hoists, elevators, conveyors, mechanized equipment, and motor vehicles.

15 USC 1263
Consumer Product Safety Act
This Act sets standards for the manufacture, processing, and labeling of products sold to U.S. consumers.

18 USC 831 et seq.
Dangerous Cargo Act
This Act restricts the import of fireworks and nuclear materials and authorizes enforcement by Customs. See 49 CFR Parts 170-171, 173, 177, 179, and 195; 46 USC 870.

21 USC 301 et seq.
Food, Drug, and Cosmetic Act
This Act prohibits deceptive practices and regulates the manufacture, sale and importation or exportation of food, drugs, cosmetics, and related products. See 21 USC 331, 381, 382.

19 CFR 12.1 et seq.; 21 CFR 1.83 et seq.
Regulations on Food, Drugs, and Cosmetics
These regulations of the Secretary of Health and Human Services and the Secretary of the Treasury govern the standards, labeling, marking, and importing of products used with food, drugs, and cosmetics.

42 USC 2077, 2111, 2122, 2131, 2155
Atomic Energy Act
These laws restrict importation and exportation of special nuclear material, atomic weapons, and byproduct material, and authorizes enforcement by Customs. See 10 CFR 30, 40, 50, 70 and 110.

42 USC 263b-263n
Radiation Control for Health and Safety Act
This Act prohibits entry of electronic products found not to be in compliance with prescribed standards. See 21 CFR Part 1005. Customs enforces this prohibition. See 19 CFR 12.90 et seq.

47 USC 302a
Devices That Interfere with Radio Reception
This law prohibits the importation of devices or home electronic equipment that fail to comply with regulations promulgated by the FCC. See 47 CFR 2.1201 et seq. and 18.119. Customs enforces the prohibition.

47 USC 303(s) and 330
Importation of Certain Television Receivers
These laws prohibit importation of television receivers that are incapable of receiving all frequencies allocated to television broadcasting and authorizes enforcement by Customs. See 47 CFR 15.61-15.72. Such receivers are subject to seizure and forfeiture if a person willfully or knowingly violates this prohibition. See 47 USC 510.

Principal Exporting Countries

The following listing includes samples of the main supplier nations of the products of this chapter. It is organized by HTSUS major heading. (Refer to "Customs Classification" above for the product codes.) Countries are listed in rank order of the value of products imported to the U.S. Statistics represent customs value entries for 1993 from the Bureau of Census, U.S. Department of Commerce.

8401—Japan, France, Germany, Croatia, Canada, United Kingdom, Cyprus, South Korea, Sweden, Mexico

8402—Canada, Finland, United Kingdom, Mexico, Colombia, South Korea, Israel, Fiji, Germany, Sweden

8403—Canada, Germany, Denmark, Netherlands, Italy, Israel, Taiwan, France, Finland, Belgium

8404—Israel, Canada, Germany, South Korea, Switzerland, United Kingdom, China, France, Japan, Finland

8405—Canada, France, Japan, Germany, United Kingdom, Sweden, Netherlands, Switzerland, Taiwan, Italy

8406—Japan, Switzerland, Germany, Canada, Austria, Sweden, United Kingdom, Italy, Israel, Poland

8407—Japan, Canada, Mexico, Germany, Brazil, United Kingdom, Belgium, Austria, Netherlands, Sweden

8408—Japan, United Kingdom, Germany, Brazil, France, Sweden, Italy, India, Finland, Belgium

8409—Japan, Canada, Mexico, Germany, Brazil, United Kingdom, Italy, Belgium, France, Taiwan

8410—Japan, Canada, Brazil, Sweden, Austria, France, Germany, Norway, United Kingdom, Mexico

8411—France, United Kingdom, Canada, Germany, Italy, Sweden, Japan, Singapore, Switzerland, South Korea

8412—Japan, United Kingdom, Canada, Germany, France, Sweden, Denmark, Italy, Finland, Israel

8413—Germany, Japan, Canada, United Kingdom, Italy, Brazil, Mexico, Sweden, France, South Korea

8414—Japan, Taiwan, China, Germany, Mexico, Brazil, United Kingdom, Thailand, Canada, Singapore

8415—Japan, Mexico, Canada, Singapore, South Korea, Malaysia, Brazil, Thailand, Germany, Switzerland

8416—Germany, Canada, United Kingdom, Italy, France, Netherlands, Denmark, Japan, Taiwan, Sweden

8417—Germany, Canada, Japan, Sweden, France, Italy, United Kingdom, Austria, Finland, Mexico

8418—Mexico, Canada, Sweden, Japan, Denmark, France, Germany, Singapore, China, Slovenia

8419—Canada, Japan, Germany, Mexico, Italy, United Kingdom, France, Finland, Sweden, Netherlands

8420—Germany, Japan, Taiwan, United Kingdom, Spain, Finland, Italy, Canada, France, Netherlands

8421—Japan, Canada, Germany, United Kingdom, Sweden, France, Mexico, Taiwan, Israel, Italy

8422—Germany, Italy, Canada, Japan, Switzerland, France, Sweden, United Kingdom, Mexico, Taiwan

8423—Japan, China, Germany, Taiwan, Switzerland, Canada, United Kingdom, Denmark, Hong Kong, Singapore

8424—Japan, Germany, Canada, Mexico, Taiwan, Italy, United Kingdom, France, Denmark, Israel

8425—China, Canada, Taiwan, Japan, Germany, United Kingdom, Mexico, France, Finland, Italy

8426—Japan, Germany, South Korea, Italy, Canada, Austria, Argentina, Finland, United Kingdom, France

8427—Canada, South Korea, United Kingdom, Japan, Germany, Ireland, Mexico, Netherlands, Sweden, Norway

8428—Japan, Canada, Mexico, Germany, Sweden, Denmark, United Kingdom, Switzerland, Italy, Netherlands

8429—Japan, United Kingdom, France, Belgium, Canada, Sweden, Germany, South Korea, Brazil, Poland

8430—Japan, Canada, Germany, United Kingdom, Finland, Italy, France, Sweden, Australia, Switzerland

8431—Japan, Canada, Germany, Mexico, United Kingdom, France, Italy, Sweden, South Korea, Belgium

8432—Canada, Italy, France, Japan, Mexico, Brazil, Germany, United Kingdom, Netherlands, South Korea

8433—Canada, Germany, Japan, France, Netherlands, United Kingdom, Italy, Australia, Mexico, Taiwan

8434—Sweden, Germany, New Zealand, United Kingdom, Denmark, Italy, France, Japan, Netherlands, Finland

8435—Italy, Germany, Switzerland, France, Portugal, South Korea, Hong Kong, Sweden, Japan, Canada

8436—Canada, Netherlands, South Africa, Germany, Sweden, United Kingdom, Finland, Israel, Italy, France

8437—Italy, Japan, United Kingdom, Germany, Switzerland, Canada, Spain, Denmark, Brazil, France

8438—Germany, Italy, Netherlands, Japan, Denmark, Switzerland, United Kingdom, France, Canada, Mexico

8439—Finland, Canada, Germany, Italy, Brazil, Sweden, France, United Kingdom, Japan, Switzerland

8440—Germany, Switzerland, United Kingdom, Portugal, Belgium, Japan, Mexico, Taiwan, Italy, Canada

8441—Germany, Switzerland, Italy, Japan, Canada, United Kingdom, France, Spain, Finland, Netherlands

8442—Israel, Germany, Japan, United Kingdom, Denmark, Belgium, Sweden, Canada, France, Singapore

8443—Germany, Japan, Italy, United Kingdom, France, Switzerland, Canada, Netherlands, Austria, Sweden

8444—Germany, Italy, Japan, Switzerland, United Kingdom, France, Austria, Taiwan, Canada, China

8445—Germany, Japan, France, Italy, Switzerland, United Kingdom, Belgium, Netherlands, Czech Rep., New Zealand

8446—Japan, Switzerland, Germany, Belgium, Italy, France, Austria, Taiwan, Netherlands, Australia

8447—Japan, Germany, Italy, Czech Rep., United Kingdom, South Korea, Spain, Taiwan, Switzerland, Sweden

8448—Germany, Switzerland, Japan, Italy, France, United Kingdom, Belgium, Canada, Taiwan, Sweden

8449—France, Germany, Austria, Portugal, Italy, Japan, Sweden, United Kingdom, Taiwan, Canada

8450—Mexico, Sweden, Germany, Japan, Canada, Belgium, Spain, Italy, Singapore, South Korea

8451—Germany, Italy, Canada, Switzerland, Japan, China, United Kingdom, South Korea, France, Taiwan

8452—Japan, Taiwan, Germany, Brazil, Switzerland, China, Italy, Sweden, France, Thailand

8453—Italy, Germany, United Kingdom, Switzerland, France, Spain, Taiwan, Canada, Mexico, Israel

8454—Japan, Canada, Germany, South Korea, Switzerland, Italy, United Kingdom, Brazil, France, Poland

8455—Japan, Germany, Italy, Canada, Sweden, United Kingdom, France, Brazil, Austria, Mexico

8456—Japan, Switzerland, Germany, United Kingdom, Thailand, Italy, Taiwan, Canada, Netherlands, Austria

8457—Japan, Germany, United Kingdom, Taiwan, Switzerland, Canada, Italy, Singapore, Thailand, South Korea

8458—Japan, Germany, Taiwan, United Kingdom, South Korea, Switzerland, China, Italy, Austria, Brazil

8459—Japan, Taiwan, Germany, Canada, Switzerland, Italy, Czech Rep., United Kingdom, China, France

8460—Japan, Germany, Switzerland, Taiwan, Italy, United Kingdom, China, Singapore, Sweden, Canada

8461—Germany, Japan, Taiwan, Canada, Italy, South Korea, Switzerland, United Kingdom, France, Netherlands

8462—Japan, Germany, Canada, Brazil, United Kingdom, Sweden, Switzerland, Italy, Belgium, Finland

8463—Germany, Japan, Switzerland, Italy, Canada, France, United Kingdom, Belgium, Taiwan, Denmark

8464—Japan, Italy, Germany, Switzerland, Israel, United Kingdom, France, Austria, Spain, Taiwan

8465—Taiwan, Germany, Italy, Japan, Canada, China, Austria, Switzerland, United Kingdom, France

8466—Japan, Germany, Canada, Switzerland, Taiwan, United Kingdom, Italy, Sweden, Israel, Spain

8467—Japan, Germany, Taiwan, Sweden, Mexico, United Kingdom, Italy, Canada, Brazil, Switzerland

8468—Japan, Ireland, United Kingdom, Canada, Germany, Taiwan, Switzerland, Italy, Sweden, Mexico

8469—Mexico, Singapore, Japan, Taiwan, Indonesia, South Korea, United Kingdom, Germany, Bulgaria, China

8470—Japan, Taiwan, China, Thailand, Malaysia, Singapore, United Kingdom, Canada, Italy, South Korea

8471—Japan, Singapore, Taiwan, South Korea, Malaysia, Thailand, Canada, United Kingdom, Mexico, China

8472—Japan, United Kingdom, China, Taiwan, Germany, Malaysia, France, Philippines, Hong Kong, Canada

8473—Japan, Taiwan, Singapore, Canada, South Korea, Hong Kong, Mexico, China, Ireland, United Kingdom

8474—Canada, Germany, United Kingdom, Denmark, Japan, South Africa, Italy, Sweden, France, Austria

8475—Japan, Netherlands, Mexico, Germany, United Kingdom, France, Italy, Hungary, Sweden, Canada

8476—Canada, Japan, United Kingdom, Taiwan, France, Switzerland, Italy, Netherlands, Mexico, Germany

8477—Japan, Germany, Canada, Italy, France, Austria, Switzerland, United Kingdom, Taiwan, Netherlands

8478—Germany, United Kingdom, Italy, Netherlands, Canada, Denmark, Ireland, Switzerland, Japan, Australia

8479—Japan, Germany, Canada, United Kingdom, Italy, Switzerland, Netherlands, France, Sweden, Belgium

8480—Canada, Japan, Portugal, Germany, Taiwan, Italy, France, Hong Kong, United Kingdom, Switzerland

8481—Japan, Mexico, Germany, Taiwan, Canada, Italy, United Kingdom, Austria, France, South Korea

8482—Japan, Germany, Canada, China, Singapore, United Kingdom, France, Taiwan, Italy, Sweden

8483—Japan, Germany, Canada, France, United Kingdom, Italy, Brazil, Belgium, Mexico, Switzerland

8484—Japan, Canada, Germany, United Kingdom, Taiwan, Mexico, Brazil, France, Sweden, Switzerland

8485—Germany, Japan, Canada, Italy, United Kingdom, Nèther-lands, France, Switzerland, Sweden, Mexico

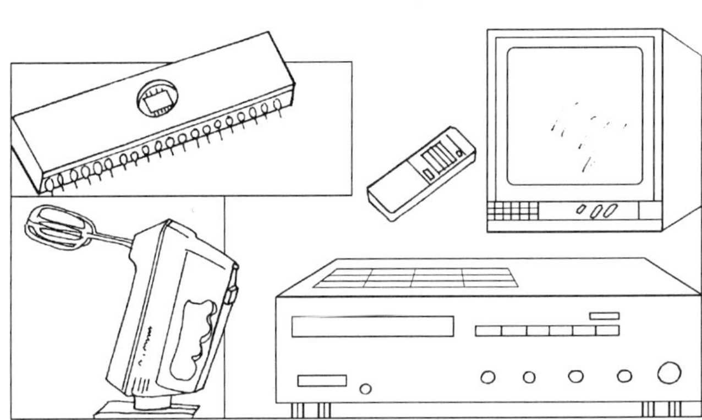

Chapter 85: Electronics and Components*

Full title: Electrical Machinery and Equipment and Parts Thereof; Sound Recorders and Reproducers, Television Image and Sound Recorders and Reproducers and Parts and Accessories of Such Articles

This chapter relates to the importation of electrically-powered products, electronics, and their components, which are classified within Chapter 85 of the Harmonized Tariff Schedule of the United States (HTSUS). Chapter 85 covers a very broad range of often highly specialized equipment, assemblies, components, and parts. The items in this chapter are those that are powered by or involve the use of electricity. Specifically, it includes electric motors and generators; transformers; electromagnets; batteries; power hand tools; electrical appliances, such as vacuum cleaners, food processors, garbage disposals, electric toothbrushes, and electric shavers; electrical starters; lighting and signaling equipment, including automotive components; flashlights; electrical industrial furnaces; lasers; water heaters, hair dryers, irons, microwave ovens, and other electric cookers; telephones and related equipment; microphones, loudspeakers, and stereo equipment; audio and video recorders and players; blank and prerecorded tapes, records, and computer disks; radio and television broadcasting, receiving, and related equipment; television sets; radars; capacitors, resistors, printed circuits, switches, panels, diodes, transistors, semiconductors, tubes, circuits, and similar components; lightbulbs; integrated electrical industrial apparatus; insulated wire; electrodes and other carbon products; insulated fittings; other miscellaneous electrical machinery; and parts of the above.

Large machinery, equipment, and appliances, especially industrial equipment, are generally classified in Commodity Index Chapter 84. For example, while many electrically-powered household appliances are covered in Chapter 85, appliances weighing more than 20 kg and such specific types of appliances as fans, clothes washers and dryers, dishwashers, pressing machines, and sewing machines are covered in Chapter 84. If you are interested in importing electric blankets, refer to Chapter 63. Consult the Commodity Index chapter for the specific product category involved for other electrically warmed articles of clothing, such as jackets (Chapter 62), socks (Chapter 61), earmuffs (Chapter 65), and boots (Chapter 65). Although assembled lightbulbs are covered in Chapter 85, the glass envelopes for such articles are found in Chapter 70. Electrically heated furniture is

*IMPORTANT: Read the Commodity Index Introduction. It is the essential framework for understanding this chapter.

covered in Chapter 94. Although the parts of the articles covered in Chapter 85 are generally included with those products, parts of general use—such as nuts and bolts, screws, and other general hardware—are classified in Chapters 72-83 by the particular material of which they are composed, if made of base metals, or in Chapter 39 if made of plastic or chapter 40 if made of rubber. Unpowered or mechanically powered hand tools are covered in Chapter 82, while specialized equipment—such as optical, scientific, medical, and other precision instruments; clocks and watches; and musical instruments—are covered respectively in Chapters 90, 91, and 92, regardless of their reliance on electrical power or components.

Key Factors

The key factors in the importation of electronics and components are:

- Compliance with U.S. Food and Drug Administration (FDA) standards and entry notification for radiation-producing devices
- Compliance with U.S. Federal Communications Commission (FCC) standards and entry notification for radio frequency devices
- Compliance with U.S Department of Energy (DOE) performance standards
- Compliance with Consumer Product Safety Commission (CPSC) and Federal Trade Commission (FTC) requirements for consumer products
- Compliance with trademark, trade name, and copyright restrictions

Although most importers utilize the services of a licensed customs broker in making their entries, and we recommend this practice, you should be aware of the regulatory, entry, and documentation issues involved in importing your product. You, as importer, are ultimately responsible for the fulfillment of any legal requirements applicable to your shipment.

General Considerations

Many electronic products and components may be imported without restrictions, permits, prior approval, special requirements, or additional paperwork. However, many others are subject to a variety of requirements enforced by a wide range of agencies, and it is necessary for importers to carefully check with the major agencies well in advance to be sure that they are in compliance with all relevant requirements for their specific electronics and component products.

Categories. From a regulatory viewpoint, many electronic devices subject to regulation fall into two general categories: those that produce radio frequency energy, and those that produce radiation. Radiation-producing electronic devices are regulated by the FDA (see addresses at end of this chapter) under the provisions of the Federal Food, Drug, and Cosmetic Act (FDCA) and the Radiation Control for Health and Safety Act of 1968 (RCHSA). Both imported and domestically produced electronic products must comply with all relevant FDA regulations. Whether you are importing a single product for personal use, or a commercial shipment for resale in the U.S., you must file an FDA Importers Entry Notice, **Form FD701** and Electronic Product Declaration, **Form FD2877** for each product type for which official standards exist. You will not be permitted to enter a shipment unless you have filed these forms. You may obtain them from FDA, National Center for Devices and Radiological Health (see addresses at end of this chapter) or from your customs broker. For an annotated diagram of FDA import procedures, refer to the "Foods" appendix on page 808.

Radio frequency (rf) devices are regulated by the FCC (see addresses at end of this chapter) under the provisions of 47 CFR Parts 2 and 15. You must file a copy of FCC **Form 740** with each shipment of rf devices. If your shipment consists of more than one type of device, you must file a separate form for each type. The form certifies that the imported model or device is either in compliance with, or is exempt from, FCC requirements, and is so labeled. An FCC entry declaration form (FCC **Form 740**) is required for products covered under FCC regulations.

Some products, such as ultrasonic therapeutic devices and television receivers, fall under the jurisdiction of both the FCC and the FDA and must comply with both sets of regulations. Although for purposes of simplicity this section will discuss the two categories as if they do not overlap, they do, and you should ascertain exactly which regulations your product is required to meet for which agency. Do not rely on one agency for information concerning the requirements of another agency. If you are in doubt as to the status of your commodity, contact both the FCC and the FDA.

Energy Efficiency Requirements. Both domestic and imported household consumer appliances must comply with applicable energy efficiency standards and labeling requirements under the Energy Policy and Conservation Act (EPCA) as amended. The DOE Consumer Products Efficiency Branch is responsible for test procedures and energy performance standards. The FTC Division of Energy and Product Information regulates household appliance labeling. You should contact these agencies (addresses below) to find out about any requirements that may be in effect at the time you anticipate making your shipment.

EPCA covers the following types of consumer products: 1) refrigerators and refrigerator-freezers; 2) freezers; 3) dishwashers; 4) clothes dryers; 5) water heaters; 6) room air conditioners; 7) home heating equipment other than furnaces; 8) television sets; 9) kitchen ranges and ovens; 10) clothes washers; 11) humidifiers and dehumidifiers; 12) central air conditioners; 13) furnaces; and 14) certain other types of household consumer appliances, as appropriate. Not all appliances are covered by requirements of both agencies.

Intellectual Property Provisions. Products such as microchips and recorded media (prerecorded tapes, records, computer software, and similar products) are subject to patent and trademark restrictions. (See "Prohibitions and Restrictions" below.) The Intellectual Property Rights (IPR) branch of U.S. Customs enforces laws pertinent to entry of such products. Importers must be prepared to show valid authorization from trademark and copyright holders. Pirated products are subject to seizure.

CPSC and FTC Regulations. Some of the products found in this section are covered by the provisions of the Consumer Product Safety Act (CPSA), which establishes standards for the manufacturing and labeling of potentially hazardous consumer products. Imported consumer products for which such standards exist must comply with the full range of requirements prescribed for domestic products. In addition, the CPSA requires all manufacturers, distributors, retailers, and others involved in the commercial handling of such products to report immediately any potentially hazardous defects or failures to conform to established standards to the CPSC for investigation and potential action. Failure to submit such a Substantial Product Hazard Report can result in action by the CPSC. Contact the CPSC (see addresses at end of this chapter) with questions regarding specific products.

Customs Classification

For customs purposes, electronics and electrical products and components are classified within Chapter 85 of HTSUS. This chapter is divided into major headings, which are further divided into subheadings, and often into sub-subheadings, each of which has its own HTSUS classification number. For example, the HTSUS number for DC generators is 8501.31.80, indicating that it is a subcategory of other DC motors and generators not exceeding 750 W (8501.31.00), which is a subcategory of the major heading electric motors and generators (excluding generating sets) (8501.00.00). There are 48 major headings in HTSUS chapter 85.

8501—Electric motors and generators (excluding generating sets)

8502—Electric generating sets and rotary converters

8503—Parts suitable for use solely or principally with the machines of heading 8501 or 8502

8504—Electrical transformers, static converters (for example, rectifiers), and inductors; parts thereof

8505—Electromagnets; permanent magnets and articles intended to become permanent magnets after magnetization; electromagnetic or permanent magnet chucks; clamps and similar holding devices; electromagnetic couplings, clutches, and brakes; electromagnetic lifting heads; parts thereof

8506—Primary cells and primary batteries; parts thereof

8507—Electric storage batteries, including separators thereof, whether or not rectangular (including square); parts thereof

8508—Electromechanical tools for working in the hand with self-contained electric motor; parts thereof

8509—Electromechanical domestic appliances, with self-contained electric motor; parts thereof

8510—Shavers and hair clippers, with self-contained electric motor; parts thereof

8511—Electrical ignition or starting equipment of a kind used for spark-ignition or compression-ignition internal combustion engines (for example, ignition magnetos, magneto-dynamos, ignition coils, spark plugs and glow plugs, starter motors); generators (for example, dynamos, alternators), and cut-outs of a kind used in conjunction with such engines; parts thereof

8512—Electrical lighting or signaling equipment (excluding articles of heading 8539), windshield wipers, defrosters, and demisters, of a kind used for cycles or motor vehicles; parts thereof

8513—Portable electric lamps designed to function by their own source of energy (for example, dry batteries, storage batteries, magnetos), other than lighting equipment of heading 8512; parts thereof

8514—Industrial or laboratory electric (including induction or dielectric) furnaces or ovens; other industrial or laboratory induction or dielectric heating equipment; parts thereof

8515—Electric (including electrically heated gas), laser or other light or photon beam, ultrasonic, electron beam, magnetic pulse or plasma arc, soldering, brazing, or welding machines and apparatus for hot spraying of metals or sintered metal carbides; parts thereof

8516—Electric instantaneous or storage water heaters and immersion heaters; electric space heating apparatus and soil heating apparatus; electrothermic hair-dressing apparatus (for example, hair dryers, hair curlers, curling tong heaters) and hand dryers; electric flatirons; other electrothermic appliances of a kind used for domestic purposes; electric heating resistors, other than those of heading 8545; parts thereof

8517—Electrical apparatus for line telephony or telegraphy, including such apparatus for carrier-current line systems; parts thereof

8518—Microphones and stands therefor; loudspeakers, whether or not mounted in their enclosures; headphones, earphones, and combined microphone/speaker sets; audio-frequency electric amplifiers; electric sound amplifier sets; parts thereof

8519—Turntables, record players, cassette players, and other sound reproducing apparatus, not incorporating a sound recording device

8520—Magnetic tape recorders and other sound recording apparatus, whether or not incorporating a sound reproducing device

8521—Video recording or reproducing apparatus, whether or not incorporating a video tuner

8522—Parts and accessories of apparatus of heading 8519 to 8521

8523—Prepared unrecorded media for sound recording or similar recording of other phenomena, other than products of chapter 37

8524—Records, tapes, and other recorded media for sound or other similarly recorded phenomena, including matrices and masters for the production of records, but excluding products of chapter 37

8525—Transmission apparatus for radiotelephony, radiotelegraphy, radiobroadcasting, or television, whether or not incorporating reception apparatus or sound recording or reproducing apparatus; television cameras

8526—Radar apparatus, radio navigational aid apparatus, and radio remote control apparatus

8527—Reception apparatus for radiotelephony, radiotelegraphy, or radiobroadcasting, whether or not combined, in the same housing, with sound recording or reproducing apparatus or a clock

8528—Television receivers (including video monitors and video projectors), whether or not incorporating radiobroadcast receivers or sound or video recording or reproducing apparatus

8529—Parts suitable for use solely or principally with the apparatus of heading 8525 to 8528

8530—Electrical signaling, safety, or traffic control equipment for railways, streetcar lines, subways, roads, inland waterways, parking facilities, port installations, or airfields (other than those of heading 8608); parts thereof

8531—Electric sound or visual signaling apparatus (for example, bells, sirens, indicator panels, burglar or fire alarms), other than those of heading 8512 or 8530; parts thereof

8532—Electrical capacitors, fixed, variable, or adjustable (pre-set); parts thereof

8533—Electrical resistors (including rheostats and potentiometers), other than heating resistors; parts thereof

8534—Printed circuits

8535—Electrical apparatus for switching or protecting electrical circuits, or for making connections to or in electrical circuits (for example, switches, fuses, lightning arrestors, voltage limiters, surge suppressors, plugs, junction boxes), for a voltage exceeding 1,000 v

8536—Electrical apparatus for switching or protecting electrical circuits, or for making connections to or in electrical circuits (for example, switches, relays, fuses, surge suppressors, plugs sockets, lamp-holders, junction boxes), for a voltage not exceeding 1,000 v

8537—Boards, panels (including numerical control panels), consoles, desks, cabinets, and other bases, equipped with two or more apparatus of heading 8535 or 8536, for electric control or the distribution of electricity, including those incorporating instruments or apparatus of chapter 90, other than switching apparatus of heading 8517

8538—Parts suitable for use solely or principally with the apparatus of heading 8535, 8536, or 8537

8539—Electrical filament or discharge lamps, including sealed beam lamp units and ultraviolet or infrared lamps; arc lamps; parts thereof

8540—Thermionic, cold cathode, or photocathode tubes (for example, vacuum or vapor or gas filled tubes, mercury arc rectifying tubes, cathode-ray tubes, television camera tubes); parts thereof

8541—Diodes, transistors, and similar semiconductor devices; photosensitive semiconductor devices, including photovoltaic cells whether or not assembled in modules or made up into panels; light-emitting diodes; mounted piezoelectric crystals; parts thereof

8542—Electronic integrated circuits and microassemblies; parts thereof

8543—Electrical machines and apparatus, having individual functions, not specified or included elsewhere in this chapter; parts thereof

8544—Insulated (including enameled or anodized) wire, cable (including coaxial cable) and other insulated electric conductors, whether or not fitted with connectors; optical fiber cables, made up of individually sheathed fibers, whether or not assembled with electric conductors or fitted with connectors

8545—Carbon electrodes, carbon brushes, lamp carbons, battery carbons, and other articles of graphite or other carbon, with or without metal, of a kind used for electrical purposes

8546—Electrical insulators of any materials

8547—Insulating fittings for electrical machines, appliances, or equipment, being fittings wholly of insulated material apart from any minor components (for example, threaded sockets) incorporated during molding solely for the purposes of assembly, other than insulators of heading 8546; electrical conduit tubing and joints therefor, of base metal lined with insulating material

8548—Electrical parts of machinery or apparatus, not specified or included elsewhere in this chapter

For more details regarding classification of the specific product you are interested in importing, consult a customs broker, the appropriate commodity specialist at your nearest customs port, or see HTSUS. HTSUS is available for purchase from the U.S. Government Printing Office (see addresses at end of this chapter), and may be found in larger public libraries. Refer to "Classification—Liquidation" on page 207 for a general discussion of customs classification.

Sample Import Duties

Import duties will vary depending on the HTSUS classification of your product. Therefore, to determine the correct amount of duties, your product must be properly classified under the HTSUS. The following sample duties are taken from the duty listings for HTSUS Chapter 85 products.

Universal AC/DC motors of an output exceeding 735 w but under 746 w (8501.20.50): 5%; AC single-phase motors of an output exceeding 375 w but not exceeding 746 w (8501.40.20): 4.2%; generating sets with spark-ignition internal combustion piston engines (502.20.00): 3%; parts for motors under 1865 w (8503.00.75): 10%; liquid dielectric transformers having a power capacity not exceeding 650 kva (8504.21.00): 2.4%; electromagnetic couplings, clutches, and brakes (8505.20.00): 3.9%; primary cells and primary batteries having an external volume exceeding 300 cm^3 (8506.20.00): 5.3%; nickel-iron storage batteries of a kind used as the primary source of electrical power for electrically powered vehicles of heading subheading 8703.90 (8507.40.40): 5.1%; power saws (8508.20.00): 2.2%; kitchen blenders (8509.40.00): 4.2%; electric shavers (8510.10.00): 4.4%; distributors and ignition coils (8511.30.00): 3.1%; parts of lighting equipment of a type used on bicycles (8512.90.40): 7.6%; flashlights (8513.10.20): 25%; induction or dielectric furnaces or ovens (8514.20.00): 2.5%; soldering irons or guns (8515.11.00): 2.5%; electric instantaneous or storage water heaters and immersion heaters (8516.10.00): 3.7%; toasters (8516.72.00): 5.3%; telephone sets (8517.10.00): 8.5%; multiple loudspeakers mounted in the same enclosure (8518.2.00): 4.9%; cassette tape recorders (8519.91.00): 3.7%; telephone answering machines (8520.20.00): 3.9%; video-cassette recorder (VCR), capable of recording (8521.10.60): 3.9%; pickup cartridges (8522.10.00): 3.9%; unrecorded magnetic tape of a width exceeding 4 mm but not exceeding 6.5 mm (8523.12.00): 4.2%; phonographic records (8524.10.00): 3.7%; video tape recordings of a width exceeding 6.5 mm but not exceeding 16 mm in cassettes (8524.23.10): 0.66 cents/linear meter; television transmitting apparatus (8525.10.20): 3.7%; radar apparatus (8526.10.00): 4.9%; radio-tape player combinations (8527.21.10): 3.7%; non-high definition, projection type television sets with a cathode-ray tube (8528.10.38): 5%; printed circuits of television tuners (8529.90.01): 5%; electrical signaling equipment for railways (8530.10.00): 2.7%; paging alert devices (8531.80.40): 2.7%; ceramic dielectric single layer capacitors (8533.23.00): 10%; fixed resistors for a power handling capacity not exceeding 20 w (8533.21.00): 6%; plastics impregnated inflexible printed circuits (8534.00.00): 5.3%; automatic circuit breakers (8535.21.00): 5.3%; relays for a voltage not exceeding 60 v (8536.41.00): 5.3%; switch panels for a voltage exceeding 1,000 v (8537.20.00): 5.3%; molded parts for switch boards (8538.90.60): 5.3%; sealed beam lamp units (8539.10.00): 3.1%; light bulbs (8539.22.80): 4%; color cathode-ray television picture tubes with a diagonal exceeding 35.56 cm (8540.11.10): 15%; diodes other than photosensitive or light-emitting diodes (8541.10.00): free; electric integrated circuits-unmounted chips of silicon (8542.11.80): free; particle accelerators (8543.10.00): 3.9%; other electric conductors of copper for a voltage exceeding 600 v (8544.59.20): 5.3%; electrodes of a kind used for furnaces (8545.11.00): 2.4%; electrical insulators of ceramics (8546.10.00): 5.8%; insulating fittings of plastics (8547.20.00): 3.7%; other parts not specified or elsewhere in this chapter (8548.00.00): 3.9%.

Entry and Documentation

The entry of merchandise is a two-part process consisting of 1) filing the documents necessary to determine whether merchandise may be released from Customs custody and 2) filing the documents that contain information for duty assessment and statistical purposes. In certain instances all documents must be filed and accepted by Customs prior to the release of the goods. Unless you have been granted an extension, you must file entry documents at a location specified by the district or area director within five working days of your shipment's date of arrival at a U.S. port of entry. These include a number of standard documents required by Customs for any entry, and:

- For radiation-producing devices, FDA Importers Entry Notice, **Form FD701** and Electronic Product Declaration **Form FD2877**
- For radio frequency devices, FCC Declaration **Form FCC 740**
- For products subject to regulation by both agencies, all three forms mentioned above
- For products subject to copyright or trademark laws, authorization from the copyright or trademark holder

After you present the entry, Customs may examine your shipment, or may waive examination. The shipment is then released provided no legal or regulatory violations have been noted. You must then file entry summary documentation and deposit estimated duties at a designated customhouse within 10 working days of your shipment's release. For a detailed description of entry procedures, standard documentation, and informal entry, see "Entry Process" on page 182.

Entry Invoice. For all articles of machinery, equipment, and apparatus, a statement is required detailing the use or method of operation of each type of machine. For machine parts, a statement is required specifying the kind of machine for which the parts are intended, or—if it is not known to the shipper—the kinds of machines for which the parts are suitable.

Prohibitions and Restrictions

Radio Frequency (rf) Devices. Under the Communications Act of 1934, as amended, all radio frequency (rf) devices are subject to FCC radio emission standards. You must file an FCC declaration FCC **Form 740** certifying that your model or device is in conformity with, will be brought into conformity with, or is exempt from the FCC requirements, for each shipment of rf devices you import. FCC standards and procedures have been developed to limit potential sources of rf interference to authorized radio services in the U.S. The FCC defines a radio frequency device as a product that emits rf energy, either intentionally or as a design byproduct. Radio frequency devices must meet specific FCC equipment authorization standards. When rf devices are imported into the U.S., a declaration is required that states that the appropriate FCC authorization has been granted. This declaration is made on FCC **Form 740**.

Equipment Authorization. FCC equipment authorization is required for certain types of rf devices imported into the U.S. Although compliance with these procedures is the responsibility of the foreign manufacturer, you should be aware of them, since noncomplying shipments will not be permitted entry. Equipment authorization procedures include: 1) type approval (requires testing of equipment sample); 2) type acceptance (requires review and evaluation of written application and equipment test report); 3) certification (requires review and evaluation of written application and equipment test report); 4) notification (requires submission of brief application); 5) verification (manufacturer tests device for compliance with FCC regulations prior to marketing, and retains test data); and 6) registration (applies to subscriber-owned and common-carrier-owned telephone devices; requires review and evaluation of written application and test report). Except for verification and registration procedures, a separate FCC **Form 731** should be filed with the FCC for each type of device for which equipment authorization is being requested. FCC **Form 730** is used for registration of telephone equipment under Part 68 of FCC rules. No application is required for verification. Fees are required for equipment authorization fillngs. Fee information is available from any FCC office or by calling (202) 643-FEES. If you would like more complete details regarding authorization procedures, contact the nearest regional FCC office, or the FCC Office of Engineering and Technology in Washington, D.C. (see addresses at end of this chapter).

Importation of Radio Frequency Devices. Each time you import a shipment of rf devices, you must file a separate FCC **Form 740** for each type of rf device represented in your shipment. Send your original completed **Form 740**(s) to the FCC Field Operations Bureau in Washington, D.C. (see addresses at end of this chapter). Attach a copy of your form(s) to the customs entry summary for your shipment, and present it to customs at the U.S. port of entry.

Some examples of rf devices requiring **Form 740** are: digital electronic weighing machinery; automatic typewriters; electronic calculating machines (not handheld); hard magnetic disc drives; cartridge-type radio-tape player for motor vehicles; microwave ovens; television cameras, receivers, and monitors; video players; video game equipment; radio receivers; digital clock radios; cordless handset telephones; and music synthesizer keyboards. For more information, contact any FCC office, or the FCC Washington headquarters (see addresses at end of this chapter).

Exclusions from Form 740 Filing Requirements. The following products do not require **Form 740**: digital watches/clocks; electronic (musical) greeting cards; battery-powered handheld calculators; and battery-powered handheld electronic games.

Radiation-producing Devices. The comprehensive Radiation Control for Health and Safety Act (RCHSA) was enacted in 1968 to protect the public from unnecessary exposure to radiation from electronic products. Administration of the law is carried out through the setting and enforcement of radiation performance standards to limit radiation emissions. The standards apply to products offered for sale or use in the U.S., whether manufactured in this country or elsewhere. Electronic products include all products or equipment capable of emitting ionizing or nonionizing radiation, or sonic, infrasonic, or ultrasonic waves. Television receivers, microwave ovens, X-ray equipment, lasers, ultraviolet lights, diathermy units, infrared heaters, ultrasonic cleaners, and particle accelerators are examples of products required to comply with RCHSA. Regulations for the enforcement of the act are published in 21 CFR Parts 1000-1050. The law is enforced by FDA's Center for Devices and Radiological Health (CDRH) (see addresses at end of this chapter).

Radiation Performance Standards and Product Certification. Performance standards are prescribed for electronic products when the FDA determines that federal regulations are necessary for the protection of the public health and safety. The standards (21 CFR Parts 1020-1050) prescribe maximum allowable radiation levels and other approaches to control of radiation emission, without specifying design features. If you are interested in importing a radiation-producing product, you should ascertain whether or not it is subject to a standard. The manufacturer of an electronic product for which there is an applicable federal performance standard must obtain certification for the product. Certification is based upon a test prescribed by the standard, or a testing program that is in accord with Good Manufacturing Practices as determined by CDRH. When considering an overseas purchase, you must determine that the product is in compliance. Certified products must bear a certification label stating that the product conforms to the applicable standard. Keep in mind that it is not as simple to identify a product that is eligible for certification but has not been certified. When in doubt, contact the FDA.

Noncomplying or Defective Products. RCHSA specifically provides that test samples may be taken from any import shipment to determine whether a product complies with an applicable standard. The FDA may—through authorization from the U.S. Customs Service—take a sample from your shipment for testing. Such samples are returned after testing is completed. If your product is discovered not to meet the provisions of an applicable standard, or if it contains any defect related to its safe use by reason of radiation emissions, the FDA will refuse entry. The manufacturer of a defective electronic product that has entered the commercial market is responsible for notifying the consumer, repairing the defect, and replacing the product or refunding the purchaser's money.

Recordkeeping. The FDA requires dealers and distributors of electronic products for which standards have been issued to maintain records. These records are intended to facilitate the location of purchasers for notification concerning defective or noncomplying devices, or to facilitate the recall of such products. In addition, manufacturers of certain electronic products designated by the regulation are required to maintain relevant product testing records and to make reports necessary to demonstrate compliance with the act.

Entry Documentation. **Form 701**, Importers Entry Notice, and **Form FD2877**, Electronic Product Declaration, are both required for each shipment of radiation-producing devices to which federal radiation performance standards apply. **Form 701** is a general FDA imports form applicable to any commodity regulated by the FDA. (For an annotated diagram of FDA import entry procedures, refer to the "Foods" appendix on page 808.) **Form 2877** must describe the compliance status of the product. You will have to affirm that the product either was 1) manufactured prior to the effective date of the applicable federal standard; 2) complies with the standard and has a label affixed by the manufacturer certifying compliance; 3) does not comply with the standard but is being imported only for purposes of research, investigation, study, demonstration, or training; or 4) does not now comply with the standard but will be brought into compliance. The provisions of RCHSA apply equally to electronic products manufactured in the U.S. and to those that are imported.

Products Covered By Radiation Performance Standards. The following products are currently covered by federal radiation performance standards. If you are considering importation of any of these products, be sure that the foreign manufacturer has obtained U.S. certification and has so labeled the items before attempting to enter a shipment into U.S. Customs territory. Uncertified products—even those that are eligible for certification—are refused entry, and any disposal or modification is undertaken at the importer's expense. Further information may be obtained from any FDA office or by referring to 21 CFR Parts 1000-1050.

Many foreign manufacturers produce electronic devices for export that conform to applicable FDA and FCC regulations. If you limit your purchases to such products and verify that the appropriate labels are affixed, you should have no difficulty with U.S. Customs.

Television Receivers. Standard effective January 16, 1970. Applies to products designed to receive and display a television picture through broadcast, cable, or closed-circuit television. Includes home television receivers, electronic viewfinders on TV cameras, TV projectors, and video monitors used with X-ray and other medical systems.

Demonstration-type Cold Cathode Gas Discharge Tubes. Standard effective May 19, 1970. Applies to tubes in which an electron flow is produced and sustained for purposes of demonstrating electron flow or X-ray production.

Microwave Ovens. Standard effective October 7, 1971. Applies to home and commercial products designed to heat or cook food through the application of electromagnetic energy.

Cabinet X-ray Systems. Standard effective April 10, 1975, except for systems designed primarily for the inspection of carry-on baggage, which became effective April 25, 1974. In addition to baggage inspection system, applies to other X-ray machines in enclosed freestanding cabinets.

Laser Products. Standard effective August 2, 1976. Amendment effective August 20, 1985, applies to all laser products, as well as products containing lasers.

Mercury Vapor Lamps. Standard effective March 8, 1980. Applies to any high intensity mercury vapor discharge lamp that is designed, intended, or promoted for illumination purposes.

Sunlamps. Standard effective May 7, 1980, amendment effective September 8, 1986, applies to sunlamp products and ultraviolet lamps intended for use in sunlamp products and intended to induce skin tanning.

Trademarks and Trade Names. Articles bearing counterfeit trademarks, or marks that copy or simulate a registered trademark of a U.S. or foreign corporation are prohibited importation, provided a copy of the U.S. trademark registration is filed with the Commissioner of Customs and recorded in the manner provided by regulations (19 CFR 133). The U.S. Customs Service also affords similar protection against unauthorized shipments bearing trade names that are recorded with customs pursuant to regulations (19 CFR 133, Subpart B). If your article bears a genuine trademark that is 1) owned by a U.S. citizen or company, 2) registered with U.S. Customs, you may not import the article without written permission from the U.S. trademark holder.

It is unlawful to import articles bearing genuine trademarks owned by a U.S. citizen or corporation without permission of the U.S. trademark owner, if the foreign and domestic trademark owners are not parent and subsidiary companies or otherwise under common ownership and control, provided the trademark has been recorded with customs.

The Customs Reform and Simplification Act of 1978 strengthened the protection afforded trademark owners against the importation of articles bearing a counterfeit mark. A "counterfeit trademark" is defined as a spurious trademark that is identical with, or substantially indistinguishable from, a registered trademark. Articles bearing a counterfeit trademark that are seized by customs and forfeited to the government may be 1) given to any federal, state, or local government agency that has established a need for the article; 2) given to a charitable institution; or 3) sold at public auction if more than 1 year has passed since forfeiture and no eligible organization has established a need for the article. The counterfeit marks must be removed before the forfeited articles may be given away or sold. If this is not feasible, the articles are destroyed. The law also provides an exemption from all restrictions on trademarked articles (limited to one of each type) accompanying a person arriving in the U.S. when the articles are for personal use and not for sale.

Copyrights. Section 602(a) of the Copyright Revision Act of 1976 provides that the importation into the U.S. of copies of a work acquired outside the U.S. without authorization of the copyright owner is an infringement of the copyright. Articles imported in violation of the import prohibitions are subject to seizure and forfeiture. Forfeited articles shall be destroyed. However, the articles may be returned to the country of export whenever customs is satisfied that there was no intentional violation. Copyright owners seeking import protection from the U.S. Customs Service must register their claim to copyright with the U.S. Copyright Office and record their registration with customs in accordance with applicable regulations (19 CFR 133, Subpart D).

Note that enforcement of copyright law has a high priority at customs, and even someone who is discovered unwittingly trying to bring in even a single copy of pirated software, audio-or video-tape, or similar article is subject to the full penalties of the applicable laws.

Country-Specific Import Restrictions

Recently, 3.5 inch floppy disks from Japan have been the subject of an antidumping action and have been banned from import into the U.S. Such actions are subject to change on relatively short notice, and the situation should be verified prior to attempting to import such products.

Marking and Labeling Requirements

FCC Requirements. All rf devices subject to FCC authorization procedures, whether manufactured within the U.S. or outside it, must bear labeling to show compliance. Devices that are not so labeled will not be permitted entry into U.S. Customs territory. For details on label wording, contact FCC (see addresses at end of this chapter).

FDA Requirements. All radiation-emitting devices for which federal standards have been determined must be certified for compliance. The manufacturer must affix a certification label to each product stating that it conforms to the applicable standard. Products requiring certification that are not so labeled will not be permitted entry.

Other Requirements. Contact the FTC (see addresses at end of this chapter) for information regarding labeling requirements.

For a general discussion of U.S. Customs marking and labeling requirements, see "Marking: Country of Origin" on page 215 and "Special Marking Requirements" on page 217.

Shipping Considerations

You will need to ensure that your goods are packaged and shipped with care to ensure that they arrive in good condition and pass smoothly through Customs. You are responsible for ensuring that the shipment is in compliance with all applicable government regulations for packaging and shipping. In most instances, you should not leave these arrangements solely to the discretion of your supplier. Careful preparation of the cargo and selection of the mode of transport can be essential to a cost-effective, timely delivery of undamaged goods. We strongly advise you to consult your shipping representative, insurance agent, or freight broker for advice on packing and shipping. Refer also to the major tab section "Packing/Shipping/Insurance" for a general discussion of packing and shipping.

Electronic products are subject to damage from excessive heat and moisture, and exposure must be guarded against. Electronic goods may be fragile, and should be carefully packed and securely stowed to avoid damage due to shifting en route.

Publications Available

The following publications may be relevant to the importation of electronics and components of Chapter 85:

The FCC Equipment Authorization Program for Radio Frequency Devices (Bulletin Number 61) and *Importation of Radio Frequency Devices* (Field Operations Bulletin Number 8) are both available from any regional FCC office (or address below).

Requirements of Laws and Regulations Enforced by the U.S. Food and Drug Administration is published by FDA and available upon request from FDA headquarters (see addresses at end of this chapter).

The *Harmonized Tariff Schedule of the United States* (HTSUS) is available from:

Government Printing Office (GPO)
Superintendent of Documents
Washington, DC 20402
(202) 512-1800 (Order line)
(202) 512-0000 (General)

The USGPO also has copies of specific laws available for purchase. The USGPO accepts credit card orders over the phone, as well as mail orders paid by credit card, a check drawn on a U.S. bank, or an international money order.

Relevant Government Agencies

Address questions regarding energy labeling of household appliances to:

Federal Trade Commission (FTC)
Division of Enforcement
601 Pennsylvania Ave. NW
Washington, DC 20580
(202) 326-3035, 326-2996

Address questions regarding FCC rules on rf devices or FCC equipment authorization to the nearest FCC regional office or to:

Federal Communications Commission (FCC)
Office of Engineering and Technology
7435 Oakland Mills Rd.
Colombia, MD 21046
(301) 725-1585

Address inquiries concerning FCC **Form 740** requirements to:

Federal Communications Commission (FCC)
Enforcement Division, Investigations Branch
1919 M Street NW, Rm. 744
Washington, DC 20554
(202) 418-1170

Address inquiries regarding importation of radiation-producing devices to either:

Food and Drug Administration (FDA)
Center for Devices and Radiological Health (CDRH)
Division of Small Manufactures Assistance
5600 Fishers Lane
Rockville, MD 20857
(800) 638-2041, (301) 638-2041

Food and Drug Administration (FDA)
Center for Food Safety and Applied Nutrition
200 C Street SW
Washington, DC 20204
(202) 205-5241, 205-5042

Address questions regarding energy performance testing and standards for household appliances to:

U.S. Department of Energy (DOE)
Building Technologies Branch
Office of Codes and Standards
1000 Independence Ave. SW
Washington, DC 20585
(202) 586-9127, 586-1510

Address questions regarding copyright and trademark laws to:

U.S. Customs Service
Office of Intellectual Property Rights
1301 Constitution Avenue NW
Washington, DC 20229
(202) 482-6960

Address questions regarding importation of electronic products to the district or port director of customs for you area. For addresses refer to "U.S. Customs District Offices" on page 62 or contact:

U.S. Customs Service
1301 Constitution Ave. NW
Washington, DC 20229
(202) 927-6724 (Information)
(202) 927-1000 (General)

Laws and Regulations

The following laws and regulations may be relevant to the importation of electronics, electrical appliances, and components. They are contained in the U.S. Code (USC) and the regulations are published in the Code of Federal Regulations (CFR), both of which may be available at larger public and law libraries. Copies of specific laws are also available from the United States Government Printing Office (address above).

42 USC 6201 et seq.
Energy Policy and Conservation Act (EPCA)
This Act authorizes adoption of standards for operating at maximum energy efficiency and prescribes labeling and testing requirements for compliance.

10 CFR Part 430
Regulations on EPCA
These regulations set test procedures and standards for measuring energy consumption of refrigerators, freezers, dishwashers, clothes washers and dryers, water heaters, air conditioners, heaters and furnaces, televisions, oven and cooking appliances, and fluorescent lamps.

15 USC 1263
Consumer Product Safety Act
This Act sets standards for the manufacture, processing, and labeling of products sold to U.S. consumers.

15 USC 1051 et seq.
Trademark Act
This Act provides, among other things, that no imported article of foreign origin that bears a name or mark calculated to induce the public to believe that it was manufactured in the United States, or in any foreign country or locality other than the country or locality where it was in fact manufactured, shall be admitted entry at any customhouse in the U.S.

17 USC 101 et seq., 602(a)
Copyright Revision Act
This law provides that the importation into the U.S. of copies of a work acquired outside the U.S. without authorization of the copyright owner is an infringement of the copyright.

8 USC 2319
Criminal Penalties for Copyright Violations
This law imposes criminal penalties on persons who are found to have violated U.S. Copyright laws.

19 CFR 133.31 et seq.
Regulations of Customs on Recordation of Copyrights, Trademarks, and Trade Names
These regulations provide procedures and requirements for registering a copyright, trademark, or trade name with U.S. Customs, as well as procedures for enforcement, forfeiture of merchandise, and assessment of monetary penalties.

21 USC 301 et seq.
Food, Drug, and Cosmetic Act
This Act prohibits deceptive practices and regulates the manufacture, sale and importation or exportation of food, drugs, cosmetics, and related products. See 21 USC 331, 381, 382.

19 CFR 12.1 et seq.; 21 CFR 1.83 et seq.
Regulations on Food, Drugs, and Cosmetics
These regulations of the Secretary of Health and Human Services and the Secretary of the Treasury govern the standards, labeling, marking, and importing of products used with food, drugs, and cosmetics.

42 USC 263b-263n
Radiation Control for Health and Safety Act
This Act prohibits entry of electronic products found not to be in compliance with prescribed standards. See 21 CFR Part 1005. Customs enforces this prohibition. See 19 CFR 12.90 et seq.

47 USC 302a
Devices That Interfere with Radio Reception
This law prohibits the importation of devices or home electronic equipment that fail to comply with regulations promulgated by the FCC. See 47 CFR 2.1201 et seq. and 18.119. Customs enforces the prohibition.

47 USC 303(s) and 330
Importation of Certain Television Receivers
These laws prohibit importation of television receivers that are incapable of receiving all frequencies allocated to television broadcasting and authorizes enforcement by Customs. See 47 CFR 15.61-15.72. Such receivers are subject to seizure and forfeiture if a person willfully or knowingly violates this prohibition. See 47 USC 510.

47 USC 605
Unauthorized Publication or Use of Communications
Customs enforces this provision which prohibits the importation or exportation of any device or equipment used primarily for the unauthorized decryption of satellite cable programming, or is intended for any other activity prohibited by 47 USC 605(a).

Principal Exporting Countries

The following listing includes samples of the main supplier nations of the products of this chapter. It is organized by HTSUS major heading. (Refer to "Customs Classification" above for the product codes.) Countries are listed in rank order of the value of products imported to the U.S. Statistics represent customs value entries for 1993 from the Bureau of Census, U.S. Department of Commerce.

8501—Japan, Mexico, Canada, Germany, China, France, United Kingdom, Taiwan, South Korea, Brazil

8502—Japan, Sweden, Germany, Italy, United Kingdom, France, Netherlands, Israel, Switzerland, Austria

8503—Mexico, Japan, Canada, Germany, France, United Kingdom, Singapore, Brazil, Switzerland, Austria

8504—Mexico, Japan, Taiwan, Canada, China, Germany, South Korea, Malaysia, Hong Kong, United Kingdom

8505—Japan, United Kingdom, Mexico, Germany, China, Malaysia, Taiwan, Costa Rica, Canada, France

8506—Japan, Indonesia, Hong Kong, Germany, Belgium, China, South Korea, Israel, Taiwan, Brazil

8507—Japan, Mexico, Taiwan, Canada, South Korea, United Kingdom, Hong Kong, Singapore, Germany, China

8508—Japan, China, Germany, Switzerland, Mexico, United Kingdom, Taiwan, Italy, Hong Kong, Sweden

8509—China, Mexico, Germany, Hong Kong, Taiwan, Japan, Canada, France, Singapore, Italy

8510—Netherlands, China, Germany, Japan, Austria, Taiwan, Ireland, Belgium, Hong Kong, United Kingdom

8511—Japan, Germany, South Korea, Taiwan, Canada, Mexico, United Kingdom, France, Hong Kong, Italy

8512—Mexico, Japan, Canada, Taiwan, Germany, China, Australia, France, Italy, Belgium

8513—China, Mexico, Thailand, Macao, Hong Kong, Taiwan, South Korea, Japan, Indonesia, Malaysia

8514—Japan, Germany, United Kingdom, Canada, Switzerland, Italy, Sweden, France, Austria, Netherlands

8515—Japan, Sweden, Canada, Germany, Switzerland, United Kingdom, Austria, Italy, Taiwan, Netherlands

8516—China, Japan, South Korea, Mexico, Thailand, Singapore, Taiwan, Canada, Germany, Malaysia

8517—Japan, Canada, Malaysia, Thailand, China, Taiwan, Israel, Mexico, Germany, South Korea

8518—Japan, Taiwan, China, South Korea, Mexico, Malaysia, Canada, Singapore, United Kingdom, Germany

8519—Japan, Mexico, China, Malaysia, Singapore, South Korea, Germany, Hong Kong, Taiwan, Thailand

8520—Japan, Malaysia, China, Mexico, Taiwan, South Korea, United Kingdom, Canada, Thailand, Hong Kong

8521—Japan, Malaysia, South Korea, Indonesia, Singapore, Thailand, China, Taiwan, Belgium, Panama

8522—Japan, China, Taiwan, Mexico, Malaysia, United Kingdom, South Korea, Hong Kong, Belgium, Germany

8523—Japan, South Korea, China, Mexico, Taiwan, Germany, Singapore, Hong Kong, Thailand, United Kingdom

8524—Canada, United Kingdom, Japan, Germany, Netherlands, Ireland, Singapore, France, Mexico, Taiwan

8525—Japan, China, Malaysia, South Korea, Mexico, Taiwan, Canada, Philippines, Hong Kong, Singapore

8526—Japan, Canada, Taiwan, Singapore, United Kingdom, China, Germany, Israel, Italy, South Korea

8527—Japan, Malaysia, China, Mexico, South Korea, Singapore, Taiwan, Philippines, Indonesia, Brazil

8528—Mexico, Malaysia, Japan, Thailand, China, South Korea, Singapore, Taiwan, Canada, Hong Kong

8529—Mexico, Japan, Singapore, Canada, Taiwan, Malaysia, United Kingdom, Thailand, China, Sweden

8530—Canada, Mexico, Israel, Germany, Taiwan, Italy, Belgium, France, Hong Kong, China

8531—Japan, Taiwan, China, Singapore, Canada, Malaysia, Philippines, Mexico, South Korea, Hong Kong

8532—Japan, Mexico, Taiwan, El Salvador, Germany, United Kingdom, South Korea, Sweden, Belgium, Canada

8533—Japan, Mexico, Taiwan, Israel, Ireland, Germany, United Kingdom, Barbados, Brazil, Costa Rica

8534—Canada, Taiwan, Japan, Hong Kong, Germany, South Korea, Thailand, Singapore, China, United Kingdom

8535—Japan, Mexico, Taiwan, Germany, Dominican Rep., Canada, China, Switzerland, Malaysia, Sweden

8536—Mexico, Japan, Germany, Canada, Taiwan, China, United Kingdom, France, Dominican Rep., Switzerland

8537—Japan, Canada, Mexico, Germany, China, United Kingdom, Singapore, Hong Kong, Malaysia, France

8538—Japan, Germany, Mexico, Canada, Switzerland, France, Taiwan, Dominican Rep., Italy, United Kingdom

8539—Japan, Mexico, South Korea, Germany, Canada, Netherlands, China, Taiwan, Hungary, United Kingdom

8540—Japan, Mexico, Taiwan, France, Italy, Germany, United Kingdom, Canada, Netherlands, Brazil

8541—Japan, Malaysia, Mexico, Taiwan, Philippines, South Korea, United Kingdom, Germany, Singapore, Hong Kong

8542—Japan, Malaysia, South Korea, Singapore, Canada, Taiwan, Philippines, Hong Kong, Thailand, United Kingdom

8543—Japan, United Kingdom, China, Taiwan, Canada, Germany, Mexico, Hong Kong, South Korea, Philippines

8544—Mexico, Taiwan, Philippines, Japan, Canada, China, Thailand, Germany, United Kingdom, Hong Kong

8545—Japan, Canada, Mexico, Germany, Italy, United Kingdom, France, Taiwan, India, Singapore

8546—Japan, Germany, Brazil, Canada, Switzerland, United Kingdom, Israel, Mexico, Taiwan, Sweden

8547—Germany, Japan, Ireland, Canada, United Kingdom, Singapore, Switzerland, Mexico, Taiwan, Netherlands

8548—Mexico, Japan, Taiwan, United Kingdom, Canada, Israel, Germany, Dominican Rep., Switzerland, South Korea

Chapter 86: Railway Equipment*

Full title: Railway or Tramway Locomotives, Rolling Stock, and Parts Thereof; Railway or Tramway Track Fixtures and Fittings and Parts Thereof; Mechanical (Including Electro-Mechanical) Traffic Signaling Equipment of All Kinds

This chapter relates to the importation of railroad equipment, which is classified within HTSUS Chapter 86 of the Harmonized Tariff Schedule of the United States (HTSUS). Specifically, it includes locomotives; self-propelled coaches; rail maintenance vehicles; rolling stock, including passenger and freight cars; parts of locomotives and rolling stock; track fittings and fixtures; and containers designed for rail and intermodal transport.

If you are interested in importing rails for track construction, refer to Commodity Index Chapter 73. Cross-ties (sleepers) are classified by their material: of wood in Chapter 44, of concrete Chapter 68. Many specialized mechanical subassemblies are covered in Chapter 84 and electrical components are found in Chapter 85, as are electrical signaling, safety, and traffic control equipment. Although Chapter 86 covers most parts and accessories, it is generally restricted to components and subassemblies, with individual parts being included in the chapters covering the type of article or the material of which it is composed—of rubber, plastics, base metals, ceramics, or glass. Instrumentation is covered in Chapter 90. Seats for vehicles are found in Chapter 94.

Key Factors

The key factors in the importation of railway equipment are:

- Compliance with all product and safety standards set by the Federal Railroad Administration (FRA)
- Compliance with all standards established by the U.S. Environmental Protection Agency (EPA) for noise and emissions

Although most importers use the services of a licensed customs broker in making their entries, and we recommend this practice, you should be aware of the regulatory, entry, and documentation issues involved in importing your product. You, as importer, are ultimately responsible for the fulfillment of any legal requirements applicable to your shipment.

General Considerations

The importation of railway equipment is relatively straightforward. However, all imports of such equipment must conform to

*IMPORTANT: Read the Commodity Index Introduction. It is the essential framework for understanding this chapter.

the product and safety standards for such articles established by the U.S. Department of Transportation's FRA. These are specific to the particular types of equipment in question, and are found in 42 CFR 200 et seq. Many of these regulations cover standards for specific types of equipment, such as the freight car safety standards, which define the types of rolling stock covered and detail standards for their components and bodies; locomotive safety standards, which do the same for locomotives; the safety appliance standard, which sets requirements for safety apparatus and features on cars; and safety glazing standards, which give particulars for windows on locomotives, passenger cars, and cabooses. Other standards are specific to certain components or categories of components, for example, covering specifications for brakes, and signal systems. Other standards are less direct, such as the track safety standards, which deal primarily with specifications for roadbed preparation and installation of track, but are specific enough that they affect the rails and auxiliary components that may be imported.

In addition, railway equipment must comply with standards established by the EPA for noise, emissions, and treatment of hazardous waste.

Customs Classification

For customs purposes railway equipment is classified within Chapter 86 of the HTSUS. The chapter is divided into major headings, which are further divided into subheadings and often into sub-subheadings, each with its own HTSUS classification number. For example, the HTSUS number for air brakes for rolling stock is 8607.21.10, indicating that it is a subcategory of brakes and parts thereof (8607.21.00), which is a subcategory of the major heading parts of railway or tramway locomotives or rolling stock (8607.00.00). There are nine major headings in HTSUS Chapter 86.

8601—Rail locomotives powered from an external source of electricity or by electric accumulators (batteries)

8602—Other rail locomotives; locomotives tenders

8603—Self-propelled railway or tramway coaches, vans, and trucks, other than those of heading 8604. This heading consists of self-contained rail vehicles powered by electricity or other power source.

8604—Railway and tramway maintenance or service vehicles, whether or not self-propelled (for example, workshops, cranes, ballast tampers, trackliners, testing coaches, and track inspectors)

8605—Railway or tramway passenger coaches, not self-propelled; luggage vans, post office coaches, and other special purpose railway or tramway coaches, not self-propelled (excluding those of heading 8604)

8606—Railway and tramway freight cars, not self-propelled

8607—Parts of railway or tramway locomotives or rolling stock

8608—Railway or tramway track fixtures and fittings; mechanical (including electro-mechanical) signaling, safety, or traffic control equipment for railway, tramways, roads, inland waterways, parking facilities, port installations, or airfields; parts of the foregoing

8609—Containers (including containers for the transport of fluids) specially designed and equipped for carriage by one or more modes of transport

For more details regarding classification of the specific product you are interested in importing, consult a customs broker, the appropriate commodity specialist at your nearest customs port, or see HTSUS. HTSUS is available for purchase from the U.S. Government Printing Office (see addresses at end of this chapter), and may be found in larger public libraries. Refer to "Classification—Liquidation" on page 207 for a general discussion of customs classification.

Sample Import Duties

Import duties vary depending on the HTSUS classification of your product. Therefore, to determine the correct amount of duties, your product must be properly classified under the HTSUS. The following sample duties are taken from the duty listings of HTSUS Chapter 86.

Rail locomotives powered from an external source of electricity (8601.10.00): 3.9%; diesel-electric locomotives (8602.10.00): 3.9%; self-propelled railway or tramway coaches, powered from an external source of electricity (8603.10.00): 6.3%; railway testing coaches (8604.00.00): 3.7%; railway or tramway passenger coaches (8605.00.00): 18%; insulated or refrigerated cars (8606.20.00): 18%; railway or tramway freight cars, open, with non-removable sides of a height exceeding 60 cm (8606.92): 18%; truck assemblies for self-propelled vehicles (8607.11.00): 3.9%; wheels, whether or not fitted with axles (8607.19.12): free; air brakes (8607.21.00): 5.5%; hooks and coupling devices for vehicles of heading 8605 or 8606 (8607.30.10): 5.5%; railway or tramway track fixtures or fittings (8608.00.00): 5.7: intermodal containers (8609.00.00): free.

Entry and Documentation

The entry of merchandise is a two-part process consisting of 1) filing the documentation necessary to determine whether merchandise may be released from Customs custody and 2) filing the documents that contain information for duty assessment and statistical purposes. In certain instances all documents must be filed and accepted by Customs prior to the release of the goods. Unless you have been granted an extension, you must file entry documents at a location specified by the district or area director within five working days of your shipment's date of arrival at a U.S. port of entry. These include a number of standard documents required by Customs for entry, and:

- Certification of compliance with FRA safety standards

After you present the entry, Customs may examine your shipment, or may waive examination. The shipment is then released provided no legal or regulatory violations have been noted. You must then file entry summary documentation and deposit estimated duties at a designated customhouse within 10 working days of your shipment's release. For a detailed description of entry procedures, standard documentation, and informal entry, see "Entry Process" on page 182.

Prohibitions and Restrictions

Locomotives, rolling stock, and ancillary equipment that do not conform to the standards established by the FRA may not be imported for use in the U.S. For example, all locomotives constructed or rebuilt after December 31, 1979 must comply with the new locomotive standards found in 49 CFR 229, including specifications for brake, coupling, suspension, and electrical, internal combustion, and steam power systems, as well as cab and other equipment standards.

Marking and Labeling Requirements

For a general discussion of U.S. Customs marking and labeling requirements, see "Marking: Country of Origin" on page 215 and "Special Marking Requirements" on page 217.

Shipping Considerations

You will need to ensure that your goods are packaged and shipped with care to ensure that they arrive in good condition and pass smoothly through Customs. You are responsible for ensuring that the shipment is in compliance with all applicable government regulations for packaging and shipping. In most instances, you should not leave these arrangements solely to the discretion of your supplier. Careful preparation of the cargo and selection of the mode of transport can be essential to a cost-effective, timely delivery of undamaged goods. We strongly advise you to consult your shipping representative, insurance agent, or freight broker for advice on packing and shipping. Refer also to the major tab section "Packing/Shipping/Insurance" for a general discussion of packing and shipping.

Railway equipment is often heavy and bulky. It must be packed and stowed carefully to ensure that it is not damaged due to shifting en route or due to exposure to heat, moisture, or other hazards.

Publications Available

The *Harmonized Tariff Schedule of the United States* (HTSUS) is available from:

Government Printing Office (GPO)
Superintendent of Documents
Washington, DC 20402
(202) 512-1800 (Order line)
(202) 512-0000 (General)

The USGPO also has copies of specific laws available for purchase. The USGPO accepts credit card orders over the phone, as well as mail orders paid by credit card, a check drawn on a U.S. bank, or an international money order.

Relevant Government Agencies

Address questions regarding DOT requirements for railway imports to:

U.S. Department of Transportation (DOT)
Federal Railroad Administration
400 Seventh Street SW
Washington, DC 20590
(202) 366-7030

Address questions regarding EPA requirements for railway equipment imports to:

Environmental Protection Agency (EPA)
Office of Air and Radiation
401 M Street SW
Washington, DC 20460
(202) 260-4996

Address questions regarding importation of railway equipment to the district or port director of Customs for you area. For addresses refer to"U.S. Customs District Offices" on page 62 or contact:

U.S. Customs Service
1301 Constitution Ave. NW
Washington, DC 20229
(202) 927-6724 (Information)
(202) 927-1000 (General)

Laws and Regulations

The following laws and regulations may be relevant to the importation of vehicles. They are contained in the U.S. Code (USC) and the regulations are published in the Code of Federal Regulations (CFR), both of which may be available at larger public and law libraries. Copies of specific laws are also available from the United States Government Printing Office (address above).

49 USC Subtitle B, Section II
Federal Railroad Administration Act
This Act establishes the FRA and authorizes that agency to govern railroads and set standards for their operations.

40 CFR 201
Regulation on Railroad Noise Standards
This regulation publishes the standards of the Railroad Noise Commission of the EPA.

49 CFR 200 et seq.
Regulation on Rail Equipment Safety
This regulation publishes the safety and design regulations for rail equipment used in the U.S.

Principal Exporting Countries

The following listing includes samples of the main supplier nations of the products of this chapter. It is organized by HTSUS major heading. (Refer to "Customs Classification" above for the product codes.) Countries are listed in rank order of the value of products imported to the U.S. Statistics represent customs value entries for 1993 from the Bureau of Census, U.S. Department of Commerce.

8601—No listing

8602—Canada

8603—Italy, Switzerland, Canada, Netherlands

8604—Canada, France, Mexico, Japan

8605—Canada

8606—Canada, Mexico, Germany

8607—Canada, Germany, Japan, Brazil, Mexico, Sweden, Austria, Poland, Italy, United Kingdom

8608—Canada, United Kingdom, Japan, Switzerland, Belgium, Italy, South Africa, Germany, Australia, Mexico

8609—Mexico, South Korea, Japan, France, Belgium, United Kingdom, Norway, Germany, Taiwan, China

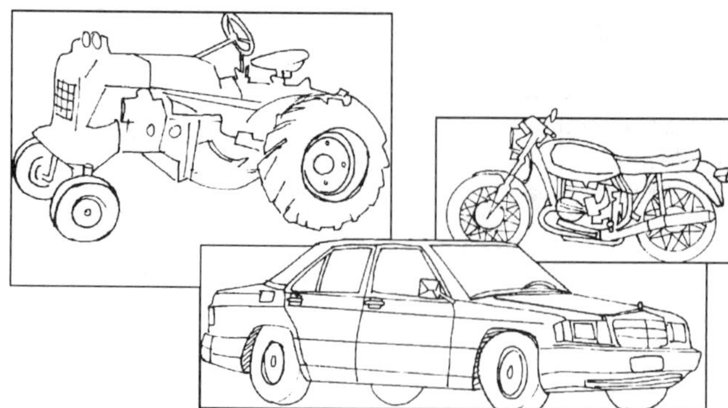

Chapter 87: Vehicles*

Full title: Vehicles Other than Railway or Tramway Rolling-Stock and Parts and Accessories Thereof

This section pertains to the importation of vehicles, which are classified within Chapter 87 of the Harmonized Tariff Schedule of the United States (HTSUS). This chapter covers a broad range of products, including tractors; buses; automobiles; trucks; special purpose vehicles, such as firetrucks; chassis fitted with engines, bodies, and most subassemblies and components for motor vehicles; self-propelled work carts; military fighting vehicles; motorcycles; bicycles; wheelchairs; baby carriages; and trailers.

Only wheeled (and some tracked) vehicles are included in Commodity Index Chapter 87. Railroads and trams running on tracks are covered in Chapter 86; watercraft are found in Chapter 89; aircraft are classified in Chapter 88; while conveyances such as sleds are covered within Chapter 95. However, children's bicycles and tricycles are included in Chapter 87. If you are interested in importing construction equipment—such as bulldozers or backhoes—loading equipment—such as forklifts—or agricultural equipment—such as plows or combines—refer to Chapter 84. Tires are covered in Chapter 40. Although Chapter 87 covers most parts and accessories, it is generally restricted to components and subassemblies, with individual parts being included in the chapters covering the type of article or the material of which it is composed—of rubber, plastics, base metals, ceramics, or glass. Seats for vehicles are found in Chapter 94. Many specialized mechanical subassemblies are covered in Chapter 84 and electrical components are found in Chapter 85.

Key Factors

The key factors in the importation of vehicles are:

- Compliance with U.S. Department of Transportation (DOT) safety standards and other regulations
- Compliance with U.S. Environmental Protection Agency (EPA) emission control standards
- Vehicles not complying with DOT standards must enter through a DOT Registered Importer (RI)
- Vehicles not complying with EPA standards must enter through an EPA Independent Commercial Importer (ICI)
- Compliance of bicycles with Consumer Product Safety Act (CPSA) safety standards and labeling requirements

*IMPORTANT: Read the Commodity Index Introduction. It is the essential framework for understanding this chapter.

Although most importers utilize the services of a licensed customs broker in making their entries, and we recommend this practice, you should be aware of the regulatory, entry, and documentation issues involved in importing your product. You, as importer, are ultimately responsible for the fulfillment of any legal requirements applicable to your shipment.

General Considerations

The DOT's National Highway Traffic Safety Administration (NHTSA) regulates importation of motor vehicles and motor vehicle equipment under the provisions of the National Traffic and Motor Vehicle Safety Act of 1966 (NTMVSA), the Motor Vehicle Information Cost Savings Act (MVICSA), and the Imported Vehicle Safety Compliance Act of 1988 (IVSCA). The Federal Motor Vehicle Safety Standards (FMVSS) are based on these three laws. The EPA regulates the importation of automobiles under the provisions of the Clean Air Act (CAA) as amended. All motor vehicles and motor vehicle equipment imported into the U.S. must meet the safety and emission-control requirements of these governmental agencies prior to entry. If you wish to import a new or used motor vehicle, you must make an appropriate declaration on DOT Declaration HS **Form 7**—in duplicate—at the port of entry whether or not it meets any or all U.S. market requirements. You can get HS **Form 7** from your customs broker, or from any U.S. Customs port office.

If you are considering importing a foreign vehicle, you should obtain the very latest DOT and EPA requirements for that specific vehicle before purchasing it. The modifications necessary to bring a nonconforming vehicle into conformity with regulations governing such issues as safety, bumper, and emission standards may require extensive reengineering; the labor, materials, storage fees, and other costs involved may be unduly high; and it may effectively be impractical or impossible to refit specific vehicles to comply. Certain models are prohibited from importation altogether, and if imported will have to be destroyed or reexported.

Independent Commercial Importers. Authorized ICIs are allowed to import only certain vehicles, based on which certificates of conformity they have obtained. The fact that an ICI may hold a certificate of conformity for a particular vehicle does not guarantee that the ICI will choose to import it, nor is it required to. Before buying or shipping any noncomplying motor vehicle, make final arrangements with an ICI, or obtain written EPA prior approval or exemption. Otherwise, Customs may assess costly storage fees at the port of entry while you take the steps necessary to render your import legal, and/or the vehicles may not be eligible for importation at all.

Bicycles. Importation of bicycles is regulated by the Consumer Product Safety Commission (CPSC) under applicable provisions of the CPSA. You do not need any permits or licenses to import bicycles, nor is any special entry paperwork required. However, you should be sure that your bicycles comply with the extensive mandatory safety standards listed in 16 CFR 1512 (see "Prohibitions and Restrictions" below). To ascertain compliance, the CPSC randomly inspects shipments of bicycles at port of entry from time to time.

Import Advisory

What you don't know about automotive imports can hurt you. Be informed. If you wish to import foreign vehicles, do your homework before you buy.

Customs Classification

For customs purposes vehicles are classified within Chapter 87 of the HTSUS. This chapter is divided into major headings, which are further divided into subheading, and often into sub-subheadings, each with its own HTSUS classification number. For example, the HTSUS number for mounted brake linings for vehicles other than agricultural tractors is 8708.31.10, indicating that it is a subcategory of brakes and servo-brakes and parts thereof (8708.31.00), which is a subcategory of the major heading parts and accessories of the motor vehicles of heading 8701 to 8705 (8708.00.00). There are 16 major headings in HTSUS Chapter 87.

8701—Tractors (other than tractors of heading 8709)

8702—Motor vehicles for the transport of 10 or more persons, including the driver

8703—Motor cars and other motor vehicles principally designed for the transport of persons (other than those of heading 8702), including station wagons and racing cars

8704—Motor vehicles for the transport of goods

8705—Special purpose motor vehicles, other than those principally designed for the transport of persons or goods (for example, wreckers, mobile cranes, firefighting vehicles, concrete mixers, road sweepers, spraying vehicles, mobile workshops, mobile radiological units)

8706—Chassis fitted with engines, for the motor vehicles of headings 8701 to 8705

8707—Bodies (including cabs) for the motor vehicles of headings 8701 to 8705

8708—Parts and accessories of the motor vehicles of headings 8701 to 8705

8709—Works trucks, self-propelled, not fitted with lifting or handling equipment, of the type used in factories, warehouses, dock areas, or airports for short distance transport of goods; tractors of the type used on railway station platforms; parts of the foregoing vehicles

8710—Tanks and other armored fighting vehicles, motorized, whether or not fitted with weapons, and parts of such vehicles

8711—Motorcycles (including mopeds) and cycles fitted with an auxiliary motor, with or without sidecars

8712—Bicycles and other cycles (including delivery cycles), not motorized

8713—Invalid carriages, whether or not motorized or otherwise mechanically propelled

8714—Parts and accessories of vehicles of headings 8711 to 8713

8715—Baby carriages (including strollers) and parts thereof

8716—Trailers and semi-trailers; other vehicles, not mechanically propelled; and parts thereof

For more details regarding classification of the specific product you are interested in importing, consult a customs broker, the appropriate commodity specialist at your nearest customs port, or see HTSUS. HTSUS is available for purchase from the U.S. Government Printing Office (see addresses at end of this chapter), and may be found in larger public libraries. Refer to "Classification—Liquidation" on page 207 for a general discussion of customs classification.

Sample Import Duties

Import duties vary depending on the HTSUS classification of your product. Therefore, to determine the correct amount of duties, your product must be properly classified under the HTSUS. The following sample duties are taken from the duty listings for HTSUS Chapter 87.

[Note: in general, completed standard vehicles are charged at a rate of 2.5%, while parts and accessories are charged at a rate of 3.1%; under provisions found in HTSUS 9903.87.00, general tariffs on trucks of subheadings 8704.10.50, 8704.21, 8704.22.50, 8704.23, 8704.31, 8704.32 or 8704.90 have been increased from 8.5% to 25%] Road tractors for use with semi-trailers (8701.20.00): 4%; log skidder tractors suitable for forestry (8701.90.00): free; diesel or semi-diesel vehicles designed for the transport of 16 or more persons (8702.10.30): 3.1%; skimobiles (8703.10.10): 2.5%; golf carts (8703.10.50): 2.5%; new passenger motor vehicles (cars) (8703.23.00): 2.5%; new passenger and specialty motor vehicles with a cylinder capacity greater than 3,000 cc (8703.24.00): 2.5%; diesel or semi-diesel ambulances with a cylinder capacity greater than 2,500 cc (8703.00): 2.5%; firefighting vehicles (8705.30.00): 3.7%; concrete mixers (8705.40.00): 3.7%; chassis with engines for passenger vehicles of heading 8703 (8706.00.15): 2.5%; bodies for passenger automobiles (8707.10.00): 2.5%; bumpers (8708.10.30): 3.1%; airbags (8708.29.10): 3.1%; mounted brake linings for nonagricultural vehicles (8708.31.50): 3.1%; gear boxes (8708.40.20): 3.1%; McPherson struts for autos (8708.80.30): 3.1%; mufflers for autos and trucks (8708. 92.50): 3.1%; clutches for agricultural vehicles (8708.93.15): free; electrical operator riding carts (8709.11.00): free; tracked military vehicles (8710.00.00): free; motorcycles with a cylinder capacity exceeding 50 cc but not exceeding 250 cc (8711.20.00): 3.7%; bicycles with a wheel diameter exceeding 63.5 cm in diameter and weighing more than 16.3 kg (8712.00.25): 5.5%; wheelchairs, not mechanically propelled (8713.10.00): 5.3%; motorcycles seats (8714.11.00): 4.2%; bicycle frames valued $600 (8714.91.20): 4.9%; wheel rims (8714.92.10): 6%; coaster brakes for bicycles (8714.94.25): 6%; baby carriages (8715.00.00): 4.4%; camper trailers (8716.10.00): 3.2%; tanker trailers or semi-trailers (8716.31.00): 3.1%.

Special Provisions. Under the provisions of 9903.87.00, the duty on trucks of subheadings 8704.10.50, 8704.21, 8704.22.50, 8704.31, 8704.32, or 8704.90 has been raised from 8.5% to 25%.

Entry and Documentation

The entry of merchandise is a two-part process consisting of 1) filing the documents necessary to determine whether merchandise may be released from Customs custody and 2) filing the documents that contain information for duty assessment and statistical purposes. In certain instances all documents must be filed and accepted by Customs prior to the release of the goods. Unless you have been granted an extension, you must file entry documents at a location specified by the district/area director within five working days of your shipment's date of arrival at a U.S. port of entry. These include a number of standard documents required by Customs for any entry, and:

- DOT Entry Declaration HS **Form 7**
- For vehicles not complying with DOT requirements: DOT bond **Form HS-474 (I-90)**
- For certain vehicles: EPA bond **Form 3520-1**

After you present the entry, Customs may examine your shipment, or may waive examination. The shipment is then released, provided no legal or regulatory violations have occurred. You must then file entry summary documentation and deposit estimated duties at a designated customhouse within 10 working days of your shipment's release. For a detailed description of entry procedures, standard documentation, and informal entry, see "Entry Process" on page 182.

Prohibitions and Restrictions

DOT Requirements—Safety, Bumper, and Theft Prevention Standards. The DOT requires that all imported motor vehicles and items of motor vehicle equipment comply with all applicable FMVSS standards in effect when these vehicles or items were manufactured. The best qualified source of safety conformance information is the vehicle's original manufacturer. Only the original manufacturer is capable of proving the date of manufacture and the state of FMVSS conformity on that date. Complying vehicles have the original manufacturer's certification permanently affixed to the vehicle or item of equipment. Customs will inspect your vehicle at the time of entry in order to determine compliance. Dealer statements and foreign registration documents are not acceptable verifications of compliance.

Temporary Importation of Noncomplying Vehicles. All temporary imports of noncomplying vehicles require advance written approval from the DOT. Various classes of vehicles and of importers are eligible for such waivers.

Motor vehicles and motor vehicle equipment that are imported solely with the intention of reexportation and that are so labeled are exempt (see 19 CFR 12.85).

Nonresidents of the U.S. may import a noncomplying foreign-registered motor vehicle for personal use for a period of time not to exceed one year. The passport number and country of issue of the nonresident importer must appear on the declaration form.

Vehicles not licensed for use on public roads that have been brought in for test, experimentation, training, demonstration, or competitive racing events are exempt. Such vehicles must be accompanied by documentation describing the purpose of importation, estimated use on public roads, and estimated time before reexport. There is a three-year maximum time limit for this kind of importation. You must obtain a special DOT waiver for periods beyond three years.

Members of the foreign military, diplomatic corps, or other official delegation temporarily stationed in the U.S. may import noncomplying vehicles for personal use. Such vehicles may be sold to another eligible individual at the end of the stay of the individual entitled to use it. Otherwise, the noncomplying vehicle must be exported when the authorized individual's tour of duty ends. Eligible members of foreign delegations must register all imported vehicles through the U.S. Department of State's Office of Foreign Missions (OFM), and must obtain an ownership title to the vehicle (good for export only) from the OFM before departing the U.S. and exporting the vehicle.

Noncomplying Vehicles Imported for Permanent Use. Unless specifically exempted, imports of noncertified or nonconforming vehicles for permanent use in the U.S., must be made under contract through a DOT-Registered Importer. Prior to the vehicle's entry, the RI will petition the NHTSA for a determination of the vehicle model and model year's eligibility for importation. (Refer to 49 CFR 593-594 for details on the eligibility process.) Once eligibility has been determined, the RI will contract to modify the vehicle to conform with all applicable safety and bumper standards. A copy of this contract must be furnished to U.S. Customs at the port of entry.

In addition, a DOT bond, **Form HS-474 (1-90)**, in the amount of 150% of the vehicle's dutiable value must be posted at the port of entry. This bond is intended to assure conformance of the vehicle within 120 days after entry. In some cases the DOT may extend the deadline to within 180 days after entry. Vehicle modification work may be performed either before or after the vehicle is imported. However, the steps for bonding and to substantiate that federal standards are being met are the same in either case.

When the vehicle has been brought up to standard, the RI certifies to the NHTSC that the modification(s) have been completed, and the bond is released. The vehicle may not be released for use or resale until 30 days after the RI has certified compliance to NHTSA, or until NHTSA has notified the importer that the vehicle and the bond may be released. In some cases NHTSA will require inspection of the vehicle to ascertain compliance.

Canadian Vehicles. The NHTSA has granted eligibility to certain Canadian-built automobiles that do not comply with applicable FMVSS but that comply with the analogous Canadian Motor Vehicle Safety Standards. These vehicles have already been cleared for importation and do not require specific authorization through NHTSA, but must still be imported as noncomplying vehicles under contract with an RI and under bond. Covered vehicles include 1) all passenger cars manufactured between January 1, 1988 and August 31, 1989 bearing a model year designation of 1988 or 1989; 2) all passenger cars manufactured on or after September 1, 1989 and equipped with an automatic restraint system by the original manufacturer that complies with FMVSS No. 208; 3) all other types of motor vehicles manufactured from January 1, 1988 on, that are certified by their original manufacturer as complying with all applicable Canadian motor vehicle safety standards, and that are of the same make, model, and model year of any vehicle originally manufactured for importation into and sale in the U.S., or originally manufactured in the U.S. for sale there, and that bear a certification of compliance with all applicable federal motor vehicle safety standards. For specific information, consult 19 CFR 10.84, or contact the DOT (see addresses at end of this chapter).

Registered Importers. If you wish to register with the DOT to import vehicles not originally manufactured to comply with applicable FMVSS, you must file a notarized Application for Registration as Importer with NHTSA. For details regarding requirements and fees, contact the NHTSA (see addresses at end of this chapter).

EPA Requirements—Emission Standards. The Clean Air Act prohibits importation into the U.S. of any motor vehicle or motor vehicle engine that does not meet EPA emission standards. Requirements have been in effect for gasoline-powered cars since 1968 and for motorcycles since 1978. These standards apply to imported vehicles whether they are new or used, made domestically or abroad, and whether or not they have been previously altered. These requirements apply to all types of vehicles—passenger cars, trucks, and other vehicles, such as campers and all-terrain vehicles—that the EPA deems are capable of being used on a public road. There are basically two vehicle categories subject to import restrictions (which are found in 19 CFR 12.73):

Vehicles Manufactured in Conformity With U.S. Emission Requirements. Anyone may import U.S.-version vehicles dating from 1971 on. Vehicles originally equipped with a catalytic converter and/or oxygen sensor and 1) that have been driven less than 50 miles; 2) are diesel fueled; or 3) have been operated only within the U.S., Canada, Mexico, Japan, Australia, Taiwan, and Grand Bahama Island may be imported without having to post a bond. (Vehicles driven outside of these countries may have had their emissions systems contaminated by leaded gasoline.) Vehicles in these categories will have U.S. emissions compliance labels in the engine compartment that will identify them as complying. If this label is missing, the importer must secure a manufacturer's statement that the particular model complies (a dealer's statement will not suffice).

Unless the vehicle meets these requirements or other specific exceptions (see below), the EPA requires that the vehicle be imported by an ICI and that the importer post a bond to ensure that the vehicle will be brought into compliance. Customs determines the amount of the bond, which is generally the value of the vehicle. If you are importing such a vehicle, you must file an EPA **Form 3520-1** (obtainable either from Customs or your bonding company) at the port of entry. The vehicle must be brought into compliance with EPA emissions standards within 120 days after entry. For specific details on options for compliance, see EPA's Automotive Imports Fact Sheet (available from EPA, address below).

Exceptions to the bond requirement include: 1) vehicles participating in Department of State, Department of Defense, or Panama Canal Commission programs approved by EPA; or 2) vehicles participating in one of the EPA-approved Manufacturers or Shippers Catalyst Control Programs. For further information contact the EPA (see addresses at end of this chapter).

Vehicles not equipped by the manufacturer with an emissions control system (model years 1968 and earlier) are not subject to import restrictions and may be imported without bond. However, you must provide proof that the vehicle was not equipped with a catalytic converter at the time of manufacture.

Vehicles Not Manufactured in Conformity With U.S. Emission Requirements. These vehicles will not be labeled as complying with U.S. emission requirements. If you wish to import such a vehicle, you must arrange for importation through an ICI holding a valid EPA Certificate of Conformity for the specific class of vehicle. ICI certificate holders are responsible for undertaking all modifications and testing required to bring the vehicle into conformance with EPA standards, and for assuring the vehicle's compliance for 5 years or 5,000 miles. For more details regarding ICIs operating in the U.S. or options for specific compliance requirements, contact the EPA (see addresses at end of this chapter) or see the Automotive Imports Fact Sheet.

Exclusions Based on Age of Vehicles or Engines. The following vehicles are excluded from EPA emission requirements and may be imported without a bond by any individual or business: 1) gasoline-fueled light-duty vehicles and light-duty trucks originally manufactured prior to January 1, 1968; 2) diesel-fueled light-duty vehicles originally manufactured prior to January 1, 1975; 3) diesel-fueled light-duty trucks originally manufactured prior to January 1, 1976; 4) motorcycles originally manufactured prior to January 1, 1978; 5) gasoline-fueled and diesel-fueled heavy-duty engines originally manufactured prior to January 1, 1970.

Racing Exclusions. Certain racing vehicles that are not capable of being operated on public roads and that are to be used only for racing events are excluded from EPA emission requirements, and may be imported by any individual or business. However, you must obtain the EPA's prior written approval prior to importation. For more information, see the Automotive Imports Fact Sheet or contact the EPA (see addresses at end of this chapter).

Miscellaneous Exemptions. Other exemptions from compliance but that require EPA's prior written permission include: 1) vehicles imported solely for repair or alteration; 2) vehicles imported for testing; 3) vehicles imported by an ICI for testing in order to obtain a certificate of conformity; 4) vehicles imported solely for display; 5) vehicles imported by individuals under circumstances of severe hardship; 6) vehicles imported by the manufacturer for national security reasons. Each of the above exemptions involves specific limitations, requirements, and documentation. For further information see the Automotive Imports Fact Sheet or contact the EPA (see addresses at end of this chapter).

Canadian Vehicles. Vehicles manufactured in Canada that are not labeled with an unconditional statement of conformity with U.S. emission standards are subject to restriction. The label may be located under the hood or in the door jamb of the vehicle. For further information see the Automotive Imports Fact Sheet or contact the EPA (see addresses at end of this chapter).

Bicycles. All bicycles and bicycle parts introduced into U.S. commerce must comply with safety regulations enumerated in 16 CFR 1512. These requirements can be divided into 1) general mechanical requirements, and 2) component-specific requirements. The regulations also prescribe specific testing procedures for steering, wheel, pedal, crank, and brake systems.

General Bicycle Mechanical Requirements. Any mechanical skills required by the consumer for assembling your bicycle must not exceed those possessed by an adult of normal intelligence and ability. Your bicycles should have no unfinished sheared metal edges or other sharp parts that are, or may be, exposed to the hands or legs. Sheared metal edges that are not rolled must be finished so as to remove any feathering of edges, burrs, or spurs caused during the shearing process. Your bicycle frame or other component should show no visible fracture as a result of prescribed testing. Attachment hardware should also be free of damage as a result of such testing.

Component-specific Bicycle Requirements. The regulation provides specific standards for: the 1) braking system; 2) steering system; 3) pedals; 4) drive chain; 5) protective guards; 6) tires; 7) wheels; 8) wheel hubs; 9) front fork; 10) fork and frame assembly; 11) seat; and 12) reflectors. Although these requirements are highly technical, and enumerating them is beyond the scope of this entry, you should be aware that the CPSC tests for and enforces them. If you are ignorant of the standards and attempt to import a noncomplying shipment, you may find that your shipment is refused entry. If your product passes Customs without inspection, but is later found to be noncomplying, you are liable for product recall. The CPSA gives the CPSC both the authority and the responsibility to protect the U.S. consumer, and to take legal action in cases when noncompliance is determined.

Substantial Product Hazard Reports. There are defect-reporting requirements for any product covered under the CPSA, including bicycles. Section 15(b) of CPSA requires any manufacturer, distributor, or retailer of such products who obtains information that reasonably supports the conclusion that such products fail to comply with an applicable consumer product safety rule or contain a defect that could create a substantial product hazard to immediately inform the Commission of the potential violation or defect. A firm's willful failure to make a Substantial Product Hazard Report can result in litigation by the CPSC.

Marking and Labeling Requirements

The DOT and the EPA each have separate labeling requirements for motor vehicles and motor vehicle equipment. Vehicles imported into the U.S. must meet the requirements of both agencies.

DOT Labeling Requirements. The DOT requires vehicles in compliance with FMVSS to have the original manufacturer's certification label permanently affixed. The label must be in English. It usually appears near the driver's door pillar or door edge. Any vehicle without such labeling is considered to be noncomplying and must be imported following the procedures outlined in the section on DOT requirements (see above). Passenger cars subject to the Federal Motor Theft Prevention Standard must be brought into compliance and have a certification label affixed before importation. These are cars listed as most likely to be stolen in Appendix A, 49 CFR Part 541, with model years beginning in 1986. Such cars must have their major parts inscribed (not merely labeled) with their original Vehicle Identification Number (VIN) before they reach the U.S. Vehicles imported for export only must also be similarly labeled. For specific details, contact DOT (see addresses at end of this chapter).

EPA Labeling Requirements. Conforming vehicles manufactured in 1968-1970 will have a label on the doorpost indicating compliance with FMVSS; those manufactured in 1971 and later will have a label in the engine compartment entitled Vehicle Emission Control Information. This label will contain the name and trademark of the manufacturer and an unconditional statement of compliance with EPA emission regulations. Motorcycles will have the label on the frame. Any vehicles manufactured from 1968 on not labeled are considered noncomplying and must be imported through procedures described in EPA Requirements section (see above). For specific details, contact the EPA (see addresses at end of this chapter).

Bicycles—Instruction Manual. If you are importing bicycles as a commercial venture, you need to be aware of the following requirements. A bicycle must have an instruction manual attached to its frame or included with the packaged unit. The manual must include at a minimum the following: 1) operations and safety instructions describing operation of the brakes and gears, cautions concerning wet-weather and night-time operation, and a guide for safe on-and off-road operation; 2) assembly instructions for accomplishing complete and proper assembly; and 3) instructions for proper maintenance of brakes, control cables, bearing adjustments, wheel adjustments, lubrication, reflectors, tires, and handlebar and seat adjustments. If such maintenance is beyond the average consumer's capability, the manual must specify locations where such maintenance service can be obtained. If the bicycle is not fully assembled and fully adjusted for the ultimate consumer, it must have the following information clearly displayed on any promotional display material and on the outside surface of the shipping carton: 1) a list of tools necessary to properly accomplish assembly and adjustment; 2) a drawing illustrating the minimum leg-length dimension of a rider, and a method of measurement of this dimension. The dimension must be readily understandable and must be based on allowing no less than one inch of clearance between the top tube of the bicycle and the ground plane, and the crotch measurement of the rider. A girl's-style frame must be specified in the same way, using a corresponding boy's model as a basis.

Mandatory Bicycle Label. Every bicycle subject to the requirements of 16 CFR 1512 must bear a marking or label securely affixed on, or to the frame of, the bicycle. The marking or label must be affixed in such a manner that it cannot be removed without being defaced or destroyed. It must identify the name of the manufacturer or private labeler. It must also bear some form of marking from which the manufacturer can identify the month and year of manufacture, or from which the private labeler can identify the manufacturer and the month and year of manufacture.

For a general discussion of U.S. Customs marking and labeling requirements, see "Marking: Country of Origin" on page 215 and "Special Marking Requirements" on page 217.

Shipping Considerations

You will need to ensure that your goods are packaged and shipped with care to ensure that they arrive in good condition and pass smoothly through Customs. You are responsible for ensuring that the shipment is in compliance with all applicable government regulations for packaging and shipping. In most instances, you should not leave these arrangements solely to the discretion of your supplier. Careful preparation of the cargo and selection of the mode of transport can be essential to a cost-effective, timely delivery of undamaged goods. We strongly advise you to consult your shipping representative, insurance agent, or freight broker for advice on packing and shipping. Refer also to the major tab section "Packing/Shipping/Insurance" for a general discussion of packing and shipping.

Vehicles must be packed and stowed carefully to ensure that they are not damaged due to shifting en route or due to exposure to heat, moisture, or other hazards.

Publications Available

The following publication may be relevant to importing vehicles. It is available from the EPA (see addresses at end of this chapter):

Automotive Imports Fact Sheet

The *Harmonized Tariff Schedule of the United States* (HTSUS) is available from:

Government Printing Office (GPO)
Superintendent of Documents
Washington, DC 20402
(202) 512-1800 (Order line)
(202) 512-0000 (General)

The USGPO also has copies of specific laws available for purchase. The USGPO accepts credit card orders over the phone, as well as mail orders paid by credit card, a check drawn on a U.S. bank, or an international money order.

Relevant Government Agencies

Address questions regarding DOT requirements for vehicle imports to:

National Highway Traffic Safety Administration
Office of Vehicle Safety Compliance
400 7th St. SW
Washington, DC 20590
(202) 366-5311, 366-2830

Address questions regarding EPA requirements for vehicle imports to:

Environmental Protection Agency (EPA)
Office of Mobile Services
401 M Street SW
Washington, DC 20460
(202) 260-3730, 260-7645

Address questions regarding bicycle regulation to:

Consumer Product Safety Commission (CPSC)
5401 Westbard Avenue
Bethesda, MD 20207
(301) 492-6580

Address questions regarding importation of vehicles to:

International Trade Administration
Office of Automotive Affairs
14th and Constitution Ave. NW, Rm. 4036
Washington, DC 20230
(202) 482-0554

Address questions regarding importation of vehicles to the district or port director of Customs for you area. For addresses see "U.S. Customs District Offices" on page 62 or contact:

U.S. Customs Service
1301 Constitution Ave. NW
Washington, DC 20229
(202) 927-6724 (Information)
(202) 927-1000 (General)

Laws and Regulations

The following laws and regulations may be relevant to the importation of vehicles. They are contained in the U.S. Code (USC) and the regulations are published in the Code of Federal Regulations (CFR), both of which may be available at larger public and law libraries. Copies of specific laws are also available from the United States Government Printing Office (address above).

15 USC 1231
Automobile Information Disclosure Act
This Act requires the labeling of automobiles and is enforced by Customs for imported vehicles.

15 USC 1391-1431
National Traffic and Motor Vehicle Safety Act of 1966
This act provides for the setting of motor vehicle safety standards by the National Highway Traffic Safety Administration (NHTSA) and prohibits the manufacture, sale, delivery, or importation of substandard vehicles. Customs assists in enforcing this Act. See 19 CFR 12.80. Temporary importations may be permitted for the purpose of bringing substandard vehicles into conformity with the safety standards (Section 1397).

15 USC 1901-1949
National Traffic and Motor Vehicle Safety Act (Bumper Standards)
This Act authorizes Customs to deny entry to any automobile failing to comply with the Act, which provides for the setting of motor vehicle bumper standards by the NHTSA, and prohibits the manufacture, sale, delivery, or importation of vehicles with bumpers that do not meet the standard. Temporary importations may be permitted for the purpose of bringing substandard vehicles into

conformity with the bumper standards (Section 1916). See 49 CFR 581 et seq.

15 USC 2021-2034
National Traffic and Motor Vehicle Safety Act (Theft Prevention)
This Act provides for the setting of motor vehicle theft prevention standards by the Secretary of Transportation concerning major automotive parts, and prohibits the manufacture, sale, delivery, or importation of vehicles that do not meet the standard. Customs will deny entry to vehicles in violation of this Act. Temporary importations may be permitted for the purpose of bringing substandard vehicles into conformity with the standards (Section 2027).

18 USC 511-512
Motor Vehicles
These laws prohibit the alteration or removal of motor vehicle identification numbers. Customs is authorized to inspect vehicles for purposes of enforcing this prohibition.

18 USC 553
Stolen Motor Vehicles
This law prohibits the importation or exportation of stolen motor vehicles, vessels, aircraft, and other mobile equipment. Customs assists in enforcing this law.

18 USC 2312 and 2313
Transportation, Sale, or Receipt of Stolen Vehicles
These laws prohibit the transportation, sale, or receipt of stolen vehicles or aircraft.

19 USC 2001 et seq.
Automotive Products Trade Act
This Act allows duty-free importation of bona fide products of Canada that are actually used in the manufacture of original automotive equipment. Customs assists in enforcing this law.

42 USC 7521-7543
Clean Air Act
This Act restricts importations of motor vehicle engines found not to be in compliance with federal motor vehicle emission standards. Customs will test and inspect engines for compliance with this Act. See 19 CFR 12.73; 40 CFR 80, 85, 86 and 600.

15 USC 1263
Consumer Product Safety Act
This Act sets standards for the manufacture, processing, and labeling of products sold to U.S. consumers.

Principal Exporting Countries

The following listing includes samples of the main supplier nations of the products of this chapter. It is organized by HTSUS major heading. (Refer to "Customs Classification" above for the product codes.) Countries are listed in rank order of the value of products imported to the U.S. Statistics represent customs value entries for 1993 from the Bureau of Census, U.S. Department of Commerce.

8701—Canada, Japan, United Kingdom, Germany, France, Italy, Belgium, Poland, Brazil, Czech Rep.

8702—Canada, Belgium, Argentina, Germany, Slovenia, Japan, United Kingdom, Finland, Venezuela, Italy

8703—Japan, Canada, Germany, Mexico, Sweden, United Kingdom, South Korea, Belgium, Australia, Italy

8704—Canada, Japan, Mexico, United Kingdom, Norway, Sweden, Germany, Australia, Belgium, France

8705—Canada, Germany, United Kingdom, Netherlands, Japan, Italy, Iceland, Spain, France, Brazil

8706—Mexico, France, United Kingdom, Canada, Japan, Brazil, Sweden, Germany, Belgium, Italy

8707—Canada, Italy, Sweden, United Kingdom, Mexico, Hungary, Japan, Norway, Austria, France

8708—Japan, Canada, Mexico, Germany, France, Taiwan, Italy, Brazil, United Kingdom, Spain

8709—Germany, France, Canada, South Korea, Japan, Italy, Taiwan, Finland, United Kingdom, Australia

8710—Canada, Germany, Netherlands, Egypt, Israel, United Kingdom, Taiwan, New Zealand, Austria, France

8711—Japan, Germany, Italy, Mexico, Austria, Slovenia, Brazil, United Kingdom, Philippines, Taiwan

8712—Taiwan, China, Japan, Hong Kong, Canada, Hungary, Italy, South Korea, India, Thailand

8713—Mexico, Taiwan, Canada, Sweden, South Korea, United Kingdom, China, France, Germany, Switzerland

8714—Japan, Taiwan, Italy, Singapore, China, Canada, France, Mexico, United Kingdom, Germany

8715—Taiwan, China, Thailand, Italy, Japan, Mexico, Sweden, Hong Kong, United Kingdom, South Korea

8716—Canada, Mexico, Taiwan, China, South Korea, Germany, United Kingdom, Israel, Malaysia, Italy

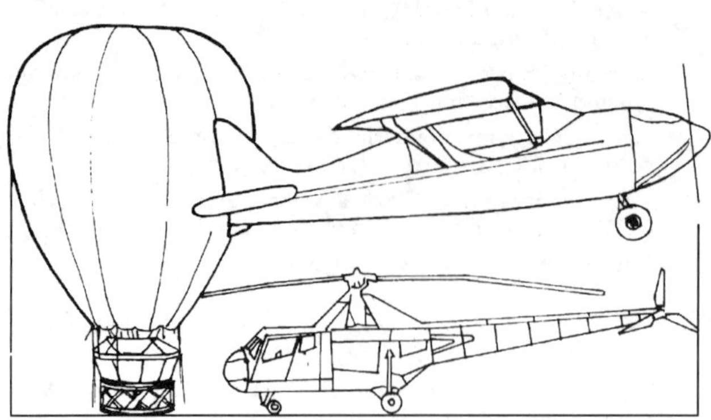

Chapter 88: Aircraft and Parts*

Full title: Aircraft, Spacecraft, and Parts Thereof

This chapter relates to the importation of aircraft and related equipment, which are classified within HTSUS Chapter 88 of the Harmonized Tariff Schedule of the United States (HTSUS). Specifically, it includes balloons, dirigibles, gliders, and similar aircraft; all other aircraft and spacecraft, including helicopters, rockets, and airplanes—whether civilian or military, or jet, turbojet, rocket, or propeller driven; parts and assemblies of these craft; parachutes; launching and recovery gear; and flight simulators and trainers.

If you are interested in importing hovercraft, refer to Commodity Index Chapter 86 if the craft are rail guided, Chapter 87 if designed to travel over both land and water, and Chapter 89 if designed to travel exclusively over water or ice. Electrical signaling, safety, and traffic control equipment are found in Chapters 85 and 86. Although Chapter 88 covers most parts and accessories, it is generally restricted to components and subassemblies, with individual parts of general use being included in the chapters covering the type of article or the material of which it is composed—of rubber, plastics, base metals, ceramics, or glass. Instrumentation is found in Chapter 90, while seats for aircraft are found in Chapter 94. Many specialized mechanical subassemblies are covered in Chapter 84 and electrical components are found in Chapter 85.

Key Factors

The key factors in the importation of aircraft are:

- Federal Aviation Administration (FAA) type certification for aircraft model to be imported
- FAA airworthiness certification for specific examples of aircraft equipment to be imported
- Compliance with quota restraints and visa requirements under U.S. Department of Commerce (DOC) Multi-Fiber Arrangements; submission of country of origin declaration; compliance with entry invoice requirements; and compliance with labeling requirements under the Textile Fiber Products Identification Act (TFPIA) for parachutes
- Compliance with U.S. Environmental Protection Agency (EPA) standards on equipment noise levels and fuel and exhaust emissions

*IMPORTANT: Read the Commodity Index Introduction. It is the essential framework for understanding this chapter.

Although most importers use the services of a licensed customs broker in making their entries, and we recommend this practice, you should be aware of the regulatory, entry, and documentation issues involved in importing your product. You, as importer, are ultimately responsible for the fulfillment of any legal requirements applicable to your shipment.

General Considerations

Product Certifications. All aircraft and related equipment used in the U.S., whether manufactured domestically or imported, must be approved by the U.S. Department of Transportation's FAA, which has established detailed and rigorous standards for such articles. Entry of aircraft or parts must include certification that the imports have received approval specifically by the FAA or from the analogous foreign authority in the country of origin—which must adhere to standards accepted by the FAA. This adherence is established through a series of bilateral agreements between the U.S. and foreign countries whereby each party agrees to comply with set rigorous standards for design, materials, manufacture, quality control procedures, and testing and oversight functions. In order to be imported into the U.S., a foreign-made aircraft model, significant component, or part must be type certified by the FAA, while specific examples of these articles must be certified (or certifiable) as airworthy. Everyone, from the manufacturer and importer to the end users, are also obligated to report any instances of specific failures, design flaws, or injuries resulting from the items imported.

An interested importer can petition the Administrator of the FAA for type certification of a product. However, it is difficult for a firm other than a major established concern to gain approval for the certification of a major new product. The materials incorporated by reference to 14 CFR, I, 1-59 catalogues technical publications by major aircraft manufacturers. Not only do are these publications officially incorporated into the regulatory standards, but they provide a de facto listing of the major countries and manufacturers from which aircraft have been authorized for type certification and import.

To receive type certification, the product must first come from a country with which the U.S. has a bilateral export-import agreement covering aircraft (this is generally restricted to the larger, well-established countries that support their own active aerospace industries). The FAA must then satisfy itself that the certification procedures in the country from which the items come is adequate to allow the FAA to accept the authority of that country's inspectors, i.e., that they comply with all necessary standards (see below). In addition, the FAA requires the submission and revue of technical specifications and data, and reserves the right to independently test the equipment.

Once a type certification has been issued, it usually remains in effect indefinitely. The Administrator of the FAA can revoke a type certification at any time on the grounds that a particular article covered by such certification is defective or if the office finds that foreign oversight has slipped to an unacceptable standard.

Standards. Regulations covering these standards are found in 14 CFR 21 et seq. in sections called Special Federal Aviation Regulations (SFAR). For example, SFAR 26 establishes the procedures for type certification approvals, while SFAR 41 governs the standards for commuter aircraft—those designed to accommodate between 10 and 19 passengers. In general, the FAA classifies aircraft into normal, utility, acrobatic, commuter, transport, manned free balloon, and special categories, with specific standards being established for each category (refer to 14 CFR Parts 23-36). Standards include compliance with mandated acceptable levels for noise, fuel consumption, and exhaust emissions.

Once type certification has been established for the product in question, importers also require airworthiness certification for the specific articles to be imported. The FAA must pass the particular examples of products as airworthy and thus eligible to be registered and/or used in the U.S. Certification by the exporting country is generally considered to constitute adequate evidence of airworthiness provided the country of origin is in compliance with FAA standards. However, importers must be prepared to submit specific technical data and/or actual products for examination and testing.

All entries under HTSUS chapter 88 must be accompanied by all necessary technical data and instruction or user manuals translated into English.

Importer Certification. Importers must be certified by the FAA to import aircraft, components, and parts. The importing firm must satisfy the FAA that it has the requisite experience, knowledge, and financial stability to be able to interpret and administer FAA requirements for entering aircraft. Once approved, importers may make an entry by entry certification, or they may make a blanket certification good for one year. A blanket certification must be filed with the district director of customs for each customs district in which the importer enters products of HTSUS Chapter 88. Renewal is by application to each affected district director prior to the expiration of the existing certification. Customs may audit sample entries to verify compliance with FAA requirements. For details refer to 19 CFR 10.183.

Environmental Issues. The EPA sets and administers standards for the environmental impact—noise, fuel, exhaust, and hazardous materials—for aircraft. All aircraft, components, and parts, including imported ones, must meet established standards with respect to these issues. The Environment and Energy Section of the FAA (see addresses at end of this chapter) is directly responsible for monitoring and enforcing these rules, and should be contacted with questions concerning aircraft-related environmental standards.

Textile Products—Parachutes. HTSUS Chapter 88 covers the importation of parachutes and related equipment, which is subject to the regulations governing the textile products used in such articles, including silk and manmade fibers. The Department of Commerce (DOC) regulates certain textile imports under the Agricultural Adjustment Act. Customs enforces textile quotas, as well as the provisions of the TFPIA. Quotas apply to certain textiles under the Multi-Fiber Arrangements (MFA), including blends of silk and/or man-made fibers. For specific information, contact the International Trade Administration's Office of Textile and Apparel (see addresses at end of this chapter). All textile imports must be accompanied by a Country of Origin Declaration. The country of origin is the country in which the material was grown, produced, or manufactured. Textile imports remain subject to country-specific quota restrictions affecting this country of origin unless they have been substantially transformed—as defined by Customs—in another country before entering the U.S. The importation of textile products is sensitive and highly regulated. Shipments of such products that do not comply exactly with all regulations will not only be denied entry, but may be seized, forfeited, and result in penalties. Always verify all procedural information, quota status, and customs rulings immediately prior to trying to enter such textile products.

Customs Classification

For customs purposes aircraft classified within Chapter 88 of the HTSUS. The chapter is divided into major headings, which are further divided into subheadings and often into sub-subheadings, each with its a own HTSUS classification number. For example, the HTSUS number for other parts for use in civil aircraft is 8803.90.90, indicating that it is a subcategory of other parts (8803.90.00), which is a subcategory of the major heading parts of goods of powered and unpowered aircraft (8803.00.00). There are five major headings in HTSUS Chapter 88.

8801—Balloons and dirigibles; gliders, hang gliders, and other non-powered aircraft

8802—Other aircraft (for example, helicopters, airplanes); spacecraft (including satellites) and spacecraft launch vehicles

8803—Parts of goods of heading 8801 and 8802

8804—Parachutes (including dirigible parachutes) and rotochutes; parts thereof and accessories thereto

8805—Aircraft launching gear; deck-arrestor or similar gear; ground flying trainers; parts of the foregoing articles

For more details regarding classification of the specific product you are interested in importing, consult a customs broker, the appropriate commodity specialist at your nearest customs port, or see HTSUS. HTSUS is available for purchase from the U.S. Government Printing Office (see addresses at end of this chapter), and may be found in larger public libraries. Refer to "Classification—Liquidation" on page 207 for a general discussion of customs classification.

Sample Import Duties

Import duties vary depending on the HTSUS classification of your product. Therefore, to determine the correct amount of duties, your product must be properly classified under the HTSUS. The following sample duties are taken from the duty listings of HTSUS Chapter 88.

Gliders and hang gliders (8801.10.00): 4.5%; balloons (8801.90.00): 5%; helicopters of an unladen weight less than 2,000 kg (8802.11.00): 5%; airplanes and other aircraft of an unladen weight not exceeding 2,000 kg (8802.20.00): 5%; airplanes and other aircraft of an unladen weight of more than 2,000 kg but not exceeding 15,000 kg (8802.30.00): 5%; airplanes and other aircraft of an unladen weight exceeding 15,000 kg (8802.40.00): 5%; spacecraft and launch vehicles (8802.50.90): 3.7%; communications satellites (8802.50.30): free; propellers, rotors, and parts thereof (8803.10.00): free; other parts of airplanes or helicopters (8803.30.00): free; parts of communications satellites (8803.90.30): free; parachutes (8804.00.00): 6%; launching gear (8805.10.00): 3.7%; flight simulators (8805.20.00): free.

Special Provisions for Spacecraft. Under heading 9808.00.80 of the HTSUS, aerospace articles imported into the U.S., either directly by the National Aeronautics and Space Administration (NASA) or by suppliers to NASA for use by the agency, may be entered duty free. This applies only to articles involved in actual launches of spacecraft, not ancillary equipment. Nor does this provision apply to communications satellites, which remain dutiable. Certification for this exemption is made the Assistant Administrator for Procurement, NASA, to the Commissioner of Customs, following the procedure outlined in 14 CFR 1217.

Entry and Documentation

The entry of merchandise is a two-part process consisting of 1) filing the documentation necessary to determine whether merchandise may be released from Customs custody and 2) filing the documents that contain information for duty assessment and statistical purposes. In certain instances all documents must be filed and accepted by Customs prior to the release of the goods. Unless you have been granted an extension, you must file entry documents at a location specified by the district or area director within five working days of your shipment's date of arrival at a U.S. port of entry. These include a number of standard documents required by Customs for entry, and:

- Federal Aviation Administration (FAA) type certification for aircraft model to be imported
- FAA airworthiness certification for aircraft equipment to be imported
- For parachutes, Country of Origin Declaration and export documentation and/or visa for textiles subject to MFA

After you present the entry, Customs may examine your shipment, or may waive examination. The shipment is then released provided no legal or regulatory violations have been noted. You must then file entry summary documentation and deposit estimated duties at a designated customhouse within 10 working days of your shipment's release. For a detailed description of entry procedures, standard documentation, and informal entry, see "Entry Process" on page 182.

Prohibitions and Restrictions

All aircraft, components, and parts must comply with detailed product and airworthiness standards. These include performance, characteristics, controllability and maneuverability, trim, stability, stalls, spins, ground and water handling ability, and miscellaneous performance elements, such as vibration and high speed operation. Structural specifications establish parameters for loads, control system, surface loads, horizontal stability/balance surface, vertical stability, ground loads, water loads, emergency landing, and fatigue. Design and construction specifications include required standards for wings, controls, landing gear, floats and hulls, personnel and cargo accommodations, pressurization, and fire protection. In addition there exist further requirements for power plants, equipment, operational limits, and markings (see "Marking and Requirements" below). All aircraft, components, and parts imported into the U.S. must conform to these specifications in every detail. These regulations are found in 14 CFR Parts 23-36.

Quotas

Restrictions on quotas under the MFA for textile materials are country-specific. Contact the U.S. Customs Quota Branch for current information regarding quotas.

Marking and Labeling Requirements

All aircraft and airframes imported into the U.S. must be labeled indelibly and in a conspicuous place (as detailed in the regulations in 14 CFR 45.11) with an airframe number. All critical assemblies and parts must be labeled indelibly with identification that include the name and number of the manufacturer.

All textile products subject to TFPIA must be marked with 1) the name and percentage by weight of the constituent fibers present in the textile product in amounts greater than 5%, in order of their predominance; 2) the name of the manufacturer or the name of the registered identification number issued by the Federal Trade Commission (FTC); and 3) the name of the country where processed. Contact the FTC (see addresses at end of this chapter) for additional information.

For a general discussion of U.S. Customs marking and labeling requirements, see "Marking: Country of Origin" on page 215 and "Special Marking Requirements" on page 217.

Shipping Considerations

You will need to ensure that your goods are packaged and shipped with care to ensure that they arrive in good condition and pass smoothly through Customs. You are responsible for ensuring that the shipment is in compliance with all applicable government regulations for packaging and shipping. In most instances, you should not leave these arrangements solely to the discretion of your supplier. Careful preparation of the cargo and selection of the mode of transport can be essential to a cost-effective, timely delivery of undamaged goods. We strongly advise you to consult your shipping representative, insurance agent, or freight broker for advice on packing and shipping. Refer also to the major tab section "Packing/Shipping/Insurance" for a general discussion of packing and shipping.

Aircraft are sometimes flown in rather than transported on other carriers. Aircraft and related equipment are often heavy and bulky. They must be packed and stowed carefully to ensure against not damage due to shifting en route or due to exposure to heat, moisture, or other hazards.

Publications Available

The *Harmonized Tariff Schedule of the United States* (HTSUS) is available from:

Government Printing Office (GPO)
Superintendent of Documents
Washington, DC 20402
(202) 512-1800 (Order line)
(202) 512-0000 (General)

The USGPO also has copies of specific laws available for purchase. The USGPO accepts credit card orders over the phone, as well as mail orders paid by credit card, a check drawn on a U.S. bank, or an international money order.

Relevant Government Agencies

Address questions regarding DOT/FAA requirements for aircraft to:

U.S. Department of Transportation (DOT)
Federal Aviation Administration
400 Seventh Street SW
Washington, DC 20590
(202) 366-5313

Address questions regarding environmental standards and regulation for aircraft to:

Federal Aviation Administration
Environment and Energy Section
800 Independence Avenue SW
Washington, DC 20591
(202) 267-3576

Address questions regarding textile requirements for aircraft-related imports to:

International Trade Administration
Office of Textile and Apparel
14th and Constitution Ave. NW, Rm. 3100
Washington, DC 20230
(202) 482-5078, 482-3737

Address questions regarding requirements under the TFPIA to:

Federal Trade Commission (FTC)
Division of Enforcement
601 Pennsylvania Ave. NW
Washington, DC 20580
(202) 326-2996 (General)
(202) 326-2841 (Textile and wool products labeling)

Address your questions regarding current textile quota information to:

U.S. Customs Service
Quota Branch
1301 Constitution Ave. NW, Rm. 2379-ICC
Washington, DC 20229
(202) 927-5850

Address questions regarding importation of aircraft to:

International Trade Administration
Office of Aerospace
14th and Constitution Ave. NW, Rm. 2122
Washington, DC 20230
(202) 482-4222

Address questions regarding importation for aircraft to the district or port director of Customs for you area. For addresses refer to "U.S. Customs District Offices" on page 62 or contact:

U.S. Customs Service
1301 Constitution Ave. NW

Washington, DC 20229
(202) 927-6724 (Information)
(202) 927-1000 (General)

Laws and Regulations

The following laws and regulations may be relevant to the importation of vehicles. They are contained in the U.S. Code (USC) and the regulations are published in the Code of Federal Regulations (CFR), both of which may be available at larger public and law libraries. Copies of specific laws are also available from the United States Government Printing Office (address above).

49 USC 106, 44501 et seq., 44701 et seq.
Federal Transportation Act
These laws establish the authority of the FAA to set procedures and specifications for aircraft, components, and parts to be used in U.S. aviation.

14 CFR 21 et seq.
Regulations of FAA on Aircraft Use
These regulations detail the procedures and specifications governing the use of aircraft, components, and parts in U.S. aviation.

7 USC 1854
Textile Trade Agreements
This act authorizes the DOC to enter into Multi-Fiber Agreements with other countries to control trade in textiles and establishes the Textile Import Program, enforced by Customs.

15 USC 70-77
Textile Fiber Products Identification Act
This act prohibits false or deceptive labeling (misbranding) and false advertising of any textile fiber products and requires all such products imported into the U.S. to be labeled in accordance with the requirements set forth in the law.

Principal Exporting Countries

The following listing includes samples of the main supplier nations of the products of this chapter. It is organized by HTSUS major heading. (Refer to "Customs Classification" above for the product codes.) Countries are listed in rank order of the value of products imported to the U.S. Statistics represent customs value entries for 1993 from the Bureau of Census, U.S. Department of Commerce.

8801—Poland, Czech Rep., South Korea, Germany, Austria, United Kingdom, China, Japan, Israel, Australia

8802—France, Canada, Netherlands, United Kingdom, Brazil, Israel, China, Germany, Italy, Sweden

8803—Canada, United Kingdom, Japan, France, Italy, Spain, Israel, Australia, Germany, Netherlands

8804—Canada, Taiwan, South Korea, United Kingdom, South Africa, Germany, Hungary, Israel, Mexico, France

8805—Canada, United Kingdom, Netherlands, France, Sweden, Israel, Germany, Australia, Denmark, Mexico

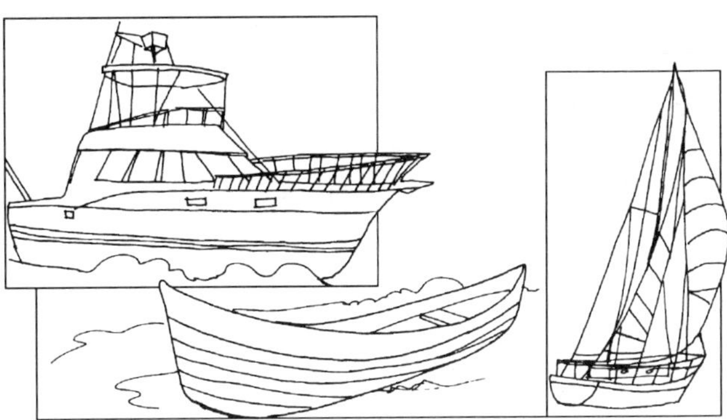

Chapter 89: Ships and Boats*

Full title: Ships, Boats, and Floating Structures

This section pertains to the importation of ships and boats, which are classified within Chapter 89 of the Harmonized Tariff Schedule of the United States (HTSUS). Specifically, it covers whole vessels, including large ships; fishing vessels; yachts and other pleasure boats; tugs; light vessels, dredges, floating docks, and drilling platforms; other vessels, such as warships and lifeboats; other floating structures, such as inflatable rafts and buoys; and vessels for scrap.

If you are interested in importing parts of or for ships or boats, refer to the Commodity Index chapter for that category of product or the specific material of which it is composed.

Key Factors

The key factors in importing ships and boats are:

- The type of boat and the purpose for which it is imported
- Compliance with U.S. Coast Guard (USCG) regulations, safety standards, and labeling requirements for boats and boat equipment

Although most importers utilize the services of a licensed customs broker in making their entries, and we recommend this practice, you should be aware of the regulatory, entry, and documentation issues involved in importing your product. You, as importer, are ultimately responsible for the fulfillment of any legal requirements applicable to your shipment.

General Considerations

U.S. Customs and USCG regulations distinguish between boats being imported permanently for commercial use or for resale, and those being imported either permanently or temporarily for personal recreational use or temporarily for purposes incidental to international trade. Customs regulations covering procedures, fees, rights, and responsibilities of vessels entering temporarily into U.S. jurisdiction are detailed in 19 CFR Part 4.

If you are importing a foreign-built pleasure boat you must notify Customs of the date the boat will arrive at the first U.S. port of entry, so that entry procedures can be completed. If you wish to import foreign-built vessels or parts thereof for resale in the U.S., you should contact the USCG Commandant (see addresses at end of this chapter) for details concerning your legal obligations.

*IMPORTANT: Read the Commodity Index Introduction. It is the essential framework for understanding this chapter.

Customs Classification

For customs purposes ships and boats are classified within Chapter 89 of HTSUS. This chapter is divided into major headings, which are further divided into subheadings, and often into subsubheadings, each with its own HTSUS classification number. For example, the HTSUS number for canoes is 8903.99.05, indicating that it is a subcategory of other—rowboats and canoes which are not of a type designed to be principally used with motors or sails (8903.99.00), which is a subcategory of the major heading yachts and other vessels for pleasure or sport (8903.0.00). There are eight major headings in HTSUS Chapter 89.

8901—Cruise ships, excursion boats, ferry boats, cargo ships, barges, and similar vessels for the transport of persons or goods

8902—Fishing vessels; factory ships and other vessels for processing or preserving fishery products

8903—Yachts and other vessels for pleasure or sports; rowboats and canoes

8904—Tugs and pusher craft

8905—Light-vessels, fire-floats, dredges, floating cranes, and other vessels the navigability of which is subsidiary to their main function; floating docks; floating or submersible drilling or production platforms

8906—Other vessels, including warships and lifeboats other than rowboats

8907—Other floating structures (for example, rafts, tanks, cofferdams, landing-stages, buoys, and beacons)

8908—Vessels and other floating structures for breaking up (scrapping)

For more details regarding classification of the specific product you are interested in importing, consult a customs broker, the appropriate commodity specialist at your nearest Customs port, or see HTSUS. HTSUS is available for purchase from the U.S. Government Printing Office (see addresses at end of this chapter), and may be found in larger public libraries. Refer to "Classification—Liquidation" on page 207 for a general discussion of customs classification.

Sample Import Duties

Foreign-registered vessels that enter U.S. territorial waters temporarily as a direct consequence of international trade or commerce are not dutiable. Yachts or other pleasure boats brought into the U.S. by nonresidents for their own use in pleasure cruising are not dutiable. Yachts or pleasure boats owned by a resident or imported for sale or charter to a resident are dutiable. The Customs duty is 1.6% for pleasure boats valued not over $15,000 and 1.9% for those valued at more than $15,000. For a new vessel, the dutiable value is normally the price paid for the vessel in the foreign port, prior to its export to the U.S., and excluding the costs of transfer. There are conditions under which an importer of a foreign-made pleasure boat is not required to pay duty. For more information see the U.S. Customs pamphlet *Pleasure Boats.* Parts of boats imported separately from the outfitted boat itself are classified by Customs according to the nature of the article—such as sails, motors, or anchors—and are subject to the duties applicable to those articles under their respective chapters.

Import duties vary depending on the HTSUS classification of your product. Therefore, to determine the correct amount of duties, your product must be properly classified under the HTSUS. The following sample duties are taken from the duty listings for HTSUS Chapter 89.

Cruise ships (8901.10.00): free; tankers (8901.20.00): free; fishing vessels (8902.00.00): free; inflatable pleasure boats (8903.10.00): 2.4%; sailboats, with or without auxiliary motor (8903.91.00): 1.5%; motorboats, other than outboard motorboats (8903.92.00): 1.5%; canoes (8903.99.05): free; row boats (8903.99.15): 4%; outboard motorboats (8903.99.20): 1.5%; tugs (8904.00.00): free; drilling platforms (8905.20.00): free; floating docks (8905.90.10): 3.7%; unfinished hulls (8906.00.10): 4.2%; buoys (8907.90.00): 3.8%; vessels or other floating structures for breaking up (8408.00.00): free.

Entry and Documentation

The entry of merchandise is a two-part process consisting of 1) filing the documents necessary to determine whether merchandise may be released from Customs custody and 2) filing the documents that contain information for duty assessment and statistical purposes. In certain instances all documents must be filed and accepted by Customs prior to the release of the goods. Unless you have been granted an extension, you must file entry documents at a location specified by the district or area director within five working days of your shipment's date of arrival at a U.S. port of entry. These include a number of standard documents required by Customs for any entry, and:

- For boats that do not comply with USCG safety standards, **Form CG-5096**
- Original bill of lading from the shipper or carrier
- Bill of sale
- Foreign registration, if any

After you present the entry, Customs may examine your shipment, or may waive examination. The shipment is then released provided no legal or regulatory violations have been noted. You must then file entry summary documentation and deposit estimated duties at a designated customhouse within 10 working days of your shipment's release. For a detailed description of entry procedures, standard documentation, and informal entry, see "Entry Process" on page 182.

Prohibitions and Restrictions

Safety Standards. Imported boats and associated equipment are subject to USCG safety regulations or standards under the Federal Boat Safety Act of 1971. Any imported boat or boat-associated equipment must meet applicable USCG safety and marine sanitation regulations before it will be allowed final entry. Details regarding these safety standards are found in USCG Consumer Fact Sheet #14. Boats without toilets or marine heads are admitted into the U.S. without further restrictions. However, if a boat has a toilet or marine head, these must either be connected to a holding tank or equipped with an operable Marine Sanitation Device (MSD) in order to be admitted. Details are found in USCG Consumer Fact Sheet #13. You can obtain copies of these fact sheets from the USCG (see addresses at end of this chapter). Regulations governing Customs treatment of entering vessels are found in 19 CFR 12.85.

Customs usually inspects boats and items of associated equipment for compliance at the port of entry. If the boat is being sailed into the U.S.—rather than shipped in by carrier—the operator is responsible for reporting to U.S. Customs immediately upon arrival to arrange for inspection.

Vessels that are foreign-built or of foreign registry may be used in the U.S. for pleasure purposes and in foreign trade with or on behalf of the U.S. However, federal law prohibits the use of such vessels in the coastwise trade, i.e. the transportation of passengers or merchandise between points in the U.S., including the carrying of fishing parties or other excursions for hire. Address questions concerning the use of foreign-built or foreign-flag vessels to the U.S. Customs Service Carrier Rulings Branch (see addresses at end of this chapter).

Noncompliance. If your boat or piece of boat-related equipment does not comply with USCG requirements, you will have to post a bond and file a declaration, **Form CG 5096**. This declaration states that the boat is not in compliance but that you, the importer, will bring it into compliance. You may obtain **Form CG 5096**

from any U.S. Customs port office. You are required to bring your boat into compliance within 180 days of filing the declaration. During this time, you may use or operate your boat or equipment only as is necessary to bring it into compliance. Once you have done all necessary work to bring it into compliance, notify the district director of Customs. You must be prepared to make available all supporting paperwork and receipts, as requested, to verify that the work has been done. The district director may also require you to deliver the boat or equipment to a specified site for a Customs inspection. When the district director is satisfied that compliance has been effected, Customs will release the bond and permit final entry. If you are unable to effect compliance within 180 days, you will have to redeliver your boat or equipment to Customs for export from the U.S. under Customs supervision.

Exemptions from Compliance. A noncomplying boat or item of related equipment is exempt from compliance under any one of the following conditions: 1) it has received a specific USCG Grant of Exemption from regulations that would otherwise apply; 2) it is entered temporarily for the purpose of exhibit, test, or participation in boat races; 3) it is owned by a member of a foreign military or government agency or public international organization on official assignment in the U.S.; or 4) it is being entered temporarily, for a period of up to one year, for repairs or alterations. The exact terms and conditions of entry will vary, but in any case you must file **Form CG 5096**.

Marking and Labeling Requirements

All boats manufactured on or after November 1, 1972 must be affixed with a Hull Identification Number (HIN) meeting USCG regulations. If your boat's foreign manufacturer has not affixed such an HIN you will have to have one assigned. You should contact the State Boating Law Administrator of the U.S. state in which your boat will be registered and used to request an HIN. To find out how to contact the appropriate Boating Law Administrator, call the Coast Guard Customer Info Line: (800) 368-5647.

All recreational boats subject to a safety standard or standards must bear either a certification label or an exemption label. Standards vary depending upon the type of boat. Contact the USCG (see addresses at end of this chapter) or the nearest district director of Customs to find out what is required for the boat you wish to import.

For a general discussion of U.S. Customs marking and labeling requirements, see "Marking: Country of Origin" on page 215 and "Special Marking Requirements" on page 217.

Shipping Considerations

You will need to ensure that your goods are packaged and shipped with care to ensure that they arrive in good condition and pass smoothly through Customs. You are responsible for ensuring that the shipment is in compliance with all applicable government regulations for packaging and shipping. In most instances, you should not leave these arrangements solely to the discretion of your supplier. Careful preparation of the cargo and selection of the mode of transport can be essential to a cost-effective, timely delivery of undamaged goods. We strongly advise you to consult your shipping representative, insurance agent, or freight broker for advice on packing and shipping. Refer also to the major tab section "Packing/Shipping/Insurance" for a general discussion of packing and shipping.

Most ships and larger boats will arrive at a U.S. port of entry under their own power. The exporter and importer must see that they are fully seaworthy prior to the transfer and voyage. Smaller vessels and other components may be packed aboard larger carriers. Care must be taken that these are stowed in such a manner as to avoid damage en route from shifting, moisture, or other hazard.

Publications Available

The U.S. Customs brochure, *Pleasure Boats*, may be relevant to the importation of ships and boats It outlines the main requirements and procedures for importing pleasure craft. It is available on request from U.S. Customs Carrier Rulings Branch (see addresses at end of this chapter).

The *Harmonized Tariff Schedule of the United States* (HTSUS) is available from:

Government Printing Office (GPO)
Superintendent of Documents
Washington, DC 20402
(202) 512-1800 (Order line)
(202) 512-0000 (General)

The USGPO also has copies of specific laws available for purchase. The USGPO accepts credit card orders over the phone, as well as mail orders paid by credit card, a check drawn on a U.S. bank, or an international money order.

Relevant Government Agencies

Address questions regarding the importation of pleasure boats to:

U.S. Coast Guard
Auxiliary Boating and Consumer Division
Recreational Boating Product Assurance Branch
2100 2nd St. SW
Washington, DC 20593
(202) 267-0984

Address questions regarding the use of foreign-built or foreign flag vessels to:

U.S. Customs Service
Carrier Rulings Branch
Franklin Court Building
1301 Constitution Ave. NW
Washington, DC 20229
(202) 482-6940

Address any other questions regarding the importation of ships or boats to the district or port director of customs for you area. For addresses refer to"U.S. Customs District Offices" on page 62 or contact:

U.S. Customs Service
1301 Constitution Ave. NW
Washington, DC 20229
(202) 927-6724 (Information)
(202) 927-1000 (General)

Laws and Regulations

The following laws and regulations may be relevant to the importation of ships and boats. The laws are contained in the U.S. Code (USC) and the regulations are published in the Code of Federal Regulations (CFR), both of which may be available at larger public and law libraries. Copies of specific laws are also available from the United States Government Printing Office (address above).

46 USC 1451 et seq.
Federal Boat Safety Act of 1971
This act establishes requirements for safety features on boats.

Principal Exporting Countries

The following listing includes samples of the main supplier nations of the products of this chapter. It is organized by HTSUS major heading. (Refer to "Customs Classification" above for the product codes.) Countries are listed in rank order of the value of products imported to the U.S. Statistics represent customs value entries for 1993 from the Bureau of Census, U.S. Department of Commerce.

8901—Norway, Canada, United Kingdom, Singapore, Russia, Germany

8902—Italy, Canada, Colombia, Russia

8903—Canada, Netherlands, Japan, Taiwan, United Kingdom, France, Italy, Singapore, Finland, New Zealand

8904—Canada

8905—Italy, Singapore, United Kingdom, Canada, Netherlands, New Zealand, Germany, Australia, Belgium, Taiwan

8906—Canada, United Kingdom, Norway, Sweden, Switzerland, Japan, Finland, Singapore, China, New Zealand

8907—United Kingdom, Canada, Norway, France, Denmark, China, Taiwan, Germany, Mexico, Italy

8908—Canada, Japan, Denmark

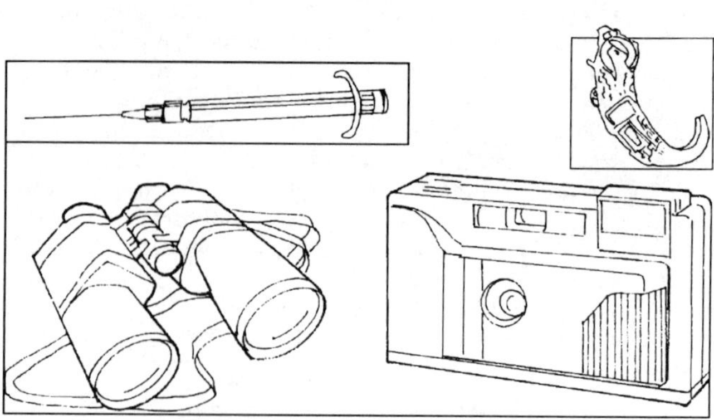

Chapter 90: Optical, Medical, and Precision Instruments*

Full title: Optical, Photographic, Cinematographic, Measuring, Checking, Precision, Medical, or Surgical Instruments and Apparatus; Parts and Accessories Thereof

This section pertains to the importation of optical, medical, and precision instruments, which are classified within Chapter 90 of the Harmonized Tariff Schedule of the United States (HTSUS). Chapter 90 encompasses a broad range of equipment, including optical fibers; lenses, prisms, and mirrors; eyeglasses, sunglasses, and goggles; binoculars and telescopes; still and movie cameras and projectors; film developing equipment; photocopiers; microscopes; magnifiers; navigational instruments; surveying instruments; scales; drafting and measuring devices; medical apparatus, equipment, and supplies; X-ray machines; testing and analytic equipment; gauges and regulators; and parts and accessories of these items.

If you are interested in importing specific components of machines made of vulcanized rubber, refer to Commodity Index Chapter 40; of leather, Chapter 42; or of textile materials, Chapters 50-63. Elastic belts and wrappings are covered in Chapters 50-63 under the materials of which they are composed. Laboratory ceramics are found in Chapter 69 and glassware in Chapter 70. Components of precious metals are covered in Chapter 71. Some associated equipment is covered in Chapter 84, while electronics not specifically listed in Chapter 90 are found in Chapter 85 (including some fiber optic cables). Timepieces are covered in Chapter 91; some medical and auxiliary furniture and light fixtures are found in Chapter 94; and toy articles of optical, medical, precision instruments are covered in Chapter 95. Parts of general use—such as screws, nuts and bolts, and nails—are classified within the headings covering the materials of which they are composed (Chapters 72-83 or Chapter 39).

Key Factors

The key factors in the importation of optical, medical, and precision instruments are:

- Compliance with U.S. Food and Drug Administration (FDA) requirements for medical devices and for radiation-producing devices
- Compliance with FDA entry notification and procedures

*IMPORTANT: Read the Commodity Index Introduction. It is the essential framework for understanding this chapter.

- Compliance with U.S. Federal Communications Commission (FCC) standards and entry notification for radio frequency devices

Although most importers utilize the services of a licensed customs broker in making their entries, and we recommend this practice, you should be aware of the regulatory, entry, and documentation issues involved in importing your product. You, as importer, are ultimately responsible for the fulfillment of any legal requirements applicable to your shipment.

General Considerations

Importation of optical products—such as cameras and binoculars—is straightforward. There are no restrictions or prohibitions. No permits, licenses, or special entry paperwork are required.

Categories. From a regulatory viewpoint, many electronic devices subject to regulation fall into two general categories: those that produce radio frequency energy, and those that produce radiation. Radiation-producing electronic devices are regulated by the FDA (see addresses at end of this chapter) under the provisions of the Federal Food, Drug, and Cosmetic Act (FDCA) and the Radiation Control for Health and Safety Act of 1968 (RCHSA). Both imported and domestically produced electronic products must comply with all relevant FDA regulations. Whether you are importing a single product for personal use, or a commercial shipment for resale in the U.S., you must file an FDA Importers Entry Notice, **Form FD701** and Electronic Product Declaration, **Form FD2877** for each product type for which official standards exist. You will not be permitted to enter a shipment unless you have filed these forms. You may obtain them from FDA, National Center for Devices and Radiological Health (see addresses at end of this chapter) or from your customs broker. For an annotated diagram of FDA import procedures, refer to the "Foods" appendix on page 808.

Radio frequency (rf) devices are regulated by the FCC (see addresses at end of this chapter) under the provisions of 47 CFR Parts 2 and 15. You must file a copy of FCC **Form 740** with each shipment of rf devices. If your shipment consists of more than one type of device, you must file a separate form for each type. The form certifies that the imported model or device is either in compliance with, or is exempt from, FCC requirements, and is so labeled. An FCC entry declaration form (FCC **Form 740**) is required for products covered under FCC regulations.

Some products, such as ultrasonic therapeutic devices and television receivers, fall under the jurisdiction of both the FCC and the FDA and must comply with both sets of regulations. Although for purposes of simplicity this section will discuss the two categories as if they do not overlap, they do, and you should ascertain exactly which regulations your product is required to meet for which agency. Do not rely on one agency for information concerning the requirements of another agency. If you are in doubt as to the status of your commodity, contact both the FCC and the FDA.

Medical Devices. Importation of medical products, including radioisotopes and radioactive materials, is regulated by the FDA, under the Federal Food, Drug, and Cosmetic Act (FDCA), as amended by the Medical Device Amendments of 1976 (MDA). MDA defines a device as any health-care product that does not achieve any of its principal intended purposes by chemical action in or on the body, or by being metabolized. For example, eyeglasses (both prescription and nonprescription) are considered medical devices, as is the syringe that injects a vaccine (although the vaccine itself is not a device).

Entry Requirements. Imported products regulated by the FDA are subject to FDA port of entry inspection. **Form FD701** is required for all such importations and may be obtained from your local FDA Import Operations office, or from FDA headquarters (see addresses at end of this chapter). The FDA also controls radiation-emitting electrical devices under the provisions of the Radiation Control for Health and Safety Act of 1968, as amended (RCHSA). An Electronic Product Declaration **Form FD2877** must be filed for every product type for which official standards exist. No medical devices (or other electronic instruments affected by the requirements) will be admitted unless these documents are filed and approved. For an annotated diagram of required FDA import procedures refer to the "Foods" appendix on page 808.

Shipment Detention. If your shipment is found to be noncomplying, it may be detained at the port of entry. In the case of products subject to FDA jurisdiction, the FDA may permit you to bring such a shipment into compliance before making a final decision regarding admittance. However, any sorting, reprocessing, or relabeling must be supervised by FDA personnel, and will be done at the importer's expense. Such conditional release to allow an importer to bring a shipment into compliance is a privilege, not a right. The FDA may consider subsequent noncomplying shipments of the same type of product to constitute abuse of the privilege and require the importer to destroy or reexport the products. To ascertain what your legal responsibilities are, you should contact these agencies regarding the specific items to be imported.

Customs Classification

For customs purposes optical, medical, and precision instruments are classified within Chapter 90 of the HTSUS. This chapter is divided into major headings, which are further divided into subheadings, and often into sub-subheadings, each of which has its own HTSUS classification number. For example, the HTSUS number for parts and accessories of X-ray tubes is 9022.90.40, indicating that it is a subcategory of other apparatus, including parts and accessories (9022.90.00), which is a subcategory of the major heading apparatus based on the use of X-rays for medical uses (9022.00.00). There are 33 major headings in HTSUS Chapter 90.

9001—Optical fibers and optical fiber bundles; optical fiber cables other than those of heading 8544; sheets and plates of polarizing material; lenses (including contact lenses), prisms, mirrors, other optical elements, of any material, unmounted, other than such elements of glass not optically worked

9002—Lenses, prisms, mirrors, and other optical elements, of any material, mounted, being parts of or fittings for instruments or apparatus, other than such elements of glass not optically worked; parts and accessories thereof

9003—Frames and mountings for spectacles, goggles, or the like, and parts thereof

9004—Spectacles, goggles, and the like, corrective, protective, or other

9005—Binoculars, monoculars, other optical telescopes, and mountings thereof; other astronomical instruments and mountings therefor, but not including instruments for radio-astronomy; parts thereof

9006—Photographic (other than cinematographic) cameras; photographic flashlight apparatus and flashbulbs other than discharge lamps of heading 8539; parts and accessories thereof

9007—Cinematographic cameras and projectors, whether or not incorporating sound recording or reproducing apparatus; parts and accessories thereof

9008—Image projectors, other than cinematographic; photographic (other than cinematographic) enlargers and reducers; parts and accessories thereof

9009—Photocopying apparatus incorporating an optical system or of the contact type and thermocopying apparatus; parts and accessories thereof

9010—Apparatus and equipment for photographic (including cinematographic) laboratories (including apparatus for the projection of circuit patterns on sensitized semiconductor materials), not specified or included elsewhere in this chapter; parts and accessories thereof

9011—Compound optical microscopes, including those for photomicrography, cinematographic, or microprojection; parts and accessories

9012—Microscopes other than optical microscopes; diffraction apparatus; parts and accessories thereof.

9013—Liquid crystal devices not constituting articles provided for more specifically in other headings; lasers, other than laser diodes; other optical appliances and instruments, not specified or included elsewhere in this chapter; parts and accessories thereof

9014—Direction finding compasses; other navigational instruments and appliances; parts and accessories thereof

9015—Surveying (including photogrammetrical surveying), hydrographic, oceanographic, hydrological, meteorological, or geophysical instruments and appliances, excluding compasses; rangefinders; parts and accessories thereof

9016—Balances of a sensitivity of a 5 cg or better, with or without weights; parts and accessories thereof

9017—Drawing, marking-out, or mathematical calculating instruments (for example, drafting machines, pantographs, protractors, drawing sets, slide rules, disc calculators); instruments for measuring length, for use in the hand (for example, measuring rods and tapes, micrometers, calipers), not specified or included elsewhere in this chapter; parts and accessories thereof

9018—Instruments and appliances used in medical, surgical, dental, or veterinary sciences, including scintigraphic apparatus, other electro-medical apparatus, and sight-testing instruments; parts and accessories

9019—Mechano-therapy appliances; massage apparatus; psychological aptitude-testing apparatus; ozone therapy, oxygen therapy, aerosol therapy, artificial respiration, or other therapeutic respiration apparatus; parts and accessories thereof

9020—Other breathing appliances and gas masks, excluding protective masks having neither mechanical parts nor replaceable filters; parts and accessories thereof

9021—Orthopedic appliances, including crutches, surgical belts, and trusses; splints and other fracture appliances; artificial parts of the body; hearing aids and other appliances which are worn or carried or implanted in the body, to compensate for a defect or disability; parts and accessories thereof

9022—Apparatus based on the use of X-rays or of alpha, beta, or gamma radiations, whether or not for medical, surgical, dental, or veterinary uses, including radiography or radiotherapy apparatus, X-ray tubes and other X-ray generators, high tension generators, control panels, and desks, screens, examination or treatment tables, chairs, and the like; parts and accessories thereof

9023—Instruments, apparatus, and models, designed for demonstrational purposes (for example, in education or exhibitions), unsuitable for other uses, and parts and accessories thereof

9024—Machines and appliances for testing the hardness, strength, compressibility, elasticity, or other mechanical properties of materials (for example, metals, woods, textiles, paper, plastics), and parts and accessories thereof

9025—Hydrometers and similar floating instruments, thermometers, pyrometers, barometers, hygrometers, and psychrometers, recording or not, and any combination of these instruments; parts and accessories thereof

9026—Instruments and apparatus for measuring or checking the flow, level, pressure, or other variables of liquids or gases (for example, flow meters, level gauges, manometers, heat meters), excluding instruments and apparatus of heading 9014, 9015, 9028, or 9032; parts and accessories thereof

9027—Instruments and apparatus for physical or chemical analysis (for example, polarimeters, refractometers, spectrometers, gas or smoke analysis apparatus); instruments and apparatus for measuring or checking viscosity, porosity, expansion, surface tension, or the like; instruments and apparatus for measuring or checking quantities of heat, sound or light (including exposure meters); microtomes; parts and accessories thereof

9028—Gas, liquid, or electricity supply or production meters, including calibrating meters thereof; parts and accessories thereof

9029—Revolution counters, production counters, taximeters, odometers, pedometers, and the like; speedometers and tachometers; other than those of heading 9014 or 9015; stroboscopes; parts and accessories thereof

9030—Oscilloscopes, spectrum analyzers, and other instruments and apparatus for measuring or checking electrical quantities, excluding meters of heading 9028; instruments and apparatus for measuring or detecting alpha, beta, gamma, X-ray, cosmic, or other ionizing radiations; parts and accessories thereof

9031—Measuring and checking instruments, appliances and machines, not specified or included elsewhere in this chapter; profile projectors; parts and accessories thereof

9032—Automatic regulating or controlling instruments and apparatus; parts and accessories thereof

9033—Parts and accessories (not specified or included elsewhere in this chapter) for machines and appliances, instruments, or apparatus of chapter 90

For more details regarding classification of the specific product you are interested in importing, consult a customs broker, the appropriate commodity specialist at your nearest customs port, or see HTSUS. HTSUS is available for purchase from the U.S. Government Printing Office (see addresses at end of this chapter), and may be found in larger public libraries. Refer to "Classification—Liquidation" on page 207 for a general discussion of Customs classification.

Sample Import Duties

Import duties vary depending on the HTSUS classification of your product. Therefore, to determine the correct amount of duties, your product must be properly classified under the HTSUS. The following sample duties are taken from the duty listings for HTSUS Chapter 90.

Optical fibers and fiber bundles (9001.10.00): 8.4%; contact lenses (9001.30.00): 5.6%; glass spectacle lenses (9001.40.00): 5.6%; objective camera lenses (9002.1,80): 6.6%; eyeglasses frames of plastic (9003.11.00): 7.2%; sunglasses (9004.10.00): 7.2%; binoculars (9005.10.00): free; optical telescopes (9005.80.40): 8%; microfilm cameras (9006.20.00): 3%; fixed focus instant cameras (9006.40.40): 4%; singles lens reflex 35 mm cameras (9006.51.00): 3%; electronic photographic flash apparatus (9006.61.00): 3.9%; movie cameras for 16 mm film (9007.11.00): 4.5%; slide projectors (9008.10.00): 7%; electrostatic photocopiers (9009.11.00): 3.7%; film developing tanks (9010.20.20): 3.8%; stereoscopic microscopes (9011.10.40): 4.9%; diffraction microscopes (9012.10.00): 4.4%; hand magnifying glasses (9013.80.20): 6.6%; optical direction finding compasses (9014.10.10): 7.9%; automatic pilots for aircraft (9014.20.40): 4.2%; electrical theodolites (9015.20.40): 4.9%; jewelers' balances (9016.00.40): 5.7%; drafting tables (9017.10.00): 4.9%; hand operated digitizers (9017.20.80): 5.8%; electrocardiographs (9018.11.30): 4.2%; syringes (9018.31.00): 8.4%; rubber catheters (9118.39.00): 4.2%; sphygmomanometers (9018.90.50): 3.4%; defibrillators (9018.90.64): 7.9%; oxygen therapy apparatus (9019.20.00): 3.7%; self-contained underwater breathing apparatus (9020.00.60): free; bone plates, screws, and nails (9021.19.40): 7.2%; hearing aids (9021.40.00): 4.2%; medical X-ray machines (9022.11.00): 2.1%; demonstration models (9023.00.00): free; metals testing apparatus (9024.10.00): 4.8%; liquid filled thermometers (9025.11.20): 17%; barometers (9025.20,80): 2.8%; hygrometers (9025.80.35): 3.9%; electricity flow meters (9026.10.20): 4.9%; gas chromatographs (9027.20.44): 4.9%; nuclear magnetic resonance instruments (9027.80.25):

4.9%; microtomes (9027.90.20): 6.2%; gas meters (9028.10.00): 45 cents each + 7%; speedometers (9029.20.40): free; cathode-ray oscilloscopes (9030.20.00): 4.9%; coordinate measuring machines (9031.40.40): 10%; thermostats (9032.10.00): 4.8%; miscellaneous parts of articles of chapter 90 not elsewhere specified (9033.00.00): 4.9%.

Entry and Documentation

The entry of merchandise is a two-part process consisting of 1) filing the documents necessary to determine whether merchandise may be released from Customs custody and 2) filing the documents that contain information for duty assessment and statistical purposes. In certain instances all documents must be filed and accepted by Customs prior to the release of the goods. Unless you have been granted an extension, you must file entry documents at a location specified by the district or area director within five working days of your shipment's date of arrival at a U.S. port of entry. These include a number of standard documents required by Customs for any entry, and:

- FDA Importers Entry Notice, **Form FD701**
- FDA Electronic Product Declaration **Form FD2877** for radiation-emitting devices
- FCC Declaration **Form 740** for radio frequency devices

After you present the entry, Customs may examine your shipment, or may waive examination. The shipment is then released provided no legal or regulatory violations have been noted. You must then file entry summary documentation and deposit estimated duties at a designated customhouse within 10 working days of your shipment's release. For a detailed description of entry procedures, standard documentation, and informal entry, see "Entry Process" on page 182.

Prohibitions and Restrictions

If you wish to import medical devices into the U.S., you should bear in mind that your products are likely to be detained if they do not comply with all applicable requirements under the FDCA.Nonprescription devices must also comply with the Fair Packaging and Labeling Act (FPLA). Manufacturers of finished devices intended for importation into the U.S. must comply with the FDA's Good Manufacturing Practice regulations. If your shipment was produced by a manufacturer that does not comply with these regulations, it may be detained at the port of entry.

Medical devices include several thousand health products, from simple articles such as thermometers, tongue depressors, and heating pads, to intrauterine contraceptive devices, heart pacemakers, and kidney dialysis machines. The term "devices" also includes components, parts, or accessories of devices, diagnostic aids such as reagents, antibiotic sensitivity discs, and test kits for invitro diagnosis of disease (e.g., diabetes), and other conditions, (e.g., pregnancy).

Classification of Devices. The FDCA, as amended, requires that the FDA classify all devices intended for human use marketed in the U.S. prior to passage of the Medical Device Amendments of 1976 (MDA) ("pre-amendment devices") into one of three regulatory classes. This ensures that each device is subject to controls appropriate for it.

Class I: General Controls. Class I products are subject only to the general controls applicable to all devices. General controls include manufacturer registration, recordkeeping requirements, labeling requirements, and Good Manufacturing Practice regulations. (See "Requirements for all devices" below.)

Class II: Performance Standards. The FDA establishes performance standards for devices for which general controls are deemed insufficient in and of themselves to ensure safety and effectiveness, and for which adequate information exists to develop such a standard. Class II devices must meet applicable FDA performance standards. Performance standards may specify materials, construction, components, ingredients, labeling, and other properties of the device. A standard may also provide for device testing to ensure that different lots of individual products conform to requirements. Regulations establishing performance standards for Class II devices are found in 21 CFR Part 861.

Class III: Premarket Approval. Unless it determines that such approval is unnecessary, the FDA requires official approval for implants and life-supporting or life-sustaining devices prior to marketing. Premarket approval applications for pre-amendment Class III devices cannot be required until 30 months after they are classified or until 90 days after a regulation calling for the application, whichever comes later. Premarket approval can also be required for other devices if general controls are deemed insufficient to ensure safety and effectiveness and there is inadequate information to establish a performance standard.

Post-MDA Devices. For purposes of regulation, there are two types of devices marketed after the passage of the MDA: those that are and those that are not substantially the same as a pre-amendment device. New devices that are substantially equivalent to a pre-amendment device are classified the same as the equivalent pre-amendment product. Those not considered substantially equivalent are automatically placed in Class III, requiring premarket approval.

Pre-amendment and post-amendment devices regarded as new drugs (e.g., soft contact lenses) prior to MDA are automatically classified in Class III. Regulations on classification of devices are found in 21 CFR 860, 862-890.

Reclassification. Any interested person may petition the FDA to reclassify a device either to lower the classification from III to II or from II to I, or in some instances to raise the classification. For example, a manufacturer may decide to submit a petition when new product information becomes available on a device, or when the FDA finds that a new product is not substantially equivalent to a pre-amendment device and thus is automatically put in Class III. The FDA may also begin a reclassification action on its own initiative. Regulations on reclassification of devices are found in 21 CFR 860, Subpart C.

Premarket Notification for New Devices. All manufacturers are required to give the FDA 90 days notice before introducing a new device on the market (Sec. 510). During the 90-day period, the FDA determines whether the device is or is not equivalent to a pre-amendment device. If the FDA determines that the device is not equivalent, it is automatically placed in Class III, and the manufacturer must provide FDA with a premarket approval application containing evidence that the device is safe and effective. The device may not be commercially distributed to the public until the FDA approves the application. However, the manufacturer may try to convince the FDA to reclassify the device by filing a reclassification petition.

Manufacturers must submit a premarket notification when introducing: 1) a new device to the market; 2) a device new to a particular manufacturer even though a similar device may already be marketed by another manufacturer; 3) a device that is a modification of an existing product if the modification has a significant impact on the safety and effectiveness of the device; or 4) an old device with a major change in intended use.

A premarket notification to the FDA must include the following information: 1) the device's trade and common name; 2) labeling and advertisements describing the device, its intended use, and directions for use; 3) the device's classification; and 4) a statement detailing the device's similarity to or difference from others on the market, accompanied by supporting data.

Premarket notification regulations are found in 21 CFR 807, Subpart E.

Requirements for All Devices. All medical devices are subject to general control requirements.

Adulteration. The FDA may initiate an enforcement action (seizure, injunction, or prosecution) to protect the public from adulterated or misbranded devices (Sec. 501). A device is considered adulterated under any of the following conditions: 1) it has been manufactured, packed, or held under insanitary conditions; 2) its container is composed of a dangerous substance; 3) it contains an unsafe color additive; 4) its quality or purity falls below that which it purports to possess; 5) it does not comply with an applicable performance standard; 6) it is a banned device; 8) it is not manufactured in accordance with Good Manufacturing Practice regulations; or 9) it is an investigational device that fails to comply with applicable requirements under investigational device regulations.

Misbranding. A device is considered misbranded under any of the following conditions (Sec. 502): 1) its labeling is false or misleading; 2) its label does not contain the name and address of manufacturer, packer, or distributor, and an accurate statement of quality of contents; 3) required information is not prominently and legibly placed on the label in English; 4) the device's established name does not appear in type at least half as large as the proprietary name used; 5) its labeling does not bear adequate directions for use and adequate warnings against unsafe use; 6) it is dangerous to health; 7) it is a restricted device and its advertisements are false or misleading or do not meet minimum requirements for disclosure of product information; 8) it is a restricted device and it is not sold, distributed, or used in compliance with regulations; 9) it does not comply with an applicable performance standard labeling requirement; 10) it was made in an establishment not registered under Section 510, or not listed under Section 510(j), or if a notice respecting a device was not provided as required by Section 510(h); or 11) there was a failure to comply with a requirement under Section 518 (notification and other remedies) or Section 519 (records and reports). General labeling requirements are found in 21 CFR 801; in vitro diagnostics labeling requirements are in 21 CFR 809.

Registration and Device Listing. Every person who owns or operates any domestic establishment engaged in manufacturing a medical device intended for human use must register that establishment and list its products with the FDA (Sec. 510). This requirement also applies to any repacker, relabeler, and initial distributor of imported devices. The following are exempted (21 CFR 807) from registration and listing: 1) manufacturers of raw materials or components used in manufacturing a finished device; 2) licensed practitioners manufacturing or altering devices solely for use in practice (physicians, dentists, optometrists, clinical laboratories, etc.); 3) pharmacies and retail outlets; 4) researchers, teachers, or analysts; 5) wholesalers or common carriers whose function is to process a previously manufactured device in order to comply with the needs of the individual consumer.

You may register by submitting a completed **Form FD2891**. To obtain this form, contact: FDA, HFZ-342 (see addresses at end of this chapter), or any FDA District Office. Regulations for registration and device listing are contained in 21 CFR 807.

Good Manufacturing Practice Regulations. Manufacturers of finished devices must comply with regulations prescribing current Good Manufacturing Practice for devices. Designed to prevent the production of defective products, these regulations include requirements for building maintenance, personnel training, recordkeeping, equipment design and maintenance, and packaging and labeling controls (21 CFR 820).

Inspection, Administrative Detention, and Records and Reports. FDA investigators are authorized to enter and inspect any factory, warehouse, or establishment where devices are manufactured, processed, packed, or held. Upon approval of the FDA District Office Director, an investigator may order a firm to detain, for a period of up to 30 days, a device that the investigator suspects is adulterated or misbranded (21 CFR 800). Manufacturers of restricted devices must permit FDA investigators to inspect the premises and documents kept there—including all records, files, papers, processes, controls, and facilities with the exception of certain financial, sales, personnel, or research data (Secs. 704 and 304). Manufacturers of all devices must permit investigators to inspect records required by Good Manufacturing Practice regulations.

Should you receive information that one of your devices has been responsible for, or is associated with, a death or serious injury, you are required to notify the FDA's Center for Devices and Radiological Health and the local FDA field office as soon as possible. Such notification must be made within five calendar days. Any other problems with devices should be reported within 15 working days.

Notification, Repairs, Replacements, and Refunds. The FDA can order manufacturers to notify the public of any product defect that could constitute a health hazard, and can order manufacturers to repair, replace, or refund the cost of these defective devices. (Sec. 518).

Banned Devices. The FDA may issue a regulation banning any device that presents a substantial deception or substantial and unreasonable risk of causing injury or illness. When a change in labeling may suffice to bring a product into compliance, manufacturers are provided the opportunity to correct the device's labeling before a ban is initiated. Where a device presents an unreasonable, direct, or substantial danger, FDA may order the ban to take effect upon publication of the proposed banning regulation. Procedural regulations are found in 21 CFR 895.

Investigational Devices. Investigational devices (Sec. 520) are those used on human subjects by qualified experts, in order to conduct investigations of device safety and effectiveness. The FDA may grant such sponsors exemptions from certain FDCA requirements that would otherwise impede their studies. If you wish to obtain such an exemption, you must file an Application for an Investigational Device Exemption with the FDA. FDA regulations designed to protect the subjects of research on investigational devices are found in 21 CFR 812 (general) and 813 (intraocular lenses).

Custom Devices. Custom devices are devices ordered by members of the health professions to conform to their own special needs or to those of their patients (e.g. certain dental devices and specially designed orthopedic footwear). These are exempt from registration and from otherwise applicable performance standards or premarket approval requirements (Sec. 520). The exemption applies only to devices not generally available to or used by other health professionals. Custom devices are not exempt from other provisions of the Act and regulations.

Procedures. The importer of medical devices into the U.S. is required to register with the FDA, just as is any domestic manufacturer of similar devices. In addition, if the shipment represents the initial importation of the device into the U.S., the manufacturer is required to file a premarket notification with the FDA. If the FDA determines that the device is in Class III and requires premarket approval prior to import, the agency will deny importation until 1) a premarket approval application is approved; or 2) the device is reclassified to Class I or Class II; or 3) an investigational device exemption is in effect. If the device is reclassified into Class I or Class II, and other applicable FDCA requirements are met, the FDA will allow importation. For more details contact the FDA (see addresses at end of this chapter).

Radiation-producing Devices. The comprehensive Radiation Control for Health and Safety Act (RCHSA) was enacted in 1968 to protect the public from unnecessary exposure to radiation from electronic products. FDA administration of the law is carried out through the setting and enforcement of radiation performance standards to limit radiation emissions. The standards apply to products offered for sale or use in the U.S., whether manufactured in this country or elsewhere. Electronic products include all products or equipment capable of emitting ionizing or nonionizing radiation, or sonic, infrasonic, or ultrasonic waves. Television receivers, microwave ovens, X-ray equipment, lasers, ultraviolet lights, diathermy units, infrared heaters, ultrasonic cleaners, and particle accelerators are examples of products required to comply with RCHSA. Regulations for the enforcement of the act are published in 21 CFR Parts 1000-1050. The law is enforced by FDA's Center for Devices and Radiological Health (CDRH) (see addresses at end of this chapter).

Radiation Performance Standards and Product Certification. Performance standards are prescribed for electronic products when the FDA determines that federal regulations are necessary for the protection of the public health and safety. The standards (21 CFR Parts 1020-1050) prescribe maximum allowable radiation levels and other approaches to control of radiation emission, without specifying design features. If you are interested in importing a radiation-producing product, you should ascertain whether or not it is subject to a standard. The manufacturer of an electronic product for which there is an applicable federal performance standard must obtain certification for the product. Certification is based upon a test prescribed by the standard, or a testing program that is in accord with Good Manufacturing Practices as determined by CDRH. When considering an overseas purchase, you must determine that the product is in compliance. Approved products must bear a certification label stating that the product conforms to the applicable standard. Keep in mind that it is not as simple to identify a product that is eligible for certification but has not been certified. When in doubt, contact the FDA.

Noncomplying or Defective Products. RCHSA specifically provides that test samples may be taken from any import shipment to determine whether a product complies with an applicable standard. The FDA may—through authorization from the U.S. Customs Service—take a sample from your shipment for testing. Such samples are returned after testing is completed. If your product is discovered not to meet the provisions of an applicable standard, or if it contains any defect related to its safe use by reason of radiation emissions, the FDA will refuse entry. The manufacturer of a defective electronic product that has entered the commercial market is responsible for notifying the consumer, repairing the defect, and replacing the product or refunding the purchaser's money.

Recordkeeping. The FDA requires dealers and distributors of electronic products for which standards have been issued to maintain records. These records are intended to facilitate the location of purchasers for notification concerning defective or noncomplying devices, or to facilitate the recall of such products. In addition, manufacturers of certain electronic products designated by the regulation are required to maintain relevant product testing records and to make reports necessary to demonstrate compliance with the act.

Products Covered by Radiation Performance Standards. The following products for medical use are currently covered by federal radiation performance standards. If you are considering importation of any of these products, be sure that the foreign manufacturer has obtained U.S. certification and has so labeled the items before attempting to enter a shipment into U.S. Customs territory. Uncertified products—even those that are eligible for certification—are refused entry, and any disposal or modification is undertaken at the importer's expense. Further information may be obtained from any FDA office or by referring to 21 CFR Parts 1000-1050.

Television Receivers. Standard effective January 15, 1970. Applies to television receivers designed to receive and display a television picture, and includes electronic viewfinders on TV cameras, TV projectors, and TV monitors used with X-ray and other medical systems.

Diagnostic X-ray Equipment. Standard effective August 1, 1974. Applies to complete diagnostic X-ray systems, as well as major components, including tube-housing assemblies, X-ray controls, high voltage X-ray generators, fluoroscopic imaging assemblies, X-ray tables, cradles, film changers, cassette holders, and beam limiting devices.

Cabinet X-ray Systems. Standard effective April 10, 1975. In addition to baggage inspection system, applies to other X-ray machines in enclosed freestanding cabinets.

Laser Products. Standard effective August 2, 1976. Amendment effective August 20, 1985, applies to all laser products, as well as products containing lasers.

Sunlamp Products and Ultraviolet Lamps for Use in Sunlamp Products. Standard May 7, 1980. Applies to all sunlamp products and ultraviolet lamps intended to induce sun-tanning.

Ultrasonic Therapy Products. Standard effective February 17, 1979. Applies to any device intended to generate and emit ultrasonic radiation for therapeutic purposes at frequencies above 16 kilohertz, or any generator or applicator designed or specifically designated for use in such a device.

Note: Many foreign manufacturers produce electronic devices for export that conform to applicable FDA and FCC regulations. If you limit your purchases to such products and verify that the appropriate labels are affixed, you should have no difficulty with U.S. Customs entry.

Radio Frequency Devices. Under the Communications Act of 1934, as amended, all radio frequency (rf) devices are subject to FCC radio emission standards. You must file an FCC declaration FCC **Form 740** certifying that your model or device is in conformity with, will be brought into conformity with, or is exempt from the FCC requirements, for each shipment of rf devices you import. FCC standards and procedures have been developed to limit potential sources of rf interference to authorized radio services in the U.S. The FCC defines a radio frequency device as a product that emits rf energy, either intentionally or as a design byproduct. Radio frequency devices must meet specific FCC equipment authorization standards. When rf devices are imported into the U.S., a declaration is required that states that the appropriate FCC authorization has been granted. This declaration is made on FCC **Form 740**.

Equipment Authorization. FCC equipment authorization is required for certain types of rf devices imported into the U.S. Although compliance with these procedures is the responsibility of the foreign manufacturer, you should be aware of them, since noncomplying shipments will not be permitted entry. Equipment authorization procedures include: 1) type approval (requires testing of equipment sample); 2) type acceptance (requires review and evaluation of written application and equipment test report); 3) certification (requires review and evaluation of written application and equipment test report); 4) notification (requires submission of brief application; 5) verification (manufacturer tests device for compliance with FCC regulations prior to marketing, and retains test data); 6) registration (applies to subscriber-owned and common-carrier-owned telephone devices; requires review and evaluation of written application and test report). Except for verification and registration procedures, a separate FCC **Form 731** should be filed with the FCC for each type of device for which equipment authorization is being requested. FCC **Form 730** is used for registration of telephone equipment under Part 68 of FCC rules. No application is required for verification. Fees are required for equipment authorization filings. Fee information is available from any FCC office or by calling the FCC Licensing Division at (800) 322-1117. If you would like more complete details regarding authorization procedures, contact the nearest regional FCC office, or the FCC Office of Engineering and Technology in Washington, D.C. (see addresses at end of this chapter).

Importation of Radio Frequency Devices. Each time you import a shipment of rf devices, you must file a separate FCC **Form 740** for each type of rf device represented in your shipment. Send your original completed **Form 740(s)** to the FCC Field Operations Bureau in Washington, D.C. (see addresses at end of this chapter). Attach a copy of your form(s) to the customs entry summary for your shipment, and present it to customs at the U.S. port of entry. For more information, contact any FCC office, or the FCC Washington headquarters (see addresses at end of this chapter).

Marking and Labeling Requirements

FDA Requirements. Labeling requirements for devices vary depending upon the device's status under the FDCA. Address questions concerning the current status of your product to the FDA Center for Devices and Radiological Health, Division of Small Manufacturers Assistance (see addresses at end of this chapter). You should provide full information concerning the device and include a copy of the proposed labeling if you are considering shipping the device within the U.S. Proposed labeling may be submitted in draft form and need not be printed.

All radiation-emitting devices for which federal standards have been determined must be certified for compliance. The manufacturer must affix a certification label to each product stating that it conforms to the applicable standard. Products requiring certification that are not so labeled will not be permitted entry.

FCC Requirements. All rf devices subject to FCC authorization procedures, whether manufactured within the U.S. or outside it, must bear labeling to show compliance. Devices that are not so labeled will not be permitted entry into U.S. Customs territory. For details on label wording, contact FCC (see addresses at end of this chapter).

For a general discussion of U.S. Customs marking and labeling requirements, see "Marking: Country of Origin" on page 215 and "Special Marking Requirements" on page 217.

Shipping Considerations

You will need to ensure that your goods are packaged and shipped with care to ensure that they arrive in good condition and pass smoothly through Customs. You are responsible for ensuring that the shipment is in compliance with all applicable government regulations for packaging and shipping. In most instances, you should not leave these arrangements solely to the discretion of your supplier. Careful preparation of the cargo and selection of the mode of transport can be essential to a cost-effective, timely delivery of undamaged goods. We strongly advise you to consult your shipping representative, insurance agent, or freight broker for advice on packing and shipping. Refer also to the major tab section "Packing/Shipping/Insurance" for a general discussion of packing and shipping.

Optical, medical, and precision instruments are usually fragile and should be securely packed and stowed to avoid damage due to shifting en route. Special care must be taken to ensure that they are adequately protected from excessive vibration, heat, humidity, or water damage.

Publications Available

The following publication explains the FDA requirements for importing optical, medical and precision instruments. It is published by the FDA and is available on request from FDA headquarters (see addresses at end of this chapter).

Requirements of Laws and Regulations Enforced by the U.S. Food and Drug Administration

The following publication may be relevant to the import of medical devices. It is published by the Center for Devices and Radiological Health, FDA (see addresses at end of this chapter).

Import of Medical Devices—A Workshop Manual (HS Publication 93-4228; $11.00)

The following bulletins may be useful for importing radio devices and are available from any regional FCC office (or address below):

FCC Equipment Authorization Program for Radio Frequency Devices (Bulletin Number 61)
Importation of Radio Frequency Devices (Field Operations Bulletin Number 8).

The *Harmonized Tariff Schedule of the United States* (HTSUS) is available from:

Government Printing Office (GPO)
Superintendent of Documents
Washington, DC 20402
(202) 512-1800 (Order line)
(202) 512-0000 (General)

The USGPO also has copies of specific laws available for purchase. The USGPO accepts credit card orders over the phone, as well as mail orders paid by credit card, a check drawn on a U.S. bank, or an international money order.

Relevant Government Agencies

Address requests for information, forms, instructions regarding establishment registration and product listing, the current status of a device, or required labeling to:

Food and Drug Administration (FDA)
Center for Devices and Radiological Health
Division of Small Manufactures Assistance
5600 Fishers Lane
Rockville, MD 20857
(800) 638-2041, (301) 638-2041

Address additional questions to:

Food and Drug Administration (FDA)
Division of Enforcement, Imports Branch
200 C Street SW
Washington, DC 20204
(202) 205-4726

Address inquiries concerning FCC **Form 740** requirements to:

Federal Communications Commission (FCC)
Enforcement Division, Investigations Branch
1919 M Street NW, Rm. 744
Washington, DC 20554
(202) 418-1170

Address questions regarding importation of optical, medical, and precision instruments to the district or port director of Customs for you area. For addresses refer to"U.S. Customs District Offices" on page 62 or contact:

U.S. Customs Service
1301 Constitution Ave. NW
Washington, DC 20229
(202) 927-6724 (Information)
(202) 927-1000 (General)

Laws and Regulations

The following laws and regulations may be relevant to the importation of optical, medical, and precision instruments. The laws are contained in the U.S. Code (USC) and the regulations are published in the code of Federal Regulations (CFR), both of which may be available at larger public and law libraries. Copies of specific laws are also available from the United States Government Printing Office (address above).

21 USC 301 et seq.
Food, Drug, and Cosmetic Act
This Act prohibits deceptive practices and regulates the manufacture, sale and importation or exportation of food, drugs, cosmetics, and related products. See 21 USC 331, 381, 382.

19 CFR 12.1 et seq.; 21 CFR 1.83 et seq.
Regulations on Food, Drugs, and Cosmetics
These regulations of the Secretary of Health and Human Services and the Secretary of the Treasury govern the standards, labeling, marking, and importing of products used with food, drugs, and cosmetics.

42 USC 263b-263n
Radiation Control for Health and Safety Act
This Act prohibits entry of electronic products found not to be in compliance with prescribed standards. See 21 CFR Part 1005. Customs enforces this prohibition. See 19 CFR 12.90 et seq.

47 USC 302a
Devices That Interfere with Radio Reception
This law prohibits the importation of devices or home electronic equipment that fail to comply with regulations promulgated by the FCC. See 47 CFR 2.1201 et seq. and 18.119. Customs enforces the prohibition.

Principal Exporting Countries

The following listing includes samples of the main supplier nations of the products of this chapter. It is organized by HTSUS major heading. (Refer to "Customs Classification" above for the product codes.) Countries are listed in rank order of the value of products imported to the U.S. Statistics represent customs value entries for 1993 from the Bureau of Census, U.S. Department of Commerce.

9001—Japan, Canada, Mexico, Ireland, Germany, Thailand, United Kingdom, Taiwan, Denmark, Singapore

9002—Japan, Germany, Canada, Taiwan, United Kingdom, South Korea, Switzerland, Singapore, Hong Kong, Sweden

9003—Italy, Japan, Hong Kong, South Korea, France, Austria, Germany, China, Mexico, Taiwan

9004—Taiwan, China, Japan, France, Italy, South Korea, Hong Kong, Austria, Canada, Germany

9005—Japan, China, Taiwan, South Korea, Hong Kong, Philippines, Germany, Canada, Russia, Thailand

9006—Japan, China, Malaysia, Hong Kong, Taiwan, United Kingdom, Mexico, Philippines, Indonesia, South Korea

9007—Germany, Japan, Taiwan, Canada, United Kingdom, France, China, Austria, Italy, Mexico

9008—Japan, Germany, Slovenia, Canada, Mexico, China, Denmark, United Kingdom, Switzerland, Austria

9009—Japan, Netherlands, Canada, Hong Kong, Thailand, Mexico, France, Germany, United Kingdom, China

9010—Japan, Netherlands, Germany, United Kingdom, Switzerland, Denmark, Italy, France, Ireland, Belgium

9011—Japan, Germany, Switzerland, China, Thailand, Israel, Hong Kong, Austria, Taiwan, United Kingdom

9012—Japan, Germany, United Kingdom, Netherlands, Israel, China, Australia, Hungary, Switzerland, South Korea

9013—Japan, Germany, South Korea, United Kingdom, China, Israel, Canada, Taiwan, Philippines, Hong Kong

9014—United Kingdom, France, Canada, Japan, Germany, Mexico, Israel, South Korea, Norway, Taiwan

9015—Japan, Israel, Switzerland, United Kingdom, France, Canada, Finland, Sweden, Netherlands, Germany

9016—Switzerland, Germany, Japan, United Kingdom, Israel, Italy, Canada, Taiwan, Spain, Hong Kong

9017—Japan, Spain, China, Taiwan, Germany, Singapore, Switzerland, United Kingdom, Canada, France

9018—Japan, Germany, Mexico, Singapore, United Kingdom, Dominican Rep., Switzerland, France, Canada, Israel

9019—Mexico, Taiwan, China, Japan, United Kingdom, Hong Kong, Sweden, Germany, Italy, Ireland

9020—United Kingdom, Japan, France, Germany, Sweden, Canada, Italy, Hong Kong, Israel, Taiwan

9021—Germany, France, Switzerland, Denmark, United Kingdom, Taiwan, Japan, Sweden, Mexico, Italy

9022—Germany, Japan, France, Netherlands, Mexico, United Kingdom, Belgium, Spain, Canada, Sweden

9023—Canada, Norway, Japan, United Kingdom, Germany, Netherlands, Israel, France, Italy, Denmark

9024—United Kingdom, Germany, Japan, Switzerland, Canada, Sweden, Italy, Denmark, Israel, France

9025—China, Mexico, Philippines, Canada, Germany, United Kingdom, Taiwan, Japan, South Korea, Hong Kong

9026—Japan, Germany, Mexico, United Kingdom, Canada, Switzerland, France, Taiwan, China, Austria

9027—Japan, Germany, United Kingdom, Canada, Switzerland, Italy, Denmark, Sweden, Australia, France

9028—Canada, Mexico, Germany, Israel, United Kingdom, Brazil, Japan, Indonesia, Switzerland, Argentina

9029—Mexico, Japan, United Kingdom, Canada, Germany, Taiwan, Hong Kong, Singapore, Austria, Finland

9030—Japan, Canada, United Kingdom, Germany, France, Taiwan, Netherlands, South Korea, Switzerland, China

9031—Japan, Germany, United Kingdom, Mexico, Canada, Israel, France, Italy, Switzerland, Belgium

9032—Mexico, Japan, Canada, Germany, United Kingdom, Philippines, Taiwan, France, China, Switzerland

9033—Singapore, Sweden, Switzerland, Japan, Mexico, Germany, France, United Kingdom, Denmark, Taiwan

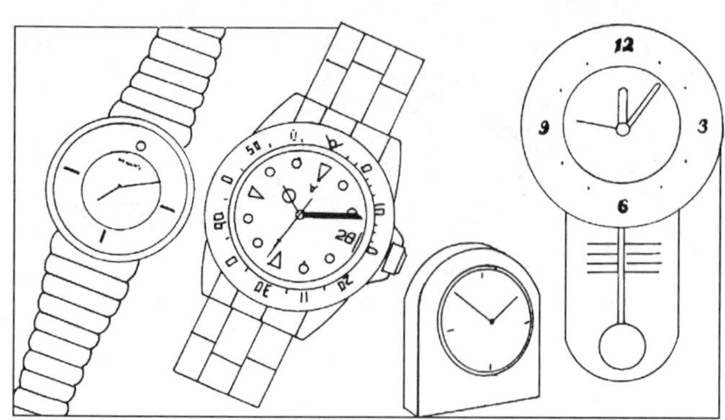

Chapter 91: Clocks and Watches*

Full title: Clocks and Watches and Parts Thereof

This section pertains to the importation of watches and clocks, their movements, and parts, which are classified within Chapter 91 of the Harmonized Tariff Schedule of the United States (HTSUS). Specifically, it includes watches and clocks of whatever variety; watch and clock movements; instrument panel clocks; alarm and other types of clocks; time clocks, time and date stamping equipment, and parking meters; time switches; watch and clock cases; watch bands; and other watch and clock parts.

If you are interested in importing watch or clock crystals, refer to Commodity Index Chapter 70; for weights, see Chapters 73-81 for the specific type of material from which they are made. Watch chains and fobs are covered in Chapter 71. Bearings are found in Chapters 73 or 84. Articles that include a clock mechanism as a subsidiary feature—such as a clock-radio—are covered in Chapter 85. Parts of general use—such as screws—are classified within the chapters covering the specific materials of which they are composed. If accessories—such as watchbands and watch batteries—are entered as part of a watch or as part of the package for use with the watch, they are classified with the watch itself; if entered separately, they are covered in the Commodity Index chapter that relates to the materials of which they are made.

Key Factors

The key factors in the importation of watches and clocks are:

- Compliance with U.S. Customs special marking requirements
- Special duty provisions for watch producers in U.S. insular possessions
- Extra information required on entry invoices

Although most importers utilize the services of a licensed customs broker in making their entries, and we recommend this practice, you should be aware of the regulatory, entry, and documentation issues involved in importing your product. You, as importer, are ultimately responsible for the fulfillment of any legal requirements applicable to your shipment.

General Considerations

Country of Origin. Watches, watch movements, clocks, and clock movements imported into the U.S. must be marked in compliance with both the usual country of origin marking required by customs, and with certain special marking requirements (see "Marking and Labeling Requirements" below) detailed in note 4 of HTSUS Chapter 91. These marking requirements are complex, stringent, and strictly monitored by customs. Customs can be expected to inspect watch and clock shipments to determine compliance. If your shipment does not comply in every respect with marking regulations, it will be denied entry.

Customs considers the origin of the watch or clock to be the origin of its movement, not the country in which it was assembled. If, for example, you wish to import a shipment of items assembled in Hong Kong whose movements were manufactured in Japan, Customs would require the items to be conspicuously labeled to indicate Japan as the country of origin. This is in addition to any requirements the country in which the item was manufactured might have regarding marking for export. The indelible special marking requirements must also be scrupulously followed. If your shipment is not in compliance with these requirements, it will be refused entry. It is virtually impossible for an importer to bring a noncomplying shipment into compliance at the port of entry. Be familiar with marking requirements and make sure the items you are considering comply before you buy them.

Insular Watch Assembly Program. The U.S. Department of Commerce's International Trade Administration (ITA) operates the Insular Watch Assembly Program. This program allows duty-free entry of watches and watch movements into the U.S. by eligible watch producers located in U.S. insular possessions—the U.S. Virgin Islands, Guam, and American Samoa—on an annual licensing basis. To import watches under this program, special documentation must be submitted to customs at the port of entry.

As detailed in note 5 of HTSUS Chapter 91, insular producers of watches may import annually-allocated quantities of product into the U.S. either duty-free or at reduced rates, depending on the percentage of foreign content. The ITA determines annual duty-free import allocations on a licensing basis. Insular watch producers wishing to receive an annual allocation must apply each year, using **Form ITA-334P**: Application for License to Enter Watches and Watch Movements into the Customs Territory of the United States. If you are issued an allocation, the ITA will send you **Form ITA-333**: License to Enter Watches and Watch Movements into the Customs Territory of the United States. This form serves as authorization to the territorial government to issue specific shipment permits to you, as well as to record the balance of your remaining duty-exemptions after each shipment permit is issued. If you hold a valid ITA license, the specific territorial government will issue you **Form ITA-340**: Permit to Enter Watches and Watch Movements into the Customs Territory of the United States. This form authorizes entry of a specified number of watches or watch movements, at a specified U.S. Customs port. It is only valid within the calendar year in which it is issued, and must be presented to Customs when you offer your shipment for entry.

If you participate in the program, you must submit **Form ITA-321P**: Mid-year Report on Watch Assembly Operations of Firms Granted a Duty-free Watch Allocation, to ITA on or before July 15 of each calendar year. In addition to duty-free allocations, you may be eligible for a Certificate of Entitlement, **Form ITA-360** authorizing duty refunds on watches entered into U.S. Customs territory. These refunds are based on specified percentages of your verified creditable wages in the insular possession.

More information concerning rules and participation in the insular watch program see HTSUS or contact the ITA's Statutory Import Programs Staff (address below.)

*IMPORTANT: Read the Commodity Index Introduction. It is the essential framework for understanding this chapter.

Customs Classification

For customs purposes watches and clocks are classified within Chapter 91 of the HTSUS. This chapter is divided into major headings, which are further divided into subheadings, and often into sub-subheadings, each with its own HTSUS classification. For example, the HTSUS number for other watches with gold-or silver-plated case is 9102.11.70, indicating that it is a subcategory of watches with a mechanical display only (9102.11.00), which is a subcategory of the major heading wrist watches, pocket watches, and other watches, including stop watches, other than those of heading 9101 (9102.00.00). There are 14 major headings in HTSUS Chapter 91.

9101—Wrist watches, pocket watches, and other watches, including stop watches, with case of precious metal or of metal clad with precious metal

9102—Wrist watches, pocket watches, or other watches, including stop watches, other than those of heading 9101

9103—Clocks with watch movements, excluding clocks of heading 9104

9104—Instrument panel clocks and clocks of a similar type for vehicles, aircraft, spacecraft, or vessels

9105—Other clocks

9106—Time of day recording apparatus and apparatus for measuring, recording, or otherwise indicating intervals of time, with clock or watch movement or with synchronous motor (for example, time registers, time recorders)

9107—Time switches with clock or watch movement or with synchronous motor

9108—Watch movements, complete and assembled

9109—Clock movements, complete and assembled

9110—Complete watch or clock movements, unassembled or partly assembled (movement sets); incomplete watch or clock movements, assembled; rough watch or clock movements

9111—Watch cases and parts thereof

9112—Clock cases and cases of a similar type for other goods of this chapter, and parts thereof

9113—Watch straps, watch bands, and watch bracelets, and parts thereof

9114—Other clock or watch parts

For more details regarding classification of the specific product you are interested in importing, consult a customs broker, the appropriate commodity specialist at your nearest customs port, or see HTSUS. HTSUS is available for purchase from the U.S. Government Printing Office (see addresses at end of this chapter), and may be found in larger public libraries. Refer to "Classification—Liquidation" on page 207 for a general discussion of customs classification.

Sample Import Duties

Import duties vary depending on the HTSUS classification of your product. Therefore, to determine the correct amount of duties, your product must be properly classified under the terms of the HTSUS. The following sample duties are taken from the duty listings for HTSUS Chapter 91.

Battery powered wrist watches having no jewels or only one jewel in the movement (9101.11.40): 51 cents each + 6.25% on the case and strap, band, or bracelet + 5.3% on the battery; wrist watches with automatic winding having more than 17 jewels in the movement (9101.21.10): 6.25%; other wrist watches having more than one jewel but not more than seven jewels in the movement (9101.29.20): 87 cents + 6.25% on the case and strap, band, or bracelet; wrist watches, battery powered, having no jewels or only one jewel in the movement with gold or silver plated case (9102.11.30): 44 cents each + 6% on the strap, band, or bracelet + 5.3% on the battery; wrist watches with opto-electric display only with straps of base metal or textile materials (9102.12.20): 3.9%; wrist watches having over 17 jewels in the movement with strap (9102.21.70): $2.19 each + 6% on the case + 14% on the strap, band, or bracelet; wrist watches with movements valued at more than $15 with strap (9102.29.45): $1.16 each + 6% on the case + 14% on the strap, band, or bracelet; clocks with battery powered watch movements and only opto-electric displays (9103.10.20): 3.9% on the movement and case + 5.3% on the battery; instrument panel clocks with clock movements measuring more than 50 mm in width or diameter valued not more than $10 each with opto-electrical display only (9104.00.05): 3.9% on the movement and case + 5.3% on the battery; battery or AC powered alarm clocks (9105.11.40): 3.9% on the movement and case + 5.3% on the battery; parking meters (9106.20.00): 45 cents each + 7% + 2.5 cents/jewel; time switches with clock or watch movements or with synchronous motor valued not more than $5 each (9107.00.40): 15 cents each + 4% + 2.5 cents/jewel; completed watch movements with automatic winding having more than 17 jewels (9108.20.40): $2.15 each; completed clock movements measuring not over 50 mm in width or diameter (9109.90.20): 30 cents each; rough watch or clock movements (9110.19.00): 9%; watch cases of base metal not clad with precious metal (9111.20.40): 4 cents each + 8.5%; clock cases of other than metal (9112.80.00): 6.9%; watch bands of textile material (9113.90.40): 9%; springs for watches (9114.10.40): 11%; assemblies for watches consisting of two or more pieces or parts fastened or joined inseparably together (9114.90.15): 9%.

Entry and Documentation

The entry of merchandise is a two-part process consisting of 1) filing the documents necessary to determine whether merchandise may be released from Customs custody and 2) filing the documents that contain information for duty assessment and statistical purposes. In certain instances all documents must be filed and accepted by Customs prior to the release of the goods. Unless you have been granted an extension, you must file entry documents at a location specified by the district or area director within five working days of your shipment's date of arrival at a U.S. port of entry. These include a number of standard documents required by Customs for any entry, and:

- For insular producers importing watches under the Insular Watch Assembly Program: **Form ITA-340**

After you present the entry, Customs may examine your shipment, or may waive examination. The shipment is then released, provided no legal or regulatory violations have occurred. You must then file entry summary documentation and deposit estimated duties at a designated customhouse within 10 working days of your shipment's release. For a detailed description of entry procedures, standard documentation, and informal entry, see "Entry Process" on page 182.

Entry Invoice. For all commercial shipments of watches and watch movements, the following information must appear on the invoice or on a separate sheet attached to and constituting a part of the invoice for each group, type, or model: 1) for watches: a thorough description of the composition of the watch cases, the bracelets, bands, or straps; the commercial description (ebauche caliber number, ligne size, and number of jewels) of the movements contained in the watches; and the type of battery (manufacturer's name and reference number), if the watch is battery-operated; 2) for watch movements: the commercial description (ebauche caliber number, ligne size, and number of jewels); if battery-operated, the type of battery (manufacturer's name and reference number); and 3) the name of the manufacturer of the exported watch movements and the name of the country in which the movements were manufactured.

Prohibitions and Restrictions

See "Country-Specific Import Restrictions" below.

Country-Specific Import Restrictions

Watches or watch movements containing any material that is the product of any country with respect to which HTSUS Column 2 rates of duty apply are not eligible for duty-free import under the Insular Watch Assembly Program.

Quotas

The U.S. Departments of Interior and Commerce administer import quotas on watches and watch movements from insular possessions admissible free of duty that are described in detail in note 5 to HTSUS Chapter 91 on a licensing basis. Information concerning licenses may be obtained from the Statutory Import Programs Staff of the International Trade Administration (see addresses at end of this chapter).

Marking and Labeling Requirements

All watches, watch movements, clocks, and clock movements imported into the U.S. must be marked in accordance with general customs country of origin markings and in accordance with regulations detailed in note 4 of HTSUS Chapter 91, specifically applicable to watch movements.

General Marking Requirements. Foreign made watches, watch movements, clocks, and clock movements must comply with the usual country of origin marking requirements. Customs considers the country of origin of watches and clocks to be the country of manufacture of the movement. The name of this country should appear either on the outside back cover or on the face of the dial and may be in the form of a sticker or label.

Special Marking Requirements. The terms "watch movement" and "clock movement" refer to devices regulated by a balance wheel and hairspring, quartz crystal, or any other system capable of determining intervals of time, with a display or system to which a mechanical display can be incorporated. "Watch movements" include those devices that do not exceed 12 mm. in thickness and 50 mm. in width, length, or diameter; "clock movements" include those devices that are larger than the watch movement dimensional specifications. The term "cases" embraces inner and outer cases, containers, and housings for movements, together with parts or pieces, such as—but not limited to—rings, feet, posts, bases, and outer frames, and any auxiliary or incidental features, that (with appropriate movements) serve to complete the watches, clocks, time switches, and other apparatus provided for in HTSUS Chapter 91. Chapter 91 requires items to be conspicuously and indelibly marked by cutting, diesinking, engraving, or stamping. Articles required to be so marked shall be denied entry unless marked in exact conformity with these requirements.

Opto-Electronic Displays. Movements with opto-electronic display only and cases designed for use with them, whether entered as separate articles or components of assembled watches or clocks, are not subject to these special marking requirements. Such items need only to be marked according to the requirements of 19 USC 1304.

Watch Movements. Watch movements must be marked on one or more of the bridges or top plates to show 1) the name of the country of manufacture, 2) the name of the manufacturer or purchaser, and 3) the number of jewels, if any.

Clock Movements. Clock movements must be marked on the most visible part of the front or back plate to show 1) the name of the country of manufacture, 2) the name of the manufacturer or purchaser, and 3) the number of jewels, if any.

Watch Cases. Watch cases must be marked on the inside or outside of the back cover to show 1) the name of the country of manufacture, and 2) the name of the manufacturer or purchaser.

Clock Cases. Clock cases and other cases must be marked on the inside or outside of the back cover to show 1) the name of the country of manufacture, and 2) the name of the manufacturer or purchaser.

For a general discussion of U.S. Customs marking and labeling requirements, see "Marking: Country of Origin" on page 215 and "Special Marking Requirements" on page 217.

Shipping Considerations

You will need to ensure that your goods are packaged and shipped with care to ensure that they arrive in good condition and pass smoothly through Customs. You are responsible for ensuring that the shipment is in compliance with all applicable government regulations for packaging and shipping. In most instances, you should not leave these arrangements solely to the discretion of your supplier. Careful preparation of the cargo and selection of the mode of transport can be essential to a cost-effective, timely delivery of undamaged goods. We strongly advise you to consult your shipping representative, insurance agent, or freight broker for advice on packing and shipping. Refer also to the major tab section "Packing/Shipping/Insurance" for a general discussion of packing and shipping.

Clocks and watches are usually fragile and should be securely packed and stowed to avoid damage due to shifting en route. Special care must be taken to ensure that they are adequately protected from excessive heat, humidity, or water damage.

Publications Available

The *Harmonized Tariff Schedule of the United States* (HTSUS) is available from:

Government Printing Office (GPO)
Superintendent of Documents
Washington, DC 20402
(202) 512-1800 (Order line)
(202) 512-0000 (General)

The USGPO also has copies of specific laws available for purchase. The USGPO accepts credit card orders over the phone, as well as mail orders paid by credit card, a check drawn on a U.S. bank, or an international money order.

Relevant Government Agencies

Address questions regarding the Insular Watch Assembly Program to:

International Trade Administration
Office of the Assistant Secretary for Import Administration
Statutory Import Programs Staff
14th and Constitution Ave. SW, Rm. 4211
Washington, DC 20230
(202) 482-1660

Address general questions regarding the importation of watches, clocks, movements, and parts to the district or port director of Customs for you area. For addresses refer to "U.S. Customs District Offices" on page 62 or contact:

U.S. Customs Service
1301 Constitution Ave. NW
Washington, DC 20229
(202) 927-6724 (Information)
(202) 927-1000 (General)

Laws and Regulations

The following laws and regulations may be relevant to the importation of watches and clocks. The laws are contained in the U.S. Code (USC) and the regulations are published in the Code of Federal Regulations (CFR), both of which may be available at larger public and law libraries. Copies of specific laws are also available from the United States Government Printing Office (address above).

19 CFR 10.181
Regulations on Refunded Duties for Watches and Movements Imported from US Insular Possessions
These regulations prescribe the process by which an importer of watches and watch movements can secure a refund of duties from Customs for imports from US insular possessions.

Principal Exporting Countries

The following listing includes samples of the main supplier nations of the products of this chapter. It is organized by HTSUS major heading. (Refer to "Customs Classification" above for the product codes.) Countries are listed in rank order of the value of products imported to the U.S. Statistics represent customs value entries for 1993 from the Bureau of Census, U.S. Department of Commerce.

9101—Switzerland, Italy, Sweden, Hong Kong, Germany, France, Japan, United Kingdom, Czech Rep., China

9102—Japan, Switzerland, Hong Kong, China, Philippines, South Korea, Thailand, Malaysia, Sweden, Singapore

9103—China, Taiwan, Hong Kong, Japan, Germany, Switzerland, Sweden, United Kingdom, Ireland, Croatia

9104—Canada, Japan, France, China, Hong Kong, Germany, South Korea, Switzerland, Singapore, Taiwan

9105—China, Taiwan, Japan, Germany, Hong Kong, Switzerland, France, South Korea, United Kingdom, Italy

9106—China, Japan, Taiwan, Hong Kong, Germany, Italy, France, Mexico, Switzerland, Canada

9107—Mexico, China, Japan, France, Singapore, Germany, Hong Kong, South Korea, Tunisia, Indonesia

9108—Switzerland, Japan, Hong Kong, China, Thailand, Philippines, Singapore, France, Germany, Malaysia

9109—Germany, Japan, Mexico, Switzerland, Taiwan, China, Thailand, Hong Kong, Tunisia, France

9110—Switzerland, Germany, Belgium, Thailand, Hong Kong, Taiwan, China, Japan, France, United Kingdom

9111—Switzerland, Hong Kong, Costa Rica, Japan, Italy, Germany, China, France, Thailand, Dominican Rep.

9112—Germany, Taiwan, Switzerland, Mexico, Colombia, Japan, China, France, Hong Kong, India

9113—Hong Kong, Switzerland, China, Italy, Austria, Germany, Costa Rica, Japan, Canada, France

9114—Switzerland, Germany, Japan, Thailand, Hong Kong, Canada, China, Taiwan, France, United Kingdom

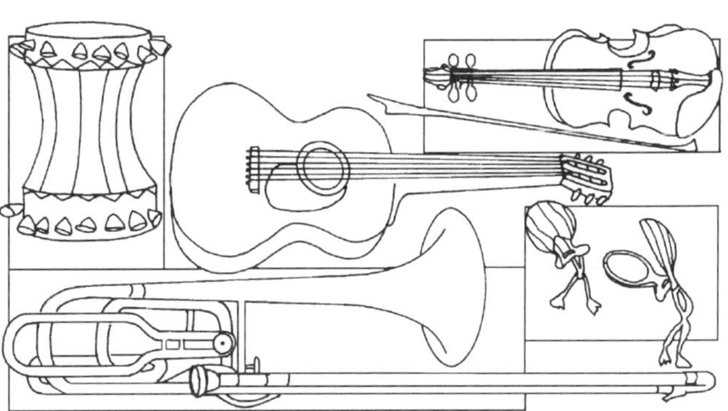

Chapter 92: Musical Instruments*

Full title: Musical Instruments; Parts and Accessories of Such Articles

This section pertains to the importation of musical instruments, which are classified within Chapter 92 of the Harmonized Tariff Schedule of the United States (HTSUS). Specifically, it includes pianos and similar instruments; other stringed instruments; other keyboard instruments; accordions; brass and woodwind instruments; percussion instruments; electrified musical instruments; music boxes, mechanical, and other instruments, such as whistles; and parts and accessories of all of the above.

If you are interested in importing electrical accessories, such as microphones, loudspeakers, headphones, switches, or similar accessories, refer to Commodity Index Chapter 85. Some specialized instrumentation is also covered under Chapter 90. Toy instruments are found within Chapter 95; brushes for cleaning instruments are covered in Chapter 96; and antique or collectors' instruments are entered under Chapter 97.

Key Factors

The key factors in the importation of musical instruments are:

- For electronic instruments, compliance with Federal Communications Commission (FCC) regulations and entry notification for radio frequency devices

Although most importers utilize the services of a licensed customs broker in making their entries, and we recommend this practice, you should be aware of the regulatory, entry, and documentation issues involved in importing your product. You, as importer, are ultimately responsible for the fulfillment of any legal requirements applicable to your shipment.

General Considerations

Importation of most musical instruments is straightforward. You do not need permits, licenses, or special entry paperwork. However, there is one important exception: importation of electronic keyboards is regulated by the FCC under the provisions of the Federal Communications Act as amended (47 USC). Other electronic instruments generally do not affect radio frequencies. However, you should consult with the FCC regional office nearest you, or contact FCC headquarters (see addresses at end of this chapter) if you have questions regarding the applicability of these regulations to your specific product.

*IMPORTANT: Read the Commodity Index Introduction. It is the essential framework for understanding this chapter.

FCC entry notification **Form 740** is required for importation of any electronic device capable of interfering with established and assigned radio frequencies. **FCC Form 740** certifies that the instruments to be entered have been tested by the manufacturer, comply with FCC radio frequency standards, and are so labeled. You must file a completed **Form 740** with the FCC for each import shipment, as well as for each type of electronic device in the shipment. Mail your completed original form to the FCC Field Operations Bureau in Washington, D.C. Present a copy of the completed form to U.S. Customs when you enter your shipment. **Form 740** is available at any regional FCC office, from FCC headquarters, or from your customs broker

Customs Classification

For customs purposes musical instruments are classified within Chapter 92 of the HTSUS. This chapter is divided into major headings, which are further divided into subheadings, and often into sub-subheadings, each with its own HTSUS classification number. For example, the HTSUS number for bagpipes is 9205.90.20, indicating that it is a subcategory of woodwind instruments (9205.90.20), which is a subcategory of the major heading other wind instruments (9205.00.00). There are nine major headings in HTSUS Chapter 92.

9201—Pianos, including player pianos; harpsichords and other keyboard stringed instruments

9202—Other string instruments (for example, guitars, violins, harps)

9203—Keyboard pipe organs; harmoniums and similar keyboard instruments with free metal reeds

9204—Accordions and similar instruments; mouth organs

9205—Other wind musical instruments (for example, clarinets, trumpets, bagpipes)

9206—Percussion musical instruments (for example, drums, xylophones, cymbals, castanets, maracas)

9207—Musical instruments the sound of which is produced, or must be amplified, electrically (for example, organs, guitars, accordions)

9208—Music boxes, fairground organs, mechanical street organs, mechanical singing birds, musical saws, and other musical instruments not falling within any other heading of this chapter; decoy calls of all kinds; whistles, call horns, and other mouth-blown sound signaling instruments

9209—Parts (for example, mechanisms for music boxes) and accessories (for example, cards, discs, and rolls for mechanical instruments) of musical instruments; metronomes, tuning forks, and pitch pipes of all kinds

For more details regarding classification of the specific product you are interested in importing, consult a customs broker, the appropriate commodity specialist at your nearest customs port, or see HTSUS. HTSUS is available for purchase from the U.S. Government Printing Office (see addresses at end of this chapter), and may be found in larger public libraries. Refer to "Classification—Liquidation" on page 207 for a general discussion of customs classification.

Sample Import Duties

Import duties vary depending on the HTSUS classification of your product. Therefore, to determine the correct amount of duties, your product must be properly classified under the HTSUS. The following sample duties are taken from the duty listings for HTSUS chapter 92.

Upright pianos (9201.10.00): 5.3%; grand pianos (9201.20.00): 5.3%; string instruments played with a bow (9202.10.00): 4.9%; guitars valued not over $100, excluding the case (9202.90.20): 6.8%; keyboard pipe organs (9203.00.40): free; piano accordions (9204.10.40): 4.7%; brass wind instruments (9205.10.00): 5.8%; clarinets (9205.90.40): 4.9%; drums (9206.00.20): 4.8%; cymbals (9206.00.20): free; electronic keyboard music synthesizers (9207.10.00): 6.8%; electric guitars (9207.90.00): 6.8%; music boxes (9208.10.00): 3.2%; metronomes (9209.10.00): 4.7%; replacement strings (9209.30.00): 4.7%; trumpet mutes (9209.99.10): 5.7%.

Entry and Documentation

The entry of merchandise is a two-part process consisting of 1) filing the documents necessary to determine whether merchandise may be released fromCustoms custody and 2) filing the documents that contain information for duty assessment and statistical purposes. In certain instances all documents must be filed and accepted by Customs prior to the release of the goods. Unless you have been granted an extension, you must file entry documents at a location specified by the district/area director within five working days of your shipment's date of arrival at a U.S. port of entry. These include a number of standard documents required by Customs for any entry, and:

- For electronic instruments, FCC **Form 740**

After you present the entry, Customs may examine your shipment, or may waive examination. The shipment is then released, provided no legal or regulatory violations have occurred. You must then file entry summary documentation and deposit estimated duties at a designated customhouse within 10 working days of your shipment's release. For a detailed description of entry procedures, standard documentation, and informal entry, see "Entry Process" on page 182.

Prohibitions and Restrictions

Electronic musical instruments not in compliance with FCC frequency regulations are not permitted into the U.S.

Marking and Labeling Requirements

Any electronic instrument of a type regulated by the FCC that is imported into the U.S. must bear a manufacturer's label certifying that it has been tested for compliance with FCC frequency standards, and is in compliance. For more details, contact the FCC.

For a general discussion of U.S. Customs marking and labeling requirements, see "Marking: Country of Origin" on page 215 and "Special Marking Requirements" on page 217.

Shipping Considerations

You will need to ensure that your goods are packaged and shipped with care to ensure that they arrive in good condition and pass smoothly through Customs. You are responsible for ensuring that the shipment is in compliance with all applicable government regulations for packaging and shipping. In most instances, you should not leave these arrangements solely to the discretion of your supplier. Careful preparation of the cargo and selection of the mode of transport can be essential to a cost-effective, timely delivery of undamaged goods. We strongly advise you to consult your shipping representative, insurance agent, or freight broker for advice on packing and shipping. Refer also to the major tab section "Packing/Shipping/Insurance" for a general discussion of packing and shipping.

Musical instruments are usually fragile and should be securely packed and stowed to avoid damage due to shifting en route. Special care must be taken to ensure that they are adequately protected from excessive heat, humidity, or water damage.

Publications Available

The *Harmonized Tariff Schedule of the United States* (HTSUS) is available from:

Government Printing Office (GPO)
Superintendent of Documents
Washington, DC 20402
(202) 512-1800 (Order line)
(202) 512-0000 (General)

The USGPO also has copies of specific laws available for purchase. The USGPO accepts credit card orders over the phone, as well as mail orders paid by credit card, a check drawn on a U.S. bank, or an international money order.

Relevant Government Agencies

Address questions regarding FCC requirements for the importation of electronic musical instruments to:

Federal Communications Commission (FCC)
Enforcement Division, Investigations Branch
1919 M Street NW, Rm. 744
Washington, DC 20554
(202) 418-1170

Address questions regarding FCC standards and testing for electronic musical instruments to:

Federal Communications Commission (FCC)
Office of Engineering and Technology
7435 Oakland Mills Rd.
Colombia, MD 21046
(301) 725-1585

Address questions regarding the importation of musical instruments to the district or port director of customs for you area. For addresses refer to"U.S. Customs District Offices" on page 62 or contact:

U.S. Customs Service
1301 Constitution Ave. NW
Washington, DC 20229
(202) 927-6724 (Information)
(202) 927-1000 (General)

Laws and Regulations

The following laws and regulations may be relevant to the importation of musical instruments. The laws are contained in the U.S. Code (USC) and the regulations are published in the Code of Federal Regulations (CFR), both of which may be available at larger public and law libraries. Copies of specific laws are also available from the United States Government Printing Office (address above).

47 USC 302a
Devices That Interfere with Radio Reception
This law prohibits the importation of devices or home electronic equipment that fail to comply with regulations promulgated by the FCC. See 47 CFR 2.1201 et seq. and 18.119. Customs enforces the prohibition.

Principal Exporting Countries

The following listing includes samples of the main supplier nations of the products of this chapter. It is organized by HTSUS major heading. (Refer to "Customs Classification" above for the product codes.) Countries are listed in rank order of the value of products imported to the U.S. Statistics represent customs value entries for 1993 from the Bureau of Census, U.S. Department of Commerce.

9201—Japan, South Korea, Germany, Czech Rep., Austria, China, Macao, Netherlands, Mexico, Russia

9202—South Korea, Taiwan, Japan, Germany, Canada, China, Mexico, Indonesia, Romania, Czech Rep.

9203—Canada, United Kingdom, Italy, Netherlands, Germany, Belgium, India, China, Japan, Ireland

9204—Germany, China, Italy, Japan, Hong Kong, Austria, Slovenia, Taiwan, Brazil, Russia

9205—Japan, Taiwan, France, Germany, United Kingdom, Czech Rep., China, Switzerland, South Korea, Hong Kong

9206—Taiwan, Japan, Canada, Thailand, Germany, United Kingdom, Switzerland, Chile, South Korea, Netherlands

9207—Japan, South Korea, Mexico, Italy, China, Taiwan, Thailand, United Kingdom, Germany, India

9208—China, Taiwan, Japan, Malaysia, Hong Kong, Sri Lanka, Thailand, Switzerland, United Kingdom, Canada

9209—Japan, Taiwan, Mexico, Germany, Italy, Hong Kong, China, United Kingdom, France, South Korea

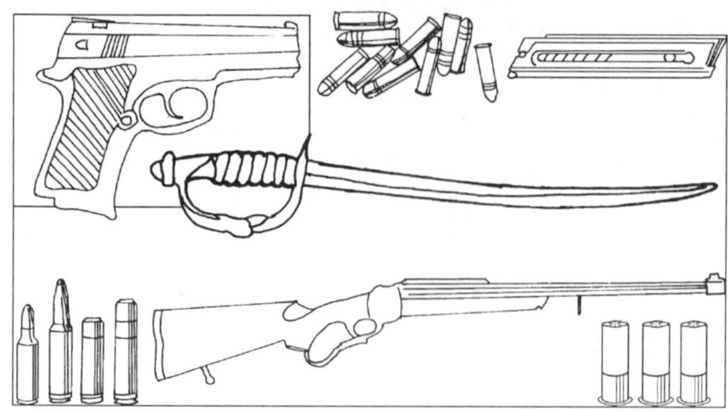

Chapter 93: Arms and Ammunition*

Full title: Arms and Ammunition; Parts and Accessories Thereof

This section pertains to the importation of arms and ammunition, which are classified within Chapter 93 of the Harmonized Tariff Schedule of the United States (HTSUS). Specifically, it includes military rifles and artillery; revolvers and pistols; sporting longarms; air, gas, and spring-fired guns; military munitions and other ammunition; military-type edged weapons, such as swords and bayonets; and miscellaneous articles fired by charges, such as ramsets, riveters, flare guns, and starters' pistols.

If you are interested in importing explosives or propellant powders not manufactured into ammunitions or munitions, refer to Commodity Index Chapter 36. Edged tools and cutlery not designed specifically for military use are covered in Chapter 82. Armored or other military vehicles are found in Chapter 87. Unless attached to firearms, telescopic sights or other optical devices are classified within and entered under Chapter 90. If you are interested in importing archery products, fencing foils, replica firearms, or related toy or novelty items, refer to Chapter 95. Collectors' pieces and antiques are covered in Chapter 97. Although the parts of articles covered in Chapter 93 are generally included with those products, other general hardware—such as nuts and bolts, screws, and other general hardware—are classified in Chapters 72-83 by the particular material of which they are composed, if made of base metals, or in Chapter 39 if made of plastic.

Key Factors

The key factors in the importation of arms and ammunition are:

- U.S. Bureau of Alcohol, Tobacco, and Firearms (BATF) import license required
- BATF import permit required
- Compliance with BATF regulations pertinent to the specific type of weapon involved

Although most importers utilize the services of a licensed customs broker in making their entries, and we recommend this practice, you should be aware of the regulatory, entry, and documentation issues involved in importing your product. You, as importer, are ultimately responsible for the fulfillment of any legal requirements applicable to your shipment.

*IMPORTANT: Read the Commodity Index Introduction. It is the essential framework for understanding this chapter.

General Considerations

The importation of arms and ammunition into the U.S. is subject to very strict and complex regulation. The information in this listing is not exhaustive. Penalties for failure to comply with regulations are serious. Before you attempt to import these items into the country, be very sure you have fulfilled all legal requirements.

BATF Regulations. Importation of firearms is strictly regulated under the Gun Control Act of 1968 (GCA) and the import provisions of the Arms Export Control Act of 1976 (AECA), which are enforced by the BATF. You must be a BATF-licensed importer to import these articles, and, with certain exceptions, only those firearms generally recognized as particularly suitable for, or readily adaptable to, sporting purposes may be imported. Except for sporting shotguns, shotgun parts, or shotgun ammunition, all firearms, ammunition, and implements of war are listed on the U.S. Munitions Import List and are subject to AECA import controls (27 CFR 47). If you wish to import items on the Munitions Import List, you must register with the BATF (see addresses at end of this chapter). Even the temporary in-transit importation of arms and ammunition destined for a destination outside the U.S. is banned unless the importer has a license from the Office of Defense Trade Control, U.S. State Department (see addresses at end of this chapter).

Firearms fall into four general categories: sporting, military, antique, and NFA (those that are regulated by the National Firearms Act, including firearms with a bore of greater than .50 caliber; machine-guns; destructive devices, such as mines and grenades; silencers; short-barreled rifles; and short-barreled shotguns). Licensing and permit requirements vary according to category. You must have an approved BATF **Form 6** Import Permit for the importation of any firearms except for antiques (firearms actually manufactured in or before 1898 are classified as antiques and require no permit). **Form 6** permits are valid for six months from the date of issue. Separate licenses are required to import explosives or munitions in bulk (**BATF F 5400.13**) or to transport them interstate (**BATF F 5400.16**). However, these licenses are not required for imports of small arms and related ammunition.

Toxic and Hazardous Substances. Shipments of products deemed toxic or hazardous must generally be in compliance with the requirements of the U.S. Environmental Protection Agency (EPA) and the U.S. Department of Transportation (DOT), including packaging, shipping, marking, and labeling requirements. Arms and ammunition are not considered chemical substances under the Toxic Substances Control Act (TSCA). However, importers are required to include a negative certification ("I certify that all chemical substances in this shipment are not subject to TSCA") with their documentation. This statement must be filed at the time of entry.

Consumer Products Regulation. The Federal Hazardous Substances Act (FHSA) imposes special controls on hazardous consumer products, which are defined as substances that are flammable, combustible, or have the potential to cause substantial personal injury during or as a proximate result of any customary or reasonably foreseeable handling or use. The Consumer Product Safety Commission (CPSC) does not require permits, special invoicing, limited entry, licenses, or any special approval process for importing hazardous consumer products into the U.S. However, if you are importing these types of products, you are responsible for ensuring that they meet all applicable FHSA and Consumer Product Safety Act (CPSA) requirements. There detailed regulations cover testing and labeling of such products. Contact the CPSC (see addresses at end of this chapter) for specific requirements on the product you are importing.

Customs Classification

For customs purposes, arms and ammunition are classified within Chapter 93 of the HTSUS. This chapter is divided into major headings, which are further divided into subheadings, and often into sub-subheadings, each of which has its own HTSUS classification number. For example, the HTSUS number for parts of rifles other than rifle barrels is 9305.90.10, indicating that it is a subcategory of parts of arms other than barrels (9305.90.00), which is a subcategory of the major heading parts and accessories of articles of headings 9301 to 9304 (9305.00.00). There are seven major heading in HTSUS Chapter 93.

9301—Military weapons, other than revolvers, pistols, and the arms of heading 9307

9302—Revolvers and pistols, other than those of heading 9303 or 9304

9303—Other firearms and similar devices which operate by the firing of an explosive charge (for example, sporting shotguns and rifles, muzzle-loading firearms, Very pistols, and other devices designed to project only signal flares; pistols and revolvers for firing blank ammunition; captive-bolt humane killers; line-throwing guns)

9304—Other arms (for example, spring, air, or gas guns and pistols, truncheons), excluding those of heading 9307

9305—Parts and accessories of articles of headings 9301 to 9304

9306—Bombs, grenades, torpedoes, mines, missiles, and similar munitions of war and parts thereof; cartridges and other ammunition and projectiles and parts thereof, including shot and cartridge wads

9307—Swords, cutlasses, bayonets, lances, and similar arms and parts thereof and scabbards and sheaths therefor

For more details regarding classification of the specific product you are interested in importing, consult a customs broker, the appropriate commodity specialist at your nearest customs port, or see HTSUS. HTSUS is available for purchase from the U.S. Government Printing Office (see addresses at end of this chapter), and may be found in larger public libraries. Refer to "Classification—Liquidation" on page 207 for a general discussion of customs classification.

Sample Import Duties

Import duties will vary depending on the HTSUS classification of your product. Therefore, to determine the correct amount of duties, your product must be properly classified under the HTSUS. The following sample duties are taken from the duty listings for HTSUS chapter 93.

Military rifles (9301.00.30): 4.7% on the value of the rifle + 20% on the value of the telescopic sight, if any; artillery pieces with a bore of more than 30 mm (118 caliber) (9301.00.90): 3.4%; revolvers or pistols (9302.00.00): 27 cents each + 6%; muzzle-loading firearms (9303.10.00): free; sporting shotguns (9303.20.00): 5.1%; sporting rifles valued over $25 but not over $50 each (9303.30.40): 7.5% on the value of the rifle + 20% on the value of the telescopic sight, if any; air rifles (9304.00.20): 7.8%; parts of revolvers or pistols (9305.10.20): 8.4%; parts of shotguns other than barrels (9305.29.10): 2.8%; cartridges for riveting (9306.10.00): 5%; shotgun shells (9306.21.00): 5%; rifle cartridges (9306.30.40): 5%; military munitions (9306.90.00): 3.6%; swords, with scabbards (9307.00.00): 5.3%.

Entry and Documentation

The entry of merchandise is a two-part process consisting of 1) filing the documents necessary to determine whether merchandise may be released from Customs custody and 2) filing the documents that contain information for duty assessment and statistical purposes. In certain instances all documents must be filed and accepted by Customs prior to the release of the goods.

Unless you have been granted an extension, you must file entry documents at a location specified by the district/area director within five working days of your shipment's date of arrival at a U.S. port of entry. These include a number of standard documents required by Customs for any entry, and:

- BATF **Form 6** Import Permit
- If importing antique firearms, documentary verification of the article's age
- Any documentation required for surplus military curio and relic firearms

After you present the entry, Customs may examine your shipment, or may waive examination. The shipment is then released, provided no legal or regulatory violations have occurred. You must then file entry summary documentation and deposit estimated duties at a designated customhouse within 10 working days of your shipment's release. For a detailed description of entry procedures, standard documentation, and informal entry, see "Entry Process" on page 182.

Prohibitions and Restrictions

The importation of arms and ammunition is highly restricted. You may import firearms on the U.S. Munitions Imports List and NFA firearms only if you have satisfied the BATF that the items are 1) for U.S. government use; 2) for scientific or research purposes; 3) for testing or use as a model by a registered manufacturer; or 4) solely for use as a sample by a registered importer or registered dealer. You must include with your permit application a detailed explanation substantiating your claim that the importation meets one of the above criteria. NFA firearms are also subject to the restrictive conditions found in 26 USC 4844 and 27 CFR 179.111.

Assault Weapons. Automatic and semi-automatic "assault" weapons—rapid fire, large clip military style firearms—are prohibited imports, and restrictions on such arms have recently been tightened further. Surplus military firearms are also a prohibited import, except for those classified as curios or relics that also meet the sporting-purpose criterion. It is unlawful to own—and therefore to import—a machine-gun (i.e. a fully automatic firearm) that was registered prior to May 19, 1986.

Surplus Military Curio and Relic Firearms. If you wish to import surplus military weapons classified as curios or relics, you must first be a licensed importer, and must then make specific application to the BATF for this category of import. The BATF will consider your application if 1) the firearms were manufactured in a non-proscribed country or area; 2) the firearms were manufactured in a proscribed country or area prior to the date the country or area became proscribed; or 3) the firearms manufactured in a proscribed country or area have been stored in a non-proscribed country or area for at least five years immediately prior to importation. (See "Country-Specific Import Restrictions" below for a list of currently proscribed countries or areas.) You must provide a certification statement with your application explaining how your proposed shipment meets the above criteria. You must also provide documentary information on the country or area of storage for the five-year period immediately prior to importation. Such information may, for example, include 1) a verifiable statement in English by a government official or any other bona fide official, agent, or custodian having knowledge of the date and place of manufacture and/or the place of storage, and whose identity and position can be verified from the information provided; 2) a warehouse receipt or other document that provides the required storage history; or 3) any other document you believe substantiates the place and date of manufacture and the place of storage. The BATF may require you to furnish additional documentation to aid in its determination of whether your import permit application should be approved. All certification statements must be sworn and executed under penalties of perjury.

Country-Specific Import Restrictions

Firearms manufactured in certain countries after certain years may not be imported into the U.S. Importation of firearms manufactured in and after the year in parentheses originating in the following countries is prohibited: Albania (1944), Bulgaria (1944), Cuba (1959), the Czech and Slovak Republics (1948), Estonia (1939), Hungary (1947), Kampuchea (Cambodia) (1975), Latvia (1939), Lithuania (1939), North Korea (1948), Outer Mongolia (1921), Poland (1947), Rumania (1947), the republics of the former Soviet Union (1917), Vietnam (1954). Many of these restrictions may be under review. You should check with customs regarding specific proposed imports.

Certain types of military rifles manufactured in the People's Republic of China are currently banned from import into the U.S.

Shipping Considerations

You will need to ensure that your goods are packaged and shipped with care to ensure that they arrive in good condition and pass smoothly through Customs. You are responsible for ensuring that the shipment is in compliance with all applicable government regulations for packaging and shipping. In most instances, you should not leave these arrangements solely to the discretion of your supplier. Careful preparation of the cargo and selection of the mode of transport can be essential to a cost-effective, timely delivery of undamaged goods. We strongly advise you to consult your shipping representative, insurance agent, or freight broker for advice on packaging and shipping. Refer also to the major tab section "Packing/Shipping/Insurance" for a general discussion of packing and shipping.

The DOT, the U.S. Coast Guard (USCG), and the U.S. Customs Service all have regulations regarding the shipment of arms and ammunition. These regulations are designed to ensure the safety of any carrier transporting weaponry as well as that of other carriers and personnel, and vary depending on the type, nature, and quantity of the product being shipped. Contact the USCG Port Captain of the shipping district into which you plan to import your product with details about type of weapon, quantity, etc., for specific USCG requirements.

Arms and ammunition must be carefully packed and stowed to not only for safety but also to avoid damage during transit. Heat and sharp blows to cargoes of munitions must be avoided, as must excessive humidity or water damage. Security of the cargo is an added concern.

Publications Available

The following publication may be relevant to the importation of arms and ammunition of Chapter 93:

Your Guide to Federal Firearms Regulation (published by BATF, address below).

The *Harmonized Tariff Schedule of the United States* (HTSUS) is available from:

Government Printing Office (GPO)
Superintendent of Documents
Washington, DC 20402
(202) 512-1800 (Order line)
(202) 512-0000 (General)

The USGPO also has copies of specific laws available for purchase. The USGPO accepts credit card orders over the phone, as well as mail orders paid by credit card, a check drawn on a U.S. bank, or an international money order.

Relevant Government Agencies

Address questions regarding BATF requirements for importation of arms and ammunition to:

Bureau of Alcohol, Tobacco and Firearms (BATF)
Firearms and Explosives Import Export Branch
650 Massachusetts Avenue
Washington, DC 20226
(202) 927-8300

Address questions concerning licensing for in-transit shipments of arms and ammunition to:

U.S. Department of State
Office of Defense Trade Control
State Dept. Annex 6
Washington, DC 20522
(703) 875-6650

Address questions on the consumer product safety aspects of importing arms and ammunition to:

U.S. Consumer Products Safety Commission (CPSC)
Division of Regulatory Management
5401 Westbard Road
Bethesda, MD 20207
(301) 492-6400

Address questions regarding the importation of arms and ammunition to the district or port director of customs for you area. For addresses refer to "U.S. Customs District Offices" on page 62 or contact:

U.S. Customs Service
1301 Constitution Ave. NW
Washington, DC 20229
(202) 927-6724 (Information)
(202) 927-1000 (General)

Laws and Regulations

The following laws and regulations may be relevant to the importation of arms and ammunition. The laws are contained in the U.S. Code (USC) and the regulations are published in the Code of Federal Regulations (CFR), both of which may be available at larger public and law libraries. Copies of specific laws are also available from the United States Government Printing Office (address above).

22 USC 2751 et seq.
Arms Export Control Act
This Act restricts the sales of arms, authorizes Presidential control over the import and export of defense articles, and creates a U.S. Munitions List, where items subject to control appear. It also prescribes licensing and registration requirements for manufacturers, exporters, and importers.

15 USC 1263
Consumer Product Safety Act
This Act sets standards for the manufacture, processing, and labeling of products sold to U.S. consumers.

18 USC 831 et seq.
Dangerous Cargo Act
This Act places import restrictions on fireworks and nuclear materials, and Customs enforces these laws. See 49 CFR Parts 170-171, 173, 177, 179, and 195; 46 USC 870

18 USC 841 et seq.
Importation of Explosive Materials
This law imposes criminal penalties for the unauthorized importation of explosive materials. Customs aids in the enforcement of this statute. See 26 CFR Part 181.

18 USC 921 et seq.
Gun Control Act
This Act restricts the importation of firearms and is enforced by Customs. See 26 CFR Part 178 and 26 CFR 251.

18 USC 960 et seq.
Exportation of Armed Vessels, Arms, Liquor, and Narcotics
These laws regulate the prerequisites to a vessel's departure and the prohibitions against exportation of armed vessels, arms, liquor, and narcotics. Customs will refuse clearance to vessels not in compliance with these laws.

18 USC 1715
National Firearms Act
This law requires all imported explosives, munitions of war, firearms, and ammunition be covered by a BATF permit. Customs will deny entry without such permit.

18 USC 2277
Explosives or Dangerous Weapons Aboard Vessels
This law prohibits the existence of explosives and dangerous weapons aboard vessels. Customs is authorized to enforce this law. See 46 USC 170.

22 USC 401 et seq.
Exportation of War Materials
This law authorizes customs seizure and forfeiture of arms, munitions of war, and other articles exported in violation of 22 CFR 127.

26 USC 5801 et seq.
Importation of Firearms
This law authorizes the BATF to regulate the importation of certain firearms into the U.S. The law further authorizes Customs to take "appropriate action" to assure compliance with 27 CFR 47, and with 27 CFR 178 and 179, as those sections concern the importation or attempted importation of articles on the U.S. Munitions Import List. The assistance rendered by Customs to the BATF generally involves the inspection of required documentation prior to the release of certain imported firearms from Customs. See 27 CFR 45.56.

Additionally, any vessel, vehicle or aircraft used to transport, carry, convey, or conceal any firearm with respect to which there has been a violation of any provision of 26 USC Chapter 53 (or any regulations issued pursuant to that chapter) is subject to seizure and forfeiture under Customs rules. See 27 CFR 179.182.

49 USC App. 781 et seq.
Contraband Seizure Act
This Act makes it unlawful to transport, conceal, or facilitate the transportation of "contraband articles," as defined in the statute (certain narcotic drugs, certain firearms, and counterfeit coins). Customs assists in seizures made by the Secret Service of any aircraft, vehicle, or vessel being used in violation of this Act. The Customs laws relating to seizure, forfeiture, remission, mitigation, etc., apply to seizures and forfeitures occurring under this Act. The Secretary of the Treasury is empowered to authorize persons to carry out provisions of this Act. See also 18 USC 8 (obligation or other security of the U.S.); 18 USC 471 et seq. (counterfeiting and forgery); 18 USC 2341 (contraband cigarettes); 21 USC 802 (narcotic drugs); 26 USC 5801 et seq. (National Firearms Act); 19 CFR 12.48 (counterfeit coins; importation prohibited); 27 CFR Parts 70, 72 (BATF Procedures and Disposition of Personal Property); 31 CFR Part 401-406 (seizure authority of Secret Service agents).

Principal Exporting Countries

The following listing includes samples of the main supplier nations of the products of this chapter. It is organized by HTSUS major heading. (Refer to "Customs Classification" above for the product codes.) Countries are listed in rank order of the value of products imported to the U.S. Statistics represent customs value entries for 1993 from the Bureau of Census, U.S. Department of Commerce.

9301—China, United Kingdom, Sweden, Germany, Russia, Ukraine, Czech Rep., Hong Kong, Israel, Brazil

9302—Austria, Germany, Brazil, Italy, Spain, Belgium, Israel, Hungary, China, Russia

9303—Italy, China, Japan, Belgium, Spain, Germany, Brazil, Russia, United Kingdom, Hungary

9304—Japan, Germany, China, South Korea, Taiwan, United Kingdom, Spain, Canada, Italy, Austria

9305—Japan, Italy, Canada, Mexico, China, Germany, Belgium, Austria, Spain, Brazil

9306—United Kingdom, China, Israel, Canada, Germany, Mexico, South Korea, Sweden, Italy, Russia

9307—Spain, Taiwan, India, China, Malaysia, Japan, Germany, Philippines, Russia, Italy

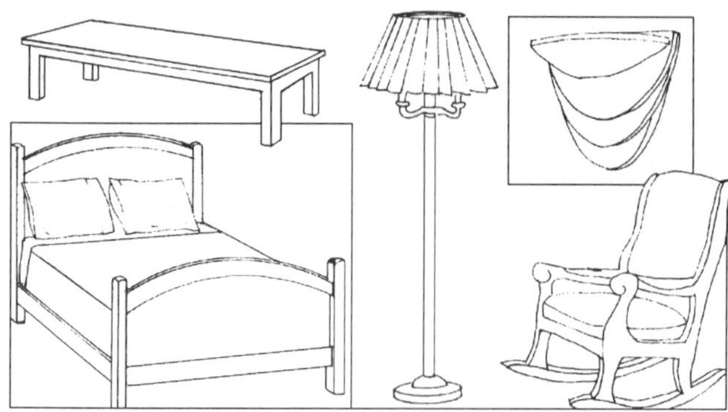

Chapter 94: Furnishings*

Full title: Furniture; Bedding, Mattresses, Mattress Supports, Cushions, and Similar Stuffed Furnishings; Lamps and Lighting Fittings, Not Elsewhere Specified or Included; Illuminated Signs, Illuminated Nameplates, and the Like; Prefabricated Buildings

This section pertains to the importation of furnishings, which are classified within Chapter 94 of the Harmonized Tariff Schedule of the United States (HTSUS). Specifically, it includes chairs of all kinds; medical and related furniture; other furniture for home, office, or other use, of whatever materials; beds, mattresses, and bedding; lighting fixtures and lamps; parts of the above items, including furnishings for vehicles; and prefabricated buildings and structures.

Although this chapter is comprehensively broad and straightforward, some related products are classified in other Commodity Index chapters. If you are interested in importing pneumatic or water mattresses, pillows, or cushions, refer to the Commodities Index chapters covering the primary material of manufacture: plastic (Chapter 39), rubber (Chapter 40), or other textile materials (Chapter 63). Mirrors designed to rest on the floor are classified in Chapter 70. Any articles involving precious metals are found in Chapter 71, Parts of general usage—such as nuts and bolts, screws, and similar fittings—are covered in the chapters pertaining to the material of which they are composed: Chapters 72-83, if of base metals, or chapter 39 if of plastics. Specific hardware fittings for furniture are found in Chapter 83. Furniture designed as parts of refrigeration units or as parts of sewing machines are found in Chapter 84, while furniture designed as parts of apparatus of Chapter 85 is also classified with those articles. Flashlights, special purpose lighting, and related fixtures are also covered in Chapter 85. Although some components of vehicles are covered in Chapter 94, the bulk of automotive components are found in Chapter 87, pertaining specifically to vehicles. Dental chairs incorporating dental appliances or spittoons are classified within Chapter 90. Furnishings of which the primary component is a clock are included in Chapter 91. Toy furniture, billiard tables and similar game articles, special furniture for shows or exhibits, and decorative furnishings are covered in Chapter 95.

*IMPORTANT: Read the Commodity Index Introduction. It is the essential framework for understanding this chapter.

Key Factors

The key factors in the importation of furnishings are:

- For cribs: compliance with Consumer Product Safety Commission (CPSC) safety standards
- For mattresses: compliance with Flammable Fabrics Act (FFA) flammability standards
- For lighting fixtures: compliance with voluntary Underwriters' Laboratory (UL) lighting standards, monitored by the Consumer Product Safety Commission (CPSC)

Although most importers utilize the services of a licensed customs broker in making their entries, and we recommend this practice, you should be aware of the regulatory, entry, and documentation issues involved in importing your product. You, as importer, are ultimately responsible for the fulfillment of any legal requirements applicable to your shipment.

General Considerations

Regulations. Chapter 94 covers a wide variety of articles within a very few headings and subheadings relative to other chapters of the HTSUS, and its classifications are generally broad and inclusive. With a few important exceptions, importation of furnishings is straightforward. No permits, licenses, or special entry paperwork are required. Infants' and children's furnishings are regulated by the CPSC, under the provisions of the Consumer Product Safety Act (CPSA). Specific restrictions, prohibitions, and requirements apply to full-size and non-full-size baby cribs under the law. (See "Prohibitions and Restrictions" below.)

Definitions. Under previous Customs regulations, furnishings had to fit on the floor or ground to be classified as furniture. However, under the HTSUS, certain furniture—including cupboards, bookcases, shelved furniture, unit furniture, seats, and beds are also considered to be furniture even if they are designed to be hung, fixed to a wall, or stand on another piece of furniture or some other architectural element.

Furniture with Textile Content. Furniture incorporating textile elements is not considered a textile quota commodity, and is not restricted by the terms of Multi-Fiber Arrangements (MFA). However, such furniture must be labeled according to provisions of the Textile Fiber Products Identification Act (TFPIA), which is administered by the Federal Trade Commission (FTC).

Textile Labeling and Invoice Requirements. You are responsible for your imported product's compliance with applicable provisions of the TFPIA. Furniture with textile components that require labeling under TFPIA must already be labeled at entry, or the shipment will be refused. (See "Marking and Labeling Requirements" below.) If you import shipments of furniture with textile components subject to TFPIA and valued at over $500, you must provide special information on the entry invoice (see "Entry and Documentation" below).

Flammability Standards. Furniture containing textile elements also falls under provisions of the Flammable Fabrics Act (FFA) administered by the CPSC. You should be aware that introduction into U.S. commerce of any item for which there is an applicable FFA standard, and that does not comply with that standard, is subject to legal action by the CPSC. If the commission believes a product does not comply with a flammability standard, it is authorized to pursue a variety of legal sanctions, including 1) seizure, condemnation, and forfeiture of the noncomplying product; 2) administrative cease-and-desist order requiring an individual or firm to stop sale and distribution of the noncomplying product; or 3) temporary injunction requiring the individual or firm to stop sale and distribution of the noncomplying product pending final disposition of the administrative cease-and-desist proceeding.

For most items of textile furniture there are at present no regulations or standards promulgated under FFA, and importation of these items is not actively monitored by CPSC. However, mattresses and mattress pads are subject to specific FFA standards, and are actively monitored by the CPSC. Importers are legally responsible for all aspects of compliance. (See "Prohibitions and Restrictions" below.)

Product Safety. The CPSC also has authority, under the Consumer Product Safety Improvement Act of 1990, to seek civil penalties against any person who knowingly violates a regulation or standard issued under section 4 of the FFA. The commission may seek a civil penalty of up to $5,000 per product involved, up to a maximum penalty of $1.25 million for any related series of violations.

The CPSC takes its responsibility for consumer protection seriously, and the wise importer will make sure that products are in compliance with applicable standards. Not only that, but persons who trade in articles covered under CPSA are responsible for making Substantial Product Hazard Reports to CPSC when they become aware that such product could have a defect that presents substantial risk of injury or death to the public.

In addition, importers of consumer products are responsible to report to the commission if: 1) a particular model of the product is the subject of at least three civil actions filed in federal or state court; 2) each suit alleges the involvement of that model in death or grievous bodily injury; and 3) at least three of the actions result in a final settlement involving the manufacturer in a judgment for the plaintiff within any one of the two-year periods specified in section 37 of CPSA.

Lighting. Importation of lighting and lighting fixtures is relatively straightforward. You do not need permits or licenses. U.S. Customs requires a breakdown, by weight, of materials composing each article (i.e. how much metal, how much glass, how much wood) for tariff classification purposes. The breakdown may appear on the invoice presented at entry, or may be attached as a separate sheet provided by the supplier.

Lighting and lighting fixtures fall under the jurisdiction of the CPSC, which administers the Consumer Product Safety Act (CPSA). CPSC does not require any special entry documentation or procedures. There are no restrictions or prohibitions under CPSA pertaining to lighting or lighting fixtures. However, voluntary UL standards have been established for indoor and outdoor lights, including Christmas lights. Manufacturers may list complying products with UL, and may mark or label those products as UL-listed, thus assuring the U.S. consumer that the products meet with voluntary compliance standards. Only products that are UL-listed may bear such labeling or marking. Though there is no federal requirement that an item be listed with UL, requirements vary by state. Certain states prohibit the sale and use of non-listed electrical products. Products that are not listed with are not necessarily noncomplying products, nor does unlisted status necessarily imply that the product is dangerous.

Consumer Product Import Surveillance Program. The CPSC monitors imports of many different types of commodities under its Import Surveillance Program. From time to time, CPSC inspects shipments to ascertain compliance with voluntary standards. In addition, Section 15 of the CPSA requires manufacturers, importers, distributors, or retailers to provide CPSC with Substantial Product Hazard Reports when a product defect is discovered that presents substantial risk of injury to the consumer. In such cases, CPSC must be notified, and remedial corrective action (i.e., a product recall) will be required. For more information regarding voluntary compliance standards for lighting and lighting fixtures, contact the CPSC (see addresses at end of this chapter).

Customs Classification

For customs purposes, furnishings are classified within Chapter 94 of the HTSUS. This chapter is divided into major headings, which are further divided into subheadings, and often into subsubheadings, each of which has its own HTSUS classification number. For example, the HTSUS number for chairs of teak is 9401.61.20, indicating that it is a subcategory of other upholstered seats with wooden frames (9401.61.00), which is a subcategory of the major heading seats, whether or not convertible into beds, and parts thereof (9401.00.00). There are six major headings in HTSUS Chapter 94.

9401—Seats (other than those of heading 9402), whether or not convertible into beds, and parts thereof

9402—Medical, surgical, dental, or veterinary furniture (for example, operating tables, examination tables, hospital beds with mechanical fittings, dentists chairs); barbers' chairs and similar chairs, having rotating as well as both reclining and elevating movements; parts of the foregoing articles

9403—Other furniture and parts thereof

9404—Mattress supports; articles of bedding and similar furnishing (for example, mattresses, quilts, eiderdowns, cushions, poufs, and pillows) fitted with springs or stuffed or of cellular rubber or plastics, whether or not covered

9405—Lamps and lighting fittings including searchlights and spotlights and parts thereof, not elsewhere specified or included; illuminated nameplates and the like, having a permanent fixed light source, and parts thereof not elsewhere specified or included

9406—Prefabricated buildings

For more details regarding classification of the specific product you are interested in importing, consult a customs broker, the appropriate commodity specialist at your nearest customs port, or see HTSUS. HTSUS is available for purchase from the U.S. Government Printing Office (see addresses at end of this chapter), and may be found in larger public libraries. Refer to "Classification—Liquidation" on page 207 for a general discussion of customs classification.

Sample Import Duties

Import duties vary depending on the HTSUS classification of your product. Therefore, to determine the correct amount of duties, your product must be properly classified under the HTSUS. The following sample duties are taken from the duty listings for HTSUS Chapter 94.

Leather upholstered seats for aircraft (9401.10.40): 4%; motor vehicles seats (9401.20.00): 3.1%; seats other than outdoor furniture (9401.40.00): 3.2%; seats of woven materials, such as rattan (9401.50.00): 5.6% through December 31, 1992, 7.5% thereafter; upholstered seats with a metal frame (9401.71.00): 4%; dentists' chairs (9402.10.00): 3.9%; hospital beds (9402.90.00): 5.3%; metal office furniture (9403.19.00): 4%; wooden office furniture (9403.30.80): 2.5%; bent wood kitchen furniture (9403.40.40): 6.6%; furniture of reinforced laminated plastics (9403.70.40): 6%; furniture used for motor vehicles (9403.90.10): 3.1%; automotive furniture of fabric other than cotton (9403.90.60): 7%; mattress supports (9404.10.00): 4%; mattresses (9404.21.00): 6%; pillows, cushions, and similar furnishings (9494.90.10): 6%; quilts (9494.90.90): 14.5%; chandeliers and wall lighting fittings, of base metal (9405.10.40): 5.7%; table, bedside, floor, desk, and other lamps, of base metal other than brass (9405.20.60): 7.6%; Christmas tree lights (9405.30.00): 8%; incandescent lamps fueled by propane, kerosene, etc. (9405.50,20): 3.7%; illuminated signs, other than those made of metal (9405.60.50): 5.3%; lamp parts, including globes, of glass (9405.91.30): 14%; prefabricated buildings of metal or plastic (9406.00.80): 5.7%.

Entry and Documentation

The entry of merchandise is a two-part process consisting of 1) filing the documents necessary to determine whether merchandise may be released from Customs custody and 2) filing the documents that contain information for duty assessment and statistical purposes. In certain instances all documents must be filed and accepted by Customs prior to the release of the goods. Unless you have been granted an extension, you must file entry documents at a location specified by the district/area director within five working days of your shipment's date of arrival at a U.S. port of entry. These include a number of standard documents required by Customs for any entry.

After you present the entry, Customs may examine your shipment, or may waive examination. The shipment is then released, provided no legal or regulatory violations have occurred. You must then file entry summary documentation and deposit estimated duties at a designated customhouse within 10 working days of your shipment's release. For a detailed description of entry procedures, standard documentation, and informal entry, see "Entry Process" on page 182.

Entry Invoice—TFPIA Requirements. All invoices for furnishings containing textiles should indicate: 1) the constituent fiber or combination of fibers in the textile fiber product, designating with equal prominence each natural or manufactured fiber in the textile fiber product by its generic name in the order of predominance by the weight thereof if the weight of such fiber is 5%or more of the total fiber weight of the product; 2) percentage of each fiber present, by weight, in the total fiber content of the textile fiber product; 3) the name, or other identification issued and registered by the FTC, of the manufacturer of the product or one or more persons subject to Section 3 of the TFPIA (15 USC 70a) with respect to such product; and 4) the name of the country where processed or manufactured.

Prohibitions and Restrictions

Although furniture designers, manufacturers, and importers usually have considerable leeway in the products they may deal in, detailed regulations and specifications do exist for specific types of furnishings, including infant furniture and bedding.

Baby Cribs. Specific standards have been adopted for baby cribs, including rail height, spacing of crib components, interior dimensions, acceptable hardware, finishing details, and instructions to be included with items that require assembly, for both full-size and non-full-size cribs. These specifications are extremely detailed and must be strictly followed. See 16 CFR 1508 and 1509.

Such items as mesh/net/screen cribs, nonrigidly constructed baby cribs, cradles (both rocker and pendulum types), car beds, baby baskets, and bassinets (also known as junior cribs) are not subject to the requirements. However, these items are regulated by the CPSC under the CPSA. If you are interested in importing them, you should be familiar with basic applicable safety regulations for items intended for use by children. For more information, contact the CPSC (see addresses at end of this chapter).

Recordkeeping. If you import cribs, you must keep and maintain the following records, for three years after production or importation of each product lot: 1) sale, 2) distribution, and 3) results of all inspections and tests conducted in accordance with 16 CFR 1508. When any CPSC officer, employee, or agent asks to see your records, you must allow full access to them, as long as the request was made at a reasonable time. If he or she needs to make copies, conduct inventories, or in any other way verify the accuracy of the records you provide, you must allow him to do so.

Mattresses and Mattress Pads. Standards have been established under the FFA for the flammability of mattresses and mattress pads. These standards are found in 16 CFR 1632. The law defines "mattress" as a ticking filled with a resilient material, used alone or in combination with other products, intended or promoted for sleeping upon. This includes, but is not limited to: adult, youth, crib, and bunk bed mattresses; futons, water beds and air mattresses that contain upholstery material between the ticking and the mattress core; any detachable mattresses used in any item of upholstered furniture, e.g. convertible sofa bed, corner group, day bed, roll-away bed, high riser, and trundle bed mattresses.

Not subject to this regulation are such items as: sleeping bags; pillows; mattress foundations; liquid-and gaseous-filled tickings such as water beds and air mattresses that do not contain upholstery material between the ticking and mattress core; upholstered furniture that does not contain a detachable mattress such as chaise lounges; drop-arm loveseats; press-back lounges; push-back sofas; sleep lounges; sofa beds (including jackknife sofa beds); sofa lounges (including glide-outs); studio couches and divans (including twin studio divans and studio beds); juvenile product pads, e.g. such as car bed, carriage basket, infant carrier and lounge, dressing table, stroller, and playpen pads; or crib bumpers.

The terms "mattress and mattress pad" will be used to refer only to those mattresses and mattress pads that are subject to the regulatory standards of the FFA.

Prototype Testing Requirements. Each manufacturer of mattresses and mattress pads intended for sale in the U.S., and all other persons or firms initially introducing such articles into U.S. commerce, must meet all applicable requirements under the FFA. This includes importers. If you are interested in importing these products, you will benefit from an awareness of general testing requirements, since no mattress or mattress pad may be introduced into U.S. commerce unless it has been subjected to prototype testing and has been certified as being in compliance. It is not within the purview of this index to outline testing procedures. If you need more information on prototype testing than what is briefly outlined below, you should contact CPSC for pertinent details.

The specified tests are designed to determine an article's ignition resistance when exposed to a lighted cigarette. The necessary testing is a premarket procedure. Therefore, no mattress or mattress pad for which a prototype has not passed the required tests may be marketed in the U.S. No failed prototype may be marketed in the U.S. unless the prototype is reworked to rectify the problem, retested, and passed in a new test.

The test method measures the ignition resistance of a mattress or mattress pad by exposing the surface to lighted cigarettes in a draft-protected environment. The surfaces to be tested include smooth, tape edge, and any quilted or tufted locations. A two-sheet test is also conducted on similar surface locations. In the latter test, the burning cigarettes are placed between the sheets. The regulation provides specific technical requirements for specimen selection and test procedures.

It should be noted that a minimum of three, and in some cases six samples must be tested for clearance of a single prototype. If even one sample fails, the whole prototype will be disqualified unless and until it is reworked, retested, and passed. Failure to comply, and especially knowing failure to comply, may result in legal penalties.

Recordkeeping. The FFA requires that every manufacturer, importer, or other person initially introducing mattresses or mattress pads into U.S. commerce maintain certain records. You must maintain records for each prototype, for as long as the prototype is in production, and/or the ticking and/or the tape edge material is being used on it. All required records must be retained for three years thereafter. You must maintain the following records: 1) manufacturing specification and description of each mattress or mattress pad prototype with an assigned prototype identification number; 2) test results for all or any of the three separate testing procedures described in the standards, as follows: prototype test (16 CFR 1632.4, 1632.5), ticking classification test (16 CFR 1632.6), and tape edge materials test (16 CFR 1637.7).

Required records common to all three tests are: Test results and details of each test performed, including a) prototype identification number; b) ticking classification (A, B, or C) if known (this is a mandatory record for ticking classification test results); c) test room conditions; d) cigarette locations; e) number of relights for each location; f) whether each cigarette location passed or failed; g) name and signature of person conducting test; and h) date of test.

In addition to the above information, records for prototype and type of edge materials tests must include: a) test supervisor's certification of standard testing procedures and result accuracy; b) photograph of the bare surface of each mattress or mattress pad tested, with each prototype identification number and a clear designation as to which part of the article was sheeted and that part was bare during testing; 3) certification from the ticking supplier, stating the ticking's classification and that the test was performed in accordance with 16 CFR 1632.6 is a valid alternative to ticking classification test result records; 4) records to support any determination that a particular material used in a prototype (other than ticking or tape edge material) did not influence the prototype's ignition resistance during testing and therefore could be substituted by another material—such record should include photographs of physical specimens; 5) manufacturing specifications and description of any new ticking or tape edge material substituted, with the identification number of the prototype involved; 6) where mattress pad laundering is required during testing procedure, details of any approved alternate laundering procedure used; 7) identification, composition, and details of the application of any flame retardant treatments employed relative to mattress pads or mattress pad components; and 8) disposition of all failing or rejected prototype mattress or mattress pads. Such records must either: a) demonstrate that the items were retested and reworked in accordance with the standard, and were in compliance prior to sale or distribution, or b) otherwise show the disposition of such items.

Exemptions. "One of a kind" mattresses are exempt from prototype testing. This is a mattress or mattress pad manufactured in accordance with either a physician's written prescription or other comparable written medical therapeutic specification, to be used in connection with the treatment or management of a named individual's physical illness or injury. Such an article must bear a warning label (see "Marking and Labeling Requirements" below). The manufacturer or importer of this type of mattress, in lieu of recordkeeping requirements named above, must keep a copy of the written prescription or other comparable written medical therapeutic specification for each mattress or mattress pad, during a period of three years, measured from the date of manufacture.

Marking and Labeling Requirements

Furniture with Textile Content. Furniture that includes a textile element must be labeled according to requirements of the Textile Fiber Products Identification Act (TFPIA). All textile products imported into the U.S. must be stamped, tagged, labeled, or otherwise marked with the following information as required by the TFPIA, unless exempt from marking (see TFPIA, Section 12): 1) the generic names and percentages by weight of the constituent fibers present in the textile fiber product, exclusive of permissible ornamentation, in amounts of more than 5% in order of predominance by weight, with any percentage of fiber or fibers required to be designated as "other fiber" or "other fibers" (including those present in amounts of 5% or less) appearing last; and 2) the name of the manufacturer or the name or registered identification number issued by the FTC of one or more persons marketing or handling the textile fiber product; and 3) the name of the country where processed. A word trademark, used as a house mark and registered with the U.S. Patent Office, may appear on labels instead of the name otherwise required, provided the owner of the trademark furnishes a copy of the registration to FTC prior to use.

The information listed above is not exhaustive. TFPIA requirements are extensive. The Act specifies such details as types of labels, means of attachment, label position on the article, package labeling, unit labeling for two-piece garments, and arrangement of information on the label; allowable fiber designations; country-of-origin indications; requirements for trim and ornamentation, linings and interlinings, and pile fabrics; sectional disclosure; use of trade names and trademarks; and requirements for swatches and samples. The FTC publishes a booklet intended to clarify TFPIA requirements to facilitate voluntary compliance in the industry (see "Publications Available" below). It is available on request, at no charge, from the FTC (see addresses at end of this chapter).

Cribs and Their Retail Cartons. Each crib and retail carton must be clearly marked to indicate: 1) name and place of business (city and state) of manufacturer, importer, distributor and/or seller; and 2) model, stock, catalog, or item number, or other numerical symbol to identify articles of identical construction, composition, and dimensions.

A warning statement regarding mattress dimensions is required both for full-size and non-full-size cribs. For the statement required on non-full-size cribs, see below. The following is the required statement for full-size cribs. It must appear both on the retail carton and the inside of the head end-panel or the top surface of the mattress support. "CAUTION: Any mattress used in this crib must be at least 27 1/4 inches by 51 5/8 inches with a thickness not exceeding 6 inches" or "CAUTION: Any mattress used in this crib must be at least 69 cm by 131 cm with a thickness not exceeding 15 cm." The marking must appear in block letters at least one-fourth inch high, must contrast sharply with the background (by color, projection, and/or indentation), and must be clearly visible and legible. Mattress dimension must be taken from seam to seam, or edge to edge where appropriate.

Crib markings must be of a permanent nature. They may be paint-stenciled, die-stamped, molded, or indelibly stamped directly on the crib, or permanently affixed, fastened, or attached to it by means of a tag, token, or other suitable medium. Markings must not be readily removable or subject to obliteration either during normal crib use or as a result of reasonably foreseeable damage or abuse.

Non-Full-Size Cribs. In addition to marking and labeling requirements outlined above, which are applicable to all cribs regardless of type or size, the following mattress caution statements are required for non-full-size cribs. The inside surface of any rectangular crib must bear the warning: "CAUTION: Any mattress used in this crib must be at least X inches long by Y inches wide and not more than Z inches thick." The manufacturer should fill the blanks with applicable dimensions complying with mattress size requirements in 16 CFR 1509.9. The inside surface of any nonrectangular crib must bear the warning: "CAUTION: Check proper fit of mattress. Should be not more than X inches thick. The maximum gap between mattress and inside of crib border (or edge) should be no more than 1 inch." The specifications should state applicable dimension to effect compliance with 16 CFR 1509.9.

Mattress and Mattress Pad Labeling Under the FFA. All mattresses and mattress pads subject to the standard must bear a permanent accessible and legible label containing the month and year of manufacture and manufacturer's location. All FFA-required label information must be set forth separately from any other label information Other information, representations, or disclosures appearing on any required or other label may not interfere with, minimize, detract from, or conflict with required information. Only the ultimate consumer may remove or mutilate any required label.

All mattress pads that contain a chemical fire retardant must be labeled with precautionary instructions to protect the pads from agents or treatments known to cause deterioration of their flame resistance. Such labels must be permanent, prominent, conspicuous, and legible. If a mattress contains a chemical fire retardant, it must be prominently, conspicuously, and legibly labeled with the letter "T."

One-of-a-kind mattresses and mattress pads must bear a permanent, conspicuous and legible label with the following statement: "WARNING: This mattress or mattress pad may be subject to ignition and hazardous smoldering from cigarettes. It was manufactured in accordance with a physician's prescription and has not been tested under the Federal Standard for the Flammability of Mattresses (FF 4-72)." This labeling must be attached to the mattress or mattress pad so as to remain on or affixed to it for the useful life of the article. It must be at least 40 square inches (250 sq. cm.) with no linear dimension less than 5 inches (12.5 cm). The letters in the word "Warning" must be no less than 0.5 inch (1.27 cm) in height. All letters on the label must be in a color that contrasts with label background. The label warning statement must also be conspicuously displayed on the invoice or other sales papers that accompany the mattress in commerce from manufacturer to final point of sale to a consumer.

For a general discussion of U.S. Customs marking and labeling requirements, see "Marking: Country of Origin" on page 215 and "Special Marking Requirements" on page 217.

Shipping Considerations

You will need to ensure that your goods are packaged and shipped with care to ensure that they arrive in good condition and pass smoothly through Customs. You are responsible for ensuring that the shipment is in compliance with all applicable government regulations for packaging and shipping. In most instances, you should not leave these arrangements solely to the discretion of your supplier. Careful preparation of the cargo and selection of the mode of transport can be essential to a cost-effective, timely delivery of undamaged goods. We strongly advise you to consult your shipping representative, insurance agent, or freight broker for advice on packing and shipping. Refer also to the major tab section "Packing/Shipping/Insurance" for a general discussion of packing and shipping.

Furnishings are goods that may be heavy, bulky, and fragile. They require careful packing and stowing to withstand the rigors of transport. Care must be taken to avoid damage due to shifting of the cargo, as well as to protect the goods from heat, humidity, or water, which can damage surfaces and components of some products.

Publications Available

The following publication may be relevant to the importation of furnishings containing textiles:

Questions and Answers Relating to the Textile Fiber Products Identification Act and Regulations

Available free of charge on request from the Federal Trade Commission (see addresses at end of this chapter), this publication is an excellent source of information written in clear lay language. We recommend that anyone interested in importing textile products but unfamiliar with the regulations obtain a copy of this booklet.

The *Harmonized Tariff Schedule of the United States* (HTSUS) is available from:

Government Printing Office (GPO)
Superintendent of Documents
Washington, DC 20402
(202) 512-1800 (Order line)
(202) 512-0000 (General)

The USGPO also has copies of specific laws available for purchase. The USGPO accepts credit card orders over the phone, as well as mail orders paid by credit card, a check drawn on a U.S. bank, or an international money order.

Relevant Government Agencies

Address questions regarding labeling requirements under TFPIA to:

Federal Trade Commission (FTC)
Division of Enforcement
601 Pennsylvania Ave. NW
Washington, DC 20580
(202) 326-2996 (General)
(202) 326-2841 (Textile and wool products labeling)

Address questions regarding FFA and/or CPSA requirements for imported furniture to:

Consumer Product Safety Commission (CPSC)
5401 Westbard Avenue
Bethesda, MD 20207
(301) 492-6580

Address questions regarding the importation of furnishings to the district or port director of customs for you area. For addresses refer to "U.S. Customs District Offices" on page 62 or contact:

U.S. Customs Service
1301 Constitution Ave. NW
Washington, DC 20229
(202) 927-6724 (Information)
(202) 927-1000 (General)

Laws and Regulations

The following laws and regulations may be relevant to the importation of furnishings. The laws are contained in the U.S. Code (USC) and the regulations are published in the Code of Federal Regulations (CFR), both of which may be available at larger public and law libraries. Copies of specific laws are also available from the United States Government Printing Office (address above).

15 USC 1263
Consumer Product Safety Act
This act gives the Consumer Product Safety Commission authority to set safety standards, testing procedures, and reporting requirements to ensure that consumer products not already covered under other regulations are not harmful.

15 USC 70-77
Textile Fiber Products Identification Act (TFPIA)
This Act prohibits false or deceptive labeling (misbranding) and false advertising of any textile fiber products and requires all textile fiber products imported into the U.S. to be labeled in accordance with the requirements set forth in the law.

19 CFR 11.12b; 16 CFR 303 et seq.
Regulations on Labeling and Marking
These regulations detail the labeling and marking requirements for textiles as specified by the CPSC and the invoice contents required by U.S. Customs for purpose of enforcing the labeling and marking rules.

15 USC 1191-1204
Flammable Fabrics Act (FFA)
This Act provides for the setting of flammability standards for fabric by the Consumer Product Safety Commission (CPSC) and for enforcement by U.S. Customs.

16 CFR 1610, 1611, 1615, 1616, 1630-1632
Regulations on Flammable Fabric Standards
These regulations specify the flammability standards adopted by the CPSC under the FFA for various types of textiles.

Principal Exporting Countries

The following listing includes samples of the main supplier nations of the products of this chapter. It is organized by HTSUS major heading. (Refer to "Customs Classification" above for the product codes.) Countries are listed in rank order of the value of products imported to the U.S. Statistics represent customs value entries for 1993 from the Bureau of Census, U.S. Department of Commerce.

9401—Canada, Mexico, Taiwan, Italy, Japan, China, Malaysia, Indonesia, Thailand, Germany

9402—Japan, United Kingdom, Sweden, Switzerland, Germany, Taiwan, Canada, France, Mexico, Italy

9403—Taiwan, Canada, Mexico, China, Italy, Thailand, Malaysia, Germany, Indonesia, Denmark

9404—China, Canada, Mexico, Taiwan, India, South Korea, Sweden, Denmark, Italy, Germany

9405—China, Taiwan, Mexico, Canada, Italy, Thailand, South Korea, Germany, Hong Kong, Philippines

9406—Japan, Canada, United Kingdom, Belgium, Germany, Ireland, Italy, Netherlands, Singapore, Mexico

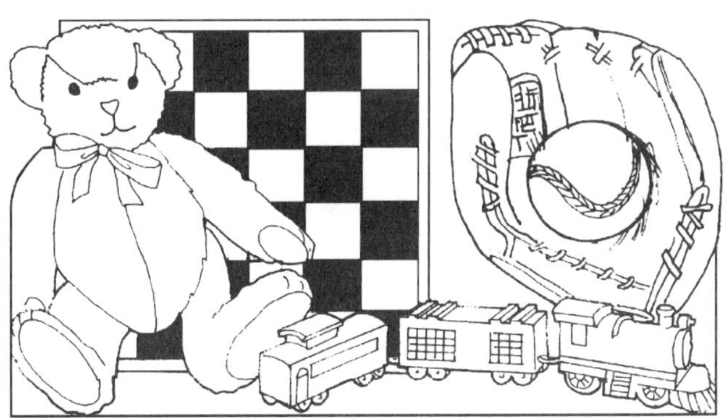

Chapter 95: Toys, Games, and Sports Equipment*

Full title: Toys, Games, and Sports Equipment; Parts and Accessories Thereof

This section pertains to the importation of toys, games, sporting goods, and related items, which are classified within Chapter 95 of the Harmonized Tariff Schedule of the United States (HTSUS). Specifically, it includes wheeled children's riding toys, dolls and other figures, stuffed toys, models, mechanical and electrically-driven toys, puzzles, games, video games and game equipment, Christmas decorations, party goods, sports equipment, swimming pools, exercise equipment, fishing equipment, and carnival rides and equipment.

If you are interested in importing hunting equipment, including firearms and ammunition, refer to Commodity Index Chapter 93. Fireworks and similar articles are covered in Chapter 36. Line not made up into fishing line is found in Chapters 39 and 42, or in the Commodity Index chapters covering the various types of textile materials (Chapters 50-63). Sports bags are covered in Chapters 42 and 43, while sports clothes are included in Chapters 61 or 62, and flags, bunting, and similar articles are covered in Chapter 63. Sports footwear and headgear are found, respectively, in Chapters 64 and 65. Walking sticks, riding crops, and similar items are covered in Chapter 66. Unmounted glass eyes for dolls or other toys are classified in Chapter 70. Electric motors, transformers, and remote control devices are found in Chapter 85. Bicycles are covered in Chapter 87 and boats in Chapter 89. Goggles and other eyewear for sports use are classified in Chapter 90. Christmas tree candles are found in Chapter 34 and Christmas tree lights in Chapter 94. Sporting arms and ammunition are covered in Chapter 93. Parts of general use—screws, nails, nuts, bolts, and washers—are covered according to the material of which they are composed: of base metals in Chapters 72-83, of plastics in Chapter 39, and of rubber in Chapter 40.

Key Factors

The key factors in the importation of games are:

- Compliance with any applicable Consumer Product Safety Commission (CPSC) safety requirements
- Compliance with U.S. Food and Drug Administration (FDA) standards and entry notification for radiation-producing electronic devices

*IMPORTANT: Read the Commodity Index Introduction. It is the essential framework for understanding this chapter.

- Compliance with U.S. Federal Communications Commission (FCC) standards and entry notification for electronic radio frequency devices
- Compliance with trademark, trade name, and copyright restrictions, where applicable

Although most importers utilize the services of a licensed customs broker in making their entries, and we recommend this practice, you should be aware of the regulatory, entry, and documentation issues involved in importing your product. You, as importer, are ultimately responsible for the fulfillment of any legal requirements applicable to your shipment.

General Considerations

CPSC Regulation. There are no permits and licenses required to import products of HTSUS chapter 95. However, toys, games, and sporting goods fall under the jurisdiction of the CPSC, which administers and enforces the Consumer Product Safety Act (CPSA), and these products must comply with CPSA's extensive safety standards. Although the CPSC does not require any special import entry documentation or procedures, there are extensive restrictions on the types of toys and related items that may be introduced into U.S. commerce. Certain types of toys are banned from import entirely; others are banned unless they meet applicable CPSA safety and testing requirements. (See "Prohibitions and Restrictions" below.) The CPSC monitors imports of many different types of commodities under its Import Surveillance Program. From time to time, shipments may be inspected at random or for cause to ascertain compliance with mandatory safety standards. Products may also be tested by CPSC in order to determine compliance.

Substantial Product Hazard Reports. Defect-reporting requirements exist for any product covered under the CPSA, including toys. Section 15(b) of CPSA requires every manufacturer, distributor, or retailer of such products, who obtains information that reasonably supports the conclusion that such products either 1) fail to comply with an applicable consumer product safety rule, or 2) contain a defect that could create a substantial product hazard, to immediately inform the CSPC of the potential violation or defect. Your willful failure to make a Substantial Product Hazard Report can result in civil litigation by the CPSC.

The Commission is rigorous in its enforcement of safety standards for toys and other articles intended for recreational use, especially by children. Seven major U.S. importers of foreign toys have recently been sued by the CPSC for infractions of safety standards, or for failing to comply with substantial product hazard reporting as required under the CPSA. U.S. Customs cooperates with CPSC by seizing shipments identified as hazardous.

Litigation is not the CPSC's first course of action in cases of noncompliance. The Commission first issues warnings, giving importers ample opportunity to correct problems. However, do not let the fact that port of entry inspections are not performed on each and every toy shipment lull you into believing that noncomplying toys may be entered into U.S. commerce if they can slip through customs. Products that do not comply can be recalled at any point. Repeated noncompliance may result in investigation by CPSC and in possible litigation. Be familiar with the regulations applicable to your product, and be sure your product is in compliance. If you have any doubts, contact the CPSC before making your purchase.

Electronic Devices. Many electronic devices subject to regulation fall into two general categories: those that produce radio frequency energy, and those that produce radiation. Radiation-producing electronic devices are regulated by the FDA (see addresses at end of this chapter) under the provisions of the Federal Food, Drug, and Cosmetic Act (FDCA) and the Radiation Control for Health and Safety Act of 1968 (RCHSA). Both imported and domestically produced electronic products must comply with all relevant FDA and FCC regulations. Whether you are importing a single product for personal use, or a commercial shipment for resale in the U.S., you must file an FDA Importers Entry Notice (**Form FD701**) and an Electronic Product Declaration (**Form FD2877**) for each product type for which official standards exist. You will not be permitted to enter a shipment unless you have filed these forms. You may obtain them from FDA, National Center for Devices and Radiological Health (see addresses at end of this chapter) or from your customs broker. For an annotated diagram of FDA import procedures, refer to the "Foods" appendix on page 808.

Radio frequency (rf) devices are regulated by the FCC (see addresses at end of this chapter) under the provisions of 47 CFR Parts 2 and 15. You must file a copy of FCC **Form 740** with each shipment of rf devices. If your shipment consists of more than one type of device, you must file a separate form for each type. The form certifies that the imported model or device is either in compliance with, or is exempt from, FCC requirements, and is so labeled.

Products that fall under the jurisdiction of both the FCC and the FDA and must comply with both sets of regulations. Do not rely on one agency for information concerning the requirements of another agency. If you are in doubt as to the status of your product, contact both the FCC and the FDA.

Copyright and Trademark Provisions. Products such as some video games or branded toys may be subject to patent and trademark restrictions. (See "Prohibitions and Restrictions" below.) The Intellectual Property Rights (IPR) branch of U.S. Customs enforces laws pertinent to entry of such products. Importers must be prepared to show valid authorization from trademark and copyright holders. Pirated products are subject to seizure.

IRS Considerations. Certain types of fishing tackle have a 10% Internal Revenue Service (IRS) tax levied in addition to customs duty rates. Customs does not collect this tax at entry, and the tax is not part of the Customs entry procedures. If you are considering importation of fishing tackle, you should contact the IRS for relevant information.

Customs Classification

For customs purposes toys, games, and sporting goods are classified within Chapter 95 of the HTSUS. This chapter is divided into major headings, which are further divided into subheadings, and often into sub-subheadings, each of which has its own HTSUS classification number. For example, the HTSUS number for stuffed dolls is 9502.10.20, indicating that it is a subcategory of dolls, whether or not dressed (9502.10.00), which is a subcategory of the major heading dolls representing only human beings and parts and accessories thereof (9502.00.00). There are eight major headings in HTSUS Chapter 95.

9501—Wheeled toys designed to be ridden by children (for example, tricycles, scooters, pedal cars); dolls' carriages and dolls' strollers; parts and accessories thereof

9502—Dolls representing only human beings and parts and accessories thereof

9503—Other toys; reduced size ("scale") models and similar recreational models, working or not; puzzles of all kinds; parts and accessories thereof

9504—Articles for arcade, table, or parlor games, including pinball machines, bagatelle, billiards, and special tables for casino games; automatic bowling alley equipment; parts and accessories thereof

9505—Festive, carnival, or other entertainment articles, including magic tricks and practical joke articles; parts and accessories thereof

9506—Articles and equipment for general physical exercises, gymnastics, athletics, other sports (including table-tennis) or outdoor games, not specified or included elsewhere in this chapter; swimming pools and wading pools; parts and accessories thereof

9507—Fishing rods, fish hooks, and other line fishing tackle; fish landing nets, butterfly nets, and similar nets; decoy "birds" (other than those of heading 9208 or 9705), and similar hunting or shooting equipment; parts and accessories thereof

9508—Merry-go-rounds, boat-swings, shooting galleries, and other fairground amusements; traveling circuses, traveling menageries, and traveling theaters; parts and accessories thereof

For more details regarding classification of the specific product you are interested in importing, consult a customs broker, the appropriate commodity specialist at your nearest Customs port, or see HTSUS. HTSUS is available for purchase from the U.S. Government Printing Office (see addresses at end of this chapter), and may be found in larger public libraries. Refer to "Classification—Liquidation" on page 207 for a general discussion of customs classification.

Sample Import Duties

Import duties vary depending on the HTSUS classification of your product. Therefore, to determine the correct amount of duties, your product must be properly classified under the HTSUS. The following sample duties are taken from the duty listing for HTSUS Chapter 95.

Chain-driven wheeled children's riding toys (9501.00.30): free; doll carriages (9501.00.60): 7.8%; stuffed dolls (9502.10.20): 12%; doll clothes and other apparel accessories (9502.91.00): 8%; electric train sets (9503.10.00): 6.8%; scale model assembly kits (9503.20.00): 6.8%; animal stuffed toys (9503.41.10): 6.8%; large scale ceramic toy tea sets (9503.70.40): free; inflatable toy balls (9503.90.50): 6.8%; home video games (9504.10.00): 3.9%; billiard tables (9504.20.60): 5.1%; playing cards (9504.40.00): 0.8 cents/pack + 0.8%; board game sets (9504.90.60): 4.6%; Christmas ornaments of glass (9505.10.10): 6.6%; party hats (9505.90.60): 3.1%; downhill skis (9506.11.40): 5.1%; golf club sets (9506.31.00): 4.9%; unstrung tennis rackets (9506.51.40): 3.9%; soccer balls (9506.62.40): free; baseballs (9506.69.20): 3%; ice skates (9606.70.40): 5.8%; exercise machines (9506.91.00): 4.6%; sleds (9506.99.45): 5.5%; fishing rod and reel sets (9507.10.00): 7.6%; snelled fish hooks (9507.20.40): 5%; artificial bait and flies (9507.90.70): 9%; fairground amusements (9508.00.00): 3.7%.

Entry and Documentation

The entry of merchandise is a two-part process consisting of 1) filing the documents necessary to determine whether merchandise may be released from Customs custody and 2) filing the documents that contain information for duty assessment and statistical purposes. In certain instances all documents must be filed and accepted by Customs prior to the release of the goods. Unless you have been granted an extension, you must file entry documents at a location specified by the district or area director within five working days of your shipment's date of arrival at a U.S. port of entry. These include a number of standard documents required by Customs for any entry, and:

- For radiation-producing devices, FDA Importers Entry Notice, **Form FD701** and Electronic Product Declaration **Form FD2877**
- For electronic devices, FCC Declaration **Form FCC 740**
- For products subject to regulation by both agencies, all three forms mentioned above
- For products subject to copyright or trademark laws, authorization from the copyright or trademark holder

After you present the entry, Customs may examine your shipment, or may waive examination. The shipment is then released provided no legal or regulatory violations have been noted. You must then file entry summary documentation and deposit estimated duties at a designated customhouse within 10 working days of your shipment's release. For a detailed description of entry procedures, standard documentation, and informal entry, see "Entry Process" on page 182.

Prohibitions and Restrictions

Potential Hazards. In general, 16 CFR 1500 seeks to prevent articles intended for children's use from presenting potential hazards resulting either from normal use or from reasonably foreseeable damage, abuse, or unintended use. To this end, the regulation prescribes stringent safety tests for toys deemed to present even a potential hazard. The tests are designed to simulate use and abuse of toys in order to determine resultant potential hazards. Regulations and tests vary depending upon the nature of the toy and the age group for which the toy is targeted. Toys not specified by the manufacturer for any particular age range are subjected to the most stringent testing composed of the procedures for all age groups. The regulation makes the following age distinctions: toys intended for use by children 1) 18 months of age or less; 2) 18 months to 36 months of age; or 3) 36 months to 96 months of age.

Toys deemed to represent a hazard under normal use or under reasonably foreseeable damage or abuse fall within three categories: 1) those that present mechanical hazards; 2) electric toys or articles that present electrical, thermal, or certain other mechanical hazards; and 3) those that are not electrical toys, but that present an electrical or thermal hazard. In addition, certain toys may be prohibited under the Federal Hazardous Substances Act (FHSA).

Mechanical Hazards. For purposes of regulation, toys present mechanical hazards by virtue of the following:

1) Toys with sharp points, sharp glass or metal edges, or sharp wires or protrusions. Hazards include possible lacerations, puncture wound injuries. Types of toys: certain rattles and pacifiers, toys with noisemaking elements, stuffed toys with certain internal and external components, certain walkers or jumpers, lawn darts. (Note: lawn darts are unconditionally banned articles; there are no exceptions and no exemptions.)

2) Toys with small parts that can become dislodged or be willfully removed by the child. Hazards: aspiration, ingestion, choking, etc. Types of toys: certain rattles and certain toys with noisemaking elements, etc.

3) Toys with exposed parts such as coil springs that may expand sufficiently to allow an infant's finger, toe, etc. to be caught between the coils and injured. Hazards: amputation, crushing, lacerations, fractures, hematomas, bruises, or other injuries to fingers, toes, or other parts of the anatomy of young children. Articles: such items as baby bouncers, walker-jumpers, baby-walkers, etc.

4) Toys with impulse-type sound at a peak pressure level at or above 138 decibels. Hazard: hearing damage; article: toy caps intended for use with toy guns (see "Caps" below).

5) Toys constructed and used as noisemakers, whereby the parts can fracture, fragment, or disassemble during use. Toys of this nature are called "clacker balls." Design and construction of these items is highly regulated (see "Clacker Balls" below).

For each mechanical hazard listed above there are provisions under the regulation by which an article which could present such hazard can be considered in compliance and safe for the child.

Baby Bouncers and Jumpers. Importers of baby bouncers, walker-jumpers, baby-walkers, or similar articles are responsible for ensuring that these products are designed and constructed in keeping with specific requirements outlined in 16 CFR 1500.86(a)(4). There are also labeling requirements for these items (see "Marking and Labeling Requirements" below). If you import these toys, you are responsible for recordkeeping identical to that required for electrical toys (see "Recordkeeping" below).

Sharp Objects. Sharp points, sharp glass, or metal edge restrictions. 16 CFR 1500 prescribes tests to determine the accessibility of any sharp points or edges, or of any sharp metal or glass edges, in toys intended for children eight years old and under. The regulation exempts from such testing toys that by reason of their function necessitate the inclusion of sharp points (e.g. sewing machines) or sharp metal or glass edges (e.g. toy scissors or toy tool kits) and that do not have any nonfunctional sharp points or glass or metal edges. Exempted toys must be conspicuously labeled (see "Marking and Labeling Requirements" below). The regulation also exempts any children's non-toy articles that meet the criteria for exempted toys (e.g. ballpoint pens, children's ice skates, and children's cutlery).

Small Parts Restrictions. The regulation bans toys or articles intended for children under the age of three years that because of small parts present a hazard of choking, aspiration, or ingestion. Articles banned if they do not comply with the CPSA's specific safety standards include, but are not limited to: squeeze toys; teethers; crib exercisers; crib gyms; crib mobiles; other toys or articles intended to be affixed to a crib, stroller, playpen, or baby carriage; pull and push toys; pounding toys; blocks and stacking sets; bathtub, wading pool, and sand toys; rocking spring and stick horses, and other figures; chimes, musical balls, and carousels; jack-in-the-box toys; stuffed plush and flocked animals and other figures; preschool toys, games, and puzzles intended for use by children under three; infant and juvenile furniture articles intended for use by children under three, such as cribs, playpens, baby bouncers, walkers, strollers, and carriages; dolls intended for use by children under three, such as baby dolls, rag dolls, and bean bag dolls; toy cars, trucks, and other vehicles intended for use by children under three. With certain exceptions, all toys or articles intended, marketed, or labeled to be entrusted to, or used by, children under three years of age are subject to this regulation.

Exemptions to Small Parts Restrictions. The following are exempt from small parts restrictions: 1) balloons; 2) books and other articles made of paper; 3) writing materials such as crayons, chalk, pencils, and pens; 4) children's clothing and accessories, such as shoelace holders and buttons; 5) grooming, feeding, and hygiene products, such as diaper pins and clips, barrettes, toothbrushes, drinking glasses, dishes, and eating utensils; 6) phonograph records; 7) modeling clay and similar products; 8) fingerpaints, watercolors, and other paint sets; 9) rattles (when in compliance with 16 CFR 1510.2) and 10) pacifiers (when in compliance with 16 CFR 1511.2(a)).

Rattles. Rattles are banned articles unless they comply with applicable requirements under the CPSA. These requirements are intended to eliminate from U.S. commerce infant rattles that may cause choking and/or suffocation because their design or construction permits them to enter an infant's mouth and become lodged in the throat. 16 CFR 1510 describes the tests required to determine compliance.

Pacifiers. Pacifiers are banned articles unless they meet requirements laid out in 16 CFR 1511. The regulation provides specifications and tests for structural integrity, guard or shield requirements, and protrusions. The attachment of ribbons, strings, cords, or other attachments, is expressly prohibited. Warning labeling is required (see "Marking and Labeling Requirements" below). In addition, rubber pacifiers containing significant levels of nitrosamines are banned hazardous substances as defined in Section 2(g) of FHSA. If you import pacifiers containing more than 60 parts per billion of nitrosamines as measured by methylene chloride extraction, the CPSC will bring an enforcement case against you.

Caps. Both paper and plastic caps for use in toy guns must be such that they do not produce peak sound pressure levels greater than 158 decibels when tested in accordance with 16 CFR 1500.47. They must bear warning labeling (see "Marking and Labeling Requirements" below). If you wish to distribute toy caps, you must notify CPSC Bureau of Compliance (CPSC address below) of your intention. You must either conduct or participate in a program to develop caps that produce a sound pressure level of not more than 138 decibels when tested in accordance with 16 CFR 1500.47. After notifying the CPSC of your intention, you must submit a progress report to the Bureau of Compliance at least once every three months concerning program status. If you are interested in importing caps, you should be aware that the prescribed maximum decibel level is under investigation, and that the regulation may be changed, pending CPSC's findings. Check with the CPSC for an update.

Clacker Balls. Clacker balls are banned unless they comply with all provisions in 16 CFR 1500.86(5)(i-vi). Clacker balls must be designed, manufactured, assembled, labeled, and tested in ways specified by the regulation (see "Marking and Labeling Requirements" below). Such articles must be tested according to regulation at time of production. Tested shipments must not exceed the failure rate outlined in the table found in 16 CFR 1500.86. Toys must be fully assembled at the time of sale. Recordkeeping requirements applicable to clacker balls are identical to those applicable to children's electrical items (see "Recordkeeping" below).

Electric Toys and Articles. Electrical toys for children include any toy, game, or other article designed, labeled, advertised, or otherwise intended for use by children, and powered by electrical current from nominal 120 volt branch circuits. Such articles are banned articles if in normal use or when subjected to reasonably foreseeable damage or abuse, the design or manufacture may: 1) cause personal injury or illness by electric shock; and/or 2) present an unreasonable risk of personal injury or illness because of heat (as from heated parts, substances, or surfaces), or because of certain mechanical hazards. Extensive manufacturing requirements specify standards for such elements of the toy as: protective coatings, mechanical assembly, structural integrity, switch mountings, insulating material, electrical design and construction, and performance.

Each manufacturer of electrical toys and articles for children must establish and maintain quality assurance programs to ensure compliance with all 16 CFR 1500 requirements. Electrical toys must be produced in accordance with detailed material specifications, production specifications, and quality assurance programs. They must be 1) constructed out of materials safe and suitable for the particular use for which the toy is intended; and 2) finished with a high degree of uniformity and as fine a grade of workmanship as is practicable in a well-equipped manufacturing establishment. Each component of a toy must comply with all applicable requirements in 16 CFR 1505. Electric toys and other children's articles require extensive labeling (see "Marking and Labeling Requirements" below).

Recordkeeping. If you import foreign electrical toys and articles, you are responsible for the compliance of your shipment. You must keep and maintain for three years after importation of each lot of toys, the following: 1) material and production specifications and description of required quality assurance program; 2) results of all inspections and tests conducted; and 3) records of sale and distribution. You are required to make these records available, upon request at reasonable times, to any officer or employee of the CPSC. You must also permit the CPSC to inspect and copy records, to make such inventories of stock as are deemed necessary, and to otherwise verify the accuracy of the records you keep.

Electrical and Thermal Hazards—Nonelectrical Toys. Kites 10 inches or greater in any dimension and constructed of aluminized polyester film, or any kite having a tail or other component consisting of a piece of aluminized polyester film 10 inches or greater in any dimension present a risk of personal injury from electric shock. Such kites conduct electricity, and may become entangled in, or otherwise contact, high voltage electric power lines. These kites are unconditionally banned, and there are no exceptions and no exemptions.

Other Hazards. Toys composed in part of flammable solids are prohibited. The regulation specifies testing whereby a substance may be determined to be "flammable." Toys painted with any coating substance containing lead are prohibited under 16 CFR 1303. There are no exceptions or exemptions associated with these prohibitions.

Exemptions. Certain articles are exempted from classification as banned hazardous substances, on condition that they are adequately labeled, and that adequate instructions and warnings are provided for safe use. They are: 1) chemistry sets and other science education sets, and their replacement components, when labeled according to 16 CFR 1500.83; 2) firecrackers designed to produce audible effects, if such effect is produced by a charge of not more than 500 milligrams of pyrotechnic composition; 3) educational materials such as art materials, preserved biological specimens, laboratory chemicals, and other articles intended and used for educational purpose; 4) liquid fuels containing more than 4% by weight of methyl alcohol, and intended for operation of miniature engines for model boats, cars, etc.; 5) novelties consisting of a mixture of polyvinyl acetate, U.S. Certified Colors, and not more than 25% by weight of acetone, and intended for blowing plastic balloons; 6) games containing, as the sole hazardous component, a self-pressurized container of soap solution or similar foam-generating mixture that has no hazardous ingredient; 7) model rocket propellant devices designed for use in light-weight, recoverable, and reusable model rockets, provided certain technical conditions laid out in the regulation (16 CFR 1500.85) are met; 8) separate delay train/or recovery system activation devices intended for use with premanufactured model rocket engines wherein all of the chemical ingredients are preloaded so the user does not handle any chemical ingredient, and are so designed that the main casing or container does not rupture during operation; 9) solid fuel pellets intended for use in miniature jet engines for propelling model jet airplanes, speedboats, etc., provided such pellets meet technical specifications in 16 CFR 1500.85(a)(10); 10) fuses intended for igniting the fuel pellets named in 9) above; 11) kits intended for construction of model rockets and jet propelled model airplanes requiring the use of difluorodichloromethane as a propellant, provided the outer carton bears a specified warning statement (see "Marking and Labeling Requirements" below.); 12) flammable wire materials intended for electro-mechanical actuation and release devices for the model kits described above, provided each wire does not exceed 15 milligrams in weight.

Radio Frequency Devices. Under the Communications Act of 1934, as amended, all radio frequency (rf) devices are subject to FCC radio emission standards. Video game players—other than battery-operated, handheld electronic games, which are exempted from the standards—are classified as rf devices and must comply with the requirements and procedures for such products. You must file an FCC declaration certifying that your model or device is in conformity with, will be brought into conformity with, or is exempt from the FCC requirements, for each shipment of rf devices you import. FCC standards and procedures have been developed to limit potential sources of rf interference to authorized radio services in the U.S. The FCC defines a radio frequency device as a product that emits rf energy, either intentionally or as a design byproduct. Radio frequency devices must meet specific FCC equipment authorization standards. When rf devices are imported into the U.S., a declaration is required that states that the appropriate FCC authorization has been granted.

Radiation-Producing Devices. The comprehensive Radiation Control for Health and Safety Act (RCHSA) was enacted in 1968 to protect the public from unnecessary exposure to radiation from electronic products. Administration of the law is carried out through the setting and enforcement of radiation performance standards to limit radiation emissions. The standards apply to products offered for sale or use in the U.S., whether manufactured in this country or elsewhere. Electronic products include all products or equipment capable of emitting ionizing or nonionizing radiation, or sonic, infrasonic, or ultrasonic waves. Few items classified within Chapter 95 are likely to be directly affected by these regulations. However, if you have any doubts about the status of your product, contact the FDA's Center for Devices and Radiological Health (CDRH) (see addresses at end of this chapter).

Trademarks and Trade Names. Articles bearing counterfeit trademarks, or marks that copy or simulate the registered trademark of a U.S. or foreign corporation are prohibited importation, provided a copy of the U.S. trademark registration has been filed with the Commissioner of Customs and recorded in the manner provided by regulations (19 CFR 133). The U.S. Customs Service also affords similar protection against unauthorized shipments bearing trade names that are recorded with customs pursuant to regulations (19 CFR 133, Subpart B). If your article bears a genuine trademark that is 1) owned by a U.S. citizen or company, 2) registered with U.S. Customs, you may not import the article without written permission from the U.S. trademark holder.

It is unlawful to import articles bearing genuine trademarks owned by a U.S. citizen or corporation without permission of the U.S. trademark owner, if the foreign and domestic trademark owners are not parent and subsidiary companies or otherwise under common ownership and control, provided such trademark has been recorded with customs.

Copyrights. Section 602(a) of the Copyright Revision Act of 1976 provides that the importation into the U.S. of copies of a work acquired outside the U.S. without authorization of the copyright owner is an infringement of the copyright. Articles imported in violation of the import prohibitions are subject to seizure and forfeiture. Forfeited articles shall be destroyed. However, the articles may be returned to the country of export whenever customs is satisfied that there was no intentional violation. Copyright owners seeking import protection from the U.S. Customs Service must register their claim to copyright with the U.S. Copyright Office and record their registration with customs in accordance with applicable regulations (19 CFR 133, Subpart D).

Note that enforcement of copyright law has a high priority at customs, and even someone who is discovered unwittingly trying to bring in even a single copy of pirated software, audio-or video-tape, or similar article is subject to the full penalties of the applicable laws.

Marking and Labeling Requirements

Toys that by reason of their functional purpose necessarily present the hazard of sharp points, or of sharp metal or glass edges, and that do not have any nonfunctional sharp points, metal or glass edges, must be so identified by a conspicuous, legible, and visible label at the time of any sale.

Pacifiers. Pacifiers must bear the following label statement legibly and conspicuously on any retail display carton containing two or more pacifiers: "Warning—Do Not Tie Pacifier Around Child's Neck As It Presents a Strangulation Danger." This statement must also appear on each individually packaged pacifier.

Caps. Both paper and plastic caps intended for use in toy guns must bear the following statement on the carton and in the accompanying literature: "WARNING—Do not fire closer than 1 foot to the ear. Do not use indoors."

Clacker Balls. Clacker balls must be conspicuously labeled with: 1) name and address of manufacturer, packer, distributor, or seller; 2) code or mark that will permit the manufacturer to identify any given batch, lot, or shipment in the future. This mark must appear on one or all of the following: the toy itself, its package, its shipping container; it must also appear on all invoices and shipping documents; 3) warning statement on the main panel of the retail container and display carton, and on any accompanying literature, to the effect that if cracks develop in a ball, or if the cord becomes frayed or loose or unfastened, use of the toy should be discontinued. An additional statement is required if a ring or loop or other holding device is present: "In use, the ring or loop must be placed around the middle finger and the two cords positioned over the forefinger and held securely between the thumb and forefinger." Any wording is permissible, as long as it provides adequate instructions and warnings to prevent the holding device from accidentally slipping out of the hand during use. All warning statements must be printed in sharply contrasting color within a borderline, and in letters at least one-quarter inch high on the main panel of the container, and at least one-eighth inch high on all accompanying literature.

Construction Kits. Kits for model rockets and jet-propelled airplanes must bear a warning on the main panel on the outer carton, in conspicuous type. The warning should state: "WARNING—Carefully read instructions and cautions before use."

Baby Walkers, Baby Bouncers, Walker-Bouncers, etc. These articles must be conspicuously labeled with the following: 1) name and address of manufacturer, packer, distributor, or seller; and 2) code mark on the article itself, its package container, and any invoices or shipping documents, which will enable the manufacturer to identify the particular model at any future time. When the manufacturer makes significant structural or design changes to a particular model, the model number must also be changed.

Electrically Operated Toys. The extensive provisions of the CPSA labeling requirements for these toys include but are not limited to the following:

General Requirements. All labeling must be prominently and conspicuously displayed under customary conditions of purchase, storage, and use. All required information must be readily visible, noticeable, clear, and, except where coding is permitted, in legible English (other languages may also be included as appropriate). Such factors governing labeling and location, type size, and contrast against background may be based on necessary condensations to provide a reasonable display.

Specific Requirements. Both the toy and its packaging must be marked to indicate: 1) electrical ratings; 2) any required precautionary statements (see below); 3) the date (month and year) of manufacture (or appropriate codes). The date may appear on the instructions provided with the toy instead of on the toy itself if the manufacturer wishes.

Markings. Markings required to be placed on the toy itself must be of a permanent nature, such as paint-stenciled, die-stamped, molded, or indelibly stamped, and should not readily wash off for any reason. All required markings on the toy and package labeling must contrast sharply with the background (whether by color, projection, or indentation) and must be readily visible and legible. There are specific minimum size requirements for type. Adequate instructions, easily understood by children of those ages for which the toy is intended, must accompany each toy. Instructions must describe applicable installation, assembly, use, cleaning, maintenance (including lubrication), and other functions as appropriate. Applicable precautions must be included, as well as information required on the labeling (except for date of manufacture if it is placed on the toy itself). Instructions must also contain a statement addressed to parents, recommending that the toy be periodically examined for potential hazards and that any parts thus found to be potentially hazardous be repaired or replaced.

If a toy is produced or assembled at more than one establishment, the toy and its shelf pack or package must have a distinctive mark (which may be in code) identifying the toy as the product of a particular establishment. A toy must be marked to indicate its rating in volts as well as in amperes and/or watts. If a toy utilizes a single motor as its only electric energy-consuming component, the electrical rating may be marked on a motor nameplate. In this case, the rating need not be marked elsewhere on the toy if the nameplate is readily visible after the motor has been installed. A toy must be rated for 1) alternating current only, 2) direct current only, or 3) both alternating and direct current. The alternating current rating must include frequency or frequency range requirement, if necessary because of a special component.

Precautionary Statements. Electrically operated toys must bear the statement: "CAUTION—ELECTRIC TOY." The following statement must appear both on accompanying instructional materials and on the upper right hand corner of the package and shelf pack display panel: "CAUTION—ELECTRIC TOY: Not recommended for children under (___) years of age. As with all electric products, precautions should be observed during handling and use to prevent electric shock." The blank in the preceding statement should be filled in by the manufacturer. In no instance may the manufacturer indicate that the article is recommended for children under eight years of age if it contains a heating element. The term "ELECTRICALLY OPERATED PRODUCT" may be substituted for the term "ELECTRIC TOY" in the case of other electrically operated products that may not be considered "toys" but are intended for use by children.

Thermal Hazards. Toys having surfaces defined in the regulation as Type C or Type D (16 CFR 1505.6(g)(2)), and that have temperatures greater than those shown in the table in 16 CFR 1505.7, are defined as "hot." Hot toys must be marked with the statement: "HOT—Do Not Touch," where readily noticeable when the hot surface is in view. When the marking is on other than the hot surface, the word "HOT" must be followed by appropriate descriptive words such as "Molten Material," "Sole Plate," or "Heating Element," and the statement "Do Not Touch." An alternative statement for a surface intended to be handheld as a functional part of the toy shall be "HOT (___) Handle Carefully." The blank should be filled in by the manufacturer with a description of the potential hazard (e.g. "Curler" or "Cooking Surface"). The regulation prescribes tests to determine temperature hazard.

Lamp Hazards. A toy with one or more replaceable incandescent lamps having a potential difference of more than 30 volts rms (42.4 volts peak) between any of its electrodes or lampholder contacts and any other part or ground, must be marked inside the lamp compartment where readily noticeable during lamp replacement with the statement: "WARNING—Do not use light bulbs larger than (___) watts." The manufacturer should fill in the blank with a number specifying the wattage rating of the lamp. Such toys must bear the statement: "WARNING—Shock Hazard. Pull plug before changing light bulb" on the outside of the lamp compartment, where the user will readily notice it before gaining access to the compartment. Toys that utilize one or more nonreplaceable incandescent lamps (other than pilot or indicator lamps) must be marked where clearly visible with the statement: "SEALED UNIT—Do not attempt to change light bulb" or an equivalent statement.

Water. If not suitable for immersion in water, a toy cooking appliance (such as a corn popper, skillet, or candy-maker) or other article that may conceivably be immersed in water, must be marked with the statement: "DANGER—To prevent electric shock, do not immerse in water; wipe clean with damp cloth," or an equivalent statement.

FCC Requirements. All rf devices subject to FCC authorization procedures, whether manufactured within the U.S. or outside it, must bear labeling to show compliance. Devices that are not so labeled will not be permitted entry into U.S. Customs territory. For details on label wording, contact FCC (see addresses at end of this chapter).

FDA Requirements. All radiation-emitting devices for which federal standards have been determined must be certified for compliance. The manufacturer must affix a certification label to each product stating that it conforms to the applicable standard. Products requiring certification that are not so labeled will not be permitted entry.

For a general discussion of U.S. Customs marking and labeling requirements, see "Marking: Country of Origin" on page 215 and "Special Marking Requirements" on page 217.

Shipping Considerations

You will need to ensure that your goods are packaged and shipped with care to ensure that they arrive in good condition and pass smoothly through Customs. You are responsible for ensuring that the shipment is in compliance with all applicable government regulations for packaging and shipping. In most instances, you should not leave these arrangements solely to the discretion of your supplier. Careful preparation of the cargo and selection of the mode of transport can be essential to a cost-effective, timely delivery of undamaged goods. We strongly advise you to consult your shipping representative, insurance agent, or freight broker for advice on packing and shipping. Refer also to the major tab section "Packing/Shipping/Insurance" for a general discussion of packing and shipping.

Toys, games, and sporting goods must be carefully packed and stowed to avoid damage en route. In addition, some more fragile components may require special handling and additional attention to protect them from heat or water damage.

Publications Available

The following publication explains the FDA requirements for importing radiation-producing products. It is published by the FDA and is available on request from FDA headquarters (see addresses at end of this chapter).

Requirements of Laws and Regulations Enforced by the U.S. Food and Drug Administration

The following bulletins may be useful for importing electronic and radio devices and are available from any regional FCC office (or address below):

FCC Equipment Authorization Program for Radio Frequency Devices (Bulletin Number 61)
Importation of Radio Frequency Devices (Field Operations Bulletin Number 8).

The *Harmonized Tariff Schedule of the United States* (HTSUS) is available from:

Government Printing Office (GPO)
Superintendent of Documents
Washington, DC 20402
(202) 512-1800 (Order line)
(202) 512-0000 (General)

The USGPO also has copies of specific laws available for purchase. The USGPO accepts credit card orders over the phone, as well as mail orders paid by credit card, a check drawn on a U.S. bank, or an international money order.

Relevant Government Agencies

Address questions regarding CPSC requirements for toys, games, and sporting goods to:

Consumer Product Safety Commission (CPSC)
5401 Westbard Avenue
Bethesda, MD 20207
(301) 492-6580

Address questions regarding FCC rules on rf devices to the nearest FCC regional office or to:

Federal Communications Commission (FCC)
Office of Engineering and Technology
7435 Oakland Mills Rd.
Colombia, MD 21046
(301) 725-1585

Address inquiries concerning FCC **Form 740** requirements to:
Federal Communications Commission (FCC)
Enforcement Division, Investigations Branch
1919 M Street NW, Rm. 744
Washington, DC 20554
(202) 418-1170

Address inquiries regarding importation of radiation-producing devices to either:

Food and Drug Administration (FDA)
Center for Devices and Radiological Health
Division of Small Manufactures Assistance
5600 Fishers Lane
Rockville, MD 20857
(800) 638-2041, (301) 638-2041
or

Food and Drug Administration (FDA)
Division of Enforcement, Imports Branch
200 C Street SW
Washington, DC 20204
(202) 205-4726

Address questions regarding copyright and trademark laws to:

U.S. Customs Service
Office of Intellectual Property Rights
1301 Constitution Avenue NW
Washington, DC 20229
(202) 482-6960

Address questions regarding the importation of toys, games, and sporting goods to the district or port director of Customs for you area. For addresses refer to"U.S. Customs District Offices" on page 62 or contact:

U.S. Customs Service
1301 Constitution Ave. NW
Washington, DC 20229
(202) 927-6724 (Information)
(202) 927-1000 (General)

Laws and Regulations

The following laws and regulations may be relevant to the importation of toys, games, and sporting goods. The laws are contained in the U.S. Code (USC) and the regulations are published in the Code of Federal Regulations (CFR), both of which may be available at larger public and law libraries. Copies of specific laws are also available from the United States Government Printing Office (address above).

15 USC 1263
Consumer Product Safety Act
This act gives the Consumer Product Safety Commission

authority to set safety standards, testing procedures, and reporting requirements to ensure that consumer products not already covered under other regulations are not harmful.

16 CFR 1500.18
Regulation of CPSC on Banned Toys
This regulation lists the types of toys banned as creating an unreasonable risk of personal injury or illness when subjected to reasonably foreseeable damage or abuse.

16 CFR 1500.50-1500.53
Regulations on Testing Methods for Toys
These regulations prescribe testing methods by which CPSC will determine whether toys intended for use by children are substantially hazardous, and therefore fall within the proscriptions of 16 CFR 1500.18.

16 CFR Part 1501
Regulations on Testing Toys for Ingestion, Choking, or Aspiration Hazards
These regulations prescribe testing methods by which CPSC will determine whether toys intended for use by children under age 3 present an unreasonable risk of choking, aspiration, or ingestion, and therefore fall within the proscriptions of 16 CFR 1500.18.

16 CFR Parts 1115, 1116
Regulations on Substantial Product Hazard Reports
These regulations outline the requirements for filing substantial product hazard reports, including persons who must file, content of reports, confidentiality, and filing procedures.

15 USC 1051 et seq.
Trademark Act
This Act provides, among other things, that no imported article of foreign origin that bears a name or mark calculated to induce the public to believe that it was manufactured in the United States, or in any foreign country or locality other than the country or locality where it was in fact manufactured, shall be admitted entry at any customhouse in the U.S.

17 USC 101 et seq., 602(a)
Copyright Revision Act
This law provides that the importation into the U.S. of copies of a work acquired outside the U.S. without authorization of the copyright owner is an infringement of the copyright.

8 USC 2319
Criminal Penalties for Copyright Violations
This law imposes criminal penalties on persons who are found to have violated U.S. Copyright laws.

19 CFR 133.31 et seq.
Regulations of Customs on Recordation of Copyrights, Trademarks, and Trade Names
These regulations provide procedures and requirements for registering a copyright, trademark, or trade name with U.S. Customs, as well as procedures for enforcement, forfeiture of merchandise, and assessment of monetary penalties.

15 USC 1261
Federal Hazardous Substances Act
This Act controls the importation of hazardous substances, sets forth prohibited imports, and authorizes various agencies to promulgate labeling, marking, and transport requirements.

49 CFR 170 et seq.
Regulations on Hazardous Materials
These regulations list all substances deemed hazardous and provide transport, marking, labeling, safety, and emergency response rules.

21 USC 301 et seq.
Food, Drug, and Cosmetic Act
This Act prohibits deceptive practices and regulates the manufacture, sale and importation or exportation of food, drugs, cosmetics, and related products. See 21 USC 331, 381, 382.

19 CFR 12.1 et seq.; 21 CFR 1.83 et seq.
Regulations on Food, Drugs, and Cosmetics
These regulations of the Secretary of Health and Human Services and the Secretary of the Treasury govern the standards, labeling, marking, and importing of products used with food, drugs, and cosmetics.

42 USC 263b-263n
Radiation Control for Health and Safety Act of 1968 as amended
Customs refuses entry to all electronic products found not to be in compliance with standards prescribed under this act. See 19 CFR 12.90 et seq.; 21 CFR Part 1005.

47 USC 302a
Devices That Interfere with Radio Reception
This law prohibits the importation of devices or home electronic equipment that fail to comply with regulations promulgated by the FCC. See 47 CFR 2.1201 et seq. and 18.119. Customs enforces the prohibition.

Principal Exporting Countries

The following listing includes samples of the main supplier nations of the products of this chapter. It is organized by HTSUS major heading. (Refer to "Customs Classification" above for the product codes.) Countries are listed in rank order of the value of products imported to the U.S. Statistics represent customs value entries for 1993 from the Bureau of Census, U.S. Department of Commerce.

9501—Taiwan, China, Mexico, Italy, South Korea, Germany, Hong Kong, Canada, Philippines, Thailand

9502—China, Malaysia, Taiwan, Macao, Indonesia, Germany, Thailand, Philippines, Mexico, Hong Kong

9503—China, Mexico, Taiwan, Thailand, Hong Kong, Macao, South Korea, Indonesia, Malaysia, Canada

9504—Japan, China, Taiwan, Hong Kong, Thailand, United Kingdom, Mexico, Malaysia, South Korea, Canada

9505—China, Taiwan, Thailand, Philippines, Hong Kong, Germany, Mexico, Sri Lanka, Italy, Canada

9506—Taiwan, China, Canada, Mexico, Japan, France, Thailand, Austria, South Korea, Italy

9507—South Korea, China, Japan, Taiwan, Sweden, Thailand, Singapore, Norway, Hong Kong, Mexico

9508—Italy, Switzerland, Canada, United Kingdom, Liechtenstein, Germany, Japan, Luxembourg, France, Netherlands

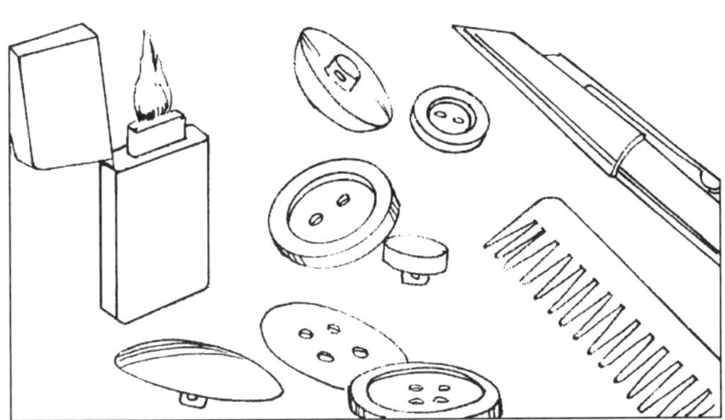

Chapter 96: Miscellaneous Manufactured Articles*

This section pertains to the importation of miscellaneous manufactured articles, which are classified within Chapter 96 of the Harmonized Tariff Schedule of the United States (HTSUS). This chapter is largely a catch-all for a variety of products that don't fit in easily in other categories. Specifically, it includes such diverse and various items as worked animal products—such as ivory, bone, horn, and coral; worked vegetable or mineral products—such as gelatins and waxes; brooms and brushes; sieves; toilet sets; buttons, zippers, and other fasteners; pens and pencils; blackboards; typewriter ribbons, cigarette lighters; smoking pipes; combs, hairpins and other hair dressing articles; misters and sprayers; vacuum bottles; and mannequins.

Various fittings and ornaments are covered in Commodity Index Chapter 96, but products for specific uses or defined articles are usually classified elsewhere. For example, if you are interested in importing pencils for cosmetic use—such as eyebrow pencils—refer to Chapter 33. Items for umbrellas and walking sticks are found in Chapter 66, while real and imitation jewelry is covered in Chapter 71. (Nevertheless, hair ornaments, whether or not they include precious metals and/or precious or semi-precious stones or pearls, are classified in Chapter 96.) Assembled cutlery is included in Chapter 82, but knife handles imported separately would enter under Chapter 96. Scientific instruments—such as special drawing pens—or special brushes for medical uses would fall within Chapter 90. If you are interested in importing antiques or works of art consisting of carved animal products, refer to Chapter 97. Parts of general use—such as nuts, bolts, screws, and nails—are classified within the chapter that applies to the materials of which they are made, Chapters 72-81 for base metals, and 39 for plastics.

Key Factors

The key factors in the importation of brushes are:

- For brushes intended for use on humans or animals: compliance with U.S. Food and Drug Administration (FDA) regulations, entry notification, and procedures
- For products made from endangered species: compliance with U.S. Fish and Wildlife Service (FWS) license, permit, country-of-origin permit, import documentation, and recordkeeping requirements
- For certain brooms and intermediate broom-making materials: restrictions and random U.S. Department of Agricultural (USDA) inspection for some species

Although most importers utilize the services of a licensed customs broker in making their entries, and we recommend this practice, you should be aware of the regulatory, entry, and documentation issues involved in importing your product. You, as importer, are ultimately responsible for the fulfillment of any legal requirements applicable to your shipment.

General Considerations

Importation of most miscellaneous manufactured products—such as hair products, buttons, and pens and pencils—is straightforward. You do not need permits or licenses, nor is special entry paperwork required.

Products Derived from Endangered Species. Importers interested in importing articles such as some hair products and other items of ivory, horn, bone, and coral should be aware of potential conflicts with endangered species regulations, which are extremely rigid. Pertinent laws and regulations include the Endangered Species Act (ESA) and the Convention on International Trade in Endangered Species of Wild Flora and Fauna (CITES), administered by the FWS (see "Prohibitions and Restrictions" below).

Brushes. Brushes fall into two categories for regulatory purposes. Those that are not used on the human body or on animals—such as scrub brushes and artists' brushes—are not regulated. If you are importing these types of brushes you need no licenses or permits, nor is any special paperwork required for entry.

Brushes or any other products intended for use on humans or animals are regulated under the Federal Food, Drug, and Cosmetic Act (FDCA), enforced by the FDA. All items, both domestic and foreign, that fall within these regulations must comply with the requirements established by the FDCA and its enforcers in every detail. Imported products regulated by the FDA are subject to FDA port of entry inspection. **Form FD701** is required for all FDA-regulated importations, and may be obtained from your local FDA Import Operations office, from FDA headquarters (see addresses at end of this chapter) or from your customs broker. For an annotated diagram of required FDA import procedures see the "Foods" appendix on page 808.

Some brush-making materials, particularly broom corn (*Sorghum vulgare* variety *technicum*), are restricted (see "Prohibitions and Restrictions" below), while others—such as some boar bristles—may be subject to endangered species regulation. Products made of broom corn are subject to random USDA port inspections. The USDA may require fumigation or other treatment to ensure that no harmful insects or plant species capable of reproducing are brought into the U.S.

Detention of Shipment. If your shipment is found to be noncomplying, it may be detained at the port of entry. In the case of products subject to FDA jurisdiction, the FDA may permit you to bring such a shipment into compliance before making a final decision regarding admittance. However, any sorting, reprocessing, or relabeling must be supervised by FDA personnel, and is done at the importer's expense. Such conditional release to allow an importer to bring a shipment into compliance is a privilege, not a right. The FDA may consider subsequent noncomplying shipments of the same type of product to constitute abuse of the privilege and require the importer to destroy or reexport the products. To ascertain what your legal responsibilities are, you should contact these agencies regarding the specific items to be imported.

*IMPORTANT: Read the Commodity Index Introduction. It is the essential framework for understanding this chapter.

Customs Classification

For customs purposes miscellaneous manufactured articles are classified within Chapter 96 of the HTSUS. This chapter is divided into major headings, which are further divided into subheadings, and often into sub-subheadings, each of which has its own HTSUS classification number. For example, the HTSUS number for hairbrushes valued over 40 cents apiece is 9603.29.80, indicating that it is a subcategory of other brushes (9603.29.00), which is a subcategory of the major heading brooms, brushes, hand operated mechanical sweepers, mops and feather dusters (9603.00.00). There are 18 major headings in HTSUS Chapter 96.

9601—Worked ivory, bone, tortoise-shell, horn, antlers, coral, mother-of-pearl, and other animal carving material, and articles of these materials (including articles obtained by molding)

9602—Worked vegetable or mineral carving material and articles of these materials; molded or carved articles of wax, of stearin, of natural gums, or natural resins, of modeling pastes, and other molded or carved articles, not elsewhere specified or included; worked, unhardened gelatin (except gelatin of heading 3503) and articles of unhardened gelatin

9603—Brooms, brushes (including brushes constituting parts of machines, appliances, or vehicles), hand-operated mechanical floor sweepers, not motorized, mops, and feather dusters; prepared knots and tufts for broom or brush making; paint pads and rollers; squeegees (other than roller squeegees)

9604—Hand sieves and hand riddles

9605—Travel sets for personal toilet, sewing, or shoe or clothes cleaning (other than manicure and pedicure sets of heading 8214)

9606—Buttons, press-fasteners, snap-fasteners, and press studs, button molds, and other parts of these articles; button blanks

9607—Slide fasteners and parts thereof

9608—Ball point pens; felt-tipped and other porous-tipped pens and markers; fountain pens, stylograph pens, and other pens; duplicating styli; propelling or sliding pencils (for example, mechanical pencils); pen-holders, pencil-holders, and similar holders; parts (including caps and clips) of the foregoing articles, other than those of heading 9609

9609—Pencils (other than those pencils of heading 9608), crayons, pencil leads, pastels, drawing charcoals, writing or drawing chalks, and tailor's chalks

9610—Slates and boards, with writing or drawing surfaces, whether or not framed

9611—Date, sealing, or numbering stamps and the like (including devices for printing or embossing labels), designed for operating in the hand; hand-operated composing sticks and hand printing sets incorporating such composing sticks

9612—Typewriter or similar ribbons, inked or otherwise prepared for giving impressions, whether or not on spools or in cartridges; ink pads, whether or not inked, with or without boxes

9613—Cigarette lighters and other lighters, whether or not mechanical or electrical, and parts thereof other than flints or wicks

9614—Smoking pipes (including pipe bowls) and cigar and cigarette holders, and parts thereof

9615—Combs, hair-slides, and the like; hairpins, curling pins, curling grips, hair-curlers, and the like, other than those of heading 8516, and parts thereof

9616—Scent sprayers and similar toilet sprayers, and mounts and heads therefor; powder puffs and pads for the application of cosmetics or toilet preparations

9617—Vacuum flasks and other vacuum vessels, complete with cases; parts thereof other than glass liners

9618—Tailors' dummies and mannequins; automatons and other animate displays used for shop window dressing

For more details regarding classification of the specific product you are interested in importing, consult a customs broker, the appropriate commodity specialist at your nearest customs port, or see HTSUS. HTSUS is available for purchase from the U.S. Government Printing Office (see addresses at end of this chapter), and may be found in larger public libraries. Refer to "Classification—Liquidation" on page 207 for a general discussion of customs classification.

Sample Import Duties

Import duties vary depending on the HTSUS classification of your product. Therefore, to determine the correct amount of duties, your product must be properly classified under the HTSUS. The following sample duties are taken from the duty listings for HTSUS Chapter 95.

Worked ivory (9601.10.00): 4.2%; coral, cut but nor set (9601.90.40): 2.1%; worked unhardened gelatin (9602.00.10): 4.2%; whiskbrooms of broom corn, valued not over 45 cents each (9603.10.10): 8%; other brooms valued over 95 cents each (9603.10.60): 32%; toothbrushes (9603.10.90): 0.2 cents each + 3.4%; artists' brushes valued over 10 cents each (9603.30.60): 3.1%; paint rollers (9603.40.20): 7.5%; feather dusters (9603.90.40): 2.8%; hand sieves (9604.00.00): 4.9%; sewing kits (9605.00.00): 8.1%; snap fasteners valued not over 20 cents per dozen (9606.10.40): 6.9%; acrylic resin plastic buttons (9606.21.40): 0.4 cents/line/gross + 6.4% [Note: a line is a button measure of 0.635 mm]; base metal buttons (9606.22.00): 5.7%; button blanks other than of casein (9606.30.80): 11.4%; plastic zippers (9607.19.00): 15%; ball point pens (9608.10.00): 0.8 cents each + 5.4%; felt-tipped pens (9608.20.00): 8%; mechanical pencils (9608.40.40): 6.5%; ball point pen refills (9608.60.00): 0.8 cents each + 5.4%; pencils and crayons (9609.10.00): 14 cents/gross +4.3%; pencil leads greater than 1.5 mm in diameter (9609.20.40): 0.5 cents/gross; chalkboards (9610.00.00): 5.1%; dating stamps (9611.00.00): 5.3%; cartridge typewriter ribbons less than 30 mm wide (9612.10.10): 4.8%; ink pads (9612.20.00): 7%; gas-fueled nonrefillable pocket lighters (9613.10.00): 10%; pipes and pipe bowls of wood or root (9614.20.40): 0.5 cents each + 4%; hard rubber or plastic combs valued not over $4.50/gross (9615.11.10); 14.4 cents/gross + 2%; nonthermic hair curling devices (9615.90.20): 8.1%; hair pins (9615.90.30): 6.1%; powder puffs (9616.20.00): 8.5%; vacuum flasks having a capacity exceeding 2 liters (9617.00.40): 8.7%; store mannequins (9618.00.00): 6.3%.

Entry and Documentation

The entry of merchandise is a two-part process consisting of 1) filing the documents necessary to determine whether merchandise may be released from Customs custody and 2) filing the documents that contain information for duty assessment and statistical purposes. In certain instances all documents must be filed and accepted by Customs prior to the release of the goods. Unless you have been granted an extension, you must file entry documents at a location specified by the district or area director within five working days of your shipment's date of arrival at a U.S. port of entry. These include a number of standard documents required by Customs for any entry, and:

- For brushes intended for use on humans or animals: FDA Importers Entry Notice, Form **FD701**
- For products made from endangered species, U.S. Fish and Wildlife Service (FWS) Import Declaration **Form 3-177**, original and 3 copies (if products are derived from exotic wildlife or endangered species)
- FWS permit or import documentation (if products are derived from exotic wildlife or endangered species)
- Permits or certificates required under Convention on International Trade in Endangered Species (CITES), Endangered Species Act (ESA), and any other regulations applicable to the particular shipment

- Where applicable, USDA import permits for brooms and broom-making materials

After you present the entry, Customs may examine your shipment, or may waive examination. The shipment is then released provided no legal or regulatory violations have been noted. You must then file entry summary documentation and deposit estimated duties at a designated customhouse within 10 working days of your shipment's release. For a detailed description of entry procedures, standard documentation, and informal entry, see "Entry Process" on page 182.

Prohibitions and Restrictions

Exotic and Endangered Species. Products of certain plants and animals are restricted or prohibited from importation because of their status under the CITES, ESA, or other U.S. laws. Additional prohibitions or restrictions may be imposed by the laws of the exporting country. You are legally responsible for fulfilling the requirements of all applicable rules and regulations. If you import or attempt to import a product in violation of such laws, whether or not you are aware of the violation, your product may be seized and you may be subject to stiff fines and/or imprisonment.

Virtually all articles made from exotic leathers or other parts of reptiles and amphibians; sea turtles; exotic tropical bird feathers or other parts; ivory from elephants or marine mammals; and coral from many Caribbean, Pacific Island, and Southeast Asian countries are prohibited entry under various endangered species laws.

Importers must provide the FWS with both the common and scientific species names for any products about which they have questions or are planning to import well in advance of the proposed importation. If you are unsure of the regulations or their applicability, check with the FWS or with the World Wildlife Fund (addresses below). Also be sure to check with the local authorities in the country you expect to import from; your embassy or consulate in that country should be able to direct you to the proper local authorities. You should be prepared to furnish full documentation to FWS or Customs personnel for any even potentially questionable product.

Country-Specific Import Restrictions

Corn and closely related plants and their parts (including those of the genus *Chionachne, Coix, Echinochloa, Eleusina, Euchleana, Miscanthus, Panicum, Pennisetum, Polytoca, Sclerachne, Setaria, Sorghum, Trilobachne,* and *Tripsicum*), including materials used in the manufacture of brooms and brushes—specifically broomcorn—are banned form importation into the U.S. if they originate from the countries listed: Africa (all countries), Australia, Bangladesh, Bhutan, Brunei, Bulgaria, Burma (Myanmar), Cambodia (Kampuchea), Hong Kong, India, Nepal, New Zealand, North Korea, Oceania, Pakistan, Papua New Guinea, People's Republic of China, Philippines, Russia and the other republics of the former Soviet Union, Singapore, South Korea, Sri Lanka, Taiwan, Thailand, and Vietnam. Corn-related products from other countries require prior USDA approval.

Quotas

The following items are subject to tariff-rate quotas:

9603.10.10—.30 Whiskbrooms wholly or in part of broom corn: in any calendar year prior to the entry, or withdrawal from the warehouse for consumption, of 61,655 dozen whiskbrooms classifiable under subheadings 9603.10.10 to 9603.10.30, inclusive: 8%; thereafter 12 cents each.

9603.10.40—.60 Brooms, wholly or in part of broom corn: in any calendar year prior to the entry or withdrawal from warehouse for consumption, of 121,478 dozen brooms classifiable under subheadings 9603.10.40 to 9603.10.60, inclusive: 8%; thereafter 32 cents each.

Marking and Labeling Requirements

For a general discussion of U.S. Customs marking and labeling requirements, see "Marking: Country of Origin" on page 215 and "Special Marking Requirements" on page 217.

Shipping Considerations

You will need to ensure that your goods are packaged and shipped with care to ensure that they arrive in good condition and pass smoothly through Customs. You are responsible for ensuring that the shipment is in compliance with all applicable government regulations for packaging and shipping. In most instances, you should not leave these arrangements solely to the discretion of your supplier. Careful preparation of the cargo and selection of the mode of transport can be essential to a cost-effective, timely delivery of undamaged goods. We strongly advise you to consult your shipping representative, insurance agent, or freight broker for advice on packing and shipping. Refer also to the major tab section "Packing/Shipping/Insurance" for a general discussion of packing and shipping.

Miscellaneous manufactured articles include a wide range of goods, some of which are fragile. They require careful packing and stowing to withstand the rigors of transport. Care must be taken to avoid damage due to shifting of the cargo, as well as to protect the goods from heat, humidity, or water, which can damage some products.

Publications Available

The following publication explains the FDA requirements for importing miscellaneous manufactured articles for sanitary use. It is published by the FDA and is available on request from FDA headquarters (see addresses at end of this chapter).

Requirements of Laws and Regulations Enforced by the U.S. Food and Drug Administration

Buyer Beware is a pamphlet published by the World Wildlife Federation. The pamphlet discusses the products that may not be imported into the U.S. because of endangered species considerations. It is available from:

World Wildlife Fund
1250 24th Street NW
Washington, DC 20037
(202) 293-4800

The *Harmonized Tariff Schedule of the United States* (HTSUS) is available from:

Government Printing Office (GPO)
Superintendent of Documents
Washington, DC 20402
(202) 512-1800 (Order line)
(202) 512-0000 (General)

The USGPO also has copies of specific laws available for purchase. The USGPO accepts credit card orders over the phone, as well as mail orders paid by credit card, a check drawn on a U.S. bank, or an international money order.

Relevant Government Agencies

Address questions regarding FDA requirements for importation of brushes for human or animal use to:

Food and Drug Administration (FDA)
Division of Enforcement, Imports Branch
200 C Street SW
Washington, DC 20204
(202) 205-4726

Address questions regarding products derived from wildlife or endangered species to:

U.S. Fish and Wildlife Service (FWS)
Office of Management Authority
4401 N. Fairfax Drive, Room 432

Arlington, VA 22203
(703) 358-2095
(800) 358-2104, (703) 358-2104 (Permits office)

Address questions regarding restrictions on brooms and broom-making materials to:

U.S. Department of Agriculture (USDA)
Animal and Plant Health Inspection Service (APHIS)
Plant Protection and Quarantine (PPQ)
Federal Building, Rm. 631
6505 Belcrest Road
Hyattsville, MD 20782
(301) 436-8645

Address questions regarding importation of miscellaneous manufactured articles to the district or port director of Customs for you area. For addresses refer to"U.S. Customs District Offices" on page 62 or contact:

U.S. Customs Service
1301 Constitution Ave. NW
Washington, DC 20229
(202) 927-6724 (Information)
(202) 927-1000 (General)

Laws and Regulations

The following laws and regulations may be relevant to the importation of miscellaneous manufactured articles. The laws are contained in the U.S. Code (USC) and the regulations are published in the Code of Federal Regulations (CFR), both of which may be available at larger public and law libraries. Copies of specific laws are also available from the United States Government Printing Office (address above).

21 USC 301 et seq.
Food, Drug, and Cosmetic Act
This Act prohibits deceptive practices and regulates the manufacture, sale and importation or exportation of food, drugs, cosmetics, and related products. See 21 USC 331, 381, 382.

19 CFR 12.1 et seq.; 21 CFR 1.83 et seq.
Regulations on Food, Drugs, and Cosmetics
These regulations of the Secretary of Health and Human Services and the Secretary of the Treasury govern the standards, labeling, marking, and importing of products used with food, drugs, and cosmetics.

Convention on International Trade in Endangered Species of Wild Fauna and Flora (CITES)
This comprehensive wildlife treaty signed by over 100 countries, including the United States, regulates and in many cases prohibits commercial imports and exports of wild animal and plant species threatened by trade.

16 USC 1531
Endangered Species Act
This Act prohibits the import and export of species listed as endangered and most species listed as threatened. It is the U.S. law that implements CITES.

16 USC 1361 et seq.
The Marine Mammal Protection Act
This Act prohibits the import of marine mammals and their parts and products. These species include whales, walruses, narwhals, seals, sea lions, sea otters, and polar bears.

19 CFR 12.26 et seq.
Regulations on Importation of Wild Animals
These regulations list the wild animals that are prohibited from importation or that require import permits.

50 CFR Parts 10, 13, and 16
Regulations of FWS for Importing Wildlife and Fish
These regulations specify the animals and animal products subject to import prohibitions and restrictions.

16 USC 3371 et seq.
Lacey Act
This Act prohibits the import of species taken, possessed, transported, or sold in violation of the law of a foreign country.

16 USC 4201
The African Elephant Conservation Act
This Act prohibits imports of carved ivory products from any country and only permits imports of whole tusks from elephants legally hunted in certain African countries.

42 USC 264 et seq.
The Plant Quarantine Act
This Act gives the Plant Protection and Quarantine branch of the USDA authority to restrict or prohibit importation of plants or their seeds found to carry specific plant pests and pathogens.

Principal Exporting Countries

The following listing includes samples of the main supplier nations of the products of this chapter. It is organized by HTSUS major heading. (Refer to "Customs Classification" above for the product codes.) Countries are listed in rank order of the value of products imported to the U.S. Statistics represent customs value entries for 1993 from the Bureau of Census, U.S. Department of Commerce.

9601—Philippines, China, India, Hong Kong, Taiwan, Italy, Thailand, Japan, Indonesia, Australia

9602—Canada, China, Belgium, Japan, Venezuela, Mexico, Israel, Colombia, Taiwan, United Kingdom

9603—China, Taiwan, South Korea, Germany, Japan, Italy, Mexico, Canada, Brazil, Thailand

9604—Mexico, China, United Kingdom, Taiwan, Italy, South Korea, Hong Kong, Germany, New Zealand, Belgium

9605—China, Hong Kong, Taiwan, South Korea, Japan, France, Thailand, Philippines, Italy, United Kingdom

9606—Taiwan, Italy, Hong Kong, Germany, Japan, South Korea, Thailand, China, Czech Rep., France

9607—Japan, Taiwan, China, Italy, South Korea, Hong Kong, Mexico, Israel, Switzerland, Indonesia

9608—Japan, Taiwan, Germany, Mexico, France, China, South Korea, United Kingdom, Italy, Indonesia

9609—China, Taiwan, Japan, Brazil, Malaysia, Indonesia, Mexico, Germany, France, United Kingdom

9610—China, Taiwan, Israel, Canada, United Kingdom, Portugal, Thailand, Japan, Hong Kong, Brazil

9611—Japan, Taiwan, China, Austria, Germany, Malaysia, Hong Kong, South Korea, Sweden, Singapore

9612—Japan, Mexico, United Kingdom, Malaysia, China, Italy, South Korea, Netherlands, Canada, Singapore

9613—Mexico, South Korea, China, France, Thailand, Japan, Netherlands, Philippines, Taiwan, Spain

9614—Italy, Greece, United Kingdom, France, Turkey, Ireland, Denmark, Spain, Netherlands, Germany

9615—China, South Korea, Taiwan, Thailand, Hong Kong, France, Mexico, Dominican Rep., United Kingdom, Italy

9616—France, Taiwan, Japan, United Kingdom, China, South Korea, Malaysia, Germany, Philippines, Italy

9617—Japan, Taiwan, Canada, Brazil, Malaysia, China, Germany, United Kingdom, Hong Kong, India

9618—China, Canada, United Kingdom, Taiwan, Italy, Denmark, France, South Korea, Mexico, Belgium

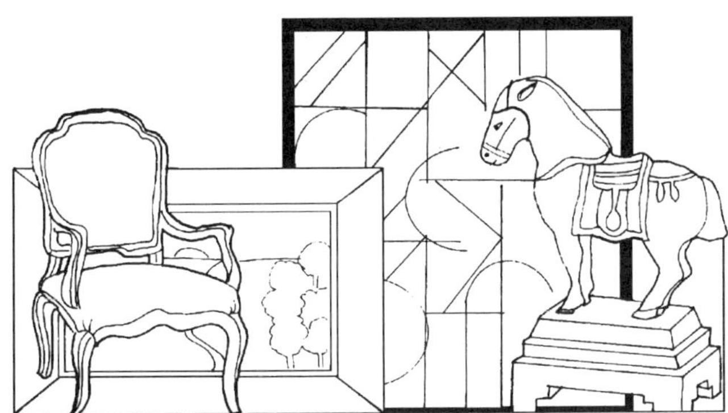

Chapter 97: Works of Art, Collector's Pieces, and Antiques*

This section pertains to the importation of works or art, collectors' pieces, and antiques, which are classified within Chapter 97 of the Harmonized Tariff Schedule of the United States (HTSUS). This rather broad category includes graphic arts—paintings, drawings, prints, and engravings—sculpture and other three dimensional art; philatelic, numismatic, and other collectible items of virtually any variety; and antique objects of at least 100 years of age.

Unused postage stamps and similar items with current use value are covered under Commodity Index Chapter 49. Theatrical scenery, backdrops, and similar articles are covered within Chapter 59 unless the artistry of the item or the reputation of the artist is such that it outweighs the value of the pieces if used in their intended manner, in which case they would be entered under Chapter 97. Unless the age or the artistry of the object is exceptional, such that it would clearly belong within Chapter 97, articles of pearls, precious or semi-precious stones, or other precious materials would be entered under Chapter 71. Articles produced in bulk for commercial purposes—including most handicrafts and many folk art objects—even if individually hand-made or finished, are entered under the category covering the materials of which they are made or the category of the article, as would be the case with any entry. This rule also applies to articles that are less than 100 years old and ineligible for entry as antiques. Neither will reproductions of existing artworks be entered as original art, except within narrowly defined limits (see "General Considerations" below).

Key Factors

The key factors in importing works of art, collectors' pieces, and antiques are:

- For artworks, documentary proof that the work is original, unique, and handmade
- Special information on invoices for certain categories of art
- If entered for exhibition only, a customs bond and additional documentation required, sale prohibited
- For antiques, proof of age (must be more than 100 years old) in order to qualify for duty-free status
- Whether or not the item is intended for personal use or resale
- If repaired, the proportion of new materials used, and to what extent the item has been transformed (affects dutiability)
- Products derived from species listed under endangered or threatened species regulation require authorization and must enter at U.S. Fish and Wildlife Service (FWS) designated ports
- Restrictions under cultural property protection convention: certification required to ensure the export of such articles was legal
- Restrictions on pre-Columbian artifacts: certification required to ensure the export of such articles was legal
- Restrictions on the importation of facsimiles of postage stamps
- Restrictions or prohibitions from other U.S. governmental agencies as applicable

Although most importers utilize the services of a licensed customs broker in making their entries, and we recommend this practice, you should be aware of the regulatory, entry, and documentation issues involved in importing your product. You, as importer, are ultimately responsible for the fulfillment of any legal requirements applicable to your shipment.

General Considerations

Works of Art. Beauty may be in the eye of the beholder, but the U.S. Customs Service has somewhat narrower and more specific criteria in mind. Customs defines a work of art as one that is an original, unique, handmade item. For items such as engravings, prints, or lithographs, the definition hinges on the execution of the master plates and the actual imprinting of the examples from them by the artist or with the artist's authorization and supervision. This definition excludes reproduction by mechanical or photochemical processes, which may place art photographs in a somewhat anomalous position, requiring additional testimony regarding their artistic nature. Customs also defines original sculpture as including the first twelve castings, replicas, or reproductions made from a sculptor's original work, model, or mold by the sculptor or by another artist whether or not the sculptor is alive at the time the castings, replicas, or reproductions are completed.

Artwork enters the U.S. duty-free. Mass-produced manufactured items that happen to be hand-painted or hand-decorated are not considered works of art, and are dutiable according to the category into which they fall. Frames and similar mountings are included along with the art, provided they are of a kind and value normally associated with those articles; otherwise they will be entered and charged separately. If you wish to import original works of art you must provide two declarations at the time of customs entry that verify the originality of the work, its maker, the fact that it is handmade, and how it was made: 1) a declaration by the artist, (or, if that is impossible, a declaration by the seller or shipper), and 2) a declaration by the importer. If this documentation is provided, the piece will invariably be entered duty-free. In some cases customs may waive the artist's or shipper's declaration, but the importer's declaration is always required. In addition, extra information may be required on the entry invoice.

Authenticity. When importing artists' proof etchings, engravings, woodcuts, lithographs, or prints made by other hand-transfer processes, be sure that they bear the genuine signature or mark of the artist as evidence of their authenticity. If they do not, you should be prepared to present some kind of documentary evidence to establish authenticity. For some imports the district director of Customs may require proof of the character of the ar-

*IMPORTANT: Read the Commodity Index Introduction. It is the essential framework for understanding this chapter.

ticle, which might include certificates from curators or other recognized authorities on art, that the imported article represents some recognized school, kind, or medium of the free fine arts.

Antiques. Customs classification of an article as "antique" is primarily an issue of dutiability, because items classified as antiques under Chapter 97 enter duty free while others are subject to duty according to their category. If you wish to enter an item as an antique, you must present adequate documentation verifying the date of production of the article in question. Antique documentation for customs purposes can be a gray area. There is no official customs certificate of antiquity. However, a letter from you stating something like "this item is more than 100 years old," will not suffice. You must obtain specific documentary verification of the item's date of manufacture. On the other hand, a certified statement from an appraiser or trade association, or even a letter from the foreign supplier, is often adequate. Some countries certify antiques, usually as part of the process of controlling their export. Where exit permits are required because of the antiquity of the item, such documents may serve as an official determination by officials of the exporting country of the age of the article. Certain items may be regulated under laws administered by governmental agencies other than U.S. Customs, and may require special additional documentation (see "Entry and Documentation" below.)

If you are entering antiques for resale in the U.S., you are subject to duties. Resellers are also subject to penalties if it is determined after entry that the items are less than 100 years old. The base rate of such penalties is 6.6%, and can rise to as high as 25%, in addition to pertinent duties. (Entries made for personal use are generally somewhat easier, and penalties do not apply on any items subsequently assessed to be less than 100 years old.) Because Customs levies duty on antique items based on the percentage of any non-antique materials used in repairs, it is important to have a record of all recent repairs or reconstructions made using non-antique materials. In some cases, if the transformation of the article is significant due to such repairs, Customs will reclassify the item as recent rather than as an antique and levy duties accordingly. Customs regulations regarding antique imports are found in 19 CFR 10.53.

Cultural Property. The Convention on the Means of Prohibiting and Preventing the Illicit Import, Export, and Transfer of Ownership of Cultural Property ("the Convention"), to which the U.S. is a signatory, was adopted by the General Conference of the United Nations Education, Scientific, and Cultural Organization (UNESCO) to provide cultural property import protection for listed countries. The Convention is designed to prevent the illicit importation of archaeological or ethnologically significant property from the listed countries. At present, 68 countries are contracting parties to the Convention. (See "Country-Specific Import Restrictions" below.)

Customs enforces regulations governing the import of cultural property found in 19 CFR 12.104. Import of cultural property not otherwise prohibited under Convention restrictions is straightforward.

Postage Stamps. Importation of foreign postage stamps into the U.S. is straightforward. You do not need permits or licenses, nor is special paperwork required. If you are importing postage stamps in current use, you are not even required to make a formal customs entry. Importation of facsimiles of U.S. postage stamps is regulated by the U.S. Secret Service (see "Prohibitions and Restrictions" below).

Used, canceled, or postage stamps not in current use valued for their collectibility are found in Chapter 97.

Articles Intended for Exhibition. If you are acting under the authority of a museum or other recognized cultural institution to import works of art, antiques, collectors' pieces, or cultural property for temporary exhibition, under the terms specified in Commodity Index Chapter 98, you will need additional documentation for your import, and you will be required to make the entry under customs bond. (Refer to "Surety" under the heading "Entry Process" on page 182 for details.) You should have an officer of your institution complete a declaration on Customs **Form 3325**. Customs may require that you produce at entry a copy of the charter of the institution you represent, or an original order from such institution authorizing you to act as its agent in making the import. You may file this extra documentation with the district director of the port of entry any time within six months of making entry. Chapter 98 entry rules specifically prohibit the sale of items entered under its provisions. If the works of art that you enter under Chapter 98 are sold or offered for sale, exposed for sale, or transferred or used in any manner contrary to regulations governing these imports, you will be required to pay duties immediately to the district director of the port of entry.

Endangered Species Items. Those interested in importing articles including materials derived from listed endangered or threatened species should be aware of potential conflicts with endangered species regulations, which are complex and extremely rigid. Pertinent laws and regulations include the Endangered Species Act (ESA) and the Convention on International Trade in Endangered Species of Wild Flora and Fauna (CITES), administered by the FWS (see "Prohibitions and Restrictions" below).

Although antiques made of or otherwise incorporating such materials are usually allowed entry if properly documented, works of art incorporating such materials are somewhat more problematical. Entries of any such materials are required to be made through designated FWS entry ports to ensure that trained personnel are available to rule on them.

Customs Classification

For customs purposes, works of art, collectors' pieces, and antiques are classified within Chapter 97 of the HTSUS. This chapter is divided into major headings, which are further divided into subheadings, and often into sub-subheadings, each of which has its own HTSUS classification number. For example, the HTSUS number for paintings, drawings, and pastels is 9701.10.00, indicating that it is a subcategory of the major heading paintings, drawings, and pastels, executed entirely by hand, other than drawings of heading 4906 and other than hand-painted or hand-decorated manufactured articles (9701.00.00). There are six major headings in HTSUS Chapter 97.

9701—Paintings, drawings, and pastels, executed entirely by hand, other than drawings of heading 4906 and other than hand-painted or hand-decorated manufactured articles; collages and similar decorative plaques; all the foregoing framed or unframed

9702—Original engravings, prints, and lithographs, framed or not framed

9703—Original sculptures and statuary, in any material

9704—Postage or revenue stamps, stamp-postmarks, first-day covers, postal stationery (stamped paper), and the like, or, if unused, not of current or new issue in the country to which they are destined

9705—Collections and collectors' pieces of zoological, botanical, mineralogical, anatomical, historical, archeological, paleontological, ethnographic, or numismatic interest

9706—Antiques of an age exceeding one hundred years

For more details regarding classification of the specific product you are interested in importing, consult a customs broker, the appropriate commodity specialist at your nearest Customs port, or see HTSUS. HTSUS is available for purchase from the U.S. Government Printing Office (see addresses at end of this chapter), and may be found in larger public libraries. Refer to "Classification—Liquidation" on page 207 for a general discussion of customs classification.

Sample Import Duties

Import duties vary depending on the HTSUS classification of your product. Therefore, to determine the correct amount of duties, your product must be properly classified under the HTSUS. There are no import duties on items classified within the headings of HTSUS Chapter 97, all of which may be entered duty-free. However, items that do not meet the specific criteria set for Chapter 97 entries are subject to regular rates of duty according to the nature of the article, i.e., printed matter, jewelry, furniture, clocks, etc. Thus there is a substantial interest on the part of importers to gain entry under Chapter 97, and a special interest on the part of Customs to insist on full justification before allowing entry under these classifications.

Entry and Documentation

The entry of merchandise is a two-part process consisting of 1) filing the documents necessary to determine whether merchandise may be released from Customs custody and 2) filing the documents that contain information for duty assessment and statistical purposes. In certain instances all documents must be filed and accepted by Customs prior to the release of the goods. Unless you have been granted an extension, you must file entry documents at a location specified by the district or area director within five working days of your shipment's date of arrival at a U.S. port of entry. These include a number of standard documents required by Customs for any entry, and:

- For works of art, artist's declaration, where possible; if artist's declaration is not possible, declaration from shipper or other authority
- Importer's declaration
- If the work is being imported by a museum or other recognized institution for exhibition only, Customs **Form 3325**, and Customs **Form 301** (entry under bond) and, occasionally a copy of the institutional charter of the importing institution, and/or original of the order from such institution to the importer or agent offering the artwork for entry
- For antiques, adequate documentation to certify that the item is more than 100 years old
- For antique firearms, Bureau of Alcohol, Tobacco, and Firearms (BATF) authorization
- If derived from endangered species, entry through FWS-designated port
- For restricted articles, country-of-export certification of legality

After you present the entry, Customs may examine your shipment, or may waive examination. The shipment is then released provided no legal or regulatory violations have been noted. You must then file entry summary documentation and deposit estimated duties at a designated customhouse within 10 working days of your shipment's release. For a detailed description of entry procedures, standard documentation, and informal entry, see "Entry Process" on page 182.

Entry Invoices. Entry invoices for works of art entered duty-free under HTSUS headings 9701.90.00, 9702.00.00, and 9703.00.00 must show whether they are originals, replicas, reproductions, or copies, and also the name of the artist, or who produced them, unless upon examination the appraiser is satisfied that such statement is not necessary to a proper determination of the facts.

Prohibitions and Restrictions

Antiques. An item classified as antique by U.S. Customs may also be an item regulated by another governmental agency, requiring separate special documentation or even licensing. For example, antique firearms are strictly regulated by the BATF (see addresses at end of this chapter). You must be licensed by that agency to import these items into the U.S. BATF import documentation requirements are complex, stringent, and highly specific.

Products derived from species of wildlife listed under endangered species laws are subject to regulation by the FWS. If, for example, you intend to import antique scrimshaw (carvings in ivory), you must do so through one of the ports designated by FWS for that purpose.

Cultural Property. Articles of cultural property documented as appertaining to the inventory of a museum, public monument, or similar institution in any Contracting Party State, deemed to be removed after April 12, 1983, or after the Contracting Party State's date of entry into the Convention, whichever date is later, are prohibited importation into the U.S.

Classification. For Convention purposes, cultural property falls into eleven categories: 1) rare collections and specimens of fauna, flora, minerals, anatomy, and objects of paleontological interest; 2) property relating to a) history—including the history of science and technology—and military and social history; b) the lives of national leaders, thinkers, scientists, artists, and other like figures; and c) events of national importance; 3) products of archaeological excavations or of archaeological discoveries; 4) elements of artistic and historical monuments or archaeological sites that have been dismembered; 5) antiquities more than 100 years old, such as inscriptions, coins, and engraved seals; 6) objects of ethnological interest; 7) property of artistic interest, such as pictures, paintings, and drawings produced entirely by hand, or original works in any material, of statuary art, sculpture, engravings, prints, lithographs, artistic assemblages, and montages; 8) rare manuscripts and incunabula, old books, documents, and publications of special interest (historical, artistic, scientific, literary, etc.), singly or in collections; 9) postage, revenue, and similar stamps, singly or in collections; 10) archives, including sound, photographic, and cinematographic archives; and 11) articles of furniture and musical instruments older than 100 years.

Archaeological or Ethnological Designation. Articles originating in Contracting Party State countries and falling into any of these categories are subject to import protection, and may be listed by a U.S. Treasury Decision as designated archaeological or ethnological materials. Articles so designated are prohibited import under the Convention on Cultural Property Implementation Act (CCPIA). Unless you can provide extensive certification ensuring that the articles are authorized for export by officials of the country of origin, any shipment of designated articles you attempt to import will be subject to seizure and forfeiture. For details regarding import restriction, exemptions, and certification requirements, see 19 CFR 12.104c.

If you are importing cultural property from any listed country, you are responsible for knowing the artifact's status under the Convention. At present, there are four countries that have designated cultural property: 1) El Salvador (prehistoric archaeological objects from the Cara Sucia Archaeological Region); 2) Bolivia (antique ceremonial textiles from Coroma); 3) Guatemala (archaeological material from the Peten Archaeological Region forming part of the remains of the ancient Maya culture; and 4) Peru (archaeological materials from the Sipan Archaeological Region forming part of the remains of the Moche culture). Treasury Decisions are published in the Federal Register. CCPIA import restrictions are generally effective for five years from the date on which the party state requests the restriction, with optional three-year extensions if a need is determined.

For more details, see 19 CFR 12.104(a-i), or contact your nearest customs port.

Pre-Columbian Monumental and Architectural Sculpture and Murals. Import restrictions apply to any stone carving or wall art that is the product of a pre-Columbian Indian culture of Belize, Bolivia, Colombia, Costa Rica, the Dominican Republic, Ecuador, El Salvador, Guatemala, Honduras, Mexico, Panama, Peru, or Venezuela. 19 CFR 12.105 lists as restricted articles: 1) such stone monuments as altars and altar bases, archways, ball court markers, basins, calendars and calendrical markers, columns, monoliths, obelisks, statues, stelae, sarcophagi, thrones, and zoomorphs; 2) such architectural structures as aqueducts, ball courts, buildings, bridges, causeways, courts, doorways, (including lintels and jambs), forts, observatories, plazas, platforms, facades, reservoirs, retaining walls, roadways, shrines, temples, tombs, walls, walkways, and wells; 3) architectural masks, decorated capstones, decorative beams of wood, frescoes, friezes, glyphs, graffiti, mosaics, moldings, or any other carving or decoration that had been part of or affixed to any monument or architectural structure, including cave paintings or designs; and 4) any fragment or part of any stone carving or wall art. The country of origin of these items is considered to be the country in which the item was initially discovered.

Pre-Columbian articles of the above categories exported from their country of origin after June 1, 1973 are prohibited import into the U.S.

You may import pre-Columbian articles provided you fulfill one of the following conditions of entry: 1) file with the district director of customs at the port of entry a certificate, issued by the government of the country of origin, certifying that the specific exportation was not made in violation of the laws of that country; 2) present satisfactory documentary or sworn testamentary evidence to the district director of customs that the article was exported from the country of origin on or before June 1, 1973; or 3) present satisfactory evidence that the article is not one covered by 19 CFR 12.105.

If you cannot produce the certificate or evidence required at the time of making entry, your shipment will be detained in Customs custody, at the risk and expense of the consignee, until the necessary documentation is presented to Customs. You must provide documentation within 90 days of shipment detention, unless other arrangements are explicitly authorized by the district director. Articles for which appropriate documentation is not presented within the required time limit are subject to forfeiture.

Philatelic Items. Facsimiles of postage stamps are prohibited entry except those for philatelic, educational, historical, or newsworthy purposes. You may obtain further information from the U.S. Secret Service (see addresses at end of this chapter).

If you are not sure whether your import is subject to restriction, check the Commodity Index under the specific item name. The district director of customs nearest you will also be able to give you information regarding possible restrictions (refer to "U.S. Customs District Offices" on page 62).

Exotic and Endangered Species. Products of certain plants and animals are restricted or prohibited from importation because of their status under the CITES, ESA, or other U.S. laws. Additional prohibitions or restrictions may be imposed by the laws of the exporting country. You are legally responsible for fulfilling the requirements of all applicable rules and regulations. If you import or attempt to import a product in violation of such laws, whether or not you are aware of the violation, your product may be seized and you may be subject to stiff fines and/or imprisonment.

Virtually all articles made from exotic leathers or other parts of reptiles and amphibians; sea turtles; exotic tropical bird feathers or other parts; ivory from elephants or marine mammals; and coral from many Caribbean, Pacific Island, and Southeast Asian countries are prohibited entry under various endangered species laws.

Importers must provide the FWS with both the common and scientific species names for any products about which you have questions or are planning to import well in advance of the proposed importation. If you are unsure of the regulations or their applicability, check with the FWS or with the World Wildlife Fund (addresses below). Also be sure to check with the local authorities in the country you expect to import from; your embassy or consulate in that country should be able to direct you to the proper local authorities. You should be prepared to furnish full documentation to FWS or Customs personnel for any even potentially questionable product.

Country-Specific Import Restrictions

Country-specific import restrictions depend upon the item in question. Endangered species regulation is country-specific. The BATF prohibits importation of firearms from certain countries. For details, see the index section pertinent to your import.

Cultural Property. The following countries are currently State Parties in the Convention on Cultural Property: Algeria, Argentina, Australia, Bangladesh, Bolivia, Brazil, Bulgaria, Burkina Faso, Byelorussia, Cameroon, Canada, Central African Republic, Colombia, Cuba, Cyprus, the Czech Republic, Democratic Kampuchea, Democratic People's Republic of Korea, Dominican Republic, Ecuador, Egypt, El Salvador, Germany, Greece, Guatemala, Guinea, Honduras, Hungary, India, Iran, Iraq, Italy, Jordan, Kuwait, Madagascar, Mali, Mauritania, Mauritius, Mexico, Nepal, Nicaragua, Niger, Nigeria, Oman, Pakistan, Panama, People's Republic of China, Peru, Poland, Portugal, Qatar, Republic of Korea, Russia, Saudi Arabia, Senegal, Slovakia, Socialist People's Libyan Arab Jamahiriya, Spain, Sri Lanka, Syrian Arab Republic, Tunisia, Turkey, Ukraine, United Republic of Tanzania, United States of America, Uruguay, the republics of the former Yugoslavia, Zaire, Zambia. Additions to and deletions from the list of State Parties are accomplished by Federal Register notice, from time to time, as the necessity arises.

Marking Requirements

Works of Art. Original works of art are exempt from country of origin marking. However, the country of origin must be conspicuously marked on the outside of the crate or packing material in which the work of art is shipped.

Antiques. Individual antique items are exempt from country of origin marking, but the country of origin must be marked on the outside of their packing or shipping crate.

For a general discussion of U.S. Customs marking and labeling requirements, see "Marking: Country of Origin" on page 215 and "Special Marking Requirements" on page 217.

Shipping Considerations

You will need to ensure that your goods are packaged and shipped with care to ensure that they arrive in good condition and pass smoothly through Customs. You are responsible for ensuring that the shipment is in compliance with all applicable government regulations for packaging and shipping. In most instances, you should not leave these arrangements solely to the discretion of your supplier. Careful preparation of the cargo and selection of the mode of transport can be essential to a cost-effective, timely delivery of undamaged goods. We strongly advise you to consult your shipping representative, insurance agent, or freight broker for advice on packing and shipping. Refer also to the major tab section "Packing/Shipping/Insurance" for a general discussion of packing and shipping.

Works of art, collectors' pieces, and antiques encompasses a wide range of items, many of which are exceedingly fragile. They require careful packing and stowing to withstand the rigors of transport. Care must be taken to avoid damage due to shifting of the cargo, as well as to protect the goods from heat, humidity, or water, which in many cases can ruin them.

Publications Available

The *Harmonized Tariff Schedule of the United States* (HTSUS) is available from:

Government Printing Office (GPO)
Superintendent of Documents
Washington, DC 20402
(202) 512-1800 (Order line)
(202) 512-0000 (General)

The USGPO also has copies of specific laws available for purchase. The USGPO accepts credit card orders over the phone, as well as mail orders paid by credit card, a check drawn on a U.S. bank, or an international money order.

Relevant Government Agencies

Address questions regarding BATF requirements for importation of antique firearms to:

Bureau of Alcohol, Tobacco and Firearms (BATF)
Firearms and Explosives Import Export Branch
650 Massachusetts Avenue
Washington, DC 20226
(202) 927-8300

Address questions regarding FWS requirements for importation of antiques or artworks derived from endangered species to:

U.S. Fish and Wildlife Service (FWS)
Office of Management Authority
4401 N. Fairfax Drive, Room 432
Arlington, VA 22203
(703) 358-2095
(800) 358-2104, (703) 358-2104 (Permits office)

Address questions regarding importation of facsimiles of U.S. postage stamps to:

U.S. Customs Service
Office of Intellectual Property Rights
1301 Constitution Avenue NW
Washington, DC 20229
(202) 482-6960

Address questions regarding the importation of works of art, collectors' pieces, and antiques to the district or port director of Customs for you area. For addresses refer to"U.S. Customs District Offices" on page 62 or contact:

U.S. Customs Service
1301 Constitution Ave. NW
Washington, DC 20229
(202) 927-6724 (Information)
(202) 927-1000 (General)

Laws and Regulations

The following laws and regulations may be relevant to the importation of works of art, collectors' pieces, and antiques. The laws are contained in the U.S. Code (USC) and the regulations are published in the Code of Federal Regulations (CFR), both of which may be available at larger public and law libraries. Copies of specific laws are also available from the United States Government Printing Office (address above).

19 CFR 10.48
Regulations of Customs for Entry as Works of Art
Customs enforces the provisions requiring documentary proof at time of entry that original works of sculpture and/or engraving are not mass produced.

19 CFR 2091 et seq.
Regulation on Importation of Pre-Columbian Art
These regulations require that all importations of Pre-Columbian art be accompanied by a certificate from the country of origin certifying that such exportation was lawful.

Convention on Cultural Property Implementation Act (CCPIA)
This act provides the implementing authority to enforce UNESCO's Convention on the Means of Prohibiting and Preventing the Illicit Import, Export, and Transfer of Ownership of Cultural Property. The U.S. Customs Service is responsible for administering its provisions.

Convention on International Trade in Endangered Species of Wild Fauna and Flora (CITES)
This comprehensive wildlife treaty signed by over 100 countries, including the United States, regulates and in many cases prohibits commercial imports and exports of wild animal and plant species threatened by trade.

16 USC 1531
Endangered Species Act
This Act prohibits the import and export of species listed as endangered and most species listed as threatened. It is the U.S. law that implements CITES.

16 USC 1361 et seq.
The Marine Mammal Protection Act
This Act prohibits the import of marine mammals and their parts and products. These species include whales, walruses, narwhals, seals, sea lions, sea otters, and polar bears.

19 CFR 12.26 et seq.
Regulations on Importation of Wild Animals
These regulations list the wild animals that are prohibited from importation or that require import permits.

50 CFR Parts 10, 13, and 16
Regulations of FWS for Importing Wildlife and Fish
These regulations specify the animals and animal products subject to import prohibitions and restrictions.

16 USC 3371 et seq.
Lacey Act
This Act prohibits the import of species taken, possessed, transported, or sold in violation of the law of a foreign country.

16 USC 4201
The African Elephant Conservation Act
This Act prohibits imports of carved ivory products from any country and only permits imports of whole tusks from elephants legally hunted in certain African countries.

Principal Exporting Countries

The following listing includes samples of the main supplier nations of the products of this chapter. It is organized by HTSUS major heading. (Refer to "Customs Classification" above for the product codes.) Countries are listed in rank order of the value of products imported to the U.S. Statistics represent customs value entries for 1993 from the Bureau of Census, U.S. Department of Commerce.

9701—Switzerland, United Kingdom, France, Spain, Germany, Hong Kong, Italy, Singapore, Netherlands, Japan

9702—United Kingdom, France, Germany, Switzerland, Spain, Hong Kong, Canada, Israel, Japan, Mexico

9703—United Kingdom, Switzerland, France, Italy, Canada, Germany, China, Hong Kong, Japan, Venezuela

9704—United Kingdom, Canada, Israel, France, Russia, Netherlands, Taiwan, Switzerland, Germany, Australia

9705—Russia, Argentina, United Kingdom, Switzerland, France, Canada, Mexico, Greece, Germany, Belgium

9706—United Kingdom, France, China, Switzerland, Italy, Netherlands, Germany, Belgium, Japan, Hong Kong

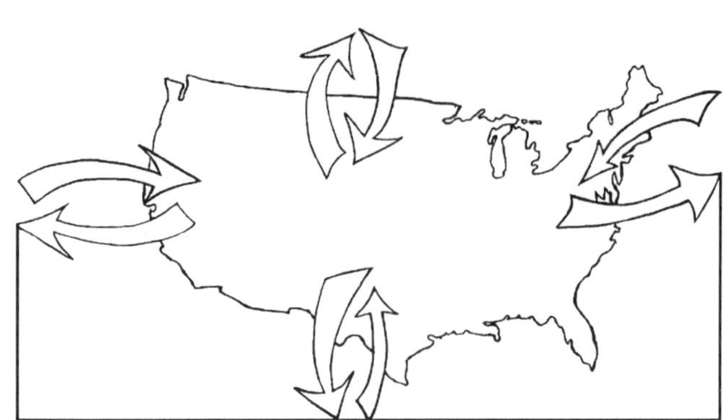

Chapter 98: Special Classification Provisions*

This chapter pertains to the importation of specific products or types of products under specified conditions and/or by specified classes of persons or other entities, which exceptions are classified within Chapter 98 of the Harmonized Tariff Schedule of the United States (HTSUS). The classification of any article that is described in any provision of this chapter will fall within the chapter—that is, this chapter takes precedence over any other potential classification of the article—as long as the article meets the conditions specified in the appropriate provisions of HTSUS Chapter 98. Any article failing to meet all of the conditions established for inclusion in HTSUS Chapter 98 will be entered under the provisions of the HTSUS chapter in which it would normally be classified absent the special conditions.

Although most importers utilize the services of a licensed customs broker in making their entries, and we recommend this practice, you should be aware of the regulatory, entry, and documentation issues involved in importing your product. You, as importer, are ultimately responsible for the fulfillment of any legal requirements applicable to your shipment.

General Considerations

HTSUS Chapter 98 is designed to cover exceptions and special circumstances as decreed by legal provisions, agency regulations, or diplomatic courtesies. Some of the provisions are highly specific, while others are broad in application. Many have extensive qualifying provisions, limits, and procedures that need to be carefully assessed to determine eligibility.

Many of the applications within HTSUS Chapter 98 represent personal or noncommercial entries that will be of little interest to importers. However, subchapters I and II cover items exported from and returned to the U.S.; III deals with containers used in international trade; VIII through X refer to imports of specifically defined official organizations for which importers may act as agents; XI through XIV cover importation of commercial samples and items under bond; XV refers to products of U.S. fisheries; and XVI includes various specific miscellaneous categories.

Any article exempted from duty under subchapters IV through VII—those pertaining to allowable personal exemptions—will also be exempted from any internal revenue taxes which would have been levied on such articles if imported under regular circumstances.

*IMPORTANT: Read the Commodity Index Introduction. It is the essential framework for understanding this chapter.

No specific authorizations are needed to import articles under the provisions of HTSUS Chapter 98. However, the importer must satisfy Customs that the entry qualifies under the terms of the specific provision of Chapter 98, which may require specific documentation. Importers should ascertain what documentation Customs will require in advance and be prepared to furnish it to facilitate their entries.

Customs Classification

For customs purposes, articles covered by special provisions are classified within Chapter 98 of the HTSUS. This chapter is divided into subchapters, which are the equivalents of the major headings of other HTSUS chapters, which are further divided into subheadings, each of which has its own HTSUS classification number. There are 17 subchapters in HTSUS Chapter 98.

9801—Articles exported and returned, not advanced or improved in condition; animals exported and returned

9802—Articles exported and returned, advanced or improved abroad

9803—Substantial containers or holders

9804—Personal exemptions extended to residents and nonresidents

9805—Personal exemptions extended to United States personnel and evacuees

9806—Personal exemptions extended to distinguished visitors and to personnel of foreign government or international organizations

9807—Other personal exemptions

9808—Importations of the United States government

9809—Importations of foreign governments and international organizations

9810—Importations of religious, educational, scientific, and other institutions

9811—Samples for soliciting orders

9812—Articles admitted free of duty under bond for permanent exhibition

9813—Articles admitted temporarily free of duty under bond

9814—Tea admitted free under bond

9815—Products of American fisheries

9816—Noncommercial importations of limited values

9817—Other special classification provisions

Sample Import Duties

Import duties vary depending on the HTSUS classification of your product. Therefore, to determine the correct amount of duties, your product must be properly classified under the HTSUS. Most articles classified within Chapter 98 are imported duty free. However, there are some specific exceptions which are summarized here:

Aircraft or other articles previously exported from the U.S. with benefit of drawback (or, in the case of aircraft of heading 9813.00.05) (9801.00.70-.80): a duty equal to the duty on the importation of like articles not previously exported, but in no case in excess of the sum of (a) any customs drawback proved to have been allowed upon such exportation and (b) the duty that would have been payable on any articles used in the manufacture or production of such articles had they not been exported (or in the case of aircraft, entered and exported under heading 9813.00.05); articles exported for repairs, alterations, or processing (9802.00.40): a duty on the value of the cost of the operations performed (value added) but not on the value of the article itself [Note: this provision applies to all subheadings of subchapter II except for 9802.00.20 and 9802.00.90, which are imported duty free, and 9802.00.80, for which see the following]; articles assembled abroad from production-ready components exported from the U.S. for such assembly (9802.00.80): a duty on the full value of the finished product less the cost of the components produced in the U.S. [Note: this provision does not apply to textile and apparel articles assembled in Mexico which are admitted duty-free]; automobiles rented abroad and brought into the country by a U.S. resident for personal use (9804.00.60): free for such temporary period as the Secretary of the Treasury may grant within the limits prescribed by law; all subheadings of subchapters 9812, 9813, and 9814: free, under bond; articles for personal or household use or as personal gifts valued at a total of no more than $1,000 retail in the country of acquisition and that accompany a person arriving in the U.S. (9816.00.20): 10% of fair retail value; articles for personal or household use as above but accompanying a person arriving from American Samoa, Guam, or the Virgin Islands (9816.00.40): 5% of fair retail value [Note: in the two preceding entries, the claimant may not have exercised this privilege within the preceding 30-day period].

Entry and Documentation

The entry of merchandise is a two-part process consisting of 1) filing the documents necessary to determine whether merchandise may be released from Customs custody and 2) filing the documents that contain information for duty assessment and statistical purposes. In certain instances all documents must be filed and accepted by Customs prior to the release of the goods. Unless you have been granted an extension, you must file entry documents at a location specified by the district or area director within five working days of your shipment's date of arrival at a U.S. port of entry. These include a number of standard documents required by Customs for any entry, and:

- Such supporting documentation as Customs may specify for the given import

After you present the entry, Customs may examine your shipment, or may waive examination. The shipment is then released provided no legal or regulatory violations have been noted. You must then file entry summary documentation and deposit estimated duties at a designated customhouse within 10 working days of your shipment's release. For a detailed description of entry procedures, standard documentation, and informal entry, see "Entry Process" on page 182.

Marking Requirements

For a general discussion of U.S. Customs marking and labeling requirements, see "Marking: Country of Origin" on page 215 and "Special Marking Requirements" on page 217.

Shipping Considerations

You will need to ensure that your goods are packaged and shipped with care to ensure that they arrive in good condition and pass smoothly through Customs. You are responsible for ensuring that the shipment is in compliance with all applicable government regulations for packaging and shipping. In most instances, you should not leave these arrangements solely to the discretion of your supplier. Careful preparation of the cargo and selection of the mode of transport can be essential to a cost-effective, timely delivery of undamaged goods. We strongly advise you to consult your shipping representative, insurance agent, or freight broker for advice on packing and shipping. Refer also to the major tab section "Packing/Shipping/Insurance" for a general discussion of packing and shipping.

Publications Available

The *Harmonized Tariff Schedule of the United States* (HTSUS) is available from:

Government Printing Office (GPO)
Superintendent of Documents
Washington, DC 20402
(202) 512-1800 (Order line)
(202) 512-0000 (General)

The USGPO also has copies of specific laws available for purchase. The USGPO accepts credit card orders over the phone, as well as mail orders paid by credit card, a check drawn on a U.S. bank, or an international money order.

Relevant Government Agencies

Address questions regarding special provisions of HTSUS Chapter 98 to the district or port director of Customs for you area. For addresses refer to "U.S. Customs District Offices" on page 62 or contact:

U.S. Customs Service
1301 Constitution Ave. NW
Washington, DC 20229
(202) 927-6724 (Information)
(202) 927-1000 (General)

Principal Exporting Countries

The following listing includes samples of the main supplier nations of some of the product categories of this chapter. It is organized by HTSUS major heading. (Refer to "Customs Classification" above for the product codes.) Countries are listed in rank order of the value of products imported to the U.S. Statistics represent customs value entries for 1993 from the Bureau of Census, U.S. Department of Commerce.

9801—Canada, Mexico, United Kingdom, Japan, Germany, Netherlands, France, Hong Kong, Switzerland, Singapore

9802—Canada, United Kingdom, Mexico, Germany, Italy, Japan, France, Sweden, Netherlands, Portugal

9808—Germany, United Kingdom, France, Japan, Italy, Canada, Netherlands, Denmark, Switzerland, Russia

9810—United Kingdom, Germany, Canada, Italy, Sweden, France, Japan, Belgium, Netherlands, Israel

9812—Germany, France, United Kingdom, Switzerland, Spain, Japan, Netherlands, Italy, China, Ghana

9814—Japan

9817—Canada, United Kingdom, Italy, Spain, Netherlands, Germany, France, New Zealand, China, Denmark

TEMPORARY AND ADDITIONAL CHANGES

Chapter 99: Temporary and Additional Changes*

Full title: Temporary Legislation; Temporary Modifications Established Pursuant to Trade Legislation; Additional Import Restrictions Established Pursuant to Section 22 of the Agricultural Adjustment Act

This chapter pertains to the importation of specific products or types of products that are subject to special and/or temporary alterations in duty rates or other customs treatment, which exceptions are classified within Chapter 99 of the Harmonized Tariff Schedule of the United States (HTSUS). The classification of any article that is described in any provision of this chapter will fall within the chapter—that is, this chapter takes precedence over any other potential classification of the article—as long as the article meets the conditions specified in the appropriate provisions of HTSUS Chapter 99. Any article failing to meet the conditions established for inclusion in HTSUS Chapter 99 will be entered under the provisions of the HTSUS chapter in which it would normally be classified absent the special conditions.

Although most importers utilize the services of a licensed customs broker in making their entries, and we recommend this practice, you should be aware of the regulatory, entry, and documentation issues involved in importing your product. You, as importer, are ultimately responsible for the fulfillment of any legal requirements applicable to your shipment.

General Considerations

Commodity Index Chapter 99 is designed to cover exceptions and special circumstances as decreed by legislative, executive, or other agency actions. All represent temporary modifications—usually a raising or lowering of applicable duty rates—to the customs treatment of products usually classified elsewhere in the HTSUS. Some of the provisions are highly specific, while others are broad in application. Many have extensive qualifying provisions, limits, and procedures that need to be carefully assessed to determine eligibility.

Products covered in **Subchapter I** are subject to cumulative duties, which are payable in addition to the normal duties levied on the items (this subchapter applies to a limited range of organic chemicals). **Subchapter II** covers temporary reductions in duty rates for the specified products. Note that the items listed in this subchapter are subject to provisions that have a specific period of applicability, the vast majority of which expired at the end of 1990 or 1992 (expired provisions are shaded).

Subchapter III pertains to import restrictions imposed by congressional action. These provisions, which primarily affect various agricultural, food, and textile products, as well as footwear and motor vehicles, are of indefinite applicability. Recent provisions that are no longer in force are shaded.

Subchapter IV covers additional restrictions on agricultural products. These restrictions are instituted by the Secretary of Agriculture in accord with the procedures established in Section 22 of the Agricultural Adjustment Act. These provisions primarily affect dairy products, such as milk and cheese, as well as peanuts, cotton, and sugar. Agricultural quotas for the products covered are also established in this subchapter.

Subchapter V covers the extensive special provisions of the U.S.-Canada Free Trade Agreement. Provisions are numerous and highly specific. Terms are also generally substantially more favorable than those allowed to most exporting countries.

Subchapter VI covers the special provisions of the North American Free Trade Agreement (NAFTA) that apply to imports to the U.S. from Mexico. These provisions are also extensive, detailed, and generally favorable.

Some specific authorizations may be needed to import articles under the provisions of HTSUS Chapter 99. The importer must satisfy Customs that the entry qualifies under the terms of the specific provision of Chapter 99, which may require specific documentation. Importers should ascertain what documentation Customs will require in advance and be prepared to furnish it to facilitate their entries.

Customs Classification

For customs purposes, articles covered by temporary special provisions are classified within Chapter 99 of the HTSUS. This chapter is divided into subchapters, which are the equivalents of the major headings of other HTSUS chapters, which are further divided into subheadings, each of which has its own HTSUS classification number. There are six subchapters in HTSUS Chapter 99.

9901—Temporary legislation providing for additional duties

9902—Temporary reductions in rates of duty

9903—Temporary modifications established pursuant to trade legislation

9904—Additional import restrictions established pursuant to Section 2 of the Agricultural Adjustment Act

9905—Temporary modifications established pursuant to the United States-Canada Free Trade Agreement

9906—Temporary modifications established pursuant to the North American Free Trade Agreement

Sample Import Duties

Import duties vary depending on the HTSUS classification of your product. Therefore, to determine the correct amount of duties, your product must be properly classified under the HTSUS. Provisions of HTSUS Chapter 99 are highly specific. Importers should carefully review the chapter for any provisions that affect their particular products.

Entry and Documentation

The entry of merchandise is a two-part process consisting of 1) filing the documents necessary to determine whether merchandise may be released from Customs custody and 2) filing the documents that contain information for duty assessment and statistical purposes. In certain instances all documents must be filed and accepted by Customs prior to the release of the goods. Unless you have been granted an extension, you must file entry

*IMPORTANT: Read the Commodity Index Introduction. It is the essential framework for understanding this chapter.

documents at a location specified by the district or area director within five working days of your shipment's date of arrival at a U.S. port of entry. These include a number of standard documents required by Customs for any entry, and:

- Such supporting documentation as Customs may specify for the given import

After you present the entry, Customs may examine your shipment, or may waive examination. The shipment is then released provided no legal or regulatory violations have been noted. You must then file entry summary documentation and deposit estimated duties at a designated customhouse within 10 working days of your shipment's release. For a detailed description of entry procedures, standard documentation, and informal entry, see "Entry Process" on page 182.

Marking Requirements

For a general discussion of U.S. Customs marking and labeling requirements, see "Marking: Country of Origin" on page 215 and "Special Marking Requirements" on page 217.

Shipping Considerations

You will need to ensure that your goods are packaged and shipped with care to ensure that they arrive in good condition and pass smoothly through Customs. You are responsible for ensuring that the shipment is in compliance with all applicable government regulations for packaging and shipping. In most instances, you should not leave these arrangements solely to the discretion of your supplier. Careful preparation of the cargo and selection of the mode of transport can be essential to a cost-effective, timely delivery of undamaged goods. We strongly advise you to consult your shipping representative, insurance agent, or freight broker for advice on packing and shipping. Refer also to the major tab section "Packing/Shipping/Insurance" for a general discussion of packing and shipping.

Publications Available

The *Harmonized Tariff Schedule of the United States* (HTSUS) is available from:

Government Printing Office (GPO)
Superintendent of Documents
Washington, DC 20402
(202) 512-1800 (Order line)
(202) 512-0000 (General)

The USGPO also has copies of specific laws available for purchase. The USGPO accepts credit card orders over the phone, as well as mail orders paid by credit card, a check drawn on a U.S. bank, or an international money order.

Relevant Government Agencies

Address questions regarding special provisions of HTSUS Chapter 99 to the district or port director of Customs for you area. For addresses refer to "U.S. Customs District Offices" on page 62 or contact:

U.S. Customs Service
1301 Constitution Ave. NW
Washington, DC 20229
(202) 927-6724 (Information)
(202) 927-1000 (General)

Laws and Regulations

Various laws and regulations may be relevant to the importation of special provisions classifications. Laws are contained in the U.S. Code (USC) and regulations are published in the Code of Federal Regulations (CFR), both of which may be available at larger public and law libraries. Copies of specific laws are also available from the United States Government Printing Office (address above).

17 USC 624
Agricultural Adjustment Act
This act, through Section 22, establishes the authority of the Secretary of Agriculture to institute quotas and other restrictions on various agricultural products.

Appendix: Foods*

This index entry presents a broad overview of general U.S. Food and Drug Administration (FDA) requirements for the importation of foods into the United States. It is by no means exhaustive, and is intended to supplement the information in the commodity index chapters dealing specifically with food and with FDA entry procedures in general, including those for products such as drugs and cosmetics. If you are interested in importing FDA-regulated products, you should read this general section, as well as any pertinent specific chapter. You should also contact all regulating agencies applicable to your product for more details.

Although most importers utilize the services of a licensed customs broker in making their entries, and we recommend this practice, you should be aware of the regulatory, entry, and documentation issues involved in importing your product. You, as importer, are ultimately responsible for the fulfillment of any legal requirements applicable to your shipment.

Importation of food is regulated primarily by the FDA, under the Federal Food, Drug, and Cosmetic Act (FDCA), the Fair Packaging and Labeling Act (FPLA), and sections of the Public Health Service Act (PHSA). FDA regulations regarding importation of foods of any kind are extensive and stringent. In addition to FDA requirements there may be U.S. Department of Agriculture (USDA) and/or National Marine Fisheries Service (NMFS) regulations pertinent to specific products. USDA or NMFS requirements will be outlined under the commodity to which they pertain.

Imported products regulated by the FDA are subject to FDA port-of-entry inspection. **Form FD701** is required for virtually all FDA-regulated importations and may be obtained from your local FDA Import Operations office, from FDA headquarters (see addresses at end of this chapter), or from your customs broker. If your shipment is found to be noncomplying with applicable laws and regulations, it may be detained at the port of entry. The FDA may permit you to bring a noncomplying shipment into compliance before a final decision is made regarding admittance. However, any sorting, reprocessing, or relabeling must be supervised by FDA personnel, and is done at the importer's expense. Conditional release of an illegal importation to allow an importer to bring it into compliance is not a right but a privilege. If you repeat noncomplying shipments of the same article, the FDA may interpret this as abuse of the privilege and require you to destroy or reexport subsequent shipments.

*IMPORTANT: Read the Commodity Index Introduction. It is the essential framework for understanding this section.

Both domestic and imported products are subject to the same legal requirements under the FDCA, FPLA, and PHSA. Since this is an importer's manual, we will consider primarily those aspects of the relevant laws which apply directly to importation. However, you should be aware that FDA requirements for interstate shipping, premarket testing, etc. directly affect your business. The fact that such information is only briefly touched on in this index is no indication of its scope, breadth, complexity, or of the potential fines, penalties, and loss of revenue which could result from ignorance of these laws. If you are interested in importing FDA-regulated products, you should become familiar with FDA regulations not only on importation but also on interstate shipping, storage, handling, packaging, etc.

Basic Requirements and Prohibitions. The FDCA prohibits importation of articles that are adulterated or misbranded. You will find detailed definitions of these terms in the text of the law. In brief, products that are defective, unsafe, filthy, or produced under insanitary conditions are considered to be adulterated. Products labeled with inadequate information or with false or misleading statements, designs, or pictures are considered misbranded. The law also prohibits distribution of any article requiring prior FDA approval if such approval has not been given. Depending upon the nature of your product, you may be required to provide required reports and to allow the FDA to inspect your facilities.

Premarket Testing and Approval. You should be aware that the FDCA and PHSA require manufacturers of certain consumer products to establish, prior to marketing, that such products meet the safety and effectiveness requirements of the law, and that they are properly labeled. Substances added to food must be "generally recognized as safe," "prior sanctioned," or approved by specific FDA regulations, based on scientific data. Samples of color additives must be tested and certified by FDA laboratories. Residues of pesticide chemicals in food commodities must not exceed safe tolerances set by the Environmental Protection Agency (EPA) and enforced by the FDA. Such premarketing clearances are based on scientific data provided by the manufacturer, subject to review and acceptance by U.S. Government scientists. For more information regarding your responsibilities as importer, contact FDA's Bioresearch Monitoring Staff (see addresses at end of this chapter).

Interstate Shipments. It is possible that an imported food product which violates one of the U.S. food laws may pass Customs without FDA sampling or detention. The fact that such a product slips through Customs undetected does not render it legal under U.S. law. You should be aware that introducing food products that violate applicable laws and regulations into U.S. commerce can have serious consequences. The FDA periodically inspects U.S. facilities and food products introduced into interstate commerce to ensure compliance with the FDCA. Penalties for violation of FDCA regulations range from fines to imprisonment. Products found to be in violation are subject to either immediate recall or to seizure by the court.

Recall may be voluntary, or may be ordered by the FDA. You may initiate voluntary recall of products by contacting the nearest FDA field office. Guidelines on industry responsibilities and FDA recall procedures can be found in 21 CFR 7. However, if you are responsible for introducing a product into U.S. commerce in violation of applicable laws and regulations, your voluntary cooperation in a recall does not relieve you of any liability for the violation.

Seizure is a civil court action taken in order to remove goods from commerce. If your goods are seized, you may 1) abandon them to the disposal of the court; 2) file a claim contesting the government's charges (thus initiating a trial); or 3) request permission to bring the goods into compliance. Seized goods may not be altered, moved, or used without permission of the court.

You will also be held responsible for all expenses incurred as a result of seizure of your goods.

Carriers of food in interstate commerce are required to use only FDA-approved equipment and support facilities. Sanitation requirements protecting passengers and crew on interstate carriers are in the regulations for Control of Communicable Disease (21 CFR 1240) and Interstate Conveyance Sanitation (21 CFR 1250). These regulations specify requirements for equipment and operations for handling food, water, and waste both on conveyances and in support facilities. For further information, contact FDA's Division of Regulatory Guidance (see addresses at end of this chapter).

Color Additives. A color additive is a dye, pigment, or other substance, whether synthetic or derived from a vegetable, animal, mineral, or other source, which imparts a color when added or applied to a food. Foods containing color additives that have not been proved safe for the particular use to FDA's satisfaction are considered adulterated under the FDCA. You will find a list of approved color additives and the conditions under which they may be safely used, including the amounts that may be used when limitations are necessary, in 21 CFR 73,74, and 81. Unless specifically exempted by regulation, each batch of color must be tested and certified by the FDA before that batch can be used in food. FDA certification is not limited to colors made by U.S. manufacturers. The FDA will consider a request by a foreign manufacturer for certification, if the request is signed by both the foreign manufacturer and an agent residing in the U.S. Certification of a color by an official agency of a foreign country will not be accepted as a substitute for certification by the FDA. Send your requests for certification or for information regarding certification procedures and regulations, to FDA Division of Color Technology (see addresses at end of this chapter).

The Federal Food, Drug, and Cosmetic Act

The FDCA is the most comprehensive food law of its kind. If you are interested in importing food products into the U.S., you should be familiar with its provisions. The following sections briefly cover principal FDCA requirements applicable to the importation of food items. These are not exhaustive, but rather are meant to give you a sense of the degree and nature of the regulation. You should address specific questions, or requests for further details to the FDA.

Health Safeguards. Adulterated food is illegal and will be refused entry. A food is considered adulterated under the following conditions: 1) it contains any added or naturally occurring poisonous or harmful substance; 2) it contains additives not determined safe by the FDA prior to use; 3) it contains residues of pesticides not authorized by, or in excess of tolerances established by EPA regulations; 4) it contains non-FDA-certified colors; 5) any part of it is filthy, putrid, or decomposed; 6) it is the product of a diseased animal or one that has died otherwise than by slaughter; 7) it has been prepared, packed, or held under insanitary conditions whereby it may have become contaminated with filth or have become harmful to health; or 8) it is in packaging material which contains a poisonous or harmful substance. Some packaging materials are considered food additives and are thus subject to regulation.

Economic Safeguards. You must not conceal damage or inferiority in foods in any manner. Food labels must not contain false or misleading statements or omit material facts required by regulation. A food must not be sold under the name of another food. A substance recognized as a valuable constituent of a food must not be omitted or abstracted in whole or in part, nor may any substance be substituted for the food. Food containers must not be so made, formed, or filled as to be misleading. If you import a food for which a standard has been established for fill-of-container, it must either comply with such requirements, or bear a label statement that it falls below such requirements.

Label Information. The law states that required label information must be conspicuously displayed and in terms that the ordinary consumer is likely to be able to read and understand under ordinary conditions of purchase and use. If the label bears representations in a foreign language it must also bear all of the required statements in English. All imported foods must be marked in English with the name of the country of origin. For details concerning type sizes and styles, location, etc. of required label information, see 21 CFR 101. What follows is a brief overview of labeling information required on packaged food.

1) The name, street address, city, state, and zip code of either the manufacturer, packer, or distributor. A foreign address may omit the zip code. Street address may be omitted if the firm is listed in a current city or telephone directory. If the food is not manufactured by the person or company whose name appears on the label, the name must be qualified by "Manufactured for," "Distributed by" or a similar expression.

2) An accurate statement of the amount of food in the package. The required units of measure are the avoirdupois pound and the U.S. gallon. Metric measurements may be used in addition to the required units of measure. The law provides specific, detailed regulations regarding position, type size, etc. of the net weight declaration. There are varieties of application, depending upon the size of package, the nature of the product, i.e., whether it is liquid or solid, etc.

3) The common or usual name of a food must appear on the principal display panel, as well as the form of the product (i.e. "chopped," "whole," "sliced," etc.)

4) Unless the food is standardized, its ingredients must be listed by their common names in order of their predominance by weight. Labeling of standardized foods need only include those ingredients which the standard makes optional. (Most ingredients in standardized foods are optional and therefore must be listed on the label.) For purposes of labeling, a food's ingredients are those individual food components which go into making a mixed food. If a certain ingredient is the characterizing one in a food, it may be required to appear as part of the name of the food (e.g., shrimp in shrimp cocktail). Food additives and colors must be listed as ingredients except in butter, cheese, and ice cream.

Nutrition Labeling. Labeling of food products must include specific nutritional information. Required information is described in 21 CFR Part 101 and is extremely complex and specific. Additional requirements for specific products and product categories may be found in other regulations as well. Nutrition labeling regulations have been substantially overhauled, with major new provisions and requirements going into effect in 1994. The minimum requirements, found in 21 CFR 101.9, include the following (see sample): 1) serving size and number of servings per package; 2) total calories and calories from fat per serving; 3) total fat and saturated fat (in grams), total cholesterol and sodium (in milligrams), total carbohydrates, dietary fiber, sugars, and protein (in grams) per serving; 4) percent of all of the constituents listed in the preceding number as a percent of the daily values based on a recommended base 2,000 calorie daily diet; 5) U.S. Recommended Daily Allowances (U.S. RDA) in percentages of certain vitamins and minerals per serving; and 6) a display of the daily values with the recommended values in grams or milligrams—depending on the constituent—for fat, saturated fat, cholesterol, sodium, carbohydrates, and dietary fiber, plus the calories per gram for fats, carbohydrates, and protein. Other nutrients recognized as essential in the human diet may be listed if they contribute at least 2% of the U.S. RDA. The regulations provide highly specific instructions for such labels, and offer several display options based on the shape, size, and other variables of the particular type of package. For further information, consult 21 CFR Part 1 or contact the FDA (see addresses at end of this chapter).

Nutrition Facts

Serving Size 1 Cup (228g)
Servings Per Container 2

Amount Per Serving	
Calories 260	Calories from Fat 120
	%Daily Value*
Total Fat 13g	20%
Saturated Fat 5g	25%
Cholesterol 30mg	10%
Sodium 660 mg	28%
Total Carbohydrate 31g	10%
Dietary Fiber 0g	0%
Sugars 5g	
Protein 5g	
Vitamin A 4% •	Vitamin C 2%
Calcium 15% •	Iron 4%

* Percent Daily Values are based on a 2,000 calorie diet, Your daily values may be higher or lower depending on your calorie needs:

	Calories:	2,000	2,500
Total Fat	Less than	65g	80g
Sat Fat	Less than	20g	25g
Cholesterol	Less than	300mg	300mg
Sodium	Less than	2,400mg	2,400mg
Total Carbohydrate		300g	375g
Dietary Fiber		25g	30g

Calories per gram:
Fat 9 • Carbohydrate 4 • Protein 4

Sample nutritional labeling.

Foods for Special Dietary Use. There are specific content labeling requirements for foods purporting to have special dietary use. Foods labeled with claims of disease prevention, treatment, mitigation, cure, or diagnosis must also comply with the drug provisions of FDCA. You should consult the detailed regulations under sections 403(j), 411, and 412 before importing foods purporting to have special dietary use.

Sanitation Requirements. FDCA regulations require that foods be produced in sanitary facilities, and be free of filth (e.g. rodent hairs and excreta, insect parts and excreta, parasitic worms). Foods containing filth are adulterated, whether or not harm to health can be shown, and whether or not such elements can be detected in the laboratory. The law requires action against illegal merchandise no matter where it may have become illegal. You should be sure that your products are packed and handled in the shipping vehicle in such a way as to prevent goods unadulterated at point of origin from spoilage or contamination en route. If your shipment is found to be contaminated at the port of entry, it will be detained. If it is contaminated after Customs entry and landing, it will be subject to the same seizure or recall proceedings used for domestic products.

Detailed description of the FDA's standard of sanitary conditions in food establishments are published in Current Good Manufacturing Practice Regulations. You may obtain a copy of these regulations from the FDA (see addresses at end of this chapter).

Food Defect Action Levels. There are no specific regulated tolerances for filth in food per se. The FDCA considers food adulterated if it consists in whole or in part of a filthy, putrid, or decomposed substance. However, your product will not be condemned because of the presence of foreign matter in amounts below the irreducible minimum after all possible precautions have been taken. The FDA's food defect action levels establish the amounts of contamination which render foods subject to enforcement action. These levels pose no hazard to health and are subject to change by the FDA. Any products which might be harmful to consumers, or which are produced in violation of FDA's Current Good Manufacturing Practice Regulations are subject to regulatory action, whether or not they exceed the defect levels. To obtain a copy of published food defect action levels, contact FDA headquarters (see addresses at end of this chapter).

Pesticide residues on raw agricultural commodities. "Raw agricultural commodity" means any food in its raw or natural state, including all unprocessed fruits, vegetables, nuts, and grains. Foods that have been washed, colored, waxed, or otherwise treated in their unpeeled natural form are considered to be unprocessed. Tolerances for pesticide residues on specific raw agricultural commodities are established, revoked, or changed, as the facts warrant such action, by EPA. Section 408 of the FDCA lists current tolerances in force. Raw products containing pesticide residues are in violation of FDCA unless: 1) the pesticide chemical has been exempted from the requirement of a residue tolerance; or 2) the residue does not exceed the tolerance established for that food.

Processed foods that contain any residue of a pesticide which is not exempted or for which no tolerance has been established are considered adulterated. If a tolerance has been established, a pesticide residue in the processed food does not adulterate the ready-to-eat food if the residue does not exceed the tolerance established for the raw agricultural commodity. If you are considering importation of foods which could contain pesticide residues, you should contact FDA's Division of Regulatory Guidance (see addresses at end of this chapter) for current information regarding tolerances.

Food additives. Any substance intended for use in producing, manufacturing, packing, processing, preparing, treating, packaging, transporting, or holding food may be considered a food additive under the FDCA. Excluded from this category are the following: 1) substances generally recognized as safe by qualified experts; 2) substances used in accordance with previous approval under FDCA, the Poultry Products Inspection Act (PPIA), or the Meat Inspection Act (MIA); 3) pesticide chemicals in or on raw agricultural products; 4) a color additive; or 5) new animal drugs. Items 3, 4, and 5 are subject to similar safety requirements of other sections of the law.

If you are not certain whether the chemicals or other ingredients used in your foods are subject to the safety clearance requirements of the Food Additives Amendment, you may seek an opinion from FDA. General principles for preparing a food additive petition are in 21 CFR 171. FDA premarket approval for food additives involves scientific studies and testing. When the FDA gives premarket approval for an additive, it issues a regulation permitting and circumscribing its use in foods. A substance cleared under the Food Additive Regulations is still subject to all the general requirements of FDCA.

IMPORTING FOODS INTO THE UNITED STATES

A Summary of the Procedures U.S. Importers Must Follow When Handling Food Products

(Shaded boxes are importer responsibilities)

1. Importer files Entry Notice with U.S. Customs.

2. FDA notified of entry.

3. FDA reviews importer's Entry Notice.

4A. FDA doesn't want sample. May Proceed Notice sent to U.S. Customs and importer.

4B. FDA wants sample. Notice of Sampling sent to U.S. Customs and importer.

5. U.S. Customs/FDA collects physical sample. Sample is analyzed by FDA.

6A. FDA finds sample in compliance. Release Notice sent to U.S. Customs and importer.

6B. FDA determines sample is violative. Notice of Detention and Hearing sent to U.S. Customs and importer.

7A. Importer responds toNotice of Hearing and Detention.

7B. Importer does not respond to Notice of Hearing & Detention.

8A. FDA holds hearing on detained product.

8B. FDA sends Notice of Refusal of Admission.

9A. Importer presents evidence indicating product is "in compliance."

9B. Importer submits application to recondition.

9C. FDA receives verification of exportation or destruction.

10A. FDA collects follow-up sample.

10B. FDA reviews importer's proposed reconditioning procedure.

11A. FDA finds sample in compliance. Release Notice sent to U.S. Customs and Importer.

11B. FDA finds sample not in compliance.

11C. FDA approves importer's reconditioning procedures.

11D. FDA disapproves importer's reconditioning proposal.

12. Importer completes all reconditioning procedures.

13. FDA conducts follow-up inspection/sample collection.

14A. FDA finds sample in compliance. Release Notice sent to U.S. Customs & importer.

14B. FDA sample not in compliance.

Food and Drug Administration, Center for Food Safety and Applied Nutrition, Industry Activities Section, Washington, DC 20204

FDA Import Procedures

1. Importer or agent files entry documents with U.S. Customs Service within five working days of the date of arrival of a shipment at a port of entry.
2. FDA is notified of an entry of regulated foods through:
   - Importers Entry Notice (FDA **Form FD 700** set) or Land Port Entry Notice (FDA **Form FD701**);
   - Copy of U.S. Customs **Form 7501**, "Summary Sheet for Consumption Entry;"
   - Copy of commercial invoice; and
   - Surety to cover potential duties, taxes, and penalties.
3. FDA reviews importer's Entry Notice (FDA **Form FD701**) to determine if a physical examination (wharf examination, sample examination) should be made.

4A. Decision is made not to collect a sample. FDA issues a May Proceed Notice (FDA **Form FD 702**) to U.S. Customs and the importer of record. The shipment is released as far as FDA is concerned.

4B. Decisions is made to collect a sample based on:

- Nature of the product,
- FDA priorities, and
- Past history of the commodity.

FDA issues a Notice of Sampling (FDA **Form FD 712**) to U.S. Customs and the importer of record. The shipment must be held intact pending further notice. A sample will be collected from the shipment. The importer of record may move the shipment from the dock to another port or warehouse (contact U.S. Customs for details).

5. FDA obtains a physical sample. The sample is sent to an FDA District Laboratory for analysis.

6A. FDA analysis finds the sample to be in compliance with requirements. FDA sends a Release Notice (FDA Form FD 717) to U.S. Customs and the importer of record.

6B. FDA analysis determines that the sample "appears to be in violation of the FDCA or other related Acts." FDA sends U.S. Customs and the importer of record a Notice of Detention and Hearing (FDA **Form FD 777**) which:

- Specifies the nature of the violation, and
- Gives the importer of record 10 working days to introduce testimony as to the admissibility of the shipment.

The hearing is the importer's only opportunity to show that the importation meets all legal requirements or to show how the shipment may be made eligible for entry.

7A. Consignee, true owner, importer of record, or a designated representative ***responds*** to the Notice of Detention and Hearing. The response permits the introduction of testimony, either orally or written, as to the admissibility of the shipment.

7B. Consignee, true owner, importer of record, or a designated representative ***neither*** responds to the Notice of Detention and Hearing ***nor*** requests an extension of the hearing period.

8A. FDA conducts a hearing concerning the admissibility of the product. The hearing is an opportunity to present relevant matters and is confined to the submission of pertinent evidence.

8B. FDA issues a Notice of Refusal of Admission (FDA **Form FD 772**) to the importer of record. This is the same person or firm who was sent a Notice of Sampling. All recipients of the Notice of Sampling and the Notice of Detention and Hearing are sent a copy of FDA **Form FD 772**.

9A. Importer of record presents evidence indicating that the product is in compliance. Certified analytical results of samples, examined by a reliable laboratory and which are within the published guidelines for levels of contaminants and defects in food for human use, may be presented.

9B. Importer of record submits an Application for Authorization to Recondition or Perform Other Action (FDA **Form FD 766**). The form requests permission to try to bring a food that is adulterated or misbranded into compliance by relabeling or other action, or by converting to a non-food use. A detailed method to bring the food into compliance must be given.

9C. FDA receives verification of the exportation or destruction of the shipment from U.S. Customs. The exportation or destruction of the merchandise listed on the Notice of Refusal of Admission is carried out under the direction of U.S. Customs.

10A. FDA collects follow-up sample to determine compliance with guidelines.

10B. FDA evaluates the reconditioning procedure proposed by the importer. A bond is required for payment of liquidated damages.

11A. FDA finds that the sample is "in compliance." A Release Notice (FDA **Form FD 717**) with the statement "Originally Detained and Now Released" is sent to U.S. Customs and the importer.

11B. FDA finds that the sample is not in compliance. The importer may either submit an Application for Authorization to Recondition or to Perform Other Action (see 9B) or, FDA will issue a Notice of Refusal of Admission (see 8B).

11C. FDA approves importer's recondition procedures. The approved application contains the statement "Merchandise Should Be Held Intact Pending the Receipt of FDA's Release Notice."

11D. FDA disapproves applicant's reconditioning procedure if past experience shows that the proposed method will not succeed. A second and final request will not be considered unless it contains meaningful changes in the reconditioning operation to ensure a reasonable chance of success. The applicant is informed on FDA **Form FD 766**.

12. Importer completes all reconditioning procedures and advises FDA that the goods are ready for inspection/sample collection.
13. FDA conducts follow-up inspection/sample collection to determine compliance with the terms of the reconditioning authorization.

14A. FDA analysis finds that the sample is in compliance A Release Notice (FDA **Form FD 717**) is sent to the importer and to U.S. Customs. The charges for FDA supervision are assessed on FDA Form **FD 790**. Copies are sent to U.S. Customs which is responsible for obtaining total payment including any expenses incurred by their personnel.

14B. FDA analysis finds that the sample is still not in compliance. Charges for FDA supervision are assessed on FDA **Form FD 790**. Copies are sent to U.S. Customs which is responsible for obtaining total payment including expenses incurred by their personnel.

Importers Can Speed Food Entries

1. Determine before shipment that the product to be imported is legal.
2. Have private laboratories examine samples of foods to be imported and certify the analysis of the processor. While not conclusive, these analyses might serve as an indication of the processor's ability to produce acceptable, legal products.
3. Become acquainted with FDA's legal requirements, before contracting for a shipment.
4. Request assistance form the FDA District Office responsible for your port of entry.
5. Know the food importing procedures described on this information sheet.

The Food Additive Regulations (21 CFR 180) list foods allowed to be artificially sweetened, and permitted amounts of such sweetener. If your product is artificially sweetened, it must be labeled as a special dietary food. Products containing saccharine must bear a warning label which states: "Use of this product may be hazardous to your health. This product contains saccharin, which has been determined to cause cancer in laboratory animals." For further information regarding food additives, contact FDA (see addresses at end of this chapter).

Food standards. 21 CFR 103-169 contains full details on FDA food standards. Standards of identity define what a given food product is, its name, its ingredients, and required label information. Standards of quality are minimum standards which specify quality requirements over and above those generally established under the FDCA. Do not confuse FDA standards of quality with USDA grades for agricultural products, and U.S. Department of the Interior (USDI) grades for fishery products. Fill-of-container standards define how full the container must be and how this is measured.

If you import a food represented as one for which a standard of identity has been promulgated, it must comply with the specifications of that standard in every respect. If your foods fall below applicable standards of quality or fill of container, you must identify it as substandard on the label. The FDA does not require identification of USDA or USDI grades on food labels, but when the label contains this information, the product must comply with the specifications for the declared grade. The terms "Fancy" or "Grade A" may be used only on the labels of those products meeting the specifications established for such grades by USDA. For more information contact FDA (see addresses at end of this chapter).

Publications Available

All FDA regulations are updated and republished annually in *Title 21, Code of Federal Regulations.* The CFR is available at law libraries and some major public libraries, and may be purchased from the U.S. Government Printing Office (USGPO). The USGPO accepts credit card orders over the phone, as well as mail orders paid by credit card, a check drawn on a U.S. bank, or an international money order.

Government Printing Office (GPO)
Superintendent of Documents
Washington, DC 20402
(202) 783-3238 (Order line)
(202) 512-0000 (General)

FDA publications explaining regulations are available upon request from the FDA at (202) 205-5241; others may be available from the USGPO (address above).

Relevant Government Agencies

Address general inquiries regarding importation of foods to:

U.S. Food and Drug Administration (FDA)
Center for Food Safety and Applied Nutrition
200 C Street SW
Washington, DC 20204
(202) 205-5241, 205-5042

U.S. Food and Drug Administration (FDA)
Center for Food Safety and Applied Nutrition
Office of Constituant Operations
200 C Street SW
Washington, DC 20204
(202) 205-4307

Address your inquiries regarding premarket testing and approval to:

U.S. Food and Drug Administration (FDA)
Center for Food Safety and Applied Nutrition
Office of Premarket Approval
200 C Street SW
Washington, DC 20204
(202) 418-3100

Address your inquiries regarding testing and certification of color additives to:

U.S. Food and Drug Administration (FDA)
Center for Food Safety and Applied Nutrition
Office of Cosmetics and Colors
200 C Street SW
Washington, DC 20204
(202) 205-4530

Address your inquiries regarding import permits for milk and cream, for interstate travel sanitation, and general regulatory questions to:

U.S. Food and Drug Administration (FDA)
Center for Food Safety and Applied Nutrition
Office of Field Programs
200 C Street SW
Washington, DC 20204
(202) 205-4187

Address your inquiries regarding canned foods to:

U.S. Food and Drug Administration (FDA)
Center for Food Safety and Applied Nutrition
Office of Constituant Operations
200 C Street SW
Washington, DC 20204
(202) 205-4307

Address your inquiries regarding the National Shellfish Sanitation Program to:

U.S. Food and Drug Administration (FDA)
Center for Food Safety and Applied Nutrition
Office of Seafood
200 C Street SW
Washington, DC 20204
(202) 418-3133

Notes:

Notes:

Canada Mexico

JAPAN China Germany

Taiwan U.K. Korea

France Italy Singapore

Malaysia Hong Kong Thailand

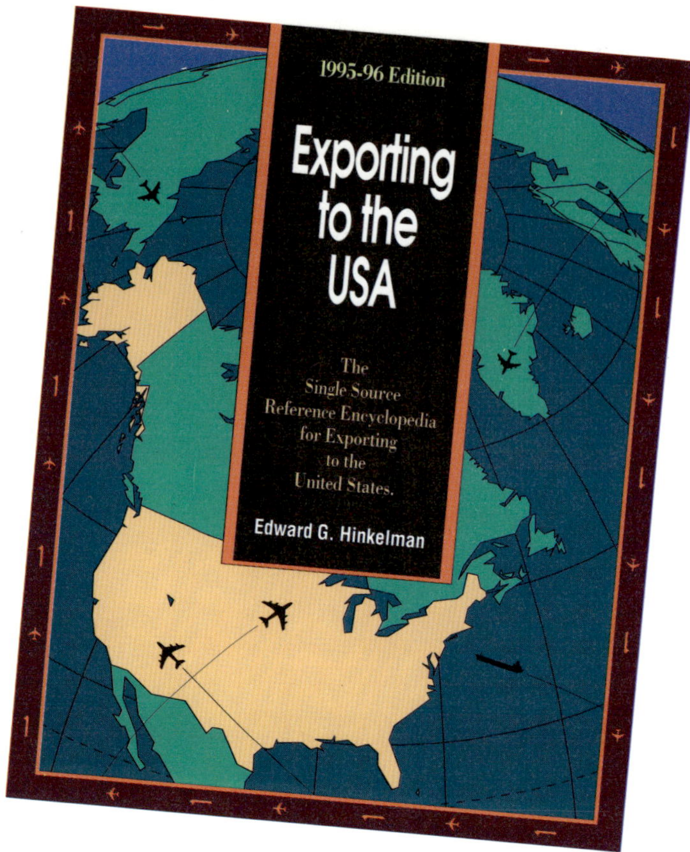

The world's largest market... awaits you!

Exporting to the USA is the most comprehensive reference available for the business of exporting goods to the United States. Extensively researched by a team of professionals, this authoritative 780-page reference is an indispensable tool for international businesses who wish to sell their products to the world's largest single economy.

Here is just some of what you will find:

Commodity Index
Exporting to the USA is the only reference available which details U.S. Customs entry procedures on a product-by-product basis. This "Commodity Index" is organized according to the 99 chapters of the Harmonized Tariff Schedule of the United States (HTSUS), the official tariff used by the U.S. Customs Service to classify and establish duties for all US imports.

Each of the 99 entries of the Commodity Index includes:

- key import factors
- general import considerations
- customs classification
- sample duty rates
- Customs entry and documentation procedures
- prohibitions, restrictions, and quotas
- country-specific limitations
- marking and labeling requirements
- shipping considerations
- publications available
- U.S. government regulating agencies
- applicable laws and regulations.
- key exporting countries

From ice and snow to nuts and bolts, from textiles to tile, from semiconductors to nuclear reactors, it's all here!

U.S. Customs Entry and Clearance
Exporting to the USA includes rock-solid information about the entire U.S. Customs entry and clearance process from the U.S. Customs Service itself. Information you can rely upon to make decisions, keep informed, and stay out of trouble.

International Banking
This section contains Swiss Bank Corporation's acclaimed guides to letters of credit and foreign exchange. Both are extremely readable and include illustrations for every step in the process.

Packing & Shipping
This section contains an extensive guide to container packing for all types of cargo, with over 80 illustrations, photos and charts. Also included is an illustrated guide to container types, and a section on international cargo insurance.

Exporting to the USA
780 pages, 8.5" x 11"
ISBN 0–885073–02–X
Hardcover, US$87.00

Professional Books for International Trade

1505 Fifth Avenue
San Rafael, CA 94901 • USA
(415) 454-9934
FAX (415) 453-7980
Order Line: (800) 833-8586

A

B

C

D

E

F

G

H

I

J

K

L

M

N

O

P

Q

R

S

T

U

V

W

X–Y–Z

Notes:

Notes: